NEW CATHOLIC
ENCYCLOPEDIA

*An International Work of Reference
on the Teachings, History, Organization,
and Activities of the Catholic Church,
and on All Institutions, Religions,
Philosophies, and Scientific and Cultural
Developments Affecting the Catholic Church
from Its Beginning to the Present.*

*Prepared by an Editorial Staff at
The Catholic University of America,
Washington, District of Columbia.*

PUBLISHERS GUILD, INC. in association with the McGRAW-HILL

Volume XVII
Supplement: Change in the Church

NEW CATHOLIC
ENCYCLOPEDIA

BOOK COMPANY   WASHINGTON, D.C., NEW YORK, N.Y.

Nihil Obstat:
Rev. William J. Hill, OP, S.T.M.
Censor Deputatus

Imprimatur:
✠ William Cardinal Baum
Archbishop of Washington
September 27, 1978

NEW CATHOLIC ENCYCLOPEDIA

Library of Congress Catalog Number: 66-22292
ISBN 0-07-0102-35X

POPE JOHN PAUL II

POPE JOHN PAUL I (Aug. 26—Sept. 28, 1978)

To His Holiness

Pope John Paul II

EDITORIAL STAFF

Foreword

The *Catholic Encyclopedia* (16 v., 1904–16; Suppl. 1922) and the *NEW CATHOLIC ENCYCLOPEDIA* (15 v., 1967; Suppl. v. 16, 1974) are the two "reference works of record" in the English language on matters Catholic. For The Catholic University of America their sponsorship stands as an achievement expressing the University's purposes of scholarship, research, and the communication of knowledge, with a Catholic motivation and spirit. The value of the achievement lies in the lasting and continuing service that these works have rendered to scholars, students, and general readers. Volumes supplementing any established reference work are in principle both desirable and to be expected. The University presents Volume 17 in the conviction that this thematic supplement is an absolute necessity.

The volume concentrates on "Change in the Church." A central reality in Catholic life and for Catholic study, the Church has become the Church that Vatican Council II has shaped, a changed Church and a Church in change. The life of the Church and the range of academic disciplines concerned are in a state of teeming vitality, in some respects of turbulence. Enough time has passed to reflect on what has happened and what may be expected. Vatican II is no longer simply a recent event; it has become an abiding and far-reaching force. Its documents have been sufficiently assimilated in thought and their import tested in practice to permit an assessment of that force and its future potential. Five Synods of Bishops have been held; the revision of liturgical rites and books is all but complete; the Church's new, conscious self-insertion into the world for the promotion of human rights and betterment is an observable and multiform fact; acceptance of the diverse ministries and gifts of the laity is expanding; the role of women in the Church is a clearly delineated issue.

Like a university an encyclopedia exists because of the conviction that reflection attentive to the past and informed about the present can develop sound knowledge and the well-founded judgments of wisdom. The character of the Church's life, present and yet to come, can never again be grasped easily or evaluated simply: the Council has acknowledged the Church to be the Pilgrim Church, *renovata sed semper renovanda*. Yet, because the Church is a reality that has a pervasive bearing on life and on knowledge, the present generation cannot leave study of today's Church to future historians. Volume 17 is a needed instrument. This new *Supplement* gathers and organizes the information generated by the ecclesial developments of the immediate past. A significant element in that information receives special attention: the documentation that has guided the process of change. The volume also provides a careful correlation with the earlier volumes of the *NEW CATHOLIC ENCYCLOPEDIA* as an aid to the perception of both the continuity and the discontinuity that mark the life of the Vatican II Church. Perhaps most importantly the articles in Volume 17 come from a significant cross-section of the People of God. Some 500 contributors of a wide and diverse background write from the experience of their own involvement in and reflection on the life of the Church. Their presentation of data and their perceptive evaluations articulate the theme of the volume in a way that will provide the reader with a sound knowledge, basic for judgment about the present and future Church.

Edmund D. Pellegrino
President
The Catholic University of America

Preface

The Editorial Board decided in 1976 on the opportuneness of a second Supplement to the *NEW CATHOLIC ENCYCLOPEDIA*, a theme-volume on "Change in the Church." Volume 17 centers on the Church as it has become and continues to be the "Vatican-Council II Church." The Supplement is self-contained, but is also designed to bring out the impact of postconciliar thought and life on earlier entries in the *ENCYCLOPEDIA*.

SCOPE. The development of the theme takes its direction and limits from a statement in the radio address, aptly called *Ecclesia Christi, lumen gentium*, by Pope John XXIII, Sept. 11, 1962, a month before Vatican II's opening. The Pope envisioned the Council's agenda as a renewed search into: the Church's inner vitality (*vitalità ad intra*), whereby it continually offers, especially to its own members, the treasures of faith that enlightens and of grace that sanctifies; and its outward vitality (*vitalità ad extra*), i.e., the Church in the face of the temporal demands and needs of peoples (ActApS 54 [1967] 680; *Discorsi, messaggi, colloqui del Santo Padre Giovanni XXIII* v. 4 [Vatican City 1963] 522). Pope John's vision was in fact borne out: the two principal documents of the Council are *Lumen gentium*, the Dogmatic Constitution on the Church, and *Gaudium et spes*, the Pastoral Constitution on the Church in the Modern World. Most of the teaching in the other conciliar documents is implicit in them; the Church's thought and life have been and continue to be consequences of the key ideas and action proposals contained in these two main documents. The election and declared programs of Popes John Paul I and II demonstrate that the Church is irreversibly the Vatican II Church; John Paul II made this particularly and vigorously clear in his homily at the Mass inaugurating his ministry as supreme pastor, Oct. 22, 1978. The contents of Volume 17 bear striking witness to the presence of powers of thought and of action in the Church that will continue to transform it in its search for renewal as the Sacrament of Christ, the Light of the World (*Lumen gentium* 1) and as the Servant Church, deeply concerned with the joys and hopes, griefs and anxieties of mankind, especially the poor (*Gaudium et spes* 1).

PLAN OF THE VOLUME. Change in the Church has included the documents and actions implementing the Council, but also modes of thought, movements, and events that have in fact emerged in the Church's life. (In Volume 17 the theological evaluation in Michael Fahey, SJ's article, "Change in the Church" offers an excellent overview of the topic of the volume. The plan of Volume 17 covers its theme in the sense of both intended and de facto change. The statement of John XXIII as well as the order and contents of *Lumen gentium* and *Gaudium et spes* suggested a first major division of the plan into matters related to the Church's inner life and those related to the Church's outreach in the ministry of justice and peace. As supplementing and, where necessary, revising or reinterpreting the contents of the *NEW CATHOLIC ENCYCLOPEDIA*, Volume 17 articulates the two main headings through a title list made up of those *ENCYCLOPEDIA* entries most directly affected by change; new titles are those required by the life of the Church since the Council. The structure and implications of *Lumen gentium* and *Gaudium et spes* have further guided organization of the close to 800 articles under ten areas with their key sub-areas as follows:

THE CHURCH IN ITS INNER LIFE:
I. *The Church Receiving the Word of God*: Revelation; Faith; Knowledge of God; Atheism; Philosophy of Religion; Theology; Theology and Philosophy.
II. *The Church in its Being*: The Church; Local Church; Parish; People of God; Universal Priesthood; Sacraments; Incorporation into the Church; Catholicity; Catholicism (U.S.): Eastern Churches; Ecumenism; Non-Christians and Nonbelievers; Mary; Ecclesiology; Christology; Sacramental Theology; Ecumenics; Mariology.
III. *The Church's Ministries*: Ministry; Apostolicity; Hierarchy; Bishops; Collegiality; Synods of Bishops; Priesthood; Deacons; Lay Ministries; Women and Ministry; The Church Sanctifying, Teaching, Ruling; Discipline; The Magisterium; Canon Law; Canonical Jurisprudence; Canonical Studies; Homiletics; Pastoral Planning.

IV. *The Church Worshiping*: Worship; Liturgy; Liturgical Art; Liturgical Books; Liturgical Languages; Liturgical Music; Liturgical Year; Liturgical Ministers; Liturgy of the Hours; Liturgy of the Sacraments; Liturgy of the Eucharist; Liturgical Blessings; Liturgiology; Liturgical Theology; Sacred Musicology; Liturgy and Anthropology.

V. *The Church's Witness of Holiness*: Call to Holiness; Contemporary Spirituality; Active Life; Contemplative Life; Priestly Formation and Spirituality; Religious Life; Lay Spirituality; Moral Theology; Spiritual Theology; Pastoral Psychology.

VI. *The Church's Witness of Evangelization*: Mission of the Church; Evangelization; Missions; Missionary Formation; Inculturation; Latin America; the African Church; Missiology; Missionary Catechetics; History of Religions; Comparative Study of Religions.

THE CHURCH'S MINISTRY OF JUSTICE AND PEACE:

VII. *The Church in the World*: Ministry of Justice and Peace; Temporal Values; Dignity of the Person, the Family, and Marriage; Community of Mankind; Human Rights; Social Thought and Social Action; Minority Rights (Ethnics; Women); Black Theology; Feminism and Theology; Social Theology; Sociology; Sociology of Religion; Theology of History.

VIII. *The Church and the Right to Life and Work*: Right to Life; Abortion; Health Care; The Aged; Death; Right to Work; Economics and Social Problems; Economic Justice; Distribution of Wealth; Church Investments; Labor; Migration; Poverty; Unemployment; Business Ethics.

IX. *The Church and Political Communities*: Church and Politics; Political Freedom; Terrorism; Prisons and Prisoners; Civil Rights; Church and State (U.S.); Church in Communist Countries; Church in Latin America; Church in the Philippines; Papal Diplomacy; Third World; International Economic Aid; Peace and War; Liberation Theology; Political Theology; Theology of Hope.

X. *The Church and Culture/Education*: Culture; Media of Social Communication; Catholic Press, Journalism and Publishing; Christian Education; Catechesis; Moral Education; Catechetical Directories; Catechisms; Adult Catechesis; Youth Catechetics; Adult Religious Education; Parochial Schools; Catholic Secondary Education; Catholic Higher Education; Ministry of Teaching; Campus Ministry; Catechetics; Theology and Philosophy in Seminaries; Theology in Catholic Colleges.

The specific entries within these ten areas include two types that call for comment. One group consists of articles on the status of related academic disciplines. These disciplines include not only the traditional sacred sciences, but also social sciences and other secular disciplines, the study of which Vatican II endorsed for their service to the Church's mission and ministry. A second group of articles covers organizations that have a bearing on the theme of the Volume. Council-inspired, new organizations or new initiatives of the old are important indicators of the Church's contemporary life. These identifying articles are mainly on organizations in the United States.

BIOGRAPHY. To maintain a policy of the *ENCYCLOPEDIA*, Volume 17 contains a selected group of biographies of personages important to the Church's life; all are deceased, with the exception of the reigning Pope.

ARRANGEMENT. The articles of Volume 17 are arranged, as throughout the *ENCYCLOPEDIA*, alphabetically by the first solid word, or, where necessary, by the second solid word; thus Association for Social Economics comes before Association of Catholic Teachers.

ABBREVIATIONS. The main abbreviations used in the Volume are bibliographical; a list of these (Reference Works and Periodicals; Documents of Paul VI; Vatican II Documents; Documents of the Synod of Bishops; NCCB Documents; Liturgical Instructions) forms part of the back matter. The abbreviations for Reference Works and Periodicals combine new sources with selected items from the bibliographical abbreviations in Volume 15. Abbreviations for Liturgical Instructions are included because their theological richness and potential for liturgical formation led contributors to cite the Instructions copiously in the text.

CROSS REFERENCES AND INDEX. The cross-reference system serves to direct the reader to related material in other articles. An asterisk before the name of person or subject (e.g., *Collegiality) indicates that there is an article of that title in the volume. A *see* reference with the term in small capitals has the same function (e.g., *see* COLLEGIALITY). When a further aspect of the subject is treated under another title, a see also reference with the term in small capitals is placed at the end of the article (e.g., *See also* COLLEGIALITY). Cross references to earlier volumes are indicated by volume and page number in parentheses following a term or relevant statement, thus (1:333). In addition to the cross-reference system the analytical index will greatly increase the reader's ability to get best use of the *ENCYCLOPEDIA*. Suggestions for the most effective use of the index are given in the Guide to Use of the Index, where correlation with the whole *ENCYCLOPEDIA* is also explained.

BIBLIOGRAPHY. Authors of articles in most cases have included bibliography; by the nature of the volume many items are from current journals and periodicals. It was left to the contributors' discretion to omit bibliography if they felt that the state of the literature provided nothing significant on a given topic.

CONTRIBUTORS. All articles are signed; the full name and identification of the some 500 contributors are given in the back matter of the volume.

APPENDIX. Because the papal and curial documents since Vatican II are so numerous and influential, an appendix assembling the principal ones chronologically has been prepared by Sister Claudia Carlen, IHM and is followed by a topical index.

ACKNOWLEDGMENTS. The Executive Editor is pleased to express grateful appreciation, first of all, to the Editorial Board. Their contributions to the planning of the volume and the benefit of consultation with them as a group and individaully have been of immense help. Much valuable assistance came also from members of USCC/NCCB, CARA, NCEA, the U.S. Mission Council, the faculty of The Catholic University of America, and other groups. A particular debt is owed to Mr. James Schellman, Assistant to the Executive Secretary of the International Commission on English in the Liturgy (ICEL) for notable assistance in the area of liturgy. The cheerfully-given and competent assistance of Carolyn Lee and Shirley Pototsky of the Catholic University Theology Library was indispensable, especially on bibliographical matters. A great debt is owed to the research, editorial, and indexing assistance of Sister Claudia Carlen, IHM, Jill C. Rees, Catherine Clarkson, and Brother Hugh D. Burns, OP. Above all it is the contributors who have created the volume; to have received their generous and able collaboration has been a high privilege and remains a treasured experience.

THE EXECUTIVE EDITOR

A

ABBEY *NULLIUS*

In keeping with the directives of Vatican II, which sought to restore monks to their ancient traditions of serving God within the confines of their monasteries (*Perfectae caritatis* 9) and to have the nature of the Church clearly manifested in the People of God belonging to the diocese (*Christus Dominus* 22–23), the territorial jurisdiction of an abbey independent of any diocese yet comprising the care of the faithful in that area (1:10) was modified by Paul VI in the motu proprio *Catholicae Ecclesiae*, Oct. 23, 1976. For the future, an abbey *nullius* is not to be established unless very unusual circumstances for the good of souls are present. Existing abbeys *nullius* are to be converted into other ecclesiastical jurisdictions or, if they lie entirely within an existing diocese, are to revert to the condition of other abbeys. Abbots who do not exercise jurisdiction over layfolk are not to receive episcopal ordination. The only U.S. abbey *nullius*, Belmont Abbey (N.C.), reverted to the condition of a simple abbey at the end of 1976.

Bibliography: ActApS 68 (1976) 694–696.

[M. J. DLOUHY]

ABBOT/ABBESS, BLESSING OF

Vatican II called for a "shining forth in its true spirit" of monastic life (*Perfectae caritatis* 9) and the revised Blessing of an Abbot or Abbess (1:10) reflects that spirit. Over the course of centuries, this monastic rite had been modified to reflect the civil and social conditions of each period. The new blessing rite emphasizes the spiritual function an abbot is called to carry out and eliminates such obsolete elements as the imposition of hands, the enthronement of the new prelate, and his blessing of the layfolk. Confusion between the role of an abbot and that of a bishop is avoided. The blessing is conferred during Mass after the Liturgy of the Word. The bishop interrogates the newly elected abbot as to his principal spiritual duties: will he observe and teach the Rule? will he instruct the monks by his example and thus lead them to God? will he administer the property of the monastery for the good of the community and the poor? After the litany has been prayed, the bishop concludes with the solemn prayer of blessing and invests the abbot with the Rule

and staff. Investiture with ring and miter is optional.

The rite for the blessing of an abbess is similar. After the Gospel and homily, the newly elected abbess is presented by two members of her community and questioned about her willingness to rule the community and care for the spiritual welfare of her religious in obedience to the pope and local bishop. After the litany has been prayed, the bishop imparts the blessing, presents her with the Rule and, if she had not received one at her profession, also a ring.

The rite of blessing was approved by Paul VI on Oct. 19, 1970 and promulgated on Nov. 9, 1970.

Bibliography: ActApS 63 (1971) 710–711. *Notitiae* 60 (Jan. 1971) 32–36.

[M. J. DLOUHY]

ABORTION (U.S. LAW)

Some observers felt that the 1973 abortion decisions of the Supreme Court did more than create a right to abort (1:30; 16:3). By devaluing unborn life because of the burdens a new life creates, the Court appeared to dignify elective abortion as a morally preferred and, perhaps, constitutionally mandated response to social problems. This assessment was to be tested in Supreme Court decisions in 1976 and 1977.

The 1976 Decisions. On July 1, 1976, the Court decided two cases with a common issue: may a state constitutionally condition an elective abortion on the consent of either the woman's husband or an unmarried minor's parents? Previous Supreme Court decisions had recognized (1) that rights "older than the Bill of Rights" inhere in the sanctity, intimacy and unity of the "bilateral" marital relationship (*Griswold v. Connecticut*, 1963), and (2) that the rights of parents to direct the upbringing of their children are of the essence of liberty (*Pierce v. Society of Sisters*, 1924). Proponents urged that spousal and parental consent statutes merely codified rights implicit in the *Griswold/Pierce* formulations. Rejecting this argument, the Court struck down a mandatory consent statute in *Planned Parenthood v. Danforth*. The Court reasoned that the state may not "delegate authority" to prevent an abortion when, under the 1973 decisions, the state itself lacks that authority. (In a companion case, *Bellotti v. Baird*, the Court refused to strike down a statute which allowed for court review of parental nonconsent.) By holding that family rights exist only by "delegation" from the states, within limits set by the judiciary, the 1976 decisions substantially eradicated the *Griswold/Pierce* doctrine of family unity *cum* liberty. That the Court was willing to take so revolutionary a step to facilitate abortion lent credibility to the earlier assessments of the 1973 decisions.

The 1977 Decisions. Given the proselytizing tenor of the 1973 and 1976 decisions, the 1977 decisions represent a startling reversal of the judicial trend. In *Maher v. Roe* and *Poelker v. Doe* (decided June 20, 1977), the Supreme Court was asked to determine whether it is unconstitutionally discriminatory to exclude non-therapeutic abortion from municipal hospitals and state medical assistance programs, while at the same time these services and benefits are extended to childbirth. Holding that a state may "make a value judgment favoring childbirth over abortion," in order to further the state's "strong and legitimate interest" in the life of the fetus, the Court found the exclusions constitutionally permissible. (A third case, *Beale v. Doe*, dealt only with interpretation of the Social Security Act.) Encouraged by the 1977 decisions, states will undoubtedly react with legislation designed to effectuate further their strong interest in protecting unborn life. Legal challenges will follow. It is difficult to foresee how courts will be able to resolve very many of these cases without exploring the nature of the state's interest in unborn life, or, to put it another way, the nature of unborn life. Are unborn children live human beings? This fundamental question of fact, which the Supreme Court sidestepped in 1973, appears ready for a comeback as a result of the 1977 decisions.

Constitutional Amendments. Hearings on proposed Human Life and States Rights amendments were held by committees of both the Senate (1974–75) and House (1976). The Senate committee declined to report out any amendment (September 17, 1975); the House committee took no action. Some in the pro-life movement have espoused a call for a national constitutional convention as a means of coercing favorable congressional action. Others point out that Congress would likely respond (if at all) with a politically pragmatic States Rights amendment, which is generally unacceptable to the pro-life movement. It has been noted too that there are no ground rules in the Constitution for delegate selection or limitation of issues at a convention. Pro-abortionists might well dominate the convention and force through a broad range of anti-life, anti-family proposals.

The Political Scene. Despite congressional inertia, the pro-life movement gained momentum. The 1976 Supreme Court decisions caused many who had been apathetic to perceive permissive abortion as a direct threat to their own families. Abortion became an issue in the 1976 presidential primaries. The government funding debate, sparked by the 1977 decisions, kept the issue before the public. A pro-life/pro-family alliance emerged in Houston in November, 1977 in opposition to extreme positions taken by the National Women's Conference held there Nov. 18–21.

Five years after the 1973 decisions, abortion remains a "hot issue" in the courts, Congress, and the political arena.

See also BISHOPS' COMMITTEE ON PRO-LIFE ACTIVITIES.

Bibliography: R. BYRN, "Judicial Imperialism," *Human Life Review* 3 (1977) 19–35 (reviewing the 1973, 1976, and 1977 decisions). HOUSE AND SENATE SUBCOMMITTEE HEARINGS, *Proposed Amendments on Abortion* (6 v., U.S. Government Printing Office, 1974–76). *National Right to Life News* 4 (Feb. 1977) (articles pro and con regarding a national constitutional convention).

[R. BYRN]

ABORTION (U.S. LAW AND MORALITY)

In 1973 the U.S. Supreme Court ruled laws against abortion in the United States unconstitutional (1:30; 16:3). Without going into detail, it can be said that the basis for this ruling was the woman's right to privacy. Although this right is not found explicitly in the Constitution, it is commonly accepted by jurists as a constitutional right. Even in civil law, however, the right to privacy is not an absolute right; it will yield to a "compelling interest" on the part of the state. But the Supreme Court did not consider the human fetus to be a compelling state interest during the first two trimesters and to be so only with certain limitations during the third. The moral theologian certainly accepts a right to privacy vis-à-vis the state and even other private persons, but he may not be willing to accept a destructive act against a human fetus as a private matter, or if it is, he may not concede that the welfare of the human fetus is not a compelling state interest. Certainly, since the beginning of the 3d century jurists in the Western world have considered abortion a valid area for penal legislation. It is difficult to see why it should suddenly be considered out of bounds. But it should be emphasized that the right to privacy upheld by the Court binds only in reference to the state and rules out any interference in abortion on the part of the state. The right does not rule out efforts by private individuals, e.g., a husband or a parent, to prevent abortions. Neither does it impose any obligation either on the state or on other private individuals to provide assistance in abortions. That the state is not obliged to fund abortions has been made explicitly clear in a more recent decision of the Court (*Maher v. Roe* and *Poelker v. Doe*, June 20, 1977). Nor does a doctor or a hospital by reason of the decision have any legal duty to provide abortion services. If they did, they would have a moral obligation to resist such an imposition.

One concern of the moral theologian is that people frequently tend to confuse legality with morality. The fact that abortion is legal in no way affects its morality. That something is done in private may put it beyond the civil law, but it does not make it morally right. There is an intimate connection between law and morality. The law may affirm an already existing moral duty, or it may even create one. But law does not cover the whole of morality. The fact that something is morally wrong does not mean that there must be a civil law against it. This is true even of ecclesiastical law; the Church does not attach an excommunication to every sin. Similarly, civil law does not penalize every immoral act. It penalizes only those acts that cause harm to the community. If wrongdoing does not harm the community, although it is still immoral, it is not a matter for penal legislation. Actually, in the past civil societies have even legalized practices, such as prostitution, which were clearly harmful to the community. The justification for such legislation was that it would be a lesser evil than prohibitive legislation which would drive the practice underground. Attempts have been made to justify legalized abortion on the same grounds, but the proponents of legalized abortion have never offered adequate proof of their position. There is no evidence, however, that this kind of reasoning was behind the Supreme Court decision. At any rate, one cannot judge abortion to be morally right because there is no law against it or because it has become legalized. Unfortunately, this is what many people who have no moral ·code of their own seem to do.

There are those who would justify abortion morally as the exercise of a woman's right over her body. They see prohibitive legislation as a violation of this right. The Supreme Court, fortunately, did not go this far. It ruled abortion legislation unconstitutional because it violated the woman's right to privacy, not her right to abortion. It says nothing about the morality of abortion. It says only that, as a private decision which does not pose a threat to the community, it should not be the subject of penal legislation. One may have good reasons for contesting this reasoning, but it does not confirm in any way a right to abortion. The basis in law for the right not to be penalized for abortion is not that the abortion is justifiable, but simply that the decision is private. There is no right to abortion based on a woman's right over her body. The fetus is not part of the woman's body. The woman would indeed have a right to self-defense (13:60,61) even against another person in unjust aggression, but theologians in the past who have tried to justify abortion on this basis have had great difficulty proving the fetus to be an unjust aggressor. Even if proved, it would apply only in those cases where the fetus was a threat to the life of the mother. It would certainly not be a basis for a general right to abortion. Moreover, even in unjust aggression theologians are reluctant to talk about a right to take the life of another; the right, rather, is one of self-defense.

A more recent decision of the Court rules that states may not impose on minors (under 18) the requirement that they get the consent of parents before an abortion (*Planned Parenthood v. Danforth*, July 1, 1976). The Court felt that this was a logical consequence of its 1973 decision. If an abortion is a private decision, the state has no right to set down any requirements (presumably for the good of the fetus) since this would constitute public interference. One who has misgivings about the original decision will not be any more at ease with this one. But, again, it should not be overinterpreted. It does not say that a parent may not try to keep a child from having an abortion. What it says is that a parental prohibition of abortion will have no legal support. A youngster, therefore, who went ahead and had an abortion without the permission or even against the wishes of her parents would not be prevented from having it by the civil law or penalized in any way. Viewed morally, the permission of a parent to have an abortion would be irrevelant; even with parental permission the abortion would be wrong. But if a child went ahead and had an abortion against the wishes of the parents, the offense would not only be against the fetus but a violation of the parent–child relationship as well: the parents have moral rights to obedience from their children.

[J. R. CONNERY]

ACOLYTE, MINISTRY OF

The ministry of acolyte was created when the minor order of acolyte was suppressed by the motu proprio, *Ministeria quaedam*, Aug. 15, 1972 (Paul VI Min-Quaedam II–IV). With the office of *reader it is one of the two universally existing forms of lay ministry. The ministry of acolyte is not limited to candidates for the Sacrament of Order but "may be committed to lay Christians" (ibid. III). Requirements for admission to the office of acolyte are: (1) the presentation of a petition freely made out and signed by the aspirant to the Ordinary (the bishop and, in clerical institutes, the major superior) who has the right to accept the petition; (2) a suitable age and special qualities to be determined by the episcopal conference; (3) a firm will to give faithful service to God and the Christian people. The ministry is conferred according to the liturgical rite of institution of acolytes found in the Roman Pontifical. "The acolyte is appointed in order to aid the deacon and to minister to the priest" (ibid. VI). His functions thus relate the acolyte to the altar; (1) he assists at the altar, by aiding the priest or deacon, at the Preparation of the Gifts in Mass; (2) assists deacons and priests at other liturgical celebrations; (3) aids in the distribution of Communion when necessary; (4) in extraordinary circumstances is entrusted with publicly exposing the Blessed Sacrament for adoration and afterward replacing it, "but not with blessing the people"; (5) may also "to the extent needed, take care of instructing other faithful who by temporary appointment assist the priest or deacon in liturgical celebrations by carrying the missal, cross, candles, etc., or by performing other such duties" (ibid.).

The exclusion of women from this ministry (ibid. VII) has had the effect of reserving this office to candidates for the Sacrament of Orders. In April 1975 the U.S. NCCB asked the Vatican to clarify what functions a girl or woman can perform at the altar in addition to reading the Scriptures and serving as an extraordinary or special minister of the Eucharist. The reply in September of that year was ambiguous and the query was sent back for clarification. The Congregation for Divine Worship simply reaffirmed that women might serve as (uninstituted) readers and as extraordinary ministers of the Eucharist. The question of institution has not been finally resolved.

Bibliography: Bishops' Committee on the Liturgy, *Study Text III, Ministries in the Church: Commentary on the Apostolic Letters of Pope Paul VI, "Ministeria quaedam" and "Ad pascendum"* (USCC Publ. Office, Washington, D.C. 1974). International Commission on English in the Liturgy, *Institution of Readers and Acolytes* (Washington, D.C. 1976). Origins 5 (1975) 370.

[J. A. GURRIERI]

ACTIVISM (SPIRITUAL LIFE)

In its widest acceptation activism is a doctrine or a policy that advocates action. An activist is one who makes use of action almost exclusively to attain his objective (1:99). If he is a radical, he usually welcomes confrontation, peaceful or otherwise, in achieving what he considers an urgent goal. As a philosophy activism teaches that the essential nature of the existent consists in its activities. In Catholic circles activism formerly denoted excessive apostolic activity exercised in the sacred ministry or among religious. Since Vatican II this negative aspect is no longer emphasized and a wider connotation is given to the term to embrace all spiritual activity, particularly in the apostolate concerning the modern world. One has only to read the Pastoral Constitution on the Church in the Modern World (*Gaudium et spes*, Dec. 7, 1965), or the Decree on the Apostolate of Lay People (*Apostolicam actuositatem*, Nov. 18, 1965), to be convinced of its new meaning. Although caution is still expressed regarding dangerous apostolic activity, a similar trend toward legitimate activism is seen in the Decree on the Appropriate Renewal of Religious Life (*Perfectae caritatis*, Oct. 28, 1965) and the Decree on the Ministry and Life of Priests (*Presbyterorum ordinis*, Dec. 7, 1965).

Historically activism, denoting excessive and even dangerous apostolic action, has undergone a rather turbulent development in the Church, beginning with the "philosophy of action" as advocated by Blondel (2:617) in modern times, which was considered suspect. Spiritual activism drew another warning from Pius XI who, communicating with the Father General of the Jesuits on June 16, 1944, used the phrase "heresy of action" for the first time; he had reference to the condemnation, Jan. 22, 1899 in *Testem benevolentiae*, a letter to Card. Gibbons, of Americanism (1:443). Active virtues were considered of greater importance than passive virtues and activity in the apostolate was evaluated in relation to its beneficent results rather than its supernatural values for the human being. Pius XII also referred to this excessive form of apostolic action in his encyclical *Menti nostrae* (ActApS 42 [1950] 677). Paul VI in an Audience of Sept. 8, 1976, once again alluded to the role of grace in the activity of man and the insufficiency of natural virtues only. "In the modern age," he said, "there has been the distinction between the passive and active virtues, as though the very distinction were enough automatically to discredit the former and exalt the latter." He goes on to say that external action only is not enough and that the necessity of prayer is an indispensable component of apostolic action ("Building the Church," *The Pope Speaks* 2, 4 [1976] 313). However that Pope Paul was not a reactionary concerning apostolic activity, especially regarding the laity, is evident from his apostolic exhortation, *Evangelii nuntiandi*, in which he shows that the primary and immediate task of lay persons is the evangelizing activity of the "vast and complicated world of politics, society and economics, as also the world of culture..." (Paul VI EvangNunt 70). This has been the tenor of the various *Synods of Bishops held in Rome after Vatican II where it has been emphasized that *evangelization and human progress are not only not opposed to each other but that they cannot be separated from each other.

See also APOSTOLIC SPIRITUALITY.

Bibliography: M. C. D'ARCY, *Humanism and Christianity* (Cleveland 1970). J. GREMILLION, *The Gospel of Peace and Justice* (New York 1976). G. GUTIERREZ, *Theology of Liberation* tr. and ed., C. Inda and J. Eagleson (Maryknoll, N.Y. 1973). W. A. KASCHMITTER, *The Spirituality of Vatican II* (Huntington, Ind. 1975). PAUL VI, *Fidelity and Relevance* (Boston 1970). L. J. PUTZ et al., eds., *Apostolic Dimensions of Religious Life* (Notre Dame, Ind. 1966). J. L. SEGUNDO, *The Liberation of Theology* (Maryknoll, N.Y. 1976).

[L. F. BACIGALUPO]

ACTIVISM, POLITICAL AND SOCIAL

Activism, seen today as a form of ministry, is a Christian presence in the world order and a committed response to the scriptural call to justice. Activism means rectifying society's oppressive conditions. It also means reconstructing society toward greater justice—creating alternatives. Religious activists assume their responsibility for history and participate in a long process that they hope will eventually achieve a more just society. Through the past 20 years, meeting people's basic needs and struggling against oppressive structures have led religious activists to a new consciousness of the need to eradicate the causes. At this point the activity often assumes a political dimension, because effecting causal change means facing national and international political power. The Church's social teachings reflect this new consciousness. Paul VI, in his "Call to Action" commemorating *Rerum novarum*'s 80th anniversary declared that the ultimate decision rests with political power. He urged churchpersons to become involved politically because "solidarity in action at this turning point in human history is a matter of urgency" (Paul VI Octog-Adven 5; cf. PopProgr 1, also *Gaudium et spes* 75).

Political structures are often unresponsive to the socio-economic systems that perpetuate an unjust distribution of resources, environmental deterioration, and the alienation, powerlessness, oppression, and marginalization of billions of people. Decision makers affirm these systems daily when they preserve the status quo, regardless of the consequences for the majority of people. Their decisions, although influenced by interests outside politics, occur in the political arena and thus necessitate organized political involvement to promote human and environmental development.

Political situations differ. Totalitarian systems require different tasks and methods. However, in those states allowing participation in the political process, the political activist's task falls into three basic categories: the people, the decision makers, and the legislative or political process.

More people need to become aware of the need to appropriate their rights, to sense their power in relation to the political process, to become an effective voice counterbalancing present power. Political activists engage the people and promote communal responsibility and solidarity. Finally, they organize for maximum political effectiveness. Meanwhile, decision makers need to explore the relationship between justice and politics, evidence concern for all people and assume their responsibility for promoting a more just society. Activists attend to this task while also affirming decision makers who already incorporate such insights into their political endeavors. In the political process, religious activists combat the sources of dehumanization by promoting concrete benefits for more people, such as adequate food, clothing, employment, health care, and participation in decisions that affect their lives. They also create legislative possibilities for new, alternative social and economic structures to insure more just relationships among people.

Effective political activity for justice has two essential elements: an adequate analysis of society's oppressive trends and contradictions, and creative options for reshaping present structures. Analyses help in preparing strategy and action. They also place political choices in a wider context, making it easier to choose, piece by piece, the injustices to be corrected with maximum effectiveness. Practicality about tactical approaches can mean emphasizing a lesser good on a short-range basis in order to achieve a long-range effect. Such choices, however, cannot compromise the ultimate goal of a more just society. Several guiding questions measure right choices. Will this approach enable more people to participate in decision making? Does it foster self-reliance and a cooperative ownership of resources? Will it effect changes in the social-economic system?

There are many ways of pursuing the social political task. Legislatively, activists run for elective office; work in the election campaigns of appropriate candidates; and form or join public-interest groups to inform and organize others, lobby decision makers, testify before governmental bodies, and submit legislation. In other areas, social-political activists initiate protests to influence public opinion and decision makers, seek appointment to administrative offices that affect policy and try to make the media responsive to society's injustice. Concern, cooperation, reflection, and openness characterize such social-political activity. Religious activists usually care about people, particularly the powerless and the underprivileged. They also realize the importance of cooperation with the people themselves and with persons and groups with similar agendas. Reciprocity characterizes their activity, engagement in a mutual struggle made possible only by sustained and coordinated effort. This spirit of cooperation often results in the formation of communities, people bonded by their social concern and committed to achieving more justice.

Most religious activists continually evaluate their activity as to goals, mode of operation, and results. Such reflection keeps them in touch with their vision and makes their activity more effective. It also ensures that their goals and methods mirror their values and the just world order they struggle to actualize. Finally, social-political activists recognize that greater justice is a long-range goal involving many uncertain decisions. Hence, they continually struggle to modify their activity in light of people's experience of injustice, the ever-changing social and political scene, and the consequences of their own actions.

See also JUSTICE AND PEACE, MINISTRY OF; NETWORK.

[V. SIXEAS]

ADVERTISING (MORAL ASPECT)

Vatican Council II did not treat in a formal way the moral aspects of advertising; the moral principles governing advertising, however, can be drawn from the Council's Decree on the Means of Social Communication (*Inter mirifica*, December 4, 1963, especially 3–12). In addition, the Council mandated that a pontifical commission for social communication be set up by the Holy See; on April 2, 1964, Pope Paul VI established The Pontifical Commission for the Means of Social Communication. This Commission issued on Jan. 29, 1971 a major pastoral instruction on the means of social communication (*Communio et progressio*, ActApS 63 [1971] 593–656), a section of which deals explicitly with advertising (59–62). More recently, May 22, 1977, Pope Paul VI in a written message took the occasion of the World Day of Social Communications to apply Christian principles to the field of advertising (ActApS 69 [1977] 333–336). For the remainder of this article *Communio et progressio* will be abbreviated to CP, and Pope Paul's address will be abbreviated to World Day.

In general, the Christian should understand the social value of advertising. "It tells the buyers of goods and services available. It thus encourages the widest dis-

tribution of products and in so doing it helps industry to develop and benefit the population" (CP 59). At the same time, advertising must never be considered immune from the moral law of God. Morality in advertising should be a primary concern of the advertising industry. "It is therefore desirable that advertisers make definite rules for themselves lest their sales methods affront human dignity or harm the community" (CP 60). In particular, the following moral principles apply in a special way to advertising: (1) *truthfulness*: "Advertising must respect the truth, taking into account accepted advertising conventions" (CP 59); (2) *respect for the dignity of the human person*: "Those forms of advertising which, without shame, exploit the sexual instincts simply to make money or which seek to penetrate into the subconscious recesses of the mind in a way that threatens the freedom of the individual ... must be shunned" (CP 60); or, to put it more positively, advertising must obey "the imperative requirement to respect the human person, his right-duty to make a responsible choice, his interior freedom ..." (World Day); (3) *social responsibility*: "Serious harm can be done if advertising and commercial pressure become so irresponsible that communities seek to rise from poverty to a reasonable standard of living in such a way as to seek this progress by satisfying wants that have been created artificially" (CP 61); or, in the words of Paul VI: "Advertising ... must take into account the common good, keep in mind the legitimate interests of others, and especially have due regard for the concrete circumstances of the integral development affecting the people to whom it addresses itself, for their cultural and economic environment, and for the level of education they have attained" (World Day).

The final point of moral concern, and one that Pope Paul considered very important, is the powerful influence that advertising exerts on the media of communication: "Advertising, moreover, takes on an ever growing importance, because in large part it finances the development of the communications media and uses them for its own purposes, directly and sometimes dangerously influencing their orientation and their freedom" (World Day). The essential freedom of the media must be safeguarded, by legislation if necessary.

Bibliography: English tr. of *Communio et progressio* in A. Flannery, ed., *Vatican Council II: The Conciliar and Postconciliar Documents* (Northport, N.Y. 1975). English translation of Pope Paul VI's message on advertising in OssRomEng May 19, 1977.

[D. L. LOWERY]

AFRICA, SOUTHERN

The countries included in this survey are: the Republic of South Africa (RSA); Namibia (South West Africa); Rhodesia (Zimbabwe); Swaziland; Lesotho; and Botswana. They embrace a vast area, more than 1 million square miles, with a population of about 28 million people. Catholics make up approximately 10 percent of that number. The gross statistics do not reflect the fundamental problem of much of the area, namely the pervasive racial segregation and discrimination by which whites have maintained domination in Africa, Rhodesia, and Namibia, despite their being a small percentage of the population of these nations. Swaziland, Lesotho, and Botswana are governed by black authorities, but are nonracist in their treatment of the white minorities. In all of them, the number of

Catholics continues to grow, although expatriate missionaries far exceed the small number of indigenous clergy and religious.

South Africa. The Catholic Church in the Republic of South Africa is organized into four archdioceses, nineteen dioceses, and three prefectures-apostolic. At present, there are 867 expatriate and 330 local born priests in South Africa. These 1,197 priests minister to a Catholic population of 1,844,270, giving an average of one priest for every 1,540 Catholics. About 80 percent of the priests are white, whereas about 80 percent of the lay Catholics are black. The total population of the country is about twenty-six million. There are about 4,000 sisters and 200 brothers in South Africa. Between them they run 325 primary schools, with 88,056 pupils, and 118 secondary schools. There are 337 sisters engaged in nursing.

The Republic of South Africa has for many years followed a policy commonly called *apartheid*, a term changed officially to "plural democracies." The policy's announced goal is the preservation of the cultural identity of each of the many "nations" which constitute the Republic. In 1977, a plan was announced which would create three parliaments: Coloured, Asian, and White. The majority of the nation's population, which is black, is to be distributed among nine "Homelands" which South Africa plans to make into Independent nations. This scheme would allot to the blacks, who constitute 71 percent of the population, 13 percent of the land. Two of these new nations have been created: Transkei (1976) and Boputhatswana (1977). Black people living outside the homelands are declared citizens of one of them according to their tribal ancestry; they cease to be citizens of South Africa itself and consequently have there only the status of migrant workers. The homeland scheme has failed to receive approbation or recognition from any nation aside from South Africa, being regarded as unjust, a denial of human rights, and a ruse to perpetuate white domination in South Africa.

World opinion was aroused to renewed vigorous denunciation of the South African government when in September 1977 Stephen Biko, a leader of the Black Consciousness Movement, died as a result of untended injuries received while he was in police custody. Following outcries of indignation, the government moved to suppress criticism within the country by jailing almost all black leaders except those appointed by the government itself, and by banning several influential white critics. (Banning-orders forbid, among other activities, speaking in public or writing for publication.) Among the imprisoned black leaders was Father Smangaliso Mkhatshwa, the acting secretary-general of the South African Catholic Bishops' Conference (SACBC). After four months of imprisonment, Mkhatshwa was released with some of the others who had been arrested in October, but was placed under severe restrictions as to his movements and activities.

The SACBC in its annual plenary meeting of February 1977 called for drastic changes in the organization of South African society to eliminate injustices and oppression. In three documents they addressed the critical situation, reform within the Church itself, and the problem of selective conscientious objection to military service. On racism they declared:

We again profess our conviction, so often repeated, that the only solution of our racial tensions consists in conceding full citizen and human rights to all persons in the Republic, not by choice on the false grounds of colour, but on the grounds of the common humanity of all men, taught by our Lord Jesus Christ. . . . It is clear that the Black people of the Republic have passed the point of no return and no temporary suppression by violence, only a just sharing of citizenship, can give hope of any safety for the children, Black or White, now growing up in the Republic, and prevent the horrors of civil war in the future (SACBC 584).

The bishops committed themselves "to give practical expression to the conviction that the Church's mission includes work for complete human liberation and to the teaching of 'Evangelii nuntiandi' that evangelization includes transforming the concrete structures that oppress people; and in the light of this, to strive that the Church be seen in solidarity with all those who work for the promotion of human dignity and the legitimate aspirations of oppressed people; on the side, therefore, of Black Consciousness, in regard both to those who promote it and those who suffer for it" (SACBC 583).

It seems clear that: (1) the Church in South Africa may be in for difficult days, since its announced policy is contrary to government policy and even illegal in several significant ways; and (2) there will be some conflict within the Church itself between the adherents of the Black Consciousness Movement (including many black priests) and white church authorities; this conflict will center around questions of tactics and confrontation with government authorities and others promoting a slower rate of change in race relations.

In April 1978, the Dutch Reformed Church of South Africa cut its ties with its "Mother Church," the Dutch Reformed Church of the Netherlands. The latter has been critical of South Africa's racial policies, while in South Africa the Church has been a principal supporter of the government. Members of the government have been predominately adherents of the Dutch Reformed Church. Branches of that Church are also organized for coloured (mixed ancestry) and black South Africans; these have been critical of the racial separation and discrimination which mark the official policy of the country.

Namibia (South-West Africa). This nation, which is in transition from dependency on the Republic of South Africa to independence, occupies about 318,000 square miles on the southwest coast of Africa, it is the size of Britain and France combined. Its new name, Namibia, is derived from the Namib Desert which stretches the length of its coast. In 1974, its population was estimated at 852,000: 753,000 Africans and Coloureds, 99,000 Europeans. The Catholic Church is not strong in Namibia, it counts only 4,000 whites, 118,000 non-Europeans. Ecclesiastically, it is divided into two vicariates-apostolic, Windhoek, the capital city, and Keetmanshoop in the south.

Namibia has had a turbulent and violent history since it became a German protectorate in 1884. In the years 1904–07, the German forces almost exterminated the Herero and Nama tribes, killing around 80,000 Africans in the aftermath of an uprising against the intruding colonialists. In 1919, the mandate was transferred from Germany to South Africa by the League of Nations. After the demise of the League, the United Nations assumed trusteeship, but this was not recognized by South Africa, which continued its occupation and control of Namibia. The UN continued to demand that South Africa withdraw and the demand was confirmed by a series of World Court rulings. In 1966, the UN General Assembly terminated South Africa's mandate and declared that Namibia is the direct responsibility of the UN. Legal and diplomatic efforts continue up to the present in various tactics designed to achieve independence and majority rule for the people of Namibia.

Meanwhile, the South West Africa Peoples' Organization (SWAPO) has been recognized by the UN as the sole authentic representative of the Namibian people. The validity of this attribution is open to some question, since SWAPO's strength is principally among the Ovambo people of the north and is not so great among the Herero, the other principal African group. The truth of the matter will become evident only when free and open political activity and elections are held. The South African Government in maintaining its possession and control of the territory has resorted to draconian emergency regulations: public meetings are prohibited without prior police permission; police may detain suspects indefinitely for interrogation; arrests, torture, and the death penalty have been commonly used to suppress opposition. South Africa has (1979) rejected a UN-supervised transition to Namibia's independence.

The Christian Churches stand at the center of the Namibian conflict. The Lutheran Churches in the country count a combined black congregation of over 300,000. Their leaders, along with Anglican and Catholic bishops, have repeatedly called for a change in South African policy and the restoration of freedom and human rights. Two Anglican bishops in succession have been expelled from the country because of their efforts on behalf of justice.

Because of its international status and the potential threat to the general peace of the area, Namibia is currently the object of serious efforts by the U.S. and other nations to achieve an independent government which would adequately and justly represent the various groups within the country without thereby perpetuating racialism and tribalism.

Botswana. Botswana is a nation of large area (230,000 sq. miles) and small population (630,000). Eighty percent of the people live along the eastern border, while the remainder of the country is the arid and semi-arid Kalahari Desert. Its government is a parliamentary democracy which permits the existence of opposition political parties. Commercial developments in Botswana operate in the Western, capitalistic model, while the tribal, communal system of property ownership prevails elsewhere. Botswana is a nonracial society, but is surrounded on all sides by territories in which white domination of the black majority has prevailed up to the present time: the Republic of South Africa, Rhodesia, and Namibia (South West Africa). It has one small contact with Namibia via a ferry across the Zambezi River at a point where the boundaries of four nations touch.

The Catholic Church in Botswana claims 21,000 adherents under a single bishop whose see is in Gaborone, the capital. Twenty-three priests, two religious brothers, fifty-one sisters, and thirty-one catechists work in the nation.

Although Botswana has great resources, both agricultural and mineral, these are barely developed. Consequently, its people are generally very poor. While the government of Botswana has committed itself firmly to the support of majority rule in South Africa, Namibia,

and Rhodesia, its economic dependence on them has made it impossible for relations to be cut. One of Botswana's principal exports is human labor: the men who leave to work in South Africa or Rhodesia and who send back some of their earnings for the support of the families left behind. Botswana's economic problems have been aggravated in recent years by the large number of refugees from Rhodesia and South Africa who have access across the long, unfortified frontiers. In the cases of some more important refugees, Botswana is merely a stopping-off point where air transportation to other, safer places can be reached. For thousands of others, Botswana is the place to stay and wait for improved conditions in the country from which the refugees have fled. International aid has met their needs to some extent, but the increasing number of clients and the delay in the arrival of aid is causing considerable suffering among the new arrivals.

Lesotho and Swaziland. Two small kingdoms survive in Southern Africa. The larger, Lesotho, embraces nearly 12,000 sq. miles and approximately 1 million people; the smaller, Swaziland, is only 6,700 sq. miles, with about 473,000 people. The presence of the Catholic Church is felt much more intensely in Lesotho, which is nearly 50 percent Catholic. There is an archbishop at Maseru, the capital, and three other bishops divide the rest of the nation. Swaziland, by contrast, counts only about 40,000 Catholics, less than 10 percent of the population. The entire country is a single diocese whose bishop lives in Manzini. All the bishops of the two nations are Africans.

Maintaining national unity has not been the major problem in these nations that it has been in almost every other African country. Each of them is inhabited almost exclusively by members of a single tribe: in Lesotho, the Basotho; in Swaziland, the Swazi. Lesotho has the problem, however, of economic survival and achieving some measure of economic independence, since it is relatively undeveloped. It is estimated that between 45–65 percent of the adult male labor force of Lesotho at any time is resident in South Africa, which surrounds the little nation completely. Swaziland, in contrast, exports little of its labor but a great deal of sugar, iron ore, wood pulp, asbestos, and fruit.

Both nations have maintained a nonracial policy which admits whites to residence and economic enterprise. Because of their intimate connection with South Africa, neither has permitted the organization of political groups aimed against that nation. The question of assisting political refugees from South Africa is a recurring one. With or without government cooperation, South African security police have occasionally captured fugitives who had made their way into Lesotho or Swaziland. Nevertheless, Lesotho is particularly suitable for escapes via international-airline flights not subject to the scrutiny or control of South African police.

The bishops of both countries are members of the South African Catholic Bishops' Conference and join in its efforts to bring about racial peace and justice in the whole region.

Rhodesia (Zimbabwe). It is extremely difficult to write anything about Rhodesia in the Autumn of 1978 which might still be valid six months or one year from that time. The political situation, which has many repercussions on the life of the Church, is in a state of flux; no one can predict with any certainty whether the nation is to be further torn by an intensified war or, on the other hand, to achieve peace and the prosperity which its resources would make possible.

Rhodesia is a medium-sized country, as African nations go: about 150,000 sq. miles, with a population of about 6,100,000 people. The racial imbalance is tremendous: 5,800,000 of those people are Africans; the remainder, some 300,000 are Europeans. The land is divided almost equally between the two groups.

The Catholic Church in Rhodesia numbers more than one-half million communicants, one archdiocese, four dioceses, and one prefecture-apostolic. Only one Ordinary, the archbishop of Salisbury, is African. The concern of the Catholic Church for issues of social justice in Rhodesia has been expressed over many years through the work of the Catholic Commission for Justice and Peace, an arm of the bishops' conference. The Commission's episcopal chairman, Bishop Donal Lamont, was expelled from the country in 1977 after his Rhodesian citizenship was withdrawn because of his criticism of the government's policies. The Commission has published *The Man in the Middle*: *Civil War in Rhodesia* (Origins 6 [1976] 267–272, excerpts) and *Rhodesia, The Propaganda War* aimed at countering the government's repeated accusations that the guerillas were "terrorists," torturing and killing innocent people. The Commission accumulated evidence, published in these booklets, that the same tactics were used by government security forces to repress its critics, even disguising government security personnel as guerillas. This tactic, unless exposed, has caused the guerillas to be blamed for inhuman treatment of villagers.

The settlement of the present civil war is complicated by tribal and personal antagonisms and ambitions. Rhodesia's arbitrarily drawn borders contain two broad linguistic groups, the Ndebele and the Shona, and several minor tribal groups. This fact makes political unity difficult to obtain, and the resulting conflict is not simply black against white.

At the time of this writing, an "internal settlement" has been reached between the white Prime Minister Ian Smith and three black leaders: Bishop Abel Muzorewa, the Reverend Ndabaningi Sithole, and Chief Jeremiah Chirau. These four men constitute an executive office during a transition period which will end when general elections are held and a new constitution becomes operative. Not included in the transition period are the two men who control the guerilla forces fighting against the Ian Smith regime: Joshua Nkomo and Robert Mugabe. Their absence and their promise to continue guerilla warfare threatens the survival of the "internal settlement."

During this protracted period of civil war, the work of the Church in Rhodesia has been severely hampered and, in some areas, brought to a standstill. Missionaries in the villages, generally speaking, have been on good terms with the guerilla forces, willy-nilly supplying them with food and medical supplies. Nevertheless, some missions have been attacked and personal injury, including death, inflicted on mission personnel. While the government attributes such acts to the communistic indoctrination received by the guerillas during their training in Mozambique, it is suspected, and in some cases documented, that the attacks were perpetrated by government forces disguised as guerillas. Due to the danger from both sides in the conflict, some missions have been deserted by their staffs until peace is restored.

Bibliography: SACBC, Statement, Origins 6 (1977) 581, 583–585. Rhodesian Catholic Bishops' Conference, "Pastoral Guidelines for a Turbulent Rhodesia," Origins 7 (1978) 477–480.

Appendix. The following is a list of name-changes for countries and/or ecclesiastical jurisdictions within countries; former place names are in parentheses, with references to earlier *New Catholic Encyclopedia* entries. Dates of creation of new dioceses or other changes are given opposite ecclesiastical jurisdictions.

ANGOLA, PEOPLE'S REPUBLIC OF (1:540)
    Benguela
    Bie (Silva Porto)
    Huambo (Nova Lisboa)   Diocese: 1970
    Lubango   Archdiocese: 1977
    Nejeira (Pereira de Eca)   Diocese: 1975
    Novo Redondo   Diocese: 1975
    Saurino (Henrique de Cervalho)   Diocese: 1975
    Serpa Pinto   Diocese: 1975
    Uige (Carmona-São Salvador)

BENIN, PEOPLE'S REPUBLIC OF (to 1975, Dahomey; 4:612)

BOTSWANA, REPUBLIC OF (to 1966, Bechuanaland; 2:212)
    Gaborone   Diocese: 1970

BURUNDI, REPUBLIC OF (2:906)

CENTRAL AFRICAN EMPIRE (to 1976, Central African Republic; 3:399)
    Bambari   Diocese: 1965
    Bouar   Diocese: 1978

CHAD, REPUBLIC OF (3:410)
    N'Djamena (Fort Lamy)   Archdiocese: 1973
    Sarh (Fort Archambault)

CONGO, PEOPLE'S REPUBLIC OF (to 1969, Congo, Republic of [Brazzaville] 4:165)

DJIBOUTI, REPUBLIC OF (to 1977, French Territory of Afars & Issas)
    Djibouti

EQUATORIAL GUINEA, REPUBLIC OF,
    Bata (Vicariate Apostolic of Rio Muni; 12:510)   Diocese: 1966
    Malabo (St. Isabel)   Diocese: 1974

GABON (6:234)
    Franceville   Diocese: 1974
    Oyem   Diocese: 1969

(THE) GAMBIA
    Banjul (Bathurst)

GHANA, REPUBLIC OF (6:460)
    Keta-He   Diocese: 1975
    Sekondi-Takoradi   Diocese: 1969
    Sunyani   Diocese: 1973

GUINEA-BISSAU, REPUBLIC OF
    Bissau   Diocese: 1977

IVORY COAST, REPUBLIC OF
    Korhogo   Diocese: 1971
    Man   Diocese: 1968

KENYA, REPUBLIC OF (8:160)
    Garissa   Prefecture Apostolic: 1978
    Kakamega   Diocese: 1978
    Lodwar   Diocese: 1978
    Machakos   Diocese: 1969
    Marsabit   Diocese: 1964
    Mombasa (Mombasa-Zanzibar)   Diocese: 1964
    Nakuru   Diocese: 1968
    Ngong   Diocese: 1978

LESOTHO, KINGDOM OF (to 1968, Basutoland; 2:162)
    Mohale's Hoek   Diocese: 1977

MADAGASCAR, DEMOCRATIC REPUBLIC OF (to 1975, Malagasy; 9:102)
    Ihosy   Diocese: 1967
    Mananjary   Diocese: 1968

MALAWI, REPUBLIC OF (9:108)
    Chiawana   Diocese: 1965
    Mangochi (Prefecture Apostolic of Fort Johnston)   Diocese: 1973

MALI, REPUBLIC OF (9:113)
    Mopti   Diocese: 1964
    San   Diocese: 1964
    Sikasso   Diocese: 1963

MOZAMBIQUE, PEOPLE'S REPUBLIC OF (10:57)
    Lichinga (Vila Cabral)
    Maputo (Lourenço Marques; 8:1033)
    Penba (Porto Amelia)
    Xai-Xai (João Belo)   Diocese: 1970

NAMIBIA (to 1966, South-West Africa; 13:485)

NIGERIA, FEDERAL REPUBLIC OF (10:466)
    Abakaliki   Diocese: 1973
    Awka   Diocese: 1977
    Ekiti (to 1972, Ado-Ekiti)   Diocese: 1972
    Idah   Prefecture Apostolic: 1968
    Ijebu-Ode   Diocese: 1969
    Illorin   Diocese: 1969
    Issele-Unu   Diocese: 1973
    Lokoja   Diocese: 1965
    Maiduguri   Diocese: 1966
    Minna   Diocese: 1973
    Sokoto   Diocese: 1964

RWANDA, REPUBLIC OF (12:765)
Kabgayi — Diocese, reduced from archdiocese: 1976
Kibungo — Diocese: 1968
Kigali — Diocese: 1976

SENEGAL, REPUBLIC OF (13:81)
Kaolack — Diocese: 1965
Saint-Louis of Senegal — Diocese: 1966
Tambacounda — Prefecture apostolic: 1970
Thies — Diocese: 1969

SIERRA LEONE, REPUBLIC OF (12:203)
Freetown & Bo — Archdiocese: 1970
Kenema — Diocese: 1970

SOMALIA (13:424)
Mogadiscio — Diocese: 1975

SOUTH AFRICA, REPUBLIC OF (13:477)
De Aar — Diocese: 1967
Klerksdorp (Prefecture Apostolic of Western Transvaal) — Diocese: 1978
Louis Trichardt-Tzaneen — Diocese: 1972

SUDAN, DEMOCRATIC REPUBLIC OF (13:773)
El Obeid — Diocese: 1974
Juba — Archdiocese: 1974
Khartoum — Archdiocese: 1974
Malakal — Diocese: 1974
Rumbek — Diocese: 1974
Tombora — Diocese: 1974
Wau — Diocese: 1974

TANZANIA, UNITED REPUBLIC OF (Tanganyika; 13:933)
Mahenge — Diocese: 1964
Mtwara (Abbacy *nullius* of Ndanga) — Diocese: 1972
Njombe — Diocese: 1968
Same — Diocese: 1978
Singida — Diocese: 1972
Songea (Abbacy *nullius* of Peramiho) — Diocese: 1969
Sumbawanga (Karema) — Diocese: 1969
Zanzibar & Pemba — Apostolic Administration: 1964

UGANDA, REPUBLIC OF (14:362)
Holma — Diocese: 1965
Jinja — Diocese: 1966
Kabale — Diocese: 1966
Kampala (succeeded Rubaga; 12:695) — Archdiocese: 1966
Lira — Diocese: 1968
Moroto — Diocese: 1965

UPPER VOLTA, REPUBLIC OF (14:474)
Diebougou — Diocese: 1968
Fada N'Gourma — Diocese: 1964
Kaya — Diocese: 1969
Nouna-Debougou — Diocese: 1975

ZAIRE, REPUBLIC OF (Democratic Republic of the Congo; Congo, Republic of [Léopoldville] 4:166)
Budjala — Diocese: 1964
Kananga (to 1972, Luluabourg; 8:1076)
Kinshasha (to 1966, Léopoldville; 8:664) — Diocese, reduced from archdiocese: 1966
Kinsangani (to 1966, Stanleyville; 13:642)
Kole — Diocese: 1967
Kolwezi — Diocese: 1971
Lubumbashi (to 1966, Elizabethville) — Archdiocese: 1959
Luiza — Diocese: 1967
Mbandaka-Bikoro (to 1966, Coquilhatville; 4:317) — Archdiocese: 1975
Mbuji-Mayi — Diocese: 1966
Mweka — Diocese: 1964

ZAMBIA, REPUBLIC OF (14:1110)
    Chipata (to 1968, Fort Jameson)
    Kasama
    Mansa (to 1967, Fort Rosebery)
    Mbala (to 1967, Abercorn)
    Ndola
    Solwezi

                                  Archdiocese: 1967

ZIMBABWE (to 1979, Rhodesia; 12:463)
    Sinoia

                                  Diocese: 1959
                                  Diocese: 1976

                                  Prefecture Apostolic: 1973

                                          [R. E. LAMBERT]

AFRICAN CHRISTIANITY

One hundred years ago the place of Christianity in Africa was extremely limited. The ancient Coptic and Ethiopian Churches survived in the Northeast but both suffered from isolation and intense traditionalism. Neither made any impact upon the rest of Africa. Elsewhere there were various settler communities and missionary endeavors, Catholic and Protestant, along the coast, but their future was far from secure and they left the greater part of the interior quite untouched. In the West and the South a genuinely African Protestant Christianity could indeed be detected. Its origins in Sierra Leone were not even missionary, dating as they did from the return of North American exiles (former slaves). Between Freetown and the Niger Delta a self-aware, articulate little network of churches had developed, led by men like Bishop Samuel Ajayi Crowther and James, "Holy", Johnson, both Anglicans. It remained a tiny rather Westernized elite, hardly considerable enough to make its impact between an increasingly numerous, white-missionary force, determined to keep the ecclesiastical reins firmly in its own hands, and the millions of the interior.

Development of the Mission Churches. From the mid-1870s there was a rapid multiplication of missions away from the coast, to be quickly followed by the colonial division of the continent. By 1900 Africa had been parcelled out politically by Britain, France, Germany, Portugal, and Belgium, and it was rapidly being divided ecclesiastically in an even more intricate manner by a mass of missionary societies of all Christian denominations. There were, nevertheless, many considerable stretches of inland Africa where almost no mission began work until well after World War I. This was particularly the case in the Sudanic belt where Islam was already fairly strongly entrenched and the colonial powers were reluctant to allow Western missionaries to penetrate.

By this time the chosen instruments of missionary growth were the school and the hospital. Through them the Churches both made a major contribution to the modernization of Africa and found tools for an increasingly massive evangelization. The progressive African had little alternative in the pursuit of advancement to entering the mission school with its dual stress upon literacy and church membership. A number of tribal societies were tending by the 1930s to take on a markedly Christian character—the Yoruba, the Igbo, the Baganda, the Bahaya, the Tutsi of Rwanda-Burundi, among others. Christianity went with the impact of European power, trade, and culture, but this impact took a wide variety of forms. If it consolidated the power and self-confidence of the Baganda and the Tutsi, it overturned the world of the Zulu, the Bakongo, and the Shona. Many other peoples were still showing relatively slight interest in the whole process, for instance the Sukuma or the Masai of Eastern Africa. Among some of the more Christianized religious conversion could soon be followed by bitter reaction and a firmly massive withdrawal from the mission Churches (particularly Protestant) into independent Churches (*see* AFRICAN INDEPENDENT CHURCH MOVEMENT). A major phenomenon among the Zulu, the Kikuyu, the Yoruba, and the Shona, the independent Church phenomenon, however hardly appeared, or if it did, hardly endured, in Uganda, Tanganyika, Rwanda-Burundi, and elsewhere.

Nevertheless, the mission Churches were showing themselves with few exceptions decidedly slow in the training of an ordained ministry and still more in the promotion of black clergy to senior positions. The Catholic Vicariate (later Diocese) of Masaka, Uganda, established with a wholly black clergy in 1939 under Msgr. Joseph Kiwanuka long remained very much an exception. Whether or not it took the form of independent Churches and open schism, almost everywhere by the 1950s there was a growing tension within the main Churches between white-missionary leadership and the quickly multiplying black membership. This tension was a natural reflection of the wider movement for political independence. It could be argued that the mission Churches were rescued from a highly critical situation by the coming of that independence to most of black Africa around 1960.

Africanization. The Churches mostly responded quickly enough to the new situation (or even anticipated it a bit) by the appointment of senior African ecclesiastics. Thus in the Catholic Church by 1962 there were more than a dozen newly appointed black archbishops able to usher in a new era, that of "Church" rather than "Mission." Missionaries did not, however, withdraw to any large extent. Indeed there were more of them in Africa in 1970 than there had been in 1960 or at any previous date. Most of the less conspicuous Catholic dioceses even continued to be led by expatriate bishops for quite a few years. Nevertheless the decisive shift in leadership was quite unmistakable by 1970. The shortage of local priests was such that almost nowhere did local bishops show any desire for foreign missionaries to withdraw and the tensions common in the 1950s were often remarkably replaced by fraternal collaboration. This has become still more evident as the Churches have come under increasing political pressure in the troubled atmosphere of the 1970s.

It was sometimes suggested before the coming of political independence that as Christianity entered black Africa in close collaboration with colonialism, it would also go out with the ending of colonialism, or at least much decline. Hitherto at least this has in no way proved to be the case. On the contrary, the growth of

African Christianity both numerically and in maturity over the last twenty years has been remarkable. The giants of Christian Africa are Zaire and Nigeria, with Tanzania, Uganda, Kenya, Ethiopia, and Ghana to back them up. Exact statistics are quite unattainable but while a total of 25 million could be reasonable for 1950, one near 100 million might be the best estimate for 1975. Roughly half of these may be Roman Catholics, the other half including the Ethiopian Orthodox, some ten million members of independent Churches, and a strong representation of almost every Protestant tradition (particularly Anglican, Lutheran, Methodist, Presbyterian, and Baptist).

The numerical growth of the ordained ministry has also been considerable and there has been a particularly large increase in the total number of Catholic major seminarians—from 1,600 in 1960 to 3,600 in 1975. This has appeared particularly striking at a time when in most parts of the world the number of seminarians has greatly declined. Nevertheless the rise in absolute numbers of the ordained remains wholly inadequate to the need. Three-quarters of the Catholic priests in black Africa are still expatriates, but their number is now falling steadily on account both of political pressures and a lack of vocations in the old sending countries. If the annual number of black ordinations has risen from a little over one hundred in the early 1960s to a little under three hundred by the late 1970s, that must be seen in a context of well over 300 dioceses. The rise, furthermore, has been predominantly in relatively few dioceses (most notably the Igbo parts of eastern Nigeria and some areas of Tanzania and Uganda). Well over two hundred dioceses still have hardly a handful of local priests and some none at all. The priest/people ratio in black Africa has been getting very rapidly worse in these years. In many places today it is something like one priest to 8,000 Catholics, worse than that of many parts of Latin America. With present policies there is absolutely no likelihood of this altering.

Basic Christian Communities. In these circumstances it is inevitable that the Catholic Church in rural Africa must go forward with a very low level of priestly ministry. Most village churches are fortunate if visited briefly by a priest once or twice a year. The staple ministry is provided instead by a catechist, probably married, and, quite probably, a local council of Christians exercising collective responsibility. For this sort of "basic Christian community" the priest is an outsider and very possibly almost an irrelevance. Indeed so many active Christians have never been married in church or are otherwise irregularly married and, therefore, ineligible for Communion that the basic community is often not and could not be a Eucharistic community. While many people have urged the importance of rectifying this pattern of things and restoring Mass and priesthood to the center of local church life by the ordination of at least some of the better trained catechists, and some episcopates have asked for permission to do so, such proposals have been steadily rejected by Rome (see CATECHISTS, MISSIONARY).

In practice the position is often not so different in other Churches despite their less rigid rules. The insistence of a relatively high level of professional training for the clergy and the problem of providing an adequate salary subsequently have tended to restrict the numbers of the ordained. In theory all the main Churches are led by professionally trained, male clergy; in practice in the villages where the heart of Christian life is to be found leadership is predominantly unprofessional, lay, and frequently female. In this the shape of a small congregation, Catholic or Anglican, may be not dissimilar to that of an independent Church.

Problems of the African Churches. Whether at grass-roots level or at that of the professional leadership, the Churches in Africa today are having to cope with three main types of problem: institutional, cultural, and political. The first has already been discussed—how to maintain and develop a viable structure for the Church in very poor societies, with a large and quickly growing membership, with few professional clergy, and an unretainable past tradition of dependence on foreign manpower and money.

Cultural Problems. The second is how to relate Christian life to the cultural world of its members. Far too little was done about this in the past. Traditional African cultures were complex, varied, and greatly different from anything familiar to Western missionaries. There was a widespread tendency on the part of the latter to condemn customs almost indiscriminately as diabolical and unclean, though this tendency was probably stronger among evangelical Protestants than among Catholics. This judgment largely derived from ignorance of the religious beliefs and symbols, the marriage customs, and the social organization of the peoples they were endeavoring to evangelize. This rather uncomprehending and rigid condemnation was frequently carried across to the older African clergy, unwillingly to depart from missionary norms but also painfully aware of the existential divide in social and moral practice between African tradition and missionary Christianity. Today this sharp divide is being challenged by such academic African theologians as John Mbiti and Bolaji Idowu, who argue instead for a profound religious and moral continuity between African traditions and Christianity. Inevitably there is some over-simplification here as well as a rejection of the rather puritanical model of Christianity asserted by missionaries as the only acceptable one. There is also some reluctance on the part of black church leadership to accept the conclusions of the scholars.

The issue of polygamy is theoretically a key one. An important and respected element in the marriage system of most traditional African societies, it was strongly condemned by nearly all missionaries so that insistence upon monogamy has often seemed little less than a mark of the Church. This missionary condemnation (one, of course, in line with the mind of the home Church) has been strongly criticized by many modern scholars, white as well as black, as not biblically based and as a sheer failure to understand African culture. Theoretically well-founded as such criticism may be, it may appear to have relatively little practical significance today. Articulate Christian women are profoundly unwilling to go back on the Church's stand against polygamy, which they see as a symbol of sexual inequality. And most bishops agree with them. Pastoral concessions to the individual are one thing; an altering of public teaching another. Moreover stable polygamy, fully entered into under customary law, is less common today than an irresponsible and temporary polygamy of the rich, which is not to be sanctioned in Africa any more than anywhere else. It could be that the theologians arguing today for cultural comprehension are fighting the battles of the 19th century at the risk of blindness to those of the 20th.

In practice while the emergence of academic "African theology" is a very necessary part of the Church's coming of age, the search for African Christian "authenticity" at this level may prove of secondary significance—the academics are too few in number and too far removed from the contemporary needs of the rural community. The ethos of the two is so different. Nevertheless polygamy remains a reality at the village level. The Christian polygamist is a common phenomenon and he may well be a congregational leader. What is most important in African Christianity is often what is least adequately recorded: the emergence of a vast "village" Christianity, a symbiosis of beliefs and practices from many sources in which spirit-possession, the fear of witches, polygamy, and the moral obligations inherent in an extended family cohere with biblical monotheism, a passion for Baptism, Christian devotional texts, and the structural relationships of a small congregation proud of its simple little church. While ecclesiastical leadership is almost bound to regret much in this development in so far as it has time to notice it, there is very little it can do about it. The vitality of African Christianity is coupled with an absence of effective control from the top.

Political Problems. Partly the absence of control from the top is the consequence of increasing political uncertainties. Church schools were largely taken over by governments around 1970 but in some cases this was at first more formal than real, for a good working cooperation remained between the two parties. Such cooperation became increasingly problematical as the 1970s advanced. Excellent relations remained in some countries, notably Kenya, Tanzania, and Zambia. Julius Nyerere particularly, a profoundly Christian thinker, developed in Tanzania a policy of *Ujamaa*, pacific village socialism, with which church leaders could cooperate most actively. Elsewhere relations often grew less amicable. Harassment might make it difficult for bishops even to meet or to travel freely round their dioceses. Archbishop Tchidimbo of Conakry was imprisoned in 1970 and for many years thereafter. Seventeen Hutu priests were executed without trial in Burundi in the fearful massacres of 1972. The Anglican Archbishop Luwum of Kampala, Uganda, was murdered in February 1977, as was Cardinal Bayenda of Brazzaville. The list could be easily extended. The increasingly tyrannical character of some governments, the Marxist fervor of others were very different things from the rather benign approach of most of the leaders of the immediately post-independence period. The instability of the situation and of the policies of many regimes has forced church leaders to limit themselves often enough to a more purely religious message coupled with a month-to-month concentration on institutional survival.

The effects of political instability and revolutionary radicalization are felt not only in the institutional field but also in the cultural. The "African theology" of the 1960s made sense within a world of middle-class, post-colonial prosperity which could afford to look back nostalgically on the precolonial past. To confront ruthless tyranny very different theologies may be needed. Certainly revolutionary Marxism is out to sweep away African tradition as well as the relics of colonialism. The

"Black theology" which has developed in South Africa, with its far greater awareness of the sin and agony of the contemporary situation and of the redeeming power of Christ, may be the theology of the future for other parts of the continent as well. Yet it is impossible to generalize or to predict. Nowhere in the world is Christianity more alive than in Africa today, but this vitality partakes of the diversity and instability characteristic of every side of the life of the continent.

Bibliography: C. G. BAËTA, ed., *Christianity in Tropical Africa* (London 1968). D. BARRETT, ed., *African Initiatives in Religion* (Nairobi 1971). C. P. GROVES, *The Planting of Christianity in Africa*, 4v. (London 1948–58). A HASTINGS, *Christian Marriage in Africa* (London 1973); *African Christianity* (London 1976); *A History of African Christianity 1950–1975* (Cambridge 1979). E. FASHOLÉ-LUKE et al., eds., *Christianity in Independent Africa* (London 1978). M. MURPHREE, *Christianity and the Shona* (London 1969). B. A. PAUW, *Christianity and Xhosa Tradition* (Cape Town 1975). T. O. RANGER and J. WELLER, eds., *Themes in the Christian History of Central Africa* (London 1975). D. REECK, *Deep Mende* (Leiden 1976). A. SHORTER, *African Culture and the Christian Church* (London 1973). J. V. TAYLOR, *The Growth of the Church in Buganda* (London 1958).

[A. HASTINGS]

AFRICAN INDEPENDENT CHURCH MOVEMENT

The term "African Independent Church" refers to religious bodies that have been formed in Africa by Africans themselves. Either they have originated as a splinter-group from a Mission Church, or they are a new creation. In any case, they are independent of Mission Churches and worldwide communions.

Extent and Origins. Independent Churches are found in all parts of sub-Saharan Africa, but they are especially numerous in West Africa, Southern Africa, and in one country of East Africa, Kenya. In some countries attempts have been made by Independent Churches to form an association, e.g. in South Africa there has been the South African Independent Churches Association. In at least one case an Independent Church has been admitted to the World Council of Churches after careful examination of its doctrine and church practice; this is an Independent Church in Zaïre, the Church of Jesus Christ on Earth through the Prophet Simon Kimbangu. Other cases are under consideration. The word "Church" is used to designate these movements in preference to the pejorative term "sect," but it must not be assumed that all these Churches are Christian. Some are "Old Testament Churches" which make little or no reference to Jesus Christ.

African Independent Churches usually owe a great deal to the personality and charisma of their founders. In some cases, membership is largely determined by a master-disciple relationship that derives from African tradition. At other times these Churches are proprietary, with a dynastic leadership patterned on traditional chiefship. Frequently African Independent Churches are identified with particular ethnic groups and owe certain aspects of their teaching to African traditional religion and cosmology. Independent Churches offer their members an intense experience of community and this is often what attracts their adherents. The older Mission Churches seem too monolithic and impersonal; their structures are complex and frightening, like those of secular governments; they do not offer a basic community experience at the local level. The Independent Churches, on the other hand, do offer their members such an experience and this local church community reinforces or substitutes for the family community, which is no longer equipped to integrate the individual into wider society. The church community does this. The bonds it creates are of a personal nature; it helps people on the margins of modern life to rise above the inadequacies of their own education and environment. It compensates for frustrations, offering an ideological brotherhood and a system of mutual help both spiritual and material. It permeates every facet of human existence and offers solutions that are acceptable to people used to living in small communities, whereas the larger church organizations are unfamiliar and unadapted. Two factors account for the success of the Independent Churches: their size which is small enough to ensure that all members are active, yet large enough to be viable; and their totalitarian character or sense of wholeness, offering the individual a new conception of the world.

However, there are several drawbacks connected with these movements. They tend to create a parallel society, cutting themselves off visibly from the rest of the world by peculiarities of dress and behaviour. They form a world within the world. Very often they tend to be particularist and anti-ecumenical and to be biblically and liturgically conservative or fundamentalist. Through their emphasis on healing, they encourage people to expect immediate cures and miraculous answers to prayer. Some of these Churches are strongly opposed to the use of hospital medicines. On the whole they neglect or misunderstand the Eucharist and the paschal mystery which it celebrates, although they place great emphasis on Baptism, often as a healing ritual.

Typology of African Independent Churches. The first serious student of the African Independent Churches was a Lutheran Bishop, Bengt Sundkler. From his research experience in South Africa Sundkler proposed a dual classification of Independent Churches as Ethiopian and Zionist types. The former stressed the African or Black character of the Church, while the latter represented a spiritual or Pentecostal category, led by an African prophet, evoking a new Israel or a new Jerusalem. This original classification has stimulated many other scholars to create typologies that rest on a variety of criteria. Probably the most useful, as well as the most theological, typology is that of Harold W. Turner. Turner distinguishes three main types: Christian, Hebraist, and Neo-Traditional.

The Christian type of Independent Church is one that closely resembles the Mission Churches in doctrine and practice. Its differences are mainly due to sociological or historical causes. The African Methodist Church (in South Africa), the Church of Simon Kimbangu (already mentioned), and perhaps the Aladura Church of the Lord in Nigeria are examples. In some cases such a Church is reabsorbed by a Mission Church. This was the case of the Ugandan African Greek Orthodox Church, a splinter group of the Anglican Church of Uganda which is now a recognized part of the Greek Orthodox Church.

The Hebraist type is one that is mainly inspired by the Old Testament, finding in the life and history of ancient Israel many parallels with the experience of rural-dwelling Africans. Such Churches have more in common with Judaism than with Christianity. Turner distinguishes two emphases: the Israelite tendency that strongly rejects magic and idolatry, while going in for joyful and ecstatic dancing; and the Judaistic tendency which emphasizes repentance, suffering, asceticism, and legal prohibitions. Both types practise healing, spirit-possession, and speaking with tongues in varying degrees and believe that their founder is a prophet or mouthpiece of God. Such Churches are the Zionist Church of Isaiah Shembe in South Africa and the African Israel Church in Nineveh of Zakoo Kivuli in Kenya.

Neo-Traditional Churches are those movements which are really new forms of traditional African religion mixed with Christian elements; they differ only in their conscious attitude towards official Christianity. Some are revivalist, bearing no grudges and offering a straightforward return to traditional sources, reinterpreted frequently in a Christian way. Others are nativistic movements, racially and ethnically conscious, which propose to purge the community of foreign religious elements. This may not, however, prevent them from exhibiting an idealistic, post-Christian interpretation of the religion they are attempting to purify and revive. Finally, there are the frankly syncretist movements that incorporate elements from Christianity and African tradition without much discernment or even integration. Examples of these movements are: *Dini ya Misambwa* (Religion of the Ancestors) of Elijah Masinde in Kenya, and the *Maria Legio* (sic) Church of Gaudencia Aoko and Simeo Ondeto, also of Kenya. This Church is an amalgam of Catholic practices—particularly those of the Legion of Mary—and *Juogi* Spirit beliefs of the Luo people. The Catholic lay apostolate movement, the Legion of Mary, with its own tightly structured organization and exclusive paraliturgy, has more than once unwittingly become a model for syncretist splinter groups. Another example is that of the *Bacwezi* movement in Western Uganda which combines Legionary piety with a revival of hero spirits, traditional to the people of Ankole.

Relationship with the Mission Churches. Although certain types of social structure favor the spontaneous growth of Independent Churches, most of these movements owe their origin to an unconscious failure on the part of the Mission Churches. They are the creation of people who are not yet at home in the modern world, people who find their old world-view unattractive, but who have not yet grasped the new, Christian outlook. They are also the creation of people who have been deeply wounded by Christian bigotry, intolerance, and aggressiveness. The dissemination of Bible translations has enabled them to go themselves to the sources and to make their own comparisons and contrasts between the religion of the missionaries and the religion they find in Scripture. Women have suffered the most or feel the most need for the kind of support offered by the Independent Churches. This explains the preponderance of women members. These movements are—in Victor Turner's terminology—"liminal movements" which correspond to a felt need in a time of upheaval and change. People transpose their frustrations onto a mystical plane and await deliverance.

For those Churches which separated from older, Mission bodies, there was what David B. Barrett has called a "flashpoint," an immediate cause, often a trivial dispute, which set a discontented convert or catechumen on the path of becoming the prophet of a new religion.

In some cases a Mission Movement has taken a benevolent attitude towards the establishment of new, independent communities. This has been true of some of the Pentecostal Churches and David M. Beckmann has put forward the interesting suggestion that the Spiritual Churches of Ghana and other parts of West Africa may be a return, in Christian guise, of African spirit-possession traditions that crossed the Atlantic with the slave trade.

Marshall W. Murphree has criticized those who see the Churches in a given society as being essentially in competition or conflict. He also rightly repudiates what he calls the "layer approach," which sees the Independent Churches as the outcome of different experiences that have overlaid one another in a time sequence. He advocates a dialectical approach that allows one to see that the different Churches, Mission and Independent, all influence one another informally and serve the varied needs of the whole community. Harold Turner detects an increase, since the 1960s, in the more formal relationships between the Independent Churches and the Missions. This has happened, for example, in West Africa where the independent movement is older and better established and where earlier antagonisms have been forgotten. In general, members of Mission Churches take one of three positions towards the African Independent Churches. The Optimistic Position is that of David B. Barrett, who sees these movements as mainly a Christian phenomenon, even an "incipient Reformation." He predicts a rapid increase which will eclipse membership of the Mission Churches by the end of the century. What may be called the Pessimistic Position is that of G. C. Oosthuizen who regards these Independent Churches as "Post-Christian" ethnocentric folk religions that are adulterating the message of the Gospel. Harold W. Turner takes a Realistic Position, which detects a growth of Christian insight in these movements and holds that they will draw nearer to official Christianity as people in Africa become more sophisticated. In the meantime, Mission Churches can learn many lessons from them about the incarnation of the Christian message in African cultures.

Independent Churches and Nationalism. In many countries of Africa those excluded from political activity can only make their comments and express their political aspirations through a church organization. African Independent Churches were focal points for rallying opposition to colonial governments, but after independence African governments have been extremely wary of them. Not a few of them have been banned as subversive, or potentially subversive. Church organization offers a training ground for those who want to enter public or political life. A great deal of current historical research is directed to the Independent Churches and the role of their leaders in nationalist movements. Examples are legion and these are merely a selection: John Chilembwe in Malawi; Tomo Nyirenda in Zambia and, more recently, Alice Lenshina and her Lumpa Church; Simon Kimbangu in Zaïre; Kinjikitile and the *Maji-Maji* movement in Tanzania; Reuben Spartas and the 1948–50 riots in Uganda; Elijah Masinde in Kenya. African Independent Churches are often essentially movements of protest—not so much against the Mission Churches, as against the prevailing social order.

Bibliography: D. B. BARRETT, *Schism and Renewal in Africa* (Nairobi 1968). D. M. BECKMANN, *Eden Revival, Spiritual Churches in Ghana* (St. Louis 1975). M.-L. MARTIN, *Kimbangu, an African Church* (London 1975). M. W. MURPHREE, *Christianity and the Shona* (London 1969). G. OOSTHUIZEN, *Post-Christianity in Africa* (Grand Rapids, Mich. 1968). T. RANGER and J. WELLER, ed., *Themes in the Christian History of Central Africa* (London 1975). B. SUNDKLER, *Bantu Prophets in South Africa* (Oxford 1961). H. W. TURNER, *African Independent Church: Aladura Church of the Lord* (2v., Oxford 1967); "A Typology for African Religious Movements," *Journal of Religion in Africa*, 1, fasc. 1 (1967) 1–34. F. B. WELBOURN and A. B. OGOT, *A Place to Feel at Home* (Oxford 1966).

[A. SHORTER]

AGED, CARE OF

A line from Robert Browning, "Grow old along with me, the best is yet to be" is frequently quoted in writings about the elderly. As the aging population increases, however, more and more people are finding that their later years are becoming the most difficult from the standpoint of finances, physical infirmities, and social interaction.

Statistics and Initiatives. Figures released by the U.S. Department of Health, Education and Welfare reveal that one in every nine persons in the U.S., in 1976, was 65 years of age or over, a total of 22.9 million people. In addition, the studies indicated that this figure was increasing at the rate of 1,510 per day so that if the current birth- and death-rate remain constant, by the year 2000 the over-65 population of the country will total 32 million or 12.2 percent of the total expected population of 262 million. This marked shift in population has an impact on the work force, the economy, politics, family life, and the general pattern of society.

The government, alert to the fact that the older population is becoming a political force and a social issue, convened the 1971 White House Conference on Aging. Professional organizations such as the American Association of Retired Persons, the largest organization in the world working for the elderly, and such volunteer organizations as the National Council on Aging are championing the cause of the nation's elderly in the areas of age-discrimination, housing, health care, inadequate income, and social neglect. The Church, too, always aware of the needs of all confided to its care, is giving greater attention to the elderly. The Fathers at Vatican Council II voiced this concern for the elderly: "The livelihood and the human dignity of those especially who are in particularly difficult circumstances because of illness or old age should be safeguarded" (*Gaudium et spes* 66; cf. *Apostolicam actuositatem* 11).

A profile of the elderly of the typical Catholic parish would reveal that those who today are among the seniors are those who grew up in a pre-Vatican II Church, with its heavy emphasis on authority, who probably attended parochial school, whose social life was probably centered on such parish activities as the sodality, altar-boy society, children of Mary. A number were immigrants who found in their parish a familiar haven amid the struggle for identity and acceptance.

Problems of the Aging. Statistical studies in gerontology vary in their findings because of numerous factors, but in general it would seem that the plight of the elderly American citizen is beset with problems brought on by inflation, the vagaries of declining health, and the loneliness associated with outliving family and friends. When the Social Security System was instituted in 1935 it was thought that the nation no longer would have an older, retired population without income. However, Social Security benefits did not keep pace with the inflated cost of living and poverty has become the lot of many old people.

Since problems of inadequate housing, medical services, nutrition, and opportunity for suitable recreation flow from insufficient income, the financial plight of the elderly must be a primary concern of those who would improve the living conditions of the nation's elderly. Their needs fall within John XXIII's statement of human rights:

> Every man has the right to life, to bodily integrity, and to the means which are suitable for the proper development of life; these are primarily food, clothing, shelter, rest, medical care, and finally the necessary social services. Therefore, a human being also has the right to security in cases of sickness, inability to work, widowhood, old age, unemployment, or in any other case in which he is deprived of the means of subsistence through no fault of his own (John XXIII PacTerr 11; cf. NCCB, *Society and the Aged* 10).

Old people, living on fixed incomes, suffer from inflation more than the general population; the continuing higher cost of fuel is but one example. Economists can quickly identify the correlation overall between rising prices and the problems of the elderly. Increased property taxes and operating costs for landlords are factors affecting the elderly as they are no longer able to maintain their own homes or lack sufficient income to pay rent or food bills. The same domino effect is evident in the rise of health-care costs that force the aged to cut back on health maintenance, in spite of private or government-sponsored, health-insurance programs. Worse than the indignities foisted on them by financial pressures is the elderly's suffering from loneliness. Because Americans are living longer than ever before, a new situation is arising where the middle-aged are becoming responsible not only for their own children, but also for the maintenance of elderly parents; it is even not uncommon to find elderly in the over 60-years bracket with one or both parents still living. In many instances the advanced elderly, whether at home or in a nursing home, feel abandoned by their relatives because no one keeps in close touch with them.

The Parish and Ministry to the Aged. The accusation of being out of touch with the elderly might also be leveled at the Church, because past efforts concentrated on youth. The Church has always addressed the needs of its people as it perceived those needs. When the American Church was an immigrant Church and when American society shifted from being agrarian to being industrial, there was a great need for orphanages, hospitals, and schools. Now an over-65 population of 22 million is a challenge calling for the Church's attention to needs that are going unmet. In the past needs were served through institutions; the emphasis today has to take a new approach since 95 per cent of those 65 and over are living in the community, 81 per cent being ambulatory. The Harris Poll has shown that the aged want opportunities to stay within the mainstream of society, to share in solving their own and society's problems; they also want to speak for themselves.

On May 5, 1976 the NCCB issued a statement, *Society and the Aged*, in which the bishops set forth both the rights of the elderly and the obligation of the Church, the family, and individuals to respect and enhance the dignity of all elderly. "This requires a rethinking of personal attitudes in the light of Gospel values. Our first task is to restore to the elderly the dignity and sense of worth which they deserve" (*Society and the Aged* 8). The hierarchy and such national agencies as the National Conference of *Catholic Charities (Commission on Aging), are in a unique position to play the role of advocate by helping to establish, develop, and influence national policy towards the old. In a basically impersonal and complex society the effectiveness of programs can be blunted. Essential is the development of strategies for humanizing service-delivery systems and for putting them within the effective reach of those to be served. Within the structure of the Church the parish is admirably adapted to the required task. Parish resources include its being of limited size and central in the life cycle. The elderly should be comfortable in the familiar parish setting.

But the parish does not automatically or ordinarily consist of a homogeneous group. Every parish has to conduct its own needs-assessment survey. This will mean a door-to-door inquiry about the elderly, their housing, health, nutrition, transportation, social activities, spiritual needs. Once the needs of its elderly are identified, the parish, rather than itself trying to answer the needs, becomes the intermediary between its old people and existing public and private service agencies. If the parish survey uncovers, for example, a large number of elderly needing hearing or sight tests, then the parish could arrange an examination day by the local public-health agency in the parish hall. Similarly the parish could ask for the services of a public-health nurse and/or a public-health aide to relieve a family's burden in caring for their frail elderly. Volunteers from the parish could assist the elderly to fill out eligibility forms for government services, which by their bureaucratic complexity frequently are daunting to old people.

Other specific services—transportation, friendly visits or phone calls, meals on wheels, day-care centers—all fall within the parish potential. But the needs of the elderly are not limited to food, clothing, and shelter; psychological, spiritual, and intellectual needs must also be met. Old age is a time of opportunity for growth and development, not just a time for decline and loss. Some people have aged successfully; their "secret" must be studied and communicated to others. New and creative ways of meeting needs must involve the elderly themselves; it is useless to set up magnificent programs, masterpieces, perhaps, of social ingenuity, and then try to force the elderly to fit the programs.

One of the great advantages of working with the elderly on a parish level is that it offers many types of intergenerational exposure. The young can get to know, to serve, and to learn from the old; the old can find joy in the buoyancy and hope of the young. Henri Nouwen writes: "When we allow our world to be divided into young, middle-aged, and old people, each calling for a specialized approach, then we are taking the real care out of caring, since the development and growth of men and women take place, first of all, by creative interaction among the generations" (Nouwen 111). A parish can offer that type of care. "Caring is the way to the other by which a healing community becomes possible" (ibid.).

Bibliography: V. L. BENGTSON, *The Social Psychology of Aging* (New York 1973). R. N. BUTLER, *Why Survive? Being Old in America* (New York 1975). R. H. DAVIS, ed., *Aging: Prospects and Issues* (Univ. of Southern California 1973). L. HARRIS AND ASSOCIATES, *The Myth and Reality of Aging in America* (Washington, D.C. 1975). V. JOSEPH, *The*

Parish and Ministry to the Aging (National Conference of Catholic Charities 1977). R. A. KALISH, *Late Adulthood: Perspectives of Human Development* (Monterey, Cal. 1975). C. S. KART and B. MANARD, *Aging in America* (New York 1976). D. C. KIMMEL, *Adulthood and Aging* (New York 1974). M. MERCEDES, *Serving Older Persons* (Washington, D.C. 1970). National Conference of Catholic Bishops, *Society and the Aged* (Washington, D.C. 1976). B. L. NEUGARTEN, *Middle Age and Aging* (Chicago 1968). H. NOUWEN and W. J. GAFFNEY, *Aging* (New York 1974). J. H. SCHULZ, *The Economics of Aging* (Belmont, Cal. 1976).

[M. J. FLYNN]

AGNOSTICISM

Agnosticism was addressed by Vatican Council II as it stands in the technological culture of today. "No doubt, today's progress can foster an exclusive emphasis on observable data, and an agnosticism about everything else . . . [including] the intimate meaning of things . . . [and] higher realities" (*Gaudium et spes* 57).

Claims. The Vatican II Fathers are not alone in noting a connection between science/technology and the decline in belief. In the preface to *Humanist Manifestos I and II* (1973), philosopher Paul Kurtz asks, "What more pressing need than to recognize in this critical age of modern science and technology that, if no deity will save us, we must save ourselves?" *Manifesto II* goes on to say: "In our judgment, the dogmas and myths of traditional religions do not . . . pass the tests of scientific evidence" (16).

A respected social-science study of beliefs and values in the U.S., reflecting popular opinion in the period just after Vatican Council II, concludes: "Two values— *salvation* and *forgiving*—stand out above all the others as the most distinctively Christian values [especially for devout churchgoers]; [whereas] the average non-believer's value profile . . . place[s] a higher value than do Christians on *equality . . . wisdom*, and on instrumental values emphasizing personal competence—being *capable, independent, intellectual,* and *logical* [elsewhere identified as the values of academics, and particularly of scientists] (Rokeach 82; cf. 128, 146).

There are two issues here. One is the accuracy of these claims; Andrew Greeley of the National Opinion Research Center (the agency that actually conducted the Rokeach survey) has concluded from his reading of the data that at least for Roman Catholics belief does not decline with an increase in education, income, or social status (Greeley). The second issue is what believers in the supernatural, especially leaders of institutional religion, ought to do about a climate of unbelief in technological culture.

The Evidence. The evidence for a link between scientific/technological rationality and agnosticism is tenuous at best. It does seem plausible and proponents of a "religion without revelation" (Julian Huxley) or such advocates of a "desupernaturalized" religion as the Unitarians predict that as culture becomes more "post-industrial" or "postmodern" religion will become more privatized, nonsupernatural, and noninstitutional (Glock and Stark, 287–288). Notable, also, for their lack of religion are several imaginative depictions of future, scientific cultures—Anthony Burgess, *A Clockwork Orange*, George Orwell, *1984*, B. F. Skinner, *Walden Two*, Kurt Vonnegut, *Player Piano*.

However, as theologian Krister Stendhal warned the Commission on the Year 2000, "It is unrealistic to believe that 'institutional religion' will fade away. . . . It is easier to make a case for the opposite. Christianity has changed immensely during its history, as have other religions; they will continue to do so, but the church and its counterparts have a basic continuity" (Bell 219).

Academic social scientists might well be projecting their values onto society generally, a danger that is sometimes recognized: "College professors, who typically place a high value on being *logical* . . . seem in their formulation of consistency and balance theories to have projected their own values . . . onto others" (Rokeach 78). The most extreme example is the so-called post-industrial thesis—best defended by John Kenneth Galbraith—according to which modern technological society is or will be increasingly run by technical experts. This theory has not gone unchallenged, especially by critics who see it as a perhaps unconscious power play by the very expert proponents in favor of their own thesis.

Another caveat is called for. Many of the reported studies of scientific unbelief seem to reflect mainly the values of academic scientists, whereas the value profile of the total technical community probably much more closely approaches that of the general culture; in any case, the technical community includes many church-goers.

Assessment of the Issues. Agnosticism is not atheism (see 1:205) and both are to be distinguished from what might be called "practicing agnosticism," i.e., a way of life in which, without its being explicitly denied, religion ceases to be practically important in the everyday lives of large numbers of people. The phenomenon is not at all peculiar to Christianity (cf. Eliade 43, 46, and passim on the loss of reverence for "sky gods" in favor of more mundane spirits which protect everyday life). Some of what is taken to be the nonbelieving attitude of technological culture may reflect an "agnosticism-of-indifference" as much as it does any agnosticism based on "scientific" values.

If it is assumed that there are relatively basic value differences that divide devout believers from nonbelievers professing a science/technology-based humanism, and if, more importantly, it is assumed that expert "postindustrialism" characterizes the belief system of ever more influential classes in "postmodern" culture, what is the "believing community," especially the Christian community, to do? Part of the task will, of course, be the quite traditional exhortation of the lax, whether science-minded or not, to greater devotion. But this is by no means the only or even the major evangelization challenge. No devout believing Christian is going to concede easily that belief in the supernatural is incompatible with the scientific method, with technical competence, or even with a culture typified by science and technology. The Fathers at Vatican II urged the faithful to "blend modern science and its theories . . . with Christian morality and doctrine," to let "their religious practice and morality . . . keep pace with their scientific knowledge and with an ever-advancing technology" (*Gaudium et spes* 62). Nonetheless, if the value-measuring social scientists are correct—if there is a fairly basic split between the value systems of devout believers and those of science-inclined nonbelievers—then the task of evangelizing important and influential segments of contemporary and future society is likely to be a challenge of the highest order.

Bibliography: D. BELL, ed., *Toward the Year 2000* (Boston 1967).

M. ELIADE, *Patterns in Comparative Religion*, tr. R. SHEED (New York 1958). J. K. GALBRAITH, *Economics and the Public Purpose* (Boston 1973). C. Y. GLOCK and R. R. STARK, *Religion and Society in Tension* (Chicago 1965). A. GREELEY, *The American Catholic* (New York 1977). M. ROKEACH, *The Nature of Human Values* (New York 1973).

[P. T. DURBIN]

ALL SOULS' DAY

The remembrance of the dead continues to be celebrated on Nov. 2 according to the new Roman Missal and Calendar but is no longer transferred to another day if it falls on Sunday (1:319). The new Missal also contains three Mass formularies, but the rubrics that each priest may offer three Masses and that the first formulary should be used for the principal Mass are omitted. (The custom of offering three Masses is still observed by some, but not all priests.) While in the second formulary the former antiphons *Requiem aeternam* are retained, all the other antiphons and the prayers express clearly the paschal character of Christian death as demanded by Vatican II's Constitution on the Sacred Liturgy (*Sacrosanctum Concilium* 81). The *sequence *Dies irae* and the final Absolution (*Libera me*) are deleted. No special readings are given. Instead, the celebrant may choose freely from the 45 readings from the Old and New Testaments given in the Sacramentary for Masses for the Dead. The color of the vestments may be black or violet, with permission given to episcopal conferences to add or substitute others according to local customs. Recitation or singing of psalms and appropriate hymns is encouraged. The final blessing, formerly omitted, is restored and in the U.S. the Sacramentary even contains a *Solemn Blessing for each of the formularies. The former special rubrics concerning omission of the kissing of the gospel book, the blessing of water, and kneeling at prayer need no longer be observed. The present liturgical celebration of All Souls' Day reminds us of the Church's teaching that those whom we commemorate are already assured of eternal glory even if they still need our prayers.

[A. CORNIDES]

ALTAR

The revised order for the dedication of *churches and altars according to the Roman rite (May 29, 1977) sums up contemporary doctrine concerning the liturgical altar. The altar is a symbol of Christ the Lord, who is the living altar of the heavenly temple (Heb 4.14; 13.10). Its function is as "the table of the sacrifice and of the paschal banquet." It is defined as the "center of the thanksgiving which is achieved through the Eucharist, to which all the other rites of the Church are in some way directed." An older tradition is restored: new churches should have only one altar, to signify the one Savior Jesus and the one Eucharist of the Church—although there may be a second altar in a separate chapel for weekday celebrations.

The Roman document, which is part of the Roman *Pontifical, repeats the 1969 norm that the altar (rather than the lectern or the Eucharistic *tabernacle) should occupy a position in the church building which is truly central and to which the attention of the entire assembly is spontaneously directed. Thus in newer churches the altar is brought forward, ideally located at the crossing, close to the congregation; it is the place where the bishop or priest (facing the congregation) and other ministers meet the assembled body of the faithful. In the restoration of older churches, if it is not desirable to remove completely the altar near the east wall of the sanctuary area, it has often been possible to retain its reredos or other altar piece, while changing its appearance so that the altar near the congregation is the central focus of the church (cf GenInstrRomMiss 259-270).

Other developments in the Roman liturgy have affected the design of altars. With the change of focus of the Liturgy of the Word—from the altar to the lectern or pulpit—the epistle and gospel ends of an oblong altar have become obsolete. This in turn has stimulated the square design of altars, smaller in dimensions, but still in proportion to the size of the church building and the sanctuary area. Such altars appropriately have the appearance of the table for the sacrificial meal (rather than looking like counters) and generally are elevated only to the extent needed for them to be the center of the assembly's attention.

See also FURNISHINGS, SACRED.

Bibliography: Bishops' Committee on the Liturgy, *Environment and Art in Catholic Worship* (Washington, D.C. 1978) 71–73.

[F. R. MCMANUS]

ALTAR BREADS

Ancient tradition, still maintained in the Eastern Churches, was to use ordinary leavened bread for Eucharist (2:779). Unleavened wafer-bread ("hosts") came into use in the West from the mid-9th century for pragmatic reasons: they kept fresh longer, clergy were prevented from using scraps of bread, and the laity were less likely to regard the Sacrament as ordinary bread.

The Roman Missal (April 6, 1969; revised, March 26, 1970) keeps the tradition of wheat bread and the Latin use of unleavened bread (GenInstrRomMissal 282) but insists that "the nature of the sign demands that the material for the eucharistic celebration appear as actual food" (ibid. 283). It is to be made so that it can be broken and shared, though in the traditional round shape; hosts are tolerated when the number of communicants or other pastoral needs require them (ibid. 283). The "Third Instruction on the Correct Implementation of the Constitution on the Liturgy" (Sept. 5, 1970; ActApS 62 [1970] 698–699) adds that the genuineness of the sign applies more to color, taste, and thickness than to shape (5).

There has been some experimentation—mid-Eastern bread, larger and thicker whole-wheat wafers, large concelebration hosts, baking by members of a parish—but little widespread change or enforcement of the legislation. Convenience, insensitivity to symbol, an inadequate sense of the sacred and of reverence, and the continued (though forbidden) practice of reserving large quantities of consecrated bread have militated against change.

Bibliography: R. M. WOOLLEY, *The Bread of the Eucharist* (London 1913). Liturgical Commission, Diocese of Providence, "Altar Bread Today," *Worship* 49 (1975) 360–365.

[J. DALLEN]

AMERICAN BOARD OF CATHOLIC MISSIONS (ABCM)

After Vatican Council II and the restructuring of the episcopal conference, ABCM (1:398) was made a standing committee of the National Conference of Catholic Bishops (NCCB). Following a subsequent reorganization of NCCB reducing the number of standing committees, ABCM ceased to be a standing committee, but NCCB continued to administer ABCM as in the past. In April, 1972 ABCM was reconstituted as a standing committee of NCCB. The seven-member committee, each member serving for three years, was chaired in 1976 and 1977 by Most Reverend John J. Sullivan, Bishop of Kansas City—St. Joseph, Missouri. Recent meetings have included exchanges of information and coordination with the Catholic Church Extension Society and the Commission for Catholic Missions Among the Colored People and Indians. In 1977 ABCM allocated diocesan grants of $2.4 million and special grants of $1.08 million, for a total of some $3.5 million.

[T. D. HINTON]

AMERICAN INDIAN CATHOLIC MISSIONS

Since Vatican Council II the Catholic missionary approach with Native American tribes has experienced both reevaluation and revitalization in light of renewed statement of church teaching and heightened Native American self-expression. Historical material on Catholic Indian Missions in the United States includes brief references in both the *Catholic Encyclopedia* and the *New Catholic Encyclopedia* (1:402).

Church Efforts. While individual Catholic Indian missions continue their ministry with the many distinctive Native American tribes in the local areas, greater emphasis is being placed on cooperative missionary activity within the churches of various tribes, as well as on diocesan, regional, and national cooperation. The *Bureau of Catholic Indian Missions continues to serve the United States Catholic missions; for legislative awareness in response to inquiries and needs of those in the field, its location in Washington, D.C. is ideal.

In May 1977, the United States Catholic Conference issued a statement by the American bishops on American Indians. The statement shares reflections on the relationship of the Catholic Church in the U.S. with American Indian peoples. The document treats the areas of faith and cultures in the Church; justice in the American experience; American Indians and the role of the Church.

In a paper, *A New Beginning*, prepared by the Social Action/Social Welfare Department of the Minnesota Catholic Conference, the Catholic bishops of Minnesota share their understanding of the relationship of the Church with Native American people. The Archdiocese of St. Paul-Minneapolis has opened a Diocesan Office of Native American Ministry and issued a Statement of Purpose and Function of the Archdiocesan American Indian Worship Committee.

Native American tribes are given financial assistance through various national, parish collections, through the Commission of Catholic Missions among the Colored and Indian People, and the Campaign for Human Development.

Religious orders continue to serve the missions by providing personnel, support, and, in a number of instances, joint action to secure justice within the various tribes of Native American people. Such activity is exemplified by the Jesuit Office of Social Ministries

and the Justice and Peace Center in Milwaukee, Wisconsin.

Some former Catholic mission schools are becoming tribally-operated, contract schools conducted by Native American school boards. Consequently, a number of missions are pioneering different approaches to cathechesis among families. A number of Catholic Indian missions are initiating or continuing dialogues between the religious leaders within the tribe and the missionary personnel. The dialogue taking place at St. Francis Mission, St. Francis, South Dakota, is perhaps a model in this regard. Permanent diaconate programs are beginning to be developed in a number of dioceses. Presently, the most defined and developed of these programs in relation to the Native American tribes can be found at the Sioux Spiritual Center in Plainsview, South Dakota.

Native American Self-Expression in the Church. The 1970s have seen several manifestations of the growing development and beginnings of self-expression of Native Americans within the Church. At the Eucharistic Congress of 1976 in Philadelphia, one of the liturgies was celebrated by a Native American priest and incorporated the liturgical expressions of several tribes. At the Detroit *Call to Action Conference there were Native American participants who brought forward their special concerns. In November 1977, a group of Catholic Native American people gathered in Marty, S.D. to establish the Federation of Catholic Indian Leaders. In February 1978, Regis College in Denver sponsored a Symposium on Plains Indian Witness to Religious Living. The 38th Annual Tekakwitha Conference was held at St. Martin's Academy in Rapid City, S.D. The annual conference is presently being revitalized to provide continuity of approach in evangelization in the areas of ministry, catechesis, liturgy, evangelical liberation, and family life. Native American Catholic Congresses, especially among the various Sioux bands, continue to bring Catholic Native Americans together for a few days of prayer and sharing.

The Native American Native Religious (NANR) formed as an association of 54 native religious priests, brothers, sisters, and permanent deacons. Forty-one associate members comprising primarily priests and religious who are not Native American, participate in the annual conference. The organization encourages development of religious life among Native American religious through shared prayer, support, and understanding by means of its annual meeting.

Religion and/or cultural research centers have been organized to deepen understanding between the various cultures. Some of the more prominent examples of such efforts include the American Indian Cultural Research Center at Blue Cloud Abbey, Marvin, S.D.; Religion Research Center at St. Labre's Mission in Ashland, Mont.; St. Stephen's Center, Wind River, Wy.; Holy Rosary at Pine Ridge, S.D. There are also a number of urban centers, such as the Chief Seattle Club in Seattle, Wash. and those found in Minneapolis, Minn. and Rapid City, S.D. These urban centers assist Native Americans living in or moving to cities. The *Marriage Encounter Movement, to help make good marriages better, is gaining acceptance among Native Americans, especially when they are led by Native American couples.

The missionary radio station, KNOM, in Nome,

Alaska, broadcasts to most of Alaska and parts of Russia. On the air 18 hours a day, the station is manned mainly by volunteers. Another station, KINI, is owned by St. Francis Mission in St. Francis, S.D. and will include programs of music, including Lakota music, local and national news, and sports. Much Native American participation is planned in the operation of this station. Mission publications, many of which are in conjunction with fund-raising efforts, include: *Red Cloud Country, Wind River Rendezvous, Padre's Trail, Morning Star People.* The *Wabanaki Alliance*, a newspaper, is published by the Division of Indian Services, an agency of the Diocesan Human Relations Services, Inc., of Maine.

Bibliography: Bureau of Catholic Indian Missions, Archives. NCCB, "The Church and American Indians," Origins 6 (1977) 766–768.

[P. A. LENZ]

ANGLICAN ORDERS

Pope Leo XIII on Sept. 18, 1896, in the Bull *Apostolicae curae*, declared that defects of both form and intention in the Anglican Ordinal of 1552 were so serious that ordinations performed according to the Anglican rite have been and are completely null and void. Pope Leo's condemnation was not simply a quibble over the fine points of the Church's sacramental discipline, but rather the Roman Catholic Church's insistence on two important matters of faith. (1) Holy Orders do not originate solely from the organizational maturation of the postapostolic Christian communities; bishops and priests exercise a commission which derives from the commission which Christ himself gave to his apostles. (2) The Eucharist is not only a source of grace and unity for Christ's followers, but a sacramental action by which the Church is associated with Christ's unique sacrifice on Calvary. The Anglican/Roman Catholic International Commission (ARCIC) claimed in 1973 that, in view of the agreement which the 18-member Commission jointly appointed by the pope and the archbishop of Canterbury had reached on essential matters concerning the doctrine of ordained ministry, the judgment expressed in *Apostolicae curae* was "put . . . in a new context." ARCIC found that the Anglican Communion and the Roman Catholic Church agreed on the two underlying matters of faith that were of such concern to Pope Leo XIII in 1896. The first matter of faith is explicitly treated in the *Agreed Statement on Ministry and Ordination*:

> Ordination denotes entry into this apostolic and God-given ministry, which serves and signifies the unity of the local churches in themselves and with one another. Every individual act of ordination is therefore an expression of the continuing apostolicity and catholicity of the whole Church. Just as the original apostles did not choose themselves but were chosen and commissioned by Jesus, so those who are ordained are called by Christ in the Church and through the Church (14).

The 1972 *Agreed Statement on Eucharistic Doctrine* deals with the second important matter of faith:

> Christ's redeeming death and resurrection took place once and for all in history. Christ's death on the cross, the culmination of his whole life of obedience, was the one, perfect and sufficient sacrifice for the sins of the world. There can be no repetition of or addition to what was accomplished once for all by Christ. Any attempt to express a nexus between the sacrifice of Christ and the eucharist must not obscure this fundamental fact of the Christian faith. Yet God has given the eucharist to his church as a means through which the atoning work of Christ on the cross is proclaimed and made effective in the life of the church. The notion of *memorial* as understood in the passover celebration at the time of Christ—i.e. the making effective in the present of an event in the past— has opened the way to a clearer

understanding of the relationship between Christ's sacrifice and the eucharist. The eucharistic memorial is no mere calling to mind of a past event or its significance, but the church's effectual proclamation of God's mighty acts. Christ instituted the eucharist as a memorial (*anamnesis*) of the totality of God's reconciling action in him. In the eucharistic prayer the church continues to make a perpetual memorial of Christ's death, and his members, united with God and one another, give thanks for all his mercies, entreat the benefits of his passion on behalf of the whole church, participate in these benefits and enter into the movement of his self-offering (5).

Despite this agreement between the Roman Catholic Church and the Anglican Communion, the Roman Catholic Church has not changed its canonical discipline in regard to the invalidity of Anglican Orders.

Bibliography: ARCIC, *The Three Agreed Statements* (SPCK and CTS, London 1978). P. F. BRADSHAW, *The Anglican Ordinal* (SPCK, London 1971). F. CLARK, "Les ordinations anglicanes, problème oecuménique" Greg 45 (1964) 60–93. E. P. ECHLIN, *The Story of Anglican Ministry* (Slough, England 1974). J. J. HUGHES, *Absolutely Null and Utterly Void* (Washington, D.C. 1968); *Stewards of the Lord: A Reappraisal of Anglican Orders* (London 1970). C. F. SCHREINER, *The Christian Priesthood of the Anglican Communion and Apostolicae Curae* (Pelham Manor, N.Y. 1974). E. YARNOLD, *Anglican Orders: A Way Forward?* (CTS, London 1977).

[H. J. RYAN]

ANGLICAN/ROMAN CATHOLIC CONSULTATION (U.S.)

The Anglican/Roman Catholic Consultation in the United States (ARC) is the official group for dialogue on the national level to foster *organic union between the Roman Catholic Church and the Episcopal Church. ARC is jointly sponsored by and reports to the Bishops' Committee on Ecumenical and Interreligious Affairs (BCEIA) of the National Conference of Catholic Bishops (NCCB) and the Joint Committee (of the House of Bishops and the House of Clerical and Lay Deputies of the General convention) on Ecumenical Relations of the Episcopal Church (JCER). The Consultation has met 22 times since its initial meeting at Washington, D.C. in June 1965. Each meeting lasts for a three-day period of shared prayer and theological research. ARC has fourteen members drawn from the clergy and laity of both Churches. The seven Roman Catholic members are appointed by the BCEIA and the seven Episcopalian members are appointed for three year terms by the JCER. The current ARC cochairmen are the Most Reverend Raymond Lessard, Roman Catholic Bishop of Savannah and the Right Reverend Arthur Vogel, Episcopal Bishop of West Missouri. The Secretaries of ARC are Rev. J. Peter Sheehan of BCEIA and Dr. Peter Day, the Ecumenical Officer of the Episcopal Church. ARC has published agreements on Eucharistic Sacrifice, pastoral programs, theological methodology, and the purpose and nature of the Church. The Consultation has also released a summary of its work which was published in January 1978 and entitled "After Twelve Years".

Bibliography: ARC, "After Twelve Years," Origins 7 (1978) 467–473. BCEIA and JCER, *Documents on Anglican Roman Catholic Relations* I, II, and III (USCC Publ. Office, Washington, D.C. 1972, 1973, and 1976). H. J. RYAN, and J. R. WRIGHT, eds., *Episcopalians and Roman Catholics Can They Ever Get Together?* (Denville, N.J. 1972). A. A. VOGEL, "In the United States," in B. and M. PAWLEY, eds., *Rome and Canterbury through Four Centuries* (New York 1975) 364–387.

[H. J. RYAN]

ANGLICAN/ROMAN CATHOLIC INTERNATIONAL COMMISSION (ARCIC)

The Anglican-Roman Catholic International Commission (ARCIC) is a group of clerical and lay scholars from the Roman Catholic Church and the Anglican Communion, its 18 members were jointly appointed in 1969 by the pope and the archbishop of Canterbury to promote and coordinate the *organic union of the Roman Catholic Church and the twenty-three autonomous Churches making up the Anglican Communion. In 1970 ARCIC met in January at Windsor Castle and during October at Venice. Since then ARCIC has met annually for a ten-day period of shared prayer and research: in 1971 ARCIC again met at Windsor; 1972 at Gazzada, Italy; 1973 at Canterbury; 1974 at Grottaferrata, Italy; 1975 at Oxford; 1976 at Venice; 1977 at Chichester; and in 1978 for the third time at Venice.

For the Roman Catholic Church the work of ARCIC is received by the Vatican Secretariat for Promoting Christian Unity and sent to the national episcopal conferences. For the Anglican Communion the Archbishop of Canterbury's Counsellors on Foreign Relations receive the work of ARCIC, which is then forwarded to the Anglican Consultative Council. The cochairmen of ARCIC are the Right Rev. Alan C. Clark, Roman Catholic Bishop of East Anglia in England, and the Most Rev. Harry R. McAdoo, Archbishop of Dublin in the Church of Ireland. The members of ARCIC come from Europe, North America, Africa, and Australia.

ARCIC had a 10-member Subcommission on the Theology of Marriage and its Application to Mixed Marriages. Under the joint chairmanship of the Most Rev. Ernest L. Unterkoefler, Roman Catholic Bishop of Charleston, S.C., and the Most Reverend George O. Simms, Archbishop of Armagh and Primate of All Ireland in the Church of Ireland, the Subcommission began its work in 1967. With the aid of thirteen consultants the Subcommission completed its work on June 27, 1975. The *Final Report* of the Subcommission was approved by ARCIC at Oxford in August 1975 and was issued in Spring 1976. The *Final Report* has been very favorably reviewed by several national episcopal conferences of the Roman Catholic Church and by some of the 23 autonomous Churches of the Anglican Communion. By the end of 1978, however, no Church had as yet altered its canonical regulations on marriage to incorporate the suggestions made in the *Final Report*.

ARCIC receives the reports and coordinates the work of 16 national and regional, official dialogue groups: Australia, Belgium, Canada, East Africa, England, France, Japan, Papua-New Guinea, Scotland, South Africa, South America (Argentina), South Pacific, Uganda, United States (ARC), Wales, and the West European Joint Working Group.

Central Issues Studied. In addition to the work of its Subcommission and its role in coordinating national and regional, official dialogues, ARCIC has its own agenda of studying the three theological areas—Eucharist, Ordained Ministry, Christian Authority in the Church—which have given rise to controversy between Rome and Canterbury since the 16th century. ARCIC is investigating these three areas in the hope of showing that at a level deeper than the polemical expressions of the past centuries the Roman Catholic Church and the Anglican Communion share substantial agreement in the Christian faith even in these areas of traditional controversy. For this aspect of the work of ARCIC the Commission has produced three Agreed Statements to be used as study documents in the national, regional, and local dialogues. They are: *The Agreed Statement on Eucharistic Doctrine* (Windsor 1971), *Ministry and Ordination: A Statement on the Doctrine of the Ministry* (Canterbury 1974), and *An Agreed Statement on Authority in the Church* (Venice 1976). These national, regional, and local dialogue groups are critically to assess the Agreed Statements and to test, improve, and clarify the consensus on doctrinal issues expressed by ARCIC in its Agreed Statements. The dialogue groups then send their written recommendations on the Agreed Statements to ARCIC.

On the basis of the recommendations received, ARCIC is at present drafting documents to supplement the Windsor Statement on Eucharist (1971) and the Canterbury Statement on Ministry and Ordination (1974). At the time of the 1978 meeting at Venice, ARCIC had not yet received a sufficient number of recommendations from the 16 official, regional dialogue groups to do more than outline the points in the Statement on Authority (1976) that seem to some of the dialogue groups to need further clarification. These points are in addition to the four issues which the Statement on Authority had already designated as the immediate theological agenda for ARCIC. Those four issues are. (1) Claims on behalf of the Roman See as commonly presented in the past have put a greater weight on the Petrine texts (Mt 16.18–19; Lk 22.31–32; Jn 21.15–17) than the texts are generally thought able to bear. (2) Does the language of "Divine right" applied by Vatican Council I to the successors of Peter imply that a Church not in union with the See of Peter is for that reason less a Church? (3) What are the implications stemming from the doctrine of infallibility of the Church when one considers the papal dogmatic definitions of Mary's Immaculate Conception and Assumption? (4) Does the claim that the pope possesses immediate jurisdiction, the limits of which are not clearly specified, open the way to its illegitimate or uncontrolled use?

Further Areas of Study. ARCIC must also study new areas of potential tension between the Roman Catholic Church and the Anglican Communion. These areas center on the role of women in ordained ministry and the life style required by corporate Christian witness to the Gospel. (1) The member Churches of the Anglican Communion in Canada, Ireland, Hong Kong, South Africa and the United States (Episcopal Church) have approved the ordination of women to the priesthood. In Hong Kong and the United States (Episcopal Church) canonically approved ordinations of women to the priesthood began to take place in January 1977. The General Convention of the Episcopal Church meeting at Minneapolis in September 1976 also approved the ordination of women to the episcopacy but as yet no woman has been ordained a bishop. Citing this issue among others as a paramount concern, some Episcopalians have split with their Church and on January 28, 1978 at Denver, Colorado, liturgically appointed four Episcopal priests as bishops of a new Anglican Church of North America. (2) The Anglican and Roman Catholic traditions seems to differ on the formation of Christian conscience especially in matters of sexual morality (marital chastity and homosexuality) and right to life issues (abortion and euthanasia).

Bibliography: ARCIC, *The Three Agreed Statements* (CTS and SPCK, London 1978). A. C. CLARK and C. DAVEY, ed., *Anglican-Roman Catholic Dialogue: The Work of the Preparatory Commission* (London 1974). H. J. RYAN, "The Canterbury Statement on Ministry and Ordination" *Worship* 47 (1974) 2–20; "Eucharist in Anglican-Roman Catholic Dialogue," *JEcumSt* 13 (1976) 233–238; "Anglicans and Roman Catholics on Authority in the Church" *America* 136 (March 5, 1977) 183–186; "Anglican-Roman Catholic Dialogue" *New Catholic World* 220 (July-August, 1977) 168–172. G. O. SIMMS and E. L. UNTERKOEFLER, eds., *Final*

Report on the Theology of Marriage and Its Application to Mixed Marriages (USCC publ. Office, Washington, D.C. 1976). E. J. YARNOLD and H. CHADWICK, *Truth and Authority* (CTS and SPCK, London 1977).

[H. J. RYAN]

APOSTOLATE OF THE LAITY (DECREE)

Vatican Council II's Decree on the Apostolate of the Laity (*Apostolicam actuositatem*, Nov. 18, 1965) in its final version is not considered a major document in opening new horizons for the layman. However, the development of the document proved to be a major contribution to the Council. The first draft of 170 pages eroded to 48 when major sections were transferred to *Lumen gentium* and *Gaudium et spes*. The major statement of the Council on the Laity is found in ch. 4 of *Lumen gentium*.

The Decree on the Laity itself does not reflect the conciliar shift in the theology of the Church, from the monarchical model with centralization of authority to a fraternal one with recognition of the diversity of gifts in the local Church. The decree rather perpetuates a patronizing clerical tone and a dualism between the secular and the sacred and between the Church and the world. It is a restatement of Pius XI's statements on Catholic Action (3:262) and Pius XII's on the lay apostolate (8:573). The decree does not capture the new basis for authority in the Church found in the Constitution on the Church: "The laity are gathered together in the People of God and make up the Body of Christ under one Head . . . The lay apostolate, however, is a participation in the saving mission of the Church itself. Through their baptism and confirmation, all are commissioned to that apostolate by the Lord himself" (*Lumen gentium* 33). This represents a turning point in the Church's own understanding of the place of the lay person in church life.

While the People of God concept pervaded the major Vatican II documents and implied a shift in the rooting of ministry in the Church from Rome to local Church, it still retained the clergy-lay distinction. Since Vatican II "laity" is becoming less acceptable as a description of those baptized into a community, which is increasingly seen as fraternal rather than hierarchical. To contrast the laity with the clergy is increasingly seen to involve elitism. Since Vatican II's efforts to ameliorate the clergy-laity distinction in its pejorative sense, which implies separation and subordination, both clergy and laity as categories are becoming less acceptable. The decline of candidates for the priesthood and the demise of lay movements are indicators that these distinctions may no longer fit current understandings of Church and ministry.

Ministry, however, is an overarching concept, capable of covering all ministries—ordained and unordained—without making one ministry subordinate to another. Ministry is both a New Testament and a post-Vatican II concept that replaces those of Catholic Action and lay apostolate.

See also MINISTRY, UNORDAINED.

Bibliography: F. KLOSTERMANN, "Decree on the Apostolate of the Laity," Vorgimler 3:273–404. J. B. SHEERIN, *Decree on the Apostolate of the Laity of Vatican Council II, Commentary* (New York 1966).

[D. J. GEANEY]

APOSTOLIC SPIRITUALITY

Apostolic spirituality is the way of life in the Spirit proper to Christians dedicated to apostolic works. Every authentic mode of Christian spirituality is centered in a life of union with the Risen Christ who remains present with the Church through the gift of his Spirit. The sources of growth in the life of the Spirit are the same for all Christians: reading and meditation on Scripture; celebration of the liturgy, especially the Eucharist; love of one another; and dedication to the mission of the Church. But perhaps the most significant factor shaping diverse modes of Christian spirituality is the attitude toward the world. Christian thought about the world has been a dialectic between "entry into" and "separation from" the world; a tension between world-affirming involvement and world-negating detachment. In Christian spirituality this tension has been expressed in the option between contemplation and action, between personal holiness and apostolic works, between prayer and service.

Vatican II. The documents of Vatican Council II offer illuminating perspectives that suggest a resolution of the traditional tension and offer principles of integration for an apostolic spirituality. The Constitution on the Church sets forth the Church as the People of God in history, a communion where human persons, through the grace of God, become brothers and sisters and manifest the presence of God's love in the world (*Lumen gentium* 9–10). The solidarity of the Church with the human family is clearly expressed in the Council's Pastoral Constitution on the Church in the Modern World: "The joy and hope, the grief and anguish of the men of our time, especially of those who are poor or afflicted in any way, are the joy and hope, the grief and anguish of the followers of Christ as well. Nothing that is genuinely human fails to find an echo in their hearts" (*Gaudium et spes* 1). Within this world-affirming perspective the Vatican documents stress the apostolic call given to all Christians by the fact of their union with Christ in Baptism. "The Christian vocation is, of its nature, a vocation to the apostolate as well" (*Apostolicam actuositatem* 2). For the laity this share in the mission of the Church is exercised in the world as well as in the Church, in the temporal order as well as in the spiritual. Lay persons share in the ministry of the Word by announcing to the world by word and witness the message of the Gospel, but the renewal of the temporal order is their distinctive task in the building of the Kingdom of God (ibid. and 6; cf. *Lumen gentium* 31).

All religious are viewed as dedicated to the welfare of the entire Church, as showing forth and witnessing Christ: in contemplation on the mountain, or proclaiming the Kingdom of God to the multitudes, or healing the sick and the maimed, or converting sinners to a good life, or blessing children and doing good to all (*Lumen gentium* 46). Withdrawal from the world characterizes the life style of religious ordered to the contemplative life, and yet even these religious serve the Church by their hidden apostolic fruitfulness.

The recognition of human values and the needs of the apostolate are principles governing the adaptation of life styles of religious institutes. Thus the spirituality of religious life has moved from a more monastic kind of spirituality which stressed withdrawal, detachment, personal holiness, and limited involvement with the world to a spirituality that seeks to integrate faith and life, contemplation in the midst of the world, the Gospel and human needs and concerns, and thus is more authentically apostolic (*Perfectae caritatis* 2).

The Council resolves the traditional tension between personal sanctification and apostolic ministry in the elaboration of this key statement of the Decree on Priestly Ministry and Life: "Priests will attain sanctity in a manner proper to them if they exercise their offices sincerely and tirelessly in the Spirit of Christ" (*Presbyterorum ordinis* 13). Further, "by assuming the role of the Good Shepherd, they will find, in the very exercise of pastoral love the bond of priestly perfection which will unify their lives and activities" (ibid. 14). (*See* PRIESTLY SPIRITUALITY.)

Reflections. Modern biblical studies have offered insights into the apostolic spiritualities of the New Testament, and the Gospel of John can shed light on the traditional tension between contemplation and action in Christian spirituality through its metaphor of the vine and the branches. "I am the vine, you are the branches. Whoever remains in me, with me in him, bears fruit in plenty; for cut off from me you can do nothing" (Jn 15.5). The disciple must be in direct relationship with Jesus who dwells within the disciple; only then can the disciple bear fruit, continue the works of Jesus, the One Sent by the Father. The ministry of the disciples is the ministry of Jesus in another mode. Just as the source of Jesus' mission is his union with the Father, and his mission is to reveal the Father, so the source of the disciples' mission is their contemplative union of love with Jesus, and they are sent to proclaim what they have heard and seen, what they have looked upon and touched.

The disciples bear witness to the life that became light in Jesus and are sent to continue Jesus' mission of drawing all people into union with the Father. The work of an apostle is to reveal that love in word and deed, but the apostle must first be a disciple—one who has walked in the presence of the Lord, who has seen the Risen Lord and believed. The essence of the apostolic mission is contemplative union with Jesus, a knowing that is loving, a recognition of the presence of God within human life. The disciples see the Lord in the midst of the world; as apostles they become his presence in the world.

Another understanding of the integrating principle of Christian life is offered by Paul: ". . . the love of God has been poured into our hearts by the Holy Spirit which has been given us" (Rom 5.5). From this intimate union grows a life of charity, the same source of energy enabling Christians to love God and one another. The apostolate is lived in faith, hope, and love, open to the gifts of the Spirit and open to the mystery of others.

Apostolic spirituality is grounded in a dialogue between the Gospel and the world. It takes seriously the exhortation to "give your full attention to the needs of persons, their problems and their searchings," and to "give witness in their midst, through prayer and action, to the Good News of justice, love, and peace." The apostle must continuously make connections between the human story and the story of Jesus and help others experience their lives as part of God's ongoing redemptive work in the world. The apostle must walk in the presence of the Lord, seeking always the mind and heart of Christ, so that care of others does not distract from God or compete with God but rather is an expression of the love of God poured forth in our hearts. Apostolic spirituality is a life of contemplative service that actualizes the healing, reconciling, redemptive presence of Jesus in the world. For the apostle, sent into the world as Jesus was sent by the Father

to identify with the human situation, contemplative union in faith and love with the Sender is essential to the fulfillment of mission. Contemplation in the midst of the human arena is an ongoing discovery of the "zone of God" in created reality, a sense of the Kingdom of justice demanding transformation of structures, and a commitment to share responsibility for the world being born anew. The life of such an apostle demands immersion in the world and times set apart for solitude, an openness to the needs of others and a zone of inner peace, a dialogue with experience and a communion with the indwelling Spirit. It demands union with the Risen Lord who stands in our midst.

[D. KENNEDY]

APOSTOLIC SUCCESSION

Apostolic succession is clearly the key issue still dividing the Christian Churches. In its small "t" traditional sense, apostolic succession means that the pope and bishops of the Catholic Church can trace the validity of their episcopal orders all the way back, in an unbroken historical sequence, to the twelve apostles (1:695). The outward sign by which this connection is both symbolized and effected is the laying on of hands at ordination. Consequently, the Catholic Church alone can claim to be "the one, true Church of Christ" since she alone has her origin in the apostolic period. This is, however, too narrow a conception.

Apostolic Succession and the Local Church. The notion of apostolic succession was first articulated in the 2d century during the Church's confrontation with Gnosticism. The latter movement insisted that salvation comes through knowledge and that such knowledge is secretly communicated to a select few. The Church's pastoral and theological leadership, especially in the person of Irenaeus, opposed this insidiously elitist concept of Christian truth by arguing that such truth is in principle available to all and that the criteria for judging and evaluating it are at once open and public. Specifically, if a teaching is consistent with the apostolic teaching, then it can be received as a reliable expression of the Gospel.

It is important to note that the witness of the apostolic Church meant the witness of *all* apostolic Churches, not any one in particular. Indeed the Church universal, whether of the apostolic period or of today, is a *communio ecclesiarum*. The Church is not simply a collectivity of individual Churches but is rather a community of Churches. Therefore, the pastoral leaders of the individual Churches are neither absolute in their own communities nor are they linked exclusively with the Church of Rome and its bishop, the pope. They are related one to another, and all together are related to the symbol of unity for the whole international network of Churches, the Bishop of Rome. In the words of Vatican II: "The collegial nature and meaning of the episcopal order found expression in the very ancient practice by which bishops appointed in the world over were linked with one another and with the Bishop of Rome by the bonds of unity, charity, and peace" (*Lumen gentium* 22). Even to this day, when a new bishop is ordained, there are three coconsecrators to dramatize the fact that he is being admitted to the one common office, the *ordo episcoporum*, and to a college. On the other hand, the ecclesial integrity of the local

Church is not thereby compromised, it is still the Body of Christ in that place. And yet it is not a living member of the Body of Christ universal unless it is at the same time in communion with all of the other Churches which constitute that Church universal. Apostolicity, like *collegiality (with which it is obviously closely connected), is the product of a kind of dialectic between the universal and the particular. And so, too, apostolic succession. It is not as if an individual bishop or an individual local Church were themselves directly linked with a particular apostle or a particular apostolic community. A bishop is not a successor of the apostles in that sense, some pious oratory notwithstanding. Rather he and his local Church are in succession to the apostles and to the apostolic communities insofar as they are part of the total college of bishops and of the total college of local Churches that together constitute the Church universal.

Degrees of Apostolic Witness. Although the apostles are dead and their unique experience unrepeatable, their witness and service are not yet finished. Their mission perdures and it perdures not only in the episcopal office but in the whole Church. The whole Church is the People of God. The whole Church is the Temple of the Holy Spirit. The whole Church is the Body of Christ. And it is the whole Church that shares in the traditional threefold mission of Christ as prophet, priest, and king (*Lumen gentium* 30). It is an unusually constricted understanding of apostolic succession, therefore, that limits it to the mission and sacred power of the apostles and bishops received and exercised by the mandate of Christ. And that narrow meaning, in turn, makes ecumenical progress on such questions as the mutual recognition of ministries, or even intercommunion, very difficult, if not finally impossible.

The Roman Catholic/Lutheran consultation in the U.S., for example, has urged the broader understanding upon their respective pastoral leaders (*see* LUTHERAN/ROMAN CATHOLIC DIALOGUE). There is no reason, from the Roman Catholic side, why certain Lutheran ministries could not be acknowledged as valid (as valid certainly as the Lutheran Churches which they serve) unless Catholics insist that ordinations are valid only when they are performed by bishops whose episcopal orders are themselves traceable in an uninterrupted line all the way back to the apostles themselves. But if this were the case, Vatican II would not have been able in the Decree on Ecumenism to describe non-Catholic Churches as "Churches" and acknowledge their members as our brothers and sisters in Christ, having "a right to be honored by the title of Christian" (*Unitatis redintegratio* 3). There are, in other words, degrees of apostolicity and of apostolic succession. The primary criterion is not validity of episcopal orders but fidelity to the word, witness, and service of the apostles and of the apostolic communities.

See also CHURCH, LOCAL (THEOLOGY).

Bibliography: W. BRENNING, SacrMundi 1:86–90. H. KÜNG, *The Church* (New York 1967); ed., *Apostolic Succession. Concilium* 34 (1968).

[R. P. MCBRIEN]

APOSTOLICITY

The NT term ἀπόστολος is rooted in the Semitic notion of delegation or authoritative representation. Its political and secular parallel today would be an ambassador or diplomat: the authority of the ambassador is in proportion to the authority and standing of the government and nation which sends him or her. So, too, the authority of the Apostles in relation to the Lord.

Witness of Word. The apostolic office had several different aspects, e.g., witnessing to the risen Lord, discipleship, but none more distinctive than the proclamation of the Gospel at the direct instruction of the Lord: "And he commanded us to preach to the people, and to testify that he is the one ordained by God to be judge of the living and the dead" (Acts 10.42). The core of this proclamation was the same as it was for Jesus himself, namely, the coming of the Kingdom of God (Mk 1.15). From the beginning the Christian community understood itself as being "built upon the foundation of the apostles and prophets, Christ Jesus himself being the cornerstone" (Eph 2.20). The Church is first *called* to discipleship (election) and then *sent* to proclaim what she has received (mission, apostolicity). She does this under the impulse of the Holy Spirit (Jn 14.16; 16.14). The link between Christ and his Apostles is so strong that the founding of the Church is sometimes ascribed to Christ (1 Cor 10.4) and at other times to the apostles (Eph 2.20).

Witness of Service. If the Church is to be faithful to her apostolic character, however, she must do more than simply maintain doctrinal orthodoxy. She must be attentive not only to the apostolic word but also to their witness and especially to their mode of service. Just as the apostles engaged in constant preaching of the Gospel, so the Church must continually refine and critically purify her own preaching. But evangelization, as the Third General Assembly of the Synod of Bishops (1974) insisted, involves more than verbal expression. It must "take account of the unceasing interplay of the Gospel and of man's concrete life, both personal and social." Indeed the Second General Assembly Synod's document *Justice in the World* (1971) declared that "action on behalf of justice and participation in the transformation of the world . . . are a constitutive dimension of the preaching of the Gospel, or, in other words, of the Church's mission for the redemption of the human race and its liberation from every oppressive situation" (Synod JustWorld, Introd. p. 34).

The apostles also engaged in sacramental ministry and in creating a fellowship of prayer. A Church conscious of its apostolic character will continually renew and reform her liturgical life and encourage new styles of community and prayer. Changes in religious congregations since Vatican II and the development of such movements as the *charismatic renewal, whatever the merits or deficiencies of particular cases, are ways by which the Church realizes her apostolicity.

Finally, an apostolic Church must minister to the world of which she is herself a part. Apostolicity is directly opposed to insularity. The Church officially represents Christ to humankind. She is in fact the fundamental Sacrament of his presence. As such she must always be open to structural and institutional change so that she may more effectively communicate what she embodies and is sent to proclaim.

Bibliography: A. JAVIERRE, SacrMundi 1:77-79. H. KÜNG, *The Church* (New York 1967). POPE PAUL VI, *Evangelii nuntiandi* (Washington 1974).

[R. P. MCBRIEN]

ARCHIVES, ECCLESIASTICAL

Church archives formally developed in the United States after the publication of the Code of Canon Law (1918), which requires every diocese to have an official depository for the preservation of church records (CIC cc. 375–378). Prior to 1918 many documents disappeared or were dispersed, out of carelessness, ignorance, lack of adequate facilities, or an unwillingness to preserve them for posterity. However, some dioceses, like those of Baltimore and St. Louis, succeeded in preserving archival materials intact. On Nov. 22, 1974 the NCCB Committee for the Bicentennial issued "A Document on Ecclesiastical Archives," stressing their importance:

> At the same time we regret that our Church's singular role in the development of our country has not been presented as fully as it deserves to be. Although books, monographs, articles, and essays on the subject of American Catholicism abound and many of them are of high scholarly and literary quality, church historians have still not penetrated to the heart of the peculiarly American experience in all too many cases, because they have not had access to the pertinent documents of bishops, dioceses, religious orders, and institutions. The difficulty is not so much that such papers are not extant, although it is true, unfortunately, that in certain known cases large holdings of important documents have been destroyed because they were mistakenly judged to be "outdated" or "useless" or "trash." The problem is rather that in many places the papers which do exist in abundance have not yet been organized for preservation and research. Consequently, on the one hand, they are not easily accessible to church historians and, on the other, they are in danger of being lost, dispersed, or damaged through lack of proper care, fire or flood, or inadvertent disposal.

The documents urged that all bishops appoint a diocesan archivist. Access to ecclesiastical papers and records was encouraged:

> Finally, we express our sincere hope that the residential bishops may be disposed to grant access to the diocesan archives without undue limitations when properly accredited ecclesiastical historians request it. The past products of such research support, we believe, the contention that serious historians, even graduate students and doctoral candidates have, with very rare exceptions, used such permission with honesty, fairness, responsibility, respect for the documents, and true Christian charity. Catholic historians have characteristically evinced a distinct pride in the persons and institutions of their Church of past generations, and, in our judgment, no bishop need fear that by opening this archives to scholarly examination, he will expose the Church's past to deliberate attempts at embarrassment.

Notable Depositories in the U.S. To check the frequent loss of church papers the University of Notre Dame, through its Archives Department, has been active in collecting personal papers of bishops, priests and Catholic laymen, as well as transcripts of American missionary letters sent to Europe. The collections include copies of letters from the United States to the Congregation for the Propagation of the Faith in Rome from 1622 to 1865. The American Catholic Historical Society Archives housed at St. Charles Seminary in Philadelphia are a mine of early Catholic Americana, including newspapers and serials. Georgetown University contains early Catholic Americana, notably the papers of John Gilmary Shea, the first scholarly historian of the Catholic Church in the United States. Recently it acquired the archival collection of Woodstock College. Between 1872 and 1927, Bishops Gibbons, Keane, and O'Connor, exercised leadership on a national level and thus their papers take on added significance. Many are now preserved in the Richmond Diocesan Archives in Virginia. The Archives of the Archdiocese of Santa Fe, NM 87501, has published a calendar of its holdings that encompasses Franciscan missionary activities and the career of Archbishop John Lamy (made famous by Willa Cather in *Death Comes for the Archbishop*). The Department of Archives at Catholic University, Washington, D.C. 20064, has noteworthy collections on labor relations and labor unions. In addition, it has assembled copies of the papers of John Carroll (1735–1815), the first bishop of Baltimore, and other materials on the early American Church. Marquette University, Milwaukee WI 53223, has an archival center for Catholic journalism in the United States.

An area of growing importance is the archives of European associations dealing with American missionary projects. The Baraga Archives of Marquette, MI 49855, has assembled materials from several countries involving the career of Bishop Baraga. The University of Notre Dame Archives owns transcripts from American mission society files in Austria, Germany, Ireland, and Italy.

A unique collection of approximately 30,000 bound manuscripts or codices representing the holdings of fifty monastic libraries in Europe is now available on microfilm at St. John's University, Collegeville, MN 56321. A major portion of the manuscript holdings of the Vatican Library on microfilm is now on deposit at St. Louis University, St. Louis, MO 63108.

Valuable collections have been assembled through the interests of religious communities and orders, like that on Franciscan history now available at the Academy of American Franciscan History, Box 3440 Washington, D.C. 20034; the collection of Dominicana at the Dominican House of Studies, 487 Michigan Ave., N.E., Washington, D.C. 20017; and the Jesuit collections at Georgetown University, Washington, D.C. 20057, at St. Louis University, St. Louis, MO 63108, and at Gonzaga University, Spokane, WA 99258.

Those concerned with Canadian church history may find central depositories at the Centre for Canadian Catholic Church History, St. Paul University, 223 Main, Ottawa, Ontario K15 IC4, Canada. The archdiocesan archives of Montreal and Quebec City contain material on the colonial history of French settlements in the United States. Additional archdiocesan archives have been established at Halifax, Ottawa, St. Boniface, Manitoba (The Pas), and Vancouver.

Though there is no current standard guide to Catholic church archives nor an inventory of unpublished material on the history of the American Catholic Church, those interested in doing further research on specific topics will want to consult *The National Union Catalog of Manuscript Collections*, a continuing series published by the Library of Congress since 1959. Here appear many entries on collections of Catholic church archives, plus valuable annual indexes and a cumulative index for reports from 1959 to 1963. Occasional articles on Catholic church records and depositories appear in the *American Archivist*, a journal sponsored by the Society of American Archivists.

Specific Subject Collections. The following is a compilation of the main depositories of church-history materials and sources primarily located in the United States. *Abbey of St. Martin*, 1077–1780: Huntington Library, San Marino, CA 91108; *Alaska Missions*: Gonzaga Univ., Spokane, WA 99258. *American Catholicism before 1842*:

Catholic Univ. Archives Washington, D.C. 20064. *Benedictines:* St. John's Univ. Archives, Collegeville, MN 56321 and St. Vincent's Archabbey Archives, Latrobe, PA 15650. Bureau of Catholic Indian Missions Archives: Marquette Univ., Milwaukee, WI 53223. *California Church History and Missions,* 1770–1955: Academy of California Church History, P.O. Box 1668, Fresno, CA 93717 and Univ. of San Francisco Archives, San Francisco, CA 94117. *Catholic Charities:* Catholic Univ. Archives, Washington, D.C. 20064. *Catholic Newspapers:* American Catholic Historical Society, St. Charles Seminary, Philadelphia, PA 19151. *Catholic Order of Foresters, St. Paul, 1894–1928:* Minnesota Historical Society, St. Paul, MN 55501. *Church in Michigan:* Detroit Public Library, Detroit, MI 48202. *Church in Minnesota:* Catholic Historical Society, St. Paul Seminary, St. Paul, MN 55501. *Church in the Mississippi Valley and in the West:* St. Louis Univ. Archives, St. Louis, MO 63108. *Church in Missouri and the Dakotas:* Conception Abbey Archives, Conception, MO 64433. *Church in Texas:* Texas Catholic Historical Society, P.O. Box 13327, Austin, TX 78711. *Church in the United States:* American Catholic Historical Society, St. Charles Seminary, Philadelphia, PA 19151. *Church in Western Pennsylvania:* Duquesne Univ. Archives, Pittsburgh, PA 15219. *Church in Wisconsin, 1695–1944:* Wisconsin State Historical Society, Madison, WI 53706.

Dominicans: Dominican House of Studies, 487 Michigan Ave., N.E., Washington, D.C. 20017. *Dublin, Ireland Mission Society:* Univ. of Notre Dame Archives, Notre Dame, IN 46556. *Franciscans:* Bancroft Library, Univ. of California, Berkeley, CA 94720, St. Bonaventure Univ. Archives, St. Bonaventure, NY 14778, John Carter Brown Library, Brown Univ., Providence, RI 02912, Academy of American Franciscan History, P.O. Box 3440, Washington, D.C. 20034 and Santa Fe Archdiocesan Archives, Santa Fe, NM 87501. *Gambell Missionaries, 1898–1906:* Alaska Historical Society, Juneau, AK 99811. *German Settlements:* St. Vincent's Archabbey Archives, Latrobe, PA 15650. *German Jesuits in America, 1611–1760:* Library of Congress, Washington, D.C. 20540. *Irish and Home Rule:* American Irish Historical Society, 991 Fifth Avenue, New York, N.Y. 10028. *Jesuits in Alaska:* Gonzaga Univ. Archives, Spokane, WA 99258.

Jesuits in California, 1768: Oscott College, Birmingham, England. *Jesuit Missions among Kickapoo and Potawami Indians:* St. Louis Univ. Archives, St. Louis, MO 63108. *Jesuits in North America, 1612–1685:* Wisconsin State Historical Society, Madison, WI 53706. *Jesuit Missions in the Northwest, 1843–1947:* Gonzaga Univ. Archives, Spokane, WA 99258 and Univ. of Alaska Museum, Fairbanks, AK 99701. *Jesuits in Oregon:* Gonzaga Univ. Archives, Spokane, WA 99258. *Jesuit Papers, Copies from Germany, Mexico, Rome, and Spain, "Jesuit Americana":* St. Louis Univ. Archives, St. Louis, MO 63108. *Latin-American Church:* Bancroft Library, Univ. of California, Berkeley, CA 94720; Museum of New Mexico, P.O. Box 2087, Santa Fe, NM 87503; and Academy of American Franciscan History, P.O. Box 3440, Washington, D.C. 20094. *Lyons* (France) *Mission Society:* Univ. of Notre Dame Archives, Notre Dame, IN 46556. *Missions in Missouri and the Dakotas, 1873–1923:* Conception Abbey Archives, Conception, MO 64437. *Munich (Germany) Mission Society:* Univ. of Notre Dame Archives, Notre Dame, IN 46556.

Oregon Missions: Oregon Historical Society, Portland, OR 97205. *Paris (France) Mission Society:* Univ. of Notre Dame Archives, Notre Dame IN 46556. *Phillipines:* Newberry Library, Chicago, IL 60610; Univ. of Michigan Library, Ann Arbor, MI 48108; Duke University Library, Durham, NC 27706; and Princeton Univ. Library, Princeton, N.J. 08540. *Representatives of the American Hierarchy in Rome, 1832–1903:* Catholic Univ. Archives, Washington, D.C. 20064. *Sisters of St. Joseph, 1850–1931:* College of St. Catherine, St. Paul, MN 55101. *Society for the Propagation of the Faith, 1822–1900:* Univ. of Notre Dame Archives, Notre Dame, IN 46556. *Spaniards in Florida and West Indies, 1783–1795:* Huntington Library, San Marino, CA 91108. *Spanish-American War Papers:* St. Joseph Central House, Emmitsburg, MD 21727. *Spanish Missions, 1776–1955:* Bowers Museum, Santa Ana, CA 92706. *Sulpicians in the United States:* St. Mary's Seminary Archives, Roland Park, MD 21210. *Texas and Southwest Missions:* Univ. of Notre Dame Archives, Notre Dame, IN 46556 and Bishop's House, Amarillo, TX 79178. *Vienna* (Austria) *Mission Society:* Univ. of Notre Dame Archives, Notre Dame, IN 46556.

[R. A. BURKE]

ASSOCIATION FOR RELIGIOUS AND VALUE ISSUES IN COUNSELING

This organization was from 1962 called the National Conference of Catholic Guidance Councils (earlier Catholic Counselors, National Conference of Diocesan Guidance Councils). The new name was adopted in 1977 to signify the current direction of the Association. A division of the American Personnel and Guidance Association (APGA), the Association has as its purposes: to integrate values and theological and philosophical content into student and pupil-personnel research and practice; to foster the development of student and pupil-personnel services, particularly values in counseling, in Catholic, private educational institutions. The Association meets annually with APGA; its own executive committee holds a Fall meeting at the office of the current president. The Association serves as a consultant agency for schools and other education-related institutions. The major emphasis is on value issues pertaining to the counseling process, on its religious dimensions, and on moral education. Membership includes the professionally qualified in the field of counseling or personnel, associates, and student members.

[D. T. DRISCOLL]

ASSOCIATION FOR SOCIAL ECONOMICS

Founded in 1942 as the Catholic Economic Association (3:267), the Association for Social Economics (ASE) is an organization of professional scholars dedicated to the study of the social and moral dimensions of economic theory and policy; it changed its name in 1971. The objectives of the ASE are: (1) to foster research centered on the reciprocal relationship between economic science and broader questions of human dignity; and (2) to assist in the formulation of economic policies consistent with the ethical values of a pluralistic society. The ASE meets in convention once a year for the presentation of scholarly papers and discussion of current developments in social economics; the annual meeting is held in conjunction with that of the American Economic Association. The ASE also acts as sponsor for programs held regularly in conjunction with the meetings of regional associations, such as the Midwest Economics Association. The official journal of the ASE is the *Review of Social Economy*, regularly published twice yearly. For the benefit of members, the ASE also publishes an annual *Newsletter* and an organ of commentary, *The Forum*. Membership is open to all persons interested in the relationship between moral questions and economic activity.

[S. T. WORLAND]

ASSOCIATION FOR THE SOCIOLOGY OF RELIGION

The Association for the Sociology of Religion (ASR) was founded in 1938 as the American Catholic Sociological Society by Rev. Ralph Gallagher, SJ and a group of leading Catholic sociologists (1:399). These Catholic sociologists had decided that they needed a learned society of their own to encourage Catholics to study sociology and to provide themselves and other Catholics with a congenial forum for developing their research. ACSS published the *American Catholic Sociological Review* (ACSR).

In the early 1960s, many members of ACSS felt that there was little or no need for just another general sociological journal but that there was a need for a scholarly journal devoted solely to research in the sociology of religion. Consequently, ACSS changed its journal into *Sociological Analysis: A Journal in the Sociology of Religion* (v. 1 1964). In 1971, ACSS voted to transform itself into the Association for the Sociology of Religion. The members thought that the suspicion prevalent in the 1930s that Catholic sociologists could not be objective, unbiased scientists had been dissipated and that the American Sociological Association was as good a general forum for them as it was for other sociologists. Since then ASR, through its meetings and publications, has been able to provide a forum for discussion and research in the sociology of religion for all sociologists, whatever their religious persuasion. In this way ASR has been able to serve both the scholarly community and the public at large by pointing to the central importance of religious belief and religious institutions in social organization and in social disorganization.

See also RELIGION, SOCIOLOGY OF.

[R. J. MCNAMARA]

ASSOCIATION OF CATHOLIC TEACHERS

The Association of Catholic Teachers, offices Philadelphia, is the oldest Catholic teachers' union in the country. The Association's Constitution was ratified, formalizing the union (ACT), in March 1966. In May 1967, the Association of Catholic Teachers voted to affiliate with the American Federation of Teachers, AFL-CIO. In February 1968, ACT was formally recognized by the Archdiocese of Philadelphia after winning 70 per cent of the vote in a representation election, held by mutual agreement between the Archdiocese and the Association, and conducted under the auspices of the St. Joseph's College Institute for Industrial Relations and its coordinator, Rev. Dennis Comey.

The Association currently represents 1200 lay teachers employed in the 30 archdiocesan high schools, as well as lay teachers in one high school in the Diocese of Trenton, New Jersey. The Association is currently involved in a representation campaign to include the 2300 elementary lay teachers in the Archdiocese. A National Labor Relations Board election was held on June 14, 1977, but the ballots are impounded pending a U.S. Supreme Court decision. ACT has been one of the prime movers behind the newly formed National Association of Catholic School Teachers; two of ACT's officers are members of the National Association Executive Committee. One of ACT's prime objectives at the present time is the passage of tuition-credit legislation which will benefit parents of students in nonpublic elementary and secondary schools.

In June 1978, the ACT disaffiliated from the American Federation of Teachers. The first Catholic teachers' union in the country to affiliate with AFT become the first to disaffiliate. The reason given was a history of insensitivity to the problems of Catholic teachers. AFT's recent all-out campaign to defeat tuition credits while demeaning nonpublic schools was the final blow to the 1150 members of the Association of Catholic Teachers. In October, 1978, ACT formally affiliated with the National Association of Catholic School Teachers.

See also TEACHERS' UNIONS, CATHOLIC.

[J. J. REILLY]

ASSOCIATION OF CONTEMPLATIVE SISTERS (ACS)

The Association of Contemplative Sisters is a national organization of women religious who are members of canonical contemplative communities and women who are pursuing, individually or in groups, newer forms of contemplative ways of life within the Church. ACS was founded by sisters from different orders in August 1969 and has grown from an original 135 members to about 600 in 1978, forming seven geographical regions. Members are from sixty-two communities representing the principal religious families, namely, Benedictine, Carmelite, Cistercian, Dominican, Maryknoll, Passionist, Poor Clare, Precious Blood, Redemptoristine, Sacramentine, Visitandine. ACS functions through delegates elected by each region, an elected governing board, and a national assembly which meets every two years.

The Association came into being four years after Vatican Council II because of an awareness on the part of sisters of the dangers of isolation, their needs in areas of formation, continuing education, government, social awareness, means of self-support and, most importantly, the enrichment of their prayer life, and the realization that renewal and growth in their orders would come about only through personal interaction and mutual collaboration.

ACS endeavors have included a program on prayer and spirituality held for six weeks during four consecutive summers, leadership training programs to aid sisters in decision-making processes within communities, a seminar on the theology of Church and law. The Association publishes a quarterly, *Contemplative Review*. A high priority of ACS from its inception has been a continuing process of communication with the Holy See, the hierarchy of the United States, and with other sisters' organizations. ACS is a member of Sisters Uniting.

[E. M. ENOCH]

ASSOCIATION OF PROFESSORS OF MISSIONS

The' Association of Professors of Missions (APM) brings together the teachers of missions throughout the United States and Canada to promote the development of the field of mission studies and the personal growth of the members themselves. Organized in 1952 in Louisville, Ky., the Association built on a previously established Fellowship of Professors of Missions from the Atlantic seaboard area. A similar Midwest Fellowship of Professors of Missions also developed at the same time. Both regional groups continue to meet annually.

From 1952 to 1972 the APM met biennially, normally at the same location and just after or prior to the meeting of the American Association of Theological Schools. Membership in the APM was initially open only to those professors of missions from institutions accredited with the American Association of Theological Schools and to other qualified persons by invitation of the executive committee. In a growing effort to be more ecumenical the reference to institutional relationship with the Association of Theological Schools was removed from the membership requirement in 1972. That same year at the time and place of the APM's biennial meeting (June 1972, Nashville), the American Society of Missiology (ASM) came into being with the help of the Association. Since 1972 the two organizations meet at the same time and place, with the APM meetings focusing more sharply on issues related to the teaching of missions. The Proceedings of the biennial meetings of the Association of Professors of Missions were published from 1952 to 1974. The publication of the Proceedings was suspended, since the ASM began in 1973 the publication of the journal, *Missiology* (135 North Oakland Street, Pasadena, CA 91101).

Bibliography: J. T. BOBERG, ed., *Proceedings: Association of Professors of Missions* (Chicago 1972 and 1974).

[J. T. BOBERG]

ATHEISM

Atheism is one of the main and most characteristic signs of our time. Never before in the history of mankind have religious belief in general and the Christian faith in particular been assailed by so many criticisms or been so radically repudiated. While in previous ages to believe in God was almost natural to man, as Vatican Council II notes, "many of our contemporaries have never recognized this intimate and vital link with God, or have explicitly rejected it" (*Gaudium et spes* 19).

Up to the beginning of the 19th century both theoretical and practical atheisms were rare exceptions. It was only after the works of such figures as Hegel, Feuerbach, Marx, Engels, Comte, Schopenhauer, Nietzsche, and Freud that atheism so entered into the field of philosophy as to become almost a common tenet of speculative thought. Philosophical atheism exercised a contagious influence and quickly all fields of science (physics, biology, astronomy etc.) were touched by it. At the same time, as a result of the new cultural outlook, of social and economic developments and, in some cases, of political pressures, for many people atheism became a new way of life.

Vatican II and Atheism. The problem of atheism was faced several times by the popes of this century, especially by Pius XI (*Divini Redemptoris*), Pius XII (*Ad Apostolorum Principis*), John XXIII (*Mater et magistra*) and Paul VI (*Ecclesiam suam*). Quite naturally the problem of atheism was also brought to the attention of the Fathers of Vatican II, who dedicated an important section of the Pastoral Constitution on the Church in the Modern World to the study of the different types of atheism, to their causes, and to the answers the Church should give to them (*Gaudium et spes* 19–21). The Council does not provide a systematic division of the different species of atheism. It speaks of two forms of atheism which take "a systematic expression": the humanistic atheism of the Western world, grounded on the assumption of the incompatibility of human freedom and dignity with religious belief; and the materialistic atheism associated with communism, grounded on economic and social reasons (ibid. 20). But it is clear that not all the forms of systematic or theoretical atheism can be reduced to these two. As a matter of fact there are many more; and almost all the species of atheism mentioned by the Council (skeptical, agnostic, scientific, positivistic etc., ibid. 19) belong to the systematic or theoretical type.

Causes. More accurate and satisfactory is the analysis of the causes of atheism provided by the Council. It rightly registers as main causes the following. (1) The mystery of God: this leads some people "to believe that man can assert absolutely nothing about him." (2) Fallacious methodologies: "Others use such a method so to scrutinize the question of God as to make it seem devoid of meaning. Many, unduly transgressing the limits of the positive sciences, contend that everything can be explained by this kind of scientific reasoning alone." (3) False humanism: "Some laud man so extravagantly that their faith in God lapses into a kind of anemia, though they seem more inclined to affirm man than to deny God . . . . They claim that this [human] freedom cannot be reconciled with the affirmation of a Lord who is author and purpose of all things." (4) Religious deviations: "Some form for themselves such a fallacious idea of God that when they repudiate this figment they are by no means rejecting the God of the Gospel." (5) The problem of evil: "Atheism results not rarely from a violent protest against the evil of this world." (6) Hedonism and materialism: "Modern civilization itself often complicates the approach to God . . . because it is excessively engrossed in earthly affairs." (7) The scandals of the believers: "To the extent that they neglect their own training in the faith, or teach erroneous doctrines, or are deficient in their religious, moral or social life, they must be said to conceal rather than reveal the authentic face of God and religion" (ibid.).

Remedies. If such are the causes of atheism, it is easy enough to discover the remedies for it. *Gaudium et spes* insists on two. The first belongs to the theoretical level and consists in showing to the atheists that religious belief, Christian faith in particular, is not against man, it does not belittle his dignity and does not hamper his freedom. "The recognition of God is in no way hostile to man's dignity, since this dignity is rooted and perfected in God . . . . A hope related to the end of time does not diminish the importance of intervening duties, but rather undergirds the acquittal of them with fresh incentives . . . . Far from diminishing man, her [the Church's] message brings to his development light, life, and freedom" (ibid. 21). The second remedy belongs to the practical level and consists in Christians giving a clear witness of faith in everyday life: "The remedy which must be applied to atheism, however, is to be sought in a proper presentation of the Church's teaching as well as in the integral life of the Church and her members.... Faith needs to prove its fruitfulness by penetrating the believer's entire life, including its worldy dimensions, and by activating him toward justice and love, especially regarding the needy" (ibid.).

Atheism as such is still condemned by the Church: "In her loyal devotion to God and men, the Church has already repudiated and cannot cease repudiating, sorrowfully but as firmly as possible, those poisonous doctrines and actions which contradict reason and the common experience of humanity" (ibid. 21). But at the same time the Church shows great concern for the atheist. She does not treat them as her enemies, but as persons who are also called to enter into the Kingdom of God: "She courteously invites atheists to examine the Gospel of Christ with an open mind" (ibid.). Also with regard to the atheists the Church adopts the same dialogical method that she has recommended for the relationships between her members and Christians separated from the Catholic Church (ibid.).

Theology and Atheism. Already before but especially during and after the Council atheism has drawn the attention of Christian philosophers and theologians, who have analyzed this very complicated phenomenon from every side: historical, social, political, anthropological, theological, and pastoral. For the problem of the evangelization of the atheists, the main positions taken by Christian philosophers and theologians can be reduced to four.

Adaptation. According to a small group of authors, who received great publicity immediately after Vatican II, under the name of theologians of "the death of God," atheism is to be taken very seriously, since in modern culture there is no longer any rational motivation for believing in God. Modern man is honestly an atheist. Therefore, according to these theologians, the best strategy in the present situation is to adapt the Gospel to his atheistic understanding of reality, by eliminating from the Christian message and from Christian life in general, the whole religious, supernatural, and divine aspect, and by stressing on the contrary its content on a humanist level, showing, at this level, how Christianity is superior to any other interpretation of reality. As St. Paul became a Jew with the Jews and a Greek with the Greeks, so the preachers of the 20th century must become atheists with atheists, abandoning "the religious hypothesis." Even when this hypothesis is dropped, Jesus has sufficient prerogatives (his love for others, his complete dedication to his neighbor, his perfect freedom etc.) to win human confidence, obedience, faith, and complete surrender. He has still sufficient claims to be considered the savior of mankind. This strategy of an "atheistic" (nonreligious) proclamation of the Gospel to an atheistic and secularized world was initially proposed by the Lutheran theologian and martyr of Nazi persecution, Dietrich Bonhoeffer. It was then followed and promoted by such "death of God" theologians as Altizer, van Buren, Robinson. After a short, passing success it was recognized that the strategy of "historical compromise" between Christianity and atheism is a failure and extremely self-defeating. In the concern (certainly a legitimate one) to make the Gospel intelligible to modern man, this compromise mutilates it in its most essential element—precisely in the religious, ultramundane, transcendent, sacred, divine element. The originality of Christ and the quality that rendered him capable of being the savior of mankind is not just that of being a supremely free man, or a man completely dedicated to others (man-for-others), but his identity of being the Son of God.

Confrontation. According to some authors the only valid strategy of the Church in the face of atheism is frontal counterposition. Atheism is seen as the extreme expression of human pride, the most detestable aberration of man's reason and heart, since only a madman or a fool can proclaim that God does not exist or that "God is dead." Therefore for a believer it is impossible to come to an agreement with atheism; it is impossible even to start a dialogue for the atheist's motivations cannot be justified nor his perspectives and language accepted. Atheism is the number-one enemy of mankind. The first condition for mankind to be able to receive the message of salvation is to abandon atheism and the human idolatry which is masked under the attractive mantle of secular humanism. Salvation is possible for the atheist only on the condition that he is converted and professes the most complete and unconditional submission to God. Among the most authoritative assertors of this strategy are Barth and Brunner, two of the major exponents of contemporary Protestant theology, and such Catholic thinkers as Maritain, Molnar, and Del Noce.

This strategy seems too drastic to many people. It forgets that every error contains at least a kernel of truth that must be patiently picked out and carefully preserved. In the second place, while admitting that to embrace the Gospel a deep conversion is always necessary, it must be clarified that this conversion does not entail sacrifice of everything human, as Barth claims. Humanity is living today under the sign of the Cross and many human achievements are in conformity with God's plan. Finally, it is necessary to distinguish between atheists and atheism. While atheism must be criticized and rejected with firm resolution, it is necessary to show the greatest understanding for atheists.

Integration. According to other theologians the most effective and appropriate strategy is that which does not eliminate either the originality of the Gospel or the reality of atheism, but tries on the contrary to preserve them both by integrating atheism into Christianity. The attempt to reach this goal consists in reducing the significance of atheism: by showing the atheist that his own view of the world, of history, of society, of man, of science, of politics etc., if developed consistently, does not exclude God at all, but, on the contrary, logically, leads to him, to his plan of salvation, to the liberation, the love, the divinization that Jesus Christ alone makes possible. There are three main versions of this strategy of *integration*: the scientific one of Teilhard de Chardin, the political one of the theologians of Latin America (Gutierrez, Assmann, Boff, etc.), and the metaphysical one of Tillich and Rahner. The first version tries to integrate into the Gospel the scientific doctrine of evolution (generally professed by scientific atheism). The second adopts the political doctrines of Marxism. The third tries to make the Gospel emerge from the idealistic metaphysics of man, conceived as an infinite capacity for self-transcendence.

The positive aspects of this strategy are obvious. It is capable of entering into dialogue with scientists, philosophers, artists, politicians who do not share a religious belief; it manages to appreciate their ways of understanding and explaining things, their social, economic, and political initiatives, their dynamism, their determination to improve our society, to change the world. But the strategy also raises serious reservations: it seems too optimistic, since it establishes a natural bridge between metaphysics, science, and politics on the one hand, and the Gospel on the other hand, ignoring the absolute qualitative difference that distinguishes God from man. In the second place, by establishing a natural, logical connection between science, politics, metaphysics, and the Gospel, it eliminates the perfectly gratuitous, absolutely new and unforeseeable character of God's plans and his intervention for the salvation of mankind by grace.

Double Conversion. According to some authors atheism implies a double distortion, namely, of the natural order and of the supernatural order. Consequently of an atheist they require a double conversion: (1) on the natural level, a conversion of mentality, which will cause him to embrace a more open view of things, so as to make room for a transcendent reality; (2) on the supernatural level, a conversion to the work of salvation that God accomplishes in Jesus Christ. A first conversion at a natural level is required because the Gospel is the proclamation of the Good News that God has saved mankind in Jesus Christ. Now, this proclamation will continue to seem absurd, aberrant, stupid as long as man remains completely shut up in himself and does not recognize any other reality except the "this-wordly" one or any other action except one that man himself carries out in history. So, a conversion of viewpoint, a change of mentality is required in the first place, to lead man to confess his own finiteness and, at the same time, to recognize his capacity for overcoming it not only horizontally but also vertically. Then he will be ready to enter into dialogue not only with his fellowmen but also with other beings superior to him, should he perceive their existence.

At this point, with the help of God's grace, the phase of the second conversion will begin: the phase in which the Gospel will no longer be considered as a fairy tale, an absurd story or mere myth, but as the truth that makes him free, restores him to health interiorly, and fills his heart with joy, since "only in the mystery of the Incarnate Word does the mystery of man take on light" (*Gaudium et spes* 22). Among the most brilliant supporters are J. Miguez Bonino, H. Urs von Balthasar, Richard Niebuhr, Henri de Lubac.

This theory is fully adequate, because it is apt to safeguard both the originality of the Gospel and the necessity of a rational basis for Christian faith. It is also fully consistent with the teachings of *Gaudium et spes*, which does not simply invite the atheist "to examine the Gospel of Christ with an open mind" and to gladly accept it (*second conversion*) but also requires from him to reject all those prejudices and fallacious methodologies that prevent him from seeing that the recognition of the reality of God does not cause any damage to the nobility and greatness of man (*first conversion*).

Marxists. Beside the discussion of atheism as it has been conducted by Protestant and Catholic theologians, an analysis of atheism has been advanced by some nonbelievers during recent years. Starting from the 1950s atheism has become a problem not only for Christian thinkers but also for the atheists themselves, especially for some philosophers (E. Bloch, R. Garaudy, M. Machovec), who profess themselves to be followers of the dialectical/historical materialism of Karl Marx. In their studies these authors do not consider religion or Christianity to be a cause of the alienation of mankind. There have been epochs and places where religion and Christianity have been used as principles of alienation; but this does not belong to their very essence. Essentially the sources of alienation spring from the nature of man and give expression to his fragmentary and incomplete existence; moreover religion and Christianity help him to overcome his deficiencies and to realize a fully reconciled existence, in a classless society. Moving from this new appreciation of religion and Christianity this group of atheists has shown great interest in the dialogue with Christian believers. In recent years meetings and congresses, where atheists and Christians convene in order to acquire a clearer and deeper understanding of each others' positions and for the search of more adequate solutions for practical problems of great concern for mankind, have become more and more frequent. It is expected that this dialogue will continue and will be intensified in the future.

Christian believers should pursue their dialogue with the atheists with a sincere, honest, and open mind, according to the spirit of true dialogue. They should never forget that dialogue, besides a theoretical moment, also includes a practical moment, during which the believer reveals the true meaning of Christian faith to the atheists in his daily actions: actions of justice, peace, and charity. This moment is extremely important. Indeed experience proves that the witness of a serious Christian life for the atheist is much more enlightening than many brilliant sermons on the beauty of the Gospel.

See also MARXISM AND CHRISTIANITY.

Bibliography: T. ALTIZER, *The Gospel of Christian Atheism* (Philadelphia 1966). H. U. VON BALTHASAR, *The God Question and Modern Man*, tr. H. Graef (New York 1967). E. BISER, *Theologie und Atheismus.* E. BLOCH, *Atheismus im Christentum* (Frankfurt 1969). P. TEILHARD DE CHARDIN, *The Phenomenon of Man*, tr. B. WALL (New York 1959). A. DEL NOCE, *Il problema dell'ateismo* (Bologna 1965). C. FABRO, *Introduzione all'ateismo moderno* (Rome 1964). R. GARAUDY, *Dieu est mort* (Paris 1962). G. GUTIERREZ, *Theology of Liberation*, tr., ed., E. INDA and J. EAGLESON (Maryknoll, N.Y. 1973). I. LEPP, *Psychoanalyse de l'athéisme moderne* (Paris 1961). H. DE LUBAC, *Le drame de l'humanisme athée* (Paris 1945). M. MACHOVEC, *Jesus für Atheisten* (Stuttgart 1972). J. MIGUEZ BONINO, *Christians and Marxists: The Mutual Challenge to Revolution* (London 1976). B. MONDIN, *Cultura, marxismo, cristianesimo* (Rome 1978). K. RAHNER, "Atheism and Implicit Christianity," *Theological Investigations* 9, tr. G. Harrison (London 1972) 145–164. J. A. T. ROBINSON, *Honest to God* (London 1963). B. WELTE, *Nietzsches Atheismus und das Christentum* (Darmstadt 1958).

[B. MONDIN]

ATTWATER, DONALD

Writer, editor; b. Dec. 24, 1892, Forest Garte, Co. Essex, England; d. Feb. 3, 1977, Storington. Of devout, Wesleyan parentage, in his youth he became, with them, an Anglican and, finally, at 18, on his own, a Catholic. After schooling in private and public institutions, he studied law but earned no degree. In the Royal Artillery during World War I, he was in Egypt and Palestine, 1916–1919. There he began an interest in Eastern

Christianity which would help to make him a writer and a specialist in studies of the Christian Orient. Among his works in this field: *The Dissident Eastern Churches* (Milwaukee 1937); *The Golden Book of Eastern Saints* (Milwaukee 1938); *Life of St. John Chrysostom* (Milwaukee 1939); *Eastern Catholic Worship* (Milwaukee 1945); *The Christian Church of the East* (Milwaukee 1947); *Saints of the East* (New York 1963).

After the war, he settled on the Isle of Caldey where he came under the influence of the Benedictines and of Eric Gill, both of whom were to mold his life. For the Benedictines, he took over the editorship of their quarterly review, *Pax*. He also edited a popular review on the liturgy, contributing many articles for it. This led to his becoming, in 1925, Associate Editor for England of the American review *Orate Fratres* (later to become *Worship*). For a time, he was also Contributing Editor for the American weekly *Commonweal*. From the inception of the *Catholic Herald*, London, he was on the staff and served as its Editor, 1935–1936. He was also Assistant Editor of a daughter paper, *The Glasgow Observer* from 1939 on. Prior to this, he became a founder of the Society for the Vernacular in English. The liturgy became one of his absorbing interests, and he was a strong voice in the liturgical movement. He wrote liturgical pieces for Catholic reviews both in England and the U.S. and, in 1961, published his *Layman's Missal*.

Attwater also authored several dictionary-type works. In 1931, e.g., he published *A Catholic Dictionary* (issued in England as *A Catholic Encyclopedic Dictionary*). His *Dictionary of Saints*, published in 1938, was later reissued as the *Penguin Dictionary of Saints* (Baltimore 1965), a continuing best seller. Earlier he had published his edition of the monumental Alban Butler-Herbert Thurston, SJ, *Lives of the Saints* (4 v., with notes and commentaries, New York 1956). During World War II, he was employed by the British Military Forces as a lecturer on current affairs. At war's end, he went on three lecture tours of the United States, and became a Visiting Lecturer at Notre Dame University.

Other of Attwater's works include: *The Catholic Church in Modern Wales* (London 1935); *The White Fathers in Africa* (London 1937); *Names and Name Days* (Milwaukee 1939); *A Dictionary of Mary* (New York 1956); *Dictionary of the Popes* (London 1965). Among his translations are: V. Solov'ev, *God, Man, and the Church*; N. A. Berdiaev, *The End of Our Time*; *Dostoievsky* (New York 1934); *Christianity and Class War* (London 1932). His last book *The Cell of Good Living* (London 1969) was a study of the life and views of Eric Gill, the artist who had influenced so deeply the renaissance of English letters of which Attwater was a part.

Bibliography: The London *Tablet* (Feb. 12, 1977) 161. *The Times* of London (Feb. 5, 1977) 18.

[P. F. MULHERN]

AUTHORITY, ECCLESIASTICAL

Vatican Council II, while remaining in fundamental continuity with Vatican I on church authority, nevertheless emphasized several aspects of the issue that had not been prominent at Vatican I nor in most textbooks of theology since (1:1115).

Communal Context. The first of these consists in Vatican II's effort to discuss authority always within the communal context—its ground and the condition of its effec-

tive exercise. Thus, before the discussion of the hierarchical structure of the Church, the Constitution on the Church has two chapters on the whole Church as Mystery and as People of God (*Lumen gentium* 1–17). Individual offices and ministries in the Church are treated in a parallel manner; the pope and individual bishops are discussed in the context of the whole episcopal college (ibid. 18–23; cf. *Christus Dominus* 1–4). The bishop is related to the corporate body of his *presbyterium* and local ministries are presented in the context of a diversity of ministries and charisms (*Lumen gentium* 27–29, 31–33, 36; *Christus Dominus* 15; *Presbyterorum ordinis* 2; *Apostolicam actuositatem* 2). These communal associations have, since the Council, received a certain institutional expression in the *Synod of Bishops, priests' senates, and diocesan and parish councils. Conciliar statements and their implementation have given concrete form and shape to the fundamental notion that all authority in the Church exists in and for the service of the whole Church-community.

Ministry. Secondly, the Council, while working with the threefold division of church authority into preaching, sacramental, and governing ministries, made an effort to overcome the rather sharp division which had been common between the power of orders and the power of *jurisdiction. All three ministerial functions were grounded and given in the Sacrament of Ordination, and the intrinsic connection between the ministry of Word, Sacrament, and community was thereby emphasized.

The "Crisis of Authority." Since the Council, and especially in the wake of the 1968 encyclical, *Humanae vitae* (16:215), a number of issues have arisen with regard to authority in the Church and particularly with regard to the *teaching authority or magisterium. Three aspects of what some have called the "crisis of authority" deserve notice: the relationships between the magisterium of pope and bishops and other bearers of the Christian message, between doctrinal authority and theological reasoning, and between the authority of the magisterium and the freedom of theologians.

(1) *Magisterium and Other Bearers of the Gospel.* Vatican II attempted to provide a balanced view of the various "authorities" that concretely bear the Christian message from generation to generation. While the Constitution on Divine Revelation affirmed that only the "living teaching office of the Church" has the "task of giving an authoritative interpretation of the Word of God," the Council also insisted that this teaching office "is not superior to the Word of God but is its servant." The magisterium was not presented as "the universal and proximate rule of faith" (by which it was once common to distinguish it from the "remote rules"—the Scriptures and tradition); rather, Scripture, tradition and magisterium are presented as "so linked and associated with one another that none of them can stand without the others and that, working together each in its own way, under the action of the Holy Spirit, they all contribute effectively to the salvation of souls" (*Dei Verbum* 10). The Council also spoke of the activity of the Holy Spirit in the whole body of the faithful by which the Church is infallibly preserved faithful (ibid. 8; *Lumen gentium* 12). Other bearers of the Christian message are also mentioned in the course of the conciliar documents: the liturgy, Christian art, the family, the examples of holy men and women, the work of theologians, etc.

In some ways, the present "crisis of authority" is the problem of working out, both theoretically and practically, the relationships among these various "authorities." It is fairly well agreed that it is a simplistic solution to subordinate all other authorities to any single one of them and that each of these bearers of Christian authority has its own distinct weight and character. It remains, however, to work out an understanding that can respect the distinctive contribution of all and within such respect to devise an ecclesiastical practice by which the pope and bishops can effectively coordinate the variety of gifts and contributions.

(2) *Doctrinal Authority and Theology.* The second question concerns the relationship between doctrinal authority and theological reasoning. It had become fairly common to distinguish sharply between these elements and to assert that the authority of official teachings is independent of the theological reasoning employed for their defense or illustration. Magisterial authority in the Church arises, it was argued, from Christ's appointment ("He who hears you hears me") and from the assistance of the Holy Spirit promised by Christ and given to pope and bishops in ordination. But, on the other hand, such assistance was acknowledged to be neither revelation nor inspiration; therefore the assistance does not excuse pope or bishops from using the ordinary means necessary to investigate the meaning of the Gospel. Today there is a noticeably greater reluctance to separate the truth or value of church pronouncements from the force of the arguments employed, especially in cases that do not involve infallibility. Much of the recent controversial literature on the magisterium revolves around the relationship between the "formal" teaching authority and the "matter" being taught.

(3) *Authority and Freedom of Inquiry.* The third relationship concerns the authority of official teachings and the freedom of theological investigation and speculation. In principle, everyone seems to acknowledge both that the pope and bishops have a distinctively grounded authority to teach and that freedom is necessary to the integrity and success of theological inquiry. The difficulties arise when the issues are particular. Two areas of controversy have arisen.

The first concerns the interpretation of the monuments of the doctrinal tradition. Scholars are now officially encouraged to apply critical-historical method to previous doctrinal determinations. This requires placing them in their historical situations and determining the concrete problematic in which they were elaborated, the questions to which they sought to reply, and the meaning and force their authors meant to give them. A certain dogmatic fundamentalism has thereby been ruled out of court and the difficulty of transposing these traditional teachings to new contexts of meaning been made uncomfortably clear. The controversies raised by this development are very similar to those that earlier centered around the question of biblical interpretation.

The second area of controversy regards the relationship between contemporary exercises of the magisterium and theological inquiry. Theologians have recently claimed considerable freedom to interpret,

question, and criticize contemporary church teachings, where these are not given infallibly. The *fallible* magisterium is understood to be an important and distinct factor in the development of the Church's sense of its message and mission; but it is not regarded as the only one nor as the necessarily determinative one (this being precisely what it means to say that it is fallible). The controversy provoked by this newly claimed freedom has prompted a mass of often bitter literature on the possibility and limits of theological dissent from official church teachings and on the relationship between the magisterium and the *theologian.

Evaluation. No theoretical or practical resolution of the controversies involved in these three issues is yet in sight. The three questions are interrelated, but perhaps the second is most basic. For it calls attention to the heart of the classic problem of authority, the relationship between its "formal" and "material" components. Until recently, Roman Catholic theology greatly stressed the formal element, as in the principle that the faithful were to inquire not so much about what was being said but about who was speaking: the truth and value of the *quod* was determined by the formal authority of the *quo.* Historical investigations have questioned the traditional basis for this position and critical theories of authority have argued that it is unbalanced. The Church's rule of faith is both the fundamental message and its authorized bearers, but the message is not known to the Church only through the magisterium. A "material" component, then, is intrinsic to an evaluation of any exercise of the teaching office and the other means by which the Church is kept in the integrity of the faith provide a norm by which the Church in any age receives or does not receive official Church pronouncements.

In the concrete, no resolution of the difficulties now being experienced can be expected without broadening the process by which official church teachings are elaborated, so that all the bearers of Christ's message are involved in the decision in ways appropriate to them. This will not mean collapsing all these bearers into an undifferentiated mass; it will mean that all the bearers will mediate each other's authority. The Church will then have most confidence that it hears Christ's word and will from pope and bishops when it knows that all the sources and bearers of the message by which it lives have been heard and have been found all to be leading it in one direction or another.

Bibliography: C. BUTLER, "Authority and the Christian Conscience," AmBenRev 24 (1974) 411–426. Y. CONGAR, "La 'Réception' comme réalité écclésiologique," RevScPhilTh 56 (1972) 369–403; "Pour une histoire du terme 'magisterium'," RevScPhilTh 60 (1976) 85–98; "Bref historique des formes du 'magistère' et ses relations avec les docteurs," ibid. 99–112. Congregation for the Doctrine of the Faith, "Mysterium Ecclesiae," ActApS 65 (1973) 396–408, tr. *Declaration in Defense of the Catholic Doctrine of the Church* . . . (USCC Publ. Office, Washington, D.C. 1973). A. DESCAMPS, "Théologie et magistère," EphemThLov 52 (1976) 82–133. A. DULLES, *The Resilient Church* (New York 1977). International Theological Commission, *Theses on the Relationship between the Ecclesiastical Magisterium and Theology* (Washington, D.C. 1977). K. RAHNER, "The Teaching Office of the Church in the Present-Day Crisis of Authority," *Theological Investigations* 12, tr. D. BOURKE (New York 1974) 3–30. T. H. SANKS, *Authority in the Church: A Study in Changing Paradigms* (Missoula, Mont. 1974). E. SCHILLEBEECKX and B. VAN IERSEL, eds., *Truth and Certainty. Concilium* 83 (New York 1973).

[J. A. KOMONCHAK]

B

BAPTISMAL FONT

The focal point of the baptistery where the Sacrament is actually administered. In early times the shape of the baptistery was largely governed by the shape of the font (as in the Baptistery of the Orthodox at Ravenna). There must be a provision for draining the font, either the whole font or that portion in which the Baptism actually occurs; but since Baptism is not a daily occurrence and a dry font is not a very meaningful symbol, it is well to have a sizable pool of water in the font and at least a slight flow of water (probably recirculated) always to be seen. Moving water is "living water," a highly meaningful symbol. With the primary importance of Baptism (the *ianua ecclesiae*) in Christian life, and in view of the number of times the faithful are reminded of their own Baptism (Easter Vigil, every Sunday Mass), it would be well to have the font of significant size and containing enough water that at least an infant could be baptized by immersion without adding more water.

[C. H. MEINBERG]

BAPTISMAL PROMISES

Baptismal promises consist in the renunciation of evil and profession of faith in the solemn celebration of Baptism and in the Easter liturgy.

Rites of Baptism. In the rite of Baptism for children, following the blessing of the baptismal water, the celebrant (priest or deacon) addresses a series of questions to the parents and godparents of the child (or children) to be baptized. To the questions they respond with a simple "I do." The dialogue, expressing the actual baptismal "promises," is a rejection of evil in its various aspects and an affirmation of belief in the chief truths of the Christian faith (BaptCh 120–123).

In this dialogue, the parents and godparents are speaking for the child (or children) about to be baptized. The procedure is a symbolic manifestation of faith for the child as yet unable to answer: "Do you reject Satan?" the celebrant asks and the child symbolically responds "I do." And so to the other questions: "And all his Satan's works?" "And all his empty promises?" In the profession of faith, according to the threefold division of the Creed, the repeated "I do" signifies the response which the to-be-baptized would

give. The faith thus expressed sums up Christian belief: in God the Father, in Jesus and his redemptive life, in the Holy Spirit who vivifies the Church towards eternal life. Celebrant and congregation then give assent to the profession of faith they have witnessed (ibid. 123).

In the Sacraments of Christian Initiation for adults, the responses are made by the one being baptized. They come as the formal expression before the community of the process of conversion during the *catechumenate (ChrInitAd 29–30). In the stages of the prolonged catechumenate there is already a process of exorcism and renunciation of non-Christian worship (ibid. 78–80) and, as part of the election of candidates, their presentation of the Creed (ibid. 183–186). At the celebration of Baptism the renunciation and profession of faith are a dialogue between celebrant and the catechumens themselves (ibid. 217–219). The same promises are made in the simplified rite of adult Baptism (ibid. 259–260). In all cases after the profession of faith the Baptism immediately follows (ibid. 219).

Easter Liturgy. The service of renewing the baptismal promises was inserted in the Easter Vigil service in the restoration ordered by Pius XII, in 1951, and is retained in the present *Sacramentary. The Easter Vigil is not a fast or "watch" before a feast, but the night celebration of the Resurrection, which, in ancient times, endured until dawn. Traditionally, Easter was the feast of Baptism, and the oldest parts of the renewed Vigil service center around it. The readings, for example, are a scriptural commentary on the meaning of the ritual of Christian initiation. In the blessing of the *baptismal water, the theme is that water, made productive by the Holy Spirit, gives birth to the divine life in man. The ritual of Baptism and also the revised ritual for Christian burial recall the relation of Baptism to the death and resurrection of Jesus; that relationship is highlighted in the feast of the Resurrection. The entire ritual of the Easter Vigil awakens the consciousness of the people of being a baptized people. The renewal of promises reinforces this consciousness, an emphasis in Vatican Council II's Constitution on the Liturgy (*Sacrosanctum Concilium* 6). The renewal of the promises by the assembly occurs after the blessing of baptismal water and the celebration of Baptism at the Easter Vigil; the renewal is also part of all the Easter-day Masses.

[P. F. MULHERN]

BAPTISMAL WATER, BLESSING OF

Baptismal water was formerly blessed in the Roman rite ordinarily only during the Holy Saturday Easter Vigil (see 14:826). The new rites for the Christian initiation of adults (promulgated Jan. 6, 1972) and for the Baptism of infants (promulgated May 15, 1969) provide for the blessing of the water during the baptismal rite itself. The ceremony of blessing the water during the Easter Vigil has been much simplified in the 1969 Roman Missal. Oils are not poured into the water, nor does the celebrant breathe on the water. The placing of the paschal candle in the water is optional. This water may be used throughout the Easter season. In the celebration of Baptism, whether of adults or infants, during the Easter season outside the Vigil service itself, a formula used for blessing the water is again used, to add the element of thanksgiving, but the actual asking of God's blessing is omitted (ChrInitAd 216, 389; BaptCh 55).

Outside the Easter season (or during the Easter season when blessed water is not available), water is blessed during the ceremony before the renunciation of Satan, profession of faith, and Baptism. Three alternative forms are provided in the rituals. The first of these very beautifully traces the symbolism of water through salvation history; the other two provide for a recurring congregational acclamation (ChrInitAd 215, 389; BaptCh 54, 223–224).

[J. DALLEN]

BAPTISTERY

The baptistery is the room or building (often the latter in early days) in which Baptism is administered. Liturgical histories show the changes that have taken place in the placement, importance, size, and design of the baptistery through the Christian centuries (2:72). Vatican Council II's Constitution on the Liturgy ordered attention to its suitability and dignity (*Sacrosanctum Concilium* 128). Today with the renewed baptismal rites, there is a tendency to place the baptistery near the sanctuary; since celebration of Christian initiation often takes place within a Mass, this location can be quite effective, tending as it does to keep the action of the initiation ceremony in focus with the action of the Mass. This also helps to emphasize the Sunday as a "little Easter" and to make the renewal of faith (Creed) more thoughtful and significant.

Bibliography: Righetti 1:342–397.

[C. H. MEINBERG]

BAPTIZED CHRISTIANS (RITE OF RECEPTION)

The Rite of Receiving Baptized Christians into Full Communion with the Catholic Church is of great ecumenical importance. It embodies the teaching of the Decree on Ecumenism of Vatican Council II that those in other ecclesiastical communities "who believe in Christ and have been properly baptized are put in some, though imperfect, communion with the Catholic Church" (*Unitatis redintegratio* 3). The purpose of this rite is to perfect that communion. In keeping with the provision of Acts 15.28, cited in the Instruction accompanying the rite (1) that no greater burden be demanded

of them than is necessary, the rite requires no abjuration of heresy for those born and baptized outside the Catholic Church, but only a profession of faith (*see* ABJURATION 1:23). The ecumenical effect is especially considered in the requirement that all appearance of triumphalism be avoided, and the suggestion that the reception Mass be celebrated with only a few relatives and friends (Rite 3b). The concern is shown in the clear statement that all repetition of Baptism, or the administration of conditional Baptism (unless there is reasonable doubt of the fact or validity of prior Baptism), is expressly prohibited (ibid. 7). Even necessary conditional Baptisms are to be conducted privately.

The rite itself takes place after the Homily at Mass and consists principally in the recitation of the Nicene Creed and the statement, "I believe and profess all that the holy Catholic Church believes, teaches, and proclaims to be revealed by God." The bishop, or the priest to whom he entrusts the celebration of the rite, receives the person with the imposition of the right hand. If the candidate has not been confirmed, the bishop or priest instead says the Confirmation prayer and administers that Sacrament. In either case the celebrant greets the one received and his name is mentioned in the General Intercessions as the Mass continues.

See also INCORPORATION INTO THE CHURCH.

Bibliography: *Rite of Reception of Baptized Christians into Full Communion with the Catholic Church* (Washington, D.C. 1973).

[L. L. MITCHELL]

BASIC CHRISTIAN COMMUNITIES

Basic Christian communities (English term for *comunidades eclesiales de base, communautés de base*; also known as mini-parishes, life-communions, neighborhood churches, grass-roots communities) are relatively small (in comparison with parishes), homogeneous groups of Christians who share common interests, values, and objectives; who search to emphasize primary, interpersonal, ongoing relationships; and who view themselves as ecclesial entities. Basic Christian communities are the form in which growing numbers of concerned peoples are structuring themselves as an alternative or a complement to the parish model of Church. Their common interests, their possibly living in the same area, and their limited numbers (from 8 to 40, some would say 100) allow members to develop close personal relationships. Generally these groups seek some concerted impact on the world and undertake apostolic options as a group. The rhythm of sacramental life varies according to group discernment and the availability of a priest or deacon. The purpose of basic Christian communities is not to be parish societies that provide services to the parish, to be study groups, or to be movements infusing church life with one special quality; but rather to hold their own identity as an ecclesial unit.

Such factors as discontent, the unavailability of a priest, impersonalism, the great distances between the members of some rural parishes, have been catalysts for the origin of some basic Christian communities. Among the positive features of these communities are: the experience of authentic community and close supportive relationships beyond the family; effective community supports and challenges to the members towards more meaningful service; a setting in which faith is deepened by the critique of the interaction between reading the

Gospel and the struggle to live as Christians; promotion of involvement in contemporary society; rapid development of many and varied ministries or services among the members; and a questioning of the parish as the only model for Church.

Basic Christian communities have become a major element of the pastoral practice of significant segments of the Catholic and Protestant Churches over the world. They are a cornerstone of much Latin American pastoral work. In many areas of Africa and Asia they are likewise a key for pastoral development. Gatherings to evaluate and advance the work are constantly held in these areas, as well as in Europe. In the United States and Canada the phenomenon is widespread and growing, but seldom an integral part of diocesan planning. Among U.S. Hispanics however, the idea has taken on marked significance. Every major document of U.S. Hispanics since 1972 has directed itself to development of basic Christian communities. Likewise, beginning in 1971 nearly every papal and synodal document on pastoral affairs has concerned itself with basic Christian communities, progressing from oblique references to cautious concern, to support and directives for their healthy development (see Paul VI EvangNunt 58).

See also COMMUNITY; MISSION (NEW TRENDS); PARISH (PASTORAL THEOLOGY).

Bibliography: T. G. BISSONNETTE, "Comunidades Eclesiales de Base: Contemporary Grass Roots Attempts to Build Ecclesial Koinonia," *Jurist* 36 (1976) 24–58. C. FLORISTAN, *Comunidad Christiana de Base* (San Antonio 1976). J. MARINS and T. TREVISAN, *Communidades Eclesiales de Base* (Bogotá 1975).

[T. G. BISSONNETTE]

BEATIFICATIONS AND CANONIZATIONS

Pope Paul VI issued two documents on competencies and procedures with regard to beatifications and canonizations.

Sanctitas Clarior. The motu proprio *Sanctitas clarior* (ActApS 61 [1969] 149–153), implementing *Lumen gentium* (40, 47, 50), was chiefly concerned with clarifying the competencies of bishops to introduce causes of servants of God for beatification. The Pope decreed that diocesan bishops (or their equivalents) must consult the Holy See before introducing a process; the Holy See decides whether the grounds are sufficient. The process of inquiry into miracles is a separate step. *Sanctitas clarior* recognizes the right of national and regional episcopal conferences to establish, after recognition by the Holy See, tribunals for investigation of processes. The individual rights of local Ordinaries within such conferences to initiate causes remain intact.

Sacra Rituum Congregatio. In May 1969 the apostolic constitution *Sacra Rituum Congregatio* (ActApS 61 [1969] 297–305) established the new Congregation for the Causes of Saints (*see* CURIA, ROMAN). The work of this Congregation is divided among three offices. The first, headed by a Secretary, has a judicial function over the institution of causes and the findings of the process. The second office is under the Promotor General of the Faith, with the function of testing and reviewing processes. The third office has historiographic and hagiographic functions.

Beatifications since 1965. (Here and in the Canonization list, the first parenthetical reference is to the *New Catholic Encyclopedia*; date of beatification/canonization follows; then reference to *Acta Apostol-*

icae Sedis and/or the English edition of *L'Osservatore Romano*.)

Barbieri, Clelia, virgin and foundress of the Little Sisters of the Suffering Virgin, Oct. 27, 1968 (ActApS 60 [1968] 680–684; OssRomEng 1968, n. 32, 2 & 8.

Berneux, Siméon *see* KOREAN MARTYRS below.

Berthieu, Jacques, priest and martyr of the Society of Jesus, Oct. 17, 1965 (ActApS 57 [1965] 817–822).

Bertoni, Gaspare, priest of the Congregation of the Holy Stigmata of Our Lord Jesus Christ, Nov. 11, 1975 (ActApS 68 [1976] 486–489; OssRomEng 1975, n. 45, 1–4.

Brou, Marie-Eugénie Milleret de, foundress of the Sisters of the Assumption of the B.V.M., Feb. 9, 1975 (ActApS 67 [1975] 244–247; OssRomEng 1975, n. 8, 6–7).

Bus, César de, priest and founder of the Fathers of Christian Doctrine (2:908) Apr. 27, 1975 (ActApS 67 [1975] 324–326; OssRomEng 1975, n. 19, 6–7).

Charbel, *see* Makhlouf, Sharbel.

Dominici, Maria Enrica, Sister of St. Ann and Providence, May 7, 1978 (OssRomEng 1978, n. 20, 1 & 8).

Droste zu Vischerung, Maria, member of the Good Shepherd Sisters, Nov. 1, 1975 (ActApS 68 [1976] 489– 492; OssRomEng 1975, n. 45, 1–4).

Febres Cordero, Michele Francisco, member of the Institute of the Brothers of Christian Instruction, Oct. 30, 1977 (OssRomEng 1977, n. 45, 3–9).

Freinademetz, John, missionary of the Society of the Divine Word in China, Oct. 19, 1975 (ActApS 68 [1976] 247–250; OssRomEng, 1975, n. 44, 6–7).

Grossi, Vincenzo, priest and founder of the Daughters of the Oratory, Nov. 1, 1975 (ActApS 68 [1976] 168–170; OssRomEng 1975, n. 45, 1–4).

Ignatius of St. Agatha, priest of the Order of Friars Minor Capuchin, Apr. 17, 1966 (ActApS 58 [1966] 351–356).

Janssen, Arnold, founder of the Society of the Divine Word (7:826) Oct. 19, 1975 (ActApS 68 [1976] 244–247; OssRomEng 1975, n. 44, 6–7).

Kasper, Katharina, foundress of the Poor Handmaids of Jesus Christ (8:133) April 19, 1978 (OssRomEng 1978, n. 17, 1 & 4).

Kolbe, Maximilian, priest of the Order of Friars Minor Conventual (16:239), Oct. 17, 1971 (ActApS 64 [1972] 401–407; OssRomEng 1971, n. 43, 8–9).

Korean Martyrs of 1866, Bishop Siméon Berneux and companions, Oct. 6, 1968 (ActApS 60 [1968] 657–661; OssRomEng 1968, n. 29, 6–8):

Siméon Berneux, bishop and vicar apostolic; Antoine Develuy, bishop and vicar apostolic; Juste de Bretenières, priest; Louis Beaulieu, priest; Pierre Henri Dorie, priest; Pierre Aumaître, priest; Martin Huin, priest; Peter Ruy Chong-ryul; John Nam Chong-sam; Peter Ch'oe Hyong; John Chun Chang-un; Mark Chung Eui-pae; Alexis U Se-yong; Luke Hwang Sok-tu; Joseph Chang Nak-so; Thomas Sohn Cha-son; Peter Cho Hwa-so; Joseph Cho Yun-ho; Peter Lee Myong-so; Bartholomew Chung Mun-ho; Peter Sohn Sonji; Peter Han Won-so; Peter Chung Won-ji; John Lee Che-hyon.

Ledóchowska, Maria Teresa, virgin and foundress of the Sodality of Peter Claver (8:601) Oct. 19, 1975 (ActApS 68 [1976] 250–254; OssRomEng 1975, n. 44, 6–7).

Leopold da Castelnovo, priest of the Order of Friars

Minor Capuchin, May 2, 1976 (ActApS 68 [1976] 548–550; OssRomEng 1976, n. 20, 6–7).

Lopez de Rivas, Mary of Jesus, virgin and nun of the Order of Discalced Carmelites, Nov. 14, 1976 (ActApS 69 [1977] 252–255; OssRomEng 1976, n. 48, 6–7).

Makhlouf, Sharbel, priest and monk of the Maronite Lebanese Order of St. Anthony, Dec. 5, 1965 (ActApS 57 [1965] 955–960); canonized Oct. 10, 1977.

Mazenod, Charles Joseph Eugène de, bishop (9:522) Oct. 19, 1975 (ActApS 68 [1976] 241–243; OssRomEng 1975, n. 44, 6–7).

Michelotti, Anna, foundress of the Congregation of the Little Servants of the Sacred Heart of Jesus for the Sick Poor, Nov. 1, 1975 (ActApS 68 [1976] 253–256; OssRomEng 1975, n. 45, 1–4).

Molas y Vollvé, María Rosa, foundress of the Sisters of Our Lord of Consolation, May 8, 1977 (OssRomEng 1977, n. 20, 2–5).

Moreno y Díaz, Ezechiel, bishop and member of the Order of Augustinian Recollects, Nov. 1, 1975 (ActApS 68 [1976] 486–489; OssRomEng 1975, n. 45, 1–4).

Moscati, Giuseppe, layman, Nov. 16, 1975 (ActApS [1976] 259–262; OssRomEng 1975, n. 48, 5–7).

Pietrantoni, Agostina, religious of the Sisters of Charity of St. Joan Antida Thouret, Nov. 12, 1972 (ActApS 65 [1973] 229–235; OssRomEng 1972, n. 47, 1–2).

Rua, Michael, priest and major superior of the Society of St. Francis de Sales, Oct. 29, 1972 (ActApS 66 [1974] 529–532; OssRomEng 1972, n. 45, 1).

Schervier, Franziska, foundress of the Franciscan Sisters of the Poor (12:1127) Apr. 28, 1974 (ActApS 66 [1974] 596–598; OssRomEng 1974, n. 19, 5–9).

Steeb, Karl, priest and founder of the Sisters of Mercy of Verona, July 6, 1975 (ActApS 67 [1975] 465–468; OssRomEng 1975, n. 29, 2–3).

Viti, Maria Fortunata, nun of the Order of St. Benedict, Oct. 8, 1967 (ActApS 59 [1967] 955–960).

Wagner, Liborius, priest and martyr (14:766) March 24, 1974 (ActApS 66 [1974] 373–375; OssRomEng 1974, n. 15, 4–5).

Wiaux, Mutien Marie, member of the Institute of the Brothers of Christian Instruction, Oct. 30, 1977 (OssRomEng 1977, n. 45. 8–9).

Wüllenweber, Theresia von (Mary of the Apostles), Oct. 13, 1968 (ActApS 60 [1968] 673–680; OssRomEng 1968, n. 30, 5).

Canonizations since 1965.
Bénilde, Christian Brother (2:311), Oct. 29, 1967 (ActApS 59 [1967] 1017–1026).

Billiart, Marie Rose Julie, virgin and foundress of the Congregation of the Sisters of Notre Dame de Namur (2:557), June 22, 1969 (ActApS 62 [1970] 144–156; OssRomEng 1969, n. 27, 6–7).

Couderc, Marie Victoire Thérèse, virgin and foundress of the Religious of the Cenacle (4:368–369), May 10, 1970 (ActApS 62 [1970] 394–402; OssRomEng 1970, n. 21, 6–7).

Deodatus of Aquitaine, martyr of the Order of Friars Minor, June 21, 1970 (ActApS 62 [1970] 488–495; OssRomEng 1970, n. 27, 5–6).

Forty Martyrs of England and Wales (9:319), Oct. 25, 1970 (ActApS 62 [1970] 745–753; OssRomEng 1970, n. 45, 6–8):

Almond, John (1:328); Arrowsmith, Edmund (1:851); Barlow, Ambrose (2:101); Boste, John (2:718–719); Briant, Alexander (2:795); Campion, Edmund (2:1115–16); Clitherow, Margaret (3:959); Evans, Philip (5:654); Garnet, Thomas (6:292); Gennings, Edmund (6:334); Gwyn, Richard (White) (6:872); Houghton, John (7:174–175); Howard, Philip (7:180); Jones, John (Buckley) (7:1097); Kemble, John (8:147); Kirby, Luke (8:204); Lawrence, Robert (8:571); Lewis, David (Charles Baker) (8:686); Line, Anne (8:771); Lloyd, John (8:946); Mayne, Cuthbert (9:520–521); Morse, Henry (9:1152); Owen, Nicholas (10:840); Paine, John (10:866); Plasden, Polydore (11:429); Plessington, John William (11:441); Reynolds, Richard (12:455); Rigby, John (12:496); Roberts, John (12:536); Roe, Alban (Bartholomew) (12:550); Sherwin, Ralph (13:174); Southwell, Robert (13:485); Southworth, John (13:486); Stone, John (13:724); Wall, John (14:776); Walpole, Henry (14:779); Ward, Margaret (14: 808); Webster, Augustine (14:840); Wells, Swithun (14:869); White, Eustace (14:893).

Jacobis, Giustino de, bishop, first apostolic vicar of Ethiopia and member of the Congregation of the Missionaries of St. Vincent de Paul (7:794), Oct. 26, 1975 (ActApS 69 [1977] 23–28; OssRomEng 1975, n. 45, 3).

John of Avila, priest and confessor (7:1029), May 31, 1970 (ActApS 62 [1970] 481–487; OssRomEng 1970, n. 24, 5).

John Baptist of the Conception, priest of the Order of the Most Holy Trinity (7:1030), May 25, 1975 (ActApS 68 [1976] 97–106; OssRomEng 1975, n. 23, 6–12).

Jornet e Ibars, Teresa, virgin and foundress of the Little Sisters of the Poor and Aged (7:1106), Jan. 27, 1974 (ActApS 68 [1976] 433–422; OssRomEng 1974, n. 6, 6–8).

López y Vicuña, Vincenta María, foundress of the Daughters of Mary Immaculate for Domestic Service (8:987), May 25, 1975 (ActApS 68 [1976] 107–112; OssRomEng 1975, n. 23, 6–12).

Makhlouf, Sharbel, priest and monk of the Maronite Lebanese order of St. Anthony, Oct. 10, 1977 (ActApS 70 [1978] 224–230; OssRomEng 1977, n. 42, 4–5); beatified Dec. 5, 1965.

Masías, John, laybrother of the Order of Preachers (9:41) Sept. 28, 1975 (ActApS 68 [1976] 443–449; OssRomEng 1975, n. 41, 6–9).

Murialdo, Leonardo, confessor and founder of the Pious Congregation of St. Joseph (10:83), May 3, 1970 (ActApS 62 [1970] 385–393; OssRomEng 1970, n. 20, 6–7).

Neumann, John Nepomucene, bishop of Philadelphia, Redemptorist (10:364), June 19, 1977 (ActApS 70 [1978] 217–223; OssRomEng 1977, n. 25, 1–3).

Nicholas Tavelić and companion-martyrs of the Order of Friars Minor (Deodatus of Aquitaine, Peter of Narbonne, and Stephen of Cuneo) June 21, 1970 (ActApS 62 [1970] 488–495; OssRomEng 1970, n. 27, 5–6).

Ogilvie, John, priest and martyr of the Society of Jesus (10:659), Oct. 12, 1976 (ActApS 69 [1977] 305–311; OssRomEng 1976, n. 43, 1–3).

Peter of Narbonne, martyr of the Order of Friars Minor, June 21, 1970 (ActApS 62 [1970] 488–495; OssRomEng 1970, n. 27, 5–6).

Plunket, Oliver, martyr and archbishop of Armagh (11:446), Oct. 12, 1975 (ActApS 69 [1977] 65–74; OssRomEng 1975, n. 42, 1).

Porras y Ayllón, Rafaela Maria, foundress of the Congregation of the Handmaids of the Sacred Heart (11:595), Jan. 23, 1977 (ActApS 69 [1977] 193–197; OssRomEng 1977, n. 5, 2–4).

Seton, Elizabeth Bayley, foundress of the Congregation of the Sisters of Charity of St. Joseph (13:136), Sept. 14, 1975 (ActApS) 68 [1976] 689–693; OssRomEng 1975, n. 38, 1–3).

Silva, Beatrice da, virgin and foundress of the Enclosed Franciscan Sisters of Mary Immaculate, Oct. 3, 1976 (ActApS 69 [1977] 129–135; OssRomEng 1976, n. 42, 6–7).

Stephen of Cuneo, martyr of the Order of Friars Minor, June 21, 1970 (ActApS 62 [1970] 488–495; OssRomEng 1970, n. 27, 5–6).

Torres Acosta, María Soledad, virgin and foundress of the Servants of Mary (14:206), Jan. 25, 1970 (ActApS 62 [1970] 81–88; OssRomEng 1970, n. 5, 12).

[H. D. BURNS]

BELGRADE CONFERENCE

The Conference on Security and Cooperation in Europe, which met in Belgrade from October 1977 to March 1978, reviewed the implementation of the 1975 *Helsinki Agreement and discussed additional steps to strengthen East-West cooperation. Representatives of 32 European nations, the United States, Canada, and the Holy See exchanged views on military security, economic and scientific cooperation, and human rights. The exhaustive review included a detailed case-by-case examination of human rights' abuses. According to the chief American delegate, Ambassador Arthur J. Goldberg, "We have expressed our concern and our regret and at times our outrage at the incidents which have occurred in direct contravention" of the Helsinki Agreement, which pledged respect for "human rights and fundamental freedoms, including the freedom of thought, conscience, religion or belief." Although the Soviet Union, East Germany, and Czechoslovakia, the principal targets of such accusations, blocked any mention of these debates in the official summary, the Belgrade Conference placed the participating states' treatment of their own citizens into the legitimate framework of international diplomacy.

The Belgrade Conference assured a continuation of the review process by scheduling a similar session at Madrid in November 1980. It also provided for additional meetings of experts to consider scientific cooperation, machinery for the peaceful settlement of international disputes, and demilitarization of the Mediterranean Sea. Thus, in spite of the differences expressed at Belgrade, the direction in international diplomacy begun at Helsinki will continue.

[R. J. GIBBONS]

BENEDICTION AND EXPOSITION OF THE BLESSED SACRAMENT

By decree of June 21, 1973 approved by Pope Paul VI, a revised "Rite of Eucharistic Exposition and Benediction" was issued by the Congregation for Divine Worship. Such exposition of the Holy Eucharist, either in the ciborium or in the monstrance, is intended to acknowledge Christ's marvelous presence in the Sacrament; it invites us to the spiritual union with our Lord that culminates in sacramental Communion; it fosters very well the worship due Jesus in spirit and in truth (HolyCommIntrod 82). The exposition service should clearly express that the cult of the Blessed Sacrament is properly related to Mass and carefully avoid anything which obscures the principal desire of Christ in instituting the Eucharist: to be with us as food, medicine and comfort (ibid.).

Only a single genuflection is now made in the presence of the Blessed Sacrament, whether reserved in the tabernacle or exposed for public adoration (ibid. 84). For exposition in the monstrance, four to six candles are lighted, as at Mass, and incense is used. For exposition in the ciborium, at least two should be lighted, and incense may be used (ibid. 85). Exposition exclusively for giving benediction is prohibited, but periods shorter than the traditional *Forty Hours Devotion are permitted provided the blessing with the Eucharist is preceded by scriptural readings, songs, prayers, and sufficient time for silent prayer (ibid. 89).

The ordinary minister is a priest or deacon wearing the humeral veil who, at the end of the period of adoration, blesses the people with the Sacrament by making the sign of the cross in silence over them with the monstrance or ciborium. Certain others, e.g. acolytes, special ministers of Communion, religious appointed by the Ordinary, may publicly expose and later repose the Eucharist, but not give the benediction (ibid. 91).

See also EUCHARIST, WORSHIP AND CUSTODY OF.

[J. M. CHAMPLIN]

BIBLE AND LITURGY

The concern of Vatican Council II to "open up the treasures of the Bible more lavishly" in the liturgy (*Sacrosanctum Concilium* 51) has been realized in the restoration of the rites for the celebration of the Eucharist, the Liturgy of the Hours, and the other Sacraments and sacramentals.

The Bible in the Mass. The Council for the Implementation of the Constitution on the Sacred Liturgy (Consilium, 16:99) in order to foster experimentation, after establishing certain general principles, authorized the use of interim weekday lectionaries prepared by episcopal conferences. These lectionaries contained a one-year cycle of Gospel readings, but a two-year cycle for the First Reading, with Old and New Testaments assigned to alternate years. In 1965 the proposal of the German hierarchy was approved, and in 1966 that of the French hierarchy, as well as a third system prepared by the Consilium itself. Many other countries adopted one of these lectionaries; in 1967 the German system was authorized for use in the United States. In the same year the Consilium also authorized particular lectionaries for use on various special occasions.

Immediately after the promulgation of the Constitution extensive preparations were undertaken for a definitive lectionary, involving wide consultation of experts in liturgy, biblical studies, catechetics, and pastoral theology. Approved in stages by the Consilium and again revised after submission to episcopal conferences, the first Synod of Bishops, and some 800 experts, the project was promulgated in 1969.

The Sunday and feast-day lectionary has returned to the ancient tradition of three readings, drawn from the Old Testament (replaced by Acts in Paschaltide), the apostolic writings, and the Gospels, respectively. A three-year cycle devotes a year to each of the Synoptics, while John is used during Paschaltide and other seasons and for part of Year B. The Old Testament Reading is chosen to correspond to the Gospel, while the epistles are read semicontinuously. Lent has a more complex pattern. Most of the New Testament and the principal texts of the Old Testament are thus proclaimed on Sundays.

The ferial lectionary proposes two readings for each day. The Gospels are arranged in a one-year cycle, while the first reading has a two-year cycle; both years alternate Old and New Testament passages except in some seasons. Both series are usually semicontinuous and thus not intended to correspond to each other.

Separate lectionaries are provided for propers and commons of saints, and for ritual and votive Masses, with a great variety of selections appropriate to the occasion. The rubrics are flexible enough to permit numerous options on many occasions.

The lectionary has also restored the ancient usage of the antiphonal psalm, which serves as Responsory to the First Reading. Proper refrains are provided for each formulary, and with carefully selected verses from an appropriate psalm or canticle. Other refrains and psalms are supplied for optional use during seasons and for commons.

The Mass lectionary has had a notable ecumenical impact: several major Protestant denominations have produced lectionaries substantially in agreement with the Roman system (*see* LECTIONARIES).

The Bible in the Liturgy of the Hours. The reading of the Bible in the Liturgy of the Hours is intended to supplement that of the Mass; it includes longer and more difficult readings and draws upon all the books of Scripture except the Gospels. Each day one long biblical reading is assigned to the Office of Readings (formerly Vigils or "Matins"), together with a nonbiblical reading, usually patristic, relating to the same theme. The system prepared for this is on a two-year cycle (GenInstrLitHor 146–152); because of its bulk, however, it was consigned to a supplement and a reduced one-year cycle was printed in the *editio typica*. The other hours contain a short biblical reading which gives trenchant expression to a particular theme.

The Liturgy of the Hours maintains the traditional importance of the Psalter, though it has eliminated three imprecatory psalms and parts of others. The psalmody of each hour has been shortened so that the Psalter is spread over four weeks, though some psalms are repeated and three historical psalms used only in some seasons. Psalms are assigned to appropriate days and hours in keeping with their content and literary character. Efforts have been made to assist the participant in understanding the psalms Christologically. Each psalm is introduced by an antiphon, a title, and a phrase from the New Testament or the Fathers pointing to its Christian meaning. New optional psalter collects are provided: consigned to a supplement in the *editio typica*, they are printed within the Psalter itself in the authorized American translation (*see* PSALTERS, VERNACULAR).

The Bible in Other Rites. The Mass lectionary contains a wide selection of Readings and Responsorial Psalms for rites normally celebrated within the Eucharist: the rites of catechumenate and adult Baptism; infant Baptism; Confirmation; Orders; Marriage; blessing of abbots and abbesses; consecration of virgins and religious profession; funerals; and dedication of churches and altars. The special books for these rites also contain lectionaries, sometimes with additional choices. Other rites, such as those for Penance and Anointing of the Sick, have separate lectionaries of their own.

Biblical Versions. In order to provide a Latin biblical text suitable for liturgical use and at the same time conformable to modern critical standards, Pope Paul VI in 1965 appointed a commission to revise the Vulgate. The Commission's work, which appeared in sections, was completed late in 1977; a one-volume edition is in preparation. Called the *Nova Vulgata*, this version has been used in the new liturgical books to the extent that it was complete at the time of their publication. Vernacular versions of Scripture can be authorized by national hierarchies for liturgical usage. Those approved for use in the United States include *The Jerusalem Bible*, *The New American Bible*, *The Revised Standard Version*, and *The Grail Psalter*.

Bible and Piety. While the reform of the liturgical rites is nearing completion, the restoration of a biblical mentality among Catholics generally is still in its initial stages. The effectiveness of increased exposure to the Scriptures in the liturgy will depend upon continuing biblical education. Serious efforts have been made to bring about a renewal of preaching through improved seminary training, workshops for priests, and production of materials for assistance in homily preparation. Biblical instruction has been introduced at all academic levels and in adult education programs. Bible reading has become common among some Catholics both individually and in groups organized for common prayer and study. Literature and audio-visual aids for biblical popularization are increasingly available.

Some tendencies in post-Vatican II Catholicism, however, have constituted a hindrance to the growth of a genuine biblical piety (*see* 2:520). The late 1960s were marked by secularizing tendencies that stressed contemporary relevance, and both teaching and preaching were to some extent diverted from a biblical orientation. In some unauthorized liturgical experimentation the Bible was entirely displaced in favor of secular texts for the Liturgy of the Word. In reaction to this, the 1970s have produced a new pietism that is generally enthusiastic about the Bible, but sometimes approaches it in a spirit of narrow fundamentalism. While Catholic biblical scholarship has continued to flourish, some signs of disenchantment with scientific study of the Bible have also appeared.

Bibliography: P. BÉGUERIE, "La Bible née de la liturgie," *Maison-Dieu* 126 (1976) 7–23. B. BOTTE and H. CAZELLES eds., *La Parole dans la liturgie* (Paris 1970). I.-H. DALMAIS, "La Bible vivante dans L'Église," *Maison-Dieu* 126 (1976) 7–23. M. MAGRASSI, "Tipologia biblica e patristica e La Liturgia della Parola, "*Rivista liturgica* 53 (1966) 165–193; "Interpretazione cristiana e liturgica della Bibbia," ibid. 55 (1968) 151–192. C. VAGAGGINI, *Theological Dimensions of the Liturgy*, tr. of 4th rev. ed., L. J. DOYLE (Collegeville, Minn. 1976). A. VERHEUL, "La service de la Parole," QuestLiturgParoiss 56 (1975) 225–256. Entire issue of *Maison-Dieu* 82 (1965).

Mass lectionary: G. FONTAINE, "Ordo lectionum Missae," *Notitiae* 5 (1969) 237–282; the same commentary in EphemLiturg 83 (1969) 436–451; "Le lectionnaire de la Messe au temps de l'Avent," *Notitiae* 7 (1971) 304–317; 364–376. Entire issue of *Maison-Dieu* 99 (1969).

Office lectionary: E. J. LENGELING, "Die Lesungen und Responsorien im neuen Stundengebet," LiturgJb 20 (1970) 231–249. A. ROSE, "La répartition des lectures bibliques dans le livre de la Liturgie des Heures," EphemLiturg 85 (1971) 281–305. C. WIÉNER, "Le lectionnaire biblique de l'office," *Maison-Dieu* 105 (1971) 103–116. For the one-year cycle, see *Notitiae* 7 (1971) 393–408; 8 (1972) 265–269; for the two-year cycle, 12 (1976) 238–248; 324–333; 378–388.

Psalmody: J. PASCHER, "Die Psalmen als Grundlage des Stundengebets," EphemLiturg 85 (1971) 260–280. J. PINELL, "Las oraciones del Salterio 'per annum' en el nuevo libro de la Liturgia de las Horas," *ibid.* 86 (1972) 354–389; 417–448, also published separately (Rome 1974). A. ROSE, "La répartition des psaumes dans le cycle liturgique," *Maison-Dieu* 105 (1971) 66–102; "La lecture chrétienne du Psautier dans la Liturgie des Heures," EphemLiturg 86 (1972) 5–30. J. G. TARRUEL, "La Nouvelle distribution du Psautier dans le 'Liturgia Horarum'," *ibid.* 87 (1973) 325–382.

Other rites: J.-B. MOLIN and G. BEQUET, "La célébration de la Parole dans le nouveau rituel du baptême des enfants," *Maison-Dieu* 98 (1969) 32–58.

Versions: J. GRIBOMONT, "La parfaite version biblique ou la quadrature du cercle," *Maison-Dieu* 118 (1974) 29–48. J. H. WESTLAKE, "The Liturgical Use of Modern Translations of the Bible," StLiturg 8 (1972) 98–118.

Attitudes toward the Bible: J. BARR, *The Bible in the Modern World* (London 1973). F. REFOULÉ, "L'exégèse en question," *Supplément* 111 (1974) 391–423.

[C. J. PEIFER]

BIBLE SERVICES

The growth of paraliturgical bible services (2:532) before Vatican Council II was due to the recognition that pastoral goals were difficult to achieve through the liturgy in its then fossilized state. While the Council recommended "sacred celebrations of the Word of God" (*Sacrosanctum Concilium* 35, 4; cf. *Inter oecumenici* 37–39, Congr. of Rites, ActApS 56 [1964] 877–900), it rendered paraliturgical services largely unnecessary by reforming the liturgical rites so as to make them accessible to the people. Since the publication of the Liturgy of the Hours and the principal sacramental rites, most pastoral needs can be satisfied by the liturgy itself (*see* BIBLE AND LITURGY).

The most important occasion for para-liturgies of the Word is to substitute for the Sunday Eucharist when a priest is not available. In such cases a deacon, or even a lay person, may be authorized by the bishop to conduct the Liturgy of the Word substantially as at Mass through to the General Intercessions, followed by the Lord's Prayer, the distribution of Communion, and the concluding Prayers. Such services have become common in places suffering from severe shortage of priests, as in parts of Latin America, especially since the authorization of the permanent diaconate and of extraordinary ministers of the Eucharist.

The new rite of Penance (1973) provides a Rite for Reconciliation of Several Penitents which includes a Celebration of the Word. Several examples are provided, and the appendix contains sample penitential services for various seasons and categories of people. Communal penance services have been introduced into many parishes and religious houses as preparation for individual confession, or even with general absolution if it has been authorized by the Ordinary.

The rite for funerals (1969) contains provisions for a vigil or Celebration of the Word for the Deceased, to be held in the home or mortuary, or even in church. It consists of introduction, psalmody, prayer, biblical readings with responsories, homily, general intercessions, and the Lord's Prayer. This official rite, which permits numerous options, should now replace the various wake services previously in use.

A similar Liturgy of the Word is provided for other rites when celebrated outside of Mass: admission to catechumenate; Baptism; Confirmation; Holy Communion; Marriage; Anointing of the Sick; institution of readers; admission to candidacy; initiation into religious life, first profession and renewal of vows.

Seasonal celebrations of the Word, e.g. in Advent, can now be supplied, in many cases, by utilizing the options permitting adaptation of the Liturgy of the Hours to the needs of the local community.

Bibliography: J. P. MEIER, "Celebration of the Word in Communal Services of Penance," *Worship* 50 (1976) 413–420. A. M. ROGUET, "Les célébrations sacrées de la Parole de Dieu," *Miscellanea liturgica Lercaro* 2 (Rome 1967) 119–132.

Examples of Bible services: A. CHAO and P. BRUNNER, *Glory to the Lord: Twenty Bible Vigils* (Collegeville, Minn. 1966). J. GALLEN, *Scripture Services: Eighteen Bible Themes Arranged for Group Use* (Collegeville, Minn. 1963), also available in Spanish.

[C. J. PEIFER]

BIBLE VERSIONS FOR LITURGY

Since the entry on Bible versions (2:425) several major versions of the entire Bible have been produced; only those approved for use in the liturgical Churches are here discussed.

The *Revised Standard Version* (RSV), including the second edition of the New Testament and the Apocrypha was published as *The New Oxford Annotated Bible* in 1973. This was twenty-one years after the first publication of the RSV (1952). The *International Consultation on English Texts (ICET) adopted the basic style of the RSV, since it retains much of the strength and flavor of earlier English versions. The RSV is acclaimed for its accuracy and freshness, having benefited from careful planning, clearly stated goals, and a board which included experts in English usage. Though technically a revision, it was in effect a new translation. An annotated edition for Catholics was issued in 1965.

The English *Jerusalem Bible* (JB) appeared in 1966. The project had been prompted by the excellence and phenomenal success of *La Bible de Jerusalem* (first one-volume edition, 1956), to which it has a complicated relationship. Critics have questioned whether JB deserves to be called "a fresh translation," especially since most of its crucial decisions accord with those of the French Bible. In the Old Testament it frequently prefers the Septuagint readings. When judged by the results, however, JB is a readable and remarkable version. The literary quality is generally maintained at a level throughout, though readers will be grateful for A. Di Lella's careful listing of deficiencies (see bibliog.).

The *New English Bible* (NEB) appeared in 1970, the result of twenty years' work by a team representing the Anglican and Protestant Churches of the British Isles. The translation is contemporary, fresh, and in no sense intended to be a revision. The New Testament is already a second edition, and the Apocrypha are included. NEB was produced with the help of a special literary panel. Despite the care expended on it, it has been heavily criticized both as to its scholarship and as to its English diction. The Old Testament is already in the process of complete revision.

The *New American Bible* (NAB) likewise appeared in

1970, the result of more than thirty years' work under Roman Catholic direction. Earlier called the *Confraternity Version*, it was to have been at first a translation of the Latin Vulgate. With the appearance of *Divino afflante Spiritu* in 1943 it was decided that all work would be done from the original texts. The translation appeared in various stages. The project gained something of an ecumenical dimension when three revisers were appointed from outside the Roman Catholic Church. NAB has been praised for many reasons—its scholarship, its adoption of standard English spellings of proper names, and its use of the Hebrew text in translating Ecclesiasticus. Its unevenness has been frequently pointed out by critics.

The *Good News Bible* (N.Y., 1976), although used at times in churches, does not appear to have received official approbation for liturgy.

Bibliography: K. R. CRIM, "Versions, English," InterDictBiblSuppl 933–938. B. AVERY, "The Revised Standard Versions," *Worship* 32 (1958) 416–419. L. WEIGLE, "The RSV of the Bible," CBQ 14 (1952) 310–318. A. DI LELLA, (on JB), CathBiblQuart 29 (1967) 148–151. F. DANKER, (on NAB), CathBiblQuart 33 (1971) 405–409. J. REUMANN, (on NAB), JBiblLit 92 (1973) 275–278. M. DAHOOD, (on NEB), *Biblica* 52 (1971) 117–123.

[J. I. HUNT]

BIBLES, COMMON

Common Bibles are interconfessional translations produced in accordance with the guidelines devised by the executive committee of the United Bible Societies and the Vatican's Secretariat for Promoting Christian Unity. They represent an ecumenical response to Vatican Council II's Dogmatic Constitution on Divine Revelation (*Dei Verbum* 22, 25) which called for a Bible produced in cooperation with separated brethren, accessible to all Christians, and with explanatory notes adapted to the interests of non-Christians as well. According to the guidelines, the deuterocanonical books and segments of books (apocrypha) would be grouped as an Intertestamental cluster between the Old and New Testaments. The entire translation was to be accomplished by a working committee, a review committee, and a consultative group, all of whose memberships were to include individuals representing the Protestant, the Roman Catholic, the Eastern Orthodox, and the Anglican traditions. In addition, the resulting translation was to be entirely clear to the mass of modern men and women. Strictly speaking, therefore, the label "common Bible" does not properly apply to the dozens of translations used interchangeably by Catholics and Protestants, including the Revised Standard Version produced by Protestants and subsequently endorsed (1966) by Catholics; or the forthcoming edition for Catholics of the Good News Bible (to include the deuterocanonical books); or the Catholic Jerusalem Bible widely accepted by Protestants; or the many volumes of the Anchor Bible whose translators, commentators and editors did not work as a team. In 1972, a French New Testament was produced in strict accordance with the guidelines, and presented to the Pope in 1973. It comprised 826 pp. including notes and introductory material. An Italian New Testament was similarly accepted by the Pope in 1976.

Bibliography: W. ABBOTT, "The Quest for a Common Bible," *Month* 37 (1967) 152–158; "The Shape of the Common Bible," *Bible Today* 37 (1968) 2553–56. J. EPSTEIN, "Toward an Ecumenical Bible," JEcumSt 8 (1971) 369–381. P.–E. LANGEVIN, "Le Nouveau Testament de la Traduction oecuménique de la Bible," *Laval théologique et philosophique* 29 (1973) 257–272.

[E. J. DILLON]

BIBLICAL THEOLOGY

This article supplements Stanley B. Marrow's comprehensive survey of the subject in the *New Catholic Encyclopedia* (2:545). It considers: the relationship between Vatican Council II and biblical theology; the nature of the discipline; and its relationship to hermeneutic.

Vatican Council II and Biblical Theology. Under the heading "The Revision of Ecclesiastical Studies" the Council's Decree on Priestly Formation directed that "Dogmatic theology should be so arranged that the biblical themes are presented first" (*Optatam totius* 16). According to this statement dogmatic theology is to begin the consideration of doctrine from Scripture and (methodologically speaking) from Scripture alone. The approach is to consist in an organic presentation of the meaning of the biblical passages that have bearing upon a particular doctrine so that a comprehensive grasp of the content and the actual state of the doctrine in Scripture is achieved. Only then is tradition (i.e., the later comprehension of biblical doctrine as it has occurred historically in the Church) to be considered. Finally, the contemporary understanding of the doctrine is to be taken up.

This conciliar directive on Scripture as the methodological starting point for dogmatic theology logically emerges from the Council's comprehension of the Bible's place in the totality of divine Revelation, outlined in the Dogmatic Constitution on Divine Revelation. Scripture itself attests to a variety of ways in which God has made himself and his will known: in historical events; in the divinely inspired understanding and communication of the religious meaning of these events; in the choice of the OT patriarchs as vehicles through whom an initial understanding of his existence and of his plan for the human race was made known; in the activity and teaching of Jesus of Nazareth, and especially in his death on the cross and his resurrection (*Dei Verbum* 1–6). In this context of variety in God's communication of himself and his will Sacred Scripture has arisen, willed by God as a perpetual record of his self-communication and in itself another form of that communication (ibid. 7). The origin of Scripture is not an accident of human history, but one of the ways in which God chooses to manifest himself and his will. Just as the OT Scriptures arose to enshrine and to continue God's self-communication to the people of Israel, so the NT Scriptures arose, again at the inspiration of God, to enshrine and continue the divine self-communication in and through Jesus Christ and through the Apostles (ibid. 7–8).

The grasp of the religious content of Scripture in terms of totality, whether the totality be fully developed doctrine or doctrine on its way to completion or contained in Scripture only inchoately, lies among the general aims of biblical theology. Vatican II accepted this particular function of the discipline and directed that it be employed in dogmatic theology.

The methodological separation of the Bible from tradition and from contemporary theology possesses evident values. The acceptance of Scripture as the starting point of doctrine helps to prevent the distortion of the meaning of the biblical text that occurs when theological conceptions and understandings of a later time are introduced into it. Second, the idea of tradition as development in the understanding of biblical doctrine becomes clearer and, at least in its positive aspect, is legitimated. Third, the foundational importance of Scripture opens the way to interaction among the various branches of theology: biblical, patristic, historical, dogmatic, moral, liturgical, and pastoral. The whole of theology, including exegesis and biblical theology, has constantly to reevaluate itself in terms of its relationship to Scripture; each branch can illumine the other out of its own experience with Scripture. Finally, seeing Scripture in its totalities provides a balanced view of its religious content and better enables those who have teaching functions in the Church to convey its meaning to their contemporaries.

The Nature of Biblical Theology. When the terms "Bible" and "theology" are merged to create the term "biblical theology," a question of meaning automatically arises. Historically, biblical theology originated out of the desire to bring the religious thought of Scripture into clear focus. Throughout its history the discipline has stood as a reaction to the inadequate relationship between dogmatic theology and Scripture, to the reduction of the content of Scripture to the phenomenon of religion as such by "the history of religion school," and to a biblical exegesis that became primarily preoccupied with linguistic, historical, archaeological, and literary considerations raised in the material of the Bible. However, the historical origins of biblical theology do not shed effective light on the nature of the discipline. The terms "Bible" and "theology," and not historical origins, are of essential significance in the determination of the discipline's nature.

The Bible is God's Word to man. It contains both his self-communication as well as the inspired writer's reflection upon that communication. Theology is the science of faith. As a science it consists in the methodological reflection upon the content of faith. In the context of this understanding of the nature of the Bible and the nature of theology, biblical theology may be understood as the methodological reflection, undertaken in the light of faith, upon the religious content of Scripture. Since the discipline has the religious content of the Bible as the object of its study, it is biblical; since it reflects upon the content of Scripture in a methodological way, it is theological: hence the term "biblical theology." As a discipline it makes the claim that methodological reflection on the religious content of Scripture for the purpose of understanding its thought in an organic manner is feasible and illuminating. It is in this claim, inherent in the discipline itself, that both the strength and weakness of biblical theology lie.

The Strength of Biblical Theology. For the materials with which it works biblical theology has necessarily to depend on exegesis. It is the science of exegesis, and not biblical theology, that achieves direct contact with the thought of the biblical author, the actual meaning the inspired writer wished to convey to his contemporary listener or reader (the literal sense of Scripture). Since the biblical writers did not present their religious conceptions in a systematic fashion, their understanding of religious themes (e.g., faith, hope, love, resurrection, judgment) must be gleaned from the results of the exegesis of those passages where these themes occur or in which they play a part. One cannot understand, for example, faith in St. Paul from single passages in his letters but only from the totality of his writings. The task of the biblical theologian is to penetrate and organize the results of exegesis so as to arrive at the

totality of the Apostle's conception of faith as he has bequeathed it to us.

When biblical theology has pursued the study of individual themes in the various authors and books of the NT as well as in the OT to the extent that the themes are present there, it has been at its fruitful best. The articles on biblical themes in modern encyclopedias of the Bible attest to the success of the discipline when it takes this approach to Scripture. In the field of the NT the discipline has enjoyed a similar success in studying the theological thought of Paul, John, and to a limited extent, the Synoptic Gospels. The letters of Paul, the Johannine literature (1–2 Jn, Jn, Rev), and the Synoptic Gospels readily lend themselves to an organic grasp of their thought, since each group of writings possesses fairly constant perspectives, ideas, and aims. The literature of the OT, however, does not contain groupings of material that derive from a single author or circle. Accordingly, in terms of literary units the theological thought of the OT has to be ascertained book-by-book and in the case of the Pentateuch with the help of the different sources that lie behind it.

The Problematic for a Biblical Theology. The strength of biblical theology consists in the tracing of individual themes throughout the Bible and in coming to grips with the thought of its literary units. In performing these functions it aims at a descriptive presentation of biblical thought, organized in a logical way, couched in modern language and resting solidly on the results of exegesis. However, these successful approaches to Scripture arrive at the conclusion that it contains different types of methodological reflection on God's self-communication. Materially speaking, it is not a unified but a divergent presentation of thought, even on the same themes. St. Paul's conception of faith, for example, and the theological use he makes of it differ from the conception of faith and the use to which it is put in the Fourth Gospel and in the Synoptic Gospels. The same differentiation exists on many themes among authors and between books in the Bible.

This factor of different "theologies" in Scripture creates a serious difficulty for the ultimate goal of biblical theology: to create a theology of the OT, of the NT, and finally of the entire Bible. As long as the discipline works with themes and literary units in Scripture, its organic presentation of the thought of Scripture remains attached to the biblical books and authors, for it bases itself on the results of exegesis. But once it attempts to overcome the factor of differentiation in the theological methodologies in Scripture, its work takes a step away from biblical books and authors to biblical categories of thought (e.g., God, man, creation, grace, sin). Although it adheres to the results of exegesis, it places these results in new contexts. Thus it creates a personal construction of the theology in the Bible. The aphorism that there are as many biblical theologies as there are biblical theologians becomes verified. How this difficulty is to be overcome, if it can be overcome, constitutes a challenge to biblical theologians. Many NT scholars simply prefer to present its theological thought in terms of its principal literary units: the Synoptic Gospels, Paul, and John. In their view the factor of differentiation simply has to be accepted as a reality in the theological methodology of Scripture.

Biblical Theology and Hermeneutic. As far as Scripture is concerned, hermeneutic involves the question of communication and understanding. The Bible is a divinely inspired, religious communication through the written word. By the very fact that it is written word it is, like all literature, confined to time, place, culture, and a particular set of addressees. The original audiences for whom it was written could normally understand it as communication more easily than people of a later time. For the latter it is communication in a translation from Hebrew and Greek, which limits understanding, and it employs thought-patterns and types of literature no longer in vogue, at least in the Western world. Therefore it requires interpretation beyond translation that will bridge the gap between ancient communication and contemporary understanding.

Exegesis and biblical theology both have a role to play in bridging the gap. The first step belongs to exegesis. It is its task to establish the original meaning of the biblical text in its own time, place, and circumstances. The second step belongs, quite naturally, to biblical theology. It organizes the results of exegesis into a total focus that brings the necessary balance to the comprehension of biblical thought. In the performance of its role in the process of the interpretation of Scripture, however, biblical theology is as historical a discipline as is exegesis. In seeking a totality in the understanding of a biblical theme or of a biblical book or author, it must adhere faithfully to the original meaning of Scripture. Exegesis is the criterion by which biblical theology is fundamentally judged. No more than exegesis may it introduce later theological conceptions or religious views into scriptural thought.

Biblical theology makes its contribution directly to those whose knowledge of the Bible has been achieved through exegetical study or through sound exegetical instruction, for they are already in position to appreciate the thematic approach to scriptural understanding as well as the approach in terms of literary units. Finally, both exegesis and biblical theology are stimulated to reexamine their assessment of scriptural data by contemporary questions having a bearing upon biblical teaching, e.g., divorce and remarriage, social responsibility, the meaning of resurrection. The biblical theologian is in good position to consider such questions from his vantage-point in order to contribute to their contemporary solution from the theological implications of Scripture. In this role the biblical theologian joins with the patristic, historical, and contemporary, systematic theologian to contribute to the mature judgment of the magisterium of the Church.

Bibliography: On *Dei verbum* ch. 1 and 2, J. RATZINGER, ch. 3, A. GRILLMEIER, Vorgrimler 3: 170–198; 199–246. On *Optatam totius* 16, J. NEUNER, Vorgrimler 2: 397–400.

Bible dictionaries: L. HARTMAN, *Encyclopedic Dictionary of the Bible* (New York 1963). IntDictBibl and IntDictBiblSuppl. J. L. MCKENZIE, *Dictionary of the Bible* (Milwaukee 1965).

Current discussion on biblical theology: W. J. HARRINGTON, *The Path of Biblical Theology* (Dublin 1973). G. HASEL, *Old Testament Theology: Basic Issues in the Current Debate* (Grand Rapids, Mich. 1972); *New Testament Theology: Basic Issues in the Current Debate* (Grand Rapids, Mich. 1978). J. L. MCKENZIE, *A Theology of the Old Testament* (New York 1974). R. H. SCHELKLE, *Theology of the New Testament*, v. 3, tr. W. A. JURGENS (Collegeville, Minn. 1973). H. SCHLIER, *The Relevance of the New Testament*, tr. W. J. O'HARA (New York 1968) 1–25.

Biblical theologies, W. G. KÜMMEL, *The Theology of the New Testament*, tr. J. E. STEELY (Nashville, Tenn. 1973). J. L. MCKENZIE, op. cit. H. RIDDERBOS, *Paul: An Outline of His Theology*, tr. J. R. DEWITT (Grand Rapids, Mich. 1975). K. H. SCHELKLE, *Theology of the New Testament*, 4 v. tr. W. A. JURGENS (Collegeville, Minn. 1971–76).

Current Protestant discussion, K. STENDAHL, IntDictBibl 1:418–432. J. BARR, IntDictBiblSuppl 104–111. B. S. CHILDS, *Biblical Theology in Crisis* (Philadelphia 1970).

[C. P. CEROKE]

BILATERAL CONSULTATIONS

The ecumenical exchanges that have come to be known as bilateral consultations are a rather recent feature of the ecumenical movement, gaining a certain prominence in the late 1960s and thereafter. Prior to that time Churches engaged in the *ecumenical movement developed their relationships to a great extent according to the conciliar pattern, which they still maintain in the World Council of Churches (WCC) and its counterpart regional and local councils. The conciliar mode brings numerous Churches together for the sake of cooperative action and the expression of Christian witness through agreed upon resolutions and policy statements. In the earlier phase the Churches were also gaining experience with and expanding the church union movement. The conciliar ecumenical pattern engages two and often several Churches in the effort to develop and adopt a plan whereby they may unite into a single, unified Church. Such a pattern of relationships still continues to the present time.

Bilateral consultations are different. First of all, they engage participants from but two Churches or two confessional families of Churches in dialogue. Such consultations are not aimed initially at expressing a common Christian faith transcending all differences and divisions. They do have the advantage of allowing for a much more detailed exploration of particular church traditions, the history of their development, and their current directions of development. The historic specificity of each particular church tradition can be taken into full account and historic divisions between two traditions can be probed with undivided attention.

The bilateral dialogues are distinguished, secondly, by their use of dialogue as an ecumenical method. The dialogic method represents an advance over previous methods of common study employed in ecumenism. Comparative *ecclesiology, one of the prior methods used, had resulted in a substantial exchange of information among ecumenists about the differing doctrinal commitments and ecclesial structures of diverse Churches. But the exchange of information did not in itself produce further agreement. What became known as *Controverstheologie*, the intensive debate of points at issue between the Churches, was also productive of voluminous scholarly exposition, although not equally so of agreement. An exercise in dialogue requires the partners not only to share what each already knows but to seek, if possible, new perspectives unknown to either previously, from which further understanding may result. Thus beyond the sharing of information and concomitant removal of mutual stereotypes and misunderstandings it is aimed at the accomplishment of agreements that can properly be said to be new. The spiritual requirements made of partners in dialogue—openness to a change of heart, sensitivity to the dynamic interrelationships of Christian truths and the way they are connected to the core of the Gospel—further exhibit the fact that dialogue is undertaken not solely as a sharing of what is known but a search for what is yet undisclosed.

The number of bilateral consultations multiplied with the impetus of Vatican Council II. To ensure broad-based contacts, representatives of the various world confessional families as well as of the WCC were invited to be present as observers at Vatican II. The Church to Church relationships that thus were established provided the matrix for continuing bilateral relationships after the Council. In 1975 over 45 such consultations were being conducted both internationally and regionally; in approximately half of these Roman Catholics participated as partners.

The cumulative achievement of these bilaterals is noteworthy. They have consolidated and expanded agreements among the Christians participating with respect to the Eucharist; they have greatly advanced mutual understanding of the nature and function of the ordained ministry; they have indicated further convergence in Christian understanding of the nature and exercise of authority in the Church. While the decision to engage in dialogue does not assure in advance that agreement will be reached, the fruitfulness of this method seems well attested in its ability to further new agreements. The method was not designed so much for decision making as for the gaining of new insight. Still further methods may have to be found to assist the Churches in coming to common decisions on the basis of the results of their engagement in bilateral dialogues.

See also ANGLICAN-ROMAN CATHOLIC CONSULTATION (U.S.); DISCIPLES OF CHRIST/ROMAN CATHOLIC CONSULTATION; LUTHERAN/ROMAN CATHOLIC CONSULTATION; ORTHODOX/ROMAN CATHOLIC DIALOGUE; PRESBYTERIAN-REFORMED/ROMAN CATHOLIC CONSULTATION; SOUTHERN BAPTIST/ROMAN CATHOLIC CONSULTATIONS; UNITED METHODIST/ROMAN CATHOLIC DIALOGUE.

[J. F. HOTCHKIN]

BISHOPS' ADVISORY COUNCIL, U.S. CATHOLIC

After Vatican Council II the bishops of the United States found it advisable and desirable in performing their pastoral responsibilities to consult with non-bishops (cf. *Lumen gentium* 27–37; *Christus Dominus* 16–18; *Presbyterorum ordinis* 7; *Apostolicam actuositatem* 20). To accomplish this and as an exercise in shared responsibility at the national level the United States Catholic Bishops' Advisory Council was created in 1969. The council is composed of sixty regional and at-large members who reflect the thinking of the total Church in America today. This microcosm of the Church is composed of twenty-four lay men and women, six priests and six bishops elected by their peers within the twelve NCCB geographical divisions of the country; six religious men and women elected by the Conference of Major Superiors of Men and the Leadership Conference of Women Religious and eighteen at-large members chosen by a committee of the Council to assure proper representation of ethnic and racial minorities, age range from college students to senior citizens, theologians, canon lawyers, permanent deacons, and members of specialized ministries. Council members are elected to serve for a term of three years. They meet as a body twice each year.

The role of the Bishops' Advisory Council in its consultative capacity is that of listening to the constituencies and staff of NCCB and USCC, engaging in dialogue with these representatives and among themselves, and making recommendations and proposals in their reports to the Administrative Committee and Administrative Board of the bishops. The bishops respond to the reports in the records of their deliberations at their meetings.

Selected members of the council are observers at the meeting of the Administrative Committee of the bishops.

[T. B. POSEY]

BISHOPS' COMMITTEE FOR ECUMENICAL AND INTERRELIGIOUS AFFAIRS (BCEIA)

In 1964 Card. Albert Meyer and Joseph Ritter along with other American bishops who had collaborated with Card. Augustin Bea (16:23) in the preparation of Vatican Council II's Decree on Ecumenism met in Rome. After discussion they recommended the establishing of a commission in the United States that would be of assistance in furthering the implementation of the Decree and other ecumenical decisions taken by the Council. On Nov. 11, 1964 the U.S. hierarchy established the Bishops' Commission for Ecumenical Affairs, as it was then called, naming Archbishop Lawrence J. Shehan of Baltimore its first chairman. Six other bishops (Brunini, Carberry, Flanagan, Helmsing, Leipzig, and Unterkoefler) made up the remaining members of the original commission. The commission elected Msgr. (now Card.) William W. Baum as its first executive director and the commission opened the office of its secretariat at the National Catholic Welfare Conference (NCWC, now U.S. Catholic Conference, USCC) building in Washington on January 7, 1965.

The purposes set for the commission at the time of its establishment were the following: (1) to interpret the conciliar Decree on Ecumenism and its application to the United States; (2) to propose guidelines, methods, and techniques for fostering prudent ecumenical dialogue and action; (3) to advise and cooperate with individual bishops on particular ecumenical problems arising within their respective dioceses and to aid in the formation of diocesan commissions for ecumenical affairs when requested; (4) to serve as coordinator for the more effective participation of the U.S. hierarchy in various aspects of the ecumenical movement within the United States. Among the plans for this last were measures to provide a point of contact with non-Catholic Christian Churches, Communities, and Ecclesiastical Conferences within the U.S.; to designate (with the approval of the local ordinary) official Catholic observers to the annual meeting of the U.S. Conference for the World Council of Churches and other similar conferences; to name permanent observer-consultants for conversations with non-Catholic, Christian-unity bodies, and to initiate dialogue with the Eastern Orthodox Church in the United States.

The wording of this original mandate indicates the caution with which the Commission set about its task. It did not anticipate the strong response of other American Churches that was so quickly forthcoming. As early as March 1965 the Commission moved to set up subcommissions to further specific relations with the Orthodox, Episcopal, Lutheran, and Reformed Churches. And in October a further subcommission was organized for contacts with the Methodist Church. Two additional subcommissions were organized for relations with the *National Council of Churches of Christ (NCCC) and with the Jewish community the same year. In addition to the bishops, thirty-three priests, six laymen, and one laywoman were invited to serve on these subcommissions.

During 1965 official actions had been taken which inaugurated the ongoing *bilateral consultations with the Lutheran, Orthodox, Episcopal, and Reformed Churches. In 1966 such meetings were inaugurated with the Methodist Church and in 1967 with American Baptist Churches and with the Christian Church (Disciples of Christ). In June 1965 the Governing Board of the NCCC invited the Commission to send observer-consultants to the meetings of the Board as well as of its departments and divisions. In 1966 regular meetings with representatives of the NCCC began. In the same year the Commission was invited to name observer-consultants to the meetings of the Consultation on Church Union (COCU; 16:101).

In addition to these direct contacts with other Christian bodies, the Commission was also active in providing assistance to the Catholic dioceses. In 1965 it published its "Interim Guidelines for Prayer in Common and *communicatio in sacris*" (superseded by Part I of the Holy See's "Ecumenical Directory" issued May 14, 1967 by the Secretariat for Promoting Christian Unity). Together with the NCWC Bureau of Information it inaugurated in the same year the publication of *Direction: Unity*, a news bulletin on ecumenism (later merged with the NCCC bulletin, *Faith and Order Trends* under the new title *Unity Trends*, and still later superseded by the Graymoor publication, *Ecumenical Trends*, as well as a new BCEIA quarterly newsletter). In 1966 it established its Commission for Education in Ecumenism, which published general guidelines on this subject and prepared material on ecumenical education in seminaries (later incorporated to a large extent in the 1971 "Program for Priestly Formation"). Also in 1966 the Commission published its "Recommendations for Diocesan Commissions for Ecumenical Affairs."

At the end of 1965 Bishop John J. Carberry had succeeded Cardinal Shehan as chairman of the Commission and eight bishops had been elected to membership on the Commission in addition to the original six. In November 1966 the National Conference of Catholic Bishops reorganized the Commission, adopting its present title and significantly expanding its work. The work of the BCEIA, under the coordination of its central office and executive director, was to be divided into the following subordinate special secretariats: secretariat for Christian unity; secretariat for Catholic-Jewish relations; secretariat for relations with non-Christian religions; and secretariat for secular humanists. These secretariats were seen as counterpart correspondents to the Holy See's Secretariats for Promoting Christian Unity, for Non-Christians, and for Non-Believers. In 1967 Rev. Edward H. Flannery was elected first executive secretary of the Secretariat for Catholic-Jewish Relations (*see* CATHOLIC JEWISH RELATIONS). The Secretariat was the first after Vatican II to publish "Guidelines for Catholic-Jewish Relations" (1967), which foreshadowed the commitment to these relations which the American bishops most recently expressed in the 1975 "Statement on Catholic-Jewish Relations: On the Occasion of the Celebration of the Tenth Anniversary of *Nostra aetate*, No. 4."

Msgr. Baum concluded his service as the executive director of the BCEIA in mid-1967. He was succeeded in the Spring of 1968 by Msgr. Bernard F. Law, who served in that capacity until 1971. Rev. John F. Hotchkin, who had joined the BCEIA staff as Msgr. Baum's assistant in 1967, then succeeded Msgr. Law as the director. Card. John J. Carberry was succeeded by

Archbishop Baum as chairman of the Committee in 1973 and he in turn was succeeded by Bishop Law in 1976. In 1974 the NCCB, at the recommendation of the BCEIA, again altered its mandate to separate from it the dialogue with secular humanists and with science and technology and to entrust this work to a newly formed *Bishops' Committee for Human Values with its own separate membership and secretariat.

The BCEIA, besides its relationships with the NCCC and the COCU has cosponsored bilateral dialogues with nine Churches and confessional families of Churches in the U.S. In addition to the Churches already mentioned, these also include meetings with the Southern Baptists and the Armenian Apostolic Church. Bishops of the Committee chair each of these consultations and annually are joined by as many as 150 theologians and other experts (priests, religious, laity) in carrying out the work of the dialogue. All of these consultations periodically publish reports of their findings and selected study papers.

[J. F. HOTCHKIN]

BISHOPS' COMMITTEE FOR HUMAN VALUES

This standing committee of the National Conference of Catholic Bishops (NCCB) has two functions. It serves as a listening post and participant in the dialogue in science, technology and values; it is the counterpart of the Vatican Secretariat for Non-Believers.

In the latter capacity the Committee seeks to increase understanding and cooperation between Catholics and secular humanists, Marxists, and atheists. It was primarily with a view to being informed on matters of science and technology, however, that Bishop Mark J. Hurley urged the National Conference of Catholic Bishops to establish the Committee in November of 1974 (*see* BISHOPS' COMMITTEE FOR ECUMENICAL AND INTER-RELIGIOUS AFFAIRS).

In the past the Church did not sufficiently recognize or value the scientific enterprise. Vatican Council II, however, exhorted Christians to join with all who search for the truth and seek to build up this world (*Gaudium et spes* 43). The Council Fathers affirmed the values inherent in scientific study and fidelity to truth in scientific inquiries (ibid. 57).

The Committee for Human Values recognizes much common ground between the Christian and the scientific traditions: their mutual spirit of inquiry; their sense of responsibility for the future; and their common commitment to humankind's welfare. The Committee attempts to contribute to serious reflection on activities and decisions in the realm of science and technology. It wishes to dialogue with the scientific community to search out the meaning of true human progress.

In the face of the awesome possibilities available through the life and natural sciences, the Church is posing many questions. What is the meaning and value of particular scientific enterprises? What ends are being served? How are our scientific discoveries being used? Increases in scientific knowledge have resulted in many benefits to society. At the same time, some investigative technologies and applications of scientific knowledge require wise and discerning choices. Recognizing that it is the guardian of a rich tradition, replete with religious and moral principles, the Church also acknowledges that it does not have a ready answer to every question.

There is clearly a twofold responsibility in matters of science and science policy. It is recognized that science has a public function and commitment. Because the scientific enterprise is not solely scientific it assumes an obligation vis-à-vis the general public—to inform them and welcome their participation in the transcientific aspects of their activities. That, of course, places a burden on the public to be informed so they can contribute to the goal of science in service of human needs. Education of the public to issues in science and technology is necessary for public participation to be responsible and effective.

The secretariat of the Committee keeps abreast of events in science and technology in order to advise the bishops of their ethical implications. It also serves as a Christian presence to the scientific community, one which communicates the Church's concern with the value dimensions of issues in science and technology. Through these initiatives the Committee attempts to clarify and assist the course science is taking.

[A. NEALE]

BISHOPS' COMMITTEE FOR LIAISON WITH THE NATIONAL OFFICE FOR BLACK CATHOLICS

In 1969 the National Conference of Catholic Bishops (NCCB), through its Liaison Committee chaired at that time by Cardinal Lawrence Shehan, began discussions with clergy and religious representing the Black Catholic community. These meetings resulted from a call by the newly established (1968) Black Catholic Clergy Caucus and the National Black Sisters' Conference for greater participation by Black Catholics in the policy-making structures of the American Catholic Church. The establishment of a central office for Black Catholics was envisioned as necessary to achieve this objective. Following initial discussions, the NCCB appointed an ad hoc committee, under the chairmanship of Bishop Peter L. Gerety (now archbishop of Newark). This committee engaged in a series of meetings with Black Catholic clergy, religious, and laity, as well as superiors of religious communities working in the Black apostolate, to determine the sentiment for such an office. With the assistance of the ad hoc committee, Black Catholics established a planning group to develop a formal proposal for the establishment of the central office. Interim funds were authorized by NCCB and the National Office for Black Catholics (NOBC) was opened in Washington, D.C. on July 1, 1970.

The Bishops' Ad Hoc Committee for Liaison with NOBC has remained in existence since that time and is the official organizational link between the NCCB and NOBC. The Committee is currently under the chairmanship of Bishop William Johnson of Orange, California. Members are Bishops Harold Perry, Joseph Francis, Eugene Marino, and Joseph McNicholas. The Committee meets at least twice yearly with representatives of the NOBC, the National Black Sisters' Conference, The National Black Catholic Lay Caucus, and the National Black Catholic Clergy Caucus. The activities of NOBC and the membership organizations are reviewed, a financial report is given, and plans for future activities are discussed. The meetings are primarily informational and form the basis for a report on NOBC given to all bishops at their semi-annual meetings. The NCCB Ad Hoc Committee for Liaison supports NOBC in special projects which NOBC undertakes. Primary among these is the annual fund-raising program, Black Catholics Concerned, an annual collection in predominantly Black parishes for the support of NOBC.

[J. M. DAVIS]

BISHOPS' COMMITTEE FOR THE CHURCH IN LATIN AMERICA

The NCCB Committee for the Church in Latin America has the responsibility of serving as the principal catalyst for service and aid to the Church in Latin America. To achieve this goal, the Committee follows the guidelines recommended to national episcopal conferences providing funds and personnel to Latin America as formulated by the General Council of the Pontifical Commission for Latin America (COGECAL). The Committee maintains liaison with and provides service to the Consejo Episcopal Latino-Americano (CELAM), the Pontifical Commission for Latin America (CAL), and its General Council, and deals with the individual episcopal conferences throughout Latin America, including the Caribbean countries and Mexico.

Such communication is essential if the committee is to respond properly to the challenge of Vatican Council II: "The development of a nation depends on human and financial aids. The citizens of each country must be prepared by education and professional training to discharge the various tasks of economic and social life. But this in turn requires the aid of foreign specialists who, when they give aid, will not act as overlords, but as helpers and fellow-workers" (*Gaudium et spes* 85). To avoid duplication in programming, the Committee works in close collaboration with other Catholic and private agencies providing financial aid to the Church in Latin America. The criteria for the allocation of funds, largely obtained through annual national, parish collections, is periodically reviewed, since the priorities of the Church in Latin America are ever changing. Particular emphasis is given to the initiation of new projects that will serve as pilot programs applicable throughout Latin America.

In concert with other approved activities within NCCB, the Committee assists in disseminating information on the realities in Latin America to assist the people in the United States to develop a clearer understanding of the problems facing the Latin American Church. Upon request, the committee also seeks qualified personnel for service. In response to a request from the bishops of Latin America, the committee offers a training program for personnel assigned to Spanish-speaking countries. Speaking the language fluently is only one essential for communication; it is also important that religious and lay personnel have a thorough preparation in such subjects as the history, the cultural, the socio-religious and socio-economic conditions of Latin America.

In all of its work the Committee seeks to respond to the exhortation of Paul VI's apostolic exhortation: "Evangelization involves an explicit message, adapted to different situations constantly being realized, about the rights and duties of every human being, about family life without which personal growth and development is hardly possible, about life in society, about international life, peace, justice and development—a message especially energetic today about liberation" (Paul VI EvangNunt 29).

[F. L. NEASON]

BISHOPS' COMMITTEE ON EVANGELIZATION

In November 1975, after a lapse of sixteen years when no national Catholic meetings had been called to wrestle with the challenge of sharing the Catholic faith with the unchurched American, an "Exploratory Consultation on Evangelizing the Eighty Million Unchurched Americans" was held at Marriottsville, Maryland. The national consultation for church leaders was sponsored by The Catholic University of America, the Glenmary Fathers, the Josephite Fathers and Brothers, the Paulist Fathers, and the United States Catholic Mission Council.

The 1974 Synod of Bishops had evangelization as its theme; Paul VI's major apostolic exhortation On Evangelization in the Modern World developed out of the Synod. With this as background, and under the gentle prodding of Archbishop Jean Jadot, Apostolic Delegate to the U.S., Bishop James Rausch, then General Secretary of the USCC/NCCB and two of his assistants, Thomas C. Kelly, OP (now Bishop and General Secretary) and Rev. Michael Sheehan, began looking for concrete ways in which to begin responding to the call for a more concentrated effort on evangelization. In their search, they discovered and warmly supported the theme and the program at Marriottsville. Four representatives from the USCC/NCCB were sent to join with the 151 bishops, clergy, religious, and laity from over forty dioceses and religious communities that met for four days in the effort to rekindle interest in this unique aspect of ministry. Archbishop Jadot celebrated the Eucharistic Liturgy on one of the days of the Consultation.

In June 1976, the "Marriottsville Group"—made up of Rev. Bernard Quinn of the Glenmary Research Center, Robert Kearns, SSJ of the Josephite Pastoral Center, Anthony Bellagamba, IMC and Sr. Ann Gormly, SSND, both of the U.S. Catholic Mission Council, Rev. Frederick Guthrie of Catholic University, and Alvin Illig, CSP—was invited to meet with Bishop Rausch, Frs. Kelly and Sheehan, and members of the staff of the USCC/NCCB to help formulate a recommendation on evangelization that could be presented to the bishops at their November 1976 meeting. Following the day-long conference, Sr. Ann Gormly, Frs. Quinn and Illig were asked to draw up a specific recommendation. This was presented to the bishops in November and the NCCB responded by calling for the establishment of NCCB Ad Hoc Committee on Evangelization.

Between November 1976 and November 1977, the USCC/NCCB assembled a group of bishops to form a new Committee on Evangelization with Archbishop Francis T. Hurley of Anchorage, Alaska as chairman. Ten other bishops volunteered to serve on this Committee: Victor Balke of Crookston, Minn; Michael Begley of Charlotte, N.C.: Joseph Daley of Harrisburg, Pa.; Joseph Francis of Newark, N.J.; James Hickey of Cleveland, Ohio; Roger Mahony of Fresno, Cal.; Edward O'Meara, National Director of the Society for the Propagation of the Faith; Raymond Pena of San Antonio, Texas; James Sullivan of Lansing, Mich.; and John Sullivan of Kansas City-St. Joseph, Missouri.

A key policy meeting was held in Arlington Heights, Ill., in June 1977. At this meeting the bishops gave more and more attention to the evangelization of the 40 percent of the American people without active church or synagogue involvement. The Committee fully acknowledged that everyone needs to be evangelized, and affirmed the American Church's evangelizing activities in the form of apostolic ministry to the 49 million active Catholics and ecumenical dialogue with the 73 million active Protestants. The Committee indicated that the Church had evangelizing structures and programs for interreligious dialogue with the 11 million members of non-Christian religions in America.

At the level of leadership represented by the USCC/NCCB, however, the Church had no specific department or committee of persons directly concerned on a full time basis with the 12 million alienated Catholics and the 68 million unchurched Americans. The new Committee on Evangelization became convinced that the time had come for the American Catholic community consciously to broaden its vision from the "nurture and the maintenance of the Catholic faith" to the "reaching out and the sharing of the Catholic faith" as called for by Pope Paul in *Evangelii nuntiandi*.

At its November 1977 meeting the American bishops formally established the NCCB Ad Hoc Committee on Evangelization, and approved as an initial step the proposal of the Committee to develop a two-year plan of action aimed at raising the public awareness of the American Catholic community to the Gospel mandate to evangelize. A national office to assist this work and to gather and share model programs of what is being done was opened in Washington with Alvin A. Illig, CSP as its first Executive Director.

In February 1978, the Administrative Committee of the USCC/NCCB invited Archbishop Francis Hurley to deliver a major presentation on evangelization before all the bishops at their May 1978 meeting in Chicago and also approved the plan to conduct during 1979 twelve regional consultations on evangelization for priests, religious and the laity.

[A. A. ILLIG]

BISHOPS' COMMITTEE ON PRIESTLY FORMATION

This standing committee of the National Conference of Catholic Bishops (NCCB) was founded in 1966. The Committee exists to advise the NCCB regarding the training of seminarians for the priesthood. The Holy See has directed that the entire formation of priests, that is, the arrangement of the seminary, its spiritual formation, and its pastoral training, should be adapted to the various circumstances found in different countries of the world. This adaptation, since it deals with very important principles, is to be carried out according to the common norms for diocesan clergy set up by the episcopal conferences and in agreement with the rules made by superiors of religious communities.

The Committee on Priestly Formation consults with experts, drafts proposals, and formulates policies. The major objectives of the Committee are threefold. The first, following on the *ratio fundamentalis* for priestly formation of the Congregation for Catholic Education (ActApS 62 [1970] 321–384), is to develop the *Program of Priestly Formation*, which is approved by both the NCCB and the same Congregation. The second is to conduct an ongoing review of the *Program of Priestly Formation* in order to provide for a revised document every five years (current *Program* 1976). The third objective is to assist the implementation of the *Program of Priestly Formation* by sending consultation teams to offer assistance and to effect interpretation and application of the *Program* in individual institutions. The Bishops' Committee maintains liaison for the NCCB with the Formation Committee of the *Conference of Major Superiors of Men and many other groups concerned with seminary education and the training of the clergy.

[D. J. PAKENHAM]

BISHOPS' COMMITTEE ON PRIESTLY LIFE AND MINISTRY

This standing committee of the National Conference of Catholic Bishops (NCCB) began in 1973 on the basis of the NCCB's Study of the American priesthood (1967–71) and was the result of a recommendation by the *ad hoc* Committee on Priestly Life and Ministry (1971–73). The Committee consists of the elected chairman, selected bishops, and a committee of advisors chosen from priests recommended by priest senates (16:41), the *Conference of Major Superiors of Men, and by bishops. There are three subcommittees: for Spiritual Renewal and Continuing Education, Priestly Affirmation and Support, and Distribution of Clergy.

The purpose of the Committee on Priestly Life and Ministry is to advise the NCCB about the concerns and needs of priests in the United States. It also facilitates the implementation of the Vatican Council II's Decree on the Ministry and Life of Priests (*Presbyterorum ordinis*), the document on the ministerial priesthood from the 1971 *Synod of Bishops, and the 1972 NCCB Study on the American Priesthood. The Secretariat for the Committee serves the Committee by research, liaison with priest senates and bishops, consultation with organizations interested in the ministerial priesthood, the drafting of Committee proposals for the NCCB, and the conducting of the general staff work of the Committee.

Since 1973 the Committee has presented the following documents to the NCCB: (1) *The Spiritual Renewal of the American Priesthood*; (2) *The Ad Hoc Committee Report on Authority, Maturity, Ministry and Scholarship*; (3) *The Program for Continuing Education of Priests*; (4) *Spiritual Direction for Priests in the USA/The Rediscovery of a Resource*; (5) *An Enquiry About Alcoholism Among Catholic Clergy*; (6) *As One Who Serves —Reflections on the Pastoral Ministry of Priests in the United States*. These publications are available from the Secretariat or USCC Publications Office, 1312 Massachusetts Avenue, N.W., Washington, D.C. 20005.

[C. A. MACDONALD]

BISHOPS' COMMITTEE ON PRO-LIFE ACTIVITIES

The Ad Hoc Committee for Pro-Life Activities of the National Conference of Catholic Bishops (NCCB) was formally established at the November, 1972 NCCB general meeting. The primary responsibilities of the Committee were to monitor events and trends in the areas of population control, abortion, euthanasia, and family life, and to conduct the annual Respect Life Program. Although these responsibilities had formerly been carried out by the USCC Family Life Division, the issues were demanding increased attention and, very often, a specific response from the NCCB. In addition, the concern to prepare for the 1974 United Nations World Population Year prompted the NCCB at the November 1972 meeting to set up a more formal and specialized unit with the formal title of the Ad Hoc Committee for Population and Pro-Life Activities. Cardinal John Cody was named Chairman and Bishops George Ahr, Juan Arzube, Walter Curtis, Francis J. Dunn, Timothy Harrington, Andrew McDonald, and Harold Perry constituted the membership.

In keeping with its mandate the Ad Hoc Committee planned to give immediate attention to the population question. This was to involve consultation with population experts and government figures, and the drafting of a statement and of educational materials for the use of the dioceses. To initiate this work and to define the responsibilities of the Committee more precisely, a planning meeting was arranged for January 23, 1973, in Chicago. On January 22, 1973, the U.S. Supreme Court issued its sweeping abortion decisions (*Roe v. Wade, Doe v. Bolton*) (*see* ABORTION, U.S. LAW) striking down the abortion laws of Texas and Georgia. These decisions asserted that abortion is a medical procedure and a woman's right to privacy in deciding to abort takes precedence over the life of the unborn child, who is not considered a person entitled to the customary constitutional protections. Moreover, the Court denied the states any power to establish laws protecting the unborn during the first six months of pregnancy and allowed regulations during the final three months only to the degree that they did not override health concerns of the mother. The health of the mother was defined broadly so as to include socio-economic concerns and matters of personal convenience, so that, in effect, the unborn child was deprived of any protection throughout the entire course of pregnancy.

The seriousness of these decisions and the timing of the Court's judgment called for immediate action and the Ad Hoc Committee issued a statement at its January 23, 1973 meeting and prepared a proposal of actions to be considered by the Administrative Committee at its February 12, 1973 session. It was clear that abortion would be equally as demanding a concern as population, and that the Ad Hoc Committee would likely continue in existence well beyond 1974.

In addition to the statement of January 23, 1973, the Committee issued *Pastoral Guidelines for the Catholic Hospital and Catholic Health Care Personnel* on April 11, 1973. Further the Committee recommended statements for release by the NCCB Administrative Committee in February and September 1973 and by the NCCB general membership in November 1973. In addition, the Committee completed its consultations and work on the *Statement on Population*, which was also issued by the NCCB on November 12, 1973. The series of statements during 1973 show the development of a general policy of opposition to the Supreme Court's decisions, and endorsement of efforts to reverse the opinions of the Court. Primary attention was given to encouraging efforts to obtain a constitutional amendment asserting that the unborn child is a person under the law and restoring to the Federal government and the states the power to enact laws restricting abortion.

As a result of a series of consultations and discussions during 1973, the Committee developed a comprehensive rationale that was enunciated in the Testimony of the U.S. Catholic Conference before the Senate Sub-Committee on Constitutional Amendments on March 7, 1974. Cardinals John Krol (Philadelphia), John Cody (Chicago), Timothy Manning (Los Angeles), and Humberto Medeiros (Boston) presented the USCC testimony in which they argued that the right to life is a basic human right that should be protected by law. The Cardinals rejected the charge that Catholics were attempting to force their moral teaching on the country and emphasized that there is a clear constitutional tradition protecting fundamental human rights that should logically extend to the unborn child from conception onward.

At the May 1975 NCCB General Meeting Cardinal Cody reviewed the activities of the Ad Hoc Committee and the completion of the work on population. He recommended that the Committee continue its work in the pro-life area and that a new chairman be appointed. Cardinal Terence Cooke (New York), who had chaired the special committee that originated the Respect Life Program in 1972, assumed the chairmanship; Archbishops Cornelius Power (Portland, Ore.) and Thomas Donnellan (Atlanta, Ga.) and Bishop Raymond Gallagher (Lafayette, Ind.) and Charles Salatka (Oklahoma City, Okla.) joined the Committee to give representation in each of the twelve regions of the country. The Committee was thereafter known as the Ad Hoc Committee for Pro-Life Activities.

In order to more clearly define the work of the Ad Hoc Committee and the activities of state Catholic conferences and dioceses, Cardinal Cooke, proposed a *Pastoral Plan for Pro-Life Activities* that was adopted at the November 1975 NCCB general meeting. The *Pastoral Plan* outlined a broad range of educational, pastoral, and public policy activities directed to restoring respect and protection for all human life. The public policy dimension included: (1) support for a constitutional amendment; (2) support for federal and state laws restricting the practice of abortion; (3) continual research leading to judicial refinement of the *Roe* and *Doe* opinions; (4) support for legislation and social programs that provide alternatives to abortion. Cardinal Cooke and Archbishop Joseph Bernardin (Cincinnati, Ohio) restated NCCB support for a constitutional amendment in testimony before the House Sub-Committee on Civil and Constitutional Rights on March 24, 1976.

Because the formation of attitudes is a long-range and demanding responsibility, the educational emphasis was increased through the annual Respect Life Program, which is sent to each of the more than 18,000 parishes each October. This Program also provides an opportunity to demonstrate consistency in supporting respect for life in such areas as poverty, health care, and support for the aged. The role of the Church in the United States in opposing permissive abortion has not been wasted. In June 1977 the U.S. Supreme Court decided that the government may legitimately favor natural childbirth over abortion and is not required to fund abortion services. The U.S. Congress enacted restrictions on federal funding of abortion consistent with the Court opinions.

The Ad Hoc Committee for Pro-Life Activities continues to give witness to the NCCB commitment to protection of human life at every stage of its existence and in every circumstance by its long-range educational programs and by its support for public policies that build respect for human life and human dignity.

See also PUBLIC POLICY ISSUES AND THE CHURCH.

Bibliography: National Conference of Catholic Bishops/U.S. Catholic Conference, *Documentation on Abortion and the Right to Life*, v. 1 (Washington, D.C. 1974); *Documentation on Abortion and the Right to Life* v. 2 (Washington, D.C. 1976); *Pastoral Plan for Pro-Life Activities* (Washington, D.C. 1975).

[J. T. MCHUGH]

BISHOPS' COMMITTEE ON THE LAITY

The Bishops' Committee on the Laity is a standing committee of the National Conference of Catholic Bishops and, as such, assumes responsibilities on behalf of the Conference in matters relating to the laity. While this standing committee was established only in 1975, the interests of the laity are not a new concern of the hierarchy. As early as 1919 it was felt that some kind of national coordinating committee was necessary—indeed, some thought, essential—as a means of communication between the bishops and the various national organizations. There was, however, a sensitive concern that the participation of the hierarchy in the coordinating committee not be so dominant as to crush the individual spirits of organizations or to create a dependency within the organizations. The earliest expression of organized, centralized lay activity in the Catholic Church in the United States was in the form of a Department of Lay Organizations. This department was a component of the National Catholic Welfare Conference (1919–66). The general objectives were to serve as an information channel and clearinghouse; to promote cooperation among clergy and laity in matters affecting the welfare of the Church and the nation; to cooperate in furthering the aims of the organizations, locally and nationally; to participate through Catholic lay-representation in national and international movements involving moral questions, and to interpret Catholic principles generally in the social and civic arenas. These objectives were largely met through the activities of the National Council of Catholic Women and the National Council of Catholic Men, until the years immediately following the conclusion of Vatican Council II. At that time, a newly structured episcopal conference came into being, namely, the National Conference of Catholic Bishops and its social service arm, the United States Catholic Conference.

With this reorganization came an ad hoc committee within the NCCB, called the Committee on the Lay Apostolate. It was this committee which oversaw the merger of the Councils of Catholic Women and Men into the *National Council of Catholic Laity (NCCL) in 1971. At the same time, the ad hoc Committee on the Lay Apostolate became a NCCB standing committee. This committee continued to elicit broad-based episcopal support for the fledgling NCCL, whose principal thrust was the training and development of parish councils throughout the country, and many parish councils subsequently became affiliate members of NCCL. When the Councils of Catholic Men and Women decided to remain autonomous organizations under the umbrella of the NCCL, the financial burden on NCCL became so great that it had to reduce staff and curtail programmatic activity. It maintained close contact, however, with the Bishops' Committee on the Lay Apostolate and began to press for some kind of focus for laity within the NCCB. In November 1975, Archbishop Edward McCarthy was elected Chairman of the Committee on the Lay Apostolate and, under his chairmanship, the Committee was reorganized and renamed the Bishops' Committee on the Laity. The new name was a clear indication that the Committee's pastoral concerns would range beyond that of organizations and movements (although including them) to the vast number of unaffiliated, or even disaffected, Catholic laity.

This reorganized Bishops' Committee on the Laity —consisting of Bishops Chavez, McKinney, Mihalik, Ottenweller, Povish, and Rausch, in addition to Archbishop McCarthy—identified its primary objective as service to the NCCB in its efforts to recognize and promote lay responsibility by the establishment of a permanent secretariat that would be a resource service available to the bishops and others for consultation, reliable information, models and assistance in developing fuller participation of the laity in the life, apostolate, and lay ministries of the Church. The secretariat was also envisioned as an education and communication service for both bishops and laity to provide vehicles for dialogue between hierarchy and people. It was felt, too, that the secretariat would insure that the role of the laity would be fully considered and recognized in the formation of policies, programs, statements and activities within the NCCB. Of major concern to the Committee was that the secretariat be an affirmation service to express and demonstrate the recognition, interest, support, and encouragement of the bishops to organizations, movements, and initiatives of the laity.

The secretariat was established at the May 1977 meeting of the NCCB in Chicago. It has, during the first year of its life, attempted to address the concerns of the Bishops' Committee on the Laity in a number of ways. It published a *Directory of Diocesan Lay Programs and Resources* in April 1978. This identifies areas throughout the Church in the U.S. where there are special programs to enable and encourage the laity to participate fully in the life and ministry of the Church and to identify also those who are the enablers. A major consultation was held, also in April 1978, between leaders of national lay organizations and movements and the Bishops' Committee on the Laity. Approximately forty different groups were represented at this historic first "gathering," which explored ways for the organizations and movements to participate in the evangelization efforts of the U.S. Church. Several smaller meetings took place around the country with people involved in the emerging lay or—as some refer to them—unordained ministries.

There are several areas likely to be of continuing concern to the Committee. One is certainly that of enabling the national lay organizations and movements to become more aware of each other's charisms and of how the different charisms enrich the total life of the Church. Another is the range of issues arising from the development of lay or unordained ministries in the broad context of committed Christian presence in the world and also in the more specialized understanding of trained service (either volunteer or paid) to the Church

and the world. The parish-renewal project, the national pastoral plan for family ministry, and the evangelization programs—all priority NCCB concerns—are likely to become, along with the subject of shared responsibility, major items on the future agenda of the Bishops' Committee on the Laity.

[D. R. LECKEY]

BISHOPS' COMMITTEE ON THE LITURGY

The Bishops' Committee on the Liturgy (BCL), called the Bishops' Commission on the Liturgical Apostolate until 1965, was established in 1958. Under a succession of chairmen, beginning with Archbishop Joseph Ritter, the Commission, principally through its secretary, carried on its work, which included the promotion of diocesan liturgical commissions, permissions to publish the *Collectio rituum*, the survey of diocesan liturgical calendars, preparation of the liturgical books in the vernacular (after 1963).

Organization of the BCL. The immediate effects of Vatican Council II's Constitution on the Liturgy (Dec. 4, 1963) on the Commission was to enlarge its concerns. In particular, during the special April 1964 meeting of the bishops, called chiefly to deal with questions of vernacular in the liturgy, it was agreed that the Commission should supervise the English versions of the liturgical books. As a specification of its ordinary responsibilities, the Commission was also directed to sponsor study sessions for seminary professors of liturgy. The role or competence of the body, however, was to be defined more precisely only in the Roman document *Inter oecumenici*, the September 1964 instructions on the proper implementation of the Council's Constitution on the Liturgy. In 1964 a secretariat was authorized and in January of 1965 it was opened to serve the standing Liturgy Committee of the National Conference of Catholic Bishops.

The BCL is headed, as a NCCB standing committee, by a chairman, elected for a three-year term. He, in turn, is to choose at most six other members to constitute the full committee. The addition of bishop-consultors is permitted, usually three in number. The Committee is assisted by a group of advisors, ordinarily chosen for diverse liturgical specializations. The designation of such advisors has been made by the chairman or by the committee.

Introduction of Revised Liturgies. Since Vatican II the BCL's major concern and responsibility has been the introduction and implementation of the revised liturgical rites in the vernacular. Of major significance are the Order of Mass, the Sacramentary, Lectionary, and the rites for the Sacraments, as well as the other official liturgical rites of the Church—Liturgy of the Hours, religious profession etc. (*see* LITURGICAL BOOKS OF THE ROMAN RITE).

In addition to overseeing the preparation and publication of these official rites, in a limited manner the BCL has undertaken publications to assist in the ongoing catechesis necessary in the process of implementation (*see* LITURGICAL CATECHESIS). In 1965, the monthly *BCL Newsletter* of the committee was first published, intended primarily for the bishops of the United States and for their diocesan liturgical commissions; it now enjoys a much broader circulation than originally envisioned. In 1973, a series of study booklets was begun to serve as commentaries on current liturgical developments (e.g. *Study Text II: Anointing and Pastoral Care of the Sick*; *Study Text IV: The Rite of Penance*). Official committee statements have been prepared to assist in the proper development of liturgical practice (e.g. 1972, *Music in Catholic Worship*; 1977, *The Sign of Peace*; 1978, *Environment and Art in Catholic Worship*). In 1975 the Committee prepared and published guidelines to assist those publishing the official liturgical books, semiofficial liturgical publications, popular participation materials, and missalettes.

Supervision over Adaptations. The newly revised liturgical books published by the Holy See, list in their introductions (*praenotanda*) matters which are proposed for adaptation by authority of the individual episcopal conferences. Examples of such adaptations, considered to be ordinary or lesser adaptations, can be found by way of example in the rites of Marriage and funeral prepared for use in the dioceses of the United States. The determination of the place proper for the ordinary celebration of the Sacrament of Penance (i.e. in the U.S. the *chapel of reconciliation) and the sign of repentance to be shown by the faithful before receiving general absolution (i.e. in the U.S. left to the pastoral discretion of the celebrant) are examples of adaptations which the introduction of the rite relegated to national episcopal conferences.

More radical or major adaptations require a faculty and the confirmation of the Holy See. Dioceses may make application for such adaptations to the BCL; the NCCB may submit requests directly to the Congregation for the Sacraments and Divine Worship. Up to now, no major adaptations of this nature have been requested or introduced into the liturgical practice for the dioceses of the United States by the National Conference of Catholic Bishops.

Bibliography: Bishops' Committee on the Liturgy; *Newsletter 1965–1975* (Washington 1977) bound volume; *Newsletter 1976–1978*, unbound issues.

[T. A. KROSNICKI]

BISHOPS' COMMITTEE ON THE PERMANENT DIACONATE

The Bishops' Committee on the Permanent Diaconate (BCPD) was established in November 1968. Its initial principal responsibilities had already been outlined by the National Conference of Catholic Bishops (NCCB). At that time three functions of the committee stood out: (1) to offer local bishops recommendations concerning concrete details of and questions about the diaconal vocation; (2) to establish a formation program including doctrinal, pastoral, and spiritual aspects of training; and (3) to review and approve plans for the use, developed by the various dioceses, of the specific ministry of the permanent diaconate (16:123).

In 1971 BCPD published *Permanent Deacons in the United States: Guidelines on their Formation and Ministry.* These guidelines remain the basic document for the implementation of the restoration of the permanent diaconate in this country. A revision and updating is planned after the completion of a projected professional survey of the diaconate in the United States.

Growth has been surprisingly rapid and strong. In 1969 there were four initial centers for training. By 1977, there were formation centers in 106 dioceses in the country with 2,387 deacons ordained and active

in a great variety of ministry, including hundreds of deacons ministering to the imprisoned, sick, disadvantaged, victims of injustice, youth, and in the catechetical apostolates. There are 2,610 candidates in training. Feasibility studies are underway in other dioceses.

The functions of BCPD and its Secretariat in the National Conference of Catholic Bishops have broadened since the original committee began operation in 1968. The motu proprio of Pope Paul VI, *Ad pascendum*, published in 1972, contained the requirement that episcopal conferences, with attention to the local situation, issue proper norms for the course of theological studies and submit them for the approval of the Congregation for Catholic Education (VIIb). This requirement is satisfied in the U.S. by a process whereby the BCPD evaluates each diocesan proposal and gives either approval or disapproval. Consequently the committee has become an official evaluative agency for programs of formation. With the growth of such local programs it has recognized the expressed need for formal evaluation of programs and in 1977 promulgated a policy for such evaluation somewhat similar to the process of evaluation provided for seminaries by the Bishops' Committee on Priestly Formation. The BCPD is the Committee of the Conference that is given general oversight of both the formation and ordained ministry of permanent deacons throughout the nation. There are normally seven bishops on the committee whose office in the Conference is staffed by an Executive Director, a deacon Staff Associate, and a secretary.

See also PERMANENT DIACONATE, FORMATION FOR.

[E. J. FIEDLER]

BISHOPS' COMMITTEE ON VOCATIONS

The Committee on Vocations of the National Conference of Catholic Bishops (NCCB; 16:312) was established as a standing committee in 1968. It exists to advise the NCCB regarding the vocation endeavors of this country and to coordinate these endeavors as stated in Vatican Council II's Decree on Priestly Formation: "The Council also directs that in accord with pontifical documents on the subject all pastoral activity on behalf of vocations should be systematically handled and unified by vocational organizations already established in the territories of each diocese, region, or nation" (*Optatam totius* 2).

The mandate given to the Committee when it was established was to cooperate with the *Conference of Major Superiors of Men (CMSM) and the *Leadership Conference of Women Religious (LCWR) in the vocational endeavor of this country. This mandate also called for the establishment of a National Office for Vocations. In conjunction with the LCWR and the CMSM, the Bishops' Committee on Vocations is the representative support of the NCCB for the *National Catholic Vocation Council.

The Bishops' Commitee on Vocations provides guidelines and assistance to vocation directors through interface with the *National Conference of Diocesan Vocation Directors, the *National Conference of Religious Vocation Directors for Men, and the *National Sisters Vocation Conference. In light of such studies the committee has published guidelines for offices of church vocations. The Bishops' Committee on Vocations also prepares the National Plan for Church

Vocations. This Plan is revised every five years, sent to the Sacred Congregation for Catholic Education in Rome, and distributed to vocation offices throughout the United States. This National Plan for Church Vocations is a compendium of varied programs of vocation promotion in the Church that have been proven worthy in individual areas and is developed in order to provide a vision for the American Church.

The Committee on Vocations also provides liaison for the NCCB with the varied organizations interested in the work of vocation promotion in the United States. It sponsors other activities on an *ad hoc* basis according to the need expressed by those involved in this work. The scope of vocations and the development of vocations for ministry in the United States has grown greatly since 1968. During these years there was a dramatic decline in the numbers of those choosing the priesthood and religious life as vocations; there has also been a rise in the number of lay persons interested in working in various areas of ministry. The promotion and coordination of vocations to the priesthood, to religious life, to the permanent diaconate, to secular institutes, and to lay ministerial vocations is a priority task of the Bishops' Committee on Vocations. Special efforts for specific promotional activities regarding vocations in the life of the Church today are extremely important; creative responses to this need are in action in many parts of the United States. The Committee strongly supports the coordinative agency for church vocations, the National Catholic Vocation Council, in order to achieve their common goals.

[D. J. PAKENHAM]

BISHOPS' COMMITTEE ON WOMEN IN SOCIETY AND THE CHURCH

Created in October 1971 for the purpose of studying questions regarding women's role in Church and society and reporting to the U.S. bishops on these matters, this NCCB Ad Hoc Committee discovered within a few years that its work needed to be both intensified and expanded. The chairman, Bishop Michael F. McAuliffe, reported in November 1975 what the tasks of the Committee involve: "(1) to study the issues; (2) to dialogue with concerned parties on the questions; and (3) to act as advocate for women by proposing policy measures and programs for consideration by the NCCB" (Origins 5[1975] 399).

Bp. McAuliffe succeeded as chairman of the Committee following Abp. Leo C. Byrne's death in 1974. Although the episcopal membership has changed somewhat from year to year, Bishops George R. Evans and Ernest L. Unterkoefler have been members since 1971. In addition, several women have met regularly with the Committee since their appointment as consultants in 1973. These are LeMay Bechtold of St. Cloud, Minn., a member of the Bishops' Advisory Council; Margaret Brennan, IHM of Monroe, Mich., a past president of the Leadership Conference of Women Religious; Agnes Cunningham, SSCM, professor of patristics at St. Mary of the Lake Seminary, Mundelein, Ill.; Loretta Favret of Silver Spring, Md., nationally active in the Family Life Movement; and, until 1977, Margaret Mealey, executive director of the National Council of Catholic Women.

The Committee has conducted meetings with various groups on such matters as women on welfare, minority women, and women in ministry. It has identified a number of substantive issues concerning women in society, including sex-role stereotyping, sexism in language, and discrimination in such areas as education, employment, and law enforcement. With regard to the status of women in the Church, Bp. McAuliffe noted in 1975 that among issues brought to the attention of the Committee with growing urgency are the following: "(1) traditional theological interpretations of the nature and role of women in family, Church, and society; (2) the possibilities for women's fuller participation in the Church's many ministries; (3) the need to include women in the decision-making processes of the Church; (4) apparent disparities in the opportunities afforded women for fuller participation in parish and diocesan life; (5) the need for women to have more direct voice in the direction of their own lives; (6) continuing obstacles raised to the growing life of the Church by prejudicial attitudes toward women on the part of both men and women, clergy and laity" (ibid. 398).

Also in 1975 the Committee emphasized the importance of research on the concept of "personhood," and especially on the question of the basis upon which traditional distinctions between feminine and masculine roles have been determined. It reiterated a cautious position on the Equal Rights Amendment, noting "certain difficulties in the amendment" and recommending that "implementation of the amendment, should it muster the necessary votes to be adopted, be scrutinized and monitored" (ibid. 399; Origins 2 [1972] 240).

During 1975 and 1976 there was discussion of a proposed office for women's concerns at the U.S. Catholic Conference. Although the proposal was eventually rejected, the Committee released in 1976 a report prepared by a task force of six women charged with articulating the concerns of women in the Church. This report identified five priority areas: changes in the processes of theologizing; broadening current images of women; reexamining traditional classification of females in the Church; examination and reformation of church processes and structures; and attention to social issues affecting the status of women (Origins 6 [1976] 69–74).

Also appearing in 1976 was a study by Committee-consultant Agnes Cunningham, SSCM, on *The Role of Women in Ecclesial Ministry: Biblical and Patristic Foundations*. There she observed that "the limitations of women's ministerial role in the Church today leads naturally to an awareness that the contemporary role of women differs markedly from that which prevailed in the early Christian centuries" (Cunningham 6). In introducing this study, which Cunningham developed at the Committee's request, Bp. McAuliffe declared: "It is the Committee's hope that reflection on the vital contribution of women to the apostolic and patristic eras of the Church will help to open new approaches to ministry for women in the contemporary era."

In 1977 the Committee conducted an informal survey of the extent to which women are involved in policy making, executive, and administrative positions in diocesan structures. With more than 100 dioceses responding, the survey indicated a general increase in the participation of women in diocesan decision-making, with a concentration of both religious and laywomen in the fields of education and social service. In his November 1977 Committee report Bp. McAuliffe voiced a hope that the data collected in the informal study will provide bishops with ideas that will "open up new avenues for applying the talents of women to the services of the Church" (Origins 7 [1977] 381). The Committee plans next, he indicated, to study the involvement of women in the life and ministries of the parish.

Bibliography: Origins, "In Context: Women in Society," 2 (1972) 240; "Office for Women's Concerns Proposed," 5 (1975) 396–400; 6 (1976) 5; "Identifying Women's Concerns," 6 (1976) 69–74; "The Positions Women Now Hold in the Church," 7 (1977) 381–384. A. CUNNINGHAM, *The Role of Women in Ecclesial Ministry: Biblical and Patristic Foundations* (USCC Publ. Office, Washington, D.C. 1976).

[A. E. PATRICK]

BISHOPS' JUSTICE PROGRAM

As an outgrowth of the American bishops *Call to Action conference, a national assembly of clergy and laity convened in 1976 to discuss questions of social justice in the United States, a plan of action and education was promulgated in May 1978 by the National Conference of Catholic Bishops. The program, entitled, "To Do The Work Of Justice," was designed by the bishops to enhance Catholic understanding of social responsibility as reflected in papal and conciliar teachings. It also serves as an invitation to the entire Church in the U.S. to join in specific activities on behalf of human rights and social justice within the period 1978–1983.

The measures called for in the NCCB plan include: a program of engaging scholars and universities in undertaking research into issues of justice and peace; the institution of educational programs on social justice in primary and secondary Catholic schools, seminaries, colleges, and universities; the establishment of a center for justice education at the U.S. Catholic Conference as well as diocesan offices for social education and advocacy; consultations on the parish and community responsibility, economic justice, and political responsibility; a major symposium on human rights; a national advocacy on behalf of the elderly; a Lenten program focusing on personal life styles; the preparation of national pastoral letters on racism and on the subject of the rights of the handicapped.

In their first response to the recommendations of the Call to Action conference, in May 1977, the bishops directed the President of the NCCB to establish an *ad hoc* committee to develop a five-year plan of action in consultation with the NCCB and USCC committees and secretariats. Archbishop John R. Roach, of St. Paul-Minneapolis, Vice President of the NCCB, was selected to serve as chairman of the *ad hoc* committee on the Call to Action Plan. During the Fall of 1977, the committees of the NCCB reviewed assigned recommendations of the Call to Action meeting and referred their evaluations and proposals for action to Archbishop Roach's committee. From these recommendations, the committee proposed the agenda encompassed by the plan, "To Do The Work of Justice."

In presenting the Plan for approval by the nation's bishops, it was noted that the suggested actions comprising the five-year plan were selected as representative of key components in the ministry for justice and peace. They were chosen, declared the bishops, because of their intrinsic significance and because they symbolized the larger range of issues that the Church is challenged to address in contemporary society. The NCCB Ad Hoc Committee on the Call to Action Plan is charged with the responsibility of reporting on the progress of the plan annually and it will coordinate an overall evaluation of the plan in terms of its impact on the Church and society, in 1983.

Bibliography: NCCB, *To Do The Work of Justice* (USCC Publ. Office, Washington, D.C. 1978).

[F. J. BUTLER]

BLACK CATHOLICS (U.S.)

Within the last decade since the death of Martin Luther King, Jr. in 1968, Black Catholics in the United States have made a dramatic shift in three areas: (1) a new self-awareness; (2) a new understanding of their Catholicism in relation to the Catholic Church in the United States; (3) a new sense of solidarity with the Black community as a whole. This new consciousness among Black Catholics is a result of the Civil Rights Movement of the 1960s and the increase of Black self-determination and Black protest movements toward the end of the same decade. This article will be confined to an analysis of trends and shifts in mentality rather than a history of specific organizations and a statistical analysis.

Self-Awareness. The new self-awareness of Black Catholics in the U.S. might be termed "a coming of age." In the past decade Black Catholics have begun to speak out on their own behalf and they have been heard. This was not the first time that such efforts at recognition had been made. Daniel Rudd (d. 1933) and the five Afro-American Catholic Congresses (1889–1894), Thomas Wyatt *Turner (d. 1978) and the formation of the Federated Colored Catholics in 1925 represent previous efforts on the part of Black Catholics to speak out with a unified voice that would be heeded by the Church and the world at large. This effort met with limited success.

All of this changed, however, when a representative number of Black priests formed the Black Catholic Clergy Caucus in April 1968. This initial meeting was held in the climate of anxiety and violence that followed the assassination of Martin Luther King, Jr. It was the first time that the Black Catholic clergy had ever had the opportunity to meet in such a large gathering to address their own problems and frustrations and to express their aspirations and hopes. The result was a series of proposals in regard to the Church and Black Catholics presented to the American bishops. These proposals were that Black priests be involved in the decision-making process on the diocesan level and within the Black community; that a more effective use be made of Black priests; that efforts be made to utilize the services of Black priests where there are none or at least the expertise of white priests attuned to the Black movement; that every effort be made to foster Black vocations; that training centers for Black ministry be set up in every diocese for those to be engaged in service within the Black community; that a Black-directed department for Black Catholic affairs be set up within the United States Catholic Conference; that Black religious be utilized as much as possible; that the permanent diaconate for Blacks be furthered; and that each diocese allot funds for establishing Black leadership training.

The long-term result was the creation of the *National Office for Black Catholics (NOBC) in 1970 as an organization speaking to the concerns of Black Catholics. At the same time the Black sisters met and organized the Black Sisters Conference and the seminarians formed the Black Seminarians Conference. The laity, finally, set up the Black Lay Caucus. Black Catholics also organized groups on the diocesan level. Out of this organization there resulted dialogue with bishops, religious superiors, and Catholic organizations. There came the realization that Black Catholics were now no longer a missionary field waiting for others to take the initiative. It was now the Black Catholic community which had to pinpoint the issues and assist the Catholic Church in the U.S. to solve the pressing problems.

Relationship to the American Church. The overall problem was the erosion of the position that the Catholic Church held in the Black community. Specifically, there was the issue of Black vocations to the priesthood and the religious life; a clearer understanding of the need for leadership within the Church for Blacks—clerical, religous, and lay; the continued existence of Catholic schools within the inner city; the adaptation of the Catholic liturgy to a Black culture; and a more concerted effort to combat racism as it appeared in certain areas of Church structure and local mentality.

Much of this discussion was initiated through the efforts of the NOBC or one of its subsidiary organizations. There were workshops on pastoral ministry and Black Liturgy. Here the remarkable efforts of the Rev. Clarence Rivers and the journal, *Freeing the Spirit*, must be mentioned. Conferences and institutes on pastoral ministry in the Black community along with seminars for the religious formation of Black candidates to the religious life were called regularly. There were Black self-help organizations like the Southern Co-operative Development Fund organized through the efforts of a Black priest, the Rev. Albert McKnight, CSSp in Louisiana.

In 1974 the NOBC issued a document relating to the subject of evangelization discussed at the 1974 *Synod of Bishops. This document, prepared by several Black Catholic organizations, was entitled *Black Perspectives on Evangelization*. It formulated concerns and suggested guidelines for a more effective evangelization in the Black community today. It was the summation by the Black Catholic community of the major issues facing the Catholic Church in the Black community in the accomplishment of her mission. As it stated, "We are at a point when our own thoughtful reflection on our collective experience and history in the Catholic Church must be incorporated into any contemporary blueprint for guiding Catholic ministry among Black people."

The ordination of three Black auxiliary bishops, the Most Rev. Joseph Howze, Joseph Francis, and Eugene Marino, were indicative of the Church's concern for the Black community. In 1966 the Most Rev. Harold Perry had been made auxiliary to the archbishop of New Orleans. Finally, the creation of the Diocese of Biloxi with the elevation of the Most Rev. Joseph Howze as its first Ordinary in 1977 gave a new pride of purpose to Black Catholics.

Solidarity with Blacks throughout the World. Finally, Black Catholics have arrived at a new sense of solidarity with the Black community both nationally and internationally. It was the clarion call of Pope Paul VI to the

African nations at Kampala in Uganda on July 31, 1969 to formulate Catholicism in terms of African culture and thereby offering to that same Church "the precious and original contribution of 'negritude' which she particularly needs in this historic hour" (ActApS 61 [1969] 577–578) that has given Black Catholics in America a sense of their particular mission and opportunity held in common by Africans everywhere. Repeated visits by members of the African hierarchy and clergy, religious, and students to this country and Afro-American Catholics to the Church in Africa have helped to raise the consciousness of American Black Catholics to the concerns and the accomplishments of Africans. There is a renewed pride in shared culture and history. This has created a new political consciousness relating to American foreign policy and efforts at liberation. This special concern of the Black Catholic community received recognition by the appointment of a Black priest, the Rev. Rollins Lambert, to the post of advisor on African Affairs at the USCC Department of Social Development and World Peace in 1975.

On the national level a much broader contact with Black Protestant Churches has taken place. Most significantly there is the attention that Black Catholic theologians, for example Rev. Edward Braxton and Joseph Nearon, are now giving to Black theology. Their task of theological discourse in the context of the Black experience and Catholic tradition will be a crucial one as the Catholic Church seeks to dialogue with the Black Church in this country.

Future Directions. Despite the fact that Black Catholics in the U.S. have undergone remarkable changes in self-awareness and self-determination and despite the fact that the Black presence in American Catholicism has roots deep in both American and Catholic history, serious problems remain to challenge the American Church in the last quarter of the 20th century. The major issue is still the commitment of the Catholic Church to Blacks in the inner city. The number of Catholic schools that close their doors within the city because of economic failure and personnel shortages has prompted many Blacks to accuse the local Church of insensitivity to the needs of ghetto children. There is the feeling that the local Church is not as willing as before to make the financial commitment to urban problems that the Church once made. There is no longer the enthusiasm among religious and clergy for active social involvement that once assured vocational commitment from the American Church as a whole.

The problem is made more serious in terms of parish organizations and parish leadership. Many formerly all-Black parishes were phased out in the 1960s as an effort toward desegregation within the Catholic Church. Black Catholics were incorporated into existing white parishes. In many instances this meant the destruction of what had been the focal point of Catholic identity for Black Catholics within the Black community. The local Black Catholic church served the same socio-cultural function as did the Black Protestant church. Many Black Catholics found anonymity if not a begrudging acceptance within the context of a white Catholic parish. For the upwardly mobile Blacks moving into the suburbs the entrance into the typical Catholic parish will probably increase. On the other hand, parishes within the central city and in certain rural areas will continue to try to restore the Black parish not as a segregated institution but as a recognized center for Black liturgical expression, Black religious leadership, and Black identity in terms of history and contemporary concerns. More concentrated efforts will have to be made in this direction so as to overcome the suspicion that the Catholic Church is an alien force within the Black community.

The Black Catholic population is increasing although at a slower rate than previously. With one million Black Catholics in the United States, Black vocations to the priesthood and the religious life remain a crucial problem. There are approximately at this time (1978) some two hundred and seventy Black priests, some one hundred brothers, and about the same number of permanent deacons; there are approximately seven hundred Black sisters. Black vocations need to be sought out in a positive way. It is here that the greatest hope for growth will be seen in the Black Catholic community. The proposal to create a Black theological center for the formation of Black priests and religious and white priests and religious for ministry within the Black community is still in the planning stage. Its implementation will doubtless affect the progress of recruitment of Black candidates.

Perhaps the most critical area for the Catholic Church in the U.S. in its relationship with racial minorities is the image that the Church presents to the world. In a multicultural, multiracial America the Black presence within the Church is scarcely discernible. Affirmative action programs remain a challenge for the American Church in terms of catholicity and worldwide credibility. In fact, it will be the peculiar vocation of Black Catholics in the U.S. in the next generation to be the American Church's sign that the Pilgrim Church everywhere is truly universal, authentically poor, and actually present to the modern world.

Bibliography: E. K. BRAXTON, "What Is 'Black Theology,' Anyway?" *The Critic* 36 (1977) 64–70. Divine Word Missionaries, J. BOBERG, ed., *The Word In the World.* '76. *Black Apostolate* (Techny, Ill. 1976). L. LUCAS, *Black Priest, White Church. Catholics and Racism* (New York 1970). R. MCCLORY, "Black Catholics. Church Losing Ground. A Personal Analysis," *National Catholic Reporter* 13 (Feb. 4, 1977); "Black Catholics II. Now For the Good News. A Personal Analysis." *National Catholic Reporter* 13 (Feb. 11, 1977); "Black Catholics III. Seeking Black Leadership. A Personal Analysis." *National Catholic Reporter* 13 (Feb. 18, 1977). National Office for Black Catholics, *Black Perspectives on Evangelization of the Modern World* (Washington, D.C. 1974); Origins 4 (1974–75) 472–479. National Office for Black Catholics and The Liturgical Conference, *This Far By Faith. American Black Worship and Its African Roots* (Washington, D.C. 1977). M. W. NICKELS, "Journey of a Black Catholic," *America* 135 (July 10, 1976) 6–8. G. SHUSTER and R. KEARNS, *Statistical Profile of Black Catholics* (Josephite Pastoral Center, Washington, D.C. 1976). D. SPALDING, "The Negro Catholic Congresses, 1889–1894," CathHistRev 52 (1966–67) 66–87.

[C. DAVIS]

BLACK THEOLOGY

There are basically two ways to account for the emergence of contemporary Black theology, one negative and the other positive. The former suggests that with the collapse of the classical religious world-view of the past and the resultant pluralism, traditional theology was shaken to its foundations and underwent an identity crisis. Somewhat nervously there poured forth a theology of hope, a *liberation theology, a feminist theology, and a Black theology. The critics of this development argued that these "new theologies" were in fact only social movements that were appropriating Chris-

tian symbols to enhance and legitimate their partisan concerns.

The positive account views the whole development from the perspective of the sociology of knowledge. This account argues that theology is in conversation with three distinct communities: (1) the Church; (2) the academy; (3) the significant socio-cultural and political movements of the day. Church theologians reflect upon the specific traditions of which they are heirs and mediators with a view to rearticulating the deepest insights of their traditions in a contemporary language. The theologian in the academy attempts to provide a sophisticated and refined account of the meaning of the Christian tradition in such a way that all reasonable people employing rigorous academic methods of the university will comprehend, if not affirm, its assertions. Theology in the socio-cultural and political context is a *praxis* theology. It seeks to point out the intrinsic relationship that obtains between the key religious symbols of a tradition and the urgent social issues of the day and thus to move people from words to deeds. Therefore in the face of the scandal of oppressed minorities in a supposedly Christian society a theology of the oppressed, a liberation theology, a Black theology develop. Black theology therefore is not contained by Protestant or Catholic doctrine. Nor is it preoccupied by the speculations and painstaking "methodologies" of the university. In its forthright opposition to the theologies of what it considers the racist attitudes of white suburban Christianity, Black theology declares itself to be the reflection of Black religionists on the Black religious experience for the enrichment of Black people. Whether or not white theologians read it, understand it, agree with it, dispute it, or ignore it is of little import. It seeks to be faithful to the "Black experience" and to translate traditional theological themes (God, Jesus, the human condition, Church and eschatology) into a language that will heighten the conciousness of the Black American so that he can transcend and transform his oppressed condition.

Origins and Proponents. While Black theology as a formal corpus is somewhat new on the theological scene, its origins are as ancient as the rich religious culture of Africa and its roots are found in the pre- and post-Civil War experiences of slaves. It found beautiful expression in spirituals, sermons, the blues, and stories of an oppressed people. While Martin Luther King, Jr. might be the admired patriarch of the present generation of Black theologians, his tempered views are not conspicuous in the writings of those who dominate the scene today. A representative list of authors, their central themes and key works, will be helpful. Eulalio Balthasar holds that white, Western theology sustains racism by supporting a color symbolism that sees white as good and black as evil (*The Dark Center: A Process Theology of Blackness*). For Albert Cleage, Jesus is, indeed, the Black Messiah (*The Black Messiah*). Cecil W. Cone points up an identity crisis in Black theology that is due to neglect of the experience of an almighty sovereign God as the point of departure for all Black theology (*The Identity Crisis in Black Theology*). James H. Cone to construct a radical Black theology of liberation joins Black power with the biblical depiction of the God of the Exodus and the New Testament Jesus, who proclaims good news to the poor, release to captives (*Black Theology and Black Power; A Black Theology of*

Liberation; God of the Oppressed). Major Jones seeks to enrich Black liberation theology by constructing a Christian ethic of freedom based on *agapé* (*Christian Ethics for Black Theology*). William Jones frames the problem of evil in the compelling question, "Is God a White racist?" (*Is God a White Racist? A Preamble to Black Theology*). J. Deotis Roberts proposes a compatibility and reconciliation of the thrust of Black liberation theology with a universal Christian vision (*A Black Political Theology*). Joseph Washington holds that the oppressed Blacks are God's chosen people (*Black Religion, The Politics of God*).

E. Balthasar is the only Catholic author. His views, while philosophically provocative, are only activist by implication. James Cone, however, continues to have the greatest impact. Cone states that his theology will differ in perspective, content, and style from the Western theological tradition transmitted from Augustine through to Barth. Therefore, with all respect to Nicaea, Chalcedon, and the Church Fathers, *homoousios* is not a *Black* question; Blacks do not ask whether Jesus is one with the Father or divine or human. These questions only arise within the "axiological perspective" of white experience. Those sharing this viewpoint like to think that their perceptions are universal; in fact, they completely ignore the millions of Christians who are oppressed by a racist society. Black theology finds its heresy and orthodoxy in the present. Jesus Christ is the liberator of the oppressed. Therefore, any theological interpretation of the Gospel in any period of history that does not proclaim Jesus as the liberator of the oppressed, must be declared heretical. Any view of the Church that neglects to see it as a people whose work and conciousness are defined by the community of the oppressed is anti-Christian.

The Catholic Church. To date the Church has given no formal or official recognition to Black theology, but this is not to say that there is no connection or impact. In the Catholic social teachings of the past decade and a half we find very similar concerns expressed in more formal and generic language. John XXIII's *Mater et magistra* and *Pacem in terris, Gaudium et spes* of Vatican Council II, and Paul VI's *Populorum progressio* and the "Message to the Peoples of Africa" all reject every form of oppression, racism, and social injustice. However these measured exhortations, deriving from a "deductive anthropology," seem tempered and remote when compared with the fiery challenge of the "inductive anthropology" of Black theology. Further, these documents stop short of advocating violence, while some proponents of Black theology suggest that violence may be the only way to overcome the oppressors.

In the U.S. more tangible signs of the impact of Black theology are to be found in the reality and the activities of the *National Office for Black Catholics. Perhaps the most significant impact of Black theology on the American Catholic scene is pastoral and in liturgy. More and more Black priests working in Black parishes are turning to Black theology for a meaningful idiom for their ministry. Many have transformed the interiors of their churches from their original ethnic Italian, Polish, Irish, or German motifs into Afro-American motifs. The pioneering liturgical music of Fr. Clarence Joseph Rivers is a further translation of Black theology.

Just as Alex Haley's *Roots* has impelled many Black people to reappropriate their lost African identity, the emergence of Black theology may well urge for many Black Catholics the reappropriation of religious experiences that transcend their Catholic tradition or the Protestant traditions from which they may be converts. One hopes that Black theology will continue to develop in such a way as to expand its notion of the "Black experience" and to address some of the philosophical implications of its assertions. One equally hopes that the Catholic Church in America will continue to develop its understanding and embracing of theological pluralism in such a way as to be enriched by the best of the literature of Black theology, which seeks to put forth the Gospel with a new and telling urgency.

Bibliography: E. P. BALTHASAR, *The Dark Center: A Process Theology of Blackness* (New York 1973). C. W. CONE, *The Identity Crisis in Black Theology* (Nashville, Tenn. 1975) J. H. CONE, *God of the Oppressed* (New York 1975); *Black Theology and Black Power* (New York 1969); *A Black Theology of Liberation* (New York 1970). M. J. JONES, *Christian Ethics for Black Theology* (New York 1974). W. R. JONES, *Is God a White Racist?* (Garden City, New York 1973). J. DEOTIS ROBERTS, *A Black Political Theology* (Philadelphia 1974). J. R. WASHINGTON JR., *Black Religion* (Boston 1965); *The Politics of God* (Boston 1967). J. GREMILLION, *The Gospel of Peace and Justice: Catholic Social Teaching since Pope John* (New York 1975).

[E. K. BRAXTON]

BLESSINGS, LITURGICAL

Blessings have traditionally been considered as a type of sacramental. According to the 1917 Code of Canon Law, "the lawful minister of sacramentals is a cleric upon whom that power has been conferred and who is not forbidden by competent authority to exercise it" (CIC c. 1146).

The Roman *Pontifical contains those blessings and consecrations either strictly reserved to the bishop or whose ordinary minister is the bishop. The Roman Ritual contains those blessings given by the priest either as an ordinary minister or as an extraordinary minister delegated by the bishop or by special indult.

Vatican Council II's Constitution on the Sacred Liturgy requested that "reserved blessings be few in number and only in favor of bishops or ordinaries: provision is also to be made that some blessings, at least in special circumstances and at the discretion of the ordinary, be given by qualified lay persons" (*Sacrosanctum Concilium* 79).

Title IX of the Roman Ritual contains three types of reserved blessings: those reserved to bishops and other Ordinaries and to priests with special faculties (Chapter IX); blessings given by priests having an apostolic indult (Chapter X); and blessings proper to certain religious communities (Chapter XI). The 1964 *Inter oecumenici,* Instruction on the Proper Implementation of the Constitution on the Sacred Liturgy from the Congregation of Rites (ActApS 56 [1964] 877–900) permits all priests to bestow the majority of these blessings. The recent revision of the sacramental and other liturgical rites has also extended to priests certain blessings once reserved to the bishop. Thus in case of necessity any priest may bless the oil used in the Anointing of the Sick. The 1977 Rite of a Dedication of a Church and Altar allows the priest to consecrate a chalice or paten (*see* CHURCHES, DEDICATION OF).

Blessings given by the deacon have also been extended. "It pertains to the office of a deacon, in so far as it may be assigned to him by competent authority, to administer Baptism solemnly, to be custodian and distributor of the Eucharist, in the name of the Church to assist at and to bless marriages, to bring Viaticum to the dying . . . to administer sacramentals, and to officiate at funeral and burial services" (*Lumen gentium* 29). Thus the deacon, whether permanent or transitional, may give the blessings contained in these sacramental rites. When he is an ordinary minister for the exposition of the Eucharist, he may bless the people with the Sacrament. He may also preside at the celebration of the Liturgy of the Hours and bestow its concluding blessing. The deacon may give only those blessings allowed him by law. Thus he presently may not bless ashes, statues, rosaries, etc.; the responsibility of the deacon in this area will be more precisely determined with the publication of the ritual of blessings which is still in preparation. The new edition of the ritual will undoubtedly contain texts not exclusively reserved to the ordained minister, to be used within a domestic setting (e.g. the blessing of children, of the family, of food).

[L. J. JOHNSON]

BROTHER, RELIGIOUS

During the post-Vatican II years there was much upheaval in the lives of religious brothers, both in clerical and lay congregations. Defections among some groups amounted to as high as 20 percent of the total membership and vocations decreased significantly. However, a certain stability has been achieved and some recent statistics indicate a gradual growth in the number of religious brothers in the United States. Three key elements in the life of religious brothers have been significantly addressed in the recent past: ministry, priestly ministry, renewal. Remarks here reflect the American scene, though much has been accomplished elsewhere, particularly in Third-World areas. (The positive impact of numbers of brothers from the Third World on international chapters of both clerical and lay congregations is widely appreciated.)

Ministry. In clerical orders, the "lay" brothers were often those who attended to the good order and maintenance of institutions and communities. They might have been attached to publications or development work, but most were involved in building and manual labor. Nonclerical congregations traditionally were maintaining a single apostolate—teaching, caring for the sick, etc. The past ten years have seen significant changes in both instances. Brothers in clerical orders have become professionals in any number of ministerial areas. Their training, therefore, can be lengthier and more academic than in the past. Very often such brothers are equal members of a team-ministry approach in various apostolates. Furthermore, despite canonical problems with a brother's becoming a major superior in clerical orders, brothers are often appointed or elected local superiors (cf. Congregation for Religious, Instruction Nov. 27, 1969, ActApS 61 [1969] 739–740). Many brothers in all-brother congregations have branched from, for instance, the traditional work of the Catholic school into broader areas of the educational apostolate. Not uncommon is the brother working in neighborhood services, campus ministry, seminary education, parish ministry, or service to disenfranchised groups. Lastly, brothers have, in this new understanding of and approach to ministry, deepened their commitments in the area of social justice. This phenomenon indicates the readiness of the brothers today to look beyond their "traditional" roles, see new needs in society and the Church, and respond accordingly.

Ordained Ministry. The question of the orders of diaconate and presbyterate with regard to brothers has been significantly discussed in recent years. Though some nonclerical orders such as the Marianists always allowed some brothers to be ordained for priestly ministry to the community and its apostolates, most nonclerical orders opted to retain an entirely lay character in their congregations. Since Vatican II and its invitation to brothers to consider the ordination of some members (*Perfectae caritatis* 10), most congregations have discussed the question on a regional and international basis. The Institute of the Brothers of the Sacred Heart has, for example, permitted each province to decide whether some of its brothers are to be ordained for priestly ministry in, primarily, its own houses. The Institute has maintained its lay character, calls its ordained members "Brother" and, in turn, they freely choose not to be major superiors after their ordination. It is emphasized that the ordained member embodies the priesthood of the community and, only with exception, will sacramentally minister outside the community. Other congregations, such as the Christian Brothers, have decided to retain their tradition of no ordained members. In clerical orders it has been possible to move from brotherhood to the ordained priesthood.

Perhaps the more pressing question in clerical orders is the development of the permanent diaconate for some brothers. Brothers are a very small percentage of the permanent deacons in the United States. Of the twelve who are (1978), some came to diaconate when they were serving in the overseas apostolate, others through a ministry in which some sacramental presence was deemed important. Most clerical orders are not actively encouraging brothers to be ordained deacons. Likewise, the Board of the *National Assembly of Religious Brothers (NARB) in 1975 affirmed that the ministries religious brothers and sisters render arise from their religious consecration (*Perfectae caritatis* 8) and, consequently, there is no need for another public call to ministry such as ordination to the permanent diaconate. Many brothers maintain that effective and genuine pastoral ministry can be done without ordination and further hold that brothers symbolize that all lay people ought to expand their presence in responsible pastoral ministry with the blessing, cooperation, and assistance of the Church.

Renewal. A third significant element in the lives of religious brothers has been in the area of renewal. Some brothers' congregations were in the forefront of changing programs of initial religious formation. From novitiate immediately following high school, the preferred sequence involved academic and life experience before the commitment of vows. Brothers have also developed extensive programs of religious and professional renewal. Professional training and updating are now the norm in clerical orders. The Sangre de Cristo Center for Renewal in New Mexico, though operated by the Brothers of the Christian Schools, is one of several places where brothers from many congregations experience lengthy programs of renewal and change, while others participate in prayer experiences or summer workshops in pastoral leadership.

Lastly, it is to be noted that through programs of renewal as also through new ministerial commitments, the brothers are developing a more significant impact in the larger Church. From a somewhat provincial attitude prior to Vatican II, the brothers are now in the mainstream of church life, and many serve important positions within the USCC, the Conference of Major Superiors of Men, and other national organizations.

Bibliography: The following studies have been prepared by the Christian Brothers and published by St. Mary's Press, Winona, Minn. *The Brothers and Their Vows* (1974); *Priestly Brothers* (1975); *Power and Authority* (1976); *Life Together: A Study of Religious Associations* (1978). D. A. FLEMING, "Report to CMSM on Brothers as Superiors in Clerical Orders," Origins 5 (1975–76) 693, 695–700.

[W. A. MOELLER]

BROWN, LEO CYRIL

Priest of the Society of Jesus, labor mediator-arbitrator, economist-educator; b. Stanberry, Ia., April 28, 1900; d. St. Louis, Mo., May 3, 1978. Leo C. Brown, SJ was the eldest of five sons of Edward P. and Mary A. (Wallace) Brown; he spent his childhood in Council Bluffs, Ia., after leaving the family farm where he was born. Both his father and he worked for Union Pacific Railroad and were active union members. After high school and World War I army service, Leo entered Creighton University, while working nights as a railroad clerk. After a year he joined the Society of Jesus at St. Stanislaus Seminary in Florissant, Mo. He received both A.B. and M.A. degrees at St. Louis University and taught at St. Louis University High and Campion High School in Prairie du Chien, Wis., where he was prefect of discipline.

He was ordained in 1934, receiving his S.T.L. from St. Louis University the following year. He entered Harvard University in 1937, receiving his Ph.D. degree in economics as a Wertheim Fellow in 1940. He returned to St. Louis University after a brief time as instructor at Regis College, Denver, Col., and founded the University's labor school in 1942, when he was also named public member of the Kansas City regional war labor board. In 1944 he became director of the Institute of Social Sciences at St. Louis University and was elected secretary-treasurer of the newly formed Catholic Economic Association. He became president in 1949, shortly after he was appointed director of the Institute of Social Order, acting regent of the School of Law, and professor of economics at St. Louis University.

By this time he had already attained national recognition as an outstanding mediator of labor disputes and was cited in *Coronet* magazine in 1955 for his work as an ad hoc arbitrator. He was a charter member of the National Academy of Arbitrators and was elected president in 1960. After serving as a member of the regional wage stabilization board during the Korean conflict, Fr. Brown was named in 1953 to the Atomic Energy Labor-Management Panel under the direction of Cyrus Ching, created by President Dwight Eisenhower to resolve disputes at AEC installations. Fr. Brown became chairman of this panel in 1968, a post he held until his death. He made extensive use of the technique of mediating to reduce the number of issues in disputes involving contract terms and then arbitrating the remaining unresolved items, in the tradition of George Taylor and William Leiserson—a technique which has come to be called "med-arb." Beginning in 1956 he served

as chairman of numerous minimum-wage committees appointed by the Secretary of Labor under the provisions of the Fair Labor Standards Act to set minimum wage rates in Puerto Rico and American Samoa. He was also appointed chairman of numerous system boards and public-law boards under the Railway Labor Act, and regularly served as arbitrator for the airline industry. He was permanent arbitrator designated in the contracts of many companies and unions and served in that capacity until his death.

In 1962 he was named staff editor of the *New Catholic Encyclopedia* for all the social sciences and personally wrote numerous articles on economic theory and history and on the labor movement and dispute resolution machinery both in the U.S. and abroad. It was during his stay in Washington, D.C. for this assignment that he formed closer ties with U.S. Department of Labor administrators so that he was designated special mediator by the Secretary of Labor in disputes ranging from the Hawaiian sugar industry and San Francisco hospitals to the Boston Metropolitan Transit Authority and AVCO in Stamford, Conn. For his work on the latter case he received a special citation from President Lyndon Johnson and in 1973 was presented with the first special mediator award by the Federal Mediation and Conciliation Service.

In 1963 he left St. Louis with the Institute of Social Order, which was renamed the Cambridge Center for Social Studies under the direction of Theodore Purcell, SJ, but five years later he returned to St. Louis University to continue mediation, arbitration, teaching, and writing until his death. In 1970, in recognition of his "contributions to industrial peace and his leadership in fostering research in social problems," he was awarded an honorary Doctor of Laws degree by Loyola University in Chicago, Ill. From 1968 until his death he was a member of the board of trustees at Marquette University in Milwaukee.

Among his writings are *Union Policies in the Leather Industry* (Harvard Press, 1947), *The Impact of the New Labor Law on Union-Management Relations* (Institute of Social Order, 1948), *The Shifting Distribution of the Rights to Manage* (Council of Profit Sharing Industries, 1950), *Tripartite Wage Determination in Puerto Rico* (Cambridge Center for Social Studies, 1966). He coauthored *Social Orientations* (Loyola University Press, 1954) along with other members of the ISO research staff, and contributed numerous articles to the ISO periodical *Social Order*. His arbitration awards are reproduced in *Labor Arbitration Reports* (Bureau of National Affairs). Other articles appear in *Review of Social Economy, Proceedings of Industrial Relations Research Association, Proceedings of National Academy of Arbitrators, Saint Louis University Law Journal, Monthly Labor Review, Hospital Progress*, and others. At the time of his death he was writing a book on mediation and arbitration.

[G. W. GRUENBERG]

BUDDHISM, CHURCH AND

For centuries contacts between Christianity and Buddhism were either nonexistent or at best fragmentary and sporadic. There were Nestorian-Buddhist contacts in China from the 7th through the 14th centuries; European missionaries were in touch with Buddhists in

Japan in the 16th, in Tibet in the 17th and 18th and then with other Buddhist countries into the 18th and 20th centuries. The 19th century began the serious scientific study of Buddhist texts by mainly secular Western scholars. But at no time have the conditions for a serious and fruitful Buddhist/Christian dialogue been as favorable as at present. For the scholarly work begun in the 19th century has provided a solid basis of information; the openness expressed in Vatican Council II has provided a favorable atmosphere; present conditions have made it possible for non-Buddhists to acquire firsthand experience of Buddhism in Asia and in the West, both from Eastern teachers and increasingly from competent Western teachers. Thousands of young Westerners have travelled to Buddhist countries and many of them have entered deeply into the Buddhist experience.

Vatican II. Although the Vatican II documents deal with Buddhism directly only once (*Nostra aetate* 2), light is shed on the nature of the Buddhist/Christian dialogue in other documents as well. The Constitution on the Church expresses more unambiguously than any previous council document the availability of eternal salvation for those who do not know the Gospel of Christ or his Church (*Lumen gentium* 16). The Decree on the Church's Missionary Activity declares that none of the good sown in the heart and minds of men is ever lost (*Ad gentes* 11) and invites Christian religious communities to reflect on how Christian religious life may be able to assimilate ascetic and contemplative traditions whose seeds were sometimes already planted by God in ancient cultures prior to the preaching of the Gospel (ibid. 18). The Decree on Ecumenism, although it speaks directly of the dialogue with other Christians, enunciates principles which can apply to other dialogues as well. Especially applicable is its frequent insistence that inner renewal on the part of Christians is a primary goal in all serious dialogue (*Unitatis redintegratio* 4, 6). Other important principles enunciated are the need for a new attitude and change of heart (ibid. 7), for serious study to understand the outlook of the dialogue partner (ibid. 9), for a theology training of future priests and bishops which is sympathetic and not polemical (ibid. 10), for doctrinal expression which does not present unnecessary obstacles to understanding (ibid. 11), and for cooperation in the work of making the world a decent place to live (ibid. 12).

Some Misconceptions. The uninformed Christian who turns his attention to Buddhism may have to correct certain popular misconceptions. While it is true, for instance, that the idea of God is absent, most notably in Theravada, Buddhism cultivates a profoundly reverent attitude toward an order of reality that is absolute and transcendent. Again, Christians sometimes dismiss Buddhism as a do-it-yourself Pelagianism, with no place for grace. Yet, while the word grace hardly occurs, particularly in Theravada, enlightenment or its equivalent does not come as a result of any human effort. Rather, when one properly disposes oneself—through diligent and persevering effort, it is true—it comes from beyond as a gift. Another popular image pictures Buddhists as idolaters, worshiping statues. But authentic Buddhism is no more inclined to adoration of images of Buddha than authentic Christianity to adoration of images of the saints. An even more pervasive Christian

suspicion is that Buddhism is a religion of despair, in which annihilation is sought through entrance into Nirvana, and responsibility for this, unreal world is abandoned. But the negative language of Buddhism, much like that of the Christian mystics and classical theologians, grows out of the conviction that ultimate reality is of a totally different order, beyond anything we can express with words. It is much like the language of St. John of the Cross, who writes of "nothing, nothing, nothing, nothing, and even on the Mount nothing." Again, Buddhist expressions like "beyond good and evil" have led some Christians to suspect antinomianism. However, an even modest acquaintance with the strong emphasis on morality in Buddhist theory and practice will despel this misconception.

Possibilities of Dialogue. Just as the dialogue with other Christians has helped Catholics to notice and correct deficiencies, to rediscover neglected elements, and develop inherent but hitherto dormant possibilities, so also the dialogue of Christianity as a whole, especially Western Christianity, with Buddhism can have possibly even deeper consequences. Some of the ways in which this renewal may take place are: (1) the rediscovery of the contemplative dimension of the whole of life, to correct a heedless, pragmatic activism; (2) a renewed respect for the mysterious incomprehensibility of God; (3) an expanded repertoire of methods of meditation and prayer, with serious attention to the part the body plays in the process; (4) a subtle and practical grasp of the workings of the mind; (5) modes of uncovering and overcoming inordinate attachments; (6) a renewed respect for the intuitive mode of knowing; (7) the correction, through a transformation of inner vision, of any shallow moralism and legalism, so that action flows spontaneously out of seeing, not fearfully out of uncomprehended compulsion; (8) a rediscovery of direct religious experience, the lack of which in workaday Christian celebrations is most frequently cited by young people as their reason for turning to Buddhist practice; and (9) a deepening of the theory and practice of nonviolence. Of course, each kind of Buddhism has its own character and some are more easily related to Christianity than others.

Because of the almost completely separate histories of Christianity and Buddhism over two millennia, cultural expressions, Scriptures, theological vocabulary, and religious symbols provide formidable barriers to dialogue. Thus the sharing of basic religious experience, particularly between Christian and Buddhist monks and contemplatives, has been of decisive importance. Such sharing of experience provides the basis on which issues of particular difficulty can be fruitfully discussed. Some such issues are God, creation, the reality of person (human or divine), reincarnation, the reality and goodness of matter, and responsibility for the world and the social order.

Bibliography: D. BERRIGAN and T. H. HANH, *The Raft Is Not the Shore* (Boston 1975). *Dialogue* (Colombo, Sri Lanka, New Series 1974–). H. DUMOULIN, "Exkurs zum Konzilstext über den Buddhismus," LexThK² Suppl 2: 482–485. Secretariatus pro non-Christianis, *À la rencontre du bouddhisme*, 2 v. (Rome 1970); *Christianity Meets Buddhism* (La Salle, Ill. 1974). H. M. ENOMIYA-LASALLE, *Zen-Way to Enlightenment* (New York 1968). A. GRAHAM, *Conversations Christian and Buddhist* (New York 1968). W. JOHNSTON, *The Still Point* (New York 1970). H. DE LUBAC, *La rencontre du bouddhisme et de l'occident* (Paris 1952). T. MERTON, *Zen and the Birds of Appetite* (New York 1970).

[D. J. O'HANLON]

BULTMANN, RUDOLF KARL

New Testament exegete and theologian, educator, author; b. Aug. 20, 1884, Wiefelstede, Oldenburg, Germany; d. July 30, 1976, Marburg/Lahn, Federal Republic of Germany. The eldest son of the Rev. Arthur Bultmann, an evangelical Lutheran pastor, and of Helene (Stern) Bultmann, Rudolf Karl Bultmann had two brothers, Peter and Arthur, and a sister, Helene. One of his brothers was killed in World War I, the other died in a Nazi concentration camp during World War II. His paternal grandfather, a Pietist, had been a missionary in Africa, and his maternal grandfather a pastor in Baden. This family information is important for an understanding of Bultmann whose family ties, especially those with his wife and three daughters, were unusually close and influential. The classical training of his gymnasium years at the Humanistisches Gymnasium in Oldenburg, 1895–1903, developed in Bultmann a deep interest in the Greek classics, classical philology, literary criticism, and in humanistic education as such. After completing his gymnasium studies, he studied theology for three semesters in Tübingen, two in Berlin, and two more in Marburg. Bultmann was influenced in Tübingen by the church historian Karl Müller, in Berlin by the Old Testament scholar Hermann Gunkel and the historian of dogma, Adolf Harnack, in Marburg by the New Testament professors Adolf Jülicher and Johannes Weiss, and the systematic theologian Wilhelm Hermann.

After he had taught for one year in the gymnasium at Oldenburg, he accepted (1907) the position of *Repetent* in the Seminarium Philippinum in Marburg where he had a scholarship to the University. He received the licentiate in theology in 1910, after submitting his thesis *Der Stil der paulinischen Predigt und die kynisch-stoische Diatribe*, a topic suggested to him by Weiss. In 1912, he received his *Habilitation* with the thesis *Die Exegese des Theodor von Mopsuestia*, a subject proposed by Jülicher. He was *Privatdozent* in New Testament exegesis at Marburg until 1916, when he became assistant professor at the University of Breslau. It was while he was at Breslau that he began to write *Die Geschichte der synoptischen Tradition* (tr., *The History of the Synoptic Tradition*, New York, 1968), in which he rigorously applied the methods of literary form criticism and historical analysis to the Synoptic Gospels in order to ascertain the earliest forms of that material known to the early Church and then to determine what part of that material may, with some confidence, be ascribed to Jesus. The book raised serious questions about the liberal theological conviction that the historical Jesus could be known through the Gospels and that he was or should be the central concern of Christian faith. This work was completed at the University of Giessen where in 1920 Bultmann had succeeded Bousset as professor. In 1921, he was appointed to a professorship at the University of Marburg where he remained until his retirement in 1951.

By 1922, then, there existed for Bultmann a kind of moral imperative to formulate a theology of the New Testament commensurate with the achievements of the historical-critical method as exemplified in *Die Geschichte der synoptischen Tradition*. The catastrophic social, cultural, and religious effects of World War I evident then in Germany, Bultmann's personal and academic disenchantment with the anthropocentric naïveté of liberal theology, among other factors, led to his efforts to develop a dialectical theology in response to the program outlined by Karl Barth in his 1919 *Commentary on Romans*. Though there is some evidence of a Neo-Kantian influence, fostered perhaps by the Marburg philosophers Cohen and Natorp, in two articles written in 1920, the dominant philosophical influence on Bultmann in formulating his theology was Martin Heidegger, who taught at Marburg from 1923 to 1928 and with whom Bultmann maintained a personally close relationship and conducted a joint seminar.

In his 1924 essay, "Die liberale Theologie und die jüngste theologische Bewegung," Bultmann claimed that Christian faith had to be associated with an absolute beyond the vicissitudes of history and hence that faith is not in fact necessarily related to the historical Jesus, but is rather dependent upon the eschatological act of God in Jesus and in the Christian kerygma. In a decisive essay of 1925, "Das Problem einer theologischen Exegese des Neuen Testaments," clearly employing the thematic categories of Heidegger, Bultmann holds that theological exegesis cannot operate from a detached neutral viewpoint, but biblical texts are rather to be accepted as statements meant to determine the existence of the reader. The subject matter of the Bible is possibilities for understanding human existence and the object of theology is nothing other than the conceptual presentation of man's existence as determined by God, that is, as man must see it in the light of Scripture.

Bultmann's assessment of the historical Jesus may be found in his 1926 work *Jesus* (tr. *Jesus and the Word*, New York 1934), in which he claimed that much that is known about the man is encrusted with myths that originated with the early Christians. Jesus was a Jewish, existentialist, apocalyptic preacher challenging his contemporaries to radical obedience in view of the imminent coming of the reign of God. Like other historical figures he challenged people's understanding of their existence but in historical fact, he is one presupposition among others for the theology of the New Testament. Thus, the historical Jesus is not of constitutive significance for theology, for Christian faith is not a response to the message of Jesus but to the Church's message about him.

Though he eschewed political involvement, Bultmann took a determined and early stand against Nazism. In 1934, he associated himself with the Confessing Church which rejected the paganism and racial teachings of Hitler's state Church and scattered throughout his articles written between 1933–60 are rejections of any exaltation of blood, nation, and race.

Although he previously had written on myth in the New Testament (e.g. in RGG, 1930), Bultmann's lecture of April 21, 1941 entitled "Neues Testament und Mythologie," given before the Gesellschaft für Evangelische Theologie in Frankfurt/Main and repeated the following June in Alpirsbach, made him a controversial figure among churchmen and biblical scholars, and gave his name high prominence in the world of theology. He distinguished between the truths contained in the Gospel and the mythological language in which they are presented. He stated that if the truth of the New Testament is to influence modern man, who cannot accept myths, the New Testament itself must be stripped of its mythological trappings and restated in language that addresses man in his existential condition. A fundamental datum of that condition is that the world of nature and history is a closed world in which God cannot directly be known. The demythologization controversy that ensued is examined in detail in Bultmann's 5-volume *Kerygma und Mythos; Ein theologisches Gespräch* (*see* DEMYTHOLOGIZING).

Among his other works are *Das Evangelium des Johannes* (1941; tr., G. R. Beasley-Murray, *The Gospel of John; A Commentary*, Philadelphia 1971); *Offenbarung und Heilsgeschehen* (1941); *Das Urchristentum im Rahmen der antiken Religion* (1949; tr., R. H. Fuller, *Primitive Christianity in Its Contemporary Setting*, Cleveland 1956); *Der alte und der neue Mensch in der Theologie des Paulus* (1964; tr. K.R.Crim, *The Old and New Man in the Letters of Paul*, Richmond, Va. 1967); and his most important three-volume work, *Theologie des Neuen Testaments* (2 v. 1948–53; tr., K. Grobel, *Theology of the New Testament*, New York 1951–55). Some of his moving sermons were published in the volume *Marburger Predigten* (1956; tr., H. Knight, *This World and Beyond*, New York 1960). His Shaffer Lectures of 1951 given at Yale were published in the volume *Jesus Christ and Mythology* (New York 1958), and his Gifford Lectures of 1955 were collected in the volume *Presence of Eternity: History of Eschatology* (New York 1957). Bultmann also had contributed articles to Kittel's *Theologisches Wörterbuch zum Neuen Testament.*

Much honored during his lifetime by honorary degrees (St. Andrews, Syracuse), by membership in academies (Oslo, Göttingen, and Heidelberg), by the Federal Republic of Germany (Grand Cross of Merit), Bultmann receives enduring tribute in the influence he has had on New Testament theologians, for whatever a theologian may think about Bultmann, his methodology and thought must be confronted by all serious scholars.

A bibliography of Bultmann's own writings may be found in R. Bultmann, *Exegetica*, E. Brinkler, ed. (Tübingen 1967). A complete bibliography is to be published soon by P. Joseph Cahill.

Bibliography: H. W. BARTSCH, ed., *Kerygma and Myth*, tr. R. H. FULLER (New York 1961); *Kerygma and Myth II* (London 1962). C. E. BRAATEN and R. A. HARRISVILLE, eds., *Kerygma and History* (Nashville 1962); *The Historical Jesus and the Kerygmatic Christ* (Nashville 1964). P. J. CAHILL, "The Theological Significance of Rudolf Bultmann" ThSt 38 (1977) 231–274. J. B. COBB, JR., *Living Options in Protestant Theology* (Philadelphia 1962). T. C. ODEN, *Radical Obedience: The Ethics of Rudolf Bultmann* (New York 1964). S. M. OGDEN, *Christ Without Myth* (New York 1961). N. PERRIN, *The Promise of Bultmann* (Philadelphia 1969). J. M. ROBINSON, *A New Quest of the Historical Jesus* (Naperville, Ill. 1959). W. SCHMITHALS, *An Introduction to the Theology of Rudolf Bultmann*, tr. J. BOWDEN (Minneapolis 1968).

[T. J. RYAN]

BUREAU OF CATHOLIC INDIAN MISSIONS

The Bureau of Catholic Indian Missions has been the central focus of the United States Catholic Church's response to missionary activity with the various tribes of Native American people since its inception in January 1874 (2:889). Rev. John B. Tennelly, SS carried forward the work of the Bureau as well as the Commission for the Catholic Missions among the Colored People and the Indians until his retirement in 1976. The work of the Commission together with its annual national collection in parishes demanded much of his time. Publication of the *Indian Sentinel* was discontinued in 1964.

Since 1976 the present director, Monsignor Paul A. Lenz, has initiated several efforts towards revitalizing the Bureau with primary emphasis on evangelization. The Bureau is being restructured as a service function and a communication link with missionary personnel. It is reestablishing in practice service to the bishops so as to intensify the Church's responsiveness to Native Americans and the awareness of their need to share fully and maturely in the life of the Church (*see* AMERICAN INDIAN CATHOLIC MISSIONS).

Transfer of the archives of the Bureau of Catholic Indian Missions—records, correspondence, reports, journals, photographs, published and unpublished materials—to Marquette University, forming the nucleus of a Marquette University Project, has been completed. The project is designed to locate, preserve and make accessible the invaluable records of the Catholic Indian Missions.

In 1977, the Bureau began the process of reestablishing credibility with mission personnel by learning how it can be of service in the present and for the future. Also in 1977 a newsletter was initiated for communication and sharing between the various missions throughout the United States. Through the encouragement of local and regional efforts in evangelization, the Bureau is giving reality to the hope expressed in the May 1977 NCCB statement "The Church and American Indians" (Origins 6 [1977] 766–768) that the efforts of the Bureau be renewed and redoubled in the coming years.

The Bureau with increased staff and service, is laying the ground work necessary to give practical implementation to these directives. In so doing, the Bureau looks to the theme of the 1974 Synod of Bishops—evangelization, given expression by Pope Paul VI in his apostolic exhortation, On Evangelization in the Modern World—as well as to continual guidance of the Spirit within the developing Churches under the direction of the bishops. The service intended by the Bureau in the present and future is "to evangelize man's culture and cultures (not in a purely decorative way, as it were, by applying a thin veneer, but in a vital way, in depth and right to their very roots), always taking the person as one's starting point and always coming back to the relationships of people among themselves and with God" (Paul VI EvangNunt 20).

[P. A. LENZ]

BURIAL (CANON LAW)

Christian burial, a right enjoyed by all the faithful, means the transfer of the body to the church, where the funeral services are celebrated, and the interment in the lawful place. It involves a religious and an ecclesial act; it benefits the soul of the deceased by way of suffrage; moreover, it consoles those who continue as pilgrims on earth and tends to draw them closer to God and to the Church. Christian burial may be denied to those who die in notorious violation of God's laws and of the public order of the Christian community (2:896).

For pastoral reasons, in order to render easier the celebration of ecclesiastical burial in the case of Catholics who have preserved their attachment to the Church and yet at the time of death are in an irregular marriage, under excommunication, or have committed suicide, the Church has revoked the restrictions of CIC

c. 1240, §1. Such Catholics must have given some signs of repentance and the granting of Christian burial must give no scandal to other members of the Christian community. A priest who seriously believes that, the above mitigation notwithstanding, in a particular case Christian burial should be denied, is first to consult the local Ordinary. Some dioceses publish detailed guidelines on Christian burial.

Public Mass or funeral rites may be celebrated for deceased non-Catholic Christians if expressly requested out of a genuinely religious motive by members of the family, by friends, or, in the case of a civil ruler, by subjects of the deceased, and if in the judgment of the local Ordinary there will be no scandal given to the faithful.

Bibliography: O'Connor-Suppl c. 1240 and c. 1241: Congregation for the Doctrine of Faith, Letter (private) May 29, 1973; Decree, Burial of Manifest Sinners Sept. 20, 1973; Decree, Public Mass for Deceased Non-Catholic Christians June 11, 1976.

[N. HALLIGAN]

BUSINESS ETHICS

Vatican Council II's Constitution on the Church in the Modern World in its section on socio-economic life, gives general principles for new developments in business ethics. The council stresses the need for justice in the business and economic community. While it urges progress in the production of goods and services, it also points out that economic development should be in the service of man and as far as possible under the control of all the people involved and not run solely by an elite or a government. Further, it calls for removing as quickly as possible the immense economic inequalities that now exist between and within nations (*Gaudium et spes* 63–72).

Developments of the 1970s. The ideals stressed by the Council for business ethics were given new emphasis by Watergate and subsequent exposures of the involvement of business in bribery and illegal political contributions. Opinion polls showed continuing decline in the prestige of business. One study by Archie Carroll (1975) regarding the internal problems of business found that middle managers often felt compelled to conform to their superiors' demands on them, even though it meant compromising personal values and standards. Regarding the overseas operations of the large American corporations, the Security & Exchange Commission called for disclosures of foreign bribes and especially of false or disguised slush-fund accounting. These disclosures in the case of Gulf Oil resulted in the ousting of the chief executive officer.

Studies. Silk and Vogel (1976), reporting on a meeting of top managers at the Conference Board, noted that businessmen were thoroughly shaken by the combination of antibusiness public sentiment and the revelation of political and corporate scandals that marked the late 1960s and the mid-1970s. They saw American businessmen slowly and painfully trying to adapt to new and unfamiliar demands, including the matter of ethics. Baumhart (1968), in a landmark study of what businessmen say and think about each others' ethics, concluded that their ethics was neither as good nor as bad as segments of the public generally believed. He described the specific problems businessmen faced and proposed practical solutions.

Brenner and Molander (1977), in an extensive replica-

tion of Baumhart's study, found businessmen disagreeing as to whether ethical standards in business had changed from the past. They seemed to be more cynical about their fellow businessmen in 1976 than they had been in 1961. They favored ethical codes (but saw them as having only limited value), accepted the idea of social responsibility as a legitimate goal for business, and ranked their customers ahead of shareholders and employees as the group to whom they felt the greatest responsibility. Baumhart interpreted these and other findings as indicating that business behavior was more ethical in 1977 than it was fifteen years before. But the expectations of the public had risen more rapidly than corporate ethical behavior. Purcell (1977), studying Dartmouth Tuck Business School Graduates over a ten-year period, found that although these young managers were often in conflict situations, they seemed generally to have acted in an ethical manner, many reporting that they were helped by having studied business ethics in graduate school.

Social Demands on Business. From the mid-1960s to the late 1970s business faced a tidal wave of social legislation of all kinds: the Civil Rights Act of 1964 with its impact on personnel policies; consumer legislation affecting marketing decisions; environmental legislation and its impact on capital spending and foreign competition, e.g., steel; employee-safety and health regulations; the shifts of social costs of all these to the user; the problem of inflation coupled with unemployment; the growth of *multinational corporation; the rapid growth in the late 1970s of shareholder proposals on socio-ethical issues brought up by public-interest advocates especially Protestant and Catholic church groups, coupled with responses by institutional investors not always supporting management. All these issues forced top management to concern itself with the corporations' impact on society, with basic ethical implications.

Responding to these movements, schools of business administration have shown growing interest in socio-ethical issues. McMahon (1975) found that about 56 per cent of graduate schools of business offered courses in the general area of the socio-ethical issues of business. Centers for business ethics sprang up at the University of Virginia, Illinois Institute of Technology, Bentley College, The Catholic University of America, Chapel Hill, North Carolina, and elsewhere. The scope of ethics had now broadened from earlier questions of pricing and honesty to include the larger social questions of race relations, pollution, product quality and safety, occupational health, arms production, violence, and also the portrayal of women and minorities on television, corporate governance and accountability, the quality of working life, and human rights abroad.

Top management faced such new problems as management incentives, the superannuated employee, privacy, disclosure, balancing the rights of the various claimants on the corporation, affirmative action versus reverse discrimination, payouts, especially abroad, market power, monopoly, oligopoly and competition, government regulation, product quality, consumer welfare, pressures on mid-managers to produce, conflict of interest.

Ad Hoc Responses. In this changed climate there was some increased sensitivity on the part of management to ethical issues manifested by greater stress on ethics in management development programs, for example, at

IBM and Allied Chemical. Another example: by 1978, about 28 corporations had explicitly-designated "ethics committees" on their boards of directors such as the Norton Company in Massachusetts, and Consolidated Natural Gas in Pittsburgh.

However, the new corporate-responsibility movement was often merely a response to the challenge of public-interest advocates rather than a self-conscious and deliberate application of ethics to business. By the end of the 1970s business had still not yet synthesized for itself the conflicting basic values as between the Enlightenment philosophy-of-science view and the Judaeo-Christian-Greco-Roman view (Cavanagh 1976; Walton 1969 and especially 1977). Conflicts continued unresolved between religious skepticism and religious faith, between means and ends, between individualism and a sense of community, between contract and status, market price and just price, competition and cooperation, etc. Part of the problem was the perennial question: is ethics really practicable for corporate decision making?

Continuing Problem—Is Ethics in Business Practical?
Some managers continue to question the wisdom and feasibility of introducing ethics explicitly into executive decision-making, inevitably asking: "Whose ethics are you talking about?". The issue calls for exploring whether ethics is too personal or too culture- and time-bound, how codes can yield practicality, whether law is the answer. Then a workable threefold ethical process for management will be outlined.

Ethics Too Personal. Ethics is said to be too personal, too individual for corporate use; private ethical preferences should not affect the policy decisions of the public corporation.

Indeed ethics does concern person-to-person honesty and fairness. But the normal manager is not schizophrenic; his private ethical values inevitably affect his corporate decisions for good or bad. Furthermore, ethics also asks questions of *public* purpose. For example, should the effects of competition on the quality of life be examined? Is too much or too little competition harmful? Are Americans wastefully consuming too much of the world's energy and resources with too little concern for development of the Third World? Should the corporation respond only to groups with power or should it respond also to the surrogate advocacy of the powerless? One virtue at the core of ethics is the notion of justice and justice by its nature concerns more than individual behavior.

Ethics Too Variable. Second, some managers see ethics as too variable or too situation-bound to have a role in management decision making.

Of course ethics is influenced by culture and time. For example, the Middle Ages condemned *all* interest taking as usury. But as Broderick (1934) points out, this proscription changed as commercial society evolved, capital became productive, and the science of economics developed. There is and must be adaptation over time in ethical thinking. But ethics also has an immutable core. Solomon Asch, a social psychologist, makes this point when he says, "We all feel that we value a thing because it has value, and not that it has value because we value it" (Asch 1953, 358). Clyde Kluckhohn, an anthropologist, went through the literature of anthropology and came out with this conclusion: "Contrary to the statement of ... extreme cultural relativity, stan-

dards and values are not completely relative to the cultures from which they derive.... To the extent that ... imperatives are universal in distribution and identical or highly similar in content, they afford the basis for agreement among the peoples of the world" (Kluckhohn 1951, 418). An expression of that agreement is the thirty articles of the United Nations Universal Bill of Human Rights adopted by the General Assembly in 1948 (7:214).

Codes of Ethics. Codes of ethics can help management to make ethics practical but they are not a panacea, even when they can be enforced on association members, something not commonly the case. Sometimes they merely relate the profession to individual clients rather than to the collective public. Nevertheless, codes clarify ethical thinking and encourage ethical behavior.

Ethics and Law. As for the relationship between ethics and law, while laws are obviously necessary, laws, government agencies, lawyers and courts cannot be involved in every management decision. The country would become bogged down by a legal bureaucracy that could ultimately produce a contempt for law. The late 1970s witnessed something of this in the medical malpractice maze. Both personal and corporate ethical practices are necessary for freedom from legalism and regulatory excesses.

A Threefold Ethical Process. Ethics can be readily used by management if decision-making includes a threefold ethical process like the following model: the examination and support of general ethical principles; the examination and support of middle-level ethical principles; the in-depth study of cases and classes of similar cases. The three are interacting tools and should be used *simultaneously*, each reinforcing or clarifying the other.

Basic Ethical Principles. These can be stated as follows. (1) People should maximize value and minimize disvalue in their actions. (2) Human life ranks much higher than animal life. (3) Persons and institutions should be just and honest in their dealings. (4) The morality of an action is determined by analysis of the values and disvalues present in the act, the circumstances inseparable from the situation, and the intention of the agent.

Most people would agree with those general principles. They are fundamental, the foundation on which ethics is built, though they have no practical value until they are specified by middle principles and case analyses. But judging cases has no ethical meaning either unless the judgments are based on fundamental ethical principles. This is where the simultaneity comes in.

Middle Ethical Principles. These ethical principles are "middle" because they are *in between*, serving as a bridge between the more general principles and specific cases. They stem both from a study of general principles and from a study of specific-case situations. Practical experience is important in formulating them. They should be held firmly as long as they promote justice; they should be modified when new situations demand it.

Most of the thirty articles of the UN Universal Declaration of Human Rights are middle ethical principles. Here are two other examples. (1) The rule of law is central, but unjust laws can exist; and there are times when a higher moral cause justifies breaking the law (most would add the proviso that the violator be willing to accept the consequences). Example: the civil disobedience of the Montgomery, Alabama bus riders. (2) Property is a vital private right, but it has a social aspect. Example: I may not build any kind of building I want, without regard for zoning laws.

There are two additional kinds of middle principles, more logical in character, that provide guidance. (3) There is a difference between a precept or commandment, saying what must be done, and a counsel, recommending the better or more selfless or saintly action. Examples: I must fulfill a contract; I may give half my income to the poor. (4) When a good action has both a good effect and a bad effect (a common conflict situation), a person may rightly perform the action provided (a) he does not directly intend the bad effect; (b) the bad effect is not a means to the good end, but is simply a side effect; and (c) the good involved is not outweighed by the bad effect. (This is the Scholastic "principle of the double effect"; an example: a pharmaceutical company may market a needed drug (that might in some cases have harmful side effects) provided the good and bad effects are carefully weighed and consumers are encouraged to take all reasonable precautions.

Specific-Case Analysis. While essential to the process of ethical reasoning, the middle-level principles are not fully usable (or perhaps even discovered) until applied to specific cases.

The middle principle just cited—"The rule of law is central, but unjust laws can exist and there are times when a higher moral cause may justify breaking the law"—immediately poses the question of when individual conscience justifies violating the law. Specific-case analyses are needed to help answer that, e.g., re civil disobedience to achieve civil rights. Another example: "Property is a vital private right, but it has a social aspect." One practical example of the issue that principle raises is the covering over of strip mines for the benefit of the people in Kentucky and West Virginia versus the resulting higher cost in electric power and perhaps fewer urban jobs in Chicago and Pittsburgh. Who is right? The tough trade-off questions between competing groups in society cannot be solved by principles alone but must also involve the continuous and careful analysis of cases and classes of cases along with the principles. The student of ethics must work closely with economists, lawyers, sociologists, psychologists, engineers, and other professionals, while keeping ethical values uppermost.

By using these three tools with deliberately studied and *simultaneous interaction*, the manager has at his disposal a practical process for ethical decision-making. Decisions will sometimes be difficult. Differences of opinion may be due to ethical pluralism. But more often they will be due to the complexity or ambiguity of the facts in specific cases. A manager—both as an individual and as a member of a management team—should follow his own (hopefully enlightened) conscience with both prudence and courage.

Future Hope—Institutionalizing Ethics on Corporate Boards. If business ethics is to be more than mere talk or public relations, ethics will need to become "institutionalized," that is, formally acknowledged and integrated into business decisions at all levels, but especially beginning with the corporate board of directors and its top management (Purcell 1978). The need is

for some directors and perhaps some officers explicitly charged with the promotion of ethics. These ethical advocates need not be philosophers in the field of ethics, but they should keep up to date on the extensive literature of ethics as applied to business.

A principal function of the corporate-board ethics-committee would be to identify generic questions of an ethical nature that should be asked routinely along with the usual legal, financial, amd marketing questions. For example: a strategic planner might ask, "If we take certain actions, what would our market share be and will we run afoul of antitrust laws? What would our discounted cash flow be?"

The ethics advocates might want to know how a given decision will affect the rights of employees versus the rights of the corporation; or whether an action help or hurt the long-run general welfare of the cities or countries (South Africa, for instance) where the company's plants are located, or, how the firm will balance the public's right to know about minority hiring and the company's right to keep competitive information confidential; or whether a new product help or hurt the environment, the conservation of energy, the quality of life, or the safety of consumers.

The corporate-ethics advocates would need to be socially sensitive enough to phrase such questions in generic terms but still keep them sufficiently practical and thus manageable for specific, top-management decisions. They will also need to "sense" ethical issues before there is a public hue and cry about them. They could help develop an ethical code for their company and encourage ethics seminars for top, middle, and lower managers in mid-career, with experience enough to perceive the ethical implications of decisions. Ethical advocates could encourage the study of ethical principles and cases in schools of business administration, some of which could perhaps help industry towards solving actual ethical problems.

If the committee were entirely composed of corporate officers, its secretary would need to be a strong and able manager who had the backing of the chief executive officer (CEO). The CEO will be a prime force in the success or failure of the ethical advocacy idea. But a board made up exclusively of *outside* directors is preferable.

Top-management executives have generally been cool to the ethical-advocacy idea. Their objections may be put into about four categories: (1) the "ethics is too subjective and variable" argument; (2) the "the only hope is law" argument; (3) the "tokenism" argument; (4) the "ethics is everybody's business but especially the CEO's business" argument. The arguments that ethics is too variable and subjective, or that law is the only hope have been answered earlier.

As for tokenism, one chief executive officer stated: "If one person is worrying about ethics, others will feel less constrained to do so on their own." But that does not necessarily follow. While ethical advocacy might be focused on one board member as secretary of the committee, the responsibility should be explicitly shared by a committee of the board.

As for "ethics is everybody's business, especially the CEO's business," what is everybody's business usually becomes nobody's business. The corporation has already institutionalized functional experts in law, finance, marketing, public relations, research, and so forth to assist the chief executive officer. The CEO does not regard law or finance as "everybody's business." Ethics is not more complex or elusive than law or economics or finance; unanimity among economists or lawyers is not a constant.

Ethics in business is not a matter of window-dressing but concerns the realistic and serious management determination to institutionalize ethics, especially at the board-room level of major American corporations. This concern will do much to bolster public confidence in the American business system. Ethical considerations can enter practically and systematically into executive decision-making both at the policy level and at lower-management levels if business is willing to experiment, to take some risks, and to be creative.

Bibliography: S. E. ASCH, *Social Psychology* (New York 1952). R. BAUMHART, *Ethics in Business* (New York 1968). S. N. BRENNER and E. A. MOLANDER, "Is the Ethics of Business Changing?" *Harvard Business Review* 55 (1977) 57–71. J. BRODERICK, *The Economic Morals of the Jesuits* (London, 1934) esp. ch. 6, "The Five Per Cent Controversy." A. B. CARROLL, "Managerial Ethics: A Post-Watergate View," *Business Horizons* (April 1975) 75–80. G. F. CAVANAGH, *American Business Values in Transition* (Englewood Cliffs, N.J. 1976). C. KLUCKHOHN, "Values and Value Orientation," in T. PARSONS and E. A. SHILS, eds., *Toward a General Theory of Action* (Cambridge, Mass., 7th ed., 1976) 418. T. F. MCMAHON, *Report on the Teaching of Socio-Ethical Issues in Collegiate Schools of Business/Public Administration* (Center for the Study of Applied Ethics, Univ. of Virginia, Charlottesville 1975). T. V. PURCELL, "Do Courses in Business Ethics Pay Off?" *California Management Review* 19 (Summer 1977) 50–58; "Institutionalizing Ethics on Corporate Boards," *Review of Social Economy* 36 (1978) 41–53. L. SILK and D. VOGEL, *Ethics and Profits* (New York 1976). United Nations, *Everyman's UN Handbook* (8th ed., New York 1968). C. WALTON, *Ethos and the Executive* (Englewood Cliffs, N.J. 1969); *The Ethics of Corporate Conduct* (Englewood Cliffs, N.J. 1977).

[T. V. PURCELL]

C

CALENDAR, COMMON LITURGICAL

The liturgical year (16:259) is not the result of a direct and conscious arrangement of the annual cycle for pedagogical purposes about some such thematic scheme as the life of Christ or salvation history. Rather, as the earlier article has shown (2:1062), it is the result of a long and complex evolution in which many cultic and cultural forces have shaped times of feast and fast into a pattern that not only celebrates the several dimensions of the Christian kerygma (8:167), but constitutes an epitome of the entire Christian tradition. Critically reviewed in the 16th cent. with widely divergent results ranging from slight to radical reform, the calendar has received fresh attention since Vatican Council II along lines manifesting more ecumenical convergence. Calendars of occidental Churches in the U.S. today agree in beginning the year with four Sundays of Advent leading to Christmas, and all observe the feast of Epiphany on January 6 or an adjacent Sunday, with the Sunday after Epiphany kept as the Baptism of Christ. Omitting the former three pre-lenten Sundays (Septuagesima, Sexagesima, Quadragesima), all begin Lent on Ash Wednesday and distinguish the days of Holy Week. Easter is celebrated for 50 days, terminated by the one-day celebration of Pentecost, from which the following Sundays are numbered.

Such are the norms for the liturgical year issued with the new Roman Calendar (1969). They were adopted by the Presbyterian *Worshipbook* (1970), the Episcopal *Proposed Book of Common Prayer* (1976), and the Lutheran *Book of Worship* (1978). The same norms govern the lectionary prepared for the Consultation on Church Union (1974), now approved for use by the Methodist Church. The Disciples of Christ and the United Church of Christ follow the calendar of the Presbyterian *Worshipbook*. In the United Kingdom, on the other hand, calendar reform began somewhat earlier and along different lines. In 1963 a Joint Liturgical Group composed of representatives of the Churches of England, Scotland, Ireland, and Wales (Anglican, Methodist, Presbyterian, Baptist, Congregationalist, and Churches of Christ, with an observer from the Roman Catholic Church) undertook the formulation of a common calendar and lectionary along new lines. The result, published in 1967, arranged the Sundays of the year thematically about three major festivals: Christmas and Easter, each preceded by nine Sundays and followed by six, and Pentecost, followed by 21 Sundays. Although the earlier (1962) calendar of the Church of South India had treated Septuagesima as the Ninth Sunday before Easter, the parallel arrangement before Christmas was an innovation of the Joint Liturgical Group. Traditional themes of Epiphany were set on the first and third Sundays after Christmas, but that feast itself did not appear. Since its publication this radical proposal has undergone further development in a more conservative direction in individual Churches. In *The Calendar and Lessons* (1969) the Church of England added feasts of Christ and of the saints, and the *Methodist Service Book* (1975) restored Epiphany and All Saints' Day. Both retain the three pre-lenten Sundays as well as the distinctive nine Sundays before Christmas, although alternative titles show that these are coming to be seen either as Sundays before Advent (Methodist) or as the last five Sundays after Trinity or Pentecost (Church of England). A period preceding Advent has also characterized the Methodist calendar in the U.S., the time after Pentecost giving way to a season of Kingdomtide from the last Sunday of August. Roman and Lutheran calendars designate the last Sunday after Pentecost as Feast of Christ the King, and the same lessons are given in other lectionaries.

While the number of observances in the sanctoral cycle (16:401) has been reduced in the reform of the Roman Calendar from 338 to 191, it has been increased in calendars of the Lutheran Church to 127 and of the Episcopal Church to 152; for both the latter these are divided between feasts (Lutheran, 30; Episcopal, 33) and optional commemorations (*see* SAINTS, MEMORIALS OF THE). Like the Roman, the Lutheran Calendar occasionally places more than one optional memorial on the same day. The General Roman Calendar has 33 feasts of fixed date (10 designated Solemnities) with others of moveable date, as well as 64 obligatory memorials. All modern calendars strongly emphasize *Sunday as a weekly feast of Christ which is accorded precedence over all but the most important feasts of fixed date, an emphasis that casts doubt on the acceptability of any universal calendar reform (such as the World Calendar), which would interrupt the independent cycle of the week.

Bibliography: R. C. D. JASPER, ed., *The Calendar and Lectionary: A Reconsideration by the Joint Liturgical Group* (London 1967). The Standing Liturgical Commission of the Episcopal Church, *The Church Year.* Prayer Book Studies 19 (New York 1970). The Inter-Lutheran Commission on Worship, *The Church Year: Calendar and Lectionary.* Contemporary Worship 6 (Minneapolis, Philadelphia and St. Louis 1973). R. NARDONE, "The Roman Calendar in Ecumenical Perspective," *Worship* 50 (1976) 238–246.

[T. J. TALLEY]

CALENDAR, LITURGICAL (U.S.)

The General Norms introducing the 1969 Universal Calendar of the Roman Church allow various countries to prepare their own particular *calendars by inserting in the general calendar observances of special importance to the individual country. After preliminary consultation the National Conference of Catholic Bishops authorized such a calendar in November 1971; it was formally approved by the Sacred Congregation for Divine Worship on December 28, 1971. The calendar includes six obligatory memorials: Elizabeth Ann Seton (Jan. 4), John Neumann (Jan. 5), Peter Claver (Sept. 9), Isaac Jogues and companions (Oct. 19), Frances Xavier Cabrini (Nov. 13), and Our Lady of Guadalupe (Dec. 12). Isidore, the patron of farmers, appears as an optional memorial (May 15). Two votive Masses are also allowed: one for Independence Day (July 4) and other civic observances, the other for Thanksgiving Day (fourth Thursday in November). A complete set of Propers is provided for the votive Masses as well as a provisional set for John Neumann. The other feasts have a proper Opening Prayer with the other texts taken from the Common. The National Conference of Catholic Bishops allows individual Ordinaries to determine which days should be observed as special times of prayer replacing the former rogation and ember observances.

See also SAINTS, MEMORIALS OF THE; MASSES, VOTIVE.

Bibliography: BCL Newsletter 5 (June–July 1969); 7 (December 1971); 8 (January–February 1972); 8 (March–April 1972); 13 (May–June 1977).

[L. J. JOHNSON]

CALENDARS, PARTICULAR

The General Norms of the 1969 Roman Calendar allow the formation of particular calendars, i.e. the insertion of special celebrations into the general calendar by individual regions, countries, dioceses, and religious families. In June 1970, the Congregation for Divine Worship issued an instruction giving specific norms for the establishment of such calendars.

Particular calendars may include saints proper to a region or religious community as well as those saints listed in the universal calendar but to whom a higher rank will be given. To insure historical credibility, proper hagiographical studies must, when necessary, be conducted regarding the life and deeds of the saint. Whenever possible, the saint should be commemorated on the day of death; otherwise, on a day of importance in the cult of the saint. If the feast already occurs in the general calendar, it should generally be observed on the same day. Permission is granted for a more solemn celebration of the saint in some parts rather than in the whole of a diocese or religious family.

In addition to commemorating those saints having a special connection with a particular diocese, the diocesan calendar may include a proper liturgical celebration of the principal and secondary patrons of the diocese as well as the anniversary of the dedication of the cathedral.

See also SAINTS, MEMORIALS OF THE.

Bibliography: Sacred Congregation for Divine Worship, "Normae universales de anno liturgico et de calendario," *Notitiae* 46 (April–June 1969) 165–176 (Eng. tr., USCC pub. v-453). "Instructio de calendariis particularibus atque officiorum et Missarum propriis recognoscendis," *Notitiae* 58 (November 1970) 348–370.

[L. J. JOHNSON]

CALL TO ACTION CONFERENCE

The Call to Action Conference, an assembly of Catholic diocesan representatives meeting under the auspices of the National Conference of Catholic Bishops (NCCB), marked the culmination of an eighteen-month national consultation on social justice. The Conference was held in Detroit, Mich., Oct. 21–23, 1976. The proceedings of the convocation in which 1,300 delegates, priests, religious, and laity from 152 dioceses participated, resulted in 182 recommendations, which in turn formed the basis of a five-year plan of social action for the Catholic Church in the United States.

The Call to Action Assembly was intended to mark the Catholic observance of the Bicentennial anniversary of the United States. The concept for the program had its genesis in 1971 with deliberations of the U.S. Catholic *Bishops' Advisory Council, a national body which provides guidance and consultation to the American bishops. The Council urged the establishment of a Church-sponsored symposium on *A Call to Action,* the English title of the encyclical *Octogesima adveniens* of Pope Paul VI on the 80th anniversary of *Rerum novarum.*

A Committee of the NCCB was formed in 1973 with a mandate to prepare a conference on social justice. Card. John F. Dearden, Archbishop of Detroit, was appointed chairman of the sixty-two member planning committee. A program of consultation leading up to the Call to Action Conference was undertaken in 1975. At the diocesan and parish level across the country the program theme of "Liberty and Justice for All" formed the basis of group discussions. At the national level the NCCB conducted seven hearings, each three days in length, and held in the cities of Washington, D.C., San Antonio, Texas, Minneapolis, Minn., Atlanta, Ga., Sacramento, Cal., Newark, N.J., and Maryknoll, New York. Sixty-five bishops joined by religious, priests, and laity took testimony from over four hundred persons who focused on particular areas of social need and church life. Included among the witnesses were homemakers, farmers, theologians, economists, social workers, union leaders, community organizers, feminists, unemployed persons, Amerindians, and Blacks, as well as many other individuals. The consultation focused on a wide variety of topics dealing with family and neighbourhood life, economic justice, internal and political affairs, the needs of minorities, the aged, women, education, cultural pluralism, world hunger, war and peace, and a multitude of other contemporary social issues. In early 1976, the concerns and recommendations raised in the program—over one million of them—were reviewed and summarized by teams of bishops, priests, religious, and laity. A series of preliminary documents on the discussion findings were prepared for the next stage of the consultation, the Detroit meeting.

The densely written recommendations of the Call to Action Conference touch upon many areas of church life and its social mission. They range from a strong condemnation of the arms race and of nuclear weaponry to just wages for teachers in Catholic parochial schools; from a concern for the viability of the small family farm to a concern for a healthy urban neighbourhood; from the subject of the new economic order as voted by the General Assembly of the United Nations to equal rights for women in the labor market.

In their initial response to the Detroit Assembly, the bishops of the United States in a 1,400 word pronouncement, affirmed in general the findings of the Call to Action meeting and the preceding bicentennial consultation. In the statement the bishops said:

> We invited this process of structured public discussion in the Church so that we might listen to the needs of our own people and through their voices come to know more specifically and to share more intimately "the joys and hopes, the griefs and the anxieties" of the people of our age. Admittedly, the process of consultation was imperfect and there are some conclusions which are problematical and in some cases untenable. This has been a source of concern. Yet, this two-year process was marked by trust and respect among nearly all who took part. It gave many people a good opportunity to speak directly to church leaders. It identified issues and a number of constructive suggestions for action. It helped dramatize how the Church and its leadership are perceived by some. We are grateful to all who shared their insights with us. We affirm our commitment to the principle of shared responsibility in the contemporary Church, and we assert our intention to improve consultation with our people.

The hierarchy went on to underscore "the direct and intimate connection between the mission of the Church and the ministry of justice," and pledged themselves to the establishment of a five-year program on social justice. To accomplish this the NCCB established a special committee on implementation and Archbishop John Roach of St. Paul-Minneapolis was appointed its chairman. The thirty-one episcopal committees of the NCCB and U.S. Catholic Conference were assigned various recommendations of the Call to Action Conference for evaluation.

Following Committee deliberations, the bishops, at their May 1978 meeting gave final approval to a program of action designed, as the bishops themselves declared, "to clarify and specify the implications for the Church in the United States of a social ministry at the service of the justice of God" (*see* BISHOPS' JUSTICE PROGRAM).

Bibliography: NCCB-USCC, *A Call to Action* (Washington, D.C. n.d.) (includes Working Papers, Resolutions, Bishops' Response, Reference Documents).

[F. BUTLER]

CAMPBELL, JAMES MARSHALL

Priest, educator; b. Warsaw, N.Y., Sept. 30, 1895; d. Washington, D.C., March 25, 1977. He was the son of William H. and Catherine (McGinnis) Campbell. He earned his B.A. at Hamilton College, Clinton, N.Y. in 1917. Awarded a Locke Fellowship in Greek, he began studies at Princeton which were interrupted by service in a machine-gun company, May 24, 1918–Feb. 24, 1919. In September 1919, still enjoying the Locke Fellowship

and later a Knights of Columbus Fellowship, Campbell enrolled at The Catholic University of America where he received an M.A. (1920) and a Ph.D. in Greek (1922). For the next four years he studied theology at the Sulpician Seminary (Theological College) and was ordained a priest by Bishop Thomas J. Shahan June 14, 1926. Campbell was named a Monsignor December 17, 1958.

For forty-six years higher education under Catholic auspices in the U.S. was influenced by Campbell. The immediate beneficiary was Catholic University. His erudite lectures, direction of doctoral dissertations for the *Catholic University Patristic Studies*—his own dissertation: *The Influence of the Second Sophistic on the Style of the Sermons of St. Basil the Great* being the second of more than one hundred—and scholarly publications, e.g., *Greek Fathers* (1930), *A Concordance of Prudentius* (1932 in collaboration with R. J. *Deferrari) focused attention on the patristic seminar under the direction of the reorganized Department of Greek and Latin. A monumental study, *Greek Attitudes toward Chastity from Homer to Plato*, the fruit of forty years of research, was impeded by illness and left unpublished because of the author's blindness.

Beginning in November 1934 Campbell's administrative talents raised the University's College of Arts and Sciences from the doldrums. As dean for the next consecutive thirty-two years he insisted on high admission standards and the successful completion of an orderly sequence of courses in the lower division. The Program of Concentration prescribing quality instruction in a chosen field, joined with the Reading List for the junior year and the Coordinating Seminar and Comprehensive Examination in the senior year, gave the College an enviable reputation. As director of the Pacific Coast Branch of Catholic University at Dominican College, San Rafael, Cal. (1932–1970) and through the University's Program of Affiliation, Campbell's impact on Catholic higher education assumed larger dimensions. As an inspector for some twenty-five years he examined most of the more than two hundred colleges, seminaries, and institutions of religious formation affiliated with Catholic University. Without prejudice to an institution's autonomy and objectives, he pointed out elements of strength and weakness and through constructive advice established genuine partnerships for excellence.

As a person Campbell was first and foremost a priest and a scholar with an exemplary devotion to duty and accuracy, a generous contributor to worthy causes, and always uneasy with honors and distinctions, however richly deserved.

Bibliography: R. J. DEFERRARI, *Memoirs of the Catholic University of America 1918–1960* (Boston 1962). M. N. MALTMAN, "Dominican College of San Rafael," *New Catholic Encyclopedia* 4:970.

[H. DRESSLER]

CAMPUS AND YOUNG ADULT MINISTRY (USCC)

The Office of Campus and Young Adult Ministries, under the Department of Education of the United States Catholic Conference (USCC), has responsibility for continuing support of these ministries in the field. Patrick H. O'Neill, OSA is director, with offices at 1312 Massachusetts Ave., N.W., Washington, D.C. 20005.

Field Services and Information have a twofold aim: to continue to serve the needs of campus ministers in building a national program for campus ministry; and to provide necessary direction and services for the developing work of young adult ministry. There are 2,500 full and part time campus ministers serving approximately 900 campus ministry centers. These men and women—religious, priests, laymen and laywomen—direct their ministry through the following services: spiritual and pastoral counseling, teaching, justice and peace programs, liturgical development, sacramental preparation, and programs related to the life of the Gospel and the university. To respond to their needs, the USCC offers a monthly newsletter, two annual campus-ministry programs of introduction for new campus ministers, an annual graduate program for experienced campus ministers, publications such as *National Guidelines for Diocesan Directors and Campus Ministers* and *National Status Report on Campus Ministry*. The National Advisory Board of Diocesan Directors of Campus Ministry is made up of thirty men and women representing the thirty ecclesiastical provinces in the U.S. and is seen as the focal point of contact with the USCC Office.

In January, 1975 the USCC Department of Education initiated the work of young adult ministry. A twenty person USCC Young Adult Board meets quarterly to give direction to this work, respond to the emerging needs of more than 150 programs and to design programs and action responses for the many diverse communities of young adults. The department publishes a quarterly newsletter *The National Young Adult Reporter* and also *Young Adult Ministry Resources*. An annual national convention, leadership-training programs, and diocesan educational consultations are among the concerns of the young adult ministry section.

[P. O'NEILL]

CAMPUS MINISTRY

Campus ministry is an essential and officially recognized component of the mission of the Church. It witnesses to the Gospel of Jesus Christ by teaching and preaching the Word of God and by gathering together the community for worship and service. Campus ministry is directed to students, faculty, administrators, staff, and those others served by universities, colleges, and other institutions of post-secondary education. It is conducted by members of the local community, which includes the ordained, religious, and lay persons—faculty, administrators, and students.

Catholic campus ministry has certain essential responsibilities. It promotes theological study and reflection on the religious nature of humankind. This ministry sustains the Christian community on campus with pastoral care and liturgical worship and helps the campus community to serve the needs of its members and the needs of the wider community. It integrates its apostolic mission with other ministries of the diocese and the local community and must raise current issues and crucial questions about faith, ethics, and modern life with the local bishop and the People of God. Since campus ministry is an expression of the Church's involvement with post-secondary education and its role in society, it must concern itself with the programs and policies of post-secondary educational institutions and the ways in which these either promote or hinder the humanization of society. Campus ministry is, then, a complex of pastoral, educational, and prophetic efforts, giving witness of the gospel message to all persons within the university and post-secondary educational milieu.

The nature of the academic enterprise and the apostolate of campus ministry requires that campus ministry be a central and integral element of the institution. Campus ministry should participate in developing the goals and objectives of the institution; it should feel responsible and be held accountable for leadership in attaining those religious goals that are properly its objective. Like the strictly academic activities of the university, campus ministry must be inspired by a profound respect for human freedom, which is an indispensable basis for human and Christian growth of personality. Only on this basis can the Catholic university form mature persons who will not tolerate a divorce between the faith that they profess and the lives that they lead, but rather will unite their human, domestic, professional, scientific, or technical endeavors into a vital synthesis with their religious values. Because of its commitment to the service of the entire university and to values, campus ministry must be especially concerned with examining from a Christian point of view, the values and norms predominant in modern society. Thus it will try to respond to the urgent appeals of people who, in many different and sometimes aberrant ways, are crying out for values and ideals that will give meaning to their lives. It will give special attention to problems that are of the most vital interest to the faith, to morality, and to the life of the Church in the contemporary world.

The pastoral goals of this work are: to raise consciousness within higher education concerning the issues of justice and peace in society and to develop programs responsive to these issues; to provide a channel both for campus ministry to witness to God's presence on the campus and for the campus community to express its experiences to the Church; to interpret and communicate the mission of campus ministry to the whole Church and the community at large; to foster the living tradition of the Roman Catholic Church on the campus through the full celebration of the liturgy and through a variety of forms of education; to develop a faith community supportive of living the Christian life in the university environment; to provide personnel, facilities and programs for human and spiritual growth for individuals in the total campus community; and, to develop ecumenical working relationships that respond to the needs of all people involved in higher education.

The distinctiveness of campus ministry is that it is Christ's ministry present in the university community. Professionals who minister to the campus share with other ministers the joys, excitements, and frustrations of the human situation, but in the distinctive setting of the university community. Higher education is perhaps the most formative agent in society today. It therefore continues to demand the fullness of the ministry, the shape and focus of which is always determined by the context in which the Church finds itself and the special needs of the institutions that are to be served.

See also CATHOLIC CAMPUS MINISTRY ASSOCIATION.

Bibliography: National Catholic Educational Association, *Campus Ministry Guidelines* (Washington, D.C. 1972; also Origins 1 [1972] 557–558, 560–561). Pontifical Council for the Laity and Congregation for Catholic Education, Joint Declaration, *Pastoral Ministry on University Campuses*, Origins 6 (1976) 197–204.

[P. O'NEILL; P. COLLINS]

CANDIDACY FOR ORDINATION (RITE OF ADMISSION)

Through the motu proprio *Ad pascendum* (Aug. 15, 1972), Paul VI instructed that a "rite of admission to candidacy for the diaconate and presbyterate" be introduced for men in the Latin Church. In some respects this rite replaces the former ceremony of tonsure (14:199), through which a lay person formally became a cleric. The "Rite of Admission to Candidacy," however, has no juridical significance; entrance into the clerical state is now deferred until a man has been ordained deacon. The admission to candidacy is thus neither a ministry nor an order, nor is it a prerequisite for seeking admission to the ministries of reader and acolyte. Rather, it is a liturgical action, celebrated either during Mass or during a celebration of the Word, in which those who intend to petition ordination to the diaconate and/or the presbyterate publicly announce their resolution in the presence of the Church, while the community prays for the strengthening and success of that resolution. A bishop, or the major superior of a clerical religious institute, presides at the celebration and officially accepts the candidates' declaration of intent. Structurally, the rite follows a pattern similar to that observed for the institution of *lay ministers, though the celebration of admission to candidacy is never to be joined to a liturgy of institution or ordination (16:323). Following the Gospel and homily, the bishop instructs the candidates about their responsibility to prepare, spiritually, academically and pastorally, for the ordained ministries of deacon and presbyter. Then the candidates are called by name and examined about their resolution to continue preparing for ordination. After the bishop has announced the Church's acceptance of the candidates' intention, the rite is concluded with prayer. Optional lectionary Readings are also provided for the celebration. Paul VI's *Ad pascendum* notes that men who aspire to the transitional diaconate may not be admitted to candidacy before they have completed twenty years of age and have begun their formal course of theological studies.

Bibliography: C. BRAGA, "'Ministeria Quaedam' Commentarius," EphemLiturg 87 (1973) 191–214; J. D. CRICHTON, *Christian Celebration: The Sacraments* (London 1973) 163–167. Pope Paul VI, "Ad Pascendum" ActApS 64 [1972] 534–540 (English tr., *Catholic Mind* 71 [January, 1973] 59–64). USCC, *Rites of Institution of Readers and Acolytes; Admission to Candidacy for the Diaconate and Presbyterate; Ordination of Deacons, Presbyters, and Bishops* (Washington, D.C. 1973).

[N. MITCHELL]

CANON LAW SOCIETY OF AMERICA

Since Vatican Council II the Canon Law Society of America (CLSA) has exercised a particularly effective influence in the American Church (16:47). As a professional society its function has been twofold: fundamental research in the pressing faith and order issues; and advocacy for renewal in church structure and in Canon Law itself. Numerous studies and proposals have assisted the leadership and people of the U.S. Church to fulfill their responsibilities in the period of post-conciliar development. Symposia, research teams and study papers broke ground in such areas as due process in canonical procedures, renewal of religious life, selection of bishops, status of women, the juridical procedures in matrimonial tribunals, and the revision of the Code of Canon Law.

Think Tank. "Now after one of the most momentous decades in the history of the Church, CLSA has felt the need to look into the future, to forecast what the Church of the next ten years will be like and to determine what the Society can do as a new stage in ecclesial life begins to emerge." To that end a Think Tank was convoked at Douglaston, New York, May 26–29, 1974. A cross section of the American Church—bishops, theologians, canonists, religious, laity, Blacks and Hispanics—were asked to read the signs of the times. In light of their hopes and fears for the future the participants arrived at a consensus on the needs of the Church and on some realistic goals responding to those needs. Three broad goals and action categories were identified. They concerned the Church as an ordered *communio* in mission to the world (*see* CHURCH AND COMMUNIO) and an expanded concept of *ministry. Dictating these goals were the issues of a newer understanding of the role of law in the Church and the fundamental nature of church governance. The results were visionary, but they were based on Pope Paul VI's directive that Canon Law must be founded in theology, not in civil law or any other current system of law. The pattern that form follow function was considered essential and therefore, since the life of the Church is primary, Canon Law must express the structuring of that life.

Vatican II presents a rich vision of the Church, particularly in its reliance on biblical imagery. Current Canon Law is based on older models and was considered inadequate for expressing the Council's teaching. The Think Tank recommended research to develop the ancient model of church organization as a *communio* to provide a tool for renewed ecclesial ordering. Today's understanding of ministry is a part of the heritage of the Church. Needless to say it was not always thus. Ministry flows from the Sacraments of Baptism and Confirmation and has wider possibilities than hitherto recognized. New and more models of ministry need to be developed in order to broaden the opportunities to meet the needs of people. The purpose of church organization and ministry is not exhausted in service to its members. Vatican II gives a vision of the Church as a "light of the world" (*Lumen gentium*), sharing the hopes and joys of all men, making present the Lord of History to the world today. The Church is in mission to the world. In its life and structure it must embody such values as justice, personal rights, the brotherly solidarity and peace to which all men are called in Christ.

The CLSA board of governors affirmed this reading and immediately sought for ways to carry it forward. A Permanent Seminar was established to do interdisciplinary research into the following areas: ecclesial models and their canonical implications; theology of mission and its canonical implications; ministry; and the ever pressing question of the indissolubility of Christian marriage. The Permanent Seminar was to look to the future and propose law based on theology; the Think Tank also noted the great need for education that would raise the consciousness of people in the Church concerning the role of law in the pastoral ministry. To do this CLSA established a continuing education committee. Thus far one project has been completed: a five-part video tape program has been produced to assist personnel in their ministry to the divorced and remarried with a filmstrip on the development of the theology and law on marriage. Since there existed a great deal of confusion in the minds of many as to the current status of the CIC as well as the many pronouncements from the Roman dicasteries (curial offices) a study was commissioned detailing the many agencies that produce the law of the Church, with an analysis of the authority or binding force to be attached to these pronouncements. A pamphlet on the findings was published in June 1975.

Another goal proposed at the Think Tank urged the CLSA to create a modus operandi whereby the total Church in America, in light of its mission to the world, could speak with secular society more effectively. Under the aegis of CLSA some forty agency personnel met at the University of Notre Dame in June 1975 to begin this task. The dialogue was profitable. Similar meetings with other groups and/or agencies are planned for the future.

Revision of the Code of Canon Law. Since 1968 CLSA has been deeply concerned about the revision of the CIC proposed by Pope John XXIII and since carried forward by Pope Paul VI. Professional critiques have been developed by task forces of specialists for all of the *schemata* of the proposed new law. These reflections have been submitted to the Pontifical Commission for the Revision of the Code of Canon Law through the National Conference of Catholic Bishops. Generally speaking CLSA has been concerned about the substance of what has been proposed in the revision, as well as about the methodology being used in proposing it. At five national conventions since 1968 CLSA has adopted resolutions expressing its continuing interest in the process. Ultimately the credibility of the Church and of its juridical order is at stake. The new Code will only achieve its purpose when, as Pope Paul VI said in 1977, the new law proves "to be an instrument most finely attuned to the life of the Church."

CLSA Committees. Much of the continuing development in juridical science and practice achieved by CLSA is the work of its committees. Current questions of interest being studied are: role of minorities (Blacks and Hispanics) in the Church; status of women in Canon Law; theology of marriage; collaboration with the Orthodox Churches; alternatives to tribunal procedures; juridical effects of charisms in religious life; and fiscal accountability in the Church. As these studies are completed their findings are published and made available through the CLSA offices.

Tribunal Assistance. The American Procedural Norms, proposed by CLSA, approved by the NCCB and granted to the U.S. Church by Pope Paul VI (*see* MARRIAGE TRIBUNALS, EXPERIMENTAL NORMS) as particular law until the new Code is promulgated, has done much to meet the pastoral and procedural concerns of tribunal personnel and enable them to minister more

effectively to the divorced and remarried. At the same time CLSA saw the need to keep its membership abreast of the developing jurisprudence and theology of marriage. To respond to this, *Annulments*, now in its third edition with some 30,000 copies in circulation around the world, was published; *Tribunal Jurisprudence*, a biennial reporter of U.S. jurisprudence, is now in its fourth volume.

Role of Law Award. The Think Tank alerted the Society to the need for an assessment of the role of law in church order. To highlight this concern and in a way to personify it CLSA established (1973) an annual Role of Law Award to be given to one of its members whose life and ministry embodied a perception of this insight. The following criteria are used in the nomination and selection process: embodiment of a pastoral attitude; commitment to research and study; participation in the revision of law; facilitation of dialogue and interchange of ideas within the Society and with other groups. Frederick R. McManus, Paul M. Boyle, CP, Raymond E. Goedert, Lawrence Wrenn, and Robert T. Kennedy have thus far been honored by their colleagues for their distinguished service.

The Canon Law Society of America was founded in 1939 at Washington, D.C. during the fiftieth anniversary celebration of the founding of The Catholic University of America. One year later the *Jurist*, a journal of canonical science, was published by the faculty of Canon Law, at The Catholic University. From 1940 through 1968 the minutes of CLSA national meetings as well as other historical data were reviewed in this journal. Since 1968 CLSA has undertaken to publish an annual volume of the proceedings of its national convention, containing all major addresses, seminars, committee reports, and minutes. CLSA also publishes a semiannual *Newsletter* for its membership. At present there are more than 1,400 members around the world—clergy, religious, laymen, and laywomen. The logo of CLSA depicts the Mosaic tablets of the Law surrounded by the flames of the Spirit with the text, ". . . In Christ Jesus, the life giving law of the Spirit, has set you free from the law of sin and death" (Rom 8.2). This indeed sets forth an ideal for the American canonist.

Bibliography: CLSA publications: W. BASSETT, ed., *The Choosing of Bishops* (Hartford 1971). J. BIECHLER, ed., *Recent Roman Replies* (Hartford 1966). P. BOYLE, ed., *Discussions of the Motu Proprio "Ecclesiae Sanctae"* (Hartford 1966); *Renewal Through General Chapters* (Hartford 1967); *Selected Passages from Religious Constitutions Dealing with the Evangelical Counsels and Community Life* (Hartford 1967). CLSA, ed., *American Procedural Norms* (Hartford 1969); *Audio Visual Learning on Marriage, Divorce, Tribunal Practice* (Hartford 1976); *Bond of Marriage* (Hartford 1968); *CLSA Critique on the Proposed Schemate* (Hartford 1975); *Canon Law on Priestly Life and Ministry* (Hartford 1973); *Future Discipline of Priestly Celibacy* (Hartford 1971); *On Due Process* (Hartford 1970); *Procedures for the Selection of Bishops in the United States* (Hartford 1973); *Provisional Plan for Choosing Bishops* (Hartford 1971); *Role of Law in the Church* (Hartford 1966); *Simplification of Procedures in Privilege of Faith and Lack of Form Cases* (Hartford 1967); *Think Tank, an Agenda for the Future* (Hartford 1974); *Toward Constitutional Development within the Church* (Hartford 1967); *Trullo Cases* (Hartford 1975). J. A. CORIDEN, ed., *Who Decides for the Church?* (Hartford 1971). E. DILLON, ed., *Matrimonial Jurisprudence, United States* (Toledo 1974). J. DOLCIAMORE, ed., *Matrimonial Jurisprudence, United States* (Toledo 1973). R. KENNEDY, ed., *Report of the Committee on Due Process* (Hartford 1969). F. MORRISEY, ed., *Canonical Significance of Papal and Curial Pronouncements* (Hartford 1974). K. O'ROURKE, ed., *Renewal through Community and Experimentation* (Hartford 1968). J. PROVOST, ed., *Church as "Communio,"* Jurist 36, 1/2 (1978). W. SCHUMACHER, ed., *Matrimonial Jurisprudence, United States* (Toledo

1975). T. STOCKER, ed., *Matrimonial Jurisprudence, United States* (Toledo 1976). E. SURGES, ed., *Recent Roman Replies* (Hartford 1967). L. WRENN, ed., *Annulments* (1st ed., Hartford 1967); *Annulments* (2d ed., Hartford 1970); *Common Sources of Nullity* (Hartford 1968).

Also J. CORIDEN, ed., *We the People of God* (Huntington, Ind. 1967); *Sexism and Church Law* (New York 1977, from CLSA 1976 Symposium on Women in the Church Law). A. MAIDA, ed., *Tribunal Reporter* (Huntington, Ind. 1970, 1973). L. WRENN, ed., *Divorce and Remarriage in the Catholic Church* (New York 1973).

[D. E. HEINTSCHEL]

CANONICAL STUDIES

The foundation for canonical studies is set forth in Vatican Council II's Decree on Priestly Formation: "in the explanation of canon law...the mystery of the Church should be kept in mind, as it was set forth in the Dogmatic Constitution on the Church..." (*Optatam totius* 16). In other words, a good perception of the mystery of the Church leads to the right understanding and sound application of law. In 1975 the Congregation for Catholic Education issued a circular letter addressed to Ordinaries of dioceses and religious communities, as well as to rectors of seminaries and religious scholasticates; it was entitled, "On the Teaching of Canon Law to Those Who Are Preparing for Priestly Ministry" (*De doctrina iuris canonici candidatis ad sacerdotium tradenda*, in *Communic* 7 [1975] 12–17).

The first part is foundational: it states the role and purpose of Canon Law in the Church. It recalls the complex nature of the Church, which is "a community of grace and a hierarchical society" that lives through the gifts of the Spirit, but operates through the structures of a human community; its very humanity requires legal norms and structures. The second part points to pastoral needs: persons expert in law are needed at every level of the ecclesial community, in the dioceses, in religious institutes, in counseling the faithful. The third part gives practical norms for the organization of studies. The following is a short summary of the norms.

In all seminaries or similar institutes, a professor of Canon Law should be appointed. In his teaching he should begin with an explanation of the theological foundations of law, but he should lead the students to learn the applications of the law in pastoral situations. He should give special attention to ecumenical issues, especially in the field of liturgy and Sacraments. He should also seek out opportunities for his students to observe in chanceries, tribunals and similar institutions. The circular letter of the Congregation sets an ideal. At present, many seminaries and scholasticates still fall short of this ideal, although improved standards are already discernible.

Bibliography: Congregation for Catholic Education, "On the Teaching of Canon Law to Those Intending to Be Priests," in Bishops' Committee on Priestly Formation, *The Program of Priestly Formation* (2d ed., Washington, D.C. 1976) Appendix IV, 156–161.

[L. ÖRSY]

CAPITAL PUNISHMENT

The U.S. Supreme Court's 1972 decision (*Furman v. Georgia*) ruled against the death penalty (16:48) because of inequities in imposing sentence. Thirty-five states and the Federal Government set about passing laws to get around the accusation of a capricious selection process and thus get around the Eighth Amendment's ban on cruel and unusual punishment. The new statutes typically required sentence of death for specified offenses. The movement in favor of the machinery of death became clear in the U.S. Supreme Court's twin decision of July 2, 1976, which banned mandatory death sentences for every murder conviction, but otherwise returned the matter on a case-by-case basis to state jurisdictions to operate within statutory sentencing guidelines. Significantly the court refused to find the death penalty unequivocally and in itself in violation of the Eighth Amendment. In practice states can impose and execute death penalties; in fact the death sentence has been carried out, e.g. in Utah, 1977. Public opinion moved in favor of death in various countries for somewhat kindred reasons: in Latin America, in France, Italy, and West Germany in response to terrorism; in England as a retaliation for the deaths resulting from the unrest in Northern Ireland and IRA bombings; and in the U.S. in the hope that it would be a deterrent against violent crime.

The Catholic Church was hampered in its attempts to counter this trend because of its long-standing position that the state has the right to inflict the death penalty for certain grave crimes; in defense of society; and to protect the lives of citizens (3:79). For pastoral reasons, however, the Canadian bishops (March 1976) passed a resolution favoring the abolition of the death penalty, at the same time calling for prison reform and the reform of the entire justice system. Its action was taken in respect for life, while it termed the death penalty a violent measure which begets violence. The NCCB, in a decision that was far from unanimous, made a simple declaration in November 1974 in opposition to the death penalty. Two years later, their position was far more clear and effective. They took as guidelines: (1) the sovereignty of God over life; (2) the duty to aid the criminal and not merely punish; (3) the awareness of human fallibility; (4) the need of reconciliation; and (5) the growing awareness of the complexity of criminal actions and motivations. Their pastoral conclusion was that the death penalty should be abolished. To oppose death in this case was consistent with the dynamic which led the Church to oppose abortion and euthanasia and the bishops urged Catholics to range themselves at the side of the Quakers, who had a long tradition of struggle in behalf of life.

Catholic writers have added that since the new mandatory laws, the number of minority persons (mostly Black) under sentence of death now comprises 60 per cent of the total (360 out of 600, as of Aug. 1976). Previously it had been 54 per cent. The deterrent rationale has come under fire from all sides as being dubious and unproven, certainly not necessary, and probably a distortion of retribution. The Irish Commission for Justice and Peace (November 1976) rejected the concept of *lex talionis* and the argument of self-protection, along with capital punishment, while at the same time urging individuals to renounce violence for whatever goals (in reference to the 1600 dead in Ulster). In the *L'Osservatore Romano* (Feb. 20, 1977), G. Concetti stated forthrightly that the right to life is "primordial and inviolable" and that the state lacks the right to take it away. In the modern understanding the state is viewed not as having absolute rights, like the divine right of kings, but more accurately as a limited mechanism with rights and powers limited even as are the rights of the citizens it represents.

Bibliography: DocCath 73 (1976) 277, 1081; 74 (1977) 139–142, 147, 187–188. B. FLANAGAN, "The Death Penalty is Immoral," *U.S. Catholic* 41 (1976) 12. NCCB Statement on Capital Punishment (USCC Publ. Office, Washington, D.C. 1977). Origins 6 (1976) 389–395. A. PAULUS, "Case against Capital Punishment," *Sisters* 47 (1976) 494–497. R. PUGSLEY, "Bringing back Death," *Commonweal* 103 (1976) 518–519.

[E. J. DILLON]

CARITAS INTERNATIONALIS

Caritas (Catholic Charities) is, within the framework of the threefold pastoral task of the Church (liturgy, evangelization, *diakonia*/service), an operational instrument of the *diakonia* of the Christian community, which, carrying out works of Christian brotherhood and sensitizing the People of God to active charity, witnesses Christ's love to all mankind. Caritas Internationalis (CI) is an international confederation of Catholic organizations for charitable and social action. The member organizations are mandated or recognized by their respective episcopal conferences principally for: social services; emergency aid; community development; animation of the Christian community towards charity and justice.

Created in its present form in 1950, upon invitation of Pius XII, CI sets forth the work of a first international organism, "Caritas Catholica," founded in 1924. CI developed rapidly, especially after Vatican Council II, counting at present (1978) 104 member-organizations in 101 countries. Affiliated members in the U.S. are the National Conference of Catholic Charities and Catholic Relief Services.

The principal aim of CI is to assist its members to promote Christian charity and social justice in the world. This means in particular: stimulating and aiding national Caritas to participate in assistance, human promotion, and integral development of the most underprivileged; studying problems and causes of poverty in the world and proposing solutions conforming with justice and the dignity of human person; fostering the foundation of new national charitable organizations; participating in the endeavors of peoples to better their individual and collective standards of living; promoting and coordinating the relief activities of its members in cases of disaster; representing its members at interdenominational and international levels; attaining cooperation with the other international aid and development organizations.

CI's supreme decisional body is the General Assembly of all member organizations, meeting every four years, and electing the president, the 5 vice-presidents (representing Africa/Middle East, Asia/Oceania, Latin America, North America, Europe), the treasurer and the 12 members of the Executive Committee. The task of the Executive Committee is to carry out the program established by the General Assembly. Standing Commissions are in charge of the sectors: Social Studies and Formation; Development and Social Services; Mutual Aid Fund; Statutes; Finances; Emergency Aid. The Bureau, composed of the president, vice-presidents, and treasurer, supervises the activities of the General Secretariat, located in Rome, as the practical executive organ of Caritas Internationalis.

Besides the general role of information, study, and documentation, CI is entrusted by its members with the coordination of their international activities in the operational field. CI has become the most relevant Catholic organization in the sector of Emergency Relief. Its involvement in the interdenominational "Joint Church Aid"-operation, airlifting during the Nigeria/Biafra civil war (1967–70) tens of thousands of tons of relief goods and saving millions of lives, its relief operations on occasion of the Bangladesh floods (1970–73), the Vietnam war (since 1954), the drought in the Sahel zone and Ethiopia (1973–75), the earthquake in Guatemala (1976) is well known. Social assistance and development aid are the most appropriate activities of the CI member-organizations. To integrate them into the overall pastoral care of the Church, by theological and social reflexion, animation, conscientization and formation, is the task of CI.

CI is in standing working relationship with the most important intergovernmental bodies, guaranteed by consultative status with ECOSOC, UNICEF, UNESCO, FAO, ILO (special list), Council of Europe; it maintains delegations in New York, Paris, Geneva, Rome, and Strasbourg. Publications include: *Intercaritas* (bi-monthly in 4 languages); *Info-sheets* (monthly); *Reports of General Assemblies*; a *Directory*. The address of the General Secretariat is Palazzo S. Calisto, Vatican City.

[G. HÜSSLER]

CATAFALQUE

The catafalque as a structure used to simulate the presence of a corpse (3:201) while not forbidden, is already practically obsolete in many places. The desire for authenticity in liturgical celebration and the authoritative suggestion that absolution be given only in the actual presence of the corpse may further hasten its disappearance.

Bibliography: *Notitiae* 7–8 (1965) 254.

[A. CORNIDES]

CATECHESIS

As the result of directions specified in Vatican Council II (1962–65) and the worldwide Synod of Bishops in Rome (1977), the term and significance of catechesis (χατήχησις) returned to the forefront in the Church's life and ministry. In its verb form (χατηχέω) catechesis appears six times in the New Testament (Lk 1.14; Acts 18.25; 21.21; Rom 2.18; 1 Cor 14.19; Gal 6.6) where its interpretation varies from "transmission" to instruction, to narration—always oral. Without employing the word itself the Letter to Hebrews briefly delineates the elements of the Christological catechesis: repentance, conversion, faith, baptism, resurrection, eternal life (Heb. 6:1–3). In fact, the canonical Gospels can be read as formal catecheses following on the proclamation of the Christian message.

History. Patristic references, e.g., Tertullian, Egeria, Jerome, etc., used the term to describe oral preparation of those seeking Baptism. Two notable facts characterize catechesis in the early Church: (1) it was integral to the Christian community's life and worship as part and parcel of the continuous ecclesial process of being Church; and (2) catechesis per se was designed for adults who were in the catechumenate, however seminal may have been their faith at that stage. As long as there was a formal catechumenate, from the 2nd to the 6th centuries there were two distinct phases to catechesis, namely, preparation for Baptism and Eucharist, and a postbaptismal disclosure of the deeper meaning of the Christian mysteries. This later phase is known as mystagogical catechesis.

With the decline of the catechumenate, catechesis almost disappeared from the Christian vocabulary. In the late medieval and Reformation periods it reappeared under a different concept and a new literary genre, "catechism." Essentially catechisms were confessional works setting forth creed, code, and cult in a form that could easily be learned and memorized. They were a far cry from the comprehensive, oral, community, adult-centered, and liturgy-scripture based context which the original term encompassed.

With the advent of printing the catechism gradually became identified as the major and almost solitary means of instructing inquirers and youthful believers in the truths of the Christian faith. The manual assumed an exaggerated role of primacy and held it for nearly four centuries. In the late 19th and early 20th centuries, however, church leaders began exploring broader possibilities of catechizing. Along with the revival of interest and scholarship in liturgy, Scripture, and the very nature of the Church as Church, catechesis became the focus of a movement intent on revitalizing the Church's inner growth and self-understanding.

The Contemporary Church. In the early 1960s the Council Fathers of Vatican II reassessed catechesis. They urged new approaches in response to the needs of the times and boldly called for directories to deal with fundamental principles of catechizing (*Christus Dominus* 44; *Apostolicam actuositatem* 10; *Ad gentes* 14). Six years later (1971) the Sacred Congregation for the Clergy published the General Catechetical Directory (GCD; *Directorium Catechisticum Generale*) in compliance with the Council's injunction. Within the decade numerous national directories appeared. The hierarchy of the United States published its catechetical directory, *Sharing the Light of Faith*, in 1979. The 1977 Synod of Bishops confirmed steps already initiated. Not only did it seem to endorse the modern catechetical movement, but it sought to provide a "new impulse to catechesis" for the contemporary Church.

"Trinitarian and Christocentric in scope and spirit, consciously emphasizing the mystery of God and the plan of salvation which leads to the Father, through the Son, in the Holy Spirit (Eph 1.3–4)" (*Sharing the Light of Faith* 47), contemporary catechesis seeks to present the Christian message in its entirety. Christ, true God and true man, his saving work carried out in his Incarnation, life, death, and resurrection, is the center of the message. The revised rites of the Sacraments, especially the Rite of Christian Initiation of Adults (1974), have given new models and special emphases to catechesis, hearkening back to early church practice and reaccentuating the close relationship of catechesis with the Church's liturgy.

Catechesis addresses, not only the intellect, but the whole person. It is education in the faith, not merely instruction *about* the faith. Deepening and maturing the faith life of individuals and the community is the aim and objective of catechesis. Maturity of faith is iden-

tified by the transformation of heart and mind, renewal and conversion (GCD 18). An ideal Christian faith is continually striving for a deeper maturity. Stated another way, being Christian implies becoming ever more maturely Christian (Rom 1.17; 6.3–4; 8.9; 9.26). As it fosters inquiry, sharing, and dialogue among believers intent on developing greater comprehension and appreciation of the mysteries of God in Christ, catechesis plays a significant part in that process of becoming. Thus, catechesis appropriately belongs to all the faithful and should continue throughout one's lifetime (*see* CONVERSION).

Catechesis is not meant for just one segment of the Church's population. Nor can a single catechesial program be expected to meet the needs and wishes of all people. Therefore adaptation is called for (GCD 5, 13). "The Christian faith must become incarnate in all cultures" (Synod '77). Through adaptation, that is, adapting to the sensitivities of age differences, diversities of cultural milieux, varieties of experiences, environments, etc., while always faithfully adhering to the timelessness of Christian truth, catechesis confronts new situations with a fresh approach.

The current documents mentioned point to the responsibility of the Christian community, parish, diocese, etc., in catechizing. Not only is the body of the faithful the principal setting and environment for catechesis, it is considered the chief catechist, instructing, forming, giving credible witness, and exemplifying the ideals of Christian commitment. Therein, all participants experience both teaching and learning moments in the ongoing sharing of faith. The community is both the medium and the message, "a sign of the wisdom and love of God that was revealed to us in Christ" (GCD 107; cf. 101, 130). The mystery of the Church, local and universal, forms part of the content and experience of catechesis.

Bibliography: Readings: Egeria, 46:3–4 in CSEL 39, p. 37. Jerome, "Epistola 50," 237. PL 22.513; "Liber Contra Joannem" 419. PL 23.364. Tertullian "Adversus Marcionem," IV, 29. PL 2.434. Studies: D. S. AMALORPAVADASS, "Nature, Purpose and Process of Catechesis," *International Catechetical Congress* (USCC Publ. Office, Washington D.C. 1971). J. AUDINET, "Catéchèse, Action d'église et culture," *Catéchèse* 62 (Jan. 1976) 53–83. M. C. BRYCE, "The Interrelationship of Liturgy and Catechesis," AmBenRev 28 (1977) 1–29. Congregation for the Clergy, *General Catechetical Directory* (USCC Publ. Office, Washington, D.C. 1971). A. EXELER, *Wesen und Aufgabe der Katechese* (Freiburg-im-Breisgau 1966). A. GANOCAY, *Becoming Christian* (New York 1976). J. A. GRASSI, *The Teacher in the Primitive Church and the Teacher Today* (Santa Clara, Cal. 1973). J. A. JUNGMANN, *Handing on the Faith*, tr. A. N. FUERST (New York 1959; 5th ed. 1968). B. L. MARTHALER, "To Teach the Faith or to Teach Theology: Dilemma for Religious Education." CathTheolSoc 31 (1976) 217–233. R. M. RUMMERY, *Catechesis and Religious Education in a Pluralist Society* (Sydney, Australia 1975). *Sharing the Light of Faith*, National Catechetical Directory, USA (USCC Publ. Office, Washington, D.C. 1979).

[M. C. BRYCE]

CATECHESIS, ADOLESCENT

Adolescent catechesis is that part of ministry to youth which is directly concerned with the communication of the message of the Gospel. Total youth ministry has seven components: the Ministry of the Word; of Worship; of Creating Community; of Guidance; of Justice and Service; of Enablement; and of Advocacy. Catechesis is placed under the Ministry of the Word.

The Ministry of the Word is the sharing of the good news of salvation as shown to us in Jesus Christ. This sharing involves elements of both evangelization and catechesis. Pope Paul VI pointed out that the Church evangelizes "when it seeks, through the power of God's Word, to convert both the personal and collective consciences of people, the activities in which they engage, and the lives and concrete milieux which are theirs" (Paul VI EvangNunt 18). For young people this evangelization most often begins with the witness of adults who are trained to work with youth and who are part of a faith-filled community which the youth are invited to enter.

The characteristics of the period of transition from childhood to adulthood make the task of the adolescent catechist a special challenge. On the one hand, young persons frequently feel confused about the meaning of life and lack the self-esteem needed for meaningful relationships with either God or other persons. This confusion is frequently manifested exteriorly by the behavior associated with adolescence: boredom, frustration, moodiness, rebellion, and apathy about religion. On the other hand, it is at this time of life that for the first time the capacity to experience the spiritual dimension of reality becomes operative. Concepts like goodness, unity, truth, and beauty begin to take on a whole new dimension: so does the concept of love and the reality of evil. While this capacity typically develops during the adolescent years, youth do not automatically use it widely. To the degree that they begin to experience spiritual insight into reality, the need to control their environment which has characterized their early years is replaced by the need to find meaning for the reality they experience, including the meaning of their own personal existence. They will value whatever gives meaning to existence and begin to reject whatever they consider superficial.

Since adolescent catechesis will fall within these two polarities, great attention must be given to the young person's search for understanding. The first educational need during this period of life is for self-discovery. Adolescents are ready now to find out for themselves, to arrive at their own conclusions. They must be given the opportunity to arrive at new understandings without pressure or without being forced to accept what they hear, read, or see. Adolescents may be expected to question, to examine the catechesis they have been given as children and this questioning frequently means that their grasp of what they have been taught is not sufficient for their developing intellectual capacities; they are in search of a grasp of truths that they may have previously accepted without understanding. During this period of growth, it is important that opportunities to question, to examine the basis for their faith-community's interpretation of the mystery of life and belief in God be provided in an unthreatening atmosphere. Presenting the truths of faith in a dogmatic fashion is counter-productive in the catechesis of adolescents; that approach not only violates good educational practice, but serves also to alienate young people from religion.

Traditionally, catechesis has been associated with a classroom model, whether in Catholic schools or parish religion classes. Today, religious educators realize that catechesis can be effectively carried out informally in small groups with adults who are genuinely concerned in joining the young people in reflecting on their lives and experiences in the light of Christian faith. Whatever the approach, the first concern of the catechist should be based on the needs of the persons involved. Putting people before programs is good pedagogy and it is especially important in the catechesis of adolescents. The typical adolescent needs to be challenged intellectually and is capable of some systematic methods of study. The inner coherence of the truths of faith, the study of Scripture, the Church, the Sacraments, and morality should be a part of the overall program. Retreats, service projects, and field trips that provide youth with experiences and opportunities to pray and reflect on the meaning of faith in daily life should all be part of a total program of youth catechesis.

[R. MCDONELL]

CATECHESIS, ADULT

Adult catechesis is a particular form of catechesis; its purpose is the same as that described by Vatican Council II for all catechesis, "to develop a living, explicit, active faith, enlightened by doctrine" (*Christus Dominus* 14), but it addresses the age group beyond adolescent years and uses strategies appropriate to their interests, needs, and manner of learning. "It deals," states the *General Catechetical Directory* (GCD), "with persons who are capable of an adherence that is fully responsible [and therefore] must be considered the chief form of catechesis. All the other forms . . . are in some way oriented to it" (GCD 20). Thus adult catechesis accepts as a basic premise that the faith of the Christian community has its normative expression in the beliefs and values of its mature members. The catechesis of children and youth, though necessary, is directed to it.

Adult catechesis is not new. Present-day emphasis represents a return in principle to the practice of the early Church which regarded catechesis as continuous even after the rites of initiation. It is a corrective to the almost exclusive concern for the catechesis of children which gradually developed as infant Baptism supplanted the ancient catechumenate. Adult catechesis is new, however, in the sense that it recognizes the special needs of Christians in the modern world and the emergence of laity into leadership positions (cf. *Gaudium et spes* 43; *Apostolicam actuositatem passim*). This article describes some of the factors which have brought adult catechesis into greater prominence, and outlines its nature and concerns.

Influencing Factors. The renewed emphasis on adult catechesis in the years after Vatican II is the result of the convergence of several independent forces and movements that had been gathering momentum for some years.

Beginnings. In the 1950s the French school of catechetics inspired by Pierre-André Liégé, OP and Joseph Colomb, SS recognized that, like all learning, catechesis has to be lifelong if it is to be effective. They stressed the need for "maturity of faith," a theme that was taken over by the 1971 GCD (cf. 20–30). In the mid-1960s a great deal of publicity surrounded the appearance of *De Nieuwe Katechismus*, commonly referred to as the "Dutch Catechism." In commissioning the work, the hierarchy of the Netherlands had made a deliberate decision to shift the focus of catechesis to adults. The spontaneous acceptance which greeted the Dutch Catechism in translation throughout the Catholic world convinced others of the need for additional works of this kind. Meanwhile in the U.S. many, like Gabriel Moran, FSC, were saying in print and public lectures that Christianity is an adult religion. In another sphere a number of social scientists (e.g., Havighurst, Peck, 1955; Erickson, 1950, 1976) had begun to investigate and advocate theories of developmental stages for adults. They identified particular needs at various ages from young adulthood through mid-life and old age. Educators like Paul Bergevin of the Univ. of Indiana described characteristics of the adult learner and began to delineate principles of adult education. Malcolm Knowles popularized the neologism, "androgogy," to distinguish it from "pedagogy," which etymologically refers to the education of children.

The convergence of these ideas ultimately yielded the text in the GCD quoted at the outset. The bishops of the U.S. cited that text in addressing the matter. In *To Teach as Jesus Did* (1972), a pastoral statement on Catholic education, they insisted that adult catechesis "is situated not at the periphery of the church's educational mission but at its center" (73). In the *national catechetical directory, *Sharing the Light of Faith* (1978), the bishops reiterated that adult catechesis is "the primary concern of the entire catechetical enterprise" (40).

Church Documents. That theme has been reinforced by several statements emanating from Rome in recent years. The most significant document to call attention to adult catechesis was the *Rite of Christian Initiation of Adults*, a decree promulgated by the Congregation for Divine Worship (1974). Vatican II had called for the restoration of the *catechumenate for adults (*Sacrosanctum Concilium* 64). Following that mandate the Congregation for Divine Worship revised for modern use the practice of the early Church, making the catechetical enterprise more clearly a responsibility of the Christian community as a whole. Comprising several distinct steps, the rite clearly respects the developmental nature of human growth and change. While the revised rite focuses on adults preparing for Baptism, Confirmation, and Eucharist, it restores the practice of *post-baptismal catechesis, referred to as "mystagogical catechesis." Thus it extends adult catechesis beyond sacramental preparation, calling for continual reflection on the mystery of Christian commitment.

The 1977 *Synod of Bishops recommended that the adult catechumenate be made normative for all catechesis. First they stated in their *Message to the People of God*, "The model for all catechesis is the baptismal catechumenate, that special formation which prepares an adult convert for the profession of his baptismal faith during the paschal vigil" (8). And in another proposal at the end of the Synod they added, "The question of introducing a catechumenate, in the precise sense, for the baptized should be carefully studied and experimented with" (*Thirty Four Propositions* 30). Specialists in androgogy agree that effective adult learning has certain characteristics: it (1) draws on the life experiences of the learner; (2) is problem oriented, i.e., it addresses specific needs, interests, and anxieties; (3) involves the learner in the planning and directing of the program; (4) aims at immediate implementation; and (5) is group centered.

The GCD shows an awareness of the other characteristics of adult learning as well. It calls for specialized catechesis at various stages of development from young adulthood   to old age (GCD 92–95). It recognizes particular circumstances and conditions in an adult's life which require special attention, e.g. preparation for marriage (ibid. 96). Given the complex demands of present-day society, the GCD says catechesis should address such issues as: (1) sociological and cultural changes; (2) moral and religious questions underlying social reform; (3) the place of social action within the Christian community; and (4) the need to ground faith in something more than emotional experiences (ibid. 97). Basically it is imperative that adult catechesis take people where and as they are as its point of departure.

Related to the growth of faith is the dynamics of conversion, which, according to the GCD, "is always present in the dynamism of Faith" (ibid. 18). Conversion is a developing reality that for Christians continues throughout a lifetime as they discover and rediscover the impact of their relationship with the Lord. It is the latter—second, third, and subsequent conversion experiences—to which catechesis has special reference. Catechesis does not stop with Baptism or with Confirmation, with graduation from high school or college, or with marriage. One author has noted that "catechesis ceases only in the beatific vision" (Kavanaugh 389). It is, in other words, integral to continuous formation in Christ, described by the French as *formation permanente*.

Community Based. Group centeredness is of particular importance in adult catechesis because of its ecclesial nature. The Christian community is alternately the learning body and teaching group. Ultimately it is the local community, through its spirit and practice, that evangelizes, catechizes, and establishes the setting and climate allowing for and nurturing the growth of all its members into full Christian maturity. Effective adult catechesis therefore presumes a community conscious of itself as Church and its own responsibility to grow and develop.

Present and past adult programs, though not always catechetical as such, prove the validity and the merit of group participation in adult learning and formation. The successes of discussion clubs of the 1940s and 1950s of the *Christian Family Movement exemplify that fact. But these had forerunners. The apostolate of Warren Mosher (1860–1906) is one example. Mosher's Catholic Reading Circles of the late 19th and early 20th century provided opportunities for people to advance their own understanding of the faith, to meet and exchange with others the insights gleaned from their readings.

The effectiveness of present programs and movements further testifies to the value of group involvement. The *Cursillo and *charismatic renewal, *Marriage Encounter, Genesis II, and the *basic Christian communities are some of these. Even the revised catechumenate's effectiveness is related to the collective participation of those aspiring to become fully Christian.

In conclusion it may be asserted that Christians possess knowledge of many things; what they often lack is coherence, unity, and comprehension of the interrelatedness of these things. Thus one of the urgent tasks for adult catechesis is to simplify, unify, and integrate Christians' knowledge, understandings, experiences, assisting them to distinguish the essential from the accidental and to contribute to a growing and formative faith life.

Bibliography: P. BERGEVIN, *A Philosophy of Adult Education* (New York 1967). M. C. BRYCE, "Hopes for the Coming Synod," *America* 137 (1977) 215–217. "Catéchèse d'Adultes" (Symposium) *Catéchèse* 42 (1971), 39–86; Congregation for the Clergy, *General Catechetical Directory* (USCC Publ Office, Washington, D.C. 1971). K. COUGHLIN, "Motivating Adults," LivLight 13 (1976) 269–298. A. KAVANAGH, "Christian Initiation for Those Baptized as Infants," LivLight 13 (1976) 387–396. M. KNOWLES, *The Adult Learner: A Neglected Species* (Houston, Texas 1973). P. LIÉGÉ, *Consider Christian Maturity* (Chicago 1965). LivLight 15 (Spring, 1978)—"Special Feature: Synod '77," 7–127. B. L. MARTHALER, "Catechetical Dimensions of Marriage Encounter," Origins 7 (1977) 130–135, G. MORAN, *Religious Body* (New York 1974). *A New Catechism* (Dutch), tr. K. SMYTH (New York 1967). D. PIVETEAU, "L'Église, les adultes et la formation permanente," *Catéchèse* 59 (1975) 161–178. NCCB, *To Teach as Jesus Did* (USCC Publ. Office, Washington, D.C. 1973); *Sharing the Light of Faith* (National Catechetical Directory) (USCC Publ. Office, Washington, D.C. 1979). M. SHEEDY, "The Reading Circle Movement," *The Champlain Educator* 23 (1904) 600.

[M. C. BRYCE]

CATECHESIS FOR CONFIRMATION AND EUCHARIST

The Introduction to the *Rite of Christian Initiation for Adults* ch. 4 provides pastoral suggestions for preparing uncatechized adults for Confirmation and Eucharist. Their situation, which is presently more common than that of unbaptized adults in many parishes in the United States, is compared to that of catechumens. Although baptized, such adults never have heard the Gospel of the saving mystery of Christ. Their situation differs from that of catechumens, however, in that their conversion is based upon the Baptism they have already received, the power of which must be unfolded (295). Their formation is modeled on that of the catechumens. It should be conformed to the liturgical year, with its final part taking place during Lent. At the Easter Vigil they profess their baptismal faith, receive Confirmation, and participate in the Eucharist. Finally, they participate with the newly baptized in the *post-baptismal catechesis.

See also CATECHUMENATE FOR ADULTS.

Bibliography: *Rite of Christian Initiation of Adults* (Washington 1974).

[L. L. MITCHELL]

CATECHETICAL CENTERS

Since the 1967 survey of catechetical centers (3:218) catechesis and catechetics have become of ever more intense interest. The Lumen Vitae center in Belgium where, under the late Georges Delcuve, SJ, many Americans were trained, was discontinued in the 1970s. The pastoral impact of the Institut Supérieure Catéchétique in Paris and Strasbourg's Centre de Pédagogie Chrétienne, in spite of their leadership in the field, has been disappointing and the problem of dechristianization remains acute. The National Catechetical Centre for England and Wales, established in 1959, is now defunct. The *East Asian Pastoral Institute in Manila, under Alphonso Nebreda, SJ and Adolfo Nicolas, SJ, successors of the founder, Johannes Hofinger, SJ, continues its work in missionary catechetics. Missionaries from every part of the Far East have been trained at the Jesuits' prestigious Ateneo de Manila, which welcomed the East Asian Pastoral Institute to its campus in the 1970's.

By the time of the *Synod of Bishops, 1977, at Rome,

with its theme "Catechetics in Our Time" the catechetical movement had taken deep root in the life of the American Church. The American delegation at the Synod made a notable contribution, well informed as it was from the broad consultation preparatory to the publication of the *National Catechetical Directory. Catechetical centers across the country had energized progress towards these achievements since the initiation of the catechetical movement in the 1950s.

By the late 1970s in the U.S. catechetical centers had advanced far beyond the pioneer office of earlier years of the Confraternity of Christian Doctrine (CCD) in Washington D.C. The United States Catholic Conference (USCC) through its Department of Education and its quarterly, the *Living Light*, and the National Forum of Religious Educators have served to sharpen the Church's focus on the central issues of religious education in the Roman Catholic tradition. Indispensable to this achievement has been the training over the years of catechetical leaders and researchers at universities like The Catholic University, Washington D.C., and Fordham University, New York. Fordham in the late 1950s and early 1960s developed the first graduate programs of prominence in the new catechetics and has since been joined by year-round and summer programs at other universities. Unlike catechetical centers in Europe, the outstanding centers in the U.S. have flowered within university settings, with still further expansion in prospect as diocesan seminaries launch religious education programs on the graduate level.

[V. M. NOVAK]

CATECHETICS

Catechetics is studied reflection on the art and ministry of catechizing (General Catechetical Directory 113). The 1977 Synod of Bishops called it "catechetical science" (OssRomEng, Nov. 17, 1977, 6). As a discipline, catechetics studies the theory, objectives, practice, principles, history, and methods of catechesis in a scientific way. It draws on allied disciplines, including theology, the social sciences, and learning theories to develop norms and criteria for evaluating catechesial activity. In short, what ethics is to ethos, and political science is to politics, catechetics is to catechesis.

Since catechesis is a form of the ministry of the Word, many of the principles found in treatises on pastoral theology and preaching also apply in catechetics. A number of works, however, can be properly classified as treatises on catechetics. St. Augustine's "First Catechetical Instruction" (*De catechizandis rudibus*), for example, presents a fully developed explanation of the nature and principles of catechesis while also giving practical advice on catechetical methods. In the late Middle Ages, Jean Gerson wrote *De parvulis trahendis ad Christum* (c. 1417) explaining the nature and defending the importance of catechesis to those who would belittle it. Like many of the better catechisms, the catechism of the Council of Trent (*Catechismus ad parochos*, The Roman Catechism, 3:231) contains a preface outlining principles and methods of catechesis. In the 19th century, Félix Dupanloup, bishop of Orléans, wrote a treatise on "the science of catechising [sic]," which was translated into English as *The Ministry of Catechising* (London 1890).

Also in the 19th century catechetics began to emerge as an academic discipline in the curriculum of seminaries. It was first seen as an aspect of pastoral theology with emphasis largely on pedagogy. Later a group of theologians and pastoral leaders at the University of Tübingen and elsewhere sought to reformulate the entire catechesial practice as it existed, expanding it from the definitional concentration on the catechism, to the broader realms of sacramental and historical dimensions of Christian life. Out of that ferment the catechetical movement rose. Four men are usually associated with its innovation: Johannes M. Sailer (1751–1832), bishop of Regensburg, considered by some as the founder of the science of pastoral theology; Bernard Heinrich Overburg (1754–1826); John Baptist Hirscher (1788–1865) of Tübingen and later of Freiburg; and Augustine Gruber (1763–1835). All four were intent on replacing the catechism with a more comprehensive catechesis. Both Overburg and Hirscher wrote manuals that broke with the prevalent pattern of catechisms in use at the time. In 1887, the *Katechetenverein* of Munich was founded. It was an association of professional theologians intent on promoting better catechesis. Two serious catechetical journals were already in publication then: *Katechetische Blätter* in 1875 and *Christlich pädagogische Blätter* followed two years later.

By the opening of the 20th century the movement had caught on and spread. Pius X's writings and exhortations, especially his encyclical *Acerbo nimis* (1905) affirmed and strengthened the impulse. Gradually the shift from method to a more wholistic incorporation of method with message and doctrine advanced to a prominent place. That was due in large part to the work of Joseph A. *Jungmann, especially his *Die Frohbotschaft und unsere Glaubensverkündigung* (1937). In 1946, G. Delcuve, a Belgian Jesuit, opened an international school, Lumen Vitae, for catechists and began circulating a quarterly periodical by the same name. A few years after that (1951), in Paris, the national hierarchy of France founded the Institut Supérieur Catéchétique, a program in higher catechetical studies. The bishops named two Sulpicians, Joseph Colomb and François Coudreau as directors. In 1960, Colomb began a similar catechetical program in Strasbourg. In England, Francis H. Drinkwater (1886–) had already initiated fresh approaches and insights into the field. In addition to his pastoral work he began publishing *The Sower* (1918); retitled *The New Sower*, that journal continues.

John Montgomery Cooper (4:298) was the first to respond to the need for the academic study of catechetics in the United States. He opened the religious education department at The Catholic University of America in 1937. The work was subsequently continued by Gerard S. Sloyan (1919–) and later by Berard L. Marthaler, OFM Conv (1927–) as leaders of catechetical thought and progress at Catholic University. Francis L. Buckley, SJ at the University of San Francisco and Vincent Novak, SJ of Fordham University in New York also contributed to the resurgence of interest in catechetics at the university level. The interdenominational Association of Professors and Researchers in Religious Education (APRRE) in the U.S. counts many Roman Catholic professors of catechetics and religious education among its members.

The number of journals concerned with "science of catechizing" is further evidence that catechetics has come into its own at the present time. In addition to the German and Belgian journals already named, there is in Italy *Catechesi* (1933), a review of pastoral catechetics under the auspices of the Salesian Catechetical Center in Turin. In the U.S. *Living Light* (1963), whose editorial policy is directed by the Department of Education, USCC, is described as "an interdisciplinary review of Christian education." *Vérité et vie* appeared in 1949 from Strasbourg. *Catéchèse* (1960) comes from the Centre national de l'enseignment religieux in Paris. The Latin American bishops are responsible for *Catequesis Latinoamericana*, which began circulating in 1968 from Asunción, Paraguay. Under the auspices of De La Salle Training College in Castle Hill, N.S.W., Australia, *Our Apostolate* began in 1952 and continues publication. The *East Asian Pastoral Institute, Manila, Philippines, publishes *Teaching All Nations* (1964).

Although its beginnings and growth can be traced through more than a hundred years, catechetics as a discipline per se is still in process. Whether as an academic discipline or simply as a description of a serious, systematic analysis of catechesis, catechetics holds an increasingly significant place in the Church's scholarly assessment of self-continuance and maintenance.

Bibliography: F. X. ARNOLD, *Pastorale theologische Blicke* (Freiburg im B. 1965). A. BOYER, *Catéchètique* (Paris 1947). J. B. COLLINS, ed., *Catechetical Documents of Pope Pius X* (Paterson, N.J. 1946). Congregation for the Clergy, *General Catechetical Directory* (USCC Publ. Office, Washington, D.C. 1971). W. CROCE, "Katechetenvereine," LexThK² 6:35. F. A. DUPANLOUP, *The Ministry of Catechising*, tr. G. FARRAN (London 1890). X. FLEURY, "Introduction," *Catéchisme historique* (Dublin 1765). H. HALBFAS, *Theory of Catechetics* (New York 1971). J. HIRSCHER, *Katechetik* (Tübingen 1831). J. HOFINGER and C. STONE, eds., *Pastoral Catechetics* (New York 1964). J. A. JUNGMANN, *Katechetik* (Freiburg im B. 1955); Eng. ed., *Handing on the Faith*, tr. A. N. FUERST (New York 1959); *The Good News: Yesterday and Today*, tr. W. HUESMAN (New York 1962). B. L. MARTHALER, *Catechetics in Context* (Huntington, Ind. 1973). A. MULLER, ed., *Catechetics for the Future. Concilium* 52 (New York 1970). Synod of Bishops, 1977, LivLight 15 (Spring 1978) entire issue.

[M. C. BRYCE]

CATECHISMS

During the mid-1970s catechisms published under Roman Catholic auspices in the U.S. and elsewhere showed marked differences in scope and format from the classic catechisms of previous centuries. Until recently catechisms had been considered primarily as children's manuals, but the new publications aim at a wider audience and move away from the terse question-answer format which characterized most manuals since Luther popularized the genre in the 16th century.

Cathechesis was and is by etymology and practice oral. Catholic post-Reformation catechisms, though written for publication, retained such oral characteristics as repetition, organization of material in numerical groupings (e.g., *seven* gifts of the Spirit), and other mnemonic devices that aided memorization. Some have argued, for example, that the success of the so-called Baltimore Catechism was due in large part to the cadence of language which made it easy to recite. The older catechisms were criticized, however, for their almost total reliance on verbal formulas and the absence of any effort to relate the question-answers to the central mysteries of Christianity or to indicate any order of priority among the questions and answers.

Vatican Council II charted a new course when it

mandated catechetical directories that would provide guidelines and principles for catechesis (*Christus Dominus* 44). The *General Catechetical Directory* issued by the Congregation for the Clergy in 1971 put special emphasis on the need for catechesis at every stage of life and linked it intimately with sacramental preparation and practice. The Directory also laid down norms for the production of catechisms in the future (119), but not all the manuals that have appeared in the U.S. in the years after Vatican II meet those specifications. Thus none claims to have been "submitted to the Apostolic See for review and approval" (ibid.).

The major "catechisms" which have appeared in recent years are designed for an adult audience and generally are full book-length. Some have been the work of an individual (Hardon, Greeley, Kevane). Some are the product of group collaboration (Dyer, ed., T. C. & R. Lawler and D. W. Wuerl, eds.). Another collaborative venture done in Europe may represent a trend of the future (Feiner and Vischer); *The Common Catechism* is an ecumenical effort by Protestants and Catholics to agree on a joint statement of the Christian faith. During the 1977 Synod of Bishops it was learned that a common text for catechesis is in use in some places in Africa.

A catechism of more official standing is the five-part text being produced in Italy under the direction of the Italian episcopal conference. It is designed according to age levels: infancy (written for parents); childhood; adolescents; young adults; and mature adults. Similar efforts are underway in Hungary, India, and elsewhere. They resemble the graded, religion series in use in schools and catechetical programs in North America insofar as the basic catechism text is supplemented with auxiliary materials including guides for parents and catechists.

See also NATIONAL CATECHETICAL DIRECTORY.

Bibliography: M. C. BRYCE, review of J. FEINER and L. VISCHER, eds., *The Common Catechism* (New York 1975) AmEcclRev 169 (1975) 567–568. Congregation for the Clergy, *General Catechetical Directory* (USCC Publ. Office, Washington, D.C. 1971). G. J. DYER, ed., *An American Catholic Catechism* (New York 1976). A. M. GREELEY, *The Great Mysteries—An Essential Catechism* (New York 1976). J. A. HARDON, *The Catholic Catechism* (Garden City, N.Y. 1975). E. KEVANE, *Creed and Catechetics* (1978). T. E. KRAMER, "The New Catechisms in Review," *New Catholic World* 219 (1976) 185–188. R. LAWLER, D. W. WUERL, and T. C. LAWLER, eds., *The Teaching of Christ—A Catholic Catechism for Adults* (Huntington, Ind. 1976). *Lumen Vitae* 32 (1977) 244. B. L. MARTHALER, "Catechisms Revisited: New Things and Old," *America* 133 (Sept. 20, 1975) 148–150.

[M. C. BRYCE]

CATECHISTS, MISSIONARY

Vatican Council II's Decree on the Church's Missionary Activity insisted on the outstanding and most necessary contribution of missionary catechists to the spread of the faith and of the Church; it calls them "co-workers of the priestly order" (*Ad gentes* 17). A renewed conception of the role of catechists, and consequently of their recruitment, training, and maintenance, is emerging everywhere since the Council. The inspiration is Vatican II's ecclesiology, insistence on the responsibility of the whole community for the Church's mission and on the need for full self-reliance of the local Churches and integration of the Gospel into their cultures. The movement of decolonialization, accompanied by growing opposition to any form of foreign dominance, the rapidly decreasing number of foreign missionaries, and the lack of local priestly vocations also have contributed to the rethinking of the pastoral structures of the church communities. An excellent and authoritative summary of the renewed conception of the catechist's role is the 1970 report of the plenary assembly of the Congregation for the Evangelization of Peoples. From this document and the studies made by the Congregation's Commission for Catechesis and Catechists, and from other important studies and reports, the following trends emerge.

(1) There is a growing awareness that the first aim of the mission is not to take care of individuals as such but to build up Christian communities responsible for the evangelization of their own milieu and for the pastoral care of their members. In these communities the catechist is no longer thought of as the priest's aide or representative, picked by the priest and sent to the community, but, in the words of the above-mentioned report: "The catechist comes from the community itself and through his special charism becomes its animator. The catechist is not simply a substitute for the priest, but in his own right is a witness to Christ in the community to which he belongs." The Commission study published in 1972 states: "His role, which was formerly centered on the pastoral care of the individual members—their religious instruction, their preparation for the sacraments, their religious practices—will address itself more and more to helping toward the building up of the Christian community; a dynamic evangelical community, open to society in full development, the leaven in the dough . . . . So the catechist must be the man of the community, sharing its responsibilities and sustained by it" (14).

(2) Therefore, as experience seems to prove, rather than there being one man as leader, in the way the catechist formerly was, there should be shared pastoral responsibilities, so that every aspect of the life of a Christian community will be better taken care of and all the members will be more involved. The catechist should be picked from among the adults already recognized as leaders in their communities.

(3) In-service training of these grass-roots catechists and leaders in seminars and regular meetings conducted by a team of specialists, with the collaboration of the local pastors, should be preferred over sending trainees away to school and thus uprooting them from their communities. This in-service training responds better to local needs than would a central school environment.

(4) Besides local catechists and leaders, a limited number of highly qualified and professional catechists will be needed for training and animating candidates. Regional pastoral-catechetical centers can provide for the training of the professionals.

(5) The grass-roots catechists and leaders should receive a canonical mission (cf. *Ad. gentes* 17) that stresses their union with the bishop and the parish priests and supports their authority. But this mission should be given only for a fixed time, after which they can be reelected or, if needs be, replaced.

(6) Catechists should not depend on the Church for their support, but should provide for their own sustenance as every other community member does. If some reimbursement is needed, the community should provide it.

(7) In many countries of Africa, Asia, and Oceania bishops give more and more faculties and respon-

sibilities to local catechists. Fear of clericalizing the best of these lay leaders keeps most bishops from ordaining them permanent deacons, as proposed in the Decree on Missions "for those who actually carry out the functions of the deacon's office" (*Ad gentes* 16). But more and more bishops also ask themselves if the same argument does not hold for ordination of the catechists to the priesthood; as many reports indicate, catechists carry out practically all the pastoral functions of the priest except for celebration of the Eucharist and administration of other Sacraments. Some bishops think priestly ordination feasible, provided the priests of this new type first prove their worth as lay leaders, so that imposing hands on them would not elevate them to a privileged clerical state or make them dependents of the Church for their sustenance (*see* AFRICAN CHRISTIANITY).

Bibliography: J. CAULWAERT, "The Ordination of Lay People to Ministries in the Church," LumV 26 (1971) 585–592; "Promoting Lay Leaders for the New Type of Ministry," *Teaching All Nations* 10 (1973) 72–76; "Ministry in Today's Christian Communities," LivWor 10 (1973) 119–127; "Lent of the Local Church and Lessons to be Learned from 'Mission Countries'," LivWor 10 n. 2 (Feb. 1974). Congregation for the Evangelization of Peoples, Commission for Catechesis and Catechetics, *The Training of Catechists* (1974). National Catechetical and Liturgical Center, Bangalore, India, *First All-India Catechetical Meeting* (1969); *Second All-India Catechetical Meeting* (1971); *Catechetical Progress in the Dioceses of India* (1971). Papstlisches Werk der Glaubensverbreitung, *The Catechist according to the Council* (Aachen 1967). M. F. PERRIN-JASSY, *Leadership* (Gaba Institute, Eldoret, Kenya 1974). Pro Mundi Vita, *Catechists*, Bulletin 36 (1971); *New Forms of Ministry in the Church*, Bulletin 50 (1974). A. SHORTER and E. KATAZA, *Missionaries to Yourselves, African Catechists Today: A Project of the Pastoral Institute of Eastern Africa* (London 1972).

[J. CAULWAERT]

CATECHUMENATE (RITE OF ADMISSION)

The Rite of Admission to the Catechumenate is the first stage of the Christian initiation of adults. It marks the candidates' first public declaration before the Church of their intention to become members. Before they can be admitted as catechumens candidates must be grounded in the basic fundamentals of the spiritual life and Christian teaching (ChrInitAd 16). Entry into the catechumenate marks their formal entry into the household of Christ (ibid. 18). According to Vatican Council II, "Catechumens who, moved by the Holy Spirit, desire with an explicit intention to be incorporated into the Church, are by that very intention joined to her" (*Lumen gentium* 14). They are therefore entitled to be married by Christian rites, and if they should die to receive Christian burial.

The Rite begins with a formal entry into the church building by the candidates and their sponsors, who are met at the door by the priest. If the candidates have practiced non-Christian religions, these may be renounced, and they are signed on the forehead and on the senses, may take a new name, and are brought into the church, where a Liturgy of the Word is celebrated. After the Gospel and Homily a Gospel book is presented to the catechumens and prayer is offered for them by the faithful (ChrtnitAd 68–95). They are then dismissed "but remain together to share their fraternal joy and spiritual experiences" (96). If the Eucharist is to be celebrated, it continues after the dismissal of the catechumens with the General Intercessions (ibid. 97).

The admission begins an extensive period of pastoral formation and discipline at the end of which they are "elected" for Baptism. The period has no fixed length

but is determined by the bishop according to circumstances (ibid. 20). Those admitted as catechumens take part in the Liturgy of the Word and receive blessings and sacramentals. They do not ordinarily participate in the Eucharist, but are dismissed after the Liturgy of the Word (ibid. 19:3).

Bibliography: M. C. BRYCE, "The Catechumenate: Past, Present and Future," AmEcclRev 160 (1969) 262–273. Murphy Center for Liturgical Research, *Made, Not Born: New Perspectives on Christian Initiation and the Catechumenate* (Notre Dame, Ind. 1976). J. WAGNER, ed, *Adult Baptism and the Catechumenate. Concilium* 22 (New York 1967).

[L. L. MITCHELL]

CATECHUMENATE FOR ADULTS

The bishops of Vatican Council II called for the restoration of the catechumenate in two separate documents. The Constitution on the Sacred Liturgy and the Decree on the Church's Missionary Activity both speak of a catechumenate comprising several distinct steps and adapted to the situation of the local Church (*Sacrosanctum Concilium* 64–66; *Ad gentes* 13–14). On January 6, 1972, the Congregation for Divine Worship issued the decree of implementation of the new Rite of Christian Initiation of Adults, allowing its immediate use in Latin and its use in the vernacular as soon as a translation was prepared and approved. The English translation was issued in 1974 in a provisional text approved for interim use in the dioceses of the United States. Since that time a gradual implementation of the new rite has begun in numerous parishes across the country.

Structure. The catechumenate is structured in four sections, each with its own character and marked by special prayers and rites. These sections correspond to the varied stages in the process of conversion.

Precatechumenate. The first stage is the period of evangelization and precatechumenate. This is a time of inquiry by the candidate and of evangelization by the Church. During this period the proclamation of the Gospel is central, leading to faith and initial conversion. Episcopal conferences may provide some kind of reception of interested inquirers beginning this stage, and pastors are to help the inquirers with suitable prayers during the precatechumenate.

Admission. A candidate who has come to faith and has decided to join the Church is formally admitted to the catechumenate in the presence of the Christian community. This rite is "of very great importance," for "the Church, carrying out its apostolic mission, admits those who intend to become members" (ChrInitAd 14). From this time on, the catechumens are considered part of the Church with the right to Christian marriage and burial (ibid. 18). This second stage may last several years and is the time of catechesis and formation. Along with doctrinal and moral instruction, the catechumens are given experience in the Christian life of prayer and service to others and are supported by the example and prayers of the faithful. Celebrations of the Word for their benefit are encouraged and they are invited to participate in the Liturgy of the Word at the Eucharist, ordinarily being dismissed before the Eucharist proper begins.

Purification. The third stage, the period of purification and enlightenment, usually coincides with Lent. It begins on the first Sunday of Lent with the rite of election, by which the candidates are accepted by the community for the celebration of the Sacraments of initiation at Easter. This stage is a period of "intense preparation of heart and spirit" (ibid. 22) for the Easter celebration and the Sacraments. It is a time of spiritual preparation more than catechesis and it is marked by the celebration of the scrutinies and the presentations. The scrutinies are ceremonies of *exorcism and prayer for the elect, celebrated on the third, fourth, and fifth Sundays of Lent. They are "intended to purify the catechumens' minds and hearts, to strengthen them against temptation, to purify their intentions, and to make firm their decision . . ." (ibid. 154). The presentations of the Creed and the Lord's Prayer are celebrated after the scrutinies. The elect are to memorize these ancient summaries of faith and prayer and render them publicly before Baptism (cf. 183). The Sacraments of initiation are properly celebrated at the Easter Vigil and as a single celebration, including Baptism, Confirmation and first Eucharist.

Mystagogia. The celebration of the Sacraments marks the full incorporation of the candidates as members of the faithful. But the rite includes a final stage for the newly baptized, the period of *postbaptismal catechesis or mystagogia. This period generally lasts until Pentecost and is a time for deeper understanding of and incorporation into the paschal mystery. It is also a time for deepening the relationships of the new members with the rest of the faithful and for frequent reception of the Eucharist. Some form of celebration around Pentecost completes this final stage. It is recommended that the newly baptized gather again on the anniversary of their Baptism, and the bishop, if he has not presided at the Sacraments of initiation, is to "make sure . . . that at least once a year he meets the newly baptized and presides at a celebration of the Eucharist" (ibid. 239).

Pastoral and Doctrinal Implications. The Rite of Christian Initiation of Adults thus represents a significant departure from former pastoral practice. Its goal is the formation of knowledgeable, active, apostolic, and prayerful members of the Church. It proposes to achieve this by careful attention to the conversion process, recognizing the varied stages in the development of faith. It seeks to pace this process in a full ritual elaboration, calling the whole community to a continual involvement in the process. The rite attempts to foster conversion by attention to various dimensions involved in a radical commitment to Christ. It recognizes the need for intellectual education, for psychological support, for social incorporation into a living community, for moral instruction, and for spiritual guidance. The use of *sponsors during the stages of the catechumenate provides for an intense personal dimension, complementing the communal emphasis in many of the ceremonies and activities. The need for adaptation on the national, diocesan, and parish levels is recognized in the rite itself (ibid. 64–67) and much remains to be done before it will be clear just how this universal rite can be used most effectively in different cultural situations.

Even prior to such adaptations, however, it is clear that this rite carries some radical and far-reaching implications for the life and ministry of the Church. Most basic of these is the renewed concept of the Church itself contained in the rite. The Church is envisioned as a strong and vibrant apostolic community, intensely involved in the living out of the death and

resurrection of Jesus and actively reaching out to evangelize and draw others into that mystery. It presumes a local parish that is a warm, supportive community of faith and prayer, willing and able to assist the catechumens in their growth in Christ.

The rite also redefines membership in the Church, following the lead of Vatican II (cf. *Lumen gentium* 14; *Ad gentes* 14). Catechumens are recognized as "joined to the Church and part of the household of Christ" (ChrInitAd 18). Though unbaptized, they are members of the Church, forming an order of catechumens distinct from the order of the faithful. Moreover, one who is not ready to become an active participant in the life and mission of the Church is not considered a suitable candidate for the Sacraments. The implications of this perspective for many baptized Christians becomes obvious as the conversion process is articulated in the public rituals of the catechumenate.

Shifts in such basic elements of ecclesiastical understanding will have ramifications in numerous areas of church life and policy. The idea of non-baptized members of the Church may eventually alter the Church's practice of *infant Baptism, perhaps allowing enrollment in the catechumenate as an option, with the Sacraments of initiation occurring after a long period of instruction and formation. The insistence in the rite on Confirmation as an integral part of initiation at the Easter Vigil may have ramifications on the common understanding and celebration of that Sacrament. The model of the catechumenate for Christian formation could have numerous implications for religious education at all age levels, perhaps leading to a more integrated experience of instruction, prayer, and *celebration. The view of ministry contained in the rite as the obligation of the community as a whole and as the responsibility of every Christian could radically influence the common understanding of ordained ministry. The very existence of an order of catechumens in the Church also alters the general view of the orders of deacon, presbyter, and bishop, along with increased emphasis on the "order of the faithful."

Further implications will become apparent as the rite is implemented generally throughout the Church. Because it touches so many areas of ecclesiastical life and policy, this implementation will necessarily be slow and uneven. It is an integral part of the process by which the post-Vatican II Church seeks to renew herself in structure and in spirit.

See also CHRISTIAN INITIATION, SACRAMENTS OF.

Bibliography: *Rite of Christian Initiation of Adults*: Provisional Text (USCC Publ. Office, Washington, D.C. 1974). *Made, Not Born*, ed. by Notre Dame Center for Pastoral Liturgy (Notre Dame, Ind. 1976). A. KAVANAGH, "The Norm of Baptism: The New Rite of Christian Initiation of Adults." *Worship* 48 (1973) 143–152. *Liturgy* 22 (Jan, 1977) (whole issue on catechumenate). L. E. MICK, "A Parish Experiment," and "Looking at the Future," *Today's Parish* 8 (1976) 37–41 and 42–43.

[L. E. MICK]

CATECHUMENS (JURIDICAL STATUS)

The restoration of the catechumenate, mandated by Vatican Council II, raises questions that have not been of functional concern in the Church for a millennium: what is the juridical status of catechumens and what are their rights and responsibilities? The Dogmatic Constitution on the Church states that "catechumens who, moved by the Holy Spirit, desire with an explicit intention to be incorporated into the Church, are by that very intention joined to her. With love and solicitude mother Church already embraces them as her own" (*Lumen gentium* 14). Catholics have become so accustomed to viewing Baptism as the means of joining the Church that the noting of a catechumen as a member of the Church requires new categories in theology and in Canon Law, and a new pastoral praxis.

The Decree on the Missionary Activity of the Church notes that "the juridical status of catechumens should be clearly defined in the new Code of Canon Law. Since they are already joined to the Church, they are already of the household of Christ and are quite frequently already living a life of faith, hope, and charity" (*Ad gentes* 14).

The 1972 Rite of Christian Initiation of Adults speaks in similar terms of catechumens as part of the Church (ChrInitAd 14, 18) and then adds that "when two catechumens marry or when a catechumen marries an unbaptized person, the appropriate rite is celebrated. One who dies during the catechumenate receives a Christian burial" (ibid. 18).

Thus, it is incumbent on the revisers of the Code of Canon Law to provide for the canonical discipline of the restored catechumenate. The 1975 draft of the proposed revision of sacramental law, however, does not offer any systematic treatment of the catechumenate. Several commentators have noted the omission: "The scheme deals in several places with adult baptism. However, there seems to be no systematic effort to provide for the restored canonical discipline of the catechumenate. This may well be because of a failure to stimulate efforts in the particular churches to revive the catechumenate. Obviously its specific form is to be determined by particular legislation. Yet its nature and importance should be specified in the Code in accord with the general thrust of the January 6, 1972 *Ordo* for adult baptism and the administration of the sacraments of initiation" (Green 276).

See also CATECHUMENATE FOR ADULTS.

Bibliography: T. GREEN, "The Revision of Sacramental Law: Perspectives on the Sacraments Other than Marriage," StCan 11 (1977) 261–327.

[L. E. MICK]

CATHOLIC ACTION

Catholic Action (3:262) as a movement or a theological concept has been laid to rest. It spanned the era between Vatican I and Vatican II. It will remain as a significant historical link between the Vatican I monarchical view of the Church and hierarchical view of ministry and Vatican II, which responds to the democratization of society and understands the Church as the People of God. Catholic Action, stripped of its political use by the Church, will remain the genius of Pius XI and Card. Joseph Cardijn. The Catholic Action movements were a successful accommodation or bridge between an ecclesiology that rooted all ministry of the Church in the hierarchy and a growing awareness of the gifts of each person to the world as a witness to the Gospel. The major Vatican II documents, on the Church, *Lumen gentium*, and on the Church in the modern world, *Gaudium et spes*, witness the shift by omitting even any reference to Catholic Action. However, the Decree on the *Apostolate of the Laity (Apostolicam actuositatem)* does pick up the thread of

Catholic Action theology, which makes it unrepresentative of the mainstream of Vatican II teaching. The shift in theology can be found especially in ch. 4 of *Lumen gentium*.

[D. J. GEANEY]

CATHOLIC CAMPUS MINISTRY ASSOCIATION

The Catholic Campus Ministry Association (CCMA), an outgrowth of the National Newman Chaplains' Association, is a professional organization founded in 1969 as an independent association of Catholic chaplains from both secular and Catholic campuses. The first President of CCMA was Rev. Charles Forsyth, OSB who in 1969 was president of the National Newman Chaplains' Association. Previous to the formation of CCMA, the Newman apostolate (10:420) dealt specifically with students and chaplains on secular campuses. One reason the National Newman Chaplains' Association became CCMA was that its membership was limited to chaplains active on the secular or non-Catholic campus. Chaplains on Catholic campuses had for the most part the traditional role of chaplain in a Catholic school, with emphasis on sacramental ministry and lack of recognition, of programming, and of financing. The formation of CCMA made it possible for all Catholic campus ministers to form one larger group and share goals and objectives.

The terms "chaplain" and "campus minister" both include the ordained clergy, vowed religious men or women, and properly assigned lay persons. Campus minister is the more widely used title and connotes the all-embracing idea of ministry developed out of Vatican Council II.

Membership in the Association is not automatic but rather the result of the free choice of each minister. At the founding of CCMA, those involved dedicated themselves: to the development of the Christian community on whatever campus they were present; to the validity of the total educative process; and to loyalty to the Church even though a direct relationship to the Church was not present. From the beginning there has been an indirect relationship to the bishops through the USCC Department of Education.

The purposes of CCMA as further developed are: (1) to provide a supportive community for its members; (2) to be a strong and coordinated voice for the Church's ministry in higher education; (3) to provide continuing education programs for its members; (4) to establish appropriate relationships with individuals and agencies in the Church and in the field of higher education; (5) to encourage ecumenical and interfaith understanding; (6) to provide guidelines and assistance for recreating campus-ministry personnel. Campus ministry has a fourfold program: religious, educational, social, and social-action. The educative role of campus ministry has become more significant in recent years because of the realization that the American Church needs an educated laity who are religiously literate.

One of the first actions taken by CCMA for continuing education of the campus ministers was the initiation of annual study weeks for the growth and development of its members. These were based on the model set up at an invitational meeting in New Orleans in January 1968 sponsored by the National Newman Chaplains'

Association. The CCMA voted to regionalize them in 1970 and two study weeks were convened in January 1971 in Boca Raton, Fla. and Phoenix, Arizona. The popularity and strength of the study weeks is evidenced by the fact that there are now three annual ones, Eastern, Western, and Midwestern, held at Christmas, Easter, and late Spring respectively and that over half the membership attends one or more of them.

CCMA reached an ecumenical milestone when it opened its membership to Protestants and invited Protestants to attend the annual study weeks as participants and resource persons. A CCMA journal, *Process*, begun in 1974, has become a learning and ministerial instrument for its members. The contributions, primarily from CCMA members, have become valuable tools for sharing ideas for personal development and programming.

Presently, CCMA consists of over 900 members with a constituency of clergy, religious priests, brothers, and sisters, lay men, lay women, and Protestant ministers. The governing body is an executive board made up of six elected members with up to three appointed members. The latter may be appointed for one year to represent a constituency not represented by an elected member, e.g., commuter colleges. A recent significant turning point came in 1977 with the appointment as executive director of Sister Margaret M. Ivers, IBVM and the establishment of a permanent executive office located at Wayne State University in Detroit. The executive director handles all the daily administrative matters of CCMA and the executive board is free to concentrate on policy decisions.

[M. M. IVERS]

CATHOLIC CHARITIES

The year 1978 marked the 250th anniversary of Catholic Charities within the present boundaries of the United States. In 1728 the French Governor of Louisiana requested the Ursuline Sisters of New Orleans to care for homeless children whose parents had been killed in an Indian attack north of the city (O'Grady 18). This became the first orphanage under any auspices and marked the beginning of institutional care, which has been one of the largest and strongest programs of Catholic Charities in this country.

The Term. Throughout this long period the work of Catholic Charities has been extensive and constant; it is important at the outset, however, to identify the term "Catholic Charities." It has many connotations and several variations; such other titles for the work have been used as "Catholic Social Services," "Catholic Welfare Bureau," "Catholic Social Concerns," "Catholic Family Services," "Human Resources Department." The concept common to all is that of service to and care of individuals and groups experiencing some physical, psychological, or social need. The types of care and service provided by Catholic Charities have varied from place to place and from time to time. At all times, however, Catholic Charities has sought to respond to need. Therefore, programs have changed as new needs have arisen or new approaches for solving old problems have been found.

Historical Summary. A lengthy quote from a National Conference of Catholic Charities (NCCC) study provides a historical summary that suggests this traditional effort to respond to need.

Historically, the early development of Catholic Charities in the United States had two main thrusts, one parochial and the other institutional.

Most religious communities have had as one of their purposes the service of those in need. It is not surprising to find that a number of specialized institutions to meet the health and social needs of people were developed under their sponsorship, especially in the latter part of the nineteenth century. Many of these were designed to preserve the faith of children, so many of whom were the neglected offspring of new immigrants who found it difficult to become acclimated to the new land.

Virtually every parish became the cultural as well as the religious center, providing for a variety of educational, social, and recreational needs of its people. In many instances, a strong ethnic flavor could be discerned in these activities. Needs of the people were met on a volunteer basis. The work of the St. Vincent de Paul Society was monumental, providing the first line of Catholic Charitable activity for many years.

In the 1920s and '30s a number of factors converged to give impetus to a new direction for the Church's Charitable effort. Up until that time, the participation of government in the relief programs was minimal. However, with the massive problems of the Depression, it became evident that voluntary philanthropy was in no way capable of meeting the staggering problems of the day. Many of the social programs which we know today had their beginnings at this moment in history, altering the course for both governmental and voluntary activity.

At the same time, social work began to develop as a profession. A struggle ensued within the Catholic Charities movement concerning the "professionalization" of Charity. At this time, Catholic Charitable activities tended to become identified with family agencies whose principal concern was child welfare, although a number also provided casework services to families as well. It was at this period that the United Fund Movement gained in momentum and many Catholic Charities organizations found themselves as partners or participants in these "once a year" campaigns.

The social mobility of Catholics also was and is a continuing factor in more recent developments. Catholics, who once made up the bulk of the poor, are now part of the mainstream of American economic life. Increasingly, the institutional systems of the Church in education, health, and social services have found themselves serving a middle- and upper-class clientele. By and large, the new poor have lacked identification with the Church.

Following World War II, a number of events occurred that called for, and would continue to call for, a different response from the Catholic Charitable Movement. Vatican II, the Civil Rights Movement, the Poverty Programs, Ecumenism—all these, to a greater or lesser degree, have had an impact upon formal Catholic Charitable activity.

Today, most Catholic Charitable agencies and institutions see themselves as part of the total community. Their clientele is anyone who is in need. Such a broadened service base along with an increase in public funding, whether from voluntary or governmental sources, has brought about a growing awareness of the need for accountability, both in terms of the quantity and quality of its service (NCCC Cadre Study 1972, 81–82).

A concrete illustration of response to emerging need is the resettlement program of Catholic Charities. This began with the resettlement of displaced persons in 1949. The need became evident, programs were developed, information was exchanged and discussions held to determine how best to continue this program. At every annual meeting of the NCCC for five years this topic was on the agenda (NCCC Proceedings). The work still continues with the resettlement of Indo-Chinese refugees.

Agencies and Services. More than forty different services are provided in the U.S. by Catholic Charities agencies and institutions. These cover the spectrum from family counseling to housing for the elderly, from child care (adoptions and foster homes) to job training, from service to unwed parents to home health care, from day care to legal aid, and many others. In addition to this direct service category, community development and social action programs are found in many places, e.g., community organization, social-justice education, advocacy, legislative activity, neighborhood centers (NCCC *Annual Survey*).

These programs are provided by 530 social service agencies in 148 of the 158 dioceses and more than 1000 institutions under diocesan or religious order auspices. Approximately 100,000 persons are involved in conducting these programs. In 1976 reports from 88 per cent of the agencies and almost 50 per cent of the institutions revealed expenditures of approximately $350 million. These funds come from Catholic Charities' appeals, diocesan grants, United Way allocations, special contributions, foundation funds, fees for service, and government grants or purchase of services (ibid. 23). Thus the Catholic Charities movement represents the social service arm of the Church, and is one of the largest, if not *the* largest, voluntary, nonprofit social-service organization in the country.

The National Conference of Catholic Charities. "The National Conference of Catholic Charities is the central organization for Catholic Charities in the United States. In the words of a brochure published by the National Conference, 'it provides a national service in our Diocesan agencies; it interprets their work on a national scale; it represents the whole of Catholic Charities on national and local issues, and today, increasingly, in international matters since it is a member of the International Conference of Catholic Charities established in Rome on December 12, 1951'" (Gavin vii). NCCR is a federation type of organization, coordinating the work of the many agencies and institutions and other programs existing on a diocesan level. It was formed in 1910 by the local units, rather than vice versa (ibid. 18). Its services are "in the nature of servicing the providers of service, viz., by gathering and distributing information; by engaging in research and making known the findings; by providing consultation; by keeping in touch with or making representations before the executive and legislative branches of Government concerning social welfare matters; by convening the membership to study problems and exchange information, to meet with experts from other organizations and other fields, to deliberate policy, and to launch action. The national (conference) should also provide impetus and direction in the convening of people, for, today, not fewer but more services are needed. And to provide more services, more people are needed. But that is only part of the reason for convening. Equally important is the unitive aspect of bringing people together to become aware of their common humanity and to work together on common tasks" (NCCC Cadre Study 31).

A thirty-nine-member board of directors governs the National Conference. The board is elected by the members, both group (agencies and institutions) and individual. A national staff, under an executive director is located in Washington, D.C. NCCC has five commissions (Commissions on Families and on Children, Commission on Aging, Commission on Services to Unwed Parents, Commission on Housing) and numerous committees, which provide leadership, direction, and service in specific areas of concern to the Catholic Charities movement.

NCCC is distinct from but closely associated with, the U.S. Catholic Conference, the official national organization of the U.S. bishops. NCCC has an episcopal liaison officer for relations with USCC and there is a working relationship between the NCCC executive director and the USCC associate general secretary. There are other working relationships and ad hoc collaboration on issues of common concern. Four national groups are allied to NCCC as Affiliated Organizations: the Society of St. Vincent de Paul, the Association of Ladies of Charity in the U.S., the National Christ Child Society, and the Diocesan Directors of Catholic Charities. Each of these has representation on the NCCC board.

In order to develop broader involvement of more people in the Catholic Charities Movement, NCCC has expanded its concept of membership and has sought to enable members to be the basic determiners of policy. This has resulted in a "Charities Congress" held on the occasion of the NCCC annual meeting. Delegates, elected in twelve NCCC regions, convene at the Congress to adopt Policy Statements and Resolutions. These provide guidance for the board in determining directions for the Conference and for the staff in conducting the day to day affairs (NCCC *By-Laws* 9–11).

Recent Developments: The Cadre Study. In 1972 the National Conference completed a two-year study and began a renewal process. The report adopted is called *Toward a Renewed Catholic Charities Movement* (informally called the "Cadre Study"). This reconfirmed the mission and commitment of Catholic Charities, and set directions for the future. In it, new theological insights were examined and the goals outlined. Of particular interest are the three "roles" described for Catholic Charities.

The Continuing Commitment to Service. "In addition to the new roles proposed for Catholic Charities . . . , there should be a continuing commitment to service. The type of service may change according to the needs of the particular time and place. There will always be people in need of services—and Catholic Charities must stand ready to serve them, being particularly concerned about those most in need. It must be at hand wherever there is oppressed humanity, wherever there are individuals in pain, wherever there are people in need of service, whether this is caused by external oppression or interpersonal family breakdown" (NCCC Cadre Study 31).

Humanizing and Transforming the Social Order. "To humanize and transform the social order entails social action, a term meaning many things to many people. Our interpretation of social action is based, quite simply, on belief in the necessity of pursuing social justice for all (and particularly for those unable to do so for themselves unaided) which, in turn, involves effecting changes in the existing social systems" (ibid. 32).

Convening the Christian Community and Other Concerned People. "The role of Convening, for our purposes, is a reaching out to others to stimulate them to social awareness and to recruit them as active partners in the pursuit of the goals of the Catholic Charities Movement" (ibid.).

Consequences. This NCCC study has guided the Catholic Charities movement for the past five years and will continue to do so for years to come. It truly has begun a renewal process in response to the call of Vatican Council II. Services of Catholic Charities have been mentioned above. The Charities Congress, including preparations for it, are part of the Convening effort. On the diocesan and local community level, members of Catholic Charities gather to analyze and debate proposed policy statements and to elect delegates to the

Congress. Other types of Convening take place on the local or regional level. As examples of such Convening one Southern diocese brought together persons from all over the diocese to discuss problems of the elderly and develop strategies for action; another held a "convening" on Family Life Ministries, aimed at strengthening family life, and bringing together parish leaders and clergy from fourteen counties.

The Role of Humanizing and Transforming the Socia Order reaffirms a long-standing commitment of Catholic Charities. NCCC has been involved in the development of the Social Security system, the federal housing program, social services legislation, immigration policy, and many other social welfare developments, both on the federal and state level. Of late it has provided testimony before Congress on national health insurance proposals, the Food Stamp Program, and the Indian Child Welfare Act. An example of this role, is the NCCC "Welfare Reform Project." This seeks not simply to improve the present welfare system but to achieve a complete overhaul that will make it more humane, more efficient, and more responsive to the needs of the poor. Through workshops, audio-visual materials, writings, and discussions, NCCC seeks to inform people about the welfare system, review the options for changes, and enlist support for action strategies. If progress is made with this project, it will indeed effect a transformation (Ryle; Corcoran).

Parish Social Ministry. The NCCC Cadre Study expresses the intent of NCCC "to serve the Church whenever she is realized—but especially in the local Christian community" (NCCC Cadre Study 29). Pursuing this intent, the Conference has begun a "Parish/Neighborhood Volunteer Project," informally called the Parish Outreach Project. It is a move to encourage central Catholic Charities agencies to engage in social ministry in new and different ways for the parish community. Doing this, Catholic Charities would be an enabler assisting the parish to develop a social-ministry program and thus have the parish provide some basic services needed in the local community or undertake action for community improvement.

The Parish Outreach Project, begun in 1976 on the national level through the help of foundation funding, is a response to needs and expectations on the local level. Already many parishes had social-ministry programs and several diocesan Catholic Charities offices had undertaken special outreach-to-parish efforts. A 1976 study identified forty-two diocesan programs, with 628 persons assigned or related to this work (Joseph and Conrad). It has grown extensively in the past two years. By 1978 the national office estimated that there are close to 100 diocesan programs involving more than 800 persons.

Ministry of Service. The NCCC approach is based on the premise that the responsibility for serving neighbor rests with each individual Christian; such responsibility has a corporate character (Bishops' Committee 29). The parish as a group forming a Christian community carries such a corporate responsibility and must sponsor a ministry of service within the parish if it is to be totally Christian. NCCC seeks to help the parish fulfill this responsibility, providing consultation, technical assistance, and back-up support. The trained NCCC staff will not only help the volunteer to do what is possible in the parish, but also will deal with those complex situations and needs which are beyond the competency of the volunteer (NCCC *Parish Outreach* 5–7).

The whole concept of "Parish Outreach," still in its beginning stages, responds to the pastoral emphasis so central in the thought of Vatican II. The concept in the U.S. looks to a return of a large measure of service functions to the parish. It becomes a special ministry in the parish and an essential part of the life of the Church: "This awareness of the Church's social mission and of the Christian's social responsibility, with the constant presence of the works of mercy in the Church, have led many to identify the ministry of service as an essential part of the life of the Church. While we cannot multiply 'ministries' indefinitely, there does seem to be validity for this particular identification. Jesus pointed to His works of mercy—giving sight to the blind, making the lame walk, etc.—as a sign that He was the Messiah, as a mark of His mission (Mt 2.2–6). Today, it must still be an essential part of the Church, and a mark of its divinely commissioned mission. It is appropriate that the parish, the basic Church community, have the ministry of service, the social ministry, firmly established as a part of parish life" (Jadot 55).

Catholic Charities, obviously, has long meant involvement in the ministry of service, as its tradition and programs indicate. So have such other groups as the St. Vincent de Paul Society and the Ladies of Charity. With the recognition of and greater emphasis on a parish service-ministry, Catholic Charities has begun to address this as a part of its mission. Its efforts to promote "Parish Outreach" manifest how this is carried out at the present time.

Publications. In 1975 NCCC undertook a major revision of its publications. One result was the launching of *Social Thought*, with the cosponsorship of The Catholic University of America's School of Social Work. It is a quarterly journal, devoted to professional consideration of contemporary social problems and to critical analysis of proposed or actual responses to these problems, especially programs of service. Other publications of the National Conference are *Charities USA*, a monthly magazine on issues and events and people in the Charities movement or of interest to members of NCCC; *Congressional Comment*, a quarterly legislative bulletin; *Parish Outreach*, a monthly bulletin on parish social-ministry; *The Annual Survey*, a compilation of statistics on diocesan Catholic Charities programs; and an annual *Directory of Agencies*.

The long history of Catholic Charities has been marked by a desire to serve, translated into practical programs to meet the needs of the poor, the disadvantaged and the distressed. The response to need and the desire to serve are expressions of the love of neighbor mandated by Jesus Christ. This service undertaking includes the broader effort of social action, advocacy, and involvement of people. The future of Catholic Charities will be motivated by the same values: service, love, and the pursuit of justice.

Bibliography: Bishops' Committee on Priestly Life and Ministry, *As One Who Serves* (Washington, D.C. 1977). L. J. CORCORAN, "A Perspective on Welfare Reform," *Charities, USA* 4 n.7 (1977) 2. D. P. GAVIN, *The National Conference of Catholic Charities, 1910–1960* (Milwaukee 1962). J. JADOT, "Building a Community through Faith and Service," *Social Thought* 3 n.4 (1977) 51–58. M. V. JOSEPH and A. P. CONRAD, *National Trends in Parish Social Ministry* (NCCC publ., Washington, D.C. 1977). National Conference of Catholic Charities, *Proceedings* (Washington,

D.C. 1948–52); *Towards a Renewed Catholic Charities Movement: A Study of the National Conference of Catholic Charities*, the "Cadre Study" (Washington, D.C. 1972); *By-Laws* (Washington, D.C. 1975); *Annual Survey* (Washington, D.C. 1976); *Parish Outreach: Building Community through Service* (Washington, D.C. 1977). J. O'GRADY, *Catholic Charities in the United States: History and Problems* (NCCC publ., Washington, D.C. 1931). E. J. RYLE, "Welfare Reform: The Carter Administration Plan," *Charities, USA* 4 n.6 (1977) 4–14.

[L. J. CORCORAN]

CATHOLIC COMMITTEE OF APPALACHIA

National attention in the early 1960s focused on the extensive poverty found in large segments of the Appalachian Mountains. Church leaders of eighteen denominations formed the Commission on Religion in Appalachia (CORA), an ecumenical group working cooperatively to alleviate some of the pressing human needs of the region. As CORA met semi-annually, the Roman Catholic component simultaneously grew and soon became an entity in itself. Bishops, laypersons, religious, and priests—all ministers in the region—soon formed the Catholic Committee of Appalachia (CCA).

Appalachia, as defined by the Appalachian Regional Commission, comprises parts of twelve states: N.Y., Pa., Ohio, Md., Ky., Va., Tenn., N.C., S.C., Ga., Miss., Ala., and all of West Virginia. It is an immense area containing 397 counties and all or part of twenty-six Catholic dioceses. Besides being the Roman Catholic caucus for CORA, CCA became an organization which bonded together Catholics working throughout the mountain chain. CCA is a membership organization whose participants are engaged in a wide variety of ministries. Together they strive to address the many needs of the area, particularly among the poor and oppressed.

The Catholic Church has few members in the more isolated mountain communities where it is often little known. It is particularly for these communities and the Catholic workers within them that the CCA exists. CCA brings to the attention of both Church and civic leaders the needs of the area and attempts to link together persons with similar concerns in rural Appalachian communities. Members of CCA in 1973 and 1974 traveled throughout the mountains listening to the people. They then asked the twenty-six ordinaries of the region to respond to what had been heard by means of a pastoral letter. In February, 1975 the pastoral letter *This Land is Home to Me* was promulgated by the Appalachian bishops.

The pastoral letter addresses itself to the powerlessness of many Appalachian people, their wide diversity, strengths, and struggles. It also addresses the misuse of land by large corporate land holders or users (*see* LAND REFORM), the overconsumption of society and the lack of control of people over their own destinies. Appalachia is seen as a microcosm of much that is happening elsewhere in the nation and world where the poor have no voice.

In the letter "liberation from every oppressive situation" is recognized as "a constitutive dimension of the preaching of the Gospel . . . , of the Church's mission" (cf. Synod JustWorld p. 34).

Besides the distribution of over 140,000 copies of "This Land is Home to Me," CCA has recently published a dialogue focuser on the pastoral letter, has researched the strip-mining issue as well as lobbied for a strong strip-mine enforcement bill, supported coal miners in their strikes at Harlan and Stearns, Ky., joined the J. P. Stevens boycott, and aided in flood recovery efforts following devastating floods in Appalachia in 1977. CCA continues to link volunteers with needed work and generally acts as a clearing house on Appalachian concerns and interests.

See also CORE APPALACHIAN MINISTRIES.

[M. S. SCANLAN]

CATHOLIC COMMITTEE ON URBAN MINISTRY (CCUM)

The Catholic Committee on Urban Ministry, located on the campus of the University of Notre Dame, is a national network of over 5,000 priests, sisters, brothers, lay persons, all of whom are involved in one or another aspect of social and pastoral ministry. They are united by the conviction that the effort to create a more human world and to achieve justice and freedom for people at home and abroad is a major task of the Church.

Primarily, CCUM is a ministry to the ministers—providing to persons and organizations in social ministry support, communication, and connection with others in similar ministries. In addition, CCUM, through its national, regional and state conferences, and summer Pastoral Institute for Social Ministry at the University of Notre Dame, is a forum for analysis of issues, for exchange of ideas in programming, for skill development and training. Primary in the focus in CCUM programming are the theology undergirding social ministry and analysis of complex justice issues and of the skills necessary to effect social change. In the words of its current chairman, Rev. Philip J. Murnion, Director of the Office of Pastoral Research of the Archdiocese of New York: "Whether working within Church institutions or not, CCUM people acknowledge their relationship to the Church and see their ministry as the extension of the Church into every field of social ministry."

Founded in 1967 by Msgr. John J. Egan of Chicago with a small group of priests engaged in urban affairs in their dioceses, CCUM remained a small informal support group until the Fall of 1970 when Msgr. Egan accepted a joint faculty appointment at Notre Dame with the Institute for Urban Studies and the Theology Department. He invited the CCUM group to the campus and challenged them either to disband the group or to shape plans for extending this core group to include the many hundreds of laity, religious, and clergy in a variety of social ministries in the United States. The decision to expand was unanimous and CCUM began to grow.

CCUM constituents were re-affirmed in their efforts by the 1971 Synod of Bishops when, in their statement on *Justice in the World*, they said: "Action on behalf of justice and participation in the transformation of the world fully appear to us as a constitutive dimension of the preaching of the Gospel." It was this "call to action" which also led the CCUM persons to take an active part in the National Conference of Catholic Bishops Bicentennial "Liberty and Justice for All" program and to work for the implementation of the Bishops' plan for social justice in the American Church.

[P. ROACH]

CATHOLIC CONFERENCE ON ETHNIC AND NEIGHBORHOOD AFFAIRS

The mission of the Catholic Conference on Ethnic and Neighborhood Affairs (CCENA) is to develop an awareness of the importance of the Catholic parish to the revitalization of neighborhoods and cities and to work for the conservation and enrichment of those fundamental ethnic values which sustain the family and respect for human life. It recognizes that the neighborhood, the parish, and ethnic cultural values are fundamentally important in building and preserving that community that the Church is called to create among all persons. Hence CCENA attempts to bring physical and financial resources to bear upon the building up of neighborhoods and parishes.

CCENA was founded in 1974 as the result of a national meeting of 250 religious leaders from 25 ethnic and parish groups in 35 cities. Begun as a special project of the *National Center for Urban Ethnic Affairs, on which it still relies for its technical assistance capabilities and moral support, CCENA is a network of ethnic and neighbourhood leaders and organizations. Its greatest achievement has been the building of parish/neighbourhood organizations in over 50 neighbourhoods in as many cities. CCENA also holds national and regional conferences on parishes and neighborhoods, acts as advocate for a greater parish/neighborhood sensitivity within the Church, and promotes recognition of the significant contribution that the Churches can and have made to American society. CCENA tries to inculcate and practice the fundamental principles of Catholic social action: personalism, pluralism, and subsidiarity. It is an affiliate of the United States Catholic Conference.

See also ETHNICITY; URBANIZATION.

[R. D. PASQUARIELLO]

CATHOLIC HOSPITAL ASSOCIATION

In July 1978 the Catholic Hospital Association (CHA; 3:268) had 638 member hospitals; these facilities had 164,403 beds and cared for more than 5.5 million patients each year. In addition CHA represented 232 long-term care facilities. Because of its increased services and expanded staff a new administration building, the third St. Louis expansion in two decades, was dedicated April 15, 1975. During the years of growth since 1965 John J. Flanagan, SJ continued to serve as executive director until being succeeded by Thomas J. Casey, SJ in 1968. In 1970 Sr. Mary Maurita Sengelaub, RSM became executive director; during her term the title was changed to "president and chief executive officer." Sr. Helen Kelley, DC took office as president Jan. 1, 1977, after a six-month orientation as executive vice-president. She served also as chairman of a two-year Study Committee, and at the end of its work announced her resignation, effective Sept. 2, 1978.

New Structures, Plans, and Programs. In response to the changing needs of its membership CHA in 1965 engaged an independent consulting organization to make a survey of central-office field activities. From the consultant's report, the Articles of Association and Bylaws were modified, amended, and simplified; both the former executive and administrative boards were replaced by a Board of Trustees, a single, combined managing-group; new council structures were de-

veloped; and many innovative programming concepts were advanced. To aid individual religious and laity serving the hospital apostolate, a task-force committee was created in 1966 to study and probe the future role of all Catholic health facilities. Several regional hearings, conducted over a four-year period, considered the challenges of ownership, trusteeship, and planning. During 1968–70 position-papers were drafted on national health issues and a series of regional seminars was sponsored, in which the educational emphasis concentrated on strengthening constituent board- and management-structures. The Association—sensitive to the external and internal forces exerting influence on membership, as well as setting the stage for future CHA service commitments—reexamined and subsequently revised its purpose and objectives. While programs of institutional-membership service continued, new activities were designed to assist corporate-level (sponsoring-group) leadership in the Catholic health system.

Catholic Health Services Leadership Program. In 1971 CHA developed a new programming concept that sharply contrasted with the traditional methods of constituent service. By unifying the combined efforts of institutional and sponsoring-group leadership, the Catholic Health Services Leadership Program began to project a process that encouraged idea and resource sharing, as well as problem-solving pools, among the religious congregations and dioceses that sponsor Catholic health facilities.

Catholic Health Assembly. The Catholic Health Assembly, which began in 1972, is the Association's principal meeting, convening the House of Delegates in annual session. The Assembly is primarily structured as a national forum to meet the apostolic, educational needs of Catholic-hospital and nursing-home chief executive officers (administrators, associates, and assistants), trustees, diocesan coordinators, directors of departments of pastoral care (including chaplains), major superiors and hospital coordinators, as well as members of apostolic study-committees, health councils, or commissions. The Assembly's week-long program, held in different sections of the United States each June, focuses on the crucial matters facing the Catholic health-care system.

Service on Medico-Moral Issues. In 1973, after two years of intensive investigation and planning, the Pope John XXIII Medical-Moral Research and Education Center was formed and began operation under a 15-member board—drawn principally from the Catholic health-apostolate. The Center was initially funded by CHA. In recent years, constituent members have expressed concern to CHA regarding long-range, complex medical-moral issues that included genetic experimentation and manipulation, transplants, the family as the basic unit of society, and, in fact, the total life-spectrum from inception through death. Therefore, the creation of the Pope John XXIII Center seemed the logical approach to the moral implications of future scientific, medical, and technological advance. Formed in the Spring of 1973, the CHA Department of Medical-Moral Affairs has been engaged in theological education to help relate to "present-day" medical-moral concerns. Staff serves as a resource pool in matters dealing with medical ethics. (In contrast, the Pope John XXIII Center is concerned with "long-range" medical-moral problems.)

Services on Government and Legislation. Two new services for membership began in 1973: a Department of Government and Legislative Services and a Department of Legal Services. Both were considered to be an integral part of CHA's pro-life strategy campaign and represented increased efforts to influence and promote favorable state and federal legislation. An early contribution of cooperative duties between departments was the preparation of model "conscience clauses" to protect Catholic institutions, physicians, and employees in state statutes pertaining to abortion. Increasing federal regulations, along with the shifting focus of the legislature and judiciary toward the health-care delivery system, made it imperative that CHA-member facilities be constantly alerted to federal developments that might affect their operations. To that end, CHA opened in September 1976, an office in Washington, D.C. to further enlarge the governmental and legal services requested by membership and to have more ready access to federal resources and information. This office monitors and analyzes legislation and federal activity dealing with regulations; opinions and hearings before such administrative agencies as the Internal Revenue Service and the Social Security Administration; and the activities of the judicial branch, including the U.S. Supreme Court and all federal courts. In particular, the office attempts to discern and identify implications of legislation and regulation-implementation on national and local levels in such areas as certificate-of-need and appropriateness review. To keep Gospel values prominent and alive in society, a principal objective is to insure that constitutional safeguards, due process, appeal, and fair-hearing procedures are contained in new and pending legislations. The gathering and analysis of information, continuing educational efforts, and field communication reflect the goals and functions of the Washington office.

Project 1980. Recognizing the swift rate of acceleration at which dramatic changes can take place in the health delivery system, CHA created "Project 1980," a vehicle for discussion and study of the projected needs of the Catholic health-apostolate and, conversely, the ways in which the Association would meet these needs. As part of its work, the Project 1980 Committee attempted both to predict and to profile membership characteristics by the year 1980. The committee felt that this initial effort would help assure that the CHA goals, strategies, and services continue to be appropriate and responsive. To begin with, the Committee compiled a list of target areas where specific and tailored programs required implementation. Those target areas touched on the Association's concern that alternative means of continuing ownership/sponsorship/management which would maintain facility identification within the Catholic Church would be available where needed; that new programs be created to deal effectively with all levels of government; that programs offered by Catholic health facilities be appropriate for the community served; and that the programs for the chronically ill and aging be expanded.

Hospital Cooperation. Considerable attention has been directed in recent years toward the need for greater cooperation among hospitals. Attention has been given to a current trend to develop systems within which hospitals and other health-care facilities will achieve greater effectiveness of operation and better provision of services to communities. Examples of such developments are found in a range of activities consisting of mergers, affiliations, shared services, trade-offs of services, and consortia. Catholic hospitals sponsored by specific religious congregations represent subsets of multihospital facilities within the total "system" of Catholic hospitals. In certain situations, "shared services" have been extensively developed to work with a particular group of hospitals—often quite widespread geographically—sponsored by one of these religious congregations. Nevertheless, a wide range in degree of centralized control exists from one religious congregation to another and such provision of "corporate services" has been confined mostly to larger religious orders sponsoring six or more hospitals. These groups have served hospitals well within their particular control. However, CHA has become increasingly concerned about those hospitals that are not part of such arrangements and which, because of lack of a solid base, are not able to achieve the benefits of cooperative efforts through such multihospital arrangements. Another dimension of Catholic hospital subgrouping is that in many cases hospitals sponsored by a religious congregation are located in quite diverse geographic areas. And therefore, the question arises as to the importance of recognizing different types of grouping of Catholic hospitals, either by civic or religious community, by geographic location, or by diocesan boundaries —or all types combined.

Long-Range Planning and Development Committee and Study Committee. In 1976 the Long-Range Planning and Development Committee, a standing committee of the CHA Board of Trustees, was charged with identifying national trends in the delivery of health-care services; with assessing future political, social, financial, and cultural factors; and with developing a recommended action plan. As an outgrowth of these deliberations, the committee was further charged to investigate the merits of retaining an independent consulting firm to analyze and evaluate the current and projected programs and services of the Association.

An in-depth, independent analysis of CHA— concentrating on how well its purpose, objectives, programs, and services were meeting the needs and expectations of its members—was undertaken by an 18-member Study Committee, chaired by the CHA president, Sister Helen Kelley. The committee was made up of most segments of the apostolate, including institutional and noninstitutional membership and sponsoring groups. Assisted by a consulting firm, the work of the committee was divided into two separate areas of concentration: an internal focus (examining the Association and its constituency) and an external perspective (the environment in which CHA functions, as influenced by government, the Church, the public, and allied health groups). In April 1978 the Association acted upon the Committee recommendations, as contained in a study entitled "Forming Christian Community for Healing." The study was a blueprint for major alterations in the CHA that would build "a clearer Catholic identity" in Catholic health-care organizations. Outlined in the committee's report to the CHA Board of Trustees were "major shifts in emphasis" to be achieved by the implementation of some 30 specific recommendations for policy and procedural changes. In calling for change, the study cited new tensions and philosophical differences which have emerged between the secular and ecclesial in health care delivery. "In no other sphere of Church life are the Church's institutions so directly and deeply a part of the secular, pluralistic society." Because of technological developments and "altered societal values," Catholic health-care leaders must confront direct challenges in such medical-moral questions as abortion, sterilization, and euthanasia. In view of such "ominous issues," the study called for "stronger and more visible theological and hierarchical support" of the Church's health-care ministry.

As to specific recommendations, the Board of Trustees approved "as a working document" a new statement of mission, but turned down recommendations that the Association change its name to the "Catholic Health Association," and move its central office to Washington. The board also approved recommendations that CHA's primary ministries be advocacy and education; that its governmental-affairs office in Washington be strengthened; that it increase its services to the aged and its long-term care facilities; and that the organization develop guidelines to help Catholic health facilities evaluate their effectiveness. In addition, the Association is presently investigating other methods to assist its constituency and sponsoring groups to develop and strengthen a renewed sense of Catholic identity.

[S. MOLDAVER]

CATHOLIC-JEWISH RELATIONS, NCCB SECRETARIAT FOR

The Secretariat for Catholic-Jewish Relations was established at the annual meeting of the American bishops in September, 1967, within the framework of the *Bishops' Committee for Ecumenical and Interreligious Affairs. Its present moderator is Bishop Francis J. Mugavero of Brooklyn. Its function is to aid the dioceses in setting up secretariats or other agencies in accordance with Vatican Council II's Declaration on Non-Christians (*Nostra aetate* 4) and the Guidelines issued January 3, 1975 by the Pontifical Commission for *Religious Relations with Judaism.

Major objectives include: (1) aid to other organizations within the Church whose work (liturgy, education, justice and peace efforts) involves Catholic-Jewish relations; (2) liaison with the Jewish community, its major religious branches and agencies; (3) work with other Christian Churches and private organizations (National Council of Churches of Christ; National Conference of Christians and Jews) for the promotion of Jewish-Christian relations; (4) promotion of scholarly dialogue and joint social action between the Catholic and Jewish communities; (5) research and publication on major developments in the field; and (6) dialogue on both the national and international levels.

Under the leadership of its first full-time Executive Secretary, Rev. Edward Flannery, the Secretariat participated in many pioneering efforts which have greatly improved Catholic-Jewish relations, for example, in sponsoring the first national Jewish-Christian Workshops ever held in this country and in assisting the bishops in the preparation of their break-through "Statement on Catholic-Jewish Relations," promulgated on November 20, 1975.

See also JEWISH/CATHOLIC RELATIONS.

[E. J. FISHER]

CATHOLIC LEAGUE FOR RELIGIOUS AND CIVIL RIGHTS

The Catholic League for Religious and Civil Rights, founded in 1973, is a civil rights and antidefamation organization serving the Catholic community in the same manner as the American Civil Liberties Union and the Anti-Defamation League of B'nai B'rith serve their respective communities. Independent of the hierarchy, the Catholic League is governed by a board of directors, consisting of lay and religious leaders. The work of the League falls into three primary categories: (1) education, promoting the rights and interests of Catholics through educational and informational programs; (2) negotiation and confrontation, challenging individuals who violate the rights and liberties of Catholics; and (3) litigation, establishing and defending the religious and civil rights of Catholics and others through legal action.

The League's first protest action was against a booklet entitled *Population Control: Whose Right to Live?*, published by the Xerox Corporation and used in many high schools. The booklet classified Paul VI's teaching on birth control as a crime against humanity. After the League threatened Xerox with legal action, the publisher agreed to discontinue sale and distribution of the book, and not to permit third parties to reprint it. The first lawsuit in which the League engaged was the defense of Dr. Frank Bolles, a Protestant physician active in the right-to-life movement in Colorado and convicted of violating state law by sending anti-abortion literature through the mail. With the help of the Catholic League, he was vindicated when the Colorado Supreme Court upheld his right to freedom of speech.

Among the League's other important legal cases were the following: *Wolfe v. Schroering* (388 F Suppl. 631 W.D. Ky.). A Federal Circuit Court upheld the right of 28 doctors and nurses from Kentucky to refuse to participate in abortions. *Doe v. Irwin* (428 F Suppl. 1198). The U.S. District Court, Southern District of N.Y., affirmed the right of parents to be notified before a state agency gives contraceptives to their minor children. *Lucido v. Cravath, Swain and Moore* (75 Civ 6341). The League is assisting an attorney who alleges that he was fired from his Wall Street law firm because of his religion and national origin. *Erzinger et al v. University of California*. This is a case pending before the Superior Court, San Diego County, in which a group of students are protesting the collection of mandatory fees to pay for elective abortions through a university health-insurance plan.

The League has helped to guarantee the right of senior citizens living in a federally-subsidized apartment complex in Cincinnati to conduct religious services on the premises, and it persuaded the Department of Housing and Urban Development to veto a prohibition against Church-related schools in Portchartrain-New Town, a federally subsidized subdivision of New Orleans, Louisiana. Among the League's successful antidefamation activities was the protest against a birth control brochure distributed by the Federal government in Latin America that contained a picture irreverent toward the Blessed Virgin. The League protests against antireligious satire in *National Lampoon* led six major advertisers to drop their advertising in that magazine and, ultimately, to an editorial policy decision to discontinue anti-religious satire.

The Catholic League has distributed nearly 1500 free sets of the audio-visual presentation *Abortion: How It Is* to Catholic and Protestant high schools and other interested organizations. It is currently engaged in a long-term study of inner-city nonpublic schools serving minority students. The results of this study will be used to demonstrate the advantages that education vouchers can bring the children of the poor.

At the beginning of 1978, the Catholic League had a nationwide membership of over 20,000. It was in the process of setting up a network of local chapters in major metropolitan areas, with chapters in Minneapolis-St. Paul and Washington, D.C. already established. Members receive a monthly newsletter and supplementary articles on issues of current importance. The Catholic League's national headquarters is located at 1100 W. Wells St., Milwaukee, Wis. 53233. The League's President and founder is Rev. Virgil C. Blum, SJ, professor of political science at Marquette University.

[V. C. BLUM]

CATHOLIC LIBRARY ASSOCIATION

The Catholic Library Association (CLA) has actively pursued its stated purpose since its founding in 1921: "to encourage the development of religious-oriented libraries as centers of Christian thought, to serve as the backbone and coordinating force of the Church's educational endeavors."

Though the purpose of the Association can be identified through its annual programs, it can most readily be seen in the ongoing activities of its committees. In 1974, CLA established the Religious-Education/Library Services Committee "to assist the Church in the United States in its task to educate the faithful by means of effective media programs and other library services." The Committee's three objectives have formed the framework of its activity: (1) to identify the role and need for a professional librarian in a diocesan, parish, regional, and area Religious Education Center; (2) to identify the role of media in the programs used in religious education; (3) to develop Standards for Diocesan Religious Education Centers and its programs, thus providing librarians with guidance and a curriculum needed for involvement in this library career.

Aided in 1975 by a grant from The Our Sunday Visitor Foundation, the Committee conducted a survey of religious education centers in Hartford, Conn. (selected as a typical urban/rural environment) and began work on several publications to meet the needs identified by committee members. The first of these publications was *Periodicals for Religious Education Centers and Parish Libraries*, a guide to magazines, newspapers, and newsletters (1976), which provides an annotated bibliography of 106 recommended publications for the religious-education center collection. *Books for Religious Education*, an annotated bibliography also published in 1976, identifies two hundred books recommended for use by children, adults, and young adults. In 1977 the committee produced the *Guide for the Organization and Operation of a Religious Resource Center*, a comprehensive handbook designed to meet the needs of a religious resource-center staff in organizing media and planning for media use in religious education. Two other publications are in preparation: *Media for Religious Education* and *Catholic Subject Headings*. The

Catholic Periodical and Literature Index, a bimonthly index of Catholic periodicals, national Catholic newspapers, and currently reviewed books by Catholics or of Catholic interest, continues to be a valuable reference resource for religious education. The official publication of the association, the *Catholic Library World* provides monthly reviews of media and articles of interest to librarians responsible for religious resource centers.

In addition to publications, the Association provides institutes for librarians working in religious-education centers at the annual convention and the local units provide encouragement and assistance on a regional level. The Catholic Library Association's commitment to religious education has been strong and consistent; its assistance has been both professional and valuable.

Bibliography: Catholic Library Association. *Handbook and Membership Directory, 1978* (Haverford, Pa. 1978).

[J. T. CORRIGAN]

CATHOLIC PEACE FELLOWSHIP

The Catholic Peace Fellowship comprises the Roman Catholic membership of the inter-religious *Fellowship of Reconciliation (FOR) and describes itself as an educational service. In fact it has also been an action group, by giving leadership in the protest movement against the Viet Nam War, by counseling Catholic conscientious objectors and draft resisters as well as by serving its principal purpose of transmitting the Catholic pacifist tradition and the teachings of the modern Church on peace.

CPF was established at the instigation of the Fellowship of Reconciliation with the help of James H. Forest, a former editor of Dorothy Day's pacifist monthly *The Catholic Worker*, principally. Fathers Daniel and Philip Berrigan, the monk Thomas Merton, sociologists Msgr. Paul Hanly Furfey and Gordon C. Zahn, among others, contributed significantly to the establishment of CPF. An office was opened at the beginning of 1965 in New York City by James Forest; he was joined four months later by Thomas C. Cornell. Together they guided the rapidly-growing group until 1968, when Cornell was imprisoned for 6 months for burning his draft certificates at a public demonstration. While he served his sentence at Danbury Federal Correctional Institution, Forest participated in the destruction of draft files in Milwaukee and was subsequently jailed for two years. Cornell then directed CPF and Forest joined FOR staff as editor of its monthly magazine *Fellowship*. He now coordinates the International FOR in Alkmaar, The Netherlands.

CPF continues to function on the educational level and was active in the Detroit *Call to Action of the Bishops' Bicentennial Observance in October 1976. The New England CPF holds an annual conference the first Saturday after each Easter. Total membership is approximately 3,000. An occasional *Bulletin* is mailed free upon request. Address 339 Lafayette St., New York, N.Y. 10012.

[T. CORNELL]

CATHOLIC PREACHING MINISTRY INTERNATIONAL

Catholic Preaching Ministry International, (CPMI) a professional organization for Catholic priests in full-time ministry of renewal through preaching in parishes and retreat houses, arose from a conference of missioners from 22 religious communities in Washington, D.C., December 1967. Its purpose is to respond to a twofold problem: the image of the professional preacher and his continuing education.

Originally called Inter-Community Association of Missioners, "Inter-Com," CPMI opens membership to priests engaged in the apostolate of preaching or vitally interested in furthering it. Annual seminars offer conferences, sharing on new programs, and mutual support. Cooperative preaching projects are designed and promoted. A quarterly newsletter reports on events special to the apostolate.

As "preaching is the primary apostolate ..." (Paul VI EcclSuam 90), CPMI developed a plan for national certification of preachers and proposed realistic standards for excellence in professional preaching. The first twelve missioners were certified in 1971; certification is renewable after five years. Peer evaluation recognizes proficiency in the art of preaching for the instruction, growth, and development of God's People.

CPMI promotes growth in the preaching apostolate through encouragement of continuing education and preaching workshops. There are plans to sponsor a national center for preaching at an outstanding university. The CPMI office is at 475 Oak Avenue, Cheshire, CT 06410.

[J. C. HUGHES]

CATHOLIC PRESS (U.S.)

This article is a review of periodical and serial publications (on books, see PUBLISHING, CATHOLIC; on issues related to Catholic journalists, see JOURNALISM, CATHOLIC). A periodical is a publication with a distinctive title which appears at regular intervals, generally oftener than once a year. The chief function of a Catholic periodical is to disseminate news about certain aspects of Christianity and the Catholic Church. A broader term, "serial," is applied to any publication issued in successive parts, usually at regular intervals. The latter technical term includes magazines, newspapers, annuals, supplements, e.g. *New Catholic Encyclopedia*, and series, e.g. *Fathers of the Church*. The survey in this article covers: the publishing rationale; periodicals; association organs; professional journals; documentary and bibliographical series; notable annuals; indexing services; and English-language serials from abroad.

Rationale. Catholic periodicals reflect a continuing belief in the value of the written word, a tradition which stretches back to the early days of Christianity when the Apostles felt the compelling impulse to compose the Gospels and Paul of Tarsus the need to pen his Letters to announce the Good News in a format appealing to an ever-widening audience. The justification for the Catholic periodical lies in the basic principle of communication: the right to information as fulfilling a need. Vatican Council II gave new meaning to this right in many ways: radically in describing the Church as the People of God, with a right therefore to mature and informed participation in Church life (cf. *Lumen gentium* 37), and in affirming the principles of collegiality and of shared responsibility and decision making. Explicitly the Council affirmed man's freedom to "search for the truth, voice his mind, and publicize it" and to have access to information about public affairs (*Gaudium et spes* 59; cf. *Inter mirifica* 5); the principle

applies a fortiori within the Church, and is expressed particularly with regard to research and exchange of ideas (*Gaudium et spes* 62). In the U.S. the level of education among Catholics is such that never before has there been a Catholic people so capable of being informed and of weighing options. This educated public needs a mass of organized religious information to stimulate and support its imagination. There is a further factor that motivates the Catholic press. At a time of decline in the number of Church-related schools, editors are dedicated to providing at least a partial solution to this gap in Christian education. Here is a place for magazines that try to present to members of the Church a forum for dialogue in which liberal and conservative, young and old, lay and clergy, can learn what others are thinking and doing. There is also a new conviction that Christian instruction should address adults, not children alone. Church members have been urged since Vatican II to look outward and become involved in relationship with other Christians and in the complex social, economic, and political problems of this age of the "Church in the World." Magazines can play a vital role in disseminating information and in promoting dialogue not only within the Christian community but, also, between it and the secular world. In no area of Christian communication-media has there been a more telling impact than in the widespread development and proliferation of serial publications. Possibly undue publicity, without adequate explanation for their failure, has been given to the demise of such standard publications as *Ave Maria* and the *Sacred Heart Messenger*. It is true that periodicals out of tune with the climate of Vatican II or that relied on blind loyalty for support have disappeared. But the rejuvenation of many serials and the genesis of many others prove that educated persons look to presentation of basics and to the support of sound scholarship. Catholic serials answer this need.

One way of illustrating the effectiveness and diffusion of the Catholic printed media in the United States is the combined circulation-data for Catholic newspapers and magazines in the following table:

TABLE: Circulation for U.S. Catholic Press*

	Number	Circulation per issue
National Newspapers	9	641,421
Diocesan Newspapers	152	5,239,921
Magazines and Journals (English language)	269	20,894,950
Foreign-Language Magazines	29	522,395
TOTALS	459	27,298,687

*Source: *Catholic Press Directory* (1977).

National Newspapers. The diocesan newspaper is uniquely American in that Catholic newspapers in other countries are national both in scope and circulation. There are, however, national Catholic weeklies in the U.S. and a wide range of editorial viewpoints. Thus the popular *National Catholic Reporter* (P.O. Box 281, Kansas City, MO 64141) is a forthright, outspoken, progressive publication that has been controversial since its beginning. Other successful weekly publications present views that extend from moderate—e.g. the *National*

Catholic Register and *Twin Circle* (1901 Avenue of the Stars, Los Angeles, CA 90067), *Our Sunday Visitor,* together with its Spanish edition, *El Visitante Dominical* (Noll Plaza, Huntington, IN 46750)—to right-wing—e.g. *The Wanderer* (128 E. 10th St., St. Paul, MN 55101). It may be noted that the editorial policies of the diocesan newspapers also evince a similar range, matching the views of the local Ordinary and the tenor of church life in each diocese.

Periodicals. Periodicals with a national circulation and influence may be divided into those of general scope and interest, mission publications, and periodicals on the spiritual and devotional life.

General Periodicals. Brilliant laymen are responsible for publishing *Commonweal* (232 Madison Ave., New York, N.Y. 10016) and *The Critic* (180 N. Wabash Ave., Chicago, IL 60601). They display a provocative editorial approach that has earned them wide respect. In the same category must be placed *America* (106 W. 56th St., New York, N.Y. 10016); the *U.S. Catholic* (221 W. Madison St., Chicago, IL 60606); *New Catholic World,* successor (v. 215) in 1972 to the venerable (1865) *Catholic World* (1865 Broadway, New York, NY 10023); *The Sign* (Monastery Place, Union City, NJ 07087); *St. Anthony Messenger* (1615 Republic St., Cincinnati, OH 45210); *Franciscan Herald* (1434 W. 51st St., Chicago, IL 60609); Liguorian (1 Liguori Rd., Liguori, MO 63057); *Catholic Digest* (P.O. Box 3090, St. Paul, MN 55165); and *Columbia,* the official organ of the Knights of Columbus (1 Columbus Plaza, New Haven, CT 06507). Others include: *Anthonian* (Patterson, N.J. 07509); *Bible Today, The* (Collegeville, MN 56321); *Catholic Charismatic* (545 Island Rd., Ramsey, N.J. 97446); *Catholic Forester Magazine* (305 W. Madison St., Chicago, IL 60606); *Catholic Woman's Journal* (3835 Westminster Pl., St. Louis, MO 63108); *Catholic Worker* (36 E. First St., New York, N.Y. 10003); *Christian Renewal News* (890 Hillcrest Dr., Pomona, CA 91768); *Cross Currents* (103 Van Houten Fields, W. Nyack, N.Y. 10994); *Ecumenist, The* (1865 Broadway, New York, N.Y. 10023); *Marriage and Family Living* (St. Meinrad, IND 47577); *Parish Monthly* (Noll Plaza, Huntington, IND 46750); *St. Anthony Messenger* (1615 Republic St., Cincinnati, OH 45210); *St. Joseph's Messenger and Advocate of the Blind* (St. Joseph's Home, P.O. Box 288, Jersey City, N.J. 07303); *Social Justice Review* the oldest Catholic journal devoted to the topic (3835 Westminister Pl., St. Louis, MO 63108).

Mission Periodicals. Impressive circulation statistics suggest that the American public has generously supported a number of mass-mailed mission magazines. This is remarkable in this era when many periodicals are threatened with financial losses. These publications continue to benefit from some kind of subsidy, usually underwritten by a religious order or community whose members volunteer service in the missions. As a result of these subsidies, missionary magazines have flourished and their format and intellectual content have earned the respect of thoughtful readers. Among these are *Catholic Near East Magazine* (1011 First Ave., New York, N.Y. 10022); *Claverite, The* (1821 Orleans Ave., New Orleans, LA 70116); *Columban Mission* (St. Columbans, NE 68056); *Crusader's Almanac, The* (1400 Quincy St. N.E., Washington, D.C. 20017); *Divine Word Missionaries* (Techny, IL 60082); *Educating in Faith* (335 Broadway, New York, N.Y. 10013); *Extension*

(1307 S. Wabash Ave., Chicago, IL 60605); *Jesuit Bulletin* (4511 W. Pine Blvd., St. Louis, MO 63108); *Josephite Harvest, The* (1130 N. Calvert St., Baltimore, MD 21202); *Marianist Missionary Report* (119 Franklin St., Dayton, OH 45402); *Maryknoll Magazine* (Maryknoll, N.Y. 10545); *Medical Mission News* (10 W. 17th St., New York, N.Y. 10011); *Mission* (366 Fifth Ave., New York, N.Y. 10001); *Mission Intercom* (1302 18th St. N.W., Washington, D.C. 20036); *Missionhurst* (4651 N. 25th St., Arlington, VA 22207); *Salesian Missions* (148 Main St., New Rochelle, N.Y. 10802); *Worldmission* (366 5th Ave., New York, N.Y. 10001).

Periodicals on Spirituality. These offer forward-looking appraisal of personal life firmly rooted in traditional spiritual principles. Among such magazines are: *Benedictines* (Mt. St. Scholastica, Atchison, KA 66002); *Blue Army of Our Lady of Fatima* (Ave Maria Institute, Washington, N.J. 07882); *Desert Call* (Spiritual Life Institute of America, Sedona, AZ 86336); *Emmanuel* (194 E. 76 St., New York, N.Y. 10021); *Eucharist* (194 E. 76 St., New York, N.Y. 10021); *Liturgy* (1221 Massachusetts Ave., N.W., Washington, D.C. 20005); *Living Worship* (1221 Massachusetts Ave., N.W., Washington, D.C. 20005); *Marian Helpers Bulletin* (Eden Hill, Stockbridge, MA 01262); *Miraculous Medal* (475 E. Chelten Ave., Philadelphia, PA 19144); *Modern Liturgy* (from 1973–77, *Folk Mass and Modern Liturgy,* Resource Publications, San Jose, CA 95129); *My Daily Visitor* (Noll Plaza, Huntington, IN 46750); *Priest* (Noll Plaza, Huntington, IN 46750); *Spiritual Life* (2131 Lincoln Rd., N.E., Washington, D.C. 20002); and *Soul* (Ave Maria Institute, Washington, N.J. 07882).

Association Publications (Newspapers, Newsletters and Magazines). Among those with a national circulation are: *Agape* (Christian Family Movement/Marriage Encounter); *Brothers Newsletter* (National Assembly of Religious Brothers); *Camillian, The* (National Association of Catholic Chaplains); *CHD Newsletter* (Campaign for Human Development); *Catholic League Newsletter* (Catholic League for Religious and Civil Rights); *Catholic Rural Life* (National Catholic Rural Life Conference); *Catholic Woman* (National Council of Catholic Women); *Charities, USA* (National Conference of Catholic Charities); *Christian Life Communicator* (National Federation of Christian Life Communities); *Christopher News Notes* (The Christophers); *Comment/Media Today* (Christian Communications Apostolate); *Commitment* (National Catholic Conference for Interracial Justice); *Communications* (U.S. Conference of Secular Institutes); *Contemplative Review* (Association of Contemplative Sisters); *Deaf Blind Weekly,* Braille (Xavier Society for the Blind); *In-Formation* (Religious Formation Conference); *Network Quarterly* (Network); *News/Views* (National Sisters Vocation Conference); *People* (National Council of Catholic Laity); *Priests—USA* (National Federation of Priests' Councils); *Probe* (National Assembly of Women Religious); *Process* (Catholic Campus Ministry Association); *Sistersharing* (National Sisters Communication Service).

Professional Journals. The surveys of scholarly journals, biblical and theological, in the *New Catholic Encyclopedia* (2:540; 14:34) do not need radical alteration as far as Catholic publications in the U.S. are concerned. One venerable journal has suspended publication, *The American Ecclesiastical Review* (v. 1–169, 1889–1975). Another regrettable loss is *Liturgical Arts*

(v. 1–40, 1931–72). *Continuum* ended publication in 1970 (v. 1–8, 1963–70). The following is a representative list: *American Benedictine Review* (1950–); *American Catholic Philosophical Association, Proceedings* (1926–); *Americas, The* (Academy of American-Franciscan History 1944–); *Anthropological Quarterly* (Catholic Anthropological Conference, 1928–50, v. 1–25; n.s. v. 26, 1953); *Bulletin of Medieval Canon Law* (v. 1, 1971, superseded *Institute of Medieval Canon Law Bulletin*, v. 1–16, 1955–70); *Bulletin of the National Guild of Catholic Psychiatrists* (1953–); *Canon Law Society of America, Proceedings* (1969–, formerly in the *Jurist*); *Catechist, The* (1967–); *Catholic Biblical Quarterly* (1939–); *Catholic Historical Review* (1916–); *Catholic Journalist, The* (Catholic Press Association of the U.S., 1949–); *Catholic Lawyer* (1955–); *Catholic Library World* (1929–); *Catholic Mind, The* (1903–); *Catholic Theological Society of America, Proceedings* (1946–); *Chicago Studies* (1962–); *Classical Bulletin* (St. Louis University, 1925–); *Classical Folia* (Catholic Classical Association, 1946–); *Counseling and Values* (v. 16, 1971–; continues *National Catholic Guidance Conference Journal*, v. 1–15, 1956–71); *Homiletic and Pastoral Review* (1900–); *Horizons* (Journal of the College Theological Society; 1974–); *Hospital Progress* (Catholic Hospital Association, 1920–); *Jurist, The* (1941–); *Linacre Quarterly* (Federation of Catholic Physicians Guilds; 1932–); *Listening; Journal of Religion and Culture* (1966–); *Living Light. An Interdisciplinary Review of Christian Education* (1964–); *Modern Schoolman* (1925–); *New Scholasticism* (1927–); *Pastoral Music* (National Association of Pastoral Musicians; 1976–); *Religion Teachers' Journal* (1967–); *Renascence* (Catholic Renascence Society; 1948–); *Review for Religious* (1942; v. 30–33, 1970–74 contain an exhaustive series, "Subject Bibliography for Religious"); *Review of Politics* (1939–); *Review of Social Economy* (Association for Social Economy, formerly Catholic Economics Association; 1942–); *Social Thought* (National Conference of Catholic Charities; 1976–); *Sociological Analysis: A Journal in the Sociology of Religion* (Association for the Sociology of Religion, formerly the Catholic Sociological Society; 1964–); *Spirituality Today* to v. 30, 1978, *Cross and Crown*): *Theological Studies* (1940–); *Theology Digest* (1953–); *Thomist* (1939–); *Thought* (1926–); *Today's Catholic Teacher* (1967–); *Worship* (1951–, superseded *Orate Fratres*, v. 1–25, 1926–51).

Documentary and Bibliographical Publications. Vatican II and its aftermath have created a greater need than ever for collections of documentation. In the U.S. that need has been outstandingly served since its inception on May 24, 1971 by *Origins* (National Catholic News Service, 1312 Massachusetts Ave. NW, Washington, D.C. 20005), published 48 times a year and containing official church documents, reports on significant addresses, news. *The Pope Speaks* (1954–) continues, published since 1975 by Our Sunday Visitor Press. A less formal but very informative resource is CRUX of the News (continuous since 1967); there are also irregular special issues, *CRUX Resources* and *CRUX Specials*. The *Canon Law Digest* (1937–) continues, Vol. 7 covering legislation to 1972 and edited now by J. I. O'Connor alone; current cumulative supplements extend to 1977. The *Jurist* and the *Review for Religious* also carry significant Roman documents on Canon Law. Specialized documentation is provided by the BCL *Newsletter*, which

in 1973 succeeded the bulletin of the Bishops Committee on the Liturgical Apostolate. (Index to 1974, R. F. Hagburn, San Francisco 1974). The Bishops' Committee for Ecumenical and Interreligious Affairs (BCEIA) has issued a *Newsletter* since 1972. Since 1973 the International Commission on English in the Liturgy *Newsletter* has announced the progress of revision and translation of liturgical books. Bibliographical documentation (in addition to the *Catholic Periodical and Literature Index*) is provided by *Religious Book Review* (1973–; successor to *Religious Book Guide*, v. 1–3, 1970–72).

Notable Annuals. The *Annuario Pontificio* comes out in an annual edition from Vatican City and has statistics for each diocese, including churches, chapels, parishes, hospitals, diocesan priests, theology and philosophy programs, number of newly ordained priests of the preceding year, number of professed religious men and women, number of areas of diocesan territories presented in square kilometers and the number of Catholics. The publication of these statistics is the greatest advance for the accumulation of universal church data. It is also a worldwide church telephone directory. Since 1972, the Central Statistics Office of the Church, an agency of the papal Secretariat of State, has issued a *Statistical Yearbook of the Church* (*Annuarium statisticum Ecclesiae*) which offers principal statistics about the presence and manifold activities of the Church throughout the world. The material is printed in three corresponding columns, Latin, French, and English. *Activities of the Holy See* (*Attività della Santa Sede*) is a yearly report, begun in 1941 and devoted to papal events, the pope's day-to-day work, audiences, messages on special occasions, meetings with diplomats, and conferences with heads of state. It also provides annual reports of various administrative divisions within the Roman Curia. The *Catholic Almanac* is an annual publication containing a wealth of useful facts and statistical data pertaining to the Church and its related organizations. The *Official Catholic Directory* encompasses a list of names of church leaders, bishops, priests, organizations, parishes, and dioceses throughout the United States. Women engaged in the Church's ministries have for some time tried to have their names listed in the *Directory* but without success.

Indexing Service. A major factor in the growing influence of periodicals is the production of a systematic list of ideas, persons, and places mentioned in some 130 serials, a compilation known as the *Catholic Periodical and Literature Index* (461 W. Lancaster Ave., Haverford, PA 19041), pointing out their locations in collected volumes, usually by year and page number. It is notably strong in its coverage of works on the Bible, church history, and general religion. Motion pictures and drama reviews are listed; there is a selection of Catholic-interest books, and a special section listing book reviews. Not least in the value of the Index is its indexing of official Catholic documents, papal curial, and diocesan, together with commentaries. The Catholic Library Association sponsors this indispensable tool.

Foreign Publications in English. Noted here are those that have special interest and circulation in the U.S. since Vatican Council II. In the newspaper category an English edition of *L'Osservatore Romano*, semi-official newspaper of the Holy See, was begun with the April 4, 1968 issue. It is an important source of documentation as well as feature pieces on current issues. Two reviews began supplements on the spiritual life that are widely read in the United States. *The Doctrine and Life Supplement* (Dublin) dates from 1961 and is devoted to articles for women religious and their spiritual directors. *The Way-Supplement* (London), begun in 1966, is devoted to special themes on the spiritual life and includes documentation sections. *The Month* (London, v. 1–186, 1864–1945, n.s. 1–45, 1949–1969) began a new series in 1970; devoted to current interest topics, it absorbed the *Dublin Review* in 1967 and the widely-circulated *Herder Correspondence* in 1970. An influential ecumenical review is *One in Christ* (v. 1, 1965) which continued the *Eastern Churches Quarterly*, from Ramsgate Abbey, England. The important catechetical center, East Asia Pastoral Institute, has published the quarterly, *Teaching All Nations*, from Manila since 1964. Another catechetical quarterly is *Lumen Vitae* published in Brussels by the International Center for Studies in Religious Education; the English edition dates from 1950. From Canada, *Studia Canonica*, begun in 1967 by the faculty of Canon Law, University of St. Paul, Ottawa, is a semiannual that is an outstanding journal on canonical studies. The English edition of *International Catholic Review* (*Internazionale Katholische Zeitschrift Communio*) was superseded by the American edition of *Communio* (1974–). The Secretariat for Promoting Christian Unity has issued *Information Service* since 1967 and the Secretariat for Non-Christians a *Bulletin* since 1966. The organ of the Pontifical Commission for the Revision of the Code of Canon Law is *Communicationes* (from 1969); that of the Commission for the Revision of the Code of Oriental Canon Law is *Nuntia* (from 1973). The Congregation for Religion and Secular Institutes publishes *Informationes SCRIS*, the English version of which, *Consecrated Life*, is published by the Institute on Religious Life (Daughters of St. Paul, Boston, Mass.). *Notitiae*, is a multilingual monthly, (v. 1, 1965) begun by the Consilium for the Implementation of the Constitution on the Sacred Liturgy and now published by the Congregation for the Sacraments and Divine Worship. *Seminarium*, begun in 1950, is now under the Congregation for Catholic Education and is particularly devoted to implementing Vatican II's Decree on Priestly Formation. An important post-Vatican II serial was *Concilium*, which began in 1965; its continuation is *Concilium: Religion in the Seventies*, begun in 1978 by the Seabury Press. In the area of documentation the English edition of *Pro Mundi Vita* on religious sociology first appeared in 1964 from the Pro Mundi Vita Center in Brussels; there is also a Pro Mundi Vita-dossier series issued irregularly on special themes. IDOC (International Documentation on the Contemporary Church) has an English language *I-Doc Bulletin* (1960), *I-Doc Catalogue of Documents* (1970), and I-Doc dossiers; the IDOC publications are the bane of cataloguers. A massive, computerized documentary-serial is *RIC*, the acronym for the Bibliographical *Repository of Christian Institutions*, from the Center of Research and Documentation on Christian Institutions (CERDIC), Faculty of Human Sciences at the University of Strasbourg. The first volume of the county-by-county bibliographical catalogue appeared in 1968; *RIC Supplements* concentrating on bibliography for specific themes began appearing for 1971–72. The Institut Bibliographique de Liturgie. Abbey of Mont-César, Louvain, since 1965 has provided an immense service to liturgical researchers,

its *Fichier bibliographique de liturgie*. This is a comprehensive bibliography, issued in card form, on 20th-century liturgical literature, including texts and periodical articles. Supplements are issued monthly. In the U.S. the *Fichier* is received by the libraries of The Catholic University of America, St. John's Abbey, Collegeville, Minn., and the University of Notre Dame.

[R. A. BURKE]

CATHOLIC RELIEF SERVICES

Catholic Relief Services—United States Catholic Conference, is the overseas relief and development agency of the American Catholic community (3:328). Organized in 1943, it has continually served the needy and deprived in other lands without regard to race, creed or color. It now operates in over 80 developing countries of the world. The basic motivation underlying the founding and continuance of Catholic Relief Services was, and is, Christian compassion for the poor. CRS programs are intended as a living expression of the love of one human for another out of love for God. Their implementation seeks: to demonstrate our Christian concern and obligation to respond to the human needs of the poor and suffering in other countries; to render assistance to impoverished people that meets their immediate needs; to support creatively self-determined community activities of people struggling to eradicate the root causes of their poverty; to collaborate with groups of good will in programs contributing to a just society in which all may freely participate—within the framework of Catholic social doctrine; to sensitize the people of the United States to their moral obligation to alleviate human suffering, to address its causes, and to further social justice.

In its ever increasing Self-Help Development Program, deliberate, planned efforts are made with developing individuals and communities overseas to eliminate the causes of poverty, hunger and disease, and produce tangible evidence of increased socio-economic participation, including enhancement of their human dignity.

[E. B. BRODERICK]

CATHOLIC THEOLOGICAL SOCIETY OF AMERICA

The Catholic Theological Society of America (CTSA) dates from 1946. Its purpose, within the context of the Roman Catholic tradition, is to promote studies and research in theology, to relate theological science to current problems, and to foster a more effective theological education, by providing a forum for an exchange of views among theologians and with scholars in other disciplines. The CTSA seeks to achieve its purpose chiefly through its annual convention in early June and through the publication of the convention *Proceedings* (ProcCTSA). It also publishes, either in the *Proceedings* or separately, various reports of research teams set up and funded by the Society. Also, each year the CTSA presents an award to some theologian for outstanding achievement in theology; originally called the Cardinal Spellman Award, it is now called the John Courtney Murray Award.

In keeping with the change and renewal occurring in the Church as a result of Vatican Council II, CTSA has also experienced change and renewal in its own activity and in its ministry to the Church. In the early 1970s the CTSA revised its Constitution. The requirements for membership were raised so that ordinarily the doctorate in the sacred sciences is required for active membership and the completion of doctoral course work is required for associate membership. At the same time during the years since Vatican II CTSA membership has increased and broadened to include a number of non-Catholic theologians, a growing number of women and lay persons, and a greater number of graduates from European and non-Catholic universities. In recent years a layman and several women religious have served on the board of directors. A religious brother and a woman religious have served as vice-president and president.

Another change in the life of CTSA concerns the format of the annual convention. The convention is now structured around some general theme bearing on theology itself and its relation to other disciplines and current problems. Besides several general sessions addressing the convention theme there are a number of smaller workshops relating the general theme to particular areas of interest, continuing seminars in certain areas promoting more effectively an ongoing exchange of views among scholars. Some of the general convention themes in the last few years have been: Catholic Theology in Social and Political Context (1975); The Divine and the Human in Christianity (1976); Theology and the Study of Religion (1977); Voices of the Church (1978).

During the past few years, especially, a number of research teams have been established by the CTSA board of directors, either on its own initiative or at the request of the members or of the American bishops. These research teams have studied the following topics: Hospital Ethics, Pastoral Activity for the Divorced and Remarried, the *Bilateral Consultations in the United States (a second research team has been commissioned to update this study), Renewal of the Sacrament of Penance, Human Sexuality, and the Status of Women in the Church. The final reports of these research teams are submitted to the board of directors, which then decides whether or not to publish the reports. The reports of the research teams mentioned just above have all been published. As stated most clearly in the foreword to the book *Human Sexuality* (the final report of the research team set up by the CTSA), the acceptance for publication of such reports does not mean that the board of directors or the members of the CTSA either approve or disapprove of the contents of the reports. It simply means that publication of these reports is judged useful for promoting continuing study and discussion on the part of the members of the CTSA and of the larger scholarly community.

A final feature of change and renewal in the life of the CTSA can be seen in its association and cooperation with other scholarly societies and groups. The CTSA is a member of the Council on the Study of Religion. Its 1972 convention was held in conjunction with the International Congress of Learned Societies in the Field of Religion. The CTSA has also collaborated with various scholarly groups such as the Canon Law Society of America and with various committees set up by the American bishops.

In all these ways the CTSA seeks to renew and revitalize itself in order to achieve its purpose in the service of the Church.

[E. H. KONERMAN]

CATHOLICISM, CULTURAL

The ideology of "newness" has often distorted our way of seeing America. It leads us to imagine that each human individual is a *tabula rasa* on which the New World was immediately impressed and falsely suggests that the Old World had no residual force. If this were true, then in two or three generations each individual would be like any other, interchangeable, each equally formed and shaped by the New World environment. But the thousand years of cultural tutelage that preceded the arrival of the immigrants in America have not been totally erased. If they had, the effects of slavery would have vanished in a generation; the experience of being Jewish would have lost all force on the educational, political, and cultural careers of individuals; each generation of Catholics—Hispanic, Eastern European, Irish, German and the rest—would be neutral with respect to Catholic cultures; and Calvinism and Puritanism would demonstrate no lasting force. The truth is that the cultures of the past retain a powerful inward, spiritual, imagistic force upon behavior of individuals today.

The Cultural Catholic. Tutelage under one or another Catholic culture has been felt by nearly one out of every three Americans. The official figure of membership in the Catholic Church is 50 million, or nearly one out of every four Americans. One may safely estimate that there are at least another 20 million who, although now unchurched or in some other Church, descend from families shaped by Catholic cultures in the past. Thus, besides the essentially religious concepts of "believing" and "practising Catholics," there is also the important concept "cultural Catholic."

There are, as Christopher Dawson pointed out, many historical variants of Catholic culture, each only analogously related to the others. Yet, just as clearly, there are distinctive features of Catholic cultures sufficient to distinguish them, even in the lives of individuals who may be unaware of the differences, from the features of other cultures. In the panorama of world religions, not all religions value history as Catholicism does; see the world as sacramental; give salvific force to the body and its resurrection; hold to the essential graciousness of nature, while recognizing its wounds; value intellect and theology as appropriate instruments of, and protections for, religious faith; maintain historical and institutional forms of worship and administration; have a strong sense of the value of community, within which the rights of persons are given a nonindividualistic content; maintain a strong tension between religious authority and individual conscience. A Catholic culture (even for those who live within it while not themselves being Catholic) does not have the same shape, spirit, emphases, or symbolic forms as a Calvinist, a Jewish, a Buddhist, or a Hindu culture.

The specific and distinctive aspects of Catholic cultures in the U.S. have been too little studied. For one thing, the host culture of the U.S. is both predominantly Protestant and Protestant in a novel way. Thus scholars have had to extend themselves simply to grasp the uniqueness of American Protestantism. They have barely, as yet, directed their attention to American Catholicism and American Judaism. Moreover, until quite recently, there does not appear to have been a sufficient mass of artists, intellectuals, and scholars who are Catholic to bring American Catholicism to full and articulate self-consciousness. Nor have American scholars or artists paid proportionate attention to the impact of Catholic cultures upon the common culture of the United States.

Impact in the U.S. A fuller and deeper study of Catholic culture in America might well become one of the fields of keenest intellectual investigation in the near future; the process has clearly begun. One reason is that Catholics play so central and critical a role in the shaping of the nation's politics. Catholics are numerous, are selectively concentrated in key states, and rank relatively high in voter participation. The great Democratic majorities amassed in support of liberal legislation since 1932 have been anchored in large Catholic majorities in key urban centers in Northern industrial states. Irish Catholics, in particular, have been disproportionately successful in politics.

To an extent heretofore too little studied, big city "machines," labor unions, and, in general, a major portion of the "progressive" politics of the last fifty years have been built, in part, upon a distinctively Catholic form of populism. Catholic urban populism is quite different from that of rural areas, whether in the South or in the Midwest. In general, the scholarly and intellectual elites charged with analyzing and describing the course of American politics have been only partly sympathetic to and often quite undiscerning about Catholic populism. "The Reformers" have often shown little comprehension of the quite different political culture of "the Regulators." A firm grasp of reality demands more exact sociological, political, and literary analyses of the Catholic cultures of America.

Although his figures are admittedly somewhat uncertain, Harold Abramson has estimated that the 50 million Catholics reported in official figures break down culturally into a configuration something like the following:

TABLE 1: Estimated Size of Catholic Ethnic Groups in the United States*

Italians	10,000,000
Irish	8,300,000
Germans	7,600,000
Poles	5,300,000
French-Canadians	5,000,000
Eastern Europeans	3,600,000
Spanish-speaking	3,500,000
English	1,500,000
Lithuanians	1,300,000
Scandinavians	200,000
Others	1,500,000
Total	47,800,000

*Abramson 19 (see bibliog.); based on 1970 estimated total Catholic population in the United States.

In political circles, the figure for Hispanic-Americans is conventionally given as 11 million, a figure considerably higher than Abramson's. Some of his other figures may also be disputed. But his thoughtful estimates do show the relatively equal proportions of the Catholic population in several key cultural groupings—Eastern European, Italian, Irish, and Hispanic—and the strong representation of German and French Catholics. These distributions suggest a mental picture somewhat different from the usual off-hand expectations.

Yet it is not so much the differences *within* the Catholic people that are, initially at least, of most significant import. So great has been the emphasis in recent generations upon the "Americanization" of Catholics, upon their assimilation into American life, that relatively little attention has been paid to their *differences from* the American norm, their distinctiveness, the extent to which America has been changed by assimilating new materials *from them*. It is even possible that the real contributions of American Catholics to the common American patrimony—their original impact upon the shape and power of "the sacred canopy" defining American reality, so to speak—is only just beginning. One reason why this might be so is that the number of American Catholics able fully to exploit American opportunities in the furtherance of their talents is only in the present generation reaching something like a proportionate distribution among the nation's elites: in literature and the academy, in cinema and the mass media, in political practise and theory, in corporations, and in some, at least, of the philanthropic foundations.

It would probably be an error to look for Catholic contributions solely, or even mainly, in strictly ecclesiastical or theological fields. Many original contributions have been *cultural*—affecting the symbolic forms through which the society understands itself, observes its proper rituals, and conducts its ordinary business. Catholics in politics, for example, seem more willing to speak openly about power and "clout" than do their more moralizing peers. Since politics is mainly about the distribution of power and money, this gain in public discourse about politics represents a contribution to the nation's realism and maturation. ("When a fella says, Tain't the money, it's the principle," Mr. Dooley wisely observed, "It's the money.") Irish novels, from James T. Farrell's *Studs Lonigan* to Edwin O'Connor's *Last Hurrah*, represent a horizon, sense of reality, and narrative form quite different from those of Jewish novels or New England-Protestant novels. The working-class liberalism of many Catholics seems to be quite different from the liberalism of American Jews and Protestants. In religious history, the spirituality of the ordinary Catholic parish—its vision of God, of the individual, the world, and the community—appears to be quite different from the spirituality of either mainline or evangelical Protestants. Catholic attitudes toward sex seem to be distinctive, not always in stereotypical ways. All these are matters deserving of clearer analysis than any now available in religio-sociological literature.

Present and Future Significance. The sociocultural shape of American life over the next thirty years is likely to be very much affected by what happens to such "mediating" institutions of daily life as the family, the neighborhood, the Churches, labor unions, schools, and voluntary associations of every sort. Over the past forty years, both the State and the larger public society have usurped more and more of the functions of the mediating institutions. Our lives, and those of our children, are far more invaded by public messages projected into every nook and cranny of the soul by the mass media. They have less and less space for privacy, intimacy, and inwardness than has ever been the case in human life before the age of technology. (Often it is this invasion which is spoken of, quite inaccurately, as "secularization.")

In these new realms of political-cultural discourse, those shaped by Catholic traditions should, at last, be able to speak with exact relevance. Walter Ong, SJ and Marshall McLuhan have explicitly drawn on Catholic traditions in their interpretations of the distinctive postmodern sensibility. The "new" language of myth and symbol, of the heart and the tacit meaning, of ritual and contemplation, has once again made ancient categories relevant. Even the postmodern sense of limits and environmental "laws" has brought back a climate in which the concept of natural law may have a renaissance.

Catholic cultures have traditionally been neither so individualistic as English Protestantism, nor so oriented toward the benevolent State as modern liberalism. Catholic traditions have normally relied for their sustenance upon those mediating institutions (especially the family) that stand between the lonely individual and the State. In such mediating communities individual Catholics have felt most at home, both theoretically and in practice. In them, Catholic intellectual and symbolic life has found its most familiar social bases. Here Catholics might be expected to make their most distinctive and articulate intellectual contributions to social theory.

As members of an international people, a people distributed through several historical eras, those Catholics who become intellectually aware of their identity may also be expected to make certain key contributions to the building up of a new understanding of world pluralism. They are already living out a form of unity across cultural boundaries and historical eras. They might therefore be expected, almost instinctively, to find symbolic forms and concepts that help to define new methods of "passing over" from one cultural context to another, for the sake of practical cooperation and more exact understanding.

The American Catholic community carries within it the largest and most highly trained intellectual and artistic elite of any branch of the Catholic people in history. Whether this new class of Catholics meets its full intellectual and practical responsibilities for the building of a new world order, the reconstruction of society within the United States, and a new creative synthesis of the Catholic spirit and the symbolic forms of American life, is a challenge against which future historians may properly take its measure. The time is auspicious. The possibilities of creativity are many. Yet there is room for many fears and many doubts whether, either in vision or in grace, there are sufficient numbers to do well all that remains to be done.

Bibliography: H. J. ABRAMSON, *Ethnic Diversity in Catholic America* (New York 1973). J. BARTON, *Peasants and Strangers: Italians, Rumanians, and Slovaks in an American City* (Cambridge, Mass. 1975). P. BERGER and R. NEUHAUS, *Empower People: The Role of Mediating Structures in Public Policy* (Washington, D.C. 1977). J. BODNAR, *Immigration and Industrialization: Ethnicity in an American Mill Town, 1870–1940* (Pittsburgh 1977). J. M. CUDDIHY, *No Offence: Civil Religion and Protestant Taste* (New York 1978). J. P. DOLAN, *The Immigrant Church—New York's Irish and German Catholics, 1815–1865* (Baltimore 1975); *Catholic Revivalism: The American Experience* (Notre Dame, Ind. 1978). A. GREELEY, *Ethnicity in the United States: A Preliminary Reconnaissance* (New York 1974); *The American Catholic: A Social Portrait* (New York 1977). V. GREENE, *Slavic Community on Strike* (Notre Dame, Ind. 1968); *For God and Country: The Rise of Polish and Lithuanian Ethnic Consciousness in the United States* (Madison, Wis. 1975). R. F. HAMILTON, *Restraining Myths: Critical Studies of United States Social Structures and Politics* (New York 1975). R. VECOLI et al., eds., *The Other Catholics* (New York forthcoming [1978]).

[M. NOVAK]

CATHOLICITY

From its very beginning in Abraham (Gn 12.3 with Sir 44.21 [LXX] and the NT passim) the Judeo-Christian tradition has understood itself to have a universal or catholic dimension. Since there is but one God, and this one God's very being is to be a gift-giver, the extent of his *philanthropia* (Ti 3.4) must be universal, extending from the original gift of the creation of the entire world (Gn ch. 1–2) to the even greater abundance of the redemption (Rom 5.12–21), the new creation in Christ (2 Cor 5.16) and in the Holy Spirit who, as the "other Paraclete" (Jn 14.16) and "the power from on high" (Lk 24.49), reveals the incomprehensibility of the divine being in itself and in its relationship to the world (Jn 3.8 with Rom 11.33–36).

If the very being of God, inwardly and outwardly, is catholic, then the theandric revelation and communication of his being with the world must also be catholic. Hence, Jesus, the original and primal Sacrament of God in the nongodly being of creation, is also necessarily catholic (which prompts theologians to designate him both the *concretum universale* and the *universale concretum*). In its own way, then, the Church, which is the Sacrament of Christ who is the Sacrament of God, must also be catholic.

History. Indeed, this term has had a privileged status in Christian theology, although it appears in neither the LXX nor the NT. Apparently Ignatius of Antioch is the first (*c.* 110) to use it to designate the Church (in *Smyr.* 8.2). Extremely worthy of note is that for him catholicity emphasizes not only quantitative extension (totality, universality), but also qualitative integrity (truth, genuineness, orthodoxy). Later Church Fathers continue this same double signification, so that the Church cannot be a small, separatist, sectarian conventicle, but must necessarily be a universal convocation and congregation of all the faithful from the four ends of the earth. This understanding peaks in St. Augustine, who never tires of contrasting the *pars Donati* with the *Catholica* (with which term as a substantive he designates the true Church 240 times in his writings between 388–430).

This same insight continues throughout the Middle Ages, especially under the rubric of the *fides catholica*, which is characterized by universal validity (orthodoxy) and universal propagation. Indeed, in its roots the Church is already catholic before it has even begun to spread geographically. Nominalism and Reformation polemics undo this twofold signification of catholic, so that it becomes an almost exclusively geographical and sociological term. This trend was intensified by the Protestant tendency to emphasize purity and by the Roman Catholic tendency to emphasize universality; there remains, therefore, the ecclesial and theological separation of what had originally been an organic unity (3:338; 339).

Lumen gentium. Against this background can best be appreciated the special ecumenical significance of Vatican Council II's Constitution on the Church in the statement: "This Church [Christ's] . . . subsists in the Catholic Church, which is governed by the successor of Peter and by the bishops . . ." (*Lumen gentium* 8). The history of the evolution and final formulation of this text heightens its significance. To be especially noted is that the Church of Christ is not simply and absolutely identified with the Roman Catholic Church. Although an earlier draft had used "is," the final text uses "subsists." The theological commission also rejected *integro modo* and *iure divino* as modifiers of *subsistit*. Furthermore, the Church of Christ is identified not as the "Roman" but simply as the "Catholic Church," and the Pope is identified as the "Successor of Peter," not as the *Romanus Pontifex*, as in the earlier, 1963 text.

Ecclesiology and Ecumenism. The import of such distinctions for theology and ecumenical dialogue is clear. First, the local Roman Church is neither equated nor confused with the Western Patriarchate nor the Church Universal; this is of special value for Eastern Christians and Churches. Second, "Churchness" is not restricted to the Roman Catholic Church; this is of special value with reference to Orthodox, Anglican, and Protestant Churches. Both points are of as yet completely unappreciated value for the theology of the local Church (see CHURCH LOCAL, [THEOLOGY]). Thus, by a strange and circuitous path, the original significance of catholicity (universality and truth) has been at least seminally evoked by the condition of the divided and thus compromised *catholica* and by the demands of the ecumenical desire. If catholic means both universal and true, then wherever some, at least, of the true is present, there must also be present at least some of the universal. The present status of the one Church and the many Churches need, then, no longer be primarily considered as the guilty product of human hubris, the disorderly chaos engendered by every sin from Adam and Eve until the present. Rather, the present status can be considered as the deficient ecclesial realization of that divine and theandric *communio* in God and Christ, whereby the one and the many, unity and diversity are shown to be not conflictive, but congenial. Thus, true unity, orthodoxy, and catholicity are possible only mutually.

For Churches other than the Roman Catholic, the force of catholicity entails a serious effort to surpass traditional sectarian tendencies, ecclesially as well as theologically. Of special note here is the *sola* syndrome, which deserves scriptural, theological, and psychological reexamination. For the Roman Catholic Church, whose very name expresses a special claim to be the *Catholica*, this likewise entails serious reform. First of all, the reform means moderation of excessive Romanist and papalist centralism and domination. The Petrine Office needs to mirror more effectively the Petrine Service, that of a corroborating brother (Lk 22.32), not of a dictating lord (1 Pt 5.3). Thus would be realized that most precious of all papal titles, *Servus Servorum Dei*. Furthermore, the ill-fated practice of excommunication, whose ecclesio-political use has caused such grief to the Church-communion, will be simply relinquished. Above all, this Roman Catholic Church, whose very title is a boast of unity in diversity and diversity in unity as well as a proclamation of the compatibility of the local and universal Church, will constantly remind itself of that *et–et*, which, in contrast to the multiform *sola* of other traditions, is its most precious note and mark. For Christians a truly catholic attitude would allow the ecumenical movement to mature, not in the return of the separated Churches to the Roman Catholic Church, but in the return of all the currently separated brothers and their Churches to the One, Holy, Catholic, and Apostolic Church.

See also INCORPORATION INTO THE CHURCH.

Bibliography: W. STÄHLIN, *Allein. Recht und Gefahr einer polemischen Formel* (Stuttgart 1950). Y. CONGAR, *After Nine Hundred Years* (New York 1959); *Dialogue Between Christians* (London 1966); *Vraie et fausse réforme dans l'Église* (2d ed., Paris 1969). H. VOLK, *Gott Alles in Allen* (Mainz 1961). H. ASMUSSEN et al., *The Unfinished Reformation* (Notre Dame 1961). P. ALTHAUS, "Sola Fide Numquam Sola," *Una Sancta* (1961) 227–235. J. MEYENDORFF, *Orthodoxy and Catholicity* (New York 1966). J. PELIKAN, *The Emergence of the Catholic Tradition* (Chicago 1971). R. EVANS, *One and Holy* (London 1972). H. URS VON BALTHASAR, *Katholisch* (Einsiedeln 1975). K. RAHNER, *Grundkurs des Glaubens* (Freiburg 1976).

[R. KRESS]

CATHOLICS UNITED FOR THE FAITH

Catholics United for the Faith Inc. (CUF) is an independent association of lay Catholics founded in response to what Vatican Council II styled the universal vocation to holiness. "All of Christ's followers . . . are invited and bound to pursue holiness," the Council declared (*Lumen gentium* 42). This means also the laity are called to further the renewal called for by the Council, which Pope Paul VI has termed an inner, personal, moral renewal. Fundamentally, CUF provides an organized framework for the laity to pursue this authentic renewal.

CUF came into being in 1968 as a direct and immediate result of the cry of Paul VI on Sept. 26 of that year: "Where is the love for the Church?" One of the conscious purposes of CUF President H. Lyman Stebbins in organizing this new lay association was to provide a rallying point and focus for all of the laity who wanted to respond in a concrete way to this appeal of the Pope. Within the first ten years of its existence, CUF had attracted more than 13,000 members from every state of the United States, every province of Canada, and even some members from abroad. Since another one of CUF's purposes is to be a united group in each locality striving to defend Catholic doctrine and morals in accordance with the magisterium, many (but not all) CUF members are organized into more than 110 local chapters throughout the U.S., 8 in Canada, and one in Australia.

In addition to prayer and personal renewal, CUF members have been consistently concerned with such topics as Catholic education, cathechetics, and liturgy and the organization has also issued a number of publications on these and similar topics. A monthly Newsletter is sent free of charge to members and contains, in addition to news of the activities of the chapters, topical articles on the Church and subjects of current interest to Catholics. Administrative offices are at 222 North Ave., New Rochelle, N.Y. 10801; associate membership is available gratis to priests and religious, and these associate members also receive the monthly CUF Newsletter.

[K. D. WHITEHEAD]

CELEBRATION AND LITURGY

When the word "celebration" first acquired widespread application to liturgical services at the time of Vatican Council II, the apparent intention was an emphasis on liturgy as a communal endeavor, requiring the active participation of the entire congregation, and as festive in character. No longer were the faithful to regard themselves as mere passive recipients of grace, nor were they to consider the Sacraments as operating in an impersonal, quasi-mechanical fashion. Since the Council scholars have considerably enriched the understanding of celebration by relating it to language, ritual, symbol, leisure, play, and contemplation—thus making it a central concept in a still evolving pastoral theology of worship.

Celebration is neither self-generated nor self-subsisting. It is called forth by birth, puberty, marriage, promotion, leave-taking, homecoming, victory, recovery from illness, death, and other such events of transition. All these occurrences produce critical dislocations in the time and space of ordinary daily life. They separate people from the safe boundaries of their individual routines, roles, and incumbencies, and expose them to the fearful yet fascinating realm of mystery. In this uncontrollable realm people are deprived of any ground of their own on which to stand. Nevertheless they do not fall, for by yielding to the mystery they are upheld and held together by the power and love of One who is revealed therein. This Other has become their sure and common ground. In this way humans are able to discover and affirm the deepest truth about themselves as persons: that by becoming vulnerable they are made strong, by surrender they are set free, by dying they are brought to life; and that their strength, freedom, and life do not come from them but from One who transcends them. This experience of the gift of life at the powerful moment of its being creatively given is what moves people to celebrate.

The festal activity of human beings at celebration, then, is nothing less than the symbol in which the innermost reality of creation is disclosed, made present, accepted, and praised. Through it the world is brought forth afresh and shown to be what it is: the revelation of One who transcends the world, but who is present to it as its ground. Only in relationship to him do all things find their meaning, significance, and truth.

Because celebration expresses relationship and meaning, it may be called language—even the highest language—for it alone communicates the truth of creation and enables it to be shared. As an expression of ultimate meaning it necessarily assumes a definite form, structure, or pattern. In other words it is a ritual act. Celebration supposes that the participants have been lifted beyond themselves by their surrender to the One who transcends them. Thus their words and deeds are not their own, but are signs of the presence and power of the One to whom they have surrendered. Celebration, therefore, is founded on self-effacement and self-transcendence. It is only degraded by self-aggrandizing expression.

Christians proclaim that God's act of raising Jesus from the dead by the power of his Spirit is the event wherein life is fully given. Through faith and Baptism they join Jesus in his death and are raised to creatively new life by the same Spirit who raised Jesus. This is the life which they gather together to celebrate and so make present in the liturgy. Liturgical celebration, therefore, is a form of symbolic action through which God reveals and accomplishes the paschal mystery in the Church and through which the Church expresses and actualizes its surrender to that mystery, thereby being constituted as the Creation of God, the Body of Christ, and the Fullness of the Holy Spirit.

Bibliography: R. GRAINGER, *The Language of the Rite* (London 1974). R. E. NEALE, *In Praise of Play: Towards a Psychology of Religion* (New York 1969). J. PIEPER, *In Tune With the World: A Theory of Festivity*, tr. R. and C. WINSTON (Chicago 1965). P. REGAN, "Liturgy and the Experience of Celebration," *Worship* 47 (1973) 592–600; "Pneumatological and Eschatological Aspects of Liturgical Celebration," *Worship* 51 (1977) 332–350. V. TURNER, "Passages, Margins, and Poverty: Religious Symbols of *Communitas*," *Worship* 46 (1972) 390–412; 482–494.

[P. REGAN]

CELIBACY (RITE OF COMMITMENT)

Among the rites of the revised Roman *Pontifical as revised after Vatican Council II there is a special rite of

"Commitment to Celibacy" *within the liturgy of ordination for deacons.* After the homily of the ordination Mass, those to become deacons are presented to the bishop, who instructs them on the duties of this ministry and asks them to declare before God and the assembled people their intention to observe celibacy permanently "for the sake of the kingdom." The rite emphasizes the choice of celibacy as an incentive toward pastoral charity and service, rather than as an ascetical ideal associated with notions of ritual or cultic purity. Mandated explicitly by the motu proprio *Ad pascendum* (Aug. 15, 1972; ActApS 64 [1972] 534–540), which laid down norms for the order of deacon in the Latin Church, this brief rite of public commitment is required of all candidates for the office (including members of religious communities), with the obvious exception of married men who are being ordained to the permanent diaconate. Since Jan. 1, 1973, therefore, the requirement of clerical celibacy is no longer attached to the subdiaconate, an office suppressed by the motu proprio of the same date, *Ministeria quaedam* (ibid. 529–534). The rite of commitment to celibacy in the liturgy of diaconal ordination should not be confused with the "Renewal of Commitment to Priestly Service," in which the bishop and presbyters of a diocese reaffirm their dedication to the pastoral service of the people at the *Chrism Mass on Holy Thursday.

Bibliography: J. D. CRICHTON, *Christian Celebration: The Sacraments* (London 1973) 163–167. Pope Paul VI, *Ad pascendum*, English tr. *Catholic Mind* 71 (1973) 59–64; *Ministeria quaedam*, ibid. 55–59. U.S. Catholic Conference, *Rite of Institution of Readers and Acolytes; Admission to Candidacy for the Diaconate and Presbyterate; Ordination of Deacons, Presbyters, and Bishops* (Washington, D.C. 1973).

[N. MITCHELL]

CELIBACY, FORMATION IN

The Congregation for Catholic Education's document, *A Guide to Formation in Priestly Celibacy* (April 11, 1974), does not treat of the speculative aspect of celibacy (3:369; 16:81) but intends to put forth concrete guidelines for the training of seminarians because of changes in culture and psychological sensitivity. The meaning of celibacy for the contemporary priest is seen in terms of its affinity with the ministerial priesthood since, as one of the evangelical counsels, it enhances his service of pastoral charity, reinforces his apostolic availability, and harmonizes with the eschatological character of the priesthood. While admitting special difficulties with the acceptance of celibacy both by modern culture and present-day seminarians, the document reaffirms the appropriateness of the link between celibacy and priesthood.

The goals of seminary training that involve formation in celibacy are threefold: human maturity, Christian maturity, and priestly maturity. Human maturity is important because seminary training does not replace human formation. Emotional stability, an integrated sexuality, and a self-control that tends toward self-improvement are necessary components in the humanization process of the seminarian. Christian maturity implies a positive self-acceptance in Christ, a view of sexuality understood in terms of self-giving, and a control of sensual passion motivated by the suffering Christ. The emotional maturity of the priest helps him to be more completely taken over by Christ. Sexual maturity for the priest presupposes growth in love and his sexual self-control demands a life-long struggle and daily renunciation.

The document, based upon some of the major insights of contemporary adolescent and humanistic psychology, straightforwardly faces the difficulties of formation and the complexity of the problem. It links sexual maturity closely with emotional maturity as a gradual and highly relational process. The demands of celibacy for life-long sacrifice, constant vigilance, and an open and integrated personality are the very requirements of true Christian love; it can never be the mere observance of a legal requirement, but must always be a way that a priest articulates his spirituality. A balanced celibate attitude does not rule out the possibility of deep and lasting relationships with women. Nor does it allow for a judgmental or punitive approach to individual sexual problems. The proper training in celibacy for the seminarian is an important preparation for his later life as a priest.

Most of the writing about celibacy since the publication of these guidelines has moved away from the concern for optional celibacy to attempts to clarify the meaning of a celibate spirituality. Hetero- and homosexual relationships, the deepening of personal affectivity, the meaning of chastity, repression and sublimation by the celibate, the presence of sexual feelings, fantasies and desires, masturbation, and sexual intercourse are some of the concrete issues addressed.

Bibliography: G. M. FOUREZ, "Christian Celibacy: A Mystery of Death and Resurrection," RevRel 31 (1972) 725–732. D. GOERGEN, *The Sexual Celibate* (New York 1974). P. S. KEANE, "The Meaning and Functioning of Sexuality in the Lives of Celibates and Virgins," RevRel 34 (1975) 277–314. W. F. KRAFT, "Celibate Genitality," RevRel 36 (1977) 600–612. Sacred Congregation for Catholic Education, *Guide to Formation in Priestly Celibacy* (USCC Publ., Washington, D.C. 1974).

[J. L. EMPEREUR]

CENSORSHIP OF BOOKS

The scope of prior censorship of books (3:392) and *imprimatur* were reduced significantly by the decree of the Congregation for the Doctrine of Faith, "De Ecclesiae pastorum vigilantia circa libros," March 7, 1975 (ActApS 67 [1975] 281–285). The rationale given for continued prior censorship was the right and duty of pastors to preserve and safeguard truths of faith and integrity of morals. The norms limit previous censorship to books of scriptural and liturgical texts and their vernacular translations, books of devotion, catechisms and works related to catechetical formation, and textbooks intended for grade, intermediate or higher school that relate to Sacred Scripture, theology, Canon Law, church history, and religious or moral studies. However, any writing displayed, sold, or given away in a church or oratory must have been published with ecclesiastical approval. Ordinarily, approval of the local Ordinary is sufficient, but liturgical books require a mandate from the episcopal conference after confirmation of the Apostolic See. The norms recommend, but do not require, secular clergy or members of institutes of perfection to have permission of their bishop or major superior to publish books on religion or morality.

Interestingly, these universal norms are in agreement with recommendations made by the National Conference of Catholic Bishops in April, 1967 and are strikingly analogous to American law on prior censorship and minors under eighteen.

Bibliography: O'Connor Suppl. through 1975 at c. 1385. F. R. MCMANUS, "Precensorship of Books," *Jurist* 35 (1975) 344–348. L. L. MCREAVY, "Revised Legislation on the 'Imprimatur' Requirement," ClergyRev 60 (1975) 463–465. W. J. NESSEL, "Prior Censorship for Young Readers," *Jurist* 29 (1969) 199–201. [W. J. NESSEL]

CENSURES, ECCLESIASTICAL

In 1973 a *Schema* or draft of the revision of Canon Law on penalties in the Church presented the latest thinking of central church authorities on ecclesiastical censures (*see* PENAL LAW, DRAFT OF).

The *Schema* retained the traditional meaning of censures as a medicinal penalty intended to lead the offender to a change of heart and changed manner of acting (3:394). The draft of the new Canon Law also retained the traditional censures of excommunication, interdict, and supension. However, a number of significant changes were proposed for the new code of Canon Law.

Excommunication will be a much stiffer penalty than in the 1917 Code (CIC). It would exclude someone from even being at Mass, would also exclude them from all participation in the life of the Church, and would cut off even such residual benefits as pensions from previous church involvement. Interdict would cut one off from only religious and sacramental life, whereas suspension would affect all other aspects of participating in church life. For clergy, this would keep them from participating as a celebrant in the Sacraments. In many ways, the *Schema* proposed new content for old terms.

The draft law would also dramatically change the way censures are lifted. Currently censures are remitted when a person repents and approaches appropriate authority in the public or external forum, or approaches a confessor in the internal forum (5:1037). Censure blocks the reception of the Sacraments, including Penance, and must be absolved before sacramental absolution can be received. The new law would separate these elements, and would permit sacramental absolution of sins even though the confessor could not absolve from the censure.

While lauding the pastoral intention of the proposed changes, canon law experts have sharply criticized the way censures are handled. The separation of external and internal fora has been done in such a way that the Sacrament of Penance would no longer bring about reconciliation with the Church. Automatic or *latae sententiae* censures are retained, despite the *Schema's* attempt at a more personal and pastoral approach.

According to published reports, the Pontifical Commission for the Revision of the Code of Canon Law has referred the question of sacramental absolution to decision by a higher authority. The Commission has decided to retain *latae sententiae* censures, and has made some modifications in the content of censures, while retaining the basic approach proposed in the 1973 draft.

The most significant practical development in ecclesiastical censures in the United States was the 1977 lifting of the automatic excommunication for remarriage after divorce. This penalty, peculiar to the United States, had been established in the last century by the Third Plenary Council of Baltimore (2:39). United States bishops petitioned the Apostolic See to confirm the vote of the bishops rescinding the automatic penalty, since the application of the penalty was somewhat questionable and did not seem to be achieving the result desired. The lifting of the automatic excommunication did not automatically restore divorced and remarried Catholics to sacramental Communion, but cleared one obstacle to more effective pastoral ministry to such persons.

Bibliography: Pontificia Commissio Codici Iuris Canonici Recognoscendo, *Schema documenti quo disciplina sanctionum seu poenarum in Ecclesia Latina denuo ordinatur* (Vatican City 1973) *(reservatum).* Coetus Studiorum de Iure Poenali, *Communic* 7 (1975) 93–97; 8 (1976) 166–183; 9 (1977) 147–174. T. J. GREEN, "Future of Penal Law in the Church," *Jurist* 35 (1975) 212–275, bibliog.

[J. H. PROVOST]

CENTER FOR APPLIED RESEARCH IN THE APOSTOLATE (CARA)

The Center for Applied Research in the Apostolate (CARA) is an independent, church-related organization founded in 1965 as a national research center for the Church and chartered as a nonprofit corporation in the District of Columbia. CARA's establishment was in response to a need recognized at the time of Vatican Council II by bishops, priests, religious, and laity for religious and social research that could assist the Church in keeping pace with the changes in the social, demographic, and economic conditions of contemporary society.

CARA's goal is: to discover, promote and apply modern techniques and scientific informational resources for practical use in a coordinate and effective approach to the Church's social and religious mission in the modern world, at home and overseas. CARA endeavors to carry out research with characteristics that are: theological, objective, practical, and future-oriented.

Initial funding for establishing CARA was provided by Card. Richard J. Cushing of Boston and many major superiors of the religious congregations of men and women. CARA receives no regular subsidy from any source. Its church-research activities are financed by gifts and grants, and by income from contract services to clients.

While CARA is an independent organization, its Board of Directors is composed of bishops, priests, religious, and laity who are in a position to represent the various segments of the Church in the U.S. and to indicate areas in need of church research. CARA's permanent staff is made up of priests, religious, and laity with academic backgrounds in the fields of theology, the social sciences, and informational systems. Supplementing the work of this staff is a network of CARA Associates, qualified professionals throughout the country who work with the Center on a project-by-project basis in areas appropriate to their qualifications.

CARA'a major areas of interest are defined by its designated programs: Church Personnel, Church Management, Pastoral Research and Planning, Education, Health Ministry, Religious Life. Each Program engages in one or more of the following four kinds of activities: (1) serving as an information-resource and documentation center for the Church in matters within the scope of the particular program; (2) undertaking applied research projects designed to help the Church at large or particular sectors within the Church; (3) helping the Church at large benefit from scientific research and modern techniques by dissemination of research through seminars and workshops; (4) on request, undertaking client-oriented research projects and services, designed to assist specific individual organizations within the Church (e.g., dioceses, parishes, religious orders, church institutions) in fulfilling their mission.

[J. V. O'CONNOR]

CENTER OF CONCERN

As a result of discussions between representatives of the United Stated Catholic Conference and leaders of the Society of Jesus, the Center of Concern was established in Washington, D.C. in 1971 as an action/reflection center to explore the complex political, economic, and social issues of the day. William F. Ryan, a Canadian Jesuit, was named its program director and Irving S. Friedman, then chief economist with the World Bank, its chairperson. The Center operates as an autonomous, public-interest group, while still maintaining strong ties to its religious origins. It defines itself as a team of people engaged in analysis, advocacy, and education on global issues of development, justice, and peace. The principal value guiding its work has been that of social justice. In particular the efforts of the Center have been directed to: (1) evaluating global policy issues with a radically open, interdisciplinary approach, readily moving back and forth between ethical, value-informed analysis, competent social science analysis, and lived experience; (2) supporting the concerns of developing nations, particularly as voiced in the United Nations and in policy discussions in North America; (3) identifying the single struggle for justice in both global and domestic issues—namely, who has power and in whose interest it is exercised; (4) integrating a commitment to social change with spiritual resources, that is, linking faith and justice.

Through its nongovernmental consultative status with the United Nations, the Center has monitored and reported on UN Conferences on trade, population, food, women, human settlements, water, unemployment, and the *new international economic order. Center staff carries on discussions with U.S. government leaders and other professional groups concerning American foreign-policy positions and circulates widely its own policy analysis, prepared in a social justice perspective. To enrich its efforts and broaden its impact, the Center is linked to a network of social action/reflection centers on this continent and around the world.

In church circles the Center carries on programs of consultation with church leaders, education for justice, and publication. It has already conducted over 1500 workshops for religious personnel and for justice and peace networks. Its chief publications have been *The Quest for Justice* (1972), *Soundings: A Task Force on Social Consciousness and Ignatian Spirituality* (1974), *Detroit and Beyond: The Continuing Quest for Justice* (1977), and *The American Journey* (1977). Among statements drafted for church leaders was the Appalachian Bishops' Pastoral, *This Land is Home to Me* (1975; *see* CATHOLIC COMMITTEE OF APPALACHIA).

In its ongoing attempt to discern "the signs of the times" and integrate faith and justice, the Center has become the secretariat for the Interreligious Peace Colloquium, whose purpose is to help Muslim, Jewish, Christian, Hindu, and Buddhist believers work together for world justice and peace. In 1978 Peter Henriot, SJ became the Center's director.

[W. F. RYAN]

CHANGE IN THE CHURCH

The ambiguity in the word "change" is reflected by the need to specify it further—does it mean a change for the better or for the worse? Change taken as healthy is progress, growth, evolution, emergence, development. Change viewed negatively is upheaval, alteration, innovation, disintegration, substitution. Change can also refer to two separate phenomena: those beyond control (e.g., change in the weather, change of life) and those resulting from intentional planning (governmental restructuring, remodeling). Admittedly it is sometimes difficult to know whether a change is inevitable or planned (e.g., fluctuating rates of currency exchange, unemployment). When planned change proceeds from moral conversion it is described as renewal, restoration, renovation, updating (*aggiornamento*). Planned change includes two aspects: a visible, structural end-product that differs in some way from what went before and a more elusive internal motivation that generates the process. In church life change proceeds from concern but it also creates concern.

Vatican Council II's Reflections on Change. The Pastoral Constitution on the Church in the Modern World of Vatican II noted the undeniable fact of change in the world and in particular the contemporary rapidity of change (*Gaudium et spes* 4–7; 54). These changes were viewed as challenges to mankind and to the Church. The text spoke of profound and rapid changes in the whole world and identified them as social, psychological, moral, and religious. About changes in the Church, actual or intended, Vatican II had little explicit to say. The Council did speak of desired changes in the liturgy (*Sacrosanctum Concilium* 1) and justified them with the proviso that they were guided "by way of appropriate and organic development" (*Orientalium Ecclesiarum* 6).

In retrospect it is regrettable that the Council did not try to explain to the broader membership in the Church what historians of Christianity and theologians had been seeing with increasing clarity: that elements of church life and doctrine had changed in the Church's history, sometimes dramatically. The Council might well have explained the fact that the Church had changed over the centuries and have given as well reasons for various developments in dogma, hierarchical institutions, sacramental practices, ways of interpreting the Scriptures. Much remained implicit in the call for *aggiornamento* as Pope John XXIII, addressing the Fathers at the opening of the Council, Oct. 11, 1962, noted: "The substance of the ancient doctrine of the deposit of faith is one thing, and the way in which it is presented is another." Earlier in a radio address on Sept. 11, 1962 Pope John had described the project of the Council, without giving examples of historical precedents, as "the Church seeking to renew itself in its inner vitality, whereby it represents the treasures of faith and grace, especially to its own members; and in its external vitality, in its ministry to men in their need of justice and peace with all the temporal problems of this changing age."

Recent Changes in the Catholic Church. Some changes in the Catholic Church, especially since the 1960s, are clearly visible to its members and even to outside observers. The most obvious changes are not necessarily the most significant ones. Furthermore, because of the double structure of change—motive and observable reshaping—there could be a perception of changes in visible structures without any understanding of the reasons behind the adaptation. Ignorant of history, some have been unaware of similar attempts at change in the past. Seven major changes can be noted in the Catholic Church in the last two decades.

Liturgy. First are the changes in the manner of celebrating the Sacraments, especially the Eucharistic Liturgy, including the introduction of the vernacular, additional Eucharistic Prayers, *Communion in the hand, new cycles of Scriptural readings (freshly translated from the original languages), freer attitudes toward rubrical directives. Sacramental liturgies such as those of Baptism, Reconciliation, and Ordination were also rewritten (*see* LITURGICAL BOOKS OF THE ROMAN RITE). Behind these changes was the desire to enrich their significative value and their intelligibility. Also intended was a wider distribution of roles among the laity to offset a previous concentration on the clergy's role. Lay readers, auxiliary (extraordinary) ministers of the Eucharist, fuller participation in liturgical prayers are instances.

Ecumenism. Second, attitudinal changes also occurred toward other Christian Churches or ecclesial Communities. This shift was symbolized by the presence of some non-Catholic observers at Vatican II, even though their influence was often indirect. Further such gestures of reconciliation took place as the kiss of peace in Jerusalem between Pope Paul VI and Patriarch Athenagoras I (1964) and their mutual lifting of the excommunications between East and West (1965). After Vatican II's Decree on Ecumenism bilateral theological conversations were initiated throughout the world between Catholics and other Christians (*see* BILATERAL CONSULTATIONS). Although the Council stated that the Church of Christ "subsists in the Catholic Church" (*Lumen gentium* 8), it did not wish to identify exclusively the Roman Catholic Church with the Church of Christ. This shift implied a reassessment of the estrangement between East and West since 1054 and a reassessment of the Protestant Reformation. Differences between Christians were seen to be frequently on the level of theological understanding rather than on the level of faith. These ecumenical developments are now leading to reopening the question of eventual official *Eucharistic sharing with other Christian Churches and even the possibility of recognizing the ordained ministry of other Churches.

Bishops in the Church. Third, the development of the collegiality of bishops and new emphasis on the synodal nature of the Church have in recent years complemented a previously highly-centralistic, papal process of decision-making which had been notable in the Catholic Church, especially since the definition of papal infallibility at Vatican I. The last decade has seen greater importance attached to the International Synod of Bishops (which remains however only an advisory agency) and the various episcopal conferences.

Evangelization and Inculturation. Fourth, changes of emphases in the manner of evangelizing and in missionary activity have developed out of an increased perception of the need to respect and appreciate various national traditions and to inculturate the Gospel message in creative ways (*see* INCULTURATION, THEOLOGICAL). In its Declaration on Non-Christian Religions the Catholic Church expressed in a new way its appreciation for the fact that non-Christian religions are in themselves a direct source of holiness for millions of people and therefore evangelization would have to dialogue with these traditions rather than simply oppose them (*Nostra aetate* 2).

Ministry of Justice. Fifth, the Catholic Church has been seen as changing, especially in certain episcopal conferences and in some dioceses, by becoming more involved in the struggle for social justice. Though prepared by such modern encyclicals as *Mater et magistra* and *Populorum progressio* this concern has drawn upon the insights of *liberation theology and the need to include a process of "conscientization" in the Church's preaching. This fact has led to some dismay and confusion in the minds of those who feel it is an undue involvement with matters political.

Pluralism. Sixth, the Catholic Church has changed by admitting legitimate diversity and pluralism in church life and theology. More and more theologians began to appeal to what has been called "model" thinking whereby different ecclesiologies are seen to be complementary and in fact present in various ways in the New Testament itself. Admitting wider pluralism has led to a broader tolerance for discussing ideas that once seemed to be at variance with official teachings of the Catholic Church. The Council had taken positions that differed from earlier official teachings (e.g., in the area of religious freedom and in interchurch cooperation). Now new theological positions, some of them seemingly provocatively novel, related to Christology, Eucharist, ministry, human sexuality, pastoral care of the divorced, etc., have been circulated. Some of these views were opposed by Vatican sources; some seemed to be restatements of Modernist positions; still they were not openly condemned with the same force they might have been fifty or even twenty-five years ago.

A New Language. Seventh, a clear attempt has been made to develop a new terminology for certain doctrinal and theological issues. Nonspecialists in the Church have not always recognized this shift but many of the new terms made their way into ordinary teaching and preaching. Such new expressions as "Petrine ministry" for papacy, "reception into full communion" instead of conversion, "general synod" instead of ecumenical council, "ecumenical marriage" instead of mixed marriage are but several examples. This shift in terminology grew out of a perception that certain words had been too sharply polemical, too remote from Scripture, too triumphalistic or juridical, or too insensitive to historical development. This led to some misunderstandings in why catechetical instruction was being adapted.

This list of seven areas of change in the Church is not exhaustive. The emergence of such new themes as "reading the signs of the times" (see Synod JustWorld p. 33; Paul VI EvangNunt 76), "discernment," "ongoing revelation," "hierarchy of truths," is noteworthy. The emergence of Catholic charismatic renewal, the reorganization of religious orders, especially those of women, new modes of training future priests, consultation of the laity have also marked these two decades.

Negative Reactions to Change. Some see change as unwarranted or disruptive innovation rather than as responsible progress. These Christians perceive changes as a disconcerting tolerance of questionable factors: decline in authority; decrease in self-abnegation; watering down of doctrines; unhealthy compromise with the value-system of the unbelieving world; false irenicism with dissident Christians through ecumenism leading to a loss of denominational identity; neurotic, restless search for change simply for the sake of change;

irresponsible, unauthorized innovations especially in the liturgy; lack of respect for past generations. These negative assessments are present in varying degrees among some Catholics, but most notably among the so-called traditionalists who have rallied around Archbishop Marcel Lefebvre. What is central to them is not their nostalgic call to return to the Tridentine Latin Mass, but their deep-seated conviction that the Church has uncritically accepted the secular ideas espoused by the French Revolution—liberty, equality, fraternity. In refutation of the traditionalists' views, others argue that in fact these persons are not traditionalists but immobilists who have succumbed to the perennial temptation to fix the Church in a particular, successful form of incarnation and to render a particular church style permanent even when an earlier situation calling for this style has ceased to exist.

Theological Reflections on Change. Theologically it can be argued that the tension about change in the Church is related to the dialectic between two aspects of the Church's nature. On the one hand, the Church is rooted in God's once-for-all, irrepeatable act in Christ and is called to preserve a unique revelation that remains normative for all generations and cultures. On the other hand, the Church is in eschatological process, called to be what it has not yet become.

"The Already-There—The Not-Yet-Realized." Since its origins the Church has assiduously guarded its traditional patrimony, the *paradōsis* handed on since the life, death, and resurrection of its founder who is "Jesus Christ the same, yesterday and today and for ever" (Heb 13.8). Many Christians read the promise made to Peter that "on this rock I will build my church and the powers of death shall not prevail against it" (Mt 16.18) as a special promise of stability and continuity. This perception of the Church's indefectibility seems to imply for them a relative sameness. Otherwise what is the point about the promise to Peter or indeed the promise of Christ that he would send the Spirit of truth as guide (cf. Jn 16.13)? Could these perceptions of God's fidelity toward the Church be compatible with the idea that the Church in any age might only partially (even inaccurately) preach the Gospel or might indeed forget something crucial to its self-understanding?

Yet belief in God's fidelity must be kept in balance with the belief in the eschatological nature of the Church, which is to say that although the Church, as also the reign of God that it helps to promote, is "already there" still it is "not yet" fully realized. The Church remains capable of development because of its vocation to grow in grace and holiness. Not only is the Church God's gift (*Gabe*) but it bears a responsibility (*Aufgabe*) to become something more. The marks or notes of the Church: one, holy, catholic, and apostolic (9:240) are not verifiable empirical data, but dimensions still to be realized. The Church is both bride of Christ but still sinful (the *casta meretrix* of the patristic tradition). The Letter to the Ephesians mentions this need for growth in the Church when it urges "building up the body of Christ, until we all attain to the unity of faith" (Eph 4.13). Ephesians suggests that just as the risen Christ at the right hand of the Father is growing into a fullness (*plērōma*) as he prepares to hand over the completed work of creation to the Father, so too the Church under grace is in labor and growing into fulness.

One of the ways that earlier theology reflected on the

tension between the unchangeable and the changeable in the Church was to distinguish between aspects that exist *iure divino* (elements of God's permanent design for the Church) and those that exist *iure humano* (resulting from human decisions for the well-ordering of the Church that could be reversible). Historical studies show that too much has been grouped under the umbrella of *ius divinum* that in fact is the result of *ius humanum*.

Limits. Clearly, despite the need for certain adaptations, there are limits to change in the Church. What can never change is its relationship with the Savior whose life, death, and resurrection makes salvation possible; the Lord's Supper as a memorial of Christ and as focal point of the Church; the importance of Baptism in Christ; the special status of the inspired Scriptures; fidelity to the moral imperatives of the New Testament. These and many other features cannot be altered at will without the Church's ceasing to be Church. But the Church's vocation to be an intelligible sign or Sacrament to believers and unbelievers of the presence of Christ to the world makes it imperative that its structural forms take on different shapes and dimensions in history (*see* CHURCH [THEOLOGY]). Otherwise the Gospel could conceivably be limited.

Uneasiness within a changing Church affords an opportunity to comprehend more profoundly the nature of faith. Faith is not meant to be a secure refuge nor a well filled with definitive answers on every conceivable question. A willingness to live with darkness and incompletion will result in better appreciating the mystery dimension of faith or what the theology of the East calls the apophatic aspect of Christianity.

Pastoral Considerations. One of the challenges to the Church today, particularly to those who exercise pastoral office, is to help Christians, especially older ones, resolve their confusion implicit in the lament: "This is not the Church I grew up in!" Such an uneasiness is not simply looking homeward toward an idealized past, but a profound malaise more acute than the disillusionment of those frustrated by the slowness of the official Church to change structures and previous decisions simply because "it has never been done before."

Several episcopal conferences, e.g., those of Holland and Ireland, have addressed the pastoral problem of change in letters that deserve wider circulation. The challenge to church leaders is to convey a new sense of continuity, one based not on structural sameness or close similarities with the past but on God's fidelity toward the Church. The Church's continuity does not rest upon empirical verifiability but upon faith inspired by hope in the presence of God. The nonhistorical, unchanging factor of the Church's existence is fundamentally God's fidelity through the grace of Christ's Spirit.

To this unchanging element is added a process of adaptive continuity springing from the Holy Spirit's remaining in the Church and through the many charisms that this Spirit bestows for the further building up of the Church. The Church as a community is called to discern, communicate, adapt, and transmit through different cultures its historical identity in Jesus Christ. Just as men and women are called to cooperate with the Creator in building up creation unto its perfection, so also are Christians responsible for the building up of the Church in this day.

Bibliography: Pastoral Letters: Bishops of Ireland (Sept. 14, 1972), "Change in the Church," *Catholic Mind* 71 (1973) 49–64. Bishops of the Netherlands (March 3, 1968), "Renewal and Confusion," *Herder Correspondence* 5 (1968) 146–148; (Feb. 10, 1976), "Vivre dans le changement," *DocCath* 73 (1976) 620–633.
Studies: W. BÜHLMANN, *The Coming of the Third Church*, tr. R. WOODHALL (Maryknoll, N.Y. 1977). P. CHIRICO, "Dynamics of Change in the Church's Self-Understanding," ThSt 39 (1978) 55–75. C. B. DALY, "Change and Continuity in the Church," IrTheolQ 39 (1972) 60–78. A. DULLES, *The Survival of Dogma* (New York 1971); "*Ius divinum* as an Ecumenical Problem," ThSt 38 (1977) 681–708. M. A. FAHEY, "Continuity in the Church amid Structural Changes," ThSt 35 (1974) 415–440. T. S. KUHN, *The Structure of Scientific Revolutions* (Chicago 1970). N. LASH, *Change in Focus. A Study of Doctrinal Change and Continuity* (London 1973). B. LONERGAN, *Method in Theology* (New York 1972). L. O'DONO-VAN, "Was Vatican II Revolutionary?" ThSt 36 (1975) 493–502. J. O'MALLEY, "Reform, Historical Consciousness and Vatican II's Aggiornamento," ThSt 32 (1971) 573–601. T. F. O'MEARA, "Philosophical Models in Ecclesiology," ThSt 39 (1978) 3–21. K. RAHNER, *The Shape of the Church to Come*, tr. E. QUINN (London 1974); "Basic Observations on the Subject of Changeable and Unchangeable Factors in the Church," *Theological Investigations* 14, tr. D. BOURKE (New York 1976) 3–23. M. SCHOOF, *A Survey of Catholic Theology, 1800–1970* (Chicago 1970).

[M. A. FAHEY]

CHAPEL OF RECONCILIATION

A special chapel for confession is not mandated or mentioned in the new (1973) Rite of Penance. But discussing the rite, Crichton says that commentators are already beginning to talk of an arrangement other than the confessional (4:136). Most of these take their cue from the notion of reconciliation, a fuller and richer concept than older ideas of Penance and confession. This can be seen in the directive to the priest to greet and welcome kindly the penitent entering for reconciliation (PenanceIntrod 41). There is a general tone of warmth in the entire ceremony. The rubric just before the absolution reads, "Then the priest extends his hands over the penitent's head (or at least extends his right hand)..." (ibid. 46). Consequently while provision is made for an alternative, the first option is for the imposition of hands. There is no possibility for the imposition of hands in the old style confessional.

The reconciliation chapel is a small room closed off from the rest of the church, accessible by a single door or by two doors (with the second door for the priest and preferably from another access). In any case the first door is for the penitent (there is no reason why the priest could not come this way earlier also). The penitent entering has an immediate choice: just ahead is a grill and kneeler and, slightly to one side, a chair or small bench (for those who cannot kneel); to the other side slightly further back than the grill there is a little table with a small crucifix and a open Bible on it and next to this a comfortable chair. The penitent always has a choice here: to take the chair by the table and face the priest; to kneel, or to sit, at the grill. The room is well, but moderately lighted, comfortable and pleasant without being luxurious. Many churches have already provided a special chapel of reconciliation.

See also PENANCE (RITE).

Bibliography: J. M. CHAMPLIN, *Together in Peace* (Notre Dame, Ind. 1975). J. D. CRICHTON, *The Ministry of Reconciliation, a Commentary on the Order of Penance* (London 1974). M. R. PRIEUR, *The Sacrament of Reconciliation Today* (Liturgical Commission, Diocese of London, Ontario 1974). E. MCM. JEEP, *The Rite of Penance, Commentaries*, v. 2, *Implementing the Rite* (Liturgical Conference, Washington, D.C. 1975).

[C. H. MEINBERG]

CHAPTERS, RELIGIOUS

The periodic gathering of religious called the chapter has always brought the dimension of democracy into the vowed life. The key decisions that mark the progress of a religious institute are normally acts of chapters (3:456). Vatican Council II emphasized this aspect of chapter when it wrote: "Let chapters and councils faithfully acquit themselves of the governing role given them; each should express in its own way the fact that all members of the community have a share in the welfare of the whole community and a responsibility for it" (*Perfectae caritatis* 14).

The most significant development in the practice of chapter is the use of the occasion as a powerful instrumentality for renewal. Sometimes called an "open chapter," a procedure is designed to involve the total membership in preparation for the chapter. By means of a sequenced series of activities, usually assemblies or small group meetings, the major areas of the community's life and apostolate are studied and discussed. The meetings are dialogical in nature rather than debates on disputed points.

Another significant development in the practice of chapter is the conceptualization that chapter is not an organizational, legislative act but a salvific event. As Eduardo Pironio, Prefect of the Sacred Congregation for Religious and Secular Institutes, wrote, Sept. 16, 1976, "A chapter is not a mere study meeting, a superficial gathering or a short-lived revision of life. A chapter is essentially a paschal celebration...a salvific event...an outstanding moment in the history of salvation that an institute must write 'not in ink, but in the Spirit of the living God, with human hearts, instead of stone' (2 Cor 3.3)" (OssRomEng [Sept. 16, 1976] 5–10). At this time the religious chapter is undergoing profound evolution in the search to make it a vital event in the life of the community. The objective of the search is to clarify the mission of the institute and to find what the Spirit is saying to the community.

[C. OVERMAN]

CHARISMATIC PRAYER

A style of Christian prayer now widespread in the Catholic Church in the wake of the charismatic movement. Related to an initial experience of the Holy Spirit, it is rooted in the conviction that prayer is a gift of God (Gr. χάρισμα; 3:460) and not the product of human striving. In the NT, the Holy Spirit, the Gift of God (Acts 2.38; Rom 5.5; Jn 4.10; 7.37–39) gives inspired utterance, whether this be such basic acclamations as "Jesus is Lord!" (1 Cor 12.3), "Come, Lord Jesus!" (Rev 22.20) and "Abba, Father!" (Gal 4.6), or inspired intercession (Rom 8.26–27), or prayer in tongues (1 Cor 14; Acts 2.1–11).

Glossolalia, or tongue-speaking, is the most celebrated aspect of charismatic prayer. As practiced among charismatics, it is used both in personal prayer and in public prayer meetings, where most often it is a spontaneous choral singing without intelligible words. Less frequently it is used in a proclamatory way by an individual, followed by an "interpretation" by someone else or sometimes by the speaker himself. As a prayer-gift, speaking in tongues is generally explained by theologians and biblical scholars who have experienced or studied the movement as a form of preconceptual prayer, that is, vocalization of a prayer of the heart (or of the spirit, as distinct from the mind, 1 Cor 14.15–16) prior to conceptualization and shaping into

understandable language—a phenomenon not without parallels in other traditional forms of prayer. That it is not, except in very rare instances, the speaking of a real human language is supported by cross-cultural linguistic studies of tongue-speaking and by Paul's teaching that the "interpretation" is equally inspired and not simply the work of a translator (1 Cor 14.13). The tongue-speaking by the Apostles on Pentecost may be understood as their actually speaking the various languages of their hearers. However, one should not overlook the emphasis in the text of Acts upon the miraculous hearing. Three times the text says *each one* (singular) heard *them* (plural) speaking *his own* (singular) language (Acts 2.6, 8, 11). This, coupled with the accusation of drunkenness to which Peter addresses his response (rather than to an unusual brilliance in languages) suggests to some scholars that Luke used the early Pauline tradition of a preconceptual prayer language and, combining it with current Jewish Pentecost traditions about the gift of the Law amid wind and fire, saw the first Christian Pentecost as the new covenant of the Spirit destined for "every nation under heaven." In any case, charismatics view the experience as one in which they yield to the Spirit praying within them. This prayer, which is essentially praise and thanksgiving (1 Cor 14.16), also disposes to a hearing of a "word of the Lord," whether this be in a scriptural reading, an interpretation, or a prophecy (usually uttered in an oracular "I" form). All of these have Pauline antecedents. Prediction is not the primary function of prophecy. Its primary function as inspired speech is the community's "upbuilding, encouragement and consolation" (1 Cor 14.3).

A further aspect of charismatic prayer is prayer for healing, whether physical or emotional, and occasional prayer for "deliverance," though in the latter case there is considerable divergence of both theory and practice within the movement (*see* HEALING, CHRISTIAN).

Elements of biblical and early Christian spirituality that the charismatic approach to prayer has pointed up are thus: (1) prayer as a gift of the Holy Spirit; (2) the primacy of praise; (3) the importance of expecting to hear God speaking in prayer; (4) the healing ministry of the Church and the role of prayer in the healing process.

Bibliography: E. ENSLEY, *Sounds of Wonder; Speaking in Tongues in Catholic Tradition* (New York 1977). F. S. MACNUTT, *Healing* (Notre Dame, Ind. 1974); *The Power to Heal* (Notre Dame, Ind. 1977). D. GELPI, *Pentecostal Piety* (New York 1972). G. T. MONTAGUE, *The Holy Spirit: Growth of a Biblical Tradition* (New York 1976); *The Spirit and His Gifts* (New York 1974). W. J. SAMARIN, *Tongues of Men and of Angels* (New York 1972).

[G. T. MONTAGUE]

CHARISMATIC RENEWAL, CATHOLIC

The Charismatic Renewal (also called the "Pentecostal Movement") has affected nearly all Christian denominations in the course of the present century. In the Catholic Church, it began from several roots, the most important of which was the Chi Rho Society at Duquesne University in 1967. From there via Notre Dame, Ind. and Ann Arbor, Mich., it then spread rapidly across the country and into the other English-speaking lands. Within five years it was worldwide, being particularly strong in the British Isles and France, also in Latin America, especially Puerto Rico.

Character of the Renewal. Accurate statistics on the

numbers involved in this movement have never been compiled. The *International Directory of Catholic Charismatic Prayer Groups* for 1977 (compiled in 1976) lists over 3,000 groups in the U.S. and Canada and about 1,600 in the rest of the world. The average membership of a group is probably not far from 40, but not all the members are Catholic, and in any case the list of charismatic groups is neither complete nor accurate.

Distinctiveness. The Charismatic Renewal is one among many church renewal movements that sprang up before and after Vatican Council II. It is distinguished from the others, first, because it is concerned primarily and directly, not with the reform of structures or institutions, but with the renewal of the Christian spirit. Secondly, it looks for renewal to be brought about, not by any technique, process, or method, nor even by some new form of devotion, but by the action of the Holy Spirit. This does not mean that methods, devotions, or techniques are despised; but simply that the Holy Spirit is regarded as the only power capable of "renewing the face of the earth." The chief aim and actual effect of the Charismatic Renewal is to make people turn to the Holy Spirit with expectant faith, and yield to his promptings with complete docility. The Renewal did not originate in an idea or a plan. It arose quite unexpectedly and spontaneously out of the religious experience of a few people who then propagated it enthusiastically. Others were drawn to seek the same experience because of the fruits which they could observe in the lives of acquaintances. Those who became involved in the movement had to reflect post factum on its meaning and develop by experimentation such methods as seemed best suited to cooperate with a work which the Holy Spirit had already set in motion.

The Charismatic Experience. The most prominent feature of the movement is the wide-scale reappearance of such charismatic phenomena as prophecy, healing, discernment of spirits, speaking in tongues, which are well known in the New Testament but have been rather uncommon since about the second century. More important are the fruits of the renewal: a lively awareness of the reality and presence of God, a sense of personal union with Jesus Christ, warm love for one's fellows, deep interior peace and joy, deliverance from habits of sin and from crippling psychological bonds, an eager desire to read Scripture, ability to pray longer and more fervently, and a new appreciation of the Sacraments, especially the Eucharist. As a result, people that had been estranged from God have been converted, flagging faith has been reanimated, and faithful Christians have been stirred up to more generous service and bold Christian witness. These effects are bound up largely with one central experience commonly known as "baptism in the Holy Spirit." This expression, although based on the language of the New Testament (Mt 4.11; Jn 1.33; Acts 1.5; 11.16; 1 Cor 12.13, etc.), is disconcerting to those many who would prefer to replace it with some term less susceptible of misinterpretation, such as "outpouring" or "release" of the Spirit. At any rate, it does not imply that the Holy Spirit is missing from sacramental Baptism. It simply designates a powerful experience of the presence and action of the Holy Spirit that introduce a person into a life of much greater dependence on his inspiration; it is often marked by the reception of charismatic gifts. Frequently this Pente-

costal grace (as it may also be called) is received through the laying on of hands with prayer, but this informal ritual is not looked upon as a sacrament, but merely as prayer in action.

Those involved in the Charismatic Renewal are generally inclined to gather for prayer meetings, often in private homes. These meetings consist largely of spontaneous prayer, singing of hymns, reading of Scripture, and sharing of experiences. The prayer meetings commonly lead to the formation of prayer groups, which meet together regularly (usually once a week). The prayer groups, in turn, have in many cases developed into communities bound together by a firm "covenant," involving the members with one another in other activities besides prayer.

Organization. Although spontaneity characterized the beginning of the movement and remains in many ways essential to it, there has been a very strong development of organization and method under the leadership of the Ann Arbor group seconded by that in South Bend. A National Service Committee directs a program of international, national and regional conferences. Supported by an Advisory Board of leaders from all over the U.S. and Canada, it effectively molds the teaching and activities of the majority of prayer groups in the country, which it has organized into regions. Through its organ, Charismatic Renewal Services, Inc., it publishes books, pamphlets, and cassette tapes, as well as the monthly review, *New Covenant.* It has elaborated a method of preparing people for the baptism in the Spirit, called "Life in the Spirit Seminars," with a follow-up program of instruction called "Christian Life Series." An International Communications Office, designed to provide information, support and coordination on a worldwide basis, was founded in Ann Arbor and later, at the suggestion of Cardinal Leo J. Suenens, transferred to his diocese of Brussels. W. Storey and J. M. Ford have strongly criticized the very organizational, authoritarian, and nondenominational direction given by South Bend and Ann Arbor. Without reacting so sharply, numerous local charismatic groups have held somewhat apart from their direction.

Although the main thrust of the Renewal seems to be more popular than profound, and more apostolic than contemplative, still it seems to be affecting the Church at all levels—clergy, laity, and religious.

Evaluation. Theologically, the Renewal does not pose any special problems, since it implies no doctrinal innovations, but simply a renewed awareness of the action of the Holy Spirit dwelling in all the faithful both to sanctify them and to equip them for service to the church community. On the pastoral level, however, when the operation of the charisms and personal experience of the Spirit become more commonplace in a community, a distinct change in the tone or tempo of Christian life can be observed. This poses a question of interpretation: should the Renewal be regarded as a recovery of a tone that should always have been present, or as the beginning of a new era in the Church's history, marked by a more manifest action of the Spirit, with perhaps a specially eschatological significance? The renewal also makes the task of distinguishing between authentic and illusory inspirations of the Spirit a much more urgent pastoral function.

Some practical problems are raised by the Renewal, most of which fall under three headings: ecumenism, enthusiasm, and relations with the Church. The ecumenical problems are mentioned in the article, *Charismatic Renewal and Ecumenism. As for enthusiasm, the Renewal unquestionably excels at producing enthusiastic Christians, something the Church sorely needs today. But religious enthusiasm has a tendency to get out of hand, as well as to foster an emotional, superficial piety, cultivating "religious experience" for its own sake and neglecting the values of silence, interiority, and contemplation.

As for relations with the Church, the Renewal is engendering new "charismatic ministries," e.g., healing, prophecy, counseling, and also "pastoral leadership," alongside the official, ordained ministry. This is in keeping with the general move toward a greater role of the laity in the modern Church, but the transition does not always occur without friction and excesses. Likewise, the charismatic prayer meetings and communities correspond to a widely felt need of *basic Christian community, and of a warmer style of worship; but carried to excess they tend in greater or lesser degree to supplant the Church in the lives of their participants. Sometimes charismatics, impressed by the powerful new experience of the Spirit which the Charismatic Renewal has brought them, but ignorant of the mighty role played by the Spirit throughout the Church's history, and insensitive to the Spirit's deep, even if not dramatic, work in ordinary Christian life, are tempted to think that the Church had lost the Spirit until the Charismatic Renewal began.

But the foregoing are problems that must be dealt with, not errors of principle. In spite of them, this movement has been received by the Catholic hierarchy more favorably than by the leadership of any other denomination. Vatican II providentially affirmed the essential principles of the Charismatic Renewal even before it began (*Lumen gentium* 4, 7, 12, 15, 34 etc.). The official statements of the bishops of the United States (1969, 1975), of Puerto Rico (1972), of Quebec (1974), of Canada (1975), of Panama (1975), and of the Antilles (1977), as well as statements by individual bishops and other religious authorities, and finally those of Pope Paul VI, have almost without exception maintained a tone of cautious encouragement. Cardinal Suenens has become the quasi-official patron of the movement at large; the Bishops' Ad Hoc Committee for the Catholic Charismatic Renewal headed by Bishop Gerard L. Frey (Lafayette, La.) was constituted to deal with the Renewal.

Bibliography: R. LAURENTIN, *Catholic Pentecostalism* (New York 1977), bibliog. K. MCDONNELL, *Charismatic Renewal and the Churches* (New York, 1976), bibliog. E. O'CONNOR, *The Pentecostal Movement in the Catholic Church* (rev. ed., Notre Dame, Ind. 1974); *Perspectives on Charismatic Renewal* (Notre Dame, Ind. 1975) bibliog.; *Pope Paul and the Spirit* (Notre Dame, Ind. 1978). K. and D. RANAGHAN, *Catholic Pentecostals* (New York 1969). L. J. SUENENS, *A New Pentecost?* (New York 1975).

[E. D. O'CONNOR]

CHARISMATIC RENEWAL AND ECUMENISM

The Charismatic Renewal has several ecumenical aspects. It has touched practically all denominations. It originated among Protestants, but in currents turning back to some of the "Catholic" values lost in the Reformation. The Holiness movement (7:53), from which it sprang directly, was a 19th-century effort to recover the values of real holiness (in John Wesley's meaning and as distinguished from the mere "imputed righteousness" involved in justification by faith alone). The laying on of hands, belief that the charisms are still actual today, and other "Catholic" attitudes and practices help to account for the fact that the early "Pentecostals" (from 1901 onward) were compelled to leave their parent Churches (chiefly Holiness, Methodist and Baptist) and form new ones, neither Protestant nor Catholic, but a "third force" (H. van Dusen).

The early Pentecostals were largely antagonistic to the established Churches, partly because of this experience, partly from the conviction that ritual, dogma, and organization impeded the free action of the Spirit. They reacted negatively to the ecumenical movement as compromising Christian faith.

But during the 1950s, the Pentecostal spirit penetrated the older Churches, members of which ("Neo-Pentecostals") insisted on staying in the Church even after becoming "charismatic." In the Catholic Church, the Charismatic Renewal (as the movement is more commonly called) originated largely under the influence of Pentecostals and Neo-Pentecostals. Many Catholics have been alarmed by this fact, as by the thesis that genuine charisms could occur outside the Church. Vatican Council II, however, in its Decree on Ecumenism has recognized that the Holy Spirit is present with his gifts among our "separated brethren"; and that what he does among them can contribute to our own edification (*Unitatis redintegratio* 3, 4). Moreover, it was promptly recognized that essential motives of the charismatic movement are in full accord with Catholic teaching.

The charismatic movement is probably the most successful locale of grass-roots ecumenism today (*see* ECUMENISM, REGIONAL AND LOCAL). Instead of discussing ecumenical theory or doctrinal differences, it brings people of various denominations to pray together in a fellowship that is not just friendly and respectful, but warm and loving. Many see it as the work of the Spirit restoring the unity of his people at a depth accessible only to him.

But this free religious intercourse of theologically untrained people has its problems. Not a few Catholics have been influenced by the old Pentecostal antipathy for ritual, dogma, and authority and some have left the Church altogether. Others have absorbed Pentecostal beliefs (e.g. about tongues) or Protestant attitudes (e.g. towards Mary, the saints, or the Sacraments). In their eagerness to overcome all sources of disunity, some have adopted views of the Church that are incompatible with Catholic faith, e.g. that "denominations," including Catholicism, are merely human attempts to realize the "true Church," an invisible entity which transcends them all. Others have encouraged illicit practices of intercommunion. Some cross-denominational groups seem to be endeavoring in effect to take the place of the Church as the congregation of believers.

These trends are only partially counterbalanced by the fact that many Pentecostals and Protestant charismatics have come to a new appreciation of the wisdom of Catholic spiritual doctrine, sacramentalism, and order. The future of the charismatic renewal in the Catholic Church depends largely on whether its tremendous ecumenical potential is cultivated in accord with a wholeheartedly Catholic vision of the Church.

[E. D. O'CONNOR]

CHARISMS IN MINISTRY

Charisms and ministry are two separate, but related phenomena. The relationship between the two is established in three areas: call, service to build up the Body of Christ, and eschatological gift.

New Testament. Speaking with reference to Israel, Paul links together both charism and call (Rom 11.29). The link between the two should not be surprising because the giving of a gift would at least imply a call to use it or to accept it. The charisms accompanying Israel's call are listed in Rom 9.45: the sonship, the glory, the covenants, the giving of the law, the worship, the promises, and the patriarchs. Likewise, in the new dispensation, the gift of apostleship, for example, entails a corresponding call to be an apostle. As regards service to build up the Body, Paul seems to place more value upon a gift destined for such a purpose, than upon a gift that serves no such function. Speaking in tongues, then, is a gift that includes the call to do so, but it is not as valuable a gift as that of interpreting such utterances (1 Cor 14.2–5). The lists of charisms in Rom 12.6–8 and 1 Cor 12.28–31 are almost exclusively keyed to this function of service.

The eschatological nature of charism will empty the possessor of any undue sense of pride or personal claims in ministry, but at the same time will give an extreme importance to the use of personal charisms in ministry. As with any gift, there is no right to a charism, but it is given here and now as a presence of the end-time in the present. If God's self-revelation to humanity in Jesus is seen as a unique event, then his particular self-revelation through the charisms of individuals should be seen as closer to the norm (cf., together, 1 Cor 12.31; 13.13; and Jn 15.12).

It is important to note that not every charism is ministerial—e.g., celibacy (1 Cor 7.7), speaking in tongues, and some of Israel's charisms noted above—and that not all ministerial charisms are of equal value. Thus, when Paul enumerates the charisms, he will sometimes grade them (e.g., 1 Cor 12.12). At the head of this list of charisms are the gifts of being apostles, prophets, and teachers—certainly a statement that ministries are charisms (also Eph 4.11–14), and that these are among the most important charisms (cf. 1 Cor 12.31; 13.13; 14.1).

Charisms in Church Ministry. The Church has been immeasurably enriched by this link between charism and ministry. Throughout the centuries, founders of religious orders have been noted for such varied charisms as care of the poor, care of the sick, care of orphans, teaching, preaching, missionary work, communal prayer, eremetical prayer. They and their followers have changed the face of the earth as profoundly as any other factor.

Vatican Council II recognized this relationship between charisms and ministry in the Dogmatic Constitution on the Church (*Lumen gentium* 12), the Decree on the Missionary Activity of the Church (*Ad gentes* 23), and especially in the Decree on the Apostolate of the Laity: "From the reception of these charisms or gifts, including those which are less dramatic, there arise for each believer the right and duty to use them in the Church and in the works for the good of mankind and for the upbuilding of the Church" (*Apostolicam actuositatem* 3).

While an opposition between charismatic ministry and institutional ministry is a false one (all ministry being charismatic), the present renewed awareness of ministry as a gift of Christ to his Church and indeed as the presence of Christ within his Church has stimulated continuing renewal and reflection. Among the more pointed issues that have arisen is one on the nature of the call to ministry itself: whether the call to ministry simply is a controlled personal attraction, verified by superiors, and then consecrated; or is the recognition by the community and its authority that gifts mark a person out to receive a mission through the bishop's consecration or other deputation.

See also MINISTRY, UNORDAINED.

Bibliography: M. LEGUILLON, "Episcopal Charisms and Personal Charisms," OssRomEng (Jan. 2, 1975) 4–5. M. SCHAEFFER, "Charism, Priesthood, and Church," *Sisters* 48 (1976) 77–87.

[P. J. LEBLANC]

CHARISMS IN RELIGIOUS LIFE

High interest in the concept of charism (3:460) as a focal element in the renewal of religious life followed closely on the promulgation of the documents of Vatican Council II. A simple reference in *Lumen gentium* (42) to the evangelical counsels as constituting a gift of God to the Church was elaborated in *Perfectae caritatis* (1) and developed still further by Paul VI's 1971 apostolic exhortation on religious life (Paul VI EvangTest 7–29). References in these documents to the "proper character of each institute," "the charisms of the founders," and "the dynamism proper to each religious family" prompted religious congregations to develop a new sense of their origins. The deepening understanding of the spirit of the founder, a renewed study of Scripture, and a keener sensitivity to the signs of the times, have become the triadic impetus for revitalizing the religious congregation.

Religious Life as Gift within the Church. Vatican Council II's Dogmatic Constitution on the Church first situates religious life ecclesially (*Lumen gentium* 43–47), then a separate decree turns to the specific renewal of religious congregations (*Perfectae caritatis*). The study of the charism that religious life is or of the charisms of particular founders is, accordingly, best done in the context of the general theology of charism within the life of the Church. Seen thus organically related to the life of the Church, the renewal proper to religious life will avoid either narrow concern for superficial differences or a diminished appreciation of the place of religious life among the rich variety of gifts given for the building up of the Body of Christ.

From the theology of charism some principles are of particular value in reflecting on the charism of religious life. These are: (1) that charisms are universally present in the Church; (2) that charisms are frequently of quite an ordinary character; (3) that charisms are apostolic, related, that is, to the building up of the Kingdom of God and given for the benefit not only of the recipient but also for others; and (4) that charisms appear in constantly new forms. These principles provide a sound basis on which a religious congregation might ground the work of research and reflection on its proper charism.

Prior to the awakened awareness of religious life as a charism, it was common to speak of the call to religious life. Sometimes the connotation was that this call to religious life carried strong meanings of duty or obligation or even of unwelcome intrusion into ordinary life. Viewed as a charism, however, religious life is seen as both gift and call. That it is a gift implies that there is a grace given as a power to fulfill joyful religious commitment for the sake of the Kingdom. The screening of candidates for religious life should include discernment of gifts that will enable the candidate to respond. That response is not merely a matter of a good and disciplined will determined to live up to an intellectualized ideal, but rather a response made with a certain ease and freedom of spirit (see VOCATION, PSYCHOLOGY OF).

Discernment of Charisms. Several ideas are used interchangeably in discussing the charism of religious life. These are "the spirit of the founder," "the spirit of the institute," "the charism of the founder," and the "founding charism." It is more useful, however, to broaden the appreciation of the various dimensions of a community's self-image by distinguishing among the aspects just named, and even to add others, rather than to make them terms interchangeable with charism. In other words, the gift that a particular congregation is to the Church is a composite of interrelated qualities. The charism of the founder is the gift and call given enabling the founder to institute a particular religious family. The events of a historical period, the particular geographic location, the cultural milieu, the ecclesial setting, the other persons who joined at the founding of the community—all of these contribute toward the characteristic spirit of the institute. The dynamism of the charism throughout the history of the congregation can be explored through the lived experience of the members, the decisions made, the roads taken and not taken. Understanding its charism requires, therefore, that an institute explore it as a continuing operation within a corporate entity in history and not as a static quality inhering in the founder alone. The charism of the present institute, the ensemble of its gifts, will be organically related to the founding persons, but it may and probably should exhibit some differences.

The sources for understanding and explicating the charism of religious life or of a particular institute are Scripture, theology of charism, foundational texts, histories, and other archival materials. To these sources must be added an examination of the contemporary needs of the People of God and a realistic assessment of the present members' capacities to respond to these needs. A search process that is reflective, discerning, and dialogic will illumine the meaning of the charism of the institute so that it might be anointed and freed for the service of God and his people.

Bibliography: L. CADA and R. FITZ, "The Recovery of Religious Life," RevRel 34 (1975) 690–718. J. C. FUTRELL, "Discovering the Founder's Charism," WaySuppl 14 (Autumn 1970) 62–70. P. KAUFMAN, "The One and the Many: Corporate Personality," *Worship* 42 (1968) 546–556. W. KOUPAL, "Charism: A Relational Concept," *Worship* 42 (1968) 539–545. PAUL VI, *Evangelica testificatio*, tr. *On the Renewal of Religious Life* (USCC Publ. Office, Washington, D.C. 1971). K. RAHNER, "Observations on the Factor of the Charismatic in the Church," *Theological Investigations* 12, tr. D. BOURKE (New York 1974) 89–97.

[G. FOLEY]

CHASUBLE

Normally worn over the alb for the celebration of the Eucharist, the chasuble has taken on various forms. (GenInstrRomMissal 81; 299). The chasuble is especially affected by the present adaptation of liturgical vestments (ibid. 304–305). The customary form immediately prior to the liturgical renewal was the Roman chasuble (3:517). Its skimpy design with often heavy ornamentation has given way to a more ample vestment of a color, fabric, and design that emphasize simplicity (see *Sacrosanctum Concilium* 124). The chasuble, like other liturgical vestments, should be designed according to the canons of art in order that its noble beauty will enhance the very celebration of the community (GenInstrRomMissal 311). These same remarks can also apply to the design of the dalmatic in the case of the deacon (ibid. 298).

See also LITURGICAL VESTMENTS.

Bibliography: B. M. RAMSEY, "The Chasuble: its History and Development to the Present Day" (Ph.D. thesis, Univ. of Tennessee 1972).

[A. D. FITZGERALD]

CHASUBLE-ALB

The chasuble-alb (*casula sine alba*) is a long and ample vestment developed in recent years for the celebrant of the Eucharist in accord with the General Instruction of the Roman Missal (304). It is to be beautiful in the fabric used and in design so as to be appropriate for the Eucharist. Its use removes any need for an alb. With this new vestment the stole is worn outside; it thus makes more evident the sign that the presiding minister acts *in persona Christi* (ibid. 4; 60). Only the stole need be of the color required for the day or season.

The chasuble-alb was authorized for use in the U.S. on May 11, 1977 with the same conditions already given for other countries (*Notitiae* 9 [1973] 96–98; 12 [1976] 312–313). It may be used in concelebrated Masses, in Masses for special groups, in celebrations outside a sacred place, and in other similar and appropriate circumstances. While the principles of the General Instruction (ibid. 81 a; 298; 299) remain in effect for the ordinary celebration of the Eucharist, they are not to diminish the need to respond to the *justes nécessités du temps présent* (*Notitiae* 9 [1973] 97). Artists and vestment makers must, therefore, continue to seek new materials and designs for the present age in order to highlight the ministry of the celebrant through the beautiful character of the vestment (GenInstrRomMissal 297).

Permission for the chasuble-alb does not remove the faculty of concelebrants to use alb and stole alone in the celebration of the Eucharist (ibid. 161).

[A. D. FITZGERALD]

CHILDREN, RELIGION AND

In the years immediately following Vatican Council II, two fundamental changes took place in the area of children and their religious life and development: first, new catechetical approaches revolutionized religious education for children; and second, a growing awareness of the potential of children to authentically experience and live the Christian life at any age level changed the liturgical approach to children.

Religious Education. In the area of catechetics, most of the United States entered the postconciliar age with the basic approach operative for many years. Centered on such books as the Baltimore Catechism, the emphasis was on memorized learning of doctrinal truths. It was presumed that even though the memorized material was probably not understood at the time, as a child grew and matured, the meaning of the truths would become apparent. The theological shifts occasioned by the Council required a new approach, with few educators prepared for the problems which ensued. While experiences differed widely throughout the country, a few general trends were seen.

First, the role of parents was brought to the front. Much more was required in terms of their time, effort, and personal involvement. Many parents, themselves confused by the religious changes, resisted the new role of primary teachers of their children in the ways of faith. Some classes for parents began to parallel the training of children, setting the stage for a later development of family-centered religious education (*see* CATECHESIS, ADULT).

The second major trend was a decided decline in the doctrinal content of texts and lectures. Instead there were attempts at emphasis on the social and community aspects of the Christian life. Reaction to this soon developed, charging that too little doctrine was being taught; that religious education had lost its Catholic character; that a general humanism was being substituted for faith. Soon curriculum guidelines such as the Green Bay Plan and Idaho Plan began to set standards for the new approaches. They in turn set the stage for the coming of the General and National Cathechetical Directories.

The third major trend of the early postconciliar Church was the reestablishing of the role of traditional Catholic customs and practices. Some, such as May and October devotions, were downplayed or dropped in some parishes; others, such as group first Communion found themselves in conflict with the emphasis on the family. Still others, such as Confirmation, became much more strongly advocated. This set the stage for the development of the liturgy for children.

Following the early reactions to the Council, the religious educators moved rapidly to correct abuses without losing the directions of the Council. Directors of religious education were appointed in thousands of parishes throughout the country. The involvement of families led to full parish-wide experiments in family-centered religious education, involving all of the family in a simultaneous learning program. The CCD program (Confraternity of Christian Doctrine), the bulwark of the 1940s and 1950s, was reworked and under the direction of thousands of volunteers, conducted classes for both teachers and children (*see* RELIGIOUS EDUCATION/CCD). The National Conference of Diocesan Directors of Religious Education/CCD was formed to coordinate their efforts. As the mid-1970s approached, the scene shifted dramatically. Thousands of paid and volunteer teachers had been trained in theology, psychology, and other disciplines related to religious education. New textbooks and programs had been introduced, correcting the early imbalances and inviting active liturgical participation as a necessary element of religious education.

Children's Liturgies. The second area of religion and children is the changes in their liturgical and spiritual lives. The theology and psychology underlying the Tridentine liturgy left no room for adaptation of the liturgy for children. Liturgy was basically the prayer of the adult Church which children attended. This was dramatically changed by Vatican II's Constitution on the Sacred Liturgy. Calling for a full document on liturgy and children (which came out in 1972 as the Directory for Masses with Children), the Council viewed children as fully capable of celebrating the Lord's Supper at their own level (*Sacrosanctum Concilium* 19 and 34).

Attempts in this direction produced a new liturgical event, Children's Liturgy. Early versions, before the publication of the Directory, were sometimes bizarre and poorly done. Soon, however, quality rapidly improved as liturgical scholars pointed out what to emphasize and what to omit, what was in good taste and what was not. A firm basis was provided by the 1972 Directory for Masses with Children (*see* MASSES WITH CHILDREN). Both before and after the publication of the Directory, various books had been written giving theory and practice for Children's Liturgy. The Directory's broad but precise guidelines enabled quality to become easily achievable both in the books about Children's Liturgy and in the celebrations of the Liturgies themselves. In the early 1970s the Vatican permitted the use of three experimental *Eucharistic Prayers for Children. These completed the necessary support material for Children's Liturgies. The underlying principle is that children should experience Jesus and that there is no more important way than in the celebration of the Mass and Sacraments. Religious educators and priests soon joined in working the religious education programs of parishes into a liturgical framework. The celebration of Sacraments became major times in the lives of both parents and children. The liturgical life enabled religious education to be not just talking about Jesus, but actually participating in his life. There are continuing problems in the integration of catechetics and liturgy in the religious life of children, but they are minor in comparison to the strides that have been made. Much was lost in the confused times immediately following the Council, but today's children are able to hear the Word of God and share in the Lord's life in ways unthought of years ago.

[W. T. FAUCHER]

CHRISM MASS

At the Chrism Mass the bishop consecrates the chrism (used in Baptism, Confirmation, and the ordination of priests and bishops) and blesses the oil of catechumens (used in prebaptismal anointing, optional in the case of infants), and the oil of the sick (used for anointing in the Sacrament of the Sick).

The Mass and its texts accent the priesthood, expressing the communion of priests with their bishop. If possible, all priests should take part in it and receive Communion. It is always concelebrated by the bishop with priests from various parts of the diocese. After the Homily priests renew their commitment to priestly service. A proper Preface (of the priesthood) is used and the whole congregation may receive Communion under both forms. The Mass is ordinarily on Holy Thursday morning, but if it would be difficult for clergy and people to gather then, it may be held earlier, though near Easter. The texts of the Mass and the rites for blessing the oils are given in the *Sacramentary of the Roman Missal with the Holy Thursday liturgy.

[J. DALLEN]

CHRISTIAN

The Vatican Council II documents make frequent reference to the kind of life and activity that should characterize those who bear the name "Christian" or "faithful of Christ" (cf. *Apostolicam actuositatem* 31; *Lumen gentium* 15, 42; *Gaudium et spes* 1, 22; *Sacrosanctum Concilium* 9; *Perfectae caritatis* 5). But the Council's expression of the dogmatic and ecclesiological force of the term is particularly noteworthy. That expression is guided by the basic statement: "The Church recognizes that in many ways she is linked with those who, being baptized, are honored with the name of Christian" (*Lumen gentium* 15). Several elaborations appear in the Council documents:

> God has gathered together as one all those who in faith look upon Jesus as the author of salvation and the source of unity and peace, and has established them as the Church, that for each and all she may be the visible sacrament of this saving unity (ibid. 9).
>
> All men are called to be part of this catholic unity of the People of God, a unity which is harbinger of the universal peace it promotes. And there belong to it or are related to it in various ways, the Catholic faithful as well as all who believe in Christ, and indeed the whole of mankind. For all men are called to salvation by the grace of God (ibid. 13).
>
> Men who believe in Christ and have been properly baptized are brought into a certain, though imperfect, communion with the Catholic Church (*Unitatis redintegratio* 3).
>
> All those justified by faith through baptism are incorporated into Christ. They therefore have a right to be honored by the title of Christian, and are properly regarded as brothers in the Lord by the sons of the Catholic Church (ibid.).

These statements make the original New Testament use of the term "Christian" important to ecumenism.

The term appears three times, in Acts 11.26, which notes, "it was in Antioch that the disciples were first called 'Christians'"; in Acts 26.8, which quotes King Agrippa's sarcastic reply to Paul, "A little more and your arguments would make a Christian of me"; and in 1 Pt 4.16, where believers are exhorted, "if anyone of you should suffer for being a Christian, then he is not to be ashamed of it." χριστιανοί is a rare and later synonym for "brothers," "disciples," and "saints," and is derived from χριστός, the Greek equivalent of the Hebrew *Masshiah* (anointed). The Hellenized Latin-*ιανος* was suffixed to indicate that those assuming the title thus formed were of the household named, the partisans, clients, or slaves of the master or κυριός thus designated. The term Christian (χριστιανός) was formed on an analogy with Ηρωδιανός (Herodian), καισαριανός (partisan of Caesar), and the family of titles bestowed by Christians themselves on heretics, such as Βασιλειδιανοί (followers of Basilides) and Νεστοριανός (Nestorian). The name was formed from the title Christ because confession that Jesus was χριστός (cf. Peter's confession, Mt 16.17) or Lord (the common Pauline formula) epitomized the believer's faith.

The only scriptural evidence regarding the origin of the name is the notice of Acts that it was first used in Antioch, and the text can be taken to mean either that the disciples invented the term or that they accepted a name already current among their pagan neighbors. Though 1 Pt 4.16 may suggest that opprobrium attached to the name Christian, the context is the writer's advice to those convicted or liable to be convicted before a Roman magistrate, and the shame which the reader is urged to bear gladly is probably that evoked by legal condemnation, especially when such condemnation implied guilt of crimes (atheism, anthropophagy) usually associated with profession of the name by opponents of the Church. There is no clear evidence that the name Christian was bestowed by antagonists of the Church, though by the end of the century it was a title of honor among Christians, a term of opprobrium among pagans.

The meaning of the name, established in part by its derivation, is clarified by consideration of the significance of the title Messiah in Jewish tradition, according to which χριστιανοί are members of the royal household of God's anointed; and by the Jewish doctrine of names, according to which names effectively represent persons and those taking the name become members of the household. Such meanings were deepened by the theology and practice of the Church, life in Christ being inaugurated by Baptism and perfected by participation in Christ's Body and Blood. That the title Christian effectively expressed the relation between Christ and his disciples is indicated by its occurrence in Pliny's account of the trial of Christians (Ep. 96), and in the *Annals* of Tacitus (15.44).

See also INCORPORATION INTO THE CHURCH.

Bibliography: E. J. BICKERMAN, "The Name of Christians," HarvThRev 42 (1949) 109–124. R. A. LIPIUS, *Über den Ursprung und den ältesten Gebrauch des Christennamens* (Jena 1873). H. B. MATTLINGLY, "The Origin of the name *Christiani*," JThSt n.s. 9(1958) 26–37. E. PETERSON, "Christianus," in *Miscellanea Giovanni Mercati* 1, StTest 121 (1946) 356–372. C. SPICQ, "Ce que signife le titre de chrétien," *Studia theologica* 15 (1961) 68–78.

[J. PATRICK]

CHRISTIAN FAMILY MOVEMENT

The Christian Family Movement (CFM) consists primarily of married couples who act together on matters affecting not only their own but other families. They meet regularly in each others' homes to discuss the application of Scripture to their lives and to investigate a social problem or situation. CFM, formally established in 1949 (3:639), originated out of a desire to understand and implement the role of the laity in the Church and out of a conviction that couples could assist each other in enhancing married and family life, as well as in contributing to the betterment of society. CFM's meaning and purpose found endorsement in the documents and spirit of Vatican Council II.

From its beginning CFM adopted and used the "Jocist technique" or social inquiry method of Observe—Judge—Act (attributed to Canon Joseph Cardijn of Belgium and the Young Catholic Workers). In this method each individual observes and gathers facts on a particular problem; the problem is judged by the group; then a practical action is agreed to be taken. The distinctive characteristic of CFM is the actions taken by its members on social issues such as international life, politics, and family life. The national organization encourages and assists in these areas principally by providing "Social Inquiry" programs.

A long series of program books using the social-inquiry method began with *For Happier Families*. More than 400,000 copies of this book were used by couples throughout the world. New program books are issued at least yearly; the many topics include family, race, politics, leisure, community, economics, international life, and others. Involvement in these programs leads to a characteristic result. Through their actions members of CFM frequently become involved in other organizations as leaders. Studies by the Univ. of Notre Dame's Sociology Dept. have shown CFM's "formation through action" programs to be unusually effective.

Another characteristic of the national movement has been the generation of several new organizations. The Foundation for International Cooperation (FIC) grew out of a CFM inquiry on foreign students. FIC fosters student exchanges and international family-to-family visiting. The concept of creative use of leisure led to CFMV—The Christian Family Mission Vacation. CFM created the *Marriage Encounter in Spain. CFM in the U.S. sponsored in 1968 a tour by more than a hundred Spanish couples and chaplains, who conducted encounters for Spanish-speaking couples throughout the country. The first Marriage Encounter in English was given following a CFM convention at Notre Dame in 1967.

In 1961 CFM was affiliated with the NCWC (now USCC) through the National Council of Catholic Men, confirming the strong ties CFM has with the Church in most dioceses.

From its inception the movement saw itself as broadly Christian and open to all Christians. There was a small but significant Protestant membership particularly in Episcopal Church parishes. In 1968 the executive committee formally declared that CFM was indeed open to all Christians and took measures to encourage expansion in Protestant Churches. Participation by Protestants slowly increased among members, committees, leaders, and staff.

CFM is administered by a board of directors comprising contact couples from ten geographical areas in the U.S., one Canadian contact couple, and four officer couples. An executive-director couple and a director of development are appointed by the board of directors. A national office is maintained at Calumet College Center, 2500 New York Avenue, Whiting, Ind. (a Chicago suburb). Records and documents of CFM are available at the library of the University of Notre Dame, Notre Dame, Indiana.

[D. AND R. MALDOON]

CHRISTIAN INITIATION, SACRAMENTS OF

The Sacraments of Christian Initiation are Baptism, Confirmation, and the Eucharist. Normatively they are celebrated together at the Easter Vigil after a Lenten period of purification and enlightenment for those preparing to receive the Sacraments. In the case of infants they are traditionally administered separately over a period of years (in the Latin Church). However administered, the three Sacraments of initiation bring us from the power of darkness to the full stature of Christ with his power to carry out the mission of the People of God, the Church, throughout the world (ChrInitGenIntrod 1–2).

Baptism. The Constitution of the Sacred Liturgy ot Vatican Council II speaks of Baptism grafting men into the paschal mystery of Christ, in which they die, are buried, and rise with him, receiving the adoption of sons (*Sacrosanctum Concilium* 6). The Dogmatic Constitution on the Church develops the theme further in its ecclesial aspect, stating that Baptism binds us not only to Christ but to his Church and its worship, through which we profess the baptismal faith before men (*Lumen gentium* 11). It is through this Sacrament that we are incorporated into Christ and formed into the holy People of God, giving to it both an individual and a social dimension. The bishop is properly its chief minister by virtue of his central position in the liturgical life of the Church (ChrInitGenIntrod 12) and he should celebrate the rite at the Easter Vigil, but parish priests, and other priests and deacons are its ordinary ministers (ibid. 11).

The descent into the baptismal water and rising from it is the sacramental expression of participation in death and rising again of Christ; by it we pass with him through death and the grave to participate in his risen life. Baptism is for Christians a new birth as children of God by adoption and grace and carries with it the forgiveness of sins and incorporation into the Church, the People of God and Body of Christ. It is the *transitus* or "passover" from death to life.

Confirmation. In the early Church (and in the Eastern Churches still) Confirmation was normatively administered with Baptism. This is re-established in the new rite for the initiation of adults and children of catechetical age. Confirmation binds the recipients more perfectly to the Church, endowing them with the special strength of the Holy Spirit (*Lumen gentium* 11). This is so that they may bear witness to Christ for the building up of his body in faith and love (ConfIntrod 2). It therefore intensifies and deepens the baptismal life and commitment, pointing those confirmed toward bearing witness to Christ. It is the reception by those baptized of the Pentecostal outpouring of the Holy Spirit, and is therefore closely connected with the paschal mystery of the Sacrament of Baptism. The Sacrament is conferred through the anointing with chrism on the forehead with the words, "Be sealed with the gift of the Holy Spirit" (ibid. 9), but the laying on of hands has an important place in the integral administration of the Sacrament, especially when it is administered by the bishop after the example of the Apostles who gave the Spirit through the laying on of their hands (ibid. 7).

In the Latin Church Confirmation is not normally administered to children below the age of seven, but permission is given for episcopal conferences to choose a more appropriate age, so that the Sacrament can be given after a more mature formation (ibid. 11). This formation is directed toward giving the witness of a Christian life and apostolate (ibid. 12). Confirmation should then be described as a focusing and intensification of the baptismal life, particularly in its apostolic and ecclesial dimensions.

The Eucharist. The third Sacrament of initiation is the Eucharist. It is the true rite of incorporation in which baptized Christians perform their distinctive liturgy as members of the Church. Not only do they receive Holy Communion for the strengthening of their own life in Christ and the showing forth of the unity of the Church which the Sacrament signifies, but they participate as sharers in Christ's priestly office in the offering of themselves with Christ in the Eucharistic Sacrifice (*Lumen gentium* 11).

The Eucharist is the final act of the drama of Christian initiation in which our participation in the paschal mystery is renewed every time we participate, as we proclaim the death of the Lord until he comes. "In the Eucharist, the neophytes who have received the dignity of the royal priesthood have an active part in the general intercessions (prayer of the faithful) and, as far as possible, in the rite of bringing the offerings to the altar. With the whole community they take part in the action of the sacrifice and they say the Lord's Prayer, thus showing the spirit of adoption as God's children which they have received in Baptism, then by receiving the body that was handed over and the blood that was shed, they confirm the gifts they have received and acquire a foretaste of eternal things" (ChrInitAd 36).

Implications. Considered together, the Sacraments of Christian Initiation, spaced by appropriate catechetical periods, take individuals who are outside the fellowship of Christ and unite them with Christ Jesus in the saving paschal mystery of his dying and rising again. They are thus reborn as children of God who call him "Abba, Father," are filled with the power of the Holy Spirit to bear witness to Christ, and are united with his Body, the Church, as members of the holy people of God—no longer separated individuals but made one with each other in him. They become that community of Christians who "united in Christ and guided by the Holy Spirit, press onward towards the kingdom of the Father and are bearers of the message of salvation intended for all men" (*Gaudium et spes* 1). Membership in this new people of which Christ is the Head binds persons closely together and reveals to human beings their high calling as made in the image of God. They are not only a people called out by God, but one with the whole of humanity to bring to it the gospel of salvation which is through Christ in the power of the Spirit.

The General Introduction on Christian Initiation repeats Catholic teaching that Baptism "may never lawfully be repeated once it has been validly celebrated, even if by fellow Christians from whom we are separated" (ChrInitGenIntrod 4); the Vatican II Decree on Ecumenism states that all who have been baptized are in "some, though imperfect, communion with the Catholic Church" (*Unitatis redintegratio* 3). This affirmation of Christian unity among the baptized is of profound ecumenical importance and is the basis for ecumenical cooperation, while the lack of Eucharistic communion with separated Christians is a sign of the incompleteness of this baptismal communion (*see* EUCHARISTIC SHARING).

The revision of the rites of Christian initiation after Vatican Council II and the emphasis placed in the new rites on the normative character of adult initiation preceded by a catechumenate and followed by a period of *post-baptismal catechesis (mystagogia) marks a distinct change in emphasis. Rather than removal of original sin, the positive effects of initiation, union with Christ, adoption as sons, outpouring of the Holy Spirit, and unity with the Church in its apostolic life and work are brought forward. The emphasis of public celebration restores to these Sacraments their proper liturgical character and keeps them from being seen as private rites addressed only to individuals. The initiation of new Christians is a primary concern of the local congregation and the whole Catholic Church.

Bibliography: L. BROCKETT, *The Theology of Baptism* (Notre Dame, Ind. 1971). J. D. CRICHTON, "The Christian Initiation of Adults: A Pastoral Opportunity," *Life and Worship* 41 (1972) 8–12. C. DAVIS, *Sacraments of Initiation: Baptism and Confirmation* (New York 1964). R. H. GUERRETTE, "The New Rite of Infant Baptism," *Worship* 43 (1969) 224–230. U. T. HOLMES, *Confirmation: The Celebration of Maturity in Christ* (New York 1975). A. KAVANAGH, "Initiation: Baptism and Confirmation," *Worship* 46 (1972) 262–275; "The Norm of Baptism: The New Rite of Christian Initiation of Adults," *Worship* 48 (1974) 143–152. R. KEIFER, "Confirmation and Christian Maturity," *Worship* 46 (1972) 601–608. A. MILNER, *Theology of Confirmation* (Notre Dame, Ind. 1971). NOTRE DAME CENTER FOR PASTORAL LITURGY, *Made, Not Born* (Notre Dame, Ind. 1976). B. NEUNHEUSER, *Baptism and Confirmation* (New York 1964). R. REDMOND, "Infant Baptism, History and Pastoral Problems," *ThSt* 30 (1969) 79–89. D. STEVICK, "Types of Baptismal Spirituality," *Worship* 47 (1973) 11–26. J. WAGNER, ed., *Adult Baptism and the Catechumenate*. Concilium 22 (New York 1967). G. WAINWRIGHT, "The Rites and Ceremonies of Christian Initiation," StLiturg 10 (1974) 2–24.

[L. L. MITCHELL]

CHRISTIAN LIFE COMMUNITIES

Christian Life Communities are the contemporary outgrowth of the over 400-year-old Sodalities of Our Lady (13:409). At the meeting of the General Council of the World Federation of Sodalities of Our Lady held in Rome, October 19–21, 1967, the delegation representing over 40 Sodality Federations voted to change the name to "Christian Life Communities." With a desire to better serve the Church and in order to renew the movement according to the spirit and the norms of Vatican Council II, the members of the World Federation prepared and put into effect new general principles, which replaced the Common Rules of 1910.

Today Christian Life Communities are renewed in that spirit and reality of Vatican II, and are forming Christians who will respond to "the more of Christian living" in their own lives and in service to the needs of the world today. Christian Life Communities aim to develop and sustain men and women, adults and youth, who commit themselves to the service of the Church and the world in every area of life. The communities are for all who feel the urgent need to unite their human life in all its dimensions with the fulness of their Christian faith. Spirituality is ecclesial, centered on Christ and a participation in the paschal mystery. The Spiritual Exercises of St. Ignatius of Loyola are a specific source and the characteristic of that spirituality.

Christian Life Community members seek to work for the reform of structures of society, to participate actively in vital efforts to eliminate the causes of injustice, to win liberation for victims of discrimination of any kind, and to strive to overcome the widening differences between rich and poor within the Church and wherever they exist.

Mary holds a special place as the model of total openness to God's Spirit which is visible in her continual cooperation in the work of Jesus, the Christ, liberator of humankind.

The international office of the Christian Life Community Movement is in Rome; the national office in the U.S. is in St. Louis, Missouri. The National Federation is a union of Christian Life Communities geographically located within the U.S., its territories and possessions. It is a nonprofit, religious, and educational service organization.

The vision of the Christian Life Communities today is expressed in the following statement: "The Leadership Community of the National Federation of Christian Life Communities has made its own the thrust given by the World Federation in its last general assembly in Manila '76, namely, 'Poor with Christ for a better service.' It is the purpose of this community, then, to make this vision come alive in this country by radicalizing in Christ—by an integrated Ignatian Spirituality—the vision, values, life styles, and commitment to action of its members and member communities, therefore coming to the fullest realization of our vocation within the American experience today." The implementation of the work of the Leadership Community is situated in six Commissions of the National Federation of Christian Life Community Movement. They are: the Vision Commission; the Youth Commission; the National Support

Commission; the Internal Renewal Commission; the Symbols and Lifestyles Commission; Change and Renewal of Society Commission. The monthly publication is the *Christian Life Communicator.*

Bibliography: Christian Life Communities, *General Principles* (St. Louis 1971).

[M. SCHIMELFENING]

CHRISTOCENTRISM

Vatican Council II repeatedly sets forth the central position of Jesus Christ in God's saving activity within human history. This Christocentrism is present as a directing principle throughout the conciliar documents, but is especially and explicitly contained in the Dogmatic Constitutions on the Church and on Divine Revelation. Thus in its opening words the first states that "Christ is the light of all nations" (*Lumen gentium* 1) and further on notes: "Before all things, however, the kingdom [of God] is clearly visible in the very person of Christ . . ." (ibid. 5). The Constitution on Divine Revelation refers to Christ as the "fullness of all revelation" (*Dei Verbum* 2). This centrality was evident also in Pope Paul VI's keynote address at the start of the Council's second session, in which the Pope stated that the Council's task was to express above all the pivotal reality of Christ to the world (ActApS 55 [1963] 846, tr. 129).

What is new in these declarations is not the doctrine itself, but a new perspective and manner of expression. Christ has always been regarded by Christians as the normative Revelation of God. In Vatican II, however, there has been a shift to a personalist point of view. All the signs which might lead a person to accept Christianity—whether these signs be Old Testament prophecies, Jesus' miracles, or the life of the Church—are reattached to Christ, who is their personal center. All these other mysteries emanate from Christ and lead back to him. He is the Sign of divine Revelation, and all partial signs can be understood only if they are referred to Christ as their source. This personalist shift, so much in keeping with contemporary culture, becomes evident by comparing the Dogmatic Constitution on Divine Revelation with Vatican I's 1870 Constitution, *Dei Filius*, on the Catholic Faith (Denz 3000–50). The statements of Vatican I on Revelation were so governed by the relationship between the natural knowledge of God and supernatural Revelation that the historical act of salvation by God in Jesus was not discussed. Instead, the Church as "a great and perpetual motive of credibility" (Denz 3013) confirms the divine origin of the Christian religion, as do a great number of "striking external signs" (Denz 3009). Vatican II, however, designated Christ "through his whole presence and through his manifestation of himself" as the principal sign of Revelation (*Dei Verbum* 4). In Christ, Revelation reaches its objective climax. As the epiphany of the Father, Christ reveals "through his words and through his deeds" the words and deeds of God in human form (ibid.).

The nature of the Church, so obviously a concern of Vatican II, must also be understood from this Christocentric and personalist viewpoint. Christ is the manifestation of God and the meaning of the Church is as a sign or Sacrament of Christ. Vatican II was characterized by a more lively awareness of the *mystery* of the Church, i.e., its transcendent horizon of meaning in Christ. The process of personalization, linking all signs of historical Revelation to Christ, is also at work in understanding the present life of the Church: rather than objective, external signs, it is individual Christians by the witness of their life and Christian communities by their love and service which speak forth the Church as the Revelation of God (see, e.g. *Lumen gentium* 3, 7–9, 36; *Gaudium et spes* 22; *Ad gentes* 3, 5).

Bibliography: B. HÄRING, *Road to Renewal, Perspectives of Vatican II* (New York 1966). R. LATOURELLE, *Christ and the Church, Signs of Salvation* (New York 1972). Paul VI, Opening Address, 2d Session, Vatican Council II, ActApS 55 (1963) 841–859; tr. *Pope Speaks* 9 (1963–64) 125–141.

[T. M. MCFADDEN]

CHRISTOLOGY

The task of expressing a faith-informed and systematic awareness of the meaning of Jesus of Nazareth as the Christ or savior has been one of the more controverted responsibilities undertaken by contemporary Christian theology. Attempts have been numerous and significantly divergent; some have been seen to be so radical in their conclusions that the Congregation for the Doctrine of the Faith in 1972 issued a Declaration to Preserve the Faith in the Incarnation and Trinity from Recent Errors (ActApS 64 [1972] 237–241). At issue, according to the Declaration, is the erroneous assertion that God was "present only in the highest degree in the human person Jesus" (Declaration 3). Thus the problem of the relationship between divinity and humanity in Jesus and the way to understand the unity of the person Jesus remains, even as during the first five centuries of Christianity, an issue that both occupies theologians and significantly affects the Christian community's faith.

Sources of the Problem. Several causes for the problematic nature of contemporary Christology should be mentioned. The science of biblical exegesis continues to illumine the meaning of the Gospel and the authentic message and role of Jesus. Two developments are particularly important: a clearer perception of Jesus' situation within the Palestinian culture of his time and the increasing recognition of the principal of the Christological titles (Son of Man, Lord, Christ, Son of God) as evolving, post-Easter response of the earliest believers rather than as claims of the historical Jesus. Thus the traditional proclamation of the divine/human relationship as constitutive of Jesus and revealed in the Scriptures must be very careful to take fully into account the various strata of New Testament composition. In addition, the classical theories of God in his relationship to the world and human history have lost the near unanimity which they had enjoyed in Christian theology. Process or neoclassical theism has begun to carve out a growing place in the theological speculation (*see* THEISM AND PROCESS THOUGHT), and a certain dissatisfaction with classical notions of person, nature, and hypostasis manifests itself in speculative systems even aside from process thought. Finally, many theologians believe that the traditional one person/two natures theory of the union of God and man in Jesus unintentionally swallows up the humanity of Jesus. According to this view, the finely balanced synthesis forged at the Council of Chalcedon (451) was not retained either in subsequent theology, especially not after the breakdown of the scholastic apogee of the 13th and 14th centuries, nor in popular preaching. Jesus came to be regarded as ahistorical, as lacking the worldview specific to his own time. Jesus' own "history of salvation," i.e., the development of his relationship to the Father within his lifetime, is obscured or rendered impossible. The charge of neo-Chalcedonianism, asserting that the typical belief of the faithful did not allow for any distinctly human operations of Jesus, has become the touchstone for several new approaches in Christology. Four of these approaches will be considered in this article: Spirit Christology, Christology from below, especially as this is exposed by Hans Küng, a process Christology, and Kasper's personalist ontology.

Spirit Christology. In the Prologue of the Fourth Gospel, an identity is proclaimed between Jesus of Nazareth and the eternal Word of God become flesh. For a variety of historical reasons, linked with the need to express Christian faith within the prevailing Hellenistic thought systems of the Mediterranean area in the first centuries of the Christian era, this Word or Logos Christology came to dominate theological reflection. The central model for reflection, even before the pivotal Council of Chalcedon, was a Logos Christology and the adoption of the Logos model at that Council assured its employment in subsequent theology. The preexistence of Jesus as the eternal Word and his complete equality with the Father were stressed. This has been termed a descending Christology: the eternal Word descends through the Incarnation to become a man and finally return to the Father. According to this model, any other approach smacked of adoptionism and compromised Jesus' divinity. As a result of these factors, another type of Christology—used far more extensively in the New Testament, especially by Paul, Luke, and John except in the Prologue—came to be nearly disregarded. This approach is called Spirit Christology, and it has recently come to receive considerable attention. The goal of Spirit Christology, however, is not to deny or even diminish the divine sonship of Jesus; the aim rather is to set forth an understanding of Jesus that is faithful to a large component of the New Testament, that better explains the relationship between Christ's divinity and humanity, and that speaks more cogently to modern awareness of God and human persons.

"Spirit" is understood here within the Old Testament perspective as God's saving presence and action, now operative in Jesus. The Gospels connect the Spirit with the earthly life of Jesus, whose whole ministry is achieved under the guidance and with the power of the Spirit. Paul connects the Spirit with the risen Lord. Thus the Spirit characterizes the whole salvific function of Jesus, and indeed his relationship to God and to humankind, since Scripture never separates his functions and relations. Logos Christology starts with the eternal Word who descends from God and becomes incarnate in Jesus; Spirit Christology begins with the man Jesus and describes him as filled with the Spirit. Contemporary Spirit Christology resumes this approach to structure an ascending Christology: the human person Jesus is filled with the Spirit of God, in whose power he lives his life, is raised from the dead, and redeems humankind. Whereas Logos Christology stresses the divinity of Jesus and is in danger of diminishing his humanity, Spirit Christology provides more centrally for the human personhood of Jesus. Clearly, however, the danger of adoptionism, i.e., that Jesus is divine functionally rather than ontologically, threatens this approach. In response, theologians who favor a Spirit Christology acknowledge that the Spirit fulfills Jesus from his very conception and therefore that Jesus is fully divine and fully human.

Piet Schoonenberg is one of the leading proponents of Spirit Christology. In his book, *The Christ* (1971) he maintained that the classical formula of Jesus being one divine person with both a divine and a human nature was inadequate. In its stead, Schoonenberg proposed that the one person, Jesus of Nazareth, is a human person and that it is possible to maintain that the Word did not preexist the Incarnation *as a person* but as an extension of God's self-expression. The Word of God comes to exist as a person in and through the Incarnation. Jesus' human person was pervaded by the Logos and the Spirit as extensions of God's person, so that Christ in his divine/human reality is only one person. Schoonenberg's position in *The Christ* is explained more fully in NCE 16:85, although he has clarified and somewhat altered his theory in a 1977 article (see bibliog.). Mindful of the 1972 Declaration by the Congregation for the Doctrine of Faith, Schoonenberg clearly asserts that the presence of God in Jesus is messianic and eschatological, i.e., supreme and definitive. He continues to maintain that the Word exists as a person only in Jesus (the enhypostasis of the Word), but also acknowledges that Jesus is enhypostatic in the Word insofar as God, being immanent, sustains and grounds every finite reality, including the human reality of Jesus.

Christology from Below. The cardinal premise of this approach is that greater correspondence to the New Testament evidence and to modern man's historical way of thinking would be achieved if Christology began with the real human being, Jesus of Nazareth, his historical reality, and his activity. Only then, and in a manner consistent with this historical evidence, can the relationship between this human being and God be explored. What is needed, according to this analysis, is not so much a classical Christology, speculatively and dogmatically concerned with ontological categories and the being of God, but historical Christology given over to the more functional descriptions of the earliest Christian message and, presumably, of Jesus himself. Christology from below aligns itself closely with Spirit Christology in grounding its formulations on the historical Jesus and his religious/cultural setting, but resists metaphysical analysis as not meaningful today, notwithstanding the legitimacy of such speculation in previous cultures. The inspiration for this Christological model seems to be post-Enlightenment Protestantism: a return to the historical Jesus and the challenge of a personal faith, much in the manner of Kierkegaard.

The focus on the historical Jesus rests on the conviction that an essential continuity obtains between the pre-Easter Jesus and the post-Easter message. An understanding of Jesus' message, more acute today—because of advances in scriptural study—than at any other time since the first century, unveils the meaning of life lived authentically in relationship with a loving Father. This message, as Jesus proclaimed it, is inextricably bound up with the Kingdom of God. Jesus bursts all the normal categories of his time to preach that God's cause is the freedom and fulfillment of man. Rather than being a religio-political theocracy or an avenging judgment, the Kingdom created by God's free act will be the establishment of absolute righteousness, unsurpassable freedom, and universal reconciliation. The absolute or eschatological future of God, therefore, is present in the words and works of Jesus. Indeed his authority in proclaiming the Kingdom is amazing; it is a completely underived, supremely personal authority. On his own account he asserts God's will, identifies himself with God's cause, and becomes the public advocate of God and man. Jesus' basic attitude is rooted in the ultimate reality which he calls God, his Father. This attitude is one of freedom that opens up a real alternative to self-centered protectiveness and demands a new awareness and a new way of life.

Hans Küng, one of the chief contemporary proponents of a Christology from below, strongly defends the uniqueness of Jesus and his absolute connection with the Kingdom of God. In Küng's view, however, the Resurrection is not a historical event in the sense that it can be verified by historical scientific methods. The miracle of the Resurrection is that God intervenes at the point where humanly everything seems to be lost; God brings new life out of death. What continues after Jesus' death is not his physiological body, but his personal identity—the lasting significance of his life and fate. According to Küng, therefore, the post-Easter titles applied to Jesus make explicit what had been implicit in the life of Jesus. The several titles are largely interchangeable, reflect the worldview of the time, and are not centrally important in the face of the definite criterion which is Jesus himself. The radical nature of Küng's position is most clearly reflected in his explanation of Jesus' preexistence. The Christian community's assertions about Jesus' preexistence were meant to justify the eschatological centrality of the living Jesus in the mythical manner acceptable to New Testament times, i.e., that a being existed before time and beyond this world but descended from God and became a man. Such a formulation is no longer credible today. Küng translates these preexistence motifs to say that from eternity there is no God other than the one who manifested himself in Jesus, that God always was and always will be as he became known in his Christ. Since this is so, Jesus has a universal significance in the light of this universal God. However God reveals himself to humankind, it will be in accord with the spirit of Jesus.

Process Christology. Extensive studies on process Christology in particular have recently been published, most notably one by John Cobb. Cobb uses the word Christ to "name what is experienced as supremely important when this is bound up with Jesus" (Cobb 17) and undertakes to forge a positive answer to the question whether Christ can continue to be relevant to this age, typified by a profane or wordly consciousness and a strong sense of pluralism in tension with the classical Christian notion of Christ's universality. Cobb predicates his answer on the characteristically process notion of creative transformation, realized both in art and theology. Christianity and Western art have evolved from identifying Christ, first, with an absolute God possessing sacred power, then with the human and suffering Jesus, and now to the point where Christ is regarded as the creative power of self-realization, the effective force of transformation in the world. In theology, also, Christ must be regarded as the transforming power of God in the world, which relativizes or refuses to make absolute every religion, every theology, every received word and image. Thus Christ becomes the principle that overcomes all exclusiveness, that opens human consciousness to every authentic religion. Christ is recognized as the drive toward creative transformation working in every aspect of life; he is the future not-yet-realized, transforming the givenness of the past from being a burden to becoming a potentiality for new creation.

This power of creative transformation may also be named the Logos. Transcendence is available in every experience as the influence of the new drawing the experience to this or that realization. But this is not a merely random or unspecified potentiality. Rather, there is order and rationality, the Logos as the absolute power of a meaningful evolution. God is present in every act as the new aim or purpose of that act, bringing emerging order and meaning. This is the Logos, which when successful becomes creative transformation. The image, Christ, is nothing else but the Logos immanent in the world. Christ means the immanence of the Logos in space: the initial aim of all occasions, normative, personal, beyond the individual, creative, present everywhere, especially in human love.

These notions of the Logos and creative transformation apply to Jesus of Nazareth. Jesus' life cannot be understood except as distinctive, a distinctiveness that cannot be reduced to that of a prophet or mystic. Instead, Jesus must be seen as the man who dared to act as God's agent. Legimately, therefore, the Christian proclaims that the Logos was incarnate in Jesus, although at the same time the Christian must acknowledge that the Logos is incarnate in all human beings who open themselves to God's creative power. How then is Jesus different? Cobb maintains that Jesus realizes a distinctive incarnation because his very selfhood was constituted by the Logos. Other persons may greatly conform to the possibility offered by the Logos, but the Logos remains a "Thou" other than the self, one force within the total amalgam that is a person's actual experience. In Jesus, however, the Logos is identical with the center of the self which orders all the elements in experience. Jesus' relation to God is not the confrontation of an "I" by a "Thou," but an identity between the personal "I" and God's creative power, the Logos. "This structure of existence would be the incarnation of the Logos in the fullest meaningful sense" (Cobb 140).

What seems to be distinctive about some recent process Christologies is that they have gone beyond the minimalist Christologies of earlier proponents like Shubert Ogden and Norman Pittenger. At least some process theologians find it legitimate to defend the absolute uniqueness of Jesus as a special act of God, not because Jesus is regarded as supremely revelatory by the Christian community, but because God's intention realized in Jesus is unique and decisive. Only if Jesus is objectively God's supreme act of self-expression would it be appropriate to receive him as God's decisive revelation.

Walter Kasper's Jesus the Christ. Kasper's study is an extremely competent and systematic presentation of Christology within the best tradition of classical, and in that sense conservative, Roman Catholic theology. His book, *Jesus the Christ*, grew out of his regular lectures at the University of Tübingen and its methodology is clear: one must examine the biblical texts within the developing reflection of the Church and in conversation with contemporary culture and philosophy. The philosophical questions cannot be avoided precisely because Christianity must be a *living* faith, its universal claim demands that it be presented in light of contemporary human questions and needs. Hence Kasper argues against Küng and all Christologies exclusively from below. The Hellenization of Jesus' message, the shift from functional to ontological categories, either within the New Testament or in the first centuries of the Church, should be regarded not as a distortion but as a necessary application of the meaning of

Jesus. Indeed, functional Christology is itself a form of ontic-Christology since it presents Jesus' functions (his mission and obedience to the Father) as the expression and realization of his being. Yet Kasper also has his differences with Karl Rahner and the transcendental Thomists, since, in Kasper's view, the transcendental analysis of consciousness can demonstrate man's openness to the infinite but cannot demonstrate that the infinite is a personal God. Philosophy must be content with this highly problematic situation and man's real nature cannot be understood until inquiry reaches a certain point called Jesus Christ. But what is true about the deficiencies of a Rahnerian approach is true of any metaphysics: Christology as an interpretation of an individual can accept a universal understanding of existence only when tested by the uniqueness of Jesus' own life and meaning. Kasper insists that the earliest Christological councils accepted this dialectic between philosophy and the Gospel and thus he defends the Christological dogma of Chalcedon as "an extremely precise version of what we encounter in Jesus' history" (Kasper 238).

The historical picture of Jesus that Kasper presents is consistent with the conclusions of modern exegesis and even the main lines of Küng's approach. But where Küng depicts the prophetic, the radical, and the challenging aspect of Jesus' message, Kasper stresses the faith, prayer, obedience, and self-giving of Jesus. Such an analysis of the New Testament message and acknowledgement of the basic validity of the patristic developments lead Kasper to structure a personalist ontology grounded in an appreciation of freedom, relation, and love. Jesus is the one who frees man to be himself because he lives, and offers others the possibility of living, a perfectly symbiotic relationship of love with God. In the last part of his study, Kasper treats the perennial affirmations about Jesus—that he is truly God, truly man, and a perfect unity—in the light of this personalist ontology.

Jesus' preexistence is strongly defended not as a projection of time backwards into eternity, but as an expression of the eschatological character of his person and task. "Since in Jesus Christ, God himself has definitively, unreservedly and unsurpassably revealed and communicated himself, Jesus is part of the definition of God's eternal nature" (ibid. 175). That eternal nature of God, revealed by Jesus, is freedom and love. In contrast to the dominant themes of today's culture, the death and resurrection of Jesus realize in a supreme way the meaning of both God and man: the individual emptying himself in love for others. Every particularity has its truth only by being assumed into a whole; the living reality must go out of itself in order to preserve itself. Against this background of divine freedom and love, the question of Jesus' humanity arises, i.e., what the coming of God in the flesh means. Kasper understands the body not as something which a person has but as that which a person is. Body is that through which a person is implanted in his environment and involved with his contemporaries. Hence body is an ambiguous phenomenon: it can be a source either for deception or authenticity. Since this is so, God's appearance in the flesh radically redeems the equivocal status of human existence and creates a real opportunity for corporeal redemption—the only redemption possible for man-as-body.

Kasper's defense of the unity between God and man in Jesus is based upon his notion of person and relation. In the concrete, a person exists only in a threefold relation:

to himself, to the world around him, and to his fellow human beings. But these relations require a basis of meaning supplied by God; God himself has to be included in the definition of the human person. Thus the union between God and man in Jesus is the fulfillment of human dynamism and openness to the infinite. Man as person is the indeterminate mediation between the divine and human; in Jesus Christ this mediation receives from God its specific form, plenitude, and perfection.

Bibliography: J. B. COBB, JR., *Christ in a Pluralistic Age* (Philadelphia 1975). Congregation for the Doctrine of the Faith, *Declaration*, tr. Origins 1 (1972) 664, 667–668. D. GRIFFIN, *Process Christology* (Philadelphia 1973). W. KASPER, *Jesus the Christ*, tr. V. GREEN (New York 1976). H. KÜNG, *On Being a Christian*, tr. E. QUINN (Garden City, N.Y. 1976). K. RAHNER, *Foundations of Christian Faith,*, tr. W. V. DYCH (New York 1978). P. SCHOONENBERG, *The Christ*, tr. D. COULING (New York 1971); "Spirit Christology and Logos Christology," *Bijdragen* 38 (1977) 350–375. D. TRACY, *Blessed Rage for Order* (New York 1975).

[T. M. MCFADDEN]

CHURCH (THEOLOGY)

"The Church as such" is a phrase that twenty years ago would evoke among Catholics the notion of a tightly organized and self-sufficient "religion" (Roman Catholicism) or even primarily its clerical cadres. This image persists, to be sure, but alongside it another nontechnical usage has gained currency, so that the word, "Church," is now taken to mean a loose-knit family of Christian denominations in informal connection and peopled by many who identify themselves only partially with "their" Church. After more than a century of losing their accustomed place in society, Christians are attempting to come to grips with their new situation and to do it in communication with each other. Even the Catholic Church finds its relationships with the other confessions, other religious and cultural traditions, and with the "secular world" to be problematical. The last-named area, the relationship of Church and world, is not necessarily the most urgent, but it is fundamental. Theologically it raises the issue of the three-cornered relationships between Church, world, and *Kingdom of God.

Church and World. In 1964, in his first encyclical, *Ecclesiam suam*, Pope Paul VI sounded the keynote of dialogue. He distinguished three groups with which the Church is engaged in dialogue, arranged in three concentric circles: first, all people, many of whom profess no religion; then those who profess non-Christian religions; and lastly fellow Christians who are not Catholics. Another striking indication of this determination of the Church to enter into the predicaments of humanity at large was that Vatican Council II, after reflecting on the nature of the Church in the Dogmatic Constitution, *Lumen gentium*, also issued a Pastoral Constitution, *Gaudium et spes*, on The Church in the Modern World (1965). In 1968 the Latin American bishops, assembled for their Second General Conference in Medellín, Colombia, carried this program still further (*see* MEDELLÍN DOCUMENTS). Such moves were disconcerting to many who looked upon the Church as a conservative force in their sense; setbacks have occurred and the danger of failure is not excluded.

At the level of theological reflection, *Lumen gentium* showed, for one thing, that the usual approach to ecclesiology was not the only acceptable one, and hence set the stage for new models or combinations of models which would give an account for "the hope that is in us"

(1 Pt 3.15) in terms adapted to contemporary understanding. In particular, *Lumen gentium* established the priority of the depth-dimension of the Church, its mystery in relation to the ultimate mystery of God's purposes for humankind. The sequence of its chapters is significant and has received much comment. After a first chapter, setting forth the mystery of the Church's role in the economy of salvation, the Council went on to biblical images and analogies of the Church in the second chapter. Here the "People of God" of the Christian dispensation was described as sharing throughout in the august gifts and missions of the Church—evangelizing, worshipping, reconciling—prior to any distinction between clergy and laity. Only then did the hierarchy (ch. 3) and the laity (ch. 4) receive separate consideration.

In the conciliar debates on the nature of the Church the call for a new relationship between Church and world expressed itself especially in the criticism of triumphalism. A triumphalist self-presentation of the Church left the impression, not only that the modern world was sick, but that the Church knew why it was ailing and had the remedies at hand to cure it, if only the world would accept them. Although understandable as Catholicism's reaction to secularizing tendencies, this attitude nevertheless involved an unwarranted extension of the hierarchy's claims to competence and damaged the Church's credibility in public opinion. The hierarchy, gathered in Council, reminded themselves and the world that "Christ carried out the work of redemption in poverty and oppression. . . . Likewise, the Church, although she needs human resources to carry out her mission, is not set up to seek earthly glory, but to proclaim, and this by her own example, humility and self-denial" (*Lumen gentium* 8). They went on to indicate that the poor and oppressed have a greater claim than others on the concern and solidarity of Christians, a principle which will never be popular in the world and which stands as a constant rebuke to the Church itself, standing as it does "always in need of purification" (ibid.).

The Church, then, is in the world and the world is in the Church. The Church is a part of humanity with certain distinguishing marks. It consists of those who aid one another to preserve the memory (or pass on the tradition) that goes back to Jesus of Nazareth and was set in motion by his life and preaching, death and resurrection. After he died, his Spirit was poured forth in the hearts of his followers, who then recognized that what he had told them about the approaching rule of God was after all "God's truth," for God had vindicated Jesus' message by raising him from the dead and making him the Christ (Acts 2.36).

Church, World, Kingdom. As the Christ, Jesus is not absent but present to those who remember and believe in him. The Christian tradition, thus set on its way through history, is not fixed solely on what happened in the past. The message of Jesus, confirmed by the cross and resurrection, concerned the present primarily in view of the future—the future salvation coming from God, what Jesus called the Kingdom or rule of God.

Hence the memory which Christians keep alive in their celebration of the Last Supper, their recourse to the Bible and their use of the Lord's Prayer is a "dangerous and liberating memory" (J. B. Metz in Küng 121). If the Church were to be defined in one

sentence, it might be the following: the Church consists of those men and women who together look back to Jesus Christ and forward to a joint eschatological salvation in the hope of the resurrection; in a classic summary, the *coetus fidelium*. This definition applies equally to groups of Christians who are in personal contact with one another and to the Church universal.

Any such definition, however, may seem to write off the masses of afflicted humanity who do not meet the requirement of more or less explicit faith. It is therefore important to bear in mind the thrust of Jesus' Kingdom-preaching as corrective of any ecclesiastical myopia or self-centeredness. It is the human race as a whole in its social interconnectedness and in its setting in the cosmos that God will transform and put right. Church people cannot afford to be triumphalistic, because they themselves are not yet definitively transformed. This will only take place in company with the rest of the world in God's eschatological consummation. The fact that Jesus' proclamation of the Kingdom led to his death and only thereby to his resurrection means that no failure on our part, no matter how great, can wrest the initiative from God's hands. It does not mean that Christians are authorized to tolerate inhuman conditions that are alleviable, if only here and there and for a time.

A model of the Church answering to these contemporary concerns is the Servant model (so called by Dulles 83–96). The sacramental model of the Church is also susceptible of development in this direction (compare *ibid.* 185–187): the Church is the sign and Sacrament of the world as the latter will be constituted in God's future. Both "Models of the Church" and "Church as Sacrament" are themes addressed by contemporary theologies of the Church.

Models of the Church. "We use models as intellectual tools. They help us to analyze and to explore reality. A model or a paradigm brings various elements together into a constellation, and the constellation arranges the elements in a new way" (O'Meara 3; somewhat analogous uses of "paradigm" appear in Kuhn; Shapere).

Typological analysis and comparison of theories is not new, but Avery Dulles has performed the service for ecclesiologies in a particularly novel and magisterial fashion in his *Models of the Church*. He shows, for instance, that thematic concepts of the Church (e.g. the People of God, the Body of Christ, the Dwelling or "workshop" of the Spirit) often take on a somewhat different bearing depending on the model in which they figure for a given ecclesiology. Vatican Council II's affirmations about the Church tend to be associated with two particular models, those of "mystical communion" and "sacrament." Indeed, many biblical and traditional themes can find some place also in the other of the five models which Dulles delineates: the Church as "herald," "servant," and institution. There is in each model, however, a controlling image or activity or other characteristic around which the themes are organized:

The institutional model makes it clear that the Church must be a structured community and that it must remain the kind of community Christ instituted. Such a community would have to include a pastoral office equipped with authority to preside over the worship of the community as such, to prescribe the limits of tolerable dissent, and to represent the community in an official way. The community model makes it evident that the church must be united to God by grace, and that in the strength of that grace its members must be lovingly united to one another. The sacramental model brings home the idea that the Church must in its visible aspects—especially in its community prayer and worship—be a sign of the continuing vitality of the grace of Christ and of hope for the redemption that he promises. The kerygmatic [herald] model accentuates the necessity for the Church to continue to herald the gospel and to move men to put their faith in Jesus as Lord and Saviour. The diaconal [servant] model points up the urgency of making the Church contribute to the transformation of the secular life of man, and of impregnating human society as a whole with the values of the Kingdom of God (Dulles 183).

Dulles leans to the opinion that the sacramental model, if properly developed, could be the most comprehensive of all. All models are inadequate to their object, but only the institutional model, of those he presents, is clearly deemed incapable of grounding an acceptable ecclesiology. To keep in mind the spectrum of available models is indispensable to any serious reflection on the Church.

Church as Sacrament. At the head of its Dogmatic Constitution on the Church Vatican II put the affirmation that Christ is the light of the world. It went on to describe the Church as "a kind of sacrament or sign and instrument of communion with God and of unity among all human beings" (*Lumen gentium* 1). To appreciate the implications of this approach takes some reflection. The Church is the sign of the world to come. Put another way, the Church is the sign of God's mystery at work in the present world. The Church, therefore, is not an end in itself, but points to the world to come, conceived as including not only church members but also the unchurched millions of all centuries. An important proviso, inherent in the idea of sacramentality as applied to the Church, is that its signifying power is liable to be deflected and curtailed by the imperfect faith of those who make up the Church.

The notion of sacramentality goes beyond that of a sign or symbol as conventionally understood, in that it denotes the presence or effectiveness in the sacrament of that which it signifies. But this presence can vary as to its mode and degree, depending on whether the sacrament at issue is Christ, the Church, the Eucharist, or one of the other six Sacraments. The Church is not itself divine as Christ is, but like Christ is a human, visible instrument destined by God to play a role in the salvation of humanity.

Bibliography: On the Church: G. C. BERKOWER, *The Church* (Grand Rapids, Mich. 1976). G. GUTIÉRREZ, *Theology of Liberation*, tr. C. INDA and J. EAGLESON (Maryknoll, N.Y. 1973). International Theological Commission, "De promotione humana et salute christiana," Greg 58 (1977) 413–430. H. KÜNG, *On Being a Christian*, tr. E. QUINN (Garden City, N.Y. 1976). R. P. MCBRIEN, *The Church: Continuing Quest* (New York 1970). Medellín Conference of Latin American Bishops, *The Church in the Present-Day Transformation of Latin America* (USCC Publ. Office, Washington, D.C. 1970). J. MOLTMANN, *Church in the Power of the Spirit*, tr. M. KOHL (New York 1977). W. PANNENBERG, "The Church and the Eschatological Kingdom," in W. PANNENBERG, A. DULLES, C. BRAATEN, *Spirit, Faith, and Church* (Philadelphia 1970) 108–123. G. PHILIPS, *L'Église et son mystère au IIe Concile du Vatican* (2 v., Paris 1967–68). K. RAHNER, *The Shape of the Church to Come*, tr. E. QUINN (New York 1974). E. SCHILLEBEECKX, *World and Church*, tr. N. D. SMITH (New York 1971); *Jesus: An Experiment in Christology* (New York in press).
On Models of the Church and Church as Sacrament: A. DULLES, *Models of the Church* (New York 1974). J.-P. JOSSUA, "Immutabilité, progrès, ou structurations multiples des doctines chrétiennes," RevScPhilTh 52 (1968) 173–200. T. S. KUHN, *The Structure of the Scientific Revolution* (Chicago 1970; with D. SCHAPERE, NCE 16:402404. T. F. O'MEARA, "Philosophical Models in Ecclesiology," ThSt 39 (1978) 3–21. O. SEMMELROTH, "Die Kirche als Sakrament des Heiles," in J. FEINER and M. LÖHRER, eds., *Das Helisgeschehen in der Gemeinde. Mysterium Salutis* 4/1 (Einsiedeln 1972) 309–356. P. SMULDERS, "L'Église sacrement du salut," in G. BARAÚNA, ed., *L'Église de Vatican II* 2 (Paris 1967) 313–338.

[P. MISNER]

CHURCH, LOCAL (THEOLOGY)

The Church is the Sacrament of the triune God's communion with humanity as this is revealed and realized in the two "advocates" of even sinful humanity, Jesus (1 Jn 2.1) and the "other paraclete," the Holy Spirit (Jn 14.26). The Church is, thus, a double communion—of God with man and of man with man (*see* CHURCH AND COMMUNIO).

Background. Although it is legitimate to speak of every "soul" as the Church (and a long tradition, especially from Origen does so), in keeping with both Judeo-Christianity's ontology of communion and sacrament and its actual history of salvation, "Church" is preferably used for the social and historical dimension of the Christian event and experience. Likewise, although it is legitimate and necessary to speak of the Church in the Old Testament (cf. Y. Congar, 1952), "Church" does become a technical term, designating a particular portion of the whole salvation-history, the time between the paschal and parousiac glorifications of Christ. Indeed, as the *Shepherd of Hermas* emphasizes, "The Church . . . is an aged woman . . . because she was created first, before all else . . . . It was for her that the world was made" (Vision 1, ch. 4, 1). This means that in reality the Church is a particular way humanity has of being. There is no abyss between humanity as natural and supernatural, created and graced. For there is no abyss between God and mankind. As the inward being of God is the communion of Father, Son and Holy Spirit, so is the being he communicates outwardly also communion, for it is his image and likeness (Gen 1.26–27). Hence, there is no conflict between the one and the many, between unity and diversity.

Acts of the Apostles. Only against this general background can the NT account of the origin, spread, and relationship of the Church and the Churches be understood. The problem is illustrated by the varied usage of the Greek term for Church, ἐκκλησία, which translates the Hebrew *qahal*, but which was perhaps deliberately chosen to distinguish the Christian Church from the Jewish synagogue (cf. Rost). Within the Christian communion, however, the term is used, without distinguishing, for the domestic, local, particular, universal Church, whether in the singular or plural. It may be taken that this semantic phenomenon confirms that the perichoresis (11:128) and the theandric communions revealed in the Trinity and the Christ are also present in their Sacrament, the Church. For the one and the many, the human and the divine, exist not as conflict, but as communion. Thus, between the universal Church and the local Church, the one Church and the many Churches, between unity and catholicity, there is also not conflict, but communion.

Originally "Church" would have referred to the Mother Church of all, Jerusalem (Acts 5.11; 8.11). Thus, the local, regional, and universal Church would simply have coincided, as well, perhaps, as the domestic Church and the Eucharistic synaxis. However, first conflict with the Jews (Acts 8.1), then persecution by Herod (Acts 12.1, 5; 13.1) and, finally, missionary activity (Acts 8.4, 25; 9.20; 10; 11.19) cause the members, and thus, the Jerusalem Church itself, to disperse. Thus, the one Church is now many Churches, but still one. This is the fact narrated, but not explained in the New Testament.

Pauline Churches. In his earliest Epistles Paul

emphasizes what can be called the domestic, local, or regional Churches (1 and 2 Thes 1.1; 1 and 2 Cor 1.1; Rom 16.1, 5, 16; 1 Cor 16.1, 19; Phlm 2). In the later Epistles the Church as universal is dominant (Eph 1.22). In Colossians (1.24; 4.15–16) the Church is both universal and particular (regional, local, domestic).

Interpretation. The term "Church" is neither univocal nor equivocal, but analogous, according to the sacramental and communitarian ontology of perichoresis revealed in the Trinity and Christ (the hypostatic union). According to this ontology, all being is symbolic, present to, and related with (other being). For this reason the local Church is not merely a part or administrative subunit of the universal Church. It is, rather, the real and symbolic presence of Church in any given time and place. Likewise, then, the universal Church is not the moral or juridic composite of all the local Churches, but their communion with one another. The many local Churches are the Sacraments of the many-gifted, one Spirit, just as the many-membered Church is the Sacrament of the one Body of Christ, the singular posterity of Abraham (Gal 3.17). Neither universal nor local Church may, then, claim exclusive rights in regard to the other. The Church, at whatever levels, exists only in and as communion.

The experience and theology of Pentecost supports this understanding, especially if the Pentecost narrative's referent is not the tower of Babel, but the contemporary rabbinic theology, which held that the Sinaitic proclamation of the Torah was immediately and universally intelligible to all mankind (cf. Kremer). Theologically, then, the local Church at Jerusalem would already have been universal. This one local Church is (already) the *Catholic* Church. The many local Churches are the epiphanies of this one Church in time and space. Here theology and reality themselves enjoy a rare and remarkable perichoresis, for it is clear in both that wherever *a* Church is, there *the* Church is—under the one condition that any given Church be in communion with the other *Churches*, and thus in communion with *the Church*.

This communion of perichoresis (presence to and relation with) and the consequent brotherly concern are illustrated by the practice of mutual visitations by delegates of the outlying local Churches and the "central" or universal Church (Acts 8.14; 15.30–35; 18.24; 19.1–7). These same texts also confirm Luke's concern to show how incipient and perhaps ecclesially deficient local Churches are brought into full communion within the Church and thus into full ecclesial existence. Apostolic visitation was continued in a certain fashion by the patristic practice of hospitality and circular letters among Churches and bishops (cf. von Hertling).

The perichoresis of universal and local Church is strikingly illustrated by an event recounted by Eusebius (*Hist. eccl.* 7.30). In 268 a Synod at Antioch, one of the principal or "head" Churches (cf. Grotz), excommunicated Paul of Samosata and elected Domnus as the new bishop. The synodal bishops then wrote to the bishops of Rome and Alexandria (also "head" Churches) an explanatory letter, which was, in turn, to be shared with the neighboring bishops: "We were therefore obliged . . . to excommunicate him and appoint another bishop in his place for the Catholic Church . . . and we are informing you of his appointment in order that you may write to him and receive from him a letter establishing communion." It is noteworthy that Domnus is designated not as bishop of Antioch, as one would expect, but as τῇ καθολικῇ ἐκκλησίᾳ (bishop of the Catholic Church). In the same vein, the ritual for the ordination of a bishop in the *Sacramentarium Veronense* (L. C. Mohlberg, ed., Rome, 1956, 119): *Tribuas eis cathedram episcopalem ad regendam ecclesiam tuam et plebem universam.* Hence, between the local and universal Church there is neither abyss nor conflict, but presence and communion.

This perichoresis of the many local Churches and the one universal Church is also illustrated by the Jerusalem Council described in Acts 15. Collegial in both attitude and procedure, this council provides the Church with a paradigm of problem-solving for all ages. The Church was then already both particular (regional) and universal, and so was the tendency to equate the "central" Church with Church pure and simple. The Mosaic Law was not the only, perhaps not even the primary problem at this council. Crucial, rather, was the manner in which conflicts would be solved, decisions made. The primary problem was the administrative and life style of the Church. The style chosen was not centralist, secretive manipulation by elitists, but universal, open deliberation by all the Churches—universal, central, regional, local—trusting in the Holy Spirit (Acts 15.28).

Church and Churches. Against this general background the following clarification and articulation of the term "Church" may be proposed.

1. *Divine Universal Church.* As Hermas pointed out, the Church is so old because God intended its existence first of all. From the very beginning all else has existed for the sake of Christ's Body, personal and sacramental. In this sense Church is but another word for God's universal saving will (1 Tm 2.4–6; Jn 3.15–18). Without this understanding of Church, all ecclesial life and theology become struggles and disputes about power and privilege. Only as the Sacrament of the divine saving will can the Church secure its legitimacy.

2. *Theandric Local Church.* Since God's will is to save his creation, and since grace does not destroy but perfects the nature originally created, the Church as the effected expression of the divine saving will is both human and divine. Since human beings exist in time and place, so must God's effective saving will; therefore, also the Church. As the Sacrament of God's salvation, the Church cannot exist only in general. Like its theandric founder, the Church must also "assume the condition of . . . and become as men are, . . . being as all men are" (Phil 2.7). Hence, the Church always exists in a concrete time and place, for it is the encounter between God and men.

Where this encounter is most palpably experienced and manifested is called the "local Church." Obviously, then, this local Church is most intensely Church in the celebration of the Eucharist, for nowhere else is the Memory and Tradition of the risen Christ (1 Co 11.23–27; 15:3), those privileged "definitions" of the Church, more precisely proclaimed and celebrated. Hence, the true center of the Church is not an office, but the Eucharist, whereby all are made the one Body of Christ (1 Cor 10.14–17). Thus are clearly invalidated all ambitions for monarchical or centralist hegemony at whatever level of ecclesiastical office. This is especially critical for a local Church which functions centrally within the order of the universal Church. Its "headship" is fundamentally the correct celebration of the Eucharist, whereby the sacramental unity of the Church is manifested and maintained. However, the Eucharist can be celebrated only locally, not universally. Hence, that central local Church, which is the focal point of unity for the whole Church, has as its decisive action precisely that which every local Church has and which can be performed only locally. Clearly, then, the local Church is not and cannot be merely an administrative subdistrict. It is, rather, the symbolic actualization and concrete appearance, in time and space, of the *divine* universal Church (not the papal universal Church). This means, of course, that the local Church is not a defective mode or limited reflection of the Church. Rather, in the local Church is present the entire Christian mystery, with the exception only of that which can be present only in the universality of the communion of all the local Churches. Fittingly at one time the offices of bishop and pastor, presently divided, tended to coincide. Thus, the "parish church" originates primarily not in the atomistic splitting of the universal Church by canonical and administrative procedures, but in the taking place or happening of the Christ-event in human culture and fact.

3. *Particular (Regional) Church.* Lest there be anarchy among the local Churches, there is need for focal points of unity. This service of unity would have been provided (perhaps originally almost spontaneously) by those principal or head Churches already noted, whose headship or principality was variously grounded. As the Church grew there was no longer only one presbyter or overseer. There was also a *gremium* or *collegium* of associates to assist in the shepherding of the flock. In today's terms, the original parish grew into a diocese, which was itself constituted by many parishes. There is, henceforth, both local Church and particular or regional Church. Both terms are valuable, since "regional" emphasizes a certain brute geographical reality, while "particular" emphasizes a certain peculiar quality attached to that geographical reality. It must be acknowledged immediately, however, that modern mobility makes it possible that there could be particular Churches with a very tenuous geographical dimension.

The early Church's awareness of the need for a practical means of maintaining and manifesting communion among local Churches is illustrated by the practice of the *fermentum*: a fragment of the host consecrated by the bishop was sent to his pastors so that their communion with him might be especially expressed in the celebration of the Eucharist. The exchange of letters among the bishops has already been noted (cf. von Hertling). Thus it is clear that the regional and particular Churches are not, as such, sectarian or divided. Rather, they are intended to allow the genius and culture peculiar to any given population to flourish also within the communion of believers in Christ. Remnants of the particular Churches are still present in the so-called canonical rites. This ambiguous term is good insofar as it emphasizes that a particular Church should have a particular way of celebrating the liturgy, especially the Eucharist. It is less desirable insofar as it obscures the necessary particularity of a particular Church's theology and catechesis—allowed, indeed, mandated by the hierarchy of truths of Vatican II (*Unitatis redintegratio* 11)—spirituality, organization, law, customs. Local, indigenous cultures must be allowed to flourish fully in the Church as long as they are not explicitly contrary to the Judeo-Christian revelation. The non-observance of this principle throughout the missionary activity of the Church is only being rectified recently (*see* MISSION [NEW TRENDS]).

Recent attempts to establish national episcopal conferences are small steps, however halting, in the direction of revitalizing the particular Churches. However, it is not to be blandly assumed that local hierarchies will necessarily be more sensitive and responsive to local needs (cf. Watermann). The regional and particular Church has suffered the greatest attrition during the process of church centralization. Even apart from the theology of the many and different gifts of the one Holy Spirit, the generally advocated social principle of subsidiarity is also valid for the Church. Failure of the regional Churches automatically means an impoverishment of the Church's life and comeliness, its attractiveness—as was clearly witnessed by the monochromatic Romanization of the liturgy in the West. Furthermore, particular Churches must not be thought of as exclusively geographical. The particular Church can also be based other than spatially—according to nationality, culture, education, sex, language, psychology, spirituality, economics. The one necessity is that the particular Church not encapsulate itself in isolation from, but open itself to communion with all other particular and local Churches, and thus with the one universal Church. Instructive here can be the experience, good and bad, of the monastery, which was regarded as an *ecclesiola*. Often the monastic community was summoned into existence by the failure of the *communio* of the great Church, by which failure a particular way of being Church had been previously frustrated. Ecclesial being is both centripetal and centrifugal. The regional and particular Churches are to be the way the local Churches have of being centrifugal. Their success has been marginal, for the centripetal movement has been predominant.

4. *Universal Papal (Petrine) Church.* If regional points of unity and particular Church organization are desirable for the local Churches, then by the same reasoning a central point of unity for all local and particular Churches cannot automatically be unacceptable. The reaction of Orthodox and Protestant to "good Pope John XXIII" and the cry of Luther even at Leipzig ("There is no doubt that the whole world would welcome such a man [a pastoral pope] with open arms and profuse tears!") hint that a central office in the Church is not as such universally rejected. Since God's saving will is universal, neither local nor regional (particular) Churches are sufficient as response and representation. There must also exist a way of being Church that reflects this universality. Traditionally this function has been assigned to the Church as Catholic (*see* CATHOLICITY). And therein is to be found the precise purpose of the papal continuation of the Petrine office—to support all the brothers (Lk 22.32), however many and wherever they may be; to be the rock-foundation of the Church, however widely spread it may be (Mt 16.16–19).

The proudest papal title and boast is to be the *servus servorum Dei*, however poorly it may have fit the facts. Certainly the point of the papacy is not hegemony, but shepherding; not uniformity, but unity.

The final theological underpinning for such an office is the Christian conviction that "our God is not a god of disorder but of peace" (1 Cor 14.25). However, as Pope Victor showed in one of the papacy's first peacemaking missions, ordering power is not readily exercised moderately and gently (Eusebius, *Hist. eccl.* 5.24). But, as Irenaeus and the other bishops showed in the same affair, abuse is to be corrected, neither ignored nor indulged. Nor does abuse destroy the abused thing.

Since the papacy is part of the sinful holy Church, a perfect papacy, although it may be preferred, is not to be postulated. Too often the choice unfortunately seems to be between what is perceived as Roman Catholicism's totalitarian monarchy and Protestantism's chaotic anarchy, although neither, apparently, is as bad as the rhetoric of the critics would have it. Vatican II is to be thanked for recalling that the universal papal (Petrine) Church is not monarchically structured (*Lumen gentium* 18–27). It is not a monarchy, for the college of bishops exists and operates not merely as a function of the papacy. Not without the papacy, of course, the college of bishops is nonetheless not to be subsumed into the papacy or into the Roman Curia. Unfortunately, the bishops do not seem to understand this. Obviously episcopal collegiality ought not to denature or obscure the unique symbolic shepherding of the papacy. But unfortunately in the history of the Church there has been too quick a recourse to the papacy. Thus has been destroyed that creative tension that must always exist in a pluriform society, if that society is to flourish. The Church is both centripetal and centrifugal and thus its communion involves both dialogue and tension between the universal (central) and local Churches. In the Roman Catholic tradition the central administrative offices of the Church are associated with the universal Church by reason of their association with the papacy. How far from serious dialogue and communion with the local and particular Churches this centralized universal Church still remains is illustrated by the conduct of the 1977 Synod of Bishops (cf. Kaufman).

Conclusion. In sum, the Church is the sacramental communion of those for whom Christ is the one mediator between God and man of God's salvation intended for all. Hence, the Church must happen and must exist according as humanity happens and exists. Thus there will be local (even domestic), regional/particular, and universal Church, corresponding to the reality of both God's saving will and man's response. The local Church is not merely an administrative subunit of the universal Church, but the most immediate and intense celebration of Church. Since Church is possible only by virtue of the divine perichoresis of the Father, Son, and Holy Spirit and the theandric perichoresis of Christ, its own being and lifestyle must also be perichoresis (presence to and relation with). Hence, salvation history consists of a threefold *communio* of perichoresis: Trinity—*Deus in se* ; Christ—*Deus in alio* ; Church—*Deus in aliis*— even the local "Church, which is his body, the fullness of him who fills the whole creation" (Eph 1.23).

Bibliography: H. URS VON BALTHASAR, *Die antirömische Affekt* (Frankfurt 1974). G. BARAÚNA, *A Igregia do Concilio Vaticano Segundo* (Rio de Janeiro 1966). Y. CONGAR, "Ecclesia ab Abel," in M. REDING, ed., *Abhandlungen über Theologie und Kirche* (Düsseldorf 1952). Y. CONGAR and B. D. DUPUY, *L'Épiscopat et l'Église universelle* (Paris 1962). J. DUNN, *Unity and Diversity in the New Testament* (Philadelphia 1977). J. FEINER and M. LÖHRER, eds., *Das Heilsgeschehen in der Gemeinde. Mysterium Salutis* 4/1 (Einsiedeln 1972). H. GROTZ, *Die Hauptkirchen des Ostens* (Rome 1964). L. VON HERTLING, *Communio: Church and Primacy in Early Christianity* (Chicago 1961). E. VON IVANKA, ed., *Handbuch des Ostkirchenkunde* (Düsseldorf 1971). L. KAUFMANN, *Orientierung* 41 (1977) 189–236. J. KREMER, *Pfingstbericht und Pfingstgeschehen* (Stuttgart 1973). H. DE LUBAC, *Les Églises particulières dans l'Église universelle* (Paris 1971). H. POTTMEYER, *Unfehlbarkeit und Souveranität* (Mainz 1975). K. RAHNER, *Theology of Pastoral Action*, tr. W. J. O'HARA (New York 1968). K. RAHNER and J. RATZINGER, *The Episcopate and the Primacy*, tr. K. BARKER et al. (New York 1962). L. ROST, *Die Verstufen von Kirche und Synagoge* (Stuttgart 1938). L. WATERMAN, *Rom, Platz des heiligen Offiziums* n.11 (Graz 1970).

[R. KRESS]

CHURCH AND COMMUNIO

Every adequate theology of the Church must begin with the proper beginning: not with Mt 16.16 (the promise of the Petrine primacy) but with 1 Tm 2.4 (the promise of universal salvation: "God our savior: he wants everyone to be saved..."). Traditionally the Church has been considered the Sacrament of this divine saving will, an insight revived by Vatican Council II in the Dogmatic Constitution on the Church: "By her relationship with Christ, the Church is a kind of sacrament or sign of intimate union with God, and of the unity of all mankind" (*Lumen gentium* 1); "through this Spirit [Christ] has established His body, the Church, as the universal sacrament of salvation" (ibid. 48). Accordingly the being of the Church is symbol and source of a twofold union—of God with man and of man with man. Hence, the Church is essentially a communion.

Ontology of Communio. Both Christ and the Church are called Sacrament, and each, analogously, is also called primal and original Sacrament (*Ursakrament*). The designation is not merely one among many others, equally valid; rather it is the key term in that ontology implicitly contained in the salvation history revealed in the Judaeo-Christian religious tradition. The meaning of Sacrament implies that the divine and the human are so compatible that they can be united in human experience as one event in which the human shares in and manifests the divine being to the world and invites it to participate in this sharing. Clearly, then, the Church can be understood only within the horizon of this Judaeo-Christian ontology.

Ontology of Salvation. Nowhere is the importance of philosophy more striking than in that ecclesiology which explains the Church as *communio* (*koinōnia*). All theology, and ecclesiology most of all, is liable to trivialize as soon as it forgets that it is essentially an answer to the fundamental human question (Man as the *Seinsfrage*), "What is it all about?" Any ecclesiology that wants to be taken seriously must start with 1 Tm 2.4 and the question of human salvation. Generally, and unfortunately, salvation is understood too narrowly, restricted to what is called either supernatural salvation or redemption. In reality, for the Judaeo-Christian ontology, salvation includes all that is customarily parcelled out as creation, grace, and glory. These three designate the three stages or degrees of created participation in uncreated being, which theologians have discerned to be implicitly revealed in the biblical account of history. Hence, the history of the world is correctly called "salvation-history."

If the importance of philosophy for theology is nowhere more obvious than here, likewise is the inadequacy of a "pagan" philosophy. Decisive for every philosophy is the perceived relation between the being of God and the being of the world. The Judaeo-Christian tradition offers the classic formulation of this mutuality in Gn 1.26–27, where the human creation is explicitly stated to be in the image and likeness of the divine creator. Although this formal insight is common to every philosophy and religion, the material content varies enormously. One need only compare typical Mesopotamian, Greco-Roman, Aryan, and Judaeo-Christian theories about the originating pattern, the deity, and the originated imitation, the world.

The Divine Being, Relationship. Since the being of God is decisive for the being of whatever is not God, the being or nature of the Judaeo-Christian God must be elucidated. The first and decisive assertion is that this God is triune, traditionally, the three Persons in one God. Thus are avoided the inadequacies inherent in both polytheism and even certain traditional monotheisms (cf. Peterson). In Greek philosophy substance denotes a being that stands on its own, that does not inhere in nor form part of another being. It tends to connote independence and even separation, apartness, isolation. Baneful results for certain religious approaches to God are obvious, for the deity becomes not only the One, but the Alone, even the Alien. The Judaeo-Christian God, on the other hand, and precisely as triune, emphatically reveals that by virtue of his divine unicity God is not reduced to the isolated and phthisic status of a monad. In Greek philosophy substance and relation tend to be mutually hostile, so that the more one really *is* (substance), the less one is related (relation). The ontology implicit in the triune God simply undoes this. For this God, substantial being is being related; relation is substance. Thus, God's very being is the relationships of the Father, Son, and Holy Spirit, for God is not first Father, and then only derivatively and subsequently Son and Holy Spirit (cf. Ratzinger). Rather, the very substance of God is originally communicated Being. Hence, all being, wherever it is in being, is inescapably "being with."

Perichoresis and Communio. In order to describe this triune God, theologians have had recourse to many images and terms. One of the happiest has been the Greek word *perichorēsis* (11:128), for it surpasses all others in indicating that in the triune God is reconciled one of the classical problems, not only of theoretical philosophy, but of practical living, namely the relation of the one and the many, of unity and diversity. Elsewhere considered contraries and even contradictories, in the triune God they are revealed to be congenial and harmonious. And this is aptly expressed by perichoresis, which comes from Greek words meaning to dance around with. If the anthropomorphism be permitted, perichoresis means that God is so full of being that his oneness is manyness, a manyness that in no way divides or separates, negates or isolates his oneness. Thus a term from "to dance" expresses God's being happy with himself, with his shared being—the being together of the Father, Son, and Holy Spirit. It is this kind of joyful unity in diversity that Genesis (especially ch. 1 and 2) wants to describe as the creation and which the Hebrew calls *shalom*.

Within this view it is perfectly "natural" that God, whose very being is communicated plenitude, should also communicate being to that which of itself is not God and, hence, which otherwise is simply not at all. To describe this communication in its various stages and degrees theologians have developed the terms creation, Christ, Church. If Christ, by his hypostatic union, is the most intense and unsurpassable instance of this theandric communication and communion of the divine with the human, then creation and Church are but the necessary antecedent and subsequent conditions: creation as the supposition and inception (protology) and Church as the consequence and completion (eschatology). Only in this context can the traditional distinction between nature and grace, the natural and the supernatural be properly understood. It is legitimate to refer to the creation as nature and to redemption and glory as grace, but only with the understanding that all being other than the simply divine is gratuitous and, hence, grace. Thus, humanity lives in a gracious world, and always has. The distinction between natural and supernatural remains legitimate only as long as it is clearly understood that the "super" refers not to God the Creator giving the gift, but to man the creature receiving the gift. The gift is being, the full "being with" that God intends to communicate. Hence, the creature's capacity for the "supernatural" does not demand supernatural life from a presumably reluctant God; rather, the generous God's desire to give creatures this superabundant life (Jn 1.16; 10.10) provides that there be a "nature" created to receive it.

Thus the dispute whether the Creed's *communio sanctorum* refers to holy things or holy persons may be historically pertinent, but is theologically and really otiose. For all being is communion in the holy being of God. And the Church is precisely where this holy communion is celebrated. As effect and symbol of God's inward communion outwardly communicated, the Church is the Sacrament of salvation. The eternal, immanent trinity is the savingly-historical, economic Trinity.

For this reason earliest theology speaks of the Church as "a people united by the unity of the Father, Son and Holy Spirit" (Cyprian, *De Orat. Domin.* 23). Tertullian says "For the Church is itself, properly and principally, the Spirit Himself, in whom there is a trinity of one divinity, Father, Son and Holy Spirit" (*De pud.* 21). These texts can be taken as but the logical development of John's assertion that God is love (1 Jn 4.8, 16). Both really and gnoseologically the salvation-historical Trinity is the immanent Trinity.

Such lengthy Trinitarian and Christological considerations may seem excessive in a discussion of the entry on the Church as *communio*. However, as soon as such insights are even obscured ecclesiology deteriorates into debates about lordship in the body politic of the Church, whereas it should be a *lectio divina* about the brotherhood of humanity in Christ celebrating the communion of man with God in the union of the Holy Spirit.

Being of the Church as Communio. If the Judaeo-Christian revelation understands that being as such is gift and communion, then it automatically follows that the being of the Church must also be gift and communion. If the divine and theandric sources of the Church are not grudging givers (Phil 2.6), then the Church must also strive for the "more" ($\pi\epsilon\rho\acute{\iota}\sigma\sigma\epsilon\upsilon\mu\alpha$) that must distinguish the followers of Christ who want to enter the Kingdom of God definitively (Mt 5.20). Has, however, the Church always been gracious with the grace of its source and founder?

Brotherhood. Furthermore, in keeping with both the *communio* ontology and Jesus' explicit mandate (Mt 23.8), there should be no lording it over, whether personal (Lk 22.24–27; 9.46) or official (1 Pt 5.3). The early Churches must have taken this to heart for they called themselves ἀδελφότης (fraternity; community of brothers). However, as is already evident in Cyprian, this ecclesial brotherliness soon begins to fade. Cyprian himself restricts the word to fellow bishops and clerics, and he is addressed by the Romans as "most blessed and glorious *Papa*" (*Ep.* 30). Soon brother is entirely restricted, henceforth an honorific title designating only clerics and monks. Late in the 4th or early in the 5th century the decline of brother as the universal designation of Christians is complete—even bishops are no longer called brother, but colleague; the episcopate no longer brotherhood, but *collegium* (from the Roman juridical *collega*).

Sacrament of Communio. Hence, although the revival of *collegiality at Vatican Council II is to be heartily greeted, the proper response is hardly unrestrained enthusiasm. For collegiality itself already marks a decline from the ecclesial brotherhood meant to be the historical Sacrament of that communion which is the divine and theandric being revealed in the Trinity and communicated in the Christ. Clearly, then, the Church cannot be a monarchy (and it never has been except in the formal distinctions of the theologians), for both the biblical text and human history persuade that monarchy is not congenial to the Judaeo-Christian ontology. Not only papal, usually the most acerbically criticized, but all ecclesiastical paternalism and clericalism are simply inconsonant with the ideals and example of Jesus, "who is the firstborn of many brothers" (Rom 8.29). Nor can the Church be content with the oligarchic pattern of church organization exemplified by the combination of Roman papacy and Roman Curia, whose reform, although promised apparently from its origin, is still awaited. Nor would the alleged internationalization of curial membership and infrequently convened Synods of Bishops achieve the desired end. Neither are democratic and republican arrangements necessarily apposite to the needs of the Church; it is not clear that they would adequately respect and represent the Church as the brotherly Sacrament of the encounter of God and man.

Since the Church has always been a more or less unconscious mélange of governmental practices adapted from the surrounding culture, a thorough demystification is needed, of past and present ideologies of ecclesiastical office. A serious attempt is needed to discover institutional and structural means of a brotherly lifestyle. For within the communion of the many-membered Body of the one Head, Christ, all governance (κυβερνήσις, 1 Cor 12.28) is the service (διακονία, Rom 12.7) of the shepherd (ποιμήν, Eph 4.12). Of course reform of personal attitudes is radically necessary, but personal attitudes without social structures are neither effective nor enduring.

Communio, Giving and Forgiving. In neither the institutions of its officials nor in the holiness of its members, however, does the Church expect paradisal innocence or utopian perfectionism. The true Church is not gnostic, but has always (Mt 12.36–43) known that it is, in the words of Augustine, a *corpus mixtum* of saints and sinners. Being *simul justa et peccatrix*—the Lutheran formula almost adopted by Vatican II in the

Dogmatic Constitution on the Church: "the Church, embracing sinners in her bosom, is at the same time holy and always in need of being purified . . ." (*Lumen gentium* 8)—the Church is aware that it is an *ecclesia reformata semper reformanda*. In the customary course of events the holiness of the Church, even as the communion of the saints, is not sinlessness, but forgiveness. For it is the Church of God, who wills not the death, but the life of the sinner (Ez 18.23); the Church of Jesus, who is the friend of sinners (Mt 11.19); and the Church of the Holy Spirit, who is the forgiveness of sins (the Postcommunion of the Roman Liturgy for Whit Tuesday, based on Jn 20.19 with Lk 20.19; 24.47 and Acts 1.8). Disastrously throughout the Church's history this precise nature of its holiness has been misunderstood, by both liberals and conservatives, reformers and integralists. The result has been presumption in those who identify the pilgrim Church with the eschatological Kingdom; despair, in those who identify the sinful Church with the Synagogue of Satan (Denz 1187). Both types are responsible for rending the seamless garment which Christ's Church is to be. Asserting their own holiness, both desert the holiness of that patient (2 Pt 3.9 with Wis 11.15–12.27), divine Wisdom which "sweetly and powerfully disposes all things" (Wis 8.1) and of whose goods and mysteries the Church is the sacramental communion. Rightly, then, the Church is most intensely Church through the Communion in the lifegiving Body received at the banquet table spread by the (incarnate) divine Wisdom himself (Prv 9.1–6; Sir 24.19–22 with Lk 22:14–20 and 1 Cor 1.19–31). The gift of the Christian Church, although simultaneously sinful and holy, still the communion of saints, illuminates the fundamental insight of the Judaeo-Christian ontology, namely, that being is both divinely given and forgiven.

A Lived Communio. The mission of this Church is to practice this ontology. In both its structure and its life the Church is to be a communion of giving and forgiving. The officer in the Church is to be a shepherd, mindful that Jesus alone is the absolute Sacrament (Jn 10.1–10) of the Divine Shepherd (Ez 34.1). Hence, popes, bishops, pastors, and leaders of whatever kind "are not dictators over your faith, but fellow workers with you for your happiness" (2 Cor 1.24), "administrators of this new covenant" (2 Cor 3.6), who coordinate the many gifts of the one Spirit for the building up of the one Body of Christ. The members are to remember that as members they are also the fellow workers, equally responsible for the completion of the Body of Christ (Col 1.24), for it is not a monarchy, but a communion. Having been loved first by God and brought into communion with him, they are all henceforth able to love others and bring them into the same communion so that the joy of all may be complete (1 Jn 4.7, 10, 19; 1.4). Thus, the new and greatest commandment is love (Jn 13.34; 15.13), but love is practiced in communion (Jn 15.1–7) and by following the way of hospitality (Rom 12:13; *philoxenia*, i.e. love of strangers). Someone who is loved cannot be a stranger; hence, the Church as communio means that neither God nor the "other" is an alien or stranger. Hence, the double commandment—for we are all, God and man, neighbors (Lk 10.29–37)—is the perfect practical proposition of the Church as communion. The crucial question, then, is always whether the Church is a generous, all-embracing, giving and forgiving host, a communion in the image and likeness of Christ and the triune God.

In sum, as the Sacrament of salvation the Church is a communion, of God with the nongodly, and then of this communioned creation within itself. This communion salvation is threefold: from ontological nothingness by the Father's empowering creation; from hamartiological nothingness by the Son's forgiving redemption; and from axiological nothingness by the Holy Spirit's gifting affirmation.

The Church as communion is created and graced humanity's celebration that between God and humanity there is not an abyss (for the abyss is only not being at all) but perichoresis—between God and man and therefore among men.

Bibliography: A. BRUNNER, *Dreifaltigkeit* (Einsiedeln 1976). J. HAMER, *The Church Is a Communio*, tr. R. MATHEWS (New York 1964). K. HEMMERLE, *Thesen zu einer trinitarischen Ontologie* (Einsiedeln 1976). M J. LE GUILLOU, *Mission et unité* (Paris 1960). H. DE LUBAC, *Catholicism*, tr. L. SHEPPARD (New York 1950). R. KRESS, *Holy Church, Sinful Church* (Canfield, Ohio 1978). E. PETERSON, "Der Monotheismus als politisches Problem," *Theologie Traktate* (Munich 1951). J. PROVOST, ed., "The Church as Communio," *Jurist* 36 (1976) 1–245, whole issue. K. RAHNER, *The Church and the Sacraments*, tr. W. J. O'HARA (New York 1963); *Vorfragen zu einem ökumenischen Amtsverstandnis* (Freiburg im B. 1974). J. RATZINGER, *The Open Circle*, tr. W. A. GLEN-DOEPEL (New York 1966); "Bemerkungen zur Frage der Charismen in der Kirche," *Die Zeit Jesu* (Freiburg im B. 1970). O. SAIER, *"Communio" in der Lehre des zweiten vatikanischen Konzil* (Munich 1973).

[R. KRESS]

CHURCH AND STATE (U.S.)

In the last decade and a half the legal history of Church-State relations in the United States (3:742) has been marked by major Supreme Court decisions with regard to both the freedom of religious exercise and the issue of the establishment of religion.

Freedom of Religious Exercise. The Supreme Court decided several issues involving conscientious challenges to military service and also a major conflict concerning Amish religious objections to compulsory schooling beyond the age of eight years.

Conscientious Objectors to War. In 1965 the Court unanimously interpreted the statutory exemption for pacifist conscientious objectors to include those who based their claim on nontheistic concepts of a supreme being or power (*U.S. v. Seeger*, 380 U.S. 163). Five years later, the Court applied the rationale of that decision to cover a conscientious objector who explicitly denied that his views on war were "religious" (*Welsh v. U.S.*, 398 U.S. 333 [1970]). The statutory exemption for pacifists was held to exclude only those whose beliefs were not deeply held and those whose beliefs rested on reasons of policy rather than religious or moral principle. Three justices dissented.

Despite many attempts by selective conscientious objectors to military service in the Vietnamese war to secure Supreme Court review of their claims, only near the end of American involvement, in 1971, did the Court decide the issue (*Gillette v. U.S.*, 401 U.S. 437). The Court there upheld the statutory exclusion of selective conscientious objectors, finding secular purposes in the exclusion. The Court also concluded that "substantial government interests" justified the burdens of military service imposed on the religious freedom of selective conscientious objectors. Justice William O. Douglas alone found the denial of exemption invidious discrimination.

The Amish and Compulsory Schooling. The Amish people object to formal schooling beyond the eighth grade as corrupting "worldliness." Although Amish parents provided informal vocational training as an alternative to conventional high-school education, Wisconsin prosecuted them for noncompliance with requirements of formal school attendance of children until 16 years of age. The Court overturned the convictions, holding that the government interest in compulsory schooling would not be substantially impaired by exempting the Amish (*Wisconsin v. Yoder*, 406 U.S. 205 [1972]). Moreover, the Court found no evidence that Amish children desired further formal schooling against the wishes of their parents, nor evidence that Amish children would be educationally handicapped if they left their communities when they came of age. Dissenting Justice Douglas alone would have remanded all but one of the cases for new hearings to ascertain the wishes of the children.

Establishment of Religion. In the last decade, the Supreme Court decided important cases involving the religious establishment clause in three main areas: (1) tax exemption of church property; (2) government aid to church-related grade and high schools; and (3) government aid to church-related colleges.

Tax Exemption. In 1970, over the sole dissent of Justice Douglas, the Court upheld tax exemptions for real and personal property used exclusively for religious, educational, or charitable purposes (*Walz v. Tax Commission*, 397 U.S. 664). Such broadly based exemptions, according to the Court, foster the community's moral and mental development and so operate neither to advance nor to inhibit religion, although Churches receive incidental economic benefits. The Court found the government involvement with religion by exemptions not to be "excessive," in part because less than what would result from taxation. Justice William J. Brennan, concurring separately, advanced two secular purposes of the exemptions: the exempted nonprofit organizations contribute to the well-being of the comtion in a pluralistic society and to diversity of association in a pluralistic society.

Aid to Parochial Schools. In 1968 the Court upheld the loan of secular textbooks by New York to all secondary, including parochial, school pupils (*Board of Education v. Allen*, 392 U.S. 236). The Court concluded that both the purpose and primary effect of the textbook loan were secular. Three justices dissented.

In 1971 the Court struck down Pennsylvania and Rhode Island programs supplementing salaries of nonpublic school teachers of secular subjects, finding "excessive entanglement" between government and religion in the required continuous surveillance (*Lemon v. Kurzman*, 403 U.S. 602). Moreover, the Court noted a broader base of entanglement in potential political divisiveness along religious lines. Only Justice Byron C. White dissented, arguing that the states were financially supporting a separable secular objective.

In 1973 the Court invalidated three New York laws providing financial assistance to nonpublic schools (*Committee for Public Education v. Nyquist*, 413 U.S. 756). One partially reimbursed nonpublic schools serving low-income families for maintenance and repair of buildings, a second partially reimbursed low-income parents for tuitions paid to nonpublic schools, and a third gave tax credits to other parents of nonpublic school pupils. All three programs were said to have a primary effect of advancing religion. Moreover, according to the Court, the tax credits would increase Church-State entanglements and would encourage political divisiveness because benefits flow primarily to parents of children attending sectarian schools. In the same year, the Court also invalidated a New York law reimbursing nonpublic schools for mandatory record-keeping and tests (*Levitt v. Committee for Public Education*, 413 U.S. 472). Three justices (Warren J. Burger, William H. Rehnquist, and White) dissented in favor of the tuition and tax credit programs, and Justice White also dissented in favor of the reimbursement programs for maintenance and mandatory services.

In 1975, over the dissent of three justices (Burger, Rehnquist, and White), the Court invalidated two Pennsylvania programs providing instructional materials to nonpublic schools on loan and auxiliary services such as counseling and therapy there by public school personnel (*Meek v. Pittenger*, 421 U.S. 349). Though the first program admittedly served secular purposes, the Court found that it primarily benefited pervasively religious institutions and so had the primary effect of advancing religion. The second program was invalidated because it would involve the "excessive entanglement" of continuous surveillance and foster political divisiveness. But over the dissents of Justices Brennan, Douglas, and Thurgood Marshall, the Court upheld on the basis of *Board of Education v. Allen*, 392 U.S. 236, a third program providing for the loan of secular textbooks to children in nonpublic schools.

In 1977 the Court reviewed six Ohio programs for nonpublic school pupils (*Wolman v. Walter*, 433 U.S. 229). The Court upheld payments for diagnostic services within nonpublic schools by public employees (over the dissent of Justice Brennan), payments for therapeutic, guidance, and remedial services by public employees off nonpublic school premises (over the dissent of Brennan and the partial dissent of Justice Marshall), and the loan of secular textbooks and payments for standardized tests in secular subjects (over the dissents of Brennan, Marshall, and Justice John P. Stevens). But the Court struck down the loan of instructional materials over the dissent of three justices (Burger, Rehnquist, and White) and payments for field-trip transportation over the dissents of four justices (Burger, Lewis F. Powell, Rehnquist, and White), holding that both programs supported the religious role of the schools.

Aid to Church-Related Colleges. Unlike aid to parochial grade and high schools, the Court has approved direct federal and state grants to church-related colleges. In 1971 the Court upheld federal construction grants to such colleges for facilities restricted to secular uses (*Tilton v. Richardson*, 403 U.S. 672). The Court there found a separable secular purpose and primary effect without "excessive entanglement" or excessive potential for political divisiveness. Justices Black, Brennan, Douglas, and Marshall dissented. In 1973, over the dissents of Brennan, Douglas, and Marshall, the Court sustained the issuance of state bonds to assist a church-related college finance construction of facilities devoted exclusively to secular uses (*Hunt v. McNair*, 413 U.S. 734). And in 1976, over the dissents of Justices Brennan, Marshall, Stevens, and Stewart, the Court upheld annual per-pupil state grants to church-related colleges for exclusively secular purposes, finding the recipient colleges not to be pervasively sectarian (*Roemer v. Board of Public Works*, 426 U.S. 736).

Summary. The Court has thus approved tax exemptions for church property and government aid to church-related colleges but disallowed most forms of government aid to church-related grade and high schools. In the course of these decisions, the Court expanded the Schempp test of secular purpose and effect (cf. *School District v. Schempp*, 374 U.S. 203, 222 [1963]) by also requiring no "excessive entanglement" and no undue potential for political divisiveness. The current justices are divided into three groups: (1) those who support aid for secular purposes to both church-related colleges and church-related grade and high schools (Burger, Rehnquist, and White); (2) those who support such aid to the colleges but not most forms of aid to the grade and high schools (Blackmun, Powell, and Stewart); and (3) those who oppose most forms of aid to both (Brennan, Marshall, and Stevens).

Bibliography: On cases of conscientious objectors to the Vietnamese war: R. J. REGAN, *Private Conscience and Public Law* (New York 1972) 33–52. On religious freedom generally: D. A. GIANNELLA, "Religious Liberty, Nonestablishment, and Doctrinal Development—Part I. The Religious Liberty Guarantee," *Harvard Law Review* 80 (1967) 1381–1431. On the religious establishment clause: J. H. CHOPER, "The Establishment Clause and Aid to Parochial Schools," *California Law Review* 56 (1968) 260–341. D. GIANNELLA, "Religious Liberty, etc.—Part II. The Nonestablishment Principle," *Harvard Law Review* 81 (1968) 513–590; "Lemon and Tilton: The Bitter and the Sweet of Church-State Entanglement," *Supreme Court Review* (1971) 147–200. P. G. KAUPER, "Public Aid for Parochial Schools and Church Colleges: The Lemon, DiCenso, and Tilton Cases," *Arizona Law Review* 13 (1971) 567–594. R. E. MORGAN, "The Establishment Clause and Sectarian Schools: A Final Installment?" *Supreme Court Review* (1971) 57–97.

[R. J. REGAN]

CHURCH AND WORLD

The fourth chapter of Vatican Council II's *Gaudium et spes* was devoted to "the role of the Church in the modern world." It describes the world as the concrete locus of God's revelatory and redemptive work, discusses the contribution which the Church can make to individuals and to society today but also what the Church can learn from the modern world, and, finally, relates the whole discussion to Christ as the Alpha and Omega of God's creative work.

In the Council's vision, the world is something more than a mere "vale of tears," simply providing the context in which individuals work out their eternal destiny. First of all, the world itself has positive value as itself God's creation. Furthermore, many of the developments which have shaped the modern world are acknowledged to be themselves good and beneficial and even as fulfilments of the saving design of a God who does not work solely within the boundaries of the Church or only for narrowly "religious" purposes. But, from another standpoint, the world is seen to be a world of man's creation. Here the governing thoughtform is not cosmocentric but anthropocentric and historical. When the world is seen as history, the way is opened to a theology which intrinsically links the doctrines of *creation and redemption; which attempts a more than merely private statement of the basic Gospel-message; which understands grace to be a liberation of man for the complete realization of his individual and social purpose; and which, therefore, does not separate (even if it distinguishes) "Church" and "world," "salvation-history" and "secular history," but acknowledges only one world, created by and for the one God, the object of Christ's love in whom it is to be brought to its own consummation.

In its proper character, then, the "world" is seen to be more than the place where man lives out his private existence. The concrete world is understood to be both constituted and mediated by meaning and value (Lonergan), a world which men have shaped and formed and which in turn forms and shapes men. As such, it has all the ambiguity of the other works of man. The contemporary world is a historical moment, whose features are neither all pleasant nor all evil. The fundamental impulses shaping its character and possibilities can be identified: the human desire to understand nature and society and to bring them both under intelligent and critical control; the effort to make the world a place for ever greater human freedom from uncontrolled nature and from unjust human domination; the weakness and sinfulness deflecting man from the high goals of such understanding and freedom; the secret workings of God's grace in individuals, societies and movements; the public word of Christian revelation mediated in and by the Church.

Such a positive and yet critical attitude towards the world founds the Church's involvement in contemporary affairs. Its concern is particularly with what man has done in and to the world, which is to say with the world as man has constructed it. In its social teaching, especially since Vatican II, the Church has acknowledged the value and necessity of scientific and technological progress for human development and liberation, but it has also warned that such progress is not an unmitigated good, but that, besides threatening nature's ecological balance, it has also served as a potential instrument of an even greater enslavement of the human heart and mind. The Church has further noted that human development has been an unequal achievement, with a small part of the race enjoying relative prosperity while the greater number struggles to reach or retain the basic necessities of life. Christian concern for social justice has, therefore, shifted its concern from problems internal to nations to the international order and has sought to enlist Christians in the difficult political and economic analyses and choices necessary for a creative and liberating activity.

A *political theology seeks to explain the Church's redemptive role in the world as that of being an "institution of critical freedom" (Metz), whose function is to keep alive the Christian vision of integral human development and freedom and to bring it to bear upon contemporary questions. In this process the Church itself will have to be judged by that vision and churchmen must ask what changes in the Church may be necessary for it to undertake that critical and emancipatory role in the world. In this interaction, one of the fundamental assertions of Vatican II is reflected, namely, that both "Church" and "world" have something to learn from one another.

Bibliography: J. B. METZ, *Theology of the World,* tr. W. GLEN-DOEPEL (New York 1969). J. GREMILLION, ed., *The Gospel of Peace and Justice: Catholic Social Teaching since Pope John* (Maryknoll, N.Y. 1976). G. GUTTIEREZ, *A Theology of Liberation: History, Politics, and Salvation,* tr. C. INDA and J. EAGLESON (Maryknoll, N.Y. 1973). B. LONERGAN, *Method in Theology* (New York 1972).

[J. A. KOMONCHAK]

CHURCH IN COMMUNIST COUNTRIES

The Christian communities in the socialist countries of Eastern Europe are stronger and more active than many Western publics surmise. Church attendance and religious observance compares favorably to Western Europe and in some instances, notably Poland, may be unparalleled elsewhere on the Continent. Only in Albania, the tiny country which is itself isolated in the socialist community, has organized religion been eliminated. The Churches, to be sure, lost their prerevolutionary or prewar wealth and institutional strength. Nonetheless they have retained and developed their structure as Churches or denominations. Theological academies are at work and religious journals are being published. Though the approach of the Soviet government to religion is paradigmatic for the other states in the East-European socialist community, their varied histories and cultures lead to great diversity in religious patterns. Thus in the German Democratic Republic theological faculties remain, as in prewar times, a regular component in a number of state universities. Similarly in Czechoslovakia and Hungary there are salaries or subsidies for clerical support from the state. Nor are party and church membership in fact always mutually exclusive. Nonetheless the fate of religion—here we are concerned chiefly with the Christian communities—in the epic reorganization of society which began in the October Revolution is still far from clear. Feudally institutionalized Churches, in East and West alike, proved anachronistic in the emergence of the modern world. The nature of, and the reasons for, the difficulties with religion in the Soviet Revolution cannot be pursued here. We can only comment briefly on the manner in which the experiences since the Revolution shape the options of Church and State in the socialist countries of Eastern Europe today.

War Era. World War II holds a pivotal position in the emergence of the system of relations prevailing today between the Churches and the State in the Soviet Union. By the eve of that holocaust, organized religion had been all but eliminated. To be sure, the Orthodox Church, as the dominant Christian body in Old Russia, had already moved, by the late 1920s, through resistance to neutrality then to active support of the Revolution. That change on the part of the Church, however, had uncertain consequences, effected as it was by a *locum tenens* (Metropolitan Sergii) of the formally vacant Moscow patriarchate. Admittedly a change in policy at the peak of the hierarchy could not immediately disengage church and peasant culture. In any case, though with fluctuations, the government until World War II pursued the original campaign to eliminate organized religion. In June 1941, with the Soviet government stunned by the sudden German invasion, Metropolitan Sergii moved quickly and publicly to rally the Russian people to the defense of the motherland. When some clerics wavered, notably in the Ukraine, and welcomed the Germans as liberators, Sergii was able further to consolidate his patriotic commitment by rebuking such action in the strongest possible terms. Whether or not the Metropolitan had so calculated, Stalin, beleaguered by the invasion, sensed the importance of religious sentiment and support in the war effort. The Kremlin reached an understanding with the Orthodox hierarchy. The Holy Synod was permitted to meet and elect a patriarch, that office having been vacant since the death of Patriarch Tikhon in 1925. In exchange for patriotic support, worship was restored and many churches reopened. The limitations of the original Leninist decrees, which limited religious expression to intramural cultic activity, were accepted by the Church.

Meanwhile various free Churches presented rather different problems. Evangelicals and Baptists, suppressed by Church and State alike under the Czars, were initially favored by the Revolution, as were various communal religious groups. These, it was assumed, would be more responsive to the political and economic goals of the new regime, a hope that rather quickly paled. The new Soviet government had required groups to register and to meet certain formal requirements, an arrangement more readily implemented with hierarchical than with decentralized or spontaneous communities. In 1944 the two main free-church groups met in Moscow and formed the All-Union Council of Evangelical Christians and Baptists (AUCECB) (an earlier Union had failed in the 1930s). Though, as in the case of the Orthodox Church, the sphere of action was defined by the requirements of the cult, the development of a strong central organ was furthered. Thus a strong AUCECB denominational headquarters has emerged in Moscow, with representatives traveling widely throughout many parts of the Soviet Union. The AUCECB is active in the Baptist World Alliance, has joined the World Council of Churches, and participates in the Christian Peace Conference (see below).

Post-War Exchange and Conflict. The new *modus vivendi* between Church and State, achieved in a war-time crisis, exemplifies, interestingly enough, important elements of "exchange and conflict" theory prevalent in the social sciences today: partners pursue possibly incompatible goals in a market context, engaging in transactions that each finds rewarding in his own terms. Retrospectively it can be said that the enormous challenges confronting Soviet diplomacy when the war ended permitted, indeed encouraged, the perpetuation of the new bargaining relationship. Both inside and outside the modified national boundaries, Soviet policy had to deal with multiple ethnic and national groups, whose particularity often included important religious elements. Here the Churches could render important service, both in exerting influence and in improving the Soviet image abroad. Though the immediate postwar flux passed within a few years, the shift to a global scale in Khrushchev's "peaceful coexistence" campaign provided new challenges.

In the new era, the Moscow Patriarchate moved actively among the family of Orthodox Churches. A theological conversation begun in Prague in the late 1950s and oriented both to the past failures of the Churches and the coming dangers of the nuclear age, quickly expanded in the 1960s into a global effort of the Soviet and other socialist-country Churches—the Christian Peace Conference (CPC). In a related move, the Russian Orthodox Church, followed by others, joined the World Council of Churches (WCC) in 1961 and sent observers to Vatican Council II. Both the CPC and the WCC provided opportunities for the establishment of contacts with the Churches of the Third World, whose ecclesiastical ties otherwise were chiefly Western.

Advantageous as the new market arrangement appears to be for the Soviet and other governments, results for the Churches have been far more ambiguous. Whatever the design of the governments, it appeared at times that contradictory policies were pursued simultaneously. Thus while central hierarchies were given enlarged arenas for action, especially abroad, pressures appeared to increase at the diocesan or local level.

Indeed during the very time that Orthodox Patriarchate took up membership in the WCC the Synod, under the direction of the state Council for Russian Orthodox Church Affairs (CROCA), adopted a change in parish structure. On the surface laudable, insofar as it increased both decentralization and lay participation, the Council proved in fact to mean a weakening of pastoral leadership and an opening into parish management by local political authorities.

This innovation brought to a head, in various "underground" Churches, an issue that had long smoldered. Lenin's decrees and the Soviet Constitution declared a strict separation of Church and State and of the Church from education. At the same time, however, all religious property, including the objects needed for cult, were turned over to local civil authorities. These were then entrusted by these same authorities to duly registered religious groups for use. Thus both registration and administrative requirements involved the civil authorities in the life of the religious communities so directly that critics could view the arrangement as violating the law on the separation of Church and State.

The implementation of the new regulations led to many irregularities at local levels in the removal of priests and the closing of churches. When parish members appealed to bishops and higher levels of the hierarchy, help was not forthcoming. The criticism mounted that the leaders of the central organs, both Orthodox and Evangelical Baptist, respectively, had compromised or even betrayed the Churches. Indeed, much to the embarrassment of the hierarchies, and of the state, criticism reached both the World Council of Churches and the United Nations. Spokesmen of the Orthodox Church were accused of lying when confronted with the problem abroad. In the case of the Evangelical-Baptist AUCECB, *initsiativniki*, the dissidents, grew strong enough to set up a Council to replace the existing one. The result may have been a wholesome one, inasmuch as the AUCECB incorporated many of the reforms the dissidents demanded.

Religious dissent meanwhile has become part of the wider current of dissent in the Soviet Union, and, to a lesser degree, elsewhere. In the ferment surrounding the Final Accords of the Helsinki Conference on European Security and Cooperation further information on the struggle of the 1960s has come to light. A 336-page manual on "Legislation concerning Religious Cults" prepared by the Council for Religious Affairs (replacing the CROCA noted above) in 1971 discloses various unpublished regulations that put dissenters in violation without their knowledge. Meanwhile state authorities have intervened in instances of local governmental abuses and Soviet atheist education has frequently been criticized from within for lack of sophistication. In such better moments, Marx and Lenin can always be quoted to the effect that the sensibilities of believers must be respected, and that religion will be overcome only when those degrading conditions which give rise to it are overcome.

Clearly then a symbiosis exists between religious communities and the State, and again between the hierarchies and the faithful. Critics such as Solzhenitsyn regard improvements of recent decades as merely tactical and no one can guarantee that harsh conditions will not return. Others, however, believe that a process of historical change is under way, that in the longer perspective new possibilities are emerging. Meanwhile the Vatican has developed a new *Ostpolitik* consistent with the latter assumption, paralleling thus the bargaining relationship between the Russian Orthodox hierarchy and the Soviet party and government. An achievement of the new Ostpolitik is an accommodation between the Vatican and Hungarian state authorities which climaxed in the 1977 reception of the First Secretary of the Hungarian Communist Party by Pope Paul VI. The other side of the coin has been a modification of papal policy vis-à-vis the Ukrainian Uniates and Lithuanian Catholics. Not surprisingly these accommodations draw criticisms of compromise to the Vatican remarkably similar to the charges of compromise which *initsiativniki* level at the official hierarchies in the Soviet Union for the concessions which they make to the Kremlin.

See also EASTERN CATHOLIC CHURCHES; UKRAINIAN RITE.

Bibliography: B. BOCIURKIW and J. W. STRONG, ed., *Religion and Atheism in the U.S.S.R. and Eastern Europe* (London 1975). M. BOURDEAUX, *Patriarch and Prophets* (New York 1970); *Religious Ferment in Russia* (London 1968). R. CONQUEST, *Religion in the USSR* (London 1968). D. J. DUNN, "Papal-Communist Detente: Motivation," *Survey* 22 (Spring, 1976) 140–154. W. G. FLETCHER, *Religion and Soviet Foreign Policy 1945–70* (London 1973); *The Russian Church Underground 1917–1970* (London 1971). M. HAYWARD and W. C. FLETCHER, ed., *Religion and the Soviet State: A Dilemma of Power* (New York 1969). G. SIMON, *Church, State and Opposition in the USSR* (Los Angeles 1974). E. WEINGÄRTNER, ed., *Church within Socialism* (Rome 1976). Also periodical documentation in *Religion in Communist Dominated Areas* (New York) and *Religion in Communist Lands* (London).

[P. PEACHEY]

CHURCH INVESTMENTS

Institutions connected with the Roman Catholic Church in the United States having investments are diocesan-related, religious congregation-sponsored or owned, or are affiliated with the Catholic Church as a health care and educational institution. In some dioceses, excess monies from parishes and other corporate entities are placed in central financial agencies for investment of the monies. In many dioceses one of the largest funds is the cemetary account. As is the case with any Catholic religious organization, investments are covered by particular laws of the institution and Canon Law.

Canon Law distinguishes two types of moral persons (associations of physical persons existing for some purpose having personality): collegiate moral persons and non-collegiate. A collegiate moral person is an association of physical persons having legal personality distinct from its members (i.e., religious orders, provinces and local houses). All property owned by a collegiate moral person is ecclesiastical property and must be administered according to the constitution of the religious community. Non-collegiate moral persons (parishes and dioceses, plus hospitals, orphanages and institutions of higher learning if erected as such by the Holy See or local ordinary) are not associations or physical persons but aggregations of goods or property having legal personality bestowed upon things that are destined to be used for a religious or charitable purpose (Crosby 20).

Since a corporation has the capacity to receive and hold property, it may acquire it in the same way as a physical person, i.e., by purchase, gift, by devise or bequest under a will. A gift is defined in the law as a "voluntary transfer of property by one to another without any consideration or compensation therefor." Such gifts can be divided into two kinds: 1) absolute gifts which have no conditions or restrictions attached except the understanding that they must be used in fulfilling the defined purposes of the institution; 2) less-than-absolute gifts which, if accepted, must be used by the donee for the use specified by the donor. Less-than-absolute gifts are part of two kinds of funds: 1) trust funds and 2) restricted funds (Crosby 21).

Catholic institutions tend to invest their monies through banks and/or brokers. While some may invest in land, most tend to place their monies in the traditional forms for security reasons: stocks, bonds, and forms of certificates of deposit. Some groups have begun investing in the options market; however, this is more speculative and, as a result, not greatly used by the average Catholic institution. Despite common opinion about the purported wealth of the Catholic Church in the U.S., investments in the stock market are part of the investments of other nonprofit institutions (churches, foundations, health care facilities and schools) which together constitute less than 5 per cent of the market.

In the mid-1970s, because of well-publicized accounts of mismanagement by various Catholic institutions, especially fundraisers, NCCB, USCC, the Conference of Major Superiors of Men, and the Leadership Conference of Women Religious created policies and guidelines for investments. At the same time, in response to investment practices of several Catholic institutions which brought them close to bankruptcy, an educational effort was launched to help Catholic institutions achieve fiscal responsibility in their investment practices (*see* FUND RAISING AND RESPONSIBILITY). Around the same time, to help Catholic institutions achieve social responsibility in their investments, the *National Catholic Coalition for Responsible Investment was inaugurated.

Bibliography: M. H. CROSBY, *Catholic Church Investments for Corporate Social Responsibility*, pamphlet (Milwaukee 1973).

[M. H. CROSBY]

CHURCH MEMBERSHIP (U.S.)

Church membership information comes from several sources. The U.S. census gathered information on religious membership in 1890, 1906, 1916, 1926, and 1936, but after that time it stopped in deference to citizen objections about separation of Church and State. Since then the only available data have come from compilations of reports from religious bodies and from public opinion polling.

Statistics. The *Yearbook of American and Canadian Churches* presents the most accurate information available on about 220 religious groups, Christian and non-Christian. Each year about half of the groups to whom the forms are sent do not return them, so the *Yearbook* prints the most recent information it has on those groups, sometimes information a decade old. Since some religious groups enumerate children as members while others do not, the *Yearbook* distinguishes "inclusive membership" from "full, communicant, or confirmed members." Many religious groups, however, do not report both figures.

The *Official Catholic Directory* publishes membership statistics gathered annually from each diocese. Usually these are based on reports from individual parishes, and the accuracy of such reports is much in question. In 1977 the Office of Pastoral Research of the Archdiocese of New York surveyed diocesan offices asking them how they arrive at the statistics sent to the *Directory*. Most said they add up parish reports, but about one-fifth make estimates based on total population of the diocese and percentage assumed to be Catholic, or based on Mass attendance, funerals, or other data.

Table: CHURCH MEMBERSHIP TRENDS IN THE
UNITED STATES, 1950 TO 1975

Year	Roman Catholic Membership	As Percentage of Total U.S. Population	
		Membership of All Religious Bodies[a]	Roman Catholic Membership[b]
1950	28,634,878	57.0	18.9
1951	29,241,580	57.3	18.9
1952	30,425,015	58.6	19.3
1953	31,648,424	59.2	19.8
1954	32,575,702	59.8	20.0
1955	33,396,647	60.4	20.3
1956	34,563,851	61.1	20.5
1957	35,846,477	60.6	20.8
1958	39,509,508	62.6	22.8
1959	40,871,302	63.1	23.0
1960	42,104,899	63.3	23.3
1961	42,876,665	63.2	23.4
1962	43,847,938	63.2	23.6
1963	44,874,371	63.9	23.8
1964	45,640,619	64.3	23.9
1965	46,246,175	64.2	23.8
1966	46,864,910	64.0	23.8
1967	47,468,333	63.6	23.9
1968	47,873,238	64.0	23.9
1969	47,872,089	63.8	23.6
1970	48,214,729	64.0	23.5
1971	48,390,990	63.5	23.4
1972	48,460,427	62.9	23.2
1973	48,465,438	62.4	23.0
1974	48,701,835	62.2	23.0
1975	48,881,872	62.0	22.9

[a]Total inclusive membership of all religious groups, Christian and non-Christian, as estimated by the editor of the *Yearbook of American and Canadian Churches* two years prior to each edition.

[b]Roman Catholic data from the *Official Catholic Directory*, listed here for one year prior to each edition.

A third source of information is two interdenominational studies done in 1952 and in 1971, in which many religious bodies cooperated in compiling statistics for each county in the U.S. In 1952, one-hundred fourteen and in 1971 fifty-three denominations participated. Nationwide public opinion polls provide additional information. The Gallup organization gathers annual data using standard questions. The 1976 figure for the percentage of adults 18 or over who say they are "a member of a church or synagogue" was 68, down 5 points since 1965. The 1976 figure for the percentage of adults who give Catholicism as their "religious preference" was 28, up 3 percentage points since 1966. These poll figures are somewhat higher than the figures produced from reports of church bodies.

Trends. The period 1945 to 1965 was one of membership growth in virtually all Christian groups, both in real numbers and also in percentage of the total U.S. population. But after 1965 a change occurred. Several mainline Protestant denominations began declining sharply in membership, especially the Episcopal Church, United Church of Christ, United Presbyterian Church, and United Methodist Church. Meanwhile some other denominations such as the Assemblies of God, Seventh Day Adventist Church, Church of the Nazarene, and Southern Baptist Convention have continued to grow steadily. The Roman Catholic Church virtually stopped growing in the early 1970s.

The reasons for the membership trends in the Protestant denominations have been much debated. Analysts have found that the declining denominations tend to be those highest in overall socio-economic status, most liberal in theology, and most open to individualism and pluralism in doctrine. By contrast, the denominations continuing to grow have lower overall socio-economic status, more conservative theology, and more rigid doctrinal and moral standards. Researchers have found that the membership trends are largely the result of shifting commitments among youth and young adults, not older adults. Since the middle 1960s, affluent, educated young adults have declined in church participation and this has most affected the denominations composed of the upper socio-economic groups.

The cessation of growth in the Roman Catholic Church is partly the result of the same value shift among youth. Also American Catholics have experienced rapid upward-social mobility and integration into all spheres of American society in the past two decades. The older immigrant mentality passed away in the 1960s and 1970s. Sometimes it is argued that Vatican Council II greatly weakened the Church, but Greeley and his associates produced strong evidence that the impact of Vatican II was more positive than negative.

Bibliography: J. CARROLL, D. JOHNSON, and M. MARTY, *Religion in America: 1950 to the Present* (New York 1978). N. DEMERATH, "Trends and Anti-Trends in Religious Change," in E. SHELDON and W. MOORE, eds., *Indicators of Social Change* (New York 1968) 349–445. E. GAUSTAD, ed. *Historical Atlas of Religion in America* (rev. ed., New York 1976). A. GREELEY, W. MCCREADY, and K. MCCOURT, *Catholic Schools in a Declining Church* (Kansas City, Mo. 1976). A. GREELEY, *The American Catholic: A Social Portrait* (New York 1977). D. JOHNSON, P. PICARD, and B. QUINN, *Churches and Church Membership in the United States 1971* (Washington, D.C. 1974) for 1972 data. National Council of Churches of Christ, *Churches and Church Membership in the United States* (New York 1956) for the 1952 data. G. SHAUGHNESSY, *Has the Immigrant Kept the Faith? A Study of Immigration and Catholic Growth in the United States 1790–1920* (New York 1925).

[D. R. HOGE]

CHURCHES, DEDICATION OF

The revised Order for the Dedication of a Church, promulgated on May 29, 1977 by the Sacred Congregation for the Sacraments and Divine Worship, continues the reform and simplification of this rite already inaugurated in 1961 (3:862). Primitively the Eucharist was the principal and often the only act of dedication. Subsequent additions to the rite gradually came to overshadow the centrality of the Eucharist, which, in turn, came to be seen as a mere appendage to the dedication. The new Order, emphasizing the Eucharist as the primary element in the dedication, places the whole rite within the framework of the Mass.

Introductory Rites. Among the Introductory Rites is the presentation of the new building to the bishop by representatives of those who contributed toward its construction. The traditional lustration, originally an exorcism of a pagan temple which was to be used for Christian worship, is now transformed into a penitential rite recalling the purification bestowed through Baptism.

Readings, Prayers and Anointings. The Liturgy of the Word begins with an optional blessing of the ambo.

Whereas the first reading is always Neh 8.1–10, the others are selected from the Lectionary's Common for the Dedication of a Church. The General Intercessions are replaced by the Litany of the Saints, formerly sung during the entry into the church. The Litany serves to introduce the deposition of the relics of martyrs or saints beneath the altar and not, as often occurred previously, in a stone placed within the altar's table. This deposition, however, is not strictly required. Faithful to Western and Eastern tradition, the new rite retains a Prayer of Dedication whereby the bishop, expressing praise and thanks, solemnly declares the community's desire to dedicate the building to God. This prayer, although reflecting certain phrases from the Ambrosian Preface for the Sunday of the Dedication, is a new composition. The rites which follow, i.e. the anointing of the altar and walls, the incensation and the illumination of the altar and church, visibly illustrate the work of Christ in his Church, especially in the Eucharist. Thus, for example, the altar is anointed as being the symbol of Christ, the Anointed One, who offered his life as a sacrifice for all.

Liturgy of the Eucharist. The celebration of the Eucharist, being the primary purpose for which church and altar have been constructed, is the principal and most ancient part of the dedication. The proper Preface, integral to the rite, views the stone temple as the sign of God's presence in Christ, in the Church, and in the heavenly Jerusalem. If there is a Blessed Sacrament chapel, the Eucharist is brought in procession to this place following the Prayer after Communion.

The Order provides another rite to be followed when, by way of exception, it has been customary to celebrate Mass in a church which has not been dedicated. Such a rite, omitting several elements of the normative form, is to be used only if the church's altar has not been dedicated and only if there has been a major change in the building's appearance or canonical status.

Bibliography: *Ordo dedicationis ecclesiae et altaris* (Typis Polyglottis Vaticanis 1977; International Commission on English in the Liturgy, "Green Book," 1978). I. M. CALABUIG, "Appunti di una lettura," *Notitiae* 13 (1977) 391–450.

[L. J. JOHNSON]

CIRCUMSTANCES, MORAL

According to traditional Catholic theology a human action derives its moral quality from both the object and the circumstances of the action (3:880). The most important circumstance is a personal or ulterior end, the agent may intend in placing the action. The moral act has its first and essential morality from the object, for instance the direct killing of an innocent person (murder), taking another's property against his reasonable will (theft), speaking contrary to one's mind (lying). The circumstances can affect the objective morality of an action in various ways. But no good circumstance, not even a good, ulterior end, can make licit an action evil *ex objecto*.

Many contemporary Catholic theologians, on the other hand, think that circumstances sometimes can make actions legitimate that are evil *ex objecto*. Such acts they term "prima facie evil," "physical evil," "ontic evil," "premoral evil," "nonmoral evil," but not necessarily "moral evil" (sin). Nonmoral evil does not become moral evil until it is taken up into the agent's intention; that is to say, it does not become moral evil if it is done for a proportionately good reason. The final

moral evaluation of an act must take into consideration all the circumstances, especially the personally intended end. Accordingly, these theologians justify certain actions that are evil *ex objecto* in certain circumstances, for instance abortion to save the life of the mother, masturbation for fertility testing, therapeutic sterilization. This means that these Catholic theologians reject the concept of "intrinsically evil acts," i.e., actions which are judged morally evil or sinful prior to a consideration of the circumstances in which they are done. Their opinion is not countenanced in church pronouncements on morality.

See also MORAL THEOLOGY (CONTEMPORARY TRENDS); MORALITY; NATURAL LAW.

Bibliography: J. FUCHS, "The Absoluteness of Moral Terms," Greg 52 (1971) 415–458. R. MCCORMICK, *Ambiguity in Moral Choice* (Milwaukee 1973).

[J. F. DEDEK]

CITIZENS FOR EDUCATIONAL FREEDOM (CEF)

A nonprofit, nonsectarian, nonpartisan organization which focuses on the primary rights of parents in education, affirmed by the Supreme Court in 1925 in the Oregon School Case (10:738). It was founded in 1959 in St. Louis and incorporated (1961) under Missouri laws by a group of citizens aroused by the disregard of these rights in public education and by financial discrimination against parents who, for conscientious reasons, patronize nonpublic schools.

CEF's slogan, "a fair share for every child," sums up its goals for nonpublic education: (1) tax benefits (credits/deductions) for tuition payments; (2) equal sharing by students in mandated programs such as the Elementary and Secondary Education Act; (3) application of the Court's "child-benefit" principle to public programs for the disadvantaged, physically handicapped, mentally retarded, and to services such as transportation and textbooks; (4) minimal control by public agencies. Public education goals include: (1) sharing by school administrators of decision-making and accountability with parents; (2) respect for religious and moral values of parents and children; (3) options for alternative education through consumer vouchers.

To achieve its goals, CEF has several programs: (1) the molding of public opinion through its quarterly, *Freedom in Education*, publication of books, pamphlets, article reprints and through speakers it provides and conferences it sponsors; (2) organization of state and local chapters to make the CEF position known to political representatives; (3) communication with members through its monthly news bulletin, *Focus*; (4) support of state and national legislation that aids the parent and student rather than institutions.

CEF has national executive offices in Washington, D.C., active federations in the more populous states, and local chapters in major metropolitan centers. As a movement it works with groups who share one or more of its specific goals. It is governed by a national board of trustees (45 members) composed of prominent citizens without regard to race, creed, or political affiliation.

[E. F. SPIERS]

CIVIL DISOBEDIENCE

May a validly promulgated civil law be flaunted? Legally? The positivist maintains, "Never." "Just law" theorists find the question more difficult (*see* CIVIL LAW). Morally? Neither Aquinas nor such recent human-rights documents of the Church as *Pacem in terris* and *Gaudium et spes* (74) maintain that there is a moral right in all circumstances to disobey an "unjust law"—public order, scandal, etc. may sometimes dictate obeying it.

Even positivists do not exclude the political or moral right in certain circumstances to disobey civil law. Still not all such violations constitute "civil disobedience." According to Rawls (364–365) civil disobedience is based not on moral obligation or divine right, but on a theory of society, the conception that society is a "scheme of cooperation among equals." In this view, civil disobedience, as distinguished from other forms of opposition to law, is "a public, nonviolent, conscientious yet political act contrary to law with the aim of bringing about a change in the law or policies of the government." One invokes neither a personal morality (such as opposition to all war) nor group interest (such as higher wages for cotters), but "the commonly shared conception of justice that underlies the political order." The civilly disobedient actor seeks to touch the "public's sense of justice." To do this, Rawls insists, the disobedience must be open, not covert. And it must be nonviolent, rather than militant (for militance attacks the legal and political order as a whole).

The broader view of civil disobedience as in H. D. Thoreau's 1848 *Civil Disobedience* (Bedau 27–48) embraces what Rawls calls "conscientious refusal," which may be grounded on discrete religious concerns rather than shared principles of justice, and may include "conscientious evasion," where the actor seeks to conceal, rather than proclaim, his deliberate violation of law (see also Zinn).

Bibliography: H. A. BEDAU, ed., *Civil Disobedience* (New York, 1969). J. RAWLS, *A Theory of Justice* (Cambridge, Mass. 1971). H. ZINN, *Disobedience and Democracy* (New York 1968). M. WALZER, *Obligations: Essays on Disobedience, War and Citizenship* (Cambridge, Mass. 1970).

[J. A. BRODERICK]

CIVIL LAW

What criteria identify the authoritative body of legal materials ordinarily conceived as binding on persons in a given organized society, principally the nation-state? What constitute criteria for identifying a particular rule as belonging within such a body of authoritative material?

Aquinas' definition of law (ST 1a2ae, 90.4), is a useful starting point for these inquiries even today: "A directive of reason promulgated by the authoritative source in a community for the common good." Although Aquinas conceived his definition as applicable analogically to eternal law, natural law, and divine and positive human law, his prime reference point is generally understood to have been human positive law, in the modern sense civil law. Two aspects of the definition have been challenged and defended ever since by jurists holding polar positions now identified roughly as "natural law theory" and "juridical positivism": the contentions that law is essentially a directive of reason, and not of will, and that law is essentially directed to the common good of a given society. Nineteenth- and twentieth-century positivists (John Austin, Hans Kelsen, Alf Ross) insist that neither of these conditions, however desirable, is a necessary attribute of civil law. With varying modulations (and special adjustments for a

constitutional society that furnishes standards against which ordinary laws must be measured), positivists generally postulate the need only for promulgation by the community's de facto source of legal power with an intention to oblige. In their view such promulgation constitutes authoritative civil law even though the product be highly unreasonable and in no way directed to achieving the "common good." Such provisions, say the positivists, may be bad law, but they are none the less "civil law." Although other contemporary jurists (Lon Fuller, Alexander d'Entreves) decline to accept their total view, this positivist position remains dominant.

Of great significance to the Catholic traditional understanding of civil law (which has been generally faithful to the Aquinas view) are the recent clarifications as to the "common good." In *Pacem in terris*, Pope John XXIII stressed it as primarily "recognizing, respecting, reconciling, protecting, and promoting the personal rights and duties of individual citizens" (58, 60, 75, 139)—a far cry from insinuated statist implications. And in Vatican Council II the common good was similarly identified as "the sum of those conditions of social life which allow social groups and their individual members relatively thorough and ready access to their own fulfillment" (*Gaudium et spes* 26, 74).

Bibliography: J. AUSTIN, *Lectures on Jurisprudence* (5th ed., London 1885); *The Province of Jurisprudence Determined* (London, New York 1954). A. P. D'ENTREVES, "The Case for Natural Law Reexamined," *Natural Law Forum* 1 (1956) 5–52. L. L. FULLER, *The Law in Quest of Itself* (Chicago 1940); *The Morality of Law* (New Haven 1965). H. KELSEN, *The Pure Theory of Law* (Berkeley, Cal. 1967). A. ROSS, *On Law and Justice* (Berkeley, Cal. 1957). R. M. UNGER, *Knowledge and Politics* (New York 1975); *Law in Modern Society* (New York 1976).

[J. A. BRODERICK]

CIVIL RELIGION

Civil religion in America today refers to a national faith that has a creed and moves the people of the nation on occasion to stand in judgment on its laws when they perceive that those laws violate what the creed affirms. It also moves people to rejoice in their nation-state when they experience it as realizing the values of the creed.

Bellah's Theory. Robert N. Bellah extracted the term "civil religion" from Rousseau's *Social Contract* (Book 4, ch. 8), where it was used with a narrower meaning to refer only to a set of beliefs that support the political authority of the State. In Rousseau's analysis, these included belief in the existence of God, life to come, the reward of virtue and the punishment of vice, with the added dictum of the "exclusion of religious intolerance." In his essay, Rousseau, as social philosopher, was recommending a way to civic harmony through supporting civic authority, a development of the ancient *pietas* (Marty, 1974). Bellah adds meaning in a new use of the term. He is shaping it to refer to something more specifically religious in the sense of transcending the law of the land yet capable of passing judgment on it. He introduced the term in 1967 as a concept for sociological analysis of a phenomenon he thought could be distinguished from several others. At that time, he said: "While some have argued that Christianity is the national faith and others, that church and synagogue celebrate only the generalized religion of the 'American Way of Life,' few have realized that there actually exists alongside of and rather clearly differentiated from the churches an elaborate and well-institutionalized civil religion in America" (Bellah, 1967). The main tenets of this faith he extracts from the *Declaration of Independence* and the *Constitution*. The central elements are the belief that God created all people equal and endowed them with certain inalienable rights (Bellah, 1976, 168). The critical quality of this religion, he claims, is that people who believe in it can call upon it as a framework from which to judge the nation when it violates the rights of people or fails to protect them in time of unrest. Thus, the test of the depth of the institutionalization of America's civil religion in the mid-1960s was to be its response to the civil-rights movement and the antiwar movement (Bellah, 1967). Writing again about civil religion in 1974, Bellah entitled his book *The Broken Covenant*. Here he speaks as prophet to a nation failing to fulfill its promise. He expresses the hope, however, that scholars who find flaws in the American system will do what Max Weber and Émile Durkheim, who preceded them in the analysis of the relationship between religion and society, did, namely, use the lecture platform to clarify the present reality and to warn their colleagues about imminent dangers their analyses reveal. Their scientific observations thereby provide social service (Bellah, 1976). To make his point clear, he refers to the behaviors of Jefferson and Lincoln as foremost spokesmen of American civil religion, reiterating "the right of revolution should the state attempt to destroy the God-given rights of the individuals" (Bellah, 1976, 167–168).

For Bellah, "civil religion at its best is a genuine apprehension of universal and transcendent religious reality as seen in or, one could almost say, as revealed through the experience of the American people." Political theorists and activists who have taken a position on separation of Church and State are disturbed by Bellah's passion and, for this reason, question his objectivity as a sociologist, claiming that the intent of his analysis is to bring about a condition of critical self-examination from the perspective of religious symbol and fervor, while they believe that the failures of State are better addressed from the perspective of cool reason and secular values (Smith; Wilson, 1971). This focus is but one dimension of the debate that currently surrounds civil religion.

The Sociological Debate. Writings of social scientists and ethicists preceded the debate by providing the books that incorporated the themes that later were analyzed as civil religion (de Tocqueville, Dewey, Tuveson, Smith). It is possible, as Prof. Mary L. Schneider of Michigan State Univ. suggests, to extract from the debate at least five definitions that provide different focuses on religion and the State or society. The first became popular in the mid-1950s, when America's common religion was described as emerging from actual life, ideals, values, ceremonies, and loyalties of the people. The suggestion was made that, out of its own ethos and history, a people can come to worship its own heritage (Warner, Williams). A second theme took the form of religious nationalism. In this perspective, the State becomes the object of religious adoration and glorification. This is a main aspect of classical *pietas*, wherein religion and patriotism are one (Dohen). Stress on the value of liberty as provided for in a democracy without dependence on a transcendent deity or even on

a spiritualized nation is described as the focus found in Dewey's *Common Faith*; here, democracy is religion. (Williams). A fourth theme is Protestant nationalism, without there being any zealous or idolatrous element to it; it simply is the fusion of Protestantism and Americanism, its moralism, individualism, pragmatism, values, and the like. This perspective characterizes any number of works but is particularly evident in Winthrop Hudson (Ahlstrom; Cuddihy).

All of these emphases, analyses, and commentaries are not the phenomenon that Bellah seeks to isolate for analysis. The fifth theme, then, is the one that characterizes his own work. Civil religion is a normative reality; it is essentially prophetic and stands over and against the folk ways of the people. It judges idolatrous tendencies of particular forms of Christianity and Judaism. In the words of Bellah, "it is of the essence of the American civil religion that it 'challenges institutional authority'" (Bellah, 1976). He locates in civil religion the prophetic function of calling the nation, including its civic leaders, to account whenever they fail to provide the members their rights as people "created equal." He includes, therefore, among the martyrs of the republic Abraham Lincoln and Martin Luther King. Bellah predicted a crisis of conscience for the nation at the time of the Vietnam War. When this did not occur, it did not disconfirm, for him, his analysis but indicated that the covenant was broken, though hope never fails. When his own writings carried the prophetic above the analytic function, his social-science colleagues chided him for his lack of objectivity (Fenn, Hammond). But religionists espoused his cause and made him the central figure of major bicentennial celebrations (Boardman and Fuchs). The debate continued, then, with two new focuses: (1) is the covenant really broken? (Novak); (2) has the focus of civil religion moved from the nation to the world society? (Neal).

While essayists were debating the reality or emergent quality of civil religion (Bourg, Richey, and Jones), some survey analysts were attempting to measure the verbalized opinions and attitudes from samples of significant size and diversity to determine whether any variable could be found with consistency that might be claimed to carry this conception of civil religion through the social consciousness of acting communities of American people. To date that research is indecisive. In some cases, the sample is too narrowly encompassed to preclude the Protestant nationalism concept (Hoge). At other times, the items are too general to conclude that civic piety is not also being measured (Christenson and Wimberley). This lack of conclusiveness is agreed to by the researchers themselves. In the late 1970s, they are inviting more empirical studies with better measures and samples before anything decisive can be claimed as causally connected with civil religion or before it can be stated that civil religion can be differentiated for analysis from any of the other concepts connected with national patriotism, with which it is so closely connected experientially (Wimberley, Cole and Hammond). To get evidence that would be convincing for the existence of the civil-religion hypothesis, one would have to find a substantial number of non-church-related believers as well as church-related ones. At the present time, the items used provide high association with church attendance but correspondingly low association with socially concerned non-church-attenders. There should be no significant difference if civil religion is an independent variable. Other research, assuming the civic-piety definitions of civil religion, examines its presence in new religious expression of the 1970s (Robbins).

Theological Interest. The intellectual and religious interest in the idea of civil religion is directly associated with a new political consciousness in modern theological speculation. (*see* POLITICAL THEOLOGY). Theologians show the need of new reflection on religion and State now that their attention has been drawn to the growing problems of a world economy that outstrips the power of the State and the corresponding need for associations of some type capable of addressing in a serious way the ethical and social problems generated by new centers of power (Baum, Neal, 1977). This political emphasis is dialectically related to the Churches' affirming the value of their plurality and social commentators' allocating religion to the private sphere with high public approval in established states only (Bell, Berger, Greeley). The emergence of more effective power centers in Third-World concentrations in the international struggle for survival brings the question of the object of civil religion into the forefront of Catholic reflection and analysis. In this context, the traditional association of Catholicism with the affirmation of hierarchy and of Protestantism, with congregationalism, shifts interest to the Judaic theme of exodus and covenant for a movement-perspective for historian, social scientist, and religionist simultaneously. From this fact derive the contemporary debates about civil religion.

Bibliography: S. AHLSTROM, "The American National Faith: Humane Yet All Too Human," in J. M. ROBINSON, ed., *Religion and the Humanizing of Man* (Council on the Study of Religion, Waterloo, Ont. 1973). G. BAUM, *Religion and Alienation* (New York 1975). R. N. BELLAH, "Civil Religion in America," *Daedalus* 96 (1967) 1–21; "American Civil Religion in the 1970's," in R. E. RICHEY and D. G. JONES, eds., *American Civil Religion* (New York 1974) 255–572; *The Broken Covenant* (New York 1975); "Response to the Panel on Civil Religion," *Sociological Analysis* 37 (Summer 1976) 153–159; "Comment on 'Bellah and the New Orthodoxy'," *Sociological Analysis* 37 (Summer 1976) 167–168. P. L. BERGER, *The Sacred Canopy: Elements of a Sociological Theory of Religion* (Garden City, N.Y. 1967). J. BERNARDIN, "Civil Religion," *Origins* 5 (1975–76) 113, 115–117. C. J. BOURG, "A Symposium on Civil Religion," *Sociological Analysis* 37 (Summer 1976) 141–159. C. CHERRY, ed., *Today's New Israel: Religious Interpretations of American Destiny* Englewood Cliffs, N.J. 1971). J. A. CHRISTENSON and R. C. WIMBERLEY, "Who Is Civil Religious?" *Sociological Analysis* 39 (Spring, 1978) 77–83. W. A. COLE and P. E. HAMMOND, "Religious Pluralism, Legal Development, and Societal Complexity: Rudimentary Forms of Civil Religion," JScStRel 13 (June, 1974) 177–189. J. M. CUDDIHY, *No Offense: Civil Religion and Protestant Taste* (New York 1978). J. DEWEY, *A Common Faith.* Terry Lectures (New Haven 1934). D. DOHEN, *Nationalism and American Catholicism* (New York 1967). A. GREELEY, *The Denominational Society* (Glenview, Ill. 1972). P. E. HAMMOND, "The Sociology of American Civil Religion: A Bibliographic Essay," *Sociological Analysis* 37 (Summer, 1976) 169–182. D. R. HOGE, "Theological Views of America among Protestants," *Sociological Analysis* 37 (Summer, 1976) 127–139. W. S. HUDSON, *Nationalism and Religion in America: Concepts of American Destiny and Mission* (New York 1970). B. KATHAN and N. FUCHS, *Civil Religion in America: A Bibliography* (New Haven 1976). M. MARTY, *The New Shape of American Religion* (New York 1959); "Two Kinds of Civil Religion," in R. E. RICHEY and D. G. JONES, *American Civil Religion* (New York 1974) 139–157. S. E. MEAD, "The Nation with the Soul of a Church," *Church History* 36 (Sept., 1967) 262–283. M. A. NEAL, "Civil Religion, Theology and Politics in America," in *America in Theological Perspective* (New York 1976); "Civil Religion and the Development of Peoples," *Journal of Religious Education* (March–April, 1976); "Rationalization or Religion: When Is Civil Religion Not Religion But Merely Civil?" in *A Socio-Theology of Letting Go* (New York 1977) 9–31. R. NEUHAUS, *Time Toward Home: the American Experiment as Revelation* (New York 1975). M. NOVAK, *Choosing Our King: Powerful Symbols in Presidential Politics* (New York 1974). T. ROBBINS et al., "The Last Civil Religion: Reverend Moon and the Unification Church," *Sociological Analysis* 37 (Summer 1976) 111–125. E. A. SMITH, ed., *The Religion of the Republic* (Philadelphia 1971). E. L. TUVESON, *Redeemer Nation: The Idea of America's Millennial Role.* (Chicago 1968). W. L. WARNER, *American Life: Dream and Reality* (Chicago 1957). R. WILLIAMS, *American Society* (New York 1970). J. F. WILSON, "A Historian's Approach to Civil Religion," in R. E. RICHEY and D. G. JONES, *American Civil Religion* (New York 1974) 115–138; "The Status of 'Civil Religion' in America," in E. A. SMITH, ed., *Civil Religion* (Philadelphia 1971) 1–21. R. C. WIMBERLEY, "Testing the Civil Religion Hypothesis," *Sociological Analysis* 37 (Winter, 1976) 341–351. M. L. SCHNEIDER, "A Catholic Perspective on American Civil Religion," in T. M. MCFADDEN, ed., *America in Theological Perspective* (New York 1976) 123–139.

[M. A. NEAL]

CLEMENS, ALPHONSE HENRY

Educator in the sociology and spirituality of the family; b. Aug. 19, 1905, St. Louis, Mo.; d. Sept. 19, 1977, Washington, D.C. Receiving his master's and doctoral degrees from St. Louis University, he then headed the department of sociology and economics at Fontbonne College in St. Louis, where he established one of the first undergraduate degree programs in family life. He also directed the department of sociology and economics and the Consumer Institute at Fontbonne. He served in the St. Louis offices of the War Labor Board, the Office of Price Administration, and the National Labor Relations Board. He married the former Bess Wolfers of Cape Girardeau in 1936, and they had two children. Joining The Catholic Univ. in 1946, he was associate professor in sociology until his retirement in 1970. There in 1951 he opened a marriage counseling center and directed graduate degree work in family life studies. He was the Director of the Air Force Chaplains' Institute in Human Relations from 1956 to 1969 and the Clergy Seminar in Family Apostolate and Marriage Counseling.

He was a member of the American Economic Society, the Catholic Economics Society, and the Executive Board of the National Catholic Conference on Family Life; he was President of the American Catholic Sociological Society, 1945–46. Dr. Clemens wrote many periodical articles, edited a number of publications about family-life education, and was editor of *Holy Family*, a magazine, 1933–35. His best known books were *Marriage and the Family, an Integrated Approach* (1957), *Design for Successful Marriage* (1964), and *The Cana Movement in the U.S.* (1953). Among many honors for his accomplishment in the marriage field, he accepted the Bishop Bartholomew Award in 1960 for outstanding work in family-life education at Catholic University.

Dr. Clemens and his wife brought the Cana Conference idea to Washington and were the first chair-couple of the Cana Movement in the archdiocese. He was instrumental in initiating several institutes on marriage and the family for clergy and laity which helped the movement across the country. Through his writing and lecturing in a scholarly and inspiring manner he gave much impetus to the growing married couples' groups of the 40s and 50s. At his retirement in 1970 he studied for the permanent diaconate program for two years. He joined the Chaplains' Staff at the Bethesda Naval Medical Center and spent long hours there as Eucharistic minister and spiritual counselor. Considered one of the foremost pioneers in this country's family apostolate he is revered by many who knew him as a deeply spiritual and zealous layman.

[K. C. ENZLER]

CLERICAL DRESS

The norms of church law governing the dress of clerics, of both the Latin and the Oriental Rites (CIC c. 361nl; ClerSanct 77, 1), outside of use in the sanctuary or liturgical functions, are presently in force, not having been revoked (3:947). Thus the cleric should wear a becoming ecclesiastical garb, according to the legitimate customs of the place and the regulations of the local Ordinary. Besides imposing a duty, the Church at the same time grants a right to clerics (deacons and priests) to a distinctive dress, which may be taken away as a penalty. The purpose of the legislation has been to encourage modest and appropriate attire for clerics in the context of the locale where they reside and/or exercise their apostolate. In some way or by some symbol, at least by the simplicity of their garb, they should be distinguishable from nonclerics. Religious clerics are also bound by the same norms when outside their houses.

In the U.S. the wearing of the black suit with a roman collar and rabat has been the standard clerical dress. However, there has been a growing practice which restricts the wearing of this garb as regards places and circumstances. This has been due partly as a result of the drastic changes in society after World War II and in the Church following Vatican Council II, partly as paralleling the wider variety in some liturgical vesture, and partly because of the influence of the change in clerical dress in other countries. Apart from acceptable recreational attire, suits of other somber colors worn with the roman collar or with the conventional shirt and tie have become more noticeable in clerical usage. Permanent deacons normally wear lay attire, except in certain instances approved in the diocese of their incardination. Male religious are exhorted to be distinguishable from the laity "by the use of the roman collar or by some other visible and appropriately distinctive sign" (O'Connor). Unless in a particular diocese the bishop in accordance with the canon has regulated clerical dress, it seems that the silence of the Ordinaries is allowing a custom to arise that relaxes the conformity heretofore prevailing.

Bibliography: Congregation for Religious and Secular Institutes, Letter (Private) Jan. 22, 1972, O'Connor 7:534–535.

[N. HALLIGAN]

CLOISTER

Adaptation of the laws for the cloister of nuns wholly dedicated to contemplation (3:359) was effected in the Eastern Churches under the authority of the patriarchs or hierarchs (motu proprio *Ecclesiae Sanctae* II, 9, 30) and in the Latin Church according to the norms of the Instruction of the Congregation of Religious and Secular Institutes, *Venite seorsum* (Aug. 15, 1969), which constitutes the prevailing law for papal enclosure. Material separation of the cloister is reaffirmed and is to be observed according to the tradition of each Institute as authenticated by the Holy See. Nuns who engage in an external apostolate follow the norms of their constitutions, the minor papal enclosure being suppressed (*Ecclesiae Sanctae* II, 32). Greater local autonomy characterizes the norms governing egress and ingress. With at least the habitual consent of the local Ordinary,

the local superioress may authorize egress: for health care provided in the locality and when necessary to accompany a sick nun; for manual labor outside of the cloister but within the monastery precincts; for the exercise of civil rights and the performance of other administrative acts. Local Ordinaries continue to enjoy the faculty to authorize other instances of egress for a just and serious reason (Paul VI PastMun 34), but for an absence exceeding three months permission of the Holy See is required.

The list of those permitted by law to enter the enclosure has been expanded to include a priest to minister to the seriously or chronically ill, a priest and servers to conduct liturgical processions, physicians and others whose services are regularly required by the monastery and, according to their statutes, the extern sisters of the monastery. All penalties for the violation of the papal cloister of nuns are suspended pending the promulgation of a new Code of Canon Law.

Conformable to the Declaration of the same Congregation (June 4, 1970), superiors general of canons regular, mendicants, and clerics regular have in many instances adjusted the observance of enclosure according to the norms of CIC c. 604. Monks, however, must continue to observe the rules of cloister set by CIC c. 598.

Bibliography: J. GALLEN, "Canon Law for Religious after Vatican II," RevRel 34 (1975) 63–66.

[W. B. RYAN]

CODE OF CANON LAW, REVISION OF

Pope John XXIII on January 25, 1959 called for the revision of the Code of Canon Law, in the same memorable address in which he announced the forthcoming Vatican Council II (ActApS 51 [1959] 68). He recalled the interrelationship between the Council, the renewal of the Church, and the reform of the Canon Law again in 1959 in his encyclical letter *Ad Petri cathedram* (ibid. 511).

The Pontifical Commission. During the first Spring inter-session of the Council, shortly before his death, March 28, 1963, Pope John formally established the Pontifical Commission for the Revision of the Code of Canon Law, with Cardinal Pietro Ciriaci as president, and forty other cardinals as members. The Commission was charged with preparing a revision of the Code of Canon Law according to the decrees and decisions of Vatican Council II. Pope Paul VI broadened the membership of the Commission by the addition of seventy consultors, an international group of experts in Canon Law and theology, in April 1964. After suspending its work during the deliberations of the Council, the Commission, including members and consultors, met on May 6, 1965, to decide the procedures to be followed, the division of labor, and the constitution of subcommissions. It was at this meeting, in the Spring that preceded the final session of the Council, that the Commission decided that the revision of the Canon Law should take the form of a new code, following the order, methodology, and spirit of the 1917 Code of Canon Law, which had been mainly the work of cardinal Pietro Gasparri. This meant that the Gasparri Code, which had been in force as the universal law of the Church for less than fifty years, would be revised and updated by the decrees of the Council. This decision, of course, precluded the possibility of a radical departure from the principles of preconciliar Canon Law.

Shortly before the close of the final session of Vatican II, on Nov. 20, 1965, Pope Paul VI solemnly inaugurated the work of the Commission for the Revision of the Code of Canon Law. The actual work of the consultors of the Commission did not begin until January 1966.

Cardinal Ciriaci divided the consultors into ten study groups to examine and review the Code and submit emendations to the cardinals. The study groups were designated according to the sections of the Gasparri Code, each to be responsible for the revision of the canons in the given sections. The study groups were assigned the revision of the canons on general norms, the sacred hierarchy, religious, laity, the Sacraments, marriage, the ecclesiastical magisterium, temporal goods, judicial procedures, and the penal law. On Jan. 15, 1966 Cardinal Ciriaci wrote to the presidents of the episcopal conferences, asking them to submit proposals for a working arrangement between the conferences and the Commission. He also asked the conferences to formulate particular suggestions for the revision of the various canons of the Code in light of the decisions of Vatican II.

With the death of Cardinal Ciriaci in December 1966, Pope Paul VI appointed the former secretary of the Council, Archbishop (later Cardinal) Pericle Felici, as the new president of the Commission. Later in 1967 Cardinal Felici increased the number of study groups to sixteen, with the addition of scholars to analyze the order of the Code and draft directive principles for the revision. Among the committees he formed were the special committee charged with drafting the fundamental constitutional law for the Church (*Lex fundamentalis*) and a committee to draft a new administrative law for the protection of the rights of the faithful.

The Work of the Commission. The Pontifical Commission for the Revision of the Code of Canon Law has submitted its policies and the progress of its work to each of the international meetings of the Synod of Bishops in Rome. These reports were accepted and approved by the Synods, not only as a general encouragement of the immense work of canonical revision, but as a particular and specific approbation of each major part of this project.

To its consultors and the episcopal delegates attending the 1967 Synod of Bishops in Rome the Commission offered a detailed position paper containing the principles it would follow in revising the Code of Canon Law. These principles were discussed in the Synod at length. The synodal bishops then approved ten general principles to guide the revision of the Canon Law.

Guiding Principles. First, rather than radically alter the law, the Commission elected basically to follow the juridical format of the 1917 Code. The new code is to be a modernization and adaptation of the Gasparri Code, with special emphasis on the definition and protection of rights and obligations of persons within the visible society of the Church. Secondly, the new code will attempt to eliminate conflicts between the internal forum, i.e., conscience, and the external forum, i.e. the public administration of the Church. The new code will be basically concerned with the external social order of the Church, not matters of individual conscience. Thirdly, the new code will be more pastoral: minimizing invalidating and incapacitating laws; emphasizing exhor-

tation over strict duty; and providing greater freedom and flexibility in general norms. Fourthly, the office of bishop will be positively cast with detailed inclusion of the bishops' individual and collegial authority in the Church. This will entail a rethinking of the institution of bishops' *faculties and powers of *dispensation. The fifth principle of the revised law is that of subsidiarity, with greater recognition of the independence and competencies of the ritual Churches, episcopal conferences, regional and local councils. The sixth principle affirms the fundamental equality of all persons in the Church and the protection of the rights of all the baptized by norms of accountability to curb arbitrary abuses of authority. The seventh principle elaborates a procedure for protecting subjective rights through judicial recourse and appeal and a new system of administrative tribunals. The eighth principle is that the new law maintain the basic territorial division of jurisdiction in the Church accepted by the 1917 Code. Extraordinary provisions will be considered in jurisdictional units wherein strict territorial delimitation should not be solely determinative. The ninth principle concerns a reduction in the penal law and a desire that ecclesiastical penalties be imposed and remitted only in the external forum (*see* PENAL LAW, DRAFT OF). Finally, the Synod approved the study proposed by the Commission of a new systematic ordering of the Code to fit the spirit of Vatican II and the scientific requisites of canonical legislation.

Consultative Procedures. Under the direction of Cardinal Felici the Commission adopted a procedure of consultation for examining the *Schemata* prepared by the various study groups. The definitive text is first transmitted to the pope for his judgment on whether it is to be forwarded to others involved in the consultative process. If the pope agrees, the text is then sent with appropriate changes and clarifications to the episcopal conferences, the offices of the Roman Curia, the Unions of Superiors General, and to the faculties of various Catholic universities. After responses are received from these sources, the individual study groups are convened to study the responses and make appropriate revisions of the text. After the necessary changes have been made, the *schemata* are then forwarded for a final revision to the cardinals of the Commission. They decide then whether or not to transmit the revised canons to the pope for his approval and decree of promulgation.

At the present writing, the full text of the following sections of the revised Code of Canon Law are in the final stage of consultation: the administrative law; the penal law; the law of the Sacraments; general norms; physical and juridical persons; clerics in general and in particular; religious; the laity and associations of the faithful; sacred times and places; divine worship; the ecclesiastical magisterium; temporalities; and the formal procedural law.

Lex Ecclesiae Fundamentalis. When Pope Paul VI solemnly inaugurated the work of the Pontifical Commission for the Revision of the Code, Nov. 20, 1965, he proposed formulating in canonical norms a basic constitutional law for the whole Church. A constitutional law, he said, though historically without precedent, would serve at the present time to clarify the ecclesiology of Vatican II and define more surely the basis of authority for the revised Canon Law. Five days later the plenary commission of cardinals decided that the project should be undertaken and made arrangements for an initial draft.

Preliminary Drafts. The first draft, entitled *Prima quaedam adumbrata propositio Codicis Ecclesiae fundamentalis,* was sent to the central Committee of consultors for study in 1966. At its annual meeting in June of that year the Committee suggested three principles to guide in drafting the constitutional law: (1) the *Lex fundamentalis* should reflect both the theological and juridical character of the Church and yet be animated by an easily discernible ecumenical spirit; (2) the notion of the Church as People of God should receive central emphasis, in accord with the teachings of Vatican II, and the rights and duties of the faithful should be delineated within this context; and (3) the *Lex* should illustrate, at least in a general way, the relationship between the Church and mankind, in terms of the Church's mission, rights, and duties vis à vis the world.

A new draft, now bearing the title *Lex Ecclesiae fundamentalis: Altera quaedam adumbratio propositionis,* was accepted by the Commission in April 1967 as a primary working document. Cardinal Felici at that time appointed a special commission of thirteen members, chaired by Msgr. W. Onclin and Fr. R. Bidagor, SJ, to solicit and evaluate further proposals to refine the document. The Synod of Bishops, meeting at the Vatican in October 1967, approved the project and accepted for further consideration this second draft of the *Lex Ecclesiae fundamentalis.* In May 1969 the Vatican Press published a revised version of this draft. The Code Commission sent this version to all the cardinalatial members of the Commission for the Revision of the Code, to the consultors of the Congregation for the Doctrine of the Faith, and to the members of the International Pontifical Theological Commission for their comments and observations.

After this round of consultation, worldwide publicity given to the project generated both controversy regarding the timeliness and content of the fundamental law and a flood of critical suggestions for its emendation. At the present writing, the Code Commission has worked through to a ninth revised version of the *Lex Ecclesiae fundamentalis* in the light of these criticisms. The Commission has proposed to the pope that the *Lex* be promulgated in conjunction with the new Code of Canon Law.

The Ninth Revised Version. The *Lex Ecclesiae fundamentalis* in its present form contains ninety-four canons arranged in three chapters.

(1) *Introduction.* After recalling the Church's divine origin, the draft describes it as both a spiritual community and a human society, requiring its own distinctive juridical order. Christ committed his mission to the Church, which it fulfills, in a sense, through the continual refinement of a rule of law. Law in the Church need not be rigidly uniform. In fact, the ecclesial community most effectively realizes its own unity by providing a diversity of order and discipline according to the various conditions and situations prevailing among the individual local Churches.

(2) *Chapter One.* The Church, primarily identified as the People of God, is described in terms of its structure and purpose. Its unity as well as its diversity are pointed up by means of this image. Although the Church exists and realizes itself in and through the various local Churches and regional groupings of Churches, it stands forth as a single, universal reality. Article 1 of Chapter One treats the question of membership in, or affiliation with, the People of God (i.e. the Church), the fundamental rights and duties common to all the faithful, and the various orders existing among the members (laity, ministers, and religious). Article 2 of Chapter One considers the divinely constituted hierarchy, established as ministers for the pastoral care of the People of God, the supreme pontiff, bishops (as a college and as individual shepherds), priests, and deacons. Their responsibilities and prerogatives are generally outlined.

(3) *Chapter Two.* Using the order commonly followed by the Vatican II documents, the draft describes the three essential functions of the Church and points out the preeminence of the sanctifying role. Chapter Two defines the teaching, sanctifying, and shepherding functions, and articulates the responsibilities on each level of church membership for the fulfillment of these roles. The rights and duties of the papacy, the bishops (collegially and individually), the priests, the deacons, and the laity, in regard to the indispensable offices of the Church, receive basic formulation.

(4) *Chapter Three.* This section considers the relationship between the Church and the world, the Church and the community of mankind, the Church and the secular order. It lays out, in a very general way, fundamental principles regarding the Church's mission, its prerogatives, and its obligations in the non-Christian world.

Bibliography: The literature on the revision of Canon Law is so vast that only a few representative works can be cited. The official publication of the Pontifical Commission for the Revision of the Code of Canon Law is *Communicationes* (Rome 1968–): See also *Principia quae Codicis Iuris Canonici recognitionem dirigant* (Typis Polyglottis Vaticanis 1967); English tr. R. G. CUNNINGHAM, *Jurist* 30 (1970) 447–455. G. ALBERIGO, ed., *Legge e Vangelo* (Istituto per le Scienze Religiose, Brescia 1972). Canon Law Society of America, "A Critique of the Revised Schema of the *Lex Fundamentalis,*" AmEcclRev 163 (1971) 3–17. P. FELICI, "*De opere Codicis Iuris Canonici recognoscendi,*" PeriodicaMorCanLiturg 64 (1975) 13–25. T. J. GREEN, "The Revision of the Code: The First Decade," *Jurist* 36 (1976) 353–441. S. KUTTNER, "The Code of Canon Law in Historical Perspective," *Jurist* 28 (1968) 129–148.

[W. W. BASSETT]

COGLEY, JOHN

Editor and author who the *New York Times* said was "generally regarded as the most prominent Roman Catholic journalist of his generation"; b. in Chicago, March 16, 1916; d. in Santa Barbara, Cal., March 28, 1976. He attended parochial schools, the Servite preparatory seminary, and Loyola University in Chicago. During the Depression he joined the Catholic Worker movement, led by Dorothy Day and Peter Maurin. For four years he was in charge of its St. Joseph House of Hospitality, Chicago, and edited the *Chicago Catholic Worker.* A nonpacifist despite his Catholic Worker connection, Cogley served in the Air Force from 1942 to 1945. After the war he was cofounder and coeditor of *Today,* the national Catholic student magazine. Leaving *Today* he took what was then an unusual step for a layman, going to the Catholic University of Fribourg, Switzerland to study theology. Back in the United States, in 1949 he became executive editor of *Commonweal,* the lay-edited journal of opinion where he was to remain as an editor for five years and as a columnist for another ten. Throughout his life he contributed to a wide variety of publications, from *Collier's* and *Look* to the *New Republic* and *America.*

The period of his career at *Commonweal* was one of the

most exciting in American religious history and Cogley was very much part of that history. Like John Courtney Murray, SJ, he did not accept the "error has no rights" proposition that was in those pre-Vatican Council days the official Roman Catholic position on Church-State. This editorial stance brought him much criticism from establishment-minded critics as well as winning him devoted readers all over the country. At Vatican Council II, of course, the more liberal position he espoused was finally vindicated. Indeed, the Council ratified much of what Cogley had always stood for, and his *Times* obituary said that "in many ways he personified an ideal that emerged from that assembly—a theologically knowledgeable layman, socially concerned, confident that Christianity is relevant to modern life." In 1955 Cogley left *Commonweal* to join the Fund for the Republic (now the Center for the Study of Democratic Institutions). His first task was to head a study of blacklisting in the entertainment industry, and his two-volume critical study of the widespread practice brought him into instant disfavor with the House Un-American Activities Committee. The Committee huffed and puffed, threatening dire consequences if he did not reveal his confidential sources. He refused and eventually the HUAC threats melted away. Becoming a permanent member of the Center, Cogley headed up the project on "Religious Institutions in a Free Society" with John Courtney Murray and Reinhold Niebuhr as consultants, and later the Center's study on "The American Character." In 1960 he served as Church-State adviser in the Kennedy presidential campaign, playing a leading role in briefing Kennedy before the crucial Houston ministers' confrontation. In 1964 he took a leave from the Center to live in Rome for a year while expanding an *Encyclopedia Brittanica* article into a book, *Religion in a Secular Age* (New York 1968), and at the same time covering the proceedings of Vatican Council II for Religious News Service, for which he received the Catholic Press Association's St. Francis de Sales Award. In 1965 he left the Center for the Study of Democratic Institutions to join the *New York Times* as religious news editor. It was a post he filled with distinction, establishing the fact that good writing could make even abstruse theological issues clear and interesting. In 1967 for reasons of health he returned to Santa Barbara and the Center, where he become a senior fellow and founding editor of the successful *Center Magazine*. In 1972 he published *Catholic America*, a popular history of the Catholic Church in this country. Among his other writings was a regular syndicated column for the Catholic diocesan press and later for the *National Catholic Reporter*.

But after *Humanae vitae*, Pope Paul's encyclical on contraception, he became increasingly uncomfortable in the Roman Catholic Church. Thereafter he gave up writing his regular weekly column, feeling that it was not right for him to be considered a Catholic writer when he could no longer support papal positions. In *A Canterbury Tale* (New York 1976), his memoirs, he later wrote: "It was now clear to me that by the time of *Humanae vitae* I no longer accepted the papal claim to infallibility.... After 1968 and that fatal encyclical, I began to look more to the Episcopal Church." By September 1973 his mind was made up and he joined the Episcopal Church. The move surprised and saddened many of his Catholic friends, but Thurston Davis,

SJ, former editor-in-chief of *America*, summed up the attitude of those who knew him: "All we know is that John Cogley was incapable of pretending to be a Roman Catholic, once he had decided that he no longer shared that faith and its official moral teaching in their fullness." In 1974 Cogley applied to the Episcopal Diocese of California for ordination to the priesthood and was accepted. He was subsequently ordained deacon but was destined not to become a priest; on March 28, 1976, he had a fatal heart attack and died, leaving his wife, Theodora, six children and four grandchildren. It was hard for his friends to believe that such a warm and vital personality had passed from their midst. For his friends and devoted readers, the titles of two columns written in his memory summed up their feelings: one, by Peter Steinfels, was called "Death of a Hero"; the other, by Robert E. Lauder, SJ, was called, simply, "Death of a Christian."

Bibliography: *New York Times Biographical Edition* 7 (1976) 337.

[J. O'GARA]

COLLEGE THEOLOGY SOCIETY

An association of college and university teachers, almost all of whom are affiliated with schools in the United States or Canada, the College Theology Society serves: to promote the teaching of theology, especially on the undergraduate level; to foster communication and exchange of information and experience relative to the study of religion through publications sponsored by the Society and through national and regional meetings; and to integrate religious studies into the rest of the undergraduate curriculum. In 1978 the Society had 750 members from over 200 colleges; a large percentage of the membership comes from the Eastern and Midwestern sections of the United States. Although full membership is open to all who teach religious thought on the college or university level or who have been awarded a graduate degree in the field, the Society has historically drawn a significant majority of its members from Catholic institutions.

The Society began in 1953 and was originally called the Society of Catholic College Teachers of Sacred Doctrine (13:396). Its development since that time has mirrored the changes that have taken place in the academic study of religion at Catholic colleges. Religious studies, as well as that branch of the discipline that concerns itself particularly with Christian theology, have increasingly come to be recognized as bona fide academic pursuits that have a legitimate place in the liberal arts curriculum (*see* RELIGIOUS EDUCATION). Within the college classroom, stress has been increasingly placed upon understanding the phenomenon of religion, or the meaning of a tradition's scriptures, or the doctrines of a Church; the academic approach is distinct from training in doctrinal orthodoxy or nurturing personal commitment. Thus, as college curricula changed in the 1960s and 1970s, so also did the College Theology Society—a change concretely illustrated by the adoption of its new name at the 1967 annual meeting. Today the Society reflects a broad range of academic inquiry, although its principal focus remains Christian theology. Its membership includes non-Catholic as well as Catholic teachers in public and religiously-affiliated institutions.

A new constitution was ratified in 1976, specifying the duties of the Society's elected officers, board of directors, and five standing committees. The annual meeting has been considerably revised and is now structured around ten areas of inquiry, e.g., speculative theology, religion and culture, world religions. In this way continuing communication among members in a particular field is encouraged. There are also several geographic regions within the Society which sponsor local meetings, often in conjunction with other professional associations. The Society is affiliated with the International Federation of Catholic Universities and the National Council on the Study of Religion. As a member of the latter, it shares executive-office facilities with other learned societies for greater coordination and cooperation in projects concerned with the field of religion.

Publications have been a strong component of the Society's efforts in recent years. An annual publication, distributed to members but also marketed as a trade book, is built around specifically solicited, theme articles: A semiannual journal, *Horizons*, begun in 1974, has proven to be exceptionally successful. With an editorial office at Villanova University and partially supported by assistance from that institution, the journal features scholarly articles, book reviews, opportunities for readers' comments on contemporary issues, and studies on effective college teaching. Circulation of *Horizons* has reached 1,250. The journal is included in the major periodical indexes. Additional publishing ventures are being planned, notably a classroom resource series in which members will collaborate to produce books designed specifically for the college student.

The Society will celebrate its 25th anniversary at its 1979 annual convention to be held at Trinity College, Washington, D.C.—the site also of its first convention. Continuity, linked with a capacity for adaptation, seems to have contributed to the vitality of the College Theology Society over the past quarter-century.

[T. M. MCFADDEN]

COLLEGIALITY

Collegiality is a term rediscovered by contemporary theologians and restored to official honor in the Dogmatic Constitution on the Church by Vatican Council II to describe the Church's mode of life, especially governance: "Together with its head, the Roman Pontiff, and never without this head, the episcopal order is the subject of supreme and full power over the universal Church" (*Lumen gentium* 22). The Council regularly interchanges the terms *collegium* (college), *ordo* (order), *corpus* (body), and *fraternitas* (brotherhood).

The Vatican II Formulation. Although collegiality was one of the most hotly debated topics at Vatican II, it is difficult to understand why. As Karl Rahner has pointed out, nothing really new was offered (LexThK^2 Suppl. 1:210, 211, 222–224). Neither the original draft (1962) of the Constitution on the Church nor the final text (1964) went beyond either current Canon Law (CIC c. 228n1) or the understanding of Vatican Council I, especially if the clarifications of Zinelli and Gasser are taken into consideration (cf. Mansi 52, 1109D-1110B; 52, 1114D; 52, 1216C), as well as Kleutgen's *relatio, De schemate* (ibid. 53, 308–332), or the 1875 *Declaratio collectiva episcoporum Germaniae* (Denz 3112–16). Hence, Rahner suggests, the real value was not *what* was said, but *that* it was said in such a solemn church council and the possibilities it opens up for future theological and ecclesial activity.

Conciliar Debate. Vatican II's doctrine on collegiality is to be greeted warmly, since it counters an illegitimate fascination with monarchy, but not as warmly as it was debated, for it is a reminder of a decline from that original brotherliness that was the ideal characteristic of Christian life and government. Greatest opposition came from certain Council Fathers and Romanist theologians, apparently still frightened by a specter which had haunted Vatican I. This was the Protestant jurisprudence of the 17th and 18th centuries which had maintained that *collegium* meant *societas aequalium* (a society of equals) and thus eliminated any and all hierarchical differentiation. Likewise invoked was Roman Law, although this clearly never asserted that a *collegium* was a *societas aequalium* (cf. Pauly-Wiss RE 4/1: 380–480). To avoid the possibility of even such capricious misunderstanding Vatican II offers *societas stabilis* as a synonym for *collegium*, (*Lumen gentium* 19).

Doctrinal History. The fears were, of course, idle, and the qualifications in no way impede or diminish collegiality as the style of life and governance in the Church. They serve only to prevent the univocal application of secular categories to the Church. The fears in fact betray an ignoring of Catholic history, both ecclesial and theological. In the 4th and 5th centuries *collegium* was a common term, designating the apostolic community, as well as the community of bishop-presbyter (priest) and of the bishops among themselves. During the 14th-19th centuries, even among those decidedly dedicated to papal primacy and even among the Italian-speaking, the concept of the collegial character of the episcopacy played a prominent role.

However, from the 12th century on a distinction between *ordo* and *jurisdictio* intensified to the point of becoming a separation. This was complicated by an undue emphasis on the cultic (and priestly) dimension of both the Church and its ordained minister or office (equated terminologically with priest), as well as a decidedly individualistic approach to priesthood and Eucharist. The ordained minister (priest, bishop) was related to the *corpus verum* (the Eucharistic Body of Christ) on the basis of ordination by the Sacrament of Holy Orders, to the *corpus mysticum* (the ecclesial Body of Christ) on the basis of appointment by (episcopal or papal) jurisdiction (cf. de Lubac). Thus scholastic theology declined to acknowledge that episcopal ordination belongs to the Sacrament of Holy Orders and attributed it solely to papal jurisdictional empowerment. Thus was the collegiality of the episcopacy and the episcopate emptied, except for a vapid, mutually benevolent intent. In such a theology the episcopal college would have to be regarded as merely the jurisdictional creation of the papacy.

The Restored Teaching. This theology was kept in the first draft (1962) of the Constitution on the Church. The final and official document (1964), however, emphatically restored the ancient understanding of collegiality as the juridical as well as moral communion of the bishops among themselves and in union with the pope, for the shepherding of the universal Church. Thus, the paragraph quoted at the beginning of this article, also states "one is constituted a member of the episcopal body by virtue of sacramental consecration and by hierachical communion with the head and members of the body" (*Lumen gentium* 22). To be noted is that communion is not only with the head, but also with the other members of the college. For collegiality is both "vertical," of bishops with pope, and "horizontal," of bishops with one another. Hence, however necessary the pope be as head, the bishops as members are not mere appendages or automatons under the papal powers. The same must also be said of the bishop and his presbyterate. Joseph Ratzinger (then theologian, now cardinal and archbishop) emphasized at the time of Council that "conciliarity is something that belongs to the essence of the Church; however it has worked historically, the conciliar principle lies at the heart of the Church and ever presses from within towards realization" (Ratzinger 180).

Among theologians two kinds of collegiality can be discerned: "from above" and "from below," depending on whether the starting point is the universal episcopal college or the local Church. Karl Rahner illustrates both: "A bishop is a bishop of a place because and *in so far* as he belongs to the supreme directive body of the Church . . ." (Rahner, *Bishops* 22). On the other hand, "For this reason, no doubt, the earliest local Church was a bishop's Church . . . . We can say that, in the sense and to the extent that the whole Church is completely present in the local Church, the Church's powers of jurisdiction and order are completely present in the local bishop . . . . But since his bishop's Church is *the* Church, in that mysterious presence of the whole in the part which is found only in the Church, impulses from above (Holy Spirit) can directly manifest Christian and ecclesiastical life in him, and through him and his Church to the whole Church" (Rahner and Ratzinger, 27, 29, 32).

The Nota Explicativa. Just as all Christians are responsible for the whole Church in their own special ways (one Holy Spirit—many, diverse gifts) so are individual bishops/episcopal college and pope/papacy all responsible, not only for their local Churches, but in their own special ways for the whole Church. Consequently, the repeated insistence before, during, and after Vatican II that the college of bishops can exist and function only in union with its head, the pope, can hardly be considered a theological and ecclesial concern. A special instance of anxiety over privilege and de facto (if not de iure) power, is the so-called *Nota explicativa praevia*, which, although termed *praevia*, was *appended* to the Dogmatic Constitution on the Church. It must be stressed that this *Nota* is not part of the official doctrine of the Council. It was and remains only part of the *acta* of the Council, enjoying only whatever authority such *acta* customarily enjoy; as one of the eminent Council participants himself indicates: "The object of the Fathers' vote was not the note . . . but the text of the Constitution . . . . The Note stands as one of clarification . . . and as so approved by the Holy Father" (Archbishop P. Parente, *L'Avvenire d'Italia* Jan. 21, 1964, 9).

Need for Development. Currently the practice of collegiality is clear neither in the documents of Vatican II, in the theories of the theologians, nor in the life of the Church. According to the Constitution on the Church, episcopal collegiality is exercised not only solemnly and extraordinarily in an ecumenical council, but also otherwise and ordinarily in the daily life of the Church. Intimations, at best, of such ordinary collegiality can be discerned in the patriarchates and national episcopal conferences. Of considerable value in this regard can be the historical studies of W. de Vries and M. J. LeGouillou (see bibliog.). Certainly one of the most urgent problems of the Church today is the articulation of collegiality in both theological theory and ecclesial practice, for the sake of the local, particular, and universal Church.

This article has focused on collegiality as the proper mode of church governance. However, even this more Christly way of ecclesial shepherding is not the real point of collegiality. Collegiality can be properly understood only in the context of the *apostolic succession. There is a sense in which the Church simply as such is the apostolic succession. In a more restricted sense apostolic succession means that the apostolic college is continued in the episcopal, the particular foundational attributes of the Twelve being excepted of course.

Hence episcopal-papal collegiality is always to be understood primarily as the means whereby the contemporary disciples of Christ, the successors of the apostolic Church, are enabled to keep alive the tradition and memory of Christ and to avoid subjection to domineering lords (1 Pt 5.3) because they are all the communion of "the many brothers of his Son" (Rom 8.29).

Bibliography: G. ALBERIGO, *Lo sviluppo della dottrina sui poteri nella chiesa universale* (Rome 1964). R. AUBERT, ed., *Le Concile et les Conciles* (Paris 1960). J. COLSON, *L'épiscopat catholique* (Paris 1963). Y. CONGAR, "Konzil als Versammlung und grundsatzliche Konziliarität der Kirche," in H. VORGRIMLER, ed., *Gott in Welt II* (Freiburg 1964) 135–165 (contains many sources). Y. CONGAR, ed., *La collégialité épiscopale* (Paris 1964). V. FAGIOLI and G. CONCETTI, eds., *La Collegialità episcopale per il futuro della Chiesa* (Florence 1969). J. GUYOT, *Études sur le sacrement de l'ordre* (Paris 1957). O. KARRER, *Um die Einheit der Christen* (Frankfurt 1953). H. KÜNG, ed., *Papal Ministry in the Church. Concilium 64* (New York 1971). J. LECUYER, *Études sur la collégialité épiscopale* (Lyons 1964). M. J. LE GUILLOU, "L'Expérience orientale de la collégialité épiscopale et ses requêtes," *Istina* 10 (1964) 111–124. H. DE LUBAC, *Corpus mysticum* (rev. ed., Paris 1949). K. RAHNER, *Bishops: Their Status and Function,* tr. E. QUINN (London 1964). K. RAHNER and J. RATZINGER, *The Episcopate and the Primacy,* tr. K. BARKER et al. (New York 1962). J. RATZINGER, *Das neue Volk Gottes* (Düsseldorf 1970). P. RUSCH, "Die kollegiale Struktur des Bischofsamtes," ZKathTh 86 (1964) 197–216. O. SEMMELROTH, "Die Lehre von der kollegialen Hirtengewalt über die Gesamtkirche," *Scholastik* 39 (1964) 161–179. D. M. STANLEY, "The New Testament Basis for the Concept of Collegiality," ThSt 25 (1964) 197–216. W. DE VRIES, "Der Episkopat auf den Synoden vor Nicäa," ThPraktQ 111 (1963) 263–275; "Die kollegiale Struktur der Kirche in den ersten Jahrhunderten," UnaS 19 (1964) 296–317.

[R. KRESS]

COLLINS, JOSEPH BURNS

Leader in catechetics in the U.S.; b. Waseca, Minn., Sept. 7, 1897; d. Washington, D.C., Jan. 23, 1975. After attending school in Waseca, he went on to study at St. Mary's College in Winona, Minn., the St. Paul Seminary in Saint Paul and the Urban University in Rome, receiving an S.T.D. in 1924. He was ordained for the Diocese of Winona in Rome May 17, 1924. Returning to the United States, he taught philosophy at St. Mary's College and the College of St Teresa in Winona, 1925–1930. He did post-graduate work at Johns Hopkins University and was awarded a Ph.D. in 1934. He taught one year at Notre Dame College of Maryland and at Sulpician Seminary in Washington, D.C., 1933–1937. His acquaintance and association with the Sulpician Fathers at St. Mary's Seminary in Baltimore led him to join the Society of Priests of Saint Sulpice in 1935. In 1937 Collins began teaching at The Catholic University of America. He became a regular faculty member in 1939 and taught moral theology and catechetics there until his retirement in 1968.

Early in his career Collins became interested in the Confraternity of Christian Doctrine as a practical solution to the problems and task of catechizing children and adults. In 1942 he became the director of the National Center for the CCD, a post he held for 25 years. Following his resignation as director in 1967, he remained at the National Center as Assistant Director and later as a consultant until his death. As director of the National Center for the CCD in the years from 1942 to 1967, Collins was a very influential figure in catechetics in the United States. For 24 years (1942–66) he edited the bi-monthly aid for catechists, *Our Parish Confraternity*. In 1964 under his leadership the National Center began to publish the quarterly catechetical journal, *The Living Light*.

He authored or edited 14 books and countless articles which appeared in such publications as *The Register, Our Sunday Visitor, American Ecclesiastical Review* and the *New Catholic Encyclopedia* (cf. Volume 15:44). Among his more important books are *Kergymatic Renewal and the CCD, Updating the CCD High School of Religion, CCD Methods and Modern Catechetics*; and *Some Guidelines for a New American Catechism*.

His long and dedicated service in the field of catechetics was recognized and rewarded in 1964 by Pope Paul VI with the Pro Ecclesia et Pontifice Medal. He also received the Benemerenti Medal in 1965. He was working on a history of the CCD at the time of his death. The first chapters were published in the *American Ecclesiastical Review* 168 (1974) 695–706; 169 (1975) 48–67; 237–255; 610–620; 690–702.

[T. E. KRAMER]

COMMISSIONS, PAPAL

Pontifical commissions (*commissiones*), councils (*consilia*), and committees (*comitatus*) are listed in the *Annuario Pontificio* as a subsection of the Roman *Curia, constituted for special needs or interests (4:13). Additions and changes have occurred during and since Vatican Council II. Included here are the Secretariats having under them important pontifical commissions; the order followed is that of the *Annuario* 1977 (1042–1080).

The *Secretariat for Promoting Christian Unity, originally created by Pope John XXIII, June 5, 1968, received final confirmation by Pope Paul VI, Aug. 15, 1967 (Paul VI RegEccl).

The Pontifical Commission for *Religious Relations with Judaism was created by Paul VI, Oct. 22, 1974. It is part of the above Secretariat and works to carry out the relations towards Judaism expressed by Vatican Council II (*Lumen gentium* 16; *Nostra aetate* 4).

The Secretariat for Non-Christians, instituted by Paul VI, May, 9, 1964 is devoted to the promotion of studies conducive to fostering relations between the Church and the Non-Christian religions (see *Lumen gentium* 16; *Nostra aetate* 2–3).

The Commission for Religous Relations with Islam was created as an adjunct of the Secretariat for Non-Christians by Paul VI, Oct. 22, 1974 and seeks to encourage relations between Christians and Islam, with the eventual cooperation of other Christian bodies (*see* ISLAMIC/ROMAN CATHOLIC DIALOGUE).

The Secretariat for Nonbelievers was instituted by Paul VI, April 9, 1965 and is devoted to the study of *atheism in its many forms and to dialogue with nonbelievers (see *Lumen gentium* 16; *Gaudium et spes* 19–21).

The Pontifical Council for the *Laity was established by Paul VI, Jan. 6, 1973 because of the emerging role of the laity in the Church (see *Lumen gentium* 30–38; 39–42; *Apostolicam actuositatem*). Established by Paul VI, Jan. 11, 1973, the Committee for the Family was affiliated with the Council for the Laity, Dec. 10, 1976. Its aim is to study and to put into unified, pastoral focus

problems of marriage and family life (see *Gaudium et spes* 47–52).

The Pontifical Commission for *Justice and Peace (*Iustitia et Pax*), established by Paul VI, Jan. 6, 1967, seeks to promote social justice among all nations, with special concern for the developing nations (see *Gaudium et spes* 73–89).

The Pontifical Commission for the Revision of the Code of Canon Law, formally instituted by John XXIII, March 25, 1963, has been in the process of preparing and submitting to the bishops of the Church proposals for a new codification of church law (*see* CODE OF CANON LAW, REVISION OF). The Pontifical Commission for the Revision of the Code of Oriental Canon Law, instituted by Paul VI, June 10, 1972, has a corresponding function, but must also formulate sections of the Eastern Churches' law that have not yet been codified (*see* ORIENTAL CODE OF CANON LAW, REVISION OF).

The Pontifical Commission for the Interpretation of the Decrees of Vatican Council II was established by Paul VI, Jan. 3, 1966 and is charged with authentic solution of questions regarding the conciliar documents.

The Pontifical Commission for Social Communications, (11:555) had its competence extended to the printed media by Paul VI, April 2, 1964. Its concern is both the social influence of the media of social communication (see ADVERTISING [MORAL ASPECTS]) and their use by the Church for its mission. Under this commission is the Vatican Film Library (*Filmoteca*), for cinematic and television material of interest to the Church.

The Pontifical Commission for *Latin America, attached to the Sacred Congregation for Bishops since 1969, dates from 1958. The General Council for Latin America was established by Paul VI, Nov. 30, 1963 for collaborative efforts between CELAM and the episcopal conferences of Europe and North America on behalf of the Churches of Latin America.

The Pontifical Commission for the Pastoral Care of Migrants and Tourists was established by Paul VI, March 19, 1970 and is also dependent on the Congregation for Bishops. Its concern is mainly for migrants and the undocumented (*see* MIGRATION, RIGHT OF).

The Pontifical Council *Cor Unum was instituted by Paul VI, July 15, 1971; its interests are human and Christian development.

The *International Theological Commission is a research adjunct of the Congregation for the *Doctrine of the Faith, established by Paul VI, April 11, 1969.

The *Pontifical Biblical Commission (11:551) was restructured by Paul VI, June 17, 1971 and made an adjunct of the Congregation for the Doctrine of the Faith.

In addition to the commissions listed there are other particular entities for the specific concerns of the curial congregations. The important Council for the Implementation of the Constitution on the Sacred Liturgy (the *Consilium*), which substantially carried out the revision of the liturgical rites and books called for by *Sacrosanctum Concilium* ceased to exist with the restructuring that formed the Congregation for the *Sacraments and Divine Worship, July 11, 1975 by decree of the apostolic constitution *Constans nobis* (ActApS 67 [1975] 417–420).

Two commissions whose work remains important to

biblical studies continue in existence. The Pontifical Abbey of St. Jerome for the Revision and Correction of the Vulgate established by Pius XI, June 15, 1933 is devoted to restoring the original reading of the Latin Vulgate text of St. Jerome. The Pontifical Commission for the New Vulgate was erected by Paul VI, Nov. 29, 1965 to prepare a new Latin text of the Bible that would take into account progress in biblical studies and provide a new and authoritative text in the universal language of the Church.

Other commissions having a more restricted scope are: the Commission for Sacred Archeology; the Committee for the Historical Sciences; the Commission for Sacred Art in Italy; the cardinalatial Committee for the Sanctuaries of Pompeii and Loreto; the Commission for Russia; the Commission for the State of Vatican City; the Permanent Commission for the Protection of Historical Monuments of the Holy See.

Bibliography: AnnPont 1977.

[J. E. RISK]

COMMITMENT

Commitment is an act of the will by which a person orients the total personality in response to a reality deemed absolute (4:14). Christian faith asserts God's self-communication in Jesus Christ as an absolute invitation to humanity addressed to the totality of human existence. This self-communication brings an actual sharing of divine life. Commitment, then, as the free and full acceptance of and witness to God's Revelation, forms an essential and characteristic element of Christian faith. It is both affirmation and activity appropriate to the recognition of the call to participate in the creative and redemptive plan of God.

The Christian engages in communal participation in this divine plan through the mission of the Church. Sacramental life concretizes the call that all receive to associate themselves with Christ in his saving mission and also elicits the response which grace inspires. The documents of Vatican Council II, stressing the Church as the Sacrament of salvation, essentially state that the commitment which the Church signifies is one of perfect charity. The individual willingly accepts the fact that love of God and love of neighbor cannot be separated. The Christian, in faith, recognizes the call to holiness which is only achieved through self-giving love. This recognition is the beginning of the actualization of the Church's mission to be a sign of the unity of humankind and of the Kingdom of God.

Individuals are to enact this faith commitment as social beings. With hope and confident freedom, the Christian is a realist regarding life in the world and seeks to bring the meaning of God's revealed promises to the variety of social situations and responsibilities in which he or she is involved. Human existence, in its varied forms and contexts, is neither denied nor tolerated but is rather the basis of an obedient faith. In both the single and married life choices, each person thus recognizes the historical character of his or her vocation in light of the Gospel. All vocation is essentially the historical responsibility undertaken in openness to God's presence in human existence.

The public profession of religious states of life specifically signifies commitment as an essential element of Christian faith. Here the person accepts a particular ecclesial structure as the chosen form of commitment to God. This structure is not the object of religious commitment but is vital to the historical efficacy of that commitment. Public by nature, the commitment is asserted as an intensification of the baptismal commitment of Christian life. Ordinarily, the evangelical counsels of poverty, chastity, and obedience are vowed perpetually to God through the Church. The perpetual nature of the vows stresses the totality more than the temporality of this commitment of men and women religious. In contemporary expression, this commitment is directed to the liberation of persons from all forms of oppression. This accounts for the plurality of forms of religious life within the Church today.

Bibliography: M. FARLEY and D. GOTTEMOELLER, "Commitment in a Changing World," RevRel 34 (1975) 846–867. K. RAHNER, Foundations of Christian Faith, tr. W. V. DYCH (New York 1978).

[C. WREN]

COMMON LIFE (CANON LAW)

The draft of the Schema of Canons on Institutes of Life Consecrated by Profession of the Evangelical Counsels contains the presently proposed legislation on common life (4:24), reflecting the emphasis since Vatican Council II. Worthy of note is the use of "fraternal life" to express more clearly the spiritual, interior, personal, social nature of the obligation intended by the law. In any religious institute fraternal life in common is to be lived according to the constitutions (c.93.1). Members of conventual institutes lead the fraternal life in common (c.114.2). In institutes of associated apostolic life (in CIC called "societies of common life," 13:384), whose members are not religious, but who support their apostolate by a bond of fraternal union (c.119), the fraternal life is to be so organized that it prepares for and steadily fosters and aids their apostolic activity (c.120).

Quoting Acts 2.42, which describes the primitive Christian community, Vatican II's Decree on the Renewal of Religious Life emphasizes the aspect of brotherhood, communal life, fellowship, union: religious, as members of Christ, should live together as brothers (Perfectae caritatis 15). The same document also observes: let all remember that chastity is preserved more securely when among the members there is true brotherly love in the common life (ibid.). Similarly, the institutes themselves should endeavour to bear collective witness to poverty; provinces and houses should share their property with one another (ibid. 13). Finally, *religious superiors should exercise authority in a spirit of service of the brethren; through their superiors religious are led to serve all their brothers in Christ, just as Christ ministered to his brothers (ibid. 14). Thus fraternal life provides the environment for brotherly solidarity, coresponsibility, subsidiarity, and a healthy pluralism.

This notion of fraternal life was expressed in Lumen gentium, n. 43. It was further developed in Ecclesiae Sanctae II, V, 25–26 and in the instruction Renovationis causam II, 15, 18, 32 and in Pope Paul's exhortation Evangelica testificatio 21, 24–26, 32, 34–36, 39–41. These official texts indicate that the unity of the brethren is to be the fruit of charity—loving one another, living for the same ideal together, sharing the same gifts, bearing the burdens of life together (Baum). The specific details of fraternal life in common in each institute must be spelled out in its statutes and must be in conformity with the nature and purpose of that institute. At profession each member must accept these statutes as his law of life and love.

The present canonical obligation to dwell together under the same roof is continued with the exceptions already allowed by law. A religious community must live in a legitimately erected religious house, which should have its own church or oratory, in which the Eucharist is celebrated and reserved, so as to be truly the center of the community (*Schema* c.97). Monks ordinarily offer their service to the divine majesty within the boundaries of the monastery (c.99). For members of canonical institutes it is recommended that they be assigned to parishes which are close together or near their principal house, as far as this is possible, in order that the regular life may be fostered (c.112.3). Yet a hermit is recognized in law as a religious, if he professes the three evangelical counsels, stabilized by vow, and has and observes his own rule of life under the guidance of the local Ordinary or of a competent religious moderator (c.92.2). Other instances when living out of community regularly is permitted may be found in faculties granted to proper superiors.

For the most part the *Schema* repeats the content of the CIC's legislation on the common life of material goods without using that expression. Thus, each institute, taking into account its own proper nature and character, should define in its constitutions the manner in which the evangelical counsel of poverty is to be observed in its own proper life style (*Schema* c.71.1). For religious the profession of poverty for the sake of the following of Christ implies complete dependence in the use and disposition of material goods as well as the giving up of at least the administration of one's own patrimony (c.95.1). Whatever the members receive for their own work, as stipend or as pension, redounds to the institute (c.95.3). The statutes for members of institutes of associated apostolic life should define the personal situation of the members with regard to temporal possessions and set down suitable norms governing their use, keeping in mind the equality of the members in the fraternity (c.121). Members of *secular institutes are not bound by the law of common life. In temporal matters they observe a mode of living in keeping with the Christian faithful, each according to his own situation (c.124). It seems that in its final revision Canon Law will have only general norms, leaving to particular law statutory specifications on fraternal life in common.

See also CODE OF CANON LAW, REVISION OF.

Bibliography: Pontifical Commission for the Revision of the Code of Canon Law, *Schema of Canons on Institutes of Life Consecrated by Profession of the Evangelical Counsels* (USCC publ. office, Washington, D.C. 1977). Congr. of Religious and Secular Institutes, Instruction, *Renovationis causam,* Eng. tr. *On Bringing up to Date the Formation for Religious Life,* WaySuppl. 7 (1968) 1–96. *Informationes SCRIS,* Eng. ed., Institute of Religious Life, ed., *Consecrated Life* (Boston 1977–). G. BAUM, *Commentary on Decree on Renewal of Religious Life of Vatican II* (New York 1966); J. BEYER, "Religious Life or Secular Institute," WaySuppl 7 (1969) 112–132; "Institutes of Apostolic Life," WaySuppl 8 (1969) 182–207; "Apostolic Poverty and Church Law," WaySuppl 9 (1970) 27–46; "Norms of the Secular Vocation," WaySuppl 12 (1971) 24–34; "Institutes of Perfection in the New Law of the Church," WaySuppl 13 (1971) 87–115; "Renewal Chapters: First Reflection," WaySuppl 14 (1971) 108–113; "The New Law of the Church for Institutes of Consecrated Life I," WaySuppl 22 (1974) 100–116; "The New Law of the Church for Institutes of Consecrated Life II," WaySuppl 23 (1974) 75–96. "Decretum Perfectae caritatis . . . commentarium," Periodica MorCanLiturg 56 (1967) 331–356; "De institutorum vitae consecratae novo iure," Periodica MorCanLiturg 63 (1974) 145–168; 179–222; 64 (1975) 363–392; 533–588; 65 (1976) 13–58, 243–296. J. GALLEN, "New Canon Law for Religious in Detail," RevRel 35 (1976) 232–250. M. SAID, "Particular Law of Institutes in Renewal of Consecrated Life," RevRel 36 (1977) 924–947.

[A. GAFFIGAN]

COMMUNICATION, USCC COMMITTEE ON

This standing committee of the United States Catholic Conference (USCC; 16:462) has responsibility and authority to review and make recommendations on objectives, plans, programs, and policies of the Communication Department (one of three major units of the USCC) for approval by the USCC's Administrative Board. The Committee also oversees implementation of such programs and policies.

A bishop is chairman and there is an equal number of episcopal and nonepiscopal members, total membership is no less than thirteen and no more than twenty-one. In addition to the chairman, two other episcopal members are elected by the membership of the corporation; the remaining bishop-members are appointed by the chairman after consultation with the other elected members and the NCCB-USCC General Secretary. Nonepiscopal members are chosen from the clergy, religious, and laity, usually for their expertise in various communication fields. A delegate of the *Conference of Major Superiors of Men regularly has a seat on the committee. Ex officio membership (non-voting) is extended to the president of the Catholic Press Association and the president of UNDA-USA, which is the U.S. chapter of *UNDA, an international Catholic association for radio and television. Members are invited to serve by the chairman after consultation with the president and the General Secretary. The term is three years, and no one may serve two consecutive terms. Staff support for the committee and the direction of the department are the responsibility of the department secretary.

The committee is responsible for reviewing the work of the USCC Communication Department, which includes National Catholic News Service, Office for Promotion & Training (Creative Services), and Office for Film and Broadcasting. It also oversees the work of the NCCB/USCC Office of Public Affairs and National Catholic Office for Information.

Programs monitored include national level church representation to the media industries; production of the USCC programs aired on the three national radio and television networks; publication of NC News, its features and picture services; "Know Your Faith," an adult religious education service; *Origins,* a weekly documentary service; *Catholic Trends,* fortnightly institutional newsletter; *American Catholic Who's Who,* a biennial biographical reference book; *Film & Broadcasting Review,* biweekly review of major motion pictures, educational films, and national television programs; *Report,* a USCC newsletter for the hierarchy; *Share,* communication newsletter for dioceses; promotion programs for national church fund-raising and public-education efforts (e.g. Campaign for Human Development, Respect Life, National Catholic Schools Week, Catholic Relief Services).

The committee, with the authority of the Administrative Board, issues formal conference statements in its own name upon approval by the General Secretary and by two-thirds of the departmental committee members.

When time or special circumstances make this impractical, the chairman, with the authorization of the president, may issue an official statement in his own name as committee chairman. The committee chairman and General Secretary may also authorize the issuance of formal conference statements by the department secretary.

Conference publications resulting from committee action have included: official U.S. translation of the Pastoral Instruction of the Pontifical Commission for the Media, *Communications: The Media, Public Opinion and Human Progress* (1971), which calls for application of the principles and norms of *Inter mirifica*, Decree on the Media of Social Communication of Vatican Council II; *Statement on Freedom of Information* (1973), a commentary on freedom of the news media, *Statement on the Family Viewing Policy of the Television Networks* (1975) which declared "unacceptable" the report of the Federal Communications Commission to the Congress on broadcast of violence, indecent and obscene material; *The Use of Modern Means of Communication as Instruments for Evangelization*, a report on original meetings of the NCCB in 1974 on this topic; a statement of the General Secretary expressing "total opposition" to advertising of contraceptive products on television, terming such a step "a gross violation of the rights of parents to guide the moral and social development of children" (1976); a petition to the FCC calling for regulation providing adequate previewing of network programs by local stations and by bonafide critics, and for investigation of the influence of program rating services on television programs; an *amicus* brief in the U.S. Court of Appeals Ninth Circuit, regarding a case arising from the networks' family viewing policy (1977).

Communication Committee chairmen have included: Most Reverends Philip M. Hannan, Archbishop of New Orleans (1968–70), John L. May, Bishop of Mobile (1971–74), Joseph L. Bernardin, Archbishop of Cincinnati (1974–75), Joseph R. Crowley, Auxiliary Bishop of Fort Wayne-South Bend (1975–).

[R. B. BEUSSE]

COMMUNION IN THE HAND

On May 29, 1969 the Congregation for Divine Worship published the instruction *Memoriale Domini* (ActApS 61 [1969] 541–545) allowing episcopal conferences to consider and vote on the restoration of the ancient practice of receiving Communion in, or on, the hand, a practice in use up to the 9th century. Pope Paul VI had judged that, if it so desired, episcopal conferences, by a two-thirds majority, could petition the Holy See for permission to restore this practice as an option. Up to 1977 about fifty episcopal conferences and individual dioceses had asked, and received, permission to introduce the option.

In November 1970, it was moved on behalf of the *Bishops' Committee on the Liturgy, that the U.S. National Conference of Catholic Bishops (NCCB) approve the following resolution:

that with the confirmation of the Apostolic See in accord with the Instruction on the Manner of Administering Holy Communion (May 29, 1969), individual bishops be authorized to permit the administration of Holy Communion into the hand of the communicant, provided:
(a) that the individual communicant be always free to indicate whether he would receive Communion in his hand or in the usual manner;

(b) that the role of the minister of Communion always be maintained by his placing the consecrated bread in the communicant's hand with the usual formula;
(c) that the introduction of the practice of administering Holy Communion in this manner be preceded in any diocese by thorough catechesis under the direction of the Ordinary and the diocesan liturgical commission.

The results of the voting were 117 in favor, 107 opposed and, since a two-thirds majority had not been obtained, the resolution was not implemented. Again in November, 1973, the motion came before the bishops. This time, after much debate, the bishops voted down the resolution 121 to 113. Finally, in the Spring of 1977, the bishops again considered the resolution and 190 of the 274 members of the NCCB voted to petition the Holy See for permission. It was received on June 17, 1977.

The feast of Christ the King, November 20, 1977, became the target date for introduction of Communion on the hand in the United States although the actual implementation was left to the judgment of the local bishop.

Throughout the implementation, there has been an effort to realize Pope Paul's desire for adequate instruction of the faithful so that the practice will "strengthen their faith" and "increase the sense of their dignity" (cf. *Memoriale Domini*). The proper context for viewing this return to an ancient practice is the Church as the Body of Christ, the Eucharist as the making present of Christ's Body and Blood under the forms of bread and wine and as a means of deepening Christ's presence in the people who form his Body and, finally, the entire Communion Rite as the immediate setting for the reception of our Lord's Eucharistic Body. If the option of Communion on the hand leads to a growing respect and reverence for Christ's presence in the Eucharist as well as in his people, then Catholics throughout the world will rediscover the wonderful truth of what it means to say "Amen" to the Body of Christ. As St. Augustine put it: "If you receive well, you are what you have received . . . Since you are the Body of Christ and his members, it is your mystery that is placed on the Lord's table; it is your mystery that you receive . . . You hear the words: 'The Body of Christ,' and you answer 'Amen.' Be therefore members of Christ, that your 'Amen' may be true . . . Be what you see, and receive what you are . . ." (Serm. 227. PL 38:1099).

Bibliography: J. J. MEGIVERN, *Concomitance and Communion* (New York 1963), The best work on this question and pp. 5–50 are invaluable for an understanding of the history of Communion as well as the factors influencing it. Bishops' Committee on the Liturgy, *The Body of Christ* (Washington, D.C. 1977). Federation of Diocesan Liturgical Commissions, *Take and Eat* (Chicago 1977).

[J. H. MCKENNA]

COMMUNION OF SAINTS

Although the Church's credal designation as a "communion of saints" dates only from the 5th century, the reality accentuated by such a title has a much longer history (4:41). Nicetas of Remesiana appears to have originated the phrase when he declared in a commentary on the baptismal creed at the turn of the 5th century that in the Christian Church we believe we "will attain to the *communion of saints*" (*De Symbolo* 10). The fact that the Latin equivalent of this phrase, *communionem sanctorum*, can mean both a "communion of saints" and a "communion of holy things" allows for a double interpretation of the original intent behind the credal formulary.

The communion of saints is both the fellowship of the faithful spanning all ages of holiness and also the participation in the Sacraments, blessings, and salutary effects of life within the Church. Certainly, the context of Nicetas's remark is personal, the communion of all righteous people who comprise the Church and who are "sanctified by faith . . . sealed in the one Spirit and made one body" in Christ. It is evident, too, from such commentaries as that of Faustus of Riez and Pseudo-Augustine that sharing in the merits of the saints and being inspired by their example to greater hope and courage figure prominently in the understanding of Church and in the mentality underpinning eventual inclusion of this title in the Apostles Creed. In the communion of saints, which is the Church, there is effected a communication of benefits between all members made possible by their mutual rootedness in Christ. Dietrich Bonhoeffer draws from this rich tradition to define the Church as "Christ existing as community" (Bonhoeffer 101). This community unites all Christians in one and the same life and in one and the same prayer. The faithful thus share in the fellowship and intercession of the saints.

This is why the Church has cultivated the memory of her dead, in particular the Blessed Virgin Mary, the apostles and martyrs and all those whose faith is recommended as an example and inspiration to the faithful of any age. They point to that final communion in Christ which constitutes the calling and ultimate delight of every Christian. The saints are likewise witnesses to the reality of God's kingdom and their lives, an additional motive for Christians to be conscious of that fraternal charity binding them to Christ and to each other in a unique fellowship enduring beyond the grave. Hope of the eventual reunion of all in God's love becomes an important theme in the liturgy as the Church venerates the memory of these saints and joins with them in offering worship to God in Christ. Because they were willing to die daily and even to lay down their lives for their brethren, their fellowship in glory is an inspiring testimony that Christian love is stronger than hatred and that life in Christ will triumph over death. Christian worship is enriched by the recollection that such prayer is offered in a closely knit communion of saints in whom Christ dwells and his body grows. For this reason "the ancient prayer *for* the apostles, prophets and martyrs became after their death a prayer *with* them in the communion of saints on behalf of the whole Church" (Thurian 2:20).

Vatican Council II portrayed this fellowship as a union of the "pilgrim Church" with the heavenly Church (*Lumen gentium* 48–51). In other words, the faithful are engaged in the same love for God and neighbor as those who have already experienced the promised resurrection. This union of holy people within the Church of today with the saints in heaven and those undergoing a purgatorial purification thus transcends death itself. The role of the saints is seen as a vital dimension of the Church's inner strength. Their example and intercessory power are recognized in her worship and in her efforts to understand the bonds which link all ages of church history to the one mediator, Christ, in whose life the Church recognizes her vocation and achieves her identity (ibid. 51). As Thurian notes, the saints are "signs of the presence and of the love of Christ" (Thurian 2:23). The Church's call to perfection is, in turn, related to the mode in which Christ brings about a union in holiness of all his members. Although the Church, as indeed the entire world, attains this perfection in fullness only when all things will be "reestablished in Christ," God has already begun to bring this about through His Spirit and through the Church in whom Christ's presence in history now continues. Through her Christian life in Sacrament and mission to the world, the Church witnesses to the meaning of that final age when God will be acknowledged as source of all holiness and his Kingdom established over all his creation (*Lumen gentium* 6; 48).

If the Church is, indeed, a communion of saints, this is because her members are united in a fellowship of holiness in which the signs of Christ's Kingdom are radiated to the world (see *Gaudium et spes* 32; 39; 43–45). The Church as communion is called to break down the barriers of nation, race, class, and culture in order to proclaim the brotherhood and sisterhood of all peoples in Jesus. The Spirit brings believers into a new sense of unity in their common life in Christ, transcending all the old sources of division, even death itself. The Christian experience of unity in Word, fellowship, Eucharist, and mission has a way of drawing people out of their paths of personal isolation into the experience of the love and communion in Christ's own love. The past of Jesus' love for people is thus relived in his new incarnational presence through his Spirit and in the fraternal love of his followers. The future offers, not the fear of death or separation, but hope and resurrection. The Christian community, as a communion of saints, is seen, therefore, as a sign of the way God extends his reconciling love to the entire world.

See also CHURCH AND COMMUNIO; HOLINESS, UNIVERSAL CALL TO.

Bibliography: K. BARTH, *Credo* (New York 1962). P. BERNARD, "Communion des Saints," DTC 3:429–454. D. BONHOEFFER, *The Communion of Saints*, tr. R. G. SMITH (New York 1963). J. HAMER, *The Church Is a Communion*, tr. R. MATHEWS (New York 1964). J. N. D. KELLY, *Early Christian Creeds* (London 1960). J. P. KIRSCH, *The Doctrine of the Communion of Saints in the Ancient Church* (St. Louis 1910). M. THURIAN, *The Eucharistic Memorial*, tr. J. G. DAVIES (2 v., Richmond, Va. 1961).

[G. B. KELLY]

COMMUNION TABLE

The place at which the laity receive Communion has varied throughout the centuries. A rather varied practice is observable in America today. If there is a place provided, one option is to use three or four small tables so designed that they harmonize with the main sanctuary furnishings (see FURNISHINGS, SACRED). This expedites the reception of Communion by large numbers without sacrificing dignity and without an undue break in the action of the Mass; it also provides a fitting place where the chalice may be placed when Communion under both kinds for large numbers is allowed.

Bibliography: Righetti 1:317–318.

[C. H. MEINBERG]

COMMUNITY

The passing of traditional society and the emergence of urban, industrial society in the West led to widespread concern among social analysts about how to promote and maintain new forms of community (4:80;

16:92) among people torn loose from familial, cultural, and moral bonds. Expectations that the solidarity of the traditional community would be replaced by a new "organic solidarity," as Émile Durkheim (4:1121) described the modern condition of interdependence, quickly faded. In his introduction to the second edition of *The Division of Labor in Society*, written in 1902, Durkheim lamented the absence of moral commitment to any common good and acknowledged the continuing need for "a whole series of secondary groups near enough to individuals to attract them strongly in their sphere of action and drag them, in this way, into the general torrent of social life." Seventy-five years later, there is even more widespread concern about the loss of community in modern life and renewed interest in the need for groups of solidarity that mediate the relationships between the individual and society.

Disintegration of Community. The transition from tradition to modernity that lies behind this condition has been a prolonged one, varying in pace from one section of the world to another and, in extension, from one part of society to another. The process inaugurated in Western society has gradually spread across the world and it is only in the second half of the 20th century that nations of the Third World have been caught up in the process. It is not surprising that these nations have attempted to avoid some of the disintegrative effects of modernization. One example of this has been the program of *Ujamaa*, the program for modernization led by Jules Nyerere in Tanzania which attempts to combine industrialization with retention of some of the communal features of tribal life. Another reflection of this concern to retain community in the process of modernization has been, as sociologist Peter Berger points out, the attraction that socialism seems to have for many developing countries because of its more directly communitarian aspects.

But the transition to modernity was not a one-step process in the West either. It was, for example, only in the last half of the 20th century that the full force of *urbanization was felt in the United States. It was only at this time that the country had distanced itself by a generation from the last wave of mass immigration of essentially rural European peoples. It was also only at this time that the occupational force became decidedly urban, with more than half the labor force in service occupations. Prior to this, the bulk of the labor force had been, first, in such rural extractive industries as farming, mining, and fishing, then in manufacturing, which required large coordinated work forces of people with little education tied to the regions where materials and power were available. Now the prevailing pattern of workers in urban jobs, in mobile service positions, in expanding government employment, and in middle-class life means that the style of modernity is not only the norm but also the characteristic experience of life in U.S. society. There remain large segments of the population, especially among Blacks and Hispanics, who are caught in poverty by not having access to the skills and power of modern urban life. Ironically, they are most likely to be found in the cities as the mobility of modern life has enabled the most urban peoples to live in the suburbs. Nonetheless, the process of modernization and its related erosion of community has been most extensively felt in the United States in the last two decades.

At this point, therefore, evidence of the disintegration of community feared by 19th-century social critics seems to be mounting. Pieces of this evidence are: accelerating crime rates; loss of family stability, as evidenced in delayed marriage, climbing divorce rates, and other signs; decline in political-party membership and in voting rates; disaffection from church life; and increased difficulty in agreeing on norms for community life that can be translated into law and public morality. Perhaps the sharpest example of the latter is in the area of laws of obscenity and sexual morality. Evidence of enduring community should be found in expressions of loyalty, fidelity, secure relationships, and common good; in fact it is precisely these virtues of community and grounds for civility that are thought to be absent from contemporary life.

Recovering Community. Expressions of concern about community may be found in attempts at establishing or recovering grounds for group solidarity. Some of these are the movements among Blacks, native Americans, Hispanic peoples, and white ethnic groups to reassert racial and ethnic identity as a basis for cooperative effort in a pluralist society (*see* ETHNICITY). Similarly, Durkheim's concern for solidarity groups, reasserted in the 1950s by Robert Nisbet, is once again the focus of attention in discussions of public policy. There is growing attention to the importance of the neighborhood as a social unit, to the significance of the family, and, in the Church, to the community life of the *parish. Among the spokespersons for a shift from a policy of relating government services and corporate life directly to the individual to a policy that would support voluntary communities in their efforts to care for their members, has been Monsignor Geno Baroni, whose *National Center for Urban Ethnic Affairs has been a major advocate for neighborhood and ethnic communities. Also, Peter Berger and Richard Neuhaus have fixed on this same theme in *To Empower People*, the opening statement of a project on strengthening communal groups, which they refer to as "mediating structures." Many other efforts to develop community have arisen, especially since the late 1960s when the centrifugal forces seemed to lead to a condition which author William L. O'Neill identified in the title of his review of the sixties, as one of "Coming Apart." These include a wide variety of communes, encounter groups, and small-group development in Church and society.

The difficulty facing anyone who would promote community life is to identify the main causes for the loss of community and the central features of community. For the Marxist, the causes are to be found in the structure of the economy and the solutions in a collectivist economic system. Others, fearing domination by more centralized control of economy and society, locate the cause in the erosion of family, neighborhood, and other voluntary communities, and propose as a solution that all government and corporate life be made more accountable to the communal elements in society. Still others locate the cause in the individuating and atomizing consequences of the combined political and philosophical revolutions of democracy and Enlightenment. Perhaps the most astute spokesperson for this view is R. M. Unger, whose work, *Knowledge and Politics*, articulates this explanation and proposes a more organic and communitarian approach to understanding and social life.

Whatever the causes of disintegration, the ingredients necessary for the integrity of community appear to be the sharing of critical values in life and important interaction with others who share and celebrate these values. If there is evidence of widespread loss of community, of what Philip Slater has called the "pursuit of loneliness," there are many signs of increased attention to the needs of community, of increased efforts at developing or restoring community, and of greater readiness to discuss the importance of shared values and the common good as bases for enduring community. These signs may be found in the spread of community-organizing efforts throughout the country, in renewed discussion of the vitality of the modern family, in explorations of ways of holding corporate life accountable to social development in local communities, and in a variety of other discussions and actions that will likely change the character of public policy and American society in the decades to come.

Bibliography: É. DURKHEIM, *The Division of Labor in Society* (New York 1964). R. NISBET, *The Quest for Community* (New York 1953). R. M. KANTER, *Commitment and Community* (Cambridge, Mass. 1972). W. L. O'NEILL, *Coming Apart* (New york 1971). P. BERGER, *Pyramids of Sacrifice* (New York 1974). R. M. UNGER, *Knowledge and Politics* (New York 1975). P. SLATER, *The Pursuit of Loneliness* (Boston 1970). P. BERGER and R. NEUHAUS, *To Empower People* (Washington, D.C. 1977).

[P. MURNION]

COMMUNITY, FORMS OF

Whether community living is a witness to renewed vitality in the post-Vatican II Church is a hard question. The answer involves the interplay of personalism and communitarianism.

Background. In the 20th-century United States personalism and communitarianism both have prominence. Sometimes they are complementary, at others in opposition. Each has its philosophical, theological, sociological, economic, and political implications. Personalism as a specific movement originated in France (1932–33) as a reaction against the rationalist concept of man and against dehumanization in an industrialized society; it entered the American intellectual stream with Emmanuel Mounier's *A Personalist Manifesto* (1938). Peter Maurin popularized its communitarian aspect in terse, graphic essays and gave it a concrete form through his communal, Green Revolution. Daniel Cohen names Maurin an early prophet of the back-to-the-land movement and cites the moral influence of Maurin and Dorothy Day, cofounders of the Catholic Worker Movement, as "far more widespread than we might imagine" (Cohen, 161). Even today the Catholic Worker Movement retains its authentic Christian respect for the dignity of the human person, in contrast to Synanon, another typical service community, that has ended in tyranny, destructive of personal freedom and responsibility (Fairfield; 334–338; 344–345; see *Time*, Dec. 26, 1977, 18).

The personalist–communitarian phenomenon was intensified by Martin Bubers's "I-Thou" existentialism. Practically unknown at the opening of the decade, Buber was in vogue by the end of the 50s. His insistence on a life of dialogue as the birthright of a human being, "for only through it can we attain authentic human existence" (Friedman, 97), gives a new dignity to the concept of community, emphasizing its formative power but also stressing the importance of personal integrity. Only when individuals are aware of their own integrity

and open to the integrity of others can true dialogue and consequent growth take place.

In the 1960s Vatican Council II stated the value of interpersonal relations (*Gaudium et spes* 23), gave attention to the church community as in *Lumen gentium* (8–16; 50–51) and to the several communities of mankind in *Gaudium et spes* (63–90), and recommended communal life to priests in *Presbyterorum ordinis* (8; cf. bibliog. NCCB, ch. 3). Over all, however, the conciliar documents gave greater stress to the dignity and freedom of the human person and to personal responsibility for self-fulfillment (cf. Paul VI PopProgr 15).

Religious Life. The conciliar emphasis on personalism, coupled with a chance circumstance, led to a strong personalist focus in the renewal of religious life. The circumstance was Erving Goffman's 1961 *Asylums*, a study of "total institutions." He based his conclusions mainly on his experience with prisoners, included some references to army and navy training, but also quoted at random from the Rule of St. Benedict and from two "unscientific" versions of religious life. The study, focusing on the likenesses between current structures of religious life and a "total institution," brought immediate reaction from many religious: first angry defensiveness, then reconsideration of the issue, and finally reluctant admission that Goffman's work contained more than a grain of truth. The focus of the renewal of religious life shifted from former concern for structure to become person-centered; the renewal was motivated, therefore, by true tenets of personalism and in preference over concern for the communitarian structure. The result often was a selfish individualism that tended to discredit authentic personalism. This, along with other polarities stemming from renewal, created many tensions in community life. The passage is one from structured-community living to true person-communities that are centers of welcome, encouragement, and challenge to all their members, regardless of age, "to become fully human and totally available to the Church and its mission" (McGoldrick, 6). American women religious, although they "are on the cutting edge of renewal" (Clark, 1), may be only halfway to the goal.

Women religious "still grapple with questions: Who are we? Who are we called to become? What hidden gifts and talents are we called to share?" (LCWR 7). But this grappling is very different from the critical, identity question of the early 70s: is there any future to religious life? Women religious know there is a future and one with strong demands on them. They must mature as persons, as women, while they search for liberating concepts of the *vows, for new directions, and for roles in ministry. They must open themselves courageously to evolving forms of community, especially those enabling both religious as individuals and religious corporate bodies to be visible forces of love and justice, to be truly in and for the world, even when this demands radical changes in life style.

The grappling itself is a sign of renewed vitality in religious life, as the LCWR *Goals for 1990* testifies. The goals mark a courageous acceptance of the challenge issued by Max Delesplesse of the International Center of Community Life, when he summoned religious to help in the "recommunitarization" of the Church, a help that presupposes decentralization of religious groups and a more complete insertion of religious into Christian communities that constitute the Church com-

munity (Delesplesse, 73–81). Buber's hope, "a reformation of society into a community of communities" (40),
gives a world dimension to this challenge. A critical
reflection on the experience of religious men reveals a
similarity of struggles and ends on a similar note for the
future—"faith-centered and hope-filled" (CMSM).

Lay Communities. Two communitarian developments
outside religious life deserve mention. The revolution
originating in 1965 and expressed in thousands of
communes by 1968, drew into the experiment with
community living both intelligent youth from affluent,
middle-class families and middle-aged professionals;
both were rebelling against the modern, profit-seeking,
consumer society and against a strictly rational, scientific view of reality. This revolution in all its ramifications is part of "a heroic effort of spiritualization"
predicted by Jacques Maritain as early as 1941 (Maritain, 129–130). A second communitarian phenomenon,
praying groups, sprang out of the alienation of post-
World War I, developed steadily in the Protestant
milieu, all through the Catholic period of emphasis on a
"Catholic mind expressed in Catholic Action," and
finally burst almost full-blown, into Catholic life in
February, 1967, as the Catholic *charismatic renewal.
The charismatic movement has a strong communitarian
thrust, evidenced by the network of covenanted communities throughout the world that maintain more or
less close relationship with the Word of God Community in Ann Arbor, Michigan.

The type of community represented by counterculture communes, covenanted Christian households,
and varied other service-oriented communities received
notice from Vatican II only in an amendment to *Schema
13* signed by twenty-four bishops, but this communitarian movement continues to pour new life into
the Church. Many of its individuals and communities
may be offering a clearer, more visible witness to the
new Pentecost than their struggling brothers and sisters
in religious life. Barriers are breaking down both within
the Church and between Churches, however, allowing
much mutual witnessing to happen.

See also BASIC CHRISTIAN COMMUNITIES.

Bibliography: T. CLARK, *New Pentecost or New Passion* (New York
1973). D. COHEN, *Not of This World* (1973). Conference of Major
Superiors of Men (CMSM), "Hope Filled Deeds and Critical
Thoughts," *Crux*, Extra (Oct. 17, 1977). M. DELESPLESSE, *The Church
Community: Leaven and Life Style*, tr. K. Russell (Ottawa 1969).
R. FAIRFIELD, *Communes U.S.A.* (Baltimore 1972). G. F. FITZGERALD,
Communes (New York 1971). M. S. FRIEDMAN, *Martin Buber, The Life of
Dialogue* (Chicago 1955). J. JUDSON, *Families of Eden* (New York 1974).
Leadership Conference of Women Religious (LCWR), *Choose Life*
(Washington, D.C. 1977). J. MARITAIN, *Ransoming the Time*, tr. H. L.
Binsse (New York 1941). R. MCGOLDRICK, "Formative Communities: A
Fuller Approach to Formation," *In-Formation* 19 special issue (Aug.,
1976). National Assembly of Women Religious (NAWR), "Com-
munities," *Probe* (Nov., 1977). National Conference of Catholic Bishops
(NCCB), *Spiritual Renewal of the American Priesthood* (Washington,
D.C. 1972). R. G. SMITH, *Martin Buber* (pa. New York 1967).

[A. E. CHESTER]

COMMUNITY, RELIGIOUS

The significance of the community aspect of religious
life has become clearer since Vatican Council II. It is
not, as some have seemed to imply, the sole justification
for religious life in the Church, but it is an essential
element, together with a standing before God in prayer
and worship, and a commitment to the People of God in
Christian service.

Community living only a few years ago seemed to
imply a certain amount of anonymity and uniformity.
Gradually a new awareness has developed among
religious men and women that community has more to
do with interpersonal relationships, with one's human
sensitivities, and with the many intangibles that change
a dwelling into a home. One of the most significant of
the changes in religious life since Vatican II has been
this development in the sense of community among
members of the various religious congregations.

There is little remnant of the attitude that all must fit
a certain mold. Persons are esteemed for themselves,
with their own personalities and gifts and idiosyncrasies;
in turn, this calls for tolerance and forgiveness, and, on
occasion, reconciliation (*see* RECONCILIATION, MINISTRY
OF). One of the consequences of this development is
that much of the structure, the predictability, the
tidiness of religious life has disappeared, replaced by
informality and greater personal concern of religious for
each other. Religious communities are more conscious
than previously that the responsibility for their own
lives and their own development is in their hands.
Communities devote considerable effort to arriving at a
consensus on goals for themselves for the year; periodically they review their progress. In the process of setting
goals, communities often practice discernment among
themselves as to the exact nature of the apostolate the
members will engage in and on the way in which surplus
funds earned by the community will be distributed
among the poor. A more difficult exercise of community
living is the occasional confrontation, called for by
circumstances, between the community and one or more
of its members. This is regarded as an expression of
concern for an erring member and an admission of the
responsibility of the community for each of those who
make up its membership. What used to be regarded as a
problem for the superior is now seen as a responsibility
of the particular group living together in a Christian
community, a religious house.

The sense of true community is such a desirable good
that many religious today, especially the younger
members, regard it as the most valued aspect of
religious life. In some cases candidates have been
disappointed in not finding Utopia (interpreted as the
ideal of community among the religious) within the
walls of the monastery or convent. Experiences of the
past ten years confirm the truth that the task of
formation of a true spirit of community is arduous and
the fruit of the personal gift of each to the service of all.
It is not a gift handed to the candidate when he or she
enters the religious community but is created by the
members themselves in their relationships with one
another. Further, the spirit of community, like all living
things, has its own laws of growth: it waxes and wanes,
it flourishes and falls on hard times, but often enough it
shows itself to be extraordinarily vital, particularly at
moments of stress.

The Gospel of Christ is epitomized in the love of
God and love of fellow man. For the religious the
first application of this law of love is within the religious community itself. Perhaps in the multitude
of changes wrought in religious life since Vatican II
the one most significant of all is in the quality of life
in community. While not so striking to outsiders as
such other changes as life-style, dress, informality, and
diversity, still improvement in the spirit of community

touches the core of the Christian vocation and is therefore the ultimate criterion as to whether or not religious life is to survive in the Church. Newer attitudes of community living are expressed in a number of congregations by the formation of smaller groupings, often without a designated superior, living among the people in residential areas. The life-style of these innovative, smaller communities is usually more informal than that in the parent house and is often characterized by more personal interaction in psychological and religious spheres and by more spontaneity in communal prayer forms (see PRAYER COMMUNITY). These communities are a form of miniature laboratory in which many of the newer ideas concerning religious life are meeting the test of practice. There have been many failures in these experimental houses; criteria for success are not yet clear, but among them are the psychological soundness of its members, the conscious effort to cultivate a spirit of community among the religious of the house, and some minimal experience as a worshiping community. A total openness to the larger civic community, in which the religious and their home are always available to others, is the single most disruptive force in the experience of these smaller experimental houses.

[W. QUINN]

COMMUNITY OF MANKIND

Under this title, Vatican Council II's Pastoral Constitution on the Church in the Modern World lays down the chief principles on which the Church bases its social teaching. These are: the intrinsically communal or social nature of man; the interdependence of individual and society; the common good defined in terms of greater personal and communal development; the primacy of the person and his rights; the social power of love and forgiveness; an ideal of social justice rooted in the fundamental equality of all men; the need to go beyond a merely individualistic morality to responsible participation in public affairs; and the ideal of the universal human solidarity revealed and realized in the Body of Christ (*Gaudium et spes* 23–32).

These principles have been reaffirmed and developed in official church teaching since the Council. Paul VI in *Populorum progressio* (1967) outlined a vision of the integral development of each person and of all persons and in *Octogesima adveniens* (1971) pressed the issue more forcefully, urging Christians to involve themselves in the needed political activities. The 1971 Synod of Bishops document, *Justice in the World*, made use of the vocabulary of the *liberation theology to relate social and political liberation to the redemptive work of Christ and the role of the Church in the world.

Continuity of Social Teaching. All four of these documents are in basic continuity with earlier Church teaching on social issues, but they also represent significant advances. The fundamental continuity consists in the principle of the primacy of the spiritual in human affairs, "spiritual" meaning not only the "religious," but also the cultural and the moral, and "primacy," not only an extrinsic relationship, but the fact that there is more to man than the material and the economic and that this "more" in man is neglected only at the price of immense human suffering and eventual frustration. From this primary affirmation flow the elements that have marked the Church's social teaching:

the defense of the dignity, rights and freedom of the individual; the affirmation of the ulterior purposes of wealth and power; the repudiation of unbridled liberalism; the denial of "ironclad" economic laws; the demand for an equitable distribution of the world's goods.

Advances in Social Teaching. There are three ways in which recent Church teaching marks an advance upon earlier documents. First, the recent documents recognize that "the social question has become worldwide" (Paul VI PopProgr 3). The key questions of social justice today do not concern only relations between capital and labor, rich and poor, within countries. The whole world is now divided into parallel groups, with whole nations now standing to the developed world as the poor and powerless workers once stood to the owners of wealth and power at the turn of the 20th century. Recent documents speak to nations as earlier ones spoke to classes and they urge the same redress of evil for whole peoples that has been attempted in social legislation on behalf of workers throughout this century.

Secondly, the recent documents teach that, if these problems are to be met, then Christians must "pass from economics to politics" and recognize that, if not the only one, still political involvement is "one demanding manner of living the Christian commitment to the service of others" (Paul VI OctogAdven 46). This development (1) precludes an artificial separation of the economic from the political and (2) encourages theologians to explore the relationship between Christian living and political activity.

The third characteristic of more recent Church teaching on social issues is that it builds on more explicitly theological bases. Earlier social teaching had constructed its argument on natural law-theory; recent documents have built on direct biblical and traditional theological grounds. They have recalled the social protests of the OT prophets and have made an effort to show that the redemptive word and work of Christ and his Church have immediate implications for the way man lives in society. Thus, Paul VI speaks of Christ working in and with those who work for social justice and warns that the very preaching of the Gospel will be ineffective "unless it is accompanied by the witness of the power of the Holy Spirit, working within the activity of Christians in the service of their brothers" (ibid. 48, 51). The 1971 Synod closely linked "the redemption of the human race and its liberation from every oppressive situation" and said that "action on behalf of justice and participation in the transformation of the world" appeared to be "a constitutive dimension of the preaching of the Gospel" (Synod JustWorld p. 34).

Mankind, Radically Social and Historical. A full theological justification of such statements and of such activity, besides building upon a "political hermeneutic" of the Scriptures and tradition, must employ a historically and socially conscious fundamental anthropology. Human existence will then be understood to be radically historical and social: we *become* and we become *together* the fully human beings we were created to be in the image of God. That historical process defines man's individual existence and his existence in society: there is a history of human existence and its goal is the full development of all human capacities, intellectual, critical, moral, and religious. Such development is also a liberation, as man struggles to overcome whatever prevents or impedes a full and authentic human life before God.

If God has created man for such authentic self-realization, then to stop or to be prevented from developing is to fall short of God's creative and redemptive purpose. Incomplete human development, consciously accepted or imposed, takes on the dimensions of sin against the Creator. Sin means being locked in the self one already is: defining responsibilities solely in terms of oneself and of one's fears and desires, refusing to self-transcend towards genuine values of love and service. Such self-imprisonment only falls short of authentic self-fulfilment, it also falls short of what God intended in creation.

This perspective enlarges the meaning perceptible in the NT description of redemption as liberation. God's redeeming word and favor break in upon the closed, sin-constructed human world and self, destroy their presuppositions and discredit their habits, and thus free man for a life lived in that self-transcending fulfilment which is the love of God and of neighbor. The freedom for which man was created again becomes a possibility, the broken image of God is restored, and men need no longer "fall short of the glory of God" (Rom 3:23).

If there is a clear sense in which this dialectic of enslaving sin and liberating grace is radically independent of our economic, social, political, and cultural situations, it also remains, as the recent church-documents remind us and the recent *political and *liberation theologies urge, that concern and work for the development and liberation of individuals and of whole peoples from economic and social misery is not only a contemporary demand of charity, but is part of the very redemptive mission of the Church. For the failure or refusal to develop towards intelligent, critical, and responsible living has its consequences on societies as well as on individuals. No less than the individual's self, the character of a social order is shaped by that great dialectic of sin and grace, of what Paul VI has called that "historical and psychological process in which constraint and freedom as well as the weight of sin and the breath of the Spirit alternate and struggle to prevail" (ibid. 37). Where the "weight of sin" and its constraints prevail, there arises what has come to be called "social sin" or "sinful social structures." These come under Gospel-judgment and need Gospel-grace in two respects. As objective realities, they embody the limited and even sinful choices of past and present generations, but they also provide the context for individual human living in which a person "is often turned away from the good and urged to evil by the social environment in which he lives and in which he is immersed from the day of his birth" (*Gaudium et spes* 25).

Unless, then, the scope of Christ's victory over falsehood and evil is to be arbitrarily restricted to the mind and heart of individuals, then the Christian message must also be addressed to the social and political embodiments of the "reign of sin." From this standpoint, the social mission of the Church is an immediate and inescapable dimension of its role as the social and historical mediation of Christ's redemptive work. The particular responsibility of a "catholic" Church is thus to make its universal claim to be God's one People not only a sign but also an instrument of that fundamental unity of the whole community of mankind before God.

Bibliography: J. GREMILLION, ed., *The Gospel of Peace and Justice: Catholic Social Teaching since Pope John* (Maryknoll, N.Y. 1976). G. GUTIERREZ, *A Theology of Liberation: History, Politics and Salvation*, tr. C. INDA and J. EAGLESON (Maryknoll, N.Y. 1973); E. J. RYLE, ed., *The Social Mission of the Church: A Theological Reflection* (National School of Social Service, Washington, D.C. n.d.).

[J. A. KOMONCHAK]

CONCELEBRATION

As it was introduced by the New Order of Mass of April 3, 1969, concelebration refers to verbally expressed joint sacramental action of several priests in celebrating the Eucharist (4:103; 16:92). The rubrics permit a limited amount of variations as well as adaptation to local customs and needs, leaving final regulations to local bishops and major religious superiors. Both the Constitution on the Sacred Liturgy (*Sacrosanctum Concilium* 57) and the declaration of the Sacred Congregation for Divine Worship on concelebration of August 7, 1972, recommend concelebration as a fuller manifestation of the unity of the priesthood, the Church, and the one Sacrifice of Christ. The basic principle of the declaration, however, is that a concelebrated Mass follows the same norms as Mass by one priest; it determines only which parts have to be said aloud, although in a subdued voice, or sung, or accompanied by gestures on the part of the concelebrants; and who are entitled to receive the corresponding stipend.

Concelebration, as practised now, reduces the need for private Masses on special occasions, makes possible a manifestation of the unity of the priesthood, and fosters awareness of this unity among priests. It stresses, however, external rather than internal participation and is sometimes felt to underscore the separation between the ministering clergy and other members of the worshipping community. It therefore raises again some practical and dogmatic questions concerning the nature of the Church, the ministry as service, the theological foundation of Mass *stipends. As an important element for liturgical renewal, concelebration may lead in time to a form of celebration that will express fully the depth and richness of doctrine contained in and to be expressed through the celebration of the Eucharist.

See also MASS, CONVENTUAL/COMMUNITY.

Bibliography: K. RAHNER and A. HÄUSSLING, *The Celebration of the Eucharist* (New York 1968). A.-M. ROGUET, "Pour une théologie de la concélébration," *Maison-Dieu* 88 (1966) 116–126. E. DEKKERS, "Concelebration: Limitations of Current Practice," *Doctrine and Life* 22 (1972) 190–202. D. POWER, "Sacramental Celebration and Liturgical Ministry," in H. SCHMIDT, ed., *Liturgy. Concilium* 72 (1972) 26–42. A. GONZÁLEZ FUENTE, "La Concelebración en peligro?" *Phase* 16 (1976) 403–410.

[A. CORNIDES]

CONCILIUM MONASTICUM IURIS CANONICI

New wine cannot be put into old wineskins. For this reason John XXIII not only called for an ecumenical council but also for a new Code of Canon Law. Even before the Council concluded its work, the *Canon Law Society of America sponsored a Concilium Monasticum Iuris Canonici to give monks around the world an opportunity to have some say in the formulation of the new law proper to them. Monastic canonists of all nations have been invited to share in its work and questionnaires have been sent to large cross sections of monastic communities.

In 1966 the Pontifical Commission for the Revision of the Code of Canon Law received the *Propositum monasticum de Codice iuris canonici recognoscendo* prepared by the Concilium. Presuming that the new Code would take the same form as the present CIC, the *Propositum* is formulated in 42 canons divided into sections, chapters, and articles as are the CIC Titles. The fundamental question put by the *Propositum* was the delineation of those who were to be included within the category of monks. Some wanted the monastic state to be identified with the contemplative state. However, the *Propositum* followed the lead of Vatican Council II which spoke of monks who "either devote themselves entirely to divine worship in a life that is hidden, or lawfully take up some apostolate or works of Christian charity" (*Perfectae caritatis* 9). Yet there was a strong desire to provide adequately for the contemplative life, and also for the eremitical way. Thus, the second section of the *Propositum: De vita monastica in specie*, has three chapters: *De vita coenobitica, De vita eremetica, De vita unice contemplativa*. The first section of the *Propositum* concerns itself with law for monasteries and federations, and such matters as admission, formation, and transfer. There was no distinct provision for nuns, for the Concilium held strongly that dispositions concerning monks are to apply equally to nuns. However it is necessary to note that active members of the Concilium have been exclusively monks with the nuns being given little opportunity to take part in the work.

The *Propositum* was one of the first concrete proposals received by the Pontifical Commission. It was taken up at the first meetings of the subcommission concerned with the section on religious life. By its presence it affirmed the right to be heard of those who were being legislated for. By its demands for a provision that fully respected the specific nature of a God-given vocation it called for a complete rethinking of this section of the CIC and an abandoning of the prevalent terminology and categories. The result has been that the *Schema canonum de institutis vitae consecratae per professionem conciliorum evangelicorum* (Canon Law for Religious) has been universally acknowledged as being the best *schema* so far produced, the one the most approximating a fulfillment of the general norms proposed for the new Code, and for some the only acceptable one.

The idea of a constitutional rather than a codified law for the Church is perfectly acceptable to monks who only look for recognition of the fact that monastic life is quite distinct from other forms of religious life and must have a distinct structure and a framework sufficiently flexible to allow the life its free development under the guidance of the Spirit. The due autonomy of the local community under its Spiritual Father is capital in this regard.

See also CODE OF CANON LAW, REVISION OF.

Bibliography: "Propositum Monasticum de Codice Iuris Canonici Recognoscendo," *Jurist* 26 (1966) 331–357; "Monastic Proposal for Canon Law," RevRel 26 (1966) 19–45. J. BEYER, "De institutorum vitae consecratae novo jure," PeriodicaMorCanLiturg 62 (1974) 145–168, 179–222; K. D. O'ROURKE, "The New Law for Religious: Principles, Content, Evaluation," RevRel 34 (1974) 23–49. M. B. PENNINGTON, "The Canonical Contemplative Life in the Apostolate of the Church Today," *Jurist* 24 (1964) 409–422; "The Integration of Monastic Law in the Revised Code," *Jurist* 25 (1965) 345–350; "Monastic and Contemplative Life and the Code of Canon Law," RevUnOttawa 36 (1967) 529–550, 757–770; "The Structure of the Section Concerning Religious Life in the Revised Code," *Jurist* 25 (1965) 271–290. M. SAID, *Progetto della riforma della legislazione codiciale "De religiosis," un giro d'orizzonte* (mss. of a talk given in 1974 to an international conference of major superiors).

[M. B. PENNINGTON]

CONFERENCE OF INTERNATIONAL CATHOLIC ORGANIZATIONS

The Conference of International Catholic Organizations (COIC) links the 29 organizations so acknowledged by the Holy See; 17 others share in COIC work as associate or guest members. Vatican Council II has set forth the mission of international Catholic organizations (*Gaudium et spes* 90; *Apostolicam actuositatem* 19), as have numerous messages addressed to COIC by Popes Pius XII, John XXIII, and Paul VI. The last, in a letter addressed to the General Assembly of the Conference in 1977, declared: "Man today is becoming more and more aware that he will not solve the problems of the times or build anything lasting unless he goes beyond the circle of narrow nationalism, is open to a diversity of cultures, and strives towards a cohesive, international solidarity. The Church is particularly alert to this issue and conscious of offering to the world a specific concept of man—a concept rooted in the universality of human nature and illumined by divine revelation. Therein lies the reason for the Church's teaching on the human family and for the Church's presence in international organizations, in whose work it is a joy to see so many of the Church's children engaged."

Coordination and close links among international Catholic organizations was the reason for the Holy See's approval of COIC in 1953. To carry out its purpose and to facilitate exchange of information research and cooperation aimed at action the Conference has created within its membership permanent Working Groups regarding a variety of issues—education, human rights, etc.—or *ad hoc* Working Groups—e.g., in connection with the Synods of Bishops, world conferences of the United Nations, etc.

The Conference participates in international affairs as belonging to the group of nongovernmental organizations having consultative status in: the UN Economic and Social Council; ILO; WHO; FAO; OAS; UNESCO; UNICEF; the Council of Europe. As an aid to its activities COIC maintains information centers in New York—International Catholic Organizations, Information Center, 323 E. 47th St., New York, N.Y. 10017; Paris—CCIC 9, rue Cler, 75007 Paris; Geneva—Centre d'Information des OIC, 1, rue de Varembé, 1200 Geneva. Within the Church COIC maintains liaison with the dicasteries of the Roman Curia and enjoys consultative status with the Pontifical Council on the Laity. It publishes trimonthly its *Bulletin de Liaison*. Headquarters are at 1 route de Jura, 1700 Fribourg, Switzerland.

[A. SCHAFTER]

CONFERENCE OF MAJOR SUPERIORS OF MEN (CMSM)

In recent years the Conference of Major Superiors of Men (16:94) has actively promoted and witnessed a rebirth in the practice of contemplative prayer. It has been instrumental in calling attention to the Western heritage of mysticism in the prayer of quiet by propagating a modern version of it, the *prayer of centering.

CMSM has sponsored the establishment of centers of this prayer across the country.

Continuing in its efforts to further the work of renewal in religious communities, the Conference has extended its energies to the areas of *second-career vocations, preretirement and retirement of men religious. It has conducted a series of workshops in this field in collaboration with national, Catholic universities and is actively engaged in cooperating with The Catholic University of America in the establishment of a Center for the Study of Preretirement and Aging.

In conjunction with the National Conference of Catholic Bishops (NCCB) and the Leadership Conference of Women Religious (LCWR), CMSM has helped to develop a set of Guidelines for Fund Raising to promote fiscal responsibility. It has also collaborated with the *National Catholic Development Conference (NCDC) in the sponsorship of workshops on financial stewardship. Cooperative measures of these types have become an essential pattern of operation among major church organizations.

Through its continuing contacts with Vatican agencies and with national conferences of religious in many countries, CMSM has set priorities on assistance to Third World countries in their evangelizing efforts. Addressing global injustices and challenging religious to respond actively to this call to be present to the poor of the world have become the central concerns of the Conference.

[D. P. SKWOR]

CONFESSION, FREQUENCY OF

Sacramental confession (4:132) presupposes that a change of heart and conduct has already begun and is sincerely purposed to be deepened and maintained. To foster greater awareness, especially by the penitent, of the abiding value and rich benefit of this Sacrament in the perfecting of Christian charity, Vatican Council II mandated a revision of the rite and formulas of the Sacrament of Penance "so that they more clearly express both the nature and effect of the sacrament" (*Sacrosanctum Concilium* 72). In the aftermath of the Council, for a variety of reasons, a remarkable decline in the number and frequency of confessions became widespread. The Sacrament ceased to retain its former central importance in the lives of many Catholics or its close link with the reception of the Eucharist.

The revised Rite of Penance (1973) reaffirmed the necessity of the Sacrament of Reconciliation. "Those who by grave sin have withdrawn from the communion of love with God are called back in the Sacrament of Penance to the life they have lost" (PenanceIntrod 7). Moreover, the revision made no change in the obligation of annual confession under the usual conditions. The new Rite seeks to make the celebration of the Sacrament more meaningful and effective for the penitent by providing more options, such as a common penitential rite with individual confession and absolution and the extraordinary situation of a general absolution, and by facilitating the penitent's greater participation in the process of making a confession.

As Pope Paul VI noted "all men who walk the earth commit at least venial sin and so-called daily sins. All, therefore, need God's mercy to set them free from sin's penal consequences" (Paul VI IndDoct 3). For this reason the revised Ritual urges frequent confession so that "those who through daily weakness fall into venial sins [might] draw strength from a repeated celebration of penance to gain full freedom of the children of God" (PenanceIntrod 7). Moreover, the Church wishes priests to recommend to the faithful frequent or devotional confessions because of the abundant benefits for Christian living. Men and women religious, solicitous for fostering their union with God, are instructed to approach the Sacrament of Penance frequently, that is, twice a month. The same norm befits clerics whose office bespeaks sanctity of life.

Bibliography: Sacred Congregation of Religious and Secular Institutes, Decree, *Dum canonicarum legum*, Dec. 8, 1970, O'Connor 531–534. Sacred Congregation for the Doctrine of Faith, Pastoral Norms on General Absolution, June 16, 1972, O'Connor 667–673. N. HALLIGAN, *The Ministry of the Celebration of the Sacraments*, v. 2, *Sacraments of Reconciliation* (Staten Island, N.Y. 1973) 97–99.

[N. HALLIGAN]

CONFESSORS OF RELIGIOUS

To foster growth in holiness and to more surely unite them with the Church in its continuing quest for conversion and renewal, the Sacred Congregation for Religious and Secular Institutes in a Decree of December 8, 1970 re-ordered and simplified the norms governing the confessors of religious (4:144), particularly religious women. All religious women and novices enjoy free access to any confessor approved in the place, the special jurisdiction for the confessor (CIC c. 876.1) being no longer required. An ordinary confessor is to be designated for monasteries devoted to the contemplative life, to houses of formation, and to larger communities. Similarly, an extraordinary confessor is to be provided for these monasteries and houses of formation without, however, the religious being obliged to present themselves to him. The designation of confessors in all cases pertains to the local Ordinary, who also determines their qualifications and duration of office. The appointment and reconfirmation in office are to be made in consultation with the community.

Where applicable these same norms apply to lay communities of religious men and dispositions of the CIC contrary to or irreconcilable with the new norms remain suspended.

[W. B. RYAN]

CONGREGATIONAL SINGING

The growth of congregational singing as an important part of American Catholic worship is a recent development (4:171), taking marked impetus from the publication of Vatican Council II's Constitution on the Sacred Liturgy in 1963. The growth is largely attributable to the strong emphasis which that document placed on the active participation of the faithful in the liturgy (*Sacrosanctum Concilium* 30). The revision of the rites themselves in order to make such participation a more integral part of the liturgy (ibid. 50–56), a more extensive use of the vernacular (ibid. 36, 54), and the redefinition of the concept of sacred music in terms of its closeness to the liturgical action as opposed to any particular style or type of music (ibid. 112) have made at least some degree of active participation in song a reality in the Roman Catholic parish of today.

In the first years following the Council the accepted norm for congregational participation was, in most parishes, the so-called four-hymn Mass. Though it originated to fill the need for congregational singing within the context of a pre-Vatican II Latin liturgy, the four-hymn "tradition" is unfortunately still all too common today. The revision of the Eucharistic Liturgy itself in 1970 made it possible to place the emphasis where it belongs—on the congregational singing of those elements that are an integral part of the liturgy. The 1972 statement from the *Bishops' Committee on the Liturgy, *Music in Catholic Worship*, indicates that there are five acclamations which ought to be sung "even at Masses in which little else is sung": the Alleluia; the Holy, Holy, Holy Lord; the Memorial Acclamation; the Great Amen; and the Doxology to the Lord's Prayer (54). Congregational participation in the processional chants at the Entrance and the Communion is also encouraged, as is the singing of the Responsorial Psalm after the first reading (ibid. 60, 63). Singing by choir or congregation is encouraged, though not demanded, at the Lord, Have Mercy; the Glory to God; the General Intercessions; the song during the Preparation of the Gifts; the Lord's Prayer; the Lamb of God; the song *after* Communion; and the recessional song (ibid. 64–74). Of these, the General Intercessions and the Lord's Prayer should, when sung, always belong to the congregation. How much music a given congregation sings is to be determined by ability and need, rather than by distinctions between high or low Mass. The choir is seen in a role supportive of congregational singing, as well as in its traditional role of singing alone.

The larger part of congregational music used in churches today is taken either from the rich tradition of Reformation hymnody or from the folk-style music that has grown up as a part of the liturgical renewal. Congregational singing of a limited repertory of Latin *Gregorian chant, while recommended for the whole Church, has been given little emphasis in the United States.

The question of hymnals and other aids to congregational participation remains a large one, though the recent publication of several fine hymnals has been encouraging (*see* HYMNS AND HYMNALS). The use of missalettes is still prevalent; it is difficult for them to include the variety of options available in the new rites while at the same time maintaining a body of familiar material. The question of a national hymnal has been discussed at length, and the Canadian bishops have actually adopted one. Though a national hymnal can provide music from different publishers in one book, it runs the risk of arresting further development. The proliferation of mimeographed hymnals at the local level, though solving many problems, has brought on the legal problem of copyright enfringement—a problem made more acute by the recent revision of the copyright laws of the United States (US Code Title 17, amended by Public Law 94–553).

Many problems remain to be solved, and a body of good congregational music is still being developed, but the last fifteen years have seen American Catholic congregations move from a relatively passive role into one in which their singing is a normal part of worship.

See also MASS, MUSIC OF.

Bibliography: L. DEISS, *Spirit and Song of the New Liturgy* (Cincinnati 1970). Bishops' Committee for Liturgy, *Music in Catholic Worship* (Washington, D.C. 1972). M. A. O'CONNOR, "The Role of Music Director in Liturgical Celebration," LivLight 14 (1977) 593–608.

[R. B. HALLER]

CONSCIENCE, FREEDOM OF

Among the most dramatic events of Vatican Council II was the conflict that ended with a large majority favoring the Declaration on Religious Freedom (*Dignitatis humanae*), thus rejecting the "thesis-hypothesis" theory on religious freedom (6:109) that had been widely accepted for a century (4:204). The Declaration produced several noteworthy results: it achieved doctrinal unity on the point that religious freedom is a universal and natural right; it eliminated a major source of tension with non-Catholics; it fostered a less triumphalist and more humble spirit among Catholics.

The Council's action also cast new light on various theological issues. The establishment of a state religion is seen to be inconsistent with full religious liberty, since it places pressures, open or subtle, on dissidents. There is at least a verbal contradiction between Pius IX's Syllabus of Errors (13:854) and the Declaration on Religious Freedom: this requires explanation in terms of the meaning of the theory of development of doctrine (16:131). Since the right to freedom of conscience results from man's dignity as a free, rational agent, which precludes that he be ever forced to act contrary to his conscience, difficult questions arise about the nature and limits of discipline within the Church; the cases of Abp. Lefebvre and Hans Küng illustrate well the range and type of issues involved. Other problems arise in regard to mixed marriages, e.g., some requirements imposed in the past are now seen to be inconsistent with the Church's due respect for individual freedom, but there remains the question of how such freedom is to be combined with safeguarding the faith.

There are also pastoral and political implications. The Council repeatedly noted that even the hint of coercion or proselytizing (*see* JEWISH/ROMAN CATHOLIC RELATIONS) was inconsonant with religious liberty, thus rejecting certain types of past missionary activities. But if the faith is only to be accepted freely, even more should it be lived freely. This entails the democratization of the Church, manifestations of which are the Synod of Bishops and the growth of parish councils. In the revision of the Lateran Pact (8:410), the Church seems ready to give up all privileges; as other concordats are similarly revised, Church-State relations and the status of the Church are going to change considerably in traditionally Catholic countries. A further consequence of full religious freedom and equal share in the common good is that where there is state-subsidized education students going to religious schools should receive as much financial support as those who do not.

Bibliography: J. LECLER et al., *Religious Freedom, Concilium* 18 (New York, 1966) with helpful bibliographical survey. E. MCDONAGH, *Freedom or Tolerance?* (Albany 1967). H. MADELIN, "La Liberté religieuse et la sphère du politique," NouvRevTh 97 (1975) 110–126, 914–939. O. MURDICK, "Religious Freedom: Some New Perceptions in Light of Vatican II," *Religious Education* (1976) 416–426. J. C. MURRAY, ed., *Religious Liberty: An End and a Beginning* (New York 1966).

[G. J. DALCOURT]

CONSEQUENCES, MORALITY OF

According to traditional Catholic theology there is an obligation to avoid even the unintended bad consequences of moral actions in so far as it is morally possible to do so (4:212). However if there is a proportionate reason for the act and it becomes morally impossible to avoid the evil consequence, this can be permitted to occur according to the principle of double effect. But according to the same principle no one may ever intend the bad consequence as an end or as a means to another good. Thus, for example, a physician may remove a cancerous uterus in a pregnant woman permitting the death of the fetus; he may not directly terminate a pregnancy even if an abortion is the only means to prevent both mother and fetus from dying.

Some contemporary Catholic theologians argue that the more fundamental principle applicable in situations where there are both good and bad consequences of an act is the rule to choose the lesser evil in such circumstances. This amounts to the application of a "consequentialist calculus." Physical evil is not the same as moral evil. Physical evil (nonmoral, premoral, ontic, prima facie evil) becomes moral evil (sin) only when it is taken up as evil into a person's intention, that is when it is intentionally caused without a proportionate reason. This does not mean that moral evil may be done in order that good may come of it. But it does mean that physical evil (as described above) may be done in order that good may come of it. One example such theologians give is that a physician may directly terminate a pregnancy to save the life of the mother, for the physical evil (death of the fetus) does not become moral evil (sin) in the presence of a proportionate reason.

See also MORALITY.

Bibliography: J. FUCHS, "The Absoluteness of Moral Terms," Greg 52 (1971) 415–458. R. MCCORMICK, *Ambiguity in Moral Choice* (Milwaukee 1973).

[J. F. DEDEK]

CONSERVATISM AND LIBERALISM, THEOLOGICAL

Application of these largely political terms to theological statements may be justly resented; yet they will be used, and the attempt must be made to see why and to see how they might be used responsibly. Expressions like "liberal" or "conservative" are especially susceptible of polemical use, and quickly degenerate into labels that are not accurate and should rather be avoided than pursued.

In the measure that theological teaching, however, reflects and affects the spirit of an age, it seems to prompt classification as conservatism or liberalism. "Conservative" and "liberal," then, do not describe theological statements or positions themselves, but rather refer to the way those statements may relate to the spirit of an age. Given that initial clarification, it is fair to say that a liberal theological stance will tend more to accommodate current intellectual movements, while a conservative posture will tend to find them alienating or threatening to theological sanity. Each position, if it is to make genuine theological assertions, must represent itself as carrying forward an authentic tradition; yet they will differ in the strategies employed to elaborate that tradition.

The differences may so polarize them that representatives of either group will come to caricature the other's position polemically. A liberal will be tempted to accuse a conservative of unwillingness to risk a nostalgic attachment to the past by confronting contemporary issues, and a conservative may look upon a liberal as one so anxious to adopt current outlooks that he cares little about the richness of the common heritage. Once these polemical uses have been invoked, the expressions "liberal" and "conservative" quickly become labels and lose descriptive force.

To classify liberal or conservative tendencies in theology with some accuracy, however, calls for attention to the earlier observation: these terms describe the ways in which theological assertions relate themselves to the surrounding intellectual currents. Thus a theological liberal will be prone to distinguish expression from substance and to regard a particular doctrinal expression as culture-bound and thus subject to revision. By contrast, a theological conservative will note how expression in words and in practices so often carry the substance of the matter that they cannot easily be revised without altering the sense of what is being passed on. Because theology is logically tied to a tradition and because traditions develop by a judicious mixture of change and of continuity, theologians will always be divided into conservatives and liberals. Furthermore, the surrounding intellectual currents may shift so that an individual may find himself in one camp or another at different times in his life.

The relatively fixed use for "theological liberalism" refers to a 19th-century movement that sought to accommodate the Scriptures to historical method in such a way as to meet current criteria for scholarly rectitude; Schleiermacher offers the most notable example (8:711). Until rather recently the tendency would have been to label Catholic counterparts "Modernists."

See also PLURALISM, THEOLOGICAL.

Bibliography: J. HITCHCOCK, *Decline and Fall of Radical Catholicism* (New York 1971). M. NOVAK, *The Open Church* (London 1964). F. SCHLEIERMACHER, *Brief Outline of the Study of Theology* (Richmond, Va. 1966).

[D. BURRELL]

CONSULTATION ON COMMON TEXTS

The origins of the Consultation on Common Texts lie in the somewhat hesitant decision of Vatican Council II to permit some use of the *vernacular in liturgy, with approved translations (*Sacrosanctum Concilium* 36). This decision led perceptive Protestants to initiate unofficial correspondence with such figures in North American Catholicism as Rev. Gerald J. Sigler and Rev. Frederick R. McManus, looking towards production of agreed common liturgical texts. The Presbyterian, Scott F. Brenner, writing in 1964, and the Lutheran, Hans Boeringer in 1966, laid the groundwork for a gathering sponsored by the Institute for Liturgical Studies at Valparaiso University (Valparaiso, Ind.) in August 1966, attended by persons from the Inter-Lutheran Commission on Worship, the Protestant Episcopal Church, the United Presbyterian Church, the Worship Commission of the Consultation on Church Union (COCU), and the International Commission on English in the Liturgy (ICEL), of the Roman Catholic Church.

The following year (1967) this group sponsored a more widely attended meeting in conjunction with the National Liturgical Week of the *Liturgical Conference, also at Valparaiso, Ind.; this became the first of several such meetings. A smaller working group on "Agreed Texts" began meeting semi-annually to prepare English translations of the Lord's Prayer and the Apostles' Creed (released in May 1968), the Nicene Creed and portions of the Ordinary of the Mass (August 1968), and to embark upon the preparation of a common Psalter for liturgical use (November 1968). Its work was first published by the Consultation on Church Union as part of *An Order for the Proclamation of the Word of God and the Celebration of the Lord's Supper* (Forward Movement Publications, Cincinnati 1968).

In 1969 the working group began using the name "Consultation on Common Texts" and concentrated on its Psalter project, leaving the earlier agenda of translations of the Lord's Prayer, the Ordinary of the Mass, the Creeds, and the Lucan Canticles to international bodies, particularly the newly formed *International Consultation on English Texts (ICET). It did serve however as a center for evaluation of ICET's texts in North America. Membership gradually became more diverse with the additional participation of Presbyterian and Methodist representatives; Canadian Churches also began to take part. The Psalter project came to fruition with *A Liturgical Psalter for the Eucharist* (Augsburg Publishing House and The Liturgical Press 1976). Translator of these fifty-some Psalms was the Rev. Professor Massey Shepherd, Jr. of the Protestant Episcopal Church in the U.S.A., who had been among the founders of the Consultation and who prepared his translation in close partnership with it (*see* PSALTERS, VERNACULAR).

At about the same time the Consultation undertook its most recent effort, namely, encouraging closer conformity in the use by various denominations of the three-year Roman Lectionary (1969). The widespread adoption of this Lectionary by Churches and congregations as diverse as Disciples of Christ, Methodist, Presbyterian, Lutheran, Episcopalian, and Roman Catholic, led the Consultation to convene a Conference on the Lectionary in Washington, D.C. in March 1978 to initiate efforts among these Churches (in both Canada and the U.S.A.) to evaluate the Lectionary, to harmonize various editions thereof, and to coordinate their calendars and use of weekly pericopes (*see* LECTIONARIES).

Thus the Consultation on Common Texts has in little more than a decade: (1) produced new texts for common use; (2) cooperated in the production of internationally agreed upon texts; (3) encouraged ecumenical agreement in the liturgical use of the Bible; and (4) served as a continuing channel for Churches both Protestant and Catholic to move ever closer together in their ways of worship.

[H. A. ALLEN]

CONTEMPLATION

Contemplation as understood by contemporary thinkers describes the state of those who seek an intuitive, integrated manner of being before the Lord. The questions that formerly necessitated the distinctions between natural/supernatural, acquired/infused, ordinary/extraordinary, ascetical/mystical contemplation do not arise today (4:258). Other approaches to the topic have become necessary, given the varying philosophies now handmaidens to theology as well as the many social sciences which have influenced it. The last two decades have witnessed a renewal in biblical research and a resurgence of interest in the classics of Western and Eastern mysticism; both movements have contributed to the emerging models for contemplation.

The search into the mystery of God's summons to a contemplative life is not confined to Catholic Christians. In writing on the nature of Revelation, some theologians show that God's epiphanies elude attempts to measure, define, or control; these writers are aware that the psychosomatic experiences concomitant with the devout life of prayer and meditation escape doctrinal boundaries. Worldwide religious dialogue between Christians and non-Christians is possible on the level of religious experiences. As the movement of God into the life of humanity is defined within particular ecclesial traditions, theological diversity is obvious and necessary. Catholic contemplatives, while acknowledging God's multiple advents in history, view contemplation as inseparable from identification with Jesus Christ, the unique and supreme Revelation of God.

Contemplative Life as Integration. Jesus accepted the mystery which was at the center of his existence; contemplatives, led by the Spirit of Jesus, open their lives to the mystery at its center where God and humanity meet. The metaphor, then, that most nearly approximates the contemplative stance is that of integration. A former metaphor was "mystical marriage." Both, though shaped in the unconscious level of different eras, suggest the same reality. It is the holistic search into the mystery of the interpenetration of the human and the divine exemplified in Jesus that consumes the contemplative's daily existence. A contemplative model develops from examining the contemplative's specific modes of articulating experiences of God, of Jesus, of the Church, of prayer, daily life, work, and leisure. To make the model tangible necessitates listening to those who recognize and respond to an integration of their lives in God and noting the similarities between their experiences and those of the great mystics and contemplatives.

Experiencing The Divine. The contemplative finds it impossible to experience God as apart from life. Having been led into a profound sense of presence known even in times of absence, the contemplative recognizes God as manifest in life's joys, struggles, summonses to change, its demands for faith, and in its slow, often imperceptible growth. The quest is for God-within-life, mysteriously and consistently present even in darkness and frustration, and for the integration of human and divine wisdom, love, and life.

Experiencing Jesus. "It is no longer I, but Jesus Who lives in me" (Gal 2.20) clearly expresses the contemplative's experience of Jesus. Identification with the Lord is seen to be erroneously limited to those instances in which Christians feel they have acted well. Authentic identification with Jesus occurs only as the pattern of dying and being raised becomes etched indelibly upon a person's existence. This dying is defined as the presence within and outside the Christian of the absurd and irrational elements of daily life, painful and ill-assorted pieces that seem to defy understanding. Faith demands of the contemplative the affirmation that precisely in this confusion and desolation lies the redemptive possibility. The darkness of the human psyche is already redeemed. The contemplative person trusts that the Word of God saves and in faith the transformation occurs. The contemplative is raised up by the power of God and is rendered able to continue in new purposes and directions toward deeper levels of integration. It is this passage through dying and being raised that brings about the identification of the contemplative with the Lord Jesus.

The Church. The Church continually reminds the contemplative that our lives are seized by God communally. The People of God know themselves by the death/rebirth cycle present in their lives and by the redemptive significance which, because of Jesus, they are able to attribute to this process. They are pilgrims moving toward God, their ultimate destination, in exodus from all that enslaves them. Jesus manifests himself in ways similar to those of the Gospel accounts of resurrection. Persons with eyes of faith perceive the Lord; others do not. Authority is understood by the contemplative as a gift entrusted temporarily to certain members of the Church for the service of all. The Sacraments are dynamic expressions of God's saving activity. As a People the Church is commanded to proclaim the Reign of God and to heal the afflicted. The contemplative, always and above all a person of the Church, has a profound sense of this mission.

Prayer. Contemplative prayer is not something a person does; it is something a person is. The words of the "Our Father" may be recited, but the attitudes expressed therein are internalized in the contemplative who is able to distinguish between meditation methods, prayers said communally or individually, and those moments in which a wordless absorption in God is present. There is no conceptualization nor self-conscious examination of being before the Lord. The contemplative simply is before the Lord in times of work and prayer, in solitude, and in relationship; the language of contemplative prayer is silence; the place of contemplative prayer is everywhere; God-within-life is the totally engaging reality. The contemplative is unable to separate sacred and secular, not through lack of careful discernment, but because everything human has been touched by the Incarnation of God. Thus the extraordinary lies within the most ordinary of events and people. "Pray always" has been actualized; the contemplative person has become the prayer.

The World. The world is not something apart from the contemplative's self. The joys and evils present in creation, as well as the redemption of creation by Jesus, are present within each one. When contemplatives are truly centered in God and self, they are most authentically in touch with the world. Thus today's contemplative feels deeply the pain of the world's injustices. The call to justice issued by church leaders strikes deeply within, calling for concern and involvement; the stance of the "guilty bystander" tears at the contemplative's conscience. It is probably accurate to state that justice in the world will be brought about by contemplative persons, those who are most deeply in touch with themselves and thus with all of humanity.

Contemporary Contemplatives. Contemplatives have known a history of misunderstanding in the Church, as only a glance at the biographies of John of the Cross, Teresa of Avila, or Meister Eckhardt shows. Yet the true contemplative has never been the member of an elitist or arcane sect. The contemplative person has been one who experiences life as more consistently integrative even in disintegrating moments. The measure of Christian holiness is charity and contemplatives can be no exception to this standard. They may be inside and outside of monasteries and cross all levels of society. God's summons to the interpenetration of the human and the divine is not limited.

The portrait of the contemplative person drawn here fits current research in mental health and psychology. The holy individual is the healthy individual. The Church has called on all to reexamine the basic dignity of the human person evident in the Scriptures. The stress on pastoral theology demands that what is written and preached corroborate contemporary religious experience and that tradition be brought forward as vital truth. Thus the current description of contemplation cannot be couched in language which prevents the faithful from being able to identify with the profound summons of God to a life of highest union in his love, lived out in the terms of ordinary daily experiences.

Bibliography: ST. AUGUSTINE, *Confessions,* tr. R. WARNER (New York 1963). H. URS VON BALTHASAR, *Prayer,* tr. A. V. LITTLEDALE (New York 1961). A. BLOOM, *Beginning to Pray* (New York 1971); *Living Prayer* (Springfield, Ill. 1975). J.-P. DE CAUSSADE, *Abandonment to Divine Providence,* tr. J. BEEVERS (Garden City, N.Y. 1975). *Cloud of Unknowing,* tr. C. WALTERS (Baltimore 1961). S. N. DASGUPTA, *Hindu Mysticism* (New York 1959). C. D. DOHERTY, *Poustinia* (Notre Dame, Ind. 1975). W. JAMES, *Varieties of Religious Experience* (New York 1958). ST. JOHN OF THE CROSS, *Complete Works,* tr. E. ALLISON PEERS (Westminster, Md. 1963); tr. K. KAVANAUGH and O. RODRIGUEZ (Washington, D.C. 1973). ST. IGNATIUS OF LOYOLA, *Spiritual Exercises,* tr. A. MATTOLA (Garden City, N.Y. 1964). R. MARITAIN, *Journal,* ed. J. MARITAIN (Albany, N.Y. 1974). T. MERTON, *Seven Storey Mountain* (New York 1945); *The Sign of Jonas* (New York 1953). K. RAHNER, *Theological Investigations* 4, tr. K. SMYTH (New York 1974) 239–252; 7, tr. D. BOURKE (New York 1972) 3–46, 72–87. A. SCHIMMEL, *Mystical Dimensions of Islam* (Chapel Hill, N.C. 1975). W. CANTWELL SMITH, *The Meaning and End of Religion* (New York 1963). ST. TERESA OF AVILA, Complete Works, tr. E. ALLISON PEERS (New York 1946). STE. THÉRÈSE DE LISIEUX, *Autobiography,* tr. R. KNOX (New York 1958). ST. THOMAS AQUINAS, *Summa theologiae* Eng.-Lat. (1a, 12.5–13), v. 3, ed. H. MCCABE (New York 1969). S. WEIL, *Waiting for God,* tr. E. CRAUFURT (repr., New York 1973).

[B. DOHERTY]

CONTINUING EDUCATION FOR MINISTRY

Different in-service training programs of continuing education for ministry have appeared on all continents since Vatican Council II. These have emerged as a high-priority response to a real need expressed by bishops, priests, and sisters everywhere. Internal and external modifications and changes in the Church's life and structures have made these new vehicles for theological updating, and personal and community renewal a most important feature of the contemporary Church. The appeal of the Council for shared responsibility and new structures of a collegial type has resulted in the establishment of synods, pastoral councils, senates, etc. New approaches to the realization of community, as evidenced by the growth of *basic Christian communities, together with a review of apostolic commitments, underscored the need for a serious investigation of biblical, theological, and other spiritual sources. The realization of effective community building at all levels of the Church can be achieved only by sound planning and organization of available resources for the promotion of continuing education.

The manner of presentation and the methodology of the various efforts in this field of continuing education have varied considerably. Very few programs have been evaluated professionally and critically. There has been a certain unevenness in the results of these in-service training efforts. Underlying presuppositions exist in each program and criteria for evaluation of these varied efforts are difficult to formulate. Financial limitations and the constraint of a lack of qualified professional personnel are typical problems. Methodologically, there has been a wide spectrum of experiences, ranging from models using a classical, deductive, teaching type, to those which employ an inductive method. In some cases a blend of two methods has been attempted, together with a particular emphasis on the group's own special needs. As regards content, and at the theological level, the most vital points of discussion can usually be reduced to Christology and ecclesiology. Social concerns and moral issues are related, at least indirectly, to these subjects. Anthropology in its several forms is an indispensable horizon.

In a world where science and technology dominate and where the processes of secularization and socialization are quickly influencing opinion, there is a pronounced tendency to look to ideologies and to their social and political counterparts, to replace traditional spiritual values. A medieval *Weltanschauung*, or dominant world view, predominant for centuries in the West, has gradually given way to new influences. Essential for present and future ministry in the Church and to the world are a deeper understanding that takes account of contemporary scientific and philosophical modes of thought, and a thorough knowledge of the past, in order to hold those elements of past, present, and future in active tension. Traditional and new ministries in the Church, where continuity in change is imperative, will depend heavily on in-service, continuing education as a requirement for professional and competent ministry.

See also MINISTRY (ECCLESIOLOGY).

[R. J. MAHOWALD]

CONVERSION

Like "ministry," "stewardship," "Christian witness," the term "conversion" has acquired a new currency and new resonances in Catholic usage. Conversion formerly meant primarily joining the Catholic Church or, secondarily, turning to an intense spiritual life from one of religious apathy or of sin (as in the case of many saints). The contemporary understanding of conversion and the issues it involves can be traced most aptly by pairing it with another term newly-prominent in Catholic circles, "evangelization." Because conversion is its objective, evangelization in its present acceptation illumines the meaning of conversion. That meaning is both a forward development in the Church and also, at many points, a recovery of the Catholic theological heritage.

Those to Be Converted. What postconciliar language refers to as evangelization Vatican Council II still spoke of as "mission." The Decree on Missions refers to the Church's missionary character as essential and describes as a basic duty of the People of God the proclaiming of the Good News of Christ to all nations (*Ad gentes* 35). Those to whom this mission is directed are those who have not received the Good News. Evangelization, then, keeps this traditional address as one of its meanings and the potential converts are the "unchurched," as Pope Paul VI made clear in his apostolic exhortation on the subject (Paul VI, EvangNunt 49–53). But the Council also began a new emphasis in its frequent use of "conversion" and the development of the conciliar ideas is one mark of the new sense the term has currently.

The "convert" is, first of all, the Church itself, the whole and each one of the People of God. As to corporate conversion, the Constitution on the Church states:

Going forward through trial and tribulation the Church is strengthened by the power of God's grace . . . so that in the weakness of the flesh she may not waver from perfect fidelity . . . , that moved by the Holy Spirit she may never cease to renew herself (*Lumen gentium* 9).

The Council also notes in reference to ecumenism the Church's "need of a change of heart that will make the yearning for unity grow and mature" (*Unitatis redintegratio* 7). Pope Paul VI took up the theme of ecclesial conversion and made it more explicit:

The Church is an evangelizer, but she begins by being evangelized herself . . . . She is the People of God immersed in the world and often tempted by idols, and she always needs to hear the proclamation of the "mighty works of God" (Acts 2.11) which converted her to the Lord; she always needs to be called together afresh by him and reunited. In brief, this means that she has a constant need of being evangelized . . . . The Second Vatican Council recalled and the 1974 Synod vigorously took up again this theme of the Church which is evangelized by constant conversion and renewal, in order to evangelize the world with credibility (Paul VI EvangNunt 15).

The Pope had said that "Evangelization is in fact the grace and vocation proper to the Church, her deepest identity . . ." The Church also, therefore, exists in order to be converted; conversion is also part of the Pilgrim Church's proper identity: "Then the People of God becomes in the world a Sign of Conversion to God" (Penance 4).

The conciliar and postconciliar teaching emphasizes, as well, individual conversion of those already members of the Church. Thus the Constitution on the Liturgy notes that people must be converted before they come to the liturgy and must be continually summoned to faith and repentance (*Sacrosanctum Concilium* 9). The Decree on Missions gives a particularly rich description of conversion as the beginning of a spiritual journey and as a progressive change of outlook and morals through the catechumenate and onward from the old to the new man (*Ad gentes* 13). The Council reminds priests that through sharing the Word of the Gospel their task is to summon all men to conversion and holiness (*Presbyterorum ordinis* 4) and points to the priests' need for a continuous "turning of heart" (ibid. 18). Pope Paul VI described *metanoia* (conversion) as the condition for approaching the Kingdom of God and as consisting in "a profound change of the whole person by which one begins to consider, judge, and arrange his life according to the holiness and love of God, made manifest in his Son" (Paul VI *Paenitemini* ActApS 58 [1966] 179). The 1971 Synod of Bishops repeated the theme: "From the beginning the Church has lived and understood the Death and Resurrection of Christ as a call by God to conversion in the faith of Christ and fraternal love" (Synod JustWorld p. 41): "The Christian lives under the law of liberty, which is a permanent call to men to turn away from self-sufficiency to confidence in God and from concern for self to a sincere love of neighbor" (ibid. p. 42). In this connection, Pope Paul laid special stress on converting the nonpracticing (Paul VI EvangNunt 56).

The theme of continuing conversion process for all Christians runs through the revised liturgy and is especially clear in the restored catechumenate and in the new rites of Penance (Reconciliation). The Introduction for the rites of the Christian initiation of adults speaks of a "first evangelization" and "precatechumenate" leading to an initial conversion to be deepened by the period of catechumenate, one of purification and enlightenment (ChrInitAd 1, 4, 9, 10). Significantly the Introduction sees the catechumenate as proceeding in the midst of the community so that the faithful reflect on the value of the paschal mystery and renew their own conversion (ibid. 4). The Sacrament of Reconciliation attests to the truth that the Church which includes within itself sinners, and is at once holy and in need of purification constantly pursues repentance and renewal (Penance 3; cf. *Lumen gentium* 8 and 12). "The genuineness of penance depends on ... heartfelt contrition. For conversion should affect a person from within so that it may progressively enlighten him and render him eventually more like Christ" (Penance 6a).

The Meaning of Conversion. Religious news writers have occasionally remarked on recent Roman Catholic attention to evangelization and personal conversion that it has very much the tone of Protestant evangelicalism. It is not inaccurate to assess the teaching and campaign on evangelization as directed toward a conversion experience, to developing Catholics who are "born-again Christians." But that assessment has to be examined.

Conversion, Personal. Conversion is being seen currently as a continuous interior process characteristic of the communal life of the Church and of each of the faithful. No less striking than the documentary statements is a phenomenon that, whether as a response to the Council or not, is part of the contemporary Church's life. Much attention has been directed toward the nonpracticing or disaffected Catholic and toward leakage in the Church's membership. But it is equally true that there has been an intensification of spirituality, of a quest for a more intimate contact with God. (Archbishop Jean Jadot pointed to "interiorization" as one of the signs of hopefulness for today's Church [Jadot, 232].) The conciliar and postconciliar documents and the actual life of the Church represent a recovery of a theological tradition. The *locus classicus* on conversion is Session VI of the Council of Trent, the Decree on Justification (Denz. 1520–83). Some of the beauty of the Tridentine teaching and of the theological heritage it represents was blurred by polemical use, whether against the Reformers or in internal theological squabbles. Still, the 20th-century Catholic should not be unmindful of Trent's striking psychological description of the conversion process (Denz 1526) or of the profoundly and positively-developed theology of conversion (or justification) already part of the Catholic heritage. Paradoxically, it must be admitted, the post-Tridentine Catholic ethos so objectified the Christian life that present perceptions about conversion amount to a recovery. The rejection of "justification by faith alone" and of personal assurance of salvation led to an emphasis on the objective efficacy of the Sacraments which obscured the truth that the Sacraments presuppose and are a sign of the recipient's personal faith. (This was acknowledged in 1978 by Msgr. Philippe Delhaye, Secretary of the International Theological Commission, in connection with the Commission's document on marriage. A notable part of that document is its declaration that without *personal* faith there can be no true, i.e. valid, Sacrament of marriage.) Even the preaching of the Word of God, always the first channel of faith and evangelization (*res eodem modo conservantur quo et creantur*; cf. Paul VI EvangNunt 22; 42), often came to be treated in practice as peripheral and perfunctory. Too seldom and too little preached was the "Gospel of Grace," that the Christian life is continually a turning to God and a turning away from sin by personal choice prompted by inner grace. The theme "turning to and turning away" marks the development of the whole of moral theology in St. Thomas Aquinas's

Summa theologiae. The turning away from God and to a created end is the essence of sin; turning to God and away from sin is the essence of the life of grace (ST 1a2ae, 72.5, 73.1, etc.). Being "converted" is never simply a state of not being in sin; it is constantly expressed in every morally good decision by the positive choice to cling trustfully to God above all. Being converted is thereby always the choice to turn away from whatever is opposed to loving God above all. That turning-to and turning-away is possible and sustained by grace: a person turns to God because God turns the person to choose him above all (ST 1a2ae, 109.6). What is true of an initial act of conversion remains true as long as "being converted" lasts. The "convert" needs always to be empowered by God. But grace moves a person *to act, to choose*, that is, to elicit an inner and personal act; the state of being a Christian can never consist in the outward observance of rites or of having a "record" free of violation of the commandments. Because turning to God under grace is always a positive choice, it is always turning away from the opposite; conversion thus means tension: the change of heart and renewal against the forces of sin, ever present, within and without. That radical continuous process is the attitude which explains listening to the Word of God and sharing in the celebration of the Sacraments. Both presuppose and nurture the always-to-be-renewed process of conversion.

Two facts in the Church's life today attest to a renewed, or retrieved, appreciation of the personal decision that being a Christian involves. One is the liturgy. The rites of Christian initiation and reconciliation already alluded to imply that they are seen as paradigmatic for the whole Christian life (ChrInitAd 21). Conversion must come at some point as a personal decision and must be renewed as such continually (see Kavanagh). Being a Christian for every adult must involve an adult act (see ChrInitAd 30). The liturgy for children is being seen more and more not on the same level as liturgy *tout court*, but as disposing children for the period when they will make the "decision for Christ." Significantly, with regard to the precatechumenate and entrance into the catechumenate, the possibility of a period of several years for being initiated is clearly acknowledged (ChrInitAd 7b). The period of evangelization towards initial conversion has as its aim "that the true desire of following Christ and seeking Baptism may mature" (ibid. 10; cf. 9). The second fact is a shift of emphasis in catechesis. Almost the whole catechetical effort of the past was directed to children and youth. The new direction is on the primary need and importance of catechizing adults, a not minor part of which is liturgical catechesis (*see* CATECHESIS, ADULT; CATECHETICS).

The Conversion Experience. Because conversion is interior and personally appropriated under grace, conversion implies another element: the experience of the divine, the experience of the saving grace of Jesus Christ. In this regard the Church has also made a recovery from a historical, pronouncedly negative attitude towards the personal, the subjective, the experiential. That negative attitude had deep roots: with the crises of Quietism and Semi-Quietism, the term "mysticism" became almost a synonym for aberrance. Another, more recent attitude toward experience is best seen in Pius X's repudiation of Modernism, the Encyclical *Pascendi Dominici gregis* (*Acta Sanctae Sedis* 41 [1907] 593–650, esp. 604–609). The condemnation rejects personal experience as the sole and absolute criterion measuring the reality of the divine. The effect of the condemnation in the era of anti-Modernism was to make religious experience suspect and to refuse it any place in theology or spirituality.

The contemporary evaluation, however, maintains that it is one thing to make personal religious experience the exclusive criterion of belief and practice, another to recognize that experience must be an ingredient in any effective belief or faithful practice. The Council points to the Church and the faithfuls' own experience as a source of the deepening grasp of divine Revelation:

> This tradition which comes from the apostles develops in the Church with the help of the Holy Spirit. For there is a growth in the understanding of the realities and the words which have been handed down. This happens through the contemplation and study made by believers,... through the intimate understanding of spiritual things they experience and through the preaching of those who have received through episcopal succession the sure gift of truth (*Dei Verbum* 8).

The point is also expressed in the following description of the *mystagogia* (post-baptismal catechumenate):

> A fuller, more fruitful understanding of the "mysteries" is acquired by the newness of the account given to the neophytes and especially by their experience of receiving the sacraments. They have been renewed in mind, have tasted more intimately the good word of God, have shared in the Holy Spirit, and have come to discover the goodness of the Lord. From this experience, which is proper to the Christian and is increased by the way he lives, they draw a new sense of the faith, the Church, and the world (ChrInitAd 38).

No one has ever been converted or stayed converted on the basis of bare obligation to keep the commandments or of simple obedience to a hierarch. It is of the nature of grace and theological charity to take hold of the person and make belief breathe with love. The reason for nonrenewal or change of mind by a decisive faith is that there is no renewal or change of heart by love. The meaning of *fides formata* in classical theology is that it is an *affective* and thereby an *effective* belief; the essence of "experience" is a love-inspired conviction. The teaching of St. Thomas that the Gifts of the Holy Spirit are to every person necessary for salvation rests on the need of a quasi-experiential knowledge deriving from the intensification of affective attachment to God in order to survive in crises—where the choice is between turning away from or turning toward God above all (ST 1a2ae, 68.2). Even if it does not appeal in its message or mood to all, the Catholic charismatic renewal is a symptom of the recovered sense of a need for experiential contact with the divine. So are the many other forms of intensifying prayer life.

If exaggeration is feared, Catholic theology has a simple, built-in safeguard against the role of experience. No one should mistake feeling to be a claim of salvation personally assured. The reality experienced is the reality of grace itself; no one can claim *certitude* of the presence of grace because grace and its effects are divine and thus the object of belief or of special revelation. There is a further heritage of theological wisdom that keeps the recognition of the positive need of experience from being an illusory search for "feeling good about God." The wisdom of the saints is a guide that the one who gives and shapes the experience is the Holy Spirit. Experience can be as negative as that of St. Thérèse. But the saints' lives are an assurance that those who believe and love receive personal conviction and trust from the Spirit.

"Born-Again Catholics." A "born-again Catholic" is a contradition in terms, if "born-again" is accepted with its history in mind. A Catholic by definition is one who is united to the Church as the Church is constituted through faith and the Sacraments of faith as a community of salvation, the Body of Christ with its invisible elements of sanctification and its visible structures. The life of conversion leads always to life lived in and through communion within the Body of Christ. The "born-again" experience in its historical emergence in Christianity is precisely anti-ecclesial. In the "gathered Church" concept of the Anabaptist and Baptist tradition, Congregationalism, and in the Holiness Movement and its sequel, Pentecostalism, the conversion experience or the once-and-for-all reception of entire sanctification, constituted true believers and only such believers constitute the Church. The once-for-all conversion experience itself had no relationship to or need of Sacraments or hierarchical ministries; indeed it involved their repudiation. Thus the Church as understood in Catholic teaching is in fact superfluous. Where there have been suggestions of aberration by charismatics, it has been in the direction of treating their own *ecclesiolae* as more "spiritual" and therefore transcending the conventional Church community. For the Catholic, the Church lives and expresses her life of evangelization and conversion in the Liturgy of the Word and of the Sacraments (Paul VI EvangNunt 47). The Catholic becomes and continues to be converted in the ecclesial community and communion. The liturgical catechesis that is so splendid an element of the instructions in the revised liturgical books seeks to bring about the personal affirmation and nurture of conversion through Word and Sacrament.

Conversion and Liberation. In a phrase cited many times in this volume the 1971 Synod of Bishops made a pronouncement on evangelization that brings out a further facet of the contemporary understanding of conversion:

> Action on behalf of justice and participation in the transformation of the world fully appear to us as a constitutive dimension (*ratio constitutiva*) of the preaching of the Gospel or, in other words, of the Church's mission for the redemption of the human race and its liberation from every oppressive situation (Synod JustWorld p. 34).

The statement has as its background the Church's new address to the world in Vatican II's Constitution on the Church in the Modern World.

"Secular" Conversion. Part I of the Constitution (*Gaudium et spes* 1–45) interprets the whole of human existence as a process of turning toward (*conversio*) genuinely human values. The import of this conversion is perhaps best captured in the word "personalization" (*Gaudium et spes* 6), which is explained in these words: "Persons and societies thirst for a full and free life worthy of man—one in which they can subject to their own welfare all that the modern world can offer them so abundantly. In addition, nations try harder every day to bring about a kind of universal community" (ibid. 9). The process of a "secular" conversion, one including a right ordering of human values, the Council describes in this way: "Man achieves his dignity when, emancipating himself from all captivity to passion he pursues his goal with a spontaneous choice of what is good..." (ibid. 17). This part of the Constitution gives full recognition

to every noble human value and aspiration, and to the need of both individuals and the economic and political communities of mankind to turn from base and self-centered aims to the adherence to and striving for true human betterment (see Paul VI Address to Diplomats). That the affirmations the Church makes with regard to the temporal order are unfeigned appears from these statements:

> They are mistaken who, knowing that we have here no abiding city but seek one to come (Heb 13.14) think that they may therefore shirk their earthly responsibilities. For they are forgetting that by the faith itself they are more than ever obliged to measure up to their duties..... Nor, on the contrary, are they less wide of the mark who think that religion consists in acts of worship alone and in the discharge of certain moral obligations, and who imagine they can plunge themselves into earthly affairs in such a way as to imply that these are altogether divorced from the religious life (ibid. 43).

This conciliar vision views the earthly history of man as calling for the development of the dignity of the person as the image of God and regards the history of mankind in its communitarian forms as the unfolding of God's plan. The vision recalls a theme prominent in classical theology because of the influence of Pseudo-Dionysius. In his works, "On the Heavenly Hierarchy," "On the Ecclesiastical Hierarchy," and "On the Divine Names" the dynamics of the universe consists in the hierarchic process of "going forth" and "return"—*proodos* and *epistrophē*. The *epistrophē* of Dionysius becomes for St. Thomas Aquinas *conversio*, the term by which he interprets the whole, dynamic order in the world of creation and of grace as a process in which God as good is turning all things back to himself. The effect of this act of God converting is the received "being converted" of all beings, above all of angels and men, to their source, the divine fontal goodness. The very vitality of human striving is the effect of God drawing all back to himself (ST 1a, 62.2; 105.5; 106.1; 1a2ae, 109.6). That view remains a theological abstraction until concretized in the actual history of salvation through Christ, the Alpha and Omega. The divine act of converting and the reception of that conversion achieve the overcoming of sin and the communication of grace by Christ. Yet the point of the classical view and of *Gaudium et spes* is that intrinsically human values are not obliterated or nullified by the history of salvation. Their expression and their validity always remain; they are both a positive groundwork for the definitive conversion through Christ and reach their full actualization by that ultimate conversion. Quoting an earlier address to the College of Cardinals (ActApS 65 [1973] 383) Paul VI declared that in fact it is only in the Christian message that modern man can find the answer to his questions and the energy for his commitment to human solidarity (Paul VI EvangNunt 3). The new dimension of the Church's position toward the world is that it is consciously historical in a way that the Dionysian and the medieval vision were not. The evangelization-liberation process means the Church's insertion into the actual condition and oppressive situation of modern man (*see also* RECONCILIATION, MINISTRY OF).

Conversion and Human Development. The Council document and the 1971 Synod's statement become translated into the issue of the relationship between evangelization (therefore conversion) and human development. The issue has become controversial, as is indicated elsewhere in this volume (*see* JUSTICE AND

PEACE, MINISTRY OF). The *Synod of Bishops, 1974, on Evangelization in the Modern World makes this summary statement: "This orientation [of the Church] toward evangelization in this present age is linked by a special bond with concern for true human development which the Church always keeps as an integral part of its mission and activity on earth" (Caprile 987). "True human development is to be understood as from God the Father and Creator, as having received its deepest roots from his Son the Redeemer, and as being poured out by the Holy Spirit in individual hearts and among men. Therefore, because they are joined intimately in the work of creation and of redemption, human development and eternal salvation cannot be separated by the activity of the Church or of any of the faithful" (ibid. 987-988).

In responding to the direction taken by the 1974 Synod, Paul VI clearly addressed the issue of evangelization and human development:

> Between evangelization and human advancement—development and liberation—there are in fact profound links. These include links of an anthropological order, because the man who is to be evangelized is not an abstract being but is subject to social and economic questions. They also include links in the theological order, since one cannot dissociate the plan of creation from the plan of Redemption. The latter plan touches the very concrete situations of injustice to be combatted and of justice to be restored. They include links of the eminently evangelical order, which is that of charity: how in fact can one proclaim the new commandment without promoting in justice and in peace the true, authentic advancement of man? ...
> We must not ignore the fact that many, even generous Christians who are sensitive to the dramatic questions involved in the problem of liberation, in their wish to commit the Church to the liberation effort are frequently tempted to reduce her mission to the dimensions of a simply temporal project. They would reduce her aims to a man-centered goal; the salvation of which she is the messenger would be reduced to material well-being. Her activity, forgetful of all spiritual and religious preoccupation, would become initiatives of the political or social order. But if this were so, the Church would lose her fundamental meaning. Her message of liberation would no longer have any originality and would easily be open to monopolization and manipulation by ideological systems and political parties. ...
> With regard to the liberation which evangelization proclaims and strives to put into practice one should rather say this: it cannot be contained in the simple and restricted dimension of economics, politics, social or cultural life; it must envisage the whole man, in all his aspects, right up to and including his openness to the absolute, even the divine absolute; it is therefore attached to a certain concept of man, to a view of man which it can never sacrifice to the needs of any strategy, practice or short-term efficiency (Paul VI EvangNunt 31-33).

From these documents it is clear that one aim of evangelization must be liberation for persons and society on the basis of Gospel values. This, as Paul VI points out, calls for another dimension of conversion:

> The Church considers it to be undoubtedly important to build up structures which are more human, more just, more respectful of the rights of the person and less oppressive and less enslaving, but she is conscious that the best structure and the most idealized system soon become inhuman if the inhuman inclinations of the human heart are not made wholesome, if those who live in these structures or who rule them do not undergo a conversion of heart and outlook (ibid. 36).

The 1971 Synod had stated similarly "Education demands a renewal of heart, a renewal based on the recognition of sin in its individual and social dimensions" (Synod JustWorld p. 46).

Nonbelievers. Implied in these documents is a twofold conversion, functioning in different order for the nonbeliever or nonpracticing and for the "already converted." Nonbelievers and the nonpracticing were the concern of both *Guadium et spes* and of *Evangelii nuntiandi*. The Council gave special attention to modern atheism, but there is a common symptom in all those alienated contemporaries: the conviction that there is no divine dimension to history and society and no relevance that God and Christ have to them personally (see Paul VI EvangNunt 55–56). The article in this volume on *atheism points out the need of a double conversion as the most effective remedy to that attitude (*see also* FOUNDATIONAL THEOLOGY). Conversion, therefore, at the level of human values, in terms of human development—whether personal or societal—is at least a logical prerequisite to the more profound conversion to God and Christ who offer eternal salvation. The possibility and the problems on the part of those who are in need of the first conversion are immense; it may be questioned whether, in fact, such a conversion ever does or can occur discretely and antecedently; in other words, is not conversion to Christ necessary before conversion to a view of the right values intrinsic to human existence can occur? But from the point of view of the Church's evangelization, its link with human development becomes clearer. To reach the nonbeliever and to create possible dispositions for any sort of conversion, the Church must preach Gospel values as liberating from every form of human oppression and debasement of the person. The message that Jesus is liberator of men, that the Gospel means an eminent fulfillment not a negation of human values is not credible if the Church is indifferent to human values. That active involvement can dispose the nonbeliever to being converted to a true sense of conscience and of genuinely human priorities. The first conversion can be a disposition to final acceptance of Christ's whole Gospel. The 1971 Synod stated: "While the Church is bound to give witness to justice, she recognizes that anyone who ventures to speak to people about justice must first be just in their eyes. Hence we might undertake an examination of the modes of action and of the possessions and life style found within the Church itself" (Synod JustWorld p. 44).

The Already "Converted." The relationship between the twofold conversion for the active and convinced Christian is of an inverse order. Conversion to Christ and effective acceptance of Gospel values must honestly embrace a conversion to justice. "Each individual gains them [the Kingdom and salvation] through a total interior renewal which the Gospel calls *metanoia*; it is a radical conversion, a profound change of mind and heart" (Paul VI EvangNunt 10). "Men frequently join together to commit injustice. It is thus only fitting that they should help each other in doing penance so that they who are freed from sin by the grace of Christ may work with all men of good will for justice and peace in the world" (Penance 5). There are two implications: The first is that there is a negation of conversion to Christ as Savior if conversion does not include the affirmation and promotion of human "secular" values. Radical conversion is involved, since the connatural attitude of the human heart includes the predominance of self-interest precisely in the areas that belong to justice. Thus Paul VI described the Holy See's working evangelically for human rights with the aim that brotherhood may replace the egoism of nation, group, race, or culture . . . the Church calls upon individuals not to shut themselves off by seeing only their particular

concerns, but to open their minds and hearts to the rights, the needs, and legitimate aspirations of others (Paul VI, Address to Diplomats 75). The second implication is allied: the interiorization of justice in all of its forms. Of all the "natural" virtues and values, justice is the most "reasonable," i.e., it most requires a rational perception of proportion, the recognition, contrary to connatural self-interest, of the rights of others. Sheer justice has, in fact, a negative implication, i.e., it is the force that keeps human beings from harming each other; its achievement has more often been the effect of law enforcement and coercive sanctions than of personal acceptance of its demands. But in its nature, as a virtue, justice requires personal assimilation, personal interiorization in the positive will to respect and to further the rights of others. The nature of grace and charity is above all interiorization, personal transformation. For the believer justice receives a new and powerful animation. That animation is a conversion, the constant rectification and renewal of will against self-interest and its positive bent upon the human well-being of others and of society. It is worth remembering a basic teaching on the need for grace as healing (*gratia sanans*), grace restoring the power to do what is at the level of simple human rectitude and decency. One of the specific needs for grace classically singled out was to fulfill the Decalogue and the Decalogue sets forth the rudimentary demands of *justice* (ST 1a2ae, 109.4). The conversion of grace leads to a conversion for justice. Culminating its remarks on the help that Christians bring to the world and human values, the Council states:

> Although by the power of the Holy Spirit the Church has remained the faithful Spouse of her Lord and has never ceased to be the sign of salvation on earth, still it is very well aware that among her members, both clerical and lay, some have been unfaithful to the Spirit of God during the course of many centuries. In the present age, too, it does not escape the Church how great a distance lies between the message she offers and the human failings of those to whom the Gospel is entrusted (*Gaudium et spes* 43).

Conversion at the level of true human values is bound up with conversion to Christ; it is the more necessary as progressively the Christian witness becomes the only convinced institutional affirmation of and activity for what is genuinely human, noble, and worthy of the human person, and of the community of mankind.

Bibliography: H. URS VON BALTHASAR, "Conversion in the New Testament," Communio 1 (1974) 47–59. Bishops, Canada, Pastoral, "De la parole aux actes." Bishops, The Netherlands," Pastoral, "La conversion et le pardon," DocCath 71 (1974) 218–227. E. BRAXTON, "The New Rites of Reconciliation in American Culture," ChSt 15 (1976) 185–198. G. CAPRILE, *Il Sinodo dei Vescovi 1974* (Rome n.d.). C. ELLIS, "Metanoia and Community," Way 12 (1972) 292–300. V. J. GENOVESI, "The Death of Love: A Radical Theology of Love," AmEcclRev 169 (1975) 87–101. A. GRAHAM, *Contemplative Christianity* (London 1975). B. HÄRING, *Evangelization Today* (Notre Dame, Inc. 1974). Z. HEIRERO, "La conversión como retorno a la armitad divina," *Estudio Agustiniano* 11 (1976) 3–44. J. HOFINGER, *Evangelization and Catechesis* (Paramus, N.J. 1976). W. J. H. HOLLERWEGE, *Evangelisation gestern und heute* (Stuttgart 1974) bibliog. J. JADOT, "Signs of Hope in the American Church," Origins 4 (1974–75) 228–232. A. KAVANAGH, "Christian Initiation for Those Baptized as Adults," LivLight 13 (1976) 387–396. M. LEGANT, *Mutation de l'Eglise et conversion personnelle* (Paris 1975). J. PASQUIER, "Experience and Conversion," Way (1977) 114–122. PAUL VI, "Address to Diplomats," Jan. 11, 1975, *Pope Speaks* 20 (1975) 71–77. D. POWER, "Confession as Ongoing Conversion," HeythropJ 13 (1977) 180–190. J. C. SAGNE, *II peccato: Alienazione o invito alla liberazione?* (Bari 1976). M. STOGRE, "Psycho-Social Theology of Conversion," WaySuppl 27 (Spring 1977) 88–99. J. THOMAS, ed., "Se convertir," *Christus* 23 (1976) 2–93, entire issue.

[T. C. O'BRIEN]

CONVERT APOSTOLATE AND ECUMENISM

Until recently, the convert apostolate could be defined as a movement dedicated to attracting non-Catholics to the Roman Catholic Church. The persons being prepared to admission to the Catholic Church were called "converts," without respect to whether they were coming from another Christian Church or from non-belief to Baptism (4:292). Today the term "convert" is explicitly rejected as an appropriate designation of an already baptized Christian welcomed into full communion. The foreword to the *Rite of Reception of Baptized Christians into Full Communion with the Catholic Church* states that "the term 'convert' properly refers to one who comes from unbelief to Christian belief. Although conversion of life is the continuing imperative of Christian believers, the concept of Christian conversion is applied only in reference to Christian initiation—through Baptism, Confirmation and the Eucharist—rather than to a subsequent change of Christian communion."

The "convert" apostolate, then, is no longer an apt title when the task in question is the preparation and reception into the Roman Catholic Church of Christians from other Churches and Ecclesial Communities. The Baptism and Christian heritage of the candidate for reception are carefully respected. Such a candidate is never to be confused with a catechumen and any appearance of triumphalism is to be avoided in the celebration of the rite of reception (ibid. Introduction 3b).

Decree on Ecumenism. The basis for this change in terminology and treatment is the teaching of the Decree on Ecumenism regarding the "certain, though imperfect, communion" which exists between baptized Christians who belong to other Churches or Ecclesial Communities and the Catholic Church (*Unitatis redintegratio* 3; cf. *Lumen gentium* 8; 15). Already united with the Catholic Church by means of faith in Christ, Baptism, and other gifts of the Holy Spirit, the Christian candidate is admitted to full communion through a special rite of reception, usually celebrated during Sunday Mass. Because this relation of "imperfect communion" is affirmed not only of individual Christians but also of Christian Churches and Ecclesial Communities separated from the Catholic Church, the question arises: should Catholics undertake to attract already-baptized Christians to this full communion? Is such an effort appropriate in the era of ecumenical relations? The Decree on Ecumenism affirms that there is no opposition between ecumenical action and the work of bringing candidates into full Catholic communion. Ecumenical action is not a new method of gaining members for the Catholic Church but a movement to reunite the Churches themselves. The work of "preparing and receiving" candidates, on the other hand, does not imply "recruiting"; it is, rather, a response to the initiative of individuals (*Unitatis redintegratio* 4).

Although the Decree on Ecumenism regards Christian Churches that are not in full communion with the Catholic Church as deficient in one way or another, and in varying degrees, it affirms that they possess many elements of salvation and are capable of leading their members to redemption in Christ (ibid. 3). This acknowledgment of the ecclesial reality of separated Churches constitutes the foundation of ecumenical dialogue and common witness.

The Decree enjoins Catholics to take several measures to promote the ecumenical movement: they should eliminate unfair judgments and misrepresentations of other Christian Churches; initiate dialogue between competent experts; join with other Christians in cooperative work for the good of humanity; come together for common prayer; and undertake vigorous self-renewal and reform. This last is identified as the primary task of Catholics (ibid. 4).

Common Witness. In addition, Catholics are directed to collaborate with other Christian Churches in giving common witness to those who do not know Christ. With Baptism and the patrimony of faith as a basis, the Churches should strive to overcome the scandal that division presents by engaging in joint missionary efforts (cf. *Ad gentes* 6; 15; 29 and Paul VI EvangNunt 77). It is only realistic, however, to acknowledge that denominational affiliation is the ordinary way in which persons express conversion to Jesus Christ through Baptism. The limits imposed on common witness by doctrinal difference, varying ecclesiologies, and conflicting ethical positions should be addressed in ecumenical dialogue in a climate of openness and mutual commitment to truth. According to Pope Paul's apostolic exhortation On Evangelization, the Catholic Church "has a lively solicitude for the Christians who are not in full communion with her. While preparing with them the unity willed by Christ, and precisely in order to realize unity in truth, she has the consciousness that she would be gravely lacking in her duty if she did not give witness before them of the fullness of the revelation whose deposit she guards" (Paul VI EvangNunt 54.3).

"Common Witness and Proselytism," a statement developed by the *Joint Working Group of the World Council of Churches and the Roman Catholic Church (May 1970), named indifference, isolation, and rivalry as the major obstacles to common Christian witness (2). It directs the Churches to respect each other's right to religious freedom. In giving witness they should seek the glory of God and not their own prestige, and they should reject any form of coercion. Especially, they must repudiate as proselytism "every unjust or uncharitable reference to the beliefs or practices of other religious communities in hope of winning adherents" (ibid. 27). Beyond this, the statement calls for a serious commitment to common witness. Churches should give priority to the evangelization of non-Christians, avoiding competition and the active recruitment of members from other Christian Churches. When a Christian freely chooses to change ecclesial allegiance in obedience to conscience, it is recommended that pastors of both Churches be consulted and be made aware of this decision (ibid. 28).

The 1966 instruction, *Matrimonii sacramentum*, eliminates all reference to the obligation previously imposed by law on a Roman Catholic partner in a mixed marriage to strive prudently for the "conversion" of the non-Catholic partner (CIC c. 1062). In 1967 Paul VI and Patriarch Athenagoras I exchanged a pledge explicitly rejecting the intention of drawing the faithful from one Church to the other. Roman Catholic participation in parish *covenant relationships and ecumenical theological clusters and the revision of regulations concerning mixed marriage are only a few evidences of the "mutual esteem and love" (*Ad gentes* 6) which today characterizes the relationships between the

Catholic Church and other Churches and Ecclesial Communities.

See also INCORPORATION INTO THE CHURCH.

Bibliography: C. J. PETER, "Ecumenism and Denominational Conversion," *Communio* 3 (1976) 188–199. *Rite of Reception of Baptized Christians into Full Communion with the Catholic Church* (Washington, D.C. 1976). Secretariat for Promoting Christian Unity, "Common Witness and Proselytism," *Information Service* 14 (April 1971) 2:18–23.

[S. BUTLER]

CONWAY, WILLIAM

Primate of Ireland; b. Jan. 22, 1913, Belfast; d. April 17, 1977, Armagh. He studied in Belfast at St. Mary's Christian Brothers' School, St. Malachy's College, and Queen's University, receiving from the latter a B.A. in English literature in 1933. He then studied theology at St. Patrick's College, Maynooth and was ordained there in 1937. He received a Doctor of Divinity degree from St. Patrick's in 1938, and a doctorate in Canon Law from the Gregorian University, Rome, in 1941. Returning to Maynooth, he served there as professor of moral theology from 1942 to 1958, the last year also as vice president. During this period he served on Government Commissions on Higher Education and on Income Tax. In 1958 Conway was consecrated titular Bishop of Neve and named auxiliary to the Archbishop of Armagh, Cardinal John D'Alton. In 1963 Conway was chosen to succeed D'Alton as Archbishop and Primate of All Ireland (the Republic and Northern Ireland), and held the post until his death. He was created cardinal in 1965 by Pope Paul VI, who also appointed him to be one of three chairmen for the 1967 Synod of Bishops and papal legate to the 1972 National Eucharistic Congress in Madras. Conway also served on the Sacred Congregation for Bishops, for the Clergy, for Catholic Education, and for the Evangelization of Peoples. He died of cancer at his residence.

Conway's service as primate covered a period of widespread violence in Northern Ireland that erupted in 1969 and continued with varying degrees of intensity throughout the rest of his life. Since the groups inflicting the violence were identified according to their association with the Catholic or Protestant communities, the conflict was commonly interpreted as a religious war. But Conway joined with the leadership of the Protestant Churches to issue united appeals for peace. Some Protestants accused him of denouncing Protestant violence more strongly than Catholic. And some Catholic critics suggested that he should have moved more boldly to implement the new spirit of Vatican II and endorse the rights of Protestants to follow their own consciences in such areas as divorce and birth control. Also controversial was his continued support of separate schools for Catholic children, which many analysts thought served to continue the alienation between Catholics and Protestants. Virtually everyone agreed, nonetheless, that Conway was personally a man of peace who took significant strides toward improving the ecumenical climate in Ireland. His cautious style of leadership was also credited with maintaining a strong sense of Catholic unity and loyalty during the post-Vatican II years when bitter controversy and abandonment of the Church were common in some other places. At the end of his tenure, surveys found nine out of ten Irish Catholics still attending Mass at least once a week. He was succeeded as Archbishop by Msgr. Tomas O'Fiaich, a native of County Armagh and president of St. Patrick's College.

[T. EARLY]

"COR UNUM," PONTIFICAL COUNCIL

The Pontifical Council "Cor Unum" for the Promotion of Human and Christian Development was established by Pope Paul VI's letter, July 15, 1971, to Cardinal Jean Villot, Papal Secretary of State (ActApS 63 [1971] 669–673). The purpose was to provide information and coordination for Catholic agencies engaged in funding relief and development projects. A few weeks earlier a hand-delivered letter from Card. Villot had announced the papal proposal for such a central agency. That announcement had been viewed as portending centralization under Roman curial control and as threatening the grass-roots exercise of *collegiality already at work in the efforts of *Caritas Internationalis and the agency for International Cooperation for Socio-Economic Development, headed by Cardinal Leo J. Suenens. The first, centered in Vienna, had been engaged successfully in short-term relief; the second, centered in Brussels, concentrated on long-term development. Both had participated since 1968 in round-table meetings with representatives of the Pontifical Commission for *Justice and Peace of the Congregation for the Evangelization of Peoples, and of SEDOS, a documentation agency of religious congregations engaged in missions.

In Germany, a chief source for relief services, such publications *Publik* and *Herder Korrespondenz* predicted a sharp decline in German offerings from fear of Vatican control of funds; warned that aid initiatives would be linked with Vatican diplomacy. Fears were expressed that episcopal solidarity would be weakened because nunciatures would intervene between recipient and donor countries; that ecclesiastical priorities would mean discrimination against non-Catholic and non-Christian groups; and that such ecumenical fund-raising as that between Catholics and Lutherans would end. The Amsterdam newspaper *De Tijd* published an interview in which the director of the Dutch Lenten Action (collecting and distributing some $65 million annually) disclosed that he had insisted, in reply to Card. Villot, on advance consultation as to aim and functioning of the proposed centralized agency, on continuance of the round table project, and on autonomy for national aid initiatives.

Unfortunately the letter establishing "Cor Unum" was promulgated before any coordinated response to Card. Villot's letter was possible. Nevertheless at his address to the moderators and members of "Cor Unum," Jan. 13, 1972 (ActApS 64 [1972] 773), Paul VI assured them that there was no threat to autonomy or to the structures already designed for cooperation. The name "Cor Unum," the Pope said, was intended to evoke the unanimity of the primitive Church. He stressed the need for efficiency and harmony, and of beneficiary participation in decisions on allocation of funds. The Pope also addressed a "Cor Unum" group on May 27, 1976 (ActApS 68 [1976] 457–458). The *Annuario Pontificio* has not, in any edition since 1971, given its customary "Note storiche" on the origin and role of "Cor Unum." There has been little mention of "Cor Unum" in the Catholic press since the controversy at its inception.

Bibliography: W. JERMAN, "Cor Unum: Return of the Monolith?" *New Blackfriars* 52 (1971) 562–568. L. DE VAUCELLES, "De Rome et de la chrétienté," *Études* 336 (Jan.–June 1971) 267–269.

[E. J. DILLON]

CORBISHLEY, THOMAS

English Jesuit, a foremost figure in England's Christian unity movement, author, journalist, broadcaster; b. Preston, May 30, 1903; d. London, March 11, 1976. He studied philosophy and theology at St. Mary's Hall, Stonyhurst, and at Heythrop College (Oxon.); as an undergraduate at Campion Hall, Oxford, he received a first in Classical Mods and Greats. Ordained in 1936, he was prefect of Jesuit students 1938–45, then at Oxford Master of Campion Hall, 1945–58. From 1958 he was Superior of the London Farm Street Church and community until 1966 and spent the remainder of his life there with a reputation as "the Priest of London." Besides writing, broadcasting, lecturing, and caring for souls, he was active in groups concerned with ecumenism, relations with Jews, humanists, and Marxists, and with the promotion of the European Community ideal. One of his favorite roles was that of Chaplain to the Catholic Institute for International Relations. He was a frequent contributor to the Jesuit review *The Month* and served on its editorial board. In addition to the many contributions he made to national and religious journals, he published many books, including: *Roman Catholicism* (1950), *Religion Is Reasonable* (1960), *Ronald Knox the Priest* (1964), *The Contemporary Christian* (1966), *The Spirituality of Teilhard de Chardin* (1971), and *The Prayer of Jesus* (1976); he also translated and edited the *Spiritual Exercises of St. Ignatius of Loyola* (1963). The masterful article "Mysticism" in v. 10 of the *New Catholic Encyclopedia* is by Corbishley.

Though he had the quality of a professional scholar, Corbishley's main contribution belonged to the realm of *haute vulgarisation*. There were two reasons for this. First, he was above all else a priest, with a rare gift for linking tradition with his own adventurous thinking and he wanted to share his vision of Christ in the world as widely as possible. Secondly, he had the kind of all-embracing mind which sought to bring the insights of theology, philosophy, history, and the arts into a unity and was therefore less inclined to strict specialization. It was first as a teacher that he revealed his Ignatian (and Teilhardian) vision in his awareness of continuity between the life of the spirit and natural creation—his understanding that the whole of creation is subsumed in Christ's redemptive dispensation, that the eternal Kingdom of God is to be quarried out of history. Many of those he taught learned the incarnational theology of Vatican Council II twenty years before it opened. The openness Corbishley showed in his ideas at a time when Roman Catholic institutions still tended to be embattled behind juridical terminology was a source of sheer liberation to his students at Oxford and of admiration throughout the University, but it could get him into mild trouble with ecclesiastical authority, especially when his impetuous, generous gestures to the "separated brethren" seemed to preempt the developing mind of the Church. "Dear Tom," wrote Cardinal Heenan once, "I write neither in sorrow nor anger but . . . ." His courteous urbanity and his gift for seeing all sides of a question at once could give the impression of trying to be all things to all men, in the less

respectable sense, and of being too open-ended to be effective. Yet all that was really at work was the charity of an enthusiast. Partly because of shyness, he walked more easily with those who could enter deeply into his thoughts—Lord Hailsham and Dr. Michael Ramsey, former Abp. of Canterbury, were among his closest friends—but few people realized how he would travel up and down the country, speaking to small audiences in church halls, students' societies, and local ecumenical groups as well as preaching his ice-breaking sermons in Westminster Abbey or St. Paul's Cathedral.

Tom Corbishley was a man who loved God and also loved the world. A friend suggests that his life can be summed up in a prayer from Teilhard's *Messe sur le Monde*: "Receive, O Lord, this all-embracing sacrifice which your whole creation, drawn by your magnetic power, offers you as another day dawns."

[H. KAY]

CORE APPALACHIAN MINISTRIES (CAM)

Core Appalachian Ministries unites the four central Appalachian Dioceses of Covington, Ky., Richmond, Va., Nashville, Tenn., and Wheeling-Charleston, W. Va. in a cooperative-regional effort of community-development ministry.

This effort is one of *community development* because the goal is to encourage a process of social action in which the people of a community organize themselves for planning and action.

The work of CAM is *ministry* because it is part of the Church's work of evangelization and liberation; it is an effort to share the good news that Jesus has made us free. That message is shared not only by word but in the action of working with people toward self-determination. The basis of this ministry is confirmed in the Gospels and in the long standing social-doctrine tradition of the Church. It is further reflected in the pastoral letter, *This Land Is Home to Me*, issued by the bishops of Appalachia in 1975: "Throughout this whole process of listening to the people, the goal, which underlies our concerns, is fundamental in the justice struggle: namely citizen control or community control. The people themselves must shape their own destiny."

The effort of CAM is a *regional* cooperation because the central dioceses share a contiguous geographical area having common problems and resources with people of a common heritage and history.

The objectives of CAM are: (1) to hear, to reflect upon, and to act in response to the concerns of the people of central Appalachia as they are communicated through the efforts of community-development workers in each of the dioceses; (2) to facilitate communication in the central Appalachian region between and among the people of the region and between people and the Church; (3) to channel resources to community groups in the region involved in self-help efforts for systematic change; (4) to reflect upon the role and work of the Church in the light of the expressed concerns of the poor.

CAM attempts to meet those objectives through: (1) community-development field work at the local level; (2) interdiocesan and interstate action; (3) diocesan executive action; (4) CAM board action.

The board of directors is composed of four members from each participating diocese, including the bishop of each diocese. The board meets twice a year.

Community-development ministry is a relatively new direction of ministry in the Church. Understanding of the intimate connection between Gospel and social responsibility grows each day. The actions that should be taken as a result of gospel presence for justice in the world are not always clear, however. Therefore, there is need to be in dialogue with a variety of people and groups to develop multiple dimensions to that understanding and search. The mode of organization in CAM reflects that stance of dialogue and search. The CAM board meetings serve as the locus of an ongoing reflective process based on three imperatives for action outlined in the Appalachian pastoral letter: (1) listen to the people; (2) carefully use scientific resources; (3) be steeped in the presence of the Spirit.

Through CAM field staff, the concrete experiences of local groups are communicated to the level of corporate church action. In this way CAM serves as a linkage system between people and people, between people and Church, between diocese and diocese.

See also CATHOLIC COMMITTEE OF APPALACHIA.

[M. M. PIGNONE]

CORPORATE SOCIAL RESPONSIBILITY

Since corporate institutions are actors on the local, state, national, and international stage, the effort to use their investments (esp. property, stocks and bonds) to promote good and avoid harm is called corporate responsibility. Stressing corporate responsibility with its investments is not an entirely new phenomenon for the Church. Protestant denominations have had long-standing decisions against investments in companies involved in tobacco, liquor, slave-related businesses or other activities contrary to their social creeds for many years.

The 1971 Synod of Bishops asked Catholic institutions to undertake an examination of the modes of acting and of the possessions and life style found within the Church itself (Synod JustWorld p. 45). The effort of its institutions (dioceses, religious congregations, foundations, schools, and health-care centers) to examine their possessions and specifically those in the form of investments, has brought the Church into a new role as advocate of social responsibility. Since 1973, under the leadership of the *National Catholic Coalition for Responsible Investment, Catholic institutions have become actively involved in promoting justice within their own institutions and, through their investments, with other institutions. Areas of special concern have related to human rights (hiring practices, discrimination) ecological matters, concentration of wealth and power, involvement of *multinational corporations in developing nations, and right-to-life concerns.

In dealing with corporations and banks with whom they have investments, Catholic groups involved in the corporate responsibility movement tend to follow an adaptation of the model offered by Jesus to those who preached conversion: talk, coalition (word of two or three witnesses), litigation (taking it to the judge), divestment (shaking the dust from the disciples feet).

[M. H. CROSBY]

COUNCIL FOR RELATIONS BETWEEN SCRSI AND IUSG

This is a consultative body established in response to the motu proprio *Ecclesiae Sanctae* (1967) II, 42, for collaboration on ongoing questions relating to religious life. First convened on June 8, 1968, it now meets approximately every month. The Council is composed of eight electees from both the *International Union of Superiors General and the *Union of Superiors General (hence is a "Council of Sixteen"), with the Cardinal prefect, secretary, and other members of the Congregation for Religious. A valuable forum for consultation, exchange of views and ongoing studies concretely connected with the current development of religious life, the Council also gives information for themes treated by the plenary sessions of the Congregation and for the triennial Synod of Bishops. Minutes are reported in the publication of the Congregation (*Informationes SCRIS*) and sent to members of the two Unions and to national conferences of religious.

Bibliography: Institute of Religious Life, ed., *Consecrated Life*, Eng. ed. of *Informationes* (Boston 1977–).

[M. LINSCOTT]

COUNSELING, PASTORAL

As a special type of counseling, pastoral counseling assumes the religious needs of the counselee and the professional ministerial background of the counselor. According to Cavanaugh (1962), it partakes of some of the elements of all forms of counseling, for it is eclectic in its methods and pragmatic in its approach. It differs from all other methods of counseling in that it includes God in the counseling relationship.

Bier (1959) refers to two elements involved in pastoral counseling as the proximate goal, which is psychological, and the ultimate goal, which is religious and pastoral. The effective combination of the two goals constitutes the characteristic features of pastoral counseling. To obtain the delicate balance between the religious and psychological dimensions of human problems has been the greatest challenge to the spiritual and psychological authenticity of the pastoral counselor.

Theological Roots. For centuries counseling was an informal art considered a prerogative of elders, heads of families and pastors, by virtue of their position and wisdom. The pastor's counsel, considered religious direction, was rooted in his theological training and his own life experiences. Grounded in this theological tradition, the guidance of the pastor was a process by which he dealt with human problems as springing from the spiritual conditions of the soul and its relationship to God. Until the 20th century that kind of helping situation was not singled out with a special name, but its position within the pastoral-care dimension of ministry was very clear.

It was within this strong theological tradition that Anton T. Boissen in 1925 began the clinical pastoral-education program for Protestant theological students. Boissen brought them to the Worcester State Hospital in Massachusetts to learn theology by deepening their insights into the problem of sin and salvation through the study of the mental patients in the hospital. Although he acknowledged the help of psychiatrists and psychologists, he insisted that his students bring theological questions to these deep crisis experiences of life. Over the years, however, more and more of the psychological influences became a part of the training.

Psychological Roots. At the turn of the century, the therapeutic movement springing from psychiatry and psychology, primarily based on Freudian theory, were viewed by the Catholic Church as alien to God and religion. Misiak and Staudt (1954) credit Thomas V. Moore (16:300) of The Catholic University of America as most influential in the 1930s in calling to account those pastors who frowned upon psychiatry as antireligious. Moore, a priest-psychiatrist, called for a revised education of the clergy which would lead them to an appreciation of the value of psychology in their pastoral work.

On April 13, 1953, Pope Pius XII addressed the Fifth International Congress of Catholic Psychotherapists in Rome and observed that psychology was capable of achieving valuable results for the religious dispositions of man. Meanwhile, the American Catholic Psychological Association, founded by William C. Bier, SJ, labored through the 1940s and 1950s to establish psychology as a valid secular science. These gradual attitude changes in the Catholic Church laid the groundwork for the powerful events of the 1960s, which would affect pastoral counseling: Vatican Council II and the major breakthrough in counseling theory, research, and practice.

Two thrusts of the Vatican II documents gave support to increasing interest in pastoral counseling: the pastoral nature of the documents, especially *Lumen gentium* and *Gaudium et spes*, and the frequent references to the use of psychological research into human behavior. Concurrently, a plethora of counseling theories and methodologies inundate every helping profession, including pastoral care. The new insights, when put into a pastoral framework, have led in general to improved understanding and education in pastoral care and also to increased interest in this aspect of Church ministry.

The initial contribution of psychology to pastoral counseling was a clearer understanding of human behavior, conscious and unconscious motivation, the psychodynamics of personality development and disorders, and knowledge of the schools of psychotherapy and counseling. Most theological seminaries have offered theoretical courses in the principles of human behavior since the 1950s.

It is only since Vatican II, however, that Catholic seminarians and priests in significant numbers have been exposed to formal training in the art of counseling. Hiltner (1975) points out it was not until after Vatican II that Catholic clergy became involved in the Association for Clinical Pastoral Education, which had been certifying clergy since the 1930s. The number and proportion of Catholics (including religious) participating in various pastoral-counseling programs in seminaries and colleges has continued to grow through the 1960s and the early 1970s.

Current Issues. Much as an adolescent struggling with his identity, in the latter part of the 1970s the profession of pastoral counseling continues to search for clarification of its purpose and identity in its ministry to the Church.

The Spiritual Dimension. With the introduction of psychodynamic psychology and counseling techniques, pastoral counseling adopted a secular, nonreligious view of man, with emphasis on interpersonal problems and societal forces as the causes of man's spiritual problems. Hendrix (1977) points out very succinctly that pastoral counseling has been content to relate psychological problems to psychological structure and interpersonal problems to interpersonal structure, but it has failed to relate spiritual problems to spiritual structure. The image of the self, the self's problem and the modes of healing, have been naturalistic. Man has been deprived of spirit by being perceived as rooted in nature and culture. Pastoral-counseling theory must be expanded to include consideration of the spiritual dimension of human development and counseling techniques modified to facilitate union with God.

The Ministry of Counseling. A second issue which needs resolution, especially within the Catholic tradition, relates to the definition of pastoral counselor. Presently, to be certified as a pastoral counselor by the American Association of Pastoral Counselors, one must be a fully ordained minister under the authority of a recognized religious communion. The counselor must be an expert in knowledge of the spiritual life and an expert in interpersonal relations. This is what Hiltner (1977) refers to as "professional ministry." In the Roman Catholic Church only a fully ordained priest can be certified as a pastoral counselor.

Unsettling questions are raised, however, when unordained Christians with competent theological and counseling background, dedicated to church ministry, cannot be recognized as professional pastoral counselors. The growing number of permanent deacons represents one group which might meet all the requirements of pastoral counselors, except the sacramental functions of presbyteral ordination. Religious women, likewise, who are prepared in theology and pastoral counseling and who serve as full-time members of parish ministry teams, press for professional certification (*see* WOMEN IN MINISTRY).

Resolution of these issues in fidelity to the essential dimensions of pastoral counseling could very well lead the profession into a healthy maturity, with a clear sense of direction and mission.

Bibliography: W. C. BIER, "Goals in Pastoral Counseling, a Catholic View" *Pastoral Psychology* 10 (Feb. 1959) 7–13. J. R. CAVANAUGH, *Fundamental Pastoral Counseling* (Milwaukee 1962). H. HENDRIX, "Pastoral Counseling in Search of a New Paradigm," *Pastoral Psychology* 25 (1977) 157–172. S. HILTNER, "Pastoral Counseling and the Church," *Journal of Pastoral Care* 31 (1977) 194–209. H. MISIAK and V. M. STAUDT, *Catholics in Psychology: A Historical Survey* (New York 1954). J. PATTON, "Editorial," *Journal of Pastoral Care* 30 (1976) 217–221. Pius XII, "On Psychotherapy and Religion: An Address," (USCC Publ. Office, Washington, D.C. 1953).

[M. M. CUNNINGHAM]

COUNSELS, EVANGELICAL

The basis for a Catholic understanding of the evangelical counsels has been broadened considerably during recent decades (4:383). Developments in both theology and the social sciences contributed to a new evaluation. We shall here highlight some of the shifts in perspective.

In theology, biblical scholarship facilitated a more authentic exegesis of crucial passages like Mk.10:21 and Lk.10:41. More generally, a rediscovered biblical anthropology stresses the integrity of the human person: Christ saved not souls, but humans, soul and body. Sexuality is seen as a high human value. A new biblical emphasis falls on the communal aspects of salvation, counteracting individualistic tendencies of the recent past. There is a growing appreciation of human nature as an unfolding reality. Static notions of perfection are being superseded by dynamic ones. All this determines a new theological outlook on the evangelical counsels.

The social sciences throw light on monasticism as a basic human phenomenon independent of the Christian tradition. Obedience, voluntary poverty, and sexual abstinence form a recurrent syndrome at the core of monasticism in Jainism, Buddhism, Hinduism. In

Shamanism, we can trace the roots of that syndrome far into prehistory. We find evidence of it, moreover, in the *Dead Sea Scrolls within a pre-Christian biblical context: the life of the Qumran Community shows close sociological resemblances to Christian observance of the evangelical counsels. Thus, Catholics and, say, Buddhists, who tended to consider their monks and nuns as super-Christians and super-Buddhists respectively, discover that "life according to the evangelical counsels" is simply one possible way of being human, differently interpreted by the various religions.

Psychology supports this, e.g., by A. Maslow's exploration of Peak Experiences, high points of mental well-being and creativity, in which there is the blissfully experienced paradox that to lose self is to find one's true identity; the paradox that solitude is at the same time oneness with all; the paradox that the answers to the deepest existential questions are found the moment one listens rather than asks. It is possible to find in these paradoxes the seed-intuitions for a life of poverty, celibacy, and obedience—voluntary poverty as progressive detachment from selfish wants in grateful self-acceptance; celibacy as a radical way of expressing that solitude of the human heart which is at the same time intimate communion with God and all creatures; obedience as tuning in on God speaking through the circumstances of one's life, as the interference of self-will is gradually reduced.

Thus, the evangelical counsels gain new significance for our time (see *Lumen gentium* 42–46; *Perfectae caritatis* 5, 12–14). Amidst the boredom of affluence, voluntary poverty witnesses to the joy that springs from needing less and being more grateful; celibacy proves that the loneliness of the "lonely crowd" can be turned into joyful solitude; obedience points toward the dimension of meaningfulness which lies beyond our preoccupation with purpose. These values are brought nearer to *all* human beings as the evangelical counsels are now seen as anchored not primarily in the Gospels, but in what Thomas Merton called an imperishable "instinct of the human heart," channeled and brought to its fulfilment when it finds its focus in Christ.

Bibliography: M. ELIADE, *Shamanism*, tr. W. R. TRASK (rev. ed., New York 1964). M. HELLDORFER, ed., *Sexuality and Brotherhood* (Lockport, Ill. 1977). A. MASLOW, *Religions, Values, and Peak Experiences* (New York 1970). F. WULF, "Decree on the Appropriate Renewal of the Religious Life," Vorgrimler 2:301–370.

[D. F. K. STEINDL-RAST]

COVENANT RELATIONSHIPS

One creative expression of parish-level ecumenism, and in some instances of diocesan-level ecumenism, is the growing practice of "covenant relationships." A covenant is an agreement between two or more local congregations of differing traditions who pledge to one another some degree of constant cooperation, collaboration, understanding, and support. What is pledged varies from place to place according to local circumstance. More specifically a covenant is an agreement between two parishes or congregations in which the members commit themselves at least to pray publicly for one another at every Sunday liturgy or worship service, to cooperate in whatever manner they decide is mutually beneficial, and to come to know and support one another in living the Christian life.

A covenant between local congregations usually involves five different areas: (1) *spiritual*—public prayer for one another in separate worship services or liturgies; ecumenical services on specific occasions during the year; and occasional sharing to the extent allowed in one another's form of worship; (2) *intellectual*—discussion groups (informal dialogue) to promote mutual understanding; shared programs for scripture study or for teaching basic Christian truths and attitudes at various age levels; (3) *moral*—cooperative programs for bringing Christian values to bear on local, national, or world problems in order to counter injustice and/or to alleviate the needs of those suffering from poverty, prejudice, discrimination, and the like; (4) *organizational*—sharing physical facilities and personnel to the extent this is permitted and helpful to both communities; (5) *social*—promotion of events (e.g., dances, picnics, holiday celebrations) that bring the members of each community into informal settings to foster personal contacts and deepen mutual appreciation of their common hopes, desires, and needs as human beings.

A covenant is one practical step toward building trust and cooperation, understanding and support on the firm foundation of prayer and faith. It is a visible, concrete response to Jesus' prayer for the unity of his disciples (Jn 17). Its formalized programs tend to define and implement ecumenical activities in an ongoing way. It can help avoid the attitude which acknowledges ecumenism as very desirable in theory but allows it to remain a dead issue on the local level. A covenant provides a vehicle for expressing unity more visibly to insure common witness, and for allowing growth in understanding the commitment to strive for Christian unity.

See also ECUMENISM, REGIONAL AND LOCAL.

[T. HORGAN]

CREATION

Vatican Council II underscored creation (4:417) as meaning the first and essential step in the unfolding of the history of salvation (*Dei Verbum* 3). Creation is viewed as directly connected with the incarnate center of the mystery of salvation, Christ the Lord (*Lumen gentium* 2, 36). The Council found the basis for the dignity of human effort in man's participation in the work of the Creator and in the realization in history of his plan (*Gaudium et spes* 34). Christian humanism originates in the dignity of human activity as a co-responsibility for the world's development shared with the divine creative and sustaining activity (ibid. 35). Citing the teaching of Vatican Council I on the harmony between the Creator and laws that govern creatures, the Council confidently asserts that there need not be any conflict between scientific investigation and faith (ibid. 36).

Theological endeavor after the Council generally has not pursued the theology of creation. Perhaps too willingly, theologians have left the questions of the origin of the universe to scientists. The latter have offered new theories about the origin of the universe: the "big bang" theory, the steady-state and continuous-creation theory, the pulsating-universe theory. Present scientific evidence seems to postulate a universe infinite in time, space, and matter. Theologians in response steadfastly assert that there can be no ultimate conflict between the doctrine of creation and scientific investigation.

Bibliography: R. BUTTERWORTH, *The Theology of Creation* (Notre Dame, Ind. 1969). G. DYER, "Creation in Double Perspective," ChSt 6 (1967) 3–25. L. GILKEY, *Maker of Heaven and Earth* (Garden City, N.Y. 1965). T. HOSINKSI, "Creation and the Origin of the Universe," *Thought* 48 (1973) 213–239; 387–403.

[D. J. EHR]

CULTURE, CHURCH AND

Culture is the ensemble of elements in man's struggle to survive and improve the state of his existence as it is developed and transmitted by the group. It develops through continuing interrelationships between the members of the group with their land, climate, and contacts with other groups. Once it is produced, it obtains an objective existence of its own—e.g., grammar, tools, customs, etc.—and will become a part of the natural world of the newcomers who are raised within the group. Culture is learned, but once it is acquired, it functions biologically because it becomes an integral part of the total and permanent identity—the *personalité de base*—of the persons of that group. Even though aspects of culture can be changed and altered, it can never be totally removed or replaced. Deep cultural traits are so persistent that they almost appear to be transmitted biologically through the genes and chromosomes.

Vatican II: A Rediscovery. In the beginning of the Church, the question of the relationship between the Gospel and other cultures had been one of the primary pastoral questions of that time—how the Greeks could become Christians without having first to become Jews (cf. Acts 10 to 15). Yet as the Christianization of Europe was completed and the period of Christendom began this question hardly came up again. The consolidation of the existing Christian culture became the overriding concern. With the beginning of the great missionary efforts in the 1500s, a few, such as Mateo Ricci (see 3:611), struggled with rather modest attempts to inculturize the Gospel, but for the most part it was taken for granted that the European, especially the Western European, expression of Christianity was Christianity itself. Thus missioners, Catholic and Protestant alike, went to new lands and attempted to make *Spanish* Christians, *English* Christians, etc., out of the new peoples they met, rather than helping them to become Asian *Christians*, African *Christians*. The Church seemed to have forgotten the original missionary formula and thus worked more for a cultural conversion than for a true evangelical conversion to the way of the Lord.

Not until the time of Vatican Council II did the question of the interrelationship between the Gospel and culture begin to be asked officially by the Church (cf. *Gaudium et spes* 53–62). Several factors contributed to this issue's becoming central. A decisive factor was certainly the presence of Council Fathers from Asia, Africa, and other so-called missionary countries. They expressed their desire to be Catholics and in full communion with the Apostolic See, but not to be forced to become some sort of second-class Europeans. A real full communion and sharing with the one and universal Church, they felt, should imply not only the adaptation of some external trappings, but also the integration of their culture and their ways of thinking. This gave rise to the importance and place of the local and particular Churches as the embodiment of the universal Church in the particular (*see* CHURCH, LOCAL [THEOLOGY]). This question was further deepened and expanded by the Council's insistence on fidelity to the founding sources of Christianity and at the same time fidelity to contemporary society. Out of this concern for fidelity, the Council Fathers and subsequent *Synods of Bishops gradually articulated the fact that the essential task of the Church is twofold: to listen constantly to the Word of God that she might constantly turn away from the idols of the world and insist on the demands of the new commandment of love; then to proclaim the Word of the Lord to all the peoples of the world in a manner truly creditable (Paul VI EvangNunt 15; cf. *Ad gentes* 5). Out of these concerns for the implantation, growth, and development of the local Churches and the need to be faithful to the way of the Lord through contemporary society and culture, the Church today is looking at the normative interrelationships between Jesus and his culture and between the first apostolic missioners (Jewish Christians) and the different cultures they encountered as they went beyond their own cultural boundaries to carry the Gospel to the worlds of the Gentiles.

Jesus and Inculturation. The key question is how Jesus functioned in relationship to his time and space. Jesus was not some sort of acultural and ahistorical "universal" person. He was deeply inculturated with his people. He was the well defined and easily recognizable Galilean from Nazareth; from here he made his way to Jerusalem, denouncing whatever in his group enslaved and rejected people by keeping them from appreciating their fundamental human dignity. Having become a Jew, Jesus did not ask his people to cease being Jews, but he did invite them to relativize and discard anything in Jewishness that was keeping them from being fully human and from appreciating their own human dignity and the dignity of others. He likewise announced a new basis for human dignity and belonging: everyone is welcomed as he is, to the Kingdom of the God who is the Father of everyone. If anyone does not want to belong, it is not because he does not qualify, but simply because he personally refuses the invitation. But Jesus' denunciation of the degrading and segregating systems created by men and the announcement of the universal Kingdom for everyone became a serious threat to all who relied on such systems for the legitimization of the exploitation of others and the preservation of their own privileged status, prestige, and power. Thus, they had to get rid of the threat—they choose their own security rather than liberation (Jn 11.48). Jesus is killed because from within his own culture he questioned and revealed structural defects that were enslaving and dehumanizing everyone. Yet in his resurrection he opened the way for the possibility of a new type of existence; he was still Jesus of Nazareth but in a radically new way, for he was now fully revealed as the Christ; he was no longer just Jesus but he was now Jesus Christ or what the Greeks preferred, the Lord.

This inculturation-denunciation-announcement (death and resurrection) is *the way* of the Incarnation. True conversion to Christ does not mean a conversion from one's cultural group to another cultural group, but a conversion within one's cultural group so as to situate oneself and live within one's people in a radically new way. The first Christians did not cease being Jews, but they transcended Judaism by becoming Christian Jews and the first Greek converts did not become Jewish Christians, but they transcended their Greek ways by becoming Greek Christians. Through the plan of the Incarnation, the Christianness will be "mestizo-ized" with Jewishness or Greekness; the converted groups are enabled to die to their own enslavements of exclusiveness and rejection and to become a new human group more open and accepting of others, to pass from enslaving particularisms to liberating catholicity.

The Current Process. There is no such person as a "pure"—universal, acultural, and ahistorical—Christian. By reason of the Incarnation/Resurrection dynamic, every Christian will be a hyphenated Christian—he will be what he is culturally, while at the same time transcending radically the cultural limitations of his group. Only through this interpenetrative process of God's way with man's cultural ways will the extremes of superficial syncretism or destructive ethnocide in the name of the Gospel be avoided and the Gospel truly implanted as the seed of the Father into the womb of the mother, into the cultural matrix of a people, to give birth to new and truly local Churches. Only through such a process will the essential catholicity of the Church be a life-generating service rather than an ethnocidal imposition. The great diversity that will result from such a process will not be detrimental to the essential unity of the Church. Rather it will contribute to the true unity in diversity of the many peoples and the many nations who in Christ transcend their own particularism and nationalisms and who, without ceasing to exist, will now situate themselves in a new way in relationship to each other—not as enemies but as equal members of the family of God. Conversion liberates cultural groups from the enslavements of exclusiveness to the mentality of openness and universality—both to give and to receive of the wealth which God has placed in all peoples.

To the degree that the culture is evangelized and cultural expressions of the Gospel begin to emerge, the culture itself will become a transmitter of the Gospel. However, the culturally transmitted Gospel is in constant need of explicit evangelization, catechesis, liturgical celebrations, and theological reflection that utilize the language, art-forms, philosophy, and wisdom of the people (*Ad gentes* 22) if the full meaning of the Christian symbols transmitted by the culture is to be appreciated. When this process stops, the Gospel begins to be equated with the culture and it loses its transforming force; it ceases to denounce sin as it exists in the structures of the group and to announce the new possibilities that break through and transcend the cultural enslavements of the group. The challenge for the Catholic Church of the United States today is that the fidelity to the most ancient tradition of the Church, a new expression of catholicity must build within the country a new Catholic Church which will not be threatened but rather welcome the great diversity of languages and ethnic traditions found within the United States. Humanly speaking, this appears as chaos, but in the power of the first Pentecost, this apparent impossibility—the new universal community inclusive of all the peoples of the earth—is precisely the challenge of the Church of the United States. Only when the Church accepts such a challenge will the original dynamism of the Gospel be restored so that she may effectively live and proclaim the Gospel in the 20th century (Paul VI EvangNunt 2 and 3).

See also INCULTURATION, THEOLOGICAL.

Bibliography: V. ELIZONDO, *Christianity and Culture: An Introduction to Pastoral Theology for the Bicultural Community* (Huntington, Ind. 1975).

[V. ELIZONDO]

CULTURE, DEVELOPMENT OF

In distinguishing it from the popular notion of culture as merely the civilized learning (generally the arts) of a privileged few, anthropologists have stressed the inclusiveness and totality of the term "culture" to comprehend *all* that is learned and shared in a particular society (i.e., *a people*) and passed down from one generation to another. The evolution of the term, which originated in England with E. B. Taylor (*Primitive Culture* 1871), and provided, then, one of the few cornerstones for a new science, cultural anthropology, suggests a process of epistemological development whereby, as Man discovers more and more about himself, culture becomes determined by the conditions of Man's increasingly sophisticated adaptation to his social and physical environments (Fried 1967). Thus it refers not to a static, unchangeable concept but to a dynamic process. Older definitions of the term "culture," a flight away from evolutionary theory into descriptive humanism, were bent on stressing specific differences between Man and animals; they emphasized the material process inherent in the concept, and saw Man as essentially *homo faber*, a toolmaker; they envisioned culture as an abstraction of human behavior, and often—misleadingly—equated it with "civilization" (in terms of the sum total of the material and intellectual equipment of a people).

Kroeber and Kluckholn collected some 160 definitions of "culture" the majority of which (some 100) were culled during the decade 1940–50, reflecting, in part, the growing complexity of the social sciences of that period but not reflecting, necessarily, any increase in the quality of the definitions (Vermeersch 10). Modern definitions, conscious of the recent work by animal behaviorists and ethnologists admit that the concept may not be exclusive to humans; they allow not only the descriptive and substantive basis of the concept but introduce also an explanatory dimension; they veer away from *abstractions* of behavior to focus more on the human group of actors "coping." Thus culture becomes yet another adaptive strategy, and a cause of human behavior, for it is the "Idea" between Man and Nature. Bennett's definition "Culture is Man's way of adapting to the environment" (Bennett 849) preserves culture as a central referent but is characteristic of the shift in definitions towards an adaptational frame. Nevertheless, for some scholars, culture has become too broad a concept to be used any longer as an analytical tool.

Whether culture should be regarded as a complete set of learned behaviors, or should refer only to those rules for social behavior which, for example, determine ideologies or codes (i.e., "tried" precedents), is a controversy which has diverted anthropologists in recent years. This controversy is in fact mirrored in different categories of definitions which often confuse culture and society e.g., those that stress mental states or processes—knowledge, ideas, beliefs, attitudes, values and morals—latent in the minds of people but *responsible* (ultimately) for behavior; and those that refer to regularly repeated patterns of behavior—habits, customs (Vermeersch, 14).

However deep the disagreement among scholars as to the relationship between the two concepts—culture and society—most agree on the definition of *culture* as the ideational system and of *society* as patterns of actual behavior. The distinction has been likened to that made by Noam Chomsky in *Aspects of the Theory of Syntax* (MIT Press, Cambridge, Mass. 1965) between competence and performance in language, in that "culture is defined as being a system of rules which is distinct from and independent of any verifiable patterns of actual, observed behavior" (Avila 525).

Thus the cultural component provides the means and mechanism for regulating the network of social relations which is the societal component. This distinction served to establish different foci for the study of the same socio-cultural phenomena, such that the British developed *social* anthropology and the North Americans developed *cultural* anthropology, in effect the same discipline. Among others, Marxist theorists specifically rejected this dichotomy, pointing out that culture is not synonymous with the superstructive but the fruit of the socio-economic base, above all the means of production. In this sense, culture came to be regarded as the social heritage, a guide and a design for living derived from a storehouse of tradition, the source of basic cultural values whose cutting edges were the norms and sanctions of daily behavior. The "storage" aspect of culture, nevertheless, lends itself to a preservative conservatism on which ethnocentrism and ideocentrism breed. Even Western anthropologists—ardent students of exotic "other cultures" (rarely, until recently, their own)—have been guilty of serial (or secondary) ethnocentrism, i.e., interpreting a people's culture through the eyes of the previous culture they studied.

Similarly, in the U.S. the melting-pot theory whereby it was thought that foreign immigrants were completely assimilated into the American way of life was falsely premised on the loss of the immigrant culture and the acquisition of a homogeneous, Anglo-based cultural tradition of the host country. The actual cultural pluralism of American society is testimony to the fact that cultures are adaptive, neither wholly preserving nor losing their social heritage, yet "coping" with the innovations required by a new cultural environment. Acculturation, in effect, is not an undirectional process; rather, it is a reciprocal interflow as a result of which new syncretic forms of culture are often produced, e.g., Afro-American "cults" such as *vodun* (more popularly, 'voodoo') in Haiti, *santeria* in Cuba, *caudonble* in Brazil, are actually new folk religions composed of a fusing of Roman Catholic beliefs about saints and West African pantheistic practices.

Bibliography: W. AVILA, "Toward a Theory of American Culture" in B. BERNARDI, ed., *The Concept and Dynamics of Culture.* (The Hague 1977). J. W. BENNETT, "Anticipation, Adaptation and the Concept of Culture in Anthropology," *Science* 192 n. 4242 (May 1976). B. BERNARDI, ed., *The Concept and Dynamics of Culture* (The Hague 1977). N. CHOMSKY, *Aspects of the Theory of Syntax* (Cambridge, Mass. 1965). M. H. FRIED, *The Evolution of Political Society: An Essay in Political Anthropology* (New York 1967). A. KROEBER and C. KLUCKHOLN, *Culture: A Critical Review of Concepts and Definitions* (Cambridge, Mass. 1952). E. B. TAYLOR, *Primitive Culture* 2 v. (London 1871; New York 1958). E. VERMEERSCH, "An Analysis of the Concept of Culture," in B. BERNARDI, ed., *The Concept and Dynamics of Culture* (The Hague 1977).

[M. KENNY]

CURIA, ROMAN

The Roman Curia, which exists to assist the pope in conducting the affairs of the universal Church (4:539),

has been reorganized by the apostolic constitution *Regimini Ecclesiae universae* (Aug. 15, 1967) and a number of subsequent documents. Divided into the Secretariat of State, Congregations, Tribunals, Secretariats, Commissions, and Offices, it is now organized as follows.

Secretariat of State. The Secretariat of State or Papal Secretariat has the task of immediately assisting the pope in governing the universal Church and in dealing with the Roman dicasteries. Within its competence are all matters entrusted to it by the pope and any matters that do not fall within the competence of other curial departments. In conjunction with the Council for the Public Affairs of the Church it supervises ecclesiastical dealings with civil governments. In the motu proprio *Quo aptius*, Feb. 27, 1973, Paul VI dissolved the Apostolic Chancery as a separate curial department and entrusted its functions to the Secretariat of State. Within the Secretariat there now exists a Chancery of Apostolic Letters charged with drafting such papal documents (4:946) as decretals, apostolic constitutions, apostolic briefs, and Latin letters. Also subordinate to the Secretariat is the General Statistics Office for the Church. The Secretariat exercises supervision over the government of Vatican City and the publication of the *Acta Apostolicae Sedis*.

The Council for the Public Affairs of the Church was formerly called the Sacred Congregation for Extraordinary Ecclesiastical Affairs. Its competence extends to all dealings between the Church and civil governments and therefore involves supervision of papal *legates. The Cardinal Prefect of the Council for the Public Affairs of the Church and the Papal Secretary of State are required to be the same person. The Secretariat of State and the Council for the Public Affairs of the Church jointly supervise the Pontifical Commission for Social Communications Media.

The Sacred Congregations. Equal juridically and exercising administrative power in the Church are the nine Sacred Congregations. Composed of cardinals and some diocesan bishops (motu proprio *Pro comperto sane*, Aug. 6, 1967), each congregation is presided over by a Cardinal Prefect, who is assisted by a Secretary and a Subsecretary, both selected by the pope.

The Sacred Congregation for the *Doctrine of the Faith was called the Holy Office until Dec. 7, 1965 (motu proprio *Integrae servandae*). It is charged with safeguarding Catholic faith and morals throughout the world. Among its functions are examining new doctrines and opinions, studying and, when necessary, reproving books sent for its examination, safeguarding the dignity of the Sacrament of Reconciliation, and processing petitions for dissolution of marriages in favor of the faith and petitions for laicization. The Congregation can employ either administrative or judicial procedure, as a given case requires. Attached to the Sacred Congregation for the Doctrine of the Faith are the *International Theological Commission, established *ad experimentum*, July 12, 1969, and the *Pontifical Biblical Commission, reorganized by *Sedula cura* June 27, 1971.

The Sacred Congregation for Oriental Churches was formerly called the Sacred Congregation for the Oriental Church. In addition to cardinals, patriarchs of the Oriental Churches, and major archbishops equivalent to patriarchs are members of this Congregation. The Congregation has as many offices as there are rites in the Oriental Churches in communion with Rome. Its competence extends to all questions which involve persons, things, or rites of the Oriental Churches. It includes a Special Commission for the Liturgy and the Pontifical Mission for Palestine.

The Sacred Congregation for Bishops was formerly called the Sacred Consistorial Congregation. Among its members ex officio are the cardinal Prefects of the Council for the Public Affairs of the Church, the Congregation for the Doctrine of the Faith, the Congregation for the Clergy, and the Congregation for Catholic Education. In places and for persons not subject to the Congregation for the Oriental Churches or the Congregation for the Evangelization of Peoples, and after consultation with the proper episcopal conferences, it creates, divides, or merges dioceses, ecclesiastical *provinces, and regions. It is also competent with respect to all questions dealing with bishops; and therefore has the responsibility of nominating bishops, apostolic administrators, and military vicars. To this Congregation are attached the Pontifical Commission for *Latin America and the Pontifical Commission for the Pastoral Care of Migrants and Tourists.

The Sacred Congregation for the Sacraments and Divine Worship has a more complicated history. *Regimini* established two congregations to deal with the Church's worship. The Sacred Congregation for the Discipline of the Sacraments was to deal with the discipline of the seven Sacraments in areas not touched by the Congregation for the Doctrine of the Faith (the doctrine on and the Sacrament of Reconciliation), the Sacred Congregation of Rites (rites and ceremonies for the celebration, administration, and reception of the Sacraments), and the Tribunals (the nullity of marriage). The Congregation of Rites was given competence in all areas directly touching the Roman and other Latin rites. It was to have two sections: a liturgical section to deal with the supervision of divine worship and a judicial section to deal with the canonization of saints. On May 8, 1969, the apostolic constitution *Sacra Rituum Congregatio* suppressed the 1967 Congregation of Rites and divided its work between two new Congregations: a Sacred Congregation for Divine Worship and a Sacred Congregation for the Causes of Saints. The Congregation for Divine Worship was competent in matters of worship, both liturgical and nonliturgical, under their ritual and pastoral aspects. It was charged with the preparation of liturgical texts, the revision of the calendar, and the interpretation of rubrics and liturgical books. On July 11, 1975, the apostolic constitution *Constans nobis* abolished both Congregations and merged their functions into a single Congregation for the Sacraments and Divine Worship, with two sections: one to deal with Sacraments, the other to deal with divine worship. The Congregation has two special Commissions. One of these processes petitions for dispensation from *ratum et non consummatum* marriages. The other handles cases involving doubts about the validity of Holy Orders.

The Sacred Congregation for the Causes of Saints became an independent Congregation on July 11, 1975. Its functions had hitherto been officially attached to the Congregation of Rites. The new Congregation deals with the Beatification of Servants of God, the Canonization of Saints, and the preservation of relics. The Congregation has three Offices. Its judicial Office processes petitions dealing with the causes of saints. The

Promotor General of the Faith has the task of upholding the law and of issuing observations or expositions or casting votes, as the law and the case requires. The third Office is a historical-hagiographical office. The Congregation for the Causes of Saints has its own Chancery.

The Sacred Congregation for the Clergy was originally called the Sacred Congregation of the Council. Its work is carried out in three Offices. The first Office promotes the spiritual, intellectual, and pastoral growth of the diocesan clergy. It supervises cathedral chapters, pastoral councils, and priests' senates. Through a special Council, it promotes the adequate distribution of clergy throughout the world. The second Office fosters the preaching of the Word of God and supervises the preparation of national and international cathechetical and pastoral directories. The third Office is concerned with the preservation and administration of the temporal goods of the Church. To the Sacred Congregation for the Clergy is attached an International Council for Catechesis.

The Sacred Congregation for Religious and Secular Institutes is divided into two sections. Its first Section deals with the affairs of religious institutes and societies of the common life (13:384) in the Latin rites. Its second Section supervises the activities of those *secular institutes. To this Congregation is attached a Council for the Relations between the Congregation and the International Unions of Superiors General.

The Sacred Congregation for the Evangelization of Peoples or the Propagation of the Faith was formerly known only by the latter title. Its competence extends to all missions established for the preaching of the Gospel throughout the world. In addition to the cardinals selected by the pope, the presiding officers of the *Secretariat for Promoting Christian Unity, the Secretariat for Non-Christians, and the Secretariat for Nonbelievers also are members of this Congregation. The Congregation has its own library and archives and is assisted by a number of commissions: for the theology, spirituality, and vitality of the missions; for the revision of various constitutions and rules governing religious institutes and seminaries under the direction of the Congregation; a pastoral commission for the study of principles and methods regarding the activity and cooperation of missionaries; a commission for catechists; a council of superiors general on the Pontifical Work of the Propagation of the Faith; a council of superiors general on the Pontifical Work of St. Peter the Apostle; a council of superiors general on the Pontifical Missionary Union; a supreme governing commission for the activities of these last three councils; and a council of superiors general for the Pontifical Work of the Holy Childhood.

The Sacred Congregation for Catholic Education was formerly the Sacred Congregation for Seminaries and Universities. Its scope includes supervision of the formation of priests and the scientific education of clerics and lay people in the faith. It is divided into three Offices. The first Office oversees the governance, discipline, and temporal administration of those seminaries not within the jurisdiction of the Congregation for the Evangelization of Peoples. The second Office supervises universities, faculties, and schools of higher studies which bear the name "Catholic" by right. The third Office cares for diocesan and parochial schools and all other Catholic schools below the rank of universities or faculties. The Congregation has a legal counsel attached to it as well as the Pontifical Office for Priestly Vocations.

Tribunals. There are three Tribunals in the Roman Curia.

The Supreme Tribunal of the Apostolic Signatura is composed of cardinals selected by the pope. A sort of Supreme Court for the Church, it has two sections. Its first Section deals with strictly judicial affairs. It oversees the administration of justice in the lower tribunals, resolves disputes about judicial competence, erects regional and interregional tribunals, hears cases involving accusations of nullity against Rotal proceedings, tries cases assigned to it by the pope, and enjoys the rights recognized by various concordats. Its second Section serves as an administrative court, resolving conflicts of competence among Roman dicasteries, dealing with questions about the exercise of administrative jurisdiction in the Church, and examining administrative questions referred to it by the pope or the congregations. The Signatura is governed by its own proper law.

The Sacred Roman *Rota, also governed by its own norms, has competence in all those areas specified in law (CIC cc. 1598, 1599, 1557. n2). It now also has jurisdiction over marriage cases between a Catholic and a non-Catholic or between two non-Catholics, whether baptized or not, whatever rite each party belongs to.

The Sacred Apostolic Penitentiary is presided over by the Cardinal Grand Penitentiary. The competence of this Tribunal embraces the whole of the internal forum. It grants favors, absolutions, dispensations, commutations, sanations, and condonations for the internal forum. Saving the competence of the Congregation for the Doctrine of the Faith on matters of doctrine, the Sacred Penitentiary is alone competent on questions concerning the granting and use of indulgences.

Secretariats. The three Secretariats are principally concerned with ecumenical affairs.

The Secretariat for Promoting Christian Unity fosters ecumenical activity among Christians. It has two Offices to deal with Oriental and Occidental issues, respectively. This Secretariat has adjoined to it the Pontifical Commission for *Religious Relations with Judaism, established Oct. 22, 1974.

The Secretariat for Non-Christians promotes dialogue with those non-Christian groups that nonetheless profess some religion. It also seeks to deepen Christians' understanding of non-Christian religions. A Commission for Religious Relations with Islam was established Oct. 22, 1974 (see ISLAMIC/ROMAN CATHOLIC DIALOGUE).

The Secretariat for Non-Believers was first established April 9, 1965 to study *atheism and to establish dialogue with those nonbelievers who were sincerely interested. After the Secretariats are the various commissions of the Curia, listed in a separate entry in this volume (see COMMISSIONS, PAPAL).

Offices. The final large grouping within the Curia is composed of the Offices. The Apostolic Camera administers the finances of the Curia and the temporal goods of the Holy See during a vacancy. Its presiding officer is the Cardinal Camerlengo. The Prefecture of the *Papal Household is in charge of the Apostolic Palace and arranges papal appointments. The Prefecture for the Economic Affairs of the Holy See, directed by a commission of three cardinals, supervises the

administration of the property of the Holy See. The Administration of the Patrimony of the Holy See has an Ordinary Section and an Extraordinary Section. Each handles the business committed to it, the latter receiving its instructions directly from the pope. The General Statistics Office of the Church, as noted, is under the direction of the Secretariat of State.

Bibliography: Pertinent documents, published in ActApS are the following: *Catholicam Christi Ecclesiam*, 59 (1967) 25–28; *Constans nobis*, 67 (1975) 417–420; *Integrae servandae*, 57 (1965) 952–955; *Pro comperto sane*, 59 (1967) 881–884; *Quo aptius*, 65 (1973) 113–116; *Regimini Ecclesiae universae*, 59 (1967) 885–928; *Regolamente generale della Curia Romana*, Feb. 2, 1968, 60 (1968) 129–176; *Sacra Rituum Congregatio*, 61 (1969) 297–305; *Sedula cura*, 63 (1971) 665–669; *Statuta "ad experimentum" Commissionis Theologicae*, 61 (1969) 540–541.

[J. G. JOHNSON]

CURSILLO MOVEMENT

The Cursillo Movement (4:548) is a movement of the Church in the area of the apostolate of the laity that has as its purpose the Christianization of the world through the apostolic action of Christian leaders in all the areas of human activity. The Movement's purpose is achieved by means of a strategy and a method.

The strategy involves seeking out (the precursillo stage) the key people in the different environments, converting them to a deeper relationship with God by having them accept their role as lay apostles (the 3-day exercise) and then linking them together for their mutual support and apostolic effectiveness (the postcursillo stage).

The weekend (*cursillo de cristianidad*) is an intensive experience in Christian community living centered on Christ and built around 15 talks (10 by laymen, 5 by priests), active participation in the discussions and related activities, the celebration of the Liturgy. The follow-up program focuses on small weekly reunions of three to five persons and larger group reunions, called *ultreyas*, in which participants share experiences and insights derived from their prayer life, study, and apostolic action.

The Movement operates within the framework of diocesan and parish pastoral plans, and functions autonomously in each diocese (120 in the U.S.) under the direction of the bishop. Responsibility for growth and effectiveness rests with a diocesan secretariat and a diocesan leaders' school, or both. By 1977, when Spain was celebrating the twenty-eighth anniversary of the first cursillo, the Movement was operative on five continents, in nearly fifty countries, with a total of 857 dioceses; there are two and one half million *cursillistas*, of whom nearly 500,000 are in the U.S.

Stability and acceptability of the Cursillo Movement by the hierarchy would not have been possible without its being accepted and encouraged by the Holy See. Paul VI was the first pope to speak about the Movement. In 1963, he named St. Paul its patron. Later in an allocution on May 28, 1966, on the occasion of the first World *Ultreya* in Rome, he noted that the Christian life contains many riches of which Christians are unaware and commended Cursillo for making it possible to recall these riches to a conscious level and its ability to enrich *cursillistas* with a *sensus ecclesiae*. He reminded the *cursillistas* that they should take the lead in renewing the world for Christ by implementing the documents of Vatican Council II.

The U.S. Movement is overseen by a national board of 24 priests and laity and Bishop Joseph Green of Adrian, Mich., who is National Episcopal Advisor to the Movement and the liaison with the National Conference of Catholic Bishops. A National Center is staffed and located in Dallas, Texas, and provides the local movements with Cursillo literature and educational material, including a monthly magazine, *Ultreya*.

The modern thrust of Cursillo in the U.S. is in terms of evangelization. It sees itself as an instrument of *evangelization for the Church in the world. The last two National Encounters (1973 and 1977) have focused on this theme and the challenge of meeting today's need for a Catholic laity that will respond individually and collectively to their vocation to be evangelizers in the world.   [G. P. HUGHES]

D

DANIÉLOU, JEAN

Theologian, patristics scholar, Jesuit, spiritual writer, bishop, and cardinal; b. May 14, 1905, Neuilly-sur-Seine near Paris; d. of a heart attack May 20, 1974 in Paris. His father, Charles Daniélou, was a deputy and minister during the Third Republic; his mother, Madeleine Clamorgan, was in her own right a woman of great spiritual and intellectual caliber. Jean Daniélou did his degree in letters at the Sorbonne, from which he graduated in 1927. He then proceeded to take up a brilliant career in Parisian literary life—for example, he did the Latin translation of Jean Cocteau's *Oedipus Rex*, written for Igor Stravinsky. On Nov. 20, 1929, he entered the novitiate of the Society of Jesus at Laval. He made his profession of vows Nov. 21 1931 and took his course of philosophy at Jersey (1931–34), he taught as the professor of rhetoric at the Collège St. Joseph in Poitiers (1934–36), and did theology at the theologate of Lyon-Fourvière (1936–39). There his mentors, Henri de Lubac and Hans Urs von Balthasar, started him in patristic studies. He was ordained to the priesthood Aug. 24, 1938. He pronounced his solemn vows in Paris, Feb. 2, 1946. The personal notes he made during this period and published as *Carnets spirituels* (1978) attest to the seriousness of his spiritual formation.

In 1941 P. Daniélou was assigned to Paris and there spent the rest of his life in intense activity as teacher, scholar of international repute, student chaplain, apostle among the intellectuals—who accepted him as one of their own—but also among all levels of people. Lastly, he became a defender of the faith in the crisis which engulfed the Church after Vatican Council II. In 1942 he published *Le Signe du Temple ou de la Présence de Dieu*. This is the small book which he always said contained the whole of his thought in embryonic form. Characteristic of the personality of its author, it shows a contemplative attitude, a taste for symbolic theology, a use of the exegetical methods of the Fathers, and a care to impart in a simple way to a vast public the riches of his spiritual life and scholarly work. Both a Hellenist and a religious, he devoted his doctoral dissertation to the spiritual doctrine of Gregory of Nyssa. This was defended successfully at the Institut Catholique in Paris (1943) and at the Sorbonne (1944). For the then-required second thesis at the Sorbonne he translated

Gregory of Nyssa's *Life of Moses* which formed later the first volume of *Sources Chrétiennes* (1944); the rapid development as well as the high scholarly quality of this collection owes much to the personal initiative of Jean Daniélou, who was its codirector with Henri de Lubac. In 1943 he became editor of *Études*. He became professor of the history of Christian origins in the faculty of theology at the Institut Catholique and was elected dean in 1961. From this chair, which he was to occupy until 1969, he formed generations of young priests, and exercised an undisputed leadership in the field of patristics.

His substantial professional achievement clearly opens several new areas. (1) Parallel to W. Volker and Hans Urs von Balthasar, he is the chief instrument of a return to St. Gregory of Nyssa. In addition to his thesis of 1944, *Platonisme et théologie mystique/Essai sur la doctrine spirituelle de Grégoire de Nysse*, he dedicated numerous articles to the subject. The most important ones are collected in *L'être et le temps chez Grégoire de Nysse* (1970). A contemplative himself, he especially studied mysticism and spiritual exegesis in Gregory. He published an anthology of these mystical texts called *La colombe et la ténèbre* (1967). As an intellectual sensitive to the problems raised by secular culture for the Christian, he set himself to study how Gregory reworked and Christianized the philosophical ideas of his day. (2) With H. de Lubac, he is the principal artisan of a rediscovery of patristic exegesis, which, like the liturgy to which it is closely bound, explores the symbolic dimension of Scripture in order to nourish the spiritual life. In particular he illumines the notion of typology which ties history and symbolism together in a specifically Christian way. Salvation history is marked by such interventions of God that the events of the Old Testament announce those of the New. They, in turn, are spread out across the ages of the Church in the sacramental and mystical life of each Christian in anticipation of full eschatological realization. Here his pertinent works, are: *Sacramentum futuri/Étude sur les origines de la typologie biblique* (1950); *Bible et liturgie; la théologie biblique des sacrements et des fêtes d'après les Pères de l'Église* (1951). (3) In his *Histoire des doctrines chrétiennes avant Nicée* (3v., *Théologie du judéo-christianisme*, 1958; *Méssage évangelique et culture hellénistique aux IIe et IIIe siècles*, 1961; and *Les origines du christianisme latin*, 1978), which is more than a history of dogma in the traditional sense, he sketches a history of Christian culture. He describes it in the light of the resources provided by the cultures surrounding it, then shows how Christian culture tests, purifies, or adopts these cultures, at times suffering the failures known as heresies. By gathering together disparate texts of the most archaic Christianity, apparently confusing in themselves, he provides the key by showing that an authentic faith expresses itself in the modality of Semitic thought. He became one of the most outstanding specialists of this rediscovered "Judaeo-Christianity." With the same care for cultural roots, yet always bearing in mind the uniqueness of the faith in order to appreciate it in its various embodiments, he dedicated a monograph to each of the two Alexandrians, *Origène* (1948) and *Philon d'Alexandrie* (1958), as well as the first part of one volume of his *Nouvelle histoire de l'Église* (1963). (4) Again, he enjoyed a notable role in the thought of his time by his critical work in *Bulletin d'histoire des origines chrétiennes*, marked by his powers of assimilation, perceptiveness, and insight. After 1946 it was published yearly, for a quarter of a century, by Daniélou, as *Recherches de Science Religieuse*.

Professionally, P. Daniélou was a historian of the early Church. However, both by family heritage and his own temperament, he was a man transformed by the zeal of the apostle, intellectually alive to every contemporary current of thought, and open to all manner of dialogue. Thus he was one of the chief inspirations behind the review *Dieu Vivant/Perspectives religieuses et philosophiques* (1945–55). In its pages there came together in a friendly milieu thinkers of every creed and philosophical persuasion. He was also much involved in the ecumenical encounter and formed lasting friendships with Orthodox Christians, Protestants (such as Oscar Cullmann), Anglicans (such as Dr. Cross) and with Jews (such as A. Chouraqui). But his own outlook was quite all-encompassing. The Cercle Saint-Jean-Baptiste was a group of young people cofounded by Daniélou with a view to the missionary vocation. He was their chaplain and he proposed to them, somewhat in the tradition of Monchanin and L. Massignon, to meet non-Christian cultures in a positive way. The aim was to form a Christianity not of individuals torn from their own culture and uprooted from their natural environment, but of Christians who were part and parcel of their actual culture, as was historically the case with the Semitic culture of the Judaeo-Christians and also that of the Graeco-Latins. He set to work to develop a theological vision flexible enough to embrace these principles, but especially to draw out all the implications related to Christian spirituality as he viewed it. The essential teaching which he gave to the Cercle Saint-Jean-Baptiste is contained in: *Le mystère du salut des nations* (1945); *Le mystère de l'Avent* (1948); *L'essai sur le mystère de l'histoire* (1953); *Les saints païens de l'Ancien Testament* (1956); *Jean-Baptiste témoin de l'Agneau* (1964); and *L'Église des apôtres* (1970). The members of the Cercle received a thorough theological and spiritual education from him. In an effort to free them from current exegetical vulgarizations, the following works emerged: *Au commencement* (1963); *Les évangiles de l'enfance* (1967); and *La résurrection* (1969). Two retreats given to the Cercle have also been published: *La Trinité et le mystère de l'existence* (1968), and *Contemplation et croissance de l'Église* (1977). They show us

the true stature of Daniélou as a spiritual theologian.

P. Daniélou exerted a great and lasting influence as chaplain to the Catholic students at the Sorbonne, and especially beginning in 1941 to the École Normale Supérieure where he ministered to the young women (at Sèvres). Out of this apostolate came *Dieu et nous* (1956) and *Approches du Christ* (1960). Up to the end of his life he kept himself in contact with the world of young people and, with calm judgment, responded to their needs, which he often anticipated. He was a man of public note, a speaker both warm and disciplined in his thought, sought after for lectures by parishes, varied Catholic groups, professional clubs, and the like, as well as for articles in the national press, and for radio and television broadcasts.

Farsightedly and very soon he saw the signs of the crisis of faith which arose in the Church and he sounded a cry of alarm in *Scandaleuse vérité* (1961). From that time on he set himself to show, without losing any of his supernatural optimism, the intellectual roots of the ambiguities of the moment and their inevitable developments—the rejection of realism, separation of religion and faith, loss of the sense of the sacred, and others. In 1962, he was called as a *peritus* to Vatican Council II by Pope John XXIII and worked on the Constitution *Gaudium et spes*. He was consecrated bishop in Paris on April 21, 1969 and created cardinal deacon by Paul VI during the consistory of April 28. He carried on with his work as professor and dean, and did not change his manner in the least. While keeping up his professional tasks, he increased the number of times he spoke out on issues of the day. Addressing both the French bishops and the public at large, he used the authority of his office to make the voice of fidelity to the Gospel heard. This fidelity had been weakened by the "reductionism" of the secularists and by those who, at least in practice, had often betrayed the Council. This struggle alienated him from the most influential part of the Catholic intelligentsia and clergy. His burning zeal expressed itself through his talent as a polemicist. He who in the past was an "avant-gardist" was rebuked for having gone over to the reactionary side. (One can only recall his article in *Études* in 1946, "Les orientations présentes de la pensée religieuse," which had provoked suspicion in Rome and unleashed the attacks of the ultra-conservatives against the "new theology," all of which amounted to a portent of the ensuing repression against even the most eminent Jesuits.) Though he rejected this charge, he could not allay the force of this hostility. He merely affirmed that, just as always, he was a free man and faithful to the Gospel, notwithstanding the pressure of factions and other schools of thought. Thus he courageously met unpopularity in the conviction that service to the Church and zeal for souls demanded it. Concerning this struggle see: *L'oraison, problème politique* (1965); *L'avenir de la religion* (1968); *Christianisme de masse ou d'élite* (1968); *Tests* (1968); *La foi de toujours et l'homme d'aujourd'hui* (1969); *Nouveaux tests* (1970); *La culture trahie par les siens* (1972); and *Pourquoi l'Église* (1972).

Bibliography: Autobiography, *Et qui est mon prochain?* (Paris 1974). A. Daniélou bibliography to 1968, D. VALENTINI, *La teologia della storia nel pensiero di J. Daniélou. Corona lateranensis* 20 (Rome 1970). His patristic writings, *Epektasis, Mélanges offerts au cardinal Jean Daniélou* (Paris 1972). Works on Judaeo-Christianity, *Recherches de science religieuse* 60 (1972) 11–18 (repr. *Judaeo-christianisme. Recherches historiques et théologiques offertes au cardinal Daniélou* (Paris 1972). A bibliography, exclusive of articles, M.-J. RONDEAU, ed., *Jean-Daniélou, 1905–1974* (Paris 1975). Studies, P. LEBEAU, *Jean Daniélou* (Paris 1967). M.-J. RONDEAU, ed., *Bulletin des Amis du cardinal Daniélou*, annual (1975–   ). On the cardinal's death, see Communio 2 (1975) 93–95; 317–319.

Works in English: *The Salvation of the Nations*, tr. A. BOUCHARD (London 1949); *Origen*, tr. W. MITCHELL (New York, 1955); *Bible and Liturgy* (Notre Dame, Ind. 1956); *God and Us*, tr. W. ROBERTS (London 1957); *The Lord of History* tr. N. ABERCROMBIE (Chicago 1958); *The Presence of God*, tr. W. ROBERTS, (Baltimore 1960); *From Shadows to Reality: Studies in the Biblical Typology of the Fathers*, tr. W. HIBBERD (Westminister, Md. 1960); *Christ and Us*, tr. W. ROBERTS (New York 1961); *The Scandal of the Truth*, tr. W. J. KERRIGAN (Baltimore 1962). *History of Early Christian Doctrines*, tr. J. A. BAKER: v. 1, *Theology of Jewish Christianity* (London and Chicago 1964); v. 2, *The Gospel Message and Hellenistic Culture* (London 1973); v. 3, *Origins of Latin Christianity* (London and Philadelphia 1977); *In the Beginning*, tr. J. L. RANDOLF (Baltimore 1965); *The Work of John the Baptist*, tr. J. A. HORN (Baltimore, 1966); *Prayer as a Political Problem*, tr. J. R. KIRWAN (New York 1967); *The Infancy Narratives*, tr. R. SHEED (New York 1968); *God's Life in Us* (Denville, N.J. 1969); *Why the Church?* tr. M. F. DE LANGE (Chicago 1975).

[M.-J. RONDEAU; B. VAN HOVE]

D'ARCY, MARTIN CYRIL

English Jesuit lecturer and author; b. Bath, 1888; d. London, Nov. 20, 1976. He was educated at Stonyhurst and joined the Society of Jesus in 1906. He read for a classical degree at Oxford (1912–16), took a double first in Mods and Greats, and subsequently won the John Locke Scholarship for his essay on Greek moral philosophy. He taught at Stonyhurst (1916–19), and was ordained in 1921. In 1923 he won the Green Moral Philosophy Prize at Oxford; later he went to Rome for a biennium in philosophy. From 1927 he was at Oxford as researcher and lecturer, then as Master of Campion Hall (1933). The new Campion Hall, designed at D'Arcy's instigation by his friend Sir Edward Lutyens, was opened in 1936. D'Arcy succeeded Fr. Cyril Martindale as the dominant Catholic radio speaker on BBC. During World War II he lectured in the U.S. and in Portugal at the request of the British government. In 1945 he was appointed provincial of the English Jesuits and took up residence at Farm Street, London, where he remained for the rest of his life. His term of office ended in 1950. In 1953 he lectured in the Far East (some of his works have been translated into Japanese) and from 1956 until the early 1970s lectured annually for some months in the U.S. In 1956 he was elected a Fellow of the Royal Society of Literature and in 1960 an honorary member of the American Academy of Arts and Sciences.

D'Arcy's outstanding books include: *The Mass and the Redemption* (1926); *Catholicism* (1927); *Christ as Priest and Redeemer* (1928); *The Spirit of Charity* (1929); *Thomas Aquinas* (1930); *Christ and the Modern Mind* (1930); *The Nature of Belief* (1931); *Mirage and Truth* (1935); *Death and Life* (1942); *The Mind and Heart of Love* (1945); *Communism and Christianity* (1956); *The Problem of Evil* (1957); *The Sense of History, Secular and Sacred* (1959); *No Absent God* (1962); *Facing God* (1966); *Facing the People* (1968); *Facing the Truth* (1969); and *Humanism and Christianity* (1971).

For his Jesuit students as later for all his brethren during his provincialate, D'Arcy stood as one opening broad horizons, in contrast with the narrow confines of strictly ecclesiastical study. He was never dogmatic, but brought to his different spheres of authority the willingness to listen and consult; he was unfailingly courteous

to the young, seeking their opinions without artificiality. He expected his men to live disciplined lives without coercive prescriptions, but his liberal ways tended to clash with the more definitive ways of Roman authorities. Moreover he was not a natural administrator and his fresh ideas at times outpaced their execution. His term as provincial was not a happy time for him. He was a man of deep spirituality and a discerning spiritual guide. He often worked far into the night and, for all his hospitality to others, his own tastes were frugal. He believed, however, in the Church's function as patron and trustee of artistic endeavor, as symbolized by the beautiful statue of St. Ignatius at Campion Hall and Eric Gill's masterly sculpture, oddly enough, of St. Martin.

Specialists are apt to say of D'Arcy that he was neither philosopher, theologian, nor historian; that he was at best a man of letters, with his rich and vivid (almost exhausting) prose, but not an original thinker. Certainly his books were full of other people's ideas and the search for "the mind of D'Arcy" could be strenuous. His originality lay, however, in his gift for integrating the beliefs and experiences of others into a new enlightenment, his refusal, as one critic put it, to leave them scattered on the ground for the birds to pick at. The essential D'Arcy appeared in *The Mind and Heart of Love* in which he sought a clue to the working of the human spirit in the duality running through creation and experience: the active and passive, egoism and sacrifice, the classical and the romantic, life and death, masculine and feminine, the dominant and the recessive, Eros and Agapē, the lion and the unicorn: *animus* the reason dominating passion, *anima* the great longing, the breakaway of desire from self. It is a book to change lives and has done so.

In *The Sense of History* D'Arcy rejected the cruder forms of the providential theory and did not attempt to verify the rise and fall of historic societies against theology. He argued, however, that out of God's Revelation and man's relation with God something could be garnered to illuminate man and his development through the ages, and to enlarge the vision of human effort and achievement. Bringing sacred and profane wisdom together, he saw human history working towards a communal fulfilment in Christ. His position was that Christians could see more in history than others and point to its destination. The historian or philosopher equipped with Christian insight could dig deeper into the evidence.

The response to D'Arcy varies as men and minds vary. For many his vision is totally unacceptable. For others the universality of his thinking offers a prophecy, a new reason for being, a preface to the theology of hope, the ground of dialogue for believer and humanist. Few who knew him will claim to have been completely untouched by his offering.

[H. KAY]

DEAD SEA SCROLLS

Since Fitzmyer's article in the *New Catholic Encyclopedia* (4:676) four more volumes of the series *Discoveries in the Judean Desert* (DiscJudDes), as well as separate editions of the Targum of Job from Cave 11 and the Enoch material from Cave 4 have appeared. Fitzmyer (1975) has recently published one of the most useful bibliographies and surveys of contents of the

Qumran documents including the texts found at Masada, Wadi Murabbaʿat, Naḥal Hever, Naḥal Ṣeʾelim, Naḥal Mishmar, and Ḥirbet Mird. His work is welcome since to date most of the Qumran material, preliminary descriptions and evaluations, must be studied from scattered periodical articles.

General Survey. The scrolls of the 11 Caves at Qumran formed in antiquity a single library belonging to a single sect, the Essenes. With the exception of the Copper Scroll (3Q15), the Qumran literature is religious in nature, even the astrological and calendaric materials. From the Hebrew canon of the OT, only the Book of Esther has still not been found and in this case it well may be that the book was avoided rather than simply not known. Most of the Apocrypha are not represented, but Cave 4 yielded four Aramaic MSS and one Hebrew MS of the Book of Tobit, supporting the long text of the Greek Sinaiticus and the Old Latin translations. Also well known at Qumran was the Book of Sirach (Ecclesiasticus). The Qumran group also had 10 copies of the various sections of Enoch in Aramaic (without the Parables) and 11 copies of the *Book of Jubilees* in Hebrew. Then there are 3 MSS of the *Testament of Levi* in Aramaic and one of the Hebrew *Testament of Nephthali*. In one scholar's judgment: "the Qumran library gives the impression of a certain selectivity, but hardly of any fine distinction between a closed canon and all other texts" (Skehan).

Of the documents from the "minor caves," Caves 2, 3, 5–10 published by Milik in DiscJudDes 3 (1962), the Copper Scroll (3Q15), dated *c.* 100 A.D., written outside Qumran in proto-Mishnaic Hebrew and telling of treasure buried around Jerusalem and Jericho, has attracted the most scholarly and nonscholarly comment. There are two main views on the immense hoard of treasure described: one that what is being described is either the actual wealth of the community (Dupont-Sommer) or that of the Jerusalem temple, hidden before or during the early siege of the city by the Romans (Rabin, Allegro); the other that 3Q15 is a type of fabulous literature, a fictional account of hidden treasure (Milik).

In 1974, the papyrologist J. O'Callaghan claimed that the tiny papyrus fragments 7Q3–18 were actually portions of NT writings (Mark, Acts, Rom, 1 Tm, Jas, 2 Pt). Most scholars have received his claims with extreme skepticism, but the issue he raised cannot simply be dismissed, although it seems most likely that these fragments are nothing more than copies of some old Greek translation of the OT.

Cave 4. The main library or the principal hiding place for the community's library at the approach of the Roman forces was Cave 4. It has yielded the most significant MSS lode: the oldest known copies of the Hebrew Bible dating back to the 3d cent. B.C.; fragments of important apocrypha preserved in later traditions; and fragments of hundreds of MSS throwing light on the beliefs and practises of the Qumran community, including copies found in Cave 1 of sectarian works. J. Allegro (1968) with the collaboration of A. A. Anderson edited the first definitive collection of fragments from Cave 4. Unfortunately, this publication must be used with caution since some fragments have not been properly identified or joined, many readings are questionable, and the numbering of the plates is confusing. Its contents are mostly exegetical para-

phrases and observations concerning individual books of the Bible (Gn, Ex, Is, Hos, Mi, Na, Zeph, Ps) or selected portions (*florilegia, testimonia*). 4Q175 (also known as 4Q *Testimonia*), dated between 100–75 B.C., is a series of biblical citations given one after another: Dt 5.28–29; Ex 20.21 (wrongly identified by Allegro as Dt 18.18–19); Nm 24.15–17; Dt 33.8–11, Jos 6.6 accompanied by a pesher taken from *The Psalms of Joshua*, a hitherto unknown work, which condemns the man of Belial and his brother. The ordering of the quotations in this MS is determined by the normal biblical order of the books. The work is not clearly a collection of messianic *testimonia* as formerly thought, since the basic theme seems more eschatological, stressing the destruction of those who do not accept the teaching of the messianic figures of the sect. Another MS from Cave 4 that has attracted attention is 4Q174 (4Q *Florilegium*) dated between 1–50 A.D., a pesher explaining three principal biblical passages (2 Sm 7.10–14; Ps 1.1; Ps 2.1) with other biblical passages cited as an aid to interpreting these principal passages. The work is not a collection of *testimonia* referring to the last days, as Allegro claims, but rather a pesher on the first lines of a series of Psalms with the passage from 2 Sm serving as an introduction glorifying David, who is thought of as the author of the Psalter. More biblical and nonbiblical MSS from Cave 4 are now available to the scholarly world through the careful editing work of R. De Vaux and J. Milik (1977).

Prior to its discovery in Cave 4, the apocryphal Enoch literature was known only in ancient translations. Now a good part of that literature has been published by J. T. Milik (1976). Fragments of this original, Aramaic–Enoch literature have also been recovered from Caves 1, 2, and 6, but the most significant material comes from Cave 4. Cave 4 has yielded seven fragmentary MSS (4QEn^{a-g}) dating from the first half of the 2d cent. to the last third of the first cent. B.C. These seven fragments preserve parts of the Book of Watchers, the Book of Dreams, and the Epistle of Enoch. Four other fragmentary MSS (4QEnAstr^{a-d}), dating from the end of the 3d cent. B.C. to the early years of the first cent. A.D., preserve a form of the Astronomical Book, greatly expanded beyond what is known of its counterpart in 1 Enoch. This work in reality formed a distinct piece of literature in antiquity and was copied in independent scrolls. It was also realized subsequently that at least two of these MSS (4QEn^c and probably 4QEn^e 2–3) contained part of another Enoch-related work, the Book of Giants, which exists in other fragmentary texts from the same cave (4QEnGiants^{a-e}?). This book has also been found to be represented among previously unidentified or misidentified fragments from other caves that had already been published in DiscJudDes 1 and 3 (two from Cave 1, 1Q23 and 24; one from Cave 2, 2Q26/1 and one from Cave 6, 6Q8). What is significant is that five parts of the Enoch literature are preserved in the Qumran fragments: The Astronomical Book; The Book of Watchers; The Book of Giants; The Book of Dreams; and The Epistle of Enoch. Significantly absent and in the past important for some NT scholars' speculations on the origins of the Son of Man title is The Book of Parables. Furthermore, the Qumran Enoch material preserves a form of that literature more elaborate and older than that known from 1 Enoch; it represents the Books of Enoch known to Palestinian

Jews of the pre-Christian and early Christian periods.

Cave 11: Psalm Scrolls. J. A. Sanders (1965) edited the definitive edition of a Psalm scroll from Cave 11 (11QPs^a) which dates from the first cent. A.D. Its special interest is to be found in the non-Psalm material that it combines with 41 of the canonical Psalms beginning with Ps 101, including two distinct compositions that have elsewhere been merged into the apocryphal Ps 151 preserved in the LXX. Also contained in 11QPs^a are Sir 51.13–30 and 2 Sm 7.23ff; two hymns known earlier from Syriac sources and now labeled Ps 154–155; three other previously unknown Psalmlike texts; and a curious prose passage crediting David with 4050 poetic works. Though the compiler's arrangement of the Psalms is different, there are slight indications that of these materials he knew the canonical order of the Psalms. A Psalmlike "Apostrophe to Zion" also found in 11QPs^a has been identified by J. Starcky as one of three nonbiblical pieces in 4QPs^f along with at least 3 canonical Psalms. In addition to the Psalm scroll edited by Sanders, Cave 11 has yielded two other Psalm scrolls (11QPs^b; 11QPsAp^a) described by J. van der Ploeg (1965; 1967), as well as a part of Lv in paleo-Hebrew script (11QLv) and a poorly preserved copy of Ez in a Hebrew text close to the Masoretic.

Cave 11: Job Targum. Years of study will be demanded before the full importance of the Aramaic targum of Job from Cave 11 for a better comprehension of the difficult Hebrew text of Job can be realized. Edited by J. van der Ploeg and A. S. van der Woude (1971), the targum contains less than one-sixth of the canonical text. Though the fragments range from Job 17.14–42.11, it is only from 37.10 on that the text is substantially intact—happily the most important part of Job. In the main, the targum is a rather literal translation of the Hebrew, but the places where it paraphrases or adds phrases are often enough those where the Hebrew text itself is suspect or scarcely intelligible. Dated from the first cent. A.D., the Cave 11 copy of the targum displays nothing that is clearly sectarian and hence the question has been raised as to whether such a text might not have been composed outside the community. If this were so, then the language used might represent a type of Aramaic employed on a wider scale than in the Essene community of Qumran where postbiblical Hebrew was used for most of the sectarian writings.

Cave 11: Melchisedek. A. S. van der Woude (1965) published a group of 13 small fragments from Cave 11 (11QMelch) which contain a number of phrases revealing new facets of the Melchisedek legend in Palestinian Judaism of the first cent. A.D. Van der Woude views the Hebrew text as an eschatological midrash on Lv 25 and other OT texts in which Melchisedek, now a heavenly being above the angels and possibly identified with the archangel Michael, is to be the deliverer of divine judgment in the last year of Jubilee, perhaps on the Day of Atonement. The associations made make the comparisons in the Epistle to the Hebrews between Jesus and Melchisedek all the more intelligible. While a direct influence of the midrash on Heb 7 is ruled out, since the latter is developed in terms of Gn 14 and Ps 110, still this text makes it understandable how the author of Hebrews could argue for the superiority of Christ the high priest over the levitical priesthood by appeal to such a figure.

Cave 11: Temple Scroll. Acquired in the summer of 1967 during the Six-Day War by Yigael Yadin (1967), the Temple Scroll from Cave 11 (11Q"TempleScroll") is the longest of the Qumran MSS, containing parts of 56 columns and measuring over twenty-eight feet. Distinctive in its contents, the scroll is concerned with four groups of subjects: (1) a large collection of Halakhoth or religious rules on such subjects as ritual cleanliness; (2) an enumeration of the required sacrifices and offerings according to the festivals; (3) detailed prescriptions for the building of the Temple, with specific measurements of the courts and technical notes on the sacrificial machinery and procedure to be followed during festivals; (4) statutes concerning the king, his bodyguard, and the mobilization plans to be adopted in the event of attack. The scribe as well as the author of the scroll seem to have been members of the Essene sect, because the special Qumran calendar is followed. Yadin cites as one of the strangest aspects of the scroll the author's belief that this work was a divine decree given by God, a Torah. This document promises to be most useful as a source of comparison of specific laws and customs of the sect with those of the biblical text.

This survey has touched upon the major publications of the last fifteen years. For many of the other scrolls not yet definitively published, the reader is referred to Fitzmyer's bibliography.

Significance for the OT. Fitzmyer's evaluation that "the Qumran variants have the greatest effect on scholarly research into the history of the OT text" retains its validity, since as contrasted with the Masoretic and Samaritan texts known from the medieval period, and with the indirect evidence of the LXX, the Qumran MSS offer a sampling and a means of probing into the antecedents of these witnesses. As a case in point, F. M. Cross Jr. finds in the Qumran MSS of the Books of Samuel a chain of evidence for a distinctive Palestinian text type, the archetype of which he would place in the 5th cent. B.C. This line of transmission is witnessed to by the Chronicler (4th cent. B.C.), by 4QSam^b (3d cent. B.C.), by 4QSam^a jointly with the proto-Lucianic LXX (1st cent. B.C.), and finally by Josephus (1st cent. A.D.). Over against this early Palestinian text with its five centuries of traceable history, Cross sets a text that would have branched off as a local text in Egypt, not later than the 4th cent. B.C. From this Egyptian text is derived the old Greek translation preserved in the Codex Vaticanus as far as 2 Sm 11.1 inclusive. More sharply divergent from the Palestinian type is the first-cent. Greek text reflected in the proto-Theodotion materials. The Hebrew supposed in these materials may generally be labeled as proto-Masoretic, close to but not identical with that of the Masoretic text. As to where these Egyptian and proto-Masoretic texts originated, Cross refers them back to a local text preserved in Babylon, 4th–2d cent. B.C., and reintroduced into Jerusalem during the Hasmonean or Herodian period. In sum, the Qumran MSS have disclosed that even in the transmission of the Hebrew text, plurality preceded unity.

Significance for Christianity. The literature of the last fifteen years has established the importance of the Qumran MSS for understanding the organization and religious practises of early Christianity and such principal spokesmen as Paul and John. More recent studies, however, have shown the promise of the scrolls for a deeper understanding of the Christology of the NT. It has already been noted that the absence of the Parables of Enoch from the 4QEn^a–g material will necessitate a reworking of the antecedents of the "Son of Man" title as used of Jesus in the NT. On the other hand, the prominence of Melchisedek as a heavenly being in 4QMelch provides a better understanding of the comparison made in the Epistle to the Hebrews. Also the case for the Semitic origins of NT titles given to Jesus has been forwarded by materials from Qumran. The title "Lord" for God was not unthinkable in Semitic usage, since the absolute use of *mare* (Lord) as a title for God has been found in 11QtgJob. Another Qumran Aramaic text that bears on the titles of Jesus is a pseudo-Danielic text from Cave 4 (4QpsDanA^a) in which the title "Son of God" turns up for the first time in a Qumran text. The text is admittedly fragmentary, but no matter what interpretation of this eventually proves acceptable, there is no doubt that the Aramaic titles found therein as applied to some human being in the apocalyptic setting of this last third of the first-cent. B.C. text will have to be taken into account in future discussions of the title used of Jesus in the NT. While the evidence of the Qumran texts affecting NT Christology bears mainly on philological aspects of the study, these are basic and no theological constructs can be proposed that do not come to terms with this evidence.

Bibliography: J. FITZMYER, *The Dead Sea Scrolls. Major Publications and Tools for Study* (Missoula, Mont. 1975) for bibliography, including unedited materials from Qumran.

Texts: J. M. ALLEGRO, *Qumran Cave 4:I (4Q158–186)*, DiscJudDes 5 (1962). M. BAILLET, J. T. MILIK, and R. DE VAUX, *Les "Petites Grottes" de Qumrân*, DiscJudDes 3 (1962). J. T. MILIK, *The Books of Enoch: Aramaic Fragments of Qumran Cave 4* (Oxford 1976). J. P. M. VAN DER PLOEG, "Le psaume XCI dans une recension de Qumrân," RevBibl 72 (1965) 210–217; "Fragments d'un manuscrit de psaumes de Qumrân (11Q Ps^b)," ibid. 74 (1967) 408–412. J. P. M. VAN DER PLOEG and A. S. VAN DER WOUDE, *Le Targum de Job de la grotte XI de Qumrân* (Leiden 1971). J. A. SANDERS, *The Psalm Scroll of Qumran Cave 11*, DiscJudDes 4 (1965).

Preliminary Description of MSS: A. S. VAN DER WOUDE, "Melchisedek als himmlische Erlösersgestalt," *Old Testament Studies* 14 (1965) 354–373. Y. YADIN, "The Temple Scroll," *Biblical Archeologist* 30 (1967) 135–139.

Translations: G. VERMES, *The Dead Sea Scrolls in English* (Baltimore 1975).

Commentaries: J. A. FITZMYER, *The Genesis Apocryphon of Qumran Cave 1* (Rome 1971). J. SANDERS, *The Dead Sea Psalms Scroll* (Ithaca, N.Y. 1967). M. SOKOLOFF, *The Targum to Job from Qumran Cave XI* (Ramat-Gan, Israel 1974).

Studies, OT: F. M. CROSS and S. TALMON, eds., *Qumran and the History of the Biblical Text* (Cambridge 1975). J. MURPHY-O'CONNOR, "The Essenes and Their History," RevBibl 81 (1974) 215–244. P. W. SKEHAN, "Texts and Versions," *Jerome Biblical Commentary* (Englewood Cliffs, N.J. 1968) 69. G. VERMES, "The Impact of the Dead Sea Scrolls on Jewish Studies during the Last Twenty-Five Years," *Journal of Jewish Studies* 26 (1975) 1–14.

Studies, NT: M. BLACK, ed., *The Scrolls and Christianity* (London 1968). J. H. CHARLESWORTH, ed., *John and Qumran* (London 1972). J. FITZMYER, *Essays on the Semitic Background of the New Testament* (London 1971); "The Contribution of Qumran Aramaic to the Study of the New Testament," NTSt 20 (1974) 382–397. J. MURPHY-O'CONNOR, ed., *Paul and Qumran* (London 1968). G. VERMES, *Jesus the Jew* (London 1974).

[T. J. RYAN]

DEATH, THEOLOGY OF

Recent years have witnessed a marked growth in serious reflection on the topic of death (4:687) by theologians as well as social scientists and humanists. As Vatican Council II's Pastoral Constitution on the Church in the Modern World has noted, "it is in the face of death that the riddle of human existence grows most

acute. Not only is man tormented by pain and by the advancing deterioration of his body, but even more so by a dread of perpetual extinction" (*Gaudium et spes* 18). Death is indeed one of those perennial questions that must be confronted anew by each generation.

Some thinkers have suggested that conditions seemingly peculiar to modern society have made important changes in the present-day understanding of the meaning of death. Among such changed conditions are: (1) the fragmentation of the family and the impoverishment of communal relationships; (2) the growing impersonality of modern society, especially in its urban settings; (3) persistent stress on the individual (as autonomously free) rather than on society as the basic social unit; (4) the increasingly pluralistic and secular character of religious beliefs; (5) the deritualization of grief and mourning practices; (6) the high valuation placed on youth and the tendency to associate death primarily with old age; (7) a pronounced emphasis on and fascination with the future, which death interrupts and cancels out; and (8) recent achievements in biomedical technology which call into question the adequacy of traditional definitions of death. It is in dialogue with these kinds of developments that recent theological reflection on the topic of death has taken place.

Death and Man's Final Option. Out of a renewed appreciation of the dignity and freedom of man, several Catholic theologians (particularly L. Boros and R. Troisfontaines) have recently argued that death is not merely that which is passively endured, but is also that which man embraces as a free and conscious agent. Thus every person (even an infant) makes a definitive decision about his or her destiny in the instance of death. Such a theory, however, is not without difficulties. Theologians critical of this position (e.g., D. Dorr, M. J. O'Connell) argue that such a theory fails because not only does such a decision at the moment of death seem more angelic than human, but the theory also is confronted with a crucial and unresolvable dilemma. Either the moral choices and the free acts prior to death are truly determinative for the person vis-à-vis God (and thus the final option is not necessary) or else the option is necessary because the earlier choices are not truly significant (which throws into question the adequacy of life's meaning as constituted by its everyday acts and choices). However, these difficulties notwithstanding, it does seem possible to affirm that man can express and seal in his death that dedication and openness to God which characterized his life. To see this type of commitment expressed in a unique and exquisite way, the Church looks to the life and death of Jesus.

Death as the Destiny of Jesus. Certain strains of traditional Catholic theology used to insist that Jesus should not have died since he was without sin. Such a conception, however, is without foundation. Even granting that it was not necessary for Jesus to have died by crucifixion, death was necessarily and implicitly in Jesus' destiny simply because he was a man and shared in the limited and finite character of the human condition.

The understanding of death not simply as that which occurs just at the end of a person's life, but as something present from the very beginning as a constitutive element of that life makes it clear that death was for Jesus and is for mankind the only possibility, amid the relativities of a finite existence, for establishing in a permanent and absolute way the direction and quality of each person's life. Thus, as K. Rahner insists, "we cannot really say that Christ could have redeemed us through any other moral act than his death, even had God been disposed to accept some other act" (Rahner 71). These comments serve to bring into sharper focus what seems clear from the testimony of Scripture, the tradition of the Church Fathers, and the general teaching of the Church, namely, that, without prejudice to the importance of the resurrection, Jesus saved man by his death and not in any other way.

However, even in light of the above rather positive statements regarding man's ability to face death with equanimity and confidence, there is no denying that death is the ever-present abyss adjacent to man's existence—that which appears as the opaque, dark and empty end which marks the close of every human life. Viewed from its dark side—so disconcertingly familiar—death dramatically magnifies the true scope and risk of faith: a reliance on God when every reason for such a reliance is challenged at its deepest level. From such a perspective the resurrection of Jesus is seen for what it truly is: an act of God for which there is no logical reason, a mysterious and elusive basis for hope in what seems a clearly hopeless situation.

Bibliography: L. BOROS, *The Mystery of Death*, tr. G. BAINBRIDGE (New York 1965). H. M. CARGAS and A. WHITE, eds., *Death and Hope* (New York 1970). B. J. COLLOPY, "Theology and Death," ThSt 39 (1978) 22–54. M. MCC. GATCH, *Death: Meaning and Mortality in Christian Thought and Contemporary Culture* (New York 1969). K. RAHNER, *On the Theology of Death*, tr. C. H. HENKEY, *Quaestiones Disputatae* 2 (New York 1961). R. TROISFONTAINES, *I Do Not Die*, tr. F. E. ALBERT (New York 1963). J. WAGNER, ed., *Reforming the Rites of Death, Concilium* 32 (New York 1968).

[J. A. LA BARGE]

DEFERRARI, ROY J.

Classic scholar and educator at The Catholic University of America, 1918–67; b. Stoneham, Mass. June 1, 1890; d. Washington, D.C. Aug. 24, 1969. He graduated from Dartmouth in 1912, received his Ph.D. from Princeton in 1915, and was a faculty member there, 1915–18. After serving in the Army Air Service in World War I, he began his half-century of work at Catholic University. As professor of Greek and Latin he helped build his Department's reputation in patristics, and on the occasion of the University's reorganization in 1930 tributes from leading centers of Greek and Latin research in England, France, Germany, Italy, and the United States testified to the quality of the Department's recent publications.

From his early years at Catholic University Deferrari was increasingly recruited as a consultant on academic administration to dozens of colleges and universities, to many members of the American hierarchy, to major superiors of numerous religious congregations in North and South America, and the Far East. At one period a thousand schools, mostly Catholic, at all levels—primary, secondary, college, and university—were being helped by him through his chairmanship of Catholic University's Committee on Affiliation. Among his other extramural activities he served on the Managing Committee of the American School of Classical Studies in Rome, The Dean's Conference of the Association of American Universities, and the Executive Committee of the Middle States Association of Colleges and Secondary Schools. After the armistice with Japan in 1945 he was included by President Truman in a mission of college educators sent to advise General McArthur on educa-

tional problems. Deferrari was awarded 13 honorary degrees and was named a Knight of St. Sylvester by Pope John XXIII. In collaboration with colleagues and students at Catholic University he produced a number of indexes and concordances: a complete index of the *Summa theologiae* of St. Thomas Aquinas, 1956, A Concordance of Lucan, 1940, A Concordance of Ovid, 1939, A Concordance of Prudentius, 1932, A Concordance of Statius, 1943.

One of his less happy productions was a translation of Denzinger's *Enchiridion symbolorum, The sources of Catholic Dogma*. A review in *Theological Studies* 17 (1957) 280–288, earnestly recommended that the volume be recalled and the whole work redone under more careful supervision. He also edited the proceedings of workshops on college curricula, college administration, and the special problems of Catholic higher education. He also produced such widely used text books as *First Year Latin* (1967), *Second Year Latin* (1948), *Third Year Latin* (1950), *Fourth Year Latin* (1953).

His *Memoirs of the Catholic University of America 1918–1960* (St. Paul Editions, Boston 1962), contains in Appendix 4 his own bibliography, pp. 441–444. His autobiography, *A Layman in Catholic Education, His Life and Times*, (St. Paul Editions, Boston 1966) does not add much to The *Memoirs*. In the *Memoirs*, Cardinal Richard J. Cushing of Boston described Dr. Deferrari as realistic, competent, and respectful of tradition, yet ever ready to change in the light of the successive needs of the times. He was associated with the series, *The Fathers of the Church, A New Translation* from its first volume in 1947, and was instrumental in its transfer to The Catholic University of America Press. He was solely responsible for the translation of several volumes of the series, especially *St. Basil, Letters, Eusebius, Ecclesiastical History, St. Ambrose, Theological and Dogmatic Works, Orosius, Against the Pagans*.

[T. HALTON]

DEMYTHOLOGIZING

P. J. Cahill concluded the earlier article on demythologizing with the remark that more work by scholars is required in order to appreciate the analogous nature of human understanding and insight which makes myth a necessary mode in the complementary dialectic of human cognition (4:763). While it is undoubtedly true that Roman Catholic biblical theology will never entirely recognize its own concerns in R. *Bultmann's demythologization program, it is nonetheless true that Catholic exegesis shares his preoccupation to seek out and express adequately and effectively for modern men and women the data of faith contained in the Bible, especially the New Testament. In all candor, Bultmann himself would have agreed that "demythologizing" is an ugly mouthful, but yet it was his way of placing the problem of locating, understanding, and interpreting myth in the broad field of hermeneutics. In this sense, his two essays on demythologizing in 1941 were preliminary steps to the major problem, the problem of hermeneutics, and research in this area by Bultmann's pupils and others, which has taken several directions, is and will continue to be of utmost significance to Catholic theology. Further, modern studies in the field of depth psychology and the history of religions have brought about a far-reaching rehabilitation of myth. Myth is rather commonly regarded today by Catholic scholars as a distinct mode of knowledge that can never be adequately reduced to rational discourse and as a mode essential to religious expression. If religion is understood as a dialogue between God and man, and if Revelation is viewed as the total process by which God draws near to man and manifests his presence, then assuredly the possibility that the divine presence might be apprehended and registered in mythical thought and symbolism must be kept open.

Among Catholic biblical scholars the thought of Mircea Eliade and Paul Ricoeur on myth has been influential in recent years. Eliade describes myth as the narration of a sacred history, relating an event that took place in primordial time, the sacred time of the beginning. Myth narrates how through the deeds of supernatural beings a reality came into existence. Myth can be known, experienced, and lived by means of recitation and ritual. The myth is lived in the sense that one is seized by the sacred, exalting power of the events recollected or reenacted. The relevance of such a description for a deeper understanding of both the Jewish Passover and the Christian Eucharist has been grasped by Catholic biblical scholars.

In his work, Paul Ricoeur has analyzed the process whereby a primal experience finds a language, assembles that language into a myth, and subsequently generates reflection on the myth, which reflection, in turn, becomes a theology. Myth, secondary symbolism according to Ricoeur, emerges from primary symbolism and develops into an elaborate, tertiary symbolic system. In the NT are found the primary symbols of sin and redemption from sin. The NT theologies accept the myth of the rebellion of the primal man, Adam, as the narrative account of the origin of the primary symbol, "sin," and accept the symbol "sin" as corresponding to a fundamental aspect of reality experienced in the world (e.g. Rom 5.12). But there is also in the NT the corresponding primary symbol of redemption from sin (e.g. Rom 5.18–21), which is based upon the death of Jesus interpreted as redemption by means of the symbolic language deriving from the suffering servant passages in Is 53, and expressing the fundamental view of mankind's situation in the light of resurrection faith. From these examples it may be seen that the type of myth or mythical symbol that is the concern of the NT and scholars is the existential myth.

The existential myth or mythical symbol comes into existence so that mankind can live meaningfully in the tension of his unlimited desire to know, his orientation toward the transcendent, and his finite capacity both to know and to achieve. Against man's permanent horizon of mystery, transcendence and the unknown, mythical symbolism provides both a necessary and realistic orientation; it provides some realistic sense of balance in the tension at the heart of all human existence, and as such is permanently a legitimate vehicle of human meaning and cognition. The existential mythical symbol is found not only in the creation myth involving Adam and the vicarious redemption found in Second Isaiah, but is also biblically expressed in the concept of cosmic salvation found in the prologue of John's Gospel and in such similar NT hymms as Phil 2.6–11; Col 1.15–20; 1 Tm 3.16; Heb 1.2–5 and 1 Pt 3.18–22. And certainly the eschatological and apocalyptic presentation of both the OT and NT fulfill the criteria of existential mythical symbolism.

The most common function of the mythical symbol in the NT is that of interpreting history. In the crucifixion narrative for example, Mark presents details taken from Ps 69 and 22, which are concerned with the righteous sufferer and God's vindication of him: Mk 15.23, the offering of wine mingled with myrrh from Ps 69.21; 15.24, the dividing of the garments from Ps 22.18; and 15.29, the mocking from Ps 22.7. These narrative details are not true at the level of factual history but are included because the crucifixion of Jesus is interpreted by Mark as the death of the righteous sufferer whom God vindicated and hence as the fulfilment of Ps 69 and 22. In an interpreted sense, however, they are true and their use illustrates how the NT narrative through the mythical symbol interprets the event. In much of the NT history (*Historie*) is presented as historic (*Geschichte*), and that history as historic involves history as historical and the historical as interpreted by the mythical symbol.

Bibliography: R. BULTMANN, "The Primitive Christian Kerygma and the Historical Jesus," in C. BRAATEN and R. H. HARRISVILLE, eds., *The Historical Jesus and the Kerygmatic Christ* (Nashville 1964) 15–42. P. J. CAHILL, "Myth and Meaning," in J. W. FLANAGIN and A. W. ROBINSON, eds., *No Famine in the Land* (Missoula, Mont. 1975) 275–291. M. ELIADE, *The Quest: History and Meaning in Religion* (Chicago 1969); *Myth and Reality*, tr. W. R. TRASK (New York 1963). H. FRIES, *Bultmann, Barth, and Catholic Theology*, tr. L. SWIDLER (Pittsburgh 1967). B. J. F. LONERGAN, *Insight: A Study of Human Understanding* (London 1958). J. L. MCKENZIE, *Myths and Realities* (Milwaukee 1963). N. PERRIN, *The Promise of Bultmann* (Philadelphia 1969); *The New Testament: An Introduction* (New York 1974). P. RICOEUR, *The Symbolism of Evil*, tr. E. BUCHANAN (Boston 1969); *Freud and Philosophy: An Essay in Interpretation*, tr. D. SAVAGE (New Haven 1970). W. SCHMITHALS, *An Introduction to the Theology of Rudolph Bultmann* (Minneapolis 1968).

[T. J. RYAN]

DEVELOPING NATIONS

The wide gap between developed and developing nations received increasing attention in the forums of world opinion during the 1970s. Only a fifth of the world's people live in the industrial countries of North America, Western Europe, and Japan, but they receive nearly two-thirds of the world's total income. The majority of the world's people live in the developing nations of Latin America, Africa, and Asia. Three-quarters of them are illiterate and one-third suffer from malnutrition. One billion people earn less than one hundred dollars per year. This disparity between rich nations and poor nations raises fundamental questions of justice and equity.

Calls for Development. The developing nations have pressed these questions vigorously in recent years. Much of the global economic framework was established while many of the developing nations were still under the colonial yoke. Now that they have gained control over their political affairs, they have claimed a larger voice in economic affairs as well. The United Nations, which proclaimed the 1970s as the Second Development Decade, convened special sessions in 1974 and 1975 to consider these questions. Throughout these deliberations, the Group of 77, which actually numbers well over a hundred developing nations, has displayed a remarkable unanimity and new-found political strength. Even more significant has been the growing recognition among the developed nations that redress of inequities in the existing economic order not only serves the interest of the developing nations, but their own interest as well.

The Church's concern for this issue stems from its ministry to the world in promoting peace and justice.

One of the pronouncements of Vatican Council II, the Pastoral Constitution on the Church in the Modern World, affirms the Church's view toward assisting developing nations. The document, in discussing ways of building up the international community, identifies excessive economic inequalities as a source of injustice and dissension among men. The universal common good requires provision of such basic human necessities as food, health, education, and employment throughout the world. Such development depends on international cooperation to provide human and financial assistance. Norms for this cooperation include the developing nations' reliance primarily on their own efforts, the advanced nations' heavy obligation to help the developing peoples, the international community's coordination and stimulation of economic growth, and avoidance of solutions militating against man's spiritual nature and development. The Council's statement advocates international cooperation particularly in the investigation of the population problem. Since relief of world poverty is "the duty of the whole People of God," the Church must be present in the community of nations and Christians should cooperate in the work of international organizations (*Gaudium et spes* 83–90).

The role of international organizations has become increasingly prominent as events have shown that alleviation of world poverty depends on structural reforms of the international economic order. No longer can it be argued that economic growth by itself will eventually eliminate poverty. To the contrary, the gap between rich and poor has widened, and even in developing nations with high rates of growth the condition of the poor has deteriorated. Some Latin American countries in particular display conspicuously unequal income distribution patterns. Economic development in such cases has benefited large landowners and the urban middle class without providing additional economic opportunities for the growing numbers of rural poor. Developing nations as a whole seek institutional changes that will provide greater opportunities to share in the growth of world income (*see* LAND REFORM; WEALTH, DISTRIBUTION OF).

Economic Problems. The global distribution of income depends on the structure of international trade and the mechanism of international payments.

Payment Deficits. Developing economies usually have to import capital goods, technology, managerial skills, and energy supplies. The major exports of most developing nations, however, consist of only a few basic commodities. Thus the world market prices of these few exports largely determine whether the poor nations can buy the imports needed for development without incurring a balance of payments deficit. The prices of basic commodities, however, are notoriously unstable, and the weak bargaining position of most developing nations may place them at a further disadvantage when exchanging their products for the diverse output of the industrial countries. With the notable exception of petroleum, price increases for raw materials have usually caused buyers to turn to other suppliers or to find substitutes.

Because unstable export earnings can disrupt development planning and development aid has been inconsistent, many developing nations have relied on foreign loans to help finance needed imports. As a result they have accumulated substantial external debts which now impose further burdens on the balance of payments. For some developing countries, external debt servicing now exceeds 20 percent of export earnings. The credit worthiness of many developing nations is also limited by the fact that they were not present for the distribution of international reserves when the *International Monetary Fund (IMF) was established in 1944, and the allocation of Special Drawing Rights, which increased official reserves overall between 1970 and 1973, followed the existing distribution. Thus, the developing nations lack both a dependable income and a financial cushion. As a result, they tend to be especially vulnerable to international economic crises, which have occurred with unprecedented frequency since 1970. The skyrocketing price of energy, the worldwide shortage of food, and the devaluations of the dollar have exerted profound shocks on developing economies. Such circumstances have made it difficult to provide for present needs, let alone plan for future development.

The Multinationals. Development planners have also encountered conflicts with *multinational corporations, which provide the technology and managerial skills required to establish manufacturing industries. More often than not, multinational corporations with operations in developing nations have refrained from sharing technology and training natives for managerial positions (*see* TECHNOLOGY, TRANSFER OF). In the case of mining industries, conflicts over prices have led developing countries to nationalize the operations of foreign companies. While this assertion of permanent sovereignty over natural resources has distressed the industrial nations, it may discourage wasteful consumption of irreplaceable resources at the expense of future generations. Developing nations have also imposed restrictions encouraging multinational corporations to form joint ventures with local concerns and to concentrate on the development of export industries.

Marketing Competition. Even when developing nations have diversified their exports by developing manufacturing industries, they have not always been able to market these products. In the industrial countries, which constitute the only important market, producers have demanded protection from this new competition. In this way too, the fate of the developing nations depends on the policies of the developed nations.

Development Programs. All of these issues received mention in the Declaration on the Establishment of a *New International Economic Order, adopted by the United Nations General Assembly on May 1, 1974. Further deliberation of all of them has taken place both within the UN and in a variety of international conferences. The UN has established a Center for Transnational Corporations, which sponsors the exchange of information, and has given consideration to a proposed code of conduct for multinational corporations. The January 1976 Jamaica Conference on the reform of the international monetary system included the developing nations as equal partners and provided for an enlargement and a more frequent review of their IMF quotas, even though it did not stabilize exchange rates or link development assistance to Special Drawing Rights, as the developing nations had hoped.

In November 1974, the World Food Conference in Rome, where papal influence contributed significantly to the discussions, focused the world's attention on the problem of *world hunger. Although the developing countries have made great strides in increasing their agricultural output, these gains have been matched by population increases. In this situation too, there is an issue of distribution as well as growth. In the U.S. where most grain is converted to animal food, annual per capita consumption of grain is 1850 pounds, compared to 400 pounds in the developing nations. When the world food supply has dwindled, the rich have satisfied their wants by bidding up the price and excluding the poor from the market. The World Food Conference agreed that more equitable sharing was necessary and recommended at least ten million tons of grain per year in food aid to the developing nations.

The most extensive dialogue of all took place in Paris between December 1975 and June 1977, at the Conference on International Economic Cooperation. Although the Paris Conference dealt with the whole spectrum of issues involved in restructuring the international economic order, it produced relatively few concrete results. The Conference committed one billion dollars, with major shares contributed by the United States and the European Community, to a Special Action Program for the urgent needs of low income countries. The industrial countries also promised to increase their annual level of official development assistance, moving toward the UN target 0.7 percent of gross national product. The Conference agreed in principle to stabilize the export earnings by establishing a Common Fund to purchase buffer stocks of raw materials. Although the negotiations on implementing the Common Fund have since broken down, this proposal and the other issues raised at the Paris Conference are now on the international diplomatic agenda and cannot be avoided.

While this multilateral dialogue continues, individual nations and institutions have also acted to increase their assistance to developing nations. Several countries, notably Canada, Sweden, and the Netherlands, have cancelled the official debts of developing nations and pledged increases in development assistance. More debt cancellations are likely in the near future. The *World Bank has redirected its aid efforts toward meeting basic human needs by improving the productivity of small farms. International charitable relief organizations, including many church-affiliated groups, have cooperated effectively to provide more efficient relief services with their limited resources. Although the challenge of world poverty is enormous, these combined efforts from many quarters offer great hope of overcoming the challenge.

Bibliography: J. AMUZEGAR, "A Requiem for the North-South Conference," *Foreign Affairs* 56 (1977) 136–159. J. N. BHAGWATI, *The New International Economic Order* (Cambridge, Mass. 1977). R. BOSSON and B. VARON, *The Mining Industry and the Developing Countries* (New York 1977). MAHDUB UL HAQ, *The Poverty Curtain* (New York 1976). R. S. MCNAMARA, *One Hundred Countries, Two Billion People* (New York 1973). O. SCHACHTER, *Sharing the World's Resources* (New York 1977).

[R. J. GIBBONS]

DEVOTIONS, POPULAR

The term "devotion" here has two related meanings. (1) It means exercises of piety (*pia* or *sacra exercitia*): public prayers, worship services, or church ceremonies —but somehow other than the official church liturgy in the strictest sense. Thus, for example, the Way of the Cross is considered a popular devotion; but the veneration of the cross on Good Friday is part of the official liturgy. (2) "Devotion" is also the general term for

themes characteristic of some of these exercises of piety, even when these have been assumed into the official liturgy. Thus, for example, the devotion to the Sacred Heart of Jesus. These devotions are called "popular" for several reasons. (1) They were designed for and practiced by ordinary people in the Church, and not mainly by religious professionals. (2) At some periods in history they have appealed to a relatively large proportion of church members. (3) They are capable of communal celebration and were often so celebrated: they are the prayer of structured groups of Christians and not only of individuals.

Counter-Reformation Origins. There are phenomena analogous to popular devotions in some Eastern and Reformation Churches, and some of what later came to be considered popular devotions can be traced to origins in the medieval West. But the category of popular devotion is above all a creation of the Counter Reformation in the Latin West. Popular devotions arose as a consequence of the codification of the Roman liturgy following the Council of Trent. The limits and content of the official liturgy were quite precisely prescribed, with a twofold result. (1) The spontaneous evolution of the rites now for the first time defined as part of the official liturgy was almost completely stifled. Thus much of the creative response of the Counter-Reformation Church to the needs of its worshipers had to be embodied in forms which supplemented or paralleled the official liturgy, now regarded as a given and not to be tampered with. (2) In time specific papal authorization came to be considered an indispensable element in constituting a form of worship as part of the official liturgy. Popular devotions, no matter how expressive of the actual worshiping consciousness of the Christian people, had to be something other than—and in a legal sense less than—the official liturgy of the Church.

This left compilers and practitioners of the devotions relatively free from official control. But many of the devotions were forced to the edges of the central mysteries of Christian worship. And some of them were couched in a literary and conceptual style too tied to the religious fashions of the moment. Conversely the official liturgy tended to become more and more remote from the living religious consciousness of Catholic worshipers.

Devotions and Vatican II. Official Roman Catholic church discipline has maintained the distinction between popular devotions and the official liturgy. The Constitution on the Liturgy of Vatican II warmly recommends popular devotions that conform to church norms and laws; the devotions form part of the actual, though extraliturgical, spiritual life of the Church. They should in every way be oriented toward the official liturgy, which is said to be by its very nature superior to any of them. Devotions, especially those celebrated in common as part of the public life of the Church, should harmonize with the seasons of the liturgical year. They are in some way derived from the liturgy, and should in turn lead people to the liturgy (*Sacrosanctum Concilium* 13).

In fact, at least in the U.S., the devotions, while they are still important in the individual prayer lives of many Catholics, have almost disappeared from the public life of the Church. Probably the hardiest survivor, the Way of the Cross, has traditionally been celebrated publicly only during Lent, and thus thoroughly accords with the church year. And the actual celebration of the official

Liturgy of the Eucharist and other Sacraments has assumed many of the characteristics—like the use of the vernacular language, light music, and a generally more colloquial style—formerly associated almost exclusively with the popular devotions.

Liturgical Origins of Devotions. There is general agreement that most of the popular devotions can be traced to some kind of origin in the classical liturgy. The complete Rosary, for example, parallels the liturgical Psalter, with one Hail Mary for each of the 150 Psalms. Until about the middle of the 16th century, the devotions tended to be patterned directly on the existing liturgy. The Little Office of the Blessed Virgin Mary, for example, until very recently the most widely used nonclerical Liturgy of the Hours, follows quite exactly the shape of the canonical Office. There are the usual hours, each with its complement of Psalms and canticles, readings, hymns, and collects. But there is only one Office, to be repeated each day of the week. Probably the next most widely distributed medieval devotion, the Hours of the Cross or Passion, is composed as a commemoration (antiphon, versicle-response, collect) to be added to each hour of the canonical Office. The commemoration relates each hour of the occurring canonical Office with a time and an event in the history of the Passion.

After the middle of the 16th century, other forms began to appear. Generally they are an adaptation for communal recitation of a form of written meditation or reflection first designed for private and individual use. Probably even these more recent forms could be shown to have some connection, even if remote, with the classical liturgy.

The basic afternoon devotion in honor of the Blessed Sacrament, until recently so prominent in the public worship life of the American Church, began as a festive conclusion to the canonical hour of Vespers. In some places the final Marian antiphon (usually *Salve Regina*) was enriched with additional prayers and songs, called "Salve devotions." In other places the Blessed Sacrament was sometimes exposed at Vespers; Eucharistic songs were sung, and the people were blessed with the reserved Sacrament. These two traditions combined and the splendid result began to rival canonical Vespers in importance and came to be celebrated independently.

Richness of Continental Devotion Forms. The international treasury of popular devotions is very rich. In some countries the devotions formed a local, episcopally approved supplement to the Roman liturgy. Polish and Hungarian diocesan rituals, for example, provided additional services to fill out the Roman program for Holy Week and Easter. Before the reform of the official Roman services, at a time when the Easter Vigil, for example, was anticipated very early on Holy Saturday morning, these colorful, obvious, and well-timed vigils and processions were far more prominent in the popular mind and at the parochial level than the relatively opaque and difficult international services. From some points of view these local devotions were better vehicles of Christian worship than the adjacent rites in the Roman books. In some local Churches, most notably the dioceses of Germany, a complete cycle of popular devotions has grown up to parallel the Roman liturgy throughout the whole church year. The texts of these devotions, of a kind almost unknown in the U.S., are edited and printed with great care and have enjoyed the

most solemn episcopal approval. Local devotions of this sort, with deep roots in the traditions of a region or institute, are said by the Vatican II Constitution on the Liturgy to have a special dignity (ibid.). Postconciliar legislation directs that such devotions, provided they are in accord with the official liturgy and the liturgical seasons, are to be treated with reverence in the formation of the clergy (*Inter oecumenici* 17; see bibliog.).

The United States. American Catholics had to be satisfied with a plainer devotional diet. The Roman Catholic Church in the U.S. assumed much of its style from the Church in England and especially in Ireland. There during the Counter-Reformation centuries, when devotion-making flourished on the Continent, the public worship life of the Church had to be kept to the bare and unobtrusive minimum because of the English penal laws.

In America the principal devotion was to the Lord present in the reserved Sacrament. Exposition of and benediction with the Blessed Sacrament typically formed the celebrational context of other devotions. Whether directed to the Lord himself or to a saint, the devotional prayers were usually recited consciously and specifically in the presence of the Lord in the Blessed Sacrament; and most of the devotions concluded with Eucharistic benediction. In a typical American Roman Catholic parish in the second quarter of this century the regular round of public common worship consisted of Mass every morning, with some form of popular devotion for Sunday afternoon and perhaps one evening during the week. The Sunday service, which earlier American church legislation had determined ought ideally to have been canonical Vespers, might consist of a Holy Hour or the Rosary during the plain seasons, prayers to the Mother of God during May (with no reference to Eastertide) and October, to Saint Joseph during March (with no reference to Lent), and to the Sacred Heart of Jesus during June. The weeknight service was often an unchanging perennial novena. Benediction would inevitably conclude all of these services. Once a year the *Forty Hours Devotion, a three-day solemnity in honor of the Blessed Sacrament, would be observed. There was little tie-in to the official church year, though Lent was and is usually marked by the public celebration of the Way of the Cross.

In the U.S. the principal reason for the demise of the devotions, which were almost exclusively afternoon functions, was the rise of the evening Mass. Church legislation has constantly emphasized the importance of corporate prayer other than the Eucharist, usually in terms of a kind of Liturgy of the Hours pastorally unfeasible for non-professionals. But there is no popular theological conviction that would lead clergy and people to choose any nonsacramental (and thus seemingly somehow "non-effective") prayer service in preference to the Mass. Once it became possible and easy to celebrate afternoon and evening Masses, the afternoon and evening devotions disappeared from parish schedules. Other reasons for the extinction of the devotions were associated with socio-economic or ethnic groupings which were dissolving or at least becoming unfashionable. There was more competition for leisure time. The official services could incorporate many appealing features of the devotions. Finally, the widespread Catholic charismatic movement responds to the need for warmth of expression and religious experience that was formerly met almost exclusively—to speak of worship services—through the devotions.

The Values in Popular Devotions. The shortcomings of the popular devotions are obvious. It does not seem possible or desirable that the conventional devotional services of the recent past should regain their former prominence in American church life. On the other hand, they were an authentic expression of the prayer life of the Church. It is appropriate to suggest perennial values that devotions have and that should continue in future forms of prayer intended for ordinary people in the Church.

(1) Popular devotions represent the continuance in the Latin West of the *cathedral* style of public prayer—the style of common worship for ordinary Christians, as distinct from the *monastic* style—the style developed among religious professionals (clerics, monks, religious, laity with a special religious interest). The cathedral style of worship did not find a place in the post-Tridentine Roman Liturgy of the Hours, which is a thoroughly monastic prayer form. Since ordinary Christians could not accommodate themselves to the official Liturgy of the Hours, their style of public prayer had to appear in other less official and seemingly peripheral forms (see LITURGY OF THE HOURS [PASTORAL ADAPTATION AND CELEBRATION]). Though the devotions are legally less than liturgical, they embody a tradition of popular liturgical prayer that dates back to the patristic age and is a precious, if not essential, part of the patrimony of the praying Church.

(2) The devotions tend to be an expression of religious experience rather than a statement about religious experience. The deep-seated bias of the Roman liturgy is to conceive and experience public worship as a concise, abstract, external, and relatively superficial statement about the way things are between God and human beings. The devotions do not suffer from that impoverishment: they are an embodiment or a way of experiencing the relationship between God and his people.

(3) The devotions are conceived as a way of enabling the worshiper to do something rather than as a way of something being done to the worshiper. They are expression rather than education: they regard the Christian as a privileged person rather than as an object of instruction.

(4) The devotions, relative to the standard official liturgy of their time, are highly ceremonialized. They are thus simultaneously available to people of a wide range in age, educational background, and degree of religious interest.

(5) The devotions are almost unvarying in form and repetition of parts is frequent even within a given service. Though they are rightly criticized for not reflecting the seasons of the church year, the devotions bear witness to the principle—so fundamental in the tradition of individual, private prayer—that variety is not the spice of prayer. The devotions are a reminder that rhythm of public and private prayer is similar and that norms for the composition of public prayers are appropriately found within the experience of those who pray.

Bibliography: Congregation of Rites, *Inter oecumenici,* ActApS 56 (1964) 877–900; tr. *Instruction for the Proper Implementation of the Constitution on the Sacred Liturgy* (USCC Publ. Office, Washington, D.C.

1964). C. DEHNE, "Roman Catholic Popular Devotions," *Worship* 49 (1975) 446–460. This article includes a basic bibliography on the subject of popular devotions, esp. notable are the works on "cathedral" and "monastic" forms of liturgy, 447, note. Paul VI EvangNunt 48.

[C. DEHNE]

DIACONATE FOR WOMEN

The restoration of the permanent diaconate (16:123) authorized by Vatican Council II in the Dogmatic Constitution on the Church (*Lumen gentium* 29) and Pope Paul VI's subsequent 1967 motu proprio *Sacrum diaconatus ordinem* stimulated the already developing interest in women's fuller participation in the ministries of the Church. The next ten years witnessed an increase in studies on women's roles in ministry in the early history of the Church, pointing up the evidence for the existence of a female diaconate. On the basis of this research, the increasing participation of women in social, economic and political life, as well as the needs of ministry today, such groups as the International Association of Women Aspiring to the Presbyteral Ministry began more actively to pursue the extension of permanent diaconate programs to women. A request prepared under the auspices of this organization was submitted to the 1974 *Synod of Bishops. At the same time, in the light of the considerable development of ministry in which women are involved, others began to question the appropriateness of the restored diaconate to the emerging aspirations of women for ministry in the Church.

Church History. Research reveals that women played important roles in the growth of the early Church to which the Scriptures attest; that, while the office of deacon was not fully developed the word *diakonos* was applied to women, as for example, to Phoebe (Rom 16.1); that by the 3d century the office of deaconess clearly existed in the Syrian Church; that the office underwent expansion in the Eastern Churches from the 3d to the 12th centuries; that it was less well constituted in the Western Church, although women were in fact ordained to the diaconate in Lower Italy and Gaul; that the ministry of women deacons was primarily in service to other women, instructing them in preparation for Baptism, anointing and assisting them in the baptismal rite, visiting and caring for them when sick, ushering them into their places in the Christian assembly; that the order diminished as the Church lost its missionary character and the practice of adult Baptism diminished; that the order of diaconate became subsumed as a step toward priesthood.

Theology of Orders. Theological studies have clarified the relation of diaconate to priesthood pointing out that, while the major orders are conferred through sacramental ordination, not all major orders entail priesthood. *Lumen gentium* states clearly that hands are imposed upon deacons not unto the priesthood but unto a ministry of service (29). Within the official church teaching that priesthood cannot be extended to women it is still possible to take a positive position on the diaconate for women, as did Archbishop Thomas J. McDonough of Louisville in an archdiocesan communication, Dec. 9, 1976. Archbishop William Borders of Baltimore in a pastoral letter on "Installing Women in Church Ministries and Positions" (Aug. 19, 1977) noted that the 1977 *Declaration on the Question of the Admission of Women to the Ministerial Priesthood* (Origins 6

[1977] 517–524) had left open the possibility of admitting women to the diaconate. He observed pointedly, "Through the providence of God the diaconate was instituted to advance the mission of Christ in the service of the people of God. The providence of God is still with us."

Petition for Diaconate. The archbishop's pastoral letter is cited along with affirmations of the Catholic Theological Society of America, the Canon Law Society of American and the Catholic Biblical Association, to support a resolution approved by the *National Association of Permanent Diaconate Directors in February 1978. The members of this independent organization requested that the *Bishops' Committee on the Permanent Diaconate petition the NCCB to seek approval from Rome for the ordination of women to the permanent diaconate in the United States.

Yet while biblical and theological reexamination supports in theory the permanent diaconate as an option for women and an openness to the possibility is evident among some members of the hierarchy, many women have turned their interest from the permanent diaconate to priesthood. The national conference "Women in Future Priesthood Now—A Call for Action," held in Detroit, Nov. 28–30, 1975, may have been a definitive turning point. In the opinion of many who are concerned about the place of women in the Church anything short of priesthood for women is a compromise in an agenda that aims at official church acknowledgment of the full personhood of women and her corresponding participation in the mission of the Church.

Women's Diaconal Ministries. The aspirations of women toward priesthood stem from the involvement of many, both lay and religious, in work that is quite clearly *diaconal*. The degree to which women have contributed to the development of church ministries is impressive. The Congregation for the Evangelization of Peoples in *The Role of Women in Evangelization* takes note of some of the functions being performed by women religious in so-called missionary countries. The document cites that in the absence of a priest sisters preside over the liturgical assembly of the faithful on Sundays and weekdays, exhorting and instructing the faithful in their Christian duties; that the presence of the sister makes possible the reservation of the Blessed Sacrament, which she is able to distribute to the people; that in some cases bishops have authorized sisters to assume permanent charge of parishes; that they administer the Sacrament of Baptism and preside at marriages as the Church's official witness. Such responsibilities carried out by women are among those for which the permanent diaconate has been reconstituted (cf. *Lumen gentium* 29).

While what is called "missionary" endeavor may be viewed as presenting unusual circumstances, calling for extraordinary means to carry out the Church's mission, it is still notable that an official Vatican commission documents the fact that women function with ecclesiastical approval in performing services that are clearly those of the restored diaconate. This may well point to the fact that opening the permanent diaconate to women is a definite possibility in the near future. Some women would view this development as an important step forward for women in the Church. Others, however, would find it limiting and inadequate. For the latter the

expanding experience of women in ministry suggests whole new approaches to the concept and structure of diaconate. It also calls into question the official Church's views on women that prevents them from sharing fully in sacramental ministry.

See also WOMEN IN MINISTRY; WOMEN IN THE CHURCH.

Bibliography: R. H. ARTHUR, "The Diaconate for Women," *Sisters Today* 43 (1972) 490–496. W. D. BORDERS, "Installing Women in Church Ministries and Positions," Origins 7 (1977) 167–170. Congregation for the Evangelization of Peoples, *Role of Women in Evangelization*, Origins 5 (1976) 702–707. A. CUNNINGHAM, *The Role of Women in Ecclesial Ministry: Biblical and Patristic Foundations.* (Washington, D.C. 1976). R. GRYSON, *The Ministry of Women in the Early Church*, tr. J. LAPORTE and M. L. HALL (Collegeville, Minn. 1976). P. HÜNERMANN, "Conclusions Regarding the Female Diaconate," ThSt 36 (1975) 325–333. "Issues of the Permanent Diaconate," Origins 7 (1978) 624. J. A. KOMONCHAK, "Theological Questions on the Ordination of Women," in A. M. GARDINER, ed., *Women and Catholic Priesthood: An Expanded View* (New York 1976) 241–257. T. J. MCDONOUGH, "Toward Mutuality. The Evolving Role of Women in the Archdiocese of Louisville," Supplement to *The Record* (Archdiocesan newspaper) Dec. 9, 1976. P. F. MURPHY, "Women in Ministry, The Future Based on Present, New Experiences," Origins 7 (1977) 267–272.

[N. FOLEY]

DIOCESE (EPARCHY)

Vatican Council II's document on bishops describes the diocese (4:871) as a section of the People of God entrusted to a bishop to be guided by him with the assistance of his clergy and to be formed into one community (*Christus Dominus* 11). Since the bishop is to form his people into a community, he must work closely with the various cooperators who assist him in governing the diocese.

Because all the priests of the diocese form one presbyterate with the bishop and should work together with him, an assembly or senate of priests should be established to represent the priests in advising the bishop. Pope Paul VI, by his apostolic letter *Ecclesiae sanctae* Aug. 6, 1966, ordered that there should be established such a council of priests in every diocese. As representing the entire presbyterate of the diocese, it should include priests in different ministries, of different regions, and of various age groups; religious priests may also be included among the members. Questions of major moment should be considered by the council. The priests council ranks as the preeminent consultative body in the diocese. Where cathedral chapters or boards of consultors exist, however, they retain their own proper functions and competency until they are revised, (Paul VI EcclSanct 15–18).

In addition to the council of priests, the Decree on the Pastoral Office of Bishops recommends establishment in each diocese of a special *pastoral council in which clergy, religious, and laity specially chosen by the bishop may participate with a consultative voice. The function of the pastoral council should be "to investigate and to weigh matters which bear on pastoral activity" (*Christus Dominus* 27). In the section of *Ecclesiae sanctae* dealing with the missions, Paul VI recommended that the pastoral council "also contribute its services to the preparation of the diocesan synod" (Paul VI EcclSanct 20).

Bibliography: Bousc-O'Connor 6:264–298, esp. 271–277; O'Connor 7:383–390. J. BEYER, "De consilio presbyterii adnotationes," PeriodicaMorCanLitur 60 (1971) 29–101; "De consilio pastorali adnotationes," PeriodicaMorCanLitur 61 (1972) 31–46.

[G. P. GRAHAM]

DIOCESES, REVISION OF

In the Decree on the Pastoral Office of Bishops Vatican Council II taught that, for a diocese to fulfill its purpose, the nature of the Church should be evident in it, the bishop should be able to carry out his pastoral functions effectively in it, and the spiritual welfare of the people should be ministered to as well as possible (*Christus Dominus* 22). On the basis of these criteria, diocesan boundaries are to be revised where necessary. On Aug. 6, 1966 Pope Paul VI, in the apostolic letter *Ecclesiae sanctae*, required that each episcopal conference examine its existing territorial divisions. If necessary, special commissions should be set up for this work. Not only should the bishops of the province or region be consulted, but lay and ecclesiastical experts should also be heard. Any actual changes are to be made by the Holy See on the recommendation of the episcopal conference. The National Conference of Catholic Bishops (16:312) has a standing Committee on Boundaries of Dioceses and Provinces.

Bibliography: Bousc-O'Connor 6:271.

[G. P. GRAHAM]

DIPLOMACY, PAPAL

The international activity of the pope (the Holy See) finds official expression in: (1) diplomatic relations with states; (2) membership in specialized governmental organizations; and (3) participation in world conferences called for specific purposes.

As of 1978 approximately 85 governments maintained diplomatic relations with the Holy See; among the ambassadors were two women (Uganda and Zambia). On July 6, 1977, President Jimmy Carter announced he had asked David McLean Walters, of Miami, a lawyer, to act as his personal representative to the Vatican. Walters, the first Catholic to be chosen by a president for this mission, followed Ambassador Henry Cabot Lodge, who had represented Presidents Nixon and Ford. The White House stated that the presidential envoy "would visit the Vatican from time to time to exchange views on international and humanitarian subjects of common interest and concern." The new envoy had his first audience with Pope Paul VI on Oct. 6, 1977. A permanent office in Rome is headed by a Foreign Service officer. It has no diplomatic status. In 1978 Robert F. Wagner, former mayor of New York, was appointed presidential envoy.

Each year, in addition to the labors of the various governmental agencies of which it is a member, or to which it sends recognized Observers, the Holy See is invited to participate in conferences on special questions. Among the most important of such assemblies in recent years was the Helsinki "Conference on Security and European Cooperation" (July 1973), with its first sequel at Belgrade (October 1977). By this invitation and others in similar cases, the sponsoring governments recognized the contribution that the Holy See can legitimately make, within its own moral and religious sphere, towards the solution of problems of peace and development. From the viewpoint of the Holy See these general issues are closely linked to the specific concerns of the Catholic Church. At the Helsinki Conference and its sequel, the papal representative laid particular stress upon religious freedom and the right of peoples to free movement of ideas and fraternal exchanges for religious purposes (*see* BELGRADE CONFERENCE; DISARMAMENT; HELSINKI AGREEMENT).

It was held by the Holy See that the observation of these two rights would be powerful conducives to distension among nations. The policy of *détente* pursued by Pope Paul VI towards the Communist regimes of Eastern Europe, however, encountered severe criticism from such dissidents as Aleksandr Solzhenitzyn. The same criticisms came also from some Catholic circles, as the Holy See multiplied contacts and negotiations with the authorities of the Communist-style regimes. The scope of these papal efforts was to secure a relative normalization of church life and in particular the appointment of bishops to sees long vacant. The most sensational gesture was the removal by Pope Paul VI of the heroic exile, Cardinal József *Mindszenty from his post as archbishop of Esztergom and primate of Hungary (Feb. 5, 1973). This paved the way for the appointment of a new primate, Archbishop (now Cardinal) Lazlo Lekai, more acceptable to the Hungarian regime. Papal policy of distension in regard to Moscow was criticized by the Ukrainian (Eastern-rite) Catholics, who are headed by the exiled Archbishop of Lviv, Cardinal (and Major Archbishop) Josyf Slipyj, the burden of whose complaint was that the pope overlooks their sufferings at the hands of Moscow, in the quest of a problematical settlement with the Soviet leaders (*see* UKRAINIAN RITE).

The Holy See is likely to persevere along this line, despite criticisms, as long as hope remains of a peaceful negotiated accord. Some progress can be seen in Czechoslovakia, where Cardinal František Tomášek has been recognized as Archbishop of Prague. But important sees are still vacant in the Slovak region. In the Baltic countries, such as Lithuania, now incorporated in the Soviet Union, such important sees as Kaunas and Kaišydorys, remain vacant, visible signs of continuing trial for Catholics of the country. Pope Paul defended his policy of distension (*Ostpolitik*) in an address to the College of Cardinals, Dec. 22, 1977: "We would like to repeat, for the benefit of those who suffer, that our ear is not deaf nor is our heart—is it necessary to insist?—insensible to the cries and the calls for help that come from these quarters. It is our pledge to continue to do all in our power to come to their help, by the roads and in the ways possible, and that appear to us more opportune and efficacious. And we would like to hope that these efforts, united to all those who love the true good of peoples, will not remain without results" (Paul VI, 1977, 47–48). Earlier on the same recurrence Dec. 22, 1972, the Pope stated his confidence in divine providence and the power of the truth "to stabilize and to re-establish everywhere, despite obstacles arising from particular ideological systems or governments, a clear and honest relationship likely to guarantee to the Church a sufficient living space" (Paul VI, 1972, 25; ActApS 65 [1973] 25).

There are no diplomatic relations with Poland for the time being. On the other hand an exchange of envoys between Yugoslavia and the Holy See has existed since 1970. The Holy See has not recognized the State of Israel but this has not prevented papal audiences to two prime ministers (Golda Meir and Menachen Begin) under their official titles. In Italy, on Dec. 3, 1976, long-standing informal negotiations towards an agreed revision of the 1929 Church-State concordat (Lateran

Pact, 8:410) were formally authorized by the Italian Parliament. Negotiations are still (1978) in progress.

Bibliography: G. BENELLI, "The Church and Communism," Address (Catholic Truth Society: London 1976). H. CARDINALE, *The Holy See and the International Order* (Gerard Cross, Bucks, England 1976). U. A. FLORIDI, *Detente versus Dissent* (1976). J. MINDSZENTY, *Memoirs* (New York 1974). PAUL VI, "Address to the Sacred College of Cardinals," Dec. 22, 1972 ActApS 65 (1973) 19–26; Dec. 22, 1978, ActApS 70 (1978) 39–48. H.-J. STEHLE, *Eastern Politics of the Vatican, 1917–1978* (Athens, Ohio 1979). Diplomatic affairs are published in the annual, *L'Attività della Santa Sede* (Vatican City), in OssRom, and in the fortnightly *La Civiltà Cattolica*.

[R. GRAHAM]

DISARMAMENT

When Vatican Council II got under way in the Fall of 1962, neither nuclear armaments nor disarmament efforts nor other social problems were on its agenda. It became apparent during the first session, however, that many Council Fathers were convinced that the Church must come to grips, in the light of Gospel teaching, with contemporary questions that were being most urgently thrust upon her by the world. The principal debates on nuclear weapons and disarmament took place at the third session (November 1964) and the fourth session (October 1965) in connection with the Schema on the Church in the Modern World.

Council Decisions. Some Catholic pacifists hoped for an outright condemnation of nuclear weapons and nuclear deterrence policy by the Council or at the very least a stern criticism of states possessing "overkill" stockpiles, even if the consequences should prove disadvantageous to the security of the Western nations. But most of the members of the Council, while determined to demonstrate a strong Christian commitment to peace and abhorrence of nuclear war, recognized that there was a difference between what the Council might do ideally and what it could be expected to call for in light of practical considerations and of the limitations on governmental leaders' initiatives in view of the existing international situation.

Pope John XXIII's *Pacem in terris*, April 11, 1963, had a considerable impact upon the climate of opinion in which the subjects of nuclear weapons and disarmament were discussed by the Council. Only about twenty of the two thousand Fathers presented their views on these issues, but several of them spoke on behalf of other bishops and they raised important questions on: the morality of nuclear weapons; the possibility of employing them against military targets in a just war or of prohibiting their use under any circumstances; the validity or invalidity of the concept of nuclear deterrence (with precisions on possession of, intention to use, and preparations to use nuclear weapons, and on declaratory policies concerning and actual use of nuclear weapons); the relationship between Christian moral imperatives and the political-technical perspectives of the problems involved; and the terrible dilemmas often facing political leaders.

The bishops realized that they themselves were not experts on matters of nuclear weapons and strategy, and that they did not have available any invited *periti* to give advice in this complex field. Nevertheless they were appalled by the danger of nuclear cataclysm and by the tragic anomaly inherent in governmental policies of threatening to destroy civilization for the purpose of defending its values and preventing war. For the most part, the Fathers were also sympathetic to the plight of governmental leaders responsible for the security of their countries against unjust aggression in a world of value conflicts where there was no effective international organization for keeping the peace and protecting the rights of nations. The text of the final document, the Pastoral Constitution on the Church in the Modern World (79–82), reflected an intention not so much to denounce governments for pursuing security policies as to exhort them to move steadily toward improving the prospects for international peace. "Insofar as men are sinful, the threat of war hangs over them, and hang over them it will until the return of Christ. But to the extent that men vanquish sin by a union of love, they will vanquish violence as well" (*Gaudium et spes* 78).

Nuclear Weapons, Deterrence, and the Arms Race. Vatican Council II lamented the fact that modern science and technology have invested warfare with a savagery far surpassing that of previous ages and reiterated the traditional Catholic teaching that the human conscience is bound permanently even in matters of war by the principles of the universal natural law. Governmental officials and experts should strive therefore to make military activity and its consequences less rather than more inhuman. But the right of governments to invoke military force under any circumstances was not unequivocally condemned. "As long as the danger of war remains and there is no competent and sufficiently powerful authority at the international level, governments cannot be denied the right to legitimate defense once every means of peaceful settlement has been exhausted" (ibid. 79). Military action is justifiable for defense, but not to subjugate other nations.

The possession of military potential does not make every military or political use of it lawful. Weapons may not be used which involve massive destruction far exceeding the bounds of legitimate defense. The Council made its own the condemnations of total war pronounced by Popes Pius XII, John XXIII and Paul VI: "Any act of war aimed indiscriminately at the destruction of entire cities or of extensive areas along with their population is a crime against God and man himself" (ibid. 80).

An early draft of *Gaudium et spes* contained the following paragraph, which proved to be the most controversial one in the debate over nuclear weapons: "Although after all the aids for peaceful discussion have been exhausted, it may not be illicit, when one's rights have been unjustly hampered, to defend those rights against unjust aggression by violence and force, nevertheless the use of arms, especially nuclear weapons, whose effects are greater than can be imagined and therefore cannot reasonably be regulated by men, exceeds all just proportion and therefore must be judged before God and man as most wicked. Every honest effort, therefore, must be made, so that not only may nuclear warfare be solemnly proscribed by all nations and alliances as an enormous crime, but also so that nuclear arms or others of like destructive force may be utterly destroyed and banned" (*The New York Times*, December 10, 1964).

The Council, however, stopped short of condemning governmental policies of deterrence based on the possession and deployment of nuclear weapons. It recognized the possibility that states may amass such weapons with the intention not of carrying out but of dissuading a surprise attack through fear of retaliation. Interventions by some American, English, and West European bishops led to the following mitigation of language in the final document: "Hence this accumulation of arms, which increases each year, also serves, in a way heretofore unknown, as a deterrent to possible enemy attack. Many regard this state of affairs as the most effective way by which peace of a sort can be maintained between nations at the present time" (*Gaudium et spes* 81). The endorsement of deterrence, however, was a grudging one. The Council did not wish to condone the arms race as a safe way to preserve a steady and authentic peace. "Rather than being eliminated thereby, the causes of war threaten to grow gradually stronger." The era of mutual deterrence is merely "an interlude granted us from above" during which ways must be found to resolve disputes in a manner more worthy of human beings (ibid.).

Pope Paul VI, in his dramatic address to the UN General Assembly on October 4, 1965, during which he uttered his famous appeal—"Never again war!"—solemnly cautioned governments against the pitfalls which inhere in policies of deterrence based upon armaments competition. Nuclear arms, he said, "engender bad dreams, feed evil sentiments, create nightmares, hostilities, and dark resolutions even before they cause any victims and ruins.... They warp the outlook of nations. So long as man remains the weak, changeable and even wicked being that he so often shows himself to be, defensive arms will, alas, be necessary. But your courage and good qualities urge you on to a study of means that can guarantee the security of international life without any recourse to arms" (*Pope Speaks* 11 [1966] 54–55).

Pope Paul also subsequently warned that nations should not rely too long upon armaments competition as a peace-preserving method. The balance-of-terror formula "may indeed have certain practical, even if exclusively negative, advantages in the short run," he told the diplomatic corps, Jan. 11, 1975, "but it is too far removed from those moral values which alone make possible the development of peace," because it leads to a "ceaseless competition for equality and eventual superiority in military strength ...." Thus it is too weak a barrier against the strong temptation to gain predominance by violent means, and "may lead to dangerous miscalculations by those who are primarily interested in justified self-defense" (*Pope Speaks* 20 [1975] 73).

The Holy See presented to the UN General Assembly, May 7, 1976, a statement on disarmament in which the armaments race, even though motivated by a concern for legitimate defense, was unreservedly condemned. Such a race does not afford security, declared the Holy See, because at the nuclear level there is already a surplus of what is needed for deterrence, and the race introduces elements of instability which could upset the balance of terror, while the proliferation of traditional or conventional weapons through the arms trade creates regional imbalances which can generate new conflicts or aggravate existing ones. Reiterating an earlier statement of Cardinal Roy, President of the Pontifical Commission for Justice and Peace ("Reflections on '*Pacem in Terris*' after Ten Years, April 7, 1973," *Pope Speaks* 18 [1973] 9–39), the 1976 statement by the Holy See notes that the "armaments race has its own inner dynamism which is independent of any feelings of aggressiveness and which is escaping the power of the state to control it. It is a machine running mad" (*Pope Speaks* 22 [1976] 245).

Arms, Economics, and World Poverty. Within recent decades, the Catholic Church has been increasingly inclined to criticize arms expenditures of governments on the grounds that they constitute a diversion of scarce resources from more worthwhile human purposes. Thus the Council termed the arms race "an utterly treacherous trap for humanity, and one which injures the poor to an intolerable degree" (*Gaudium et spes* 81). Nearly a year before the Council came to a close, Pope Paul, speaking at the International Eucharistic Congress in Bombay, Dec. 4, 1964, had exhorted every nation to "contribute even a part of its expenditure for arms to a great world fund for the relief of the many problems of nutrition, clothing, shelter and medical care which affect so many peoples" (*Pope Speaks* 10 [1965] 152). In an address to the UN Food and Agriculture Organization (FAO), Nov. 16, 1970, the Pope lamented the wastefulness of war budgets, noting that nations devote fabulous sums to armaments and undertake costly technological ventures merely for the sake of prestige when the sums so squandered could save more than one country from poverty (*Pope Speaks* 15 [1970] 346–347). Speaking to the diplomatic corps, Jan. 10, 1972, he rejected as an un-Christian motivation the argument that arms production is needed to prevent mass unemployment, since there exist many other pent-up economic demands for constructive works to eliminate the scourges of hunger, ignorance, and disease (*Pope Speaks* 16 [1971] 309–311). The arms race, he told the 1974 Synod of Bishops, is a "costly madness for the world" (*Pope Speaks* 19 [1974] 218).

All of these themes were reiterated in the Holy See's Statement on Disarmament of 1976, in which the arms race was scored as an injustice and a form of theft: "The evident contradiction between the waste involved in the overproduction of the machinery of war and the vast number of unsatisfied vital needs (in the developing countries; in the poor and marginalized members of the prosperous societies) is already an act of aggression against those who are the victims.... This act of aggression is criminal: these weapons, even if never used, are, by their high cost, starving the poor to death" (*Pope Speaks* 22 [1976] 243–244). The Statement expressed confidence in the ability of industrial societies, given proper planning, to adjust from military to civilian employment without net increases in unemployment.

Disarmament and Arms-Control Negotiations. Vatican II did not call upon governments to disarm unilaterally but to work toward reciprocal disarmament "proceeding at an equal pace according to agreement, and backed up by authentic and workable safeguards" (*Gaudium et spes* 82). Pope Paul on subsequent occasions reiterated the call for negotiated, controlled disarmament, as he did in his letter to the UN Secretary General, Oct. 4, 1970, marking the 25th anniversary of the world body (*Pope Speaks* 15 [1970] 205–206). While never expecting any government to place itself in an unfair security position by disarming unilaterally, the Pope yet expressed the hope that governments will dare to take initiatives to break the vicious cycle of the arms race (address to the FAO already cited) and that policymakers will look upon their counterparts in other countries not as probable aggressors but as possible future collaborators, capable of doing good for the building of a more human world. (Address to the Diplomatic Corps, Jan. 10, 1972, *Pope Speaks* 16 [1971] 309–311).

Before the Vatican Council had begun, the Soviet Union and the United States had each submitted a proposal for general and complete disarmament (GCD) to the United Nations. But for a variety of reasons—not so much economic as political, technical and strategic—the superpowers had been unwilling or unable to make progress toward GCD. During the years of the Council, and partly because they recognized the dangers of their confrontation in the Cuban Missile Crisis, the superpowers shifted their diplomatic efforts to more modest arms-control measures, beginning with the Partial Nuclear Test Ban Treaty. This was followed by the Outer Space Treaty of 1967 and the Non-Proliferation Treaty of 1968. Speaking to the College of Cardinals on June 24, 1968, Pope Paul called the latter treaty "an indispensable first step toward further measures along the way to universal disarmament" (*Pope Speaks* 13 [1968] 217) despite numerous limitations that might keep some governments from giving it unconditional support. The Pope's *caveat* undoubtedly referred to objections that the treaty curbed "horizontal proliferation" (to additional States) but not "vertical proliferation" (by the nuclear-weapon powers), and discriminated against the civilian nuclear activities of non-nuclear-weapon States. Interested in exerting a constructive diplomatic presence on the arms-control scene, the Holy See acceded in 1966 to the Geneva Protocol Outlawing Gas and Bacteriological Warfare, in 1967 to the Outer Space Treaty, and in 1971 to the Non-Proliferation Treaty.

The American bishops in their Pastoral "Human Life in Our Day," Nov. 15, 1968, expressed concern lest the U.S. decision to deploy a "thin" antiballistic missile system be a prelude to the building of a "thick" ABM system, which might trigger an action-reaction process and upset the existing strategic balance. Four years later, in the SALT Accords signed in Moscow, the United States and the Soviet Union agreed to limit themselves to only a low level ABM capability. Subsequently the U.S. abandoned its ABM program entirely.

The Catholic Church, speaking through popes and diplomatic legates of the Holy See, the Pontifical Commission on World Justice and Peace and several national episcopal conferences, has increasingly criticized the arms race as unnecessary, unsafe, and unjust. Strategic theorists may contend that the "overkill" hypothesis is not relevant for analysis in a rapidly changing technological environment in which governments, in the absence of negotiated, symmetrical agreements, will inevitably seek security and equilibrium through the development of new weapons systems or qualitative improvements in existing ones. Economists may doubt that major budgetary savings, if they could be achieved in the military sector as a result of disarmament, would really be allocated to the worthy purposes which the Church advocates. But the Church disdains to enter into sophisticated theoretical disputes over strategy, politics, and economics. Without condemning governments for their legitimate worries about defense in a world that lacks an effective peace-keeping authority, the Church persistently warns the nations not to carry their security apprehensions so far as to fuel the military-technological competition to the point of madness. She urges governments to act in a manner designed to foster mutual trust, so that they may reduce the levels of their own suspicions, fears, and military expenditures, and—in both the industrially advanced and less developed nations—reallocate their resources to the alleviation of poverty and the promotion of genuine human development. Only by so urging, patiently and prudently, can the Church continue to bear witness to her divine mission and to the Christian humanist values of justice and peace.

[J. E. DOUGHERTY]

DISCIPLES OF CHRIST/ROMAN CATHOLIC DIALOGUE

Dialogue was proposed informally by Dr. George G. Beazley, President of the Council of Unity of the Christian Church/Disciples of Christ, and Mgr. (now Card.) William Baum, then Secretary of the Bishops' Committee for Ecumenical and Interreligious Affairs, in December 1966 and an initial meeting was held March 16–17, 1967 at Christian Theological Seminary in Indianapolis. Bilateral conversations continued in two series, covering in the first (Sept. 25, 1967–April 26, 1969) the nature of unity, the Eucharist, pastoral problems of intermarriage, and the ministry; and in the second (Nov. 3, 1970–June 28, 1972) the parish in the Consultation on Church Union (COCU) plan, Baptism and Confirmation, and postbaptismal sin and reconciliation. The conversations were abetted by the ecumenical mandate of Vatican Council II, the lack of any history of polemical encounter between Roman Catholics and Disciples, and the absence among Disciples of a dogmatic tradition framed in reaction to late medieval Catholic theology.

Several areas of broad agreement were identified. Both groups accept the authority of Scripture and share the conviction that the Church is intended by Jesus Christ to enjoy visible unity. For both Disciples and Roman Catholics, the Eucharist is the central and characteristic action of the Church. The belief that the Sacraments of Baptism and the Eucharist are efficacious as well as symbolic, normative in Roman Catholic sacramental theology, is widely held by Disciples.

At the conclusion of the second series of conversations "An Adventure in Understanding," a declaration summarizing the progress of the bilateral consultations, was published. This document, with the papers prepared by members of the conversations over a five-year period, provided the basis for joint action constituting the Disciples of Christ/Roman Catholic International Commission for Dialogue, which held its first meeting at Indianapolis, Sept. 22–27, 1977.

Bibliography: Documents, *Mid-Stream* 6 (Winter 1967) 50–66; 7 (Winter 1968); 12 (Winter–Summer 1972). G. G. BEAZLEY, JR., "Catholic/Disciple Bilateral Conversations: An Analysis of Agreements and Areas of Difference," *Mid-Stream* 12 (Winter–Summer 1972) 192–206; W. J. JARMAN and P. D. MORRIS, "Roman Catholic/Disciple Dialogue: An Adventure in Understanding," *Mid-Stream* 12 (Winter–Summer 1972) 5–15. P. D. MORRIS, "Disciples of Christ-Roman Catholic Dialogue," *New Catholic World* 220 (July–Aug. 1977) 196–201.

[J. PATRICK]

DISCIPLINE, ECCLESIASTICAL

Ecclesiastical discipline consists of the application of a set of practical rules, composed by the Church for the universal guidance of Christian behavior (4:895). These rules, as distinguished from dogmatic formulations, are embodied in articles of Canon Law. They include precepts, and sanctions, to guide the Church's theological, moral, social, and liturgical life. They are administered through the pastoral care of local diocesan bishops. Diocesan bishops share the one priesthood of Christ in collegial union with the pope in solicitude for the instruction and direction of the universal Church. Their brother priests, religious, and laity of the diocese share in the priesthood of Christ in their concern for the life of the Church.

Organized cooperation in church discipline is furthered through annual meetings of national episcopal conferences (16:157) and occasional universal councils of the Church, as well as through papally mandated *Synods of Bishops on specified topics. Since Vatican Council II (1963–65) emphases in ecclesiastical discipline are on pastoral approaches to promotion of the spiritual life of the Church rather than on legal approaches. Bishops are to prepare general directories for the people of their own dioceses suited to local conditions. As directed by the Decree on the Pastoral Office of Bishops, the present Code of Canon Law is being revised to support these emphases according to the principles given in the conciliar decree (*Christus Dominus* 44).

Present Discipline. As it affects the Latin Church the present discipline is basically embodied in the Code of Canon Law (*Codex iuris canonici*, CIC), which was promulgated in 1917 and became effective May 19, 1918. Since 1918, laws issued by the Holy See can be found in the *Acta Apostolicae Sedis*, its official organ for the promulgation and/or publication of decrees, decisions, pronouncements, encyclical letters, etc. (CIC c. 9). However, in addition to this official publication, private documents are sent to bishops and religious superiors in various countries. These are often reprinted in publications of a less official nature. The Bouscaren-O'Connor *Canon Law Digest* (since v. 7 continued by O'Connor alone) is one such publication that serves as a source for information on existing law.

Book One of the CIC, which contains the general principles of law, for the most part remains unchanged, as do certain precepts pertaining to temporal goods, marriage courts, and general concepts on crimes and penalties. Other precepts of the CIC technically remain in effect unless officially abrogated or derogated, but these are to be interpreted in the light of conciliar and post-conciliar documents. (See address of Cardinal Pericle Felici, Synod of Bishops, October 18, 1974, in the organ of the Commission for the Revision of the Code of Canon Law, *Communicationes* 6 [1974] 157). The 1918 CIC is not to be considered as the decisive expression of ecclesiastical law today, but it provides the basic standards for interpretation and the general context of any legislation.

Present Spirit. Christian life must have its sanctions, precepts, and normative directives. Only when these are rightly understood will they be regarded as essential to Christian living. These are to be directives of a way of life which love given by the Spirit prompts. As the Christian lives by faith and dependence upon fellow Christians it is important that the Father remind us by the Church's laws of all that life in the Church means. The conciliar Dogmatic Constitution on Divine Revela-

tion makes clear that the Church's doctrinal magisterium in exercising its office as teacher of the faithful "is not above the word of God, but serves it, teaching only what has been handed on, listening to it devoutly, guarding it scrupulously, and explaining it faithfully ... with the help of the Holy Spirit" (*Dei Verbum* 10).

The purpose of every law Christ enunciated was to secure man's perfect conformity with God's will. Vatican II brought into focus the "law of the Spirit" as a loving knowledge within the heart, enabling the Christian to know connaturally the Father's will, desire it, and carry it out (*Dei Verbum* 5). In God's plan Christians are to learn their dependence on the Spirit of Christ by experiencing a need for his divergent movement in other members of the community. Often individuals receive direction from the action of the Holy Spirit in another.

See also CODE OF CANON LAW, REVISION OF; JURISPRUDENCE, CANONICAL.

Bibliography: M. AHERN, "Law and the Gospel, " in J. E. BIECHLER, ed., *Law for Liberty* (Baltimore 1967) 93–108. N. EDELBY et al., eds., *Canon Law Postconciliar Thoughts: Renewal and Reform of Canon Law. Concilium* 28 (New York 1967). F. G. MORRISEY "The Role of Canon Law Today," ChSt 15 (1967) 236–253.

[M. M. MODDE]

DISPENSATIONS

With regard to dispensations from general laws as granted by diocesan bishops (4:905), Vatican Council II established the system of reservations to replace the system of asking the Holy See for *faculties. The diocesan bishop now can dispense his own faithful from a general law of the Church except when a reservation of the dispensation has been made by the Church's supreme authority. No longer must a bishop always rely on a faculty from the Holy See before he can dispense.

Source of the Bishop's Authority. According to Vatican II, bishops are endowed with a sacred power (*Lumen gentium* 18), received through episcopal consecration or ordination, which also confers the ministries of sanctifying, teaching, and governing (ibid 21). However, these ministries can be exercised only in hierarchical communion with the pope and the other members of the college of bishops (ibid. 21, 22). Once given the canonical mission of being the head of a diocese, usually directly by the pope (ibid. 24), as successors of the Apostles, bishops enjoy inherently (*per se*) all the ordinary, proper, and immediate power required for exercising their pastoral ministry (*Christus Dominus* 8 a).

Bishops govern their dioceses as Christ's vicars and legates and in his name. Yet their sacred power can be circumscribed within certain limits by the Church's supreme authority. They are not regarded as the pope's vicars, for the habitual, daily care of the faithful is entrusted completely to them. Nor can their sacred power be destroyed by the supreme and universal power, for the Holy Spirit unfailingly preserves the form of government established by Christ in his Church (*Lumen gentium* 27).

Dispensing Authority. According to Vatican II, for each diocesan bishop the faculty exists to dispense from a general law and in a particular case the faithful over whom he exercises authority according to the norm of law as often as he judges the dispensation to be for their spiritual welfare, unless a special reservation has been made by the Church's supreme authority (*Christus*

Dominus 8 b). The source for this dispensing authority is the bishop's sacred power, which he exercises fully once he is given his particular canonical mission. He is free to dispense from a general law, following the above conditions and as long as the Church's supreme authority has not in some way reserved the dispensation.

Implementation. *Christus Dominus* 8 b applies to the residential or diocesan bishop of the Latin Church and of the Eastern Churches. Paul VI interpreted and implemented *Christus Dominus* for the Latin Church in *De episcoporum muneribus* (June 15, 1966) and for the Eastern Churches in *Episcopalis potestatis* (May 2, 1967). With the exception of variations in the latter, these two apostolic letters parallel each other in their provisions.

In both documents, Paul VI defined various terms, the most important of which is *general laws of the Church*. These are disciplinary laws which *prescribe or prohibit* and are enacted by the Church's supreme authority to bind everywhere those for whom they are made. Beyond the scope of the bishop's dispensing authority are constitutive laws, procedural laws, permissions, indults, faculties, and absolutions. Divine law—natural and positive—is beyond this dispensing authority, for only the pope as Vicar of Christ can dispense from divine law. In *De episcoporum muneribus* and *Episcopalis potestatis* Paul VI reserved to himself the dispensation from a number of general laws, considered to be very seriously binding upon the faithful. It can be reasonably assumed that these are disciplinary laws which prescribe or prohibit.

Canon 81. *Christus Dominus* 8 b derogates or partially changes CIC c. 81 so that the diocesan bishop (the residential bishop and his equivalents in law) can dispense in a particular case when recourse to the Holy See is difficult, simultaneously grave harm in delay exists, and the dispensation is one from which the Holy See usually dispenses. The term "Ordinaries" in Canon 81 refers to diocesan bishops and major superiors of exempt clerical communities. *Christus Dominus* 8 b refers only to bishops of dioceses, while *De episcoporum muneribus* and *Episcopalis potestatis* extend the term "diocesan bishops" not only to residential bishops but also to others equated in law to them. None of the documents extends the dispensing authority to major superiors of exempt clerical communities; hence, c. 81 remains in full force in all its provisions for these major superiors.

Bibliography: T. BAUERFEIND, "The Source of the Bishop's Jurisdiction: A Historical Survey of Canonical Mission" (J.C.L. dissertation, The Catholic Univ. of America, 1971). J. BRYS, *De dispensatione in iure canonico* (Bruges 1925). L. CAPIELLO, *De ordinariorum dispensandi facultate ad normam canonis 81* (CUA CLS 323; Washington, D.C. 1952). S. KUBIK, *Invalidity of Dispensations according to Canon 84.1* (CUA CLS 340; Washington, D.C. 1953). R. RYAN, *The Authority of the Residential Bishop in the Latin Rite to Dispense from the General Laws of the Church* (CUA CLS 482; Washington, D.C. 1973).

[R. R. RYAN]

DIVORCED AND SEPARATED CATHOLICS

With a pastoral inventiveness characteristic of American Catholicism, a vital, growing ministry to and by divorced Catholics has been developing in recent years. Divorce among Catholics was a fairly rare phenomenon until the 1960s, but in that decade the divorce rates in the society as a whole began a sharp rise: By the mid-60s it was clear that Catholics were divorcing almost as much as the population at large and by the early 1970s some observers began to perceive that Catholics who had refrained from divorcing years before were now taking advantage of reduced social and religious barriers and choosing to divorce. The 1978 estimate is that there were at least 6 million ever-divorced Catholic persons in the U.S. and at least half of them were in second marriages. In 1977 more than one million American marriages ended in divorce for the third year in a row and Catholics made up at least 20 percent of that total. Demographers at the U.S. Census Bureau predicted that of all Americans currently marrying almost 40 percent would eventually divorce and that 80 percent of those would eventually remarry.

Ministry to the Divorced. Widespread divorce among Catholics posed difficult pastoral problems for the American Church. Besides taking a personal toll on the divorced and their families, it became a threat to a Church with a strong history of family and marital stability. Even though there had been several Catholic organizations for some years that provided spiritual support for divorced women (the Júdeans, the Fabiolas, and some retreat programs), contemporary divorce ministry began to develop fully in the early 1970s. In retrospect it is easy to understand why: divorce was beginning to touch almost every Catholic parish and almost every Catholic family and was raising confusing issues about the divorced person's place in the Church community. At the same time the helping professions were just beginning to examine the experience of divorced persons and for the first time to design special strategies for help through the traumatic transition.

The support group for men and women going through divorce formed at the Paulist Center in Boston in early 1972 became the model of the developing new ministry. The Paulist Center group positioned divorced persons themselves as the primary helpers of one another and proved that supportive community at the time of marital breakdown can help facilitate a good recovery. Annual conferences at the Boston Center in 1972, 1973, and 1974 attracted growing numbers of clergy, professionals, and divorced people. In 1975 with about 300 representatives present from twenty states and Canada, the North American Conference of Separated and Divorced Catholics (NACSDC) was formed to connect the mushrooming number of divorce groups.

NACSDC has become a clearinghouse for resources and materials on divorce ministry, provides education and lay leadership training, and publishes a quarterly newsletter, *Divorce*. It is structured with a board of divorced persons themselves representing the twelve USCC regions plus two Canadian regions. In July 1978 it held its eighth annual conference at the Univ. of Notre Dame, and regional conferences were held in seven of the U.S. regions and Canada. The Beginning Experience, a weekend recovery-model for divorced persons and widows, fashioned after Marriage Encounter by Sr. Josephine Stewert of Forth Worth, Texas, is now offering its program in 35 U.S. dioceses. This weekend model draws the recently divorced into divorce ministry, and then moves them into the continuing support groups.

Church Initiatives. The removal by Pope Paul VI in November 1977 of the automatic excommunication imposed in the U.S. on the divorced entering a second marriage was a major achievement for the divorced Catholics movement. This unfortunate law had helped create a negative climate in the American Catholic community towards the divorced and caused many of them to become alienated from the Church. Important efforts in a number of American dioceses have recently sought to reach out to the millions of disaffected divorced and divorced/remarried Catholics. The American procedural norms for the speedier processing of marriage annulments has created a dramatic upsurge in the number of annulments granted in the U.S. from about 700 in 1967 to almost 20,000 in 1977 (see MARRIAGE TRIBUNALS). Even though this canonical process has enabled thousands of second-marriage Catholics to have their new marriages accepted by the Church, it has barely touched the massive number of failed Catholic marriages. Where it is impossible to resolve a marital situation canonically, pastors are increasingly resorting to the approved means of the Church in the internal forum to reconcile many such Catholics. The patient work of many canonists, theologians, and pastors has prepared the way for this growing process of reconciliation to the Eucharist underway in the American Church (see MARRIAGE [CANON LAW]).

The NCCB issued in 1978 a Pastoral Plan on the Family which called for the development of divorced Catholics ministry in every diocese and commended the unique ministry of divorced Catholics to each other. At least eight U.S. dioceses now have full-time staff persons directing this ministry (Baltimore, Newark, Rochester, Toledo, Cincinnati, Minneapolis-St. Paul, Columbus, and Miami), while others have appointed priest chaplains (Cleveland, Des Moines, Hartford, Camden, Louisville, and Orlando). Family life offices in many other dioceses now consider divorce ministry an integral part of their total service to families. There are now about 400 Divorced Catholic Groups in the U.S. and Canada, located in parishes, Newman Centers, retreat houses, and schools. New ones seem to form every day.

Bibliography: International Theological Commission, "Propositions on the Doctrine of Christian Marriage," Origins 8 (1978) 235–239. NCCB, *Plan of Pastoral Action for Family Ministry* (USCC Publ. Office, Washington, D.C. 1978). R. S. WEISS, *Marital Separation* (New York 1975). L. G. WRENN, *Divorce and Remarriage in the Catholic Church* (New York 1973). J. J. YOUNG, *Ministering to the Divorced Catholic* (New York 1978).

[J. J. YOUNG]

DOCTRINE OF THE FAITH, CONGREGATION FOR THE

Formerly called the Holy Office (4:944), this Congregation of the Roman *Curia received its new name and program in 1965 from Paul VI's motu proprio *Integrae servandae* (ActApS 57 [1965] 952–955). Juridically on a par with other curial congregations, it yet has a primacy both of age and of responsibilities—in the words of Paul VI, "it deals with the most important affairs of the Roman Curia" (ibid. 953). The workings of the Congregation were further outlined in the apostolic constitution reorganizing the Curia, *Regimini Ecclesiae* (ActApS 59 [1967] 897–899). As the auxiliary of the Church's ordinary magisterium it is entrusted with the double mission of promoting and of safeguarding the Church's doctrine on faith and morality.

Purpose and Spirit. Acting in accord with the fresh vision of the Church renewed by Vatican Council II Pope Paul, in the 1965 motu proprio, emphasized the positive need for promoting the doctrine of the faith as

the best way "to correct error, to recall with gentleness those who stray to the right path, and to give new strength to the heralds of the gospel" (*Integrae servandae* 95.3). The stress he placed on "charity which casts out fear" (1 Jn 4.18) seems a marked contrast to the previous inquisitorial spirit. At the same time the twelve articles of *Integrae servandae* make clear that charity itself would still require the Congregation to exercise its previous surveillance over matters of faith and morality and, when necessary, to condemn erroneous doctrine. In a word, the mandate of the Pope to the Congregation was "to speak the truth in a spirit of love" (Eph 4.15).

Make-Up of the Congregation. The constitution *Regimini Ecclesiae* adapted the composition of the Congregation to that of the other Vatican dicasteries. Previously the pontiff himself bore the title of prefect, though generally affairs were actually conducted by the secretary with the assistance of the assessor, the commissioner, and other lesser officials. Now the Congregation is presided over by a cardinal prefect, assisted by the secretary, the under-secretary, and the *promotor iustitiae*. Cardinals and bishops appointed by the pope constitute the official membership of the Congregation. Its day-to-day work is carried on by a staff, divided into four sections (doctrinal, matrimonial, sacerdotal, and disciplinary), each with a secondary major official at its head.

In matters of major importance the Congregation is assisted by a group of consultors, formed of the secretaries of seven other congregations together with priest theologians of various nations chosen by the Holy See for proficiency in specific areas of doctrine. With the secretary of the Congregation as chairman this group meets every Monday to discuss the matter referred to it and to give a consultative *votum*. Episcopal members resident in Rome, in their Wednesday meeting, discuss the same material and the views of the consultors to draw up a deliberative *votum* to be presented to the pope as the considered view of the Congregation. Every two years the cardinal and bishop members, resident in or away from Rome, meet for a plenary session to discuss the affairs of the Congregation and to chart its course.

Work and Procedures. According to *Integrae servandae* the Congregation's first task is to promote the Church's doctrine of faith and morality by providing helpful guidelines for the authentic development of theology. This responsibility involves the examination of new trends in theology with a view to sponsoring them if they are sound and correcting them if they are contrary to the principles of faith. This work is greatly helped by the annual meetings of the *International Theological and Biblical Commissions under the presidency of the cardinal prefect. Concomitantly the Congregation carries out its responsibility in other areas: in the appraisal and, if necessary, the condemnation of questionable doctrinal writings; in decisions on matrimonial cases involving the favor of the faith (9:289); in judgment on canonical crimes against faith and the Sacrament of Reconciliation; in the study of requests for laicization presented by priests. The Congregation must also deal with whatever doctrinal matters the pope, the other dicasteries, or local Ordinaries refer to it through the cardinal secretary of state.

Judgment in doctrinal areas involves not only much study within the Congregation but also the beneficial use of expert scholarship outside the Congregation. In a meeting each Saturday the office personnel decides which questions can be resolved by the staff itself and which need more careful study. In accord with *Integrae servandae* matters of major importance are submitted to several specialists in various countries with a request for a full memorandum on the question under discussion. The response of these scholars provides a wealth of expert information for study by episcopal members and consultors. The time consumed in securing this assistance from specialists inevitably causes delay in the making of final decisions; however, recourse to the Church's scholars is necessary if the decisions of the Congregation are to be responsible and well-founded. Whenever the final judgment involves a judicial process that could result in condemnation, the individuals concerned as also their Ordinaries are informed so that they may prepare a defense. If this right is waived the Congregation itself appoints a fully competent advocate to represent the defendant.

The Oath of Secrecy. Previously the members, the consultors, and the staff of the Holy Office were bound by oath under penalty of reserved major excommunication to observe silence on all aspects of their work. Today the oath is still in force, but the nature and extent of its obligation, now free of the previous penalty, are identical with the moral obligations of "the common secret" and of *papal secrecy, binding on the whole Roman Curia. In requiring this oath the Church provides a prudent implementation of the natural law of fiduciary silence operative in many areas of the Congregation's work.

Bibliography: AnnPont 1978:993–995; 1465–1466. F. M. CAPPELLO, *De Curia Romana* 1 (Rome 1911) 57–108. N. DEL RE, *La Curia Romana. Lineamenti storici giuridici* (3d ed., Rome 1970). J. HAMER, "Structures, Procedure, and Mission of the Congregation for the Doctrine of the Faith," OssRomEng 31 (Aug. 1, 1974) 6–9; "In the Service of the Magisterium: The Evolution of a Congregation," *Jurist* 37 (1977) 340–357. E. HESTON, *The Holy See at Work* (Milwaukee 1950). V. MARTIN, *Les Congrégations romaines* (Paris 1930) 40–63. U. NAVARETTE, "Commentarium litterarum apostolicarum . . . quibus S.C.S. Officii nomen et ordo immutantur," PeriodicaMorCanLiturg 55 (1966) 610–652.

[B. M. AHERN]

DÖPFNER, JULIUS

Cardinal; b. Aug. 26, 1913, Hausen, Germany; d. Munich, July 25, 1976. After courses in philosophy and theology in Rome, he was ordained there Oct. 29, 1939, for the Diocese of Würzburg. Two years later, he received the doctorate in theology at the Gregorian University, and was assigned to Schweinfurt, where he was chaplain to thousands of displaced person's from East Germany who were seeking a home. During the postwar years, while on the staff of the diocesan seminary, he promoted cooperative housing for the numerous war refugees. Named bishop of Würzburg by Pius XII, he was ordained in the local cathedral, Oct. 14, 1948. He was transferred to the Diocese of Berlin on Jan. 17, 1957. There he labored to achieve a sense of unity between the Catholics of West and East Berlin, and was renowned as a rebuilder of the churches destroyed during the war.

Created a cardinal by John XXIII, Dec. 15, 1958, he was then named Archbishop of Munich and Freising. Here, as a leading figure of the German hierarchy, Döpfner had a significant role in the preparations for Vatican Council II. In June 1960, e.g., he chaired the gathering of German bishops on preparations for the Council. Thereafter, he was named a member of the Central Preparatory Commission and, at the same time, to the Committee on Technical Arrangements. During the first session he became a member of the Secretariat for Extraordinary Matters and was also appointed to the Commission for Coordination. For the succeeding sessions, with Cardinals Agagianian, Lercaro, and Suenens, he was named by the Holy Father to the key post of Moderator of the Council. In his various positions in the administration of the Council, he was frequently heard. In addition his was a familiar voice during important debates in the Council chamber.

Few were the important topics on which he was not heard. He entered the debate, e.g., on the Church, on Bishops, on Religious, on Priestly Formation, on Vocations. Most importantly, probably, was his influence on the framing of *Lumen gentium*, esp. by insistence on the need to go beyond a legalistic concept of the Church and to stress the Church *as mystery*. Sanctity, he pointed out, is bestowed on man through the mediation of Christ *and* of the Church, insofar as it is the primordial Sacrament of Christ. Later he was involved with a number of other cardinals in the delicate issues of religious freedom and the Church's relationship with Judaism.

Between the sessions of the Council, Döpfner organized and conducted numerous episcopal gatherings, notably the meeting of the European bishops at Fulda in August 1963. With the end of the Council, he continued to be associated with its programs. In 1963 he was named to the Commission for the Revision of the Code of Canon Law and became a familiar figure at the meetings of the Synod of Bishops. In 1967, e.g., he was present as a representative of the Conference of German Bishops. His interventions were numerous and he was named to the Commission for the Study of Doctrinal Errors. Then, as president of the German hierarchy, he took part in the extraordinary sessions of 1969. In 1970, he was elected a member of the Council of the General Secretariat of the Synod of Bishops and continued active in the 1971 and 1974 Synods. In addition, he was a member of the Congregations for the Oriental Churches, Clergy, the Evangelization of Peoples, and Catholic Education. Vast was the concourse of those who, on word of his sudden death, besieged the hospital chapel where his remains lay. Fitting tribute to a churchman who liked to tell that he was the son of a shoemaker.

Bibliography: H. FESQUET, *The Drama of Vatican II*, tr. B. MURCHLAND (New York 1967). OssRomEng 31 (435) July 29, 1976, 8; 36 (436) Aug. 5, 1976, 2. Vorgrimler *passim*.

[P. F. MULHERN]

DYING, CARE OF

Because dying persons have gained the status of teacher in contemporary culture, dying is seen now as a process rather than as a solitary moment at the termination of a life (*see* DEATH, THEOLOGY OF) Dr. Elisabeth Kübler-Ross, a pioneer of interest in care of the dying, has attempted to chart five stages in the death process of terminally ill patients: denial and isolation, anger, bargaining, depression, and acceptance. Each calls for a different form of relating and care from medical personnel, family, and religious pastors.

Physicians have become more willing to consider a

patient's right to know the true nature of his condition. The fact, manner, and place of telling this to the patient are an important aspect of care of the dying. Physicians have also become able to admit the limitations of their profession. The care of terminal patients is less often interpreted as requiring the use of every possible means to prolong life. Not only extraordinary means of preserving life are being rejected but even sometimes what would be considered ordinary means. In extreme cases, mercy death or *euthanasia, consisting of a positive intervention to accelerate death, is seen by some theoreticians as falling within the province of care of the dying. There are Catholic writers on both sides of the mercy-death debate.

Extreme suffering of the terminally ill is no longer considered as inevitable by most medical personnel or as salvific by most religious people. Alleviation of pain has become the goal of care. Even the use of such drugs as heroin and marijuana are becoming acceptable for this purpose. As medical technology and techniques develop, the procedure of triage also is involved in care of the dying. Triage, once considered a necessity only on the battlefield, is the process of allocating scarce medical resources and thus preferring some persons' lives as more valuable than others. Triage is potentially involved in the choosing of which patient will receive an organ transplant and in the assignment of patients to modern technological medical resources.

The question of the proper place to care for the dying is being reevaluated. More dying patients want to complete the dying process at home rather than in a hospital. Yet they require specialized services and potent pain-killing drugs. England has spearheaded a development of hospices—homes specifically designed to meet the needs and desires of dying patients—where dying can be a humane experience. The hospice idea is being taken up in some cities of the United States (see Rossman).

Finally, there has been increased awareness of the need for all persons to explore their own fears of death, not only to help deal with the grief connected to the death of a loved one, but also to help a person integrate his or her death into life.

Bibliography: E. KÜBLER-ROSS, *On Death and Dying* (New York 1969). D. C. MAGUIRE, *Death by Choice* (New York 1974). R. NEALE, *The Art of Dying* (New York 1973). P. RAMSEY, *The Patient as Person* (New Haven 1970). P. ROSSMAN, *Hospice* (New York 1977). S. STODDARD, *The Hospice Movement* (New York 1978).

[M. R. MAGUIRE]

E

EAST ASIAN PASTORAL INSTITUTE (EAPI)

The East Asian Pastoral Institute, Manila, Philippines, is a renewal center that seeks to serve Asian and Pacific local Churches. Its founder was Austrian Johannes Hofinger, SJ, formerly a seminary professor in China. Expelled by Communists, in 1953 he began the EAPI in old quonset huts, publishing from here and lecturing in Asia, the Pacific, U.S., Africa, Europe. He organized international catechetical-liturgical study weeks at Nijmegen, Holland (1959), Eichstatt, Germany (1960), Bangkok, Thailand (1962), Katigondo, Africa (1964), Manila (1967), Medellín, Colombia (1968). Asian bishops and religious superiors often urged a pastoral program in Asia, since studying in Europe was expensive and deculturizing. East Asian Jesuit provincials realized the need; on August 15, 1965 Fr. General Pedro Arrupe reconstituted the Institute and named its first Director, Alfonso M. Nebreda, SJ, a Basque and pastoral theologian with experience in Japan. The Ateneo de Manila University offered an apt site. While a building was being constructed, the first course began, in borrowed quarters, September 1, 1966.

The participants, about seventy-five, come from almost every Asian and Pacific country, with some from Africa. They are men, women, religious, lay, priests; average age is forty, apostolic experience averages at least five years but most have more, so that each course totals about a thousand years. The main course begins September 1st, ends March 31st. Subjects offered are in four main divisions: the theological spectrum, behavioral sciences, Asian and Pacific scene, the audio-visual world. The common language is English. The total program's aim is spiritual renewal, theological reflection, pastoral effectiveness, pursued through interpersonal, intercultural, interdisciplinary approaches, resulting in information, formation, transformation. Building community is central. All participants live in, and are expected to know how to build Christian communities at home because they have experienced this particular academic, intercultural, coeducational community of believers.

The resident staff, about fifteen, is Jesuit, lay, diocesan priests, men and women religious. The Jesuit and non-Jesuit Central Board determines policies. Administration is collegial, from the Central Board/Director down to departments/committees. Ultimate jurisdiction remains with Jesuit East Asian assistancy provincials. The teaching staff, about forty, comes from the EAPI, from the Philippines, Sri Lanka, Taiwan, Indonesia, Japan, New Zealand, U.S., Rome, and elsewhere. Again they are Jesuits, laity, men and women religious. Asian and Pacific research is fostered. Some graduates do a thesis for an M.A. civil degree from the Ateneo University, of which the EAPI is a federated unit.

In its first thirteen years the EAPI sent forth one thousand graduates. Seven became bishops. Others are generals, provincials, superiors, diocesan directors of catechetics and liturgy, cooperators in schools, parishes, social works. Several have founded local pastoral institutes. In summers the EAPI has conducted seven one-month courses for over six hundred priests, and continues also two-month, audio-visual training programs. Asian and Pacific bishops at times request further help within their countries. The EAPI staff therefore goes out to conduct courses for bishops and priests, lay people and religious.

Publications: *Teaching All Nations*, a quarterly, reached in 1978 its fifteenth year, *Good Tidings*, a bi-monthly, its seventeenth. The Christian Communities Program (CCP) issues religious education booklets, adopted by many Philippine dioceses and used as a model in other cultures.

After building up the EAPI as Director for thirteen years, Fr. Nebreda in 1978 was succeeded by Adolfo Nicolas, SJ.

Bibliography: A. M. NEBREDA, SJ, LumV 21 (1966) 566–577 and 29 (1974) 453–458; G. S. MELIS, LumV 24 (1969) 505–514.

[F. X. CLARK]

EASTERN CATHOLIC CHURCHES

The life of the Eastern Catholic Churches during the 1970s was difficult in the East European nations under Communism, and precarious in the Near East because of the struggle between Israel and the Arabs. Christianity was attacked by an attempt made in Egypt to pass a law making apostasy from Islam a capital crime (1976), while Israel enacted a law (1977) punishing with heavy fines and five years of prison anyone who offers "material inducement" to an Israeli to change his religion. The

South Indian Churches of the Malabarians and Malankarians continue to advance rapidly. The Eastern Catholic immigrants in the U.S.A., Canada, Brazil, Argentina and Australia made valiant efforts to defend themselves against defection to the Latin Rite by building up their ecclesiastical organization.

The Pontifical Oriental Institute (11:557) in Rome, the foremost center of such studies in the world, continues its research and educational task, now divided into two schools, one of Eastern ecclesiastical studies and the other the School of Eastern Canon Law. Besides 51 doctoral candidates, there were 57 postgraduate students and 90 others from 32 nations. The number of alumni from the Orthodox Churches is growing, including the Soviet Union, and some have now reached the episcopacy in their Church.

Unresolved Problems. The demand of the Eastern Catholics to be regarded as autonomous, particular Churches, has not been honored by the Roman Curia. The warm, official recognition of the non-Catholic Eastern Churches by Vatican Council II (*Unitatis redintegratio* 14–18) and publicly shown over the years to their representatives by Pope Paul VI and the spokesmen of the Curia, has not been matched in respect to the Eastern Catholic Churches. Acceptance of the existence of particular Churches and of some autonomy could be the interpretation of Vatican II's *Lumen gentium* (13) in respect to the universal Church, and of the whole of *Orientalium Ecclesiarum* in relationship to the Eastern Churches. Such an interpretation has found no encouragement, though the matter was again brought up at the 1974 Synod of Bishops by Archbishop Maxim Hermaniuk, Metropolitan of the Ukrainian Catholic Church in Canada, and other representatives of the Eastern Churches.

Pope and Patriarchs. The Eastern Catholic patriarchs have rejected the option to be members of the college of cardinals, following in rank at once after the six cardinal bishops. They wish to see the Eastern patriarchs associated at a level of quasi-equality with the chief patriarch of the West, the pope and bishop of Rome. The only remaining Eastern patriarch created cardinal (1965) is the Coptic patriarch (Stephanous I Sidarous). They do not wish to participate as members of a conclave that elects the pope; they would reserve this to the clergy of the Diocese of Rome, represented by the cardinals. The Eastern patriarchs prefer to view the cardinals not as electing the pope who is also the bishop of Rome but rather as electing the bishop of Rome who as such is also the pope. In matters concerning the Diocese of Rome and the Latin Rite Church, the cardinals shall have precedence, but in affairs of the universal Church, the first place after the Roman Pontiff is to be accorded to the Eastern patriarchs. The Latin Rite patriarchs (Venice, Jerusalem, Lisbon), not enjoying patriarchal jurisdiction, do not come into the question.

Recodification of Eastern Canon Law. The work was begun in 1935. Four parts of a future code had been promulgated (Marriage Law 1949, Judicial Procedure 1950, Law of Religious 1952, Constitutional Law and On Persons 1957) before Vatican II. The Council suspended the work and then subjected the law to a wholesale revision. Established by Paul VI in 1972, the Pontifical Commission for the Revision of the Code of Oriental Canon Law has made public the drafts of several parts of the future code in an annual periodical

Nuntia (since 1974). Principles of codification of the law on the patriarchal and archiepiscopal Churches has provoked criticism as expressed in a circular letter (1977) by Cardinal Joseph Slipyj, head of the Ukrainian Church. The idea of one common code for all Eastern Catholic Churches is inappropriate since each Church is a legal entity of a sovereign nature. The promulgation of an Oriental Code should be an act of that Eastern Church and not of the Roman pontiff alone. The People of God should have a part in the management of their Church, as in the election of their patriarch. Ecumenical considerations and the legislative efforts of the Eastern Orthodox Churches have been neglected. Eastern and non-Catholic Western Christian Churches could never be induced to unite with Rome on terms of autonomy as narrow as those accorded to the Eastern Catholic Churches. The most objectionable feature is the continued denial of jurisdiction to the Eastern Churches outside the Near East and Eastern Europe.

Life of the Churches. A meeting of the Byzantine Rite Byelorussian clergy, with Bishop Cheslav Shipovich presiding, held in Rome (1977), resolved to request the Holy See to appoint, with appeal to the constitution of Byelorussia and the Helsinki Agreement, speedily a Byelorussian bishop for Byelorussia.

Coptic Catholic Patriarchate. With 4 dioceses (160 priests, 115,000 members) this has the distinction of being the only Uniate group accepted by the Orthodox counterpart. At the express request of the Coptic Orthodox Patriarchate, the auxiliary bishop and one priest from the Coptic Catholic Patriarchate were appointed to the Mixed Commission of Theologians, which held its first meeting in the Orthodox Patriarchate under the joint presidency of both patriarchs.

Greece. The tiny community of Byzantine Rite Catholics (16 priests, 2,500 faithful alongside a Latin Rite Church with 12 dioceses, 37 parishes, 60 priests, 43,000 faithful) was ruled by a bishop as apostolic exarch. After his death in 1974 a forceful move was sponsored by the Orthodox Church of Greece against conferring episcopal dignity on a new exarch. Rome, however, decided not to heed the protest and appointed Anargios Printesis as exarch with ordination as bishop of Athens in 1975.

Hungarian Byzantine Rite. The Dioceses of Hajdudorogh (124 parishes, 175 priests, 300,000 members) and the Apostolic Exarchy of Miskolc (28 parishes, 34 priests, 23,000 members) finally received a bishop and auxiliary bishop in 1975, after the Communist government had given its assent to end a five-year vacancy.

Malabarians. The largest group of St. Thomas Christians in Kerala (South India), this Church, dating from apostolic times, originally dependent on the East Syrian (Chaldean) Church, is the most flourishing Eastern Catholic Church (2,700 priests, 2.2 million members). The Malabarians had been forbidden to preach the Gospel among the non-Christians of India, this being reserved to Latin Rite Christians, present in India only from the 16th century. Vatican Council II gave equal rights to the Eastern Churches in missionary endeavors (*Orientalium Ecclesiarum* 4). The Malabarian Church was then assigned missionary areas, which were later (1977) established as dioceses; the Church thus has two provinces with 17 dioceses and is therefore a candidate for elevation as a major archiepiscopate or patriarchate.

Maronites. The Patriarch of Antioch of the Maronites (15 dioceses within and 3 outside—U.S., Brazil,

Australia—the patriarchate, 1.5 million members) occupies the position of an ethnarch because the Maronites constitute with minor Christian groups one half of the population of Lebanon. The delicate apportionment of political power between the Christians and Moslems, established in the constitution, was disturbed by the influx of 400,000 Moslem refugees from Israel-occupied Palestine. In the internal war of 1976 45 Maronite churches were destroyed and many Maronites were among the estimated 65,000 victims. Fr. Sharbel, in the world Youssef Makhlouf (1828–98), a Maronite priest and hermit, was declared a saint by Pope Paul VI (1977), the first one from the Eastern Churches to be canonized by an act of a pope. His shrine in Anaya (Lebanon) is visited by Christians and Moslems.

Melkites. The vicar of the Melkite Patriarch of Antioch (17 dioceses within and 2—U.S., Brazil—outside the patriarchate; 600,000 members) in the Diocese of Jerusalem, Archbishop Ilarion Capucci, was arrested by the Israeli authorities and sentenced in 1974 to a 12-year term for smuggling arms for the Arab liberation forces. His liberation was a condition stipulated by every Arab terrorist group. At the intervention of the Vatican, Israel released Abp. Capucci in 1977 and the pope assigned him to be visitor of the Melkite communities in South America. Because of him the loyalty of Arab Christians to the common Arab cause will now be perceived with less skepticism by the Moslem majority.

Romanians. The absorption of the Byzantine Rite Catholic Romanians by the Romanian Orthodox Church, to which they were forcefully subjected in 1948, is progressing, according to private information. Several former Catholic priests have been appointed Orthodox bishops, and Catholic clergy have received preferential treatment because of being better educated than the majority of the Orthodox clergy. The strangely subdued protests from Rome against the annexation to the Orthodox Church by brutal coercion has been explained by some observers as signal to the Romanian Catholics to give up the struggle. There are now only some 15,000 Byzantine Rite Romanian Catholics left from a Church that counted 1.6 million in 1948.

Slovaks. The Diocese of Prešov in Slovakia was reconstituted during the Dubček thaw (1968) when the faithful could shake off Eastern Orthodox affiliation imposed by the Communist government (1950) and again profess Catholicism. 217 parishes, 235 priests, 315,000 members and administration is under a provisional Ordinary, a priest. Auxiliary Bishop Vasil Hopko, released after 12 years of incarceration, died in 1976, leaving the diocese without an ordaining prelate.

Ukrainian Catholics. The head of the Ukrainian Catholic Church, the largest Eastern Church before World War II (4 million in 1943—in the free world now 15 dioceses, 1 million members), is Cardinal Joseph Slipyj. He has declared his Church to be of patriarchal rank, and continues to build up a net of subsidiary centers of the Ukrainian Catholic University of St. Clement with headquarters in Rome, an institution for the preservation of the Ukrainian religious and cultural heritage (*see* UKRAINIAN RITE).

Yugoslavs. The Byzantine Rite Catholics in Yugoslavia are of Croatian, Ukrainian, Russine, Macedonian, Romanian ethnic extraction, joined in the Diocese of Krizevci (57 parishes, 63 priests, 60,000 members). The faithful in Macedonia (5 parishes, 5,000 members) has the Latin Rite bishop of Skopje-Prizren, who is a Byzantine Rite priest, as apostolic visitor. The Diocese of Krizevci is administered by Msgr. Gabrijel Bukatko, who is also the Latin Rite Archbishop of Belgrade.

Eastern Catholics in the United States. The Maronites have transferred the seat of the Diocese of St. Maron (est. 1972) from Detroit to Brooklyn, N.Y. (50 parishes, 65 priests, 30,000 members).

The Apostolic Exarchy of Melkites in the U.S.A. was transformed into the Eparchy of Newton, Mass. (30 parishes, 54 priests, 22,000 members), under the immediate jurisdiction of the pope. The Melkite Patriarch vindicated the right of the patriarchate to jurisdiction over all Melkites in the world, not yet recognized by Rome, by issuing a separate decree of erection and by installing the bishop himself in the presence of the apostolic delegate to the United States. In affirmation of his jurisdiction, Patriarch Maximos V in Canada ordained (1977) a married man to the priesthood against the contrary norm of Rome that there should be no married clergy outside the Near East.

The Ruthenian Byzantine Rite Metropolia (ecclesiastical province) of Pittsburgh, Pa. and the Dioceses of Passaic, N.J. and Parma, Ohio (218 parishes, 256 priests, 279,000 members), which have under their jurisdiction also the Byzantine Rite Slovaks, Hungarians, and Croats, were successful in establishing new parishes in the South (Florida) and West (California, Arizona, Colorado, New Mexico, Alaska) in response to the general internal migration in the U.S.A., in spite of a dearth of priestly vocations and heavy losses to the Latin Rite of faithful who settle out of reach of Ruthenian parishes.

The Ukrainian Metropolia of Philadelphia, Pa. with the Dioceses of Stamford, Conn., and St. Nicholas of Chicago (196 parishes, 240 priests, 272,000 faithful) was disturbed by agitation in connection with the movement for a Ukrainian patriarchate, with violent demonstrations at the ordination of two bishops (1971) and the establishment of parishes independent of the diocesan bishops. The development of church life is seriously hampered by a dearth of vocations and a superannuated clergy, of whom 40 percent are over 65 and 70 percent over 50 years of age.

The Armenians (6 communities), Byelorussians (1), Chaldeans (3), Russians (6) are under the Latin Rite bishops, as are also the Byzantine Rite Romanians (15 churches), whose wish to have a bishop of their own has not yet been satisfied.

Eastern Catholics in Canada. Only the Ukrainians have a hierarchy of their own, the Metropolia of Winnipeg and the Dioceses of Edmonton, Alta., New Westminster, B.C., Saskatoon, Sask., and Toronto, Ont. (240 parishes, 241 priests, 240,000 members), having under their jurisdiction also the Ruthenians, Hungarians, and Slovaks, though the latter have an auxiliary bishop in Toronto as apostolic visitor. Numerous new parishes are being constantly organized in larger cities, especially in Winnipeg and Toronto, for the faithful leaving the farms and for those migrating to the suburbs. Yet, the future is bleak because the communities are relatively small and distant from each other. The Church needs, therefore, a larger number of priests, while at the same time the clergy is superannuated, and there is an insufficient number of celibate vocations. The older people are unwilling to abandon the concept of a married pastoral clergy as they had known it in Europe and also in Canada up to recent times. Opposition was reinforced by the discussion of the same problem going on in the Latin Rite Church.

[V. J. POSPISHIL]

EBLA

Ebla is the ancient name of Tell Mardīkh, a major archeological site in northern Syria, located between Aleppo and Hama, excavated since 1964 by a team of the Missione Archeologia Italiana in Syria, under the direction of Paolo Matthiae. The site was occupied intermittently and to varying degrees from the 4th millennium B.C. on; the major occupational phases date from the mid-3d to the mid-2d millennium. Early work on the site (1964–1973) focused on the early 2d-millennium (Middle Bronze Age) settlement, an important early contemporary of the great kingdoms of Aleppo, Mari, and Hammurapi's Babylon. Subsequent study has aimed at 3d-millennium materials; in addition to further exploration of public buildings, recent work has yielded major epigraphic finds. In and around the royal palace on the acropolis of the city, archeologists have found about 7,000 cuneiform tablets. Information contained in the tablets, in combination with the rich context of excavation, is pointing the way to an increasing appreciation of the complexities of inland Syrian culture and history.

Ebla was a major urban center in mid-3d millennium Syria (13:894); the horizons of its vast textile trade included Palestine, Mesopotamia, Elam (southwestern Iran), and southern Anatolia. Its more restricted, cultural affiliations are not entirely clear: Mesopotamian elements coexist with features known from later distinctive Syro-Palestinian traditions. The Eblaite synthesis of artistic and ideological materials is unique and often original; the forms of writing depend in part on the Mesopotamian Kish tradition attested at Abu Sālabīkh and Farᶜah (near Nippur) and pre-Sargonic Mari. Firm dating of the Royal Palace has been difficult. Ceramic and plastic materials indicate that the basic occupation, of about a century and a half, belonged to the 24th–23d centuries; evidence of writing favors a higher date, perhaps as high as the 27th–26th centuries. If the lower dates are correct, then the period of Ebla's greatest power coincided with that of the empire of Sargon (I) of Akkad and his descendants. His grandson Naram-Sin would be the destroyer of Ebla. The higher dates would make Ebla contemporary with the Early Dynastic powers of Sumer.

Five kings of Ebla are known by name. The greatest of them was Ebrium (Ebrum), whose name is similar to that of Abraham's forbear, Eber (1:32; 10:1097). The kings of Ebla generated extensive diplomatic and commercial relations throughout the Near East. They exerted economic and political influence on neighboring cities, and occasionally embarked on military ventures to secure trading privileges and other concessions. The commercial and diplomatic life of Ebla assured that the archives contain many place names. In Syria-Palestine, the existence in the 3d millennium of some great urban sites has been demonstrated; notable among these are Ugarit, Damascus, Sidon, Hazor, Megiddo, Lachish, Ashdod, Gaza, and Jerusalem. The Cities of the Plain of Genesis are mentioned in a trade itinerary in the order in which they occur in the Bible. The region around Ebla includes many places with names similar to those of Abraham's ancestors, e.g., Haran and Mahor.

The religion was a form of Canaanite polytheism with minor, Mesopotamian elements intermingled. Chief gods include Dagan (Hebrew Dagon), Rasap (Phoenician Reshef), Sipish (Ugaritic Shapash); the cultus was sacrificial. Outside religious texts and records, the gods occur in personal names, e.g., Ibbi-Sipish, "(The sun god) Sipish has called (me)." Many personal names have the common divine element 'il, and may be compared with identical or similar names in the Bible, e.g., mi-ka-il, biblical mîkā'ēl. The institution of prophecy existed at Ebla.

The tablets of Ebla are in the cuneiform (wedge-shaped) script developed by the Sumerians (13:788). Some of the tablets are in the Sumerian language; a number, however, reveal that the scribes of Ebla had adapted the cuneiform script to the writing of Eblaic, the local Semitic language (13:77). Still others are bilingual vocabularies matching Sumerian logograms and Semitic words. Texts from Ebla concern matters economic (taxes, textiles), administrative (rations, royal edicts), historical (treaties, tribute payments), juridical (purchases, punishments), literary (stories, hymns, proverbs), and scholarly (lists of word and signs). Giovanni Pettinato, the epigrapher at Tell Mardīkh, describes the Eblaic language as Old Canaanite, a close relative of Hebrew and Phoenician; other scholars have suggested that a more complex description is indicated.

Both the language and culture of Ebla are related to those of the Bible and as work proceeds the ties will become clearer. Ebla will shed light on biblical language, and literary and legal texts, and on the patriarchal age. It may be that the standard Middle Bronze Age dates for Abraham will have to be raised to the mid-3d millennium, if the apparent links between the Ebla tablets, Genesis 14 and archeological evidence from sites around the Dead Sea are confirmed.

See also MARI (9:204).

Bibliography: For popular reports, see, from 1976 on, *Biblical Archeologist*; for scholarly reports, *Syro-Mesopotamian Studies* and *Orientalia*.

[D. N. FREEDMAN]

ECCLESIOLOGY

The field or subdiscipline of theology which treats of the Church is ecclesiology (5:34). Two main factors have dominated its development since the close of Vatican Council II in 1965: the ecumenical dialogue of representatives of the various Christian Churches and the re-examined relationships between Christians as church members and the rest of humanity, whether considered under the religious aspect or the secular. Since Pope John opened the windows, it is more difficult to think about the Church without reference to those outside. (Nor is the atmosphere of polarization within the Roman Catholic Church to be overlooked, which pits those who regard Vatican II's reforms as the utmost limit against those who feel the Council did not go far enough.)

Approaches. An unparalleled concentration on ecclesiological themes took place as a result of Vatican II. Much of it is conceived in the framework of Christian ecumenism, as in Hans Küng's book, *The Church*. A particular forte of his is the integration of contemporary scripture studies into theology; an important focus of his work, therefore, although characteristic also of many other authors, is the recovery of the normative beginnings of church life as found in the New Testament. Absorbed in overcoming the Catholic-Protestant division by drawing on the ultimate sources cherished by both, Küng paid scant attention to the service which the Church may be called upon to render to the world at large.

The series, entitled *Mysterium Salutis*, a monumental systematics involving a whole group of theologians, attempts to situate the Church vis-à-vis world history through a salvation-history approach. It is based firmly on a sacramental view of the Church, a view which seems inexhaustible in its fecundity and most congenial to the Catholic mind.

Issues. Certain questions have received particular attention in recent ecclesiology. One is the paradigmatic shift which can be discerned between pre-Vatican II and post-Vatican II ecclesiology. The very emphases and order of the first three chapters of the Council's Dogmatic Constitution on the Church break with the conventions of the recent past. The newly prominent theme of the Church as People of God now rivals the previous emphasis on Church as Body of Christ. All this suggests another likely approach to ecclesiology, one centered on the Holy Spirit's role in the Church (Mühlen), and the use of multiple models of Church in elaborating an adequate ecclesiology.

Other prominent themes are the mission or purpose of the Church, which has to be thought through again; ecclesial community at the level of personal contact (*basic Christian communities, comunidades de base*); the gap between reform-minded theological reflections and actual reform measures or lack of them in practice; human rights as an object worthy of the Church's struggle not only for itself but for the world at large (*see* POLITICAL THEOLOGY, LIBERATION THEOLOGY); and declericalization of the Church.

The extended discussion of church authority in all its aspects seems to indicate the need to bring up for scrutiny some deeply rooted presuppositions of conventional thinking about the Church. For instance, what some have called, in a debatable simplification, the "Constantinian era" of the Church, still present in its effects, may be a hindrance to realizing a good theory or even more, an appropriate practice, of church authority today (*see* AUTHORITY, ECCLESIASTICAL).

Bibliography: G. BARAUNA, ed., *L'Église de Vatican II* (Paris 1966–67). J. COMBLIN, *The Meaning of Mission* (Maryknoll, N.Y. 1977). Y. CONGAR, *Ministères et communion écclésiale* (Paris 1971). B. COOKE, *Ministry to Word and Sacraments: History and Theology* (Philadelphia 1976). A. DULLES, *The Resilient Church* (Garden City, N.Y. 1977). M. A. FAHEY, "A Changing Ecclesiology in a Changing Church," ThSt 38 (1977) 754–762. J. FEINER and M. LÖHRER, eds., *Mysterium Salutis* v. 4/1 and 4/2 (Einsiedeln 1972–73). International Theological Commission, *Theses on the Relationship between the Ecclesiastical Magisterium and Theology* (Washington, D.C. 1977); "De promotione humana et salute christiana," Greg 58 (1977) 413–430. H. KÜNG, *The Church*, tr. R. and R. OCKENDEN (New York 1967). R. MCBRIEN, *Do We Need the Church?* (New York 1969). H. MÜHLEN, *Una Persona Mystica* (3d ed., Paderborn 1968). G. TAVARD, *The Pilgrim Church* (New York 1967). Vorgrimler *passim*.

[P. MISNER]

ECONOMIC AID, INTERNATIONAL

International economic aid transfers in the thirty years following World War II played a major role in the revitalization of the war-devastated economies of Western Europe and Japan, and in the rate of aggregate economic growth achieved by many of the developing nations of Africa, Asia, and Latin America. In some instances, e.g. South Korea, Taiwan, and Brazil, aid contributed to such rapid rates of economic growth that many observers now classify these nations as having reached or moved over the line between developing and developed economies. These achievements, however, are not uniformly distributed among developing countries and in 1975 when the United States per capita income was over $7,000, forty countries had per capita incomes of less than $300 and another sixteen countries had per capita incomes ranging between $300 and $500. Thus the basis of the moral imperative for economic-aid transfers from richer nations to poorer nations remains (see 5:43) and it has been strongly reenunciated both in the Pastoral Constitution on the Church in the Modern World of Vatican Council II (*Gaudium et spes* 86) and in Pope Paul VI's social encyclical on human development (Paul VI PopProgr 49).

Methods and Objectives. While the basic moral considerations regarding international economic aid have not changed in the last decade, the methods and the recipients of aid have changed significantly. In the 1950s and 1960s the general notion concerning methods and recipients involved the receiving nation as a whole, the objective of aid being the stimulation of national economic growth. It was then assumed that if growth was increased, the benefits of growth would "trickle down" to the poorest individuals within the nation. In order to maximize this growth, aid was generally provided to enlarge either the basic infrastructure of the economy (railroads, ports, electric generating facilities, etc.) or to expand the manufacturing sector, particularly in regard to industries that related to international trade (that is, either import-competing or export-generating industries).

Events of the early 1970s shifted the orientation as to who should receive aid and what kind of aid should be provided. The food shortfalls of the first part of the decade made it quite clear that many of the developing nations are living on the edge of a precarious food supply. At the same time studies of the development process indicated that while economic growth had been achieved at very high historic rates in the majority of developing countries, the distribution of income within these countries was often becoming more inequitable, with the poorest members of these societies becoming not only relatively but absolutely poorer. These two developments shifted the emphasis in foreign aid from industrial to agricultural development and from economic growth in general to economic growth aimed at impacting directly on the "poorest of the poor." This shift was manifested in the development of a new aid-granting criterion, termed "basic human needs," which focuses on attempting to provide minimum food, clothing, shelter, health, education, and the like to the lowest income groups in developing countries.

Official Development Assistance. Unfortunately the shift in emphasis toward the poorest sectors of the developing world has occurred at the same time as a significant shift in the financial contributions of the developed nations away from true aid and towards more commercial forms of financial flows. Between the start of the United Nations First Development Decade in 1960 and the end of 1977, Official Development Assistance (ODA)—economic-aid transfers that involve either outright gifts or grants, or carry very low interest payments and a very long period before repayments begin and/or are completed—rose from $5.2 billion to $14.8 billion; but this increase was not large enough to offset the rate of increase of world prices. Consequently, ODA in real value was less in 1977 than it was in 1961, even though the developed nations were richer and the needs of the poorest developing nations were greater. With regard to achieving international justice, what is even more disturbing is that real ODA contributions have fallen consistently since 1972.

Real output in the richer nations rose at an annual rate of almost five percent between 1960 and 1977 and thus the proportion devoted to ODA declined sharply from 0.52 percent of output to 0.31 percent. This trend was the exact opposite of what the United Nations was trying to achieve when it set forth a target for resource transfers of one percent of the gross national product of developed countries, of which 0.7 percent was to be in the form of official development assistance. While all developed nations of the nonsocialist world accepted this target in principle (the socialist nations of Eastern Europe and the Soviet Union have not and in reality they provide very little economic assistance outside of their own bloc), only a few, Sweden being the most consistent, have met the goal. Some, including the United States, have not yet even settled on a date when the goal should be met.

Debt Problems. The failure of ODA to grow in the 1960s and 1970s meant that official development-aid per person in developing countries fell very dramatically as the rate of population growth remained relatively high. This resulted in most of these countries being forced to turn to nonconcessional financial flows. In the 1960s nonconcessional flows came to equal official development assistance, but following the increase in oil prices in 1974, nonconcessional flows, particularly from the private banking sector, rose very rapidly. By 1977 they accounted for two-thirds of all net financial flows to developing countries. Inasmuch as nonconcessional flows carry higher interest rates and more stringent repayment provisions, the shift from ODA to nonconcessional flows resulted in a major increase in the foreign debt of developing countries. In 1976 the United Nations Conference on Trade and Development (UNCTAD) estimated that if loans from private markets continued to make good the shortfalls in official development-assistance needed by developing countries, then by 1980 developing countries as a whole (excluding oil-exporting nations) will have to devote fifty percent of all of their export earnings just to handle the service on past debt. To many observers, including the proponents of a *New International Economic Order, this "debt burden" has built into it the seeds of disaster for the lowest-income countries and conceivably for the higher-income countries because of what default on these past loans might mean for the private banking community.

Proposals for the Future. Because of the needs of developing countries and because of the inherent instability of the present system of financial transfers, a change in the economic-aid transfers from developed to developing nations has recently been proposed. It is argued that resource transfers should be separated from the totally voluntary area of present and past programs, which make them completely dependent upon the fluctuating political will of individual developed countries.

Instead what is envisioned is some form of self-financing that will insulate economic aid from abrupt changes and, therefore, will allow recipients to plan more effectively. Proposals put forth to achieve such an end include: use of the allocation of Special Drawing Rights by the *International Monetary Fund; the development of world taxes on international pollutants; the development of a system of taxes on *multinational corporations; a small tax on all exports; and/or taxes or fees on commercial activities arising from such areas common to the world as international sea beds, outer space, or the polar regions.

Bibliography: Overseas Development Council, *Global Justice & Development: Report of the Aspen Interreligious Consultation* (Washington, D.C. 1975). K. P. SAUVANT and H. HASENPFLUG, eds., *The New International Economic Order: Confrontation or Cooperation between North and South* (Boulder, Col. 1977) Part 4.

[J. J. MURPHY]

ECUMENICAL INSTITUTES AND CENTERS

The institutes and centers established over the past fifty years to train persons and supply resources for the ecumenical movement's special needs are generally of two types: those engaged in training theologians and conducting theological studies in view of the conversations and growing relationships between the Churches (*see* ECUMENICS); and those engaged in promoting ecumenical activities for a particular Church or across denominational lines. In 1978 there were approximately two hundred and fifty such institutes and centers throughout the world.

History. The first actual ecumenical institute was and still is attached to the Benedictine community at Chevetogne, Belgium (3:556). Founded in 1926 by Dom Lambert Beauduin (2:199) to develop Roman Catholic-Eastern Orthodox contacts and promote spiritual ecumenism, it is now committed to contacts and conversations with all Christians but with emphasis on Eastern Christianity. Since 1927 the monks of Chevetogne have published *Irénikon*, the first strictly ecumenical journal. When the ecumenical movement took on more identifiable form with the establishment of the World Council of Churches (WCC) in 1948, ecumenical institutes began to proliferate. This was particularly true in Germany where the experience of persecution during the Hitler regime gave Christians a renewed sense of common relationship. German institutes almost invariably are associated with university faculties of theology. Their purpose is to prepare clergy and teachers in the principles and practice of ecumenism or to conduct research on specific ecumenical issues and concerns.

In other places in Europe institutes and centers were developed to assist the official Church in ecumenical mission. The more prominent of these are the St. Willebrord Vereniging (1948) in the Netherlands, established to advise the Dutch Roman Catholic hierarchy; the *Centre d'études oecuméniques* (1965) in Strasbourg, France, organized to do research for the Lutheran World Federation; and the *Institut oecuménique* at Bossey, Switzerland (1946), the WCC study center. With the entrance of the Roman Catholic Church into the mainstream of the ecumenical movement during Vatican Council II, several episcopal conferences established centers to provide them with services, resources, and personnel for ecumenical ministry. Among these are the John XXIII Center in Manila, The Philippines (1968) and the *Centre d'oecuménisme* in Montréal, Canada (1963).

In other parts of the world, and notably of the Third World, ecumenical institutes and centers manifest the special concerns of local Churches or of the region. The Institute on Church and Society in Ibadan, Nigeria (1964), exists "... to stimulate the search for a deeper understanding of Christian responsibility..." and witness in Church and society in general. The Ecumenical Christian Centre of Bangalore, India (1963) is concerned with enabling the people of India to understand social change and participate actively in nation-building. The *Centre Chrétien d'études Maghrébines* in El-Biar, Algeria, (1961) seeks to contribute to "... those who want to know Muslims better in order to render Christian service in North Africa." Today the term "ecumenical center or institute" indicates more than a concern for inter-Christian unity. It reflects the ultimate goal of the ecumenical movement, that is, that Christians should be a sign of that unity which is possible for all humanity.

Ecumenical institutes and centers sponsored by Roman Catholics notably stress spiritual ecumenism among their other concerns. This is so because of the influence of Fr. Paul Wattson (14:828) of Graymoor, New York, the originator of the Church Unity Octave (1908), and Abbé Paul Couturier (3:422) of Lyons, France, who adapted the Octave (1934) into the *Week of Prayer for Christian Unity (January 18–25) which is now a universal Christian observance.

The United States. In the U.S. six of the existing twenty-one ecumenical institutes and centers are related to or under Roman Catholic sponsorship. Three of these demonstrate the variety that exists among ecumenical institutes and centers:

The Institute for Ecumenical and Cultural Research at St. John's University, Collegeville, Minnesota. It was conceived as a study center and established in 1967 by Kilian McDonnell, OSB. It is a place where scholars sensitive to cultural trends can develop their theses respecting the interplay of human experience (society) and religious aspirations (Church), as well as their impact on belief, worship, and spiritually-motivated action. The Institute is composed of resident fellows from all religious persuasions who live and work in the environment of a Benedictine community and a university faculty. The Institute each year has at least ten resident fellows who engage in ecumenical studies and projects done individually but in the context of community living. The Institute also develops research programs requiring collective and interdisciplinary study and sponsors conferences, conversations, or colloquia on matters of particular interest to theologians or of importance to church people generally. The results of the Institute's scholarly research are published in books, journals, and theses. The Institute itself publishes a modest quarterly, *Ecumenical Newsletter.*

The Graymoor Ecumenical Institute. It was founded in 1967 by the Atonement Friars at their headquarters in Garrison, N.Y., as a place where people of all faiths can come to discuss issues that confront the Churches and are on "the cutting edge" of Christian life today. The Institute sponsors conferences, seminars, and consultations of ecumenical concern and annually publishes the results as "The Graymoor Papers" in the *Journal of Ecumenical Studies*, published by Temple University in Philadelphia. The Institute's own publication is *Ecumenical Trends*, a monthly, which contains documentation, informational articles, and notices on the ecumenical movement, especially in North America. The Graymoor Ecumenical Institute also is an ecumenical action center which emphasizes local, congregational/parish-level ecumenism (*see* ECUMENISM, REGIONAL AND LOCAL). Annually, in cooperation with the Faith and Order Commission of the National Council of Churches and the Roman Catholic Bishops' Committee for Ecumenical and Interreligious Affairs, it produces and distributes throughout the U.S. prayer leaflets and resource booklets for the yearly observance of the Week of Prayer for Christian Unity. The Atonement Friars who staff the Institute, with the advice of an interdenominational consultative board, also publish study guides on the agreed statements resulting from the *bilateral consultations in the U.S. and other resources for ecumenical involvement on the parish level. To encourage the local clergy in their ecumenical responsibilities the Institute sponsors the Ecumenical Clergy Association, a spiritual fellowship open to all Christian clergy and lay affiliates. The Association's newsletter, *At/One/Ment* lists resources, events, and approaches that help foster local-level ecumenism and encourages prayer for those ecumenically involved.

The John XXIII Ecumenical Center at Fordham University in New York City. It was founded in 1951 as the Russian Center. Its origin can be traced to the Jesuit mission in Shanghai, China (1941–47), where the Jesuits ministered to the White Russian colony. With the advance of the Communist forces in 1949 the White Russian colony and the Jesuits had to flee. The Jesuits resettled on the Fordham Campus and under the leadership of Frederick Wilcock, SJ developed the Russian Center. For fourteen years prior to 1950 the university had sponsored conferences on Eastern Rite Catholicism; the small band of Jesuits from Shanghai took responsibility for that program. They also taught at the university's newly-established Institute of Russian Studies, aided Russian displaced persons, began publishing and lecturing on the Eastern Churches, initiated dialogues with Orthodox theologians, and trained seminarians for ministry among Eastern Rite Catholics.

In 1963 Pope John XXIII gave permission for the Center to change its name, in favor of his own papal title, not to indicate any movement away from work among Russians, but to reflect the broadened possibilities in ecumenical work and Eastern Christian studies. Today the Center is more academic than pastoral in orientation and is not exclusively Jesuit-staffed. In 1966 the Center launched the Fordham lectures on Byzantine Christian Heritage; in 1971 this became the Summer Institute, now the principal activity of the Center. The Center conducts an advanced degree program on Eastern Christian studies, covering liturgy, spirituality, theology, history, and Canon Law, with emphasis on patristics. During the winter months staff members engage in and direct research programs. The Center publishes the only Roman Catholic journal in the United States concerned exclusively with Eastern Churches, *Diakonia*, whose documentation and chronicles of American Eastern Orthodoxy make it a valuable ecumenical journal for informing the vast majority of Western Christians in the U.S. about the reality and contribution of the small but great Churches of Eastern Christianity.

Bibliography: Friars of the Atonement, Centro Pro Unione, *Ecumenism Around the World* (2d ed. Rome 1974).

[T. HORGAN]

ECUMENICAL MARRIAGES, PASTORAL CARE OF

Vatican Council II in its third session submitted to Pope Paul VI the issue of a revision of church law regarding mixed marriages, and in particular those marriages in which one partner is a Roman Catholic, the other a baptized member of another Christian Church. It became obvious that the principles in the Decree on Ecumenism needed to be applied to this pastoral situation. The urgency of such reconsideration was pressed in several bilateral and interconfessional conversations.

Church Law. The decree of the Congregation for the Oriental Churches, *Crescens matrimoniorum* on Orthodox-Catholic marriages, Feb. 22, 1967 (ActApS 59 [1967] 165–166) and the motu proprio *Matrimonia mixta*, Jan. 7, 1970 (ActApS 62 [1970] 257–263) contain the revised legislation. In general, the changes reflect a positive evaluation of the status of the non-Catholic Christian partner, of that partner's Church, and of that partner's freedom of conscience. The possibility that a mixed marriage between two baptized Christians (now often referred to, though not in official documents, as an "interchurch," "ecumenical," or "interconfessional" marriage) might help in reestablishing Christian unity is explicitly adverted to. Neither in doctrine nor in law is such a marriage placed on the same level as one between a Catholic and an unbaptized person. The interchurch marriage is a Sacrament; it involves a "certain communion of spiritual benefits." The special character of the interchurch marriage is strongly underlined in the Jan. 1, 1971 NCCB statement on implementing *Matrimonia mixta*.

According to the new legislation, Roman Catholics may not licitly contract marriage with baptized non-Catholics without securing a dispensation from the local Ordinary. Those applying are asked to declare their readiness to remove all dangers to faith and to promise to do all in their power to see that their children are baptized and brought up in the Catholic Church. The first declaration appears necessary as a condition for granting the dispensation; the promise regarding the Catholic upbringing of the children does not. Rather it is a solemn reminder of the Catholic's grave obligation. The revised law notes that both husband and wife are bound by the responsibility of the children's upbringing. The nature of a joint decision excludes the possibility that the outcome is "within the power" of one partner. The Catholic is expected to fulfill the promise "as far as possible" within the concrete situation.

Pastoral Care. The basic principle of pastoral care for interchurch marriages is that both Churches should be equally involved. *Matrimonia mixta* exhorts pastors to form "relationships of sincere openness and enlightened confidence" with pastors of other Christian Churches. They are directed to foster the unity, based on Baptism, of interchurch couples and families.

Joint pastoral care should begin with preparation of the couple for marriage. In addition to instruction regarding the nature of Christian marriage, opportunity should be provided for each partner to become acquainted with the beliefs and practices of the other's Church. They should attend each other's services on occasion; each should be encouraged to remain faithful to his or her own religious tradition.

With a dispensation from the local Ordinary, Roman Catholics may be married in the church of the non-Catholic Christian. (The directives of the various episcopal conferences vary widely as to the circumstances which warrant such a dispensation.) In this case, the wedding is according to the order of the church where it is held; ideally, the pastors of both churches would have a role in the service.

Joint pastoral care and occasional worship in each other's church should continue after the wedding. The husband and wife will come to feel a special kinship with the partner's Christian tradition. The love that binds them may help to bring members of their congregations together in understanding and love. In their own family, a "domestic church," the hoped-for unity of Christians will be prefigured. Although the children of the interchurch marriage should have a clear affiliation with only one Church, they may also have a spiritual link with the other parent's Church. In their religious education and experience of worship they should be enriched by both Christian traditions.

Pastoral movements which direct and support interchurch couples now flourish in England and Wales, Ireland, Holland, France, Germany, Switzerland, and Italy. Regular reports on these movements are provided in the periodical *One in Christ*. The Association of Interchurch Families (England) holds annual retreats; a group centered in Lyons publishes a journal, *Foyers mixtes*. A kit for counselling interchurch couples has been developed ecumenically in Canada. The Massachusetts Commission on Christian Unity published a noteworthy booklet of practical guidelines, *Living the Faith You Share*.

Episcopal directives vary widely. In Holland, provision for Eucharistic sharing was made as early as 1968. The bishops of Strasbourg and Metz have more recently identified conditions under which interchurch couples and families might share the Eucharist in both the Catholic and the Protestant Churches. Similar directives were adopted by the Swiss episcopal conference. Bishop George Hammes of Superior, Wis. provided for the admission of non-Catholic Christian spouses to Communion on special family occasions.

The theological and pastoral questions continue to be discussed in ecumenical dialogues (Anglican-Roman Catholic, Methodist-Roman Catholic, Orthodox-Roman Catholic, and the Lutheran/Reformed/Roman Catholic consultations).

Bibliography: P. DORA, "Ecumenical Marriages: In Need of Pastoral Care," EcumTr 6 (1977) 65–72. M. HURLEY, ed., *Beyond Tolerance* (London 1975). E. LYNCH, "Mixed Marriages in the Aftermath of 'Matrimonia mixta,'" JEcumSt 11 (1974) 637–659; "Interchurch Marriages Ten Years On," *One in Christ* 14:1 (1978). NCCB, *On the Implementation of the Apostolic Letter on Mixed Marriages* (USCC Publ. Office, Washington, D.C. 1971).

[S. BUTLER]

ECUMENICAL MOVEMENT

The main emphasis in this article will be on Roman Catholic participation since 1973 in the ecumenical movement (5:96; 16:139), which is understood as the process of reconciling divided Christians. This understanding of the ecumenical movement is somewhat broader than the generally accepted view of ecumenism as a movement to achieve the organic unity of the Churches and somewhat less comprehensive than the idea of a "wider ecumenism," which concerns relations not only between Christians and adherents of other world living religions but also between Christians and nonbelievers. During the years 1973–1977, the ecumenical movement was characterized by: increasing convergence on heretofore highly-disputed questions, both doctrinal and moral; a strengthening of ecumenical cooperation on the local and regional levels; a heightened consciousness about the continuing role of potentially or actually divisive factors in the midst of growing Christian unity; a sense of having achieved some maturity as a movement; and a concomitant impression of ambiguity about the ecumenical future, at least among professional ecumenists.

Survey. The period 1973–1977 saw increasing consensus on previously disputed doctrinal and moral issues among participants in the *bilateral consultations and similar conversations held between Roman Catholics and Christians of other Churches and communities. The most prolific bilateral dialogues were those between Roman Catholics and Anglicans on the international (ARCIC) and the national (ARC) levels. The Anglican/ Roman Catholic International Commission produced *Ministry and Ordination: A Statement on the Doctrine of the Ministry* ("The Canterbury Statement," 1973) and *Authority in the Church: A Statement on the Question of Authority, Its Nature, Exercise and Implications* ("The Venice Statement," 1977). A special international Anglican-Roman Catholic Commission on the Theology of Marriage and Its Application to Mixed Marriages also issued its *Final Report* in June 1975. In addition, the Joint Commission on Anglican-Roman Catholic Relations in the U.S.A. published an *Agreed Statement on the Purpose and Mission of the Church* (1975) as well as a formal response (1974) to ARCIC's "Canterbury Statement" from a North American perspective.

Agreed statements between Roman Catholics and several other Christian Churches and communities also marked this period of growing consensus on previously disputed doctrinal and moral issues. Lutherans and Roman Catholics in the United States released a *Common Statement on Ministry and the Universal Church* (1974) which came from a bilateral dialogue cosponsored by the U.S.A. National Committee of the Lutheran World Federation and the U.S. Roman Catholic Bishops' Committee for Ecumenical and Interreligious Affairs (BCEIA). In the previous year (1973), the two sponsoring agencies had encouraged joint Lutheran-Roman Catholic (Augsburg Publishing Co., Paulist Press) publication of a background study, *Peter in the New Testament*, in preparation for the common statement on ministry and the universal Church (*see* LUTHERAN/ROMAN CATHOLIC DIALOGUE). Conversations conducted from 1972–1975 by the Joint Commission of the Roman Catholic Church and the World Methodist Council were summarized in a 1976 document entitled "Growth in Understanding," while the *United Methodist-Roman Catholic Dialogue/ U.S.A. issued a *Report on Holiness and Spirituality of the Ordained Ministry* (1976). The national Orthodox-Roman Catholic Consultation produced agreed statements on respect for life (1974), the Church (1974), the

principle of economy (1976; cf. 754), and the pastoral office (1976). *An Adventure in Understanding: Roman Catholic-Disciples Dialogue, 1967–1973* (1974) reviewed six years of intensive dialogue sponsored by the Council on Christian Unity of the Christian Church (Disciples of Christ) and the BCEIA and helped prepare the ground for an international dialogue scheduled to begin in 1978. On a less extensive level, the Baptist-Roman Catholic Regional Conference published the papers and proceedings of a consultation on *The Church Inside and Out* held in 1974. Finally, in the U.S. the Presbyterian-Reformed/Roman Catholic Consultation published a statement, *The Unity We Seek* (1977), in which numerous practical recommendations to improve relations between these Churches were proposed, including shared ministries, shared Eucharist on certain occasions, democratization of church structures, local covenant communities, and expanded educational programs for laity and clergy. A number of these recommendations for the local-regional level that resulted from the Presbyterian-Reformed/Roman Catholic dialogue are already being implemented or being planned in various parts of the world (*see* ECUMENISM, REGIONAL AND LOCAL).

Advances. Considered to have begun in 1910 with the World Missionary Conference in Edinburgh, the ecumenical movement has taken multiple forms during its brief existence. One of its major expressions has been through councils of Churches, world, national and regional-local. Roman Catholics belong to some local and state councils of Churches and participate in many activities and agencies of the National Council of Churches of Christ in the U.S.A. (NCCC) and the World Council of Churches (WCC), particularly in their respective Commissions on Faith and Order. Roman Catholics were therefore able to celebrate and share in the general sense of "having come of age" when the WCC marked its 25th anniversary in 1973, as did the NCCC in 1975. The 50th anniversary of the Faith and Order Movement in 1977 was also marked by widespread Roman Catholic participation in the celebrative events around the world. Official Roman Catholic observers were noticeably present at the Fifth Assembly of the WCC held in Nairobi, Kenya, during late 1975.

For their part, Roman Catholics observed the tenth anniversary of the promulgation of Vatican II's Decree on Ecumenism (*Unitatis redintegratio*) in 1974 and Declaration on the Relation of the Church to Non-Christian Religions (*Nostra aetate*) in 1975. As a result of celebrating all these events, Roman Catholics have gained a sense of having matured somewhat in their new role as an official partner in the ecumenical movement. On the more practical level, Roman Catholics now generally try to make their intramural events and organizations as ecumenical as possible. This trend was particularly evident when a Committee for the Participation of Other Christians was formed and duly funded on the occasion of the Eucharistic Congress held in Philadelphia during 1976. The growth of stable and productive ecumenical institutes and centers within the Roman Catholic Church itself is another instance of the increasing ecumenical maturity which has marked the post-Vatican II era (*see* ECUMENICAL INSTITUTES AND CENTERS).

Obstacles. Despite the many ecumenical advances made in the period 1973–1977, numerous obstacles to ecumenical growth and progress remain solidly in the way for Roman Catholics in their relationships with other Christians. Issues like the ordination of women, abortion, sexuality, and especially homosexuality, such Marian doctrines as the Immaculate Conception and the Assumption of the Blessed Virgin, and so-called 'non-theological/moral' factors like the dramatic rise of conservatively-oriented groups inside the various Christian Churches, all constitute points of serious contention and barriers to be overcome as Roman Catholics mature even further in their ecumenical relationships with other Christians and with one another inside the Roman Catholic Church itself.

For these reasons many Roman Catholic Christians are ambiguous about the ecumenical future and pose searching questions that must eventually be confronted. Ecumenically-concerned Roman Catholics are presently asking questions. Is there a future for ecumenism when the dominant socio-cultural trends are strongly adverse to the ecumenical enterprise? Granted that the bilateral dialogues have produced marvelous consensus statements on previously divisive doctrinal and moral issues, do such statements represent any real ecumenical advance when the church officials to whom the documents are directed do little or nothing to implement them in a practical way? Although impressive ecumenical advance is occurring on the local-regional levels, the question is how to involve the majority of Christians who, on the one hand, are apathetic and indifferent towards ecumenism or, on the other, are frustrated and alienated by the slow pace and lack of dramatic results in the arena of local-regional ecumenism.

While the Roman Catholic Church has a general sense of having reached some measure of maturity in the ecumenical movement, ecumenists ask how to handle the more widespread and perhaps more significant trend toward anti-institutionalism, especially regarding church authorities, which has developed among Roman Catholics, particularly young people. What is the meaning of the seeming inability by many Christian Churches both to accommodate intramural diversities, healthy and otherwise, and to handle dissidence in its several forms successfully enough to avoid actual schisms and further divisions among the Christian Churches? In sum, many ecumenical Roman Catholics at the end of the 1970s are asking if ecumenism has any future at all and if it does, how and in what forms ecumenism will survive into the next century.

Bibliography: Anglican/Roman Catholic Commission on the Theology of Marriage and Its Application to Mixed Marriages, *Final Report* (USCC Publ. Office, Washington, D.C. 1976). Anglican-Roman Catholic Commission/U.S., *ARC-DOC*, I–IV (Documents on Anglican-Roman Catholic Relations) (USCC Publ. Office, Washington, D.C.). Baptist-Catholic Regional Conference, *The Church Inside and Out* (USCC Publ. Office, Washington, D.C. 1974). *Consultation on Church Union—A Catholic Perspective* (USCC Publ. Office, Washington, D.C. 1970). N. EHRENSTROM and G. GASSMANN, *Confessions in Dialogue: A Survey of Bilateral Conversations among World Confessional Families, 1959–1974* (3d rev. ed. Geneva 1975). P. C. EMPIE and T. AUSTIN MURPHY, *Papal Primacy and the Universal Church. Lutherans and Catholics in Dialogue* 5 (Minneapolis 1974). M. HURLEY, *Praying For Unity: A Handbook of Studies, Meditations and Prayers* (Dublin 1963). J. W. KENNEDY, *Nairobi 1975: A First-Hand Report of the Fifth Assembly of the World Council of Churches* (Cincinnati 1976). Lutheran-Roman Catholic Theological Consultation, *Lutherans and Catholics in Dialogue*, 1–5 (USCC Publ. Office, Washington, D.C.). Roman Catholic/Presbyterian-Reformed Consultation, *The Unity We Seek* (New York 1977). L. SWIDLER, ed., *The Eucharist in Ecumenical Dialogue* (New York 1976). United Methodist-Roman Catholic Dialogue/U.S.A., *Holiness and Spirituality of the Ordained Ministry* (USCC Publ. Office, Washington, D.C. 1976). N. H. VANDERWERF, *The Times Were Very Full: A Perspective on the First 25 Years of the National Council of the Churches of Christ in the United States of America, 1950–1975* (New York 1975).

[C. V. LAFONTAINE]

ECUMENICS

There is no expert consensus on what ecumenics is or entails, except that it may be defined tautologically as the study of ecumenism and/or the ecumenical movement in their several different meanings.

Interpretations. There are as many understandings of ecumenics as there are ways to view ecumenism and the ecumenical movement. Some maintain that ecumenics is a separate discipline with its own principles, method, and content. For others it is either a subfield of Christian theology or a qualitative dimension characterizing all aspects of Christian theology. Regarding subject matter, ecumenics is said by some to concern only those efforts at mutual understanding and eventual unity that occur among Christians and their Churches. Others describe the subject matter as extending to the relationship between Christians and members of other living world religions. A few would define ecumenics in terms of reconciliation and mutual understanding between believers and nonbelievers. Ecumenics is therefore presently engaged in a process of self-definition, just as ecumenism and the ecumenical movement are also being defined and redefined.

Institutes of Study. The several understandings of ecumenics are reflected institutionally and structurally in various ways. For those viewing ecumenics as a separate, though still not perfectly demarcated discipline, there exist schools and institutes of ecumenics such as The Ecumenical Institute at Bossey, Switzerland, sponsored by the World Council of Churches. The Ecumenical Institute is "a study and research center which serves as a place of encounter between the Gospel and our world within an ecumenical context where men and women may deepen their understanding of questions affecting the renewal, witness and unity of the Church." Perhaps even more highly and specifically organized is the Irish School of Ecumenics in Dublin which is "an academic study center with a systematically organized program of courses in various aspects of the movement for Christian unity leading to a Master of Arts degree." For those to whom ecumenics is a subfield or even a dimension of Christian theology, there are centers and faculties specializing in ecumenics such as the Institut Supérieur d'Études Oecuméniques in Paris which is a university institute for ecumenical formation and research whose aim is "to form researchers, professors for theological faculties, seminaries and study centers, and promoters of the ecumenical movement." Similar to the Institut Supérieur are the Johann Adam Möhler Institut für Okumenik in Paderborn, and the Institute for Ecumenical and Cultural Research at Collegeville, Minnesota.

Specialized institutes, centers, and organizations reflect the various understandings of subject matter with which ecumenics can be concerned. There is, for example, The Ecumenical Christian Center in Bangalore, India, which is a "research, study and inspirational center for Christians of all persuasions and non-Christians from all walks of life as well"; the John XXIII Center of Fordham University, which specializes in the study of the Eastern Churches; the NCC Center for the Study of Japanese Religious in Kyoto; the Center Mi-ca-el in Montreal, Canada, whose main interest is Judaeo-Christian relations; and the Centre Chrétien d'études Maghrebines in El-Biar, Algeria, whose purpose is "to contribute to the formation of those who want to know Muslims better in order to render Christian service in North Africa."

Theological Themes. The generalized institutes for ecumenics and ecumenical studies do not, of course, confine their academic endeavors merely to the study of dogmatic theology in relation to ecumenism and the ecumenical movement. Biblical sciences, history, ethics, sociology, anthropology, political science, economics, philosophy, and the fine arts are some of the major disciplines which contribute to and are incorporated into the enterprise of ecumenics. Related and complementary are seminars and reflection/action sessions which emphasize ecumenical field-work, practical training in an ecumenical situation, e.g., in a covenanted parish, a local council of Churches, or an ecumenical task force on hunger.

In the area directly related to Christian dogmatic theology, several emphases and trends have either continued or emerged since 1970. Foremost has been the study of ecumenical dialogue as such, its nature, characteristics, methods, and limitations. Work also continues in ecclesiology to determine more precisely the relation of the Roman Catholic Church to other Christian communities; in Christology and soteriology to specify more exactly the nature of non-Christian salvation; in sacramentology to describe more definitively the divine presence in the Sacraments as those are related to Christian persons and communities existing in a state of division; in eschatology to relate Christian life style and moral behavior to common principles arising from a biblical and apocalyptic ambiance. Similar endeavors proceed in missiology, liturgics, and spirituality, thus making ecumenics an indispensable enterprise, however the discipline may be defined or described.

Bibliography: N. EHRENSTROM and G. GASSMANN, *Confessions in Dialogue* (3d rev. ed., Geneva 1975). G. HASENHUTTL and J. BROSSEDER, "Ecumenical Theology," SacrMundi 2:202–207. H. KÜNG, ed., *The Future of Ecumenism. Concilium* 44 (Paramus, N.J. 1969). Secretariat for Promoting Christian Unity, *Directory for the Application of the Decisions of the Second Vatican Council concerning Ecumenical Matters Part II: Ecumenism* (Washington, D.C. 1970); *Reflections and Suggestions concerning Ecumenical Dialogue* (Washington, D.C. 1970).

[C. V. LAFONTAINE]

ECUMENISM, REGIONAL AND LOCAL

Church leaders and theologians repeatedly have urged Christians to be ecumenically involved at all levels because, as the Decree on Ecumenism noted, "Concern for restoring unity pertains to the whole Church, faithful and clergy alike" (*Unitatis redintegratio* 5). Without total involvement ecumenism can not attain its goals. Progress at every level of Church life has occurred since the publication of the Decree on Ecumenism, but progress has been slow at the regional and local levels because of isolationary habits and antiprogressive attitudes among some Roman Catholics. However, sufficient progress had been made by 1975 that the Pontifical Secretariat for Promoting Christian Unity issued *Guidelines for Ecumenical Collaboration at the Regional, National and Local Levels.* To a great

extent this document reflected what had already been achieved in the U.S. and elsewhere.

Regional Ecumenism. Following a brief exposition of the Roman Catholic understanding of "local Church" the Vatican document outlined specific guidelines for programs of sharing prayer and worship; for a common biblical apostolate; for joint pastoral care, particularly in hospitals and to persons in mixed marriages (*see* ECUMENICAL MARRIAGES, PASTORAL CARE OF); for the common use of church facilities; for collaboration in Christian education programs and use of the media; and for social action and human development programs. The document gave particular support to and urged Roman Catholic participation in Christian councils and councils of Churches.

Collaboration by Roman Catholics in these areas has been evident, but so sporadic that those committed to practical ecumenism experience frustration and sometimes have tried to force reaction, if not action, regarding intercommunion, mixed marriages, and participation in social action programs. As a result local leadership has sometimes become very cautious. In recent years, too, councils of Churches in the United States have come under heavy criticism, being called solely social gospel agencies, and are themselves undergoing renewal. This situation has hindered Roman Catholic collaboration. Another practical difficulty is to find a way for Roman Catholics precisely as such to relate to interchurch agencies and other Churches in a corporate manner. Nevertheless church leaders consistently, even though cautiously, urge Roman Catholic participation in regional and local ecumenism. The foremost Roman Catholic expression of this effort is the National Association of Diocesan Ecumenical Directors whose purposes are "to stimulate an exchange of ideas, experiences and evaluations among Roman Catholic ecumenical officers, to promote programs which further the work of Christian Unity and interreligious cooperation, and to cooperate with the national Bishops' Committee for Ecumenical and Interreligious Affairs."

Local Ecumenism. The parish-level ecumenism, however, has been more fruitful for Roman Catholics than have other areas of ecumenical activity. Common prayer and bible-study programs, pulpit exchanges living-room dialogues, summer bible schools and youth programs, Christian outreach services in the neighbourhood or town, and "open house" programs between Roman Catholic parishes and other local congregations have a ten-year history in the United States. Parish or local-level ecumenism for Roman Catholics implies sharing one's belief, tradition, and commitment to service with other Christians on the congregational level. Although this level of ecumenical involvement certainly can and probably will become more widespread in the future, it already should be recognized as a significant development for the ecumenical movement in the United States.

One creative expression of parish-level ecumenism, and in some instances of diocesan-level ecumenism, is the growing practice of "covenant relationships." A covenant is an agreement between two or more local congregations of differing traditions who pledge to one another some degree of constant cooperation, collaboration, understanding, and support.

See also COVENANT RELATIONSHIPS; EUCHARISTIC SHARING.

Bibliography: D. BOWMAN, ed., *U.S. Catholic Ecumenism—Ten Years Later* (USCC Publ. Office, Washington, D.C. 1975). T. HORGAN and A. GOUTHRO, *Parish Ecumenism* (Garrison, N.Y. 1977). Secretariat for Promoting Christian Unity, *Guidelines for Collaboration at the Regional, National, and Local Levels* (USCC Publ. Office, Washington, D.C. 1975).

[T. HORGAN]

EDUCATION, HUMAN RIGHT TO

Post-World War II discussion of human rights has generally included the right to education. Earlier both secular and ecclesiastical sources emphasized the concurrent rights of family, Church, and State in education. Pius XI's Encyclical, *On the Christian Education of Youth*, described, with approbation, the Church's historic role in education—the monastic and cathedral schools and the flowering of that cultural leadership in the medieval universities. Further, the Pope argued both from St. Thomas Aquinas and Leo XIII that nature itself required the development of human potential so as to enable man to achieve his final salvation as an individual and also to contribute to societal peace and harmony. Pius XI observed that education "is essentially a social and not a mere individual activity," one in which complementary roles are played by family, Church, and State. This 1929 document appears as a stepping stone toward understanding the right to education as an individual's right in the teaching of Pius XII, the United Nations Charter, and the statements of Vatican Council II, John XXIII, and Paul VI.

The Individual's Right. In a Christmas Eve radio address in 1942, Pius XII stated: "All men of whatever race, condition, or age, in virtue of their dignity as human persons, have an inalienable right to education" (ActApS 35 [1943] 5–8). This view is clearly consistent with the Dec. 10, 1948 UN Declaration on Human Rights in which the right to education is affirmed. On Nov. 20, 1959, in the UN Declaration on the Rights of the Child, this human right was made even more explicit.

Parallel with these international affirmations of such a "right" was the Church's expanding concept of its foundation. The Vatican II Declaration on Christian Education repeats Pius XI almost verbatim; but the Constitution on the Church in the Modern World, the writings of John XXIII, the 1971 Synod of Bishops, and Paul VI's, *Populorum progressio*, pay new attention to the relationship between education and social justice. While acknowledging that true education is oriented toward man's final end, Pope John emphasized that a human right, such as that of the right to education, arises from the inherent dignity of the human person and its meaning is open to continual revision:

> By the natural law every human being has the right to respect for his person, to his good reputation; the right to freedom in searching for truth and in expressing and communicating his opinions, and in pursuit of art, within the limits laid down by the moral order and the common good; and he has the right to be informed truthfully about public events. The natural law also gives man the right to share in the benefits of culture, and therefore the right to a basic education and to technical and professional training in keeping with the stage of educational development in the country to which he belongs. Every effort should be made to ensure that persons be enabled, on the basis of merit, to go on to higher studies, so that, as far as possible, they may occupy posts and take on responsibilities in human society in accordance with their natural gifts and the skills they have acquired (John XXIII PacTerr 12).

As he had already done in *Mater et magistra*, Pope John links right to education and the development of a just society. He points out that it is through human society that persons "should share their knowledge, be able to exercise their rights and fulfill their obligations, be inspired to seek spiritual values, mutually derive genuine pleasure from the beautiful of whatever order it be, always be readily disposed to pass on to others the best of their own cultural heritage, and eagerly strive to make their own the spiritual achievements of others" (ibid. 36).

Persons, therefore, must be educated if they are to contribute to this cultural evolution of society. The individual citizen must also be empowered to share in the benefits of economic life and in the decision-making processes of his government. The Pope argues for education as a condition necessary for fulfilling a person's duties to society. This is a recognition of a relationship specifying the right to be educated: the level of the educational opportunities varies with the level of society. The Pope insists, however, that there should be no impediment to full opportunity arising from race, sex, or economic handicap. Thus, without minimizing the importance of education in the faith, Pope John does give a greater autonomy to cultural development than does earlier papal teaching.

Relying on the concept of the common good as a basic factor in determining the right to education, because education is linked to cultural contexts, Vatican II amplifies Pope John's point:

> 'Because of the closer bonds of human interdependence and their spread over the whole world, we are today witnessing a widening of the role of the common good, which is the sum total of social conditions which allow people, either as groups or as individuals, to reach their fulfillment more fully and more easily.... At the same time, however, there is a growing awareness of the sublime dignity of the human person, who stands above all things and whose rights and duties are universal and inviolable. He ought, therefore, to have ready access to all that is necessary for *living a genuinely human life*: for example, food, clothing, housing, the right freely to choose his state of life and set up a family, *the right to education*, to work, to his good name, to respect, to proper knowledge, the right to act according to the dictates of conscience, and to safeguard his privacy and rightful freedom even in matters of religion' (*Gaudium et spes* 26; emphasis added).

A Right in Social Justice. The growing recognition expressed is that if man is to be truly free, he must play the major role in his own self-development or liberation. Because he has the need to realize his own potential fully he has a right to tools or opportunities strengthening that capacity. The Council links that point to the basic requirements of justice:

> Great numbers of people are acutely conscious of being deprived of the world's goods through injustice and unfair distribution and are vehemently demanding their share of them. Developing nations like the recently independent states are anxious to share in the political and economic benefits of modern civilization and to play their part freely in the world, but they are hampered by their economic dependence on the rapidly expanding richer nations and the ever-widening gap between them. The hungry nations cry out to their affluent neighbors; women claim parity with men in fact as well as of rights, where they have not already obtained it; farmers and workers insist not just on the necessities of life, but also on the opportunity to develop by their labor their personal talents and to play their due role in organizing economic, social, political, and cultural life. Now for the first time in history, people are not afraid to think that *cultural benefits are for all* and *should be available to everybody* (ibid. 9; emphasis added).

The document's statement in regard to culture further illumines the right to an education. "It is one of the properties of the human person that he can achieve true and full humanity only by means of culture, that is through the cultivation of the goods and values of nature. Whenever, therefore, there is a question of human life, nature and culture are intimately linked together. The word 'culture' in the general sense refers to all those things which go to the refining and developing of man's diverse mental and physical endowments" (ibid. 53). The whole of Chapter 2 of Part II then expands on this notion. The clear statement on the need to provide the opportunities for all persons to come into direct and vital contact with their own cultural roots expresses precisely the role of education.

The 1968 Medellín Documents of the bishops of Latin America placed the right to education within the framework of building a just society: "Education is actually the key instrument for liberating the masses from all servitude and for causing them to ascend 'from less human to more human conditions'." This particular goal of education, according to some commentators, may require that it be countercultural. The 1971 Synod of Bishops recognized that aspect of it when they wrote: "Accordingly educational methods should therefore be such, that men are taught to live life in its encompassing reality and according to the evangelical principles of personal and social morality, which find expression in vital Christian witness" (Synod JustWorld 45–46). It called for an education which would nurture people "thirsting for justice" and pointed out that an education which made men more "human" would free them from the manipulation of others (ibid. 46). The bishops of the United States in their pastoral letter, *To Teach As Jesus Did*, saw true education as dependent upon the building of Christian community within the educational institution: "Through education men must be moved to build community in all areas of life; they can do this best if they have learned the meaning of community by experiencing it" (To Teach 23). Education in the general humanistic sense and in the more traditionally understood Christian sense thus come together in the whole educative process.

Right to Higher Education. There is a shift in perspective from the right of the family, the Church, and the State to educate the child to the right of the child (or adult) to be educated. The change dramatizes the need to recognize the inherent dignity of all persons and to empower them in the work of self-development. Increasing technological and scientific knowledge dictates longer years and broader horizons for educational experience.

Third-World persons, it can be argued from John XXIII and Vatican II, even have a right to "higher education." That is implicit in Pope John: "And since our present age is one of outstanding scientific and technical progress and excellence, one will not be able to enter these organizations [those which affect economic, social, cultural, political decisions] and work effectively from within unless he is scientifically competent, technically capable, and skilled in the practice of his own profession" (John XXIII PacTerr 148).

The Vatican II documents provide these telling statements:

> Accordingly, while one may not neglect primary and intermediate schools, which provide the basis of education, one should attach considerable importance to those establishments which are particularly necessary nowadays, such as professional and technical colleges, institutes for adult education and for the promotion of social work, institutions for those who require special care on account of some natural handicap, and training colleges for teachers of religion and of the other branches of education .... The Sacred Synod earnestly recommends the establishment of Catholic universities and faculties strategically distributed throughout the world, but they should be noteworthy not so much for their numbers as for their high standards. Entry to them should be made easy for students of great promise but of modest resources, and especially for those from newly developed countries (*Gravissimum educationis* 9, 10).
>
> Furthermore, when man works in the fields of philosophy, history, mathematics and science and cultivates the arts, he can greatly contribute towards bringing the human race to a higher understanding of truth, goodness, and beauty, to points of view having universal value ....
>
> Every effort should be made to provide for those who are capable of it the opportunity to pursue higher studies so that as far as possible they may engage in the functions and services, and play the role in society, most in keeping with their talents and the skills they acquire .... We must do everything possible to make all persons aware of their right to culture and their duty to develop themselves culturally and to help their fellows" (*Gaudium et spes* 57, 60).

In the less developed, or deliberately underdeveloped nations, the right may be limited for the time being to a more basic training needed for economic well-being. Nevertheless, it is to be expected that in coming years the right will be expanded to include the same cultural benefits and similar levels of preparation for participation in political and economic life now characterizing developed countries. It seems safe to conclude that while the primary right to education is a universal human right, the particular kind of education in question depends on the expectations and possibilities of individual societies. But the ideal to be pursued is the fullest possible realization of each person's potential and the kind of education that will nurture it.

[A. GALLIN]

EMPLOYEES/EMPLOYERS, MORAL OBLIGATIONS OF

In its Pastoral Constitution on the Church in the Modern World, Vatican Council II provides an excellent summary of, and commentary on, previous papal social teaching concerning the economic order (*Gaudium et spes* 63–72). While it is evident that the Council is concerned about the moral obligations of employees and employers (5:327), it does not address itself to these obligations in a series of neat prescriptions, but rather highlights certain basic moral principles and draws some practical conclusions.

The most significant principle concerns the intrinsic value of human work. "Human work ... surpasses all other elements of economic life" (ibid. 67). The reason for this is that human work "comes immediately from the human person who as it were impresses his seal on the things of nature and reduces them to his will. By his work a man ordinarily provides for himself and his family, associates with others as brothers and renders them service; he can exercise genuine charity and be a partner in the work of bringing divine creation to perfection" (ibid.). It follows that the human person should take his work seriously, that man "has the duty to work loyally" and that men should "devote their time and energy to the performance of their work with a due sense of responsibility" (ibid.). It also follows that men have a *right to work, and "it is the duty of society to see to it that, according to the prevailing circumstances, all citizens have the opportunity of finding employment" (ibid.).

The Council does not enter into a formal discussion of the just wage, but it clearly states the fundamental moral principle: "Remuneration for work should guarantee man the opportunity to provide a dignified livelihood for himself and his family ..." (ibid.). The Council is at great pains to offset any economic theory that would organize and direct work in such a way as to make it dehumanizing: "But it too often happens, even today, that workers are almost enslaved by the work they do" (ibid.). The Council insists on the following moral norms: (1) work should be accommodated to the worker, to his needs as a person, with special consideration for family life, sex and age; (2) work should provide the opportunity for the worker to develop his personality and his peculiar talents; (3) work should provide sufficient rest and leisure so that workers can "cultivate their family, cultural, social, and religious life" (ibid.). The Council repeats a principle emphasized in John XXIII's encyclical, *Mater et magistra*, that all, including workers, should be allowed actively to participate in the administration of the enterprise (ibid. 68).

Finally, *Gaudium et spes* makes its own what has become traditional Catholic moral teaching on two significant questions. (1) It defends "the right of workers to form themselves into associations which truly represent them"; the worker should be allowed to take part in such associations without the fear of reprisals on the part of the employer (ibid.). The Council says nothing about the dispute on whether a worker is in some way morally obliged to join such associations. (2) It affirms the right to strike: "but the strike remains even in the circumstances of today a necessary (although ultimate) means for the defense of workers' rights and the satisfaction of their lawful aspirations" (ibid.). At the same time, Christian morality clearly demands that "all should strive to arrive at peaceful settlements and all should engage in sincere discussions" and "effect reconciliation as soon as possible" (ibid.).

See also BUSINESS ETHICS.

Bibliography: P. J. RIGA, *The Church Made Relevant* (Notre Dame, Ind. 1967). J. GREMILLION, *The Gospel of Peace and Justice* (Maryknoll, N.Y. 1976).

[D. L. LOWERY]

EPISCOPACY (SPIRITUAL THEOLOGY)

While everyone in the Church is called to holiness (1 Thes 3.3; Eph 1.4) St. Thomas Aquinas taught that those who solemnly and permanently bind themselves to the public promotion of the works of holiness belong to the "state of perfection." Bishops have primacy in this special state because they take on, as "the fountainheads of perfection in the Church" (ST 2a2ae, 184.5 *sed contra*), the pastoral responsibility of working for the salvation of others (ibid. 185, 4. ad 1). This teaching of St. Thomas crystalizes that of the Fathers. The *Didascalia Apostolorum* (2, 25) affirmed: "You ..., O bishops, are to your people priests and prophets, and princes and leaders and kings, and mediators between God and his faithful, and receivers of the word and preachers and proclaimers thereof, and knowers of the Scriptures and of the utterances of God, and witnesses of His will, who bear the sins of all, and are to give answer for all." The Fathers also taught that the bishop must possess the fulness of contemplation (cf. Julianus Pomerius, *De vita contemplativa* 1, 13) and of an activity directed toward the enlightenment and guidance of his subjects. From the bishop, as from the visible sign of the invisible presence of Christ in his Church, there flows the power of orders and of jurisdiction to all within his territory. To him belongs the responsibility

for administering the Sacraments, for preaching, teaching, judging, and governing. Vatican Council II's Dogmatic Constitution on the Church reaffirms this: "... bishops channel the fulness of Christ's holiness in many ways and abundantly" (*Lumen gentium* 26). By reason of episcopal ordination, "those chosen for the fulness of the priesthood are gifted with sacramental grace enabling them to exercise a perfect role of pastoral charity through prayers, sacrifice, and preaching, as through every form of a bishop's care and service. They are enabled to lay down their life for their sheep fearlessly, and, made a model for their flock (cf. 1 Pt 5, 3) can lead the Church to ever-increasing holiness through their own example" (ibid. 41). While the "state of perfection" is postulated by the Church's essential holiness, those ordained to bring others to sanctity must themselves possess an already acquired perfection: "for when the head languishes, the members have no vigor" (St. Gregory the Great, *Liber regulae pastoralis* 2, 7). St. John Chrysostom said that a bishop would have to be "as pure as if he were standing in the heavens themselves" (*On The Priesthood* 3, 4). Thus St. Cyprian taught (*Ep.* 67, 2) that for the office of bishop there should be chosen only "unblemished and upright priests, who holily and worthily offering sacrifices to God, may be heard in the prayers which they make for the safety of the Lord's people."

[T. C. KELLY]

EPISCOPAL VICAR

With the promulgation of Vatican Council II's Decree on the Bishops' Pastoral Office, the new office of episcopal vicar was established in the Church. The Decree sets forth the canonical structure of the office (*Christus Dominus* 23, 26–27), which is further clarified motu proprio by Pope Paul VI (Paul VI EcclSanct I, 14). Both documents stress that the purpose of the office of episcopal vicar is to allow the fullest collaboration possible in the responsibility and authority of the local Ordinary.

Historically, there has always been within the Church various offices to help the bishop by sharing responsibility in areas of his pastoral authority. The Fathers of Vatican II were sensitive to the need both for unity within dioceses and for meeting the diversification of responsibilities without further multiplying auxiliary and coadjutor bishops. The new office of episcopal vicar is meant to respond to this requirement by empowering the person in this office to do all the bishop does, except ordain. Limitations can be placed upon the office by the bishop, who retains ultimate control; still the office provides for achieving maximum collaboration and utilization of episcopal powers.

The episcopal vicar can be appointed only by a diocesan bishop (however, the Apostolic See in the letters of nomination can itself name a bishop's episcopal vicar). Unless he is an auxiliary bishop, the vicar must be appointed for a term of office and is removable at the will of the bishop (Paul VI EcclSanct 14 §5). Moreover, there is no stipulation made as to the number of episcopal vicars named in a given diocese. The paramount principle is that the purpose of having episcopal vicars is for the further good and ordering of a diocese. Therefore, the number of such vicars would be dependent on the needs of the diocese, *iuxta peculiares loci necessitates* (ibid. §1).

The authority of the episcopal vicar within the area of his competency is of the same kind as that of the vicar general in common law (*Christus Dominus* 27). He may also execute rescripts, unless a different arrangement has been made or they are granted to the bishop by reason of his personal qualification (Paul VI EcclSanct I, 14, §2). The power of dispensation enjoyed by bishops according to CIC c. 81, 82 and Paul VI's *De episcoporum muneribus* (1966) is granted to the episcopal vicar, as are the episcopal faculties set forth in the Pope's *Pastorale munus* (1963).

The authority and consent of the local Ordinary is still preserved in virtue of *Ecclesiae sanctae*. In areas of assigned competency, no matter whether it be part of the diocese or a specific apostolate, the episcopal vicar does exercise ordinary authority; thus, he is not a delegate of the bishop. Frequent communication with the local Ordinary is of paramount importance. He is not to act contrary to the mind or will of the local Ordinary, but rather conform with the bishop's policies (Paul VI EcclSanct I, 14). The vicar cannot overrule the bishop, but the bishop can overrule him. The needs of a given diocese allow for a great flexibility in the responsibilities an episcopal vicar could have: such areas as religious, clergy, different canonical rites, language or minority groups, education, ecumenism, financial administration, cathechesis. The possibilities not only insure a meeting of needs but also strengthen the bonds of collaboration with the Ordinary.

Bibliography: W. BASSETT, "The Office of Episcopal Vicar," *Jurist* 28 (1968) 425–469. T. CUNNINGHAM, "The Episcopal Vicar," *Irish Theological Record* 109 (1968) 421–429. V. DE PAOLIS, "De vicario episcopali secundum decretum Concilii Vaticani II *Christus Dominus*," PeriodicaMorCanLiturg 56 (1967) 309–330. G. GRAHAM, "The Power of Bishops in Recent Documents," *Jurist* 28 (1968) 425–469.

[J. A. BARNHISER]

EQUALITY

From its inception, the Christian religion has endorsed the concept of human equality (5.497). Philosophically, it bases the tenet on the shared possession of a human nature essentially the same for every person. Theologically, it perceives equality in the universal application of redemption to every person of every age and in every stage of life. The first supplies a note of essential identity; the second, a source of supreme dignity. The combination of the two evokes an inference of moral and religious rights, together with correlative obligations, and so establishes a reciprocal order of justice.

Vatican Council II, in its Pastoral Constitution on the Church in the Modern World reaffirms this ancient tradition, but then adds a novel dimension by relating equality to social justice. It refuses to place the blame for existing inequalities exclusively on individuals. Social institutions and cultural patterns of behavior must be indicted for instilling and perpetuating many social inequities. A reform of these agencies, therefore, is as necessary as a reform of personal habits, for public acts of discrimination, no less than private injustices, are a frustration of the divine purpose and a source of scandal, social injustice and international unrest (*Gaudium et spes* 29).

By way of illustration, the document singles out the contemporary unequal status of women sanctioned and preserved by so many discriminatory laws, customs, and attitudes (ibid.). In so doing, it, perhaps, inadvertently invites the women of the world to expect a more equal share in the Church's ministry and priesthood. Explanations offered to show that these demands are impossible of fulfillment have excited mixed reactions (*see* WOMEN, ORDINATION OF; WOMEN IN THE CHURCH). In a similar context, the Church has not yet determined to what extent and in what way the laity can share more equally in the ruling power of ecclesiastical jurisdiction (*see* MINISTRY [ECCLESIOLOGY]; LAITY, VOCATION OF).

The disregard for human equality manifested in the 1973 U.S. Supreme Court decision on abortion (*see* ABORTION [U.S. LAW]) explains much of the protest arising from Catholics and others. The failure of the government to protect human life in its earliest stages opens a new area for public discrimination based on age and physical condition. This concession to the real but selfish interests of the more powerful is regarded as an unconscionable compromise of the basic principle of equal protection of the law reminiscent of the 1857 Dred Scott decision and its restrictive definition of a legal person, and as presenting a serious threat to the essential rights of the insane, incurably ill, and unwanted aged. Legalized abortion and euthanasia are, therefore, opposed as attempts to institutionalize an unjust denial of human equality and equal dignity. Other areas of social discrimination attracting the attention of religious organizations today are discernible in *interracial justice, labor-management relations, health-care delivery, criminal treatment, worldwide food distribution, educational and employment opportunities, and housing. Because of the magnitude and scope of existing social inequities, *Gaudium et spes* recognizes that reforms will be slow in coming and difficult of achievement. In striving to overcome their natural resistance to change, institutions, like individuals, must be "accommodated by degrees to the highest of all realities, spiritual ones" (ibid.).

[P. A. WOELFL]

EQUALITY IN THE CHURCH

Equality in the Church is intimately connected with a dynamic process of democratization. Those who urge this process believe that it is necessary for the credibility of the Church today. The process must begin with the local Church because the reality of the Church is found in the event of the individual community. The plurality of communities implied becomes a unity by a common belief in Jesus Christ and by the attempt of Christians to orient their lives according to the Gospel message. Vatican Council II strongly stated the principle of equality based on all members' sharing in a union of grace and salvation in Christ (*Lumen gentium* 32).

The Church, a True Community. Equality in the Church, as a matter of social justice, is opposed to any form of oppression or domination. In the concrete, power and authority in the Church are to be exercised in the way that Jesus used them, that is, as a service to others. Authority in the Church cannot be paternalistic or patriarchal. Not that there is no place for authority or people with power in the Church, but the authority must always be responsible (*see* AUTHORITY, ECCLESIASTICAL).

Whatever authority and power in the Church mean, they cannot oppose the freedom of a Christian to live as a man or a woman. The freedom that comes with the acceptance of Revelation and Jesus Christ as Lord relativizes all such distinctions as nationality, sex, race, and social status (*Lumen gentium* 32). The Gospel does not allow for the presence of power structures that create positions of dependence or subordination in the Church. Christ has overcome alienation between persons and the Church must therefore be a truly human community. The Church cannot oppose the struggle for human dignity. Whenever the Church assembles it should be clear to all that redemption has been achieved in Christ. For this to be so, the Church needs to manifest clearly its concern for the happiness and salvation of others in the way the community works and worships together.

Expressions of Equality. The freedom Christ gives is to be reflected in the image of the Church. Among the characteristics of this image of the Church the following four are particularly necessary.

(1) All members of the Church are to contribute to the building of the Church in a collegial manner. The Church is not an institution for the purpose of providing some service as in the case of an insurance company. The Church is not like a family ruled over by a despotic father, but more like a mature community of brothers and sisters. There cannot be two classes of society in the Church, the rulers and the ruled. The vision of the clergy and the laity into two distinct social categories is questionable. Co-responsibility of all the members of the community has to be institutionalized by means of some form of elected body which works in conjunction with the leaders of the community.

(2) The life of the Christian community is necessarily public in character. Official proceedings affecting its life should be made generally available to all the members of the community. A comprehensive pattern of communications is, consequently, a prerequisite. The flow of information must be both ways and not merely from the leaders to the ordinary members of the community. Since the Church is not totalitarian, public criticism is a necessary part of its dynamism and purpose. This criticism should be given some legitimate institutional form.

(3) The fulfillment of the Church's ministry demands ministerial offices. Those who have the gifts for these offices should be so recognized by the community. At present the most obvious example of the lack of equality in the Church is the total exclusion of women from ordained ministry. Leaders should be elected in collaboration with the community. The leaders of the Church and the rest of the community are bound to mutual cooperation. Accountability is a normal corollary of the exercise of office; the exercise of power in the Christian community ought to be constantly checked and verified. Decisions about matters of great importance should not be made unilaterally by the one holding office, but in cooperation with the whole community.

(4) The local Church should possess its own autonomy. Excessive centralization based upon the model of a monarchy conflicts with the equality of the Christian. The relationship between the local and the universal Church is governed by the principle of subsidiarity. In order to be the Sacrament of the world, the Church must be a unity in plurality (*see* CHURCH, LOCAL [THEOLOGY]).

Bibliography: A. CUNNINGHAM, *The Role of Women in Ecclesial Ministry: Biblical and Patristic Foundations* (Washington, D.C. 1976). B. VAN IERSEL and R. MURPHY, Eds., *Office and Ministry in the Church. Concilium* 80 (New York 1972). A. MÜLLER, ed., *Democratization of the Church. Concilium 63* (New York 1971).

[J. L. EMPEREUR]

ESCHATOLOGY

Few areas of theology have seen such an extensive development in the post-conciliar period as has eschatology (5:524). The shift from a one-sided concentration on the salvation of the individual to a reflection on cosmic eschatology that had gained considerable momentum before Vatican Council II has become commonplace.

Theological Aspects. Although eschatology remains necessarily bipolar, most theologians today refuse to separate the final fulfillment of the person from the redemption of the universe. Recent treatises on the meaning of *death shed new light on this polarity. The tendency to envisage Christ's Second Coming or parousia as a catastrophic event predetermined by God to take place at a wholly unexpected moment has given way to a more evolutionary concept. Rather than terminating history, eschatology is now generally viewed as its fulfillment in terms of the Christian maturity implied in the notion of Pleroma (9:129). The content of this fulfillment has been developed in a variety of ways which can be only briefly summarized here.

Parallel with emphasis on the cosmic dimensions of eschatology, there has been a decided acceleration in the trend toward incarnational, as opposed to soteriological, theology. The redemption of the world is envisaged more and more in terms of its gradual divinization. In the phraseology of Karl Rahner (EncTheol, see bibliog.), the self-communication of God, which finds its peak moment in the Incarnation, is one side of the coin; the other side is the transfiguration, rather than annihilation, of creation through self-transcendence. This approach involves a deeper recognition of the continuity between mankind and nature, between the spiritual and the material. This recognition has led to a much more positive evaluation of secularization theology, with an increasing reliance on the data of the social sciences and technology.

These trends in eschatology stem, at least remotely, from a notably increasing *Christocentrism in theology. Not only is more attention being given to the humanity of Christ, but emphasis on his resurrected state as *normative* dominates the field of eschatology. Although the biblical concept of resurrection implies a bodily dimension, it is essentially a transhistorical event consisting in the radical transformation of the deceased *person* and a mystical integration into the risen body of Christ. As Léon-Dufour states it, "Jesus Christ is both a person into whom the universe is drawn, and the universe made personal in him" (241). The Eucharist is understood more clearly as *the* eschatological Sacrament, in which the consecrated bread and wine are seen as foreshadowings of what the whole world will have become and when (in the opinion of some theologians) the surface of his Mystical Body will have been transformed into the recognizable image of his glorified countenance.

Consequences. The vital role of human persons in the shaping of the future is a central theme of contemporary eschatology. Increasing stress is placed on the Christian community's obligation to assume responsibility for promoting social justice so that the world may become the vehicle of the *Kingdom of God. The injunctions of Vatican II's *Gaudium et spes* have been taken literally by a significant segment of Catholics for whom the corporal works of mercy, together with the abolition of war, social injustice, and discrimination are no longer merely salutary practices but categorical imperatives. As evidence, it should be noted that support of the peace movement at a variety of clerical and lay levels was instrumental in the decision to withdraw U.S. troops from Vietnam. Priests and members of religious orders have sought and obtained election to the U.S. Congress and other political offices which were formerly out of bounds. Men and women belonging to ten different religious orders work together in Chicago at "8th Day," a center founded in 1974 for the purpose of building coalitions and helping to educate and organize for political influence in the area of social justice.

The mid-1970's have also seen an expansion of organizations supporting ethnic and other oppressed groups in their fight for equality of civil opportunities. Originating in Latin America, a *liberation theology flourishes throughout the Western Hemisphere. Widespread, but not universal, backing has been given by Catholics to the Equal Rights Amendment. At their Dec. 1977 meeting, major superiors of four leading religious leadership organizations (Leadership Conference of Women Religious, Conference of Major Superiors of Men, *Confederacion Latino-Americano de Religiosos, Conférence Religieuse Canadienne*) declared that the promotion of justice for the poor and oppressed is a primary aim of religious life. And even though this decade has witnessed a certain "privatization" of morality, especially in the field of human sexuality, there has been strong support among Catholics for the antiabortion struggle. One final voice must be added to the Church's prophetic witness, that of E. F. Schumacher, the late British economist, whose book protesting the strangling, depersonalizing complexity of big business has become a bestseller in the U.S.

The post-conciliar era has seen the continued influence of radical existentialism. Although the valuable insights of R. *Bultmann's realized eschatology have, in general, been modified and integrated into the mainstream of biblical hermeneutics, extremist positions continue to exert a significant appeal. In 1977 a group of British theologians published an anthology of essays to popularize a radical demythologizing of Christology: "Jesus was . . . 'a man approved by God' . . . the later conception of him as God incarnate, the Second Person of the Holy Trinity living a human life, is a mythological or poetic way of expressing his significance for us" (Hick, ix). More nuanced in their approach to eschatology are process theology (16:365) and the theology of *hope proposed by the Protestant theologian, Jürgen Moltmann. In a recent book, Moltmann follows Dietrich Bonhoeffer's pattern of prognosis, playing down church structure in favor of voluntary fellowships energized by the Spirit's charismata. Speculations regarding the possibility of man himself effecting the parousia, e.g. by medically produced immortality, seem far-fetched.

See also HISTORY AND ESCHATOLOGY (16:210); GOD, TRANSCENDENCE AND IMMANENCE OF (16:194); HERMENEUTICS (CONTEMPORARY) (16:206).

Bibliography: EncTheol 434, 1450. J. C. HAUGHEY, ed., *The Faith That Does Justice* (New York 1977) esp. ch. 8. J. HICK, Ed., *The Myth of God Incarnate* (Philadelphia 1977). X. LÉON-DUFOUR, *Resurrection and the Message of Jesus*, tr. R. N. WILSON (New York 1974). G. MARTELET, *The Risen Christ and the Eucharistic World* (New York 1976). E. F. SCHUMACHER, *Small Is Beautiful* (New York 1973). Philadelphia (41st) Eucharistic Congress, *Jesus, the Living Bread* (Plainfield, N.J. 1976).

[M. K. HOPKINS]

ESCRIVÁ DE BALAGUER Y ALBÁS, JOSÉ MARÍA

Founder of Opus Dei (10:709); b. Barbastro, Spain, Jan. 9, 1902, d. Rome, June 26, 1975. After high school he studied at the School of Law of the Univ. of Saragossa, subsequently receiving the doctorate in law from the Univ. of Madrid. He studied for the priesthood in Saragossa and was ordained on March 28, 1925. Later he received a doctorate in theology from the Pontifical Lateran University, Rome. His priestly work began in rural parishes and was continued in the slums of Saragossa and Madrid, among university students and people from a wide variety of backgrounds. On Oct. 2, 1928 he founded Opus Dei, an association whose object is to spread Christian doctrine and virtues in all environments of social and professional life. Its spirituality consists in seeking the fullness of Christian life through the members' sanctification of the practice of their own profession or occupation in the world. Opus Dei itself carries out only works of spiritual direction and apostolate; its members enjoy the same complete freedom and independence in their professional activities as any other citizen. Currently (1978) the association is established on every continent with more than 70,000 members of 80 nationalities.

In 1946 Msgr. Escrivá de Balaguer moved his residence to Rome and travelled throughout Europe to prepare and consolidate the apostolic work of Opus Dei. Between 1970 and 1975 he carried out an extensive work of preaching and catechetical instruction in practically every country of Latin America and in various European nations. In addition to historical, juridical, and theological writings, he is the author of widely read spiritual books including *The Way* (Chicago 1954), *Holy Rosary* (Chicago 1953), *Conversations with Msgr. Escrivá de Balaguer* (Shannon 1968), *Christ Is Passing By* (Chicago 1974), *Friends of God* (in press; Spanish Madrid 1977), and *La Abadesa de las Huelgas* (Madrid 1944). *The Way*, first published in 1934 under the title *Consideraciones espirituales*, by 1977 had sold 2,680,000 copies in 34 languages. His successor, elected unanimously on Sept. 15, 1975, is the Very Rev. Alvaro del Portillo y Diez de Sollano.

Bibliography: S. BERNAL, *Msgr. Josemaria Escrivá de Balaguer* (London and New York 1977). A. BYRNE: *Sanctifying Ordinary Work* (New York 1975). J. THIERRY, *Opus Dei, a Close-Up* (Cortland, N.Y. 1975).

[M. M. KENNEDY]

ETHNICITY

While there is no general agreement on the referent of the term "ethnicity," it is widely used, indicating that it points to a reality of particular relevance to American society. In its narrowest sense, the term refers to group and individual identity based on national origins. More broadly, it refers to group consciousness based on an assumed or real common origin, which can therefore include the factors of religion, language, or region of the world. Most broadly, ethnicity refers to diversity in

American society, which includes the nuance of the interaction of those groups defined by the term.

The significance of ethnicity lies in its reference to the salience of group identity for society in general. Americans can and do act in groups and identify themselves in group terms. Ethnic-group identity is not the same as identity through membership in a voluntary group. The characteristics of ethnic-group identity tend to perdure, that is, for example, Polish-American traits remain throughout life, whether the individual consciously chooses to identify with them or not. Voluntary-group membership is an association by intention, terminating with the end of the intention. Ethnicity, on the other hand, refers to enduring factors, sometimes called "primordial ties" or "givens"—kinship connections, religious identity, language, and those particular cultural or social patterns associated with a particular geographical place.

Ethnicity is a worldwide phenomenon. The Basques, French Canadians, Walloons, Ibos, the Sherazi, Lebanese Muslims, Irish Catholics are by reason of religion, national origin, language, or geography ethnic groups. But ethnicity is distinct in each country, which is to say that ethnic identity is contextual. Being an Italian-American or an American Catholic is very different from being simply Italian or an Italian Catholic, though all these designations share some traits.

Ethnicity is important because it helps provide coherence, meaning, value, and order to individual, family, and group life. It satisfies the individual psychological need of identity definition. It serves the social function of establishing, preserving, and inculcating basic values and norms. It has the political function of allowing individuals to organize into interest groups to exercise their political rights. Finally, it serves the important cultural function of maintaining traditions and institutions.

Vatican Council II, in affirming that when persons consciously take part in social groups they are carrying out the design of God, also affirms the value of ethnicity (*Gaudium et spes* 55–57). Moreover, it makes the right to full cultural development, to which ethnicity is integral (ibid. 55), an issue of social justice because persons can only achieve authentic and complete humanity through culture (ibid. 59). The function of the Church is to recognize and help implement the full cultural development of individuals and groups, so that all might participate in the cultural benefits that allow the fulfillment of the human race (ibid. 60–62).

Bibliography: N. GLAZER and D. P. MOYNIHAN, *Ethnicity: Theory and Experience* (Cambridge, Mass. 1975). M. GORDON, *Assimilation in American Life* (New York 1964). A. M. GREELEY, *Ethnicity in the United States* (New York 1974).

[R. D. PASQUARIELLO]

ETHNICS, RIGHTS OF

The entirety of the Judaeo-Christian tradition proclaims the intrinsic rights of minorities within any population. This tradition moreover proclaims ethnic and cultural pluralism as values for humankind. One can show this from Sacred Scripture by moving from the ancient Hebrew laws protecting the alien to the words on community in multiplicity placed by the Book of Revelation in the mouths of the saints: "By your blood you did ransom men for God from every tribe and tongue and people and nation and have made them a kingdom and priests to our God" (Rev 5.9–10). Awareness of these elements and their practical implementation have not, however, always been explicit or faithful. Official church pronouncements have emphasized them carefully only recently and a broader consciousness of them among the church's leaders and people has facilitated proper activity on behalf of minority rights.

Vatican Council II's documents offer many authoritative ecclesiastical statements relative to the rights of diverse ethnic and cultural groups within a society. Especially forceful on the point is the Pastoral Constitution on the Church in the Modern World (*Gaudium et spes* 53, 60, 73). Council, Roman documents, and the statements of national episcopal conferences, the American in particular, have repeatedly enunciated and developed the point that societal unity finds itself furthered by encouragement of ethnic and cultural pluralism. Many actions on the part of church institutions and individual Catholics in these years carry dramatic instruction on the values in question. To mention just three: liturgical reform has universally declared ethnic and cultural pluralism to be right; racial and other such forms of segregation along with required conformity to ruling ethnocultural patterns have, at least in principle, ended in churches, schools, and other church agencies; the Church's voice has been and remains often loud in advocacy for the rights of minorities and for the maintenance of ethnic and cultural identity with more than ghetto forms.

That the United States is a polyethnic and multicultural nation is an empirical given; that this datum has not been honored and respected as it should be is now widely acknowledged as fact. The abandonment of melting-pot mythology nationally has resulted at least partly from awareness that it masked domination of all others by particular amalgams of ethnic and cultural values. This abandonment has compelled many, first, to plead for, then, to demand overthrowal of systems that oppress minority ethnic and cultural values and, finally, to require that these values be systemically encouraged as integral to the U.S. self-assessment, rather than merely peripheral and only incidental. (The self-image to be desired may be exemplified by way of contrast with such illustrations as the *Saturday Evening Post* covers of just a few years ago. For their dominant Waspish imagery one could substitute a set of images that depict the differences among peoples seriously and with equal mythic honor, not simply as quaint or as the eccentric irrelevancies of background nonparticipants.) The right of peoples in this nation to a developed ethnic and cultural diversity is not only compatible with the Gospel and Catholic doctrine, but is, as indicated above, the official teaching of the Church. Catholics, then, in this country possess an obligation to champion the fight for ethnic rights. Men and women of whatever ethnic origin or cultural pattern must permit in federal, state, and local laws and in their application nothing that hinders or penalizes ethnic or cultural diversity, but must rather promote all that will respect and encourage sound pluralism.

[M. PAREDES]

EUCHARIST, WORSHIP AND CUSTODY OF

On the Feast of Corpus Christi, June 21, 1973, the Congregation of Divine Worship revised the regulations regarding "Holy Communion and the Worship of the

Eucharist Outside Mass." This article reflects the teaching of the decree concerning the holy hour, perpetual and nocturnal adoration, spiritual communion, and Eucharistic processions and congresses.

Principles. "The celebration of the eucharist is the center of the entire Christian life... The other sacraments, all the ministries of the Church, and the works of the apostolate are united with the eucharist and are directed toward it... The celebration of the eucharist in the sacrifice of the Mass is truly the origin and goal of the worship which is shown to the eucharist outside Mass" (HolyCommIntrod 1–2). On the other hand, "the sacrament is not to be less the object of adoration because it was instituted by Christ the Lord to be received as food... The eucharistic mystery must be considered in its fulness, both in the celebration of Mass and in the worship of the Sacrament, which is reserved after Mass to extend the grace of the sacrifice. The primary and original reason for reservation of the eucharist is viaticum. The secondary reasons are the giving of communion and the adoration of our Lord Jesus Christ" (ibid. 3–5). On the meaning of Real Presence the decree repeats what Vatican Council II's Constitution on Liturgy (*Sacrosanctum Concilium* 7), Paul VI's encyclical *Mysterium fidei* (1965), and the 1967 instruction of the Congregation of Rites, *Eucharisticum Mysterium* 55 (ActApS 59 [1967] 568–569), have taught concerning the chief ways in which Christ is present in his Church. And "this presence of Christ under the appearance of bread and wine is called real, not to exclude other kinds of presence as if they were not real, but because it is real *par excellence*.... It is highly recommended that the place [for the reservation of the Eucharist] be suitable also for private adoration and prayer, so that the faithful may easily, fruitfully, and constantly honor the Lord through personal worship" (HolyCommIntrod. 6, 9).

The introduction also notes that because "the eucharistic sacrifice is the source and culmination of the whole Christian life, ... devotions should be in harmony with the sacred liturgy, take their origin from the liturgy, and lead the people back to the liturgy.... The faithful should remember that this presence... is directed toward sacramental and spiritual communion... The faithful should make every effort to worship Christ the Lord in the sacrament, depending upon the circumstances of their own life. Pastors should encourage them in this by example and word" (ibid. 79, 80).

Exposition. "During the exposition of the Blessed Sacrament, the celebration of Mass is prohibited in the body of the church... The celebration of the eucharistic mystery includes in a more perfect way the internal communion to which exposition seeks to lead the faithful" (ibid. 83). When solemn exposition of the blessed sacrament takes place for a short period of time (such as a few hours or less), it is "to be arranged in such a way that the blessing with the eucharist is preceded by a suitable period of readings of the word of God, songs, prayers, and sufficient time for silent prayer" (ibid. 89) The document also notes that some religious communities and other groups have the practice of perpetual Eucharistic adoration or adoration over extended periods of time. When the whole community takes part in adoration with readings, songs, and silent worship this will promote the spirit of unity and brotherhood which the eucharist signifies and effects.

Adoration by one or two members of the community in turn "is also highly commended... The worshippers pray to the Lord in the name of the Church" (ibid. 90). Whenever exposition with the monstrance is to extend over a long period, a throne in an elevated position, but not be too lofty or distant, may be used (ibid. 93).

Processions and Congresses. It is for the local Ordinary to judge whether Eucharistic processions are opportune in today's circumstances (ibid. 101). Eucharistic congresses should be regarded as a kind of station "to which a particular community invites an entire local Church, or to which an individual local Church invites other Churches of a single region or nation or even of the entire world" (ibid. 109). Specialists ought to make research beforehand "which will lead to the consideration of genuine needs and foster the progress of theological studies and the good of the local Church" (ibid. 110). One of the primary concerns must be "research and promotion of social undertakings for human development and the proper distribution of property..." (ibid. 111 c). The celebration will include "an opportunity for common prayers and extended adoration in the presence of the blessed sacrament exposed at designated churches" (ibid. 112 c).

The main thrust of the liturgy on the celebration of the Lord's Supper and, perhaps most of all, the emphasis placed on the importance of the active apostolate in the 1960s account for the fact that Eucharistic devotions outside Mass are much less popular now than they were. Confraternities (or "pious unions") which promote these devotions have lost the major portion of their membership (e.g., the People's and the Priests' Eucharistic Leagues, the Nocturnal Adoration Society, the once flourishing but now defunct Catholic Youth Adoration). The practice of perpetual, and particularly nocturnal, adoration has ceased in many of the communities of congregations that formerly were characterized by this devotion (e.g., the Congregation of the Blessed Sacrament). Now they normally pray their holy hour at a fixed time, either before they begin or after they return from their ministerial functions.

See also BENEDICTION AND EXPOSITION OF THE BLESSED SACRAMENT; FORTY HOURS DEVOTION; HOLY COMMUNION, RITES OF.

[F. COSTA]

EUCHARISTIC PRAYERS

A Eucharistic Prayer is a lyric and ecstatic summary prayer-statement of what it means for the Church to celebrate the Eucharist. The prayer makes a statement which is Eucharistic in the fullest sense, one that is theological, Christological, and ecclesiological. As public prayer, the manner of statement is evocative language. The Prayer is designed to speak for and to the entire praying assembly, i.e., it is designed both to express the faith of the assembly and to deepen it by calling it to its most fundamental reality. Eucharistic Prayers have traditionally emanated from local Churches, developing out of the self-understanding of those Churches over long periods of time. There are four set Eucharistic Prayers in the new *Sacramentary.

Eucharistic Prayer I. This, the Roman Canon, is the traditional Eucharistic Prayer of the Roman Rite. Eucharistic Prayers II–IV were introduced with the revised Order of Mass in 1969. Eucharistic Prayer I only gradually came to be used in all the Catholic Churches of the Christian West, though an early version of it was already being used at Milan in the latter part of the 4th century. By *c*. 600 the Prayer had achieved its present form. Stylistically, the Prayer is cast in the sonorous court rhetoric of the late Roman Empire. Unlike other classic Eucharistic Prayers, the Roman Canon is almost entirely cast as a prayer of petition, except for its *Preface and Holy, Holy, Holy. Another distinctive mark of the Prayer is its allowance for variability—most notably in the Preface, but also in its other segments. Apart from the Preface-Sanctus, the Prayer is cast as a petition that by its offering of the gifts of bread and wine the Church will be sanctified.

Theologically, the Prayer reflects a perspective akin to that of the Letter to the Hebrews. The earthly Church is seen as conjoined to the heavenly Church and the prayer for the assembly expands into prayer for others. The Church is seen as in communion with the ascended Lord and his triumphant Church, and yet its earthly members pursue their pilgrim way as sinners, trusting in the mercy of God. The references to the sacrifices of Abel, Abraham, and Melchisidek, as also the numerous commemorations of the Apostles and martyrs, reflect the sense of being encouraged by the heavenly "cloud of witnesses." The medium of this communion between the earthly and heavenly Church is the offered gifts. They are seen as being taken to the heavenly altar, so that those who share them receive the Body and Blood of Christ and share in the life of his saints. A unique feature of the Prayer is its singling out the recitation of the institution narrative as a consecratory moment: the narrative is preceded by a petition that the offered gifts may become for us the Body and Blood of Christ.

Eucharistic Prayer II. This is based on the Eucharistic Prayer from the *Apostolic Tradition* (*c*. 215) usually attributed to Hippolytus of Rome. The distinctive feature of the original is its portrayal of Christ as God's servant who by the work of the Spirit forms by his passion, death, and resurrection a new people as servants of God. The first part of the Prayer, praising God for Christ as servant, is integrally linked to the Anamnesis (calling to mind), which identifies the Church's self-offering with the offering of Christ, "We give you thanks for counting us worthy to stand in your presence and serve you." These distinctive features are somewhat obscured in the Sacramentary's adaptation. The introduction of a Sanctus after the praise of God and the inclusion of an invocation that the bread and wine be consecrated by the power of the Spirit before the institution narrative, are features which separate the praise from the offering. Virtually all distinctive features of the original prayer are obliterated when its proper Preface is not used.

Eucharistic Prayer III. This is best understood as an adaptation of Prayer I, but with a structure more intelligible to a contemporary congregation, and substituting for the ecclesiology and Christology of the Letter to the Hebrews the reconciliation theology of that to the Colossians. By so doing, Prayer III articulates a more cosmic vision of the economy of salvation and offsets the impression given by the Roman Canon that it is only Christians who are worthy of the Church's attention in prayer. Like Prayer II, Prayer III precedes the institution narrative with an invocation for consecration of the bread and the wine. The Anamnesis (seg-

ment after the institution narrative) of Prayer III is unusual, offering as it does Christ's sacrifice with no mention of the bread and cup. The balanced expressions of the Roman Canon, affirming both the Real Presence of Christ and the function of the bread and wine as signs, are discarded in favor of a literal realism hitherto unknown in Catholic prayer patterns.

Eucharistic Prayer IV. This represents an adaptation of the anaphora of St. Basil, used in both Byzantine and Coptic rites and probably emanating from Antioch in the 4th century. The distinctive feature of this Prayer is its cosmic sweep, moving from the awesome reality of God to creation through the history of salvation to the parousia. Somewhat more successfully than Prayers II and III, it incorporates a theology of the Holy Spirit as integral to the Prayer and thus as integral to a Christian world-view. Somewhat alien to the structure of this type of prayer, however, is the inclusion of an invocation for the coming of the Spirit (Epiclesis) upon the gifts before the institution narrative—a "correction" of the original Prayer not in harmony with the statement of Vatican Council II's Constitution on the Liturgy that all rites are of equal value (*Sacrosanctum Concilium* 4).

Bibliography: A. HÄNGGI and I. PAHL, *Prex Eucharistica* (Fribourg 1968) complete bibliog. J. JUNGMANN, *The Mass of the Roman Rite*, 2 v. tr. F. A. BRUNNER (New York 1949) v. 2; *The Eucharistic Prayer*, tr. R. L. BATLEY (New York 1956). C. VAGGAGINI, *The Canon of the Mass and Liturgical Reform*, tr. P. COUGHLAN (Staten Island, N.Y. 1967). J. B. RYAN, *The Eucharistic Prayers, a Study in Contemporary Liturgy* (New York 1974). L. SOUBIGOU, *A Commentary on the Prefaces and Eucharistic Prayers of the Roman Missal*, tr. J. A. OTTO (Collegeville, Minn. 1971).

[R. A. KEIFER]

EUCHARISTIC PRAYERS FOR SPECIAL OCCASIONS

The Eucharistic Prayers for Reconciliation were originally designed for use during the 1975 year of reconciliation, but permission to use them has not been rescinded. The Eucharistic Prayers for Masses with Children were approved for trial use in 1974; permission for their use has been extended beyond the initial three-year trial period. Other Eucharistic Prayers have been approved at the request of episcopal conferences for specific regions and occasions.

For Reconciliation. The Eucharistic Prayers for Reconciliation retain the same structure as the Eucharistic Prayers of the Sacramentary. The first part of Prayer I for reconciliation is essentially a conflation of materials from Prayers II and IV of the Sacramentary. Material from the post-Sanctus of Prayer IV is incorporated into the Preface. The institution narrative is introduced by material about the paschal mystery from Prayer II. The result is that this prayer can best be seen as an improved version of Prayer II, with the institution narrative evoking the whole paschal mystery and not merely the Last Supper. Prayer II for reconciliation is less tied to biblical and traditional phrasing, but what it gains in a contemporized immediacy it also loses in richness. There is a glibness of expression that strikes the ear as excessively optimistic about peace in the world. Neither Eucharistic Prayer for Reconciliation eases basic problems already present in prayers II–IV of the Sacramentary.

Masses with Children. The Eucharistic Prayers for Masses with Children are structured in the same fashion as prayers II–IV of the Sacramentary. In a number of important ways, however, these prayers show significant improvement. The General Instruction in the Sacramentary states that the Eucharistic Prayer expresses the prayer of the whole Church and that by means of the Eucharistic Prayer, the whole Church offers the Eucharist (GenInstrRomMissal 54). These Prayers are richly interspersed with acclamations, and their language is less contrived. The result is Prayers more readily audible to a contemporary congregation and more readily experienced as prayers in which they share fully.

Another improvement is the moving of the people's Anamnesis Acclamation to a position following the celebrant's Anamnesis. This placement both clarifies the meaning of the Anamnesis and the function of the Acclamation. The purpose of the Anamnesis is to express the Church's offering of the Eucharist and by way of acclamation the congregation expresses its share in that offering. Since the celebrant speaks on behalf of the congregation and in its name, it is more appropriate that the Acclamation should follow the celebrant's praying of the Anamnesis. The celebrant's praying leads naturally to the climactic finale of the whole congregation's acclamatory expressing of that act of offering. The role of both priest and people is much more effectively signed in this Prayer structure.

In view of the improvements upon the Sacramentary Prayers which the Prayers for Masses with Children represent, it needs to be asked whether they should not serve as models for future development of the Eucharistic Prayer.

See also MASSES WITH CHILDREN.

[R. A. KEIFER]

EUCHARISTIC SHARING
(INTERCOMMUNION)

The appropriateness of divided Christians nonetheless celebrating together and sharing in the Eucharist, occasionally or regularly, and that not simply on the basis of a spontaneous personal decision but with eventual official approbation, has been widely discussed and debated in the last fifteen years. Roman Catholic theological writing on Eucharistic sharing is now widespread, although begun later than the work of the World Council of Churches, the Anglican Church, or those Churches that officially permit open communion. When the *New Catholic Encyclopedia* was published (1967) there was no entry at all on "intercommunion"; in its first supplement., v. 16 in 1974 Eucharistic hospitality was treated in the context of the article on the ecumenical movement (16:147), which summarized the Vatican II Decree on Ecumenism (1964) and the three follow-up directives of the Secretariat for Promoting Christian Unity (1967, 1972, 1973). What is added here are further terminological clarifications about Communion, reference to recent episcopal guidelines, *bilateral consultations, and a growing uneasiness about the correctness of the presuppositions within which the possibility of Eucharistic sharing is discussed. There can be no definitive statement on Eucharistic hospitality or intercommunion precisely when a new consensus on this question may possibly be emerging in the Catholic community that could alter the present disciplinary legislation. The preference of a growing number of theologians, for the terms "Eucharistic hospitality" or "sharing" over the ambiguous and tautological word "intercommunion" is followed here.

Communion in the New Testament. Communion is a multivalent religious term. Communion (κοινωνία) was one of several expressions St. Paul used to express the most intimate union of a Christian with God and consequently with other believers through the salvific power of Christ's Spirit. Paul's formula of blessing, recently incorporated into the Roman Liturgy as an opening greeting, relates communion with grace and love: "The grace (χάρις) of the Lord Jesus Christ and the love (ἀγάπη) of the God and the communion/fellowship (koinōnia) of the Holy Spirit [is/be] with you all" (2 Cor 13.13). Paul found *koinōnia* to be a useful image for the mystery of God's love made visible in Christ's Incarnation. Secondarily, Paul treated the ecclesiological implications of this communion in terms of sharing with one another in the Church. The main focus was the relationship between God and believer rather than a description about common faith affirmations. God is seen as calling the Christian into communion with his Son (1 Cor 1.9). The divine initiative results in our being made communicants with Christ (2 Cor 1.7; Phil 3.10) and in the divine nature (2 Pt 1.4; 1 Jn 1.3,6). Paul did recognize that communion has a double effect: grace is bestowed to draw the individual closer to God, but grace also builds up Church unity. Quite concretely and in an extended sense, *koinōnia* could also refer to financial relief or aid provided to needy members of other Churches (2 Cor 9.13; Rom 15.26; Heb 13.16) as an outward expression of Christians' participation in the Spirit. Paul also calls sharing in the Body and Blood of Christ at the Lord's Supper a *koinōnia* (1 Cor 10.16) and this Eucharistic reference has been important in subsequent usage. To "receive communion" meant to "partake of the Eucharist." The New Testament word *koinōnia* was rendered variously in the Latin Vulgate as *communicatio*, *societas*, *participatio*, *collatio*, and only once as *communio* (Heb 13.16).

Later Meanings of Communion. As with many words in ecclesiastical usage, the term "communion" was to undergo a shift in emphasis. With the rise of monepiscopacy and concern for ecclesial solidarity against heterodox teachers, communion often referred to the bond uniting bishops and faithful with each other or that bond uniting the faithful among themselves locally or across a wide geographical extension. By the late 4th century, probably first in Latin, the expression *communio sanctorum* was added to creeds (St. Jerome's *Confession* of 378; the Council of Nîmes, 394); it may refer either to sharing with the saints (*sancti*) or sharing in the holy mysteries (*sancta*) preeminently Baptism and Eucharist. Ecclesial communion between local Churches was expressed variously, as, e.g., participating in synods, sharing in the installation of bishops for neighboring Churches, or offering the Eucharist to travellers from a distant Church provided they bore *litterae communicatoriae*, a certificate of good standing in their native Church.

Vatican Council II strongly emphasized the ecclesial dimension of communion when it noted that some Churches are not in *plena communio* with the Catholic Church (*Unitatis redintegratio* 4; 14; 17; *Orientalium Ecclesiarum* 4; 30). The Council also spoke of *communio ecclesiastica* (*Unitatis redintegratio* 3; 4; 20; 21) or *communio hierarchica* (*Lumen gentium* 22; *Christus Dominus* 5). Pope Paul VI in addressing Patriarch Athenagoras I, Oct. 26, 1967, spoke of the "profound and mysterious communion" existing between the Orthodox and the Roman Catholic Church (*Tomos agapēs* n. 190). The wide spectrum of usages for "communion" explains the growing preference for the term "shared Eucharist." Through God's salvific initiative, through shared faith in the Lordship of Christ, through Baptism and a shared vision of Christian life, *inter-communion* exists even among members of divided Churches.

Official Attitudes toward Eucharistic Hospitality. Vatican II spoke of "the wonderful sacrament of the Eucharist by which the unity of the Church is both signified and brought about" (*Unitatis redintegratio* 2). The Catholic position on Eucharistic sharing expressed at the Council and subsequently reiterated is that such sharing should normally take place only when it signifies already existing unity. Shared Eucharist, so it is argued, should not take place indiscriminately as a means for achieving unity. The precondition is doctrinal unity, not that unity in Christ already present through Baptism, which is presumed. If shared Eucharist were more widely and officially practiced, closer doctrinal unity, it is feared, will never be achieved. But since Vatican II did not treat of Eucharistic hospitality in detail but set down only broad norms for *communicatio in sacris* (ibid. 5–12), the directives do not appear definitive. As further ecumenical explorations about the nature of belief in the Eucharist take place, the Catholic Church will have to reevaluate its directives. This could be done at an ecumenical council with representatives of the major Christian Churches. Another possibility would be to encourage decisions first at diocesan or national levels. Currently the Catholic Church is open to individual Orthodox, Anglican or Protestant Christians participating in the Eucharist celebrated in the Catholic Church under very special conditions, but it does not in principle allow reciprocity whereby Catholics may receive the Eucharist in other Churches except Orthodox. Before admitting mutuality the Catholic Church would first have to recognize the validity of ordinations in Churches lacking what has been called *apostolic succession and it would also need to state unequivocally its conviction that Christ is "really" sacramentally present in other Eucharistic celebrations. In light of previous official teaching and certain papal decisions, e.g. Leo XIII's bull *Apostolicae curae* on Anglican Orders (1:696), such a major reevaluation cannot be taken without full deliberation. A conversion of attitudes would be necessary as well as careful pastoral catechesis to avoid popular confusion and distress.

Recent Episcopal Guidelines. During the 1970s several episcopal directives were published envisaging special local situations and establishing the possibility of wider Eucharistic sharing. Noteworthy among these directives are those of Bishop Elchinger of Strasbourg (1972) and the Swiss Synod (1975). The Strasbourg directive addresses partners in mixed marriages (*foyers mixtes*), but does permit and encourage under proper circumstances even reciprocal Eucharistic sharing. In the U.S. guidelines were published by Bishop George A. Hammes of Superior, Wisconsin (1973) and Archbishop Peter L. Gerety of Newark (1978). They are somewhat restricted in scope, concerned with individuals and not groups and only with non-Catholics' reception of the Eucharist in the Catholic Church. Typical of the conditions for Eucharistic sharing are those laid down by the Newark guidelines. Non-Catholics who wish to receive Communion in the Catholic Church must experience a serious spiritual need; have no recourse to a minister of

their own community for a significant time or reason; spontaneously and freely ask to receive Communion; have a faith in the Eucharist conforming to Catholic belief; have a proper disposition, be leading a worthy life, and be free in their own ecclesial community to request admission to the Eucharist in another Church. The Newark directive allows priests to decide whether these conditions are met without conferring with the local bishop. These guidelines have been criticized as requiring onerous procedures and as marked by triumphalistic language.

Theological Reactions. A strong tide of feeling has been rising in some quarters of the Catholic Church that official intercommunion should be approved without further delay. Indeed some assert that the onus of proof now lies with those who wish to postpone a decision in favor of official Eucharistic hospitality. The particular types of objections brought against the present Catholic reluctance to approve Eucharistic sharing are as follows. The Eucharist is a Sacrament of healing and not an ecclesial celebration of doctrinal unity. Christ in his Eucharistic presence is the source and strength of the drive to unity no less than its goal. Second, Christians of principal Churches do in fact share the essential Christian doctrines enshrined in the creeds of the earliest centuries. Again, since the Reformation much development and clarification have taken place in theology and in practices of popular piety within various Churches. Growth in theological understanding, symbolized in such consensus statements as the Windsor Document (1971) of the *Anglican-Roman Catholic International Commission or the U.S. Lutheran/Roman Catholic agreement on the Eucharist, has been notable (*see* LUTHERAN/ROMAN CATHOLIC DIALOGUE). If these consensus statements are accurate, which seems to be the case, and if they are to be adopted officially as common descriptions of Eucharistic belief, then sharing not only on an individual basis would seem to be possible. Fourth, it is argued that one should not reduce to a system of regulations a dynamic sacramental principle. Furthermore, every Church shares the ambiguity of all human understanding so that some serious disagreement in the articulation of belief is still compatible with Eucharistic sharing. A sixth objection concerns the implied equal status of the sign-character and cause-character of the Sacraments that underlies the current Vatican position that inevitably leads to an impasse. Finally, the Lord's Supper, precisely as *Lord's* Supper, is not the place to practice church discipline but should be seen as a sign of the messianic banquet open to a much wider circle.

Recent Developments. In sermons given in April 1977 and January 1978 the Archbishop of Canterbury, Donald Coggan, raised the question for Anglicans and Roman Catholics whether the time had not now arrived when such a measure of agreement on so many fundamentals of the Gospel does exist that a relationship of shared communion could be encouraged by the leadership of both Churches. Noting the increased incidence of unofficial intercommunion among Anglicans and Catholics in various parts of the world, Coggan asked whether perhaps the Holy Spirit is not speaking to the leadership of the Churches through the voice of people who see the scandal of disunity. He argued that underlying differences of doctrine, of expression, of explanation is a failure to repent of the way Anglicans and Catholics have injured one another in the past. These public statements were noted by Pope Paul VI and the English Cardinal Archbishop of Westminster, Basil Hume, but no formal acceptance or rejection has as yet taken place. In October 1978, at the time of his installation, Pope John Paul II met with Abp. Coggan, but the following month warned against haste in regard to Eucharistic sharing.

As officials of the Catholic Church continue to ponder this central question of ecumenism, it has become clearer that Eucharistic sharing is a modern problem not soluble simply by appeal to precedents from earlier days. The issue revolves around a question of pastoral care and governance rather than around insuperable doctrinal factors. Change would occasion shock and resistance in some quarters; delay would cause disillusionment and tensions with church authorities. How specifically the Catholic Church will resolve this dilemma in the future cannot be foreseen.

See also CHURCH AND COMMUNIO.

Bibliography: Church documents in addition to the Vatican II decrees: *Tomos agapēs* (Vatican City 1971), esp. the exchanges between Pope Paul VI and Patriarch Athenagoras I, as well as other Orthodox-RC papers. Secretariat for Promoting Christian Unity, "Directory Concerning Ecumenical Matters. Part One" [dated May 14, 1967], Flannery 483–501 (also USCC Publ. Office); "On Admitting Other Christians to Eucharistic Communion in the Catholic Church" [dated June 1, 1972], Flannery 554–559 (also USCC Publ. Office); "Note Interpretating the Instruction" [dated Oct. 17, 1973], Flannery 560–563.
Episcopal Directives: L. A. ELCHINGER, Bishop of Strasbourg, "Eucharistic Hospitality for Interchurch Marriages" [dated Nov. 30, 1972], *One in Christ* 9 (1973) 371–380; "Further Reflections" [dated Jan. 25, 1973], ibid. 380–387. G. A. HAMMES, Bishop of Superior, Wis., "Pastoral Letter on Eucharistic Sharing" [dated Mar. 22, 1973], *One in Christ* 9 (1973) 401–404; Swiss Interdiocesan Synodal Assembly, "Pastoral Instruction Concerning Eucharistic Hospitality" [dated Mar. 1, 1975], *One in Christ* 11 (1975) 376–382. P. L. GERETY, Archbishop of Newark, N.J., "The Pastoral Reasons for Eucharistic Sharing" [dated Feb. 9, 1978], Origins 7 (1978) 534–540.
Bibliographies: G. PIGAULT and J. SCHLICK, *Eucharist and Eucharistic Hospitality: International Bibliography 1971–73* (Strasbourg 1974). J. B. BRANTSCHEN and P. SELVATICO, in H. STIRNIMANN, ed., *Interkommunion. Hoffnungen zu bedenken* (Fribourg 1971) 77–149.
Studies: V. VAJTA, "*Intercommunion*" *avec Rome?* (Paris 1970). G. KREMS and R. MUMM, eds., *Evangelisch-Katholische Abendmahlsgemeinschaft?* (Regensburg 1971). A. PÜTZ, *Interkommunion und Einheit* (Trier 1971). "Beyond Intercommunion," *Faith & Order, Louvain 1971,* Faith and Order paper n. 59 (Geneva 1971) 54–77. *Modern Eucharistic Agreement* (London 1973). J. KENT and R. MURRAY, eds., *Church Membership and Intercommunion* (Denville, N.J. 1973). Institute for Ecumenical Research, Strasbourg, "Eucharistic Hospitality. A Statement on Lutheran-Roman Catholic Intercommunion," *One in Christ* 9 (1973) 388–401. A. HASTINGS, "Is There Room for Reciprocal Intercommunion between Catholics and Anglicans?" *One in Christ* 9 (1973) 337–353. K. HEIN, *Eucharist and Excommunication. A Study in Early Christian Doctrine and Discipline* (Bern 1973). R. MUMM and M. LIENHARD, eds., *Eucharistische Gastfreundschaft* (Kassel 1974). J. PRUISKEN, *Interkommunion im Prozess* (Essen 1974). R. BOECKLER, ed., *Interkommunion-Konziliarität* (Stuttgart 1974). R. ERNI and D. PAPANDREOU, *Eucharistiegemeinschaft. Der Standpunkt der Orthodoxie* (Fribourg 1974). J. HOFFMANN, "Theological Reflections on the Directives of the Bishop of Strasbourg concerning Exceptional Cases of Eucharistic Hospitality," *One in Christ* 11 (1975) 266–281. E. LANNE, "L'Eucharistie dans la recherche oecuménique actuelle," *Irénikon* 48 (1975) 201–214. N. EHRENSTRÖM and G. GASSMANN, *Confessions in Dialogue: A Survey of Bilateral Conversations Among World Confessional Families* (3d rev. ed. Geneva 1975). J. PROVOST, ed., "The Church as Communion," *Jurist* 36 (1976) 1–245, esp. M. A. FAHEY, "Ecclesial Community as Communion," 4–23. L. SWIDLER, ed., *The Eucharist in Ecumenical Dialogue,* JEcumSt 13.2 (1976) 191–344. F. J. VAN BEECK, "Intercommunion: A Note on Norms," *One in Christ* 12 (1976) 124–141. A. DULLES, "Eucharistic Sharing as an Ecumenical Problem," in *The Resilient Church* (New York 1977) 153–171. D. COGGAN, Archbishop of Canterbury, "Call for Eucharistic Sharing," Origins 7 (1978) 23–25. "The Pope and the Archbishop of Canterbury: Joint Statement," Origins 7 (1978) 25–26. R. MURRAY, "Intercommunion: A Turning-point?" *Tablet* [London] 232 (1978) 126–128.

[M. A. FAHEY]

EUTHANASIA

Current debate often confuses "letting die"—or, better, refraining from harmful efforts to prolong life (*see* LIFE, PROLONGATION OF)—with "putting to death" dying, comatose, or seriously defective persons, commonly called "mercy-killing" or *active* euthanasia. This debate has been intensified by the defense of legalized abortion on the ground that "quality not quantity of life counts." Two competing value-systems underlie this current debate. Humanism regards human organisms as the product of nonteleological, natural forces that become of value only through socialization. Fetuses do not yet have such value, seriously defective children are incapable of receiving it, and permanently mentally incapacitated adults have lost it. Such humans are of no value to themselves and their care and even their suffering presence injures the quality of life of socially functioning persons. Hence such unfortunates retain only the "right not to live" or "to die with dignity."

In contrast, such monotheistic value systems as Christianity hold humans to be of value because they are unique creations of God and will eternally remain living in personal relation to him; from this relation all social relations flow. However, this personal value requires full development through mutual sharing in society. Although children and permanent defectives are chiefly receivers of care, they also enhance the quality of social life: the moral growth of a society is ordinarily achieved only by courageous suffering, compassionate caring, and intelligent efforts to remove the causes of suffering without destroying the persons who suffer. For Christians suicide, including consent to be put to death to escape such trials, is rejection of the gift of life and the opportunity for personal and social growth. To put innocent persons to death as an escape from the burden of their care or the pain of compassion is to reject the very purpose of society, which is mutual care.

Currently certain Catholic moralists propose to revise moral theology by eliminating the concept of exceptionless moral norms so as to solve all conflict situations by weighing the predominance of values or disvalues ("the principle of proportion"). They accordingly are discussing whether in some ethical conflicts active euthanasia might be the best solution. Nevertheless, leaders of this trend are very hesitant to conclude that in fact the values to be achieved by euthanasia could be sufficient to outweigh the great harm to the fundamental respect for the unique dignity of every human person.

Bibliography: B. ASHLEY and K. O'ROURKE, *Health Care Ethics* (St. Louis 1978). J. F. DEDEK, *Contemporary Medical Ethics* (New York 1975) 137–155. R. A. MCCORMICK, "Moral Notes," ThST 34 (1975) 53–102. D. MAGUIRE, *Death by Choice* (New York 1974). W. E. MAY, *Human Existence, Medicine and Ethics* (Chicago 1977) 131–158. P. RAMSEY, *Patient as Person* (New Haven 1970).

[B. M. ASHLEY]

EVANGELIZATION

On December 8, 1975, Pope Paul VI issued a 20,000 word Apostolic Exhortation, Evangelization in the Modern World (*Evangelii nuntiandi*), the first document devoted exclusively to that topic. The document marks a phase in the life and even language of the Church's mission.

Evangelii Nuntiandi, Documentation. The exhortation is, as the name implies, more of a call for renewed dedication to the task of preaching the Gospel in its entirety than a theological delineation of the ministry of evangelization itself. While containing rich possibilities for future theological development, it seeks primarily to show how the Church is "equipped to proclaim the Gospel and to put it into people's hearts with conviction, freedom of spirit and effectiveness" (Paul VI EvangNunt 4). Evangelization seeks to make all humanity new: "The Church evangelizes when she seeks to convert, solely through the divine power of the Message she proclaims, both the personal and collective consciences of people, the activities in which they engage, and the lives and concrete milieux which are theirs" (ibid. 18).

This new thrust towards evangelization is the climax of a rather sudden evolution in the Church's theology of preaching from that espoused by Pius XII in *Mediator Dei* issued in 1947. The first phase of this evolution is evident in the documents of Vatican Council II, which was convened by Pope John XXIII in 1962 to make the Church of the twentieth century ever better-fitted for proclaiming the Gospel to the people of the twentieth century. As a result of the decline of the Church in Europe and prodded by the trauma of the Second World War, the Council placed the responsibility for promoting the faith on pastors of souls, whereas *Mediator Dei* had left the matter of spiritual growth in the hands of the faithful themselves.

In 1947, speaking of the necessity of personal piety for fruitful participation in the liturgy, Pope Pius XII had written in *Mediator Dei* that the faithful "are strictly required to put their own lips to the fountain, imbibe and absorb for themselves, the life-giving water, and rid themselves personally of anything that might hinder its nutritive effect in their souls" (31). The Pope also referred to the readings from Scripture and the homily at Mass only as things "enhancing the majesty of this great Sacrifice" (101). However, in the Constitution on the Sacred Liturgy Vatican II states: "It is the duty (of pastors of souls) to ensure that the faithful take part fully aware of what they are doing, actively engaged in the rite, and enriched by its effects" (*Sacrosanctum Concilium* 1). The Decree on the Ministry and Life of Priests repeats this understanding when it states as the purpose which priests pursue by their ministry "that men knowingly, freely and gratefully accept what God has achieved perfectly through Christ and manifest it in their whole lives" (*Presbyterorum ordinis* 2). Furthermore, the *homily is no longer a mere enhancement of the liturgy, but an integral part of it (*Sacrosanctum Concilium* 56). The unremitting seriousness of the crisis of faith was again acknowledged in 1967 when, on June 29, Pope Paul VI called for a special Year of Faith in which the Church "rethinks its reason for being and refinds its native energy."

During this period the concept of the missionary activity of the Church also evolved. The Decree on the Missionary Activity of the Church of Vatican Council II recognized a distinction between the work of an established local Church in spreading the Gospel and the work of the missions "in certain territories recognized by the Holy See" (*Ad gentes* 6). In these latter places, "The specific purpose of missionary activity is evangelization and the planting of the Church among those peoples and groups where she has not yet taken root" (ibid.). Once established, however, the local Church and its native clergy have the responsibility of evangelizing, unless changed conditions call for the

Church Universal to undertake renewed missionary activity. On August 15, 1967, this traditional distinction between missionary activity and evangelization was blurred somewhat when the Sacred Congregation for the Propagation of the Faith in charge of these missionary activities was renamed the Sacred Congregation for the Evangelization of Peoples or Propagation of the Faith, though its competency remained limited to designated territories.

Paul VI took the most vigorous step yet to promote evangelization by convoking the 1974 *Synod of Bishops to deal with it. Although many problems in evangelization were aired during the Synod, and the bishops spoke vigorously in favor of it, no real theological or pastoral progress was made toward directing the activities of the Church. Instead the bishops asked the Pope to reflect on the synodal discussions and then to provide the Church with new directions and impulses for the evangelization of the modern world. *Evangelii nuntiandi* was his response to their request. Firmly linking his teaching to the principles enunciated in the documents of Vatican II (Paul VI EvangNunt 59), he extends the understanding of their consequences; the most innovative aspect of the document is the Pope's insistence that it is the duty of all members of the Church to evangelize because evangelization "is the essential mission of the Church" (ibid. 14).

Reflections. Evangelization is the term used by the Church to identify the communication of the Gospel of Jesus Christ to all people through its various ministries. It is a derivative of the Greek for *good news*, which implies victory over one's enemies and the dawn of a new age characterized by liberation, joy, and peace under kingly rule. In the NT Jesus Christ is presented as both the Herald who proclaims the good news (Lk 4.18, 43) and as himself being the Good News (Lk 2.10). He is the Word of God coming in power to effect salvation (Jn 1.1–14). Through his life, death and resurrection, Jesus definitively overcame sin and death and brings eternal life to those who enter into the Kingdom of God by placing their faith and trust in him (cf. Lk 12.32; Acts 10.36–43; Rom 5.1–11, 6.9–11; Eph 2.5, 6; 1 Pt 4:6). While Jesus' own ministry of announcing the kingdom was limited to the Jews, his specially chosen apostles were commanded to carry his message of salvation to the entire world (Mt 28.18–20; Mk 16.16). Hence today evangelization refers to the mission of the Church to spread the Kingdom of God throughout the world through the preaching of the Word of God, the celebration of the Sacraments of Christ and the living out of a life of love in the Holy Spirit under the guidance of the Church.

Because the term evangelization has not been part of common theological usage, it has yet to be precisely defined in contemporary thought and tends to embrace many disparate elements. As used by the Roman Catholic Church, however, evangelization is quite distinct from the *evangelism* that flows from the 18th-century pietistic movement in Europe and was shaped in the United States by American Protestant revivalism. Nevertheless, Catholic evangelization shares some common features with evangelism: emphasis on the Scriptures, personal witness, and the necessity of faith. It differs from evangelism in that it also stresses the importance of the hierarchical Church with its sacramental and magisterial life and social witness. Current interest in evangelization has quickened because of the recognition of static Church growth, declining sacramental practice, and lack of significant social impact. While actual statistical studies vary somewhat in their findings, in 1975 the Church Universal accounted for only 18.3 percent of the world's population and 22 percent of the U.S. population. At the same time, in the U.S. between 38 and 50 percent of the population is estimated to be "unchurched." Church growth in the U.S. in 1977 through adult Baptisms was less than 18 percent and infant Baptisms have declined 30 percent since 1966. In addition, less than half the Catholics in the U.S. regularly attend Mass and the failure to reach vast portions of the young in religious education programs is a major concern.

Since the emphasis on evangelization as the "essential mission of the Church" is still so new to the 20th-century Catholic Church, it is difficult to discern the directions it will take or the problems it will encounter. Nevertheless, certain difficulties have already been noted in the United States. (1) There is a need for effective models for evangelization in the Catholic tradition. Protestant models, being in so many cases nonhierarchical, cannot be fruitfully translated directly into Catholic ministries. (2) Seminaries are not currently prepared to offer formal training in either a theology of evangelization or practical evangelization ministry; hence, institutional activities in this area are still many years off. (3) American optimism with its emphasis on the innate goodness of the human person becoming operative when the person is freed from the oppression of disease, economic deprivation, and social injustice makes it difficult to communicate the importance and necessity of faith in Jesus Christ for even truly human living. (4) The 1977 *Synod of Bishops addressed itself to the problem of catechesis. As in the case of evangelization, no clear theological statements resulted; yet, the need for developing the relationships between evangelization and catechesis was acknowledged and subsequent papal leadership in this area is expected.

See also MISSION OF THE CHURCH; MISSION (NEW TRENDS); PREACHING.

Bibliography: Paul VI, On Evangelization in the Modern World: Apostolic Exhortation *Evangelii nuntiandi* (USCC Publ. Office, Washington, D.C. 1976). D. BOHN, *Evangelization In America* (New York 1977). J. BURKE, *Gospel Power* (New York 1978). D. B. BURRELL and F. KANE, *Evangelization In The American Context* (Notre Dame, Ind. 1976). J. R. HALE, *Who Are The Unchurched?* (Washington, D.C. 1977). J. HOFINGER, *Evangelization and Catechesis* (New York 1976).

[J. BURKE]

EVANGELIZATION, PROGRAMS OF

At the end of the 1970s two events dominate the national evangelization scene in the American Catholic Church. The first is the National Congress on Evangelization celebrated in Minneapolis in August 1977, sponsored by the *Word of God Institute. Twelve hundred bishops, priests, deacons, religious, and lay people participated in an intensive three-day program featuring preachers and biblical scholars who proclaimed major gospel themes related to evangelization. In addition, experts in various ministries conducted special workshops to explore methods of evangelization. As a result, church leaders as well as individual Christians left with a renewed commitment to evangelization. In writing of the Congress, Cardinal Jean Villot, Vatican Secretary of State said: "The Holy Father is confident that the National Congress will provide an excellent opportunity for deep and prayerful reflection on God's word and on the task of evangelization that is shared by all who belong to Jesus Christ.... His Holiness ... looks forward to seeing sound programs in evangelization being fostered, through the grace of God, as a concrete result of the Congress" (Letter to Abp. John R. Roach, July 14, 1977).

The second significant event was the opening of the National Office of the *Bishops' Committee on Evangelization in November 1977, in Washington, D.C., to serve as headquarters for a two-year plan of action. The aim was: (1) to stimulate within the Catholic community a prayerful ministry to the churchless and alienated in the U.S., that is to those who have never been part of any Church and to those who become alienated from the faith they once had; (2) to act as a central agency in the gathering and dissemination of information about programs and resources for evangelization.

Other than these two national undertakings, evangelization is currently limited to local programs of either ecclesiastical or lay sponsorship.

While twenty dioceses have established offices of evangelization, the programs they have initiated at this point are still modest and the response to them has been limited. Diocesan programs for the most part reflect a sincere desire to channel the work of existing offices and structures of the diocese into new directions under the general heading of evangelization. For some, it is only a matter of applying a new label to old programs; others have undertaken more innovative projects, especially in terms of mass-media appeals. However, in the one significant effort reported, the media appeal was a distinct disappointment.

To a great extent, the ecclesiastical programs still reflect a concern more with church members, presently active or alienated, than with those who have never been a member of any Church. Programs stress the traditional methods of home visits, renewed liturgies, special workshops, and adult education classes. Parochial schools continue to consume the major portion of church resources and evangelization as a distinct category has not yet become a significant budgetary item. In keeping with this lack of emphasis on evangelization, the 1977 Official Catholic Directory reports only 79,627 converts for the entire United States. With a total Catholic population of 49,325,752, this figure represents only a 0.16 percent conversion rate.

Lay movements in evangelization are generally uncoordinated and highly individualistic; whether such programs are resulting in actual conversions to the Roman Catholic Church is questionable and unfortunately statistics revealing their conversion rate are unavailable. Although the lay programs vary widely in their approach to evangelization, the Protestant evangelical practice of "knocking on doors" and distributing tracts does not seem to have become common among Roman Catholics; the individuals doing it report using Protestant materials because of the dearth of Roman Catholic tracts.

While the *charismatic renewal movement has shown great vitality in the life of the Church in the decade of the '70s, it has not yet, as a whole, made serious efforts to evangelize. Other movements, such as the *Cursillo, *Marriage Encounter, etc., are beginning to turn their attention to evangelization, but for the most part, these programs, too, are concerned with those who already believe in Jesus Christ. The Legion of Mary, by contrast, has a significant thrust towards evangelization with one of their programs meriting special attention, *Peregrinatio pro Christo*, which utilizes home visits and bible study. Perhaps this last is indicative of possible new programs in evangelization because of the growing interest in the Bible among Roman Catholics and the formation of increasing numbers of bible-study and bible-sharing groups. The National Council of Catholic Women is making a continuing effort to promote the formation of bible-sharing groups among its membership as part of their ongoing education in the faith with the hope that eventually it will lead to local programs of evangelization.

Seminaries have not yet established courses in the theology of evangelization or training programs in evangelizing techniques, although some seminarians are being used by dioceses in their diocesan programs on an occasional basis. Until *preaching as the primary means of evangelization is stressed in the theological reflection and pastoral practice of the Church and is significantly incorporated into the formation of its future priests, major changes in the Church's programs to evangelize cannot be expected.

[J. BURKE]

EXORCISM

In liturgy and theology an exorcism is the Church's prayer that the power of God's Holy Spirit free a person from sin and evil and from subjection to the devil, the spirit of evil (5:748). In popular understanding exorcism generally refers to the driving out of a demon who has possessed a person. The Church, however, is reluctant to admit supernatural possession in particular cases, since most apparent cases can be explained by pathological conditions. Both modern biblical scholarship and current psychological theory and practice are inclined to admit a supernatural explanation only when a natural explanation has been proven impossible. A practical indication of this reluctance is the 1972 abolition of the office of exorcist with the other minor orders (Paul VI MinQuaedam).

Exorcisms in the form of prayers for protection from evil do remain in the baptismal rituals. The Rite for Infant Baptism (*Ordo Baptismi parvulorum*, May 15, 1969; second *editio typica*, June 24, 1973), for example, contains a prayer of exorcism at the end of the prayer of the faithful and litany, prior to the (optional) anointing with the oil of catechumens (which functioned historically as an exorcism). But where the first edition spoke of freedom from the power of darkness (*a potestate tenebrarum*) the second speaks rather of "original sin" (*ab originalis culpae labe*, BaptCh 49).

More elaborate exorcisms may be found in the Rite of Christian Initiation of Adults. Exorcism is described as showing "the true nature of the spiritual life as a battle between flesh and spirit" (ChrInitAd 101) and the formulas (ibid. 113–118; 373) speak of preservation from sin and evil. The scrutinies, intended to purify and strengthen the candidate (ibid. 154), contain rites of exorcism whereby "the Church teaches the elect about the mystery of Christ who frees from sin. By exorcism they are freed from the effects of sin and from the influence of the devil, and they are strengthened in their spiritual journey and open their hearts to receive the gifts of the Savior"

(ibid. 156). The ritual's formulas (ibid. 164, 171, 178, 379, 383, 387) reflect this understanding.

Similarly, the blessing of *baptismal water in the rituals and the blessing of water at the beginning of the order of Mass in the Sacramentary no longer contain an exorcism of water (or of the salt, use of which is optional).

Scepticism regarding demonic possession and de-emphasis of exorcism in no way imply denial of the power of evil customarily spoken of as the devil or Satan.

Bibliography: R. BÉRAUDY, "Scrutinies and Exorcisms," in J. WAGNER, ed., *Adult Baptism and the Catechumenate. Concilium* 22 (1967) 57–61. J. CORTÉS and F. GATTI, *The Case against Possessions and Exorcisms* (New York 1975). L. MITCHELL, *Baptismal Anointing* (London 1966). R. WOODS, *The Occult Revolution* (New York 1971).

[J. DALLEN]

EXPERIMENTATION, MEDICAL

The present article presupposes the definition of medical experimentation and the statement of the basic applicable ethical principles outlined in the earlier article in the *New Catholic Encyclopedia* (5:756).

Medical and Public Concern. Medical research and experimentation have provided the physician with considerably improved methods for dealing with human disease and dysfunction. Among these are: antimicrobial agents for a variety of infectious diseases; organ transplantation for dealing with total kidney failure and selected heart conditions; better surgical techniques for repair of injuries to tissue and bone; chemotherapy and radiation therapy for cancer control; sophisticated diagnostic techniques such as computerized tomography (CAT); ultrasonography and numerous other laboratory tests which provide to the physician more precise information about the condition of his patient; and a host of drugs to deal more effectively with hypertension, anxiety, pain, hormonal deficiencies, allergies, and many other human dysfunctions.

As the benefits of medical research became more evident in everyday life, increased funding has provided the means for still more research. Thus, national support (Federal, state, industrial and private nonprofit) for health research and disease in 1961 was $1.1 billion while for 1976 it was about $5.1 billion, representing approximately 3.6 per cent of a total health cost of $141.1 billion (National Institutes of Health 1977-Basic Data).

Parallel with the increase in medical research has been an augmentation in the medical profession's concern about the ethical aspects of human experimentation. One measure of this increased interest is the notable increase in the number of publications in the medical literature which deal with the ethical dimensions of human experimentation. Interest has also been aroused with the revelation of several apparently flagrant examples of the violation of basic human rights associated with medical research. Such occurrences, it must be stressed, are rare.

Governmental Action. In 1974 Congress passed and the President signed into law, the National Research Act, establishing the National Commission for the Protection of Human Subjects of Biomedical and the Behavioral Research (Title II of Public Law 93–348). The eleven-member Commission assumed the task of: (1) identifying the basic ethical principles which should undergird research involving human subjects; (2) developing appropriate guidelines; (3) making recommendations for administrative action to the Secretary of the Department of Health, Education, and Welfare (HEW). In current practice these regulations apply only to those research and development projects which are funded by HEW.

An earlier set of HEW regulations had been published Dec. 1, 1971: "The Institutional Guide to HEW Policy on Protection of Human Subjects." The policy therein set forth was continued and developed in the later regulations. The HEW regulations currently (1978) in force were developed gradually as the National Commission completed a study and made recommendations to the Secretary of HEW. Part of a refinement process included, and continues to include, consultation with the scientific community and interested public groups or individuals.

The basic regulation governing the protection of human subjects in biomedical and behavioral research were published in the *Federal Register*, May 30, 1974. These regulations required, among other items, that: (1) the risks be outweighed by the sum of benefits to the subject and the importance of the knowledge to be gained; (2) the rights and welfare of the subject be adequately protected; (3) legally effective, informed consent be obtained; (4) the research be reviewed at timely intervals. Other regulations governing research when the subjects are fetuses, pregnant women, or the products of *in vitro* fertilization were issued Aug. 8, 1975. These were modified and augmented by regulations published Jan. 11, 1978. Proposed policies governing the use of psychosurgery in practice and research were issued May 23, 1977, while publication of and invitation of public comment on the report and recommendations of the National Commission regarding research involving children appeared in the *Federal Register*, Jan. 13, 1978.

Church Teaching. Vatican Council II and Popes John XXIII and Paul VI in the area of medical research have primarily applied and reinforced what Pope Pius XII had already said at some length. In his address to the Pontifical Academy of Sciences, April 27, 1968, Pope Paul VI stated: ". . . the Holy See intends to show that the Catholic Church respects scientific research, recognizes its freedom within its own domain, and looks forward eagerly to its present and future conquests" (*The Pope Speaks* 13 [1968] 108). In an earlier address to Pediatric Cardiologists the Pope stated the supreme rule for medical practice and research: ". . . that man is . . . 'the subject, the basis and the end' of life in society . . . ." (May 12, 1967; *The Pope Speaks* 12 [1967] 365). The Pope's abiding concern is shown when he addressed the European Association of Hospital Doctors, April 28, 1973 and noted the need to ". . . reconcile legitimate and necessary research with the personal rights of the patient, who can never be sacrificed as if the matter involved merely a part of humanity ordained to the good of the whole" (*Pope Speaks* 18 [1973] 69–71). Finally, Pope Paul reiterated his central theme: "In this field of medical ethics, we would like once more to stress its foundation: unconditional respect for life, from its beginning" (Paul VI to the doctors of Flanders, April 23, 1977, OssRom May 5, 1977, 9).

From these quotations and other papal statements it is evident that the magisterium relative to medical research asserts three main points. (1) Medical research is necessary and good but must be for the true welfare of human beings. (2) Human life must be respected by the individual and others at all stages of its existence; therefore, research risks are to be limited by the requirements of justice and charity. (3) Human persons are individually of inestimable value and may not under any conditions be used as mere

means; consequently, informed and free consent is an absolute condition for human experimentation.

Informed Consent. In practice, perhaps the area of greatest difficulty is the process of obtaining truly informed and freely given consent from the potential research subject. Government regulations provide a framework and a mechanism to assure some degree of compliance with the regulations. Nonetheless, ultimately the protection of the subject's basic human rights devolves on those doing the research. The assessment of the risk/benefit ratio depends much on the experimenter's own understanding of the research about to be undertaken. Obtaining appropriate informed consent from the potential research subjects rests in large measure on the researcher's having an attitude of profound respect towards human beings and on his ability to express the expected benefits and reasonably anticipated hazards in a manner that adequately informs and freely elicits the appropriate consent. Special groups such as the poor, the sick, employees, medical and graduate students are considered to be "consent prone" and require particular care to assure the absence of coercion. Other groups such as fetuses, the mentally retarded, children, and prisoners are especially vulnerable and thus are generally inappropriate for human experimentation, unless there be serious need and additional safeguards are rigorously enforced.

Bibliography: T. L. BEAUCHAMP and L. WALTERS, *Contemporary Issues in Bioethics* (Belmont, Cal. 1978). R. L. BOGOMOLNY, *Human Experimentation* (Dallas 1976). C. FRIED, *Medical Experimentation: Personal Integrity and Social Policy* (New York 1974). B. H. GRAY, *Human Subjects in Medical Experimentation* (New York 1975). N. HERSHEY and R. D. MILLER, *Human Experimentation and the Law* (Germantown, Md. 1976). J. KATZ, *Experimentation with Human Beings* (New York 1972). W. E. MAY, *Human Existence, Medicine and Ethics* (Chicago 1977). National Academy of Sciences, *Experiments and Research with Humans: Values in Conflict* (Washington, D.C. 1975). T. J. O'DONNELL, *Medicine and Christian Morality* (New York 1976). P. RAMSEY, *The Patient As Person* (New Haven and London 1970). S. J. REISER, A. J. DYCK, and W. J. CURRAN, *Ethics in Medicine, Historical Perspectives and Contemporary Concerns* (Cambridge, Mass. 1977). J. J. SHINNERS, *The Morality of Medical Experimentation on Living Human Subjects in the Light of Recent Papal Pronouncements* (Washington, D.C. 1958). M. B. VISSCHER, *Ethical Constraints and Imperatives in Medical Research* (Springfield, Ill. 1975).

[A. S. MORACZEWSKI]

EXTRAORDINARY MINISTERS OF THE EUCHARIST

Extraordinary ministers of the Eucharist are those who distribute the Eucharist on any occasion when the bishop, priest, deacon, or instituted acolyte is unable to fulfill this function for whatever reason. The instituted *acolyte is by his office a special minister of the Eucharist. His function is outlined in Paul VI's motu proprio, Aug. 15, 1972, on ministries (Paul VI MinQuaedam VI). However, pastoral experience revealed that the need for extraordinary ministers of the Eucharist is not sufficiently met even by the ministry of acolyte. The 1978 provisional English text for the rite of commissioning these ministers calls them "Special Ministers of Holy Communion." Church history showed that in addition to bishop, priest, and deacon lay people administered Communion under certain circumstances up until the 8th century. This historical evidence coupled with a renewed ecclesiology and theology of Baptism as well as extreme pastoral need led many individual bishops and episcopal conferences to request the Holy See to authorize in their dioceses or territories lay ministers of the Eucharist.

Fidei custos. According to Canon Law, the ministry of dispensing the Eucharist was normally reserved to priests and deacons (CIC c. 845). On March 10, 1966 the Congregation for the Sacraments issued an Instruction on the Minister of Eucharistic Communion When Priest and Deacon Are Absent (*Fidei custos*) amending this canon and allowing residential bishops and other designated ecclesiastical authorities to ask for the faculty to permit suitable persons under their jurisdiction to administer Communion to themselves and to the faithful. The faculty was granted for a three-year period, after which the experience was to be evaluated. The Congregation for the Discipline of the Sacraments granted this faculty to the U.S. National Conference of Catholic Bishops on March 9, 1971, for one year and, upon request extended the concession on Jan. 18, 1972.

Immensae caritatis. On Jan. 29, 1973 the Congregation for Divine Worship's Instruction Facilitating Sacramental Communion in Particular Circumstances (*Immensae caritatis*) outlined for the Latin rite norms for extraordinary ministries, Communion twice on the same day, mitigation of the Eucharistic fast for the sick and the aged, and *Communion in the hand. Appended to this document were rites for deputing extraordinary ministers. *Immensae caritatis* recognized that a lack of sufficient ministers for the Eucharist can occur when there is a large number of communicants at Mass and, outside of Mass, when there are many sick who require the Eucharist.

Conditions. The use of special ministers applies under the conditions that follow. (1) In case of true need, the local Ordinary has the faculty to permit a qualified person to act as an extraordinary minister for a specific occasion, for a time or, in the case of necessity, in some permanent way. (2) The local Ordinary has the faculty to permit individual priests exercising their sacred office to appoint a qualified person to distribute Holy Communion on a specific occasion, in case of genuine need. (3) These faculties may be subdelegated to auxiliary bishops, *episcopal vicars, and episcopal delegates. (4) There is a suggested order for choosing the extraordinary ministers, e.g. religious before laity; men before women, but it may be altered for prudential reasons. (5) In religious houses, superiors or their vicars may exercise the office of distributing Communion in the appropriate circumstances. (6) When possible, the extraordinary minister should receive the mandate according to the rite appended to the instruction.

Exercise of This Ministry. The spread of the use of extraordinary ministers responds to liturgical and pastoral needs. It has its theological basis in the common priesthood of the faithful, distinct from the ordained priesthood. Since the Eucharistic assembly provides for its own needs, the special ministers are to be used only at those Masses in which they fully participate. They are not to be assigned and waiting somewhere to distribute Communion at several celebrations. Large congregations require as many such ministers as are needed for all the Masses without any one having to assist at more than one Mass.

In parishes with no resident priest, the extraordinary minister may be appointed to distribute Communion on Sunday and even on weekdays. Where there are many sick to whom Communion is to be distributed, the special ministers have the task, not only to bring the Eucharist for Communion, but in some way link this Eucharist to the parish Mass. The Sacred Congregation for Divine Worship has issued rites for *Holy Communion outside Mass and for the administration of Communion and viaticum to the sick by an extraordinary minister.

Bibliography: Bishops' Committee on the Liturgy, *Study Text I: Holy Communion (Immensae caritatis)* (Washington, D.C. 1973). EncDocLit, *Immensae caritatis* 915–920; *De sacra communione et cultu mysterii eucharistici extra missam* 951–964 (tr., Flannery 242–253); *Fidei custos,* Eng. text, O'Connor 7: 645–648; cf. BCL Newsletter 7 (1971) 1; 8 (1972) 1 J. KOLESAR, *Ministers of Life: The Role of Lay Ministers of the Eucharist* (Phoenix, Ariz. 1973).

[J. B. RYAN]

EXTRAORDINARY MINISTERS OF THE EUCHARIST (RITE OF INSTITUTION)

The instruction *Immensae caritatis*, issued by the Congregation for the Discipline of the Sacraments, January 29, 1973, contains the appendix, Rite for Commissioning an Extraordinary Minister of Holy Communion and Rite for the Designation of a Minister of Holy Communion on a Particular Occasion.

The first rite may be carried out during Mass or outside Mass, with the people present. At Mass, the rite is structured as follows. (1) The homily presents the pastoral reasons for the office of extraordinary minister. (2) Presenting to the people the ministers-elect, the celebrant stresses that their lives must be worthy of the task they are given to perform. (3) The ministers-elect indicate their willingness to undertake the office and to reverence and care for the Eucharist they will administer. (4) The congregation prays for the ministers-elect and the celebrant recites a special prayer for them. (5) An invocation for the designated ministers is added to the General Intercessions.

The designated ministers bring the plate with the bread to the altar at the Preparation of the Gifts. At Communion they may receive under both kinds.

Outside of Mass, the suggested rite opens with a song, a greeting by the celebrant and a brief Liturgy of the Word, either using the texts and chants of the liturgy of the day or from suggested texts appended to the rite. The rite continues as in points (2) and (3) above. The rite concludes with a blessing, a dismissal, and a song.

In cases of necessity for a special minister to be delegated for a particular occasion the rite is brief. During Mass at the Breaking of the Bread the designated person goes to the altar and, after the Lamb of God, is blessed by the celebrant with the words: "Today you are to distribute the body and blood of Christ to your brothers and sisters. May the Lord + bless you, N." The minister responds: "Amen."

Bibliography: Bishops' Committee on the Liturgy, *Study Text 1: Holy Communion (Immensae caritatis)* (Washington, D.C. 1973).

[J. B. RYAN]

FACULTIES, BISHOPS'

A faculty in its legal sense means the power, privilege, or permission that a competent ecclesiastical superior grants to a subordinate for the performance of an act which the subordinate is otherwise incapable of doing validly or is prohibited by law from doing licitly. In granting a faculty, the superior extends the exercise of his own jurisdiction by sharing it with a subordinate.

Habitual Faculties. A particular faculty is given for use in specific cases and for definite persons. On the other hand, a habitual faculty is given at large to be used in favor of indeterminate persons. A habitual faculty which is granted permanently or for a definite period of time or for a certain number of cases is considered to be a privilege beside the law (*praeter legem*). Unless in its concession it was otherwise provided for, or the person was chosen for personal qualifications, a habitual faculty conceded to a diocesan bishop or to another Ordinary, does not expire with the expiration of the authority of the Ordinary to whom it was conceded, even though he has begun to make use of it, but it passes over to whichever Ordinary suceeds him in government. Unless otherwise provided for, or the person was chosen for personal qualities, a habitual faculty granted to a diocesan bishop belongs likewise to his vicar general and, within the limits of his competency, to his *episcopal vicar. A faculty granted to a subordinate carries with it other powers which are necessary for its use. Therefore, a habitual faculty once granted also includes the power to remove obstacles, if there be any, which impede the execution of the favor, in order to achieve the effect of obtaining the favor.

Episcopal Faculties. Prior to Vatican Council II, the practical employment of habitual faculties was most conspicuous in the granting of the Quinquennial Faculties by the Congregation for Bishops on the occasion of the Ordinary's five-year report (5:787). Quinquennial Faculties were granted to anyone classified as an "Ordinary" in CIC C. 198.1, that is, to residential bishops, abbots or prelates *nullius*, vicars, prefects, and administrators apostolic, and all those who during a vacancy succeed or are duly appointed to replace the above-mentioned officers, even temporarily.

The traditional Quinquennial Faculties have been made superfluous by various documents issuing from the Holy See since Vatican Council II extending episcopal powers. A letter from the Apostolic Delegate to the U.S. (Aug. 6, 1977) informed the American bishops that in an audience of July 9, 1977 the Holy Father confirmed until revision of the Code of Canon Law the few faculties not elsewhere granted and that the Congregation for Bishops would no longer issue an Index of Quinquennial Faculties.

An understanding of the granting of faculties to bishops presupposes awareness of the distinction between diocesan bishops—in the *Code* of *Canon Law* they are called "residential"; according to Vatican II, however, they should be called "diocesan" (*Christus Dominus* 11)—and titular bishops; these last are further divided into those who hold office in a certain diocese, namely, coadjutor bishops and auxiliary bishops, and those who are simply titular bishops and have another role to fulfill for the good of some portion of the People of God, or for several particular Churches or even the universal Church. Coadjutor and auxiliary bishops should be granted those faculties necessary for rendering their work more effective and for safeguarding the dignity proper to bishops. If there is no provision for it in the letter of nomination, the diocesan bishop is to appoint his auxiliary or auxiliaries as vicars general or at least as episcopal vicars. Unless competent authority has otherwise provided, the faculties which auxiliary bishops have by law do not cease when the office of the diocesan bishop comes to an end. A coadjutor bishop with the right of succession must always be named vicar general by the diocesan bishop. In particular cases competent authority can grant the coadjutor even more extensive faculties.

The most important office in the diocesan curia is that of vicar general. However, as often as the proper government of the diocese requires it, one or more episcopal vicars can be named by the bishop. These automatically enjoy the same authority which the common law grants the vicar general, but only for a certain part of the diocese, or for the faithful of a determined rite. The vicar general and episcopal vicar have no legislative power in the diocese, but only executive power, namely for performing acts within the competence of the diocesan bishop, excepting those acts which the diocesan bishop may reserve to himself or which by law require a special mandate of the diocesan bishop.

Changes in Bishops' Faculties. Pope Paul VI, in the apostolic letter motu proprio, *Pastorale munus*, Nov. 30, 1963 (ActApS 56 [1964] 5–12) granted extensive faculties and privileges to local Ordinaries in order to meet growing needs and existing necessities in dioceses throughout the world. Since the grant deals with exceptional faculties, they cannot be delegated by bishops to others than the coadjutor, the auxiliaries and the vicar general, unless in the concession of the individual faculties another provision is expressly made.

In a subsequent extension of the faculties the Holy See allowed Ordinaries in the United States to delegate the faculties of *Pastorale munus* to the chancellor of the diocese, and to episcopal vicars where the bishop had no vicar general. Furthermore, the Sacred Congregation for Bishops can and has granted to Ordinaries the power to delegate faculties to priests other than the chancellor (e.g. vice-chancellors). In accordance with the rule of existing laws, faculties which belong by right to diocesan bishops belong also by right to vicars and prefects apostolic, administrators apostolic, abbots and prelates *nullius*. Even though vicars and prefects apostolic cannot appoint a vicar general, still each of them can lawfully delegate to the vicar general the faculties in question (Bousc-O'Connor 6:385–386). The faculties and privileges of *Pastorale munus* became effective Dec. 8, 1963.

Pastorale munus also extended certain privileges to all bishops, both diocesan and titular, which faculties become effective upon receipt of authentic notice of their canonical appointment.

The motu proprio *De Episcoporum muneribus* of June 15, 1966 (ActApS 58 [1966] 467–472) established norms for the dispensing powers of bishops. The instrument notes that the Vatican II gives to bishops the faculty, among others, to dispense in particular cases from the general laws of the Church the faithful over whom they exercise authority according to law, whenever they judge that it would be for their spiritual good, unless a special reservation has been made by the supreme authority (*Christus Dominus* 8b). The motu proprio makes a list for the Latin Church of those general laws whose dispensation is reserved to the Holy See. The document indicates that *Christus Dominus* 8b derogates only from CIC c. 81. (The term diocesan bishop includes members of the hierarchy who are equivalent to them in law.)

Many faculties were also given to bishops by Pope Paul VI through various Congregations, such as the Sacred Congregation for Religious and Secular Institutes and the Sacred Congregation for the Sacraments and Divine Worship. Such faculties are usually communicated through the Sacred Congregation for Bishops.

The Aug. 6, 1966 motu proprio *Ecclesiae Sanctae* (ActApS 58 (1966) 757–787) presented norms established by the Holy Father for the implementation of some of the important decrees of Vatican II, including *Christus Dominus*, the Decree on the Pastoral Office of Bishops (cf. Paul VI EcclSanct I, 13–14 on faculties). These norms went into effect on October 11, 1966.

To bishops, as successors of the Apostles in the dioceses entrusted to them, there belongs *per se* all the ordinary, proper, and immediate authority which is required for the exercise of their pastoral office (cf. *Lumen gentium* 21; *Christus Dominus* 3). However, the Roman Pontiff, who exercises supreme, full, and immediate power in the universal Church, recognizing the pastoral needs of the People of God, continues to share his authority and jurisdiction by imparting to bishops faculties needed to discharge more efficiently and effectively their pastoral office.

Bibliography: A. J. BEVILACQUA, *Episcopal Faculties since Vatican Council II* (Brooklyn 1971). Bousc-O'Connor 6:370–388; 394–400. A. G. CICOGNANI, *Canon Law*, tr. J. M. O'HARA and F. J. BRENNAN (rev. ed. Philadelphia 1935). J. DE REAPER, "Pastorale Munus: Commentary," IrEcclRec 104 (1965) 110-143. G. P. GRAHAM, "The Power of Bishops in Recent Documents," *Jurist*, 28 (1968) 425–448. W. J. LA DUE, "De Episcoporum Muneribus," *Jurist*, 27 (1967) 413–425. PAUL VI, *Pastorale munus*, tr. *Granting Special Faculties and Privileges to Local Ordinaries; De Episcoporum muneribus*, tr. *On the Power to Grant Dispensations* (USCC Publ. Office, Washington, D.C. 1963; 1966). F. TIMMERMANS, "New Faculties and Privileges Granted to Bishops," *Clergy Monthly* 28 (1964) 41–52; 267; 268.

[A. J. QUINN]

FAITH, ACT OF

Faith, the name for the response to revelation, is never faith in the abstract but a human act in a *special* situation, social condition, and historical period (5:799). What characterizes faith at the present time is the forms it takes in the context of contemporary atheism, secularism, and religious pluralism, which, as Vatican Council II's Constitution on the Church in the Modern World notes, put belief to a test and refine it (*Gaudium et spes* 19–21). The confrontation is partially due not only to the intrinsic difficulty of faith but also to the neglect or failure of Christians to live up to the Gospel ideal of witnessing to Christ. At the same time present-day problems challenge believers to lead a stronger and purer life of faith. The varieties of contemporary *atheism grew out of the 18th-century Enlightenment and the declaration of the "death of God," with human reason and freedom declaimed in God's stead. Man is tempted to believe in his own inevitable progress and perfectibility to the point of an assurance that he can create the world and take destiny into his own hands. To this secular "faith" the universe no longer reflects God; he is increasingly irrelevant to and absent from it. Man has passed from a divinized into a hominized world, into a post-Christian or dechristianized age.

Is real faith, then, possible in a secularized age? The secularism begotten of scientific and technological progress and a sense of human mastery of the world can be beneficial to the Christian faith. It no longer identifies God with the once humanly uncontrollable forces of nature. An earlier and less enlightened faith may have hidden rather than revealed the true face of God. The chief object of the Christian faith remains the same—but through secularization God has been made to recede from the world and to appear more transcendent than ever. The act of faith puts a positive construction upon the rise of secular society and seeks the meaning of the Gospel within it. It looks less to the signs of *space* than to the signs of the *times*, where God proves himself to be the Lord of history. The Christian draws on the heritage of faith to find the answers to the existential questions of the order, meaning, and goal of life.

While there is the shift away from a medieval Christian view, away from a spatial to a temporal view of reality, the act of faith today is no less intellectual than formerly. Even when it does not grapple with questions of the truth and verifiability of how God rules all things "from above," or with a set of propositions for belief, it still has to perceive and acknowledge the mysterious presence of the living God within the events of time. Man is made more responsible to God for the world and society. He is to trust that the unseen is more real than the seen.

In accordance with the New Testament term for faith, πιστεύειν, which can mean "to rely on, to trust" as well as "to believe," the element of trust looms larger in the life of faith today. Faith involves risk, insecurity, uncertainty, doubt, a Kierkegaardian "leap" into a future that rests with God. It dictates a reliance on the will of the God who knows what is best for human fulfillment. Faith is not only an act of obedience, made once-for-all, but a lifetime commitment to the divine summons. Convinced that the Word of God is trustworthy, the believer faces the unpredictable and incalculable future with courage. He cannot weather the present-day crisis of culture without "a more personal and explicit adherence to faith," which will instill him with "a more vivid sense of God" (*Gaudium et spes* 7).

The fact that a child is born into a Christian family, baptized, educated in his environment, does not dispense him from making a free, personal, adult life-decision for or against Christ; he will act upon that decision seriously, superficially, or not at all. The ratification is not so much a matter of a single act or acts as of a basic, life-long orientation to the whole of reality with its values, including God, Christ, his Church.

The total and unconditional surrender to God in the act of faith precludes an exclusively intellectualist view but does not exempt the Catholic from orthodoxy (see Vatican II, *Dei Verbum* 5). It is inaccurate to say that belief stems merely from the will to believe, without consideration of the truths normative for faith. So-called ortho-praxis without orthodoxy will not check the decline or forestall the loss of religious faith. The Catholic ideal is to fuse the two, doctrine and practice: faith ought to be a visible quality of human life, a character development. Genuine faith should affect the whole man and the totality of human living, even if it would be foolish to expect the perfect correlation of belief with life and action.

If faith and secular life are not to be left polarized, then Christians must take the fact of a pluralist world into account. The Christian faith brings home a transcendent way of life rather than a source of theoretical doctrine. A way of life is familial, social, historical, ecclesial. So it is possible for Christians to live together and witness to Christ on the basis of a love-inspired faith. Without disregarding the ecclesial framework of their faith, they must realize they have major interfaith areas where they can live and work for unity of faith. Faith, living and active, leads to the religious experience of love, and love will attract believers spontaneously to the same values, to a sense of what is morally good in interpersonal relationships, to a share in that connatural knowledge which faith and love—the resonance of love in faith's act—make of transcendence, unity, and fidelity.

Bibliography: L. DEWART, *The Future of Belief: Theism in a World Come of Age* (New York 1966). R. PANIKKAR, "Faith—A Constitutive Dimension of Man," JEcumSt 8 (1971) 223–254. K. RAHNER, *Do You Believe in God?* (New York 1969). B. SIZEMORE, JR., "Christian Faith in a Pluralistic World," JEcumSt 13 (1976) 405–419. P. SURLIS, ed., *Faith: Its Nature and Meaning* (Dublin 1972). C. WILLIAMS, *Faith in a Secular Age* (New York 1966).

[J. FICHTNER]

FAMILY

Development of the Church's understanding of family within its pastoral mission has been greatly accelerated since Vatican Council II's major treatment of this topic. Beginning with the Constitution on the Church, where the concept of "domestic church" (*ecclesia domestica*) is emphasized (*Lumen gentium* 11), the renewal of the Church's appreciation for the place of the family within its total life was principally brought out in the Pastoral Constitution on the Church in the Modern World.

Vatican II Teaching. In treating of areas of special concern, the Council sets forth in sections 47–52 an extensive treatment of the family and Christian marriage. At the outset, the document establishes the importance of the issue: "The well-being of the individual person and of human and Christian society is intimately linked with the healthy condition of that community produced by marriage and family. Hence, Christians and all who hold this community in high esteem sincerely rejoice in the various ways by which people today find help in fostering this community of love and perfecting its life, and by which spouses and parents are assisted in their lofty calling" (*Gaudium et spes* 47). The Constitution indicates serious dangers that threaten the family and voices confidence in the strength within this basic institution (ibid.). In section 48 the sanctity of marriage and family life is examined; section 49 treats the special nature of conjugal love; 50 and 51 deal with parenthood and the need to harmonize conjugal love with a respect for life; finally, section 52 expands on the notion of family itself and lays the basis for a deeper development of the Church's pastoral ministry in this area.

In addition Vatican II's Decree on the Apostolate of the Laity sketches the social role for the Christian family. The Decree urges couples and family members to "cooperate with men of good will to ensure the preservation of these rights (i.e., parental right to educate their children and the lawful independence of the family) in civil legislation, and to make sure that attention is paid to the needs of the family in government policies regarding housing, the education of children, working conditions, social security and taxes; and that in decisions affecting migrants, their right to live together as a family is safeguarded" (*Apostolicam actuositatem* 11). This same decree also expands on other apostolic activities to be appropriately undertaken by families.

Pope Paul VI. After Vatican II, the family and Christian marriage were extensively treated by Pope Paul VI in several documents, including the encyclical, *Humanae vitae* (1968), an address, May 4, 1970, to the Teams of Our Lady (ActApS 62 [1970] 428–437) and in his 1975 apostolic exhortation On Evangelization in the Modern World. In his writings and pronouncements, Paul VI emphasized the importance of the "domestic Church" and the nature of pastoral ministry that involves the family.

In the apostolic exhortation Paul VI again referred to the designation of family as "the Church of the home." In elaborating on the theme, he wrote: "This means that there should be found in every Christian family the various aspects of the entire Church" (Paul VI EvangNunt 71). This family's mission and the ministry which proceeds from it is explained: "In a family which is conscious of this mission, all the members evangelize and are evangelized. The parents not only communicate the Gospel to their children, but from their children, they can, themselves, receive the same Gospel as deeply lived by them. And such a family becomes the evangelizer of many other families, and of the neighborhood of which it forms a part" (ibid.). This coincides with the teaching of Vatican II on the apostolic mission of the laity in the Church, which states: "For that very purpose, He made them His witnesses and gave them understanding of the faith and the grace of speech, so that the power of the gospel might shine forth in their daily social and family lives." (*Lumen gentium* 35).

In the mid-1970s, in order to respond to the need for pastoral ministry directly affecting families, Paul VI established a Committee for the Family. In the press announcement of the Committee's formation in January 1973, the following description of the Committee's purpose was offered: "In the face of the generalization of the problems and the diversity of the situations, there is lacking in the Church an ecclesial institution of universal character, charged with the task of gathering, promoting and coordinating, within an overall pastoral vision, the efforts that are being made within the area of the family." On March 13, 1974, Paul VI addressed the Committee membership and specifically called for moving beyond study and reflection to pastoral action in this area. He indicated that the Committee should devote itself to the promotion of centers of reflection, action and witness to the Christian understanding of family relations (ActApS 66 [1974] 232–234). In 1975, the topic for the Committee's study was the sacramentality of marriage. The 1976 motu proprio *Apostolatus peragendi* (ActApS 68 [1976] 700–703) refers to the Pontifical Committee. This document determined that the work of the Committee was to be carried out in close collaboration with the Pontifical Council for the Laity, while keeping its own structure and identity.

In 1978, the Committee issued a document entitled *The Family in the Pastoral Activity of the Church* in which the mission of the Committee was further delineated and the status of family pastoral activity in the Church was examined. This report summarized the situation of the family apostolate on the level of episcopal conferences and, also, explored the situation of movements, organizations, and centers that assist in the Church's promotion of family life. In this report, the Committee concluded with emphasis on the vital nature of the family within the Church's ministry: "Pastoral concern for marriage and the family has become one of the most essential aspects of the apostolate today. That which occurs in the family has a primary effect on the life of the Church in the world." In conclusion, it points out: "This is the time to present the family as the center of the pastoral reflection of the Church. It is all the more so in that various forms of renewal proclaim that they have great need of the family in order to be able to pass to the level of action. If the Church evangelizes and sanctifies the family, the family will, in turn, construct and sanctify the Church" (Committee for the Family 24).

The American Bishops. In the United States the action by the United States Catholic Conference has been greatly expanded by the May, 1978, approval of a *Plan of Pastoral Action for Family Ministry.* This Plan was made in response to recommendations made principally from the USCC Ad Hoc Commission on Marriage and Family Life, constituted in November 1975 and headed by Archbishop John R. Quinn. The *Plan of Pastoral Action* calls for a major renewal of the Church's effort to development of a more effective and articulated pastoral ministry for families. It does this by calling for an extensive process of pastoral listening and planning, the designation of 1980 as a "Family Year" for the Catholic community, and setting aside the 1980s as a decade of pastoral study and development.

Bibliography: Committee for the Family, *The Family in the Pastoral Activity of the Church* (USCC Publ. Office, Washington, D.C. 1978; D. CONROY, ed., *Curriculum Outline and Resources on Family Ministry* (Washington, D.C. 1977). R. HAUGHTON, "A Family's Ministry," Origins 5 (1975). NCCB, *Plan of Pastoral Action for Family Ministry* (USCC Publ. Office, Washington, D.C. 1978). PAUL VI, "Allocution to Équipes de Notre Dame" May 4, 1970, in *The Teachings of Pope Paul VI, 1970* (USCC Publ. Office, Washington, D.C. 1971) 166–176; "Address to the Committee on the Family," *Pope Speaks* 19 (1974–75) 15–17; *Apostolatus peragendi*, motu proprio, tr. *Pope Speaks* 22 (1977) 26–29.

[D. CONROY]

FAMILY (EDUCATIONAL ROLE)

The educational role or mission of the family was highlighted in the teachings of Vatican Council II. The Declaration on Christian Education stressed the role of parents as "the first and foremost educators of their children" (*Gravissimum educationis* 3). This teaching is consistent with the teachings of Pius XI in his encyclicals *Divini illius Magister* and *Mit brennender Sorge* as well as that of Pius XII in his allocution to the first national congress of the Italian Association of Catholic Teachers (September 8, 1956).

Vatican II Teaching. This same Vatican II document further points out: "For it devolves on parents to create a family atmosphere so animated with love and reverence for God and men that a well-rounded personal and social development will be fostered among the children (ibid.)." Hence, the family is the first school of those social virtues which every society needs. The Declaration then relates the primary educational role of the family to the society as a whole by indicating that "certain rights and duties belong to civil society," because of the need to arrange for the common good within the society itself. It specifies certain ways in which this duty to promote the education of the young is able to be carried out: overseeing the duties of parents and others who are charged with educational responsibility; implementation of the principle of subsidiarity; completing the educational task when parental and other efforts are insufficient; building schools in accord with the needs of society (ibid.).

The Church's own educational role is also specified. The responsibility to announce the Gospel and communicate the life of Christ in its fulness to those who believe also gives the Church a unique title in complementing the family's role in education (ibid.).

In the Pastoral Constitution on the Church in the Modern World, the Council Fathers also clarified the family's educational role. In facing the contemporary difficulty within the present world setting, of fostering a well-rounded education involving "the ideal of 'the universal man'" the family's proper attitude toward this role is indicated. The Constitution states: "The family is, as it were, the primary mother and nurse of this attitude. There, in an atmosphere of love, children can more easily learn the true structure of reality" (*Gaudium et spes* 61).

The American Bishops. In the United States specification of the family's role with regard to religious education and the catechesis of the children has come about especially in connection with the work of the 1977 *Synod of Bishops and the preparation of a *National Catechetical Directory for the United States. In a position paper (written intervention) submitted by the National Conference of Catholic Bishops of the United States to the 1977 Synod of Bishops, the family's role in catechesis was more extensively outlined. The further development of the family's part in the catechetical process is seen as crucial for the future of catechetics. This document also indicated the more recent development of total *family ministry, which includes evangelization, prayer, and social ministry along with catechesis as integral to the family's mission (NCCB, Synod 75–78).

Additional teaching by the bishops of the United States in their pastoral letter on Christian education, *To Teach as Jesus Did* (1972), pointed to the need for the family to play a vital role in catechetical formation. The pastoral letter pointed out: "In seeking to instill understanding of the Christian family's role, family life education must employ such means as premarital instruction and marriage counseling, study, prayer and action groups for couples, and other adult programs which married persons themselves may plan and conduct in collaboration with Church leadership" (NCCB, To Teach 51).

Furthermore, in the final draft of the National Catechetical Directory (NCD), as approved by the National Conference of Catholic Bishops in November 1977, there is ample reference to the important role of the family in catechesis. In Chapter 1, the family's crucial task is explained, "Family and community are also extremely important in the catechetical process. While other factors are involved (e.g., age, sex, size of community, present study of religion, parental approval of the friends of their children, etc.), the impact of parents is primary among the human factors which influence this process. This is the principal reason for the current emphasis on preparation for parenthood and parent education, as well as a subsidiary motive for adult education" (NCD 25).

Educational efforts within dioceses have led in the 1970s to a more direct concern for the role of the parents and the family in the catechetical process. Family sacramental preparation programs and various other forms of family-centered catechesis have been tried extensively. Moreover, the *Plan of Pastoral Action for Family Ministry*, approved by the United States bishops in May 1978, pointed out the role of parents as "the primary catechists of their children" and called for the extensive development of family educational ministry.

Bibliography: NCCB, *To Teach as Jesus Did* (USCC Publ. Office, Washington, D.C. 1972); National Catechetical Directory, "Sharing the Light of Faith"; *Synod of Bishops 1977* (USCC Publ. Office, Washington, D.C. 1978); *Plan of Pastoral Action for Family Ministry* (USCC Publ. Office, Washington, D.C. 1978). J. L. THOMAS, *The American Catholic Family* (Washington, D.C. 1974).

[D. CONROY]

FAMILY MINISTRY

Vatican Council II devoted special attention to the family (*Gaudium et spes* 47–52) because healthy marital and family relationships are of deep pastoral concern for the Church. The *Pastoral Plan of Action for Family Ministry*, of the NCCB, passed at the May 1978 meeting of the bishops in Chicago, expresses a fundamental pastoral priority in the Church in both the enrichment of sound families and the healing of families who are hurting. It also begins a process of planning and implementation whereby the real Christian and human needs of families will be met by effective expressions of ministry.

Four Steps in Ministry. This process involves four steps which are to bring the Church into a more effective ministerial relationship with its families. The first step is one of listening to the families themselves as they seek to express their own particular charisms as well as the difficulties they perceive in the working out of their full Christian potential. This step also involves a raising of awareness in the Church of the sacramental nature of marriage and family life. The Church, like a competent counselor, first establishes the real conditions under which it will attempt to serve the ones in need.

The second step enables families to care honestly for themselves and others. It seeks to point out that the Christian life has an active, loving dimension which must be communicated externally. Church life is fundamentally an active caring. The Church, as an expression of God's care and concern in the world, attempts to extend that care by empowering its members to help themselves and to move out to meet the needs of others. This care is to extend also toward the betterment of the social structures of which family life is a part.

The third step flows from the sense of mission which is fundamental to the Christian life wherever it is actualized. The Plan speaks not only of the ministry done by a professionally trained person, for example, a marriage counselor or a family therapist, but also, to the ministry of the lay person. The Plan describes a like-to-like ministry, for example of married couples assisting the engaged in preparing for marriage, parents creating support groups for each other; widows ministering to others who have been drawn into similar life circumstances. The underlying idea is that ministry is not reserved to a special stratum of church personnel, but rather it is a characteristic of all who are Christian. Further, ministry ought to gain expression in the ordinary situations of people's lives.

The fourth step is the call to establish whatever structures are judged necessary to accomplish the fullest extension of family-life ministry. These structures are not to be ends in themselves, but are intended to facilitate and free persons for effective ministry. It is also necessary that training be a part of ministry so that the real needs of persons be met.

Professional Counseling. Marital and family ministry may demand formal counseling so as to bring the individuals into a more effective life of relationship. This may involve some form of family therapy where the concern is for the total relational structure of the family unit. It is based on a belief that the family is a social system of interlocking and dynamic parts. To deal sufficiently with the difficulties of any single member of the family, it is necessary to acknowledge the effects operating from the total system. Personal, individual problems are seen to be usually family problems and a resolution of the problems will necessarily involve the whole family in some way.

In recent years there has developed a section of marriage therapy related specifically to the sexual area of life. Provided that the means employed in dealing with the problems are in accord with authentic Catholic moral thought, then the individual or couple can feel justified in seeking such counsel. Clinics have been established to deal with sexual dysfunction under the general auspices of the Church in some parts of the country. This form of helping couples can certainly be seen as a valid form of healing ministry.

The Christian life is a life of sharing; it is a life where interdependence is admitted, even celebrated. With marriage and family life being one of the most common and fundamental structures where the Christian life is lived in all its concreteness and incarnationality, it is appropriate that Christians, in particular, move to assist each other, and those outside the Church, in the betterment of marriage and family life. This may involve support, counseling, or merely being with others in the affirmation of the fundamental Christian goodness of being married and being a family person.

Bibliography: NCCB, *Pastoral Plan of Action for Family Ministry* (USCC Publ. Office, Washington, D.C. 1978).

[D. M. THOMAS]

FAMILY SERVICES, CATHOLIC

Family-life agencies, under the name "Family Life Bureau" or a similar name, exist in most of the dioceses in the United States. These diocesan agencies maintain a close tie with the NCCB/USCC offices concerned with marriage and family life. Diocesan directors and staff meet regionally for interrelationship and exchange of programming ideas and educational initiatives. National conventions and workshops for directors, through sociological and philosophical presentations by experts are a resource for continuing professional education, policy formation, and evaluation of trends. Family services can be grouped logically into their three main spheres: preparation for marriage; growth in family living; therapy for family crises.

Preparation for Marriage. Preparation for marriage is largely concentrated on Pre-Cana conferences, held frequently during the year in parish locations around the diocese, with a team of priest, doctor, and four couples to host, teach, and moderate for the program. Training sessions are held for the speaker couples. Some attempts are now being made to conduct Pre-Canas on a parish basis, taking four couples through a series of evenings at the home of a married couple. Pre-Cana itself is not enough. There should be more remote and earlier preparation, starting with courses for life education in primary and upper grades. Many high schools and CCD programs have good courses. Parish programs are available for parents' discussion on sex education for their children at home and in school. Engaged Encounter involves the engaged couples in a weekend away with other couples and a team of married couple and priest, to concentrate on deeper preparation of the Sacrament and good communication in marriage.

Growth in Family Living. Under the growth-in-family-living aspect are Cana Clubs, Teams of Our Lady, Christian Family Movement action-groups, Post-Cana for the widowed, and Marriage Encounter. There is an organization for separated and divorced Catholics and there are programs on parent-teen communications, human sexuality, prayer and the middle years of marriage offered to parishes in a package designed for a family renewal series. Family Masses, couple-and-family-retreats and days of recollection are also promoted. Annual golden- and silver-wedding jubilee ceremonies are held in many places. Respect Life Month and the March for Life are advertised and supported.

Family planning clinics teach safe, effective, and morally acceptable methods of responsible parenthood. Couples are instructed and guided in their use of the basic body temperature and the newer ovulation methods. This individual counseling is followed up with chart-guidance as long as desired. Parish informational programs in *natural family planning and high school classes on fertility awareness are also becoming popular. Records of some clinics show over 98 percent effectiveness of this symptothermal combination of methods.

Family Therapy Activities. Family therapy activities, include referral service for family counseling, help for diocesan priests to get some professional training in this field. Para-counseling techniques are offered in courses to permanent deacons and their wives so that their availability on the parish level may provide some initial counseling and referral, often in cases which are not yet in crisis.

The diocesan Catholic Charities Offices, which are well-established social-work agencies, give direct service to Catholic families and children. This includes casework service, temporary financial assistance, placement in institutions, group homes and adoptions, and service to unwed mothers. The agencies provide family counseling and services to the elderly and refugees.

Much of family-life education takes place in the family itself, so it is important to reach parents with programs and help. It is impossible to estimate the great amount of such inspiration and training that is done by the couples-movement already mentioned and by the volunteers for these movements who contribute so much time and energy to the work of the family apostolate. The witness value alone is tremendous.

Most diocesan family life agencies have small staffs and budgets, but with the approval of the new "Plan for Family Ministry" (that is, *to* and *by* families) by the U.S. Bishops in their Chicago meeting of May 1978, there should be considerably more diocesan and parochial effort toward attention to this basic group of society. This will be a fulfillment of frequent papal and conciliar statements on the importance of the family in the life of the Church.

[K. C. ENZLER]

FEDERATION OF DIOCESAN LITURGICAL COMMISSIONS (FDLC)

The Federation of Diocesan Liturgical Commissions (FDLC) has undergone little structural or constitutional change since it first convened in Pittsburgh in 1969 (16:180). Its official address changed from Pueblo, Col. to Pevely, Mo. to Chicago, Ill. where the present office of its administration is located. It continues to share in the sponsorship of an annual meeting of diocesan liturgical commissions each October. In structure these meetings have changed from a conference to a convention format. A booklet is prepared each February on the convention topic for diocesan and regional (12 regions) discussion. Action and nonaction statements submitted to the national meeting deal with liturgical topics that are debated and voted on at the convention. As a result of these votes the priority issues are acted upon by the board for implementation.

The Federation is concerned with the pastoral aspects of liturgy and has been influential in bringing about: the option of *Communion in the hand (1977); a greater concern for liturgical courses both in seminaries and in continuing education programs for clergy; the presence of full-time liturgical personnel trained in liturgical theology in most large dioceses. In 1971 it published the *Prayer of Christians*, an interim breviary used until publication (1974) of the four-volume, International Commission on English in the Liturgy translation of the Liturgy of the Hours.

Through its standing music committee the FDLC assisted in the *Bishops' Committee on the Liturgy's publication of "Music in Catholic Worship" (1972) and conducted a vast investigation into the possibility of a National Hymnal. This effort led to the publication of three good hymnals and service books by independent publishers that are replacing disposable participation materials in the United States (*see* HYMNS AND HYMNALS). An art and architecture committee has raised the consciousness of bishops and pastors to the necessity of professional competence in the design and redesign of spaces for community worship. Materials of background theology were published by FDLC to assist the liturgical catechesis introducing of the Sacraments of Anointing the Sick, Reconciliation, and Communion in the hand. Aimed at parish liturgical committees, these tools assisted a smooth transition from the older to the revised rituals of ministering Sacraments. The FDLC looks to better leadership among the many Hispanic cultures in the country through trained Hispanic liturgists working with the bishops. It has active committees dealing with: rural liturgical problems, evangelization, communal absolution, and the justice of music copyrights.

[J. L. CUNNINGHAM]

FEENEY, LEONARD

Poet, essayist, founder and superior of a religious congregation of men and women, b. Lynn, Mass., Feb. 15, 1897, and d. Still River, Mass., Jan. 30, 1978. Trained in Jesuit schools, he entered the Society in 1914 and after completing seminary studies did graduate work at Oxford. He was ordained at Weston College in 1928.

Feeney quickly attracted attention in the Catholic literary world with his first book of poetry, *In Towns and Little Towns* (1927). This was followed over the next twenty years by a great variety of writings: essays, short stories, sketches, biography, dramatizations, and more poetry. Educated "in the hard school of wonder," as he put it, he was entranced with "the earthliness of heavenly things and the heavenliness of earthly things." With his buoyant, paradoxical style he was called by many the "American G. K. Chesterton." Among Feeney's popular books were: *In Towns and Little Towns* (1927); *Fish on Friday* (1934); *Boundaries* (1936); *Riddle and Reverie* (1936); *Song for a Listener* (1936); *You'd Better Come Quietly* (1939); *Survival Till Seventeen* (1941); *The Leonard Feeney Omnibus* (1943); *Your Second Childhood* (1945).

One of Feeney's outstanding characteristics was his insistence on the primacy of doctrine as the source of theology and devotion. "And by the way/Speaking of how to pray,/Dogmas come first, not liturgies." Frank Sheed, a long-time friend and one of his publishers, said of his writings, "For Father Feeney, dogma is not only true; it is breathlessly exciting. That is his special vocation—to make his readers feel the thrill." Besides contributing to Catholic periodicals and broadcasting on "The Catholic Hour," Feeney was also literary editor of *America*, president of the Catholic Poetry Society of America, and in demand as a lecturer. In 1943, at the height of his literary and lecturing career, he was assigned as permanent chaplain to St. Benedict Center, an intellectual and spiritual forum for Harvard and Radcliffe students, founded in 1940 by Catherine Goddard Clarke. Every Thursday he gave lectures on the panorama of the Catholic faith, interspersed with lively anecdotes and comical impersonations, justifying one critic's comment that he was "as Catholic as St. Thomas Aquinas and as American as Mark Twain." Like Chesterton, whom he called a "A tank of paradoxygen," he was adroit at impromptu versifying and punning. "If one is a Catholic," he wrote, "one cannot think without being cosmical or without being comical either, because the faith links all realities together and fills the world with surprises." His love of dogma made Feeney come out in the open when it was unfashionable to do so and insist that the doctrine, *extra ecclesiam nulla salus*, must he held and professed without compromise. This stand bred a reaction which led to ecclesiastical censures on him and his followers.

On Jan. 17, 1949, with Catherine Goddard Clarke, he founded a religious community of men and women. In 1958, the community moved from Cambridge, Mass., to a farm in Still River, Mass., where they were better able to follow a monastic life of prayer, study, and manual labor according to the Benedictine spirit, which had for years fascinated Feeney. In 1972, through the efforts of Bishop Bernard J. Flanagan of Worcester, Cardinal Humberto Medeiros of Boston, and Cardinal John Wright of the Congregation for the Clergy, all ecclesiastical censures against Father Feeney were removed. Subsequently the majority of the members of the community were reconciled with the Church.

In its obituary editorial, *The Catholic Free Press* of Worcester said: "Father Feeney, . . . because of the clarity of his thought, won for himself a lasting place in the history of the Church in America . . . . What he said, what he was, what he did, was part of the history of his times. If he had an overconsuming fault—and how we wish this could be said of more of us!—it was that he possessed a love for the Church, for Jesus and Mary, that could not and would not be compromised."

[S. M. CLARE]

FELLOWSHIP OF CATHOLIC SCHOLARS

Concerned that many Catholic scholars were becoming immersed within their own research; that scholarly disciplines were becoming monolithic and unrelated to other disciplines; that each seemed to be growing less positively related to the magisterium of the Church; a group of lay, religious, and priest scholars formed the Fellowship of Catholic Scholars, incorporated early in 1978. The purpose of the Fellowship is to elicit interdisciplinary scholarship and cooperation in the support, promotion, and defense of the ecclesiastical magisterium in its teaching of the Catholic faith. Membership requires at least the equivalent of an advanced academic degree, recommendation by two other members, and election by the Board of Directors. Nonvoting associate and honorary members who share Fellowship goals are also accepted. The Fellowship publishes a Newsletter (v. 1, 1978), plans to publish symposia, and holds scholarly conventions. Its mailing center is at St. John's University, Jamaica, New York,

11439. Its first president was Ronald Lawler OFM Cap., Ph.D., of The Catholic University of America. Its first convention theme, Catholic Faith and Human Life, was addressed by several internationally known scholars.

Bibliography: Fellowship of Catholic Scholars, *Articles of Incorporation, and By-Laws* (Washington, D.C. 1978).

[H. V. SATTLER]

FELLOWSHIP OF RECONCILIATION

The Fellowship of Reconciliation (FOR) was founded in England on the eve of World War I in 1914. The founding energy was supplied by the German Lutheran pastor and Christian socialist leader Friederich Siegmund-Schultze and the English Quaker leader Henry Hodgkin. Both determined that their pacifism would have to survive the war. The following year the FOR was established in the U.S. as a membership organization of religious pacifists. Other groups have been established since; there are now twenty-seven national groups and an International FOR headquartered in Alkmaar, The Netherlands.

During World War I FOR efforts on behalf of conscientious objectors led to the creation of the American Civil Liberties Bureau (now Union). During the 1920s and 30s leading Protestant churchmen were attracted in large numbers to the FOR. Norman Thomas and Reinhold Niebuhr were early executive secretaries. A. J. Muste, another executive secretary, was able to inject new forms of militant, nonviolent action into the labor movement (the sit-down strike) that led to success where failure had been the rule. In 1940 FOR established as a project the Congress of Racial Equality (CORE), and started the first racially integrated sit-ins at segregated restaurants.

During World War II the FOR counselled conscientious objectors and maintained the pacifist witness. In 1947 the FOR sent a racially integrated team into the upper South to test regulations governing interstate transportation. Participants found themselves for a month on a chain-gang. FOR member Martin Luther King, Jr. called upon FOR for assistance in the earliest years of the Montgomery bus boycott in 1957. FOR thus became the principal ally of the Southern Christian Leadership Conference.

FOR members were among the first to protest the Viet Nam War, organizing vigils, study teams to South Viet Nam, servicing conscientious objectors and draft-resisters, and finally lending leadership to the organization of the mass demonstrations that marked the end of public support for the war. During the war period the membership grew rapidly and for the first time Roman Catholics and Jews joined in significant numbers. Among the most active of the religious groupings within the Fellowship has been the *Catholic Peace Fellowship. The FOR numbered 25,202 members in 1978. Headquarters is at Box 271, Nyack, NY 10960.

[T. C. CORNELL]

FEMINISM AND CHRISTIAN THEOLOGY

In every age there are new vistas to explore as Christians seek to understand the relationship between a vision revealed in the symbols and stories of the Christian tradition and the cultural forms that shape and misshape human existence. As a people whose understanding of God's Revelation grows through the slow and sometimes painful processes of history, Christians are constantly called to read the signs of the times and be ready for new insights into the meaning of faith. Of the many areas currently effecting just such a radical rethinking of the Christian tradition, one stands out in bold relief on the theological horizon: the feminist critique of Christian theology. If theology is a pattern of understanding enabling the believer to hold together faith and experience, say the feminists, is not adequate to the questions of a newly conscious people.

State of the Question. The exact nature of the difficulties has been variously described. An early statement of the problem was that a theology developed almost exclusively by men, while appropriate for them, cannot assist women, because it is not addressed to women's social and historical situation nor shaped by women's experiences (Goldstein). Critics of this persuasion call for a "supplemental" theology that will reflect the "feminine factor" and communicate God's Revelation to women precisely as women (Mount).

In recent years this way of approaching the problem has been superseded by a more radical statement of the question and a more serious challenge to the tradition. Calling itself a "post-Christian feminism," the newer school of thought defines the problem this way: traditional theology is hopeless because the Christian religion is irredeemably sexist. Believing that Christianity defines woman as inferior, these critics charge that it has been a prime factor in the oppression of women throughout history. By offering a male image of God, a male savior, and life in a male-dominated community, they argue, Christianity requires of women an alienation from self that is ultimately destructive (Daly). Such a position goes far beyond the call for a "supplemental" theology; it demands a new religion to replace a Christianity seen as fundamentally misogynist. There is a tragic irony to this way of viewing the crisis: by identifying traditional *interpretations* of Christianity with Christian *Revelation itself*, thinkers of this school have conceded that the way men have interpreted the symbols and stories of the Christian religion is the only right way. Despite this failing, post-Christian feminists have made an invaluable contribution to the contemporary debate, for they have demonstrated the need for a new apologetic that can answer their devastating accusation.

A third way of viewing the theological crisis is to say that traditional theology needs to be reformed for the sake of women and men alike, because in addition to giving women a false sense of inferiority, it has given men a sense of superiority equally false. Making a fundamental distinction between the Word of God and the Word of Man, these critics call for a thoroughgoing revision of the theological viewpoint (Burghardt). The struggle over questions related to the "second sex" has driven some theologians back to the sources to seek there authentic Revelation about the daughters of God. This re-viewing of Scripture and tradition has issued already in fresh insights into the stories of creation and redemption, historical interpretation of the symbols of liberation, and a renewed vision of that community of equals to which Christian poetry, if not Christian history, points.

From this there emerges the barest outline of a new

Christian anthropology. Many of the details are yet to be worked out, but the literature extant provides a base for suggesting the following as essential parts of the whole.

Creation for Community. The feminist revisitation of Genesis, while recognizing the residues of the patriarchal society in which it was born, notes that the myth reveals a vision of woman that is nonetheless an exalted one (Trible, Brueggemann). The woman owes her existence to God's intervention and power; she is created in the divine image and blessed by divine approbation, being called "very good" (GN 1.26, 31). Alone of all other creatures she is a match for the man, capable of drawing forth from him a cry of delight and desire (Gn 2.23). Like her partner, she is called by the Lord God, and commissioned with the care of the earth (Gn 1.28–30). The import of the opening chapters of Genesis and their depiction of the world before sin is, then, a glimpse of the human vocation: Adam and Eve, the woman and the man are created for *communion* with each other and with God.

Generations of male theologians have taught that the woman, being created second, is subject to the man in the divine order of creation. The structure of the myth does not support such an interpretation. It is only after both the man and the woman have ruptured their relationship with God that the woman is named by the man and cursed with the fateful words that she will long for her husband and he will lord it over her (Gn 3.16, 20). Male domination and female subordination play no part in the stage of innocence; they stem, therefore, not from God's will but from human failure; male domination can be interpreted to be a result of sin.

Redemption for Community. This interpretation of God's vision preserved in the Old Testament is born out in the new image of Jesus that feminist exegetes are discovering (Swidler, Collins, Ruether [1974]). Reconstructing the ways in which Jesus rejected traditional taboos associated with women (Mt 9.20), called upon their experiences in his preaching (Lk 13.20; 15.8–10), and invited them to a discipleship transcending the restrictions of Jewish law and cult (Jn 4.1–39), these studies hint of a new dimension to the story of redemption. If the subordination of women is a result of sin, then this form of human alienation from God's intentions must be an object of Jesus' salvific mission. It must be, the logic of the argument continues, that Jesus' redeeming power will manifest itself in the new community created under the guidance of the Spirit so that the sinful human tendency to categorize by sex is corrected: difference between the sexes need no longer mean preference or power-domination.

Liberation for Community. Such an interpretation of the historical fact of the subordination of women—that it derives not from the will of God but from sinful human structures on which God has passed judgment in the person of Jesus—can provide a theological foundation for: (1) a critique of the theological tradition; (2) a critique of cultural forms; (3) the construction of a new theological synthesis; and (4) the reformation of human institutions through engagement in the social struggles of the day.

As Christian understanding grows in time, so does the appropriation in time of the implications of Jesus' redemptive action. Redemption becomes liberation when people not only believe in the vision, but act on it.

Therefore, feminists theologians argue, the current women's movement will be truly liberating if it arouses Christians to engage in the struggle for women's equality while at the same time shaping the image of equality to the vision of the Gospel (Russell, Collins).

Symbols for the New Community. If human beings live and act in large measure out of imagination, then the symbols and stories that shape the human image of the world also shape life in that world. One theologian has called attention to the power of a single image by pointing out that it was Christian meditation on men as sons of God that gradually destroyed all theologies based on class, or race, or nation (Lynch). This insight serves to highlight the dilemma of the feminist facing the Christian tradition. To some extent there *can* still be a theology built upon and biased by *sex* because of traditional ways of understanding the incarnation of God in a male human being, and because the image of "men" as "sons of God" has left undeveloped the implications of this incarnation for "women" who want to be "daughters" of God. Yet, if the alienation from self that feminists have described in such convincing detail is to be healed in the Christian religion, there must be a way for a woman to find God in *her*self and love *her*. That is, there must be a way to understand the being of woman as participating in the *imago Dei* that is the foundation and in Jesus' "sonship" that is the crown of theological anthropology. The dilemma cannot be bypassed with an appeal to women to think of "man" as generic. The problem runs deeper.

Current attempts to deal with the problem go in two directions. The first stresses that God is a spirit and that the Christian life is primarily life in the Spirit (Ruether [1974]). The difficulty with this emphasis is that it intensifies another problem to which feminists are increasingly sensitive: the flight from woman's body in Christian thought and, in fact, the general prejudice against bodily life's being worthy of theological reflection. A second direction is toward a reappropriation of Mariological symbols (Ruether [1975]). This approach seems in many ways more promising, but it will surely entail the painstaking, perhaps painful, work of demythologizing.

See also WOMEN IN THE CHURCH.

Bibliography: W. A. BRUEGGEMANN, "Of the Same Flesh and Bone: Gen. 2:33a," CathBiblQuart 32 (1970) 532–542. W. BURGHARDT, ed., *Woman, New Dimensions* (New York 1977). A. Y. COLLINS, "An Inclusive Biblical Anthropology," *Theology Today* 34 (1978) 358–369. S. D. COLLINS, *A Different Heaven and Earth* (Valley Forge, Pa. 1974). M. DALY, *Beyond God the Father* (Boston 1973). V. GOLDSTEIN, "The Human Situation: A Feminine Viewpoint," *Journal of Religion* 40 (1960) 100–112. W. LYNCH, *Images of Faith* (Notre Dame, Ind. 1973). D. MACE and G. HAGMEIER, "Equalitarianism and Male Dominance: A Catholic-Protestant Dialogue on Changing Religious Concepts," *Pastoral Psychology* 20 (1969) 49–62. E. MOUNT, "The Feminine Factor," *Soundings* 13 (1970) 379–396. R. R. RUETHER, *New Woman New Earth, Sexist Ideologies and Human Liberation* (New York 1975). R. R. RUETHER, ed., *Religion and Sexism* (New York 1974). L. M. RUSSELL, *Human Liberation in a Feminist Perspective* (Philadelphia 1974). L. SWIDLER, "Jesus Was A Feminist," *New Catholic World* 212 (1971) 177–183. P. TRIBLE, "Depatriarchalizing in Biblical Interpretation," *Journal of the American Academy of Religion* 41 (1973) 30–49.

[M. A. O'NEILL]

FETAL RESEARCH

Fetal research is any medical *experimentation that involves a human fetus (i.e., the product of conception from fertilization until expulsion or extraction from the uterus). Once the living fetus is outside the womb, it is properly an infant, whether premature or full term.

With some exceptions, Federal regulations governing fetal research follow the recommendations of the National Commission for the Protection of Human Subjects of Biomedical and Behavioral Research whose study had shown that fetal research had in the past contributed significantly to the understanding, diagnosis, and treatment of fetal and neonatal dysfunctions. (See *Federal Register*, Aug. 8, 1975; Jan. 13, 1977.)

The human fetus is truly a subject, not an object. Notwithstanding the ancient theories (and modern versions) of delayed animation, a review of the evidence and line of argumentation urges the conclusion that the human fetus is a human *person* from the instant of conception. Consequently, the fetus is the subject of basic and inalienable rights pertaining to life; the fetus therefore, cannot be the subject of any research which endangers life or health. In making an assessment of such risk, no distinction may be made among an aborted fetus, one selected for abortion, or one being allowed to develop to term.

Fetal research should be directed to the benefit of the individual fetus or entail no, or minimal, risk. Informed consent should be obtained from the mother except where she had previously granted permission for an elective abortion. In these circumstances, appropriate consent from a court-appointed guardian is necessary. Informed consent should also be obtained from the father, except where the procedure is in response to the health needs of the mother, or the father cannot be contacted within a reasonable time.

Bibliography: E. F. DIAMOND, "Redefining the Issues in Fetal Experimentation," *Linacre Quarterly* 44 (1977) 148–154. A. R. DI IANNI, "Is the Fetus a Person?" AmEcclRev 168 (1974) 309–326. D. G. MCCARTHY and A. S. MORACZEWSKI, *An Ethical Evaluation of Fetal Experimentation*. Report of the Task Force on Fetal Experimentation, Pope John XXIII Medical-Moral Research and Education Center (St. Louis 1976). R. A. MCCORMICK, "Fetal Research Morality, and Public Policy," *Hastings Center Report* 5 (1975) 26–31. National Commission for the Protection of Human Subject of Biomedical and Behavioral Research, *Report and Recommendations: Research on the Fetus* (Bethesda, Md. 1975). K. O'ROURKE, "An Ethical Evaluation of Federal Norms for Fetal Research," *Linacre Quarterly* 43 (1976) 17–24. J. J. QUINN, "Christianity Views Fetal Research," *Linacre Quarterly* 45 (1978) 55–63. P. RAMSEY, *The Ethics of Fetal Research* (New Haven 1975). H. O. TIEFEL, "The Cost of Fetal Research: Ethical Considerations," *New England Journal of Medicine* 294 (1976) 85–90. L. WALTERS, "Ethical Issues in Experimentation on the Human Fetus," *Journal of Religious Ethics* 2 (1974) 33–54.

[A. S. MORACZEWSKI]

FIRST COMMUNION, CELEBRATION OF

The liturgical celebration of First Communion is a golden opportunity to further develop the adult faith-community where a child can grow; to encourage the family's participation in the event through their liturgical involvement; to heighten children's appreciation of the uniqueness of this special day in their life. Several options are open for celebration of First Communion.

Individual First Reception within a Sunday Liturgy. There are ways of involvement in the liturgy itself that can help the celebration be meaningful and special for the child, yet not encumber the adult Sunday liturgy.

Before the liturgy begins, the lector or a parent can mention the child's name or even read a few sentences about the child. This is also a good opportunity to remind the community of the importance of their support and example (*see* PARISH [COMMUNITY OF WORSHIP]). The family should sit together in the front pew; pews

can also be reserved for close family and friends. The child and parents can be seated before Mass or may choose to be involved in the Entrance Procession. In the Entrance Procession, the first communicant may process into church with the celebrant, with the family accompanying. The child could carry a candle, especially a candle with special significance, e.g., the candle received at Baptism. The parents could contact the person responsible for the music and request hymns that have a special significance for the child. Since it is an adult Sunday liturgy, songs used should be appropriate to the action of the Mass and should be familiar to the congregation. Any solo or child's song should be sung before Mass or as one of the Communion songs.

At the General Intercessions the child can be remembered in a special petition composed by either the family or the celebrant. For the Presentation of the Gifts the family may bring the gifts to the altar. After this they may return to their seats or they could approach the sanctuary and stand either around or at a place close to the altar, remaining there until after they have received Communion. At the Sign of Peace it would be appropriate for the family members to extend the greeting to the congregation. It is especially meaningful for the celebrant to make a special effort to come and greet the family and child. At Communion the child and family should receive before others in the congregation have begun to move toward Communion stations. The child and family may receive under both kinds; care needs to be taken, however, that the child is comfortable with this. Sensitivity should be extended to family members who may not feel comfortable approaching the Eucharist or who cannot receive with the child. Perhaps the celebrant could place his hands on the head of the person who will not be receiving and give a special blessing. Similar action could be included for family members who are too young to be receiving the Eucharist.

Before the Final Blessing the celebrant can invite the child forward to receive the Communion certificate and the celebrant's congratulations. He may also present the child with a gift from the parish, such as a New Testament. (Many inexpensive paperbacks in a child's language are available.) At the Recessional the family may leave with the celebrant or remain in their seats. The congregation may be invited to offer their congratulations to the child before leaving the church.

Solemn and Group Reception. The opportunity is provided at some time toward the end of the year or on Holy Thursday for all the children to come together for a Solemn First Communion. This allows children whose parents could not, or would not, participate as a family to be easily integrated. Many of the same options elaborated above could be used here with a few alterations suited to the size of the group.

Group reception refers to small groups of children who at designated dates throughout the year, may make their First Communion together. Most of the same liturgical options listed above would apply. The children could enter as a group with the celebrant, but then go and sit in a reserved pew with their parents.

Home Mass. There are a variety of views here, depending on local customs. Some feel First Communions are not reserved for family and a few friends but involve the church community. It is held that the major Feast Day, Sunday, should be the day for such a festive church celebration. Others contend that the family and a few friends are the major community for such a small child and that a home liturgy is more intimate and personal.

If such a liturgy is chosen the options are wide and varied, depending once again on diocese, parish, celebrant, family. To suggest a few: (1) parents welcome those gathered; (2) no processions—all may be gathered informally; (3) family members may be involved in all Readings; (4) music is entirely up to the family; (5) the child can be referred to frequently throughout the Liturgy.

See also CHILDREN, RELIGION AND; MASSES WITH CHILDREN.

Bibliography: Archdiocese of St. Paul-Minneapolis; *The Family, The Child, and First Communion* (1971). J. BENZSCHAWEL and J. VILLOTTI, "Some Helpful Ideas for Celebrating First Communion," *Religion Teachers Journal* 8 (1975) 16–17. Congregation for Divine Worship, *Directory for Masses with Children* (USCC Publ. Office, Washington, D.C. 1973). Congregation of Rites, Instruction, *Eucharisticum Mysterium*, May 25, 1967, tr. *On Eucharistic Worship* (USCC Publ. Office, Washington, D.C. 1967) especially art. 14 and 32.

[J. VILLOTTI BIEDNZYCKI]

FIRST CONFESSION

The practice of deferring children's first confession until some time after first Communion dates back to the early 1960s in the United States. Many religious educators believed that since seven-year-old children were capable of only an external rather than a relational understanding of sin, their initiation into sacramental Penance was premature at that age. Some argued further that since children of that age had not developed a sense of group dependency, they could not comprehend Penance as an expression of reconciliation to a community. In general authorities in the field accepted the converging theological and psychological evidence that strongly suggested the positive advantages of a later age for first confession. Since the Code of Canon Law nowhere demanded that children go to confession before first Communion, there seemed to be no real juridical problem in changing the order of the reception of the two Sacraments. Parishes around the country began adopting the newer practice. A survey conducted in 1972 by the U.S. Catholic Conference concluded: "On the average, 52% of the parishes across the nation were estimated to have opted for prior reception of first Communion."

Vatican Declarations. Doubts concerning the legitimacy of the newer practice began to arise in 1972 following the publication of the *General Catethetical Directory* by the Sacred Congregation for the Clergy. An appendix to the Directory stated that the age for both confession and Communion is about the seventh year and concluded that "the Holy See judges it fitting that the practice now in force in the Church of putting confession ahead of first Communion should be retained." The directory added that in regions where the newer practice had already been introduced, the bishops should consult with the Holy See if they wished to continue the practice.

At their meeting in November 1972 the American bishops voted to ask the Holy See to continue postponing first confession so they could evaluate the pastoral effectiveness of the new order of reception of Eucharist and Penance. Their request was not directly answered.

In May 1973, however, a brief declaration was issued jointly by the Congregation for the Clergy and the Congregation for the Sacraments (ActApS 65 [1973] 410; tr. Origins 3 [1973] 100). The declaration stated that all experiments that permitted first Communion before first confession were to cease.

The declaration did not, however, end all discussion, and the subject was again considered at the November 1973 meeting of the American bishops. They took the position that the declaration should be given a "pastoral interpretation which is rather broad, so that the impression of obligation to confess before first Communion would not be insisted upon." Meanwhile the Canadian bishops had requested that the Holy See clarify the meaning of the declaration. They were informed that the declaration "does not aim at compelling or regimenting every child to receive first penance before first Communion or to foster conditions which would prevent children from receiving the sacrament of penance before their first Communion ... but to emphasize that during the one and same initiation period, children should be given a positive and pastoral catechetical preparation for these two sacraments." The Holy See was concerned that children's right to the Sacrament of Penance be respected. Accordingly it insisted that children be given sufficient catechesis so that they could realistically exercise that right. Children had the right but not the obligation to confess before first Communion and pastors and catechists ought to respect that right.

The matter finally seemed to be settled. But then in May of 1977 the two Roman congregations sent a letter to all bishops stating that the Sacraments of Penance and Eucharist should be received in the order designated in Pius X's 1910 decree, *Quam singulari*, that is, confession before first Communion. An appendix to the 1977 letter offered an official negative reply to the question of whether as a general rule first Communion might be received before first confession.

Interpretation. Some have interpreted this latest communiqué as a definitive interpretation of the law, which, it is claimed, now requires that as a rule children must receive the Sacrament of Penance prior to being admitted to first Communion. Several objections are offered against this strict interpretation of the law. First of all it is evident that the recent Roman documents on this question did not intend to enact new legislation but merely to insist that the old legislation of *Quam singulari* be observed. *Quam singulari* did not, in fact, consider the precise question of whether children were required to confess before first Communion; its concern was with the rights of seven-year-old children to be admitted to the Sacraments of Penance and Eucharist. The only mention of obligation in the 1910 decree had to do with the obligation of annual confession and Communion. It should be noted, however, that the law of annual confession was always interpreted as binding only those who were guilty of mortal sin. Furthermore, even if *Quam singulari* had obliged children to confession before first Communion, this obligation would have been abrogated with the promulgation of the Code of Canon Law in 1917. The Code, which replaced the preceding corpus of church legislation, contains no directives concerning the necessity of confession before first Communion.

Secondly, the 1977 letter from the Holy See concedes:

"It is not necessary to add that the strict obligation of confession should be understood according to the traditional teaching of the Church." The traditional teaching of the Church is that one is obliged to confess before Communion only if conscious of mortal sin. No one, including a seven-year-old sinner, is obliged to make a devotional confession before being permitted to receive the Eucharist.

Thirdly, the Code states quite plainly that "every baptized person who is not prohibited by law can and ought to be admitted to Holy Communion" (CIC c. 852). Thus the Church guarantees the fundamental right to all its members to full participation in the Eucharistic banquet unless there is some juridical prohibition. The surrounding canons specify in detail those whom the law prohibits from Communion. Included are the excommunicated, those of manifestly infamous repute, those without the use of reason, and so forth. Not included on the list of those barred from Communion are children who have not made a devotional confession. Children have, therefore, the same right as other Catholics to receive the Eucharist and so have no obligation to go to confession if they are not in the state of mortal sin.

In summary, the Church affirms the right of all who have attained the age of discretion to be admitted to the Sacrament of Reconciliation. Since this right can be exercised only if children have some understanding of the Sacrament, recent Roman documents insist that the children be given adequate catechesis on Penance before first Communion. Because children of seven are normally incapable of committing serious sin, they are not bound by canon 856 which obliges those guilty of mortal sin to make a sacramental confession before receiving Holy Communion. It is disputed whether the recent, cited documents from the Holy See oblige children to the Sacrament of Reconciliation before first Communion. In practice, then, parents, pastors and catechists are free to advise children to defer first confession until a later time provided that they respect the children's right to choose to receive sacramental Penance before first Communion.

Bibliography: F. BUCKLEY, *Children and God: Communion, Confession and Confirmation* (Denville, N.J. 1974); "First Confession Before or After First Communion?" HomPastRev 72 (1972) 49–56. J. CUNNINGHAM, "First Sacraments and the Synod on Catechetics," *America* 137 (1977) 211–215. J. HARDON, "First Confession: an Historical and Theological Analysis," *Église et théologie* 1 (1972) 69–110. B. MARTHALER, *Catechetics in Context* (Huntington, Ind. 1974) 260–281. L. ORSY, "The Sins of Those Little Ones," *America* 129 (1973) 438–441. T. SULLIVAN, "The First Confession: Law and Catechesis," *America* 137 (1977) 128–131; "What Age for First Confession?" *America* 129 (1973) 110–113. U.S. Catholic Conference, *A Study Paper for First Confession* (Washington, D.C. 1973). J. J. WRIGHT, "The New Catechetical Directory and Initiation to the Sacraments of Penance and Eucharist," HomPastRev 72 (Dec. 1971) 7–24.

[T. F. SULLIVAN]

FOCOLARE MOVEMENT

The Worldwide Focolare Movement (Work of Mary) embodies a specific form of spirituality best described as the Gospel seen from the perspective of unity; the aim is to strive for that unity for which Jesus prayed on the night before he died. Focolare had its origin in 1943 in Trent, Italy, when a young school teacher, Chiara Lubich, together with a few young women, amid the devastation of World War II, came to see that there is but one reality that can never fail and can, therefore, become the ideal of life. That ideal is

God, who is love. They began together to live each moment as if it were the last moment of their lives. Soon many people, attracted by the mutual love they saw, began to live the same life.

In 1962 Focolare was initially approved by Pope John XXIII, and received the continued blessing of Pope Paul VI, who on Feb. 8, 1978, said to a group of its members: "Be faithful to your inspiration which is so modern and so fruitful." Now the Movement exists in every continent and came into special prominence in 1977 when its foundress, Chiara Lubich, was awarded the Templeton Prize for progress in religion.

The spirituality of the Focolare Movement bears a striking kinship with the spirit of Vatican Council II. The Council frequently recalls the promise of Jesus to be present wherever two or more are united in his name (Mt 18.20). The Council's stress on unity is well known: "For the promotion of unity belongs to the innermost nature of the Church" (*Gaudium et spes* 42). These are only two of the fundamental points of the spirituality of the Movement.

The Focolare Movement has many branches, some of which are movements in their own right, though animated by an identical spirituality and represented in the General Coordinating Council of Focolare in Rome and locally. At the heart are the Focolarini, single men and women living in separate communities called Focolare Centers. Following the evangelical counsels of poverty, chastity, and obedience, the Focolarini work as other lay persons in regular jobs and professions. Their goal is to achieve unity among themselves through a mutual, daily practice of charity. Some married persons, while continuing to live in their families, participate fully in the life of the Focolare Centers. The married Focolarini are the backbone of the New Family Movement, which aims at bringing the Focolare spirit of unity into family life. Also part of the Focolare Movement are the Volunteers, who are totally committed to the Focolare spirit and aim at transforming all human realities according to the spirit of the Gospel. The Volunteers are the backbone of the New Humanity Movement, which aims at renewing all fields of human activity.

The young generations make up three Movements known as the Gen (New Generation). They are divided according to their age into the Gen II for teenagers and young adults; Gen III for children; and the Gen IV for the little ones. The Gen are the backbone of the Youth Movement and they have committed themselves to living the Gospel message of love and use all possible means, such as music, sports, art, and so on to share their ideal with others.

The priests' Movement is made up of diocesan priests committed to living the Focolare spirituality. Often the life of unity of these priests brings about a transformation of parish life. These parishes form the New Parish Movement. Seminarians living this spirit make up the GenS (Gen Seminarians).

Men and women religious can also be associated with Focolare, while continuing to live in their own communities. Focolare spirituality helps them to see how the specific charism of their founders can be lived in the present time. They also cultivate a rapport of unity with other religious orders and congregations. Young religious living this spirit form the GenR (Gen Religious).

Wherever the Focolare Movement exists various ecumenical activities take place. Of particular interest is the Ecumenical Center of Ottmaring, Germany, where Lutherans and Catholics work together, though they live in separate communities. The Movement is present throughout the Christian world and has also spread among non-Christian religions.

Every year summer meetings, called Mariapolis (City of Mary), are held for those who wish to come into contact with Focolare. The goal of the Mariapolis is to generate the presence of Christ in the community through the practice of mutual and constant charity. Permanent Mariapolises exist in Italy, Africa, Argentina, and Brazil.

The Movement operates New City Press, and also publishes *Living City*, a monthly magazine devoted to the spirituality of the Movement. In North America there are Focolare Centers in New York, Chicago, Boston, San Antonio, and Toronto.

Bibliography: S. C. LORIT et al., *Focolare after 30 Years* (New York 1976). C. LUBICH, *That All Men Be One* (London and New York 1973).

[R. D. TETREAU]

FORTY HOURS DEVOTION

By decree of June 21, 1973 the Congregation for Divine Worship issued a revised ritual, "Holy Communion and Worship of the Eucharist Outside Mass." It does not specifically mention the Forty Hours Devotion (5:1036). Instead, the document simply recommends with the local Ordinary's consent and when suitable numbers of people will be present, in churches where the Eucharist is regularly reserved, solemn exposition of the Blessed Sacrament once a year for an extended, even if not strictly continuous period of time. Thus, the local worship community may reflect more profoundly upon the Eucharistic mystery and adore Christ in the Sacrament (HolyCommIntrod 86). When uninterrupted exposition is not possible because of too few worshipers, the Blessed Sacrament may be replaced in the tabernacle during the scheduled periods of adoration, but no more often than twice each day (ibid. 88).

The host should be consecrated in the Mass which immediately precedes the exposition and after Communion placed in the monstrance upon the altar. Mass ends with the prayer after Communion and the concluding rites are omitted. The priest then may locate the Blessed Sacrament on an elevated, but not too lofty or distant throne, and incense it (ibid 93–94). Prayers, scriptural readings, religious silence, homilies or exhortations, congregational singing, and part of the Liturgy of the Hours should be employed during the exposition to direct the faithful's attention to the worship of Christ the Lord (ibid. 95–96). This extended exposition is interrupted for Masses celebrated through that period (ibid. 83).

[J. M. CHAMPLIN]

FOUNDATIONAL THEOLOGY

Recent decades have seen a shift in Europe from apologetics to fundamental theology, from defense of one's position to more ecumenical study of common ground, from stress on objective proofs to focus on existential decision, from an argument prior to faith to an appropriation within faith of its conditions and basis.

Diverse Approaches. But within this general agreement there is much diversity. Rahner conceives a part of systematic theology which is formal in its study of permanent basic structures of saving history, and fundamental in relating these structures to those of the human mind. Geffré sees fundamental theology as the critical and hermeneutical function of all theology. Bouillard would still try to assemble general principles to keep fundamental theology from becoming an omnium-gatherum. As to material content, Geffré, after Rahner, would stress anthropology, while Bouillard would make the doctrine of God focal. Many speak in this context of dialogue with the world, and Fries lists a dozen partners in such dialogue, from world religions and Marxism to literature and natural science. The topic now, however, is foundational theology, which would not differ etymologically from fundamental theology but in now-developing usage refers to a quite distinct approach for which it will be useful to reserve a distinct term. This article will adopt that convention and will study the foundational theology of B. Lonergan, with whose work the term has become especially associated.

Lonergan: Foundations, A Task of Theology. Lonergan sees eight tasks for theology, four of them a study of and encounter with the past (research, interpretation, history, dialectic), and four in which the theologian takes a personal stand. "Foundations" as a *specific task* is fifth in the list, the first in the second set of four, followed by doctrines, systematics, and communications (*Method* 127–133). But this specific task provides foundations only in a limited measure, "not of the whole of theology, but of the three last specialties" and "not the whole foundation of these ... but just the added foundation needed to move from ... indirect discourse ... to ... direct" (ibid. 267). In the *broader* sense of foundations there is a twofold base, "the normative pattern of our conscious and intentional operations" (ibid. 19), and religious conversion conceived as "God's gift of his love and man's consent" (ibid. 289). The two are related as "basic anthropological" and "specifically religious component" (ibid. 25), and together form "a rock on which one can build" (ibid. 19, text and note). Each is existentially operative but can be objectified, the pattern of operations in "transcendental method" (ibid. 13–20), and religious conversion (which "grounds both moral and intellectual conversion," ibid. 283) in the functional specialty called foundations (ibid. 130).

Foundational Reality. Within this speciality there is a distinction between foundational reality and foundational theology. The reality is the threefold conversion, but this "is not foundational in the sense that it offers the premises from which all desirable conclusions are to be drawn. [It] is, not a set of propositions that a theologian utters, but a fundamental and momentous change in the human reality that a theologian is" (ibid. 270). And so "foundations present, not doctrines [on the true religion, on Christ the divine legate], but the horizon within which the meaning of doctrines can be apprehended. Just as in religious living 'a man who is unspiritual refuses what belongs to the Spirit of God; it is folly to him; he cannot grasp it' (1 Cor 2.14), so in theological reflection on religious living there have to be distinguished the horizons within which religious doctrines can or cannot be apprehended" (ibid. 131).

In its application to the new context of theology (empirical, dynamic, concrete, historical, adaptable—as opposed to deductive, static, abstract, universal, invariable), this seems quite new, in line with the present stress on orthopraxis as source for orthodoxy. But as psychological wisdom it is comparatively old: not only is there the Pauline doctrine Lonergan quotes, but Aristotle had said that "the end appears to each man in a form answering to his character" (*Nic. Eth.* 1114a), and Aquinas repeated this: *Qualis unusquisque est, talis finis videtur ei* (ST 1a2ae, 58.5; a point basic in St. Thomas's idea of knowledge by connaturality). Both Aristotle and Aquinas (ibid. 1a, 83.1, obj. 5) made this an objection against liberty, but neither denied its positive truth. Lonergan has turned the objection into a positive principle and extended its application to all that lies within the human horizon. When horizons are dialectically opposed, "What in one is found intelligible, in another is unintelligible. What for one is true, for another is false. What for one is good, for another is evil" (*Method* 236). Hence, "Genuine objectivity is the fruit of authentic subjectivity" (ibid. 292), and method uses "foundations as a criterion for deciding between the alternatives offered by dialectic" (ibid. 349).

Expression of Foundational Reality. When we move from the foundational reality to its expression (ibid. 267), we come finally to language, "the vehicle in which meaning becomes most fully articulated" (ibid. 112), and so to categories.

Categories. Categories derive from foundations in two ways corresponding to the twofold base: there is a "base for general theological categories in transcendental method" (ibid. 283), and a base for special ones in God's gift of his love effecting religious conversion (ibid. 283–284). General categories refer to: patterns of experience; conscious operations within the patterns; levels and manners of operating; realms of meaning and worlds meant; heuristic structures for accumulating operations; differentiations of consciousness; states of conversion and non-conversion; dialectically opposed positions and counter-positions, etc. (ibid. 286–287). Special theological categories will be a vast manifold radiating out "from the initial theological category of conversion to the community of the converted, to its traditions, to its origins, to its destiny, to its God" ("Bernard Lonergan Responds" 232; see also *Method* 290–291). But within this framework, which provides "a transcultural base" open to "universal communication" (*Method* 282), one must expect great diversity; while Catholic theology, with its tradition on God's universal salvific will, will tend to regard the foundational reality as common to mankind, differences in consciousness and conversion will give "a pluralism in the expression of the same fundamental stance and, once theology develops, a multiplicity of the theologies that express the same faith" (*Method* 271).

Doctrines and Truth. From categories we turn to doctrines and the question of truth and need still another distinction. For there is a doctrine that may be "just the objectification of the gift of God's love" (ibid. 119). Here, our "actuated orientation towards the mystery of love and awe . . . may be objectified as a clouded revelation of absolute intelligence and intelligibility, absolute truth and reality, absolute goodness and holiness" (ibid. 115–116). Since religious experience is not solitary, religious community will form, communities will endure, their expressions become traditional, and the religion have a history (ibid. 118). Though Lonergan does not spell this out, one can conceive the formation in this way of a set of religious doctrines which would have their basic criterion of truth in the authenticity of the

believing subjects and would not have to relate this truth to that given in the very Word of God himself. But there may also be, as in Israel and Christianity, "a personal entrance of God himself into history, a communication of God to his people . . . . Then not only the inner word that is God's gift of his love but also the outer word of the religious tradition comes from God" (ibid. 119). Here is a new sense of "doctrines" and new questions arise, crucial for Lonergan's approach: What relation has our twofold foundation to these doctrines already on the scene? What relation do doctrines divinely given have to those we might creatively formulate? What are the roles, respectively, of loyalty and criticism in regard to doctrines from the past?

A first step is to give up our claim to possess eternal truths: "They exist, but only in the eternal and unchanging mind of God" (*A Second Collection* 193). The dogmas that formulate for us the truth in Revelation are subject to the historicity that characterizes all human thought and action (*Method* 324–326). What is permanent in dogma attaches to the meaning and not to the formula, even though the meaning is not apart from a verbal formulation (ibid. 323). Another step (not explicit in Lonergan) might be to realize that in each originating case of divinely given truth there was something like an objectification of an inner word and so some community between ourselves and a Moses or a Paul.

First Phase Theology. This is liberating in a general way, but for positions on particular elements of our tradition we must turn to the first phase of theology: research, interpretation, history, dialectic (ibid. 325–326). For the positive side of this phase is to receive from the past, "to harken to the word . . . ." And so "one engages in *lectio divina* . . . assimilates tradition . . . encounters the past," and the result is "a theology *in oratione obliqua* that tells what Paul and John, Augustine and Aquinas, and anyone else had to say about God and the economy of salvation" (ibid. 133). But there is a critical aspect too. Believers can become inauthentic, and "the unauthenticity of individuals becomes the unauthenticity of a tradition" (ibid. 80); the interpreter "has to be critical not merely of his author but also of the tradition that has formed his own mind" (ibid. 162); and, those "brought up in an unauthentic tradition, can become authentic human beings and authentic Christians only by purifying their tradition" (ibid. 299). Thus, there is "evaluational history that decides on the legitimacy of developments" (ibid. 320; see 302, 312), and dialectic which "deploys both the truth reached and the errors disseminated in the past" (ibid. 299).

Both parts of the foundation, transcendental method and objectified conversion, are relevant here, though in different ways. For first-phase theology is directly based on transcendental method, the four precepts of which now become: assemble the data; interpret its meaning; judge what was going forward; and evaluate options (ibid. 133–135). Conversion is not a requisite or explicitly involved in the *procedures* of this phase, for "anyone can do research, interpret, write history, line up opposed positions" (ibid. 268); but, "though believers and agnostics follow the same methods, they will not attain the same results. For in interpreting texts and in resolving historical problems, one's results are a function, not only of the data and the procedures, but also of the whole previous development of one's understanding" ("Bernard Lonergan Responds" 227–228). So converted and unconverted will arrive at different histories, different interpretations, and follow different styles in research; these differences "become the center of attention in dialectic. There they will be reduced to their roots. But the reduction itself will only reveal the converted with one set of roots and the unconverted with a number of different sets" (*Method* 271).

The danger of second-phase positions unduly influencing first-phase investigations is recognized (ibid. 143), but it is vital that conversion does not destroy the objective character of truth. The converted subject "still needs truth.... The truth he needs is still the truth attained in accord with the exigencies of rational consciousness. But now his pursuit of it is all the more secure because he has been armed against bias" (ibid. 242). Thus, apologists retain their role; they cannot be efficacious, for they do not bestow God's gift; still, "They must be accurate, illuminating, cogent. Otherwise they offer a stone to one asking for bread" (ibid. 123).

Commitment to God's Word. The critical approach of first-phase theology is, however, to be combined with an attitude of loyal commitment to the Word that comes to us from God (ibid. 298, 323–324, 331, 332). The economy of this give and take (not elaborated in *Method*) is perhaps not subject to rigid control, but should be likened to the twin forces of initial propulsion and gravitation that hold an object in orbit round the earth, though that orbit constantly changes with the changing relation of the forces. Two points may offer some reassurance here. One is Newman's advice on "the true way of learning," to begin with global acceptance and reject error as you discover it, rather than to begin with a universal doubt and then hope to achieve truth (*Grammar* 377). Another is the proposal to transpose rather than to discard formulas from the past: "There are the transpositions that theological thought has to develop if religion is to retain its identity and yet at the same time find access into the minds and hearts of men of all cultures and classes" (Lonergan, *Method* 132–133). It is just such transposition that the second phase of theology can accomplish on the basis of the specialty, foundations; as Nicea transposed into the conciliar consubstantiality the Pauline attribution of Yahweh's glory to the Son, so we must transpose Nicea into what is appropriate in our time.

The Ultimacy of the Foundations. Our last question asks in what sense these foundations provide a first in principles, an ultimate in regress. For Lonergan, then, both of the foundational realities are self-justifying and unassailable. The dynamism of incarnate spirit which, objectified, becomes transcendental method provides "natural inevitabilities and spontaneities that constitute the possibility of knowing, not by demonstrating that one can know, but pragmatically by engaging one in the process. Nor in the last resort can one reach a deeper foundation than that pragmatic engagement. Even to seek it involves a vicious circle...." Again, "The critical spirit ... is a self-assertive spontaneity that demands sufficient reason for all else but offers no justification for its demanding" (Insight 332). To put it comprehensively, we are dealing with "the demands of the human spirit: be attentive, be intelligent, be reasonable, be responsible, be in love" (Method 268).

Similarly, the religious foundation, as reality, is unassailable. Being in love with God, and so loving in an unrestricted manner, "provides the real criterion by which all else is to be judged; and consequently one has only to experience it in oneself or witness it in others, to find in it its own justification" (ibid. 283–284). It is gift. "Only God can give that gift, and the gift itself is self-justifying" (ibid. 123). In what sense it is ours to accept or reject the gift, how the Donor might enlist our cooperation in the one case, whether he might withdraw the gift in the other—all these are real questions for the theologian, but their solution will not affect the foundational reality. If the gift is present and operative, one objectifies it for foundations; if it is not present, one will operate on the basis of the native dynamism of spirit; if that is not present, one will not be reading this article.

Other questions multiply. There is the question whether Christianity involves a new religious conversion—this will depend on how radically one understands religious conversion. There is the question of how one deals with "unbelievers"—this in turn will depend on one's nature/grace doctrine, whether the initial salutary orientation is given with creation or occurs as an unpredictable event. There is no space for these questions here, no space either to relate this article to the foundational theology being developed by Protestant theologians, or to discuss the positions taken vis-à-vis Lonergan's foundations by those who have been influenced by his thought. (For example, R. Doran would accept foundations in the subjectivity of the believer, but would enlarge the field of subjectivity to include a psychic conversion; D. Tracy, on the other hand, would not make the believer's faith an intrinsic factor in foundations and, perhaps in sign of this difference, retains the more familiar nomenclature, "fundamental theology.")

Bibliography: H. BOUILLARD, "La tâche actuelle de la théologie fondamentale," *Le Point Théologique* 2 (Paris 1972) 7–49. R. DORAN, *Subject and Psyche: Ricoeur, Jung, and the Search for Foundations* (Washington 1977). H. FRIES, "Fundamental Theology Today," TheolDig 24 (1976) 275–279. C. GEFFRÉ, *A New Age in Theology* (New York 1975) ch. 1. B. LONERGAN, *Insight: A Study of Human Understanding* (London 1957); *Method in Theology* (London 1972); "Bernard Lonergan Responds," in P. MCSHANE, ed., *Foundations of Theology* (Dublin, London 1971) 223–234; *A Second Collection* (London 1974). J. B. METZ, ed., *The Development of Fundamental Theology. Concilium* 46 (New York 1969). J. H. NEWMAN, *An Essay in Aid of a Grammar of Assent* (London 1930). K. RAHNER, "Formale und fundamentale Theologie," LexThK[2] 4:205–206; *Theological Investigations* 1, tr. C. ERNST (Baltimore 1961) 1–18; 19–37. D. TRACY, *Blessed Rage for Order: The New Pluralism in Theology* (New York 1975).

[F. E. CROWE]

FRANKFURT SCHOOL

The Frankfurt School, most famous for its Critical Theory, was conceived in 1922 by Felix Weil. His family fortune provided for both the inauguration of the Frankfurt Institute of Social Research in Frankfurt, Germany and the financial independence necessary for its members to perform the envisaged social research and theoretical speculation both there and elsewhere, especially in the United States, during the period of exile caused by Nazism. Officially erected in 1923, the Institute only began to develop the approach which later characterized it in 1930 under the leadership of Max Horkheimer (1895–1973). He remained director of the Institute until his retirement. He and Theodor Adorno (1903–1969) are most closely identified with both the Institute and the development of its Critical Theory. Among others associated with the institute, although all have gone their separate ways, the more well known are W. Benjamin, F. Pollock, and especially in the United States, P. Tillich, E. Fromm, H. Marcuse, and J. Habermas.

General Theory. In order to produce a new critical theory, the Frankfurt School attempted a fusion of Marx's socio-economic with Freud's psychoanalytic critique. Originally directed precisely against the capitalist economic system and its concomitant implicit ontology, the new Critical Theory soon widened its scope to include the "whole (of reality)," which it deemed to be a "totally administered world," and, hence, destructive of individual human persons, their freedom, their pleasure, their being. Thus, "the (empirical) whole is the untrue." Consequently, Critical Theory rejected both the more recent positivism, empiricism, and scientism as well as the older classical metaphysical systems, because both inherently tend to accept and equate any given particular state of reality with reality pure and simple. According to Critical Theory, the malaise of modern man is rooted specifically in the Enlightenment, but can be traced all the way back to the dawn of human consciousness and reflective thinking. The exploitation of nature and the alienation of humanity involved in this beginning have intensified steadfastly and culminated in the capitalist economic system, whose own proper fruit has been the mass culture and consumer civilization, so typical of the West, but inexorably infecting all mankind. The result is the total and seemingly incurable alienation of man—not only economic, social, cultural, but also ontological.

A Theological Dimension. Although some thinkers associated with the Frankfurt School have remained steadfastly atheistic, there is discernible in the writings of especially Benjamin and the later Horkheimer and Adorno what has been termed a theological dimension. Thus Adorno and Horkheimer have been led to the conclusion that, since "the whole is the untrue," the appeal to or "longing for the entirely other" is not absolutely reprobate, although it "is, to be sure, a nonscientific wish." However, on the basis of their fear of and opposition to the cheap reconciliation advocated in customary metaphysical systems (German Idealism) and the reduction of everything to the status of means in contemporary empiricist scientism, they remain decidedly dedicated to their Negative Dialectic. By it alone can the temptation to absolutize the present moment be overcome. Thus their admittedly impressive achievement remains but a negative critique. Hence their noble aim of overcoming the split in human consciousness, of reconciling subject and object, person and nature, of restoring paradise (the influence, however implicit and unreflective, of the Jewish background of many members of the Frankfurt School ought never be overlooked) was essentially beyond attainment. The thin line between Judeo-Christian negative theology and rationalist agnosticism is strikingly manifest in their thought.

Writings. Horkheimer and Adorno not only thought together, they also wrote together *Dialectic of Enlightenment* (New York 1944, 1972). The foundation of Critical Theory, as well as of all their later writings, was provided by that book along with Horkheimer's *Eclipse of Reason* (New York 1947, 1974) and Adorno's *Minima Moralia* (Frankfurt, 1951, 1976). Their entire work can be viewed, as they themselves viewed it, as

"a critique of philosophy, and therefore (it) refuses to abandon philosophy." Their journey, starting in the culture of assimilated German Jewry, took them through classical Greek and modern European philosophy as well as the Marxist and Freudian critiques to a head-on confrontation with contemporary mass-consumer culture, created by technological rationalism. They were philosophers characterized by a refusal to accept human suffering, by a demand for justice in a world where injustice at least seems to triumph. Hence they were led to define the human being as the "Longing for the Entirely Other," the title of what may be termed Horkheimer's last will and testament (*Die Sehnsucht nach dem ganz Anderen*, Hamburg 1970). For theistic thinkers their writings are clearly an inspiration and a challenge, for the philosophy of religion an especially fertile source of new insights about the transcendent, both human and divine.

Bibliography: Suhrkamp Verlag of Frankfurt, Germany, has published the collected works of T. Adorno and is publishing those of M. Horkheimer. T. ADORNO, *Negative Dialectics* (New York 1972); *Jargon of Authenticity* (Evanston 1973). T. ADORNO et al., *The Positivist Dispute in German Sociology* (New York 1976). M. HORKHEIMER, *Die Sehnsucht nach dem ganz Anderen* (Hamburg, 1979); *Critical Theory* (New York 1972); *Critique of Instrumental Reason* (New York 1974). M. JAY, *The Dialectical Imagination* (Boston 1973). K. OPPENS et al., *Über Theodor W. Adorno* (Frankfurt 1970). H. SCHWEPPENHÄUSER, ed., *Theodor W. Adorno zum Gedachtnis* (Frankfurt 1971).

[R. KRESS]

FUND RAISING AND ACCOUNTABILITY

Since Vatican Council II, several internal and external forces—in many respects unrelated—have converged to create in the Church in the U.S. a situation in which a document dealing with accountability in fund raising, with far-reaching ramifications for the Church, was formulated. The NCCB at its general meeting in Washington, D.C. in November 1977 approved and promulgated *Principles and Guidelines for Fund Raising in the United States by Arch/Dioceses, Arch/Diocesan Agencies and Religious Institutes*. It sets down norms for the right exercise of accountability in the entire field of fund raising in the Church.

Background. Within the Church there had been for a long time concern for procedures whereby dioceses and religious institutes would disclose to their donors and to the public the amounts of funds received and how they were disbursed. Moreover, efforts were underway to make all appeals ethical beyond reproach, using methods in good taste, and having a theologically sound motivation. These concerns proved to be well-founded. Isolated incidents of mismanagement of funds came to light in different parts of the country in both dioceses and religious institutes.

A second force was the consultation involving the NCCB, the Conference of Major Superiors of Men (CMSM), and the Leadership Conference of Women Religious (LCWR) together with other Catholic organizations with expertise in this field, for the purpose of developing a body of principles and guidelines. This process was in line with the declaration of the apostolic letter of Pope Paul VI on implementation of Vatican II. The Pope states: "The episcopal conference of any country can, after consultation with the interested religious superiors, establish norms for seeking alms which must be observed by all religious" (Paul VI EcclSanct I, 27).

A third force was the Federal Government. Bills were introduced in Congress which would require nonprofit, tax-exempt institutions and private, charitable organizations to make public disclosure of their fund-raising activities. Perhaps the most publicized was the Wilson Bill (H.R.41). Its special focus was on charitable organizations which "solicit in any manner or through any means a remittance of a contribution by mail." This bill is being strongly opposed. Opponents see such legislation as unwarranted intervention on the part of government in a nongovernment matter and a violation of the traditional doctrine of separation of Church and State. The newly self-developed and self-imposed body of regulatory norms for accountability in the Church is a clear expression of the means whereby the Church will conduct its own self-surveillance without government interference.

The document consists of four parts; each begins with a principle which is first explained theologically and pastorally, then concretized into specific guidelines. The four parts are on: Stewardship; Religious Authority; Accountability; and Techniques. The guidelines follow.

Stewardship Guidelines:

1. The fund-raising appeal should be directed toward motivating the faithful to participate in apostolic works in fulfillment of their responsibility to share with others.
2. No organization should ask the faithful to fund its total and absolute security. Nor should an organization engage in fund-raising efforts for undefined future needs.
3. The trust relationship between donor and fundraiser requires that funds collected be used for the intended purpose and not be absorbed by excessive fund-raising costs.
4. Appeals for funds must be straightforward and honest, respectful, and based on sound theological principles. The donor must be informed how the donated funds will be used and assured that the funds given are used for the purpose intended and that restrictions stated by the donor will be observed.

Religious Authority Guidelines:

1. Religious institutes and diocesan agencies should observe those prescriptions of Canon Law and their own regulations which require approval of major superiors and/or the Ordinary of the place to solicit funds.
2. The approval of fund raising by proper authority should express the purpose for which the funds are raised and the methods to be used in raising them. Effective control of fund-raising programs should be maintained through periodic review and, where necessary, appropriate sanction.
3. Religious or diocesan agencies may not proceed in the collection of funds by public subscription without the consent of the Ordinaries of those places where the funds are collected...
4. Major superiors of religious institutes should, as a moral duty, provide the Ordinary of the place where the fund raising originates with significant information about the fund-raising programs and the apostolates they support.

Accountability Guidelines:

1. Accountability requires the fundraiser to provide timely reports on the extent to which promises expressed or implied in the solicitation of funds have been fulfilled.
2. Fund-raising reports should be prepared in scope and design to meet the particular concerns of those to whom reports are due: namely, the governing body and membership of the fund-raising organization itself, religious authorities who approved and must monitor the fund-raising effort, donors to the particular organization and the giving public at large, and those who are beneficiaries of the funds given.
3. Fund-raising reports should provide both financial information and a review of the apostolic work for which the funds were raised. The availability of these reports to benefactors on a regular basis or on reasonable request should be publicized.
4. Fund-raising organizations should provide their governing bodies with an annual audit prepared in accordance with generally accepted accounting principles, and, where size warrants, by a certified public accountant.
5. All financial reports of a fundraiser should be consistent with the annual audit. At minimum, a fundraiser's report, regardless of scope, should set forth the amount of money collected, the cost of conducting the fund-raising effort, and the amount and use of the funds disbursed.
6. Donations should be acknowledged with promptness; reasonable requests from donors for information about their particular gift should be met.

Implementation Guidelines:

1. Local Ordinaries and major superiors, within their respective jurisdiction, should exercise control over fund-raising activities to achieve conformity with these guidelines. Particularly in response to formal complaints, legitimate charges and remedy abuses, even to the point, when necessary, of terminating a fund-raising program.
2. In virtue of their endorsement of these guidelines, the National Conference of Catholic Bishops, the Leadership Conference of Women Religious and the Conference of Major Superiors of Men agree to assist their respective constituencies in achieving appropriate control of fund-raising activities and in obtaining effective sanction for abuses. Accordingly, each Conference will, through its President:
   (a) promulgate these guidelines and other suitable norms for responsible fund raising;
   (b) help correct abuses through
      i) cooperative efforts with the responsible authorities
      ii) a meeting of the Presidents of the three Conferences (NCCB, LCWR, CMSM), to collaborate on further action should an abuse on the part of a member of these constituencies not be resolved by the member's responsible authority.

Comment. Fr. Andrew Greeley in his syndicated column summed up the thoughts of many on the Church's accountability in all financial matters in these words: "We need such accountability not because there is great wealth or great abuse but because in the absence of accountability, wealth and abuse will always be suspected." The *Principles and Guidelines* are fundamentally a sound, concise statement, representative of a broad spectrum of concern and positive ideas. However, one major shortcoming is found in the statement on stewardship; it tends to narrow the concept of stewardship and leads the uncritical reader to equate stewardship with fund raising. In reality, stewardship as a wholly biblical concept conveys the dynamic of man's management of all God's material *and spiritual* gifts, and as a pastoral concept encompasses all ministries. It is the opinion of many, including some bishops, that the opening paragraphs on stewardship should have contained a clarification wherein a distinction is made between Stewardship of Treasure, and Stewardship of Time and Talent (*see* NATIONAL CATHOLIC STEWARDSHIP COUNCIL).

[F. A. NOVAK]

FURNISHINGS, SACRED

Vatican Council II's Constitution on the Liturgy devotes most of its Chapter 2 to sacred art and furnishings (*Sacrosanctum Concilium* 122–128). The meaning and use of liturgical furnishings are defined in the new Roman Missal (1971) in relation to the worship of the Christian assembly (GenInstrRomMissal 257). "Noble simplicity . . . should be a major factor in selecting furnishings" (ibid. 287). Because of a relation to the ways in which Christ is present in the liturgy (ibid 7; cf. *Eucharisticum mysterium* 3f; HolyCommIntrod 6) the altar, ambo, and celebrant's chair are special points of focus for the worshiping community. The adaptability of the worship space for the celebration of Sacraments other than the Eucharist and for common prayer is not to be ignored. All furnishings serve the active participation of the faithful, enhancing their faith-expression by artistic quality and liturgical appropriateness (GenInstr-RomMissal 253). They are not restricted by recent church documents to any particular design, style, or material (ibid 287–288), but are to be signs of openness to the world in which we live, fulfilling their purpose according to "the genius and traditions of each people" (ibid 287).

For the Assembly. Furnishings should both manifest the unity of the full assembly and facilitate the exercise of individual roles (ibid 257). The relationship between the seating and the sanctuary should convey a feeling of oneness, facilitating participation in the liturgy both "by seeing and by understanding everything" (ibid 273), without hindering appropriate movement. Provision for kneeling is not required (ibid 21), thus allowing for more flexible seating furnishings.

The celebrant's chair should be designed so that, in appearance and position, it will heighten and focus the presiding role of the celebrant without seeming distant or dominating. Other seating for ministers should be in harmony with the more significant furnishings, permitting the convenient exercise of these ministries in the assembly (ibid. 271). The organ, for example, should be situated where it can best strengthen the community in singing (ibid. 275).

The strength of design and the beauty of the altar should naturally point to its central significance. Its unique role as a special sign of fellowship in Christ should not be diminished by numerous minor altars; it should not be encumbered by decorations or unnecessarily distracting objects (ibid. 276). Flowers, for example, may be placed anywhere in the church to add a sense of joy and festivity; placed only on or near the altar, however, they could obstruct participation or distract. A single altar cloth is to be used on the altar to enhance the impression it makes on the faithful as the Lord's table (ibid. 268). Different materials or colors may be used as long as they do not veil the meaning and function of the Lord's table (ibid 268, 311). Relics may be placed in or under the altar as long as they are of proven authenticity (ibid 266).

The Word of God is to be proclaimed from a single ambo (pulpit) so that "the attention of the person may be easily directed to that place" (ibid. 272). By design and placement it should signify the importance of the Word of God and fittingly relate to the other sanctuary furnishings. It should have a solid appearance and an artistic value that will not normally invite covering by banners. A lectern for the cantor or commentator should not rival the ambo for attention; it is more appropriate that the lectern be movable (ibid. 68, 272).

Other Furnishings. A credence table for setting the sacred vessels and for purifying them after Communion should be conveniently located in or near the sanctuary area (ibid. 80). Often a table for the gifts is also necessary. It is located near the back of the church and, not being merely utilitarian, it should not be left cluttered when not in use.

Candles find their meaning in the living flame that they provide in the celebration. Not merely decorations of the altar, they are signs of reverence and solemnity. Candles and candlesticks should be proportioned to the place and arranged so that they do not "block the view of what is happening at the altar or what is placed on it" (ibid. 269). The number of candles may vary, according to the solemnity of the celebration, from two to seven (ibid. 179; HolyCommIntrod 85). The candles used in processions or at the proclamation of the Gospel may be the same ones used for the Eucharist. No specific material is prescribed as long as they provide a lively flame without being smoky or unpleasant; substitution of electric lights is not permitted (*Notitiae* 10 [1974] 80). The paschal candle is a special sign of Christ, light to all peoples (Lk 2.32). As the flame from which the faithful receive the light of life (Jn 8.12), the same candle should be used in the service of light for the Easter vigil and for baptisms throughout the year. It should be of appropriate size and beauty (*Environment and Art* 90; see bibliog.).

A single cross is required in the area of worship. It may be a permanent cross suspended over the altar or behind it, but it may also be a processional cross capable of being located in different places according to the celebration. If a cross is near the altar it should not diminish visibility of the Eucharistic action, nor should it compete with other significant furnishings for attention.

Images of Christ, Mary, and the saints continue to be a part of the environment of worship. They should be appropriate expressions of the Christian mystery and not distract from the actual celebration (GenInstrRom-Missal 278), but lend meaning to the total surroundings. They may be permanent, such as a statue, or temporary, such as cloth hangings that set a mood for a season or for a celebration. The introduction of temporary images can help children perceive God's deeds more easily and be a support for their prayer (*Directory of Masses with Children* 35).

Stations of the cross foster the devotion of the faithful without having an overly prominent place in the church. They may be placed in a separate part of the church, for example, in the chapel of reservation. Their design should be simple, clearly evoking the mystery they represent.

Other items such as cruets for water and wine, corporal, purificator, chalice veil (which may always be white), and censer all retain their traditional place among liturgical furnishings (GenInstrRomMissal 80, 82). A bell is no longer required, but may be rung shortly before the Consecration and at each elevation (ibid. 109).

Bibliography: Bishops' Committee on the Liturgy, *Environment and Art in Catholic Worship* (USCC Publ. Office, Washington, D.C. 1978). Congregation for Divine Worship, *Eucharisticum mysterium*, Instruction of May 25, 1967 (ActApS 59 [1967] 539–537; Eng. tr. *On Eucharistic Worship*, USCC Publ. Office, Washington, D.C. 1967); *Directorium de Missis cum pueris* Nov. 1, 1973 (ActApS 66 [1974] 30–46; Eng. tr. *Directory for Masses with Children*, USCC Publ. Office, Washington, D.C. 1974). Episcopal Liturgical Commissions of Ireland, *Building and Reorganization of Churches* (Dublin 1972). Liturgical Commission, Diocese of Wilmington, *Guidelines to Design or Renovate a Church* (Wilmington, Del. 1968). J. WHITE, "Liturgy and the Language of Space," *Worship* 52 (1978) 57–66.

[A. D. FITZGERALD]

G

GENERAL INTERCESSIONS

Christian tradition has always given an important place to intercessory prayer. St. Paul exhorts to the offering of "prayers, petitions, intercessions and thanksgiving for all: for kings and all in authority, so that we may be able to live quiet and peaceful lives in the full practice of religion and of morality" (1 Tm 2.1–4). Intercessory prayer is a natural part of the liturgy in which the Church, in the name of Christ, continues to offer the prayer and petition which he poured out in the days of his earthly life. Already by the 2d century the origins of the General Intercessions appear. St. Justin Martyr writes (c. 155) that "on the Lord's day, after the reading of Scripture and the homily, all stand and offer the prayers" (*First Apology* 67). Vatican Council II's Constitution on the Liturgy called for the restoration of these General Intercessions which in the course of time had disappeared from the Roman Mass (*Sacrosanctum Concilium* 53).

At Mass. The structure of the General Intercessions (also called the Prayer of the Faithful, but less appropriately, see De Clerck 310) has three parts. First, after the Homily the one presiding invites the people to pray. Second, the deacon (or another person) announces the intentions to the people and they pray for that intention in silence or by a common response, recited or sung. Third, the one presiding concludes with a prayer (GenInstrRomMissal 47). As a rule the sequence of intentions is: (1) for the needs of the Church; (2) for public authorities and the salvation of the world; (3) for those oppressed by any need; and (4) for the local community (ibid. 46).

Liturgy of the Hours. The Church praises God throughout the course of the day by celebrating the Liturgy of the Hours. The tradition does not separate praise of God from petition and "often enough praise turns somehow to petition" (GenInstrLitHor 179). Consequently, the General Intercessions have been restored to Morning and Evening Prayer, however with some nuance to avoid repetition of the petitions at Mass. The intentions at Morning Prayer are to consecrate the day to God (ibid. 181); those at Evening Prayer stress thanksgiving for graces received during the day. The intentions found in the *Hours Book* are addressed directly to God (rather than to the people, as at Mass) so that the wording is suitable for both common celebration and private recitation (ibid. 190). Although "the Liturgy of the Hours, like other liturgical actions, is not something private but belongs to the whole body of the Church" (ibid. 20), it must be acknowledged that it is still often prayed privately. In every case, however, the petitions should be linked with praise of God and acknowledgement of his glory or with a reference to the history of salvation, as in the Lord's Prayer (ibid. 185).

Bibliography: Consilium, *De Oratione Communi seu Fidelium: Natura, momentum ac structura. Criteria atque specimina coetibus territorialibus episcoporum proposita* (Vatican City 1966). P. DE CLERCK, *La "prière universelle" dans les liturgies latines anciennes: Témoignages patristiques et textes liturgiques*. Liturgiewissenschaftliche Quellen und Forschungen, band 62 (Münster, Westfalen 1977).

[T. RICHSTATTER]

GENOCIDE

Genocide is the crime of destroying the lives, liberty, property, and culture of an entire racial, ethnic, political, or other human group (6:336). The characteristic quality of genocide is the intent on the part of the perpetrator of destroying the target group "as such." The 1948 Genocide Convention leaves enforcement to the individual states parties to the agreement. The United States has still (1978) not ratified the convention but the crime of genocide, first identified as the crux of the count of Crimes Against Humanity at Nuremberg, is firmly established in customary international law (7:576).

The most important instance of an individual being tried for the crime of genocide is the trial of Adolf Eichmann by Israeli courts in 1961–62. The Genocide Convention provides that, "Persons charged with genocide ... shall be tried by a competent tribunal of the state in the territory of which the act was committed, or by such international penal tribunal as may have jurisdiction with respect to the contracting parties . . . ." Israel did not exist as a state when the crimes with which Eichmann was charged occurred, but claimed jurisdiction: (1) on grounds of a universal jurisdiction over such international criminals as war criminals and pirates; (2) under the protective principle whereby a state may claim jurisdiction over acts having an injurious effect on its security and vital interests. The Israeli courts held that the connection between the State of

Israel and the Jewish people was such that genocide committed against Jews prior to Israel's establishment fell under Israeli jurisdiction.

Genocide as a term has been overused and abused. The U.S. was accused of genocide in the Vietnam War because of the great loss of life, social dislocation, and material destruction caused. Nuclear deterrence and war are often condemned as genocidal by nature. Given genocidal intent, a war could constitute genocide; however, the conduct of war is generally judged on the basis of the principles of proportion and discrimination (*see* WAR, MORALITY OF). Genocide is not a concept relevant to war unless a belligerent is attacking a people or group "as such," not for reasons of legitimate military necessity but as a matter of lethal discrimination.

In the absence of an international criminal system, states can do little but protest against the genocidal policies pursued by other states except, as in the Eichmann case, when one of the criminals is brought into their jurisdiction. The more extreme alternative of military or other intervention, as in the case of the Indian invasion of East Pakistan to help the Bengalis evict Pakistan and to form the new state of Bangladesh, is severely limited by international law restrictions on the use of armed coercion even in a just cause. Protests have been made against alleged genocidal policies in a number of countries, e.g., Rwanda (Tutsis, 1962–64); Nigeria (Ibos, 1966–67 and during the unsuccessful secession of Biafra, 1967–70); Uganda (Acholi and Langi, 1971; Baganda and Ankole, 1972; Ugandan Christians increasingly by 1977, all under the repressive Amin regime); Burundi (Hutus, 1972); Paraguay (Aché Indians, 1970–78); and Pakistan (Bengalis in East Pakistan, now Bangladesh, 1971). Characterization of these policies as genocide is complicated by the context of civil and tribal warfare in which most of the atrocities and repression occur. In all of these situations there were clear violations of human rights but whether they constituted genocide as defined by the 1948 Convention is doubtful.

The suppression of a revolt by the Tibetan people against the Chinese Communists in 1959 led to UN inquiries and protests. In this connection, a report of the International Commission of Jurists (a nongovernmental organization having consultative status in the UN) found "a systematic design to eradicate the separate national, cultural and religious life of Tibet . . . at least . . . a prima facie case of genocide against the People's Republic of China."

Bibliography: R. ARENS, ed., *Genocide in Paraguay* (Philadelphia 1976). P. N. DROST, *Genocide*, v. 2 of *The Crime of State* (Leyden 1959). R. HILBERG, *The Destruction of the European Jews* (Chicago 1961; rev. ed. New York 1973). D. HILLS, *The White Pumpkin* (London 1975) [Uganda under Amin]. Israel, District Court of Jerusalem, December 12, 1961; Supreme Court, May 29, 1962, Attorney General of Israel v. Eichmann, in E. Lauterpacht, ed., *International Law Reports* 36 (London 1968) 5–344. Panel, "Biafra, Bengal, and Beyond: International Responsibility and Genocidal Conflict," *Proceedings of the Sixty-Sixth Annual Meeting of the American Society of International Law* in *American Journal of International Law* 66 (1972) 89–108. M. M. WHITEMAN, ed., *Digest of International Law* (15 v., Washington, D.C. 1963–73) 11:848–874.

[W. V. O'BRIEN]

GILBY, THOMAS

English Dominican theologian, author, editor; b. Birmingham, Dec. 18, 1902; d. Cambridge, Nov. 29, 1975. Thomas Gilby was a member of Emmanuel College, Cambridge, when he chose to become a Dominican in 1919. After ordination (1926) he did graduate work at Louvain in philosophy. His career divided into three periods. He was a lector at Hawkesyard Priory (Staffordshire) and Blackfriars, Oxford; until 1935, he was also an editor and frequent contributor for *Blackfriars*. His views on marriage and political issues (e.g. the Spanish Civil War) were not approved by some of his confreres. To this period belong his *Poetic Experience* (1934), *Marriage and Morals* (1936, pseudonym T. G. Wayne; repr. 1952). Next came his service as chaplain in the Royal Navy (1939–48) with a full experience of naval warfare and a period as representative of the British government lecturing in American universities. During the war he wrote, on logic, *Barbara Celarent* (1949) and, on epistemology, *The Phoenix and the Turtle* (1950). From 1948 until his death his home was Blackfriars, Cambridge, as a subject and for several terms as prior. He raised funds for and designed a cloister-hall-library addition. This was also the most productive literary period of his life: *Between Community and Society* (1953); *Principality and Polity* (1958, in the U.S., *Political Thought of St. Thomas Aquinas*); also a novel, *Up the Green River* (1955) and a military history, *Britain at Arms: A Scrapbook from Queen Anne to the Present Day* (1953). His articles on prudence and on charity in the *New Catholic Encyclopedia* are particularly noteworthy.

Above all, he began and completed his most lasting work, as editor, translator, annotator, and commentator for St. Thomas Aquinas's writing. He began modestly with an arrangement, translation, and annotation of *St. Thomas Aquinas, Philosophical Texts* (1955, frequently reprinted) and the less well known, *St. Thomas Aquinas, Theological Texts* (1955). With the encouragement and support of Sir Oliver Crosthwaite-Eyre, chairman of Eyre and Spottiswoode, Publishers, Fr. Thomas undertook the English-Latin edition of the *Summa theologiae* (60 v., 1965–76) which occupied him until the eve of his death. He personally translated, edited, and annotated v. 1, 5, 8, 16, 17, 18, 28, 36, 43, 44, 59. But as General Editor he literally handled every page of copy and proof for each of the 60 volumes. He personally presented the first volume to Pope Paul VI, Dec. 1963, but did not live to see the presentation to Pope Paul of the last volume published (v. 48), in May 1976. The first volume, ST 1a, 1, on the nature of theology (*sacra doctrina*), v. 8 on the metaphysics of creation, and v. 18 on fundamental moral theology are masterpieces and a treasure for all who would seek to recapture some of the riches of Catholic theology. All through his life Thomas Gilby was dedicated to a quiet convert apostolate, to reconciling the strayed, and to counseling the anguished. He was a man of simplicity, of unfailing courtesy, good humor and wit, of immense loyalty to the Church, to his brethren, and to his friends. While Fr. Thomas often wished that he could have directed his energies to the contemporary theological issues, that divine providence in which he trusted absolutely shaped his life so that his great theological wisdom and humane insight, which might otherwise have never been preserved, are there to be shared in the pages of "the Gilby *Summa*." He died suddenly, but not unexpectedly, among his own in the Blackfriars refectory.

[T. C. O'BRIEN]

GOOD CONSCIENCE PROCEDURES

The reconciliation of individual conscience and religious authority has occasioned considerable discussion concerning divorced and remarried Catholics who seek recognition in the internal forum of their marital status in order to permit the reception of Penance and the Eucharist. Although modernized canonical procedures and updated jurisprudence have made it possible for many petitions of nullity to be handled by regional tribunals, cases still remain unresolved because of lack of sufficient grounds or unverifiable evidence. There is no ready solution or canonical procedure for the handling of this complex problem. Cases may be referred to the Sacred Penitentiary in Rome, which has jurisdiction in matters pertaining to the private arena of conscience and the confessional. "Good conscience procedures" refers to the personal decision of those in a canonically unresolved marital irregularity to receive the Sacraments.

Changes both in society and the Church have engendered a tendency to emancipate conscience more and more from the formative influence of anything but personal insights, separate graces, and private judgments. Individuals need better guidance than the laissez-faire "act according to conscience." Conscience and authority not merely admit of reconciliation; they demand one another. When both are functioning rightly there can be no conflict between them since both have their origin in God.

In the formation of conscience the Christian faithful must carefully attend to the certain doctrine of the Church and not simply act as unguided reason dictates. If conflict arises between a person's sincere judgment and the magisterium, the presumption of truth favors the latter. "In matters of faith and morals, the bishops speak in the name of Christ and the faithful are to accept their teaching and adhere to it with a religious assent of soul" (*Lumen gentium* 25).

Bibliography: N. CROTTY, "Conscience and Superego: A Key Distinction," ThSt 32 (1971) 30–47. B. HÄRING, *The Law of Christ*, v. 1, tr. E. G. KAISER (Westminister, Md. 1961). J. MCGRATH et al., "Good Conscience Procedures," Origins 2 (1972) 254–256. L. ORSY et al., *Jurist* 30 (1970) 1–74. ProcCLSA 35 (1973).

[J. MCGRATH]

GREGORIAN CHANT

This article will consider recent official statements on Gregorian chant (6:756) as well as its use in the American Church. Pope Paul VI's "Letter to Bishops on the Minimum Repertoire of Plain Chant" was promulgated in 1974, along with a small booklet of chants entitled *Jubilate Deo*. Both letter and booklet ostensibly fulfilled a directive of Vatican Council II's Constitution on the Sacred Liturgy (*Sacrosanctum Concilium* 54; cf. MusicamSacram 47), which insisted on the vocal participation of the laity in parts of the Latin Ordinary of the mass. F. McManus wrote that the reason for the insertion of this statement into the paragraph was so that Christians ". . . should be able to employ it [Latin] on the occasions when they come together from different countries in places of pilgrimage or during international congresses." Although the "Letter" gave other reasons for learning chant, e.g., its cultural and pedagogical value for monks, religious and seminarians and its fundamental role in understanding all sacred music, the primary purpose for printing the booklet of chants was the 1975 Holy Year, at which a large, international gathering of pilgrims was expected in Rome.

In *Jubilate Deo* there are three kinds of music: chants for the Ordinary of the Mass, chants for exposition and benediction of the Blessed Sacrament, and chants for Marian devotions. Several miscellaneous pieces are also included, e.g., the *Te Deum* and the antiphon *Tu es Petrus*. This brief repertoire, though relatively familiar, does not represent the classic body of Gregorian chant—the Propers—nor does it implement other Vatican II demands, such as the preservation and cultivation of the treasury of sacred music (*Sacrosanctum Concilium* 114).

Some authors claim that chant holds "pride of place" with relationship to all other music used in the liturgy. Several official documents, however, present a more realistic view. The General Instruction on the Liturgy of the Hours (1971) states: "In liturgical celebrations sung in Latin Gregorian chant, as proper to the Roman liturgy, should be given pride of place, other things being equal" (GenInstrLitHor 274, a direct quotation from MusicamSacram 50). Neither Gregorian chant nor the immense repertoire of sacred music that came after it was intended for popular vocal participation. Execution was left to skilled performers. Today, consequently, a full use of chant or Renaissance polyphony in liturgy reduces the congregation to almost total silence. Except for a few churches where "concert" Masses of chant and polyphony are celebrated, there is no place where the vast majority of American Catholics have any contact with liturgical music from the past.

At the same time interest in medieval music is at an all-time high, as evidenced in scholarly research, by performances of this kind of music on recordings and in the concert hall, and in the influence of the past upon contemporary musical composition. Relative to music for liturgy there are, besides the already well-known Gelineau psalm-tones and other psalm-tone formulas dependent upon modal theory, a number of new compositions that utilize Latin chant and/or chant techniques, e.g., several of the works of the Roman Catholic C.A. Peloquin or of the Episcopalian Richard Proulx (both published by G.I.A. Publications, Inc., Chicago). With these composers the goal is to create a music that is both ancient and at the same time modern, a music that catches the ear of the Christian worshiper today. The journal *Sacred Music* publishes reports on use of Gregorian chant in American churches as well as articles on its use even for vernacular liturgy.

See also MUSIC, SACRED (LEGISLATION); MASS, LATIN CHANTS FOR.

Bibliography: *Jubilate Deo: Cantus gregoriani faciliores quos fideles discant oportet ad mentem constitutionis concilii Vaticani II de sacra liturgia* (Washington, D.C. 1974). Both a pew edition and an accompaniment edition were published by G.I.A. Publications, Inc. (Chicago 1974). F. R. MCMANUS, *Sacramental Liturgy* (New York 1967) 81–91.

[F. C. QUINN]

H

HAYDEN, JEROME

Benedictine monk, priest, psychiatrist, b. Dec. 2, 1902, Pittsburgh, Pa., d. July 18, 1977, Brighton, Massachusetts. James Edward Hayden completed his undergraduate and graduate studies at the Univ. of Pittsburgh, where he gained the doctorate in medicine in 1927. After some years on the medical school faculty he next went to the Univ. of Louvain where he was awarded the doctorate in philosophy in 1939. After briefly resuming his medical practice and teaching in Pittsburgh, Dr. Hayden became a monk at St. Anselm's Benedictine monastery in Washington D.C. in 1943, taking the name Jerome. After monastic and theological studies he was ordained, Feb. 11, 1947. To specialize in psychiatry and its harmonization with theology he studied at The Catholic Univ. of America, the Univ. of Montreal, and McGill University. He joined the faculty of the Department of Psychiatry and Psychology at Catholic Univ. in 1949, and at this time became president and director of St. Gertrude's School for retarded girls in Washington.

In 1957 Cardinal Richard J. Cushing asked Fr. Jerome's monastic superiors to allow him to come to Boston to found a Catholic institute for psychiatry. This project responded to Fr. Jerome's deepest aspirations and was to become his life's work. The institute was legally incorporated in July 1957 and its twofold purpose was, in Fr. Jerome's words: "to marshall the forces of religion and the psychological sciences in the promotion of mental health through the prevention, early detection and treatment of illnesses of the emotionally maladjusted; and the harmonization of the valid findings of the broad field of psychiatry and the philosophical and theological approaches, for the better understanding of man's nature and of his temporal needs and achieving his eternal destiny." To this he devoted all the energy and talents of the remaining years of his life. The financial support of the Cardinal never came and Fr. Jerome bore the economic burden of the institute as well as the direction of its professional and clinical work. These heavy responsibilities prevented much of the scholarly research and publication for which he was qualified, but he did contribute important articles to such periodicals as the *Bulletin of the Guild of Catholic Psychiatrists*, and the *Proceedings of the Catholic Theological Society of America*. He lectured to large audiences in the Eastern U.S., and in Rome during Vatican Council II addressed groups of bishops on the subject of mental health and the priesthood. With all this, Fr. Jerome kept up the demanding practice of individual therapy, and helped a great number of souls. While intensely concerned with intellectual and professional goals, he remained a man of deep, simple piety, with a lifelong devotion to the Blessed Mother. It was characteristic that he named the institute which was his life's work Marsalin, a title he composed from the words *Maria Salus Infirmorum*.

[A. BOULTWOOD]

HEALING, CHRISTIAN

The wave of renewal in the Church in response to Vatican Council II has reawakened, along with other charismatic manifestations, an emphasis on the healing presence of the risen Christ. Simultaneously throughout the world, the past decade has seen a growing interest in spiritual healing, some of it under religious auspices, some frankly atheistic and naturalistic. Essentially two things continue to distinguish Christian healing from that of other religions and disciplines: first, it is centered in an awareness of a personal presence as its source, the person of the risen Jesus Christ; second, it flows directly out of a community of prayer and the sacramental system.

Theology and Practice. Renewal of interest in prayer for healing, especially among ecumenical prayer groups, has stimulated a reformulation of the theology of healing, both theoretical and practical. Increasing development and refinement can be expected as the interaction between new experiences and speculation on these experiences continues to bring theology abreast of the intense movement of the Spirit throughout the Church. Most notable among changes in the practical order is that healing prayer is no longer the almost exclusive domain of saints and special shrines. Christians throughout the world are praying with renewed faith in the healing presence of Jesus Christ and expecting his direct response to their prayer. Ecumenical sharing among Christians has tempered extremes in denominational attitudes toward healing prayer. Protestants, strong in their fundamental faith in words of the Gospel, especially Mk 11.24, that whatever is asked for in prayer will be done, are challenging and stimulating Catholics to new dimensions of faith. Catholics, on their part, in demonstrating the power for healing present in the Sacraments and in the gift of love connected with Eucharistic prayer, are drawing increasing numbers of Protestants toward sacramental and communal forms of prayer.

Miracles and proof of personal holiness are not important preoccupations in this new emphasis on praying for wholeness. Christians, rather, see themselves cooperating with a constantly creative God, who has made himself available to the sufferings of mankind (Mk 1.15 and Mt 18.19–20). Prayer for healing is an acceptance of Christ's directive to his followers to love one another as he has loved them (Jn 15.12). It flows out of that union which involves laying down life itself for one another in Christian community. But its efficacy depends far less on the holiness of the ones praying than on the faithfulness of the Word of God and his desire to share his life with us (Jn 10.10).

As Christian laymen join in prayer for healing, persons with special healing gifts emerge in the parish communities. Some of these have special gifts in praying for physical healing; others minister more effectively to emotional suffering. Sharing in the healing ministry of Christ is an essential part, however, of the life of every believing Christian, just as it was an important manifestation of the divine presence in the life of Jesus himself (Jn 14.12–13). Christian healing incorporates attitudes of compassionate love, faith in Jesus Christ, obedience to the full Gospel message, and humble reverence before the mysteries of life, death, and suffering. Its primary purpose is to reveal the Father's love and to glorify his goodness in the life he has shared with his creation.

Ministers and theologians of Christian healing continue to debate the reasons some persons are healed, some are only improved, and some do not respond at all to prayers for healing (MacNutt, 1974, ch. 18). There is, nevertheless, a great reluctance to accept sickness as "sent by God" for the "good of the soul." While redemptive suffering will always have an honored place in Christian life, sickness itself is an evil which all members of the Church are called to prevent and eradicate as far as they are able. Efforts to improve spiritual methods of preventing and healing sickness are an even more vital part of Christian life than efforts on the scientific level.

Christian Healing and the Medical Sciences. The past decade has seen a definitive swing in both medical and philosophical thinking toward the acceptance of man as a unified being, in whom body, soul, and spirit constantly interact (ibid. ch. 11, 17). Thus, interdisciplinary cooperation between medical professionals, psychologists, and clerics is increasing steadily. One growing phenomenon is the Christian healing clinic or hospital in which medical doctors, psychologists, and pastoral ministers cooperate in the care of individual patients. Most healing is a process involving a time and sequence known only to God. It calls for a community of persons, professional and lay, willing to spend time with those who suffer and love them into wholeness, using the best medical and spiritual means available. Church-related health services pledge themselves to minister on all levels to the sick and disabled, providing a witness of Gospel values through an environment of love and

respect for human dignity, especially important in the experience of death. Entered into with faith and joyful acceptance when it is ultimately seen to be the will of God, a Christian death, graced by the Sacraments, is the most complete healing of all, an entrance into the eternal fullness of life won for all Christians by Christ on Calvary.

Inner Healing. One of the most significant voices in the broadening arena of healing, Mrs. Agnes Sanford, an Episcopalian, has launched a movement in prayer for spiritual and emotional ills, called "the healing of memories" or "inner healing." Through prayer the process brings an individual's emotional problems and sufferings into contact with Jesus' perfect love. Through his healing action, the affirming love of God satisfies those universal needs in a person's spirit that human beings have been unwilling or unable to touch with love. That part of the individual psyche traumatized or wounded by sin—the person's own sin or the sins of others—is healed and brought into the life of grace. Prayer for inner healing is especially effective in conjunction with psychological counseling and the Sacrament of Reconciliation. It usually involves an effort on the part of the one suffering to forgive God, self, and others for the failures and disappointments in his life, along with a resolve to take responsibility for the direction of that life. Such healing adds a powerful dimension to the treatment of homosexuals, alcoholics, and victims of other compulsions who are seeking to form new patterns of behavior. It is often accompanied by a spontaneous healing on the physical level, indicating the close interaction between body and spirit.

Healing and the Sacraments. In a special way, the Sacraments have flourished in their healing aspects since Vatican II. The renaming and ritual revision of two important channels of healing, the Sacraments of Reconciliation and of Anointing, reflect a more positive emphasis on Christ's will for all to become whole in body and spirit. In administering the Sacrament of Reconciliation, the priest has new opportunities to spend time with the penitent, discovering with the help of the Holy Spirit the root causes of sin. He is thus able to encourage penitents to realize the spiritual and emotional healing available to them as they enter into the forgiving love of Jesus and the Father. The Sacrament of Anointing in its new format places more emphasis on the building of faith for direct physical healing in the sick person, as is clear from its ritual formula: "May the Lord, who frees you from sin, save you and raise you up." By making this Sacrament available to persons other than those in imminent danger of death, the Church reaffirms its belief in the restorative power of her anointing, in accordance with Js 5.14–16.

Throughout the centuries the healing Sacrament par excellence has been the Eucharist, a daily occasion for Christians to enter into greater wholeness on all levels, spiritual, emotional, and physical. Special Masses for healing, sometimes combined with the Sacrament of Anointing for the sick, are held in some parishes to call the attention of the faithful to the healing power of the Eucharistic Liturgy. Christian healing, which finds its culmination in the Eucharistic celebration of a community gathered in love and prayer, extends beyond personal concerns for bodily and spiritual fulfillment: it calls Christians to work and prayer for the unity of the

Body of Christ and the healing of society. As Christians cooperate actively with the liberating grace of the Creator Spirit, allowing themselves to be reformed into the image of the Father, made whole only to be broken open in the service of life, they will be freed to respond to the challenge of bringing healing to the whole of creation, the formation of a just society on earth.

Bibliography: M. KELSEY, *Healing and Christianity* (New York 1973). M. and D. LINN, *Healing of Memories* (New York 1974); *Healing Life's Hurts* (New York 1978). F. MACNUTT, *Healing* (Notre Dame, Ind. 1974); *Power to Heal* (Notre Dame, Ind. 1977). G. MALONEY, *Jesus, Set Me Free* (Denville, N.J. 1977). B. MARTIN, *The Healing Ministry in the Church* (Richmond, Va. 1960). A. SANFORD, *The Healing Gifts of the Spirit* (Philadelphia 1966); *The Healing Light* (Plainfield, N.J. 1972); *Creation Waits* (Plainfield, N.J. 1978). J. SANFORD, *Healing and Wholeness* (New York 1977). M. SCANLAN, *The Power in Penance* (Notre Dame, Ind. 1972); *Inner Healing* (New York 1974); M. SCANLAN and A. T. SHIELDS, *And Their Eyes Were Opened* (Ann Arbor, Mich. 1976). B. SHLEMON, *Healing Prayer* (Notre Dame, Ind. 1976). B. SHLEMON, M. and D. LINN, *To Heal as Jesus Did* (Notre Dame, Ind. 1978). R. STAPLETON, *The Gift of Inner Healing* (Waco, Texas 1976). B. TYRELL, *Christotherapy* (New York 1975).

[J. HILL]

HEALTH CARE AND THE CHURCH

The Church's role in the provision of health care services is rooted in Jesus' ministry of healing. During his earthly life, he set an example of compassionate care by ministering to both physical and spiritual needs. The Gospels reflect that he showed the deepest sympathy for those suffering from illness and disability and included them with the poor and oppressed with whom he shared his "Good News." The physician Luke describes again and again Jesus the healer, who reached out to the sick and "laid his hand upon each" and "cured them" (Lk 4.40). Furthermore, he admonished his disciples to do likewise. Down through the centuries, Christians have dedicated their lives to the service of the sick. Historically, this work has had two aspects. On the sacramental level, it has offered the Anointing of the Sick and pastoral care to those who suffered illness. On the level of physiological care, the Church has established and operated health institutions and programs; in fact, the Church exercised the pioneering effort in this field. Long before health care became a specific governmental concern, it already had been given a high place in the Church's list of priorities. Many of the hospitals the world over were Church-sponsored. Today, in the United States alone, due primarily to the efforts of religious communities of women, the Catholic Church is the largest single presence in the voluntary health care sector. It operates 669 general hospitals, an additional 90 "special hospitals" as well as approximately 200 long-term care or nursing home facilities (*Official Catholic Directory 1978*). The extensiveness of this involvement is even more striking when one considers the individual, valuable contributions made by religious and laity alike in the various health professions and paraprofessions (*see* HOSPITALS, CATHOLIC).

Health Care, A Ministry of Justice. Much of the early Church commitment in health care can be viewed as apostolic works of mercy and charity to the poor, the aged, the infirm, and the dispossessed. Programs and facilities were established to meet the needs of these persons. Contemporarily the provision of health care services is seen as an integral part of the Church's social ministry and a matter of social justice. The right to health care, long articulated by philosophers as a basic human right, has been strongly upheld by the Church in the 20th century. Most recently, Pope John XXIII reaffirmed this when he said: "Beginning our discussion of the rights of man, we see that every man has the right to life, to bodily integrity, and the means which are necessary and suitable for the proper development of life. These means are primarily food, clothing, shelter, rest, medical care and finally, the necessary social services" (John XXIII PacTerr 11).

In the U.S., this right is currently the subject of careful scrutiny as well as heated debate, occasioned by rising costs and technological advances in the treatment of disease. Through the efforts of dedicated men and women in both the public and voluntary sectors, Americans in general, receive good health care. However, this does not obscure the fact that there are failures and inadequacies in the system when viewed from a perspective of social and distributive justice. Paradoxically, though the U.S. spends far more on health care than any other country, it lags significantly behind many industrialized nations according to certain accepted health indices, such as infant mortality and male life expectancy (Hu; World Population Bureau). One primary reason proffered for the disparity between expenditures and results is that health care benefits are not equally distributed throughout the population. In certain areas, for instance, the rural South or the inner cities, citizens are denied basic health services because these services are either unavailable or inaccessible. Likewise, people can find themselves lacking health care simply for financial reasons or because of the presence of cultural barriers. These issues are now being addressed by increased participation by government in health care delivery and financing.

Current Problems and Directions. The problems of the larger system are experienced by the Catholic health care system, which finds itself in a period of transition, anguishing over its own identity and the role it should play in the future delivery of health care services. The declining numbers of religious women in health care, financial problems, the deterioration of facilities, and population changes, have led some Catholic hospitals to relocate from the inner cities to the suburbs, thus eliminating the opportunity they once enjoyed to serve the poor and the alienated. These changes coupled with a greater emphasis on technology, make it difficult to distinguish some Catholic institutions from their secular counterparts. These changes as well as the impetus given to social justice by Vatican Council II, have stimulated the hierarchy, religious congregations, and the leadership of Catholic health programs to reexamine the role of Catholic health institutions in light of the signs of the times.

A pastoral letter on health is being developed by the American bishops at the present time. In its formative stages, the focus is on the social justice dimension of health care ministry. The draft document calls for the health care apostolate to be faithful to the healing mission of Jesus. Recognizing the great contribution of Catholic hospitals, it suggests that energies now be devoted to the development of alternative health care models that can provide the broadest range of services to the greatest number of people. Holistic health care centers that make simultaneous provision for physical, emotional, and spiritual aid; hospices that offer humane, personalized care for the terminally ill; and expanded health education programs that foster a stronger self-care orientation for ordinary people are mentioned as examples. Catholic health professionals are challenged to respond creatively in the allocation of scarce health resources and urged to give priority to those persons and geographic areas that are drastically under-served. The growth of publicly financed health care in the United States as well as continued debate over national health insurance schemes, is addressed by calling for a well-articulated, comprehensive national health policy that is based upon social justice principles and that recognizes each person's basic dignity and right to health care. It also recommends that the policy and subsequent program development should involve full citizen participation at every level.

In the recently published (1978), "Forming Christian Community for Healing," the final report of the study for future directions of the *Catholic Hospital Association, a similar social justice thrust is evident. The development of new constituencies is encouraged particularly those that focus on the aged, the unborn, the alienated, and the dispossessed. The health pastoral and the Association report provide encouragement and support to the individual and institutional efforts that are a renewed witness to the Gospel values in the health world today.

Bibliography: T. HU, ed., *International Health Costs and Expenditures*, U.S. Department of Health, Education and Welfare, HEW Publ. (NIH) 76–1067 (Washington, D.C. 1976). World Population Reference Bureau, Inc., "1976 World Population Data Sheet" (Washington, D.C. 1976).

[E. BALDWIN]

HEIDEGGER, MARTIN

Martin Heidegger (5:733) died on May 26, 1976 and was buried in Messkirch, the place of his birth nearly 87 years before (Sept. 26, 1889); according to his wish the funeral was held by his nephew, Heinrich Heidegger. Bernard Welte, professor of the Catholic theological faculty at the Univ. of Freiburg im Breisgau, where Heidegger began and ended his teaching life, spoke at the grave ("Seeking and Finding," *Listening* 12 n. 3 [1977] 106–109).

Writings. Two-thirds of Heidegger's writings remain unpublished; he made arrangements for the definitive edition, being published by Klostermann; see F.-W. von Herrmann, "Observations on the Definitive Collected Works of Martin Heidegger," *Universitas* 17 n. 1 (1975) 29–37. The edition is divided into four parts: (1) already published works, 1914–70, with Heidegger's marginalia (already available and of special interest are the marginalia to *Sein und Zeit*, also in the Niemeyer edition, 14 Aufl., 1977); (2) the lectures, Marburg, 1923–28, Freiburg, 1928–44 (it has not been decided whether the Freiburg lectures, 1916–23, will be included; already available and of special interest for the appropriation of Aristotle and Husserl and its role in the novelty of *Sein und Zeit* are the lectures of the winter semester, 1925–26, v. 21, and the summer semester, 1927, v. 24, a version of the "missing" *Sein und Zeit* 1/3); (3) the unpublished essays, 1919–67; (4) preparations and sketches, reconsiderations and indications. The remarks of the editor of each volume will be useful for interpreting the text (see, e.g., the Collected-Works, v. 2, edition of *Sein und Zeit*). The lectures on Plato's *Sophistes*, winter semester, 1924–25, introduced by an interpretation of Aristotle's *Nichomachean Ethics* 6, will be of special interest.

Biographical Material. An introduction to Heidegger's life and work, with photographs, biographical and bibliographical data: Walter Biemel, *Martin Heidegger: An Illustrated Study*, tr. J. L. Mehta from the German of 1973 (New York 1976); also H.-M. Sass, *Heidegger-Bibliographie* and *Materialien zu einer Heidegger-Bibliographie* (Meisenheim am Glan 1968 and 1975). An indispensable instrument, especially because of the references to themes of *Sein und Zeit* in later works: H. Feick, *Index zu Heideggers 'Sein und Zeit'* (2 Aufl., Tübingen 1968). Other biographical sources: T. Sheehan, "Heidegger's Early Years: Fragments for a Philosophical Biography," *Listening* 12 n. 3 (1977) 3–20; Hannah Arendt, "Martin Heidegger at Eighty," *New York Review of Books* Oct. 21, 1971 (German in *Merkur* Oct. 1969); Hans-Georg Gadamer's essays, recollections, remarks: "Die Frage Martin Heideggers," (Heidelberg Academy of Sciences 1969); *Kleine Schriften* 1 and 3 (Tübingen 1967 and 1972; some of this material is translated in David E. Linge, tr. and ed., *Philosophical Hermeneutics*, Berkeley, Cal. 1976—see esp. 202–205 and 224–227); *Hegels Dialektik* (Tübingen 1971); "Nur wer mitgeht, weiss, dass es ein Weg ist," *Frankfurter Allgemeine Zeitung*, Sept. 28, 1974; "Plato und Heidegger," *Der Idealismus und seine Gegenwart. Festschrift für Werner Marx zum 65. Geburtstag.* hrsg. von U. Guzzoni et al. (Hamburg 1976); *Philosophische Lehrjahre* (Tübingen 1977); *Philosophie in Selbstdarstellung* 3, hrsg. von L. J. Pongratz (Hamburg 1977). Karl Jaspers on Heidegger, *Philosophische Autobiographie* (erweiterte Neuausgabe, Munich 1977). "A Giving of Accounts: Jacob Klein and Leo Strauss," *The College* 22 n. 1 (Annapolis and Santa Fe 1970) 1–5. *Erinnerung an Martin Heidegger* hrsg. G. Neske (Pfullingen 1977).

Autobiographical. Heidegger's self-presentation: *Antrittsrede* (Heidelberg Academy of Sciences 1957); also in part in the preface to *Frühe Schriften* (Frankfurt am Main 1972); the letter to the author (1962), W. J. Richardson, *Heidegger: Through Phenomenology to Thought* (The Hague 1963); and "Mein Weg in die Phänomenologie" (1963), *Zur Sache des Denkens* (Tübingen 1969; tr. in *On Time and Being*, New York 1972). Statements by Heidegger on his rectorship at the Univ. of Freiburg, 1933–34: his *Spiegel* interview, Sept. 23, 1966, published May 31, 1976 and translated in *Philosophy Today* 20 n. 3/4 (1976) 267–284; K. A. Moehling, "Martin Heidegger and the Nazi Party: An Examination" (Ph.D. thesis, Dept. of History, n. 72–79, 319, Northern Illinois Univ. 1972) Appendix B and C (Heidegger letters of 1945, marred by errors in transcription); Moehling writes in *Listening* 12 n. 3 (1977) 93: "... the veracity of the two 1945 letters and the 1966 interview is sustained by the conclusions of the independent investigation Freiburg University conducted in 1945."; see also F. Fédier, "Trois attaques contre Heidegger," *Critique* 234 (1966) 883–904.

Three documents worthy of note: "A Discussion between Ernst Cassirer and Martin Heidegger," (1929) in N. Langiulli, ed., *The Existentialist Tradition* (New York 1971); Heidegger's letter to Husserl, Oct. 22, 1927, in *Husserliana* 9:600–602; and "Über das Zeitverständnis in der Phänomeologie und im Denken der Seinsfrage," *Phänomenologie—lebendig oder tot? Zum 30. Todesjahr Edmund Husserls*, hrsg. von H. Gehrig, Veröffentlichungen der katholischen Akademie der Erzdiözese Freiburg, 18 (Karlsruhe 1969); see also

Husserliana 10:353, 22–23 and Fink, Nov. 24, 1931, in Dorion Cairns, *Conversations with Husserl and Fink*, (The Hague 1976).

Heidegger and Theology. On Heidegger and theology see the lecture (1927–28) and the letter in *Phänomenologie und Theologie* (Frankfurt am Main 1970); "Gespräch mit Martin Heidegger" (1953) in *Anstösse: Berichte aus der Arbeit der evangelischen Akademie Hofgeismar*, hrsg. von H. Noack (Karlsruhe 1954), tr. in J. G. Hart and J. C. Maraldo. *The Piety of Thinking* (Bloomington, Ind. 1976). See also *La Quinzaine littéraire* 196 (1974) 3: "La foi n'a pas besoin de la pensée de l'être." Tributes by Karl Rahner and Heinrich Ott appear in *Martin Heidegger im Gespräch*, hrsg. von R. Wisser (Freiburg im B. 1970). For Rahner's existential-transcendental (mis)interpretation of Heidegger, see "The Concept of Existential Philosophy in Heidegger," *Philosophy Today* 13 n. 2/4 (1969) 125–137; Rahner approved the translation from the French, published in 1940; the German of his article is "nowhere available." A remarkable use of Heidegger in a theological context: Hans Urs von Balthasar, *Herrlichkeit, Dritter Band/Erster Teil: Im Raum der Metaphysik 3* (Einsiedeln 1965); see also Heinrich Ott, *Denken und Sein. Der Weg Martin Heideggers und der Weg der Theologie* (Zollikon 1959); Walter Strolz., *Menschen als Gottesfrage* (Pfullingen 1965). E. Schillebeeckx, "Toward a Catholic Use of Hermeneutics," in *God the Future of Man*, tr. N. D. Smith (New York 1968) 1–50 describes Heidegger as "the philosopher behind the whole of modern theology (and thus comparable to Aristotle, the philosopher who, via Arabic philosophy, was behind the whole 'new theology' of the Middle Ages)..." (14; see Scotus, Prologus to the *Ordinatio*, 12, Note).

Some issues relevant to theology which Heidegger has freshened and opened up are: the circumincession of past and future—recapitualtion and anticipation; the unity of concealing and revealing in origin, tradition, and consummation; hermeneutics as the way of being (and not merely the form of understanding) of Scripture and Sacrament; prethematic horizon and thematization of horizon; the reserved availability of the questioned in the question, the questioning, and the questioner; God's not being reducible to the one lordliest being among all other beings.

The unavailability and obscurity in symbol and mystery are not to be reduced to an absence to be overcome by a presencing (manifesting, grasping, dominating: getting all together into a commanding view). The *lēthē* (hiddenness) in *alētheia* (truthing), hiddenness withheld in emergence, withdrawn in gift, is saving plenitude, not privation (not recalcitrance to wresting): *lēthē* as *Verbergung* is *Bergung*. Heidegger's way opens up the interplay of absence/presencing and hiddenness/manifesting (clarification: clearing *up*, making clear *to*) toward appropriation of the gift of taking place in the space clear *of* that cleared *away* interplay: the way from *Versprechen im Entzug* to *Erörterung in die Lichtung*.

[T. PRUFER]

HELSINKI AGREEMENT

The Final Act of the Conference on Security and Cooperation in Europe, signed at Helsinki on Aug. 1, 1975, represented significant progress toward both the reduction of international tensions and the recognition of *human rights. Several provisions of the agreement

promised improved relations between the nations of Eastern and Western Europe, whose ideological differences have obstructed a permanent peace settlement since the end of World War II. The participants in the conference, including the Holy See, the United States, Canada, the Soviet Union, and 31 other European nations, agreed: to respect the sovereign equality, inviolable frontiers, and territorial integrity of the other signatories; to refrain from the use of force; to settle disputes by peaceful means; and not to intervene in one another's internal affairs. These confidence-building affirmations enhanced the sense of security for European states.

The signatories of the Final Act also promised to "respect human rights and fundamental freedoms, including the freedom of thought, conscience, religion or belief" and to promote the effective exercise of all rights and freedoms "which derive from the inherent dignity of the human person and are essential for his free and full development." Within this framework the participating states pledged to "respect the freedom of the individual to profess and practice, alone or in communion with others, religion or belief acting in accordance with the dictates of his own conscience." Other provisions of the Helsinki Agreement pledged cooperation in such humanitarian endeavors as reunification of families, easier travel, and expanded cultural contacts, and in freer exchanges of information between countries.

To assure the execution of these commitments and to facilitate further progress, the Helsinki Agreement provided for additional meetings to consider these questions and specified Belgrade as the location for the first of these meetings in 1977.

See also *BELGRADE CONFERENCE.

[R. J. GIBBONS]

HIERARCHY

The word "hierarchy" usually refers to the episcopacy, though sometimes it includes the three degrees of the ordained ministry (6:1097). It is not a term of great antiquity, and though used at first to speak of spiritual realities it has in effect come to underline the powers of bishops and the distinction between clergy and laity. Studies in patristics and in the New Testament have made it clear that there are better ways of expressing the relation of bishops to the faithful. One such example are the well-known words of St Augustine: "I am a bishop for your sake, I am a Christian together with you" (*Sermo* 340, 1; PL 38.1483). This refers back to a time when a man's official position did not of itself guarantee his authority; it was expected that he enjoyed the spiritual authority of the man of God, who gives himself in loving service for the people. With a similar understanding of its mission the episcopacy undertook the work of Vatican Council II. This is reflected in the message to the world published early in the first session: "Far from turning us away from our tasks on earth, our adherence to Christ in faith, hope and love commits us wholly to the service of our brethren, in imitation of our beloved Master who came not to be ministered unto but to minister." This understanding of the ordained ministry is written into the documents of the Council, starting with the chapter on the hierarchy in the Constitution on the Church (*Lumen gentium* 18–27; cf. *Christus Dominus* 16). The bishops' mission is to serve and not to be served. Their powers of order and jurisdiction are equally affirmed. In a context, however, of service they appear as tools of service, to be used for the good of the Church by men endowed with the Spirit.

See also MINISTRY (ECCLESIOLOGY).

Bibliography: Abbott 3–7. Y. CONGAR, *Power and Poverty in the Church*, tr. J. NICHOLSON (Baltimore 1964).

[D. N. POWER]

HIGHER EDUCATION, CATHOLIC

In perhaps no other area of Catholic life were the crises and uncertainties of the Church after Vatican Council II so pronounced and acute as in higher education. The educational crisis had in fact preceded the Council, in that there was already much self-examination and self-criticism in Catholic academic circles by the mid-1950s. The conciliar reforms accelerated that process. (Although Catholic institutions of higher education, distinct from seminaries, exist in many parts of the world, by far the largest and most ambitious system is found in North America.)

Crisis of the 1960s. The sources of this crisis were multiple, and no list could be exhaustive. A few of the more important causes were: the concern whether Catholic institutions maintained academic standards as rigorous as those in the better secular schools; the charge that Catholic colleges and universities fostered a provincial mentality in their students, shielding them from worldly influences and not acquainting them adequately with the fullness of modern culture; changing attitudes on the part of many of the faculty and students of these institutions; a crisis in Catholic theology and philosophy that forced a rethinking of the essential nature and mission of the schools; radical changes in Western society itself, which inevitably affected the educational institutions; financial difficulties and fears for survival; crises within the religious orders operating the schools. These factors made themselves felt in a variety of ways and provoked a variety of responses.

Curricula and Faculty. Beginning already before 1960 there was conscious effort by many colleges and universities to diversify their curricula and faculty. Non-Catholics had taught at such institutions for years, but now they were recruited in larger numbers and by set policy, precisely in order to make these institutions more diverse and open. Catholic institutions also began to adopt academic criteria that were commonly recognized throughout the educational world. According to these criteria, faculty were to be hired and rewarded primarily on the basis of measurable competence in their disciplines—the prestige of their earned degrees, their publications, and their teaching skills. Once hired, faculty were to enjoy full academic freedom within the limits of their professional competence. Religious belief as a criterion, although not totally discounted, tended to be deemphasized.

These hiring practices were one aspect of a new policy of seeking to make Catholic institutions more "open to the world." By about 1960 it was less and less common to refrain from assigning readings from books on the Index or from dealing with non-Christian thinkers in a largely negative way. Many faculty began to question whether there existed a distinctively Catholic approach to sociology, psychology, philosophy, or other disciplines. Often disciplines were taught little differently from the way they might be taught in secular schools. Increasingly professors in Catholic institutions were people who had taken their advanced training in secular schools.

Theology and Philosophy. The reforms of Vatican II forced a further rethinking of the role of Catholic institutions, generally tending to make them still more open and ecumenical. New approaches to theology appealed less to the traditions and dogmas of the Church and emphasized instead personal or communal religious experience as the source of belief. Theology came to be less identifiably Catholic, and some theologians argued that religious education should be ecumenical in the broadest sense. Both in theology and philosophy the authority of St. Thomas Aquinas, which had been dominant in the curricula for decades, was now greatly deemphasized (*see* THOMISM). Instructors came increasingly to believe that a systematic approach was no longer possible and that some kind of ecclecticism was necessary (*see* PLURALISM, THEOLOGICAL).

Social and Political Issues. The internal crisis of the Church was paralleled by a nearly global crisis of authority and identity affecting many of the institutions of the world, especially in the West. In the U.S. the movement against the war in Vietnam, and the criticism of many other political and social realities that accompanied it, affected attitudes towards education as well. The colleges' role *in loco parentis* was abandoned under pressure. Sweeping curricular reforms, sometimes involving an end to all required courses, were introduced. There was a great increase in social action of all kinds, ranging from violent confrontations with the authorities to peaceful tutoring projects in aid of underprivileged children.

Financial Crises. By the early 1970s a threatening financial crisis was the most serious challenge to most Catholic schools. Educational costs had risen enormously. The number of students choosing to attend college levelled off after several decades of constant increase. Many private institutions found difficulty in competing with well-funded state schools. Catholic educational leaders struggled to obtain various kinds of public aid in the face of the persistent court decisions that either forbade or severely limited such aid. Predictions that throughout the 1980s the college-going population would decline precipitously led to further anxieties.

Personnel Crisis. The post-conciliar changes in the Church deeply affected religious orders, who were the operators of the majority of American Catholic colleges and universities. Of the thousands of religious who left their orders, most were of the generation that was just assuming positions of responsibility and were especially from among those who had been given advanced academic training. Thus many orders no longer found themselves able to staff their schools adequately. Among religious who remained in their communities there was much uncertainty regarding the proper roles of either the schools or the communities themselves.

Individual institutions were affected by all this in a variety of ways. St. John's University in New York City in 1966 became the first American Catholic school to experience a faculty strike. Later it was one of several New York institutions which refused to accept state money for fear of being forced to compromise their religious identity. Saint Louis University, Jesuit-run for almost 150 years, became the first Catholic institution to grant control to a predominantly lay board, although it insisted still on its Catholic and Jesuit character. Fordham University in New York and a number of other schools in New York State ceased, as a condition of qualifying for state aid, to designate themselves officially as Catholic. In the early 1970s one of the country's best known Catholic women's colleges, Manhattanville College, Purchase, N.Y., was given up by the Religious of the Sacred Heart and officially secularized. A Black who was also a Protestant minister was appointed president. Dozens of smaller Catholic colleges closed their doors completely. Some traditionally prestigious institutions like the University of Notre Dame and Georgetown University, despite some difficulties, continued to flourish financially and in enrollment.

Reassessment and Prospects. The mid-1970s brought still another period of reassessment to most Catholic institutions, this time a reassessment of the often frenetic changes that had occurred over the previous two decades. A few institutions had successfully made the transition from religious to secular. Most Catholic educators expressed the belief, however, that the survival of their schools depended in great part on their continuing to be identifiably religious in character in order to provide a clear cut alternative to state-supported colleges.

The problems connected with this stance were many. Had the changes that had already occurred been so far-reaching as to be almost irreversible? Was there sufficient unity of belief among faculty and students to make the religious emphasis viable in practice? How could the commitment to openness and academic freedom be reconciled with the desire to maintain an institutional philosophy? Would the acceptance of public money, which many institutions regarded as essential to their survival, necessarily prevent the continuation of a meaningful religious character? Who would set the tone for this Catholic presence as the proportion of professed religious on most faculties continued to decline?

As smaller Catholic colleges continued to close their doors in the late 1970s, a few new ones—Thomas Aquinas College, Calabasas, Cal., for example, or Cardinal Newman College (1976) in St. Louis, Mo.—were being founded by traditionalist Catholics who believed that the secularization process in the established schools was irreversible. Some older institutions, like the University of San Francisco, began the experiment of offering students the option of a traditionally structured Catholic liberal arts curriculum embracing spiritual and moral as well as purely academic concerns (*see* HIGHER EDUCATION, LIBERAL ARTS IN).

Facing the 1980s, most American colleges anticipate the possibility of a drop in enrollment because of the decline in the college-age population. The possibility of attracting increased numbers of older persons back to the campuses has been widely discussed. Vocational objectives—the desire that academic programs be directly related to careers and offer prospects of employment after graduation—are dominant almost everywhere.

Catholic institutions see themselves as able to respond to these needs but also rely on their being able to provide students with certain things for which secular institutions are perhaps not well equipped—a strong sense of social justice and responsibility that rests on an understanding of human beings as God's creatures; an awareness of the spiritual dimensions of reality; the opportunity for worship; the systematic exploration and deepening of the life of faith; and the sense of being a link with and a part of the continuing Christian tradition.

Bibliography: R. HASSENGER, ed., *The Shape of Catholic Higher Education* (Chicago 1967). J. HITCHCOCK, "How Is a College or University Catholic in Practice?" *Delta Epsilon Sigma Bulletin* 20 (1975) 40–53. E. MANIER and J. W. HOUCK, eds., *Academic Freedom and the Catholic University* (Notre Dame, Ind. 1967). NCEA, "The Catholic University in the Modern World," *College Newsletter* 35 (1973) 1–10. P. H. RATTERMAN, *The Emerging Catholic University* (New York 1968). P. C. REINDERT, *The Urban Catholic University* (New York 1970).

[J. HITCHCOCK]

HIGHER EDUCATION, CHURCH AND

There have been significant changes in the U.S. Catholic college and university since Vatican Council II. Among other changes are a different perception of their role and a different way of relating to the official Church.

Factors of Change. Before examining the Church relationship of the almost 250 colleges and universities that are Catholic, it is useful to glance at the events which triggered the changes of the last decades.

(1) Supported by the GI Bill thousands of young men and women swelled the enrollments of Catholic colleges. Existing institutions were expanded, new ones were founded, many previously single-sex colleges became coeducational. All higher education began to boom; so did that portion that was Catholic—and as the path to careers for first-generation college youth.

(2) To serve the needs of growing student bodies, many new faculty were added. In a seller's market those with graduate degrees were in short supply. In many Catholic colleges there was a feeling that graduates of Ivy League and other prominent public universities would introduce a new element of academic excellence not previously enjoyed. The significance of this development lay in the fact that these new faculty and administration recruits did not come out of a Catholic academic tradition and often had neither understanding nor appreciation of it.

(3) The youth revolution of the 1960s changed significantly the relationships of youth to their elders, to value standards, and to society's institutions. Along with the rest Catholic colleges and universities bore the full brunt of the revolution. This era simply created new situations not previously faced. Results were particularly seen in changed governance structures, weakened core curricula and academic requirements, relaxation if not abolition of rigid discipline patterns, and significantly changed life styles of the students. While the pendulum began to swing back in the 1970s from the more extreme practices of the previous decade, the effects of the youth revolution lived on.

(4) To the social ferment of the 1960s was added the big "Catholic event," the convening of Vatican Council II, which sketched out new directions and emphases for the Church. The emphases on shared authority, on accountability, on liberty of conscience, on the Church as Christian community, on ecumenism, and on updated liturgies, etc., created new expectations, anxieties, and tensions. The waves from the Council also washed the shores of Catholic colleges and universities, already seeking to cope with other change forces. The "new" theology came into vogue as manual theology gave way to the new directions emanating from the Council and from European universities.

(5) A final factor creating the environment for the Catholic college and university was the entrance of government-aid programs into higher education. Inflationary pressures sent costs in an upward spiral. The gap widened between tuitions at private-sector institutions and in subsidized public colleges. Without government aid, many private colleges and universities would have been forced from the market. In *Tilton v. Richardson* (1971) 403 U.S. 672 the Supreme Court upheld the constitutionality of federal grants and loans for construction; in *Roemer et al. v. Board of Public Works of Maryland et al.* (1976) 426 U.S. 736, of noncategorical state grants. Nevertheless the aid to Church-related colleges or universities required the institutions to be very circumspect in their relations to sponsoring religious bodies (see Wilson).

Relationship to Church Authority. Funding was but one of the reasons most colleges moved a legal arm's length from their sponsors. Educational leaders felt the Church-renewal process suggested a clearer distinction between Church and academe. Although religious orders and dioceses retained a leadership or sponsorship role in their colleges, most of the institutions became separate corporations and added lay persons to their boards and their administrations (see Fox and McGrath).

While the movements just described were influencing the American scene and creating a changed relationship of the Catholic college with the Church, an international development has emerged in the form of the activities of the International Federation of Catholic Universities. At the special request of Pope Paul VI, this organization took on new life. After regional meetings around the world had produced initial drafts of a new statement on the role and mission of Catholic universities, an authoritative document, "The Catholic University in the Modern World," was produced at a Congress in Rome in November 1972, convened by the Sacred Congregation for Catholic Education (see bibliog. NCEA).

The document clearly summoned Catholic universities to perform their service of intellectual leadership to the Church and to the world. The highest academic standards are to be pursued. There is a clear acknowledgment of the different ways in which institutions carry out their mission, conditioned by their national and cultural heritage. Even the way the institutions relate to the Church is subject to different traditions and practices. While the document speaks of "the university," it is clear that its applicability extends to those institutions in the United States classified as colleges. The document has had a significant effect on both institutions and Church leadership, calling the former to a renewal of mission, and cautioning the latter to respect the independence of Catholic higher education.

In 1976 the College and University Department of the National Catholic Educational Association (called since Feb. 1978 the Association of Catholic Colleges and Universities) produced another statement, "Relations of American Catholic Colleges and Universities with the Church" (see bibliog.). It had a more limited objective than the 1972 Roman document and stressed the need to understand the American academic and legal environment in which Catholic colleges and universities seek to provide an authentic service to the Church community. After noting the extraordinary variety among Catholic colleges and universities, ranging from large urban universities with multiple schools and faculties, to small, largely residential liberal arts colleges, women's colleges, and two-year institutions, the document takes pains to describe the unique organization of American higher education. Legal structures of control and ownership and the roles of regional and discipline-based accrediting groups, which are not typical in other countries, are mentioned. Catholic identity of the institutions is reaffirmed in a summary listing of the many ways in which service is given to the Catholic community, e.g., in fostering theological research and study, building faith communities, encouraging ecumenical activities and providing a forum for dialogue on important issues within the Church. Given the unique manner in which Catholic colleges relate to the American Church because of their history and the restrictions of American constitutional law, the most important function of the entire document is to point out to those in the Church outside the U.S. that a relationship with Church authority that stresses leadership rather than juridical control is not only possible but has proven to be successful.

Initiatives on Catholic Identity. The issue of Catholic identity has been addressed with seriousness and increasing frequency by Catholic higher education leadership. Academic communities utilized lengthy consultative processes, involving all campus groups, to craft new statements of mission. The National Catholic Educational Assn. College and University Department (Association) focused on identity issues in annual meetings and publications, aided by generous support from the Delta Episilon Sigma Honor Society (see Borders, Ellis, Hitchcock, Orsy).

The interest in candid exploration of identity and Church relationship issues has not been confined to the academies. The General Secretary of the United States Catholic Conference assembled leadership from Catholic honor societies to further the discussion—an action warmly received by the scholars; the then USCC General Secretary, Bishop James S. Rausch, convened the first meeting, June 17, 1974. The focal point of those discussions has been research on matters of special concern to the Church, the absence of which has occasioned criticism of Catholic universities. The same need was expressed during and following the *Call to Action Conference, sponsored by the American bishops in the bicentennial year.

The dialogue was fueled by a widely publicized symposium held at Notre Dame in January 1976, titled "Evangelization in the American Context," but which really centered on discussions between bishops and scholars/administrators on relationships of higher education and the Church (see Burrell and Kane).

Less widely known, but also of importance, has been a small group called the Bishops and Presidents Committee which began to meet in the Fall of 1974. Structured as a nonofficial body composed of an equal number of hierarchy and presidents, it has functioned well as a liaison between Catholic leaders with a shared interest in Catholic higher education, but who view it from different perspectives in the Church.

Several financial pressures affecting all private higher education in the U.S. in the 1970's have not made it easier to sharpen the focus on Catholic identity and to renew the Catholic college and university—a process, it should be added, which is never finished. Examination, dialogue, and renewal continue in Catholic higher education. If anything is clear, it is that in the U.S. there is a real pluralism among Catholic colleges and universities in the way they perceive their Catholic identity. Whether traditional or progressive, whether focused on orthodoxy or on service, whether emphasizing the Catholic academic tradition of the past or trying to carve out a new role in a more ecumenical period, there is life and hope in Catholic higher education.

Bibliography: W. D. BORDERS, "Call to Action: Response from Catholic Colleges and Universities As Community," *Delta Epsilon Sigma Bulletin* 22 (May 1977) 40–48. D. B. BURRELL and F. KANE, *Evangelization in the American Context* (Notre Dame, Ind. 1976). J. T. ELLIS, "To Lead, To Follow, or To Drift? American Catholic Higher Education in 1976: A Personal View," *Delta Epsilon Sigma Bulletin* 21 (1976) 40–66. M. FOX, "Confident, Cordial and Critical," *Occasional Papers on Catholic Higher Education*, NCEA, 1 n. 1 (July 1975) 14–18. J. F. HITCHCOCK, "How is a College of University Catholic in Practice?" *Delta Epsilon Sigma Bulletin* 20 (1975) 40–53. J. J. MCGRATH, *Catholic Institutions in the United States: Canonical and Civil Law Status* (Washington, D.C. 1968). NCEA, "The Catholic University in the Modern World," *College Newsletter* 35, n. 3 (March 1973); *Occasional Papers on Catholic Higher Education* 2, n. 1 (April 1976). L. M. ORSY, "Interaction between University and Church," *Delta Epsilon Sigma Bulletin* 19 (1974) 40–61. USCC, *Call to Action* (Washington, D.C. n.d.). C. H. WILSON, *Tilton v. Richardson, The Search for Sectarianism in Education* (Association of American Colleges, Washington, D.C. 1971).

[J. F. MURPHY]

HIGHER EDUCATION, LIBERAL ARTS IN

The liberal arts include a variety of subjects of study, most of which are based in the humanities and all of which are distinguished by the fact that they are not directed to the mastery of professional knowledge or skills. They are more concerned with living than with making a living. In American four-year liberal arts colleges, which stand between the secondary school and the graduate or professional school, the liberal arts form the core of the curriculum and provide what is described as "general education." This usually includes such subjects as literature, philosophy, history, fine arts, mathematics. Frequently, it may also include some exposure to one or more scientific disciplines, together with at least a basic introduction to a foreign language and culture. Many liberal arts colleges in the U.S. exist as the undergraduate divisions of large universities. Some seven or eight hundred of them are, however, typically small, independent institutions, operating as public trusts controlled by a governing board under a charter granted by the state. Many are Church-related and the greatest number of these are conducted under Catholic auspices. Indeed, the four-year liberal arts college is the form most commonly taken by Catholic higher education in America.

Gaudium et spes. That contemporary Catholic higher education should continue its traditional concern with the liberal arts seems to be called for by Vatican Council II's Pastoral Constitution on the Church in the Modern World. This document speaks of the deep cultural shift taking place in modern times and of the subsequent need for wisdom, which comes not from technical proficiency alone, but from those things that serve to perfect the intellect and enable man to surpass the world of mere things and to deal not only with new knowledge but also with determining what is of lasting worth; to harmonize new knowledge with an education nourished by classical studies as adapted to various traditions. The document speaks of this as a new age in human history and points to the need to direct cultural life wisely in relation to the forces of dynamic social conflict and the powers unleashed by science in order to avoid the destruction of both the old and the new aspects of civilized life (*Gaudium et spes* 53–62).

To understand the possible constructive role of the liberal arts in Catholic higher education within the cultural context described in *Gaudium et spes* and in order to appreciate both the potentialities and the limitations of liberal arts studies, it is essential to see them in their historical perspective, particularly as they relate to the life of Catholicism and the cultures it has affected or actually created.

History of the Liberal Arts Tradition. The concept of liberal arts education had its origins in pre-Socratic Greece, where it may have developed especially in the school of Pythagoras. In the *Politics* Aristotle takes it to be axiomatic that there is a kind of education essential for the intellectual development of free men, one not directed to any other end. The important parts of this "liberal" or free man's education are said to be reading and writing, gymnastics, music, and drawing; yet any one of these might lose its "liberal" quality if it were pursued for some menial or servile end. The social assumptions of Aristotle's world limited the study of the liberal arts to free men—in a slave-state system to the few who could enjoy the leisure necessary to both wisdom and virtue. Nonetheless, he clearly established a bond between study pursued for its own sake and the true life of freedom.

With the advent of Christianity, some of the Church Fathers were clearly suspicious of the value to Christians of studies associated with the liberal arts. What, it was asked, had Athens to do with Jerusalem? St. Jerome, for example, abjured his studies of the Latin classics, for one could not be at once a Christian and a "Ciceronian." Yet, other ancient Christian writers thought otherwise and, like St. Basil the Great, advised that the literature of pre-Christian antiquity should be read by young persons since it contained much valuable knowledge about human experience and God's working in history. Even St. Augustine, who said that poetry could be "the devil's wine," nevertheless commended the liberal arts as belonging to the new free people, the *liberi Dei*, as the means to prepare themselves to read the Scriptures, attain wisdom, and fit their minds to contemplate the truths of their new freedom.

In medieval universities, with their faculties of law, theology, and medicine, the liberal arts were regarded as preparatory intellectual disciplines. They were the core of preprofessional education: the trivium (grammar, rhetoric, logic) and the quadrivium (arithmetic, geometry, music, and astronomy). St. Thomas Aquinas in his commentary on Boethius, *De Trinitate* (5.1 and 3) saw the liberal arts as outlined in Hugh of St. Victor's *Didascalicon* as preparing the intellect to deal with the truly "free" sciences of metaphysics and theology.

The concept of the liberal arts which is traditional in American colleges is more "literary" than that of the medieval schoolmen because it owes much of its development to the work of the Christian humanists of the Renaissance, of whom Erasmus and St. Thomas More are examples. The humanists were so named because they were concerned with the *studia humanitatis*, the term for the Greek and Latin linguistic and literary studies of students in the late medieval universities who did not wish to follow the professional courses of the faculties of medicine, law, or theology. Thus the

"Humanities" were not directed to any professional training and eventually they formed the core of modern liberal arts education.

From the Renaissance, then, came the concept of liberal arts studies as mainly those concerned with the classical languages and literature. But the Renaissance humanists frequently also conceived of the liberal arts as the best practical program of education for a future member of the ruling class. Roger Ascham (1515–68), a distinguished humanist and the tutor of the future Queen Elizabeth I, especially stressed the importance of classical studies. Even so pragmatic a Renaissance man as Francis Bacon (1561–1626) observed that men of practical experience may serve well enough in particular instances but that it takes men learned in history, literature, philosophy, mathematics, logic, and rhetoric to manage great affairs and develop national policy. The humanist theory of the liberally educated gentleman combined with the Puritan demand for a learned ministry to produce the first examples of the American liberal arts college at Harvard and Yale. In colonial times, the curricula of these institutions, especially designed to prepare young men for the ministry, typically included Latin, Greek, Hebrew, logic, mathematics, natural and moral philosophy.

The American Catholic Tradition. Georgetown was founded in 1786 as the first of a number of Catholic liberal arts colleges primarily established as preparatory schools for the seminary with a curriculum derived from the Jesuit secondary schools of Europe, which placed major emphasis upon Greek and Latin studies. Almost from their outset, however, the Catholic colleges responded to the new and changing culture of the U.S., which was heavily influenced by English Protestant traditions. Indeed the Catholic liberal arts colleges were in many ways missionary institutions in what was often an alien and hostile setting. As the 19th century advanced, American Catholic colleges increasingly responded to demands for so-called practical courses in English, business, and science. They were more and more serving an immigrant population, interested not only in the education of priests but also in joining the American middle class. Yet, like their non-Catholic counterparts, they held to the basic theory that their primary purpose was to provide that intellectual development to be derived from the study of the liberal arts, with the study of the classics continuing preeminent.

The thesis that intellectual development was the goal of liberal arts education had its greatest spokesman in Cardinal Newman, whose *The Idea of a University* appeared in 1852 in the form of a series of lectures related to the projected founding of a Catholic university in Dublin. Newman conceived of liberal arts education as having for its purpose "nothing more or less than intellectual excellence." This was at once an ambitious and a modest concept, for it set forth the goal of developing the highest and most distinctive human capability while it also recognized its own limitations. For example, Newman, who gave theology a central and integrating role in the university, nonetheless insisted that the kind of education he called "liberal" could not in itself produce generations of educated, practicing Catholics. It could not, he said, be expected to "contend against those giants, the passion and pride of man." Unlike his great contemporary, Matthew Arnold, he did not expect the study of "humane letters" to be the source of the "sweetness and light" of moral and aesthetic values. The most to be expected of the liberally educated gentleman, as Newman envisioned him, was that having cultivated his intellect, he would know the art of social life and have a certain "fitness for the world."

Present and Future Value. Of course, the world for which Newman's product of a liberal education was to be "fit" was that of established wealth, public service, and abundant leisure associated with a relatively small group of Victorian English gentlemen. Like Aristotle or the Renaissance humanists, Newman saw liberal arts education as an experience suited to a ruling class. Indeed it has been left to relatively recent times, and principally to American higher education, to attempt to continue to cultivate and develop the study of the liberal arts, for they serve man's own vision of his identity and the quality of his life. They also attempt to put liberal arts studies in a "democratic" framework and to be concerned with their "relevance" to upward social mobility. Such concerns have been quite characteristic of American Catholic liberal arts colleges. These colleges typically describe themselves as having goals of helping students to discover their aptitudes, with a view to preparing them to undertake vocational or professional studies or to hold positions of management. Moreover, they also stress their concern to perform these services for persons of every social class and background.

It is, however, widely acknowledged that in the contemporary world a major task of the liberal arts colleges must be increasingly that of developing in students a balanced critical competence through the strategy of inquiry provided by such disciplines as history, literature, and philosophy. Beyond all such considerations, however, is the evident need for a sense of roots, of cultural identity among those who must cope with a world in which rapid change quickly makes mere professional competence obsolete. Even more deeply felt is the increasing desire to share with others of diverse cultures simply what it means, and has always meant, to be human. To such concerns, especially among the young, liberal arts studies address themselves, with a power uniquely their own.

As *Gaudium et spes* observes, it is essential today to bridge the gaps between the specialized areas of information so as to determine not only how they relate to one another but also to make certain that care is taken to "safeguard man's powers of contemplation and wonder which lead to wisdom" (*Gaudium et spes* 55). It is most important to those involved in Catholic higher education to continue to cultivate and develop the study of the liberal arts, for they serve man's own vision of his identity and the quality of his life. They also contribute to the preservation and development of what *Gaudium et spes* calls the "notion of the human person as a totality in which predominate values of intellect, will, conscience, and brotherhood ... established by the Creator and wondrously restored and elevated in Christ" (ibid. 61).

Bibliography: D. BELL, *The Reforming of General Education* (New York 1966). H. S. BROWN and L. B. MAYHEW, *American Higher Education* (Center for Applied Research in Education, New York 1965). D. DAICHES, *The Idea of a New University* (London 1964). S. GRAUBARD, ed., *Daedalus* 103 n. 4 (1974), whole issue (Proceedings, American Academy of Arts and Sciences). M. HADAS, *Old Wine, New Bottles* (New York 1962). R. HASSENGER, ed., *The Shape of Catholic Higher Education*

(Chicago 1967). R. M. HUTCHINS, *Higher Learning in America* (New Haven 1936). J. MARITAIN, *Education at the Crossroads* (New Haven 1943). E. W. POWER, *A History of Catholic Higher Education in the United States* (Milwaukee 1958). M. VAN DOREN, *Liberal Education* (New York 1943).

[P. VAN K. THOMSON]

HIGHER EDUCATION AND ECUMENISM

The strong ecumenical thrust of Vatican Council II has resulted in a variety of ecumenical activities at United States Catholic colleges and universities.

(1) Because the colleges had faculties trained in theology and religious studies, many of them in the theologically creative years surrounding the Council, they were able to respond quickly to the call for ecumenical courses. Through such programs Catholic students have been introduced to the other religious traditions.

(2) Many colleges have added non-Catholic theologians on part-time or full-time appointments, not only to teach their own denominational theology, but to assist in teaching standard courses in Scripture, history of Christian Churches, and cross disciplinary courses in such fields as sociology and psychology of religion.

(3) Catholic colleges have often responded to the religious needs of students from other Communions by adding representatives from those denominations to *campus ministry teams.

(4) Non-Catholic faculty and staff members are common on the Catholic campus. However, many denominational colleges are considering the extent to which a "critical mass" from the sponsoring Church is needed in order to maintain denominational identity and mission. There is growing agreement on the need to have a strong core from the sponsoring body as well as some from other Churches. Colleges are trying to face two problems. How can preferential hiring be done in the face of affirmative-action and civil-rights legislation, regulation, and judicial decisions? How can the institution pursue ecumenical objectives while transmitting its own denominational heritage?

(5) Catholic colleges and universities have also become active in consortia with neighboring institutions, thereby providing for cross-registration of students and joint faculty appointments. The most prominent examples have been those involving theologates which have established independent but linked programs at places as diverse as Chicago and Berkeley.

(6) Special mention should also be made of ecumenical institutes such as those at St. John's Univ. in Collegeville, Minn. and Seton Hall Univ. in South Orange, New Jersey. On the international level the University of Notre Dame has established the Ecumenical Institute in Jerusalem.

(7) On the national level, the staff of the Association of Catholic Colleges and Universities meet regularly with their counterparts in the higher education associations of other denominations, seeking to understand the various forms of Christian higher education, to cooperate in joint efforts and to present to the Churches and the general public an example of joint ecumenical effort in Christian higher education.

[J. F. MURPHY]

HIGHER EDUCATION AND GOVERNMENT FUNDS

American higher education has been historically noted for its mix of public and private institutions, sponsorship and control of which range from large, publicly-supported research universities established by state legislatures with public governing boards to small liberal arts colleges privately supported by individual religious denominations or congregations. The influence of government, state and federal, extends across the entire range of such institutions and is exercised principally through financial support of students and institutions, and through direct and indirect regulation and control.

Support from the States. Financial support of institutions and of students by individual states and by the federal government has a long history. During the 17th century, for example, public assistance from the colonial government was the largest single source of revenues for the nation's oldest university, Harvard, a privately controlled institution. Since the earliest days of its existence the federal government has left primary responsibility for financial support of higher education to individual states and to private initiative. As a result the role of higher education in federal policy has tended to remain instrumental to other national priorities. In 1787, for example, the Northwest Ordinance earmarked income from the sale or rental of territorial lands to support the establishment of colleges, universities, and seminaries as an inducement to attract settlers. The Justin Morrill Acts of 1862 and 1890 sought to promote economic development of new states by authorizing the establishment of land-grant colleges with income from the sale of federal lands granted to the states in order to educate working classes in practical skills related to agriculture and mechanical arts. Even as recently as the late 1970s the movement to give taxpayers income tax credits for tuition payments was prompted largely by a perceived need for middle-income tax relief.

The primary responsibility of the states for direct government-funding of higher education as well as the institutional direction of that support is reflected in the fact that by 1975, 76 percent of all degree-credit students in American higher education were enrolled in the public-sector institutions of the fifty states. Nevertheless, federal financial support of both public and private institutions and their students has risen rapidly since World War II with the increased public perception of higher education as instrumental in the pursuit of social and economic goals of national policy.

Federal Support. The Serviceman's Readjustment Act of 1944, "GI Bill," established a precedent-setting relationship between equality of opportunity as a social policy and access to higher education as an instrument of that policy. In the GI Bill the target group of students eligible for financial support was World War II veterans from a much wider range of social classes and economic levels than was represented in the student bodies of American colleges and universities in pre-war years. By 1955, more than 2.2 million veterans, one out of seven, had taken advantage of the opportunity to study for a degree in public and private colleges and universities. The GI Bill was the forerunner of a series of laws designed to expand student access to higher education, culminating in the Higher Education Amendments of 1972, which in effect affirmed a federal policy of universal higher education and thereby acknowledged the right of all Americans to educational opportunity beyond elementary and secondary levels (*see* EDUCATION, HUMAN RIGHT TO). Subsequent legislative proposals for federal student-aid have indicated increasing concern with financial problems not only of student access to some higher education, but also of effective student choice among public and private institutions. This concern has been exacerbated by the persistent inflation of the 1970s, which has widened the gap between relatively high tuition costs of privately supported institutions and the lower tuition charges of state-financed colleges and universities.

Recipients of Federal Support. By the last half of the 1970s access to higher education became an established part of federal policies of equality of opportunity for racial minorities, women, the economically disadvantaged, the handicapped, and other target groups. In the 1979 federal budget the amount requested for undergraduate- and graduate-student assistance alone was well over 8.5 billion dollars, approximately four times the total federal appropriation for all purpose in higher education in 1963. The most common forms of federal aid to colleges and university students are direct grants and loans, subsidy of student employment, and subsidized bank loans for educational expenses. Including the major programs of student financial assistance the federal government funds more than 425 educational programs in 13 cabinet departments and other federal agencies. Although less federal spending is channelled directly to colleges and universities than to the students within those institutions, the growth in direct payments to institutions is substantial, having tripled between 1963 and 1974, from approximately 1.5 billion dollars to about 4.5 billion dollars.

Close to half these expenditures by the federal government are directed to research and development within educational institutions. The launching of Sputnik by the USSR in 1957 on the heels of the "cold war" raised fears of scientific and educational unpreparedness in the United States. The result was a sharp escalation in government support of basic and applied research in colleges and universities, which became further identified as resources for the solution of national problems. Federal spending for basic science and related graduate education grew from under 140 million dollars in 1953 to a peak of just under 3 billion dollars in 1967, declining thereafter to 2.2 billion dollars in 1975. It should be noted that research and development funds have tended to be concentrated among relatively few colleges and universities. A group of 100 universities, about $2/3$ public and $1/3$ private, whose membership varies only slightly from year to year, consistently receives over 85 percent of such funds. Much less federal funding is allocated to colleges and universities for improvement in the quality of undergraduate education, although at least some of the efforts of such agencies as the U.S. Office of Education, the Fund for the Improvement of Postsecondary Education, and the National Endowment for the Humanities are directed to improvements in the quality of programs and instruction in higher education.

Government Regulation. Government control and regulation of institutions of higher education are generally less direct in the U.S. than elsewhere. As indicated, the federal government has historically left the primary responsibility for creation, funding, and control of educational institutions to the states. The states in turn have typically exercised their prerogatives through establishment and funding of public colleges and universities

governed by boards separate from legislative and executive state agencies. Both state-aid and state-regulation of private colleges and universities, although varying considerably among states, have not been notably significant features of American higher education, with a possible exception of the widespread exemption from state and local taxation of property and revenues. Recently, however, federal regulations pertaining to federally-mandated social programs have begun to be applied to both public and private colleges and universities. Colleges and universities, for example, are now responsible for compliance with regulations governing: labor relations; equal opportunity and affirmative action in hiring of minorities, women and the handicapped; operation of pension plans; and standards of occupational health and safety and of environmental protection. However, corresponding financial assistance to meet the cost of complying with such regulations has not generally accompanied the growth in regulation.

For purposes of both federal financial assistance and regulation by the federal government Church-related colleges and universities generally have rights and responsibilities similar to those of other private institutions. A succession of decisions in federal courts supports the notion that the religious influence in Church-related colleges and universities is not so pervasive as to rule out all constitutional eligibility for federal funding. Hence, unlike most programs in religious elementary and secondary schools, many activities of Church-related colleges and universities can qualify for relevant federal financial assistance by meeting appropriate tests of religious neutrality. State constitutions and courts, however, vary considerably in restrictions placed upon the eligibility of these institutions for state financial assistance.

See also CHURCH AND STATE (U.S.); HIGHER EDUCATION, CHURCH AND.

[E. BARTELL]

HILDEBRAND, DIETRICH VON

Catholic philosopher and moral theologian, outspoken defender of traditional Catholic teaching, b. in Italy, 1889, d. New Rochelle, N.Y., Jan. 30, 1977. His father Adolph (1847–1921) was a sculptor, his paternal grandfather Bruno (1812–78), a political economist. Von Hildebrand received his doctorate in philosophy from the University of Göttingen, Germany (1912), was converted to Catholicism in 1914, and was a professor on the faculty of the University of Munich from 1924. When Hitler came to power in 1933 von Hildebrand, known to be anti-Nazi, was forced to flee to Florence. Later he joined the faculty of the University of Vienna, but when Austria fell he escaped and joined the faculty of the Catholic University of Toulouse, France. With the fall of France he went to Spain and then to the U.S. where he joined the Fordham University faculty in 1942. He was professor of philosophy there until his retirement in 1960. By the time he had become emeritus he had already written 30 books and more than 100 articles on philosophy and morality. Among his main works *Christian Ethics* (1952) and *True Morality and Its Counterfeits* (1955) were especially praised. In the era of Vatican II in quick succession appeared his *The Sacred Heart* (1965) and *Man and Woman* (1966), as well as two books coauthored by his wife (the former Alice Jourdain), a philosophy teacher at Hunter College: *The*

Art of Living (1965) and *Morality and Situation Ethics* (1966). Next came his strong summons to Catholic conservatives, *Trojan Horse in the City of God* (1967), a refutation of secularism and what he described as contemporary errors and horrors. Later he published his defense of Paul VI's encyclical *Humanae vitae* (1969) in his *In Defense of Purity* (1970) and *Celibacy and the Crisis of Faith* (1971).

Von Hildebrand's early writings reflect three dominant influences: the phenomenology of his professor E. Husserl, his own conversion to Catholicism, and the ethical approach of M. Schelers. Von Hildebrand's later writings were an attempt to respond to what he considered the most serious crisis in the entire history of the Church. In an interview granted to E. Wakin (May 1969) he insisted there could be no change in the revealed doctrine of the Church, only development, in Newman's sense of making explicit what was implicit. While von Hildebrand rejoiced over Vatican II's attempts to vivify mere convention and eliminate bureaucratic legalism, he deplored such other results as the loss of a sense of the supernatural and the eagerness to cater to the values of a desacralized, dehumanized, and depersonalized world. Progressives, he maintained, absolutize current views and relativize traditional orthodoxy. The greatest service the Church can render the world is to help individual souls progress in sanctity. St. Francis of Assisi is the model; he did not set out to change the world, but to follow Christ; by doing that, he did change the world. What is needed are a few great saints who would reverse all secularist and liberal trends and reinstate the true orthodox faith.

Bibliography: E. WAKIN, *U.S. Catholic* 34 (1969) 6–13.

[E. J. DILLON]

HINDUISM, CHURCH AND

Rather than describe the historical or sociological relationships between Hinduism and the Church, this article surveys the change taking place in the understanding of the problem itself. An exposition of three major facts linked to this change leads to an indication of three major features of the new understanding. Two introductory remarks are needed to situate the analysis. (1) "India" cannot refer to Hindu India alone (Islam and many other religions are very much alive), nor can "the Church" mean Roman Catholicism only (about fifty percent of Indian Christians profess allegiance to Rome). (2) The changes to be described are still too recent to have reached the majority of the people. Most people, Hindus and Christians alike, still hold to the "old" views; there are even fundamentalist revivals on both sides. Yet the signs of the times point in the direction explored here.

Three Factors for Change. About a century ago, Hindus saw Hinduism as the many-faceted, eternal, and everlasting order, *sanātana dharma*, while Christians saw it as a "false religion." On the other hand, while Christians saw the Church as the depositary of divine Revelation, center of the only true, universal, and transcultural religion, Hindus saw Christianity merely as another foreign "religion" attempting to supplant Hinduism. This situation, grossly oversimplified for heuristic purposes, has been undermined by three factors.

(1) *Culture Consciousness.* Since World War I the increasing conviction has arisen that no human culture, including its religious component, can encompass the universal range of human experience. Though the Church stresses her divine origin and divine mandate, the necessity of emphasizing her own historicity in order to affirm her identity makes it clear that she cannot disentangle herself from her own cultural patterns. This consciousness has awakened worldwide: other religions and cultures are better known and appreciated; similarities and differences are being seen in more irenic perspectives. Tolerance begins to appear not only as a practical necessity but as a theoretical virtue. "Pluralism" is another key word, though rather ambivalent. By and large, "exclusivity," once considered almost the criterion of truth, a seal of divine Revelation ("we" and "only we" have the full truth, salvation, grace, divine assistance, etc.), no longer has such positive appeal. On the contrary it seems that when something can be proven to be universally human, it is now believed to be true and valid.

(2) *The Independence of the Indian Subcontinent.* Independence (1947) has contributed effectively to the change of perspective in the mutual evaluations of Hinduism and Christianity in general. The Indian Constitution declared India a "secular state": religions would be free but no religion would have any privilege, nor would the religious factor influence the running of state affairs. Thus the de facto linking of Britain and the Western powers with Christianity began slowly to disappear, changing the perspective on the problem. Relations between Hinduism and the Church more and more became simply dealings between concrete institutions. Christians had begun to realize that a global conversion to Christianity was unlikely. Furthermore, the relative number of Christians was rapidly decreasing vis à vis the growth of world population. The Church, which once represented a majority of people and wielded much power, was now becoming a minor factor in world affairs. In India, as elsewhere, the aspect of service to humanity was coming increasingly to the fore; conversion to her fold is no longer the Church's major driving force, and the spiritual aspect of *metanoia* is acquiring its central importance.

Emphasis is laid upon the fact that one should not cease to be Indian in becoming Christian. But as the distinction Indian/Hindu is subtle or nonexistent for a Hindu, the Hinduization of the Church proceeded at a greater pace than before. "Acculturation," "accommodation" or "adaptation" remains one of the most acute problems in the Church today (*see* INCULTURATION, THEOLOGICAL). The distinction between religion and culture has become very blurred. In a period of world decolonization, a new reflection on the nature of Hinduism and the Church was bound to come. The process is still very much alive.

(3) *Vatican Council II* (1963–65). For the first time in conciliar history an ecumenical council emphasized the harmony among the religious urges of mankind and the positive features of the different religions of the world. Vatican II documents stress that "all men are called to the new People of God," (*Lumen gentium* 13) and even quote St. John Chrysostom, saying: "He who sits in Rome knows that the Indians are his members" (ibid.). The same document recognizes various degrees of belonging to this People, and that religions are related to it in diverse ways (ibid. 16), though any truth and good among the nations is held to be "an evangelical preparation" (ibid.). The Declaration on the Relation of the

Church to Non-Christian Religions acknowledges that since ancient times there has been "a certain perception of the mysterious power" that hovers over cosmic and human events (*Nostra aetate* 2). Hinduism is described in this text as the contemplation of divine Mystery expressed in the inextinguishable fecundity of myths and explored by deep philosophical effort; Hinduism seeks liberation through an ascetic way of life, profound meditation, or loving confidence in God (ibid.). Here again, "The Catholic Church does not reject anything which is true and holy in these religions," and Catholics should even "acknowledge, preserve and promote the spiritual goods" of other religious traditions (ibid.).

In short, since the turn of the century there has been a change in the self-understanding of Man's religiousness. The confluence of the aforementioned three factors has contributed to the three changes now to be enumerated.

Three Features of New Understanding. Rather than entering into controversial issues, we shall describe the present situation as it appears to a phenomenological analysis.

1. *Convergence of Purpose.* Most scholars in the matter agree that the fundamental dimension of the Church is Mystery, Sacrament, be this interpreted as the Mystical Body of the risen Christ, the Eucharist, Human Service or even the Urge to Liberation. Worth remembering is the insistence with which Pius XII changed the word "Christianity" in all his documentary drafts to the word "Church." The relationship of the Church with Hinduism in this case is not primarily that of one religion or ideology to another religion or way of life, but that of two (or more) living organisms dealing with common problems, seen from different viewpoints, solved perhaps by complementary means. The relationship transcends the sociological realm of being different communities and becomes instead one of convening to explore areas of possible common effort for the *liberation*—both *sōtēria* and *moksha*—of Man. The simile of the salt does not tell Christians to transform all into salt, but to collaborate in order to enhance the quality of human life.

2. *Openness to Dialogue.* "Hinduism" is an existential term linking a bundle of religions which originated in the Subcontinent and have not repudiated Hinduism's mythical origin. Many contemporary Hindu schools and a prevailing Hindu mentality no longer necessarily see the Church as a menace to their existence, although they do not believe she is what she claims to be. The relationship is not between two compact blocs, because Hinduism has hardly ever been compact and because the Church now seems to present as many faces as does Hinduism itself. This has permitted the two to enter into fruitful dialogue on the doctrinal level, leading to better mutual understanding, even to mutual fertilization. Despite exceptions, the general tone seems to be one of mutual curiosity in exploring an unknown future.

3. *Force of Nostra Aetate.* One of the few condemnations issuing from Vatican II (*Ecclesia reprobat*) occurs in its Declaration on the Relationship of the Church to Non-Christian Religions, precisely condemning discrimination against or harassment of any human being because of race, color, class, or religion (*Nostra aetate* 5). This practically amounts to official recognition of religious pluralism. Over against this background three events may help situate the Church in her actual relations with Hinduism in the post-Vatican II era.

(a) In 1964 the 38th International Eucharistic Congress was celebrated in Bombay with the presence of Pope Paul VI, the vice-president of India, and other religious and civil authorities. It was a public recognition that the Church should not be identified with an aggressive "religion" trying to undermine the Hindu way of life. The concurrent theological congress addressed itself to "Christian Revelation and Non-Christian Religions." The congress triggered some reactions that helped to clarify issues as well as deepen problems.

(b) In 1969 the *All-India Seminar on the Church in India Today* (prepared since the *All-India Study Week*, "Indian Culture and the Fulness of Christ" celebrated in Madras in 1956), represented the affirmation of the Church in contemporary India and the sociological acceptance of the status quo within a secular state. The seminar stressed not only the vitality of the Church but her role in India in peaceful ecumenical and universal collaboration for the nation and the world. Everywhere, voices were raised against any ghettoizing mentality, either in theory or in practice.

(c) In 1971 within the more popular celebrations of the 19th centenary of the death of St. Thomas, the Apostle of India, an International Theological Conference was convened in Nagpur. There, perhaps for the first time in the history of the Roman Church, Indian voices predominated and the new understanding of the Church was discussed with all the theological details for bridging the gulf between an exclusivistic Church, having the monopoly on truth, and an amorphous one, having no other mission than to help the development of the nation. The general topic was evangelization. As a follow-up of this Congress and of the 1969 seminar, a "Research Seminar on Non-Biblical Scriptures" took place in 1974 and in 1976 two further seminars on the "Ministries in the Church in India"—the first an effort *ad extra*, and the second an essay to look *ad intra*. Both meetings raised controversy and can be considered milestones on the way of the Church in her search for identity among the peoples of the world—in this case the peoples of India.

Bibliography: The bibliography is immense. Preference has been given to Indian publications but doctrinal studies on particular issues have in general been disregarded. D. S. AMALORPAVADASS, ed., *Research Seminar on Non-Biblical Scriptures* (National Biblical Catechetical and Liturgical Centre, Bangalore 1974). Over thirty papers plus reports on the several workshops. Most, if not all the authors, were Roman Catholics living in India. "No Scripture can be identified with the Word of God as such, which is a living reality" (p. 669). The official declaration speaks of "a radical reorientation of the Indian Church" (p. 693). *Ministries in the Church in India. Research Seminar and Pastoral Consultation* (New Delhi, C.B.C.I. Centre, 1976). Over thirty research papers and reports of the several workshops, followed by a "Pastoral Consultation." "The Church, like her Lord and Master, . . . has been aware from the very beginning of her existence that she is a serving community and that her mission is to be at the service of the world" (Preamble of the conclusion of the Research Seminar p. 511). G. H. ANDERSON, *Asian Voices in Christian Theology.* (Maryknoll, N.Y. 1976). Although India is only one of the nine countries studied, the book situates the Christian Protestant reflection of Asian theology today. R. BOYD, *An Introduction to Indian Christian Theology* (Madras: The Diocesan Press 1969). J. B. CHETHIMATTAM, ed., *Unique and Universal. An Introduction to Indian Theology* (Centre for the Study of World Religions, Dharmaran College, Bangalore 1972). Seventeen essays reflecting on the meaning of theologizing in an Indian context today. J. DESROCHES, *Christ the Liberator* (Centre for Social Action, Bangalore 1977). D. J. ELWOOD, ed., *What Asian Christians Are Thinking. A Theological Source Book* (New Day Publ., Quezon City, Philippines 1976). Essays by thirty Asian Christians covering topics from theology in Asia to Man and Nature, God and Revelation, Religious Pluralism and Theologies of Mission, Development and Liberation. G. GISPERT-SAUCH, ed., *God's Word among Men. Theological Essays in Honour of Joseph Putz, SJ* (Vidyajyoti, Institute of Religious Studies, Delhi 1973).

Festschrift in honor of four European Jesuits: J. Putz, J. Bayart, J. Volcksert and P. De Letter, who have spent their lives in India as theologians. Twenty-two authors write on the meaning of Listening, Reflecting, Contemplating, or Proclaiming the Word. C. HARGREAVES, *Asian Christian Thinking. Studies in a Metaphor and its Message* (Indian Society for Promoting Chrisian Knowledge, Delhi; Christian Literature Society, Madras; Lucknow Publishing House, Lucknow; Zodiac Press, Delhi 1972). N. MINZ, *Mahatma Gandhi and Hindu-Christian Dialogue* (The Christian Literature Society, Madras 1970). J. NEUNER, ed., *Christian Revelation and World Religions*. Introduction by J. Neuner, contributions by H. Küng, P. Fransen, J. Masson, R. Panikkar (London 1967). Contains the four papers delivered at the Theological Conference of the Eucharistic Congress in Bombay, plus an Introduction and the Conclusions of the Conference. "The Christian attitude is not one of judgement or condemnation; it is an attitude of witnessing, and prayer for and with the world" (p. 24). R. PANIKKAR, *Māyā e Apocalisse. L'incontro dell'Induismo e del Cristianesimo* (Rome 1966); *Kerygma und Indien. Zur heilsgeschichtlichen Problematik der christlichen Begegnung mit Indien* (Hamburg 1967). PUNJABI UNIVERSITY, Patiala. *Christianity.* Contributors: Mathew John, V. C. Samuel, Parmananda Divarkar, R. Panikkar. Five Indian Christians write on (1) the Bible; (2) the Faith; (3) Christianity, Ethics; (4) Prayer, Worship and Mystical Experience; (5) Christianity and World Religions, following the identical format of the four other books in the series, the others being on Hinduism, Buddhism, Islam and Sikhism. J. PATHRAPANKAL, ed., *Service and Salvation. Nagpur Theological Conference on Evangelization.* (Theological Publications in India, Bangalore 1973). Thirty-seven presentations from the point of view of Mission, Bible, Theology of World Religions, Evangelization, and Dialogue, by Roman Catholic authors. T. PAUL, ed., *The Emerging Culture in India. Father Zacharias Lectures 1974* (Pontifical Institute of Theology and Philosophy, Alwaye, Kerala 1975). A dozen essays on the problem of Modern Culture in India, from different perspectives. M. M. THOMAS, *The Acknowledged Christ of the Indian Renanaissance.* (The Christian Institute for the Study of Religion and Society, Bangalore 1970).

[R. PANIKKAR]

HISPANIC AFFAIRS, NCCB/USCC SECRETARIAT FOR

The essential mission of the Secretariat for Hispanic Affairs is to assist the National Conference of Catholic Bishops (NCCB) and the United States Catholic Conference (USCC) in responding to the pastoral needs of Hispanics. The Secretariat also serves as staff to the Bishops' Ad Hoc Committee for Hispanic Affairs.

Archbishop Robert E. Lucey had established an office for Hispanics in San Antonio in 1945. In 1968 that office was moved to the Bishops' Conference in Washington, D.C. to provide nationwide service. Under its director, Pablo Sedillo, Jr., this Division for the Spanish-speaking within the Dept. of Social Development experienced a growth in staff and a change in direction from merely social and material assistance to an integral pastoral approach. In 1974, the Division was elevated to a National Secretariat for the Spanish speaking and in 1978 the name was changed to the NCCB/USCC Secretariat for Hispanic Affairs. These changes underscore the importance and growing work of the National office.

The Secretariat organized and coordinated two historic National *Encuentros* (meetings) in 1972 and 1977 and helped with more than 30 regional and diocesan *Encuentros* in the intervening years. Between 1972 and 1977 the Secretariat actively helped in the establishment of more than 100 diocesan offices for Hispanics and the organization of the country into six Hispanic regional offices: Northeast, Southeast, Midwest, Northwest, Southeast, and Far West. The Secretariat has pursued a process of concientization of Hispanics to their values and potential, education in faith, and promotion of lay leadership. It has provided services to dioceses and regions in pastoral planning, migrant-farmworker ministry, workshops in the formation of basic Christian communities, and other assistance in research, confer-

ences, and publications to help the promotion and pastoral development of Hispanics.

To continue its work the Secretariat now consists of five professional staff members: Director, Research Assistant, Pastoral Specialist, Migrant Specialist, and Communications/Education Specialist. Together they carry out the task of advocacy within the various structures of the Bishops' Conference, especially in what refers to the implementation of the *II Encuentro Nacional Hispano de Pastoral*. The coordination of the Hispanic apostolate at the national level is carried out by maintaining close communication and periodic meetings with the six Hispanic regional offices. They in turn help coordinate the work of the diocesan offices for Hispanics. The task of coordination also includes maintaining communications with such Hispanic apostolic movements as the Spanish Cursillo and Movimiento Familiar Cristiano (MFC), Hispanic national organizations such as PADRES, Hermanas, and the newly formed National Hispanic Youth Task Force, as well as such other institutes as the Mexican American Cultural Center (MACC) in San Antonio, the Northeast Pastoral Institute in New York and the Midwest Hispanic Institute at Mundelein College, Chicago.

See also HISPANICS IN THE U.S.   [M. L. GASTÓN]

HISPANICS IN THE U.S.

By "Hispanics" or *Hispanos* are understood persons who themselves or whose parents and/or ancestors are of Mexican, Chicano, Puerto Rican, Cuban, Dominican, Central or South American, or Spanish descent. Although such other terms as *Latino* and "Latin American" are still in use, "Hispanics" has become the most acceptable, all-inclusive designation for the second largest identifiable minority in the United States.

Estimates of the number of Hispanics now in the U.S. range from the figure of 12 million, as reported by the U.S. Census Bureau in 1975 (correcting the extremely low and widely contested figure of 9 million shown in the 1970 census), to the more commonly accepted figure of 16 million. But neither figure takes into account Puerto Ricans, who are U.S. citizens and number around three million. In addition there are some 3 million persons in the country without legal documentation, commonly called "illegal aliens" (the preferred term is "undocumented workers" or "undocumented immigrants"). In all, therefore, there are close to 20 million persons in the U.S. who may be identified as Hispanic Americans. Comparison of these figures with the 1965-estimate of 6 million makes it evident that the Hispanic population has increased considerably in the last 10–15 years through births and immigration and that the increase will continue. Not surprisingly, then, population experts have suggested that by 1990 sixty-seven percent of the U.S. population will be of Hispanic background.

The present Hispanic population divides as follows according to origin: 57 percent Mexican; 16 percent Puerto Rican; 7 percent Cuban; 7 percent Central or South American; and 13 percent Spanish or other Spanish-speaking. Though Hispanics share many elements of culture including a common language, similar values, customs, and religion, each major group has its own distinct characteristics.

Mexican Americans. The people longest in the U.S. are those members of the Mexican-American population who call themselves *Hispanos* or "Spanish Americans." These are the descendants of the original Spanish settlers who came to New Mexico in 1598, to Texas in the 17th century, and to California beginning with the start of the Franciscan missions in 1769. When the Southwest was taken away from Mexico in 1848, there were 75,000 settlers in that vast territory—60,000 in New Mexico, 10,000 in California, and 5,000 in Texas. They have been close-knit people, their lives circumscribed by the local village and the extended-family group; their isolation from the Anglo-American community led to the preservation of old customs to a greater degree than among other Hispanic groups. But the growth of industrialization in the Southwest and the tremendous increase of the Mexican population in that area has led increasingly to the grouping of these people with the whole Mexican-American population in the Southwest.

The largest tide of Mexicans coming to the U.S. occurred during the Mexican Revolution (1808–21), the bloodiest civil war in this hemisphere. Hundreds of thousands of refugees were driven across the border by the tides of war. In the U.S. millions of acres of land in the West had come under irrigation, the railroads were being built, and mining areas were opening—all of which created a great need for labor. The World Wars added to the demand for workers. Subsequently the population explosion in Mexico and the continuing demand of the U.S. economic system for cheap labor have continued to keep the tide of immigrants flowing. About half of the early 5 million residents of Mexican descent live in Texas and most of the remainder in other Southwestern states. Today, every 5th Texan is of Mexican origin. Los Angeles has 1.5 million Mexican Americans and, after Mexico City, is the second largest "Mexican" city. Although it is true that the Southwest is where most Mexican Americans live, there are Mexican Americans in the Midwest, Northeast, and the Southeast, especially where families drop out of the migrant streams to settle down. In Chicago there are now more Mexican Americans then Puerto Ricans.

Many Mexican Americans have made considerable progress in education, social mobility, in the professions, and in politics—electing their own candidates to offices on local, state, and national levels. In the Catholic Church, five of the eight Hispanic bishops are of Mexican-American descent. Yet of all the Hispanic groups Mexican Americans are still the ones with the greatest rural population and the lowest educational levels (23 percent of persons 25 years or over have completed less than 5 years of school). They are second only to the Puerto Ricans in percentage of families earning less than the poverty income of $5,000 annually. Many of them remain migrant agricultural workers, suffering under wretched housing and working conditions, police brutality, and continued discrimination. Because of the violent discrimination which the Mexican Americans had suffered over 130 years as a "conquered people," as some historians labeled them, many had almost come to accept the inferiority which had been enforced upon them for so long. Only in recent years have they begun to discover their history, to see themselves as a worthy and unique people, and to demand the dignity and respect due them.

Puerto Ricans. The second largest group of Hispanics in the U.S. began migrating to the mainland when the U.S. took over the Island of Puerto Rico after the Spanish-American War in 1899. After citizenship was conferred on Puerto Ricans in 1917, many were recruited to work in war industries and others were inducted into military service. The great migration began, however, after World War II and continued through 1968. Then the flow began to reverse: between 1972 and 1976 a total of 200,000 returned to the island; in 1977 a net, return-migration of 40,000 was recorded.

The reasons the Puerto Ricans came to the mainland were economic. A mere 35 years after the U.S. took over the island in 1899, fully 80 percent of the land ownership had passed into North-American hands. Without land there was little to keep the Puerto Rican peasant back home. Further, this small island had become overpopulated with a ratio of 900 persons per square mile. Today Puerto Ricans are in every state of the union, with the heaviest concentrations in New York City (1,000,000), Chicago (about 250,000), and other Northeastern cities.

The Puerto Ricans are the poorest Hispanic ethnic group in America. The income of 38.8 percent of Puerto Rican families falls below the poverty level. Puerto Ricans share with Mexican Americans the deep wound of oppression and of never having led self-determined lives. Puerto Rico has never been an independent country, but went from Spanish subjugation to a discriminatory existence under U.S. rule. Some of the problems encountered by the majority of Puerto Ricans who are urban dwellers are unemployment, discrimination, lack of good, bilingual education, poor housing, and language and cultural barriers caused by lack of respect for their cultural values and traditions.

Cubans. The history of Americans of Cuban origin goes back to the 19th century. Cuban colonies have existed in the U.S., especially in the Tampa, Fla. area, since the beginning of Cuba's struggle for independence from Spain in 1868. In fact Cubans had been on the mainland since the founding of St. Augustine, Fla. in 1565, because this settlement had strong ties with Cuba until Florida was taken over by the U.S. in 1821. By 1924 more than 5,000 Cuban immigrants were reported. The unrest and persecution in Cuba under President Fulgencio Batista brought thousands to the U.S. in the decade ending in 1959; however, it was not until Fidel Castro seized power in Cuba in 1959 that the major exodus began. Since 1959 about 10 percent of Cuba's population has left the island, with 90 percent ending up in the United States. From 1959 to 1977 nearly 700,000 Cubans have legally migrated to the U.S., by 1980 it is estimated that close to 950,000 persons of Cuban origin or descent will be U.S. residents. The Eastern-seaboard states have attracted the bulk of Cuban migration, close to 85 percent. About 50 percent of the Cubans settled in South Florida, 30 percent in the New York-New Jersey area, 8 percent in California, 7 percent in Chicago and 4 percent in Puerto Rico. The rest are scattered throughout the nation.

Contrary to popular belief, Cuban immigrants were not all of the upper middle class. In fact blue-collar workers form a larger proportion in the exodus than in the population still in Cuba. Among the refugees 35.5 percent were blue-collar workers; when the agricultural workers and fishermen are added, Cubans of this economic level make up 41.3 percent. The Cubans are the oldest Hispanic population, with a median age of

37.7, eight years older than the general U.S. median (29). The median age for Mexican Americans is 20.8 and for Puerto Ricans 20.4. Of the three major Hispanic groups in the U.S., the Cubans have the highest median income per family—$11,773. One reason is that Cubans have the highest percentage of women in the work force, as well as the highest proportion of professional and technical workers.

Others of Hispanic Origin. Besides these three major groups, there are close to two million other Hispanics in the U.S.; of these 80,000 are of Central and South American origin and 1.3 million are from "other Spanish" origin. Included in these two categories are some 400,000 Dominicans, living mainly in the Northeast, and tens of thousands of Colombians, Argentinians, Ecuadorians, Salvatorians, and sizable colonies from every other Latin-American nation. These immigrants share many of the characteristics of the three major groups discussed above, as well as those religious and cultural values treated below.

Cultural and Religious Values. Although Hispanics are not a completely homogeneous population, they share many elements of culture, including a common language, similar values and customs, and one religion.

The Family. One of the most cherished of Hispanic values is the family, which in turn is the preserver of many other traditional values: a marked degree of appreciation and love of children, a special love for the mother, a deep reverence and compassion for the aged. Hospitality is an art learned as a matter of course in the Hispanic homes and is a genuine concern for the visitor and often for the stranger. *El honor* of the person and the family is still a strong force and more than likely is a carry-over from the Spanish heritage.

Popular piety. Otherwise known as "popular religiosity," popular piety runs deep in Hispanic peoples. Each Hispanic people has its own devotion to Mary and the saints: Mary is popular under the titles of *Guadalupe, Pilar, Caridad del Cobre, San Juan de los Lagos*; Saint John the Baptist is the patron saint of Puerto Ricans. Popular religiosity should not be viewed simply as an emotive religious expression or an escape from commitment. Family religion (as opposed to the official ritual of the Church) can, at times, be seen as a subtle and quiet, yet strong protest against what a minority group may be tolerating in an atmosphere of oppression. Among Cubans and Puerto Ricans there has been a revival of practices especially of the Lacumi religion brought by slaves from Africa centuries ago, now called *Santeria* (a syncretism of polytheistic and Christian elements) and spiritism. Yet so much of Catholicism is interwoven into the culture of Hispanics that they retain a sense of loyalty even when they engage in such alien cults. Because of the lack of care and services that ideally would be provided by the Catholic Church, many Protestant groups, especially the store-front, evangelical sects, have made great inroads into Hispanic Catholicism. Yet the transition to Protestantism is never made, it seems, without a sense of loss.

The U.S. Church and Hispanics. The past five years have shown a mounting quest for unity and cooperation among the Hispanic groups, in order to obtain greater response from the State and from the Church in the areas of housing, bilingual education, political representation, and equal opportunity for employment and social services. As greater numbers of Hispanics became more educated and more conscious of their dignity and talents, there is greater participation and involvement in many areas of public life.

In 1972 the U.S. bishops sponsored the *I Encuentro Nacional*, a national meeting of 250 bishops and leaders in the Hispanic apostolate. The main purpose of the *Encuentro* was to study the situation of Hispanic Catholics, to present solutions to the many social and religious problems that beset them, and to try to formulate a coordinated pastoral plan on the national level. At the time there were only 30 diocesan offices for Hispanics and only one Hispanic bishop. In the years following the *I Encuentro*, the episcopal Division for the Spanish-Speaking was elevated to the Secretariat for Hispanic Affairs, both for the NCCB and the USCC. Increased services to migrant farmworkers were developed; the formation of *basic Christian communities among Hispanics was promoted (there are now more than 600 of these communities throughout the country). By 1978 offices for Hispanics had been created in 120 dioceses; there are now 8 Hispanic bishops and three Regional Hispanic Institutes providing education and leadership training. The country is divided into six Hispanic regions, four of which have full-time Regional Directors and offices. Hispanics were actively involved in the Call to Action Conference and in the International Eucharistic Congress, both in 1976.

In August 1977 the *II Encuentro Nacional Hispano de Pastoral* brought together 1,200 Hispanics, among them the eight Hispanic bishops and many other bishops and cardinals with large Hispanic populations in their dioceses, to evaluate and continue the pastoral planning begun at the *I Encuentro* in 1972.

Fruit of a nationwide, grass-roots consultation process, the Conclusions approved at the *II Encuentro* represented the voice of reflection groups involving more than 100,000 Hispanic Catholics throughout the country. The Conclusions dealing with evangelization, ministries, human rights, integral education, political responsibility, and unity in pluralism, contain the guidelines for the Hispanic ministry for years to come. A special task force of bishops from various NCCB and USCC Commitees has been formed to study the Conclusions and prepare recommendations for their implementation. One of the Conclusions already approved by the bishops was the establishment of a national Hispanic Youth Task Force to study the specific needs of the Hispanic youth for their evangelization.

In 1978 the Secretariat for Hispanic Affairs, which functions in conjunction with the Bishops' Ad Hoc Committee for Hispanic Affairs, organized an Ad Hoc National Advisory Committee to provide regular input from the various regions and from such national movements as Cursillo and Movimiento Familiar Cristiano, from such national organizations as *PADRES and *Las Hermanas, and other Hispanic institutes. All continue their involvement in coordinating and unifying pastoral service for Hispanics.

See also CULTURE, CHURCH AND; ETHNICITY; ETHNICS, RIGHTS OF.

Bibliography: Reports: Cuban National Planning Council (CNPC): P. J. PROBIAS and L. CASAL, "The Cuban Minority in the U.S.: Preliminary Report on Need Identification and Program Evaluation" (Boca Raton, Fla. 1973); A. HERNANDEZ, "The Cuban Minority in the U.S.: Final Report on Need Identification and Program Evaluation" (Washington, D.C. 1974). NCCB/USCC Secretariat for Hispanic Affairs: F. PONCE, "Hispanics in the United States: A Statistical Survey" (USCC Publ.

Office, Washington, D.C. 1977). U.S. Bureau of the Census—Current Population Reports: "Population Characteristics, Persons of Spanish Origin in the U.S. March 1973" Advance Report (Washington, D.C. 1973); "Population Characteristics, Persons of Spanish Origin in the U.S., March 1976" Advance Report (Washington, D.C. 1976). U.S. Commission on Civil Rights, Report, *Puerto Ricans in the Continental United States: An Uncertain Future* (Washington, D.C. 1976).

Studies: J. P. FITZPATRICK, *Puerto Rican-Americans: The Meaning of Migration to the Mainland* (Englewood Cliffs, N.J. 1971); *Hispanic Americans and the Church in the Northeast* (New York 1977). Mexican American Cultural Center (MACC): R. RAMIREZ, "La Familia, Channel of Faith and Culture" (San Antonio 1978); also other MACC publications on Mexican Americans. NCCB/USCC Secretariat for Hispanic Affairs: *Conclusions of the II Encuentro Nacional Hispano de Pastoral* (USCC Publ. Office, Washington, D.C. 1977); F. PONCE, "The Segundo Encuentro: A Challenge to the Church" (USCC Publ. Office, Washington, D.C. 1977); M. SANDOVAL, *Hispanic Challenges to the Church* (USCC Publ. Office, Washington, D.C., forthcoming [1978]).

[M. L. GASTÓN]

HISTORICAL THEOLOGY

Historical theology as a scholarly discipline is difficult to define. An acceptable working definition might be "the genetic study of Christian faith and doctrine" (Pelikan xiii). But such study has been differently designated in recent centuries, with varying content and consequent confusion. The time-honored term for the genetic history of faith and doctrine is *history of dogma*, where "dogma" is sometimes restricted to basic orthodox affirmations of the Christian Church (e.g., Trinity), sometimes used more loosely to include less central doctrines. In the latter sense, *history of theology* is a term consecrated by long usage. *History of Christian thought* adds to dogmas and doctrines what we call ethics, as well as Christian reflection on other problems both of thought and of society (e.g., politics or such philosophical issues as the problem of universals). *Historical theology* itself has been used not only for the genetic study of faith and doctrine, but for the entire study of the history of the Church, and occasionally for all those theological and paratheological disciplines whose method is historical. One understanding of *positive theology* has been the study of Scripture and church history. Some see *history of Christian doctrine* as the clearest term; for it distinguishes the field from general church history and from other branches of church history, e.g., history of liturgy or of Canon Law.

Development of the Discipline. The development of the discipline has been influenced from two quarters: (1) the movement of theology, especially its stances toward doctrinal continuity and change; (2) the evolution of the historical method. If the definitive Word God spoke in Christ has been deposited with the Church, then, as early orthodoxy saw it, doctrinal change could only be distortion. In consequence, historical theology in the patristic period is largely a matter of documenting the apostolic succession of dioceses and dogmas, and the cataloguing of sects and heresies, rather than the genetic study of the mainstream of Christian doctrine (cf., e.g., the works of Irenaeus, Eusebius, Epiphanius). In this context the prevailing theological attitude came to be enshrined in the classic axiom of Vincent of Lérins: "one must take the greatest possible care to believe what has been believed everywhere, ever, by everyone (*quod ubique, quod semper, quod ab omnibus creditum est*)" (*Commonitoria* 2). Tradition was the touchstone, innovation the automatic enemy. "Let nothing be innovated," Stephen I wrote to Cyprian, "beyond what has been handed down" (Cyprian, *Ep.* 74).

In the Middle Ages the *Sic et non* theological method (e.g., in Abelard and in its refinement by Aquinas) uncovered apparent contradictions in what had been accepted as patristic consensus. But the method is more important for the questions it raised than for the answers it proposed. It did not make use of historical criteria to account for the theological variations it was attempting to explain.

The Reformation controversies, while confronting the crucial allegation of a cleavage between primitive Christianity and the Catholic tradition, still pursued history polemically and evaluated change dogmatically. The task of historical scholarship was to prove that the adversary was guilty of innovation, had broken from authoritative Scripture or unvarying tradition, and therefore was doctrinally in error. In this sense the Reformation and Counter-Reformation outlook was closer to patristic and medieval than to modern historiography. On the other hand, a new temper and method were beginning to show: a more profound probing of the past and a growing sense of the pluralism of the past. In addition, the more objective methodology of Renaissance humanism, especially in the area of secular history, could not but affect, if only gradually, the confessional search for the Church's historical and doctrinal roots.

In the Enlightenment climate of the 18th century, both on the Continent and in Great Britain, the scholarly study of church history increasingly emancipated itself from ecclesiastical sponsorship and began to define itself as an academic discipline. But the golden age of historical theology was the 19th century. This for two reasons. First, research in Christian theology came to be dominated by the modern historical method, particularly by the historical investigation of the New Testament and of the development of dogma. Here some of the more influential figures, for all their recognized inadequacies, are Ferdinand Christian Baur, Johann Adam Möhler, John Henry Newman, and the most erudite and eloquent spokesman for historical theology, Adolf von Harnack, with his utter commitment to the historical method as the primary means for analyzing Christian doctrine. Each faced frankly and knowledgeably the inevitable tension between history and tradition or faith commitment. Second, critical editions of the source material, e.g., patristic texts, built more extensively and profoundly upon the remarkable editions produced in the previous three centuries, stimulated in part by many discoveries of lost works, particularly from the earliest period and in Oriental languages (e.g., Syriac, Georgian, Coptic). Such editions and discoveries have increased at a remarkable rate in the 20th century and historical research has been intensified through comprehensive study of individual writers and the history of individual words and ideas.

Present Views: Content and Method. The present task of historical theology is not easily expressed. The basic issues are content and method. For some, the subject matter is what the Church has believed, taught, and confessed on the basis of the Word of God. Besides admitted ambiguities ("Church," "Word of God"), such a definition restricts the discipline unduly to what the various confessions regard as dogmas or their equivalent. It is hard to see how historical theology can disregard the genetic study of theologoumena (e.g., speculations on the human knowledge or ignorance of

Christ, on religious freedom, on the human person as image of God) and moral issues (e.g., abortion, social justice). Historical theology's subject matter should be broad enough to embrace whatever in thought, belief, and life can properly be termed Christian and has a history.

Equally controversial is the discipline's methodology. For some scholars, the one legitimate demand on historical theology is that it be sound history, that it follow the canons of acceptable historical method, presumably determined nontheologically. Others would accept this for a *history of theology*, but are persuaded that a discipline which calls itself *historical theology* cannot disregard theological presuppositions that make for a ceaseless dialectical interaction between faith and history and in fact affect one's interpretation of the past.

The issue so put involves the relationship between historical and systematic or dogmatic theology. Contemporary reflection sees them as inseparable, yet distinct. For Gerhard Ebeling, these are two aspects of the same hermeneutic task of theology: their common concern is the concrete event of the Word of God; their common task to foster effective contemporary proclamation. Historical theology is primarily concerned to determine the *traditum*: what was handed down and how. Dogmatic theology focuses on the contemporary observance of the tradition, participates in the *actus tradendi*, the tradition of a present and continuous event. As essentially systematic, it must show how all genuine theological statements are necessarily related to one another and to the reality they bring to understanding. Historical theology exercises a "disturbing" function: it upsets established prejudices, forces the dogmatic theologian to face uncomfortable facts and forgotten truths.

Wolfhart Pannenberg argues that, since Christianity is essentially a process, a history, the tasks involved in describing the essence and truth of Christianity can only be performed within a historical theology, provided that, while remaining historical, it adopt a systematic approach. Such a historical theology, he believes, would end "the opposition between historical and systematic theology." In the present theological situation, however, a "special" systematic theology is necessary in addition to the historical disciplines.

Bibliography: G. EBELING, *Theology and Proclamation: Dialogue with Bultmann* (Philadelphia 1966) 22–31. W. PANNENBERG, *Theology and the Philosophy of Science* (Philadelphia 1976) 371–381, 418–420. J. PELIKAN, *Historical Theology: Continuity and Change in Christian Doctrine* (New York 1971). J. RATZINGER, *Das Problem der Dogmengeschichte in der Sicht der katholischen Theologie* (Cologne 1966). G. H. WILLIAMS, "Church History: From Historical Theology to the Theology of History," in A. S. NASH, ed., *Protestant Thought in the Twentieth Century: Whence and Whither?* (New York 1951) 145–178.

[W. J. BURGHARDT]

HISTORY, PHILOSOPHY AND THEOLOGY OF

The expression "philosophy of history" is here used to mean any comprehensive design for the entire course of history, like those proposed by Vico, Hegel, and Toynbee, whereas "theology of history" further specifies the design or plan by including God in the explanation. "Philosophy of history" is a term which is also sometimes used by philosophers to denote an examination of the historian's methods, especially in their hermeneutical, epistemological, and evaluative aspects. This "critical" philosophy of history, practically

undeveloped until impetus was given it by Dilthey, Croce, Collingwood, and others in the 20th century, has often been employed to refute and to criticize those philosophies or theologies of history that have proposed designs for the course of history. Philosophy of history in this second sense plays no role in the documents of Vatican Council II.

The Historical Perspective of Vatican II. The Council does not explicitly espouse any particular philosophy or theology which attempts to expose a design for the course of history. Nonetheless, the official documents of the Council take more notice of history than those of any previous council, and, hence, they at least implicitly deal with the process of the story of mankind. The Constitution on the Church, though it never loses sight of the transcendent nature of the Church, insists that the Church truly enters human history (*Lumen gentium* 8, 9). The introductory paragraphs of the Constitution on the Church in the Modern World even attempt an assessment of the current historical situation and venture the judgment that the human race has entered "a new age of history" (*Gaudium et spes* 4). This judgment concurs with, and probably reflects, the conviction Pope John XXIII expressed in *Humanae salutis*, his apostolic constitution, Dec. 25, 1961, convoking the Council, which stated that human society was "on the edge of a new era." Other documents of the Council, especially when they deal with real or seeming changes in doctrine and discipline, evince a similar awareness of historical context and process. The desire to bring the Church up to date and to make it more effective in the contemporary world was the pervasive theme of the Council, as the term *aggiornamento* suggests. Such a desire in itself indicated an awareness of historical and cultural change and made possible the Council's adoption of "accommodation to the times" as its theme. Previous councils tended to assess change negatively and, in principle, to resist it in the Church.

Vatican II's attention to history was a response to the more general application of historical methods and categories to the kind of study of religion that had gained great momentum in the 19th century, especially in Protestant circles, and that in the 20th century characterized biblical, patristic, and liturgical scholarship also among Catholics. The impetus for the Council's attention to history was, in fact, derived from such scholarship rather than from systematic theology, where a rather ahistorical Neo-Thomism prevailed for the most part. Simply by taking account of history, the Council virtually assumed the obligation to make some statements about its course or design. The pastoral nature of the Council and the fact that its decrees were documents formulated in committee precluded the possibility that any single point of view would prevail to the exclusion of others. Nonetheless, certain features of the Council's appreciation of history can be singled out as more typical than others.

Conciliar Evaluations of History. First of all, the Council assesses the course of history and the current "age" with considerable optimism, speaking of its social, scientific, technological "progress" (cf. *Gravissimum educationis* Introd. and 1; *Apostolicam actuositatem* 1; *Gaudium et spes* 57. For qualification of this optimism cf. *Apostolicam actuositatem* 7; *Presbyterorum ordinis* 17 and 22; *Gaudium et spes* 10, 15, and 37). Although it recognizes the ambiguities and ambivalence of the human condition, it gives relatively little support to those philosophies or theologies of history that view the story of mankind as a decline from an earlier and better condition. Secondly, the Council consistently maintains that the course of history is under providential guidance (*Lumen gentium* 23) and it occasionally employs the Eusebian description of the historical process as a "preparation for the Gospel" (*Lumen gentium* 16), as an unfolding of a divine plan, which presumably has a beginning, middle, and end (*Dei Verbum* 2–3, 11, 14). The Council asserts, for instance, that Christ is the key, the center, and the purpose of the whole of human history (*Gaudium et spes* 10). Eschatological expectations for history are expressed in that same document (ibid. 39, 45). Thirdly, Vatican II evidences a strong sense of continuity with the past and a desire to remain faithful to it. Continuity of faith, of spiritual gift, and of evangelical tradition from the primitive Church to the present is often asserted, despite recognition that considerable change has taken place through the centuries (*Lumen gentium* 9, 21, 23, 33, 39, 50, 51; *Perfectae caritatis* 1, 9; *Apostolicam actuositatem* 8; *Ad gentes* 5). Fourthly, the Council often makes use of forward-looking terms like progress, evolution, and maturation to describe how continuity has been maintained while change has occurred (*Gaudium et spes* 6, 54; cf. above on optimism). When these terms are applied to doctrine, (*Lumen gentium* 12; 55; *Unitatis redintegratio* 24; *Optatam totius* 11; *Dei Verbum* 7; *Apostolicam actuositatem* 3; *Dignitatis humanae* 1, 9, 12; *Gaudium et spes* 63) they quite inevitably suggest the viewpoint of scholars influenced by Newman's Essay on the *Development of Christian Doctrine* and by the renewed interest in the doctrine of the Mystical Body of Christ, which was widespread in Catholic circles for several decades before the convocation of the Council. In both instances, an organic model of change is implied. The evolutionary model for the development of the cosmos expounded by Teilhard de Chardin was probably also an influence (cf. *Gaudium et spes* 39, 45).

Thus there is considerable effort in the documents of the Council to break away from a style of historical thinking which would see the Church as immune to process or change, as if it moved through history unaffected by history. This effort in some instances even intimates a breakdown of the traditional dichotomy in ecclesiastical documents between the Church and the Christian people, which allowed the Church to be without fault and untouched by history while the Christian people sinned and were subject to the "injuries of time." The use of terms like "the People of God" to designate the Church, especially in *Lumen gentium*, is seen by some scholars as indicating this change in mentality.

By acknowledging the phenomenon of historical change and by legislating or encouraging a number of modifications in liturgy and discipline, the Council in effect raises the problem of how any given change might be tested as authentically continuous with the tradition in question. The Council responds to this practical and theological problem only generically by insisting upon the necessity of remaining faithful to the original inspiration of the tradition. It thus promoted experimentation in practice and it imposed upon theologians in an urgent way the task of further reflection upon this aspect of philosophy or theology of history.

Bibliography: L. J. O'DONOVAN, "Was Vatican II Evolutionary?" ThSt 36 (1975) 493–502. J. W. O'MALLEY, "Reform, Historical Consciousness, and Vatican II's Aggiornamento," ThSt 32 (1971) 573–601.

[J. W. O'MALLEY]

HISTORY OF RELIGIONS

History of religions, though its concerns had been anticipated by ancient historians and ethnographers, medieval chroniclers of Islam's expansion into the Mediterranean, explorers and the missionaries who followed in their wake, and *philosophes* of the Enlightenment, only emerged as a distinct academic field in the late 19th century. The burst of activity in Oriental studies and linguistics sparked a thorough reconsideration of religion and mythology. Through his own work (editing and translating Sanskrit texts), his editorial efforts (the *Sacred Books of the East* series), and his advocacy of the new "Science of Religions" (*Religionswissenschaft*) F. Max Müller (1823–1900) provided a decisive impetus. His own theories (on solar mythology and on religion as a "disease of language," e.g.) have fallen from favor, but Müller's goals of organizing the field and specifying its methodology remain primary concerns.

Because of its scope: "nothing short of scholarly inquiry into the nature and structure of the religious experience of the human race and its diverse manifestations in history" (J. Kitagawa), history of religions has always had to rely upon the findings of other disciplines. Mircea Eliade's survey of the field since 1912, in which the major contributions of sociology, anthropology, and psychology are duly noted, highlights the degree of that dependence. In an attempt to secure the position of his field, Eliade describes it as a "total discipline" which integrates the results obtained by other approaches but which, unlike them, seeks to bring out the "autonomous value" of religious phenomena as "spiritual creations." Like others in the field, Eliade claims that the meaning of religious phenomena is not exhausted by anthropological, psychological, or sociological interpretations; it remains to interpret religious phenomena *as such*. That involves understanding both of particular historical manifestations and of "the transhistorical content a religious datum reveals throughout history" (Eliade). History of religions seeks to unite historical and systematic perspectives on its subject matter.

Attempts to achieve that blend have provoked various criticisms. Area specialists have eyed historians of religions' transhistorical categories warily and have sometimes questioned their philological training. G. van der Leeuw, C. J. Bleeker, and other phenomenologists of religions have split off their pursuit of systematic categories from the purely historical study of religions. Historians of religions themselves, building on the notion that a discipline is defined by a distinct methodology, have criticized the idea of a "total discipline" as an imprecise umbrella designation with no clear research agenda.

The relationship of history of religions to theological disciplines has also been broached. Both H. Kraemer and S. Radharkrishnan, for example, have questioned whether the value-free stance of history of religions is possible or even desirable; they would substitute a perspective on other religions which explicitly incorporates the observer's own viewpoint as a standard for comparison. Van der Leeuw sees his work as a phenomenologist as propaedeutic to his task as a theologian. Others, like F.

Heiler, have seen history of religions as promoting the unity of all religious traditions. Throughout this century the oppositions between historical and systematic understanding and between objectivity and involvement have prevented a consensus on the scope and method of the field from emerging. As a result, several schools, each with its own vision of the field, have dominated. At Chicago, J. Wach, his student J. Kitagawa, and Eliade have advocated the integral understanding of religious data; in Holland van der Leeuw and Bleeker have favored the phenomenological approach; Scandinavian scholars have stressed the interdependence of myth and ritual and the strict historical approach.

Despite the lack of consensus, certain accomplishments can be noted. From his own distinctive approach Eliade himself has produced masterful studies of yoga and shamanism. His elucidation of the role of myths, rites and symbols in the creation of sacred space and sacred time has had wide influence and has motivated a number of specific studies. The phenomenologists have proposed a rich and nuanced classification of religious phenomena, though they have risked blurring the distinctiveness of specific historical forms. By rooting his interest in the present, rather than in Eliade's determinative primordial past, W. C. Smith has effectively portrayed the deep personal impact and continuing vitality of religious traditions as lived. Specific research animated by work in history of religions can be found in countless journals and monographs, but until Müller's original goals are more fully accomplished their cumulative impression will be diminished as history of religions remains "an area of scholarly pursuit in search for a definition of itself" (P. Ashby).

The documents of Vatican Council II have prompted a greater Catholic attention to this discipline (cf., e.g., *Lumen gentium* 16; *Gaudium et spes* 92; *Ad gentes* 26; *Nostra aetate* 2).

See also MISSIONARY FORMATION.

Bibliography: Works on method: P. H. ASHBY, "The History of Religions," in P. RAMSEY, ed., *Religion* (Englewood Cliffs, N.J. 1965) 1–49. R. D. BAIRD, *Category Formation and the History of Religions* (The Hague 1971). M. ELIADE and J. M. KITAGAWA, eds., *The History of Religions: Essays in Methodology* (Chicago 1959). M. ELIADE, *The Quest* (Chicago 1969). J. S. HELFER, ed., *On Method in the History of Religions, History and Theory,* Beiheft 8 (Middletown, Conn. 1968). H. PENNER and E. YONAN, "Is a Science of Religion Possible?" *Journal of Religion* 52 (1972) 107–133.

Studies: C. J. BLEEKER and G. WINDGREN, eds., *Historia religionum* 1 (Leiden 1969); 2 (Leiden 1971). M. ELIADE, *Patterns in Comparative Religion* (New York 1958); *Yoga: Immortality and Freedom* (2d ed., Princeton 1969); *Shamanism: Archaic Techniques of Ecstasy* (Princeton 1964). R. PETTAZZONI, *Essays on the History of Religions* (Leiden 1954). J. Z. SMITH, *Map is Not Territory* (Leiden 1978). G. VAN DER LEEUW, *Religion in Essence and Manifestations* (2 v., New York 1963).

Histories: J. DE VRIES, *The Study of Religion: A Historical Approach* (New York 1967). E. J. SHARPE, *Comparative Religion: A History* (London 1975).

[E. V. GALLAGHER]

HOLINESS, UNIVERSAL CALL TO

A prominent element in the current resurgence of theological concern for the laity in the Church is the theme of genuine sanctity as meant for everyone. The egalitarian atmosphere of the day was a natural preparation for the emphasis of Vatican Council II on the biblical idea of complete holiness to be found in all vocations of life. The doctrine of the universal call is not new in the Church. Early patristic literature commonly assumes that all biblical themes (except radical poverty and dedicated virginity) are meant for all classes of people. However, with the rise of the religious orders many people began to identify the highest reaches of holiness with those persons who renounced property and family for a single-minded pursuit of the kingdom. This popular identification never became part of Catholic teaching, but at the same time the universal call to holiness was not prominent in the ordinary proclamation of the Church in everyday parish life. Yet it was implied in the canonization of lay saints and it was explicit in the liturgical texts. For example, the original Latin text for the feast of St. Teresa of Avila prays that we, all of us, "always be nourished by the food of her heavenly teaching and enkindled by it with the desire for true sanctity," and on the feast of St. John of the Cross the liturgy prays that we may "imitate him always." Likewise the declaration of these saints as universal doctors indicates the universal applicability of their teaching. Nonetheless, the popular preaching in typical parishes hardly emphasized the Church's genuine mind.

Teaching of Vatican Council II. The Council devoted the whole of Chapter 5 in *Lumen gentium* to the universal call to holiness; this same teaching is also found repeatedly and with a rich diversity of expression in other documents. All the disciples are to be holy and give the witness of a holy life (*Lumen gentium* 10, 32, 39). The faithful of every condition are called to that perfect holiness by which the Father is perfect (ibid. 11). They have the obligation, not simply an invitation, to strive for the perfection of their own state in life (ibid. 42; *Unitatis redintegratio* 4), and they are therefore to grow to the mature measure of the fullness of Christ himself (*Sacrosanctum Concilium* 2). The Council presents Jesus as the author and consummator of the universal call in his teaching that everyone is to be perfect (Mt 5.48) and in the greatest of all commandments addressed to all men, a total love for God with entire heart, soul and mind (Lk 10.27). All the faithful are to practice the spirit of evangelical poverty and therefore to achieve a detachment from this world and its riches (*Lumen gentium* 42). They are to come to the aid of the poor not only from their superfluities but also from their needed resources, a radical doctrine indeed (*Gaudium et spes* 69, 88). The Decree on the Laity states that they are consecrated as holy people both to offer spiritual sacrifices in everything and also to witness to Christ throughout the world (*Apostolicam actuositatem* 3). They too are to progress in holiness through a generous dedication to spreading the kingdom, through meditation on the word of God and through the other spiritual aids available in the Church (ibid. 4; *Dei Verbum* 25). They are likewise to carry the cross and live the spirit of the beatitudes (*Apostolicam actuositatem* 4).

This universal call is implied in another conciliar theme, namely, that the Church herself is filled with holiness because she has Christ. He fills the whole body of the Church with the riches of his glory, and so she receives her "full growth in God" (Col 2.19). Because in Jesus resides the fullness of divinity, each of us is to attain our fulfillment in him, not just a partial perfection (Col 2.9). The Ephesians are to be filled with "the utter fullness of God" (Eph 3.19; *Lumen gentium* 7). Even here on earth the members of the Church are to experience divine mysteries, "the things that are above." (Ps 34.8; 1 Pt 1.8; 2.3; *Lumen gentium* 6; *Sacrosanctum Concilium* 10).

Conciliar teaching also points to a striking, specific theme: each vocation is to be the locus of profound intimacy with God, for the Council assumes mystical prayer to be found in all classes in the Church as a normal development of the grace life. The modern layperson must be concerned with developing the life of contemplation (*Gaudium et spes* 56, 59); the new creation and genuine holiness are to be found in the laity (*Ad gentes* 21). The first and most important obligation of lay people is to live a profoundly Christian life (ibid. 36). They as well as all others in the Church pray continually (*Sacrosanctum Concilium* 12), burn with love during the liturgical celebrations, and taste fully the paschal mysteries (ibid. 10). Active religious no less than the cloistered are assumed to be "thoroughly enriched with mystical treasures" (*Ad gentes* 18), while all priests are to "abound in contemplation" (*Lumen gentium* 41). Though all priests and laity can and must seek perfection, yet the former are bound to acquire that perfection under the new title of their configuration to Christ in the Sacrament of Ordination and in their sacred ministry (*Presbyterorum ordinis* 12). Seminarians are to learn to live in intimate familiarity with the indwelling Trinity (*Optatam totius* 8) and the entirety of seminary life is to be penetrated with prayerful silence as a preparation for the kind of life priests themselves are to live (ibid. 11). The Council again speaks of mystical experience for all in the Church when it describes all the faithful as growing in understanding divine realities through their contemplation and study and experience of them (*Dei Verbum* 8). No ecumenical council of the past approaches this last one in the frequency of mention and the strength of what it says about contemplation and mysticism in the Church's life.

Biblical Basis. This teaching of the Church is rooted in Scripture. All holiness takes its origin and finds its exemplar in the transcendent otherness of the Lord God. He is majestic in holiness, a worker of wonders (Ex 15.11). Men become sanctified only because he first is the all holy one (Lv 11.44). A special people is consecrated, set apart from all other nations because they belong to the holy Lord (Lv 20.26), the one who alone is holy (1 Sm 2.2). He is *the* Holy One (Is 40.25), and so he is named holy (Lk 1.49). It is this holiness of God that requires his human handiwork to be holy (Lv 19.2). When Isaiah looks upon the thrice Holy One whose glory fills the earth, he feels lost, for he is a man with unclean lips (Is 6.1–5). God's people are to be holy in all they do because the Holy One has called them (1 Pt 1.15–16). Those who have tasted the very goodness of this God are living stones which make up the spiritual house in which he dwells and consequently are a royal, priestly, holy nation (1 Pt 2.3–9).

The God of revelation is a God of totality, never a God of fractions. All men and women, not just a small elite, are called to love with their whole hearts, souls, minds (Lk 10.27). No one can be a disciple unless he renounces all he possesses, not simply most of it (Lk 14.33). In community his followers are to be not merely cordial and helpful but completely one as the Father and Son are one (Jn 17.21–23). In showing mercy all are to be perfect as the heavenly Father is perfect (Mt 5.48). All are to be transformed from glory to glory into the very image of the Lord (2 Cor 3.18), and to try to be as pure as he is (1 Jn 3.3). All are to be holy and spotless, for all are God's work of art (Eph 1.4; 2.10). Love and knowledge are to increase without end and thus to reach perfect goodness (Phil 1.9–11). Scripture never gives the impression that this complete sanctity is meant for a small favored group only. Though vocations in life differ in the facility with which they lead to holiness, there is no difference in the goal.

Nature of This Holiness. The universal call does not bear simply on a moral rectitude, a polishing up of a Platonic, Aristotelian, or other, merely natural ethic. According to Scripture it is a transformation, a deification, a revolution, an exchange, a losing of one's old self to find a new self. It is a being filled with a divine knowledge, love, joy, peace that surpasses understanding (Phil 4.4,7; 1 Pt 1.8). It is a new creation which eye has not seen nor ear heard, nor the heart imagined (1 Cor 2.9). It is an "utter and blissful perfection" to which men come freely (*Gaudium et spes* 17). It is one and the same holiness in all persons, even though there are differing degrees of it and vocational paths which lead to it (*Lumen gentium* 41).

By definition holiness is not mediocrity. To speak of the universal call to holiness is to speak of a universal call to saintliness. It is a call to what traditionally has been described as heroic virtue (14:709). That man or woman is holy who lives the theological virtues (faith, hope, love) and the moral virtues (humility, fortitude, chastity, justice, patience and the others) to an eminent degree not attainable by human resources alone. The canonized saints are exemplars of this heroic goodness. Their lives are replete with illustrations of the joyous fullness with which men are to live. When the Church canonizes men and women and when she celebrates them in the liturgy and calls for the imitation of their goodness, she is reiterating the universal call to holiness. What this universal call means in the concrete can also be seen in the mystic's description of the transformation that occurs in the person who has grown to the highest development of prayerful contemplation. St. John of the Cross describes traits of this growth: one loves God in everything; his excessive impulses disappear; his emotions are peaceful and he loses useless desires; he enjoys an undisturbable peace and a habitual joy in the divine presence; his actions are "bathed in love" and are done with an amazing strength; his union with God is as the union of a candle flame with the sun.

Implications. The two-way theory of sanctity seems no longer tenable. This latecomer in the history of theology held that there are two ways to sanctity: one is the active, ascetic, ordinary way; the other is the passive, mystical, extraordinary way. Both Scripture and Vatican Council II make it clear that there is only one way to complete holiness, a way to which all men and women are invited. It is a way that has active and passive elements, ascetical and mystical developments. However, both Scripture and Vatican II (as well as the Council of Trent) do teach that there are different vocational paths leading to the one holiness and that those paths differ in effectiveness. Virginity consecrated to Christ more easily enables one to give the Lord undivided attention, to pursue the radical demands of the kingdom (1 Cor 7.32–35; Lk 18.29–30; *Optatam totius* 10). The Church does not say that a given religious is superior in holiness to a given married person, but she does say that the radical surrender of all that the world yearns for is a privileged, superior way of life because it bestows an immense freedom from impediments to achieving the "one thing necessary."

The holiness to which all are called is ecclesial and objective, not simply individual and subjective. The universal call includes the objective call and obligation to enter and remain in the Catholic Church which Christ has made necessary for salvation (*Lumen gentium* 14). It is true that the Holy Spirit does operate with his sanctifying power outside the boundaries of the Church (ibid. 15) and that he can lead to holiness those in good faith. Yet in objective fact one may not try to separate adherence to Christ from adherence to his Church: "he who hears you, hears me; he who rejects you, rejects me" (Lk 10:16).

The diverse spiritualities in the Church (religious—and its kinds—married, priestly, charismatic, etc.) include all elements of evangelical holiness; they are characterized by differing emphases and life styles, but all lead to the one holiness.

Bibliography: Paul VI, OssRomEng, July 17, 1975, 1; Oct. 16, 1975, 10. K. TRUHLAR, J. SPLETT and K. HEMMERLE, EncTheol 635–641. T. DUBAY, *Authenticity* (Denville, N.J. 1977).

[T. DUBAY]

HOLINESS OF THE CHURCH

Since Vatican Council II there have been two noteworthy developments in the theological discussion of the classical note of the Church, its holiness (7:54). One development bears on the sacramentality of the Church as sign of salvation and it is under this model especially that recent thinking centers its attention. The other development is a renewed interest in the universal call to holiness, a subject of considerable relevance to the Church as sacred temple of the Spirit.

The subject of the Church's holiness comes up frequently in the thought of Vatican Council II. The documents speak of the holy Church, the holy temple, a holy nation, the holy People of God, holy Mother Church, the holy Catholic Church (*Lumen gentium* 2, 5, 6, 9, 12; *Sacrosanctum Concilium* 60, 102, 103, 122; *Unitatis redintegratio* 2; *Orientalium ecclesiarum* 2; *Gravissimum educationis* introd.; *Dei Verbum* 19). We find the traditional theme of the creedal notes of the Church as "one, holy, catholic and apostolic" (*Lumen gentium* 8; *Christus Dominus* 11) together with the contemporary theme of the Church as the universal Sacrament of salvation in which we acquire sanctity (*Lumen gentium* 48; *Ad gentes* 1, 5). She has come forth from the side of the dying Christ as a "wondrous sacrament" (*Sacrosanctum Concilium* 5) and his light shines brightly on her countenance (*Lumen gentium* 1, 15). She functions like a sacrament in that she is both a sign and an instrument of a double holiness-union, namely with God and with neighbor (ibid. 1). Salt of the earth and light of the world, she is holy in her life and worship and work, a sign of the divine presence in the world (*Ad gentes* 1, 15).

The Church is not adequately seen until it is seen as divine as well as human (*Sacrosanctum Concilium* 2). The very core of her holiness, a core that pervades the whole, is the multiple presence of Jesus in her liturgical celebrations: in the Mass, in the person of the priest and under the Eucharistic species; in the Sacraments, in the biblical word and in the praying and singing faithful (ibid. 7). The Church is the holy temple of the Spirit, the dwelling place for God on earth (ibid. 2). She is led not by mere human hopes and reasonings but by the Lord's Spirit who continually sanctifies her by indwelling, by praying on behalf of the faithful, by guiding her to all truth, by unifying her, by adorning her with charismatic gifts and fruits, by keeping her freshly youthful in the power of the Gospel, by renewing her and uniting her to her Spouse (*Gaudium et spes* 11; *Lumen gentium* 4). Thus the faithful are to grow to deep holiness, "profoundly penetrated by the Spirit of Christ" (*Ad gentes* 11).

Closely allied with this divine indwelling theme is the Church as holy because she produces holiness. Although many elements of sanctification are found outside the visible structure of the Church (*Lumen gentium* 8), yet she alone possesses the totality and fullness of these means of salvation (*Ad gentes* 6; *Unitatis redintegratio* 4). "It is only through Christ's Catholic Church, which is 'the all-embracing means of salvation,' that [the separated brethren] can benefit fully from the means of salvation," for the Lord entrusted all his blessings to the apostolic college alone (ibid. 3). From the liturgy grace is poured forth as from a fountain and the faithful are set on fire with love (*Sacrosanctum Concilium* 10).

This mark of the Church is not an angelism. Human persons are likewise part of the "wondrous sacrament." The Church is always and in every century freshly youthful in her saints. Even the structural elements sanctify by their sacramental, proclaiming, governing functions, and by their own prayer and example (*Lumen gentium* 26–27). The Decree on the Apostolate of the Laity repeatedly stresses that ordinary faithful bring the Gospel spirit into the secular sphere, but the effects of grace especially appear in the practice of the evangelical counsels either privately undertaken or in a canonically recognized religious institute (*Lumen gentium* 39). Among these counsels virginity-celibacy is eminent because it makes pursuing God easier through an undivided heart (ibid. 42). Although religious life does not belong to the hierarchical element in the Church, it does belong inseparably to her life and holiness (ibid. 44). Members of these institutes enrich the life of the Church, identify with her in their apostolic undertakings, lend luster to her by their holiness, live and image the Church's wedded union to Christ (*Perfectae caritatis* 1, 2, 7, 12).

It is not commonly noted that the Church's holiness is implicitly contained in the biblical image of her being the virgin bride of the Lord. An ideal virgin bride is untainted, pure, wholly centered on her beloved, a model of undivided attention. Thus the Church is a virgin bride (2 Cor 11.2), worthy of her lord, and living in perfect fidelity (*Lumen gentium* 6, 9). Although individuals fail, the Church herself never fails in the integrity of her faith, hope, love. Through the gifts in her members she is a spouse adorned for her husband (Rev 21.2; *Perfectae caritatis* 1). From these gifts and undivided devotion to her Lord it follows that the Church is holy in her continual prayer. She is a holy nation called by God out of darkness to sing his praises (1 Pt 2.9; *Sacrosanctum Concilium* 14). This she does ceaselessly through celebrating the Eucharist through all time zones of the world, through praying the Liturgy of the Hours, and through the private prayer of her members. Thus the Church makes holy the whole course of day and night over the face of the planet. She is the "voice of the bride singing to her bridegroom" (ibid. 84). This is why the contemplative life with its abundance of mystical treasures "belongs to the fullness of the Church's presence" and is to be established everywhere (*Ad gentes* 18). That Vatican Council II speaks of contemplation and prayer no less than eighty times (aside from references to liturgy) is indicative of the place prayer occupies in the mind of the contemporary Church.

Paradoxically the Church is holy and yet needing to be purified and renewed (*Lumen gentium* 8; *Unitatis redintegratio* 6). Failure of the members to live fervently dims the radiance of the Church's image in the world (ibid. 4) and so her sanctity, while real, is imperfect on earth (*Lumen gentium* 48). It is a growing holiness, for the Holy Spirit purifies and renews her ceaselessly (ibid. 3, 5; *Sacrosanctum Concilium* 2; *Gaudium et spes* 21). Yet at the same time the Church is the "spotless spouse of the spotless Lamb" and "indefectibly holy" (*Lumen gentium* 6, 39). The paradox is partially explained by the fact that in Mary the Church has "already reached that perfection by which she is without spot or wrinkle" (ibid. 65). The Mother of Jesus is at this moment the image of what the whole Church is to be when her holiness achieves its full perfection and completion in heaven (ibid. 2, 48, 68).

If the Church of the future is reduced to a diaspora situation in more regions of the world, her mark of holiness will become still more relevant as a light shining in darkness, the kind of light that draws the heart as well as the mind.

Bibliography: B. KLOPPENBURG, *Ecclesiology of Vatican II* (Chicago 1974); R. LAWLER, D. WUERL and T. LAWLER, *The Teaching of Christ* (Huntington, Ind. 1976) 196–200.

[T. DUBAY]

HOLLIS, (MAURICE) CHRISTOPHER

Writer, editor, politician; b. Axbridge, England, March 2, 1903; d. Mells, Somerset, England, May 6, 1977. His father, Anglican bishop of Taunton, England, had been headmaster of Wells Theological College; his mother was a writer of Anglican histories and stories which continue to command an audience. Hollis went to Eton on scholarship and, while there, won further scholarships to Oxford. As a student at the University (Balliol College), he fell under the influence of Bernard Shaw, and, especially, of Belloc and Chesterton. During his last year at Oxford, at twenty-two, he became a Catholic. He next took part in an extended debating tour, as a member of the Oxford Union, in company with Douglas Woodruff and Malcolm McDonald, visiting the United States, New Zealand, and Australia. For the ten years following, 1925–35, he was an instructor at Stonyhurst, a Jesuit college in Lancashire.

His first book, *The American Heresy* (1930), about assorted American political figures, belongs to this period, as do his *Thomas More* (1934), *St. Ignatius* (1931), and *The Monstrous Regiment* (1930) on Queen Elizabeth and her times. His next two books marked the economic phase of his miscellaneous interests. *On the Breakdown of Money* (1937) and *The Two Nations* (1935), were effects of the influence on his mind of McNair Wilson, then a correspondent of the *Times*. These led to his "American period," 1935–39, when he was lecturing in economics at the Univ. of Notre Dame. These years saw, too, the appearance, in the form of letters, of a series on foreign issues of the day: *Foreigners Aren't Fools*; *Foreigners Aren't Knaves*; and *We Aren't So Dumb*. The war brought him back to England. After a term as instructor at Downside Abbey School, he entered the Royal Air Force. By a rather unusual arrangement, he worked as an intelligence officer by night, and, by day, supervised the Catholic publishing house, Burns & Oates. Somehow, at the same time, he wrote his most successful work, *Death of a Gentleman* (1945).

At war's end, Douglas Jerrold, who had brought Hollis into Burns & Oates, got him into forming a company, Hollis and Carter, for the publication of books on education. This also was the political phase of his life; he became the Conservative member of parliament for Devizes, held the seat for ten years, and then gave it up, undefeated. As an MP he had played a part in the abolition of capital punishment for murder. In his last years he joined the Liberal Party. From 1936 until his death, he was a director of the London *Tablet* and up to a few weeks before his death, he contributed numerous signed articles and reviews to that publication. Meanwhile he was a regular contributor to the obituary columns of the London *Times*. For years, under Malcolm Muggeridge, he was on the board of *Punch*, writing for it a parliamentary sketch.

His literary output, mostly Catholic in character, was very extensive. Among his better known works: *Erasmus* (Milwaukee 1933); *Lenin* (Milwaukee 1938); *G. K. Chesterton* (London 1950); *Evelyn Waugh* (London and New York 1954); *The Achievements of Vatican II* (New York 1967); *Newman and the Modern World* (New York 1968); *The Mind of Chesterton* (Coral Gables, Fla. 1970).

Bibliography: *Tablet* (London), May 14, 1977, 466–467; *Times* (London), May 9, 1977, 16.

[P. F. MULHERN]

HOLY COMMUNION, RITES OF

On June 21, 1973, the Congregation for Divine Worship published a section of the Roman Ritual entitled, "Holy Communion and Worship of the Eucharist Outside of Mass." The text included three distinct parts: Holy Communion outside of Mass; administration of Communion and Viaticum to the sick by an extraordinary minister; forms of worship of the Eucharist—exposition, Benediction, processions, congresses. Both the Congregation for Divine Worship's promulgating decree and the General Introduction to the rite itself supply theological bases and practical guidelines for Communion and Eucharistic worship outside Mass.

Celebration of the Eucharist within Mass is the true origin and purpose of worship shown to the Eucharist outside Mass (HolyCommIntrod 2). The principal reason for reserving the Sacrament after Mass is to unite, through sacramental Communion, the faithful unable to participate in Mass, especially the sick and aged, with Christ and the offering of his Sacrifice (ibid. 5). Sacramental Communion during Mass is the more perfect participation in the Eucharist and therefore the faithful should be encouraged to receive Communion during the actual Eucharistic celebration (ibid. 13). Nevertheless, those prevented from being present should be refreshed with the Eucharist even outside Mass. In that way they realize they are united not only with the Lord's Sacrifice but also with the community itself and are supported by the love of their brothers and sisters (ibid. 14). This is true particularly of the sick and aged who should be given the opportunity to receive frequently, even daily, above all during the Easter season (ibid.).

Communion outside Mass. Communion may be given outside Mass on any day or at any hour except for certain restrictions during Holy Week (ibid. 16). The priest, deacon, acolyte, or specially designated minister distributes Communion to the faithful. A corporal, communion plate, and candles as well as appropriate vesture for the minister are needed. Communion is given in the customary way to each individual (ibid. 17–20). A celebration of the Word accompanies this rite so the faithful by hearing God's Word learn that the marvels it proclaims reach their climax in the paschal mystery of which the Mass is a sacramental memorial and in which they share by Communion (ibid. 26). A scriptural greeting and penitential rite similar to the procedure at Mass begins the service. A Liturgy of the Word follows with one or more readings, a homily, and general intercessions. A list of suitable passages is provided in the ritual (ibid. 27–29). This word celebration may be abbreviated or adjusted to meet the circumstances (ibid. 42). The ciborium or pyx is then removed and placed on the altar. The minister genuflects, introduces the Our Father and sign of peace, genuflects again, and shows the host to the people, reciting the usual formula (ibid. 30–35). After distribution of Communion, the minister returns remaining hosts to the tabernacle, genuflects, pauses for an optional period of silence or the singing of a song, then concludes with a final prayer and blessing (ibid. 36–39).

Communion for the Sick. A priest or deacon distributing Communion to the ill observes the ritual prescribed in the Rite of Anointing and Pastoral Care of the Sick. When an acolyte or duly appointed extraordinary minister performs this function, the special rite contained in the 1973 document is used (ibid. 54). In such instances, the procedure described above is basically followed with the following few modifications now noted. Those who cannot receive Communion in the form of bread may receive it in the form of wine, but the Precious Blood must be carried to the sick person in such a way as to eliminate all danger of spilling (ibid. 55). The sign of peace is omitted. The minister crosses himself or herself while invoking, instead of bestowing, God's blessing on all present (ibid. 63).

Communion by an Extraordinary Minister. When a priest or deacon is present, the extraordinary minister receives Communion from him, then assists in the usual way with the distribution of hosts. If a priest or deacon is not present, the extraordinary minister conducts the rite outlined above for Communion outside Mass with the few minor verbal changes specified in the ritual.

[J. M. CHAMPLIN]

HOLY OILS AND CHRISM

The three oils continuing in use for the Church's worship are the oil of catechumens, the oil of the sick, and chrism. The section of the revised Roman Pontifical entitled, *Ordo benedicendi oleum catechumenorum et infirmorum et conficiendi chrisma* (hereafter Ordo) prepared by the Congregation for Divine Worship was promulgated by Pope Paul VI on Dec. 3, 1970. The English translation, approved in final form in 1972, is contained as Appendix II in the American Sacramentary. The new rite is a revision, rearrangement, and simplification of the earlier rites.

The matter for the oils is olive oil or other plant oil (Ordo 3); perfume is added to make the chrism aromatic (ibid. 4), which may be prepared before the rite (ibid. 5). The rite takes place during the Chrism Mass on Holy Thursday morning or near the end of Lent; the rites may be grouped together as ending the Liturgy of the Word or in the traditional places (the oil of the sick was traditionally blessed before the conclusion of the Eucharistic Prayer and the oil of catechumens and the chrism after Communion; ibid. 11–12).

The consecration of chrism is reserved to the bishop (ibid. 6), but the oil of catechumens may be blessed by the priest during the rites of adult catechumenate (ibid. 7; the anointing preliminary to the Baptism of infants may only be omitted in the U.S. if the minister deems it pastorally necessary or desirable—BaptCh 51); the oil of the sick may be blessed by the priest in necessity (Ordo 8b). Oils are no longer used in blessing baptismal water. By the decree *Pientissima mater Ecclesia* of the Congregation of Rites, March 4, 1965 (ActApS 57 [1965] 409) bishops may permit priests to carry the oil of the sick with them in case of possible need.

The prayers of blessing stress the purpose for which the oils will be used. The longer and more developed prayer for the consecration of the chrism (two alternative forms are provided) traces the use of oil in salvation history: this blessing is concelebrated by the priests who concelebrate the Mass. (Breathing on the oil is an optional gesture.)

[J. DALLEN]

HOLY SPIRIT

Impetus to a greater appreciation of role of the Holy Spirit in the Christian life (7:98) has come through the *charismatic renewal. While better classified as a renewal *in* the Holy Spirit than a devotion *to* him, the movement stresses the experiential nature of faith and finds support in those Scripture passages that speak of the gift of the Holy Spirit.

Baptism in the Holy Spirit. Stress is laid on an initial experience popularly called the "baptism in the Holy Spirit," accompanied by the expectation of some charismatic manifestation, such as praying in tongues or prophecy. Precedents for this relationship between the Holy Spirit as Gift and the gifts of the Holy Spirit (7:99) are seen especially in Acts. How the charisms and the Sacraments of *Christian Initiation are related is a matter of current theological discussion. In practice, the "baptism in the Holy Spirit" (also sometimes referred to as "infilling" or "release" of the Holy Spirit) is experienced as a new departure in the Christian life effected usually through prayer and the laying on of hands by other Christians. The central and unique characteristic of the charismatic movement is the relation perceived between this renewal in the Holy Spirit and the charisms. With the encouragement of Paul (1 Cor 14.1), the gifts are actively sought. Those listed in 1 Cor 12–14 are held to be available today, such as tongues, prophecy, healing, the word of knowledge, the word of wisdom (*see* CHARISMATIC PRAYER). Yielding to these gifts is seen as a way of cooperating with the renewing work of the Spirit.

Theological Explanations. Among the theological explanations of this relationship, there are those who would explain it as an unfolding of the sacramental grace particularly of Baptism and Confirmation. Note is taken of the fact that the reception of the Spirit in Acts is always accompanied by a charismatic manifestation. Others seek an understanding of the relationship in a more general theology of grace, for which the praying community as such would be sufficient ecclesial cause. In discussing the missions of the divine persons, specifically the sending of the Son and the Spirit into the soul of the Christian, St. Thomas Aquinas says that such a sending "is especially seen in that kind of increase of grace whereby a person moves forward into some new act or some new state of grace: as, for example, when a person moves forward into the grace of working miracles, or of prophecy, or out of the burning love of God offers his life as a martyr, or renounces all his possessions, or undertakes some other such heroic act" (ST 1a, 43.6 ad 2). It is significant that the sending he speaks of is not the initial sending but a subsequent "breakthrough" into a new experience of grace. It is further significant that the examples Aquinas gives of such an *innovatio* or *profectus* are connected with charismatic manifestation. These two aspects correspond to the charismatic experience as it is described and lived today by many Christians. It further appears that the division of grace into sanctifying (*gratia gratum faciens*) and charismatic (*gratia gratis data*), which in the past often led to a disregard for the latter in favor of the former, should be made with great caution, since what is aimed at building up the Church will normally also be related to a personal growth in grace (ibid. 43.3 ad 4). To seek the gifts and to yield to them may thus be as important an exercise for spiritual growth as practices of asceticism. The gifts are, at any rate, calculated to expand the community's experience of God as gift.

Though the charisms are sought as particular manifestations of the Spirit, the charismatic movement has a strong Christocentric devotional base, so that the Holy Spirit appears more as a power moving the Church through his gifts than as an object of devotion in himself.

Bibliography: D. L. GELPI, *Charism and Sacrament: A Theology of Christian Conversion* (New York 1976). K. MCDONNELL, *The Holy Spirit and Power: The Catholic Charismatic Renewal* (New York 1975). G. T. MONTAGUE, *The Spirit and His Gifts* (New York 1974); *The Holy Spirit: Growth of a Biblical Tradition* (New York 1976). E. D. O'CONNOR, *Perspectives on Charismatic Renewal* (Notre Dame, Ind. 1975) extensive bibliography. L. J. SUENENS, *A New Pentecost?* (New York 1975); *Theological and Pastoral Orientations on the Catholic Charismatic Renewal* (Notre Dame, Ind. 1974). F. SULLIVAN, "The Baptism in the Holy Spirit and Christian Tradition," *New Covenant* 3 (May 1974) 30.

[G. T. MONTAGUE]

HOMILETICS

Homiletics is the body of knowledge concerned with the theology and practice of preaching (7:111). In a seminary curriculum homiletics is considered a part of pastoral studies along with Canon Law, religious education, pastoral leadership and counselling (*Bishops' Committee on Priestly Formation, *Program of Priestly Formation* [1977] n. 148–155). The purpose of instruction in homiletics is to assure "that each seminarian acquires professional competency in those areas of communication which are integral to the public utterance of the spoken word" (ibid. 150).

Since Vatican Council II there have been significant changes in the teaching of homiletics in Catholic seminaries. These changes have been a result of a number of factors. Probably the most important one is the renewed emphasis on preaching within the Catholic

Church. The Decree on the Ministry and Life of Priests states that the proclamation of the Word of God through preaching is the most important duty of the priest (*Presbyterorum ordinis* 4). Contemporary theology of preaching views preaching not as a message about faith, but as the occasion *for an actual salvific meeting* between God and man. "In still another way yet more truly . . . (God) is present in the Church as she preaches, since the Gospel proclaimed is the Word of God, which is preached only in the name and by the authority of Christ and with his presence . . ." (Paul VI MystFid; ActApS 57 [1965] 763).

A second factor has been the general decline in the public's unquestioning acceptance of institutional authority. In the Church one of the results has been a more vocal laity who feel freer to criticize the quality of preaching and the qualifications of preachers. This has been accentuated by the ecumenical movement which has familiarized Catholic clergy and laity with the centrality of preaching in the Protestant tradition in contrast to its lack of emphasis in the Catholic tradition.

The final factor has been a change in the field of speech education. Public speaking, which provided the traditional framework for instruction in homiletics, has now been situated within the broader spectrum of communication. Public speaking is seen as but one form of public communication, and to be not even the most important form. All introductory speech sequences now include intrapersonal, interpersonal, and mass communication.

Curricular Elements. At present there is no standard homiletics curriculum. Yet there is a consensus that an effective program of instruction in homiletics must include the following elements.

The Person as Preacher. From both a theological and a communications viewpoint the preacher is central to the preaching task. The homily in essence must be a witness to a saving encounter between God and the preacher. Thus his spiritual life is an essential part of preaching. The preacher must learn to be honest about his own concerns, failures, and successes. This portion of the course must provide the seminarian with tools for self-analysis and a setting for rededication in faith.

Theology and Preaching. The preacher must understand the importance of preaching in God's salvific plan. Preaching is the normative link between God and man. He must be aware of the kerygmatic nature of preaching in which Christ actually meets men through the preaching event (Ebeling). In another vein, instruction in practical exegesis must be given in which a biblical passage is analyzed not only for its theological but also its "homiletic" content.

Preaching as Communication. An overview of research in communication is crucial for effective preaching. A course would cover such topics as speaker credibility, persuasion, attitudes, dissonance theories. A preacher must know his congregation. Thus he must be provided with proper tools for audience analysis. These include strategies for overcoming audience barriers to the message. According to communication theory this is one of the most neglected and most important areas of preaching.

Homily Preparation and Evaluation. The elements of the traditional speech course are still essential for the preacher. Its format can be based upon the classical rhetorical canons (invention, arrangement, style, memory, and delivery) or on other contemporary arrangements. The element of added importance today is a full treatment of homily evaluation through individual critiques, video and audio taping, and critique teams.

New Forms of Preaching. While instruction in special forms of preaching (retreats, cursillos, etc.) has been a peripheral part of the curriculum in homiletics, being introduced are such types of preaching as dialogue homilies (chancel and congregational), multi-media homilies, and the use of radio and television. While these forms will not replace the traditional preaching format, they remain important to the preacher.

See also PREACHING.

Bibliography: G. EBELING, *Theology and Proclamation: Dialogue with Bultmann* (Philadelphia 1966). R. HOWE, *The Miracle of Dialogue* (New York 1963); *Partners in Preaching: Clergy and Laity in Dialogue* (New York 1967). J. JUNGMANN, *The Good News Yesterday and Today* (New York 1962). W. MALCOMSON, *The Preaching Event* (Philadelphia 1968). K. RAHNER, ed., *The Renewal of Preaching: Theory and Practice* (New York 1968). D. RANDOLPH, *The Renewal of Preaching: A New Homiletic Based on the New Hermeneutic* (Philadelphia 1969). C. REID, *The Empty Pulpit* (New York 1967). G. ROXBURGH, ed., *Clergy in Communication* (4 v., Ottawa 1970). W. THOMPSON and G. BENNET, *Dialogue Preaching: The Shared Sermon* (Valley Forge 1969).

[A. STEICHEN]

HOMILY

One of the most significant developments in the life of the Church after Vatican Council II has been the restoration of the Homily to its privileged place within the Eucharistic Liturgy and, indeed, within the liturgies of all the Sacraments. The Homily originally designated a type of familiar, artless discourse used in explaining the scriptural readings during Christian worship. From the time of Origen it came to mean a commentary on some portion of Scripture and, later, any kind of sermon to the Christian people in connection with the Eucharist. As the term is used in the Constitution on the Liturgy (*Sacrosanctum Concilium* 52) and in the instructions and decrees implementing that basic charter of liturgical reform, the Homily signifies a pastoral reflection on the liturgical texts near the end of the Liturgy of the Word. The Constitution insists on the vital relationship between Word and Sacrament within the Eucharistic celebration and to this end decrees: (1) "more ample, more varied and more suitable readings from Sacred Scripture," and (2) a sermon or homily drawing its content "mainly from scriptural and liturgical sources" and directed toward a deeper understanding of "the mystery of Christ ever made present and active in us," especially in the liturgical celebration itself (ibid. 34).

In this view the Homily is conceived of not merely as a catechetical instruction located within the Eucharistic Liturgy; rather, it is conceived of primarily as a pastoral reflection on the mystery actually being celebrated in the liturgical event, an event which is a kind of peak moment in the ongoing mystery of the believer's new life in Christ. This same view of the importance and the chief function of the Homily has prevailed in the post-conciliar development of the other Sacraments; it is reflected in the new rituals for Baptism, Penance, Matrimony, and the Anointing of the Sick. The ritual for each of these Sacraments calls for a Homily following selected scriptural Readings, based on the Readings, and directed towards a greater understanding of, and therefore a greater participation in, the sacramental mystery itself. The new regime of the Sacraments, therefore, calls for the closest possible integration of the

ministry of Word and Sacrament, in order to bring about a more perfect interiorization of the Christian mystery itself, a mystery revealed in the Word, symbolized in Sacrament, and lived out in the faith-life of a believer continually inspired and energized by Word and Sacrament.

See also PREACHING.

Bibliography: E. ECHLIN, *Priest as Preacher*, (Cork 1973). J. HOFINGER, *Evangelization and Catechesis*, (New York 1976).

[T. D. ROVER]

HOMOSEXUALITY

During the 12 years elapsing since the article on homosexuality appeared in *The New Catholic Encyclopedia* (7:116) the author has developed his thought along the lines that follow.

Psychological Factors. Several notable points emerge from psychology in regard to homosexuality.

Male and Female Homosexuality. Research tends to stress more the differences between lesbians and male homosexuals. Causal factors in the genesis of lesbianism are more unknown than in that of male homosexuals and the condition itself seems to emerge later. Lesbians, moreover, tend to form more permanent unions under more private circumstances, while the male homosexuals tend to the bar and bath cultures with less concern for privacy. Unlike many male homosexuals who throughout life avoid any attempt at physical intimacy with the other sex, lesbians have histories of prior attempts to relate intimately to males before they turn to a lesbian way of life; they give greater value to psychological intimacy and companionship than to the physical pleasure of the relationship; and once one woman has formed a stable union with another, it is more likely to be permanent than the union of male homosexuals. Again, the lesbian seems to feel more keenly the lack of children than her male counterpart and some seek children through artificial insemination. The incidence of alcoholism among male homosexuals is much higher, as high as 50 percent in some studies. In February 1976 the national gay newspaper, *The Advocate*, described the pandemic proportions of the problem among males in the Los Angeles area. In the civil rights struggle male homosexuals stress their rights as *gays*; lesbians, on the other hand, emphasize their rights as *women*. Finally, many of the differences between heterosexual males and females are repeated in the relationships between male homosexuals and lesbians with this qualification: there is minimal attraction between male homosexuals and lesbians. In all these psychological analyses the data is incomplete and further research will disclose other facets of this phenomenon.

Overtness. Willingness to admit overt homosexual behavior has increased over the past decade for a variety of reasons: propaganda of many homosexual organizations that "gay is good"; the impact of a situationist ethic which sees in homosexual behavior an alternate life style to marriage and to celibacy; the encouragement which many homosexuals receive from other homosexuals to declare publicly that they are homosexual in life style. Militant homosexuals hope by encouraging secret homosexuals to declare themselves to acquire a strong political influence.

Evaluation. Opposing the tendency among many American psychiatrists to regard the homosexual condition as at most a simple personality disorder for those disturbed by it (referendum of American Psychiatric Association, 1974) Dr. Ruth Tiffany Barnhouse regards homosexuality as a serious psychological problem. With other psychiatrists, Barnhouse analyzes this complex psychodynamic in terms of problems of unsatisfied dependence, of unresolved power issues, and of fear of heterosexuality. Highly competitive societies tend to produce a greater number of homosexuals than do the less competitive, so that it is not surprising that the dependency or power motivations may be prominent in the development of homosexuality. Unlike the Freudians, however, Barnhouse does not hold that the origins of homosexuality are sealed in the first six years of life, important as these years are. Experiences throughout the latency period (roughly from six to twelve years of age) are also important, particularly in peer relationships and in the experiences of competitiveness and aggressiveness. The environment of the adolescent also has a crucial impact upon sexual orientation. At this time both sexes undergo sexual-identity confusion—they do not know how to be adult members of their own sex and without this knowledge it is extremely difficult to know how to approach the opposite sex. Not surprisingly, they usually go through a period of associating principally, if not exclusively, with members of their own sex. While many may engage in some homosexual activity with no lasting effects, a few may trigger unresolved difficulties from earlier stages, thereby precipitating a more serious homosexual commitment, but not necessarily a lasting one. The additional impact of a power-oriented culture confuses the male adolescent still further. In this situation the young man may be seduced by the milieu, choosing homosexual behavior, which he perceives to be approved by the culture. Barnhouse's study has important pastoral implications for the young. It shows the immorality of propaganda advocating a homosexual way of life, the need for intensive guidance and spiritual direction, and the greater hope that, with professional and spiritual guidance, the sexual reorientation of such young people can be accomplished. (On the latter point see bibliog: S. B. Hadden.)

Morality. In the 1966 *New Catholic Encyclopedia* article the argument from Scripture was based upon a series of both OT and NT texts (Lv 18.22; 20.3; Rom 1.27; 1 Cor 6.9–10; and 1 Tim 1.9–10). Although the cited texts remain a legitimate argument, a much better argument can be drawn from the teaching of both Scripture and Christian tradition on the nature of human sexuality and marriage. That teaching asserts that genital sexual expression between a man and woman should take place only in marriage and that marriage is a permanent, exclusive, procreative, and loving union. Apart from the intention of man and woman, sexual intercourse has a twofold meaning: it is an act of union with the beloved and it is procreative. These unitive and procreative meanings are distinct, but inseparable. Neither may be excluded, although for various reasons the procreative may not be achieved. Christian marriage, then, is the norm of sexual expression and all other forms of sexuality, whether between man and woman or between members of the same sex, must be evaluated in the light of the same teaching. This position cannot accept homosexual acts, because they cannot fulfill any procreative purpose and because they run counter to the complementary natures of man and woman. On the other hand, Scripture, both OT and NT, confirms the heterosexual union of man and woman in procreation. The Genesis description (1.27–28; 2.18–24) is concerned with man and woman forming the first family, and Eph 5.21–33 describes the way in which the relationship between man and woman is like that between Christ and his Church.

From the earliest times to the present day the teaching of the Church has been at one with Scripture on this point. Within the last decade, however, challenges of this doctrine have arisen. Some moralists, including those within the Catholic Church, have proposed that a homosexual way of life, particularly if it involves a stable relationship, is an alternative life style. It is assumed that no one can be a complete person without the experience of genital expression and that the human body may be used in any way that is pleasing to the lovers. Since it is the quality of the love relationship that counts, it does not matter whether such love exists between members of the same or of the opposite sex. These and other arguments in favor of homosexual activity have been confronted by the Congregation for the Doctrine of Faith in its *Declaration on Certain Questions Concerning Sexual Ethics* (1975), by *Principles to Guide Confessors in Questions of Homsexuality* (1973) of the National Conference of Catholic Bishops' Committee on Pastoral Research and Practice, and by *To Live in Christ Jesus* (1976), pastoral letter of the National Conference of Catholic Bishops. The 1976 pastoral supports the basic human rights of homosexuals, while reaffirming the Church's stand against homosexual actions. It adds that "the Christian community should provide them a special degree of pastoral understanding and care." In the exercise of his civil rights, however, the homosexual should realize that they are limited by the rights of others, particularly in the sensitive area of teaching on the elementary and secondary levels.

Pastoral Care. Deeper understanding of the dynamics of human sexuality has contributed to pastoral programs for homosexual persons that are concerned with helping them to form chaste friendships with both homosexuals and heterosexuals. The homosexual is shown that there is a difference between the human need for intimacy and for genital expression. Chastity is proposed as a form of charity and as a quality of human friendship; the fact that chastity is a divine gift is also stressed. But it is a gift expressed within a spiritual plan of life which must be worked out by the homosexual under the guidance of a spiritual director. In this way the chaste life has become achievable in the lives of many homosexuals.

There is urgent need for more research on the etiology of female homosexual tendencies and for the development of group programs. These will offer both the male and the female homosexual a sense of supportive community. This will help them live chastely within an environment which in its predominant heterosexual orientation does not understand the interior dispositions of the homosexual.

Bibliography: ANOMALY (pseudonym) *The Invert and His Social Adjustment* (rev. ed. Baltimore 1948). A sound case for abstinence. D. S. BAILEY, *Homosexuality and the Western Christian Tradition* (London 1955). Much valuable research, but must be read in light of more recent scriptural criticism. R. T. BARNHOUSE, *Homosexuality: A Symbolic Confusion* (New York 1977). J. R. CAVANAGH, *Counseling the Homosexual*

(Huntington, Ind. 1977). Updating of author's *Counseling the Invert* (Milwaukee 1966). D. CORY, "Homosexuality," *Encyclopedia of Sexual Behavior*, A. Ellis and A. Abarbanel, eds. (New York 1973) 485–493. Stresses subjective approach of a sociologist. C. E. CURRAN, "Dialogue with the Homophile Community: the Morality of Homosexuality", in *Catholic Theology in Dialogue* (Notre Dame, Ind. 1972) 184–219. A. DAVIDSON, *The Returns of Love: Letters of a Christian Homosexual* (Downers Grove, Ill. 1970). J. DOMINIAN, "Helping the Homosexual," *St. Anthony Messenger* (June, 1973) 14–19. A. GUINDON, *The Sexual Language* (Ottawa 1976) 299–377. A good phenomenological approach, but settles for steady partnership among homosexuals. J. F. HARVEY, "Morality and Pastoral Treatment of Homosexuality," *Continuum* 5 (1967) 279–297; "The Controversy Concerning the Psychology and Morality of Homosexuality," *American Ecclesiastical Review* 167 (1973) 602–629; "Female Homosexuality," *Linacre Quarterly* 36 (1969) 100–106; "Homosexual Marriages," *Marriage and Family Living* 56 (1974) 18–23; "Changes in Nomenclature and Their Probable Effect" in J. R. Cavanagh, ed. *Counseling the Homosexual* (Huntington, Ind. 1977) 30–36; "Contemporary Theological Views," *ibid.* 222–238; "Chastity and the Homosexual," *The Priest* 33 (1977) 10–16. S. B. HADDEN, "Male Homosexuality," *Pennsylvania Medicine* 70 (1967) 78–80; "The Homosexual Group: Formation and Beginnings," *Group Process* 7 (1976) 81–92. L. HATTERER, *Changing Homosexuality in the Male* (New York 1970). A thorough clinical study of over two hundred male homosexuals. A. KARLEN, *Sexuality and Homosexuality: A New View* (New York 1971). Excellent work. A. KOSNIK et al., *Human Sexuality* (New York 1977) 186–218. J. J. MCNEILL, *The Church and the Homosexual* (Kansas City, Mo. 1976). Representative of the position that homosexual unions are natural for some. L. OVESEY, *Pseudohomosexuality* (New York 1969). Pioneering exploration of the two nonsexual motivations in the development of homosexuality, namely, dependency and power; hence, the term "pseudohomosexuality." W. N. PITTENGER, *Making Sexuality Human* (Philadelphia 1970); *Time for Consent* (London 1970). A. PLÉ, "L'homosexualité, approches morales et pastorales," *Vie Spirituelle, Suppl.* 25 (1972) 340–354. W. SIMON and J. H. GAGNON, "The Lesbians: A Preliminary Overview," *Sexual Deviance* (New York 1967) 247–282. C. SOCARIDES, *The Overt Homosexual* (New York 1968). Good bibliography of psychoanalytic literature on the subject. R. W. WELTGE, ed., *The Same Sex; An Appraisal of Homosexuality* (Philadelphia 1969). Contemporary Protestant views.

[J. F. HARVEY]

HOPE, THEOLOGY OF

"Theology of hope" is the name of a movement which gained international attention in 1964 with the publication of *Theologie der Hoffnung* by Jürgen Moltmann, a Reformed theologian now teaching at the Univ. of Tübingen. The Lutheran theologian Wolfhart Pannenberg and the Roman Catholics Johannes Metz and Karl Rahner have since allied themselves with the movement.

Ernst Bloch, Philosophy of Hope. The name and movement were inspired by the philosophy of hope of the East German Marxist Ernst Bloch, especially in his 3-v., *Das Prinzip Hoffnung* (1959). That work made Moltmann realize that hope in the future of history was a thoroughly biblical principle left undeveloped in Christian theology. He concluded that a theology based on that hope would remain faithful to the biblical message and yet speak meaningfully to modern man, since it shared with him his alienation from the past and his instinctive drive for meaning from the future. Moltmann sought to integrate three basic themes: the theology of eschatology of Karl Barth, Otto Weber, Hans-Joachim Iwand, Gerhard von Rad, and Ernst Käsemann, to which he had been introduced during his studies at the University of Göttingen 1948–57; the theology of the apostolate of J. C. Hoekendijk and especially of Arnold van Ruler (both of whom Moltmann studied, 1956–58), who made history meaningful in Christianity by combining with eschatology a social and political mission to the world as preparation for the *Kingdom of God; and Bloch's philosophy of hope based on Hegel and Marx, which would serve largely

as a philosophical and conceptual system of historical process useful for elucidating the biblical revelation.

Bloch, a Jew, was himself fundamentally inspired by the Judeo-Christian revelation transmitted to him through the theology of Thomas Münzer (10:79) and Joachim of Fiore (7:990), which he interpreted in "left-wing" Aristotelian-Marxist categories. Bloch once summarized his whole philosophy as "S is not yet P"; by this he meant that subject is not yet predicate, or being is not yet what it can be. He saw being as essentially dynamically oriented toward its essence or utopia, i.e., what it is capable of becoming when its potentialities reach fulfilment. This drive entails a dialectical process of history, now largely conducted by man, where the "not-yet" of the *futurum* is educed purely from the latencies and tendencies of creative matter. The present is the "front-line" between the unfinished past, transcended because it is not yet the "kingdom of freedom," and the "kingdom" or the "home of identity," where man and nature will be perfectly reconciled. History is the open-ended "exodus" of the "not-yet" of being-matter, striving to overcome the possibility of falling into Nothingness by realizing the All. The objectively-real possibilities of the future reside in the "core" of matter yearning to be set free. It is this yearning which Bloch finds expressed in the data of man's phantasies and daydreams, in his basic hunger and love drives, in his literary, musical, and religious utopias. The ontological substratum pervading all these, however, is hope. Christianity has finally brought it to light as the human-eschatological messianic drive inherent in all reality. Bloch is grateful to Jesus and Christianity, he says, for turning the transcendent God into a vacuum and replacing him with the human messiah and ultimately with the undiscovered hidden future realization of man and the world in "eschatological brotherhood." Christ left behind a community of love to act as a steward of the messianic hope by serving as the building material and city of the future kingdom.

Jürgen Moltmann, Theology of Hope. In spite of Bloch's heavy influence, there remain a number of radically dissociating elements in Moltmann's thought. While Moltmann's theology of hope is essentially rooted in the perception that, from beginning to end, "Christianity is eschatology, is hope" (*Theology of Hope* 16), his systematic expression of the contents of this perception belies accommodation with Bloch and process theology. Like Bloch, Moltmann speaks of the future as the "mode of God's being." Unlike Bloch, Moltmann roots the nature of this future in the God who really exists "ahead of us in the horizons of the future opened to us" by his history of promise. Unlike Bloch, Moltmann speaks of the future as *adventus (parousia) Dei*, the arrival from ahead of us of "the God of the coming kingdom," whose reality, glory, and divinity are made known from the experience of his future in its transforming effect upon the past and the present. History is not built upon utopian wish-fulfilment of what can emerge from the "eternal process of the becoming and begetting of being," but is the continuing anticipation, in the past and the present, of the "not-yet"—the radically "new" and transforming future "which is neither in its reality nor in its potentiality already in existence" (*Future of Hope* 10–15). Whereas *futurum* can never be completely new, *adventus* is full of the infinite possibilities possible only to God and thereby pointing always toward him. It thus creates an ever-advancing "front-line" between the past which is "obsolete and passing" (the Old) and that which has never before been (the New).

Christian eschatology speaks of the future of God only from its reality-prolepsis in Christ's death and resurrection. In that event, God anticipated his future kingdom of *life out of death* and thereby created history as the time of hope. The glory of resurrection, however, shines forth in history from the crucified Christ and only there. The cross of Christ thus becomes the historical form of the resurrection and the kingdom of life with God becomes the future hope of the cross "until he comes." Since Christ rose from the dead, his death on the cross marks God's final judgment upon all that contradicts the future of freedom. Christ's present reign takes place in the historical dialectic of the cross-resurrection event that already mediates to the godless and godforsaken world under the conditions of the present liberation from enslavement to sin and death.

The "front-line" of the future of new life occurs in history wherever the power and significance of the Christ event continue to be mediated to a dying world. This takes place in the proclamation of the Gospel, which, as Word-prolepsis of the eschatological hope of the kingdom to the poor, mediates hope itself. The sacrament of hope is further mediated to history in the creation of the Christian community of hope wherever, as the new People of God, it overcomes contradiction with the future kingdom it manifests. Hope is, finally, present wherever, as "creative, battling, and loving obedience" (*Future of Hope* 38) it transforms personal life and social, political, and cosmic orders in anticipation of the coming new world. Thus, in a mission of service to the world in the spirit of Christ's "self-renouncing love," the Christian extends into the world the power of hope as the ontological force of the kingdom in history.

Hope is thus the power of faith which sets history in motion and gives it all its vitality. What is grounded in faith becomes effective through hope in the form of love of all reality in the service of its new birth. In its own way, Moltmann's theology of hope replaces a static metaphysics of being with a dynamic "metaphysics" of the Christ event, whose branches are visible in more recent developments in *political and *liberation theology.

Karl Rahner. Theology of hope finds expression in more recent writings of Karl Rahner, who endeavors to extract hope from its subordinate position to faith and love in traditional scholastic theology by seeing it as an enduring power of *dispossession of self* in radical self-commitment to the absolutely uncontrollable and utterly incalculable transcendence of the God of truth and love. This eschatological hope is that by which the individual knows that the promise of salvation, definitively offered to all in Christ's radical act of hope on the cross, is concretely conferred upon the individual as the promise of *his* salvation. On the basis of *Lumen gentium* 35 Rahner argues that this hope in the absolute future of God must express its self-dispossession outwardly in the "permanent transformation of the framework of secular life" (*Theological Investigations* 10, 256). In its continually revolutionary attitude toward petrified historical and social structures, Christian hope in practice obeys God's command to hope in his absolute future, sets out ever anew in an exodus toward that future, and sustains the future by making it real.

Vatican Council II gave official sanction to the "Eschatological Nature of the Pilgrim Church," the title of *Lumen gentium* ch. 7. The Church is seen as carrying on the mission of preparing for the "promised restoration" which has "already begun in Christ" and is "already anticipated in some real way" in the "imperfect holiness" of the Church (*Lumen gentium* 48). The "joys and hopes" of this age are the "joys and hopes ... of the followers of Christ" (*Gaudium et spes* 1) until "there is a new heaven and a new earth" (*Lumen gentium* 48). The "children of promise" are obliged to express their hope in the glory to come "in their daily social and family life" by continually turning it toward God and wrestling it from the forces of evil (ibid. 35). In their service to the total human community in every temporal labor and joy, the faithful "consecrate the world itself to God" and "lead their brother men to that King whom to serve is to reign" (ibid. 34–36).

See also ESCHATOLOGY; PROGRESS; THEOLOGY AND HISTORY.

Bibliography: E. BLOCH, *Das Prinzip Hoffnung* (3 v. Frankfurt 1967); *Man on his Own*, tr. E. B. ASHTON (New York 1970); *A Philosophy of the Future*, tr. J. CUMMING (New York 1970). C. E. BRAATEN, *The Future of God* (New York 1969). W. H. CAPPS, *Time Invades the Cathedral* (Philadelphia 1970). M. D. MEEKS, *Origins of the Theology of Hope* (Philadelphia 1970). M. D. MEEKS, *Theology of the World*, tr. W. GLEN-DOEPEL (New World 1969). J. MOLTMANN, *Theology of Hope*, tr. J. W. LEITCH (New York 1967); *Religion, Revolution, and the Future*, tr. M. D. MEEKS (New York 1969); "Theology as Eschatology," in F. HERZOG, ed., *The Future of Hope* (New York 1970) 1–50; *Hope and Planning*, tr. M. CLARKSON (London 1971); *The Experiment of Hope*, tr. M. D. MEEKS (Philadelphia 1975). W. PANNENBERG, "The God of Hope," tr. G. H. KEHM, in *Basic Questions in Theology* 2 (Philadelphia 1971) 234–249. K. RAHNER, *Theological Investigations* 10, tr. D. BOURKE (New York 1973) 235–289. O. WEBER, *Grundlagen der Dogmatik*, 2 v. (Neukirchen/Moers 1955–62).

[M. R. TRIPOLE]

HOSPITALS, CATHOLIC

There are 650 hospitals in the United States operated under the auspices of the Catholic Church—about 20 percent of the private, not-for-profit hospitals in the country. Most Catholic hospitals are sponsored by religious women, but 7 are sponsored by religious brothers, and about 20 by dioceses. There are (1978) about 180 fewer Catholic hospitals than there were ten years ago but the number of beds has increased by some ten thousand.

Significance of Statistics. The increased number of beds is a sign that the larger hospitals are progressing and serving the changing health needs of the population. The decline in number indicates that many small rural Catholic hospitals have closed because of the same conditions that have forced other small rural hospitals to close: a lack of physicians willing to practice in rural areas and of funds for sophisticated equipment and higher salaries that in the U.S. are a part of providing health care. A decline in religious vocations and a desire for other ministries have also been factors in leading religious congregations to close or give up sponsorship of some health facilities.

One statistic demonstrates the change that has occurred in Catholic hospital ministry in the last ten years: in 1967, about eight percent of the chief executive officers were lay people; today, over fifty percent are lay people. Thus lay responsibility and participation in this ministry has increased considerably and efforts are being made to incorporate the laity more fully into this ministry. Models for lay sponsorship of Catholic health care facilities, for example, are being developed.

Moreover, most Catholic hospitals have lay people serving with religious on the boards of trustees, a responsibility exercised by the laity only rarely ten years ago.

The Mission of Healing. Like all other institutions in the Church, the Catholic hospitals in the U.S. have responded to the call for renewal and deeper Christian commitment sounded by Vatican Council II. As a result, in recent years there has been intense self-questioning and a search for Christian identity, both on the part of people responsible for Catholic health care facilities and on the part of individuals engaged actively in this ministry. Under the leadership of the *Catholic Hospital Association, a greater sense of mission and self-understanding is present in the personnel, administrators, and sponsors of Catholic hospitals. That mission is to witness in the power of the Spirit to the abiding presence and healing ministry of Jesus Christ. Thus, quality health care provided in a Christian manner is the main purpose of the Catholic hospital.

In establishing Catholic hospitals, it is not the intent of the Church or Catholic sponsoring groups to set up a separate system of health care for Catholics. While this may have been the motivation in times past, today it is clear that Catholic hospitals are open to people of all denominations whether as patients, physicians, or employees. What the Church does attempt to do through Catholic hospitals is to penetrate, not parallel, secular society. An important purpose of Catholic institutions, as Vatican II explains it, is "to serve as a leaven and as a kind of soul for human society as it is renewed in Christ and transformed into God's family" (*Gaudium et spes* 40). Thus, the Catholic hospital seeks to be a place where the excellence of medical care, provided according to Christian principles, will help the Gospel spirit permeate and improve the temporal order. That does not mean denial, destruction, or replacement, but an enrichment, inspiration, enlightenment of the temporal with the values of Christ lived realistically through people and institutions with professional competence and Christian commitment. Thus, Catholic health facilities seek to "strengthen the seams of human society and imbue the everyday activity of man with a deeper meaning and importance" (*Gaudium et spes* 40). In a health-care setting, several values contained in the Gospels can be communicated to people more effectively than in other forms of human endeavor; for example, the Christian concept of suffering and death and of the dignity of individuals. The personnel of a Catholic hospital, then, should seek to treat every person with equal respect, realizing the worth of every human life and respecting the gift of life that God has given each person. The meaning of suffering and death should be explained in word and action to patients, as well as the interactive relationship in the human person between body and soul. In sum, Catholic health care facilities seek to give more than quality medical care, though this is the basis for their existence.

Social Justice. Another purpose of Catholic health care facilities lies in the realm of social justice. As the 1971 Synod of Bishops stated: "Action on behalf of justice and participation in the transformation of the world fully appear to us as a constitutive dimension of the preaching of the Gospel or, in other words, of the Church's mission for the redemption of the human race and its liberation from every oppressive situation" (Synod JustWorld p. 34). In the past, Christian spiritual-

ity often emphasized resignation or acceptance of oppression; often, no other course was available. Today, however, the teaching of the Church makes it clear that Christians should try to change the institutions that oppress or humiliate people. For Christians and Christian institutions in the field of medical care, there are many factors that could be improved: the emphasis upon remedial rather than preventive care; the continuing escalation of health-care costs; the limited access of the poor to health care; the need of some form of health insurance for all Americans; the involvement of state legislatures in determining the time of death and the treatment of dying patients; and the technological practice of medicine. Because of the numbers both of Catholic health care facilities and of Catholic and other Christian personnel, some unified effort at improving the system of health care in the country should be developed. The Catholic Hospital Association, as a result of its recent self-analysis, seeks to bring these institutions and individuals into a working relationship so that the responsibility of working for a better society may be fulfilled.

Pastoral Care. Another feature and distinguishing mark of the Catholic hospital is the presence of a pastoral-care program. In times past, the Catholic hospital was looked upon, more or less, as an extension of the Catholic parish; the chaplain at the hospital ministered only to the Catholic patients and his presence was looked upon as a convenience. Moreover, the only person associated with pastoral care was a priest. Today, the situation is entirely different. Pastoral care is a service in the Catholic hospitals not as an extension of the parish but rather because spiritual health is looked upon as an integral element in human health: a person cannot be healthy unless there is an effort to heal the spiritual and emotional as well as physiological needs. Pastoral care in a Catholic hospital is concerned about patients of all faiths; often there are chaplains of other denominations on the pastoral team. Moreover, counselors and pastoral visitors, often sisters or lay people, are part of the pastoral staff. People associated with pastoral-care departments are given special training so that they may be effective members of the health care group. Sacramental ministry is still an integral part of pastoral care, but the pastoral department offers many more services today than in the past and functions not as an adjunct to health care but as an integral part of the healing process. This is the meaning of the phrase that Catholic hospitals seek "to heal the whole person."

Conclusion. Throughout history there has been an effort on the part of Christians to carry on Jesus' healing ministry. Early efforts were directed toward home care alone; later on, when society became more complex, hospitals were organized and religious orders founded with their total apostolate the care of the sick. At first, these hospitals were mainly concerned with helping people, especially the poor, die in an atmosphere of Christian concern and comfort. In recent years, when the practice of medicine became more sophisticated and when the hospital became the center of the health care profession, the purpose and surrounding of the hospital changed considerably. With new concepts of hospital and of medical care there is more potential to heal and restore health, more opportunity to prevent disease. Though care for the poor is still a concern of Catholic hospitals, the health of all society is the primary concern. With all the changes, however, the purpose of

Catholic hospitals remains in accord with the Church's mission to bring the person of the healing Christ to people, to penetrate society with Christian values, and to work for a better society by striving for social justice in the field of health care.

Bibliography: American Hospital Association, *Hospitals in the 1980s* (Chicago 1977). Catholic Hospital Association, K. D. O'ROURKE, ed., *The Mission of Healing* (St. Louis 1976); *New Approaches and Orientations* (St. Louis 1977).

[K. D. O'ROURKE]

HOUSE OF AFFIRMATION

The House of Affirmation Inc., International Therapeutic Center for Clergy and Religious began as an outgrowth of the Worcester Consulting Center for Clergy and Religious. This was established in 1970 in response to the expressed needs of the religious professionals in the diocese, with the enthusiastic support of the Most Reverend Bernard J. Flanagan, Bishop of Worcester. The impact of Vatican Council II had been strongly felt by both clergy and religious, who had to meet increased pressures from the demands of decentralization and responsible involvement in social and ecclesial issues. The services of the Consulting Center provided a religious professional the opportunity for self-discovery through the contemporary approaches of psychiatry and psychology in dialogue with theological developments. At the suggestion of the Interim Senate for Religious Sr. Anna Polcino, SCMM, MD, a physician, surgeon and psychiatrist then working at the Worcester State Hospital, and Rev. Thomas A. Kane, Ph.D., D.P.S., then completing postgraduate work in psychology, became codirectors of the Consulting Center.

The overriding goal of the Consulting Center was to help clients become fully human, consistently free persons within the context of their ecclesial calling and social insertion. Sister Anna and Father Kane undertook to meet this goal through a threefold program of service, education, and research. After two full years of operation, however, it became apparent that the outpatient facilities were not sufficient for some religious and clergy who had come to the Consulting Center; there was definite need for an intensive residential treatment program. The House of Affirmation became a reality in October 1973 when the doors were opened to its first residents in Whitinsville, Massachusetts. Sr. Anna assumed the responsibility of psychiatric director of therapy and Fr. Kane, that of executive director. The residential center pursues the same goals as the Consulting Center, namely, service, education, and research. In 1974 a Boston office of the House of Affirmation opened and is directed by James P. Madden, CSC; in 1977 a second residential center was opened in Montara, California directed by Bernard J. Bush, SJ and Edwin J. Franasiak, MD; the third center was opened in Knowle, England in 1978, under the direction of Sr. Fiona Vallance.

The variety of programs offered by the House of Affirmation include residential psychotheological therapy, outpatient therapy, career and candidate assessment, consultation to religious communities, an internship leading to a master's degree in psychology, creative potential-development courses, and a publishing division to disseminate literature of interest to religious professionals. The House of Affirmation is neither a place of confinement nor a haven for "rest and recreation"; rather, it is a miniature social-religious community planned and controlled to facilitate the social learning of its residents. The professional staff members have accepted as the general goal of psychotherapy to help the "unfree," childishly dependent person become a genuine adult capable of "responding affirmatively to life, people and society" (Dalrymple, 10). The focus is on self-understanding and insight-building of an immediate and current nature in view of helping the individual to grasp the meaning of his existence in its historical totality. Ultimately, the mentally healthy client will attain freedom to choose, maturity in outlook, and responsible independence.

See also PSYCHOTHEOLOGICAL THERAPY.

Bibliography: J. DALRYMPLE, *The Christian Affirmation* (Denville, N.J. 1971). T. A. KANE, *The Healing Touch of Affirmation* (Whitinsville, Mass. 1976).

[T. A. KANE]

HOUSES OF PRAYER

Houses of prayer came into existence as one response to Pope John XXIII's call for a new Pentecost. Aware of their need for a more authentic prayer life to answer this call, in 1962 many religious women consulted Bernard Häring, CSSR. After conferring with some contemplatives, he came up with the challenge that apostolic religious "drink from their own well." His simple suggestion was that at least one house of a congregation form a rhythm of life determined by the needs of prayer alone—a place where members could step aside from their ordinary apostolic pace to find their own rhythm of the spirit; a place open to the needs of the community, the Church, and the world. He called this a "house of prayer," as in Isaiah, "I will make them joyful in my house of prayer" (56.7).

Fr. Häring presented the idea to the Conference of Major Superiors of Women (CMSW) at their 1965 meeting, but translation of the idea into a definite movement of the Spirit came quite accidentally. An item in the February 1968 newsletter of the CMSW called for some way of facilitating intercommunity cooperation. Sister Margaret Brennan of the Immaculate Heart of Mary Sisters, Monroe, Mich. volunteered for the assignment; significant developmental steps followed. In February 1968 a Clearing Center was opened in Monroe. In August a Conference on Contemplative Living in the Contemporary World was begun and representatives from ninety-five North American congregations developed a working rationale. In October seven members from the Monroe Conference met with Thomas Merton, OCSO at Redwoods, Cal.; he believed that the house of prayer would be central in the reexamination and recovery of the identity of all contemporary religious life. In 1969 HOPE '69 (House of Prayer Experience) a summer experimental program involving nineteen congregations, tested the rationale and shared the results through a report, *Exploring Inner Space*. In September 1970 Visitation House (The Lord's Barn) opened in Monroe and Kresge House opened in Detroit as an intercommunity orientation center offering an experiental program. At Thanksgiving in 1974 an Evaluative Conference held in Monroe made clear that the house of prayer was in actuality a new form of religious living in the Church today.

The House of Prayer Movement, however, was not organized; rather it developed in the spirit of Abraham one step at a time in faith, taking risks, letting things happen. The result was a multiplication of summer HOPE programs and a constantly increasing number of ongoing houses of prayer. Some seventy-five listed in the *Annual Directory* (1976) illustrate the variety: community-sponsored or intercommunity and/or mixed-community staffed; charismatic; stressing ministry or contemplation; offering Eastern or Western spirituality. The existential nature of their development makes classification difficult. The character of a house of prayer depends upon the charism of its core members and on their response to the needs that converge upon them. The outreach may extend to sisters, priests, brothers; to students, lay adults, ecumenical groups. The form of service is similar: days or weekends of varied prayer experiences, private or guided retreats, spiritual direction. A special evidence of vitality is the disappearance of traditional barriers between congregations, between men and women, religious and lay, between Catholic, Protestant, Buddhist, Hindu, or Jew.

The house of prayer idea has reached Mexico, England, France, Australia, the Philippines, and various parts of Africa. Through hundreds of letters and guests from all over the world, the orientation center has given help, encouragement, experience. Sister Mary Jo Maher, IHM visited all the outstanding spiritual leaders in Brazil, published articles in the leading Portuguese periodicals, and helped to organize HOPE programs. A HOPE program in Jerusalem, begun in 1973, continues to concentrate on Christian–Moslem–Jewish dialogue (Marie Goldstein, RSHM, HOPE Ecumenical Seminar, P.O.B. 19056, Jerusalem). Two contemplatives who gave encouragement and practical help are Sister Lilla Marie, MM, of the Maryknoll Cloister and Brother David Steindl-Rast, OSB, from the Monastery of Mt. Saviour in Elmira, New York.

Bibliography: *Annual Directory of Houses of Prayer, Crux* (Albany 1976, 1977). A. E. CHESTER, *Prayer Now* (Albany 1975). B. HÄRING, *Acting on the Word* (New York 1968).

[A. E. CHESTER]

HUMAN ACT

Morality has bearing only on human subjects and their properly human activity; thus the treatise on human acts has always been an important prelude in the study of moral theology (7:206).

Traditional Meaning. Within the Catholic tradition, a human act has always been seen contrasted with "an act of man." The latter term is used to describe actions which are common to both humans and animals; the former term is employed to refer only to those acts which can be performed by human beings. In most manuals of moral theology, a human act is defined as any action that issues from a person acting freely and with antecedent knowledge of the end or purpose of the act itself and with accompanying advertence. Human acts, therefore, are not to be confused with merely instinctive or inadvertent actions. Rather, they are the free and deliberate acts that set human beings off as being proper moral agents.

Before an action can be described as human, some dimensions of knowledge and freedom must be present in the actor; cognitive and volitional factors are essential. A fully human action presupposes some knowledge of the goodness or badness of the proposed action and some freedom of the will. The will's act proceeds in the light of the knowledge of the end or goal to be achieved. Every human act, therefore, presupposes knowledge. The formal object of the will is goodness and value; it is the function of the intellect or reason to indicate the good and to assess value. Thus human acts have their root in the spiritual center of the human person, i.e. in insight and in freedom.

Intellect and will do not exist in a vacuum, but in persons who are unique in themselves and involved in concretely differing situations. Both the classical and contemporary approaches to moral theology have, therefore, recognized the existence of modifying factors influencing human intellection and volition. Both approaches have always appreciated the fact that there are impediments to the due and proper working of both intellect and will; that the intellect may judge incorrectly or perversely and the will be influenced in its choice of moral good by its own inclinations to evil; that free election and free choice undergo serious inward and outward interference. The classical approach to moral theology distinguished between "actual obstacles" to the functioning of intellect and will and "habitual obstacles." The former, it saw as transient; the latter, it saw as permanent. The "actual" obstacles were usually listed as ignorance, passion, fear, and violence; the "habitual" obstacles were generally enumerated as evil propensities of the will, acquired evil habits, an incorrect sense of values, and mental aberrations.

Contemporary Interpretation. The contemporary approach to moral theology, while in no way denying the modifying factors singled out by the classical approach, treats the matter from a somewhat different point of view. Contemporary moralists distinguish between conceptual cognition and evaluative cognition, and between the will's philosophical (radical or seminal) freedom and its psychological (situational or achieved) freedom. According to contemporary authors, to be fully human, cognition must be both conceptual and evaluative. Conceptual cognition expresses what the object is; evaluative cognition appraises the value the object has. Thus, it is possible for a person to know that something is wrong inasmuch as that is what is taught by Church or society (conceptual cognition) and yet, for some reason or another, have serious difficulty in being able to appreciate why the contemplated action is wrong for him or her in this particular context (evaluative cognition). The fact that the projected action is wrong makes no great impression or at least makes far less impression than it ordinarily would. Thus, despite sufficient conceptual knowledge that a contemplated action is wrong, imputability would be measured rather in proportion to the evaluative knowledge that has been disturbed or suppressed.

It is also the opinion of many contemporary authors that to be fully human in its exercise, the will must be free both philosophically and psychologically. Philosophical freedom is the power, given certain prerequisites of knowledge and motivation, of saying yes or no freely to a proposed action or of choosing freely between two alternative courses. It means that at the time the choice was made, the person could have made the opposite choice even though with difficulty or repugnance. Psychological freedom is a freedom from obstacles and pressures that make the exercise of philosophical freedom difficult. Philosophical freedom is *freedom to determine* its own choices; psychological freedom is *freedom from the obstacles*, pressures, and impediments which make choices difficult. In the minds of some contemporaries, the classical tradition in moral theology seemed to take for granted the human person's freedom as a perfectly autonomous power of decision hindered in the exercise of its sovereignty only accidentally by factors that are rather exceptional. Contemporary authors seem to be less reluctant to admit that freedom of the will can be influenced only in exceptional cases. They tend to see human freedom as "freedom in situation" and they insist that the dialectic between freedom and determinism is essential for every human action.

Many contemporary moralists indicate the presence in all of the human person's actions of a determinism traceable to three sources—the biological, the social, and the psychological. They point out that recent discoveries of neurosurgery, endocrinology, and the use of drugs have demonstrated the influence of biological factors on the freedom of moral action. The pressure of society can also exert great influence on free activity and pressure groups and pressure factors have enormous determining potential in contemporary society. Finally, studies in depth psychology reveal constant neuroticizing factors under which many people live within the course of their growth and development as human beings.

In the human act, the cognitive and the volitional are completely necessary. The moral agent must have knowledge and he or she must have freedom. Authors have always been conscious of the fact that both elements can be seriously influenced by many factors both extrinsic and intrinsic to the human agent. However, the extent of this influence has ever been and remains seriously problematical. In this area as in many others which deal with human activity, the moral theologian has to be critically and judiciously aware of the discoveries of the empirical sciences. What they establish about the power to know and the freedom to choose can have considerable impact on knowledge of what constitutes the human act and this, in turn, has serious implications for theological teaching on such central matters as moral imputability and conscience formation.

Bibliography: J. FORD and G. KELLY, *Contemporary Moral Theology* 1 (Paramus, N.J. 1958) 174–312. J. FUCHS, *Human Values and Christian Morality*, tr. M. H. HEELAN (Dublin 1970), esp. "Basic Freedom and Morality," 92–111. E. MCDONAGH, "Towards a Christian Theology of Morality: The Moral Subject," IrTheolQ 39 (1972) 3–22. L. MONDEN, *Sin, Liberty and Law* (New York 1965) 19–72. G. REGAN, *New Trends in Moral Theology* (New York 1971) 187–207.

[J. A. O'DONOHOE]

HUMAN DEVELOPMENT

Human development is a process enabling people to take responsibility for the direction of their own lives and to guide themselves, within a social context, toward the one ultimate destiny intended by their Creator. The Christian concept of human development considers the human person as an integrated whole with one ultimate vocation. In this concept the ideal is that each person retain and nurture a constant movement towards that final goal. Within the notion of human development lies a recognition of the fact that human beings can achieve this ultimate objective only by acting according to a

knowing and free choice, and, in an ever increasing degree, by taking personal responsibility for the direction of their own lives. Man is left "in the hand of his own counsel" (Eccl 15.14) so that he can seek his Creator spontaneously (*Gaudium et spes* 17). This authentic freedom reflects the *imago Dei* within and it is only in freedom that human persons can develop their potentials and direct themselves towards their divine destiny.

The social circumstances into which many people are born and live often prevent them from developing their own potentials and pursuing the divine purposes set for them. Human freedom and personal responsibility—so necessary for authentic human development—are greatly diminished for people in extreme poverty. Because so many persons exist in dehumanizing living and working conditions, they are deprived of all but a minimal possibility of acting on their own initiative and responsibility. Ill-fed, inhumanly housed, illiterate, without jobs, and deprived of political power, they lack the necessary means of acquiring responsibility and moral dignity, and of furthering their own human development (Synod JustWorld p. 36). The life-long movement of individual persons towards their ultimate end unfolds within a social context. Born into community, and by nature social, they depend on and must relate to human community in order to develop their inborn potentials (Paul VI PopProgr 15). The manner in which the social order is structured directly affects the quality of human relationships, progress in developing potentials, and movement toward this ultimate end. While true human development includes personal conversion and constant turning towards God and neighbor, it also requires that there be made available such basic necessities for leading a truly human life as food, clothing, decent housing, education, dignified employment, participation in the political process. The lack of such necessities presents obstacles to human development that ultimately result from unjust social policies and structures within society.

The Campaign for Human Development under the U.S. episcopal conference represents one effort to bring about changes in social structures and to foster just social relationships. This working for justice, working for human development, has been recognized as a constitutive dimension of the preaching of the Gospel—it represents an integral part of the Church's mission (Synod JustWorld p. 34). The Campaign for Human Development is one approach to the realization of this ministry. For human development today requires changes in those systems and structures of society which oppress and stifle individuals, and which make it impossible for persons—individually and collectively—to act upon their own initiative and take responsibility for the quality and direction of their lives.

Bibliography: Campaign for Human Development, *Source Book on Poverty, Development, and Justice* (Washington, D.C. 1973).

[B. EVANS]

HUMAN LIFE AND NATURAL FAMILY PLANNING FOUNDATION

The forerunner of The Human Life and Natural Family Planning Foundation was incorporated in 1969 as The Human Life Foundation. It was established following a November 1968 vote of the American Catholic bishops in response to the appeal of Pope Paul VI to world scientists for research to improve methods of child spacing in keeping with the tenets of his encyclical, *Humanae vitae.*

The Corporation is organized exclusively to sponsor, through funding pursuant to contracts entered into with qualified persons, scientific research, experimentation, investigation, and analysis pertaining to the following areas: the generation of human life and reproductive physiology (including ovulation, spermatogenesis, factors influencing the transmission of life at the ovulant stage and at the stage of fertilization, fertilization, nidation); the beginning of human life; psychological and physiological ramifications of the human sexual act; medical implications of human-fertility control; implications of human-fertility control in relation to social and economic pressures upon family life and in relation to demographic problems; termination of the existence of the conceptus by abortion and otherwise; what constitutes abortion; abortifacients; what constitutes the end of human life; euthanasia; biological significance of the term "human"; medical and social implications of human transplantation.

The Foundation makes available to the public scientific knowledge derived from such scientific research, experimentation, investigation, and analysis, and sponsors or carries out educational programs related to the foregoing areas. It also cooperates with other organizations and persons performing related research and education.

An initial grant of $800,000 from the American bishops was directed into research of many different types. A grant to Fairfield University established the base line for the 1970s on the effectiveness of the Sympto-Thermal method of natural family planning in actual use in Canada, France, Colombia, Mauritius, and the United States (Tolor, Rice, and Lanctot). Another grant to Rudolf Vollman, M.D., of Switzerland, led to the publication of a definitive new book on the human menstrual cycle (Vollman). Josef Roetzer, M.D., of Vienna, worked under a Foundation grant to evaluate utilization of natural methods by his own patients and developed refinements on the Sympto-Thermal method with effectiveness comparable to the most popular artificial contraceptives (Roetzer and Keefe).

In January 1972 the Foundation cosponsored with the National Institute of Child Health and Human Development an international meeting of scientists and natural-family-planning experts to exchange information on the practice and potential of the methods (Uricchio and Williams). A year later a grant from the U.S. Agency for International Development made possible a second international meeting in Washington, D.C. to focus on methods of teaching natural approaches to fertility control. This meeting set the groundwork for the formation of the International Federation for Family Life Promotion, an international organization of natural-family-planning units in 50 countries and also the Natural Family Planning Federation of America.

Both of these international meetings underscored the need for a disciplined approach to the training of American natural-family-planning teachers as the condition for successful application of the methods in the United States. In 1974 a grant was made to the Foundation by the Health Services Administration of the U.S. Dept. of Health, Education, and Welfare (HEW) to develop the outline for such a teaching curriculum. By 1975, when the Foundation again convened an interna-

tional symposium in Boston, Mass., both the curriculum outline and a plan for a rigorous American test of the two most popular methods had been completed and were presented to HEW and the World Health Organization (WHO) authorities. Shortly thereafter, HEW funded full development of the curriculum and necessary educational aids through the Health Services Administration and adopted the comparative study of the Sympto-Thermal and Ovulation methods in the Archdiocese of Los Angeles under a grant of $1,400,000 from the National Institute of Child Health and Human Development. Starting from a base of the original Foundation curriculum outline, WHO initiated research on a cross-cultural teaching curriculum and adopted the study outline used in the Archdiocese of Los Angeles for a WHO study of these two methods in Colombia, South America.

Development of the curriculum and the growth of the popularity of natural methods in the U.S. after 1975, resulted in two new programs for the Foundation. One, the library and communications center, was directed toward the exchange of accurate information in the family-planning and scientific communities as well as the acquisition of key educational materials from around the world for review by teachers. This center has been influential in providing correct terminology and current information to the nationwide population-library network. A second program, a collaborative effort involving teachers, physicians, and scientific investigators, resulted in the creation of a publishing division. In addition to its own educational materials, the Foundation prepares the publications of the International Federation under a special contract.

Although the Foundation saw its role as separate from the National Family Planning Federation of America for several years, it became evident in 1977 that the two organizations would be more effective as a single unit. In November 1977 the lay members of the Federation board were elected to the Foundation board and the new Human Life and Natural Family Planning Foundation combined the strengths of both. Edward B. Hanify of Boston, founding chairman of the original Foundation board, continues as president and chairman of the board of the expanded Foundation. The 23-member board includes educators, physicians, a psychiatrist, a social scientist, business executives, and attorneys.

In May 1978, the Foundation cosponsored with the *Bishops' Committee on Pro-Life Activities a 10-year report meeting in New York City to assess the progress of the decade following the publication of the encyclical letter *Humanae vitae.* This meeting concluded with a general session to draft a 5-year plan for future development of natural family planning in the United States. Also in 1978 HEW launched a series of research and educational programs intended to make natural methods more generally available in the United States. Foundation personnel and board members were instrumental in the conduct of many of these programs.

Bibliography: J. ROETZER and V. F. KEEFE, *Fine Points of the Symptothermic Method of Natural Family Planning*, A. Zimmerman, ed. (Human Life Center, Collegeville, Minn. 1977). A. TOLOR, F. J. RICE, and C. A. LANCTOT, "Personality Patterns of Couples Practicing the Temperature-Rhythm Method of Birth Control," *The Journal of Sex Research* 11 (1975) 2:119–133. R. F. VOLLMAN, "The Menstrual Cycle," in E. A. FRIEDMAN, ed., *Major Problems In Obstetrics and Gynecology* 7 (Philadelphia 1977). W. A. URICCHIO and M. K. WILLIAMS, eds., *Proceedings of a*

Research Conference on Natural Family Planning (The Human Life Foundation, Washington, D.C. 1973).

[L. J. KANE]

HUMAN RIGHTS

In 1948 the General Assembly of the United Nations proclaimed the Universal Declaration of Human Rights "as a common standard of achievement for all peoples and all nations." The Declaration affirms the civil and political rights traditionally valued in Western democracies: the rights to life, liberty, security of person, property, association, freedom from arbitrary arrest and imprisonment, etc. It also includes the social, economic, and cultural rights more recently emphasized in socialist societies: the rights to food, clothing, shelter, health, work, education, social security, etc. Both kinds of rights are grounded in the fact that "All human beings are born free and equal in dignity. They are endowed with reason and conscience and should act towards one another in a spirit of brotherhood" (Art. 1).

Widespread concern that this Declaration be translated into action was one of the "signs of the times" which shaped the deliberations and conclusions of Vatican Council II. Echoing Pope John XXIII's encyclical *Pacem in terris*, the Council observed that "there is a growing awareness of the exalted dignity proper to the human person since he stands above all things, and his rights and duties are universal and inviolable. Therefore, there must be made available to all men everything necessary for leading a life truly human, such as food, clothing, and shelter; the right to choose a state of life freely and to found a family, the right to education, to employment, to a good reputation, to respect, to appropriate information, to activity in accord with the upright norms of one's own conscience, to protection of privacy and to rightful freedom in matters religious too" (*Gaudium et spes* 26). In the years since these statements were made important developments in the human rights area have taken place in both secular society and in the Churches.

The Context of Renewed Concern. Interest in the promotion of human rights has been stimulated by a growing awareness that they are violated in many parts of the world.

The World. The number of authoritarian regimes in Latin America, Africa, and Asia has increased dramatically during this period. These governments frequently appeal to the need to protect national security as a justification for states of emergency or siege in which such basic constitutional guarantees as *habeas corpus* are suspended. The widespread use of torture and summary imprisonment as a means of social control has been carefully documented by Amnesty International (a nongovernmental organization which received the Nobel Peace Prize for its work in 1977). Violations of rights to religious freedom, freedom of movement, and free speech in Eastern Europe and the Soviet Union have been widely publicized. A pledge to respect rights "which derive from the inherent dignity of the human person and are essential for his free and full development" was included in the Final Act of the Conference on Security and Cooperation in Europe held in Helsinki in 1975 (see HELSINKI AGREEMENT). This pledge has formally introduced questions of violations of human rights into superpower politics and diplomacy. The right to self-determination for the black majorities in South

Africa, Zimbabwe (Rhodesia), and Namibia (Southwest Africa) has become an important economic and political issue both on the continent of Africa and internationally (*see* AFRICA, SOUTHERN). The UN conferences on population and on food (1974) underscored the lack of protection accorded rights to fulfillment of basic human needs for a majority of the world's population. Reaffirmation of the importance of social and economic rights provided moral backing for proposals for the creation of a *New International Economic Order at the Sixth and Seventh Special Sessions of the UN General Assembly (1974 and 1975). Both public and private agencies concerned with world economic development such as the *World Bank, the Club of Rome, and the Overseas Development Council have begun to advocate an international development strategy designed to meet the basic human needs and protect the minimal rights to subsistence of the world's poorest people. Despite all these important developments, however, the UN Declaration still remains a "standard of achievement" rather than a fulfilled reality in many parts of the world.

The United States. In the U.S. discussion of the protection of human rights has also developed in significant new ways. The Carter administration introduced human rights considerations into U.S. foreign policy in a highly visible way. The U.S. Congress has approved legislation outlawing military and economic aid to "any country which engages in a consistent pattern of gross violations of internationally recognized human rights unless such aid directly benefits the needy." The policy implications of these actions have been subject to heated discussion. On the domestic front the debate about how the rights of minorities are to be protected has been similarly intense and new developments have been notable. The equal protection clause of the U.S. Constitution has been interpreted in a way which calls for affirmative action by government to assure that blacks and other minorities have access to social goods (e.g., education, jobs) which they have been denied by traditional patterns of discrimination. Others have argued that this leads to a form of "reverse discrimination" against whites, though this position is more difficult to sustain from both a moral and legal point of view. The debate has also been vigorous over a proposed Equal Rights Amendment to the Constitution which would outlaw denial or abridgement of rights under the law on account of sex. This amendment and a number of judicial decisions concerning discrimination against women are manifestations of one of the most important new developments in human rights area: the modern women's movement. Strident conflict over the relationship between the rights of women in the area of abortion and the rights of nascent human life has been a particularly visible manifestation of the difficulty which societies can have in their efforts to translate human rights into social policy. The same difficulty is evident in the growing discussions of the rights of homosexuals, the rights of those who are physically sick, mentally retarded or psychologically disturbed, and the rights of those who are dying.

In short, the past decade has produced important new awareness of the significance of the claims of human dignity and human rights throughout the world. At the same time, the knowledge that these claims are often denied in practice has increased. The difficulty of formulating both a coherent theory of human rights and consistent social policies for their protection has become more evident than ever before.

Developments in Roman Catholic Rights-Theory. The classic statement of Roman Catholic thought on human rights in the modern period is Pope John XXIII's encyclical *Pacem in terris* (1963). In its approach the foundation of all rights is the inviolable dignity of the human person. From a theological point of view this dignity is seen as a consequence of the fact that all persons are created in the image of God, have been redeemed by Jesus Christ, and are called to a destiny beyond history. Philosophically considered, this dignity is rooted in the fact that persons are endowed with freedom and reason. Their ability to think and to choose, their experienced obligation to discriminate between good and evil actions, and their hopes which always exceed the present moment—all these indicate that persons are more than things and should be treated accordingly. Thus, though their ultimate warrant for human dignity and rights in Catholic thought is theological, human dignity and rights are also grounded in an analysis of the person which is intelligible apart from Christian faith. Respect for human dignity in concrete historical, natural, and social relationships calls for definite forms of action and social organization. Such particularized demands of human dignity are called human rights. *Pacem in terris* presents a list of these rights which approximately parallels that contained in the UN Universal Declaration. This list includes both the negative immunities from social or political interference characteristic of the liberal tradition (life, liberty, property) and the positive entitlements to the fulfillment of basic human needs stressed in socialist societies (food, shelter, health care, work, education, etc.). The duty to protect these rights is an obligation both to refrain from violating the dignity of others and to positively come to the aid of others when failure to do so would result in the destruction of their dignity. Thus the modern Catholic rights-theory as synthesized by *Pacem in terris* sees rights as correlative with duties. These duties obligate individuals, society, and the state. Rights are not created by the state but are rather to be recognized and guaranteed by it. All persons are obligated to contribute "to the establishment of a civic order in which rights and duties are progressively more sincerely and effectively acknowledged and fulfilled" (John XXIII PacTerris 31).

Advance in Basic Principles. Since Vatican II this understanding of human rights has been retained, but it has been nuanced and developed in significant ways. The Declaration on Religious Freedom explicitly states that the Council "intends to develop the doctrine of recent Popes on the inviolable rights of the human person and on the constitutional order of society" (*Dignitatis humanae* 1). This statement is remarkable for its acknowledgment of the possibility of change in the fundamental principles of Catholic social ethics. Emphasis on the dynamic and developing nature of the demands of human dignity has been characteristic of Catholic rights-theory since the Council. The principal result of the new attention to the historical conditions of the time has been an emphasis on the interlocking connections between the various human rights. This interconnectedness is the result of the increasing importance of complex social structures in the lives of individual persons and smaller associations. The protection

of personal dignity cannot take place apart from careful attention to the way powerful economic, social, and political systems shape and impinge on persons and groups. Such structural interdependence is particularly important in efforts to secure the rights of the poor in the less developed countries.

The Rights of Development and Participation. Beginning with Pope Paul VI's encyclical letter *Populorum progressio* (1967), Catholic discussion of human rights has given increasing attention to the socio-economic rights of the poor of the Third World and to the structural changes in the international economy which respect for these rights demands (*see* THIRD WORLD, CHURCH AND).

At the 1971 Synod of Bishops the interconnection of all human rights and the power of large-scale structures of social organization led to the affirmation of the fundamental importance of the "right to development" as a guiding principle in all discussion of human rights. The Synod defined this right as "a dynamic interpenetration of all those fundamental human rights upon which the aspirations of individuals and nations are based" (Synod JustWorld p. 37). This right, therefore, should not be regarded simply as an additional right to be added to the lists which were presented in the Universal Declaration and in *Pacem in terris*. Its emergence clarifies the way in which the concept of human rights is increasingly dependent on an analysis of the predominant institutional patterns of human interaction—economic, political, technological, and ecological. In the words of the Synod, "The strong drive toward global unity, the unequal distribution which places decisions concerning three-quarters of income, investment, and trade in the hands of one-third of the human race, namely the more developed part, the insufficiency of merely economic progress, and the new recognition of the material limits of the biosphere—all this makes us aware that in today's world new modes of understanding human dignity are arising" (ibid. p. 36). This analysis of the present situation calls in a new way for the protection of every person's "right to participation" in the institutions which can threaten or enhance his or her human dignity.

Thus in the postconciliar period the rights to development and to participation have become integrating concepts in Roman Catholic thinking on human rights. They have opened the way to the further incorporation of insights from socialist thought on the importance of social and economic rights and of structures of economic power in the present world situation. They have also provided a basis for renewed activity by the Catholic Church in opposition to those authoritarian regimes which frequently appeal to the need for national security as a justification for social patterns which effectively dominate large segments of the population and deny them any genuine form of economic and political participation (*see* LATIN AMERICA, CHURCH IN; PHILIPPINES, CHURCH IN). The rights to development and participation have provided a basis for criticism of both capitalist and socialist ideologies whenever these are used to marginalize people economically or silence them politically. The other more classical rights (both liberal and socialist) are seen as specifications of these two fundamental norms of contemporary Roman Catholic rights-theory.

Renewal of a Theology of Human Rights. These

developments have been supported not only by a changed analysis of the social situation but by a renewal of the theological framework of Catholic social thinking. Traditional Catholic social ethics has been rooted in natural law thinking and has appealed to reason rather than Revelation as its primary methodological norm. This commitment to the use of reason, including both philosophy and the social sciences, has been vigorously sustained since the Council in discussions of human rights. At the same time the ambiguities of the notion of *natural law have been more explicitly recognized than in the past. In his 1971 "Call to Action" Paul VI took note of the fact that "the human sciences are a condition at once indispensable and inadequate for a better understanding of what is human" (Paul VI OctogAdven 40). They are indispensable because the concrete conditions and possibilities for the protection of human dignity and rights cannot be known without careful use of human reasoning and analysis. They are inadequate because social, scientific and philosophical reasoning can grasp only partial aspects of the full reality of human existence. Thus since the Council the plurality of visions of the normatively human which exists in the world has been increasingly recognized. While continuing to propose an approach to human rights that is rooted in claims about the nature of the human person, contemporary Catholic teachings have made it much more explicit that Christian faith has influenced its understanding of human nature. Thus, as Vatican II put it, "By virtue of the gospel committed to her, the Church proclaims the rights of man. She acknowledges and greatly esteems the dynamic movements of today by which these rights are everywhere fostered" (*Gaudium et spes* 41). This development in Catholic-rights theory is not simply methodological. It has had the substantive consequence of reinforcing the tradition's stress on human solidarity and on the rights of the poor and the marginalized. By developing its approach to human dignity and rights from the perspectives of both the Christian Gospel and human understanding, contemporary Catholic thought has come to give practical priority to the dignity and rights of the poor, the oppressed, and the victimized. This new emphasis has not replaced that of John XXIII and his predecessors but rather gives it a new religious depth and practical orientation.

Developments in the Protestant Churches. The same social threats to human dignity that have stimulated increasing concern for human rights in secular society and in the Roman Catholic Church have brought about a growing discussion of human rights in a number of Protestant Churches and ecumenical groups. The World Council of Churches (WCC) conducted an important *Consultation on Human Rights and Christian Responsibility* in St. Pölten, Austria in 1974. The topic of human rights was a major focus of the WCC Assembly in Nairobi in 1975. In 1970 the World Alliance of Reformed Churches (WARC) began a serious investigation of the "Theological Basis of Human Rights and the Liberation of Human Beings," a process which culminated at a Theological Consultation in London in 1976 and at the Centennial Consultation of WARC in Scotland in 1977. In 1970 at Évian, France, the Lutheran World Federation (LWF) summoned the Churches "to search for ways, means, and opportunities of enabling their members to study the Universal Declaration of Human Rights and to undertake the application of this declaration in the national life of their member Churches." In 1976 the Department of Studies of the LWF convened an important Consultation on the Theology of Human Rights. In commemoration of the 25th anniversary of the Universal Declaration in 1973, the World Council of Churches and the Pontifical Commission for Justice and Peace issued a joint appeal to the Churches on the subject of human rights.

Developments in Protestant Thought. These events give evidence of significant developments in Protestant thinking on the subject of human rights. Because of traditional Protestant preference for biblical rather than natural-law approaches to ethics, the theological task of determining a contemporary Christian approach to human rights has been greater for Protestantism than for Roman Catholicism. The same preference has enabled Protestant theologians to see close links between the more biblically-based liberation theologies and the language of human rights. In general the Protestant discussions of human rights have stressed the analogies between the Christian vision of the Kingdom of God and the kind of human society in which persons are fully respected. Negatively, they have emphasized the sinful propensity of human beings which leads to the absolutizing of particular social systems or ideologies. By stressing human sinfulness in this way the Protestant thinkers argue for the need continually to liberate both individuals and social systems from enslavement to that which is not truly human. The defense of human rights is a continual protest against such enslavement.

Ecumenical Consensus. There are important signs, therefore, of movement toward greater theological consensus between Roman Catholics and Protestants on the foundations of social morality and the Christian contribution to the social order. In adopting human rights as appropriate categories for understanding this contribution Protestantism is moving closer to traditional Catholic thought. At the same time, by making its biblical and theological bases clearer Catholicism is moving toward what has been a traditionally more Protestant approach. In the years ahead it is to be hoped that these theological developments will continue and that genuinely ecumenical action in defense of human rights will intensify. Such progress will continue if the Churches remain responsive to the economic and political realities of secular society and to both the liberal and socialist strands in the debate about human rights, while deepening their understanding of the political implications of Christian faith.

Bibliography: M. COHEN, T. NAGEL, and T. SCANLON, eds., *Equality and Preferential Treatment* (Princeton 1977). Commission of the Churches on International Affairs (WCC), *Human Rights and Christian Responsibility*, 2 v. (Geneva 1974). A. COX, *The Role of the Supreme Court in American Government* (New York 1976). R. DWORKIN, *Taking Rights Seriously* (Cambridge, Mass. 1977). J. FEINBERG, *Social Philosophy* (Englewood Cliffs, N.J. 1973). J. GREMILLION, ed., *The Gospel of Peace and Justice: Catholic Social Teaching since Pope John* (Maryknoll, N.Y. 1976). LADOC, *Latin American Bishops Discuss Human Rights*, 2 v., LADOC Keyhole Series n. 15 and 16 (Washington, D.C. 1977). A. O. MILLER, ed., *A Christian Declaration on Human Rights* (Grand Rapids 1977). Pontifical Commission for Justice and Peace, "The Church and Human Rights," OSSRomEng, Oct. 23, 30; Nov. 6, 13, 1975. D. D. RAPHAEL, ed., *Political Theory and the Rights of Man* (Bloomington, Ind. 1967). L. B. SOHN and T. BRUEGGENTHAL, eds., *Basic Documents on International Protection of Human Rights* (Indianapolis 1973). Theological Studies Department of the Federation of Protestant Churches in the German Democratic Republic, "Theological Aspects of Human

Rights," *WCC Exchange* n. 6 (December 1977). H.-E. TÖDT, "Theological Reflections on the Foundations of Human Rights," *Lutheran World* 1/1977, 44–58. V. VAN DYKE, *Human Rights, the United States and the World Community* (New York 1970). E. and M. WEINGÄRTNER, eds., *Human Rights Is More than Human Rights: A Primer for Churches on Security and Cooperation in Europe*, IDOC Europe Dossier Five (Rome 1977). Yale Task Force on Population Ethics, "Moral Claims, Human Rights and Population Policies," ThSt 35 (1974) 83–113.

[D. HOLLENBACH]

HUTCHINS, ROBERT MAYNARD

American writer, editor, and educator, b. Brooklyn, N.Y., January 17, 1899, d. Santa Barbara, Cal., May 16, 1977. He attended Oberlin College, in Ohio, where his father, a Presbyterian minister, had been professor of theology. During World War I Hutchins interrupted his education and served in the ambulance service for the Italian and United States armies. He was later graduated from Yale University (1921) and Yale Law School (1925), where he was subsequently named dean (1927). He was named president of the University of Chicago in 1929 and remained until 1951. He introduced a curriculum based on the "Great Books"; his views clashed with the prevailing empiricism and pragmatism, and he especially opposed the idea that the university was a place to learn a trade. Through Mortimer J. Adler he became attached to the classics and to the thought of St. Thomas Aquinas. Hutchins vigorously defended academic freedom and led the opposition to faculty loyalty oaths. He played a significant role in the development of the atomic bomb. At the request of the U.S. government (1940), he invited the nation's foremost scientists to Chicago for what was called the Metallurgical Project. He gave final approval to the tests carried out secretly under the university stadium, Dec. 2, 1942, which resulted in the first controlled, self-sustaining nuclear chain reaction.

In 1951 Hutchins became associate director of the Ford Foundation, and in 1954 the president of the Fund for the Republic, whose main objective was the defense of civil liberties. In 1959 he founded at Santa Barbara the Center for the Study of Democratic Institutions, intended as a community of scholars in serious dialogue on serious issues. The Center was aided by a $10 million grant from Chester Carlson of Xerox Corporation. Hutchins retired as the Center's chairman in 1974, but then resumed the presidency in 1975 when there was a real threat of insolvency and many staff members were dismissed and a separate branch was set up in Chicago. From 1943 he had been chairman of the Board of Editors of *Encyclopaedia Britannica* and a director for Encyclopaedia Britannica, Inc.; besides editing the *Great Books*, he coedited with Mortimer J. Adler (from 1961) the annual supplement: *The Great Ideas Today*. Of special religious significance among the latter was the 1967 issue, which consisted of a symposium on the theme, Religionless Christianity, with Harvey Cox, E. L. Mascall, Martin E. Marty, and M.-D. Chenu among the participants. Part 3 of the 1969 issue includes Étienne Gilson's article on the idea of God and the difficulties of atheism. Hutchins' own writings include: *No Friendly Voice* (1936); *The Higher Learning in America* (1936); *Education for Freedom* (1943); *The University of Utopia* (1953); and *The Learning Society* (1968).

[E. J. DILLON]

HYMNOLOGY

Hymnology is that discipline which is concerned with the historical and scientific study of the hymn, from both a textual and musical point of view. Hymns have been a part of Christian worship from its very beginnings. Originally the word seems to have been used to describe any song in praise of God—scriptural or not, stanzaic or free. Later it came to be applied in a more restrictive sense to any nonscriptural, religious poem in strophic form, usually in a regular meter, and set to a relatively simple melody (7:287).

The extensive repertoire of Christian hymnody provides a large body of available material, much of which remains untapped, while at the same time providing the basis for insights into such current problems as variety in the liturgy and adaptation of the liturgy to the various cultures of local Churches (*see* LITURGY AND LOCAL CHURCHES). The sheer number of hymns from patristic and medieval sources is staggering. The *Analecta hymnica medii aevi* (G. Dreves and C. Blume, ed., Leipzig 1886–1922) contains fifty-five large volumes of Latin hymn texts and it is not complete. Study of the theology, literary form, and poetic approach to the truths of the faith as it is found in these hymns provides insights valuable for today. Modern poetic translations of these hymns, most of which have never been translated, would not only add variety to contemporary worship, but would also provide witness to the faith of Christians in earlier centuries.

Study of the vernacular hymnody of the past, whether of medieval Germany, 15th-century England, or 16th-century Germany or France, can prove useful in solving the problems of vernacular hymnody today. Many recent hymnals have drawn upon hymnological research to provide hymns from previously neglected areas: the work of such 17th-century English religious poets as George Herbert, the lesser known hymns of such great 18th-century hymn writers as Isaac Watts and the Wesleys, and the hymns of such 19th-century authors as John Keble or John Henry Newman.

The study and collection of hymn tunes is also important to hymnology. Of special value are collections of hymns in plainchant style, Lutheran chorales, and tunes from the French metrical psalters. The study of such tunes provides insight into what makes a singable tune and into the process of adapting older melodies as well as popular and folk melodies to contemporary use. The study of spirituals, evangelical songs, and other folk genres provides necessary insights into the adaptation of worship music to various cultures, as well as to the development of authentic forms of worship in a more popular vein.

In addition to the materials listed below mention should also be made of other important work in recent years. The work of the Hymn Society of America, both in its published papers and in its periodical, *The Hymn*, remains indispensable to hymnology. The continued excellent work of Erik Routley, especially his more recent articles in *The Hymn* and in *Worship*, to say nothing of his many earlier publications, provide a valuable hymnological resource. J. Vincent Higgenson's *Handbook of American Catholic Hymnals*, published (1976) by the Hymn Society of America provides an excellent and comprehensive study of a long-neglected area. The forthcoming publication of a *Dictionary of American Hymnology* under the leadership of Leonard Ellinwood will certainly be an important hymnological event.

Bibliography: W. H. FRERE, *Historical Edition of "Hymns Ancient and Modern"* (London 1909). M. FROST, ed, *Historical Companion to "Hymns Ancient and Modern"* (London 1962). *The Hymnal 1940, Companion* (3d. ed. rev., New York 1951). G. P. JACKSON, *Spiritual Folk Songs of Early America* (New York n.d.). H. A. L. JEFFERSON, *Hymns in Christian Worship* (London 1950). B. STÄBLEIN, "Hymnus," MusGG 6:987–1032). O. WESTENDORF, "The State of Catholic Hymnody," *The Hymn* 28 (1977) 54–60.

[R. B. HALLER]

HYMNS AND HYMNALS

It is not much more than a decade since the able and comprehensive *New Catholic Encyclopedia* article was written (7:295). During that time developments have been so great and changes so swift that it is here possible only to mark the major trends and, in a manner not normal in a reference work, to guess at future probabilities.

Change. The most noticeable change in Catholic habits concerning hymnody is the very liberal interpretation of the instructions of Vatican Council II in respect of vernacular songs. The active participation of the people was encouraged by the Constitution on Sacred Liturgy; and this has been partly interpreted as a licence to use hymnody of non-Catholic origins. Congregational hymnody is essentially a Protestant invention when it is associated with liturgy, and its fountainhead was Martin Luther. It must be made quite clear that before his time the laity was not deprived of communal religious song. But communal religious song was not part of the liturgy: Luther's contribution was to make it so. This means that hymnody in English and German (its two classic living languages) reached its maturity in a Protestant environment. It does not mean, however, that Protestant hymnody often, or even normally, expressed ideas and doctrine repugnant to Catholics. Therefore it was natural that with the new liberation of hymnody Catholics should take advantage of the readymade repertory. As a consequence of this, to mention only two examples, the English Catholic hymnal, *Praise the Lord* (1972) uses Protestant originals for 40 per cent of its 334 hymns and *Worship II* (1975), the American hymnal, for 60 per cent (185) of its 306 uses Protestant originals.

The years under review (1965–77) have been years of unresolved tension, and the direction of that tension is illustrated in two quotations:

> The Church recognizes Gregorian chant as being specially suited to the Roman Liturgy. Therefore, other things being equal, it should be given pride of place in liturgical services (Vatican II, *Sacrosanctum Concilium* 116). All means must be used to promote singing by the people. New forms of music suited to different mentalities and to modern tastes should also be approved by the episcopal conference (*Liturgicae instaurationes* 3c; 3d Instruction on the Proper Implementation of the Constitution on the Liturgy, Congr. for Divine Worship, Sept. 5, 1970; ActApS 62 [1970] 692–704]).

If the translation correctly interprets the mind of the Constitution, we have here a pair of instructions which demand considerable skill if they are to be harmonized. What is clear is that in practice the carrying out of the second instruction has been done largely at the expense of the first.

Catholic Hymnals. Since 1965 a large number of hymnals for local and for more general use has been published. Among these are, in the U.S., *The Missouri Catholic Hymnal* (1969), *The People's Mass Book* (1970), *The Johannine Hymnal* (1970), *Worship* (1971), *The Catholic Hymnal* (1974), *The Vatican II Hymnal* (1974), *Pray Together Hymnal* (1975), *The Catholic Liturgy Book* (1975), *Worship II* (1975) and *We Celebrate with Song* (1976). Not all of these reach the standard of typography, precision, and editorial care that are found in the best of them, and some show evidence of hasty compilation. But these are only a few—representing perhaps the most and the least satisfactory—of the hymnals which the explosion since 1965 had produced.

Canada's best example is *The Catholic Book of Worship* (1972) and England has produced *The Parish Hymnal* (1969), *The New Catholic Hymn Book* (1971), *Praise the Lord* (1972), and *A Song in Season* (1976).

Mention must also be made of the music ministry of the *Centre Nationale de Pastorale Liturgique* in Paris, which has been introducing hymnody, mostly in the form of responsive canticles, to French-speaking Catholics, under the leadership of Didier Rimaud and Joseph Gélineau.

Non-Catholic Hymnody. American hymnals from other communions during our decade include the Lutheran *Worship Supplement* (1969), *Hymnal for Christian Worship* (American Baptists and Disciples, 1970), *More Hymns and Spiritual Songs* (Episcopal, 1971), the Mennonite *Worship Hymnal* and *Christian Hymnal* (1971, 1972), the Presbyterian *Worshipbook* (1972), *The Covenant Hymnal* (1973), *Hymns for the Living Church* (1974), *The Book of Worship for U.S. Forces* (1974), *The Hymnal of the United Church of Christ* (1975), *The Baptist Hymnal* (Southern Baptist Convention, 1975), *Westminster Praise* (1976), and *Ecumenical Praise* (1977). A new hymnal for the Lutherans is, at the time of writing, projected.

In Canada there have appeared the *Hymn Book* (for the Episcopal Church and the United Church of Canada, 1971) and the Presbyterian *Book of Praise* (1972). In Great Britain this decade has mostly been the decade of "Supplements"—small selections amplifying but not superseding existing full-size books. The hardbound new hymnals have been *The Cambridge Hymnal* (1967), *Church Hymnary, Third Edition* (1973), *Christian Worship* (1976), *The Grace Hymnal* (1977). Two important books for young people have appeared: *Youth Praise* (1966) and *Psalm Praise* (1974). The "Supplements" are *Hymns and Songs* (Methodist, 1969), *100 Hymns for To-day* (Anglican, 1969), *New Church Praise* (United Reformed Church, 1975), *Praise for To-day* (Baptist, 1975), and *English Praise* (Anglican, 1976).

Perhaps the most unusual event during the period was the publication in 1974 for the fourth and greatly enlarged edition of the international hymn book, *Cantate Domino*, containing (as did its predecessors since the first in 1924) hymns from a wide variety of cultures, all printed in several languages, and itself having been much enriched because in this edition for the first time Catholics participated.

A glance at these books, together with a great number of small occasional, experimental publications, indicates the speed at which things have moved. The cultural restlessness of the second half of the 20th century is a nontheological fact with which Vatican II itself had to wrestle: it has produced much that is trivial and ephemeral and much also that is likely to be a permanent enrichment of the literature. Among authors of new texts the American Martin Franzmann (1907–76) and Ford L. Battles deserve special mention: among the British, Frederick Pratt Green, Fred Kaan, Brian Wren, Michael Hewlett and Timothy Dudley-Smith seem to be in greatest demand. The Scottish priest James Quinn, has done special service in editing *Hymns for All Seasons* (1969), a compilation of his own texts and translations upon which most later editors have drawn.

The Future. The original article predicted a National Hymnal for American Catholics. At the moment of writing this prospect has receded; it is too early yet to attempt a fusion of all the cultures represented in modern American Catholicism, especially in an age in which the existence of racial and ethnic Catholic groups is a fact of life. That article also commends the development of new hymns in 20th-century styles. We should now have to say that much depends on whose style is being commended—that of rebellious and concerned youth, that of Mr Calvin Hampton (for whom see *Worship-II*) or that of Richard Dirksen, whose setting of "Rejoice, ye pure in heart" (1974) is certainly the finest example of modern use of the traditional style. The 20th century is more enigmatic than was thought in 1965, and predictions about even the near future are too subjective and unreliable to attempt here. What we can say with some assurance is that while deviations (some creative, some ephemeral) from the traditional line of hymnody have appeared and will continue to appear—and without them hymnody will become overly pedagogic and conservative—the main line of hymnody is producing a steady stream of excellent material in words and music. Some of the less durable material has already fallen by the wayside: yet the contribution of such folk-artists as Sydney Carter (*Green Print for Song*, 1973) and some of the minstrels from Friends of the English Liturgy Publications in California can now be seen to have had a permanent effect, while the use of modern language, without the abandonment of scriptural ideas, has now become almost universally accepted by contemporary writers. All will in the end be well if according to the spirit of Vatican II Scripture and doctrine are always kept at the center and the hymnody of the people is kept as universal and as satisfying to the widest possible number of temperaments, from cultivated to innocent, as it can be.

Bibliography: E. ROUTLEY, "Contemporary Catholic Hymnody in Its Wider Setting: The Larger Hymnals," *Worship* 47 (1973) 194–221, 258–273, 322–337, 417–423.

[E. ROUTLEY]

I

IMPOTENCE

In the *New Catholic Encyclopedia* (7:403) J. J. Brenkle, in his comprehensive treatment of marital impotence and sterility, quotes Vlaming-Bender that: "It is certain that impotence is the incapacity of that specific act which is the proper object of the marriage contract" (Vlaming-Bender, *Praelectiones Juris Matrimonii* [4th ed., Bussum 1950] 174). But Brenkle points out that "to make the definition workable, the essential components of marital intercourse need to be specified." He subsequently refers to the canonical controversy as to whether or not *verum semen* (the male ejaculate) must contain components developed in the testicles. Brenkle gives an excellent review of the reasons behind the controversy and the disparity between the apparent doctrinal convictions of the Congregation for the Doctrine of the Faith and the juridical practice of the Roman Rota.

The Rota followed the opinion that even though the absence of healthy or developed spermatozoa in the ejaculate constituted only sterility, the proper concept of "true semen" required at least something in the ejaculate that had developed in at least one testicle. Thus the Rota considered the vasectomized male as not only sterile, but also impotent, whereas certain responses of the Congregation for the Doctrine of the Faith indicated that a grossly normal ejaculate, even if consisting only of fluid from the prostate, the seminal vesicles and various other glands, was sufficient for the canonical concept of *verum semen*.

Finally, on May 13, 1977, the Congregation for the Doctrine of the Faith, clearly exercising its doctrinal competence and with the explicit approval of Pope Paul VI, stated that the authentic teaching of the Church is that while impotence is indeed an impediment to marriage, the concept of canonical potency does not necessarily require in the ejaculate anything that has been produced in the testicles (ActApS 69 [1977] 426).

While the decree in no way implies approval of vasectomy as a contraceptive sterilization, it does declare, as Catholic teaching, that the vasectomized male is capable of the marriage act provided erection, penetration, and the ejaculation of secretions from the prostate, seminal vesicles, and various other glands be possible. Even more significantly, while the decree does not explicitly mention that this is likewise true of the castrate, it is clearly implied and the implication is confirmed by earlier replies of the same Congregation, which explicitly dealt with cases of castration (see Silvestrelli). Current clinical experience with androgen hormone therapy in cases of castration indicates the practicality of this teaching.

Bibliography: A. SILVESTRELLI, "Circa l'impotenza e l'inconsumazione nella giurisprudenza canonica anche del S. Ufficio," *Monitor ecclesiasticus* 98 (1973) 112–130.

[T. J. O'DONNELL]

INCARDINATION AND EXCARDINATION

The Fathers at Vatican Council II expressed concern about the distribution of clergy throughout the world, and they determined that the norms of excardination and incardination (7:409) should be revised to meet the pastoral needs of the Church (*Presbyterorum ordinis* 10). Two papal documents have simplified and reformed the institution of incardination. The motu proprio *Ecclesiae Sanctae* (Aug. 6, 1966) required seminarians to be instructed about the needs of the whole Church and directed Ordinaries to permit clerics to transfer to another diocese temporarily or permanently. After working in another diocese for five years, a cleric may manifest an intention to be incardinated by writing to his own Ordinary and the Ordinary of the guest diocese. Unless one of the Ordinaries expresses his opposition in writing within four months, the cleric becomes incardinated by law in the new diocese (Paul VI EcclSanct I:1–5). A further simplification of incardination provided by *Ad pascendum* (Aug. 15, 1972) determined that entrance into the clerical state and incardination are now brought about simply by ordination to the diaconate (Paul VI AdPasc IX).

[J. G. JOHNSON]

INCORPORATION INTO THE CHURCH (MEMBERSHIP)

In any contemporary discussion on "belonging to the Church" the first point to be stressed is that Vatican Council II's Dogmatic Constitution on the Church (*Lumen gentium*) advisedly dropped the terms "member" and "membership." The first schema of the *Constitutio de Ecclesia* had, in keeping with Pius XII's

1943 encyclical, *Mystici Corporis Christi*, employed the terms. But in its final form *Lumen gentium* used instead "incorporation," a notion at once more precise and more flexible. The deliberate substitution is clear from a comparison of *Lumen gentium*, art. 14 with the 1962 schema, art. 9, and the 1963 schema, art. 8. Likewise, the idea of *votum Ecclesiae* (intention of the Church—Abbott) did not keep the meaning given to it (in line with the thought of St. Robert Bellarmine) during the discussions of Vatican Council I (Mansi 53:311–312), in *Mystici Corporis Christi*, and in the Holy Office's letter to the archbishop of Boston regarding the "Feeney Case" (Denz 3870). The expression *votum Ecclesiae* retained that "classical" meaning only in the passage on catechumens (*Lumen gentium* 14.3). The application of *votum Ecclesiae* to non-Catholics reflects an entirely different viewpoint (*Lumen gentium* 15.2; 8.2—*ad unitatem catholicam impellunt*, "these elements or gifts properly belonging to the Church of Christ possess an inner dynamism toward Catholic unity" [Abbott]).

The setting aside of the idea of membership in favor of that of incorporation has called for the development of a carefully nuanced vocabulary, consistent with Vatican II ecclesiology. With regard to Catholics, *Lumen gentium* uses "being incorporated" (*incorporatio*), qualifying the term with the adverb "fully" (*plene*) and emphasizing that full incorporation requires the presence of the Holy Spirit (*Lumen gentium* 14.2). For non-Catholics and catechumens, the Constitution speaks of their being linked (*conjunctio*) to the Church, again carefully stressing the role of the Holy Spirit in each case (*Lumen gentium* 14.3; 15.2). As for non-Christians the Constitution uses "being related" (*ordinantur*), a term that suggests a dynamic relationship, an orientation towards the Church (*Lumen gentium* 16). Every shade of difference in meaning among these terms is important. But the terms acquire their full force only in the light of the most authoritative commentaries on them, the Decree on Ecumenism and the Declaration on the Relationship of the Church to non-Christian Religions. Then, supposing the nuances indicated, the richness of such expressions as the following becomes clear: "Churches and ecclesial Communities" (*Unitatis redintegratio* 3.3; cf. *Lumen gentium* 15.1); "separated brethren" (brothers divided; *Unitatis redintegratio* 3.4); separated Churches and ecclesial Communities (*Unitatis redintegratio* 3.4); "full communion"—"imperfect communion" (ibid. 3.1).

The Force of "Incorporation." Commentators on the conciliar texts have perhaps not paid enough attention to the fact that, although tightly linked, the terms *incorporatio* (*Lumen gentium*) and *communio* (*Unitatis redintegratio*) are not synonymous. The main focus of "incorporation" is on individuals as such and although *Lumen gentium* (15) does make passing reference to the ecclesial standing of groups as such, that is not its primary emphasis. The main bearing of "communion," on the contrary, is on groups as such, in their relation to the Catholic Church and to each other. It is of some interest to point out that *Lumen gentium* (14.2; 14.1) uses the term *communio* to indicate union ("unity of communion"—Abbott) with the successor of St. Peter, but that in *Unitatis redintegratio* the term "communion" takes on the traditional sense of the *koinōnia*, the fellowship, of the Churches (*Unitatis redintegratio* 3.4).

In this respect, the Decree on Ecumenism is richer than the Constitution on the Church: it acknowledges a genuine salvific value in Churches and ecclesial Communities as such (i.e. not merely in the ecclesial elements or vestiges existing in them).

Every ecclesial tradition affirms that incorporation in Christ involves a core element, known only by God, which consists in the presence within a person of the love of God poured forth by the Holy Spirit (Rom 5.5). This element is so important that without it there exists no full and complete incorporation, possessing every guarantee of authenticity (see *Lumen gentium* 14.2, a capital text on the point). This spiritual, interior incorporation often occurs before Baptism (see St. Thomas Aquinas ST 3, 66.11 & 13 on baptism of desire and of blood) and at times even without any explicit knowledge of the mystery of Christ (*Lumen gentium* 16).

Here it should be stressed that when they speak formally of incorporation into the Church, most ecclesial traditions—even those which do not give prominence to the Sacraments—acknowledge that its accomplishment is normally through Baptism. The gift of the Holy Spirit which is the inner mark of belonging to the Body of Christ is made ordinarily to those who seal their faith in Jesus Christ by Baptism. Admittedly some Christian bodies born during or after the Reformation are silent on the point. The more ancient Christian traditions, however, are unanimous here, even though they may explain differently the connection between the sacramental rite and the inner incorporation or may not all recognize the validity of Baptism administered in ways other than their own.

Every person baptized in a true Baptism belongs to the Body of Christ and therefore to the Church. One of the most important consequences of Vatican II ecclesiology is the break with Bellarmine's viewpoint, repeated in *Mystici Corporis Christi*, which in fact limited true belonging to the Church to those baptized within the Catholic community. For Vatican II every genuine Baptism truly brings incorporation into Christ and the Church. Even though divided, the Church is single (*Unica Christi Ecclesia*, *Lumen gentium* 8.1) and Baptism brings entrance into the single (though divided) Church. This is the profound implication of the expression "the one single Baptism of the one single Church." *Lumen gentium* refrains from stating that the Church *is* the Catholic Church; it chooses rather to affirm that the "Church subsists in the Catholic Church" (*subsistit in; Lumen gentium* 8). The precise reason of this choice is to give recognition to the presence of genuinely ecclesial elements in the non-Catholic bodies which the document, further on, designates as "Churches or ecclesial Communities." (The 1964 *schema* of the *Constitutio de Ecclesia* has this: "*loco 'est' 1.21, dicitur 'subsistit in' ut expressio melius concordet cum affirmatione de elementis ecclesialibus quae alibi adsunt.*") The implication is that in these "Churches and ecclesial Communities" the Church (the *single* Church) is present. Therefore those who by Baptism belong to these bodies and within them live in faithfulness to the Spirit, relying on the elements of genuinely evangelical life they find there (*Lumen gentium* 8.2; 15.1 & 2; *Unitatis redintegratio* 3), by that same belonging also belong to the single Church.

Given the viewpoint of the conciliar documents (which in their own way mark a return to Aquinas's insistence on the interiority of incorporation into

Christ—ST 3a, 8.3), it is extremely important to keep in mind that belonging to the single Church comes about in and through belonging to the "Churches and ecclesial Communities." These bear within them elements of sanctification and of truth which make it possible for the baptized to live according to the Gospel. Therefore the value of each "Church or ecclesial Community" as such is not set aside—treated, that is, as meaningless or purely incidental. Moreover, the Council refuses to conceive the incorporation as though it were an unmediated action of the Holy Spirit, between the Spirit and each individual alone. However far from being what the Catholic Church regards as the true form of the Church, every ecclesial Community is the locus of a genuine incorporation into the single Church. Acknowledgement of that fact is an implication of the idea of "incomplete communion"; the accent falls on "communion," the noun, rather than on "incomplete," the adjective, and clearly the term "communion" should not be taken to mean anything other than the "communion" that incorporation in Christ brings about (see Bertrams; Hamer; Kasper; Lanne; McDonnell; McGovern).

Incorporation through Baptism means, then, incorporation into the single Church. The Church, however, exists now as divided, disunited. *Lumen gentium* and the other conciliar documents which explicitate its ecclesiology, affirm that incorporation, while real, does not have the same completeness in all Churches and ecclesial Communities. The documents add that incorporation has this fulness only in the Catholic Church (*Lumen gentium* 8.2 [*subsistit in* passage]; *Unitatis redintegratio* 3.5). To illustrate let us give an image: a graft can be made onto a living body, yet for some reason not receive all the vigor and strength of the body because of some defect or lack in the way the grafting onto the whole organism is done. In the belief of the Catholic Church the baptized person fully (*plene*) incorporated into the Church is the one who shares truly in the Eucharist (i.e. as one having charity), within a community whose bishop, ordained in the apostolic succession, is in communion with the bishop of Rome (except for the last part the Catholic Church is at one with the Orthodox Churches in this understanding).

Two Views of the Church. To grasp the meaning of this Catholic position, it is important to recall the difference between two views of the Church, the "Catholic" view—that of Roman Catholics, the Orthodox, and some Anglicans—and the Protestant one. The Protestant view considers the Church essentially in its invisible reality (its *res* in the Scholastics' vocabulary). It looks immediately at what God works in the heart "of all who love the Lord Jesus Christ in sincerity and whose names are known only to God" (Moss 2,41). Thus, the focus is on the effect of grace and the mysterious bond existing here and now between the glorified Christ and each sincere believer. Such a reading of the reality of the Church, therefore, centers on realized sanctification, that is on the invisible communion of all who are in grace. Outward signs—the Sacraments, the institutional Church—have a value of mere instrumentality, no more. All those who confess Christ—and thereby may *possibly* be sanctified—have the possibility of existing within the ecclesial plenitude to the degree that charity is alive in them. It is impossible, therefore, to take institutional elements as the index of degrees of ecclesiology.

The Catholic view is altogether different. The reality of the Church must be seen as consisting *at once and inseparably* of what Christ works here and now within the faithful and of the institutional elements established from the outset by the apostolic community, the interpreter of Christ's will. From the day of Christ's resurrection to the day of his second coming the Church, taken in its total reality, is the *Sacramentum salutis*, i.e., the expression of all that salvation implies—not only the inner presence of grace, but also the channels of grace. These instruments also are saving gifts of God and constitutives of the manifestation of his grace. The Church received its identity at once from its inner, mysterious reality (its *res*) and from the visible means (the *sacramentum*) of which it is the bearer. For the Church is, in the present world, the Body of Christ, to be seen always as tightly bound to the Jesus of the Incarnation—the eternal Son of the Father, but also the One Sent to give to men along with the event of salvation the means for entering into that salvation.

Full Incorporation. This makes clear the meaning of the important statement of the Constitution on the Church: "They are *fully* incorporated into the society of the Church who, possessing the Spirit of Christ, accept her *entire* system and all the means of salvation given to her" (*Lumen gentium* 14.2). Full incorporation comes about where the spiritual reality (the possession of the Spirit of Christ) and the entirety of visible, essential elements are present. To be joined only to the visible institution without charity is not to be "in the heart of the Church" (ibid.); to possess charity without holding fast to the outward, institutional and essential elements is not to belong totally to the reality of the Sacrament that the Church is. The two aspects of incorporation into the Church, the spiritual and the visible, are, as it were, interfused. Among the factors that together give the Church its outward manifestation, the institutional aspect is inseparable from the communal profession of faith and from sharing in the Sacraments, above all in the Eucharistic *synaxis*. The Eucharist is the unifying center in which come together, within the *communio* of the Body of Christ, the communion of the profession of faith and the communion with the apostolic ministry, whose *centrum unitatis* is the bishop of Rome. Incorporation achieves in the Eucharist its full measure.

This understanding of the incorporation in Christ and the Church allows for breaking away from the Counter-Reformation positions maintaining that there is no genuine belonging to the Church other than within the Catholic community, bound fast to the pope (Bellarminus, *De conciliis* 3, 2 [ed. Fevre 1870] v. 2. 316–318). That conception remained in the thought of *Mystici Corporis*; use of the term "membership" made difficult any sort of nuancing. But thanks to its ecclesiology—prepared by the renewal of patristic studies and the ecumenical dialogue—Vatican II was able to affirm at the same time that Churches or ecclesial Communities separated from the Catholic Church are part of the *single* Church, and that nevertheless incorporation in Christ and his Church possesses within the Catholic Church the fulness that it does not have elsewhere.

It is appropriate to mention here without going more deeply into it, a conviction spreading in many Catholic quarters engaged with other Christians in a common witness. Briefly put it is this: life takes precedence over institution. The position is midway between the Protestant view of the Church of the elect and the Catholic view which stresses the institution. The position represents an attachment to a *res*, human fidelity to the Gospel, and a refusal to attribute to the aspect of the Church as *sacramentum* the importance given to it by *Lumen gentium* (see Congar). This conviction is often the concomitant of ecumenical initiatives described by the unfortunate label "secular ecumenism." In the face of. this trend several theologians—notably those active in campus ministry in France and those in some mission countries—have been considering the need to introduce, even into the Catholic Church, a set of degrees of belonging to the Church. The first would be a kind of catechumenate, prolonged and completely rethought. The idea, however, does not call into question the basic view of incorporation into the Church that has been here presented.

Bibliography: W. BERTRAMS, "De gradibus communionis in doctrina Concilii Vaticani II" Greg 47 (1966) 286–305. Y.-M. CONGAR, "What Belonging to the Church Has Come to Mean," Communio 4 (1977) 146–160. J. HAMER, "La terminologie ecclésiologique de Vatican II et les ministères protestants," DocCath 53 (1971) 625–628. W. KASPER, "Der ekklesiologische Charakter der nichtkatholischen Kirchen," ThQsch 145 (1965) 42–62. E. LANNE, "Le Mystère de l'Église et de son unité," Irénikon 46 (1973) 298–342. K. MCDONNELL, "The Concept of Church in the Documents of Vatican II as Applied to Protestant Denominations," Lutherans and Catholics in Dialogue—IV, Eucharist and Ministry (Minneapolis 1970) 307–324. J. O. MCGOVERN, The Church in the Churches (Washington, D.C. 1968). C. B. MOSS, What Do We Mean by Reunion (London 1953).

[J. M. R. TILLARD]

INCULTURATION, THEOLOGICAL

The term "inculturation" is a neologism of current theological language. It identifies a concept which theologians have found necessary in dealing with worldwide Christian experience. Both term and concept appear to have been taken from cultural anthropology, where "acculturation" means measurable changes in artifacts, customs, and beliefs consequent upon contact between two disparate cultures; and "enculturation" (introduced by M. J. Herskovits, 20th-century American anthropologist) means the life-long learning process through which persons introject their own cultures. Generally, theologians use "acculturation" or "acculturization" (much less frequent) to mean the bringing of a preexistent body of truth to another culture. The word reflects the earlier concepts, "accommodation," "indigenization," and "adaptation." Theologians' use of "inculturation" is more complicated. The concept usually suggests, first, that every culture owns true and beautiful religious elements before the Word is proclaimed within it. Then, it suggests that the Word can be effectively proclaimed only upon condition that evangelization is preceded by a thorough-going comprehension, immersion into, and adoption of the culture itself by those who are to proclaim the Word. Finally, it suggests that the act of faith-commitment itself will be culturally shaped, and, similarly, the consequent articulations of faith in theologies, ecclesiologies, and ascetical practices and theories. The term is applied to evangelization and to catechesis as well, as it was at the *Synod of Bishops of 1977.

"Inculturation" applied to the act of faith and to theology is hardly a univocal concept, but its application does show patterns. In Latin America, it generally refers to the inclusion into the theological enterprise of socioeconomic and political analysis; in Africa, of tribal cultures evolving into nationalisms; in India, of the great religions as they function in excruciating societal conditions. The presumption is becoming more common that the Church in Europe inculturated the Word into a monarchical ecclesiological system and into scholastic (Aristotelian, Platonic, and, currently, existential) philosophies and theologies. Finally, the implications of this concept of inculturation are immediately plain in such issues as theological *pluralism; the interpretation of traditional doctrines on the *depositum fidei*; ecclesiology, and particularly on the matter of the magisterium; in liturgical languages and rites.

The concept is rooted most recently in Vatican Council II documents—*Lumen gentium, Gaudium et spes*, and *Ad gentes*—and it was extensively developed in Paul VI's *Evangelii nuntiandi* (*see* EVANGELIZATION). It is so recent, however, that there is no true bibliography on the topic. However, the papers delivered at the Dar es Salaam, Tanzania, meeting of Third World theologians should be consulted, in S. Torres and V. Fabella, eds., *The Emergent Gospel* (Maryknoll, N.Y. 1978).

See also LITURGY AND LOCAL CHURCHES; MISSION (NEW TRENDS); MISSIOLOGY.

[J. A. TETLOW]

INDIFFERENTISM

Reviewing the explicit rejection of indifferentism by Pius X in the Syllabus of Errors (Denz 2915–18), Vatican Council II employed a pastoral approach and reappraised: *communicatio in sacris*; irreligious indifferentism; irenicism; and religious freedom.

Communicatio in sacris. This means common worship (*i.e.*, sharing in the official, public prayer of a Church). The Decree on Ecumenism replaced the strict attitude of Canon Law (*e.g.*, CIC c. 732; 1258; 2319), which prohibited active participation on the grounds that other Christian communities lacked the character of a Church. Reversing this position, the Decree recommended a discriminating (not general) participation in the worship and Sacraments of other Churches (*Unitatis redintegratio* 8), particularly the separated Eastern Churches (cf. *Orientalium Ecclesiarum* 26–29; Ecumenical Directory of the Secretariat for Unity, Part I, 39–54). The Decree provided two principles for avoiding religious indifferentism: first, liturgical worship and the Sacraments signify an already existing—even if not perfect—unity of the Church and thus general participation cannot be applied in most cases; second, as a means of grace for the faithful, liturgical worship and the Sacraments also contribute to the growth of unity (*see* EUCHARISTIC SHARING).

Irreligious Indifferentism. Such indifferentism may be divided into postulatory atheism of the West and atheistic communism of the East. The pastoral Constitution on the Church in the Modern World places atheism in its treatment on the question of man: that is, atheism is not considered from a metaphysical or epistemological perspective but is viewed in terms of an authentic desire for true humanism (*Gaudium et spes* 19–21). Postulatory atheism stresses the absence of God and the value of man alone on the existential level. Disregarding the economic and political aspects of atheistic communism of the East, the Decree refers to previous repudiations of communism; it then urges the Church to reflect on its own defective humanism and its role in the growth of Marxism. Irreligious indifferentism thus has its roots more in man's attempt to become truly human than in any positive act against God or religious institutions. Since Vatican II, a Third World *liberation theology has attempted to develop humanistic principles (based on the dignity of man and his freedom as a Christian) that seek to avoid both postulatory atheism and atheistic communism (*see* ATHEISM; MARXISM AND CHRISTIANITY).

Irenicism. As a conciliatory approach to doctrine, irenicism may be true or false. The Decree on Ecumenism rejects false irenicism, or the partial disclosure or diluting of tenets on either side of a dialogue to achieve peaceful union; it is contrary to the spirit of ecumenism and leads to mutual deception. On the contrary, the Decree encourages true irenicism, which avoids polemics, practices brotherly love, recognizes goodness and truth wherever found and emphasizes common aspects and presents Catholic doctrine more profoundly, more precisely, and more fully in a mutually understandable language (*Unitatis redintegratio* 11).

Religious Freedom. The Declaration on Religious Freedom basing its position on the dignity of the human person (fully known only in the light of Revelation), insisted on two negatively stated rights: (1) no man may be compelled in the religious sphere to act in a manner contrary to his conscience; (2) within due limits no one may be prevented from acting in accordance with his conscience (*Dignitatis humanae* 2). The document considers only the moral dimensions of religious freedom—rights whose object is freedom from coercion but not the content of religious faith—and thus does not pass judgment on the problems of the true or the erroneous conscience. Regardless of former practices, a person today, whether believer or nonbeliever, has the right not to be prevented from practicing his religion, whether privately or publicly. Religious freedom thus leads to religious pluralism which, however, is not to be confused with religious indifference; religious pluralism is based on the right to profess and practice one's religion and makes no value judgment on truth and error; religious indifference, however, suggests that all religions equally possess truth and thus have equal value.

Bibliography: J. FEINER, "Decree on Ecumenism," Vogrimler 2: 57–164. H. HOECK, "Decree on Eastern Catholic Churches," ibid. 1: 307–331. N. MOLINSKI, "Indifferentism," SacrMundi 3: 120–121, P. PAVAN, "Declaration on Human Freedom," Vorgrimler 4: 49–86. J. RATZINGER, "Pastoral Constitution on the Church in the Modern World," Part One, Introd. and ch. 1, "Dignity of the Human Person," ibid. 5: 115–163. Secretariat for Promoting Christian Unity, *Directorium . . . de re oecumenica, Pars I,* ActApS 59 (1967) 574–592, tr. *Directory for the Application of the Decisions of the Second Vatican Council concerning Ecumenical Matters,* Part I (USCC Publ. Office, Washington, D.C. 1967).

[T. F. MCMAHON]

INFALLIBILITY

In Catholic teaching infallibility is believed to be a guarantee given to the Church of immunity from distorting the truths of faith and, as defined by Vatican Council I (Denz 3074), a guarantee of this same immunity given when the pope teaches *ex cathedra* (7:496; 16:220).

Status of Theology. Three moments can be detected in the modern discussion on infallibility. (1) The textbook moment in which the teaching of Vatican I on papal infallibility was proclaimed; the conditions of its exercise were detailed and, almost unconsciously by some, but more consciously by others, extensions were made as to the scope of infallibility. The last involved both broadening the object of infallibility to include so-called secondary objects and broadening the exercise of infallibility from *ex cathedra* pronouncements to include the teaching of the ordinary magisterium of the pope.

(2) The moment of denial emerged clearly at the beginning of the 1970s when the textbook view became subject to two forms of attack. The first, most prominently typified by Hans Küng, denied the validity of the received doctrine on various grounds: the doctrine was contradicted by the many historical errors of the papacy; it did not take into account the historically conditioned nature of all statements; it could not be shown to have any basis in Scripture; it was propounded by Vatican I, a council that looked to a highly rational model of truth now known to be inadequate. Küng proposed replacing the older notion of "propositional infallibility" with a dynamic notion of the Church, which, despite specific errors, continuously persists in the path toward greater truth. The second form of attack, typified by Brian Tierney, attacked the infallibility doctrine on the grounds that the reasons for which it was first formulated were defective. So defective were they, argued Tierney, that the Church should now have the courage to reject the erroneous doctrine that has stemmed from them. The writings of both Küng and Tierney evidenced the zeal of the crusader and the partisanship of the polemicist.

(3) The philosophical moment began from the premise that the revelation of God appears in a never-to-be-surpassed fullness in Christ's humanity; all God's gifts to the Church are summed up in him. If there is an infallibility in the Church, it must in some way pertain to Christ's humanity and to the human nature that the Church's members share with him. These considerations are at the bottom of a new approach to the question of infallibility. This approach studies the process of human understanding, the conditions of human certitude, the kinds of truth open to certitude, and the manner in which the quality of understanding is influenced by the knower's experience and in turn affects that experience. This approach is manifested in the composite work edited by E. Castelli and in the work of P. Chirico (see bibliog.).

Principles of the new approach. (1) Some Christian truths are of universal saving significance: they are of such a nature that any person of any era or culture who appropriates them and lives by them will move toward Christian fulfilment. Thus: two great commandments are of universal saving significance; the exact location of Christ's birth is not.

(2) Infallibility is always bound to truths of universal saving significance. Insofar as the whole of the faithful possesses, at least implicitly, such truths, the body of believers can be said to be endowed with *passive infallibility*. Insofar as church leaders explicitly grasp the truths by which the whole Church lives, they have the charism of *active infallibility*. The conditions under which a pope or a general council teach infallibly are not merely legal conditions externally proclaimed at the desire of Church leaders; rather, they are those conditions of personal self-realization by which the consciousness of the church leaders expands to embrace the truths that are universal in the Church.

(3) Active or conscious infallibility is a quality of a mind or of minds, for only a mind can grasp the universal. Statements that reflect an understanding of the universal truths of the Church are relative, time-conditioned, and therefore subject to verbal revision.

(4) The basic function of infallibility is to indicate the universal traits that characterize the Church and bestow on it its identity. Only when the Church as a whole has begun to accept it does a trait's identification become a genuine possibility. Hence, infallibility is not a tool for solving disputed questions in the Church. It is far more the culminating act of a process by which the Church, having realized an enduring truth in the breadth of its membership, now comes to recognize explicitly the meaning of that realization.

Bibliography: B. TIERNEY, *Origins of Papal Infallibility, 1150–1350* (Leiden 1972). G. HUGHES, "Infallibility in Morals," ThSt 34 (1973) 415–428, J. T. FORD, "Infallibility: Who Won the Debate?" CathThSoc 31 (1976) 179–192. P. CHIRICO, *Infallibility: The Crossroads of Doctrine* (Kansas City 1977). E. Castelli, ed., *L'Infalibilité: son aspect philosophique et théologigue* (Paris 1970). Also bibliog. 16:222.

[P. CHIRICO]

INFANT BAPTISM AND COMMUNION

Since Vatican Council II, increasing emphasis has been given to the integrity of the Christian initiation ritual, comprising the Sacraments of Baptism, Confirmation, and First Eucharist. This is most clearly evident in the Rite of Christian Initiation of Adults (27–36), but has also influenced the Rite of Confirmation and the Rite of Baptism for Children. This principle of integral celebration has raised some basic questions in the minds of scholars and of parents and parish priests: Should the Church continue to baptize infants; if so, should we also confirm and communicate infants?

Infant Baptism is a long-standing practice in the Church, perhaps dating from apostolic times. Most commentators today accept the *validity* of infant Baptism, but some question its pastoral effectiveness (16:21). Confronted with the problem of baptized Catholics who do not seem committed to Christ or to the Church, some have suggested that Baptism be delayed until a true conversion is experienced. The restoration of the *catechumenate for adults has also led to the suggestion that infants might be enrolled in the catechumenate, thus becoming members of the Church, with the Sacraments of initiation celebrated at a later age (*see also* INCORPORATION INTO THE CHURCH). On the other hand, concern for integral celebration of the Sacraments of initiation has also led to consideration of infant Confirmation and Communion, conferred in the same celebration as infant Baptism.

In the ancient practice of the Church, infants, like adults, received all three Sacraments in the same celebration. Even when Confirmation began to be delayed in the West because of the insistence on the bishop's being the minister of Confirmation, infant Communion was still maintained. The practice seems to have been universal until about 1200 and did not cease altogether in the West until the 16th century, following the Council of Trent. In the Eastern Church, the custom of infant Communion (and Confirmation) has been maintained even to the present time.

The current focus of the question, then, is not on the *possibility* of infant Confirmation and Communion, but on its pastoral advisability. In this question, as with the question of infant Baptism, the underlying issue is how conversion to Christ and commitment to the Christian way of life can best be fostered in the lives of those being initiated into the Church. All questions of age and of ritual integrity are ultimately dependent on that issue.

Bibliography: E. BRAND, "Baptism and Communion of Infants: A Lutheran View," *Worship* 50 (1976) 29–42. C. CRAWFORD, "Infant Communion: Past Tradition and Present Practice," ThSt 31 (1970) 523–536. J. C. D. FISHER, *Christian Initiation: Baptism in the Medieval West* (London 1965). R. GUERRETTE, "Ecclesiology and Infant Baptism," *Worship*, (1970) 433–437. J. JEREMIAS, *Infant Baptism in the First Four Centuries* (London 1960); *The Origins of Infant Baptism* (Naperville, Ill. 1963). A. KAVANAGH, "The Norm of Baptism: The New Rite of Christian Initiation of Adults," *Worship* 48 (1974) 143–152. C. KIESLING, "Infant Baptism," *Worship* 42 (1968) 617–626. D. PERRY, "Let's Stop Baptizing Babies," *U.S. Catholic* 37 (1972) 14–15. R. X. REDMOND. "Infant Baptism, History and Pastoral Problems," ThSt 30 (1969) 79–89.

[L. MICK]

INITIATION OF CHILDREN OF CATECHETICAL AGE (RITE)

This special adaptation of the *Rite of Christian Initiation of Adults* is provided as ch. 5 of that document for use with unbaptized children old enough to be taught who are presented, usually with a Confirmation or First Communion class, to receive Christian Initiation. The rite treats them as children, not as either infants or adults, and provides a three-stage initiation. First, they are made catechumens (ChrInitAd 314–329) in a simple rite in which the children express their desire to be baptized and the parents give their consent. They are signed with the cross and given a Gospel book. Second, a penitential rite (scrutiny) is performed, perhaps when the baptized members of the class receive Penance (ibid. 330–342). The third stage is the celebration of the Sacraments of *Christian Initiation (ibid. 343–368).

[L. L. MITCHELL]

INSTITUTE FOR CONTINUING THEOLOGICAL EDUCATION

The Institute for Continuing Theological Education began in Rome, in 1970, at Casa Santa Maria, the graduate house of studies of the Pontifical North American College. The programs had the approval of the NCCB Committee for the College. Participation was limited to priests in pastoral ministry, as a means of providing an in-service training program for personal and community renewal. An ideal was seen as a group of diocesan and religious priests from the U.S., usually about 35 in number, with between 10 and 30 years of pastoral experience in the ministry. The syllabus was organized generally around the needs expressed by the priests themselves and each three-month session was evaluated by them, as well as by the committee for the Institute, which was composed of participating lecturers. Increased demands changed the program from a single three-month session to biannual sessions. Contact with the Roman Curia, World Council of Churches, and study-pilgrimages in the Holy Land were additional and varying features of this program.

After a period of experimentation a successful nuclear curriculum was developed. Currents of philosophical thought affecting theology today, Old and New Testament biblical theology themes, special emphasis on Christological and ecclesiological questions, sacramental and moral theological themes, constituted the content of the Institute program.

Growing out of this experience, and related to the content and method of this program, theological consultations were organized for U.S. bishops. The first session of one month was held in Rome in 1974, another session in 1975, and a third in 1978. Several similar efforts to duplicate the Institute were undertaken in North America and Europe, in order to provide for a growing need for updating.

See also CONTINUING EDUCATION FOR MINISTRY.

[R. J. MAHOWALD]

INSTITUTE FOR THE STUDY OF ATHEISM

The Institute for the study of Atheism (*Istituto Superiore per lo studio dell'ateismo*) is a branch of the faculty of philosophy in the Pontifical Urban University (*Pontificia Università Urbaniana*), Rome. It was officially inaugurated by Card. Franz König, President of the Secretariat for Nonbelievers, with a lecture on "The Bankruptcy of 'Scientific' Atheism", on February 14, 1977.

The Director of the Institute is Prof. Battista Mondin. The Institute pursues a double aim: (1) preparation of clergy, religious, and laity for an intelligent dialogue with today's cultural expressions, which often are atheistic; (2) elaboration of pastoral methods responding to the attitudes of nonbelievers. The programs are directed towards the analysis of the causes of the spread of atheism in the modern world, of the main types of theoretical and practical atheism, of the basic works of the philosophers who developed atheistic views, and of the remedies that can be found against what Plato already called the "worst of all evils." The program is distributed over a period of three years, during which the students are given the opportunity to attend thirty different courses (at least ten each year). Some of the course titles are: Philosophy of Religion and Atheism; Foundations of Religious Belief; Theological Language and Atheism; Doctrine of the Church and Atheism; Psychoanalysis and Atheism; Historico-critical Genesis of Atheism; Atheism and Neo-Marxism; Atheism as Provisional Condition in Martin Heidegger; Atheism in Contemporary Philosophy; Italian Communism; Geography of Atheism; Atheism and Secularization.

The courses are conducted by some of the best renowned authorities in the field. Some belong to the Secretariat for Non-Believers (Vincenzo Miano, Franziskus Skoda, Bernard Jacqueline); some belong to the staff of the Urban University (Luigi Bogliolo, Cornelio Fabro, Matteo Aiassa, Giuseppe Dalla Torre, Tommaso Federici); and some to the State University of Rome (Armando Rigobello). The Institute grants a licentiate (M.A.) and a doctorate (Ph.D.) in philosophy with specialization in the field of atheism.

[B. MONDIN]

INSTITUTE ON RELIGIOUS LIFE

The Institute on Religious Life is a national service organization, established at the opening of the 1975 Holy Year, to make better known and esteemed the indispensable role in the Church of those called by God to the consecration of religious life, to foster a more effective understanding of and adherence to the Church's teaching on religious life, to assist religious communities in their efforts to implement the process of renewal and adaptation called for by Vatican Council II, and to promote religious vocations. In this undertaking a board of directors, drawn from bishops, priests, religious men and women, and laity are assisted by an episcopal advisory board.

Foundation of the Institute resulted from a growing concern among many bishops, priests, religious, and lay people regarding the modern world's spiritual crisis and what was seen as a consequent harmful effect on religious life itself and on the apostolic works of religious congregations. From its inception the Institute recognized that the secularization challenge resulting in polarizing tensions and statistical impoverishment related to numbers, vocations, and apostolic works was not to be confronted with negative criticism nor with any approach that would be divisive. On the contrary, the Institute was to emphasize a positive approach of service, support, healing, and reconciliation. At the same time, such efforts were to be based on the conviction that vibrant and fruitful religious life could only be that in accord with the mind and will of the Church.

Dedicated to the Sacred Heart of Jesus and the Immaculate Heart of Mary, the Institute strives to fulfill its ideal of service by prayer and sacrifice, by study and research, by advice and consultation, by publicity and communication. A quarterly newsletter, *Religious Life*, is sent to the various categories of membership—voting, associate, affiliate, and auxiliary. One Institute communication project involves translation and dissemination to English speaking lands of *Consecrated Life*, a vernacular edition (Daughters of St. Paul, Boston) of the official bulletin *Informationes* initiated by the Sacred Congregation for Religious and Secular Institutes in 1975.

The National Office and Information Center for the Institute on Religious Life is located at 4200 North Austin Avenue, Chicago, Illinois 60634.   [J. J. HOGAN]

INSTITUTION OF READERS AND ACOLYTES (RITE)

Pope Paul VI's apostolic letter *Ministeria quaedam* (Aug. 15, 1972) mandated a number of changes in the rites by which persons are designated for nonclerical ministries in the Latin Church. First, the letter suppressed the offices of porter, exorcist and subdeacon, while it retained those of reader (lector) and acolyte. Secondly, some significant changes of vocabulary appeared: reader and acolyte are no longer called "minor orders" but "ministries"; the liturgy in which these offices are assigned is not an "ordination" but an "institution." Thirdly, the ministries of reader and acolyte are no longer exclusively restricted to students preparing for ordination to the presbyterate; they are open to lay people as well, though women are specifically excluded from institution as readers or acolytes. Finally, men preparing for diaconate, permanent or transitional, and for the presbyterate, must first be instituted as readers and acolytes, unless a special dispensation has been sought and received.

The liturgy of institution for both ministries is structurally the same. The rite takes place during Mass (acolytes, readers) or during a Liturgy of the Word (readers). After the Gospel and Homily the candidates are called by the bishop, who gives a short instruction on the responsibilities of the ministry. Readers are reminded that they must read the Scriptures in the liturgical assembly, instruct persons in the faith, and prepare them for the Sacraments. Readers may also announce the intentions for the General Intercessions and assist in directing congregational singing. Acolytes are instructed to assist the priests and deacons at the Eucharist, give Holy Communion to the faithful as an "auxiliary minister" and bring the Eucharist to the ill. Following this instruction the bishop blesses the ministers with prayer and presents them with signs of their service (a vessel of bread and wine for the acolytes; a Bible for the readers). The new Roman Missal (*Sacramentary*) provides a special Mass formula for the rites of institution ("Ritual Mass for the Ministers of the Church").

It should also be noted that *Ministeria quaedam* gives national episcopal conferences the option of recognizing further forms of lay ministry in the Church. Such ministries need not be purely liturgical; they may include works of social service and pastoral charity in the local community. The role of women in such future ministries seems to remain open, even after the publication of the "Declaration on the Question of the Admission of Women to the Ministerial Priesthood," published by the Congregation for the Doctrine of the Faith on Jan. 17, 1977 (*see* WOMEN IN MINISTRY).

Bibliography: R. BERAUDY, "Les Ministères institues dans 'Ministeria Quaedam' et 'Ad Pascendum'," *Maison-Dieu* 115 (1973) 86–96. C. BRAGA, "Ministeria quaedam" (Commentarius) EphemLiturg 87 (1973) 191–214. F. BUSSINI, "Les églises et leurs ministères," *Maison-Dieu* 115 (1973) 107–132. J. D. CRICHTON, *Christian Celebration: The Sacraments* (London 1973) 163–167. Paul VI, "Ministeria quaedam," ActApS 64 (1972) 529–534. Sacred Congregation for the Doctrine of the Faith, "Declaratio circa quaestionem admissionis mulierum ad sacerdotium ministeriale," ActApS 69 (1977) 98–116 (Eng. tr. *Catholic Mind* 75 [1977] 52–64). United States Catholic Conference, *Rite of Institution of Readers and Acolytes; Admission to Candidacy for the Diaconate and Presbyterate; Ordination of Deacons, Presbyters, and Bishops,* revised by decree of Vatican Council II (Washington 1973).

[N. MITCHELL]

INTERNATIONAL CATHOLIC MIGRATION COMMISSION

In response to the need for coordination of Catholic migration and refugee services on a worldwide basis, the International Catholic Migration Commission (ICMC) was established in 1951 with headquarters in Geneva. ICMC is an operational organization carrying out programs for people on the move, especially refugees, in 45 countries of the world. Programs consist of counselling and all types of social assistance prior to emigration, departure arrangements (including travel loans, reception and job placement on arrival), as well as assistance in finding homes. By the end of 1977, ICMC had granted travel loans in the amount of approximately 50 million dollars, thereby assisting hundreds of thousands of uprooted people to find a country of permanent resettlement. The Commission has recently been working to an increasing extent in countries of the Third World.

The policy-making organ of the Commission, the ICMC Council, meets once a year to determine the priorities of the organization. Every three years the Council elects the President and other officers of the Governing Committee. Mr. John E. McCarthy, Director of Migration and Refugee Services/USCC, became President of the Commission in September 1977.

ICMC maintains regular contacts with international organizations and represents Catholic affiliates at international conferences. It cooperates especially with two intergovernmental organizations, the Office of the United Nations High Commissioner for Refugees (UNHCR) and the Intergovernmental Committee for European Migration (ICEM) and has consultative status with the Council of Europe and the UN Economic and Social Council. ICMC has contracts with intergovernmental and governmental agencies which provide funds for worldwide resettlement programmes.

See also MIGRATION, INTERNATIONAL.

[E. WINKLER]

INTERNATIONAL COMMISSION ON ENGLISH IN THE LITURGY (ICEL)

In 1962 during the first session of Vatican Council II, a small group of English and American bishops, realizing that the use of the vernacular in the liturgy was about to be sanctioned to some degree, informally discussed the possibility of providing common texts for all English-speaking Catholics. Further discussion of this possibility continued among a widening group of English-speaking bishops during 1963. In October of that year bishops representing ten episcopal conferences met in the English College at Rome under the chairmanship of Archbishop Francis Grimshaw of England to lay plans for the work of the International Commission on English in the Liturgy. The following conferences were represented at that meeting: Australia, Canada, England and Wales, India, Ireland, New Zealand, Pakistan, Scotland, South Africa, and the United States. In 1967 an eleventh member, the conference of bishops of the Philippines, joined the original group.

Founding of ICEL. The International Commission on English in the Liturgy originating in Rome at the heart of the Council was the first response of a number of conferences sharing the same language to the directive of the Constitution on the Sacred Liturgy: "... it is for the competent territorial ecclesiastical authority ..., to decide whether, and to what extent, the vernacular is to be used. Their decrees are to be approved, that is, confirmed, by the Apostolic See. And whenever it seems called for, this authority is to consult with bishops of neighboring regions that have the same language (*Sacrosanctum Concilium* 36.3)." The Council's wish that countries sharing the same language should work together was more forcefully underscored in a letter dated Oct. 16, 1964 of Cardinal Giacomo Lercaro, president of the Consilium for the Implementation of the Constitution on the Sacred Liturgy, to the presidents of conferences of bishops. In that letter Cardinal Lercaro stated that international commissions should be established by conferences of bishops sharing the same language to make one text for all. The pioneering work of ICEL can thus be seen as the inspiration for the several other language commissions which were established at the direction of the Holy See.

In 1964 the bishops of ICEL prepared a formal mandate for the work to be undertaken as a common effort. This mandate, already anticipating the creation of a committee of experts to oversee the ICEL program, was addressed to the International Advisory Committee on English in the Liturgy. The mandate was submitted to each of the constituent conferences of bishops and was ratified by all of them in 1964. A formal constitution was adopted in the same year. The principal element in the constitution is the structured plan to relate the International Episcopal Committee on English in the Liturgy and the International Advisory Committee on English in the Liturgy as two distinct entities within the single organizations.

It was also in 1964 that the bishops of ICEL invited various experts, priests and lay people, to join them in their deliberations as they began to make definite plans towards the production of English vernacular texts which, it was hoped, would be acceptable to each of the member conferences. These experts who constituted the original Advisory Committee met for the first time in London during January 1965 and again, with the bishops, in Rome in November 1965. They represented the various specializations which would be necessary in developing a vernacular liturgy: liturgists, classical scholars, patrologists, English scholars, musicians. At a later stage biblical experts were also consulted. Since 1965 the work of ICEL has depended heavily on the talents of numerous English-speaking people, representative of these several areas of scholarship. It is the function of the Advisory Committee to oversee the work of ICEL and to advise the bishops after a careful review of the proposed translations and projects.

Structure and Work. The Episcopal Board (originally, Committee) of ICEL is the governing body of ICEL. Each conference designates one bishop as its representative on the board. All projects and translations, having been endorsed by the Advisory Committee, must be submitted to the Episcopal Board for final approval. When a text has been approved by a two-thirds majority vote of the Episcopal Board it is then submitted to the separate conferences for the vote of their individual members. In addition to presenting the texts to their conferences, the members of the Episcopal Board regularly report to their conferences on the continuing work of ICEL as well as on proposals for future work. The eleven members of the Episcopal Board also serve as the board of trustees of the civil corporation, the International Committee on English in the Liturgy, Inc., which was established under Canadian law in 1967 to protect the copyright of the ICEL texts. The legal safeguard provided by copyrighting the texts helps to preserve the literary and liturgical integrity of the texts under the authority given to the bishops by Vatican II. The ICEL copyright also helps to promote the availability of the texts to all the English-speaking countries through the international conventions of copyright law.

The daily activities of ICEL are carried on through a secretariat which was established in Washington, D. C. in 1965. The work of the secretariat is directed by an executive secretary who is immediately responsible to the Advisory Committee and ultimately to the Episcopal Board.

The Episcopal Board and Advisory Committee issued two booklets, *English for the Mass* (1966) and *English for the Mass: Part II* (1967), which gave various sample translations of the Order of the Mass and the proper parts of the Mass. In order to assist them in the pioneering work of translating the Latin liturgy into English, the bishops and specialists invited comments from "all who are interested in the liturgy, not only Roman Catholics, but also members of other Christian bodies."

The first liturgical text issued by ICEL was the translation of the Roman Canon (Eucharistic Prayer I) which was presented to the conferences of bishops in 1967. This work was the product of many draft proposals and careful deliberation by the Advisory Committee and Episcopal Board. In the process of reaching the final draft hundreds of consultants, specialists in the various disciplines represented on the Advisory Committee, were asked to submit comments. In addition, all of the bishops of the English-speaking world were invited to give their comments after studying the draft. Since ICEL's beginnings consultation has played a major part in the ICEL process. The generous participation of these many bishops, priests, religious, and lay people has served to make the work more representative of the individual conferences and has insured that the texts will be acceptable in each of the separate countries. The publication of the Roman Canon has been followed by twenty-one translations of the rites revised at the direction of Vatican II. Although each of these works involved wide consultation and the reworking of a number of drafts, the texts which stand out, in terms of the magnitude of work involved, as the principal accomplishments of ICEL are the *Roman Missal* (1974) and *The Liturgy of the Hours* (1975–76). Since 1969 ICEL's norms of translation have been closely based upon the principles set down in the *Instruction on Translation of Liturgical Texts* issued by the Consilium for the Implementation of the Constitution on the Sacred Liturgy (*Notitiae* 5 [1969] 3–12).

With major portions of its work of translation completed, ICEL in 1976 established three subcommittees to insure that the special competencies required for the second phase of ICEL's work would be available. Work on the second phase of the program had already begun several years before and the Advisory Committee had almost from the first relied on a structure of ad hoc subcommittees. It was, however, only in 1976 that a plan for the establishment of three standing subcommittees, altogether distinct from the Advisory Committee though working under its direction, was devised and put into operation. The second phase of the ICEL program, endorsed by its Episcopal Board, is primarily directed to three general services: (1) the provision of music for the revised rites; (2) the provision of original texts, composed in the vernacular, in accord with the norms laid down in the revised Roman books; (3) the reordering of the revised Roman books to make them more pastorally effective for the celebration of the rites in the English-speaking countries. To this end the Advisory Committee established the following standing subcommittees: the subcommittee on music; the subcommittee on translations, revisions, and original texts; the subcommittee for the presentation of texts. The work of providing commentaries on the individual rites and other pastoral aids was also begun by ICEL as part of the second phase of its program.

A major undertaking of ICEL in the future will be an exacting reappraisal of all English liturgical texts, beginning with those issued in ICEL's first years. This process will consider each text and subject it to a rigid analysis in light of the comments and criticisms which have been made over the years. The systematic evaluation of the texts from each rite will require at least a year in each instance depending on the length of the rite. It is expected that the entire process will require more than a decade to complete.

In addition to the member conferences there are also fifteen associate-member conferences of ICEL. Since 1963 the following bishops have served as chairmen of ICEL: Archbishop Grimshaw (1963–65); Archbishop Paul J. Hallinan of the United States (1965); Cardinal Gordon J. Gray of Scotland (1965–71); Archbishop G. Emmett Carter of Canada (1971–75); Archbishop Denis E. Hurley of South Africa (1975–).

See also LITURGICAL BOOKS OF THE ROMAN RITE.

[J. R. PAGE]

INTERNATIONAL CONFEDERATION OF CHRISTIAN FAMILY MOVEMENTS (ICCFM)

The International Confederation of Christian Family Movements is composed of groups of families from every continent who accept the propositions that the family is the basic unit of society and that strong families and the enduring values they bring to modern society are vitally needed. The first conference of the ICCFM was held in 1966 at Caracas, Venezuela. In 1977 at an International Assembly in the Philippines, the Movement reconfirmed the characteristics of Christian Family Movements. The Christian Family Movement is an ecumenical, lay-movement. As participants in a Christian movement, member families rejoice that they are called to be bearers of the Good News of Jesus Christ. As families they have a challenge to go beyond their own individual families to participate in a mission to the families in their communities and the wider world. As dedicated to a movement they see that they must redirect themselves to involvement in the socio-economic, moral-religious, and political needs of families. Through the inquiry process families discover that throughout the world there is widespread poverty, insufficient income, undernourishment, ill-health, inadequate housing, unemployment, helplessness, discrimination, and social disorder. Alongside the decision to become involved in these deep human needs is a commitment to act against the causes which are embedded in unjust social and economic systems.

[P. CROWLEY]

INTERNATIONAL CONSULTATION ON ENGLISH TEXTS (ICET)

The International Consultation on English Texts is to be distinguished from the Roman Catholic body, *International Commission on English in the Liturgy (ICEL), which exists to achieve an English version of liturgical texts and with a view toward their ecumenical possibilities. After some informal contacts ICEL invited a number of representatives of other English-speaking Churches from various countries to meet their representatives and in 1969 ICET was formed. The secretary of ICEL has always been its secretary, but ICET is an independent, ecumenical body. It has made use of work done by various *ad hoc* groups.

The need for ICET arose from two causes. First, the Roman Catholic Church, putting its liturgies officially into English for the first time, did not feel bound by the texts of the Anglican *Book of Common Prayer*, which other non-Anglican Churches had largely followed. Secondly, the Churches which had long used these texts, felt the need to modernize them (especially to address God as "you"). It seemed sensible that the Churches should do this together for parts of the liturgy they have in common.

In 1970 ICET published *Prayers We Have in Common*, containing in Category A the Lord's Prayer, the Apostles' and Nicene Creeds, the Glory to God, Holy, Holy, Holy, and the Glory Be to the Father. These texts had been under discussion for some considerable time, and the ICET had reached agreement about them. They were therefore presented to the Churches for experimental use over an extended period, perhaps for several years. *Prayers We Have in Common* also included in Category B texts on which it was still working: Sursum Corda, Agnus Dei, and Te Deum. Both sets of texts had brief explanatory commentaries. In 1971 the booklet appeared in an enlarged and revised edition. All the texts were now in the same category. The only major changes were to items formerly in Category B, with corresponding changes in the commentary. The Lucan canticles (Magnificat, Benedictus, Nunc dimittis) were added. The American version of this (1972) further altered two lines in the Te Deum. In 1974 ICET met again, to consider what improvements had been suggested by the actual use of the texts. As a result, the *Prayers We Have in Common* appeared again in 1975 in a second revised edition, and now included the Lord Have Mercy (Kyrie), and a new note on changes necessary in musical settings. The commentary, though containing much of its original material, naturally defended the changes made.

ICEL has for the most part simply adopted the ICET texts and commends them as if they were its own, and so the Roman Catholic Church in English-speaking countries uses most of them. Most of the other major Churches use them also, especially in the Liturgy of the Eucharist. The chief exception is the Lord's Prayer, on which it is difficult to reach agreement. Some Churches, even while addressing God in general as "you," still retain the traditional "thou" version in this prayer, only slightly modified. Others are still experimenting with forms of the "you" version different from the ICET form. Apart from this, *Prayers We Have in Common* has found general acceptance and there are no plans for its further revision.

Bibliography: International Consultation on English Texts, *Prayers We Have in Common* (London and Philadelphia 1970; enlarged and rev. ed. London 1971, Philadelphia 1972; 2d and rev. ed. London and Philadelphia 1975).

[A. R. GEORGE]

INTERNATIONAL LIAISON

International Liaison is the United States Catholic Coordinating Center for Lay Volunteer Ministries and is an affiliate of the United States Catholic Conference. Headquarters are in Washington, D.C. The work of the International Liaison is to engage itself in mission participation and awareness, and to: (1) poll the missions each year to ascertain their needs for lay expertise; (2) maintain constant contact with the U.S. dioceses; (3) indicate urgent and immediate, as well as projected needs of missions; (4) list such needs in the annual publication, *The Response*, distributed to the laity directly through the International Liaison, Vocation offices, Propagation of the Faith offices, lay apostolate offices, campus ministry groups, and various colleges and universities; (5) maintain contact with sister organizations throughout the world; (6) refer candidates for placement, training, and screening; (7) assist missions in whatever way possible to expedite Vatican II's decrees on direct lay participation in the total life of the Church; (8) act as the central coordinating center for the various sending and receiving International Liaison Coalition members to engage in catechesis for lay ministries.

[M. R. PARATORE]

INTERNATIONAL MONETARY FUND (IMF)

The International Monetary Fund was established in 1945 as an independent international organization to promote worldwide monetary cooperation and a freer system of world trade and payments as a means of helping its members, now numbering 132 states, to achieve economic growth, high levels of employment, and improved standards of living. To this end IMF's main function is to see that its member states follow exchange practices that facilitate balance of payment adjustment. It provides reserve credit for the purpose of assuring that the adjustment itself does not cause disruption by being too precipitous or by being undertaken in response to transient difficulties. The IMF is a specialized agency of the United Nations (UN) under Article 57 of the UN Charter and has special authority to cooperate with other international organizations and to make arrangements for that purpose. The Fund as an institution possesses full juridical personality, including the power to contract, acquire and dispose of property and to initiate legal proceedings. It also enjoys certain specified privileges and immunities. Its headquarters are in Washington, D.C.

The IMF Articles of Agreement, which are in effect its constitution, entered into force on December 27, 1945. Thus: (1) a new international institution came into existence; (2) the member countries of IMF became subject to new rules of public international law, the observance of which IMF supervises; and (3) IMF acquired assets, consisting of gold and the currencies of members, which it administers in accordance with its Articles. The First Amendment to the IMF Articles of Agreement took effect July 28, 1969. It gave IMF the authority to create a new monetary reserve asset, the special drawing right (SDR), to meet the global needs of monetary authorities for international liquidity without having to rely on further acquisition of gold or reserve assets. The SDR is the first international reserve asset to be created by a decision of the world community. The Articles require that, in any decision to allocate (i.e., to issue or create) SDRs, the IMF shall seek to meet the long-term global needs for additional reserve assets.

A proposed Second Amendment to the IMF Articles has been submitted to members and is well on its way to acceptance or ratification. The Amendment states that IMF shall supervise the international monetary system in order to insure its effective cooperation and the compliance of members with their obligations on exchange policies and practices. The Resolution approving the proposed Amendment was adopted by the Board of Governors on April 30, 1976. The Amendment's entry into force, together with members' accep-

tance of the increase in total quotas from SDR 29 billion to the SDR 39 billion agreed under the Sixth General Review of Quotas, will increase the number and importance of the IMF enabling powers and give its members greater flexibility in the choice of exchange rate arrangements, subject at all times to certain general obligations and to IMF surveillance. The proposed amendment also provides for a reduction in the role of gold in the international monetary system.

The IMF Articles of Agreement provide that all power shall be vested in the Board of Governors, consisting of one Governor and one alternate appointed by each member. The Board normally meets once a year for review and for consideration of future policy. The Governors may also vote on specific questions by mail. In supervising the management and adaptations of the international monetary system, the Board is advised by a 20-nation ministerial level Interim Committee established in 1974, which will serve until a permanent and representative Council of Governors with decision-making powers is set up under the terms of the proposed Second Amendment. The Governors have delegated many of their executive powers to 20 Executive Directors who are responsible for the day-to-day operations of IMF and are in continuous session in Washington under the Chairmanship of the Managing Director. Five of the Executive Directors are appointed by the five members having the largest quota, and the others are elected by the Governors of their constituencies.

[J. H. REID]

INTERNATIONAL THEOLOGICAL COMMISSION

The institution of this new Vatican commission was announced by Pope Paul VI in the consistory of April 28, 1969, as his response to recommendations made during Vatican Council II and the specific proposal of the 1967 Synod of Bishops (ActApS 61 [1969] 431–432; cf. 713–716). The function of the Commission is "to study doctrinal questions of major importance in order to offer advisory assistance to the Holy See and, in particular, the Congregation for the Doctrine of the Faith" (Statutes, ibid. 540–541). The Commission, therefore, has only a consultative and not a deliberative voice in the functioning of the ordinary magisterium of the Church.

Format. The Commission is constituted of thirty members chosen by the pope from names recommended by the cardinal prefect of the Congregation for the Doctrine of the Faith after consultation with the national episcopal conferences. The members, representing various nations and diverse schools of theology, are chosen for their proficiency in one or other of the theological disciplines and for their fidelity to the magisterium. Their five-year appointment may be renewed for another quinquennium. The president of the commission is the prefect of the same Congregation; he is assisted by a secretary-general.

Function and Procedures. Because the Commission meets only once a year for a week, its work focuses on the clarification of urgent doctrinal principles rather than on precise points of doctrinal practice. These annual meetings are complemented by the continuing research of committees and the contributions solicited from other experts. The resultant documents, set forth in the form of theses or in a more extensive cursive style, are first submitted to the pope and the Congregation for the Doctrine of the Faith. Afterwards they are most often made public as a service to the bishops and theologians of the Church. Such publications are frequently accompanied by commentaries prepared by individual members of the Commission. To date, the commission has published documents on: the sacerdotal ministry (1971); the unity of faith and theological pluralism (1972); the apostolicity of the Church and apostolic succession (1973); criteria for the knowledge of Christian morality (1974); the relation between the magisterium and theologians (1975); Christian salvation and human progress (1976); and marriage (1977).

Bibliography: AnnPont 1978: 1073; 1466–1467. Documents from the Commission and matters relevant to it are published, from 1969, in OssRom and DocCath (under the index title "Actes du Saint Siège"); English translations appear in Origins. The USCC has published, *Theses on the Relationship between the Ecclesiastical Magisterium and Theologians*, with commentary by O. Semmelroth and K. Lehmann (Washington, D.C. 1977).

[B. M. AHERN]

INTERNATIONAL UNION OF SUPERIORS GENERAL (WOMEN)

The International Union of Superiors General (UISG) is an organization of pontifical right, established by the Congregation for Religious, Dec. 8, 1965 to respond to Vatican Council II, *Perfectae caritatis* 23, and to efforts of superiors general of women's congregations to create an association for mutual collaboration, sharing, and support, centered in Rome but with two-way communication with religious sisters throughout the world. UISG aims to foster at the international level the continuous renewal of the life and mission of religious sisters in the Church through their superiors general by research and reflection, by collaboration with the Congregation for Religious and Secular Institutes (SCRSI), by representation on ecclesial and international bodies, and by appropriate communication and evaluation. It represents approximately 2,400 superiors general of women's congregations of apostolic life. Since the first general assembly in 1967 (statutes revised 1973), the UISG has operated through triennial assemblies of approximately 100 locally elected delegates across the world, annual meetings of an intercontinental council of 28 members (19 elected by the assembly, 9 appointed by the SCRSI), regular meetings of an executive committee of eight based in Rome, and a permanent secretariat. It is juridically recognized by the Italian state (Decree 1296, Dec. 10, 1971).

The Union sponsors annual international meetings in Rome. It participates in many ecclesial initiatives involving women religious and is their representative on the Council for Relations with the SCRSI. In a style that is prayerful, effective and sisterly, UISG tries to combine three main thrusts of service: primarily, up-to-date world awareness, through its councillors, of trends in the evolution of sisters' religious life; conjointly, reflection on these through permanent or *ad hoc* commissions, larger meetings, and a quarterly bulletin; complementarily, enrichment of input through relations with ecclesial and national bodies and with national conferences of religious. It maintains ongoing collaboration with the *Union of Superiors General (Men).

Bibliography: UISG, *Bulletin* 30 (1973) 29.

[M. LINSCOTT]

INTERNATIONAL UNION OF THE CATHOLIC PRESS

In 1977 the International Union of the Catholic Press, known as UCIP after its name in French, observed its 50th anniversary by convening the Eleventh World Congress of the Catholic Press in Vienna. Several hundred delegates from all continents took part.

UCIP includes five federations and five regional bureaus. They are the International Federation of Catholic Journalists, International Federation of Catholic Dailies and Periodicals, International Federation of Catholic Press Agencies, International Federation of Catholic Teachers and Researchers in the Science and Techniques of Information, International Federation of Church Press Associations; the bureaus are for Latin America, South Asia, Southeast Asia, East Asia, and Africa. Its president is Louis Meerts, editor-in-chief of *Gazet van Antwerpen* in Antwerp, Belgium. Its secretary-general is Rev. Pierre Chevalier and its headquarters are at 10 Avenue de la Gare-des-Eaux-Vives, Geneva.

The UCIP program for 1979–80 includes a strong emphasis on training journalists and supporting the growth of periodicals and news services in the Third World. In 1977 UCIP began to work for "A new order of information" in the Third World, one "not imposed from without." Father Chevalier wrote that the new order of information "must bring more respect for justice and more love into a domain that is too often ruled by egoism and domination."

[A. E. P. WALL]

INTERNATIONAL WOMEN'S YEAR, WORLD CONFERENCE FOR THE

The first worldwide conference focusing on women, their problems, and aspirations was held under United Nations auspices in Mexico City, June 19–July 2, 1975, midway through International Women's Year (IWY). The IWY Conference, like IWY itself, resulted from the work of the UN Commission on the Status of Women, established in 1946. The Commission surfaced a growing global consciousness of injustices toward women. The critical issues of the early 1970s, including the hunger crisis, turned development experts attention to women's roles in developing countries. At the same time women in the developed countries were growing in their awareness of being victims of economic, political, and social inequities and of the unjust economic and political system that had developed worldwide under male leadership.

The Conference. Over 6,000 persons attending the Mexico City meeting worked toward the goals of: (1) promoting equality among women and men; (2) integrating women fully into the process of socio-economic development; and (3) increasing women's contribution to the effort for world peace. The IWY Conference was held in two sections: a government Conference and an unofficial Tribune. The former, with delegates from 133 nations, and 149 other UN recognized bodies, prepared a World Plan of Action and approved a statement of principles, the "Declaration of Mexico." Both documents and the conference debate covered issues ranging from the links between the international economic order and the poverty faced by women in developing nations to the need for the greater participation of women in public affairs and of men in family life.

The Plan of Action was adopted by consensus with reservations and two abstentions. The United States registered reservations with the Plan because of statements on the *new international economic order and voted against the Declaration because of paragraphs linking Zionism to racism. The Vatican, along with China, abstained from the consensus on the Plan and on the Declaration because of their statements on procreation. At the Tribune, women, freed of governmental restraints, used discussions, art, and the media to explore their own situation. Although the Tribune was the setting for challenge and conflict, it was also an occasion for participation and sharing as women from totally different backgrounds learned of one another's concerns, fears, and dreams.

The Impact of the Conference. The Conference was an important stimulus in the struggle of women seeking justice. In preparing for it, the UN, national governments, and nongovernmental institutions were forced to look more closely at women, the roles they fill, and the heavy burdens they bear. The Plan of Action spelled out concrete actions which people and governments need to undertake if women are to be free to make their potential contributions to world society. The Plan set a ten year time line for action. It called for a conference in 1980 to evaluate progress and to plan strategies for further action. Tribune sessions set the stage for establishing networks, monitoring progress, and sharing information.

Since the Conference the UN has designated 1976–85 as United Nations Decade for Women: Equality, Development and Peace in order to promote and facilitate the World Plan of Action. Nations and UN regional groups have also drawn up appropriate Plans of Action. Societies have become more conscious of the harmful impact of male-dominated structures as the actual activities and burdens of women have become better known. The discord and conflict that have occurred will continue as women struggle for change. However, the struggle is accompanied by the hope that changes in women's self-image, in more equitable and thus stronger family structures and in increased opportunities for women, will lead to societies that treat women and men more justly.

Bibliography: E. BOULDING, *Women in the Twentieth Century World* (New York 1976); *Women and World Development* (Washington, D.C. 1976); *United Nations Meeting in Mexico* (New York 1975).

[M. BURKE]

INTERRACIAL JUSTICE

Moral theologians have commonly raised the ethical concept of justice as one of the four cardinal virtues (as used by ancient philosophers) to a more complex, theological notion embracing commutative, distributive, and legal aspects. The totality for them describes a harmony between the rights and duties of individuals, the communities of which they are members or citizens, and the whole of a nation or even of all human society. Such harmony reflects the justice of God Himself, or right order ($\delta\iota\kappa\alpha\iota\sigma\sigma\acute{\upsilon}\nu\eta$ of the Scriptures).

Concept of Interracial Justice. Interracial Justice enters the picture both to describe all racial discrimination leading to denial of rights and as a subspecies of social justice, a term itself of relatively recent vintage,

owing much of its acceptance to frequent use in papal encyclicals and other church documents on social order (e.g. Pius XI *Quadragesimo anno*, ActApS 23 [1931] 177–288). As an instance of social justice interracial justice in its positive aspects is an integral part of the social teachings of the Church. When racism or even individual racial prejudice prompt the denial of another's strict individual right to life and liberty, the offense is not specified by the motive but by the rights deprived, so that such offenses are violation of *commutative* justice. When the goal is the promotion and protection of the rights of social groups or "races," the object bears on the common or social good, and the virtue is more properly termed interracial justice, as a form of social justice.

History. The classic modern denial of justice because of race is, of course, Nazism. The theory of *Mein Kampf* and the genocidal practices of Hitler's Germany combine to offer a picture of outrages committed against the lives, liberty, and property of millions of human beings in the name of an Aryan-Master Race theory. Pope Pius XI's insightful, but unfortunately neglected, encyclical, *Mit brennender Sorge*, in 1937, against Nazi philosophy, detailed how the scriptural revelation of the oneness of the human race has been confirmed by the sciences, history, natural philosophy, and common law. In sum, the Catholic teaching is an expression also of the scientific conviction: there is no master race, no inferior race—there is but one human race. There are no basic variations on the theme of human nature, though differences, properly termed accidental, occur within all groups in such discernible qualities as health, strength, mental ability, social position, or economic status.

The Hitlerian deviation from acceptance of the unity of the human race and the basic dignity of every human person as creature of God had precedents through the ages, e.g., in the widespread practice of slavery which subjugated some human groups to others, most often as the result of victory in wars. In the U.S., however nuanced the practice in various regions and because of the varied outlooks of slave owners, the institution of slavery deprived Blacks (and often others) of their basic liberties and civil rights until after the Civil War. Institutionalized injustice on the basis of race was largely overcome by the passage (1865) of the 13th Amendment of the U.S. Constitution prohibiting "involuntary servitude," and the 14th (1868) denying to individual states the right to make or enforce any law "abridging life, liberty or pursuit of happiness." It was not, however, until 1964 that Federal law was to prohibit discrimination in employment, and only in 1968 did the nation enact a National Fair Housing Act.

Catholic Teaching. Theoretically, justice can demand minimal obedience, i.e. giving to each his due as understood by some mathematical standard or verified against a rigid set of words, as in a contract. For the Christian, justice is inseparable from love and more is required than the respect for the irreducible objective rights. All forms of justice, in the full Christian meaning, are integrated with the love due to the person–creditor, and hence oblige beyond the impersonalities of matter, money, or the like.

The authoritative teachings of the popes and of Vatican Council II on the evil of racism have their counterparts, for the American scene, in numerous NCCB pastorals and in statements of many individual bishops. The admittedly less than vigorous, often divided, and therefore highly ambiguous leadership of early American history, even beyond Civil War days, has been succeeded by forthright and unanimous teaching, especially in such recent episcopal documents as *Discrimination and the Christian Conscience* (1958) and *The National Race Crisis* (1968). The latter is especially notable, for besides renewing their moral condemnation of racial prejudice and discrimination, the bishops recognized that "racist attitudes and consequent discrimination exist, not only in the hearts of humans but in the fabric of their institutions" and outlined a campaign against institutional racism as well as against public and private acts of discrimination. Among tasks of unfinished business of the Catholic community the bishops listed "the total eradication of any elements of discrimination in our parishes, schools, hospitals, homes for the aged, and similar institutions." Catholics "of every color and ethnic group" were called on to "ally themselves with religious and civic programs" to demonstrate love of neighbor in deeds. Among goals to be won for previously deprived minorities were: quality education, "especially for traditional victims of discrimination"; job opportunities, "essential to insuring self-respect and family life"; decent housing, without segregation by race; public and private assistance (welfare) that "respects the dignity of persons and the integrity of families." To these principal concerns there were added references to the need for adequate health care and the destruction of the white segregationist mentality which the National Commission on Civil Disorders (Kerner Report) had called responsible for the racial crisis of the Sixties.

Present Realities: Rather than probe the many and various theories of "race," it is more profitable for the guidance of consciences to detail the chief categories careful observers discuss as subject to the most violations of interracial justice on the American scene. The U.S. Equal Employment Opportunity Commission simply enumerates four general groups which regularly suffer from racial discrimination: *Blacks* (not of Hispanic origin); *Hispanics* (all persons of Mexican, Puerto Rican, Cuban, Central or South American, or other Spanish culture or origin); *Asians or Pacific Islanders* (all persons having origins in any of the original people of the Far East, Southeast Asia or the Pacific Islands); *American or Alaskan Natives (Indians)* (all persons having origins in any of the original peoples of North America).

Inclusion in such groups may occur because a person externally appears to belong, subjectively identifies with, or is regarded in the community as belonging. Clearly identification in and by the community is the principal way of designation. It is not therefore by "race" in any scientific sense, but sometimes by color, sometimes by physical characteristics, often enough by language facility or by national origin. Not to be overlooked in the broad spectrum of racial injustice are the sins occasioned by ethnic differences at least so far as these lead to attacks on strict rights. Civil laws usually prohibit discrimination on the basis of "race, color, religion, sex, or national origin." The moral law considers unjust racial discrimination sinful, and affirmatively demands both interracial justice and the love of other humans such discrimination violates.

A pastoral on racism is planned by the NCCB for 1978, both because of the continuing discrimination and the failure of civil laws to overcome it, and as a further response to the recommendations on race and ethnicity emerging from the nationwide Bicentennial consultations of 1976 (*Call to Action). Within the Church, leadership to obtain minority rights is exercised by such groups as the *National Office of Black Catholics (NOBC), the USCC Secretariat for *Hispanic Affairs, and the *National Catholic Conference for Interracial Justice (NCCIJ). Most dioceses have Justice and Peace commissions which strive for racial harmony and numerous religious congregations have social justice committees. Emerging as the vehicle for broad lay participation in the ministry of racial justice efforts are the social concerns committees of parish councils. To achieve the common goal of interracial justice collaboration is vital on the national and regional levels with such proven minority leadership groups as NAACP, Urban League, Leadership Conference for Civil Rights, PADRES, Las Hermanas, and American Indian Rights Movement.

Bibliography: J. LA FARGE, *Catholic Viewpoint on Race Relations* (New York 1956). J. T. LEONARD, *Theology and Race Relations* (Milwaukee 1963). V. MAINELLI, ed., *Social Justice: The Catholic Position* (Washington, D.C. 1975) documents. G. MYRDAL, *An American Dilemma: The Negro Problem and Modern Democracy* (2 v., New York 1944). National Catholic Conference for Interracial Justice, NCCIJ, *Catholic Schools and Racial Integration* (Washington, D.C. 1975).

[A. J. WELSH]

ISLAMIC/ROMAN CATHOLIC DIALOGUE

Dialogue between the Church and Islam is as old as Islam itself. In fact, there is a sense in which it had, in Mohammed's young manhood, a pre-Islamic background. Even if the Bahira legend (2:16–17) were for the most part unreliable, it is certain that Mohammed had many early contacts with Christians of various persuasions and degrees of erudition, and that the "first Hegira" of Muslims, fleeing persecution from the ruling aristocrats of Mecca, was specifically to the Christian *Negus* (emperor) of Abyssinia in 615. Mohammed clearly incorporated selected Christianity, such as he understood it, into Islam and Koran 5:85 says in words attributed to God: "You will discover that those who are most implacable in their hatred of the Muslims are the Jews and the pagans, while those nearest to them in affection are those who profess to be Christians. That is because there are priests and monks among them, and they are free of pride." Ultimately, however, both the Jews and the Christians, as "people of the Book" (i.e., the Bible), were accorded a status as privileged minorities within the Isalmic world or, more accurately, "protected" minorities, in return for payment of special taxes.

Early dialogue, apart from the business of the street or increasingly actual submission (the meaning of *Islām*) to Islamic rule, concentrated upon basic theological issues. St. John Damascene and those associated with him and his tradition are the first major figures. In the Latin Middle Ages Peter the Venerable of Cluny and Bl. Raymond Lull stand out in sharp contrast to the worst in the crusading mentality. In later times more realistic, if occasionally eccentric dialogue developed within the context of European colonialism.

By the time of Vatican Council II, the Islamic/Roman Catholic dialogue had progressed to an extent far in advance of Islamic relations with other Christian communities and in a notable manner which set it in the context of Christian ecumenism. That was due in the main to such figures as Charles Lavigérie, founder of the White Fathers, Charles de Foucauld, founder of the Little Brothers and Little Sisters of Jesus, and Louis Massignon, the Islamologist of the Collège de France. Their spiritual disciples, particularly Dominican and Franciscan friars, had been meeting in Rome to study and reappraise the dialogue (*Les Journées romaines*) for several years, and therefore the preparatory statement on Islam, a product of the statement on the Jews, itself an original part of the eventual Decree on Ecumenism, was comparatively easy to prepare. What the Council requested the Supreme Pontiff to declare in 1965 was quite a bit less than what was originally proposed by the preparatory commission; it was finally worded:

> The Church also regards the Muslims with esteem. They adore the only God, living and sustaining, merciful and all-powerful, the creator of heaven and earth, who has revealed himself to mankind. They strive wholeheartedly to submit themselves to his inscrutable decrees, just as Abraham, to whom the Islamic faith willingly links itself, submitted himself to God. Although they do not acknowledge Jesus as God, nevertheless they revere him as a prophet, and pay honor to his Virgin Mother, at times devoutly calling upon her intercession. Furthermore, they look forward to Judgement Day, when God will give their just rewards to men raised from the dead. For that reason they respect the moral life and worship God most particularly in the form of prayer, almsgiving, and fasting. However in view of the fact that not a few disagreements and enmities have arisen, over the course of the centuries, between Christians and Muslims, this Sacred Synod urges everyone to forget the past history of these matters and to work sincerely for mutual understanding, for justice for all mankind in the social order, good things for them in the moral order, and peace and freedom for all (*Nostra aetate* 3: cf. *Lumen gentium* 16).

Even before the statement was promulgated, a Secretariat for Non-Christians had been created by Pope Paul VI in 1964 and its Islamic division was the first to be complemented and to produce guidelines for contemporary dialogue between Roman Catholics and Muslims. These guidelines were responded to and followed by many initiatives, details of which are recorded in the *Bulletin* of the Secretariat. It might be said that the initiatives progressed slowly and not without serious reversals. The first were local; the next were international. More than one hundred formal dialogues or "conversations" were reported during the first three years. Those in Africa, Southeast Asia, and America seemed to afford special signs of success, as did the increasing participation of Non-Catholic Christians,

bound now, it appeared, in a common cause uniting them all. The worldwide consultors met in plenary sessions in Rome and Paris; it was finally apparent that Islamic/Roman Catholic dialogue had been reverently and reliably established and promised to be permanent.

During the late 1960s and early 1970s new forms of dialogue began to develop, ranging from "visits" to the *madrasah* (Islamic school) to powerful theological disputations in the sundry academic arenas of the world. In February 1976 a remarkable dialogue took place in Tripoli, Libyan Arab Republic, in which the Christian religion was represented principally by a delegation from the Vatican led by Cardinal Sergio Pignedoli. Several statements, political in nature and involving the Arab-Israeli conflict, were intruded into a final declaration that partially had to be repudiated by both sides. The dangers inherent in such statements being included in the dialogue were now fully apparent. Since then, a good measure of harmony has been established in Islamic/Roman Catholic dialogue through a careful differentiation of outlooks and objectives. With the help of various parent organizations, not a few brave universities, and many persistent individuals, both Christians and Muslims, the dialogue has taken place with most conspicuous success during the later 1970s in Jerusalem, Rome, London, Paris, Madrid, Granada, New York, Toronto, Chicago, Salt Lake City, Los Angeles, Lima, Honolulu, Kyoto, Singapore, Dacca, New Delhi, Lahore, Tehran, and Beirut. Although uneven in form and content, these gatherings have significantly advanced mutual understanding on all intellectual and social levels.

Bibliography: The best general bibliographies on the subject are those of J. DÉJEUX and R. CASPAR, *Proche-Orient Chrétien* 16 (1966) and R. CASPAR, *Parole et mission* 33, 34 (1966). Work of the subsequent years is scattered in innumerable articles and notices in journals, for the most part. The *Bulletin* of the Secretariat for Non-Christians is a most valuable source, therefore. N. A. DANIEL, *Islam and the West* (Edinburgh 1958) is an excellent background source. The works of Louis Massignon aid in understanding the background of much of the recent dialogue; see also G. BASETTI-SANI, *Louis Massignon* (Chicago 1974). The proceedings of most of the dialogues referred to above have been published. A "Task Force on Christian-Muslim Relations" was established by the Duncan Black Macdonald Center at the Hartford Seminary Foundation in Hartford, Conn. in 1977 and appears to be emerging as a major coordinating body for the dialogue in America. *Guidelines for Dialogue with Muslims* (Vatican City 1968; multilingual editions) remains the norm by which Roman Catholic dialogue is pursued.

[J. KRITZECK]

J

JAEGER, LORENZ

German Cardinal, archbishop and ecumenist; b. Halle, Sept. 23, 1892; d. Paderborn, Apr. 2, 1975. An ordinary soldier during World War I, he was ordained to the priesthood in 1922. After 19 years in teaching and other pastoral ministries he was ordained bishop of Paderborn in 1941. In the consistory of Feb. 22, 1965 he became a cardinal. Especially interested in ecumenism, Cardinal Jaeger, along with Cardinal Bea, was influential in the establishment of the Secretariat for Promoting Christian Unity. He was also a member of the Preparatory Commission for Vatican Council II and a frequent intervener in conciliar discussions. Earlier (Jan. 18, 1957) in his own diocese he founded the "Johann-Adam-Möhler-Institut für Konfessions and Diasporakunde" (the Johann Adam Möhler Institute), one of the world's foremost centers for ecumenical study, research, and publication. Its quarterly journal, *Catholica*, is one of the most authoritative in the Roman Catholic-Protestant (especially Lutheran and Calvanist) theological dialogue.

The Institute's goals reflect Cardinal Jaeger's own interests and activities: scholarly research and description of the doctrine, worship and life of those Christian Churches separated from Rome, especially the Reformation Confessional Churches; the presentation of the Catholic faith in its fullness as the response to the questions posed by the Reformation; and the sharing of the results of these scholarly investigations with those engaged in other pastoral activity.

In addition to his episcopal and ecumenical activities, he was also a general spokesman for the German hierarchy on a wide range of other subjects, especially on pastoral care, on the status of women in civil and ecclesial society, on students, and intellectuals. He played a significant role in the reconstruction of the German Church and nation after World War II.

His ecumenical outlook and insight are well illustrated in his pre-Vatican II *The Ecumenical Council, the Church and Christendom*, tr. A. V. LITTLEDALE (New York 1961) and his commentary on Vatican II's Decree On Ecumenism, *A Stand On Ecumenism: The Council's Decree*, tr. H. GRAEF (New York 1965).

[R KRESS]

JEWISH/ROMAN CATHOLIC RELATIONS

When this issue was discussed in an earlier article in the *New Catholic Encyclopedia* its author could point only to "minimal progress" (16:144). Recent years have seen dramatic improvement.

Dialogue and Initiatives. Nationally, the NCCB Secretariat for *Catholic-Jewish Relations has fostered successful Dialogue Workshops (Dayton, 1973; Memphis, 1975; Detroit, 1977; Los Angeles, 1978) that have explored our common heritage and established patterns for future work. Academic programs, such as Seton Hall's Institute for Judaeo-Christian Studies and Temple University's Holocaust Studies program, provide an ongoing forum for scholarly exchange. Increasing numbers now participate in local dialogue groups throughout the country.

The strong response of church leaders to the Yom Kippur War and to the sad attempt in the UN to identify Zionism with racism gave reassurance to the Jewish community of Christian commitment to the State of Israel's right to exist in security. Recent textbook studies show improvement in the treatment of Jews and Judaism in Catholic teaching, though problems persist in regard, e.g., to the New Testament protrayal of the Pharisees and of the Crucifixion.

Statements from episcopal conferences—the French (1973), the American (1967, 1975)—and the *Guidelines* of the Pontifical Commission for Religious Relations with Judaism (issued Jan. 3, 1975), are among advances in understanding accomplished since Vatican Council II. These statements point to a "permanent vocation" of Judaism in God's plan and call for Christians "to learn by what essential traits the Jews define themselves." Deploring the "de-Judaization" process which began in the primitive Church, the American bishops have called for a positive theology of Judaism based on the teachings of Romans 9–11. Such moves toward a theological stance accommodated to the continuing religious vitality of the Jewish people have been reciprocated from the Jewish side in a renewed interest in Jesus and in positive rabbinic views of Christianity. The Talmudic teaching on the "Noahide" covenant between God and all humanity (Gen *Rabbah* 34; *b. Sanhedrin* 56a) has been appealed to as a framework for a new Jewish appreciation of Christianity's role in spreading the knowledge of the one God among "the nations."

Issues. Catholic scholars are beginning to see the dialogue as a necessity for the Church's own self-understanding rather than merely as an exercise in good will. The 1975 Vatican Guidelines noted that it is "when pondering her own mystery" that the Church encounters the mystery of Israel. Even such potentially divisive topics as abortion and parochial school aid, are now being surfaced and discussed in the dialogue. The International Catholic/Jewish Liaison Committee, founded in Rome in 1970, holds annual meetings of increasing importance. Its members are chosen, from the Jewish side, by the International Jewish Committee for Interreligious Consultations (IJCIC) and, from the Catholic side, by the pope after consulting with the Vatican Secretariat for Promoting Christian Unity.

A paper presented to its Venice meeting (1977) has been considered an important breakthrough on the subject of "The Mission and Witness of the Church." Delivered by Prof. Tomaso Federici of the Pontifical Urban University, the paper clearly distinguishes witness and proselytism. While the former belongs to the essential nature of the Church following the command to make known the name of the one God among all peoples, the latter, tainted as it is with such historical practices as forced Baptism and cultural pressure, should be excluded from present Christian practice. Dialogue between the Church and the Jewish people should be entered into "without mental reservation" or underlying conversionary intent.

The modern State of Israel has proven to be an apt setting for dialogue. Here, for the first time in centuries, it is the Christian community that is the minority in a majority Jewish culture. While the situation involves many uncertainties, relations between appointed representatives of the various communities began as early as 1957 with the founding of the Interfaith Committee. Scholarly dialogue, as embodied in the Jerusalem Rainbow Group and the Ecumenical Theological Research Fraternity, has proven most helpful in analyzing areas both of commonality and of divergence between the two traditions. The special link between People and Land in Judaism, for example, has received profound study. A consistent, though only partially successful effort has been made to include Moslem representatives.

While numerous challenges remain for the dialogue, and while severe tests may be ahead, especially over the volatile Middle East situation (*see* MIDDLE EAST, CHURCH AND), the prevailing mood should be judged, on both sides, as one of cautious optimism. Steady and measured progress, despite obstacles that a decade ago appeared insurmountable, are vindicating such hopes.

Bibliography: Major Catholic and Protestant statements are contained in H. Croner, ed., *Stepping Stones to Further Jewish-Christian Relations* (London, New York 1977). Documentation service on the subject is provided by Société internationale de documentation Judéo-Chrétienne (SIDIC) *Journal*, Eng. tr. (Via del Plebiscito 112, 00186, Rome, Italy). Pontifical Commission for Religious Relations with Judaism, *Guidelines*, Origins 4 (1974–75) 463–464; ActApS 67 (1975) 73–79.

[E. J. FISHER]

JOHN PAUL I, POPE

Pontificate Aug. 26–Sept. 28, 1978; b. Albino Luciani at Forno di Canale (Diocese of Belluno), Italy, Oct. 17, 1912. He was born into a poor family, his father having been forced at one period to migrate to Switzerland for work. After studies in the minor seminary at Feltre and the major seminary at Belluno, and ordination on July 7, 1935, Fr. Luciani completed his doctorate in theology at the Gregorianum in Rome in 1937. He served briefly as a parish priest at Forno di Canale and Agerdo, then from 1937–47 was professor of theology, Canon Law, and history of sacred art at the Belluno Seminary, for a time serving also as vice-rector. While continuing to teach, he also became in 1947 pro-chancellor of the diocese, then vicar-general. On Dec. 15, 1958 he was named to the See of Vittorio-Veneto and ordained bishop by John XXIII at St. Peter's Dec. 27, 1958. He participated in Vatican Council II and his commitment to its spirit of renewal was expressed in a pastoral letter to his diocese in 1967, "Notes on the Council."

Bp. Luciani was named patriarch of Venice by Pope Paul VI, Dec. 15, 1969; he took possession of his see on Feb. 3, 1970. He was created cardinal by Paul VI at the consistory of March 5, 1973, with San Marco, Piazza Venezia, as his titular church. His election in the conclave after Paul VI's death was surprising because of its swiftness and was welcomed because of Pope John Paul I's warmth and simplicity. He did away with the traditional papal coronation and was installed as supreme pastor by receiving the archiepiscopal pallium on Sept. 3, 1978; the Pope referred to the ceremony simply as the inauguration of his pastoral ministry. The program Pope John Paul outlined the day after his election proposed the following: to continue to put into effect the heritage of Vatican Council II; to preserve the integrity of church discipline in the lives of priests and faithful; to remind the entire Church that the first duty is evangelization; to continue the ecumenical thrust, without compromising doctrine but without hesitancy; to pursue with patience but firmness the serene and constructive dialogue of Paul VI for pastoral action; to support every laudable and worthy initiative for world peace.

The Pope did not live to carry out this program; the Church and the world were shocked by his sudden death. His "September Papacy" had brought fulfilment to the longing in peoples' hearts for a person and a leader who radiated joy, holiness, simple goodness. His passing left the hope that the response to his brief pontificate would be remembered by his successors and by every pastor in the Church.

[T. C. O'BRIEN]

JOHN PAUL II, POPE

Elected pope Oct. 16, 1978; b. Karol Wojtyla, May 18, 1920, in Wadowice, an industrial town in the Archdiocese of Krakow, Poland. For the first time since the Dutch pope, Adrian VI (1522–23), a non-Italian, in the person of Cardinal Wojtyla, was elected to the papacy, the decision coming on the second day of the conclave following the sudden death of Pope John Paul I. Karol Wojtyla knew poverty as a child and during high school went to work in order to help his family. In 1938 he entered the Jagiellonian University, Krakow, concentrating on poetry and drama. During the Nazi occupation he worked in a quarry, then in a chemical plant, where he became a spokesman for better working conditions. Beginning in 1942 he decided that his vocation was to the priesthood and, because the Nazis had closed the Krakow seminary, studied theology secretly. After the War he was able to complete his studies in the seminary and was ordained on Nov. 1, 1946. During the next two years he earned a doctorate in Rome, with R. Garrigou-Lagrange as his director at the Angelicum (now the University of St. Thomas Aquinas), his thesis being entitled, "Quaestio fidei apud S. Joannem a Cruce" (published in part in *Collectanea theologica* 21 [1950] 418–468). He returned to Krakow and was assigned to pastoral work in parishes and with university students. He also gained a doctorate in theology. In 1953 he began to lecture in ethics and moral theology in Krakow, and in 1954 at the Catholic University of Lublin. Fr. Wojtyla became recognized in the academic world through the more than 300 articles he published in scholarly journals, especially in the area of Christian ethics. In the progress of his own thought he integrated the methods and insights of phenomenology with his strong grounding in the thought of St. Thomas Aquinas. He was especially interested in the phenomenological system of Max Scheler (1874–1928). His commitment to the vision of St. Thomas came out during Vatican Council II; during the discussion on *Gaudium et spes* he remarked on the supreme importance to culture of philosophic wisdom, "the study of the philosophy of being, which consists in the natural contemplation of created things and which finds in them their first cause, God" (*Acta* v. 4, pt. 3, 350).

On July 4, 1958 Pius XII named Fr. Wojtyla titular bishop of Ombi (ancient Egypt) and auxiliary to Archbishop Eugene Baziak, Administrator Apostolic of Krakow. (The see had been vacant from 1951 because of obstruction by the communist regime.) The new bishop was consecrated on Sept. 28, 1958. On Jan. 13, 1964 Pope Paul VI named him archbishop of Krakow and on June 26, 1967 created him cardinal, with the title of S. Cesário al Palatino. During Vatican II he was a prominent spokesman for the Polish Church. Since the Council he has been completely dedicated to its implementation. In 1972 he published a book on the foundations of Vatican II renewal. He participated in all assemblies of the Synod of Bishops and was elected one of the three members for Europe on the Synodal *Consilium*. He was vice-president of the Polish episcopal conference, president of its committees on ecclesiastical studies and on the laity; in March 1978 he issued the report of the doctrinal committee critical of the communist regime's imposition of materialism and secularism, in violation of the cultural and religious heritage of the Polish people. With Cardinal Stefan Wyszinski, the Polish Primate, Cardinal Wojtyla became a leading figure in the Polish Church's stand for its own rights.

Pope John Paul II at the beginning of his ministry as supreme pastor showed himself to be a magnetic personality, conveying the impression of strength in mind and in spirit, of warmth and spontaneity, and of deep faith supported by firm theological convictions. Announcement of his election was greeted with surprise; yet he was well-known to his peers. His addresses and written interventions during the Council and the Synod assemblies, his published monographs, and his leadership as archbishop were all matters of record. He was known in the U.S. from visits, the latest in 1976 to the Philadelphia Eucharistic Congress. The conclave elected a pastor dedicated to the programs of Vatican II and thereby repudiated any movement to efface the image of the Church traced by the Council or to draw the Church back from the paths charted by the Council.

Vatican II Ecclesiology. The Pope's statements at Vatican II, at the meetings of the Synod of Bishops, and in a notable address in Rome to a Symposium of European Bishops, Oct. 14–18, 1975, provide a clear profile of his convinced espousal of the key ideas and aims of the Council. He saw the vision of the Council as taking in two dimensions of the Church: the Church *ad intra* and the Church *ad extra*: "The fact that the Church emerges simultaneously along these two dimensions, *ad intra* and *ad extra*, also means that it necessarily lives *in statu missionis*; that it must tirelessly carry out the burden of the mission which wells up from the very trinitarian depths of God; that through this mission it must constantly penetrate man and his world as leaven, to lead him to his eschatological consummation. Vatican II reminded us that the Church is found 'within' the world and that the world is not totally 'out' of the Church. . . . The categories *ad intra* and *ad extra* are not there to separate or polarize but to coordinate firmly in the faith the whole contemporary Church" (Wojtyla, 1976, 270).

Church ad extra. With regard to the *ad extra* dimension, the Archbishop of Krakow's most influential intervention at Vatican II was in the deliberations over *Gaudium et spes*, the Pastoral Constitution on the Church in the Modern World. He expressed the fundamental motivation of the Church's mission to man in this contemporary world: "Every pastoral initiative, every apostolate, of priests and laity alike, has as its purpose that the human person in every relationship—with self, with others, with the world—should perceive and actually express the truth of the human being's integral vocation" (*Acta* v. 4, pt. 2, 660). The personalism so characteristic of his thought he perceived as the Gospel understanding of the worth and dignity of man and that was the basis on which he wished the conciliar affirmation of religious freedom to be expressed (ibid. 11–13). He also gave clear enunti-ation to the total range of the Church's mission on behalf of human dignity. "The way in which God, through the Cross, has made the work of creation become part of the work of Redemption has settled forever how the Church accepts the meaning of the term 'world'; the Church's service brings to the world truth and morality, but always in accord with the transcendence that Redemption means" (ibid. 661).

Church ad intra. With regard to the vision of the Church *ad intra*, Cardinal Wojtyla in the 1975 Symposium gave as a simple "definition" of the Church, "that community in which the Word of the living God meets the response of living men" (Wojtyla, 1976, 265). The response is faith and the Cardinal, basing himself on vatican II (*Dei Verbum* 5), said of faith: ". . . we would say that the faith is the response of the whole person to the Word of God—a response given to God in the community of the Church. The personal and inner *credo* of Christians is always some kind of sharing in the communitarian *credo* of the Church" (ibid. 264).

The primary model of the Church for his understanding of the community of faith is that of the Church as *communio*. In the 1969 assembly of the Synod of bishops, he pointed out, Oct. 15, 1969, that *communio* surpasses the idea of community or cooperation; *communio* underlines the relationships of person to person in both their outward exchange of helps and service and in the inner sharing between the persons themselves

(Caprile, 1970, 121). On the occasion of his first formal address as pope, Oct. 17, 1978, to the cardinals, John Paul II referred to a Council statement on collegiality that "by divine revelation and the requirements of their apostolic office, each bishop in concert with his fellow bishops is responsible for the whole Church" (*Christus Dominus* 6). He had already made it clear in the 1969 Synod that collegiality is a primary element in the Church's life because it is so closely linked with the nature of the Church as *communio*: "the *communio* of the faithful in the Church ought to be expressed in the *communio* of the local Churches" (Caprile 1970, 121). He continued by stating that the idea and practice of collegiality can and must be fruitfully developed in complete accord with Vatican II. That implies the search for "the spirit of *communio* with the bishop's brethren in the episcopate—an exchange of ideas, of labors, of initiatives, in the spirit of dialogue and service, in collaboration with the Pope" (ibid. 121–122; cf. Caprile, 1972, pt. 1, 419; pt. 2, 873; 945–946).

The 1975 address, "Bishops as Servants of the Faith," is a rich expression of how Pope John Paul II perceives the dynamics of the Church as *communio*. The following are examples:

> One of the crucial decisions of Vatican II was to place the chapter on the People of God [in *Lumen gentium*] before that of the hierarchical ordering of the Church. It is in this frame that we have to consider the problem of episcopal service of the faith, not only in relationship to Christ and the Apostles, but also in its links with the People of God and in the light of the inner constitution which this People has received and continues to receive from Christ, thanks to its sharing in the Priesthood, Prophecy, and Kingship. Such constitution involves a very close, indeed organic, link with the mission entrusted personally and collegially to the Apostles, the same mission which is now continued by Bishops. Bishops must always understand and carry out their service of the faith in the Church in relationship to this sharing of the triple office of Christ, (a sharing) which the whole people of God receives. They must therefore be the priests, the "high priests" of the Church, with all the presbyters and deacons, without forgetting the common priesthood of the faithful.... Bishops must understand and live their position in the Church *in communione*. This means that this is not a one-way situation. Bishops, like priests and deacons, are tied to their people by the gift of Christ and it is only on the basis of this communion that their "own gift" becomes a reality (Wojtyla, 1976, 265–266).

> ...We must firmly assign priority to the live proclamation and announcement of the Gospel, of the kerygma, over official teaching—in the whole life of the Church but particularly in the specific ministry of Bishops.... As regards the contents of the proclamation, it is not primarily a question of the presentation of dogmas but of the announcement of the Gospel as a message with the Mystery of Christ as its core. The purpose of the proclamation of the Word is, above all, that of showing man the way to salvation and the activation of God's plan in Christ.... We must also add that proclamation should render faith "actual and faithful" to those to whom it is addressed by keeping an eye on the human experiences and real problems of modern man. But the main force of the proclamation resides in that transmission where, in some way, man disappears to make room for the Spirit of God (ibid. 269–270).

> The episcopal service of the faith, both as regards proclamation and the magisterium and as regards other priestly and pastoral ministries, must somehow be accessible in the two dimensions of the emergence of the Church *ad intra* and *ad extra*. It must converge with the mission of the Church towards our "brothers in the faith" (Gal 6.10) and towards those who, for some reason or other are "outside" (ibid. 271).

Evangelization. At the 1974 Synod of Bishops, devoted to the subject of evangelization, Cardinal Wojtyla was a key figure. He was the *relator* for the second part of the document synthesizing the synodal discussions on contemporary evangelization (*De evangelizatione mundi huius temporis. Pars altera*, text in Caprile 1975, 991–1006; summary, 559–565). He was also at the center of the difficult debates surrounding the final *declaratio* of the assembly (ibid. 1011–16). Because of the priority Pope Paul VI gave to evangelization in the Church today, Cardinal Wojtyla's personal remarks at the close of his *relatio* on Oct. 14, 1974 are noteworthy. He brought out the ambiguity, but also the emerging sense of "evangelization" as a term covering the whole mission of the Church. He emphasized that the main concerns of the synodal discussions had been: indigenization or inculturation of the Gospel; liberation in its theological, ethical, and social aspects; secularization and secularism; programmatic atheism. Perhaps the most striking statement is this: "We must be mindful, both for theological reflection and for further work on evangelization, of the supremely important truth that the whole theology of evangelization has had its origin not simply in a teaching but in a mandate. The mandate of Jesus Christ which rests on and evidences the salvific will of God, is this: 'Going therefore teach all nations .... preach the Gospel to every creature' (Mt 28.14). The issue therefore is not one simply of an empirical description of evangelization or of submitting it to theological analysis, but of fulfilling Christ's mandate—and in a way that is both theological and pastoral" (ibid. 1003–04). Significantly, in this age of ecumenical cooperation, the Cardinal spiritedly urged his confreres to keep in mind the words of Philip Potter, Secretary General of the World Council of Churches, on the need for contemporary evangelization to preserve the unity due to the message of salvation, so that the universal Church's voice, and its care and concern for the world's salvation become one in all the particular and local Churches (ibid. 1005).

The record of the thought and the life of Pope John Paul II fully justifies the surge of confidence that welled up in the Church as the first reaction to its new supreme pastor, who so clearly and staunchly offers himself as bishop-servant of the faith.

Bibliography: *Acta synodalia sacrosancti Concilii Oecumenici Vaticani Secundi*, v. 4, pt. 2 and 3 (Vatican City 1977). G. Caprile. *Il Sinodo dei Vescovi. Prima assemblea straordinaria (11–28 ottobre, 1969)* (Rome 1970); *Il Sinodo dei Vescovi. Seconda assemblea generale* (30 settembre–6 novembre 1971) pt. 1 and 2 (Rome 1972); *Il Sinodo dei Vescovi. Terza assemblea generale (27 settembre–26 ottobre 1974)* (Rome 1975). K. KLOŚAK, ed., *Logos Ethos* (Krakow 1971) 29–30, bibliography of Cardinal Wojtyla to 1970. K. WOJTYLA, "Bishops as Servants of the Faith," IrTheolQ 43 (1976) 260–273, translation of the 1975 address to the Symposium of European Bishops; "The Structure of Self-Determination as Core of the Theory of Person," Atti del Congresso Internazionale, *Tomasso d'Aquino nel suo centenaio settimo*. v. 1 *L'Huomo* (Naples 1978) 37–44. Also OssRom 262, special ed. Nov. 12, 1978, with Wojtyla bibliog. p. 3.

[T. C. O'BRIEN]

JOINT COMMITTEE OF CATHOLIC LEARNED SOCIETIES

In June 1974 the first probings were made to test the feasibility of establishing some kind of relationship between the National Conference of Catholic Bishops (NCCB) and the American Catholic scholarly community. The Joint Committee of Catholic Learned Societies (JCCLS) was established with the adoption of by-laws on April 3, 1975. The committee is composed of officially delegated members from the following professional societies: American Catholic Historical Association; American Catholic Philosophical Association; *Canon Law Society of America; Catholic Biblical Association; *Catholic Theological Society of America; *College Theology Society; and the North American Academy of Liturgy.

The by-laws set forth the following purpose for the Committee: to establish a cooperative effort and promote an attitude of mutual confidence between the Catholic scholarly community and all parts of the Christian community; to provide a means of communicating information and ideas from the scholarly community to the bishops on matters of concern to their work in the Church; to receive indications from the NCCB and to implement areas of scholarly works needed by the Church on the many levels of its pastoral work; to carry out, on the part of the societies themselves, work needed in order to understand and respond to problems in contemporary Christian life. Since its foundation three major projects have been undertaken by the joint membership.

A group of some twenty-five scholars prepared briefs on the critical issue proposed by the bishops' pastoral letter on moral values. The drafting committee from the NCCB met with the scholars over three days in Washington, D.C. to hear their presentation. This consultation had its effect upon the draft of the document, issued in 1976, *To Live in Christ Jesus.*

The senior NCCB staff officers reviewed their needs in the area of research during 1976. The many recognized issues tended to coalesce into three areas; the Church, its structure, ministries, and Sacraments; Christian family life; and the Church in the contemporary world. JCCLS appointed three subcommittees from the participating societies to review these and to propose specific projects for study. Research has begun in some areas, particularly in family life and the question of ministry.

The need for clarification of the role of the scholar in the Church has been continuously recognized in the meetings of the JCCLS with the NCCB. In early 1976 it was decided to prepare for a colloquium involving scholars and bishops to speak to the issue of the relationship of the magisterium and the scholarly community.

The Joint Committee meets semi-annually. An effort is made to have one of the meetings at the time of the November meeting of the USCC-NCCB so that the committee can meet with the designated liaison bishop and the USCC and NCCB staffs. An annual JCCLS Newsletter is also published.

[D. E. HEINTSCHEL]

JOINT ROMAN CATHOLIC/WORLD-METHODIST COMMISSION

The Eleventh World Methodist Council, assembled in London in August 1966, set up an eleven-man ecumenical committee for World Methodism. This group in its entirety took part in the first five-year series of annual conversations with Catholic bishops and theologians chosen by the Pontifical Secretariat for Promoting Christian Unity.

Like most other bilateral dialogues, that with the World Methodist Council arose out of the presence (quite regular and generous) of their observers at Vatican Council II. The Council had an appeal for Methodists for two main reasons. (1) It was a "pastoral" rather than a "dogmatic" council: Methodism has been little concerned with precise definition (cf. Dublin Report 71: "Methodist doctrine has received little official formulation and exists rather as an undefined tradition."), but more with pastoral action—mainly through preaching, hymn singing, the "class"—aimed at

personal sanctification. (2) The council's concern with spirituality and with personal holiness not only attracted Methodists but revealed to them unsuspected affinities with their own tradition and ideals.

The results of the first series of conversations were embodied in a lengthy report prepared in time for the 1971 Methodist Council at Denver, Colorado and simultaneously submitted to the Roman Catholic authorities. Not only were three Roman Catholic observers invited to Denver, but Cardinal Jan Willebrands, president of the Secretariat for Promoting Christian Unity, was asked to give the keynote address at the ecumenical evening. In the address he carefully analyzed a growing relationship and a dialogue in which he had himself taken part until he was made president and cardinal a year earlier. The Denver Report ended by recommending a modified type of dialogue with a small joint commission (five-a-side) which should aim to stimulate, coordinate, and review work done by experts throughout the world.

This new style involved an act of faith in the general interest and readiness for cooperation in Methodist-Catholic dialogue throughout the two world communities—an act of faith which proved only partly justified. However, enough cooperation was forthcoming (notably in Great Britain) to ensure that the next quinquennial report (the Dublin Report of 1976) should show advance in all the themes treated except that of Authority in the Church. This issue the Denver Report had interestingly set out, focussing on the basic relations of authority-love-freedom-individual conscience rather than, as in the Anglican dialogue, on the history of the institutionalizing of authority within the Church. In the current third five-year series of conversations begun at Bad Soden, Germany in October 1977, a theologically stronger commission has planned a series of annual reports under the general theme of "The Holy Spirit, Holiness & Humanity."

Methodism has no history of formal separation from Rome, but being an offshoot of Anglicanism it inherited the main Anglican doctrinal convictions and aversions, though in a less academic style. Thus while the traditional Reformation differences have had their place and the Anglican/Roman Catholic dialogue on Eucharist, Ministry, and Authority has been closely followed, they have not excluded such other more positively treated themes as Spirituality, Common Witness and Salvation Today, Christian Home and Family. The consciousness of a "shared inheritance" between Methodists and Catholics centers largely on their common concern for personal sanctification. The more historically-minded Methodist is aware also of a strong Eucharistic tradition (expressed classically in Charles Wesley's hymns) which needs to be revived. There is much good will between Methodists and Catholics everywhere, but those closely engaged in dialogue are probably agreed that its objectives have become less sharp during the decade of its course, and the prospect of practical steps towards any form of union remains remote. The loose nature of the World Methodist Council as a world body, compared with the Church of Rome, makes it difficult to envisage any formal approach to unity at that level, but as the spirit of dialogue and common witness grows and spreads there may well be a growing together of local Churches and communities in sufficient numbers and intensity to compel the attention of Rome and in some way of World Methodism.

See also UNITED METHODIST/ROMAN CATHOLIC DIALOGUE.

Bibliography: Denver and Dublin reports in *Proceedings of World Methodist Council* (1971, 1976).

[W. T. PURDY]

JOINT WORKING GROUP OF THE WORLD COUNCIL OF CHURCHES AND THE ROMAN CATHOLIC CHURCH

When Vatican Council II gave new expression to the Catholic understanding of Christian unity and committed the Roman Catholic Church to participation in the ecumenical movement, the question inevitably arose as to how the Church would relate to the World Council of Churches. In February 1965, after numerous preliminary conversations between Rome and Geneva, it was decided to set up a commission of experts, to be known as the Joint Working Group, in order to explore the possibilities of dialogue and collaboration and to work out the principles and methods to be employed. Initially composed of fourteen members nominated by its two parent bodies, the Joint Working Group was authorized to make recommendations rather than decisions, bearing in mind that the Roman Catholic Church is a Church, while the World Council is a fellowship of Churches and cannot speak for its members.

Since 1965 the Joint Working Group has explored a wide range of topics, such as the unity of the Church, the nature of ecumenism and dialogue, the connection between bilateral and multilateral ecumenical conversations (the Working Group does not deal with the former), the *Week of Prayer for Christian Unity, proselytism, mixed marriages, an agreed date for Easter, evangelization, the role of the laity, justice and peace, emergency relief and development aid, translation and distribution of the Bible, human rights, common catechetical programs, and the promotion of religious liberty. In addition, the Working Group has sponsored theological studies on "Common Witness and Proselytism" and "Catholicity and Apostolicity," and has fostered such developments as Roman Catholic membership in the World Council's Faith and Order Commission, consultative relations with its Commission on World Mission and Evangelism and Christian Medical Commission, and the founding in 1968 by the World Council and the Holy See of the Joint Committee on Society, Development and Peace (SODEPAX).

The Joint Working Group's study of the possibility of Roman Catholic membership in the World Council of Churches was published in 1972; by that time, however, it was clear that no such application would be made in the near future. Since then, the Working Group has sought to intensify and evaluate collaboration between its parent bodies and to discover promising new possibilities for the development of the ecumenical movement. The Working Group is now (as of 1976) composed of eighteen members, who meet annually, and is immediately related to the Vatican's Secretariat for Promoting Christian Unity and to the General Secretariat of the World Council. The importance of the Joint Working Group lies in the visibility it gives to the Roman Catholic-World Council relationship of mutual ecumenical commitment and in the way it enables this relationship to find practical expression.

Bibliography: L. VISCHER, "The Activities of the Joint Working Group Between the Roman Catholic Church and the World Council of Churches 1965–1969," EcumRev 22 (1970) 36–69. *Reports of the Joint Working Group*, published in *Information Service* (Rome, Secretariat for Promoting Christian Unity), esp. 32 (1976/III).

[J. A. LUCAL]

JOURNALISM, CATHOLIC

By the time Vatican Council II closed in December 1965 it had stimulated millions of words in the press, but few journalists could foresee what the Council would ultimately mean to the Church and to the Catholic press. There was some disappointment in the 1963 Council Decree on the Means of Social Communication (*Inter mirifica*), which seemed hasty and even superficial to some journalists, but whatever disappointment may have existed diminished substantially when the Pontifical Commission for the Media of Social Communication published its Pastoral Instruction on the application of the decree (*Communio et progressio*, June 3, 1971).

The Pastoral Instruction described the communications media as "powerful instruments for progress." More important, it firmly advanced the idea of the free flow of information: "If public opinion is to emerge in the proper manner, it is absolutely essential that there be freedom to express ideas and attitudes. In accordance with the express teaching of the Second Vatican Council it is necessary unequivocally to declare that freedom of speech for individuals and groups must be permitted so long as the common good and public morality be not endangered" (26).

Editorial Policies. For many editors, the Council was a signal to broaden the scope of their coverage of the news and to publish articles exploring such controversial subjects as the role of authority, homosexuality, the ordination of women to priesthood. But there were differing reactions, because the Catholic press reflects many cultures, nationalities and attitudes. It includes magazines of both relatively general and quite specialized interests; the well-organized diocesan weekly newspapers of the U.S. and Canada and the weekly or monthly periodicals of the Third World, often poorly financed; Catholic dailies in Europe and independent national weeklies in the United States.

In the U.S. in particular, some Catholic editors modeled their diocesan newspapers after secular dailies, sometimes publishing news stories and editorials severely critical of church practices and institutions. Other editors sought to present news and views reflecting the positions of their own bishops and the hierarchy in general. The *National Catholic Reporter* gained a relatively large circulation as it explored new journalistic territory, sometimes to the dismay of individual bishops and others. Then, for reasons that may be argued for years to come, its circulation began to slide and by 1978 was no more than half of its peak figure.

Statistics. The most accurate circulation figures within the worldwide Catholic press are maintained by the Catholic Press Association of the United States and Canada. They show that not all of the expectations of Catholic journalists were fulfilled by the Council. The Catholic Press Directory shows that in 1962, the Council's first year, there were 545 Catholic newspapers and magazines in the United States and Canada with a total circulation of 28,429,488. By the Council's last year, 1965, there were 542 periodicals with a combined circulation that had grown to 28,944,724. But the 1978 Catholic Press Directory lists 471 publications and a circulation of 26,968,785—a drop of nearly 2 million in 13 post-Council years. However, some periodicals are beginning to show healthy increases.

Freedom of Information. The concern in many parts of the world is not limited to circulation growth, but to the ability of the Catholic press to operate freely in the face of governmental pressures. Some journalists have been arrested, some publications censored, and there have been many reports of more indirect pressures. These relate to access to newsprint and advertising, and to an understanding that publication of material offensive to governmental authorities will bring difficulties. The free flow of news is not allowed in the Soviet Union, the Peoples Republic of China, and other countries with governments hostile to religion. But free and open coverage of news is difficult in some countries with large Catholic populations. These include Brazil, Chile, Cuba, the Philippines, and South Korea. Journalists have problems, at least occasionally, in Argentina, El Salvador, Nicaragua, Panama, Paraguay, Peru, Poland, and Uruguay.

The International Federation of Catholic Press Agencies, in a report published at the Eleventh World Congress of the Catholic Press in Vienna in the Fall of 1977, said that the Catholic press "remains on the defensive in significant areas of today's world. Direct and indirect pressures by governments often affect the economic health of newspapers and the personal welfare of journalists. Unofficial pressure groups at times are able to exert a chilling influence on the reporting of news." Journalists in several countries covered by the report said that they believe their personal mail is sometimes censored, making it awkward for them to discuss their problems with others. In the Third World especially, the Catholic press often is weak financially, especially vulnerable to pressures, and incapable of protecting its rights. In some instances editors decide that it is better to engage in self-censorship than to have their periodicals shut down.

But the Catholic press remains vigorous in many places, notably the U.S., Canada, Britain, Germany, Italy, Austria, France, Belgium, and the Netherlands. There is a small Catholic press in Ireland. Australia includes magazines and diocesan newspapers. There is an irregular underground Catholic publication in Lithuania and there are impressive efforts to strengthen the Catholic press in Africa, India, and other parts of Asia. Many Catholic periodicals are independently owned and edited; some are "Catholic" in the sense that a U.S. daily might describe itself as editorially "Democratic" or "Republican." That is, they reflect a Catholic viewpoint but are not attached to the Church and feel free to take positions not supported by the hierarchy.

Influence. The most elaborate survey of readers of Catholic periodicals was undertaken in 1978 by the Gallup Organization for the Catholic Press Association. It found that 63 percent of Catholics who label their religious beliefs "very important" had read their diocesan newspaper within the preceding twelve months. The poll showed that Catholic publications have a strong influence among their readers, but that nonreaders are heavily influenced by the secular press and television. It also found that Catholic-press readers are more inclined

toward ecumenism than the national profiles and they give greater support to post-Council changes.

In summary, the Council opened new areas of coverage for the Catholic press and a new sense of freedom. This freedom is limited in some instances by bishops who also are publishers and it is restricted in some instances by governments. An overall decline in circulation followed the Council, but there are signs of renewed growth in many areas. The Catholic press ranges from the official Vatican daily to independent periodicals that frequently criticize the Church, sometimes in strident terms. Financial problems abound, as they do throughout the Church. But few Catholic editors are critical of the Council, and most appear to be satisfied that the Council broadened the foundations for growth and service.

Bibliography: Pontifical Commission for the Media of Social Communication, *Pastoral Instruction on the Media, Public Opinion, and Human Progress* (USCC Publ. Office, Washington, D.C. 1971).

[A. E. P. WALL]

JOURNET, CHARLES

Swiss cardinal and theologian; b. Vernier near Geneva, Jan. 26, 1891, d. Fribourg, Apr. 15, 1975. After classical studies in Geneva and Mariahilf College, Schwyz, and St. Michael's College, Fribourg, he entered the diocesan major seminary in Fribourg. Ordained to the priesthood on July 15, 1917, he was appointed professor of dogmatic theology in the same seminary on Sept. 25, 1924 and remained on the faculty until 1970. In 1926 he founded the theological journal *Nova et vetera*, of which he remained the editor for most of his career. In 1965 he was named titular archbishop and cardinal. He was a member of the preconciliar theological commission for Vatican Council II. In addition to his theological teaching and writing he was also active in other pastoral activities in both Geneva and Fribourg.

He is customarily identified with the Thomism practiced by J. Maritain, E. Gilson, and the French Dominicans generally. Indeed, he describes his masterwork as "a comprehensive work in which I hope to explain the church, from the standpoint of speculative theology, in terms of the four causes from which she results—efficient, material, formal and final. This work is to be in four books" (*The Church of the Word Incarnate. An Essay in Speculative Theology.* v. 1, *The Apostolic Hierarchy*, tr. by A. H. C. DOWNES [New York 1955] xxv). Unfortunately only this first volume appeared in English. The original French, *L'Église du Verbe incarné* was published in Paris by Desclée de Brouwer et Cie. from 1941 on. Although ecclesiology was his speciality, Cardinal Journet's works indicate his other interests: *L'Esprit du Protestantisme* (Paris 1925) and *L'Union des Églises* (Paris 1927); mysticism and the knowledge of God, *The Dark Knowledge of God*, tr. J. F. Anderson (London 1948) and *Introduction á la Théologie* (Paris 1947); and the Christian-Muslim dialogue, *Théologie de l'Église* (Paris 1958) and "Qui est membre de l'Église," *Nova et vetera* 36 (1961) 199–203, which are still significant. Journet and Yves Congar carried on a prolonged discussion about the status of the sinner in the holy Church from 1953 when Congar reviewed v. 2 of *La Théologie du Verbe incarné*. These reviews and other remarks by Congar have been collected in Journet's *Sainte Église* (Paris 1963) 618–669. According to Journet, as late as 1965, "the church is indeed not without *sinners*, but it is without *sin*." See his "Il carattere teandrico della Chiesa fonte di tensione permanente," in G. Baraúna, ed., *La Chiesa del Vaticano II* (Florence 1965) 361. Congar, on the other hand, correctly asserts that the Church itself is sinful, thus avoiding awkward distinctions between sinful member and holy Church, which end up making the Church not a real, historical People of God, but an imaginary construct.

Cardinal Journet will be justly remembered for his contributions to the theological model of the Church as the Mystical Body of Christ. His Thomistic background enabled him to maintain the balance between the Church's visible and invisible dimensions, which had been so severely sundered in previous theology. Likewise, his Thomistic sacramental insight enabled him to understand that the ecclesial institution and structure form the *sacramentum* of the more mystical inner life of grace of the Church. His ecclesiology was a significant contribution to the spirit and theology which matured at Vatican II.

Journet is perhaps found by the generation after his death to be too conceptualist, too "scholastic," too beholden to abstract thought. His true spirit, however, is better indicated by the dedication of his masterwork not only to the Doctors Augustine and Thomas but also to the Virgin Catherine of Siena, and especially by a quotation from the Persian Bisthami which concludes his *The Dark Knowledge of God* (122): "For thirty years I travelled in search of God, and when, at the end of this time, I opened my eyes, I saw that it was He Who sought me. A voice cried to me: O Abu Yazid, what is it you desire? I replied: I desire to desire nothing, for I am the desired and You are He Who desires!"

Bibliography: S. JAKI, *Les tendances nouvelles de l'écclésiologie* (Rome 1957).

[R. KRESS]

JUDAISM AND THE EARLY CHURCH

Christianity was initially a movement of a few Jewish followers of Jesus, driven by the conviction that this recently crucified Jesus had been raised from the dead, that he would soon return as the agent of God's "Reign" (the definitive gesture of mercy and judgment toward his people) now already beginning, and that the Good News—and warning—of this was to be spread immediately. As a result of a series of crises, this movement, originally completely Jewish (Jesus and his disciples all having been Palestinian Jews), became within a century largely Gentile, though of course preserving a massive Jewish heritage. The fact that in the course of this development the movement acquired an ambivalent and even a negative attitude toward the Judaism out of which it had grown is one of Christianity's questionable heritages, one on which a good deal of light has recently been shed and to which serious attempts at rethinking have begun to be applied since Vatican Council II's Declaration on Non-Christian Religions (*Nostra aetate* 4).

"Hebrews" and "Hellenists." The initial crisis seems almost certainly to have been the execution of Jesus (at the hands of the Romans, with probable help from aristocratic Jewish collaborators), and the apparent failure of his cause. Some of those originally attracted to him, together with those who were opposed, were persuaded that the movement had failed; their expecta-

tions for the reign of God, or for the coming of his Messiah (such expectations among the Palestinian Jews of the time were many and quite varied) had not been fulfilled. Others however, led by those to whom the risen Jesus had appeared, were convinced that the movement was to continue. In an attempt to make sense of and to account for the death of Jesus (the idea of his death as "saving" event did not arise until later), his followers began to "search the Scriptures" and were able to find biblical passages which appeared to them to have predicted or explained it, and led them eventually toward a conception of the blindness and sinfulness of those of their fellow Jews who had not accepted Jesus.

Within the ranks of the growing numbers of Jews in the Jesus movement who resolved to continue, there was no unanimity as to how to proceed. The fragmentary and late account in Acts 6–8, the essentials of which seem to be historically trustworthy, points to a fairly serious difference between "Hellenists" and "Hebrews" at an early stage. The "Hebrews" seem to have been Jewish in roughly the same ways as most Jerusalem Jews (Temple-worship, sabbath-observance, etc.), and apparently saw no reason to abandon their Jewishness. They were, of course, conscious of themselves as a group apart in some sense, because of their allegiance to Jesus. The "Hellenists," on the other hand, appear to have been Jews who also spoke Greek and whose life in the diaspora led to an ambivalent attitude toward the Temple (Stephen's speech in Acts 7) and, somewhat later, about the Law. Their activity apparently led to Stephen's death and their expulsion from Jerusalem. Their move to Antioch soon led to the Gentile mission there. But the "Hebrews" in the Jesus movement remained in Jerusalem. Thus there was an initial break, but only between *some* Jewish followers of Jesus ("Hellenists") and *some* other Jews.

The Issue of Gentile Converts. A more serious crisis—probably still within the first decade—revolved around the admission of Gentiles into the movement and especially the question of the conditions under which they were to be admitted. Several positions soon developed. (1) Gentiles were to be admitted, but only on the condition of complete observance of the Law, including circumcision (Paul's opponents in Galatians; the "men from Judaea" in Acts 15.1); their stance seems to have been predicated on the belief that the Law was from God and that men had no right to change it. (2) Gentiles were to be admitted without circumcision, but were to "abstain from what had been sacrificed to idols, from blood, from what is strangled, and from unchastity" (Acts 15.29; also 15.20 and 21.25); this is the position represented as the decision of the "Apostolic Council" of Jerusalem in Acts 15 and seems to have been the actual practice of the Gentile communities known to the author of Luke/Acts. The narrative in Acts is unclear as to whether this means that Gentile converts were to observe the Law, but in a form modified for them or whether it means that Gentiles are admitted without the Law, but with a few concessions by way of compromise. (3) Gentiles are to be admitted freely, with absolutely no Law or no conditions imposed (this was the position of Paul, especially in Gal. 2). All three positions were decisions worked out by Jewish members of the Jesus movement about the admission of Gentiles. None of the three suggests that the Law should not be observed by Jewish followers of Jesus.

Positions (1) and (2) seem agreed that the Law continues to bind in some sense; positions (2) and (3) are agreed that circumcision is not required of Gentile converts. Ultimately "Christianity" (the name is applied later, in Antioch, by outsiders—Acts 11.26) became predominantly Gentile and Paul's position became the standard; but it was initially a minority position and all three were "Christian" positions. One unfortunate consequence of the crisis was that Paul's polemic, especially in Galatians and Romans, came later to be accepted as "the" Christian position. In this polemic, his position (which he associates with faith in Jesus, but which is read as though he is talking about "Christianity") is that of freedom, of maturity, of life; the position of his opponents (the belief that the Law was required of all, but which is later read as "Judaism") is that of slavery, of immaturity, and of death. It led Irenaeus, in the late 2d century, and most of the Christian writers who followed him, to see Jewish Christianity (Christians who observed the Law) as "heretical"—a position Paul would not have shared. More tragically, it has led many Christians to think of Judaism as a "slavish" observance of the Law and of value only as a "preparation" for Christianity.

The Jewish Revolts. The disastrous Jewish revolt against Rome (66–70 A.D.), together with elements in its aftermath, constitutes an unparalleled turning point. The majority (or perhaps all) of the Jewish Christians seem not to have taken part in the war. But because they were still largely regarded as Jews, both in their own estimation and in the view of many of their fellow Palestinians, their nonparticipation was resented by the more nationalistic and militant Zealots, at least. The same thing happened again in the Jewish war (again against Rome) led by Bar Kochba in 132–135. On the other hand, there seems to have been some suspicion, on the part of certain Roman officials, that the Christians, as a "Messianic" Jewish sect, were every bit as revolutionary as many other Jews. Whatever the cause and extent of the suspicion, it led many Christians, both Jewish and Gentile, to find ways to dissociate themselves from Judaism generally. Two subsequent Jewish revolts (115–117 in the provinces and the aforementioned Bar Kochba revolt in Palestine only sharpened this motive for dissociation, for "de-Judaizing."

From the Jewish side the most important effect of the war and of the destruction of Jerusalem and the Temple in 70 A.D. was the formation of the Pharisaic/rabbinic academy at Jamnia (Yavneh). This assembly, led initially by Yohanan ben Zakkai, laid the foundations for the rabbinic and talmudic Judaism that has continued to the present time. It seems that shortly after the formation of the academy, an attempt was made (perhaps in the 80s) to arrest the centrifugal forces which presented the danger of tearing post-70 Judaism to pieces. "Nazarenes" (followers of Jesus who continued their synagogue affiliation) and others were expelled from the synagogue communities and traces of this are found in the Gospels of Matthew and John, each written shortly after this expulsion and, it appears, partly in heated response to it (cf. Mt 5.10–12; 10.16–33; 22.6; 23.29–39; John 9.22; 12.42; 16.2). Matthew's version of the parables of the wicked tenants (Mt 21.33–41) and the wedding feast (Mt 22.1–10) has Jews being punished and even killed by God and replaced by (Gentile?) Christians. Matthew's Passion or trial narrative is kinder to

Pilate than Mark's and much more antagonistic to Jews ("And *all the people* answered: his blood be upon us and upon our children!" Mt 27.25). John frequently describes Jesus' opponents as "the Jews" (instead of scribes or pharisees) and can draw a contrast between Jesus and Moses as a kind of "theme" of the Gospel ("the Law was given through Moses, but grace and truth came through Jesus Christ." Jn 1.17); Jewish rejection of Jesus is deep, if not complete ("his own people received him not." Jn 1.11). For John, the Law is responsible for Jesus' death ("We have a Law and by that Law he must die." Jn 19.7); and the Passion narrative is climaxed by the Jewish rejection of Jesus—and God—as king ("We have no king but Caesar." Jn 19.15). All of this is of course intelligible as the product of the heat of polemic, but at least the use to which such texts have been put is finally being re-examined.

Patristic Literature. By the end of the first century, and despite the continuing existence of Jewish Christianity (until at least the 4th century, but now looked on as "heretical"), Church and Synagogue were separated.

Competition with Judaism. Disputation and (rarely) dialogue continued and treatises were written "Against the Jews" (by Justin, Tertullian, Hippolytus, Cyprian, John Chrysostom, Cyril, and Augustine, to name only the more noteworthy). They usually took the form of grouping a series of biblical quotations (proof-texts or "testimonies") around a set of themes which these texts were interpreted to "prove" (e.g. the Messiahship of Jesus; the appropriateness of Jesus' death; the perennial sinfulness and blindness of Jews; the replacement of Jews by Gentile Christians as God's people and heirs of the promises; the transcending of the Law and its provisions: circumcision, Temple-sacrifice, sabbath-observance, and the like). The anti-Judaism manifest in these writings was ironically prevented from dying out precisely because Judaism did not, as many Christians expected, "die"; it remained a vital and serious competitor of Christianity until well after Constantine and the formation of the "Christian" empire in the 4th century.

The Christian Apologia. In addition to the actual competition with Judaism, two other issues developed early on and both kept the anti-Judaism alive and reinforced it. The first was the standard Roman objection to Christians that they had no status and no rights because they were such recent arrivals on the religious scene of the Mediterranean world. The typical Christian response to this objection (found in Justin, Tertullian, Origen, and Eusebius) was that Christianity was the "true" (or, sometimes, "new") Israel; that Jews had lost their right to their books (the "Old" Testament) and their history because of their sinfulness and their rejection of their Messiah (Christians pointed to the Roman destruction of Jerusalem as "proof" of this) and that these books and this history were in reality *Christian* books and *Christian* history. Christians were not, therefore, new arrivals; Jewish roots were by right now theirs. Thus Christian roots in the Roman Empire were purchased at the expense of Jews.

The second issue was raised by Marcion, the 2d-century (*c.* 140) writer who not only rejected the Law of Moses (as did most Gentile Christians), but thought it consistent with a Pauline conception of the "newness" of Christianity to reject the "Old" Testament (because it contained the Law) and even the "old" God (i.e. the God who had, according to the Bible, enacted the Law in the first place). Jesus, for Marcion, came completely unannounced and unprepared for, as the representative of (or the incarnation of) a "new," previously unknown, higher God, a God of love and mercy. The Christian response to Marcion (developed especially by Justin, Irenaeus, and Tertullian) was to argue that: (1) the inferiority of the Law does not prove the inferiority of the God who enacted it; it was rather the sinfulness of the Jews God was then forced to deal with that accounts for the existence of the Law formerly and its rejection today (e.g. Jews who were "prone to gluttony" needed food prohibitions; "idolatrous" Jews needed sacrifices to remind them of the true God: Tertullian *Against Marcion* 2.18–22); and (2) the fact that the Jews of Jesus' time did not accept him does not mean that he came "unannounced," or as representative of a new God; rather the "blindness" of the Jews, their unwillingness to understand perfectly clear OT prophecies, accounts for Jesus' rejection. Here again the Christian teaching on the one God and on Jesus as his Messiah are defended at the expense of Jews and Judaism.

Conclusion. The anti-Judaism had a deleterious effect on Christianity and Christian theology (e.g. a "triumphalistic" willingness to see radical reform as something God may have wanted in "Old" Testament times, but not now, in the time of "fulfillment"). But it had the even more tragic effect of maintaining and reinforcing, throughout most of Christian history, an attitude that since Judaism had by God's plan been replaced, it had no longer any right to exist. It is a short step, and one that has too often been taken, to the attitude that Jews have no right to exist. Because the seeds of such contempt can be found in Christian origins and in the New Testament literature that Christians treasure most deeply, the task of constructing a Christian theology that is not inherently (if subtly) anti-Jewish will be difficult. But it must be done.

See also JEWISH/ROMAN CATHOLIC RELATIONS.

Bibliography: W. D. DAVIES, *Paul and Rabbinic Judaism* (3d ed., London 1970). J. FITZMYER, *Essays on the Semitic Background of the NT* (London 1971) 271–303; 435–480. D. R. A. HARE, *The Theme of Jewish Persecution of Christians in the Gospel according to St. Matthew* (Cambridge 1967). J. L. MARTYN, *History and Theology in the Fourth Gospel* (New York 1968). J. M. ROBINSON and H. KOESTER, *Trajectories through Early Christianity* (Philadelphia 1971) 114–157. R. RUETHER, *Faith and Fratricide* (New York 1974). E. P. SANDERS, *Paul and Palestinian Judaism* (Philadelphia 1977). M. SIMON, *Verus Israel* (Paris 1948, repr. Paris 1964). G. SLOYAN, *Jesus on Trial* (Philadelphia 1973). G. THEISSEN, *Sociology of Early Palestinian Christianity*, tr. J. BOWDEN (Philadelphia 1978). R. WILKEN, *Judaism and the Early Christian Mind* (New Haven 1971).
[D. F. EFROYMSON]

JÚDEAN SOCIETY

A lay ministry proclaimed in 1975 by Pope Paul VI as a "true and just apostolate." The Júdean Society is a self-help and mutual-help program to ease the pain of divorce and to encourage the divorced Catholic woman to remain in harmony with the Church. The Steps to Effective Living program authored by the foundress, F. A. Miller, serves as the format for groups meeting in private homes, and has the *imprimatur* of Archbishop Joseph T. McGucken of San Francisco. This lay ministry offers personal growth and development through spiritual, emotional, and social support. An intense self-discovery program aids members wishing an official marriage investigation. Divorce prevention,

enrichment of life after divorce, preparation for second marriage are services rendered through lectures, workshops, retreats, and small group meetings. Founded in 1952 it incorporated in 1966 as a national non-profit organization depending on private contributions and is governed by a 13 member council. Groups and chapters form as needed and the Society is represented in various dioceses across the U.S. and in two foreign countries.

[F. A. MILLER]

JUNGMANN, JOSEF ANDREAS

Austrian Jesuit, inspirer of the liturgical and catechetical renewal; b. Sand near Taufers, South Tirol (pre-World-War I Austria), Nov. 16, 1889; d. Innsbruck, Jan. 26, 1975. After theological studies in the diocesan seminary of Brixen, S. Tirol, he was ordained July 27, 1913. His work as assistant pastor in Niedervintl and Gossensasz, before becoming a Jesuit, Sept. 13, 1917, contributed substantially to the basically pastoral orientation of his later scientific work. From 1925 at the University of Innsbruck, he taught pastoral theology, catechetics, and liturgy until 1963, with interruption 1938–45 when Hitler closed the theology faculty of the university. Jungmann was also editor, 1926–63, of *Zeitschrift für katholische Theologie* (again with the interruption, 1938–45). After having contributed through his writing to create the general theological and pastoral climate for Vatican Council II, he was chosen, Aug. 25, 1960, to be a member of the conciliar Preparatory Commission. He continued his intensive and dedicated work during the Council as a highly esteemed *peritus* of the Commission for Liturgy and after the Council as consultor of the Consilium (the commission entrusted with the implementation of the Constitution on the Liturgy).

Superb mastery of his subject, penetrating, well-balanced, and impartial judgment, an exceptional gift of inspiration for sound and timely developments within the Church, especially in the fields of liturgy and preaching, deep respect for the achievements of others who engaged in the same field of studies, and his proverbial modesty—all won Jungmann many friends and enthusiastic admirers. *Festschriften* of his colleagues, friends, and former students on his 60th, 70th, and 80th birthday, as well as honors conferred by his country, manifested the great and general appreciation of him and his work. Jungmann's special talent consisted in letting the past teach an understanding and right evaluation of the present and point to right solutions for the future. Although outstanding in historical research, he was never lost in its details nor ever pursued history for its own sake. Solid historical research was for him the indispensable tool for a right assessment of the present condition of the Christian community and its need of genuine, penetrating renewal. His deep faith and his imperturbable adherence to the Church did not prevent him from seeing clearly and presenting with respectful objectivity unhealthy and harmful trends and developments of the past in Christian worship and preaching. The mere fact that, e.g., the leaders of the Church authorized and contributed to an ever-decreasing active participation of the people in the official worship of the Church, does not prove that this development was healthy and guided by the Holy Spirit. It is the special merit of Jungmann that, with his thorough historical studies combined with deep understanding of the conditions of authentic historical development, he undermined any simplistic interpretation of the Church's guidance by the Holy Spirit and opened the way to the needed, thorough reform. At first many, including also prominent leaders of the Church, considered Jungmann to be unorthodox; but soon the weight of his incontestable reasons and also his modest and prudent presentation achieved general recognition and admiration. Without the self-sacrificing work of forerunners like Jungmann the reform as initiated by Vatican II could never have happened.

Writings. Although his 1924 doctoral thesis (never published) dealt with the catechesis on grace in the early Church, the field of Jungmann's special studies was liturgy and in particular the history of the Latin liturgy and the problems of an authentic liturgical renewal. His very first book *Die Stellung Christi im liturgischen Gebet* (1925; tr. *The Place of Christ in Liturgical Prayer*, 1965) is a masterpiece of his own method. Through a thorough study of the official worship of the Church it delineates, although only implicitly, the much-needed renewal of devotional prayer. Similarly, he paved the way for the timely renewal of the rites of Penance in *Die lateinischen Buszriten* (1932). His *Die liturgische Feier. Grundsätzliches und Geschichtliches über Formgesetze der Liturgie* (1938; 4th rev. ed. 1965) is a precious study on the nature and form of authentic liturgical celebration outside of sacramental liturgy; it appeared in English as *The Liturgy of the Word* (1966). In *Gewordene Liturgie* (1940) the best of Jungmann's numerous articles reached a larger audience. The academic exile imposed by Hitler Jungmann used for preparing his main work, which made him suddenly world famous, *Missarum Sollemnia. Eine genetische Erklärung der römischen Messe* (2 v., 1948; 5th ed. 1965). It was soon translated in all major European languages: the complete English tr. of F. A. Brunner, *The Mass of the Roman Rite* (2 v., New York 1950) was followed by an abridgement by C. Riepe (1 v., New York 1959). Probably more than any other single book, *Missarum Sollemnia* prepared for and favored the conciliar reform of the Latin liturgy. Another significant work was *Der Gottesdienst der Kirche* (1955, 3d ed. 1962; tr. *Public Worship*, 1957). The lectures Jungmann gave in Summer 1949 at Notre Dame University appeared first in English as *Early Liturgy to the Time of Gregory the Great* (1959; Ger. 1967). *Liturgisches Erbe und pastorale Gegenwart* (1960) collects articles and conferences of general interest into one volume. The last two books, *Christliches Gebet im Wandel und Bestand* (1969) and *Messe im Gottesvolk. Ein nachkonziliarer Durchblick durch Missarum Sollemnia* (1970) are the crowning conclusion of an extremely rich and intensive literary activity: 304 books and articles, not counting some 800 shorter reviews of books. After Jungmann's death appeared *The Mass, an Historical, Theological and Pastoral Survey* (1976).

Because his masterful research and towering authority were almost exclusively in the history of liturgy and liturgical renewal, one may easily overlook Jungmann's momentous contribution to the renewal of catechesis and preaching. He is the acknowledged initiator and most prominent exponent of the second phase of modern catechetics known as kerygmatic renewal. It led to a shift of emphasis from method to content in all forms of the ministry of the Word. The kerygmatic approach means that any authentic announcing of God's word to young and old alike must concentrate on the good news of salvation by which God challenges sinful man to a new life in Christ. How biblical, liturgical, and kerygmatic renewal must be seen and actualized as partial aspects of a thorough integral pastoral renewal Jungmann showed best in his classic *Die Frohbotschaft und unsere Glaubensverkündigung* (1936); abridged English ed. *The Good News Yesterday and Today*, 1962, tr. W. A. Huesman, with essays, ed. J. Hofinger, appraising its contribution to pastoral renewal. When the book appeared it was so much ahead of the times that only swift withdrawal from the market could save it from ecclesiastical condemnation. But it had served its purpose. Hardly any other book anticipated and prepared for Vatican II's pastoral renewal as much as Jungmann's controversial book. During the Council, without any further opposition, its revised edition appeared: *Glaubensverkündigung im Lichte der Frohbotschaft* (1963; Eng. tr. *Announcing the Word of God*, 1967). Great influence was also exerted by *Katechetik. Aufgabe und Methode der religiösen Unterweisung* (1953; 5th ed. 1968; Eng. tr. *Handing On the Faith*, 1959). His *Christus als Mittelpunkt religiöser Erziehung* (1939) brings out the central position of Christ in genuine catechesis.

Bibliography: B. FISCHER and H. B. MEYER, eds., *J. A. Jungmann, Ein Leben für Liturgie und Kerygma* (Innsbruck 1975) complete list of Jungmann's writings, 156–207. J. HOFINGER, "J. A. Jungmann," LivLight 13 (1976) 350–359. *Festschriften:* F. X. ARNOLD and B. FISCHER, eds., *Die Messe in der Glaubensverkündigung* (Freiburg 1950; 2d ed. 1953). B. FISCHER and J. WAGNER, eds., *Paschatis Sollemnia. Studien zu Osterfeier und Osterfrömmigkeit* (Freiburg 1959). For Jungmann's 80th birthday, a separate issue of ZKathTh 91 (1969) 249–516.

[J. HOFINGER]

JURISDICTION (CANON LAW)

The pastoral concern of Vatican Council II gives a clearer vision on the developing concept of jurisdiction (8:61). Jurisdiction belongs to the *mission* of the Church. The Council considers jurisdiction as the power/ability to teach and to guide the People of God. Christ invested this power in the apostolic college with the pope as the head and the center of unity. As head of the college the pope has the personal task and responsibility to guide the People of God. In union with him the apostolic college has the same duty and responsibility.

Jurisdiction deals with the Church's tasks of teaching and guiding, which are inseparable from the task of sanctification. These three aspects are so closely connected that they are conferred simultaneously: "Episcopal consecration confers, together with the office of sanctifying, the duty also of teaching and ruling, which, however, of their very nature can be exercised only in hierarchical communion with the head and the members of the college" (*Lumen gentium* 21). Thus there are two elements in jurisdiction, the ontological element, conferred in episcopal ordination, and the authority to execute this power. This *executio potestatis* (or perhaps *potestas executionis*) is conferred in the commission given for a specific task. The pope as the head of the apostolic college has the personal authority of teaching and guiding the Church universal. Vatican II teaches that individual bishops share in the office of teaching and guiding the Church as a whole (*Christus Dominus* 6), but they have an "ordinary, proper and immediate authority" (ibid. 8) over the territorial Church assigned to them (*see* CHURCH, LOCAL [THEOLOGY]). The concern for the whole Church is in varying degrees expressed in national episcopal conferences and in the Synod of Bishops.

Jurisdiction as the task of teaching and guiding (shepherding), belongs to the *Church's* mission and includes the laity together with the hierarchy (*Lumen gentium* 30) because the laity "share in the priestly, prophetic and royal office of Christ" (*Apostolicam actuositatem* 2). This is not merely a participation in the mission of the hierarchy but "by their very vocation, they [the laity] seek the kingdom of God" (*Lumen gentium* 31; *Gaudium et spes* 11). The task of the laity is the integration of religious values and culture (*Gaudium et spes* 62), which is a direct sharing in the Church's task of teaching. The laity do not have a task independent from the hierarchy. They are not ontologically commissioned to teaching and guiding, nor do they share in ordained priesthood, but they are called to participate in the *total* mission of the Church (*see* LAITY, VOCATION OF). The extent to which jurisdiction (the power to teach and to guide) can be delegated to them is still subject to further study.

The major points in the teaching of Vatican II are the unity of the tasks of sanctification and jurisdiction; the strengthening of cooperation between individual bishops and between the bishops and the pope. The teaching deepens the role and participation of the laity. Jurisdiction becomes more closely linked to sanctification and faith than to organization.

Bibliography: F. COCCOPALMERIO, "De collegialitate episcopali," PeriodicaMorCanLiturg 62 (1973) 69–98. J. J. CUNEO, "Jurisdiction and Authority: *Missio* and *Munera*" (MS., Bridgeport, Conn. 1977). F. DANEELS, "De participatione laicorum in Ecclesiae muneribus iuxta 'Schema emendatum Legis Ecclesiae Fundamentalis'" PeriodicaMorCanLiturg 62 (1973) 99–115. A. DULLES, *The Resilient Church* (New York 1975). Pontifical Commission for the Revision of the Code of Canon Law, *Schema emendatum legis Ecclesiae fundamentalis* (Rome 1970). K. RAHNER, *The Shape of the Church to Come*, tr. E. QUINN (New York 1975). A. ZIRKEL, *Executio potestatis: Zur Lehre Gratians von der geistliche Gewalt* (St. Ottilien 1975).

[C. J. VAN DER POEL]

JURISPRUDENCE, CANONICAL

In general, the Church's legal life since the end of Vatican Council II has been marked by a steady effort to translate the doctrinal and pastoral insights of the Council into practical norms of action and renewed constitutional structures. The task is of extraordinary magnitude; many more years will be needed to bring it to completion. An overall evaluation of the process is not possible presently for lack of the historical perspective that good judgment requires. It is possible, however, to report even now on the main trends and movements that are taking place. They can be grouped under: (1) implementation of the Council through legislation; (2) preparations for a new Code of Canon Law; (3) developments in interpretation.

(1) **Implementation of the Council through Legislation.** Selected examples of new laws can well illustrate present legislative trends.

The Council's renewed understanding of the episcopal office was soon followed by new norms concerning the faculties and privileges of bishops in Paul VI's motu proprio, *Pastorale munus* (ActApS 56 [1964] 5–12) and their power to dispense from universal laws in the motu proprio, *De Episcoporum muneribus* (ibid. 58 [1966] 467–472); also, structures for the Synod of Bishops were

established by the motu proprio, *Apostolica sollicitudo* (ibid. 57 [1965] 775–780). As a consequence, a significant shift has taken place away from heavy centralization of ecclesial power in Rome toward a more even distribution of it in the particular Churches. An apostolic constitution to reform the structures of the Roman Curia *Regimini Ecclesiae universae* (ibid. 59 [1967] 885–928) opened the door for a more efficient and internationally-representative central administration.

The ecumenical pronouncements of the Council inspired new laws to promote the unity of Christians. Symbolic but illustrative of the new trend was the removal on Dec. 7, 1965, by Paul VI in the apostolic letter, *Ambulate in dilectione* (ibid. 58 [1966] 40–41), of the sentence of excommunication pronounced in 1054 against the Patriarch of Constantinople, Michael Cerularius. The severity of the norms concerning mixed marriages between Catholics and non-Catholic Christians was tempered (*Matrimonii sacramentum*, ibid. 58 [1966] 235–239; *Crescens matrimoniorum*, ibid. 59 [1967] 165–166).

The motu proprio, *Ecclesiae Sanctae* (ibid. 58 [1966] 757–787), has given practical norms for the implementation of the desire of the Council to reform the administration of dioceses, to affirm episcopal conferences, to renew religious life, and to give new impulse to the missionary activities of the Church.

The internal life of the Church has not been neglected. The apostolic constitution *Paenitemini* (ibid. 177–198) has given a new direction to the penitential and devotional discipline. New laws concerning virtually every aspect of liturgy have been promulgated at a fairly rapid rate; they are too numerous to be mentioned by titles (collected to 1973 in EnchDocLit).

Legislative activity was more intense during the four or five years following the Council. Then, implementation slowed down. The last few years could be described more as a period of waiting for the publication of a revised body of universal laws, possibly in the form of a new Code.

(2) **Preparations for a New Code of Canon Law.** The Pontifical Commission for the Revision of the Code of Canon Law was established by Pope John XXIII in 1963. From 1969 onward, the Commission has issued regular, although rather sparse, reports (*Communicationes*) on the progress of the work. The Commission is guided by the principle that, apart from a Fundamental Law (*Lex fundamentalis*) of general character, there should be a new Code divided into seven books, following substantially the pattern of the Code of Canon Law of 1917. The projected seven titles are: *General Norms, The People of God* (i.e. Law of Persons), *Teaching Office of the Church, Sanctifying Office of the Church, Law of Property, Penalties,* and *Protection of Rights and Procedures.* The first drafts on Fundamental Law, Consecrated Life, Sacraments, Penalties, and Protection of Rights and Procedures have already been submitted to the various episcopal conferences, departments of the Roman Curia, and ecclesiastical faculties for their opinions. The remaining drafts were sent to the same persons or organizations early in 1978, and the answers are due within the same year.

No information has been published about the procedure that the Commission intends to follow after the first critical evaluation has been received, if indeed precise plans have been formulated at all. It is conceivable that, after this first consultation, the law will be promulgated in its final form, or that a second draft will be submitted to the same or other persons for further evaluation. At any rate, the known project shows that the goal of the Holy See is to promulgate, eventually, a new and unified Code of Canon Law. However, the possibility of successive statutory legislation on diverse topics cannot be definitely excluded.

As far as it is known, the worldwide response to the legislative drafts has been mixed. The majority of the bishops formally approved of the Fundamental Law, but many did so with serious reservations. Theologians and canonists have voiced their own criticism of it. Some of the other drafts have been better received, some have provoked significant opposition. Nonetheless, it is important to note that, for the first time in the history of the Church, there is a widespread and thorough consultation in regard to a vast project of universal legislation.

Conflicts in conceiving the reform of Canon Law seem to be inevitable, at this point in history. In fact, it is reasonable to ask if these postconciliar years are the best time for building up a new body of laws, a new *Corpus iuris canonici*. The transformation initiated by the Council cannot but be slow in such a worldwide body as the Catholic Church. The minds of the faithful, and also of the experts in theology and law, are often divided; therefore, a new *Corpus* is likely to represent a series of compromises between contending opinions. Laws born from such conflicts may serve a temporary purpose, but they do not have lasting value. Perhaps the aim of the reform should not be to create a new Code, but should rather be to follow the humble path initiated after the Council, that is, the path of partial statutory legislation for divers topics, according to existing needs.

(3) **Developments in Interpretation.** The transition from the old law of the Code into a new one inspired by the Council has created its own specific problems of interpretation. Technically, the old law remains valid until changed, yet, when the intent of the legislator is clearly to change, even to the point where the details of the new law are known, it is not equitable any more to ask the community to observe the law in the same way as before. A statement often voiced today is that Canon Law does not exist any more. The true state of things is that many laws concerned with minor points of discipline, or with devotional observances, are indeed falling into desuetude, but the great constitutional structures of the Church are firmly established and operating with a certain smooth efficiency. In general, however, it is true that laws are interpreted in a new spirit.

Theological reflections have an impact on determining the meaning of the laws. Certainly, the gap between the canonical and the theological sciences has been too large. In trying to remedy the situation, some thinkers are now going so far as to virtually identify Canon Law with theology. Some others take a more moderate approach, respect the autonomy of each discipline, but hold that without good theology there is no right interpretation. Paul VI has stressed such an approach in his official addresses to professional groups of canon lawyers (see ActApS 65 [1973] 95–103 and Origins 2 [1973] 587–588, 593–595). Scholarly studies on the theological foundations of law are being published regularly. They have already brought about a better understanding of the role of law in the Church.

In the last decade, philosophical reflections on the nature of law have been less intense among canon lawyers, even to the point of neglect—a regrettable omission, due probably to increasing interest in theology. The result is that, to date, Canon Law has drawn no profit from the extensive studies concerning epistemological questions, nor has it benefited from the abundant research in hermeneutics. Consequently, it continues to work with a cognitional theory, inherited from the Middle Ages, which is less than satisfactory for solving modern problems about mental states, such as knowledge and ignorance, doubt and error; also, it operates on the hypothesis of a sharp distinction between the human faculties of mind and will. The theory is insufficient to explain the data of consciousness and causes serious problems in judging human actions, especially when their validity is at stake, as often happens in the case of marriages. The lack of awareness of the hermeneutical problem still impedes the emergence of a more historical and flexible interpretation of laws. Eventually, and inevitably, new philosophical insights will penetrate and significantly transform the science of Canon Law, as has already happened in biblical exegesis and theological reflection.

There is also an increasing awareness that law cannot be properly understood without help from such other human sciences as sociology, anthropology, and psychology. There is, however, little research and writing on the relationship of law to these sciences. The difficulties and tensions experienced in this period of transition are likely to have a positive impact on the development of the science of Canon Law. Its isolation has already come to an end. Its steady contact with other disciplines will bring new insights in understanding the role of law, and will have to make its application more intelligent and equitable.

See also CODE OF CANON LAW, REVISION OF.

Bibliography: The most complete, but unofficial, collection of recent legislation is: X. OCHOA, *Leges Ecclesiae post Codicem iuris canonici editae*, v. 3–4 (Rome 1972–74). For English translations see appropriate volumes of Bousc-O'Connor. Some writings concerning legislation and interpretation after Vatican II: V. MOSIEK, *Verfassungsrecht der lateinischen Kirche* (2v., Freiburg 1974–78). U. NAVARRETE, ed., *Ius Populi Dei*, 3 v. (Rome 1972). L. ORSY, "The Canons on Ecclesiastical Laws Revisited: Glossae on Canons 9–24," *Jurist* 37 (1977) 112–159. V. RAMALLO, *El derecho y el misterio de la Iglesia* (Rome 1972). A. SCHEUERMANN and G. MAY, eds., *Ius Sacrum* (Munich 1969).

[L. ÖRSY]

JUSTICE, EDUCATION FOR

The 1971 Synod of Bishops meeting in Rome gave to the Christian world a mandate "to educate for justice" and declared that "action on behalf of justice and participation in the transformation of the world" is a "constitutive dimension" of the preaching of the Gospel (Synod JustWorld Introd. p. 34). Rather than encourage a narrow individualism or a mentality which exalts possessions, education for justice is to be a freeing process, enabling those who are educated to judge and act in accord with Gospel values. It is an education that forms individuals committed to work for justice for all humankind. To achieve this, "educational method must be such as to teach men [and women] to live their lives in its entire reality and in accord with the evangelical principles of personal and social morality which are expressed in the vital witness of one's life" (ibid. p. 46).

Vatican Council II. The Vatican Council II in its Pastoral Constitution on the Church in the Modern World states: "The social order and its development must always work to the benefit of the human person.... It requires constant improvement. It must be founded on truth, built on justice, and animated by love; in freedom it should grow every day toward a more humane balance. An improvement in attitudes and numerous changes in society will have to take place if these objectives are to be gained" (*Gaudium et spes* 26). This is a description of both the need and the goal of an education for justice.

Justice education should increase awareness of the interdependence of nations and of individuals. To do this it will include a global perspective and a searching for ways to provide a better quality of life for all. Such an education requires a curriculum rooted in the Gospel values of peace, justice, human rights, the dignity of each person, and the brotherhood of the human race. It requires a methodology both cognitive and affective and one which will help those educated develop a sense of responsibility for their own lives and a concern for the lives of others. It requires an educational structure that will allow opportunities for students to learn how to maximize their political influence as citizens. The structures, policies, and relationships that create the environment within which the academic endeavors take place must offer witness to these values.

Synod of Bishops, 1971. The goals and objectives of an education for justice are clearly stated in the 1971 Synod document. It will demand a renewal of heart based on a recognition of sin in its individual and social aspects. Objectives will include a truly and entirely human way of life in justice, love and simplicity. Another goal is the awakening of a critical sense that will lead to reflection on contemporary society and its values and the motivation of men and women to renounce these values when they cease to promote justice for all persons. Justice education should be a continuing education that reaches persons of every age. It should be such an experience as to enable persons to take control of their own destinies and should result in communities that are truly human. Finally, it is a practical education which comes through action, participation, and vital contact with the reality of injustice. In the developing countries, the principal aim of an education for justice should be to awaken consciences to a knowledge of the concrete situation and to a call to secure a total improvement (Synod JustWorld pp. 46–47).

Family and School. Education for justice should be imparted first in the family, where the child's socialization process begins and where the child perceives value models. The content of this education necessarily involves respect for the dignity of the person. Since world justice is the concern, it is in the family that the unity of the entire human family must be seriously affirmed. This education will continue in the schools where students at every age will learn the rich teachings on social justice that are part of the Christian tradition and are to be found throughout the Scriptures as well as in the teachings of the Fathers of the Church and in the encyclicals and pastoral statements of modern popes and bishops. This education must be extended also to the adult community in which study, prayer, and reflection on these teachings will bear fruit in "authentic witness on behalf of justice" (Mainelli, para. 1070) in both the social and political spheres as well as in personal life-style and social behavior.

Catholic schools today can implement this mandate "to educate for justice" in a variety of ways. Ideally, an interdisciplinary approach will involve teachers and students in a united effort. Such issues as world hunger, ecology, population, human rights, racism, development, international trade policy, war, and domestic violence can be integrated into the science and language-arts class as well as into social studies and religion classes. Social action programs bring students into personal contact with the realities of injustice. Skills of non-violent conflict-resolution can be taught even to very young children and alternatives to violence can be explored. Whatever methodology a school adopts to educate for justice, the essential goal remains: to so integrate the values of justice and peace into the total school environment that students of every age will be led to the realization that an integral part of the Christian vocation is concern for justice and participation in bringing about a more just society and a better quality of life for people everywhere.

Bibliography: V. MAINELLI, ed., *Social Justice: The Catholic Position* (Washington, D.C. 1975)

[V. GROVER]

JUSTICE AND PEACE, MINISTRY OF

A principal feature of the post-Vatican Council II Church has been an intensified, almost qualitatively new, degree of sociopolitical involvement in the name of justice and peace. The forms of involvement and the issues vary, but the abiding witness to "the Gospel of peace and justice," as Joseph Gremillion has phrased it, is undeniable. In Latin America, since the Medellín Conference (1968) the Church has become the principal defender of human dignity and human rights in the face of a pattern of authoritarian military regimes which have ruled the continent in the last decade (*see* LATIN AMERICA, CHURCH IN). In East Asia the Church in South Korea and the Philippines is locked in on-going conflict with the respective governments on questions of social justice and human rights (*see* PHILIPPINES, CHURCH IN). In Rhodesia and South Africa the institutional Church is a key element in the struggle for racial justice and social transformation (*see* AFRICA, SOUTHERN). In Poland the Church remains a solitary bulwark, prevailing still in a classic Church-State conflict. In the United States, issues of civil rights, the migrant farm workers, illegal aliens, the Vietnam war, and the nuclear arms race have found the Church a visible and vocal participant.

The list of specific forms of active involvement could be extended substantially, but the purpose of this essay is not to describe Catholic participation in the work of justice and peace, but to offer a theological analysis of what impels Christians and the Church as an institution to enter the sociopolitical arena. The response to this question can be divided into a theological, an ecclesiological, and a moral explanation, with special emphasis given to post-Vatican II contributions to these themes.

Theological Explanation. The theological foundation of all of the Church's specific actions in the social ministry is defined in Vatican II's Pastoral Constitution on the Church in the Modern World. The Church, says the Council, should stand as the "sign and safeguard of the transcendence of the human person" (*Gaudium et spes* 76). Briefly stated, the protection and promotion of the dignity of the person form the basis of all of the Church's social ministry. The dignity of the person, grounded theologically in the doctrine of the person as the *imago Dei*, and philosophically in the spiritual nature of the person (ibid. 12), is articulated in Catholic teaching by a doctrine of the rights and responsibilities of each person as the direct consequence of human dignity. Since the protection and promotion of human rights, as well as the consistent fulfillment of human duties, are related to the social structure in which the person lives, the Church's commitment to human dignity, rights, and responsibilities requires that it exercise a ministry of justice and peace designed to address the political, economic, and social structure in the name of the person. To use the words of Pius XII in the 1943 Christmas message, "the person should be the foundation, the end and the agent of the social system" (cf. ActApS 35 [1943] 12–13).

The theological grounding of the social ministry of the Church has been clearly and consistently stated throughout the 20th century in the tradition of the papal social encyclicals. The strength of pre-Vatican II documents lay in their sophisticated mix of theological and philosophical themes, yielding a body of moral and social doctrine at once strong and subtle. The liability of the traditional social teaching lay in its underdeveloped ecclesiology. Little attention was paid in the social teaching of Leo XIII, Pius XI, or even Pius XII, to delineating a clear link between the social ministry of the Church and the nature and mission of the Church. The principal contribution of the conciliar and postconciliar period to the social ministry has been to close the ecclesiological gap in the social teaching.

The Ecclesiological Issue. The basic ecclesiological statement is found in the Pastoral Constitution. The significance of the document lies less in any sentence, paragraph, or passage than in its fundamental affirmation that a total ecclesiology requires not only the reflection *ad intra* of *Lumen gentium*, the Dogmatic Constitution on the Church, but also a correlative explanation of "the presence and function of the Church in the world today" (*Gaudium et spes* 2). The view of the Council was that the specific mission of the Church is religious in its nature and purpose, yet that in pursuing this religious ministry the Church contributes to three sociopolitical objectives: (1) protecting the dignity of the person; (2) fostering the unity of the human family; and (3) informing human activity with deeper meaning and purpose. These activities, the basic themes of justice and peace ministry, are endowed with religious significance by *Gaudium et spes* and are described as flowing from the very nature of the Church's mission and ministry. When this line is drawn the entire social teaching of the Church takes on new significance, because it has been placed in an explicitly theological framework. The theological design shaped by the Pastoral Constitution was not simply a conciliar achievement; the Council initiated a process of postconciliar reflection on the nature and ministry of the Church *ad extra*, "in the world of today." On the level of theological reflection the postconciliar dynamic can be traced through the emergence of *liberation theology and *political theology (quite distinct orientations, but with a common origin). Even more concretely, the influence of the Pastoral Constitution can be found in the successive international Synods of Bishops held in Rome periodically since the Council.

The 1971 Synod of Bishops. The substantial relationship between the Pastoral Constitution and the 1971 Synod's document *Justice in the World* is manifest in the strong ecclesiological tenor of the Synod's statement. The passage which has made this document a *locus classicus* in postconciliar theology is principally an ecclesiological affirmation: "Action on behalf of justice and participation in the transformation of the world fully appear to us as a constitutive dimension of the preaching of the Gospel, or, in other words, of the Church's mission for the redemption of the human race and its liberation from every oppressive situation" (Synod JustWorld p. 34). The value of this statement lies in its specificity; it identifies the social ministry (action for justice and transformation of the world) as constitutive, i.e., central to the mission of the Church. The specificity of the passage has made it useful but also controversial; the controversy is the product of the strength of the assertion. Adjectives like "constitutive" are used rarely and carefully in Catholic theology. All agree, for example, that the celebration of the Sacraments and the preaching of the Gospel are constitutive dimensions of ministry. It is not forcing the synodal text to see in it a movement of theological development, from implicit to explicit affirmation, in which the prophetic theme of justice contained in the preaching of the Gospel has been made an explicit element in defining the mission of the Church. Reaction against such an interpretation has provoked controversy over the synodal text. The debate surfaced in the 1974 *Synod of Bishops on evangelization.

The 1974 Synod of Bishops. In his opening address, Sept. 27, 1974, to the 1974 Synod Pope Paul VI posed the issue of how the sociopolitical involvement of the Church was to be understood in the total work of evangelization. The Holy Father was not, however, simply posing a question; he was stating a position based on trends he perceived among Christians involved in the Church's social apostolate: "Very often they are urged to forget the priority that their message of salvation must have and thus to reduce their own action to more sociological or political activity, and the message of the church to a man-centered and temporal message. Hence, the need to restate clearly the specifically religious quality of evangelization" (Paul VI ActApS 562, USCC 4–5). This opening statement placed the issue raised by the 1971 Synod at the heart of the 1974 Synod's work. The debate in the session on evangelization served more to intensify the theological discussion than to settle the question with precision. It was clear from many voices in the debate that the ministry of justice and peace has become an integral dimension of the work of evangelization (see Caprile 893–894, 903–904, 981–990, 1011–16; Gremillion 597–598). This witness, arising from apostolic involvement and finding expression in the synodal debate, illustrated how the daily life of the Church both contributed to and called for a clarification of the theological understanding of the role and function of the justice and peace ministry in the broader mission of the Church.

Evangelii Nuntiandi. The final product of the 1974 Synod was Pope Paul's apostolic exhortation, *Evangelii nuntiandi*, On Evangelization in the Modern World. Although the categories used in this notable document are not identical with those of *Gaudium et spes* or *Justice in the World*, the substantive issue is the same—how to relate the religious mission of the Church to its work for human dignity and the transformation of the world. In the 1974 letter the Holy Father cast the problem in terms of the link between evangelization, human development, and liberation (Paul VI Evang-Nunt 25–39). His concern seemed to be that some members of the Church would identify the content of evangelization with development or liberation or at least give the latter primacy of place. In response, he distinguished between primary and secondary dimensions of evangelization. The primary dimension is directed toward "the Kingdom of God, before anything else, in its fully theological meaning..." (ibid. 32, quoting the opening address to the Synod). In addition, evangelization must include an explicit message, "about the rights and duties of every human being, about family life...., about life in society, about international life, peace, justice and development—a message especially energetic today about liberation" (ibid. 29). The papal letter makes clear that the sociopolitical objectives should not subordinate the transcendent-eschatological dimensions of evangelization, but it is not so clear on how to state the positive linkage of the two dimensions of evangelization.

The International Theological Commission. The evidence that this question of relationship among the principal components of the Church's ministry is a continuing concern is provided by the *International Theological Commission (ITC) in its study entitled, *Declaration on Human Development and Christian Salvation* (1977). This document, described as an extension of the theological perspective of *Gaudium et spes*, addresses the question of development and salvation in its broadest categories. Several alternative formulations of the question are listed: the relationship of human activity and Christian hope; of building the Kingdom and human progress; of divine grace and human activity; of the interpretation of the heavenly and earthly cities. The emphasis of the Theological Commission is to affirm a basic unity of these terms, yet to advise that in the postconciliar period so much attention has been given to joining them that rigorous efforts must be made to illustrate their qualitative differences. The Commission explicitly admits that the 1971 Synod's statement about justice and peace activity being constitutive of the mission of the Church "is still controversial." The Commission defines "constitutive" (*ratio constitutiva*) in the language of the 1974 Synod, as "integral but nonessential" (ITC 4b). The tendency here is to draw back from the full force of the original text, but it is a tendency not a final word. The Church continues to be in the midst of an exciting debate about its mission in the world.

The purpose of this rather detailed exegesis of the debate since 1971 has been to illuminate an important issue but to avoid becoming a prisoner of distinctions. The significance of the debate initiated by the Pastoral Constitution and *Justice in the World* can be appreciated only by recognizing how the absence of a clear ecclesiological statement about the ministry of justice and peace has in the past confined such activity to a marginal position in the Church's ministry. Catholicism has been possessed of a strong social doctrine but a less than adequate understanding of how to relate the objectives of that doctrine to the total activity of the Church. This question, one of theological understanding and pastoral priorities, affects the Church's daily life

and witness. It will not be settled by a precise definition, but it will be affected in the long run by the categories used to state and explain the Church's ministry. The concern of theologians and others should not be to discern the exact weight to be accorded social ministry *vs.* sacramental activity or to adjudicate the issue of the primary *vs.* the secondary aspects of evangelization. The need of the moment, to be served by drawing on the magisterial statements and theological work since Vatican II, is a task of integration and systematization that will make available to the People of God at all levels an understanding of the Church's ministry as simultaneously rooted in a transcendent faith yet yielding a daily involvement in the works of justice and peace.

The Moral Consideration. The theological question specifies the basis of the Church's concern in all sociopolitical involvement; the ecclesiological question relates to why the Church pursues the ministry of justice and peace. The moral question identifies the content of Catholic social teaching. In describing this it is important to distinguish what the teaching is not from what it is. Catholic social teaching is not a blueprint for the reform of society; it is clearly not a ready-made plan whose implementation simply requires enough sufficiently good-willed people. On the contrary the content of the social teaching offers a broad theological-philosophical framework of analysis for examining the principal social and structural issues of the age. Only some guidelines for interpreting the moral content of the tradition of the Church's social teaching can be given here.

Sources. First, it is necessary to identify the *locus* of the teaching. Catholic social teaching should be distinguished from the wider topic of the social implications of biblical faith. The latter is found in the teaching of the prophets, in the New Testament as it develops and deepens the prophetic message, and in the life and history of the Church as it understands itself as a community in history. Within the framework of these themes, the social teaching, *stricte dicta*, has emerged in the last century in a series of papal, conciliar, and synodal statements reaching from Leo XIII's, *On the Condition of Labor* (*Rerum novarum*; 1891) through to Paul VI's *On Evangelization in the Modern World* (1976). Between these texts lie Pius XI's *Reconstructing the Social Order* (*Quadragesimo anno*; 1931); Pius XII's Pentecost (1941) and Christmas Addresses (1939–57); John XXIII's *Christianity and Social Progress* (*Mater et magistra*; 1961) and *Peace on Earth* (*Pacem in terris*; 1963); Vatican II's Pastoral Constitution on the Church in the Modern World (1965) and the Declaration on Religious Freedom (*Dignitatis humanae*; 1965); Paul VI's The Progress of Peoples (*Populorum progressio*; 1967) and The Eightieth Year (*Octogesima adveniens*; 1971); and finally, the 1971 Synod's *Justice in the World*.

Stages of Development. Second, this chronological recitation of the texts can be given a more analytical structure by distinguishing three periods of development in the social tradition. The first phase is a response by the Church to the problems posed by the Industrial Revolution. The key texts are those of Leo XIII and Pius XI; the principal issues are the role of the government in society and the economy, the right of laborers to organize, the principle of a just wage, and the Church's critique of both capitalism and socialism. The second phase emerges during World War II and continues to the present; it is the internationalization of Catholic social teaching as the Church confronts the growing material interdependence of the world and seeks to provide a moral framework for the political, economic, and strategic issues facing the human community. The key texts are those of Pius XII, John XXIII, and Paul VI as well as those of the Council and the Synods. The principal issues are the political-juridical organization of the international community, the demands of international social justice in determining the rules and relationships of international economic policy, as well as the moral issues raised by nuclear weapons and the way they require a reevaluation of the morality of warfare. The third phase is represented by Paul VI's apostolic letter *Octogesima adveniens* (1971). This rich document addresses the "new social questions." On the one hand, it analyzes the issues faced in a particularly acute way by postindustrial societies, marked by intensifying urbanization, high-scale technology and industrialization, and massive communication networks. On the other hand, the letter returns to the theme of how postindustrial and developing societies are related internationally. The focus of the document is on the kinds of organization competing for primacy in society and the philosophical currents which shape the alternative types of sociopolitical order. A striking element in the document is the more nuanced presentation and evaluation of Marxism offered by Paul VI (*see* MARXISM AND CHRISTIANITY).

Conceptual Framework, Principles. Third, an analysis of the social teaching yields a mix of substantive concepts and procedural principles which provide Catholic thought its continuity throughout different ages and geographical regions. The conceptual structure begins with the dignity of the person, elaborated in terms of a complex of rights and duties protecting and promoting the welfare of the person. This basic insight is then joined with a theory of state and society which distinguishes these entities, but affirms both as natural (therefore necessary) extensions of the social nature of the person. Specifically, Catholic teaching, with its basis in Aquinas, identifies three natural communities to which every person belongs: the family, the state, and the human community. Authority is a necessary element in any society, but the structure and functioning of authority should be evaluated in terms of another substantive concept, the common good. The content of the common good is defined in terms of the dignity, rights, and responsibilities of the person; it is the complex of spiritual, material, and temporal conditions needed in society so that each person might live in dignity (cf. *Gaudium et spes* 74). The concept of the common good applies to both national and international life and the requirements of the common good provide one determinant of the scope and structure of authority needed to govern society justly.

The procedural principles of Catholic social teaching address the question of the scope and structure of authority in society; they are regulatory principles, open to continuing scrutiny and adjustment in changing circumstances. They set Catholic theory apart from both a laissez-faire view of the state and a totalitarian conception of state power. The dominant principle is that of subsidiarity, explicated by Pius XI in 1931 (cf. 13:762). The presumption of the principle is in favor of decentralized authority, personal and local initiative; it seeks

to preserve a legitimate ambit of freedom for the person and forms of voluntary association in society. A correlative notion, to some degree a countervailing idea, is Pope John's discussion of *socialization in 1961. The presumption in this concept is that the satisfaction of certain basic needs for the citizenry as a whole may require an extension of the power of the state; this idea seeks to legitimate the use of centralized authority when other means of satisfying human needs are inadequate. Taken in tandem, subsidiarity and socialization provide Catholic thought with a framework for adjudicating the continuing question of the proper role of authority in society.

Justice within. Fourth, a significant postconciliar development in the social teaching is found in *Justice in the World's* application of social justice norms to the inner life of the Church. In the words of the Synod, "anyone who ventures to speak to people about justice must first be just in their eyes" (Synod JustWorld p. 44). This statement opens a whole range of questions regarding ecclesiastical institutions, procedures, and use of material goods, all assessed in light of the Church's own normative teaching on justice and peace.

Within this threefold framework of theological, ecclesiological, and moral reflection Catholic social teaching develops and provides the foundation for the Church's work of justice and peace. The postconciliar period has been a particularly fruitful time of development and the dynamic shows no sign of subsiding.

Bibliography: G. CAPRILE, *Il Sinodo dei Vescovi 1974* (Rome n.d.). J. COLEMAN, "Vision and Praxis in American Theology," ThSt 37 (1976) 3–40. J. GREMILLION, *The Gospel of Peace and Justice* (Maryknoll, N.Y. 1976). G. GUTTIEREZ, *Theology of Liberation*, tr. C. INDA and J. EAGLESON (Maryknoll, N.Y. 1973). J. HAUGHEY, ed., *The Faith That Does Justice* (New York 1977). International Theological Commission, *Declaration on Human Development and Christian Salvation* (USCC Publ. Office, Washington, D.C. 1977). J. METZ, *Theology of the World*, tr. W. GLEN-DOEPEL (New York 1969). J. C. MURRAY, "The Issue of Church and State at Vatican II," ThSt 27 (1966) 580–606. PAUL VI, Address at the Opening of the 1974 Synod of Bishops, ActApS 66 (1974) 557–564, tr. USCC, *Synod of Bishops—1974* (USCC Publ. Office, Washington, D.C. 1975) 1–6.

[J. B. HEHIR]

JUSTICE AND PEACE, PONTIFICAL COMMISSION FOR

Pope Paul VI established this entity of the Roman Curia experimentally by the motu proprio *Catholicam Christi Ecclesiam*, Jan. 6, 1967 (ActApS 59 [1967] 28). He restructured it definitively by the motu proprio *Iustitiam et pacem* of Dec. 10, 1976 (ActApS 68 [1976] 700–703). The Commission is intended to implement Vatican Council II's Constitution on the Church in the Modern World (*Gaudium et spes* 90) and from its inception has worked in conjunction with the Pontifical Council for the *Laity, established at the same time. The task of the Commission is to study the concrete problems of justice, peace, and human rights, to intensify awareness of the doctrinal and pastoral dimensions of such problems, and to animate in Catholics a sense of responsibility in these matters. The Commission has close ties with national episcopal conferences, with their national committees on justice and peace, and collaborates with other Christian and non-Christian world agencies with similar aims (*see* SODEPAX). The Commission seeks to act in harmony with the papal Secretariat of State, but some tensions have arisen. The Commission's occasional confrontational approach contrasts with the Secretariat's dominant concern to appeal to the good will of established governments and ruling elites.

Members and consultants of the Commission serve five-year terms and meet in general assembly once a year. Important interventions have included its working paper on the Church and human rights, on the 25th anniversary of the United Nations Universal Declaration of Human Rights (1975); its endorsement of the goals of the *New International Economic Order, urging the poor nations to assume power and take initiative in constructing a new economic order (1977); its paper addressed to the Conference on the Law of the Sea, in which it backed the UN declaration that the sea is the common patrimony of humanity. The Commission urged that the seas' resources be available first to poorer nations (1977). Archbishop (now Cardinal) Maurice Roy of Quebec was the first head of both the Commission on Justice and Peace and the Council for the Laity. The secretariat of the Commission is housed in the Trastevere slum district of Rome. Its present head is Archbishop Bernardin Gantin of Dahomey, the first African to head a curial agency.

Bibliography: AnnPont 1978:1052–1053; 1480. "Déterminant les structures définitives de la Commission Pontificale Justice et Paix," DocCath 74 (1977) 6–7, "La Déstination universelle des biens," ibid. 757–760.

[E. J. DILLON]

K

KELLER, JAMES G.

Founder of The Christophers; b. Oakland, Calif., June 27, 1900; d. New York City, Feb. 7, 1977. Educated in public schools and for seven years at St. Patrick's Seminary, Menlo Park, Calif. he joined Maryknoll in September 1921. Most of his studies during the major seminary years were at The Catholic Univ. of America (S.T.B., 1924, and M.A., 1925). He was a member of the Maryknoll class of 1925 and was ordained August 15, 1925 at his parish church, St. Francis de Sales in Oakland. He founded The Christophers in 1945 out of the conviction that each person can do something, with God's help, to change the world for the better. The name "Christopher" taken from the Greek meaning "Christ-bearer," sums up the missionary character of the movement.

Tirelessly Keller proclaimed the Christopher ideal that "you can change the world" by stimulating millions to show personal responsibility and individual initiative in raising the standards of all phases of human endeavor. He stressed in particular those fields of influence that affect the common good of all—government, education, labor-management relations, literature and entertainment. His book, *You Can Change the World*, published in 1948, was a best seller. To bring the message of positive, constructive action to the widest audience possible, he launched *Christopher News Notes*—published 7 times a year, sent gratis to 750,000 persons; weekly radio and television programs; a one-minute inspirational radio spot-broadcast daily; a yearly Christopher book; a daily newspaper column called "Three Minutes a Day"; and the Christopher Awards—in recognition of writers, producers, and directors in literature, motion pictures, and television whose works attest to the highest values of the human spirit. To accentuate the positive as the Christopher objective, he adopted as the Christopher motto the Chinese proverb, "Better to light one candle than to curse the darkness"; the Prayer of St. Francis as the Christopher Prayer; and stressed the biblical injunction from St. Paul, "Be not overcome by evil, but overcome evil with good" (Rom 12.21). A man of prayer, great hope and vision, he was consumed with the idea of reaching as many people as he could in his lifetime with the love and truth of Christ. A victim of Parkinson's Disease, he retired as director of The Christophers in 1969, but remained as consultant up until the last year of his life. In January 1976, he received the Benemerenti Medal from Pope Paul VI, in recognition of his service, during 50 years as a priest, to the Christophers and to the Maryknoll Fathers. His autobiography, *To Light a Candle*, has helped to light myriad candles of hope and joy in the hearts of men and women everywhere. Christopher activities are still conducted today from the headquarters in New York City at 12 E. 48th Street, with the Rev. John T. Catoir as Director.

[THE CHRISTOPHERS]

KINGDOM OF GOD

Scripture scholars and writers in Christology have probed the theme, Kingdom of God (8:188, 191) in many fine recent studies. They have provided a better understanding of the Gospel message but also an enriched theology of the Church and of the core activity of the Church, the liturgy. Since the term occurs frequently in the documents of Vatican Council II, liturgical prayers, and Sunday homilies, the purpose of this article is to reflect briefly on the meaning of this phrase, as the core of Christ's message in the Gospel, as manifested by the Church in the world today and as experienced in liturgical worship.

The Kingdom of God, Core of Christ's Teaching. There are instances in the Gospel in which the eschatological character of the Kingdom of God is referred to, e.g.—"thy kingdom come." (Mt 6.10), but the main thrust of this phrase in the preaching of Christ has to do with the here and now: "The time is fulfilled, and the kingdom of God is at hand, repent and believe the gospel" (Mk 1.15; cf. Mt 4.17; 10.7; Lk 10.9, 11). The Kingdom is not a place but rather the new manifestation or presence of God's sovereignty. This presence begins with Jesus himself, God coming among men. By his very presence in the flesh and in power he can say, "the kingdom of God is at hand." Through his teaching Jesus opens a new era of understanding God and his relationship to men. He calls God, *Abba* (Mk 14.36), a familiar title for "father"—one who is close to men in love and forgiveness. He is not God the law-giver of the Jews or the fullness of moral goodness of the Greek system, but a creative goodness that makes others good by a contagious love. The God proclaimed by Jesus is not that of the philosopher, the unmoved mover or unchangeable source of being, but the living God of love and justice. This God shows forth his glory and kingship by his sovereign freedom to love and to forgive. In this he shows that he is God and not man (Hos 11.9).

The Kingdom of God begins with each person who accepts the Gospel message—the loving forgiveness of the Father. "The kingdom of God is within you." (Lk 17.21). This calls for action (δύναμις); a creative power to share this loving forgiveness with others. The Kingdom then makes itself felt in the acceptance of human beings by each other, in taking down social barriers and prejudices, in new unrestricted communication among men in brotherly concern, and the sharing of sadness and joy. The whole of Christ's redemptive work may therefore be summed up as revealing and establishing the love of the Father among men, the Kingdom of God.

The Kingdom of God Manifested in the Church. The community of those who have accepted the Gospel message, "the kingdom of God is at hand," is called the Church (cf. Lk 12.32, the "Little Flock"). The Church acts through the presence and power of Christ who sent it into the world to continue to proclaim and effect the reign of God until the day of its perfection. Just as Christ is the incarnation and effective sign of God's power and glory in the world, so the visible Church is the sign and instrument of the Holy Spirit and his saving power among men. The Church is then in a real sense a Sacrament; it is both the sign or manifestation of the Kingdom among men and at the same time realizes or effects what it signifies (see CHURCH [THEOLOGY]).

Entrance into the Church signifies the beginning of the new life of the Kingdom that is within (cf. Rom 6, 3–11). Again, this life is one of power (δύναμις) to transform the world into the universal Kingdom "of truth and life, a kingdom of holiness and grace, a kingdom of justice, peace and love" (Preface of Christ the King). This is why, although there is a clear distinction between earthly progress and the increase of the Kingdom of Christ, earthly progress is of vital concern to the Kingdom of God in so far as it can contribute to the better ordering of human society (*Gaudium et spes* 39). It would be inaccurate to identify the Kingdom with the Church just as it would have been inaccurate to have identified it with Israel. Christ has given the Church the duty of witnessing to the Kingdom and of forming and safeguarding the faith of those who wish to enter it, but the Church and the Kingdom will be commensurate only at the end of time.

The Kingdom Experienced in Liturgical Worship. The core of Christ's teaching was the proclamation of the Kingdom of God—God's historical and eschatological action in which he saves his people. Thus the Anamnesis of God's saving activity in the Eucharistic Liturgy becomes quite clearly not only the community's recall of the wondrous deeds that the Lord has wrought on their behalf in the past but includes likewise a consciousness of his presence with the hope that their gracious Lord will continue to exercise his power for them. Liturgical worship acknowledges him as Lord, and brings renewed awareness of the presence of his saving power through Word and Sacrament. If then, the Kingdom of God is God's divine activity, the way to celebrate the Kingdom is to celebrate what he has done.

The Kingdom of God can be only perceived through faith that God is at work in our midst (Lk 18.10; 17.11; 18.35; Jn 9.35; Lk 8.10; Lk 17.21). However, to acknowledge him, to worship him is not enough. Jesus has admonished that only those who do the will of the Father as he has done will enter into the Kingdom. Those who carry on the activity of Jesus, of bringing God's concern to all people regardless of nation, race, sex, or social situation—these are doing the will of the Father, and will enter the Kingdom of God. In the words of Vatican II, "This eucharistic celebration, to be full and sincere, ought to lead on the one hand to the various works of charity and mutual help, and on the other hand to missionary activity and the various forms of Christian witness" (*Presbyterorum ordinis* 6).

Bibliography: J. E. BRUNS, "The Kingdom of God," Ecumenist 2 (1964) 80–82. C. DAVIS, "The Vatican Constitution on the Church," ClergyRev 50 (1965) 264–282. J. GALLEN, "A Pastoral-Liturgical View of Penance Today," *Worship* 45 (1971) 132–150. A. GEORGE, "La Règne de Dieu d'après les Évangiles Synoptiques," VieSpirit 110 (1964) 43–54. W. KASPER, *Jesus the Christ* (New York 1976). K. MCDONNELL, "Themes in Ecclesiology and Liturgy from Vatican II," *Worship* (1967) 66–84. K. MCNAMARA, "The Mystery of the Church," IrEcclRec 106 (1966) 82–103. N. PERRIN, *The Kingdom of God in the Teaching of Jesus* (Philadelphia 1963). G. PHILIPS, *L'Église et son mystère au deuxième Concile du Vaticain* (Paris-Tournai 1967). R. SCHNACKENBURG, *God's Rule and Kingdom*, tr. J. MURRAY (New York 1963).

[E. L. DEPRIEST]

KNOWLES, DAVID

English monk, historian; b. on the feast of St. Michael, Sept. 29, 1896 at Eastfield, Studley, in Warwickshire; d. Nov. 21, 1974 in Chichester. Christened Michael Clive, he received the name David as a Benedictine. Knowles' scholarly reputation rests principally on his work as a historian of pre-Reformation English monasticism; his *opus magnum* is *The Monastic Order in England; a History of its Development from the Times of St Dunstan to the Fourth Lateran Council, 943–1216* (Cambridge 1940; 2d ed., 1963). The 3-v. *The Religious Orders in England* (Cambridge 1956, 1957, 1959) completed his history of the religious orders in England up to and inclusive of the Reformation; this work is not of the same exceptional stature as his *Monastic Order.*

Knowles was educated in the school at Downside Abbey where he became a novice in 1914 and where he pronounced simple vows in 1915 and solemn vows in 1918. From 1919 to 1922 he studied classical languages and philosophy at Cambridge as a member of Christ's College. He was ordained priest July 9, 1922. During the academic year of 1922–23 he studied theology at Sant' Anselmo, Rome. Upon his return to Downside Abbey, Dom David took up a number of duties, e.g., as teacher of classics in the school, temporary novice master in 1928, and master over the junior monks, from 1929–33. He became the editor of the *Downside Review* to which he made many contributions. His first book, *The American Civil War . . .* (Oxford 1926) was the result of a lifelong enthusiasm, but he never visited North America, despite many invitations to lecture.

Dom David was the leader of a group of monks at Downside who sought to initiate a new foundation of a contemplative character. Permission for this foundation was refused by the abbot of Downside and by the Congregation of Religious (1934). As a result Father David lived from 1933 to 1939 in a form of exile at

Ealing Abbey, London. In 1939 the tension of these years culminated in a nervous breakdown. Without permission Father David left the jurisdiction of Downside, an action which incurred for him a canonical suspension. Later Abbot Cuthbert Butler (now Bishop Butler) arranged for Dom David's position to be regularized as an exclaustration, a condition which perdured until his death. This arrangement made it possible for Dom David to live outside his monastery and yet remain a Benedictine in good standing. Despite this tragedy in his life, Dom David always deeply cherished his calling as a Benedictine and he maintained an affection for Downside Abbey. The monks of Saint Leo Abbey, Florida, reissued Dom David's booklet, *The Benedictines* . . . (Saint Leo, Florida 1962), which had appeared years before (London 1929; reprinted New York 1930) because these monks considered this essay to be the "nearly perfect exposition" of Benedictine monasticism.

Knowles' reputation as historian was spreading. In November 1941 he was awarded the honorary degree of Doctor of Letters by Cambridge, and in 1944 he became a Fellow of Peterhouse and thereafter his ascent up the ladder of academic success was rapid: University Lecturer at Cambridge in 1946, professor of medieval history in 1947, and in 1954 Regius Professor of Modern History in the University, a position he held until his retirement in 1963.

Father David was a man of slight physical build but with an intense and strong inner spirit. He was quiet and even austere, but possessed a gentle humor. His inner strength made possible his extraordinary productivity, but it also had a hand in the tragedy of his life. Moreover, this quiet strength was discernible in his carefully prepared and dignified lectures which held both seasoned scholars and undergraduates spellbound. Father David, as he was known to his friends, was a reserved man, but this reserve did not prevent his warmth and charm from coming through clearly in his lectures and especially in personal conversation and correspondence.

As an author David Knowles was perhaps the finest stylist of modern historians writing in English. He wrote to be clear and he always was so; yet his writings were rich in apt figures of speech and in literary allusions. He may have been at his very best in his assessment of character, a topic that he took up in his now-famous inaugural lecture as Regius Professor. However, he demanded at times too much of those about whom he wrote, as he did of himself, a characteristic that no doubt played a part in difficulties with his Abbey. His characterizations of Thomas Becket, Bernard of Clairvaux, Lord Macaulay, Cardinal Gasquet, and Dom Edward Cuthbert Butler are modern classics in character evaluation.

Throughout his life, Father David was intensely interested in the life and study of mysticism. In the former he had a personal abiding interest. His writings on mysticism, however, are narrow in scope and not of the same caliber as his work as a monastic historian. The personal quality of his passion for mysticism may have prevented his writings on it from achieving the quality of his historical writings.

Bibliographies of Father David's writings indicate the exceptional productivity of a monk whose way of life was both highly disciplined and austere. This prolificness did not abate in his years of retirement. What did emerge in his later years was a firmly conservative concern over the changes taking place in the Catholic Church and in what he considered to be its crisis of authority. He expressed this concern avidly and eloquently in a number of articles written in retirement. Dom David composed an autobiography which will not be published in the near future nor will it be accessible to researchers till a later date, a decision made by his literary executors. In considering the life of David Knowles as a monastic historian, one cannot escape a comparison with Dom Jean Mabillon, the 17th-century Maurist whom he so admired. In addition, what Dom David wrote of Dom Edward Cuthbert Butler (1858–1934) is surely an even more apt description of himself: ". . . he will long be remembered as the most remarkable English Benedictine scholar and historian of his time" (*The Historian and Character and Other Essays* [Cambridge 1963] 362).

Bibliography: For lists of the writings of Knowles, 1919–1962: D. KNOWLES, *The Historian and Character and Other Essays* (Cambridge 1963) 363–373; for 1963–1974 with supplement for 1932–1962: A. STACPOOLE, "The Making of a Monastic Historian—III," *Ampleforth Journal* 80 (1975) 51–55. Biographical studies: C. N. L. BROOKE, "David Knowles, 1896–1974," *Proceedings of the British Academy* 61 (1976) 439–477 K. J. EGAN, "Dom David Knowles, (1896–1974)," AmBenRev. 27 (1976) 235–246. W. A. PANTIN, "Curriculum Vitae," in D. KNOWLES *The Historian and Character. . .* xvii–xxviii. A. STACPOOLE, "The Making of a Monastic Historian—I, II, III," *Ampleforth Journal* 80, Parts I and II (1975) 71–91; 19–38; 48–55.

[K. J. EGAN]

L

LABOR MOVEMENT

The long-standing Catholic commitment to labor (8:232) declined in the late post-World War II period, especially in the United States. This was true of both church social documents and of social ministry. A new structural situation, however, may now revive Catholic concern in this area and link it with development interests that have been more central in recent years.

The Catholic Labor Heritage. When the early industrial revolution swept much of the First World (the nations of the North Atlantic community), it unleashed great injustice upon the new working classes. The Church challenged early industrial life, often called laissez-faire capitalism, in a series of official teachings beginning with Pope Leo XIII's encyclical, *Rerum novarum* (1891). Catholic teaching also attacked the opposite tendency still present in society, namely socialism. Catholic concern for labor in this period grew out of both genuine feeling for the sufferings of workers and institutional self-defense against antireligious socialist movements. Briefly the early Catholic social strategy of the industrial era focused on class conflicts between capital and labor in the industrial centers and somewhat later on the national East-West conflict between the liberal and Communist countries. The underlying ideology appropriated by Catholicism rejected the socialist vision. Rather it endorsed liberal reform movements, often under the call for a "Third Way."

Labor movements which fitted into this perspective received Catholic support. Sometimes, as in much of Europe, this required creating confessional Catholic unions because socialist elements were so strong. Other times, as with the United States, Catholic support could be given to this tendency within secular labor movements. Here a key vehicle of the Catholic strategy was the Association of Catholic Trade Unionists, founded in 1937 but going into decline in the post-war period.

Decline of Catholic Labor Interest. In the post-World War II period, new social conditions arose which altered the Catholic social strategy and weakened attention to labor questions. Within the industrial centers of the First World, capital and labor seemed to move toward balance. There were many reasons for this. The consolidation of capital in large corporations had enabled workers also to consolidate their power in strong unions. The new union strength forced collective bargaining as a widely accepted procedure and also pressured the new regulatory state to adopt such benevolent welfare policies as social security, minimum wage, and unemployment compensation. Also, technological advances deepened mass-consumerism. This was especially true in the United States, which emerged from World War II in a position of industrial hegemony, able to subsidize internal prosperity by international expansion and by a controlling voice over the post-war international economic order. Finally, internal socialist movements waned again especially in the United States. Thus, for many reasons, class tensions between capital and labor became less acute.

Similarly new conditions were emerging in the international East-West conflict between the First World and the Communist Second World. The eventual nuclear balance of terror made secular and church leaders look for peaceful coexistence. As the Communist consolidation of power was accepted, Catholic leadership began diplomatic engagement with Eastern socialist states (*see* DIPLOMACY, PAPAL). Thus the Catholic East-West strategy shifted from confrontation to bargaining, in the hope of maximizing church leverage in a difficult but permanent situation.

The most important change in the new period, however, was the growing Catholic focus on the Third World—the development question, which was phrased in national and community terms, and not in class or labor-movement terms. In the post-war period a new spirit swept over the South of the globe, long marginalized from the industrial centers. Scores of colonial nations gained independence and numerous new states emerged. First World industry, now growing into mature transnational enterprises, penetrated Latin America, Asia, and to a lesser degree Africa. Industrialization, or "development" seemed to be coming to the poor countries. Since this area housed the world's greatest poverty and the majority of humanity (with highest rates of population growth), and since growing consciousness of the colonial legacy made this area ripe for Communist penetration, Catholic social concern rapidly focused on the Third World. The North-South axis of geopolitical tension between rich and poor nations displaced the East-West axis of tension between liberal and Communist nations.

New Catholic Social Teaching. All three shifts—the reduction of capital/labor class conflict in the First World, the search for peaceful coexistence East-West, and new North-South neocolonial tensions—precipitated a new stage in Catholic social teaching.

Papal Teaching. The conditions of industrial labor received only minimal attention; the two main questions of North-South justice and East-West peace were addressed respectively by Pope John XXIII' encyclicals *Mater et magistra* (1961) and *Pacem in terris* (1963). Both themes came to center stage in Vatican Council II's Constitution on the Church in the Modern World (*Gaudium et spes*, 1965). Subsequently Pope Paul VI set up the Pontifical Commission for *Justice and Peace to work in these areas. His later encyclical "On the Development of Peoples" (*Populorum progressio*, 1967) became its Magna Carta. In response, a Catholic "Justice and Peace" network of social thought and action began to emerge worldwide.

Community-Development Issues. The shift was not only international, however, since community-development issues, other than traditional labor concerns, began to be addressed within industrial societies. Primary attention was given to internal marginalized sectors—rural life and agricultural workers, the urban poor, racial and ethnic minorities, and women—as well as hostility toward war and the military-industrial complex. In the United States, new movements burst upon the public in the 1960s—the civil rights movement, the anti-poverty crusade, the anti-war movement, the student New Left—and later the women's movement and the ecology movement. At first, labor was sometimes seen as an ally, but often as an enemy, especially in matters of affirmative action and the war in Vietman. More important, the organizing thrust itself had shifted from the producer side where labor is organized, to the consumer side of community organization and to public interest-constituency work. Recently, however, many assumptions behind these movements are being reexamined. This reexamination opens on the possibility of a creative integration of old and new concerns in a fresh vision and strategy.

Possibility of a New Integration. The objective foundation for an integration of post-war social movements with classic labor concerns lies in the new structural situation taking shape.

Transnational Capitalism. This situation differs from the localized laissez-faire capitalism of the early industrial era and from the national social welfare or corporate capitalisms of the recent past. It can briefly be described as a maturing transnational capitalism, which is abandoning social welfare benevolence, restoring laissez-faire principles on a global market scale, and converting nation-states into key vehicles of competitive and often repressive economic coordination. Central to this structural change is, of course, the global spread of industrialization by transnational corporations and transnational banks (private and public). This tendency is most advanced in the many right-wing authoritarian "National Security States" of the Third World. Authoritarian socialist states are also well positioned for integration into this new structure. So far, many First-World nations have been only moderately affected by the changing structures. They are moving away from Keynsian economic policies by tolerating wide margins of *unemployment, by attempting to reduce deficit

spending and social welfare programs, as well as by furthering the centralization of political power with new corporate/government linkages and growing roles for national security agencies. In the United States, the impact has been felt most in the fiscal crisis of the cities, especially in the Northeast quadrant—the nation's old industrial base. This sector has been thrown into competition with the new industrial base rising in the South and Southwest (the "Sun Belt"), a domestic echo of the global North-South tensions precipitated by the new mobility of capital.

Labor Concerns. In this new situation, labor movements become both a primary target of groups seeking to restructure society in a more exploitive and repressive direction and the immediate concern of groups seeking to defend the basic human needs and basic human rights of ordinary working people. Little by little, therefore, Catholic social activists have found themselves drawn back to labor concerns—beginning with the struggle of the farmworkers (*see* MIGRANT FARMWORKERS), the Farah boycott, and recently the organizing drive in the New South (centering in the textile industry, with the J. P. Stevens Co. as the main focus). But since the market is now transnational, the labor question also becomes international. The repression of labor movements in Third World countries like Chile, Brazil, or the Philippines is a global Catholic concern, increasingly seen as linked to the new mechanisms of capital accumulation on a global scale—mechanisms which are beginning to operate in the U.S. as well.

Possible Developments. Should a revival of Catholic labor concern be near, it will undoubtedly be marked by both continuity and discontinuity with the heritage of the past. Similar to the earlier period, a new wave of Catholic labor concern would probably stress the need for a new social order, the primacy of social and industrial unionism, the need to organize the unorganized, and similar issues. In contrast to the past, however, it might also highlight several new themes: a probing of humanistic resources from the socialist tradition; close linkages with community development movements, both here and in the Third World, particularly those doing community or consumer organizing among the urban and rural poor; economic conversion to peaceful production in place of a growing military-industrial complex; a central role for marginalized races and ethnic groups, and especially for women; and finally an analysis and strategy which will locate the capital/labor conflict within the international context of the maturing transnational market system.

Should the revival take this form, the development orientation of Catholic social action during the 1960s would be creatively fused with the labor orientation of the earlier Catholic style. The major question remaining, however, is what organizational form can be the carrier of such a new Catholic thrust.

Bibliography: S. AMIN, "Toward a Structural Crisis of World Capitalism," *Socialist Review* 5, n. 1 (1975). N. BETTEN, *Catholic Activism and the Industrial Worker* (Gainesville, Fla. 1976). J. GREMILLION, *The Gospel of Justice and Peace: Catholic Social Teaching Since Pope John* (Maryknoll, N.Y. 1976). J. HOLLAND, *The American Journey* (New York 1976). D. J. O'BRIEN and T. A. SHANNON, eds., *Renewing the Earth: Catholic Documents on Peace, Justice, and Liberation* (Garden City, N.Y. 1977).

[J. HOLLAND]

LAITY (THEOLOGY)

Vatican Council II's 1964 Constitution on the Church, with its unprecedented theological treatise on status, rights, and functions of the lay Christian (*Lumen gentium* ch. 4), was complemented one year later by two other extensive statements of particular relevance to a theology of the laity: the Decree on the Apostolate of Lay People (*Apostolicam actuositatem*) and the Pastoral Constitution on the Church in the Modern World (*Gaudium et spes*). The first elaborates upon the apostolic obligations incumbent on all Christians and describes in some detail the two areas in which lay persons, by reason of their Christian vocation, are called to extend the salvific mission of Christ. It states rather severely that any member of the Body of Christ "who does not work at the growth of the body to the extent of his possibilities must be considered useless both to the Church and to himself" (*Apostolicam actuositatem* 2), but in context the rigor of this statement is softened by the document's realistic understanding of the layperson's "possibilities." These are to be found both within the ecclesial structure and in the temporal order. Thus, within the ecclesial structure: "The hierarchy entrusts the laity with certain charges more closely connected with the duties of pastors: in the teaching of Christian doctrine, in certain liturgical actions, in the care of souls" (ibid. 24), and "the laity should develop the habit ... of bringing before the ecclesial community their own problems, world problems, and questions relative to man's salvation, to examine them together and solve them by general discussion" (ibid. 10).

But it is the temporal order, especially, in which lay Christians will find their distinctive apostolate, the various spheres of which are studied in both documents. Of singular importance for the theology of the laity is the frequent acknowledgment of the intrinsic value of the world and the autonomy of secular pursuits. Thus: "All that goes to make up the temporal order: personal and family values, culture, economic interests, the trades and professions, institutions of the political community, international relations, and so on, as well as their gradual development—all these are not merely helps to man's last end; they possess a value of their own, placed in them by God, whether considered individually or as parts of the integral temporal structure ..." (ibid. 7). *Gaudium et spes* reflects with enthusiasm on the layperson's dedication to the advancement of secular concerns as the fulfilment of God's will (*Gaudium et spes* 43). This vision must be shared by the entire ecclesial community; pastors are urged "to set forth clearly the principles concerning the purpose of creation" (*Apostolicam actuositatem* 7); the spirituality of the lay Christian must be rooted and developed in this conviction (ibid. 4). Thus a developing "theology of secularity" is intimately related to the theology of the laity.

See also MINISTRY, UNORDAINED.

Bibliography: J. METZ, *Theology of the World*, tr. W. Glen-Doepel (New York 1969).

[W. J. EGAN]

LAITY, FORMATION OF

Vatican Council II envisioned the laity as playing an essential role in the task of Christian renewal, the core-purpose of the Council. Its Decree on the Aposto-late of the Laity, which treated the laity's vocation, evangelical service and apostolic goals, emphasized the need for lay people to receive the appropriate training or "formation" for the work they do in and for the Church (*Apostolicam actuositatem* 28–32). In addition to the knowledge and skills necessary for a particular occupation, lay persons need theological education if their apostolic witness is to be intellectually supported by a sound understanding of religious truth (*Gaudium et spes* 62).

In the United States, the types and levels of lay theological formation are in fact quite varied. Since Vatican II many lay people have completed the requisite theological studies for full-time professional positions in the Church. Many parishes, for example, have instituted programs of religious education that are supervised by lay persons who have earned advanced degrees in theology. Similarly, many lay people are teaching religious studies at every level—from grade school to graduate school. In addition, lay persons serve as directors of liturgy and music in churches or work in administrative and research positions in church-related institutions. Correspondingly, the laity have countless opportunities to participate in various theologically oriented programs, ranging from the traditional to the innovative: adult education classes, retreat conferences, bible-study sessions, renewal workshops, ecumenical dialogues, charismatic meetings. In general, this recent interest in theological formation can be seen as one aspect of the laity's effort to deepen their understanding of the Gospel and to share the Christian message with others.

[J. T. FORD]

LAITY, PONTIFICAL COUNCIL FOR THE

The Pontifical Council for the Laity is a Vatican curial entity established definitively as Pontifical by Paul VI's motu proprio *Apostolatus peragendi* (Dec. 10, 1976). Previously, by the motu proprio *Catholicam Christi Ecclesiam* (Jan. 6, 1976), the Pope had tentatively established the experimental Council of the Laity along with the Pontifical Commission for *Justice and Peace, both under the direction of Cardinal Maurice Roy of Quebec. The Council was an attempt to implement Vatican Council II's Decree on the Apostolate of the Laity (*Apostolicam actuositatem* 26). It was also a papal follow-up to the encyclical *Populorum progressio* and attempted to integrate the laity into the Church's official organisms and activities. The goal was to reach the many well-intentioned Catholics in every country and in every milieu who are not yet fully aware of their responsibilities as Christians in the Church and world of today.

The Council's original presidential team consisted of two archbishops, a monsignor, a layman, and a laywoman. However, the various elements of the Curia found it hard to assimilate this new lay presence. In an address to the 6th plenary session (1972), the Pope felt constrained to remind members of the Council that it was not their role to issue directives, which was the sphere proper to the episcopate. He also defined their center of concern to be such issues as the evolution of the family cell and respect for life. Such matters as the proper management of social, economic, or political structures are the business of the Commission on Justice and

Peace. When the new and definitive structure of the Council was revealed in 1976, it had as its president Cardinal Opilio Rossi, and a presidential committee of three other cardinals—Ugo Poletti, Eduardo Pironio, and Joseph Schröffer. The vice-president was a bishop and the secretary was a monsignor. Thus no layperson would represent the Council in interdepartmental meetings of the Curia. The latest *Annuario Pontificio* (1978) includes among the Council's concerns observance of ecclesiastical laws which pertain to the laity. The Council must have a permanent committee for the family.

The Pope has encouraged the council to foster such clerically-inspired lay initiatives as sodalities, pious associations, secular institutes, and third order groups. The Council's principal document to date is its working paper on pastoral action in the university milieu (Feb. 1977). Despite its limited acceptance by traditional curialists, the Council is looked on as a hopeful sign by its mere existence. The members have contributed information for the activities of the Commission for Justice and Peace, whose activist bishops and priests have greater access to higher authority in the Vatican.

Bibliography: AnnPont 1978: 1049–51; 1481; ActApS 59 (1968) 416–417; 64 (1972) 678–681; 68 (1976) 696–700.

[E. J. DILLON]

LAITY, VOCATION OF

Questions having to do with the laity's vocation (8:330) have been raised frequently in the wake of Vatican Council II, occasioned both by positions taken in conciliar documents and by developing perceptions of what it means for the Church to be in the world. To what are lay people in the Church called? Who issues the call? How is the call answered? Such questions cannot be answered briefly; the intent here is to uncover and expose a principle that seems to become clearer as the Council recedes into the past and the Church moves into the future.

Laity in the Church. The term, "lay people in the Church," suggests two interpretive observations. The term may imply their belonging by plenary right to the People of God who constitute, in the era of the New Covenant, the Body of Christ. This is the emphasis in the Dogmatic Consitution on the Church, where the laity's share in Christ's priestly, prophetic, and royal dignities is described (*Lumen gentium* 34–36). Second, the term may raise the issue of how lay people are distinguished in the Church from those who, in modern times, are called "clergy and religious."

With reference to the first interpretation of the term, the relevant observation is that any and all ecclesial vocations are based on vital union with God through Christ. What makes the Church as such alive is its union in Christ and the conscious realization of this union gives impetus to every authentic ecclesial initiative.

The second interpretation of "lay people in the Church" as implying the distinction between laity and clergy or religious helps pinpoint the question, to *what* are lay people in the Church called?, for it triggers the further question: what should be seen as peculiar about the laity's realization of vital union with God in Christ?

If the above distinction (laity vs. clergy and religious) is somehow real and not merely a juridical fiction, the question is more than fanciful. A rational approach to it, moreover, involves seriously comparing the laity's

experience of God with that of the clergy and religious. And if the witness of lay people and of contemporary theologians is to be believed, the peculiar quality of the lay experience of God and his love consists in its being *secular*. Apparently this means that it is an experience that occurs in the world and through the world (where the term, *world*, stands for the temporal or, as we are wont to say, the natural order). The world so understood includes and is even centered in the way people realize and assimilate what is happening to them, especially in their relationships with other people, whether familial, social, economic, or political. Thus the lay experience of God means the realization of the divine presence in and through daily life—which consists in the temporal affairs of family and other more or less intimate communities, as well as transactions which are, on the surface, less human.

Again it should be noted that if the world, as it is marred by sin, be viewed as a whole, a great, even preponderant segment of the experience indicated could be described as dehumanizing and consequently as not at all a setting open to the experience of God. Yet the witness of those who are believers and who manifest the signs of vital union with God is that *everything* in the temporal order, whether it be the obvious source of joy and hope or the apparent source of grief, anxiety, and depression, bears the divine as immediately attainable in faith and as such is the way in which God is or can be experienced here and now.

This is a great mystery and is, therefore, patient of many and various descriptions, some of which would seem to border even on the denial that anyone can experience God in the secular milieu. Thus, for example, there are those who speak of the "death of God," and are referring to the experience of God's absence from the world (personal and/or external) in which, to all appearances, the evil of sin prevails (*see* ATHEISM).

Vatican II, the Lay Experience. Once the lay experience of God is certified, so to speak, the original question of the laity's vocation opens up somewhat. Throughout the Council's Constitution on the Church and Decree on the Apostolate of the Laity, where the laity's vocation is touched on, the constant directive is twofold: (a) to bring to men the message and grace of Christ; (b) to penetrate and perfect the temporal sphere with the spirit of the Gospel (see e.g., *Apostolicam actuositatem* 5; *Lumen gentium* 34, where the phrase is "[consecration of] the world to God"; cf. *Gaudium et spes* 43). Of these two tasks the second obviously corresponds to the experience focussed on here. When it is asked, therefore, to *what* lay-people in the Church are called, the response, in the first place—and this is close to being specific in some technical sense—is *to the experience of God itself in and through the world*. This experience is what consecrates the world to God; and by this experience the temporal sphere is "penetrated and perfected," because lay people are not separate from the temporal sphere as observers looking down on a scene that unfolds without their involvement. Rather they belong to the temporal sphere as agents, who by their very mode of being (i.e., in their experience as lay people) transform their sector of that sphere (private or public) into something which, of itself, it is not.

This is such a simple truth and appears so obvious upon reflection, that it might be dismissed as not even worth considering. Such is not the case, however, because from this principle, as a starting point, the vocation of the laity clearly emerges as consisting not merely in being competent in the world, but in discovering and experiencing God in whatever is done or undergone. Such a discovery, moreover, is what keeps the life of lay people on an even keel and is the seed of the peace which is to be shared with all men of goodwill. Where it is lacking it is evident that people are being overwhelmed by anxiety and depression.

Fundamentally, then, the vocation of the laity in the Church is an organic outgrowth of their being in the world as believers and, in that condition, discovering the mystery of God's gift of himself. What comes out of that experience may very well be regulated in the Church by those who exercise authority. Bishops, moreover, may invite and should encourage lay people to bring forward their wisdom and gifts for the work of bringing to people the message and grace of Christ (*Lumen gentium* 37; *Christus Dominus* 17). Laity may even share in aspects of the ecclesial ministry which, at least in modern times, have been reserved to the clergy. Such leadership and coordination of efforts on the part of the hierarchy, however, are secondary to what has been here described as the core element of the vocation of the laity: having, enjoying, and sharing the experience of God in and through what is, of itself, secular, albeit permeated with the presence of the God who wills to bestow himself upon man.

Bibliography: Y. M. CONGAR, *Christians Active in the World* (New York 1968). G. GUTIERREZ, *A Theology of Liberation* (Maryknoll, N.Y. 1973). G. PHILIPS, *Achieving Christian Maturity* (Chicago 1966). K. RAHNER, *Christian of the Future* (New York 1967).

[M. SCHEPERS]

LAITY IN CANON LAW

The substance and form of the revised canonical legislation on the laity approach their final version. Indications to date verify that the Pontifical Commission for the Revision of the Code of Canon Law has given rightful attention to Vatican Council II's Dogmatic Constitution on the Church, *Lumen gentium*, as the principally appropriate basis for the content of the coming law. The form of this law, particularly as to the number of canons, will be influenced no doubt by the specific content of the statutes and by the interrelating content pattern of the revised legislation (8:327).

By way of projection, there is the expectation of a group of canons in the new law which relate generally to the status of the laity as a distinctive body of persons already sharing the basic rights and duties of all believers in the Church. These basic rights and duties, rooted in the incorporation of all believers into Christ and the People of God through Baptism, will be described, delineated, and concretized in those more general statutes. In their content these norms will provide the frame of reference for other more specific canons affecting the laity's juridical status. That frame of reference will be the fundamental, Christian, individual equality of all believers in dignity and action relative to the over-all building up of the Body of Christ and the universal call to *holiness.

The more specific canons will relate directly to the laity's singular responsibility to foster the Kingdom of God, especially through the ordering of temporal goods in accord with divine purposes (*see* LAITY, VOCATION OF THE). In this regard the legitimate autonomy of the temporal order and the personal freedom and responsibility of the laity may well be affirmed, as also their right to acquire a fuller knowledge of the sacred sciences and to use this knowledge in their service to the Church (*see* LAITY, FORMATION OF). Explicit treatment may be given also to the laity's right and duty to be involved in the apostolate individually and corporately.

Another set of canons will consider "Associations of the Faithful." Statutes can be expected containing fundamental, juridical principles delineating the respective associations' relationship to ecclesiastical authority. The statutes will undoubtedly give evidence of the Church's due respect for the right of the laity to form associations. The principle of subsidiarity will certainly affect the content of the revised norms.

Bibliography: T. J. GREEN, "The Revision of the Code: The First Decade," *Jurist* 36 (1976) 399–404.

[D. E. ADAMS]

LAND REFORM

Within developing countries the poorest of the poor are to be found among rural, landless workers and sharecroppers, renters, or owner-operators with extremely small plots of land. Therefore social programs that are to deal effectively with the problem of severe poverty in these countries must somehow reach this rural labor force. Land reform is perhaps the single most powerful policy measure available for improving the economic conditions of these groups. The crucial role of this measure in achieving improved living standards for the rural poor is recognized in the strong statement on land reform contained in Vatican Council II's Constitution on the Church in the Modern World (*Gaudium et spes* 71).

The Economics of Land Reform. Land reform may be defined as the redistribution of land from the owners of large estates to rural laborers, especially those already working on the land. Sometimes the term "agrarian reform" is used to denote broader programs that include in addition a full set of complementary actions, such as the provision of seeds and fertilizers and marketing networks. Land reform may involve compensation paid to former owners or it may be without compensation. It may involve the creation of a new farm structure, based on numerous family farms of modest size, or may lead to a postreform structure of large cooperative or state farms. The political context will ultimately determine not only decisions on alternatives such as these but also whether land reform takes place at all.

Increasingly economists are viewing land reform as a nearly unique measure that can achieve two goals simultaneously: increased "equity" (or improved relative economic position of the poor) and increased agricultural production. The potential for raising agricultural production stems from the fact that large private estates tend to use their land less fully than do small family farms. Production per unit of land area is lower on large farms than on small, even after compensating for differences in land quality. Large owners may hold tracts of land idle or sparsely grazed because they view the land as a means of holding a real asset for portfolio investment purposes rather than for agricultural production. When inflation is rampant and securities markets are poorly developed, land is an especially attractive asset for holding wealth.

Even where large estates do farm the land, their economic incentives lead them to use their land less fully than small farms. They must hire workers at the going wage rate, while small family farms employ unpaid family members, who place a lower implicit valuation on their labor than the outside wage rate (because full-time wage employment is not available). Therefore labor is cheaper for small farms than for large estates. Also, owners of large estates implicitly view the cost of their land as low, while the cost of extra land is high to the small farm. The result of these divergences in prices of land and labor is that the large estate has incentives to use relatively little labor on its land, while small farms apply considerably more labor per unit of land available. Other economic forces, such as the exercise of monopoly power by large farms over local access to land and, accordingly, over the wage of labor, lead in the same direction. With a land-tenure structure composed of large estates alongside numerous small farms (called in Latin America the *latifundio-minifundio* complex), there results a waste of resources in the economy. Land lies underused in large estates; labor is crowded excessively onto the remaining land in tiny plots. Agricultural production therefore can be raised by restructuring the landholding pattern so that the excess labor on small farms and in the landless labor force can be combined with the underused land in large estates. In this process, rural employment will also rise because of the more intensive use of labor by small, postreform units.

Where the agrarian structure is based on tenant (sharecropper or rental) establishments dispersed uniformly into already small operational units (as in prereform Japan, Korea, and Taiwan), land reform consists of transforming tenants into owners. Although the size structure of actual operations changes little in this type of reform, there tends to be a positive effect on production, as ownership gives a more direct incentive to those who work the land.

One possible economic difficulty with land redistribution is that for some products there might be economies of scale, making large-scale production more efficient than small-scale. In fact, the notion of economies of scale has been cited as the basis for favoring as a postreform structure large collective or cooperative farms rather than moderate family farms. There is little evidence, however, in support of economies of scale in agriculture. Unlike industry, agriculture tends to be just as efficient on a small-scale basis as on the basis of large-scale operations. Heavy farm machinery that might require large-scale operations will usually be inappropriate for developing countries where labor is plentiful and capital scarce. Empirical studies of even plantation sectors, such as sugar cane, tend to show that small-scale production is just as efficient as large.

Land reform may reduce production temporarily if implementation is poor. Long periods of uncertainty prior to full implementation will discourage investment on those farms likely to be expropriated. Moreover, distribution networks for marketing and for farm inputs may be so disrupted as to require the government to provide new networks if production is to be maintained or increased. Furthermore, because poor farmers consume a higher share of their output, the marketable surplus available for use in the cities or for export may decline, although the rise to be expected in output will tend to provide a margin for increased on-farm consumption.

Land Reform in Practice. Historical experience with land reform provides some guide to its potential for improving the standard of living of the rural poor and, at the same time, increasing overall agricultural production. Perhaps the salient lesson from historical experience, however, is that thoroughgoing land reforms require an extremely powerful political force to overcome the opposition of existing rural interests. The cases of Japan, Taiwan, and Korea illustrate this point. Occupation authorities forced postwar land reform in Japan; in postwar Korea, land left by the Japanese was available for expropriation, and in Taiwan the regime from the mainland found it desirable to consolidate its rural support by distributing land from indigenous elites to rural workers. These three cases also illustrate the more equitable income distributions achievable through land reform, and the high levels of production and growth that may be reached with a small-scale agricultural structure.

In Latin America, Mexico (after the Revolution in 1910) and Bolivia (after the 1952 revolution) are the classic cases of sweeping land reform. Here, prereform structures were the *latifundio-minifundio* complex. In both cases, agricultural production eventually rose after reform, although severe political disturbances, uncertain application for reform in the initial years (especially in Mexico before 1930), and some diversion of production from the marketed surplus to on-farm consumption, caused an interim period of disruption in agricultural supply. Within the last decade relatively extensive land reform has been carried out in Peru and applied but later reversed in Chile. In these two cases it appears that the imposition of large state or cooperative farms as the postreform structure caused problems of poor incentives for workers, relative to what would have been achievable under a small family-farm organization for reformed agriculture. Elsewhere in most of Latin America (except for Cuba), land reform has remained largely on paper. In these countries, land reform is thwarted by political power of landed interests. In addition, technocrats often prefer the large "modern" farm over an administratively awkward reformed structure of small farms.

In the Middle East, land reform in Egypt essentially involved a transfer of rental income but little production change on the large irrigated farms; in Iran, a relatively extensive redistribution of land transferred income while at least maintaining production; but land reform in Iraq was less successful, in part because of a long period of uncertainty in its application. In sub-Saharan Africa the problem of land tenure has been primarily one of establishing land-use and ownership patterns that can circumvent the disincentives inherent in communal use of land, often on a nomadic basis.

The Potential. Fundamentally land reform is a social and political issue. It alters rural political relationships, in some cases terminating feudal practices that involve human bondage. In addition, however, land reform has major economic implications. With proper implementation, the economic benefits of land reform should be especially large in much of Latin America and sizable gains should also be possible in such Asian countries as India, Pakistan, and the Philippines. In sub-Saharan Africa, where land-tenure patterns have not evolved into a structure of private ownership of large farms alongside small establishments, land redistribution per se is less important than the establishment of workers' private rights to land as a means of raising incentives for modern practices. In all regions, and especially Africa, improvement in agricultural techniques has a high priority and measures for land reform must be accompanied by the adequate delivery of improved seeds, fertilizer, and other inputs in order to assure the full realization of potential output gains.

See also WEALTH, DISTRIBUTION OF.

Bibliography: R. A. BERRY and W. R. CLINE, *Agrarian Structure and Productivity in Developing Countries* (Johns Hopkins Univ. Press, Baltimore, 1979).

[W. R. CLINE]

LA PIRA, GIORGIO

Italian political leader, professor, and social organizer; b. Pozzallo, Italy, Jan. 9, 1904; d. Florence, July 8, 1977. One of the "little professors" who dominated the Christian Democratic Party's left-wing, Giorgio La Pira forged much of the theory of social Catholicism in postwar Italy. His unique personality, which generated considerable controversy, further enhanced the impact of his ideas. He was widely admired as a "lay monk" because of his ardent faith, ascetic manner, and incessant charitable projects, but his conviction and independence sometimes vexed his colleagues and enraged his opponents.

La Pira, who had been a professor of Roman law at the University of Florence since 1933, became a national political figure in the aftermath of World War II. Elected to the Constituent Assembly as a Christian Democratic representative, he served on the subcommission which drafted the constitutional provisions establishing the independence of the Church in Italy. Even the large Italian Communist Party supported this arrangement, in part because of La Pira's desire for collaboration. When in the midst of the Cold War, the Christian Democrats instead took a hard line against Communism, La Pira reminded his party of the need to establish a more just social order inspired by Christianity. To this end he advocated a "crusade on poverty." The efforts of the Minister of Labor, Amintore Fanfani, and his Undersecretary, La Pira, resulted in the enactment of a state housing program for workers. However, most of La Pira's proposals for social reform, like his concept of Europe as a third force in world affairs, found little favor among Christian Democratic leaders intent on increased productivity and closer alignment with the United States through NATO.

In 1951 he left the national scene to become Mayor of Florence, a post he held for ten of the next thirteen years. In that position he continued his dialogue with local Communist leaders, strove to improve the welfare of the lower classes, and promoted world peace even when his activities embarrassed his fellow Christian Democrats in the national government. He organized the International Congress for Peace and Christian Civilization and the Mediterranean Congress of Florence and served as the president of both groups. His commentary on John XXIII's encyclical *Mater et magistra* applauded its concern for social justice and peace. When the government banned the antiwar film *Non Uccidere* from the theaters in 1961, La Pira arranged to have it shown in a public building in Florence. This step led to a confrontation with the prefect, the chief of police, the minister of the interior, and the prime minister, in which the mayor prevailed by citing St. Paul, the Gospels, Thomas à Kempis, and the

Church Fathers. The ultimate embarrassment to his party resulted from La Pira's peace efforts during the Vietnam War. When he returned from a private visit to Hanoi in December 1965, his impressions were officially conveyed to Washington by Fanfani, who was Foreign Minister at the time. At the height of right-wing attacks on such attempts at mediation, La Pira criticized the U.S. Secretary of State in an interview which had been arranged by Mrs. Fanfani because she thought that her friend's eloquence and sincerity would convert his critics. Fanfani resigned because of the controversy, but La Pira characteristically never budged from his beliefs.

Bibliography: G. GALLI and P. FACCHI, *La sinistra democristiana* (Milan 1962). L. C. WEBB, *Church and State in Italy 1947–1957* (Melbourne 1958). F. R. WILLIS, *Italy Chooses Europe* (New York 1971). M. ROMANA DE GASPERI, ed., *De Gasperi Scrive* 2 v. (Brescia 1974).

[R. J. GIBBONS]

LAS HERMANAS

Las Hermanas (Sp., sisters) is a group of religious and lay women of Hispanic and non-Hispanic origin who actively minister to the needs of Hispanics and who together grow in awareness of their cultural and religious heritage in order to function better as Church for the good of all. In accordance with their Constitutions, Las Hermanas propose to be present to the constantly changing needs of the Hispanic people, and, as a group, aim to support each one of its members in appreciation for and an expression of their Hispanic culture and religious values.

Las Hermanas agenda has developed over an eight-year period. The founding meeting was held in April 1971 in Houston, Texas. Hermanas met for the Second National Assembly in Sante Fe, New Mexico in November of the same year. The Third National Assembly met near Chicago (a team-concept government was formed, replacing president, vice-president, secretary and treasurer). The Fourth National Assembly met in Los Angeles, California in August 1973 and in August 1974 the Fifth National Assembly met in Bonner Springs, Kansas. The Sixth National Assembly was held in New York City in 1975, the Seventh the following year in Denver, Colorado where Hermanas made a retreat with Gustavo Gutierrez, author of *A Theology of Liberation*, and the Eighth National Assembly was held in Detroit, Michigan in 1977. In 1978, Las Hermanas and PADRES are holding a joint retreat-assembly in El Paso, Texas, on the theme, "Together in Ministry."

Las Hermanas, as an organization, has a National Coordinating Team of three Hermanas elected for two years each and who represent the organization nationally. In each state or region where Hermanas live and work, there are state or regional coordinators, depending on the number of Hermanas, and locally Hermanas meet to respond to local needs. A national newsletter, *Informes*, keeps them informed of current issues affecting the Spanish-speaking across the country and Hermanas involvement in them. The ministry of Hermanas is expressed in present historical circumstances by an attitude of support and challenge among themselves and by action as an informing agent and pressure group among non-Hispanics. Goals are to engage Hispanic sisters in active ministry among Hispanics, to make more effective those non-Hispanics in the Hispanic apostolate, to encourage and help one another in the task of cultural identification, to share understanding and insights and to give supporting evidence of injustice when it becomes necessary. The aim of Las Hermanas is to share and to work toward a more just society, which, divested of some of its prejudices, will view cultural diversity not as a threat, but as a creative expression of human genius. To achieve this, an Hermana, as an individual or as a member of a local chapter, acts as an advocate for her people in her religious community and/or in her professional work. The national projects of the organization are the corporate response of Las Hermanas to their purposes and goals. Each Hermana shares in these projects through direct involvement or through monetary and/or moral support by formal membership in the organization.

National projects include: *Proyecto Mexico*, a scholarship program to assist Hispanic sisters exchange service positions in domestic work for a more direct involvement in the Hispanic apostolate; *Awareness and Cultural Workshops*, these are of several types designed to sensitize participants to the needs of the Spanish-speaking; *Leadership/Issue Discernment Workshops*, a process which facilitates the formation of a critical conscience in grass-roots communities; *Convivencias de promoción*, a spiritual development program of retreats, conferences, and in-service evangelization projects for parish workers.

Each Hermana determines the degree and mode of her involvement, but her fundamental stance and orientation is that of service, advocacy, and identification with the Hispanic people. Hermanas are presently involved in educational endeavors, pastoral ministry, ministry to the farmworkers and migrant workers, the undocumented, the imprisoned, half-way houses for women, unwed mothers, battered women, bilingual and bicultural programs, formation programs for Hispanics, hospital work, vicariates, administration of Spanish offices, and in many other fields related to the Spanish apostolate. Through this diversity the organization seeks to meet the varied needs of the Hispanic peoples in the U.S. Catholic Church. "United in Prayer and Action" is the motto of Las Hermanas; these women hope to help keep Christ alive in the modern day Catholic Church in the United States and hope to bring to light the deep faith of the Hispanic people who make up such a large portion of the American Catholic Church.

[M. CASTAÑEDA]

LATIN AMERICA, CHURCH IN

While the contributions of most of the Latin American Churches to Vatican Council II were slight, the Council's impact on them in both internal and external aspects was tremendous. These Churches had been somewhat isolated from the debate and questioning elsewhere which anticipated the Council and were thus unable to contribute in an active and informed manner to most themes under conciliar discussion. The Latin American Churches were, for the most part, still located in relatively stable societies in which the Catholic religion was assumed to be the faith of the overwhelming majority and where the State was expected to support the Church in its very broadly defined role. The Churches pursued such largely traditional roles as promoting an other-worldly, pietistic religion, administering large institutions such as schools for the upper classes,

and staunchly opposing Communism, thereby remaining in alliance with conservative political parties and groups.

Signs of Change for Social Reform. In a continent of tremendous disparities and variations, however, there were exceptions, most notably the Churches in Brazil and Chile where the theology of such European figures as Henri de Lubac, M.-D. Chenu, and Emmanuel Mounier found support and the sociological approach of Louis Joseph Lebret provided the data whereby the Church and its surrounding reality could be questioned. In these two countries a process of questioning was initiated in the 1950s. Modern theological themes were contrasted with a bleak social and economic reality, and decisions were made at the national level which sought to reorient the Church's role in society. Catholic Action played an important part in this reorientation, but whereas in Chile it evolved into the Christian Democratic Party, in Brazil it became more radical and founded Ação Popular (Popular Action). Sectors of the hierarchy in these countries also supported the Church's redirection by making national and regional statements in favor of such themes as agrarian reform, just wages, and structural changes in society and by actually assisting in the organization of movements to promote change. In both countries the official Church promoted rural education with the intention of giving peasants basic literacy in a manner designed to develop their consciousness as humans with rights. Further, bishops from Brazil and Chile were instrumental in founding CELAM (Latin American Bishops' Conference) in 1955 which, while beginning with a somewhat conservative orientation, did grow in its service function and was later to assist the evolution of other hierarchies. It must be stressed that these changes in the Churches in Brazil and Chile took place while both countries were functioning as open and democratic political systems.

Social Change in the 1960s. These two precursors were notable exceptions. Throughout the rest of the continent there was little questioning and even less activity before Vatican II. However, in the early 1960s it became apparent that ecclesiastical change was in the air. Latin America contains 40 percent of the world's Catholics and is peculiarly the Church's own "Third World," the inhabitants merely existing and in miserable conditions. In that era change had to come about in the face of the pressures of industrialization and urbanization; moreover, the example of the Cuban revolution, which by 1961 had turned Marxist, was a sobering perspective for both the Catholic Church and the U.S. government. The response of the latter was the Alliance for Progress as a support for those democratic governments which at that time were emerging from dictatorships. Vatican II, particularly in *Gaudium et spes* would have much to say to this process of change, and even before it convened Pope John XXIII addressed CELAM in 1958 (ActApS 50 [1958] 997–1005) and wrote a letter to the Latin American bishops in 1961 (ibid. 54 [1962] 28–31) in which he called upon the bishops to become aware of the situation on the continent and prepare the Church to assist in change. In this context, then, of general lack of preparation, tremendous demands, and the specific requests of Pope John the impact of the Council was bound to be important. As its spirit of dialogue, openness, collegiality, and emphasis on the laity spread throughout the continent, the

Church increasingly assumed a function of service and the institution everywhere began to take account of itself and its role in society. This process was heavily assisted from abroad in terms both of reflection and research, and was coordinated at the regional level through the structures and institutes of CELAM.

The more specifically socio-political thrust in this process of renewal and reform was given added momentum by Pope Paul VI in his 1967 encyclical *Populorum progressio*, which admitted the possibility of revolution, and by the letter of the Jesuit general, Fr. Pedro Arrupe, December 1966, encouraging Jesuits to become more involved in assisting change in society. Of no little importance was the response of the Churches in Europe and North America, which, as they too reflected on the messages of the Council, sent great numbers of personnel to Latin America with clearly defined commitments to assist the people. All of these trends promoted an awareness of the Church's past role and developed a commitment for it to act in multiple ways to change itself and society.

The Medellín Conference 1968. Undoubtedly the culmination of the questioning and the commitment was the Second General Conference of CELAM held in Medellín, Colombia, August 1968. The conference had been called at the request of Pope Paul and was attended by 150 bishops from all over the continent. It was, as Dom Helder Camara has stated, "the symbol of an effort to bring to fruition on our continent the great conclusions . . . of Vatican II." In the conclusions, published in English as *The Church in the Present Day Transformation of Latin America in the Light of the Council*, the bishops recognized that the structural underdevelopment of the continent was due to its condition of economic dependency. They further denounced institutionalized violence, demanded transformations, and committed the Church to participate in the liberation of the poor. The Churches in Latin America, then, had speedily come a long way from the pre-Council era. It would appear that they had come even further in view of the formulation of *liberation theology in this same period and the response to it not only of certain groups of priests and nuns but even of a number of bishops.

The *Medellín documents, however, did not necessarily imply subsequent action once the bishops returned to their dioceses, nor action by religious congregations still ensconced in their various institutions. The Colombian bishops did not adhere to the conclusions, issuing their own statement instead. As it became clear that many bishops were not actively committed to applying the conclusions of Medellín some of the priests' groups which had been forming since the Council and had by that time adopted the theology of liberation as a common framework, sought to pressure the bishops. ONIS, (*Oficina Nacional de Información Social*) in Peru and the Movement of Priests for the Third World in Argentina would appear to have had some success, but the Golconda Group in Colombia was isolated and groups elsewhere were smaller and less representative. The clergy and laity of Christians for Socialism in Chile attempted to push the Chilean bishops into a position close to the theology of liberation, but failed, whereas in Brazil several very progressive bishops took it upon themselves to promote very advanced positions. Throughout the continent, (with the glaring exception of

Colombia), however, a process of change and renewal did take place, even if not up to the expectations of the Medellín conclusions, and the Church's socio-political role was reflected upon and at times changed.

Reactionary Military Regimes. While the Church was assuming a progressive orientation the governments were moving in the opposite direction. In the early 1960s it appeared as though revolution in Latin America was a real possibility; but by 1967 and the death of Che Guevara this was largely ruled out. Early in the decade democracy also seemed possible and was for a time aided by the Alliance for Progress until 1965 and the American invasion of the Dominican Republic, at which point the commitment of the U.S. also disappeared. Increasingly throughout the continent the military took power. Beginning with Brazil in 1964, then in Argentina in 1966, Bolivia in 1971, Uruguay in 1972, and Chile in 1973 the generals assumed control, so that whereas in 1961 there was but one military dictatorship (Paraguay) in South America, by 1973 the only democracies left were Colombia and Venezuela. What is more, these were not traditional military regimes that Latin America had known on and off during one hundred and fifty years of independence, but something very different and pernicious. In the face of industrialization and urbanization, real or imagined guerrilla threats, and with support of the U.S., the military regimes everywhere developed doctrines of national security to justify their assuming total power and to eliminate threats through a type of internal war. They rely on their ideological formulations not only to categorize all dissent as subversion that must be expurgated but also to justify indefinite periods in power. The military dictatorships' concern is not to return power to democratically elected civilians, which they have fully purged anyway, but to maintain control and direct the processes of modernization as they see fit. In these endeavors they have received direct support from the U.S. government and ample resources, mainly from the Trilateral countries.

The implications for the Church, as it absorbed the social teachings of the Council and attempted to implement some aspects of the Medellín conclusions, are great. While it directed its attentions to miserable living conditions, unjust wages, and generally attempted to help the poor, the governments were increasingly closing off all channels of representation and criticism. Thus the activities of the Churches, or sectors of them, have increasingly been defined as subversive by national governments and there are now continent-wide military strategies to deal with "subversion in the Church." Aggravating this situation is the fact that as all channels of participation are eliminated, the Church, with its institutional basis, residue of legitimacy, and international links, is increasingly seen by the people as the only organization they can look to for support and assistance. It is difficult to imagine within the Churches a process equivalent to the military coup that could reverse the stated commitment to the people. In consequence it is most likely that tensions and conflicts with the governments will continue as long as these military regimes maintain their present colorations. There are, of course, varying degrees of implementation of the commitment to the people. An observer visiting Latin America today, ten years after Medellín, would find a high degree of implementation in Brazil, Chile, El Salvador, Nicaragua, and Paraguay and very little in

Colombia and Uruguay; the other countries are somewhere in between. Variations also exist within any one country. Even in Brazil, whose hierarchy maintains a generally high degree of unity on progressive positions, very advanced positions are assumed in such dioceses as Crateus, Goias, João Pessoa, and Olinda/Recife, and more conservative positions are taken throughout much of the South of the country, with the bishop of Diamantina, D. Geraldo de Proença Sigaud, publicly attacking some of his brother bishops as Communists. In conservative Colombia the bishop of Buenaventura is on a par with the progressive Brazilians as is the bishop of Riobamba in Ecuador. The Church most certainly is not a monolith either throughout the continents or within any one country. There is, however, a continuing tendency to fulfill the commitment of Medellín and this leads to conflicts with the militaries and other elements favoring the status quo.

Church-State Conflicts. It should be pointed out that there have always been conflicts between elements in the Church and governments in Latin America. But, whereas in the past these conflicts normally centered around anticlerical governments trying to strip the Church of inherited privileges, today they are between populist Churches ridding themselves of privileges and repressive governments desirous of church support for the status quo. As long as the Church does not question these regimes and the unequal distribution of power and benefits there are no conflicts. The Church, or elements within it, is attacked when it assumes progressive positions. The conflicts today are centered on three main areas or issues.

Human Rights. The general area of human rights is undoubtedly where the most publicized conflicts between Church and State arise. By definition, the military governments are *de facto* as opposed to *de jure* in their legitimacy and even when they have formulated their own constitutions, they still rely heavily on decree laws and other exceptional means of control. In ruling "above the law" they also without exception ignore the procedural defenses of human rights developed in the West during centuries and either engage directly in their violation or create the conditions whereby others can do so. In waging the internal war against those defined as subversives, the military regimes have created a climate where human rights are meaningless and torture and intimidation are standard. In most countries, therefore, flagrant violations of human rights in the form of torture and imprisonment without charges take place. Since Medellín and its recognition of the structures of institutionalized violence there is also a growing awareness in the Churches that human rights are denied by the mere fact that people are not allowed opportunities for anything more than survival, let alone self-betterment. This awareness was most dramatically signalled in May 1973 by the publication in Brazil of two regional episcopal statements to commemorate the 25th anniversary of the UN Universal Declaration of Human Rights and the 10th anniversary of *Pacem in terris*. These two statements, from the Northeast and the Center-West, emphasized the international and national causes for the marginalization of vast sectors of the population—a situation in which they could enjoy no human rights. The two aspects of violation of human rights—the unintentional through structures of violence and the intentional by means of torture—have been combined in national episcopal statements from Brazil in 1976 and 1977, indicating that there is now a high degree of unity within that hierarchy. A number of other hierarchies, including those of Argentina, Chile, El Salvador, Nicaragua, and Paraguay, have also made statements in 1976 and 1977 in favor of human rights and against their violation both in specific instances and generalized situations. What is more, in these same countries, groups and institutes, frequently ecumenical, have been formed to investigate specific instances of the violation of human rights and to provide assistance to those most directly concerned. The importance of the statements and activities is not only that it helps those immediately involved and indicates the option of the Church, but, just as importantly, that it calls international attention to these violations and may possibly lead to some positive pressures by foreign governments.

Land Use. An issue that is becoming increasingly important concerns the ownership and use of land. Since colonial times land has been extremely unequally distributed in Latin America. Today rapid increases in population and the pressures of modernization to exploit the land more fully in forms that are capital-intensive has caused an increased maldistribution of property and throughout the continent peasants are being forced off the land. This is especially serious as those investing in land are not middle-level farmers but rather large banks and corporations, national and international, who see its value mainly in growing export crops, the benefits of which are unlikely to reach those being forced off. What is more, the pattern of industrialization pursued all over the continent is capital-intensive so those losing the land are also unlikely to find jobs in the industrial sector. The result is that large percentages of the population are increasingly marginalized, even while the continent modernizes. The Churches in the countries of Brazil, Chile, El Salvador, Mexico, Paraguay, and Peru have spoken out in favor of the peasants and in Brazil, El Salvador, and Paraguay have established organizations to assist them in keeping their land. The Churches, in criticizing the implications of peasants losing their land, must refer beyond the laws of the governments, which permit and indeed encourage this process, to more abstract principles firmly based on Catholic doctrine (*see* LAND REFORM).

The Indigenous Peoples. Another issue of increasing importance that is related to the ownership and use of the land is that of the indigenous people found in about half the countries. The Church's historical role regarding these peoples has been ambiguous, but during the years since Medellín the role has been to assist the Indians to keep their land threatened by expanding modernization and preserve their cultures threatened by modern consumer society. These efforts are taking place mainly in Brazil, Mexico, Paraguay, and Peru and there have now been a number of continent-wide meetings of Indians supported by the Churches to develop strategies for general application.

Related Areas. In addition to these three predominant areas of Church concern and frequent conflict there are also the related ones of democratization, urban marginality, and the nature of education. Indeed, it is impossible to isolate the issues as they ultimately lead to the nature of the modernizing process being promoted by the military regimes on the continent. To criticize and to work in one area immediately leads to all the others; thus the Church's statements necessarily follow the path of the Brazilian ones in questioning the whole nature of modernization and its impact on the people. Since the military regimes have their goals clearly defined, they are not responsive to the prophetic criticism and questioning of the Churches, much less to their organizing the people for social change. Thus throughout the continent torture and repression have gone from the lower classes, to the middle classes, and entered into the Church with direct impact on laity, clergy, and even bishops. Either through direct government action or by unleashing a certain "white terror," priests have been killed in Argentina, Brazil, Chile, El Salvador, Mexico, and Panama quite specifically for their work with the people. Bishops have been threatened throughout, attacked and abused in Brazil, and seventeen were arrested in Ecuador in 1976. As the option to speak out for and work with the people has become more defined, the residue of legitimacy the military has been willing to grant the Church has also disappeared. It is now widely recognized that the subversive movement has even penetrated the Church.

The process of conflict that erupts with greater or lesser virulence in approximately half the countries takes forms ranging from veiled threats against individuals within the Church to out-and-out frontal attacks leading to exile or even death. Generally those military governments which align themselves clearly with the Western bloc of nations and continually refer to their defense of Western Civilization are unwilling to take on the Church as a clearly defined enemy as has been the case in the Eastern bloc. Rather, the attacks are from the edges and are normally subtle. There is, however, a process at hand whereby, as the roles of these modernizing states expand and conflicts continue, the Church's capabilities are being forcibly reduced to a point that little resembles the colonial legacy of structures running throughout all sectors of society. The Church loses its radio stations and newspapers, finds less and less support for such institutions as its schools, and sees increased taxes on what properties it has remaining. As this occurs its traditional resources for influence are diminished or eliminated and many in the Church are disturbed that it will lose all prominence and power. However, Medellín also supported the formation of *basic Christian communities whereby the Church decentralizes from diocesan and parish structures, and discards large institutions completely, to work more closely with people in their various strata. These communities are forming very quickly in Brazil, Chile, Honduras, and Paraguay and appear to be a structure that can finally penetrate most milieus in most countries. Thus as the Church loses its older encumbrances with their weight of history and finally squarely faces the shortage of clergy, it is forced to rely increasingly on the people. Rather than assume a monopoly over the population through the formalistic administration of Sacraments, the Church works more with the people in whose name it has spoken for so long.

Today more than ever before the processes of change in the Latin American Churches take place because of a dynamic within them as they recognize their future roles in these societies. Whereas the change initiated with the Council took place largely from the outside, today there is an indigenous process at work that seems likely to continue, irrespective of outside events.

Bibliography: T. C. BRUNEAU, *The Political Transformation of the Brazilian Catholic Church* (London 1974). CELAM, *The Church in the Present Day Transformation of Latin America in the Light of the Council* (Bogota 1970; USCC Publ. Office, Washington, D.C. 1970). E. DUSSEL, *History and the Theology of Liberation: A Latin American Perspective* (Maryknoll, N.Y. 1976). G. GUTIERREZ, *A Theology of Liberation. History, Politics, and Salvation,* tr. C. INDA and I. EAGLESON (Maryknoll, N.Y. 1973). D. LEVINE and A. WILDE, "The Catholic Church, 'Politics' and Violence: The Colombian Case," *Review of Politics* 39 (1977) 220–239. T. O'DEA, *The Catholic Crisis* (Boston 1968). T. G. SANDERS, "The Church in Latin America," *Foreign Affairs* 48, n. 2 (1970) 285–299. T. H. SANKS and B. H. SMITH, "Liberation Ecclesiology: Praxis, Theory, Praxis," ThSt 38 (1977) 3–38. B. H. SMITH, "Religion and Social Change: Classical Theories and New Formulations in the Context of Recent Developments in Latin America," *Latin American Research Review* 10 n. 2 (Summer 1975) 3–34. USCC *Latin American Documentation* (Washington, D.C. 1972–78). I. VALLIER, *Catholicism, Social Control, and Modernization in Latin America* (Englewood Cliffs, N.J. 1970).

[T. C. BRUNEAU]

LATIN AMERICA, EVANGELIZATION IN

Translating Christ's message of eternal love into the temporal world of Latin America is a challenge of unending complexity, as the region's bishops have conceded from colonial times to the present. That difficulty is no less real today than it was for the Spanish friars who accompanied the conquistadores five hundred years ago. They were beset then with problems of cultural differences, of popular religion, of dealing with political realities—the same problems, in somewhat altered form, which face Catholic evangelizers today. Modern evangelization problems in Latin America can be discussed from the historical standpoint, in light of recent ecclesial developments, and in the context of contemporary political events.

History. The evangelism which was the unifying principle of the early colonial years was immersed in the Tridentine, Counter-Reformation mentality of deep mystical faith, devotion to the Virgin Mary, sacramental perception of worship, and of realism towards Christ's passion and death. Such early missionaries as Fray Bartolomé de Las Casas, O.P. championed the cause of native Indians, and there were early evangelizing attempts—as at the Second Council of Lima in 1582–83—to make the strange Christian faith more comprehensible to the Indians by means of catechism translations and instructions in their native tongue. But many of the missioners from Europe failed to initiate such efforts, and the natural wall between native peoples and colonizing priests was never satisfactorily breached as far as the masses were concerned. When socio-political developments in the 1800s resulted in the stratification of class divisions, a break in Church-State cooperation, and the expulsion of Jesuit missioners, the gap was not only widened, but made almost permanent. The evangelization process faced staggering problems: dioceses were leaderless; priests were in short supply; many of the intellectually elite left the Church; and popular religiosity—in which church doctrine, often barely recognizable, was blended with elements of Indian and African worship traditions—emerged as a potent force among the people.

Not until the present century, did the Latin American Church—partly in response to a growing secularization—begin to grow in openness, foster international ties, and attempt to develop new models of evangelization. Despite its enthusiasm for reaching out to the poor and oppressed, however, it still faces many of the old problems. Not the least of them is a chronic shortage of native priests, resulting in a continued reliance on foreign missioners.

Ecclesial Developments. The bishops of Latin America had met jointly once before—in Rome in 1899, at the invitation of Pope Leo XIII—but their meeting in Rio de Janeiro in 1955 was of far more significance. It resulted in the formation of CELAM (Consejo Episcopal Latinoamericano), the permanent conference of bishops from Central and South America that would coordinate church activities in the years ahead. A second major result of the Rio de Janeiro meeting was a decision to explore ways of revitalizing the Church's presence throughout Latin America, leading in turn to the development of large-scale pastoral planning. (The forerunner of such long-range projects was the Movement of Natal, formed in Brazil's Northeast in 1948. It urged de-emphasis of the multiplication of traditional evangelizing efforts in parishes and schools in favor of creative, new pastoral activity geared to the masses.)

If the new evangelizing effort drew its framework from CELAM, it received its vitality from Vatican Council II and the second major conference of inter-American bishops, held in 1968 at Medellín, Colombia. Latin America had a relatively minor role in Vatican II preparations, but felt its impact with particular force. To a degree, the Council legitimized new Latin American developments, the roots of change reflected in the work of philosophers such as Brazil's Paulo Freire. The 1960s were also years of increasing secularization, which combined with the new sense of freedom in the Church to produce a crisis in the priesthood—which in turn slowed the progress of evangelizing efforts.

The Latin American bishops addressed these and a wide range of other problems at Medellín, a meeting planned by CELAM to adapt the teachings of Vatican II to Latin America. Pope Paul VI personally launched the conference, urging its 130 delegates to "effort, daring, and sacrifice." Telling them of his "exact awareness of this blessed hour," the Pope said the time and the place demanded "something new and something great." The Medellín conclusions had a decidedly liberal—if not revolutionary—tone, particularly in social and economic areas. In dealing with questions of evangelization (one unit considered evangelization of the masses, another evangelization of the elite), delegates urged a respect for popular religion as symbolic both of cultural strength and protest against oppression; called for strengthening the permanent diaconate and growth of *basic Christian communities (*comunidades de base*); sought renewed attention to pastoral planning directed to the entire spectrum of church membership. The presence of foreign missioners was welcome, delegates agreed, but they must conduct their evangelizing in accordance with local-Church planning.

The CELAM Study (1974). Under CELAM and other agencies, many post-Medellín meetings have studied the Church's evangelizing role, especially toward the masses of indigenous people. CELAM's major effort in studying evangelization was preparation of a study document for the 1974 *Synod of Bishops, convened on the theme of evangelization. The CELAM document recommended new attention to "the Easter mystery," since Latin American tradition placed such emphasis on

Christ's death. Previously, the document noted, Latin American evangelization had been focused on the cross; new attention must be given to "the joy of Christ's rising." Marian devotions— "one of the most striking traits of the Latin American soul"—must be maintained, said the study document, but should be redirected, purified where necessary, and incorporated into the center of the Paschal Mystery. In that way, the paper said, "Marian devotions can be made into a permanent source of evangelization."

The 1974 document urged that evangelization be permeated with a sense of history; that it attempt to discern the active presence of God in individual cultures; that it not stop at the level of proclamation, but move on to call forth an explicit faith response. There is an intimate relation between evangelization and human development, the document noted, but the latter "cannot be regarded as a substitute for the ardous task of explicitly evangelizing."

In discussing evangelizing agents, the CELAM study mentions use of modern means of social communication (the radio has been of special importance in reaching people in sparsely-settled, remote areas) and the basic Christian communities encouraged at Medellín.

Comunidades de Base. The spread of these communities has been one of the most dynamic features of Latin American evangelization. Nurtured in the *liberation-theology spirit popularized by the Peruvian, Gustavo Gutierrez, and utilizing the techniques of concientization advanced by Freire, the communities are simply small groups of people with some common denominator—people from the same neighborhood, most frequently—who meet informally with a discussion leader to reflect on their lives and their problems within the framework of Christian principles. They first emerged in three widely separated areas—Brazil, Chile and Panama—and by the late 1960s had spread throughout Latin America. They multiplied as rapidly as they did, according to Father José Marins of the Latin American Pastoral Institute at Medellín, "because Christians suddenly realized that they had to evangelize the people of their continent who had been baptized but had no real contact with sacramental life or the word of God, no community oneness."

Leaders of basic Christian communities may be priests or sisters, but far more often they are laymen, reflecting yet another phenomenon of postconciliar evangelization in Latin America—the rapid growth of new lay ministries. Catechists, animators, announcers of faith, coordinators of reflection groups—by whatever name they are known—they have emerged as a prophetic expression of the real faith of the people. These lay people—encouraged and trained, frequently, by foreign missioners schooled in the new approach—serve as spiritual catalysts within their communities: teaching, preaching, bringing the Sacraments, representing Christ. In some cases, Rome has been petitioned to permit their ordination—waiving celibacy requirements where necessary—but the petitions have been rejected on grounds of insufficient education and lack of theological training (*see* AFRICAN CHRISTIANITY). The wording of Rome's decisions in these matters, in turn, has tended to expand the gulf between the organized Church and the natives in the areas involved. "We are educated," they argue, "in our own culture."

Their cause is one of several taken up by progressive

elements, who charge that the Medellín spirit has been abandoned in favor of more traditional approaches to evangelization and other church concerns. One such voice is that of Dom Helder Camara, archbishop of Olinda-Recife, Brazil, known to the world for his efforts on behalf of the poor and oppressed.

Political Developments. Camara challenged CELAM to "transform Medellín into a source of inspiration" for pastoral action along social lines, and the CELAM document on evangelization spoke of a "yearning for integral liberation." But its approach was cautionary: it warned priests against letting the evangelizing mission be absorbed or supplanted by political commitments.

Some theologians want evangelization to take a direct political stance. If there is injustice at the levels of economics, politics, culture and learning, argues Segundo Galilea, "evangelization must fight to restore justice and put wealth, power and knowledge at the service of brotherhood. This is true liberation." José Comblin sees the Church's vigorous defense of human rights as "the very substance of the Jesus message." There had been earlier complaints that the Medellín spirit toward evangelization was being ignored in many areas of Latin America. As CELAM officials prepared for the third general conference of Latin American bishops—to be held in Puebla, Mexico, in February, 1979—tensions along these lines deepened, and complaints grew more open. The Puebla deliberations seemed destined to foretell much about the future direction of evangelization in Latin America—whether it will continue along the bold new paths charted at Medellín or return to more traditional lines.

Bibliography: J. M. BONINO, "Popular Piety in Latin America." LADOC 7, n. 5 (May–June 1977) 30–41. H. CAMARA, "Socio-Political Conflict in Latin America," LADOC 7, n. 3 (Jan.–Feb. 1977) 38–43. CELAM, *The Church in the Present-Day Transformation of Latin America in the Light of the Council* (The Medellín Conclusions) (Washington, D.C. 1973); Certain Aspects of Evangelization in Latin America. Suggestions for Reflections Offered by CELAM to the Forthcoming Synod. Prepared by CELAM's Theological-Pastoral Study Team, 1974 (unpublished). L. M. COLONNESE, ed., *Conscientization for Liberation* (Washington, D.C. 1971). J. COMBLIN, *The Meaning of Mission*, tr. J. DRURY (Maryknoll, N.Y. 1977); "The Church in Latin America after Vatican II," LADOC 7, n. 3 (Jan.–Feb. 1977) 1–31; "The Church and the National Security System," LADOC 6, n. 28 (May–June 1976) 1–23. J. J. CONSIDINE, ed., *The Church in the New Latin America* (Notre Dame, Ind. 1964). Encounter of the Church with the Indigenous People of Latin America, Pro Mundi Vita 52 (1974) special issue. C. A. FREI, "The Church We Want." *Cross Currents* 26 (1976) 3–10. S. GALILEA, "Evangelization of the Poor." LADOC 7, n. 5 (May–June 1977) 46–54. G. GUTIERREZ, *A Theology of Liberation*, tr. C. INDA and J. EAGLESON (Maryknoll, N.Y. 1973). G. MACEOIN, *Latin America: The Eleventh Hour* (New York 1962); *Revolution Next Door* (New York 1971); "Latin America in Search of Liberation," *Cross Currents* 21 (1971) entire issue. J. MARINS, "Basic Christian Communities." *Concilio* (Madrid) April, 1975. C. PALMES, "Basic Ecclesial Communities and Religious Leadership in Latin America," Pro Mundi Vita 50 (1974) 77–79. R. POBLETE, "Forms of Ministry in the Church of Chile," Pro Mundi Vita 50 (1974) 34–37. S. SHAPIRO, ed., *Integration of Man and Society in Latin America* (Notre Dame, Ind. 1967). USCC, *Priests and Religious for Latin America* (Washington, D.C. 1971).   [G. M. COSTELLO]

LATIN AMERICA, PONTIFICAL COMMISSION FOR

The Pontifical Commission for Latin America (CLA) was created as part of the Roman Curia by Pius XII, April 19, 1958, for study and unified action regarding Latin American Catholic life with its many challenges. The Commission was intended to foster collaboration among concerned curial departments. More recently its main purpose seems to be centered on the activities of

CELAM (*Consejo Episcopal Latinoamericano*) and of the various national episcopal conferences in order to assist with personnel and funds. By act of Paul VI, Nov. 30, 1963 the Commission was conjoined with the General Council for Latin America, an umbrella organization that includes representatives of CELAM, European and North American development agencies, and the International Unions of Superiors General. In July 1969 the Commission became part of the Congregation for Bishops. While the Church in Latin America is not classified as a mission Church, the Congregation for Bishops emphasizes the need of foreign personnel and resources. In addition, Paul VI's address to the fourth (1968) and fifth (1969) sessions of the General Council stressed recruitment of more priests, religious, and laity from Europe and North America for service in Latin America (ActApS60 [1968] 207–209; 61 [1969] 513–514). The CLA seems to have lost any leverage vis-à-vis CELAM; this was apparent at the Medellín Conference (1968), when the presence of Cardinal Zamore, then head of CLA, did not succeed in moving CELAM in the direction signaled by the Vatican (see MEDELLÍN DOCUMENTS). In some ways the Latin American bishops have attained an unprecedented autonomy and thus the CLA is left with a largely monitoring role.

Bibliography: AnnPont 1978:1064–1066; 1467. D. E. MUTCHLER, *The Church as a Political Factor in Latin America* (New York 1971) 104, 109–112, 117–118, 121–122.   [E. J. DILLON]

LATIN AMERICAN CONSULTATION FOR THEOLOGY IN THE AMERICAS

The Latin American Consultation for Theology in the Americas was organized by Sergio Torres, a priest from Chile presently working in the United States, and with the ecumenical support of various Churches. Its first conference was held in Detroit, Aug. 17–24, 1975. The 200 participants included theologians, social activists, and social scientists from the entire Western Hemisphere. The Consultation was planned to initiate serious dialogue between, on the one hand, the exponents of *liberation theology from Latin America and of *Black Theology, minority groups within the United States, namely Hispanics, Native Americans and women, and on the other hand, white theologians of the U.S. and Canada. The objective was to search out the meaning of liberation theology in the "First World."

One of the main challenges of the Consultation was the discovery of a common language which would make authentic dialogue possible among very diverse participants. Latin Americans were challenged by the Blacks to "put their own house in order" with respect to nonwhite minorities before they "preached" to North America. Latin Americans often expressed their fear that Black Theology had already bought into the U.S. oppressive system of economics. Both parties appeared as oppressors to the minorities, whose causes were relegated to a secondary agenda. North American establishment theology demonstrated no creativity in theology, in understanding history, or in appreciating the conditions of the people.   [V. ELIZONDO]

LATIN LITURGY ASSOCIATION

An organization founded in 1975 to promote the use of the Latin liturgy, *Novus ordo*, principally in the

United States. The group was formed in response to what seem to its founders to be widespread confusion about the Latin liturgy in America. Many people equate the *Latin Mass with the Tridentine Mass, superseded since Vatican Council II. Thus the use of Latin is either deemed to be impermissible or is associated with groups which repudiate the authority of the Council (*see* TRADITIONALIST MOVEMENT, CATHOLIC).

The Latin Liturgy Association calls attention to the Council's specific urgings that the Latin language not only be preserved in worship but that the laity be encouraged to learn the appropriate parts (*Sacrosanctum Concilium* 36), an exhortation to which Pope Paul VI also added his own voice (Paul VI MissRom). The Association is especially anxious to preserve the rich musical heritage of the Latin liturgy.

The first chairman of the Association is James Hitchcock, professor of history at Saint Louis University. Members of the advisory board include such prominent persons in the American religious and cultural scene as Michael Novak, Paul Hume, William F. Buckley Jr., John Lukacs, Clare Booth Luce, and Paul Henry Lang. The Association enjoys close relations with the Association for the Latin Liturgy in Great Britain, although there is no official tie between the two groups.

[J. HITCHCOCK]

LATIN MASS

The Constitution on the Sacred Liturgy of Vatican Council II expresses a twofold intention for the liturgical language of the Roman rite. The reform of the liturgy should both preserve the use of the Latin language and at the same time provide for celebration in vernacular tongues (*Sacrosanctum Concilium* 36). During the Council itself, Consilium, a study group of scholars, pastors, and bishops, was formed to carry out this legislated reform. Reviewing the voluminous liturgical research of the preceding half-century, the Consilium revised all liturgical books of the Roman rite, including the Roman Missal. This revision, spanning a decade, was limited to providing new Latin editions of all the rites; vernacular translations have been subsequently produced under the auspices of territorial episcopal conferences around the world (*see* INTERNATIONAL COMMISSION ON ENGLISH IN THE LITURGY).

The Consilium completed the new Order of Mass by 1969 and this new Latin Mass was approved by Pope Paul VI on April 3, 1969. In his Apostolic Constitution *Missale Romanum* the Holy Father stated that the new edition of the Latin Mass replaces the 1570 Missal of Pius V and that the so-called Tridentine Latin Mass is no longer to be used.

Although most Roman Catholics have celebrated the new Mass only in their own vernacular, the new rite can be and often is celebrated in Latin. The universal nature of the Roman Church often brings Catholics from diverse linguistic and cultural backgrounds together for common worship. A tradition of sixteen centuries of liturgical Latin provides such multilingual assemblies with a rich store of texts and music to unite the People of God in Eucharistic praise. The 1969 *Missale Romanum* comprises the best selection of such texts and Gregorian melodies.

A helpful and growing practice for local parishes is to teach the community simple Gregorian-chant settings for the Ordinary parts of the Mass, the *Kyrie, Gloria, Credo, Sanctus, Agnus Dei,* and *Pater Noster.* Occasional singing in Latin of such selections from the *Graduale Romanum* reminds the faithful of the universality of the Church and even predisposes them for international assemblies of Catholic worship. Choirs may enrich the Mass with other more challenging Gregorian or polyphonic settings for Latin texts.

Congregations which, in spite of the contrary legislation, insist on the permanent and unchanging practice of the Tridentine Latin Mass engage in religious nostalgia. The true catholicity of the Church is a universality in history, and anthropologists observe that the great rituals of world religions inevitably evolve and change in the course of history.

The only provisional exception for the continued use of the Tridentine Mass is stated in an October 24, 1974 letter from the Congregation for Divine Worship. Elderly, infirm priests who might experience difficulty in observing the new Order of Mass may use the *Missale Romanum* of Pius V, i.e., the Tridentine Mass, when no congregation is present.

See also CATHOLIC TRADITIONALIST MOVEMENT.

Bibliography: PAUL VI, MissRom. BCL Newsletter, 8 (1972) 7, 8; 10 (1974) 3; 11 (1975) 1, 9, 10.

[J. T. KELLEY]

LAVANOUX, MAURICE ÉMILE

Artist, editor, critic; b. New York, N.Y., June 10, 1894; d. New York, N.Y., Oct. 21, 1974. He received a bilingual education, studying in Montreal (1906–11), at Columbia University (1912–17), Atelier Laloux, Paris (1919–20). A volunteer for military service in the French army in World War I, he worked in offices of Gustaf Steinback and of Maginnis and Walsh, Boston, as draftsman and researcher, acquiring vast experience in the planning and construction of churches. In 1928 he invited a group of architects, artists, and clergymen interested in liturgical arts to several meetings at Portsmouth Priory, Newport, R.I.; from this emerged the Liturgical Arts Society. In 1932 he launched *Liturgical Arts Quarterly* with Harry Lorin Binsse as managing editor. Lavanoux served as editor and secretary until the magazine was discontinued in 1972 for lack of funds.

During the 40 years that he published the *Quarterly* Lavanoux became internationally respected among artists and scholars associated with the liturgical movement. He lectured on church art and architecture in universities and seminaries throughout the U.S., Canada, and in Europe. His world travels were constantly geared to the study of new developments in the field and the establishment of personal contacts that might enrich editorial contributions to the *Quarterly*. It gradually took on an international character that provided leadership throughout the Church. Early, too, Lavanoux associated his work with the ecumenical movement, and he became highly respected in Protestant and Jewish circles.

While almost all of his publishing energies were focused on the *Quarterly*, a considerable opus in itself, Lavanoux also edited A. Henze and T. Filthout, *Contemporary Church Art* (1956) and contributed an important introduction to A. Christ-Janer and M. M. Foley, *Modern Church Architecture* (1962). He served on juries for competitions sponsored by the American Institute of Architecture, the Cardinal Lercaro Awards, Columbia and Princeton Universities' schools of architecture. He also served as adviser to architecture students at Columbia. He was consultant on many ecclesiastical buildings and contributed articles to many magazines.

Though Lavanoux lived and worked in financial conditions that most people would reckon to be penury, thanks to an uncompromising attitude on principles, he was occasionally the recipient of honors. In 1967 he was made a Knight Commander of St. Gregory; in 1968 he received an Honorary Citation of membership from the American Institute of Architects; he received honorary doctorates from St. Vincent's College (Latrobe, Pa., 1946), Georgetown University (1964), St. Bonaventure University (1968), Loyola University (New Orleans, 1971), and The Catholic University of America (1972). While his years of enforced retirement, following the discontinuance of the *Quarterly*, were fraught with disappointment, he continued to work for the improvement of standards in liturgical art and assumed the editorship of *Stained Glass* magazine. He also threw himself more energetically than ever into the work of the Contemporary Christian Art Gallery (New York City). Following his quiet death at home, tributes appeared in many journals, both religious and secular. While many stressed that Vatican Council II and its Constitution on the Sacred Liturgy (to which he had substantially contributed) had put the seal on his life's work, he himself had felt that the work was just beginning. His last editorial in *Liturgical Arts Quarterly* reaffirmed that "this is not a dream. It assumes sincerity, humility, cooperation, a knowledge that can overcome invincible ignorance." Those long associated with Maurice Lavanoux felt that these words were truthfully autobiographical.

[C. J. MCNASPY]

LAW, CHRISTIAN

The Gospel made flesh in Jesus Christ and proclaimed by his Church is completely opposed to a legalism that would impose intolerable burdens on men and identify righteousness with fidelity to external observances. Yet this Gospel is by no means antinomian or lawless. Indeed, lawlessness (*anomia*) is portrayed in the New Testament as an inner hardening of heart preventing entrance into the Reign or Kingdom of God (cf. Mt 7.23; 13.41; 23.28, 33; 2 Cor 6.14; 1 Jn 3.4). Far from annulling God's law, the Gospel makes it even more urgent and compelling. The Christian is "subject to the law of Christ," literally *in the law of Christ* (1 Cor 9.21), for it is this law, "the law of the Spirit of life in Christ Jesus," that has set the Christian "free from the law of sin and death" (Rom 8.2).

Classical Theology. The principal, defining characteristic of the law of Christ is that "it is the very grace of the Holy Spirit, given to those who believe in Christ"; in this "the whole power" of the law of the Gospel consists (Thomas Aquinas, ST 1a2ae, 106.1). Thus the law of the Gospel, Christian law, is both first and foremost a law of life. It communicates to men the inward power to be virtuous (*ibid.* 107.1), that is, to love the good and to order their loves so that they love the Good, God, above all (cf. ST 1a2ae, 55–67; 2a2ae, 23). This law is thus a law of life-giving love and love-giving life, making friendship with God, and through him with all men, possible.

The life- and love-giving law of grace is given in and through the humanity of the incarnate Word. The grace springing forth from Christ is thus fittingly mediated in an incarnate way, through the Sacraments, and it finds concrete, visible expression in an incarnate way, through deeds or human acts. Thus the law of the Gospel does enjoin external works that are necessarily required by the inner life of grace-filled friendship with God and it does likewise prohibit external works or deeds that are by their very nature opposed to this kind of life (ST 1a2ae, 108.1). One who believes in Christ, one who has become one body with Christ through Baptism (cf. 1 Cor 6), is inwardly moved by the Spirit of life and love to express the love of God and neighbor by freely and joyously choosing to do what this love demands and to refrain from doing what this love proscribes (cf. ST 1a2ae, 107.1 ad 2 "per se in ea inclinantur, non quasi in extranea, sed quasi in propria"; 108.1 ad 2; 108.2).

Augustine and Aquinas both teach that the Sermon on the Mount "contains all that a Christian needs to conduct his life." The Sermon does more than propose a set of ideals, for through it Christ bids and empowers his disciples to order their desires and loves so that they may act in loving obedience to God (Augustine, *De Serm. Dom. in Monte*, 1, 1. PL 34, 1231; St. Thomas, ST 1a2ae, 108.3).

Contemporary Theology. The foregoing account of the Gospel and Christian law, rooted in the classical theological tradition of Augustine and Aquinas, is undergoing serious rethinking today. Some contemporary writers, such as Herbert McCabe, while acknowledging the legitimacy of the term "law" as applied to the Gospel and admitting the validity of absolute prohibitions, suggest that perhaps the meaning of the Gospel of grace can be communicated more efficaciously today by speaking of it as a new "language" or way of understanding and expressing ourselves than as a "law," with the legalistic connotations that this term possesses.

Others, for example Charles Curran, express concern that this more classical way of viewing the law of the Gospel is too unhistorical, i.e., too little concerned with the historical and cultural circumstances in which both the Gospel and theology emerged and also too little concerned with the eschatological tension of the Christian life and the reality of sin.

Another group of contemporary authors, e.g. Richard McCormick, Josef Fuchs, Bruno Schüller, believe that no concrete external deeds are of such a nature that they are intrinsically opposed to the inner demands of the Gospel of grace—a belief that seems to be expressed clearly enough in Aquinas (cf. ST 1a2ae, 108.2 along with 1a2ae, 20.2). This group is sharply challenged by other contemporary writers, principally Germain Grisez and John Finnis. The debate here, although principally conducted in discussions over the meaning of *natural law, has obvious implications for a proper understanding of the the Gospel and Christian law insofar as there can be no genuine contradiction between the two but rather a deepening of the understanding of natural law in the light of the Gospel.

Despite these contemporary concerns, theologians still concur with Aquinas in holding that the Gospel, the law of grace, the law of Christ for his faithful, is first and foremost a law that gives life and love and inwardly transfigures and transforms human life.

Bibliography: C. CURRAN, "The Relevancy of the Gospel Ethic," in

Themes in Fundamental Moral Theology. (Notre Dame Ind. 1977) 5–26. J. FINNIS, "Natural Law and Unnatural Acts," HeythropJ 11 (1970) 365–387. J. FUCHS, "The Absoluteness of Moral Norms." Greg 52 (1971) 415–458. B. HÄRING, *The Law of Christ* v. 1 (Westminister, Md. 1961) 252–266. G. GRISEZ, "Toward a Consistent Natural-Law Ethics of Killing," *American Journal of Jurisprudence* 15 (1970) 64–96. H. MCCABE, *What Is Ethics All About?* (Washington, D.C. 1969); in England published as *Love, Law, and Language* (London 1968). R. MCCORMICK, "Notes on Moral Theology," ThSt 33 (1972) 68–86; 39 (1978) 79–104. W. E. MAY, "The Moral Meaning of Human Acts," HomPastRev 78 (Oct. 1978) 10–21. W. KASPER, "Law and Gospel," SacrMundi 3:297–299. B. SCHÜLLER, "Direkte Tötung-indirekte Tötung," *Theologie und Philosophie* 47 (1972) 341–357. Thomas Aquinas St., ST 1a2ae, 106–108; also *In Hebraeos* 8, lect. 2; *In Romanos* 6 lect. 3.

[W. E. MAY]

LAY MINISTERS (RITE OF INSTITUTION)

By the apostolic letter, *Ministeria quaedam*, issued motu proprio Aug. 15, 1972, Pope Paul VI reformed the discipline of liturgical ministries for the Latin Church. On the same day, in another apostolic letter, *Ad pascendum*, the Pope set down norms for the order of deacon, transitional and permanent. New rites were prepared by the Congregation for Divine Worship for the institution of readers and acolytes, for the admission to candidacy for ordination as deacons and priests, and for the commitment to celibacy.

Ministeria quaedam. This motu proprio abolished first tonsure, the minor orders of porter, lector, exorcist and acolyte, and the order of subdeacon, and created two lay liturgical ministries (no longer designated as "minor orders"), reader and acolyte. Entrance into the clerical state is joined to ordination to the diaconate (Paul VI MinQuaedam I,II). The reasons for this reformation of the Church's ministries were many: (a) "while the Second Vatican Council was in preparation, many pastors of the Church requested that the minor orders and subdiaconate should be reexamined"; (b) many of the tasks and functions of the minor orders had fallen into disuse; (c) "the general and orderly renewal of the liturgy" required the restructuring of the ministries necessary for a reformed liturgy (ibid.). The ultimate rationale was stated in the Constitution on the Sacred Liturgy: "in liturgical celebrations each person, minister or layman, who has an office to perform, should do all, and only, those parts which pertain to this office by the nature of the rite and the principles of the liturgy" (*Sacrosanctum Concilium* 28). The offices to be preserved from the ancient minor orders and from the subdiaconate were the ministries of the Word and of the altar. However the door was left open for the creation of new ministries: "Besides the offices common to the Latin Church there is nothing to prevent episcopal conferences from requesting others of the Apostolic See" which those conferences judge necessary or useful for local reasons (Paul VI MinQuaedam IV). Other ministries might be the office of catechist (especially in the light of the revised Rite of Christian Initiation of Adults), exorcist, porter, and a ministry of music.

Elements of the Rite. The rite of institution of readers and the rite of institution of acolytes are similar. Readers and acolytes are instituted by the bishop, or the major superior of a clerical religious institute, during Mass or during a celebration of the Word of God after the Gospel is read (Institution 1). The structure of the rite is as follows. (1) Calling of the Candidates: the candidates are called by name, and each answers: "Present." (2) Instruction: after the Homily, the bishop instructs the candidates on the nature of the ministry into which they are about to be instituted. (3) Invitation to prayer and the Prayer: the bishop invites all present to pray for the candidates; all pray briefly in silence. Then the bishop continues by calling upon God to bless the candidates who have been chosen for the ministry, and to strengthen them in the functions they are about to undertake. (4) Institution: each candidate then goes to the bishop and is handed the sign of his ministry, a Bible in the case of readers, a vessel with bread or wine, in the case of acolytes. If the institution takes place at Mass, the Mass continues as usual. When acolytes are instituted, some may assist at the altar in the Preparation of Gifts. Readings and Psalms are provided in the rite for use in the celebration of institution.

Bibliography: *The Roman Pontifical: The Institution of Readers and Acolytes* (Washington, D.C. 1976). Bishops' Committee on the Liturgy, *Study Text III. Ministries in the Church: A Commentary on the Apostolic Letters of Pope Paul VI "Ministeria Quaedam" and "Ad Pascendum"* (Washington, D.C. 1974).

[J. A. GURRIERI]

LAY MISSIONARIES

There have always been lay missionaries in the U.S. Catholic Church mission effort (8:577). Until rather recently, however, there was little organization or recorded history of these lay missionary endeavors. Usually the lay missionary was a person with a specialized competence, e.g., as a doctor, nurse, engineer. He or she was engaged on an ad hoc basis with a particular mission society of priests or sisters. After Vatican Council II a new orientation and impetus were prompted by the Decree on the Apostolate of the Laity and the Decree on the Missionary Activity of the Church. Although before Vatican II there had been some organization of the lay apostolate, e.g., Catholic Action, YCS, YCW, the specific movement of lay organizations in mission work was initiated through the inspiration of these documents.

During the 1960s, a great many lay missionary groups were founded: Catholic Lay Mission Corps (Texas), Association for International Development (New Jersey), International Catholic Auxiliaries (Illinois), Women Volunteers for Africa (Washington), Frontline Apostolate (Ohio), etc. The first recorded groups (1961) were the Society of Our Lady of the Most Holy Trinity, which was founded by the Reverend James Flanagan in Santa Fe, New Mexico, and Extension Lay Volunteers, founded in Kansas City by the Reverend John Sullivan (now bishop of Kansas City-St. Joseph, Mo.) which began work in Oklahoma and later extended its activity throughout the country. In the early 1960s, the Papal Volunteers for Latin America (PAVLA) was founded and was viewed as the counterpart overseas of Extension Volunteers, in a Peace Corps-Vista analogy.

Such groups differed in many ways. Some were founded by priests or religious societies; some were composed of lay people only. Some were mission-sending organizations; others were mission centers or mission-related organizations that received personnel. Some groups worked only in this country; others were engaged in mission work overseas.

Most of the above-mentioned groups suffered a severe decline or ceased to exist by the end of the 1960s. Many reasons for the decline are given. Often the missionary clergy and religious did not offer firm moral support to the laity. The lay people were viewed as offering inexpensive labor or as potential vocations to the priesthood or the religious life. There was little screening and little or inadequate preparation of the volunteers. At times, job descriptions were unclear; consequently, the receiving missionaries, unable to perceive the need for the particular talents of the new personnel, did not know how to utilize them. Also, in the official Church, there seemed to be a lack of interest. Confusion reigned as to the role of the laity in mission. The integration of evangelization and *human development was not universally accepted. Furthermore, the motivation of the volunteers may have left something to be desired. Many seemed more interested in social and political involvement than in witnessing to the Good News of Christ. Thus the rejection of colonialism and U.S. domination in many parts of the world caused numerous lay missionaries to feel unwanted and disillusioned.

In the 1970s a reappraisal and reorganization began. In 1973, *International Liaison (U.S. Catholic Coordinating Conference for Lay Volunteer Ministries), which had been organized in 1963 as an office of the Archdiocese of Newark, expanded its operation to serve as a referral center on a national basis. It was incorporated in 1975 and formed a coalition of the major sending and receiving groups of lay missionaries in the United States. In 1977, the office was moved to Washington, D.C., and affiliated with the USCC as the official center for lay missionary activity of the U.S. Catholic Church.

Today the Church has matured and is more prepared than it was earlier to welcome the active participation of the laity in world mission. Mission societies, such as Maryknoll, have developed sophisticated programs to recruit, screen, and train lay personnel. The new vision requires a word about terminology. Lay people in mission prefer not to be referred to as "lay missionaries," because the expression could seem to indicate their role to be inferior to that of the religious or priest missionary. They see themselves simply as missionaries, without the need to categorize. Even the word "volunteer" is not entirely acceptable. How can people be said to "volunteer" when they do what they are called to do by reason of their Baptism? Again, many do not like the expression "lay ministry," as it connotes an imperfect clerical state, they much prefer to speak of their "services."

The role of mission is to witness to the Church's total concern for the entire person; the Christian message is intrinsically tied in with temporal as well as spiritual salvation. Hence the laity are not to replace the religious or clergy in mission, but to complement them, as they exercise their skills and training in teaching, agronomy, cooperatives, medicine, and so on. Today the status of lay people is recognized and valued in its own right within the context of bearing Christian witness, either by direct evangelization or by the utilization of technical expertise and skills.

See also LAITY, VOCATION OF; MISSION (NEW TRENDS).

[A. BELLAGAMBA]

LAY SPIRITUALITY

The progression of ideas in this article is linked by an underlying coherence: the Church, seeking to renew itself, encourages its members to reflect upon the orientation that the Holy Spirit gives to the inner, divine life in the faithful. Significant statements contained in Vatican Council II's Constitution on the Church in the Modern World and in the Decree on the Apostolate of the Laity guide this synthesis (see also *Sacrosanctum Concilium* 26–40; *Christus Dominus* 16–18; *Gravissimum educationis* 3, 5, 7; *Ad gentes* 15, 21, 41).

Unity in Diversity. The Christian is defined as one born "from above," for everything begins with the new birth of water and the Spirit (Jn 3.5). Through Baptism the believer is called to a superior way of living, to a life according to an inner, divine, and vivifying principle, the Holy Spirit. This is the baptismal reality of every Christian. In this sense, there is only one spirituality in the Church, one founded on the πνεῦμα, the Holy Spirit.

The source of all forms of Christian living is the Spirit of Christ, Christian spirituality being, as L. Bouyer specifies, the study of the reactions that the objects of faith raise in the religious consciousness (Bouyer, *History* 1, viii). There is only one life by the Spirit, although innumerable manifestations of his inspiration, e.g. such recent expressions of the spiritual life as the *secular institutes, the communities of Charles de Foucauld, the *Missionaries of Charity of Teresa of Calcutta. In the differentiation of unity lies the symmetry and splendor of the twelve-gated heavenly Jerusalem. The Holy Spirit reveals the power of his oneness in the diversity of tongues (Acts 2) and the multiplicity of charisms (1 Cor 12. 4–7). Origen says repeatedly that there must be various viewpoints in the Church so that the fullness of the one Word can blossom forth in human form. The divergence of roles corresponds to God's allotment of his gifts. The Spirit who "breathes where he wills" (Jn 3.8), "singles out his gifts to each one according to his own will" (1 Cor 12.4–11; cf. Eph 4.11–13). The varieties are thus determined from on high and have as sole objective the unity of the Body of Christ. Through different charisms, "one and the same Spirit" builds up the whole Christ (cf. 1 Cor 12.11). To some contemporaries, so easily convinced that the Holy Spirit is at work in them as individuals, it is difficult to explain that he is active in them for the building up of the whole Church. This same situation St. Paul had to face with the Corinthians. From the reception of these very gifts, which have as source the Holy Spirit himself (these *charismata* are thus really *pneumatika* according to Paul), arises for each believer the duty to use them for the benefit of the Christian community (see *Apostolicam actuositatem* 3).

The fundamental problem confronting Paul in Corinth was that of division in the Church. Today's essential task is to comprehend the meaning of the unity of the Mystical Body. This requires first discovery of the unifying role of the Spirit within the lives and in the particular functions of all the members of Christ's Body. Dissonance has no place in the Church. For failure to coordinate various functions causes division in Christ himself (1 Cor 1.13) into whose Body all were baptized in "one Spirit" (1 Cor 12.13). Until the Spirit is present and active in each member, he cannot reside in all fullness within the Body of Christ (cf. 1 Cor 3.16–17).

The basic model prior to all differentiation is that of the Church herself as the "Bride without blemish or wrinkle," chosen by Christ for himself, typified in Mary, the immaculate mother and bride. Mary combines all states of life: virginity and motherhood, the married and religious, the lay and the priestly. She, who knew how to probe the Word of God (cf. Lk 2.51) revealed the attitude that underlies all individual charisms. Her "Behold the handmaid of the Lord" becomes the expression of the all-renouncing and thus redeeming love modelled on that of Christ, the Servant of God. In her, the Church contemplates the ideal she herself "desires and hopes to be" (*Sacrosanctum Concilium* 103). In the unceasing stream of the one spirituality in the Church, lay spirituality corresponds to the particular Pentecostal mission that incorporates the laity into the work of salvation. Christ in his glory bestows offices, charisms (Eph 4.7f.), gifts in proportion to faith (cf. Rom 12.3–8). For all must "practice the truth in love, and so grow up in all ways into Christ, who is the Head; by him the whole Body is fitted and joined together, every joint adding its own strength"; it is in the building up of this Body "in love," that constitutes the work of the Holy Spirit (Eph 4.15–16).

Vocation of the Baptized. What is unique about Christianity, compared to other religions, is that its Head is forever present and living: Christ is "the true vine" (Jn 15), that fullness of Being to whom the believer is organically united. Grafted into Christ at Baptism, the believer cannot live or die except *in Chrsito Jesu* (cf. Rom 6.4–5). On these grounds every mature Christian has the strict obligation to attain some awareness of this religious reality.

The term "lay" does not mean "unsacred." Derived from the Greek substantive *laos*, people, it is found in the Scriptures as a designation for the People of God: *laos theou* (Congar 3–27; Tucci). In the baptismal perspective, the lay vocation has both a negative and a positive aspect: renunciation of Satan and commitment to Christ. Christ alone can free a person from the spirit of evil, yet he will not do so unless the believer is willing to cooperate. To renounce Satan, "all his works and empty promises," is to renounce all temptations of the "flesh" inasmuch as disoriented instincts desensitize a person to the call of the divine Spirit. It means to renounce every good thing that is a potential "idol," that could take the inner place reserved only for the supreme good, God himself. The baptismal renunciation is, thus, the acceptance of the Cross, which must henceforth shape the Christian life, whatever form it takes (Bouyer, *Introduction* 163–184). Acceptance of the Cross is the precondition for positive commitment to Christ. Commitment is the response to the Revelation of the divine love that created man, that saves, and that never ceases its search and summons. Commitment becomes the means of thanksgiving for this very love.

The two aspects mentioned constitute the foundation of the spiritual ascension of the baptized, called to become the temple of the Holy Spirit and invited together into a Mystical Body, the Church, which is the participation in the society of the Holy Trinity, built by the Spirit, who is the mutual Love of Father and Son.

It is a dogmatic certainty that human action can be sanctified: "Whatever you do," says St. Paul, "do it in the name of our Lord Jesus Christ" (Col 3.17). The Apostle who invented the formula, *in Christo Jesu*, expressed the conviction that every act must be done in union with Christ. He thus left the series, *compati, collaborare, commori, con-resuscitare* . . . meaning that the Christian becomes the extension of Christ (on *in Christo* and verbs with the Greek prefix, *sun*, see

Cothenet). In consequence, the state of life and type of work the believer selects provide him with the cross, uniquely his own, and the activity he is destined to supernaturalize and to take as his share in the work of transfiguration by the Holy Spirit. By the acceptance of the Cross and participation in the creative work of the Spirit, the baptized prolongs mystically through time the mystery of Christ. For the Passover of Christ is not the final act of the incarnate mystery; it begins his work and opens a way. The redemptive act inaugurates the Christian experience. The vocation of the layman cannot be one of creativity only, the Cross being only for the consecrated few. Every Christian life has a redemptive role; "it fills up" what otherwise would be lacking to the Passion of Christ, for his Body which is the Church (Col 1.24). And having "put on Christ," having received the gift of the Spirit, every believer has been transformed into "a new creation" (cf. Gal 6.15; 2 Cor 5.17). The mystery of Christ does not excuse from participation in his Passion; on the contrary, in the union of the Christic Body, it anticipates the "hour" of the believer and renders it efficacious.

At Baptism Christ, the archetype of all Christian existence, gives a particular "form" to the life of all the faithful (Rom 6.3–12). The *forma servi* (Phil 2.7 and 8; cf. Mt 20.27–28) becomes the *forma gregis* (1 Pt 5.3 and 5). The Christian commitment is a call to give one's life for Christ; to accept the last place in foolishness and contempt, as "the scum of the earth" (1 Cor 4.10–13); that self-giving alone becomes the fountain of spiritual fecundity in the world. At Baptism, in the waters of the world, the baptized's life becomes an endless immersion in Christ. But it is in the Eucharist that Christ's Spirit invades and gives this form to all Christian living. For it is a *communio*, an exchange of life surrendered, of divine life shared.

The Spirit of holiness that Christians receive in the Sacraments leads them not only to a constant struggle in the world against the spirit of evil, but to overcome evil with good (Rom 12.21). By their baptismal vocation, the Christian laity are a "substitute for Christ" (Cerfaux 88) where Christ most needs to be, if he is not there yet or is there no longer.

Called to Holiness. The Vatican II declaration that the root reason for "human dignity lies in man's call to communion with God," affirms the excellency of his spiritual nature (*Gaudium et spes* 19; cf. *Lumen gentium* 39–42). For man was destined to a life of friendship with God. Centuries before the messianic age, Israel treasured the prophecies of Jeremiah (31, 31–34), Ezekiel (36, 23–37, 14) and Joel (3.1–5). At Pentecost, this hope fulfilled becomes the reality of the New Covenant. Faithful to his promise, God pours the power of his Spirit, who in transforming the heart of man, creates a new heaven and a new earth. The Apostles' experience of this gift marks the beginning of Christianity.

At present, when so much is expected of everyone on the level of professional performance, the Church acknowledges the urgency of bringing "all men to full union with Christ" (*Lumen gentium* 1). For all men have received the means to live beyond themselves. Baptized "in one Spirit," they are called to form with Christ "one Body" (1 Cor 12.13). With his all-surpassing perfection Christ, in whom dwells "the fullness of divinity," (Col 2.9) fills the whole Body with the riches of his glory (cf. Eph 1.18–23; *Lumen gentium* 7; Pius XII *Mystici Cor-*

poris 208). God told Moses that the Israelites had to be holy: "for I, Yahweh your God, am holy" (Lv 19.2). It was a requirement based on the very relation established between the community and the Lord. Christ, "the holy one of God" (Jn 6.69; cf. Lk 1.35; 4.34; Mk 1.24; Acts 3.14; 4.27) calls everyone to the perfection of the Father: "You therefore are to be perfect, even as your heavenly Father is perfect" (Mt 5.48). The Church reminds us that his call is addressed to all believers, at all times, with no less impact or emphasis: "Christian holiness is not a privilege for the few, but the duty common to all; it falls not only upon those who have been endowed in a special way with spiritual qualities and divine gifts, but binds every Christian. For God himself has imposed this command: 'Be therefore perfect as your heavenly Father is perfect'" (Pius XI 288).

St. Paul reveals that the presence of the Holy Spirit in the Christian demands holiness. Therefore, in his eschatological teaching to the converts of Thessalonika, he explains that it is by the Spirit and the effect of saintliness he brings about in their lives, that they will distinguish themselves from those who do not "know God" (1 Thes 4.1–8; cf. Eph 1.4);the Parousia and the necessity for vigilance are the background of this, the Apostle's first letter.

In Pauline terminology, perfection is more a pursuit than a goal (cf. Phil 3.15; Huby 34). It is "the perfection that comes through faith in Christ" (Phil 3.9), a quality that must imbue all Christian behavior, because it means acting in accordance with God's will (Col 4, 12). "To make every man perfect in Christ" (Col 1.28), is St. Paul's purpose (De la Potterie and Lyonnet 197–219). Christian perfection cannot be reduced to mere ethical behavior. Holiness is primarily a call to share in the transcendence of God, his "otherness," which is intimately related to his glory. For this holiness, according to Rudolf Otto, there is only one appropriate expression: *mysterium tremendum* (Otto 12). He explains that this complex term derived from the Hebrew qādôsh (in Greek ἅγιος; in Latin *sanctus*), constitutes "the real innermost core" of every religion, "and without it no religion would be worthy of the name" (Otto 6).

In the Christian perspective, through sin man became alienated from God; the divine image in him was distorted. Thus, from ch. 3 in Genesis the whole movement of Revelation is oriented towards restoring man's original and existential union with God. This is accomplished as a mystical union with Christ in which he becomes the source of divine life communicated through his Spirit. In salvation history, God unfolds the "hidden purpose of his will," his design concerning human destiny, the assimilation of man into the stream of his own triune life. Thus the Constitution on Divine Revelation begins with the reaffirmation that through Christ, the Word made flesh, man has access to the Father in the Holy Spirit and comes to share in the divine nature (*Dei verbum* 2; cf. Eph 2.18; 2 Pt 1.4). Christ, the divine Word, not only unveils these expectations but fulfills what God has promised. Through his Spirit, Christ accomplishes now in believers what he did for mankind on the Cross.

The spiritual doctrine of St. Paul is briefly stated in Romans: "Through his resurrection from the dead (Jesus) has been constituted Son of God with power according to the spirit of holiness" (Rom 1.4; see Procksch). In his letters, St. Paul repeatedly affirms that the risen Christ, eminently holy in his glorified humanness, works powerfully through his Spirit to justify and to make holy all those who believe that God raised him from the dead: "who was given up to death for our sins and was raised to life to justify us" (Rom 4.25). This doctrine is echoed in Eucharistic Prayer III: "Father, all life, all holiness come from you through your Son, Jesus Christ our Lord by the working of the Holy Spirit." The onward, irresistible thrust of the Spirit, leads men to holiness. Through the Sacraments, the Eucharist in particular, the Spirit interiorizes more and more the saving action of Christ. Yet its perception is not easy, for the believer "walks by faith and not by sight" (2 Cor 5.7). The Christian proceeds in the chiaroscuro of faith toward the full radiance of God's glory.

Through his own religious experience Paul believed that the eschatological age had come; that life in Christ meant life in the Spirit. The old order, that of the Law of Israel, was gone. It had been replaced by what Paul called "the law of the spirit of life in Christ Jesus" (Rom 8.2). This gift of God is, far more demanding than the Law of Moses, for unless the "law of the spirit" is interiorly assimilated, it is without effect, dead. The Spirit must give a "form" to the character and conduct of the believer. St. Paul therefore does not hesitate to identify "power of the Spirit" with the "strong convictions" of the faithful at Thessalonika (1 Thes 1.5).

Those of the New Covenant encounter God as they make their own dispositions of Christ on the Cross. Only then, do they experience the power of the Spirit of the Risen Lord (Phil 3.10) and are guided inwardly by his Spirit (cf. Gal 5.23–26). Unlike Moses who, reflecting God's glory, had to cover his face, they "with unveiled faces," fully alive with the inner presence of the Spirit, are called to contemplate the glory of the risen Christ. Today, when the fascination of the world blinds, the need is to contemplate the glory of Christ, the Lord. This contemplation brings about transformation into the likeness of God, the radiance of the Christian's whole being with the glory of God that shines on the face of Christ (cf. 2 Cor 3.18; 4.6). If "the Spirit bears witness that we are children of God" (Rom 8.16), the entire life of the Christian must become the expression of this reality which the world cannot see, but which the Christian truly is (Rom 8.29 and 1 Jn 3.2).

In the course of history the Church has been animated by the holiness of those members who, following their respective type of Gospel perfection, have contributed to its splendor. By their lives they witness to the immeasurable love of Christ "whose power, working in us, can do infinitely more than we can ask or imagine" (Eph 3.19–21).

The Layman: Sign of the Sacred in the Secular City. The Church states that believers today bear some responsibility for the spread of atheism, because they lack an awareness of their faith. Their very competence in a profane skill renders this deficiency in the religious sphere more flagrant. Christians contribute to atheism, Vatican II declares, because they "conceal rather than reveal the authentic face of God and religion" (*Gaudium et spes* 19).

To discover the essence of God, one must know the totally disinterested love (cf. 1 Jn 4.8) proper to the invisible Father. "Christ died for us while we were still sinners..." (Rom 5.8). Only the Cross reveals the transcending love of God. Now the Holy Spirit "pours out into our hearts" this unique "*agapē* of God" (Rom 5.5). The Spirit can give the love which is "beyond all knowledge," for he is the principle of divine love and divine life. The theological distinction between Giver and gift comes in later Augustinian doctrine, yet the elements for such development are clearly present in St. Paul. This love is the condition of all other gifts, for it is the communication and foundation itself of the Spirit. The self-forgetting *agapē*, which Paul eloquently describes, corresponds equally to the heart of Christ and to the Christ-love in the heart of the believer (1 Cor 13.4–7). Thus, at the outset of the Christian era, this love was the sign by which Christ's disciples could be recognized (Jn 13.35). St. Paul presents the self-sacrificing love of Christ as the key to the whole redemptive mystery. For it is the only way to encounter God in the unique way He has chosen to encounter man (Ahern 210).

As modern man masters matter, he experiences a thirst to discover his own depth. He aspires to attain an infinite dimension, a fulfillment. As he denounces pharisaism or legalism, he searches for a transparency in the Christian heart that would disclose the love of Christ at work. In the mature Christian divine love becomes the sign of salvation accomplished. It is the mystery to discover; it should be perceived as that living love, supreme gift of the Spirit, which not only transforms the believer into a child of God, but changes his environment into a divine milieu. The role of the layman is precisely to be a sign of this *agapē* and to let it diffuse its radiance in the world.

Transformation. "In the human nature which he united to Himself," Christ, the divine Word, redeemed man and transformed him into "a new creation" by His own death and resurrection (*Lumen gentium* 7; Rom 6.4; cf. Gal 6.15; 2 Cor 5.17; see Rey). Through the Spirit, "the pledge of our inheritance" (Eph 1.14), man is renewed from within. This renewal St. Paul reveals as a transformation *in Christo Jesu* (cf. Eph 4.23–24). It is the experience which consists in the emptying of human consciousness and the effusion of the Holy Spirit. In this sense, one can indeed define the Holy Spirit as: "Christ assimilable" (Maranche 38).

St. Paul tries to explain: while the "outer man" fails, the spiritual "inner man" grows through grace and "is renewed day by day" (2 Cor 4, 16–5, 5; Eph 3.16; Rom 7.22; cf. J.-B. Colon, DTC 11:2406). It is the transition from the psychic to the spiritual man; he who lets Christ, the life-giving Spirit, act within himself (1 Cor 15.45–49; cf. 1 Cor 13.11). It is the "spiritual" man who is, for the apostle, the "mature" Christian. Transformation, according to St. Paul, begins with one's judgment (Eph 4.23; Rom 12.2). The more it is renewed in the image of the Creator, the more the believer progresses in "true knowledge" and attains the wisdom that Paul describes in his first letter to the Corinthians (ch. 1 and 2; cf. Col 3.10). This special gnosis is revealed through the Cross, by the Spirit. For the Spirit searches the depths of God and penetrates the heart of man. The transformed Christian thus attains a new vision which corresponds to the *sophia en musterio*. He is able to discern God's Spirit and interpret spiritual realities, for the Spirit has formed in him "the mind of Christ" (1 Cor 2.12–16; cf. Rom. 8.27). To "Christ's mind" consequently, corresponds a different scale of values; the excellency of spirit over instinct, the eternal over the

transitory. Death represents a gain for anyone to whom "to live is Christ" (cf. Phil 1.21; Gal 2.19–20). To lose one's life for the Gospel, is to save it. The committed Christian lives beyond himself, "in Christ." For this reason at all times in the world, he is both a source of attraction and a stimulating irritant.

His life, bearing testimony to this *agapē*, reveals therefore, the achievement of an ideal toward which every one secretly aspires. In the secular city, where society slides into spiritual decadence, it points to a transcendence, to a call from above. As a sign of the sacred, the vocation of the layman is linked to the gift of grace. But it depends on him to remove every obstacle so that his life becomes the sign of the continuing transfiguration by the power of the Spirit. Precisely because the believer holds within himself the mystery of this sacred and living Love, in the world, he can never be of the world. In the words of the prayer of the primitive Christianity of the *Didache*, quoted recently by Karl Rahner, the faithful lives "letting-the-world-go-by" so that grace may come (Rahner 79). The "mature" Christian thus heralds here and now the presence of the divine. The layman must live this mystery of the divine love in the spirit of humility and must diffuse it in the spirit of boldness.

The above are the general underlying principles of a spirituality for the laity. There are excellent studies relative to these particulars: the married state, the perspectives of holiness within one's work, and "the sacrament of the brother" (Bouyer, *Introduction*; Teilhard de Chardin; von Balthasar). In all instances, the believer makes visible something of the reality of Jesus Christ and of his Kingdom in heaven. He is the sacred sign of the Father's love that cannot remain closed, but is open and passing into the world. No one has ever seen God, but through his Spirit, he pours his own love into us. Thus abiding in us; perfecting and radiating charity within us (cf. 1 Jn 4.12). In this manner, with his own love, God progressively, slowly, creates the Christian anew into "a man after (his) own heart" (cf. Acts 13.22–24; 1 Sm 13.14). He alone is able to build a society of divine life and divine love. Only he can prepare the Kingdom of God by engaging in temporal affairs and, as *Lumen gentium* states, "by ordering them according to the plan of God" (*Lumen gentium* 31). For he carries out his responsibilities "in such a way that they . . . always start out, develop and persist according to Christ's mind" (ibid.).

Apostleship. The vocation of the baptized is not only a call to holiness, but also to apostleship. The theme of Vatican II's Decree on the Apostolate of the Laity is that, endowed with the Spirit of the risen Christ they must participate in the saving mission of the Church itself. The fundamental law of the apostle will always be: "the power of God deployed in weakness" (2 Cor 12.9–10); the disciple perceives ever anew the experience of the fragile vessel that holds and discloses a treasure (2 Cor 4.7). Having received from the Spirit the love of Christ poured into the heart, the believer acquires an awareness which consists more in knowing how one is loved by the other, than in knowing the other that one loves (cf. Gal 4.9). Progressively, he discovers the vast dimensions of divine love ("the breadth and the length, the height and the depth of the love of Christ" Eph 3.18 and 19). Thus, the world becomes his mission. This was the mystery of the division of fire on the day of Pentecost. And the same Spirit that scatters, unites. For the Spirit creates the community or *koinōnia*. This summit of the experience of faith is realized especially through the Eucharist. Those partaking of the one bread are assimilated into the one Body of Christ; by drinking the blood of Christ, they drink his own Spirit (1 Cor 10.16 and 17). In the Eucharist, having "tasted to their full of the paschal mysteries," the faithful are inspired to become "of one heart in love" (*Sacrosanctum Concilium* 10).

When the work which the Father had given the Son to do was accomplished, the Holy Spirit was sent that he might sanctify the Church and that all believers would have access to the Father through Christ in one Spirit (cf. Eph 2.18; 4.4; 1 Cor 6.17 and 12.13). This growth and this unity are foretold in the Lord's words concerning his death on the Cross: "And when I am lifted up from the earth, I shall draw all men to myself" (Jn 12.32).

This is how the Kingdom of God, although hidden, grows through the power of the Spirit. When Christ was glorified, he communicated his Spirit, the power that would enable his disciples to subject all created things to the Father "so that God may be all in all" (cf. 1 Cor 15.27–28). The laity, through their labor in profane fields, must in consequence contribute not only to the moral improvement of mankind, but to the liberation from oppression, the establishment of peace and the promotion of culture (*Gaudium et spes* 53–62). For all secular spheres are God's dominion. The call of the laity is to imbue human activity with spiritual values to prepare the soil for the seed of the Word of God. This is their participation in the third office of Christ: his Kingship (cf *Lumen gentium* 31; Congar). All creation, must be delivered from its slavery to corruption (cf. Rom 8.21). Then it will be in the hands of men, provided they are one with Christ, for Christ is God's (cf. 1 Cor 3.23). The future of the universe is therefore, closely linked to the reign of charity. The transformation of the world depending on the indwelling mystery of divine love in the faithful. This explains why the layman, citizen of heaven, is not asked to flee from the world. Indeed, because he is a citzen of heaven he is capable of bringing the world to its destiny.

In the theology of St. Paul, the redemptive work is one of a new creation (Benoit 303) where Christians, conformed to the likeness of the Son, the firstborn of many brothers, (cf. Rom 8.29; Col 3.10–14), in turn, make up that "new man" which represents all renewed and reconciled humanity that Christ "recapitulates" (Eph Ch. 1–3; cf. Col 3.10–11). Christ, the fullness of the Godhead, fulfills himself in the Church, his body (cf. Eph 1.23). All the faithful grow into one holy temple where God lives in the Spirit (Eph 2.22). In this way, the believer is called to form the "perfect Man" that must attain his adult age with the fullness, *plēroma*, of Christ himself (cf. Eph 4.4–16).

The Fathers of the Church, faithful to the doctrine of the Apostle, present a synthesis of the experience of faith in the building up of "this Man spread about over the whole earth" (Augustine, *Enarr. in Ps. 122.* PL 37, 1650). Henri de Lubac writes that in this "perfect Man," this "New Man," the chef d'oeuvre of the Spirit toward which tend the convergent efforts of all, consists the essence and the last word of the Mystery of Christ (de Lubac 13).

Conclusion. In the wasteland of secularism, the layman witnesses to the new, eternal life acquired by Redemption and to the creative and fulfilling power of divine love. The Spirit does not lead to a passive pietism. Constantly drawing on the source of grace, the layman grows in holiness as he cooperates with the will of the heavenly Father and reveals through his earthly activities the love with which God has loved the world. "Filled with the Spirit" (Eph 5.18), the faithful penetrate ever more deeply into the Mystery of Christ and are committed more intimately to the building up of his Body. As sign of the transcendence of divine love, the layman on his earthly pilgrimage to eternal beatitude, represents the new creation. By the charity which "abides" (1 Cor 13.13), the faithful build on earth the total Christ, who already reigns in heaven. This is the viewpoint in the concluding paragraph of *Lumen gentium* on the laity: "Each individual layman must be a witness before the world to the resurrection and life of the Lord Jesus, and a sign of the living God. All together, and each one to the best of his ability, must nourish the world with spiritual fruits... They must diffuse in the world the spirit which animates those poor, meek, and peace-makers whom the Lord in the Gospel proclaimed blessed.... In a word: 'What the soul is in the body, let Christians be in the world'" (*Ep. ad Diognetum* 6, ed. Funk 1,400) (*Lumen gentium* 38).

Bibliography: Biblical and patristic studies: J. B. BAUER, "Die Wortgeschichte von 'laicus'," ZKathTh 81 (1959) 224–228. P. BENOIT, *Exegèse et théologie* 3 (Paris 1968). L. BOUYER in *History of Christian Spirituality*, v. 1, *The Spirituality of the New Testament and the Fathers* (New York 1978). L. CERFAUX, *The Christian in the Theology of St. Paul*, tr. L. SOIRON (New York 1967). P. CHANTRAINE, "Le Suffix grec '-ikos'," *Études sur le vocabulaire grec* 3 (Paris 1956) 97–171. E. COTHENET," "Sacred Scripture: St. Paul," in E. MALATESTA, ed., *Imitating Christ*, v. 5 of Religious Experience Series (St. Meinrad, Ind. 1974) 18–26. J. HUBY, *Saint Paul, Épîtres de la captivité. Verbum salutis* 8 (rev. ed. Paris 1947). M. JOURJON, "Les premiers emplois du mot 'laïc' dans la littérature patristique," LumV 65 (1963) 37–42. I. DE LA POTTERIE and S. LYONNET, *The Christian Lives by the Spirit*, tr. J. MORRISS, (Staten Island, N.Y. 1971). O. PROCKSCH, ἀγιωσύνη Kittel ThW (Engl) 1:114–115. B. REY, *Crées dans le Christ Jésus. Lectio divina* 42 (Paris 1966). H. STRATHMANN and R. MEYER, λαος Kittel ThW (Engl) 4:29–57. G. THILS, *Christian Holiness*, tr. J. L. FARRAND (Tielt, Belgium 1961).

On "Unity in Diversity": H. URS VON BALTHASAR," The One Spirituality of the Church," TheolDig 10 (1962) 189–195. L. BOUYER, *Introduction to Spirituality* (Collegeville, Minn. 1961). L. BOUYER, et al., *History of Christian Spirituality*. v. 1, *The Spirituality of the New Testament and the Fathers* (New York 1978). L. COGNET, *Introduction à la vie chrétienne* 3 v. (Paris 1967). U. GAMBA, *Spiritualità del Concilio* 2 v. (Rovigo, Italy 1974). J. GAUTIER et al., eds., *Some Schools of Catholic Spirituality*, tr. K. SULLIVAN (New York 1959). J. MACQUARRIE, *Paths in Spirituality* (New York 1972). G. PHILIPS, *Role of the Laity in the Church*, tr. J. R. GILBERT and J. W. MOUDRY (Chicago 1956). K. RAHNER, *Theological Investigations* 3, tr. K. and H. KRUGER (Baltimore 1967) and 7, tr. D. BOURKE (New York 1971). C. DUQUOC, ed., *Spirituality in Church and World. Concilium* 9 (New York 1965) esp. F. VANDER BROUCKE, "Spirituality and Spiritualities," 45–60. C. DUQUOC, ed., *Spirituality in the Secular City. Concilium* 19 (New York 1966). H. VAN ZELLER, *The Current of Spirituality* (Springfield, Ill. 1970).

On the vocation of the baptized: F. X. ARNOLD, "Bleibt der Laie eine Stiefkind der Kirche?" *Hochland* 46 (1954) 401–412, 524–533. L. BOUYER, *Introduction to Spirituality* (Collegeville, Minn. 1961) 163–184. Y. M.-J. CONGAR, *Lay People in the Church*, tr. D. ATTWATER (Westminister, Md. 1965), bibliog. 3–27; "Laïcs et mission dans l'Église," LumV 63 (May–July 1965) and 65 (Nov.–Dec. 1963) entire issues. K. MCNAMARA, "Aspects of the Layman's Role in the Mystical Body," IrTheolQ 25 (1968) 124–143. G. PHILIPS, "La vocation apostolique du laïc," *Revue ecclésiastique de Liège* 44 (1957) 321–340. R. SPIAZZI, *La Missione dei laici* (Rome 1951). A. SUSTAR, "Der Laie in der Kirche," in J. FEINER, J. TRÜTSCH, and F. BOCKLE, eds. *Fragen der Theologie heute* (Einisiedeln 1957) 519–548. R. TUCCI, "Recenti pubblicazioni sui 'laici' nella Chiesa," *La civiltà cattolica* 109.2 (1958) 178–190.

On the Call to Holiness: R. OTTO, *The Idea of the Holy*, tr. J. W. HARVEY (New York 1969). PIUS XI, Homily, May 20, 1934, ActApS 26 (1934)

287–289. PIUS XII, *Mystici Corporis Christi*, ActApS 35 (1943) 193–248. O. PROCKSCH, op. cit.

On "the Layman . . . in the Secular City": B. AHERN, "The Law of the Spirit of Holiness," in E. MALATESTA, ed., *The Spirit of God in Christian Life* (New York 1977). H. URS VON BALTHASAR, *The God Question and Modern Man*, tr. H. GRAEF (New York 1967). H. DE LUBAC, *Catholicism*, tr. L. C. SHEPPARD (New York 1976). A. MARANCHE, *Je crois en Jésus-Christ aujourd'hui* (Paris 1968). T. MERTON, *The New Man* (London 1976). P. TEILHARD DE CHARDIN, *The Divine Milieu* (New York 1960).

[M. ADRIAZOLA]

LEADERSHIP CONFERENCE OF WOMEN RELIGIOUS OF THE U.S.A. (LCWR)

During the Holy Year 1950, major superiors from the entire world gathered in Rome to participate in the First General Congress of the States of Perfection. For women major superiors of the U.S.A. this meeting began a chain of events leading to the establishment of the Leadership Conference of Women Religious of the U.S.A., initially known as the Conference of Religious Superiors of Women's Institutes in the U.S.A. (CMSW). In 1952 the Holy See established a commission of General Superiors of Orders of Men and Women. The first committee for women religious in the U.S. planned the National Congress of Religious of the U.S.A., held in South Bend in 1952. That same year participants in the meeting also attended the First World Congress of Mothers General in Rome. All these events furthered the movement towards a national conference. In 1956 the first statutes of CMSW were adopted; the following year the first chairperson of the organization was elected. In 1959 the Holy See gave the Conference formal approbation. The bylaws, revised in 1971, were approved by the Sacred Congregation for Religious and Secular Institutes in 1972.

The Conference, as an organization with pontifical status, exercises moral power in relationship to its members. The autonomy of each congregation is preserved. The Conference possesses authority sufficient for its organizational purposes. Membership in the LCWR is open to the chief administrative officers of all institutes, provinces, and regions of women religious in the U.S. and territorial possessions. The current membership is drawn from approximately 370 congregations.

The primary purpose of the Conference is to assist these members "personally, collectively and corporately in developing creative and responsive leadership and in undertaking those forms of service consonant with the evolving Gospel mission of women religious in the world through the Church" (Bylaws 11.1). From its inception the LCWR has manifested five priorities in its programs and activities: the development of an apostolic spirituality which sees religious as vitally involved in the mission of the Church; action for justice; the fullest participation of women in ecclesial and civic life; the promotion of leadership; and collaboration with other groups of similar orientation. Early in the history of the organization significant research was undertaken through a project known as the *Sisters Survey*. Through a questionnaire disseminated in 1967, data were collected on: the changing structures of religious orders; preferred apostolic services, life styles, and theologies; and participation in adaptation/renewal processes after Vatican II. Participating in the study were 139,000 sisters, from 301 different congregations. Currently, the Conference emphasizes four goals as expressions of its

enduring priorities: to articulate a contemporary theology of religious life; to provide for its own members and for others an education to justice leading to systemic change; to involve itself in work and study regarding women's issues; and to move towards maximum collaboration.

Organizationally the LCWR is divided into fifteen geographic regions. The members gather annually in national assembly, which constitutes the legislative body of the Conference. Between assemblies the LCWR is governed by a national board and the executive committee of that board. The board is composed of five national officers, one representative from each region, and the executive director. The Conference is administered by a national secretariat located in Washington, D.C. The LCWR works in close collaboration with the Conference of Major Superiors of Men (CMSM). The LCWR and the National Conference of Catholic Bishops (NCCB), through their respective liaison committees, maintain communication and share in projects of mutual concern. Through Sisters Uniting, a committee composed of representatives from each U.S. sisters' organization, the LCWR seeks to be in solidarity with sisters-at-large. As a symbol of its concern for the world community and its need to know that community, the LCWR has secured nongovernmental status through the Office of Public Information at the United Nations.

Bibliography: *Bylaws of the Leadership Conference of Women Religious of the United States of America* (Washington, D.C. 1972). LCWR, *New Visions, New Roles: Women in the Church* (Washington, D.C. 1975); *Status and Roles of Women: Another Perspective* (Washington, D.C. 1976). M. M. MODDE, "A Canonical Study of the Leadership Conference of Women Religious (LCWR) of the United States of America" (doctoral dissertation, The Catholic University of America, Washington, D.C. 1977).

[M. D. TURNER]

LEAKAGE IN CHURCH MEMBERSHIP

Leakage refers to partial or total estrangement, voluntary or involuntary, from the practice of the Catholic faith (8:588). A useful typology includes the following: (1) *The Alienated:* those who are irregular or marginal in religious practice but retain their affiliation with the Catholic Church; (2) *The Dormant:* those who have ceased to practice altogether but retain their affiliation with the Catholic Church; (3) *The Unchurched:* those baptized as infants but not reared in the Church as well as those born of Catholic parents but never baptized; (4) *The Disidentified:* those who were reared in the Church but no longer identify themselves as Catholics.

Sources of Data. In 1929 Shaughnessy conjectured in a methodologically weak study that vast numbers of immigrants had been lost to the Church. Until recently, there have been no empirically sound national studies of Roman Catholic leakage per se; hence scientific interpretation consisted of cautious inferences made from parochial and diocesan reports, census materials, national surveys of church attendance, and several intensive studies of parish communities.

Standard Sources. The "traditional" sources were as follows: (1) *The Official Catholic Directory:* however questionable the reliability of the diocesan statistical summaries published annually by P. J. Kenedy and Sons (Greeley notes that it underestimates Catholics by between eight and ten million people), the reported total Catholic population and the number of infant Baptisms have been compared with the Bureau of Census Data on expressed religious preferences and birth rates among the American people. (2) *U.S. Census Data:* questions on religious preference are no longer asked in the decennial census; however, in 1957 the Bureau of Census did make a sample inquiry of the religious preferences of all persons fourteen years of age and over. The results, when compared with figures from *The Official Catholic Directory*, revealed discrepancies from which estimates of leakage were inferred. (3) *Surveys and Polls:* another source of data was the series of national surveys by opinion-polling agencies, based on random samples, reporting church attendance for Catholics since 1952. The reliability of the findings tended to be confirmed by their general similarity. Several diocesan or state-wide volunteer surveys of religious preferences and/or practice, together with local surveys on the parish level, provided hints as to the possible extent of leakage. (4) *Parish Studies:* exhaustive studies of American parochial communities have been few (e.g., Fichter, Schuyler), but they provided limited data on local leakage, obtained through house-to-house surveys and through internal correlations of infant Baptisms, First Communions, and Confirmations.

On the basis of these "traditional" sources, it was estimated that leakage was as low as 8 percent, if the meaning of leakage was limited to the voluntary abandonment of the faith by persons reared as Catholics or as high as 30 percent if the definition was broadened to include those who were baptized but never reared in the faith.

Scientific Sources. The "current" and by far more reliable sources of data are likely to provide not only statistical profiles of leakage but also analyses of causal and associated factors. The principal sources include the following: (1) *Specialized Studies.* In recent years a number of methodologically sophisticated studies have appeared which explore variously the possible linkages between leakage and such variables as age, family background, education, the religiousness of the spouse, religious experience, attitudes toward doctrine and authority, etc. (e.g., Kotre, Zelan, Caplovitz, Greeley). (2) *Polls.* The opinion-polling agencies (e.g., Gallup, Roper) have continued to take national soundings on religious beliefs and church attendance. Unfortunately the questions are often too broad to yield the nuanced information required for an understanding of the multidimensionality of religious behavior. (3) *Survey Research.* The National Opinion Research Center (NORC) has gathered the most comprehensive and sophisticated survey data presently available. The Center has provided information on the several dimensions of religiosity, namely ritualistic (e.g., church attendance), ideological (belief structure), experiential (affective component), and consequential (the behavioral outcomes of belief). It also attempts to examine in some depth the factors that are linked to various levels of religious behavior. In recent years NORC's Annual General Social Survey has provided an up-to-date profile of American religious behavior.

Conclusions. Given the limitations of the results of survey research, the following are tentative conclusions:

(1) The Alienated. When religious practice and beliefs are used as measures of orthodoxy, it is clear that a pro-

cess of erosion has been under way in the era since Vatican Council II. Weekly Mass attendance declined from 72 percent in 1963 to 42 percent in 1977, with only one-third of all Catholic males as regulars and one-fourth of men and women under thirty in weekly attendance. Furthermore, a growing proportion of Catholics no longer supported one or another aspect of the Church's traditional sexual ethic, such as the teachings on methods of family limitation, abortion, sterilization, premarital sex, and the remarriage of the divorced. (In the mid-1970s about one-half of Catholics rejected the Church's right to teach authoritatively on race and on birth control, although they maintained a level of religious practice similar to that of the general Catholic population.) The decline in devotion and belief was significantly greater among Catholics who were thirty or younger.

What factors are associated with religious alienation? (a) In recent studies, age correlates with religious behavior, with under-thirty Catholics less devout than their juniors and their elders. Why the association exists is not presently clear, although it has been attributed both to the influence of the youth counterculture and to disenchantment with church authority and sexual ethics issues. (b) Family background is a weighty influence upon adult religious behavior; thus family tensions in childhood correlate negatively with adult religiosity. (c) Of all the predictors of religious behavior, the religiousness of the spouse has proved to be the single most important at a time when the family is in transition; thus the alienated are likely to be married to less religious spouses. (d) In some measure religious or "mystical" experiences contribute to support orthodox practice. (e) However, one of the most controversial conclusions is that "one could account for all the change in Catholic religious behavior on a number of variables in the decade after the Second Vatican Council by the changing attitudes on sexuality and papal authority." It must be noted that the claim is more modest than it might appear, i.e., that changing attitudes account for change in behavior but not for the behavior itself. (f) Such current variables as poor sermons, clericalism, sexual ethics, and certain doctrines are associated with alienated behavior.

In ranking the relative influence of the above factors, present evidence indicates that background influences weigh more heavily than current issues; that age and religiousness of one's spouse are more significant than the religiousness of one's family; and that among current factors certain doctrines, sexual issues, and sermons are weightier influences than attitudes toward feminism and clericalism.

(2) The Dormant. It seems reasonable to classify as dormant the more than one-quarter of American Catholics who never went to church in 1977 according to NORC's General Social Survey. Two-fifths of those under thirty did not attend church and almost half the men under thirty went to Mass only once a year or less. It appears that the same dynamics that affect the religious behavior of alienated Catholics are operative in the behavior of the dormant.

(3) The Unchurched. It is not possible at present to offer precise figures as to the number of those baptized as infants but never reared in the Church, as well as those born of Catholic parent(s) but never baptized. Until research addresses its questions specifically to this

category of the estranged, speculation based on indirect evidence will have to do. (One study, defining the unchurched as those who have no formal religious affiliation or those who go to church less than once a year, concludes that one-fifth of all Americans are unchurched. A non-religious family background, marriage to an unreligious spouse and rejection of basic religious propositions are the principal factors associated with the phenomenon of unchurchedness.)

(4) The Disidentified. The progressive rate of apostasy is reflected in the data-sets available from several NORC files and one University of Michigan Survey Research Center file, namely, 8 percent in 1955, 14 percent in 1973, and 16.5 percent in 1977. The highest rates of withdrawal are found among the young and the college educated, although there has been an increase at all age levels and in all populations. What factors are associated with disidentification? Exogamous (mixed) marriage emerges as the most powerful predictor of disidentification, although the precise relationship between the two variables is unclear. After religiously mixed marriage, the most important factors linked to apostasy are a previous divorce, low confidence in the clergy, and certain liberal political attitudes.

It is clear that partial and total estrangement from Catholic practice and belief has increased significantly in recent years. In juridical terms, this means that the Catholic Church is sustaining substantive losses. In terms of the Church's future, it means that tomorrow's membership ranks will be markedly thinner. In theological terms, the meaning depends upon one's theological perspective; thus one "school" will view the trend as evidence of calamitous loss, whereas other "schools," while not discounting the element of loss, will speak of the rise of communal Catholics, the purification of the Church of milieu-Christians, and prophetic disaffiliation.

Bibliography: D. CAPLOVITZ, *The Religious Dropouts: Apostasy among College Graduates* (Beverly Hills, Cal. 1977). A. M. GREELEY, W. C. MCCREADY and K. MCCOURT, *Catholic Schools in a Declining Church* (Kansas City, Mo. 1976). J. KOTRE, *A View from the Border: A Social Psychological Study of Current Catholicism* (Chicago 1971). W. C. MCCREADY, "Faith of Our Fathers: A Study of the Process of Religious Socialization" (Ph.D. Dissertation, U. of Illinois at Chicago Arch, 1972). W. C. MCCREADY with A. M. GREELEY, *The Ultimate Values of the American Population* (Beverly Hills, Cal. 1976). J. ZELAN, "Religious Apostasy, Higher Education and Occupational Choice," *Sociology of Education* 41 (Fall 1968) 370–378.

[R. M. BROOKS]

LECTIONARIES

Although several interesting attempts have been made at finding calendrical patterns in the Gospels which would make them primitive lectionaries in themselves, the oldest extant description of the Eucharistic synaxis only records that at Rome in the 2d century, "the memoirs of the apostles or the writings of the prophets are read as long as time permits" (Justin, *Apologia* 1.67). Still, the assignment of definite passages developed with the emergence of Christian feasts and seasons so that established lectionaries are known by the 4th century, although these do not cover the entire year but only special times. The neutral periods between seem to have been given to course reading following the order of the canonical texts. While questions remain with regard to Rome and some Oriental Churches, the most common pattern consisted of three readings: Old Testament, Epistle (or Acts), and Gospel. In the early Middle Ages, however, the OT

reading disappeared from the ordinary Sunday liturgy and this, together with the closer organization of the annual cycle, left much of the Scripture unread in the course of the year, a fault which was further exacerbated by later overdevelopment of the sanctoral cycle. Therefore, one of the major concerns of Vatican Council II's Constitution on the Sacred Liturgy that "the treasures of the Bible are to be opened up more lavishly so that a richer fare may be provided for the faithful at the table of God's word. In this way a more representative part of the Sacred Scriptures will be read to the people in the course of a prescribed number of years" (*Sacrosanctum Concilium* 51).

The Council's design was completed in 1969 with the promulgation (on May 25) of a revised lectionary which includes: (1) readings from the OT, Epistles and Gospels for every Sunday, varying over a three-year cycle; (2) a daily lectionary of two readings over an annual cycle (two year cycle for weeks *per annum*); (3) a Proper and Common of saints with three readings and wide choice in the Common; and (4) provision for ritual Masses, Masses for various occasions, and votive Masses.

While present Lutheran and Episcopal lectionaries provide for the third and fourth of these categories (and the Episcopal for lenten weekdays), the Sunday lectionary has especially commended itself to other Christian traditions in North America. The lectionary in the Presbyterian *Worshipbook* (1970) is based on the Roman and that version has been adopted by the United Church of Christ and the Disciples of Christ. Similar versions are found in the (Episcopal) *Proposed Book of Common Prayer* (1976) and the forthcoming *Lutheran Book of Worship*, both lectionaries having been established in 1973. In 1974 the Commission on Worship of the Consultation on Church Union (COCU) produced a lectionary which attempts to present a consensus of the Roman, Presbyterian, Episcopal and Lutheran versions, and this has been adopted by the United Methodist Church.

In all of these the synoptic Gospels are read in order, Matthew in Year A (begun with Advent in years divisible by 3), Mark in Year B, and Luke in Year C; readings from John occur in each year. Apart from variations in festal calendars, the chief difference in these lectionaries lies in the various methods of articulating the neutral zones after Epiphany and Pentecost. For the Roman Lectionary these are a series of 34 weeks *per annum* which are used in order after Epiphany and then resumed after Pentecost. The others have separate series after Epiphany and after Pentecost, but differ in ways of assigning the latter to Sundays of a given year. Lutheran, Episcopal, and COCU lectionaries assign the Transfiguration to the Last Sunday after Epiphany as transition to Lent and all save the Presbyterian have the readings for Christ the King (Roman Lectionary) on the Last Sunday after Pentecost.

Less ecumenical accord is to be found in the United Kingdom, however, where lectionaries other than the Roman have followed the initiatives of the Joint Liturgical Group (*see* CALENDAR, COMMON LITURGICAL). While the Anglican lectionary, first published in 1967 and subsequently revised, appoints the usual three lessons for each Sunday, these vary over a cycle of two rather than three years. Further, this lectionary is built on a series of "themes" assigned to the several Sundays, the theme being brought out especially by a "controlling" lesson with the other two readings being selected to support it. For the 9 Sundays before Christmas the controlling lesson is that from the OT; from Christmas to Pentecost it is the Gospel; and for the time after Pentecost it is the Epistle. The lectionary of the (English) *Methodist Service Book* follows the original study closely, but proposals before the Church of England at present will depart from it in some respects while holding to the basic design of the Joint Liturgical Group.

See also LITURGICAL BOOKS OF THE ROMAN RITE.

Bibliography: C. WIÉNER, "Présentation du nouveau lectionnaire," *Maison-Dieu* 99 (1969) 28–49. M.-L. GUILLAUMIN, "Problèmes pastoraux du nouveau lectionnaire," *Maison-Dieu* 99 (1969) 77–87. *The Calendar, Lectionary and Rules to Order the Service 1976*. A Report by the Liturgical Commission of the General Synod of the Church of England (London 1976). *A Lectionary*. Prepared by the Commission on Worship of The Consultation on Church Union (Princeton, N.J. 1974).

[T. J. TALLEY]

LEGATES, PAPAL

Paul VI in the motu proprio of June 24, 1969, *Sollicitudo omnium ecclesiarum* redefined the meaning and function of papal legates. They are ecclesiastics, especially bishops, who are entrusted with the task of personally and stably representing the pope in various countries and regions. The term "legate" applies to a number of different kinds of officials. Apostolic delegates are the personal representatives of the pope to local Churches. Nuncios, pronuncios, or internuncios represent the Holy See to the civil governments of the territories in which they serve as well as to the local Church there. Occasionally a papal mission is appointed to deal with a specific issue in a given country. Both lay people and clerics can be sent as delegates or observers to international conferences; these, too, are papal legates; but their office is not treated in detail in general canonical legislation.

A legate expresses the pope's concern for the good of the nation in which he serves, especially with respect to questions of peace and the development of peoples. He is charged with protecting the legitimate interests of the Church in her dealings with the civil government. Occasionally and bearing in mind the advice of local bishops, he enters into negotiations with the civil government about questions of concern to both Church and State. Within the limits of his mandate and in close association with the bishops and patriarchs of the region, the legate promotes ecumenical dialogue. Being under the direction of the cardinal secretary of state and the prefect of the Council for the Public Affairs of the Church, the legate reports directly to them about all his activities.

Other duties of the legate are more closely allied with internal affairs. He informs the Holy See about the spiritual condition of the local Church and communicates and interprets papal documents and curial deliberations to the local Church. He is the facilitator of the process whereby candidates for the episcopacy are selected; and he forwards their names to the proper Roman dicasteries, together with an accurate indication of which candidate seems most suitable. The legate also has the duty of studying the question of the creation, division, and suppression of dioceses. He will inform the proper Roman dicastery of the episcopal conference's recommendations on the matter.

The legate is advised to give generous assistance and counsel to individual residential bishops. Although not himself a member of the national episcopal conference, he generally attends its sessions. He is to be notified in advance of its agenda and is to inform the Holy See about it. The legate exercises similar functions with respect to religious superiors and the national conferences of religious. Whenever no official delegate or observer has been appointed to an international conference within his territory, the legate is to pursue the business of the conference, informing the Holy See of its progress. Delegates or observers at an international conference are to complete the mission entrusted to them after consulting with the legate in whose territory they happen to be.

The legation (offices of the papal legate) itself has certain legal privileges. It is exempt from the jurisdiction of the local Ordinary and the legate can grant faculties for use in the oratory of the legation. The legate has the right to bless the people and to celebrate the Liturgy of the Hours in all churches within his territory. He takes precedence over all patriarchs, archbishops, and bishops within his territory, but not over cardinals. All of these rights aim at making clear the dignity of the office of the legate and at enabling him to perform his duties more easily.

Bibliography: PAUL VI, *Sollicitudo omnium ecclesiarum*, ActApS 61 (1969) 471–484.

[J. G. JOHNSON]

LEONINE COMMISSION

This is the editorial group entrusted in 1879 by Pope Leo XIII as the *Commissio Leonina pro editione critica operum Sancti Thomae de Aquino*. Among the marks of maturing scholarship in the American Church are the creation of an American Section of the Commission in Feb. 1965 and the appointment on Oct. 30, 1976 of the American Dominican, William A. Wallace, as *praeses* (Director General) of the whole Commission. The work of the Commission, begun in 1880, rapidly resulted by 1906 in 3 folio volumes of St. Thomas's commentaries on Aristotle (logic, natural philosophy) and in 8 folio volumes of his *Summa theologiae*. But thereafter until 1948 only the *Summa contra gentiles* (1930) and an index volume (1948) were issued, because of the two World Wars and the Great Depression. A reorganization in 1948, however, and in the 1960s financial support from the St. Thomas Aquinas Foundation in the U.S. have led to rapid progress in the last decade. The following works have appeared:

t. 22 *Q.D. de veritate* (3 v. 1970–1976);

t. 26 *Expositio super Job* (1965);

t. 40 *Contra errores Graecorum; De rationibus fidei; De forma absolutionis; De substantiis separatis; Super Decretalem;*

t. 41 *Contra impugnantes Dei cultum et religionem; De perfectione spiritualis vitae; Contra doctrinam retrahentium a religione* (1970);

t. 43 *De principiis naturae; De aeternitate mundi; De motu cordis; De mixtione elementorum; De operationibus occultis naturae; De iudiciis astrorum; De sortibus; De unitate intellectus; De ente et essentia; De fallaciis; De propositionibus modalibus* (1976);

t. 47 *Sententia libri Ethicorum* (1969);

t. 48 *Sententia libri Politicorum; Tabula libri Ethicorum* (1971).

The following volumes are in press:

t. 23 *Q.D. de malo* (2 v.);
t. 42 *Compendium theologiae; De articulis fidei, etc.*;
t. 44 *De decem praeceptis; Super Credo; Sermones*;
t. 45 *Sententia libri De anima; Sententia librorum De sensu et sensato et De memoria et reminiscentia*;
t. 46 *Sententia Aristotelis Metaphysicae* (3 v.).

The American section, assigned to edit the Commentary on Aristotle's *Metaphysics*, operated at Yale University from 1965 until 1977, when its facilities were transferred to The Catholic University of America. Its task was one of unusual difficulty because of the complexity of the MSS tradition for the *Sententia libri Aristotelis Metaphysicae*, but the work has now been completed. The next undertaking of the American section will be Aquinas's commentaries on Book Three of the *Sentences* of Peter Lombard, works of Boethius, and Pseudo-Dionysius, *On the Divine Names*.

[T. C. O'BRIEN]

LERCARO, GIACOMO

Archbishop and cardinal, leader in social action and liturgical reform; b. Quinto al Mare, Archdiocese of Genoa, Oct. 28, 1891; d. Bologna, Oct. 18, 1976. Ordained July 25, 1914, he became archbishop of Ravenna in 1947 and of Bologna from 1947 until resigning in 1968; he was created cardinal Jan. 12, 1953. As archbishop he was faced at Ravenna and Bologna with Communist ascendancy after World War II; he became a recognized leader in combining evangelization of the worker with strong advocacy and pursuit of programs representing Catholic principles of social justice. He showed no interest in dogmatic condemnations of Marxism, but chose rather the course of positive preaching of the Gospel in its full meaning. He became the champion of liturgical reform, but again in conjunction with the Church's mission to the poor; he was convinced that the Church of Christ is at once the praying Church and the Church of those in need. As both liturgical and social reformer he was regarded with some uneasiness by conservative episcopal colleagues. His place as a key figure in Vatican Council II was won, therefore, rather against the odds. He was not chosen by the Italian episcopate even as a nominee for the liturgical commission, in spite of his established reputation. Yet simply by his quiet but effective interventions at key points in the conciliar debates he exercised a strong shaping hand on reform of the liturgy, the restatement of the Church's nature, the formation of the Synod of Bishops, the declaration on religious freedom, promotion of ecumenical collaboration and positive relations with the Jewish people, and on the statement of the Church's role in the social, economic, and political life of the modern world. Paul VI appointed Cardinal Lercaro to prepare the formation of the postconciliar commission to implement the Constitution on the Liturgy, *Sacrosanctum Concilium*; from 1964 to 1968 he headed the Consilium. With its secretary, Annibale Bugnini, he was responsible for initiating the process that has led to the revision of the texts for the Roman liturgy; the pastorally reformed service books and their accompanying instructions are witness to the spirit Card. Lercaro infused into the reform of the liturgy. Yet his task did not progress without the murmuring and sometimes the outcry of those who felt that the purity of the Latin liturgy was being violated. In 1968 he resigned from the Consilium and from the See of Bologna.

Cardinal Lercaro was "a holy bishop, intelligent and learned, humble and zealous. He appeared mild and meek before his adversaries; he was certainly strong in his proclamation of the values of the gospel and his dedication to the forms, beauty, and inner spirit of the Christian liturgy (McManus)."

Bibliography: F. R. MCMANUS, "Cardinal Giacomo Lercaro," *Liturgy* 21 (Dec. 1976) 292.

[T. C. O'BRIEN]

LIBERATION THEOLOGY

The term "liberation theology" covers a diversity of theological movements. Historically and specifically, it refers to a recent theological line of thought within Latin America that focuses on the political, economic, and ideological causes of social inequality and makes liberation rather than development its central theological, economic, and political category. It not only analyzes the concrete Latin American situation, but it argues that all theology should begin by analyzing its concrete social situation and by returning to its religious sources for means to rectify it. Some of the ideas of liberation theology were taken up by the Second General Conference of the Latin American Episcopate (CELAM) that met in Medellín, Colombia in 1968. The *Medellín documents describe the institutional violence and the exploitive relations of dependency in the social situation and they point to the need for cultural and economic liberation.

In a more extended sense, liberation theology refers to any theological movement making the criticism of oppression and the support of liberation integral to the theological task itself. Black theology and feminist theology are therefore seen as major types of liberation theology. The term has also been appropriated by American Indians, ethnics, and other minority groups. Because of its relationship with specific groups, some view liberation theology negatively as simply a specific cultural movement in which specific groups appeal to religious beliefs in order to legitimate their particular agenda and goals.

Common Methodology of Liberation Theologies. In its more fundamental and extended meaning, liberation theology refers to a theological method. Notwithstanding the diversity of liberation theologies they share a common theological methodology. This methodology brings to the fore within theology an awareness of the sociology of knowledge, since it underscores the interrelation between theory and praxis. It outlines the social and cultural conditions of theological concepts and institutional patterns. Therefore, it encourages theology to become more self-reflective about the socio-political basis of its religious symbols and their consequential praxis. It advocates a practical as well as theoretical role for theology as a discipline. Several basic traits constitute the common methodology of liberation theology.

Starting Point. The starting-point of liberation theology is an analysis of the concrete socio-political situation and the uncovering of the discrimination, alienation, and oppression within it. The discrepancy between the rich and poor within individual countries and between the advanced and developing nations leads Latin American liberation theology to single out the relations of dependency between nations as the cause of this inequality. It therefore censures theories of development reinforcing rather than correcting the exploitation. It therefore demands liberation and not development. Feminist theology argues that the discrimination against women in society and Church is not only factual, but has been given cultural and religious legitimation. Black theology not only points to socio-economic discrimination, but also underscores its cultural causes. All liberation theologies therefore undertake to demonstrate by their analysis of the concrete situation not only the existence of discrimination or oppression, but also its economic and cultural causes.

Reflection on the Religious Tradition. Secondly, liberation theology studies the religious tradition in relation to this contemporary analysis and experience which provides a new perspective for reading and interpreting the tradition. Does the tradition support or allow the unjust situation? Or does it work against it? Much of Latin-American liberation theology examines how the Church's mission has been understood. Has the distinction between priests and laity led to a dichotomy in which the priest has a spiritual mission and the laity a worldly one without much interrelation? Has the Church's mission been bifurcated by separating its salvific function from its concern for the world? Feminist theology describes how masculine language and patriarchal images have specified the religious understanding of God and how anthropological misconceptions have become institutionalized as religious taboos. Black theology not only uncovers how the oppression of blacks has been legitimated in church history, but also shows how fundamental images of blackness and whiteness have led to this oppression. In each liberation theology, therefore, the present experience and analysis of injustices has led to a critique not only of the present but also the past with its cultural and religious traditions.

The Reconstructive Task. Thirdly, liberation theology proposes that theology has the twofold constructive task of retrieval and reinterpretation. Theology should retrieve those forgotten religious symbols or neglected ecclesial practices that could serve to overcome the oppression. It equally proposes a fundamental reinterpretation of traditional religious symbols and beliefs that legitimate oppression or discrimination. Latin-American liberation theology seeks not only to retrieve the public dimension of faith and the political mission of the Church, but also to reinterpret traditional conceptions of sin, grace, salvation history, and eschatology. Sin is reinterpreted as social sin in reference to social structures. Development—political, cultural, and economic—is related to God's Kingdom not merely as sign, image, or anticipation, but as a causal relation that underscores continuity and fulfillment. Black theology discovers in black experience, history, and culture the resources to overcome alienations. It reinterprets traditional conceptions of divine providence, suffering, and salvation. Feminist theology retrieves images of the femininity of God and views of the equality of the sexes within the history of religions and Christianity. It also reinterprets traditional religious symbols and beliefs. It does not simply urge that sexist language be excluded from biblical, liturgical, and theological texts, but seeks to revise dominant images of God. Likewise it suggests that the traditional conceptions of original sin as pride or the desire for power often expresses masculine rather than feminine experience (see FEMINISM AND CHRISTIAN THEOLOGY).

Praxis as Criterion. Fourthly liberation theologies make concrete praxis not only a goal but also a criterion of theological method. Present experience and praxis provide not only a source from which tradition is questioned, but also a criterion by which the truth of theological affirmations can be judged. Much diversity exists among liberation theologians in regard to the norm of theological affirmations. Within Black theology James Cone takes a Barthian position, where J. Deotis Roberts is more Tillichean. Often Latin American liberation theologies so underscore the primacy of praxis that their positions could be described as a sort of theological consequentialism. Feminist theology along with the others places a premium on personal experience and partisan commitment as a source and criterion of theological affirmations. Since all liberation theologies focus on the relation between theory and praxis, they emphasize the significance of praxis as a source and goal. They demand that theology concern itself with concrete social and political goals. Moreover, these goals should be more than those established by the present structures of society. Instead they should involve a restructuring of society itself. Only if society is restructured and its culture revised, they believe, can their visions of emancipation and liberation be achieved.

Criticisms. Both the individual liberation theologies and the common methodological basis have been criticized, the criticisms centering on the question of criteria and goals. Firstly, since liberation theologies strive to eliminate social discrimination and political oppression, they are criticized for identifying the Church's mission as an immanent socio-political goal rather than as a transcendent, eschatological end. Secondly, since liberation theology appeals to personal experience as a source and norm of theological reflection, it is criticized for replacing objectivity with partisanship. Thirdly, since the goal of liberation is a standard by which the religious tradition is evaluated, it is objected that such a standard is unspecified unless one already has a vision of what constitutes genuine liberation. In response liberation theologians strive to show how precisely the transcendence of the Christian vision contributes to political reform and how this vision provides the ultimate norm of theological reflection and praxis. Its aim is not to eliminate transcendence, but to link this transcedence with social, political, and cultural reform.

See also BLACK THEOLOGY; LATIN AMERICA, CHURCH IN ; POLITICAL THEOLOGY.

Bibliography: General surveys of Latin American theology and liberation theology: H. ASSMANN, *Theology for a Nomad Church* (New York 1976), J. MIGUEZ BONINO, *Doing Theology in a Revolutionary Situation* (Philadelphia 1975). F. FIORENZA, "Latin American Liberation Theology," *Interpretation* 28 n. 4 (1974) 441–457. G. GUTIERREZ, *A Theology of Liberation*, tr. C. INDA and J. EAGLESON (New York 1973). J. SEGUNDO, *A Theology for Artisans of a New Humanity*, tr. J. DRURY (5 v., New York 1973); *The Liberation of Theology* tr. J. DRURY (New York 1976). History of the movement: E. DUSSEL, *History and Theology of Liberation* (New York 1976). Documents of a conference bringing all liberation theologies of North America together: S. TORRES and J. EAGLESON, *Theology in the Americas* (New York 1976).

[F. SCHÜSSLER FIORENZA]

LIFE, PROLONGATION OF

In the Karen Quinlan case the Supreme Court of New Jersey, March 31, 1976 ruled (on the basis of the "right of privacy") that, under certain conditions, physicians who judge a comatose patient will never regain consciousness may discontinue use of a respirator to prolong life. Miss Quinlan continued breathing without the respirator. This case aroused controversy on two issues.

First, it is debated how to define human life and death. The answer is important also to determine when organs for transplantation can be "harvested" from a newly-dead body. Catholic moralists generally continue to hold that the decision is best left to medical prudence based on *concurrent* signs. While admitting the cessation of spontaneous brain functions ("brain-death") is an important criterion, they deplore the recent attempts of some states to define death exclusively by this one sign.

Second, the traditional distinction of *ordinary*, obligatory means from *extraordinary*, non-obligatory means of medical treatment is under debate. Most agree that ordinary care includes oral feeding, hygiene, and easily administered medication; while extraordinary means are to be judged not absolutely but *relatively* to the patient's condition and the resources of those obligated to care.

The underlying principle which limits the obligation to prolong life is that the proper goal of medical treatment is not experimentation, nor the avoidance of difficult, prudential decisions, but the true benefit of the patient. To initiate or continue artificial means of prolonging life which cannot restore specifically human functioning, or which do so only at the price of a constant absorption in the struggle to live (as in prolonged use of kidney dialysis for some, repeated resuscitation, etc.) does not seem really to benefit the patient. Hence the patient is not obliged to consent to such treatment, nor are guardians or physicians obliged to provide it, at the expense of their availability for other duties.

While some moralists today raise the question whether in some cases such "permitting to die" is significantly different from "putting to death" most maintain this distinction as valid and important (*see* EUTHANASIA). In the present case, however, the issue is not precisely whether to "let die," but rather whether it is reasonable to use medical techniques which do not benefit the patient.

Bibliography: R. BRANSON et al., "The Quinlan Decision," *Hastings Center Report* 6 (1976) 8–22. D. J. HORAN, "The Quinlan Case," *Linacre Quarterly* 44 (1977) 168–176. R. A. MCCORMICK, "Notes on Moral Theology," ThSt 37 (1976) 70–119. G. MEILANDER, "The Distinction between Killing and Allowing to Die," ThSt 37 (1976) 467–470. P. RAMSEY, *Patient as Person* (New Haven, Conn. 1970).

[B. M. ASHLEY]

LITANY (LITURGICAL USE)

A litany is a form of public prayer wherein a leader expresses a series of petitions or invocations, to each of which the congregation responds with a set formula —for example, "Lord, have mercy" or "pray for us" (8:789–790). "Litany" has also been used to designate a procession with petitionary prayer, such as those of the rogation days (12: 551).

Litanies in the Mass. Litanies are found in the Roman Mass and in other rites. An ancient example is the *Oratio fidelium* (Prayer of the Faithful) with its Greek response, *Kyrie eleison* (Lord, have mercy) and *Christe eleison* (Christ, have mercy). By the time of Gregory the Great (590–604) this litany had been moved from the end of the Mass of the Catechumens (now known as the Liturgy of the Word) to near the beginning, but the invocations had been lost, with only the responses

remaining. These remained a prominent musical element of the Mass until recent liturgical reforms (8:789). In the 1969 Roman Missal a communal penitential rite was introduced for the first time. In the first form of this rite a modified *Confiteor* is used, followed by "Lord, have mercy," "Christ, have mercy," and "Lord, have mercy," twice each (rather than three times each as in the Tridentine Mass), once by the celebrant and once by the congregation. (This may be in Greek or in the vernacular.) In the third form of this rite three invocations are addressed to Christ—a number are provided in the Sacramentary and others may be composed and used—and given the same responses (GenInstrRomMissal 29–30). The ancient Prayer of the Faithful has also been restored (the preferred name is *General Intercessions), although there is no set form or response. Petition is to be made for the needs of the Church, public authorities and the salvation of the world, those in need, and the local community (ibid. 45–47).

The *Agnus Dei* (Lamb of God) is another ancient litany in the Mass. Originally sung during the Breaking of Bread and repeated as often as necessary, it came to be reduced to a pre-Communion song, repeated only three times. In the 1969 Missal it is again to accompany the Breaking of Bread and is repeated as often as necessary (ibid. 56e). A new translation by the *International Consultation on English Texts, representing major English-speaking Churches, expresses the meaning of "Lamb of God" through paraphrase: "bearer of our sins," "redeemer of the world" (*Prayers We Have in Common* [Philadelphia 1975]).

The Litany of Saints. Reforms initiated by Vatican II have also produced new forms of the Litany of the Saints, the most important non-Eucharistic litany. Published March 21, 1969 by the Congregation of Rites in conjunction with the new Roman Calendar, it consists of two simplified forms, a longer one for ordinary use in public intercessions and processions and a shorter one for special occasions during Mass, such as the Easter Vigil and ordinations. The one for solemn intercessions includes prayer to God, invocations of the saints, invocation of Christ, prayer for various needs, and a conclusion. Variation is permitted in both: other saints may be added and invocations appropriate to the occasion. The uniformity in the Litany established by the reform of Pius V has thus been transcended.

Other officially approved litanies (Loreto, Holy Name, Sacred Heart, Saint Joseph, Most Precious Blood) have not been affected by liturgical reforms; the first of these, the Marian Litany of Loreto, has been most frequently in public use in this country.

[J. DALLEN]

LITURGICAL BOOKS OF THE ROMAN RITE

At the heart of the liturgical renewal instituted by Vatican Council II is the principle of restoring to all the faithful "that full, conscious, and active participation in liturgical celebrations which is ... their right and duty by reason of their baptism" (*Sacrosanctum Concilium* 14). A major element in the implementation of this principle has been and continues to be the provision of liturgical texts in the major vernacular languages in accordance with the Constitution on the Liturgy (ibid. 36). This directive and paragraph 40 of the Sept. 26,

1964 Instruction of the Congregation of Rites *Inter oecumenici* (ActApS 56 [1964] 877–900) place the responsibility for the translation of liturgical texts from Latin into the vernacular languages with the episcopal conferences. Once produced, these translations become the official text within a nation or region only after they have received confirmation by the Holy See.

In drafting Article 36 the Council Fathers expressed the need for cooperation among regions which share a common language (*Sacrosanctum Concilium* 36:3). A number of English-speaking bishops present at the Vatican Council formed the *International Commission on English in the Liturgy (ICEL). This commission now represents more than twenty member and associate-member conferences of bishops where English is spoken.

The process of translation employed by ICEL involves broad consultation. The initial draft of a rite is prepared under the direction of ICEL's Advisory Committee, a body of specialists in various fields. It is then issued as a Green Book or provisional text to all of the participating episcopal conferences for comment and criticism. On the basis of this consultation a revised text is prepared and submitted to the Episcopal Board. This board constitutes ICEL's governing body and is comprised of bishop-representatives from each of the member conferences. If the bishops approve the text, it is then issued to the conferences as a White Book or final draft. However, the conferences remain free to accept or reject the ICEL text.

Revised Liturgical Books through 1978. The following is a list of all of the revised liturgical books of the Roman rite (8:890; 16:256). They are given in the chronological order in which they appeared in the Latin *editio typica*, and their date of issue as a Green Book or White Book by ICEL is indicated.

1. *De ordinatione diaconi, presbyteris et episcopi* (April 15, 1968):
   Green Book: Rites of Ordinations of Deacons, Presbyters, and Bishops, 1969;
   White Book: Ordination of Deacons, Priests, and Bishops, 1975.
2. *Ordo celebrandi matrimonium* (March 19, 1969):
   Green Book: Rite of Marriage, 1969;
   White Book: Rite of Marriage, 1969.
3. *Missale Romanum* (April 3, 1969; 2d ed., March 27, 1975):
   Green Book: The Revised Roman Missal, 1971;
   White Book: The Roman Missal, 1973 (*see* SACRAMENTARY).
4. *Ordo baptismi parvulorum* (May 15, 1969; 2d ed. March 27, 1977):
   Green Book: The Baptism of Children, 1969;
   White Book: Rite of Baptism for Children, 1969.
5. *Ordo lectionum missae* (May 25, 1969):
   Green Book: Lectionary for Mass, 1969;
   White Book: Lectionary for Mass, 1969.
6. *Ordo exsequiarum* (April 15, 1969):
   Green Book: Order of Funerals for Adults, 1967;
   White Book: Rite of Funerals, 1970.
7. *Ordo professionis religiosae* (Feb. 2, 1970):
   Green Book: The Revised Rite of Religious Profession, 1971;
   White Book: Rite of Religious Profession, 1974.

8. *Ordo consecrationis virginum* (May 31, 1970):
   Green Book: The Revised Rites of Consecration to a Life of Virginity and Blessing of Oils, 1971;
   White Book: Rite of Consecration to a Life of Virginity, 1975.
9. *Ordo benedictionis abbatis et abbatissae* (Nov. 9, 1970):
   Green Book: The Revised Rite of Blessing of an Abbot and Abbess, 1971;
   White Book: Rite of Blessing of an Abbot or Abbess, 1975.
10. *Ordo benedicendi olea et conficiendi chrisma* (Dec. 3, 1970):
    Green Book: The Revised Rite of Blessing of Oils, 1971;
    White Book: Rite of the Blessing of Oils, Rite of Consecrating the Chrism, 1972.
11. *Liturgia Horarum* (April 11, 1971):
    Green Book: The Liturgy of the Hours, 1974;
    White Book: The Liturgy of the Hours, 1974.
12. *Ordo confirmationis* (Aug. 22, 1971):
    Green Book: The Revised Order of Confirmation, 1971;
    White Book: Rite of Confirmation, 1975.
13. *Ordo initiationis christianae adultorum* (Jan. 6, 1972):
    Green Book: Rite of Christian Initiation of Adults, 1974;
    White Book: (in preparation).
14. *De institutione lectorum et acolythorum, de sacro caelibatu amplectendo, de admissione inter candidatos ad diaconatum et presbyteratum* (Dec. 3, 1972):
    Green Book: Rite of Institution of Readers and Acolytes, Admission to Candidacy for the Diaconate and Presbyterate, Commitment to Celibacy, 1973;
    White Book: Institution of Readers and Acolytes, Admission to Candidacy for Ordination as Deacons and Priests, Commitment to Celibacy, 1976.
15. *Ordo unctionis infirmorum eorumque pastoralis curae* (Dec. 7, 1972):
    Green Book: Rite of Anointing and Pastoral Care of the Sick, 1973;
    White Book: (in preparation).
16. *Ritus ad deputandum ministrum extraordinarium sacrae communionis distribuendae* (Jan. 29, 1973):
    Green Book: Rite of Commissioning Special Ministers of Holy Communion, 1978.
17. *De sacra communione et cultu mysterii eucharistici extra missam* (June 21, 1973):
    White Book: Holy Communion and Worship of the Eucharist outside Mass, 1974.
18. *Ordo paenitentiae* (Dec. 2, 1973):
    Green Book: Rite of Penance, 1974;
    White Book: Rite of Penance, 1974.
19. *Preces eucharisticae pro missis cum pueris et de reconciliatione* (Nov. 1, 1974):
    Green Book: Eucharistic Prayers for Masses of

Reconciliation, Eucharistic Prayers for Masses with Children, 1975.

20. *Ordo dedicationis ecclesiae et altaris* (May 29, 1977):

Green Book: Dedication of a Church and an Altar (1978).

ICEL in 1978 published the Roman Pontifical, a compilation of the rites listed in which a bishop is the minister (*see* PONTIFICAL, ROMAN). In addition to the ICEL texts listed, several episcopal conferences have made use of their prerogative to produce their own translations. The books thus produced are: (1) the *Roman Missal* and the *Rite of Funerals*, produced by the National Liturgical Commission of England and Wales in 1968 and 1971 respectively; and (2) *The Divine Office*, produced by the hierarchies of Australia, England and Wales, and Ireland in 1974.

The Revisions and Liturgical Renewal. An important document for understanding the complex challenge of developing a vernacular liturgical language is the *Instruction on Translation of Liturgical Texts*, issued by the Consilium for the Implementation of the Constitution on the Sacred Liturgy, on Jan. 25, 1969 (*Notitiae* [1968] 3–12). In a farsighted few sentences, the Instruction lays out the parameters of the task: "...it is not sufficient that a liturgical translation merely reproduce the expressions and ideas of the original text. Rather it must faithfully communicate to a given people, and in their own language, that which the Church by means of this given text originally intended to communicate to another people in another time. A faithful translation, therefore, cannot be judged on the basis of individual words: the total context of this specific act of communication must be kept in mind, as well as the literary form proper to the respective language" (6). The Instruction then recommends that a liturgical translation must take into account the true meaning of the text, its communicability for the particular congregation, and its intended use as spoken communication in the liturgical assembly (*see* LITURGICAL TEXTS, TRANSLATION OF).

Finally, the introductions to the new liturgical books are an indispensable source for understanding the breadth of the present renewal. In each circumstance choices as to texts, song, movement, and environment are to be made in order to suit the particular liturgical celebration to the community which gathers for it. These decisions are left variously to episcopal conferences, diocesan Ordinaries, and the individual priest celebrant. However, to further insure the "full, conscious, and active participation" of the faithful, it is assumed that the priest will make these choices in consultation with the other ministers and the people whom he serves (see GenInstrRomMissal 313).

In these introductions, the various aspects of the Church's sacramental ministry which these rites express are presented within a richly consistent and comprehensible theological framework. All of the rites draw their power and significance from the Paschal Mystery of Jesus Christ and each is treated as a particular expression of this seminal event. Because of their pastoral and theological presentation, the introductions provide instructive and meditative reading, both for those who bear liturgical-pastoral responsibility in the Christian community and for students of the liturgical renewal of the Second Vatican Council.   [J. M. SCHELLMAN]

LITURGICAL CATECHESIS

Liturgical catechesis is either religious teaching about the liturgy or the religious teaching embodied in the liturgy. Postconciliar documents on catechetics and on the liturgy have stressed the importance of both kinds of liturgical catechesis. Special initiation into the meaning and style of Christian worship is obviously needed for beginners in the Christian life, whether children or adult converts. And all worshipers have deserved from their pastors some special liturgical education during the time of transition from the former to a renewed liturgical observance. On the other hand, an aim of the liturgical reforms mandated by Vatican Council II has been so to simplify and clarify the liturgy that the need for explanations of the rites is greatly diminished. From this perspective the most important single reform of the Roman liturgy has been the translation of ritual texts into modern vernacular languages.

Conscious and active participation in liturgical celebrations constitutes the principal continuing catechetical experience of most Catholics. And it is the experience of the *whole* of Christian worship—not just of its expressly didactic moments—which forms the Christian understanding. Even so the Christian liturgy is characterized by a specifically—though not solely—didactic moment: the complex of Bible readings, songs, and preaching called the Liturgy of the Word. Postconciliar reforms have amplified and enriched this portion of the Roman liturgy more than any other. In the new Mass Lectionary the more important parts of both Testaments are parceled out for systematic public reading in one-, two-, and three-year cycles. Many alternative readings are provided in the Commons of the Saints and for ritual and votive Masses, and the celebrant is given wide discretion in the choice of readings. The Lectionary for the Liturgy of the Hours has undergone similar revision. All the Sacraments are now preceded by some kind of Liturgy of the Word, even in private and individualized circumstances. Preaching, to be understood as an integral part of a specific liturgical celebration and not as an extraneous element, is expected at Sunday and holy day Masses and at all ordinary communal celebrations of the other Sacraments.

Other postconciliar enhancements of the catechetical potential of the Roman liturgy may be mentioned. In all rites the celebrant may intervene at transitional moments to help the worshipers enter more fully into the celebration. Among the new sacramental rites, those for infant Baptism and Marriage especially show a very strong didactic bias; the Rite for the Christian Initiation of Adults intends a constant meshing of formal instruction and liturgical celebration at each stage along the way to complete sacramental incorporation into the Church. Introductions to each of the new rites summarize the pastoral and doctrinal considerations operative in the reforms, and thus provide valuable resources for those responsible for liturgical catechesis. The Directory for Masses with Children (*Pueros baptizatos*, 1973) gives official approbation to simplifications and adaptations of the Mass intended to make the celebration more apt for groups of young children, for whom the standard liturgy may be frustrating and confusing (*see* MASSES WITH CHILDREN).

[C. DEHNE]

LITURGICAL COMMISSIONS, DIOCESAN AND NATIONAL

Liturgical Commissions came into being as a direct mandate of Vatican Council II's Constitution on the Sacred Liturgy: "Likewise, by way of advancing the liturgical apostolate, every diocese is to have a commission on the sacred liturgy under the direction of the bishop" (*Sacrosanctum Concilium* 45). Larger dioceses, utilizing their greater resources, were first to begin naming people to commissions and to begin active work. Some dioceses had an almost inoperative commission until models of operation began to develop.

The founding of the *Federation of Diocesan Liturgical Commissions (FDLC) in 1968 provided great impetus and enabled many of the dioceses of the country to form functioning commissions of their own. By the mid-1970s, almost every diocese had an active commission of some type.

Commission structures vary greatly, normally dependent on the importance the bishop and diocese attach to liturgy, but somewhat dependent on size. There are three main types of structure. (1) A growing number of dioceses use the term "office of worship," and have a full-time staff. In some dioceses this is related to a commission, in others, the staff has assumed the role of commissions. (2) The second form is the commission, usually made up of religious, priests, and laity functioning directly under the bishop. This is the most common form. In dioceses where there is a pastoral council the commission may have a relationship with that body. (3) In a few dioceses the commission is only a committee of the priests' senate.

The functions of a diocesan commission fall into five main areas: (1) developing and promoting liturgical spirituality and knowledge in priests and seminarians; (2) setting the agenda for FDLC work both nationally and regionally; (3) educating religious and laity in the revised rites and establishing training programs for lay ministers. (4) implementing new rites; (5) researching and evaluating existing rites with a view to future American adaptation.

At the present time in the U.S. there is no national liturgical commission (see *Sacrosanctum Concilium* 44), the functions of that group being handled by the FDLC and the Bishops' Committee on the Liturgy, along with the recognized liturgical centers.

Liturgical commissions have been very successful in updating the Church and working for quality in worship. Normal obstacles include lack of awareness of the theology underlying liturgy, the absence of liturgical spirituality in the American Catholic tradition, and even occasional opposition. The majority of people have been very interested and supportive—priests, religious, and laity. Programs for readers, lay ministers of the Eucharist, and liturgy planning have reached millions. Many liturgy commissions are also responsible for music and art within a diocese. Much has been done nationally through the FDLC Music Committee and the *National Association of Pastoral Musicians, with valuable results on the diocesan question. Most commissions have also been involved with the issue of music-copyright laws within dioceses. Few dioceses have been able to provide the people with an effective art commission. The liturgical commissions have provided what work has been done in art and architecture, but much remains to be done. Liturgical commissions and offices of worship are still in the process of creating modes of operation and clarifying structures. Much change can still be expected in this area before all the ways of implementing the Council directives have been explored.

[W. T. FAUCHER]

LITURGICAL COMMITTEES, PARISH

One of the standing committees on every parish council should be the liturgical committee. This group of people is charged with the tasks of seeing to the effective carrying out of proper roles by those who minister in worship and of planning together Eucharistic, sacramental, and other prayer forms according to the liturgical calendar and consistent with local prayer needs.

Membership on the committee can vary but should consist of a priest and the parish musician (organist or song director; *see* MINISTER OF MUSIC). Other persons involved in parochial worship should also be included e.g. the religious education director, deacon, coordinators of other ministries (lectors, ushers, servers, cantors, special ministers of the Eucharist, altar society, those charged with youth and children's liturgies and baptismal programs). All persons should have or be given a background in *liturgical theology. They should know and have access to the liturgical books so that their planning will be consistent with the demands of the Church in its ritual worship.

Liturgical planning is a prayerful process wherein the prayers and readings are considered in the context of the season as celebrated for particular groups within a parish. Such planning need not be thematic (BCL Newsletter 10 [1974] 137–138, which contains the translation of A. Bugnini, *Notitiae* 10 [1974] 137–138). Choices of art forms: songs, visuals, decorations, movement of people, and ritual actions should be made by the committee. Selection of persons to fulfill the various ministries should be made so that the end result and final purpose of planning is prayerful celebration for the entire parish.

Bibliography: Department of Worship, Archdiocese of Detroit. *Implementation Guide of Parish Worship Commission* (Detroit 1976). *Liturgy Committee Handbook* (A Nine-week Study Guide), The Liturgical Conference (Washington, D.C. 1971). *There are Different Ministries*, The Liturgical Conference (Washington, D.C. 1975).

[J. L. CUNNINGHAM]

LITURGICAL CONFERENCE

From its beginnings in 1940 until 1960 this voluntary membership association was known chiefly for its sponsorship of an annual Liturgical Week in the United States or Canada, for the influence of some of its leaders on developments in the Church, and for its periodical bulletin providing communication among Roman Catholics concerned about the vitality and pastoral character of liturgical celebration (8:892). The origins of a Bishops' Commission on the Liturgical Apostolate in 1958 and of an office and secretariat in 1964 were not without the influence of Liturgical Conference leaders, some of whom were involved also in preparatory work for Vatican Council II and in its proceedings.

The establishment of a central office and staff in Washington, D.C. in 1960 and the tremendous impetus given to all movements for ecclesial reform and renewal by the Council led to an expansion of the Liturgical Conference's membership as well as its activities and services. Liturgical Weeks drew large numbers of people during the conciliar years, peaking at about 15,000. An extensive publications program was launched to explain conciliar reforms, offer popular background for them, and suggest ways of implementation. This "Parish Worship Program" (1964) of books, kits, pamphlets was followed by the publication of a popular commentary on the Constitution on the Sacred Liturgy (1965). Regional groups developed in New England, the Southeast, and the Southwest, and began to have annual meetings.

At the same time, ecumenical activity was accelerating. A number of Anglican, Lutheran, and Protestant liturgiologists and liturgical practitioners had become involved in Liturgical Conference activities and dialogue. They appeared in the one-day institutes preceding Liturgical Weeks and then in the programs of the Weeks themselves. Some were nominated and elected to the board of directors. Since the association is governed by a board of directors elected by the membership, this development opened both membership and leadership to all Christians who share the Conference's concerns. The Liturgical Conference's character changed from a voluntary association serving the Churches in communion with Rome to one that is consciously and deliberately ecumenical.

The membership bulletin developed by several stages into a bi-monthly journal, *Liturgy*. A number of new periodical services were begun: *Living Worship* and *Homily Service*, which continue in 1978; *Parish Council, Today Songs for Today's People,* and *Major Feasts and Seasons*, which were temporary services. Specialized meetings, sponsored by the Liturgical Conference, on church architecture and liturgical music resulted in books. Proceedings of the Liturgical Weeks continued to appear as annual volumes through 1967. The Weeks themselves continued through 1969, resuming in 1975, and beginning again on an annual basis in 1977.

Corresponding to the rapid postconciliar development of liturgical renewal and with the evolving ecumenical character of the association, the range of publications broadened. Problems of adapting reformed rites were addressed in the 1970 *Manual of Celebration* and its *Supplement One*, and in *Celebrating Baptism*; children's need for ritual experience in *Children's Liturgies* and *Signs, Songs and Stories*; small group liturgies in *There's No Place Like People*; ways of integrating family and household prayer with parish worship in *Parishes and Families*. A number of filmstrips were done in cooperation with other agencies to educate for sacramental worship and the church year. The *Liturgy Committee Handbook* was published in 1971, the first of a series of manuals for liturgy planners and ministers that by 1978 included *The Lector's Guide* (1973); *The Ministry of Music* (1975); *There Are Different Ministries* (1975); *Strong, Loving and Wise: Presiding in Liturgy* (1976); *The Spirit Moves: A Handbook of Dance and Prayer* (1976); and *Touchstones for Liturgical Ministers* (1978), a series of brief summary guidelines.

A kit of materials for encouraging and guiding parish planners in a restoration of Lent-Easter as appropriate seasons for climaxing the catechumenate (especially for adult candidates in the course of the whole community's annual experience of prayer sharing and faith sharing in

small groups) was published as *From Ashes to Easter: Design for Parish Renewal. Simple Gifts* was a two-volume collection of articles from *Liturgy; Dry Bones,* from *Living Worship; The Rites of People,* a popular study of ritual questions. Three volumes, by different authors, examine *The Rite of Penance*: I *Understanding the Document*; II *Implementing the Rite*; III *Background and Directions.* The particular gifts and contribution of black religious experience in the U.S. is the subject of *This Far by Faith: American Black Worship and its African Roots. It Is Your Own Mystery: A Guide to the Communion Rite* examines the central part of a Eucharistic Liturgy historically and pastorally.

The Liturgical Conference also offers workshops on most of these subjects and engages its staff members in consultation for special liturgical events. These efforts, the publications mentioned above, correspondence with members and others, Liturgical Weeks, specialized seminars—all are part of the Liturgical Conference's continuing service to all the Churches as an educational, a motivating, and an advocacy force.

[R. W. HOVDA]

LITURGICAL EDUCATION IN SEMINARIES

Vatican Council II, aware of the need for competent leadership in the liturgical reform, speaks of the continuing formation of priests who "are to be helped by every suitable means to a fuller understanding of what they are about when they perform sacred rites, to live the liturgical life and to share it with the faithful entrusted to their care" (*Sacrosanctum Concilium* 18). Such trained leadership cannot be fully achieved in one generation; the development of liturgical life will largely be in the hands of future leaders of communal worship. When the Council Fathers speak of full participation of the laity as the heart of the liturgical life, they immediately add that "it is absolutely essential . . . that steps be taken to ensure the liturgical training of the clergy" (ibid. 14). Seminary professors must be properly trained in the study of liturgy and offer courses in liturgics which are "to be ranked among the compulsory and major courses in seminaries and religious houses"; seminaries and religious houses are to be permeated with a liturgical spirituality (ibid. 15–17). Moreover, in theological faculties the study of liturgy "is to rank among the principal courses. It is to be taught under its theological, historical, spiritual, pastoral, and juridicial aspects" (ibid. 16). Other theological disciplines are to be taught in such a way as to connect each one to the liturgy.

Guidelines Proposed. How are these mandates, absolutely essential to the liturgical renewal, being implemented? The *Ratio fundamentalis institutionis sacerdotalis (Basic Plan for Priestly Formation),* issued March 16, 1970, by the Sacred Congregation for Catholic Education, offers guiding norms to the national episcopal conferences for the implementation of directives from the documents of Vatican II applicable to seminary formation. The *Ratio fundamentalis* touches upon a number of liturgical questions in seminary formation: (1) liturgical life as foundation and growth factor in spiritual formation (14); (2) daily celebration of Eucharist, "the center of the whole life of the seminary" (52);

(3) "a sound variety in the manner of participation" in liturgy so that seminarians not only make personal spiritual progress, "but also be prepared practically . . . for their future ministry and liturgical apostolate" (52); (4) formation for understanding, reverencing and praying the Liturgy of the Hours (53); (5) instruction which assists in linking liturgy with daily life, with all forms of the apostolate and with Christian witness (53); (6) the study of liturgy as a principal theological discipline, linked with other subjects "in order that the students may realize how the salvation mysteries are rendered present and operative in the liturgical ceremonies" (79); (7) the study of the texts and rites of Oriental and Western liturgies as theological fonts (79); and (8) a practical understanding of liturgical options and of "what is changeable and what is, by divine institution, liturgically immutable" (79).

In the United States the National Conference of Catholic Bishops issued the first edition of *The Program of Priestly Formation* in 1971. It contains two elements regarding liturgy which surpass the *Ratio fundamentalis*: a strong emphasis on providing training in leadership skills for presiding at the liturgy (45b, 74c, 138), and adaptation of the liturgy and its music to the specific needs of college-age seminarians (358). In the second edition of *The Program for Priestly Formation* (1976) strong emphasis is placed on the following dimensions of the liturgical formation of seminarians: (1) the role of liturgy in the continuing process of conversion which is the foundation of all Christian life, and especially that of the presbyter (35–36); (2) integration of the Eucharist into daily life (38–39); (3) Eucharist and public celebration of the Liturgy of the Hours as formative of seminary community and as preparatory for ministry within parochial communities (37, 40); (4) instruction in art, music, and communication so that the ministers can create a proper atmosphere for celebration (146); and (5) other practical instruction, e.g. experience in working with liturgy teams or committees, and understanding the importance of parental involvement in sacramental preparation (147).

Actual Status. Despite the positive support of official documents for sound liturgical formation and instruction in seminaries, a survey on liturgical training of seminarians jointly conducted by the Seminary Research Department of the Center for Applied Research in the Apostolate (CARA) and the Bishop's Committee on the Liturgy (1973) revealed the following: (1) in most seminaries the study of liturgy is at best that of an ancillary discipline; usually it is merely a subdivision of sacramental theology; (2) few seminaries have even one full-time person with an advanced degree in liturgy; (3) professors of liturgy have little influence upon seminary praxis or the training of celebrants; (4) such fundamental areas as the liturgical year, the meaning of Sunday, or the liturgical use of Scripture are not addressed; (5) not all seminary faculties understand that liturgy is by nature an integrative discipline, affecting many areas of seminary study and practice. Similar criticism surfaced at a meeting of the Partners-in-Dialogue Program with Seminary Personnel at the Murphy Center for Liturgical Research (now the Notre Dame Center for Pastoral Liturgy), University of Notre Dame, March 15–16, 1976.

With the revision of the liturgical books now complete a more systematic approach can be taken to address the problem. The Federation of Diocesan Liturgical Commissions is in the process of writing a liturgical supplement for the next revision of *The Program of Priestly Formation* (1980–81). This supplement will be the result of wide consultation and it will include detailed instruction on the role of liturgy in seminary life, models for academic courses involving curricular interrelatedness, field-education programming, and the pastoral and practical dimensions of presidential style.

See also LITURGICAL THEOLOGY; THEOLOGY AND LITURGY.

Bibliography: "CARA Seminary Survey, Teaching Liturgy," Origins 4 (1974) 209, 211–217. Congregation for Catholic Education, *The Basic Plan for Priestly Formation, Ratio fundamentalis* . . . (USCC Publ. Office, Washington, D.C. 1970). NCCB, *The Program of Priestly Formation* (USCC Publ. Office, Washington, D.C., 1st ed. 1971; 2d ed., 1976).

[D. W. KROUSE]

LITURGICAL EXPERIMENTATION

Liturgical renewal involves a twofold process. According to Vatican Council II's Consitution on the Liturgy, the rites must be purified of those elements which are "out of harmony with the inner nature of the liturgy or which have become less suitable in the course of time" (*Sacrosanctum Concilium* 21). However, the liturgy must also be adapted to the temperament and traditions of peoples (ibid. 37–40). "Even in the liturgy, the Church does not wish to impose a rigid uniformity in matters which do not involve the faith or the good of the whole community. Rather does she respect and foster the qualities and talents of the various races and nations" (ibid. 37).

This cultural incarnation of the texts and rites must follow the general liturgical principles given in numbers 21 to 46 of the Constitution. "In order that sound tradition be retained, and yet the way remain open to legitimate progress, a careful investigation—theological, historical, and pastoral—should always be made into each part of the liturgy which is to be revised. Care must be taken that new forms grow organically from forms already existing" (ibid. 23).

The bishops are to be aided in this work by institutes for *pastoral liturgy which are to promote the studies and experiments necessary to adapt the liturgy to the people (ibid. 44). Furthermore, each celebrating community is to "experiment" in the sense that they have the responsibility to use fully and intelligently the freedoms given in the introductions to the new rites.

See also LITURGICAL LAWS, AUTHORITY OF; LITURGY (STRUCTURAL ELEMENTS).

[T. RICHSTATTER]

LITURGICAL GESTURES

Any act or movement of the human body becomes a gesture when it gives expression to meaning within an interpersonal relationship. Liturgical gestures in their turn express specific meanings within the relationship between God and human persons in community celebrations (8:894). Vatican Council II in the Constitution on Liturgy gave clear directives that liturgical gestures be expressive of the divine realities that they signify, and at the same time that these gestures be adapted to contemporary needs (*Sacrosanctum Concilium* 21, 62; *Gaudium et spes* 4–10 shows that implementation means more than simply changing a former ritual for a revised one).

It is evident that Baptism by immersion more clearly

expresses the inner faith reality of dying and rising with Christ (*Sacrosanctum Concilium* 6), than does Baptism by pouring a trickle of water on the forehead. Christian Initiation admits the non-Christian into the mysteries of Christ and into the faith community as well (ChrInitAd 19, 2). This is expressed very well when celebrant and members of the assembly—at least sponsors and catechists—sign each of the five senses of the candidate when he/she is admitted to the first step of the catechumenate (ibid. 85).

The General Instruction of the Roman Missal also concerns itself with Vatican II's call for more authentic liturgical gestures. The kiss of peace has been reinstated as an expression of the state of full reconciliation and forgiveness (GenInstrRomMissal 56, b). There is mention that "the sign of Communion," as the eschatological banquet, "is more complete when given under both kinds" (ibid. 240). Also "the nature of the sign demands that the material for the Eucharistic celebration appear as actual food" (ibid. 283).

Emphasis on the gesture of laying on of hands in the Sacrament of Reconciliation further carries out the Council's concern for meaningful gestures. The *Praenotanda* of the revised Rite of Penance, give the directive: ". . . the priest extends his hands or at least his right hand, over the penitent and pronounces the formula of absolution" (PenanceIntrod 19). This gesture is encouraging as it reassures the penitent in a kindly human way of safety from evil by the power of Jesus' death and resurrection. Such directives on meaningful gestures exemplify the richness of the instructions accompanying the liturgical rites in their revisions since Vatican II.

Bibliography: J. D. CRICHTON, *Christian Celebrations*, v. 1, *The Mass* (London 1971), v. 2, *The Sacraments* (London, 1973). M. HELLWIG, *The Meaning of the Sacraments* (Cincinnati, Ohio 1972). L. MITCHELL, *Meaning of Ritual* (New York 1977).

[M. P. ELLENBRACHT]

LITURGICAL LAWS, AUTHORITY OF

The early Church Fathers were profoundly aware that the Sacraments give the Church its very structure; this liturgical structuring of the Church has been reaffirmed by Vatican Council II. The Constitution on the Church states that the organic structure of the Church is brought into operation by means of the Sacraments (*Lumen gentium* 11). The Constitution on the Liturgy states that it is through the liturgy that the true nature of the Church is made visible (*Sacrosanctum Concilium* 2).

Because of this intimate relation between the liturgy and the Church, the Council states that the regulation of the liturgy depends on the Apostolic See, episcopal conferences, and the local bishop. "No other person, not even a priest, may add, remove, or change anything in the liturgy on his own authority" (ibid. 22). This statement is taken from *Mediator Dei*, encyclical of Pope Pius XII published in 1947. If the authority of the Church over the liturgy is reaffirmed with words taken from *Mediator Dei*, that authority over liturgical matters is now exercised in a much different manner than under Pius XII.

Formerly the Church presumed that if each detail of the rite was carefully performed, the entire ceremony would accomplish its purpose. Today the General Instructions and Introductions to the new liturgical rites look first of all to the end to be achieved by the rite and to its overall effect. The new rubrics give the reasons and the purpose of the new legislation. Clearly there is growing awareness that the liturgy is concerned not only with "things" but with actions, persons, and relationships. These are not so easily governed by the style of precise, detailed laws which were formerly the norm. For example, the Rite of Baptism states that the celebration "should reflect the joy of the Resurrection" (ChrInitGenIntrod 6). The Rite of Marriage directs the priest to "first of all strengthen and nourish the faith of those about to be married" (MarriageIntrod 7). The Rite of Funerals states that "priests should be especially aware of their responsibility to those present, whether Catholic or non-Catholic, who never or almost never take part in the eucharist or seem to have lost their faith. Priests must remember that they are ministers of Christ's Gospel to all" (FuneralsIntrod 18). The rite also states that "in general, all the texts of the rite are interchangeable and may be chosen, with the help of the community or family, to reflect the individual situation" (ibid. 24). It is indeed difficult for anyone with a real pastoral sense to be "disobedient" to such "rubrics" as these.

However, the new rites are not primarily concerned with freedom but with responsibility. The same funeral rite states: "if an individual prayer or other text is clearly not appropriate to the circumstances of the deceased person, it is the responsibility of the priest to make the necessary adaptations" (ibid. 24). Again and again the new rites stress that those leading the celebration are responsible for the proper functioning of the celebration. The Constitution on the Liturgy itself states that "pastors of souls must realize that, when the liturgy is celebrated, something more is required than the laws governing valid and lawful celebration. It is their duty also to ensure that the faithful take part fully aware of what they are doing, actively engaged in the rite and enriched by it" (*Sacrosanctum Concilium* 11).

Although the new rites may seem to give the celebrating community much more freedom than formerly, the new laws also demand that these freedoms be used wisely in order that the purpose of the rite be accomplished. Those planning and leading the celebration need to be aware of the general principles of the liturgical reform and to be familiar with the introductions to the new rites and the "General Instructions." They should do all in their power to assure that the celebration is a manifestation of the nature of the true Church, for it is from this fact that liturgical laws derive their authority.

See also LITURGICAL EXPERIMENTATION; LITURGY (STRUCTURAL ELEMENTS); RUBRICS.

Bibliography: A. COYLE and D. BONNER, *The Church Under Tension* (New York 1972). F. MCMANUS, "Liturgical Law and Difficult Cases," *Worship* 48 (1974) 347–366. T. RICHSTATTER, *Liturgical Law Today: New Style, New Spirit* (Chicago 1977). J. ROTELLE, "Liturgy and Authority," *Worship* 47 (1973) 514–526.

[T. RICHSTATTER]

LITURGICAL MOVEMENT, CATHOLIC

For all intents and purposes, the promotion of the liturgy as a "movement" or an "apostolate" in the Catholic Church ceased with the publication in 1963 of the Constitution on the Sacred Liturgy by Vatican Council II. This was the crowning achievement of the liturgical movement and the fulfillment of the hopes and dreams of those visionaries who spent their lives for the day when the official Church would validate their teaching (8:900). The Constitution endorsed the efforts of the pioneers but it only marked the beginning of the work to be undertaken by the Church universal. The document approved on Dec. 4, 1963 established the liturgical agenda for decades to come—liturgy was to become a priority concern of the Church. National liturgical commissions; institutes for pastoral liturgy; trained experts in worship, music, art and pastoral practice; cultural adaptations were all called for (*Sacrosanctum Concilium* 44). The Consilium for the Implementation of the Constitution on the Sacred Liturgy, a commission of experts, was established in 1964 to carry out the revisions of the Roman liturgical books (16:99). Except for the section of the Roman Ritual on blessings all of the Church's liturgical books were published in their Latin revisions before 1978.

Each language group has been charged with the task of translating the Latin edition into the vernacular (*see* LITURGICAL TEXTS, TRANSLATION OF). These translations must be approved by each episcopal conference and confirmed by the Sacred Congregation for the Sacraments and Divine Worship. Actual sacramental formulae are approved by the Holy Father for each language group. In 1963 the English-speaking world formed the *International Commission on English in the Liturgy (ICEL) which was incorporated in Canada (1967) with Washington, D.C. as the site of its secretariat.

In the U.S., the Bishops' Commission on the Liturgical Apostolate was formed in 1958 and is now called the *Bishops Committee on the Liturgy (BCL) with a full time secretariat. As dioceses established liturgical commissions in keeping with the directive of the Constitution (*Sacrosanctum Concilium* 44), the *Federation of Diocesan Liturgical Commissions (FDLC) came into existence in 1969 to promote leadership in pastoral liturgy. Two members are elected from each of twelve regions in the country to serve on a board of directors. Together with the BCL and a local diocese, the FDLC sponsors a national commission meeting annually. It has promoted the appointment of full-time-trained liturgical personnel in most large dioceses in the country.

The U.S. has more academically qualified liturgists than any other country and as a result the *North American Academy of Liturgy (NAAL) was established out of an initial meeting in 1973. The Academy has a Constitution and a working agreement with the liturgical journal, *Worship*, to publish the proceedings of its annual meeting. The BCL has also designated certain places as centers for liturgical research. The following continue to hold this designation: Notre Dame Center for Pastoral Liturgy (1970); St. John's, Collegeville (1970); the Center for Pastoral Liturgy at The Catholic University of America (1976); and the Mexican American Cultural Center (1976).

The *Liturgical Conference, which had been in the vanguard of the liturgical movement through its sponsorship of the National Liturgical Conferences each year, continues to be a membership organization. Lately it has serviced the needs of parish liturgical committees and ministers through the publication of background and practical materials as well as through workshops. It has also revived the National Liturgical Weeks on a much smaller scale Princeton (1975); Iowa City (1977).

In the area of the arts, a Composers' Forum for Catholic Worship was established in 1970 to promote the composition of new music, but was discontinued in 1977. With the demise of the National Catholic Music Educators Association there was formed in 1976 a *National Association of Pastoral Musicians to include both pastors and musicians. The BCL document *Music in Catholic Worship* (1972) did much to promote good music in liturgy and has led to a similar BCL publication, *Environment and Art in Catholic Worship* (1978), to guide the design and redesign of space for worship. After lengthy and broad-based consultation carried out by the music subcommittee of the FDLC, it was agreed that a national hymnal would be unwelcome, but the end result has been a number of good hymnals replacing the periodical disposable materials for parochial participation (*see* HYMNS AND HYMNALS; HYMNOLOGY).

Although the official worship books have been revised and liturgical expertise is available, the effects of the liturgical changes have been unevenly experienced to date. Liturgy is no longer a movement, rather it is integrally a part of the pastoral ministry of the Church.

Bibliography: A. BUGNINI, "Movimento liturgico o Pastorale liturgica," *Notitiae* 10 (1974) 137–138; Origins 3 (1974) 551–552. F. MCMANUS, "State of the Liturgy," Origins 2 (1972) 301, 303–304, 310–312. Bishops' Committee on the Liturgy, *Newsletter* (Washington, D.C. 1964–). *Liturgy*, Liturgical Conference (Washington, D.C. 1956).

[J. L. CUNNINGHAM]

LITURGICAL MOVEMENT AND ECUMENISM

Just as forms of worship constituted an index to the divergence of Christian bodies from one another in the 16th and following centuries, so in our own time liturgical reforms, proceeding almost simultaneously in most of the Churches of the West, have been at once symptomatic of growing ecumenical convergence and important influences on that movement. Following upon the ecumenical initiatives of Vatican Council II, the Consilium for the Implementation of the Constitution on the Sacred Liturgy (16:99) invited observers from other traditions to be present at work on the reform of the Calendar and Lectionary, and the *International Commission on English in the Liturgy (ICEL), charged with the preparation of authorized English translations of the new Latin liturgical documents, was assisted in its work by consultants enlisted from other Churches to review draft translations from an ecumenical viewpoint. One of the more important examples of ecumenical cooperation in liturgical reform has been the work of the *International Consultation on English Texts (ICET), a cooperative drafting of modern English versions of frequently used liturgical texts by representatives of the Anglican, Baptist, Congregational, Lutheran, Methodist, Presbyterian, and Roman Catholic Churches in England, Ireland, Scotland, Wales, Canada, Australia, South Africa, and the United States. Since 1969 this group of twenty-five scholars, in regular consultation with the bodies represented, has produced and revised texts of the Lord's Prayer, the Creeds, and the ordinary chants of the Eucharist and divine office, texts which have been widely adopted in recent liturgical reforms. An unofficial ecumenical group in the U.S. has proposed a *Common Eucharistic Prayer* already adopted by the Episcopal Church and under consideration by others.

Apart from such work toward textual agreement, augmented by significant consensus on the Calendar and Lectionary, there is evident as well widespread agreement regarding the structure of services, especially the Eucharist. This common structure for the Eucharist, based on historical studies, appeared already in the rite published in 1950 or the union of Anglicans, Congregationalists, Methodists, and Presbyterians as the Church of South India. This rite, influenced by an earlier but seldom used Anglican rite for Bombay, was widely acclaimed by liturgical scholars and many of its features (e.g., three readings, intercessory prayer before the presentation of the gifts, the sign of peace, the memorial acclamation in the Eucharistic Prayer) have become almost standard in modern liturgies. It should be noted, however, that the use of such new liturgies is optional in many of the Churches, so that much of the apparent consensus is more a promise than a present reality.

Beyond liturgical practice, the historical and theological insights of the liturgical movement have contributed greatly to the doctrinal accord emerging in ecumenical dialogues, especially in such areas as Eucharist and ministry; but here, too, much remains in the realm of promise.

Bibliography: International Consultation on English Texts, *Prayers We Have in Common* (Philadelphia 1975). Church of South India, *The Book of Common Worship* (London 1963). A. CLARK, ed., *Modern Eucharistic Agreement* (London 1973). T. S. GARRETT, *Worship in the Church of South India. Ecumenical Studies in Worship 2* (Richmond, Va. 1958). H. J. RYAN and J. R. WRIGHT, eds., *Episcopalians and Roman Catholics: Can They Ever Get Together?* (Denville, N.J. 1972).

[T. J. TALLEY]

LITURGICAL MUSIC

The renewal of liturgical music in the Church (10:97) takes its immediate origins from Vatican Council II, the Constitution on the Sacred Liturgy, which sets out the general principles of the renewal.

Conciliar Guidelines. Three areas in particular have assumed prominence in the years since the Council: the active participation of the faithful in the liturgy; the character and language of the rites themselves; and the cultural adaptation of the liturgy to different peoples.

Participation and Music. Active participation of the faithful, in which music plays a vital part, the Council presents as a norm: the faithful should take part in the liturgy "by means of acclamations, responses, Psalms, antiphons, hymns, as well as by actions, gestures, and bodily attitudes . . . and at the proper time, a reverent silence" (*Sacrosanctum Concilium* 30). A liturgy in which the faithful remain largely passive is to be replaced by one in which "whether as a minister or one of the faithful each person who has an office to perform should carry out all and only those parts which pertain to that office by the nature of the rite and the norms of the liturgy" (ibid. 28). Thus acolytes, readers, commentators, and members of the choir are all seen as fulfilling a genuine liturgical function (ibid. 29).

Rites and Texts. The rites themselves are to be characterized by a noble simplicity, and to be short, clear, free from useless repetition, and within the peoples' power of comprehension so that little explanation is required (ibid. 34). The question of language has assumed great importance since the Council and has given rise to certain problems, especially in the area of liturgical music, where the mere translation of texts is

only a beginning. What the Council Fathers seem originally to have envisioned was a basic retention of the Latin language combined with a somewhat wider use of the vernacular, especially in the readings, directives, and in some prayers and chants (ibid. 36). *Gregorian chant was still to have been given "pride of place, other things being equal" (ibid. 116). The years since the Council, however, have seen a much greater role being given to the vernacular, largely for valid pastoral reasons, with a consequent lessening of the traditional role of Latin and Gregorian chant.

Inculturation. The Constitution also provides basic principles for the cultural adaptation of the liturgy to various peoples (*see* INCULTURATION, THEOLOGICAL). A rigid uniformity is to be avoided—rather the qualities and talents of various races and nations are to be respected and fostered (ibid. 37). When revising the liturgical books, provision is to be made for legitimate variations and adaptations for different groups, regions, and peoples, especially in mission lands (ibid. 38; *see* LITURGY AND LOCAL CHURCHES). For liturgical music, an important principle for cultural adaptation was the recognition that one cannot, especially in a cross-cultural context, define sacred music in terms restricted to a given style or repertoire. Instead the criterion is to be how closely the music is connected with the liturgical action. The Church thus approves "all forms of true art which have the requisite qualities, and admits them into divine worship" (ibid. 112). Though the pipe organ is still said to be held in high esteem, other instruments are to be admitted for use in worship as long as they are appropriate for sacred use, in accord with the dignity of worship, and are conducive to the edification of the faithful (ibid. 120). The sacred music of the past, chant as well as other types, is to be preserved, however, and choirs are to be assiduously developed (ibid. 114). Education in liturgical music is stressed, especially in seminaries and Catholic institutions, and composers are encouraged to write music, not only for large choirs but also for smaller choirs and the congregation (ibid. 115 and 121; *see* HYMNOLOGY; MUSICOLOGY, SACRED; CONGREGATIONAL SINGING).

Post-Conciliar Directives. The first important post-conciliar guidelines on music in the liturgy are contained in the Congregation of Rites 1967 instruction, *Musicam sacram* (ActApS 59 [1967] 300–320). Though it was in many ways an interim document, important guidelines were given for singing in the vernacular (MusSacr 47–48; 57–61), for greater choice in the selection of elements to be sung (ibid. 7), and for greater participation of the congregation, especially in the singing of such elements as the Responsorial Psalm, the Holy, Holy, Holy, and the Lord's Prayer (ibid. 29–36). A new rite for the Mass as well as a completely new lectionary were prepared and introduced in 1970. The "General Instruction of the Roman Missal," which accompanied the publication of the texts of the new rite, is of particular value to the liturgical musician—especially chapter two (GenInstrRomMissal 7–57) in which the various elements of the rite are explained, specifying the role of music in each.

Bishops' Committee on Liturgy. In 1967 the NCCB had also issued a statement on the place of music in Eucharistic celebrations. Revised and published by the Bishops' Committee on the Liturgy in 1972 as *Music in Catholic Worship*, this document remains what is probably the best statement on the role of music in the liturgy issued since the Council. The document underlines the "preeminent importance" of music in the liturgy (BCL Music 23) and locates it among those signs and symbols which serve to express the faith of the worshiping community. Good celebrations are seen to foster and nourish that faith, poor celebrations to weaken and destroy it (ibid. 6). Special emphasis is placed on: the ministerial role of music in the liturgy (ibid. 23); the necessity for careful planning which involves separate but coordinated judgments on musical, liturgical, and pastoral aspects (ibid. 25–41); and the role which music can play in each of the elements of the liturgical action (ibid. 50–78). Active participation is to be implemented in liturgical planning, in the singing of those elements that are by their nature congregational, and in the emphasis placed on the role of cantor, choir members, and instrumentalists. Signs used in the rites, and music is such a sign, are to be simple and comprehensible, humanly attractive, meaningful, and appealing to the community of worshipers (ibid. 7). Though the use of Latin is mentioned in several places (ibid. 27, 28, 76), the primary referent is obviously vernacular liturgy. Cultural adaptation is mentioned only briefly (ibid. 28 and 41).

Specific Documents. There have been no other general statements or instructions on liturgical music, though a number of more specific documents contain sections on music. The *General Instruction on the Liturgy of the Hours* published in 1970, makes clear the importance of this prayer as the prayer of the entire Church (GenInstrLitHor ch. 1) and gives specific directions for its communal celebration in song (ibid. ch. 5). Norms for the use of music at benediction and exposition are contained in the 1973 *Instruction on Holy Communion and Worship of the Eucharistic Mystery Outside Mass* (93–100). The place of music in Masses for children is set forth in the 1973 *Directory for Children's Masses* (30–32). The way in which music is incorporated into communal penance celebrations is described in the 1973 instruction which accompanied the publication of the new rites of Penance (PenanceIntrod ch. 2 and 3). All of the above instructions except that on the Liturgy of the Hours are found in A. Flannery, ed., *Vatican Council II: the Conciliar and Post Conciliar Documents* (Northport, N.Y. 1975). In 1974 three books were published which provide for the use of Latin chant in the new liturgy where desirable: from the Congregation for Divine Worship, *Jubilate Deo* (Vatican City 1974), containing the minimum repertoire of Gregorian chant for congregations (see Origins 4 [1974] 45–47, accompanying letter to NCCB); *Graduale Romanum* (Solesmes 1974), the full gradual for the new rite; and *Graduale simplex* (Rome 1974), a revised and augmented edition of the collection of simpler Mass chants for use in smaller churches.

Organizations. Since Vatican II a number of organizations have come into existence or grown considerably in order to provide for the needs of a renewed liturgy. Supervision and coordination of the liturgical renewal in the U.S. is provided in large part by the work of the *Bishops' Committee on the Liturgy. The work of individual diocesan liturgical commissions is supported and coordinated by the *Federation of Diocesan Liturgical Commissions. The *International Commission on English in the Liturgy (ICEL) is concerned with the preparation of suitable texts in the vernacular.

Among a number of organizations involved in the renewal of liturgy and music, the Bishops' Committee on the Liturgy has designated six official centers for liturgical research: the Notre Dame Center for Pastoral Liturgy (Formerly the Murphy Center for Liturgical Research) in Notre Dame, Ind.; St. John's University, Collegeville, Minn.; the *Mexican American Cultural Center in San Antonio, Texas; the Center for Pastoral Liturgy at The Catholic University of America in Washington, D.C. Other centers important for liturgical music are the *National Association for Pastoral Musicians, founded in Washington, D.C. in 1976, and the *National Office for Black Catholics (NOBC), begun in 1968. Of particular importance to research are the *North American Academy of Liturgy, a Christian ecumenical organization of professional liturgists, musicians, and persons in related fields; and the Hill Monastic Manuscript Library at St. John's University in Collegeville, Minnesota.

Study and Research Centers. In the area of education a number of programs are available to liturgical musicians. Full graduate programs in liturgical studies exist at St. John's University, Collegeville; the University of Notre Dame; and The Catholic University of America. Programs devoted specifically to liturgical music are found at Catholic University; St. Joseph's College in Rensselaer, Ind.; Duquesne University in Pittsburgh; and at Yale University. In addition to these full time programs a number of workshops are given throughout the country by individual dioceses and by various other organizations, among which should be mentioned the World Library of Sacred Music, the Center for Pastoral Liturgy at Catholic University, and the Notre Dame Center for Pastoral Liturgy. At one time the Pius X School of Liturgical Music (11:418; *see* WARD, JUSTINE), Manhattanville College in Purchase N.Y. played an active role in the education of liturgical musicians, but it has, in recent years, become inactive.

Publishers and Publications. Publishers of liturgical music have also grown in the years since the Council. Among the more important publishers specializing in music for Roman Catholic liturgy are: G.I.A. Publications, Inc.; World Library of Sacred Music (now a part of J. S. Paluch, Inc.); F.E.L. Inc., the Liturgical Press; North American Liturgy Resources; and Worship Resources, Inc. Many larger publishers maintain sacred music catalogs as well.

The number of periodicals concerned with liturgy and liturgical music has increased dramatically since the Council. The first, and still one of the most important is *Worship*, now the official organ of the North American Academy of Liturgy as well. Other important periodicals include: *Liturgy*, a publication of the Liturgical Conference; *Sacred Music*, from the Church Music Association of America; *Modern Liturgy*; *Pastoral Music*, from the National Association of Pastoral Musicians; *Freeing the Spirit*, published by the NOBC; and, from England, *Music and Liturgy*. Among other Christian or ecumenical journals, special mention should be made of *The Hymn*, published by the Hymn Society of America. Two publications are of particular importance for the liturgical musician since they have an official status. These are *Notitiae*, published by the Sacred Congregation for Divine Worship and the Sacraments; and the BCL *Newsletter*, which contains directives and guidelines for the Church in the United States.

The Future. The decade and a half since the promulgation of *Sacrosanctum Concilium* has seen the completion of the revision of the rites themselves, and the beginning of their implementation and development. The recent (August 1977) approval on an experimental basis of the Ministry of Music as an official ministry of the Church in the United States points to a real recognition of the importance of the role of the liturgical musician. Among the desired developments for the future are: greater cooperation and sharing among liturgists and liturgical musicians; better education in the field of liturgical music at all levels; greater balance between the use of traditional and newer elements in the liturgy; continuing growth in the quality and amount of liturgical music available; and a constant awareness that growth and excellence in liturgical music must always be seen in a context of faith and prayer.

Bibliography: R. J. BUTLER, "A Decade of Harmony and Discord in Church Music," LivLight 4 (1977) 14, 580–592. L. DEISS, *Spirit and Song of the New Liturgy* (Cincinnati 1970). J. GÉLINEAU, *Voices and Instruments in Christian Worship* (Collegeville, Minn. 1964). M. GILLIGAN, *How to Prepare Mass* (Oak Park, Ill. 1972). E. GUTFREUND, *With Lyre, Harp and a Flatpick: the Folk Musician at Worship* (Cincinnati 1973). B. HUIJBERS, *The Performing Audience: Vernacular Liturgy and Musical Style* (Cincinnati 1974).

[R. B. HALLER]

LITURGICAL REFORM

The program of liturgical reform (8:908; 16:260) projected by the Second Vatican Council was delineated in its Constitution on the Sacred Liturgy, promulgated Dec. 4, 1963.

Principles of Liturgical Reform. The paramount purpose of this reform was to restore to the faithful "that full, intelligent, active part in liturgical celebrations which the nature of the liturgy itself requires, and which, in virtue of their Baptism, is their right and duty" (*Sacrosanctum Concilium* 14). This essentially pastoral concern as the supreme norm for liturgical reform is repeated over and over throughout the Constitution, and is given solid doctrinal support in the rich theological introduction on the nature of the liturgy and its importance in the life of the Church (ibid. 5–13). This theological and pastoral foundation for reform, likewise prefaced to each of the seven remaining chapters of the Constitution, was to become one of the insistent and increasingly profound characteristics of the major documents of liturgical reform. Posited on the assumption that the liturgy consists of "a part that is unchangeable because it is divinely instituted and of parts that can be changed," the reform clearly involved giving to "texts and rites a form that will express clearly the sacred content they are meant to signify, a form such that the Christian people will be able to grasp this content as easily as possible and share in it in a full, active, congregational celebration" (ibid. 21).

Three areas were explicitly singled out for a revision based on an understanding that liturgical services were "not private activities, but celebrations of the Church" (ibid. 26): (1) the hierarchical and communal nature of the liturgy, by which the diverse ministerial roles of the entire liturgical assembly were to be fostered (ibid. 26–32); (2) the pastoral and didactic nature of the liturgy, by which, through the clear, concise, and simple conjuncture of word and rite, the faith of the partici-

pants is nourished (ibid. 33–36); (3) the cultural diversity of various groups, regions and peoples, which, while still preserving the "substantial unity of the Roman rite," would profit by "legitimate variations and adaptations" (ibid. 37–40). In light of the pastoral and theological objectives of the Constitution, these were the three fundamental directional principles that were to govern the reform of the Eucharistic Liturgy, rites for the other Sacraments and sacramentals, the Liturgy of the Hours, the calendar, church music, and sacred art.

Vehicles of Reform. To carry out this reform, Paul VI established, Jan. 25, 1965, a commission known as the Consilium for the Implementation of the Constitution on the Liturgy, under the direction of Cardinal Giacomo *Lercaro. This body of highly-qualified experts retained its quasi-autonomous identity until late in 1969, when it was reconstituted as the Special Commission for the Completion of the Liturgical Reform within the newly created Congregation for Divine Worship, with Cardinal Benno Gut as first prefect. From July 11, 1975 competency for liturgical reform passed to the newly constituted Congregation of *Sacraments and Divine Worship, with Cardinal James Knox as prefect. Whereas the overall revision of the Roman liturgy was centralized under the direction of the Holy See, legitimate adaptation was to be channelled through the competent regional and national episcopal conferences. In the U.S. the liturgical reform has been under the guidance of the *Bishops' Committee on the Liturgy, which, since 1970, has been in consultation with the *Federation of Diocesan Liturgical Commissions. The English translations of the Latin *editio typica* of the various reformed liturgies have been provided by a separate entity under the English-speaking episcopate, the *International Commission on English in the Liturgy.

Major Achievements of Liturgical Reform. The reform of the liturgical books mandated by the Constitution (*Sacrosanctum Concilium* 25) is now substantially complete. Sections of the first part of the Roman Pontifical which appeared earlier have now been republished in an integral compilation, and a major section of the second part, rites for the dedication of a Church, was promulgated in May, 1977 (*see* CHURCHES, DEDICATION OF). The episcopal ceremonial still remains, at this date, unavailable, as do the Roman Ritual section on blessings and the Roman Martyrology. But it does at last seem that the enormous task begun by the Consilium is nearing its conclusion. Granted that the reforms are the result of lengthy and laborious study, debate, and compromise, and that they themselves must undergo periodic revision, it is nevertheless possible at this point to make a general assessment of some of the major achievements of the liturgical reform envisioned by Vatican Council II.

(1) *The Liturgy, Locus of Encounter.* Fundamental throughout the entire liturgical reform is the conviction that the Church celebrates in her liturgy, through ritual transposition, the Trinitarian economy of salvation, celebrating, that is, the mysteries "in which are set forth the victory and triumph of his death, and also giving thanks to God for his inexpressible gift in Christ Jesus, in praise of his glory through the power of the Holy Spirit" (ibid. 6). The dialogic perception of the liturgy as being the locus par excellence where God speaks to his people through Christ and where they, in return, respond to the Father by actualizing the priestly mission

of the same Christ is expressed not only in the Constitution (ibid. 7), but also in the theological statements introducing the reformed rites. In this regard, the General Instruction on the Roman Missal, the General Instruction of the Liturgy of the Hours, the General Norms for the Liturgical Year and the Calendar, for example, mark an extraordinary advance over the juridical, rubrical directives of the analogous sections of the unreformed books. This theological understanding of the liturgy as being "the very exercise of the priestly office of Jesus Christ" and therefore "preeminently a sacred action, the efficacy of which no other act of the Church can equal on the same basis and to the same degree" (ibid. 7) is what underlies the Church's repeated emphasis on liturgical reform.

(2) *Other Theological Aspects.* The *ressourcement* (return to sources) of the reform also brought with it a rediscovery or restoration of certain theological aspects of the Christian tradition which through the centuries had fallen into the background: the totality of the paschal mystery in every liturgical celebration; the multimodal presence of Christ in all of the liturgy and not only in the Eucharistic elements; the Trinitarian economy of prayer to the Father, through the Son, in the power of the Spirit; the role of the Holy Spirit in the formation and sanctification of the Church as People of God set apart to sing his praises within their assembly; the eschatological hope of the pilgrim Church awaiting the day of the Lord; liturgical remembrance of the deeds of the Lord of history and their recovery in the Kingdom; the relationship of faith, repentance, conversion, reconciliation and their sacramental realization; the incarnational and worldly dimension of Christian life; and many more areas which have hardly begun to be explored. In no small measure is this theological recovery due to the Constitution's stipulation (ibid. 92) that the Scriptures be made readily accessible in greater fullness, and that patristic and other ecclesiastical writers be represented more authentically.

(3) *The Liturgy, Prayer of the Whole People.* The hierarchical and ecclesial aspect of the liturgy described in the Constitution (ibid. 26–32) has restored the precious value that liturgy is not the private province of the clergy, but is indeed the prayer of the whole people who, while under the leadership of the ordained minister, all exercise the shared priesthood of Christ. In this context, the multiple functions of readers, cantors, acolytes and other ministers, as well as the active participation of the congregation are to be regarded as a true liturgical ministry.

(4) *A Pastoral Liturgy.* Regarding the pastoral and didactic nature of the liturgy (ibid. 33–36), three reformed areas have produced incalculable benefits: introduction of the vernacular far beyond the expectations of the conciliar Fathers; restoration of the Liturgy of the Word almost to the point of surfeit; and transparency of rite. More than any other change, perhaps, the use of the vernacular has made the liturgy into an active and conscious part of Christian spirituality. In place of the spare rites of the Tridentine liturgy there is now accessible to the people in their own language a copious, amplified liturgy with God's Word poured forth in abundance. The use of the mother tongue consequently makes immediately available the astonishing increase of Scripture reading, not only in the admirable Lectionary at Mass with its several cycles of judiciously selected pericopes and responsorial psalms, but also in the cycle of readings prepared for the Liturgy of the Hours and the sacramental celebrations, so that every liturgy allows God to speak to his people and Christ to proclaim the good news (ibid. 33). Drawing upon this source, the *homily, regarded as an integral part of the liturgy, will be "like a proclamation of God's mighty deeds in redemptive history" (ibid. 35), with the mystery of Christ always present and at work in the Church. In addition, catechetical insights, brief commentaries, and instructions are encouraged to make of the prescribed liturgy a more cohesive and effective celebration. Finally, the ritual symbolic actions and gestures have been pared down so that the dominant liturgical symbol becomes more immediately understandable, pruned of its former repetitive and allegorical overlayering.

(5) *Adaptation and Inculturation.* The most revolutionary liturgical reform, in comparison with the previous four-hundred-year static uniformity, has been, without doubt, the acceptance of the principle of liturgical adaptation required by the needs and cultural differences of various groups, regions, and peoples (ibid. 38). Instances of group adaptation have been the publication of guidelines for Mass with special groups (May 15, 1969), and deaf-mutes (June 26, 1970), and a Directory for *Masses with Children (Nov. 1, 1973). Regarding cultural adaptation, the *Praenotanda* of the reformed liturgical books make special provision for regional adjustments to be determined by episcopal conferences, a norm which has been liberally applied, notably in the funeral liturgy and in the marriage rites. Translation of the *editio typica* into a multitude of vernacular languages has brought along with it its own peculiar requirements of linguistic and literary adaptation (*see* LITURGICAL TEXTS, TRANSLATION OF).

Further Demands of Liturgical Reform. If the first phase of liturgical reform is virtually complete, viz., revision of the liturgical books, it is evident—judging from worldwide indications during the past decade— that the second, and collateral, phase, that of celebration and experiential transposition, has hardly begun. The problems emerging from this stage of implementation and reform can be reduced to two large areas, both interrelated, which can be sketched here only in broad terms: the process of assimilation and interiorization, and the process of cultural adaptation and creativity.

Assimilation and Interiorization. Liturgical forms and reforms have as their purpose personal, ecclesial, and societal transformation; liturgy exists for man, not man for the liturgy. The reform of the liturgical books, which is, after all, an institutional reform, must be consonant with the goal outlined in the Constitution: to increase the faith and vigor of Christian life for all those who believe in Christ (ibid. 1). To transpose the printed letter of a prescribed rite to a joyful, communal celebration which has the power to renew Christian life requires a whole complexus of celebrational skills, not only on the part of all the liturgical ministers, but also, and above all, on the part of the priest celebrant. If liturgy is prayer, it must become the most prayerful experience possible; if liturgy is the actualization of the salvific mystery-presence of Christ, then it must also create an environment where the mystical contact with the utterly numinous Holy One is not only possible, but surely established. If liturgy is the "summit towards which the Church's activity tends, it must also be the fountain from which all its vitality flows" (ibid. 10). In this sense, liturgy provides the source and point of return for the Church's mission of evangelization and working towards a kingdom of justice and peace in the world; and as the process of assimilation and interiorization continues, liturgy will become more and more the transforming ritual of those who want to celebrate their communion of faith in an alien and increasingly desacralized world.

Cultural Adaptation and Creativity. Perhaps the most difficult question to deal with is how to resolve, or keep in creative tension, the dialectic between "the substantial unity of the Roman rite" (ibid. 38) and the pluralistic drives of cultural hegemony. Related to this is the difficulty posed by the working principle that "new forms should grow organically from those already existing" (ibid. 23) and the hard facts of cultural, spatial, and historical discontinuity between the disparate sources of the Catholic liturgical tradition and the increasing fragmentation of any unified religious *optique.* Liturgical adaptation (16:255), then, is not simply a matter of a few slight variations in an otherwise uniformly received liturgy, nor even of more liberal adjustments in the style of celebration, liturgical vesture, space, and accoutrements. What is involved is a move towards regaining the cultural sources of ritual creativity, symbolic expression, linguistic, musical, and other artistic charisms indigenous to each distinctive cultural group, race, or region (*see* LITURGY AND LOCAL CHURCHES). In other words, the parameters of liturgical reform are vast indeed, and this present age, with all its baggage, is barely moving toward the horizon.

Bibliography: D. BONDIOLI et al., "Situazione della liturgia riformata e futuro della pastorale liturgica," *Rivista di Pastorale Liturgica* 13 (1976) 3–36. W. J. BURGHARDT, "A Theologian's Challenge to Liturgy," ThSt 35 (1974) 233–248. D. DYE, "Statut et fonctionnement du 'rituel' dans la pastorale liturgique en France après Vatican II," *Maison-Dieu* 125 (1976) 133–165. P. M. GY, "La reforme liturgique de Trente et celle de Vatican II," *Maison-Dieu* 128 (1976) 61–75. R. KACZYNSKI, ed., *Enchiridion documentorum instaurationis liturgicae, I (1963–1973)* (Turin 1976) with suppl., "Documenta instaurationis liturgicae," *Notitiae* 12 (1976) 355–356. E. J. LENGELING, "Tradition und Fortschritt in der Liturgie," LiturgJb 25 (1975) 201–223. I. OÑATIBIA, "Dieciseis años de intensa evolución litúrgica: 1961–77," *Phase* 17 (1977) 189–217. Sacred Congregation for the Sacraments and Divine Worship, *Notitiae n. 113: Indices generales annorum 1965–1975* (Vatican City 1976). H. SCHMIDT, "Liturgy and Modern Society—Analysis of the Current Situation," in H. SCHMIDT, ed., *Liturgy in Transition: Concilium 62* (New York 1971) 14–29. H. SCHMIDT and D. POWER, eds., *Politics and Liturgy: Concilium 92* (New York 1974). R. G. WEAKLAND, "The 'Sacred' and Liturgical Renewal," *Worship* 49 (1975) 512–529.

[G. M. COLESS]

LITURGICAL RITES

For many English-speaking Christians the Roman rite is synonymous with the worship of the Catholic Church. However, the Roman rite is only one of many rites. The first centuries of Christianity witnessed a great diversity of liturgical formulas. The bishop had to improvise the liturgical prayers even as he had to improvise many other aspects of his office. During the 4th to the 8th centuries written texts began to be used; those of the major episcopal cities quite naturally received a certain prominence and thus there developed around these principal sees a common liturgical practice: a liturgical rite.

The Roman rite was originally the liturgy of the city of Rome. It spread very early throughout Italy. St.

Ambrose writes that he follows the Roman usage (rite); however, he insists that it is reasonable to adopt some practices from other Churches also (*De sacramentis,* 3.1.5). The Roman rite spread across the Alps and was carried by the missionaries to England and Ireland and Germany. Finally, Charlemagne imposed it on the Empire. The rite underwent certain changes as it spread across Europe. Some of these local adaptations and customs found their way back to Rome itself and influenced the liturgy there. The invention of the printing press and the reform of the Council of Trent were the two major factors which reduced the diversity within the Roman rite; however, certain variations continued to exist, for example, in the rites of religious orders, such as the Dominicans, the Carthusians, and the Premonstratensians.

The ecclesiastical province of Milan has preserved to this day its own way of celebrating the liturgy: the Ambrosian rite. Spain developed a Latin liturgy fundamentally different from that of Rome: the Mozarabic or Visigothic rite (Spain was dominated by the Visigoths from the 5th to 7th centuries). This Spanish liturgy, however, was replaced by the Roman rite by order of Gregory VII towards the end of the 11th century and is now celebrated only in certain churches of the diocese of Toledo and in one chapel of the cathedral.

The attitude of Rome toward these variations within its rite has changed in the course of the centuries. At first there was a rather liberal attitude as witnessed in Bede's *History of the English Church and People.* Bede perhaps indicates the 8th-century attitude when, in answer to a question by Augustine of Canterbury as to why some Churches in Gaul say Mass differently than in Rome, he has Pope Gregory respond: "My brother, you are familiar with the usage of the Roman Church. If you have found customs, whether in the Church of Rome or of Gaul or any other that may be more acceptable to God, I wish you to make a careful selection of them and teach the Church of the English. Things should not be loved for the sake of places, but places for the sake of good things. Therefore select from each of the Churches whatever things are devout, religious, and right" (*History* 1.27). In the course of time, this tolerant attitude changed: first for political reasons, and then because of a certain understanding of the relationship of liturgy to doctrine which seemed to demand that unity of faith required a uniformity of liturgical practice.

Vatican Council II's Constitution on the Sacred Liturgy states that "the Church holds all lawfully recognized rites to be of equal right and dignity; that she wishes to preserve them in the future and to foster them in every way. The Council also desires that, where necessary, the rites be revised carefully in the light of sound tradition, and that they be given new vigor to meet present-day circumstances and needs" (*Sacrosanctum Concilium* 4). The practical norms given in the Constitution were to be understood as applying only to the Roman rite, however, the principles of liturgical reform were to be applied to the worship of the whole Church (ibid. 3). The task of applying the general principles and revising the rites to meet present-day circumstances is currently being carried out in the various rites within the Latin tradition. It is not an easy task. Often liturgical elements which have been hallowed by traditional use have to be changed to meet the prayer needs of contemporary Christians. In some cases the Roman rite is seen to be more fitting than the variants. Some, for example the Dominicans, have decided to adopt the Roman rite. Others are revising their rites. Spring 1976 marked the publication of the revised Ambrosian Missal. The new missal of Milan manifests the distinctive features of the ancient Ambrosian rite while, at the same time, showing the fruits of contemporary liturgical study.

In all this work, Bede's principle holds true: rites should not be imposed because of their origin or antiquity; rather we must select from our traditions those things which are "devout, religious, and right."

Bibliography: B. BOTT, "Rites et familles liturgiques," *L'Église en Prière* (Paris 1965). A. KING, *Liturgies of the Religious Orders* (London 1955). "The New Ambrosian Missal," BCL Newsletter 13 (January 1977) 50–51.

[T. RICHSTATTER]

LITURGICAL TEXTS, TRANSLATION OF

The fifty years before Vatican Council II saw the publication in the West of countless people's missals enabling the laity to follow the Latin liturgy in translation. When, however, after the Council it was no longer a question of following the liturgy with the aid of a book but of actively participating in a living, vernacular liturgy, two important considerations arose: the translation of texts had to be in an idiom which would speak directly to the contemporary person; and some degree of uniformity was desirable among those countries which shared a common language. In an effort to achieve this the various language groups set up committees to supervise the translation of liturgical texts. In the English-speaking world this committee was called the *International Committee (later, Commission) on English in the Liturgy (ICEL). It is subtitled "A Joint Commission of Catholic Bishops' Conferences" and consists of an episcopal board, representing eleven countries, and an Advisory Committee of experts in various disciplines, namely, liturgy, Scripture, theology, pastoral studies, language, literature, and sacred music. It is incorporated in Toronto, Canada. Washington, D.C. is the site of its executive secretariat.

The first meeting of ICEL's Advisory Committee was in London in February 1965, when first principles of liturgical translation were discussed and formulated. These were further discussed at a full meeting in Rome in November of the same year and were published by the secretariat in a booklet entitled *English for the Mass* (March 16, 1966). The booklet offered sample translations of the common texts of the Mass and invited comments from the public at large. Over four thousand replies were received. A further booklet, *English for the Mass: Part II* (Feb. 1967) was then published, submitting for criticism various selected texts from the proper prayers, prefaces, readings, and psalms. In 1968 came the publication of another booklet entitled *Towards a Translation of the Lord's Prayer in Contemporary English—Biblical and Patristic Considerations*. The very many replies elicited by these publications resulted in the compilation of a list of valued consultors from every part of the English-speaking world to whom preliminary drafts of translations could be sent for criticism before a final text was agreed. It also ensured a high degree of ecumenical cooperation which led to the setting up in April 1969 of the *International Consultation on English Texts (ICET). The results of their combined effort have been published in various editions of *Prayers We Have in Common*. These texts have since been adopted by many of the participating Churches.

Meanwhile the combined experience of liturgical translators in every language group throughout the world was gradually serving to clarify the fundamental principles involved in liturgical translation, with the result that the Consilium for the Implementation of the Constitution on the Sacred Liturgy was able to issue on January 25, 1969 an *Instruction on Translation of Liturgical Texts* (*Notitiae* 5 [1969] 3–12) which went a long way towards systematizing liturgical translation everywhere. This Instruction may be summarised as follows.

(1) The true meaning of the original text must be rendered in the translation. This means that in some instances a critical text of the passage to be translated must first be established. Latin terms must be considered in the light of their historical and liturgical uses. The unit of meaning is not the individual word but the whole passage.

(2) The translation must be intelligible to the average participant in the liturgy, hence the accuracy and value of a translation can only be assessed in terms of the general principles relating to verbal communication. The language should be that in common use. Where, as often happens, there is no word in common use that exactly corresponds to the biblical or liturgical sense of the term to be translated, the nearest suitable word must be chosen. In many modern languages a biblical or liturgical language will have to be created by use. A translation of a liturgical text will often require "cautious adaptation."

(3) Liturgical texts vary in their literary genre; each genre demands an appropriate style of translation. Prayer differs from proclamation, and the liturgical prayers themselves vary in style, from the succinct, chiseled form of the *orationes* or Collects to the much more expansive and discursive style of the Eucharistic Prayers. The Prefaces are lyrical passages quite unique in their conception. Other texts are poetic in character and require very sensitive handling. Hence there can be no such thing as a common liturgical or sacral style. Particular care is needed with texts that are intended to be sung. A purely literal translation of a hymn is obviously out of the question. Normally an entirely fresh rendering will have to be made—one which accords with the musical and choral traditions of a particular language group.

(4) The translation of Scripture passages intended for reading in a liturgical context poses special problems. The sacredness of the text requires a high degree of conformity with the biblical passages in the Latin original (Inst. *Inter oecumenici* 40a). A paraphrase of a difficult text in order to make it more intelligible, or the insertion of words or explanatory phrases, is not permissible. This is the task of catechesis and the homily. On the other hand, responses and antiphons, even though they come from Scripture, are in a special category. There are many passages that are not simply from the Vulgate text, but are liturgical accommodations of the Scriptures, adapted so as to relate a scriptural text to a particular moment in the liturgy or to a particular feast or season. Hence the translation should be similarly nuanced. If it is not possible to do

this in translation, an episcopal conference may choose other texts to serve the same end. The fact that these texts are intended for singing as well as for recitation may also necessitate a certain adaptation.

A letter of the Congregation for Divine Worship, Oct. 25, 1973 (ActApS 66 [1974] 98–99) included the following: the approval of the essential formulas of the Sacraments the Pope reserves to himself; approval of translations requires that they conform to the Latin text.

Inevitably the use of the vernacular in liturgy brings with it the problems of a changing, living language. ICEL is committed to reviewing its translations at least once every ten years.

See also VERNACULAR IN LITURGY.

Bibliography: L. BOUYER, *Rite and Man: The Sense of the Sacral and Christian Liturgy* (London 1963). C. MOHRMANN, *Liturgical Latin: Its Origins and Character* (Washington 1957). M. RICHARDS, *The Liturgy in England* (London 1966). R. SNYDER, *Contemporary Celebration* (Nashville and New York 1971). D. B. STEVICK, *Language in Worship* (New York 1970).

[H. E. WINSTONE]

LITURGICAL THEOLOGY

The theological task arising from Christian worship is multifaceted. Its starting point is neither dogmatic affirmation, nor, strictly speaking, liturgical text, but rather the living Church actively engaged in the worship of God. Likewise, its final goal is not merely to understand the various dimensions of worship, but in addition to return that understanding to the Church's life and prayer.

Place and Character. Liturgical theology must intersect with other branches of theology, e.g., ecclesiology, Christology, and soteriology, particularly insofar as their own theological truth unfolds in the act of worship. It must examine current and past liturgical texts, as expressions of theological understanding and as texts whose meaning and purpose is to be activated as Christian worship. Liturgical theology must engage many disciplines and many methodologies, but its enduring concrete focus on the living worship of the Church is both its unifying principle and its distinguishing characteristic.

As a branch of theology it is both systematic and pastoral. It is systematic in that it explores the doctrines of faith which liturgy articulates in its own way (*lex orandi est lex credendi*) and examines these doctrines in relation to their other formulations. Liturgical theology also explores fundamental theological questions relating faith to prayer and Revelation to proclamation. It is pastoral because liturgical theology always speaks from and to the Church at prayer. It cannot rest content with the inner logic of a reflective methodology. The truth which unfolds in liturgical theology must finally be validated in the experience of worship itself.

Development. Liturgical theology evolves upon several relationships which hold between faith, the liturgical event, and reflective theology. These can be specified as: faith related to liturgy and liturgy related to theology.

Faith and Liturgy. A dialectic relationship exists between faith and liturgy. Vatican Council II in the Constitution on Sacred Liturgy articulated the dual movement of this dialectic when it affirmed that liturgy expresses faith (movement from faith to liturgy) and, at the same time, instructs or informs faith (movement from liturgy to faith) (*Sacrosanctum Con-*

cilium 59). Liturgical theology must engage both movements of this dialectic.

The first movement is addressed in the attempt to understand the inner contours of the faith experience as it comes to expression in symbolic action. This is a complex hermeneutical task, partially fulfilled by phenomenological description, e.g., describing the inner movement of Eucharistic Prayers and the full significance as commitment and surrender of the people's *Amen.* The task is further advanced by anthropological and psychological studies into the nature and behavior of ritual, and by investigations into the power of language to evoke affections, motivation, and commitment (*see* LITURGY AND ANTHROPOLOGY). In short, liturgical theology at this point attempts to determine the conditions under which people successfully enter and engage in liturgical prayer, and the dynamics by which faith seeks ever new modes of liturgical expression.

Liturgical theology likewise seeks to understand the effect liturgy has upon faith. Vatican II gives two directions for this investigation: "In the liturgy the sanctification of man is manifested by signs perceptible to the senses, and is effected in a way which is proper to each of these signs..." (ibid. 7). *Sanctification* signals all that God in Christ has done and continues to do *for us.* It embraces liberation from sin, growth in holiness, and a promise of final victory over death. Vatican II affirms that this is not a mysterious, behind-the-scenes activity of God. Rather, it is spoken to human awareness and accomplished in human life in recognizable ways.

Liturgical theology seeks therefore to understand the liturgy as accomplishing this twofold function, viz., to *manifest* and *effect* sanctification. For the first, it attempts to understand the nature of proclamation with deep respect for the mystery of God, the evocative thrust of symbolic language, and the cognitive dimension of human awareness. For the second, it investigates the profound truths of the Christian faith, conscious that not only is the liturgy the place where these truths unfold, but that the inner dynamics of the liturgy reveal the process by which they unfold.

Liturgy and Theology. A similar dialectic relationship exists between liturgy and theology, which liturgical theology likewise investigates. The movement toward theology recognizes the liturgy as a privileged source (*locus theologicus*) for understanding the Church, its sacramental actions, and its fundamental creeds. This line of investigation is perhaps the most developed, and represents the original scope of liturgical theology (*see* LITURGIOLOGY 8:921). The Introductions and texts for the revised rites encourage this kind of investigation, since they embody far more of the Church's rich tradition than the liturgical books they replace.

The converse movement toward the liturgy involves the return of theological insight to the Church at prayer. Reflective theology brings forth explanation which, by the very fact that the liturgy continues to be celebrated in the Church, must likewise take on the nature of promise. The truth of theology must be sought in worship, and its function to give faith something to look for in worship needs to be understood well. Theology's return to worship is the final task of liturgical theology.

See also THEOLOGY AND LITURGY with bibliography.

[P. E. FINK]

LITURGICAL VESSELS

Liturgical vessels are to be fashioned in keeping with their liturgical function (GenInstrRomMissal 295). Their use in the celebration should not distract but rather truly express the meaning of the action taking place. Thus is the artist to see to it that the liturgical vessels are also adapted "to the taste and customs of the various regional cultures" (ibid. 295). The materials chosen should be solid and lasting, "esteemed as valuable" in the region where they are to be used. (ibid. 290). In their culture they can stimulate the faith they express by their noble and beautiful qualities as well as in their sacred use. Sacred vessels, even if they are not made of gold, are blessed according to the formulas found in liturgical books (GenInstrRomMissal 296). The blessing for the chalice and paten is found in the *Rite for the Dedication of a Church and Altar* (ch. 7), now being prepared for publication in English (BCL Newsletter 14 [1978] 107). They may be blessed by a priest and oil is no longer to be used. The word "blessing" is preferred to "consecration" in this context, the latter term being served for the Eucharist. They may be blessed outside of Mass, but it is preferable that their blessing be immediately related to their use in the Eucharistic Liturgy.

Just as the blessing cup and the one loaf (1 Cor 10.16) are central to the Eucharistic celebration, so too are the chalice and paten of primary importance (GenInstrRomMissal 290). Modern chalices, in diminishing the prominence of the long stem, have a unified design and a larger cup. The use of natural materials and the lack of external ornamentation aim at a certain simplicity. The cup is to be made from a material that is impermeable to liquids at least on the inside (ibid. 291). The base, however, can be made of any solid and worthy material. Gold-plating may have to be used for the cup on metals that tarnish or oxidize (ibid. 294).

The paten, or other vessels intended to hold the Eucharistic bread, may be made from "any material locally held in esteem as suitable for use in worship—for example, ebony and certain hardwoods" (ibid. 292). The paten should be large enough to serve the needs of the gathered community so that numerous vessels do not have to be used regularly for the celebration. A Communion bowl may also be used instead of (or with) the paten (ibid. 80c). The ciborium, which is used for the reservation of the Eucharist, should not look like a vessel for drinking. It might also be smaller since the faithful are to receive hosts consecrated at the same Mass (ibid. 56h).

There is no prescribed shape or material for the monstrance used for benediction. (HolyCommIntrod 85; 92–94). A ciborium may be used instead of a monstrance. The use of a Communion plate is not prescribed (cf. GenInstrRomMissal 117). Other vessels such as censer, cruets, sprinkler, containers for oil have not been the object of any change—as long as their use and appearance enhances rather than distracts from the celebration. Here, as elsewhere, good artistry should predominate (ibid. 312).

The use of a tube or a spoon for Communion under both kinds is an indicated possibility, without however prescription of material or form (ibid. 248–252).

Bibliography: BCL Environment and Art 96–97.

[A. D. FITZGERALD]

LITURGICAL VESTMENTS

Vestments worn in the celebration of the liturgy help to distinguish the various ministerial roles and also enhance the expressive quality of a common faith (GenInstrRomMissal 297). Ministers are thus to wear the vesture proper to their ministry so that the diversity of functions in the liturgy may be clearly signified (cf. ibid.) Liturgical vestments that have a beautiful quality will inspire noble sentiments in those present, helping them to heighten awareness of their dignity as God's children (Gal 3.22; Col 3.10). Vestments are to be examples of genuine Christian art (Congregation of Rites, *Inter oecumenici* 13) and can be especially significant in celebrations with children, helping them to appreciate God's wonderful works in creation.

Particular Norms. The materials chosen for liturgical vestments are to correspond to the dignity of the liturgy and of the persons who wear them (GenInstrRomMissal 305). New materials or designs can be proposed by episcopal conferences according to the needs and customs of their region. (ibid. 304, 305). There seems to be a tendency to adopt vestments that are both more ample in form and less gaudy. Because they express the grace and joy of the Christian celebration, their beautiful character is to be in the choice and design of the fabric rather than in eye-catching or added ornamentation (ibid. 306). Renewal of the various visual aspects of the liturgy, rather than stopping with externals, helps to stimulate faith by giving it expression in signs that can be shared in response to God (BCL Music 5; Environment and Art 20).

Alb. The basic liturgical vestment is the alb; it can be tailored so that a cincture or an amice need not be worn (GenInstrRomMissal 81, 298). The alb is worn with other vestments, such as the stole, chasuble, or dalmatic, depending upon the particular celebration or the minister who wears them. The alb may also be replaced by a cassock and surplice according to the particular situation (ibid. 298; HolyCommIntrod 20). The alb may also be worn today by lay ministers (*see* CHASUBLE-ALB).

Stole. The vestment of ordained ministers, the stole is generally worn with a chasuble or dalmatic (GenInstrRomMissal 81). The deacon is to wear it over his left shoulder, joined on his right side, while bishop and priest wear it around their neck and hanging straight down in front (ibid. 302). When there are not enough vestments for numerous concelebrants, they may simply wear an appropriate stole over the alb (ibid. 161; cf. *Notitiae* 3 [1967] 192–193).

Cope. The cope is worn for solemn occasions, especially in processions (GenInstrRomMissal 302; HolyCommIntrod 105). Cope and humeral veil (*Notitiae* 5 [1969] 327) are worn by the minister who gives the blessing during the celebration of benediction (HolyCommIntrod 92–93). It may also be used at the celebration of the Liturgy of the Hours, even by several ministers (GenInstrLitHor 255). The use of a maniple in the liturgy is suspended (*Tres abhinc annos* May 4, 1967; *Notitiae* 3 [1967] 192). The biretta is nowhere mentioned in the General Instruction of the Roman Missal. For the particulars on the vesture of the bishop see *Notitiae* 4 (1968) 224–226; 246–252; 307–311; 312–324.

Liturgical Colors. A variety of color in the celebration of the liturgy helps to provide a richer expression of faith. The color of the vestments can evoke some aspect of the mystery being celebrated; variation in the color used can highlight the progressive character of the liturgical year and of the Christian life as well (GenInstrRomMissal 307). The specific colors used are the result of long-standing custom in the Roman Church. Since the perception of color is a cultural matter, adaptation to the needs and taste of the people is suggested to episcopal conferences (ibid. 308).

The usual colors are white, red, green, and purple, each one relating to some moment of the liturgical year or to specific feasts. Black may still be used for funeral Masses and rose for the third Sunday of Advent and the fourth Sunday of Lent (ibid. 308). Current adaptation finds variation in fabrics of more than one color and in shades of color as well. Chasuble and stole, for example, need not match exactly in color as long as they complement one another.

Other kinds of options allow for the use of the special vestments for festive occasions even if they are not the color of the day (ibid. 309). An appropriate color is to be used for votive Masses, but the color of the day or season may also be used (ibid. 310). The veil for the chalice may always be white. (ibid. 80).

Bibliography: BLC Music; BCL Environmental and Art. Congregation for Divine Worship, *Directory for Masses With Children* (USCC Publ. Office, Washington, D.C. 1973); Congregation of Rites, *Inter oecumenici*, Sept. 6, 1964, ActApS 56 (1964) 877–900, tr. *Instruction on the Proper Implementation of the Constitution on the Sacred Liturgy* (USCC Publ. Office, Washington, D.C. 1964); *Tres abhinc annos*, May 4, 1967, ActAps 59 (1967) 442–448, tr. *On the Correct Implementation of the Constitution on the Sacred Liturgy*, Further Instruction (USCC Publ. Office, Washington, D.C. 1967). E. HAULOTTE, *Signification de vêtements selon la Bible.* Collection de théologie 65 (Paris 1966). R. PAQUIER, *The Dynamics of Worship*, tr. D. MACLEOD (Philadelphia 1967) 135–146. C. E. POCKNEE, *Liturgical Vesture: Its Origins and Development* (Westminister, Md. 1961).

[A. D. FITZGERALD]

LITURGIOLOGY

The goal of liturgical studies taken as a whole remains the faith-filled worship, *in actu*, of the Church. Consciousness of the various dimensions of this task continues to evolve, and is raised to a new level with the promulgation of new liturgical texts. Regarded by many liturgical scholars as the climax of reform, but only the first step in renewal, the new texts mark a turning point in the strategy and tactics of liturgical scholarship (*see* LITURGICAL REFORM).

Official reform has restored for the worship of the Church richness from the tradition that had been badly mutilated or entirely lost in the course of history. Renewal is its complement and completion. It involves the passage of that richness into the living prayer of the Church, and the inner transformation, both personal and communal, which that passage will effect. The new rituals recognize the mutual interrelationship between faith and its liturgical expression, and their flexibility promises to allow the two to evolve together.

On the road to reform it was necessary to unearth earlier forms of Christian worship and to understand their patterns of evolution (*see* LITURGY [HISTORICAL DEVELOPMENT]). It was also necessary to locate liturgical science in the mainstream of theological activity. Liturgiology (8:919) in its modern development sought to bring liturgical studies from the periphery to the center. Vatican Council II confirmed this centrality (*see* THEOLOGY AND LITURGY). Focus on renewal recognizes the liturgical event as the concrete

meeting place of faith and theological reflection, influencing and influenced by both. *Liturgical theology is emerging as a part of theology concerned with this threefold relationship, including within its own broadening scope the concerns of liturgical science or liturgiology.

Bibliography: See bibliog. for Theology and Liturgy.

[P. E. FINK]

LITURGY

Vatican Council II in The Constitution on the Sacred Liturgy (Dec. 4, 1963) describes liturgy as the carrying out of the work of redemption, especially in the paschal mystery (*Sacrosanctum Concilium* 2, 6); the exercise of the priestly office of Christ (ibid. 7); the "presentation of man's sanctification under the guise of signs perceptible by the senses" (ibid.); and a sacred action surpassing all others because it is the action of Christ the priest and of his Body the Church (ibid.). The liturgy is viewed as a foretaste of the heavenly liturgy (ibid. 8), "the summit toward which the activity of the Church is directed"; and the "fount from which all her power flows" (ibid. 10). Liturgy is seen as the source of grace and sanctification in Christ as well as the glorification of God (ibid.). Thus the constitution builds upon and goes beyond Pope Pius XII's definition of liturgy as the "public worship of the Mystical Body, Head and members" (*Mediator Dei* 20).

Liturgical Life. The approach of Vatican II to the liturgy has had far-reaching consequences in the practical life and work of the Church. The liturgy of the Church is more than a particular activity of the community; it is the very life force of the Church and is intimately connected with its identity.

Pope Paul VI took evangelization as "the grace and vocation proper to the Church, her deepest identity" and then went on to describe evangelization by its relationship to liturgy: the Church "exists in order to evangelize, that is to say in order to preach and teach, to be the channel of the gift of grace, to reconcile sinners with God, and to perpetuate Christ's sacrifice in the Mass, which is the memorial of his death and resurrection" (Paul VI EvangNunt 14). The direction underscored is one of greater integration of liturgy and life, of the formal activity of the community in worship and all other dimensions of the Christian life. There is a certain resonance taking place in the contemporary development of the liturgical life and the classic notion of liturgy (cf. Liturgy: History of the Word 8:928). Expressed obversely, liturgy and the practical living of the Christian life in mission and apostolate are different sides of the same coin. One without the other is an incomplete expression of Christianity.

Liturgical Participation. It follows that full and active liturgical participation (8:906) "by all the people is the aim to be considered before all else, for it is the primary and indispensable source from which the faithful are to derive the true Christian spirit" (*Sacrosanctum Concilium* 14). Such participation has steadily grown since 1963. The new Roman Missal stresses the participation of the faithful in the Mass by taking "their own proper part in it and thus gain its fruits more fully" (GenInstrRomMissal 2). Participation "is demanded by the very nature of the celebration, and is the right and duty of Christians by reason of their baptism" (ibid. 3; cf. 4, 5, 7). The same document elaborates the ecclesial nature of the Eucharistic assembly (ibid. 62) and identifies the special ministries the faithful are called to exercise in the liturgy (ibid. 63–73). The same emphasis on communal participation and on the variety of ministerial roles is found in the introductory statements of the other revised rituals.

Key elements in the question of participation are its quality and its motivation. There is sociological indication that these elements are improving (cf. McCready). While fewer American Catholics are attending Sunday Mass as compared with statistics in 1963, the majority of those who continue to attend have positive attitudes regarding their participation and the role expected of them in the reformed liturgy. Gradually the following norm is being implemented on the local level: "All concerned should work together in preparing the ceremonies, pastoral arrangements, and music for each celebration. They should work under the direction of the rector and should consult the people about the parts which belong to them" (GenInstrRomMissal 73).

Participation of the people is not only a matter of including the community in acclamation, song, gesture, and other responses. New forms of communication of the Word and new means of enriching popular response are being developed and encouraged. For example, the Bishops' Committee on Liturgy (BCL) in its document *Environment and Art in Catholic Worship* (1978) instructs on the use of audio-visuals in the liturgy: "It is safe to say that a new church building or renovation project should make provision for screens and/or walls which will make the projection of films, slides and filmstrips visible to the entire assembly, as well as an audio system capable of fine electronic reproduction of sound" (104). The committee goes on to say that there are two ways in which such media may be used to enhance celebration and participation: "(1) visual media may be used to create an environment for the liturgical action, surrounding the rite with appropriate form; (2) visual and audio media may be used to assist in the communication of appropriate content, a use which requires great delicacy and a careful, balanced integration into the liturgy taken as a whole" (106).

Liturgy as Witness and as Formative. Sensitivity to quality in liturgical celebration is paramount in any liturgical endeavor. In 1972 the BCL insisted with bold frankness that "good celebrations foster and nourish faith. Poor celebrations weaken and destroy faith" (BCL Music 6). Liturgy is a witness to the faith of the celebrating community. As such it must express a living faith within the membership of the community, a faith which in turn can be shared with others at the celebration as well as in the practicalities of daily life. In particular such faith must be present in the liturgical ministers of the celebration. Their primary role as leaders of the praying community demands a personal transparency which leads others to a deeper faith response.

Liturgy is also the source of faith in so far as it forms the faith experience and response of the community. Liturgical expression is thus intimately connected with the divine initiative which imparts the gift of faith. The reception and perception of that gift is directly influenced by the modality of the vehicle which imparts and proclaims its presence, i.e. the liturgical celebration.

Liturgical expression is thus rooted in what a given faith community is. It points to and helps form in a principal way what it should be eschatologically and shapes the practical living of the community.

Bibliography: BCL, Music; BCL Environment and Art. W.C.MCCREADY, *Changing Attitudes of American Catholics toward the Liturgy: 1963 to 1974* (Collegeville, Minn. 1975).

[D. W. KROUSE]

LITURGY (HISTORICAL DEVELOPMENT)

To supplement the earlier considerations in the *New Catholic Encyclopedia* (8:938) this article develops the relation of historical learning to *liturgical reform.

Historical Studies and the Tridentine Liturgy. Knowledge of the historical development of the liturgy has been a key factor in the actual reform and renewal of the liturgy since the 16th century. Certain factors account for the appearance at that time of a high regard for the lessons of history: the invention of printing and consequent accessibility of works from earlier times; the quickening of historical interest and skills ushered in by the Renaissance; and the challenges of the 16th-century Reformers, who wanted to measure contemporary church life by the norm of Scripture and the early Church.

Obviously, the inchoate stage of patristics, church history, and liturgical studies made them only partially reliable as guides for reform; moreover, Reformers and Catholics both subordinated the argument from history to other considerations and often to polemics. But the principle of discrimination among liturgical usages based on a study of accounts of and texts from earlier times was unmistakably operative. Pius V, in the Bull, *Quo primum tempore*, July 14, 1570, which introduced the reformed *Missale Romanum*, referred to the study of the sources whereby the basic form was disengaged from distorting accretions. Unfortunately Pius V also envisioned a complete adherence to the revised liturgical books and these were expected to serve as the standard of liturgical worship for generations to come. In keeping with this spirit, the curial body set up by his successor, Sixtus V—the Sacred Congregation of Rites—likewise was to serve merely a regulative function. Hence, as further discoveries were made of ancient liturgical documents, there was no way in which this increase in knowledge could have an effect in the evolution of liturgical practice.

The result of this policy was a liturgy which remained largely invariable for the 400 years from the Council of Trent to Vatican Council II. Another effect of the policy was a favorable climate for the pursuit of historical studies in liturgy, at least as these studies were considered to have "archeological" interest. In connection with the flowering of positive theology in the 17th century, scholars like Denis Petau or Petavius (11:199), Jean Morin (9:1149), and the Maurists (9:508) uncovered lost documents and added greatly to the knowledge of various stages of liturgical history.

The 19th Century. Only in the 19th century, however, does there appear, in addition to the critical tools of historical research, an appreciation of development—so necessary a part of what is now recognized as the modern historical consciousness. This was an invaluable aid in interpreting scanty sources and reconstructing a plausible history. Moreover, the four decades embracing the turn of the present century saw the finding or deciphering of several invaluable documents from the early centuries (*Didache, Apostolic Tradition, Pere-*

grinatio Etheriae, Testamentum Domini, the *Euchologion* of Serapion, and the catechetical instructions of Theodore of Mopsuestia) that have profoundly reshaped the understanding of the practices of the early generations of Christians. Most of these documents derive from a time which antedates the final settlement in the major liturgical families. Throughout the 17th, 18th, and 19th centuries the later books of non-Western liturgies had been studied, but only more recently has the technique of comparative study been refined to the point where it yields mutually enriching results. Finally, a series of critical editions and studies of extant material of the Roman and Gallican tradition has established beyond doubt the major stages of development, diffusion, and alteration of Rome's liturgy.

The vast increase of knowledge about the liturgy in the early Church, its central role, the communal character of its celebration, and the variability of its forms stood in dramatic contrast with the prevailing style of post-Tridentine offering of Mass and conferral of Sacraments. Only in the nonliturgical devotions was there a vibrant engagement of the congregation. From the early decades of the 19th century date the first stirrings of a movement to bring the riches of this new knowledge of liturgy to bear on the life of the worshiping congregation. Initially, the primary goal was a renewal of interest in and love for the liturgy as actually celebrated according to the post-Tridentine books. Eventually, however, the desirability of further liturgical reform was raised as an important pastoral question. By the early 20th century scholars had achieved a remarkable consensus on the reconstruction of liturgical development in the first three Christian centuries and this provided an unprecedented standard of judgment for identifying later accretions and distortions. For many, the principal focus of discussion was the issue of introducing the vernacular into liturgical services. More perceptive liturgiologists, on the other hand, perceived incalculable ramifications in the change to the use of language that would be generally understood, for they knew well how much of Trent's program had not yet been accomplished when measured against information acquired since the Tridentine reforms.

Pius XII and Liturgy. The Holy See became involved in liturgical reform to an increasing extent throughout the present century. After some early initiatives on the part of Leo XIII (1902) and Pius XI (1930) to establish a historical section in the Congregation of Rites, Pius XII (1948) set up a Pontifical Commission for the General Restoration of the Liturgy with the reform of the liturgical books as its goal. Pius XII had acknowledged the significant advance in liturgical knowledge in his Encyclical Letter, *Mediator Dei* (1947). He especially applauded those aspects which resulted in a deepening of liturgical spirituality. He warned against an excessive attachment to past practices, and "archeologism," whereby everything ancient would be ipso facto recommended for current practice. Moreover, he noted that later developments in liturgical practices were also instituted under the guidance of the Holy Spirit and not to be lightly rejected. Finally, he issued a stern warning against private initiative in liturgical reform, noting that the sole competence for such action rests with the Holy See.

The program of Pius XII made some notable advances in the 1950s: restoration of the Paschal Vigil and general reform of Holy Week; allowing evening Masses with a modification of the laws of fasting; and a simplification of the rubrics of the Missal and Breviary. But on the issue of the use of the vernacular, the policy was very hesitant regarding new concessions.

Historical Studies and Vatican II's Liturgical Renewal. In many ways, the liturgical reform and renewal initiated by the Vatican Council II was in continuity with the work of Pius XII and his predecessors. Like them, the Council acknowledged the usefulness of historical information but insisted on pastoral considerations as a final arbiter in determining various features of renewal. In many instances, those very factors which were adopted because they promised a quickening of people's involvement in and appreciation for the liturgy represent a restoration of features dominant in early Christian liturgy: general use of the vernacular, active participation, and diversification of roles. That does not mean that the reforms were adopted because of the early Church, yet the knowledge of historical precedent was an invaluable aid in assuring a broad sense of continuity when bold steps were taken.

Eucharistic Liturgy. It was in the Liturgy of the Eucharist that the impact of the vernacular and active participation of the congregation was first and most widely experienced, because the Sunday Eucharist is the most regular contact the majority of Catholics have with the liturgy. A considerable degree of simplification in the prayers and ritual gestures of the celebrant (kisses, bows, signs of the cross, tones of voice) enabled the major elements of the Mass to stand out more clearly. This is especially true of the *Eucharistic Prayers, whose unitary character is clearer than before. The provision of additional texts—rather than the single, mandatory Roman Canon (Eucharistic Prayer I)— captures something of the variability which characterized the earliest stages of liturgical development. Eucharistic Prayer II is an edited version of the prayer found in the 3d-century *Apostolic Tradition* of St. Hippolytus (6:1141). The position of the celebrant both at the chair and at the altar (where he is permitted to face the people) now makes his leadership of the people's prayer more effective. The restoration of the Prayer of the Faithful insures that the special cares and concerns of the congregation as well as the worldwide Church are explicitly included in Sunday and feast-day celebrations. Finally, many features of the Communion rite have been adjusted to enhance its symbolic impact (kneeling to receive not mandatory, using bread which looks like bread and is consecrated at the Mass in which it is received, receiving from the cup—and add to these the subsequent adoption of *Communion in the hand and the use of lay ministers of distribution). In all these cases, the assurance that the "new" practices were really a recovery of usages characteristic of the Church's liturgy for the first several hundred years has been an indispensable component of the *liturgical catechesis preparatory for change in liturgy.

Christian Initiation. For the rites of Christian Initiation, the debt to historical scholarship is especially evident in the integral view of the Sacraments of *Christian Initiation (Baptism, Confirmation, Eucharist), in the restoration of the *catechumenate for adults and in the liturgical and ministerial ramifications of adult initiation as a central concern of the Church. The situation of adult converts most readily allows for the conferral of the three Sacraments of Initiation in one liturgical celebration, preferably at the Paschal Vigil, and it is deemed to be of such importance that provision has been made for this to be done, even when the bishop is not present and a presbyter is presiding. In the case of the restoration of catechumenate (the Council confirming, thereby, an action of John XXIII), no doubt the recent experience of mission countries was persuasive. But it also recaptures a vision of church organisation well known to students of liturgical history. Accordingly, the local Church is comprised of various groups of "orders," one of which includes all those preparing to be received through Baptism as members of the "order of the laity." In the revised Rite of Christian Initiation of Adults all the members of the Church are invited to take some part in the overall program of preparation. This is especially true during Lent, the season in which the themes of conversion, faith, and Baptism reveal the prominent role that initiatory activity had in the original organization of the liturgical year.

Rites of Reconciliation. In the reform of the Rite of Penance, several "recoveries" are noteworthy. First, the baptismal character of the Sacrament is emphasized, particularly when it is celebrated during Lent. In the teaching of the Introduction to the Rite and in the wording of the prayers, an unmistakable focus on reconciliation highlights the connection of this Sacrament (as also is the case with Baptism) with the mission of Jesus and his saving redemption. The new provisions for communal services of reconciliation manifest the ecclesial dimension, both of the effects of sin and of the remedy for sin—an explicit teaching of the Council (*Lumen gentium* 11)—and a restoration of a patristic understanding of the Sacrament. Finally, an enlarged notion of ministry (Penance 8) carries this further.

Other Revisions. The revision of the rites for Holy Orders has likewise benefited from and fostered a vision of church life that has much in common with the patristic age. The restoration of the diaconate on a permanent basis has facilitated an understanding of the threefold organization of ordained ministry: the order of bishops, the order of presbyters, and the order of deacons. By ordination a layman is received into an "order" of people within the Church who, corporately and individually, have special responsibilities. Such a collegial vision has also been fostered by the restoration, on a wide basis, of the practice of *concelebration of the Eucharist and by the laying on of hands on the part of all bishops who are present for the ordination of a new bishop. The threefold organization of ordained ministry has also been made clearer by the suppression of some of the steps toward priesthood (subdiaconate, porter, exorcist) and the extension of nonordained ministries to candidates who will never seek ordained ministry. In the revised liturgy of ordination, the focus on the central gesture of imposition of hands and its accompanying prayer is much clearer. This prayer, in the case of episcopal ordination, is now an edited version of the prayer for the ordination of a bishop found in *Apostolic Tradition*—a restoration of immense ecumenical significance, in view of the widespread use of this prayer in other Christian traditions which have ordained bishops.

In the post-Vatican II reform of the Christian Calendar, knowledge of the origins of usages has given valuable perspective. This is especially evident in the prominence given to the *Sunday celebration, and in the arrangement of observances in Holy Week.

By no means is this an exhaustive inventory of items in the post-Vatican II reform which reflect an awareness of earlier stages in the long historical development of the liturgy. Numerous examples of prayer texts and ritual provisions for other liturgical situations (e.g. anointings, dedications) could be added. Yet the impact of careful and painstaking historical research on the ambitious Vatican II program of liturgical reform is unmistakable. It indicates that the work of scholars over the last century was a necessary and providential preparation for the current renewal.

Not only does the implementation of the new liturgical provisions offer an opportunity for a quickening of church life in keeping with the best features traceable in the works of the Fathers, it also accomplishes another stated goal of Vatican II, viz. to foster the unity of the Church (*Sacrosanctum Concilium* 1). To the extent that Catholic liturgical practice returns to a condition that prevailed before the major divisions and a similar development takes place in other Christian Churches, one can have reason to hope for a full restoration of ecumenical unity.

Bibliography: B. BOTTE, "Tradition apostolique et Canon romain," *Maison-Dieu* 87 (1966) 52–61; "L'Ordination de l'évêque," *Maison-Dieu* 98 (1969) 113–126. L. BOUYER, *Liturgical Piety* (Notre Dame 1954). M. CNUDDE, "L'Ordination des diacres," *Maison-Dieu* 98 (1969) 73–94. H. JEDIN, "Das Konzil von Trient und die Reform der liturgischen Bücher," EphemLiturg 59 (1945) 5–38. J. JUNGMANN, *The Mass of the Roman Rite: Its Origins and Development* (2 v., New York 1950); *The Early Liturgy* (Notre Dame, Ind. 1959). A. KAVANAGH, "The Norm of Baptism: The New Rite of Christian Initiation of Adults," *Worship* 48 (1974) 143–152, 318–335. R. KEIFER and F. MCMANUS, *The Rite of Penance Commentaries.* v. 1 *Understanding the Document* (Washington 1975). B. KLEINHEYER, "L'Ordination des prêtres," *Maison Dieu* 98 (1969) 95–112. H. MANDERS, "Tradition and Renewal: The New Roman Anaphoras," *Worship* 42 (1968) 578–586. A. ROSE, "La prière de consécration pour l'ordination épiscopale," *Maison-Dieu* 98 (1969) 127–142.

[G. H. PATER]

LITURGY (STRUCTURAL ELEMENTS)

The principal development in the past decade with regard to the structural elements of the liturgy is the growing awareness that these signs must be functional. The elements themselves are much the same as those listed in the earlier article in the *New Catholic Encyclopedia* (8:939), namely, words, actions, and things. The thrust of Vatican Council II was not to give us new symbols so much as to make existing symbols authentic and expressive of the spiritual realities they effect. The Constitution on the Liturgy states that "in the restoration of the liturgy, both texts and rites should be drawn up so as to express more clearly the holy things which they signify. The Christian people, as far as is possible, should be able to understand them with ease and take part in them fully, actively, and as a community" (*Sacrosanctum Concilium* 21). "The rites should be distinguished by a noble simplicity. They should be short, clear, and free from useless repetitions. They should be within the people's power of comprehension, and normally should not require much explanation" (ibid. 34).

The Council described the liturgy as "the means by which we are enabled to express and manifest the mystery of Christ and the real nature of the true Church" (ibid. 2). The past decade has brought greater awareness of the mysterious, communitarian nature of the Church, the People of God, and of the liturgy as the means by which this Church becomes visible to the world. If the liturgy is to express this reality accurately, the structural elements of the liturgy—things, actions, words—must be truly functional.

Things and Actions as Signs. The documents implementing the Constitution on the Liturgy, evince a gradual and growing realization of the necessity of working to make liturgical signs authentic and expressive. First in importance are the signs of bread and wine. "The nature of the sign demands that the material for the Eucharistic celebration appear as actual food. The gesture of breaking the bread, as the Eucharist was called in apostolic times, will more clearly show the Eucharist as a sign of unity and charity, since one bread is being distributed among the members of one family" (GenInstrRomMissal 283).

"The sign of communion is more complete when given under both kinds—bread and wine—since in that form the sign of the Eucharistic meal appears more clearly. The intention of Christ that the new and eternal covenant be ratified in his Blood is better expressed, as is the relation of the Eucharistic banquet to the heavenly banquet" (ibid. 240). It is true (now as formerly) that Christ is present even under the form of bread without the wine; but now that the value of the sign itself is seen, the instructions can state that "the faithful should be urged to drink from the cup, for this brings out the sign of the Eucharistic meal more fully" (ibid. 241).

In all the liturgical rites it is urged that signs be used which speak clearly of the spiritual reality. "Father, you give us grace through sacramental signs, which tell us of the wonders of your unseen power" (ChrInitAdult 215). The new Rite for Baptism urges us to use expressive signs. "The rite of immersion is more suitable as a symbol of participation in the death and resurrection of Christ" (ChrInitGenIntrod 22). Even those signs which are not as central to the sacramental system as eating, drinking, breaking bread, immersion, are to be authentic and performed with care. For example the clothing after Baptism is a sign (as is clear from the accompanying prayer, ChrInitAdult 225) that the baptized has become a new creation and has been clothed in Christ. The putting on of a real garment is a sign of this real "clothing in Christ." To give the baptized merely a small cloth symbolizing a garment, as was often done formerly, weakens the symbolism; there was only a hint of the garment which is a sign of the reality.

Words and Language. The function of words and language in the liturgy has also undergone a change in the last decade. Formerly, liturgical words were spoken to God; sermons and pious devotions nourished the faithful. Now there is a growing awareness that the liturgy is both the worship of God and the means of his communication to his people. This change in emphasis has brought with it the possibility and the importance of using a language which can actually communicate.

Furthermore, there is a movement away from considering the words themselves in isolation from their function as signs. The revised rites insist on concern not only with the text itself, but with the proclamation of the text. "The tone of voice should correspond to the nature of the text, which may be a reading, a prayer, an instruction, an acclamation or a song; the tone also depends on the form of celebration and the solemnity of the assembly" (GenInstrRomMissal 18). The rubrics have begun to be concerned not just with the words, but with communication arts.

Another important development during the past decade is the appearance of directives which state that something is to be said "in these or similar words." The function of the text to communicate takes precedence over specific words. Directives have also appeared which give the end to be achieved without indicating specific words. For example, in the Rite of Marriage: "At the appointed time, the priest goes to the door of the church and meets the bride and bridegroom in a friendly manner, showing that the Church shares in their joy" (Marriage 19). No specific words are given; the directive merely indicates the function of the greeting without giving the words to be used.

The past decade, then, has seen a new emphasis placed on the function of the structural elements of the liturgy. The words, actions, and things employed in worship must have the power to express the inner nature of the Church and to carry out its external ministry. It is through the liturgy "that the faithful express and manifest the real nature of the true Church" (*Sacrosanctum Concilium* 2) and it is through the liturgy "that the sanctification of men and women in Christ, and the glorification of God (to which all other activities of the Church are directed) are achieved with maximum effectiveness" (ibid. 10).

Bibliography: The first and most important source material is the Introductions and General Instructions to the new rites themselves.

[T. RICHSTATTER]

LITURGY AND ANTHROPOLOGY

The Roman Catholic liturgical reform mandated by Vatican Council II's Constitution on the Sacred Liturgy (1963) inaugurated a rapid sequence of changes in the official liturgical rites of the Church. Catholic worshipers and sympathetic observers noted the impact of the ritual changes most directly in the celebration of the Mass, the Church's central liturgical action. Vernacular languages replaced Latin as the language of public prayer; some ritual actions were eliminated altogether, others were constricted; unfamiliar new elements emerged.

Principles enunciated in the Vatican II document guided the work of those postconciliar groups charged with the revision of the books of liturgical rites. Among the general norms was the requirement that careful investigation—theological, historical, and pastoral—should be made into each part of the liturgy to be revised (*Sacrosanctum Concilium* 23). The availability of historical information and theological analysis developed during a century-old liturgical movement clearly facilitated the work of the revision of the Roman liturgy. Less attention had been given to the question of what might be considered adequate pastoral research.

The Relevance of Social-Cultural Anthropology. European liturgical publications of the conciliar and postconciliar era reflect a measure of interest in sociology and psychology as the human or social sciences basic to pastoral research in liturgy. There is little evidence that the discipline of social-cultural anthropology was perceived as significant for pastoral research either in Europe or North America during the first decade of reform. Subsequently anthropologists of the Anglo-American school concerned with the human consequences of the displacement of familiar religious symbols pressed the issue.

The field of social-cultural anthropology gives evidence of an operating consensus to work with Clifford Geertz's definition that "religion is: (1) a system of symbols which acts to (2) establish powerful, pervasive, and long-lasting moods and motivations in men by (3) formulating conceptions of a general order of existence and (4) clothing these conceptions with such an aura of facticity that (5) the moods and motivations seem uniquely realistic." This operating definition does not address the question of foundations of faith, but focuses on observable symbolic behaviors which give expression to and sustain the living faith of a people.

British anthropologist Mary Douglas was one of the first to question the orientation of official liturgical reform from the viewpoint of her discipline. In *Natural Symbols* (1970) she suggested that reformers of the Roman Catholic liturgy lacked profound insight into the social significance and power of corporate and public symbolic rites, and so they were doing unwitting harm to liturgy. In 1972 Victor W. Turner, then of the University of Chicago, restated the challenge to official liturgical reform in a two-part article in *Worship*, observing that on the basis of its results the official reform seemed to rise from the premises of a narrow positivism and to take an exclusively structural-functional approach to ritual action, to the detriment of the spiritual well-being of the Catholic people.

At the 1975 meeting of the newly-formed *North American Academy of Liturgy the issue of methodological presuppositions in liturgical studies was raised. Members of the Academy, trained for the most part as historians of liturgy and sacramental theologians, were disposed to encourage interdisciplinary study and so established a working seminar on ritual studies within the Academy. That seminar has not matured sufficiently in 1978 to yield anything more than preliminary exploratory essays. Nevertheless, the foundations have been set for dialogue between social-cultural anthropologists and liturgiologists on the nature of ritual symbols and the ritual process.

In the U.S. a major interpreter of the discipline of social-cultural anthropology for theology in general and liturgical studies in particular has been Urban T. Holmes, dean of the Episcopal School of Theology at the University of the South. Holmes has mediated and interpreted the work of scholars of the Manchester school of situational analysis, among them Turner, Shlomo Deschen, and Sally Falk Moore. The basic methods of inquiry of the Manchester school promise to have bearing on uncovering in a new way the intimate relation between the eccesiology, Christology, and eschatology of the Christian assembly and the actual forms of its liturgical celebrations.

Issues Arising from Liturgical Reform. The intimate relation between doctrine and worship has traditionally been acknowledged in the axiom *lex orandi lex credendi*. In the past era of fixed and stable rites, uniformly performed, it was more easily declared that the objective character of the Roman liturgy expressed an objective and uniform Catholic understanding of the doctrines of the Church, of the work of Christ, and of human destiny. The postconciliar emphasis on the reg-

ional and the local Church and the desirability of appropriate adaptation introduced diversity and subjectivity and prescriptive principles in the manner of celebrating the Eucharist and the other rites of the Church (*see* LITURGY AND LOCAL CHURCHES). As a result, study of contemporary liturgical reform and its pastoral and theological impact requires newer methods for gathering, analyzing, and interpreting data on the Church gathered for public worship. Researchers must be prepared to deal with the liturgy not only as it is set out in liturgical books, but as it is actually celebrated.

Situational Analysis of Ritual Celebration. The approach of situational analysis in ritual studies acknowledges but is not limited by the assumptions, goals, and methods of structural analysis as these were outlined by Claude Lévi–Strauss. Structural analysis is concerned with constants and universals. Situational analysis investigates the actual ritual performance as historical and social event. It considers the particular use and meaning of ritual symbols within a given performance while acknowledging the essential complexity and ambiguity of an effective ritual symbol. It notes the relationship of the ritual performance to the social structures of the performing group, and the phenomenon of ritual change within the ritual process. Situational analysis is designed to deal with variables as well as constants in the study and interpretation of ritual action.

Investigation of Ritual Symbols. Several distinct methods for investigating the actual use and meaning of ritual symbols within a given ritual performance or liturgical action have been developed within the complex discipline of social-cultural anthropology. Each yields specific types of data. Turner, for example, proceeds by way of a three-part investigation of the exegetical, positional, and operational use of dominant and instrumental ritual symbols. He defines ritual symbols as the smallest units, verbal or nonverbal, of a ritual action. Gregory Bateson's theory of metalanguage explores repetition and redundancy within multiple nonverbal codes and planes of communication. He is interested in the capacity of symbolic interaction to express the truth of complex relationships in condensed forms. With the work of Bateson the field of social-cultural anthropology crosses into the fields of social psychology and communication theory, other disciplines which investigate public symbolic action and ritual performance.

Investigation of Ritual Change. In its present state social-cultural anthropology has also developed approaches to the investigation of the phenomenon of ritual change. Shlomo Deshen rejects the sociological category of secularization as inadequate to account generally for the phenomenon of symbolic change within religious institutions, since religious institutions normally have mechanisms to enable and legitimate change. Instead he has identified four possible modes of ritual and symbolic change, namely, eradication or abandonment, creation, innovation, and profanation, and he finds significance in the circumstances which surround each of these modes of symbolic change. Turner explores the matter within a broader framework. He identifies four phases in that social movement he calls social drama: (1) the breach of established social relations within a group; (2) the emergence of a crisis which sets out publicly the true state of affairs within a group; (3) redressive action, that is, an attempt to reestablish equilibrium frequently through creative use of common symbols; and (4) the reintegration of the disturbed group or a formal acknowledgement of its rupture.

Within this framework, Turner proposes a hypothesis to account for the occasional breakdown of the power of traditional symbols to express and unify a group. Among the circumstances which surround and contribute to ritual change there is, according to Turner, either a rejection of the traditional normative demands associated with the symbol(s) or a loss of the emotional force, positive or negative, formerly emanating from the symbol. The loss of a sense of meaning, feeling, or value, for whatever reason, is judged to cause alienation from rituals and institutions which have been the bearers of those realities.

On a closely related question, Victor Turner and Urban Holmes have both employed the work of Mihali Czikszentmihalyi on "flow" in play to analyze and interpret the phenomenon of malaise which has often set in among both clergy and laity when they self-consciously celebrate the reformed liturgical rites. Their preliminary explorations promise to have significance for pastoral dimensions of liturgical renewal generally. As is the case with most other aspects of the interaction between liturgical studies and social-cultural anthropology, the development and refinement of hypotheses interpreting the present pastoral situation in the celebration of the reformed Roman Catholic liturgy are dependent on extended case studies and network analysis. Another decade should see significant advances being made in the use of the methods of the emerging discipline of social-cultural anthropology with liturgical studies.

See also LITURGICAL REFORM.

Bibliography: G. BATESON, *Steps to an Ecology of Mind* (New York 1972). S. DESHEN and M. SHAKEID, *The Predicament of Homecoming* (Ithaca, N.Y. 1974). C. GEERTZ, *The Interpretation of Cultures* (New York 1973). U. T. HOLMES, "What Has Manchester To Do with Jerusalem?" *Anglican Theological Review* 59 (1977) 79–97; U. T. HOLMES, "Ritual and the Social Drama," *Worship* 51 (1977) 197–213. G. V. LARDNER, "Communication Theory and Liturgical Research," *Worship* 51 (1977) 299–307. V. W. TURNER, "Forms of Symbolic Action: Introduction" in ROBERT F. SPENCER ed., *Forms of Symbolic Action* (Seattle 1969); "Passages, Margins, and Poverty: Religious Symbols of Communitas," *Worship* 46 (1972) 390–472, 482–494; *Dramas, Fields, and Metaphors: Symbolic Action in Human Society* (Ithaca, N.Y. 1974).

[M. COLLINS]

LITURGY AND LOCAL CHURCHES

The rich diversity of liturgical forms that can be traced back to New Testament times gave way, in the course of the centuries, and for various reasons, to the fixed and even rigid uniformity of the Latin Mass that Catholics all over the world knew as the unchanging and even unchangeable expression of their one faith. Vatican Council II opened a great range of new possibilities in its decision to allow the vernacular into Catholic worship and this led to a spate of translations everywhere. However, Vatican II went much further than recommending translation of the existing Mass rite. It also radically reformed the rite and stated the need for research in adapting worship to particular cultures. Although the Constitution on the Liturgy was an early product of the Council and was unable to use the developing ideas about the Church and human culture that emerged more clearly in *Ad gentes* and *Gaudium et spes*, for example, it does stress the need for "adapta-tion": "Provided that the substantial unity of the Roman rite is preserved, provision shall be made, when revising the liturgical books, for legitimate variations and adaptations to different groups, regions and peoples, especially in mission countries" (*Sacrosanctum Concilium* 38). It also envisages the need for more radical adaptation in certain areas, especially when it calls for episcopal conferences "to carefully and prudently consider which elements from the traditions and cultures of individual peoples might appropriately be admitted into divine worship" (ibid. 40.1). The third Instruction on the Implementation of the Constitution is more explicit: "If wider adaptations are needed, . . . —the bishops should make a detailed study of the culture, traditions and special pastoral needs of their people" (*Liturgicae instaurationes* 12).

Partly as a result of these invitations, and partly as a result of the general change in the Church's approach to non-Western cultures, leaders in the Church throughout the world have begun the long process of finding ways of making worship more meaningful to people who belong to a non-Western culture. A new image of the Church at worship is emerging, that of a unity in diversity.

In Africa, the first signs of this new image were seen in matters such as the introduction of traditional instruments, like the drum, and traditional actions, like the dance, into the liturgy. In Zaire, a new rite for the Mass was drawn up, using various African gestures and symbols, as well as more concrete formulations of prayers: sin is like "the insect that sucks our life-blood from us," for example. In fact, the word "adaptation" is no longer satisfactory, as the African Bishops pointed out in a declaration at the 1974 Synod of Bishops when they rejected as outdated and inadequate the "theology of adaptation" and opted instead for a "theology of incarnation" (*see* INCULTURATION, THEOLOGICAL).

In India, also, something new is coming to light, manifest in the Rite of Mass for India, which uses traditional Hindu gestures and symbols, as well as having one of the readings in the Liturgy of the Word from the Sacred Writings of India, the "Indian Old Testament." The prayers of the Mass are expressed in an idiom familiar to Indian tradition, for example, the blessing: "May God the indweller in the cave of your heart animate you with his life." This liturgy is, in the words of an Indian theologian, a proof of how the Church in India is passing from "importing and copying to creativity and originality" (D. S. Amalorpavadass).

The kind of research called for by Vatican II is increasing but it is still too early to look for tangible results. In Tanzania, for example, a national committee for research into African culture is doing some interesting work. Their starting-point was expressed in these words, in 1975, worth quoting because they give a good "definition" of inculturation: "The mission process . . . is not fundamentally one of 'adapting' a Christian culture to the needs and forms of expression of a non-Christian culture, a process of translation only. Rather it is a creative process in which a new Christian culture comes into being." Several Eucharistic Prayers have been composed at the AMECEA Pastoral Institute, using African prayer forms, for purposes of study. One can say that study is the key word at the moment, but one can hope for concrete results in the not too distant future, if the liturgy is to be made truly meaningful in African cultures. Indeed, the same is true of Europe and America, as Cardinal Marty pointed out in 1975.

The principle of localizing and the ecclesiology of the Church as a *communio* of local Churches, mean that each people should be able to worship the Father through the Son in the One Spirit according to their own authentic traditions. In fact, it is only through concrete examples that the expression "Liturgy and Local Churches" can be made clear. The principles are established in the idea of "inculturation," but liturgy is basically an action, an event. For this reason two other examples may be given: one, the Sunday Mass in Ndjong Melen, Cameroun, which is a liturgical celebration in the flamboyant and festive spirit of West Africa—a great crowd liturgy from which the cathedrals of the West could take some hints about popular participation. The second example is of a study project going on in Turkana, in North-Western Kenya, among the Turkana nomads. Fr. Tony Barrett, an Irish missionary, has worked out an experimental ritual for Baptism, Confirmation, and Marriage, as well as rites for birth and death, using the structure of Turkana initiation rites and other rites of passage. The exciting possibilities of this kind of thing—one being the fact that a fresh expression of the Christian faith in such a context can illuminate elements of Christianity that have been obscured in the Western culture by producing "flowers that have never been seen before" (Cardinal Maurice Otunga at the 1977 Synod of Bishops)—should counter-balance the lack of enthusiasm in Rome for radical liturgical experiments, largely as a reaction to the Abp. Lefebvre affair.

See also CHURCH, LOCAL (THEOLOGY); MISSIONARY ADAPTATION.

Bibliography: A bibliography is difficult to give because of the developing situation in these matters. Three periodicals may be mentioned as good sources of latest developments: *Vidyajyoti*, Institute of Religious Studies, Delhi, India; *AFER*, AMECEA Pastoral Institute, Eldoret, Kenya; *Worship*, Collegeville, Minnesota. See also: A. BARRETT, *Incarnating the Church in Turkana* (Gaba Publications, Eldoret, Kenya 1978). B. BURKI, *L'Assembleé dominicale* (Immensee 1976). Congregation for Divine Worship, *Liturgicae instaurationes* (ActApS 62 [1978] 692–704); tr. *Third Instruction for the Correct Implementation of the Constitution on the Sacred Liturgy* (USCC Publ. Office, Washington, D.C. 1970). B. LUYKX, *Culte Chrétien en Afrique* (Immensee 1974). A. SHORTER, *African Culture and the Christian Church* (London 1973).

[B. HEARNE]

LITURGY OF THE HOURS (PASTORAL ADAPTATION AND CELEBRATION)

Without frequent and fervent prayer the life of the Christian soon can easily become directionless and empty. In the absence of *communal* prayer, relying solely on private devotion, Christian witness becomes individualistic and ultimately devoid of any ecclesial sense. The development of the Liturgy of the Hours (or Divine Office) through the ages was predicated on the necessity for Christians to gather as often as possible not only to sanctify the day through the celebration of various hours, but to strengthen the community's capacity and resolve to give witness to Christ as the gathered faithful. So "like all liturgical celebrations, the Liturgy of the Hours is not a private act. As a public sign of the Church. it belongs to the whole Church and has impact on all its members" (GenInstrLitHor 20). By its very nature the Liturgy of the Hours is a communal action of the Church, since it is the Church's daily round of prayer celebrated in common. Private recitation of any or all of the hours is always exceptional rather than

normative. The primary responsibility of "those in sacred orders or with a special canonical mission" is to direct and preside over the prayer of the community (ibid. 23). The obligation of bishops, priests, and deacons to pray the hours is linked to their duty to assure the celebration of this liturgy by local communities, particularly on Sundays and solemnities. Deacons and priests, together with parish liturgy planning teams, ought to devise programs of creative catechesis and implementation of the Liturgy of the Hours, aware of the possibilities and needs of the particular parish. Pastoral adaptation of the hours, as well as parish catechesis on the Office, should draw its direction from the General Instruction on the Liturgy of the Hours, a theological and pastoral document.

Parish Catechesis on the Liturgy of the Hours. Parishes have learned from recent experience in the implementation of new liturgical rites that catechesis is not only desirable but necessary before and during that implementation. While the Liturgy of the Hours, particularly Morning and Evening Prayer, does not represent a great innovation, American Catholics do not have much recent experience with this form of common prayer. Especially is this true of the common recitation or singing of the Psalms. Experience with the Responsorial Psalm in the Eucharistic Liturgy demonstrates the need for a thorough-going catechesis on the nature of the Psalms, the tradition of their use in the Church's liturgy, and the various forms of singing them. Thus instruction on psalmody will benefit the celebration of the Eucharist as well as the Office. The General Instruction of the Liturgy of the Hours provides a sound basis for parish catechesis since it offers a pastoral theology of the praying Church. Central is the relationship between prayer and witness: "When one takes part in the Liturgy of the Hours, he contributes in a hidden way to the growth of God's people, for he makes the apostolate more fruitful" (ibid. 18). Frequent communal prayer is therefore intrinsic to parish life, for such prayer strengthens and nourishes the resolve of the Church to persevere in its witness to Christ in the world. "Prayer is of the very essence of the Church. The Church is a community and should express in prayer its communal nature" (ibid. 19). Some of the following principles and themes might be included in a parish catechesis:

(1) the relationship of communal prayer and Christian witness (ibid. 19);

(2) the consecration of time and the sanctification of the Church (ibid. 10–11, 14);

(3) the Liturgy of the Hours as preparation for the Eucharist (ibid. 12);

(4) participation in Christ's priestly work of praise (ibid. 13, 15–16);

(5) developing the prayer of supplication and intercession (ibid. 17);

(6) the Psalms as Christian prayer, and the nature of psalmody (ibid. 100–109, 121–139);

(7) the place of God's Word, its reading, and celebration in the life of the Church (ibid. 140–158);

(8) the nature of the various hours of prayer, and the intrinsic importance of Morning and Evening Prayer;

(9) finally, the celebration of the liturgical year through the Liturgy of the Hours.

These are only some of the themes with which a pastoral catechesis on the Liturgy of the Hours might deal. The General Instruction is rich in a great variety of subjects and ought to be studied carefully.

Pastoral Considerations in the Implementation of the Hours. "Perhaps the most difficult and challenging task is to make the liturgy of the hours in fact and practice, as well as in theory and doctrine, the prayer of the entire Church" (BCL, *A Call to Prayer*). Extraordinary efforts are indeed required to implement the celebration of the communal prayer of the Church. Likewise hard pastoral questions regarding the priority of prayer in individual parishes need to be asked. One such question involves scheduling. Given the current pastoral practice of daily Eucharists, for example, when does one schedule and celebrate Morning and Evening Prayer, "the hinges of the Office," in a local parish?

(1) *Scheduling the Hours.* Obviously the most important days for celebrating the hours are Sundays and solemnities; secondarily, feasts and weekdays. The greatest obstacle, oddly enough, is the multiplicity of Masses on those days. Parishes need to reexamine their Mass schedules in order to strike a proper balance between the principles of convenience and the presence of a community at the Eucharist. Too often in large urban or suburban parishes weekday and Sunday Eucharists are multiplied in the name of convenience for the people, when in fact very few people are present at certain celebrations, especially in the early morning hours. The question of stipends and support of the clergy, a legitimate concern, frequently intervenes in the problem of scheduling. The Eucharist needs to be scheduled according to need and the actual presence of an assembly. Once that is accomplished, Morning and Evening Prayer may take their proper places. The liturgical day ought to begin, especially on Sundays, with Morning Prayer and conclude with Evening Prayer. For example, Sundays might begin with Evening Prayer I ("First Vespers") on Saturday before the anticipated Masses and might be celebrated as a vigil to prepare those who are present for the Sunday Eucharist. Late Sunday evening may seem more suitable nowadays for the celebration of Evening Prayer II, rather than late afternoon as in the past. However, this may vary from place to place. A possible schedule for Sundays and solemnities in the medium- or large-size parish might look something like the following:

Evening Prayer I—5:00 P.M. (Saturday)
Eucharist(s)—from 5:30 onward
Morning Prayer—at 8:00 A.M. (Sunday)
Eucharists—from 8:30 A.M. onwards
Evening Prayer II—at 4:00 P.M. or 5:00 P.M. after the last evening Mass.

Such a schedule, of course, is merely theoretical. A parish needs to take into consideration the scheduling of Baptisms and Marriages (usually on Sunday afternoons) before it can create a schedule of prayer and Eucharist in its Sunday celebration. Weekdays will be easier to schedule if it is borne in mind that the day begins with Morning Prayer and ends with Evening Prayer, and Masses are not needlessly multiplied in between.

(2) *Which Hours to Celebrate?* As Morning and Evening Prayer are the hinges of the Church's daily round of prayer, they are naturally the most important of all when scheduling the celebration of the hours. However, the other hours of the Office should find some place in a parish's prayer life. Daytime Prayer (mid-morning, mid-day, or mid-afternoon) and Night Prayer (Compline) are as easily celebrated by small groups as they are by large groups. Rather than beginning a parish meeting "with a prayer," one of the hours might be recited or sung. Thus an evening parents' meeting might end with Night Prayer; a school faculty meeting in the afternoon might end or begin with one of the daytime hours. Even on a diocesan level, those who plan meetings and congresses ought seriously to consider solemn celebration of one of the hours instead of the Eucharist, especially on weekends; in this way people are not taken away from their parish Eucharistic celebration. Even the Office of Readings can be profitably celebrated in a parish on important occasions, since it enables people to delve more deeply into the Scripture and become acquainted with the rich theological tradition which the second reading of that Office represents. Marian, Eucharistic, and other devotions can be carefully joined to the celebration of some of the hours from time to time.

(3) *Who leads the Celebration of the Hours?* Those who are obliged to the Office also have the responsibility to lead the people in its celebration. Thus priests and deacons, and even the bishop in his cathedral, should lead in the celebration of each of the hours. However, the leadership of prayer in the celebration of the Liturgy of the Hours is not limited to those in Orders. Lay men and women and religious should be trained in the ministry of prayer-leadership to assure the daily celebration of the hours. Families should likewise be encouraged to pray the hours at home, especially Morning, Evening and/or Night Prayer.

(4) *Participation Materials.* The publication of materials suitable for the celebration of the hours is still in process. While the 4-v. edition of the Liturgy of the Hours and its one-volume excerpt, *Christian Prayer*, are available, these are too expensive for most parishes. However, excerpts from the hours are being published and made available. Parish liturgy committees should investigate what is available. A few hymnals include Morning and Evening Prayer for all Sundays and solemnities and should be examined for their inclusion when a parish is deciding to purchase a hymnal-service book. If parishes wish to edit their own collection, consultation with the diocesan liturgical commission, especially with regard to copyrights held by ICEL and various other publishers, must occur. However, as more parishes begin to celebrate the Church's common prayer more and better materials will be made available.

(5) *Musical Choices.* In celebrating any of the hours, planners ought to keep in mind certain principles with regard to music. Obviously the hymn which begins Morning or Evening Prayer must be sung and must reflect the character of the feast. A choice must be made with regard to *psalmody, to sing or not to sing the Psalms, to use Psalm tones (e.g. Gregorian, Anglican, Gélineau, etc.), or metric Psalms. If Psalm tones are chosen, then the type of psalmody is important; responsorial, antiphonal, or *indirectum*. While the Psalms need not be sung on weekdays, it would seem inappropriate merely to recite them on Sundays and solemnities. In parish celebration consideration ought to be given to the question of using a constant repertory of Psalms, rather than varying them every day. As with the Eucharist, care, planning and competent musical leadership are required. The simplest of chants are quite accessible to most congregations nowadays and ought not to be rejected out of hand as too difficult or out of date (*see* LITURGY OF THE HOURS, CHANTS OF). Music in the Liturgy of the Hours is not ornamental—the Psalms are songs before all else—for the "sung celebration of the Divine Office is the form which best accords with the nature of this prayer" (GenInstrLitHor 268).

(6) *Ritual Elements in the Celebration of the Hours.*

The celebration of any of the hours may be as simple or as elaborate as the needs of a particular community or occasion may require. The use of such ritual elements as water, light, incense, flowers, processional banners, vestments, or electronic media (e.g., visuals) ought carefully to be integrated in the celebration of the Office and in the proper places. For example, the use of incense is traditional during the singing of the *Magnificat* or *Benedictus*. At times incense may be used as a penitential act in the celebration of Evening Prayer. A light service or *lucernarium* can sometimes be joined to Evening Prayer as well, just as a rite of sprinkling to recall Baptism might find an occasional place in Morning Prayer.

(7) *Other Occasions in Celebrating the Hours Solemnly.* There are many occasions when the Liturgy of the Hours ought to be celebrated with solemnity, not as an alternative to the Eucharist, but rather as more fitting than the Eucharist. (a) At ecumenical gatherings, such as are held during the *Week of Prayer for Christian Unity or on Thanksgiving Day, Christians from many different backgrounds can draw on the common tradition of Morning or Evening Prayer of the various Churches to create a truly ecumenical and unifying service of prayer. Many of the Churches are in the process of revising or already have revised their rites for the Liturgy of the Hours. These revisions, as with the Roman Catholic reform of the Office, are based on the common tradition and demonstrate an already achieved liturgical unity. Thus an ecumenical gathering ought to be celebrated in this Liturgy that all can call their own and in which unity may already be perceived. (b) During the seasons of Advent, Epiphany, Lent, and Easter special celebrations of Morning or Evening Prayer, or even the Office of Readings, might be adapted without prejudice to the normal celebration of the hours or the Eucharist. For example, on the third Sunday of Advent the celebration of Evening Prayer might be lengthened and adapted to resemble a ceremony of lessons and carols. An Evening Prayer in Lent might be joined to a celebration of the Stations of the Cross. Evening Prayer on the feast of the Epiphany might include a dramatic reading or dramatization (through dance, mime, etc.) of the theophany of the Messiah. During Eastertide, a longer Office of Readings might be devised for the neophytes during their *mystagogia*, stressing the communal nature of their newly acquired faith. Such adaptations, of course, ought to be accomplished without doing harm to the course of prayer or the liturgical year as provided in the liturgical books and must be carefully planned.

The Liturgy of the Hours as Family Prayer. The need for families to pray together is important not only that children might grow up in an atmosphere of prayer and devotion, but also because through prayer a family can find nourishment for its faith and strength for its unity. The Liturgy of the Hours is not the panacea people are looking for to preserve the family (there are no such panacaeas), but it does provide, especially in the "little hours" (Daytime Prayer and Night Prayer), a varying form of prayer for parents and children that is adaptable to the needs of each particular family. Members of the family can participate in Night Prayer, for example, in a variety of ways. The Psalm is constant for each day of the week. The *Nunc dimittis* (Canticle of Simeon) is unchanging. After a while these invariables can be

learned by heart and become a part of each person's "repertory" of prayer. The Marian antiphons at the end of Night Prayer, like the opening hymn, can be easily sung by a family. Prayerful silence is likewise learned from this prayer, as is a sense of penitence and reflection on the day's activities during the examination of conscience. Instead of a hastily recited formula for grace before meals, Prayer at Midday might be recited in common around the table before the start of Sunday dinner. The celebration of the Liturgy of the Hours by a family has many merits, e.g. familiarity and use of the Psalms as Christian prayer, the singing of simple hymns, but most of all the development of prayer in the life of a child that prepares the child for Sunday worship and eventually for Christian witness.

Communal Prayer and Personal Prayer. The goal of the Liturgy of the Hours is the development and growth of a praying Church, a Church united to the communion of saints who worship in the presence of God. Communal prayer ultimately develops an intense life of personal prayer. The Liturgy of the Hours will always need to be adapted; thus Paul VI noted that the 1971 revision has provided "various forms of celebration that can be accomodated to the various groups, with their differing needs" (Paul VI LaudCant 1). There is no opposition between communal and personal prayer, especially when the latter draws its nourishment from the former. "When the prayer of the the the Office becomes real personal prayer, then the bonds that unite Liturgy and the whole of Christian life are manifested more clearly. The whole life of the faithful, during the single hours of the day and the night, constitutes a *leitourgia*, as it were, with which they offer themselves in a service of love to God and to men, adhering to the action of Christ, who, by staying among us and offering himself, sanctified the lives of all men" (ibid. 8).

Bibliography: BCL, *A Call to Prayer. The Liturgy of the Hours* (USCC Publ. Office, Washington, D.C. 1977). P. BOTZ, "Praying the Psalms," *Worship* 46 (1972) 204–213. Congregation for Divine Worship and the Sacraments, *General Instruction of the Liturgy of the Hours* (USCC Publ. Office, Washington, D.C. 1975). J. D. CRICHTON, *Christian Celebration: The Prayer of the Church* (London 1976). PAUL VI, *Laudis Canticum*, ActApS 63 (1971) 527–535; tr. *Laudis Canticum. Apostolic Constitution on the Breviary* (USCC Publ. Office, Washington, D.C. 1977). F. C. QUINN, "Music and the Prayer of Praise," *Worship* 46 (1972) 214–219. A. M. ROGUET, *The Liturgy of the Hours: the General Instruction with Commentary*, tr. P. COUGHLAN and P. PURDUE (Collegeville, Minn. 1974). W. G. STOREY, "The Liturgy of the Hours: Principles and Practice," *Worship* 49 (1972) 194–203; "Parish Worship: The Liturgy of the Hours," *Worship* 49 (1975) 2–12. W. G. STOREY, et al., eds., *Morning Praise and Evensong. A Liturgy of the Hours in Musical Setting* (Notre Dame, Ind. 1973).

[J. A. GURRIERI]

LITURGY OF THE HOURS, CHANTS OF

Although many religious and monastic communities are experimenting with the use of music in the Liturgy of the Hours (4:920), the following article will be concerned with that music which is readily accessible and directed to the ordinary Christian community. Two factors must be borne in mind: at the present time the available music is limited; diverse Christian communities have different requirements relative to the "shape" of the office and the music used in it. For example, the needs of monastic communities can hardly be equated with the needs of parish communities.

The 1973 publication, *Morning Praise and Evensong,* is a presentation of the "hinge" hours of the office in a musical setting and only intended for communal celebration. A variation on its pattern, with different music, was published in *The Catholic Liturgy Book* (1975), a service book and hymnal. Both Episcopalian and Lutheran communions have been influenced by the ritual patterns of *Morning Praise and Evensong*; along with their revisions of liturgical prayer they are developing music for it.

The English-language versions of the office following the pattern of the normative *Liturgia horarum* (a pattern slightly different from *Morning Prayer* . . .) and providing music, or at least texts that can easily be sung, fall into two groups: (1) temporary translations of the Liturgy of the Hours; and (2) officially approved translations of the *editio typica*. Two editions of the "interim breviaries," now no longer to be used, were published in English; both were employed for liturgical prayer in the U.S., i.e., *The Prayer of the Church* (1970), printed in Great Britain, and *Prayer of Christians* (1971), published in the U.S. under the auspices of the *Federation of Diocesan Liturgical Commissions (FDLC). Each of these books printed hymn texts that could be sung, although the hymns found in the American edition were better suited to the Eucharistic Liturgy.

The officially approved translation for the U.S., *The Liturgy of the Hours*, was published in four volumes, 1975–76. A British edition, published in three volumes as *The Divine Office* (1974), is not approved for use in the United States. The American edition, a translation by the International Commission for English in the Liturgy (ICEL), became obligatory Nov. 27, 1977. It includes no music but does print hymn texts that can be sung. Several editions of a one-volume reduction of the four volume *Liturgy of the Hours*, all titled *Christian Prayer* (1976), contain actual music for hymn texts, music for the Ordinary, and musical settings for the psalms. Several of the OT and NT canticles are also set to music, along with the Gospel canticles and a selection of antiphons for the Christian year. The music was commissioned and gathered by ICEL, which promises more such music in the future. In 1978 ICEL published organ accompaniments for the hymns and service music of *Christian Prayer*.

Certain questions arise from this survey of the music easily available for celebration of the office. (1) There are plentiful hymn texts and tunes for the office. There is a definite need, however, for more contemporary settings of both words and music.

(2) With the exception of the few settings of OT and NT canticles that employ a refrain technique, music provided for psalms (and canticles) is typically that of the psalm-tones, a music demanding alternating choirs, a liturgical practice of monasteries, not parishes. New approaches to psalmody should be a concern; more canticle settings are also needed. If it is true that psalms cannot always be understood and prayed if they are not sung or if there is no reference to music (GenInstr-LitHor 121–123; 278–279), then it seems desirable to commission the production of a new liturgical psalter that respects the poetic quality of each psalm and, at the same time, that is intended to be set to music.

(3) At present pastoral celebrations of the Liturgy of the Hours is not a general practice of Catholic Christians. Much of the music provided—and even perhaps the pattern of the normative office—is directed more to monks or religious than to clergy and laity. Moreover, official publications of the divine-office music strive to satisfy two distinct modes of prayer: individual (devotional) prayer and communal (liturgical) prayer (*see* LITURGY OF THE HOURS [PASTORAL ADAPTATION AND CELEBRATION]).

(4) Several options are available for getting music and texts into the hands of the people; the FDLC, for example, published a pamphlet, *Advent Evening Prayer* (1977), making available a musical setting of Evening Prayer for the four Sundays of Advent. Catholic hymnals and service books should not be printed unless they contain texts and music for the hours. Missalettes could be enlarged by the publishers in order to contain parts of the office.

Over the next decade a time of musical creativity and experimentation is called for. But a creative approach to liturgical sung prayer might never occur if the normative pattern and texts of the Liturgy of the Hours are always demanded. For example, the antiphons in the official translation are quite often much too long to be used with a musical setting; a suspicion might arise that some of these longer texts were provided because the compilers assumed the office would ordinarily be read and, consequently, that textual elaboration was demanded.

Bibliography (Chronological): *The Prayer of the Church: Interim Version of the Roman Breviary* (London 1970). *Prayer of Christians: American Interim Breviary* (New York 1971). F. C. QUINN, "Music and the Prayer of Praise," *Worship* 46 (1972) 214–219. W. G. STOREY, F. C. QUINN, and D. F. WRIGHT, *Morning Praise and Evensong: A Liturgy of the Hours in Musical Setting* (Notre Dame, Ind. 1973). *The Divine Office: The Liturgy of the Hours According to the Roman Rite* (3 v., London 1974). *The Catholic Liturgy Book: The People's Complete Service Book* (Baltimore 1975). *The Liturgy of the Hours according to the Roman Rite* (4 v., New York 1975–76). *Christian Prayer* (Baltimore, Collegeville, Minn. and New York 1976). *Daily Prayer of the Church*, Contemporary Worship 9, Prepared by the Inter-Lutheran Commission on Worship for Provisional Use (Minneapolis 1976). *The Proposed Book of Common Prayer, according to the Use of the Episcopal Church* (Kingsport, Tenn. 1977). FDLC, *Advent Evening Prayer* (Chicago 1977).

[F. C. QUINN]

LOVE (THEOLOGY)

In classical Catholic theology love was understood as the supernatural or theological virtue of charity and its acts. Through divinely infused charity a person is oriented directly to the goodness of God as he is in himself, and God is loved for his own sake; the self and others are loved inasmuch as they potentially or actually participate in the divine goodness.

Since charity intends God as he is in himself rather than as only Creator of the universe, it was understood to be distinct from natural love of God, based on natural knowledge of him as source of the universe. Accordingly, charity presupposes the supernatural knowledge of God that is faith, which in turn exists only as a response to a free, supernatural, divine revelation.

Even this most rudimentary statement of the meaning of charity in classical theology discloses that the concept, "charity," is inseparably bound to the meanings of such other concepts as natural love, natural knowledge, faith, revelation, the natural and the supernatural. Charity is analyzed and its meaning employed as a part of a theological conceptual system; its meaning is assigned in conjunction with the assignments of other meanings within the system.

The direction of contemporary theology that was established by Vatican Council II has passed from a classical worldview and into historical consciousness. That has brought about theological developments of the concepts inseparably bound to the notion of charity in classical theology. The meaning of charity itself, it is therefore clear, must evolve similarly.

In the textbook way of pursuing theology the principal treatise on charity has traditionally been part of moral theology, a discipline oriented in the past to the preparation of confessors. The orientation towards *praxis*, it is now generally recognized, was conducive to understanding the Christian life in a minimalistic way. The Christian life as presented in the textbook setting is the life of the precepts or commandments. It is distinct from the life of the counsels, which was classified also as the life of striving for perfection and was studied in another discipline, ascetical theology.

As an element of Christian life, charity did not escape the minimalizing tendency in the science of the life of the precepts. Moral theologians generally maintained that Christ's new law of charity added no moral precepts in a material sense to those already contained in the Decalogue; charity, rather, brought a new "form" to acts in accord with those precepts. Thus moral theology tailored charity to fit the life of the precepts. While the face of charity in ascetical theology was generous and self-sacrificing, mirroring the countenance of its crucified Lord, the face of charity in moral theology was often egocentric and self-serving. Moralists saw charity as love, first, for God; secondly, for self; and only thirdly, for neighbor. Since the Christian life studied by ascetical theology was considered to be extraordinary, and since biblical research had not yet come into existence, the moralists' understanding of charity prevailed in classical Catholic theology.

Models for Understanding Charity. Three models or ways of understanding charity are now discernible in theology. They can be called potency–act, I-Thou, and self-transcendence respectively.

Potency–Act Model. The potency–act model of charity prevailed in moral theology from its beginnings as an independent discipline until the period of Vatican Council II. Basic to this model is the notion that love is an act of the intellectual appetite, the will. Man desires happiness, and his beatitude in the order of salvation is the beatific vision of the divine essence, in which man's supernaturally elevated intellectual appetite for the perfect good is completely fulfilled. Love for God is radically love for the perfect good, which God in himself is and to which the human intellectual appetite is ordered, at least when supernaturally elevated by charity. The neighbor is loved inasmuch as she or he is related to the divine goodness.

The strength of the potency–act model is its insistence on God's transcendence. If God is understood as the perfect, universal good, which totally satisfies the human appetite and in which alone the beatitude of man consists (ST 1a2ae, 2.8), there can be no tendency toward the false immanentism inclined to seek God only as present in the neighbor and not also as the transcendent Mystery and to reduce religion to social service in the secular city.

Nevertheless, this model has several limitations. The uniqueness of the person of the neighbor seems to be undervalued and ultimately superfluous. If the neighbor is loved only inasmuch as he or she participates in the divine goodness, it is difficult to explain how the neighbor is loved precisely inasmuch as he or she is not God but a unique person in his or her "otherness" in

relation to God. How or why the neighbor can be loved for his or her own sake is not readily explicable, and there is a tendency to regard the neighbor as a means to one's own final end. St. Thomas himself concluded that the perfection of charity essential to beatitude does not necessarily include a perfection of charity for the neighbor: even if there were only one soul enjoying God, it would be perfectly happy (*beata*) without a neighbor to love (ibid. 4.8 ad 3).

Another disadvantage of this model is its anthropocentrism. Man is (obediential) potency for the beatific vision, in which God is apprehended directly. God as the perfect good is seen as man's fulfillment, the fulfillment of the human appetite. The charge of regarding God here as a function of man cannot be completely escaped. A theocentric view of reality, it seems, would see man at the ultimate goal of love as a "function" of God.

A third disadvantage is demonstrated by the history of the use of this model. The model is individualistic and hardly conducive to the development of a social consciousness that strives toward the reign of God in working to ameliorate the social order on earth.

I–Thou Model. The second model of charity, the I–Thou, differs from the first in that it sees the love for "a concrete Thou" (Rahner) rather than an explicit love for God as the primary, fundamental act of charity. The love for a human Thou, according to this model, is the human and moral act par excellence. In it a person comes to himself or herself, fulfills his or her personal nature and freedom, and actuates himself or herself totally as a person in relation to all reality. The genuine love for a human Thou, moreover, is a supernatural act of charity and intends, implicitly and unthematically, God as he is in himself; and this implicit intending of God is the basic act of love for God.

Unlike the potency–act model, the I–Thou model emphasizes that love is an interpersonal relation and that, rather than rationally objectifiable goods, persons themselves in their ultimately mysterious depths are intended by love. This model makes clear also that a person is loved for his or her own sake as the unique individual that he or she is. Hence there is little tendency to regard the neighbor as a means to one's own beatitude. Love is seen here also as issuing from the mysterious core of the human spirit, touched by the Spirit of God, where a person freely disposes of herself or himself. As the notion that love is an act of the intellectual appetite is basic to the first model, basic to the second is the idea that love is the personal act par excellence of freely disposing of oneself.

A limitation of the I–Thou model, shared in its own way by the first model, is that it seems to portray a "cheap grace" of personal fulfillment. Fulfillment appears to be located prematurely in the I–Thou relation. To be sure, the love for a human Thou is seen as placing the one who loves in an authentic relation to all reality. What is not indicated, however, is that one who stands in authentic relation to all reality must experience an exigency to work toward the transformation of the social order of the world. Precisely because the person loving a human Thou is seen as actuating herself or himself in the totality of her or his person, it is unclear that authentic universal, social community could add anything essential to the personal fulfillment already realized in the I–Thou communion.

Self-Transcendence Model. A third model sees charity as self-transcendence. Whereas the second model emerged in the decade before Vatican Council II, the third began to appear, chiefly in *liberation theology, only in the decade following the Council. Still undeveloped, the self-transcendence model sees man, somewhat in the manner of Eastern mysticism, as oriented to transcend himself. Its view differs from Eastern mysticism, however, in that personal individuality is won, not lost, in self-transcendence.

While the potency–act model sees man as an active potency for the good, which, when attained, actuates and fulfills him, the self-transcendence model sees him more as a passive potency, capable of being annexed, indeed through his own cooperation, to the reality greater than himself that envelops him. Man needs to be "converted" (Lonergan) to reality; he must allow himself to be annexed to reality through authentic relations to it. Knowledge, according to this model, is less a drawing of reality into the mind and an actuation of the self (*intellectus quodammodo omnia*) and more a process of allowing the self to be annexed or joined, in an authentic (cognitive) relation, to the totality of what is. Similarly, love is seen as a state of conversion to reality, in which a person allows herself or himself to be united, in an authentic personal (affective and effective) relation, to the whole of reality.

Defense of the Self-Transcendence Model. The third model seems to possess the strengths but none of the weaknesses of the other two models. The idea of love as the self transcending itself through authentic personal union with the totality of reality, like the first model, certainly safeguards the transcendence of God. Indeed the third model reverses the anthropocentrism of the first and locates the individual properly within the totality of reality, seeing him or her as ultimately annexed to God himself.

Like the I–Thou model, the self-transcendence model sees love as issuing from the depths of a person, from the core of personal freedom; moreover, it recognizes that the basic act of love is the I–Thou relation and that love is directed to the Thou in the mysterious, nonobjectifiable depths of his or her person. However, the third model also makes it clear that the fulfillment experienced in the love for a human Thou is merely relative and that personal fulfillment is ultimately to be found only in the fulfillment of the totality of reality. Only the self-transcendence model, seeing the individual as called to be annexed authentically to the whole of reality, makes clear that the individual's fulfillment is ultimately inseparable from the beatitude of all mankind. Love according to this model becomes, in a word, the seeking of the Kingdom of God. It becomes an active concern to transform the world by working to transform society into authentic community. And when charity is understood as personal commitment to the reign of God, the unity of love for God and love for neighbor is seen in a new, more intimate and universal dimension, concealed from the eyes of the first and second models.

Bibliography: G. GILLEMAN, *The Primacy of Charity in Moral Theology,* tr. W. RYAN and A. VACHON (Westminister, Md. 1959). B. HÄRING, *The Law of Christ* (Westminster 1964) 2:83–107, 351–469. R. JOHANN, *The Meaning of Love* (Westminster 1959). B. LONERGAN, *Method in Theology* (New York 1972) 101–124, 237–244. K. RAHNER, *Theological Investigations* 5 (Baltimore and London 1966) 439–459; 6 (London and New York 1974) 231–249. N. RIGALI, "Toward a Moral Theology of Social Consciousness," Hor 4 (1977) 169–181. P. TEILHARD DE CHARDIN, *The Phenomenon of Man,* tr. B. WALL (New York and Evanston, Ind. 1959) 237–290.

[N. RIGALI]

LUNN, ARNOLD

Catholic convert and apologist, England's leading authority on skiing, b. Madras, India, April 18, 1888; d., London June 3, 1974. His father was Sir Harry Lunn, who was a Methodist missionary in India, later worked for the Thomas Cook travel agency, and in 1906 formed a successful tour business of his own. His mother was an Irish Protestant devoted to Sinn Fein and Irish independence. Lunn in 1908 founded the Alpine Ski Club and from 1919 was editor of the British Ski Year Book. He introduced the modern slalom course in Muerren, Switzerland, in 1922, thus creating the modern Alpine slalom race. For 15 years (1924–39) he was a member of the executive committee of the Féderation Internationale de Ski (FIS) and later (1946–49) was chairman of the International Downhill Ski Racing Committee.

One particular experience of an Alpine sunset Lunn credited with awakening in him a sense of the spiritual and the supernatural, in his *The Swiss and Their Mountains* (1963). Lunn's formal education took place at Harrow and at Balliol College, Oxford. He wrote of his conversion in *Now I See* (London 1934). His defense of Catholicism usually involved collaboration with a friend, such as Ronald Knox; or with friendly foes, such as the Anglican Garith Lean, or the philosopher C. E. M. Joad, or the scientist J. B. S. Haldane. Lunn's books often took the form of debates. In addition to *Difficulties* (1932, with Ronald Knox), there should be mentioned his *Science and the Supernatural* (1935, with J. B. S. Haldane), and *Christian Counterattack* (1969, with Garith Lean). His reputation as a conservative made him especially useful in World War II, when he traveled extensively in Spain, Portugal, Latin America, and the United States, as a spokesman for Britain and the defense of Christian civilization against Nazism.

While refusing to become an alarmist after Vatican Council II, he was annoyed by some secularist trends, and especially saddened by events in the United States. He spoke and continued writing against the new morality, e.g., in *The New Morality*, with G. Lean (rev. ed., London 1967), which he viewed as a accommodation of the Christian code to secularist sensibilities, a preoccupation with social problems, and a general revolt against authority. The real division, as he saw it, was not between liberals and conservatives, but between those who are and those who are not intimidated by dominant fashions of secularism. He refused to tone down differences between various Christian communions, but was in favor of a militant ecumenism, in which all would band together to reverse the triumphant advance of secularism. He summed up his approach (in an article in the *Tablet* dated the day before his death) by citing Augustine: Love men, slay errors.

Bibliography: A. LUNN, *Come What May* (Boston 1941) autobiography. *Tablet* 221 (1967) 90–91, 132–133; 224 (1970) 544; 227 (1973) 654; 228 (1974) 527.

[E. J. DILLON]

LUTHERAN/REFORMED/ROMAN CATHOLIC STUDY COMMISSION

From 1971 to 1976 an international group, representatives of the Lutheran World Federation, the World Alliance of Reformed Churches, and the Vatican's

Secretariat for Promoting Christian Unity, met several times for the purpose of dialogue on the issue signified in their full title: Roman Catholic/Lutheran/Reformed Study Commission on "The Theology of Marriage and the Problems of Mixed Marriages."

At their final meeting in Venice, April 25 to May 2, 1976, they approved a report on their discussions and findings. The participants unanimously affirmed "the permanence and lifelong character of marriage...on the ground of the Christian Gospel in the gift of Christ and his grace." Nevertheless sharp divergences remained between the Catholic and the Protestant sides on the question of indissolubility and of divorce and remarriage.

Although the papal motu proprio of 1970, *Matrimonia mixta* (see 16:283), allows more practical cooperation than is generally realized, some canonical requirements which remain in force seemed to the Commission to be less than ideal, ecumenically speaking. (On ecumenism and the theology of marriage *see also* ANGLICAN/ROMAN CATHOLIC INTERNATIONAL COMMISSION.)

Bibliography: Commission Report, "The Theology of Marriage and the Problem of Mixed Marriages," Origins 7 (1978) 481–494. N. EHRENSTRÖM and G. GASSMANN, *Confessions in Dialogue* (3d ed., Geneva 1975) 33–36.

[P. MISNER]

LUTHERAN/ROMAN CATHOLIC DIALOGUE

Since Vatican Council II many *bilateral consultations or conversations have developed on an official level between representatives of different Churches. The Lutheran/Roman Catholic dialogue, as comprising official conversations in this sense with appointed discussion partners who convene on a planned basis, got started especially early in the United States and issued a first set of papers and conclusions on the status of the Nicene Creed as dogma already in 1965.

International. On the international level, the Joint Lutheran/Roman Catholic Study Commission on "The Gospel and the Church" held five meetings from November 1967 to February 1971. These resulted in an important joint statement, called the "Malta Report" (MR) after the site of the final meeting at which it was adopted. The Commission was able to overcome some divisive issues of such long standing that more than half of its thirteen members wondered whether it was not time to take some large steps towards unity, possibly a mutual recognition of one another's ordained ministry or permission for intercommunion on specific occasions. The "Malta Report" seems destined to be regarded as a milestone in Lutheran/Catholic relations.

A successor group was formed soon afterwards to take up where the Study Commission had left off. It is called the "Roman Catholic-Lutheran Joint Working Group" or the "International Commission" and holds a plenary session about once a year. One of its goals is to elicit and evaluate responses to the MR from theological faculties, Lutheran Churches and Roman Catholic episcopal conferences around the world. An initial evaluation made in 1975 had only a limited number of responses with which to work. For the rest, the International Commission has taken up particular questions which were either not treated in the MR or required further consideration.

Thus, at the 1974 meeting in Rome, the significance of the world for the self-understanding of the Church was taken up again with reference to the theology of liberation; the same theme had been of critical importance in setting a common frame of reference for the original Commission, whose report devotes a whole section to "the Gospel and the World." At the same meeting it was decided to set up a subcommittee to prepare a common study on the Lord's Supper. This was discussed at the 1976 meeting at Liebfrauenberg near Strasbourg and was in nearly final form for the 1977 meeting at Paderborn. When issued, it is expected to claim that far-reaching agreement on Eucharistic doctrine may be found between Lutherans and Catholics. The International Commission is also working on the question of the ordained ministry, with particular attention to the episcopate, and on the question of the unity of the Church. Regarding the latter, there was a preliminary discussion in Liebfrauenberg on different "models of church unity," each with its positive elements.

Dialogue in the U.S. The American conversations have been even more remarkable, especially when taken in conjunction with the contributions of American theologians to the MR. (For an account of the American dialogue up to 1973, i.e. including the first four volumes of *Lutherans and Catholics in Dialogue*, see 16:265.)

In March 1974 the U.S. Lutheran/Catholic dialogue group released the text of its "Joint Statement on Papal Primacy." Soon thereafter it published the statement, together with several studies that had been submitted in the course of its deliberations, in *Papal Primacy and the Universal Church*. The Joint Statement is followed by the "Reflections" of the Lutheran participants on the one hand and the Catholic participants on the other. Total agreement was, of course, not achieved: the Catholic spokesmen expressed their conviction that the papal form of ministry is divinely willed; the Lutherans, for their part, would not admit that, except *a posteriori*—insofar as a pope's actions would show him to be acting in a ministerial capacity for all Christians.

Nevertheless, the degree to which the differences have been narrowed is widely recognized as potentially epoch-making, depending on the extent and the manner in which the group's methods and conclusions are accepted. This is not the first question which the U.S. Lutheran/Catholic Consultation has moved off dead center and placed on the agenda of church bodies as a real, and not merely utopian, possibility. In 1967 it had urged that the Lutheran doctrine of the Lord's Supper be recognized as sound by Catholics and vice versa; in 1970, that consideration be given to the mutual recognition of ministries (both, be it noted, in advance of the MR). Then, in 1974, the appointed participants came to the much more conditional conclusion, that the papacy, *if renewed in the light of the Gospel*, might perform a service to the Church at large which all Christians would be obliged to acknowledge. Such considerations seem almost as if meant to be a response to Pope Paul VI's frequent avowals that the papacy is the greatest obstacle on the ecumenical horizon today (*see* PRIMACY OF THE POPE).

From 1974 through 1978 the American dialogue group wrestled with the thorny issue of infallibility, papal and ecclesial. In the course of these discussions, a pattern of differences based on varying understandings of justification has been surmised. The participants have therefore decided to examine the question of justification in the next round of meetings. In this way they are taking up a classical issue between Lutherans and

Catholics, one treated briefly in the MR but never expressly placed on the agenda in the American conversations.

Bibliography: "Report of the Joint Lutheran/Roman Catholic Study Commission on 'The Gospel and the Church': Malta, 1971," *Lutheran World* 19 (1972) 259–273. "Lutheran-Catholic Dialogue" (Joint Statement on Papal Primacy), Origins 3 (1974) 585–600. N. EHRRENSTRÖM and G. GASSMANN, eds., *Confessions in Dialogue* (3d, rev. ed., Geneva 1975).

P. C. EMPIE and T. A. MURPHY, eds., *Papal Primacy and the Universal Church. Lutherans and Catholics in Dialogue* 5 (Minneapolis 1974). G. A. LINDBECK, "Lutherans and the Papacy," JEcumSt 13 (1976) 368–378. H. MEYER, "Das Papstamt in lutherische Sicht," in H. STIRNIMANN and L. VISCHER, eds., *Papsttum und Petrusdienst* (Frankfurt 1975) 73–90. H. MEYER, H. SCHÜTTE, and H. J. MUND, *Katholische Anerkennung des Augsburgischen Bekenntnisses* (Frankfurt 1977). C. J. PETER, "Ambiguity, Criticism and Promise," *New Catholic World* 220 (1977) 187–190. Secretariat for Promoting Christian Unity, *Information Service* 35 (1977) 5.

[P. MISNER]

M

MARIOLOGY

The period, 1972–78, showed a two-fold orientation in Mariology: continuation of the directions of Vatican Council II; new areas, as explorations in the devotional life of the faithful. Study was spurred by important papal documents and joint pastorals by national episcopal conferences, as in the United States, the NCCB's *Behold Your Mother. Woman of Faith* (Nov. 21, 1973), Switzerland (1973), Puerto Rico (1976), and Poland (1977).

Pope Paul VI's apostolic exhortation *Marialis cultus* (Feb. 1, 1974), "for the right ordering and development of devotion to the Blessed Virgin Mary," showed Mary's place in the revised Western liturgy and included significant points on anthropology, on the Virgin Mary in respect to women's rights, and on human dignity. Study sessions were held in conjunction with popular manifestations, as at the 14-day Marian Congress in Sydney, Australia, September 1976.

The seventh international Mariological Congress was held at Rome, May, 1975, on Marian cult in the era from 1100 to 1500. Catholic charismatics held their first international meeting in Rome at the same time; their Marian congress was on "Our Lady and the Holy Spirit." The eighth international Marian Congress is planned for Saragossa, Spain, October 1979, on Marian cult in the ecumenically sensitive 16th century. Organizer of these congresses and publisher of the proceedings is the Rome-based International Pontifical Marian Academy, headed until his death in 1977 by C. Balic, OFM, now by P. Melada, OFM.

National societies concerned with Marian theology continued to meet, for example, French (*Bulletin de la soliété française d'études mariales*), Spanish (*Estudios Marianos*), Canadian (French-speaking, occasional publication) and American (*Marian Studies*). The recent topics of the French society illustrate current concerns: "Mary's place in religious congregations of Marian Inspiration" (1972); "Mary and the Question of Women" (1973 and 1974); and "Representations of Mary in Popular Piety, Historically, Iconographically, and Psychologically" (1976 and 1977). The Spanish society has reached its 40th volume of proceedings; recent themes have been: "The Psychology of Mary" (1972); "Mary and the Mystery of the Church" (1973); "Marian Dogmas and the Interpretation of Dogma" (1976).

Popular cult of the Virgin Mary is being more and more investigated: origins and significance of folk devotion in various cultures, both in the Old World (pilgrimage sites and shrines like Czestochowa and Lourdes, more visited than ever), and in the New World (Guadalupe, Argentina, and other countries). An associated theme is the place of Mary in the "way of beauty," complementing the "way of the intellect," as Pope Paul suggested to the Roman congress of May, 1975.

Marian Library Studies (Dayton), the international *Marianum* (Rome) and *Ephemerides Mariologicae* (Madrid), and other periodicals, both technical and general, illustrate present centers of Mariological interest: popular piety; Scripture, especially the infancy narratives; catechetics; ecumenism; Mary as model of the Church, e.g., in medieval studies, St. Bernard of Clairvaux, Isaac of Stella, and other 12th-century Cistercians.

An American branch of the Ecumenical Society of the Blessed Virgin Mary, founded in England, 1967, was established in 1976 and has been meeting twice a year, with Anglican, Presbyterian, Orthodox, Baptist, and Catholic participation. A theologian in the Reformed tradition, Dr. J. A. Ross Mackenzie (Union Theological Seminary, Richmond, Virginia) received the president's patronal medal at Catholic University, Washington, D.C., December 7, 1977. The medal, founded in 1974, recognizes promotion of study and veneration of Mary (previous recipients were Archbishop Fulton J. Sheen, Mother Mary Claudia, IHM, and Theodore Koehler, SM, curator of the Marian Library at the University of Dayton).

From the Mariological Society of America articles in *Marian Studies*, reflect the growing ecumenical interest: 1975, Ross Mackenzie and B. de Margerie, SJ.; 1976, F. M. Jelly, OP, and D. Dietz, OMI, on the hierarchy of truths (16:208); 1977, John T. Ford, CSC, on *sensus fidelium* in Cardinal Newman; 1978, R. H. Fuller, on *theotokos* in the New Testament, and Ross Mackenzie on the New Eve. An offshoot of the Lutheran-Roman Catholic consultations in the United

States is an interdenominational project resulted in a book, *Mary in the New Testament* (New York 1978), similar to *Peter in the New Testament* (New York 1975).

Bibliography: E. R. CARROLL, "A Survey of Recent Marian Theology," annually, in *Marian Studies*, most recent 29 (1978); "Theology on the Virgin Mary," ThSt 37 (1976) 253–289; "Mariology, " in G. DYER, ed., *An American Catholic Catechism* (New York 1976). F. JELLY in J. C. LAWLER, D. W. WUERL, and R. LAWLER, eds., *The Teaching of Christ. A Catholic Catechism for Adults* (Huntington, Ind. 1976). R. LAURENTIN, "Bulletin sur la Vierge Marie," every second year in *Revue des sciences philosophiques et théologiques*, most recent 69 (1976). J. C. DE SATGÉ, *Down to Earth: The New Protestant Vision of the Virgin Mary* (Wilmington, N.C. 1976), by an English Anglican member of the Ecumenical Society of the BVM, which publishes several conferences yearly, available from the Secretary, 237 Fulham Palace Rd., London SW6 6UB. Papers from the society's international conference, Birmingham, 1975 are in E. YARNOLD et al., "God and Mary," WaySuppl 25 (1975). The American chapter of the Society has published, D. G. DAWE, *From ·Dysfunction to Disbelief: the Virgin Mary in Reformed Theology* (1977), available from the Society's offices, National Shrine, 4th and Michigan Ave. NE, Washington, D.C. 20017.

[E. R. CARROLL]

MARRIAGE (CANON LAW)

Since 1966 the principal changes that have taken place in the Canon Law of marriage (9:271) have been in four areas: (1) marriage preparation; (2) mixed marriages; (3) the procedural law governing the adjudication of marriage annulments; and (4) the jurisprudence relative to the requirements for a valid marriage.

Marriage Preparation. The 1918 Code of Canon Law, in treating marriage, contained a section of sixteen canons (CIC cc. 1019–34) entitled "Concerning Those Things Which Should Precede the Celebration, Especially the Banns." On June 29, 1941 the Sacred Congregation of the Sacraments issued an *Instruction* (Bousc-O'Connor 2:253–276), detailing how those canons were to be implemented. The canons along with the Instruction, were, until well into the 1960s, the principal legislative enactments that influenced parish priests in preparing people for marriage. Both enactments tended to be legalistic; their major preoccupation being with the detection of impediments. Each of them (c. 1033, *Instruction* n. 8) recommended, more or less incidentally, that there be some instruction in Christian doctrine, particularly regarding marriage, but the chief concern seems to have been with legalities. Occasionally the *Instruction* offered quaint advice: after the priest who performed the wedding sent the notification of marriage to the church of Baptism, he was advised "not to rest" (*is vero non acquiescat*) until he received word from the church of Baptism that the notification had indeed been entered into the baptismal register. But, in general, the *Instruction* took a hard attitude towards priests who did not obtain all the necessary permissions and complete all the necessary forms: Ordinaries were told that "they should not fail to inflict upon negligent pastors, especially upon habitual offenders, canonical penalties in accordance with c. 2222, §1, including suspension *a divinis*" (*Instruction* n. 12). Few if any priests seem to have been suspended because of their neglect of the *Instruction*, but it also seems true that, as a result of the *Instruction*, few couples received any genuine preparation for marriage.

There was, undoubtedly, less need a generation or two ago for genuine preparation, but in recent years the divorce rate has risen sharply virtually all over the world and there is a growing awareness that marriage is a state of life that demands not only considerable maturity in the spouses but also some prior insights into the challenges and problems of marriage and some basic vocational skills.

Vatican Council II in the Constitution on the Church in the Modern World recommended that programs of instruction be initiated to strengthen and prepare people for married life (*Gaudium et spes* 52) and beginning in the 1960s one diocese after another in the U.S. began to issue local legislation designed to insure that marriages celebrated in the Church have reasonable prospects for success. Initially those diocesan programs referred only to the marriages of teenagers, usually requiring some counselling or at least some evaluation of people below a certain age, to determine whether the parties had reached a basic maturity. Gradually, however, the programs have been expanded. Many dioceses now have regulations that refer to all couples planning to marry, irrespective of their age. Frequently a waiting period of several months is required, during which both an assessment process and a formation process are conducted. The assessment process often involves a rather thorough premarital inventory aimed at determining the ability and/or compatibility of the parties relative to such things as personal adjustment, communication, interests, finances, children, and sexuality. The formation process attempts to impart marital skills and to heighten appreciation of the dignity and holiness of marriage. In those instances where the couple does not demonstrate an adequate readiness for marriage, the Catholic ceremony is postponed. There are instances, of late, where the dioceses of an ecclesiastical province or of a state are banding together and issuing common legislation for the entire region. Thus there is a first step, perhaps, towards a unified marriage preparation law for the nation, as suggested by c. 250 of the 1975 schema of the revised Canon Law on the Sacraments (*see* CODE OF CANON LAW, REVISION OF).

Mixed Marriages. According to the Code of Canon Law, when a Catholic married a non-Catholic, certain *cautiones*, that is to say, guarantees or promises were required. More specifically, the non-Catholic party was obliged to promise to remove all danger of perversion from the Catholic party and both parties had to guarantee that all children born of the marriage would be baptized and educated only in the Catholic Faith (CIC c. 1061). Many authors regarded these guarantees as required by divine law, and therefore beyond the power of the Church to dispense. It was furthermore expected that, even in a mixed marriage, the consent of the parties would always be exchanged before a Catholic priest (c. 1094) and never before a non-Catholic minister or rabbi, even by way of a secondary ceremony (CIC c. 1063). Catholics who attempted marriage before a minister were excommunicated (CIC c. 2319).

Matrimonii Sacramentum. On March 18, 1966, however, the Congregation for the Doctrine of the Faith, convinced that it was now "advisable that the rigor of the present law on mixed marriages be mitigated," issued the instructiom *Matrimonii sacramentum* (Bousc-O'Connor 6:592–597). This instruction did several things. It abrogated retroactively the censure incurred by a Catholic for attempting marriage before a non-Catholic minister. It welcomed the minister into the sanctuary during the Catholic ceremony and invited, or at least permitted, him to offer an exhortation, prayers, and congratulations at the conclusion of the ceremony. Where there were "difficulties" with the marriage taking place before the Catholic priest rather than a minister, the Ordinary was advised to refer the case to the Holy See, suggesting that in individual cases and given the proper circumstances, Rome was ready to permit Catholics to marry before the minister of the non-Catholic spouse. *Matrimonii sacramentum* also altered the promises to be made by the non-Catholic. The odious promise "to remove all danger of perversion" was dropped altogether and the promise regarding the children was changed from a positive to a negative one. It was, in other words, no longer expected that non-Catholics would promise to baptize and educate the children in the Catholic faith, but only that they would not prevent their Catholic spouse from doing so. And even here the requirement was not absolute. Non-Catholics were only "invited" to make that promise. Where they could not do so in good conscience, the Ordinary was, once again, advised to refer the case to Rome.

For the next four years, until the issuance of the decree *Matrimonia mixta* (March 31, 1970) the Congregation for the Doctrine of the Faith responded to individual requests regarding the two issues of dispensing from the form, that is to say, the requirement that marital consent be expressed before a Catholic priest, and dispensing from the guarantees.

As regards the form of marriage, a typical case presented to the Congregation might involve the irrevocable opposition to a Catholic ceremony on the part of the non-Catholic's parents, or perhaps the fact that the non-Catholic party had a parent, relative, or even close friend who was a minister and who desired to perform the ceremony. In such cases the Congregation generally responded by permitting the Ordinary to dispense from the form according to his own discretion (Bousc-O'Connor 6:627–630).

The form of marriage as it applies to a marriage between a Catholic and an Orthodox was, meanwhile, following special rules. The Decree of the Second Vatican Council on Oriental Churches, dated November 21, 1964 (ibid. 6, 7–19) had, in effect, extended the form of marriage to include the Orthodox priest whenever an Eastern Rite Catholic married an Orthodox (*Orientalium ecclesiarum* 18). On Feb. 22, 1967, by the decree *Crescens Matrimonium* of the Congregation for the Oriental Church (Bousc-O'Connor 6:605–606), the same extension of the form was recognized in the case of a *Latin* Catholic marrying an Orthodox. In both cases it was expected that, for lawfulness, the Catholic party would obtain permission for the ceremony to take place before the Orthodox priest, but as for validity even without that permission the ceremony would be recognized. For the Latin rite Catholic this became effective March 25, 1967.

As regards requests made to the Congregation for the Doctrine of the Faith between March 1966 and March 1970 for a dispensation from the guarantees, a typical case might involve, e.g., a Lutheran woman, wishing to marry a Catholic man but intent on baptizing and bringing up the children as Lutherans. The case might be further complicated by the fact that the woman was a devout Lutheran, while the man had a more tenuous relationship to his Church. The woman could not, in good conscience, promise to allow her husband to bring up the children as Catholics, and the man, respecting her conscience, could not, therefore, honestly make his promise either. Such requests were generally granted by the Congregation "provided that the Catholic party seriously promises that he will provide, in as far as he shall be able, for the children to be baptized and educated as Catholics." In many cases it was clear that there was no realistic hope that the children would in fact be reared as Catholics, but Rome nonetheless always insisted that the Catholic party at least be disposed to do whatever was possible (ibid. 6:597–604).

Matrimonia Mixta. The decree *Matrimonia mixta*, dated March 31, 1970 (O'Connor 7:711–717), went several steps beyond the provisions of *Matrimonii sacramentum* and the interim practice. It dropped altogether any promise, even a negative one, to be made by the non-Catholic party; while a double promise was expected of the Catholic, first that "he is prepared to remove the dangers of defecting from the faith," and, secondly, that "he will do all he can in his power to have all offspring baptized and educated in the Catholic Church," this latter promise to be interpreted presumably in light of the *praxis Curiae* prior to the decree. It was, however, no longer necessary to send such requests to Rome. The decree acknowledged that, where the promises were made, the local Ordinary was empowered to grant the dispensation. The decree likewise acknowledged that the local Ordinary had the right to dispense from the canonical form in the case of a mixed marriage, but it left to the episcopal conference the establishment of norms that would insure a desirable uniformity within a given country in regard to many of the details involved in a mixed marriage.

Over the next several months various episcopal conferences around the world issued their particular norms implementing *Matrimonia mixta*. Those for the United States were dated November 16, 1970 (O'Connor 7:718–740) and, among other things, recommended that the Catholic promises be expressed in the formula "I reaffirm my faith in Jesus Christ and, with God's help, intend to continue living that faith in the Catholic Church. I promise to do all in my power to share the faith I have received with our children by having them baptized and reared as Catholics."

The prescriptions of this instruction *Matrimonia mixta*, as detailed by the particular norms of episcopal conferences, remain the current law governing mixed marriages.

Annulment Procedures. In the mid-1960s, U.S. Tribunals were granting about 300 annulments per year. By the mid-1970s, that number had risen to 18,000 per year. Perhaps the most important, if somewhat intangible, reason for this dramatic increase in annulments is that, since Vatican II, the Church has seen itself, to a degree it previously had not, as a Church called to embrace sinners and to seek and save what was lost (*Lumen gentium* 8). There is, consequently, a heightened interest in reaching out to divorced people and in providing them a place in the Catholic community.

A second reason for the annulment explosion is the need occasioned by the soaring divorce rate. In 1975 the number of divorces in this country exceeded, for the first time, one million; and that was more than double the divorces granted ten years earlier. This has naturally resulted in more and more Catholic people approaching their Church for a decision on their right to remarry.

But besides the interest and the need, there is a third reason that explains the phenomenon, and that is the increased efficiency of the tribunals themselves. There are, undoubtedly, many factors that have contributed to that efficiency, but chief among them is the American Procedural Norms (*see* MARRIAGE TRIBUNALS, EXPERIMENTAL NORMS), commonly referred to as the APN, a set of guidelines that simplified and streamlined the mechanics of obtaining an annulment (O'Connor 7:950–966).

U.S. Tribunal Norms. The core of the APN is its three principal features, namely: (a) the right of a petitioner to approach his or her own diocese for a decision (the universal law of the Church does not automatically permit this); (b) the faculty permitting an annulment to be granted by one judge (the universal law generally requires three); and (c) the annulment's becoming final following the decision of only one ecclesiastical court whenever an appeal is judged clearly superfluous (the universal law requires that every affirmative decision in first instance be reviewed by an appeal court).

The procedural norms first went into effect on July 1, 1970. They were granted only to the U.S., and for an experimental period of three years. On June 20, 1973, almost on the eve of their expiration date, the APN were renewed for one year by Rome. The extension, however, was granted with obvious reluctance, and with the clear understanding that the extra year of grace was granted only in order to facilitate the orderly transition back to the universal law. July 1, 1974 was to mark the final termination of what had apparently been, in the eyes of Rome, an unsuccessful experiment (O'Connor Suppl c. 1960).

On May 22, 1974, however, the Council for Public Affairs of the Church, "having considered the matter more maturely," and under considerable pressure from the American episcopate, once again renewed the APN, this time "until a new system of procedure in marriage cases is promulgated for the Latin Church" (ibid.).

Causas Matrimoniales. In 1970, shortly after the APN were first granted, several other countries, Australia, Belgium, England, and Canada, petitioned for and eventually received permission to modify somewhat the annulment process in their respective countries. Partly, no doubt, to curtail further requests of this kind and to maintain some uniformity in judicial proceedings around the globe, and partly to reduce "the excessive lengthiness of matrimonial processes," Pope Paul VI, on March 28, 1971, issued the apostolic letter *Causas matrimoniales* (O'Connor 7:969–974). This letter promulgated new procedural law for the universal Church in the same areas that had come to be regarded as the core of the APN. In each of the three areas, however, *Causas matrimoniales* settled on a compromise between the 1918 procedural law and the 1970 APN. Briefly, the compromises were these: (a) the residence of the petitioner is not a source of competence but the place where most of the proofs are collected (often the same as the petitioner's residence) is, providing certain permissions are obtained; (b) in individual cases, the episcopal conference can permit one judge to decide a case; and (c) appeal is required, but the appellate procedure is simplified.

Schema of Procedural Law. On November 3, 1976 a draft of that new system of procedural law entitled

Schema canonum de modo procedendi pro tutela iurium seu de processibus was submitted for evaluation to the bishops of the world. In the three critical areas, it repeated almost verbatim (cc. 337, 24, and 347 of the *Schema*) the compromises that had been reached in *Causas matrimoniales.* That these compromises would be included in a schema that appeared as late as 1976 suggests a determined perseverance on the part of the Roman Curia regarding the compromises and an adamant intent to maintain them as the universal law of the Church, without admitting of exceptions. On the other hand, criticism of the schema was substantial. Circumstances differ, of course, from nation to nation, so that the various episcopal conferences around the world have responded to the schema in various ways. In general, however, the American episcopate remains convinced that the compromises of the schema would leave American matrimonial tribunals ill equipped to deal with the American problem; and indications are that the United States episcopate will give its vigorous support to the continuance of the "experimental" procedural norms. Nevertheless the future of procedural law and probably of the American tribunal system as it now exists remains uncertain.

Jurisprudence. As the term is commonly used jurisprudence is applied, legal matrimonology. It is, in other words the application of the science of marriage to the question of marriage validity. Its concern is with such basic, rather philosophical questions, as: what is the essence of marriage? what are the indispensable qualities that must exist in the two people in order for them to be fit subjects for marriage? what actions are required by the couple in order to enter marriage? It is called jurisprudence because it is exercised in a judicial setting by jurists or judges who have been called upon to determine whether all the absolute essentials are or are not present in a given marriage; to determine, in other words, whether or not a particular marriage is valid.

Like every science, jurisprudence is dynamic and in a state of constant evolution, but traditionally, in discernible ways: by developing new principles; by restoring old principles after a period of dormancy; by utilizing existing principles previously ignored; by expanding, refining, or contracting prevailing principles; by explicitating what had been implicit or by giving a new emphasis to a principle; and also by a change in circumstances that results in a new application of an old principle. Although jurisprudence is never static, some periods of history are more dynamic than others, and this is certainly true of the past couple of decades, during which jurisprudence has developed with extraordinary rapidity in a number of areas. The following are some examples of that development, listed according to their evolutionary style.

Contraction. An example of jurisprudence evolving by the restriction of a principle may have been occasioned by the so called "Vasectomy Decree" of May 13, 1977 (ActApS 69 [1977] 426; *see* IMPOTENCE). It is perhaps too early to say for sure but it is the opinion of some that this decree of the Congregation for the Doctrine of the Faith relative to the "impotence which prohibits marriage" (*impotentia, quae matrimonium dirimit*) may result in church courts' taking a more restricted view of what constitutes male impotence. The gist of the decree is that if a man can perform sexually, he should be regarded as potent, even though his ejaculate contains no spermatozoa. Such men, vasectomized men, for example, were considered by chanceries *ante factum* not to be barred from marriage as far as the impediment of impotence was concerned. If, however, the marriage later ended in divorce, tribunals were accustomed, if petitioned *post factum*, to declare the marriage null on the grounds that the man was not capable of performing "those acts which are per se apt for the generation of offspring" and should therefore be regarded as impotent. Tribunals in other words, have always had a wider view of impotence than have chanceries. There is some speculation, however, that since Pope Paul VI personally approved the "Vasectomy Decree," tribunals will now adopt the more restricted chancery notion. Should this prove true it would be an example of jurisprudence evolving by contraction.

Restoration. The most important and dramatic development in jurisprudence in recent years was effected by restoring an old principle that had, for many years, been dormant. It concerns the most fundamental of all jurisprudential problems: what is the essence of marriage? The Code of Canon Law (CIC c. 1081 §2), P. Gasparri, *De Matrimonio*, n. 776, practically all of the manualists, and Rotal decisions for many years held that the essence of marriage consists in what might be called the right to the joining of *bodies*, or, more accurately, the right to those acts which are per se apt for the generation of offspring. The right to the joining of *souls*, on the other hand, i.e. the right to a personal, conjugal communion was regarded as pertaining not to the essence of marriage, but only to its wholeness or integrity.

In recent years, however, a host of Rotal decisions have come to consider the right to the community of life as pertaining not merely to the integrity but to the very essence of marriage. This insight is endorsed not only in decisions of the Roman Rota and the Apostolic Signatura but also in the 1975 *Schema canonum* proposed for revised law on the Sacraments, in which the new canon 1081 §2 is adjusted to read: "Matrimonial consent is that acts of the will whereby a man and a woman by means of a mutual covenant constitute with one another a communion of conjugal life which is perpetual and exclusive and which by its very nature is ordered to the procreating and education of children" (c. 295 §2).

Although this development in jurisprudence has been heralded as an innovation, resulting largely from Vatican II, it is, in fact, rather a restoration of an older jurisprudence, reflected with limpid clarity in the works of such distinguished canonists as Tomas Sanchez (12:1040), who published in 1602, and Franz Schmalzgrueber (12:1137), who wrote about a century later.

The impact and ramifications of recognizing the right to the community of life as part of the essence of marriage have been profound and extensive. Previously, people were regarded as lacking the basic, stable capacity for marriage only by reason of genital impotence, that is to say, only when they were unable to exchange the right to the joining of *bodies*. Now, however, people are also considered to lack the capacity for marriage when they are radically incapable, by reason of some mental disorder or emotional immaturity, of exchanging the right to the joining of *souls*.

According to this jurisprudence, a tribunal will declare a marriage null when it has determined that one spouse, even though of "sound mind" at the time of the ceremony, nevertheless lacked, at that time, the capacity to enter with the other person into a lifelong union that would be characterized by at least minimal caring and sharing.

This ground now accounts for more than 90 per cent of all annulments granted in the U.S., perhaps 17,000 or more per year, and although most canonists are convinced that it is a legitimate jurisprudential development as well as a useful pastoral tool, its long term effect on marriage stability and family life has also become for some a source of concern and even alarm.

Expansion. Substantial error has always been regarded as a ground of nullity (CIC c. 1083). Traditionally, however, the term "substantial error" referred, for all practical purposes only to the case where, on the wedding day, a groom or bride mistakenly married the wrong physical person, a person physically different from the one he or she intended to marry. In recent years, however, this ground has been expanded to include the situation where one party fraudulently conceals from the other a serious defect, flaw, or deficiency, some important quality which the other party has a right to know. A man, for example, knowingly has an illness which will soon disable him but he conceals this from his fiancee because he fears that, if told, she might not marry him. Or he conceals from her the fact that he is a carrier of a genetic disease, or that he has been in a previous civil marriage and perhaps even has children, or that he is homosexual. Current jurisprudence regards as null marriages under such conditions because the deceived person was in substantial error. The meaning is not simply that there is a question of mistaken identity, but that the person taken in marriage was of a substantially different character than was known.

Utilization. An invalid marriage can be validated in either one of two ways, by sanation (*sanatio in radice*) or by so-called simple convalidation. The law and jurisprudence on the simple convalidation has always been clear and demanding. Two things are required for validity. First of all, both parties must personally recognize the first ceremony as invalid, and secondly, since they have not effectively taken each other as husband and wife in any previous ceremony, they must do so at the time of the convalidation (CIC c. 1134). A simple convalidation, in other words, is not a mere blessing or a mere confirmation or reiteration of a former exchange of rights; it involves a new marital consent distinct from the former, inefficacious one. Since most non-Catholics, and even some Catholics, would not, in fact, view the ceremony this way, validations involving such people should properly be effected not by simple convalidation but rather by sanation.

In fact, however, the practice, at least in the U.S., was, for many years, to validate such unions by simple convalidation; and this improper practice undoubtedly resulted in a great many invalid convalidations. Although, in theory, there has been no jurisprudential change over the years on this point, nevertheless, the traditional jurisprudence was, in practice, almost universally unknown or ignored and was only rarely applied to a particular marriage. Since the early 1970s, however, most American ecclesiastical courts have been disposed to declare null convalidations that were entered by people who regarded them as church formalities or blessings or the sacramentalizing of an already valid marriage. And this new practice has, in effect, constituted a genuine evolution in jurisprudence by utilization of existing law.

Application. Evolution by utilization is one thing; evolution by application is another. The former occurs where both the law and the circumstances remain exactly the same, but the law, after a period of being ignored, is newly utilized. Evolution by application, on the other hand, occurs where the circumstances or cultural conditions change and provide new applications for the law. The jurisprudence on the conditioned marriage provides an example of this. Jurists have always regarded a marriage as conditioned and therefore nullified whenever a party attached such excessive importance to a particular circumstance that he or she rated it higher than marriage itself and really did not want the marriage without the all-precious circumstance. Traditionally this circumstance was usually something very specific and was most often suggested by the culture in which the marriage took place. A man, for example, might condition a marriage by intending to marry only a virgin; or a woman, by intending to marry only a man who would convert to the Catholic faith. The present culture, with its emphasis on personalist values, has created a new application for the old principle. Young people today are inclined to attach excessive importance to personal fulfillment in marriage. Indeed some, perhaps many, are intending, at least implicitly, to enter marriage only if it is personally fulfiling. This is to condition a marriage just as surely as the man of a different time and place and culture conditioned marriage by intending to marry only a virgin. Thus, in a sense, a new jurisprudence emerges, but only in its application.

A second example of jurisprudence evolving by application is in the area of an intention against perpetuity. It has always been recognized that a person who enters marriage while reserving the right to divorce should the marriage prove unhappy, enters marriage invalidly. Jurists used to think, however, that that law had a narrow application; now they understand it to have a broad application. This change has resulted chiefly from the divorce mentality so prevalent today. Again, jurists used to be of the opinion that a person's opinion favoring the admissibility of divorce was virtually irrelevant when judging the validity of a specific marriage. In theory, in other words, a person might believe divorce acceptable, but in practice should be presumed to have entered marriage for life, regardless of that belief. Personal opinions were seen as residing purely in the mind and as quite separate from the will or intentions. Today, however, such an evaluation is no longer tenable. Clearly the divorce mentality has now become such an active part of a vicious circle that the mentality itself is now clearly contributing to the increase in actual divorces. Personal belief, therefore, or perhaps more accurately, the degree to which a person has subscribed to the divorce mentality, is now seen as extremely relevant, not perhaps decisive in itself of marriage nullity but certainly highly significant. This is another example of jurisprudence evolving by applying an old law to a new cultural context.

Bibliography: J. T. BURTCHAELL, *Marriage Among Christians, A Curious Tradition* (Notre Dame, Ind. 1977). T. J. GREEN, "The American Procedural Norms—An Assessment," StCan 8 (1974) 317–374. J. HOTCHKIN, "Mixed Marriage: Review," HomPastRev 81 (1971) 335–347. L. G. WRENN, *Annulments* (1st ed. Hartford 1967; 2d ed. Hartford 1970; 3d ed. Toledo, Ohio 1978); *Divorce and Remarriage in the Catholic Church* (New York 1973). *See also* bibliography for CANON LAW SOCIETY OF AMERICA.

[L. G. WRENN]

MARRIAGE, INDISSOLUBILITY OF

Vatican Council II presented a vision of the Church's self-understanding and applied that vision to many areas of church life, especially to those of pastoral concern. The Constitution on the Church in the Modern World recognizes that marriage is a pastoral problem of special urgency and that contemporary social atmosphere threatens and negates many of the values taught by the Church on marriage, its indissolubility or permanence in particular. The Council Fathers responded to the anxious consciences caused by the social atmosphere and the "plague of divorce" (*Gaudium et spes* 47) by reaffirming in a nonpolemical manner the teaching of the Church on marriage. The Council Fathers taught that marriage is a community of love rooted in irrevocable personal consent from which a lasting relationship arises. They stressed that the existence of the sacred bond produced by this consent no longer depends on human decision alone (ibid. 48). The Decree on the Apostolate of the Laity reminds married couples that, "it is the supreme task of their apostolate to manifest and prove by their own way of life the unbreakable and sacred character of the marriage bond" (*Apostolicam actuositatem* 11).

The authentic teaching on any point of doctrine is mediated to the community by the teaching authority of the Church. An awareness of the data forming the context of the Church's teaching is necessary to understand the teaching itself and the contemporary stance of the Church toward indissolubility. The data falls into the following general categories: biblical evidence, historical evidence and the teaching of the magisterium.

Biblical Evidence. The New Testament texts cited to support the Church's teaching that marriage is indissoluble are: Mt 5.31–32; 19.3–12; Mk 10.2–12; Lk 16.18; 1 Cor 7.10–16. In their analyses biblical experts feel the texts represent four mutually independent traditions of Jesus' teaching on the indissolubility of marriage. The authors conclude to the certainty that there was a teaching of Jesus against divorce in quite absolute terms. (1) In Lk 16.18, Mt 5.32 and Mk 10.11 there are variant forms of Jesus' saying that marriage after divorce is adultery. Each text speaks of the indissolubility of marriage. Matthew, in his Palestinian context considers the question from the viewpoint of the husband. Luke and Mark, making adaptations for their own communities, speak of divorce in a non-Jewish context and delineate the rights of the wife regarding divorce. (2) The confrontation between Jesus and the Pharisees over divorce described in Mk 10.12 (questions regarding the licitness of divorce) and in Mt 19.3–12 (assuming the fact of divorce but raising questions about the grounds for divorce) shows Jesus quoting Genesis (Gn 1.27; 2.24) and teaching that the arrival of the Kingdom of God in himself opens men's eyes to the full understanding of God's will in creation. One of these perceptions present "from the beginning" is that marriage is not a merely human institution, but it is God's will that husband and wife become "one flesh" (flesh meaning the entire human being and thereby implying more than sexual union). The exceptive clause of Mt 19.9 shows the author adapting the saying of the Lord to the mores of a society in which adultery (*porneia*) had long been accepted as making divorce mandatory, not optional. Biblical experts point out the text of Mt 9.12 reinforces Jesus' teaching on indissolubility, since Mt shows that faith binds the believer to the creational decree not to remarry, but to become "eunuchs" for the sake of the Kingdom. (3) In 1 Cor 7.10–16, Paul confirms the teaching of the Synoptic Gospels that marriage must not be dissolved. Regarding mixed marriages, however, Paul apparently feels he cannot impose Jesus' prohibition of divorce and remarriage on unbelievers. Most exegetes feel in the case of the dissolution of marriage to an unbeliever, the Christian is free to remarry (the Pauline Privilege).

Historical Evidence. The historical evidence on indissolubility based on patristic, conciliar, and papal teaching has been examined in detail on many occasions (see bibliog.). Although there is no universal scholarly agreement on the interpretation and ecclesiological significance of individual citations, the following statements are certainly justified on the basis of the historical evidence. (1) The historical evidence as a whole strongly supports the proposition that marriage is indissoluble. (2) After five centuries of common witness to the indissolubility of marriage a difference appeared in the witness of the Church in the East and the Church in the West. The Church in the West was constant in the witness to the tradition; the Church in the East began to accept the practice of divorce and remarriage for reasons of adultery. (3) In 1563 the Council of Trent presented the authentic teaching of the Church on indissolubility (Denz 1805, 1807) and this teaching has governed practice in the Western Church to the present day.

Magisterium. The teaching of the magisterium has been consistent since the Council of Trent. (1) Regarding consummated sacramental marriages the teaching is absolute—this type of marriage cannot be dissolved for any reason by any authority. (A canonical annulment is not a divorce but an authentic declaration that there has never been a valid marriage in a particular case.) (2) Regarding nonconsummated sacramental marriages and nonsacramental marriages, the teaching of the Church is that they are not absolutely indissoluble. The Church does dissolve these marriages through papal dispensation. The most recent statement of the papacy on the question of indissolubility was in response to the contemporary discussion that "marriage could die if love ceases." Addressing the Roman Rota, Feb. 9, 1976, Pope Paul VI, without underestimating the importance of love, repeated the traditional teaching of the Church and stressed the permanence of the sacred bond of marriage (ActApS 68 [1976] 204–208).

See also MARRIAGE (CANON LAW).

Bibliography: A. AMBROZIC, "Indissolubility of Marriage in the New Testament: Law or Ideal?" StCan 6 (1972) 269–288. W. BASSETT, ed., *The Bond of Marriage* (Notre Dame, Ind. 1968). A. BEVILACQUA, "The History of the Indissolubility of Marriage," CathThSoc 22 (1967) 253–306. G. JOYCE, *Christian Marriage* (London 1948). J. NOONAN Jr., *Power to Dissolve* (Cambridge, Mass. 1972). PAUL VI, "Defending the Stability of Marriage," Origins 5 (1976) 614–616. V. POSPISHIL, *Divorce and Remarriage: Toward a New Catholic Teaching* (New York 1967). E. SCHILLEBEECKX, *Marriage: Human Reality and Saving Mystery* (New York 1965). B. VAWTER, "Divorce and the New Testament," CathBiblQuart 34 (1977) 528–542. L. WRENN, ed., *Divorce and Remarriage* (New York 1973). International Theological Commission, "Propositions on the Doctrine of Christian Marriage," Origins 8 (1978) 235–239.

[E. J. GILBERT]

MARRIAGE ENCOUNTER

Marriage Encounter, both a program and a movement, is an opportunity for married couples to explore their lives in the presence of God. Although the term "encounter" signifies a confrontation or even a clash, Marriage Encounter (a literal translation of the Spanish *Encuentro Conjugal*) means "to rediscover" or "to meet again." The program, which usually takes place on a weekend, helps couples to search for and rediscover their vision of love. With this program, God's presence is essential, because the gift of love given by the couple becomes fruitful only in God's presence through the discovery of the place of God within their lives. This belief, then, underlies Marriage Encounter's conviction of the sacredness of the covenant, the Sacrament, of marriage. Fr. Gabriel Calvo, the founder of Mariage Encounter, puts it this way: "There is within each couple a divine energy of love. It has to be released by a deep sharing between husband and wife, through the communication of their feelings and of the whole of their lives together. It cannot be done in just one moment."

The Marriage-Encounter weekend provides the first moment for this release of the energy of love. During the weekend, the couples have the opportunity to search their own lives for their feelings, dreams, and desires. As they share, the Lord's presence enables the release of the energy of love. Also, as they share, they come to the discovery of God's vision for marriage, which, simply stated, is a call to become united with each other and with God.

Marriage Encounter has its origins in Spain in 1953 through the combined efforts of Fr. Calvo and several married couples. (Mercedes and Jamie Ferrer; José and Marguerite Pick; Diego and Fina Bartimeo). The inspiration of the "Marriage Teams of Pope Pius XII" came from the weekly talks then being given by Pope Pius XII to newly married couples in Rome. Fr. Calvo and the couples would first read the Pope's talk, along with several verses from Scripture. Then, after searching their own individual life's experience, each couple would meet to share their reflections. Afterwards, the couples would meet as a group and share these common reflections to deepen their commitment to marriage and the family. The papal talks and the reflections that flowed out of them eventually became the core topics for the presentations that are still given on Marriage Encounter weekends. The first *Encuentro Conjugal* was held in Barcelona in 1962. The program began in the U.S. in 1967, under the aegis of the Christian Family Movement. Marriage Encounter has also spread in Latin America, Europe, and Asia.

Within this initial group was also developed the method of communicating—a presentation based on the experience of life, a reflection on each individual's life experience, followed by a mutual sharing of this individual reflection. This is the method of dialogue as it is now practiced within Marriage Encounter, as well as such other offshoots as Family Encounter, *Retorno*, Priests' Encounter, Engaged Encounter. The method is best summarized in another statement of Fr. Calvo: "There is no unity without reconciliation. There is no reconciliation without communication. There is no communication without first encountering (discovering) oneself."

Marriage Encounter has had a powerful impact on thousands of couples and enabled them to renew their commitment to marriage as a ministry. Because of Marriage Encounter, these same couples who in the past saw their lives more as confusion, now see their marriages as the means for grace and life for themselves and others. Inspired by this vision, they possess a new understanding of the Gospel and its meaning for everyday life. Ultimately, however, the final goal of Marriage Encounter is much broader than the couples themselves. There is a natural outflow of love from the couple to family, relatives, friends and, finally, to the larger communities of Church and society. Through the gift of self, there occurs an inner conversion both in the individual and the couple. This conversion becomes the basis of understanding and acceptance, out of which flows the unity of love. Marriage Encounter does not teach a technique, because it presents its method as a free sharing which can be accepted or rejected. Marriage Encounter helps a couple to explore their experience of life. As they share this individual experience, they begin a journey, a search toward unity with each other and with the wider community in order to build together the new creation promised by Jesus Christ. Together, couples and their families join in a new Exodus toward the promised land which will be built on the foundation of love they have rediscovered.

See also NATIONAL MARRIAGE ENCOUNTER; WORLDWIDE MARRIAGE ENCOUNTER.

[T. HILL]

MARRIAGE TRIBUNALS, EXPERIMENTAL NORMS FOR

A primary postconciliar canonical concern has been reforming the law governing marriage nullity cases. Two values are basic: reverence for the sacredness of marriage and respect for the dignity and rights of Christians. Both Vatican Council II and the 1967 Synod of Bishops called for a simplified, shortened, and expeditious marriage nullity process. The 1968 *Canon Law Society of America convention approved 27 norms geared to expediting marriage cases in the United States. They addressed some of the most critical problems facing tribunals, e.g., personnel deficiencies, length of process, etc. The norms were endorsed with some modifications by the American bishops in 1969 and authorized by the Holy See for a 3-year experimental period beginning in July, 1970.

The provisions of universal procedural law of the CIC remain in effect except where the norms specifically modify them. The norms are not mandatory but rather are strongly encouraged for more efficient administration of justice.

The norms were to cease in July, 1973. However, after an initial Holy See refusal to renew them, the combined efforts of American bishops and canonists brought about in 1974 their continued authorization until the revision of the universal procedural law (O'Connor-Suppl c. 1960).

A revised procedural law schema was sent to the bishops in 1976 for evaluation. It has been sharply criticized, since it would eliminate some American norms that have been indispensable in meeting the legitimate expectations of people approaching tribunals. The issue however is still unresolved.

Among such critical norms are the following: norm 3 expediting one-judge tribunal options and norm 7 empowering the court of the petitioner's residence to handle his case. The first helps to deal with the problem of a lack of trained personnel; the second attempts to respond to the demands of an increasingly mobile society. Perhaps the most significant change has been norm 23, II, permitting waiver of the former mandatory appeal whenever the truth has been adequately served by a first instance nullity decision and a second hearing of a case would be superfluous.

Bibliography: Official Sources, "American Procedural Norms," *Jurist* 30c(1970) 363–368. L. DEL AMO, "Procedimiento matrimonial canónico en experimentación," *Lex Ecclesiae: Estudios en honor del Dr. Marcelino Cabreros de Anta* (Salamanca 1972) 461–542. T. GREEN, "The American Precedural Norms...an Assessment" StCan 8 (1974) 317–348. C. LEFEBVRE, "De procedura in causis matrimonialibus concessa conferentiae episcopali USA," PeriodicaMorCanLiturg 59 (1970) 563–592. L. WRENN, "The American Procedural Norms," AmEcclRev 165 (1971) 175–186.

[T. J. GREEN]

MARTIN, MARY

Foundress of the Medical Missionaries of Mary; b. Marie Helena Martin, in Dublin, Ireland, April 25, 1892; d. Jan. 27, 1975, Drogheda, Ireland. During World War I, she trained as a Voluntary Aid Defense nurse and was posted to hospitals at Malta and in France, during which time she became inspired to continue her healing work after the war. It became her dream to found a religious congregation and do medical work as a missionary. Hearing of an opportunity to work in a mission in Calabar, South Nigeria, she trained in midwifery in Dublin and went to Africa for three years, primarily caring for women and maternity cases. Her commitment to the life of a religious healer deepened, but she had many years to wait until the Holy See decided to let religious do obstetrics and surgery. Miss Martin and two companions received religious training from the Benedictines of Glenstal Abbey, Co. Limerick, in return for their housekeeping services at the Abbey school. The Abbey was founded in honor of Dom Columba Marmion who had always been a spiritual inspiration for Miss Martin.

Permission for religious to practice medicine came in 1936 with the instruction *Constans ac sedula* of the Congregation for the Propagation of the Faith and in May of that year the Holy See gave its consent to the founding of a new congregation. Miss Martin and her two companions sailed for Calabar in early 1937, but soon after arrival she contracted malaria and nearly died. Her sickbed profession, April 4, 1937 in Port Harcourt, marked the founding of the Medical Missionaries of Mary. Still severely ill, Sister Mary of the Incarnation, or Mother Mary, had to leave Africa under medical instructions never to return. Her two companions remained behind in noviceship and worked to build the first mission.

At home and improved in health, Mother Mary's efforts were turned to getting support for her fledgling congregation. Her brother gave her a house called Rosemount in Dublin to be a house of studies for the new novices, and in December 1938, the novitiate at Collon, Co. Louth, was canonically erected and five novices received. The following December, a maternity hospital, Our Lady of Lourdes, was opened in Drogheda. The congregation, growing rapidly, needed a larger novitiate by 1940, and a new one was built in Drogheda, which also is the motherhouse. In 1942, the hospital received state recognition as a training school for sister-midwives, and today the International Missionary Training Hospital is in full operation.

Mother Mary continued as mother general until January 1969 when she resigned. She was confined to bed for many of her last years and died at the motherhouse. Much of the growth and success of the Medical Missionaries of Mary throughout the world was due to the unflagging zeal of Mother Martin, who was able to excite the interest and cooperation of many supporters and vocations. Her community continues to expand, working on four continents with over 25 mission hospitals, many out-patient clinics and field stations.

[A. M. HUBBARD]

MARXISM AND CHRISTIANITY

Marxism is a system of ideas, first enunciated by Karl Marx, then developed and embodied by world-wide Communist Party movements. Much of the controversy about the compatibility of Marxism and Christianity revolves around the issue of which of the doctrines associated with Marxism are really essential to it.

Historical Opposition. Since its inception, Marxism has appeared to be the very antithesis of Christianity. Its atheism scorned God and religion. Its materialism denied the soul and after life. Its determinism negated free will. Its revolutionary strategy promoted class antagonisms and violent overthrow of the state. Its socialism would take away the right to private property, and with it, the incentive to work. Stalinist Russia seemed clearly to prove how destructive these ideas were in practice. Marxist theory became Communist reality; the terms became identified. Pope Pius XI denounced Communism as "intrinsically evil" in his encyclical *Divini Redemptoris* (1937). Communist takeovers in Eastern Europe and China after World War II brought religious persecution and imprisonments. Cardinal *Mindszenty of Hungary symbolized the Church's resistance to Communism.

Changing Attitudes. In recent years a dramatic change has occurred. A growing number of Christians are calling for openness to Marxism or even espousing it. Bishop Helder Camara of Olinda-Recife, Brazil called for a synthesis of Marxism and Christianity like the synthesis St. Thomas Aquinas achieved between Aristotle and Christianity in the Middle Ages. In Latin America *liberation theology has often adopted a Marxist perspective, arguing that Christianity must recognize the reality of class struggle and side with the poor and oppressed against the rich. In Italy, growing numbers of Catholics have advocated a Communist government for their country and have even joined the Communist Party. In Chile, the Marxist-socialist regime of Salvador Allende (1970–73) won the active support of some Christian groups and led to the founding of an international group, Christians for Socialism. In England, "New Left" Catholics have gone so far as to argue that Christians *should* be Marxists, that the only truly Christ-

ian response in the current world situation is to join in the struggle for revolutionary socialism.

Church Pronouncements. These stances have provoked some conflict within the Church and warnings on the part of bishops. But they have also led to important distinctions made in official church documents about socialism and Marxism. Pope Paul VI, in his "Call to Action" letter, May 14, 1971, drew several important distinctions about Marxism and socialism. He asserted that a Christian "cannot adhere to the Marxist ideology, to its atheistic materialism, to its dialectic of violence, and to the way it absorbs individual freedom in the collectivity, at the same time denying all transcendence to man and his personal and collective history . . ." (Paul VI OctogAdven 26). But the Pope also distinguished between "historical movements" (e.g., socialism) which have many positive social and economic goals, and the "false philosophical teachings" (e.g., atheism) which first prompted these movements and on which they still draw (ibid. 30). Then, with specific reference to Marxism, Paul noted that some Christians are calling for rapprochement with Marxism, pointing to a "certain splintering of Marxism" which had always appeared to have a unitary ideology based on atheistic materialism. He notes the quite different meanings given to Marxism: as the practice of class struggle; as collective political power under a single party; as an ideology based on historical materialism; and finally as a "scientific activity, as a rigorous method of examining social and political reality, and as the rational link, tested by history, between theoretical knowledge and the practice of revolutionary transformation" (ibid. 33). But Pope Paul cautioned that Marxist analysis and ideology have always been linked together and have led to totalitarian societies (ibid. 34).

Two important statements by groups of Catholic bishops have drawn upon these distinctions made by Paul VI. The permanent council of the French episcopacy, in late June 1977, declared Marxism and Christianity theoretically incompatible, citing as the main reasons for this judgment Marxist atheism, materialism, and its claim to a "monopoly" of scientific truth. But the declaration also manifested a sophisticated awareness of different types of Marxism and different levels of Christian adherence to Marxist ideas and strategies. It called for continued dialogue with the Marxist world and included no condemnation of the economic goals of socialism. The bishops of the Antilles, on Nov. 21, 1975, presented what they saw as "the current teaching of the Catholic Church on socialism." First, they noted that private property is not an absolute right; the goods of the earth are for all. "It follows from this that any society in which a few control most of the wealth and the masses are left in want is a sinful society." Second, they argued that the Catholic Church does not condemn indiscriminately all forms of socialism. It has condemned particular aspects of socialism—denial of God and the spiritual, the insistence on the need for class warfare, and the suppression of all types of private property. But there are other forms of socialism in the world. Third, in looking at socialism, Marxism, or capitalism, one should carefully distinguish between basic aspirations, ideologies, and concrete historical movements.

Reasons for Shift in Attitudes. Three developments in recent years help to explain these shifting attitudes toward Marxism. First, the Church has given new stress to the achievement of a just society as part of its essential mission. Vatican Council II in *Gaudium et spes* spoke of the Church's involvement in the world and of the need to transform it. The social encyclicals of John XXIII and Paul VI and the 1971 Synod of Bishops made "justice in the world" a focus of concern. Biblical studies have focused on God acting in history, and God as the "liberator of the oppressed" (Synod JustWorld p. 41). In Europe *political theology and in Latin America liberation theology have given further impetus to the quest for justice. Second, several political-economic developments have contributed to the change: the growing importance of Third World countries; the growing awareness of the severity of world hunger and of the great disparity in distribution of wealth; the failure of "development" policies (e.g., foreign aid, transfer of technology) to improve the situation of poor nations and the discontent in many First World countries with the prevailing, capitalist economic system (*see* NEW INTERNATIONAL ECONOMIC ORDER). Third, changes within Marxism/Communism have contributed to a reevaluation. The Allende regime in Chile seems to have respected religious liberty. Eurocommunist leaders, such as Enrico Berlinguer in Italy, have promised full respect for religious liberties and to seek socialism through democratic rather than revolutionary means. Church officials and the Communist Parties in Eastern Europe have, perhaps by necessity, developed more "accommodation" to each other. Critical Marxists have undertaken reevaluations of Marx's thought on issues of freedom, democracy, and religion.

Arguments for Marxism. The question remains: why are some Christians turning to Marxism? There are, first of all, certain concerns, values, and aspirations which Marxists and Christians hold in common. (1) The Marxist critique of capitalism and imperialism, while carried out "scientifically," evokes a strong moral sense from its condemnation of an economic system which appears to profit the rich at the expense of the masses. Correspondingly, in the biblical tradition there are strong denunciations of injustice, of oppression of the poor by the rich. (2) The Marxist critique looks to the emancipation of the poor, the exploited, the proletariat. Moreover it sees this emancipation as the direction history must take—a revolutionary struggle leading to a new and more humane society. But also in the Judeo-Christian heritage God identifies with the poor and acts in history for their liberation. Yahweh leads the Israelites out of bondage from Egypt; Jesus proclaims as his mission "to set the downtrodden free" (Lk 4.11) and bases salvation on a response to the hungry and needy of the world (Mt 25). (3) The Marxist solution is to work for the radical transformation of society by replacing the capitalist economic system with a socialist system of public ownership in which all will work and share in harmony. This same goal seems also reflected in the biblical promises of "a new heaven and a new earth" and the Christian concern for building a community of love and concern in which all can share the goods of the earth.

But there are also reasons why some Christians have explicitly chosen Marxism rather than some separate, specifically Christian alternative. The Bible could not offer concrete solutions to 20th-century problems. The social teachings of the Church, these Christians argue,

relied without success on moral appeals to owners and rulers to change. They find in Marxism the "tools" needed to effect real change: a method of analysis which gets to the root, economic causes of injustice in the world; an important ideological critique which points out elements of church doctrine and practice that tend to reinforce the *status quo* (e.g., an overstress on peace and unity); the importance of praxis, a commitment to social change by taking the side of the poor in their struggles; and a vision of what human society should be—men and women working together and sharing together out of a sense of mutual concern.

This "Christian-Marxist" outlook is growing, but is shared by a still-small minority within the Church. Critics charge that this outlook "idolatrizes" Marxism and overlooks the historical record of Communism in practice. Marxist Communism, these critics argue, has a long and inhumane record of religious persecution, of oppressive political rule, and of very limited achievements in attaining the promised goals of economic equality and social harmony. Other critics would challenge Marxism's claim to be "scientific" or Christian efforts to equate God's liberating action in history with Marxist socialism.

Are Marxism and Christianity Compatible? The Key Issues. But the most persistent issues, the questions most often raised about the compatibility or incompatibility of Marxism and Christianity, are those noted by Pope Paul VI regarding Marxism—its atheism, its materialism, its stress on class struggle and violence, the absorption of individual freedom in a collectivity. Critics see Marxism as inseparable from these elements; advocates believe they are either not essential to Marxism (e.g., atheism) or not incompatible with Christianity (e.g., class struggle). The following is a brief examination of these issues.

(1) *Atheism.* Marx himself was clearly an atheist and charged that religion was "the opium of the people." Most Communist parties have insisted on atheism as essential for membership and view religion as both an obstacle to social change and as an unscientific superstition. But some neo-Marxists have recognized that religion can be a stimulus for social change, a "protest against suffering," as even Marx noted. Some critical Marxists hold that the historical reasons for insisting on atheism no longer obtain and hence that atheism is not essential to Marxism.

(2) *Philosophical Materialism.* Marx's colleague Friedrich Engels made materialism an essential part of Marxism. He argued that the origin of the world and the origin of mind can be explained by matter in motion without reference to God or soul. All that exists is a product of matter. But one can argue that Marx used the word "materialism" to stress economic factors in history and that the achievement of a new socialist society does not depend on the espousing of philosophical materialism. The critical, practical issue may be what a Marxist regime determines is essential—whether it will impose atheism and materialism as a privileged ideology or whether it will respect a plurality of religious and philosophic views.

(3) *Class Struggle and Violence.* The idea that capitalism creates class divisions between those who own and control the means of production and those who work for them is certainly essential to Marxism. Any effort to change the system radically will involve struggle. But

the difficulty in evaluating whether such struggle is compatible with Christianity stems from an ambiguity about what class struggle involves. Liquidation of a class or incitement of hatred against a class would certainly seem incompatible with Christianity. But risking hostility by standing with the poor and opposing injustice would not be.

The issues of violence raises a different set of difficulties. Some Marxists would argue that socialism can be brought about without revolutionary violence, by democratic means, at least in some countries. Where violence does appear to be the "last resort," some Christians would argue there is just cause for its use, viz., to resist an intolerable oppression. Christian pacifists, on the other hand, would reject violence as never permissible.

(4) *The Loss of Individual Freedom.* Critics of Marxism argue that Communism has led in practice to a one-Party rule and the suppression of freedom. Other critics see any socialist economy as inevitably creating an impersonal, bureaucratic state in which the individual has little to say. Critics of capitalism, on the other hand, argue that all real decision-making power rests in the hands of the ruling class, and that capitalism suppresses the most basic freedom, viz., the right to work and to share equally in the results of one's labor. Critical Marxists argue that "true Marxism," what Marx himself intended, was a democratic, participatory socialism in which each individual shares in the political and economic decisions which affect his/her life. Ultimately the issue of whether Marxism and Christianity are compatible may only be resolved by the concrete directions each movement takes in the years ahead.

See also ATHEISM; DIPLOMACY, PAPAL.

Bibliography: J. MIGUEZ BONINO, *Christians and Marxists* (Grand Rapids, Mich. 1975). H. CHAMBRE, *Christianity and Communism* tr. R. F. TREVETT (New York 1960). G. GIRARDI, *Marxism and Christianity* (New York 1968). P. HEBBLETHWAITE, *The Christian-Marxist Dialogue* (New York 1977). G. GUTIERREZ, *A Theology of Liberation* tr. C. INDA and J. EAGLESON (Maryknoll, N.Y. 1973). J.-B. METZ and J.-P. JOSSUA, eds., *Christianity and Socialism* (New York 1977). J. MIRANDA, *Marx and the Bible* (Maryknoll, N.Y. 1974). J. L. SEGUNDO, *The Liberation of Theology,* tr. J. DRURY (Maryknoll, N.Y. 1976). D. VREE, *On Synthesizing Marxism and Christianity* (New York 1976).

[A. F. MCGOVERN]

MARY AND THE CHURCH

Recent years have witnessed further developments of Vatican Council II's Marian doctrine in the Dogmatic Constitution on the Church (*Lumen gentium* ch. 8). It was most significant for the renewal of Mariology and of devotion to Mary that the Council Fathers voted, Oct. 29, 1963, in favor of making the Marian schema a part of the document on the Church. The very title of the chapter, "The Blessed Virgin Mary, Mother of God, in the Mystery of Christ and the Church," placed her in close relationship with her Son (Christocentric Mariology) and with his Mystical Body (ecclesiotypical Mariology). This is the proper setting in which to assess Mary's role in the work of Redemption. The true ecumenical importance of the Council's decision is derived not from minimizing her place in Catholic faith and piety, but from emphasizing a sharing-oriented Mariology instead of one that is privilege-centered.

The Mary-Church Analogy. As the postconciliar era progresses, the Marian dogmas are contemplated more and more in accord with Vatican II's teaching on the "hierarchy of truths" in the Decree on Ecumenism:

"When comparing doctrines with one another, they [Catholic theologians] should remember that in Catholic doctrine there exists an order or hierarchy of truths, since they vary in their relation to the foundation of the Christian faith" (*Unitatis redintegratio* 11). This foundation is the central Christian dogma of the redemptive Incarnation whereby the triune God is revealed. Under the impetus of Vatican II the theology of Mary stresses the truth that her special graces and prerogatives are to be seen as primarily for the sake of her Son and his redeemed-redeeming Body, the Church. Divine Revelation about Mary makes the central mysteries of faith more intelligible and meaningful for Christian living.

The Christocentric and ecclesiotypical emphases of contemporary Mariology are mutually complementary and not in conflict. For Mary cannot be related to Christ without being intimately associated with the ecclesial Body that he received through his redemptive activity. At the same time, she is the archetype of the Church only because her unique relationship with Christ is the basis for the Church's share in his redeeming work (see Semmelroth 1963, esp. 80–88). Consequently, concentration upon the ecclesiotypical significance of Marian doctrine and devotion should not obscure their basic Christocentric character.

Theologians today are more inclined to include the Mary-Church analogy within the basic Marian idea or fundamental principle of Mariology. "Her concrete motherhood with regard to Christ, the redeeming God-man, freely accepted in faith—her fully committed divine motherhood—this is both the key to the full understanding of the Marian mystery and the basic Mariological principle, which is concretely identical with Mary's objectively and subjectively unique state of being redeemed" (Schillebeeckx 106). Within one organic principle the two emphases are contained, i.e., both the Christocentric (Mary's "fully committed divine motherhood"), and the ecclesiotypical (her "objectively and subjectively unique state of being redeemed"). Her vocation to be the mother of the Word incarnate must be considered in close connection with the graces that reveal her calling to be the prototype of the Church.

Immaculate Conception. Accordingly, Mary's Immaculate Conception is God's special favor preparing her to accept freely the invitation to be the Reedeemer's mother and so to share in the redemption. Following St. Bernard, St. Thomas Aquinas taught that her consent was given "in place of the whole human race" (ST 3a, 30.1). Because she was so completely receptive to God's loving plan, the members of Christ's Body can receive the fruits of Christ's redeeming love into their own lives. Being the first fruit of her Son's Redemption, Mary is uniquely redeemed *objectively* (preservation from all sin through the grace of the Immaculate Conception). Responding to her vocation with total commitment, she is uniquely redeemed *subjectively.* Since she received the Savior into her own life of loving faith, Mary cooperated maternally in Christ's objective redemption of the human race. Indeed Christ alone is the Redeemer who reconciles the world to the Father in the Holy Spirit. Mary's "fully committed divine motherhood," however, gives her free act of identifying with his objective redemption a redemptive meaning and value for all the members of the Church.

Divine Maternity. The truth that Mary's motherhood of Christ is both bridal and virginal has rich ecclesiotypical significance (see Semmelroth 1963, esp. 117–142). Her vocal *fiat* of free consent at the annunciation and her silent *fiat* at the foot of the cross make Mary the spiritual bride of the Redeemer. In her compassion she received the fruits of her Son's sacrifice both for her own redemption and for that of the whole Church. Concomitantly, and as a result of this creative receptivity to grace, her bridal motherhood is also virginal. Her maternal fruitfulness cannot come from human power but from the breath of the Holy Spirit. Had she conceived Christ other than as a virgin, her bridal relationship with the *Logos* incarnate would have been obscured. Without her perpetual virginity, the revelation of her complete and continuous fidelity to Christ and his messianic mission would have been blurred. Mary then is the archetype of the Church as the Church is also the virginal bride of Christ. As the community of persons redeemed by him, the Church is called to be constantly faithful to his word. The Immaculate Conception is the perfect exemplar of a grace-filled Church. As the sacramental community called to mediate Redemption to the world, the Church also images the bridal motherhood of Mary. The Assumption makes her "the sign of sure hope, and comfort for the pilgrim people of God" (*Lumen gentium* 68–69). All the Marian dogmas, therefore, converge toward a theological and prayerful contemplation of Mary as the archetype of the Church.

As bridal and virginal mothers, both Mary and the Church are to be dynamically united together with the Holy Spirit. The sole source of their spiritual fecundity is the abiding presence and activity of the risen Lord's Spirit. A closer connection between Mariology and Pneumatology will contribute greatly to a balanced Christology, ecclesiology, and Christian anthropology. Much remains to be done in this regard, especially by theologians of the Western Church who have begun to study more seriously the magnificent heritage of the Eastern tradition on the Holy Spirit.

New Eve. A portion of the patristic patrimony common to East and West is the image of Mary as the New Eve. Its rediscovery, under the special inspiration of Cardinal Newman's Marian writings, has led to a renewed research into the witness of the Fathers who made use of this image in their teaching about Mary. After the Scriptures, it reflects the most ancient meditation upon Mary and is a very fertile source of the Mary-Church analogy and typology. The National Conference of Catholic Bishops (NCCB) in the pastoral on the Blessed Virgin Mary points out: "Even more anciently, the Church was regarded as the 'New Eve.' The Church is the bride of Christ, formed from his side in the sleep of death on the cross, as the first Eve was formed by God from the side of the sleeping Adam" (NCCB 41). From her earliest days the Church has seen herself symbolized in Mary and has come to understand her mysterious self more profoundly in light of Mary as archetype. Mary "personifies" all that the Church is and hopes to become.

The impact of an ecclesiotypical Mariology upon Marian devotion has been most salutary. Pope Paul VI in his apostolic exhortation for the right ordinary and development of devotion to the Blessed Virgin Mary, stated: "She is worthy of imitation because she was the first and most perfect of Christ's disciples. All of this has

a permanent and universal exemplary value" (Paul VI 35). Mary, of course, is not an exemplar in the sense of being a stereotyped blueprint upon which contemporary Christians are to model their lives. Nevertheless, if Christians are to mature as members of Christ's living Body, the Church, they must prayerfully penetrate the perennial meaning of Mary-like faith, courage, concern, constancy, etc.

Still a stumbling block for many, especially members of other Christian Churches, is the concept of Mary's mediation and intercession. It seems to interfere with the unique mediatorship of Christ. Vatican II's Marian chapter clearly teaches: "Mary's function as mother of men in no way obscures or diminishes this unique mediation of Christ, but rather shows its power" (*Lumen gentium* 60). Reconceptualization of the mystery must remove from Mary's mediatory role any image of her being a go-between, as though the risen Lord were made remote. Such a misconception misses the basic meaning of the Incarnation and true grandeur of Mary, namely, that God the Son has chosen to become man in her and to be an abiding presence among men in his risen humanity forever. Her spiritual motherhood primarily helps dispose believers to encounter the ever-present Christ more intimately in their daily Christian lives. Both by her example as archetype of the Church and by her intercessory ministry in glory, Mary enlightens and inspires her spiritual children to grow more docile to the direct action of her Son's spirit and to cooperate more generously with the special graces of God's redeeming love.

Bibliography: R. E. BROWN et al., eds., *Mary in the New Testament* (New York, Philadelphia, Toronto 1978). E. R. CARROLL, *Understanding the Mother of Jesus* (Wilmington, Del. 1978). J. C. DE SATGÉ, *Down to Earth: The New Protestant Vision of Mary* (Wilmington, N.C. 1976). L. DEISS, *Mary, Daughter of Sion* tr. B. T. BLAIR (Collegeville, Minn. 1972). D. FLANAGAN, *The Theology of Mary* (Hales Corners, Wis. 1978). F. M. JELLY, "Marian Dogmas within Vatican II's Hierarchy of Truths," *Marian Studies* 27 (1976) 17–40; "The Mother of Jesus," and "Mary, Mother and Model of the Church" in R. LAWLER, D. W. WUERL, and T. C. LAWLER, eds., *The Teaching of Christ: A Catholic Catechism for Adults* (Huntington, Ind. 1976). G. F. KIRWIN, "Mary's Salvific Role Compared with That of the Church," *Marian Studies* 25 (1974) 29–43. T. A. KOEHLER, "Mary's Spiritual Maternity after the Second Vatican Council," *Marian Studies* 23 (1972) 39–68. J. A. R. MACKENZIE, "The Patristic Witness to the Virgin Mary as the New Eve," *Marian Studies* 29 (1978) 67–78. G. A. MALONEY, *Mary: The Womb of God* (Danville, N.J. 1976). J. H. NEWMAN, *The New Eve* (Westminister, Md. 1952). PAUL VI, *Marialis cultus*, apostolic exhortation, Feb. 2, 1974, ActApS 66 (1974) 113–168; tr. *Devotion to the Blessed Virgin Mary* (USCC Publ. Office, Washington, D.C. 1974). E. SCHILLEBEECKX, *Mary, Mother of the Redemption*, tr. N. D. SMITH (New York 1964). A. SCHMEMANN, "Our Lady and the Holy Spirit," *Marian Studies* 23 (1972) 69–78. O. SEMMELROTH, *Mary, Archetype of the Church*, tr. M. VON EROES and J. DEVLIN (New York 1963); "Dogmatic Constitution on the Church, Chapter 8," Vorgrimler, 1:285–296 (New York 1967).

[F. M. JELLY]

MASS, CONVENTUAL/COMMUNITY

The 1969 Roman Missal recognizes the central place of the conventual or community Mass of a religious house, college of canons, or other ecclesial community; it also broadens the meaning of the conventual Mass—part of the choral liturgy—to include the Mass at which any type of community worships together (GenInstRomMissal 76). The community Mass is not one of the special "forms of celebration" outlined in the Instruction, but it does have certain norms to enhance and express its communitarian character. All community members should exercise the ministry for which they have received an ordination or institution; presbyters should concelebrate; there should be singing; participants may receive Communion under both kinds. With regard particularly to concelebration, its practice is emphasized as desirable, in conformity with the recommendations of *Eucharisticum Mysterium* (47), the Instruction of the Congregation of Rites, May 25, 1967 (ActAPS 59 [1967] 565). All priests who have no pastoral charge to celebrate the Eucharist for the faithful should concelebrate the community Mass; even those who do have such an obligation may receive Communion. A later Declaration of the Congregation for Divine Worship, Aug. 7, 1972 (ActApS 64 [1972] 561–563) indicates that those with an obligation to a pastoral celebration, may also concelebrate the community Mass.

[T. C. O'BRIEN]

MASS, LATIN CHANTS FOR

According to Vatican Council II's Constitution on the Sacred Liturgy (1963), "Liturgical worship is given a more noble form when the divine offices are celebrated solemnly in song, with the assistance of sacred ministers and the active participation of the people" (*Sacrosanctum Concilium* 113). The Constitution further states: "The typical edition of the books of Gregorian Chant is to be completed; and a more critical edition is to be prepared to those books already published since the restoration by St. Pius X. It is desirable also that an edition be prepared containing simpler melodies, for use in small churches" (ibid. 117).

The initial effort to implement these directives is seen in the publication, *Missae in quarta periodo Concilii Oecumenici Vaticani II celebrandae*, used at the daily Masses during the Council. It contained seven formularies of Proper chants for Masses of the Holy Spirit and formularies for the September Ember days, Advent, feasts of the Blessed Virgin Mary, the Apostles, martyrs, and confessors. This was followed by *Variations for Holy Week*, published March 7, 1965, which contained simple chants for the Chrism Mass of Holy Thursday as alternatives to the full Proper chants of the *Graduale Romanum* and the *Missale Romanum*.

Two decrees of the Congregation of Rites, Dec. 14, 1964 (ActApS 57 [1965] 407–408) approved the publication of the *Kyriale simplex* (*editio typica*, Vatican City 1965) and the *Cantus* (Vatican City 1965). The *Kyriale* contains: *Asperges* (Tones I and II); *Vidi aquam; Kyrie* I, II, III, IV, and V; *Credo* I, II, III, and IV; chants for the concluding rite; and two settings of the Pater Noster. The *Cantus* provides simple arrangements of the chants sung by the celebrant.

A further decree of the Congregation of Rites, Sept. 3, 1967 (*Notitiae* 3, 1967) approved the publication of the *Graduale simplex in usum minorum ecclesiarum* (Vatican City 1967). This was intended for churches which find it difficult to perform the more ornate melodies of the *Graduale Romanum* correctly. It was designed to be used in combination with the *Graduale Romanum* and provided simple Latin antiphons and melodies for the four Proper chants of the Mass, offering alternatives for sung Masses.

The revisions of the General Calendar, the Lectionary, and the Sacramentary brought about the need for the revision of the *Graduale Romanum*. The decree of the Congregation for Divine Worship, June 24, 1972 (ActApS 65 [1973] 274) approved the *Ordo cantus Missae* (*editio typica*, Vatican City 1972) that was to serve the function of

indicating what Latin chants found in the *Graduale Romanum* might be used in the liturgy on any specific date according to the revised General Calendar. In 1974, the revision of the *Graduale Romanum, Graduale Sacrosanctae Romanae Ecclesiae de tempore et de sanctis*, was published (Abbatia Sancti Petri De Solesmis 1974). The booklet *Jubilate Deo* (Vatican City 1974) contains a minimum repertoire of familiar Latin chants and was intended to facilitate music at such international celebrations as the Holy Year or Eucharistic Congresses, to promote congregational singing, and to guard and foster the artistic worth of Gregorian Chant—as well as to exemplify the unity of the Church.

[M. A. O'CONNOR]

MASS, MUSIC OF

"Many and varied musical patterns are now possible within the Liturgical structure" states the document of the *Bishop's Committee on the Liturgy, Music in Catholic Worship* (1972). According to present legislation, every part of the Roman Mass may be sung (except those private prayers of the celebrant to be spoken in a quiet voice). What should be sung depends on the musical, liturgical, and pastoral judgment of a specific celebration. Musical liturgy is normative, i.e., the norm for the Roman Mass is a celebration in which music is used.

The Introductory Rites. The parts preceding the Liturgy of the Word, viz., the Entrance, Greeting, Penitential Rite, Gloria, and Opening Prayer, assist the assembled people to become a worshiping community and to prepare themselves for the entire celebration. Central to the Entrance rite is a procession. The Entrance Song enhances the procession in gathering the community. The Prayer concludes the procession and the Entrance rite. Proper antiphons are given to be used with appropriate psalm verses. These may be replaced by the chants of the Simple Gradual (*Graduale simplex* Rome 1974), by other psalms and antiphons, or by other fitting songs.

The Greeting, the Lord Have Mercy and the Gloria may be sung in several variations but each should be used to enrich the entrance rite and not merely to extend it.

The Lord Have Mercy traditionally was in a litany form, a form important to the understanding of the liturgical action of intercession itself. The Gloria has traditionally been composed as a song, although recent settings by Alexander Peloquin and others have successfully developed an antiphonal style for easy congregational participation (*see* HYMNOLOGY; HYMNS AND HYMNALS).

Liturgy of the Word. Central to the Liturgy of the Word is the proclaiming of the Scriptures. Various styles of music (and silence) are utilized to enrich and highlight the Readings from the Scriptures. First, the worshiping community hears the Scriptures in the First Reading and indicates that the message has been accepted by responding its assent and prayer through an appropriate Responsorial Psalm. The new Lectionary lists 900 refrains in its determination to match the content of such psalms to the theme of the reading. Selected seasonal refrains are also offered in the Lectionary for the congregation unable to learn a new response every week. Silence is the response to the

Second Reading. The Alleluia and Verse is the acclamation of paschal joy serving both as a reflection upon the Word of God proclaimed and a preparation for the Gospel. After the cantor or choir sings the Alleluia, the people customarily repeat it. Then a single proper Verse is sung by the cantor or choir, and all repeat the Alleluia. If it is not sung, the Alleluia is omitted. During Lent a brief Verse of acclamatory character replaces the. Alleluia and is sung in the same way.

The Prayer of the Faithful (General Intercessions) is designed as a litany. "Litanies are often more effective when sung" (BCL Music 74). The repetition of melody and rhythm draws the people together in a strong and unified response. Current practice has fostered spontaneous prayer and individual and personalized intentions, rather than the general intercessory character which would be emphasized by a sung form.

Effective use of singing the Scriptures or the Creed, while permissible, have met with limited success and therefore appear to be reserved for special situations.

Liturgy of the Eucharist. Music for the Eucharistic Liturgy is meant to match the three main segments of the Liturgy.

Preparation of the Gifts. Preceding the important Eucharistic Prayer of Blessing is a simple rite preparatory of the gifts to be used, the table, and, in fact, of the worshiping community, for the Eucharistic Action. Various methods may be chosen for this preparation, from a simple gathering of people to the altar, to a formal procession presenting the gifts. Music chosen will vary according to the action chosen, but "scale, rhythm, and proportion" are critical here. Antiphonal psalm, song, choir motet, instrumental music may be appropriate to the action selected.

The Eucharistic Prayer of Blessing. The Eucharistic Prayer of Blessing, which may be sung, is normally interspersed with the community's affirmation and acclamation. The opening dialogue of the Preface initiates an exchange, the Holy, Holy, Holy affirms the congregations' awareness of the one act of praise by joining the hymn of the angels quoted from Isaiah's vision, the Memorial Acclamation makes memory of the Lord's suffering and glorification with an expression of faith in his coming, and the Great Amen affirms the entire act of praise and blessing of the Eucharist by the congregation. When sung, each acclamation adds solemnity and richness to the congregation's participation and to the unity of the celebration. Various textual variations of the Holy, Holy, Holy and the Memorial Acclamation and Great Amen have been successfully repeated and augmented to emphasize their importance.

The *Eucharist Prayers for children add additional acclamations which normally are sung to further enrich the congregational participation in the celebration.

The Communion Rite. The Communion rite is composed of the Lord's Prayer (sung by priest and people), the Sign of Peace (without song), the Breaking of the Bread (accompanied by the singing of the Lamb of God), the Communion (accompanied by the procession with song) [a period of silence and/or song] and the Communion Prayer (chanted or recited by the priest). "Those elements [of the Communion rite] are primary which show forth signs that the first fruit of the Eucharist is the unity of the Body of Christ, Christians loving Christ through loving one another." Music properly selected, therefore, supports and emphasizes

this truth. The principal texts are the Lord's Prayer, the song during the Communion procession, and the Prayer after Communion. The Lamb of God is a litany which is to accompany the important action of the Breaking of the Bread.

The Concluding Rite. A recessional song not included within the rite itself is optional. Usually it is a hymn, chosen for its appropriateness to the theme of the day's liturgy or to the liturgical season.

See also SACRAMENTARY, MUSIC OF.   [V. FUNK]

MASSES, VOTIVE

In addition to the liturgical cycle of Sundays and feasts, the Roman Missal and Lectionary of Paul VI (1969) provide prayers and readings for Masses to be offered in response to various pastoral situations. There are three kinds of such occasional Masses: Ritual Masses for the celebration of certain Sacraments, Masses for Various Needs and Occasions, and Votive Masses (GenInstrRomMissal 326–341). In the former *Missale Romanum* of Pius V (1570), as well as in most sacramentaries from the Roman tradition, the term *Missae votivae* referred to all three varieties of such occasional Masses. In the present Missal (Sacramentary), however, the term Votive Mass refers only to fifteen Masses which celebrate such objects of devotion as the Sacred Heart, the Holy Name, the Precious Blood, the Holy Spirit, the Virgin Mary, St. Joseph, and the Apostles. In addition, the new Missal contains forty-six Masses for Various Needs and Occasions, and a great variety of Ritual Masses.

The Votive Masses may be celebrated on the following days of the liturgical year: (1) on weekdays in ordinary time when there is either an optional memorial of a saint or no memorial (*see* SAINTS, MEMORIALS OF); (2) on obligatory memorials of saints, on weekdays of Advent, of Christmastime and of the Easter Season, only in the case of genuine pastoral need; and (3) by permission of the bishop, when serious need or pastoral advantage dictates, on any day except the Sundays of Advent, Lent and the Easter Season, Ash Wednesday, and during Holy Week. These same directives also apply for Masses for Various Needs and Occasions.

The practice of Votive Masses grew during the Middle Ages after the genesis of the liturgical calendar. Christians who had a special devotion to Jesus, Mary, or a saint would ask priests to offer Masses of petition or thanksgiving in the spirit of that devotion. The faithful would also request Masses for special needs or situations that arose in their daily lives and in society. Ritual Masses also arose from the sacramental needs of the people.

Bibliography: J. D. CRICHTON, *Christian Celebration: The Mass* (London 1971). G. DIX, *The Shape of the Liturgy* (London 1945). J. JUNGMANN, *Mass of the Roman Rite* (New York 1951, 1955).

[J. T. KELLEY]

MASSES FOR THE DEAD

The funeral masses in the New Roman Missal (*see* SACRAMENTARY) express more clearly the paschal character of Christian death, fulfilling the directives of Vatican Council II, Constitution on the Sacred Liturgy (*Sacrosanctum Concilium* 81–82). The texts of the antiphons, prayers, and readings emphasize the joy of the Resurrection and the hope of eternal life, while elements expressing fear of judgment, such as the sequence *Dies irae* and the absolution *Libera me, Domine* are deleted, the latter being replaced by a "Final Commendation and Farewell." Beautiful antiphons from the NT were added to the traditional *Requiem aeternam* (12:384). The instructions manifest a thorough pastoral concern and great flexibility, encourage the celebrant to select and arrange appropriate prayers and readings from among the formularies presented, and admonish him to take into consideration the circumstances of death, the sorrow of the family and the persons present, including those of other faiths and nonpractising Catholics (GenInstrRomMissal 336–341).

The Sacramentary includes 13 complete Mass formularies and a large number of prayers with the provision that all texts are interchangeable. There are 4 formularies for Mass on the day of burial, which may be celebrated on all days except solemnities and the Sundays of Advent, Lent, and Easter; 5 formularies for anniversary Masses, which are permitted on days of obligatory memorials (*see* SAINTS, MEMORIALS OF) and weekdays other than Ash Wednesday and Holy Week; one formulary for the funeral Mass of baptized children and one for a child who died before Baptism. The formularies for funeral and anniversary Masses include special texts for the Easter season but permit that the Alleluia of the antiphons be omitted if considered inappropriate. The Sacramentary offers the celebrant a choice from among 45 readings from the Old and New Testaments and 5 Prefaces. Psalms and songs are recommended as well as the homily (not a eulogy) and reception of Communion by the relatives. Incense and holy water can be used, but preferably only once. The color of the vestments can be black or violet, to which the national episcopal conferences may add others according to local customs. A later declaration by the Consilium explains that the general rubrics can be followed with regard to the kissing of the gospel book, the blessing of water, and standing during prayer (*Notitiae* 4 [1968] 136). A solemn final blessing is even included in the American Sacramentary.

Notwithstanding the joyful message of the new Masses, priests are cautioned against "too frequent celebration of Masses for the dead, lest they fail to open to the faithful the richness of the Word of God contained in the daily readings and because any Mass may be offered for the living as well as for deceased persons" (GenInstrRomMissal 316). The new Masses for the dead require careful preparation and execution but offer an excellent opportunity to impart instruction and spiritual formation on the meaning of Christian life and death.

Bibliography: *Notitiae* 4 (1968) 64–69, 136. H. ASHWORTH, "The Prayers for the Dead in the Missal of Pope Paul VI," EphemLit 85 (1971) 1–15. P.-M. GY, "Le Nouveau rituel romain des funérailles," *Maison-Dieu* 101 (1970) 15–32. J. P. MEIER, "Catholic Funerals in the Light of Scripture," *Worship* 48 (1974) 93–98.

[A. CORNIDES]

MASSES WITH CHILDREN

Before the liturgical reforms of Vatican Council II, priests and educators exercised much imagination to keep children occupied while the Mass was being celebrated. Hymns appropriate to children were sung, special prayers were recited, and modified forms of the dialogue Mass were encouraged. Since Vatican II, however, ways have been sought explicitly to adapt the Mass to children. The impetus for such adaptation was fostered by the Constitution on the Sacred Liturgy which proposed the ideal of active participation for all Christians and legitimate variations and adaptations to different groups, regions and peoples so that they might comprehend the rites they celebrate (*Sacrosanctum Concilium* 19, 34, 38).

History. At the first Synod of Bishops meeting in Rome, 1967, Cardinal G. *Lercaro, President of the Consilium for the Implementation of the Liturgy, enunciated the idea that it was not a question of composing an entirely new Eucharistic Liturgy but of abridging or omitting certain elements and of choosing certain texts better adapted to children.

In 1969 the Sacred Congregation for Divine Worship issued the *Instruction on Masses for Special Groups* (*Actio pastoralis*; see bibliog.), which encouraged the pastoral care of smaller groups so as to deepen and intensify their Christian life in keeping with their needs and their stage of development. However, the Instruction did not address the specific question of Masses with children.

Many requests from priests, catechists, bishops, and episcopal conferences asked the Holy See to give norms for celebrating Masses with children. In 1971 the Congregation for Divine Worship wrote the heads of liturgical commissions to find out their experiences and wishes in the matter. Fifty liturgical commissions from all over the world responded and requested a simpler structure for Masses with children, greater flexibility, texts adapted to their level, and greater opportunity for more active participation. The Congregation appointed Dr. Balthasar Fischer of the liturgical institute at Trier to head the committee which, after gathering its own data, submitted its report to the Congregation. On November 21, 1973, the *Directory for Masses With Children* was issued as a supplement to the General Instruction of the revised Roman Missal. By children are understood those who have not yet entered the period of preadolescence.

Character and Structure. The *Directory's* purpose is not to prescribe rules. Rather it gives general orientations indicating certain limits to adaptation and proposing doctrinal and pastoral reflections for the consideration of the different countries of the world. It is up to episcopal conferences to make further adaptations based on the considerations of the *Directory*.

Preparatory Directives. The *Directory* is divided into three chapters: I. The Introduction of Children to the Eucharistic Celebration; II. Masses with Adults in Which Children also Participate; and III. Masses with Children in Which Only a Few Adults Participate.

In Chapter I, the *Directory* recognizes that children are to be introduced to the Eucharistic celebration in various ways. Especially important is their experience at home and at school of those human values reflected in the liturgy, namely, community activity, the exchange of greetings, the capacity to listen, how to seek and grant pardon, how to express gratitude, experiences of meals with friends, and the festive celebration of special occasions.

Eucharistic catechesis will adapt itself to the age, psychological condition, and social situation of children. The family, the Christian community and the Catholic school all have their role to play in developing the spiritual capacity of children, who are introduced to the liturgy at the same time that they are led to give an increasing response to the Gospel in their daily lives (*see* CHILDREN, RELIGION AND).

Chapter II treats of the experience of children at the Sunday Mass where adults are in the majority. Even here, however, the *Directory* urges that the children be recognized in some way and suggests certain adaptations to allow them to participate and experience participation.

Liturgy for Children. By far, the greatest part of the *Directory* is devoted to Chapter III. Masses with children in which only some adults participate (not as monitors) are recommended, especially during the week. At these Masses attention is to be paid to the participation of the children by having them assist in preparing the celebration and fulfilling certain roles during it. If the priest finds it difficult to adapt himself to the mentality of the children, one of the other adult participants may speak to them in his place after the Gospel. Depending on the circumstances, such places and times of the Eucharistic celebration are to be selected that will allow the kind of liturgy suitable to children. The *Directory* discourages, for example, large groups of children at weekday Mass and Mass everyday for the same children.

Careful preparation of these liturgies for children with attention to singing, music, gestures, actions, visual elements, and silence is urged. As for the rites and texts of the Mass, the *Directory* urges sensible adaptations that do not violate the general structure of the Mass. Suggestions are made for the introductory rite, the reading and explanation of the Word of God, the *Presidential Prayers, and Communion with the rites before and after it.

The *Directory*, in recommending that the priest choose Presidential Prayers suited to children or adapted to them, insists that moral exhortation or a childish manner of speech be avoided. With regard to a special Lectionary, the *Bishops' Committee on the Liturgy, while waiting to prepare its own official Lectionary, has for the meantime endorsed the three-volume *Lectionary for Children's Mass* (New York, Pueblo Press, 1974, 1976), which while preserving the original sense and style, uses translations suited to children and shortens some readings. Scripture is never to be omitted at Masses with children but the number of readings may be reduced and more appropriate biblical selections may be substituted for those assigned.

As intimated in the *Directory* (52), three new *Eucharistic Prayers were soon prepared for Masses with children. These were made available in November, 1974, by the Congregation for Worship. The prayers appeared in their approved English translation June 15, 1975, to be used on an experimental basis for three years. These Eucharistic Prayers maintain the general structure of a Eucharistic Prayer while adapting the language to children, not only by making the language simple without being childish but particularly by using references to the everyday world of children. The Prayers also seek to give greater opportunities for children to respond by acclamation. The texts of these prayers carry out in practice many of the directional and practical ideas offered in the *Directory*.

The Bishops' Committee on the Liturgy is presently

evaluating pastoral experience with the 1973 *Directory* and the 1974 Eucharistic Prayers.

Bibliography: M. COLLINS, "Ritual Symbols: Something Human Between Us and God, Reflections on the Directory for Masses With Children," LivLight 12 (1975) 438–448. R. Kaczynski, ed., *Enchiridion documentorum instaurationis liturgicae I 1963–1973* (Turin 1976). *Actio pastoralis* 573–577; *Directorium de missis cum pueris* 968–980. *Eucharistic Prayers for Masses With Children and for Masses With Reconciliation. Provisional Text,* tr. International Commission on English in the Liturgy (Washington, D.C. 1975). R. KACZYNSKI, "Commentarium," *Notitiae* 10 (1974) 22–28. A. TOS, ed., *Lectionary for Children's Mass* (3 v., New York 1974, 1976).

[J. B. RYAN]

MEAGHER, PAUL KEVIN

Dominican moral theologian and editor; b. Clarion, Pa. May 14, 1907; d. Washington, D.C. Jan. 2, 1977. His family moved to Portland, Ore. and he joined the Holy Name Province of Dominicans at Ross, Cal. in 1924. His novitate was spent in St. Rose Priory, Springfield, Ky.; his philosophy course at River Forest, Ill and Benicia, Cal.; he completed his theology at the Collegio Angelico (now the University of St. Thomas Aquinas) in Rome and at Blackfriars, Oxford, where he was ordained by Bp. Alban Goodier, May 30, 1931. At Blackfriars his mentor was Thomas Gilby, OP and the two became life-long friends and collaborators. There also Fr. Meagher and Fr. Gerald Vann, OP became friends; in later years they coauthored *The Temptations of Christ* (London 1966; first published as *Stones Are Bread*, London 1957). Throughout his life Fr. Meagher's most striking personal quality was his capacity for friendship, marked by his loyalty, compassion, generosity, and respect for others.

His teaching career was spent chiefly at St. Albert's College, Oakland, Cal., house of studies of his province. He was professor of moral theology, *lector primarius* (1946), and, when it became a *studium generale* (1949), regent of studies. He received the highest Dominican degree in 1946, being made Master of Sacred Theology by Master General Emmanuel Suárez. During these teaching years Fr. Meagher was confessor and spiritual director to the Dominican students, preached retreats, lectured in theology to many communities of women. He also taught at the Dominican College of San Rafael and assisted in establishing there in 1946 a graduate program in theology.

Fr. Meagher left St. Albert's in 1961 to join Thomas Gilby at Blackfriars, Cambridge in launching the 60-volume English-Latin edition, *St. Thomas Aquinas, Summa theologiae* (completed in 1976). The following year, however, he took on the editorship of the area on moral theology for the *New Catholic Encyclopedia* at the request of Card. Patrick O'Boyle and Rev. John P. Whalen, managing editor. The keenness and depth of Fr. Meagher's knowledge assured the balanced and clear coverage that mark the NCE in this area of controversy and change. In 1967 he received the annual Cardinal Spellman award for excellence in theology. From 1966 to 1970 he conceived, planned, and was editor-in-chief of the dictionary program of Corpus Instrumentorum, Inc. This work, suspended for a period between 1970–73, led to the publication of the *Encyclopedic Dictionary of Religion* (3v. 1979), on which he worked until the eve of his death in spite of ill-health. The period 1970–77 was also one of great pastoral activity, in which he delighted, at St. Mary's Oneonta, N.Y. (1970–73), then at St. Mark's, Hyattsville, Md. (1973–77). He was revered as a preacher of strength and clarity, and sought out as a sympathetic and wise confessor and spiritual director. His funeral was held at St Mark's and he was buried in St. Dominic's Cemetery, Benicia, California.

[P. KELLY]

MEDELLÍN DOCUMENTS

The Medellín Documents are the promulgated official results of CELAM (Consejo Episcopal Latino-Americano), the general assembly of bishops of all Latin America convened in Medellín, Colombia, in August–September 1968. The assembly was only the second such general episcopal conference ever held on the soil of Latin America, and the first since Vatican Council II. Often compared with Vatican Council II, Medellín in its impact was similarly crucial in shaping the modern discussions and contemporary agenda of the Latin American Church. The conference centered from the outset on the themes of revolution and class conflict. The working document for the CELAM meeting had been circulated to the bishops and made public two months before the assembly convened. This working draft is of considerable importance in itself and caused a furore that determined which issues the bishops must face to retain any credibility with the young, the militants, and the most vocal clergy. The working draft is a pale reflection of the kinds of radical agenda communicated to the preparatory committee by groups of Latin American priests and laity. The working document had been forwarded to Rome for a critique and Rome had objected to its excessive concern with secular issues, but the document was circulated without incorporating Rome's objections. Pope Paul VI had already determined to attend the opening session of the conference in conjunction with his attendance at the Eucharistic Congress then being held that year in Bogotá. On three occasions the Pope tried to dissuade the bishops from encouraging the militants who were interpreting the papal teaching set forth in *Populorum progressio* as condoning the resort to violence in resisting injustice. The Pope's efforts were not completely successful.

The final documents of the conference incorporated the substance of the working draft in its descriptions of the tragic condition of the social order in most of Latin America; were unsparing in the condemnations of the imperialist powers and the violence of capitalism; agreed with papal emphases that the Church's main effort should be to appeal to the consciences of the ruling elites and that resort to violent resistance usually brings more suffering to the poor and may lead to newer forms of oppression. But especially in the section on peace the conference condemned the use of force by the ruling classes to repress opposition, characterized the current state of Latin America as a state of oppression and established violence, and seconded the teaching of *Populorum progressio* that insurrection is legitimate in the face of evident and prolonged tyranny that attacks fundamental human rights and dangerously injures the common good. Various documents, including the report on pastoral planning for the different groups, cite favorably the social consciousness of revolutionary elites, in contrast to the insensitivity of traditionalist Catholics. The document on poverty calls for a new life-style for clergy and a new Church that will continue the painful process of turning from a position of support for the privileged minority to one of identity with the impoverished majority.

See also LATIN AMERICA, CHURCH IN.

Bibliography: *The Church in the Present-Day Transformation of Latin America in the Light of the Council II Conclusions* (English tr. of the Medellín Documents, USCC Publ. Office, Washington, D.C. 1968). *Between Honesty and Hope*, tr. J. Drury, Maryknoll Documentation Series (Maryknoll, N.Y. 1970) 171–277. A. GHEERBRANT, *The Rebel Church in Latin America* (London 1974). E. MUTCHLER, *The Church as a Political Factor in Latin America* (New York 1971), esp. 98–130.

[E. J. DILLON]

MEDIA IN EDUCATION

From the earliest times the Church has used the arts to communicate the Gospel message, and to lift the minds and hearts of her members through the beauty of music, poetry, architecture, and painting to the source of the true and the beautiful, which is in God Himself. The wall inscriptions by the early Christians in the catacombs, the beauty of the medieval cathedrals, the canvasses of Michaelanglo, Fra Angelico, and El Greco are all attempts to portray the spiritual in a manner more vivid than words. Stained glass, mosaics, painting, and sculpture have been used to tell stories of the saints, martyrs, and virgins. Music, poetry, dance, drama, architecture, and other art forms have all served catechetical purposes.

The communications revolution has affected all of man's life today, including his perception of the spiritual, and has profound implications for the teaching of religion. Although the written word still forms the core of the standard educational process, frequently visual and audio-visual materials are being used to make learning interesting to young people and to involve them more totally in the learning experience. Media materials may be as simple as the classroom chalk board or as sophisticated as tape recorders, slide and movie projectors, and record players. Most of these materials are now available to almost every classroom teacher. Visual materials such as outlines and diagrams on the chalk board can serve to make a lesson clearer or be used in summary of the material presented. Text book illustrations, pictures, charts, diagrams, and maps are all helpful in encouraging students to visualize concepts.

The use of films, film strips, and records are very effective in the catechesis of both children and adults. These must be well planned in advance and be closely related to the material they accompany. They can be very helpful in: (1) encouraging students to be interested in a topic; (2) providing a vicarious experience of a part of life not yet encountered or an opportunity to reflect on some life experience; (3) helping the students clarify their values through discussion of a visual or auditory experience they have shared.

Television can also be a rich resource for the clarification of Christian values. People can live faith more fully when the stories of Scripture and tradition become their own stories. Television can offer the construct for these stories against which their lives and work can be evaluated. In addition, every major issue of society shows up on television. By reflecting on these moral issues and by raising important value questions television can become a catalyst for discussion. It presents the stories against which people can learn to contrast and compare the faith story of their own lives.

Although media offers great potential for transmitting the Gospel message there are also inherent challenges and problems in relating the media to the message. Every art form has its own integrity and requires special interpretation. Although not every catechist need be a media expert, all should have some understanding of the impact of media on their work. A message translated from word to media is no longer an abstraction, but an event; a story has become someone's life and must be handled with sensitivity as an experience of sharing among human beings who are struggling for an understanding of life and of faith itself.

[R. MCDONELL]

MEDIA OF SOCIAL COMMUNICATION AND EVANGELIZATION

The Church from the very beginning has used media of communication to proclaim the Christian message. For centuries religious themes have been depicted in painting, mosaics, stained glass, and sculpture, in architecture, music, poetry, drama, and other forms. Thus the Church has naturally and with precedent turned to the modern mass media of communication—press, television, radio, films, etc.—as instruments for evangelization as well as instruction.

Conciliar and Postconciliar Teaching. Vatican Council II, for example, expressed its interest in this subject in the Decree on the Instruments of Social Communication, which states that the Church "judges it part of her duty to preach the news of redemption with the aid of the instruments of social communication" (*Inter mirifica* 3). A more detailed treatment of the role of media in evangelization is contained in *Communio et progressio*, the Pastoral Instruction on the Media of Social Communication, published in 1971 by the Pontifical Commission for the Media of Social Communication. In its section on "The Use of the Media for Giving the Good News," this document links the Church's use of media to its response to Christ's mandate to teach all nations; notes that media offer new opportunities for confronting people with the Gospel; points out the need for technical skill and professional excellence in the use of media for religious purposes; and emphasizes that media-efforts merit increased attention by the Church in pastoral planning and the allocation of resources (126–134).

A considerable impetus was given to study, discussion, and action in this area by the 1974 *Synod of Bishops, which dealt with evangelization. In the Spring of that year, for example, the U.S. National Conference of Catholic Bishops devoted twelve regional meetings to consideration of the theme "The Use of Modern Means of Communication as Instruments for Evangelization." This was the fullest consideration of communications media ever undertaken by the episcopal conference of the United States.

In his apostolic exhortation On Evangelization in the Modern World, published in 1975 in response to the Synod, Pope Paul VI also discussed the role of media. While concluding that "the Church would feel guilty before the Lord if she did not utilize these powerful means" in efforts to evangelize, the Pope at the same time pointed to an apparent anomaly: the purpose of evangelization via mass media is to "reach vast numbers of people"—yet to do so in a way that touches "each individual . . . as though he were the only person being addressed." Leaving unanswered the question of whether and how this can be done, Paul went on to observe that, along with the "collective proclamation of the Gospel," the Church must continue to engage in "person-to-person" evangelization (Paul VI EvangNunt 45–46).

Problems of Implementation. Not surprisingly, practice has preceded and outstripped theorizing concerning media and evangelization. In the U.S., for example, Abp. Fulton J. Sheen was an early and noteworthy pioneer in the use of radio and television for evangelistic purposes; during the 1950s in particular he won nationwide attention with a series of weekly TV lectures on religious topics. Internationally, the Catholic communication organization *UNDA has for a long time devoted particular attention to media as tools of evangelization. Also, in a number of missionary and Third-World countries the Church has for many years made extensive use of broadcast media, especially radio, to overcome the problems of distance and a shortage of personnel.

In the U.S., however, the most extensive and dramatic use of mass media for evangelization has in recent years been made, not by Catholics, but by such Protestant evangelists as Billy Graham and Oral Roberts. Conservative Protestant denominations and religious bodies currently devote far larger resources to electronic media than does the Catholic Church or, for that matter, than do the mainline non-Catholic Churches and church bodies. This has been a factor in stimulating renewed interest in the subject among Catholics.

At the present time the use of media for evangelization is a matter of continuing concern to various elements of the NCCB and the USCC, as well as to national, regional, and diocesan church communication groups and communicators. Since the 1974 NCCB regional meetings, the subject has been discussed on several occasions in general sessions by the bishops. Up to this time, however, initiation of large-scale new efforts, over and above those already been carried on by the USCC *Communication Department and other church communication entities, has been deferred pending the identification of new funding sources. In December 1978 the NCCB voted in favor of a national annual collection to support media evangelization.

This points to a major practical problem. Most media efforts are expensive. In regard to broadcast media especially, potential costs include not only program production but the purchase of air time. While some religious groups active in evangelistic programming have sufficient funds for this purpose (and have begun to develop their own broadcasting networks), Catholic broadcasting efforts must generally rely on free, "public-service" air time donated by commercial networks and stations and ordinarily made at less desirable hours of the day.

The use of mass media for evangelization also raises a number of other questions. What audience or combination of audiences is envisaged? What mix of media (electronic and print, secular and church-related) is to be used? How, if at all, are efforts at evangelization by media to be coordinated with the "person-to-person" evangelization whose importance was underlined by Paul VI in *Evangelii nuntiandi*?

Despite unresolved questions and problems, however, it is reasonable to anticipate increased experimentation and further significant developments, both theoretical and practical, in the use of media for evangelization during the years ahead. As *Communio et progressio* puts it: "Christ commanded the Apostles and their successors to 'teach all nations' (Mt 28.19), to be 'the light of the world' (Mt. 5.14) and to announce the Good News in all places at all times. During his life on earth, Christ showed himself to be the perfect Communicator, while the Apostles used what means of social communication were available in their time. It is now necessary that the same message be carried by the means of social communication that are available today" (11).

Bibliography: Pontifical Commission for the Media of Social Communication, *Communio et progressio*, Eng. tr., *Communications: Pastoral Instruction on the Media, Public Opinion and Human Progress* (USCC Publ. Office, Washington, D.C. 1971).

[R. SHAW]

MEDIA OF SOCIAL COMMUNICATION AND THE CHURCH

The Church and the media of social communication (9:559) was the subject of the Pastoral Instruction *Communio et progressio*, ordered by Vatican Council II's decree on the topic (*Inter mirifica* 23) and written over a seven-year period by the Pontifical Commission for Social Communication after wide consultation. The Instruction was issued May 23, 1971 (ActAps 63 [1971] 593–656; USCC, *The Media: Public Opinion and Human Progress*).

Communio et Progressio. "The unity and advancement of men," the Instruction states, "are the chief aims of social communication and of all the means it uses" (*Communio et progressio* 1). Press, cinema, radio and television offer "a great round table" so that people can participate "in a world wide exchange in search of brotherhood and cooperation." The media enable every person to be "a partner in the business of the human race" (ibid. 19).

Although critical questions about the media are raised—concentration of power, possible encouragement of mental idleness and passivity, the incessant appeal to emotion, sapping reason (ibid. 21)—the approach of *Communio et progressio* is overwhelmingly positive. The media are seen as "gifts of God" (ibid. 2), helping people "share their knowledge and unify their creative work" to build "the earthy city" (ibid. 7). God first communicated with man. Jesus revealed Himself "as the perfect communicator" and ordered his disciples to spread the Glad Tidings "from the roof tops" (ibid. 10, 11). The media can "tear down the barriers that time and space have erected between men," help eliminate illiteracy and promote education, enable all to enjoy "the delights of culture and leisure, keep in touch with reality," and bring "far away times and places within their grasp" (ibid. 20).

"Public opinion is an essential expression of human nature organized in a society" (ibid. 25) and the media provide "a public forum where every man may exchange ideas" (ibid. 24). A person has a right, then, to be informed and to inform (ibid. 33–48). "But the right to information . . . has to be reconciled with other rights," e.g., the privacy of individual and family (ibid. 42). The instruction discusses the problems of portraying evil (ibid. 57, 58) and the "real social benefits" of advertising (ibid. 59), as well as its bad effects when misused (ibid. 60). Education regarding the media is called for so that the receivers may be discriminating and critical. They must be active rather than passive and "insist on voicing their views" (ibid. 81).

The last part of the document discusses what Catholics can contribute to the media and what they receive. The media help the Church understand "contemporary opinions and attitudes" and read "the signs of the times" and "reveal herself to the modern world." They also "foster dialogue within the Church" (ibid. 125). "Since the Church is a living body, she needs public opinion in order to sustain a giving and taking between her members. Without this, she cannot advance in thought and action" (ibid. 115). "Catholics should be aware of the real freedom to speak their minds which stems from a 'feeling for the faith' and from love" (ibid. 116). While Catholics follow the magisterium, they can and should engage in free research so that they can better understand revealed truths or explain them to a society subject to incessant change. "This free dialogue within the Church does no injury to her unity and solidarity" (ibid. 117). Scientific investigations, however, must be distinguished from public dissemination of findings. New opinions sometimes circulate "too soon and in the wrong places" (ibid. 118). The news and works of the Church should be characterized by "integrity, truth and openness" (ibid. 121).

The strengths and challenges for Catholics of the printed word, cinema, radio, television, and the theater are considered. The importance of research, national and diocesan offices for the media, press offices and public relations are all noted.

Media and the Church in the U.S. As one response to *Communio et progressio* the U.S. bishops made "The Use of the Modern Means of Communications as Instruments of Evangelization" (Documentation, USCC, Washington, D.C. 1974) the topic of their Spring, 1974, regional meetings. Some 40 recommendations came from these meetings, but no funds were appropriated to implement them. The USCC Department of Communication proposed a national collection to place "Media at the Service of the Gospel," but it failed to win approval at the November 1977 and 1978 NCCB meetings; approval was later voted by mail.

Currently, according to the 1977 *Catholic Press Directory*, there are nine national and 143 diocesan newspapers in the U.S. and Canada and 298 Catholic magazines with a total circulation of 26,818,099 (*see* CATHOLIC PRESS, U.S.). There are some 70 Catholic book publishers in the U.S. (*see* PUBLISHING, CATHOLIC). The majority of dioceses have personnel assigned to public information and communications. Some produce their own radio and TV shows, as well as use the material of such national syndicators as the Christophers, Maryknoll, Franciscan Communications Center, Paulist Productions, the Jesuits' *Sacred Heart Program* and the Passionists' *Crossroads* and Spanish version *Encuentro*. The USCC *Communication Committee, through its Office of Film and Broadcasting, works with networks in producing both radio and TV programs. In instructional TV the Catholic Television Network has been established in Boston, Brooklyn, Chicago, Los Angeles, Miami, Milwaukee, New York, Rockville Centre, and San Francisco.

Active organizations serving Catholics and the media

are the Catholic Press Association; the Association of Catholic Television and Radio Syndicators; UNDA-U.S.A. for Catholic broadcasters and allied communicators; Catholic Actors' Guild of America, Inc.; and the Catholic Communications Foundation.

[J. HARRINGTON]

MEDICAL ETHICS

In the last few years there has been a change in the texture of medical ethics, particularly from a Catholic viewpoint. The factors contributing to this change are many, complex, and not easily identifiable.

Forces of Change. Among the better recognized elements are: the responses of both medical science and Church to a rapidly growing technology; the impact of value pluralism which marks contemporary society; concern for patient's rights against medical authoritarianism; and developing revitalization of the faith dimension in secular life.

Technological Advance. The rapid expansion of scientific knowledge especially in the area of electronics, computers, molecular biology, and immunology, and their respective applications to medicine, has resulted in problems which were not considered earlier in medical ethics. The proliferation of ethical issues has led to the emergence of the new field of bioethics (16:28). The presence of two apparently distinct disciplines dealing with overlapping areas of concern has resulted in some confusion about the names and areas of applicability. Thus such terms appear as, "medical ethics," "medical-morals," "bioethics," and "biomedical ethics." The consequence is the tendency to use these terms almost interchangeably. Another consequence has been the avoidance of these terms in the titles of their books by some contemporary authors. Thus the titles of Häring, May, McFadden, and O'Donnell (bibliog.).

Value Pluralism. A survey of the writings in the field of medical ethics (or bioethics) reveals that two value-groups tend to predominate: the one which seeks to incorporate a Christian viewpoint and the other which espouses secular humanism. Frequently those fitting into the first category invoke the teachings of the Catholic Church, sometimes as overriding and decisive, in other instances simply as supportive. Those favoring a secular-humanistic approach do not necessarily deny religious values—even if their stance is "negatively neutral"—but seem rather to be concerned about meeting the needs of the broader public, one characterized by a homogenization of values. For secular humanists man is the standard; their advocacy is of values that would be most acceptable to the majority of the concerned public.

Increased Concern for Patients' Rights. The issue of human rights, dramatically focused by post-World War II revelations, continues to generate increased attention and an urge to action. Rapidly escalating health costs have raised grave concern on the part of public and government alike that the health benefits of high medical technology are being outweighed by the cost of supporting sophisticated medicine. Questions are being asked about the wisdom of allowing technology to dominate the practice of medicine. Additional support for such questions and concerns is the collective impact of popular entertainment forms—television and film—which have begun to dramatize the dangers of a runaway technology. Many fear that medical technology is taking too dominant a role in medicine. Instead of the comforting presence of the nurse at the bedside, there is instead the cold watchful eye of the television camera; between patient and physician complicated instrumentation intervenes. The patient fears that the clinical judgment of the physician will be replaced by impersonal responses of the computer. More frequently than before it is heard that physicians are praised for their technical skills but with reservations about their "bedside manner." Scientific medicine is at times contrasted with humanistic medicine.

A few voices, like those of Ivan Illich and Thomas Szasz, are raised to challenge what they perceive as a medical tyranny over health. They question whether modern medicine is truly effective in the treatment of disease. In the midst of medical advances the question is raised about the rights of the patients. Indeed, there has been a move toward codifications of a "Bill of Patient Rights."

Taken together, these various factors have succeeded in alerting the public as well as the medical profession to the state of affairs in which the rights of the patient may have been very gradually and almost silently eroded. Questions, too, are raised about who makes the decision in a medical context. Towards clarification, distinctions are proposed between one set of decisions, *medical* decisions, which properly pertain to the physician, and *personal* decisions regarding life and health, which belong to the patient as a basic right. These controversies, however, have been viewed by some as ultimately constructive for both physician and patient because they promote a more precise definition of roles.

Increased Concern for the Faith Dimension. In concert with the elucidation of patient rights and respect for the human person there has been growing articulation of the role of faith in daily life. Somewhat apart from both the medical and religious establishments there has been an increase in the popularity of faith healing which is largely associated with those involved in the charismatic renewal within the various faith communities. Such activity among believers is one indication of an increased awareness of the faith dimension in health and sickness.

Another indication of the same awareness has been the initiative taken by groups within the Church, but not as part of the official structure, to meet specific faith problems. In the recent past Catholic hospitals found themselves in the midst of painful and complex medical-moral problems for which there had been no adequate preparation. After consultation with medical and ecclesiastical representatives, the Catholic Hospital Association founded the Pope John XXIII Medical-Moral Research and Education Center for the purpose of studying the long-range medical-moral issues arising as a result of advances in science and medicine. Other groups were formed to meet a different set of problems: The Institute for Theological Encounter with Science and Technology, and The Human Life Center. Such existing organizations, as the National Federation of Catholic Physicians Guilds and the National Catholic Pharmacists Guild, also responded to the newer ethical issues.

The official Church has itself acted vigorously to meet the developing ethical concerns by the establishment of a number of Bishops' committees. Thus as part of the NCCB there are currently (January 1978) Bishops'

PATRIARCH ATHENAGORAS I with POPE PAUL VI, (Oct., 1967) (N.C. Pictures)

ARCHBISHOP MICHAEL RAMSEY of Canterbury with Pope Paul VI, Sistine Chapel
(March, 1966) (N.C. Pictures)

(Above) St. Joseph's Church, St. Joseph,
Minn., Baptistery and font. (Below) Font
has pool about 8″ deep and a constantly
trickling overflow, symbol of living water.
(Photos, Cloud H. Meinberg, OSB.)

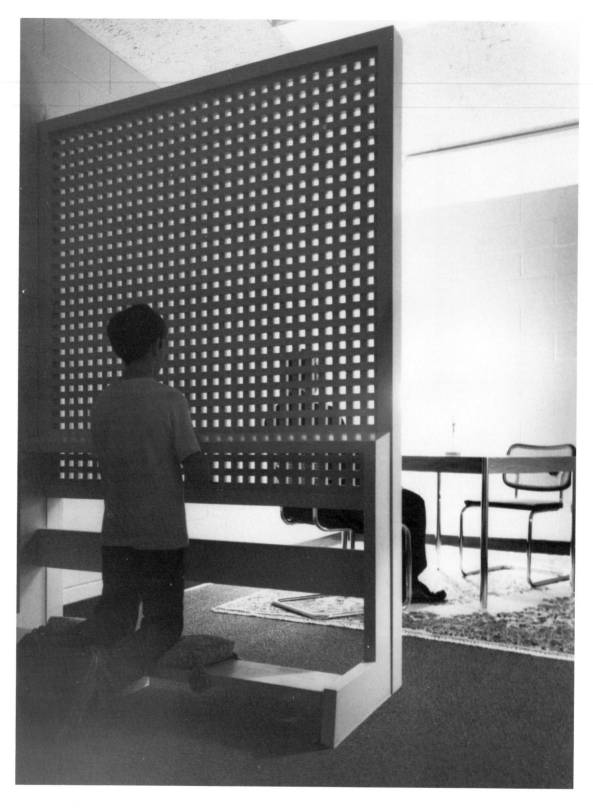

Chapel of Reconciliation, for traditional manner of confession (Photo, Larry Hoyt, as in J. M. Champlin, *Together in Peace*).

Chapel of Reconciliation for face-to-face confession (Photo, Larry Hoyt, as in J. M. Champlin, *Together in Peace*).

Children's Mass, St. Joseph's Church Sanctuary, St. Joseph, Minn. (Photo, Cloud H. Meinberg, OSB).

Communion Table, with slab of same white marble as altar, St. John's Abbey Church, Collegeville, Minn. (Photo, Cloud H. Meinberg, OSB).

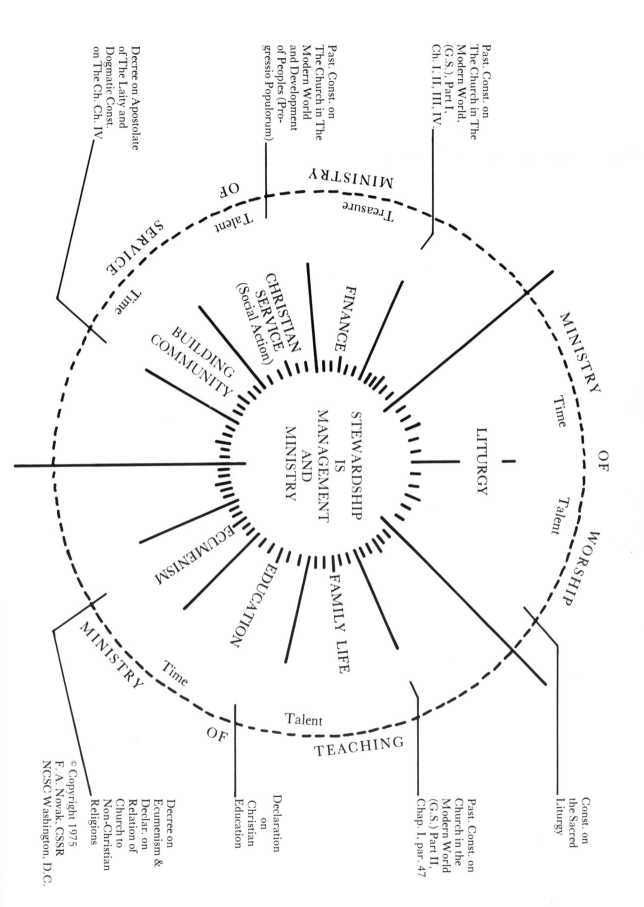

TOTAL STEWARDSHIP CONCEPT

Past. Const. on The Church in The Modern World, (G.S.), Part I, Ch. I; II, III, IV.

Past. Const. on The Church in The Modern World and Development of Peoples (Pro-gressio Populorum)

Decree on Apostolate of The Laity and Dogmatic Const. on The Ch. Ch. IV

MINISTRY OF SERVICE

Talent

Treasure

Time

MINISTRY

MINISTRY OF WORSHIP

Time

Talent

LITURGY

CHRISTIAN SERVICE (Social Action)

FINANCE

BUILDING COMMUNITY

STEWARDSHIP IS MANAGEMENT AND MINISTRY

ECUMENISM

EDUCATION

FAMILY LIFE

MINISTRY

Time

Talent

OF

TEACHING

Const. on the Sacred Liturgy

Past. Const. on Church in the Modern World (G.S.) Part II, Chap. I, par. 47

Decree on Ecumenism & Declar. on Relation of Church to Non-Christian Religions

Declaration on Christian Education

CHRISTIAN STEWARDSHIP IN SYMBOLS

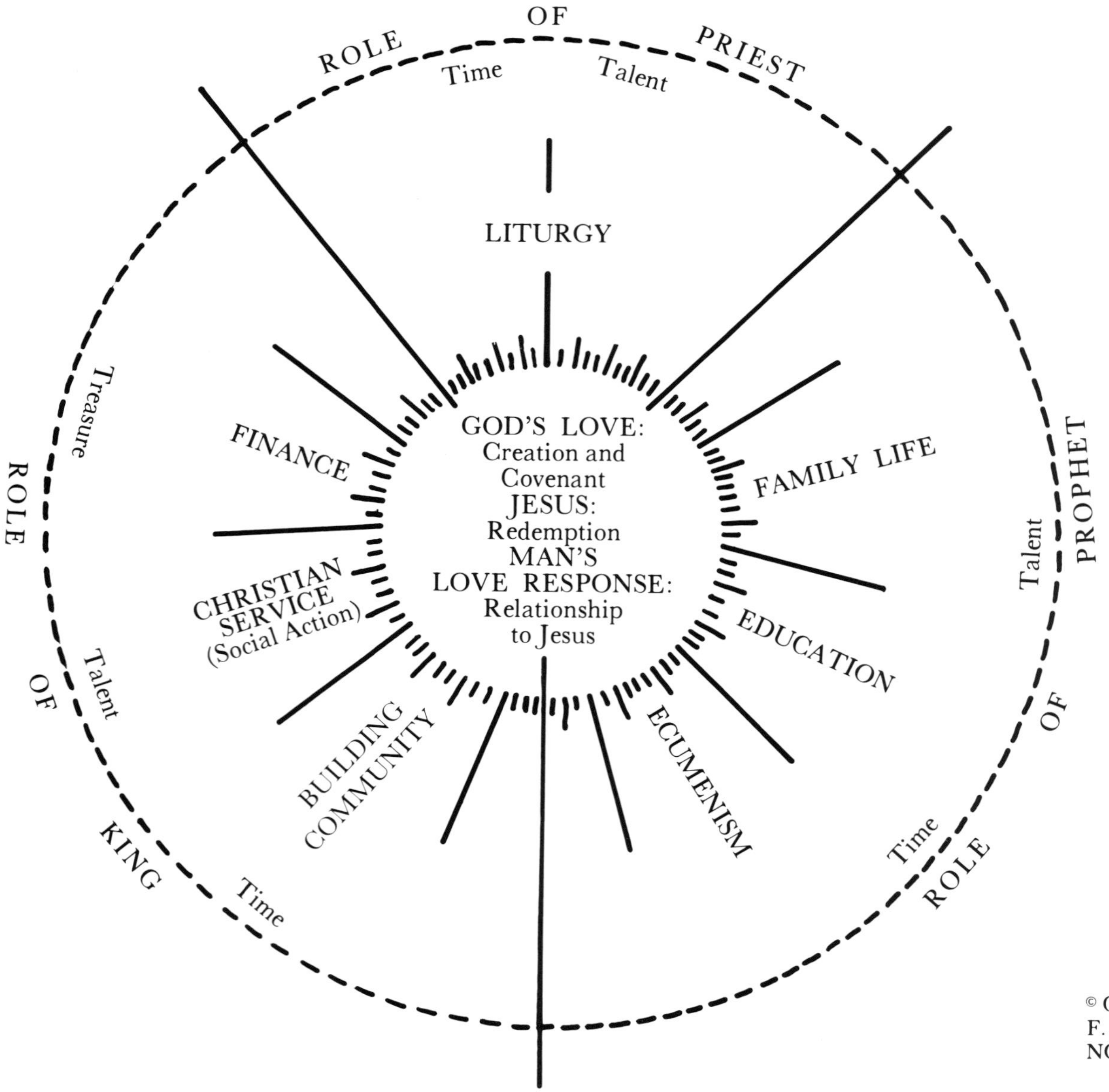

PROPHET

ROLE OF

Talent

Time

PRIEST

OF

Talent

ROLE

Time

ROLE

FAMILY LIFE

EDUCATION

ECUMENISM

LITURGY

GOD'S LOVE:
Creation and
Covenant
JESUS:
Redemption
MAN'S
LOVE RESPONSE:
Relationship
to Jesus

BUILDING
COMMUNITY

FINANCE

CHRISTIAN
SERVICE
(Social Action)

Time

Treasure

Talent

KING

OF

ROLE

Committees on Doctrine; Human Values; and Pro-Life Activities. Pertaining to the USCC is the sub-committee on Health which is part of the USCC Committee on Social Development and World Peace. Although all of these committees, in one way or another, have a concern and interest in medical-moral issues, it is the Committee on Doctrine that has been given the special responsibility to deal with medical-moral issues. In addition to these committees, the Church's concern for the faith dimension in health and sickness is witnessed by its increased openness in testifying before congressional committees on issues it feels must be defended against legislation invasive of the basic rights of individuals.

Publications. Evidence of growth and vitality within the Church has been the increased number of periodicals which seek to deal with medical-moral issues from a Catholic perspective. Some deal exclusively with ethical issues in medicine, others are concerned with broader issues in health care. A representative list includes *The Linacre Quarterly, Hospital Progress, The Medical-Moral Newsletter, Ethics and Medics, Love, Life, Death Issues.*

Important Current Topics. Clearly the current concerns of medical ethics go beyond what was traditionally its proper domain. Today writers on the topic of ethical issues in medicine do not consider themselves bound by the earlier parameters. The topics found under the heading of bioethics are now part and parcel of the publications of those who were once identified as medical ethicists. Of special concern today are such issues of distributive justice as the equitable allocation of scarce medical resources and the right to health care. The right to privacy as increasingly challenged by data banks and the questions of genetic diagnosis and counseling are other topics. The question of personal freedom surfaces when the issue of behavioral control in its many forms is considered. The acute problems associated with recombinant DNA techniques in particular, and with genetic engineering in general, raise questions about the limits of human dominion over self and nature.

Bibliography: B. ASHLEY and K. O'ROURKE, *Health Care Ethics: A Theological Analysis* (St. Louis 1978). B. HÄRING, *Ethics of Manipulation* (New York 1975); *Medical Ethics* (South Bend, Ind. 1973). W. E. MAY, *Human Existence, Medicine and Ethics* (Chicago 1977). C. J. MCFADDEN, *The Dignity of Life* (Indiana 1976). T. J. O'DONNELL, *Medicine and Christian Morality* (New York 1976). J. F. DEDEK, *Contemporary Medical Ethics* (New York 1975).

[A. S. MORACZEWSKI]

MEDICAL PERSONNEL, MORAL OBLIGATIONS OF

Though "medical personnel" is often used to refer only to physicians, in this context the term designates any person associated with the ministry of health care, whether physician, nurse, hospital administrator, or associated personnel. Many of the moral obligations of medical or health-care personnel are contained in the USCC's Ethical and Religious Directives for Catholic Health Facilities, but there are other responsibilities which must be considered as well.

"The Ethical and Religious Directives for Catholic Health Facilities." The *Ethical and Religious Directives for Catholic Health Facilities*, often called "The Directives," are a set of rules and standards for Catholic health-care facilities and for the people who conduct them and work in them. The standards have been developed over the last thirty years in an effort to have a uniform set of moral norms for Catholic health-care facilities and Catholic health-care personnel in the United States. The *Directives* are revised from time to time, the latest complete revision occurring in 1971 and minor revisions in 1973 and 1975. The present *Directives* were issued under the authority of the United States Catholic Conference (USCC) in November 1971, after having been approved by the Committee on Doctrine of the National Conference of Catholic Bishops (NCCB). The USCC may make recommendations for individual dioceses, but only the local Ordinary can make laws. Hence, the *Directives*, as a whole, do not have force until they are promulgated by the local Ordinary. However, some of the *Directives* oblige in conscience even if they have not been promulgated, because they embody the teachings of the Church or prohibit acts that are intrinsically evil. For example, even if the *Directives* are not promulgated in a particular diocese, it would still be wrong to perform abortions or direct sterilizations in Catholic health-care facilities because these actions are contrary to the moral law and prohibited by the teaching of the Church. At present, the *Directives* have been promulgated in almost every U.S. diocese. Primarily, the *Ethical and Religious Directives* apply to facilities conducted under the auspices of the Catholic Church. Thus they are addressed principally to the sponsoring groups, boards of trustees, administrators, and personnel of Catholic hospitals and nursing homes. However, because of the matter which they treat some of the *Directives* would apply to Catholics no matter where they might be offering health care.

Content. The *Directives* are divided into a Preamble and two sections, the first mainly concerned with the morality of specific medical procedures and the second with the religious care of patients. Though some *Directives* are prohibitions, for example, those against abortion and direct sterilization, many are positive norms for ensuring that Catholic health-care facilities and their personnel will offer health care for the whole person, that is, health care that serves the patient's spiritual and emotional as well as physiological well-being.

Clearly, all aspects of the complete, Christian health-care facility cannot be treated in a short document of 43 *Directives*. Thus, the *Directives* should be considered as the basic minimum, not the full expression of what it means to be a Catholic health-care facility. Even if a health-care facility observes the *Ethical and Religious Directives*, there are other obligations of which it must be aware if it is to be Catholic in the full sense of the term (cf. Catholic Hospital Association, *Evaluative Criteria for Catholic Health Care Facilities* [St. Louis 1978]). Copies of the *Directives* may be obtained from the United States Catholic Conference, Publications Department, 1312 Massachusetts Avenue, NW, Washington, DC, 20005.

Application. The *Ethical and Religious Directives*, like any other moral or legal teaching of the Church, need interpretation in order to be applied accurately. Usually interpretation will be simple and within the competence of responsible people associated with the Catholic health-care facility, but when help is needed the local Ordinary or diocesan director of health affairs should be consulted. The Ordinary should always be consulted if there is a possibility of scandal or if officials of the health-care facility consider using the principle of material cooperation.

Because the *Directives* contain statements which are drawn from the ordinary teaching of the Church and because they are promulgated for observance by the local Ordinary, individual Catholics should receive them with "loyal submission of intellect and will" (*Lumen gentium* 25). Such submission does not rule out the possibility of dissent by an individual, however, provided that the matter in question does not pertain to the extraordinary or infallible teaching power of the Church and that the general norms for dissent in conscience are followed.

The health-care facility, considered as a moral person, however, does not have the right, it seems, to dissent from the *Directives*. The Catholic facility is founded to witness not only to the healing ministry of Jesus Christ but also to the teaching ministry of Christ as carried on through the Church (cf. *Ethical and Religious Directives*, Preamble). Thus, the Catholic health-care facility would seem to be denying its reason for existence if it were to dissent to the teaching of the *Directives*. Certainly, if a facility did dissent publicly from their specific norms, the local Ordinary could declare such a facility to be no longer Catholic. Because the actions of moral persons are conducted by individual persons, acting alone or in council, the moral obligation of ensuring that the *Directives* are observed always falls back upon the individual.

Rights of Conscience. The U.S. Congress, through the Church amendment (42 U.S.C. Section 300a-7) has recognized the rights of conscience of Catholic and other private health-care facilities and the people who are associated with these institutions—the so-called conscience clauses. Thus, no Catholic facility can be directed to perform a medical or surgical procedure contrary to the *Ethical and Religious Directives*. This legislative acknowledgment of conscience rights is not the concession of a privilege, but recognition of a right flowing from the dignity of conscience and the pluralistic make-up of American society.

Other Moral Obligations. In addition to the moral obligations stated in the *Ethical and Religious Directives*, Catholic health-care personnel, whether associated with Catholic facilities or not, have additional moral responsibilities. These arise from the nature of the service that health-care professionals offer and from the needs of individuals and society. For example, increasing technology tends to make health-care professionals forget about the worth of the individual person; Catholic professionals should help to humanize their care. Moreover, the availability of health-care and health-care education is a problem in the United States; only through dedicated service by professionals will those in rural or poor urban areas get the care and education they need. The shortcomings and inequities of the American health-care system are well documented in many recent studies. In general, Catholic personnel should work to overcome the injustices associated with health care.

Health-care professionals also have the responsibility to work for social justice; they must try to change the system that oppresses people and makes it impossible for them to receive adequate medical care. The papal encyclicals point to adequate medical care as a human right because of the nature of the human person (John XXIII PacTerr 11). Since medical care contributes importantly to good health, Catholics in the field should consider it a moral obligation to help make sure that adequate care is available for all.

Lastly, in order to fulfill their profession worthily, Catholics engaged in health care should study the ethical issues involved and be as well versed in ethics and morality as they are in the technical and scientific aspects of their vocations.

Bibliography: B. ASHELY and K. O'ROURKE, *The Ethics of Health Care* (St. Louis 1978). I. ILLICH, *Medical Nemesis* (New York 1976). USCC, *The Ethical and Religious Directives for Catholic Health Care Facilities* (Washington, DC 1971; rev. ed. 1975).

[K. O'ROURKE]

METAPHYSICS

A dozen years ago the principal interest of metaphysics lay chiefly in a search for method, e.g., philosophical analysis, descriptive metaphysics, and phenomenology. Accordingly, this pushed temporarily into the background the major metaphysical questions themselves. Then, too, in the decade of the turbulent 1960s, social-political involvement worked against speculative thought and metaphysics became as unfashionable as life philosophy became fashionable. When coupled with the results of pluralism in society, in the Church and especially in Catholic academe (e.g., enrollment of more non-Catholics, of minority groups, women, etc.), these factors make plain that old views on the validity and meaningfulness of metaphysics would no longer obtain (9:727; 7:31). What kind of changes were to take place?

Changed Views. First of all, thinkers who had been provincial were goaded into broadening their outlook and began to realize that metaphysics in its historical style of system building patterned on exclusively Greek thought patterns was only one among many approaches possible; others perhaps might be more productive for contemporary needs. Previous position statements were reexamined and absolutist claims were viewed in their cultural context.

Secondly, there began a trend toward interdisciplinary thinking provoking numerous attitudinal changes toward metaphysics, its domain, methodology, and truth claims. The insights of psychology, for example, placed man, rather than being, at the center of metaphysics. The sociology of knowledge clearly indicated that both thinking and cultural factors were heavily influenced by societal horizons. (Interestingly enough, such disparate thinkers as Plato and Marx claimed this long ago.) Then, too, hermeneutics, employed so successfully in biblical studies, worked its way into metaphysics. Especially noteworthy for their influence on metaphysics today are philosophy of religion and Eastern religions, both vitally concerned with the problem of transcendence.

Thirdly, aesthetics, a category long neglected by theology and philosophy both, became an important vehicle for metaphysical enquiry. As metaphysics became less a system-building enterprise and more a personal search, the metaphysical quest turned into a revelation of the human condition. Metaphysicians were surprised to find this human condition well described, documented, and addressed in aesthetics. Heidegger's poetry, Marcel's drama and music, Sartre's essays on playful freedom, and von Balthazar's privileged religious discourse are clear examples of extraordinary metaphysical sensitivity.

Current Interests and Directions. Pluralism, then, together with attitudinal changes and different focuses of interest, changed the quest for, and meaning of metaphysics in a relatively short period of time. Although it is hazardous to be specific here (the sole safe prediction is only that continuing change will occur), the following may be proposed as a summary of the current situation in metaphysics.

Metaphysics as a comprehensive and all-embracing system worked out by speculative thought is no longer in the forefront of philosophy. Thomistic metaphysics, for example, at least as formerly taught in the curriculum, is of diminished interest, even in its "updated" form of transcendental Thomism (16:449). However, a renewed interest in ontology, namely, an attempt to probe structures and essences is quite current. (Instructive here is the nearly complete shift taken by such philosophers as Chomsky, Quine, Strawson and Kripke, who, in their quest for the answer to the problem of universals, hearken back to positions strikingly similar to medieval realism.) Further, in a time caught up in the acceleration of change, emphasis has shifted from a philosophy of *being* to a philosophy of *becoming*; this explains the continued interest in Hegelian descriptions of reality. Lastly, because of its attention to the human condition, there is a growing influence and acceptance of the phenomenological method in metaphysical enquiry.

It is fairly safe to say that while metaphysics as a system no longer dominates the philosophical scene, metaphysical questions spark increasing interest. These questions, however, will continue to be of import only to the extent that they are seen as germane to the human condition. This explains a resurrected interest in Nietzsche. The question of freedom remains a lively one and accounts for a continuing interest in Sartre and Heidegger and a rising one in Ricoeur. The search for its transcendent base moves the enquirer into the God problem, an area where metaphysics is viewed as being directional but not probative. Lastly, the issue of appearance and reality and the general involvement of man in structuring the world remain prominent. It is a hopeful sign that while metaphysical systems may come and go, the enduring questions of metaphysics remain, questions which although never totally resolved, nonetheless themselves point to human participation in reality itself.

See also PLURALISM, PHILOSOPHICAL.

Bibliography: A. J. AYER, *Metaphysics and Common Sense* (San Francisco 1970). R. ARMSTRONG, *Metaphysics and British Empiricism* (Lincoln, Neb. 1970). H.-G. GADAMER, *Truth and Method*, tr. and ed. G. BARDEN and J. CUMMING (New York 1975). E. LEVINAS, *Totality and Infinity*, tr. A. LINGUIS (Pittsburg 1970). B. LONGERAN, "Metaphysics as Horizon," Greg 44 (1963) 307–318. J. MARIAS, *Metaphysical Anthropology*, tr. F. LOPEZ-MORILLAS (University Park, Pa. 1971). I. RAMSEY, ed., *Prospects for Metaphysics* (London 1961). L. VERSENYT, *Heidegger, Being and Truth* (New Haven 1965).

[G. F. KREYCHE]

MEXICAN-AMERICAN CULTURAL CENTER

The idea for the Mexican-American Cultural Center (MACC) was initiated by *PADRES in February 1971 and it was officially launched by the Texas Catholic Conference in September 1971. The first programs started in June 1972. Since that time over 6000 students from throughout the U.S. and other countries have followed MACC programs.

The purpose of MACC is to serve as a center of continuing research, education, and leadership formation in the field of bilingual and bicultural relations in the United States. Through its work the MACC seeks to promote the betterment of the Hispanics in the United States, especially the Mexican Americans, through understanding, appreciation, and action. In order to carry out its task, the Center is divided into four institutes.

The Institute of Religion in Culture conducts courses and develops materials which take into account the historical-cultural situation of the Mexican-American and the teachings of the Church on culture and social justice. The Center has been designated as one of the official centers of liturgical research and implementation by the National Conference of Catholic Bishops.

The Institute of Language conducts research into the spoken languages of the frontier regions of the United States and conducts intensive courses in Spanish and in English which are especially designed for people who will be working in the Hispanic apostolate.

The Institute of Leadership Development seeks to identify and prepare local neighborhood leaders so that they might be more effective in the work of their communities. The Institute of Publications publishes the products of the research of MACC's teams and distributes them and other related materials.

The MACC also provides specialized programs for seminarians and for missioners preparing to go to Latin America, and offers consultation services to various pastoral groups.

[V. ELIZONDO]

MIDDLE EAST, CHURCH AND

In the decades since the establishment of the modern State of Israel the Church has frequently addressed itself to the thorny and seemingly intractable problems of the Middle East. The conflict that exists between Israel and her Arab neighbors involves political, military, and religious factors that have a long and complex history. The burden of resolving that conflict falls primarily on the principal agents, but characteristics unique to the Middle East invite the intercession of other states and other communities. Jerusalem and the Holy Places are of special concern to representatives of the three great monotheistic faiths that hold them sacred. The strategic importance of the region and the danger that a local conflict could erupt into a more devastating war, involving even the superpowers, compels the interest of other countries. Against this background the Church has continuously asserted the need for wise negotiations that would bring peace to the beleaguered people of the area and give special status to Jerusalem.

Almost immediately after he was elected Pope Paul VI spoke out on issues related to the Middle East, sometimes formulating general principles, sometimes speaking to specific events. He reiterated the explicit message of previous papal statements, calling attention to the special status of Jerusalem and the need for international guarantees. As an earnest of his concern he visited Jerusalem—the first pope to do so—in 1964.

Paul continued to express these concerns when he received high-ranking representatives of Israel: Minister of Foreign Affairs Abba Eban in 1969; Prime Minister Golda Meir, the first Israeli Prime Minister to visit the Vatican, in 1973; and, most recently, in 1978 Minister of Foreign Affairs Moshe Dayan.

Although the distance between the papal and the Israeli positions on Jerusalem remains significant, it has not stood in the way of the increased understanding and respect that has developed between the Catholic Church and the Jewish community in recent years. For example, when the Pontifical Commissions for *Religious Relations with Judaism issued a set of guidelines for Catholics in 1975, it recommended joint Catholic-Jewish work for social justice at local, national and international levels. Although it failed to mention the State of Israel, as some Jewish spokesmen pointed out, it was welcomed by Jews in Israel and other countries.

In messages to and in meetings with leaders of the Arab countries, of the Soviet Union and of the United States, and in international meetings, Paul VI reaffirmed the need for fair negotiations that would weigh the rights and legitimate interests of all sides, including the populations that fled their lands in recent decades. Speaking to the Sacred College of Cardinals in 1975 he referred to the legitimate rights of Palestinians without, however, specifying the extent of those rights.

In the Fall of 1975 the UN General Assembly approved a resolution declaring Zionism to be a form of racial discrimination. In the ensuing debate the Vatican delegate to the UN was one of those who strongly opposed that resolution. At about the same time, in a quite unrelated incident, a Vatican representative rejected the same proposition. In February, 1976, a Vatican Commission cosponsored, with the Arab Socialist Union of Libya, an Islamic-Christian conference in Tripoli. Because of organizational confusion the closing declaration referred to Zionism as a "racial aggressive movement." The Vatican representative disclaimed and repudiated the declaration because of this and other unconsidered assertions.

One sign of the improved relation between the Church and Israel involved Archbishop Hilarion Capucci, the head of the Greek Catholic Church in Jerusalem. In the early months of 1974 Arab terrorists killed a number of Israelis and in August of that year the Syrian-born archbishop, who was allowed to leave and reenter Israel without customs inspection, was arrested and jailed on charges of smuggling arms to terrorists. At the end of 1977, in response to Pope Paul's letter to the President of Israel, the archbishop was released.

These closer relations between the Church and the worldwide Jewish community will make it easier to consider in a constructive way possible causes of misunderstanding, for example the controversial new Israeli law that went into effect on April 1, 1978. The law, which makes it a prison offense to offer or accept material inducements to convert to another religion, has been criticized by liberal Jews and Christians in Israel and other countries, the president of the American Jewish Committee fearing that it would hinder "mutual trust and close relationships and a consequent danger of the loss of solid support Israel enjoys from [Christian] constituencies."

When, in the Fall of 1977, Egyptian President Anwar el-Sadat made his trip to Jerusalem, Pope Paul warmly greeted this remarkable step, calling it "a sign of peace." He again expressed those general principles, which have never wavered, concerning Jerusalem and the need for all the peoples of the Middle East to live in peace and security, with respect for the rights of all.

Although the pope, of course, speaks as the head of the Catholic Church, other voices within the Church have spoken to the issues of the Middle East. Because the United States plays such an important role in the area, the positions of Christian and Jewish communities in the U.S. are very important. It is noteworthy, therefore, that the 1973 resolutions of the United States Catholic Conference, "Toward Peace in the Middle East," was widely praised by people who hold differing positions and equally noteworthy that the comprehensive political solution it outlined remains applicable today.

The renewal of terrorism inspired by the Palestinian Liberation Organization and the reprisal that brought Israeli troops to southern Lebanon in the Spring of 1978 have diminished the hopes for peace inspired by the Sadat visit. Paul and his successors have been compelled to deplore both terrorism and the destruction caused by the strong reprisal, and to recall the goal of peace that still eludes the peoples of the Middle East.

See also ISLAMIC/ROMAN CATHOLIC DIALOGUE; JEWISH/ROMAN CATHOLIC RELATIONS.

Bibliography: USCC, *Towards Peace in the Middle East* (USCC Publ. Office, Washington, D.C. 1973).

[J. FINN]

MIGRANT FARMWORKERS (U.S.)

Migrant farmworkers as a distinct social and economic group began to emerge during the 1930s and the 1940s when the American agricultural system began to be revolutionized. This revolution was influenced partly by the Great Depression and the Dust Bowl of the 1930s and more importantly by agricultural mechanization and scientific methods introduced in the 1930s and 1940s. Subsequent changes in the present time have produced the more recent phenomenon of "agribusiness" and the gradual decline in the number of migrant farmworkers.

For the migrant farmworker each government and controlling agency or organization uses its own specific and limiting definition. In general, however, a migrant farmworker is one who harvests crops by traveling from place to place either within a state's boundaries or across state lines or both. Working side by side with migrants in the fields are seasonal farmworkers who usually harvest in a small, defined area close to their homes. Statistics regarding the migrant farmworkers are either nonexistent or completely inaccurate and unreliable. Even the federal agencies, including the Departments of Agriculture and Labor, do not defend the accuracy of their statistical data and analyses. The numbers, therefore may stand anywhere between 250 thousand and 2 million migrant and seasonal farmworkers. The ethnic and racial make-up of the migrants is similar to that of the general population, but with larger percentages of Mexican-Americans, Puerto Ricans, Blacks, Filipinos, and Poor Whites. A recent influx of Carribean peoples is now influencing the migrant population of the Northeast United States. Regardless of racial or ethnic background most migrants subsist below the national poverty income level established by the federal Office of Economic Opportunity.

As can be inferred from this lack of official recognition, the migrants remain a marginated people, living outside the main currents of American life. The fact that special programs, often inadequate and dehumanizing, are set up for migrants during their sojourn in particular areas of the nation only adds to their marginality and classification as "outsiders." Even the Churches, including the Roman Catholic Church, fail to integrate these migrant peoples into their permanent worshiping communities, but prefer to set up separate and patronizing programs for them. As a result, the migrants do not receive the necessary material, physical, and spiritual care that they so desperately need. These conditions exist not only in the states to which the migrants travel during harvest times, but also in their states of origin.

The largest of the four great migrant streams is out of the Lower Rio Grande Valley in Southeast Texas to virtually every part of the nation, but more especially to the Midwestern and Northwestern states. The East Coast stream originates in the home-base state of Florida and flows up the Coast even into Canada. Merging with this stream is one originating in Puerto Rico and the other Carribean islands and flowing into Florida and on up the Coast or directly into the Northeastern states. Finally, there is the California stream which primarily remains within that state with minor flows into the adjacent states to the east and north. Intrastate migrants can be found in Hawaii and even in Alaska. Thus, every state of the nation receives or supports migrant farmworkers who, however, tend to remain invisible to the general population, on the margin of or excluded from the life of society.

Injustices. Marginality and exclusion lead to many injustices and discriminatory practices. Vatican Council II addresses itself to the just rights, obligations, and treatment of workers, including farmworkers and those who migrate (*Gaudium et spes* 63–72; *Apostolicam actuositatem* 11). Many workers now have protection under the law through watchdog interventions and practices of the federal and state governments as well as that of labor unions. Migrant farmworkers, however, are regularly excluded from such protection by direct or indirect actions and laws, nonenforcement of existing laws, or sheer unconcern.

As a result migrants are subjected to the vilest living conditions, especially when they are following the crops. They are deprived of toilet facilities, safety precautions, and legitimate bargaining power. They must endure slave wages, insecticide and herbicide sprayings, and restrictions in their freedom of movement. Child labor is common and in some places sanctioned by law. Indeed, 63 per cent of all migrants are under sixteen years of age, the majority of whom work the fields as adults; some are as young as five and six years old. This child labor results in erratic or nonexistent education; 90 per cent of migrant children may not finish high school. Most migrants have only a fourth-grade education.

As for health, it is estimated that between 85 and 90 per cent of migrants suffer from malnutrition, especially in their early childhood years; and these are the people who keep the rest of America alive by harvesting and providing its food. Naturally, such malnutrition causes maldevelopment and in some cases brain damage.

There remain high incidences of diseases which, for the general American population, have been virtually done away with.

Pastoral care for migrants is minimal and inconsistent. Because the migrant is forced to work when the crop is ready, church attendance, religious education programs, and spiritual consultations are sporadic and lead church ministers to conclude unjustly that migrants are not a "religious" people. Quite the contrary is evident if pastoral care takes into consideration the plight, unique life style, and culture of the migrant farmworker. However, while the Church is beginning to understand the migrant a little better, not much is being done to implement effective programs and realistic pastoral apostolates for the migrants, which often clash with the more conventional approaches in pastoral care.

Programs and Problems. The USCC Secretariat for Hispanic Affairs has a migrant specialist office to research the needs of the migrant farmworkers. The USCC/NCCB sponsors National Farmworker Week in May and also supports the organizing efforts of farmworker unions. Many dioceses and archdioceses have seasonal migrant programs. However, little work is being done to assess the culture and life-style of the migrants and their migratory patterns in order to coordinate and implement appropriate apostolates and programs on the national and regional levels and, more urgently, between receiving states and the home-base states. Migrants themselves, especially parents, are almost never consulted in the planning of services or programs aimed at their needs. Thus, many of these services and programs miss the mark out of sheer ignorance of the real needs and concerns of the people they are supposed to be helping.

In recent years the phenomenon of undocumented farmworkers has complicated the situation of the domestic migrant farmworker, especially in the border states of the Southwest. The undocumented workers who are seeking relief from the unjust and oppressive labor conditions of their own country (most come from Mexico) enter the United States, thinking conditions to be better. Because of the accustomed lower standard of living of undocumented workers and the unprotected wage scale of the farming industry growers hire them instead of the domestic migrants at lower wages and so avoid the necessity of ameliorating working and living conditions. Domestic migrants, therefore, suffer from unemployment and, while the undocumented rarely seek relief through federal and state welfare programs, more citizen-migrants are forced to avail themselves of these services. Thus, a vicious and unjust cycle of oppression and misery and exploitation continues.

A fundamental answer to the migrant farmworker's plight is unionization. Vatican II explains the right of workers to organize into labor unions in order to secure and protect their rights to just living and working conditions (*Gaudium et spes* 68). In the U.S., however, and notably in the agricultural states of the South and Southwest where most migrant and seasonal farmworkers live and work, this right to organize is effectively minimized and even preempted by Right to Work laws favoring "agribusiness" owners. Many Churches, especially the Roman Catholic Church and the National Farm Worker Ministry, officially support the efforts of farmworkers to organize into labor unions. This support is clearly evidenced in the struggles of Cesar Chavez'

United Farm Workers of America in California and Florida, Antonio Orendain's Texas Farm Workers, and Baldemar Velasquez' Farm Labor Organizing Committee in the Midwest. Such movements, originating with the farmworkers themselves, not only advance the causes of justice in the lives of the migrants and agribusiness, but help to raise the migrants' self-esteem and enrich their self-image greatly. The farmworkers cry of "*Si, se puede*," has profound meaning for social justice and change.

The issues of grave injustice touched upon are complex and intricate and many times controversial and contested. But even a superficial review of the farm-labor system and the institution of migrancy reveals a highly unsatisfactory set of circumstances. The injustice inherent in the American farm-labor system ought to be a concern to all Americans, all of whom profit in a significant, material way from the present unjust system. And, while the correction of this system is for all an obligation of personal justice, it is of much more binding force for the Churches. Like the Apostle James (5.1–6), the Church must raise its prophetic voice loud and clear against the system which allows and perpetuates such gross social injustice, and it must take up the cause of the migrant farmworkers of America, the American *Anawin* of God, in order to secure for them the social and human rights of which the nation boasts.

[G. B. DYER]

MIGRATION, INTERNATIONAL

The transfer of residence from one country to another on a more or less permanent basis can take place between two countries of the same continent (intracontinental migration) or between two different continents (overseas migration). In recent years, improved travel facilities and increased international economic links have created greater mobility; migration thus often takes the form of temporary work abroad without the initial intention of permanent resettlement.

Motivation. All migration is basically the result of unsatisfactory conditions in the home country and the hope that migration will be an improvement. Usually a distinction is made between economic motivation and fear of persecution. In the first case, the migrant decides to leave his home country because of the impossibility of earning an adequate living for himself and his family. This migration is always directed to countries with a higher standard of living. Political and religious persecution of individuals or social, ethnic, or tribal groups continues to occur in many countries of the world. Fear of persecution motivates many people to flee at the risk of their lives without knowing to which country they may eventually migrate.

Migration Regulation. Although the right to migrate ("right to liberty of movement and the freedom to leave any country, including one's own") is included in the UN Universal Declaration of Human Rights (1948), national legislation restricts the freedom of migration. Legislation in all countries lays down conditions that must be fulfilled and sets numerical and other limitations. Certain countries facilitate the immigration of refugees, but the definition of who is a refugee differs. Unemployment and economic setbacks may lead to restrictions or suspension of immigration. Some countries deny outright the right to emigrate to their citizens.

Freedom of movement is granted to nationals of the European Community (Common Market) by virtue of a multilateral agreement. In other instances, migration is subject to regulations laid down on a bilateral basis. Restrictions on immigration make it impossible for millions of unemployed people to obtain an immigration visa. Illegal immigration has thus assumed considerable proportions in recent years. Illegal immigration is a serious problem to the host country and places the immigrant in a marginal situation without rights to social security, normal pay, or family reunion.

History and Volume of International Migration. Migration is a phenomenon as old as mankind. The largest international migration of more recent times took place during the 19th century. Approximately 50 million Europeans migrated to North America, 20 million to Latin America, and 17 million to South Africa and Australia during that century. During the same period about 16 million Africans were moved to America and some 11 million Chinese and 5 million Indians to East Africa and America. After World War II, 1.5 million displaced persons emigrated, mainly to North America and in lesser numbers to Australia and Latin America. Although migration continues to take place, there is particular emphasis on certain movements at certain periods. In the 1950s the accent was on national migration from European countries to the United States, Canada, and Australia. The 1960s were marked by large-scale movements of migrants between countries of the same continent that involved, for example, 12 million people in Europe. This phase of migration ended with the 1973 oil crisis which created economic difficulties and unemployment. During all this time, there has been a continuing influx of refugees from Eastern Europe. Following the change of regime in Cuba, some 650,000 persons left that country and migrated to the United States. The change of government in Chile in 1973 caused an important refugee migration and the end of the war in Indochina was followed by a mass exodus from Vietnam, Cambodia, and Laos, which still continues. Politically unsettled conditions and persecution have led to mass migration movements on the African continent involving 1.5 million people.

Church Concern in International Migration. The interest of the Church in international migration has expressed itself far back in history and numerous papal statements and church documents have stressed the importance of active assistance by church services to those compelled to leave their homelands. Following Vatican Council II, the motu proprio, *Pastoralis migratorum cura*, of Pope Paul VI in 1969 (ActApS 61 [1969] 601–603) updated the norms on the pastoral care of migrants reviewed in the light of the Council, the evolution of human mobility, and new forms of migration. The first part of this Instruction lays down general principles on such social and religious implications of the migration phenomenon as the fundamental rights of human beings and service for the common good, expressed, e.g., by duties of migrants towards the host community. Reflecting the basic directives of Vatican Council II, the Instruction on care of migrants also closely associates laymen in the work of the Church and outlines the precise tasks assigned to them.

The overall pastoral care of people on the move has been entrusted to the Pontifical Commission for Migration (itinerant people) and Tourism created by Paul VI's motu propio, *Apostolicae caritatis* of March 1970 (ActApS 62 [1970] 193–197). In the field of social assistance to migrants and refugees, the Church's tasks are performed by the *International Catholic Migration Commission, an organization concerned with the problem of population movements and the migration of refugees and nationals. This coordinating agency of Catholic migration services in 45 countries was created in 1951 at the instigation of the Holy See. At the national level, there are Church-related services to migrants in most emigration and immigration countries. Those services provide counselling before departure, assistance in obtaining visas, travel arrangements, and arrival-notification of the Catholic agency in the receiving country so that appropriate reception services can be made available. In countries without existing government services for immigrants, the Catholic agency through a network of diocesan offices finds homes and jobs for those who arrive.

The Church has always been particularly concerned for the family in migration. Separation of families is often a consequence of migration and through Catholic services everything possible is done to reunite split families.

[E. WINKLER]

MIGRATION, RIGHT OF

The clear and consistent teaching of the Church affirms that "every human being has the right to freedom of movement and of residence within the confines of his own country; and, where there are just reasons for it, the right to emigrate to other countries and take up residence there. The fact that one is a citizen of a particular state does not detract in any way from his membership of the human family as a whole, nor from his citizenship of the world community" (John XXIII PacTerr 25). The Pastoral Constitution on the Church in the Modern World points out the various causes and reasons which can lead men to the decision to justly leave their homeland in favor of a land offering more equitable solutions to their economic, political and social problems (*Gaudium et spes* 65, 66, 84).

Christian Principles. The biblical foundations for the right to migrate form a basic theme in the Old Testament. Beginning with God's entrusting of his creation to man and woman (Gn 1.28), the Bible teaches that God formed his chosen People through the migration of Abraham (Gn ch. 12 and 13). With the Exodus experience the Old Testament recognizes the rights of the migrant and the obligations one has toward the alien migrant. These same rights and obligations then become part of the Law (Ex 3.9–10; Lv 19.33–34; and Dt 10.17–19). Thus, an attitude and behavior pattern is set up among the Jewish people toward the migrant (Is 58.6–7; Ps 146; Sir 3.28–4.10).

The New Testament reiterates the Jewish Law in more general terms, certainly with the intention of establishing the universality of a common brotherhood and sisterhood of men and women and common heritage from God. God is recognized as the source and owner of all creation, the care and use of which is entrusted to men and women (Mt 6.25–34; Jn 19.9–11; Acts 4.32–35). The example of Jesus, as the refugee (Mt 2.13–15) and as the immigrant (Mt 2.19–33), suffices to give us the clear NT message on the right to migrate, as do the many travels of the Apostles and disciples of Jesus.

The constant teaching of the Fathers, doctors and theologians of the Church on the right to migrate is presented by St. Thomas Aquinas in the consideration of the common right to this worlds' resources (ST 2a2ae, 66.1–2). In the *Instruction on the Pastoral Care of People Who Migrate* (Congregation for Bishops, 1969; ActApS 61 [1969] 614–643) it is explicitly stated that "this right (to migrate) pertains not only to individual persons, but to whole families as well" (7; cf. Synod JustWorld pp. 38–39).

Problems. While the Church's position on migration remains clear, the problem of 50 million world migrants remains a serious problem of a dimension affecting almost every nation and state of the world. Migrant peoples are a "sign of the times" in the formal sense of Vatican Council II. God reveals his message of liberation in these times through the ongoing events of world societies. Surely migration is one of these revelations and migrants themselves are witnesses to and victims of a world in turmoil and change. The Christian and social implications of this phenomenon are great, especially for the wealthier societies of the world and most specifically for the United States.

Because of the gross injustices and inequities of the world economic and political systems the right to migrate is being violated. The movements of individuals and families within countries (*see* MIGRANT FARMWORKERS, U.S.) and across international boundaries for legitimate and just reasons are being limited and in many cases prohibited by the oppressive and self-interested motives of many governments. Naturally this affects the poor and the oppressed much more than the rich and powerful. Yet it is precisely the poor and the oppressed who, for economic, political, and social reasons, have the greatest need to migrate in order to improve their human condition. The rich and powerful many times use their right to free and almost unrestricted movement through tourism, international residency, and business trips to further oppress, either directly or indirectly, those already suffering human and social degradation. These flagrant violations of the right to migrate create serious moral problems in modern societies and demand prophetic and practical responses from national and regional Churches through the voices of their hierarchies.

The right to migrate is clearly a right flowing from the human nature of man and is endorsed along with its obligations by the Christian Church within the Judeo-Christian tradition. The Church in this tradition also clearly defines the just response of host communities to the person and needs of the domestic migrant and the foreign immigrant with or without proper documentation (*see* MIGRATION, INTERNATIONAL).

[G. B. DYER]

MIGRATION AND REFUGEE SERVICES OF THE USCC

Although the Catholic Church of the United States has been assisting migrants and refugees since the nation's founding, the first coordinated approach was instituted in 1921 when under the auspices of the then National Catholic Welfare Conference a Department of Immigration was founded. This Department of Immigration received a new mandate in 1965 and became the Migration and Refugee Services of the United States Catholic Conference (MRS).

This new organization encompassed the refugee resettlement activities previously carried on by *Catholic Relief Services and the activities of the Catholic Committee for Refugees, which provided support of programs for orphans, religious, and professional refugees and immigrants. Through the cooperation and coordinated activities of the Catholic Church of the United States, it has been possible for MRS to provide resettlement opportunities for over one million people over the past 30 years. These refugee movements included those displaced in the aftermath of World War II, those who fled the revolutions in Hungary, Czechoslovakia, and Cuba, the displaced of the Middle East, and those still being cared for by Southeast Asian Refugee Program.

At the present time, MRS is identified as the world's largest private agency in the migration field. Through a series of 8 regional offices and 40 diocesan components, MRS provides direct case work assistance in the immigration and migration field to approximately 200,000 persons each year. MRS actively coordinates its worldwide activities through the Geneva-based *International Catholic Migration Commission. MRS also acts in a consulting capacity to the legislative and administrative structures of the U.S. Government in the field of immigration and refugee affairs. All the services of MRS-USCC are provided without charge and without reference to the nationality, race, religious or political convictions of those served.

[J. E. MCCARTHY]

MINDSZENTY, JÓZSEF

Cardinal-archbishop of Esztergom, primate of Hungary; b. March 29, 1892, Mindszent, Hungary; d. May 6, 1975, Vienna, Austria. For a major part of his long and distinguished career in the Church, Cardinal Mindszenty personified the struggle for religious freedom under the Communist regimes of Eastern Europe. From the time of his 1949 show trial and imprisonment by the Communist rulers of Hungary, through his release during the 1956 Hungarian Revolution and his long self-imposed imprisonment in the American legation in Budapest, to his eventual exile from Hungary, his personal fate symbolized the current condition of Church-State relations.

The political convulsions which afflicted Hungary during his lifetime inevitably drew Cardinal Mindszenty into public affairs. His village of Mindszent, where his family owned a small farm, had changed little under centuries of Habsburg rule, but his studies for the priesthood opened the wider world of classical learning. By the time of his ordination, June 12, 1915, World War I had begun to dissolve many traditional social and political relationships as well as to impose extraordinary demands on his services as a curate, teacher, newspaper editor, and community advisor. The loss of the war and the overthrow of the Habsburg monarchy left a political vacuum in Hungary. The activities of the young priest on behalf of the newly formed Christian Party brought him into disfavor with both Count Károlyi's moderate leftist government and its successor, Béla Kun's short-lived Hungarian Soviet Republic. The shift to the rightist policies of Admiral Horthy's regency allowed twenty-five years of dedicated parish work in Zalaegerszeg with politics overshadowed by concern for the community and the schools.

His elevation to the episcopate in March 1944 as Bishop of Veszprém brought Mindszenty to a position of national leadership while the country was again suffering the ravages of a world war, which Hungary had entered as an ally of Nazi Germany. When the Hungarian government imitated the Nazi persecution of Jews, the Hungarian bishops vigorously protested the violation of innate human rights. Recognizing that the war was hopelessly lost, the government negotiated an armistice in October 1944, but German forces installed a puppet regime in Hungary to continue the fighting. Bishop Mindszenty presented a memorandum, signed by all the bishops of western Hungary, urging the new premier, Ferenc Szálasi, to end the senseless destruction Because of this memorandum, the Szálasi regime arrested Bishop Mindszenty. He remained a prisoner until the complete German withdrawal from Hungary in April 1945.

The end of the war left Hungary devastated and disillusioned. Bishop Mindszenty, who became archbishop of Esztergom in September and a cardinal in February 1946, organized relief efforts to overcome the food shortages, to treat the widespread illnesses, and to provide for refugees. His determination to uphold the traditional constitutional authority of the Archbishop of Esztergom led Cardinal Mindszenty to issue increasingly outspoken warnings about the threats facing the newly established democratic regime. As the Hungarian Communists consolidated their power by gradually eliminating other parties, the Church became the last focal point of resistance and the prime target of hostile propaganda. Cardinal Mindszenty's protest of the nationalization of Catholic schools in 1948 led to his ultimate conflict with the regime. He was arrested on December 26 and placed on trial in February 1949. The public trial of the Primate of Hungary demonstrated that no one could resist the will of the regime. After forced confessions from the Cardinal and a mass of fabricated evidence against him, the court found Cardinal Mindszenty guilty of treason and sentenced him to life imprisonment. The harassment of the Church also included the arrest of other bishops, the cessation of religious instruction, and the dissolution of religious orders.

The 1956 Revolution in Hungary freed Cardinal Mindszenty on October 30. When the populace enthusiastically welcomed his return to Budapest the next day, the government of Imre Nagy hastily declared the previous legal actions void. In a radio address, Nov. 3, Cardinal Mindszenty justified the revolution as a fight for freedom. He advocated neutrality, democratic elections under international control, private ownership, and religious freedom, but he carefully avoided lending support to Nagy's government or any other political faction. Less than eight hours after his speech, Soviet troops occupied Budapest and crushed the revolution. When the Soviet troops arrived, Cardinal Mindszenty sought refuge nearby in the U.S. legation. He received asylum and remained for fifteen years in spite of the protests of the Hungarian government and papal entreaties to accept a post in the Roman Curia. The Hungarian Primate believed his persistence called attention to the oppression of Hungarian Catholics, but it also obstructed Vatican efforts to reach an accommodation with the Communist regime. At the urging of Pope Paul VI, he left Hungary in September 1971 and took up residence at the Hungarian seminary in Vienna. Fifteen months before his death he unwillingly relinquished his position as Archbishop of Esztergom, while sternly proclaiming his disagreement with the Vatican pursuit of improved Church-State relations in Hungary, which allowed the appointment of new bishops. Citing examples of continued restrictions on the Hungarian Church, he announced characteristically, "In these grave circumstances Cardinal Mindszenty cannot abdicate."

Bibliography: B. KOVRIG, *The Hungarian People's Republic* (Baltimore 1970). J. MINDSZENTY, *Memoirs* (New York 1974). G. N. SHUSTER, *In Silence I Speak* (New York 1956). F. A. VALI, *Rift and Revolt in Hungary* (Cambridge, Mass, 1961).

[R. J. GIBBONS]

MINISTER OF MUSIC

"Minister of Music" is a title slowly acquiring common usage in the Roman communion, and at this state in its history, it does not enjoy a clearly defined and well-developed meaning. However, some trends can be seen to emerge from current practice.

Presently, according to popular usage, the title "minister of music" is being given to the organist, the cantor, the choir director, as well as the director of the folk-music program, depending on circumstances. All these are leadership positions, and some would limit the term to these particular roles. There is, however, another trend in the use of this term. It would include all those involved in the total music ministry program, such as all the members of the choir, as opposed to the director only. Further, the composer and the publisher have distinct roles to play in the development of music in worship, for the one is the creator of the music with which the local community will pray, while the other makes the music available in an attractive and accessible format.

Only time will tell which direction the term will finally take, for much depends on a clearer understanding of what ministry is. A very distinct possibility of development, however, is that used by non-Roman Churches, where the minister of music is the person ultimately responsible for the entire music program within a given worshiping community. Normally this person will be regarded as a professional in the true sense of the term, and will be salaried. At the same time, the minister will bring to the position a competence demonstrated by specialized training, most often attested to by academic degrees. This trend should prove the most beneficial in terms of bringing quality musicianship to the praying community.

Musical competence, however, remains only a part of the total picture of what constitutes the role of the minister of music. For this person is not only a minister of *music*, but is, as well, a minister within liturgy, and is thus a minister of the praying, worshiping community. What this means in actual practice is that the music minister brings to this position not only professional competence, but is also prepared to work within liturgical structures. He/she will take the liturgical facet of the total ministry as seriously as the musical demands and will seek to acquire the necessary skills needed for the position. The minister must be constantly aware of the delicate role this position assumes, as the ministry itself undertakes the position of facilitator of prayer through music in the midst of the assembled community. Liturgical-prayer expectations place new responsibilities on the minister of music, who can never act as a musician only, but must be a vital part of the total praying community.

The art and craft of music will be at the service of the liturgy, which means that certain expectations will be made of the competence of the musician and the music used. To be this serving person means, then, to be sensitive to the community and to the moments of prayer in which this community engages when participating in the liturgy.

The prayer of the Church properly served, coupled with competence properly recompensed, will increasingly mark the minister of music who will unite the skills of a craft with the prayer-life of the Church. Whatever direction the varied understandings of the ministry of music may take in the future, these two criteria will most assuredly be decisively present in the final picture.

See also LITURGICAL MUSIC.

Bibliography: Bishops' Committee on the Liturgy, *Music in Catholic Worship* (USCC Publ. Office, Washington, D.C. 1972).

[L. DURST]

MINISTRIES, LAY

The lay ministries, as distinguished from the sacred ministries, are those which are not entered through a sacramental ordination, but rather through an "institution." The currently recognized ministries for which such a rite exists are the ministries of lector or reader and acolyte.

While prior to the 1972 reform (by Paul VI in the motu proprios *Ministeria quaedam* and *Ad pascendum*) these ministries, along with those of porter and exorcist, were classified as minor orders and conferred through an ordination; the reform has returned to the more ancient practice of institution. The purpose of this change is to revive the value of these ministries as permanent in church life, instead of having them be merely a stage toward priestly ordination. They are ministries of lay people, not of clerics. In spite of this, the motu propios still provide for the institution of candidates for presbyteral and diaconal ordination into these ministries. The reason for this is strictly pedagogical, arising from a desire to provide such candidates with this type of formational and training experience and to indicate the developmental nature of diaconal and presbyteral preparation.

The ministry of reader, in addition to the responsibility of proclaiming the Scriptures in the liturgical assembly, includes the responsibility of preparing the faithful to receive the Sacraments. The ministry of acolyte, in addition to the responsibility of service in sacramental celebrations, includes the responsibility of distributing Communion if there is need, and of training other faithful who have liturgical functions.

While current church discipline permits the institution of women into neither ministry, such a prohibition is not to be interpreted as forbidding or discouraging women from performing the functions of reader or *extra-ordinary minister of the Eucharist. This clarification, printed in *l'Osservatore Romano* on Oct. 6, 1972 (p. 2), went on to say that no decision had been made about admitting women to these institutions, but that the prohibition had been retained pending further investigation.

There is an openness to the further development of lay ministries. *Ministeria quaedam* speaks of this in two ways. First it speaks of the possible reestablishment of previously existing ministries, such as porter and exorcist. Apart from New Testament times, other lay ministries which received varying degrees of recognition within the Church were those of catechist, cantor, widow, grave-digger, confessor, and subdeacon (until 1207 when it made a major order, now abolished). Second, it speaks of the possible establishment of a ministry of charity in cases where deacons do not exist, or this work is not being done by deacons. This notation is important because it indicates the Church's willingness not only to break new ground, but also to go beyond the liturgical/ritual categories of ministry.

In the U.S. there is a formal ministry, that of *minister of music, now recognized, and discussion of that of catechist in the future. Outside the U.S., the growth of Sunday worship assemblies without the presidency of a priest or deacon, especially in France, Central and South America could well provide another opportunity for the development of a new formal lay ministry.

See also MINISTRY, UNORDAINED; WOMEN IN MINISTRY.

[P. J. LEBLANC]

MINISTRIES, SACRED

The sacred ministries, as distinguished from the lay ministries, are those which are entered through sacramental ordination. The two forms of ministry belong to the way the People of God share in the universal priesthood (*Lumen gentium* 9–11). These are three: the ministry of deacon, the ministry of priest or presbyter, and the ministry of bishop. Since the reform of 1972 (Paul VI MinQuaedam; AdPasc), the ministry of subdeacon no longer exists.

The ministry of deacon, in accord with the wishes of Vatican Council II has been restored as a ministry in its own right, and no longer serves simply as a ceremonial function or as a stage prior to ordination as a presbyter. The requirement of celibacy is no longer linked to this order (*Lumen gentium* 29; see 16:123).

Presbyters form a collegial body under the headship of their bishop. Together, bishops and their priests assume responsibility for and the direction of the pastoral care of a local Church, both internally building up the Church, and bearing witness to the world at large through their life-style and work of evangelization. As their numbers grow, and their ministry becomes more established, permanent deacons too will participate in this responsibility.

See also PRIESTHOOD, UNIVERSAL.

[P. J. LEBLANC]

MINISTRY (ECCLESIOLOGY)

In its teaching on the ministry, Vatican Council II incorporated several elements from theologians who in the preceding decades had given renewed meaning to that word (see *Lumen gentium* 20, 21, 24, 32; *Gaudium et spes* 21). Since the Council there has been a further rediscovery of the New Testament vocabulary of gift and service. This has given rise to a growing awareness of the diversity and plurality of ministries in the Church, and of their importance for the Church's vitality.

Vocabulary. In early Latin translations of the NT *ministerium* and its cognates were used to translate διακονία and its cognates, as well as the less frequent λειτουργία. The best English rendering of *diakonia* is the word "service." The NT uses the term for activities in the Church which issue from the graces of the Spirit and build up the body of the faithful. The less commonly used *leitourgia* intimates that these activities bear the character of true worship, since they build up the priestly people in whom God is glorified.

In ecclesiastical usage *ministerium* came to be used almost exclusively of the ordained members of the Church. It took on connotations of power and official authority which the original Greek term does not possess. This use of words is itself a sign of the growing tendency to reduce the laity to a passive role in the Church and to confide mission and responsibility predominantly to the clergy. Vatican II gave sanction to a trend to reverse this situation that had begun earlier in the century. In its documents the Council continued to reserve the vocabulary of ministry for bishops, presbyters, and deacons, while using terms such as *munus*, *missio*, *charisma*, *apostolatus* and *officium* for the works of the laity. By reason of such usage, it was able to maintain a distinction between the role of ordained ministers and that of the laity, while at the same time recognizing the active part which the latter have in the mission of the Church and in service to the community. Furthermore, the Council recalled the original meaning of ministry or *diakonia* and stressed the need for the ordained to model their ministry on the service of Jesus Christ. Since then, there has been even greater attention given to the use of the word *diakonia* in the NT sources, and a deeper examination of the relation between the ministries of the laity and those of the ordained.

Origin of Ministries. The many ministries derive from the charisms, or gifts of service, which are given by the Spirit. The coordination of these gifts to the service of the common good is also the work of the Spirit. Every ministry is modelled on that of Jesus Christ (cf. Lk 22.24–27) and all power (ἐξουσία) in the Church is a share in his power (cf. Mt 28.18–20). The good of the Church and its mission requires order and leadership. The early Church turned to the Twelve (known by Luke as Apostles) or to their immediate associates, such as Paul, for this service.

That much, in brief, is the position which emerges from an exegesis of the New Testament. When little attention was given to the ministries of lay persons, it was enough for theology to explain that the power and authority of the bishops derive from the mission given by Christ to the Apostles. Given a broader concept of ministry, theology has to take other factors into account and offer a different synthesis. Three converging principles may serve this purpose. They are the Pauline teaching on the Body, the relation of all ministries to the model of the Twelve, and the action of the Spirit in the Church through time.

Pauline Teaching. The Pauline image of the Body expresses the Church's relation to Christ and his Spirit and is an effective image of her unity in plurality. Amongst other things, it brings home the corporate nature of her life and mission, as well as the personal share which each member has in the gifts of the Body and service to its life. On the basis of this image Vatican II can refer to the Church as the *sacramentum seu signum et instrumentum intimae cum Deo unionis totiusque generis humani unitatis* ("sacrament or sign of intimate union with God and of the unity of all mankind" *Lumen gentium* 1.1). Ministries contribute to the reality and witness of this corporate life and mission.

Apostles as Model. The Twelve are an eschatological image of the Church of the New Covenant, which, filled with the Holy Spirit as foretold by the Prophets, takes part in the banquet prepared by God for the Christ. Being likewise the Apostles sent by Christ, they transmit not only a life of discipleship and faith but also the mission which they received from him. Ministries in the Church derive from this mission and are modelled on that of the Twelve, in whom the early community found exemplars of disciple, pastor, and missionary.

Action of the Spirit. It follows from this that ministry is by the gift of the Spirit a share in the mission and saving power (*exousia*) of God in Christ. The intervention of the Spirit is necessary, since it is the role of the Spirit to keep alive the historical remembrance of Christ and the Twelve, while at the same time providing for that newness of creation which each epoch requires. Indeed, the remembrance is itself a source of fresh creativity, since it gives the Church an eschatological focus on history, a grasp that the Church is always an event, and the realization that she lives constantly under the judgment of God and in his hope.

A conclusion to draw from this eschatological model is that a call to mission and service is already given in the Sacraments of initiation whereby a person becomes a member of the eschatological community. Vatican Council II recognizes this in many ways, not least in its Decree on Priestly Ministry when it implies that ordination specifies the mission already given at initiation (*Presbyterorum ordinis* 1.2). Of every adult Christian it can be said that her/his call is determined by the gifts of the Spirit, of which there is a guarantee in the Sacraments of initiation. For some, these are given special recognition and a new sacramental role through the Sacrament of Order.

Classification of Ministries. Different classifications or typologies of ministries are offered to explain their respective contributions to the life of the Church. The division offered by the Council is based on the theology of the triple office of Christ, namely, that of Priest, Prophet, and King. The works of both laity and ordained ministers are diversified in terms of their participation in one or other of these offices (*Lumen gentium* 9–12).

Another classification, more descriptive in character, is based more directly on the New Testament. It distinguishes ministries of word, sacrament, and care, drawing either from the listings of ministries (e.g. Rom 12.6–8; 1 Cor 12.4–11.28–31; Eph 4.11) or from what is known in other ways, of life in the NT Church. The principal ministries of the word are those of the apostles, the prophets, and the teachers, but the listings cited would also allow inclusion of such gifts as exhortation, tongues, and the discernment of spirits from the listings quoted. Of the ministry of sacrament or worship little specific is said in the New Testament. The foundation on which such ministry is explained naturally lies in what is said of the Eucharist and Baptism, and some would also draw from texts on the presidency of communities (e.g. Rom 12.8; Heb 13.17.23), but this is rather uncertain ground. An important feature in this classification is the recognition given to the ministries of care. The category includes the service of tables (cf. Acts 6.1–6), the care of the sick (cf. Jas 5.13–16), the widow and the orphan (cf. Acts 6.1–6; Jas 1.27), healing (1 Cor 12.10), and the administration of community goods (cf. 1 Cor 12.28 on administrators and helpers). Sometimes in theology the NT word *diakonia* is used for this category alone instead of being employed for all ministries. The works falling into this category have equal status with the ministries of word and liturgy. Hence they are not to be judged inferior or less necessary. Their exercise in the life of the Church today is not a mere repetition of New Testament days, but takes on new needs and new forms.

Another classification of ministries distinguishes them by way of their relation to those aspects of the Church's life that are designated by the Greek words μαρτύρια, διάκονία, and κοινονία (witness, service, communion). A similar distinction refers them to the Church's mission to evangelize, to the inner life of each community, and to the relations fostered between communities. This is to take up the notes of the Church which are its apostolicity, its unity, and its catholicity, and to relate ministries to them.

Clearly, no classification of ministries is adequate or exhaustive, nor may it be used to restrict development of new ministries or new ways of exercising old ones. A first limitation to be found in every classification is that some ministries overlap the types given. Thus the promotion of justice and peace could be classed under word, since it pertains to prophecy and to teaching, but it could also be classified under care, since it promotes human welfare in Christ's name. A second limitation to any typology is that the types may not appear to be comprehensive. Thus in the second classification mentioned, some would posit judgment as a fourth class of ministry, while others include it under word and still others place it under sacrament, relating it thus to the Sacrament of binding and loosing. Awareness of these shortcomings is a reminder that theology's task is to understand the wonders of the Church's variety in unity, not to establish stringent categories.

Ordained Ministry. Both history and dogma distinguish between ordained ministry and other ministries. It is less clear where the nature of this distinction resides. Given the new respect for lay ministries the question has become a more acute one in recent theology (*see* MINISTRY, UNORDAINED; LAITY, VOCATION OF). Many things are involved in the discussion, including the nature of ecclesiastical *authority, the offices reserved to the ordained, the purpose of the Sacrament of Order for the life of the Church, and the structure internal to the Sacrament. It is now more commonly recognized that the theology of Order derives from the theology of the Church and not vice versa as in an earlier system. Likewise, the authority of Order has to be related to common responsibility and mission of the community and is incomprehensible outside that context.

The call to ordained ministry comes as a special call from Christ and the Spirit, but it is mediated through the Church and requires sacramental incorporation into the ministerial college to be effective. How this mediation is to be effected is both a practical and a theological crux. The intervention of the episcopacy as the normal way of proceeding is not in question. It is more difficult to determine the just part played by the faithful in the choice of ministers and in the transmission of office. It is also difficult to assess situations where leadership and sacramental presidency have been assumed or granted outside the normal channels of episcopal succession.

Ordained ministers are certainly not mere delegates of the community. To say this would be to deny the unique source of power in Christ and the Spirit. At the same time, a rigid identification of episcopal succession with *apostolic succession ignores all other authority and ministry in the Church and has serious practical as well as theological consequences. To express the delicacy of the relationship between the ordained minister and the community, some recent theology prefers images or concepts of leadership and presidency to those of power and *jurisdiction. It is further pointed out that the authority of office is normally grounded in the spiritual authority of the person to whom the office is confided. Those dogmas which affirm that the power of Christ works in the Sacraments despite the unworthiness of the minister speak to unhealthy situations to give assurance that the grace of Christ is not rendered void by bad ministers, but such dogmas do not constitute the basic principles for a theology of Order.

When the Eucharist is taken as the central point and summation of the Church's life and mystery, then the liturgical presidency of the ordained minister can be understood as the focal point of the community's relation to the Trinity. Ministry and authority are thus related to the service of the Church as a communion in faith and worship (see CHURCH AND COMMUNIO). There is room also in this image for a proper recognition of the power and spiritual authority of the nonordained ministries, since the word presidency does not suggest a monopoly of worship. It is rather the encouragement, the recognition, and the ordering in unity and harmony of all ministries, relating them in the liturgy to the communion of the Church and the glory of the Father.

Lay Ministries. Besides the multiple problems concerning the relation of ordained to common ministries, the Church today also discusses the institutionalization of some lay ministries. This means a designation to a particular function, made by the hierarchy at some level and recognized as a common procedure rather than as a unique instance. Specifically, the motu proprio of Paul VI, *Ministeria quaedam* (ActApS 64 [1972] 529–534), promoted the institutionalization of the functions of acolyte and lector for the universal Church. It also urged local episcopates to consider the need for other ministries deserving of similar recognition in their respective constituencies. Hence there are movements towards setting up formal appointment to the ministries of catechist, psalmist, marriage counsellor, or even that of lay president in communities which have no resident ordained pastor.

This practice may be either promotional or restrictive, or perhaps a combination of both. While the intention of *Ministeria quaedam* was to promote a wider share of the laity in liturgical and catechetical roles, its implementation at times appears restrictive. This is all too easily the case when it is supplemented by the appointment of *extraordinary ministers of the Eucharist. It can very easily happen that what of its nature belongs to all is in practice confined to the few, in the interests of what is deemed better order. To take the Lord's Body to other Christians and to read God's Word in the liturgy are offices which of their nature can be carried out by any mature Christian. At the moment some disciplinary measures may be needed to regulate this, but in the long run the phase of lay ministering marked by the institutionalization of these offices can only be temporary.

The question then remains whether similar procedures might be used to promote other ministries,

particularly urgent for the life and mission of the Church at a given time and in a given place. Coming readily to mind is the need to promote ministries that work for justice or those that take up the call to dialogue with other religions. Whether the process of institutionalization can ever fully avoid forms of neo-clericalism is an open question. Hence it may be more fitting to think in terms of a testing and discernment of gifts and ministries within communities and of their subsequent incorporation into the communion of faith and worship through prayer and mutual encouragement.

Bibliography: Y.-M. CONGAR, *Ministères et communion ecclésiale* (Paris 1971). B. COOKE, *Ministry to Word and Sacraments. History and Theology* (Philadelphia 1976). J. DELORME, ed., *Le Ministère et les ministères selon le Nouveau Testament. Dossier exégétique et réflexion théologique* (Paris 1974).

[D. N. POWER]

MINISTRY, EDUCATION FOR

Prior to Vatican Council II, the term "ministry" was popularly used to refer to positions of leadership in Protestant Churches (9:870). Among Roman Catholics, such words as "priesthood" and "hierarchy" were more familiar; more significantly, the status of the ordained was sharply distinguished, both in theology and in fact, from the position of the laity in the Church. Since Vatican II, the laity has increasingly come to share with the clergy in many different ministries. Simultaneously, postconciliar theology has tended to focus on the ministry of Christ and to relate all other forms of ministry to his. Thus, the current usage of "ministry" encompasses the whole spectrum of Christian service and witness, of both the ordained and the non-ordained.

Wider Scope. This shift in postconciliar thought and practice is reflected in the changes in education for ministry in the United States. Before Vatican II, the programs offered by most Catholic schools of theology were primarily geared to preparing seminarians for ordination to the priesthood; members of religious communities who were preparing for apostolates that did not require ordination usually enrolled in separate programs; relatively few programs were available for lay people. After Vatican II and a decrease in vocations to the priesthood and religious life, positions formerly held by clerics and religious began to be filled by qualified lay people; in addition, new forms of ministry developed in response to a broad variety of needs within the postconciliar Church. For example, the decision in 1968 to introduce the permanent diaconate (16:123) in the United States necessarily led to the establishment of training programs for deacon-candidates. Simultaneously, other types of programs were initiated for people who wished to prepare for nonordained ministries: many schools of theology began graduate programs designed for those working in religious education; some universities inaugurated programs in such areas as liturgy and music, spirituality and counseling, and church administration.

Programs for Praxis. Along with new academic curricula, numerous experience-based programs also appeared. Some of these programs are designed to introduce beginning students to the practical dimensions of ministerial work; other programs are intended to help experienced ministers improve their professional competence. Accordingly, programs vary widely in their goals and their educational methodologies. On the premise that ministry is the art of caring for others, some programs concentrate on teaching techniques that will enable ministers to work more effectively; other programs, however, recognizing that ministry requires a blending of theory and practice, are concerned with aiding ministers in achieving a personal integration of their theological learning and their ministerial life. For example, clinical pastoral education, offered by the departments of pastoral care in many hospitals, not only trains people to minister to the sick and dying but also encourages the spiritual growth of the trainees; many seminaries now require their students to participate in such clinical training. Other on-scene programs are directly concerned with alleviating the needs and developing the resources of poverty-stricken people in inner-city or rural areas; during vacation periods, many college students volunteer for such diversified projects as tutoring children, constructing homes, giving medical assistance, and providing legal aid. Programs training for ethnic ministries, either in this country or overseas, emphasize speaking-fluency in a foreign language and cross-cultural understanding; such programs frequently enroll lay volunteers as well as priests and religious.

Diversity in Instruction. In comparison with the past, the most prominent characteristic of ministerial education in the postconciliar church is diversity. On the instructional level, programs of study have been considerably revised and, in many places, totally new programs have been introduced. For example, theological instruction, which formerly followed a scholastic approach, now utilizes a plurality of methodologies (see PLURALISM, THEOLOGICAL); supervised pastoral fieldwork, which formerly was lacking in most schools, is now widely accepted as an integral component of ministerial formation. Simultaneously, institutional relationships have been expanded; for example, the introduction of pastoral programs has brought theological schools into closer contact with the parishes and other institutions, where students work in off-campus ministries. Similarly, ecumenism has motivated cooperation in ministerial education; in many places, arrangements have been made for the exchange of professors and the cross-registration of students from neighboring schools of different religious traditions. The most striking sign of diversity, however, is visibly personified by the student body in many schools of theology: among those preparing for the priesthood are not only recent graduates of college seminaries but also men of various ages who have had other occupations; in addition to candidates for the permanent diaconate, priests on sabbatical are updating their education; religious sisters and brothers, along with lay men and women, are preparing for future work in the Church.

In sum, theological schools are also "training centers for ministry," where students from a cross-section of the Church are educated in preparation for a diversity of future ministries.

See also LAITY, FORMATION OF; MISSIONARY FORMATION; PERMANENT DIACONATE, FORMATION FOR; PHILOSOPHY IN SEMINARIES; THEOLOGY IN SEMINARIES: WOMEN, THEOLOGICAL FORMATION OF.

Bibliography: The National Conference of Catholic Bishops has provided normative guidelines for the operation of seminaries in *The Program of Priestly Formation* (Washington, D.C. 1971); 2d rev. ed., 1976). Current developments in ministerial education are regularly discussed in the *Seminary Newsletter*, issued by the Seminary Department of the National Catholic Educational Association (Washington, D.C.) and in *Theological Education* (Vandalia, Ohio), published by the Association of Theological Schools in the United States and Canada; both these organizations also issue occasional publications concerned with current topics in ministerial education.

[J. T. FORD]

MINISTRY, UNORDAINED

The word "ministry" does not appear in the indexes of Abbott or Flannery, the two main English collections of Vatican Council II documents, even though the term is prominent, e.g., in *Lumen gentium*. Only in the postconciliar era has the meaning of ministry been appreciated and explored fully in Catholic theology. The earlier article in the *New Catholic Encyclopedia* (9:871) dealt with ministry as a Protestant term. The Council of Trent in reacting to the Reformers emphasized priesthood to the point that other leadership roles in the Church were in practice nonexistent. *Catholic Action and the apostolate of the laity were attempts in this century to reclaim some leadership for laity. However, the theology of Vatican I prevailed; the theological structure of the Church was still monarchical and all leadership was vested in the hierarchy; the layman participated through delegation. The full membership of all in the Church was restored through the theology of Vatican II. While Vatican II still used the clergy-laity distinction, it laid the ground for its elimination by rooting ministry not in the hierarchy but in the total Church, the People of God (cf. *Lumen gentium* 9–12).

There is a current reaction to the clergy-laity distinction as implying that all authority rests in the hierarchy, with elitism and abuses of clericalism as the results. Laity became defined negatively, as non-priest. When Vatican II used "People of God" as the overarching description of the Church, "laity," which is from λαός, Greek word for people, had not been reestablished as a positive word. The term was still laden with a history of subordination.

"Ministry" is the term which captures many of the subsequent shifts in theology (see MINISTRY). The Church itself is increasingly understood as a community in which the faith and its expression in service are vested primarily in the community and secondarily in its individual members. It is primarily the community which offers faith and service and not simply individual, delegated members. Second, membership in the Church comes through Baptism and Confirmation which bring the recipient to full life in the Church, in which ministry (or mission) is a constitutive part. This represents a shift from a view that saw Baptism as giving recipients a right to receive the other Sacraments, a position of passivity, and the Sacrament of Order alone as giving the power to a few to confer the Sacraments on the many. Baptism is now understood as entry to full membership and a call to mission or ministry (see HOLINESS, UNIVERSAL CALL TO; PRIESTHOOD, UNIVERSAL).

Ministry as a positive concept which embraces all the services performed in faith by the members of the community in their public and private life and as members acting in the name of their particular church community (see CHURCH, LOCAL). The theology of ministry flows from the theology of gift or charism, a reality rooted in Pauline theology and reasserted currently (see CHARISMS IN MINISTRY). The shift is away from emphasis on the power of the institution and towards the diverse works of the Spirit in each member of the community.

Ministry has the advantage of being a term of biblical origin and at the same time of being capable of expressing the styles and content of service in the Church without implying subordination or clericalism. There are three frames of reference for the idea of ministry that can be distinguished without being neatly compartmentalized and without one's subordination to the other: (1) ministry to the world, (2) ministries within the local Church, (3) the special ministry which confers office.

Ministry to the World. Ministry to the world is service in the name of Jesus Christ and involves an inner call experienced and acted on. Ministry so taken may have the form of witness in favor of some cause of justice or of simple performance of the tasks of daily life in reverence, joy, and peace. Those who see such a ministry to the world as a call, a response to a deeper power in life, do not ask for the Church to authenticate this call. That call is the actualization of their vocation as Christians. The prophets were people who ministered but without legitimating credentials; they relied on a deep inner source, the power of God, for authentication.

Ministries in the Local Church. Ministries in or to the Church are the action of people who perform services in the local Church. If Church itself is seen as ministry to the world, then ministries within the local Church are in this sense also ministries to the world. In the post-Tridentine Church the priesthood absorbed all ministries. Others served within the Church not by their baptismal commitment or the discernment of the local Church but by the nod of the pastor. He, not the community, was the legitimator of all ministries. In the U.S. today the Catholic charismatic movement has introduced "gift" into the Catholic vocabulary and raised the challenge that the local Church recognize ministering gifts. Increasingly, works people do in the name of the Church are being seen as ministries: visiting the sick, hospitality, directing retreats, care of the aged. The number is without limit. The local church community is able to name the gift and offer the possessor of it the credentials to act in its name. This is done implicitly by acknowledgement of the service or explicitly by community approval in a church ritual. The universal Church has begun to move in this latter direction, with the formal institution into the ministries of reader and acolyte (see MINISTRIES, LAY). Other church-approved ministries are envisioned (see MINISTER OF MUSIC).

With the recognition of ministry to the world as a call of God and the institution into ministries through ritual, ordination to the ministries of deacon, priest, and bishop is set in a larger and less exclusive context than earlier, one that puts aside a dichotomy between priest and lay person.

Ministry Conferring Office. However special and different in kind and nature from the ministries of people in secular life and from ministries of lay people in the church community, the ordained ministries are above all ministries of the Church, not the special possession of a person. The deacon, priest, or bishop acts for the community. He presides at community events; he does not perform community events in the name of a personal priesthood. He speaks for the community rather than to it. In New Testament terms, he is one gifted member of the community; the community affirms this gift, as it does the unique gifts given to each person in the local community.

Bibliography: H. LEGRAND, "Ministries: Main Lines of Research in Catholic Theology," *Pro Mundi Vita* 50 (Brussels 1974) 7–16.

[D. J. GEANEY]

MISSIOLOGY

Missiology is the systematized study of the mission of the Church and of the ways in which its mission is carried out (9:900). There are major changes and development in its meaning since Vatican Council II.

Vatican II and Missiology. Vatican Council II marked a new era in Catholic mission theory (see MISSION OF THE CHURCH). Among the most significant missiological ideas of the Council were: the Church as missionary by her very nature; the personal responsibility of every Christian for missionary action; unity in diversity as the form of catholicity most consistent with the nature of the Church; human betterment in all its forms as a major and integral part of the missionary task; ecumenical and interfaith understanding and cooperation as an officially approved direction to be followed in missionary situations. Closely related to these ideas was the Council's emphasis on "the signs of the times," on the central role of the Holy Spirit in evangelization and planting of Churches, on decentralization of church authority, and on declericalization. Although all of the conciliar documents might be said to be relevant to the Church's missionary task (e.g., *Sacrosanctum Concilium*, in its insistence on liturgical adaptation; *Nostra aetate*, in its respect for such non-Christian religions as Buddhism, Hinduism, and Islam; *Unitatis redintegratio* in its appreciation of ecumenical understanding and cooperation), the most important contributions to missiology were the Dogmatic Constitution on the Church (*Lumen gentium*), the Pastoral Constitution on the Church in the Modern World (*Gaudium et spes*), and the conciliar decree focused specifically on mission activity, *Ad gentes*.

Post-Conciliar Missiological Thought and Practice. The basic sources of information regarding post-conciliar missiological thought are: (1) the various preparatory and other documents connected with the 1974 *Synod of Bishops on evangelization, especially Pope Paul VI's Apostolic Exhortation *Evangelii nuntiandi* (Dec. 8, 1975); (2) the thought and practice of the various regional Churches; (3) contemporary missiological literature; (4) current trends in missionary training, planning, and research.

The 1974 Synod of Bishops on Evangelization. Although the Synod concluded with only a short and disappointing declaration, many months of invaluable preparation, on the national and regional levels, preceded the meeting. The synodal documents, especially Pope Paul VI's synthesis of the Synod in *Evangelii nuntiandi*, proved to be a useful vehicle for reaffirming, clarifying, and concretizing the various Vatican II ideas on the basis of almost a decade of worldwide experience.

The first value of these documents lies in the fact that they reaffirm and reinforce such important conciliar statements as the need to respect the individual's conscience, the need for the whole Church to be mobilized and engaged in evangelism, the closeness of the relationship between liberation and evangelization, the necessity of local self-determination, and the salvific influence of Christ outside the Church.

Moreover, the Synod and related documents have

served to clarify certain issues which have become of special concern during and after Vatican II, for example, the fact that an understanding of mission must not be limited to mission lands, since the real meaning of mission embraces the whole secularized and de-Christianized world community as well. Or again, as Pope Paul VI warned at the close of the Synod, while stressing diversity in the Church, one must not lose sight of the need for unity; while appreciating the need for small, close, and sympathetic communities (*comunidades de base; see* BASIC CHRISTIAN COMMUNITIES), one must not overlook the importance of *universal* identity; while developing local theologies, one must continue to appreciate the *entire* Gospel and *all* of Revelation. Or, as Pope Paul VI explained a year later in his *Evangelii nuntiandi*, qualitative rather than quantitative growth of the Church is of primary importance; and, by way of further clarification, the Church can effectively evangelize only when it is itself genuinely renewed and when its testimony is active.

The third contribution made by the Synod was the concretization of some significant missiological theory, for instance, how to recognize the authentic signs of God's presence in our times, how to make the best possible use of the laity in the life of the Church, and how to form "a small basic Christian community" where there was a great shortage of priests.

The Direction Taken by Regional Churches. A second important source of information regarding recent missiological developments is the actual practice of the various regional Churches, perhaps best illustrated by Latin American, African, and U.S. efforts.

CELAM (Consejo Episcopal LatinoAmericano), the continental council of Latin American episcopal conferences, has looked upon the mission of the Church as evangelization *and* humanization. With this double goal in view, pastoral plans and new structures for Latin America have been developed. There is today a new awareness of the presence of the Holy Spirit in Latin America and a dramatic spread of the charismatic movement. A rapid growth in bible study and reflection in terms of the specific local needs and cultural heritage is now taking place, with the social dimension of sin, and Christ as sole and true liberator, coming into focus in a very meaningful way and as never before (*see* LATIN AMERICA, CHURCH IN).

African Churches have chosen a somewhat similar direction. As in Latin America, the African Church has witnessed a new awareness of the Holy Spirit and a spread of the charismatic movement. The chief emphasis, however, is contextualization and indigenization—in a word, the emphasis is on Africanization of the African Church (*see* AFRICAN CHRISTIANITY).

One of the earliest practical responses to Vatican II in the U.S. was the establishment of the *U.S. Catholic Mission Council, representing the American hierarchy, mission agencies, and religious and lay missionary groups. One of the very first steps taken by this council was the issuance of an important missiological statement ("The Whole Missionary Church," June 8, 1971), which identifies concretely the consequences for the U.S. Catholic Church flowing from the declaration of Vatican II that all bishops share a collegial responsibility for church growth and that every Christian—priest, religious, lay—personally shares in the missionary task. A statement by the major superiors of U.S. men and women religious addressed to the U.S. Catholic Mission Council in May 1976 marked a further advance in U.S. Catholic missiological thinking. In the joint statement of the *Conference of Major Superiors of Men (CMSM) and the *Leadership Conference of Women Religious (LCWR) entitled "Our Hopes and Concerns for Mission" the one concern of the superiors that seemed to be facing American mission efforts today was the danger of a missiological myopia—isolation, self-centeredness, and a timid, limited, and shallow understanding of the missionary responsibility. The central hope of the superiors included the following points. (1) The U.S. mission effort should respond creatively and enthusiastically "to the *cri de coeur* for self-determination," not in a token manner but, as *Evangelii nuntiandi* puts it, "in depth and right to the roots" of cultures—true self-determination calling for creative liturgy, genuinely indigenous faith expressions, new authentic methods of theologizing and the type of economic and social liberation which the suffering people themselves longed for. (2) The American Church should not work so much *for* newer Churches as *with* them. (3) The American missionary effort should seek not only to give but to receive, not only to enrich but to be enriched. According to the statement of the religious superiors, such hopes and concerns presupposed close cooperation with the hierarchy, internal renewal within religious institutes themselves, new formational programs for religious (including the development of a sense of global responsibility and an opportunity for practical apostolic experience in a culture other than one's own), and an openness to diversification of ministries and lifestyles. The statement suggested that one-time missionary Churches should be invited to send personnel to the American Church with a view to enriching America. Emphasized, too, was the fact that lay leadership must, at all times, be genuine leadership, a leadership that is not a mere substitute or temporary measure for a shortage of priests. The statement pointed out also that active advocacy of such causes as peace, justice, and human betterment should be regarded as a legitimate and important missionary role for priests and religious.

Missiological Literature. A third source of information regarding post-conciliar trends in missiology is current professional literature, which might best be described as generally pastoral rather than theoretical in nature, often ecumenical in scope and application, and not seldom confused and contradictory.

Although some excellent, strictly theoretical literature has appeared in the post-Vatican II period, modern missiology seems to be oriented more toward such pastoral and practical problems as secularization, liberation, revolution, peace and justice, humanization, and dialogue with non-Christians.

Perhaps the main missiological thrust in recent literature has been in the direction of local theologies—theologies that are the result of interdisciplinary efforts and that are viewed both as *scientia* and as *praxis*. One form of local theology, the so-called *liberation theology, has become a major force in Latin American church life, and its influence is strongly felt among U.S. Black Christians (*see* BLACK THEOLOGY). Another form of local theology, the biblical, "dynamic equivalent" model, has, so far, had little response from Catholic missiologists. According to the proponents of this model, the essential and universally valid core of

Gospel truths must be "translated" into the local cultural forms of newer Churches in such a way that the resulting response of the local Church is equivalent to that of the early New Testament Christian communities. A basic assumption of the model is that the Gospel is concerned primarily with the meanings it wishes to convey rather than with the forms it uses to convey the meanings. Among Catholics, the main advancement in contextualization is seen in the abandonment of the former superficial type of "missionary adaptation" as a partial tool for communicating the Gospel and in the adoption of genuine accommodation as the very goal of mission. Instead of the former token adaptation, the Gospel is "incarnated," i.e., the Gospel takes on flesh of the particular time and place in the fullest sense of the term. The chief agent of conversion in incarnational adaptation is not the sending-Church but the local community itself under the guidance of the Holy Spirit and in constant dialogue with the universal Church (see INCULTURATION, THEOLOGICAL).

Missiology today no longer seems to reflect any particular "school" of thought, e.g., Münster, Louvain. On the contrary, missiological publications reveal a broad spectrum of views and approaches corresponding to the diversity found in professional missiological associations, workshops, and conferences, now tending to be ecumenical in scope. Thus, the American Society of Missiology and the Association of Professors of Missions—the two professional associations of missiologists in the United States—and the International Association for Mission Studies are all ecumenical. The leading professional missiological periodical in the U.S. today is *Missiology*, a publication that is nondenominational and that has considerable Catholic participation. The leading Catholic publishers of missiological works in the U.S. are Orbis Books of Maryknoll and the Paulist Press, both publishers having a broad ecumenical outlook.

Modern missiological writings, while showing an openness to new ideas, are often confused and contradictory—in a word, still searching, still in transition. The general tendency toward radical theologizing that occurred soon after Vatican II has affected missiology no less than it has all theological reflection. In the late 1950s, the age-old problem regarding the salvation of unbelievers had once again been revived by Karl Rahner's theory of the "anonymous Christian." The subsequent confusion and controversy regarding the salvific nature of non-Christian religions continued during and beyond Vatican II. The emphasis of the Council on pluriformity, local cultural heritage, freedom of conscience, respect for the values in non-Christian religions, and the availability of God's grace outside the visible Church seemed to be saying to some missiologists far more than had been intended by the Council. Some missiological writings have claimed that the purpose of missionary action was "to make the Hindu a better Hindu, and the Mohammedan a better Mohammedan." In the words of Gregory Baum for instance, the missionary's main task may not be to convert people to Christ but to lead them "to cling more faithfully to the best of their religion's tradition and to live the full personal and social implications of their religion more authentically (Baum 46)." While some missiologists have tended to agree with R. Schlette and Hans Küng that pagan religions are actually the "normal" and

"ordinary" means of salvation, others, like Henri de Lubac, have rejected any such substitute for Revelation or the Church. The worldwide calls for self-determination especially in the Third World and the support which these calls received from Vatican II have led a few isolated Catholic missiologists to propose a moratorium, a temporary halt to all foreign funding and personnel so as to enable the newer Churches to develop their own strength and selfhood without outside interference and control. Only by such a drastic measure would a missionary Church be free to experience Christ and to express this experience in accord with its real needs and cultural heritage. Similarly, the strong emphasis placed on liberation and development throughout the world has made some missiologists wonder—despite the emphasis of Vatican II to the contrary (*Ad gentes* 6) and despite the efforts at the 1974 Synod of Bishops on evangelization to clarify the relationship between development and evangelization —whether today's missionaries are not meant primarily to be humanizers rather than evangelizers. Such examples of confusion and contradiction might of course, be multiplied, so that the label "transitional" attached to much of the post-conciliar writings seems well justified.

Training, Research, and Planning. Another important indicator of modern missiological trends is the direction that present-day missionary training, research, and planning are taking. Only a few decades ago—despite papal directives to the contrary—the training of missionaries even in strictly mission-sending societies was more or less identical with that given to church personnel being prepared for activities in their homelands. Vatican II sought to correct the situation (*Ad gentes* 26, 34) by insisting that special premission as well as field training be given to missionaries. Emphasized was a thorough understanding of the principle of "unity in diversity" and a good grounding in such disciplines as ethnology, sociology, comparative religion, history of religions, and missiology. Missiology is described by *Ad gentes* as knowledge about "the teachings and norms of the Church concerning missionary activity . . . what roads the heralds of the Gospel have run in the course of centuries, and also what is the present condition of the missions, and what methods are considered more effective at the present time" (*Ad gentes* 26). Some missionaries, *Ad gentes* suggests, should be given an opportunity for professional training in these disciplines, while centers for pastoral planning and special institutes for professional study and research in such fields as missiology, ethnology, linguistics, and the scientific study of religions should be established (*Ad gentes* 34).

The response to Vatican II in this regard generally has been quite positive. Today, training programs in cross-cultural sensitivity are the rule rather than the exception for missionaries and local church leaders. Field experience in a culture other than their own has become a part of many theological training programs for future missionaries. Graduate degrees in cultural anthropology, linguistics, missiology and other missionary-related fields are now being pursued as perhaps never before. In many mission areas, practical mission-orientation as well as updating and continuing education for missionaries and local leaders are now a matter of policy. Centers for pastoral research, planning, and training have been established in Asia, Africa, Oceania, and Latin America. It is from this new trend in training, research and planning that one might expect the greatest development in Missiology in the future.

See also MISSIONARY FORMATION; MISSION PLANNING.

Bibliography: G. H. ANDERSON and T. F. STRANSKY, eds., *Mission Trends* (New York; Grand Rapids, Mich. 1974–76) Nos. 1–3. G. H. ANDERSON, "Mission Research, Writing, and Publishing," in W. J. DUNKER and W. JO KANG, eds., *The Future of the Christian World Mission* (Grand Rapids 1971). *Basic Communities in the Church, Pro Mundi Vita* (September 1976). G. BAUM, "Mission and Power: A Reply," *Ecumenist* 11 (1973) 44–46. R. PIERCE BEAVER, ed., *The Gospel and Frontier Peoples* (Pasadena 1973). D. BOHR, *Evangelization in America* (New York 1977). J. COMBLIN, *The Meaning of Mission: Jesus, Christians and the Wayfaring Church*, tr. J. Drury (Maryknoll, N.Y. 1977). G. GUTIERREZ, *A Theology of Liberation* (Maryknoll, N.Y. 1973). P. DAMBORIENA, "Aspects of the Missionary Crisis in Roman Catholicism," in W. J. DUNKER and W. JO KANG, eds., *The Future of the Christian World Mission* (Grand Rapids, Mich. 1971). F. GLASSER, "Missiology—What's It All About?" *Missiology* 6 (1978) 2–10. "Hopes and Concerns for Mission" (CMSM/LCWR presentation for USCMC Annual Assembly, May 1976. Washington, D.C.). L. LUZBETAK, *The Church and Cultures: An Applied Anthropology for the Religious Worker* (Pasadena, 4th pr., 1977); "Two Centuries of Cultural Adaptation in American Church Action: Praise, Censure or Challenge?" *Missiology* 5 (1977) 51–72; "Understanding 'Cross-Cultural Sensitivity': An Aid to the Identification of Objectives and Tasks of Missionary Training," *Verbum SVD* (1975) 3–25. *Missions in Theological Education: Proceedings Twelfth Biennial Meeting, Association of Professors of Missions* (Wheaton College, Wheaton, Ill., June 9–10, 1970). "The Whole Missionary Church: A Statement by the United States Catholic Mission Council, June 8, 1971" (Washington, D.C. 1971). PAUL VI, *Evangelii nuntiandi*, Eng. tr., *On Evangelization in the Modern World* (USCC Publ. Office, Washington, D.C. 1976). T. RYAN, "Contemporary Roman Catholic Understanding of Mission," in R. PIERCE BEAVER, ed., *American Missions in Bicentennial Perspective* (Pasadena 1977). "Shifting Concepts of Mission," *Occasional Bulletin of Missionary Research* (entire July 1977 issue). R. SCHREITER, "The Anonymous Christian and Christology," *Missiology* (1978) 29–52. S. TORRES and J. EAGLESON, eds., *Theology in the Americas* (Maryknoll, N.Y. 1976).

[L. LUZBETAK]

MISSION (NEW TRENDS)

The notions of mission and missionary activity in 1977 involve far more complex and sophisticated ideas than a generation ago. A concise explanation of the meaning of primary concepts and of terms in their current usage is essential to an understanding of mission in the Church.

From the outset, a distinction should be made between "missionary activity" and "mission." In the Vatican Council II's Decree on the Church's Missionary Activity, the conciliar Fathers affirm that "the pilgrim Church is missionary by her very nature" (*Ad gentes* 2) and that "this mission is a continuing one" (ibid. 5). "Missionary activity," on the other hand, is an expression used in a more limited, geographical sense: "The specific purpose of this missionary activity is evangelization and the planting of the Church among those peoples and groups where she has not yet taken root" (ibid. 6).

Reverse Mission, Mutuality of Mission, and Mission to the Six Continents. The term "reverse mission" is often confused with the idea of mutuality of mission. Some prefer not to use the expression because, they claim, it connotes paternalism. It is acceptable, however, if it is taken to mean the role the returned missioner assumes in the Church of his native country. Out of his experience with other cultures and other expressions of Christian faith he can make a valuable contribution to the education of Catholic people in his homeland. He can bring them to an awareness of the social, political, and economic injustice prevalent in the Third World; to an awareness of the enrichment of faith deriving from contact with the Church in other parts of the world.

"Mutuality of mission" refers to the current trend in the Church to refer to mission as a situation of reciprocity, mutual assistance. The Church is present virtually throughout the world and all Christians can and should be exercising mission toward others. But they can also be the recipients of mission. Third World speakers can do much to sensitize Christians in North America and Europe to the plight of the many who suffer physical hunger, racial discrimination, political oppression; to the need for a more equitable distribution of wealth; to the dangers of consumerism and materialism. In a not-too-distant future, missionaries from Asia and Africa may be working in post-Christian countries of Europe and the Americas.

The expression "mission to the six continents" is a term used to highlight the fact that mission is not limited to geographical areas. There are large segments of the world population outside the traditional "mission" countries who need the Gospel message, i.e., the missions to the "unchurched" in North and South America and Europe, the many peoples living under totalitarian regimes, migrants, and the marginated poor.

The Integral Concept of Mission and Evangelization. It is evident from numerous statements of Pope Paul VI and the Synods of Bishops that the mission of the Church is an evangelization directed toward the whole man. The missioner attempts to reach men and women, not only by the explicit preaching of the Word, but also by the witness of his life, by championing the cause of justice in an effort to effect the total liberation of men, by promoting human advancement and development in all spheres of society (Paul VI EvangNunt 30–31). Evangelization involves the prophetic proclamation of hope in the promise made by God in Jesus Christ. This prophetic role extends to the here and now of everyday life in the form of denunciation of injustice. There is no dichotomy between evangelization and humanization; they are different aspects of the same reality. The 1971 Synod of Bishops declared that "action on behalf of justice and participation in the transformation of the world fully appear to us as a constitutive dimension of the preaching of the Gospel, that is, of the mission of the Church for the redemption of the human race and its liberation from every oppressive situation." (Synod JustWorld Introd. p. 34).

In the future, more stress may be put on human development. If evangelization, seen as preaching of the Word only, does not animate that development, it will be left aside. Preaching should reveal, in a radical way, the dignity and deep meaning of man's relationship with his neighbor, without excluding explicit teaching about God and faith in him. It is no longer necessary to make the customary distinction between direct and indirect missionary methods. Into this context, fits the term "salvation." Vatican II described the Church as the "universal sacrament of salvation" (*Gaudium et spes* 45). Salvation is that toward which all men aspire but which, for the present, none possesses fully. Such salvation is not purely spiritual; in the fullest sense of the term, it implies redemption from political and social injustices and transformation of sinful structures. "Universal" indicates that salvation is for all men and not simply for those in the Church.

Moratorium. Some Protestant churchmen (WCC assembly in Bangkok, 1973; Lausanne Covenant, 1974; All Africa Conference of Churches in Lusaka, 1974) have suggested that the Churches of the Third World consider calling a halt to the flow of missionary personnel and funds from other countries—at least for a period. For Third World Christians, such a moratorium would mean taking full responsibility for the work of the Church in their own country and continent and a commitment to support it and its mission. In the Catholic Church the idea has been discussed at the grass-roots level, but no official statement or concrete proposals have been forthcoming. However, the desired goals of moratorium are considered laudable, i.e., to discover an authentic indigenous form of Christianity which can in turn enrich all the Churches of the world; to encourage local Churches to abandon dependent attitudes; to help local Churches to establish their own priorities and become missionary Churches themselves; and to enable mission-sending Churches to reexamine the nature of their mission and their future relationship with other Churches.

Pluralism in Mission. From the earliest beginnings of Christianity there was great variety in liturgy and discipline in the various regions where the Church was first established. Differences in cultural and theological formation, as well as in the psychological and national tendencies of the people, contributed to the formation of different Churches, e.g., Syrian, Coptic, Egyptian. The eighteen existing canonical rites of the Catholic Church are a remnant sign of that primitive diversity. The Apostles and their disciples carried the bare essentials of the Gospel message to various areas of the Mediterranean world where it was accepted and incarnated into the cultural milieu of particular peoples. Liturgy, theology, discipline then developed as characteristic of the local Church.

An incarnational model of mission is espoused by many missiologists and missioners today. It is no longer enough to speak of adaptation, to which many often gave only lip-service. Paul VI speaks of evangelizing "man's culture and cultures (not in a purely decorative way as it were by applying a thin veneer, but in a vital way, in depth, and right to their very roots), in the wide and rich sense which these terms have in *Gaudium et spes*" (Paul VI EvangNunt 20; cf. *Gaudium et spes* 53). African bishops have spoken of the need, not so much to Christianize Africa, but to Africanize Christianity. The consequences and implications of a truly radical incarnation of Christianity in the many cultures of the world are many and not easily foreseeable. A great pluralism in the unity of Christian faith is foreseeable; many local Churches with their own creative liturgies, indigenous expressions of faith, and new methods of theologizing. One beneficial effect might be a revitalized, lived expression of Christian ethics, since experience teaches that moral theology changes. If a Christian ethics is to be deeply influential in the normal functioning of existing cultures, its expression must come from inside those cultures. These questions must be posed: what is the essential, core message of the Gospel without which Christianity cannot exist? what are the accretions derived from European or North American cultural influence? As concrete examples, it can be asked: are bread and wine the only matter permitted in confecting the Eucharist? is polygamy always contrary to the saving message of Christ? (*see* INCULTURATION, THEOLOGICAL; LITURGY AND LOCAL CHURCHES).

The Importance of the Local Church. In the Decree on the Missionary Activity of the Church the Fathers of Vatican II emphasized the importance of the local Church: "The specific purpose of . . . missionary activity is evangelization and the planting of the Church among those peoples and groups where she has not yet taken root . . . In this missionary activity of the Church various stages are sometimes found side by side: first, that of the beginning or planting, then that of newness or youth. When these stages have passed, the Church's missionary activity does not cease. Rather, there lies upon the particular Churches which are already set up the duty of continuing this activity and of preaching the Gospel to those still outside (*Ad gentes* 6; see 19–27). Today it can be said that throughout almost all the so-called "mission world," the local Church has been planted for some time; e.g., there are more Catholic Christians in the continent of Africa than there are in the U.S. (Africa more than 49 million; U.S. about 48 million).

A clear sign that the local Churches are indeed coming of age is the increased number of episcopal conferences. Forty-nine of the ninety-five conferences listed in the 1977 edition of the *Annuario Pontificio* are under the Sacred Congregation for the Evangelization of Peoples. This number does not include the more than sixteen conferences of Latin America and the Philippines. Fuller maturation of local Churches has often coincided with the independence of many new nations, especially in Africa (*see* AFRICAN CHRISTIANITY). National pride has come to the fore. The hierarchy, clergy, and laity in these countries have realized the importance of self-sufficiency and independence in the ecclesial sphere as well. The role of the expatriate missionary is now being seen in a new and different light. Local Churches are becoming acutely aware of the need to inculturate or indigenize all aspects of church life, e.g., liturgy, theology, pastoral practice, ecclesiastical structures.

New ministries of worship, teaching, service, e.g., the permanent diaconate community leadership, roles in *basic Christian communities, etc., are of key concern. They have tended to become a possible area of friction because, as new types of ministry have developed in response to local needs, traditional forms have been called into question. In some areas the new and the old are seen as complementary, while in others they are seen as antagonistic.

The idea, developed by Vatican II, that the local Church as well ought to be missionary, has become the only possible basis of mission in many countries, e.g., Burma, India, and the Sudan, where it is difficult, if not impossible, for foreign missionaries to immigrate. This situation highlights a sadly neglected facet of ecclesiology: that the two vital functions of the Church, pastoral and missionary, are interdependent and should stimulate each other (*see* CHURCH, LOCAL, [THEOLOGY]).

Mission and Ecumenism. One of the greatest obstacles to the spread of the Kingdom among non-Christians has been the centuries-old division among those who profess to be followers of Christ. Groups of missionaries of different Christian denominations, instead of cooperating in a spirit of common witness, have been and are now divided by rivalry in many parts of the world. A heightened awareness of this fact has given impetus to ecumenical efforts in the mission field. Endeavors worthy of note are religious instruction in common, the shared use of church buildings, e.g., in

East Africa, cooperative projects in community development, e.g., CODEL (Coordination in Development), joint renewal programs, sharing of information and research centers in the mission-sending countries, and cooperation in the biblical apostolate. The solid base for these endeavors must be the goal of common Christian witness.

Vital to the success of the ecumenical movement in mission is the total rejection of proselytism, which Tommaso Federici defines as "any sort of witness and preaching which in any way constitutes a physical, moral, psychological, or cultural constraint on individuals and communities, such as might in any way destroy or even simply reduce their personal judgement, free will, and full autonomy of decision at the personal or community level." ("Study Outline on the Mission and Witness of the Church," *Face to Face, An Interreligious Bulletin* 3–4 [1977] 23). Profound study of this definition should give members of all Christian Churches pause for thought regarding certain past and, in some places, current methods of evangelization, e.g., the indoctrination and Baptism of prepuberty children.

The New Role of the Expatriate Missionary and Mission Societies. The first task of the expatriate missionary is that of inculturation. He must attempt to become integrated into the cultural, religious, and social milieu of the people among whom he lives and works. What is now new and different is that he views himself as exercising a subsidiary and supportive role vis-à-vis his indigenous colleagues, be they bishop, priest, deacon, catechist, or lay minister. Not of secondary importance is the obligation he feels to witness to the universality of the Gospel message in a local, often provincial, situation. At times this duty may involve the prophetic teaching of the transcultural and suprahistorical message of the Gospel to an ethnocentric local Church.

The role of missionary societies is at present more undecided than unclear. These societies are attempting new commitments within and beyond their traditional mission areas. There is a general tendency to avoid creating large groupings of society personnel in any one area, so as not to stifle the emerging local Church. Small units of mission society personnel are welcomed into an area by the local Church, in order that they may introduce new initiatives and approaches to mission (cf. *Ad gentes* 30–34). In their home countries, many mission societies, such as Maryknoll, are promoting the establishment of research centers, the operation of documentation and information centers, the formulation of planning procedures, and the preparation of operational plans. They also support national and international organizations such as SEDOS (*Servizio di Documentazione e Studi*), *Pro Mundi Vita*, CARA (Center of Applied Research for the Apostolate), and the Catholic Mission Councils. There is general agreement that greater cooperation and coordination among the mission societies throughout the world is most desirable and would produce excellent results.

Dialogue as Mission. Dialogue as mission is the strategy being emphasized in those parts of the world where Christianity encounters the other great religions. Freedom of conscience, revelation understood as the opening up of human consciousness in contact with the divine, universality of salvation even outside the visible communion with the Church are three themes preeminent in the concept of dialogue as mission. The goal of missionary activity, therefore, is to be seen as the fulfillment of any true and authentic religion through conversion.

In principle, the gospel message in no way aims to destroy anything that is properly valid in the religious experience of men of all faiths. There is a positive desire for dialogue, whether with other Christian Churches, with worshipers of the God of Abraham (Jews and Moslems), with adherents of the world religions, or even, with the appropriate analogy, with atheists. This intention was clearly outlined in Vatican Council II (*Unitatis redintegratio; Nostra aetate*), and by Paul VI in his encyclical *Ecclesiam suam* (1964). There remains the problem of "reconciling respect for individuals and civilizations and sincere dialogue with them ... with the universalism of the mission entrusted to the Church." Missionaries must learn to listen before claiming any right to speak. The insights of other religions can enrich the missionary as they offer him new possibilities of expression and encourage the development of latent talents. The role of the missionary, then, is one of catalyst, attempting to assist in the birth of something one alone cannot produce—a new community of God.

Basic Christian Communities in Mission. For some time, Catholic Christians in Latin America and Africa have been experimenting with small groups of believers, much smaller and more localized than the typical parish, who pray, study their faith, and share a common life together. Not only is the basic community an alternative when no priest is available; even when there is a priest, Christians find their faith renewed when they meet to worship in the intimacy of small groups. Lay leadership and initiative are fostered. Lay leaders direct the Liturgy of the Word, baptize, and when allowed by bishops, officiate at weddings, and distribute Holy Communion. This form of structuring allows for a wide variety of ministries, e.g., visiting the sick, teaching the faith to children, organizing cooperatives.

Inculturation and Missionary Efforts. As a reaction to the ethnocentrism practised in the past by the expatriate missionary in many parts of the world and in response to reflection on the missionary stance of the early Church and St. Paul (cf. Acts ch. 15; Gal ch. 2), the process of inculturation of missionary efforts is currently being reassessed. Authors differ in their use of terminology, i.e., "inculturation," "acculturation," or "incarnation." What is meant is that, like Jesus and the Apostles of the early Church, the expatriate missionary must undergo a threefold process when exercising a transcultural ministry. (1) Jesus, aware of his own identity in the godhead, became a Jewish man in Jewish society. The missionary, also secure in his cultural identity, must attempt to become one of the indigenous population by learning the language, history, culture, and religious values of the people. (2) Jesus lived and grew as a Jew. The missionary must also live and grow with his people. He must absorb their mentality and insert himself into the society and the local Church. (3) Jesus assumed a prophetic role. He perceived the evil in his society and denounced it. So also the missionary must attempt to discern the evils in society and, together with the local Church, correct them. He will be unable to find the right answers unless he himself, within the limits of the humanly possible, becomes integrated into the societal milieu and sees the Gospel through the eyes of his people without the encumbrance of his own cultural background. The three phases of this process may occur simultaneously, and they constitute an ongoing conversion (*metanoia*) essential to any effective missionary effort.

Bibliography: G. H. ANDERSON and T. F. STRANSKY, eds., *Mission Trends No. 2* (New York and Grand Rapids 1975). G. H. ANDERSON, ed., *Occasional Bulletin of Missionary Research* 1, No. 3 (Ventnor, N.J. 1977). W. BÜHLMANN, *The Coming of the Third Church* (Maryknoll, N.Y. 1977). The LADOC 'Keyhole' Series, ed. Latin American Documentation, USCC (Washington, D.C. 1976). E. HILLMAN, *Polygamy Reconsidered* (Maryknoll, N.Y. 1975). J. J. SHIELDS, *Attitudes of American Women Religious Towards the Concept of Mission* (Washington, D.C. 1977 private printing). J. L. SEGUNDO, *The Community Called Church* (Maryknoll, N.Y. 1968).

[C. M. FEIL]

MISSION OF THE CHURCH

Christ commanded his Church to continue his mission on earth and to help bring it to completion. To speak of the mission of the Church, therefore, is actually to speak of the still-unaccomplished mission of Christ Himself. This mission is twofold. There is the general or universal mission of the Church, a concern for the whole world and for all human needs in the sense of Vatican Council II's Dogmatic Constitution on the Church and the Pastoral Constitution on the Church in the Modern World. An integral part of this general mission is a special mandate: "to make disciples of all nations" (Mt 28.19), to evangelize and to plant new Churches wherever Christ is not yet known, a topic treated especially in the Decree on the Church's Missionary Activity (*Ad gentes*). The present concern is the second mission.

The Decree describes the purpose of this special mission as "evangelization and the planting of the Church among those peoples and groups where she has not yet taken root" (*Ad gentes* 6), namely, among the more than two billion non-Christian peoples living especially, but not exclusively, in the so-called "mission countries" of Asia, Africa, and Oceania. Insisting that this particular form of mission has a strong biblical base, the document carefully avoids confusing this mandate with other apostolates, such as "pastoral activity exercised among the faithful" and "undertakings aimed at restoring unity among Christians" (ibid. 6).

In recent decades, as emphasized in *Gaudium et spes* (4–10), profound changes have entered the world, giving rise to numberless complex problems with direct bearing on the Church's general as well as special worldmission. But with new problems came new insights, important rediscoveries, and new emphases. A new direction for missionary action was set by Vatican II. Although *Ad gentes* is the document that is devoted specifically to missionary activities, the other Vatican II documents throw important light on the missionary task as well. In fact, two of them, *Lumen gentium* and *Gaudium et spes*, are regarded by some missiologists as even more significant for missionary Churches than *Ad gentes* itself.

The question that the present article seeks to answer is: What were the leading conciliar ideas that have most affected present-day missionary thought and practice? Although other evaluations are possible, any such listing would have to include the following fundamental insights and emphases: (1) the Church as missionary *by her very nature*; (2) the *whole* Church as missionary; (3) self-determination and pluriformity as a basic missio-

nary policy; (4) human betterment as a major and integral part of the missionary task; (5) ecumenical and interfaith understanding as official missionary policy. These ideas have been further developed especially by the 1974 Synod of Bishops (Rome, Oct. 1974), Pope Paul VI's Apostolic Exhortation on Evangelization in the World (*Evangelii nuntiandi*) of Dec. 8, 1975 and various regional conferences of bishops, and in recent missiological literature (*see* MISSIOLOGY).

The Church, Missionary by her Very Nature. Nothing could be more basic to missonary thought and practice than the nature of the Church and her mission. It is for this reason that the Dogmatic Constitution on the Church is hailed as the most momentous missionary achievement of Vatican II, although it leaves many questions unanswered. *Lumen gentium* is a self-portrait, a theological self-understanding, in which the universality of the Church and its missionary nature stand out in bold relief. The very title of the document, "The Light of Nations," proclaims this basic characteristic. Throughout, *Lumen gentium* speaks in terms of a mission to the whole world which includes a special mandate "to proclaim and to spread among all peoples the Kingdom of Christ and of God and to be, on earth, the initial budding forth of that kingdom . . ." (*Lumen gentium* 5). The Council's preferred title for the Church is "People of God," a title that has a distinctly universal and missionary connotation (ibid. 9–17).

Using *Lumen Gentium* as a theological basis, the Decree on the Missionary Activity of the Church declares clearly that "the pilgrim Church is missionary by *her very nature*," that "missionary activity wells from the Church's *innermost nature*," and therefore "evangelization is a *basic duty* of the People of God" (*Ad gentes* 1, 2, 6; emphasis added).

The Whole Church as Missionary. Another emphasis of major importance for mission theory and practice was the Council's understanding regarding the responsibility for missionary action. The traditional view had been that missionary action was primarily the responsibility of the pope, a responsibility carried out by "specialists" within the Church called "missionaries." Vatican II, however, introduced a new emphasis: not only was the Church missionary by her inner nature but "the whole Church is missionary" (*Ad gentes* 35). The bishops share a collegial responsibility for the spreading of Christ's Kingdom in mission lands. "All bishops, as members of the body of bishops succeeding to the College of Apostles, are consecrated not just for some one diocese, but for the salvation of the entire world. The mandate of Christ to preach the Gospel to every creature (Mk 16.15) primarily and immediately concerns them, with Peter and under Peter" (ibid. 38). All priests, "as collaborators of the order of bishops," share in the bishops' special responsibility for missionary activities and, therefore, the life of every priest "has also been consecrated to the service of the missions" (ibid. 39). Every religious (ibid. 40) and every lay man and lay woman (ibid. 41) participates in this responsibility. This responsibility is not some sort of vague, indirect, and remote involvement on the part of the members of the Church but is, as ch. 6 of *Ad gentes* emphasizes, a very personal responsibility, each member carrying out a distinct missionary role according to his or her charism and particular situation (ibid. 35–41; *Lumen gentium* 17). The clear trend of the Council toward decentralization and declericalization has contributed greatly to this express widening of missionary involvement and responsibility.

Unity in Diversity: Self-Determination and Pluriformity. "Unity in diversity" was not a new idea with Vatican II. What was new was rather the emphasis, the depth of understanding, and the concreteness and seriousness about implementation. Until Vatican II, cultural adaptation (1:120–123) had been mostly superficial, paternalistic, and ethnocentric. The sending, rather than the receiving, Church had been regarded as the main agent in church planting. The decision-makers were usually the expatriate missionaries and Roman authorities. The formation of an indigenous clergy and of lay leaders had, to a greater or lesser degree, been encouraged, but the choice of such clerical and lay leaders and their formation had been almost invariably in accord with Western, rather than local patterns. It took Vatican II to concretize the meaning of "missionary adaptation" and local "self-determination." The Council felt that the faith expressions of a local Christian community had to come from the people's own experience of Christ and from their own cultural heritage.

Underlying the readiness to adopt pluriformity was the Council's recognition of the importance of the role of the Holy Spirit in forming Christian communities (*Gaudium et spes* 40; *Lumen gentium* 8; *Ad gentes* 2–5). There was also the Council's awareness of "the signs of the times"—signs that called for decentralization and self-determination not only in the world but within the framework of the Church as well. The post-World War II liberation movements and the new sense of human dignity as well as the growing national and ethnic pride evident throughout the world were important factors contributing to the increase of authority and responsibility of local bishops and regional episcopal conferences. Also contributing to this new development was the presence at the Council of the many bishops from mission lands which served as a constant reminder of the human diversity that existed in the Church. Consequently, worship, missionary methods, and training of clergy were to be tailored to the local situation (cf. *Sacrosanctum Concilium* 37–40, 107, 128; *Lumen gentium* 13, 16, 17; *Gaudium et spes* 53, 58; *Ad gentes* 10, 11, 15, 16, 22). Such sciences as sociology, anthropology, psychology, missiology, comparative religion, and history of religions were proposed as particularly useful for incarnating the Church in the given time and place (cf. *Ad gentes* 6, 34; *Nostra aetate* 2).

Human Betterment as a Missionary Responsibility. The basic constitution of the Kingdom of God is love—God's love for all mankind and man's love for God and for one another. The Church is a "sacrament" and "sign" of this love (*Lumen gentium* 1, 48; *Ad gentes* 1). Although the Church as an institution is not the immediate and proper power for realizing the humanization of the world in the concrete (*Gaudium et spes* 42, *Ad gentes* 12) all human needs of all mankind are the concern of the Church and form an integral part of the missionary task. If the universal mission of the Church is important anywhere in the world, it is important especially in the developing nations. In fact, *Gaudium et spes* in many, if not most, instances seems to have the Third World in mind, which largely coincides with the so-called "mission countries." At times human better-

ment may require particular emphasis as a part of the mission method or as a form of preevangelization. At times, such involvement may be required solely by reason of the Church's universal mission of service to all mankind (*Ad gentes* 6, 12). However, it should be noted that development, liberation, and all forms of human betterment, treated in great detail and with deep human understanding and emphasis by *Gaudium et Spes*, are not to be identified with missionary activity as such. Not social action but evangelization and planting of Churches are the primary concern of missionary action (*Ad gentes* 6).

Ecumenical and Interfaith Understanding and Cooperation. In preconciliar times, cooperation with "separated brethren" in mission work, although not unknown, was nonetheless rare. The Decrees on Missionary Activity (*Ad gentes* 15, 29) and on Ecumenism (*Unitatis redintegratio* 10) urge brotherly understanding and collaboration in missionary work to the extent common Christian beliefs will allow. Non-Christian religions had been traditionally regarded as superstitious, idolatrous, and by their very nature evil. It took encyclicals like Pope John XXIII's *Mater et magistra* and *Pacem in terris* and Pope Paul VI's *Progressio populorum*, and especially the Council itself, to make dialogue with all men of good will and inter-faith cooperation a definite policy. *Lumen gentium* points out that God's grace, without making Christ, the Church, or missionary action unnecessary, is available at all times and places, grace being mediated in many cases through the individual's conscience, sincere desire, culture, or the non-Christian religion itself. Such religions call for respect and a certain openness with a view to discovering and appreciating how God and his grace may already be operative in the non-Christian community (*Lumen gentium* 9, 14–16).

Conclusion. Although the ideas outlined have not actually originated at Vatican Council II, they are nevertheless rightly associated with the Council and referred to as "conciliar". In the Council particular ideas were rediscovered, clarified, placed on a solid biblical basis, set in a new perspective, emphasis or depth previously unknown, and/or concretized, opening the door for further missiological development and actual implementation.

Bibliography: D. BOHR, *Evangelization in America* (New York 1977). L. LUZBETAK, "Two Centuries of Cultural Adaptation in American Church Action: Praise, Censure or Challenge," *Missiology* 5 (January 1977) 51–72. T. RYAN, "Contemporary Roman Catholic Understanding of Mission," in R. PIERCE BEAVER, ed., *American Missions in Bicentennial Perspective* (Pasadena 1977). K. RAHNER, "The Mission of the Church and the Humanizing of the World," *Doctrine and Life* 21 (1971) 171–178; 231–242.

[L. LUZBETAK]

MISSION PLANNING

Church planning rests on a set of rather profound assumptions. It assumes both a certain self-understanding by the Church and a capacity to be insightful about the surrounding world. To plan is to assume that the immediate future is not divinely and unalterably fixed, but in large measure has been entrusted to the Church's creative activity. Church planning as experienced in the U.S. relies on the conviction that God takes seriously humanity's role in constructing and providing for its tomorrow. The Church has always planned its life and work. Vatican Council II simply encouraged the use of planning as an explicit process that describes what the

Church can and should be able to accomplish in the future (see *Ad gentes* 28–34). Postconciliar directives have precised this encouragement.

In specifying the bishop's role in his diocese, the *Directory on the Pastoral Ministry of Bishops* urges them to "establish a general plan or program of action for the whole diocese" (*Directory* 148). Preparation for this planning is to include both lay consultation and the use of research findings. This *Directory* presents specific guidelines for those who prepare and implement plans. Also competence, scope of activities, work assessment, technical training, spirituality, and utilization of select social sciences by these Church planners are discussed (ibid. 209).

Mission and Pastoral Planning. Planning in the Church furthers, through scientific planning skills, the universal mission to bring the Gospel effectively to *all people*. Mission planning and its companion discipline, *pastoral planning, are distinguished by their emphasis on one of two tasks.

The first is to spread or extend the Gospel to all people. This is called, somewhat erroneously, mission activity in its strict or narrow sense. Planning associated with mission effort of this sort is termed "mission planning." A second, intensifying and deepening function concentrates on the effectiveness aspect of the universal mission and is commonly known as pastoral ministry; pastoral planning serves this pastoral ministry. Unfortunately, "missionary" is a term sometimes used interchangeably with "pastoral" even when the ministry so described deepens and does not spread the faith. Implied is a broad understanding of mission or missionary.

Insofar as a specific form of pastoral ministry furthers the universal mission of the Church, it participates in the mission of Christ and the Church. It is quite another thing to say that this is *missionary* work. The whole apostolic action of the Church participates in Christ's own mission. Still, "we must not forget or undervalue the essential aspect of this mandate: the mission *ad gentes*" (Paul VI "Message"). In its understanding of missionary activity, Vatican Council II stressed the centrality of spreading the Gospel: "The specific purpose of this missionary activity is evangelization and the planting of the Church among those people and groups where she has not yet taken root" (*Ad gentes* 6). Paul VI clearly articulates the need to deepen the faith in dechristianized parts of the world, but balanced this stress by noting that spreading the Gospel to all nations was the Church's "deepest inspiration" (Paul VI EvangNunt 50). Therefore, mission planning and pastoral planning concentrate on two essential, complementary but quite different tasks in the Church's life. The differences stem from the priority each gives to one of two vital church activities; mission planning is that form of planning that concentrates its efforts on the missionary activity of the Church.

Mission planning is primarily identified with overseas apostolates. This, however, is not an essential element. All overseas apostolates are not missionary; all missionary apostolates are not necessarily overseas. Planning (and research) offices of the Glenmary Missioners and the Josephites are examples of religious institutes in the U.S. supporting home missionary activity (Sullivan 80). The extensive study of the unchurched being conducted in this country offers the hope of a stronger engagement by dioceses in the extension of the Gospel to those who have not heard (Gallup 1978). Thus, concentration of planning efforts on *spreading* the Gospel to the peoples is the essential element of mission planning.

Vatican II and Mission Planning. The Decree on the Missionary Activity of the Church is the Council's plan for missionary activity. Essentially, the document offers a structural or organizational plan. Fourteen church groupings related to the missionary effort, ranging from the Congregation for the Evangelization of Peoples (Propagation of the Faith) and episcopal conferences to pastoral councils and religious institutes are touched on in turn. Proper relationships between these groups are traced; a long list of mission-related tasks is treated, e.g., vocations, reports, knowledge of mission peoples, funding.

Even a cursory review of the missionary effort's organizational and structural development since the Council indicates considerable progress. The leadership in the Congregation for Evangelization has been broadened and internationalized (Bühlman 194). The Congregation's nomination of native bishops and encouragement of indigenization have done much for the establishment of the local Church (ibid.). When Vatican II opened in 1962, there were eleven national episcopal conferences in lands under the direction of the Congregation for Evangelization. A 1977 listing showed forty-nine such Conferences (AnnPont [1962] 773–778; [1977] 922–938).

An impressive attempt to incorporate the principles of Vatican II in a regional plan was the second Episcopal Conference of Latin America (CELAM) in 1968 at Medellín, Colombia. Medellín gave a new urgency to the work of CELAM and the various religious institutes of sociology that had developed in Latin America beginning in the late 1950s. The new awareness of justice issues brought to North America by South American exponents of *liberation theology can be traced to Medellín (*see* MEDELLÍN DOCUMENTS).

Status of Mission Planning. Behind this more institutional aspect of mission planning is the mandate to proclaim the Gospel to the ends of the earth. Mission planning has as its central purpose the formation of new responses to this mandate. The Decree on Missionary Activity presents successive stages of mission effort having as an ultimate end the progressive expansion of the Church: (1) building and planting of the Church; (2) assisting the new and youthful Church; (3) continuing to preach the Gospel to the as-yet-unreached (*Ad gentes* 6). In this context, to define concretely the time and circumstances of engagement and disengagement in mission works becomes the central concern. From this starting point stem closely related issues that mission planning struggles with today: (1) facilitation of preaching the Gospel to non-Christians in a given culture (*see* INCULTURATION, THEOLOGICAL); (2) formation of local lay leaders (*see* CATECHISTS, MISSIONARY); (3) creation of self-directing, self-sustaining and self-propagating Christian communities (*see* BASIC CHRISTIAN COMMUNITIES); (4) advancement of human dignity; (5) search for new and effective missionary approaches; (6) support for communal and spiritual growth of missioners themselves; (7) inculcation of a missionary concern in the new Churches (Catholic Foreign Mission Society 41–42 G).

At some point a more general approach to planning in the Church becomes a specific series of interlocking steps or processes. Four or five processes for planning are identified in the US. Catholic Church by the National Pastoral Planning Conference. Missionaries from the U.S. are probably most experienced with a process derived from some formulation of "Management by Objectives." While the labels, sequence, and importance of steps vary considerably, mission-planning models based on Management by Objectives tend to include: (1) reflection on a theology of mission and the group's sense of purpose; (2) a study of pertinent aspects of the natural and human environments; (3) an assessment of human and material resources available; (4) an identification of needs; (5) a goal-setting procedure; (6) a method of holding people accountable for their contribution to the group effort; (7) a regular evaluation and periodic updating of the plan.

Limitations and Challenges. Planning is not a panacea; it offers a modest hope that in the Church limited human insight will deal effectively with the complexities involved in important decisions. Because goals of the Church are less tangible than those of business or government, use of "secular" tools designed for the more concrete becomes complex. The mystery of the Church imposes real limitations on the very human planning enterprise, but, paradoxically, overstatement of the mystery prompts some to plan only for the most immediate objectives.

Mission planning has some unique difficulties. A cross-cultural model designed in North America can be viewed as a form of standardization commonly accepted in some areas of human progress. Or, it can be perceived as a subtle imposition of one culture upon another. Frequently planning models are initially designed for Western business enterprises, then later adapted for Church use. In Third-World countries, because so much suffering is attributed to Western businesses, a planning process can be categorically discredited through a certain guilt by association.

Despite these very real difficulties, mission planning can make a solid contribution to the Church's missionary effort. The Gospel has reached less than half the peoples of our time. Most of the unchristianized are located where the population is growing the fastest and people suffer the most from misery and world injustices. It is estimated that less than ten percent of the Church's priests are engaged in proclaiming the Gospel directly among nonbelievers (Bühlman 252). Age-levels of both women and men missioners have increased drastically since Vatican II. Personnel and financial resources of mission institutes can be expected to become increasingly restricted. Such factors complicate a normally difficult missionary experience of leaving a people and/or a culture for a new work. Simultaneously, the lay-mission movement shows marked signs of vitality and must be given a full share in the missionary effort (*see* LAY MISSIONARIES). Missionary activity makes demands on local leaders of newly developed Churches. Barely established in their own right, they receive a missionary mandate asking them to effect a gradual disengagement of experienced foreign missioners, to include mission work in their own plans, and to release funds and personnel to further missionary activity elsewhere.

The future of missionary activity requires difficult decisions. It is the ministry of mission planning to assist with these decisions and their implementation.

See also MISSION (NEW TRENDS).

Bibliography: W. BÜHLMAN, *The Coming of the Third Church* (Maryknoll, N.Y. 1977). Catholic Foreign Mission Society of America, "Inter-1972). Congregation for Bishops, *Directory on the Pastoral Ministry of Bishops* (Ottawa 1974). Paul VI, "Message for Mission Sunday (Oct. 23, 1977)," *Omnis Terra* 87, n. 2 (Nov. 1977) 2. Gallup Survey, Ecumenically sponsored by over 30 Churches and church organizations, "Report of the Ad Hoc Committee on Research, Peggy L. Shriver, Convener: Backgrounds, Values, and Interests of Churchless Americans, Draft II, Aug. 6, 1977" (photocopied). E. M. SULLIVAN, *Applied Research and Planning for Mission: The Experience of Catholic Dioceses.* (Center for Applied Research in the Apostolate, Washington, D.C. 1977).

[W. R. HEADLEY]

MISSIONARIES OF CHARITY

The Missionaries of Charity are a religious community founded in India in 1948 by the famed Mother Teresa of Calcutta. The sisters of the new community in many ways resemble conventional nuns, with their distinctive garb, vows, and strict community life. Their uniqueness comes from their fourth vow, the vow of compassion: to share the life of the abandoned poor and work exclusively with the destitute, the abandoned, the orphaned, the misshapen, the plague-stricken, lepers, prisoners, and prostitutes. This fourth vow attempts to keep the community faithful to the original vision and experience of its founder. Mother Teresa is the former Agnes Gonxha Bojaxhiu, the daughter of an Albanian grocer. She was born August 27, 1910 in the town of Skopje, in what is now Yugoslavia. At the age of 14, she learned of the work done in India by the Irish Sisters of Loretto. At the age of 17, she was accepted by that community and sailed for India where, as Sister Teresa, she took her first vows May 24, 1928. At the age of 36, after 18 years as a Sister of Loretto, she found herself in a Catholic school in Calcutta teaching the children of the upper middle-class. Then she experienced a distinct calling, a vocation within a vocation, to leave the safety of the convent and help the poor of Calcutta while living among them. She assigns the call to the night of September 10, 1946, when she was on a train from Calcutta to Darjeeling en route to a spiritual retreat. Upon her return to Calcutta she did not at first receive support to follow the call; but a year later she received the necessary permission from her superior general to implement her vision. She took a room in the home of a government employee and worked on a rule of life for her new community. Her first postulant was a 19-year-old Bengali girl, Shubashini Das, who became Sister Agnes. The small circle of compassionate young Indian girls who were attracted to Mother Teresa undertook as one of their first tasks the establishment of a home for the dying people brought in from the streets of Calcutta. They made use of a vacant pilgrim hostel of a Hindu temple, which they soon equipped with 200 cots. The fledgling community soon had 60 centers for Calcutta's poor and 70 more in other cities of India. Maintaining the tradition of seeking out the abandoned poor, the community spread beyond India, to Sri Lanka and Bangladesh, and to Tanzania, Yemen, the Gaza Strip, Mauritius, Australia, England, Ireland, Venezuela, Italy, Jordan, and the United States. In 25 years the community, grown to 750 members, ministers to 7,500 destitute children in 60 schools; numberless patients in 213 dispensaries; 47,000 lepers in 54 clinics; 1600 abandoned and orphaned children in 20 homes; 3,400 dying and destitute adults in 23 homes. When Mother Teresa proposed setting up a center in the slums of Rome, she was reminded that there were already thousands of nuns in Rome looking for suitable work. Her response was: "We'll help them find it."

She and her sisters chose as their center one of a cluster of the more stable type of slum barracks (*barrachi*) in the Borgata Latina of Rome, in the shadow of the Torre Fiscale, not far from the arches of the Claudian aqueduct off the Appian Way. In Tamora, East Africa, the sisters sleep on pallets all in the same room, in an abandoned, crumbling mud-walled building. They eat the same food they beg and prepare for their poor people. While Mother Teresa was in Rome in 1971, attending the meeting of the major superiors of religious, she begged for temporary volunteers from other communities to help such struggling communities as the group of her seven sisters in Amman, Jordan, who daily tend the wounded, aging, and abandoned Bedouins in the Kharami Beggar Camp in the Jordan Valley.

Wherever they live the sisters' garb reflects their Indian origins: a white Indian sari trimmed in blue and made of cheap cotton. The brothers were founded in 1963. Brother Andrew, a former Jesuit priest from Australia, heads the brothers in Calcutta and is called the order's general servant. There are 160 professed brothers and novices in India, and another 14 in Los Angeles, Cal., where they came at the invitation of the archdiocese in 1975, after their houses in Vietnam and Cambodia were closed. In Los Angeles they live among and serve the skid-row alcoholics, the drifters, the sick and elderly living alone or in nursing homes, and immigrant Mexican families. They leave the problem of societal change to others, following Mother Teresa's dictum: there are plenty of people around to do the big things; the Missionaries of Charity will do the little things that few are willing to do.

Bibliography: G. GORRÉE, *For the Love of God*, tr. P. SPEAKMAN (London 1974); *Love without Boundaries*, tr. P. SPEAKMAN (Huntington, Ind. 1976). J. GONZÁLEZ-BALADO, *Cristo en los Arrabales* (Barcelona 1974). M. MUGGERIDGE, *Something Beautiful for God* (London 1971).

[E. J. DILLON]

MISSIONARY

Vatican Council II pointed toward today's radical renewal of the meaning of missionary (9:907). Upon the whole Church there rests, by divine mandate, the duty of going out into the whole world and preaching the Gospel to every creature; the whole Church is missionary and the work of evangelization is a basic duty of the People of God (see *Lumen gentium* 17; *Ad gentes* 5–8). The missionary is any and every one who is continually being evangelized and converted to Christ and is thus committed to the liberating, loving, and saving mission of the people of God. The missionary is the Christian who allows the witness of the Spirit to shine through her or his activity and who manifests "God's will and the fulfillment of that will in the world and in world history" (*Ad gentes* 9).

Against this background, for the missionary dialogue, development, and liberation of men and women from injustice of all kinds are not simply means to an end but actually fundamental parts of that end—salvation. The Christ-missionary carries on Christ's and his Spirit's work of evangelization: the proclamation of salvation from sin, liberation from everything unjustly oppressive to humans, the development of the human person in all personal and communal dimensions, and renewal of all human structures through interaction with the Good News. As a result of these insights the missionary, both to his or her own local Church or to other local Churches must: (1) carry on mission as an ecclesial activity demanding teamwork with others representing the full vocational wealth of God's people; (2) be sent from and received by local Churches to increase the incarnational possibilities of Christ and his Spirit; (3) work always in dialogue with others continually evangelizing and being evangelized themselves; and (4) actively go out to others especially the poor and the outcast.

[J. P. MEEHAN]

MISSIONARY ADAPTATION

The question of inculturation or indigenization (the term adaptation sounds rather paternalistic and suggests pragmatic adjustment) in mission countries would not have come up with so much force and urgency had the missionary policy and practice in the recent past been in keeping with the sound tradition of the Church.

That ancient and venerable tradition had it that, like Jesus Christ, the Church would identify herself fully with the language, customs, and traditions (in short, culture) of the people to whom she brings the good news. Thus though the early Church had a Jewish expression, the first ecumenical council of Jerusalem vindicated the position of St. Paul championing the cause of indigenization against the Judaizers who wanted to impose Jewish practices on the Gentile converts (cf. Gal, Acts 15). Thus the Gospel permeated the Graeco-Roman, East Syrian, Egyptian, Slav, and finally the European cultures and helped the emergence of local Churches, indigenized in these places.

Because of various reasons and historical circumstances the Church became more and more identified with one particular cultural expression. As a result, missionary work from the 15th century onwards meant, instead of announcing the Gospel in the culture of the mission countries, the transplanting of the already-developed, Western cultural expressions of the Gospel. The new Christians in the mission countries also accepted the faith along with its Western cultural expressions and identified them as Christian culture in contrast to native culture, all the elements of which were branded as non-Christian and pagan. Thus Christianization meant Westernization, alienation of Christians from their own culture, social milieux, religious traditions, and their drifting away from the mainstream of national life. Missionary work was looked upon by others as aggression; preaching was translated as proselytism and conversion as abandonment of all that converts cherished, most especially their cultural and religious heritage.

It is in this context and background that the movement for indigenization started again in the Church, modelling missionary policy and practice on the original and authentic tradition of the Church, and still further on the incarnation of Jesus Christ. This involved a fresh theological understanding of the nature and mission of the Church in the world as embodied in the documents of Vatican Council II, especially *Gaudium et spes, Lumen gentium, Nostra aetate,* and *Ad gentes.* Like Christ (Jn 1, 1–18; Col 1, 15, 20; 1 Cor 15, 28) the Church must assume, save, gather, unify, and consecrate to God everything, including religions and cultures. The

Church must enable everyone and everything to pass through the incarnation, death, and resurrection of Christ. Everything should be purified of the taints of sin and all that is true and good should be recognized and appreciated as the seed of God's Word. In this way Christ fulfils everything and gathers to himself all that belongs to him.

Thus the Church in each place will be the actualization and localization of all that the Church means: through Jesus Christ proclaiming the Good News of salvation; gathering men of different languages and cultures, profession, and sex into the unity of faith and Baptism through the Spirit for the celebration of Eucharist in order to make of them one body, a *koinōnia*. Then the Church sends them as sign and instrument of God's Kingdom to function as servants of mankind in the concrete circumstances of history and particular life-situations of a people. In this way the Church will realize her catholicity and universality. She will be incarnated in every place and people but at the same time she will not in any way be bound up with any particular culture.

Indigenization belongs to the very core of the Church. The mission of the Church to proclaim the Good News and to incarnate this Gospel in the local culture are not two successive actions but a single and simultaneous movement. For Gospel and culture are not two static entities preserved in separate compartments without any mutual influence. On the contrary, like the divinity and humanity of Christ, they interact on one another, leading to a new synthesis for the enrichment of both without endangering each's identity. There is no such thing as a pure Gospel except as incarnated in a particular culture. The Good News to be properly experienced as such needs to be expressed in the local culture. Local cultures as a result become themselves Christian cultures and thus are purified and ennobled.

Indigenization involves and affects sensible and external forms, like the vernacular translations of the Bible and spiritual books, and original compositions; the formation of the local clergy; adaptations of the social customs and habits; incarnation of the Gospel in concrete life-situations and in every sphere of personal and family life, in social and civic activities, in economic and political life of the place. The Gospel has also to be expressed through the art forms of the countries instead of those introduced from abroad. Indigenization also means the evolution and development of local theology, trying to understand and express the Christian faith and experience in the categories, thought-patterns, cultural and religious heritage of the place. It also involves spiritual forms, like Christian spirituality and liturgy. All these are interconnected and people may start the process of indigenization from different areas provided one leads to the other.

The process initiated by Christ continues in the Church of today, more faithfully and vigorously after Vatican II; this process will end: all belong to us, the Church, we all belong to Christ, and Christ humanly will belong to God when he places at the feet of his Father all that he has recapitulated. Then the Father will be all in all; (1 Cor 3, 23; 15, 28) and then the goal of God's plan will be fulfilled, to be the praise of the glory of his grace (Eph 1.6).

See also MISSION (NEW TRENDS).

[D. S. AMALORPAVADASS]

MISSIONARY FORMATION

Every follower of Christ is a missionary. For this reason all evangelization is itself missionary formation and requires a lifetime to be completed. Here, however, missionary formation will focus primarily on the formation of those men and women called by Christ "to go, therefore..." and sent to witness and serve among peoples and local Churches other than their own (9.920). These intercultural and/or foreign missionaries are those who go to learn more about Christ as he discloses himself in different cultures. By living in the midst of others they become more aware of the Christ to whom they witness and in whom they are born again. Missionaries share the message of Christ with the people of today in their concrete totality.

Measure of Formation. The work of the missionary is a demanding one. The process for selecting missionaries should also be demanding and challenging. Mission requires men and women of deep humanity. They should be healthy, balanced persons, psychologically sound, free from false defenses and inhibitions; they should be persons who have achieved a human maturity in which they find joy and persons who share warmth and openness with others. This openness implies the willingness to be present to people. It implies openness to being crucified in mind, heart, and body without crucifying; to being imposed upon without imposing; to loving without being loved; to serving without being served; and to witnessing without being appreciated. Such persons are capable of establishing and maintaining the peace-sharing and deep relationships needed with fellow workers and other peoples they encounter in dialogue. Upon this human base the Spirit builds. The missionary, like Christ, is called to act in every event in the most human way possible. On this base too, the specific mission gifts and competencies can be cultivated.

Vatican II. Missionary formation under the impetus of Vatican Council II has undergone considerable reform and continues to show a need for more renewal. The same forces released by the Council, which encouraged all sectors of God's people to move more responsively to the modern world, have influenced the renewal of missionary formation. This renewal has taken and must continue taking place in all elements of formation: method, timing, place, and content. To renew these elements attention must be given to "the signs of the times" in the light of the Gospel. Some of the more evident of these signs can be discovered in the human actions of missionaries today. (1) The mission of Christ is a transcultural one, implying dialogue with the deep respect for other cultures and peoples. (2) The mission of Christ is primarily to the poor and their struggle for justice and peace. (3) The mission of Christ is one of service to all people. (4) The mission of Christ emphasizes local leadership and thus points to decreasing leadership positions for foreigners. (5) The mission of Christ is proclaimed and developed within community, as all members come to perform their proper ministries. (6) The mission of Christ is basically one of evangelization and transformation of human relationships. (7) The mission of Christ is a continuing process of initiation into the ministry and the mystery of Christ's transcultural mission. (8) The mission of Christ requires missionaries ready and willing to move on.

Method. The appearance of these signs at this time in

history, along with the continually increasing evidence that the methodology of learning is as important if not more important than the content, points toward an ever greater utilization of experiential learning in preparation for mission ministry. Experiential learning becomes even more crucial in view of some research facts: (1) that the human and emotional elements of overseas work are as important as technical skills in the success of a mission; (2) that overseas personnel are more likely to be deficient in the human aspects of performance than in the technical skills; (3) that the gravest problems for overseas workers are emotional and interpersonal (Harrison and Hopkins).

Because of this, overseas training or an intercultural experience within the mission candidate's own country is not only important, today it is a necessity. Training of this type will continue to increase simply because it is the best model for a life of continuing educational growth and development. For the missionary overseas, this process of learning becomes one with the process of theology and mission. The process consists in: (1) diagnosing, in dialogue with others, what is going on in human reality; (2) selecting a particular human situation for witness of service in the light of the Gospel; (3) creating or choosing a method of responding to the need; (4) taking action within a community situation; (5) rechecking the action by repeating the process. All the elements amount to this: what does the human reality say about God, about self and about other peoples? what must be done in consequence?

While participating in this process within the real human context, the learner experiences and learns to deal with the emotional impact of reality on self and others. Ideas and values have to be translated into direct action with all the risks and difficulties involved. At the same time the learner must influence others to action through leadership.

Within this type of training, leaders encourage experience and experimentation, support the learner, encourage risk taking, and help the learner discover roads to goals without inordinate dependence on experts. The context provides an environment in which the intense spiritual growth needed by the missionary can develop. Long term spiritual direction within a life of personal and communal prayer and within the experiences of ministry will foster personal reflection on the working of and growth in the Spirit. In wonder and awe the missionary is humbled before the workings of the Lord in and through the people, their values, and their customs. There can be in this process the discernment and assimilation of God's revelation as mediated by the people at hand.

Duration. The most evident change in missionary formation recently is the clear and unequivocal recognition that this formation is a lifetime process, involving the growth, development, and maturing of the total person. In order to improve language and cultural learning, missionary candidates are being placed as soon as possible overseas, after a short orientation program. Important elements in the overseas training programs are the availability of trained formation people there and the readiness of candidates to face the multiple cultural shocks.

Setting. The best place for mission training is in the overseas environment in which the candidate will eventually work; second to this is a similar overseas area; and a third choice is some environment at home, different from the candidate's own, and creating the experience of being an alien. Some provision must be made for the experiencing of cultural shock under supervised conditions. When present realities require mission training in traditional educational institutions, extended periods of field education combined with good supervision and regular pastoral reflection become absolutely necessary.

Content. The content of missionary formation is quite fluid. It changes rapidly with the changing times and the changing conditions of the world and its peoples. Some areas of questioning remain fairly constant; each area implies questions requiring individual responses. As a Christian, how does one stand personally before God and how is one able and willing to live out that stance in the reality of many tensions? What is discipleship, apostleship, and mission? As a human: how closely is one in touch with one's sexuality and emotions: anger, fear, love, depression when exposed to the conditions of cultural shock? how is one affirmed? As a community member, does one feel valued and at home, respected, and accepted in the community of peers and of associates? As an individual person, how does one integrate all of these aspects into one's personality? As a missionary, what differences must one be prepared to meet?

Such issues differentiate the content of formation programs. The main areas of the program are these: (1) theological education to appreciate thoroughly both the universality of the mission of Christ and its particularity and diversity as well as to understand Christ's mission to the world; (2) mission history and methods; (3) knowledge of transcultural relationships, sensitivity to differences in peoples and cultures, and a general knowledge of cultural anthropology; (4) practical training in linguistics, communications, educational methods, evangelization, community-building, and special skills; (5) training for leadership; team training, how to work through and with others; (6) political judgment: how to assess in terms of Gospel truth the political realities without being naive; good analysis skills for determining and understanding reality; (7) preparation to live and cooperate when necessary with other systems: e.g. socialism, dictatorships; (8) preparation to live and work with the poor.

One fact remains, given the direction of mission today, missionary formation must continue to critique and renew itself in the light of God's Word.

See also MISSIOLOGY.

Bibliography: J. COMBLIN, *The Meaning of Mission*, tr. J. DRURY (Maryknoll 1977). R. HARRISON and R. HOPKINS, "The Design of Cross-Cultural Training: An Alternative to the University Model," *Journal of Applied Behavioral Sciences* 3 (1967) 431–460. K. KOYAMA, *No Handle on the Cross* (Maryknoll 1976). Irish Missionary Union, *Education for Mission* (Dublin 1971). PAUL VI, *On Evangelization in the Modern World* (Washington, D.C. 1976).

[J. P. MEEHAN]

MISSIONS, CATHOLIC (U.S.)

In considering the missionary effort of the U.S. Catholic Church throughout the world, this article uses the term "missionaries" in its generally accepted sense, including American Catholics engaged overseas not only in the primary and subsequent stages of evangelization but also in the closely related areas of community service and development.

Current Status. American Catholic personnel serve in

112 countries outside the 48 contiguous states. There are 2,882 religious priests, 630 brothers, 2,781 sisters, and 42 seminarians in the field. There are 251 mission-sending groups. Sixty-eight dioceses sponsor 182 diocesan priests. Eighteen organizations and 10 dioceses sponsor 243 lay personnel overseas. Countries with the largest number of U.S. missionary personnel are the Philippines (472), Brazil (468), Peru (448), and a large number in the continent of Africa (1,003). Of men religious, the Jesuit and Maryknoll Fathers and Brothers have the largest number of U.S. missionaries abroad (647 and 607 respectively). Of the 182 mission-sending groups of women religious, again, Maryknoll with 466 has by far the largest number of U.S. personnel.

Decline. In 1932, there were 866 U.S. Catholic missionaries working in foreign countries. In 1963, the number had increased to 7,000; in 1964, to 8,126; and in 1968, to 9,655, the peak. Thereafter a decline occurred. In the tumultuous period of the late 1960s the U.S. Catholic Church did not go unaffected. 1970 was the watershed, the year of the first decline in the number of missionaries (8,373); there has been a steady drop since then. Nor has the number of lay missionaries increased. There were practically no lay missioners in 1932. In 1958, there were 96; 328 in 1970. They had peaked in 1966 (549). In 1977, there were 368, of this number includes 125 persons who were employed by the Catholic Relief Services (*see* LAY MISSIONARIES).

Causes. There are some clear reasons for this decline. The attitude of young people changed vis-à-vis foreign mission. The romantic aura which was attached to "adventurous" foreign mission work was lost following wider travel, Peace-Corps or military experience overseas, and exposure to foreign cultures through the mass media. Young people no longer clearly perceived the idealistic challenge associated with the physical sacrifice involved in mission work because of an amelioration of missionaries' living conditions. Concern for the many problem areas in the U.S., for example, in Appalachia, in the human rights issue, deemphasized interest in foreign mission. Many countries tightened restrictions on the entry of missionaries within their borders, for example, South Africa, Nigeria after the Biafran War, the Sudan, India, Nepal, and Burma. The factors which created loss of vocations among the young in general during this period, could also be applied to the question of missionary vocations. That many missionary priests, brothers, and sisters chose the state of marriage and left the field was another serious reason for the decline.

New Hopes. Although the number of U.S. foreign missionaries has declined and continues to do so, there is cause for optimism. The number of vocations to the priesthood and religious life throughout the world is uneven. While vocations have decreased in the United States and Western Europe, there has been dramatic growth in other countries, for example, Nigeria, Uganda, and Poland. Just as here in the U.S., so also abroad, such new roles in church ministry are emerging as extraordinary ministers of the Eucharist, married permanent deacons, and catechists who are assuming more and more responsibility in building Christian community. In many parts of the world the lack of priests has created a more self-reliant Church, less dependent on foreign influence and aid. So too, in the areas of health, social services, education, and community development, the indigenous people are becoming more self-sufficient precisely because of the lack of trained overseas personnel. This is all to the good. However, it should be noted that Baptism confers on the laity both the right and the obligation to be involved in missionary work. Greater progress has been made in involving the laity in a self-reliant Church where missioners recognized that right, even before the decline in the number of priests and religious.

Since Vatican Council II, there has been a gradual but nonetheless effective effort on the part of Christian Churches to collaborate in the mission field. Much useless duplication has been eliminated, and the scandal of division has lessened because of the new ecumenical dimension of mission.

Another encouraging phenomenon in recent years has been the struggle for social justice and the liberation of oppressed people in the Third World. Many missionaries have become involved in bettering the plight of the marginated in such countries as Brazil, South Africa, Nicaragua, the Philippines. There is also a growing awareness in the U.S. that concern for social justice must be viewed on a worldwide scale. The Detroit *Call to Action Conference (1976) recommends that "bishops and missionary societies initiate a mission program with the following elements. (1) Invite indigenous representatives of the Third World to raise critical consciousness of the people of the United States regarding their situation, in order to engage us in solidarity with their aspirations and struggle for justice and peace. (2) Plans should be completed by the mission societies and the NCCB/USCC for utilizing returning missionaries more advantageously in justice and peace education programs" (*A Call to Action, "Humankind,"* 72).

Bibliography: U.S. Mission Council, *Mission Handbook 1977* (Washington, D.C. 1977). USCC Publ. Office, *A Call to Action* (Washington, D.C. 1977).

[A. BELLAGAMBA]

MISSIONS AND ECUMENISM

Among Protestants, the primary impulse for the budding of the ecumenical movement in the 20th century originated in a missionary concern, symbolized by the first World Missionary Conference, Edinburgh, 1910: because denominational divisiveness, characteristic of the European and North American missionary enterprise, corrodes the witness of the Christian message in Africa, Latin America and Asia, it is imperative that at least a common future strategy be developed to avoid overlap, duplication, and the competition of the past. A permanent structured continuation of this concern became (1921) the International Missionary Council, which helped mission groups coordinate activities and develop corporate strategies. But this pragmatic need led inexorably to the conclusion that concern for mission cannot be separated, even structurally, from concern for church unity in faith and practice. The IMC, in 1961, merged with the World Council of Churches.

In the Roman Catholic Church, on the other hand, ecumenism had found its initial impetus not in this practical mission-imperative but in a new search into the ecclesiological issue: the one Church, yet many Churches? Vatican Council II articulated the theological response in the Constitution *Lumen gentium* (esp. 15) and in the Decree on Ecumenism. The response informed the guidelines for the reshaping of Catholic attitudes and practices. The Decree on Ecumenism also links the restoration of unity among all Christians to mission: [All Christians] "proclaim themselves to be disciples of the Lord, but their convictions clash, as though Christ himself were divided (cf. 1 Cor 1.13). Without doubt, this discord openly contradicts the will of Christ, provides a stumbling block (*scandalum*) to the world, and inflicts damage on the most holy cause of proclaiming the Gospel to every creature" (*Unitatis redintegratio* 1). Bearing the burden of divisions, the Christian Communions have not been a clear sign of Christ's one people, so it has been hard for the world to believe (Jn 13.35; 17.21). The mandate for mission is a mandate for "unanimous witness" and presently for "common witness" to whatever divine gifts of truth and life Christians already share in common (cf. *Ad gentes* 6; Paul VI EvangNunt 77).

Thus, Protestants, Orthodox, and Roman Catholics now accept at least the umbrella working principle: Mission in unity, Unity in mission. The understanding and application of this principle of synthesis, however, still varies, within as well as between the Communions, because of a lack of adequate consensus about the meaning and priorities of missionary activity, and about the divinely revealed shape of the unity of the Church.

More specific areas of discussion in the context of mission are salvation and conversion; the relation of the Church to the Kingdom; evangelization and social, economic, political, and cultural development; the encounter with people of other world faiths or of secular ideologies; indigenization of local Churches in worship, religious education, moral disciplines, and authority structures; traditional religious values vis-à-vis modernization through technology and urbanization; the missionary nature and structure of a local congregation; and the stewardship and role of foreign personnel and monies.

In the 1970s, ecumenical consensus, or lack of it, on these topics was all reconsidered because of the theological ferment in Asia, Latin America, and Africa, which are quickly becoming the new centers of worldwide influence in theological construction. Here is found heightened confidence in self-development and less interest in imported church quarrels, especially if they had been forged long ago (the East/West schism; the Reformation and Counter Reformation), and are still stated in Western religious approaches, cultural assumptions, and methodologies of philosophy and theology. The new emerging theologies, articulated, for example, by the Ecumenical Association of Third World Theologians (established in 1976), of which Roman Catholics are active participants, are already influencing missionary understanding and practice, also in the context of local and universal church unity.

Increased ecumenical collaboration or common witness is seen in the defense of human rights and the promotion of religious freedom (with the decrease of pejorative proselytism among Christians); the struggle for economical, social, and racial justice; the promotion of international understanding, the limitation of armaments and maintenance of peace; campaigns against illiteracy, hunger, alcoholism, and drug traffic; medical and health services; relief and aid to victims of natural disasters; and mass communications. Also to be noted is the collaboration in the production, publication and distribution of joint translations of the Scriptures (*see*

BIBLES COMMON) and in shared catechetical materials, seminaries, and training programs for laity and clergy.

Structurally, ecumenical cooperation is found in Roman Catholic participation in the commissions and programs of the World Council of Churches, especially its Commission on World Mission and Evangelism; of the Asian Christian Council; the All Africa Conference of Churches; national church councils, of which an increasing number have local Catholic Churches as full members, e.g., Christian Council of Kenya and the Caribbean Council; and in more local ecumenical organizations of Churches or of special interest groups.

Bibliography: G. ANDERSON and T. F. STRANSKY, eds., *Mission Trends*, v. 1, 2, 3, 4 (New York 1974, 1975, 1976, 1978). "Common Witness and Proselytism: A Study Document from the Joint Working Group between the Roman Catholic Church and the World Council of Churches," EcumRev 23 (1971) 3–20. H. VAN DUSEN, *One Great Ground of Hope: Christian Mission Christian Unity* (Philadelphia 1961). B. LAMBERT, *Ecumenism: Theology and History* (New York 1967). M.-J. LE GUILLOU, *Mission et unité*, 2 v. (Paris 1960). R. ROUSE and STEPHEN C. NEILL, eds., *A History of the Ecumenical Movement*, v. 1 (Philadelphia 1967) esp. ch. 8, 15; H. E. FEY, ed., v. 3 (London 1970). Secretariat for Promoting Christian Unity, *Ecumenical Collaboration at the Regional, National and Local Levels* (USCC Publ. Office, Washington, D.C. 1975).

[T. F. STRANSKY]

MONASTICISM, CONTEMPORARY

Monasticism in the contemporary world would appear to be a venerable institution in danger of extinction. At a time of deep and rapid cultural transformation there is something quaint and romantic about the ancient monastic ideal. But monasticism's very age attests to its resilience and adaptability. And the reason for that elastic quality of monastic witness was suggested by Vatican Council II which urged all religious to strive for renewal by rediscovering the spirit of their founders (*Perfectae caritatis* 2, 6; cf. Paul VI EvangTest 11). When this mandate is followed, it is found that the spirit of the monastic founders was surprisingly open and pioneering, quite prepared to deal with and to shape a rapidly changing world, whether theirs or today's.

The Monastic Witness. The monastic phenomenon in the Church finds expression not only in such highly visible monastic orders as the Benedictines or Cistercians, but also in many other groups or individuals who cherish monastic values and whose lives manifest in various ways a monastic witness. Their witness often expresses a certain element of stability that could easily be mistaken for a desire to preserve the past at all cost. But the deepest monastic instinct, as reflected in the earliest monastic literature, is for a prophetic witness. The monk, like the biblical prophet, commits himself to the Transcendent. Far from being wedded to traditional structures, he creates a tension as he challenges structures and institutions that have become too political or too conservative. Thus, the prophets of Israel challenged the kings and the established religion as they bore courageous witness to the countercultural demands of the Covenant. They were, in their own day, powerful forces for change, and the same is true of the monastic founders.

To say that the monastic instinct is prophetic and therefore opposed to rigidly conservative or sclerotic attitudes and open to all changes that prepare a transient world for the Kingdom is not to say that all modern monasteries and convents have been responding adequately to that instinct. In fact, many monastic institutions have become so involved in various works and projects that they find themselves too readily at ease with a secular society dominated by a value system devised to reward productivity and tending to be oblivious of religious considerations. Accordingly, renewal for monastic orders has been a painful and costly process. It would be too facile to say that the recent significant erosion in membership has been due simply to a lack of authentic monastic goals, but confusion about monastic identity certainly has been an important factor. And there appear to be stirrings of new life now as the demands of renewal have led to a rediscovery of monastic identity and of a witness that is more in keeping with the original prophetic vocation.

Renewal. The characteristics of this renewed spirit are manifold and diverse but the following appear to be particularly evident. Firstly, at a time when man has learned not only how to amass information but also how to computerize and communicate it with amazing speed, the monk is affirming the presence of mystery and is rejoicing in it as a sign of God's reality. Monastic prayer is a celebration of mystery, an expression of joyful trust in a life that need not make perfect sense, an act of hope in a world that tries to forget its own transience. Many young people who have become disillusioned with technology and bureaucracy turn to religious forms of life that are in the monastic tradition. If these seekers do not always find their way to the traditional monastic institutions, it may be because these institutions are not as devoted to mystery as they might be.

Secondly, the prayerful celebration of mystery finds ready expression in a communal form of life because respect for mystery in persons leads inevitably to a convergence of views, interests, and aspirations. Such a witness to the possibility of sharing in mutual trust and support is a powerful witness in a world weary of war and violence. This dimension of monastic witness is particularly attractive to that generation which has been sensitized to the threat of nuclear destruction.

Finally, monks are also finding their ancient witness to be surprisingly contemporary as they revive their interest in the mystery of all creation, an interest that flowers in the traditional monastic devotion to the arts. This recognition of the hidden beauty of nature is especially appropriate at a time when men and women are everywhere striving to curb and repair the abuse of their environment. The monks taught Europe how to farm as well as how to read and modern monks are rediscovering the mystery of nature at a time when the delicate beauty of the natural universe needs special protection.

World Monasticism. Internationally, monasticism continues to show its extraordinary powers of adaptation as it helps to shape the religious ideals of the emerging peoples of the Third World. In Africa, it provides a structure for communal identity that transcends tribal divisions and resists a productivity ideal that is foreign to that culture. Communal liturgy serves as a unifying and healing force for a time of difficult transition. In Asia, monasticism has always found a ready welcome. Contemporary monastic witness there strives to complement a traditionally private and contemplative preference with a keener sense of social awareness. In South America, monasticism strives to be a progressive but temperate influence for social justice in a situation where impatient and violent action seems inevitable. These varied forms and emphases of monastic witness are all consistent with the fundamental monastic quest for a Transcendent that can be reached, not outside of history nor by rejecting the positive values of creation, but within temporal realities by a search for and a celebration of the mystery that God has put at the heart of all being. However, since the fullness of the mystery is in God and at the end of history, the monk today, as formerly, will be most of all a hopeful and expectant believer, affirming creation but watching the horizon.

Bibliography: D. DUMM, "Monasticism and Contemporary Culture," AmBenRev 26 (1975) 125–141; "Work and Leisure: Biblical Perspectives," AmBenRev 28 (1977) 334–350. L. MERTON, "Monastic Vocation and Modern Thought," *Monastic Studies* 4 (1966) 17–54. R. WEAKLAND, "Monastic Renewal," *New Blackfriars* 46 (1965) 511–516.

[D. R. DUMM]

MONOGENISM AND POLYGENISM

Since Pius XII's encyclical *Humani generis* in 1950 the official position of the magisterium has changed but slightly from the teaching that all mankind has descended from a single pair of original ancestors (monogenism, 9:1063). Paul VI, in an allocution (1966) to a group of theologians, observed that polygenism (the scientific hypothesis that the human race is the result of multiple origins; 11:539) has not been scientifically demonstrated and cannot be admitted if it involves the denial of *original sin.

Subsequently, theologians remain sharply divided on the issue, though a growing number seem to hold that polygenism does not conflict with a genuine Catholic understanding of original sin, and hence should be left open for the freedom of scientific pursuit to demonstrate or reject. Karl Rahner, e.g., has reversed his earlier opinion which clearly favored monogenism. Monogenism, he argues, has not been defined by the Church and its theological note or qualification is in doubt. He sees the magisterium to be in the same position on polygenism that it was with the evolutionary concept of hominization between 1850 and 1900. This concept in those days was not "free" to be held and it appeared as if the magisterium allowed no change. Rahner explicitly sets forth and substantiates the thesis that "in the present state of theology and science it cannot be proved that polygenism conflicts with orthodox teaching on original sin, and that it would be better if the magisterium refrained from censuring polygenism" (64). Bruce Vawter is even more definite: "Whether mankind originated in monogenism or polygenism is a question which only science can answer; it is not a theological question" (90). Certainly this is the growing view of exegetes and theologians, though the positive coherence of polygenism with the traditional concept of original sin has not yet been satisfactorily elaborated.

Bibliography: Z. ALZEGHY, "Development in the Doctrinal Formulation of the Church concerning the Theory of Evolution," in J. METZ, ed., *The Evolving World and Theology*, Concilium 26 (1967) 25–33. J. L. CONNER, "Original Sin: Contemporary Approaches," ThSt 29 (1969) 215–240. B. MCDERMOTT, "Theology of Original Sin: Recent Developments," ThSt 38 (1977) 478–512. J. MACKEY, *Original Sin and Christian Anthropology* (Washington, D.C. 1969). K. RAHNER, "Evolution and Original Sin," in J. METZ, ed., *The Evolving World and Theology*, Concilium 26 (1967) 61–73. G. VANDERVELDE, *Original Sin: Two Major Trends in Contemporary Roman Catholic Reinterpretation* (Amsterdam 1975). B. VAWTER, *On Genesis: A New Reading* (Garden City, N.Y. 1977).

[D. J. EHR]

MONSIGNOR

Use of the title of monsignor (9:1070) has been altered somewhat by the Instruction of the Papal Secretariat of State, *Ut sive sollicite*, March 31, 1969 (ActApS 61 [1969] 334–340). The title may continue to be used of bishops, who, along with the superior prelates of the offices of the Roman Curia without episcopal rank, the Auditors of the Roman Rota, the Promotor General of Justice and the Defender of the Bond of the Apostolic Signatura, the Apostolic Prothonotaries *de numero* and the four Clerics of the Camera, may be addressed as "Most Reverend." For lesser prelates (supernumerary apostolic prothonotaries, prelates of honor, and chaplains of His Holiness), the distinction between "Right Reverend" and "Very Reverend" has been abolished. For them, the title may be preceded where appropriate by "Reverend."

See also PAPAL HOUSEHOLD; PRELATES, HONORARY.

[B. C. GERHARDT]

MORAL DEVELOPMENT

A capacity to judge responsibly in moral matters is an adult attribute which represents a long and gradual development. Jean Piaget, a pioneer in the study of child development, began research in this area.

Piaget. While the principal interest of Piaget's research was the child's acquisition of the mental structures that lead to logical and creative thinking, Piaget also contributed two valuable conclusions to the analysis of moral judgment. (1) Piaget saw that children first relate to their parents or to adults according to a unilateral respect (of inferior to superior) which begets a morality of obedience called *heteronomy.* The locus of responsibility is outside the person in heteronomy and submission to another's judgment is always characterized by some ambivalence, including both affection and hostility, sympathy and aggression. This characterizes children generally before the age of seven or eight. Later, children arrive at new moral relationships based on mutual respect in peer cooperation; this leads to a dawning *autonomy.* In this phase, a sense of fairness prevails over obedience and a capacity arises to modify or establish rules by consensus. Heteronomy and autonomy coexist in persons, relative to the unilateral or mutual relationships which characterize given situations. (2) Piaget saw that heteronomy leads to an attitude called *moral realism* according to which responsibility is evaluated relative to rules or laws alone. Moral realism judges the seriousness of an act in material terms according to the extent of damage done, independent of the intention of the agent. As autonomous thinking develops, the child likewise acquires an appreciation for the significance of intentions.

These findings are significant in providing parents and educators with a realistic estimate of the child's capacity for moral responsibility at the early stages. A child cannot be expected to understand the reasons for moral actions in the period of heteronomy.

Kohlberg. Harvard psychologist Lawrence Kohlberg has devised a theory which provides greater detail in the description of moral development. In his investigations, Kohlberg identified six orientations toward moral judgment which he found to represent universal stages applicable to all persons. Each stage represents a restructuring of the idea of right and wrong, from infancy to moral maturity.

At the beginning, there is the *preconventional level* containing stage one: the *punishment/obedience orientation,* where avoiding punishment and deferring to superior power alone are relevant; and stage two: the *instrumental-relativist orientation,* where a kind of self-interested bargaining guides moral perception. Next comes the *conventional level* containing stage three: "*good boy-nice girl*" *orientation,* where earning approval of significant persons matters most; and stage four: the *law and order orientation,* where fixed rules and the social status quo control moral perception. Finally comes the *post-conventional level* containing stage five: the *social-contract orientation,* where continued respect for legal authority is modified by a recognition of the human origins of the social order and the possibility of changing law for the sake of personal and social needs; and stage six: the *universal ethical-principle orientation,* where the right is perceived by an inner experience of conscience expressed in terms of the golden rule or the categorical imperative.

Kohlberg contends that these stages are universal and invariant: one cannot get to later stages without going through each of the earlier ones. Subjects cannot understand moral reasoning more than one stage beyond their own, yet they are attracted to the stage just one beyond themselves (which allows for this theory to claim validity as a strategy for moral education). It is cognitive disequilibrium—the inability to make sense of a moral situation—in a given stage that promotes the rethinking that leads to stage advance.

Difficulties and Contributions. Both Kohlberg and Piaget limit their moral perspectives to reasoning about rules. Piaget says, "All morality consists in a system of rules, and the essence of all morality is to be sought for in the respect which the individual acquires for these rules" (Piaget, 13). Many philosophers and theologians claim broader dimensions for morality than that (*see* MORAL EDUCATION). Among the elements of these theories that have been criticized are: Kohlberg's claim that there is only one virtue, justice (Peters, Philibert); the pancultural adequacy of Kohlberg's theory (Simpson); the research base for stages five and six (Kurtines and Greif, Sullivan); and the exclusively cognitive focus of Kohlberg's research (Sullivan). Yet the work of Piaget and Kohlberg has undoubtedly introduced a new epoch in moral education, demonstrating that certain dimensions of moral experience are developmental, empirically perceptible, and susceptible to strategies for stage advance.

Bibliography: R. DUSKA and M. WHELAN, *Moral Development: A Guide to Piaget and Kohlberg* (New York 1975). L. KOHLBERG, "Stage and Sequence: The Cognitive Developmental Approach to Socialization," in D. A. GOSLIN, ed. *Handbook of Socialization Theory and Research,* (Chicago 1969). W. KURTINES and E. B. GREIF, "The Development of Moral Thought: Review and Evaluation of Kohlberg's Approach," *Psychological Bulletin* 81 (1974) 453–470. R. S. PETERS, "Moral Developments: A Plea for Pluralism," in T. MISCHEL, ed. *Cognitive Development and Epistemology* (New York 1971). P. J. PHILIBERT, "Lawrence Kohlberg's Use of Virtue," *International Philosophical Quarterly* 15 (1975) 455–479. J. PIAGET, *The Moral Judgment of the Child* (New York 1965). E. L. SIMPSON, "Moral Development Research: A Case of Scientific Cultural Bias," *Human Development* 17 (1974) 81–106 E. V. SULLIVAN, *Moral Learning* (New York 1975); "A Study of Kohlberg's Structural Theory of Moral Development: A Critique of Liberal Social Science Ideology," *Human Development* 20 (1977) 352–376.

[P. J. PHILIBERT]

MORAL EDUCATION

Moral education comprises a lifelong process, influenced by many agencies in society, which promotes growth in responsibility and freedom.

Teaching of Vatican II. Vatican Council II's Declaration on Christian Education stresses the importance of moral education (*Gravissimum educationis* 7) by placing the issue in the context of changing social conditions. The ordinary faithful have an increasingly important part to play in the political and economic life of society; their social influence is amplified by developments in technology and social communication (ibid. Intro.). The Declaration acknowledging advances in psychology and pedagogy, envisages the creation of means to "develop harmoniously [young people's] physical, moral, and intellectual qualities" to the end that they will acquire "a more perfect sense of responsibility in the proper development of their own lives . . . and in the pursuit of liberty" (ibid. 1).

As an agency which seeks to achieve this end, the Catholic school must strive to do the following: (1) provide an atmosphere enlivened by the freedom of the Gospel and by a spirit of charity; (2) help adolescents interpret their personality development in a manner coherent with the "new creation" they have become in Baptism; and (3) relate human culture to the mystery of salvation so that the Catholic student will "contribute effectively to the welfare of the world of men" and become "the saving leaven in the community" (ibid. 8). Clearly, the Declaration sees moral education as developing persons who exercise their capacities as dynamic moral agents, who accept moral accountability for what they do, who take responsibility for others in relationship with them, and who arrive at a personal autonomy and freedom helpful to the human community.

Dimensions of Morality. Moral responsibility represents the maturation of the many dimensions in personal growth, not just a single dimension. It involves the capacity to decide (including initiative, experience, accountability, and caring) as well as the capacity to judge well (including understanding, fairness, and empathy). Moreover, moral education includes a proper orientation toward many levels of value.

Transcendent values. These represent the person's orientation of his life to the Author of life. Here the *religious conscience* gives testimony to a personal experience of the reality of God, to the enduring meaning of moral striving, and to a person's *vocation* to a special state in life. This level of values is altogether transempirical.

Social values. These represent the rules, order, roles, and customs of a person's culture. Persons gradually develop a capacity to relate to these values in flexible and creative ways, and this development is empirically measurable (*see* MORAL DEVELOPMENT).

Personal Values. These represent the person's relationship to self-actualization, to the maturation of personal skills and talents, and to the free acceptance and exercise of personal potential for initiative, leadership, and creativity. A good orientation toward all of these dimensions is necessary for integral moral education.

Means for Moral Education. Most important for the moral education of the child are the example, character,

and discipline of parents and family. Schools will supplement the influence of the family, but cannot be expected to provide an orientation to responsibility when this is lacking in the home. The sharing of a common vision of what is good, with family, friends, and an ecclesial community, is the most dynamic means for value formation. Likewise, only the exercise of responsibility and initiative will develop the *personal value orientation* necessary for the development of a mature autonomy and a personal freedom.

Bibliography: J. GUSTAFSON, "Education for Moral Responsibility," in N. F. SIZER and T. R. SIZER, eds. *Moral Education* (Cambridge, Mass. 1970). R. T. HALL and J. U. DAVIS, *Moral Education in Theory and Practice* (Buffalo 1975). T. LICKONA, ed., *Moral Development and Behavior* (New York 1976). USCC Department of Education, *Moral Education and Christian Conscience* (Washington, D.C. 1977).

[P. J. PHILIBERT]

MORAL THEOLOGY (CONTEMPORARY TRENDS)

Since the conclusion of Vatican Council II Catholic theological thinking and writing have changed more than in any similar period in history. Trends mentioned in the earlier volumes of the *New Catholic Encyclopedia* (9:1122; cf. 16:302) as merely beginning to exert an influence on Catholic theologians have either rapidly spread or practically disappeared. Much of what can be said of moral theology in this regard applies proportionately to systematic theology as well (*see* THEOLOGY). Change in moral theology can be considered, first, as to underlying presuppositions and methodology in approach; secondly, as to a shift in topics given prominence.

Changes in Approach. These are evident with regard to the nature and resources (*loci*) of theology and the philosophical categories incorporated.

Authority of the Magisterium. One of the most far-reaching changes has occurred in the attitude of many theologians towards the teaching authority of the pope and bishops. A strong factor influencing many in this direction was the premature publication in 1967 of the report of the papal commission appointed to study the birth-control question. The report advised Pope Paul VI to relax considerably the previous official teaching of the magisterium on the use of contraceptives in marriage. The report apparently led many theologians to judge that the Pope would follow the commission's recommendation. When *Humanae vitae* finally appeared in 1968, many of these theologians expressed disappointment and dissent even before reading the text of the encyclical (16:215). At first, most dissenters were still willing to attribute a presumption of truth to ordinary papal teaching, but for many this has come down to giving no more presumption of truth to papal teaching than would be given to any individual theologian writing on the same subjects. For them, the authority of ordinary papal teaching is only as strong as the arguments presented in that teaching.

Interpretations of Vatican II. Vatican II stressed the dignity of man as a norm in moral thought (*Optatam totius* 17; cf. *Gaudium et spes* 12–17). Some theologians have exaggerated the central place of man to the point of embracing a form of secular humanism or anthropocentrism. They make no mention of God or Jesus, and seemingly take no account of spiritual realities. Man's own self-fulfillment has become their norm of morality. The Council recommended acquaintance with modern findings of science (*Gaudium et spes* 62; *Optatam totius* 15; *Christus Dominus* 17). Some have carried this to the point of creating moral norms from sociological or psychological data, instead of using such findings as complementary material.

Philosophical Influences. Vatican II also recommended that all priests become familiar with modern philosophies so as to be able to converse with modern educated people (*Optatam totius* 17). But many divergences from traditional or official teaching of the magisterium have resulted from an unrestrained adoption of some modern philosophies. Existentialism and its moral counterpart, situation ethics, were mentioned in the previous survey as influencing many non-Catholic moralists and only a few Catholic. In the intervening years, the influence has become widespread among Catholic writers as well. A. N. Whitehead's process philosophy together with the popularity of P. Teilhard de Chardin and further paleontological findings have influenced many writers explicitly or at least implicitly to a belief that all things are in a state of flux, including human beings and their morality. This seemingly has led many writers, popular rather than professional moralists, to consider all change as progress and so to accept any new opinion as true and reject older teaching as false or at least suspect. Phenomenalism and empiricism have also influenced some Catholic moralists to the extent of accepting as true only what can be verified by personal experience (*see* PERSONALISM).

New systems, influenced more or less by one or more of these philosophies, and explicitly proposed by only one or two Catholic moralists, include consequentialism, which judges the morality of an act by its short- and long-range effects; proportionalism, which judges an act moral as long as the positive values outweigh the disvalues; the principle of the "overriding right," which would justify an exception to an apparently universal negative principle when an important or overriding right demanded it; a theology of compromise, which would make exceptions to what are considered moral absolutes for individuals who find a precept too hard to observe. These systems hold that "the end justifies the means" if the proper weight of positive values in the "end" outweighs the disvalues in the "means."

Pluralism. Adverting to their own deviation from magisterial teaching, many appeal to the approval of a certain legitimate pluralism in theology and philosophy. Paul VI many times insisted that legitimate pluralism consists of a variety of approach, methodology or emphasis; that pluralism in the sense of contradictory doctrine is not legitimate. Other dissenters maintain that their new views are a development of doctrine rather than a denial of it. Pope Paul taught that legitimate development of doctrine should lead to a fuller understanding or better expression or a new application of traditional doctrine, not a reversal or denial of it.

Use of Scripture. Contrary to a previous trend, many recent writers of the types mentioned above ignore the teachings of Scripture entirely. Others, claiming to follow the findings of historical criticism, judge that all moral teaching in the Bible was completely determined by historical and cultural factors, and so is not normative today.

Naturalistic Approaches. Similarly, while in the pre-vious survey, a return to more theological and less philosophical approaches was noted, much recent writing ignores all theological sources. Although expressing contempt for natural law theories, many use only natural reasoning in establishing their conclusions. Instead of the nature or will of God or Christ as the ultimate norm of morality, many have turned to the individual's personal integration and self-development according to each person's own experience of what this development and integration of personality entails.

These general trends are found in varying degree and in varying combinations in a sizable portion of recent writing in the field of moral theology.

Topics Treated in Recent Moral Literature. Besides greater changes since the Council in presuppositions, approaches, and methodologies among Catholic moral theologians, there has also been a greater quantity of publication of books and articles on moral questions. In spite of the expressed desire of the Holy See for revised textbooks or manuals of moral theology for seminary classes, there has been almost nothing in this line in English-speaking countries and relatively little elsewhere. Most of the books have been collections of articles or lectures previously published in periodicals, either by one author or by a number. These writings have treated many parts of moral theology. Some treat old questions with new approaches, others treat newly arisen or revived problems. Professional moral theologians, who, for the most part, are professors in seminaries or universities, have treated mainly matters of fundamental moral principles and the fields of sexuality and bioethics or medical morality. More general social-moral questions have been treated rather by sociologists, economists, ecologists, journalists, and others. Naturally there has been overlapping in both directions.

Questions of Fundamental Moral. Much of moral theological literature concerns such basic questions as: what is morality? what are the norms of morality? can there be a specifically Christian morality, and if so, how will it differ from non-christian morality? (*see* MORALITY; MORALITY, CHRISTIAN.)

Bioethics. The U.S. Supreme Court decisions on abortion (*see* ABORTION [U.S. LAW]) and the resultant reaction in the increase in pro-life activities have occasioned writing on the right to life of the unborn, as well as on the morality of experimentation on aborted fetuses, both those that survive the abortion procedure and those that do not. This in turn has led to much discussion of experimentation on intrauterine fetuses destined for abortion, and from there to the question of experimentation on any fetus, and, finally, on children below the age of responsible consent (*see* EXPERIMENTATION, MEDICAL; FETAL RESEARCH; MEDICAL ETHICS).

So-called death-with-dignity laws have brought forth new moral discussion in America and elsewhere on the old problems of *euthanasia and the use of ordinary and extraordinary means of preserving or prolonging life. Accompanying this discussion has been a good deal of pastoral treatment of attitudes toward death and dying and towards helping those who face imminent death (*see* DYING, CARE OF). Newly discovered possibilities of genetic engineering have opened up a new field of moral investigation and thought which promises to engage moralists more and more as the biological knowledge and practical expertise increase.

Sexual Morality. The so-called sexual revolution with

its widespread social acceptance of divorce and re-marriage, of homosexual activities, of pre- and extra-marital sex, of explicit public sexual performances and writings, has been the occasion of a great deal of writing both by professional moral theologians and others. Some have denied, others have defended basic tradi-tional Christian sexual morality. The Sacred Congrega-tion for the Doctrine of the Faith and a number of national episcopal conferences as well as many indi-vidual bishops have issued documents defending tradi-tional Catholic teaching on *sexual morality (*see* HOMOSEXUALITY).

Social-Moral Questions. Whereas in the period of the previous survey, racial discrimination was a prominent subject, discrimination on the basis of sex or sexual orientation has recently been more discussed. So-called reverse discrimination also arose as a topic during the latter part of this period.

*Capital punishment, *multinational corporations, the armaments race, ecology, nuclear power plants, the world food problem, union organization of Catholic school teachers are social topics with moral overtones that have evoked much comment. So also scandals in high political offices and in the management of religious finances (*see* BUSINESS ETHICS; DISARMAMENT; LABOR MOVEMENT; TEACHERS' UNIONS, CATHOLIC; WORLD HUNGER). Systemic civil and economic oppression of large portions of nations has engendered a systematic *liberation theology, especially in Latin America. As with all such general titles, liberation theology includes varying degrees of opinions regarding revolution and Marxism as possible solutions to the problem.

Conclusion. Most of what has been reported in this survey is in the nature of dissent from traditional Catholic teaching. Such widespread dissent among Catholic theologians is relatively new and is more newsworthy than defense of traditional doctrine. But, besides the pope and the bishops, there are many moral theologians, both Catholic and non-Catholic, who defend traditional morality, even though their position receives less publicity. It is an interesting sidelight that Catholic physicians have defended magisterial teaching on medical-moral issues against some professional moralists, who sought to liberate them. A number of colleges, seminaries, and organizations of laity and of scholars have been established to promote the teaching and defending of traditional Catholic theology. Some of these tend to be reactionary, but most are moderate.

Bibliography: H. ALLARD, "Recent Work in Moral Theology: In Defense of Objective Morality," *Clergy Review* 61 (1976) 191–195. C. E. CURRAN, "Present State of Moral Theology," ThSt 34 (1973) 446–467. T. DUBAY, "A Critical Appraisal of the State of Moral Theology," ThSt 35 (1974) 482–506. G. ERMECKE, "Krise der Moral–Krise der Moral-theologie," *Theologie und Glaube* 64 (1974) 338–356. R. MCCORMICK, "Notes on Moral Theology," ThSt 36 (1975) 77–129, esp. 77–117; 37 (1976) 70–119, esp. 71–87; 38 (1977) 57–114. V. MCNAMARA, "Approach-ing Christian Morality," *Furrow* 28 (1977) 213–220. G. TAVARD, "Evolu-tion in Moral Theology," *Catholic World* 203 (April, 1966) 29–32.

[J. J. FARRAHER]

MORALITY

The earlier article on morality in the *New Catholic Encyclopedia* (9:1129) treated elements on which practi-cally all Catholic writers in the fields of ethics and moral theology at the time were in agreement. Such agree-ment is no longer universal. The present article will treat the same matter with later divergences in view,

adding comments on the related questions of moral obligation and moral absolutes.

Definition. Morality can refer to actions, as, the morality of prizefighting, or to the way human beings perform actions, as, the morality of John Doe. In any case, morality is the quality of actions or agents by which they are in conformity or lack of conformity with certain norms of human conduct.

Ethical Positions and Norms. A presupposed philosophy and/or theology will affect what kind of moral norms, if any, are to be considered. Moral theology or Christian ethics will differ from moral philosophy or philosophical ethics according to the sources of knowing such norms; and each will differ according to the different philosophy or theology upon which each is based (for some of this variety, *see* MORAL THEOLOGY [CONTEMPORARY TRENDS]).

All Catholic moralists and, in fact, all professedly Christian and theistic moralists should agree fundamen-tally that man's ultimate end is somehow connected with his Creator. In other words, that moral goodness means conformity in some way with the nature or will of God. Divergences occur in determining more proxi-mate norms for learning what is or is not in conformity with man's ultimate end. For Catholics, a more proxi-mate objective norm has been the nature of man as created by God, with all his relationships: to God, to fellow human beings, and to himself, as known by reason and by revelation interpreted by the living teaching authority of the Church. But at present not all Catholic writers agree even on these points.

Many modern writers propose man's self-development as a norm, understanding such develop-ment to include a greater degree of knowledge, a balanced personality, and a comfortable degree of self-satisfaction and enjoyment. There is a great divergence in judging what these terms mean, in judging which acts or objects really contribute to such develop-ment, and even in judging what sort of norm or faculty may be used to discover which acts or objects will promote proper development. Self-development can well be a norm for judging the morality of actions even in accord with traditional Catholic thought, if measured by a full understanding of what is for the best welfare of the self in relation to the ultimate end.

Species of Morality. The distinction of the morality of actions into good, bad, or indifferent in kind, as well as the distinction between intrinsic and extrinsic morality, has been widely neglected, especially with a blurring of the distinction between subjective and objective moral-ity. While all Catholic moralists have always agreed and still agree that the most decisive element in human morality is in the person, some modern moralists refuse to consider a distinction between this morality in the agent and a morality attributed analogously to certain described actions.

Determinants. The position of such moralists has led them to deny that morality can ever be legitimately attributed to any acts objectively considered, unless such acts are described by such a prejudicial term as "murder," which implies *unjust* killing. Some such writers fail to realize that the older distinction between the *object* and the *circumstances* of a moral action did not necessarily mean that the *object* signified some kind of physical action without any circumstances. Even the term "killing" necessarily includes more content than just a physical act; in ordinary usage it denotes an act by which a living being is deprived of life. Even in times past, all Catholic moralists agreed that there was no absolute moral imperative against all killing, nor even against all killing of a human being. But in times past all did agree that the direct killing of an innocent human being was always immoral—at least apart from a certain command of the Creator who possesses ultimate dominion over all of creation.

The traditional use of the term "circumstances" as a determinant of morality beyond the object, referred to circumstances which could affect the morality of an action, other than those included in the definition of the object or act.

Objective and Subjective Morality. The modern objection that morality is never present apart from the intention of the agent misses the essential idea of the distinction between objective (or material) and subjective (or formal) morality. It is certainly true that morality is essentially in the act of the human will, but that does not mean that there cannot be a proper but derived use of the term with regard to objects and circumstances. When traditional Catholic moralists speak of an object or of an object with certain defined circumstances, as intrinsically or objectively evil in a moral sense, it is understood that this means that it would be morally wrong to intend such an action in such defined circumstances, regardless of further circumstances or intention.

Moral and Physical Evil. In considering the object of a human action, Catholic moralists have always recognized a difference in the meaning of moral evil and physical evil, although at times some have used the terms in a confused way. Evil, in general, was understood to mean the lack of something which should be present. To speak of physical evil was to speak merely of such a lack in the physical make-up of things; a lack of conformity to what some reality should normally be. Thus, a human being with only four fingers on one hand, or with six fingers, was said to be lacking conformity with what should normally be the number of fingers on a human hand, with no reference to morality. It was understood that ordinarily it would also be morally evil for one human being to inflict such a physical evil on another human being, although it was generally admitted that circumstances and intention could alter the matter. Thus, it was commonly agreed that amputation or excision of a part of the human body can be morally good in circumstances in which that part constitutes a threat to the whole human organism. For this reason, the loss of a finger was not considered a moral evil even in a remote sense, but only a physical evil, which it would be illicit to intend unless there were a good reason for doing so. On the other hand, the direct killing of an innocent human being was considered an objectively immoral action, whose only imaginable justification could be a direct command of the Creator who had the absolute dominion over human life.

Some modern moralists, including some Catholic theologians, avoid this sort of terminology. They prefer to use terms like "ontic," "premoral," "non-moral" evil to include, apparently, what traditional Catholic terminology classed as "objective" or "intrinsic" moral evil, but also to include what traditional terminology called "physical" evil. As mentioned above, there was

some confusion between the terms "physical evil" and "objective moral evil" in some older manuals, especially in the treatment of the so-called principle of double effect (4:1020), at least in their examples. But this does not prove that the distinction itself is useless.

Values and Disvalues. Instead of speaking of moral good and evil, many modern Catholic moralists prefer to follow what had previously been mainly non-Catholic philosophical terminology and speak rather of values to be achieved or preserved and of disvalues to be avoided. Practically speaking, the use of the terms "values" and "disvalues" in morality differs little if at all from the older terminology among Catholic moralists of *good* and *evil* in morality (see VALUE, PHILOSOPHY OF, 14:527 and related articles).

Again difficulties and divergences arise in determining the norm or norms for judging what is a value and what is a disvalue, as well as in determining whether there are any disvalues so great that they may never be directly chosen as a means of achieving certain positive values. All admit that many human choices involve both values and disvalues, good and evil.

Often overlooked are values in what might be called a religious or spiritual sense. These can include the value of self-denial and sacrifice (the Cross); the value of patient suffering; the value of helping others even at a seeming loss (disvalue?) to oneself; in general, the value of submission to God; and, finally, the value of achieving the real end of man's existence (union with God) even at the cost of losing the greatest of merely human values. Nevertheless, even some who neglect man's relation to God, still recognize some of these values as helps towards character development.

Moral Absolutes. What was explained above as objective moral evil is the basis of most moral absolutes (16:301). When the more traditional moralists state that an action is objectively morally evil, they mean that such an action would be morally wrong as a direct object of a human will in all imaginable circumstances in the ordinary course of affairs. Accordingly, although all killing involves some form of physical evil to a living being, it was and is not considered absolutely morally evil objectively, but needs further determination by at least some added circumstances. On the other hand, the killing of an innocent human being was and is considered a moral evil, even though the traditional principle of double effect would, under certain conditions, allow such a killing to be the unintended but foreseen event of a directly willed action. On the contrary, the direct killing of a cat would not be considered an objective moral evil, even though it is a physical evil for the cat. It could be a moral evil or a moral good for the killer depending on further circumstances as well as on the intent. To deny that there are any objective moral absolutes is tantamount to saying that it is impossible to describe any action in such a way that in no imaginable further circumstances in the ordinary course of affairs could such an action be justified, and any person who felt justified in doing such an action would be laboring under a misapprehension or false conscience.

Some who profess to deny the possibility of moral absolutes actually restrict such a judgment to personal morality and especially sexual morality, while insisting on absolutes in social matters. For example, the same writer may voice an opinion that premarital sex, masturbation, adultery, and homosexual acts can be morally good in some circumstances, but that the use of nuclear armaments or even nuclear power sources are absolutely immoral.

The Notion of Moral Obligation. The previous *New Catholic Encyclopedia* article on obligation (10:614–17) strongly emphasizes the connection of moral obligation, and thus of morality, with the relationship of man to his Creator. This is often overlooked in modern discussions of morality. In an analysis of the meanings of "ought," "must," and similar words, some common-sense ideas are often neglected. An instance of such an idea is that notions of obligation are concerned with a sort of conditioned necessity, and do not always have a tie-in with morality. For example, to say that a bridge player who bids four spades *must* take ten tricks, has nothing directly to do with morality. It only suggests that if he does not take ten tricks, he has failed in that round of play. So also with the *obligation* of religious rules in most religious orders and congregations. To say that a religious *must* keep silence, means that if he/she does not keep proper silence, he/she is not fulfilling the perfection of that form of life, but it does not imply any sin. Most regulations in business enterprises are similar. *If* one wishes to remain a member of the organization in good standing, one *must* follow such regulations. To fail to do so does not imply immorality, but may endanger the person's position in the organization. The condition implied in moral obligations might be stated: if you wish to achieve the purpose for which you exist, you must do certain things and you must avoid doing certain other things.

Bibliography: H. ALLARD, "Recent Work in Moral Theology: In Defense of Objective Morality," *Clergy Review* 61 (1976) 191–195. S. FAGAN, "No More Sin?" *Catholic Mind* 75 (Jan. 1977) 29–40 (reprinted from *Doctrine and Life* 26 [1976] 375–388). T. GILBY, ed., *Principles of Morality* in *St. Thomas Aquinas, Summa Theologiae* (60 v., London, New York 1965–1976) v. 18. R. MCCORMICK, "Notes on Moral Theology," ThSt 29 (1968) 679–741, esp. 707–718; 32 (1971) 66–122, esp. 66–80; 34 (1973) 53–102, esp. 53–65; 36 (1975) 77–129, esp. 84–100; 37 (1976) 70–119, esp. 71–87; 38 (1977) 57–114, esp. 58–84; all of which give many further references. V. MCNAMARA, "Approaches to Christian Morality," *Catholic Mind* 75 (Oct. 1977) 30–37 (reprinted from: "Approaching Christian Morality," *Furrow* 28 [1977] 213–220).

[J. J. FARRAHER]

MORALITY, CHRISTIAN

During the past decade a sharp debate among moralists, Protestant, Catholic, and Anglo-Catholic, has arisen over the meaning of a "Christian" morality. Those engaged in the dispute agree that one can rightly speak of a "Christian" morality in distinction to a "Jewish" or "Buddhist" or "humanist" morality, but they differ over the way in which a morality can be properly termed "Christian."

The Debate. On the one side can be ranged a group of writers who believe that morality can be "Christian" only in a formal, intentional sense but not in the sense that it provides the believer with a normative content specifically distinct from that of other moralities. Among the writers espousing this position are Jean-Marie Aubert, Franz Böckle, Francesco Compagnoni, Charles E. Curran, Josef Fuchs, James Gustafson, Dietmar Mieth, Richard A. McCormick, John Macquarrie and Bruno Schüller. On the other side are those who hold that a Christian morality differs from other kinds of morality not only because of its formal intentionality but also because of its normative or material content.

Among the principal exponents of this view are René Coste, Gustav Ermecke, Johannes Gründel, Josef Ratzinger, Norbert Rigali, N. H. G. Robinson, Dionigi Tettamanzi, and Hans Urs Von Balthasar.

Arguments. Advocates of the first position admit that in the concrete, because of the reality of sin and its effect on individuals and societies, some specific norms of morality may be unknown or less discernible for persons not formally included within the community of those who accept the revelation given in and through Jesus Christ. Yet such authors argue that the categorical or material content of the moral life incarnated in Christ and preached by the Church is fundamentally and substantively human or a morality of humanity. Authentic human morality, in their judgment, demands that the individual person live in responsiveness to God and his neighbor, working with others and striving with them to build up the world and humanity. Christian morality is, accordingly, human morality in its fullness, and there is no reason to think that non-Christians are intrinsically incapable of reaching the same norms of conduct, both personal and social, that the Christian finds in the sources of revelation. The consequence is that there is no material content specific to a Christian morality. What specifies a morality as "Christian" is the horizon or mentality in which concrete material norms are understood; the moral dictates that the Christian knows with an explicit Christian dimension, however, can be known by all men.

Advocates of the second position stress first the newness of the human as revealed in Jesus. They insist that for the Christian the divine love manifested definitively in Christ must become the standard of human love. They emphasize, secondly, the reliability of faith as opposed to human reason and (at least the Catholics in this group) insist on the need for the Christian to live the life that is preached by the magisterium of the Church. In concrete, existential fact, they argue, the Christian has obligations that are not incumbent on the non-Christian, obligations such as turning the other cheek, being willing to be self-sacrificing when the times require it, and, for the Catholic Christian, being willing to form conscience in accord with the authentic teaching of the Church's magisterium.

Authors in the first group are willing to admit with those in the second group that Baptism brings into being a "new man" in Christ so that to the new Christian *esse* there corresponds a new Christian *agere*. Still in their judgment (as set forth perhaps most vigorously by Fuchs and Schüller) this affects not the *what* that the Christian is to do or not do, for this *what* is something that, in principle, can be known by all who sincerely struggle for the truth. Rather it has to do with the *how* and the *why* the Christian will do what he knows to be good and right.

Proponents of the first view argue that those in the second group fail to distinguish, first, between hortatory and normative ethics in speaking of the newness of the human as manifested in Christ and, second, between the basis of the truth of a normative judgment and the way in which the truth comes to be known. Once these distinctions are made, they urge, it becomes more readily apparent that the material content, the *what*, of Christian morality can, in principle and in fact, be present in other moralities as well.

Comparison. The debate between these two groups continues. The first group seeks to emphasize the basic continuity between a Christian morality and what Macquarrie terms the "moral strivings of mankind." The second group, while by no means denying this continuity, is concerned to show that the morality manifested in Christ truly transfigures the human and imposes upon the believer obligations that simply cannot be experienced by the non-Christian.

It is somewhat paradoxical that the majority of the authors holding for a "Christian" morality only in a formal, intentional sense are among the leading critics of older Roman Catholic approaches for their failure to take seriously the reality of sin and the insights into the human provided by the Scriptures.

Although the writers in the second group have difficulty in specifying concretely the content of Christian morality, their contention that there are special norms obligating Christians in their existential lives that do not in fact oblige non-Christians—e.g., the obligation to bear witness, the obligation (for the Catholic) to heed the teaching of the Church in forming conscience—needs to be seriously considered. Perhaps one could say, in support of the first group, that such existential norms are, in principle, implicit in the meaning of the "human" and become explicit only within the horizon of an explicit faith. If this be the case, then the debate between the two groups might in the end be viewed as somewhat misplaced.

Bibliography: J. M. AUBERT, "La Spécificité de la morale chrétienne selon S. Thomas," VieSpiritSuppl 23 (1970) 55–73. H. URS VON BALTHASAR, "Obedience in the Church," in *Problems of the Church Today* (Washington, D.C. 1976) 93–100. F. BÖCKLE, "Was ist das Proprium einer christliche Ethik?" *Zeitschrift für Evangelische Ethik* 11 (1967) 148–158. R. COSTE, "Loi naturelle et loi évangélique," NouvRevTh 92 (1970) 76–89. F. COMPAGNONI, *La specificità della morale cristiana* (Bologna 1972). C. E. CURRAN, "Dialogue With Humanism: Is There a Distinctively Christian Ethics?" in *Catholic Moral Theology in Dialogue* (Notre Dame, Ind. 1970); "Catholic Ethics, Christian Ethics, and Human Ethics," in *Ongoing Revision* (Notre Dame, Ind. 1975) 1–36. G. ERMECKE, "Das Problem der Universalität oder Allgemeingültigkeit sittlicher Normen innerweltlicher Lebensgestaltung" *Münchener theologische Zeitschrift* 24 (1973) 1–24. J. FUCHS, *Human Values and Christian Morality* (Dublin 1970) esp. 112–147; "Gibt es eine spezifisch christliche Moral?" *Stimmen der Zeit* 95 (1970) 99–112 (found also in *Esiste una morale cristiana?* [Rome 1970] 13–44); "Esiste una morale non-cristiana?" *Rassegni di teologia* 14 (1973) 361–373. J. GRÜNDEL, "Ethik ohne Normen? Zur Begründung und Struktur christlicher Ethik," in J. Gründel and H. Von Oyen, Eds., *Ethik ohne Normen* (Freiburg 1970). J. GUSTAFSON, *Can Ethics Be Christian?* (Chicago 1975). J. MACQUARRIE, *Three Issues in Ethics* (New York 1970). R. A. MCCORMICK, "Notes on Moral Theology," ThSt 32 (1971) 71–78; 38 (1977) 58–70; "The Insights of the Judeo-Christian Tradition and the Development of an Ethical Code," in E. Kennedy, ed., *Human Rights and Psychology* (New York 1975) 23–36. D. MIETH, "Autonome Moral im christlichen Kontext," *Orientierung* 40 (1976) 31–34. J. RATZINGER, *Prinzipien christliche Moral* (Einsiedeln 1975) abridged translation without notes, "Magisterium of the Church, Faith, Morality," in *Problems of the Church Today* (Washington, D.C. 1976) 74–84. N. RIGALI, "On Christian Ethics," ChSt 10 (1971) 227–247; "The Historical Meaning of *Humanae Vitae*," ChSt 15 (1976) 127–138. N. H. G. ROBINSON, *The Groundwork of Christian Ethics* (Grand Rapids, Mich. 1972). B. SCHÜLLER, "Typen ethischer Argumentation in der katholischen Moraltheologie," *Theologie und Philosophie* 45 (1970) 74–104; "Zur Diskussion über das Proprium einer christlicher Ethik," *Theologie und Philosphie* 51 (1976) 321–343. D. TETTAMANZI, "Esiste un'etica cristiana?" *La Scuola Cattolica* 99 (1971) 163–193.

[W. E. MAY]

MORALITY IN MEDIA, INC.

Morality in Media is a national, interfaith organization working against the traffic in pornography constitutionally and effectively, and for media based on love, truth, and good taste. Morality in Media acts as an information and communications center, disseminating information on the problem and then channeling response. A major project of Morality in Media is the National Obscenity Law Center (NOLC), a clearinghouse of information on obscenity-law cases and materials, for prosecutors and other interested attorneys.

Morality in Media was founded in 1962, as Operation Yorkville (New York City), by three clergymen, brought together by their mutual concern for children and youth. Policy today is formed by a Board of Directors of twenty-four, representing many viewpoints, creeds, and professions. The National Planning Board is manned by top-level leaders of business, industry, labor, and the arts. The organization is interfaith, nonpolitical, and anticensorship and the first full-time professionally staffed organization of its kind. The president of the organization, Rev. Morton A. Hill, SJ, was appointed in 1968 by President Lyndon B. Johnson to the Presidential Commission on Obscenity and Pornography. Fr. Hill coauthored the Hill-Link Report of that commission, which was cited several times in the U.S. Supreme Court's 1973 landmark obscenity decisions.

The National headquarters of Morality in Media is at 475 Riverside Drive, New York, N.Y. 10027. The organization has state affiliates in Louisana, Michigan, Minnesota, Massachusetts, California, and western New York. There are also unincorporated units (chapters) in many areas of the country. The organization's income consists of gifts from concerned persons.

[M. A. HILL]

MOVEMENT FOR A BETTER WORLD

Founded by Riccardo Lombardi, SJ some 25 years ago, the Movement for a Better World (MBW; 10:56) has, since its most recent International Meeting (1975), centered on consolidating membership and deepening commitment to places in greatest need: e.g. Rhodesia, Uganda, Upper Volta, Zaire. In all there are 33 centers throughout the world; in some countries service has been extended to ecumenical circles. Animation of reflection is a high priority. MBW focussed its international reflection on the State of the World and the meaning of the Kingdom of God during 1976–1977. During 1978 attention is being given to new images of the parish.

In the United States, MBW has existed for 15 years (headquarters, Silver Spring, Md.). Animating the life of parish communities is still a high priority. To promote a long-term commitment the teams are developing a process which incorporates prospective planning into the "Retreat of the Christian Community," the basic MBW course/retreat, and an extended presence as spiritual directors for groups. Commitment to the process of renewal in a diocese is important. Presently there is a mountain-team working in Appalachia, associated with the Wheeling-Charleston Diocese. The objective is to call forth a deeper awareness of and consequent sense of responsibility for improving the quality of commitment to the Christian life among all people—religious, clergy, laity—together.

There is a steady development of further participation in the process of renewal that is happening within religious communities. MBW is meeting religious communities at a new point where there is great concern for the new image of the American religious, a release of the hidden energies of religious commitment for service to/with the world of today and tomorrow through the identification and development of new models of community.

Paul VI recalled that the first step in evangelization is the renewal of the Church itself (Paul VI EvangNunt 15). The witness of this process by others has the power to change hearts. It is to furthering this that members of MBW are committed.

[P. M. HARTIGAN]

MULTINATIONAL CORPORATIONS

"Multinational Corporations" (MNCs)—a term used here synonymously with "Transnational Corporations," the term used in United Nations' literature—are enterprises which own or control production or service facilities outside the country in which they are based. They are not always incorporated or private; they can also be cooperatives or state-owned entities. The typical MNC is a large-sized, predominantly oligopolistic firm or bank having sales, loans, or deposits running into hundreds of millions of dollars and based in a rich developed country but with affiliates spread over several countries, both rich and poor.

Recent Growth. MNCs are not new on the world scene. Prototypes, like the East India Company, date back several centuries when they were the arms of colonial governments. By the end of the 19th century they had developed the main features of the modern MNC—concentration of economic and financial power and internationalization of economic production and trade, building on an international division of labor. Since World War II the MNCs have known explosive growth, first in manufacturing and more recently in banking. Between 1950 and 1974, the percentage of total U.S. sales in manufactures accounted for by U.S. MNCs jumped from 17 to 62 percent; in the non-Communist world the percentage of total sales in manufactures accounted for by MNCs jumped from 8 to 22 percent. Similarly, in the decade 1965–75, American multinational banks increased almost threefold their outstanding loans and deposits to $30 billion and $24 billion respectively. The total sales of the bigger MNCs now far exceed the total annual income of many if not most of the poor countries with which they deal. Although the U.S. still accounts for half of the MNCs, more and more countries are spawning their own, including Russia, which now has about 40 MNCs operating in 13 non-Communist countries. The MNCs are still concentrated in developed countries, with less than one-third of their activities located in developing countries.

Power and Problems. The great power of the MNC derives largely from its ability to use finance, technology, and advanced marketing skills to integrate production on a worldwide scale. If its great size raises fears, so also does its worldview that threatens to overshadow the role of the nation-state. In many countries the MNCs make social decisions about communications, employment, consumption patterns, urban growth, transportation, etc., as byproducts of their global profit-maximizing strategies. They are today, in fact, national and international planners by default.

That the MNCs have at times used their great power irresponsibly is clear from colonial times, with the ab-uses of ITT in Chile only a more shocking recent example. But abuse of power is not peculiar to MNCs. Because they are the most evident carriers of the modern process of industrialization and interdependence they are naturally blamed for the failures of the process, which begets economic hegemony for the few and economic dependence for the majority. But the crux of the problem lies in the fact that, in the foreseeable future, no nation can accept lightly to have inside its borders an entity that is exposed to the direct commands of outsiders—particularly if those outsiders have a different ideology or worldview or are citizens of a powerful neocolonial power.

Most people admit the MNCs unique contribution to technological and market know-how and management as well as to economic growth measured narrowly in terms of economic production. Even the Soviet bloc has come to rely increasingly on Western MNC know-how. Some foresee stringent international codes, courts, and social audits as sufficient to make the MNCs accountable for their use of vast economic and political power. (The UN has a Special Commission on Transnational Corporations trying to draft an acceptable code.) Others believe that in a world of scarcity the MNC can have only a limited role, because of its innate compulsion to indiscriminate, resource-using growth. More recently responsible scholars in the US have argued that, in its present form, the MNC is destructive of democracy because it is not politically accountable for its share of political power.

Developing Nations. But it is in the poorer developing countries that MNC's role is most contradictory. Thus far they contribute to the enrichment of 5 to 20 percent of the people but perform an absolute disservice to the human conditions of the majority by not serving their basic human needs. Such needs are simply outside today's world market. MNCs also sponge up scarce local savings for their own use and make poor countries still more dependent on rich countries for finance and technology. Finally, they propagate a consumer ideology to the masses which is destined to create explosive frustrations by the very luxury and elite-oriented economic structures they are helping to put in place. This consumer ideology threatens to destroy the principal source of spiritual strength needed for effective political change, namely a people's own sense of worth and dignity. Ironically, in today's capital-intensive, MNC economy, almost two billion people are not needed to produce its goods nor have they the money to consume them.

Any final judgment on the MNCs will turn on one's worldview and priorities, on one's relative weighting of increased economic production as against meeting the basic human needs of the poor—and in what time frame. It will also depend on whether one sees development narrowly as an economic process rather than more broadly as also a political process that allows people to organize their own society to serve their basic needs, rather than being persuaded to accept the MNC model of development on the grounds that any other alternative is too costly. The unanswered question remains: Can the MNCs once again prove versatile enough to evolve a creative and indispensable role for themselves in a national and international climate that is changing and becoming more concerned for the poor majority of the world's people?

Catholic Teaching. Successive popes (for example: Pius XI, in *Quadragesimo anno* 105, 109; Paul VI *Populorum progressio* 26) have condemned excessive concentration of economic power and "the imperialism of money." Paul VI saw in MNCs potential for "a new and abusive form of economic domination" (Paul VI OctogAdven 41). The 1971 Synod of Bishops was concerned with the structured injustice and dependency patterns of modern economy (Synod JustWorld pp. 36–37) and several episcopal conferences, especially the second general conference of the Latin American bishops at Medellín, Colombia, 1968 (*see* MEDELLÍN DOCUMENTS) have explicitly deplored the "unchecked control" of foreign economic interests that keep poor economies permanently dependent.

In general, Catholic social teaching raises a flag against unaccountable economic and political power—whether attached to private ownership or not—and fosters the participation of all people in shaping the economic circumstances of their lives. The structures of world economy must be centered on meeting the basic human needs of all people—especially the poor.

Bibliography: R. J. BARNET and R. E. MULLER, *Global Reach* (New York 1974). Department of Social Development and World Peace USCC, *Development-Dependency: The Role of the Multinational Corporations* (Washington, D.C. 1974). R. GILPIN, *US Power and the Multinational Corporation* (New York 1975). C. E. LINDBLOM, *Politics and Markets* (New York 1977). R. VERNON, *Storm over the Multinationals* (Cambridge, Mass. 1977).

[W. F. RYAN]

MUSIC, SACRED (LEGISLATION)

As part of liturgical renewal the universal legislation on sacred music (10:129) consists chiefly of three major documents: chapter six, "Sacred Music" of the Constitution on the Sacred Liturgy (December 4, 1963) of Vatican Council II; *Instruction on Music* (*Musicam sacram*, March 5, 1967) by the Congregation of Rites in conjunction with the Consilium (the post-conciliar commission on the reform of the liturgy); "General Instruction of the *Missale Romanum*" (April 6, 1969) published in the U.S. in the *Sacramentary (see* GenInstrRomMissal 25, 26, 36, 67, 274, 275).

Within the United States, the following documents have been inssued: *The Place of Music in Eucharistic Worship* (November 1968) by the *Bishops Committee on the Liturgy (BCL); a revised edition entitled *Music in Catholic Worship* (1972) by the BCL; "Foreword to the General Instruction" and "Appendix to the General Instruction for the Dioceses of the United States of America," (1969) in the Sacramentary.

Major Norms. The Vatican II document reaffirms that music in liturgy is greater than any other art, and the liturgical action is given a more noble form when sacred rites are solemnized in song (*Sacrosanctum Concilium* 112). It emphasizes simultaneously the importance of choirs and congregational participation (ibid. 118), of Gregorian chant and other types of music (ibid. 116), of pipe organs and other instruments (ibid. 120), of local musical traditions and new compositions (ibid. 119, 121).

Musicam sacram began the discussion of the distinction, or lack of, between High Mass and Low Mass. It eliminates the requirement for all parts of the liturgy to be sung when any parts are sung, recommending instead varied degrees of participation with the intention of fostering congregational participation in the singing. It establishes these important new principles. Some parts of liturgy are designed to be sung and are defective without song. "Solemnity" of worship is redefined, to mean not on ornate singing but worthy and religious celebration. Masterworks designated unsuited for Eucharistic Liturgy should be utilized in devotions. The office of cantor is recognized again. The distinction of ordinary parts for the people, proper parts for the choir is eliminated. The Instruction develops fully the need to respect the musical heritage of the past "in sung liturgical services celebrated in Latin," but it does so, not to preserve the bad tradition of non-participating congregations, but rather to encourage participation in those unique multinational situations where Latin is a common language (*see* LATIN MASS).

The General Instruction of the *Missale Romanum* provides a detailed statement on the places for singing in the Eucharistic Liturgy. The first presumption of the entire Instruction is a liturgy that is sung. The cantor is designated as an official minister of the Eucharistic Liturgy. Official chants are included for the priest's chants—the Prayers, the Prefaces, conclusion of the Eucharist Prayer—and for some congregational chants, viz., the Holy, Holy, Holy, the Memorial Acclamations, the Our Father, the Greeting and Response.

The Appendix to the General Instruction for the Dioceses in the United States in the Sacramentary provides that in addition to the Entrance Antiphon and Psalm of the Roman Gradual, other collections of psalms and antiphons in English, including psalms arranged in responsorial form, metrical and similar versions be approved, provided they are selected in harmony with the liturgical season, feast, or occasion. This principle is also applied to the song at the Presentation of the Gifts and Communion song, but specifically excluded is the Responsorial Psalm. Thus, hymns developed in other religious traditions are officially authorized for use as part of the Roman Mass (*see* HYMNOLOGY; HYMNS AND HYMNALS).

Music in Catholic Worship (the revised version of *The Place of Music in Eucharistic Worship*) is preeminently pastoral rather than legal in tone and purpose. It establishes a series of principles in the theology of worship, including this: "Good celebrations foster and nourish faith. Poor celebrations weaken and destroy faith." The planning process is detailed, urging both celebrant and musician to participate. As guitars and other instruments increased in usage at liturgies, the BCL document addressed the question of secular and sacred music. The document suggests that a threefold judgment is needed: a musical judgment (is the music good music?) a liturgical judgment (is it appropriate for this part of the liturgy?) and a pastoral judgment (is it appropriate for this congregation celebrating?). *Music in Catholic Worship* also gives a simple, yet concise consideration to the liturgical structure of the Eucharist, placing each part in proportion or in scale to each other part. The result provides special emphasis for the Procession and Opening Prayer of the Introductory Rite, the Reading of and Response to the Word of God, the Eucharistic Prayer, and the Rite of Communion with the Lord's Prayer, the Communion Procession, and the Postcommunion Prayer.

While abandoning the distinction between High Mass and Low Mass and between ordinary and proper parts of the Mass completely, the BCL document divides the music of the liturgy into musical categories appropriate to the liturgical usage: Acclamations (Alleluia, Holy, Holy, Holy, Memorial Acclamation, the Great Amen, the Doxology to the Lord's Prayer), the Processional Songs (the Entrance Song, the Communion Song), Responsorial Psalms, Ordinary Chants (Lord, Have Mercy, Glory to God, Lord's Prayer, Lamb of God, Profession of Faith), and Supplementary Songs (Song at the Presentation of Gifts, the Psalm after Communion, Recessional Song, and the Litanies).

Bibliography: Texts of *Musican sacram* ActApS 59 (1967) 300–320; Eng. tr., *On Music in the Liturgy* (USCC Publ. Office, Washington, D.C. 1967). Bishops' Committee on Liturgy, *Place of Music in Eucharistic Worship* (USCC Publ. Office, Washington, D.C. 1968); *Music in Catholic Worship* (USCC Publ. Office, Washington, D.C. 1972).

[V. FUNK]

MUSICOLOGY, SACRED

The importance of musicology to the liturgical musician of today has been emphasized by the recent change in the attitude which the Church has taken toward an understanding of what is meant by sacred music. Vatican Council II's Constitution on the Sacred Liturgy states: "Sacred music is to be considered the more holy, the more closely connected it is with the liturgical action . . . the Church indeed approves of all forms of true art which have the requisite qualities, and admits them into divine worship" (*Sacrosanctum Concilium* 112). From a position which limited sacred music to certain styles within a rather narrow range set by Western European tastes and practices, the Church now admits all forms of true art into the liturgy, and judges their suitability, indeed their very holiness, from the viewpoint of the closeness of the connection of such music with the liturgical action. From being limited to a rather specific body of music, with special emphasis placed on chant and sacred polyphony, the church musician is now encouraged to use music from a wide variety of historical and cultural milieus, provided only that it is good music which can be connected closely with the liturgical action, and is not inimical to it (ibid. 114–121).

In the United States a more specific requirement for greater competence has been placed on the liturgical musician by the 1972 statement of the *Bishops' Committee on the Liturgy, Music in Catholic Worship* (Washington, D.C. 1972), which gives to the liturgical musician an important role in liturgical planning. The document speaks of a necessary threefold judgment (musical, liturgical, and pastoral) which must be made (25). The musical judgment, described as basic and primary, is to be made by competent musicians who are to judge whether or not the music is technically, aesthetically, and expressively good (26).

Sacred Musicology. Musicology, as it is concerned with the scientific, historical and analytical research involved in all aspects of sacred and liturgical music, can be of assistance to the liturgical musician in making the judgments described above. It can provide assistance in a number of specific areas. Studies in music history and stylistic analysis can provide the basis upon which to make a judgment of the true musical value of a piece of music. Good critical editions of the great music of the past can increase both the quantity and the variety of sacred music available for liturgical use. Studies in the area of performance practice can provide the musician

with principles and suggestions as to how a work, once chosen, should actually perform. A specialized and rapidly growing area of musicology is concerned with the rebuilding of early musical instruments or the construction of authentic copies. Finally, the area of ethnomusicology is concerned with research into the rich area of music cultures other than our own—an area of research which is of great importance in the adaptation of liturgy and music to the genius of peoples of various cultural backgrounds (*see* LITURGY AND LOCAL CHURCHES).

Resources on Musical Style. Musicological studies in the area of history and theory are so diverse and so numerous that only a very general view of the materials available can be presented here. In order for the church musician to be able to make a decision as to the value of a given musical work, he should be able not only to play or sing the work, but also to compare it with other works and to make some kind of analysis of it, especially in terms of style. There are numerous articles written in musicological journals concerning stylistic analysis, but two rather general works can be of great assistance to the musician in judging a given piece of music: Richard Crocker, *A History of Musical Style* (New York 1966), and Jan LaRue, *Guidelines for Style Analysis* (New York 1970). Various studies and works that take a more historical approach can also be of value. For more specific studies found in periodicals the church musician should consult the *Music Index* or *RILM Abstracts.* Among the more important musicological periodicals are: the *Journal of the American Musicological Society,* the *Musical Quarterly, Music and Letters, Acta Musicologica,* and *Musica Disciplina,* the last, concerned especially with music of the Renaissance. Studies in Gregorian chant can be found in *Études Grégoriennes, Revue Grégorienne* and the articles of *Paléographie musicale.* Important publications in other languages include such journals as: the *Revue de musicologie, Revue Belge de musicologie, Annales musicologiques, Die Musikforschung,* and *Archiv für Musikwissenschaft.*

Editions of Music. Critical editions, whether of performance or study editions, are usually of two types: collected editions or series, frequently of works from a single period or a given region; and the complete works or *opera omnia* of a single composer. Among the important major collected editions which contain sacred music are: *Denkmäler de Tonkunst in Österreich* (DTO) and *Denkmäler deutscher Tonkunst* (DdT)—editions of the works of Austrian and German composers respectively. The latter series has been continued as *Das Erbe deutscher Musik.* The sacred music of English composers has been collected especially in two series: *Musica Brittanica,* containing works ranging from the Middle Ages to the 19th century, and *Tudor Church Music.* Important collections containing sacred music from France are *Le Pupitre,* which, though emphasizing the music of the Baroque, also contains music from other periods; and *Monuments de la musique française au temps de la Renaissance.* Among series limited to works of a given period, mention should be made of *Polyphonic Music of the Fourteenth Century* and the monumental *Corpus mensurabilis musicae,* which principally contains the work of Renaissance composers. In order to discover what composers are to be found in a particular series and where in the series their work is found, three sources should be consulted: the *Harvard Dictionary of Music*, W. Apel, ed. (2d ed. rev., Cambridge, Mass. 1969) under the entry, "Editions, Historical"; Anna Harriet Heyer, *Historical Sets, Collected Editions and Monuments of Music* (Chicago 1969); and Sydney Robinson Charles, *Handbook of Music and Music Literature in Sets and Series* (New York 1972).

Rather than being issued as a part of a larger collection, many composers' works are issued as the complete works of that composer alone. Among the most important editions of the works of major composers who have written sacred music are: the *Neue Bach Ausgabe*, the *Hallische Handel Ausgabe*, the *Neue Mozart Ausgabe*, and the *J. Haydn Werke*. The complete works of other important composers of sacred music which have been published in more or less critical editions include: complete works of Josquin Desprez, Johannes Ockeghem, Jacob Obrecht, Palestrina, Orlando di Lasso, William Byrd, Claudio Monteverdi, Heinrich Schütz, and many others. A more comprehensive listing may be found in the Charles *Handbook* mentioned above.

Resources on Performance Practice. The question of performance practice is an important one for the church musician. Musical compositions from different periods cannot be performed in the same way, for each age approached the questions involved with performance in different ways. In this century, and especially since World War II, a great deal of research has gone into studies of the performance practices of almost every period of music history. Today, for example, it is relatively easy for a musician to discover how many singers were used on a voice part at the time of Dufay or of Palestrina, or what principles of ornamentation should be used for works of Bach as opposed to works of Couperin. Indeed, if a musician is interested, he can find something written on the performance practice associated with almost any work he might choose to do. Even if a performance of total historical accuracy is not the goal, knowing something of the practice of the period from which a work comes is important for an artistic and beautiful performance. Again, there are many articles concerning specific problems of performance practice in the musicological journals, but one book which should be mentioned as particularly useful is Thurston Dart, *The Interpretation of Music* (New York 1963). Texts in English translation of performance treatises contemporary with music of various periods are available in Oliver Strunk, *Source Readings in Music History* (New York 1950).

On Musical Instruments. Musicological studies into the musical style and performance practices of various periods of music history have led to the realization that often the very instruments necessary for authentic performances have not been available. This has led to the development of a twofold craft which has grown considerably since its inception in the latter decades of the 19th century. Through the pioneering work of such scholars and instrument builders as Arnold Dolmetsch, craftsmen began to restore early musical instruments to playing condition and also to build new instruments that were accurate reproductions of the instruments of earlier periods. Two important centers, one at the Smithsonian Institution in Washington, D.C. and the other at Yale University, are, along with a number of

other centers, involved today in the restoration and building of early musical instruments. There is even a periodical, the *Galpin Society Journal*, concerned with this aspect of musicology. Today it is possible not only to hear performances on instruments contemporary with the music being performed, but to obtain authentic copies of such instruments. Pipe organs with classical voicing or tracker action are becoming almost commonplace. Older organs in this country, instead of being sold or scrapped, are being restored to their original condition. The sound of a well-built harpsichord or a consort of recorders is becoming more commonplace in churches today. The use of such instruments is certainly in accord with the desire for legitimate variety which characterizes contemporary liturgy, to say nothing of the search for authenticity and beauty.

Ethnomusicological Studies. Finally, mention should be made of the importance of ethnomusicological studies in the context of contemporary worship. Since the recognition by Vatican II of the variety of cultural and musical tradition within the Church universal (*see Sacrosanctum Concilium* 119), the importance of the study of music of other cultures has been underlined. In the U.S. this is true especially because of its rich cultural heritage: the culture of Black Americans, the American Indian culture, the culture of a growing Spanish and Latin American population, and the many contemporary cultural expressions having their roots in the authentic folk culture of the American past. Awareness of this rich heritage has only recently begun, but already serious studies are being undertaken. Among the more important projects, mention should be made of the work of the *National Office for Black Catholics and of the *Mexican American Cultural Center in San Antonio, Texas. More scholarly studies can be found in such periodicals as *Ethnomusicology* and such individual works as Eileen Southern, *The Music of Black Americans, a History* (New York 1971) and the studies of such scholars as Gilbert Chase (Latin American music) and Bruno Nettl (folk music). Important to a study of the religious folk music of the American past is the pioneering work done by George Pullen Jackson. More current and detailed studies are listed in *RILM Abstracts* or the *Music Index*.

Bibliography: F. BLUME, *Protestant Church Music* (London 1975). K. FELLERER, ed., *Geschichte der katholischen Kirchenmusik*, vol. 1, *Von den Anfängen bis zum Tridentinum* (Kassel 1972). J. GÉLINEAU, *Voices and Instruments in Christian Worship*, tr. C. HOWELL (Collegeville, Minn. 1964). H. ULRICH, *Survey of Choral Music* (New York 1973). G. VAN DER LEEUW, *Sacred and Profane Beauty, the Holy in Art* (New York 1963).

[R. B. HALLER]

MYSTICISM

One of the features of contemporary religion which will almost certainly have enduring effects on the Church is the comparatively recent but widely noted awakening of interest in myticism (10:175). Although the term itself has been applied to an unmanageably broad range of phenomena, it primarily refers to the direct intuition of ultimate reality and a concomitant conviction of intimacy or identity with it. In theistic traditions mysticism usually avoids suggestions of identity with God and expresses its goal in terms of a love relationship of the closest kind. Descriptions of the relationship between the soul and God which suggest identity rather than intimacy have frequently resulted in accusations of heterodoxy and this, coupled with the subjectively authoritative nature of the mystical experience, has tainted the phenomenon with suspicions of esotericism and idiosyncracy.

Studies and Experiments. Current interest in mysticism is both theoretical and practical, is not limited to the educated or initiated, and is ecumenical or cross-cultural in its orientation. An adequate assessment of the current situation needs to consider more than the spectacular or exotic features, which, in the long view of Christian history, suggest the déjà vu rather than innovation. Particular notice should be taken of new directions in Christian spirituality, presaged by current mystical language and symbolism. Furthermore, its rather broad theoretical base adds a dimension to the contemporary renascence of mysticism which promps more serious reflection and indicates that Christian spirituality may be in the process of significant modification.

Scholarly or theoretical interest in mysticism has been steady and fruitful, even if not intense, throughout the present century. William James' chapter "Mysticism" in his *Varieties of Religious Experience* (1902), with its observation that mysticism discloses a realm of consciousness beyond the rational, gave an unremitting impetus to the study of mysticism by the behavioral and social sciences and to the continuing dialogue within and among these disciplines. The comparative study of *religions has considerably improved the comprehension of a notoriously elusive subject. Even the well-known experimental attempts to induce mystical experiences by means of drugs have led to meaningful distinctions between the religious goal of spiritual endeavor and its occasional exotic sensory accompaniments. Reasonable facsimiles of the latter can be artifically stimulated and this fact, itself well known for centuries, has reemphasized the age-old cautions of the spiritual masters against overvaluation of emotional states.

Interest in mysticism as experiential also follows behavioral science's concerns with the role and function of emotion generally, especially in its capacity to add richness and depth to life. Proliferation of sensitivity clinics and awareness institutes of indescribable variety is some indication of a general search for emotional fulfillment, a datum which corroborates theoretical observations. The successful quest for more intense feelings of personal intimacy as well as for a closer relationship with nature and life generally, has made the so-called peak experience, described by Abraham Maslow, less extraordinary. In 1973 the National Opinion Research Center reported that about 25 percent of the Catholics it surveyed and about 50 percent of the Protestants acknowledged having mystical experiences.

Developments in Theology. In the theological sphere of theory, modern Christian theologians unlike their medieval predecessors, have not given much attention to the mystical emphasis. Post-Tridentine Catholic theology with its defensive stress on ritual efficacy and ecclesiastical authority felt compelled to relegate mysticism to the exotic realm inhabited by a few "chosen souls" on the way to "infused contemplation." Mainline Protestant theology had little need for mystical vision because "this worldly," mundane activity was not seen to have any causal relationship to salvation and hence did not need to be transcended. Protestantism represented a "this-worldly asceticism" rather than an "other-worldly mysticism" in Max Weber's categories.

The antimysticism of Karl Barth and Emile Brunner reflect this emphasis.

Current theological interest in mysticism owes much to ecumenical developments. Mystical traditions within the major religions seem to share so much common ground that ecumenical endeavor frequently appears superfluous. Recent exponents of the view that at their highest, mystical levels, the world religions are, in reality, one religion (e.g. A. Huxley, F. Schuon, and S. Radakrishnan) have understandably been criticized for glossing over precious and essential distinctions, but their positions do highlight areas of almost ready-made religious unity. Conceptions of the Absolute and, even more so, descriptions of ineffable experience, tend linguistically to converge as they approach what they perceive to be their respective goals.

In its ecumenical concerns Christian theology has begun what promises to be an enormously fruitful discussion with comparative-religions studies. Mystical worldviews as well as mystical practices are three major preoccupations among comparative-religions scholars which have already stimulated some development in Christian mystical theology. Jungian psychology has also proved to be an important partner to this multileveled conversation. William Johnston's works on Zen and Christian mysticism offer a distinguished example of the theological enrichment available from such comparative studies. Robert Zaehner's comparative studies of Hindu, Muslim, and Christian mysticism have also made an enormous contribution, not only by way of generating scholarly interest in the subject but also by reason of his clarification of similarities and differences.

Some support is given scholarly concerns by widespread popular interest in Zen and Yoga. The faddish nature of the popular brands is often obvious but the very fact of concern or curiosity and especially its breadth could signal substantial readjustment in overall religious orientation. At the very least it indicates a dissatisfaction with religious resources traditionally available in the Christian West. Even though such forms as Yoga and techniques as Transcendental Meditation assert their nonreligious nature and are allegedly compatible with the traditional faiths, it is apparent that all but the merely physical ("Yoga as exercise") do clash in some way with traditional Christianity (*see* YOGA, CHRISTIAN).

Significance for Christian Spirituality. From the two distinguishing and mutually inseparable marks of the mystical phenomenon, namely its experiential emphasis and its unitive worldview, several observations relative to contemporary Christian spirituality suggest themselves. To some extent these two marks or characteristics correspond to the correlative symbols, Self and Universe, and any decided enlargement of consciousness in either area would elicit a corresponding reaction toward maintaining intimacy and cohesion between the two. Historical periods witnessing significant world expansion and its corresponding threat to intellectual and psychological cosmos are invariably accompanied by a rise in mystical experience and a more comprehensive religious worldview.

The mystical vision of Teilhard de Chardin accommodates an impressive range of recent world-expanding discovery, stretching from paleontology's substantial revisions regarding human origins all the way to nuclear theory and space travel. With the affirmation characteristic of the mystic and an immanentism at times nearly indistinguishable from pantheism, he offers a spirituality in his *The Divine Milieu* which meshes with contempory valuations of nature, science, and technology and which, in its cosmic sweep, is little disturbed by the hairsplitting details that exercised traditional dogmatic and moral theology. His vision offers Christians, both Protestant and Catholic, an affirmative valuation of work and invention, of learning and recreation. For Teilhard as well as for his kindred spirit in India, Sri Aurobindo Ghose, all these activities are inherently religious and need no ritual blessing or specific intention to make them so. Matter itself is raised to the plane of the spiritual and this *coincidentia oppositorum* finds resonance in the social sphere where the mystical and the prophetic become one in the cause of social reform.

Contrary to many popular images, the mystical religious mode is not extraordinary and is not for reclusive types. As James and others have asserted, there is a mystical dimension in all serious and sincere religion. Contemporary religion's emphasis on social problems, its deemphasis of institutional and clerical prerogatives, its diminished enthusiasm for laws, forms, and ritual all bear upon the current interest in mysticism. Even rather ordinary or commonplace religious experience can be personally transforming and authoritative and, because of its immediacy, tends to reduce dependence on institutional structures and to call into question their very relevance. This helps explain the apparent inner freedom as well as the specific orientation of such famous innovators and reformers as Paul, Bernard, Catherine of Siena, Eckhart, and Cusanus.

Teilhard's is by no means the only mystical vision influencing contemporary spirituality. An approach that can be thought of as a personalist emphasis forming a salutary counterbalance to Teilhard's universalism is the I-Thou religious vision of Martin Buber. Despite Buber's demurrer, his spiritual approach bears all the necessary marks of the mystical mode: it is experiential, comprehensive, immediate, and transforming. Buber's influence upon Catholic spirituality continues to be both deep and broad. Thomas Merton's life and example have been influential in sustaining an interest in contemplative spirituality and he himself embodied the cross-cultural emphasis mentioned above. His last days were spent in Asia pursuing the mystic ideal. He is significant not so much for the power of his vision as for the orientation and persistence of his quest. Finally, mention should be made of Simone Weil, a mystic of powerful and awe-inspiring conviction, whose importance for the spirituality of the future should not be minimized. As visionaries all of these shared a deep engagement in the world and have helped set the tone for a spirituality of personalism and human concern, global in its orientation and resource, affirmative in its assessment of nature and action.

See also CONTEMPLATION; PRAYER.

Bibliography: M. L. FURSE, *Mysticism: Window on a World View* (Nashville 1977). G. HARKNESS, *Mysticism: Its Meaning and Message* (Nashville 1973). W. JOHNSTON, *The Still Point: Reflections on Zen and Christian Mysticism* (New York 1977). R. ZAEHNER, *Corcordant Discord* (Oxford 1970; *Evolution in Religion* (Oxford 1971); *Mysticism, Sacred and Profane* (New York 1961); *Zen, Drugs, and Mysticism* (New York 1973).

[J. E. BIECHLER]

N

NATIONAL APOSTOLATE FOR THE MENTALLY RETARDED (NAMR)

In the 1960s and 1970s the Church became more aware of the vast number of mentally retarded people who were isolated from participation in its life. This isolation deprived 3 per cent of the population from contributing their special gifts of ministry and from receiving the special gifts of others. In 1961 the first murmur of a National Apostolate for the Mentally Retarded was heard at the Inter-American CCD Congress in Dallas, Texas. After a series of meetings of a core group, the constitution was approved at a meeting in West Hartford, Conn. (1967) and there in August 1970 the first NAMR conference was held. The first president was Rev. Matthew M. Pasaniello of New Jersey. The National Apostolate for the Mentally Retarded was incorporated in 1973 and officially established its office in Trinity College, Washington, D.C.

In accord with the pressing needs of mentally retarded people the preamble of NAMR's Constitution states:

> The mentally retarded are an integral part of society, equal to other men, and persons possessing a fundamental value and dignity. They are recipients of what the Church offers, and contributors to it by virtue of their individual value and of the positive Christian attitudes they stimulate in others.

The purposes of the NAMR are: (1) to promote for the mentally retarded an authentic participation in the life of the Church; (2) to enhance the personal growth of the retarded, as well as nonretarded persons by their participation in each other's lives, and by nonretarded persons benefiting from the simplicity and the prophetic role of retarded ones; (3) to take steps on a national and local level to bring to public manifestation the contribution, especially the spiritual and interpersonal one, of retarded people to society.

Annually, there is a membership conference in various sections of the United States. The members—parents, teachers, chaplains, nurses, administrators, DREs, volunteers, and professionals from other areas—attend workshops, liturgies, and lectures which highlight key areas and future trends in the field of catechesis and mental retardation (Brooklyn, 1976—Liberation); (San Diego, 1977—Genetic Counselling); (Wisconsin, 1978—The Family). A business meeting of the members approves the priorities established by the Board of Directors (15–20 from regions throughout the United States). The priorities established for 1977–78 are: (1) to work toward offices of ministry to the handicapped on a national and a diocesan level; (2) to establish and maintain communication with international and national Catholic groups and publications, so as to effect attitudinal change regarding mentally retarded persons, as well as with local groups and individuals; (3) to foster, on a parish, diocesan, and national level, liturgical participation, since the liturgical celebration is the experience whereby the disabled, the family, and the church community interact in a public manifestation; (4) to continue a NAMR newsletter and journal for the development of pastoral services in the U.S. on a planned basis, for the dissemination of approved models of pastoral service, and as a religious information service on relevant topics for local groups.

NAMR officers, president, president-elect, secretary, and treasurer, are elected at the annual meeting. The Executive director (currently, Bro. Joseph Moloney, OSF) discharges duties of the Board between annual meetings. All who participate in the spiritual, mental, or physical development of the mentally retarded are eligible for membership. Membership brings full participation in the work and publications of NAMR as well as access to consultant services and advocacy efforts on behalf of the mentally retarded.

During the conference in 1977 the membership unanimously endorsed the following proposal:

> WHEREAS NAMR is committed to defending and advocating the rights of people with handicapping conditions;
> WHEREAS NAMR is committed to assuring the rights of people with handicapping conditions as equal members of the Church:
> Be it resolved that since all archdioceses and dioceses of the United States are divided according to deaneries or regions that the Catholic Church give tangible evidence and witness of its concern for people with handicapping conditions by designating at least one parish in each region or deanery as accessible to people with handicapping conditions, by providing proper accessibility and accommodations such as wheel chair ramps, toilet facilities, signed liturgies, and other such necessary measures as a sign of its good will and intent.
> Be it further resolved that all parish churches in the United States should begin to remove any and all barriers that prevent people with handicapping conditions from participating fully in the life of the Church.

The impact of this proposal on mentally retarded and handicapped people can be gauged from the positive responses by dioceses throughout the United States.

[J. MOLONEY]

NATIONAL ASSEMBLY OF RELIGIOUS BROTHERS (NARB)

The National Assembly of Religious Brothers was organized in 1971. NARB is the only organization in the American Church designed specifically to be of service to brothers. The organization is composed of individual memberships from brothers throughout the United States and from many foreign countries. NARB is directed by a national board and elected officers. An executive Secretary conducts the daily business of a national office.

Brothers Newsletter, edited by Brother Damian Carroll, C.P., is published quarterly. It has an open subscription policy. *Brothers Bulletin* is published bimonthly for NARB members. An annual national meeting is sponsored in different sections of the United States. The organization projects a strong national image for the religious brother, and maintains a close working relationship with virtually every national Catholic Church organization.

In relation to the needs of the Church and to the needs of brothers today for continued growth in their religious life and in their service to the mission of the Church, the National Assembly of Religious Brothers fosters these goals: to encourage the development of the spiritual life of all brothers; to promote increased awareness among brothers of their ministerial power for good; to publicize the unique vocation of brothers; to provide a means for brothers to help shape the future of religious life; to heighten brothers' concern with and involvement in the needs of the Church and society; to improve communication among brothers and to provide liaison with the various organizations of the Catholic Church.

[W. BILTON]

NATIONAL ASSEMBLY OF WOMEN RELIGIOUS (NAWR)

The National Assembly of Women Religious is a movement/organization which attempts to mobilize around justice issues grass-roots religious women and associates, through diocesan councils and individual memberships. Since its origins as a national organization in 1970, NAWR has provided a corporate voice for sisters to speak on ecclesial and societal issues of concern and a forum to share resources and vision. Responding to the movement of the Church toward social justice, NAWR at its House of Delegates Meeting in Minneapolis in 1972, adopted a ministry of justice vision and goal which continue to express the direction of the group: "We commit ourselves to a ministry of justice by the continuous use of our organized power to effect local and national policy for the liberation of all peoples from oppression and to work actively to promote respect for all human life and to insure effective participation of people in decisions which affect their lives."

NAWR carries out its justice-education and action projects through its Chicago-based national office, its annual convention and House of Delegates, its local and regional programs, its monthly publications, *Probe* and *Trends*, and its three published books, *Women in Ministry* (Chicago 1973), *Gospel Dimensions of Ministry* (Chicago 1974), and *Lifestyle* (Chicago 1975). In November 1977 NAWR chose a two-pronged emphasis on justice for women in the Church and for economi-

cally oppressed women. To encourage the bonding of women NAWR presently admits to full membership not only women religious, but all women who share its goals.

[K. KEATING]

NATIONAL ASSOCIATION OF LAITY

Formation of the National Association of Laity (NAL)—until 1972, "of Laymen"—was inspired by the initiatives of Pope John XXIII and Vatican Council II's opening to democratic ideals. NAL, meeting some hierarchical resistance, was incorporated in Texas in 1967 as an independent entity to expedite the carrying out of Vatican II mandates.

To these ends NAL worked with social movements and with single-purpose groups and coalitions to curb racism, sexism, war, the arms race and to foster optional clerical celibacy, "due process" machinery, diversity in liturgies, women's ordination, collective bargaining rights, and professional academic standards. NAL demanded that church officials periodically report budgets, income, and wealth. Wide publicity stirred journalists to cover church finances and the NCCB to recommend public financial reports.

NAL took a position against the NCCB attempts to secure government funds for parochial schools and to reverse legislation of abortion (see ABORTION, U.S. LAW). NAL helped defeat "parochiaid," notably in *Lemon v. Kurtzman*, 403 US 602 (1971), and to unite civic, religious, and educational agencies against it founded PEARL (Public Education and Religious Liberty, Inc.).

NAL has supported opposition to *Humanae vitae* as well as declarations that episcopal leadership in matters of sexual morality is bankrupt and that NCCB public policy statements are a threat to ecumenism. NAL has also joined with pro-abortion groups, e.g., Religious Coalition for Abortion Rights and Catholics for Free Choice.

NAL submitted to the bishops a plan for a national *pastoral council, called for by Vatican II (*Apostolicam actuositatem* 26). However, since 1973, the Holy See has halted implementation. NAL has also reacted against the step constituting the Council of the *Laity as pontifical and the grounds for the Vatican declaration against women's ordination. NAL saw many of its own objectives reflected in the 1976 *Call to Action Conference.

Because of negative response to its objectives from bishops and others, NAL chapters have dropped from twenty-nine to fourteen, membership from 25,000 (1973) to 1300 (1978). The decline correlates with 1978 National Opinion Research Center reports of a drop in Catholic church attendance from a rate of 72 percent to one of 42 percent between 1962 to 1977.

The NAL president has said that there is hope; that history spurns cultures politically democratic but ecclesiastically authoritarian and guarantees Vatican II prophetic mandates.

[J. T. SKEHAN]

NATIONAL ASSOCIATION OF PASTORAL MUSICIANS (NPM)

A national membership organization founded in 1976 for the improvement of music within the parish, with special emphasis on liturgical music. Membership includes both parish musician and parish clergy, with a unique interest in the practical issues facing the practicing musician and the parish clergy. As an association of musicians and clergy, its stated purposes are: (1) to provide support for the practicing parish musicians through improved repertoire, through increased knowledge of the role of music in the liturgy, through practical helps for effective participation in the parish liturgical-committee planning of music; (2) to provide a forum for advocating musical excellence in liturgical celebrations; (3) to provide a vehicle for disseminating evaluations of new and current musical selections; and (4) to assist diocesan and parish level efforts in improving the quality of and interest in parish music.

Pastoral Music, a magazine published six times a year for the membership, contains feature articles, information on liturgy and planning, and critical reviews and evaluation of the music of worship. Additional services include NPM Hotline which assists musicians seeking positions and parishes looking for musicians; NPM Cassettes which provide demonstration recordings of music contained in official liturgical books, NPM Training Workshops, educational tours, and an annual national convention. Affiliated with the United States Catholic Conference, the association is led by an 18-member Board of Directors. The National Office is located at 1029 Vermont Avenue, N.W., Washington, D.C. 20005.

[V. FUNK]

NATIONAL ASSOCIATION OF PERMANENT DIACONATE DIRECTORS

This professional association of directors of permanent diaconate programs was established in February 1977. Its purposes are the following: to promote effective communication and facilitate the exchange of information and resources among the members; to develop professional expertise among members and to promote research, training, and self-evaluation procedures; to foster members' accountability to the Church, the *Bishops' Committee on the Permanent Diaconate, to permanent deacons, and to one another; to facilitate communication with the Bishops' Committee on the Permanent Diaconate; to respond to the particular needs of permanent diaconate programs as they serve the Church; to encourage and participate in programs of pastoral research and study toward the constant renewal of the permanent diaconate; to cooperate with individuals and organizations working in the pastoral service of the People of God; to seek and propose ways and means for effective implementation of solutions to national and regional problems relating to the permanent diaconate, its service, and pastoral needs; to encourage regional and national groupings of permanent deacons pursuing common goals in the structure of the American Church.

[P. MCCASLIN]

NATIONAL BLACK SISTERS' CONFERENCE

The occasion of the 10th annual National Black Sisters' Conference was used as an appropriate time to review its beginning. The first National Black Sisters' Conference (NBSC) was held in August 1968 at Mount Mercy (now Carlow) College, Pittsburgh, under the inspiration and direction of Sister Martin de Porres Grey, RSM and the Pittsburgh Sisters of Mercy. Sister Martin de Porres had had the opportunity to attend the first Black Catholic Clergy Caucus (NBCCC), held earlier in that year. At this meeting, some members of the NBCCC encouraged Sister Martin de Porres to organize Black Sisters throughout the country. Receiving the support of the bishop of Pittsburgh and also that of her religious community, Sister Martin de Porres helped the NBSC take form and direction. The NBSC is incorporated in Pennsylvania as a nonprofit organization. Following that first historic meeting, the annual conferences have been held in the following places: 1969, University of Dayton; 1970, University of Notre Dame; 1971, Carlow College; 1972, Spalding College, Louisville; 1973, Loyola University, New Orleans; 1974, Atlanta; 1975, Milwaukee; 1976, Gwynedd-Mercy College, Gwynedd Valley, Pa.; 1977, Xavier Center, Convent Station, N.J.; 1978, University of Southern California. Headquarters of NBSC are at 3508 Fifth Ave., Pittsburgh, PA, 15213.

The NBSC has dedicated itself to providing professional and spiritual enrichment for Black Catholic religious women through retreats and workshops unique to the black experience, so that they might more effectively serve the black community in their respective capacities. Through the Conference, black religious women strive to share vision and expertise in order to confront individual and institutional racism and injustice found in society and in the Church. They strive to work for the liberation of black people; to be a source of encouragement, inspiration, support, power, and challenge to one another; to discover black cultural and spiritual roots; and to be a catalyst for change.

The source of support is found not only in the physical presence of one another but more especially in the spiritual and religious life that is their mutual life-experience, commitment, fellowship, and cooperative action. A short summary which encapsulated the feeling of the first conference reads as follows: "Our first National Black Sisters' Conference brought together all shades and hues of blackness: the very ready sisters and the not so ready ones...we prayed, worshiped, talked, studied, sang and lived together experiencing unforgettably the tremendous vital force of being one in Christ. United in Him and glorifying in the special joy that we realize is a precious privilege of black religious women, we began to understand more clearly and appreciate more fully the meaning of being black, beautiful and beloved in God" (*Celibate Black Commitment* 6).

The future of black vocations is very strong and vibrant and can be found in the approximately 125 active members. With encouragement, prayer, and a constant realization of the current and ever present needs of the world for dedicated people, the religious life style will continue. The sisters are involved in various works in the areas of education, health care, parish ministry, and others. All in all the NBSC knows that the more exposure blacks have to authentic black religious and priests, the greater is the possibility for an increase in the response to God's call.

Bibliography: NBSC, *Celibate Black Commitment*, Report on the Third Annual National Black Sisters' Conference (Pittsburgh, Pa. 1971).

[C. M. BILLINGS]

NATIONAL CAMPUS MINISTRY ASSOCIATION

The National Campus Ministry Association (NCMA) is an ecumenical, voluntary association of campus ministers. Membership is open to all persons engaged in or related to ministry in higher education, including college and university ministers, pastors, and chaplains; the personnel of campus ministry agencies; university and college-town pastors; and faculty and administrative personnel with special interest in campus ministry. The work of the Association is sustained by membership dues and by occasional grants for special projects.

NCMA was founded in 1965, replacing a group of separate Protestant denominational campus ministry associations. From the outset it was the desire of the founders that the Association become even more broadly ecumenical. That desire has been realized insofar as a number of persons who hold membership in continuing denominational associations and special interest groups of campus ministers are also active in NCMA. The Association was formally constituted during an inaugural convocation, held at Michigan State University, when those present, affirming that they were "called to oneness in Christ; called to one field of ministry and mission in higher education; convinced of the importance of the service of the church in higher education and of higher education to the church; confident that together we may minister more adequately to those whom we are called to serve," joined in covenant to establish the NCMA. At the same time, the constituting members made provision for the regular election of an executive committee to facilitate the work of the Association and set down five purposes, all of which continue to guide the NCMA.

First, NCMA seeks "to foster the educational development of members" through the sponsorship of national and regional NCMA meetings and continuing education events, the publication of information about educational conferences and resources in the quarterly *NCMA Newsletter*, and the preparation and distribution of occasional study documents by and/or for the membership.

Second, in its attempt "to facilitate approaches with other individuals and agencies of the churches to ministry and mission in higher education," NCMA is a frequent partner of denominational and ecumenical agencies in mounting special projects of education and ministry, and in the past year has cosponsored with other church, community, and education organizations such events as the Changing Family Conference and the National Conference on Men and Masculinity.

Third, in pursuit of its commitment "to listen to and speak to the church and to the university," NCMA seeks to provide occasions and processes whereby its members and their colleagues can study, discuss, and speak out on issues of importance to Church, university, and society. For example, an Association task force is currently distributing study materials and planning a series of regional forums in which persons from Church and university will jointly examine the ethical implications of recombinant DNA research.

Fourth, NCMA seeks "to advance ecumenical understanding" by encouraging the development of regional ecumenical events and networks among campus ministers and their constituents, through participation in the Coordinating Council of Professional Religious Associations in Higher Education, and in its cosponsorship —from their inception—of the national Ecumenical Campus Ministry Conferences.

Fifth, NCMA works "to provide a supportive fellowship for members." The publication of placement opportunities in its newsletter, the occasional publication of a membership directory, with detailed information about members' involvements and interests, and the sponsorship of meetings and continuing education events are all ways in which NCMA attempts to build a network of support among its members.

[R. R. PARSONAGE]

NATIONAL CATECHETICAL DIRECTORY (U.S.)

On Nov. 17, 1977, after four intensive sessions of discussion and amending the text, the U.S. National Conference of Catholic Bishops (NCCB) in general assembly in Washington, D.C., voted over-whelmingly—216 to 12—to accept the document *Sharing the Light of Faith. National Catechetical Directory for Catholics of the United States.* This text was submitted to Rome for review and was approved by the Congregation for the Clergy on Oct. 30, 1978. Publication of the *Directory* in March 1979 is a pivotal event in the history of catechetics in the United States. It is of such major moment that it has often been compared in importance to the printing of the Baltimore Catechism in 1885. *Sharing the Light of Faith* marks a transitional point in catechesis in this country. It gives official approval to the adaptation of catechetical materials—printed and audio-visual—to their intended audiences. In summary, it legitimizes the sound developments that have taken place in the secular and sacred sciences as they have been incorporated into catechetics, particularly during the past 20 years.

Description. *Sharing the Light of Faith* is a handbook containing directives (norms, standards) and guidelines (recommendations, suggestions) for the catechesis of all Catholics of all ages (cradle to grave) and in all circumstances of life. It is designed to serve as a foundation or base for the development of catechetical materials for such persons as the handicapped (physical, emotional, mental); the various racial, cultural, and ethnic groups that enrich the nation and Church; families, parents (married and single), the divorced and widowed; pre-school and elementary-age children, secondary age youth, young adults, adults and the aged; the various geographical regions, including the inner city and urban, suburban, and rural areas. In addition, it deals with the catechesis of those in military service and those in residential facilities as diverse as hospitals, nursing homes, and prisons. In brief, an attempt was made to relate catechesis to every time and circumstance of life in contemporary U.S. society.

In addition to proposing catechesis as a lifelong process, the *Directory* identifies adult catechesis as the chief form of catechesis, for without a vibrant, deep-rooted faith among adults very little if anything can be expected of the rest of the community.

Background. *Sharing the Light of Faith* has its roots in Vatican Council II and in the General Catechetical Directory (GCD; *see* CATECHETICAL DIRECTORIES, 16:53). The Decree on the Pastoral Office of Bishops proposed the preparation of a general catechetical directory dealing with fundamental, universally applicable principles (*Christus Dominus* 44). The GCD, prepared over a period of approximately five years (1966–71), by the Congregation for the Clergy, with the assistance of a number of scholars from all over the world, was approved by Pope Paul VI on March 18, 1971. In keeping with the views expressed by individual commissions and some Vatican II members, the GCD urged the preparation of directories to apply the universal catechetical principles to the particular conditions and circumstances of each nation or group of nations with similar needs.

Plans for the writing of a national directory for the U.S., elaborated by a special committee of the Department of Education, United States Catholic Conference, were approved by the bishops in general assembly in Atlanta, Georgia, in April 1972, before the GCD text became available in this country.

Committees and Staff. The plan approved by the bishops contained provisions for several levels of responsibility in preparing the National Catechetical Directory. One committee, consisting of eight bishops, established policy and reviewed the text and the process at every phase of the project. This committee was chaired by Archbishop John F. Whealon of Hartford, Connecticut. Working under the direction of the Bishops' Committee of Policy and Review was a Directory Committee composed of 12 persons: four bishops, two laywomen, one layman, two women religious, one brother, one religious priest, and one diocesan priest. This committee was the first ever to be associated with bishops in making decisions regarding the teaching mission of the Church as expressed in its catechetical ministry. Staff consisted of two persons selected (as was the directory Committee) after a broad, nationwide consultation. They were Msgr. Wilfrid H. Paradis, Director, and Sister Mariella Frye, MHSH, Associate Director.

Consultation Process. *Sharing the Light of Faith* was the first major document produced by the bishops of the United States through a process of consultation. Between late 1973 and early 1977, three extensive consultations were held with interested groups or individuals as well as with hundreds of scholars. During the three consultations—one prior to the writing of the first draft and the other two on the first and second drafts respectively—approximately 100,000 recommendations were submitted, involving hundreds of thousands of persons. A minimum of 20,000 meetings were also held across the country to discuss the document in its phases of development. Well over one million copies of the various versions were distributed in both English and Spanish during the project. The volume of responses was so great that a computer was used for the first time in the history of the U.S. Catholic Church to record and to assist in the analysis of the recommendations received during the second consultation. The *Directory* was also the subject of regional meetings of bishops in Spring 1975, during which hundreds of laity, religious, and clergy joined them to discuss catechetical needs. These consultations remain the most extensive ever accomplished by the Catholic Church of the United States and perhaps in the world.

Participation of the Eastern Catholic Churches. Another first in the preparation of the *Directory* was the involvement of the Eastern Catholic Churches with jurisdictions in the United States: the Ukrainians, Ruthenians, and Melkites of the Byzantine tradition, and the Maronites of the Antiochene tradition. Though the *Directory* was written largely from the perspective of the Western Church, special effort was made to inform and interest all Catholics concerning the rich diversity found within Catholic unity.

Audience and Authority. *Sharing the Light of Faith* was prepared particularly for those responsible for catechesis in the United States. Among those who will benefit, directly or indirectly, are parents and guardians exercising their responsibilities as the primary educators of children; professional and paraprofessional catechists at all levels; men and women religious; deacons and priests involved in this ministry; and members of diocesan- and parish-council education committees or boards with catechetical duties. The *Directory* is of basic importance to writers and publishers of catechetical texts and other materials for catechesis.

The *Directory* draws its authority from the fact that it is an official statement of the National Conference of Catholic Bishops and that it has been fully reviewed and approved by the Holy See, through the Congregation for the Clergy. Not all parts of the document are of equal weight. Only those parts that deal with the teaching of the Church in regard to revelation (Chapter III) and the Christian message (parts of Chapters V and VI), and the norms and criteria for teaching these (art. 47) are normative and are thus to be observed by all.

The other portions of the *Directory* are also important, but the treatment of such matters as stages of human development, methodology, catechetical roles and training, organization and structures, resources, is subject to change in light of new knowledge or different circumstances. This is also the first document ever approved by the U.S. bishops that provides for an evaluation and periodic updating. The evaluation, to determine the effectiveness of the *Directory*, will take place approximately five years after its approval by the Holy See. The updating will be periodic in order to adjust the text to cultural changes, better methodologies, and to new church documents that have catechetical implications.

Outline of the Directory. The *Directory* consists of a preface, 11 chapters, a conclusion, and two brief appendices.

The *Preface* gives some background information on the *Directory*, such as the collaboration between the Eastern and Western Churches in its development, the consultation process, and its sources, audience, and authority. A second part provides a brief background to contemporary catechesis, including the hopeful signs as well as modern problems in catechesis in the United States.

Chapter I is entitled *Some Cultural and Religious Characteristics Affecting Catechesis* in the United States. This chapter immediately places catechesis in the context of reality, that is the situation—both good and bad—in which society finds itself. It touches upon such matters as diversity (racial, cultural, and ethnic, the many religions, theological pluralism) and science and technology. One part gives a brief profile of U.S. Catholics and another reviews the findings of professional surveys regarding the family and home in this country.

Chapter II, *The Catechetical Ministry of the Church,*

distinguishes catechesis from the other forms of the ministry of the Word and discusses the forms, sources, signs, and criteria of catechesis itself.

Chapter III, *Revelation, Faith and Catechesis*, marks the distinctions and links between public revelation (ending with the apostolic age) and the other ways in which God communicates and manifests himself today. The second part of the chapter deals with the characteristics of the response of faith, a free gift from God. A final part provides some helpful guidelines for catechizing about revelation.

Chapter IV, *The Church and Catechesis*, reviews the various meanings of Church—a mystery of divine love, People of God, One Body in Christ, servant, pilgrim, sign of the Kingdom, hierarchical society, etc. Part B is a pastoral and practically helpful guide to catechists with regard to other Christian Churches, the Jewish people, Moslems, the other religions, and those who profess no religion.

Chapter V, *Principal Elements of the Christian Message for Catechesis*, is a heavily revised and edited version of the NCCB, *Basic Teachings for Catholic Religious Education* (see CATECHETICS, 16:54) which takes into account the U.S. Bishops' pastoral letter *To Live in Christ Jesus* and the theology and practice of the revised Roman Missal and the instructions and rituals of the other revised liturgical books on the Sacraments.

Chapter VI, *Catechesis for a Worshiping Community*, establishes the relationship between liturgy and catechesis; provides theological and catechetical norms and recommendations regarding the seven Sacraments; reflects on liturgical catechesis of those with special needs (children, youth, cultural groups, etc); deals rather extensively with catechesis for prayer and the liturgical year, and; concludes with the place of sacred art and the Sacraments in catechesis.

Chapter VII, entitled *Catechesis for Social Ministry*, states that social justice is an essential element of the Gospel message and that of the Church (Synod Just-World p. 34), and consequently that it must be a dimension of all catechesis, adapted to age and circumstances of life. After summarizing the biblical and moral bases of social ministry and describing its relationship to the mission of the Church, the text enumerates an extensive number of contemporary national and international social problems that are of concern to the Church.

Chapter VIII, *Catechesis toward Maturity in Faith*, explains the relationship of faith and human development; summarizes the stages of human development, from cradle to grave (emphasizing the priority of adult catechesis); describes the process of conscience formation; gives directions for education in sexuality; provides guidelines for the catechesis of persons with special needs, and; reports on some significant factors affecting catechesis in this country.

Chapter IX, *Catechetical Personnel*, describes the ideal qualities of catechists and reviews their roles and preparation. It begins with the role of parents and progresses to that of the bishop and his diocesan staff.

Chapter X, entitled *Organization for Catechesis*, enumerates some organizational principles (subsidiarity, shared responsibility, person-centeredness in accountability, planning, evaluation, etc.), and deals successively with the catechetical responsibilities of parishes, dioceses, provinces, regions, and the national office. The roles of seminaries, colleges, and universities are also considered, as are those of special settings, such as convalescent or nursing homes, child-care institutions, hospitals, prisons, juvenile homes.

Chapter XI, *Catechetical Resources*, after establishing the priority of human resources, discusses the use of the various kinds of instructional materials, particularly the media of radio, television, and the press. It stresses the need for "media literacy" and the training of media users as well as producers. Finally, this chapter mandates that all catechetical textbooks and other materials are to be prepared or evaluated (if they are already on the market) according to the criteria and guidelines contained in *Sharing the Light of Faith*. This is to be done by "those responsible for catechetics," and the appropriate offices of the United States Catholic Conference will be available to assist in this regard.

The *Directory* ends with a brief *Conclusion* indicating the hopes for this document, and with two appendices listing the Ten Commandments and the contemporary precepts of the Church.

Bibliography: Congregation for the Clergy, *General Catechetical Directory* (USCC Publ. Office, Washington, D.C. 1971). NCCB, *Basic Teachings for Catholic Religious Education; To Teach as Jesus Did; To Live in Christ Jesus* (USCC Publ. Office, Washington, D.C. 1971; 1972; 1976).

[W. H. PARADIS]

NATIONAL CATHOLIC COALITION FOR RESPONSIBLE INVESTMENT

The National Catholic Coalition for Responsible Investment (NCCRI) was begun in February 1973 as a joint project of the National Federation of Priests Councils, the Leadership Conference of Women Religious, the Conference of Major Superiors of Men, the National Assembly of Women Religious, the Catholic Committee on Urban Ministry, and the National Catholic Conference for Interracial Justice. Coordinators of NCCRI since its foundation have been Revs. Eugene Boyle, Donald Bargen, OMI, and Michael Crosby, OFM Cap. NCCRI has a twofold purpose: to educate Catholic institutions about the desirability and manner of becoming involved in *corporate social responsibility; and to facilitate the effort of Catholic institutions in their involvement.

The educational component of NCCRI was given in over five hundred Catholic dioceses, religious congregations, schools, and health-care centers in seventeen regional meetings since 1973. As a result of most of these seminars, regional coalitions were formed to achieve the second goal of NCCRI, the active effort of Catholic institutions in the corporate responsibility movement. By 1978 ten regions, comprising over one hundred and fifty portfolio-holding Catholic institutions, became actively involved through membership in the Interfaith Center on Corporate Responsibility (ICCR) in New York, a joint project of both NCCRI-related organizations and major Protestant denominations and agencies. In 1977, Sister Regina Murphy, SC, was elected the first Catholic chairperson of ICCR.

NCCRI publishes a monthly newsletter available from its headquarters at 3900 North Third Street, Milwaukee, Wisconsin 53212, entitled *Catholic Church Investments for Corporate Social Responsibility*.

[M. CROSBY]

NATIONAL CATHOLIC CONFERENCE FOR INTERRACIAL JUSTICE (NCCIJ)

Founded in 1960 at Chicago as a federation of, and national resource center for, Catholic Interracial Councils, NCCIJ now has its national office in Washington, D.C. It is a source of publications, program aids, and training skills available to interracial councils and diocesan social justice offices for the promotion of racial harmony. During the 1960s NCCIJ served as catalyst and secretariat for the first National Conference on Religion and Race (Chicago 1963) and for Catholic participation in the widespread demonstrations and other programs designed to achieve the federal Civil Rights acts of 1964 and 1968. Project Equality, an NCCIJ initiative formed to channel the buying power of Catholic agencies and institutions towards equal employment opportunity suppliers of products and services, is now an independent, national, and interreligious organization. NCCIJ is supported by contributions from individual and organization members, general appeals, and foundation grants. The Conference includes bishops, religious, and laity on its policy-making board, but it is an autonomous body, although approved by official Catholic leadership. NCCIJ's present priorities respond, by publications, national and regional workshops and seminars, to the pressing problems of all the minorities disadvantaged by discrimination: Blacks, Hispanics, Native Americans, and Asian-Americans. In the late 1970s, full, fair and equal opportunity employment, and Catholic school integration have been the Conference's major areas of concern. Special emphasis is put on efforts to have the Church's own practices conform to the principles of social justice that Catholics accept and proclaim. The Conference makes its services available to all, regardless of race, color, religion, or national origin.

Bridge-building between the White majorities and Black minorities was the original rationale for Catholic Interracial Councils (CIC), the movement begun in the 1930s under the guidance of the late John LaFarge, SJ. The pioneer effort in the New York City area led to imitation elsewhere, until a CIC was to be found in almost every large urban area. The National Catholic Conference for Interracial Justice was established to coordinate the effort of the Councils, although each maintains its independence.

Varied and intensive governmental programs, together with the emergence of the Black Power movement of the 1960s, led to less emphasis on maintaining private interracial coalitions of volunteer members and consequently to fewer Catholic interracial councils. On the other hand, more and better official diocesan efforts were mounted to create vehicles of Catholic response to the needs of all disadvantaged minorities, especially Hispanics, Native Americans, and Asian Americans as well as Blacks. The national office of NCCIJ, correspondingly, survives with original purposes intact but with a new emphasis and relevant responsibility to serve as a bridge-builder and resource center for both Interracial Councils and those Catholic state and diocesan agencies which combat racial discrimination. At the national level, NCCIJ strives to be effective, by itself and in coalition with other civil rights and community groups (esp. NAACP, the National Office of Black Catholics, and those involved in the Spanish-speaking apostolate), in assuring the passage and enforcement of federal legislation guaranteeing equal rights and opportunities for all people, regardless of race, color, or national origin, in the areas of employment housing, education, welfare, and health care. Two perspectives are aggressively maintained: (1) racial justice is a moral issue, transcending economics and politics; (2) the ministry to achieve interracial justice is not limited to a particular group, but is an obligation shared by all, with special responsibilities on Christians who recognize the universality of redemption and brotherhood in Jesus Christ.

See also INTERRACIAL JUSTICE.

[A. J. WELSH]

NATIONAL CATHOLIC DEVELOPMENT CONFERENCE

The National Catholic Development Conference, Inc. (NCDC) was founded in 1968 for the purpose of assisting its members in developing ethical and successful methods of fund raising. Voting membership is open to those Catholic institutions listed in the *Official Catholic Directory*. In January 1978 active member institutions numbered 197 and included dioceses, religious orders and provinces, hospitals, and educational institutions. Nonvoting membership and affiliation is open to those individuals and institutions who are not eligible for active membership.

The professional beginnings of the NCDC can be traced back to 1955 when a group of mission procurators and development directors began meeting under the aegis of the Mission Secretariat in Washington, D.C. In the early 1960s members of the Catholic Press Association (CPA) with fund-raising concerns began to hold annual meetings. They called themselves the Catholic Fund-Raising Conference and met in conjunction with the CPA convention. Directly out of this group the NCDC was formed. It was incorporated in New York State, March 5, 1968. Its present offices are at 119 North Park Avenue, Rockville Centre, New York 11570. The year following its incorporation, the NCDC drew up its *Precepts of Stewardship*, a set of ethical guidelines for fund raising. Nine in number, these deal with such points as the requirement of official church approval, integrity in business associations, and the good taste and sound theology which must be associated with religious fund raising. Conditions for membership include adherence to these *Precepts* and to the 1977 NCCB *Principles and Guidelines for Fund Raising in the United States* (*see* FUND RAISING AND ACCOUNTABILITY). The annual highlight of the Conference's activities is its development convention, held usually in September, and attracting 400–500 attendees. The Conference's services to members include a continuing education program, several periodicals and, most recently, a public-information program established to compile and disseminate material on fund-raising institutions and their programs.

The NCDC maintains a liaison with the episcopal and religious conferences of the U.S., and it represents its members on postal-affairs committees and before legislative groups.

See also NATIONAL CATHOLIC STEWARDSHIP COUNCIL.

[E. DILL]

NATIONAL CATHOLIC EDUCATIONAL ASSOCIATION (NCEA)

The National Catholic Educational Association in the past decade responded to the many changes in the Catholic Church usually symbolized by Vatican Council II. A new understanding and vision of Catholic education developed. The old quantitative goal of the Plenary Councils of Baltimore (2:24), "Every Child in a Catholic School," was gradually replaced with a more qualitative goal: a good Catholic education for all.

The former definition of Catholic education as synonymous with Catholic schools gave way to a more diversified, more balanced, more realistic vision of Catholic education. There is acceptance of the fact that not every Catholic child can or will attend a Catholic school; not all Catholic youth will attend high school; and even less will attend Catholic colleges; adults need continuing education; and both the aged and preschool children need specialized programs. Catholic education is now a broad concept signifying a variety of religious educational programs for a diversified Catholic constituency. It is best described by the phrase: a Christian Educational Community, embracing the three interlocking dimensions of (1) the message revealed by God; (2) community of the Holy Spirit; (3) service to all.

At the same time, there developed an increased recognition of the primary rights of parents in the education of their children, both in the policy-making processes of Catholic education and in close-working partnerships with the professional religious educators.

The National Catholic Education Association has not merely responded to these changes, but has actually helped cause their development. In 1972 the Department of Religious Education was established, called the National Forum of Religious Educators, under the direction of Alfred McBride, OPraem. Within the department are sections for diocesan directors of religious education, parish directors, and elementary, secondary and college teachers of religion. The long-standing NCEA Commission of Continuing Education was formally incorporated into this new department. Likewise, the NCEA Commission of Boards of Education under the directorship of Dr. Mary-Angela Harper was raised to the status of a department to increase the image of parental involvement in decision-making and provide greater service to members of school boards and boards of education.

In 1974 the NCEA established a new commission for parents, called the National Forum of Catholic Parent Organizations. Its purpose is to foster the development of local home and school associations, promote cooperation between parents and teachers, assist parents in their own role as educators and promote public support for private schools.

To promote better external relations, the NCEA Department of Colleges and Universities, without changing status as an NCEA department, adopted the new title, Association of Catholic Colleges and Universities.

When C. Albert Koob, OPraem, NCEA president, suffered a serious accident in October 1972, Rev. John F. Meyers, executive director of the Department of Chief Administrators of Catholic Education, was named acting president. He later was elected president when Fr. Kroob resigned in June 1974. In 1975 the Board of Directors elected Bishop Cletus O'Donnell of Madison, Wis. to replace Bishop Raymond Gallagher of Lafayette-in-Indiana as chairman of the Board. After three consecutive terms, Bishop O'Donnell was succeeded by Archbishop Joseph Bernardin, March 28, 1978.

Since 1970 NCEA has published the quarterly *Momentum* and many other publications on special areas and interests.

Bibliography: Congregation for Catholic Education, *The Catholic School* (USCC Publ. Office, Washington, D.C. 1977). A. GREELEY, W. C. MCCREADY and K. MCCOURT, *Catholic Schools in a Declining Church* (Kansas City, Mo. 1976). C. A. KOOB and R. SHAW, *S.O.S. for Catholic Schools* (New York 1970). A. MCBRIDE, *Creative Teaching in Christian Education* (Boston 1978). NCCB, *To Teach as Jesus Did* (Washington, D.C. 1973). F. F. PLUDE, *The Flickering Light—What's Happening to Catholic Schools?* (New York 1974).

[J. F. MEYERS]

NATIONAL CATHOLIC STEWARDSHIP COUNCIL

The National Catholic Stewardship Council (NCSC) had its origin, more by accident than design, in a 1962 meeting in St. Louis, organized by Rev. Paul Kaletta, of diocesan directors of development on their concerns. Since 1965, meetings have been held annually. The group first called itself the National Association of Diocesan Financing, then the National Council of Diocesan Support Programs, and adopted the present name, National Catholic Stewardship Council in 1968. The formulation of a constitution and by-laws and the election of the first officers occurred in 1967. The episcopal moderators have been Bishops Albert Zuroweste (Belleville) 1967–74, from 1971–74, co-moderator with Edward E. Swanstrom (auxiliary, New York); and William G. Connare (Greensburg) 1974 to the present. Rev. Robert Deming (Kansas City-St. Joseph) was first executive secretary and the Kansas City chancery the first, temporary headquarters.

Following this organizational move, early progress included the Publications Committee's *Parish Stewardship Educational Program*, known as the "red kit" because of its red cover. It furnished parishes with implementation instructions, sample letters, sermons, General Intercessions, bulletin copy, and bibliography. It offered a three-weekend stewardship program whereby, parishioners received a biblical and spiritual concept of stewardship (first week), introduction to stewardship of time and talent (second week—after which they were invited to carry out an apostolate of their choice), and to stewardship of money (third week—after which they were asked to sign a pledge to contribute a certain amount of money to their church each week).

During his chairmanship of the NCSC, 1972–74, Msgr. Charles Grahmann (San Antonio) undertook other progressive steps. Listening to grass-roots voices, he became aware of three needs: (1) to expand the NCSC operation by giving more emphasis to Stewardship of Time and Talent; (2) to move the office to Washington, D.C. in order to form a relationship with the USCC-NCCB; and (3) to find a full-time executive director to carry out the Executive Board's policies in a professional manner. At the tenth annual conference in Tucson in October 1973, participants voted to support all three areas and Msgr. Grahmann engineered the process whereby these needs were met.

On February 4, 1974, Francis A. Novak, CSSR, then

engaged in stewardship work in the Diocese of Grand Rapids, was elected NCSC's first full-time executive director. His mandate was to develop catechetical and pastoral programs on the total concept of stewardship.

In 1975, the NCSC published its first major program, *Stewardship of Money, A Manual for Parishes*, as an answer to requests from Ordinaries, development directors, pastors and lay persons on parish and pastoral councils for assistance to solve parochial and diocesan fund-raising problems. A tested, successful, do-it-yourself program, *Stewardship of Money* is a seven-step procedure with emphasis on the biblical teaching of returning to God a proportion of his material gifts, on Vatican II's doctrine of co-responsibility, on active liturgical participation in the celebration of the Eucharist, especially in the Presentation of the Gifts, and on the mechanics of successful fund raising.

NCSC's second major program was published in 1976, *Stewardship of Time and Talent, A Parish Manual for Lay Ministries*. In four parts, it presents a "Plan and Program" for the development of lay ministries; a "Theology of Stewardship"; a catechesis of Lay Ministries based ont the threefold roles of Jesus as Priest, Prophet and King, and the Christian's parallel roles in the Ministries of Worship, of Teaching and of Service; Part Four presents a process for conducting parish adult education, parish council study sessions, and young adult Confirmation classes. A homiletic-pastoral approach is recommended to priests to synchronize weekend preaching with these education courses.

The NCSC office has coordinators in the 12 U.S. episcopal regions to promote membership and full participation. Stewardship programs have been set up in many dioceses. Membership embraces 114 dioceses, through personal contact with bishops by Rev. David Sheldon (St. Cloud). NCSC conducts stewardship seminars and workshops for continuing education of priests, lay institutes for ministry, pastoral and parish councils, and religious communities. The annual national conference promotes understanding of stewardship, particularly for newcomers. The NCSC office urges building community in the parish by home visitation as a kingly ministry of service in response to Paul VI's exhortation that one-on-one "personal contact" is "indispensable" (Paul VI EvangNunt 46). NCSC has contributed over 30 phrases, expressions, and terms to the National Catechetical Directory on stewardship. It has participated in the development of the NCCB *Principles and Guidelines for Fund Raising* (1977). Publications include a brochure on NCSC as a service organization to dioceses and parishes, and a visual fold-out for use in CCD and adult religious education; there is a free periodical tabloid, *Stewardship Information* (SIS). The Fr. Paul Kaletta award, established in 1975 to recognize notable contributions to stewardship, has been awarded to Msgr. Luigi Ligutti (1975), Robert Derek (1976), Bishop Edward E. Swanstrom (1977), and Msgr. Don Hughes (1978).

The immediate pastoral objectives of the NCSC are succinctly stated in the following paragraph placed in the 1978 *Official Catholic Directory*: "This office promotes the biblical concept of total Christian stewardship in the contemporary Church. It implements Stewardship of Time, Talent and Treasure in dioceses and parishes by providing self-help pastoral programs in adult education for the development of lay ministry and the spiritualizing of church fund raising. Following the dual principle of shared responsibility and accountability, it serves bishops, priests, religious, pastoral and parish councils, religious education directors, religious communities, special groups and individuals."

Bibliography: R. A. BRUNGS, *A Priestly People* (Staten Island, N.Y. 1964). Y. CONGAR, *Lay People in the Church. A Study for a Theology of the Laity*, tr. D. ATTWATER (Westminster, Md. 1957). J. GUITTON, *The Church and the Laity*, tr. M. G. CARROLL (Staten Island, N.Y. 1965). NCSC Publications: *Stewardship of Time and Talent, A Parish Manual for Lay Ministries* (1976); *Stewardship of Money, A Manual for Parishes* (1975); *Money as an Offertory Gift* (1977); *Stewardship: Symbolic Presence of the Christ Event for the Church Today* (1976).

[F. A. NOVAK]

NATIONAL CATHOLIC VOCATION COUNCIL (NCVC)

Established in August 1976, NCVC strives to give the Church in the United States visible withess of the mutual collaboration of the national vocation organizations of men and women. Membership is by organization, not by individual participation. The original organizations represented are: the *National Conference of Religious Vocation Directors of Men, the *National Sisters Vocation Conference, the *National Conference of Diocesan Vocation Directors, and Serra International. Each of the organizations has two members on the Council's board of directors. Also on the board are representatives from the National Conference of Catholic Bishops, the *Leadership Conference of Women Religious, and the *Conference of Major Superiors of Men.

The objectives of the NCVC are: to facilitate substantive exchange among national vocation organizations of men and women; to help members of each organization to become more effective vocation ministers; to bring about a mutual understanding—among member organizations—productive of unified efforts toward appreciation of and commitment to Church vocations.

Two early programs sponsored by the NCVC were the national Church Vocations Awareness Week and the biennial educational conference for all men and women concerned with church vocations work. The Council's office, located in Chicago, Illinois, is a source for information and literature on Church vocations generally.

[J. A. DONAHUE]

NATIONAL CENTER FOR URBAN ETHNIC AFFAIRS (NCUEA)

The National Center for Urban Ethnic Affairs was established as a response to the intensifying urban crises and the need to develop and legitimize ethnic, racial, and cultural diversity in American society. NCUEA believes that public and private institutions have neglected the legitimate concerns of many ethnic and working-class communities in developing meaningful public social policy.

The Center was initially developed in 1969 under the sponsorship of the Urban Task Force of the United States Catholic Conference. It was founded in 1970 by Msgr. Geno C. Baroni, who was among the first to recognize the key role of working-class and ethnic Americans and among the first to bring national attention to their problems. The Center, with the help of Ford Foundations funds, began by initiating a cooperative relationship with over thirty major Northern cities through technical assistance to their community organizations in program development.

The goals of NCUEA are to assist working class and ethnic groups to develop the community and neighborhood structures and leadership which will enable them to meet their legitimate needs most effectively; to lay the groundwork for possible cooperative efforts between black, brown, and ethnic groups on issues of mutual self-interest; to provide information and research services to these groups; and to advocate for an increased public policy sensitivity to the crucial importance of the community and neighborhood sector of urban society.

In 1978, NCUEA's staff of about 60 persons with a rich variety of ethnic and neighborhood expertise were working with more than 150 neighborhood organizations in 50 cities in the United States. The Center has a National Neighborhood Training Institute which trains community leaders in neighborhood organizing and revitalization. In addition it supplies technical assistance in the areas of building neighborhood organizations, housing, community-development credit unions, neighborhood drug prevention, neighborhood economic revitalization, neighborhood planning, and community crime prevention.

Long an advocate of cultural justice, NCUEA has the largest ethnic heritage studies resource center in the country. Through the instrumentality of NCUEA, Congress passed the Home Mortgage Disclosure Act of 1975 as an important first step in the fight against discriminatory mortgage lending (redlining). It also was involved in the establishment of the National Neighborhood Commission, and is helping to make federal urban policy sensitive to neighborhood issues.

NCUEA is unique in that it recognizes the importance of ethnicity and of religious organizations, particularly the Catholic Church, in revitalizing neighborhoods and in saving cities. The *Catholic Conference on Ethnic and Neighborhood Affairs was founded on the basis of an initiative of NCUEA which maintains an office of ethnic affairs and an office of religious affairs.

NCUEA is an independent, non-profit organization affiliated with the United States Catholic Conference. Robert J. Corletta is its current president.

See also ETHNICITY; URBANIZATION.

[R. PASQUARIELLO]

NATIONAL COALITION OF AMERICAN NUNS (NCAN)

The National Coalition of American Nuns was founded July 4, 1969 in Chicago by one hundred nuns who had gathered to discuss in a three-day conference the issues related to "Sisters' Survival Strategies." The founder was Sister Margaret Traxler, SSND, who with the networks represented by the sisters present, organized to "study, work and speak out on issues related to human rights and social justice." The first issue taken for consideration was the dismissal of Professor Mary Daly from Boston College. This was eventually resolved, but the members of NCAN organized a board of directors who then set up the guidelines for continuing action and programming of the new group.

This was the first feminist organization of nuns in the Church and the sisters, while affirming their membership in both the Church and their respective religious communities, nevertheless insisted on the complete autonomy of their religious institutes and asked all clerics and clerical groups both in Rome and in local jurisdictions to allow religious women to control the dynamics of their internal renewal processes and to open wider ministries to women. In its 1970 statement on the status of women in the Church, NCAN called for an international "alert" so that churchmen might realize the "growing correlation between Catholic women's disenchantment with the Church and the worldwide women's movement." In 1970, NCAN was among the first to call for ordination of women.

The board consists of 24 sisters from all over the U.S. and from various religious communities. The board members have always financed their own attendance at the board meetings and each has always been free to speak in the name of NCAN provided that in the general board discussions, there is consensus on the general direction of the position taken. The flexibility thus arrived at makes possible a rapid response to crisis in human-rights and social-justice issues; for example, NCAN was the first Catholic group to oppose the neutron bomb and the B-1 bomber. The group has consistently maintained a peace program and unswerving positions on interracial justice. When close to one hundred groups joined with the Leadership Conference on Civil Rights during the Supreme Court consideration (1977) of the Bakke Case, NCAN called for continual affirmative action and said that after two more centuries of affirmative action the Supreme Court might morally alter current employment and education guidelines. Like most church-related organizations of women, NCAN looks to its own membership for financial support, but foundation assistance has been generous. Two Protestant women's groups and one Jewish women's sisterhood have given grants to NCAN for its social action agenda.

The presidents of NCAN have been: Sister Margaret Traxler, SSND, Sister Ann Gillen, SHCJ, Sister Dorothy Donnelly, CSJ, Sister Judith Schloegel, CSJ, and the present officers, (1978–79) Sister Andrea Lee, SFCC and Sister Donna Quinn, OP, vice president.

[M. TRAXLER]

NATIONAL CONFERENCE OF DIOCESAN DIRECTORS OF RELIGIOUS EDUCATION/CCD

The National Conference of Diocesan Directors of Religious Education-CCD (NCDD) was organized in 1966 and has grown to include approximately 95 percent of the dioceses in the United States. The purposes of the NCDD are to foster growth of its members as professional religious education directors, and to provide a means for promoting an integrated pastoral catechetical ministry in the Church. The NCDD is organized according to the structure of ecclesiastical provinces in the United States. Voting membership is offered to diocesan directors, associate and/or assistant directors of religious education. Affiliate and associate memberships are also available.

The membership has an annual meeting in the Spring. The policy, direction, and general programming of the Conference are the responsibility of a board of directors, elected by and representing the provincial groupings of directors. The board meets three times a year: in

January, at the annual meeting, and in October. The officers, elected by the membership every two years at the annual meeting, form the executive committee of the board, which is empowered to act as necessary between board meetings. The executive secretary manages the day-to-day functioning of the organization. The office is in Washington, D.C. at the USCC Dept. of Education.

[W. WASSMUTH]

NATIONAL CONFERENCE OF DIOCESAN VOCATION DIRECTORS (NCDVD)

The National Conference of Diocesan Vocation directors began officially in October 1965, at the second national convention in Pittsburgh, when the Associations of Diocesan Vocation Directors of the Eastern Seaboard Association and of the West-Midwest voted to merge into a single national vocations organization. A national meeting had been held in Cincinnati in 1962, but the merger and election of officers in 1965, with Rev. J. Edward Duggan of Chicago as the first president, marked the beginning of a strong growth process. A tentative Constitution, adopted at the 1966 convention in Milwaukee, was formally approved at the Denver convention in 1971, with further provisions planned for 1978–79.

As NCDVD grew from seventy-five members to a membership of three-hundred-fifty, further structuring became necessary. In 1976 a resolution was passed approving a national office for the organization and in October, 1977, the central office was established in Chicago with Rev. Dennis H. Hoffman of Duluth as the first Executive Director.

As its purpose NCDVD has the promotion and preservation of priestly and/or religious vocations, and the support of its members in their own vocations by providing opportunities for personal and spiritual growth. It educates its members for the vocations apostolate by providing training in skills necessary for screening and selecting candidates and directing their growth.

NCDVD encourages defining "vocation" as "a call by God to ministry in the Church," a call given not merely to those ordained or professed, but to all.

See also NATIONAL CATHOLIC VOCATIONS COUNCIL; VOCATION, CLERICAL; VOCATION, RELIGIOUS.

[D. H. HOFFMAN]

NATIONAL CONFERENCE OF RELIGIOUS VOCATION DIRECTORS OF MEN

The National Conference of Religious Vocation Directors of Men, established in 1969, is composed of three member organizations: Eastern Religious Vocation Directors Association (ERVDA); Midwest Religious Vocation Directors Association (MRVDA); and Western Vocation Directors Association (WVDA). Its purposes are: (1) to coordinate and enhance the activities of member organizations; (2) to initiate programs at the national level that respond to needs in the area of church vocations; (3) to speak officially for its combined member organizations; (4) to serve as a member of the *National Catholic Vocation Council (NCVC); (5) to act as official liaison between its member organizations and other national organizations, especially the *Conference of Major Superiors of Men

(CMSM). The Conference sponsors a national convention biannually and publishes a quarterly, Call to Growth/Ministry, as well as an annual directory. Chicago is the site of Conference headquarters.

[C. ST. JAMES]

NATIONAL CONFERENCE OF VICARS FOR RELIGIOUS

The National Conference of Vicars for Religious (NCVR) is an organization of men and women who serve their dioceses in the United States as the representative (vicar or delegate) of the bishop to the religious of the diocese. The Conference began informally in 1967 with a gathering of several vicars in River Forest, Ill. to seek ways to better serve in their ministry to religious. In 1970 a formal Constitution was adopted and in 1976 the following mission statement was formulated at the annual assembly: "In the context of the Ministry of the Church, the Conference of Vicars for Religious sees itself as an enabling, supportive group to foster the education of Vicars for Religious in the service of stimulating the prophetic vocation for Religious life."

The NCVR is divided into four regions, which hold regional meetings in the Fall of the year. The national assembly is held annually in March. All vicars, associate vicars, and delegates for religious are eligible for membership. The NCVR has an active membership (attendance at either regional or national meetings) of about 100 men and women. One of the most significant developments in its history is the inclusion of a growing number of religious women in the office of vicar for religious. Many dioceses have both a sister and a priest (one diocese now has a brother) in the office.

In 1974 and in 1978 the NCVR held its national assembly in Rome at the invitation of the Congregation for Religious and Secular Institutes (CRSI). These meetings provided an opportunity for an exchange of ideas, problems, directions, and opportunities for mutual collaboration between the vicars and the officials of the Congregation.

Among the themes which were the subject of the most recent dialogues between the NCVR and CRSI were on the New Law for Consecrated Life, Issues of Separation, Women in Ministry, New Models of Committed Life, Relationship between the Local Church and Religious, and The Theology and Language of the Vows. These topics were presented by various men and women vicars and represented the vicars' experience in their ministry to and their relationship with American religious. This most recent meeting provided an opportunity for vicars to present to CRSI a picture of American religious life as seen from the point of view of those men and women who represent the local Church in relationship with American religious.

The members of NCVR are of varying backgrounds, men and women with graduate degrees in such disciplines as Canon Law, theology, spirituality, philosophy, history. They also come from a wide variety of ministerial experiences in education, parochial ministry, formation, chancery administration, health care; some are former major superiors of religious congregation of women. Vicars for religious find that their ministry is one of mutuality, in so far as they receive as much as they bring to the religious with whom they are associated.

[J. A. GALANTE]

NATIONAL COUNCIL OF CATHOLIC LAITY (NCCL)

The National Council of Catholic Laity was created in 1971 by the National Council of Catholic Women and the National Council of Catholic Men so that direction, guidance, and unity might be given to all existing lay organizations in the United States.

When created, the objectives of NCCL were: to intensify the efforts of the Catholic laity in the U.S.; to mobilize and coordinate efforts of the laity to bring full life and meaning to the role of the laity in the mission of the Church; to be a medium through which the laity might speak on matters of common concern; to cooperate with other national and international organizations in the solution of modern day problems; and to cooperate with the clergy, religious, and bishops in fulfilling the mission of the Church.

In the seven years of its existence, NCCL has contributed to the development of parish councils through service and publications; it has worked to make Catholic laity more conscious of their role and responsibility as People of God; it has attempted to help laity recognize their role in the secular marketplace as a form of lay ministry. As contributors to a national dialogue among bishops, priests, religious, and other lay groups, NCCL has also been active in ecumenical dialogue with national leaders of other Churches and movements. It cosponsored five seminars on criminal rights and criminal justice with seven national organizations; it held the first nationwide Human Rights and Justice Week in the U.S., October 16–22, 1977; and it furnished liturgical and educational materials to educate others on the violations of human rights. NCCL requested in 1975 that a "focal point for lay concerns" be established within the National Conference of Catholic Bishops. The bishops of the United States voted to establish a Secretariat of the Laity. As this new secretariat develops, the design of NCCL will change so that it will be ready to respond to new demands for responsible lay action and study.

See also BISHOPS' COMMITTEE ON THE LAITY.

[J. ECKSTEIN]

NATIONAL COUNCIL OF CHURCHES OF CHRIST, U.S.A. (NCCC-USA)

The NCCC is the national expression of the ecumenical movement as it exists in 31 Protestant and Eastern Orthodox Churches in the United States. Its preamble reads, "The NCCC-USA is a cooperative agency of Christian communions seeking to fulfill the mission to which God calls them. The member communions, responding to the Gospel revealed in the Scriptures, confess Jesus, the Incarnate Son of God, as Saviour and Lord. Relying on the transforming power of the Holy Spirit, the Council works to bring churches into a life-giving fellowship, an independent witness, study and action to the glory of God and in service to all creation."

In 1972 the United States Catholic Conference published a "Report on Possible Roman Catholic Membership in the NCCC," done by a blue-ribbon committee, which included three Catholic bishops and two presidents of Churches. It was sent to all Catholic dioceses for study and feed-back. The *Report* made no decision, of course, but did draw conclusions: The

NCCC–USA should continue as "a precious heritage from which American Christianity could continue to draw profit," and "nearly every argument in favor of the continuance of the NCCC (or a comparable successor) is also an argument for Roman Catholic membership. We believe that if the documents of Vatican II are the valid expression of what the Roman Catholic Church is and intends to be—as can scarcely be denied—Roman Catholic ecclesiological principles are in substantial accord with the aims and methods of the NCCC. This being so, it would seem that the arguments for Roman Catholic membership in the NCCC are as strong as the arguments for membership in the case of many of the other member churches" (*Report* p. 30).

No decision has ever been publicly taken on the *Report*, although the long silence on it seems to be an equivalent negative. The Bishops' Commission on Ecumenical and Interreligious Affairs (BCEIA) continues full membership in the Faith and Order Commission (theology) of the NCCC. National staff of the NCCB–USCC encounter their counterparts from the NCCC at frequent meetings and cooperate often in projects of mutual interest and support. Special areas of such cooperation recently have been overseas relief, domestic disasters, witness for human rights, many aspects of religious education, and the media. The General Secretary of the NCCC–USA regularly meets with the General Secretary of NCCB–USCC to discuss opportunities and problems. Frequently these meetings include the Vice-President of the Synagogue Council of America.

Across the nation, Catholic dioceses, parishes, and organizations share life and ecumenical agencies at their levels. About 58 dioceses have full membership in local ecumenical agencies, and the number steadily grows. The NCCC Commission on Regional and Local Ecumenism focuses national attention on these subnational units and enjoys good working relationships with BCEIA, including a bishop's regular attendance at meetings. Among the "related movements" in which NCCC constituency and Roman Catholics meet are: Church Women United, the Interfaith Center for Corporate Responsibility, and the Interreligious Foundation for Community Organization.

All national organizations seem to be undergoing crises and reorganizations. Both the NCCC and the USCC have experienced these. Perhaps once the consolidation has been achieved, the Catholic Church in its national expression will return to the "Report on Possible Membership in the NCCC," and again consider a more active, national ecumenical life.

[D. J. BOWMAN]

NATIONAL FEDERATION OF CATHOLIC PHYSICIANS' GUILDS

The National Federation of Catholic Physicians' Guilds, founded in 1932 in New York City, has as its purposes: service to Christ's message by applying accurate information to difficult medico-moral problems; and service in Christian charity.

Currently Guild members are urged to participate widely in parish and diocesan activities—sex education or awareness, natural family planning and pre-Cana programs, Birthright, AAI, pro-life activities, defense of the family and of marriage, and of chastity itself. Members also participate in media programs involving discussions of abortion, contraception, homosexuality, sterilization, euthanasia (by whatever term), biogenetic engineering, so that they may lend their expertise to the teaching of the Church's magisterium.

The publication produced by the Federation of Catholic Physicians' Guilds is the *Linacre Quarterly*, named for Thomas Linacre, a distinguished physician of the 16th century. A journal of the ethics and philosophy of medical practice in support of the magisterium, it serves the needs of the increasing number of physicians who have had minimal exposure to Catholic teaching and assists all readers through its medico-moral discussions. The National Federation has recently formed medico-moral teams to be placed at the disposal of the American bishops to discuss current medico-moral issues of interest to hospital staffs, guilds, clergy, seminarians, religious, and interested laity. In the past 15 years a concerted attempt has been made to protect the Christian concept that suffering and death are not enemies. Member physicians agree that they may be as difficult as they are inevitable but that the corporal works of mercy are no more outdated than are the spiritual.

A spiritual exercise in the form of a retreat or a day of recollection is held yearly, usually on the feast of the guild's patron, St. Luke. Currently there are approximately 100 guilds and 6,000 members.

[W. A. LYNCH]

NATIONAL FEDERATION OF SPIRITUAL DIRECTORS

The National Federation of Spiritual Directors is a coalition of three regional organizations of seminary and religious spiritual directors: Eastern Regional Conference of Seminary Spiritual Directors; Midwest Association of Spiritual Directors; and Western Association of Spiritual Directors.

Interest in a national federation was expressed during a meeting of formation personnel sponsored by St. Meinrad's Seminary, St. Meinrad, Ind. in June 1971. The Federation was formally constituted in June 1973 at St. John Vianney Seminary in East Aurora, N.Y. for the purpose of facilitating cooperation and collaboration among those charged with the particular responsibilities of priestly and religious spiritual formation in the United States. The executive board is composed of the president of each regional association and two other members elected at large. Biennial meetings have been held at St. Thomas Seminary, Denver in 1975 and the Pontifical College Josephinum, Worthington, Ohio in 1977. Membership in one of the regional associations includes membership in the National Federation.

[J. W. TROESTER]

NATIONAL MARRIAGE ENCOUNTER

National Marriage Encounter, like all other expressions of *Marriage Encounter, owes its origins to Rev. Gabriel Calvo and the first English-speaking Encounter given in the United States at the University of Notre Dame in 1967, at the end of the Christian Family Movement convention. To maintain a consistent approach to the Encounter weekend, as well as to provide a central clearing house for ideas, a national board was elected in 1969. However, the New York group, under the leader-

ship of Charles Gallagher, took a different approach to the Encounter and the New York group split off from National Marriage Encounter in 1971 (*see* WORLDWIDE MARRIAGE ENCOUNTER).

National Marriage Encounter has remained true to the original goal of Fr. Calvo, namely, the renewal of marriage. Moreover, it has maintained an ecumenical stance, rather than founding Encounters for various faith traditions. The national board is composed of member couples and clergy from many geographical areas. Its executive team is made up of a couple and a clergyman elected to serve for two years.

[T. HILL]

NATIONAL OFFICE FOR BLACK CATHOLICS

The National Office for Black Catholics (NOBC) was established in 1970. It was the result of two years of discussion and planning between Black Catholic clergy, religious and lay persons, and the National Conference of Catholic Bishops (NCCB). The purpose of the National Office for Black Catholics is (1) to work toward strengthening and developing the Church in the Black Community, (2) to increase the participation of Black Catholics in the total Church, and (3) to motivate the Church to work more effectively towards eliminating racism within the Church and American Society. NOBC represents the one million *Black Catholics in the United States. Although it is not a membership organization, it is structured in such a way that all segments of the Black Catholic community can have input into its programs and policies, and communication can be easily maintained. A Board of Directors composed of lay persons (9), religious sisters (3), and representatives of the Black Catholic clergy (3) regulates the activities of the organization. Board members are elected from among the constituents of five Black Catholic organizations: The National Black Catholic Clergy Caucus, The National Black Catholic Lay Caucus, The National Black Sisters Conference, the Knights of St. Peter Claver, and the Ladies Auxiliary, Knights of St. Peter Claver.

Programs are maintained in Pastoral Ministry in the Black Community, Culture and Worship, Church Vocations, Education, and Leadership Development. NOBC endeavors to respond to the needs of Black Catholics by offering programs to parishes, dioceses, and on the national level. It also undertakes special projects designed to bring the Black perspective to contemporary concerns of the Church. It has published a document on evangelization in the Black community, a filmstrip entitled "Black Married Love," and is sponsoring research in the area of religious education and catechetics. The Office sponsors two publications: *Freeing the Spirit*, a quarterly magazine, and *Impact*, a monthly newsletter. It has produced an album of Black religious music, "Freeing the Spirit," as well as *This Far by Faith* and *Soulful Worship*, two books on worship in the Black Community.

The National Office for Black Catholics is recognized by the National Conference of Catholic Bishops, Ad-Hoc Committee for Liaison with NOBC. It is listed in the Official Catholic Directory. Mr. Walter Hubbard (Seatle, WA) is currently president of the Board of Directors. The executive director is Bro. Cyprian Lamar Rowe, FMS. NOBC is located at 1234 Massachusetts Ave., N.W., Washington, D.C. 20005.

[J. M. DAVIS]

NATIONAL ORGANIZATION FOR CONTINUING EDUCATION OF ROMAN CATHOLIC CLERGY (NOCERCC)

NOCERCC was founded at a conference sponsored by the National Federation of Priests' Councils in 1973. After that time NOCERCC became an independent organization governed by an elected president and a board of directors, each elected from one of the twelve episcopal regions of the National Conference of Catholic Bishops (NCCB), plus one representative from religious communities. Full membership is limited to dioceses and religious provinces; affiliate membership comprises universities and agencies offering resources in continuing education. NOCERCC promotes continuing education of priests by: providing research, resources and training for continuing education directors of dioceses and religious communities and to committees of the NCCB; encouraging supradiocesan and regional cooperation of directors of continuing education; maintaining liaison with ecumenical groups; sponsoring an annual convention. NOCERCC has funded research projects and developed programs in: priestly spirituality, preaching, policies on alcoholism, social justice, management and leadership styles, shared ministry, sexuality, seminary training, use of video, and models of parish planning.

Bibliography: National Conference of Catholic Bishops, *Program of Continuing Education of Priests* (Washington, D.C. 1973). E. E. LARKIN, and G. T. BROCCOLO, eds., *Spiritual Renewal of the American Priesthood* (Washington, D.C. 1972).

[J. B. DUNNING]

NATIONAL PASTORAL PLANNING CONFERENCE

Starting in 1973 as an annual event, the National Pastoral Planning Conference in 1976 became an association of diocesan pastoral-planning offices and of individuals active in the ministry of *pastoral planning in the Church. The association is devoted to the development of *pastoral planning at all levels of the U.S. Church—assisting those in this ministry, providing training and a forum for information sharing, and representing pastoral planners to other national organizations. It is an outgrowth of a series of seminars, workshops, and regional meetings on pastoral planning sponsored by the *Center for Applied Research in the Apostolate (CARA) and others over the years 1971–1973. About 90–95 persons attend the annual conventions, representing about 30–45 dioceses and national organizations and proceedings have been published for every convention except the first (1973). The Conference is governed by a twelve-member coordinating committee, half of whom are elected annually on a rotating basis.

Bibliography: National Pastoral Planning Conference, *Proceedings* (Pittsburgh 1974; Washington, D.C. 1975, 1976, 1977); *Resource Bulletin* (Pittsburgh 1977).

[E. M. SULLIVAN]

NATIONAL SISTERS COMMUNICATIONS SERVICE

The National Sisters Communications Service (NSCS) was established to stimulate the effective use of mass communications in and by communities of religious women. Its goal is to articulate a communications philosophy for contemporary religious life and to raise among religious congregations and organizations awareness of ways that planned and professional communications/public-relations efforts can help apostolates and ministries, vocation education, and the administration of the congregation internally and externally.

Based in Los Angeles, the NSCS offers a variety of programs, publications, and projects dealing with mass communications in religious life and ministry. It publishes *Media & Values*, a quarterly review of modern media and its effect on human values, and *Sistersharing*, a how-to newsletter explaining practical media skills for newsletters, brochures, radio and television. NSCS also conducts: workshops/seminars, in religious media skills and organizations; job clearinghouse linking talented sister-communicators with job openings and internships in the ministry of communications. *Let Your Light Shine* is the title of its evaluation/consultation services for congregational publications.

In addition, NSCS serves a network of sisters and religious congregations concerned about media issues and the use of media by religious orders. Established in 1975 by a task force from the Leadership Congress of Women Religious, the National Sisters Vocation Conference, and the Sister (now Religious) Formation Conference, the Service currently has a nine-member board of directors and a three-person national staff. The central office of NSCS is at 1962 S. Shenandoah, Los Angeles, CA 90034.

[E. THOMAN]

NATIONAL SISTERS VOCATION CONFERENCE (NSVC)

Aware that changes precipitated by Vatican Council II as well as by converging societal and cultural factors were influencing its membership, the Conference of Major Superiors of Women (*see* LEADERSHIP CONFERENCE OF WOMEN RELIGIOUS) called in 1965 for establishment of a "working committee" on vocations. With the candidate and prospective candidate to religious life in mind, this committee was to address a twofold objective: to facilitate the work of major superiors and vocation directors faced with the task of comprehending and interpreting the meanings of religious life in a decade when these meanings seemed most elusive; and to determine what supports might be provided for vocation personnel burdened with the expectations of candidate, religious community, and Church. Evolving in 1967 from being a working committee into an independent, national organization, the NSVC continued to address these issues through efforts in research, education, consultation, and affirmation.

Sisters' dissatisfaction with speculation regarding vocations, and their insistence upon availability of reliable information, prompted research. With cooperation from the leadership in women's communities and in consultation with vocation and formation personnel, NSVC gathered previously unavailable data on entrances and departures and completed a two-phased study on women who had left religious life (*see* RELIGIOUS INSTITUTES, DEPARTURES FROM). By undertaking and financing its own studies and by encouraging and occasionally publishing the studies of others, NSVC proposed to serve its 1,500 members and fifteen regions by gaining access to more complete and accurate information on vocation-related issues. The Conference anticipates future research and educative efforts based on a policy of broad consultation. Canonists, medical doctors, psychologists, theologians, and others will be invited to address NSVC regional and national meetings.

Continuing education is further facilitated through a newsletter which deals with such topics as: vocations among minority peoples; older, widowed, and divorced candidates; contemplative vocations; extended membership programs; women religious in diocesan vocation offices; communications and media.

However actively engaged in work with candidates to priesthood and religious life, NSVC does not regard itself as a "recruitment" organization. It stresses, instead, its role in vocation-education among laypersons, religious, and clergy striving to listen and respond to the Lord whose call is persistent, audible, and compelling.

Bibliography: Publications of NSVC: M. M. MODDE, *Study on Entrances & Departures in Religious Communities of Women in the United States 1965–1972* (Chicago 1973); *Study on Entrances & Departures in Religious Communities of Women in the United States 1972–1974* (Chicago 1974). M. M. MODDE and J. P. KOVAL, *Phase I: Research Project on Women Who Have Left Religious Communities* (Chicago 1975); *Phase II: Women Who Have Left Religious Communities* (Chicago 1976). NSVC, *Vocation Personnel: Communities of Women Religious* (Chicago 1977). S. M. SCHNEIDERS, *Spiritual Direction: Reflections on a Contemporary Ministry* (Berkeley 1977).

[D. M. CARR]

NATURAL FAMILY PLANNING

Natural family planning, the monitoring of changes in the human female menstrual cycle to achieve or avoid pregnancy, also is known as "fertility awareness" or "periodic abstinence." The term "rhythm," frequently confused with modern natural methods, refers to a now obsolete form of family planning based upon calendar calculations. Considerable misunderstanding surrounds reports in medical and population journals when the term "rhythm" is used to describe all of the natural methods, whereas it is but one of many.

Methods. The original calendar-based methods of predicting a woman's time of maximum fertility were reported independently in Japan and Germany in the early 1930s by Drs. K. Ogino and H. Knaus (see bibliog.). Although their formulas differ slightly, their names are almost always linked as developing the Ogino-Knaus Calendar Method. These approaches, based upon accurate records of the length of past fertility cycles to predict ovulation in future cycles, were accepted by the Church as licit for families having serious reason to limit their fertility.

By the mid-1930s Dr. Rudolf F. Vollman was teaching an early form of natural family planning based upon changes in basal body temperature (see bibliog.). A pure form of basal body temperature monitoring, in which the couple abstains in the menstrual cycle until after temperature readings indicate ovulation has occurred, was rated in 1970 as one of the most effective methods of family planning by Christopher Tietze, M.D., of the Population Council (see bibliog.). Vollman and others advanced experiments with natural methods including other signs that would indicate the period of fertility.

Although the first publications linking changes in cervical mucus discharge appeared as early as the Ogino-Knaus papers in 1933 (see Séguy), it was another thirty years before popular use of this symptom was promoted by Bonomi in Italy, Keefe in the United

States, and the Drs. John J. and Evelyn L. Billings of Australia. Supported by research conducted in Australia by J. B. Brown and H. G. Burger (see bibliog.), the Doctors Billings developed a formal teaching approach for the utilization of cervical-mucus changes to identify the fertile period. Known interchangeably as the Billings or Ovulation Method, the cervical-mucus approach to the prediction of the time of maximum fertility in the human female spread rapidly throughout the world during the 1970s.

Effectiveness. Although both the World Health Organization (WHO) and the U.S. Department of Health, Education, and Welfare (HEW) launched long-term studies of the Ovulation Method and the Sympto-Thermal Method before the mid-1970s, controversy still surrounds the relative effectiveness of the two approaches.

The Basal Body Temperature approach, requiring abstinence from the beginning of menses in a given cycle until after ovulation has passed, traditionally is employed only by couples highly motivated to avoid pregnancy through observance of demanding rules. The Sympto-Thermal Method evolved rapidly during the 1970s reflecting the influence of the Drs. Billings and earlier work by Dr. Edward Keefe of the United States on self-observation of the cervix (see bibliog.). Formal teaching programs under the leadership of Dr. Guy of France and the SERENA organization of Canada developed methods of teaching nuances in fertility symptoms. In the mid-1970s serious efforts were made by Josef Roetzer, M.D. of Austria and others to incorporate as many of the fertility signs as possible in new refinements of the methods. Similar efforts continued in the U.S. in the Couple-to-Couple League where John and Sheila Kippley incorporated breastfeeding as a major component of their Natural Family Planning program (see bibliog.).

Research Initiatives. In response to a growing public demand for natural methods in the U.S., the Human Life Foundation, established as a research and educational Foundation in 1969 by the U.S. bishops, entered into contracts with HEW to develop an effective curriculum and teacher-training system for the Ovulation, Basal Body Temperature and Sympto-Thermal Methods. Drs. Mary Catherine Martin and Leo Min, developers of the curriculum-testing system of the Foundation, assisted WHO to launch a similar curriculum effort for use in different cultural situations around the world.

Worldwide interest in cooperation between Natural Family Planning organizations led to the formation in 1974 of the International Federation for Family Life Promotion. The Federation held its first International Congress in Cali, Colombia in 1977. American agencies formed the Natural Family Planning Federation of America in 1974. The American Federation and the Human Life Foundation formed a single organization in 1977 named the *Human Life and Natural Family Planning Foundation.

It is anticipated that effectiveness studies on the natural methods will continue well into the 1980s. Biological foundations of the temperature-based and cervical-mucus based methods indicate a potential for effectiveness in the same range as the most effective of the artificial contraceptives. Educational approaches are being developed to convey accurately the means by which human fertility can be monitored through fertility-awareness systems. The motivation of any individual couple to follow the rules remains as a primary determinant of the effectiveness of any of the natural methods. Research on the viability of sperm and better indicators of the days of female fertility continue in dozens of nations. Improvement in the educational techniques, the ability of couples to reinforce others in confronting questions of motivation and abstinence, and new developments of research promise to make the natural methods more acceptable to the general population.

Bibliography: E. L. & J. J. BILLINGS, J. B. BROWN, H. G. BURGER, "Symptoms and Hormonal Changes Accompanying Ovulation," *Lancet* 1 (1972) 282–284. E. F. KEEFE, "Self-Observation of the Cervix to Distinguish Days of Possible Fertility," *Bulletin of the Sloane Hospital for Women* 8 (1962) 129–136. J. and S. KIPPLEY, *The Art of Natural Family Planning* (Couple-to-Couple League, Cincinnati 1977). H. KNAUS, "Die periodische Frucht- und Unfruchtbarkeit des Weibes," *Zentralblatt für Gynäkologie* 57 (1933) 1393–1408. K. OGINO, "Über den Konzeptionstermin des Weibes und seine Anwendung in der Praxis," *Zentralblatt für Gynäkologie* 56 (1932) 721–732. J. SÉGUY et al., "Determining the Fertile Time," *Reproduction*, Institute for the Study of Human Reproduction, Univ. of Santo Tomás, Manila (June 1976). C. TIETZE, "Ranking of Contraceptive Methods by Levels of Effectiveness," *Advances in Planned Parenthood* 6 (1970) 117–126. R. F. VOLLMAN, "Über Fertilität und Sterilität der Frau innerhalb des Menstruationcyclus," *Archiv für Gynäkologie* 182 (1953) 602–622.

[L. J. KANE]

NATURAL LAW

Until the late 1950s the notion of the natural law found in textbooks, both philosophical and theological, in use in Roman Catholic schools was fundamentally the same (10:251). Human nature, adequately considered, i.e., considered in its essential relations to self, to neighbor, and to God, was the objective foundation of the natural law. An analysis of this nature and its essential relations could yield a knowledge both of general principles and of specific, concrete and immutable norms, both positive and negative. These norms could then be applied to specific situations by a judgment of conscience.

Today this neoscholastic notion of the natural law (perhaps, as Grisez has argued, rooted in Suárez) is commonly repudiated, both by those who seek to replace the natural law with what they regard as more adequate fundamental notions and by those who try, in differing ways, to rehabilitate the notion of the natural law. They reject the neoscholastic notion because in their judgment it is overly rationalistic and deductive in character and incapable of adequately meeting challenges such as those offered by developments in philosophy, theology, sociology, psychology, cultural anthropology.

Attention here will focus on some of the more significant efforts to rehabilitate the natural law, prescinding from a consideration of those who, although in some ways sympathetic to the natural law, prefer to replace it with other categories such as "human experience" (C. Curran), "responsible relationality" (R. Johann), or an "empirical calculation of values" (J. Milhaven). Among efforts to rehabilitate the natural law two broad types can be discerned, each represented by authors who agree on some basic issues, although they differ widely and at times significantly from one another on specifics.

Mutable Nature Explanations. One group of writers attempts to rethink the natural law on the belief that the principal defect in previous natural-law theories was a lack of historicity, a failure to recognize that human nature itself is essentially and not merely accidentally changeable. These writers, among whom may be included John Macquarrie, Philip Selznick, Charles Fay, William Luijpen, and the later (post 1970) Michael B. Crowe, stress the fact that such currents of contemporary thought, as existentialism, phenomenology, and personalism, although agreeing on hardly anything else, insist that human existence is inescapably conditioned by historicity. For them historicity is so central to human existence that it imposes the conclusion that man himself changes intrinsically, so that "human nature" today is a nature essentially different in many ways from what it was in the past.

Such writers regard natural law to be basically human rationality, as this provides a certain "directionality" in the midst of change, assuring some kind of continuity. There can thus be some immutably valid general principles of the natural law, such as *good is to be done and evil is to be avoided*, but specific, concrete norms determining the meaning of "good" and "evil" can be valid for only a given period within the historicity of human-nature-on-the-go. The view of these writers on the natural law is congenial with the position of Josef Fuchs, Bruno Schüller, Richard A. McCormick, and others that there are no absolute, negative, universal prohibitions but at best "virtually exceptionless" rules of conduct.

Immutable Nature Explanations. Another group of writers, represented by Germain Grisez, John Finnis, R. H. Armstrong, Dario Composta, Eric D'Arcy, and the "early" Michael B. Crowe, argues that the demise of conventional natural-law theory by no means leads to the view that human nature itself changes essentially. For them human nature, although dynamic in character and by no means static, is essentially unchangeable and rooted in it are basic inclinations toward real goods of human persons. Appealing to the thought of Aquinas and to the findings of contemporary psychology and anthropology, these writers stress the significance of the Thomistic distinction between speculative and practical thinking. They argue that goods known consciously, toward which there is a dynamic orientation in virtue of natural, human inclinations, give rise both to basic primary principles of the natural law and to specific norms grounded in these principles. Although the conditions in which human persons exist change and so entail growth in the understanding of the meaning of specific norms, these writers hold that there are true absolute, negative, universal prohibitions.

Significantly the early Crowe, in interpreting the Thomistic statement *natura autem hominis est mutabilis* (ST 2a2ae, 57.2 ad 1), appealed to the context in which Aquinas makes that statement to show that it ought not be understood as indicating any change intrinsic to human nature. The later Crowe, in arguing for substantial change within historical human nature, appealed to the statement but not to the teaching that is its context.

Vatican Council II, although using the term itself sparingly, explicitly appeals to natural law to support a specific condemnation of obliteration bombing (*Gaudium et spes* 79) and elsewhere refers to the reality of natural law as man's living participation in "the highest norm of human life," God's eternal and divine law (*Dignitatis humanae* 3).

Bibliography: R. A. ARMSTRONG, *Primary and Secondary Precepts in Thomistic Natural Law Teaching* (The Hague 1966). D. COMPOSTA, *Natura e razione: studio sulle inclinazioni naturali in rapporto al diritto naturale* (Zurich 1971). M. B. CROWE, "Human Nature—Immutable or Mutable," IrTheolQ 30 (1963) 204–231; "The Pursuit of Natural Law," IrTheolQ 44 (1977) 3–29. C. CURRAN, *Catholic Moral Theology in Dialogue* (Notre Dame, Ind. 1972) 116–122, 124–130, 136–139. E. D'ARCY, *Human Acts: An Essay on their Moral Evaluation* (Oxford 1963). C. FAY, "Human Evolution: A Challenge to Thomistic Ethics," *International Philosophical Quarterly* 2 (1962) 50–80. J. FINNIS, "Natural Law and Unnatural Acts," Heythrop J 11 (1970) 365–387. J. FUCHS, "The Absoluteness of Moral Terms," Greg 52 (1971) 415–458. G. GRISEZ, *Contraception and the Natural Law* (Milwaukee 1964) ch. 3; *Abortion: The Myths, the Realities, and the Arguments* (New York 1970) ch. 6; "The First Principle of Practical Reason: A Commentary on the *Summa theologiae* 1a2ae, question 94, article 2," *Natural Law Forum* 10 (1965) 168–201, repr. in abridged form in A. KENNY, ed., *Aquinas: A Collection of Critical Essays* (New York 1969) 340–382. R. O. JOHANN, *Building the Human* (New York 1968). W. LUIJPEN, *Phenomenology of Natural Law* (Pittsburgh 1967). R. A. MCCORMICK, *Ambiguity in Moral Choice* (Milwaukee 1973). J. MACQUARRIE, *Three Issues in Ethics* (New York 1970) ch. 5. W. E. MAY, "The Natural Law, Conscience, and Developmental Psychology," Communio 2 (1975) 3–31. J. G. MILHAVEN, "Objective Moral Evaluation of Consequences," ThSt 32 (1971) 407–430. B. SCHÜLLER, "Direkte Tötung–indirekete Tötung," *Theologie und Philosophie* 47 (1972) 341–357. P. SELZNICK, "Sociology and Natural Law," *Natural Law Forum* 6 (1961) 84–108, repr. in J. COGLEY, ed., *Natural Law and Modern Society* (New York, Cleveland 1962) 154–193.

[W. E. MAY]

NETWORK

A religious lobby for just legislation, seeking to make Congress more responsive to the needs of all people, particularly the poor, the hungry, the jobless, and the marginalized. The Network ideal is cooperative effort—grass roots groups organized to gather data and interact with members of Congress and their constituents at the congressional district and state levels. As a religious lobby, Network engages in the struggle for a more just society in response to the scriptural call to justice. Moreover, members try to integrate these values into their lifestyle, legislative efforts, organizational activity, theological reflection, and spirituality. A national staff coordinates these efforts; engages in legislative research; communicates with members of Congress and their staffs; works in coalition with other public interest groups; publishes a monthly newsletter and a quarterly—to inform members on current legislation and to provide indepth analyses of Network issues and theological reflection on political ministry; and conducts workshops throughout the country on the legislative process, on organizing, and on issues. Network chooses issues currently before Congress that involve local people in decisions affecting their lives and that have potential for creating more just systems or for surfacing alternatives to present structures.

A national task force of 47 women religious from a variety of congregations began Network in 1971, because they believed influencing national legislation was essential to effecting significant structural and systematic change.

[V. SIXEAS]

NEW INTERNATIONAL ECONOMIC ORDER

Distinction must be made at the outset between the official United Nation's New International Economic Order (NIEO) and various versions of a new international economic order offered by various private bodies around the world. The latter, however, generally takes as point of reference the UN's NIEO.

Origins and Objectives. The call for a NIEO issues from the Sixth Special Session of the UN on "Problems of Raw Materials and Development," held in April 1974 in New York. The agenda for that session was presented by the so-called Group of 77 (developing nations, numbering 77 at the first United Nations Conference on Trade and Development [UNCTAD] Geneva, 1974; now they number over 100). That session was marked by direct confrontation between the rich industrial nations of the West (hereafter designated as North) and the Group of 77 (hereafter designated South). One year later, under the same auspices the Seventh Special Session on "Development and International Cooperation" was held to review virtually the same agenda. This time the North chose to be more cooperative and to recognize the economic reasoning behind much that the Group of 77 proposed.

The substance of the demands made by the South at both sessions was the following: control by a nation of its own resources; greater transfer of financial resources from the North to the South; monetary and trade changes; stabilization of prices of the South's raw materials at remunerative levels; the indexation of these prices against industrial prices; a code of conduct for *multinational corporations; and finally transfer of *technology at fair prices.

In the view of the South the objective of these proposals was to bring about a New Deal for the Third World. The Old Deal of international economic relations they saw as one of unequal power with consequent domination and exploitation of the poor nations by the rich. In the UN's First Development Decade and even in the first years of the Second—early 1970s—emphasis had been on catching up or closing the gap between rich nations and poor nations. Catching up with the West was the model proposed in the Report of the Commission on Development chaired by Lester Pearson, a report for the UN on development prospects for the Second Development Decade, and published as *Partners in Development* (New York 1961). Typical of the literature presenting capitalism as model was W. W. Rostow, *Stages of Economic Growth* (2d ed., Cambridge 1971). By 1974 the world community had begun to realize that catching up with the material wealth of the West might not be very important or even desirable, at least for those who opted for a different kind of national purpose. But what was seen as needed by all nations was the right to equal opportunity to pursue their own development in self-reliance.

Changing the Imbalance of Economic Power. The structural changes called for in the two special sessions were seen by the South as required to redress the unfair balance of power. This would require, not just the limited tinkering with the system which was all the North would accept. It would require essential overhaul of trade, monetary relations, aid, debt, technology, and investment, for it was in these directions that the North's preponderance of power was felt.

From the several disparities in power one will serve to illustrate the obstacles posed, namely, trade. Widely even in the North and generally in the South, the international trade system is seen to benefit the North disproportionately. Classical trade theory claims that the poor nations gain from the rising prosperity of the rich and that trade is the mechanism of that transfer. As the rich grow in industrial prosperity they require more raw materials. This causes prices of these materials to rise, creating a second benefit for the developing nations. Also as labor costs rise in the industrialized world, investors shift their investment to the developing countries where labor costs are lower. This investment launches the poor world into industrialization. Then, too, in a system of free exchange, the Third World is at liberty to move its labor as well as its capital into the industrial North.

However, such freedom of labor is extremely limited in today's world—except for the Third World's professionally trained people, the so-called brain drain. Unskilled workers do migrate from South to North in Europe, where however, they are forced to return home when recession occurs. The U.S. tries to turn back Mexican migrant workers ("wetbacks"). · Meanwhile, though there is a good deal of investment in the South, the North's investment tends to follow previous investment, that is, to move into other industrialized countries. And its multinational corporations produce, not for the needs of the people, but to satisfy the desires of the monied few.

If the actual flow of factors of production—labor and capital—little resembles the theoretical model, the same in the view of the South must be said of the flow of raw materials and manufactured goods. The North is able to keep out of its markets competitive products of the South.

This power is most acutely felt with respect to processed goods. The North permits coffee and cocoa beans to enter duty-free because this suits the needs of the North's manufacturers of coffee and cocoa products. But it levels high duties on ground coffee and cocoa. This means that the highly lucrative processing goes exclusively to the already rich North. If the North were prepared to permit processed goods to enter free of high duties, the South would stand to gain as much as $150 billion annually. That must be contrasted with 1977's $10 billion of aid received from the North. Industrial goods and other manufacturers that compete with sensitive industries tend equally to be excluded from entry into markets of the North. Presently the developing world produces only 7 per cent of the world's total of industrial goods.

NIEO and Development. What, then, do the developing nations seek in the UN's NIEO? First, control over their own resources so that they can have a self-reliant development. This principle they fought for especially in the negotiations which in 1974 resulted in the UN Charter of Economic Rights and Duties of States, a principle accepted by the North in general, but with opposition to settling compensation for expropriation of foreign investment on the developing country's own terms and adjudication of disputes exclusively according to its law. Control of resources has been extended by most nations to cover adjacent seas outward to 200 miles.

Next, the South seeks equality of opportunity, an equality they believe is negated when their goods are barred from entry on fair terms to Northern markets. They ask that their share of world trade in manufactures be lifted to 25 per cent by 1985 and that their processed goods enter more freely. Thirdly, they want fairer terms of trade: this is the relation between the prices of what they sell and what they buy. They want better pricing of the food, fertilizers, and industrial goods they must buy from the North (as well as oil from OPEC). Hence in

the Sixth Special Session they proposed indexation. This demand they muted in the subsequent Seventh Special Session because of unyielding opposition from the North. To achieve better prices they proposed two roads. The first is to imitate the success of OPEC by creating "mini-opecs" for bauxite, copper, coffee, etc.—a line offering limited possibilities because the substitutability factor is low in oil, high in most other raw materials. The second is commodity agreements and these lead to the issue of the central piece of the Group of 77 strategy, which is UNCTAD's Integrated Commodity Program.

Commodity Agreements. The heart of this program remains UNCTAD's perennial effort to achieve commodity agreements on some eighteen raw materials, metals, and tropical beverages; the agreements would embrace remunerative prices within limited, stable boundaries of fluctuation. As never before, UNCTAD seeks to reconcile the divergent interests of producer nations (seeking higher prices or earnings) and consumer nations (seeking fair, if not lower prices). But while resistant to negotiating prices higher than what they interpret to be long-run equilibrium prices, the North is now prepared to negotiate stabilization. The principal reason is that its concern for assurance of supplies may be conditioned by price stability. Also, the North is now more prepared than ever before to entertain the idea of helping to finance the buffer stocks of the commodities in question, a necessary instrument for stabilization. To finance these buffers UNCTAD proposes a Common Fund (CF). The CF would lend to the managers of the separate commodities so that they could acquire buffer stocks. The CF would be repaid as stocks were sold off.

Compensatory Financing. Compensatory Financing is another plank in the Integrated Commodity Program. This is a lending facility which tides nations producing commodities over periods of drop in normal earnings. The *International Monetary Fund already operates such facilities. UNCTAD calls only for enlargement of these. It would finally ask the IMF or the *World Bank to help poor countries diversify as world demand for their raw materials eases off with the discovery of synthetic substitutes.

Viewing many of these proposals as either ill-conceived or costly, the North (with an agenda that preferred focus on its energy problems and need of assured supplies of raw materials) tried in the Paris Conference on International Economic Cooperation (CIEC) begun in January 1976 to head off UNCTAD's Fourth Conference, scheduled for May 1976. With the demise of CIEC in June 1977 with little to show for the 18 months' effort, the theater whether of confrontation or cooperation between North and South again becomes UNCTAD. That program, as already seen, centers on agreements for 18 commodities and is to be concluded by December 1978. Progress on those negotiations is slow and there is nothing to report at the moment of this writing.

The Debt Situation. One other problem of the Third World's non-oil producing countries occupies UNCTAD's attention. This is their debt. Since 1973 oil prices have risen six times over the price of that year (food and fertilizer price rises added to the traumatic rise in debt). External debt of the non-oil-producing states 1977/1978 was running at $150–200 billion. The huge deficits on current account will continue over some years. That leaves the question how the developing nations can confront their annual deficits, which in the best of hypotheses run at $20–26 billion (the best hypothesis being that the North would double its concessional aid from today's $10–12 billion to $20–24 billion, presently an extremely unlikely prospect). Deficits of the poorest countries will be increasingly met by governmental and intergovernmental loans like the IMF's Supplementary Financing. Such middle-income countries as Brazil, Zaire, Peru, Taiwan, are increasingly turning to private banks of the North, which have thus far met their needs. At UNCTAD IV measures to reduce the burden of the South were proposed: across-the-board concellation of officially-held debt for the poorest nations; across-the-board moratorium on debt-servicing for the most seriously affected by oil prices; across-the-board rescheduling of commercial debt. The majority of the rich nations rejected all across-the-board treatment and expressed readiness only for case by case investigation. Were the rich countries prepared to double their aid, as just mentioned, this would take care of the debt situation of the poorest. But they are no more disposed to do this than to go the route of cancellation, moratorium, and rescheduling on terms that appear in the eyes of the South to meet the situation realistically.

Prospect. Readers who for the poor nations seek a development with social justice, self-reliance, and peoples' participation will find this report discouraging. Equally so, those who believe that interdependence calls for sharing in solidarity and management of scarce resources through functional authorities at world level. On the positive side, there is, first, the fact that agreement on all sides grows as to facts and analysis of causes and remedies. A spectrum exists, stretching from Center-right (but not extreme right) to Center-left (but not extreme left). The convergence accepts fundamentals of the UN's NIEO but not all specifics. In addition, it agrees that development must be from the bottom up, a people's own, firmly rooted in rural development, respecting the essential place and role of women, and seeking to serve basic needs with political freedom.

See also DEVELOPING NATIONS; THIRD WORLD, CHURCH AND.

Bibliography: M. UL HAQ *The Poverty Curtain: Choices For the Third World* (New York 1976). Dag Hammarskjold Foundation, *What Now: Another Development* (Stockholm 1975). E. F. SCHUMACHER *Small Is Beautiful: A Study of Economics As If People Mattered* (London 1973). J. S. SINGH *A New International Economic Order: Toward a Fair Redistribution of the World's Resources* (New York 1977). Contains all pertinent UN documents. J. TINBERGEN, coordinator, *Reshaping the International Order* (New York 1976).

[P. LAND]

NONCANONICAL COMMUNITIES

Noncanonical communities are groups of persons within the Roman Catholic Church having an internal unity but no legal constitution as collegial moral persons under ecclesiastical law. Canonical communities are constituted as collegial moral persons by ecclesiastical law and are governed by the precepts of Canon Law relative to religious institutes.

Noncanonical communities, a new phenomenon of church life since the late 1960s, choose not to accept the legal personality of a collegial moral person. Lives of the members are governed by the ecclesiastical laws pertinent to all members of the Church. There are approximately sixty noncanonical communities in the United States. Some of the groups are ecumenical in structure and membership often consists of both men and women.

Forty-four former Glenmary sisters were among the earliest noncanonical communities. Organized in August 1967, as the Federation of Communities in Service (FOCIS), the members committed themselves as a lay group to serve Appalachian people in the four regions of Chicago, Cincinnati, Tennessee, Virginia-West Virginia.

The Sisters for Christian Community (SFCC), organized in 1970 by Lillana Kopp, is one of the largest noncanonical communities. Most of the members reside in the United States, but also included are members in several foreign countries. The duration of commitment to the community and its form in SFCC is according to the desire of the individual member, who is united not by rule nor constitution but by concern and communication. The majority of SFCC members were formerly members of canonical institutes. The group numbers over 200 members.

Another large noncanonical community is the Immaculate Heart Community, which, in 1971, separated from the canonical institute of the California Institute of the Sisters of the Most Holy and Immaculate Heart of the Blessed Virgin Mary. The group, which numbered 300 at the time of separation, was headed by Anita Caspary.

Bibliography: B. BAHL, "'FOCIS' Upon the People Which is Our Bread," in M. TRAXLER, ed., *New Works for New Nuns* (St. Louis 1968) 66–70. W. BERTRAMS, *Quaestiones fundamentales iuris canonici* (Rome 1969) 299–311. L. KOPP, "Are Religious Congregations Dying? Symptoms of Organizational Aging and Bureau-ectomy," in *Sisters for Christian Community* (privately circulated 1972). L. ORSY, "The Immediate Future of Religious Life," in K. D. O'ROURKE, ed., *Religious Life in the 70's* (Dubuque, Iowa n.d.). "IHM," *Crux of the News* 22 (Jan 1971) 3.

[M. M. MODDE]

NORRIS, JAMES JOSEPH

Lay leader and international expert on relief, refugee, and migration problems; b. Roselle Park, N.J., Aug. 10, 1907; d. Rumson, N.J. Nov. 17, 1976. Norris was the only layman invited to address a plenary session of Vatican Council II. On Nov. 5, 1964, Norris spoke to the assembled Council Fathers during the debate on the Pastoral Constitution on the Church in the Modern World. Speaking in Latin, Norris told the assembly: "Poverty—one of the oldest and deepest problems that confronts the Christian conscience—has taken a new shape, new dimensions, and new urgency in the last decade ... because modern science, medicine, and technology have helped to bring about a single economy, a neighborhood that is interdependent, but largely lacking the institutions and the policies that express solidarity, compassion and human obligation."

One result of the address was the inclusion in the final draft of the Constitution of a proposal to establish a church agency or office which would secure full Catholic participation in the world-wide attack on poverty. Pope Paul VI responded to this proposal by inaugurating the Pontifical Commission for *Justice and Peace, Jan. 6, 1967. National justice and peace commissions were set up subsequently around the world.

For more than 30 years of his life, Norris was deeply committed to combatting the problems of poverty and injustice. His actions and efforts on the international level helped shape the Church's awareness of her role in modern society in these areas. Norris served as European director of Catholic Relief Services (CRS) from 1946 to 1959, helping in the rebuilding of the Church and national communities in Europe in the post-World War II period. From 1959 to his death he served as assistant to the executive director of CRS as that agency of the American bishops turned its energies from a recovered Europe to the Third World countries, whose emergence were proving to be among the greatest challenges of the period.

In the same years, Norris was intensely active in the establishment of the International Catholic Migration Commission (ICMC) working closely with Msgr. Giovanni Battista Montini, then papal Substitute Secretary of State and later to become Pope Paul VI. He was a founding father of the ICMC and served as its president from 1951 to 1976. In its first 25 years of existence, the ICMC assisted more than 200,000 migrants and refugees with loans of $40 million. In both his roles as a key official in the work of CRS and the ICMC, Norris pressed church officials to utilize the strength and stability of the Church to implement Christian principles on an international level as well as to make Catholics themselves more aware of their obligations in justice and charity to the less fortunate throughout the world.

A month before his death, Norris was the first American to be awarded by the UN High Commissioner for Refugees the Fridtjof Nanzen Medal, an award to persons who have distinguished themselves in helping solve problems of refugees and migrants on a world scale. Norris was the first layman to be named an official escort on Pope Paul VI's flight to Geneva in June 1966 to visit the International Labor Organization and the World Council of Churches. Pope Paul also named him a member of the Pontifical Commission for Justice and Peace and for the Pontifical Commission *"Cor Unum" and designated him as the Vatican's representative at the funeral of Martin Luther King.

Norris was a graduate of The Catholic University of America and attended Fordham University School of Social Service. He served as a commander in the U.S. Naval Armed Guard during World War II. Besides numerous papal and national honors, Norris received honorary degrees from four American Catholic universities. At the time of his death he was survived by his wife Amanda and four sons.

[J. C. O'NEILL]

NORTH AMERICAN ACADEMY OF LITURGY

The North American Academy of Liturgy (NAAL) is an ecumenical association of specialists in Christian liturgy and related arts and disciplines. The Academy's purposes are: to provide channels for mutual professional assistance and for the sharing of methods and resources; to exchange technical information concerning research projects and activities of the members; to foster liturgical research, publication, and dialogue at a scholarly level; to encourage exchanges with individuals and communities of other religious traditions; and to communicate the activities of the Academy through the publication of annual proceedings.

Admission to the NAAL is restricted to persons of demonstrated competence in liturgical studies and to specialists in allied areas who contribute to the understanding of worship in a significant way. The Academy consists of Members, who have established and demonstrated their competence in the fields of liturgy and related areas, and Associates, who evidence a developing contribution in the field of liturgical studies and related areas.

The groundwork for the founding of the Academy was laid in December 1973. To honor the 10th anniversary of Vatican Council II's Constitution on the Sacred Liturgy, a conference for 70 people working in the field of liturgy was sponsored by *Theological Studies* at the Franciscan Renewal Center, Scottsdale, Arizona. The conveners of the conference were Walter Burghardt, SJ, and John Gallen, SJ. Travel costs and conference expenses were underwritten by the Friends of the Franciscan Renewal Center.

At the end of this conference, the group decided to meet a year later in January 1975, at the University of Notre Dame, Indiana, to continue its discussion and reflection and to found an official organization. At the end of the Notre Dame conference, the first officers of the Academy committee were elected: John Gallen, SJ, President, Rev. Daniel Stevick, Vice-President, Dr. John Barry Ryan, Secretary-Treasurer, Mary Collins, OSB, and Mr. Robert Rambusch, delegates. The president serves for one year and is succeeded by the vice-president. After Father Gallen, the presidents have been Rev. Daniel Stevick (1976), Rev. Charles Gusmer (1977), the Rev. James White (1978). Gerard Austin, OP is current vice-president (1978).

From its inception the Academy has presented the Berakah Award to honor a person who has made outstanding contributions in the field of liturgy. The recipients have been Aidan Kavanagh, OSB (1976), Godfrey Diekmann, OSB (1977), and Rev. Massey Hamilton Shepherd (1978). The liturgical journal *Worship* serves as the organ of the NAAL and publishes the annual proceedings. As of January 1978, total membership in the Academy was 236, of whom 141 were Members and 95 Associate Members. In 1977, the Academy was incorporated as a not-for-profit organization in the State of New Jersey.

Bibliography: M. COLLINS, "Liturgy in America: The Scottsdale Conference," *Worship* 48 (1974) 66–80. Papers connected with the Scottsdale Conference, ThSt 35 (1974) 233–311. Proceedings of NAAL Meetings, *Worship* 50 n. 4 (1976), 51 n. 4 (1977), 52 n. 4 (1978).

[J. B. RYAN]

NORTHEAST REGIONAL PASTORAL CENTER FOR HISPANICS

At Trinity College, Washington, D.C., June 19–22, 1972, the *Primer Encuentro Nacional Hispano de Pastoral* was sponsored by the USCC Secretariat for Hispanic Affairs. The purpose of this Encuentro was to begin the development of a pastoral plan for the Hispanic-American community, which at that time comprised approximately one-quarter of the Catholic population of the United States.

The first national *encuentro* responded to a number of initiatives taking place throughout the country and especially to the strong desire of many for a national pastoral plan for the Spanish speaking. Delegates to the meeting included bishops, their official delegates, and other persons with responsibility for the Spanish-speaking apostolate. The *encuentro* was organized around seven workshops, which covered the essential elements of a pastoral plan. Among the many conclusions reached were the following: that regional *encuentros* be held periodically with the goal of promoting awareness and concern for the Spanish-speaking and the development and coordination of the personnel and resources of the dioceses of the region on behalf of the Spanish-speaking; and that regional pastoral offices be established throughout the U.S. to coordinate pastoral planning and programs.

In February 1973 at a meeting for religious-education personnel in the Hispanic apostolate of the Northeast, it was decided that a Northeast Regional *Encuentro* should be held as soon as possible. The purpose was the formation of a Northeast Regional Pastoral Center for Hispanics and a study of the existing pastoral ministry in the Northeast which would lead to a coordinated regional plan of action. Interested persons from throughout the Northeast met regularly to conduct the necessary studies and to carry out procedures for the creation of the first Northeast regional *encuentro*. Questionnaires were sent to all the dioceses of the region in order to create a plan of pastoral action matched to actual conditions. The first Northeast regional *encuentro* was held, Nov. 29–Dec. 1, 1974, at Mount Marie, Holyoke, Mass. and brought together bishops, priests, religious, and laity engaged in the Spanish-speaking apostolate.

The first purpose of this *encuentro* was to bring together the Hispanic community of the region in a spirit of ecclesial community and dialogue so as to examine the reality of the Hispanic apostolate and to devise solutions to its problems. The *encuentro* also took the steps that led to the establishment of the Northeast Regional Pastoral Center for Hispanics (*Centro de Pastoral Hispana para El Nordeste*), with headquarters in New York. The Center has as its purpose planning, coordination, formation of, and information on the Spanish-speaking apostolate in the Northeast. It serves to give an authentic representation of the Hispanic apostolate at all levels.

[M. PAREDES]

NORTHERN IRELAND

The Churches in Northern Ireland are in a unique situation politically. All of them cover the entire island; there is no ecclesiastical border replicating the political one. The headquarters of all four major Churches are in the North, as are most of the members of the three largest "Protestant" Churches. And to top it all, the political divisions up until recently have almost duplicated those of the two general Christian traditions.

Of the 1,500,000 citizens of Northern Ireland a million belong to one of the Protestant traditions; probably 98 percent have identified themselves as Unionists, or Loyalists, wanting union between the six counties and the United Kingdom. 500,000 belong to the Roman Catholic tradition; probably 98 percent have identified themselves as Nationalists or Republicans, wanting an eventual "united Ireland" of some kind. These divisions are not neat and have changed notably since 1972 when the British suspended the local Northern Ireland government and instituted Direct Rule from London; but they serve to illustrate both the problem of the Churches within the political communities and their opportunity. The Churches, not being limited to one politi-

cal or geographical area, can easily bring people together. Many of their ministers have experience in both the Republic and in Northern Ireland.

The most notable recent statement by the Churches about their relationships to the political community, is in *Violence in Ireland: A Report to the Churches* (Belfast and Dublin 1976; to be published by Paulist Press in 1979.) A Joint Working Party co-chaired by Methodist Dr. Eric Gallagher and Roman Catholic Bishop Cahal Daly spent five years on the study; it has been accepted as a generally accurate and sensitive treatment of a basic community problem. The *Report* poses the central question: what is the relation of the Churches to the political situation in Northern Ireland in recent years? A candid prenote is given; "There exists a religious dimension to the quarrel" (20). Religious hostility still combines with political loyalty and cultural diversity to keep the people apart.

Violence in the community brings the Church-State problem to the fore. The Churches have in general called for support of the legal government; to the extremist Republicans this identifies them with the oppressor. But the Churches have also warned against institutional violence and occasional (perhaps frequent) mistreatment by legal officials; to the extreme Loyalists this identifies them with the gunmen. Obviously, the Churches as such cannot support any one political party. How then can they fulfil their ministry of reconciliation in a politically divided community? Northern Ireland offers a vexed and long-drawn-out example of the problem, with little prospect of a solution as of late 1978.

The *Report* acknowledges that Christians share largely in responsibility for the increased violence, and that Churches must be willing to sacrifice "positions of privilege in society" in pursuing justice. This would entail great changes in both North and South. In December 1974 the Church Leaders' Peace Campaign involved the four in meetings with both Prime Ministers as well as the Secretary of State for Northern Ireland. The Feakle meeting of a group of Protestant ministers with the Provisional Irish Republican Army showed how practical steps could reinforce exhortation; it resulted in a cease-fire which lasted six months and which ended only when the Provos decided the British were no longer willing to cooperate.

The Churches have strongly supported many lay-oriented groups working for reconciliation within the divided community: The Corrymeela and Glencree Centres, Peace Point Belfast and Dublin, Protestant and Catholic Encounter (PACE), Women Together, Working for Peace—and many community associations across the province. The Inter-Church Emergency Fund for Ireland, whose committee includes official Roman Catholics as well as delegates from the Irish Council of Churches, helps many peace-making local enterprises get started. The Reconciliation Ireland Fund, cosponsored by the National Council of Churches of Christ in the USA Ireland Program and Pax Christi USA, channels funds to it. One hoped-for goal is the establishment of a Christian Center for Social Investigation to study causes for injustice all over the island and formulate guidelines for concerted action in the civic arena.

The *Report* notes: "The churches can together stand for all political proposals that clearly attack injustice within the community...." "...all political leaders should be encouraged to see their task as that of reaching a just agreement with their opponents rather than of achieving victory over them; . . . to this end they should be open to any reasonable settlement proposed" (88). The *Report* urges people to use their votes to encourage politicians "to see things that way"! It ends with an acknowledgment of the need for the divided Churches to act together in all conscientious ways, so as to give an example of reconciliation for this divided society.

The Roman Catholic Church baptizes 80 percent of the people on the island; most of these are faith-filled and faithful. The other Churches in Ireland take their Christianity equally seriously. They give hope for political justice and peace with reconciliation, despite the past.   [D. J. BOWMAN]

NOVITIATE

The renewal Instruction *Renovationis causam* issued by the Congregation for Religious and Secular Institutes, Jan. 6, 1969 (ActApS 61 [1969] 103–120), substantially modified the law concerning *religious formation (*Renovationis causam* 10–32). Given for religious in the strict sense, the experimental norms sought to adapt the program to the mentality, living conditions, and apostolic demands of the present day, while preserving the nature and purpose of each institute. Apart from exceptional circumstances, the implementation was committed to the general chapters of the institutes.

Three phases of religious formation are considered. A period of preliminary probation, mandatory in some institutes as the postulancy (CIC c. 539.1), serves to effect a gradual transition from lay life and to promote the intellectual and emotional development of the candidate. The novitiate or second phase marks the beginning of the religious life (10:456). Authorization of the Holy See no longer being required (CIC c. 554), the superior general with the consent of the council can erect the novitiate house. In institutes divided into provinces the same authority may erect several novitiates in the same province. Moreover, in the interest of the formation program the superior general may temporarily transfer the novitiate to another house of the institute.

For validity the novitiate year must last for twelve months but it no longer need be continuous (CIC c. 555. 1.2°). With the approval of the general chapter by a two-thirds vote, novices may spend periods of formative activity away from the novitiate. The order and computation of these times follows special norms and must not be counted for the twelve months required for validity. To provide for this type of formation a variety of programs has been developed in the U.S., not only by individual institutes but also on an intercommunity basis, with some programs involving men and women of the same religious family.

Excluding such periods of formative activities, absences from the novitiate group or house exceeding three months invalidates the novitiate. The major superior may require that shorter absences be made up. Finally, contrary to the previous norm (CIC c. 558) in those institutes having different categories of religious (e.g., clerical and nonclerical) the novitiate made for one class is valid for the other.

The third phase or that of final probation follows the novitiate and must last for not less than three nor more than nine years. By way of innovation *Renovationis causam* permits the general chapter by a two-thirds vote

to adopt a new type of bond or promise in place of the traditional, temporary vow. This new form must be related to the practice of the evangelical counsels and the observance of the constitutions and other regulations of the institute. For a just reason the major superior may permit anticipation of temporary commitment but not by more than fifteen days.

With the exception of the norms concerning the three-months absence from the novitiate, the anticipation of temporary vows, and the validity of the novitiate for diverse categories of religious, the Instruction does not apply to nuns dedicated exclusively to the contemplative life.

Bibliography: Congregation for Religious and Secular Institutes, Instruction, *Renovationis causam*, tr. *On Renewal of Religious Formation* (USCC Publ. Office, Washington, D.C. 1969). Also Flannery 645–652. J. GALLEN, "Comments on the Instruction on Formation," RevRel 28 (1969) 886–906. WaySuppl 7 and 8 (1969).

                                                        [W. B. RYAN]

NUNS, CONTEMPLATIVE

Pius XII's 1950 apostolic constitution *Sponsa Christi* (ActApS 43 [1951] 5–37) gave the first clear direction toward a new openness and concern that might give renewed vigor to the contemplative life and its meaning in a Church that is called to act out of the reflection on the working of God among his people. This constitution invited nuns of similar traditions to federate, to find meaningful work commensurate with their vocation, and to reevaluate seriously their formation programs in keeping with their gifts (13:615). The momentum generated by *Sponsa Christi* and the growth process it initiated became a strong force in the renewal of religious life called for by Vatican Council II in *Perfectae caritatis*.

This Decree on the Renewal of Religious life called for a modification of papal cloister for nuns, according to the needs of time and place together with the elimination of outdated customs (*Perfectae caritatis* 16). Once again a new note was sounded, but not an altogether unfamiliar one as *Sponsa Christi* had already developed a reflective process in regard to a renewal growing from the experience and the insights of contemplative nuns themselves.

Paul VI's motu proprio *Ecclesiae Sanctae*, was issued in August 1966 to provide practical norms for implementing the broader directives for renewal found in *Perfectae caritatis* (Paul VI EcclSanctae II). Unhappily, it would seem, the motu proprio began a process that determined the type of modification that was to be allowed for nuns and limited the very possibility of adaptation according to time and place, precluding as well any significant attention being given to the experience of the nuns themselves. This was evidenced by the introduction of the term "material separation" as an essential constituent of contemplative life (ibid. 31).

In August 1969, the instruction *Venite seorsum* was issued by the Congregation for Religious and Secular Institutes (ActApS 61 [1969] 674–690). This instruction, along with its norms, which were to constitute the general law on enclosure for all nuns, does affirm that the institutes have the right to draw up their own particular law of enclosure for papal approval (*Venite seorsum* VII, 1). However, a highly restrictive rule (ibid. 4) of material separation in chapel and parlor areas offered only a possible modification of traditional canonical regulations.

Further difficulties clouded the process of renewal in that the wording of nuns' constitutions was centralized on an international basis and entrusted to the direction of the first orders, that is, the male counterparts. Moreover, contemplative nuns were restricted in regard to attendance at meetings and forming associations among their own and other traditions at which experience might be shared and a desired cooperation in areas of renewal fostered (ibid. 12). Without a doubt some of the restrictive legislation in *Venite seorsum* reflected the polarization common to all renewing processes in the Church and not exclusive to contemplative nuns seeking to understand and implement the process of renewal.

In the late 1960s, the *Association of Contemplative Sisters was formed in the United States for a grass-roots initiative. Although not formally recognized by the Congregation for Religious, its membership, while small, has representatives from almost half the contemplative communities in the United States. Its goals have as their focus to explore the meaning of contemplative life today while safeguarding its essential charism.

What has guided a significant number of contemplative women in these last ten years has not only been what decisions and actions were to be made or taken, but more essentially, what mode of acting could be found that would heighten their acute and profound pastoral perceptions and sense of responsibility to the Church.

Bibliography: Congregation for Religious and Secular Institutes, *Venite seorsum*, tr. *On the Contemplative Life and the Enclosure of Nuns* (USCC Publ. Office, Washington, D.C., 1969), also Flannery 656–676.

[M. BRENNAN]

OFFICE, ECCLESIASTICAL

Vatican Council II's Decree on the Ministry and Life of Priests, in putting into secondary place the so-called benefice system with regard to offices in the Church, states "...the main consideration in law will be accorded to the ecclesiatical office itself. From now on such an office should be understood as any function which has been permanently assigned and is to be exercised for a spiritual purpose" (*Presbyterorum ordinis* 20). Office in the Church signifies a continuing or permanent function, persisting beyond the tenure time-limits of a particular person. Exercise of ecclesiastical office, given its spiritual object, is radically a consequence of Baptism. The ecclesiology of Vatican II emphasizes that Baptism incorporates a person into the Church and constitutes the basis for each member's sharing in Christ's priestly, kingly, and prophetic office (*Lumen gentium* 9–12; cf. *Apostolicam actuositatem* 2). On this basis students of Vatican II see in the statement of *Presbyterorum ordinis* regarding office the opening of competency for ecclesiastical office to lay people. This accessibility is understood within the context of Vatican II's delineation of the laity-clergy distinction in the Constitution on the Church (*Lumen gentum* 10, 12) and in the Decree on the Apostolate of the Laity (*Apostolicam actuositatem* 2–3). The division of material in the schemata of the proposed revision of the Code of Canon Law reflect this new understanding of ecclesiastical office (Green 372–373).

Competency for and the scope of office are circumscribed by ecclesiastical law or by divine law. Every lay person, by virtue of Baptism into Christ and by Confirmation, is committed to the fulfillment of the mission of Christ. Clerics, by virtue of specific ordination, are committed to specific ministries or the exercise of the orders which they have received. Current Canon Law limits the assignment of ecclesiastical office to clerics (CIC c. 153nl). The Code lists four conditions that must be included if ecclesiastical office is taken in the strict sense, namely, that it be: permanently established; established by law, divine or ecclesiastical; conferred according to law; and that it carry with it some participation in ecclesiastical power, either of Order or of jurisdiction (CIC c. 147–152). Among those having office in this strict sense are a bishop, pastor, vicar general, and an officialis or a vice-officialis of a matrimonial tribunal.

Historically in the Church lay persons did hold ecclesiastical offices. In time a reaction against this practice developed into the post-Tridentine position prevailing in the Code of Canon Law. The clarification of Vatican II represents a deepened understanding of office in the Church and implicitly indicates that office in the broader sense need not be directly aligned with the power of Orders. Lay men and women are being commissioned to participate in the Church's teaching functions, to share in certain liturgical functions, to administer church goods, and to perform specified offices in chanceries and tribunals. These functions will come under the name of office, thus involving the laity in the Church's apostolate. The notion of lay persons as part of a collegiate tribunal, as indicated in Pope Paul VI's 1971 motu proprio, *Causas matrimoniales* (V–VII; ActApS 63 [1971] 443–444; O'Connor 7:971–972), means that in this qualified instance the lay judge holds office for the case to which the judge is assigned. Offices involving sacred powers, however, remain rooted in ordination and cannot be conferred except through or as a consequence of ordination.

As the richness of Vatican II's understanding of the proper functions or role of the laity in the mission of the Church evolves in the decades ahead, the newer understanding of the proper functions of office may apply to catechists, readers, musicians, extraordinary ministers of Communion, lay business-managers of a diocese, notaries, and perhaps judges in matrimonial causes. Offices held by lay persons, which do not involve Orders or jurisdiction per se, will be based upon a fuller understanding of the implications of Baptism and participation in the mission of Christ.

Bibliography: F. DANEELS, *De subjecto officii ecclesiastici attenta doctrina Concilii Vaticani II*, AnalGreg 192 (1973) (cf. review, W. J. LA DUE, *Jurist* 34 (1974) 428–429). T. J. GREEN, "Revision of the Code," *Jurist* 36 (1976) 353–441.

[D. M. BROOKE]

OFFICE OF THE DEAD

The Office of the Dead is a special office of the revised Roman breviary, no longer, as it was from the time of Pius V, of obligation to certain clerics and religious with solemn vows. Today, the office is used principally in connection with the funeral services of clerics and religious. In some places, mostly in Latin countries, it is also commonly used in connection with the funerals of the laity, especially in "month's mind," and anniversary commemorations.

In the Roman breviary, revised according to the Constitution on the Sacred Liturgy (*Sacrosanctum Concilium* 83–101) and which has appeared in Latin and in several authorized translations since 1970, there is one office of the dead. This office in the revised breviary is much different from the one it has replaced.

The one Office of the Dead is to be used for the Liturgy of the Hours on All Souls' Day (November 2) as well as on the occasion of funerals. The rubrics for All Souls' Day note that the *Dies irae* (dropped from funeral Masses) may be used at the various hours and that the first reading in the Office of Readings is to be taken from the common Office of the Dead. This office furnishes a much wider selection of readings than formerly, each with its own response. The second reading and its response are proper to the Office of All Souls' Day, the only strictly proper part of that office. If All Souls' Day occurs on Sunday, the usual Sunday office is to be said, except where the office is recited with the people. In that case, the Office of the Dead is to be used.

The structure of the current Office of the Dead follows the structure of other offices throughout the breviary. There are, e.g., in the present Office of the Dead: the Office of Readings, Morning Prayer, Daytime Prayer, Midmorning Prayer, Midday Prayer, and—a new departure—Night Prayer. The psalmody, antiphons included, for the Office of Readings, Morning Prayer, 1st and 2d Evening Prayer, is proper. The psalmody for Midmorning, Midday, and Midafternoon Prayer is taken from the Complementary Psalmody used during the year, but the antiphons are proper. The Night Prayer is taken from the office of Sunday.

The notable changes in the themes and tone of the Office of the Dead are a reflection of the changes of the entire liturgy for the dead. There is, e.g., a new emphasis on the spirit of Christian joy to be found in the hymns especially, with their reference to Christ as the Lord of the Resurrection. The directive of Vatican II (*Sacrosanctum Concilium* 81) finds its echo particularly in the Readings with their Responses, which are drawn, copiously, from the New Testament. Throughout there is a greater emphasis on the victory and joy of the resurrection, rather than on the fears and sorrows of death and judgment. The change seems summed up in the fact that the exultant alleluia rings through many of the hymns, and the doxology, "Glory be to the Father, etc.," concludes each psalm rather than the former "Eternal rest grant unto them, O Lord."

Bibliography: *The Liturgy of the Hours* (English translation prepared by the International Commission on English in the Liturgy; New York 1976).

[P. F. MULHERN]

ORGANIC UNION

Organic union is the goal of many of the Churches participating in the effort to restore Christian unity. There is, however, no consensus concerning the precise nature of organic union.

The more common Roman Catholic view does not demand complete institutional uniformity, but envisions the whole Christian Church as a communion (*communio*) of Churches, each maintaining its own traditions of theology, liturgy, spirituality, and discipline while preserving the unity of faith and the unique divine constitution of the universal Church (*Lumen gentium* 23).

Often this communion of Churches is described as a communion of *typoi*, i.e., communities with ".... a long coherent tradition, commanding men's love and loyalty, creating and sustaining a harmonious and organic whole of complementary elements, each of which supports and strengthens the other..." (*Documents on Anglican/Roman Catholic Relations I*, 39). Each of the *typoi* subsists in the Church of Christ preserving unity-in-diversity and diversity-in-unity. Each Church in the totality is a living, historical community gathered together in the name of Christ by faith and Baptism. In each Church there is faithfulness, first, to the essential content of the apostolic proclamation, second, to the perpetuation of the apostolic mission heralded by Jesus to bring all persons into God's Kingdom, and, finally, to the divine gifts for continuing the faith-life throughout the ages (such as the Scriptures and ministries).

In summary, organic union can be described as the visible, full, canonical, and ecclesiastical union of sister Churches (*typoi*) subsisting in the Church of Christ, while retaining their own theological, liturgical, spiritual, and disciplinary traditions. The precise dimensions of this diversity-in-unity remain the object of intense prayer, study, dialogue, and action by the Churches.

Bibliography: E. LANNE, "Pluralism and Unity: the Possibility of a Variety of 'Typologies' within the Same Ecclesial Allegiance," *One-in-Christ* 6 (1970) 430–451; "The Unity of the Church in the Work of Faith and Order," *One-In-Christ* 12 (1976) 34–57. Faith and Order, *What Kind of Unity?* paper n. 69 (Geneva 1974); *Uniting in Hope*, paper n. 72 (Geneva 1974). J. WILLEBRANDS, "Address in Cambridge, England," *Documents on Anglican/Roman Catholic Relations I* (USCC Publ. Office, Washington, D.C. 1972) 32–41.

[A. LAUBENTHAL]

ORIENTAL CODE OF CANON LAW, REVISION OF

The Churches of the Near East and of Eastern Europe derive their religious and canonical traditions from the ancient patriarchal sources: Byzantium, Jerusalem, Antioch, and Alexandria. The later influence of Armenia and Russia, plus the elaborations of such great medieval Byzantine canonists as Balsamon, Zonaris, and Blasteros, added to the traditions of ecclesiastical law, but did not substantially alter their primary orientation.

Modern History. Beginning in the 17th century and continuing through the 19th, as individual Eastern Churches came into union or sought to strengthen their existing ties with the Holy See, various popes, particularly Benedict XIV and Pius IX, promulgated special canonical legislation for these Churches to follow (10:763). The adaptation of Roman Canon Law for use in the particular Eastern rites led to a gradual Latin hybridization of the Canon Law of the Eastern Catholic Churches. When in 1917 the Code of Canon Law exempted the Eastern Churches from its legislation (CIC c. 1), each Eastern Church in union with Rome in effect was left with its own Canon Law, an amalgam comprising a core of the ancient Canon Law of its own patriarchal tradition plus an overlay of relatively modern Roman Canon Law.

In 1929 Pope Pius XI began the task of developing a single code to bring canonical unity to the discipline of all the Eastern Churches. He assigned the task of preparing a new codification to a commission of cardinals, which in turn supervised the work of two independent commissions. One commission was composed of scholars, who were to collect and publish the sources of the Canon Law of all the Eastern Churches. The second commission had the task of a preliminary drafting of new canons for the future code. The work of the first commission still continues, with nearly 50 volumes published now in the series *Fonti della Codificazione Orientale Canonica*. In 1935 the second commission was charged with the actual preparation of a new code. It became the *Commissio pontificia ad redigendum "Codicem iuris canonici orientalis."* World War II interrupted the work of the Commission.

After the War, however, Pope Pius XII promulgated four successive parts of the new codification. On Feb. 22, 1949 he enacted the first of the new canons, the matrimonial law, in the motu proprio *Crebrae allatae* (ActApS 41 [1949] 89–119). The law of procedure was promulgated next in the motu proprio *Solicitudinem nostram* (Jan. 6, 1950; ActApS 42 (1950) 5–120); the law of religious life, temporal goods, and the definition of terms, in the motu proprio *Postquam apostolicis litteris* (Feb. 9, 1952; ActApS 44 [1952] 65–152) and the law of rites and persons, in the motu proprio *Cleri sanctitati* (Jan. 2, 1957; ActApS 49 [1957] 433–603). All these canons were written in Latin and conceived on the model of the Latin Code of Canon Law. Though there were allowances for local variations, the new codification seriously extended the Latinization of the Canon Law of the Eastern Catholic Churches. Immediately prior to Vatican Council II, therefore, both Catholic and Orthodox authorities expressed grave uneasiness about the new law and its fundamental purposes.

The Post-Vatican II Revision. Debate during Vatican II led to sharp criticism of the existing codification. The Eastern bishops and theologians reacted against both the Latinization of the Canon Law of the Eastern Catholic Churches and the attempt to homogenize their traditions within the single code. The Decree on the Eastern Catholic Churches, therefore, called for a fundamental reform in the Canon Law. The Council mandated the restoration of the ancient canonical traditions and the preservation of that which is distinctive to the Eastern Churches (*Orientalium Ecclesiarum* 5 and 6). The Council rejected the basic premise of the Pius XII codification, namely, the desirability and feasibility of unifying the Canon Law of all the Eastern Churches on the model of the Latin Code. It stated that each Church is to be governed by its own special Canon Law (ibid. 5). The mandate of the Council required a radical change from the recent past.

Pope Paul VI on June 10, 1972, set up a new Commission for the Revision of the Code of Oriental Canon Law (*Nuntia* 1[1973]2). Consultors were appointed and study groups were formed to explore all phases of revision. As its first plenary assembly, March 18–23, 1974, the Commission adopted principles to guide the revision. The *Norme per la recognizione del Diritto Canonico Orientale* stress, among other things, that the New Oriental Canon Law should be for all the Eastern Catholic Churches, that it be truly faithful to the Eastern traditions, ecumenical, juridical, and pastoral in nature, with particular attention paid to the principle of subsidiarity, to the function of the laity, and to the particular rites and

Churches. Work on revising the Canon Law for the Eastern Churches at the present time is far from complete and fundamental differences of opinion regarding the thrust and comprehensiveness of the revised Canon Law have yet to be resolved.

Bibliography: The official publication of the Pontifical Commission for the Revision of the Code of Oriental Canon Law in *Nuntia* (1973–   ). *Jurist* 37 (1977) 171–180, from *Nuntia* 3 (1976) the list of "Documents of the Apostolic See Pertaining to Easterners published after the Second Vatican Council" and the Commission's own "Guidelines for the Revision of the Code of Oriental Canon Law" (*Nuntia* 3:18–24).

[W. W. BASSETT]

ORIGINAL SIN

Theological interest in the doctrine of original sin has continued unabated among Roman Catholics since 1965 (10:776). The discussion of the meaning of the doctrine extended beyond specialists when Pope Paul VI invited a group of theologians to Nemi, Italy in July 1966 to explore the status of the doctrine in the light of modern science. In 1968 the public eye was drawn to the controversy surrounding the appearance of *Het Nieuwe Katechismus* (the Dutch Catechism). A commission of cardinals was formed to examine the catechism and in the supplement they authorized were included their corrections of the catechism's treatment of original sin. The present article will restrict itself to a consideration of the salient features of the recent discussion among theologians.

The Principal Position. Some theologians view original sin as distinct from personal sin, and, in the tradition of St. Anselm and St. Thomas Aquinas, assert that original sin consists formally in the privation of the sanctifying grace which, according to the will of the self-communicating Creator, should have been transmitted down through history by the "sacrament" of the human family. Because God in the communication of his holy Pneuma can sanctify the human creature even prior to his or her exercise of freedom, so, too, the absence of that Pneuma where it should have been communicated is a privation in the moral-religious order ("guilt") even prior to the exercise of freedom. Such privation is guilt in a real but analogous sense. This radical, negative condition of human existence prior to the personal exercise of freedom is uncovered only by reflection on the depth and breadth of the redemption wrought by Jesus Christ. Indeed, that redemption, while itself having a history, reaches its unsurpassable climax in the life, death, and resurrection of Christ and the sending of his Spirit. Because of Jesus Christ, all of human existence is redeemed and this redemption qualifies the beginning and entire span of every person's life. In this perspective being in original sin and being-justified/redeemed are not chronologically distinguishable, but rather co-determinants of the situation of each person's freedom. Baptism is entrance into the eschatological victory of Jesus Christ as mediated unfailingly by his Church (Rahner; Weger; Segundo).

In the justified the ambiguity of existence is overcome in the sense that the double condition with which they enter human history is now transformed so that the fundamental orientation of their lives is one—life in and for God in Christ and his Spirit. This does not mean that there are no secondary, but not fundamental, dimensions of the person which are in conflict with the fundamental graced orientation of the person's life.

"Negative concupiscence" is the term classically designating these secondary resistances to grace which the justified person cannot altogether master. Struggle with them can be a way in which one shares in the Paschal Mystery.

Central to the Church's conviction regarding original sin is the correlative affirmation of the necessity of Baptism for justification. It is not unfair to observe that among contemporary theologians who affirm the traditional distinction between original sin and personal sin there is a tendency to de-absolutize the necessity of Baptism, not only for adults but also for infants. Justification occurs for them as well through the historical mediation of Christ and his Church but in the theologically "marginal" case of unbaptized infants who die the possibility of life with God is not excluded. Indeed, one theologian suggests that perhaps any gesture of acceptance into the human community can be viewed as this mediation of justification in the case of unbaptized infants who die, precisely because of the universal presence of Christ's victorious grace (Rahner).

Difficulties. The difficulty which faces those theologians who view original sin and being-redeemed as two simultaneous dimensions of historical human existence from the moment of birth is that they are affirming a simultaneous privation of grace (through "Adam" and the sin of the world) and the presence of grace (through Christ and his Church). Of course, these dimensions are ultimate and are not constituted by the empirical mixture of grace and sin found in the environment of each person. Nonetheless, in order to keep this assertion of a twofold condition that is not temporally successive but simultaneous (prior to justification) from involving a theological contradiction, it would be necessary to show how original sin is an actuality in human history even when in principle it has been overcome. The only appropriate way of asserting the concreteness of original sin is to describe it as embraced and contained by the yet more powerful saving deed of Christ. To speak of original sin as a reality holding sway all by itself is to speak abstractly.

A second difficulty which arises in regard to theologians who maintain that original sin consists formally in the privation of justifying and sanctifying grace is that they are thus able to consider it a passive *habitus* that determines the situation of human freedom but that is not interior to freedom itself. The legitimate desire to distinguish carefully between original and personal sin lies behind this definition of original sin. Still, one may ask whether such a definition, which takes the condition of original sin to be a state of impotency and not a state of both impotency *and* unwillingness, has said enough. To be sure, the notion of a prevoluntary unwillingness is paradoxical at best, but the biblical picture of sin, where it is a *potestas* as well as a *privatio*, should caution against striving simply for clarity of concept here. Certain authors are alive to this difficulty, for example, Piet Smulders, Charles Baumgartner, Maurizio Flick, and Zoltan Alszeghy.

Those theologians who identify original sin and personal sin are equivalently denying the Roman Catholic problematic. They seem to neglect the depth of human solidarity (A. Vanneste, U. Baumann).

Bibliography: On Catholic teaching: K. RAHNER, SacrMundi 4:328–334. PAUL VI, "Original Sin and Modern Science," *Pope Speaks* 11 (1966) 229–235. E. DHANIS and J. VISSER, *The Supplement to a New Catechism*, tr. K. SMYTH, in *A New Catechism, Catholic Faith for Adults,* authorized edition (New York 1969) 511–574.
Theologians: U. BAUMANN, *Erbsünde? Ihr traditionelles Verständnis in der Krise heutiger Theologie* (Freiburg 1970). C. BAUMGARTNER, *Le péché originel* (Paris 1969). J. L. CONNOR, "Original Sin: Contemporary Approaches," ThSt 29 (1968) 215–240. D. FERNANDEZ, *El pecado original, ¿ mito o realidad?* (Valencia 1973). M. FLICK and Z. ALSZEGHY, *Il peccato originale* (Brescia 1972). P. GRELOT, *Péché originel et la rédemption, à partir de l'épître aux Romains* (Paris 1973). H. HAAG, "The Original Sin Discussion, 1966–1971," JEcumSt 10 (1973) 259–289. S. MACISAAC, *Freud and Original Sin* (New York 1974). B. MCDERMOTT, "The Theology of Original Sin: Recent Developments," ThSt 38 (1977) 478–512. K. RAHNER, "Erbsünde und Monogenismus" in K.-H. WEGER, *Theologie der Erbsünde* (Freiburg 1970); "The Sin of Adam," *Theological Investigations* 11, tr. D. BOURKE (New York 1974) 247–262; *Vorfragen zu einem ökumenischen Amtsverständnis* (Freiburg 1974), P. RICOEUR, *The Symbolism of Evil* (Boston 1969); "Guilt, Ethics and Religion" in *The Conflict of Interpretations* (Evanston 1974) 425–439; "'Original Sin': A Study in Meaning," ibid. 269–286. L. SABOURIN, "Original Sin Reappraised," BTB 3 (1973) 41–81. A. SCHMIED, "Konvergenzen in der Diskussion um die Erbsünde," *Theologie der Gegenwart* 17 (1974) 144–156. K. SCHMITZ-MOORMANN, *Die Erbsünde: Überholte Vorstellungbleibender Glaube* (Freiburg 1969). J. L. SEGUNDO, *Evolution and Guilt* (Maryknoll, N.Y. 1974, P. SMULDERS, *The Design of Teilhard de Chardin: An Essay in Theological Reflection* (Westminster, Md. 1967). G. VANDERVELDE, *Original Sin: Two Contemporary Roman Catholic Approaches* (Amsterdam 1975). A. VANNESTE, *The Dogma of Original Sin* (Brussels 1975).

[B. O. MCDERMOTT]

ORTHODOX/ROMAN CATHOLIC CONSULTATION

Responsive to the ecumenical spirit awakened by the Vatican Council II's Decree on Ecumenism, *Unitatis redintegratio*, Pope Paul VI and Patriarch Athenagoras I issued, Dec. 7, 1965, a common statement of regret concerning the 1054 mutual excommunication incident. Soon thereafter the two spiritual leaders exchanged visits. Speaking in the patriarchal cathedral in Istanbul on July 25, 1967, Pope Paul stressed that the Orthodox and the Roman Catholic Churches were "sister Churches." Then, together in St. Peter's Basilica in Rome, Oct. 28, 1967, they urged a halt to past animosities and called for cooperation in scholarly, pastoral, and charitable works. These events form the background for the Orthodox/Roman Catholic Consultation in the United States.

History. This *bilateral consultation, the first of its kind between Orthodox and Roman Catholics in modern times, was officially established by the *Bishops' Committee for Ecumenical and Interreligious Affairs (BCEIA) in collaboration with the Standing Conference of Canonical Orthodox Bishops of America (SCOBA). Its assigned purpose was twofold: to provide useful data for the respective episcopal conferences on basic theological issues; to give advice to both Churches on practical ways of working together toward solving common pastoral problems.

During its infancy the Consultation was co-chaired by Archbishop Iakovos, Primate of the Greek Orthodox Church of North and South America, and Bishop Bernard Flanagan of Worcester, Massachusetts. Since 1973 Cardinal William Baum, Archbishop of Washington, D.C., has been Bishop Flanagan's successor. Though varied through the years, the membership has been drawn from biblical exegetes, canonists, historians, liturgists, and systematic theologians belonging to both Churches.

The first organizational meeting was held on Dec. 9, 1965, in Worcester. Since then the Consultation has met an additional sixteen times at irregular intervals, usually once or twice a year. Only in 1972 was it unsuccessful in effecting an encounter. A trend has emerged in the past four years, favoring a fixed biannual schedule for meetings.

Many theological and pastoral topics have been studied during the past fourteen years. As areas of consensus developed from the discussion of research papers prepared by individual members, the participants cooperated to work out agreed statements. These documents were submitted to the respective authorities through the BCEIA and SCOBA and then released to the press. Thus far the consultation has composed and issued six Agreed or Joint Statements: *On the Holy Eucharist* (Dec. 13, 1969); *On Mixed Marriages* (Nov. 4, 1971); *On Respect for Life* (May 24, 1974); *On the Church* (Dec. 10, 1974); *On the Pastoral Office* (May 19, 1976); and *On Unity and Divine Economy* (May 19, 1976). An easy access to these documents is provided by the ecumenical journal *Diakonia*, published in New York by the John XXIII Ecumenical Center.

Issues of Dialogue. Though numerous the subjects investigated can be grouped under four headings: the Eucharist, Christian Marriage, the Church and the Pastoral Office. The theological and ecumenical implications of each will be sketched briefly.

The Eucharist. The Eucharist emerged as a theme at the second meeting, held in New York City, Sept. 29, 1966, and remained in the limelight through several subsequent sessions. This topic was debated not only in the context of worship and of sacramental sharing, but also in close connection with reflection on the Church and the Pastoral Office. The studies and statements on these subjects indicate a basic harmony between Orthodox and Roman Catholics on key points: the meaning of the Eucharistic celebration; the necessity of pastoral office (bishop or presbyter) for the realization of the Church's Eucharistic celebration; and the essential rite required to express both the meaning of the Eucharist and its relationship to the Church. In spite of this unity of belief, the Consultation concedes that a further unity of love covering the whole range of essentials to Christian life is needed to enable regular *Eucharistic sharing between Orthodox and Roman Catholics.

Former obstacles to dialogue—such as the theological disputes centering on the role of the *epiklēsis* (the invocation of the Holy Spirit) or the institution narrative in the Eucharistic Prayer, and on the doctrine or transsubstantiation—were omitted in the agreed statement on the Eucharist. They were seen as being outside the necessary assent of faith required for church unity and Eucharistic sharing.

The need of pastoral office for the Eucharistic celebration stems from the fact that this office is an essential element of the structure of the Church as manifesting and realizing itself in the Eucharist.

Christian Marriage. From the beginning the theme of Christian marriage has been a constant preoccupation, appearing in ten different sessions. The topic was scrutinized from the following angles: the sacramental nature of Marriage and its liturgical celebration; marriages between Orthodox and Roman Catholics; the minister of marriage; indissolubility of marriage; ethical issues related to marriage; the pastoral care of the divorced and of those in troubled marriages.

On the sacramental nature of Marriage, a full agreement was reached on one point. In Christian Marriage a basically human situation is assumed into the life of faith. Thus the marriage partners have the vocation to live the kind of relationship existing between Christ and his Church (Eph 5.31–35). In this way they witness to the world God's love for all mankind.

On a more practical level, some progress was made concerning the pastoral care of "mixed marriages." The agreed statement on the subject urges that couples planning such a marriage seek counsel from pastors of both traditions. The area where counseling is especially important is the Christian education of the children. The final decision in this matter, according to the statement, belong to the couple, but only after informed deliberation. Respect for each other's religious tradition, mutual support, and shared responsibility in the spiritual upbringing of the children—these are strongly advised by the Consultation. Because traditional Orthodox theology teaches that the priest (not the couple) is the minister of the Sacrament, the statement suggests that marriages between Orthodox and Roman Catholics should normally take place before an Orthodox priest.

Since the two Churches approach the question of divorce and remarriage from different standpoints, the Consultation has attained no consensus on the subject. Likewise the discussion on ethical issues (artificial birth control and artificial insemination, for instance) has produced no agreement because theologians within both traditions remain at odds. The Consultation, however, did formulate a statement on respect for life. In it they deplore the decisions of the United States Supreme Court which failed to recognize the rights of the unborn.

Finally, regarding the pastoral care of the divorced, the Consultation has concentrated its study on the healing process which would enable such Christians to participate more fully in the life of their respective communities.

The Church. Aware that the main theological barriers to unity lie in the sphere of ecclesiology, the Consultation has examined the subject on nine occasions. Its brief theological statement takes its starting point in the mystery of the Trinity. Observing that the Church has its prototype in the Trinity, where both a distinction of persons and a unity of love exist, the statement concludes that the Church too must base its unity on love rather than on external law. The Spirit's presence, source of love in the Church and its real ground for continuity, finds visible expression in historical forms: Scripture, the Sacraments, and ministry, ordained in apostolic succession. These historical forms are found in the concrete local Church, where the community gathered around its bishop and other ministers realizes and expresses most profoundly its true and independent existence as Church in the Eucharistic celebration. Nonetheless it remains interdependent in relation to other Churches which possess the same Spirit of Christ.

Though a hierarchy among the interdependent Churches is acknowledged, it does not eliminate the fundamental equality of all Churches. At this point Orthodox and Roman Catholic ecclesiologies part company. Orthodox theologians do recognize a primacy (and also the Church's infallibility), but their understanding of such issues differs from the teaching of Vatican Council I.

The agreed statement *On Unity and Divine Economy*, finally, emphasizes that the recognition of another Church as Church involves a process of discerning its present ecclesial status. It calls for a continued effort by both Churches to discern the real basis for recognition of each other as "sister Churches" and as celebrants of the same Sacraments.

Pastoral Office. Besides indicating several theological conclusions shared by both traditions, the statement on the pastoral office introduced some recent trends in Roman Catholic theology. Unlike past theologians of both traditions, some modern Catholics insist that the pastor represents directly the faith of the Church and only indirectly Christ, who is the source of that faith. They also argue that women can be ordained to the pastoral office. Concerning life style and celibacy, theologians of the two traditions face different problems.

Assessments. The positive results of the Consultation are apparent. But the dialogue must expand both on the international scene and on the local-parish level. A new step was taken in the Sistine Chapel on Dec. 14, 1975. There Metropolitan Meliton of Chalcedon announced that the Ecumenical Patriarch Demetrios I had formed a special Inter-Orthodox Theological Commission to initiate a formal dialogue with Rome. Deeply enthused, Pope Paul VI entrusted the Secretariat for Promoting Christian Unity with the task of establishing a similar commission of Roman Catholic theologians. Such meetings of Roman Catholic theologians, however, are no substitute for local gatherings where the faithful of both traditions can begin to experience their unity in Christ.

Bibliography: M. AGHIORGHOUSSIS and E. J. KILMARTIN, "The Holy Eucharist in Ecumenical Dialogue," JEcumSt 13 (1976) 203–221. M. FAHEY, "Rapports entre Orthodoxes et Catholiques Romains en Amérique du Nord," *Église canadienne* 11 (1977) 179–180. E. J. KILMARTIN, "Orthodox-Roman Catholic Consultation in the U.S.A., *New Catholic World* 220 (1977) 179–186.

[C. C. MENARD]

P

PACEM IN TERRIS INSTITUTE

The founding of the Pacem in Terris Institute at Manhattan College (New York) was directly inspired by Pope John XXIII's historic encyclical *Pacem in terris* (1963). The purposes of the founding were to promote peace education and research and sponsor conferences on peace-related themes. An additional purpose of the Institute was to offer students an alternative to ROTC programs through the establishment of peace education courses.

The Institute achieved its goal of establishing peace education courses with the founding of the Peace Studies Institute in 1971. The Peace Studies program offers some thirty courses in peace and justice areas, includes practical field work at such organizations as the United Nations, the American Arbitration Association, with peace groups and with those laboring for justice in New York's ghettos. Courses are from almost every discipline and include: the Economics of Peace, War, Peace and the Arts, International Organizations, The Anatomy of Peace, Philosophies of War and Peace, Religious Dimensions of Peace, Theologies of Liberation, Social Problems Seminar, and War and Violence in Western Literature. The program leads to a B.A. degree in Peace Studies.

The Pacem in Terris Institute also hosts conferences on education for peace, social justice, specific conflict situations (e.g., Northern Ireland), and disarmament. The *Journal of Peace Studies* is also published by the Institute and includes research articles on various topics. Similar programs have also been founded at other colleges and universities although few are degree programs. Specifically, it is the goal of Pacem in Terris to help every Catholic college and university develop courses in justice and peace.

[J. J. FAHEY]

PADRES

PADRES (*Padres Asociados para Derechos Religiosos, Educativos y Sociales*) emerged in the period of ferment after Vatican Council II and of the social activism in the 1960s. It was born as a priests' fraternal association, and specifically of Chicano priests, out of painful frustration, lack of voice within ecclesiastical structures, and the isolation felt by a number of Chicano priests in San Antonio, Texas. But it was originated as something far more than a fraternal club; its concern was eventually to make its voice heard in solidarity with the Mexican-American people, who were in the throes of suffering enormous injustices.

During 1969 Fr. Rafael Ruiz of San Antonio, the first national chairman of PADRES, contacted other Mexican-American priests throughout the country. The first national gathering of priests, laity, and religious—Anglo and Hispano—met in Tucson, Ariz. in February 1970. Other priests involved in the Spanish-speaking ministry were invited as associate members of the newly formed group of Chicano PADRES. The national center was set up at San Antonio. Every second year PADRES calls its full, associate, and honorary members to a congress for the election of officers and for a review of priorities. At the *encuentros*, also convoked every second year, members meet to share experiences in Hispano ministry within the supportive and reflective atmosphere of their association.

The first purpose of PADRES has been to form a support system among religious leaders, including priests, brothers, deacons, seminarians, and laity in the Hispano ministry. It has been the concern of PADRES to encourage and help its members grow more conscious of their mission to serve among the poor and to announce Christ's justice.

As the second purpose for its existence PADRES tries fundamentally and practically, to help its members to work more effectively on behalf of the Hispanic in an advocacy and supportive kind of ministry. Thus, it advocates the rights—social, educational, cultural, and religious—of Hispanics to be full and equal sharers in the one Christ and the Church; the right to participate fully in the life and ministry of the Church; the right to be free from any type of oppressions within or outside the Church.

[M. R. MARTINEZ]

PAPAL HOUSEHOLD

On March 28, 1968 Pope Paul VI issued the motu proprio *Pontificalis domus* (ActApS 60 [1968] 305–315) on the papal household (10:975). This apostolic letter reorganizes the pontifical "court"—an office of the Roman *Curia (Prefettura della Casa Pontificia)*—, eliminating honorary offices and hereditary titles formerly given to clerics and laymen and replacing them with titles recognizing people having special tasks in the Church and at the Vatican.

The document distinguishes two parts in the pontifical household. One is the "pontifical chapel" (*Cappella pontificia*); the other, the "pontifical family" or household (*Famiglia pontificia*). The pontifical chapel includes persons with whom the pope as supreme priest prays, especially in solemn rites. The pontifical family is made up of those persons closely cooperating with the pope in governing as head of the Church and sovereign of the State of Vatican City.

Among the major specifics of reform are the following. No office in the household is to be hereditary. The former titles of nobility conferred on the two prince assistants at the pontifical throne (1:962) are eliminated; henceforth these assistants have the title "honor guards of the pope." All members of the household are to be appointed by the pope and the direction of the household is under the new office, Prefect of the Apostolic Palace.

The pontifical chapel still includes cardinals residing in Rome, prelates of the Roman Curia, and bishops having the title of Assistants at the Pontifical Throne. The document abrogates the previous entitlement of a number of ecclesiastics to be members of the pontifical chapel. Among those were the Palatine Cardinals, Palatine Prelates, the Majordomo of His Holiness, the Minister of the Interior, the Commander of the Order of the Holy Spirit, Also eliminated are such titles as Master of the Chamber, College of Mace Bearers, Master of the Horse, Master of Supplies, Postmaster General, Bearer of the Golden Rose.

The new document adds to the pontifical chapel the pastors of Rome's parishes, (men) members of the Pontifical Council for the Laity, and of the Pontifical Commission for Justice and Peace. Other ex officio members are the secretaries of the Secretariats for Christian Unity, Non-Christian Religions, and Nonbelievers, as well as the president of the Pontifical Commission for the Media of Social Communications.

The pontifical family is made up of two groups, ecclesiastics and laymen. Changes among ecclesiastics include the titles: Almoner of His Holiness, formerly the Secret Almoner; Vicar General for Vatican City, formerly the Sacristan of His Holiness (*Praefectus sacrarii apostolici*); the Pontifical *Doctor theologus*, formerly the Master of the Sacred Palace. Among laymen in the pontifical family the motu proprio designated the Commandants of the Honor Guard of His Holiness (formerly the Noble Guard) and of the Honorary Palatine Guard; but both these guards have since been abolished by letter of Paul VI to Card. Jean Villot, Secretary of State, Sept. 14, 1970 (ActApS 62 [1970] 587–588).

The motu proprio also stipulates that the only honorary *prelates or honorary ecclesiastical titles are to be: Prothonotaries Apostolic (*de numero* and *super numero*) Honorary Prelates of His Holiness, and Chaplains of His Holiness.

Bibliography: AnnPont 1978: 1087–1095; 1489–1500.

[R. J. MURPHY]

PAPAL SECRECY

The norms currently governing matters subject to secrecy in Church affairs are contained in the Instruc-

tion issued by the Papal Secretariat of State, *Secreta continere* on Feb. 4, 1974 (see CIC c. 242).

In the Church there are areas in which the imprudent divulging of certain kinds of information could hinder the Church's effective performance of her mission, injure the common good, or violate private rights. For this reason the Church, like other organizations, has norms protecting the confidentiality of certain kinds of information. *Papal secrecy* (*secretum pontificium*) is the classification used in those areas in which the Holy See regards confidentiality as being of the highest importance. The term replaces the older "secret of the Holy Office."

In some areas the need for secrecy is immediately apparent. Persons denounced for offences against the Sacrament of Reconciliation have the right to have their reputations guarded against the effects of disclosure throughout the process of investigation. The same is true in the case of doctrines or publications being investigated by the Congregation for the Doctrine of the Faith. Official information concerning the creation of cardinals, the appointment of bishops and their equivalents, and curial appointments is also kept secret. Codes and coded correspondence, official but secret information dealt with by the Secretariat of State or the Council for the Public Affairs of the Church, and anything placed under secrecy by the pope, a cardinal prefect of a department, or a papal representative are also protected.

Once a matter is determined to be protected by papal secrecy, all those who deal with it officially are bound to observe the secrecy. If a person becomes aware of such a matter accidentally but is morally certain that it is secret, he, too, is bound to observe secrecy. The obligation to keep a papal secret is a grave one. If a violation of papal secrecy becomes known in the external forum, the delinquent is to be tried either by a special papal commission or by his own competent superior; if found guilty, he falls subject to penalties proportionate to the gravity of the offense and the seriousness of the damage he has done. Dependents of the Roman Curia are subject to additional sanctions determined by General Regulations.

If someone is to be admitted to papal secrecy for official reasons, the Instruction provides the formulary for an oath that he will keep secret all those matters that are protected by papal secrecy, that he will never regard it as licit to reveal anything so protected, no matter what the circumstances, and that if he should have doubts about whether a given matter is protected, he will resolve the doubts in favor of secrecy.

Bibliography: Papal Secretariat of State, *Secreta continere*, ActApS 66 (1974) 89–92; tr., Origins 4 (1974–1975) 9–11. An earlier instruction, *Communio et progressio* (June 24, 1968), has not been published.

[J. G. JOHNSON]

PARENTS AND CHILDREN

Concern for the quality of Christian parenthood has developed in recent years particularly because of the insights of Vatican Council II. The documents on the Laity, Christian Education, and the Church in the Modern World have all contributed to a rich theological understanding of parenthood. With the personalistic emphasis of the Council, parents are viewed as the primary instruments of God in contributing to the human and Christian development of the young.

Vatican Council II. The Christian family is a unique milieu in the way that it concretizes the presence of God for children as well as their parents. In the Decree on the Apostolate of the Laity parents are viewed as "the first to communicate the faith to their children." (*Apostolicam actuositatem* 11). They do this by word and action or, more to the point, by the very fact that the Christian home is a dwelling place for God's presence. It is, in the words of that same document, "the domestic sanctuary of the Church" (*ibid*). It should also be noted that it is primarily by the mutual affection and concern that is embodied in Christian family life, that this presence of God is most realized. Empowered by that love in the home, the persons of the family can go out to serve the needs of the wider community.

Parents are educators of their children, but in a very special sense. Parents are primarily responsible for the personal and social growth of their children and their role in this matter is so decisive "that scarcely anything can compensate for their failure in it" (*Gravissimum educationis* 3). The human growth is seen as interrelated with the Christian development that is proper to particular stages of human development. The Council documents emphasize that the beginnings of both human and Christian life will ordinarily occur in the context of the parent-child relationship.

The first communication of the Gospel message, i.e., primary evangelization, will ordinarily take place in the context of family life, in the "domestic Church" (*Lumen gentium* 11). Parents are privileged instruments of God in bringing their children to an awareness of the God who loves and cares for them and has created them for eternal life with himself. "Graced with the dignity and office of fatherhood and motherhood" parents are chosen by God to bring new persons not only into life, but into life with himself (*Gaudium et spes* 48).

Implications. The responsibilities of parenthood are of no small significance, and should not be undertaken without serious reflection. Couples must be responsible in not only their actual parenting, but in their choices to become parents. Christian conjugal love is not self-serving, but an altruistic expression of love between spouses in all the dimensions of their relationship, physical, psychological, and spiritual. Therefore, there exists an intrinsic relationship between loving the spouse and a desire to express that love in such a way that it issues in the life of a new person. In the clear words of the Council, "marriage and conjugal love are by their nature ordained toward the begetting and education of children" (ibid. 50). It is out of their love for each other, in particular, as that love is expressed in the marital act, that new life comes into the world. And their marital love from Christian understanding is more than simply a human expression; it incarnates the reality of God's love. Therefore, the new life which is realized is also an expression of God's love. Parents can be appreciated as participants in God's continuing creation of new life, a designation of great significance and responsibility.

It should also be sensed that parenting is a joint action of wife and husband. While it took many centuries to appreciate the full meaning of the joint contribution of each parent in a biological sense, there is a recent, greater awareness of the special contribution that father and mother make to human and Christian development. Both parents communicate to their children a sense of value in their being loved and accepted for who they are

in themselves. Each contributes to their children's sense of sexual identity and appropriate role behavior. This comes both in the teaching and the living out of a particular sexual identity. Much the same can be said about religious development. The child's sense of the goodness of life and of relationships grows from an awareness of the love present in the relation between the parents. The witnessing of the vitality of the religious life of the parents assists children in the formulation of their own sense of the religious dimension of life.

The very identity of the human person is forged in the fires of family life. The creation and maintaining of open, supporting, and loving relationships within the family is an ideal of both human and Christian significance. The ideal is often absent and there is no other way to describe the failure to reach that ideal than as tragedy. Signs of hope are, nevertheless, a growing appreciation on the part of the Christian and human community of the importance of family life, a growing body of literature and insights into how better to develop skills for parenting, and the training of professionals to assist parents and families in a better realization of their potential.

Bibliography: K. S. BERNHARDT, *Being a Parent: Unchanging Values in a Changing World* (Toronto 1970). S. C. CALLAHAN, *Parenting: Principles and Politics of Parenthood* (Garden City, N.Y. 1973). D. CURRAN, *In the Beginning There Were Parents* (Minneapolis 1978). K. KENISTON, and the Carnegie Council on Children, *All Our Children: The American Family Under Pressure* (New York 1977). J. G. QUESNELL, *Holy Terrors and Holy Parents* (Chicago 1975). G. SCHOMP, *Parent/Child/God: Bringing You Closer Together* (Cincinnati 1977).

[D. M. THOMAS]

PARISH

The concept of the parish as the basic unit of ecclesiastical organization within the Catholic Church has been with us so long that it is difficult to conceive of its absence. A study of its history, however, brings to light the fact that the parish as it is today, a territorial entity with its own proper pastor and defined boundaries, was all but unknown in the Church up until the 10th or 11th century.

History. Before that time the only basic subdivision of ecclesiastical administration was the diocese; the bishop was the only individual charged with the administration of a defined territory and juridically responsible for the care of souls within his jurisdiction. He presided over the celebration of the Eucharist and was the ordinary minister of the Sacraments to his people. Priests and deacons shared in his ministry as helpers, but had no territorial responsibility for regional subdivisions of the diocese. Even in those places where other churches besides the episcopal church existed the power of priests and deacons entrusted with their care was greatly restricted. The churches they served were considered simply to be extensions of the local bishop's own "city" parish, which was, in fact, coterminous with the diocese itself.

The period from the 10th to the 13th centuries saw, with the expansion of the Church in Europe, the gradual development of several churches within the same city, each with its own body of clergy, who gradually became jurisdictionally independent of the bishop. These satellite churches were considered as benefices with the clergy serving them enjoying legal title to the revenues derived therefrom, but even in these cases there was no real concept of the territorial integrity of the parish. No geographic boundaries were imposed and the people were free to come and go to the church of their choice with no moral obligation imposed on the faithful to "belong" to the church nearest their place of residence. No "pastor" was required by church law to take specific responsibility for the people living within a certain geographic area.

To correct some of the abuses engendered by this rather loose system of ecclesiastical organization the Council of Trent decreed (Session 24, ch. 13–14) that every local Ordinary was to set up on his diocese clearly defined boundaries for churches and to see to it that the clergy assigned to these "parishes" assume specific responsibility for the spiritual care of the people living there (cf. Schroeder 204). It was further decreed that the people could lawfully receive the Sacraments only from the pastor of their own territorial parish and that each parish was to be assigned its own permanent parish priest.

Canon Law. This concept of parish—a territorial entity with definite boundaries and its own proper pastor assigned by the local bishop with the care of souls within it—became normative from Trent on. The 1917 Code reaffirms this territorial and juridical concept of the parish entity when it states: "The territory of every diocese is to be divided into distinct territorial parts; to each part is to be assigned its own church with a definite part of the population, and its own rector as the proper pastor of that territory is to be put in charge for the necessary care of souls" (CIC c. 216 n. 1; cf. Bousc-Ellis 151). The Code further reinforces this concept of a parish as primarily a territorial entity by stating (ibid. n. 4) that any future exceptions to this rule, as in the case of nonterritorial, "national" parishes, or territorial parishes exclusively for the use of a certain national group to the exclusion of others, could only be erected by special apostolic indult, and not by the authority of the local bishop alone. Clearly, this understanding of parish based upon its definition as a territorial entity, promulgated by the Church from the 13th century onward, is a strictly juridical and legalistic one. It has had little to do with any other elements that might have provided a binding force amongst a group of people and has rested almost entirely upon the idea that the basis of the sacramental community in the Church is geographic locale.

Vatican II Emphases. The documents of Vatican Council II have marked a move away from this almost exclusively juridical and legalistic focus, restoring to the concept of parish a more liturgical and sacramental emphasis. They have further restored the diocese to its more ancient position of the basic element of church structure (*see* CHURCH, LOCAL) and the bishop to his role as chief sign of unity and solidarity of faith amongst the people. The local parish is described, in the Constitution on the Sacred Liturgy, more as a Eucharistic and sacramental community than as a territorial entity, whose *raison d'être* derives not so much from the responsibility and right of the pastor to care for those under his charge as from the impossibility of the local bishop's being always and everywhere present to his people for the celebration of the liturgy. Two paragraphs of this document clearly show a different focus on the concept of parish than is evident in Canon Law:

The bishop is to be considered the high priest of his flock. In a certain sense it is from him that the faithful who are under his care derive and maintain their life in Christ.

Therefore all should hold in very high esteem the liturgical life of the diocese which centers around the bishop, especially in his cathedral church. Let them be persuaded that the Church reveals herself most clearly when the full complement of God's holy people, united in prayer and in common liturgical service (especially the Eucharist), exercise a thorough and active participation at the very altar where the bishop presides in the company of his priests and other assistants (*Sacrosanctum Concilium* 41).

But because it is impossible for the bishop always and everywhere to preside over the whole flock in his Church, he cannot do other than establish lesser groupings of the faithful. Among these, parishes set up locally under a pastor who takes the place of the bishop are the most important; for in a certain way they represent the visible Church as it is established throughout the world.

Therefore the liturgical life of the parish and its relationship with the bishop must be fostered in the thinking and practice of both laity and clergy; efforts also must be made to encourage a sense of community within the parish, above all in the common celebration of the Sunday Mass (*Sacrosanctum Concilium* 42).

What this quotation expresses is a move away from a strictly administrative and legalistic concept of the parish to one that is more theological and sacramental. In many ways this is a new development, since it is an attempt to recover the spiritual and social basis of Christian community within the context of a legal entity that arose much later in the history of the Church. The net result has been something of a dilemma for those interested in the field of ecclesiology and parish ministry. On the one hand it is clear that geography is not the basis of Christian community, on the other hand it is equally clear that no Christian community can exist for any extended period of time without some grounding in *place*. Even in the early Church, when communities were smaller and structure was simpler, the idea of the Church community finding its sacramental and social expression around a bishop who was connected with a definite place was essential. The question today seems to be whether or not new ways can be found of building that sense of Christian community amongst people, based upon the more ancient tradition of liturgy and ministry, without reducing its expression to merely legalistic and geographic formulas.

Current Experiments. Recent years have seen some attempts to find viable alternatives to the strictly geographical definition of parish. These have generally fallen into two types of experiments: attempts to restructure existing geographic parishes in ways that emphasize more clearly the sacramental and ministerial elements of Christian community; and attempts to form communities bound together by sacramental and/or ministerial commitments, but without any specific geographic location. Put in another way, these two basic types could be classified either as experiments in flexible forms of liturgical and ministerial expression within a defined location (for example, the boundaries of a geographic parish), or as flexible locations for people drawn together by a common style of liturgy or shared interest in a specific form of ministry (so called "floating parishes").

It is yet too early to tell whether either of these experimental forms of parish will become established well enough to presage a new era in parish life. In the U.S., at least, attempts along these lines have been somewhat isolated, depending more on the creativity and personality of individuals than on any concerted efforts by the hierarchy to encourage their development. A cursory review of experiments in new forms of parish life seems to indicate, however, that those of the first kind (greater flexibility of forms and ministries within established geographic boundaries) have been more successful and longer lasting than those of the second kind (the non-territorial "floating parishes").

It is safe to say, nevertheless, that recent developments in theology, liturgy, and ministry within the Church have led to a reevaluation of traditional and somewhat limited concepts of parish, and are gradually leading in the direction of redefining it to fit the changing needs of modern life. In the U.S., at least, the greater mobility of the population, particularly in urban areas, and their increasing awareness of alternative "styles" of parish life are gradually eroding the previously well defined concept of the geographic parish. People are more and more gravitating to those parishes which best suit their spiritual and social needs; parishes themselves are developing greater individuality of ministry and liturgical expression. It well may be that in years to come the idea of parish as it was previously understood in Canon Law will have to be changed to fit a new, far less juridical and legalistic, and far more sacramental and ministerial concept of Church.

Meanwhile it behooves those involved in parish ministry to consider carefully the standpoint from which they approach their work. Clinging too closely to the geographic and legalistic concept of the parish can result in a subservience of people's needs to historical forms and structures. On the other hand, the too rapid abandonment of traditional concepts of parish structure can leave people rootless and confused, spiritually and psychologically incapable of a rapid adaptation to novel, and sometimes untested, forms of parish life. As with most questions of this nature, the solution seems to lie somewhere in the middle. The tradition of the Church over the past seven centuries has proved the wisdom of territorial "placeness" as a stabilizing influence upon parish structure, but the needs of people today, especially in more advanced and mobile cultures, call for renewed efforts to revitalize the sacramental, social, and ministerial aspects of parish life in order to put spiritual flesh upon the bare bones of parish structure and ecclesiastical order.

Bibliography: J. D. ANDERSON, *To Come Alive! New Proposal for Revitalizing the Local Church,* (New York 1973). A. BLOCHLINGER, *The Modern Parish Community,* tr. G. STEVENS (New York 1965). M. BORDE-LON, ed., *The Parish in a Time of Change* (Notre Dame, Ind. 1967). S. B. CLARK, *Building Christian Communities, Strategies for Renewing the Church,* (Notre Dame, Ind. 1972). R. CURRIER, *Restructuring the Parish* (Chicago 1967). C. FLORISTAN, *The Parish—Eucharistic Community,* tr. J. F. BYRNE (Notre Dame, Ind. 1964). J. FOSTER, *Requiem for a Parish* (Westminister, Md. 1962). W. L. GRICHTING, *Parish Structure and Climate in an Era of Change, a Sociologist's Inquiry* (Center for Applied Research in the Apostolate, Washington, D.C. 1969). S. J. KILIAN, *Theological Models for the Parish* (New York 1977). L. L. LUTZBETAK, *The Church in the Changing City* (Techny, Ill. 1966). C. J. NUESSE and T. J. HARTE, eds., *The Sociology of the Parish* (Milwaukee 1951). J. O'GARA, ed., *The Postconciliar Parish* (New York 1967). H. RAHNER, *The Parish from Theology to Practice,* tr. R. KRESS (Westminister, Md. 1958). H. J. SCHROEDER, *Canons and Decrees of the Council of Trent* (St. Louis 1960). L. R. WARD, *The Living Parish* (Notre Dame, Ind. 1959). M. M. WINTER, *Blueprint for a Working Church, A Study in New Pastoral Structures* (St. Meinrad, Ind. 1973).

[B. C. JEWITT]

PARISH (COMMUNITY)

As part of a more general trend toward concern for the basic communal units of society, there is increased interest in the Church in the life of the local parish (10:1017). In society, this general concern is reflected in growing attention to the integrity of the family, the neighborhood, and the various neighborhood associations that provide society with basic communal net-works within which people find support and direction for life. The related Church interest in the parish may better be described as coming under an interest in the "local" Church, that is, the church within each particular locale, with all of the social, cultural, and economic factors that constitute the character of each locale (*see* CHURCH, LOCAL [THEOLOGY]. After a decade in U.S. society in which local communities were responding to national movements and government programs and in which church communities were responding to the reform initiatives coming from both national movements and universal-church directives implementing Vatican Council II, the initiative has passed back to the parish.

Emphases on Communal Life. One of the signals of this shift of focus was the intervention of Bishop Albert H. Ottenweller, now bishop of Steubenville, Ohio, then auxiliary of Toledo, Ohio, at the 1975 meeting of the National Conference of Catholic Bishops. Bishop Ottenweller pleaded for attention to the communal life of the local parish in contrast to the increasingly organizational thrust resulting from parishes' having to respond to continuous programmatic initiatives from dioceses and national offices. The intervention struck a deeply responsive chord throughout the American Church, because it spoke for all those concerns about community life which are deeply felt by parishioners and parish staffs alike.

In the face of extensive alienation from the Church, variously attributed to difficulty with church teaching or to problems of a more general erosion of a community of faith, moral positions, and mutual support, parishes are attempting to find ways to relate more directly to the structures of people's lives and to foster reflection on shared issues in contemporary life. Consequently, while it may be said that there is a revival in the parish as a unity, that interest in the parish and its relation to local community life has led to movements in two directions from the parish as a base. First, there is growing interest in development of smaller communal groups within the parish which can provide for parishioners a circle of trust where there can be reflection on faith, Scripture, family and work lives, and common concerns related to their shared socio-economic condition. This development is occurring throughout the world and perhaps the Latin American expression of it as the development of *communidades de base* (*see* BASIC CHRISTIAN COMMUNITIES) has best defined the movement. On the other hand, there are also signs of increased interparish activity, sometimes referred to as an attempt at "area Church." Here clusters of parishes, either defined as a region, vicariate, or other area by the bishop or grouping themselves spontaneously, attempt to relate church life to some larger socio-political unit of which they are a part. This leads to development of shared programs, establishment of common policies (e.g., regarding the administration of the Sacraments), sharing of resources, and collaborative involvement in community life, especially through the sponsorship of community organizations that will deal with community issues and community power.

Individual and Communal Development. Part of the concern of the parish, as the unity in which the life of the Church takes root and is experienced as a living community, is to combine new ways of promoting the life of faith as a matter of individual, personal commitment with the fostering of activities that engage the Church in the work of general human development. The former concern is reflected both in more careful approaches to the administration of the Sacraments as well as in the charismatic and other prayer movements and a host of "encounter" activities designed, at least in part, to stimulate deep personal conversion and commitment. These include the *Cursillo de Cristianidad, *Marriage Encounter, and a variety of encounter activities related to youth. This tendency is matched by a somewhat contrary one of reaching out to a broad community of human concern and of opening the parish church to include activity with people covering a broad range of levels of belief and commitment so that they can collaborate in areas of human development. Another expression of this same tension in parochial church life is the attempt to combine support for clear norms of belief and behavior, e.g., permanent marriage and stable family life, with care for those unable to fulfill these norms, e.g., ministry to divorced and separated Catholics. Parish communities are attempting to deal with these tensions and to combine both dimensions of religious belonging.

Lay Decision-Making and Ministry. A further development in parish life is the expansion and clarification of responsibility for decision-making and ministry in the Church. The most general development of shared responsibility for decision-making is through parish councils. At the same time, there is a general movement also toward more shared decision-making in the administration of the parish through a more team-like approach to relationships in the parish staff. With respect to broader participation in the ministry of the Church, there has been a proliferation of ministries, those of the permanent deacons, directors of religious education, extraordinary ministers of the Eucharist, ministers of music, youth ministers, and various forms of social service and social action ministry, from one-to-one care to community organizing efforts. This expansion of participation in ministry has led to increased interest in the development of training programs for lay ministry, to increased use of sisters in general pastoral ministry, and to increased attempts to clarify the respective responsibilities of the various ministers in the parish.

The years ahead will undoubtedly see increased efforts to develop a more integrated approach to the parish, one that will articulate the relationships among these various developments regarding the scope of the parish, the mission of the parish to the local community, sharing of responsibility for planning and ministry, and the nature of the parish as a community of both standards for life and reconciliation. To be expected also is a further reshaping of the parish in relation to smaller and larger communities as it attempts to relate clearly to the general community life of each locale.

Bibliography: S. J. KILLIAN, *Theological Models for the Parish* (Staten Island, N.Y. 1977). L. MAINELLI, ed., "The Parish and the Diakonia," Symposium, *Social Thought* 1 (National Conference of Catholic Charities, Washington, D.C. 1975) 11–99. J. RÉMY et al., "Les Paroisses: mort lente ou renouveau," Symposium, LumV 25 (1975) 5–92.

[P. MURNION]

PARISH (COMMUNITY OF WORSHIP)

In the division of jurisdiction within the Church, a diocese is divided into parochial communities usually by territory but also by nationality. Persons living within specified boundaries are automatically affiliated with the parish assigned to that area. Thus it has been common, especially in urban areas, for Catholic people to identify their home according to the parish where they belong.

The emphasis in the liturgical reform has been on the worshiping *community* rather than upon individual people at prayer. The assumption is that people already recognize themselves as a *community* of baptized persons even before they gather for worship. Given the present sociological situation in most urban and suburban areas especially, it is impossible to suppose the existence of a *community* on the basis of geography (or nationality) alone. Most people recognize nothing in common with their neighbors. Thus those in charge of parochial ministry have the very difficult task of celebrating Sacraments using the official books of the Church which assume the presence of a *community* prior to assembly.

Christian people are most evidently "Church" when they gather together as an assembly for worship. Their common bond is Baptism. The revised rituals of the Church insist that Sacraments be celebrated in the local parish: infant Baptism should normally be celebrated in the parish church (BaptCh 10) and except in danger of death should not be celebrated in private houses (ibid. 12). Although people may not recognize themselves as a community prior to worship in some areas, the liturgical reform offers the possibility of building community within the assembly so as to break down the isolation many people experience as a result of their "padlocked" daily existence in many cities.

The rites of Christian Initiation publicly celebrate the stages of the *catechumenate for adults and assumes that catechists and sponsors come from the community. This experience of an order (or special class) of people within the Church enables parishioners to come to grips with their own identity and come into contact with their Christian roots. The ritual stresses both pastoral and lay responsibility for the proper instruction of parents before infant Baptism (ibid. 7.1). Ministerial roles exercised by lay persons should help break down the walls of isolation which inhibit community. The minister of music rehearses before celebrations so that disparate voices become one voice of praise whether in choir or congregation. One who reads the Word of God as lector should ideally live that Word as a member of the community before and after assembly. *Extraordinary ministers of the Eucharist are recognizable persons eliciting an act of belief at the moment of reception, reaching out to bring the Sacraments to the sick within the parish, but they also live within the area of the parish with relationships and daily interchange.

There are important horizontal movements which necessitate interaction within the assembled community. The exchange of the sign of peace is most effective since it is not only a sign of unification prior to Eucharist but also a classical gesture of reconciliation in common experience. Recited prayers also have their own effect: "I confess . . . to you my brothers and sisters that I have sinned . . ." should not be said in the Penitential Rite at Mass after Mass without the effect of public confession being realized. Parental preparations before Baptism and first Sacraments and group marriage preparations can and do form friendships based on common purpose and interests. The horizontal movement that takes place non-verbally when people see each other in well designed gathering areas during worship should make community a reality.

In the United States there have been experiments with nonterritorial parishes gathering people with common concerns and interests who may not live within a given area. Some of these have worked but other factors in the American living experience such as neighborhood schools, organized little league, voter registration, civic events, reinforce the neighborhood concept even in the face of mobility of people and easy transportation.

The parish has for too long been identified with the church building itself or the clergy. Realization of the theological concept of people as Church will occur when parishioners have actual voice in decisions; give leadership through ministry (e.g. permanent deacons); gain insight through sharing of prayer. Good worship can help realize actual community as individual talents become part of celebration and the neighborhood everyday-living situations become applications of the proclaimed Word.

See also LITURGICAL COMMITTEES, PARISH.

[J. L. CUNNINGHAM]

PARISH, SOCIOLOGY OF

The decline of interest in the parish on the part of sociologists was foretold accurately by John D. Donovan in his contribution in 1967 to the *New Catholic Encyclopedia* (10:1019). Almost none of the work done in subsequent years by sociologists, at home or abroad, whether or not by Catholics, has focused on the parish or congregation as the unit of analysis.

The Shift from Parish Research. Meanwhile, the sociology of *religion has flourished as an area of specialization. In the case of American Catholic sociologists, as Donovan remarked, the "... parish has been replaced by concern with the whole subculture of American Catholicism." This is in tune with the concerns of American sociologists in general, who conceptualize religion in terms of a broad set of cultural values rather than as belonging to a concrete social group. This shift of levels of sociological concern might be said to parallel important events actually taking place in the society. For Catholics, Vatican Council II and its aftermath have called attention dramatically to the adequacy of what might be labelled the Catholic *worldview* in modern society: the theological questions raised about the entire institutional structure might seem more profound than parochial problems. Similarly, the values of the wider American society have been challenged by the tumultuous events of the 1960s and 1970s. Religious and spiritual phenomena have a heightened visibility, but sociological interest in them appears to be centered around what such an awakening of religious consciousness may portend for all the institutions of the society.

Parish Research Possibilities. It is not intended to imply with this description, however facile, of the state of the sociology of religion that the research directions being pursued are not fruitful. There are some considerations, nevertheless, which suggest that abandoning the parish as a locus of study may lead to the neglect of some important elements of social reality. What follows is a list of items, based on the observations of fellow sociologists, which form a frankly eclectic research agenda. It is by no means exhaustive, nor is it

guaranteed to be more productive than the research mentioned. It is based on the sociological assumption that interaction at the level of the concrete social group, in this case the parish, may be illuminating. It is also based on the premise that social forms which no longer seem relevant especially in times of rapid social or cultural change, have an unusual knack for persistence. The forms may not correspond to the ideal as seen from another point of view. Sociologists, however, should be appropriately skeptical in accepting the going wisdom and be willing to invest their research efforts on a variety of levels.

(1) *Modes of Religious Commitment.* The research of Andrew M. Greeley and his colleagues has documented the continued commitment of Catholics to the parochial school while support for other forms of involvement, e.g., rituals or submission to clerical authority, have been less than enthusiastic or have dwindled altogether. Such selectivity probably is lamentable from a canonical viewpoint, but it may be a fertile field in which sociologists can understand the way in which a significant number of American Catholics make their religious commitment. "Communal Catholics" is the effective label Greeley employs to describe them. There is a need to know much more empirical detail about such modes of religious belonging.

(2) *Parish History Revisited.* There is a question related to the first item; it is not at all clear whether or not the situation with respect to the parish is something entirely new. The school, for example, may have been the central element of belonging to the territorial parish all along from the viewpoint of the parishioners. Historical data might be available which would shed more light on the matter, so that sociologists should not have to accept uncritically nostalgic or romantic descriptions of what the parish was imagined to have been. Too often the parish history has been written from the official perspective and not that of the occupants of the pews. Historians are beginning to compensate for this omission and they are uncovering the possibility of important regional variations (see Dolan). This should come as no surprise in view of observed differences from country to country in the part the parish plays in the life of peoples of varying cultural traditions.

(3) *Persistent Ethnicity.* Variation in cultural traditions with regard to the parish is, of course, present within the whole of American society. Even under the rash and hazardous hypothesis that the process of acculturation would ultimately make of American Catholicism a seamless web, ethnic pockets persist in the United States in which both territorial and national parishes operate. The shape of these is hardly documented and their import is largely ignored, despite, for example, the continued immigration of sizable numbers of Spanish-speaking and Spanish-surname persons and of persons from various countries in the Orient.

(4) *Alternative Parishes.* Territorial parishes may be losing members among those within their geographical boundaries, but there is considerable evidence that alternative parishes develop. This can involve crossing parish lines in search of attractive liturgies elsewhere or developing home liturgies. The social networks which both lead to and are outcomes of these activities are mostly unexplored. Both their quality and their quantity remain unknowns.

(5) *New Wine in Old Skins.* Akin to the preceding

is the possibility that old parishes may themselves develop alternative styles of relating to their neighborhoods. There has been considerable impetus for this from clergy, who are painfully aware of the need for new directions. The innovative process may be abetted both by decentralization of ecclesiastical political power and by the quest for or persistence of community in some urban areas. Whether or not the parishes respond effectively can scarcely be predicted, given the paucity of studies.

Conclusion. Sociologists will recognize that the research tools appropriate for a renewed sociology of the parish, as intimated in these items, are those most frequently employed by ethnographers. The strategies are necessarily those called "qualitative," since the emphasis is clearly on getting at the meanings of the parish in the lives of various participants. These meanings may bear no resemblance to current blithe assumptions.

See also SOCIAL HISTORY.

Bibliography: J. P. DOLAN, *The Immigrant Church: New York's Irish and German Catholics, 1815–1865* (Baltimore 1975); *The American Experience: 1830–1900* (Notre Dame, Ind. 1978). A. M. GREELEY, *The Communal Catholic* (New York 1976). A. M. GREELEY et al., *Catholic Schools in a Declining Church* (Kansas City 1976). C. Y. GLOCK and R. N. BELLAH, eds., *The New Religious Consciousness* (Berkeley 1976). J. W. SANDERS, *The Education of an Urban Minority, Catholics in Chicago, 1833–1965* (New York 1977).

[R. LANE]

PARISH COUNCILS

Nowhere did the Second Vatican Council spell out the role and functioning of the parish council (16:330) as it did for the diocesan pastoral council, although after discussing the diocesan council the Decree on the Apostolate of Lay People further called for councils of clergy, religious, and laity to be established "at parochial, interparochial, interdiocesan level, and also on the national and international plane" which would "assist the Church's apostolic work, whether in the field of evangelization and sanctification or in the fields of charity, social relations, and the rest" (*Apostolicam actuositatem* 26).

The *Directory on the Pastoral Ministry of Bishops*, issued in 1973, provides further guidance regarding parish councils. It speaks first in the context of administration of church property, urging the bishop to erect councils in every parish, on which laity of administrative ability, character, and zeal are to be included, which will deliberate on such matters as plans and budget and check and make public the financial account at the end of the year or the completion of a project (69). Later, however, it speaks expressly of parish *pastoral* councils: the bishop will consider that kind of parish best in which (among other things) "laymen, according to the office given them, take part in the parish pastoral council . . ." (179); during his pastoral visitation the bishop should look into the parish pastoral council (168); to make the work of the diocesan pastoral council more effective he can require a parish pastoral council to be set up in every parish "and that these be aligned with the diocesan council" (204); the "diocesan and parish councils can be of great help in fostering a sense of community among the laity and in promoting their zeal for the apostolate" (147).

Development of parish councils has been a top concern of diocesan pastoral councils, and in most dioceses over 70 percent of the parishes have a council, while in many all or nearly all do. Guidelines from a number of dioceses have been published in *Origins*, (Springfield, Mass. in 1972; Buffalo and Boston in 1973; Louisville, St. Paul-Minneapolis, and Newark in 1976; San Diego and Columbus in 1977; Cleveland in 1978), and these present a picture of the parish council as the unifying structure of the Christian community, representative of it as a whole, serving as a principal means for sharing of responsibility for ministry and for decision-making. If decision-making is not to be mere crisis management, however, and if the council is to be truly a pastoral one, it must become involved in some form of *pastoral planning. In many dioceses there are specialized offices under various names providing organizational development services to parish councils; two of the commonest activities of diocesan pastoral-planning offices in fact relate to assisting councils and helping parishes develop goal-setting systems. Since 1974, diocesan personnel concerned with parish councils have been meeting nationally on an annual basis.

See also PASTORAL COUNCILS, DIOCESAN.

Bibliography: Congregation for Bishops, *Directory on the Pastoral Ministry of Bishops* (Ottawa 1974).

[E. M. SULLIVAN]

PARISH RENEWAL

Parish renewal is never a completed task but an ongoing process, a continual effort by staff, lay leaders, and people to keep the parish in touch with the culture and situation in which it resides, and at the same time, to keep the parish responsive to the promptings of the Lord in its midst.

Forms of Renewal. Since parish renewal is related to the local situation, the form that renewal takes will be as varied as the people and community it serves. The renewal of a campus-ministry center, for instance, will present a different picture than a Spanish-speaking parish in a large city or a rural parish in a small town. But since it is the same Lord who calls the parish to renewal and the same Gospel message that the people are called to respond to, there are common elements to parish renewal, no matter where it is located or what people it serves.

One common element of parish renewal is that the people are the focus of renewal, not the buildings or parish structure. These latter exist only as a means for helping the people understand their faith commitment and sense of community. The People of God, as Vatican Council II emphasized, are the primary focus of the Church and parish.

A second common element of parish renewal is that the People of God have a responsibility to continue the work of Christ on earth. All the parishioners are called to be ministers of the Gospel, not just the staff and lay leaders. Parish renewal is dependent on how well the people grasp this fact: that they belong to the parish, not because it provides a safer or easier path to heaven, but because the people become part of a community of worship and service. Each member of the parish shares the responsibility of worshipping the Lord in communal prayer and Eucharist and of serving one another and those outside of the parish community who are in need.

Means of Renewal. How does a parish go about the task of renewal? The ways are limited only by the creativity and imagination of the leaders and people. Some elements are the following.

Good Leaders. The first step toward renewal is inspiring and open leadership. The pastor is still the most influential agent of renewal. This is changing, and in some places a team approach shares this leadership role. But if there is to be any lasting renewal, it must be encouraged, supported-and continued by the parish staff, and especially by the pastor. The pastor and staff must be the models of parish renewal for the community.

Small Groups. Parish renewal is more easily accomplished by working with small groups of people, one group at a time. There are more opportunities for sharing and personal commitment. Some places have divided the parish into small subunits, while others have used existing groups and worked toward renewal with each one. Whatever method is used, it is important to begin with a core group and let that be the model for renewal. This core group then works with other small groups and in this way renewal is communicated throughout the parish.

Resources. Successful renewal depends on how well a parish draws on the resources that exist both within and outside the parish. Too often the talents and experience of the parishioners are passed over and not recognized or encouraged; but it is just these talents and insights that nourish parish renewal. The people feel they are a part of the process to the extent that their own resources are utilized. There are also many resources provided by the Church, through diocesan offices, publications, and independent services. These should be used on a continual basis. Sharing ideas, programs, successes, and failures with other parishes in the area is also a valuable resource.

The Word. The best means toward parish renewal and one often overlooked, is the power of the Word in and among the parish community. It is the realization that the parish does not have to accomplish renewal on its own. The parish community has the promise of the Gospel that Christ has sent the Spirit into its midst to guide and strengthen its efforts. The secret of a successful parish renewal is to let the message of Christ sink into the lives and liturgies of the parish community and let it work its effect there.

[T. P. SWEETSER]

PAROCHIAL SCHOOLS, CATHOLIC ELEMENTARY

To the phenomenon of Catholic parochial education, begun earlier, the Third Plenary Council of Baltimore in 1884, added impetus by mandating that every Catholic child be educated in a Catholic school. The massive effort that followed grew well into this century. In 1967, even then one of the early declining years in enrollment, there were 4,291,466 elementary students attending 10,528 elementary parochial schools. By 1977, the student enrollment had decreased further by 43.8 percent to 2,412,223 students; the number of elementary schools had decreased by 23.7 percent to 8,035.

Decline and Causes. The decline in enrollment coincided with the deliberations of Vatican Council II and publication of its Declaration on Christian Education (Oct. 28, 1965), which proclaimed that parents "should enjoy the fullest liberty in their choice of school"

(*Gravissimum educationis* 6) and that the Catholic school "is still of vital importance even in our times" (ibid. 8). Thus Catholic parents were reminded of their duty "to send their children to Catholic schools wherever this is possible, to give Catholic schools all the support in their power, and to cooperate with them in their work for the good of their children" (ibid.).

Yet, Catholic schools continued to decrease at a critical rate. The decline was not seen as a result of consolidations or the elimination of small inefficient units. It was seen in one 1971 study as the inevitable consequence of profound and extensive social and religious changes that have been revolutionary in character, extremely rapid in tempo, and unforeseen. One cause was summarized in the transformation of the American Catholic into the Catholic American. American Catholics had passed from being the uneducated, economically deprived, socially isolated and politically powerless into becoming part of the American mainstream. Secondly, the once-closed Catholic Church was becoming open to theological pluralism and the authority of the individual conscience, ecumenism, and the democratization of ecclesial structures. Thirdly, the Catholic school itself was changing. It was no longer a sisters' school: between 1967 and 1971, full-time religious women teaching in Catholic elementary schools decreased by 12,040 (19 percent) while full-time lay teachers increased by 14,374 (32 percent). Nor was the school any longer viewed as the only agency for religious education. Education at all age levels and in different settings was becoming of interest. Furthermore, efforts to consolidate a number of schools removed the parochial connection from Catholic elementary schooling. The school was looked to by Catholic Americans for superiority, not only in the religious, personal, and social areas of education, but also in the academic, physical, and practical. There was also fear that the voluntary financial resources of parishes were too regressive to sustain the needed progressive Catholic school. The future looked bleak; the bleakness appeared to be a self-fulfilling prophecy.

Bishops' Pastoral Message. In 1972, the NCCB pastoral message on Catholic education, *To Teach As Jesus Did,* called Catholic schools "the fullest and best opportunity to realize the threefold purpose (doctrine, community, service) of Christian education among children and young people" (To Teach 101). The message recalled Vatican II's conviction that the Catholic school "retains its immense importance in the circumstances of our times" and that Catholic parents have the duty to support the school. The school was cited as unique, contemporary, and oriented to Christian service, an instrument of forming Christians, of building community, of responding to human needs. The pastoral, acknowledged the crisis of an educational system shrinking by reason of complex sociological, demographic and psychological factors. It called the Catholic community, nonetheless, to renew its purpose in the Catholic school, to reorganize the school as needs arose, to be open to a Catholic school of the future very different from the school of the past.

Catholic educators received the pastoral enthusiastically as a message reassuring the value of the Catholic school and directing an era of educational opportunities and variety. It still remains an important resource of confirmation and influence in Catholic education.

The Greeley Study. In 1976 Greeley, McCready, and McCourt published *Catholic Schools in a Declining Church*. As "a study of value-oriented education under the stress of social change," it became a new and controversial resource in considering the crisis of a shrinking system. It presented a paradox to the American Catholic Church in its research on the Catholic school. In short, the Catholic value-oriented schools survived the forces of change, especially those within the Church, quite well. Yet, the study concluded, they remain in serious trouble. Catholic schools emerged as more important to a Church in trauma than they had been to a Church unchanged. The Church was seen as affected by two forces: the positive force of Vatican II and the negative force of the encyclical *Humanae vitae* (1968). Two-thirds of the respondents in the Study were found to endorse the conciliar changes: 87 percent of them, for example, approved English in the liturgy and about two-thirds were seen as willing to endorse such changes as a married clergy in the Church. Those who supported change showed higher levels of religious behavior than those who opposed change. The negative force, however, accounted for changes in sexual attitudes and in attitudes towards the papacy. American Catholicism was seen to have deteriorated as a result of the encyclical. The Council alone would have produced an increase of about one-sixth in Catholic religious behavior; the birth-control encyclical would have affected about a fifty percent decline in religious behavior. In combination, the forces brought about a decline in Catholic religious behavior of about one-third.

In this duel of forces, Catholic schools fared well. In the conclusion of the Greeley study's chapter on "Value-Oriented Education and Social Change," it was stated that those who experienced value-oriented education in such schools are somewhat more likely to accept change in the value-teaching institution in which the change occurs. While the dynamics of deterioration in American Catholicism maintained, Catholic schooling—especially among those who experienced more than ten years of its influence—restrained and softened the erosion. Specifically, in such matters relating to the Church's structure as active involvement in the institution, financial contributions to it, and favorable attitudes towards its leaders, the relationship between value-education and adult behavior was found to increase. The relationship between Catholic education and private ritual behavior such as daily prayer also was increased. Yet value-oriented education was found to be less influential on public ritual behavior (Mass attendance and reception of Sacraments) and of no influence on matters of sexual orthodoxy. Catholic education had, however, emerged as a more important predictor of adult religiousness than parent religiousness. Catholic schools were seen as more important in forming the religious behavior of men than the schools were found to be ten years before and they slowed the rate of religiousness-decline in both men and those under thirty. Catholic schools, then, prevented losses where they were most likely to occur and worked to influence men, the more effective religious socializers, and the young, the institution's hope for the future.

Eighty percent of the American Catholic population favored continuance of Catholic schools. Eighty percent were cited as willing to contribute more money to support a local parochial school. Fifty-two percent of this population continue to view religious instruction as the major advantage of Catholic schooling. The general Catholic population cited better discipline and better education as two other main advantages. Catholic respondents whose children attend Catholic schools cited the same three advantages, but placed better education as the first reason for enrolling their children in these schools. While their reasons for favoring Catholic schools differed in priority between the general population and the enrolling-parent group, Catholics expressed their support for Catholic education and, of all levels of education, tended most to support elementary Catholic schooling. Furthermore, in the midst of a changing Church, they overwhelmingly approved new methods in religious education, sex education in schools, and the presence of lay teachers in school faculties. The Catholic school emerged, not only as a stabilizing instrument of the institutional Church, but as a recognized asset among the membership of the Church. The study concluded that the American Catholic population continues to support its schools strongly; that unused fiscal resources are available to keep the schools in existence; that the schools in fact are more effective now than in the past; and that they are more important to the Church in its time of trauma and transition than in times of peace and stability.

Despite the strength of the Catholic school for Church and for parent, the decline in the number of schools and attendance continues. The study suggests that the principal reason is the unavailability of Catholic schools and the non-construction of new schools. It further suggests that the unavailability stems from the nonresponsive decision-making structure of the Church's leadership. Any change in policy towards new school construction will occur only when leadership becomes more open to the desire of its membership and when membership assumes an active role in making decisions. Without these changes, the decline of Catholic education will go on.

The NCEA Response. In June 1976 the National Catholic Educational Association (NCEA) called for a Symposium on Catholic Education to consider the study just cited, to react to it, and to determine recommendations for the immediate future of Catholic education. A commentary on the Symposium proceedings cited twenty-three recommendations. The highest priority stated was the need to improve the process of decision-making in the Church. Seven of the recommendations urged greater participation in decision-making. With the creation of school boards and parish councils and the emergence of lay administrators coincidental with changing policies in religious communities, the decision by bishops and pastors becomes relative to the influences of many people. A balance of deliberative authority is needed. Implicit in decision-making are the values of individual conscience and pluralism and the design of a curriculum reflective of such values. Besides participative decision-making at all levels, the recommendations contained three other major themes: the centrality of the religious/moral character; the need to meet the modern world on its own terms; the need for further research and development. NCEA responded by citing eight themes of priority for future activities: religious education and the formation of conscience in a pluralistic Church;

participatory decision-making; public relations; moral education or value formation; the community of faith; family education; finances; the consideration of a research center; the use of the media.

Legal Handicaps of Parents. The predominant concern for Catholic education continues to be the maintenance of the Catholic school. One scholar on nonpublic education considers it important to focus on private educational "options" rather than on "schools." While the American bishops opened the way to "options" in their 1972 pastoral message, there remain legal handicaps in the exercise of such options. Private-school parents are doubly taxed to fund public education and to provide funds for the alternative, private schooling they have chosen. The question must be asked whether true freedom of choice is not constrained, even when Church-related institutions are involved, by forced taxation for public educational services.

The "child-benefit" theory derived from the 1947 *Everson v. School Board* (330 U.S. 1; 5:658) provided an understanding of service to the child (transportation to Church-related schools) not in conflict with the establishment-of-religion clause. Between 1947 and 1968, it was assumed that the U.S. Supreme Court would not approve grants directly made to religious schools—grants of sizable benefits or grants funding central functions of such schools. In 1968 *Board of Education v. Allen* (392 U.S. 236) provided, however, constitutional approval for the provision of state-purchased textbooks to children of nonpublic schools. The case seemed to infer that secular functions of these schools could be state-supported. However, in 1971, the Supreme Court in a decision, favoring Lemon for Pennsylvania, *Lemon v. Kurzman* (403 U.S. 602), and Di Censo for Rhode Island (see 316 Federal Supplement 112), raised the criterion of "excessive entanglement" by the state in affairs of religious institutions. The extent of this criterion was clarified in 1975 when the Court decided in a Pennsylvania case, *Meek v. Pettenger* (421 U.S. 349), that textbooks still were permitted, but that no other services (e.g. counselling) could be provided by public school personnel for pupils in religious schools.

In the light of recent cases, parents may choose to enroll their children in nonpublic schools and support those schools. Until parents may participate in a broad-based voucher plan, or until the state permits some degree of tax relief as tax credits for tuition paid, or until all schools are financed by the clients choosing them, the practice of government continues to delimit rather than to expand parental freedom in educational choices (*see* CHURCH AND STATE).

Outlook. The National Catholic Educational Association reports (1978) that the decline of schools and enrollment continues, but at a slower rate. From 1976–77 to 1977–78, 58 elementary schools closed, a 0.7 percent decline. In the same time, the elementary population decreased by 2.5 percent, a loss of 62,000 pupils, more than the loss of the previous year, but a small decrease considering the decline of school-age children. The average school size for elementary schools has decreased from 328 in 1972–73 to 294 in 1977–78.

For the future, the relationship of the strength of parental support, the costs of private education, the extent of governmental participation, and the stance of Catholic leadership must be weighed as the maintenance, options, and growth of Catholic education and its major formal program, the elementary school, are considered.

Bibliography: Center for Field Research and School Services at Boston College: Compilers, *Issues of Aid to Nonpublic Schools* 4 v., v. 2, *The Social and Religious Sources of the Crisis in Catholic Schools* (Boston 1971). Curriculum Information Center, Inc., W. GANLEY, ed., *Catholic Schools in America* (Denver 1978). L. R. GARY, et al., *The Collapse of Nonpublic Education: Rumor or Reality?* (1971). A. M. GREELEY, W. C. MCCREADY, and K. MCCOURT, *Catholic Schools in a Declining Church* (Kansas City, Mo. 1976). R. N. LYNCH, ed., Symposium on Catholic Education, *Momentum* 7 (1976) whole issue, in part a reaction to the Greeley study. NCCB, *To Teach as Jesus Did* (USCC Publ. Office Washington, D.C. 1972). National Society for the Study of Education, *The Courts and Education* (Chicago 1978). Office of Educational Research, University of Notre Dame, *Economic Problems of Nonpublic Schools* (Notre Dame, Ind. 1971).

[R. J. SHUDA]

PASTORAL COUNCILS, DIOCESAN

Normative directives relating to the development and functioning of diocesan pastoral councils are covered in the earlier entry in the *New Catholic Encyclopedia* (16:125); this article has a complementary empirical focus on developments to 1978.

Within a year of the close of Vatican Council II, ten U.S. dioceses had established pastoral councils and the number increased steadily in subsequent years, although not every council has survived to the present. By 1977, just over half of the American dioceses had a council, and others were in development.

Membership. According to figures available on 81 dioceses in 1977, council size ranged from 16 to over 300 members, with a median of 31. About one-tenth had fewer than 20 and a similar number had over 100 members. More detailed data from 60 dioceses reported by Marceaux in 1975 indicated that in about one-quarter of the cases all members were elected, and in about one-tenth all were appointed; usually, however, there was a mix, with elected members being in the majority about 80 percent of the time. Membership of the average council consisted of the bishop (in some cases, two or more bishops), and about seven diocesan priests, four or five sisters, fourteen laymen, and seven laywomen. (The same pattern had been found in 1969.) In over three-fourths of the cases the number of laymen exceeded that of laywomen, with about twice as many laymen as laywomen in about half of the councils. Just over one-half of the councils included religious priests (an average of two or three), about one-third had a brother, and just five councils had a deacon. About half had representation of college students (averaging about two students) and about a third had high school students (averaging between three and four). About one-half of the councils met quarterly, with the majority of the remainder meeting more frequently (up to 24 times a year).

Competence. Marceaux's study found that finances, Sacraments, liturgy, social action, youth, and vocations were the major areas with which councils had concerned themselves. Specific examples of council activities included: assisting parish councils to organize; evaluating diocesan departments; maintaining parishes lacking a resident priest; establishing diocesan goals; organizing due process boards; developing guidelines for ethical diocesan investments; settling conflicts between parish councils and pastors; and formulating diocesan policy for teen-age marriages. A 1972 survey had found that assistance in development of parish councils was the most frequently mentioned work (mentioned by 37 percent of the councils), others being the diocesan school system, diocesan budget and finances, diocesan priorities, internal operation and development of the council itself, social action, lay responsibilities, due process procedures, and liturgical matters.

Councils and Pastoral Planning. The role of the council in relation to *pastoral planning is indicated by the 1973 *Directory on the Pastoral Ministry of Bishops*: "...the council furnishes the judgments necessary to enable the diocesan community to plan its pastoral program systematically and to fulfill it effectively" (204) A 1976 study by the *Center for Applied Research in the Apostolate (CARA) found that the most intensive single area of effort on the part of diocesan planning offices was assistance in the development of the pastoral council, to which it frequently served as staff. Since 1974 there have been annual national conferences of persons concerned with diocesan and parish councils, and a total of 73 dioceses had participated through 1977. The steering committee for that conference has initiated regional workshops and has scheduled the 1979 conference jointly with the *National Pastoral Planning Conference, whose members have a primary interest in shared-responsibility mechanisms in the Church.

Bibliography: Congregation for Bishops, *Directory on the Pastoral Ministry of Bishops* (Ottawa 1974). Congregation for the Clergy, "Patterns in Local Pastoral Councils" (complete text of circular letter of Jan. 25, 1973), Origins 3 (1973) 186–190. R. HOWES, ed., *Diocesan Pastoral Council: Papers Delivered at CARA Symposium 1* (Washington 1971). J. MARCEAUX, "The Diocesan Pastoral Council: Conciliar and Post-Conciliar Development of Its Competence and Composition" (JCL thesis, The Catholic University of America, Washington, D.C. 1975). National Council of Catholic Men, *Diocesan Pastoral Council: Proceedings, Bergamo Conference 15–17 March 1970* (Washington, D.C. 1970). F. R. SHEA, "A Bishop Suspends his Pastoral Council," Origins 6 (1976) 229–234. U.S. Catholic Bishops' Advisory Council, Steering Committee for a National Pastoral Council, *A Survey on Diocesan Pastoral Councils in the United States of America* (USCC Publ. Office, Washington, D.C. 1975).

[E. M. SULLIVAN]

PASTORAL COUNCILS, REGIONAL AND NATIONAL

Pastoral Councils, which involve a representative group of clergy, religious, and laity in shared decision making, are treated in several places in the documents of Vatican Council II. The Decree on the Apostolate of the Laity, calls for diocesan councils that would include the laity and goes on to add that councils of this type should be established, as far as possible, also on the parochial, interparochial, and interdiocesan level as well as in the national and international sphere (*Apostolicam actuositatem* 26).

Parish councils and diocesan pastoral councils are widespread and continue to develop in their effectiveness. Councils on the other levels, in particular, regional and national councils, have not enjoyed a similar development. In large part, this lack of growth is due to the fact that the identity of Catholics with levels of church governance beyond parish and diocese has not been strong. In the early 1970s the episcopal conference of the United States (NCCB) held regional meetings of bishops which frequently involved clergy, religious, and laity; but these regional meetings were discontinued in favor of two, rather than just one, national meetings.

The Holy See. Another reason that regional councils have not had significant development is that the Holy See has discouraged their establishment at this time. In a circular letter dated January 25, 1973 (Origins 3 [1973] 186–190) par. 12, the Congregation for the Clergy expresses the judgment, made after consultation with episcopal conferences and other Roman Congregations, that it is not now opportune, to institute pastoral councils on the interdiocesan, provincial, regional, national, or international level. The circular letter, however, urged the continued promotion of diocesan pastoral councils.

Similar Bodies. There are, nevertheless, a number of bodies which have begun to function in a manner similar to councils on the regional or state level. State Catholic Conferences, church agencies composed of the dioceses of a given state, often resemble councils in their organization and function. The twenty-seven State Catholic Conferences (16:431) rely heavily upon the talents of the laity, clergy, and religious as regards the decision-making process.

On the national level, in 1969 the NCCB established the U.S. Catholic *Bishops' Advisory Council, which is composed of bishops, priests, religious, and laity elected by their peers from the different regions of the country. While not a national pastoral council, the Advisory Council is deeply involved in the process of decision-making employed by the NCCB and provides the Church with a vehicle for shared responsibility. Considerable study was undertaken from 1970 until 1974 by the Advisory Council on the feasibility of a national pastoral council. The results of these studies and promotional efforts were not encouraging and there is no plan for such a council in the foreseeable future.

While the Pontifical Council for the *Laity has organized international meetings at Rome several times since Vatican II, no effort has been made to promote councils on the international level. It is likely that major developments regarding councils will continue to be on the parish and diocesan levels.

Bibliography: M. J. SHEEHAN and R. SHAW, eds. *Shared Responsibility at Work: The Catholic Bishops' Advisory Council 1969–1974* (Washington, D.C. 1975). USCC Advisory Council Steering Committee, *National Pastoral Council: Pro and Con*, Proceedings of an Interdisciplinary Consultation, Aug. 28–30, 1970 (Washington, D.C. 1971).

[M. J. SHEEHAN]

PASTORAL LITURGY, INSTITUTES FOR

Pastoral liturgy is the process of active and conscious participation by Christian people in the celebration of ecclesial worship of God. Its roots are seen in the liturgical movement set forth by Dom Lambert Beauduin, OSB, in Belgium at the outset of this century (2:199). It took more concrete form with the establishment of the *Centre de Pastorale Liturgique* in Paris in 1943. It reached full bloom with the International Congress at Assisi and Rome, September 18–22, 1956. It was formally recognized and endorsed by the Vatican Council II in the Constitution on the Sacred Liturgy, December 4, 1963.

That document noted that "Mother Church earnestly desires that all the faithful should be led to that full, conscious, and active participation in liturgical celebrations which is demanded by the very nature of the liturgy" (*Sacrosanctum Concilium* 14). Chapter one continues with a call for education of clergy and promotion of pastoral-liturgical life at the diocesan and parish level. It concludes with a call for national liturgical commissions assisted by "some kind of Institute for Pastoral Liturgy" and, at the diocesan level, commissions in liturgy, music, and sacred art working together or fused as one (ibid. 44–45). The decade that followed saw the establishment of such institutes throughout the world. Each country took a different approach to this call; a survey of some will show the variety of structures and identify some basic elements.

Europe and Asia. France is the prototype. The *Centre de Pastorale Liturgique*, established in 1943, was renamed after the Council document the *Centre National de Pastorale Liturgique* (4, Avenue Vavin, 75406 Paris). It continues to provide an academic base through collaboration with the *Institut Supérieur de Liturgie* at the *Institut Catholique de Paris* while it maintains a pastoral service to the bishops, dioceses, and parishes of France with a variety of programs. Pierre-Marie Gy, OP has been the guiding force of both the *Centre* and the *Institut*. The work of both can be seen in the journals, *La Maison Dieu* and *Notes de Pastorale Liturgique*.

Other institutes of significance in Europe include the academic pontifical international institute, *San Anselmo* (Via di Porta Lavernale, 19, Rome), the academic and pastoral *Liturgisches Institut* (Jesuitenstrasse, 5500, Trier, West Germany), and the pastoral Mt. St. Anne's Liturgy Center (Portarlington, County Laois, Ireland). Other institutes function at local levels such as the pastoral St. Thomas More Centre for Pastoral Liturgy (9 Henry Rd., London N4 2LH) and the Pastoral Liturgy Centre (40 North Woodside Rd., Glasgow, G4 9NB, Scotland).

Among institutes in other countries the most significant, perhaps, is the National Biblical, Catechetical, and Liturgical Centre (Post Bag 557, Bangalore-560005, India) under the direction of Rev. D. S. Amalorpavadass. The *East Asian Pastoral Institute, Manila is also an important center.

North America. In Canada an office was established, the National Liturgical Office (90 Parent Avenue, Ottawa, Ontario K1N 7B1) with Rev. Leonard Sullivan, director. In the United States a variety of structures addressed the pastoral liturgical task. The *Liturgical Conference (1221 Massachusetts Avenue N.W., Washington, D.C. 20005) is a voluntary organization addressing the question since 1940. For several years before the Council, the Bishops' Committee on the Liturgical Apostolate functioned within the NCWC. Under the NCCB–USCC, the Bishops' Committee on the Liturgy (BCL) was established in 1965. For 10 years Rev. Frederick R. McManus served as director of the Secretariat of the BCL (1312 Massachusetts Avenue N.W., Washington, D.C. 20005); the present director is Rev. John Rotelle, OSA.

Dioceses across the country established commissions and these have federated and meet annually since 1969. The *Federation of Diocesan Liturgical Commissions (1307 South Wabash Avenue, Chicago, Illinois 60605) provides commissions with guides and aids in pastoral liturgy and is represented on the advisory committee of the BCL. Acamedicians have banded together in the *North American Academy of Liturgy. Academic programs flourish at St. John's University (Collegeville, Minnesota 56321), Notre Dame University (South Bend,

Indiana 46556), The Catholic University of America (Washington, D.C. 20064), The Jesuit School of Theology (1735 LeRoy Avenue, Berkeley, California 94709) and St. Joseph's College (Rensselaer, Indiana 47978).

In this context the BCL recognized the need for major centers of pastoral-liturgical research and designated several existing centers officially. The initial centers designated were the Woodstock Center for Religion and Worship in New York, the Liturgical Studies Program of Notre Dame, and St. John's University in Collegeville. The Woodstock Center functioned from 1969 to 1975. At Notre Dame the Murphy Center for Liturgical Research was established in 1971; this was renamed, in 1977, the Notre Dame Center for Pastoral Liturgy.

In 1971 the BCL designated the Composers' Forum for Catholic Worship which functioned until 1977 (*see* NATIONAL ASSOCIATION OF PASTORAL MUSICIANS). In 1974 the *Mexican American Cultural Center (3019 West French Street, San Antonio, Texas 78228) was designated by the BCL. In 1975 the Center for Pastoral Liturgy was established at The Catholic University of America and was designated by the BCL in 1976.

Bibliography: P. DUPLOYE, *Origines du Centre de Pastorale Liturgique 1943–1949* (Paris 1968). "Centers of Liturgical Research: The United States of America," *Notitiae* 12 (1976) 203–211. *The Assisi Papers.* Proceedings of the First International Congress of Pastoral Liturgy, Assisi-Rome, September 18–22, 1956 (Collegeville 1956).

[R. J. BUTLER]

PASTORAL MINISTRIES

Pastoral ministry involves bringing Christ's Gospel and grace to men and also the promotion of genuine human values *(Directory on the Pastoral Ministry of Bishops,* 103–105; cf. Vatican Council II, *Apostolicam actuositatem* 5). It is a responsibility of all and requires the cooperation of all under the direction of the bishop, who, as leader and minister of the apostolate, is responsible for overall *pastoral planning and coordination.

Priestly Ministries. The ministry of ordained priests is different in kind from that of lay people: priests are coworkers with the bishop and sharers with him in the priesthood; their ministry, like his, involves proclamation of the Word of God through preaching and in other ways, presiding at worship, and serving the Christian and wider community. The specific ministry of priests can take many forms. The 1969–70 study of priests commissioned by the American bishops found that 83 percent of diocesan and 46 percent of religious priests spent at least one day a week in parish work; other works involving at least one day a week for diocesan priests included teaching in grade or high school (18 percent), counseling (16 percent), religious instruction (14 percent), institutional chaplaincies (10 percent), and social work (8 percent). One of every three priests in 1977 was a pastor (a proportion that is increasing as the number of parishes increases and the number of priests declines), and the primary context of pastoral ministry is clearly the parish.

Shared Responsibility for Ministry. As servant-leader of the community, the role of the priest is to be an example of the call of all to servanthood (ministry), to challenge the community to be what it should be, and to evoke leadership from it. Although not all priests are comfortable with the new style of leadership implied for them, shared responsibility for ministry has begun to find expression in new relationships between pastors and other priests, in acceptance of the ministry of the nonordained and in *parish councils. Going beyond the idea of "associate pastors," some dioceses have established team ministries in which more than one priest coequally care for the parish. An objective study of 31 such teams in one diocese found them to be more rewarding to their priest-members than the traditional arrangement, and productive of pastoral care apparently as good or even better than formerly. A broader concept of team ministry includes nonpriests, such as permanent deacons and nonordained persons both women and men, religious and lay, and there has been a growth of such pastoral teams in both parochial and nonparochial settings (e.g., campus ministry, hospitals). Increasing recognition of nonordained ministry is based both on theological grounds and on awareness of the declining number of priests, which could imply great changes at the grass-roots level in the future. Other trends in ministry include an increasing professionalization of ministry (e.g., certification of chaplains, doctor of ministry programs), and increasing recognition of the role of *women in ministry. Most persons in full time ministry are undoubtedly women, especially women religious, who have in particular shown great interest in new pastoral roles as the scope of ministries available to them (e.g., associate pastor in some dioceses) has increased.

See also LAITY, VOCATION OF; MINISTRY (ECCLE-SIOLOGY); MINISTRY, UNORDAINED; PASTORAL PLANNING.

Bibliography: Bishops' Committee on Priestly Life and Ministry, *As One Who Serves: Reflections on the Pastoral Ministry of Priests in the United States* (Washington 1977). Center for Applied Research in the Apostolate (CARA), "Team Ministry: The Hartford Model," Origins 5 (1975) 193–202. Congregation for Bishops, *Directory on the Pastoral Ministry of Bishops* (Ottawa 1974). J. A. CORIDEN, "Laying the Groundwork for Future Ministries," Origins 4 (1974) 401–410. V. JOSEPH and C. PRZYBILLA, "Preparation for New Ministries: A Futuristic View," RevRel 36 (1977) 844–857. F. A. NOVAK, *Stewardship of Time and Talent: A Manual for Lay Ministries* (Washington 1976). Pro Mundi Vita, *New Forms of Ministry in Christian Communities*, Bulletin 50 (1974) 3–95.

[E. M. SULLIVAN]

PASTORAL PLANNING

In the era since Vatican Council II research has enriched the meaning of planning for the many areas of the Church's pastoral mission.

Planning. Planning in general refers to the specification of a preferred future and selection of the means to bring it about. Insofar as they determine what they wish to do and how to do it, people and organizations generally plan, but the term "planning" usually implies a more formalized approach to the development of either a specific plan or the continuing generation of plans. Advantages of plans are that they specify for all what is to be done and how diverse activities are to be brought together in a coherent way to do it. Plans of action also provide a basis for subsequent comparison with what actually happens in order to take timely corrective steps or to improve decision-making and action in the future. Specific plans, however, are less important than a planning system, which gives an organization the capability of ensuring that its activities are continually focused in an integrated way on its essential mission despite internal and external changes. Specific plans are made obsolete by time or events, but a planning system ensures that they are superseded by new ones as needed. Good planning is also based on study and research regarding preferences for the future, the current situation and

trends, and what factors must be dealt with (and in what way) to bring about the desired future if the projection of trends implies a future different from that desired. In recent years government and private organizations—both profit and nonprofit, the latter including dioceses, congregations of religious and entire Protestant denominations—have given increasing attention to planning, often under the direction of an official expressly charged with coordination of planning and using an explicitly prescribed planning system. The evaluation component of a planning system is especially important for nonprofit organizations, which lack the pressures toward effectiveness and efficiency generated by marketplace economics.

Pastoral Planning. Pastoral planning is planning directed toward carrying out the pastoral mission of the Church. The term has been used to describe planning by the bishops collectively (e.g., development of a national pastoral plan opposing abortion), by dioceses, by religious congregations, or by groups of parishes or individual parishes. Some specifically religious reasons given for planning in the Church are that it is good *stewardship; it involves a process of discernment and true asceticism; it builds on the virtue of hope; and its future orientation is an expression of the very nature of the Pilgrim Church.

The specific purpose of applied research in the apostolate is to aid planning. The documents of Vatican II stress such research in support of the pastoral mission of the Church (*Christus Dominus* 17; *Ad gentes* 26, 34, 41; *Gaudium et spes* 62) and in particular urge *mission planning (*Ad gentes* 29). The 1973 *Directory on the Pastoral Ministry of Bishops* not only stresses applied research (102, 141) but also an organized plan or program of united pastoral action in each diocese, which should be collegially drawn up in writing after suitable information has been gathered and trends projected (103-105, 148–150, 209). The report of the American Bishops' Ad Hoc Committee for Priestly Life and Ministry (1973) recommended that dioceses and parishes establish priorities through consultation, research, and planning, and recommended pastoral planning as worthy of further attention by a permanent *Bishops' Committee on Priestly Life and Ministry.

Diocesan Pastoral Planning. The first diocesan planning office in the U.S. was founded within a year of the ending of the Council and followed a city planning model. Several others were founded in the late 1960s with diverse emphases, but in the 1970s there was acceleration in the development of diocesan planning efforts, a growing acceptance of the term "pastoral planning" as distinct from ordinary organizational or administrative planning, and establishment of the National Pastoral Planning Conference (1973). By 1976, a total of 32 American dioceses had a pastoral-research or pastoral-planning office, team, or other unit in operation, most having been founded in 1973 or later. Another 19 dioceses were moving or seemed likely to move in that direction, and yet another 21 were considering it or had expressed interest in the idea—a total of 70 dioceses in all. (A survey of religious major superiors found at least 110 congregations or provinces that reported having a research or planning unit, and another 50 that planned to establish one.)

Objectives. A 1976 study of 28 of the 32 dioceses with notable ongoing research or planning efforts found common characteristics of diocesan pastoral planning to be a holistic concern with the total mission of the Church in the diocese and concern with the implementation of shared responsibility and the mobilization of human resources for fulfillment of that mission. All were (or planned to be) involved in some form of goal-setting, and all but one explicitly emphasized a faith-centered approach to planning, stressing, e.g., the role of prayer, the spirituality of planning. Most frequently cited reason for initiating the effort was the implementation of shared responsibility: planning methods objectify goals and assumptions about the future so that people can deal with them, and hence planning is an appropriate activity for such shared responsibility organs as *pastoral councils and *parish councils. At the same time, setting of objectives (concrete, attainable, measurable goals) is a means of developing a counter-balancing accountability for whether or not goals are realized.

Functioning. The essential role of a diocesan planning office is to ensure that planning for the pastoral mission of the diocese is done, which is different from doing all of the planning itself. The work of the diocesan research and planning offices was found to fall under the following headings: (1) helping the diocese in its overall planning through development of a planning system, helping to establish diocesan priorities, ad hoc consultation to the bishop, etc.; (2) assisting in the development and/or functioning of the diocesan pastoral council; (3) helping parishes through the development of parish goal-setting and renewal programs and parish-council development; and, more generally, (4) helping people learn to work together more effectively. As the last suggests, efforts of pastoral planners bear many similarities to what is termed "organizational development" in secular circles.

Bibliography: Congregation of Bishops, *Directory on the Pastoral Ministry of Bishops* (Ottawa 1974). J. DREHER, "Pastoral Planning for Accountability," Origins 3 (1973) 182–186. L. GELINEAU, "Discoveries in Renewal," Origins 6 (1976) 421–429. J. HOGAN, "Pastoral Directions in a Local Church," Origins 5 (1976) 469–481. J. JADOT, "Effective Pastoral Planning," Origins 4 (1975) 73–75. G. M. POPE and B. QUINN, *Planning for Planning: Perspectives on Diocesan Research and Planning* (Washington, D.C. 1972). E. M. SULLIVAN, *Applied Research and Planning for Mission: The Experience of Catholic Dioceses* (Washington, D.C. 1976); "Diocesan Pastoral Planning Today," Origins 7 (1977) 108–112.

[E. M. SULLIVAN]

PASTORAL PSYCHOLOGY

The earlier *New Catholic Encyclopedia* article (10:1078) clearly set forth the definition of pastoral psychology, its subject matter, goals, and techniques. The present article will attempt to describe recent developments in this field together with some of the theoretical issues that are emerging.

Developments. The most obvious development in pastoral psychology over the past ten years has been its ready acceptance as a legitimate discipline in the field of pastoral care. Nearly all seminaries in the U.S. now require some studies in pastoral psychology and many of them provide opportunities for clinical pastoral education in accredited and supervised settings. It is taken for granted that students for the priesthood need an understanding of personality dynamics in order to minister effectively in the contemporary Church. Moreover, the methods of pastoral psychology are being employed not only to aid parishioners, but likewise in the very formation of priests and religious. Another development is the application to groups of the techniques used in helping individuals. Furthermore, there is a marked tendency to draw upon the writings of Protestant authors in the field of pastoral psychology, many of whom have made this their special area of expertise. There is, finally, a growing sophistication in this discipline among both Catholic and Protestant writers. Thus, there is a clearer awareness that psychology itself is not a monolithic discipline with a single body of scientifically verified data about human behavior. Rather, there are various "schools" within psychology, all attempting to explain phenomena that are often unclear and even contradictory. This has forced pastoral psychology to rethink some of its assumptions and to be cautious about making uncritical applications of psychology to pastoral care. This issue will be taken up at the end of the article.

Techniques. Though the discipline of psychology clearly has relevance for both liturgy and religious education, this discussion will be limited to three contemporary movements in pastoral care: counseling, discernment of spirits, and group dynamics.

Pastoral Counseling. Counseling continues to be an important service Catholics seek from their pastoral minister (whether priest, religious, or lay person). In accord with Vatican Council II's emphasis on personal freedom and responsibility, the minister is seen less as one who gives advice and solutions, and more as one who enables the counselee to gain self-understanding and come to a solution on the basis of available options. In this process, moral and spiritual values are not neglected, but are brought fully into the context of the counselee's life situation. This need not be a lengthy process and current literature in the field highlights the validity of short-term pastoral counseling (see Clinebell, 1966; Curran; Kennedy). There is, moreover, a growing tendency to connect pastoral counseling with spiritual direction. Since the minister is frequently called upon to do both (sometimes with the same individual), an understanding of the similarities and differences between the two functions is most useful. Another development has been the adaptation of general pastoral counseling methods to such specific problem areas as premarital pregnancy, alcoholism, marriage counseling, grief, and terminal illness (see Clinebell, 1976; Dicks).

Discernment of Spirits. One of the early insights of scientific psychology was that religious behavior can be motivated by distortions and conflicts within the personality as well as by authentic spiritual strivings. Thus, a given religious idea or practice (or a network of them) might be either consistent with wholesome human development or deviant from it. A major task of pastoral psychology, then, has been to aid in the differentiation of healthy from unhealthy forms of religious behavior and to develop adequate criteria for making this differentiation. It is important for pastoral ministers to be able to distinguish, for example, between true and false religious conversion, between normal and neurotic guilt, between genuine mystical experiences and ecstatic states produced by mind-expanding drugs, between authentic religious commitment and mere formalism or conformity. A considerable body of literature in this area has been produced in the past decade, much of it in *The Journal of Religion and Health* and *The Journal of Pastoral Care* (see also Oates; Pable). In classic theological terms, the question being addressed is: "Is this person being moved by divine grace or by some other influence, such as egoism, self-deception, or the spirit of evil?" This task has also been extended to the discernment of vocation (*see* VOCATION, PSYCHOLOGY OF). In the recent decade, more and more seminaries and religious communities have made use of psychological testing and interviewing in order to assess more clearly the candidate's motivation and fitness for choosing priesthood or religious life (see Coville et al.; Rulla).

Group Dynamics. Perhaps the most controversial development in pastoral psychology has been the increased utilization of group-dynamics techniques in spiritual formation and in pastoral care. Within psychology itself the study of small-group processes moved rapidly in this decade from the academic laboratory to the popular arena, usually in the form of "sensitivity training" or "group encounter" sessions. Seminaries and religious communities were quick to see in these techniques some possibilities for overcoming the impersonalism and artificial barriers often found in institutional settings. At times these techniques, which called for a high level of self-revelation, were felt to be threatening and coercive. More recently, however, the approach has been modified to emphasize training in communication skills to foster mutual support and deal with interpersonal conflict. These skills include trust formation, empathic listening, self-disclosure, expression of emotions as well as ideas, giving and receiving support, and constructive confrontation (see Egan). Meanwhile, group dynamics were being implemented in lay renewal movements within the Church, e.g., *Cursillo, *Marriage Encounter. At present there has been no large-scale effort to adapt these techniques to the traditional parish structure. Some parishes, however, are drawing upon the experience of Protestant Churches in ministering to groups with particular needs—high school youth, single adults, the separated and divorced, the bereaved, the elderly. People who are undergoing crisis or transition in life are helped to form "growth groups" in which they can find creative ways of dealing with their situation (see Clinebell, 1972; Reid).

Critical Reflection. In the past decade it has become clearer that neither theology nor pastoral care can afford to ignore the data of the behavioral sciences. The converse, however, has also become apparent: the behavioral sciences cannot provide adequate answers for theological and pastoral questions. The reason for this was stated above: the data of these sciences is often tentative and uncertain. Hence, pastoral psychology cannot be the bare application of psychological findings to pastoral problems. Rather, its method must be critical and dialectical: pastoral ministry must allow its assumptions and techniques to be critiqued by psychology; at the same time, because it is anchored in theology, pastoral ministry is able to critique psychology and to raise questions that are beyond the scope of psychology. Psychology may be able to demonstrate that a certain counseling method is more effective in increasing an individual's self-awareness, but it cannot say whether self-awareness is the highest or the only value in human experience. In the dialogue between theology and psychology the two disciplines must retain their autonomy, lest they slip into a careless sort of reductionism. Finally, students of pastoral psychology are coming to realize that psychological dynamics alone are insufficient to understand human behavior and that individuals are deeply affected by the societal context in which they live. As a result, pastoral psychology is being complemented by the study of "pastoral sociology," the study of social and cultural conditions as they affect the faith life of Christians. This trilateral analysis of the human condition—theological, psychological, and sociological—can be seen as the natural, predictable outcome of the principles enunciated in the documents of Vatican Council II.

Bibliography: H. CLINEBELL, *Basic Types of Pastoral Counseling* (Nashville 1966); *The People Dynamic* (N.Y. 1972), H. CLINEBELL, ed., "Creative Pastoral Care and Counselling Series" (Philadelphia 1976–). W. COVILLE et al., *Assessment of Candidates for the Religious Life* (Washington 1968). C. A. CURRAN, *Religious Values in Counseling and Psychotherapy* (New York 1969). R. DICKS, ed., "Successful Pastoral Counseling Series" (Philadelphia 1967). G. EGAN, *Face to Face* (Monterey 1973). E. KENNEDY, *On Becoming a Counselor* (New York 1977). W. OATES, *When Religion Gets Sick* (Philadelphia 1971); *The Psychology of Religion* (Waco, Texas 1973). M. PABLE, "Religion: Healthy and Unhealthy," *The Priest* 33 (1977) 19–22. C. REID, *Groups Alive—Church Alive* (N.Y. 1969). L. RULLA, *Depth Psychology and Vocation* (Chicago 1971).

[M. PABLE]

PATRISTICS

Patristics (patrology; 10:1112), the study of the literature of Christian antiquity, has been marked by modest but solid advances. Not only do older series of texts and translations continue, but new series (*Corpus Christianorum: Series graeca; Oxford Early Christian Texts*) have appeared, together with new or more readily accessible research tools (e.g. G. W. H. Lampe, ed., *Patristic Greek Lexicon*, the Strasbourg Centre's *Biblia patristica*, indexing biblical citations and allusions in early Christian writers). Of unparalleled importance is the long-delayed publication of the texts and translations of the Gnostic writings of Nag Hammadi in Egypt, providing firsthand evidence of the range of Gnostic ideas opposed by so many Church Fathers, and now allowing some of the material to be seen more accurately as a development of traditions to be found in the NT and earlier (e.g. the collections of the "sayings" of Jesus).

Among the emphases of recent historical scholarship have been: less interest in using the Fathers as supports for particular theological or ecclesiological positions; greater concern for understanding than for the application of such categories as "orthodox" and "heritical"; increased sophistication in the exploratory use of philosophical, psychological, and sociological analytical tools to deepen and freshen that understanding; heightened sensitivity to and appreciation of the rich diversity revealed in early Christian literature, not only among the Fathers but also between them and their opponents (many of whose writings have not been preserved); broadened interest in the concrete ways of being human and of being religious of the men and women who produced, read, and preserved (and sometimes destroyed) the writings of the Church of the first few centuries.

Vatican Council II has endorsed the study of the Fathers, pointing to our gaining a deepened sense of how the Scriptures have been used in the Church (*Dei Verbum* 23) and our retrieving a more inclusive, more "ecumenical" spirituality (*Unitatis redintegratio* 15). But Christians have also become more aware of certain other fairly common positions of the patristic era which have contributed to an unfortunate heritage, demanding serious reexamination today. These positions or attitudes of many of the Fathers would include: a pervasive anti-Judaism; an ambivalence toward sexuality and toward the human body; an antifeminism, understandable but regrettable nonetheless; a Christology which only infrequently took adequate account of the humanity of Jesus; and, especially after Constantine, a political and ecclesiastical "triumphalism" of a kind which, since Vatican II, can be more readily acknowledged and transcended.

Bibliography: W. BAUER, *Orthodoxy and Heresy in Earliest Christianity*, R. KRAFT and G. KRODEL, eds. (Philadelphia 1971). P. BROWN, *Augustine of Hippo* (Berkeley 1967). W. J. BURGHARDT, "The Literature of Christian Antiquity," ThSt 24 (1963) 437–463; 33 (1972) 253–284; 37 (1976) 425–455; 38 (1977) 762–767. J. DANIÉLOU, *History of Early Christianity*, 3 v., tr. J. BOWDEN, v. 1, *Theology of Jewish Christianity* (London and Chicago 1964); v. 2, *The Gospel Message and the Hellenistic Culture* (London 1973); v. 3, *Origins of Latin Christianity* (London and Philadelphia 1977). A. GRILLMEIER, *Christ in Christian Tradition*, tr. J. BOWDEN (2d rev. ed. Atlanta 1976). E. HENNECKE, W. SCHNEEMELCHER, and R. MCL. WILSON, eds., *New Testament Apocrypha* 2 v., tr. A. J. B. HIGGINS, et al. (Philadelphia 1963–64). J. N. D. KELLY, *Jerome* (London 1975). J. J. PELIKAN, *The Christian Tradition*, v. 1, *The Emergence of the Catholic Tradition* (Chicago 1971). J. M. ROBINSON, ed., *The Nag Hammadi Library* (Claremont, Cal. 1977). J. M. ROBINSON and H. KOESTER, *Trajectories through Early Christianity* (Philadelphia 1971). M. SIMON, *Verus Israel* (Paris 1948; repr. Paris 1964).

[D. P. EFROYMSON]

PAUL VI, POPE

Pontificate June 21, 1963–Aug. 6, 1978. The Montini papacy, will go down in history as momentous; elected supreme pastor of the Roman Catholic Church and 263rd successor to Peter as bishop of Rome, Pope Paul VI took his place in a line of religious leaders whose dedication to their spiritual obligations was total. Among his predecessors were great saints and acknowledged sinners, men of vision and a few fools. But the vast majority were good men with high religious ideals. Such was Paul VI. Nevertheless, a certain ambiguity stalked his pontificate (11:16; 16:333).

Admirers credited his apparently bifocal attitude toward human progress to his concept of the Church as "in but not of this world." As priest, papal diplomat, Vatican prelate, archbishop of Milan, and pope, Giovanni Battista Montini was a man of clear vision and decisive action. He was also sensitive, of an Italian temperament, extremely intelligent, introspective, reserved, endowed with a keen but quiet sense of humor. He possessed a guardedly effusive penchant for friendship which he had indulged in his younger days, but which he curbed as he mounted the ladder of ecclesiastical preferment. Lacking the ultimate quality of truly great pontiffs—there have been perhaps five or six—, Paul will go down in history as one of the most innovative popes ever to have sat on the chair of the Fisherman. He carried out the evolutionary policies of the two outstanding pontiffs who preceded him, Pius XII (1939–58), whom he served as personal secretary, aid, and advisor, and John XXIII (1958–63), who created him a cardinal, and prepared the way for his selection as pope.

Upon his election Giovanni Battista Montini was confronted with the impossible task of replacing the man, John XXIII, whose passing had been hailed as "a death in the household of mankind." Yet shortly before his death John had indicated that the man who could best carry out the Johannine revolution in the Church was the Cardinal of Milan. In appearance delicate and frail, where John had been robust and hearty, Pope Paul seemed reserved and diffident. But he immediately belied the appearances. Accepting the tremendous responsibility of the spiritual leadership of some 600 million Catholics, he called himself Paul to demonstrate his intention to pursue a vigorous papal policy open to the world. He likewise announced his decision to continue Vatican Council II, setting the date for the opening of the second session of that momentous assembly for Sept. 29, 1963. In word and action he quickly assured the world that it had a new, vigorous pope.

Prepapal Career. Born of a middle-class family in Brescia, Northern Italy, Sept. 26, 1898, Giovanni Battista Montini had a Church-oriented childhood. His father, Giorgio, was a banker and agricultural entrepreneur who controlled a local newspaper, *Il Cittadino*, and championed Catholic causes. His mother, Giudetta, was a delicate but determined activist involved in social and charitable enterprises. Much of young Montini's childhood was directed by his paternal grandmother and aunt. Never robust as a boy, he attended private schools, came under the spiritual and intellectual influence of the Oratorian humanist, Fr. Giulio Bevilacqua (in old age created cardinal by Pope Paul), failed the physical examination when called to the army, and spent most of World War I in charitable activities and studying theology at home, being ordained a priest in 1920.

He registered at the University of Rome in 1921 to take graduate studies in literature, but was quickly matriculated in the Pontifical Academy of Noble Ecclesiastics when Msgr. (later Cardinal) Giuseppe Pizzardo discovered that Montini's father was a member of the Italian parliament. An unforgettable impression was made on the young priest serving in the papal curia from 1924 among fascist-leaning prelates when his father and the Aventine group of parliamentarians were physically assaulted by Mussolini's henchmen. He had his own difficulties with government repression in protecting the Catholic university-students, whom he aided as chaplain and spiritual guide. A man of wide literary and religious interests, he collected the conferences he gave in Catholic circles in three books published as spiritual guides for university graduates before World War II. He translated Jacques Maritain's *Three Reformers* into Italian, developed an ear for classical music, and was a voracious reader with a retentive memory, as Jean Guitton has demonstrated in his book of dialogues with Pope Paul (see Guitton). Limited to curial activities in 1937, Montini's world vision was kept wide as he served as secretary to Cardinal Eugenio Pacelli, accompanying him on a visit to Budapest, and becoming his factotum when the Cardinal-Secretary of State emerged from the conclave of 1939 as Pope Pius XII. During World War II Montini was entrusted with organizing the papal information service for tracing prisoners of war and refugees in league with the international Red Cross and supervising Vatican aid and relief activities. In the postwar period, together with Msgr. Domenico Tardini, Montini presided over the Holy See's internal and external affairs—from 1944, Pius served as his own secretary of state, using the two monsignors as his "inside and outside" men. Montini dealt with the conditions of the war refugees, international migration problems, and aid and rehabilitation projects, using U.S. War Relief Services for direct contact with the United Nations Organizations and the International Refugee Organization. He also supported the bid of the papal nuncio in Paris, Archbishop Angelo Roncalli, to have the Holy See involved with UNESCO despite the antireligious bias of that agency's original staff.

In December 1954, as the result of a power play within the Vatican (Montini had championed a *disimpegno*, a gradual withdrawing of Vatican influence from Italian politics in keeping with the aim of Premier Alcide De Gasperi and Don Luigi Sturzo), he was relieved of his position as personal advisor to Pope Pius and consecrated archbishop of Milan. Though he was "moved up in order to be moved out," his elevation to the See of Milan proved to be a stepping stone on his way to the papacy. It gave him necessary pastoral experience and brought him into close contact with the patriarch of Venice, Angelo Giuseppe Roncalli. When the latter was elected pope in October 1958 as John XXIII, his first move was to make Montini a cardinal.

Pontificate. He lacked John's insouciance, apparent neglect of nonessentials, ebullient humor, and ability to mollify opposition, but Montini had long shared John's vision of a renewal of the Church and the courageous determination to break out of the Vatican and see and be seen by the world. John's journey's were confined to walking tours in Rome, visits to hospitals, jails, orphanges, dying friends, and a train ride to Loreto in the Abruzzi mountains. Paul covered the globe.

Papal Diplomacy. In ten major flights he visited the Holy Land, India, Turkey, the United Nations in New York, Bogotá in Colombia, Kampala in Uganda, and then made a globe trotting voyage to the Phillippines, Australia, Samoa, Indonesia, Hong Kong, and Singapore. He also visited Portugal and Geneva, and crisscrossed Italy from Taranto to Sardinia. On all these occasions he was accompanied by the press, went out of his way to visit poverty-stricken areas, and proved a most accommodating visitor. His one great disappointment was the refusal of the Polish government under Gomulka to welcome him to Warsaw for the thousanth anniversary of the founding of the Polish nation. In 1923 had served the first six months of his diplomatic career in Warsaw and wanted to return to demonstrate his affection for the Polish people. However, the communist rulers, at odds with Cardinal Stefan Wyszyński and most of the nation's Catholics (95 percent of the population), feared his presence would destroy their own credibility. They were correct; the Pope had the satisfaction of seeing the papal proverb, *qui mange le pape en meurt* "who bites the pope, dies of it"), justified with the subsequent fall of the Gomulka regime and the need the new Gierek government felt of enlisting Card. Wysziński's support.

In his dealing with the communist countries, Pope Paul followed John's example, distinguishing between an atheistic ideology that had to be condemned and the working out in the historical order of an economic and political structure that the Church could tolerate. Thus he was able to receive in audience such communist leaders as President Podgorny and Foreign Minister Andre Gromyko of Russia, President Tito of Yugoslavia, Premier Ceausescu of Rumania, and other ministers of the Polish, Hungarian, Rumanian, and Bulgarian governments. Exiles from these lands also were horrified to see the Pope welcome representatives of the Orthodox Churches from countries where Catholics had been violently forced to join these schismatic communions. But Paul was convinced that the good of souls in these regions demanded extraordinary measures and infinite charity, the Pope giving the lead. He was thus able to work out a modus vivendi or détente with all the Iron-Curtain countries except Albania for the restoration of the Catholic hierarchy and the functioning of the Church.

Paul's diplomatic policy did not enjoy the full support of the Roman Curia, nor of a considerable portion of the Church's hierarchy. To exiles from the communist countries he seemed to be selling out their martyred brethren in his attempt to follow John's so-called opening to the left. But from the start of his reign Paul had made overtures to the communist bloc, including continental China. He refused to allow the Fathers of Vatican II to pass condemnations on individuals or nations, thus gravely offending lay and clerical Catholics who had suffered for their faith. The Ukranian cardinal, Josef Slipyj, released from Soviet prison in deference to Pope John in 1962, openly criticized Paul's policies, declaring that in ten years of freedom in Rome he suffered more than in his twenty years in custody in Russia. The Hungarian primate, Cardinal József Mindszenty, who finally left his refuge in the American embassy in Budapest in 1971, defied the papal request that he resign his title as archbishop of Esztergom, forcing the Pope to remove him, in order, as the Vatican stated, to allow for the proper functioning of the Hungarian Church. In general, Paul had followed a policy of accomodation, careful howver to have his voice heard in favor of justice and decency, and against oppression and genocide.

Church Life. Paul's first encyclical, *Ecclesiam suam* (Paths of the Church, 1964), had outlined the proportions of the dialogue he felt it was the Church's duty to conduct with itself, with other Christians, and with believers and nonbelievers of all the world. In his conduct of the Council, he pursued this aim. From the start he championed the idea of clarifying the position of the bishops as successors to the Apostles, and therefore as associated with the pope in a collegial responsibility for the governance of the universal Church. He wanted the Council to produce a clear program of development for the Church tomorrow. Hence he fought for unequivocal declarations on ecumenism, the attitude of Christians toward the Jews, the identification of the Church's spiritual essence with its commitment to the social, economic, and political problems of today's world. In bringing Vatican Council II to a successful close, Dec. 8, 1965, Paul seemed determined to pursue its immediate implementation. Two days before, he had abolished the old Holy Office with its outmoded inquisition and Index of Forbidden Books, replacing this office of moral and doctrinal surveillance with the Congregation for the Doctrine of the Faith. However, he retained the old staff with the conservative "watchdog," Card. Alfredo Ottaviani, at its head. Then instead of taking advantage of the momentum created by the Council's activities, he was persuaded to slow down its implementation. A man intent on precise and orderly administrative procedures, Paul evidently felt that the less theologically-aware and more staid members of the Church should not be exposed to the shock of immediate change in the liturgy, new attitudes in approaches to non-Christians, and a fundamental reorientation in seminary training, the religious life, and the overall workings of the everyday Church.

Instant historians are convinced that this sudden change of pace was a fatal mistake. It disappointed activists within the Church who had been reading the conciliar documents and preparing for swift action. Paul's calculated risk in declaring a *vacatio legis*—a cooling-off period—resulted in a reaction whereby adventuresome clerics and laity broke out with innumerable experiments in the liturgy, a worldwide series of confrontations with bishops, revolt in the seminaries and within religious orders and societies. These people had jumped to the conclusion that the Council's constitutions and decrees promulgated by pope and bishops now constituted the mind of the Church. They attempted to force a showdown between traditionalists and innovators. Thus, much of Paul's pontificate was plagued with rebellious actions, leading him frequently to deplore the fact that the pope was not being obeyed. His habit of touching on all aspects of a question in his sermons and speeches worsened his public image, for the press invariably reported a pessimistic sentence or paragraph as characteristic of his attitude, whereas his message was usually uplifting and hopeful.

Paul's vigorous but orderly pursuit of the reform of the Roman *Curia will certainly be one of his most important achievements. One of his first acts was to abolish the old Roman aristocracy, telling its members, many of whom were involved in social scandals, that the Church could no longer do anything for them. He reduced the pomp and circumstance of Vatican protocol. Gone are the flamboyant retinues, the papal zouaves and guards, the glittering ceremonial that accompanied papal functions in St. Peter's or in the reception of political luminaries. The Pope appeared in elegant but modest robes, carrying a reed-like crozier on liturgical occasions, accompanied by a few necessary attendants, usually on foot. During the fuel shortage, he drove to the Lateran basilica in a horse-drawn carriage. And in his visits to local parishes he tried to get as close to the people as possible.

Through the apostolic constitution *Regimini Ecclesiae universae* (1967) and the motu proprio *Pontificalis domus* (1968), five years after assuming the papal office, Paul had radically changed the complexion of the administration of the Curia (*see* PAPAL HOUSEHOLD). He reduced the number of Italian heads of curial congregations—the equivalent of cabinet offices—to four; brought in a Frenchman, Cardinal Jean Villot, as papal secretary of state; appointed a Yugoslav, Cardinal Franjo Seper, as prefect of the Congregation for the Doctrine of the Faith; a Brazilian, Cardinal Agnelo Rossi, as prefect of the Congregation for Evangelization; an American, Cardinal John Wright, as prefect of the Congregation for the Clergy; and a Canadian, Cardinal Maurice Roy, as head of both the Secretariat for the Laity and the Pontifical Commission for Justice and Peace. He introduced rulings to force bishops to retire at seventy-five; limited curial appointments to five years without the right to reappointment; and, before departing for the Far East in December 1970, he decreed that cardinals,

on reaching their eightieth birthday, were excluded from voting in papal elections, at once eliminating twenty-five members of the sacred college.

Meanwhile, in keeping with recommendations of the Council, he had summoned the International Assemblies of the Synod of Bishops that in 1967, 1969, 1971, 1974, and 1977 brought to the Vatican diocesan bishops from around the world to discuss and help settle specific problems facing the postconciliar Church. Elected by national or regional episcopal conferences, these prelates convened with the heads of the curial offices under the guidance of the Pontiff. In 1967 they decided that heresy was not an immediate danger; in 1969 they discussed the use and abuse of authority; and in 1971, they dealt with priestly ministry and problems of social and economic justice; in 1974 and 1977 they treated of the Church's call to evangelization and its catechetical practices. To give permanency to the Synodal assemblies, Pope Paul instituted a Synodal Secretariat in Rome, to which fifteen prelates selected by the bishops on a revolving basis were attached and given the task of implementing former and preparing the agenda for future synods.

In his creation of cardinals, Pope Paul attempted to give the Church a truly international look. He made cardinals in such sparsely Catholic areas as Karachi, Pakistan; Osaka, Japan; Nairobi, Kenya; Seoul, Korea; Brazzaville, Congo; and Apia, in the Samoan Islands.

Paul defused a series of confrontations posed by the progressive wing of the Dutch Church, by individual theologians such as Hans Küng and Ivan Illich, and by priest-groups in Latin America, Europe, and Italy. He gave no encouragement to rightist movements and opposed so-called Catholic countries, such as Spain, Portugal, Brazil, for their intransigently capitalistic attitudes. He removed the conservative Cardinal Giuseppe Siri of Genoa, from chairmanship of the Italian episcopal conference and gave free rein to the conference's deliberations.

Although at the start of his reign, curial officials did interfere in Italian political affairs, he gradually withdrew. While clearly enunciating the Church's opposition to divorce, he did not intervene directly in the battle over Italy's divorce law. Concerned with the sad state of his own Diocese of Rome, Paul induced the archbishop of Spoleto, Ugo Poletti, to head the Vicariate of Rome and, on making him cardinal, gave him *carte blanche* to do a radical job of pastoral reorganization.

Although offended by the stance taken by the Belgian cardinal, Leo J. Suenens, who in 1969 demanded a more profound implementation of the Council, reform in the selection of bishops, and a democratization of papal elections, Paul did prepare the way for a new elective system. He suggested, but did not carry into practice, the possibility that bishops who were not cardinals, but had been elected members of the Secretariat for the Synod of Bishops, and non-cardinal patriarchs of the Oriental Churches be allowed to vote in a papal election (*see* POPE, ELECTION OF). This move pointed to a democratization of the Church's hierarchical structure and could be used in a future federation with the Oriental Orthodox and the Protestant Churches.

Paul's reputation as a progressive pope was seriously damaged by his Credo of the People of God (*Sollemni hac liturgia*) in 1968 with its conservative theology, his encyclical *Humanae vitae* (1968) outlawing artificial means of birth control, and his decision to hold the line on clerical celibacy for the Western Church in the encyclical *Sacerdotalis caelibatus* (1967). While he favored the participation of women in ecclesiastical offices and decision making, he strenuously opposed their ordination to the diaconate or priesthood. On all these issues he felt that as the supreme pastor his obligation was to preserve the Church's ancient traditions. In the birth-control decision Paul went against the official advice of a papal commission on population and family life, and raised the charge that he was indifferent to the miseries of individual married couples and the unfed masses of mankind. While he did back the few bishops who severely disciplined priests for opposing the encyclical, Paul did not indulge in such condemnations himself. While he seemed to feel a mystical need to uphold the Church's pro-natalist position, he did little to curb the episcopal conferences that broadly interpreted the pastoral teaching of the encyclical itself, stating that the Pope proposed a high ideal, but that if in conscience people could not live up to that ideal, they should not consider themselves in sin. This was the stand not only of the Dutch, Mexican, and Canadian bishops, but of the French and Italian as well. Paul's concern for traditional papal authority and the right to life confused his attitude toward the problem of overpopulation. He ran the risk of having the Church accused of failing mankind at a crucial crisis. He did call for a "rational control of births" insisting on the right of parents and not governments to decide the number of children they should have. On the tenth anniversary of the encyclical in July 1978, he maintained he had made a correct decision, but cautioned pastors and confessors to a pastoral implementation of the teaching.

Human Betterment and Peace. Paul's progressive attitudes are revealed in his encyclical On the Development of Peoples (*Progressio populorum*, 1967) and his apostolic letter, A Call to Action (*Octogesima adveniens*, 1971). These were radical documents, dealing with the world's social, economic, and political structures. Not merely did he deplore war—at the UN Assembly in New York, he cried: "No more war! War, never again!"—but he condemned injustice, governmental violence, and economic exploitation. He said plainly that governments that supported economic systems, keeping the majority of their people in degradation, were guilty of violence. Asked in Bogotá if this meant that the revolutionary overthrow of such regimes was justified, he replied that "violence was not in keeping with the Gospel." Pope Paul did condemn the use of torture, the deprivation of human rights, and the continued exploitation of the poor in Latin America, where for centuries the Church was identified with the establishment. In Kampala, Uganda he called for the Africanization of the Church. He warned against the possibility of genocide after the civil war in Nigeria, condemned the savagery of civil strife in Uganda, and showed great displeasure over the failure of the American bishops to follow his lead in condemning the bombardment of Vietnam. Following his trip to the Holy Land in 1964, he showed a nuanced attitude toward the State of Israel. He welcomed Golda Meir and Jewish leaders to the Vatican, called for a special status for Jerusalem, but did not accept diplomatic relations with Israel, mainly out of deference to the Oriental Rite Catholics—Copts, Maronites, and Melchites—headquartered in the Arab countries. On most theological matters, Paul followed a traditional line. Nevertheless, he strongly encouraged ecumenical relations with other Churches and religious, himself praying with their leaders.

Paul VI died suddenly on Sunday evening, Aug. 6, 1978, in his summer residence at Castelgondolfo, of heart failure. Behind him he left a legacy of change such as had not been accomplished by any of his predecessors in a thousand years. In updating the Church, he seemed to consider his function as similar to that of Moses, leading his people to the brink of the promised land—Pope John's "reducing of the Church to the simple structure it had when it left the hands of Christ." But Paul VI was too much of a Roman to take the Church into the twenty-first century. That task he was content to leave to his successors.

Bibliography: J. GUITTON, *The Pope Speaks: Dialogue with Jean Guitton*, tr. A. and C. FREMANTLE (New York 1968). PAUL VI, *Teachings of Pope Paul VI 1968–1975*, 9 v. (Vatican City, 1968–1975; USCC Publ. Office, Washington, D.C.).

[F. X. MURPHY]

PAX CHRISTI

Pax Christi is the International Catholic Movement for Peace founded after World War II by Bishop Théas of Lourdes to promote reconciliation between the French and Germans. The organization, which is recognized by the Holy See, has fourteen national sections and is rapidly expanding to Third-World nations. The international movement is concerned with disarmament, East-West relations, and social justice. Its headquarters are in Antwerp, Belgium and Bishop Luigi Bettazi of Ivrea, Italy is International President with Cardinal Bernard Alfrink as Honorary President.

Pax Christi was organized in the U.S. in 1973 "to establish peacemaking as a priority for the American Catholic Church." It is composed of bishops, laity, priests, and religious and has as its priorities nuclear and general disarmament, the primacy of conscience in relation to the draft and military spending, the creation of a just world-order, the examination of militarism in Catholic education, and the creation of Christian alternatives to violence. Auxiliary Bishop Thomas Gumbleton of Detroit is President of Pax Christi, U.S.A. (1234 Washington Blvd., Detroit, Michigan 48226).

[J. J. FAHEY]

PEACE, INTERNATIONAL

While the Church has been involved in the problem of international peace for the past two millennia, its teachings on this subject have never been so complete and explicit as in the past thirty years (10:38). Pope Pius XII, who spoke often on international peace, stated the basis for a Catholic perspective on international relations: "Order between political communities must be built upon the unshakable and unchangeable rock of the moral law, made manifest in the order of nature by the Creator Himself and by Him engraved on the hearts of men with letters that may never be effaced..." (Radio Message, Christmas Eve, 1941, ActApS 34 [1942] 16). Today the Church continues to base its hopes for international peace on the natural law and the biblical vocation to prophetic justice and charity. The following themes are the salient principles of the Catholic view on international peace.

(1) *A redeemed human nature is the basis of the search for peace.* While the Church fully recognizes the sin that exists in human nature it also holds that the centrality of God's creation and Christ's redemption can bring about a more perfect world. In the words of Vatican Council II: "But only God, who created man to His own image and ransomed him from sin, provides a fully adequate answer to these questions. This He does through what He has revealed in Christ His Son, who became man. Whoever follows after Christ, the perfect man, becomes himself more of a man" (*Gaudium et spes* 41).

(2) *Peace is a positive concept which implies justice and development.* Whereas the word *pax* connotes an essentially negative definition of peace, the Hebrew word *shalom* means total spiritual and physical development: "Peace is not merely the absence of war. Nor can it be reduced solely to the maintenance of a balance of power between enemies. Nor is it brought about by dictatorship. Instead, it is rightly and appropriately called 'an enterprise of justice' (Is 32.7). Peace results from that harmony built into human society by its divine Founder, and actualized by men as they thirst after ever greater justice" (ibid. 78). Pope Paul VI echoed these words in his encyclical on human development under the theme, "Development is the new name for peace" (Paul VI PopProgr 76–80).

(3) *Negotiation—not war—should be the means of settling disputes.* John XXIII stated that "men are becoming more and more convinced that disputes which arise between states should not be resolved by recourse to arms, but rather by negotiation" (John XXIII PacTerr 126). This teaching is also found in *Gaudium et spes* (80–82) and was the entire theme of Pope Paul VI's historic address (Oct. 4, 1965) to the United Nations (see bibliog.). The Church, however, does not rule out "the right to legitimate defense once every means of peaceful settlement has been exhausted" and holds that soldiers can make a "genuine contribution to the establishment of peace" as long as they are "agents of security and freedom" (*Gaudium et spes* 79). However, the 1971 Synod of Bishops stated: "It is absolutely necessary that international conflicts should not be settled by war . . ." and called for "a strategy of nonviolence" as well as the recognition of conscientious objection in each nation (Synod JustWorld p. 49).

(4) *Total war is condemned.* The Fathers of Vatican II sought to "undertake an evaluation of war with an entirely new attitude" and stated: "Any act of war aimed indiscriminately at the destruction of entire cities or of extensive areas along with their population is a crime against God and man himself. It merits unequivocal and unhesitating condemnation" (*Gaudium et spes* 80). This, the only condemnation of Vatican II was recently stated again in the testimony of the Holy See to the United Nations on disarmament (submitted on May 7, 1976; see bibliog.).

(5) *The arms race is condemned.* The Fathers of Vatican II called the arms race "an utterly treacherous trap for humanity, and one which injures the poor to an intolerable degree" (*Gaudium et spes* 81). While the Fathers did not specifically condemn the possession of scientific weapons for deterrence they did observe that deterrence "is not a safe way to perserve a steady

peace" (ibid. 81). Further, the testimony of the Holy See to the United Nations (1976) condemns the arms race, calling it a "perversion of peace" (Holy See 48) and concerning deterrence states that "the present situation of would-be security is to be condemned" (ibid. 49). The Vatican testimony also refers to the arms race as "*in itself an act of aggression* against those who are the victims of it. It is an act of aggression which amounts to a crime, for *even then they are not used*, by their cost alone *armaments kill the poor by causing them to starve*" (ibid. 47).

(6) *Disarmament is the path to peace.* Pope John urged that "the arms race should cease; that the stockpiles which exist in various countries should be reduced equally and simultaneously by the parties concerned; that nuclear weapons should be banned; and that a general agreement should eventually be reached about progressive disarmament and an effective method of control" (John XXIII PacTerr 112). This sentiment was also expressed in *Gaudium et spes* (82), in *Justice in the World* (p. 49), in Pope Paul's various World Day of Peace messages, as well as in the 1976 testimony of the Holy See to the United Nations: "We must find substitutes for war, by providing alternative wars to be won. Disarmament is inseparable from the other goals of unity, justice, harmony, and development of the whole 'human family.' The victory of disarmament is none other than the victory of peace" (Holy See 55).

(7) *An international public authority must be established to foster true international peace.* It is the Church's view that there can be no true international peace, security, justice, or disarmament without a public authority to pursue these goals through cooperation and trust. John XXIII called for the creation of such an authority: "A public authority, having worldwide power and endowed with the proper means for the efficacious pursuit of its objective . . . must be set up by common accord and not imposed by force" (John XXIII PacTerr 138). It is John's view that this public authority is an implementation of the principle of subsidiarity: "This means that the public authority of the world community must tackle and solve problems of an economic, social, political, or cultural character which are posed by the universal common good" (ibid. 140). Vatican II reiterated the Pope's view: "Hence it is now necessary for the family of nations to create for themselves an order which corresponds to modern obligations, particularly with reference to those numerous regions still laboring under intolerable need" (*Gaudium et spes* 84). Paul VI as well called for the creation of a world authority. "With all Our heart, We encourage these (international) organizations which have undertaken this collaboration for the development of peoples of the world, and Our wish is that they grow in prestige and authority. 'Your vocation' as We said to the representatives of the United Nations in New York, 'is to bring not some people but all peoples to treat each other as brothers . . . . Who does not see the necessity of thus establishing progressively a world authority, capable of acting effectively in the juridical and political sectors?'" (Paul VI PopProgr 78). The 1971 Synod of Bishops also endorsed the UN and international organizations because "they are the beginning of a system capable of restraining the armaments race, discouraging trade in weapons, securing disarmament and settling conflicts by

peaceful methods of legal action, arbitration and international police action" (Synod JustWorld p. 49).

In these and other Church statements there is clear opposition to war as a sure method of attaining peace. Rather, international peace must be built up by following the mandates of natural law, the biblical quest for peace with justice, economic and political justice, and the creation of a global authority which alone can mediate conflicts between nations in a nonviolent manner—a manner consistent with the Peace of Christ.

Bibliography: J. J. FAHEY, *The Arms Race and the Church: A Theological Pastoral Reflection* (Pax Christi Publ., New York 1977). HOLY SEE, "The Role of the United Nations and Disarmament" (1976 Testimony to the UN), *Catholic Mind* 75 (April 1977) 46–55; also in *Pope Speaks* 22 (1977) 243–259. G. and P. MISCHE, *Toward a Human World Order* (New York 1977). PAUL VI, "Address to the General Assembly of the United Nations," *Pope Speaks* 11 (1965) 47–57; World Day of Peace Messages, *Pope Speaks* 12 (1967) 329–330; 14 (1969) 311–315; 16 (1971) 349–352; 17 (1972–73) 11–15; 18 (1973) 352–356; 19 (1974–75) 341–346; 22 (1977) 38–45; 23 (1978) 35–41.

[J. J. FAHEY]

PEEBLES, BERNARD MANN

American classicist and patrologist, b. Norfolk, Jan. 1, 1906, d. Washington, D.C., Nov. 22, 1976. He was the son of John Kevan Peebles and Sallie Feild Mann. He was educated at Hampden-Sydney College and the University of Virginia (A.B., 1926), Harvard University (M.A., 1928, Ph.D., 1940). From 1932–34 he was a Fellow in the School of Classical Studies at the American Academy in Rome and he was received into the Catholic Church at that time. He taught at the University of Virginia, 1928–29; Fordham University, 1934–35; 1939–41; Harvard, 1937–39; St. John's College, Annapolis, Md. 1941–48; The Catholic University of America, 1948–1971. He took a leave of absence from St. John's College, 1942–45, for duty in the U.S. Army. He was staff sergeant in the European Theatre of Operations, mainly as chief clerk, Subcommission for Monuments, Fine Arts, and Archives, Allied Commission, Italy. He was decorated with the Bronze Star (U.S.) and the British Empire Medal.

Peebles was chairman of the department of Greek and Latin at Catholic University, 1962–70, retired from full time teaching in 1971, but remained active in teaching and editorial capacities. He was editor of *The Fathers of the Church*, series (1968–), an editor of *Traditio*, a member of the American Philological Association, the Mediaeval Academy of America, the Archaeological Institute of America, The Renaissance Society of America, the Association d'études patristiques, the Catholic Commission on Intellectual and Cultural Affairs. He was also an officer of the Patristic Society of North America (Committee on Awards). His specialty was classical and medieval Latin and patristics and he published many papers in those fields and a book, *The Poet Prudentius* (New York, 1951) (Boston College Candlemas Lectures). He contributed as coeditor with E. K. Rand to *Servianorum in Vergilii carmina commentariorum* v. 2 (Lancaster, Pa. 1946) (American Philological Monographs). His interest in Sulpicius Severus' *Vita Sancti Martini* extended from his first publication in 1934 to a posthumous publication in *Paradoxis* (New York 1977). His translation, *Life of St. Martin, Letters, Dialogues* in *Fathers of the Church*, v. 7 (New York 1949) 77–254 is by far one of the better translations of that series. He was hailed by many scholars to be the world's authority on St. Martin of Tours.

He was mild mannered, with a passion for exactness of language, led a simple life in the Washington inner city, made many friends with the common people, loved by all alike. At the time of his murder at the hands of a street assailant he was working on the definitive edition of Sulpicius Severus for the *Corpus Christianorum*. He had been a Benedictine Oblate and was buried in the habit in the family plot in Petersburg, Virginia.

Bibliography: G. MARC'HADOUR, "In Memoriam Bernard Mann Peebles (d. 22 Nov. 1976)," *Moreana* 14 (1977) 79–88.

[R. T. MEYER]

PENAL LAW, DRAFT OF

From 1966 to 1970 a committee of the Pontifical Commission for the Revision of Canon Law worked on a revision of penal law. A draft of revised canons was sent to the bishops for evaluation in December 1973.

The draft contained three sections: (1) *Praenotanda* articulating its key orientations and changes from the CIC; (2) a proposed motu propio, *Humanum consortium*, introducing the canons; and (3) 73 canons, of which 47 dealt with offenses and penalties in general and 26 with penalties for specific offenses.

Key Points. The following key points were affirmed in the *Praenotanda* and in *Humanum consortium*. Penal law is necessary in the Church as in any well-ordered society. Yet ecclesial penalties are unique, given the Church's salvific character. They are geared to preserving the Church's spiritual-moral integrity and fostering the good of the one violating Church law.

There have been different understandings of the significance of Church penalties historically. The draft attempts to be faithful to Vatican Council II principles and respond to changing pastoral needs.

Pastoral considerations call for the application of penalties only as a last resort when other legal-pastoral remedies have failed. Such penalties are not to be destructive of persons but rather are to respect human dignity and rights. Church authority should be pastorally sensitive in dealing with violators of the law.

The number of penalties is significantly reduced. Likewise they are confined to the external forum thereby minimizing conflict between the fora.

The draft views a certain legal uniformity as advantageous. Yet it is unnecessary that all offenses be specified in universal law. The principle of subsidiarity suggests that universal law clarify only those offenses so incompatible with the Christian life as to require uniform punishment, everywhere.

Evaluation. The *Canon Law Society of America's evaluation of the draft is both positive and negative. Positively speaking, the draft is less legalistic than the CIC. *Humanum consortium* at least attempts a theological rationale of the law. The simplification and reduction of penalties, their limitation to the external forum and their use only as a last resort are pastorally beneficial. The provision of greater options for legislators below the universal level is helpful.

Negatively speaking, however, there are notable methodological and substantive objections to the draft. Methodologically problematic are the lack of broad consultation in the draft's formulation and the extremely short time (3 months) allotted the bishops for evaluation. Furthermore, it is difficult to evaluate penal law apart from the other revised drafts as yet unpublished.

Substantively speaking the draft assumes the validity of penal law whereas changed circumstances require a persuasive theological rationale. Simplifying and reducing penalties are pastorally insufficient. Rather the continuing viability of penal institutes such as *latae sententiae* penalties must be reassessed. The protection afforded individual believers seems inadequate, e.g. absence of clear statement of exigencies of due process before application of penalties; present tribunal inadequacies in terms of personnel and resources. Furthermore, changing socio-cultural-theological patterns suggest more extensive investigation of the practical efficacy of Church penalties today.

The Code Commission committee is presently reworking the draft in light of the comments received from around the world. Hence promulgation of the revised penal law has been delayed indefinitely.

Bibliography: Official Documents: Pontificia Commissio Codici Juris Canonici Recognoscendo, *Schema documenti quo disciplina sanctionum seu poenarum in Ecclesia Latina denuo ordinatur* (Vatican City 1973); *Communic* 2 (1970) 99–107; 194–195; 8 (1976) 166–183; 9 (1977) 147–174 (reports on work of committee on penal law reform).
Commentaries: T. GREEN, "The Future of Penal Law in the Church," *Jurist* 35 (1975) 212–275; et al, "Report of Canon Law Society Task Force," ProcCLSA (1974) 130–140. V. DE PAOLIS, "Animadversiones ad Schema documenti quo disciplina sanctionum seu poenarum in Ecclesia Latina denuo ordinatur," PeriodicaMorCanLiturg 63 (1974) 489–507. J. PROVOST, "Revision of Book V of the Code of Canon Law," StCan 9 (1975) 135–152. A. SCHEURMANN, "Das Schema 1973 für das Kommende kirkliche Strafrecht," *Archiv für katholisches Kirchenrecht* 143 (1974) 3–63.
[T. J. GREEN]

PENAL POWER OF THE CHURCH

The most significant statement about penal power in the Church (11:68) since the Vatican Council II is the 1973 *Schema* or draft of the revision of Canon Law on crime and punishment in the Church.

Meaning. The introduction to the *Schema* argues that every visible, human society has penal law. The Church, as a society, is entitled to penal law, but this must be accommodated to this specific type of society. The possibility for such a penal law is demonstrated from the practice of St. Paul, the tradition of the Church, and the concern of recent popes.

Three specific purposes for Church penal law are listed. (1) The Church is concerned with the total good of its children, since it is a society of the supernatural order. (2) It is concerned not only with communicating this good to them, but also with conserving them in the way of salvation and keeping them from leaving it. (3) The Church is also concerned for the restoration of good order when it has been violated.

This penal power is expressed by certain deterrent types of penalties or censures; and in "expiatory" punishments, formerly known as vindictive, to repair the social order.

The *Schema* views the exercise of penal power in pastoral rather than governmental terms. What this means in practice is to be determined according to the situation of various peoples, since the relative seriousness of various actions varies according to cultural and social factors.

Unresolved Issues. The document leaves unresolved several underlying issues which are currently debated on the penal power of the Church.

1. *The Basis of Penal Power.* The underlying basis for penal law given in the *Schema* is the societal nature of the Church. The document does not appeal to the power to "bind and loose," whose significance for penal power is questioned by exegetes and theologians. However, the societal concept of Church is itself questionable as the basis for ecclesiastical law, in light of Pope Paul's Feb. 8, 1973 speech to the Roman Rota (ActApS 65 [1973] 93–103; cf. *Lumen gentium* 8–9). The Pope emphasized the Church as the Sacrament of Christ, saw juridical activity of the Church in terms of the sign of the Sacrament of Salvation, and stressed the juridical aspect of the Church must manifest and be of service to the life of the Spirit lived by the faithful. The implications of the sacramental rather than societal approach have not been worked out in the area of penal law.

2. *Nature.* The nature of penal power in the Church is described in legal terms, but in practice this power is exercised more in a family or military sense. This continues to raise questions on whether the penal power is limited by requirements of due process; on the meaning of "scandal," a key element in the application of penalties; and on the role of automatic penalties (*latae sententiae*).

3. *Extent.* The extension of penal power in the 1917 CIC applied to both internal and external fora. The 1973 *Schema* restricts penal power to the external forum. Yet many claim it fails to come to grips with Vatican II's statements on freedom of conscience and the right to public expression of opinion, and with the principle of legitimate diversity proposed in ecumenical dialogue. The relationship of the internal and external fora is debated among canonists and the solution offered by the *Schema* appears unacceptable because it leads to sacramental and ecclesiological paradoxes.

Bibliography: PAUL VI, "Address to the Roman Rota," *Jurist* 34 (1974) 1–9. Pontificia Commissio Codici Iuris Canonici Recognoscendo, *Schema documenti quo disciplina sanctionum seu peonarum in Ecclesia Latina denuo ordinatur* (Vatican 1973) (*reservatum*). Coetus studiorun de Iure Poenali *Communic* 7 (1975) 93–97; 8 (1976) 166–183; 9 (1977) 147–174. T. J. GREEN, "Future of Penal Law in the Church," *Jurist* 35 (1975) 212–275.
[J. H. PROVOST]

PENANCE (RITE)

The mandate for the reform of the Sacrament of Penance is contained in the Constitution on the Sacred Liturgy of Vatican Council II: "The rite and formulae of Penance are to be revised so that they more clearly express both the nature and effect of the sacrament" (*Sacrosanctum Concilium* 72). The reformed rite is the work of the experts and the bishops of the *Consilium ad exsequendam constitutionem de sacra liturgia* (Consilium), the Congregation for Divine Worship, and a number of other departments of the Holy See.

No ritual reform emanating from Vatican II received more thorough or lengthy scrutiny. Exhaustive research on doctrinal, historical, liturgical, and pastoral matters extended from 1966 through 1970, with the preliminary publication delayed until the Congregation for the Doctrine of the Faith could issue its pastoral norms on general absolution on June 16, 1972 (ActApS 64 [1972] 510–514). Bearing the date of Dec. 2, 1973 the Rite was made public with the approval of the Holy Father, Feb. 7, 1974.

The Rites of Reconciliation. The new Rite of Penance has three distinct ritual forms: the rite for reconciliation of individual penitents (Penance 15–21); the rite for reconciliation of several penitents with individual confession and absolution (ibid. 22–30); and the rite for reconciliation of several penitents with general confession and absolution (ibid. 31–37).

Reconciliation of Individual Penitents. The form for

reconciling individual penitents consists of five basic elements (Penance 15–21). The reception of the penitent by the minister consists of three parts: (1) a greeting by which the priest welcomes the penitent in a warm and kindly manner; (2) the sign of the cross by the penitent and priest; (3) an invitation to the penitent to trust in God, to which the penitent gives an Amen. A reading of the Word of God may be chosen by either the priest or the penitent. Then follows confession of sins and acceptance of satisfaction (act of penance) which should be keyed to the penitent's need and circumstance. Next the prayer of the penitent (expression of sorrow) and the priest's absolution. The former may be one of several fixed forms or in the penitents own words; the form of absolution retains the traditional "I absolve you..." with a prologue expressing the trinitariam aspect of salvation history and the ecclesial nature of forgiveness. The rite concluded with a proclamation of praise to God and a dismissal.

Reconciliation of Several Penitents. The rite for reconciling several penitents with individual confession and absolution has four major elements (Penance 22–30). The introductory rites consists of a psalm and antiphon or some other appropriate song, a greeting by the presiding priest or bishop, a brief word of explanation, and an opening prayer. The celebration of the Word of God may be as complete as a Sunday Liturgy of the Word or as simple as one reading (preferably a Gospel), a homily developing the Scripture that should call the penitent to an examination of conscience and a turning away from sin and to God; sin's being an offense against the whole body of the Church should be recalled. The examination of conscience may be assisted by brief statements or litanic prayer by one of the ministers. The rite of reconciliation is made up of a general confession of sins (modeled after the first Penitential Rite in the Mass liturgy), a litany or song, and the Lord's Prayer; the individual confession of sin includes counsel by the minister, a suitable act of satisfaction, and absolution accompanied by the imposition of hands. After all who wish to do so have confessed, all are invited to give thanks and praise to God for his mercy, to continue their efforts at conversion in relation to the community of believers and to raise their minds and hearts in thanksgiving to God. The service is concluded by a blessing and a dismissal.

Pastoral experience with this second form of the Rite of Penance has indicated that because of the length of time it takes to celebrate prayerfully the individual confessions required in this form of the Sacrament (particularly when the assembly is large) it seems to be pastorally advisable to bring the entire communal celebration to its proper conclusion with the blessing and dismissal, and only then to attend to those who desire individual confession and absolution. When this procedure is followed, care should be taken that the proper emphasis be given to the ecclesial nature of the particular parts of the rite so as not to diminish the desired impact of ecclesial or communal nature of the Sacrament.

Reconciliation with General Confession and General Absolution. The rite for the reconciliation of several penitents with general confession and absolution (Penance 31–37) follows the format of the rite for reconciliation of several penitents with individual confession and absolution through the introduction rites and the Liturgy of the Word. During the homily the priest explains to those desiring to receive general absolution the following points concerning their proper disposition:

the necessity for sorrow for their sins and an ongoing conversion to Christ and away from sin; the need for restitution or reparation of harm done; and the requirement that all serious sins be confessed individually at the proper time. A suitable form of satisfaction (act of penance) should be proposed to all penitents, with the proviso that each individual may add some more suitable act if they so desire.

A notable difference is that there is no suggestion that some form of examination of conscience be used at this juncture in the rite. For whatever reason, not known to this author, the examination of conscience is not mentioned. This certainly could not mean that the examination of conscience is not to be used, particularly if such a procedure is warranted by pastoral judgment. In such case the suggestion that the faithful be helped by brief statements or a short litany may be followed.

For the general confession the priest invites those who desire general absolution to indicate their intention by some visible sign, e.g., kneeling, bowing their heads, or some other sign to be determined by the episcopal conference. The penitents are then led through a general formula for confession. A litany or appropriate song may follow according to the format of the communal rite with private confession. This section always concludes with the Lord's Prayer. The presiding priest then gives absolution with his hands extended over the penitents either in the form of a *solemn blessing or as a prayer-over-the-people. In each instance the essential words established for the form of absolution conclude the prayer of general absolution.

The whole rite is brought to a conclusion by the priest inviting all to thank God and to acknowledge his mercy, the singing of a suitable song or hymn, and the blessing and dismissal of all the penitents. Another difference between this rite and the previous rite with private confession and absolution is the omission of a concluding prayer of thanksgiving to God for his mercy.

In keeping with the principles enunciated in Vatican II's Constitution on the Liturgy for a richer use of sacred Scripture and a wider choice of prayers, greetings and blessings (*Sacrosanctum Concilium* 35), this new Rite of Penance provides a rich fare, with options pertaining to all facets of each of the three liturgical forms of this new rite (Penance, ch. 4, 67–214). There is certainly no encouragement or cause given for the dreary repetition of the same prayers and readings which in the past so frequently characterized much of the sacramental liturgy.

The text for the Rite of Penance also contains Appendix I, an absolution from censures and dispensation from irregularity, and Appendix II, "Sample Penitential Services" (cf. Penance 36–37), a wide selection of extrasacramental or paraliturgical celebrations for the seasons of Lent and Advent, and for other common celebrations for different circumstances and ages and conditions of people.

Theology of the Rites of Reconciliation. One of the most important developments in the reform or renewal of the Sacrament of Penance is the emphasis given to resituating the Sacrament within the community of God's People assembled.

Reconciliation. The rite for reconciliation of individual penitents in many of the prayers, readings, and dismissal emphasizes the communal nature of sin and reconciliation. The same point is thoroughly stressed in the two communal rites of the Sacrament as well as the highly recommended penitential celebrations. The object of the Sacrament of Penance is reconciliation with God, with the Church, and with the whole community of brothers and sisters. In this context the ultimate purpose of the Sacrament of Penance is clarified: to foster the love of God above all things and commitment totally to him in and through concern for a neighbor.

Elements of the Sacrament. There are four basic elements in the Sacrament of Penance: contrition or sorrow for sin; confession of sin or the true acknowledgment of sin and the need of God's forgiveness; the act of penance or satisfaction, i.e., reparation for injury done to God or neighbor; the sign of absolution through which God grants pardon in response to a commitment to an open-ended conversion.

The first of these elements, contrition or sorrow for sin, is best expressed in the sincere change of heart required of all Christians as they continue their process of conversion to that day when they are united with Christ in the *parousia.* The second, the confession of sin, is that act by which the penitent with an open heart shares with the minister those transgressions that diminish life in Christ or alienate from Christ. The third element is the acceptance of the act of penance or satisfaction. This act requires conversion and is fulfilled by the willing performance of a proper act of reparation. Whenever possible the type or extent of this satisfaction should be adapted to the personal need and circumstances of the penitent, i.e., an act that would be helpful not only by way of reparation, but for the growth and development of the penitent in the search for unity in Christ. The Sacrament of Penance, especially the act of penance and contrition, is first a remedy for sin and then a help for the renewal of life in Christ. The final element is absolution given by the proper minister. Through the authority of the Church and the sign of absolution God extends pardon to the sinner who manifests a change of heart and accepts what is required for the remedy for sin and spiritual renewal.

Repentance for Sin. The Sacrament of Penance operates within the polarity of two extremes. One is grave sin, the sin of those who have withdrawn from the communion of love with God and are in need of restoration to the communion in Christ they had abandoned by their action. The other is the sin of those who, through human frailty, fall into lesser sin and who seek strength, courage, and growth through the celebration of the Sacrament.

With respect to mortal sins, it is the command of the Council of Trent (Denz 1707) that the faithful confess each and every grave sin that they recall in their examination of conscience. The recommendation of frequent and careful celebration of the Sacrament for growth in Christ and constant conversion is also to be emphasized so that it does not become a mere ritual repetition of a physical exercise, but a serious striving to bring to perfection the grace and life received in Baptism.

Ministries of Reconciliation. In the Sacrament of Penance or Reconciliation there are three basic offices or ministries: of the faith community of God's People assembled; of the penitent who comes seeking God's love and forgiveness; and of the ordained minister representing the Church as he presides at the celebration.

In keeping with the renewed emphasis on the communal nature of this Sacrament, the role in reconciliation of the faith community, the Church, the priestly People of God, is not to be diminished, minimized, or ignored. The Church not only calls sinners to repentance by the proclamation of the Word of God, it also intercedes for sinners and assists them with solicitous care to acknowledge their sins so as to obtain God's mercy, who alone can forgive sin. In this context the assembly of God's people become an instrument in the conversion and reconciliation of the penitent, thus fulfilling the ministry entrusted by Christ to his disciples and to the whole Church to the end of time.

Without a doubt the action of the penitent in the celebration of this Sacrament is of the greatest importance. The penitent is to approach the Sacrament with proper disposition, full of sorrow and determined to resume the process of conversion, confess his/her sin, accept the work of satisfaction and share in the reconciliation offered.

The proper minister of the Sacrament of Penance is a bishop or a priest. This ministry is exercised by proclaiming the Word of God and thereby calling the faithful to conversion and reconciliation and absolving those who seek God's loving mercy. In the name of Christ, by the power of the Holy Spirit and on behalf of the Church, they declare and grant forgiveness of sin to those who respond faithfully to this call to repentance. The Sacrament is brought to completion through the words of absolution spoken by the minister in the name of Christ and his Church and through the work of satisfaction accomplished by the penitent.

The Need and Problem of Catechesis. To set forth the mechanics of the new Rite of Penance and to explain the ritual development is one matter and quite necessary. But that is not so necessary as the task of highlighting the great need for the development of those deeper attitudes which have to do with "knowing" Christ in the true biblical sense, the understanding of Church, and how the priestly People of God form it, and the richer meaning of the love-relationship to God and to neighbor. What must be understood, if there is to be any real positive spiritual growth in relation to the Sacrament of Penance, is that a great deal more has to be changed and understood to the point of living it than the ritual texts and actions.

For the most part the response of adult Catholics to "change" in their prayer and worship life has been admirable. It speaks well of their basic faith and evidences a genuine willingness to follow good leadership when it is offered. In view of how far the Church has moved in the past twelve to fifteen years, the results are amazing. This progress can be compared to the relatively simple task of reforming the rites and producing the ritual texts and publishing the books. But reform has just begun, if reform be understood not as the transitional reform mandated by Vatican Council II but as the constant ongoing reform that must be part of the life style of the living, Pilgrim Church.

The mechanics come relatively easy and this has been adequately demonstrated. The tougher task has to do with the change in attitudes required in all interpersonal relationships, particularly in the love relationship with the Father, in Christ and through the Holy Spirit. A great deal of this difficulty stems from the general background and religious training most present-day adult Catholics were exposed to in their early formative years of primary and secondary religious instruction. There is more involved in this problem than the content of this religious education; it also has to do with the normal development of the learning capacity of the person and the truth that "adult education" has not been an area of strength in the Church in the United States (*see* CATECHESIS, ADULT).

In an attempt to break through the confusion involved in the current dilemma confronting pastoral ministry teams as they seek to keep the reform moving, three factors seem to dominate. First, for a high percentage of humankind the powers of abstraction, analysis, and synthesis are only at the developmental stage during the time a person is passing through adolescence. Secondly, it is safe to state that the greater proportion of adult Catholics do not go beyond the secondary level in formal Catholic education. Thirdly, there seems to be adequate evidence that a high percentage of adult Catholics have not developed (in matters pertaining to religion) much beyond the level of their formal religious education.

If this analysis reflects the real situation, and evidence indicates that it does, then those actively engaged in pastoral ministry and those who form policy in the Church are faced with a considerably more complex situation than providing texts and ritual reform. The issue goes well beyond the liturgy of prayer, worship, and Sacrament to the motivation of Christian commitment, to what prompts the believer to express faith by prayer, worship, and way of living. The challenge is to lead believers to understand and to take seriously what is begun by their Christian initiation; to perceive conversion as a lifetime undertaking that finds its completion in the *eschaton*.

Two solutions seem to suggest themselves. One is that adult education, with special emphasis on adult formation, be taken seriously at all levels in the Church to the extent that a much larger proportion of personnel, time, out-of-the-pocket money and capital investment be allocated to this essential work. The second is that in parochial schools and in all other forms of religious education for children, the movement be continued away from what has been called the reification of the Sacraments and all spiritual relationships, and from that static notion of what it means to be a Christian. The direction must be toward emphasizing the reality of the interpersonal encounter with the Father, in Christ, and through the Holy Spirit as believers form and act as Church.

Bibliography: *Rituale Romanum. Ordo Paenitentiae* (Typis Polyglottis Vaticanis 1974), tr. *Rite of Penance.* Study ed. (USCC Publ. Office, Washington, D.C. 1975). Bishops Committee on the Liturgy, *Study Text IV, Rite of Penance* (USCC Publ. Office, Washington, D.C. 1975) with bibliog. Bishops Committee on Pastoral Research and Practices, *Guidelines for General Sacramental Absolution* (USCC Publ. Office, Washington, D.C., n.d.). Catholic Theological Society of America, *Renewal of the Sacrament of Penance* (1975) with bibliog. Congregation for the Doctrine of the Faith, *Normae pastorales . . .,* tr., *Pastoral Norms concerning the Administration of General Sacramental Absolution* (USCC Publ. Office, Washington, D.C. 1972). R. KEIFER and F. R. MCMANUS, *The Rite of Penance: Commentaries,* v. 1, *Understanding the Document* (The Liturgical Conference, Washington, D.C. 1975). J. D. SHAUGHNESSY, *The New Rite of Penance* (National Catholic Reporter Celebration) (Kansas City, Mo. 1976).

[J. D. SHAUGHNESSY]

PENANCE, COMMUNAL CELEBRATION OF

One of the great breakthroughs at Vatican Council II was the documentary implementation of the ecclesial or communal nature of the Sacraments and their celebration. Prompted by the rediscovery of the social dimensions of Catholic doctrine, the Council set down norms relating to the hierarchic and communal nature of the prayer and worship life of believers (*see* WORSHIP, COMMUNAL). Thus: "Liturgical services are not private functions but are celebrations of the Church . . . liturgical services pertain to the whole Body of the Church" (*Sacrosanctum Concilium* 26); ". . . rites which are meant to be celebrated in common, with the faithful present and actively participating, should as far as possible be celebrated in that way (ecclesially) rather than by an individual and quasi-privately" (ibid. 27). This emphasis on the social nature of the Sacraments was made explicit with reference to the Sacrament of Penance when the same document states: "The rite and formulae of Penance are to be revised so that they more clearly express both the nature and the effect of the sacrament" (ibid. 72).

The operative words here are "nature and effect." In the first place, the Sacrament of Penance is by its very nature that means by which one who has been baptized into the Body of Christ but has become a sinner, reenters the flowing stream of opposition to sin and is reconciled to Christ and the Church. Reconciliation takes place by means of God's mercy—expressed in the Paschal Mystery of the dying and rising of Christ—combined with a spirit of true contrition and change-of-heart (*metanoia*).

In both nature and effect the Sacrament of Penance calls for communal celebration. From the very nature of Baptism it should be evident that Christians are not redeemed in isolation but are incorporated into Christ and made one with all believers who ". . . reform and are baptized" (Acts 2.28). When sin separates a believer from Christ and the Church, reconciliation is not established in isolation but in and with the whole Body of Christ in its head and its members. Such reconciliation can only be properly expressed within the assembly of God's People gathered in prayer and worship. Both Baptism and Penance stand in a similar relation to Eucharist. Baptism, as the first act in Christian initiation, finds its perfection at the Table of the Lord in the one Bread and the one Cup that make partakers one in Christ and in each other. So the Christian who has become alienated from the Table will find reentry available through the Sacrament of Penance to that same unity all faithful believers find in the banquet of the Lord. Such reentry calls for communal celebration; it cannot be expressed in any other form.

The Sacrament of Penance releases the believer from sin against God and neighbor when there is the will to repent and ". . . avoid this sin" (Jn 8.3). By its very nature sin is social. The most private sin cannot be isolated from the believer's incorporation in the Body of Christ, the People of God; the devastation of sin reverberates through the whole Body and cries out for response in and with the people assembled for prayer and song.

Further man is by his very nature social and every aspect of his being demands that he acknowledge the social dimensions of his creatureliness. Created as a member of a social body, redeemed within the People of God, initiated into the Body of Christ, and by sin alienated from fellowship with Christ and his Body, the believer can be reconciled only within this fellowship by the combined power of the mercy of God and the loving concern of the brethren. Regardless of what form the

Sacrament of Penance takes it cannot be separated from its social implications, and because it is a Sacrament (signifiying and making present what it effects) it cries out for its ecclesial dimension and its communal celebration.

Bibliography: *Rituale Romanum. Ordo Paenitentiae* (Typis Polyglottis Vaticanis 1974), tr. *Rite of Penance.* Study ed. (USCC Publ. Office, Washington, D.C., n.d.). Bishops Committee on the Liturgy, *Study Text IV, Rite of Penance* (USCC Publ. Office, Washington, D. C. 1975), with bibliog. Bishops Committee on Pastoral Research and Practices, *Guidelines for General Sacramental Absolution* (USCC Publ. Office, Washington, D.C., n.d.). Catholic Theological Society of America, *Renewal of the Sacrament of Penance* (1975) with bibliog. Congregation for the Doctrine of the Faith, *Normae pastorales circa absolutionem generali modo impertiendam* (ActApS 64 [1972] 510–514), tr., *Pastoral Norms concerning the Administration of General Sacramental Absolution* (USCC Publ. Office, Washington, D.C. 1972). J. DALLEN, "A Decade of Discussion on the Reform of Penance, 1963–1973" (S.T.D. thesis, The Catholic University of America, Washington, D.C. 1973). R. KEIFER and F. R. MCMANUS, *The Rite of Penance: Commentaries*, v. 1, *Understanding the Document* (The Liturgical Conference, Washington, D.C. 1975). J. D. SHAUGHNESSY, *The New Rite of Penance* (National Catholic Reporter Celebration) (Kansas City, Mo. 1976).

[J. D. SHAUGHNESSY]

PEOPLE OF GOD

Vatican Council II wisely adopted this term (11:111) as its generic designation of the Church, thereby opening the door to various levels of degrees of "membership." Although avoiding this latter term, the Council documents envisage Catholics as "incorporated," non-Catholic Christians as "linked" or "joined," and non-Christians as "related" to the Church (*Lumen gentium* 14–16; *Unitatis redintegratio* 3). Post-conciliar developments in theology and the *ecumenical movement have vindicated the choice of this term (*see* INCORPORATION INTO THE CHURCH).

The Catholic Community. Within the Catholic community the People of God have responded to this title by the assumption of new roles, notably in the Eucharistic celebration: permanent deacons, readers, commentators, and lay ministers of Communion. Team ministries have become commonplace, often including persons of both sexes. Catholic education and communications have witnessed an increase in lay leadership. Lay spirituality, though developing along its own proper lines, has been freed of the "double standard" of perfection which relegated it to a lower level of holiness than that demanded of priests and religious. The charismatic renewal—including the healing ministry—has proven to be a gallant ally in promoting ecumenically shared prayer. Simultaneously, the People of God (including bishops) manifest a much greater tolerance of pluralism in nonessential doctrines and practices.

Ecumenism. In relationship to the world, Catholicism (and, in fact, Christianity at large) continues to operate on the remnant principle: a minority group serving as God's catalyst. In fulffillment of this role, Catholics began the post-conciliar era by accelerating their ecumenical activity in reciprocity with Protestant denominations. Fruitful dialogue in the late 1960s and 70s resulted in several dogmatic statements of agreement between Catholics and certain Protestant groups. Some of these statements are included in the appendix of The Common Catechism, the publication of which is itself an ecumenical milestone (*see* CATECHISMS). Attention was focused away from what divides the various denominations toward how to live and teach the Christian message to the world.

By the middle of the 1970s, however, ecumenism had lost much of its momentum; it was clear that common social action (e.g., participation in the antiwar and anti-abortion movements) was not of itself an ecumenical panacea. Indeed, these causes often served to expose unresolved doctrinal differences. Just as the previous decade had revealed the limitations of the institutional dimension of the People of God, so have the 1970s shown the ecumenical limitations of the servant model of ecclesiology. The continued viability and quest for unity of the Christian community demands that, open to the Spirit, it continues to renew and to blend the many elements by which it legitimately recapitulates the People of God.

See also KINGDOM OF GOD.

Bibliography: EncTheol 1204. A. DULLES, *Models of the Church* (New York 1974). J. FEINER and L. VISCHER, eds., *The Common Catechism* (New York 1975). K. RAHNER, *The Shape of the Church to Come*, tr. E. QUINN (New York 1974).

[M. K. HOPKINS]

PERFECTION, SPIRITUAL

It might be truer to say there has been a virtual revolution rather than a simple renewal in the concept and experience of spiritual perfection among Catholics since the time the earlier article on spiritual perfection was written for the *New Catholic Encyclopedia* (11:126). Spirituality had not only suffered a divorce from theology with the emergence of the scholastic era, but the Catholic, indeed the Western contemplative tradition was virtually lost in the 16th century. It might even be said that spirituality was subjected to the same bondsmen as theology, for when mystics sought to express themselves as persons of their times seeking to speak to their times, they constructed elaborate mazes similar to the constructs of scholastic theology. One who entered upon the way to spiritual perfection had to expect to thread slowly through the maze, studying zealously the manuals and going step by step. The approach was a far cry from the rich personal sharing of a 12th-century spiritual father like William of Saint Thierry (14:938), who in his treatise, *On the Nature and Dignity of Love* would outline the stages of spiritual growth using the analogy of natural growth: infancy, childhood, youth, maturity, and old age, and then say: "It must be remembered, however, that the stages of love are not like the rungs of a ladder. All the degrees of love work together, another's experience may well differ from mine." With Vatican Council II the "scholastic parenthesis" (Dom Jean Leclercq) was closed and the universal call to *holiness was again sounded. This not only meant that the contemplative and mystic life is seen as open to all, but to the whole of each person.

The Charismatic Way. The most forceful actual learning experience in this area for the Catholic community has been the charismatic movement. Here, mystical graces of transient union (to use the recent classical terminology) are being poured out on those who seek with humble faith, especially when their seeking is joined by the prayers of brothers and sisters offered with a laying on of hands. The charismatics respond literally to—ask and you shall receive, the openness of the NT Church to the Spirit daringly reembraced, the whole person (the lay person exercising his universal priesthood) engaged in spiritual ministry.

Gifts, ordinary and extraordinary, are freely being received and exercised by simple people (and by those not readily thought of as simple, such as bishops and university professors) who have not ordinarily gone through the various stages of spiritual growth or climbed the mountain described by the classic authors of recent centuries. Those who are receiving these gifts and exercising them effectively are, at another level of their being, sometimes still struggling with quite naked passions. Spiritual guides have had to rethink their way of guidance and themselves be open to new ways of spiritual experience in order to be able to minister in an effectual and comprehensive way to the evolving Catholic community.

Eastern Mysticism. Not all Catholics have been attracted to the rather enthusiastic, often somewhat emotional and in general rather extroverted expression of spirituality that characterizes the charismatic movement in the Catholic Church in this decade. The call to inner presence and transcendence has been strong and has been equally challenging to the Christian community. The already mentioned general loss of the contemplative tradition in the West has left the Church ill prepared to meet this attraction. As a result large numbers, especially among the young but certainly not exclusively, have gone outside their own tradition to seek spiritual masters, especially among Eastern religions. The sometimes facile and generally effective methods found to enter into inner silence are being gradually integrated into traditional Western Christian understanding and practice. As a result Christians who perhaps have done little to grow in faith, Christian hope, and divine love are sometimes spending periods regularly each day in states of mind that can be described as contemplative. The danger of quietism is very evident here. There is the danger, too, that people will allow a refreshing and peaceful *natural* contemplation to replace prayer in their lives. On the other hand, to create a complete dichotomy between this kind of experience ahd the development of prayer would be a great disservice and not promote the evangelical precept to pray without ceasing (1 Thes 5.17). Conceptual faith needs to be nourished so that the natural contemplative experience can be motivated by the desire for communion with the loving God of Revelation and the Absolute, encountered in the transcendental experience, be identified as the Triune God and be embraced with a personal love. Hence reading especially of the Sacred Scriptures geared toward building up faith and a faith response in love is imperative. Whether the contemplative experience attained by the use of techniques or natural methods is truly prayer in the particular case can best be discerned, as our Lord said, by its fruits in the life of the meditator. If those fruits which Saint Paul speaks of as the fruits of the Spirit—love, joy, peace, patience, kindness, goodness, faithfulness, gentleness, self-control (Gal. 5.22–23)—are *all* growing, then the meditator can confidently be encouraged. There is need to place a certain emphasis on the "all" for a certain natural sense of goodness and peace can be readily acquired by regular periods of a deep inner quiet having no necessary bearing on a growing relation with God.

Return to Catholic Sources. The fact that other traditions are readily offering Christians simple means to enter into an attractive contemplative experience challenges the Catholic community to make its own contemplative tradition more available. Practical ways of entering into simple prayer such as are found in *The Cloud of Unknowing* (3:962) John Cassian, and other traditional writings need to be brought forward. If from the outset a person can learn a way fully informed by Christian faith and love, progress will probably be more direct and easier than if the person learns a method of contemplation in another tradition and then has to integrate it into the understanding of reality deriving from Christian faith.

Conclusion. It should not be surprising that these recent years have seen such a change in the way of entering upon and progressing along the way of spiritual perfection. Prayer is essentially communing with God. Christian perfection is essentially responding to reality as it is known with a special fullness through Revelation. But the present age has seen a dramatic shift in the way of responding to reality and of communicating. The Western world where Christianity has been based and has largely found its expression has passed from being a primarily conceptual civilization based on the printed word to becoming a more integral experiential culture. Thus the initial impulse will be to experience God rather than to read and think about him.

Although new ways have emerged in the pursuit of spiritual perfection—which are in actual fact more consonant with what has prevailed in earlier ages of the Church—the essence of spiritual perfection for the Christian has in no way changed. It still lies in a union of will with God. And the essence of the way is the same: Deny yourself, take up your cross daily and follow me (Lk 9.23). Certain experiences more commonly associated during the recent centuries with later stages of the spiritual journey are now appearing earlier and even as initial experiences. In practice this seems to be good not only in that it seems to correspond to a shift in culture but also because it seems to be facilitating the response to the call made by Vatican II—the universal call to *holiness.

Bibliography: J.-M. DÉCHANET, *William of Saint Thierry: The Man and His Work*, Cistercian Studies 10, tr. R. STRACHAN (Spencer, Mass. 1972). W. JOHNSTON, *The Mysticism of the Cloud of Unknowing* (New York 1973). W. JOHNSTON, ed., *The Cloud of Unknowing* (New York 1973). D. KNOWLES, *The English Mystical Tradition* (New York 1961). T. MERTON, *Contemplative Prayer* (New York 1969); *The New Man* (New York 1961). E. O'CONNOR, *The Pentecostal Movement in the Catholic Church* (Notre Dame, Ind. 1971). M. B. PENNINGTON, *Daily We Touch Him* (New York 1977). S. SPENCER, *Mysticism in World Religion* (London 1963).

[M. B. PENNINGTON]

PERMANENT DIACONATE, FORMATION FOR

Candidates for the permanent diaconate (16:123) are selected on merit; their maturity, quality of service, openness of mind, spirituality, are already demonstrable from the record of their experience. Middle-aged (or older), established in their work or professions, frequently married with families, candidates arrive at the point of diaconate formation with a wealth of learning and the wisdom of experience.

Origin of Programs. Although the early programs of formation were guided by seminary programs for priests or even by graduate programs for lay theologians, it soon became apparent that the formation of permanent deacons required a new process of ecclesial training. Basic education for these men, including basic helping skills, had already been woven into a demonstrated spirituality of service in the Church. Already recognized for excellence as community men, and screened for admission on that basis, they begin three years (recently, the normal length) of formation already prepared for the "call" of the Church to ordained service. The official ceremony of candidacy happens sometime during the first year as a sign of intention: unless the unexpected occurs, the candidate intends to request ordination and the bishop intends to ordain him. The formation program is viewed as a process of reflection, the enrichment of a station already secured in the Church; it is not viewed primarily as a process of initiation with ordination as a concluding rite of passage into the ministry of the hierarchy.

The bishops of the U.S. published guidelines for the formation of permanent deacons in 1971, wisely having called upon the experience of the thirteen programs then in existence. The document acknowledges the varieties of service and the opportunity still to be explored for this new ministry. National guidelines are general principles to be applied locally. Dioceses establishing programs of formation submit their plans to be approved by the *Bishops' Committee on the Permanent Diaconate, after which continuing evaluation is expected at the local level to guide adaptations of the program as experience and new situations may suggest.

Components of Programs. Although designs of programs vary considerably across the country, there are several common components: a process of evaluation and selection of candidates; orientation to the formation experience; developmental learning phases; skill-development training; and the evaluation of candidates for ordination. Several principles are also universal: that formation is a life-long commitment for which the three years only lay a foundation; that formation is directed to a quality of life and all its activities, not merely to the functions or part-time ministries to which the deacon may be assigned; that formation of a married person includes those with whom he is intimately related, spouse and family; that formation is directed to the growth of the human person in all dimensions—human, social, and spiritual; that formation implies the full participation of the candidate and engages him in all aspects of his life (family, job, civic responsibilities), quite beyond attendance at seminars and other structured learning activities provided by the formation staff.

Selection of Candidates. Selection of candidates is a crucial first stage for any program. The difficulty is compounded by the fact that not every well-intentioned, interested inquirer can be welcomed into the program. Among the many ministries in the Church, permanent diaconate is only one. This is reflected in the recent expansion of some programs to include formation in a variety of lay *ministries as well as the diaconate (e.g. the Diocese of Green Bay, Wisconsin). Diaconate requires a permanent commitment and the quality of ordained service; not *more* than lay service, but of a quality *other than* the laity provide. Stability of marriage, maturity, present situations of stress, employment history, attitude about the Church presently in transition, motivation and self-image, health factors, record of service, reputation in the community—these and other factors converge in the search for deacons who are reflective servants of faith and justice-in-action.

All programs require the participation of the wives during the early stages of the formation program. Most programs urge wives to continue throughout the three years, and provide growth activities for the families as well. Experience with the formation process has a profound effect, intended for individuals, marriages and the lives of families. To include the natural social unit (family) in the formation design is to encourage a most significant resource for personal growth and to avoid what could be a diastrous new source of tension between the deacon and his family.

Academic Formation. Several learning phases of formation are variously designed, no diocesan program duplicating another. Each locale, each formation group, each program staff is creative, as theological, doctrinal, spiritual, and ministerial topics become integrated during the phases of learning, some given more room for development in one phase than in others. Although a curriculum of subjects is more evident in some programs than in others, several basic emphases are common: the discipline of personal reflection, especially the ability to reflect critically within a Christian tradition; historical orientation to the formation of the basic exegetical skills for informed study of biblical literature; orientation to the historical developments leading to Vatican II and beyond, including ecumenism and ecclesial involvement in justice issues; the development of pastoral skills, both general and specialized to each person's gifts. The learning phases progress along a continuum: a new awareness of self and others, a deepened perception of daily experience in the context of God's living presence, new ability to express the fundamentals of Christian belief, and a theology of the Church's mission in today's world.

Evaluation of Candidates. No academic grading system is used to evaluate progress. Candidates demonstrate their progress through the quality of their participation in the group discussions and in their effectiveness with home assignments. Candidates appraise themselves with reference to personal goals which they have formulated with assistance from the staff. Growth is recognized as new insight progresses into new behaviors, personal and social. Supervision of skills often involves personal learning contacts through which the candidates structure opportunities to expand and develop their repertoire of helping skills. Although supervision begins early in the process, the third year is frequently an extended practicum for ministerial activities and during which advice and critique are readily available.

Evaluation of these learning phases has been constant during the brief history of the program; seldom does a new class of candidates merely repeat previous designs. The *National Association of Permanent Diaconate Directors was organized in 1976 for the expressed purpose of safeguarding the quality of diaconate training, especially to provide a forum for the exchange of ideas and resources. Each region, rural or urban, and each culture has its own reflection in the formation design; each new group personalizes that design for a maximum impact with its members. Directors and staffs of programs facilitate the group process of learning; each member retains responsibility for his own growth, thus the constant need for evaluation at all levels of the formation effort.

Continuing Formation. Formation programs continue beyond the ordination of permanent deacons. Their continuing competence as well as an evolving professionalism for their ministry require deacons to organize structures through which they can be accountable. Certification of ministry is one such structure widely discussed. Most dioceses have organized councils or associations of deacons intended to safeguard the permanence of their commitment and the quality of their lives. Deacons are also convening regional and national conferences through which small groups from around the country can consolidate their early efforts through the support and inspiration of one another.

Bibliography: Archdiocese of Chicago, *Permanent Diaconate Program* (Chicago 1973). Archidiocese of Washington, *The Permanent Diaconate, Formation Program* (Washington, D.C. 1977). Bishops' Committee on the Permanent Diaconate, *Permanent Deacons in the United States, Guidelines on Their Formation and Ministry* (Washington, D.C. 1971). Diocese of Des Moines, *Guidelines: The Ministry of Deacons* (Des Moines, 1974).

[D. J. WEILAND]

PERSON, DIGNITY OF

There has been a centuries-long and worldwide evolution of reverence for the human person, whose dignity has become one of the primary values in living and leading the human experience in many fields including religion, politics, education, and social justice. The Fathers of the Second Vatican Council in their document on the Church in the Modern World summarized the renewal of reverence for the human person in this way:

> There is a growing awareness of the exalted dignity proper to the human person, since he stands above all things, and his rights and duties are universal and inviolable. Therefore, there must be made available to all men everything necessary for leading a life truly human, such as food, clothing, and shelter; the right to choose a state of life freely and to found a family, the right to education, to employment, to a good reputation, to respect, to appropriate information, to activity in accord with the upright norm of one's own conscience, to protection of privacy and to rightful freedom in matters religious too.
>
> Hence, the social order and its development must unceasingly work to the benefit of the human person if the disposition of affairs is to be subordinate to the personal realm and not contrariwise, as the Lord indicated when He said that the Sabbath was made for man, and not man for the Sabbath.
>
> This social order requires constant improvement. It must be founded on truth, built on justice, and animated by love; in freedom it should grow every day toward a more humane balance. An improvement in society will have to take place if these objectives are to be gained.
>
> God's Spirit, who with a marvelous providence directs the unfolding of time and renews the face of the earth, is not absent from this development. The ferment of the gospel, too, has aroused and continues to arouse in man's heart the irresistible requirements of his dignity (*Gaudium et spes* 26).

In these historic and authoritative words the Fathers of the Council boldly summarized the renewal of respect for the dignity of the human person and, at the same time, indicated that this dignity must be nurtured and supported in practice and with Gospel fidelity.

As if to reaffirm their conviction and teaching the Fathers of the Council again addressed the dignity of the person in the Declaration on Religious Freedom:

> A sense of the dignity of the human person has been impressing itself more and more deeply on the consciousness of contemporary man. And the demand is increasingly made that men should act on their own judgment, enjoying and making use of a responsible freedom, not driven by coercion but motivated by a sense of duty. The demand is also made that constitutional limits should be set to the powers of government, in order that there may be no encroachment on the rightful freedom of the person and of associations (*Dignitatis humanae* 1).

These statements of the Vatican Council have had already and will continue to have a creative and governing effect on the life of the People of God. They have already influenced the American Catholic Church through its 1976 *Call to Action Conference. That Conference issued a document on Personhood which declared:

> In its contemporary renewal, the Catholic Church has made its own this preoccupation of men and women with discovering, affirming and vindicating their dignity and worth. Arising from such developments as improved communications and the influence of modern psychology, this emphasis on personalism has considerable significance for Christian life. Concern for human rights and freedoms has become a central element of Catholic social teaching, influencing the Church's attitude toward war, political organization and social justice. Personal growth and human development have become intertwined; the achievement of justice and the growth of persons have become part of a single effort to free humankind from the bondage of ignorance, poverty, oppression, and sin. In pastoral practice and Church teaching alike, the Catholic Church around the world has come to understand, in the words of the 1974 Synod of Bishops, that the mission of the Church "involves defending and promoting the dignity and fundamental rights of the human person."

This Conference also pointed out the areas of personal rights that should be included in the pursuit of human dignity. Persons are entitled, at least, to food, clothing, shelter, health care, and fulfilling economic opportunity in accordance with their needs. Persons in the Church have right and consequent responsibilities including the right to freedom of conscience, freedom of speech, freedom of assembly, and freedom to participate in the life and ministry of the Christian community on a nondiscriminatory basis.

Many are deprived of their right to life, to bodily integrity, and to the means which are necessary and suitable for the proper development of life. In his encyclical letter, On the Development of Peoples (*Populorum progressio*) Pope Paul VI addressed himself to these needs with his opening words:

> The development of peoples has the Church's close attention, particularly the development of those who are striving to escape from hunger, misery; endemic diseases and ignorance; of those who are looking for a wider share in the benefits of civilization and a more active improvement of their human qualities; of those who are aiming purposefully at their complete fulfillment. Following on the Second Vatican Ecumenical Council a renewed consciousness of the demands of the Gospel makes it her duty to put herself at the service of all, to help them grasp their serious problem in all its dimensions, and to convince them that solidarity in action at this turning point in human history is a matter of urgency (Paul VI PopProgr 1).

The principle of the dignity of the human person has been firmly stated in the teachings of the Church. The process by which this principle is achieved is already and will continue to be in effect in the Church and in society. The principle is inalienable and the process of pursuing it is irreversible. Each person's own reflection and experience leads to a progressively deeper realization and actualization of personal dignity. This is one of the basic needs and life goals placed in persons by the Creator. The Church and the institutions of society both are stronger as they facilitate the achievement of personal dignity for their members. Individuals are, in turn, stronger as they participate in communities that are committed to the principle of personal worth and the process whereby this worth is achieved. Human freedom with responsibility is the most effective means available to society and to persons for achieving the dignity of the human person.

[K. J. PIERRE]

PERSONALISM

In general, personalism refers to a type of thinking that begins with or focuses on the dignity and uniqueness of the human person. It stands in contrast to conceptual schemas whose preoccupation is "the nature of things," or even "human nature" understood as an abstract, universal, and relatively static reality. Personalistic modes of thinking are found today in all categories of theological writing, both dogmatic and moral, as well as in much contemporary philosophical work (on personalism as a specific philosophy, *see* 11:172).

Personalism manifests itself both in style of writing and in content. This article limits itself to theology, with particular emphasis upon moral theology, and will discuss, first, the characteristics of a personalistic style; then personalism as involving particular theological content; finally, some major representatives of personalistic theology.

The Personalist Style. Contemporary theology has become increasingly conscious of the fact that it exists to serve the members of the Church, that successful theology must be characterized both by an internal logical coherence and by a consonance with the faith-experience of people. This consciousness has led to a style of theological writing that is dialogic rather than apodictic. Such writing starts with the experience of believing persons and develops its theological insights inductively. Similarly, the conclusions are expressed in the ordinary language of people and tested once again against their experience. This rhythm of inductive thinking and experiential testing is a major characteristic of the personalistic style in theology.

Another characteristic lies in the kind of questions pursued. Personalism suggests that theology should attend to the real questions that believing people ask and should be less concerned with those which, while relevant to logical completeness, are not really experienced as important. Thus, for example, personalistic theology would discuss the Mass less in terms of its sacrificial relationship to Calvary and more in terms of its function in the lives of people, as the setting of their worship, nourishment, and communion. It would analyze the Trinity less in terms of its inner constitution and more in terms of ways the three Persons are present to and affect the lives of believers.

Content. But if personalism implies a theological style, it also refers to a particular body of teaching, or at least to a particular emphasis. The content or emphasis reveals itself chiefly in the way human beings and the world are understood.

Human beings are, to be redundant, viewed as persons. This means they are viewed as active and, to some extent, self-creating beings. They do not find fulfillment by passively accepting the facts of a situation, but by intelligently and aggressively shaping those facts and thus making them tools for the achievement of their own ends. Human persons are the reality which, by being present in the world, make everything different. Because of their capacities of intellect and will, of imagining and choosing new possibilities, of transcending self and situation in favor of something radically new, persons truly participate in the creating of the world. Indeed, that is the duty of persons. So, for example, the natural moral law is understood by personalism not to demand that human beings accept the "facts of life," but that they responsibly use human reason in the shaping of life toward humane ends.

It follows from this that personalism sees human persons as unique and individual in important ways. Individuality is not a secondary concept, a slight nuancing of the shared reality of "human nature." Rather the uniqueness of the individual is substantial, affecting the meaning of the person and of moral obligations. But for personalism, individuality does not mean isolation. It also recognizes that persons are relational beings, shaped by involvements with other persons and in turn shaping others by their actions.

This understanding of human beings as persons, as active, unique, and relational, leads to a different understanding also of the world. It sees the world as open-ended, as changing, as dynamic rather than static. In other words, personalism takes the idea of history seriously. It acknowledges that time is a linear rather than a cyclic factor in human life. Thus it concedes the unpredictability of the future. This sense of history, in turn, leads personalistic theology, and especially moral theology, to a certain humility in the formulation of convictions. There is a tentativeness in the way moral norms are articulated, an openness to revision in dogmatic statements. While sometimes an impression of cowardice or waffling may be given, actually a central personalistic conviction is at issue: we cannot guess the future, we can only deal with the present, because human persons are cocreators in a radically historical world.

Personalist Theologians. In Catholic theology, both dogmatic and moral, perhaps the key figure in the development of personalism is Karl Rahner. Rahner, in turn, has been strongly influenced by German existential philosophy, and especially by M. *Heidegger. Similar lines of thought are also pursued by Coreth, M. Blondel, Macmurray, and in a more psychological style, Binswanger. The implications of personalism for moral theology have most thoroughly been developed by Bernard Häring, though they are present as well in the writings of Joseph Fuchs, Charles Curran, Richard McCormick, Schüller, and others. Gregory Baum and Avery Dulles are also noteworthy for their use of personalistic style and, in some cases, content.

It is worth noting that Vatican Council II evidenced a familiarity with and sympathy for personalism. The selection of topics and the language of *Lumen gentium, Dei Verbum*, and *Sacrosanctum Concilium* all reflect the personalistic style; *Gaudium et spes* very explicitly endorses personalism both in style and content.

Bibliography: B. HÄRING, *Morality is for Persons* (New York 1971). T. O'CONNELL, *Principles for a Catholic Morality* (New York 1978). K. RAHNER, "On the Question of a Formal Existential Ethics," *Theological Investigations* 2, tr. K.-H. KRUGER (Baltimore 1963) 217–234; "Theology of Freedom," ibid. 6, tr. K.-H. and B. KRUGER (Baltimore 1969) 178–196; "The Experiment with Men," ibid. 9, tr. G. HARRISON (New York 1972) 205–224; *Hearers of the World*, tr. M. RICHARDS (New York 1969).

[T. E. O'CONNELL]

PHILIPPINES, CHURCH IN

In the years since its close, Vatican Council II has inspired many dynamic changes within the Philippine Church. Not the least of these has been the growing commitment on the part of an increasing number of bishops, priests, religious, and laity to addressing the problems of social injustice. This commitment has not only been in word, but more significantly in action. There have been two dramatic effects: from without the Church has suffered persecution by the martial law government of President Ferdinand Marcos; within the Church there has been a growing division, especially evident among the hierarchy.

Church Initiatives. Motivated by such documents as *Gaudium et spes* and *Lumen gentium*, the Catholic Bishops' Conference of the Philippines (CBCP) sponsored (1967) the National Rural Congress. The Congress brought together participants from all sectors of the Church to discuss the theme, "The Church Goes to the Barrios." The follow-up of this significant meeting was given to the then newly formed National Secretariat of Social Action (NASSA), the action arm of the Episcopal Commission on Social Action.

During the next three years, NASSA set upon the task of promoting and assisting the setting up of diocesan social action centers, to motivate and give organizational support to the Church's efforts at involvement in the service of total human development. Through this period, and until late 1972, there rapidly developed numerous church-motivated credit unions, cooperatives, leadership training programs for farmers, workers, and youth, as well as adult-education programs in such areas as literacy, family life, farming, and paramedical skills. There was an evident and enthusiastic growth in grass-root movements and organizations among poorer classes of Filipinos, such as among farmers, workers, slum-dwellers, and youth. From these efforts there evolved three regional counterparts of NASSA. A country-wide network was formed, operating on parish, diocesan, regional, and national levels.

In terms of evolving church structures growing out of Vatican II, and in response to concrete and expressed need, small, grass-root, *basic Christian communities (Comunidades de base)* have developed in many parts of the country. Of special significance has been the establishment of the Mindanao-Sulu Pastoral Conference and Secretariat (MSPCS) by the bishops of the Mindanao region. Participated in by all sectors of the Church, this regional body seeks to promote the integral development of Church, including action on behalf of justice as constitutive to living the Gospel.

Declaration of Martial Law. President Ferdinand Marcos declared martial law on Sept. 21, 1972 in order to "save the Republic and reform the society." The very security of the state was threatened, according to Marcos, by the activities of the New Peoples' Army (NPA), the armed wing of the Maoist Communist Party of the Philippines. Much of the general unrest however, according to some, was largely attributable to the corruption evident in government during the period preceeding martial law, which measurably contributed to an increasingly more desperate economic situation in the country. Several violent bombings occurred in the Manila area in the months just before martial law was declared. A reported assassination attempt upon the life of Defense Secretary Juan Ponce Enrile was the immediate pretext for the Marcos' martial-law declaration.

Upon declaring martial law, Marcos virtually put the finishing touches on a new Constitution which was in the process of being drafted by an elected Constitutional Convention. Especially controversial were "transitory provisions" incorporated into the Constitution, supposedly to govern the transition period between the old and new Constitutions. In effect, these articles gave Marcos all power, without limit of time, provided under both Constitutions. In January 1973, the new Constitution was reportedly approved by over 90 percent of the voters in a referendum carried out under the conditions of martial law, with the effective curtailment of the freedoms of the media, speech, and assembly.

Situation in the Country. Economically, there has been a 40 percent increase in the GNP since Martial Law, but a decrease of 40 percent in the real wages of workers. In order to encourage foreign investment by *multinational corporations, Marcos has provided for some of the most liberal enticements for foreign investment in the world: availability of capital-investment funds from local bank sources; up to 100 percent repatriation of profits; the tight restriction and control of labor organizations; and the prohibition by law of strikes and demonstrations. Transnational corporations, especially those based in the U.S. and Japan, have largely increased their investments since 1972. Most investors can recover both their capital investment, plus an adequate profit in only three years, to make their investment risk worthwhile. In the meantime the conditions of most Filipino workers have deteriorated.

With a 100 percent increase in U.S. economic and military aid since the beginning of martial law, Marcos is effectively supported by the U.S. in its continuation. With such support, he has been able to increase the numbers in his military from 50,000 to more than 150,000 in six years. The U.S. maintains some twenty military establishments in the Philippines, including the largest Air Force and Navy bases outside of the U.S. The Defense Department is second only to the Philippine Government in the number of persons it employs. This includes 40,000 U.S. citizens, and about the same number of Filipinos. The U.S. State Department defends its support of the Marcos Government and its continued presence there on the declared need for national security.

The human rights situation in the country is deplorable, as has been verified by investigations conducted by such respected groups as Amnesty International, the International Commission of Jurists (based on missions to the Philippines of William J. Butler, Esq., Professor John P. Humphrey, and G. E. Bisson, Esq.), and the Association of Major Religious Superiors in the Philippines (AMRSP). The media are government-controlled. The writ of habeas corpus has been suspended. The rights of free speech and assembly are severely restricted by law. Since martial law there has been a minimum of 60,000 persons arrested for political reasons. The present number of political detainees is estimated to be as high as 6,000 and, according to the Amnesty Report, 70 percent of the political prisoners interviewed claim to have been tortured. There are documented cases of persons who have disappeared, as well as many who have died violently while in government detention. Reflecting on the conclusions of those who conducted the investigation, the Amnesty Report states: "The delegates' unavoidable conclusion was that torture was used freely and with extreme cruelty, often over long periods. In particular, torture was used systematically against those who had no means of appeal to influential friends or established institutions" (Amnesty Report p. 12). Land reform, considered by Marcos as the keystone for the success of "The New Society" he seeks to construct under the aegis of martial law, has largely been a failure.

Militarily, the Philippine Government is involved in a virtual war in the southern region of Mindanao against a rebel Moslem force called the Moro National Liberation Front (MNLF). In a war that has resulted in the death of more than 50,000 combatants and civilians since martial law, the government has failed to resolve the situation. Some informed persons consider that, rather than being a solution, the martial-law government exacerbates the problem, which has its roots in many years of neglect and abuse by the government towards the Moslem peoples. The Moslems constitute about five percent of the total population and are concentrated in several southern provinces.

The Church: Persecution and Division. The Church in the Philippines and the martial-law government of President Marcos are on a collision course. Right from the beginning of martial law, missionary priests have been deported. Filipino priests, religious, and lay people have been arrested and detained, suspected of and charged with subversion. Even some bishops have been listed as subversives. A few church radio stations and periodicals have been closed. Some church leaders have been the object of intimidation and ridiculed in the government-controlled press. Indeed, the Church has been the object of persecution because of its action on behalf of justice.

It would be inaccurate, however, to consider the Church as united in its criticism of the abuses of the martial-law government. While there have been statements published by the bishops through the Catholic Bishops' Conference of the Philippines (CBCP) which have called for justice and consideration for human rights, there has been inconsistency between what is stated and what actually is done. The most recent critical statement made by a majority of the bishops was a pastoral letter entitled, "The Bond of Love in Proclaiming the Good News," published in January 1977. Critical of several current abuses by the government, it asserted the right and obligation of the Church to evangelize, which included actions for the liberation of all that oppresses man.

The bishops, numbering about eighty, can be distinguished on the basis of their stance in the face of martial law. Some 12 percent would openly support the Marcos regime. Another group would be openly critical, both in word and action, regarding martial law; they would represent 25 percent. The largest group, about 62 percent, would hesitate to oppose martial law openly, save for occasional joint statements.

The papal nuncio, Bishop Bruno Torpigliani, praised the martial law government in a public address in 1975. He defended his position, when questioned, by saying that his job is to establish good relations with the government so that the Church can remain free.

The Association of Major Religious Superiors of the Philippines (AMRSP) has been significantly active on behalf of justice. They have organized several task forces to deal with such particular issues as political detainees and have published revealing reports on such matters as the condition of workers and the treatment of prisoners. The government closed AMRSP's mimeographed periodical, "The Signs of the Times." The Association's activities have infuriated both the Government and conservative elements in the Church. Several members of the AMRSP board have been indicted for alleged subversive reasons. The AMRSP was reprimanded in a 1976 letter to the bishops, jointly signed by Cardinal Sebastiano Baggio for the Congregations for Bishops, and Cardinal Eduardo Pironio for the Congregation for Religious and Secular Institutes.

On Nov. 4, 1976, eighteen bishops signed and published a significant document entitled, "*Ut omnes unum sint*," which clearly stated the division in the Church. They quite candidly illustrated the dichotomy between the lack of action on behalf of justice on the part of several bishops, and the teachings of Vatican II, papal encyclicals, and statements of the Synod of Bishops, and their own CBCP statements. They indicated that the notion of the Church itself underlied this division by stating: "For, in the final analysis, the different approaches we take with regard to martial law, and its dictatorial form of government, comes down to how we understand the Church, even more crucially, how we operate pastorally from this basic understanding."

Conclusion. Bishop Francisco Claver, SJ, Ordinary of the Prelature of Malaybalay in Mindanao and one of the most clear voices on behalf of justice in the Philippines today, clarifies the basis of the Church-State conflict by saying the government's "attempt at total control of political processes, its distaste of dissent and criticism, its new-found ideology of national security and its violent practice of the same... all directly contravene what the Church understands by total human development and its consequent stress on human dignity and freedom, inviolable human rights, shared responsibility, people participation in decisions of state, etc."

In conclusion, there is a healthy dynamism in the Philippine Church. There is a struggle to make the Church a sign of hope in a socio-political and socio-economic context oppressive of human rights and human dignity. This has resulted in actual persecution of the Church from without, and serious tension within. The Church is in the process of dynamic but painful growth.

AMRSP Documentation on the Philippine Situation is available through Friends of the Filipino People, 110 Maryland Ave. NE, Washington, D.C. 20002.

Bibliography: Amnesty International, *Report on an Amnesty International Mission to the Republic of the Philippines* (2d ed., London 1977). Association of Major Religious Superiors in the Philippines, *Political Detainees in the Philippines,* Books 1 and 2 (Manila 1976, 1977). Center for International Policy, *Human Rights and U.S. Foreign Assistance Program.* Fiscal year 1978, Part 2 *East Asia* (Washington, D.C. 1977). International Commission of Jurists, *The Decline of Democracy in the Philippines* (Geneva 1977).

[T. J. MARTÍ]

PHILOSOPHY IN SEMINARIES

The study of philosophy is a constitutive, not a luxury, in the process of priestly formation. The priest is the preacher of the Gospel, not the teacher of a theology and not the proponent of a particular philosophy. His primary dependence is on the Holy Spirit. However, the priest's faith and personal maturity, his understanding of God and of prayer, his grasp of pastoral responsibilities and opportunities, in great measure depend on the philosophical components of his seminary formation. The effective preacher must learn to appropriate for himself the Catholic tradition and interpret it intelligently to his contemporaries. To accomplish this, he needs some appreciation of the philosophical principle imbedded in the tradition. It is true that scattered voices from the tradition, and some voices currently, warn against the dangerous mingling of the wine of the Gospel and the water of philosophical wisdom. By and large, however, the many differing voices of the tradition recognize a style of epistemology and ontology resident in the scriptural Word of God. This is the philosophical principle made necessary by the very nature of Catholic faith in God as transcendent Creator of all that is. Vatican Council II has recognized the centrality of this principle and thus the important role of philosophy in the work of priestly formation. Accordingly, the Council called for a profound reform in the seminary teaching of philosophy. The purpose of this article is to make reference to this call of the Council and to examine its implementation as seen in the documents that are normative for seminaries in the United States.

The Council. Vatican II suggests the manifold goals of seminary philosophical studies. They are to lead the student to a coherent understanding of man, the world, and God, to be gained by conjoining a diligent study of the Christian philosophical heritage and a serious exploration of modern and contemporary philosophical and scientific developments. This will prepare the student to enter into dialogue with his contemporaries (*Optatam totius* 15). This vision of philosophy gives expanded significance to the study of the history of philosophy through which the student can hopefully gain a critical ability to distinguish between what is true and what is false in historical philosophical movements (ibid.). Good teachers, well-trained in the method of philosophy, can so present their discipline that their students discover both an ardent love for the pursuit of truth and a realistic awareness of the limits of human understanding (ibid.). It is essential that philosophical studies make evident the intimate connection between philosophy's central concerns and the most pressing problems of human life, especially as these problems exercise special influence in the U.S. and lie at the root of many faith-problems today. Ideally philosophy and theology should be better integrated in the seminary academic program so that a more harmonious relationship could relate the concerns of philosophy to the mystery of Christ "which affects the whole history of the human race, influences the Church continuously and is mainly exercised by the priestly ministry" (ibid. 14).

Congregation for Catholic Education. This bold and imaginative plan for philosophy in seminaries has not yet been carried out with great success. A 1972 letter from the Congregation for Catholic Education, *On the Study of Philosophy in Seminaries*, expressed the matter this way: "Although the Second Vatican Council drew out with clarity certain fundamental lines for the proper revival of philosophical teaching, today six years after the Council, we have to unfortunately admit that not all seminaries are following these lines wished by the Church" (p. 153). There is little reason to suggest that the situation is any different in 1978. The reasons for this state of affairs are numerous and complex. Some in the scientific community deny to philosophy a scientific existence independent of the positive sciences. Some in the theological community bypass philosophy by insisting that the theological disciplines be undertaken exclusively in terms of historical method. The contemporary pluralism in philosophy can be a source of great difficulty for teachers of philosophy. The cultural climate, at the present time so hostile to metaphysical reflection, can be a source of great difficulty for students. These reasons, and others besides, suggest the judgment that, philosophically speaking, *Optatam totius* has offered seminary administrators and educators the best of programs at the worst of times.

Need for Philosophical Formation. Why is philosophy important in a program of priestly formation? The more obvious answers are philosophical and theological. The less obvious—but emphasized in the documentation—are spiritual and pastoral. First of all, philosophy enjoys its own intellectual autonomy; its study is a value in its own right. Philosophy is essential for the development of the mature, liberally educated person who can transcend his own times and culture, who can critique and synthesize the kinds of knowledge that constitute human learning, and who refuses to leave unexamined the foundational issues of being, truth, and goodness, the question of God, and the nature and dignity of the human being. Further, philosophy renders irreplaceable service to the work of theology. It is true that theology today has many dialogue partners, but it is also true that philosophical theology precedes all other theologies. The philosopher-theologian is obviously at work in systematic theology. Perhaps less obviously, philosophy is present when the theologian interprets a text, biblical or postbiblical; when the theologian reconstructs a historical situation or mentality; when the theologian communicates theological teaching to different peoples in different cultures. Good philosophy in seminaries today will enable students of theology to deal critically with theological pluralism, develop models for systematic reflection on the mysteries of faith, and speak to contemporary men and women in a manner neither alienated nor alienating.

Philosophy renders important service to faith and to pastoral ministry. The seminarian must have the confidence that he can be both a believer and a contemporary, intelligent person; that he can deal with the order of grace without downgrading the first creation; that he can deal with the order of nature without diminishing the transcendence of the new creation; that he can relate the world to God in such a way that prayer is possible and religious obedience is reasonable. The tasks here are deeply philosophical. Finally, philosophy renders important service to pastoral ministry. Sound philosophical training can enable the pastor to dialogue with his contemporaries in terms of his and their faith-problems without succumbing to relativism and agnosticism. It can embolden the pastor to utilize the good results of the social sciences without falling victim to the unacceptable presuppositions that have often accompanied their development. In the midst of an always changing culture, philosophy can provide the pastor with stability and a sense of direction as he deals with the irreligious rationalism and the irrational religiosity which seem to be the only options viable for so many in our times.

Program Content. What is to be said about content in a seminary program of philosophy? The student must be taught to philosophize but to philosophize within the realist, personalist, theistic perspectives of the Christian philosophical heritage. The Church can have no official philosophy; the Church, however, cannot be indifferent to philosophy in that some philosophies are not compatible with the profession of Catholic faith. The letter of the Congregation for Catholic Education states that a basic curriculum should contain a realist theory of knowledge that offers a point of departure for ontology; an ontology that leads to a philosophy of God; an anthropology that safeguards authentic spirituality and grounds a theocentric ethic that also includes the social dimension of man (p. 154). It is in this context that reference can be made to St. Thomas Aquinas. After much debate Vatican II recommended the "tutelage" of St. Thomas (*Optatam totius* 16). The bishops' *Program of Priestly Formation* makes similar recommendations (138, 389). It would seem to be a question of tradition and innovation; in method and in content St. Thomas dealt masterfully with this question in his day. He can be of exceptional help with similar but more complex questions of the present.

Programs of priestly formation are making excellent progress in the theological areas of academics, spirituality, and field education. They are not making such progress in the realm of philosophy. This could be a fatal flaw because theological renewal, in the long run, demands philosophical renewal as an essential element. Theology in seminaries depends in great measure on philosophy in seminaries.

See also PLURALISM, PHILOSOPHICAL; THEOLOGY IN SEMINARIES.

Bibliography: Bishops' Committee on Priestly Formation, *The Program of Priestly Formation* (2d ed., USCC Publ. Office Washington, D.C. 1976) and Appendix III, Congregation for Catholic Education, "On the Study of Philosophy in Seminaries," 145–155. R. D. LAWLER, ed., *Philosophy in Priestly Formation* (Washington, D.C. 1978).

[J. J. CONNELLY]

PLANNED PARENTHOOD

After a complex and shifting history, the birth control movement became national in the mid-teens of this century and gave rise to Margaret Sanger's National (later American) Birth Control League. The goal was to liberate women, stabilize the family, produce wanted and healthy babies, eliminate prostitution, and so improve society generally. Birth control was viewed as a means of avoiding abortions; an early slogan read: "Sanger is here. Sanger says no abortions." Therefore, the League worked to make birth control information and materials universally available, to establish birth control clinics, and to obtain the corresponding permissive legislation. In the 1920s the movement achieved a high degree of respectability and the support of physicians, clergy and the public. The Catholic Church, however, remained firm in its condemnation of artificial birth control. In the period from the 1920s up to World War II, the goals and the activities of the League broadened to cover all aspects of family and sexual life. The League began to view family planning as social planning, leading to an overall public policy on population, a shift expressed in the change of name (1942) to "The Planned Parenthood Federation of America." The Federation was a national center with which local groups, agencies, and clinics could affiliate, yet in many cases without surrendering all local autonomy. In 1978 there were 200 affiliates and 729 affiliated clinics (reaching more than half a million people each year)

with 20,000 volunteers at work in 200 communities in 42 states.

After World War II Planned Parenthood made significant contributions in medical research, in providing medical services, counseling and assistance, in promoting accurate sex-knowledge, in achieving welfare legislation, and in combating venereal disease. Planned Parenthood received almost universal acceptance and was given increasing support. Many Catholics continued to oppose its promotion of artificial birth control, but the impression made on most people was outstandingly good.

From the 1960s there was an increasing reliance on governmental financial support. Beginning with an $8,000 grant in 1965, direct federal support grew to an estimated $175 million in 1975, a figure projected to $250 million by 1980. This financed an enormous increase in activities and gave Planned Parenthood a major influence in legislation and governmental planning. Thus, Planned Parenthood's major support now comes from taxpayers' money. Private gifts average $175,000 annually.

Conscious of their financial capability and their prestigious reputation and influence, leaders and workers began in the 1970s to think of effecting massive social changes which would accept the sexual "revolution" of the 1960s and transform the views of society to accord with that revolution. In "A Five Year Plan: 1976–1980 for the Federation" adopted Oct. 22, 1975 the Federation proclaimed itself as "the nation's foremost agent of social change in the area of reproductive health and well-being." As such it undertakes an all-embracing campaign for "modifying attitudes, behavior changes, and/or skills" and getting rid of "the arbitrary and outmoded restrictions—legal, regulatory and cultural—which continue to limit the individual's freedom of choice in fertility matters." On abortion the program aims at "making ... contraception, abortion and sterilization available and fully accessible to all." In 1975 Planned Parenthood clinics accounted for 35,000 abortions; the plan is to increase this number to 80,000 abortions by 1980. The Federation's lawyers have been active in the pro-abortion suits before the Supreme Court, e.g. *Planned Parenthood v. Danforth* (*see* ABORTION U.S. LAW). The purpose is essentially, therefore, to destroy Judaeo-Christian ethics in all matters relating to "reproduction and fertility," that is, in all sexual matters.

The Five-Year Plan calls for using all the influence of the movement at all levels ("with the service program, our ability to command authority in the councils where national decisions are made, is immeasurably enhanced"), all its affiliates, all its clinics, and all its volunteers to achieve its overall goal of social change. All activities are "complementary parts of a single national strategy.... Our medical service, for example, is not a distinct and separate strategy from our role as 'catalyst' or change agent; it is part of it." The strategy calls for infiltrating and enlisting for the grand national goal, the media, professional organizations, educational institutions, civil-liberty groups, churches, and health and welfare agencies, public and private.

The prime target groups are the poor and teenagers. To reach the young, sex education in school is to be taken over or informed by Planned Parenthood; teen clubs are to be established to reach teenagers directly and independently of their parents. There is widespread evidence that Planned Parenthood has been successful in these endeavors. An enormous amount of material—lectures, films, printed matter—has been prepared and distributed. This propaganda, much of it arguably pornographic, includes sound information on venereal disease, contraceptive devices, and the physiology of sex, but the main message is that sexual activity involves no moral issue, but that one should love "carefully" to avoid unwanted pregnancy and venereal disease. If pregnancy occurs, then abortion is the appropriate remedy. Religious objections are sometimes noted, but moral and personality dimensions are generally ignored.

However morally neutral Planned Parenthood claims to be (and this is the grounds on which it is admitted to the public schools), its propaganda in fact promotes ethical views and at least indirectly approves and encourages sexual activity, even at early ages. It is imposing its own moral views and its own social goals upon the young and the poor. Faye Wattleton, the current (1978) president of Planned Parenthood, has announced a national leadership role in lobbying for abortion. This is an open repudiation of moral neutrality and a declaration of war on the pro-life movement. It is an enormously difficult task to prevent the imposition of the doctrinaire ethical and sociological goals of the current leadership of Planned Parenthood while preserving its beneficial medical and social services.

Bibliography: L. CORSA, JR., "The United States," in B. BERELSON, ed., *Family Planning and Population Programs* (Chicago 1966) ch. 20. "A Five-Year Plan: 1976–1980 for the Planned Parenthood Federation of America, Inc." This was never published; it was duplicated, apparently for internal use only. L. GORDON, *Woman's Body, Woman's Right* (New York 1976). R. J. HENLE, "The Grand Target: A Sex-Free Society" (Milwaukee, October, 1977), supplement to the *Newsletter*, Catholic League for Religious and Civil Rights; *Our Sunday Visitor* 66 n. 39 (Jan. 22, 1978). M. J. HUTH, "The Birth Control Movement in the United States" (Ph.D. dissertation, Saint Louis 1955), one of the most comprehensive studies for the period up to 1950. M. C. SCHWARTZ, "Bringing the Sexual Revolution Home: Planned Parenthood's 'Five-Year Plan'," *Our Sunday Visitor* 138, n. 6 (Feb. 18, 1978) 114–116. B. SUITERS, *Be Brave and Angry* (London 1973) chronicles of the International Planned Parenthood Federation.

[R. J. HENLE]

PLURALISM, PHILOSOPHICAL

Pluralism in philosophy refers to the fact that philosophy is not one but many, i.e., that throughout history there have been a diversity of philosophical systems, many contradicting each other, but all laying some claim to validity or truth (11:448). Since reality is one, in the sense that only one universe is being studied, and truth is also one, in the sense that all men are seeking a correct knowledge of that universe, it would appear that there should be only one philosophy and only one system of thought corresponding to the reality men study. As a matter of fact, however, philosophers do not agree—in the way in which scientists, say, seem to agree about their disciplines. Philosophies are divided into various schools or systems, and a student is formed in one school or other, usually developing a partisan loyalty in the process, and thenceforth setting himself in opposition to philosophers of other schools. This has always been something of a scandal for beginners in philosophy, but in recent years among Catholics the very idea of such a pluralism has taken on a different value and significance. Since Vatican Council II many have come to regard pluralism as desirable, something to be fostered in the philosophical and theological

training of future priests. This new attitude, and particularly toward philosophical pluralism in relation to contemporary theology, is the concern here.

Advocacy of Pluralism. The benign view of pluralism is not a direct consequence of any teaching of Vatican II, but seems rather to be part of a more general cultural pluralism (*see* PLURALISM, SOCIAL AND CULTURAL) that characterizes Western civilization in the late 20th century. Contemporary culture exhibits a variety of life styles and worldviews, including an especially broad diversity of religious beliefs and moral codes, and since philosophy is a part of culture, or at least seems historically and culturally conditioned, it too is being persuaded to admit a variety of options in intellectual commitment. Even science, philosophy's erstwhile competitor, has come under similar pressures. Recent work in the sociology of knowledge, and especially studies focusing on scientific revolutions (16: 402), have underscored the fallibilism in what many regard as the modern mind's greatest achievement, pointing to elements of subjectivism and relativism that underlie scientific methods hitherto regarded as completely objective and leading to certain results. Moreover Catholic theology, possibly influenced by ecumenical concerns, has become increasingly less certain of its character as an epistemic science in the scholastic sense (12:1190); seeking to model itself on contemporary thought patterns, it tends now to take the *Geisteswissenschaften* as a paradigm for its own development (*see* THEOLOGY). The weakening of knowledge claims is thus pervasive in the 3d quarter of the 20th century: emphasis is placed on personal, situational, and evolving viewpoints; reality is seen as structured by the knowing subject and his horizons; and pragmatic or coherence theories of truth are competing, even in Catholic circles, with the hitherto universally accepted correspondence account of Aristotle and Aquinas (14:327). Since science and theology have thus been effectively reduced to the status of dialectics (4:843), a general atmosphere has been created for philosophy to follow suit. Frederick Sontag, for example, sees the proper role of philosophy in theology to be one of relinquishing certitudes and becoming "more flexible" so as to provide a variety of alternatives for the development of theologies that are themselves unsure of their principles and procedures (Sontag 24). In such a climate of opinion it is not difficult to see why systematic theology in the present day is in danger of extinction or at best of being reduced to a language game or hypothetico-deductive system that can enjoy only some degree of probability. Nor is it difficult to see why Catholic philosophers are being urged to multiply thought systems for their beleaguered theological colleagues and thus go along with them in embracing pluralism as a viable option.

Reactions of Catholic Philosophers. It is difficult to make generalizations concerning the reactions of Catholic philosophers in the U.S. to this development. On the positive side, in the last decade or so the members of the American Catholic Philosophical Association (1:398) have entered into dialogue with every significant philosophical movement in the Americas and on the Eurasian continent in an attempt to benefit from any elements of truth such movements may contain. There has been a general mellowing of the fierce loyalties that used to divide Thomists, Suarezians, and Scotists, and individuals are now more identified with their subjects of specialization or the methods they find more congenial for elaborating their results. On the negative side, possibly because they have lived with pluralism for a longer time and take it as a constant occupational hazard when philosophizing, they are not much enamored of the values it has to offer the Catholic intellectual. Pragmatism, evolutionism, existentialism, idealism, and other forms of subjectivism have been the objects of their devastating critiques for too long to hold out much hope for future development. Finally, because of the very nature of their discipline, Catholic philosophers are confident in the power of reason to arrive at truth and certitude, and thus are hardly attracted to a fideism (5:908) that despairs of attaining any rational certitudes and leaves all commitment at the level of faith alone. This possibly explains why they are generally more conservative than present-day Catholic theologians and tend to be content with the Aristotelian-Thomistic or critical realist synthesis, while still actively confronting alternative systems of thought to deepen their basic insights and commitments.

Professors, Catholic Colleges. Statistical information in support of such generalizations is meager. A survey of teachers of philosophy in Catholic colleges made in 1966 showed that 60 per cent then identified themselves as Thomists, 20 per cent as having an existentialist-phenomenological orientation, 10 per cent as being analytically oriented, and the remainder divided among process philosophers of the Whiteheadian or Teilhardian variety, pragmatists, and adherents of other schools (McMullin). Undoubtedly, with the decline of Thomism in the colleges (*see* THOMISM), these statistics have shifted during the past decade. Within Thomism itself there has been a growth of interest in transcendental methods (Kantian and Hegelian), in phenomenological methods (Husserlian and Heideggerian), and in analytical methods (linguistic and Wittgensteinian). Interest has also grown in the personal and the practical, to say nothing of the historical. It should be noted, however, that these changes do not necessarily involve radical shifts in the content of philosophy or in its systematic character. Rather they are changes in methods or styles of philosophizing, some of which are better adapted than others to treating particular subject matters. Perhaps it is not surprising that those working in metaphysics and natural theology are more attracted to the transcendental; that those specializing in the philosophy of man are exploring the phenomenological; and that philosophers of science are more conversant with the analytical. But withal the core content of philosophy changes very slowly: different styles and methods lead inevitably to different terminologies, yet the truths conveyed differ but little except in the semantics of their expression.

Seminary Professors. A more recent survey of the philosophical backgrounds sought in Catholic seminarians beginning theology, published in 1974, may shed more light on the kind of pluralism now found in American seminaries. J. R. Fenili circulated a questionnaire to about 60 seminaries and elicited responses from over 900 professors; some of his queries evoked the names of specific philosophers with whom professors believed students needed an acquaintance for understanding course content; other queries were more generic, designed to gauge the professors' estimate of the importance of philosophy for theology or of their

conceptions of philosophy itself. In the tabulated results Aquinas came out far in advance of any other author and was especially cited by those teaching systematic and historical theology; Heidegger made a surprisingly good showing, partially because of the preferences registered by Scripture professors; and Kant, Aristotle, and Plato were grouped close behind in the number of times mentioned (see Table below). Philosophy was uniformly regarded as important for the professors' discipline, with the predictable exception of those engaged in pastoral and field training. And philosophy itself was conceived on the scholastic model, but with emphasis placed on personal reflection and appropriation. Significantly there was practically no support for linguistic or analytical philosophy as it is taught in most non-Catholic institutions in the United States. The rank-ordering of preferred philosophers, based on those who indicated these (slightly over 300), was as follows:

Rank	Author	Times Mentioned
1	Aquinas	218
2	Heidegger	125
3	Kant	121
4	Aristotle	104
5	Plato	99
6	Hegel	69
7	Augustine	49
8	Whitehead	40
9	Lonergan	39
10	Marcel	28
11	Rahner	24
12	Marx	24
13	Buber	23
14	Kierkegaard	22
15	Sartre	20
16	Maritain	19
17	Descartes	16
18	Husserl	16
19	Dewey	14
20	Wittgenstein	14

Church Guidelines. Turning to ecclesiastical guidelines, in an authoritative instruction issued in 1976 entitled *The Theological Formation of Future Priests*, the Sacred Congregation for Catholic Education reiterated the teaching of Vatican II that "the perenially valid patrimony of Christian thought, and especially of St. Thomas" assures primary importance when selecting the philosophy to be employed in theology. Then, explicitly addressing the problem of philosophical pluralism, the document reads:

In certain circumstances the Church can accept a healthy philosophical pluralism arising from different regions, different cultures, and mentalities, and expressed perhaps in different ways, since the same truth can be reached in different ways, and can be presented and expounded in different ways. On the other hand, it is not at all possible for her to accept a philosophical pluralism which compromises the fundamental truths connected with Revelation such as is apt to occur in certain philosophies influenced by historical relativism and materialistic or idealistic immanentism (52).

Having thus implicitly rejected historicism, idealism, dialectical materialism, and philosophies denying absolutes such as evolutionism, pragmatism, and situationism, the instruction goes on to again endorse Aquinas's philosophical synthesis. It does so on this basis:

His philosophy clearly explains and harmonizes the first principles of natural truth with Revelation, not in any static form but with the dynamism that is peculiar to St. Thomas and which renders possible a continual and renewed synthesis of the valid conclusions of traditional thought and the advances made by modern thought (53).

Of the five solutions to the problem of philosophical pluralism given in the earlier treatment in the *New*

Catholic Encyclopedia (11:450), it is perhaps noteworthy that the foregoing texts focus on two that meet the needs of the Church in the present day: (1) the solution stressing that philosophy is not an eclectic collection of different systems, but rather a continuous and gradual development of a *philosophia perennis* that gives an increasingly more adequate explanation of reality; and (2) the solution admitting the diversity and opposition of many philosophies, but insisting that whatever validity these have as philosophies lies in their being different expressions from different viewpoints and by different methods of one ultimate truth.

Evaluation. Both of these solutions are compatible with philosophy's being historical and having a history, for no one would deny that it is a product of man's intellectual activity elaborated in the course of time. To explain how this can be so it may be helpful to draw a distinction between (1) philosophy achieved (*in facto esse*) and (2) the same discipline in the process of becoming or of formation (*in fieri*). The goal of philosophy achieved is true and certain knowledge. This does not mean that every subject investigated by philosophers permits of absolutely certain judgment; it does mean, however, that the philosopher seeks truth and that there are some starting points available to him on which his search for truth can be solidly grounded. His thought may remain ever open to further extension and development, and yet it is not subject to change with regard to first principles and other self-evident truths on which this development is based, except in the sense that these come to be more deeply comprehended and understood with the passage of time. To the extent that the philosopher is able to arrive at truth and certitude with regard to matters that are not immediately evident, and to this extent alone, he possesses philosophy achieved. Once achieved, moreover, such philosophy is unchangeable and timeless and so can be said to stand outside of history. In the process of becoming, on the other hand, philosophy must be identified with the temporal flux of its formation and with the stages at which man's mind arrives in its pursuit of truth. It is in this developing sense that philosophy is historied and stands within time. This distinction once understood, clearly being historied is not a property of philosophy as true and certain knowledge, but rather as a type of knowledge that develops and comes more perfectly into being in different cultures and throughout time. A further distinction emerges between (1) philosophy and (2) history of philosophy. Philosophy, once achieved, is not concerned with what men have said, but rather with propounding and defending the truth about the matters they consider and this in ways that permit the widest variety of conceptualizations and formulations. History of philosophy, on the other hand, is concerned with ascertaining the truth of what men have said in their efforts to come to the possession of the truth they have sought, and continue to seek, both individually and collectively. Both studies can be pursued in a healthy atmosphere of pluralism that does not compromise the faith, and it is in this sense that the Church accepts pluralism in the education of its future priests.

See also PLURALISM, THEOLOGICAL; THOMISM. *Also* ANALYTICAL PHILOSOPHY (1:470); ECLECTICISM (5:40); EXISTENTIALISM (5:730); HERMENEUTICS (CONTEMPORARY) (16:206); PHENOMENOLOGY (11:256); PHILOSOPHERS, CONTEMPORARY (16:341); PHILOSOPHY (11:249); PHILOSOPHY, HISTORY OF (11:299); PHILOSOPHY, RECENT DEVELOPMENTS IN (16:348); PRAGMATISM (11:663); RELIGIOUS LANGUAGE (16:383).

Bibliography: Congregation for Catholic Education, *The Theological Formation of Future Priests* (USCC Publ., Washington, D.C. 1976). J. R. FENILI, "The Role of Philosophy as a Preparation for Theological Studies for Catholic Seminarians" (Ph.D. thesis, Marquette Univ. 1974). L. E. LOEMKER, "Perennial Philosophy," *Dictionary of the History of Ideas* (New York 1973). E. MCMULLIN, "Who Are We?" ProcAmCathPhilAs 41 (1967) 1–16. F. SONTAG, *The Future of Theology: A Philosophical Basis for Contemporary Protestant Thought* (Philadelphia 1969). W. A. WALLACE, *The Elements of Philosophy: A Compendium for Philosophers and Theologians* (Staten Island, N.Y. 1977).

[W. A. WALLACE]

PLURALISM, SOCIAL AND CULTURAL

In the Pastoral Constitution, on the Church in the Modern World, Vatican Council II strongly affirmed the principle of cultural pluralism as a fundamental ideal of the Church. One entire chapter is devoted to culture in its sociological and ethnological sense as the customs which constitute the proper patrimony of distinct human communities (*Gaudium et spes* 53–62). The Constitution acknowledges the social and technological forces which bring about a uniformity of culture, and foresees a more universal human culture developing which "will promote and express the unity of the human race to the degree that it preserves the particular features of the different cultures" (ibid. 54). The document asserts clearly that God speaks to his children in a manner adapted to different places and peoples. The Church, therefore, "is not bound exclusively and indissolubly to any race or nation; . . . she can enter into communion with various cultural modes, to her own enrichment and theirs too" (ibid. 58). The Constitution acknowledges the development of culture as necessary for the fulfilment of God's image in the human person, and sees the possibility through culture of liberating all humans from the bondage of ignorance (ibid. 59–60). There is a special comment on the need to extend the benefits of culture to women so that they may fulfil their proper role in human society (ibid. 60). It asks Christians to keep in contact with the creative members of the human family so that the benefits of cultural developments may enrich the life of the Church (ibid. 62).

The Constitution represents a historic moment in which the Church has addressed itself decisively to the problem of the relationship of faith to culture, and has clearly stated, in the context of contemporary social science, that faith must never be identified with any particular culture. This was the problem that challenged the early Church when some of the first Christians insisted that, in order to be Christians, all gentiles had to adopt the Hebrew way of life. The issue was clearly settled by the revelation to Saint Peter at Joppa (Acts ch. 10) and in the first Council of Jerusalem (Acts 15.6–30) but it has troubled the Church throughout history. All peoples have a strong tendency to identify their cultural style with God's will and Revelation. In preaching the Gospel, they often think they are communicating the Christian faith when in actuality they are imposing their own cultural expression of it on others.

Increased understanding of the importance of culture and sensitivity to its deep relationship to personal identity and security have resulted in a reawakening in people of pride in their cultural background and resistance to those who seek to change it, especially in the name of the Gospel. The influence of the Constitution is reflected in a growing interest in indigenous customs and practices. Popular piety and folk practices are being respectfully studied, and their relationship to a person's elemental commitment to God is being carefully explored.

The influence of the Constitution can also be seen in the resolutions of the first national assembly of Catholics in the United States, the *Call to Action Conference (1976), instigated by the U.S. bishops on "Liberty and Justice for All." The Conference called for a recognition of the importance of cultural pluralism to the life of the Church and recommended that serious efforts be made to enable Catholics of different cultural traditions to retain these traditions, and to enjoy a pastoral care adapted to their customs and style of life.

The Constitution does not overlook the serious problems associated with culture and faith, either in correcting evils which exist in many cultures, ". . . a humanism which is merely earth-bound and even contrary to religion itself" (*Gaudium et spes* 56), or in preserving great human patrimonies in the presence of rapid change: "How can the vitality and growth of a new culture be fostered without the loss of living fidelity to the heritage of tradition?" (ibid.).

See also ETHNICITY; INCULTURATION, THEOLOGICAL.

Bibliography: *A Call to Action. Conference of U.S. Bishops on Liberty and Justice for All* (USCC Publ. Office, Washington, D.C. 1977) 39–48.

[J. P. FITZPATRICK]

PLURALISM, THEOLOGICAL

There are many religions and many religious languages. Within a religion with a more or less common language for transcendence there are variations in language. Thus there are significant differences between Mahayana and Hinayana Buddhism, and between the Churches and sects of Christianity. Some of these variations in religious language are doctrinally formulated; so the *sola scriptura* and *sola fides* doctrines of the Reformation Churches and the ecclesiological doctrines of Roman Catholicism. Within such traditions marked by doctrinal differences there are theologies, or reflection upon the doctrines, which understand the same doctrines differently, such as Liberal and Conservative Protestant understandings of the doctrine of biblical inspiration, or the various theological schools of the Roman Catholic tradition. Pluralism is a matter of historical fact in religions, in doctrines within wide religious traditions, and in theological interpretations within doctrinal traditions. Here the concern is with theological pluralism.

While theological pluralism has always existed within Christianity (witness the divergent interpretations of the work and person of Jesus in New Testament Christianity), contemporary pluralism is qualitatively different from that which preceded it. Today's Church is faced, in the opinion of one Catholic theologian, with an "insurmountable theological pluralism" (Rahner). Whereas in the past one might dismiss those with whom one disagreed as stupid or heretical, or take disagreement to be temporary and to be resolved by argument, the present, divided state of theology seems irremediable.

Implications of Uniformity. A reflection on contemporary theological pluralism might begin with the question: what would theological unity mean? It would mean that all theologians understand the chief Christian doctrines and symbols in exactly the same way. It would mean a theological orthodoxy parallel to and representing the doctrinal language of a tradition. It would mean, in effect, what occurred in Roman Catholicism between the Modernist crisis at the beginning of the 20th century and the eve of the Second Vatican Council. For some this is a *desideratum*, for it would assure the unity, not to say uniformity, of expression in Catholic Christianity.

Such uniformity of interpretation is possible in the contemporary context only under certain contrary-to-fact conditions: (1) that there has been no significant change in the cultural criteria of meaning, truth, and value from that culture in which the original message was preached and the doctrines were framed; (2) that the ecclesial body itself is culturally homogeneous; (3) that there is an ecclesiastical coherence, discipline, and persuasive force sufficient to ensure uniformity available; (4) that theology is understood and accepted as the voice of another ministry in the Church; (5) that the act of theological understanding is equated with proclamation and creed. Such conditions have obtained in various combinations in Christian Churches at one time or another. When and where the contrary conditions obtain there is bound to be enunciated notably different theological understandings of Scripture and creeds, as well as of the function and nature of theology itself.

Since the contrary conditions obtain in the Catholic Church today, the establishment of uniformity of theological utterance as an ideal and an ecclesiastical rule would mean the reduction of theology to beliefs. The result would be either the rebirth of theology under another name—the need to interpret is constant—or the linguistic and religious corruption of the Church. It is taken by many theologians as an ethical *dictum* that understanding cannot be forced or prescribed, nor can language be made to bow without being corrupted. Although thinking can and should be reverent, it can obey only the dynamism of its questions and answer only to data and further questions. The question, then, is whether uniformity in theology is necessary for the unity of the Church. Many claim that it is not, yet how it is not remains a problem.

Reasons for Pluralism. What brings about this "insurmountable theological pluralism"? First, the profound change in the cultural context of theology, from what is termed classical to contemporary culture: the dissolution of a common world of suppositions, principles, methods, philosophies, and sciences, and the gradual formation of a radically different complex of these elements. When the cultural context of beliefs and practices changes, beliefs are necessarily and in varying degrees reformulated or else the change in culture is denied or denounced. The formulations of Christian faith of an earlier culture were conditioned by that matrix as well as by the reality intended in the formulations. As the expressions of early Jewish Christianity would have mystified medieval Christians and been scored as heretical, so the doctrinal formulations of Nicean and post-Nicean Christianity are rendered unintelligible in a new context until interpreted anew (for example, such doctrines as original sin and transubstantiation, and such terms as "nature" and "person" in the Trinitarian doctrines). In such circumstances church authority is unable to bind theological understanding to operate in an alien context—witness such papal attempts at binding as *Humani generis, Mysterium fidei,* and *Humanae vitae.*

Secondly, pluralism in theology follows from varying differentiations of consciousness, for the objectifications of faith vary as do the realms of human meaning. Thus common-sense religious language, the control of such language exercised in doctrines, and the theoretical consciousness expressed in theology may well intend the same meaning but differ significantly in expression.

Finally, pluralism in theology can follow from the different degrees of religious, moral, and intellectual conversion of members of the Church. The most radical pluralism, that most fraught with tragic consequences of utter fragmentation for the Church, is that which can be met only by conversion of mind and heart (Lonergan).

Theological Pluralism and Church Unity. What are the limits of theological pluralism? How is church unity to be maintained in the face of theological pluralism? How can there be one Gospel and many understandings of that Gospel? Theologians can hardly deny to the Church of which they themselves are members the right to draw boundaries by asking the question of the meaning of its own preaching and to reject some understandings as inadequate, incorrect, and even, in the limit, heretical. The authority of the pastoral office is not abolished by pluralism. But a new form of the understanding and exercise of that office is demanded in a new state of affairs. Theologians share responsibility for the maintenance of unity by taking the historic creeds and the authentic affirmations of the Church's faith as seriously as they wish their own role in articulating that faith to be taken. The chief ministerial officers of the Church on their side need to be acutely informed theologically and to be extraordinarily delicate in their search for church unity in belief and action (*see* THEOLOGIAN).

The unity of the Church rests on the scriptural and credal language, on common worship and action, and above all on the unifying power of the Holy Spirit poured out. Undoubtedly faith is a verbal event. It has its language and cannot be relegated to some prethematic and unformulated attitude, given simply with human existence itself. Church unity is maintained in an ongoing dialectic of belief and practice, not through the isolation of one from the other. Unity rests on both the act of God gracing persons and communities with his Holy Spirit and on Jesus Christ as his "external Word," on conversion of heart, and on the gospel message delivered in preaching, Scripture, creeds, and ministerial teaching. It is not classical culture or the expressions of that culture in beliefs that makes the Church one, but a unity of inner and outer word differently expressed in different cultures and by differently differentiated consciousness (Lonergan). The pluralisms of communications and common-sense expression and the pluralism resulting from differentiated consciousness are not the crucial problems of church unity; the problem is rather the pluralism resulting from the absence of religious, moral, and intellectual conversion on the part of church leaders and theologians.

To a certain extent the problem of church unity is political, for the interests, tasks and needs of the ministerial and theological offices in the Church do not always coincide. The Catholic Church has much to learn and to accomplish in this regard. This can be done in practice only by hard intellectual work and high seriousness on the part of theologians and careful exercise of office on the part of church leaders. In the present situation what needs most attention on both sides is the development of a new understanding of the function of theology in relation to the Church and its ministerial offices and important changes in the conditions under which these offices are exercised.

Bibliography: A. DULLES, *The Survival of Dogma* (Garden City, New York 1971); *The Resilient Church: The Necessity and Limits of Adaptation* (Garden City, New York 1977). B. F. J. LONERGAN, *Method in Theology* (New York 1972). K. RAHNER, "Pluralism in Theology and the Unity of the Creed in the Church," *Theological Investigations* v. 11, tr. D. BOURKE (New York 1974) 19–26. D. TRACY, *Blessed Rage for Order: The New Pluralism in Theology* (New York 1975).

[W. M. SHEA]

POLITICAL COMMUNITIES

The political community is a human grouping capable of satisfying the basic needs of its members, relatively autonomous in the conduct of its internal and external affairs, characterized by territory and a single principal authority responsible for the welfare and good order of the whole. If politics is viewed dynamically within a community or society, it is the process of authoritative values-allocation which directly (or indirectly through the laws that program social interaction) provides for human needs and desires. Functionally the political system makes binding, sanctioned decisions for the community, while structurally it consists of those roles and offices, institutions, activities, groups and persons who contribute to making or implementing such decisions, or to determining their precise meaning and application.

Church Teaching. Vatican II's Pastoral Constitution on the Church in the Modern World devotes Part II ch. 4 to the life of the political community "in its manifold expressions" (*Gaudium et spes* 73–77). It views the political community as the complex, relatively self-sufficient and functionally diversified social matrix (community or society) possessed of authoritative and lawful government. Although censuring disordered individualism and collectivism and affirming as the norm a personalistic and communitarian image of society, based on strong family units, the Council recognizes that an extended range of institutional and constitutional forms based on diverse historical and cultural conditions and experiences may satisfy the exigencies of justice and order.

Political communities exist for the common good and are responsible for their own internal organization, regulating the relations of citizens among themselves and with public authority. *Authority* is needed to unify and dispose the energies of the citizens toward the common good, primarily as a moral force relying on the citizens' free and conscientious performance of their functional roles. Both constitutional form and mode of selecting leaders (i.e. authorities or public decision-makers) belong to the citizens, but government must always be limited by moral principle and by citizens' natural and civil rights (including rights of free assembly, common action, expression of opinion, private and public profession and religion).

Paul VI in his "Call to Action" apostolic letter of 1971 speaks of politics as the realm of ultimate decision, a "natural and necessary link for ensuring the cohesion of the social body" creating "conditions required for man's true and complete good, including his spiritual end" (Paul VI OctogAdven 46). The Pope, echoing St. Thomas Aquinas, perceives political activity not as a remedy for disorder, sin, and evil but the functioning of a social complex in view of the common welfare, in which the liberties of individuals, families and subsidiary groups, decisionally autonomous in their proper spheres, are respected. The common good, the object or final cause of the political community is, "the sum of those conditions of social life which allow social groups and their individual members relatively thorough and ready access to their own fulfillment..." (Vatican Council II, *Gaudium et spes* 26).

Perhaps the most significant element in recent Catholic thought on the political community as expressed in the social messages of Pius XII, John XXIII, Paul VI, the Synods of Bishops, the declarations of Vatican II, and the messages of continental and national episcopal conferences has been an unprecedented affirmation of and emphasis on individual and group freedom and responsibility. Given the rapid rise in the average level of education, increasing access to information, the widespread use of participative and representative modes of decision-making, and the sensitivity of public officials to responsibly articulated demands, much of mankind is moving from the position of a manipulated social mass towards a considerable personal and group autonomy and accountability within functionally and geographically limited areas—from being an object to being a subject of history.

As population, geographic extension, and functional complexity increase political communities capable of satisfying the full range of human needs may exist at the local, regional, national, international, and universal or global levels. In terms of the principle of subsidiarity (13:762), according to which decisions should be made at the lowest hierarchical level competent, political decision-makers at each level are properly concerned with harmonizing and facilitating the activities and interactions of the lesser communities within their jurisdiction, stimulating their welfare through appropriate institutional mechanisms, readjusting and even reconstituting the rules of the game when structural inequities and inadequacies are revealed. In this vision of a pluralistic world order no political authority is deemed omnicompetent in the sense of having a right to intervene in every detail of the life and allocative processes of lesser communities, nor should any possess unrestricted power.

World Community. Although the recent social documents of the Church clearly conceive of the "political community" primarily at the nation-state level, no state is competent to deal with the common good of the whole human family, linked as it is now by exchanges of agricultural commodities, raw materials and manufactured products, the means of interpersonal and social communication, and the movement of persons. The contemporary world, bound by an increasingly dense web of economic, social, scientific and cultural interdependencies, urgently requires the development of an international political authority to provide, at the highest level, for the security, welfare and more equitable distribution of the earth's bounty within "a single world community."

Much recent Catholic thought has been directed at expressing the moral and functional requisites of such a global community (*Gaudium et spes* 77–90) and its mode of articulation in terms of: politico-juridical guarantees of the integrity of lesser communities; and of pluralism in institutional and constitutional forms, in civilization and cultural commitment, in language and ethnic identity, in patterns of action, production and consumption—all within the limits required by the common welfare of the whole of mankind.

Over and over, in varying contexts, the Church has urged Christians to help build the world, to enter a "new age in human history" with the self-awareness needful to spiritual and moral maturity. Concretely the Christian is asked to work strenuously on behalf of certain policies at the national and international levels: a humane and civic culture, based on freedom of inquiry and expression, and favorable to personal dignity and free from discrimination; such means of self-improvment for all as the benefits of literacy, a basic culture and the opportunity for higher studies; the satisfaction of legitimate desires for economic goods and services fostered by private and group initiatives and enhanced productivity; scientific and technological progress and adaptation; prudence and equity in the distribution and use of the earth's resources.

Reflection. The organically unified yet highly pluralistic, ethnically and culturally diversified world community envisaged in recent Catholic thought resembles the model of the *Respublica Christiana* conceived and partially achieved in medieval Europe. However, culturally, intellectually, and religiously it is a more open society, providing for universal, wide-ranging, juridically protected human and civil rights and characterized by a high level of personal freedom and small group autonomy. In such a global community every person and group, every authority is constrained by local or more universal moral consensuses and legal norms as well as limited but effective powers of enforcement at each echelon.

From such a vision the common welfare at every level of political community takes on a dynamic aspect. As populations shift from rural to urban settings, as the cultural levels and functional competencies of communities change over time and are diversified by age cohort, as the possibilities for weal and woe of new technologies and the instruments of social communication are explored, as economic and political institutions are modified and new ones invented to satisfy the exigencies of global development, as traditional cultures strive to retain what is perennial and valid in the context of an ecumenical culture—the concrete realization of the common good must change. In a rapidly moving world the conditions and significance of optimal personal and group self-realization vary over time, and the notion of the common welfare encompasses even the developmental process itself under "forward looking" human control (see Paul VI OctogAdven 37). At the level of the international political community papal pronouncement have praised such functional groups as the International Labor Office and the Food and Agricultural Organization, while Vatican II sees in such functional agencies "the first attempts to lay international foundations under the whole human community for solving the critical problems of our age..." (*Gaudium et spes* 84).

In 1965 Paul VI addressed the United Nations as an

incipient international authority which could develop into a guidance mechanism for the world community while *Gaudium et spes* refers to the international community as competent to make and implement decisions (86). Certainly world peace is conceived as far more than a mere absence of warfare or a balance of power based on threat and fear, preparedness and deterrence. As in every community it is an order of justice based on the protection and preservation of personal and group rights and values, shared access to the earth's bounty, mutual respect and a renunciation of violence and terror. In the contemporary world this requires renouncing weapons of mass destruction directed at cities and civil populations. But no political authority may neglect reality. The renunciation of the instruments of violence in the global community must be mutual, not unilateral. Equally, at this level, justice requires facilitating increased productivity, increasingly complex and articulated institutions, and vastly increased access to cultural goods by the populations of the emerging nations. In his 1967 social encyclical Paul VI could remark, "Development is the new name for peace" (Paul VI PopProgr 76) and thereby imply a dynamic order, a process of building the earth as an ever more just and equitable human community.

See also COMMUNITY OF MANKIND; POLITICS, CHURCH AND. *Also* POLITICAL PHILOSOPHY (11:510); POLITICAL SCIENCE (11:516); STATE, THE (13:644).

Bibliography: T. GILBY, *Between Community and Society* (London 1953). F. I. GREENSTEIN and N. W. POLSBY, eds., *Handbook of Political Science* (Reading, Mass., 1975), esp. v. 3, *Macropolitical Theory*; v. 4, *Non-Governmental Politics*; v. 5, *Governmental Institutions and Processes*; v. 8, *International Politics*. J. GREMILLION, *The Gospel of Peace and Justice—Catholic Social Teaching since Pope John* (Maryknoll, N.Y. 1976). J. MESSNER, *Social Ethics* (St. Louis 1964). G. and P. MISCHE, *Toward a Human World Order* (New York 1977). R. NISBET, *Community and Power* (New York 1962).

[C. R. DECHERT]

POLITICAL THEOLOGY

Political theology has two distinct meanings. Firstly, it is the implicit or explicit use of religious symbols to interpret, to justify, or to criticize political events, systems, or units. As implicit, it is almost coexistent with religion. As explicit, political theology is a distinct division of theology which in middle Stoicism was distinguished from mythic and natural theology. In the European Enlightenment and Catholic Restoration, it was contrasted with the notion of *civil religion, and in the 1960s it was a theological response to existentialism that stressed the public significance of Christian eschatology. Secondly, in its other meaning, political theology stands for a foundational theology that analyzes the interrelation between political patterns and religious beliefs. Their mutual influence is studied to uncover the meaning, truth, and practice of religious symbols.

Historical Analysis. Although both meanings of political theology are quite clear, political theology has often been confused with political ethics or has often been identified either with traditionalism or with *liberation theology. A historical survey will underscore its distinctive meaning.

Antiquity. In middle Stoicism, political theology appears along with mythic and natural theology as parts of a tripartite division. This Hellenistic division became current in Roman theology when Pontifex Quintus Mucius Scaevola argued for the necessity of political theology as a defense of the Roman civil religion. This tripartite division is elaborated by Marcus Terentius Varro (116–27 B.C.) in his *Antiquities*, a major source of information about the tripartite division. Since it is no longer extant, it must be reconstructed from Tertullian's *Ad nationes* and Augustine's *De Civitate Dei* and their discussions of political theology. In this tripartite division, each theology has a specific source, locus, and theme. Mythic theology consists of the poet's narration of divine stories and its locus is the theatre. Natural theology consists of the philosophical world views propounded by the philosophers in their schools. Political theology is attributed to priests and statesmen; its locus is the cities. Varro distinguishes between uncertain and certain gods, elucidates a natural theology, and gives an allegorical interpretation of Roman myths in order to salvage and defend the Roman political theology.

Both Tertullian and Augustine criticize political theology. For Tertullian, valid theology demands criteria of certitude, morality, and universality. Political theology lacks universality, for each city has its own religion. Augustine's criticisms are much more fundamental. Political theology rests upon a mythic theology. If the myths and fables are false, then the political theology is invalid. Likewise it is only as valid as its underlying metaphysical or natural theology. Augustine's analysis and critique contributes several insights. Political theology along with natural and mythic theology are viewed as three fundamentally distinct ways of speaking of God. They are distinct, but are radically intertwined. Moreover, Augustine challenges the adequacy of utilitarianism as a theological criterion of political theology. He argues against the immanence of the Roman natural theology and confronts political theology with his eschatological conception of the City of God.

Enlightenment and Restoration. Distinct evaluations of political theology appear in the Enlightenment and Catholic Restoration. The tripartite division of theology is cited by such leading representatives of the Enlightenment as H. Grotius (1583–1645), E. Lord Herbert of Cherbury (1581–1648), P. Bayle (1647–1706), G. Vico (1668–1744) and M. Diderot (1713–1784). Just as they criticize positive religion and seek to replace it with a natural religion, so too do they criticize political theology. Rousseau introduces "civil religion" as a replacement for the confessional political theologies. It should become the basis of the social contract and should encourage citizens to love their civil duties and sacrifice themselves for them. Since the religious wars were seen as the consequences of confessional political theologies, a natural civil religion would avoid such strife. Nevertheless the notion of civil religion faces a dilemma since the particularity demanded by a civil religion is undercut by the universality of natural religion. Social utility and universal truth are often in conflict.

The Catholic Restoration, represented by Catholic nobility in exile, not only elaborated but also defended a political theology. J. Donoso Cortes (1809–53), Louis G. A. de Bonald (1754–1840), Joseph de Maistre (1773–1821), Carl Ludwig von Haller (1768–1854), and the early Félicité Lamennais (1782–1854) constitute this restoration and can all be classed under the heading of seeking to reconstitute society on the basis of religion.

They perceived the interrelation between political ideas and religious ideas and asserted that changes in religious and philosophical worldviews led to changes in political patterns. Therefore, they saw the French Revolution as a result of the Enlightenment and criticized both. Against the Enlightenment they argued that no natural religion exists, but only positive religions. Only a positive religion, not a civil religion could demonstrate its utility for the state. They developed an apologetic for the social necessity of positive religion, gave primacy to the social over the individual, and suggested political utility and common consent as social criteria of theological affirmations. Their political theology underscored the sinfulness of human nature, the need for strong authority, and the Lordship of God and Christ.

Current Usage. In Germany the term political theology was used in the 1960s by Johannes B. Metz to characterize a distinct theological approach and endeavor. It expressed a theological response to the secularization and privatization of religion in industrialized, technocratic societies. Against the individualism and subjectivism of existential theology and philosophy, political theology argued that existentialism failed to come to grips with the privatizing tendencies of modern society. In fact, it only reinforced and justified them. Political theology was therefore proposed primarily as a public theology or political hermeneutics that sought to draw out the public significance and practical import of religious symbols. It especially sought to retrieve the meaning of eschatology as a source of critique and amelioration in the socio-political order (*see* HOPE, THEOLOGY OF).

Since political theology underscores the public significance of faith, it turned toward analyzing the questions of hermeneutics and the theory-practice relation. It sought to distinguish itself from previous Constantinian political theologies and to elaborate a post-Enlightenment conception of theology's relation to political practice. These issues moved political theology in the direction of fundamental theology.

Systematic Clarification. The historical survey indicates that, despite diverse uses, political theology primarily refers to the implicit or explicit use of religious symbols to legitimate or to criticize political reality. The contemporary use of political theology as response to the Marxist critique is an important shift, for whereas previously political theology justified and legitimated political systems, now it was ordered to their critique.

Although the Enlightenment distinguished between a confessional political theology and a natural civil religion, in general political theology refers to the reflective theological attempt to justify or to defend civil or political religions. But in its most recent usage, political theology was appropriated precisely as an explicit theological criticism of civil or political religions, even though some would see the civil religion itself as exercising a critical function within a country. This meaning of political theology distinguishes it quite clearly from political ethics and liberation theology.

Distinct from Political Ethics. Political ethics focuses on deontic judgments of moral obligation or on aretaic judgments of moral value and rightness; political theology analyzes how religious symbols either legitimate or criticize a political and social order. To the extent, however, that any symbolic vision leads to concrete action, it needs to be complemented by ethical reflection. On this point the advocates of political theology disagree; some demand that a specifically theological ethic as an integral part of the religious vision link theory and practice; others claim that the pluralism of modern society demands a more universal rational ethic.

Distinct from Liberation Theology. Political theology, moreover, differs from liberation theology as the general from the specific. Liberation theology is a specific political theology insofar as it is usually linked with a specific group (Blacks, women, minority groups, underprivileged nations). These appeal to their specific experiences; they then analyze their religious tradition in relation to their experience, and, drawing on their tradition, they propose a concrete vision and praxis of liberation. Since liberation theology is theoretically and practically concerned with the interrelation between religious symbols and political praxis, it is a political theology, but its methodic basis is formed by a specific experience as a starting-point and is ordered to particular political and social goals.

A Foundational Theology. In addition to its primary meaning, political theology has come to be understood as a foundational theology. As such its primary concern is not the practical application of religious symbols, but the analytical and reconstructive task of studying the pragmatics of religious symbols. It investigates their origin, development and use in relation to the socio-political order. Political theology so understood seeks to come to terms with the sociology of religion and the sociology of knowledge insofar as these affect the foundations of faith and the basis of theology. It thereby extends the histroical-critical method into a socio-critical method. Whereas the historical-critical method studies the historical context of diverse texts, political theology analyzes the social conditions and political effects of religious beliefs. Political theology would therefore come to grips with a Weberian analysis of the correlation between social status and religious beliefs, with a Durkheimian analysis of the correlation between religious and political patterns of organization, and with the Marxist analysis of the possible ideological function of religion. This foundational task would make systematic theology and theological ethics more explicitly self-reflective of their basis. Its method would not be simply hermeneutical or transcendental, but rather reconstructive, since it would take into account the history of the intertwinement of the religious and the socio-political.

Bibliography: G. BAUM, *Religion and Alienation* (New York 1975). W. R. COATES, *God in Public. Political Theology beyond Niebuhr* (Grand Rapids, Mich. 1974). H. FELD, et al., *Dogma und Politik* (Mainz 1973). A. FIERRO, *The Militant Gospel: An Analysis of Contemporary Political Theologies* (New York 1978). F. FIORENZA, "'Political Theology': An Historical Analysis," TheolDig 25 (1977) 317–334, "Political Theology as Foundational Theology," CathThSoc 32 (1977) 142–177. R. D. JOHNS, *Man in the World. The Theology of Johannes Baptist Metz* (Missoula, Mont. 1976). A. KEE, ed., *A Reader in Political Theology* (Philadelphia 1974). J. B. METZ, *Theology of the World* tr. W. GLEN-DOEPEL, (New York 1969); *Glaube in Geschichte und Gesellschaft* (Mainz 1977), H. PEUKERT, ed., *Diskussion zur 'politischen Theologie'* (Mainz 1969), C. SCHMITT, *Politische Theologie* (Berlin 1922). *Politische Theologie, II* (Berlin 1970), D. SÖLLE, *Political Theology* (Stuttgart 1976) excellent bibliog. S. WOLIN, *Politics and Vision* (Boston 1960). M. XHAUFFLAIRE, *La Théologie politique* (Paris 1972). See also bibliog. for Liberation Theology.

[F. SCHÜSSLER FIORENZA]

POLITICS, CHURCH AND

The relation between the Church as the People of God and civil authority has been a continuing concern of Christians from the beginning. Christ was born in Bethlehem because of an edict of Augustus. He spent his earliest childhood in Egypt, a refugee from a homicidal prince. His own and Israel's acceptance (Jn 19.15) of Roman jurisdiction in the matter of the crucifixion has been construed as a confirmation of the Roman Empire's authority, however unjustly exercised by its magistrate (Dante, *De monarchia* 2, 11–12). The religious crime (blasphemy), meriting death under Jewish law, before Pilate became a charge of treason and subversion (Lk 23.14). Christ's basic position regarding civil authority was enunciated in his response: "Then give to Caesar what is Caesar's, but give to God what is God's" (Mt 23.21), and in his reply to Pilate: "You would have no power over me whatever unless it were given you from above" (Jn 19.11). Both St. Peter and St. Paul in their lives and words confirm the Christians's obedience to civil authority within the limits of conscience (Pt 2.13–15; Rom 13.1–5). Initially, as members of a Jewish sect, Christians presumably enjoyed the recognition and religious immunities enjoyed by the Jews in the Roman Empire. But well before the end of the 1st century Christians were expelled from the synagogue and the Neronian persecution showed early the resistance of Rome's civic mentality to Christians. Their civil obedience was coupled with moral independence. The demand for an internal liberty beyond the reach of public authority was manifested by accepting martyrdom as the ultimate manifestation of spiritual freedom. The intimate union of civil and religious authority that characterized a more primitive world was transcended. The priest-king, emperor-*pontifex*, was replaced by two authorities, two communities, each claiming allegiance of the citizen-Christian, potentially capable of working together for human temporal welfare and spiritual betterment, yet also in a creative tension. Within that cultural area ranging from Britain to North Africa and the frontiers of Persia and the Arabian desert, the Christian community thrived, affirming ancient virtues of hearth and polity in a society increasingly egoistic and hedonistic in outlook. The last and most sanguinary persecution, under Diocletian (284–305), proved both the universal presence and the mettle of the Christian community. Then the policy of Constantine (306–337) sought to engage the Christian community in the task of Roman imperial survival.

Historical Development. State neutrality in matters religious gave way in the 4th century to Christianity's becoming the religion of the Empire. The Emperors Gratian (367–383) and Theodosius (379–395) declined the traditional title *pontifex maximus* and by the 5th century St. Augustine (354–430), in *The City of God*, detached the fate of Rome from the fate of the Church and with his notion of the "two cities" formed Christian thought on Church-State relations for a millennium and more. The Church in the person of St. Ambrose (339–397), could effectively censure the Emperor Theodosius.

Emergence of Papal Political Power. While Church and Empire were increasingly identified in the East, the political chaos of the former Western Empire in the premedieval period both permitted and required an affirmation of ecclesiastical autonomy. Pope Gelasius (492–496) enunciated the doctrine of the "two swords," affirming the autonomy of civil and ecclesiastical authority each in its own sphere. The withdrawal of Byzantine

power from central Italy required that the popes assume temporal jurisdiction over what become the Papal States. The consciously supranational religious policies of Pope St. Gregory I (590–604) were principally expressed by sending St. Augustine to England, which, in turn, became the missionary source of the German Church. Pepin (751–768) affirmed the temporal sovereignty of the Papal States while his son Charlemagne (768–814) received imperial status and leadership of the Christian commonwealth though papal coronation as Roman Emperor, to the chagrin of Eastern Christians, emperor and patriarch alike. Both politically and culturally the Church had entered a period during which it would largely stimulate the development of European civilization and become identified with it.

In early medieval Europe the Church and churchmen, heirs of classical culture and moral authorities in the community, proved valuable for civil administration. As a result there arose the investitures controversy in which the Holy See successfully reclaimed from the Holy Roman Empire the right to name bishops and bestow the symbols of their office. Innocent III (1198–1216) and Boniface VIII (1294–1303) recalled the responsibility of the Church to pass moral judgments on the acts of civil authority, a formidable power when exercised in a Christian society and backed by the sanctions of interdict or excommunication. The exercise of moral authority by Gregory VII (1073–85) in his victory over the Emperor Henry IV (1056–1106) regarding lay investiture could not in the longer run compete with the enhanced political power, legal pretensions based on the revived *Codex iuris civilis*, and ability to mobilize public opinion possessed by the rulers of Europe's emerging nation-states. The papacy's uncertain contest with Frederick II of Sicily in the early 13th century was followed by Philip the Fair's brutal effort to put down Boniface VIII, culminating in Nogaret's outrageous behavior at Anagni and Clement V's (1305–14) effective capitulation to Philip in the matter of the suppression of the Templars followed by the Babylonian Captivity at Avignon. Utilization of secular military force in the service of Christendom, most notably in the Crusades and the suppression of the Albigensians, proved a mixed blessing. The integrity of Western Christendom was perpetuated for several centuries at the cost of alienating the Eastern Church and too closely linking the exercise of the rising military capability of Europe's national states to religious justifications for its use. Post-Reformation Europe instrumentalized religious sentiments for centuries in the pursuit of the most blatant commercial, nationalistic, and dynastic interests. The Inquisition, begun to combat heresy, became in effect a counterintelligence service and thought police for the Spanish crown, while the British intelligence service largely devoted its efforts from the time of Walsingham (1532–90) to the defeat of Charles Edward Stuart at Culloden (1746) to foiling efforts at a Catholic restoration.

Loss of Temporal Power. The Catholic princes of Europe supported the Counter Reformation for reasons of faith and policy, and supported or permitted missionary efforts in New France and New Spain, South America, Africa, India, Japan, China, and Southeast Asia. In turn, these states could instrumentalize religion to a degree, exercise such controls on the life of the national Churches evident in Gallicanism and

Josephinism, and even force such concessions as the suppression of the Jesuits by Clement XIV in 1773. The Enlightenment of the 18th century effectively secularized and de-Christianized Europe's intellectual establishment and a substantial part of its social and political elite. French revolutionary *élan* harnessed to Napoleon's dream of secular empire deprived the Church of both its traditional privileges and its temporal sovereignty. Political liberalism and laissez-faire economic policies, as well as rapidly expanding commerce and industry were alienating, rendering insecure, and spiritually impoverishing a large part of Europe's tradition-based artisan and peasant population, while radical socialism, egalitarian and atheistically humanist in spirit, preached social revolution. The Papal States, restored after Napoleon's defeat, had become an anachronism in the presence of the aggressive nationalist push for the unification of the peoples of the Italian peninsula led by Piedmont. Pius IX's (1846–78) brief flirtation with liberalism at the beginning of his reign bred disillusion and a reaffirmation of the Church's traditional doctrine on society, polity, and Church-State relations in the Syllabus of Errors (1864). Vatican Council I affirmed papal infallibility and adjourned sine die as the armies of the House of Savoy moved to occupy Rome and to strip the Church of its last vestige of political autonomy under a unilaterally imposed Law of Guarantees that would seek to make the papacy a dependent of the newly unified, secular Italian state. The recognition of the Church's sovereignty and territorial integrity in the Lateran Pacts of 1929 permitted a reaffirmation of the Church's political identity and independence, and permitted more extensive diplomatic relations with governments on behalf of religion. Vatican City's negligible population largely relieve it of the onus of civil administration and the administration of criminal justice, which might render it vulnerable to public opinion aroused by not-always-friendly governments and media of communication.

The Modern Popes on Politics. The loss of temporal authority and the dominant 19th-century Western intellectual and political consensus on the social and political irrelevance of the Church were countered by Leo XIII (1878–1903), who, in a series of declarations, affirmed the legitimacy of modern representative political institutions and modes of social organization as well as the need for Christians and Catholics to take an affirmative role in them. Encouragement of Thomism as a unifying philosophic synthesis (*Aeterni Patris*, 1879) and the incisive social critique of *Rerum novarum* (1891) provided the basis for modern Catholic thought and action designed to influence society primarily through the civic action of the believer in his role as a citizen and economically productive member of the community. Christian Democracy as an ideological and organizational alternative to liberalism and socialism had won approval in the encyclical *Graves de communi re* (1901), and took on clear form as a viable political movement in Germany, Belgium, Switzerland, and Italy in the early 1900s. It came to dominate Western European politics during the twenty-year period of reconstruction after World War II and could show some successes in Latin America. The personalist and communitarian social message of *Rerum novarum* was recalled in a special way in *Quadragesimo anno* (1931) of Pius XI (1922–39), *Mater et magistra* (1961) of John XXIII

(1958–63), and again in Paul VI's "Call to Action," the apostolic letter, *Octogesima adveniens* (1971).

Pope Benedict XV's (1914–22) anguish over a secularized Christendom's suicidal and "useless slaughter" evoked the consternation of the principal belligerents in World War I. Pius XI's concern over an onslaught of totalitarianism and religious persecution found expression in the encyclical *Divini Redemptoris* (1937), condemning atheistic communism, and in the letters *Non abbiamo bisogno* (1931) and *Mit brennender Sorge* (1937) directed at the Italian Fascists and German National Socialists.

Pius XII, whose pleas for peace in 1939 went unheeded, during World War II put the weight of his moral authority behind representative governments with juridical guarantees of civil liberties. The dominant role of the Christian Democrats in Italian, German, Belgian, and Dutch politics for two decades after World War II was conditioned both by their aconfessionality and the frequent need for liberal and/or socialist allies in cabinet coalitions. German and Dutch Christian Democracy, for example, depend on strong Protestant electoral support for their success. The Christian Democratic *Mouvement Républicain Populaire* in postwar France had a leftward policy-orientation yet counted on electoral support from traditionally oriented Catholics and foundered a few years after the Gaullist educational reform of 1959 resolved longstanding Catholic grievances regarding state support for Church-related schools. Italian Catholic Action was mobilized in support of *Democrazia cristiana* through the capillary "civic committees" and only moved to regain its autonomy and essentially religious role at the end of the 1960s.

The Church's affirmation of its autonomy as a community of the spirit and as both a moral force and critic of the ethical and ideological positions dominant in modern Western thought and society gained increasing credibility as the imperial self-assurance, industry and cultural *élan* of 19th-century Europe and North America foundered on the two World Wars, depression, totalitarianism of right and left, and the process of decolonialization, and a demonstrated loss of nerve in the series of challenges provided by emerging nationalism and aggressive communist expansion. Pius XII brought the papacy back to a level of influence, intellectual and moral prestige unimaginable a century before. His successor, John XXIII, seemed personally to exemplify to a worldwide constituency created by the mass media a dimension of Christian simplicity and paternal human concern. His emphasis on *aggiornamento* brought major developments and greater universality to the Church's social doctrine in the encyclicals *Mater et magistra* (1961) and *Pacem in terris* (1963), while his calling Vatican Council II provided an opportunity to assess with full awareness and at great length the nature and role of the Church confronting the challenge of modernity. This was done in relatively peaceful times, without the imminent threat of armed heresy, yet clearly amid manifest religious and cultural malaise in the West with the conciliars' awareness of world unity and of a new world-order being born.

Contemporary Teaching. Historically the Church has rejected the liberal notion that unrestricted human freedom is a good thing in itself, rather maintaining that evil and error have no rights and may be permitted or accepted in society only in order to avoid greater evils. Liberty turned to moral license and freedom used to subvert the social order or to spread falsehood and mis-information have been conceived as perversions of right order. Yet the Church has recognized that two orders, that of God and that of the world, coexist and inter-penetrate one another, and that there is a strong and persistent presence of moral evil, wilful disordering ac-tivity, in the world. In the practical order both the in-stitutional Church and the individual Christian must adjust to the abuses of right order, the outrages of power, or the blandishments of license as tests of spiritual commitment and opportunities for the exercise of virtue.

Pope Paul VI. In Paul VI's first encyclical (1964) the Church is represented as the "mother of the whole human family and minister to its salvation" (Paul VI EcclSuam 1) constantly striving to win over to itself human society (ibid 10). "In the world but not of it" (Jn 17.15), the Church does not subscribe to any set political theory but strives for just, rational, and peaceful (i.e. well-ordered) relations among states. The Church considers itself the channel of Christ's gifts of truth and grace in which Christ lives and through which he teaches, governs, and sanctifies men. In order to sanctify the world the Church must live in it, and living in it, is, in its members, "influenced and guided by the world." Its members imbibe the world's culture, "are subject to its laws, adopt its customs" (ibid 42). This relationship creates problems, as it always has. The Church claims institutional freedom and the right to communicate the Gospel to all men, while affirming basic individual and family freedoms, the need for social justice and a public order conducive (or at least innocuous) to men's moral, intellectual, and cultural growth. Sometimes the State is unfavorable to friendly dialogue. It may permit or sup-port a corrupt, lascivious, materialistic, and hedonistic system of public values. It may even formally deny God and oppress the Church as has been the case in states espousing and applying an ideology of atheistic com-munism. Yet even here John XXIII had earlier opened the door to the Church's dialogue with *all* the world. Clearly referring to Marxism (and perhaps liberalism as well) in *Pacem in terris* he remarked: ". . . make a clear distinction between false philosophical teachings . . . and movements . . . even if these movements owe their ins-piration to these false tenets. While the teaching . . . is no longer subject to change, the movements, precisely because they take place in the midst of changing conditions, are readily susceptible of change. Besides, who can deny that those movements . . . contain elements that are positive and deserving of approval?" (John XXIII PacTerr 159). Enjoining prudent cooperation in the pursuit of common social goals that are "honorable and useful" he adds "that the Church has the right and the duty not only to safeguard the principles of ethics and religion, but also to intervene authoritatively with her children in the temporal sphere when there is a question of judging the application of those principles to concrete cases" (ibid. 160).

The Church's mission is directed to all peoples. Encompassing the earth in widening circles, it seeks to attract men of good will in every culture and society; non-Catholic Christians, Israel and Islam worshipping the same God, members of the great Eastern religious families, and all men honestly seeking to know the truth and do what is right. The Church has no illusions "that man is naturally good and self-sufficient" (Paul VI EcclSuam 59), but rejects pessimism and offers men and societies hope that their vices, weaknesses, and moral ailments are not incurable if remedy is sought in free-dom and sincerity. Vatican Council II's Dogmatic Cons-titution on the Church states that the Church "receives the mission to proclaim and to establish among all peoples the kingdom of Christ and of God" (*Lumen gen-tium* 5). The Church is conceived as both a spiritual community (Mystical Body) and a visible community, a society with formal hierarchical roles and organization, destined to promote a universal peace, reconciling the multiplicity of nations and customs and cultures in the unity of charity. Membership in this body encourages political and civic responsibility, progress in human and Christian liberty, and a commitment to justice, that is a more fitting distribution of created goods (ibid 36). Nor is this moral and civic responsibility conceived statically, but rather dynamically in terms of a process of restoring the world to God. This is a "pilgrim Church" tested and proved by a continuous confrontation with disordered values and the disordering acts of the wicked. The Church "dwells among creatures who groan and travail in pain, in need of power to stand up against the wiles of the devil and resist the evil day" (ibid 48).

Gaudium et spes. Vatican Council II's Pastoral Cons-titution on the Church in the Modern World expresses the role of the Church in human society in stark terms when it affirms that Christ broke the "stranglehold of personified evil [*Malignus*]" so that the "world might be fashioned anew according to God's design" (*Gaudium et spes* 2). However this "design" is not spelled out beforehand; rather it is the product of a "more mature and personal exercise of liberty" by men in a multiplic-ity of legitimate political, communal, and cultural ex-pressions consonant with human nature, allowing social groups and their individual members access to their own fulfillment within a kind of universal community that encompasses the whole human family (ibid). Although the Church often provided a principal vehicle for in-troduction of Western culture in the Orient, Africa and the New World, a major achievement of recent popes and of Vatican II has been the clear and explicit affir-mation that the Church transcends any single cultural area and can provide the moral and spiritual cement for a pluralistic world in which what is true and useful, good and beautiful in every tradition may be preserved as an integral part of the patrimony of mankind.

The diffidence and denial of the world, a pseudo-spirituality, and an unwillingness to participate in the affairs of the world by Christians, owing to a sense of impotence and too great a sensitivity to its evils, must be replaced by a willingness "to work for the rightful betterment of this world" (ibid. 21). This is appro-priately linked to a forceful repudiation of the pride and unrealistic folly of an atheistic humanism mistakenly seeking a genuine and total emancipation of humanity wrought solely by human effort (ibid. 20).

The Church no longer looks back nostalgically to an elite of Christian knights and princes at the Western end of the Eurasian landmass or to a parochial alliance of throne and altar, but accepts the fundamentally populist bias of so much Catholic social thought since the Middle Ages, that governments are founded on the consent of the citizens and that "praise is due to those national procedures which allow the largest possible number of citizens to participate in public affairs with genuine free-dom" (ibid. 31).

The Christian message binds men to build the world, to contribute to a better ordering of human society, to progress, in large part by attending to the welfare of others. This constrictive approach repudiates that spirit of vanity and malice which distorts and perverts human energies intended for the service of God and man. The "world" in this latter sense does exist and in it the Church serves a "saving and eschatological purpose." Composed of men, "members of the earthly city" the Church forms a visible assembly and a spiritual community that repudiates the bondage which results from sin and fosters the true, good, and just elements in every culture and a wide variety of institutions in vital synthesis with religious values (ibid. 40).

Although the Church has no autonomous mission in the political, economic, or social order, the Christian seeks "to see that the divine law is inscribed in the life of the earthly city" (ibid. 42). As human society develops the self-awareness needful to spiritual and moral maturity, individual Christians and Christian communities in the context of their own nations and cultures must play a conscious role in the decision-process, political and economic, so that policy may enhance personal dignity, reduce unjust discrimination, broaden access to cultural goods (including higher education), facilitate self-improvement, and guarantee basic rights (ibid. 43; 60). More specifically, human rights include the right to food, clothing, shelter, choice of state of life, founding a family, education, employement, good reputation, respect; appropriate information, activity in accord with the upright norms of individual conscience, protection of privacy, rightful freedom in matters religious (ibid. 26), migration (ibid. 66), inquiry and expression (ibid. 62).

In a well-ordered modern society created goods should abound for all men on a reasonable basis and, given the social nature of wealth as a gift of God rendered fruitful by human thought and effort, its benefits should be extended to the whole human family while the exigencies of present consumption are balanced with the anticipated needs of future generations (ibid. 69). Christians are encouraged to undertake "the difficult but most honorable art of politics" in an effort to harmonize authority with freedom, personal initiative with social responsibility, the exigencies of moral unity in group and functional multiplicity at every level of political community with solidarity in the cultural, racial, and ethnic diversity that must characterize a prosperous and humanly fulfilling world order (ibid. 75).

Society as a whole must be informed, leavened, reconstructed by individual and group initiatives founded on the Christian conscience. But such actions are distinct from what is done in the name of the Church and in union with the hierarchy (ibid. 76). As the Church consciously affirms its willingness to live and operate in a nationally and culturally pluralistic world, serving as sign and safeguard of the transcendence of the human person, it will no longer permit itself to be confused with any given political community, constitutional form, or social system (ibid. 76). The Church and political community, each it its proper sphere "are mutually independent and self-governing" while "each serves the personal and social vocation of the same human beings." The institutional Church's instruments of policy are the "means and helps proper to the gospel," differing in many respects from the supports of the "earthly city" and ultimately "depend on the power of God" (ibid.). Although she employs the things of time the Church does not rely on privileges conferred by civil authority and may even renounce acquired rights on occasion in order to preserve or gain the moral autonomy essential for the exercise of her rights, "always and everywhere legitimate: to preach the faith with freedom; to teach her social doctrine; to discharge her duty among men without hindrance; and to pass moral judgments, even on matters touching the political order" (ibid.). Considering the historical record of Church-State relations, this declaration is already considered a repudiation of many past actions and practices, and an opening to a future in which the Church plays an increasing international role in freedom.

Although the Church had seemed to take sides in the Cold War following World War II and Paul VI continued to condemn atheistic communism, the voice of an independent Church transcends party and polity, representing the moral interest of the whole human community. *Gaudium et spes* itself enunciates the universal Church's condemnation of injustice, savagery, deceit and subversion, terrorism and genocide, weapons of mass destruction directed against civil populations and cultural values, coercion of conscience, neglect or violation of human and civil rights, institutionalized economic and social inequities on a global scale (ibid. 78–81). While affirming that the "Church must be thoroughly present in the midst of the community of nations" both institutionally and in the persons of informed Christians, *Gaudium et spes* suggests the broad outline of a global political community based on freedom and diversity yet possessed of a universal public authority endowed with effective power to safeguard the security and rights of men and nations and sustain a just order (ibid. 89).

Reflection and Assessment. The postconciliar vision of an ecumenical order in which Church and a global polity coexist and interpenetrate recalls the medieval ideal of the *Respublica Christiana* in which the broadest range of self-governing communities and peoples, legitimate activities and interests interacted under the dual, effective, yet limited authorities of emperor and pope. In the far more complex contemporary world, abandoning any pretension to an enforced ideological or religious consensus in the Vatican II Declaration on Religious Freedom (*Dignitatis humanae*), the Church has presented a model of a mature world-order characterized by a level of well-being that obviates the coercive effects of physical need, in which men are sustained and supported by both civil and spiritual authorities in their efforts at personal fulfillment, in which men make or unmake themselves and others consciously, willfully, in communities. The model reflects a dynamic *process* in which the two cities, founded on two loves, interact and by a series of individual and social choices exhibit their distinctness. Paul VI's "Call to Action" embraces the notion of a social world in process toward global unity in multiplicity. Christian communities are "to analyze with objectivity the situation which is proper to their own country," and "discern the options and commitments which are called for in order to bring about the social, political, and economic changes . . . needed" (Paul VI OctogAdven 4).

In seeking the peace that grows from just social structures, conscious meliorative transformation of institutions must be sought at every level, a process for which constructive Utopian thinking is to be encouraged. Such thinking, by envisaging concrete institutional alternatives rather than verbalizing the abstract categories of ideology, provides "some kind of foreshadowing of the new age" (ibid. 37) and may contribute to social decision-making.

The contemporary Church has put itself clearly on record that today's social organization and the mechanisms of decision, especially at the global level, no longer correspond to the objective requirements of the universal common good. Unjust social structures at every level try the virtues of obedience and patience engendered by faith but "the present situation must be faced with courage and the injustices linked with it fought against and overcome" (Paul VI PopProgr 32). Yet the Church and its members are not the vanguard of violent revolution. Prudent action, the ability to wait out even the worst abuses of public authority and private greed, are conjoined with active work for structures altered in view of a clearer concept of man, his needs, and his destiny. Traditional emphasis on the common good, consensus, cooperation, participation, collective order, reconciliation, mutual love and forbearance contrast to ideologies based on class and intergroup conflict, adversary relations, continuous protest, and even attacks on the "social texture itself."

By cutting political and temporal ties, commitments, and dependencies the Church's institutional denunciations of unjust privilege, immoral military, economic, and social policies gain increased force at both the national and international levels. The Holy See's participation in international conferences on such issues as the environment (Stockholm 1972) and population (Bucharest 1975) has given voice to concepts and value orientations alternative to those dominant in the industrial West and has evoked an unanticipated resonance in the developing nations and among members of the socialist world. North and South America's bishops in separate assemblies have taken issue with civil authorities on such matters as nuclear deterrence, conscientious objection to bearing arms, unjust conditions of labor, the use of torture, and antisocial behavior by the privileged, including inordinate foreign political or economic control of the destinies of entire peoples. The *Synods of Bishops periodically "gathered from the whole world" add their voice to the plea for peace and justice, peoples' control of their own development and destiny, personal and group responsibility for the common good with concrete suggestions at the global level that all governments ratify and observe the United Nations Declaration of Human Rights, that strategies of non-violence be fostered, that effective economic power be decentralized and shared, that international functional agencies and agreements be strengthened (see SynodJustWorld pp. 49–51).

At every level from the individual members of the Church through parish, diocese, national, and regional episcopal conferences to its central authorities a continuous action of constructive effort and institution-building, of intellectual and practical contribution to policy-making and the political process has been initiated. In a mature world the Church and society relate to one another with increasing self-awareness. Building the city of God is seen to imply action, creating the public institutional conditions in which men's right choice is made easier and more likely, ultimately in the existential option for, or against, God.

See also POLITICAL PARTIES, CATHOLIC (11:509); POLITICAL PHILOSOPHY (11:510); POLITICAL THOUGHT, HISTORY OF (11:515); SOCIAL JUSTICE (13:318); SOCIAL MOVEMENTS, CATHOLIC (13:321); SOCIAL THOUGHT, PAPAL (13:352); STATE, THE (13:644).

Bibliography: A. I. ABELL, ed., *American Catholic Thought on Social Questions* (Indianapolis 1968). R. W. and A. J. CARLYLE, *A History of Medieval Political Theory in the West* 6 v. (London, 1903–36). I. GIORDANI, *Il messagio sociale del Cristianesimo* (Rome 1963). J. GREMILLION, *The Gospel of Peace and Justice—Catholic Social Teaching since Pope John* (Maryknoll, N.Y. 1976). D. J. O'BRIEN and T. A. SHANNON, eds., *Renewing the Earth—Catholic Documents on Peace, Justice and Liberation* (Garden City, N.Y. 1977). H. ROMMEN, *The State in Catholic Thought* (St Louis 1945). L. STURZO, *Church and State* (New York 1939). E. VOEGELIN, *Science, Politics and Gnosticism* (Chicago 1968).

[C. R. DECHERT]

PONTIFICAL, ROMAN

Most of the rites of the *Pontificale Romanum*, the liturgical book containing rites at which a bishop ordinarily officiates, have been revised, in keeping with the directives of Vatican Council II (*Sacrosanctum Concilium* 25, 71, 76, 80). Translations of these, prepared by the *International Commission on English in the Liturgy (ICEL), were first published separately (*see* LITURGICAL BOOKS OF THE ROMAN RITE); in 1978 the *Roman Pontifical*, Part I, appeared as a compilation of these rites. Except for two additions the book corresponds in scope to the *Pontificale Romanum*, of Clement VIII, promulgated in 1596 in compliance with the decree of the Council of Trent on the matter (Session 25, Dec. 4, 1563; in *Conciliorum oecumenicorum decreta* 3d ed., p. 797). The translations of the rites prepared by ICEL were first approved by English-speaking episcopal conferences and published by their decree, which had been confirmed by the Holy See; the essential formulas of the Sacraments of Confirmation and Orders, however, have their approval directly from the pope, to whom Paul VI reserved versions of sacramental formulas.

The following are the contents of the 1978 *Roman Pontifical*. Part One contains rites for the celebration of the Sacraments of Christian Initiation, Baptism, Confirmation, and the Eucharist, along with the rites of admission to the catechumenate and reception of baptized Christians to full communion. At all of these rites the accompanying instructions recommend that the bishop preside (although priests may and often do so). Part Two is on the institution of lay ministers, specifically of readers and acolytes. Part Three contains the rites of ordination of deacons, presbyters, and bishops; also of admission to candidacy for diaconate and presbyterate and of commitment to celibacy (the latter as a part of diaconal ordination for unmarried men). Part Four comprises blessings for persons publicly dedicated to God: the rite of consecration to a life of virginity, the blessing of an abbot or abbess. In addition the *Roman Pontifical* contains two other rites, belonging to Part II of the *Pontificale:* the Blessing of Holy Oils and Consecration of Chrism (English, 1972) and the rite for the dedication of a church and altar (English version in preparation). The new *Roman Pontifical* is the official and authoritative text for all the Latin-rite dioceses of the English-speaking countries.

[T. C. O'BRIEN]

PONTIFICAL BIBLICAL COMMISSION

The Pontifical Biblical Commission, in the preconciliar Church was often ignored by Catholic scholars, liberated by Pius XII's encyclical (1943) on biblical studies, *Divino afflante spiritu* (4:925). Paul VI's restructuring of the Commission by the motu proprio *Sedula cura*, June 27, 1971 (ActApS 63 [1971] 665–669) implementing Vatican Council II's *Dei Verbum*, was regarded with relief by many scholars. The apostolic letter stresses continuity and states the purpose of the Commission to be assistance to exegetes and theologians in equipping the ministers of the Word for their task of making available the treasures of Scripture, under the tutelage and guardianship of the ecclesiastical magisterium. The main changes include the following. The Commission is linked with the Congregation for the Doctrine of the Faith; decisions of the Commission are submitted to that Congregation and to the pope for any possible use or promulgation. The president of the Commission is the cardinal prefect of the Congregation for the Doctrine of the Faith; Members of the Commission, instead of being Roman cardinals serving for life as in the past, are to be biblical scholars chosen from various schools and nations to serve a five-year term; their number is not to exceed 20; non-Catholics can serve as consultants to various task-forces. There is an annual plenary session and members are bound by norms of secrecy. They are to respond to questions forwarded to them from around the world and to be available to aid both scholars and scholarship.

Pope Paul VI's address to the first plenary session of the new Commission (March 14, 1974) made favorable mention of various modern critical methods and categories familiar to exegetes (form criticism, *Redaktiongeschichte*, theological pluralism), but warned against unilateral research in solitude and a narrow rationalism of method. He reminded exegetes they are part of a team that includes pastors, theologians of other areas of competence, and jurists. New norms for examinations and degrees in biblical studies were issued by the Commission Dec. 7, 1974 (ActApS 67 [1975] 153–158). An illustration of the progressive bent of the new Commission is its June 1976 declaration that Scripture is not enough to exclude women from priesthood.

[E. J. DILLON]

POPE, ELECTION OF

The apostolic constitution *Romano pontifici eligendo* of Pope Paul VI (Oct. 1, 1975; ActApS 67 [1975] 609–645) introduces numerous changes in the legislation regarding papal elections, while retaining many traditional elements (11:572).

Electors, Cardinals only. In addresses given on March 5, 1973 and March 24, 1973, Paul VI announced his intention of consulting interested persons to see whether Oriental patriarchs who were not cardinals, as well as the members of the Council of the General Secretariat of the Synod of Bishops should participate in papal elections. The results of the consultation were not conclusive and, hence, only those persons who have been named cardinals of the Church were to be electors (*Romano pontifici eligendo* 33).

Number and Age of Electors. The number of electors is limited now to 120. While formerly the number of cardinals was fixed at 70, each cardinal could bring two or three assistants to the conclave. Presently, only in exceptional cases may an infirmarian accompany an elector, thus reducing the overall number of participants (ibid. 33, 45). Following upon the prescriptions of the motu proprio *Ingravescentem aetatem* of Nov. 21, 1970 only those cardinals who have not completed their eightieth year of age are eligible to vote in papal elections (ibid. 33).

The Conclave. The conclave is not required for validity (ibid. 41), but is to be understood as a carefully determined place, a kind of sacred retreat, where the cardinal electors choose the supreme pontiff and where they remain day and night until the election is complete (ibid. 42). Cardinals may now leave the conclave for serious reasons (ibid. 40). New norms regarding the observance of secrecy provide for an examination of the premises to determine whether listening devices or other such instruments have been introduced into the quarters (ibid. 55, 61). These precautions, as well as the other norms, have two purposes: to ensure a free election and to provide for a rapid carrying out of the business to be transacted.

Method of Election. Three forms of election are retained: acclamation by all electors, compromise giving certain electors authority to act in the name of all, and election by ballot. If the Roman pontiff is to be chosen by this last method, two-thirds of the votes plus one are required (ibid. 65). John XXIII had reduced the number of required votes to two-thirds in the motu proprio of Sept. 5, 1962, *Summi Pontificis electio*.

Episcopal Character. If the newly elected pope is a bishop, he is immediately bishop of Rome and head of the episcopal college. He possesses and can exercise full and supreme power over the universal Church. If, however, the elected person does not possess the episcopal character, he is to be immediately ordained a bishop. This change is in line with Vatican Council II's teaching on the unity that is to exist between the power of Orders and the power of jurisdiction (*Lumen gentium* 22).

Period of Prayer. If no person is elected after three days of voting, a day is to be allowed to pass without voting (*Romano pontifici eligendo* 76). The electors are to pray and may converse freely among themselves. Two other such days are foreseen if the ballots are not conclusive. After this point, forms of compromise may be adopted.

Pastoral Dimensions. The cardinals are strongly exhorted not to be guided by likes or dislikes in electing the pope, but to vote for the person whom they judge most fit to rule the universal Church (ibid 85). Likewise, the entire Church is to be united in a special way with those who are electing a supreme pontiff: the election is to be considered the action of the entire Church, and, thus, prayers are to be offered in every city and in other places as well for the successful outcome of the election (ibid. 85).

Other Simplifications. Matters of lesser importance include changes in the various excommunications to be levied against those who do not observe secrecy (ibid. 46, 58) and prescriptions regarding photographs to be taken of the deceased pontiff (ibid. 30). An ecumenical council or a synod of bishops that may have been in progress at the death of a pope is automatically suspended pending authorization by the newly elected pontiff to proceed (ibid. 34).

Bibliography: C. LEFEBVRE, "La Constitution apostolique 'Romano Pontifici Eligendo' (1er octobre 1975)," *L'Année canonique* 21 (1977) 233–238. Paul VI, *Romano pontifici eligendo*, Eng. tr., "The Election of the Roman Pontiff," *Pope Speaks* 22 (1976–77) 64–89. J. SÁNCHEZ Y SÁNCHEZ, "La constitución apostólica 'Romano Pontifici eligendo' de S.S. el Papa Pablo VI," *Revista española de derecho canónico* 31 (1975) 387–394.

[F. G. MORRISEY]

POPULATION EXPLOSION

In recent years the seriousness of the population problem has become clearer and clearer. The world population—1,000 million in 1830, 1,600 million in 1900, reaching its second billion in 1930, its third in 1961, and its fourth in 1975—appears to grow exponentially, i.e. each generation producing a new generation larger than itself. At the present rate the world population doubles every 35 years, and the United Nations' estimate for the year 2000 is *c.* 6,400 million. This population growth is not evenly spread over the globe. Grosso modo the increase is sharpest—averaging about 3 percent—in the developing countries, which are least able to support this increased population: Latin America, Africa, Asia. In the developed world—North America, Europe, U.S.S.R., Australia—increase ranges from 0.4 to one percent. Since only about one-fourth of the world population lives in developed countries, the largest proportion of births occurs in the Third World: 80 percent of all births take place in developing countries. The most immediate reason for this rapid increase is the vast improvement of health care and disease control, e.g., malaria, one of the most potent killing diseases, has been wiped out since World War II.

Improved health care has caused the death rate to go down—people live longer—and infant mortality has declined drastically. This means that more babies grow up to be parents. Hence an exponential growth pattern.

Population and Development. The fact that the population explosion affects the developing countries most not only creates very serious problems—hunger, poverty—but the continuing high birthrates seem to be a function of lower development. Paradoxically, in many developing countries, the situation of near-starvation poverty does not create a motivation to limit family size. Family-planning programs have been largely unsuccessful. The motivation to have fewer children apparently can be expected only after a certain level of development has been reached (United Nations' Threshold Hypothesis). Therefore, the population problem has to be seen in the wider context of socio-economic and cultural development, and cannot be isolated as a separate problem. While reduction of family size is obviously necessary, realistically it has to be pursued as part of a program of development.

The population explosion is a problem on two levels. First of all, the earth is finite and there must be a limit to the number of people the planet can sustain, though it may be hard to say where this limit is. Thus, certainly in the long run, the population cannot keep growing. Secondly, and for present purposes more importantly, the present condition of distribution of wealth and resources is such that the human race cannot adequately take care of the people. The birthrates are high where the availability of food, clothing, and shelter is low. While 80 percent of the births take place in the Third World, 80 percent of the world's produced wealth is consumed by 20 percent of the world's population. At least 20 percent of the Third World's people are underfed, and 60 percent have deficient diets. The vast majority of babies are born into a situation of poverty, hunger, and destitution. The most urgent task at this point is to provide all people with an opportunity to live a humanly dignified life.

Population and the Church. The main emphasis in the Church's response to the population problem is clearly on the need for a new international economic and social order, built on justice and peace. In Pope Paul VI's words: "Development is the new word for Peace" (Paul VI PopProgr 87). The responsibility of the developed nations for the developing nations is heavily stressed in this teaching. The Church has, however, been hesitant to support direct interference with the procreation process through various methods of birth control. Pope John XXIII in 1961 noted the population problem, but in his view a conflict between population and available resources was excluded by God's Providence, and by subduing the earth and international cooperation the human race would be able to solve the problems without limiting procreation (John XXIII MatMagis 185-199). It is perhaps significant that in *Pacem in terris* (1963) the Pope did not repeat this teaching. Vatican Council II gave attention to the population problem and included the interests of temporal society among the criteria for responsible parenthood, while reaffirming the right of the parents to determine the size of their family (*Gaudium et spes* 50, 87). In 1967 Pope Paul VI, in *Populorum progressio* (1967, n. 37) recognized the right of governments to try to check population growth, provided that the right to marry and to have children remains intact, as well as the right of the parents to decide how many children they want. Responsibility toward the community has to inform such decisions (Paul VI PopProgr 37). In *Humanae vitae* (1968) the Pope maintained, however, that only rhythm is an allowable method of birth control. Concerning this teaching there is widespread dissent within the Catholic Church, not only among the laity, but among the clergy and the hierarchy. Whatever the outcome of that issue, it is clear that the more decisive problem is not that of birth control but of development.

Bibliography: The literature is overwhelming. A short history of world population can be found in C. M. CIPPOLA, *The Economic History of World Population*, (7th ed., New York 1978). A general overview of the problems and a guide to further bibliography in A. MCCORMACK et al., ThSt 35 (1974) 3–70, entire issue. For official Church teaching: J. GREMILLION, *The Gospel of Peace and Justice* (New York 1975), which gives the text of the more important documents with a good introduction. Recommended is also: *Action Taken at Bucharest*, the resolutions of the UN World Population Conference, Bucharest, 1974 (UN Publication, New York 1975).

[T. M. STEEMAN]

POSTBAPTISMAL CATECHESIS (MYSTAGOGIA)

Postbaptismal catechesis (mystagogia) is the final period of the initiation of adults (ChrInitAd 37). During this period the meaning of the Sacraments is explained to those who have newly received them. When Baptisms take place at the Easter Vigil, the mystagogia are held at the Sunday Masses of the Easter season (ibid. 40). No specific ceremonies are prescribed for this period, save that the neophytes maintain a special place among the faithful and are mentioned in the homily and the

General Intercessions (ibid. 236). The purpose of the mystagogia is to enable the newly baptized to draw from their sacramental experience a new sense of the faith, the Church, and the world (ibid. 38). The families of the neophytes, their godparents, and the entire congregation share in this experience with them, but a heavy responsibility must fall upon the "mystagogue," the person (normally the pastor) who opens to them the mysteries of faith.

It was at the mystagogia that St. Ambrose, St. Cyril of Jerusalem, and other Church Fathers preached their classic homilies on the Christian Sacraments, opening their meaning to those who were newly frequenting them. It is here that the Church has traditionally taught the meaning of the sacramental life in Christ. For the Church today the period remains one of great importance both pastorally and pedagogically. It requires the active participation not only of the newly baptized and the pastor, but of the whole congregation, for it incorporates the newly baptized into the community of the faithful and places instruction in the meaning of the Sacraments in the context of their frequent reception. In this way the newly baptized can deepen and enrich their own experience of the Sacraments by a clear exposition of the Sacraments' inner meaning for their own lives and that of the whole Church and a showing forth of that meaning in the actual community life of the Church.

Bibliography: H. RILEY, *The Rite of Christian Initiation* (Regensburg 1971). E. YARNHOLD, *The Awe-Inspiring Rites of Initiation* (Slough, England 1971).

[L. L. MITCHELL]

POVERTY

The word and concept of poverty have diverse connotations in Christian history. Poverty is seen as both a blessing and an evil, as a condition or way of life to be sought after and as a result of sin in the world needing to be healed. Fundamentally poverty describes a lack of material resources or money, resulting in debilitation of basic human development. Modern social science explains it as the consequence of a low standard of living, an insufficient level of basic goods and services (food, housing, clothing, medical care) necessary to sustain a minimally decent life. Lack of sufficient education, of employment, of capital goods, or of political influence are correlates of poverty and reveal some of its causes.

In Christian tradition, poverty is also understood as a quality of spiritual and social life which is voluntarily embraced in imitation of the Lord Jesus Christ. One of the evangelical counsels and virtues set out by Jesus in the Sermon on the Mount, poverty of spirit results from a radical trust in the power and providence of God to care for his people. It claims no other security than God and avoids the potential distraction or illusions of physical control and self-sufficiency as impediments to spiritual awareness and social solidarity. The virtue of poverty does not primarily mean a negative renunciation of the world but a liberating, positive condition.

These two perspectives in Christian tradition have often resulted in ambivalence among Christians as they consider their pastoral responsibility to poor and oppressed people. It is necessary in the modern Church to understand that the two attitudes towards poverty are not only concordant but complementary. Moreover, it is necessary that believers become familiar with the significant body of doctrine and theology calling for the redemption of societal values and institutions as history moves towards the consummation of Christ's Kingdom.

Socio-Economic Analysis. The social problem of poverty refers to a lack of basic human needs which undermines the health, morale, and social order in a society. The definition of poverty is relative to social expectations and cultural standards. In Western societies severe deprivation is understood to lead to apathy, inability to work or to be creative, malnutrition, retardation, high infant mortality rates, early average age-at-death rates for adults, and other visible physical effects. Deprivation is often measured by the minimal monetary costs of basic needs.

Statistics. In the U.S., for example, a minimal diet for a four-person urban family in 1978 cost about $2,000 a year and the other needs were estimated to cost twice as much. Thus, an income/budget level of approximately $6,000 (40 percent of median family income) was considered necessary for subsistence living in an urban area for a four-person family. Using a sliding scale relative to region and family size the U.S. Government estimated that 25 million persons (12 percent of the population) lived in poverty in 1978. Another 10 million or more belonged to families with marginal income; many of these are known from government five-year studies to move into or out of poverty every couple of years, depending upon employment or illness. Other studies, such as the President's Commission on Income Maintenance in 1969, set the poverty level higher, insisting upon the figure of one-half the median family-income in a society. By such a figure upwards of 50 million or almost 25 percent of the U.S. population is poor and has been so constantly since 1910. Percentages of the population in poverty were much higher among Black, Hispanic, elderly, single-female-parent families, and children (over 20 percent as a group) than among other groupings in 1978.

The measure of poverty internationally is more difficult to standardize. Costs of goods and services vary greatly, as do cultural expectations; data-collection methods and systems are inconsistent and variable. Nonetheless, it was estimated in 1978 that over one billion persons suffered hunger or malnutrition; 4 million persons would die of starvation; 25–40 percent of the labor force in half the world's countries were unemployed or underemployed, and by conservative standards, 50 percent of the world's 3 billion population was poor at the level of deprivation. The poorest 40 of the 115 developing countries were widely considered to have neither primary products nor industrial potential with which to bargain in the world's trade markets.

Causes Suggested in the U.S. Theories which establish cause for the continuance and growth of poverty are complex and diverse. In the U.S. several factors seem crucial.

(1) Change from an evenly mixed, rural-urban pattern of residence to a predominantly urban one. This was brought on by technological displacement of rural workers; the demise of primary industries in certain regions; the rapid demise of family-owned farms and the spread of corporate agribusiness in farming; absentee land-ownership patterns, where conglomerate banking, real estate or industrial concerns are buying up

more and more land in rural America and changing its economies.

(2) The work force has expanded to include more young persons, especially racial-cultural minority groups, and women (as second-income earners in families or as career-seeking workers).

(3) The percentage of elderly has increased; they suffer enforced obsolescence in industrial or agricultural society; retirement-security programs are inadequate to stay even with cost-of-living changes and the numbers of persons drawing pensions.

(4) The numbers and percentage of single, female-headed families, has grown concomitantly; severe strains on traditional family structure have created large numbers of economically dependent families.

(5) Economic production systems have become increasingly dominated by large conglomerate corporations, the results being artifically-high price structures in consumer goods, a tendency towards automation and more capital-intensive labor force, and domination of small-area economies by nonresident owners. Less than two percent of U.S. industrial corporations control 75 percent of all manufacturing assets. In such situations local job structures and commerce systems are vulnerable to major dislocation because of relocation of industries, outflow of earnings, and the resultant disinvestment of a local economy.

(6) Low-paying, insecure job structure persists in the bottom third of the American economy and is characterized by low or rigid skill mobility in the work force and vulnerability to seasonal or random layoffs.

(7) The pattern of disadvantage continues among racial minorities and among women generally, in aggregate income and education levels, as well as in pay levels for equivalent educational and occupational categories. In short, an apparent racial and sexual discrimination persists in the economy. This discriminatory pattern applies to unemployment rates also, with unemployment among minority workers running consistently twice as high as among whites.

(8) Underlying all of these phenomena is the consistent fact that distribution of income and wealth in the U.S. has been askew since 1910. The bottom half of the U.S. population earns about 3 percent of all national income; the top half earns 63 percent. The bottom 20 percent of the population has earned between four and five percent of national income for sixty years, while the top 20 percent has earned more than 40 percent consistently. While there has been some redistribution within the middle 60 percent of the population (middle class), there has been none at the bottom. Ownership of capital, land, and productive assets is even more unbalanced. The wealthiest five percent of the population owns approximately 50 percent of all personal wealth. The bottom 60 percent owns less than five percent. As long as the economic and political control accompanying ownership remains distributed in such a concentrated way, it is unlikely that there can be significant results in any effort to distribute the national income in a more proportional manner. Strategies of more effective progressive taxation, worker ownership and capitalization of industries, guaranteed annual income, and national full employment are among many ways suggested to resolve the causes listed above.

Causes in the Third World. Factors causing poverty in the Third World include: (1) historically lower levels of industrialization, socio-economic organization, and specialization; (2) cultural patterns of land ownership, income distribution, and control of wealth which do not stress domestic investment but overseas investment or consumption; (3) climatic conditions and topography, plus lack of transportation infrastructure, which impede maximum use of potential agricultural resources; (4) labor-extensive inefficient agricultural systems; (5) lack of technological skills and methods suited to indigenous conditions and the appropriate development of the people; (6) social and economic controls and even domination as a result of colonial-era patterns of education, status, and investment; (7) dependence upon foreign markets and systems for capitalization, which often brings severe political strain in domestic government from heavy foreign pressure; (8) population growth at a pace more rapid than the agricultural or economic systems can support because of medical science's lowering of death rates; (9) outflow of net payments because of dependency upon foreign foodstuffs and foreign capital; (10) social stress from rapid industrialization and urbanization. Millions of the unemployed and landless rural inhabitants are now moving to worse squalor and poverty in the burgeoning urban areas of the Third World.

The network of dependence and consequent foreign control in which many Third World nations find themselves leads down a road of further indebtedness, domestic conflict and a widening gap between the economic strength of the wealthy nations and that of the poor Third World nations. The application of Western "development" economics has falsely presumed an efficient agricultural system, which is often not present, and a socio-cultural environment in which education, labor, and investment patterns operate similarly to Western societies. Since this is not the case, Third World economists and social ethicists have been calling for new models of development, more appropriate to the social development and control of their peoples. Democratic planning, transfer of *technology in ways which do not strengthen or maintain control by already dominant international or domestic parties, and changes in cultural values must converge so as to allow appropriate human and social developments enabling citizens of poor nations to assume control of their own affairs. Among Latin-American social ethicists, this school of development thought is associated with *liberation theology.

Poverty as a Virtue. The God of Hebrew Scriptures is consistently presented as God of the poor and oppressed. God's little ones, the bent-over ones, the *anawim*, are especially destined to be blessed by Yahweh. Scriptural studies seem to have concluded that the "poverty" here presented is essentially an attitude towards one's own power and pride. The *anawim* are not pretentious, do not invest their hopes for life and a future in their own strength or possessions. Instead, they trust in Yahweh and turn their fate completely over to him. Naturally, poor and oppressed persons, lacking options have a clearer recourse to God. It is, of course, possible to be poor socio-economically and yet mean or avaricious. Therefore, poverty of spirit does not necessarily require physical poverty. However, it is clear that in the Old Testament the two were correlated, because the wealthy and powerful, those who did not share their goods with open hands and act as stewards of creation, were described as fools who would be brought low by Yahweh. They trusted in the power and wealth of the world, and were not obedient to God or his covenants. It is also clear that God's covenant expected sharing and hospitality—the poor would be lifted up by the stewardship of their brothers, who were moved to share goods by their *spiritual poverty*.

Jesus' life style and preaching clarify the spiritual poverty to which Christians are called. He lived a simple life, in keeping with his rural-tradesman unbringing and career as a wandering preacher. He held no property or wealth, but shared freely. Nevertheless, he seemingly was not destitute and accepted the sharing of disciples and admirers, even if they were wealthy tax-collectors for the Romans. Jesus pictures himself as one who came singing and dancing. Therefore, the "poverty of spirit" Jesus embodies is an attitude of sharing, trust, and gratitude. Rather than mere detachment from physical goods or power, as religious poverty has often been portrayed, Jesus' poverty of spirit is an act of faith in his Father's providence and the coming Kingdom and an attitude of oneness with other people. So it is to be with followers of Jesus. The virtue of poverty does not require destitution, but brotherhood with other Christians and the poor. Such an unpretentious, childlike attitude towards life makes a person open to the truth of salvation Jesus came to reveal. Therefore, poverty of spirit is both a social and personal religious disposition necessary for salvation.

The early Church adopted a communal living style and an "effective" vow of poverty (really, of community) in imitation of the Lord, but also because their expectation that the end of the world and second coming of Christ were imminent. There was simply no use vesting one's future in the things of this life. As the Church moved into the Middle Ages, teachings about social mores and stewardship grew with the Church's role as societal, institutional religion and mainstay of education and historical studies. Possessions and earthly goals are seen by the Fathers of the Church to be gifts of God. They are destined for universal uses. The Christian is bound to give away superfluous goods, both to share with the poor as an act of love, and to adopt an ascetical ideal of love of God and heavenly things. However, the right to and necessity of private property is affirmed. Two schools of thought emerge. Poverty is seen as an inward spirit of sharing and inward detachment from possessions (this view was set forth especially in efforts at moral theology for society and the laity), and poverty as a vow, a way of life, expressed in communal living, seen in the rise of monasticism.

Diversity of interpretation has always characterized the concrete ethical application of the virtue of poverty to economics, personal sustenance, the morality of riches and luxury, the evaluation of banking, investment, profits. In any case, the virtue of poverty becomes especially important in reflecting upon the value basis of modern industrial society, and the pastoral responsibility of Christians to the poor.

The Church's Social Doctrine. Since modern social conditions began to develop during the Industrial Revolution, the Church has evolved a strong body of social doctrine which outlines the Christian responsibility towards poverty. Beginning with *Rerum novarum* of Pope Leo XIII in 1891, and continuing through the 1974 Synod of Bishops' statement on human rights, principles

for moral evaluation of society and life style have been set out. These include the following tenets. (1) Private property is a right of all persons, which also carries the responsibility to share one's wealth and goods with the poor (John XXIII PacTerr). It is not an absolute and unconditional right, therefore. No one may hoard for his use what he does not need when others lack necessities (Paul VI PopProgr). (2) All workers have a right to a living wage sufficient to give the worker and his family a standard of living in keeping with the dignity of the human person (John XXIII PacTerr 17). (3) All persons have the right to life, to bodily integrity, and to the means which are suitable for the proper development of life; these are primarily food, clothing, housing, rest, medical care, and the necessary social services. Therefore a human being has the right to security in case of sickness, inability to work, widowhood, old age, unemployment (ibid. 9). (4) As people seek justice and unite in charity, created goods should abound for them on a reasonable basis. All other rights, including those of property and free commerce, are to be subordinated to this principle. It is a grave and urgent social duty to redirect them to their primary finality (Paul VI PopProgr 22). (5) It is the distribution of goods among the people and their social human development as free, creative persons, which is the chief moral principle by which economies are to be evaluated. Production, profitability, wealth, efficiency, are to serve this other goal. (John XXIII MatMagis 73). (6) Jobs must be created and technical education provided, to ensure a sufficient number of decent jobs for all who want to and should work (*Gaudium et spes* 66). (7) People are obliged to come to the relief of the poor, and not merely out of their superfluous goods. All individuals and governments are to undertake a genuine sharing of goods. These goods should assist poor individuals and nations to help and develop themselves (ibid. 69). (8) Development must contain both economic growth and participative decision-making. It must be done in ways appropriate for the integral human development of persons and nations, and not be dominated by a few persons or nations (ibid. 59, and 65; Synod JustWorld pp. 36–38). (9) Structures of domination, control, oppression of workers or of poor nations, are sinful, and Christians have an absolute responsibility to work for their change (Synod JustWorld pp. 41–43). (10) The Church as an institution, Christians as individuals, and Western nations, must critically evaluate their life style, possessions, and consumption patterns. This includes bishops and priests. Unless this is done, the Gospel message of love and justice will have difficulty gaining credibility in the world (ibid.). (11) Wealthy people and nations should give away fixed percentages of their annual wealth, be willing to pay higher prices for raw materials, allow more imports from Third World countries, surrender some of their power in trade and monetary decisions, simplify their use of material resources and energy, and end the sinful arms race (ibid. pp. 35–36; Paul VI, Address to Vatican Diplomatic Corps, 1972). (12) Action on behalf of justice and participation in the transformation of the world fully appears to be a constitutive, inherent part of proclaiming the Gospel, of the Church's mission to redeem the human race (Synod JustWorld p. 34). Love implies an absolute demand for social justice (ibid. p. 42).

It seems impossible for a Catholic to be indifferent or

uninvolved in working for the alleviation of poverty and for the establishment of justice among peoples and nations. The key is the ability to develop new systems of support and sustenance which will enable Christians to surrender freely more of their goods and power. This effort is immeasurably complex. But it begins with a very simple passion and virtue, love of the Lord, trust in his power, and consequent willingness to share with others. In short, the poverty of spirit and virtue of community so clear in Christian heritage is more than ever before needed, for it is the key to the alleviation of physical poverty and human oppression. Social justice, in the end, will only be achieved through the voluntary selflessness of the powerful and the wealthy, joining with the assertion of human dignity and power of the oppressed.

Bibliography: A. GELIN, *The Poor of Yahweh.* (Collegeville, Minn. 1964). J. GREMILLION, *The Gospel of Peace and Justice*, Maryknoll, (N.Y. 1976). D. GOULET, *The Cruel Choice: A New Concept in the Theory of Development* (New York 1975). G. MYRDAL, *The Challenge of World Poverty* (New York 1970). F. PERELLA, *Poverty in American Democracy: A Study of Social Power.* Campaign for Human Development, U.S. Catholic Conference (Washington, D.C. 1974). F. PERELLA and M. PROCOPIO, *Poverty Profile U.S.A.* (Paramus, N.J. 1975). E. TROELTSCH, *The Social Teachings of the Christian Churches* v. 1 (New York 1960).

[F. PERELLA]

PRAYER

Many Catholics are aware that various methods of meditation are taught—and practiced with great personal satisfaction—by nonreligious organizations. Meditation, once considered a special activity reserved for great saints and secluded monks, is now packaged and marketed. This both intrigues and confuses many Christians, and now they are compelled to investigate, rediscover, and experience their own rich heritage of prayer and meditation. Because of the efforts of various educational programs, the doctrinal and moral teaching of Vatican Council II, is being absorbed gradually by the Catholic community. But the renewal of the Church must also include the area of spirituality. A need is increasingly expressed for *practical* instruction in the disciplines of prayer and meditation (11:667).

The spiritual vitality of the Christian community is currently augmented by the charismatic movement, but its style and ambience do not possess universal appeal. Along with the charismatic movement other forms of prayer renewal are taking place: the directed retreat, scriptural, shared prayer, and a specific effort toward the development of a personal prayer life, based on both traditional Christian meditational practices and the spiritual wisdom and experiences of other religious traditions.

Means to Prayer Life. An appeal for the rediscovery and adaptation of the Christian traditions of meditation can be partially understood in the light of the radical reform of the Church's liturgy over the last fifteen years. The Eucharistic celebration has changed, for understandably good reasons, from a passive, quiet, "contemplative" experience to a word-filled, vernacular celebration, requiring singing, responding, and "...full, conscious, and active participation..." (*Sacrosanctum Concilium* 14). This new order of the Mass leaves, it is often said, "no time for prayer." A nostalgia for the "old liturgy," the loss of an expression of personal piety to which private devotions previously responded and the apparent emphasis in preaching and teaching on

uniquely theological and social issues, encourages many contemporary authors and religious instructors to respond to the need for a practical spiritual program. A contemporary, syncretistic movement is emerging which both encourages and demystifies the practice of meditation and contemplation; it seeks to place the experiences of many different religious traditions at the disposal of its students. The findings of the modern social sciences, especially psychology, and more specifically the work of Carl Jung also contribute to the movement (see Kelsey).

The Life-Journal. Because of the principle that in prayer the Lord is best approached in honesty and self-knowledge, a diary or life-journal is often recommended as a resource for attaining this self-understanding. A continuous writing experience, which aids the meditator in investigating and evaluating life experiences, spiritual progress and goals, which provides a vehicle for remembering and healing the past, and which encourages reflection on the interior life, can be seen as a healthy experience and a helpful contribution to self-understanding and personal growth. The method of the "Intensive Journal" of Ira Progoff is one complete, detailed and easily learned system enjoying a deserved popularity.

Spiritual Direction. Many people consider the role of the spiritual director essential for spiritual progress, although there is a great deal of variety in the understanding of this very traditional role. Definitions range from that of a prayer-partner or friend, to that of an experienced, spiritual adept who actively guides or directs the interior life of another. There is no doubt that spiritual progress can be facilitated through submission to an objective, enlightened, and interested critique. Spiritual direction also serves as a check against delusion, spiritual pride, and false mysticism.

Yoga. The Yoga discipline known as *hatha yoga*, namely, the Yoga which trains the body, can be understood as a physical discipline for making the body a fit instrument in the act of prayer. Not only is the practice of *hatha yoga* a form of asceticism, it can also lead to a greater integration of body and spirit, a physical and spiritual calming, and a sense of well-being. Because of its special emphasis on proper breathing, *hatha yoga* can be a very useful preparation for serious meditation (see Déchanet).

Meditation. Meditation is a discipline which should be practiced regularly and consistently. Periods of from ten to twenty minutes, twice a day, are usually recommended for the beginner (see Le Shan).

Beginning. The novice should learn to calm the mind, first of all, by trying to empty it of all thoughts and concentrating solely on breathing. While seemingly a very frustrating exercise, practice of a few weeks brings noticeable progress. Then the beginning meditator can attempt to deal more specifically with "spiritual" considerations. For some people the goal is the prayer of silence, in which the meditator attempts to create within the self a space for the Holy Spirit to operate (see Slade; Johnston, 1974). For others, material from life's experiences, imagination, and fantasy are the stuff of meditation (see Kelsey).

The Mantra; Jesus Prayer. The *mantra* is the most useful and common technique for any form of meditation. A *mantra* is a word, or a group of words, which serve as an object for concentration. A *mantra* could, nevertheless, be anything which serves to hold the attention of the mind: a holy picture, a statue, a rosary, or whatever. Simple words or things serve the beginner best. A word or a phrase from familiar and appreciated sections of Scripture or the liturgy serve very well as *mantras*. Examples of this sort of *mantra* are: *alleluia*, *amen*, "Glory to God," "Your will be done," "Your kingdom come," "Speak, Lord, your servant listens." (1 Sm 3.10), "Lord, you search me and you know me." (Ps 139.1), "The kingdom of God is within you." (Lk 17.21), "Blessed are the pure in heart." (Mt 5.8), "Be still and know that I am God," (Ps 46.10), "Lord, have mercy." Perhaps the most famous *mantra* in the Christian tradition is the one so faithfully preserved by the Eastern Churches and known as the Jesus Prayer (7:971). While the Jesus Prayer has many forms, it is often expressed in English as, "Lord, Jesus Christ, Son of the living God, have mercy on me, a sinner" (see French).

The *mantra* word or phrase is repeated over and over, rhythmically and in harmony with the breathing, while one is seated in a comfortable position, with the back straight, the eyes closed and the body as relaxed as possible (aided, perhaps, by a preceding *hatha yoga* session). The effects of this sort of meditation differ according to individuals, but the most common experiences include a calmer, more spiritual outlook, a sense of physical and spiritual well-being, a sense of harmony with the Lord and his creation, and a more positive attitude toward others.

Daily Liturgical Prayer. One traditional treasury of prayer that has yet to reach a desired fulness of public experience and expression is the Liturgy of the Hours. This very ancient prayer tradition, which began as a popular, public prayer gathering of both laity and clergy (see Mateos), consists simply, as St. Paul noted, of "...psalms, hymns and inspired songs to God" (Col 3.16). This psalter-prayer tradition suffered a decrease in popularity for many reasons, among them its gradual monastic and clerical appropriation and a growing series of complicated additions, which quickly overshadowed the simplicity of the above Pauline description. Doubtless, too, the recent legislation easing both fasting regulations and the hours at which Mass may be celebrated, increased the practice of frequent Eucharistic celebrations and eclipsed any other form of public prayer in the parochial setting.

Now there are many simplified breviaries and psalters available. Unfortunately, their use is almost exclusively by clergy and religious in a private or semiprivate situation. The public celebration of Morning and Evening Prayer in the parish church remains an important goal for all who are sensitive to the need for varied prayer experiences. Certainly, the public celebration of the Liturgy of the Hours, with its emphasis on the psalms and canticles of Scripture and its collections of biblical readings, would provide a very special forum for preaching on prayer. The Liturgy of the Hours requires a certain scriptural culture which is somewhat lacking to today; such a lack can be remedied through education and exposure. There remains a need for a simple, musically pointed, inexpensive breviary-psalter for public use. But the greatest need is to popularize this traditional form of public prayer (*see* LITURGY OF THE HOURS [PASTORAL CELEBRATION]).

The Christian community is a pluralistic social group and must be tolerant of many diverse expressions of its unifying faith. Christians are now returning to Scripture and Tradition as resources for personal spiritual growth. Most people are convinced that both public, liturgical prayer and a deeply personal relationship with the Lord are necessary to sustain the gift of faith. The calls to evangelize and "to prepare the way of the Lord" (Mt 3.3) must be responded to by a continual dialogue with the Lord. St. Paul's admonition to "keep on praying" (Rom 12.12) goads every Christian to invest in a dynamic friendship with God, manifested by continual prayer and meditation.

Bibliography: Bishops' Committee on Priestly Life and Ministry, *Spiritual Direction for Priests in the U.S.A.: The Rediscovery of a Resource* (Washington 1977). P. CARRINGTON, *Freedom in Meditation* (New York 1965). J. M. DÉCHANET, *Christian Yoga*, tr. R. HINDMARSH (New York 1972); *The Way of a Pilgrim and The Pilgrim Continues His Way*, tr. R. M. FRENCH (New York 1965). A. GRAHAM, *Contemplative Christianity, an Approach to the Realities of Religion* (New York 1974). B. GRIFFITHS, *Return to the Center* (Springfield, Ill. 1976). F. C. HAPPOLD, *Prayer and Meditation, their Nature and Practice* (Middlesex, England 1963); *Mysticism: A Study and an Anthology* (Middlesex, England 1963); *The Journey Inwards, a Simple Introduction to the Practice of Contemplative Meditation by Normal People* (Atlanta 1975). C. HUMPHREYS, *Concentration and Meditation: A Manual of Mind Development* (Baltimore 1968). W. JOHNSTON, *Christian Zen* (New York 1971); *Silent Music: The Science of Meditation* (New York 1974). M. T. KELSEY, *The Other Side of Silence, a Guide to Christian Meditation* (New York 1976). L. LE SHAN, *How to Meditate* (New York 1974). J. MATEOS, "The Origins of the Divine Office." *Worship* 41 (1967) 477–484. I. PROGOFF, *At a Journal Workshop, the Basic Text and Guide for Using the Intensive Journal* (New York 1975). H. SLADE, *Exploration into Contemplative Prayer* (New York 1975).

[C. ANTONSEN]

PRAYER, COMMUNITY

Prayer in religious communities as a corporate activity has during the last decade undergone a diminution in the length of time given to this exercise, but simultaneously it has been intensified in its response to personal needs. The renewal effort has taken to heart the principle of Vatican Council II that "the manner of ...praying...should be suitably adapted to the physical and psychological conditions of today's religious" (*Perfectae caritatis* 3). Prayer forms in community are characterized by ritual and freedom. As a general rule religious gather for the Liturgy of the Hours, usually morning and evening, using a text such as *Christian Prayer: The Liturgy of the Hours* (New York 1976). At the same time variety is occasionally introduced by selected readings, songs, spontaneous petitions, shared prayer (a free form in which participants express their ideas and reactions to a biblical reading); even visual aids may be used. The objective is to meet the needs of those who find the formulae of ritual prayer less meaningful.

Ritual common prayer has the value of satisfying the requirement of the group to express social worship. Strong encouragement is frequently given to the members to go beyond the scheduled prayer time and to design voluntarily such forms of common prayer as shared and *charismatic prayer. Prayer activities of this kind, while open to all, usually involve a small part of the total membership.

Some communities still gather for periods of common meditation. Generally, however, the members are left free to satisfy this requirement on their own.

From the direction community prayer has taken the indication is that the degree of participation in prayer has increased. It is difficult to say, however, at this time whether or not religious have experienced any growth in the deeper or contemplative aspects of prayer. In his exhortation on evangelization Pope Paul VI wonders: "Is [the Church] more ardent in contemplation and adoration and more zealous in missionary, charitable and liberating action?" (Paul VI EvangNunt 76). Has the root of the apostolate, namely, contemplation, reached out to give sound foundation for Christian zeal?

What is clear is that religious give evidence of having an esteem for contemplative prayer. Many institutes have established *houses of prayer. Usually a few members take up residence in these houses and others come for short periods for solitude, reflection, and the reading of the Scriptures.

Another indication is the practice of directed *retreats. Many communities endorse the practice either by providing the opportunity to their members or actually directing the retreats. Lasting from five to thirty days this form of retreat consists mostly of silence, reflection, and reading of the Scriptures. The growing popularity of the nonpreached retreat is evidently a healthy reaction to the very active lives of most religious and the surfeit of meetings and renewal exercises.

The picture of community prayer is spotty. There are many positive signs, however, that religious are internalizing the necessary connection between prayer and the vitality of the vowed life. "Do not forget," said Pope Paul VI in his apostolic exhortation, "the witness of history: faithfulness to prayer or its abandonment are the test of the vitality or decadence of the religious life" (ibid. 42). By and large religious are not forgetful of this witness of history.

[C. OVERMAN]

PRAYER OF CENTERING

The prayer of centering is a process of turning inward to gather the faculties to a center in the depths of the self. The integration of body, mind, and spirit in a point of stillness releases deeper levels of consciousness and opens the self to more contemplative union with God, not as an object of meditation but as a presence within and the source of all being. In contemporary writing on Christian prayer the term "centering" reflects the influence of Eastern spirituality and depth psychology and suggests the action of a potter bringing clay into a spinning, unwobbling pivot on the wheel. Commonly used techniques to facilitate centering are rhythmical breathing, process meditation, the use of a mantra, mandala, or sacred symbol, and the repetition of the Jesus Prayer.

See also CONTEMPLATION; PRAYER.

Bibliography: B. GRIFFITHS, *Return to the Center* (Springfield, Ill. 1976) 16–39. W. JOHNSTON, *The Still Point* (New York 1970) 67–85; *Silent Music* (New York 1974) 55–67. M. KELSEY, *The Other Side of Silence* (New York 1976) 93–122. G. MALONEY, *Inward Stillness* (Denville, N.J. 1976) 39–54. I. PROGOFF, *The Well and the Cathedral* (New York 1971). M. C. RICHARDS, *Centering in Pottery, Poetry, and the Person* (Middletown, Conn. 1964) 9–56.

[D. KENNEDY]

PREACHING

The theology of preaching, like the theology of Church, to which it is closely related, does not change substantially, although fresh historical circumstances and thoughtful reflection provide fresh insights into traditional theory and practice. The two main theological sources for this mature reflection on the contempor-

ary status of the Church and the preaching act are the documents of Vatican Council II plus the postconciliar documents implementing the conciliar decrees, and the apostolic exhortation On Evangelization in the Modern World (*Evangelii nuntiandi*) issued by Pope Paul VI, Dec. 8, 1975. Both sources tend, on the one hand, to reaffirm the traditional notion of preaching as "mystery, magistracy and ministry: the very mystery of God and His ways communicated to men through a preacher exercising his ministry efficaciously in the Church under the living impulse of the Spirit" (*New Catholic Encyclopedia* 11: 698). On the other hand, each source reflects certain contemporary emphases in both theory and practice as "the Church of the twentieth century" tries, in the words of John XXIII opening Vatican II, Oct. 11, 1962, to make itself "better fitted for proclaiming the Gospel to the people of the twentieth century" (ActApS 54 [1969] 792).

The Documents of Vatican II. The first document of the Council, the Constitution on the Sacred Liturgy, deals with three fundamental aspects of preaching as it relates to the mystery of Christ and the Church: (1) it reaffirms the primacy of the work of preaching in the mission of Jesus and his followers (*Sacrosanctum Concilium* 6); (2) it reaffirms also the necessity of preaching as the unique instrument of faith and conversion (ibid. 9), thus providing the basis for that intense "evangelical" preaching which is a notable feature of the ministry of the Word in the postconciliar world; (3) it designates the privileged place for preaching within the liturgical celebration itself, that is, in the *Homily, by means of which "the mysteries of the faith and the guiding principles of the Christian life are expounded" (ibid. 52). Specific guidelines for liturgical preaching include the regrounding of the Homily in the scriptural Readings and its restored status as the natural climax of the Liturgy of the Word. In the light of developments since the Council it is clear that the rehabilitation of the Homily is one of the chief fruits of the Council in the conjoined areas of worship and preaching.

It should be noted, moreover, that in the various instructions and decrees implementing liturgical reform after the Council the Homily is conceived of as an integral part not only of the Eucharist but of the other Sacraments as well; and the new rituals for each of the Sacraments reflect this conception and this concern. Baptism, even when celebrated outside of Mass, has its own Liturgy of the Word and its own Homily; the same procedure is indicated for the rite of Penance when it is celebrated for more than one penitent and for the rite of Matrimony when celebrated outside of Mass; even the rite of Anointing of the Sick calls for a brief explanation of the scriptural texts when circumstances permit. The Homily following sacred Readings is now an integral part of the entire sacramental ritual, so that liturgical reform may be said to be governed everywhere by the necessary union of Word and Sacrament—*contactus fidei, contactus sacramenti* (cf. ST 3a, 48.6 ad 2)—in order to bring about a true interiorization of the sacramental encounter with Christ.

The documents of Vatican II are very rich also in their sensitivity to the ecclesial character of the preaching act and to the widespread sharing of the prophetic ministry throughout the Church. As in the Decree on the Church's Missionary Activity (*Ad gentes* 3) so in the Constitution on the Church the task of the

Church is seen as always centered on the act of proc-laiming the Gospel (*Lumen gentium* 17). This same Constitution, as well as other conciliar documents, clearly identifies those who are called upon to exercise this central ministry of preaching. First, bishops are said to "receive from the Lord . . . the mission to teach all nations and to preach the Gospel to every creature" (ibid. 24). More particularly they are to "preach to the people commited to them the faith to be believed and put into practice" (ibid. 25). According to the Decree on the Pastoral Office of Bishops, their prophetic mission is shared by pastors who are "cooperators of the bishop" in preaching and catechetical instruction (*Christus Dominus* 30), as well as by priests and lay people. "By the power of the sacrament of Orders . . . they (priests) are consecrated to preach the Gospel . . . and to announce the divine Word to all" (ibid 28). According to an emphasis characteristic of the documents of Vat-ican II the laity also are designated as "witnesses" of the faith and "powerful proclaimers of a faith in things to be hoped for" (ibid. 35). The role of the laity as preachers is also affirmed in the Decree on the Aposto-late of the Laity (*Apostolicam actuositatem*) wherein lay people are said to share in "the prophetic office of the Church," not only "by their efforts to permeate and perfect the secular order of things with the spirit of the Gospel" but also by their more direct efforts "to bring the news of the Gospel and the ways of holiness to mankind" (*Apostolicam actuositatem* 2). The final document of Vatican II, the Pastoral Constitution on the Church in the Modern World underlines the same prophetic mission of the laity, a mission not only "to penetrate the world with a Christian spirit" but also "to be witnesses to Christ in all things in the midst of human society" (*Gaudium et spes* 43).

Along with the rehabilitation of the Homily, there-fore, this may be designated as one of the most distinc-tive developments in the prophetic mission of Church after Vatican II, namely, the growth of the phenomenon of lay preaching. In practice this phenomenon covers a whole range of paraliturgical preaching, much of it very informal and spontaneous. Such "preaching" is usually based upon Scripture and can take the form of "teaching" or "sharing" or "witnessing," the last-named having to do with the confession of personal experiences that have challenged or restored or deepened a person's faith. It is evident that the term "preaching" as it includes communications such as these takes on a very broad signification. It ceases to be restricted to public proclamation of the mysteries deriving from episcopal mandate and as-sociated with clerical ministry. Preaching becomes, rather, any public communication of faith by any believer under a right and an impulse deriving from the baptismal character itself and, even more urgently, from Confirmation. Moreover, the rightful and fruitful exer-cise of such a ministry should be looked upon as normal in the Church, granted a right understanding of the dynamism of Baptism and Confirmation and a right understanding of the act of preaching as a charism or grace-of-words given by the Spirit in the Church for the building up of the Church in faith and love. Further-more, in addition to these informal modes of the ministry of the Word bishops may clearly broaden the range and class of mandated public preachers by de-signating lay persons of both sexes for the task, just as

bishops often designate such persons as ministers of the Eucharist.

The Apostolic Exhortation on Evangelization. The second major source for contemporary insight into a theology of preaching is the apostolic exhortation On Evangelization in the Modern World, issued by Pope Paul VI and inspired by the Third General Assembly of the Synod of Bishops (1974), which concentrated on evangelization. In this document the term "evan-gelization" has both a specific and a general meaning: specifically, it refers to the initial proclamation of the Word of God or the Good News aimed at conversion (Paul VI EvangNunt 10); in other contexts it refers to any exercise of the ministry of the Word. The specific meaning of *evangelization, however, and the stress upon that meaning in the document reflect a growing awareness that Christian ministry is exercised today in an increasingly non-Christian and non-religious environment, so that preaching must be first defined as the call to conversion. Under this aspect preaching in the Catholic sector tends to link with the evangelical character of those forms of Protestant preaching which focus almost entirely upon the call to conversion and spiritual rebirth.

While the apostolic exhortation reflects this specific need and this specific mode of preaching, the entire document provides, in addition, a vital and eloquent restatement of the chief elements in a theology of preaching.

(1) The character of the preaching act is Christologi-cal after the example of the preaching of Jesus, the first evangelizer, and as the historical extension of his preaching (ibid. 7).

(2) An ecclesial character marks the act of preaching. The exhortation insists that evangelization or the proc-lamation of the Good News "constitutes the essential mission of the Church . . . which exists in order to evan-gelize" (ibid. 14). Preaching is never "an individual or isolated act; it is one that is deeply ecclesial" (ibid. 60).

(3) The preaching act is charismatic in so far as the Holy Spirit is its principal agent and the new humanity generated by the Spirit its very goal and purpose (ibid 75). In an authentic theology of preaching it is the Spirit who moves both the preacher to preach efficaciously and the hearer to respond with a living faith.

(4) The content is revealed or God-given, a content which, however diversely expressed (the Love of the Father, the Good News, Salvation, Jesus himself) touches principally on "a transcendent and eschatologi-cal salvation" (ibid. 27), though secondarily and conse-quently on human liberation here and now from tem-poral evils (ibid. 31–38).

(5) Preaching is ministry, a ministry pertaining to the whole Church and to each of its parts. It pertains, first, to the ordained ministry of pope (ibid. 67), bishops and priests (ibid. 68); and to religious according to the silent witness of example or the overt witness of proclamation (ibid. 69). The document stresses also the ministry of the laity (ibid. 70), in virtue both of their presence in the midst of temporal affairs and of their direct service to the ecclesial community (ibid. 73). In this sense the apostolic exhortation supports the distinctive stress in the documents of Vatican II on the role of the laity in proclaiming the Good News and extending the King-dom of Christ.

(6) Preaching as a ministry calls for such special vir-

tues and qualities as the witness of a holy life (ibid. 76), the spirit of unity and amity among believers (ibid. 77), great reverence for truth (ibid. 78), authentic love for those to whom the Gospel is proclaimed (ibid. 79), and that spiritual fervor which makes the preaching of the Good News a matter of urgent personal necessity (ibid. 80).

(7) Finally, preaching is an act of discernment and accommodation, an act in which the specific character, needs, and life-situation of the hearers affect the mode of proclamation (ibid. 51–57; 62–63), though without prejudice to the universality of the preaching mandate (ibid. 49), or the claims of the universal Church (ibid. 64), or the unimpaired content of revealed truth expressed by the magisterium (ibid. 65).

In conclusion, it may be said that while the documents of Vatican II and the apostolic exhortation on evangelization clearly and persuasively restate a traditional theology of preaching—its source, its purpose, its content, its agency, both divine and human—these same documents give special emphasis and provide special insight into three distinct areas or concerns in the contemporary regime of preaching: (1) the importance of conversional preaching, or the initial moment in the proclamation of the Gospel; (2) the restoration or renewal of liturgical (homiletic) preaching, not only during the celebration of the Eucharist but as an integral part of the entire sacramental system; (3) the phenomenon of lay preaching grounded in the baptismal character of the believer and as the expression of the distinctive role of the laity in communicating the Gospel in the modern world.

Bibliography: E. ECHLIN, *Priest as Preacher* (Cork 1973). J. HOFINGER, *Evangelization and Catechesis* (New York 1976).

[T. D. ROVER]

PREAMBLES OF FAITH

Preambles of faith are those elements of the faith and reason context which can be considered as logically independent from the assent of faith and which guarantee that man is rationally and responsibly invited to accept Jesus Christ as God's authentic saving presence for him as well as for the whole world (11:702). Historically they meant either a set of abstract, supposedly universally valid, metaphysical truths (e.g., the existence of a personal God, spiritual nature of man, the possibility of transcendental method and knowledge; see Lonergan) logically preceding faith (in the sense that their denial would mean necessarily the falsehood of revelation), or a complex of signs of credibility (miracles and prophecies) which could, through rational inference, prove the divine origin of the Christian revelation. In the 1960s the a priori conditions of faith were sought in the historical dimension of human existence experienced as transcendental openness to the absolute mystery of being and thus predisposing man to accept the revelation of God-man as the concrete historical and social realization as well as the historical, objective expression of his existential openness (see Bouillard, Rahner, Darlap). As a consequence Rahner takes for a starting point of the way to faith man as the potential believer who, thanks to the abiding presence of the eschatological Christ-event in the world, is already in possession of what he is to believe, e.g., God's self-communication in Jesus Christ. Preambles of faith are therefore an implicit faith as an abiding feature of man's existence oriented to explicit faith as to its objective and conscious self-expression in the society of believers.

Since man discovers more and more the unlimited varieties of his own historical tradition, and thus a common philosophical ground for all believers and unbelievers is found extremely difficult, and moreover since implicit faith is neither empirically nor historically provable, in the 1970s the preambles of faith were sought rather in the empirical fact of the already existing believing community (the community of those who believe that Jesus is God and Saviour—the Church) as both word-event and context-event in which the revelation-faith dialogue between God and man can take place (Horvath). This conception of the preambles of faith does not assume any philosophical notion of human existence or religion in general by determining a priori which philosophy or religion should be the most adequate for man. It takes the community of believers as God-given, Christ-sign-event—which includes as its subsets the pre-Christian Jewish tradition, the historical Jesus' self-and-God revelational life, particularly his faith-raising power, his death and resurrection and the purpose of his Church's activity—as puzzling datum, strong enough to raise in man questions concerning God's personal presence in Jesus Christ. As a way to faith the starting point is therefore not so much the abstract unity of mankind, but rather the existing concrete diversity of believers and unbelievers who for a better understanding of and respect for the existing human reality-complex, through reflective dialogue try to creatively transform their "I and you believe" into "We believe." The task of the Church as God-given, inviting word-event is consequently to bring forth constantly the preambles of faith by raising questions and creating the context of love in which God's *words* answering the aroused, questioning man can be perceived in man's consciousness as the answering word of *God* (cf. 1 Thes 2.13; Vatican Council II, *Dignitatis humanae* 3; Horvath 96–105).

Bibliography: J. ALFARO, "Preambles of Faith," SacrMundi 2:324–326. H. BOUILLARD, *The Logic of Faith* (New York 1967). A. DARLAP, "Theologie der Heilsgeschichte," *Mysterium Salutis* 1 (Einsiedeln 1965) 1–156. T. HORVATH, *Faith Under Scrutiny* (Notre Dame 1975). B. J. F. LONERGAN, *Insight, A Study of Human Understanding* (London 1957). K. RAHNER, "A Way to Faith," SacrMundi 2:310–317.

[T. HORVATH]

PREFACE

In recent years the thrust of studies concerning the Preface in the Eucharistic Liturgy has been to insist upon its organic and integral relationship to the following prayer. The "General Instruction of the Roman Missal," first issued in 1969, indicates the official ecclesiastical acceptance of the assertion of the liturgical historians that the so-called Preface, with its opening dialogue, is an integral part of the *Eucharistic Prayer:

The eucharistic prayer, a prayer of thanksgiving and sanctification, is the center and high point of the entire celebration. In an introductory dialogue the priest invites the people to lift their hearts to God in prayer and thanks; he unites them with himself in the prayer he addresses in their name to the Father through Jesus Christ. The meaning of the prayer is that the whole congregation joins Christ in acknowledging the works of God and in offering the sacrifice (GenInstrRomMissal 54).

The chief elements of the eucharistic prayer are these: a) *Thanksgiving* (expressed especially in the preface): in the name of the entire people of God, the priest praises the Father and gives him thanks for the work of salvation or for some special aspect of it in keeping with the day, feast, or season. b) *Acclamation*: united with the angels, the congregation sings or recites the *Sanctus*. This acclamation forms part of the eucharistic prayer, and all the people join with the priest in the singing or reciting it . . . (ibid. 55).

History. Recent historical studies suggest more strongly than ever that the earliest anaphoras or Eucharistic Prayers were structured after the Jewish *Berakah* (or after-dinner thanksgiving) of the time of Christ, which was composed of a threefold, interconnected theme: (1) a statement of praise and adoration addressed to God as the creator and provider of food; (2) a solemn declaration of thanks to God for his redeeming actions in sacred history; and (3) a prayer of petition, asking God to continue to bestow his mercy and care on the people of Israel. Apparently, two types of Eucharistic Prayer developed, one within a basically Eastern tradition, which retained the tripartite form of the original, the other, more Western tradition, which assumed a bipartite pattern in which the first two parts of the original Jewish rite (praise and thanksgiving) coalesced into the initial "thanksgiving" that came to be known as the *Praefatio*, and which tended both to be variable according to the occasion and the feast and to appear somewhat isolated from the later supplication by reason of the *Sanctus* acclamation.

Pastoral Implications. The pastoral implications of this reassessment of the central role of the Preface, especially for providing both the general and the specific themes to be celebrated in a specific Eucharist are perhaps best to be noted in the later English editions of the Roman Missal itself. In its "Index of Prefaces" of the *Sacramentary there are eighty-four listed for various seasons, feasts, and occasions; most are provided with subtitles which rather clearly summarize the doctrinal or theological contents. Moreover, the impression is given that the further composition of other Prefaces suited to particular circumstances may be the rule rather than the exception.

The season cycle of the liturgical year has been quite liberally enriched by additional formulas which strive to bring out with increasing subtlety the thematic evolution of both the Christmas cycle and the Easter cycle. Thus, for example, the Advent-Christmas-Epiphany season now has 7 Prefaces; the Lent-Passion-Easter-Ascension-Pentecost cycle has 21. For Sundays in ordinary time there is a variety of 8 Prefaces, while 6 are for weekdays.

The sanctoral cycle is similarly enriched. The feasts and mysteries of the Lord account for 13 new formulas, while there are 16 for the feasts of the saints. Certain other celebrations have also been provided with their own Prefaces, e.g., marriage, religious profession, Christian burial, such civic observances as Independence Day and Thansgiving.

Bibliography: D. DUFRASNE, "Les Nouvelles prières eucharistiques: réflexions critiques et catéchèse," *Paroisse et liturgies* 5 (1968) 433–453. L. SOUBIGOU, *A Commentary on the Prefaces and the Eucharistic Prayers of the Roman Missal*, tr. J. OTTO (Collegeville, Minn. 1971). T. TALLEY, "The Eucharistic Prayer: Directions for Development," *Worship* 51 (1977) 316–325.

[D. GRABNER]

PREJUDICE

Two historic documents of Vatican Council II are related to the Church's effort to correct problems of prejudice among peoples of the world in general and among Catholics in particular. The first is the Declaration on the Relationship of the Church to Non-Christian Religions; and the second is the Declaration on Religious Freedom.

The first deals explicitly with non-Christian religions, calls attention to the many deep religious qualities they have in common with Christianity, and encourages a dialogue in which Christians will become aware of the values in Non-Christian religions. The more significant statement relates to the Jews, acknowledges the common heritage, corrects the misconception that the Jews have been repudiated or cursed. In what has been recognized as a significant historic statement: "The Church repudiates all persecutions against any man . . . she deplores the hatred, persecutions and displays of anti-semitism directed against the Jews at any time and from any source" (*Nostra aetate* 4). The Church rejected, "as foreign to the mind of Christ any discrimination against men or harassment of them because of their race, color, condition of life or religion" (ibid. 5).

One consequence of the Declaration was the effort to correct statements and language in liturgical or instructional texts which referred disparagingly to the Jews. It has also promoted the ecumenical efforts to identify the religious beliefs, values, and practices which the many faiths share in common and to study ways whereby these could eventually lead to a greater religious unity of the human family.

Extensive efforts have been made through pontifical commissions and local bishops' committees on interreligious affairs, and Non-Christian religions to maintain a dialogue which explores areas of agreement and difference and has resulted in steps toward understanding.

The second Declaration states the relationship of the Church to secular society and strongly affirms the freedom of the person in matters of religious belief and practices: ". . . all men are to be immune from coercion on the part of individuals and social groups and of any human power, in such wise that, in matters religious, no one is to be forced to act in a manner contrary to his own beliefs" (*Dignitatis humanae* 2). This same freedom was asserted for groups as well as individuals (ibid. 4).

Historically religion has always been closely related to problems of prejudice and discrimination (11:731–733). The explicit affirmation of the conciliar documents is the insistence on freedom from discrimination and prejudice. By calling attention to religious beliefs and practices shared in common, the Declarations seek to withdraw any religious orientation from becoming the basis for rationalizing prejudice or rejection of another person.

In relation to human freedom, the effort to give expression to the guidance of these Declarations is found in the increasing effort of Christians, as well as others, to correct racism and discrimination. In the first general assembly of Catholics in the U.S. at the *Call to Action conference (1976) of the U.S. bishops on "Liberty and Justice for all," demands were very strong for the rejection of any forms of racism, or discrimination on the basis of color, sex or nationality. It is a common practice of dioceses and church organizations now to make a public declaration of their support for various forms of affirmative-action programs, designed to eliminate discrimination.

See also ATHEISM; BUDDHISM, CHURCH AND; HINDUISM, CHURCH AND; JEWISH/ROMAN CATHOLIC RELATIONS.

Bibliography: NCCB/USCC, *A Call to Action* (USCC Publ. Office, Washington, D.C. 1977) esp. 39–53.

[J. P. FITZPATRICK]

PRELATES, HONORARY

Until recently honorary prelates (11:735) were more numerous; now they include only the categories of Apostolic Prothonotaries (numerary and supernumerary), Honorary Prelates of His Holiness, and Chaplains of His Holiness. All other categories have been abolished by the motu proprio *Pontificalis domus* of Pope Paul VI, March 28, 1968 (*see* PAPAL HOUSEHOLD). All are appointed by the pope and continue to form part of the pontifical family as well as the pontifical chapel, where their functions are regulated by the Prefect of the Apostolic Palace. Their rights and privileges continue to be governed by existing papal documents. Their dress has been simplified by the Instruction of the Papal Secretariat of State, *Ut sive sollicite*, March 31, 1969 (ActApS 61 [1969] 334–340).

Apostolic Prothonotaries *de numero* are those seven who, like the original *Notarii in Urbe*, collect and care for the records of consistories, councils, canonizations and sign papal documents. As dress the purple cassock, the purple mantelletta, the rochet, the red-trimmed black cassock without cape, the purple sash with fringes of silk at the two ends, the purple *ferraiuolo* (non-obligatory), and the red tuft on the biretta are all retained. Apart from the seven-member college there are now only supernumerary Apostolic Prothonotaries. As dress the purple cassock, the red-trimmed black cassock without cape, the sash with fringes and the purple *ferraiuolo* (non-obligatory) are retained. When appropriate, the unpleated surplice (cotta) can be worn over the purple cassock, instead of the rochet.

Honorary Prelates of His Holiness were formerly known as domestic prelates. Except for the *ferraiuolo*, their dress is the same as that for supernumerary Apostolic Prothonotaries. Chaplains of His Holiness were formerly known as Papal chamberlains or supernumerary privy chamberlains of His Holiness. Dress consists of the purple-trimmed black cassock with purple sash, to be used also in sacred ceremonies.

[B. C. GERHARDT]

PRESBYTERIAN-REFORMED/ROMAN CATHOLIC CONSULTATION

The *bilateral consultation between representatives of the North American Area Council of the World Alliance of Reformed Churches and the *Bishops' Committee for Ecumenical and Interreligious Affairs began in 1965 under the chairmanship of the Rev. Dr. Andrew Harsanyi of the World Alliance and the Most Rev. Ernest L. Unterkoefler, Bishop of Charleston, S.C.

First Round. The first round consisted of thirteen three-day meetings held from 1965 until 1971, in which the Theological Section and the Worship and Mission Section met concurrently.

Theological Section. The Theological Section studied the development of doctrine within the two traditions; this led to a concern about the diverse structure of ministry and the questions of episcopacy and papacy. Two preliminary statements on ministry were developed and published, as were subsequent statements, in the *Journal of Ecumenical Studies.*

The final statement on "Ministry in the Church" was approved at the October 1971, meeting in Richmond, Virginia. Beginning with the ministry of Jesus this document discusses the ministry of the whole Church and of ordained ministers, specific issues concerning women in ordained ministry, celibate and married representatives in ministry, and the monarchical and congregational structure of ministry, and the Presbyterian/Reformed and the Roman Catholic understandings of apostolic succession and infallibility. In conclusion it offers eight practical recommendations including these: (1) that each tradition affirm in some appropriate way that Christ is present and at work in the ministries of each tradition; (2) that specific occasions be designated for Eucharistic sharing; and (3) that further ecumenical learning and experience be encouraged on the grass-roots level (*see* ECUMENISM, REGIONAL AND LOCAL).

Ministry and Worship Section. Meanwhile the Worship and Mission Section pursued a study of worship in the two traditions from which emerged the more specific issues of inter-Christian marriage, marriage itself, divorce, and the role of women in the Church. A preliminary statement on women in the Church was published in 1970. After four semiannual meetings in which numerous women testified to the discrimination against women in Church and society, the final statement, "Women in the Church," was approved in October 1971. This document sets out the urgent reasons for the Churches to take initiatives to remedy injustice to women. It recommends full and equal participation of women in decision-making in the Churches, the ordaining of qualified women, and the establishment of theological study committees on this issue in Churches presently prohibiting the ordination of women. It also recommends that the parent bodies of the Consultation fund an Ecumenical Commission on Women to facilitate the implementation of these recommendations.

Second Round. The Second Round of the Consultation began in October 1972. The two previous Sections were merged and new members added from the fields of church history and sociology. A three-year plan was designed with the goal of describing as clearly as possible the unity sought by the Churches involved. In January 1973 a subcommittee spent a week in Columbus, Ohio, studying firsthand the ecumenical situation there. At the final meeting of this round in May 1975, (the 19th meeting since the Consultation began in 1965), the joint statement, *The Unity We Seek* was reviewed and approved.

The Church. The four sections of this joint statement correspond to the four topics examined by four subgroups of the Consultation during the preceding two years. The first section, "The Mission and Nature of the Church of Christ," considers the model of the Church as the People of God and proposes the typology of the Church as a "communion of communions" (*see* CHURCH AND COMMUNIO).

Creed and Structures. The second section, "The Unity We Seek in Belief," recommends the development of common credal statements in the present to parallel those held jointly from earlier centuries, like the Apostles' and the Nicene Creeds. The third section, "The Unity We Seek in Structure," envisions a transition period moving toward new structures not yet clear.

It repeats the eight practical recommendations from the ministry document of the First Round and adds such other recommendations as the acceptance of one another's members by the Churches.

Worship. The final section, "The Unity We Seek in Worship," suggests the recognition of a plurality of forms of worship as authentically Christian, the forming of new communities of worship, and the need for full participation and integrity in Christian worship. It concludes with recommendations for dialogue on the Eucharist, reeducation in the teaching about the Eucharist, congregations making covenants for some common worship, education about each other's worship, and a nationwide Year of Ecumenical Worship in 1980 or later.

Third Round. The Third Round of the Consultation begin in October, 1976, with another reorganization adding new representatives in the field of Christian ethics while retaining some previous participants for the sake of continuity. The round is focusing on contemporary ethical issues. The Consultation will study two moral questions from an ecumenical viewpoint to discover where agreement and disagreement are real or apparent. The first question is corporate in nature and one upon which the Churches represented are in basic agreement, namely, human rights and economic justice. The second question is one which is more personal in nature and upon which the Churches seem to disagree, namely, the moral permissibility of abortion.

If the Third Round follows the three-year schedule of the Second Round, this ethical dialogue will be completed in May 1979. As of October 1977 the Consultation had not attempted to publish any formal statements but had reached consensus on an informal statement declaring that human rights are rooted in and conferred by God and discernible also by those who are not consciously confessing Christians.

Bibliography: *The Unity We Seek* (New York 1977). This contains an Introduction offering a more complete history of the First and Second Rounds of the Consultation and bibliographical references to all papers published by participants. Other joint statements were published as follows in JEcumSt: First Round, Preliminary Statement on Ministry, 5 (1968) 462–465; 7 (1970) 686–690; "Ministry in the Church," 9 (1972) 589–612; Preliminary Statement on Women, 7 (1970) 690–691; "Women in the Church," 9 (1972) 235–241.

[D. G. MCCARTHY]

PRESIDENTIAL PRAYERS

Prayers in the name of the entire worshiping assembly, recited by the presider at Mass, celebration of the Sacraments, the Liturgy of the Hours, and other liturgical gatherings are termed "Presidential Prayers" (GenInstrRomMissal 10–12). In virtue of a calling to preside, whether through ordination or deputation of some other form, the presider has a special role to perform. He or she invites everyone present to pray and then, frequently after pausing for a moment of silence, pronounces a particular prayer, to which the group usually assents by the response "Amen." These prayers are to be spoken in a loud, clear voice; no music or song is allowed during them (ibid. 12).

Several instances of this leadership and ministerial role occur in the Eucharistic Liturgy: the Opening Prayer of Mass, the conclusion of the General Intercessions or Prayer of the Faithful, the Prayer over the Gifts, the Prayer after Communion and—on occasion—the Prayer over the People. Through all of

these both the theme of the celebration and particular junctures of the Eucharist acquire distinct prayer forms. Foremost among the Presidential Prayers, however, is the *Eucharistic Prayer, the hymn of thanksgiving and praise offered to God so as to make present the paschal mystery for all who gather together to celebrate it.

In the Sacramentary the General Instruction allows for a certain degree of flexibility in the choice of prayers according to the composition of the worshipping group and in harmony with the occasion of their praying together. One help toward such flexibility in the American Sacramentary is an alternative text for the Opening Prayer on Sundays and major feast days. On those days the prayer on the left side of the page is a faithful but not literal translation of the corresponding Latin prayer in the *Missale Romanum*; the one on the right is an alternative Prayer suggested by the Latin text and in harmony with its theme. The presider is free to choose either text according to the circumstances of the celebration he is leading.

See also SACRAMENTARY.

Bibliography: R. HOVDA, *Strong, Loving and Wise: Presiding in Liturgy* (Washington 1976). G. SOBRERO, "La Prière présidentielle," in J. GÉLINEAU, ed., *Dans vos assemblées* (Paris 1971) 259–277.

[J. SULLIVAN]

PRIEST AND PRIESTHOOD, CHRISTIAN

Biblical and historical scholarship indicates that the concrete priesthood of no epoch, including the biblical epoch, has normative value. However, a study of the concrete priesthood of all ages and of the theologies of these lived priesthoods, can yield the various, culturally conditioned notions of actual priesthood. Then it is possible to theorize from what has been common to the operative priesthood so as to reach a transcultural notion of the priestly ministry that would contain the enduring elements of the historical priesthood (11:768; 16:362).

Priesthood in the New Testament. The New Testament rarely uses priestly categories. The Gospels never call Christ a priest (ἱερεύς) and never say he offered sacrifice. St. Paul never uses the words *hiereus* (priest) or ἀρχιερεύς (high priest). Nowhere in the New Testament is a priestly title given to ministers of the Church. Just a few texts speak of Christians as priests (1 Pt 2.5, 9; Ap 1.6; 5.10; 20.6). Only Hebrews consistently calls Christ *hiereus* and *archiereus*. A basic reason for this New Testament reticence is that as Jews the early Christians possessed a priesthood and an understanding of it that did not accord with the reality of ministry exemplified in Christ and his followers. The Old Testament priesthood was still flourishing in the early days of the Church, and that priesthood still ministered to Christians who considered themselves not so much as the New Israel as the renewed Israel. Further, at this time the function of the Old Testament priesthood was largely cultic; it dealt with the offering of temple sacrifices, the rituals of purification, and the rituals of blessing. The ministry of Christ and that of his disciples, however, were evidently not purely cultic ministries, but proclamations in word and deed of the Kingdom of God, far more pastoral than cultic. The term *hiereus* simply did not accord with what these ministries were.

Christ proclaimed the Kingdom by word and action. He preached the good news that with his arrival the continuous inbreak of the goodness of the Father and his overflowing love for mankind had reached supreme expression. This new inbreak was not just expressed in sayings and parables; it was made visible in acts of power—miraculous cures, exorcisms, the pardoning of sinners, sitting at table with the dregs of society. So identified did Christ become with the Kingdom that to proclaim it he went to his death. And because of his total expression of the Kingdom in the weakness of his earthly life, the Father raised him up as the all powerful Lord through whom the blessings of the Kingdom would be forever bestowed on mankind. As risen, he was and is, in the phrase of Origen, the Kingdom personified.

The proclamation of the Kingdom by Christ put before men the challenge of discipleship, of being converted by accepting the outpouring of the Kingdom into their whole beings. Further, it led to his calling of some men who would minister to others by promoting the spread of the good news of the Kingdom far and wide and fostering the unity of those disciples who received the message. The ways in which this ministry was exercised varied according to the capacities of individuals and the needs of the people being evangelized. In the early days after the resurrection diverse ministries arose spontaneously and possessed great fluidity. To the classical triad, apostles, prophets, and teachers (1 Cor 12.28; Eph 4.11), were added those who had the gift of tongues, healers, miracle workers, administrators, evangelists, and the like. The one ministry that in reality if not in name did persist throughout most of the New Testament period was the ministry of overseer or supervisor of the growth and unity of the community and its various ministries. Thus James led the Church at Jerusalem and Paul directed the many Churches he had founded; later there appeared Timothy and Titus, roving sub-apostles, as well as the overseers (ἐπίσκοποι) and elders (πρεσβύτεροι) who are present in Acts and the pastoral epistles.

The beginning of the process by which priestly terminology was applied to Christ and his followers appears in Hebrews. By the time this letter was written the division between the Church and Israel had been sharpened. Further, the old temple with its ritual and priesthood had been destroyed. Hence, the author of Hebrews found it possible to replace the old cult and priesthood with a new cult and a new priest. The old rites were ritual, exterior, and conventional; to them is opposed a worship by Christ which is real, personal, and existential. He is the perfect high priest by the total offering of himself which was consummated on the cross, an offering in which priest and victim coalesce to form the perfect sacrifice. By his obedience unto death he is perfected, raised up by the Father, and he enters into the fullness of priesthood.

Moreover, by the same activity which makes him to be a priest forever, Christ also makes of his followers a priestly people. In Hebrews, τελειόω (make perfect) designates the consecration of Christ as priest. Further, the very offering by which he is perfected and consecrated is also the act by which his disciples are perfected and consecrated. "By virtue of that one offering he has perfected (teleioō) forever those whom he sanctifies" (Heb 10.14). In short, by his lifelong obedience supremely expressed in death, Christ becomes the great high priest so united to those he saves that they become a priestly people.

Thus, the reality described in the Gospels—the proclamation of the kingdom of God in word and act which led to Christ's death and resurrection and which challenged men to discipleship—is the same reality under other terms which Hebrews describes as the perfecting and consecration of Christ and his followers. Hence, it became possible to apply priestly terminology to the faithful in 1 Peter and in the Apocalypse; and after the New Testament period the Church applied priestly terminology to those who ministered to the priestly people in signing forth for them the one mediator, Jesus Christ, and in uniting them with one another in him.

Priesthood in the later Church. After the New Testament period a number of ministries continued along with the overseeing ministry. Soon the single bishop emerged in each place as the overseer of the community, the unifier, *the* priest. He presided over the priestly life of the Church and over the Eucharist, which expressed the great act by which Christ was perfected as priest and by which he made a priestly people. Eventually the bishop sent out members of his group of advisers (the elders or presbyters) to the outlying towns where these men then exercised a ministry similar to that of the bishop but on a smaller scale. Thus, they became "little bishops," priests in their own right who were responsible to the sending bishop. Soon, other ministries were swallowed up by the two priestly orders.

Towards the end of the first millennium a distance opened up between the priesthood and the priestly people it was called to serve. The priesthood came to be seen as a reality by itself. Priesthood was eventually defined in terms of the power to consecrate the host and thus apart from a pastoral ministry, even though the best priests were always pastorally oriented. At one time there were even "Mass priests," ordained primarily to celebrate Mass. And since priests of all degrees from the ordinary pastor up to the pope were equal in their power to consecrate, juridical categories had to be introduced to explain the various grades of priestly ministry. In a certain sense the Church had returned to the Old Testament cultic notion of priesthood.

Modern Questions. With pastoral work being taken to mean the building up of the Church as the priestly people around Christ by facilitating the internalization of the values of the Christian tradition, then increasingly the priestly ministry is viewed as the overseeing pastoral ministry. In the light of this basic insight favored by Vatican Council II, some long-standing problems can be more successfully handled. First, priestly ordination becomes the event by which an individual is inducted into a community of overseeing pastors at one of two levels (bishop or priest) through a mutual commitment of the Church (in the person of the ordaining prelate) and the ordinand. Hence, there is a distinction between the ordinary priest and the bishop in the very area that constitutes them both as priests. Secondly, by ordination the priest is empowered to preside at the Eucharist because the Eucharist is the primary activity of the pastoral ministry: it is the symbolic expression of that corporate worshiping spirit which is the goal of Christian existence. The priest is the overseer of the Eucharist to the extent that he is the overseer of the pastoral life of the Church which the Eucharist epitomizes. The bishop's Eucharist is thus *the* Eucharist of the diocese in a sense that the Eucharist of the simple priest is not (see CHURCH, LOCAL [THEOLOGY]). Thirdly, *jurisdiction is not creative of priestly powers; it is the orderly way in which already empowered individuals are assigned to specific communities (a parish or a diocese) or given the right to exercise certain priestly powers (e.g. hear confessions) with regard to designated persons. Fourthly, to ask whether women can be ordained is to ask whether the mutual commitment of individual and Church that gives rise to the overseeing pastoral ministry is possible between the Church and women of a given place and time (*see* WOMEN, ORDINATION OF; WOMEN IN MINISTRY). It was not possible in the past. Is it possible now? Fifthly, other ministries have place in the Church as specialized needs multiply. The overseeing ministry of the priest with regard to these ministries is to harmonize them towards unity.

See also MINISTRY (ECCLESIOLOGY).

Bibliography: J. BLENKINSOPP, *Celibacy, Ministry, Church* (New York 1968). P. BONY, É. COTHENET, et al., *Le Ministère et les Ministères selon le Nouveau Testament* (Paris 1974). R. BROWN, *Priest and Bishop* (New York 1970). B. COOKE, *Ministry to Word and Sacraments* (Philadelphia 1976). J. T. ELLIS, ed., *The Catholic Priest in the United States: Historical Investigations* (Collegeville 1971). E. E. LARKIN and G. T. BROCCOLO, eds., *Spiritual Renewal of the American Priesthood* (Washington, D.C. 1973). K. RAHNER, *The Priesthood* (New York 1973). A. VANHOYE, "Sacerdoce commun et sacerdoce ministériel. Distinction et rapports," NouvRevTh 97 (1975) 193–207.

[P. CHIRICO]

PRIESTHOOD, UNIVERSAL

The Church can be described as priestly because when Christ communicated his mission, that is, his destiny and Spirit, to his followers, he gave his priestly character to their very human existence now informed by his Spirit. This amounts to saying that the Church can have no other purpose than the orientation of the risen Christ. This is the general priesthood which all Christians share in common because of their baptismal entry into the community; its purpose is the nurturing of the community at the level of faith (see *Lumen gentium* 7–11). The mission of Christ is to establish the Kingdom of his Father. Because this Kingdom is coextensive with the acknowledgment and acceptance of God, Christ's mission intends the establishing of a worshipping community. Christ's priesthood is essentially accomplished in his being the Sacrament at once of God's gift to men, of human acceptance of God, and of the gift of self to God. The reason that the priestly and the sacramental are synonymous in the case of the Christian community is that Christ accomplishes his priestly mission in his existing sacramentality which is the Church. This priestly character is more basic than any power to act, even to celebrate the Eucharist.

A Priestly People. The priesthood of the Christian community is not similar to an office or function. Nor is it simply a quality possessed because the community was founded in virtue of Christ's priestly Sacrifice on the cross. This community priesthood is its basic directionality and finality. Just as in the case of Jesus Christ, the Christian community is priestly because it is sacramental. Because it is the Body of Christ, in everything that it says and does it gives witness to the presence of Christ. It is a proclamation of Christ's saving love and fidelity through its own loving and faithful concern. Men and women, consequently, are Christians to the extent that they give themselves in faith and love to Christ and to each other. Through the living sacrifice of their lives they become the Sacrament of Christ's own sacrificial offering to all people.

The priesthood of faith-sharing is exercised by some kind of public profession of this faith. That is why the priestly character of the community demands liturgical expression. All Christians as priests are called upon and empowered to profess their faith sacramentally in Christian worship. Their baptismal, priestly character cannot be defined within the limits of some specific function; it is the pervasive character of Christian living that is meant to condition the whole life of faith and grace. The Church is priestly through and through, in all its aspects, all its ministries, all its institutions and members. No one aspect or agency of the Church has a monopoly on the priesthood. The life of the Church is so rich and its priestly character so manifold that no one ministry can exhaust them. From this multiplicity springs the diversity of ministries that expresses and keeps alive the manifold aspects of the community's reality.

The Universal and the Special Priesthood. The universal priesthood is different from the priesthood that applies to the special ministry in the Church ritualized by the ordination rite. The special priesthood means direction to some specific function which enables the community to express more adequately its own communal priesthood. Special ministry functions as a Sacrament within a Sacrament. Those who possess special ministry are not more priestly than other Christians but they are called upon to give special sacramental expression to the paschal mystery so that the community can more fully celebrate its priestly character. The priestly character of the Church demands a special ministry dedicated to liturgical leadership. Liturgical ministry certainly does not exhaust the priestly ministry of the Church. All ministry must be priestly because the very dynamism of the Church is priestly. But there is a special affinity between liturgical leadership and the priesthood of the community because the liturgy brings that priesthood, that sacramental character of the whole Church, to its highest expression. Special ministry, especially the liturgical ministry, is an intensification of the common priesthood of all Christians. It flows from the community and exists for the community. To affirm the necessity of a liturgical ministry in the Church does not imply a split between an institutionalized and a charismatic form of that ministry.

See also WORSHIP, COMMUNAL.

Bibliography: B. COOKE, *Ministry to Word and Sacraments* (Philadelphia 1976).

[J. L. EMPEREUR]

PRIESTLY FORMATION

Vatican Council II's Decree on Priestly Formation initiating a renewal in the training of priests is rooted in the ecclesiology of the Dogmatic Constitution on the Church and of the Pastoral Constitution on the Church in the Modern World. It sketches a broad plan for seminaries and mandates each national hierarchy to establish its own detailed program of priestly formation, adapted to local needs and subject to regular revision (*Optatam totius* 22). In answer to a request of the 1967 Synod of Bishops the Sacred Congregation for Catholic Education drew up the "Basic Plan" (*Ratio fundamentalis institutionis sacerdotalis*, 1970), which has become normative for the more specific documents on priestly formation of each national episcopal conference. In 1971 the NCCB issued its first *Program of Priestly Formation*, which carried the approval of the Sacred

Congregation for Catholic Education for a period of five years. This program was superseded by a slightly revised second edition in 1976; a more extensive revision is planned for 1981.

Optatam Totius. This decree of Vatican II underlined values which have guided subsequent legislation on priestly formation. It stressed that the primary objective of the seminary is pastoral formation. The chief element of such formation is training for the ministry of the Word, and this is to be accompanied by training in worship and sanctification and also in pastoral service. Formation is to be adapted to the needs of the local Church. The candidate is to be given a solid spiritual formation which will ground him in an ecclesial identity, promote the development of priestly virtues, and assist him to become an integrated Christian person. His intellectual formation should value the historical approach; it should coordinate the study of philosophy and theology; it should impart a knowledge of other Christian communities. Studies should be preceded by an introductory course on the mystery of salvation which will provide an integrating framework for the total program. Indeed, the integration of all formational elements around the goal of pastoral formation is the central thrust of the decree.

The Ratio Fundamentalis and the American Bishops' Program of Priestly Formation. These contain institutional principles and principles relative to personal formation.

Seminaries. Among the institutional principles are the following. (1) Seminaries as institutions of specialized formation for priestly ministry continue to be viable and necessary. (2) The distinction between the priesthood of the faithful and the sacramental priesthood must be preserved (*see* PRIESTHOOD, UNIVERSAL); the unique features of sacramental ministry should dictate the controlling structures of seminary programs. (3) There are institutional factors each seminary should possess— "a community inspired by charity, open to modern needs, and organically constructed, i.e. one in which the authority of the lawful superior is effectively exercised with the mind and after the example of Christ; where all help to insure to the students real development of human and Christian maturity; where there is opportunity to begin experience of the priestly state through relationships both of brotherly fellowship and hierarchic dependence; where the doctrine of the priesthood is clearly expounded by teachers deputed by the bishop himself, and at the same time there is presented what priestly life means and all that is looked for in a priest . . . lastly, there should be the possibility of testing a priestly vocation, and making certain of it by positive signs and qualities." (4) Advanced seminary academic programs should encompass at least two years of philosophy and four years of theology. (5) Within the limits of the broad institutional principles set out in the two documents, local seminaries are allowed to use initiative and creativity in organizing programs.

Seminarians: Personal Formation. Within the institution certain formative principles should operate. (1) The goal of the formation process is the fostering of the individual Christian virtues and the pastoral skills that will enable the candidate to lead in the building of the Christian community under the bishop; formation is the process of internalizing the values which characterize a priest. (2) This process takes place when the candidate actualizes the values of priesthood in an integrated way. Thus, he is to be given the opportunity to experience living with his brothers, serving others in a pastoral capacity under supervision, and leading a prayerful existence under conditions in which challenging theological study enables him to see the Christian meaning of what he is doing. In other words, the key in formation is experience, in an initial manner, of the basic elements of priesthood under conditions that facilitate theological reflection upon what has happened. (3) What must be imparted above all is not simply content but a method; the candidate must learn how to learn and know how to grow as a priest.

Present Problems in Formation. Unresolved difficulties remain. There is lacking a sufficiently nuanced transcultural notion of priesthood to provide criteria that facilitate the selection and evaluation of candidates and that enable priests who internalize them to retain and harmoniously develop their identity despite changes in life style and pastoral practice. A pastoral priestly spirituality needs to be developed. For the most part the residue of a monastic spirituality characterizes seminary programs.

Formation involves many stages of growth; expectations and criteria for the various stages need to be worked out. If the law on priestly celibacy remains, there must be developed a more nuanced theology of celibacy. The qualities of the fruitful celibate, appropriate screening procedures to detect these qualities, the means of growing in these qualities, and the manner in which celibacy relates to priesthood need further investigation (*see* CELIBACY, FORMATION IN). Programs must take into account the increased complexity of modern life and the consequent wide variety of unintegrated experiences produced in even the best candidates. As a result, it usually takes longer for seminarians to reach the stage when they can fully commit themselves; later ordination must be encouraged rather than seen as the exception.

Because the future priest will face a constantly changing world, his training must stress the virtues of creativity and initiative out of a traditional understanding. A method of teaching theology must be devised which facilitates the integration of the various elements of the program. At present, pastoral, spiritual, and theological formation are somewhat divorced from one another. In particular, the academic component often treats largely of questions that learned theologians debate, not the questions with which real life confronts the tradition; the spiritual program often helps the subject develop apart from pastoral concerns; and pastoral supervision is frequently unconnected with genuine theological values. What is needed is a theology that will enable the student to discover the operational value to traditional formulations, their bearing on experience and life. With such a theology, the integration of the elements of the seminary program could become a reality. Spirituality would then become the process by which candidates individually internalize the values pointed to by the doctrines studied. And pastoral formation would be the effort to unify the Christian community by fostering the corporate internalization of those same values.

A way must be found to slow the pace of seminary life, to allow time for assimilation, to avoid the confusion and frustration that result from the present tendency to demand too many things of the candidate at once. The future priest will have to know how to aid and correlate the work of a multiplicity of specialized ministers in the Church. Hence, consideration must be given to the possibility of forming priests in conjunction with the forming of other ministers. Study must be given to the place of women and nonpriests in priestly formation.

Such issues command attention to three broader institutional questions. (1) How can initial formation to priesthood prepare for and be correlated with structures dedicated to the continuing priestly formation needed today? (2) What can be done to establish a variety of formation programs to train appropriately the diverse types of candidates found now? (3) What specific principles govern the formation of priests at theological clusters, in houses of formation, in congregation-based training programs, and in other systems that depart from the traditional seminary structure described in the *Ratio fundamentalis*?

Bibliography: Congregation for Catholic Education, *The Basic Plan for Priestly Formation* (Washington, D.C. 1971). Bishops' Committee on Priestly Life and Ministry, *The Program of Priestly Formation* (2d ed. Washington, D.C. 1976). E. E. LARKIN and G. T. BROCCOLO, eds., *Spiritual Renewal of the American Priesthood* (Washington, D.C. 1973). J.M.LEE and L. J. PUTZ, *Seminary Education in a Time of Change* (Notre Dame, Ind. 1965). D. M. MURPHY, ed., *Personal Development and Formation* (Washington, D.C. 1975).

[P. CHIRICO]

PRIESTLY SPIRITUALITY

The conciliar Decree on the Ministry and Life of Priests, opened the door to a ministerial or *apostolic spirituality (*Presbyterorum ordinis* 13–14). This theme was clearly stated in principle in the decree of the 1971 Synod of Bishops, *The Ministerial Priesthood* (21), and developed for the American scene in the *Spiritual Renewal of the American Priesthood* (1972, henceforth SRAP). This last document received wide acclaim among priests as a fair account of their own experience and a realistic approach to a spirituality appropriate to their lives.

The Development of SRAP. The bishops commissioned SRAP as a follow-up to their research projects on the priesthood in the late 1960s. A mass of material was made available through psychological, sociological, historical, scriptural, and theological investigations. SRAP was conceived less as a further study on either an empirical or research basis than as a reflection on the actual experience of priesthood in the context of spirituality. It was intended to be a practical tool to help priests deal with the new understandings of their life and ministry uncovered by the studies.

A subcommittee was appointed by the *Bishops' Committee on Priestly Life and Ministry to prepare a statement. Most of the members were part of the team of priests who had given workshops on prayer renewal for priests during the two previous years under the sponsorship of the National Federation of Priests' Councils. The whole subcommittee agreed that the new document should not be a theoretical treatise but an invitation to action. It was to be a call, not the final word, and priestly spirituality would unfold as lived experience in answer to challenge rather than as a ready-made program of spiritual exercises. The projected text was to endeavor to uncover the already existing sources of spiritual growth inherent in the daily lives of priests

and encourage them to develop their own individual spirituality.

Interaction and Prayer. The call in SRAP is to interaction. For all Christians today this is par excellence the means of growth. Interaction is interpersonal involvement. It means dialogue, sharing, doing things together. It takes place in the interplay with contemporary culture, in the relationships in ministry, in friendships and community, and in prayer. These four areas are the first four chapters of the book. Interaction flourishes when it originates in true friendship and the felt experience of community based on faith principles. The quality of life that emerges out of these deep relationships and small vibrant community tends to transfer itself to other sectors of life. For this reason chapter 3, which discusses depth relationships, is the key chapter. The emphasis on the human and the horizontal is of a piece with the times and makes SRAP very contemporary.

This approach represents a shift from the tendency of the recent past to oppose action and spirituality and to identify spirituality with prayer (*see* ACTIVISM). SRAP sees prayer as the heart of spirituality insofar as prayer is a person's whole relationship with God; personal action, i.e., action which springs out of lives that have matured through the give and take of multiple relationships, nourishes this prayer. Formal prayer is precisely one such personal action: highest on the scale of interactions, it is an important priority in the life of a priest.

The fifth and final chapter relates interaction to prayer in this deeper sense. Interaction, whether in acts of prayer or encounters with people, flows out of "the love of God poured into our hearts by the Holy Spirit who is given to us" (Rom 5.5). As the expression of that love it nurtures the original gift. Spiritual renewal moves between these poles of interaction and love of God; together they form a spiral movement reaching up to God.

In ch. 2 to 4 SRAP discusses liturgical prayer, shared prayer, and prayer alone. But its interest goes beyond prayers to prayer itself, which it sees as the underlying relationship to Father, Son, and Holy Spirit. All interaction contributes to the deepening of this union with God and explicit reference to God is by no means the most significant factor. The mysterious depth dimension of existence is transcendent and eschatological; it might be called spirituality in its pure state. But it manifests itself in multiple incarnations. All of life is the stuff of spirituality.

Models of Spirituality. Spiritual writing constantly struggles to express the relation between the outside and the inside elements of spiritual life. The spiritual journey is a movement from the without of things to the within, not by abandoning one for the other but by allowing the latter to perfect the former. SRAP uses two models to illustrate this passage. One is the Paschal Mystery of death and resurrection, and the other is the action-contemplation dyad of Western mysticism.

The priest's whole life reveals the dynamic of death and resurrection. He grows by dying to selfishness and indifference, to slavery, passion, and prejudice, to weakness and fear and by coming alive in love and freedom, in openness, courage and healthy interdependence with his fellow human beings. These are some ways he experiences "the power of Christ's resurrection and the fellowship of his suffering" and thereby comes to "know Christ," the center of all things (Phil 3.10).

Knowing Christ experientially is *contemplation, whereas action is the outer expression of that loving knowledge. The essence of spiritual growth is the raising of this contemplative quality of human life. Interaction contributes to this, both because of its ultimate rooting in God and because it touches the profound interpersonal character of the human that has surfaced currently. Rugged individualism has proved bankrupt and interdependence is the recognized human condition. SRAP tries to structure the spiritual life on this insight. Contemplative union remains the ideal, but it is attainable when a person becomes humanly whole through wholesome relationships with fellow men and women.

The interrelational activities that are the door to spiritual growth are responses to the Spirit at each moment. Discernment of how to organize life, where to act, what to do is a personal issue; discernment of spirits can no longer be relegated to extraordinary cases; it becomes an ordinary need.

Conclusion. The approach to priestly spirituality in SRAP has notably influenced other NCCB publications. Thus *The Program of Continuing Education of Priests* (1973) articulates the same principles as does *Spiritual Direction for Priests in the U.S.A.* (1977) in particular areas. The latest document, *As One who Serves* (1977), reflects on the priesthood as rooted in the risen, indwelling Christ and as expressed in the Church as *communio*; these two foundations undergird the two principal thrusts of SRAP's spirituality, prayer as union with Christ and interaction as the Christian's life.

To what extent has this spirituality been assimilated by the clergy and the seminaries? At this point it is perhaps too early to say. But impressions from retreats, study days, and workshops in spirituality, all of which have undergone a second spring in the last few years, indicate that the new spirituality speaks to the times. The priestly spirituality that is current today is a return to sources, to the priest's basic condition as a man and as a Christian, the resultant effort and reflection tend to be less particular, less privileged, less sacred, more authentic and down to earth. Here as in other areas of church life and teaching today, the priest stands beside and not above his brothers and sisters in the Lord.

Bibliography: American Association of Theological Schools, Task Force on Spiritual Development, *Voyage, Vision, Venture, A Report on Spiritual Development* (Dayton, Ohio 1972). Bishops' Committee on Priestly Life and Ministry, *The Program of Continuing Education of Priests* (USCC Publ. Office, Washington, D.C. 1973); *As One Who Serves: Reflections on the Pastoral Ministry of Priests in the U.S.* (USCC Publ. Office, Washington, D.C. 1977). L. J. CAMELI, *Spiritual Direction for Priests in the United States* (USCC Publ. Office, Washington, D.C. 1977). E. E. LARKIN and G. T. BROCCOLO, eds., *Spiritual Renewal of the American Priesthood* USCC Publ. Office, Washington, D.C. 1972). Synod of Bishops 1971, *The Ministerial Priesthood* (USCC Publ. Office, Washington, D.C. 1972).

[E. E. LARKIN]

PRIMACY OF THE POPE

The papal primacy describes the supreme authority wielded by the pope in all matters of discipline and communion in the Roman Catholic Church, insofar as he wishes to engage the full extent of his jurisdiction. Vatican Council I (1870) declared this primacy of the pope to be a dogma; Vatican Council II (1962–65) incorporated this teaching into its doctrine on the Church and the office of bishops (cf *Lumen gentium* 18; *Christus Dominus* 2).

After Vatican II some theologians went on treating papal primacy as if it were an instance of absolute monarchy in the Church; others, representing the mainstream, developed the consequences of episcopal *collegiality for the exercise of papal primacy; and a third group went further in stressing the contingent aspects of the historical development leading up to Vatican I. Above all, difficulties in the practical exercise of papal and curial authority became keenly felt, as in the controversy after *Humanae vitae* (1968).

Nevertheless certain helpful insights have been recognized as germane to the question of papal primacy, at least by those engaged in ecumenical conversations. Thus the gradual historical formation of the papal office and the fact that the Petrine responsibility for the whole Church was initially discharged by nonpapal forms of ministry, suggest the corollary that the papacy need not stay frozen forever in the state envisaged by Vatican I.

The search goes forward, therefore, for models of universal service and authority (that is to say, of Petrine primacy) more appropriate to the nature of Christianity and answering more closely to the Church's present needs. Meanwhile Christians of non-Catholic traditions are becoming more disposed to see in the papacy an institution of considerable potential for strengthening worldwide Christian communion.

See also LUTHERAN/ROMAN CATHOLIC DIALOGUE.

Bibliography: H. URS VON BALTHASAR, *Der antirömische Affekt* (Freiburg i. Br. 1974). A. BRANDENBURG and H. J. URBAN, ed., *Petrus und Papst* (Münster 1977). Y. CONGAR, "Die Apostolische Kirche" in J. FEINER and M. LÖHRER, eds., *Mysterium Salutis* 4.1 (Einsiedeln 1972) 570–594. B. D. DUBUY, "Theologie der kirchlichen Amter" ibid. 4/2 (1973) 488–523, esp. 501–505. H. KÜNG, ed., *Papal Ministry in the Church. Concilium 64* (1971). P. J. MCCORD, ed., *A Pope for All Christians?* (New York 1976). P. MISNER, "Papal Primacy in a Pluriform Polity," JEcumSt 11 (1974) 239–260. G. TAVARD, "Is the Papacy an Object of Faith?" *One in Christ* 13 (1977) 220–228. J. M. R. TILLARD, "The Horizon of the 'Primacy' of the Bishop of Rome," ibid 12 (1976) 5–33.

[P. MISNER]

PRISONS AND PRISONERS

The level of crime in the United States is alarmingly high. In 1976, for example, more than 18,000 people were murdered; 56,000 women were reported to have been the victims of forcible or attempted rape; there were 400,000 robberies and 3,000,000 burglaries. The prison and jail population figures are equally alarming. The estimated prison population in the U.S. is 534,000, an increase of 106,000 in two years. The Federal Bureau of Prisons' population has risen by 47 percent since 1970, and the minority population in prisons increased 111 percent, so that minority persons make up 65 percent of the total federal prison population. These people are housed in an estimated 5,780 correctional facilities. In 1975, it cost an average of $23.40 per day to provide food, clothing, education and rehabilitation resources for one inmate, resulting in a conservative estimate of $6,000 to $12,000 per inmate annually, with some states spending up to $24,000 a year per inmate. This means that the total cost of inmate care and custody for 1975 was $3.84 billion. More correctional facilities are being built with 1,067 new facilities either proposed or under construction. Of these, 702 have reported a construction cost of $4 billion, with an average cost of $5.72 million per facility, or up to $50,000 per cell.

Prison Ministry. How does the Church respond to the Gospel challenge to minister to the imprisoned? The thrust of contemporary prison ministry is twofold. On one level, church members engaged in this essential aspect of social justice ministry work to change the system, to attack the systemic roots of crime and the economic and environmental factors which lead many to choose criminal activity as the most feasible survival option. On another level, recognizing that to change a deeply ingrained system requires a complex blend of time as well as political, social, and economic strategizing and that people are trapped in the system as it exists now, the Church works to improve conditions in the courts and the correctional facilities.

Support for the National Moratorium on Prison Construction comes from a number of concerned Catholic groups, religious and lay. *The National Coalition of American Nuns (NCAN), for example, has issued a statement decrying the decision to build more prisons as a solution to the crime wave. NCAN claims that little is accomplished in a prison to make the incarcerated person not return to the same crime pattern as before, while there is ample evidence that the fact of imprisonment is a heavy contributor to postrelease criminal activity. Noting that only 11 percent of persons committed to federal prisons were incarcerated for robbery and violent crimes, it appears clear that the vast majority of the prison population do not constitute a threat to society. NCAN has offered a number of alternatives to building more prisons, suggestions which are more creative and constructive than a reliance on prisons as places of punishment.

Alternatives to Prison. One of NCAN's suggestions is being implemented by several Catholic and non-Catholic groups, among them Heartline of Detroit. This is the concept of a halfway house. An alternative to full-term imprisonment, a halfway house is much less debilitating, and helps to ease an inmate back into a productive life. It allows an offender to spend time working or studying in society, but with the guidance of concerned, caring individuals.

Another alternative to incarceration involves the development of probationary programs involving jobs, counseling, etc., which are community-based. For example, a Minnesota program puts persons convicted of property crimes on probation with the provision that the offender and the victim work out a mutually satisfactory mode of recompense. The recidivism rate of this program is only half the national average.

Other groups have accepted the view of Jack Nagel, that there is a close correlation between poverty and incarceration rates. For every one percent increase in unemployment rates, 2,664 more crimes per 100,000 population will be committed. Thus, for an average state of four million people, a one percent decline in unemployment would prevent more than 10,000 index crimes per year. Nagel has put it simply, "to reduce crime, provide jobs." Social-justice groups throughout the country are working towards full employment to solve this and other societal ills.

Individuals and organizations are actively encouraging state and federal legislatures to support other alternatives to incarceration. Some of these alternatives include decriminalization of victimless crimes, use of work-release and study-release programs, pretrial intervention, restitution, and community service orders. In each case the Gospel message of setting free the captives is central; free in a physical sense but, equally important, free to be fully human, reconciled with society, free to live lives of dignity and integrity in a caring community. As the 1978 USCC statement, *A Community Response to Crime*, claims, "As Christians, we have a particular responsibility to see that the message communicated to the offender and to the community reflects Christian principles, including the right to life and human dignity; responsibility to protect the rights of all persons; mercy and compassion for the less fortunate; forgiveness of those who offended or harmed us; and the openness of a loving and healing community" (USCC 35, Origins 598).

The Christian community's responsibility to the victims of crime should not be underestimated or displaced by concern for the offender. Legislative enactment in several states provide means by which financial, medicine and psychological support can be offered to victims of serious crime. There is much healing needed in the area, though, particularly among the poor, women and the elderly who are so often the victims of crime. The Church's responsibility here is clear and the challenge for more widespread involvement in the area of social-justice ministry needs to be met fully and compassionately.

Assistance to Prisoners. The second level of thrust is that of making the courts and the prisons and jails more humane. "In the sight of God, correction of the offender has to take preference over punishment, for the Lord came to save and not to condemn" (ibid. 47; Origins 599). Most prisons have visiting rights for chaplains, the larger ones often having full-time chaplains. A lot of what they do could not be said to be directly related to "religious" aspects of the inmate's lives, but it concerns them as pastors, as it deals with the total person. Chaplains often work as counsellors, advocates, or simply as persons who care enough to listen and help where possible. Many lay people are also involved in visiting programs, like the Chicago based program, "Sister on the outside for the sister on the inside."

The words, "Remember those in prison as if you were there with them" (Heb 13.3) have led many to work in prisons offering educational, psychological, and legal assistance. One such group is the Institute of Women Today which sponsors workshops in job-training, psychological support, and legal aid at Alderson and Lexington prisons for women. The team members go to prison to bring the good message of law and basic rights, to heal and unite, to free and make ready for greater freedom.

The concern for the incarcerated carries beyond the institution. Several groups minister to ex-offenders, in support groups, and employment and education resource programs. One such group is the Benedict Center for Criminal Justice, Milwaukee.

Concern needs to be community-wide, and community-based. Sensitivity to an imperative to replace lethargy with constructive action and misunderstanding with understanding is needed. A Church struggling to build a community of faith, must strive to recognize social responsibility on the part of both the community and the offender, and urge creative acceptance of this responsibility. The Christian community will then become a truly healing place where both offenders and victims of crime can experience that the Good News means they are accepted, loved, supported and challenged to become all the Lord has called them to be. It is a Gospel challenge, and a creative and courageous response will make it possible.

Bibliography: American Friends Service Committee, *Struggle for Justice* (New York 1971). Missouri Coalition for Correctional Justice,

"Statement of Opposition to New Jail and Prison Construction" (Jefferson City 1977). J. NAGEL, *Crime and Incarceration: A Reanalysis* (Philadelphia 1977). W. NAGEL, *The New Red Barn* (New York 1973). National Moratorium on Prison Construction, *Jericho* (Washington, D.C. 1976–78). Prison Research Education Action Project, *Instead of Prisons* (Syracuse 1976). M. TRAXLER, "The Institute of Women Today" in A. Wheeler and M. Wortman, eds., *The Roads They Made* (Chicago 1977). United Presbyterian Church, *Justice and the Imprisoned* (New York 1972). USCC, Committee on Social Development and World Peace, *A Community Response to Crime* (USCC Publ. Office, Washington, D.C. 1978), also Origins 7 (1978) 593, 595–604.

[A. LEE]

PRO MUNDI VITA

Pro Mundi Vita is a Catholic research center located in Brussels, founded by M. Versteeg OFM, at Tilburg, Holland, in 1960. It took its name from the theme of the Eucharistic Congress held that same year in Munich, *Pro mundi vita* (for the life of the world, Jn 6.51).

The original purpose was to provide information on distressed areas and thus to regulate distribution of missionary personnel. It moved to Brussels in 1963, the same year that it summoned the first International Congress to Essen, the diocese of the institute's protector, Bishop Franz Hengsbach. Two hundred participants—bishops, religious superiors, priests, religious, and laity—attended this pivotal event. The Abbé Houtart, director of the Center for Socio-Religious Research in Brussels, emphasized the two stages in missionary activities: preevangelization and evangelization. The first must be addressed before the second can be attempted. Dom Helder Camara followed with the comment that Latin America's need is not more priests, but development; and he insisted evangelization cannot occur until the man of today is met in his personal and communal problems of life. A layman, C.-M. Thoen, manager of the Catholic Institute for Social Research in The Hague, widened the concept of "distressed area" to include northern France as well as Bolivia, or wherever the Church's development has hardly commenced, has become stagnant, or is menaced.

Since the move to Brussels, the institute has been headed by P. Jan Kerkhofs, SJ and reflects some of his background. He teaches sociology of religion in the theology faculty at Louvain and is the international chaplain of the International Christian Union of Business Executives (UNIAPAC).

Pro Mundi Vita, similar to the think-tank phenomenon in corporate life, combines theology with the results of such social sciences as anthropology and sociology to study the Church's needs, aspirations, and tendencies. Since 1973 it has issued *Pro Mundi Vita*, a quarterly bulletin on new forms of ministry: team, part-time, specialized, ministry for married couples, and on women as priests. The bulletins deal with such issues as bioethics, sexuality, and old age.

Publications are sent to 3,000 Catholic Bishops, some non-Catholic Church leaders, 6,000 religious superiors, and 1,000 opinion-formers and theology institutes. Since 1960 Pro Mundi Vita has produced 60 different studies in five languages: English, French, Spanish, German, and Dutch, in addition to 47 special reports (dossiers) on particular issues in particular countries. Most of its annual budget of $300,000 comes from West European Lenten funds and private contributions. Special funding is sought for special projects; the Raskob Foundation funded the recent study of Thailand. The ecumenical project investigating apartheid in South Africa, as well as special projects in Burundi, the Central African Republic, and Ghana, are paid for by the episcopal conference or the religious order that requested them. The institute is presently engaged in a study exploring new ways to fulfill the episcopal role and a study of China, conducted jointly with the Lutheran World Federation. The latter is focusing on the sense of community, service of people, and the struggle against selfishness in the People's Republic. The institute has accomplished much with a staff of just six religious and two lay persons. Of special interest, and an example of the seriousness and excellence of its work, is the book edited by J. Kerkhofs, *Modern Mission Dialogue, Theory and Practice* (1969).

Bibliography: B. J. MULHEARN, "The Distress of the Church and the Task of the Religious," HeythropJ 6 (1965) 351–352.

[E. J. DILLON]

PROFESSION OF FAITH (THE CREED)

The traditional mode for the Profession of Faith and that employed in the liturgy in a more restrictive but significant sense since the revision of the Roman rite is the creed (4:436). Two creeds are used in the liturgy at present.

Nicene Creed. The Nicene Creed is used on Sundays and solemnities, and in solemn local celebrations. It is to be recited or sung by all as a response to the Word of God (GenInstrRomMissal 43–44). On the feasts of the Annunciation of the Lord and Christmas, during the words "by the power of the Holy Spirit/he was born of the Virgin Mary, and became man" all kneel. On other occasions a deep bow is made (ibid. 98).

Because of the nature of this Creed, its length and character as statement, the recommendation has been made "that it be spoken in declamatory fashion rather than sung. Further, if it is sung, it might be more effective if it takes the form of a musical declamation rather than that of an extensive and involved musical structure" (BCL Music 69); the General Instruction of the Roman Missal suggests that it be sung alternately (ibid. 44).

Apostles' Creed. The Apostles' Creed is designated for use at more limited times, although in some countries it is used as an optional alternative to the Nicene Creed. In liturgies with children, if the profession of faith is used at the close of the Liturgy of the Word, the Apostles' Creed may be chosen, especially because it is part of their catechetical formation (*see* MASSES WITH CHILDREN). Further, in 1965, the Consilium, Roman postconciliar liturgical commission, authorized the use of the Apostles' Creed in sign language for deaf congregations.

With the suppression of the hour of Prime from the Liturgy of the Hours by Vatican Council II (*Sacrosanctum Concilium* 89d), the Athanasian Creed (1:995) has been dropped from liturgical usage in the Roman rite.

[L. DURST]

PROGRESS

Vatican Council II gave more official church attention than ever before to the inherent value of human activity in the world (11:834). Nevertheless, advances within such activity must be measured by their contribution to "human progress" in terms of whatever promotes the "exalted dignity proper to the human person" and establishes a social order founded in freedom, truth, justice, and love.

Affirmation of Progress. The ultimate norm of human activity involves its harmonization with "the divine plan and will" in the scheme of salvation history. Man, created in God's image, was mandated "to subject to himself the earth and all that it contains, and to govern the world with justice and holiness," so that the "triumphs of the human race" might be seen as a "a sign of God's greatness and the flowering of His own mysterious design," and all men might come to acknowledge him as "Lord and Creator of all" (*Gaudium et spes* 33–36). Such activity not only conquers the reign of sin, but also serves to "prepare the field of the world for the seed of the Word of God." Christians, who share in Christ's priestly office, know that all their daily activities, "if carried out in the Spirit," become "spiritual sacrifices" by which the world is consecrated to God. Through these actions, Christ "will progressively illumine the whole of human society with His saving light." Thus Christians, "even when preoccupied with temporal cares ... perform eminently valuable work on behalf of bringing the gospel to the world" and leading the human community "to that King whom to serve is to reign" (*Lumen gentium* 34–36).

Progress and the Kingdom. The precise nature of the relationship between earthly progress and the final Kingdom of God has exercised theologians for centuries. Among contemporary theologians, Hans Küng holds that man can only "prepare himself and hold himself in readiness" for the gift of the Kingdom (Küng 49). But Johannes B. Metz argues the Christian is a "coworker" in the building of the Kingdom and must even now "form this world into the eschatological city of God" (Metz 94–95). Avery Dulles, following K. Rahner, suggests that the final Kingdom will "be the work of God, dependent on his initiative," though it will not come until man's efforts to create it have gone their limit (Dulles 114). Rahner further argues that human history "constructs its own final and definitive state." What man achieves endures, although "radically transformed," as "the *work* of love" realized in history (Rahner 270).

Perhaps nowhere more than in *Gaudium et spes* 39 (cf. also *Lumen gentium* 48) does Vatican II attempt to correlate "earthly progress" with the "growth of Christ's Kingdom." It insists that Christians' expectation of a new earth" intensifies their concern to cultivate this one. The growing human family gives "some kind of foreshadowing of the new age," in that "the values of human dignity, brotherhood and freedom, and indeed all the good fruits of our nature and enterprise" will be found again in the kingdom, though "freed of stain, burnished and transfigured." The document affirms that, insofar as earthly progress "can contribute to the better ordering of human society, it is of vital concern to the Kingdom of God," but it shies away from indicating the exact relationship between the two.

Theologians agree in general that man must act to create a world order that seeks correspondence with the final Kingdom of God. Insofar as man does this, he may hope in the experience of God's Kingdom, here and beyond. Insofar as he fails to do this, man is responsible for the lack of the presence of the Kingdom in history. Nevertheless, progress in all orders of human activity is not identical with the coming of God's Kingdom, which remains forever a gift not consequent upon human action.

See HOPE, THEOLOGY OF.

Bibliography: H. KÜNG, *The Church*, tr. Ray and Rosaleen Ockenden (New York 1967). J. B. METZ, *Theology of the World*, tr. W. GLEN-DOEPEL (New York 1969). K. RAHNER, *Theological Investigations* 10, tr. D. BOURKE (New York 1973) esp. 260–272. A. DULLES, *Models of the Church* (New York 1974).

[M. R. TRIPOLE]

PROPERTY, PRIVATE

Vatican Council II's Pastoral Constitution on the Church in the Modern World (*Gaudium et spes*) reaffirmed traditional Catholic teaching on private property while deepening and modernizing that teaching.

The Right Affirmed. The centrality of the right to the use of material goods as the necessary means for man's perfection is restated: "God intended the earth and all it contains for the use of every human being and people" (*Gaudium et spes* 69). This traditional conception of the right of access to material things undergirds the right to their stable personal possession, since a regime of widely distributed private property "contributes to the expression of personality. They furnish men with an occasion for exercising their role in society." Ownership provides everyone with an area of independence and should be regarded as an extension of human freedom ...." And "constitutes a prerequisite for civil liberties" inasmuch as "it adds incentives for carrying out one's functions and duties" (ibid. 71).

The Fathers of the Council were aware of the need of adapting this static, abstract, and almost metaphysical conception of property rights, based largely on the realities of an agricultural society, to contemporary realities. Thus, they were aware of the need of *land reform, speaking of "gigantic rural estates which are only moderately cultivated or lie completely idle for sake of profit," while "the majority of the people are either without land or have only small holdings" (ibid. 71). They acknowledge that in some traditional societies "the communal purpose of earthly goods [can] be partially satisfied through the customs and traditions proper to a community," and in modern industrial societies that "a body of social institutions dealing with insurance and security can, for its part, make the common purpose of earthly goods effective," but cautioning that "care be taken lest, because of such provisions the citizenry fall into a kind of sluggishness toward society and reject the burdens of office and of public service" (ibid. 69).

The Need for Adjustments. Private property has traditionally been defended by the Church against the threat of collectivism, its wide distribution urged to overcome class conflict and to achieve a greater measure of justice in the domestic society. More recently, the emphasis has been on reducing the glaring inequalities in the global community. "Today," wrote Pope Paul VI in his encyclical On the Development of Peoples: "the principal fact we must all recognize is that the social question has become worldwide" (Paul VI PopProgr 3). The reference is to the emergence of what came to be known as the Third World and the growing consciousness of the shocking disparity of income of the North and South of the planet. Robert McNamara, President of the *World Bank, in his 1976 Report revealed the extent of this disparity: the per capita income of the developed countries was $5,500 per annum while that of the poorest countries, comprising

1.2 billion people, averages under $150 annually. Moreover, asserts Pope Paul's encyclical, "the imbalance is on the increase" by the very workings of the prevailing economic disorder (ibid.) On the basis of the common purpose of created things, Vatican II urged a productive system at "the service of man and indeed of the whole man, viewed in terms of his material needs and the demands of his intellectual, moral, spiritual and religious life. And when we say man, we mean every man whatsoever and every group of men, of whatever race and from whatever part of the world" (*Gaudium et spes* 64). Pope Paul incorporated into his encyclical the stern injunction of Vatican II: "Advanced nations have a very heavy obligation to help the developing nations" (Paul VI PopProgr 48).

Specific Areas of Control. Such an emphasis on *stewardship of earthly goods mocks the attitude, whether personal or national, that what is mine is mine and I can do with it as I choose. Increasingly, the need of social control of property is seen in legislation restraining air, water, and noise pollution, abuses in the strip mining of coal, of efforts to insure access by the public to ocean beaches (only about four percent of the 59,167 miles of coastline of the continental United States is open to the public) and of the proper disposition of the vast mineral wealth at the bottom of the open sea, declared by the United Nations to be the heritage of mankind—a statement endorsed in 1977 by the Pontifical Commission for Justice and Peace. There is, as well, the increasing pressure of population on limited resources. As Paul VI exclaimed in an address to the representatives of non-Christian religions at the Bombay Eucharistic Congress (1964), "Man must meet man, nation meet nation, as children of God. In this mutual understanding and friendship, in this sacred communion, we must also work together to build the common future of the human race" *Pope Speaks* 10 (1964) 153.

And so there must be a transfer of resources, both financial and technological, from the rich to the poorer countries (*see* TECHNOLOGY, TRANSFER OF), a greater equality in trade relations so that the prices of the raw materials of the underdeveloped nations are not gravely discounted by the rising prices for the manufactures of the developed nations (*see* NEW INTERNATIONAL ECONOMIC ORDER), a World Fund created, from a universal, progressive tax, as an expression of human solidarity and a mechanism of planetary social justice. In an apostolic letter, "A Call to Action," On the occasion of the eightieth anniversary of the encyclical *Rerum novarum*, Pope Paul pointed to "new economic powers...the multinational enterprises which by the concentration and flexibility of their means can conduct autonomous strategies which are largely independent of national political powers and therefore not subject to control from the point of view of the common good" (Paul VI, OctogAdven 44).

But all these suggestions and cautions are vain if a halt is not put to the arms race whose cost in global terms in 1977 has been estimated at $350 billion, an increasing proportion of which is spent by the poorer nations, an expenditure which makes hopes of resources (and the human will) for universal social betterment illusory (*see* DISARMAMENT). Vatican II declared emphatically: "While extravagant funds are being spent for the furnishing of ever new weapons, an adequate remedy cannot be provided for the multiple miseries afflicting the whole modern world. . . . the arms race is an utterly treacherous trap for humanity and one which injures the poor to an intolerable degree" (*Gaudium et spes* 81).

Catholic thought on private property, then, recognizes the historical evolution of forces, the ambiguity of analyses, the multiplicity and interaction of political and economic forces at play; in his Call to Action the Pope eschewed the temptation "to utter a unified message and to put forward a solution which has universal validity" (Paul VI OctogAdven 4). The 1971 Synod of Bishops reminded all: "It does not belong to the Church, insofar as it is a hierarchical institution, to offer technical solutions in the social, economic and political sphere concerning justice in the world. Her true mission implies the defense and promotion of dignity and the fundamental rights of the human person" (Synod JustWorld p. 43).

Perhaps the chief contribution of Catholic teaching on the issue of ownership is the declaration of Vatican II: "For man is the source, the center and the purpose of all socio-economic life" (*Gaudium et spes* 63). Here is the test of all systems, stimulus for all strivings for greater justice.

Bibliography: R. HEYER, ed., "Stewardship and Property," *New Catholic World* 220 (1977) 212–259.

[E. DUFF]

PROVINCE AND REGION, ECCLESIASTICAL

In the years after Vatican Council II there has been a growing emphasis on regions in the Church. The Council, with its doctrine of the *collegiality, marked a turning point toward a greater cooperation of bishops, within regions, i.e. nations and subnational areas. The principal fruit of this new emphasis on regions and nations in the Church has been the establishment of national episcopal conferences. These conferences constitute a step in the decentralization of the Church and provide for a new style in the relations of bishops with the Holy See. The powers given to the conferences go beyond the powers of individual bishops, and the conferences can make laws or juridically-binding decisions in certain circumstances. Some of the tasks set before the episcopal conferences deal with the pastoral problems of their own territories. Other tasks relate to the assistance which the episcopal conferences may give to the pope in the government of the universal Church. The episcopal conferences are composed only of bishops and of ecclesiastics who are equated with them in law. Other persons can be invited by an episcopal conference in accord with its statutes but only in individual matters and only with a consultative vote.

In the U.S. the National Conference of Catholic Bishops (NCCB) is a canonical entity operating in accordance with the Vatican II's Decree on the Pastoral Office of Bishops (*Christus Dominus* 36–38). It was established by the U.S. hierarchy on Nov. 14, 1966, as the successor to the annual meetings of the bishops which began during World War I. The statutes of the NCCB were approved by the Holy See on Dec. 19, 1970 and its bylaws were approved by a majority of the members of the NCCB on Nov. 15, 1972 (16:312). The Catholic bishops of the United States also established a civil corporation, the United States Catholic Conference, incorporated under the laws of the District of Columbia. Its bylaws were approved by a majority of its members on Nov. 14, 1972 (16:462). With the introduction of vernacular liturgy, the episcopal conferences have been given responsibility for preparing texts to be approved by the Holy See. In addition, the episcopal conferences have been made responsible for choosing representatives to the worldwide Synod of Bishops which meets periodically in Rome.

Vatican II also favored regionalization in the Church by requiring that, as a general rule, all dioceses should be attached to an ecclesiastical province and be subject to the metropolitan jurisdiction of the archbishop (*see* ABBEY NULLIUS). Wherever advantageous, ecclesiastical provinces should be grouped into regions. The episcopal conferences should make recommendations to the Holy See concerning the boundaries of such provinces and regions (*Christus Dominus* 39–40).

Bibliography: O'Connor 7:290–292; 292; 293–302; 303–313. P. HUIZING, "The Structure of Episcopal Conferences," *Jurist* 28 (1968) 163–176 with bibliog. B. PRINCE, "Episcopal Conferences and Collegiality," StCan 2 (1968) 125–132.

[G. P. GRAHAM]

PSALMODY

Recent modifications in psalmody (11:935), whether in the Liturgy of the Hours or as part of the Eucharist, aim at more intelligent and fruitful participation on the part of the entire congregation, at times in conjunction with the choir.

In the work of Joseph Gélineau, SJ, there is "special attention to the rhythmic structure of the poetry of the Psalms." This in turn has allowed a sung or recited psalmody respecting the analogy between Hebrew tonic rhythm and that of modern languages (especially French and English). Père Gélineau has greatly modified his original work (e.g., his melody for Psalm 23). There are settings for all the canonical Psalms in *The Psalms: Singing Version* (New York 1968), where six groups of tones are provided.

Widely used for Entrance Song, Responsorial Psalm, Presentation of the Gifts, and Gradual, Offertory, and Communion is *Biblical Hymns and Psalms* by Lucien Deiss, CSSp (2 v., Cincinnati 1965 and 1971). Many of these are quite simple and can be easily learned by entire congregations.

In *Morning Praise and Evensong: A Liturgy of the Hours in Musical Setting*, by William G. Story et. al. (Notre Dame, Ind. 1973) there is a considerable variety in Psalm-settings. These are but samplings illustrating psalmody's transitional stages in most of the liturgical Churches.

Bibliography: J. A. EMERTON (chairman), *The Psalms. A New Translation for Worship.* Pointed Edition (London 1977). M. H. SHEPHERD, *The Psalms in Christian Worship: A Practical Guide* (Minneapolis 1976), with extensive up-to-date bibliography of work produced within various liturgical Churches.

[J. I. HUNT]

PSALTERS, VERNACULAR (LITURGY)

During the past fifteen years a number of vernacular Psalters have appeared. Some are simply parts of complete Bibles, although specialists on the Psalms were usually entrusted with the translations; many, however, have been produced independently. Of these some aimed primarily at fidelity to the Hebrew text with less concern for readability and singability; others have aimed rather at these latter qualities even while making an effort to be generally faithful to the original text. It should be pointed out that the Masoretic Text quite frequently offers a reading that defies simple translation. Hence translators have resorted to the ancient versions (especially to the Septuagint), to Semitic philology (often Ugaritic), and at times to conjectural emendation. Here only Psalters actually used in liturgical Churches will be noted, but the *Bibliography* refers to others.

Enjoying very wide popularity in the English-speaking world is the *Grail Psalter* (New York 1968). It is based on the second edition of *Les Psaumes* (Paris 1955), as prepared for the fascicle edition of *La Sainte Bible*, the French Jerusalem Bible, with the collaboration of Joseph Gélineau, SJ. The English adaptation was begun in 1954 by a team of biblical, literary, and musical experts. It first appeared in 1963, and has since appeared in a *Singing Version*. The *Grail Psalter* wished to let the Psalms speak their own message in a form as close as possible to that of the original Hebrew. It should be stated, however, that this version, following the lead of the specially prepared *Psautier* of the French Jerusalem Bible, often favors Septuagint readings and has a marked Christian orientation. It lends itself well to both recitation and singing. Ironically however its pleasant English has in fact lost something of the force and explosiveness of the original. With the exception of Psalm 95, this Psalter appears in the *Liturgy of the Hours* (New York 1975).

The Psalms from the *New American Bible* (1970) are used, e.g. in *The Prayer of Christians* (New York 1971). The translation is generally solid, even if quite traditional in tone and options. It has been noted that insufficient attention was given in this version to English rhythm and that consequently it has proved inferior for choral usage.

The Psalms, by the Monks of Mount Angel Abbey (Mt. Angel, Oregon, rev. ed., 1975), although not widely used, is unique among liturgical Psalters. Largely the work of Bonaventure Zerr, OSB, this translation is heavily dependent upon, though not subservient to, the version produced by Mitchell Dahood, SJ. No effort has been made at Christian orientation; this Psalter is Hebrew in tone and quality, and might even be termed Canaanite. There is a primitive and rugged character about it. It draws heavily upon Semitic philology (especially Ugaritic) in explaining difficult Hebrew passages.

The Psalms in the *Proposed Book of Common Prayer* (New York 1977) were produced by a team for choral use in the Episcopal Church. The translation is generally reliable and is proving adequate for recitation. Its effort to demasculinize the Psalter (e.g. "Happy are they..." rather than "Happy is the man..." in Psalm 1) is unique among Psalters.

Available in either pointed or non-pointed editions, *The Psalms: A New Translation for Worship* (London 1977), is a version produced by an interfaith English team under the chairmanship of John A. Emerton of Cambridge. The varied skills brought to the production of this Psalter augur well for its future.

Bibliography: M. GREENBERG et al., *The Book of Psalms. A New Translation according to the Traditional Hebrew Text* (Philadelphia 1972). R. S. HANSON, *The Psalms in Modern Speech for Public and Private Use* (3 v., Philadelphia 1968). *Ökumenische Übersetzung der Bibel, Die Psalmen* (Stuttgart 1976). *The Psalms for Modern Man in Today's English Version* (New York 1970) now incorporated into the *Good News Bible* (New York 1976). M. H. SHEPHERD, *The Psalms in Christian*

Worship: A Practical Guide (Minneapolis 1976) good bibliog.; *A Liturgical Psalter for the Christian Year* (Minneapolis 1976) selected Psalms, prepared with the assistance of the *Consultation on Common Texts.

[J. I. HUNT]

PSYCHOTHEOLOGICAL THERAPY

Combining the data of the psychological sciences and the relatively new idea of psychotheology or Christotherapy, the House of Affirmation, Whitinsville, Mass., has created a program, the psychotheological therapeutic community, to serve the needs of celibate clergy and religious. The program offers a model for dealing with issues and needs faced by religious professionals.

Philosophy of the House of Affirmation. The philosophy underlying the House of Affirmation's existence and operation can be succinctly stated as: treatment of the whole person in a wholly therapeutic environment. Mental health professionals adhering to this basic philosophy meet a real challenge when their clientele is constituted by other professionals whose religious values are central to vocational choice and identity. Religious men and women have chosen a celibate way of life. Because that way of life jars with the usual Freudian model of therapy, an alternative form of psychological help had to evolve to meet the needs of this relatively important and clearly delineated sociological group of celibate religious professionals. A group situation provides a favorable environment for the social relearning that constitutes therapy. Modern psychology emphasizes the tremendous power of the environment in shaping human development and behavior. In "milieu therapy," the expectancies and attitudes of the treatment staff are central to bringing about social rehabilitation but the psychotheological community concept of the House of Affirmation goes beyond this milieu therapy with its inherent psychoanalytic orientation and reductionism. There is an existential concern with rediscovering the living person amid the compartmentalization and dehumanization of modern culture. Interest centers on reality as immediately experienced by the person with the accent on the interpersonal character of the client's experience. The therapetuic community supplies the type of impartial or accepting reactions from others that favor social learning. Further, the therapeutic environment prevents further disorganization in the client's behavior by reducing his intense anxieties.

The treatment philosophy of the House of Affirmation is affirmation of the whole person. Affirmation is the positive response to the recognized goodness of the other (Pieper); it is an experience of a kind of relationship that is creative of the person. The opposite of affirmation is denial or nonrecognition and nonresponse to the other. The effect of denial is psychic annihilation (Bush). Nonaffirmed persons have generally experienced deprivation of affection in childhood, which is later reinforced by the impersonality and task-orientation of religious life. When personal worth is unrecognized and unacknowledged by others, the religious comes to believe that he or she has no value. The nonaffirmed person can go through the motions of a productive life and even outwardly look happy, but much of the appearance is pretense; inside there is anxiety, fear, insecurity, feelings of worthlessness, and depression. Efforts to boost self and reassurances from others do not seem to touch the deeper core where the

unrest lies. The negative feelings then produce such self-deflating behavior as attention-seeking, physical complaints, excessive busyness, hostility masked by a cheerful façade, addictions, futile attempts to please others, conflict with peers and authorities, and compulsive sexual acting-out. Such behavior serves only to increase loneliness and guilt-laden depression.

These problems are not cured by intensified spiritual practices or facile reassurances that one is "OK," but by another person's genuine love that is felt and makes no demands. Such unqualified love creates a nonthreatening environment where the person feels secure enough simply "to be." An atmosphere of consistent affirmation gives the necessary personal space and freedom for each person to develop his or her human identity as the base on which to build religious and community identities.

Psychotheological Therapeutic Community. The House of Affirmation has developed a unique model in its psychotheological therapeutic community. The expression "psychotheological community" (Polcino 1974) implies a quest for communion with God and with man. Personhood, it is agreed, can only be realized in community and this phenomenological aspect of man's human predicament aligns the model with the existential therapeutic movement. It seeks to analyze the structure of the religious professional's human existence in view of understanding the reality underlying the person's being-in-crisis. It is concerned with the profound dimensions of the emotional and spiritual temper of contemporary human beings. The importance of community receives emphasis in current psychological literature. Stern and Marino state that "religion and psychotherapy encourage community engagement with life; both can be distorted to emphasize a kind of pulling back in order to ensure personal safety. Insofar as they foster openness, they become true protectors of the role that love can play in cementing human relationships, and consequently, the reconciliation of society. The establishment of relationships is the first step in establishing the community. As a stranger becomes familiar, we are in a better position to reach out to him, to join our lives more closely. Our differences will never disappear and we will find it necessary to sacrifice a degree of autonomy" (Stern and Marino 66). Each person in the community remains a unique individual. A person may grow and change in the community but will retain personal identity. Personal union of community members serves to bring out and enrich what is uniquely true of each individual. "Growth in community will be effected by all those active and passive elements that created favorable conditions for the growth of unity and charity: openness, receptivity, sharing, giving, receiving. Community connotes oneness without loss of identity, a sharing in the interiority of another without the sacrifice of personal integrity" (Turner 309–310).

The adaptations recommended and wrought by Vatican Council II have changed the pattern of environmental demands on Christians at large, but even more intensely on formally professed religious men and women. Some have adjusted quickly and almost with eagerness to these changes, while others have been floundering in the insecurity of a slow and painful assimilation of change. The poignant experience of confusion, doubt, and sense of loss has taxed the adaptive capacity of many, who, cut off from safe moorings, question their identity and authenticity in what they consider an uncharted land. The postconciliar period demands maturity and balance on the part of those chosen to minister to the People of God especially because much risk is involved.

The Dogmatic Constitution on the Church, emphasized the aspect of community when it spoke of the Church as a "sign and sacrament of man's union with God and of the unity of the whole human race" (*Lumen gentium* 1). The religious community as such cannot form the person, although it should provide a setting in which the individual human being can emerge as a fully functioning adult. For too long religious communities of men and women as well as priests in rectories have had a task-oriented rather than a person-oriented environment. Yet personal development is a basic prerequisite to a meaningful life in society at large and in the local community where the celibate lives. This follows logically from the principle that love of self precedes love of others. However, I can only know myself if another reveals me to myself, just as I can only come to a real love of self when I come to the realization that I am affirmed by another (Kane, 1976, 41). Likewise, a person finds meaning and sense of identity in and through others. The person-oriented group helps toward a realization of personhood when, through the truth and goodness of confreres, a person's own powers of knowing and loving are released. In the therapeutic community of the House of Affirmation, a resident can formulate his own reactions, share them in social communication and thus become aware that others also experience the same anxieties. By sharing reactions with peers, the resident is practicing the very techniques of social interaction in which he has typically remained unskilled. In the reactions of peers with whom he shares his daily activities, the resident finds the acceptance, support, protection, challenge and competition that enable him to develop more valid self-reactions. In addition the therapeutic milieu provides the opportunity for social interaction among residents and staff.

The life of celibates can be viewed as an ongoing process of interaction with the religious, social, and natural forces that make up their environment. The meaning that life assumes for celibates depends on their personal response to these forces. The celibate community constitutes a union of persons who participate in a common love-response to the call of Christ (Beha 21). The key to a proper understanding of community lies in participation, which becomes a unifying force and, at the same time, allows for individual differences. Is not willingness to receive from him one of the dearest gifts one can give to another? Participation characterizes the relationship of individuals united by love in community. All encounters assume meaning in that context; they become avenues to change.

The difference their presence makes in the overall community process gives meaning to the lives of celibates. Being human really means that a person comes to grips, in a creative way, with a concrete life-situation. The experience of here-and-now is crucial, for life is today—not yesterday or tomorrow. The same applies in the therapeutic situation, be it individual or group: the ongoing, immediate experience of residents and therapists as they interact becomes the phenomenological focus in therapy. The total phenomena experienced at any moment are what describe the human existential situation; thus the experienced event is what is brought to therapy. Listening to another as a person, looking into his or her eyes, mind, and heart with deep sympathy, feeling that this person is suffering, is appealing to us as a person—is this not affirmative response to Christ's summons: "Love one another as I have loved you" (Jn 13.34)?

The call to Christian life is ideally expressed in the experience of the Eucharist which is the community experience par excellence. The Eucharist builds up a community of faith, and so it stands at the very center of the psychotheological community; it reveals the solidarity of all members in Christ. It is the same solidarity that is expressed in the opening words of the Pastoral Constitution on the Church in the Modern World, "The joys and hopes, the sorrows and worries of the men of our time are ours" (*Gaudium et spes* 1).

The House of Affirmation has thus accepted the challenge of the Fathers of Vatican II who urge, in the same document the appropriate use "not only of theological principles, but also of the findings of the secular sciences, especially of psychology and sociology" (ibid. 62) to help the faithful live their faith in a more thorough and mature way. In its Decree on the Appropriate Renewal of the Religious Life, the Council pursued the same line of thought: "The manner of living, praying, and working should be suitably adapted to the physical and psychological conditions of today's religious . . . to the needs of the apostolate, the requirements of a given culture, and to the social and economic circumstances" (*Perfectae caritatis* 3). In the article pertaining to chastity, religious are urged to "take advantage of those natural helps which favor mental and bodily health . . . . Everyone should remember that chastity has stronger safeguards in a community when true fraternal love thrives among its members" (ibid. 12). Celibate religious professionals who are trained in psychiatry and psychology can bring to bear their own experience in coming to a better understanding of the emotional problems of religious and priestly life today. Such is the case in the two outpatient Consulting Centers and in the residential treatment centers of the House of Affirmation.

For too long celibates have been frustrated when seeking professional help, since they were limited to psychiatrists and psychologists who had little understanding of the religious commitment; the misconceptions that could arise often deterred religious and priests from seeking psychiatric-psychological help. The House of Affirmation residential treatment center has been set up to minimize the threat and the possible alienation attendant on presenting oneself to a professional-type establishment. A homelike atmosphere has been developed that has proved most therapeutic, that prepares the individual to respond to therapy in a very positive manner, and that contrasts with the resistance that is frequently found when a priest or religious becomes the patient of a lay therapist.

An individual priest, sister, brother, deacon, or seminarian may be referred to the House of Affirmation for the purpose of coming to a better understanding of emotional problems and/or to resolve them. However, clients are always informed that unless they come of their own free will, therapy will be of little avail. No resident is accepted for treatment on the mere recommendation of religious superiors; the applicant must indicate willingness to come for therapy. The principle of confidentiality is crucial to the operation of the House of Affirmation; privacy is maintained at all times. This has produced a sense of security and trust and the clientele has grown geometrically. Since the inception of the House of Affirmation, stress has been put on its purpose: not so much to keep the celibate in the religious or priestly life as to give help towards becoming truly human and consistently free. Through therapy, the client can come to a personal decision about the future. In the course of therapy, clients come to view their experience in wider perspective and to gain a better future orientation. Self-growth demands that they have something to aim for, a goal which can be brought into reality through committed action. The individual's task will then be to actualize this possibility, to make it a reality. As clients begin to respond to their feelings, they see possibilities for the future and make attempts to achieve these; by so doing they increase responsible independence in their lives.

Many of the problems that have been presented at the consulting centers and at the residential centers have been classified as deprivation syndromes and as what Freud has described as repressive neurosis. In the first case, lack of love and acceptance (lack of affirmation) has crippled the psychological functioning of individuals; as to repressive neurosis, priests and religious are encountered who have made excessive use of the defense mechanism known as intellectualization. Many of these individuals are not aware of their emotions and have even repressed anger in their life as celibates. The repression in this instance often came about by faulty training that presented the emotion of anger as "unvirtuous," an emotion not to be expressed at any time. Yet Christ found it appropriate to express His emotions: "The angry man who picked up a cord to drive the buyers and sellers out of the temple, who wept in sadness over Jerusalem, who was bathed in sweat before His arrest was not a stoical, emotionless man" (Dalrymple 111). Through therapy, individual clients become aware of their emotions, are informed that their emotions are basically good, and are encouraged to express them in a healthy way within the context of a celibate life. Individual therapy is supported by group therapy where anger-feelings may be expressed and accepted as such. The reeducative process is somewhat long and painful but it results in a more personally satisfying and productive life. Having been affirmed by a significant other in the course of individual therapy and, in turn, affirming others, the healed resident knows and feels who he is. He finds that he is different from others but that he is acceptable, that he belongs in community, that he is contributing to it and changing it. He has come to realize that there is a unique place for him in society, that he has a unique contribution to make to it, that he can choose freely to do and to love (Kane, 1974, 75–76).

The effectiveness of this model has already been substantiated by inhouse research. It is very likely that it will find still further support for its claims with the passage of time.

Bibliography: H. M. BAHA, *Living Community* (Milwaukee 1967). B. J. BUSH, *Coping: Issues of Emotional Living in An Age of Stress For Clergy and Religious* (Whitinsville, Mass. 1976); "Healing Grace," *The Way* 16 (1976) 189–198. J. DALRYMPLE, *The Christian Affirmation* (Denville, N.J. 1971). J. L. HART, "Uses and Abuses of Religion," *Bulletin*, National Guild of Catholic Psychiatrists 22 (1976) 50–57. G. L. JEAN, "Affirmation: Healing in Community," RevRel 34 (1975) 535–541. T. A. KANE, *The Healing Touch of Affirmation* (Whitinsville, Mass. 1976); *Who Controls Me?* (Hicksville, N.Y. 1974); "The House of Affirmation," *Brothers' Newsletter* 17 (1975). J. P. MADDEN, *Loneliness: Issues of Emotional Living in An Age of Stress For Clergy and Religious* (Whitinsville, Mass. 1977). J. PIEPER, *About Love*, tr. R. and C. WINSTON (Chicago 1974). A. POLCINO, "Psychotheological Community," *The Priest* 31 (1974) 19–21; "A Psychotheological Therapeutic Community for the Religious Professional," *Bulletin*, National Guild of Catholic Psychiatrists 22 (1976) 40–49; *Intimacy: Issues of Emotional Living in An Age of Stress For Clergy and Religious* (Whitinsville, Mass. 1978). E. M. STERN and B. G. MARINO, *Psychotheology* (New York 1970). M. D. TURNER, "The American Sister Today," in *The Changing Sister* (Notre Dame, Ind. 1965). B. J. TYRELL, *Christotherapy: Healing through Enlightenment* (New York 1975); "Christotherapy: A Concrete Instance of a Christian Psychotherapy," *Bulletin*, National Guild of Catholic Psychiatrists 23 (1977) 54–73.

[T. A. KANE]

PUBLIC OPINION

Opinions are stated reactions toward particular events, persons or institutions. They are more specific than attitudes, which are stated reactions toward classes of events, persons, or institutions and tend to be more enduring. Public opinion refers to opinions toward specific events, persons, or institutions held by large populations and relevant to specific issues of public interest.

Study of Public Opinion. The study of public opinion has been most vigorous in the United States where political ideology stresses the responsiveness of political institutions to the opinions of citizens. Not all opinions held by citizens, however, necessarily concern students of public opinion. For instance, while most adults entertain opinions on child-rearing practices, these opinions concern students of public opinion only if they become directly relevant to public policy. The study of public opinion rests importantly upon systematic sampling techniques which allow, within specifiable limits of error, valid estimates of the distribution of mass opinions on specific issues and upon opinion-measurement techniques that allow the assessment of the intensity of opinions. Public-opinion study has traditionally focused upon public-policy issues. The widespread dissemination of techniques for its sampling and measurement, however, has led to the polling of opinions within organized subgroups in societies. The aim is to provide the leaders of these subgroups additional information for guiding decision-making about their own internal affairs and their relations with other institutions in that society. Labor unions, corporations, and Churches, among others, now utilize these techniques among members in order to ascertain shape and intensity of opinions concerning issues of interest.

The majority of any population will, when asked, express opinions on any specific issues. But it has been repeatedly demonstrated that the vast majority of citizens, even in the most highly educated nations, are primarily concerned with such personal problems as health, financial, and family worries. It is primarily those individuals who have in some fashion solved these personal problems in some enduring manner who regularly attend to issues beyond their private concerns and knowledgeably develop opinions about events, persons, and institutions beyond their own personal experience. This finding underlies several important characteristics of public opinion.

Findings on Public Opinion. First, highly educated and economically secure citizens are generally better informed about public issues than are less educated and poorer citizens. For all citizens, opinions on issues are shaped by experience, social background, and childhood socialization as well as by information and perceived interests. Transcending the problems of day-to-day survival allows more attention to the more distant issues of public policy. Second, it is in interaction with others, not in isolation, that most opinions are formed. The information utilized in opinion formation follows a two-step process where the most attentive citizens develop opinions and communicate them to less attentive citizens. This fact emphasizes the crucial role of social organization in the development of coherent public opinion on any issue. Voluntary organizations, political parties, pressure groups, church groups, neighborhood clubs, and parent groups, among others, serve to inform and shape the opinions of members through interaction and the articulation of positions by opinion leaders. Third, under certain circumstances public opinion can be highly unstable since many are ill-informed on issues, many issues are beyond the personal experience of the majority of people, and respected leaders have not systematically articulated public positions. Fourth, public opinion does not generally demonstrate the coherence across issues which general understandings of a liberal to conservative ideological spectrum would lead one to expect. This has led some students of public opinion to describe it as schizoid in that apparently conflicting opinions can be held with some intensity. The more attentive, however, display more coherence. Fifth, the mass media in modern societies are not particularly effective in directly manipulating public opinion on issues where opinions are strongly held and based upon some knowledge. Extensive research has shown that when citizens do attend to these media of communication they normally attend to those positions which they find most congenial and ignore views which are at variance with their own. Sixth, public opinion bears a rather erratic relationship to actual policy formation unless attention is paid to the social organization of the holders of the opinion. The more organized the holders of some opinion are, the more the opinion can be expected to bear directly upon decisions. Leaders do, however, attend to potentially organizable opinion and anticipate latent public opinion.

Finally, opinions on specific issues are not a good indication of how people are likely to behave. Even intensely held opinions on an issue do not mean, for most, that any personal action will be taken related to the issue. Organized channels which allow action upon opinions with relative ease and which provide other benefits to participants encourage action based upon public opinion. To the extent to which such channels are lacking, leaders can afford to pay less attention to public opinion.

Bibliography: H. L. CHILD, *Public Opinion: Nature, Formation and Role* (Princeton 1965). W. P. DAVISON, "Public Opinion," *International Encyclopedia of the Social Sciences*, D. Sills, ed. (New York 1968) 188–197. V. O. KEY, *Public Opinion and American Democracy* (New York 1961).

[J. D. MCCARTHY]

PUBLIC POLICY ISSUES AND THE CHURCH

From very early times theoretical and practical questions raised about the Church's role in relation to public policy issues have been answered by its members in a variety of ways. Their responses have ranged from principled indifference to the secular order, as a result of eschatological preoccupations or the conviction that the transcendent character of God's Kingdom called for such an approach, to some form of theocratic totalitarianism, in which the distinction between doctrine and polity was blurred to the vanishing point. In the United States the Church has generally sought a middle ground, conditioned by U.S. constitutional tradition and the realities of social and political conditions in this country.

History. In the early years of the Republic the small Catholic community was principally concerned with internal problems and with the need for acceptance by the larger, sometimes hostile non-Catholic society. As Catholics grew in numbers and strength, however, the Church began to take a more active role.

School issues—Protestant influence in public schools and government support of Catholic schools—triggered much of this response. For example, the Pastoral Letter of the Fourth Provincial Council of Baltimore (1840) addressed the problem of Protestant influence at length. In this document the bishops also offered certain general observations on political matters, especially the responsible use of the ballot, while disclaiming partisan intent in terms which suggest anxiety lest even mild comments, coming from them, would be misinterpreted ("You cannot, therefore, attribute our monition to any political bias, nor entertain the suspicion that it is meant to produce any political effect.")

The sophistication and self-confidence of Catholic leadership increased in the years that followed. By the end of World War I the bishops felt sufficiently secure to propose, without apology, a sweeping "Program of Social Reconstruction" (1919) treating jobs, wages, child labor, housing, social security, and much more. Growing willingness to exercise a public-policy role was also reflected in the creation, in the same year, of the National Catholic Welfare Council (later Conference), an outgrowth of the National Catholic War Council.

Since then much of the activity of the Church in the United States in relation to public policy has been identified with NCWC and with the two organizations which succeeded it in 1966, the National Conference of Catholic Bishops (NCCB) and the United States Catholic Conference (USCC). Of comparable significance has been the emergence, particularly since the 1960s, of State Catholic Conferences which articulate Catholic views on legislation and public policy at the state level. In 1977 such agencies existed in 28 states (16:431).

The scope of Church concern is very nearly as broad as the contemporary public policy agenda itself. In recent years, for instance, the bishops have issued collective statements and undertaken programs dealing with such matters as abortion, population, education, health care, communications, war and defense policy, refugees, foreign aid, human rights, civil rights, housing, employment, the aged, the reform of correctional institutions, farm policy, food policy, poverty, race, and crime.

Rationale. Theorizing about the Church's role in relation to public policy has also continued. A typical contemporary formulation on the subject was provided by the USCC Administrative Board in a statement issued in February 1976: "The Church's participation in public affairs is not a threat to the political process or to genuine pluralism, but an affirmation of their importance. The Church recognizes the right of all, including the Church itself, to be heard in the formulation of public policy."

A number of questions continue to be debated. These include the relative priority which the Church should assign to particular public policy issues in its own activities; the appropriate form for Church activity (simplistically, teaching *versus* political action); how specific the Church should be in advocating or opposing particular public policy positions and the extent and nature of the obligation thus imposed on the consciences of Catholics; and what processes should be employed in forming and expressing the Church's position with respect to public policy questions. It is universally agreed, however, that the Catholic Church, like other Churches and religious groups, has a legitimate role to play in relation to public policy.

Bibliography: J. T. ELLIS, *American Catholicism* (Chicago 1955). H. J. NOLAN, ed., *Pastoral Letters of the American Hierarchy, 1792–1970* (Huntington, Ind. 1971). USCC and NCCB statements, published by the USCC Publications Office, Washington, D.C.

[R. SHAW]

PUBLISHING, CATHOLIC (U.S.)

The golden age of Catholic publishing in America did not last long but authors, booksellers, and readers enjoyed the brief, bright period. Its beginning can be dated exactly: the Fall of 1948 when Thomas Merton's *The Seven Storey Mountain* was published and immediately appeared on all the bestseller lists to the surprise of almost everyone.

Golden Age. Until the 1940s, Catholic publishing had been mostly a matter of a few old-line Catholic houses offering worthy but often pious and dull tomes, drearily presented in unappealing format. They were to be found on the shelves of church-goods dealers, who were seldom interested in the so-called apostolate of the printed word. The spectacular success of *The Seven Storey Mountain* persuaded other general publishers that Catholic books had a market. Doubleday launched Image Books and a Catholic department under the guidance of John Delaney (whose influence on Catholic publishing in the twentieth century has been more important than that of any other single individual). Random House brought forth *The Basic Writings of Saint Thomas*, edited by Anton Pegis, and the success of that hefty two-volume work prompted *The Basic Writings of Saint Augustine*, also edited by Pegis. Farrar, Straus & Cudahy, under the guidance of Sheila Cudahy, launched Vision Books, a series of fine juvenile biographies and began issuing exceptional Catholic books for adults. Pantheon, Harper's, Scribner's, Harcourt Brace, Little Brown, and other important general publishers were soon featuring at least one book a season of particular interest to Catholic readers. Fiction, biography, poetry, spirituality, reference, juvenile—almost every category was represented. Some of the writers—Graham Greene, Sigrid Undset, Evelyn Waugh, Paul Horgan, François Mauriac—had achieved their reputations earlier, but for the first time American Catholic readers embraced them as their own. Thomas Merton continued his brilliant prose and poetry (hampered sometimes by Trappist censors) and readers regularly welcomed books by Frank Sheed and Maisie Ward Sheed, J. F. Powers, Ronald Knox, Hubert van Zeller,

Andrew Greeley, Flannery O'Connor, Louis Evely, Karl Stern, Eugene Kennedy, Walker Percy, Henri Daniel-Rops, Fulton Sheen, and John L. McKenzie, as well as lesser lights.

The demand for Catholic books accelerated so quickly that before long almost any and every Catholic book seemed to sell. Even the traditional Catholic houses were reborn as they pulled themselves into the 20th century and struggled for their share of the market, justly complaining that after all, they had sponsored Catholic books when the going was rough and now deserved some gratitude as well as sales.

Decline. So successful did Catholic publishing become that few realized a decline had set in soon after Vatican Council II. The first evidence that not only had Catholic publishing in America stopped growing but that the problems were radical was the death of the backlist, that is, of older titles still in print. One of the characteristics of Catholic publishing was that even books by little-known writers on specialized subjects continued to find an audience. But with the changes resulting from the Council, these as well as standard works became, or seemed to become, outdated, and readers would have none of them. Hagiography, for example, always a staple of Catholic reading, began to disappear and within a few years it was difficult to find biographies of even the more popular saints. Like the famous stock market crash of 1929, the bottom dropped out of Catholic publishing almost overnight. One by one the most famous names in Catholic publishing ceased to exist or were taken over by other publishers. Among those now gone are Pustet, Benziger, Bruce, B. Herder, Kenedy, Newman—all of whom were featured in the last *New Catholic Encyclopedia* survey of Catholic publishing. Sheed & Ward is now Sheed Andrews & McMeel; Fides is now Fides/Claretian; Herder and Herder is now part of Seabury. With two exceptions (Doubleday, and to a lesser extent, Harper & Row), general publishers lost their interest in Catholic books when they saw what had happened to sales and now a Catholic book on their list is a rarity.

What brought about this change in Catholic publishing from boom to depression? What brought about an end to the bright days that no one believed would ever end? Numerous factors, including the economy and cultural currents can be cited but probably the most important reasons are as follows.

(1) Catholic publishing in America, even at its best, was never broad-based in its appeal. The better educated Catholic tended to be a liberal Catholic and readers of Catholic books, magazines, and newspapers were mostly from this group. Conservative Catholics have never been major book buyers, unlike the fundamentalist Protestants, except for the works of Fulton Sheen and devotional classics. Liberal readers who had embraced Thomas Merton, Graham Greene and Evelyn Waugh were the first to realize the potential of Vatican II, the first to welcome writings of Hans Küng and to make possible his first triumphal tour of America. Unfortunately, they were also the first to become disillusioned with the pace of reform and even with the Church. Often their disillusionment led to severing their connections with the institutional Church or at least to their ceasing active participation and becoming what Andrew Greeley has called "Communal Catholics." In any event, they ceased buying Catholic books—just as

they ceased buying contemporary religious art and almost wiped out a whole industry.

(2) It soon became apparent that publishers and booksellers had not sufficiently appreciated the importance of Catholic nuns as readers. Everyone realized, of course, that nuns read avidly, that the best gift to give a nun was a Catholic book, and that they had both the time and the money to support Catholic literature. What was not realized was that nuns not only bought books themselves but influenced others to buy and to read. When the radical changes in religious life began, Catholic reading was an inevitable casualty. No longer were sisters restricted in their leisure hours or in their leisure activities. And even more crucial, the estimated 40,000 sisters who left the convent since the end of Vatican Council II (as well as the several thousand priests who are no longer active) represent many thousands of once fervent Catholic book-buyers whose interests have been diverted elsewhere.

(3) The same factors that adversely affected Catholic book publishing worked against Catholic magazines and newspapers which had grown in quantity and quality through the 1940s and 1950s. After peaking sometime in 1960, circulation for both magazines and newspapers plummeted (the *National Catholic Reporter*, for example, declined from nearly 100,000 to less than 40,000) and many publications, unable to stand the shock, gave up. This crisis was another blow for Catholic books because it limited still further the already circumscribed media for publicity, advertising, and book reviews. It became more difficult and more expensive to reach that rare Catholic who was interested in buying and reading Catholic books.

(4) A similar pattern prevailed in Catholic education. Catholic elementary schools, high schools, colleges and universities were flourishing until—again in the terrible 60s—students, for one reason or another, began to go to public or secular schools. Many schools closed; all faced budget problems. The Catholic school market which had been the support of every Catholic publisher and bookseller could no longer be depended on. Even when schools received funds from the state to purchase books, regulations prevented these funds being utilized for religious books.

(5) Three factors that were not peculiar to Catholic publishing, although they possibly hurt Catholic publishing more than most because of its weakened condition, were inflation, television, and the popularity of the paperback. Cost of publishing and bookselling spiraled faster than the price of books—not that publishers and booksellers would not have liked to raise their prices as quickly and as high as others, but they dared not do so because they feared customer resistance. All-absorbing television took more and more free time from adults and almost completely put an end to the "reading child." Paperbacks proved to be a boon to readers, but small publishers and booksellers found it difficult to adjust to a unit sale so much less than they were accustomed to.

The Present and the Future. Most observers would likely agree, that the 70s saw a lessening in the rate of decline that had plagued Catholic publishing in the previous decade and the achievement of some sort of plateau. While the situation today could not be considered cheerful, it is far better than many had feared. A notable characteristic of this present period is the dramatic change in areas of Catholic reader-interest as reflected by book sales. With certain exceptions—a few writers can still attract readers, no matter the subject—many traditional topics seem to have lost their appeal: Canon Law, liturgical changes, and other affairs of the Church; "Catholic fiction"; anything labeled "theology"; and philosophy. Books about the Bible, the Bible itself, and what might be called old-fashioned spiritual meditations have managed to keep their readership during the renewal. However, contemporary Catholics seem most interested in probing vital, basic questions—the existence of God, the immortality of the soul, the divinity of Christ—as well as in problems of individual values and morality. Writers who combine psychology and religion ordinarily find a receptive audience.

Obviously the future of American Catholic publishing depends on the reading habits and preferences of today's young Catholics. The prognosis is not optimistic. For evidence, if the polls are to be believed, there is the pervasive lack of interest in any kind of reading among young people and the continuing disillusionment with the institutional Church, of many of them. In addition, there is an alarming scarcity of young and of new, not-so-young writers, although the present is a period that can boast of John Shea, Donald Goergen, David Tracy, John and Michael Garvey, Tad Guzie, Piers Paul Read, Michael McCauley, James Carroll, William McCready, Patricia Noone, Tom McHale, Richard Woods, and John Heagle. Finally, all of the change and the turmoil may have had one positive result: the contribution of Catholic publishing to the growth and well-being of the Church in America—and, conversely, the harm inflicted when Catholic publishing is, for whatever reason, restricted—should be obvious, as a result of the past decade, to even the most obtuse observer.

[D. HERR]

R

RAIMONDI, LUIGI

Cardinal, eighth Apostolic Delegate to the U.S.; b. Oct. 25, 1912 in Lussito d'Acqui, a small town in the Piedmont region of northern Italy; d. June 24, 1975 in Rome. At a young age he entered the seminary of the Diocese of Acqui where he received his classical, philosophical and theological training in preparation for the priesthood. He was ordained a priest in Acqui, June 6, 1936.

Immediately after ordination, Fr. Raimondi was sent to Rome by his bishop in order to pursue graduate studies leading to doctorates in Canon Law and theology. He obtained both at the Pontifical Gregorian University in 1938. While pursuing these studies, he also prepared for a career in the diplomatic service of the Holy See as a student of the Pontifical Ecclesiastical Academy (then the Pontificia Accademia dei Nobili Ecclesiastici). In August 1938, he received his first diplomatic assignment as Secretary of the apostolic nunciature in Guatemala.

In 1942, Monsignor Raimondi became the Auditor of the Apostolic Delegation in Washington. He served in this capacity throughout World War II until he was named chargé d'affaires of the Holy See's mission in New Delhi, India. While in Washington, Monsignor Raimondi worked for the then Apostolic Delegate, Archbishop Amleto Cicognani, and had an opportunity to travel extensively throughout the United States. On Dec. 15, 1953, Monsignor Raimondi was appointed titular archbishop of Tarsus and Apostolic Nuncio to Haiti. In 1957, he was transferred to Mexico to become Apostolic Delegate to the Church in that country. Ten years later, June 30, 1967, Pope Paul VI named Archbishop Raimondi the eighth Italian prelate to become Apostolic Delegate to the American Catholic Church.

During a term of almost six years Archbishop Raimondi ordained twenty-two new bishops, installed others as residential bishops, and oversaw the establishment of twelve new dioceses and three new archdioceses. His pastoral duties took him to virtually every part of the country and even as far as the Trust Territory of the Pacific and Alaska. Archbishop Raimondi represented Pope Paul VI at the funerals of Senator Robert F. Kennedy in 1968 and former President Dwight D. Eisenhower in 1969. The years of Archbishop Raimondi's tenure were highlighted by the tensions confronting the Church as it groped through the immediate post-conciliar era. As Apostolic Delegate, Archbishop Raimondi found himself dealing with these situations within the American Catholic Church from his position of papal authority which he understood to be a function of love and pastoral solicitude.

When Paul VI created thirty new cardinals on March 5, 1973, the Apostolic Delegate in the U.S. was among them. Shortly thereafter, Cardinal Raimondi was appointed by the Holy Father to be Prefect of the Sacred Congregation for Saints' Causes. In the brief time that Cardinal Raimondi served in this office, he took a very special interest in furthering the canonization process of both Mother Elizabeth Ann Seton, who was to become America's first native saint (1975), and Bishop John Nepomucene Neumann, the fourth bishop of Philadelphia, canonized in 1977. On June 24, 1975, Cardinal Raimondi was suddenly and fatally stricken with a heart attack at the Vatican.

[J. M. WHALEN]

READER, MINISTRY OF

The ministry of reader is one of the two universally accepted forms of lay ministries in the Church. In the Latin Church it has replaced the minor order of lector suppressed in the apostolic letter *Ministeria quaedam* issued by Pope Paul VI motu proprio on Aug. 15, 1972. At the present time only men may be instituted into this ministry by the Ordinary (the bishop, and in clerical institutes, the major superior) according to the liturgical rite of institution of readers. Requirements for admission into the ministry of reader are: (1) the presentation of a petition freely made out and signed by the aspirant to the Ordinary who has the right to accept the petition; (2) a suitable age and special qualities to be determined by the episcopal conference; (3) a firm will to give faithful service to God and the Christian people (Paul VI MinQuaedam VIII). The reader is appointed and instituted to fulfill the following functions in the liturgy: (1) to read the lessons from sacred Scripture, except for the Gospel, in the Mass and other liturgical celebrations; (2) to recite the psalm between the readings when there is no psalmist; (3) to present the intentions for the General Intercessions in the absence of the deacon or cantor; (4) to direct the singing and the participation of the faithful. The reader "may also instruct the faithful for the worthy reception of the sacraments," (and) "take care of preparing other faithful who by a temporary appointment are to read the Scriptures in liturgical celebrations" (ibid. V). To assure the authenticity of this ministry's exercise, *Ministeria quaedam* directed episcopal conferences to set suitable intervals [interstices] which "should be observed between the conferring of the ministries of reader and acolyte whenever more than one ministry is conferred on the same person" (ibid. X). The NCCB set the interval between the two institutions as six months at its regular meeting in November 1973. While institution in the lay ministries is required before diaconal ordination, it is not limited to candidates for the order of deacon or priest. However, the exclusion of women from institution in the ministry of reader has made of this office a step before ordination in the U.S. and in many other countries, much as the former minor order of lector was a step on the way to priesthood. Both women and men without formal institution may fulfill all the functions of an instituted reader without restriction.

See also LAY MINISTRIES (RITE OF INSTITUTION).

Bibliography: *The Institution of Readers*, Eng. tr., ICEL (Washington, D.C. 1976). Bishops' Committee on the Liturgy, *Study Text III, Ministries in the Church: Commentary on the Apostolic Letters of Pope Paul VI, "Ministeria quaedam" and "Ad pascendum"* (Washington, D.C. 1974); *Newsletter* 11 (1975) 4. *Notitiae* 60 (1971) 20.

[J. A. GURRIERI]

REASON, AGE OF

The practice of children receiving the Sacraments of Penance and the Eucharist for the first time at about the age of seven, dates from the decree of the Congregation for the Sacraments, *Quam singulari*, Aug. 8, 1910 (ActApS 2 [1910] 577–583; Denz 3530–36). The decree carried out St. Pius X's rejection of the earlier practice of deferring first Communion until the age of 10 or 12 and his encouragement of Eucharistic piety through frequent Communion (see *Sacra Tridentina Synodus*, Denz 3375–83). In inspiration *Quam singulari* was a concession (see Denz 3535–36) giving to children rights previously denied. To justify admission of children to the Sacraments, the decree required that the child be able to discriminate between the Eucharist and ordinary bread; have a rudimentary knowledge of the teachings of faith. The child was deemed to have attained the age of discretion or reason (12:118) around the seventh year—in some cases before, in some after. Judgment on this was left to parents, pastors, confessors, and teachers.

In the early 1960s, the practice of first Confession and in a day or so first Communion began to be challenged by some parents, pastors, and religion teachers. An initial experiment placed first Confession about a month before first Communion. This was to instruct the child of the proper role of each of the two Sacraments. However, from the mid 1960s, the reception of first Communion, received around the seventh year of age, and the deferral of first Confession to later years, e.g., ninth or tenth year, was practiced widely.

Among the reasons for this practice, one had to do with an essential part of the Sacrament of Penance; namely, "sufficient matter," i.e. that there be some sin or sins to be absolved. For a child could have the first use of reason and be able to discern the Eucharist from

common bread and so qualify for his first Communion without either having committed sins or without being really guilty because of a lack of moral judgment. Not being guilty of sin, the young child was not capable of contrition, nor, in consequence, of receiving the Sacrament of Penance; an awareness sufficient for first Communion is not necessarily sufficient for first Confession. Moreover, later first Confession was considered more spiritually and psychologically beneficial.

However, on April 11, 1971, the Holy See, through the Sacred Congregation for the Clergy, decreed that first Confession before first Communion was to be restored. But it recognized the new practice of first Communion without Confession, permitting it to continue as an "experiment" (ActApS 64 [1971] 173–176). Two years later, on May 24, 1973, Rome decreed that the experiments of the last two years must stop and that the early decree of 1910, *Quam singulari*, was to be everywhere observed (ibid 65 [1973] 410). This prohibition was reiterated by Rome in a response on May 20, 1977 (ibid. 69 [1977] 427).

See also FIRST CONFESSION.

[A. BURROUGHS]

RECONCILIATION, MINISTRY OF

The ministry of reconciliation is a phrase that summarizes the economy of salvation. God's design is a "coming from" and a "return" to him. The "let the world be" of creation is at the same time the "let God be all in all" of the eschaton. Salvation history is the story of God committing himself more and more deeply to his creation that it might achieve perfect reconciliation with him. At the center of this plan is the Incarnation. Jesus Christ is the completely comprehensive reality that embraces all of creation. All things achieve their purpose, their right ordering, by being ordered to the Incarnate Word who has become not simply part of creation, but its center (Eph 1.9–10). The "already" of the reconciliation accomplished by Christ must be balanced off by the "not yet" of his second coming. In the time between, the ministry of reconciliation continues and the Church exists as the Sacrament and agent of this redemptive work.

Objectives. The objective of this ministry is more than the juxtaposition of created realities in peaceful coexistence. Rather it is a radical and definitive reordering that can be accomplished only in Christ, the ontological principle of unity. Creatures are reconciled with one another because they are reconciled with God. Paul is clear on this point when writing to the quarrelsome Corinthians. In seeking their reconciliation with one another and with him, he asked that they participate more deeply in the profound reconciliation achieved by Christ (2 Cor 5.16–21).

Vatican Council II speaks of reconciliation in a variety of contexts (unity among Christians, peace among nations, sacrament of reconciliation) but the primary referent is always the fundamental reconciliation achieved by Christ. While it is fully achieved only in relationship to God, this cannot excuse Christians from dealing directly with one another in seeking unity. The commandments to love God and love neighbor are in fact one (Mt 22.34–40). The ministry of reconciliation, then, involves not only an individual's relationship to God, not only bringing others to him, but also the personal relationship with others.

Exercise of Reconciliation. God has taken the decisive initiative in exercising the ministry of reconciliation, and human efforts must always be seen as a participation in this. This means not only passive openness but a positive initiative toward reconciliation. In saying that we should leave our gift at the altar and first become reconciled, the Lord is talking about reconciliation with a person who has something *against* us (Mt 5.23–24). Christians are called upon to take the initiative in reaching out as salt, light, leaven, ministers of Christ's reconciliation to the world.

Full reconciliation will be achieved only in the Kingdom, but the call is to achieve partial realizations during this time between the Lord's first and second coming. Results may be incomplete and transitory, but they serve as anticipations of the Kingdom. The incomplete and imperfect nature of reconciliation during this present journeying raises a major difficulty. Reconciliation very often seems illogical, premature, prophetic. The logical inclination would be to wait until perfect at-one-ment is achieved, when all things will fit together as they should. Christ, however, called upon his followers to engage in this ministry now, to be forgiving, to build peace and unity even in this imperfect state (contrast the attitude of the brother of the prodigal son). The first Eucharistic Prayer for Masses of Reconciliation carries the reminder that now is the time of reconciliation.

Ministry of the Community. Christian communities, as communities, exercise a ministry of reconciliation partly by being a sign and foreshadowing of the unity of the Kingdom. That is why the current disunity among Christians presents such a monumental problem. Called to be a sign of reconciliation, Christianity has made the world spectator to its own divisions for nearly the last millennium. Given the central place of the ministry of reconciliation, the unity of Christians has to count as one of the highest priorities. Ecumenical developments hold promise. Yet, while interdenominational unity appears to be increasing, intradenominational unity is becoming a serious concern. Disunity is not to be confused with healthy diversity and plurality which actually serve to enhance unity; Christian communities are experiencing fragmentation and polarization at various levels.

These problems have to be taken as seriously as Paul took them at Corinth. The Christian community exercises its ministry of reconciliation most forcefully when its unity has no apparent reason other than Christ, when people worship together celebrating bonds of oneness that go deeper than the differences that normally keep people at odds—differing political views, race, culture, prejudice.

The Ordained Ministry. The ministry of reconciliation exercised by public ministers in the Church brings with it additional considerations. The public minister is called upon to forego certain rights as an individual Christian in order to serve the wider community. The attitude of the Apostle Paul must prevail—the attempt to be all things to all people. This is not to be taken in the sense of having all the answers or holding all the resources, but precisely in the sense of serving the cause of unity. "I became like a Jew to the Jews. . . . To those bound by the law I became like one who is bound. . . . To those not subject to the law I became like one not subject to it. . . . To the weak I became a weak person . . ." (1 Cor 9.20–22).

In its Decree on the Ministry and Life of Priests Vatican Council II says that, in the interest of building the Christian community, priests are never to put themselves at the service of any ideology or human faction (*Presbyterorum ordinis* 6). The 1971 Synod of Bishops, in its document on the Ministerial Priesthood makes a similar point in reference to political involvement: "But since political options are by nature contingent and never in an entirely adequate and perennial way interpret the Gospel, the priest, who is the witness of things to come, must keep a certain distance from any political office or involvement" (Synod MinPr p. 21).

This "certain distance" from causes that can interfere with the ministry of reconciliation presents various problems. On the one hand, true peace requires justice and development (Paul VI PopProgr 87) and the Church cannot remain silent or removed from all issues. On the other hand the Church cannot claim competence in all secular affairs and specific solutions should not be confused with the Gospel message (*Gaudium et spes* 54, cf. Synod JustWorld pp. 42–43). In this matter one has but to recall how the Church, at the time of the Reformation, was closely allied with national and political interests, and the effects that this had.

The Church must be conscious of her distinctive role as a reconciler, i.e. ministering a gift that goes much deeper than practical solutions. It is often when the Church is least of the world that it can do most for the world. This must always be motivated not by the self-interest of the Church, but rather in the interests of placing itself more fully at the service of the world in the ministry of reconciliation.

Bibliography: J.-F. COLLANGE, "Appel à la réconciliation," *Énigmes de la deuxième Epître aux Corinthiens* (Cambridge 1972) 18:226–280. Y. M.-J. CONGAR, *Sainte Église* (Paris 1964). R. COSTE, "Le prêtre et la politique," NouvRevTn 94 (1972) 912–932. Pro Mundi Vita, *New Forms of Ministries in Christian Communities* Bulletin 50, (Brussels 1974). PAUL VI, *On Reconciliation,* Apostolic Exhortation, *Paterna cum benevolentia,* Dec. 8, 1974 (USCC Publ. Office, Washington, D.C. n.d.).

[K. UNTENER]

RECONCILIATION WITH THE COMMUNITY

Contemporary theology closely relates reconciliation with God and reconciliation with the Church-community both in the Sacraments of Initiation and in the Sacrament of Penance, called now the Sacrament of Reconciliation.

Movement away from a view of the Church as an external, juridical organization to a view of Church as *communio* or communitarian and as Sacrament leads to seeing it as the locus of reconciliation. The visible community is the Sacrament of humanity's reconciliation with God in and through Christ; the Church's mission and ministry is thus one of reconciliation. Belonging to that community is sacramentally actualized for an individual in Baptism, which initiates into the community of salvation and brings forgiveness of all sin.

The Church must also deal with the fact of postbaptismal sin in its members. The ministry of reconciliation belongs to the whole Church, although its ordained ministers have a unique and essential role within this ministry. The Church's ministerial assistance to the penitent sinner in the conversion process and the Church's authoritative prayer are the action and prayer of Christ its Head. The Sacrament of Penance or Reconciliation thus exists for reconciliation both with God (12:129) and with the Church.

Sacramental Theology. This double reconciliation was largely ignored and forgotten from the early Middle Ages until this century. Scholastic theology generally concluded that the *res et sacramentum* of Penance (the immediate effect of the Sacrament and the sign also of the grace of forgiveness from God; 12:813) was the penitent's interior repentance. B. M. Xiberta y Roqueta's *Clavis Ecclesiae* (Rome 1922) began the movement away from this position and by the time of Vatican Council II theologians generally agreed that reconciliation with the Church is the means to reconciliation with God. The Council parallels the two without deciding the question of causality (*Lumen gentium* 11; *Presbyterorum ordinis* 5). The Council emphasizes the ecclesial aspect of all sins, insists that in the Sacrament there is always reconciliation with the Church, states that the action of the Church in the Sacrament goes beyond absolution, and sees the whole Church involved in the Sacrament.

Today almost all theologians who see reconciliation with the Church as an effect of the Sacrament regard that reconciliation to be the *res et sacramentum*. Some questions, however, remain: is this true in the case of venial sin? how is the relationship with the Church affected by sin and how, in the case of mortal sin, is the effect of sin different from excommunication? how does the teaching on reconciliation apply to a devotional confession?

Liturgical Expression. The Rite of Penance (*Ordo Paenitentiae*, Dec. 2, 1973) in general adopts the reconciliation model of redemption, conversion, and penance and the communitarian view of the Church, as does the Rite of Christian Initiation of Adults (*Ordo initiationis Christianae adultorum*, Jan. 6, 1972; cf. ChrInitAd 1–26). The Rite of Penance regards reconciliation with the Church as an effect of the Sacrament (Penance 4, 5, 31) and endeavors to express this in the sacramental rituals, particularly through emphasis on the communal forms of celebration. While making no statement on the *res et sacramentum*, the Rite seems to see reconciliation with God as flowing from and consequent upon the renewal of grace obtained through reconciliation with the Church (cf. esp. ibid. 2, in the Latin). Reconciliation with the Church, symbolized through the imposition of hands, restores the penitent to the community in which the Spirit of Jesus is active (ibid. 5, 6d, 9a, 19, 24) and thus reinserts the penitent into the paschal mystery (ibid. 1, 2, 7, 19): the broken covenant is remade because the penitent is restored to the covenant-community (ibid. 5, 6d). The Rite thus appears open to the interpretation that reconciliation with the Church is the *res et sacramentum* of reconciliation with God, the symbolic reality and immediate effect of the Sacrament.

See also PENANCE, COMMUNAL CELEBRATION OF.

Bibliography: K. RAHNER, "Penance as an Additional Act of Reconciliation with the Church," *Theological Investigations* 10 (New York 1973) 125–149. J. DALLEN, "The Reform of Penance" (S. T. D. dissertation, The Catholic University of America, 1976). W. BEINERT, "Die ekklesiale Dimension der christlichen Busse," *Catholica* 27 (1973) 45–68. B. COOKE, "The Social Aspect of the Sacrament of Penance," ProcCTSA 22 (1967) 173–183. D. DONNELLY, "The Role of Community in the Sacrament of Penance" (Ph.D. dissertation, Claremont, 1971).

[J. DALLEN]

RELATIVISM

It is a normal feature of growing up to come to recognize that one's own experience or thought patterns are not the measure for all others. It is yet more startling, however, to be forced to acknowledge that no objective norm is easily ascertainable either. One who is startled by such a realization begins to call himself a "relativist." His initial hopes for a standard have been dashed, so he is left with the conviction that no standards are applicable: everything depends on one's point of view.

There is merit to this position, of course, since much of what people claim to be the case depends on their personal perspective. Yet if everything asserted were so affected, ordinary conversation would be impossible. So a pure relativism—in theology or anywhere else—becomes self-defeating, while a moderate form bespeaks appreciation of widely different perspectives. Such a moderate relativism is sometimes called "perspectivism"; and even "soft perspectivism," to distinguish it from "hard perspectivism" (which sounds very much like pure relativism).

The force of these distinctions in theological inquiry lies in developing an awareness of what contributions different cultures can make to a continuing tradition. Since theological interpretations themselves reflect a particular outlook, and yet become embodied in the tradition itself, it behooves a theologian to approach different cultures with a lively sense of their "otherness." Relative to their sophistication regarding, say, the range of human affections, he may be quite ignorant. So he might find himself making assertions that sound quite outrageous in the new cultural context. This realization will impel such a person to seek for ways of translating from one context to another, and may even lead him to a fresh understanding of the assertion itself. A healthy sense of *relativity* leads to development, but only in the measure that it prompts a continuing quest for understanding; abandonment of that quest is what constitutes *relativism*.

Bibliography: J. MCCLENDON and J. SMITH, *Understanding Religious Convictions* (Notre Dame, Ind. 1975). B. WILSON, ed., *Rationality* (Oxford 1970), esp. P. WINCH, "Understanding a Primitive Society,"

[D. BURRELL]

RELATIVISM, MORAL

The term "relativism" (12:220) is often associated with certain styles of moral reasoning common in contemporary literature. However, the term, as it is used, has two quite different meanings which should be carefully distinguished.

Relativism as Subjectivism. First, moral relativism can be taken as synonymous with, or at least correlative to, subjectivism, with the moral subject or agent as the sole criterion of right or wrong. A relativistic moral theory, in this sense, would be a theory denying objective morality as a whole. For it contends that the sole and exclusive source of moral value is the intention of the agent, the person's inner commitment to behaving out of loving or generous motives. Relativism, then, identifies morality with motivation; it sees the virtues as descriptions of styles of moral intending rather than as characteristics of moral action. And thus it rejects entirely the concept of "intrinsic value" as a constituent of moral judgment.

Relativism of this first sort is identified with the work of Joseph Fletcher. And, as Fletcher himself affirms, it is reductively a form of philosophical nominalism. For it claims that the objective moral value denominating specific acts does not really reside in those acts, but solely in the intentions. Arbitrarily a "name" (moral classification) is projected onto modes of behavior.

Relativism with Objective Morality. Relativism, however, can have quite a different meaning: in this second meaning it is a moral theory that sees moral value as objective but not unchanging. This sort of relativism affirms that moral value is not solely the product of human intention, that actions have value in and of themselves. But it refuses to conclude that the value of specific actions is always, in all contexts, exactly the same. Rather it affirms that an action wrong in one context might well be right in another. The reasoning involved is that morality precisely requires doing what is truly good; what is good in one context, however, might not be good in another. Thus, for example, responsible use of money would be quite different for the married man of limited means and the wealthy bachelor; proper sexual behavior is quite different for the married woman and the single woman. In these cases, then, it can be said that moral value is "relative," but relative to the facts of the case, not purely to the intention of the agent.

This second sort of relativism does not reject objective morality; it rejects immutable morality. Its ultimate basis is the belief that the world is a dynamic, not static reality and that moral value is consequently also changeable, though always objective. This kind of relativism is held by the vast majority of Catholic moralists writing today. It is, in fact, a characteristic of the Catholic tradition of moral theology, though the extent to which it is affirmed has varied among authors and periods. And as a fundamental approach for morality, it can be rooted in Thomas Aquinas's concern for finality (final cause, teleology).

Debates regarding the extent to which morality is relative (in this second sense) are not really debates about morality at all. They are debates about the nature of the world. If the world is static, then moral values will be rather absolute and unchanging. If, however, the world is dynamic and evolving, then moral values will be seen more as objective-but-relative.

Bibliography: C. CURRAN, "Natural Law," and "Utilitarianism, Consequentialism, and Moral Theology," *Themes in Fundamental Moral Theology* (Notre Dame, Ind. 1977) 27–80, 121–144. J. FLETCHER, *Situation Ethics* (Philadelphia 1966). J. FLETCHER and H. MCCABE, "The New Morality," *Commonweal* 84 (Jan. 14, 1966) 427–440. J. FUCHS, *Human Values and Christian Morality* (Dublin 1970). R. MCCORMICK, *Ambiguity in Moral Choice* (Milwaukee 1974); "Notes on Moral Theology," ThSt 32 (1971) 80–97; 35 (1975) 85–100. T. O'CONNELL, *Principles for a Catholic Morality* (New York 1978).

[T. E. O'CONNELL]

RELIGION, PHILOSOPHY OF

Philosophy of religion is reason's tribute to the religious quest of the race and to the contributions to this quest made by the great religious or quasi-religious traditions. It is a critical reflection on religious experience as philosophy of science is on scientific and technological processes, philosophy of art on aesthetic creativity, and philosophy of morals on ethical theory and practice. Like these it asks about the source and status of the foundational convictions or experiences, the logic and meaning of all their further implications, and the relationship of this whole body.

In 1781, in the preface to his famous *Critique of Pure Reason*, Immanuel Kant served the summons of his age upon religion, that it should appear before the court of reason or otherwise forfeit that respect which reason shows only to those who can stand its free and open examination. This summons signalled the end of reason's role as the handmaid of faith, the faculty which, in its philosophical function, provided the preambles to the faith: from natural theology the knowledge of God's existence and attributes and from positive apologetics, the proof of the most basic claims about Jesus. Many Christians to this day have ignored both the summons and the signal. Convinced that the new challenge from the so-called Age of Reason would simply destroy the faith it pretended to analyze, they continued to refurbish their proofs of God's existence and their arguments for Jesus' veracity.

As this sorry disagreement continued it began to appear that the attack upon the arguments for God's existence was not the most destructive element to emerge from the Age of Reason and the defense of natural theology in its most stringent form (as strict proofs of God's existence and attributes) was not the best response for even the most conservative of Christian spokesmen to make. Were the proofs of God's existence really cogent? More seriously, did the God who appeared at the conclusion of an argument in natural theology bear anything more than the most formal resemblance to the Father of Jesus Christ?

In any case, as Feuerbach's phenomenally successful *The Essence of Christianity* soon made clear, the thrust of the critique of traditional Christianity in the Age of Reason was toward a radically humanistic reinterpretation of Christianity itself, rather than against faith's preambles. Feuerbach cherished the religious instinct; he simply wanted to direct it to its proper goal, namely, the future of humanity, rather than have it alienated toward a totally other God. He did not wish to be called an atheist and he pointed out that, after all, it was Christians who first began to talk literally about a God-Man. This humanization or secularization of Christianity has been the central column of the Western critique of traditional Christianity from Hegel, through Marx, down to the recent Death-of-God movement.

So it is no longer a fight between the proponents of faith and reason and the proponents of reason alone. Faith now appears on both sides of the divide, as necessary to the new "atheist" as it was to the traditional believer. Existentialist philosophers acknowledge this in their way, if only in their borrowing of their key terms for human existence from the religious philosopher, S. Kierkegaard. Linguistic philosophers acknowledge it also, if only in A. J. Ayer's determination to avoid being called an atheist as fervently as he avoids being called a believer. The question now concerns the nature of faith in human life, the criteria on which it could be judged, and, above all, the heights or depths to which it could legitimately go or be drawn. Once this is seen to be the question, philosophy of religion comes into its own.

Unlike natural theology, which it now subsumes—by asking, e.g., whether proofs of God's existence play any real part in people's faith—and corresponding to the changeover from the comparative study of religions to the history of religions, it respects the uniqueness of the religious or quasi-religious traditions with which it deals. Questions about the possible coincidences between the great religions or quasi-religions (e.g., Marxism) at some depth—for example, their understanding of God, or their conception of the goal of human history—come at the end and are not assumed at the beginning. Compared to theology, philosophy of religion is more questioning where theology is more explanatory.

Though it still in practice bears many of the scars of the recent tragic clashes between faith and reason in Western culture—it often perpetuates obsolete objections to faith instead of being truly critical, in the positive sense of searching out the true strengths and weaknesses of a stated position—philosophy of religion at its best recalls the older, the major and saner part of the Western religious tradition, where theology and philosophy, reason and faith, formed an organic unity, and where the quest for wisdom was seen in all its range as the quest for God. Such was the vision, for instance, of the recent scientist, philosopher, and man of faith, Pierre Teilhard de Chardin. Truth may transcend reason, as Swami Nikhilananda said of Vedanta, but it is never illogical.

Bibliography: L. FEUERBACH, *The Essence of Christianity* (London 1881). A. FLEW and A. MACINTYRE, *New Essays in Philosophical Theology* (New York 1955). G. W. F. HEGEL, *Lectures on the Philosophy of Religion* (London 1895). J. HICK, *Philosophy of Religion* (Englewood Cliffs, N.J. 1973). I. KANT, *Religion within the Limits of Reason Alone* (New York 1960). S. KIERKEGAARD, *Philosophical Fragments* (Princeton 1936). J. P. MACKEY, *The Problems of Religious Faith* (Chicago 1972). K. MARX and F. ENGELS, *On Religion* (Moscow 1955). P. TEILHARD DE CHARDIN, *The Phenomenon of Man* (London 1959). P. TILLICH, *The Courage To Be* (New Haven 1952). G. VAHANIAN, *The Death of God* (New York 1957).

[J. P. MACKEY]

RELIGION, PSYCHOLOGY OF

The study of psychological phenomena of religion has been marked by four developments since Vatican Council II. Whereas in 1950 Allport remarked that empirical psychology began with the study of religion but soon abandoned it, a recent bibliography of the psychology of religion has 2773 listings, the majority published since 1960. Moreover, the discipline displays a more critical attitude toward itself, with sharper evaluation of its research designs and conclusions. It shows a more open attitude of trying to understand religion rather than explain it away, as for example, in studies in mysticism and charismatic experiences. Finally, clinical and empirical study of religion enjoys greater professional status. The American Psychological Association granted divisional status in 1975 to Psychologists Interested in Religious Issues.

The Church also shows modified attitudes. Vatican II acknowledged the auxiliary value of psychology for more effective pastoral care and a more mature living of the faith (*Gaudium et spes* 5, 54, 62). Increased reliance on psychology is apparent in many areas, particularly in assessment of candidates for religious vocations (*see* VOCATION, PSYCHOLOGY OF), *pastoral counseling, catechesis, and the work of marriage tribunals (*see* MARRIAGE [CANON LAW]).

Marriage. The Council restored emphasis in understanding marriage as the interpersonal union of the partners and their actions (*Gaudium et spes* 48). This convenantal and communal focus implied the vital importance of the psychological functioning of the partners and their twofold capacity for the act of consent and for the object of consent. Thus, the notion of consummation extends beyond sexual aspects to the psychological facets of the interpersonal union. Consequently, there has been greater collaboration between clergy and psychologists, and other experts in allied fields, in marriage preparation programs. Marriage tribunals have elicited the opinions of clinicians with greater frequency in assessing the validity of marriages presented to church courts.

Religious Education and Moral Development. The Council directed that Christian doctrine be presented to all age levels in a manner which coordinates teaching with the abilities and level of those being instructed, and urged the use of psychological advances to assist moral and intellectual formation (*Christus Dominus* 14, 30; *Gravissimum educationis* 1).

Perhaps the most significant advances in the psychology of religion come from research in cognitive development, the study of how children organize their experience (*see* MORAL DEVELOPMENT; MORAL EDUCATION). Building on Piaget's (1950) seminal work, researchers of the past two decades have refined the understanding of the structures or operations of the intellect, that is, the qualitatively different ways by which children think as they progress from simplistic to sophisticated modes of cognition. The developing comprehension of religious and related concepts has been the subject matter of manifold studies which trace the progressive capacity of youth to understand such ideas as God, prayer, the Bible, Eucharistic Presence, death, hell, and resurrection.

Researchers also have explored moral thinking. Their findings have been woven into a theory of developmental moral thinking which parallels, yet differs from, thinking about the physical world, and is pertinent to the religious educator in the development of conscience. Kohlberg (1968) has proposed a six-stage theory of moral judgment, a sequence which he holds to be crosscultural and invariant. Other investigators have pursued the cognitive and noncognitive factors which facilitate moral development. Integral to this topic is the study of values, and their subjective reordering with age.

Fowler (1976) has widened the search for patterns/structures of thinking to faith orientation and awareness. He has proposed a provisional stage-theory of the sequential modes of thinking and valuing by which a person deals with the content of a faith.

Clinical studies and social psychology research on attitude formation have provided greater appreciation of the function of affective or emotional life in religious development, and a deeper understanding of religious formation as it is an interpersonal encounter rather than simply a cognitive transmission. At times, however, findings have been precipitately and injudiciously applied to catechesis.

Other Moral Issues. Clinical psychology has reworked its understanding of responsibility and guilt and redressed an earlier trend to see guilt mainly as neurotic functioning. Mowrer (1961) was the first psychologist of stature to point out that authentic guilt, when repressed, is at the core of some psychological problems. Others also restored balance by citing guilt as a primary factor in human growth, and in delineating the varieties of guilt in the formation and dynamics of conscience.

The Council reproved antisemitism and discrimination and called for brotherhood and the solidarity of all peoples (*Nostra aetate* 4; *Apostolicam actuositatem* 14), no doubt aware that early studies found an association between prejudice and religious membership. Various studies pursued Allport's (1967) operational definitions of extrinsic and intrinsic faith—faith which subtly serves primarily for personal reassurance and security, as distinct from faith which motivates a person to transcend self-centered ends. The results of studies indicate that the person of intrinsic faith is among the most tolerant. Research has further differentiated the types of religious orientation. While confirming from another perspective the traditional insights of spiritual writers regarding mixed motivation and the need of purification of spirit, scientific research contributes to specification of the many levels and dimensions of religiosity and seemingly "simple faith."

Dying and death, long shunned as topics of psychological studies, have shown a five-hundredfold increase of entries in *Psychological Abstracts* since 1964. Studies of the dynamics of dying persons and those involved with them, and of the relation of religious orientation and attitudes toward death, provide valuable insights for pastoral ministry.

Bibliography: G. ALLPORT, *The Individual and His Religion* (New York 1950). D. CAPPS, L. RAMBO and P. RANSOHOFF, eds., *Psychology of Religion: An Annotated Bibliography* (Detroit 1976). P. PRUYSER, *A Dynamic Psychology of Religion* (New York 1968). G. SCOBIE, *Psychology of Religion* (New York 1975). M. P. STROMMEN, ed., *Research on Religious Development* (New York 1971).

Religious experience: R. W. HOOD, "Forms of Religious Commitment and Intense Religious Experience," RevRelRes 15 (1973) 29–36; "Conceptual Criticisms of Regressive Explanations of Mysticism" RevRelRes 17 (1976) 179–188. J. P. KIHLDAHL, *The Psychology of Speaking in Tongues* (New York 1972).

Vocational assessment: W. C. BIER, ed., *Psychological Testing for Ministerial Selection* (New York 1970). W. J. COVILLE et al., *Assessment of Candidates for the Religious Life* (Washington 1968). V. HERR, *The Personality of Seminarians* (New York 1969). L. M. RULLA, *Depth Psychology and Vocation* (Chicago 1971). C. A. WEISGERBER, *Testing the Seminarian: A Review of Research* (Washington 1977).

Pastoral counseling: R. H. COX and E. M. PATTISON, eds., *Religious Systems and Psychotherapy* (Springfield, Ill. 1973). C. E. CURRAN, *Counseling and Psychotherapy: The Pursuit of Values* (New York 1968); *Religious Values in Counseling and Psychotherapy* (New York 1969). D. FARNSWORTH and F. BRACELAND, eds., *Psychiatry, the Clergy and Pastoral Counseling* (Collegeville, Minn. 1969). R. VAUGHN, *An Introduction to Religious Counseling* (Englewood Cliffs, N.J. 1969). E. WEITZEL, ed., *Contemporary Pastoral Counseling* (New York 1969).

Psychological assessment of marriage: CANON LAW SOCIETY OF AMERICA, *Matrimonial Jurisprudence U.S.A.* (Toledo, Ohio 1973). J. T. FINNEGAN, "When is a Marriage Indissoluble?" *Jurist* 37 (1968) 358–374. L. WRENN, *Annulments* (3d ed., Toledo 1978).

Studies related to catechesis/conscience: D. DE PALMA and J. FOLEY, eds., *Moral Development: Current Theory and Research* (Hillsdale, N.J. 1976). J. W. FOWLER, "Stages in Faith: The Structural Developmental Approach" in T. HENNESSY, ed., *Values and Moral Development* (New York 1976) 173–211. T. HENNESSY, ed., *Values and Moral Development* (New York 1976). M. KELSEY, "The Place of Affect in Religious Education," LumV 26 (1976) 68–80. L. KOHLBERG, "Moral Development," *International Encyclopedia of the Social Sciences* 10 (1968) 483–494. T. LICKONA, ed., *Moral Development and Behavior* (New York 1976). C. ELLIS NELSON, *Conscience: Theological and Psychological Perspectives* (New York 1976). J. PIAGET, *The Psychology of Intelligence* (New York 1950). M. ROKEACH, *The Nature of Human Values* (New York 1973).

Guilt: J. A. KNIGHT, *Conscience and Guilt* (New York 1969). K. MENNINGER, *Whatever Became of Sin?* (New York 1973). O. H. MOWRER, *The Crisis in Psychiatry and Religion* (Princeton 1961). E. V. STEIN, *Guilt: Theory and Therapy* (Philadelphia 1968). A. ULEYN, *Is It I, Lord?*, tr. Mary Ilford (New York 1968).

Religious orientation/discrimination: R. O. ALLEN and B. SPILKA, "Committed and Consensual Religion: A Specification of Religion-Prejudice Relationships," JScStRel 6 (1967) 191–206. G. ALLPORT and J. M. ROSS, "Personal Religious Orientation and Prejudice," *Journal of Personality and Social Psychology* 5 (1967) 432–443. J. DITTES, "Religion, Prejudice, and Personality," in M. P. STROMMEN, ed., *Research on Religious Development* (New York 1971) 355–390. R. L. GORSUCH and D. ALESHIRE, "Christian Faith and Ethnic Prejudice: A Review and Interpretation of Research," JScStRel 13 (1974) 281–307. B. O'CONNELL, "Dimensions of Religiosity Among Catholics," *Review of Religious Research* 16 (1975) 198–207. B. SPILKA and B. MINTON, "Defining Personal Religion:

Psychometric, Cognitive and Instrumental Dimensions." Paper presented at 1975 convention of Society for the Scientific Study of Religion, Milwaukee, Oct. 24. R. STARK and C. GLOCK, *American Piety: The Nature of Religious Commitment* (Berkeley 1968).

Thanatology: H. FEIFEL, ed., *The Meaning of Death* (New York 1959). A. GODIN, "Has Death Changed?" LumV (1971) 407–430. R. D. KAHOE and R. F. DUNN, "The Fear of Death and Religious Attitudes and Behavior," JScStRel 14 (1975) 379–382. E. KÜBLER-ROSS, *On Death and Dying* (New York 1969); *Death: The Final State of Growth* (Englewood Cliffs, N.J. 1975). B. SPILKA et al., "Death and Personal Faith: A Psychometric Investigation," JScStRel 16 (1977) 169–178. A. WEISMAN, *On Dying and Denying* (New York 1972).

[J. KEEFE]

RELIGION, SOCIOLOGY OF

Through their research and writing, sociologists of religion are instrumental in informing the public, including churchmen, of changes occurring in society that are relevant to religious institutions (cf. Vatican II *Gaudium et spes* 62; *Christus Dominus* 17, which speaks of "pastoral sociology"). On a broad level, they analyze a variety of nonreligious trends within society which have an impact on religious belief and public practice, in other words, the relationship between religious institutions and other institutions within society. They also examine such specifically religious trends as varying levels of individual religiosity. Finally, they concern themselves with those social processes and structural characteristics affecting religious behavior, for example, characteristics of religious organizations that have bearing on religious orientations of members.

Studies on Religious Orientation. This last and more particular area of study may provide insights in areas of immediate concern to the *pastoral ministry, as research here has recently concerned characteristics of new members. The decline in church attendance and membership from the late 1950s to the mid-1970s has stimulated interest among church administrators desiring to attract new members. The findings by Reginald W. Bibby and Merlin Brinkerhoff, who studied churches in a western Canadian community, indicated that new members of evangelical churches were primarily transfers from other evangelical churches or were children of members. There were few "outside" converts, thus suggesting that evangelistic efforts are more successful for lapsed members or those who are part of a structural network, for example, friends or spouses of members. The studies of Catholic Pentecostals also suggest the importance of network.

Of course, the decline in membership is also due in part to churchlike- rather than sect-like religious organizations losing their young people as well as their geographically mobile members. It can be observed that major changes are occurring in the American religious orientation, in the general relationship between attitude toward authority and conventional society on the one hand and the religious order on the other.

In this connection, the church historian Sidney Ahlstrom aptly notes that the students of the 1970s who read Will Herberg's *Protestant-Catholic-Jew,* published in 1955, "find that world so remote from their own experience that they confuse it with the world of Tolkien's *Lord of the Rings*." These students received their religious education in the 1960s when attitudes and life styles were so changed from the 1950s that even religion provided little basis for continuity. Ahlstrom notes that clergy and laity recognized "a disjunction between received tradition and present belief." Peter Berger wrote that the religious institutions no longer were in charge of the "ultimate, overarching symbols" of life, that is, religion now does not provide the basic interpretation of life as experienced by man. Furthermore, as Ahlstrom notes, in the 1960s "the religious establishment was apprehended as both conventional and authoritarian." The 1960s witnessed a turning away from such institutions by significant groups of Americans, especially those of—but not limited to—the counterculture. For generational change and for new West Coast religious movements the work by Robert Wuthnow and the volume edited by Charles Glock and Robert Bellah are instructive.

Studies on Change and Reform. Even this recent era of rejection now seems to be fading in memory as reaction to the 1960s has set in. Evangelical Protestantism and Catholic Pentecostalism thrive (on the former see the work by David Moberg). Michael Harrison wrote in 1974 that the Catholic Pentecostal movement was stimulated by disillusionment with political activism on campus and by a "heightened concern with personal growth." Meredith McGuire interpreted its growth as response to the insecurity of change brought about by Vatican Council II. Harrison, McGuire, and Joseph Fichter found that those attracted to the movement were economically comfortable and well-educated. Prophecy, testimony, which is a central commitment mechanism, and fellowship provide authority and order as well as the security and personal development found in such small communities. Fichter noted in 1976 that the reformation of the Church involves adaptation, or structural and institutional reform, and renewal, or the "interior renovation of the spirit." The charismatics fit the latter category. As Rodney Stark and Charles Glock have assessed, individual salvation-experience does not particularly lead Christians toward cleansing the world of its social evils, rather, salvation addresses individual shortcomings.

In the summer 1977 issue of *Sociological Analysis*, a symposium on the late Thomas F. O'Dea, Fichter observed that, in the years following the Council, voices for structural reform came to be replaced by those calling for personal conversion and sanctity, with this orientation providing a simplistic and fatalistic view of change that undermines collective effort at reform. He wrote that the critical test of Vatican II was the extent to which the traditional ecclesiastical system could "give way to a multi-faceted system of government." His assessment is that adaptation is taking place at the grass roots with official pronouncements being disregarded, Catholic women pushing for equality (here see the article by Ruth Wallace), and laymen (but not laywomen) controlling the Pentecostal movement.

Significance of Sociological Studies. This article was begun by noting that there are at least three perspectives for studying religion in society—religion as a social institution, religion as a personal attribute, and the religious organization. Kenneth Westhues writes that at the first, macro-level, studies are highly abstract, while at the second, micro-level, research fixes on random samples of individuals. These two perspectives do not have as much payoff as the third one (viewing the religious organization) for studying the relationship between religion and social change. When religion causes change it does so in the form of the religious organization, but, as has been noted, the trend of the 1970s is toward

more personal religion, for example, the Catholic Pentecostal movement. Without the careful marshalling of resources, religious organizations are likely to find that they have less impact in bringing about any structural change in society in the early 1980s.

See also CHURCH MEMBERSHIP (U.S.).

Bibliography: S. E. AHLSTROM, "National Trauma and Changing Religious Values," *Daedalus* 107 (Winter 1978) 13–29. R. W. BIBBY and M. B. BRINKERHOFF, "The Circulation of the Saints: A Study of People Who Join Conservative Churches," JScStRel 12 (1973) 273–283; "Sources of Religious Involvement: Issues for Future Empirical Investigation," RevRelRes 15 (1974) 71–79; "When Proselytizing Fails: An Organizational Analysis," *Sociological Analysis* 35 (1974) 189–200. J. H. FICHTER, *The Catholic Cult of the Paraclete* (New York 1975); "The Catholic Laity and the Charismatic Renewal: Is This the Reformation?" *Thought* 51 (1976) 123–134; "Restructuring Catholicism," *Sociological Analysis* 38 (1977) 154–164. C. Y. GLOCK and R. BELLAH, eds., *The New Religious Consciousness* (Berkeley 1976). M. I. HARRISON, "Sources of Recruitment to Catholic Pentecostalism," JScStRel 13 (1974) 49–64; "The Maintenance of Enthusiasm: Involvement in a New Religious Movement," *Sociological Analysis* 36 (1975) 150–160. M. B. MCGUIRE, "An Interpretive Comparison of Elements of the Pentecostal and Underground Church Movements in American Catholicism," *Sociological Analysis* 35 (1974) 57–76; "Toward a Sociological Interpretation of the 'Catholic Pentecostal' Movement," RevRelRes 16 (1975) 94–104; "The Social Context of Prophecy: 'Word-Gifts' of the Spirit among Catholic Pentecostals," ibid. 18 (1977) 134–147; "Testimony as a Commitment Mechanism in Catholic Pentecostal Prayer Groups," JScStRel 16 (1977) 165–168. D. O. MOBERG, *The Great Reversal* (rev. ed., Philadelphia 1977). R. STARK and C. Y. GLOCK, "Prejudice and the Churches," in C. Y. GLOCK and E. SIEGELMAN, eds., *Prejudice U.S.A.* (New York 1969) 70–95. R. A. WALLACE, "Bringing Women In: Marginality in the Churches," *Sociological Analysis* 36 (1975) 291–303. K. WESTHUES, "The Church in Opposition," *Sociological Analysis* 37 (1976) 299–314. R. WUTHNOW, "Recent Patterns of Secularization: A Problem of Generations?" AmSocRev 41 (1976) 850–867.

[H. M. NELSEN]

RELIGION, TEACHER OF

Anyone entrusted with religious instruction and formation of others may be called a teacher of religion (12:268). Present catechetical literature and ecclesial documents, e.g. Vatican Council II and the 1971 General Catechetical Directory (GCD) use the term "catechist" as synonymous with religion teacher, but generally the term "catechist" means a religion teacher working outside of schools in such catechetical programs as CCD, in adult catechumenate, and missionary catechesis. The theologian is teacher of religion but in a specific and more academic sense (*see* THEOLOGIAN).

Who are Teachers? The postconciliar era is characterized by its awareness of the special conciliar recognition of the Christian parents as the "first and foremost" educators of their children (*Gravissimum educationis* 3; see also GCD 75). Outside of the family there is now a much larger enrollment of lay people in the catechetical apostolate, especially as teachers of religion in Catholic schools. The replacement of the religious by lay teachers requires special care for the right selection and solid formation of catechetical personnel. In the case of religious who teach religion, selection and formation is to a high degree assured and provided by their community. Unquestionably lay persons can do excellent work as teachers of religion. The problems are: how to interest and select the necessary number of truly dedicated laity able and willing to serve as religion teachers; how to provide them with a thorough spiritual and professional formation; and how to assure their further vocational progress and perseverance.

Each state of life, that of the lay Christian and of the religious, has its special advantages for the catechetical service; the lay catechist has above all a particular power of witness to Christian life within the world of today to which most students are called. But it cannot be expected that lay catechists with little or no spiritual formation can share their faith with the same religious vigor as religious, with their long and intensive spiritual training. Yet what, in the present situation of universal and deep-rooted secularism is needed most, is exactly the religious depth and dedication of the religion teacher.

More than in preconciliar times now also all instruction by priests is viewed as evangelizing catechesis, his ordination conferring not only sacramental power but also a place in and obligation to the ministry of the Word. The priest's teaching within the Eucharistic Liturgy is to be considered as the most significant and most efficient form of adult catechesis.

The difficult and often critical religious situation of today demands close collaboration of all who work in the catechetical apostolate. A closer, more efficient collaboration of religion teachers with the Christian parents remains one of the most pressing catechetical problems.

Inspired by the ecclesial insights of Vatican II, postconciliar pastoral theology shows deeper awareness of the community dimension of the entire ministry of the Word. Typical in this regard is the very definition of catechesis in the GCD characterizing catechesis as "ecclesial action" (21). It is finally the action of the risen Lord who acts through and within his saving community.

Although not all Christians are supposed to work as religion teachers in the technical sense, Vatican II stressed with unprecedented emphasis that all Christians are to be "fellow-workers of the truth" (3 Jn 8). Together with the clergy "they play a very important role" in the ministry of the Word, a contribution which "does not consist only in the witness of one's way of life (*Apostolicam actuositatem* 6).

Ministry of the Teacher. The task of the religion teacher is to "lead both communities and individual members of the faithful to maturity of faith" (GCD 21). By this a threefold aspect of the ministry of the Word receives its merited new emphasis.

(1) *Guidance to Authentic Faith.* Faith here means, of course, not just the assent to "truths revealed by God" (Baltimore Catechism), but man's free response to God's loving challenge to a life of friendship with him. In the words of Vatican II, by such faith man "entrusts his whole self freely to God offering the full submission of intellect and will (*Dei Verbum* 2 and 5). Guidance to such faith obviously requires from the religion teacher the correct presentation of God's message of salvation as transmitted by the Church. It categorically excludes any substitution of the catechist's private religious opinions for and any confusing mingling of them with the revealed Word of God. Faithful transmission, however, demands more than correct teaching on the particular doctrines of faith. Being God's heralds religion teachers must concentrate above all on the central idea of the message entrusted to them and present particular doctrines according to their due place in God's loving invitation to a new life in and with Christ. The very term "religion *teacher*" may easily mislead to a harmful overemphasis on the task of imparting solid religious knowledge. However important that may be, biblical and conciliar understanding

of faith as total surrender to God in trust and love demands emphasis upon the other dimensions of the task. As heralds religion teachers not only teach but proclaim God's message of salvation, in order to convince listeners of its all-importance for man. As witnesses they share their own faith experience with others, leading them to a genuine experience of faith. As educators they form others, guiding them to a life of authentic faith. The example, living word, and personal guidance of the religion teacher is much more important than texts or other tools (see GCD 71). Audiovisuals, in particular, must never be misunderstood as substitutes for the indispensable personal contribution of the religion teacher.

(2) *Aiming at Mature Faith.* Earlier catechesis as well as preconciliar ecclesial directives on it, was too child-centred. Catechesis did not sufficiently take into account the fact that faith is supposed to grow to a maturity which cannot be reached during childhood, children being incapable of the true insight and commitment indispensable for maturity of faith. Religious education that confines itself to children is bound to fail. Therefore "catechesis for adults . . . must be considered the chief form of catechesis. All the other forms, which are indeed necessary, are in some way oriented to it" (GCD 20).

(3) *Building up a Community of Faith.* "In catechesis, especially in that of adolescents and adults, the importance of the group is becoming greater and greater" (GCD 76). The religion teacher must lead the group to the genuine acceptance, expression, and experience of faith, he must form communities which give to the individual Christians the necessary inspiration and support for their Christian life.

The Religion Teacher and the Teaching Office of the Church. Catholic religion teachers consider all their catechetical activity as a participation in the teamwork of Christ, who continues his teaching office within and through his community. This conviction of faith challenges religion teachers to a willing integration into this community and its activity and to accept faithfully the directions Christ gives through the teaching office of the Church. The acceptance regards both the right understanding of the faith transmitted and the special way in which faith should be transmitted. Religion teachers will, of course, clearly distinguish different degrees of authority, but a lower degree of authority does not imply that its directions may be taken lightly. Obviously whenever the teaching office of the Church decides matters of faith the religion teacher is supposed to follow these directives faithfully. The main church directives for the catechetical work are now set out in catechetical directories (GCD 1971; National Catechetical Directory for the U.S., 1979).

Formation. A more adequate formation was one of the main demands of the catechetical renewal long before Vatican II. Church authorities were somewhat slow in realizing the urgency of this demand. The Council insists above all on a solid formation of missionary catechists (*Ad gentes* 17, 26). The GCD is categoric in demanding that ecclesiastic authorities consider the formation of all religion teachers "both lay and religious, and also of Christian parents" as a matter of "greatest importance" (15).

With regard to the kind of formation given to catechists the Council puts the main stress clearly on its theological and spiritual dimension, but also explicitly requires the study of catechetical method and pastoral practice. With the present situation of an ever more thoroughly secularized culture and widespread doctrinal insecurity and confusion, concentration on the theological and spiritual is more urgent than ever. But in order to succeed the formation must also give due attention to the human aspects of the catechist's activity as teacher and educator. The formation must help catechists to see and to accept catechetical activity as a real vocation; it must imbue them with deep respect for and love of the Church and willingness to accept her guidance. The doctrinal formation must enable religion teachers to distinguish clearly theological opinions, hypotheses, and interpretations from the essential content of the Christian faith and to see all doctrines of faith in the light of God's saving love with their relevance for an authentic Christian life. In their formation religion teachers must acquire a solid understanding and a deep practical appreciation of Scripture and liturgy. They must also learn to use valid contributions of contemporary theology for a better understanding of the Christian faith. Until now there seems to be acute danger that the strictly spiritual aspect of catechetical formation is not yet given its due emphasis. Especially in this age, mature faith which shapes all the activity of the catechist and confers on it its apostolic dynamism cannot simply be supposed. Religion teachers who are not men and women of prayer simply cannot lead others to a living and lasting personal encounter with God.

See also CATECHESIS; CATECHISTS, MISSIONARY.

Bibliography: It is significant for the present situation of catechetics that, in spite of the abundance of present catechetical literature, books and essays on the religion teacher as such are rare, most especially with regard to personal and spiritual formation.
Congregation for Catholic Education, *General Catechetical Directory* (Washington, D.C. 1971) 108–124. NCCB, *National Cathechetical Directory for the Catholics of the United States* (Washington, D.C. 1978) 166–186. D. CONWAY, *Forming Catechists* (New York 1966). J. HOFINGER, *You Are My Witnesses* (Huntington, Ind. 1977).

[J. HOFINGER]

RELIGION, VIRTUE OF

Unless worship is a truthful reflection of life and a faithful expression of spiritual vitality, it is empty ritual. The virtue of religion gives worship its inner dynamism by cultivating reverence, devotion, and prayer (12:270). Since Vatican Council II there has been a continuing shift from a focus on the essences of things, to an existential outlook. Man has become the center of his universe and the value of things is often measured critically and humanistically. In this age a virtue claiming something as due in justice to God is often unpopular; yet the deterioration of the moral edifice reflects the neglect of reverence for God.

One task of the Church today, therefore, is to rediscover the meaning of the virtue of religion *for us*. Perhaps an appreciation of the virtue's humanizing effects will help to give it more importance. Sacrifice is the most important act of the virtue of religion because it symbolizes the total gift of oneself to God. Vatican II sees the Sacrifice of the Mass (Liturgy) as the summit and the source of the Christian life (*Sacrosanctum Concilium* 10). Because the Christian Sacrifice is the saving action of Christ and the Church, it is of surpassing excellence and effectiveness (ibid. 7). Liturgy is impor-

tant, therefore, because it is the supreme moment of self-offering together with Christ. It reflects the Christian's life and activity for the neighbor, and expresses inner love and devotion for God. A Christian shares in the Sacrifice not so much because of the inspiration derived, as for the opportunity for self-surrender the Liturgy provides.

Vatican II also emphasized the need for both private and liturgical prayer (ibid. 12, 13); the one does not eliminate the need for the other. Rather they are mutually helpful and complementary, and are equally necessary. Many hope the popular *charismatic renewal will help restore the place of personal prayer, as the liturgical movement of a generation ago restored the central position of liturgy. Religion is the inner life of worship. A clear grasp of its importance and its generous practice will give fuller life to liturgy.

Bibliography: H. SCHMIDT, ed., *Liturgy in Transition. Concilium* 62 (New York 1971).

[E. FALARDEAU]

RELIGIONS, COMPARATIVE STUDY OF

"Comparative religions" is understood here in the broader, nondisciplinary sense in order to include some important contributions of the past two decades. While the concept of function, which focussed on the relation of religious phenomena to their social and cultural contexts, was a prominent tool in the study of religions throughout the first half of this century, in recent research it has been eclipsed by a concern with "structure," the logical relationships obtaining among religious phenomena within a specific context.

Though he did field work in South America, C. Lévi-Strauss, the leading proponent of structuralist anthropology, is interested primarily in the universal structures of the human mind. He seeks the unconscious framework of relations which underlies superficial facts. Lévi-Strauss characterizes primitive thought not by its intellectual poverty but by its demand for order, and has pursued the "logics of myth" in his four volumes of *Mythologiques* by showing "not how men think in myths, but how myths operate in men's minds without their being aware of the fact." His slighting of context has been criticized, but Lévi-Strauss' bold comparative endeavor merits serious attention.

Mary Douglas, though less concerned with universal structures, has illuminated the conceptions of order which inform beliefs about pollution and taboo in societies as diverse as those of ancient Israel and contemporary Africa. Building on the idea that "dirt" is essentially something that is out of place, she has shown that those beliefs "have as their main function to impose system on an inherently untidy reality." She also argues, in *Natural Symbols*, that particular visions of the social order will be expressed in characteristic attitudes toward the body in a given culture.

Like Douglas, Victor Turner proposes a theoretical approach which facilitates comparisons of a broad range of data. Enlarging upon A. van Gennep's observation that most rituals display a threefold structure of separation-transition-reincorporation, Turner has concentrated on the qualities of the middle phase. During that "limited period," all structures typical of daily life are suspended; the actors become a homogeneous group, and the feeling of *communitas* which the ritual engenders confirms both the underlying sentiment of essential equality and the necessity for role- and status-differentiation in society. Turner also discusses how particular symbols can be manipulated to convey ideological messages in *rites de passage* and other cultural situations.

Georges Dumézil echoes the concern with system in his work on Indo-European mythology. An adherent of *la méthode sociologique*, Dumézil has found a remarkable coherence of outlook in the mythical literature of ancient India, Iran, Italy, Germany, Scandinavia, and Ireland. He identifies as the principle of coherence the tripartite division of human and divine society into royal, warrior, and cultivator strata. Though the specifically Indo-European character of that ideology has been questioned, the main lines of Dumézil's challenging synthesis remain unshaken.

Among others in sociology, B. Wilson, through his studies on various contemporary religious movements, has influenced comparative studies of religions. Others might be mentioned, but those examples from several disciplines serve to confirm the persistence of a long-standing task for *Religionswissenschaft*. Despite its periodic claims to autonomy, it has always had and must continue to incorporate the findings of any discipline which seriously attempts the study of religions.

Bibliography: M. DOUGLAS, *Natural Symbols* (London 1970); *Purity and Danger* (London 1966); ed., *Rule and Meanings* (Harmondsworth, England 1973). G. DUMÉZIL, *L'idéologie tripartite des Indo-Européens* (Brussels 1958); *Mythe et épopée* 1 (Paris 1968); 2 (Paris 1971); 3 (Paris 1973). E. LEACH, *Claude Levi-Strauss* (New York 1970). C. LÉVI-STRAUSS, *The Savage Mind* (Chicago 1966); *Structural Anthropology* 1 (New York 1963); 2 (New York 1976). C. S. LITTLETON, *The New Comparative Mythology* (rev. ed., Berkeley 1973). J. Z. SMITH, "Birth Upside Down or Right Side Up?" *History of Religions* 9 (1970) 281–303; "Adde Parvum Parvo Magnus Acervus Erit," *History of Religions* 11 (1971) 67–90. V. TURNER, *The Forest of Symbols* (Ithaca, N.Y. 1967); *The Ritual Process* (Chicago 1969); *Dramas, Fields, and Metaphors* (Ithaca, N.Y. 1975). B. WILSON, *Sects and Society* (London 1961); *Magic and the Millennium* (London 1973); *Contemporary Transformations of Religion* (London 1976).

[E. V. GALLAGHER]

RELIGIOUS (MEN)

Changes in religious communities of men since Vatican Council II have been extensive and profound. A once coherent form of life, convincing rationale, and effective ministry have given way to significant developments in all three areas. Religious life, which is described in the Code of Canon Law as "a stable form of life in the Church" (CIC c. 482), has been modified considerably.

Adaptations. Immediately after Vatican II, most religious congregations took seriously the directive of the Decree on the Renewal of Religious Life that all aspects of their lives and state were to be examined and where necessary adapted to the needs of the times (*Perfectae caritatis* 2). Religious communities utilized more readily than before the methods and insights of the secular disciplines to help them in the process of adaptation: management theory and practice, personnel practices, sensitivity training for individuals and communities, communications seminars, psychological and sociological workshops for both superiors and rank-and-file members. These complemented the traditional resources of spiritual *retreats, which now took on such new forms as the directed private retreat, the *prayer of centering, the intensive spiritual journal (*see* PRAYER), and workshops on prayer, community and ministry.

The extensive experimentation so characteristic of the years immediately after the Council has lessened, but some of the changes introduced at that time have now become quite widely accepted. Diversity in prayer forms is almost the norm; varied ministry, such as care for migrants, housing, political action, or care for those addicted to drugs, is common, even within a single congregation that formerly might have been engaged in one dominant corporate ministry. While rather large communities of men religious had become a norm in the U.S. up to the 1950s, small groupings of religious, often living in residential neighborhoods, are now not unusual.

Present Status. Religious life among American men today is characterized by diversity, informality, personalism, and a search for authenticity. No longer is there an ideal model of the monk, for there is such an emphasis on the autonomy of the person, for the genuine personal response, that there is little of the communal image still discernible. Community life is not routinized or dominated by external requirements of place, dress, and ministry. Rather, it strives to accentuate the human needs and gifts of each of its members, living together in community for the mutual support that community provides. More and more there is a distinction drawn between the community as the home of the religious and the community as the corporate group engaged in a particular ministry.

In the case of the active religious orders, there has been a marked lessening of the influence of formal, traditional community prayer, but this factor has been balanced in many cases by the development of newer prayer forms marked by diversity, spontaneity, and brevity (*see* PRAYER, COMMUNITY). There has been a decreased interest in the divine office and the liturgy as prayer forms, but an increase in scriptural prayer services and various forms of shared prayer. In general, however, religious men as a group do not seem to have been a major influence in the *charismatic prayer movement in the Church.

Contrasting attitudes towards the process of renewal created a noticeable polarization in many institutes after Vatican II. At present these tensions have lessened considerably, except in a few isolated cases. The crisis of authority has eased, also, with the general acceptance of the concept of shared responsibility of all members of the community.

Problems. The present condition of religious life of men, at least as far as externals are concerned, is cause for concern. The flood of those leaving the life has subsided, but a certain number continue to leave. The number of religious in particular congregations has almost universally decreased and the average age of members continues to advance; new members are not sufficiently numerous to offset these trends. The diversity of ministries, some of which were ill-conceived and poorly planned and therefore doomed to failure from the start, has lessened the visible impact of particular congregations.

New members tend to be far fewer than before and considerably older upon entry. This latter fact is explained in part by the policy of most congregations not to accept candidates as young as they once did (*see* VOCATION, RELIGIOUS). Although life in community and a commitment to prayer are the stock-in-trade of religious congregations of men, and these very elements are frequently spoken of as having special appeal to young people today (witness the success of some of the Eastern religious groups), it has not followed that vocations to religious communities of men have been as numerous as previously was the case.

Search for a Model. Both the Church itself and religious life in the Church can be explained, interpreted, and understood by means of models which, since Vatican II, have been in a state of development. Models of the Church seem clearer than those of religious life. Indeed, one of the more serious lacks experienced by many is that of a theology of religious life which preserves the traditional values, especially the importance of the vows, and integrates the newer experiences of religious men since Vatican II. Among the more successful of the models of religious life are those which see it as a prophetic community or as a Gospel-centered form of life in the Church.

In the prophetic image the religious stands as a sign of contradiction to the mores and value-judgments of the times; proclaims instead a reliance on truths of revelation that are disconcerting, challenging, as demanding as the prophets of old.

In the Gospel-community image the religious community is viewed as a group especially committed to reading and reflecting on the Word of God and finding appropriate community expression of its response to this meditation in life style, proclamation, and ministry to the People of God.

Although these and other models offer promise, they individually or taken as a whole do not yet meet wide acceptance. Religious life today is an unsolved riddle in the life of the Church; the more so in that few religious are satisfied with current explanations and many continue to search out one or more models that will reflect their own experiences in religious living.

Developments of the past ten years among religious men in the U.S. have caused some to question the viability of this form of life in the Church for the future. There is reasonable cause for concern, for the related factors of advancing age and fewer new members offer matter for serious reflection. Some find grounds for optimism in the Vatican II expression that religious life "while not entering into the hierarchical structure of the Church, belongs undeniably to her life and holiness" (*Lumen gentium* 44). Others see the renewal of the life of prayer, a more significant ministry, and a more authentic community life as harbingers of better times.

Bibliography: D. A. FLEMING, ed., "Hope-filled Deeds and Critical Thought: The Experience of U.S. American Men Religious and Their Need to Reflect on It," Crux (Oct. 17, 1977).

[W. QUINN]

RELIGIOUS (WOMEN)

Probably no one element of religious life has changed more in the years since Vatican Council II than that which can be referred to as "life style." While the term is a simple one, it arises out of all those elements, both complex and profound, which motivate and energize women religious individually and which give meaning and substance to the life they share with each other. The concept has been shaped by new understandings of authority/obedience; current studies on the development of the human psyche; the dedicated pursuit of collegiality and subsidiarity in their lived experience; a new consciousness of the role of women in

the Church and in society; and a rededication to Gospel values.

In the years before Vatican II, the life style of most women religious could be described almost identically. A fixed horarium included early rising, early Mass, silence at meals, a common recreation period, prescribed common prayers and spiritual reading, solemn silence and early retiring. Sisters were identified by the habit they wore; their congregations, by the particular apostolate of the members. Sisters lived in convents on the same property as the hospitals or schools they staffed; they obeyed the person designated as "superior." Lay persons were rarely admitted to the convent beyond the chapel and parlors; sisters were seldom engaged in activities unrelated to their primary work. The life style, in general, reinforced the concept learned in novitiates that sisters were not "of the world."

In the years following Vatican II, women religious responded to the challenge of the Decree on the Appropriate Renewal of Religious Life, "adaptation and renewal in the spirit of their founding inspiration" (*Perfectae caritatis* 2). The effects of that challenge have been both spiritual and structural renewal resulting in a new vitality among sisters apparent in the expansion of their ministries and in their community life as well.

Community and the Counsels. Community, as a value, has been reaffirmed, although the goals and priorities of local communities differ widely. Communities tend to be smaller than in the past and in those circumstances where large numbers of sisters live together, they usually gravitate to smaller groups for prayer and support. Many sisters continue to live in convents, although small groups may be found living in apartments or rented houses. Personal and/or apostolic reasons for such innovative living-arrangements are recognized and honored by most congregations of women religious. One may also expect to find living together sisters associated with the local school or hospital and other sisters who work in neighboring parishes, diocesan offices, or outside the institutional Church as advocates for social justice. A phenomenon of the postconcilliar period is the intercommunity living situation that brings together members of several congregations of women religious and, occasionally, a lay volunteer or two who share common goals and values with the sisters.

Through their consecrated celibacy, women religious witness to a fullness of life in Christ which overflows into a sharing of life with others. They are therefore called to grow in their capacity for friendship with women and men whose lives touch and enrich their own. The convents of today are more recognizable as homes. Community rooms have become living rooms, open to friends and co-workers for recreation and meetings, and frequently are havens for the dejected and despairing among those to whom the sisters minister. Unused portions of some convents have been changed into parish offices and other facilities, thereby increasing the potential for activity within the once sacrosanct quarters of the sisters. Many sisters, in addition to involvement in their primary work, exercise leadership in interfaith efforts for social justice and in professional organizations. An expanded vision of the mission of the Church and participation in it has led others into more assertive roles, seeking a voice in those decisions which affect their lives as women of the Church.

A growing imitation of Christ as poor continues to be a common aspiration among the women who follow him today. New understandings of the vow of poverty in terms of simple living have become apparent in the life style of sisters as the witness of frugality gains acceptance. Such a witness offers a countervalue to the consumer society in which they live. Sisters aspire to greater simplicity as they deepen their understanding of what it means to "follow Christ," not only in the service which they give, but in the manner in which they live. A cause for tension within many sisters is the practical need frequently to request higher stipends in order to provide adequate care of elderly sisters, while at the same time they themselves espouse a life style of living on less, a paradox not readily understood by the casual observer.

New insights into the development of the human psyche and recognition that choice is essential to human existence, have influenced the understanding of obedience and authority with resultant changes evident in the manner of living in community. Sisters, reaffirming their commitment to do God's will, recognize that this is made known through a variety of voices and circumstances. Therefore the role of superior has undergone considerable revision as collegiality and subsidiarity are seriously practiced. Religious congregations continue to experiment with new or modified forms of authority both in their governmental structures and in the community life of local groups of sisters (*see* RELIGIOUS SUPERIORS).

Prayer Life. The impact of Scripture study and the renewed interest in prayer and meditation, so apparent among Christians and non-Christians alike, have had their influence in the lives of women religious as well. In addition to community prayers, many sisters participate regularly in shared prayer groups with the local communities and with the wider communities of parish or charismatic groups. Sisters take advantage of many options for the Eucharist when these are offered within their own or neighboring parishes and frequently are leaders in planning meaningful worship. Meditation and spiritual reading, formerly done in common and in prescribed places, are now done individually at the sister's convenience and in the place she finds most conducive to contemplation. The long prescribed annual retreat has become a more integrated part of the daily life of women religious as many participate in an individually directed retreat and prolong that experience through prayer and reflection on its content during the course of the year. Gaining increasing respect among women religious, as the pace of life has intensified, are Asian modes of meditation and popular interest in them has progressed from fad to serious practice for many sisters (*see* PRAYER).

Manner of Dress. While contemporary women religious would agree that they are to be witnesses of the Good News of Jesus Christ in both their service and in their manner of life, they are not agreed that a distinctive habit is necessarily the sign of their witness, as evidenced by the greater rarity of religious garb. Sisters who wear contemporary dress hold that their foundresses wore the simple dress of their day and that the way one lives her life, rather than anything she might wear, is the sign that she is committed to Gospel values. Some wear pins or rings symbolic of their commitment or to identify them as members of a particular congregation.

A number of sisters continue to value the habit as sign, but have substituted for the long habit a uniform type of street-length dress, with or without a veil. Still others retain the traditional habit. There is more to habit, however, than sign value. The choices made to wear or to lay aside a distinctive dress can indicate some basic differences in the theology of religious life prevalent among congregations of women religious—one example only of the growing pluralism which is found within the Church today.

In the years since Vatican II, women religious have learned that they are continually being formed and reformed by Jesus Christ and by their sisters and brothers in Christ. This ever-in-process formation fosters a religious life which indeed reflects the living organism of a renewed Church, the People of God.

Bibliography: P. ARUPE, "The Unarguable Witness of Austerity," Origins 7 (1977) 417–423. L. CADA and R. FITZ, "The Recovery of Religious Life," RevRel 34 (1976) 690–718. J. CHITTISTER, *Climb Along the Cutting Edge* (New York 1977). M. COLGAN, "Nuns and the Women's Movement," Origins 4 (1975) 593–596. J. K. DOYLE, *Choose Life*, Leadership Conference of Women Religious Publication (Washington, D.C. 1977). G. FOLEY, "Crisis and Opportunity in Religious Life," Origins 6 (1976) 219–223. J. M. R. TILLARD, *A Gospel Path* (Brussels 1975).

[J. K. DOYLE]

RELIGIOUS, CONSTITUTIONS OF

Vatican Council II, in its Decree on the Appropriate Renewal of the Religious Life, stipulated that "the way in which communities are governed should also be re-examined in the light of standards adapted to the physical and psychological conditions of today's religious, and also, to the extent required by the nature of each community, to the needs of the apostolate, the requirements of a given culture, the social and economic circumstances anywhere.... For this reason, constitutions, directories, custom books ... and similar compilations are to be suitably revised and brought into harmony with the documents of this sacred Synod" (*Perfectae caritatis* 3).

Ecclesiae Sanctae. The precise procedure whereby this revision of religious constitutions (12:276) is to be effected is contained in part I of section II of Pope Paul VI's motu proprio, *Ecclesiae Sanctae*, Aug. 6, 1966. The revision of the constitutions cannot affect the purpose, nature, or character of the institute. As a rule, such change cannot comprise the common law of the Church but some experiments contrary to the common law have been authorized by the Sacred Congregation for Religious and Secular Institutes (see, e.g. Bouscaren-O'Connor 6, 7 and Suppl on canon 593). Primarily, then, the revision of the legal norms of constitutions is limited to the disciplinary provisions that have their existence totally and solely from the constitutions.

Contrary to the pre-Vatican II norms which prohibited textual citations from Scripture, the Fathers, and ascetical theology to be incorporated, constitutions must now have either a separate document (constitution) setting forth "the evangelical and theological principles concerning the religious life and its union with the Church" and another constitution listing the juridical norms; or one constitution giving first the evangelical and theological principles followed immediately by the juridical norms flowing from or based upon those principles. Consequently, constitutions today must not be "a text which is only juridical or merely exhortatory." Further, "the fundamental code of each institute should exclude whatever is already obsolete, or subject to change with the customs of the time, or corresponds merely to local usages" (Paul VI EcclSanct II 12–14).

Schema for Revision of CIC. The canons in the scheme for the proposed code of Canon Law on religious life give far greater importance to constitutions as the deciding norm in many matters of religious life. The schema readily gives the impression that the constitutions will be the ordinary rule and the canons of the code the exception. Almost no restrictions are placed on the provisions of the constitutions. This fact gives rise to trepidation, since laxity in one or more forms can very easily be introduced into daily living by incorporation into constitutions. In 1901 the Sacred Congregation for Bishops and Regulars (one of the predecessors of the present-day Sacred Congregation for Religious and Secular Institutes) drew up a set of norms to indicate both what was to be included and excluded from constitutions and served as the pattern for all religious institutes of simple vows. No such norms have been issued for post-Vatican II constitutions, with the result that an opinion has risen that communities can put whatever they want into constitutions. However, the Sacred Congregation for Religious and for Secular Institutes, in practice, is not supporting such belief, because, when reviewing proposed constitutions for approval, even on a temporary basis, it has made both positive and negative observations on the contents of such proposed constitutions (see e.g. Bouscaren-O'Connor 6, 7 and Suppl on canon 501). Whether or not a set of norms comparable to those of 1901 will result from such observations remains to be seen.

Bibliography: Bousc-O'Connor 6:286–287; 7:477–478. J. F. GALLEN, "Constitutions Without Canons," RevRel 27 (1968) 452–508; "Proper Juridical Articles of Constitutions," 27 (1968) 623–640; "Writing Constitutions," 33 (1974) 1323–1338; "Typical Constitutions," 34 (1975) 191–223; "Canon Law for Religious After Vatican II: Writing Constitutions," 35 (1976) 102–111; "Writing Constitutions," 36 (1977) 773–787. I. SCHAEFER, De religiosis (Rome 1947).

[J. I. O'CONNOR]

RELIGIOUS, EXEMPTION OF

The notion of exemption of religious (12:278) was somewhat narrowed by Vatican Council II in its Decree on the Pastoral Office of Bishops, so that it "applies chiefly to the internal order of [religious] communities" and not to "those things which pertain to the public exercise of divine worship (except where differences in rites are concerned), the care of souls, sacred preaching intended for the people, the religious and moral education of the Christian faithful, especially of children, catechetical instruction, and liturgical formation" (*Christus Dominus* 35, 3 and 4). Pope Paul VI's motu proprio of Aug. 6, 1966, *Ecclesiae Sanctae*, spells out the provisions of the Vatican II decree, e.g., all religious, including the exempt, are bound by the laws, decrees and ordinances enacted concerning the sacred apostolate and pastoral and social action; public use of all the means of social communication according to Vatican II's Decree on Social Communication (*Inter mirifica* 20–21); attendance at public shows; enrollment or cooperation with prohibited societies or associations; ecclesiastical attire; fund raising (Paul VI EcclSanct I, 24–28). However, Vatican II says nothing about revoking privileges that some religious institutes have in at least some of those areas. Moreover, Vatican II states that exemption applies "chiefly" to the internal order of

communities; it does not say "solely." Further, in his motu proprio, Paul VI stated: "Religious should zealously promote the works which are proper or peculiar to their institute, that is, those which with the approval of the Apostolic See were undertaken either from the very foundation of the institute or by reason of venerable traditions, and were afterwards defined and regulated by the constitutions and other particular laws of the institute, giving special consideration to the spiritual needs of the diocese and maintaining fraternal accord with the diocesan clergy and with other institutes engaged in similar work" (ibid. I, 28). This provision of the motu proprio certainly indicates that such works, since approved by the Apostolic See, are exempt from the jurisdiction of local Ordinaries. Using this same principle, the Sacred Congregation for Religious on Jan. 26, 1959 had defended the right of a religious institute to teach religion in its schools against an effort of a particular local Ordinary to place restrictions, even though the particular religious institute did not otherwise possess the privilege of exemption. Therefore, even today, the precise limitations of exemption of religious are still not clear.

Bibliography: Bousc-O'Connor 5, 6. J. D. O'BRIEN, *Exemption of Religious in Church Law* (Milwaukee 1943).

[J. I. O'CONNOR]

RELIGIOUS EDUCATION

Religious education is understood in several ways. As a generic term it serves as an umbrella for a variety of pedagogical activities associated in one way or another with religion, e.g., formation, instruction, socialization, schooling, moral development, catechesis, bible study, teaching theology. In recent years it has also acquired a specific meaning, describing a particular field or discipline of academic study which investigates the theory and practice of the activities mentioned. In this latter sense religious education is perceived as "a special work demanding focused scholarship, unique training programs, and personnel" (Lee 8).

Origins of the Discipline. Several factors caused scholars to take a more systematic and theoretical approach to religious education. By the end of the 19th century the public school, a firm support of the Protestant tradition in the U.S., was well on its way toward secularization. The burden of religious education, therefore, fell more and more on the family, Churches, Sunday and vacation schools, and similar institutions. Such Protestant writers as George Albert Coe, Paul Vieth, William Clayton Bower, Luther Weigle, Lewis Sherrill, H. Shelton Smith, and James Smart subjected religious education endeavors to a critical examination. In Roman Catholic circles a certain dissatisfaction with the conventional method of rote memorization of the catechism, the emergence of kerygmatic theology (8:169) in the 1930s, and the blossoming of the liturgical movement in the 1950s raised theoretical questions about the nature and purpose of religious education. The need to address theoretical issues became more clearly defined in the 1960s when The Catholic University of America, Marquette, Fordham, Notre Dame, and other Catholic universities began to offer graduate programs.

Theoretical Approaches. It is possible to identify four

theoretical approaches to religious education among contemporary Roman Catholic writers.

The Theological Approach. This accepts the premise of the General Catechetical Directory (16:53) that religious education is a form of the ministry of the Word (GCD 17). The nature and purpose of religious education are defined in terms of transmitting creed, code, and cult. Religion is carried on under the direction of the Church's teaching authority.

The Social Science Approach. The designation describes religious education as the process by which religious behavior is facilitated. It argues that religious education must be grounded in learning theory and the empirical research of the social sciences. It emphasizes teaching or instruction which is defined as a prime means "of promoting learning more rapidly, of helping to effect the retention of learned behaviors for a longer period, and facilitating the translation of learned behaviors into the personal lifestyle of the student" (Lee 8).

The Socialization Approach. A third approach sees religious education as a process of socialization. The term is used, by different authors, to mean: (1) the nurture of a personal religious identity and integrity; (2) the process whereby a person is initiated and assimilated into a particular religious community; or (3) the acquisition of a religious symbol system. The first understands socialization as it is used by psychologists; the second as in sociology; and the third as in anthropology, where it is also called acculturation. Religious educators who take this approach insist to a greater or lesser degree on all three aspects.

The Educational Approach. This theory holds that education is essentially religious. In this context education is carefully distinguished and sometimes totally dissociated from schooling. Education is understood as the systematic planning of experience for growth in human understanding. It is religious insofar as it examines the deepest meaning of the origin and destiny of the world and finds its expression in social gestures— symbols and behaviors.

Evaluation. The differences in these four approaches can be most readily seen in the way they define the relationship of religion to education. The theological model takes religion—creeds, code, and cult—as the content to be taught; its educational philosophy and procedures are largely unexamined. The social-science model puts religion and education in dialogue with one another so that religious education is responsive to psychology, sociology, and anthropology, as well as to theology. The socialization model takes creed, code, and cult not so much as the content but as the means whereby individuals and communities acquire religious identity in a particular tradition; they create what they represent. The educational model separates institutional religion from education so that while Christian education and catechesis are legitimate ministries of the Church, they are not properly speaking dimensions of religious education.

While this taxonomy is based on the works of contemporary Catholic authors, there are also Protestant scholars who advocate each of the above approaches. Whatever must be said of the philosophical assumptions and theories which underlie them, in practice these approaches are not mutually exclusive.

Bibliography: H. W. BURGESS, *An Invitation to Religious Education* (Mishawaka, Ind. 1975). J. M. LEE, *The Shape of Religious Instruction* (Dayton 1971). M. J. TAYLOR, ed., *Foundations for Christian Education in an Era of Change* (Nashville 1976). P. O'HARE, ed., *Foundations of Religious Education* (New York 1978).

[B. L. MARTHALER]

RELIGIOUS EDUCATION/CCD

The character and role of the program called Religious Education/CCD (Confraternity of Christian Doctrine; 4:155) is changing significantly during the 1970s. From being simply an alternative to the Catholic school as an instructional process confined to children and youth, the program now includes also informal learning experiences. Further, programs are being fashioned for such new groupings as the family and the handicapped, and are being designed to fit the special cultural and multicultural circumstances within which people live their lives. These changes have given rise to new forms of teaching and learning experiences along with new languages and new skills.

A Share in Ministries. The change in character and function of religious education/CCD coincides with its assuming a broader purpose in the life of church communities. It is developing new relationships with all the pastoral ministries in the Church. Past relationship with ministries was an effort confined mostly to the catechetical ministry for children and youth. The CCD program tended to be the whole of that catechetical effort and catechetical objectives were expected to be fulfilled by formal, religious instruction within a CCD structure. The current renewal of catechesis as a form of the ministry of the Word (General Catechetical Directory 17–18) is showing catechesis to be broader than formal religious instruction and to include all those activities of a given believing community that respond to inquiry about the faith-life of the community and prepare for incorporation into it. The final draft of the *National Catechetical Directory states that the components of catechesis "include sharing faith life, experiencing liturgical worship, taking part in Christian service, and participating in religious instruction" (39). Consequently, religious education/CCD as a teaching/learning process becomes one of a number of components of the catechetical ministry and, as such, finds that its objectives are not ends in themselves, but are means towards the broader objectives of catechesis. As a partner it functions along with other agencies of a community of faith in the work of receiving persons into the community and incorporating all members of the community ever deeper into its mystery of union with the Lord.

Religious education/CCD is not, however, limited to the ministry of catechesis. It is also a participant in the other forms of the ministry of the Word, e.g., evangelization, homiletics, and theology, serving to carry out their objectives. Likewise, religious education/CCD is a component of the ministries of worship and service, providing for awareness and understanding of these activities and for the development of skills in persons serving in them (*see* LITURGICAL CATECHESIS).

The NCCB pastoral message on Catholic education *To Teach as Jesus Did* sums up the role of religious education/CCD when it states:

The educational mission of the Church is an integrated ministry embracing three interlocking dimensions: the message revealed by God (*didachē*), which the Church proclaims; fellowship in the life of the Holy Spirit (*koinonia*); service to the Christian community and the entire human community (*diakonia*). While these three essential elements can be separated for the sake of analysis, they are joined in the one educational ministry. Each educational program or institution under Church sponsorship is obliged to contribute in its own way to the realization of the threefold purpose within the total educational ministry. Other conceptual frameworks can also be employed to present and analyze the Church's educational mission but this one has several advantages: It corresponds to a long tradition and also meets exceptionally well the educational needs and aspirations of men and women in our time" (To Teach 14).

Religious Education/CCD Directors. The current status of religious education/CCD is further revealed in the role of diocesan directors of religious education. Every diocese in the United States has an office for religious education and a person designated as director. A rapidly growing number of parishes likewise have a director of religious education. Directors are generally charged with providing a coordinated, comprehensive, and appropriate program of religious education for all groupings of persons that are within or being incorporated into local church communities. The number of groupings of people identified as unique and calling for religious-education opportunities specially adapted to their needs has increased significantly. The new groupings are categorized in various ways: by age, e.g., adults, senior citizens; by culture, e.g., Hispanics and Native Americans; by social units, e.g., the family, singles; by special needs, e.g., the handicapped, the mentally retarded.

Many of these groupings are being approached pastorally in terms of whole ministries and directors of religious education/CCD are being asked to provide religious education as a component of larger and more comprehensive ministerial constructs. These developments have generated the need to design models of religious education that are both appropriate to and effective for these newly forming groups and also are consistent and integrated with the other forms of ministry being provided for them. The current movement to relocate religious education/CCD within and as servant to the whole church community and all its ministries is regarded as a needed and positive advance; it does tend, however, toward fragmentation. Directors of religious education/CCD now have a greater challenge to maintain the integrity and substance of programs fashioned and implemented for various groupings, but also to correlate them with their more comprehensive pastoral ministries.

There is growing pressure on the current planning processes and organizational structures that create and maintain religious education/CCD efforts as these efforts take new shape and locations. The question of whether current planning processes and structures are adequate is being voiced more often and more loudly. It appears to be one of the greatest concerns for religious education/CCD and its directors in the immediate future. National coordination and assistance are provided by religious education/CCD, a section within the USCC Department of Education, which changed to its present name in 1969 (formerly the National Center of CCD).

[R. P. STAMSCHROR]

RELIGIOUS FORMATION

Religious Formation is a lifelong process or condition providing means for growth and development toward complete integration of the personality in relation to self, to others, and to God. Because of the human condition, all spiritual development is bounded and conditioned, enhanced and strengthened, developed and explained by culture and history. The religious person is of necessity submerged in the historical process; spiritual growth must take place within this process. This requires awareness, acceptance, and practice; that entails a structure, a plan, and a system to execute the plan.

Personal Integration. Formation considered as a process must involve a personal assimilation of the Christian experience. This assimilation demands an ever deepening knowledge of Revelation, which is rooted in sacred Scripture and the living tradition of the Church; and there must develop along with this knowledge the ability to reflect upon and to discern the apostolic realities and possibilities of each experiential situation. Experiential awareness is the key to formation: experience that is spiritual, personal, vivid, rooted in faith and nourished by prayer and celebration of the Eucharist. Apostolic growth will depend upon the quality of life and its environment.

Persons in their earlier years of formation in religious life need to come to know themselves and to accept responsibility for themselves, and to be in touch with authentic conditions of human life, of human needs, aspirations, and suffering. They must have a genuine experience of these conditions, of living and sharing with those in need. Religious communities are meant to be an environment in which real conversion or *metanoia* can occur, so that evangelical truth, simplicity, and loyalty to Gospel-choices can be made. Fidelity and faith in Jesus Christ must fashion lives and lead to true growth. Personal integration means an ordered progress to maturity in the life of the Spirit and in the apostolic mission of the Church, in order to give a total commitment to Christ and Church, and at the same time to develop a sense of personal responsibility and inner freedom.

Continuing Education. Life-long learning is that quality of life characterized by an openness to self, to others, and to the world, which facilitates learning at any time, anywhere, using whatever data may be available and appropriate. Persons in ministry need to maintain a growing competence in relating biblical and theological insights to issues of contemporary life. Persons in ministry need to grow in understanding of self as person, as minister, and as member of corporate and social structures. Persons in ministry need also to maintain a growing awareness of the changes and developments in society and of their impact on human life. Programs of continuing education are aimed at helping those in formation to recognize and to assist others to recognize their own gifts, in order to share more fully in the one ministry of the Church.

The continual process of formation is not a question of ages and stages, but a movement in faith through various moments of life, the deaths and resurrections of Christian experience and ministry. New approaches, models, and structures are needed to encourage persons to share their own sacred histories. Sabbatical programs, houses of prayer, pastoral training centers, and of courses in theology, religious studies, spirituality, and contemporary understandings of the behavioral sciences are all part of the continuing development. Concerns of this formation include values and belief clarification; prayer—mystical, communal, and liturgical; personality structures—relationships, alienation, permanence, and change, apostolic spirituality; the meaning of aloneness and loneliness; of mission, ministry, work, retirement, and of death.

Religious need to be able to create and to participate in communities that are formative. At the present time, religious women in particular are bonding with all other women, in order that the present women's movement may bring about true liberation for all, both men and women. Integration is the key-word in on-going formation—the integration of action/contemplation, of mission/consecration; of being/doing, which, in a soul informed by the power and presence of God, will reveal and express to all, by word and by work, a living faith in Christ.

Bibliography: Literature remains tentative as the process of renewal develops. A bibliographical collection: St. Louis University, Dept. of Theological Studies: Institute of Religious Formation, *Bibliography of Religious Formation Readings* (rev. ed., St. Louis 1977). Congregation of Religious and Secular Institutes, *Renovationis causam*, Instruction Feb. 13, 1969, ActApS 51 (1969) 103–120; tr., *On Renewal of Religious Formation* (USCC Publ. Office, Washington, D.C. 1969); Flannery 634–655. M. FARLEY and D. GOTTEMOELLER, "Commitment in a Changing World," RevRel 34 (1975) 846–867. Leadership Conference of Women Religious, Report: *Ongoing Formation of Religious* (Washington, D.C. 1976). D. M. STANLEY, *Faith and the Religious Life* (New York 1971). J. WALSH, ed., "Principles of Religious Formation," WaySuppl 34 (Fall 1977) 5–92.

[C. PRZYBILLA]

RELIGIOUS FORMATION CONFERENCE

The Religious Formation Conference, known from 1951 to 1976 as the Sister Formation Conference (13:261) through its National Office in Washington, D.C. and its sixteen regional conferences throughout the United States, seeks to be a forum for exchange and a center for communication and sharing of resources.

On Sept. 1, 1976, the sphere of service of the twenty-five-year-old Conference widened, when with its new name, the Religious Formation Conference enlarged its membership to include personnel, men and women, engaged in initial and ongoing formation, of religious and secular institutes and noncanonical communities. The Conference has as its purpose to assist the work of spiritual, professional, and personal formation of religious by developing effective formation personnel; by encouraging the formation of communities that can work effectively within the Church to carry on the mission of Jesus; and by providing to formation personnel a means to speak, hear, and act collectively within the Church.

The bylaws of the Conference define formation as "an on-going process by which the Holy Spirit forms the Christian through consecration to an evangelical way of life within the Church in order to work more effectively to build up the kingdom of Christ." Each person bears the primary responsibility for personal growth and formation, and each is also responsible for giving support to others as they seek to develop personal character and individual talents. The community facilitates the personal and professional development of its members particularly through formation programs.

Through the years the Conference has maintained its fidelity of commitment to initial formation, while expanding its efforts, especially after the 1969 instruction of the Congregation of Religious and Secular Institutes, *Renovationis causam* (ActAps 51 [1969]

103–120), to include continuing education and formation. With its interest in the dynamics of formation ministry, the Conference is concerned that a sustaining support-system be established and maintained within the community for persons engaged in this ministry. In addition, the Conference assists communities to develop an understanding of their own contemporary mission-spirituality (global mission) and to express that understanding in their present-day ministries.

[C. PRZYBILLA]

RELIGIOUS FREEDOM

In any current Catholic analysis of religious freedom the fundamental starting point must be the Declaration on Religious Freedom promulgated by Vatican Council II, Dec. 7, 1965. The document clarifies three issues related to religious freedom: development of doctrine, dignity of the person, the relationship between the person's rights and the common good.

Development of Doctrine. The acceptance of the meaning of the development of doctrine in the Constitution on the Church (see *Lumen gentium* 8) and of the modes of its expression in the Decree on Ecumenism (*Unitatis redintegratio* 11–12) made the Council comfortable in its acceptance of religious freedom. "Truth is to be sought after in a manner proper to the dignity of the human person and his social nature" (*Dignitatis humanae* 2). Implicitly this abandons the axiomatic position that error has no rights, which put an emphasis on truth as a possession of the Church to be handed out paternalistically. The position of *Dignitatis humanae* puts the emphasis on a search for truth worthy of personal dignity. The issue of religious freedom is taken out of the realm of moral, censorious judgment and put into the context of the rights in justice consequent upon the integrity of the person. The Church's commission from Christ is a mission to persons and it includes recognition of the truth possessed by all peoples of all cultures and the possibility of incorporating that truth into the life and teaching of the Church universal. The early Church succeeded in respecting the values and philosophies of those to whom it preached the Gospel; the rapidity with which the Church became Greek, Roman, or African in its first century is evidence. In more recent centuries the Church claimed a right to privileged status under the law because it is the one true Church established by Christ. During the most active period of European colonization, the Church was unable to value the philosophies and theologies or the cultures of the Orient, Africa, and the Americas. Only recently has there emerged a recognition of the deep loss this narrow view of reality has cost all the members of the Church, the descendants both of the explorers and the explored. The recognition of the presence of truth and holiness in other Christian Churches (*Unitatis redintegratio* 13–15), in Non-Christian Religions (ibid. 16; *Nostra aetate* 2), and among all men of good will (*Unitatis redintegratio* 16) indicates an essential meaning of religious freedom. Because of human dignity, the person's acceptance of truth must be interior "free of psychological coercion" (*Dignitatis humanae* 2). The right to integrity in accepting and in the way of accepting must be respected. Doctrine cannot be imposed. The Church's own proclamation of the Gospel is understood as compatible with every genuine assent to truth (ibid. 3).

Dignity of the Person. The dignity of the person made in the image and likeness of God requires that the person be free from coercion. A person cannot in justice be forced to act against beliefs held or be denied the opportunity to act according to those beliefs. Coercion, a violation of basic human dignity, in any area, but especially in religious choices, is odious to 20th-century people, who have developed a self-understanding based upon awareness of personal worth and self-definition (*Dignitatis humanae* 2).

The Church, not only claims the fundamental right of its members to religious freedom, but makes the same demand for all people (ibid. 4, 13). However, there are distinctions. The Church asserts her self-understanding as the one true religion. This statement of belief in no way waters down the Church's statement on a religious freedom based on the fundamental dignity of all persons, but rather, strengthens it. The strong statement of self-understanding by the Church makes clear its point of view and challenges others to assert theirs. To proclaim what is Catholic is not to demean what is not Catholic. Reconciliation is never achieved by disowning self, but only by being self-determined. What the Church is affirming is that inherent in human dignity is the right of each person to be self-determined.

Personal Rights and the Common Good. Religious freedom is a subset of freedom, and political freedom is closely related to freedom of religion. The role of Government is to facilitate freedom and to limit it only in the rare cases where the unmistakable common good is involved. The conciliar declaration contains the most important general principle for any free society: ". . ., the usages of society are to be the usages of freedom in their full range. These require that the freedom of man be respected as far as possible, and curtailed only when and in so far as necessary" (*Dignitatis humanae* 7). For the first time in any official document the Church proclaims the equality of all citizens: "Finally, government is to see to it that the equality of citizens before the law, which is itself an element of the common welfare, is never violated for religious reasons whether openly or covertly" (ibid. 6).

Pope Leo XIII, while continuing the traditional claims for the one, true Church, did make one important contribution to the development of doctrine. He led the Church to a "creative return to its traditions and sources, a crucial necessity if authentic doctrinal development is to take place" (see Carter 340). During some of the most violent days of World War II in 1941, 1942, and 1943, Pope Pius XII challenged societal institutions to respect the dignity of the person, and he challenged persons to live in responsible freedom. The whole focus of religious freedom had changed from one of moralistic judgments about abstract truth to rights in justice based upon the dignity of the person. John XXIII defended personal rights to religious freedom (*Pacem in terris* 14) and rejected the position that error cancels personal rights (ibid. 158).

Implications. While a culminating point on religious freedom, *Dignitatis humanae* has many unexplored ramifications for ecumenism and for Catholics themselves. The Catholic Church addressed the whole world in *Dignitatis humanae*, challenging all to good will. The Catholic Church admits for the first time officially that non-Catholics also have and are seeking the truth. Non-Catholics recognize that the assertion on the part of the Church that it is the one true Church established by Christ is part of its self-definition. Clarity regarding self-definition makes for good dialogue. Protestants can relate theologically to the statements regarding coercion, free response to the Spirit, and centrality of Christ. The contributions to clarification of the meaning of religious community will help Protestants with an aspect of their faith with which they are struggling. Non-Christians also can relate to the Church's statements regarding religious freedom. They had always resented that which was, from their point of view, the Church's hard line. No person of good will can be offended by conviction and free human choice.

The most unexplored area in which the proclamation on religious freedom applies is to Catholics themselves. It has always been a part of Catholic self-understanding that the Church is universal, but historical situations have made the Church culturally Western. All non-Western peoples have had to take on Western ways or reject the Church. They had to make the choice of giving up their own cultures and becoming transculturalized in order to become Catholic. Only recently has the Church, once more, recognized the values in cultures other than Western. It cannot be forgotten that following a religion is one of the most culturally-tied practices in a person's experience. Justice demands that cultural values and practices be honored in every corner of the world by the Church. Recognizing and implementing this responsibility which justice enjoins might be the single most important consequence of the Church's proclamation of religious freedom.

See also INCULTURATION, THEOLOGICAL.

Bibliography: M. CARTER, "*Dignitatis humanae*, Declaration on Religious Freedom," *Jurist* 36 (1976) 338–352.

[M. CARTER]

RELIGIOUS INSTITUTES, DEPARTURES FROM

The majority of religious institutes have experienced more changes in the decade following Vatican Council II than at any other time since their foundation. Perhaps the most dramatic and significant of these changes is in membership, particularly the decrease of membership through the resignation of religious from religious life.

Statistics. In 1952 statistics show that the number of women religious in the United States was 156,696. After a twenty-seven year span statistics reveal the number of sisters in the U.S. in 1977 to be 130,804. This is a net drop of 28 per cent from the peak year of 1966 when sisters numbered 181,421. The drop represents four times the departure rate of priests in the past decade. Moreover, the number of women entering religious institutes decreased 81 per cent between the period, 1966–1975. Studies have not yet determined what portion of decrease is due to deaths of members and what portion to resignation from religious life through either dispensation or termination of vows. However, in a regional sample study completed in 1974, communities attributed 62 per cent of their total departures to resignation and 38 per cent to deaths.

Findings. Although research shows the resignation phenomenon in religious to be due to many varied factors, some striking personal and institutional factors are emerging. In a survey of 1,400 former women religious, 69 per cent indicated that personal and interpersonal stress played the largest role in their decision; 54 per cent cited organizational stress. A major stress factor was the inability of these religious to challenge their previous vocational choices in a new way when the possibility for vocational changes came.

Resignation from religious life can also be attributed to the fact that the once clear norms and social roles for religious within the Church no longer exist. External conditions influencing this transition in religious life include major shifts in secular culture, which ultimately resulted in crises that affected the Church and its self-understanding. A prolonged period of external cultural breakdown and of internal organizational change and role disintegration weakened individual commitment to a way of life perceived as no longer stable or predictable.

The history of religious life reveals that the contemporary situation is not unprecedented. Religious life through the ages has had a cyclic configuration with periods of expansion and vitality succeeded by periods of declining membership and attendant loss of the impact of religious on church life. Major changes in both the life style and the mission of religious institutes have occurred at times of natural organizational growth and more so at times of major cultural shifts.

Ultimately, the combined factors of personal and organizational stress, normal and social-role disintegration, cultural shifts, and ecclesiastical reconstitution which account for resignation of religious are the result of value shifts within individuals which evade statistical measurement. History, however, offers the assurance that the valuing of the holy in man persists and finds an organized mode of expression.

Bibliography: J. M. BECKER, "Changes in U.S. Jesuit Membership, 1958–1975: A symposium Section 1, The Statistics and a Tentative Analysis," *Studies in the Spirituality of Jesuits* 9:1 and 2 (St. Louis 1977) 1–104. P. L. DOUGHERTY, "Religious Life and the 'Signs of the Time'," *America* 134 (1976) 156–158. H. R. F. EBAUGH, *Out of the Cloister, A Study of Organizational Dilemmas* (Austin, Tex. 1977). P. L. FITZ and L. J. CADA, "The Recovery of Religious Life," RevRel 34 (1975) 690–718. R. HOSTIE, *Vie et mort des ordres religieux: approches psychosociologiques* (Paris 1972). P. HUIZING and W. BASSETT, eds., *The Future of Religious Life, Concilium* 97 (New York 1974–75). M. M. MODDE, *Study on Entrances and Departures in Religious Communities of Women in the United States January 1, 1972–May 1, 1974* (Chicago 1974). M. M. MODDE and J. P. KOVAL, *Phase II, Women Who Have Left Religious Communities* (Chicago 1976). C. W. TAGESON, *Report on Study of Church Vocations Phase I: Status and Prospects* (Notre Dame, Ind. 1974).

[M. M. MODDE]

RELIGIOUS LIFE, ADAPTATION OF

Vatican Council II's Decree on the Appropriate Renewal of Religious Life indicates that renewal involves two simultaneous processes: (1) a continuous return to the sources of all Christian life and to the original inspiration behind a given community; and (2) an adjustment of the community to the changed conditions of the times (*Perfectae caritatis* 2). Five principles are proposed to guide these processes: the Gospel as the supreme law; the safeguarding of the spirit of the founder and heritage of the community; the fostering of the enterprises and objectives of the Church in all fields; the promotion of an awareness of contemporary human conditions and needs of the Church; the caution that changes will fail unless a renewal of spirit gives life to them (ibid. a–e).

In the light of this double process and of the proposed principles which should guide such renewal, an attempt may be made to articulate the experience of this past decade in order to assess the present and to look forward to some possible developments in the future.

Pre-Vatican II Background. As background, two important Roman documents need to be cited, as well as the growing professionalism regarding service roles within the congregations themselves. In 1900, Pope Leo XIII's apostolic constitution, *Conditae a Christo* (*Acta Sanctae Sedis* 33 [1900–01] 341–347) gave official recognition to apostolic congregations of women with simple vows. With rare exception, most active religious until that time had no such affirmation. In 1917, the Code of Canon Law included a section on religious life. The legislation, while attempting to safeguard and clarify the role of religious women, was extremely restrictive, strictly juridical, and full of unnecessary detail; it also imposed a number of cloistered elements which in the long run led to a loss of identity and spirit for these congregations. These elements were incorporated into the constitutions regulating the lives of religious women to the smallest detail.

Within religious congregations themselves, the need for professionalism in the teaching and health ministries in the 1950s led to the growth of the Sister Formation movement, a grass-roots initiative towards an integration of human, spiritual, and professional formation in order to gain a self-reflective awareness within religious congregations regarding their own obligation in service (*see* RELIGIOUS FORMATION CONFERENCE). At the same time, under the aegis of the Congregation for Religious, the Conference of Major Superiors of Women was established, drawing together the leadership of religious congregations in the promotion of common goals and objectives for a deeper understanding and preservation of their role in the Church.

On the eve of Vatican II then, religious congregations of women had already begun, in an initial way, the processes which would contribute to an articulation of their role in the renewing Church.

The Renewal Experience. *Perfectae caritatis*, as has been noted, challenged religious to renew a deeper understanding of the quality of their lives and the nature of their mission. Special renewal chapters to be held within three years according to the motu proprio *Ecclesiae Sanctae* (II, I. 1–6), which also gave further guidelines for implementation of *Perfectae caritatis*. In order to adjust to modern conditions experimentations in community life, forms of prayer, religious garb, religious formation, and government structures were undertaken by all religious congregations in varying degrees and with different rates of acceleration.

Perhaps even more influential than *Perfectae caritatis* on the understanding of mission was the Council's challenge ". . . that the joys, sorrows, hopes and fears of the whole human family were also the joys, sorrows, hopes and fears of the Church" (*Gaudium et spes* 1) and the more particular apostolic exhortation of Pope Paul VI, June 29, 1971, to religious themselves to answer the cry of the poor (Paul VI EvangTest 17). As a result, together with the Council imperative, from *Pacem in terris*, to read the signs of the times (*Gaudium et spes* 4; *Presbyterorum ordinis* 9) numbers of religious congregations diversified their ministries, in accord with a widening concept of mission. This resulted in large numbers moving away from strictly institutional and corporate apostolates. In this movement and development, religious appealed to their own reflected experience as well as to the spirit of their founders or foundresses whose original inspiration was, almost without exception, to answer needs not yet adequately met either by the Church or society.

The attempts at renewal and renovation however were not marked by an easy transition. Differing ecclesiologies operative among the Council Fathers themselves and evidenced within the conciliar documents were experienced by religious as a whole and within the individual congregations themselves. Conflicting ideologies tended to polarize the movement of renewal in the latter half of the past decade even as it did in the Church generally. Efforts at clarification brought painful confrontation with the official Church and generated tensions often as destructive as they were creative. As religious enter a second decade in the post-Vatican II Church, they do so with a realism and a hope born of an experience that has been costly but clarifying in defining their role in view of possible and continued developments.

Ecclesial documents and papal teaching on the Church's imperative that the promotion of justice is a constitutive element in the preaching of the Gospel (cf. Synod JustWorld p. 34), have opened new doors and wider vistas to the deeper understanding of the life and mission of religious in apostolic congregations.

International meetings with religious from Third World countries, greater involvement in social problems of justice and human development in the U.S., as well as more extensive collaboration with the laity in sensing the evolution and emergence of their role in assuming a responsibility for the mission of the Church, have further modified and sharpened a vision for shaping the future.

Possible developments and directions for the years to come will engage religious in areas that will continue to touch the quality of their lives and the understanding of their mission. In particular, according to the 1977–78 Focus goals of the *Leadership Conference of Women Religious, areas of highest priority and deepest concern will be: to articulate a contemporary theology of religious life; effect an education for justice that leads to systematic change; promote study, prayer, and action on the Women's issue; and move toward interdependence with other groups and persons.

[M. BRENNAN]

RELIGIOUS LIFE, RENEWAL OF

The directives for the renewal of religious life are contained in the comprehensive motu proprio of Pope Paul VI, *Ecclesiae Sanctae* (Aug. 6, 1966). This precise document lists the norms for implementing four decrees of Vatican Council II: those on bishops, priests, religious, and on missionary activity. Of the four groups of people involved, only the religious were given a direct command with a time table and a program for renewal (see Flannery). Within three years of the apostolic letter every religious institute was to have convoked an extraordinary general chapter for renewal. The precise purpose of this meeting was to rewrite religious rules and constitutions in accord with the decrees and directives of Vatican II. Furthermore, the manner of preparation and participation in the renewal program was also mandated;

the maximum participation feasible was to be fostered within each institute. Thus began a gigantic worldwide movement of religious men and women to review, revise, correct, rewrite, and reinterpret the fundamental documents of their institutes in the first phase of renewal.

Perfectae caritatis. The Decree on the Appropriate Renewal of Religious Life was very definite on the comprehensive nature of the renewal program. No area, no custom, no rule or regulation was exempt from its range. The entire manner of living together, of praying together, of governing and being governed was to be adapted to the changed conditions of the times, the needs of the Church, and the requirements of a given culture. This in itself was an enormous challenge. To it was added a further and even more demanding dimension: all the above was to be accomplished in the light of the sociological, psychological, and economic needs of contemporary religious, seen as distinct persons in the context of a total society, ecclesial and civic, to which they fully belonged. This in itself was a breakthrough. Religious, especially women religious, were accustomed to being treated and considered as a kind of faceless, uniform mass of people. Five principles were given to guide the renewal in each community: the first four related the community to the Gospel, to the Church and the world, and to the original inspiration and charism of the institute; the fifth firmly asserted the primacy of the spiritual in all stages of *aggiornamento* (*Perfectae caritatis* 2–3). Religious leaders were cautioned not to interpret the decree on religious life too narrowly but rather to see it in relationship to the other more significant renewal documents, and above all to the keystone of the entire reform, *Lumen gentium*, the Dogmatic Constitution on the Church.

To the credit of the religious, no other group in the Church responded to the call for reform and renewal as immediately, as vigorously, or with such extraordinary and costly effort. This was true of religious throughout the world. The result was unparalleled in church history. Previous renewal efforts sprang from one or another individual, charismatic reformer a Francis of Assisi or a Teresa of Avila. Now the entire religious population of the world formed a network of prayer and communication, of study and research in a gigantic movement to reinterpret charism, life, and mission. The aim was to respond better to a rapidly-changing world and a renewing Church caught up in a cultural revolution, the full dimensions of which are not yet discernible.

Facing a Crisis: Departures and Decline in Vocations. As this movement was just getting underway an unexpected and unprecedented phenomenon occured throughout the Americas and Europe that startled churchmen and laity alike within and beyond the Catholic Church. An exodus of both men and women from religious life occurred, suddenly and in the large numbers; this was coupled with an equally sharp decline in vocations, especially among women. Both the departures and the drop in vocations have been thoroughly examined and documented in a variety of studies (see Ellis, Greeley, Kennedy, Modde). The effect of the two phenomena on the renewal effort was not altogether negative. In fact the positive results may, in the long-run, prove the experience to have been most salutary.

The negative effects were quite immediate: the curtailment and/or abandonment of traditional ministries, particularly in the health-care and teaching fields.

Schools closed, hospitals were handed over to lay administration, clinics abandoned. An imbalance in age groups occurred, with an ever-increasing older population and a fast-dwindling number of younger religious. The maintenance of large institutions once built to house hundreds and now half empty, posed serious financial problems. The lack of personnel to respond to new demands in ministry, new needs in formation and in continuing education taxed administrations inside and outside the institutes. For many of these a severe crisis in leadership emerged.

The tension created by the imperatives for renewal on the one hand and the striking exodus and decline on the other produced wide disturbance. Severe disagreement and divisions sprang up within communities, particularly those less open to renewal and more conservative and traditional in attitude and practice. In many cases splits occurred, with large numbers of religious forming new, autonomous groups. In other cases smaller groups merged with other communities or completely disappeared. The picture of religious life at the end of the 1960s was rather discouraging. As one writer expressed it, "Whatever its causes, there is little doubt that present-day religious life in the United States is in a considerable state of confusion, searching, experimentation, modification, alteration, reaction, and plain inertia" (Quinn 282).

Rarely before in its long history had religious life been put so severely to the test. The experience was humbling. Recourse to prayer, reliance on the Spirit, and the marshalling of inner resources evoked a positive response. The work for renewal continued with an even greater persistence both in facing the most complex issues and in searching for reasonable solutions. The issues were substantial: the very meaning of commitment by vow in a final and perpetual bond; the rights of the individual; the creation of community; the use and abuse of authority; corporate identity and personal integrity; unity and pluralism; the choice of ministry; the limits of social and political engagement, and a stronger voice in church affairs. For women religious there was also the "nonissue" that was continually seen as a real issue in many quarters, the religious habit.

It is important to note that leadership both in identifying the issues and providing viable alternative solutions came not from among the male religious, as was usual in the past, but from the women. Particularly in the U.S., the Church witnessed a new and significant development as courageous women of the Church manifested a deeper perception of the Gospel imperative, a more sensitive concern for the needs of the poor, a keener ability to read the "signs of the times" and a capacity to respond with more daring and vigor than their male counterparts. The initiative was seen especially in the areas of government, formation, ministry, and social and political involvement.

Resources for Implementing Renewal. As the 1970s continued it was clear to all that the renewal of the religious life was not a question of rewriting rules and constitutions, of buttressing former ways with new arguments, but rather of fashioning a new life style in accord with a much needed development in the theology of religious consecration. It became clear that religious life as such was in the process of a vast transformation from a past social and ecclesial culture with its particular manner of interpreting the vows, of experiencing community, and of participating in ministry to a newer and different mode, based on richer insights both, and primarily, in theology and Scripture and also in the understanding of person through a reliance on the advances of the behavioral sciences in a new and different social and ecclesial context.

Two further perceptions emerged: the radical nature of renewal and the totality of change. The transition would be neither brief nor easy. Renewal itself becomes a continuing process, a way of life and growth. The earlier terms "experiment" and "experimentation" gave way to the more enriching and more demanding concepts of "process-development," "regular, evaluative procedures," "systems of accountability," and to an openness to new ideas in the effort at continuing revitalization and direction. Formation was no longer an experience of youth but a process for all ages.

New organizations on the national and international level were developed to carry the movement forward. The most important of these are the national conferences of religious, canonically constituted and recognized bodies officially representing all the religious of a country before the hierarchy of the nation and the Holy See. Both these latter maintain fixed liaison with the conferences, allowing for an immediate dialogue, clarification of issues, and greater cooperation on significant goals and purposes. While some nations have one single conference for both male and female religious—e.g., Canada, in the Canadian Religious Conference (CRC) and South America in the Confederación Latinoamericana de Religiosos (CLAR), the United States maintains two conferences: The Leadership Conference of Women Religious (LCWR) and the Conference of Major Superiors of Men (CMSM). In recent years increased collaboration between these distinct conferences, led to their first joint assembly at Cleveland in August 1978. The Cleveland meeting has come to be regarded as one of the most significant gatherings of religious in the entire history of the American Church. This is so not only because of the sense of unity, of purposeful direction, and of strength that was evident, but more significantly because of the commitment to an effective response to the Church's call to make justice a constitutive part of preaching of the Gospel. The meeting evidenced dedication, through personal and corporate activity and through specific programs, to the defence of the powerless, poor, and oppressed in the U.S. and in other parts of the world.

A further and very significant step to forward the renewal process has been the collaboration among the conferences of religious of South America, the United States, and Canada. These groups have held three meetings, the Inter-American Conference of Religious, at Mexico City, Feb. 8–12, 1971, at Bogotá, Colombia, Oct. 27–Nov. 3, 1974 and at Montreal, Nov. 19–25, 1977. As the Cleveland Assembly marks a turning point in the history of religious life in the U.S., so the Third Inter-American Conference at Montreal holds a similar significance in the development of cooperation and collaboration and welcome interdependence among the religious of all the Americas (see CRC).

Important among other national organizations that have given direct and significant help in the renewal for American religious are the Religious Formation Conference, the Conference of the Vicars for Religious, the Center for Applied Research in the Apostolate

(CARA), Washington, D.C. and the Center for Planned Change, St. Louis.

On the international level reference must be made to two organizations in Rome: the Union of Superiors General for men religious founded and approved by the Sacred Congregation for Religious and Secular Institutes in 1962 and the International Union of Superiors General for women religious founded and approved by the same Congregation in 1965. From humble and difficult beginnings these two conferences have become very significant forces for renewal in the Church and in religious life. Besides their continuing studies and research, they conduct annual seminars and study days. Through elected representatives they meet monthly with the Congregation for Religious and with the Sacred Congregation for the Evangelization of Peoples.

Effects of the Renewal. The effects of the renewal are to be found principally in these areas: government, formation, and ministry.

Government. Government has moved toward an increased democratization of structures from the generalate level to the local community and has involved principles of decentralization, subsidiarity, delegation of authority, and accountability. The decision-making process has been carefully constructed so as to allow the utmost participation. New forms of leadership have evolved that see the role of the superior more in terms of animating and inspiring than in commanding and directing. The term "superior" itself has been abandoned by many orders since it savors of an inferior or subordinate relationship between leaders and members in favor of such more contemporary terms as "president," "director," "moderator," or "coordinator" (*see* RELIGIOUS SUPERIORS).

Religious have learned much from the administrative sciences and have engaged professional services to reorganize their systems and train their leaders. Of primary importance is the introduction of pastoral planning. One of the most promising signs for the future is the effort being made to coordinate religious-life planning with diocesan pastoral planning. This, however, is at a very early stage of development.

Religious Formation. It was a foregone conclusion that the formation of future religious would become a matter of primary concern in the renewal program. The first major document on religious life after the Council, the Instruction by the Congregation of Religious, *Renovationis causam*, Jan. 6, 1969 gave detailed guidance in this significant area. At the present writing (1978) a new and further developed instruction is about to be published by the Sacred Congregation for Religious and Secular Institutes, based on a worldwide survey of the effectiveness of the earlier document and the need evidenced for greater attention to a formation that is at once genuinely human and soundly theological.

Ministry. In the area of ministry, the renewal of religious life has had its most startling effect upon the Church and society. Suddenly religious were discovered in new and unexpected places: in inner city ghettos, in migrant worker camps, in prisons, in halfway houses for the cure of drug addicts and alcoholics, in the halls of Congress as lobbyists for justice and truth, in centers of learning—conducting seminars and workshops for bishops and priests, in the center of parochial life—reforming structures and liturgies, in prayer centers as directors of the spiritual life, and in other settings, as servants for the larger Church, beyond the limits and interests of the local, diocesan, and parochial community. First attempts in these new directions produced many errors as enthusiasts wandered all too quickly into unknown fields without guidance or perception. Gradually, new groups of religious have been prepared to respond to new needs in Church and society with adequate screening and proper training. While safeguarding the right of the community to describe and accept corporate ministries, the diverse gifts and talents of the individual religious are increasingly recognized and scope for individual preference, in dialogue with community through increasingly-more-professional, personnel-board-systems, is now the accepted course. A key principle in the process is spiritual discernment, that is, the mutual effort on the part of the individual religious as well as of the administration to discover the will of God.

Community Life and Its Expansion. Two other phenomena need to be reported as products of the age of renewal. The first is the surprisingly large number of new initiatives in community living based on the Gospel. These new initiatives are of three kinds: entirely new groups without a previous experience of traditional religious life; groups of religious separating from a parent group to begin an autonomous existence; and mixed groups formed from former religious of many different congregations. The future of these new beginnings is not yet certain. What is certain is the presence of the Spirit calling to newer forms and expressions of the aims and ideals of religious life (*see* NONCANONICAL COMMUNITIES).

A second phenomenon is the new attraction toward the religious life among members of the laity and the willingness of religious to develop new forms of membership that engage men and women, married and single, in various degrees of effective participation in the life and ministry of the community apart from religious profession of vows. In some instances this participation includes the right to active membership in the chapters of the community even on the provincial and generalate level.

Facing the 1980s the religious in the U.S.A. seem more self-assured, calm and confident. The turmoil of the 1960s gave way to the arduous efforts of revitalization and restructuralization of the 1970s. Better acquainted with renewal processes, more confident in handling conflict, humbler before the Spirit, they walk among God's people grateful for the distinct gift that is theirs to be a prophetic voice and faithful servant.

See also MONASTICISM, CONTEMPORARY; NUNS, CONTEMPLATIVE; CHARISMS IN RELIGIOUS LIFE; NOVITIATE; VOCATION, RELIGIOUS.

Bibliography: CRC, *Religious Life Tomorrow, Donum Dei* 24 (Ottawa 1978). J. T. ELLIS, *The Catholic Priest in the United States: Historical Investigation* (USCC Publ. Office, Washington, D.C. 1972). A. M. GREELEY, *The Catholic Priest in the United States: Scoiological Investigation* (USCC Publ. Office, Washington, D.C. 1972). Flannery 624–633, 1033–37, documents on renewal (1962–74). E. C. KENNEDY and J. HECKLER, *The Catholic Priest in the United States: Psychological Investigation* (USCC Publ. Office, Washington, D.C. 1972). M. M. MODDE, *Study on Entrances, Departures in Religious Communities of Women in the United States, 1965–72 and 1972–74* (Chicago, Ill. 1977). W. QUINN, "American Religious Life Today," *Sisters Today* 43 (1972) 282–287 (report on seven regional workshops for men and women religious on renewal).

[C. J. YUHAUS]

RELIGIOUS RELATIONS WITH JUDAISM, PONTIFICAL COMMISSION FOR

The Pontifical Commission for Religious Relations with Judaism was established as part of the Roman Curia by Paul VI Oct. 22, 1974, under the presidency of Cardinal Johannes Willebrands. It is linked to the Secretariat for Promoting Christian Unity, but has its own secretariat, which produces a periodical and an information service in English and French. The purpose of the Commission is to promote and foster religious dialogue between Catholics and Jews, and is open to collaboration in this area with other Christians. It intends to be available as a consulting resource to other branches of the Curia whose collaboration it seeks in translating into reality Vatican Council II's Declaration on the Relationship of the Church with Non-Christian Religions.

The Commission produced *Guidelines*, which were made public in January 1975, for implementing the conciliar guidelines (ActApS 67[1975] 73–79; Origins 4[1975]463–464). While it condemned antisemitism and cited the Holocaust, Jewish spokesmen considered that it did not truly reflect the actual Jewish-Catholic dialogue in circles outside the Vatican. The Vatican seems unable to take to heart the relation between people and land in Judaism; to date the Vatican has not recognized Israel diplomatically. The Commission secretary did attend the recent meeting of the International Liaison Committee between the Catholic Church and Judaism (Venice, March 1977), at which Professor Federici of St. Anselm and the Urbaniana in Rome expressly excluded proselytism and conversion-seeking in dealing with Jews and Judaism.

Bibliography: C. ANGELL, "Catholic-Jewish Relations Since Nostra Aetate," *America* 133 (1975) 298–301. AnnPont (1977) 1044, 1476. L. BLUE, "Christians and Jews," *The Tablet* 229 (1975) 54–55. "Communiqué officiel de la rencontre du comité international de liaison entre l'Église Catholique et le Judaisme," DocCath 74 (1977) 421–423. "A Turning Point in History," *The Tablet* 229 (1975) 49–50.

[E. J. DILLON]

RELIGIOUS SUPERIORS

The history of the Church has witnessed a succession of controlling images of religious life, each tending to have its own way of understanding the role of the superior.

Historical Models. For the first monks of the desert, the superior was above all the spiritual director and teacher of holiness. This role was prolonged in medieval monasticism, but gradually the abbot came to be regarded more as a feudal lord, the father of the extended monastic family, to whom the monks owed son-like obedience and loyalty. In the mendicant orders, the superior was seen somewhat more democratically, as a "prior" or "guardian" who was to have a special pastoral concern for the community, but who was subject to periodic reevaluation by the community and who was expected to return to the ranks of the ordinary friars once his term of office expired. In Counter-Reformation foundations the religious was often conceived in military terms, as one ready and available to wage the earthly battles of the Church and superiors were correspondingly seen as "generals," who were to expect exact and disciplined obedience in the service of apostolic ends. In the period after the French Revolution, religious tended above all to be builders of Christian institutions, such as schools and hospitals, and superiors were looked on in large measure as the "administrators" and "directors" of these institutions, able to direct the religious in a life of service within ecclesiastical institutions. Of course these images tend to intermingle in every concrete situation and the evolution of the understanding of religious superiorship has proceeded more by addition than by simple replacement of images. But the accent has clearly shifted through the centuries.

Perfectae caritatis. Vatican Council II combines the theological tradition with modern psychological and organizational thought in its brief description of the role of the religious superior in the Decree on the Renewal of Religious Life. The Council recalls that faith presents religious superiors as "God's representatives," who guide religious "to the service of all their brothers in Christ." It asserts that obedience to superiors assures among religious "a firmer commitment to the ministry of the Church" and helps them "achieve the mature measure of the fullness of Christ." At the same time, the Council endorses the heightened sense of personal freedom and maturity characteristic of contemporary thought, exhorting all religious to "bring to the execution of commands and to the discharge of assignments entrusted to them the resources of their minds and wills, and their gifts of nature and grace." Thus religious obedience will "not diminish the dignity of the human person but will rather lead it to maturity in consequence of that enlarged freedom which belongs to the children of God." Superiors, for their part, are exhorted by the Council Fathers to "be docile to God's will in the exercise of office" and to "use authority in a spirit of service," governing the religious "as God's own children" and manifesting "the charity with which God loves them." Thus, assuring a high "regard for their human personality," the superior "will make it easier for them to obey gladly." Superiors are furthermore exhorted to "give the kind of leadership that will encourage religious to bring an active and responsible obedience to the offices they shoulder and the activities they undertake." Listening willingly to the views and concerns of the religious, the superior should "encourage them to make a personal contribution to the welfare of the community and of the Church" (*Perfectae caritatis* 14).

Contemporary Understanding of Religious Life. In these and similar comments, the Council was in fact acknowledging a movement toward a new controlling image of religious life. This new image can be articulated by describing the religious as a member of a "community of prophetic service." Because of the communitarian dimension, the religious ideally possesses a strong sense of the ecclesial community and offers the witness of close-knit communion in charity for the sake of the Kingdom. As prophetic, the religious will aim to proclaim in word and action the message of the Gospel and denounce both perrsonal and social sin in the concrete, adopting a life-style at variance with the norms of comfortable society in order to incarnate the Gospel message. For the sake of service, the religious will dedicate his or her life and energy to Church and world in response to constantly evolving needs.

This new controlling image views the superior as the "animator" of such a community of prophetic service, less one who unilaterally issues commands than one who seeks in a pastoral way: to keep the community aware of its mission; to offer encouragement, challenge, support, and personal interest in each of its members; to facilitate the confrontation between contemporary needs and the sources of the group's identity and effectiveness (Scripture, Church tradition, the charism of each congregation); and to work for the renewal and adaptation of the life of the community.

Characteristics of Superiors. Leadership offered by religious superiors in this perspective is marked by four characteristics: participation, communal discernment, subsidiary, and accountability. *Participation* consists in the involvement of all members, as much as possible, in making, carrying out, and evaluating decisions. *Communal discernment* is the community effort to discover God's will by considering situations and events in the light of faith and by sharing the results of this reflection in an atmosphere of prayer and discussion. The principle of *subsidiarity* places decision-making at the level which is most competent and closest to the point where the impact of the decision will be felt. *Accountability* requires openness and mutual responsibility between superiors and their fellow religious in a free and open flow of information and evaluation.

Certainly not all religious superiors work from the model articulated here, and quite evidently the present is still a period of transition from older to newer models. The focus on the religious superior as "animator" of a "community of prophetic service" seems to be taking hold ever more prominently, however, in the thinking of chapters, congresses and study-sessions of religious, and in publications on the theology and practice of religious obedience and authority since Vatican Council II.

It may be noted that this conception of religious superiorship is not necessarily tied to the holding of hierarchical office in the Church. The ministry of the superior within a religious institute is that of maintaining and promoting the fidelity of the institute to its charism and the adaptation and renewal of the institute in order to actualize its charism more fully. The most fundamental qualification of the superior, therefore, should be the ability to stimulate and actualize the efforts of the members to live out their charism. Thus, in institutes of both ordained and nonordained members, there does not seem to be any a priori and universally applicable reason for restricting the role of superiors to the ordained members (although in particular cases this restriction may be required by concrete historical and sociological circumstances or by the specific charism of the institute). In practice, many institutes have opened up the role of superior much more widely to nonclerical members since Vatican II.

Bibliography: G. CUSSON et al., *Community Spiritual Leadership* (Ottawa 1971). Q. HAKENEWERTH, *For the Sake of the Kingdom* (Collegeville 1971). D. KNOWLES, *From Pachomius to Ignatius* (Oxford 1966). L. ÖRSY, *Open to the Spirit* (Denville, N.J. 1968). R. VOILLAUME, *Religious Life in Today's World* (Ottawa 1970).

[D. A. FLEMING]

RESURRECTION NARRATIVES IN THE NEW TESTAMENT

Faith in the resurrection of Jesus of Nazareth as the divinely caused aftermath of his ministry and crucifixion that established him as Jewish Messiah and reigning Lord of the universe permeates the thought of the NT. Apart from the resurrection-faith, there would have been no Christian community, no NT, and scarcely any historical memory of Jesus of Nazareth. The NT contains a variety of literary formulations of this resurrection-faith: discourses, termed "kerygmatic speeches" (Acts 2.14–36; 3.12–26; 4.8–12; 5.29–32; 10.34–43; 13.16–41) that assert and substantiate the resurrection-claim; confessional formulae (Phil 2.11; Rom 10.8b–9; 1 Cor 12.3; Rom 8.34; 1 Thes 1.9–10; Rom 1.1–5) expressing the Christian community's conviction of the resurrection; a tradition of the original apostolic witness (1 Cor 15.3–5) not only testifying to the resurrection but explaining its religious significance; Christological hymns (Phil 2.6–11; Col 1.15–20; Eph 1.20–22; 1 Tim 3.16; 1 Pt 1.18–22; Heb 1.3–4) inspired by the resurrection-faith; prophecies of death and resurrection (Mk 8.31; 9.31; 10.32–34 and parallel places) ascribed to Jesus himself; and finally narratives concerning the resurrection that form the conclusion of each Gospel (Mk 16.1–8, 9–20; Lk 24.1–53; Mt 28.1–28; Jn 20.1–29; 21.1–23).

The resurrection narratives with which each Gospel closes contain material not present in the kerygmatic speeches, confessional formulae, traditional apostolic testimony, Christological hymns and Gospel prophecies. This narrative material invariably follows the same pattern—a visit of women to the tomb of Jesus followed by accounts of appearances of the risen Christ. The accounts of the women's visit differ considerably in detail and the appearance stories in each Gospel are entirely different from the same type of stories in the other three Gospels.

The differences between the resurrection narratives and other formulations of the resurrection-faith in the NT have presented a persistent challenge to NT scholarship. Vatican Council II encouraged biblical scholars to pursue their research for the purpose of bringing the religious meaning of the Scriptures into ever sharper focus (*Dei Verbum* 23). With this objective in view contemporary NT scholarship has undertaken a critical reassessment of the NT material bearing on the resurrection of Christ. This article concerns itself first with Paul's use of the apostolic tradition in 1 Cor 15.1–8 and secondly with the kerygmatic speeches in Acts. Consideration of this material supplies the actual NT foundation for the understanding of the resurrection narratives. Finally, the article makes an assessment of the resurrection narratives themselves.

1 Cor 15.1–8 and the Resurrection Narratives. From the standpoint of the chronology of NT literature 1 Cor 15.1–8 is the earliest written statement concerning the apostolic testimony to the resurrection of Christ. Writing about 54–56 A.D., St. Paul uses the apostolic tradition to address himself to the question of the resurrection of the dead, in which some Corinthian Christians had lost faith (1 Cor 15.12). He reminds them that the resurrection-faith that created their community did not involve the acceptance of a marvelous display of divine power simply in favor of the crucified Jesus of Nazareth by means of which a personal glorious afterlife was granted him. What was proclaimed to them and what they accepted was that Christ "died for our sins according to the Scriptures," i.e., Christ accepted the death of the cross as God's will for the remission of sins of which all peoples throughout human history are guilty, as the OT makes clear (1 Cor 15.1–3); and that Christ "was raised . . . according to the Scriptures," an event that occurred and was made known in time ("on the third day"), 1 Cor 15.4, i.e., the manifestation of the resurrection of Christ had for its purpose God's communicating to people like themselves that in Christ's death and resurrection he was carrying to completion his plan to save humanity from the disastrous effects of sin, of which death is the chief (1 Cor 15.54–57). To deny the resurrection of the dead as the beginning of an everlasting afterlife in the full integrity of the person is to remove all religious significance from God's act in raising Christ and to render Christian faith in his person meaningless: "If there is no resurrection of the dead, Christ himself has not been raised" (1 Cor 15.13), i.e., if the dead are not restored to a life with God as the final result of the remission of their sins, neither was Christ himself restored to a life with God, for it was the prevalence of sin itself that caused his death. If Christ did not overcome the sins that caused his death, he did not overcome death and consequently was not raised.

But according to the apostolic testimony Christ was in reality raised from the dead (1 Cor 15.20), the divine sign that he did overcome sin and death. That God in fact raised him from the dead was manifested to Cephas and to the Twelve (1 Cor 15.5). To this testimony of the original apostles, the Twelve, Paul adds a list of others who had a similar experience of the risen Christ through which they understood his overcoming of sin and death: the five hundred brethren (1 Cor 15.6); James, the administrator of the Jerusalem community; and "all the apostles," probably a different group from the Twelve, who because of their experience of the risen Christ were mandated apostles by the Twelve. Paul concludes by adding himself to the list of apostolic witnesses to Christ's resurrection and its religious significance, a fact of which, no doubt, he had already informed the Corinthians when he established their community.

NT scholars disagree as to whether 1 Cor 15.3–5 alludes to, or shows that, Paul was aware of the tradition of the empty tomb. His text certainly makes no clear allusion to this tradition. The fact that the Jewish conception of the human person required both body and spirit and that on this basis the Apostle would naturally have assumed an empty tomb, does not constitute an argument for a reference in 1 Cor 15.4 ("he was buried") to the specific tradition of the empty tomb in the resurrection narratives. It seems to be a necessary inference that in Paul's understanding the apostolic preaching of the resurrection of Christ did not incorporate the datum of the empty tomb.

Although in 1 Cor 15.5–8 Paul insists that the resurrection-faith is based upon the testimony of witnesses to the risen Christ, he makes no reference to accounts of the experiences of the witnesses. The Greek verb *ōphthē* used successively in each verse of the passage to designate a particular, personal, and special encounter with the risen Christ by Cephas, the Twelve, the five hundred brethren, James, all the apostles, and Paul can be translated "was seen by" or "appeared." Even if with the majority of NT scholars one prefers "appeared," one cannot deduce the nature of the appearances from this verb. The most that can be concluded from it is that the experience of the risen Christ to which the verb makes reference had both objective and subjective elements, i.e., the verb implies more than a mere internal visionary experience, but does not necessarily imply the same kind of objective presence of Christ that was the recipients' experience of the objective presence

of the historical Jesus. From the fact that the experiences of the risen Christ were apparently different in nature from their experience of the historical Jesus it does not follow that they were any less intense and meaningful than the encounter with the Jesus of the ministry. The effect upon Paul of his experience of the risen Christ on the road to Damascus (Acts 9.1–9; 22.6–11; 26.12–18)—the intensity of his apostolic life (1 Cor 9.1–27) and his steadfastness in the face of extreme hardship (2 Cor 11.22–29)—shows that the encounter with the risen Christ could be more intense and meaningful than even a daily relationship with the Jesus of the ministry.

The lack of reference to accounts of the appearances of the risen Christ in 1 Cor 15.5–8 indicates that the original apostolic proclamation of the resurrection did not include a narrative form recapitulating these appearances. Since in the final analysis the apostolic preaching of the resurrection rested on the authority of God (cf. 1 Cor 15.15), the recital of appearances of the risen Christ would add nothing substantial to the assertion of his resurrection. Such recitals would have diverted attention away from the risen Christ to the Twelve and the phenomenon of their experiences of him.

The Kerygmatic Speeches in Acts and the Resurrection Narratives. Lk-Acts contain the perimeters of the NT resurrection-faith without any attempt on the author's part to fuse them. Luke's Gospel ends with the narrative form of the women's visit to the tomb followed by appearance narratives (Lk 24.1–53). Although Acts 1.3 speaks in strong terms of the appearances of the risen Christ to the Twelve, the kerygmatic speeches (cf. the listing above) make no mention of actual appearances. Nor do they make any reference to the empty tomb.

The material of the kerygmatic speeches coheres with the Pauline formulation of the apostolic proclamation in 1 Cor 15.3–5. Each of the speeches contains the same central assertion: "God raised Jesus" (Acts 2.32; 3.15; 4.10; 5.30; 10.40; 13.30). In 1 Cor 15.4 the formulation in the passive mood ("was raised on the third day . . .") is the Jewish way of avoiding the use of the divine name while clearly attributing the action to God. Thus in the kerygmatic formulations of both Paul and Luke the resurrection of Christ is placed outside the sphere of human observation and investigation. Its reality is declared to be knowable only if one accepts it as a communication of God, its author.

In Acts Luke chooses the Greek term *martyres*, witnesses, to characterize the role of the Twelve toward the risen Christ. In the Greek world the term *martys*, witness, carried both the sense of "eyewitness," or of one who could testify to a fact from personal experience, as well as the meaning of expert testimony in the case where testimony concerned truths not empirically verifiable and requiring special knowledge or education. Utilizing this twofold meaning of *martys*, Luke depicts the Twelve as witnesses to the risen Christ from divinely given personal experience of him and from divinely endowed insight into the religious meaning of his resurrection (Acts 2.32–36; 3.15–23; 5.32; 10.40–43; 13.31). In 1 Cor 15.3–8 Paul combines *ōphthē*, "appeared," with use of the dative case for the persons to whom the manifestation of the risen Christ was made. Thus he clearly has the idea, though not the language, of witnesses to the risen Christ. When in 1 Cor 15.3 he observes, "I handed on to you what I also received" concerning Christ's death for sin and his resurrection, both according to the Scriptures, he is referring to the divinely endowed insight of Cephas and the Twelve as a group into the religious meaning of Christ's resurrection. In substance the concept of the apostolic preaching in the Lucan speeches and in Paul's formulation of it in 1 Cor 15 are in harmony. Whereas Paul, aiming in 1 Cor 15.1–8 to focus attention on the personal relationship created by Christ's death and resurrection between Christ and every human being, contents himself with a sweeping reference to the OT Scriptures as manifesting God's will fulfilled in Christ, Luke, whose purpose in Acts is to describe the apostolic address to nonbelievers, cites the OT Scriptures explicitly (e.g., Ps 16.8–11 in Acts 2.25–28; Ps 110.1 in Acts 2.34–35; Dt 18.15–16 in Acts 3.22–23).

Conclusion. According to 1 Cor 15.1–8 and Luke's presentation of the kerygmatic speeches in Acts, the resurrection-faith of the NT Christian communities originated from the authoritative assertion of the Twelve, of Paul, and of other apostles that they had been the recipients of a divinely caused experience of the risen Christ. The salient thrust of their testimony was that the risen Christ reigned in the realm of God, a vantage point from which he demanded the faith and adherence of humanity. The orientation of the apostolic preaching was toward the otherworldly status and power of the risen Christ. It did not direct attention to the actual experiences of the witnesses who were the recipients of God's self-communication concerning his action toward the crucified, dead, and buried Jesus of Nazareth.

Nonetheless, Paul's use of *ōphthē* and Luke's of *martys* to convey the connection between the apostolic assertion of the resurrection and the experience on which the assertion was based imply a relationship between the original preachers of the resurrection-event and the person of the risen Christ. This terminology of Paul and Luke has traditionally led theologians to conclude that a real experience of the risen Christ was the root cause of the apostolic testimony to his resurrection. The experience itself was the creative force that produced the resurrection-faith, first in the apostles, next through them in others who became the Christian community. In recent years some exegetes and theologians have proposed a different interpretation of the NT data: that it was the teaching of the historical Jesus that produced the resurrection-faith, either by way of theological reflection upon his historical teaching and person together with a factor of divine revelation somehow associated with the theological reflection, or simply by way of theological reflection upon the memory of Jesus of Nazareth and his religious significance. This interpretation of the NT data, while in some respects worthy of further discussion, is not as yet sufficiently well-founded or developed to be given serious consideration here. Its principal value is that it points to the usefulness of taking seriously the question of the interaction between the resurrection-faith of the apostles and their experience of the historical Jesus. It remains to be seen whether this particular avenue of research will succeed in contributing to the understanding of the origin of the resurrection-faith in the NT.

The Resurrection Narratives. It is already clear that these narratives as well as their component parts did not originate for the purpose of creating a faith-community centered on the risen Christ. As is the case with the four Gospels as a whole, the resurrection narratives are addressed to Christian communities whose faith in Jesus Christ is established, and, in the particular instance of his resurrection, on the ground of the apostolic testimony. The evangelists composed the four Gospels in order to support the faith of Christians. In general they have the same objective in the resurrection narratives.

(1) *The Women's Visit to the Tomb of Jesus.* The visit is narrated in Mk 16.1–8; Lk 24.1–10; Mt 28.1–8; Jn 20.1–2. The differences of detail in each evangelist's presentation of the women's visit to Jesus' tomb are remarkable. In Mk 16.1 they proceed to the tomb "to anoint him"; in Lk 24.1 they bring "spices" or "aromatic oils," but for what particular purpose is not stated; in Mt 28.1 they come to "view" or possibly "to observe" the tomb; in Jn 20.1 Mary Magdalene simply "comes" to the tomb. In Mk 16.3 the women are concerned about the difficulty of rolling back the heavy stone sealing the tomb, a detail not included in the other three accounts. In Mk 16.4 and Lk 24.2, when they find the tomb open, they enter it; but in Jn 20.1–2 Mary Magdalene, making the same discovery, does not enter it. In Mt 28.1–4 the women's entrance to the tomb is blocked by an angel, who subsequently, however, invites them to determine for themselves that it is empty (Mt 28.6).

The dress of the angels varies from one Gospel to another. Mk 16.5 describes a young man dressed simply in white—a figure unconvincingly explained by some NT scholars as a representative of the risen Christ or of a Christian neophyte; Lk 24.4 speaks of two angels in shining garments, while Mt 28.3 depicts a figure whose facial features are like lightning and whose clothing is snow-white; Jn 20.12 laconically notes the presence of two angels dressed simply in white.

The function of the angels varies in the four Gospel accounts of the women's visit to the tomb. In Mk 16.6 and Mt 28.6 the angel informs the women of the empty tomb, whereas in Lk 24.3 and Jn 20.11–13 the women make the discovery themselves. In Mk 16.7 and Mt 28.7 the angel instructs the women to inform Jesus' disciples of his resurrection and that they will see him in Galilee; in Lk 24.6–7 the women are reminded of Jesus' prophecies of his crucifixion and resurrection on the third day as if these prophecies in Lk 9.22; 9.43–44; 18.31–34 were directed to the women. In Jn 20.13 the angels makes no response to Mary Magdalene's plaint that Jesus' body had been stolen from the tomb.

The women's reaction to the angelic message at the tomb varies from Gospel to Gospel: in Mk 16.8 they flee from the tomb in fear and astonishment and "say nothing to anyone"; in Lk 24.9–10 they report their experience at the tomb to the apostles; in Mt 28.8 they leave the tomb in a holy fear but with joy and set out to report to Jesus' disciples; in Jn 20. 13–14 Mary Magdalene poses no question to the angels concerning the whereabouts of Jesus' body, her main concern.

The variations among the evangelists in their depiction of the women's visit to Jesus' tomb, remarkable as they are in themselves, become even more astonishing in the light of the fact that Luke and Matthew availed themselves of the Gospel of Mk as a source and guideline for the composition of their own Gospels (a literary relationship among the synoptic evangelists that the majority of contemporary NT scholars consider to be established). On this supposition it follows that neither Luke nor Matthew viewed their variations from Mk as anything other than instructive for the faith of the Christian community.

The single constant in the four Gospel accounts of the women's visit to the tomb is their discovery that it was open and empty. In John's Gospel Mary Magdalene eventually verifies the emptiness of the tomb, her original inference (Jn 20.1–2), by personal inspection (Jn 20.11–13). Contemporary NT scholars continue to debate the historical veracity of the tradition of the open-empty tomb. Unlike the resurrection of Christ and the apostolic experience of the person of the risen Christ, the tradition of the open-empty tomb is a direct object of historical assessment.

Since the tradition was not put forward by the apostolic preaching as a basis for the resurrection-faith, its origin cannot be accounted for out of such a purpose. In all four Gospels the open-empty tomb is linked with the accounts of Jesus' burial. Although it was Roman practice to leave the corpse of the crucified to decompose on the cross or to be devoured by animals, the Roman authority, having regard for Jewish sensibilities concerning the respect due a human corpse (cf. Dt 21.22–23), permitted immediate burial of crucified Jews. Jn 19.31 has certain (unnamed) leaders of the Jews requesting Pilate to have the *crurifragium*, the breaking of the legs, performed upon Jesus and the two men crucified with him, so as to hasten their deaths and permit their burial before the Sabbath (in Jn, also the feast of the Passover). It was perhaps as a member of this delegation from the Sanhedrin that Joseph of Arimathea sought and received from Pilate charge of Jesus' corpse. At least in Judea it lay within the jurisdiction of the Roman procurator to grant the corpse of the crucified Jew to relatives or friends for the purpose of interment.

Joseph was not a relative or friend of Jesus (in Mk 15.43 he is a "prominent counsellor"; in Lk 23.50 he is a "counsellor, a good and just man"; in Mt 27.57 he is a disciple of Jesus; in Jn 19.38 he is a secret disciple). On what precise grounds he won custody of the corpse from the procurator can only be conjectured, for the evangelists supply no information on this point. In the case of one executed for a political offense, as was Jesus on suspicion of sedition, the procurator ordinarily refused such a request when it was made by one who was not a relative of the deceased. Perhaps the fact that Pilate acceded to Joseph's petition is one of the reasons why the evangelists emphasize Pilate's judgment that Jesus was innocent of sedition (Mk 15.12–15; Lk 23.13–16; Mt 27.18–19, 23–24; Jn 19.4–6). Since the Jews considered the burial of their dead, even of those executed in connection with violations of the OT Law, to be a sacred duty, it is not surprising that Joseph, as a member of the Sanhedrin, a man of stature and, as a Jew, a man of religious concern, (Mk 15.43) assumed a responsibility that Jesus' relatives and friends were unwilling or unable to undertake. Those adjudicated to be violators of the OT Law, as was the case with Jesus (Mk 14.62–64 and parallels) and the two robbers crucified with him (Lv 19.13), were normally interred in a burial ground reserved for them and located at some distance from the city where executions took place.

Among the Jews burials on the Sabbath were strictly forbidden: Joseph's choice of his own tomb (Mt 27.59–60) provided a site close enough to Golgotha that permitted interment before the Sabbath. The two robbers may have been buried with Pilate's consent by relatives or friends also near Golgotha.

The Gospel depiction of Jesus' burial is in accord with both Roman and Jewish practice concerning the final disposition of the corpse of a crucified Jew. The opinion that the burial took place in the burial ground reserved for criminals, advanced by a minority of NT scholars, lacks substantiation in the evidence. Further, on this hypothesis the women's presence as witnesses to the burial in Joseph's tomb (Mk 15.47; Lk 23.55; Mt 27.61) becomes difficult to explain, since women's testimony was not considered of value either in Jewish or Roman culture. Their testimony was simply inadequate to supplant the supposed fact of burial in a common graveyard in favor of an honorable interment in Joseph's tomb.

From a historical point of view there is no reason to dispute the accuracy of the statements in the Synoptic Gospels attributing to the women knowledge of the location of Jesus' tomb (Mk 16.1; Lk 24.1; Mt 28.1; cf. also Jn 20.1) with which each evangelist begins his account of the women's visit. The differences among the evangelists on the women's motives for visiting the tomb may well be due in part to an actual difference of motives among them and in part to the discrepancies of detail among witnesses with which historians are familiar. It was established Jewish custom to honor the tombs of the dead. Since Jesus had in fact received honorable burial, but without any marks of affection or respect from his followers, it is not unnatural that these women, who had witnessed the humiliation of the cross (Mk 15.40; Lk 23.49; Mt 27.55–56; Jn 19.25), were determined somehow to compensate for this deficiency, whether by placing aromatic materials at the tomb or, should it have turned out to be possible, around the enshrouded corpse of Jesus. Each evangelist's mention of the women's motives serves to concentrate attention upon the unexpected drama of their visit: their objectives could not be carried out, for the tomb was open and empty. Only Mt (28.2) offers the explanation that it was an angel who opened the tomb. The other evangelists leave the reader to share in the women's mystification at this turn of events (Mk 16.3–4; Lk 24.2; Jn 20.1–2).

In the Synoptic Gospels the explanation for the open-empty tomb is made by an angel or angels: the crucified Jesus has been raised by God. The angelic announcement then looks backward to prophecies ascribed to Jesus (in Lk and Mt to the passion-resurrection prophecies; in Mk to the reunion in Galilee spoken of in 14.28) and forward to his appearances to his disciples (Mk 16.6–7; Lk 24.5–7; Mt 28.5–7). The tradition of the women's discovery of the open-empty tomb (upon which the resurrection narrative of the Fourth Gospel at first centers its entire attention, Jn 20.1–13) is interpreted in the Synoptic Gospels by use of the apostolic proclamation that the crucified Jesus was buried and raised by God (cf. 1 Cor 15.4). The Twelve, the original proclaimers of this divine act, are replaced by angels: whether the proclamation be apostolic or angelic it is the message of God. On this note Mark's Gospel whether by design or by accident, originally concluded (Mk 16.1–8). The evangelist's stress on the women's silence (Mk 16.8; "...they said nothing to anyone...") need not be understood in a sense so absolute as to exclude "the disciples and Peter" (Mk 16.7). Neither Luke (24.9) nor Matthew (28.8) took Mk 16.8 to mean that the women did not report their experience at the tomb to the disciples and Peter. For Mark the women are witnesses to the burial of Jesus and to the open-empty tomb, but they are not among the original apostolic witnesses to Christ's resurrection, a function reserved to the disciples and Peter (cf. Mk 13.9–11).

Luke's inclusion of a reaction of skepticism in response to the women's report (Lk 24.9, 11, 22–24) may be in part theologically motivated (to exclude the discovery of the open-empty tomb as a basis for the apostolic proclamation of Christ's resurrection) and in part a literary technique to introduce the reader to the lengthy account of the appearance of the risen Christ to the two disciples on the way to Emmaus. Jn 20.3–10 presents a favorable reaction to Magdalene's report: in consequence of it Peter and the beloved disciple visit the tomb and are impressed by the fact that the cloths that had enshrouded Jesus' corpse are lying neatly in place. Lk 24.12 (a passage that contemporary textual critics incline to accept as authentic) reflects the same tradition, but told of Peter alone. Matthew's Gospel does not include a reaction of Jesus' disciples to the report intended by the women (Mt 28.8).

Mt 28.4 interweaves the story of the guarding of Jesus' tomb (Mt 27.62–66) with the women's visit. This evangelist's portrayal of the women's visit is set in the context of apocalyptic, a literary technique that emphasized the revelatory aspect of an event and intimated its special importance for the future. Apocalyptic features in Mt's portrayal of the women's visit are the earthquake, the descent of the angel of the Lord, the OT representative of Yahweh (Mt 28.2), the lightning-like appearance of the angel's facial features (Mt 28.3), and the paralysis of the guards (Mt 28.4). The address of the apocalyptic angel to the women appointing them emissaries to Jesus' disciples (Mt 28.5–7) places greater emphasis on their function as witnesses than is the case in the other three Gospels. Perhaps Matthew intended to contrast the women's acceptance of the resurrection-proclamation and its rejection by certain leaders of the Jewish community.

The guarding of the tomb (requested by a Jewish leadership unaware of Jesus' passion-resurrection prophecies, and not until the day after his burial), the defeat of the guards by the apocalyptic angel (a pre-Matthean or Matthean figure depicted to interpret the open-empty tomb), and therefore the payment of the guards to secure their silence (Mt 28.11–15) cannot be understood as historical data. Since this material, however, is taken seriously in Mt, the possibility suggests itself that neither the Christian story of the guarding of the tomb nor the Jewish story of the disciples' theft of the corpse nor the Christian story of the payment of the guards were originally historical assertions but forms of theological debate, probably (but not necessarily) over the religious significance of the open-empty tomb. But what precisely such a theological debate might have centered upon is not presently ascertainable.

(2) *The Christophanies.* Appearances of the risen Christ are described in Mk 16.7; Lk 24.13–53; Mt 28.9–10; 16–20; Jn 20.11–18; 19–29; 21.1–23. (a) *Mk*

16.7. Some contemporary NT scholars interpret the "seeing" of the risen Christ by the disciples and Peter (Mk 16.7a) as a reference to the parousia, to occur in Galilee. The text, however, refers the reader to Mk 14.28: "But after I am raised I will go before you into Galilee." When Mk 16.7b observes, "....there," i.e., in Galilee, "you will see him as he told you," the reference is simply to Christ now risen from the dead. Parousia-passages speak of "seeing" the Son of Man (Mk 14.62; 13.26), i.e., the risen Christ in the role of judge. Before the judgment at the parousia is to take place the disciples' function is to preach the risen Christ who demands faith now (Mk 13.9–11), a situation that is to be evaluated when he appears as the Son of Man of Dn 7.13–14 for the final judgment (Mk 13.26). Mk 16.7 speaks of the disciples and Peter seeing the risen Christ as the prelude to their mission of Mk 13.9–11. The language of Mk 16.7 has at least one christophany in view, as is also the case with each person or groups of persons mentioned in 1 Cor 15.5–8 and in the kerygmatic speeches in Acts. It is not possible to determine whether or not Mark intended to record a christophany as the conclusion to his Gospel. However peculiar it may seem that his Gospel does in fact conclude without a christophany, this omission accords with the form of the apostolic proclamation in 1 Cor 15.5–8 and in the kerygmatic speeches in Acts where it is sufficient for the audience to know that christophanies have occurred. It has also to be kept in mind that Mark's readers could easily have been in possession of a tradition of one or several christophanies to which the evangelist simply chose to allude.

(b) *Lk 24.13–32.* The Appearance to the Disciples on the Way to Emmaus is a narrative quite skillfully written. It is linked to the women's visit to the tomb (the two disciples discount the women's report on the ground that no one has seen Jesus alive, Lk 24.22–24) and to the appearance to Peter from which the Eleven and others have learned of Jesus' resurrection (Lk 24.33-34). Paradoxically, the disciples who refuse the women's report because Jesus has not been seen alive do not recognize him (Lk 24.16). Their surprise that the traveler who now accompanies them is apparently unaware of the importance of the crucifixion and death of Jesus of Nazareth (Lk 24.18–21) is matched by the traveler's surprise that they have not understood the tragedy of this prophet in terms of the OT Scriptures (Lk 24.25–27). The disciples' sadness (Lk 24.17) begins to dissipate as a result of their confrontation with the Scriptures under the guidance of the traveler (Lk 24.28–29). The meal to which they had been looking forward in his company terminates when bread is broken and given them by the traveler: the mysteriousness of nonrecognition becomes the mysteriousness of recognition; but with recognition he vanishes from their sight (Lk 24.30–31). Their report at Jerusalem is overshadowed by the announcement of the Eleven and others that "the Lord has really been raised and has appeared to Simon" (Lk 24.34).

In this narrative of Luke the experience of the two disciples surpasses that of the women, who do not see the risen Christ but have a vision of angels affirming "that he was alive" (Lk 24.23). But it falls short of the experience of Simon to whom "the Lord...appeared" (Lk 24.34). Luke uses the verb *ōphthē* of the appearance, as does Paul in 1 Cor 15.5–8 of all the appearances he mentions. In Paul this verb supposes that

Christ appears as one who has received a glorious afterlife from which he reigns over the Christian community. The two disciples discover at Emmaus that Jesus of Nazareth (Lk 24.19) is indeed alive. But Peter discovers that he is alive and raised by God as "the Lord." The two disciples recognize him; Peter understands also his identity.

The Emmaus narrative has to be understood within the limitation placed upon it by Luke. The two disciples only begin to perceive that the suffering of Jesus possesses religious meaning when the traveler explains the Scriptures to them (Lk 24.25–27). Even when they did not recognize him, his explanation cast the suffering of Jesus of Nazareth in a new and impressive light (Lk 24.32). Their recognition of him at "the breaking of the bread" (Lk 24.30–31, 35) is certainly a Eucharistic allusion, but does not imply the fullness of understanding. Rather the fullness of understanding is a requirement for a share in the Eucharistic meal. It is this understanding they begin to acquire from the declaration of the disciples at Jerusalem that "the Lord . . . has appeared to Simon."

As NT scholars have shown, Luke composed the Emmaus narrative from at least two sources. He also reworked these sources to highlight the historical ministry of Jesus (Lk 24.19), the passion-resurrection prophecies (Lk 24.20, 21b), the Christian use of the OT Scriptures (Lk 24.25–27), the Eucharist (Lk 24.35), and the apostolic proclamation of the resurrection of Christ (Lk 24.34). Thus his Emmaus narrative presents a compendium of factors that are essential to the formation of Christian faith. Luke was more interested in the religious significance of the Emmaus appearance than in the phenomenon of the appearance itself.

(c) *Lk 24.36–53.* The Appearance to the Eleven is a narrative composed of three distinct parts: the appearance of the risen Christ (Lk 24.36–43); the mission mandate (Lk 24.44–49; and the departure of Christ (Lk 24.50–53). To maintain the literary continuity of his resurrection narrative as a whole Luke places this appearance-story in the context of the report of the Emmaus disciples (Lk 24.36). The story is concerned with the disciples' recognition of Christ as corporeally risen and objectively present before them: it is not his spirit or a phantom that they see (cf. Acts 23.9), as the marks of his wounds attest (Lk 24.39a); nor are they undergoing a subjective vision, for they can touch him if they wish (Lk 24.39b). Jesus eating broiled fish before them (Lk 24.41–43) is obviously intended by Luke to indicate his bodily resurrection, but how this implication follows is unclear unless one supposes that as the host he shared the fish with them (cf. Acts 10.41). Since the story as a whole is introduced by mention of the disciples' panic and fright, a strange reaction in view of their knowledge of two appearances of Jesus, it becomes all the more clear that Luke wishes to emphasize the corporeal and objective reality of these appearances of the risen Christ especially because he has had to acknowledge the Emmaus disciples' passage from non-recognition to recognition.

The mission mandate is a compressed summary of the kerygmatic speeches in Acts, followed by mention of the gift of the Holy Spirit enabling the disciples to perform the mission (Lk 24.49; cf. Acts 1.5 for the meaning of the "promise of the Father").

The departure scene seems to be introduced with the priestly blessing of the risen Christ (cf. Heb 8.1; Sir 50.19–21). Whether there is explicit mention of an ascension in Lk 24.51 ("he was taken up to heaven") depends upon the authenticity of this clause in the Greek text. The reading has the support of good MSS, of Acts 1.2, and Lk 24.52a ("they fell down to do him reverence"), which is consistent with it.

(d) *Mt 28.9–10.* The Appearance to the Women seems, from a literary standpoint, a poorly placed christophany. Mary Magdalene and "the other Mary" (Mt 28.1) have been instructed by the angel to inform the disciples of Jesus' resurrection and of a meeting with them in Galilee. As they are on their way to fulfill this commission Jesus appears to them. Two observations may be made on the literary location of this brief narrative. In both Lk and Jn the appearance of Christ to the Eleven (or Twelve), Jesus' chosen disciples, is preceded by a christophany to others that prepares the Eleven for the experience of the risen Christ: the Emmaus disciples in Lk, who report to the Eleven and Mary Magdalene in Jn, who also makes a report (Jn 20.18). It seems then that Matthew's literary location of the appearance to the women follows a tradition that christophanies were first experienced by those outside the group constituting Jesus' chosen disciples and reported to them. Secondly, the instruction of the risen Christ to the women speaks of "my brethren" (Mt 28.10), not of the "disciples" as in Mt 28.7. "Brethren" is the common Christian term in the NT for a fraternal relationship. Consequently, the message of the risen Christ from the women to the disciples implies his forgiveness of their desertion of him. As in Lk and Jn a prior christophany in Mt prepares for the appearance of the risen Christ to his chosen disciples.

(e) *Mt 28.16–20.* This Appearance to the Eleven in Mt presents the most solemn christophany in the resurrection-narratives. It takes place on an undesignated mountain in Galilee (a favorite place for significant events in Mt: Jesus' temptation, 4.8; the Sermon on the Mount, 5.1; Jesus' prayer after the feeding of the five thousand and before the sea-walking, 14.23; Jesus' healing of a multitude of sick, 15.29; and the Transfiguration, 17.1). What precise symbolism, if any, the evangelist attached to the mountain is undetermined. Strangely, at the appearance of Christ the Eleven worship him but some "doubted." The majority of NT scholars no longer interpret this doubt by translating "had doubted" (impermissible in view of the aorist tense of the Greek verb). Some consider it to be a reference to earlier doubts among the Eleven; but if such was the evangelist's viewpoint, it is difficult to understand why he did not indicate that the doubts were now dissipated. A plausible explanation is that Matthew makes use of the tradition of doubt among Jesus' disciples concerning his resurrection to criticize the doubts of the Christian community of his own time, a point that may also be made in Mk 16.14.

The words of the risen Christ portray a structure of the Christian community that combines divine and human authority: the full authority of the risen Christ residing in the realm of God is shared in history by the Eleven. In turn they are to share it by making disciples in all nations. These disciples are to be united to the triune God through Baptism; and, beginning with the Eleven, whatever Jesus has taught (as recorded in Mt) is to be carried out by the Eleven and by the disciples in all the nations. In this very mission the risen Christ will be mysteriously present as long as human history endures. The text of this mandate in Mt 28.18–20 is related to Dn 7.13–14 and probably also to Ps 110.1. The exact conceptual relationship between these OT passages and this passage in Mt remains, however, uncertain.

(f) *Jn 20.11–18*. The Appearance to Mary Magdalene is a christophany in which the theme of nonrecognition occurs. But unlike Luke's Emmaus-narrative it is given a practical explanation: Magdalene takes Jesus for the gardener because she assumes that he is dead and that his corpse has been taken from the tomb and buried elsewhere (Jn 20.11–15). Her recognition occurs when Jesus calls her by name (Jn 20.16). Since there has been a previous conversation, it is not simply the sound of Jesus' voice that causes the recognition but his knowledge of her. While in Lk the mysteriousness lies in the nonrecognition, in Jn it lies in the recognition. Evidently, Magdalene assumes that the risen Christ is to resume his past relationship with his disciples (probably, the import of "Don't cling to me," Jn 20.17). Jesus corrects her assumption by instructing her to inform his disciples that he is ascending to his Father. By focusing attention on the ascension the evangelist prepares the way for Jesus' gift of the Spirit to the Twelve.

(g) *Jn 20.19–29*. The Appearance to the Disciples and to Thomas concludes the Fourth Gospel. In the narrative of the appearance to the disciples (Jn 20.19–23) their recognition of the risen Christ results from the perception of his wounds, at the sight of which the disciples rejoice (Jn 20.20). Their recognition and rejoicing are theologically based: in Jn the cross is the beginning of Jesus' glorification (Jn 13.31–32) and by means of it he will attract the world to himself (Jn 12.32). With his appearance to them the disciples begin to understand the truth of his words and rejoice that he is about to achieve this goal. However, the achievement is to be brought about in history by themselves. Having understood the religious significance of the cross and resurrection, they are capable of receiving and exercising the mission mandate (Jn 20.21–23): they are given the Spirit so that they might exercise discernment and authority to forgive men's sins or to withold forgiveness in the name of Christ, a power that the evangelist leaves unspecified and therefore probably conceives broadly. The fact that he makes no mention of Jesus' departure suggests that he wishes to give particular prominence to the mission mandate.

The narrative of the appearance to the unbelieving Thomas (Jn 20.24–29) is a dramatic conclusion to the Gospel, which has been written in support of Christian faith: "... that you may believe that Jesus is the Christ, the Son of God ..." (cf. Jn 20.30–31). The drama results from his absence when the christophany occurred. He refuses the disciples' testimony to the christophany and its religious significance, taking the position that unless he has the opportunity to judge for himself and on his own terms, he will not believe (Jn 20.24–25). The occurrence of the subsequent christophany with the disciples again behind locked doors (Jn 20.26; cf. Jn 20.19) does not mean that the risen Christ physically passed through locked doors, but that the physical construction of things does not preclude his objective presence. The reality and communicative force of Christ's presence are so compelling that Thomas makes the supreme confession: "My Lord and my God" (Jn 20.28).

In the opinion of contemporary NT scholars the story of the unbelieving Thomas was inspired by the tradition of the doubt among the Twelve (Lk 24.41; Mt 28.17; Mk 16.14) and the difficulties of some Christians in holding to the resurrection-faith at a time when the original witnesses to the risen Christ had died out. It was of course always known that actual witnesses were few in number and that the resurrection-faith arose out of the apostolic testimony. The story of the unbelieving Thomas dwells upon the latter fact: that it was through the apostolic word, accepted as the word of God (cf. 1 Thess 2.13), that the Christian community originated. Although the original witnesses are no longer with the community, the power of their word remains with it. The blessing or *macarism* (a Jewish way of speaking of one's good fortune in having accepted God's word, cf. Lk 1.45; 10.23) that concludes the story (Jn 20.29) does not contrast those who believed as the result of a christophany with those who believed without having experienced a christophany. The blessing is an instruction that both groups of believers are equally fortunate. The resurrection-faith lies at the heart of the Christian community, and both groups enjoy the same understanding of it. The double manner of its origin is the work of God.

(h) *Jn 21.1–23*. The narrative of the Appearance to the Disciples at the Sea of Tiberias is an addition to the Fourth Gospel, made (unlike Mk 16.9–20) before its publication, as its universal presence in the MS tradition shows. Generally speaking, its purpose is to reflect upon the roles played by Simon Peter and the beloved disciple of the Fourth Gospel (Jn 13.23; 19.26; 20.2) in the development of the Christian community. The supposition of the narrative is that both Simon Peter and the beloved disciple are dead. It is composed of two parts: an account of the appearance of the risen Christ on the shore of the Sea of Tiberias—a later name for the Sea of Galilee—(Jn 21.1–14); and an account of a conversation between Christ and Simon Peter on this occasion (Jn 21.15–23).

The appearance of Christ is set in the context of a fishing scene and in the framework of the disciples' nonrecognition of him. When he suggests where they should cast the net, they do not recognize him. But after a strikingly large catch (Jn 21.6), the beloved disciple realizes that the person on the shore is "the Lord" and so informs Simon Peter (Jn 21.7). Once on shore and breakfasting at Christ's invitation, the group of disciples recognize him (Jn 21.12). The principal point of the story is that the beloved disciple leads Simon Peter to the recognition of the risen Christ. NT scholars recognize a Eucharistic allusion in Jesus' giving of the bread and fish to the disciples (Jn 21.13), but perhaps the allusion occurs by way of reference to Jn 6.11, where Jesus performs the same action for the purpose of the feeding of the five thousand. After the feeding an instruction of Jesus follows, ending in a confession by Simon Peter (Jn 6.68–69). An instruction of Jesus now follows that focuses on Simon Peter.

The instruction is a mission mandate directed to Peter alone as in Mt 16.18–19. Three times Jesus requires him to confess his devotion, now to the risen Christ (almost certainly an allusion to the insistent tradition of his triple denial); and three times Jesus commands him to care for those who believe in him—imaged as "lambs" and "sheep"—(Jn 21.15–17). Since the leading function here given Peter is conveyed in symbolic language, its exact nature and extent cannot be set out in neat, concrete terms. It is acknowledged that his performance of the role of shepherd given him led to his martyrdom (Jn 21.18–19). The role of the beloved disciple, on the other hand, was to serve Christ in another way, one that involved preaching and teaching but not martyrdom. It is probable that the conversation between Jesus and Peter in Jn 21.21–23 has the purpose of presenting John the Apostle as one who, like Peter, but without Peter's specific mandate from Christ, exercised a pastoral ministry of preaching and teaching that is of enduring significance for the Christian community and to which the Fourth Gospel stands as the lasting witness.

Concluding Observations. The resurrection narratives contain no allegations or claims that in themselves constitute an object of historical research. From beginning to end the narratives are theological statement. Behind them lies an assumption of divine action in history. But this assumption is neither systematic nor unsystematic philosophical or theological speculation. It is an assumption unrelated to any religious thought, whether philosophical or theological, including the thought of the OT Scriptures and of Judaism itself, that preceded it. The assumption is specific: that God raised Jesus of Nazareth who was crucified, died, and was buried as a seditionist under Pontius Pilate and manifested him to be reigning in his own realm as the salvific Lord of creation. The assumption itself is historically undemonstrable: only its context, the crucifixion of Jesus of Nazareth on grounds of sedition, is an object of historical evaluation. Although the assumption itself was not the net result of religious speculation of any kind and was not presented in terms of the historically demonstrable, it was not without its own historical context: the assertions of specific people to be the divine appointees to witness to the risen Christ and to his religious reign. Except on the assumption of the divine action in history testified to by specific people as divinely appointed witnesses, a testimony that is presumed to be accepted, the resurrection narratives carry neither conviction nor intelligible meaning.

Once the presupposition of the resurrection narratives is accepted, however, they acquire meaning that is both forceful and challenging. The sequel to the burial of Jesus of Nazareth in accordance with the customs of the time is the natural mystery of the open-empty tomb. But the resurrection narratives do not permit this natural mystery to hold the field of thought. It is elevated to the plane of the resurrection itself by angelic messengers: a natural explanation for this natural mystery is denied from the outset. Even in John's Gospel the empty tomb is not a cause for weeping (Jn 20.13). The resurrection narratives show no interest in supplying data that leave no room for doubt about the empty tomb. They reflect a point of view that it was more important to provide a theological explanation for this phenomenon than to supply historical information guaranteeing the emptiness of the tomb. The fact that a theological explanation was invariably offered shows at least that it was the Christian conviction that the tomb was found to be empty.

The variety of the christophanies reveals the same theological preoccupation as the variety of the accounts of the empty tomb: a phenomenon occurred that also required interpretation. In the instance of the christophanies the phenomenon was the personal manifesta-tion of the risen Christ to chosen witnesses. The content of the christophanies as they exist in the resurrection narratives seems to be due in part to the function carried out in their lifetimes by at least some of the recipients and in part to the catechetical needs of the Christian community. There is no need to assume that the risen Christ parceled out specific directions to a variety of people who then compared notes. St. Paul asserts that after his experience of the risen Christ on the road to Damascus he felt no need to consult with the apostles in Jerusalem (Gal 1.15–17). That some form of communication took place between the risen Christ and the chosen witnesses is plausible and is indicated by Luke (Acts 1.3; 10.41). But such communication could bear only upon the immediate future and would in itself require interpretation in the course of time. The fact that the resurrection narratives offer a variety of interpretations of christophanies indicates that the appearances of the risen Christ took place, but in such a way as to require interpretation.

The literary classification of the christophanies remains unsettled. They have been categorized according to their setting (Jerusalem or Galilee), according to their content (recognition or mission), and according to their purpose (personal or apostolic).

Bibliography: P. BENOIT, *Passion et Résurrection du Seigneur* (Paris 1966). J. BLINZLER, "Die Grablegung Christi," in E. DHANIS, ed., *Resurrexit: Actes du Symposium International sur la Résurrection de Jésus* (Rome, 1974) 56–107. E. L. BODE, *The First Easter Morning* (Rome 1970). R. E. BROWN, *The Virginal Conception and Bodily Resurrection of Jesus* (New York 1973); *The Gospel according to John, XIII–XXI* (New York 1970). C. H. DODD, "The Appearance of the Risen Christ: A Study in Form-Criticism of the Gospels," *More New Testament Studies* (Grand Rapids, Mich. 1968). R. H. FULLER, *The Formation of the Resurrection Narratives* (New York 1971). J. P. GALVIN, "Resurrection as *Theologia crucis Jesu*: The Foundational Christology of Rudolf Pesch," ThSt 38 (1977) 513–524. X. LÉON-DUFOUR, *Résurrection de Jésus et méssage pascal* (Paris 1971). W. MARXSEN, *The Resurrection of Jesus of Nazareth* (Philadelphia 1970). C. F. D. MOULE, ed., *The Significance of the Message of the Resurrection for Faith in Jesus Christ* (Naperville, Ill. 1968). B. RIGAUX, *Dieu l'a ressuscité: Exégèse et théologie biblique* (Gembloux, Belgium 1973). L. SCHENKE, *Auferstehungsverkündigung und leeres Grab* (Stuttgart 1968). P. SEIDENSTICKER, *Die Auferstehung Jesu in der Botschafft der Evangelisten* (Stuttgart 1967). H. STRATHMANN, "*Martys*," Kittel ThW Eng 4:474-508. P. DE SURGY, P. GRELOT, et al., *La Résurrection du Christ et l'exégèse moderne* (Paris 1969).

[C. P. CEROKE]

RETREATS

Recent developments in the retreat movement raise anew the question of what a retreat is (12:428). Despite the wide variety of types noted below there is no cogent reason for departing from the historical development of retreats as of one piece with biblical wilderness experiences. In the old dispensation the wilderness was a privileged place for meeting Yahweh and in the new, Jesus not only spent forty days in prayerful solitude but even during his years of active ministry habitually spent long hours at prayer. Early monks made Lent itself a long retreat and monastic hospitality and medieval pilgrimages afforded the opportunity for favored encounters with God. Men and women will always need at given intervals to remove themselves from the trivialities of daily existence in order to face up more radically to the Word of God and the ultimate reason they exist. After a comparatively brief pendulum swing to "speaking retreats" there is now a return to an appreciation for silence and solitude. This return is a testimony to the soundness of the traditional concept of retreats.

Vatican Council II. The impetus given to the current retreat movement by the Council was not mainly by way of explicit statement but rather of the many renewal themes it proposed and encouraged: the deepening of the laity's spiritual life; the renewal of both liturgy and law; the updating of priestly and religious life; the purification of all classes; intensification of prayer for all men and women; increased attention to proclaiming and pondering the revealed Word. Yet the Council did refer explicitly to retreats at least three times. Bishops are to encourage priests to renew their spiritual lives from time to time by participating in retreats and other special meetings (*Christus Dominus* 16). Retreats are recommended to priests as of "greatest worth" for the faithful fulfillment of their ministry (*Presbyterorum ordinis* 18). The laity, too, are to find "periods of recollection" and "spiritual exercises" as aids for deepening their lives and furthering their apostolic endeavors (*Apostolicam actuositatem* 32).

Types of Retreats. Current approaches to the retreat experience vary considerably. In the private planned retreat a director arranges a plan and the person spends his days alone but following this guidance. The private unplanned experience is precisely what the name indicates. A charismatic retreat emphasizes elements popular in the movement: singing, praying in groups, healing services, proclaiming and sharing the biblical Word in the group (*see* CHARISMATIC RENEWAL, CATHOLIC). A dialogue retreat includes full discussion of what has been presented by the leader. The directed retreat is characterized by the one-to-one guidance given by a director to the retreatant; it is a combination of much prayerful solitude with daily spiritual direction. The traditional proclaimed retreat is still the most widespread. In it there is usually a combination of lectures, prayerful solitude and a more or less limited opportunity for spiritual direction.

Considerable variety is likewise found both in specialized groupings and in retreat locales. There are retreats organized for the married, the divorced, the single; for teenagers and for couples planning marriage; for alcoholics and for ethnic groups; for religious and for priests. These exercises can be held in a retreat house, a "spiritual center" sponsored by a religious institute, a desert or forest hermitage, a monastery or administrative religious headquarters, a boarding school during vacation time, a *house of prayer in an active religious congregation. In length of time a retreat may be one day, a week, a month or even a year. The retreat exercises may be directed by one person or by a team of two or more members.

The Future and its Problems. Though there is considerable interest in retreats among the laity, it remains true that only a fraction have ever made a retreat; a vast pool is yet to be tapped. There is the allied problem of the scarcity of directors capable of leading others into the widely desired area of advanced prayer. This perennial problem is rendered especially acute with the growth of the directed retreat, since the availability of well-trained and experienced directors is restricted to still fewer persons. The attempts to meet this shortage by special one-month or one-year courses are inadequate to real needs. Brief courses can hardly produce competency.

Bibliography: T. DUBAY, "Retreat Problematics: Traditional, Dialogue, Directed, Thematic," RevRel 33 (1974) 573–589. H. SMITH, "The Nature and Value of a Directed Retreat," RevRel 32 (1973) 490–497. E. YARNOLD et al., WaySuppl 16 (1972).

[T. DUBAY]

REUNION OF CHURCHES

The visible unity of the Churches continues to be the goal of the ecumenical movement. The Churches view present disunity as disobedience to the will of Christ. Unity is no longer viewed simply as the movement from confessional divisions to the manifestation of visible unity. The ecumenical movement is seen as part of the larger and on-going imperative for the Church to make real the unity it speaks of in the Creed. History remains the ever-changing setting in which the Churches have to discover and manifest unity in the never-ending process of renewal.

Preliminary Considerations. For many the question which is giving shape to the ecumenical movement is: what is the Church for? The answer given to this question often groups church members into transconfessional families and at times causes polarization. Such developments call into question the very identity of Christian faith and the Church. Other factors such as shared experiences, common spirituality, common interests, common demands, etc. play an important role in developing a concept of unity. Any viable concept of unity must take seriously both the present historical demands and the different confessional traditions in light of the biblical witness.

Concepts of Unity. In light of the above factors it is understandable that Churches bring different understandings of unity into the ecumenical movement. Some stress the spiritual dimensions of unity, others the living tradition, others the episcopal structure, others the Gospel rightly preached and the Sacraments rightly administered, and still others common goals and a common willingness to serve the mission of Christ.

The Churches are engaged in the quest for a unity model that will incorporate the legitimate aspects of the various concepts. There is no advance blueprint. And even when a stage of unity is reached it in turn must be transcended. The Church is always on the way (*in via*). Churches agree that the starting point must be the recognition that unity has already been *given* in Jesus Christ. Christ *remains* the source and center of ecclesiastical communion. Unity has not been wholly lost but has to be made visible where it has been obscured, to be recovered to the extent it has been lost, to be maintained where it is threatened, and to be brought to complete conformity to the will of Christ. *Ecclesial conversion* is essential. Further, it is agreed that unity does not mean uniformity but that it requires diversity-in-unity and unity-in-diversity. A majority of Churches agree that unity must be a visible unity in one faith expressed in a variety of forms, that it must be a unity involving communion in one Eucharistic fellowship, and that it must be a unity expressed in worship, in common life in Christ, and in Christian witness and service to the world.

Organic Union. There is a growing consensus that this unity in faith, fellowship, worship, and service must be embodied within an organic body expressed in a variety of forms. *Organic union* is seen as the goal of the ecumenical movement. However, there is no agreement about its precise meaning. Organic union is interpreted in a broad sense by those Churches which accord full recognition to each others' ministries, and which practice full *Eucharistic sharing without demanding any change in their respective historical structures. Others interpret it as entailing a new fellowship with its own identity. Still others, mostly Roman Catholic, envision organic union as the visible, full, canonical, and ecclesiastical union of sister Churches (*typoi*) subsisting in the Church of Christ while retaining those theological, liturgical, spiritual, and disciplinary traditions which are judged to be consistent with the demands of God's Revelation as mirrored in Scripture and tradition.

Conciliar Fellowship. Because organic union is judged as being too static by some observers it is complemented by the concept of *conciliar fellowship*. In this concept the one Church is seen as a conciliar fellowship of local Churches which are themselves truly united. Each local Church possesses, in communion with the others, the fullness of catholicity, witnesses to the same apostolic faith, and therefore recognizes the others as belonging to the same Church of Christ and guided by the same Spirit.

Admittedly the above concepts and models are ambiguous and require clarification by the prayer, study, dialogue, and action of the Churches.

See also INCORPORATION INTO THE CHURCH (MEMBERSHIP).

Bibliography: M. FAHEY, "Ecclesial Community as Communion," *Jurist* 36 (1976) 4–23. Faith and Order, *What Kind of Unity?*, paper n. 69 (Geneva 1974); *Uniting in Hope*, paper n. 72 (Geneva 1974). F. LANNE, "Pluralism and Unity: the Possibility of a Variety of 'Typologies' within the Same Ecclesial Allegiance," *One-in-Christ* 6 (1970) 430–451; "The Unity of the Church in the Work of Faith and Order," *One-in-Christ* 12 (1976) 34–57. J. MACQUARRIE, *Christian Unity and Christian Diversity* (Philadelphia 1975). L. NEWBIGIN, "The Form and Structure of the Visible Unity of the Church," *One-in-Christ* 13 (1977) 107–126. O. PATON, ed., *Breaking Barriers: Nairobi, 1975* (London 1976). H. RYAN, "The Path to Unity," Origins 7 (1968) 714–719. J. WILLEBRANDS, "Address in Cambridge, England," *Documents on Anglican/Roman Catholic Relations I* (USCC Publ. Office, Washington, D.C. 1972) 32–41.

[A. LAUBENTHAL]

REVELATION, CONCEPT OF (IN THE BIBLE)

The Dogmatic Constitution on Divine Revelation adopted by the Vatican Council II in 1965 represents a decisive advance in Catholic thinking on the nature of divine Revelation in that the view of Revelation found therein may be characterized as concrete rather than abstract; historical rather than philosophical; biblical rather than scholastic; ecumenical rather than controversial; and interpersonal rather than propositional. This article will confine itself to a presentation and commentary on paragraphs 2–6 of the Constitution, which reflect the Catholic theological evaluation of the concept of Revelation as contained in the Bible.

Conciliar Teaching. The theocentric emphasis of paragraphs 2–6 is announced in the opening paragraph which declares Revelation to be of divine origin, unconditionally derived from God's goodness and wisdom rather than solicited by the need of men. While theocentric in essence, this Revelation is nonetheless an invitation to man to communion with God. The constitutive elements of divine Revelation are both the deeds wrought by God and found in both the Old and New Testaments and the words by which God himself wills his works to be understood (*Dei Verbum* 2). This interconnection of deeds and words is insisted upon throughout *Dei Verbum*. God does not reveal Himself

through words only, but they are inseparably linked with God's deeds and with the fulfillment of his plan for man's salvation. The fulfillment of God's plan is to be found in the Christ-event, in the God-man who supremely fulfills by the total fact of his presence and public declaration of himself, by the words and deeds through which he completed his mission, especially his death and resurrection, and finally by sending the Spirit of Truth (ibid. 4). The Christ-event, in turn, had been prepared for from the very beginning of mankind's history by a series of crucial historical epiphanies and faith-filled interpretations, such as the call of Abraham, the Exodus, the Sinai event, the Babylonian Captivity, and the Return from the exile (ibid. 3). Considering mankind, the recipient of divine Revelations, *Dei Verbum* stresses the role of faith, affirming that it is for man to abandon himself freely and entirely to God in faith, and that the Holy Spirit, who moves man toward faith, unceasingly perfects it by his gifts that the understanding of divine Revelation may be more complete (ibid. 5).

Biblical and Systematic Theology. As promulgated, the Constitution raises many questions and has received from both biblical and systematic theologians considerations that elucidate more fully the nature of Revelation. If *Dei Verbum* seems to view Revelation theocentrically and faith rather passively, theologians today see both Revelation and faith in dialogical interaction, wherein the believer responds creatively to the self-manifestation of God, not simply in the depths of his own subjectivity, but in cosmos and history. Verbal Revelation, then, is a disciplined response to the divine self-manifestation made under the aegis of faith within a community and a tradition. The historical epiphanies of God's Revelation whether in the Exodus or in the deeds of Jesus call for interpretation by those inwardly disposed to penetrate their profound significance and communicate them to those disposed to believe. In the Old Testament, it was the prophets who, from the time of Moses, spoke from their faith and called Israel to share their vision and its practical demands. The Christian Church in turn was founded upon the inspired interpretation given to the words and deeds of Jesus by the prophetic leaders of the apostolic community.

Revelation whether in the Old or New Testaments is not prior but subsequent to faith, that is to say, it presupposes an interpretation by a believing and inspired prophet of the events in which God discloses himself. Revelation is the divine component of faith, enabling faith to be faith for a particular believer and a believing community.

The biblical accounts are interpreted in the special sense that they present the past from the point of view of a faith stance and frequently reconstruct the external events to bring out their faith meaning. In the Bible, therefore, it is not surprising that event and interpretation, deed and word are so intertwined that in many cases the deed is no longer knowable apart from the interpretation given to it. As may be seen from the New Testament itself, the role of the Church in relation to Revelation is decisive. The Church as the community of Christian faith is both the matrix and itself the very product of the special Revelation which it accepts and proclaims, the self-Revelation of God in his own Son.

Bibliography: G. BAUM, *Man Becoming* (New York 1970); A. DULLES, *Revelation Theology: A History* (New York 1969); "The Problem of

Revelation," CathThSoc 29 (1974) 77–106. R. LATOURELLE, *Theology of Revelation* (New York 1968). J. P. MACKEY, *The Problems of Religious Faith* (Dublin 1972). L. MONDEN, *Faith: Can Man Still Believe?* (New York 1970). G. MORAN, *The Present Revelation* (New York 1972). G. O'COLLINS, *Foundations of Theology* (Chicago 1971). W. PANNENBERG, *Revelation as History* (New York 1968). K. RAHNER, *Theological Investigations*, v. 4, 5 (Baltimore 1966). K. RAHNER with J. RATZINGER, *Revelation and Tradition* (New York 1966). H. R. SCHLETTE, *Epiphany as History* (London 1969).

[T. J. RYAN]

REVELATION, FONTS OF

Vatican Council II took up this question in the light of the debate in the 1950s about whether Catholics, in loyalty to the Council of Trent, are obliged to hold that certain revealed truths are given not in Scripture but only in apostolic Tradition.

Vatican II, Dei Verbum. Because this debate had been inconclusive Vatican II, in the Constitution on Divine Revelation, refrained from saying that there are any revealed truths known by Tradition alone, although it did say that Tradition is necessary at least for the assurance with which the Church knows some revealed truths (*Dei Verbum* 9). The Council did not directly answer the question whether all revealed truth is somehow contained in Scripture, but it implied that the question as previously formulated rested on a flawed view of both Scripture and Tradition. These sources, according to the Council, are not to be viewed statically as collections of propositional truths, but dynamically as ways in which God converses with his People (ibid. 8, 21). The two sources, moreover, are inseparable, and thus constitute one composite source. The Scriptures, themselves a crystallization of early tradition, are continually handed down ("traditioned") in the Church. Tradition is found in the total life and practice of the praying and believing Church, rather than simply in written and oral statements. Regarding the relative dignity of Scripture and Tradition, the Constitution taught that the Scriptures, "since they are inspired, really are the word of God" and are "the soul of sacred theology" (ibid. 24). Tradition, however, is to be received with the same reverence as Scripture (ibid. 9). "Together with Tradition" (but never without Tradition) Scripture is the supreme norm of Christian life and belief (ibid. 21, 24).

Post-Vatican II Theological Reflections. Since the Council, a number of Catholic theologians have been concerned with responding to the objection of certain Protestants, including Karl Barth, to the effect that by not accepting the superiority of Scripture over Tradition, the Catholic Church really makes itself the norm of its own faith and thus fails in obedience to the Word of God. These Catholic theologians assert that Scripture, as the original normative expression of the faith, has a certain critical function over against all other expressions. Thus there is a sense in which Catholics, as well as Protestants, can speak of Scripture as being the supreme criterion (*norma non normata*).

In recent years Catholic theologians have tended to qualify, without contradicting, the common assertion that Scripture and Tradition are the two fonts of revelation. Vatican II, returning to the perspectives of the Council of Trent (Denz 1501), pointed out that neither Scripture nor Tradition is a "font" in the sense of being an originative source of revelation. Both of them derive from "the same divine wellspring" (*Dei Verbum* 9), namely, God's revelation in Christ, a mystery infinitely

richer than any human attestation to it. Protestant and Catholic theologians, in the 1960s and 1970s, have focused anew on Jesus Christ as the true source of the Gospel. Although one cannot bypass Scripture and Tradition, since practically all available information about Jesus somehow derives from these sources, still the modern reader is not abjectly dependent on what these sources overtly say. Statements about God in Scripture and Tradition, even though they enjoy a certain divine protection against error, are limited insofar as they reflect a finite human understanding; they were composed under the stress of particular historical situations and are embodied in the imperfect forms of human language. By critical hermeneutics contemporary theologians seek to liberate past statements of the faith from the limitations that can be detected in them and to restate the divine message in accordance with the presuppositions, concerns, thought forms, and linguistic conventions of the present day. Thus Scripture and Tradition, while they continue to function as authorities, are being used in a sophisticated way to give fuller access to the mystery of God in Christ.

Further, theologians are now asking whether Scripture and Tradition are the only fonts of revelation. Going back to the biblical idea that God constantly reveals himself in creation (Rom 1.20), some point out that this "cosmic" revelation, imparted with the help of the Holy Spirit, is not merely natural (*see* CREATION). Because the Holy Spirit is at work beyond the visible limits of the Christian community, Christians should be alert for evidences of cosmic and historical revelation in living faiths other than Christianity.

Even when discussing revelation as given in the Church, recent theologians, following up certain indications of Vatican II, call attention to the importance of contemporary experience as a medium of God's self-communication. Thanks to the Holy Spirit, it is possible to be aware of the divine presence in human hearts and in contemporary history. Vatican II pointed out the necessity of "scrutinizing the signs of the times and interpreting them in the light of the gospel" (*Gaudium et spes* 4). It added that through interpreting the many voices of our age the Church can always achieve a deeper penetration of revealed truth (ibid. 44). Going slightly beyond the formal teaching of the Council, some writers suggest that the "signs of the times" deserve to be recognized as a distinct theological source, to be utilized in the interpretation of Scripture and Tradition.

Finally it is being pointed out, especially by advocates of *political theology and *liberation theology, that neither Scripture nor Tradition will deliver its true message to those who stand aside in an attitude of detached contemplation. For a genuine understanding of the Gospel one must participate in the process of which the Gospel speaks. In this sense it may be said that right conduct ("orthopraxis") is the norm of right thinking ("orthodoxy"). In order to distinguish judiciously between God's revelation and the historically conditioned forms in which it comes to us, and to see the Gospel in its contemporary relevance, one must be committed to the Christian life and to the mission of the Church today.

Theology since Vatican II, therefore, has moved beyond the preconciliar debate regarding the authority of Scripture and Tradition, considered as distinct repositories of revealed truth. While accepting the teaching of Vatican II regarding the inseparability of Scripture and Tradition, recent theology attempts to achieve a richer and more vital contact with Christ and the Gospel by recognizing the limitations of all human expressions of revelation, by drawing on contemporary religious experience, by pondering the "signs of the times," and by consulting persons actively engaged in Christian witness and mission.

Bibliography: W. KASPER, *Glaube und Geschichte* (Mainz 1970) 159–186. G. MORAN, "Revelation, Fonts of," NCE 12: 439–440 with bibliog. W. PANNENBERG, *Basic Questions in Theology* 1, tr. G. H. KEHM (Philadelphia 1970) 1–14, 137–181. K. RAHNER, "Scripture and Tradition," SacrMundi 6:54–57 with bibliog.   [A. DULLES]

RIGHT TO WORK

The right to work, like all true human rights, follows from the natural law, which requires, according to St. Thomas, the preservation of life itself (ST 1a2ae, 94.2). Accordingly, the Church has long maintained that it is both man's duty and his right to work and thereby to provide the goods of life for himself and his family (12:498).

Catholic Social Teaching. Pope Leo XIII taught that work "is *necessary*, because man has need of the fruit of his labors to preserve his life, and nature itself, which must be most strictly obeyed, commands him to preserve it" (*Rerum novarum* 62). Drawing on his predecessor, John XXIII emphasized the same point: "Every man has the right to life, to bodily integrity, and to the means which are suitable for the proper development of life; . . ." (*Pacem in terris* 11). Therefore, "it is clear that man has a right by the natural law not only to an opportunity to work, but also to go about his work without coercion" (ibid. 18).

Vatican Council II in the Constitution on the Church in the Modern World added that "through labor offered to God man is associated with the redemptive work of Jesus Christ, who conferred an eminent dignity on labor when at Nazareth He worked with His own hands. From this there follows for every man the duty of working faithfully and also the right to work" (*Gaudium et spes* 67).

The right to work is complemented, moreover, by the right of workers to join together in associations. Pope Pius XI declared that "just as inhabitants of a town are wont to found associations with the widest diversity of purposes, which each is quite free to join or not, so those engaged in the same industry or profession will combine with one another into associations equally free for purposes connected in some manner with the pursuit of the calling itself" (*Quadragesimo anno* 87).

Status of the Issue in the U.S. In the United States, the term "right to work" likewise refers to the right of a person to work without hindrance. In conjunction with the natural right of association, this has come to mean the right of the individual to work regardless of his affiliation or nonaffiliation with a labor union. Hence, for instance, federal law prohibits the so-called yellow-dog contract requiring employees to refrain from union activity as a condition of employment. Similarly, under Section 14(b) of the Taft-Hartley Act, individual states retain the power further to protect their citizens' right to work by outlawing "union shop" contracts which force persons to join or support unions as a condition of continued employment. Section 1 of North Carolina's

Right-to-Work law, for example, states that ". . . the right of persons to work shall not be denied or abridged on account of membership or non-membership in any labor union or labor organization or association." Right to Work laws in nineteen other states make a similar guarantee.

Opponents of Right-to-Work laws—including most union officials and some Catholic publicists—deny that compulsory unionism violates natural law. They argue that the right to work without joining a union is not absolute, but is subject to reasonable qualification, including membership in an employee organization. In their view, a labor union, like the state, is a special organization; they say it performs a necessary social function by legitimately representing the best interests of all workers during collective bargaining. Like a government, therefore, the union needs and has a moral claim to the support of those workers without exception. Refusal to join the union is considered unreasonable, and therefore, in the words of Msgr. John Ryan, even "[the closed shop] will not violate the right of the nonunionist, even if it prevents him from obtaining any employment"—even if, in effect, it denies him the means of sustaining his own life and the lives of his family.

This argument has been neither condemned nor officially sanctioned by the Church. But Catholic advocates of Right-to-Work laws cite papal encyclicals and natural law teaching to refute compulsory unionism. As they see it, nature gives priority to life and only a good higher than life itself can rightfully interfere with the divine charge to preserve that life. A union, whatever its merits, is not such a good; it is a private organization—not a government—and it exists solely for the sake of workers, not the reverse. Only the workers, in their individual capacities, can determine whether or not the union serves their interests. Right-to-Work laws, it is argued, guarantee workers this freedom.

Bibliography: T. R. HAGGARD, *Compulsory Unionism, the NLRB, and the Courts* (Philadelphia 1977). E. A. KELLER, *The Case for Right-to-Work Laws* (Chicago 1956). J. A. RYAN, "Moral Aspects of Labour Unions," CE 8:724–728.   [R. F. SMITH]

RITUAL, ROMAN

Vatican Council II directed the revision of all the liturgical books of the Roman rite (*Sacrosanctum Concilium* 25); with respect to the *Rituale Romanum* the Council directed that local or regional rituals be prepared in harmony with the decreed, new Roman Ritual (ibid. 63, *iuxta novam Ritualis Romani editionem*, an expression chosen to avoid "conformity with" or "based upon"). There has not yet appeared in single collection the revision of the *Rituale Romanum*, but the revision of the rites covered by its titles has been completed and the texts published, with the exception of the titles on blessings and on processions, litanies, and the like. With reference to the revised Latin texts the correlation of local rituals with the *Rituale Romanum* has been assured by the submission for confirmation to the Holy See of the vernacular texts for the various liturgical rites. In English the rites have appeared separately and in various collections, the texts being those prepared by ICEL. A "pocket-size" ritual is not desirable, since it would mean omitting the theologically rich instructions and optional readings accompanying the rites. The creation of regional rituals, as distinct undertakings, has only barely begun, although the vernacular editions of parts of the ritual include some adaptations and additional elements.

See also LITURGICAL BOOKS OF THE ROMAN RITE.

[T. C. O'BRIEN]

ROBERTS, THOMAS D'ESTERRE

Archbishop of Bombay (1937–50), outspoken defender of the importance of personal conscience and intelligent obedience, b. March 7, 1893 in Le Havre, d. Feb. 28, 1976 in London. He was the son of a British consul descended from a line of French Huguenots. His father became a Catholic in 1900 and Thomas was educated at the Jesuit college in Liverpool. He entered the Society of Jesus Sept. 7, 1909 and was ordained to the priesthood Sept. 20, 1925. After teaching at Jesuit colleges at Preston and Beaumont, followed by a term as rector of St. Francis Xavier's College, Liverpool, he was appointed archbishop of Bombay in 1937, an appointment he first learned about from reading a local newspaper.

The See of Bombay at the time of his appointment had a long history of ecclesiastical divisions. The Portuguese, the original colonizers, had received from the Holy See the privileges of *padroado* protectorate, the government's right to approve ecclesiastical appointments. With Bombay under British rule, an agreement was reached that the archbishop would be alternately English and Portuguese. The sharp rivalries among the different factions within the archdiocese Abp. Roberts sought to overcome first, by personal diplomacy with the Portuguese government in Lisbon and then by reorganizing parish boundaries. He initiated a wide-ranging program of social services, with particular emphasis on the needs of women, soldiers, and sailors. He also wrote a series of letters to children in the local newspaper that became an effective vehicle of instruction for young and old.

Above all, Abp. Roberts recognized that at a time of nationalistic aspirations for independence, the Church in Bombay should eventually be guided by an Indian archbishop. He pressed this view on the Holy See and, in 1946, an Indian, Valerian Gracias (later Cardinal), was appointed auxiliary. Bp. Gracias quickly assumed the day-to-day administration of the archdiocese as Abp. Roberts deliberately absented himself. When, in 1950, Bp. Gracias was officially named archbishop, Roberts returned to England.

In the next 25 years he became known as an unconventional churchman who labored indefatigably for such causes as disarmament and world peace, for a rethinking of church teaching on artificial contraception, and for the rights of personal conscience. In 1954 he published *Black Popes–Authority: Its Uses and Abuses*, a small volume which attracted attention for its frank criticism of secular and ecclesiastical authoritarianism. He urged the need for "intelligent obedience," which he understood to be a characteristically Jesuit and Ignatian ideal. One of the most painful episodes in his life was his delation to Rome (1960) by the apostolic delegate for his views and public statements. Abp. Roberts, insisting that most of the charges were untrue, urged a full and impartial hearing. Although Pope John XXIII promised such a hearing, it never was held. Roberts was not satisfied with assurances that he had been vindicated simply because the matter had not been pursued. Instead, he contrasted the standards of fairness found in English Common Law with the secrecy of ecclesiastical procedures, where there was never reparation of the damage done to personal reputation.

Through the years of Vatican Council II (1962–65), Abp. Roberts called for reform of the Roman Curia. Although he never did speak in the formal sessions of the Council (despite his request to do so), he became a popular figure at the press briefings outside of the formal sessions. He sought to have the Council issue a strong condemnation of all nuclear weapons, to support the rights of conscientious objectors to war, and urged reexamination of the teaching on artificial contraception, since he was convinced that the absolute ban on all contraception imposed heavy burdens on many Catholic families. The last issue brought him into conflict with members of the English hierarchy, in particular, Card. John Heenan, in 1964. Abp. Roberts had admitted publicly that he simply could not understand the rational arguments for the prohibition of all artificial contraception. Card. Heenan defended the traditional ban and lamented the fact that the faithful were being misled by some of their shepherds. The establishment of a special commission by Pope Paul VI to study the question was seen by some as a vindication of the questions raised by Roberts. The encyclical *Humanae vitae*, issued in 1968, however, reiterated the traditional teaching.

Although considered by some to be a "maverick bishop," Abp. Roberts was a man with a rare sense of the ridiculous and the absurd, and his sense of humor appealed even to those who disagreed with him. He was also a pastor of extraordinary warmth and sensitivity to human suffering, and many who came in contact with him through retreats in England and the U.S., and also through personal counseling at the Jesuit residence in Farm Street in London, found him a great source of faith. In addition to *Black Popes*, he wrote a foreword to *Nuclear Weapons and Christian Conscience* (1961) and contributions to *Problems of Authority* (1962), *Objections to Roman Catholicism* (1963) and *Contraception and Holiness* (1963). His last book was *The Diary of Bathsheba* (1970).

Bibliography: D. A. HURN, *Archbishop Roberts, SJ–His Life and Writings* (London 1966).

[J. A. O'HARE]

ROTA, ROMAN

The Roman Rota, a tribunal of the Roman *Curia (12:683) concerned with marriage, has recently modified its matrimonial jurisprudence. Rotal jurisprudence relative to matrimonial consent has been based on CIC c. 1081. This canon states that the free consent of the parties is the personal element which constitutes marriage. That consent, however, must be given by persons who are legally capable of rendering such consent; otherwise, the marriage is invalid.

The diriment (invalidating) matrimonial impediments listed in the Code (CIC cc. 1067–80) delineate the consensual capacity legally required and are the traditionally recognized grounds on which a formal annulment is granted should one of these impediments be proved to have existed at the time of the marriage ceremony. Despite the fact that insanity (*amentia*) is not specifically enumerated among these diriment impediments, insanity has always been admitted as a grounds for nullity.

Recently, the Rota has admitted certain emotional or psychological states less pathologic and debilitating than insanity as grounds for nullity. This jurisprudence appears to be a more precise understanding of the diriment impediments found in c. 1067 (i.e., biological nonage) and in c. 1068 (i.e., sexual impotency). Viewing marriage as being basically a unique interpersonal relationship or convenant with offspring as its "crowning glory" rather than a contract or union directed primarily to the procreation of offspring has led to this understanding (cf. Vatican II, *Gaudium et spes* 48). Thus, psychological nonage or immaturity as well as psychological or psychiatric inability to comprehend, undertake, or fulfill the basic terms of this unique interpersonal relationship from the beginning are both seen as grounds for nullity.

It must be noted, however, that recent jurisprudence also cautions that grounds for nullity do not necessarily exist simply because conjugal love is absent or has ceased or because a marriage has failed. This caution was explicitly contained in Pope Paul VI's address to the Rota, Feb. 9, 1976 (ActApS 68 [1976] 204–208) and in a decision of the Apostolic Signature dated Nov. 29, 1975 (O'Connor Suppl on c. 1081, pp. 8, 63–84).

Bibliography: M. E. LAVIN, "The Rotal Decision before Serrano, 5 April 1973..." *Jurist* 36 (1976) 302–316. Paul VI, Address to Rota, tr. Origins 5 (1976) 614–616. W. A. SCHUMACHER, "Interpersonal Communication in Marriage," StCan 9 (1975) 15–35; "The Importance of Interpersonal Relations in Marriage," StCan 10 (1976) 75–112. J.-M. SERRANO-RUIZ, "Le droit à la communauté de vie et d'amour conjugal comme objet du consentement matrimonial...," StCan 10 (1976) 271–301. Also cf. the decisions of L. Anné, Feb. 25, 1969, *Monitor ecclesiasticus* 96 (1971) 21–38; of L. Anné, July 22, 1969 (unpublished, prot. n. 8971), and of C. Lefebvre, March 1, 1969, *Il Diritto ecclesiastico* 81 (1970) 219–234.

[M. E. LAVIN]

RUBRICS

The word "rubrics" refers to the directions and instructions for celebrating a liturgical rite. The word comes from the Latin word *rubrica*—a type of red earth which could be used as a coloring agent. From the 8th or 9th century in liturgical books the text of the prayers is in black ink and the indications for ceremonies and gestures is in red ink (*rubrica*). By the 14th century the term "rubrics" indicates the liturgical laws and directives. *Lege rubrum si vis intelligere nigrum*—If you want to understand the black (the prayers), read the red (the rubrics, the directives).

The Roman Missal promulgated in 1570 by Pius V carried the rubrics as front matter. The Missal began with an *Ordo Missae*, listing the rubrics to be observed in the celebration of Mass. The last instance of this tradition is the decree *Nuper edita*, Jan. 27, 1965. After this date there is a radical change. The new Roman Missal promulgated by Paul VI, April 3, 1969, begins not with a list of rubrics but with an *Institutio generalis*—an instruction giving not only rubrics, but the reasons for the laws, the function of the prayers and ceremonies, and explanations helping an intelligent, devout and fruitful celebration. This new form of introduction—to the Missal, and to all the revised rites—indicates a radical change in perspective and is designed to encourage a new school of thought—a new spirit. Vatican Council II's document on the liturgy teaches that "when the liturgy is celebrated, something more is required than the mere observance of the laws governing valid and licit celebration" (*Sacrosanctum Concilium* 11).

See also LITURGICAL LAWS, AUTHORITY OF.

Bibliography: A. BUGNINI, "Rubriche," EncCatt 10:1427–1429. A. G. MARTIMORT, *L'Église en prière* (Paris, Rome 1965). T. RICHSTATTER, *Liturgical Law Today* (Chicago 1977).

[T. RICHSTATTER]

S

SACRAMENTAL THEOLOGY

Since Vatican Council II there is still no comprehensive development in the general theology of the Sacraments (16:399). Nonetheless, there has been considerable restructuring of the discipline (12:789).

Methodology. To avoid an understanding of the Sacraments as epiphenomenal to human life, greater efforts have been made by theologians to relate each of the Sacraments to some existential aspect of human life: e.g., relating Baptism with the experience of initiation with all the dynamics and implications this involves; relating the Eucharist to the human experience of people-eating-together and of all the factors, cognitive and non-cognitive which this implies. Such efforts have given an incarnational or in-secularizing stamp to sacramental theology and have rendered the meaning of the Sacraments more personally understandable. The influence of phenomenology is quite evident in all this, particularly in the phenomenological analysis of the human meaning of realities as contrasted with merely their entitative dimension. Nonetheless, this approach, healthy as it is, must be complemented by a Christological methodology. The roots of sacramental theology lie in an understanding of Christ as the original Sacrament. This background alone makes it possible to speak of the Church as Sacrament, a Sacrament of the Christ-event. And only against this twofold sacramental background does the sacramentality of the individual Sacraments become theologically meaningful. This entire approach enriches sacramental theology by laying bare its interconnectedness with both Christology and ecclesiology. Moreover, the results of decades of painstaking research on the history of the various Sacraments have, in the contemporary period, provided the theologian with a vista of the sacramental life of the Church broader and more varied than that of the scholastic, Counter-Reformation or 19th-century theologian. The interplay of these three methodologies, phenomenological, Christological, and historical, has left a clear imprint on the character of current sacramental theology.

Ecumenical Dialogue. As contemporary ecumenical dialogue continues, the Churches see more clearly what are the central issues and factors within sacramental theology and what are the more secondary areas of theological interpretation. Concentration in this dialogue, of course, has been on Baptism, Eucharist, Orders, and Marriage, but the other Sacraments have not been untouched. In the Catholic pursuit of sacramental theology more emphasis has been given to the positive elements and insights found in the sacramental theology of Protestant traditions (e.g. the emphasis on the Word and on the Spirit). Concern and interest in the Eastern Orthodox sacramental tradition has likewise enriched the contemporary work in this field (e.g., Sacraments as Mysteries). Two elements deserve notice regarding this ecumenical dialogue: first, the real presence of Christ within each of the Sacraments has been put more sharply into focus; secondly, the almost clear acceptance of each Church's Baptism has raised the theological issue regarding the nonacceptance of Eucharistic hospitality, since Baptism welcomes a person into Eucharistic community (*see* EUCHARISTIC SHARING).

Sacraments and Society. *Liberation theology embodies a considerable amount of study of and emphasis on the social dimension of both Church and Sacrament. To date the more fundamental work has been done in the area of ecclesiology, but the more the Church is seen in its social context and as a sign or Sacrament for a given social milieu, the more sacramental theology is being restructured accordingly. Sacraments are meaningful only within a community and it is precisely here that both the social dimension and the social crisis of sacramental theology become clear. Sacraments are meant to nourish and enrich the community, but the quality of the community itself is at stake. If a community remains indifferent to glaring human inequities and if the sacramental life of the Church continues with no change in the community vis-à-vis concrete human needs, then the question of sacramental efficacy becomes acute. Even though sacramental theology is not the same as sacramental action, but only a reflection on and an elaboration of that action, sacramental theology today must address itself to the concrete, existential questions regarding the way in which sacramental action both is and should be one of the factors creating a truly Christian community.

Sacraments and Spirituality. The growing interest in spirituality has also affected the theology of the Sacraments, insofar as more concern has been placed on the Sacraments as prayer. Rather than the classical analysis by structural elements (matter, form, minister, subject), sacramental theology is beginning to root itself in a more basic structure, namely that of communal and personal prayer. The contemporary theological approach to grace as relational and not as a "thing" shows its influence here with the emphasis on the Sacrament as a prayerful encounter or relation both with Christ and with God.

Bibliography: M. AMALDOSS, "Sémiologie et sacrement," *Maison-Dieu* 114 (1973) 7–35. B. COOKE, *Ministry to Word and Sacraments* (Philadelphia 1976). P.-M. GY, "Problèmes de théologie sacramentaire," *Maison-Dieu* 110 (1972) 129–142. B. LEE, *The Becoming of the Church* (New York 1974). C. MAYER, "Transformation der Gesellschaft mit Hilfe der Sakramente," ThQschr 155 (1975) 144–149. K. OSBORNE, "Methodology and the Christian Sacraments," *Worship* 48 (1974) 536–549. F. SCHUPP, *Glaube–Kultur–Symbol* (Düsseldorf 1974). A. VERGOTE, "La réalisation symbolique dans l'expression cultuelle," *Maison-Dieu* 111 (1972) 110–131.

[K. B. OSBORNE]

SACRAMENTARY

A sacramentary is the book of the presider's prayers for the celebration of the Eucharist and other Sacraments or rites celebrated at Mass (*see* PRESIDENTIAL PRAYERS). From about the 5th century the Church has used sacramentaries for the ministers of the Eucharist (12:792–800). In the Middle Ages such other service books as lectionaries and collections of chants were combined with the priest's sacramentary in a process which eventually resulted in the full (or "plenary") Roman Missal (9:897) known until the liturgical reform called for by Vatican Council II.

The Sacramentary Text. In the current usage of the Roman rite the Sacramentary has again become an entity unto itself for Eucharistic celebrations along with the Mass Lectionary and the *Graduale Romanum* (for music). The reestablished existence of the Sacramentary flows from one of the main intuitions of Vatican II's Constitution on the Sacred Liturgy, which requires that "each person, minister or layman, who has an active role to perform [in the liturgy], should not do all, but only those parts which pertain to his office by the nature of the rite" (*Sacrosanctum Concilium* 28; also GenInstrRomMissal 58). As a result, specific books pertain to specific functions of the service. Now an entirely proper distinction between the role of the priest and the roles of other members of the liturgical assembly is assured, with correction of that absorption of other people's participation by the presider sanctioned by the full missal. Regarding terminology, the United States and Canada have adopted the title "Sacramentary," while other English-speaking countries have assigned the title "Roman Missal" to this same book, containing the one standard translation of the pertinent parts of the 1969 *Missale Romanum* (*see* INTERNATIONAL COMMISSION ON ENGLISH IN THE LITURGY; LITURGICAL BOOKS OF THE ROMAN RITE).

The current American Sacramentary was approved by the National Conference of Catholic Bishops in November 1973, confirmed by the Holy See the following year, and went into effective use on Dec. 1, 1974, First Sunday of Advent. The book contains several introductory documents: along with the decrees of promulgation there are an American Foreword; the General Instruction of the Roman Missal and its American Appendix; the General Norms for the Liturgical Year along with the General Roman Calendar and the Proper Calendar for the United States; the Directory for Masses with Children; and a Table of Movable Feasts. Following the introductory material are the main sections of texts prayed by the presider at Mass and their responses: the Proper of Seasons; Order of Mass; Proper of Saints; Commons (of Pastors, Martyrs; Blessed Virgin, etc.); Ritual Masses; Masses and Prayers for Various Needs and Occasions; Votive Masses; Masses for the Dead; and four Appendices (that include musical settings to some texts and the Order of Mass in Latin).

General Instruction. In its present state the Sacramentary presents a changed picture of the celebration of Mass in accord with Vatican II's call for reform. Differences in structure, forms, and terminology have resulted from a decade or more of revision. The General Instruction, which gives both outline and guiding principles of the celebration, provides rich insights into the extent of the transformations which the Consilium for the Implementation of the Constitution on the Liturgy first, then the Congregation for Divine Worship carried out and brought to term. This General Instruction takes the place of the *Ritus servandus* and of the other rubrical directives that the old full Roman Missal contained. There is a marked, great difference in spirit and approach between the two texts. Whereas the old rubrics were concerned with the fine details of ritual and with what the priest did at the altar, the new Instruction can easily be described as a liturgical document of primary importance. It goes far beyond rubrical directives and sets out the nature of Eucharistic celebration. As is the case with the introductions to other postconciliar rites, its assigned task is to explain as well as describe and thus fulfill a theological-pastoral function along with its indicative role. Each major section is prefaced by a theological statement about the Mass or that part of it for which directives are given.

The General Instruction contains eight chapters. The first is an introduction which stresses the importance and dignity of the Eucharistic celebration. The second reviews the various elements of the celebration, its structure and parts. The third illustrates the roles of everyone taking part in the celebration—priest, people, and ministers. The fourth sets out the various forms of the Mass, and also contains norms for Communion under both kinds. The fifth treats of the arrangement of the church building as the place of celebration. The sixth covers what is needed for the celebration—furnishings, instruments, and vestments. The seventh provides instructions for the choice of texts at Mass—readings, chants, prayers; it also indicates the possibility of adaptation and options. The eighth and final chapter concerns Votice Masses, Masses for the Dead, Ritual Masses, Masses for Special Occasions. Chapters two and four will serve as the basis for discussion of the following two topics.

Structure of the Mass. Two main parts form the heart of the Mass, viz., the Liturgy of the Word and the Liturgy of the Eucharist; they are preceded by a set of introductory rites and followed by concluding rites.

Introductory Rites. The introductory rites provide for an Entrance Song, Greeting, Penitential Rite (with several invocations proper to the American Sacramentary), *Kyrie, Gloria,* and Opening Prayer or Collect. At Sunday liturgies the Sprinkling with Water may replace the Penitential Rite and serve as a reminder of Baptism. Taken together, all these actions set a tone of beginning, introduction and preparation for what follows.

Liturgy of the Word. Scripture Readings (two during the week and three on Sundays and solemnities) are the central parts of the Liturgy of the Word, which culminates in the Gospel. A Responsorial Psalm with its accompanying Antiphon and the Alleluia with its verse are the chants between the Readings. If not sung, the Alleluia and Verse may be omitted, but the Psalm is always to be included. A Homily after the Gospel then draws lessons for Christian living from the scriptural passages and links their message to the overall Eucharistic mystery being celebrated at Mass. Two remaining actions of the Liturgy of the Word are the recitation of the Profession of Faith or Creed on Sundays and solemnities, and the General Intercessions or Prayer of the Faithful (according to the fourfold outline of intentions: for the needs of the Church; for public authorities and the salvation of the world; for those oppressed by any need; and for the local community; these are sometimes called Bidding Prayers).

Liturgy of the Eucharist. As sort of a transition to, but actually part of, the Liturgy of the Eucharist, the Preparation of the Gifts takes the place of what was formerly called the "Offertory." The Prayer over the Gifts by the presider concludes this preparatory period (during which incensation of the altar, the gifts and the assembly may take place). Then the *Eucharistic Prayer begins with its chief elements of: thanksgiving (expressed especially in the *Preface which starts with an opening dialogue); "Holy, Holy" Acclamation; the Epiclesis or Invocation for the Spirit's Power to render both the gifts and those who receive them holy; the Narrative of Institution and Consecration; the Anamnesis or Recalling of Christ's passion, resurrection, ascension and—in four of the official Eucharistic Prayers now in use throughout the Roman rite—second coming in glory; the Offering; the Intercessions; and Final Doxology, which is concluded by the people's Amen. The Communion rite next concludes the Liturgy of the Eucharist. It involves the Lord's Prayer; Rite or Sign of Peace; Breaking of the Bread and Commingling accompanied by the "Lamb of God" verses; private preparation of the Priest; showing of the Eucharistic bread to the people and their prayer; personal Communion of the priest preceding the reception of the Eucharist by the people during which the Communion Antiphon or some other suitable song is chanted. A period of silent prayer or some song follows, and finally a Prayer after Communion is said by the presider, in which he petitions for the effects of the mystery just celebrated.

Concluding Rites. Two parts of the concluding rite are the Blessing (sometimes given in a solemn form) and the Dismissal of the members of the congregation (*see* SOLEMN BLESSING AND PRAYER OVER THE PEOPLE).

Chapter 2 of the General Instruction also includes several paragraphs on the "Elements of the Mass." Noteworthy items among those elements are "Reading and Explaining the Word of God," "Importance of Singing," "Actions and Postures," and "Silence" considered to be a means of promoting a sense of recollection, meditation on the Word proclaimed to the worshipping assembly, and prayer (*see* SILENCE IN WORSHIP).

Forms of the Mass. Gone from the Sacramentary are differences in the forms of celebrating Mass based on the degree of solemnity, as was the case with the "low,"

"high" and "solemn high" Masses of former liturgical practice. In their place the General Instruction gives three new modes of celebration and ranks them in a descending order of normal liturgical occurrence: "Mass with a Congregation," "Concelebrated Mass," and "Mass without a Congregation."

The first of these three forms of the Mass envisions a more "common form" usually celebrated in most parishes, and another form with a deacon assisting the priest presider.

*Concelebration by several priests is a restoration of an ancient usage that is only occasionally celebrated in parishes, while it seems more appropriate in houses of religious where several priests reside.

Finally, Mass celebrated without a congregation present, but always with at least one minister present "except in serious necessity," is described briefly by the closing numbers of Chapter 4 of the General Instruction.

Further Developments. Since the Sacramentary went into use in 1974 its sections related to other rites still undergoing revision have been changing their formulation and ritual contents. A second edition of the Latin *Editio typica* of the *Missale Romanum* was issued on March 27, 1975 and this new edition incorporated changes in liturgical usage promulgated before that date.

Adaptations called for by local developments and conditions in the U.S. have also modified some sections of the Sacramentary, and a revised edition will bring the book up to date. Fundamental modifications will not be made, but the very occurrence will show that the rate of liturgical reform can be expected to remain constant as assimilation by clergy and people of the revised rites of Mass and other liturgical forms takes place.

Bibliography: P. COUGHLAN, *The New Mass, a Pastoral Guide* (Washington, D.C. 1969). J. D. CRICHTON, *Christian Celebration: The Mass* (London 1971). P. JOUNEL, "Le Missel de Paul VI," *Maison-Dieu* 103 (1970) 16–45.

[J. SULLIVAN]

SACRAMENTARY, MUSIC OF

Singing should be used extensively at Mass, depending upon the talents and abilities of those who are participating, both the presiding ministers and the entire congregation (*see* MASS, MUSIC OF). Although it is not necessary to sing all parts which may be sung, the General Instruction in the Sacramentary urges that priorities be established and that preference be given to "the more significant parts, especially those which are sung by the priest or ministers with the people responding or those to be sung by the priest and people together" (GenInstrRomMissal 19). In keeping with these recommendations and in order to provide a setting which might become familiar to the clergy, it was decided to include a musical arrangement of the ministerial chants in the 1974 Sacramentary.

Development. A subcommittee was appointed by the International Commission on English in the Liturgy (ICEL) and an initial draft of the main dialogues and acclamations was prepared. The first meeting of this subcommittee took place in Rome in November 1972. At that time the basic work was done on the Prefaces, leaving the music of Holy Week, the Memorial Acclamations, and the remainder of the Prefaces to be completed. The draft was sent for criticism to approximately thirty musicians representing the English-speaking regions of the Church.

As a result of the comments received it was decided that three projects would be undertaken: the first was to be based on an attempt to preserve the Gregorian counterpart in the melodies (*see* GREGORIAN CHANT); the second, based on free rhythm, chantlike, but without having Gregorian melodies as a point of departure; and the third, a more contemporary setting, probably using measured rhythm.

A composer was commissioned to carry out the first project. The 1970 *editio typica* of the *Missale Romanum*, supplemented by material for the same, and printed in the *editio typica*, *Ordo cantus Missae* (Typis Polyglottis Vaticanis, 1972) was used as a point of reference. The English text had already been officially determined in consultation with the music experts of the ICEL Advisory Committee. (It should be noted that two members of the committee—Rev. Percy Jones of Australia and Rev. Stephen Somerville of Canada—were chosen precisely for their musical expertise.) An attempt was made to devise a formula that would be parallel to the Gregorian but suitable to support the English text and which, in addition, would enhance and respect the genius of the English language. The unmusicality of many of the official translations, and the fact that the English text is quite different from the Latin equivalent in verbal structure, made the task a difficult one. Upon completion, the project was submitted to the Music Advisory Committee where a number of revisions were made.

The adaptation is related to Gregorian yet distinct enough not to warrant another chant version. To date, the second and third projects have not been undertaken.

The Music. Music is included in three sections of the Sacramentary.

(1) In the Order of Mass with a Congregation are included:

(a) one setting of the Introductory Dialogue to the Preface, including the responses of the people; one setting of the "Holy, Holy" (encouraging the celebrant to sing this part with the people);

(b) the chants of the Prefaces of the Eucharistic Prayer for every text (84);

(c) one setting of the Acclamation "Christ has died . . .";

(d) in the Communion rite, one setting of the Our Father, Deliver Us, and Doxology.

(2) In the Proper, a setting of the Good Friday Reproaches and the music for the Easter Vigil.

(3) The Music Appendix includes:

(a) one setting of each of the four Eucharistic Prayers;

(b) three settings of the Greeting, two of the Penitential Rite; one Opening Prayer; one Prayer over the Gifts and Prayer after Communion; five versions of the General Intercessions;

(c) one setting of each Acclamation; an alternate setting of the Lord's Prayer; the Rite of Peace; two Concluding Rites; two Prayers over the People; and three forms of the Dismissal Rite;

(d) Tone I and II Introductory Dialogue and Preface I of Advent;

(e) Invitation to the Lord's Prayer—I, II, III;

(f) Rite of Peace, Concluding Rite, and verses before the Blessing by the Bishop.

The Music Appendix was made optional and includes various settings taken from earlier liturgical books approved by NCCB. The American, English, Irish, Australian, and Canadian editions include the appendix. The Indian edition includes only the music for Holy Week and the Response and Doxology within the Order of Mass with a Congregation. The Canadian edition prints a unique musical notation within the arrangement of the Eucharistic Prayers. The inclusion of the musical arrangements is an effort to encourage the clergy to make use of song in order to highlight those parts that are more important. It is hoped that the third proposed project will be undertaken in the near future in order to provide further encouragement.

See also CONGREGATIONAL SINGING; LITURGICAL MUSIC; MUSICOLOGY, SACRED.

[M. A. O'CONNOR]

SACRAMENTS (THEOLOGY)

The main directions and problems in the theology of each Sacrament will be sketched with concentration on the ecclesial nature of each of them in accordance with the emphasis in Vatican Council II's Constitution on the Church, namely the way in which the Sacraments constitute the People of God (*Lumen gentium* 11).

Baptism. Two points continue to recur in contemporary theological discussion on Baptism: first, a deeper understanding of Baptism as an initiation of a new member into the Christian community; and secondly a deeper integration of faith, both on the part of the one baptized and on the part of the Christian community as a totality.

As regards the first point, the insights gathered from contemporary biblical and historical scholarship on Baptism in the early Church help to put in focus the nature of initiation. It is certainly not a question of slavishly returning to an ancient baptismal ritual, but rather of incorporating the essential qualities of Baptism into a contemporary theological framework. Early baptismal liturgy and theology stressed the role of the community and today there is a clear effort to de-privatize both the theology and practice of Baptism (*see* CHRISTIAN INITIATION, SACRAMENTS OF).

As regards the second point, considerable theological discussion has centered on the element of faith: faith when there is question of *infant Baptism; faith when there is question of an adult Baptism either within a predominantly Christian culture or within a predominantly non-Christian culture. The faith in question is that of the recipient, the family, and the community. The entire discussion is controlled by the understanding that Baptism is an *initiation* into a faith community. Two implications of this have merited a great deal of discussion: ecumenically, the mutual acceptance of Baptism by the various Churches raises the issue of the acceptance or nonacceptance to Eucharistic hospitality as well; secondly, the whole process of Christian initiation is not being limited to Baptism, but taken as a catechumenate, Baptism, Confirmation, and Eucharist united into an integrated process.

*Original sin has played a central issue in all these discussions, and there are theologians who generally retain the traditional teaching of the Church on this matter as well as theologians who consider original sin so detrimental to theological thought that they wish to remove it from theological dialogue.

Confirmation. The relationship between Baptism and Confirmation continues to be problematic for contemporary theology. Theologians and liturgical scholars tend to go in two different directions: there are those who see an extremely close unity between the two

Sacraments, with the result that a protracted catechumenate during infancy and childhood is being stressed so that a personal faith commitment can be made with the reception of these two Sacraments. Others see less unity and stress the adult profession of faith as a centering theological element for Confirmation, thus allowing Baptism at an early age, even in infancy, and placing Confirmation at an age later than customary in the Western Church.

In contemporary theological discussion on Confirmation, there is also an emphasis on the outpouring of the Holy Spirit in both Baptism and Confirmation as a corrective to statements by some adherents of the *charismatic renewal that are seen as misleading.

Reconciliation. Since Vatican II the renewal of the Sacrament of Penance has centered theological discussion around the idea of reconciliation. The main factors involved in this are: the Christian community as always in need of purification and at all times welcoming sinners into its membership; the lifelong need of conversion on the part of the individual Christian; the sacramental celebration of reconciliation as a major moment in this process of conversion; the understanding of sin as an offense against both God and the community, and, correspondingly, of reconciliation with both God and the community.

A Theological Problem. A new theology of reconciliation is found in the Introduction of the 1973 *Ordo Paenitentiae*; it calls upon the priest-minister to be much more than a judge. He is to enter more deeply into the role of a spiritual director and guide. Yet this directive is somewhat thwarted by the threefold form of the Sacrament of Reconciliation and the theologian is left in a somewhat ambivalent state. The first form (one to one) places great weight on spiritual direction; the second and third forms (liturgical celebrations of the community) place a greater emphasis on the community as a reconciling community, than on the penitent-confessor relation. This disjuncture between the private-personal (historically the Celtic form) and the public-communal (historically the Graeco-Roman form) cannot but leave the theologian at a loss as to their integration.

Positive Gains. A number of important achievements have been made, however, by the renewal of the Sacrament. First of all, there is clearly a pronounced prayer-character to the entire sacramental celebration, which involves a greater integration of the theology of prayer and a theology of sacramental reconciliation. Secondly, there is a greater emphasis on the social nature of sin. Contemporary theological discussion on the theological nature of sin has, of course, affected the understanding of this Sacrament, but the deprivatization of sin is clearly an enrichment of theology on sin and on reconciliation. Thirdly, the Sacrament of Reconciliation is solidly placed within the ambit of forming a reconciling, Christian community. Sparked to some degree by *liberation theology, this emphasis brings out the intimate bond between Sacrament and the quality of Christian community.

Even granting all these achievements, nonetheless, the most acute question that will be raised theologically in the decades to come is this: why confess to a priest at all? Theologians have already seen the acuteness of this question and have begun to address it.

Eucharist. The Eucharist is seen as part of initiation into the Christian community and this has helped to integrate Baptism, Confirmation, and Eucharist. It has also helped to highlight the role of the Christian community in the Eucharistic celebration. Theology on the Eucharist has clearly changed and some of the changes are due to the following factors: an enlarged notion of sacramentality (Christ as the original Sacrament, the Church as the Sacrament of the Christ-event); the confrontation between classical Eucharistic theology (transubstantiation) and contemporary molecular and atomic science (one of the major influences behind the discussion on transsignification; 16:1); the stress on the social nature of the Sacrament of the Eucharist is important to ecumenism (cf. World Council of Churches, *One Baptism, One Eucharist and a Mutually Recognized Ministry*, 1975), and it is also stressed in the writings of *liberation theology.

On the doctrine of the Real Presence, the influence of contemporary phenomenology has played an important role. Basic to an understanding of the Real Presence is the phenomenon of human presence: a presence offered and a presence accepted; a presence that is not so much an either-or situation as a more-or-less situation. The connection between the Real Presence of Christ in the Eucharist and the Real Presence of Christ in the proclamation of the Word and the gathering of the faithful in prayer (cf. HolyCommIntrod 6), is still being investigated. The sign of this presence of Christ in the Eucharist today is not seen so much in the consecrated bread and wine as such, but in the Eucharistic meal, i.e., people-eating-together, which enhances the communal aspect of this Sacrament.

Discussion also continues on the Eucharist within the ecumenical *bilateral consultations and gains have been made in reaching a consensus on fundamental aspects of Eucharistic theology: on sacrifice, memorial, and Real Presence. These discussions have helped participants to sort out essentials from issues of secondary rank in Eucharistic teaching.

Anointing of the Sick. Since Vatican II the theology of the Anointing of the Sick has been guided by the transfer from death to sickness as focus. Contemporary studies on the history of this Sacrament have aided considerably in enlarging the theological considerations for this Sacrament, but a retardant is the fact that there has not yet appeared a developed theology of sickness.

The connection between this Sacrament and the forgiveness of sin, which became central during the latter part of the Carolingian renaissance, brought with it a clericalization of the Sacrament. Earlier lay-anointing had been widespread throughout the Church up until that time. That presents the contemporary theologian with still another area for clarification: the relationship between anointing and the forgiveness of sin. Some light may thereby be shed on the present restriction of the Sacrament only to priestly ministry.

Here too stress on the communal celebration of this Sacrament, following *Lumen gentium*, indicates far more the fact that the Sacraments really are of the community and do constitute the People of God.

Order and Ministry. Phenomenologically, contemporary theology on the Sacrament of Order sees the issue of *ministry to be service rather than power. The study of service among human beings leads also to the study of service as exercised by Jesus. Indeed, the center of Christian priestliness lies in the priestliness of Jesus himself as he is human. As God, Jesus is not a priest; but as man he is, and even more he is the one and only priest. All other priestliness is only a Sacrament of that one and only priestliness. The sacramentality of ministry is a basis for a genuine spirituality of ministry, since it clearly makes priestliness sacramental, i.e., a mystery of faith (cf. *Lumen gentium* 10–12).

Historical studies on the Sacrament of Order have helped present a better picture of an emergent ministry within the Church and a diversified pattern of ministry. Of importance is the connection Vatican II makes between priestly ministry and Christ as the sanctifier, teacher, and leader. The bishop, having the fulness of the priestly ministry, is so described, but the priest as well shares in each of these functions. The close relationship between episcopacy and priesthood is clear, but in both instances it is Christ who is the direct source of ministry; there is no question of the priest as a delegate of the bishop (cf. *Christus Dominus* 2; *Presbyterorum ordinis* 1).

The entire question of ministry has been the subject of ecumenical discussion, which has raised such issues as the meaning of *apostolic succession, the possibility of presbyteral ordination of women, and the meaning of the primacy of Peter and the *primacy of the pope. A further question which has arisen is the relationship between the universal *priesthood of all believers and the ministerial priesthood.

Marriage. The theology of marriage has been enriched by a number of historical studies on its development within the Christian framework. This history has indicated a great divergence of practice, which necessarily leads to a reconsideration of the theology of the Sacrament of Marriage. A second issue which has become a matter of discussion is the issue of *natural law. Since this was one of the bases for the classical approach to marriage, a change in an understanding of natural law cannot help but nuance the contemporary theology of marriage. Of importance to the question of the theology of marriage is the matter of the indissolubility of marriage or the question of divorce and remarriage. Here, too, much work has been done in rethinking New Testament passages and of historical data on this matter.

Central to a theology of marriage is the love of Christ for the Church, the reality of which Marriage is a Sacrament. Some theologians have seen this marital bond of love as one of covenant, but this has not been widely accepted.

Bibliography: L. BOFF, *Kleine Sakramentenlehre* (Düsseldorf 1975); "O que significa propriamente o sacramento," *Revista eclesiastica brazileira* 34 (1974) 860–895. B. COOKE, *Ministry to Word and Sacraments* (Philadelphia 1976). F. MCMANUS, "The Sacraments of the Church," ChSt 15 (1976) 349–371. K. OSBORNE, "Ministry as Sacrament," *Church-Ministry-Liturgy* (Helsinki 1977).

[K. OSBORNE]

SACRAMENTS AND DIVINE WORSHIP, CONGREGATION FOR THE

On July 11, 1975, Pope Paul VI established a new Roman Congregation for the Sacraments and Divine Worship by the apostolic constitution *Constans nobis* (ActApS 67 [1975] 417–420). This was done by formally suppressing two existing congregations of the Roman Curia and uniting their functions: the Congregation for the Discipline of the Sacraments, founded by Pope St. Pius X in 1908, and the Congregation for Divine Worship, founded by Paul VI in 1969. (The latter dicastery had resulted from a division of the Congregation of Sacred Rites, founded in 1588 by Pope Sixtus V; it assumed the liturgical responsibilities of the 16th-century Congregation and was in effect a successor of the postconciliar Consilium for the Implementation of the Constitution on the Liturgy.)

The new Congregation has a section for the Sacraments and a smaller section for the liturgy, with the respective scopes and competencies of the two merged dicasteries. The move was taken in the light of the close relationship of matters treated and may be expected gradually to eliminate the false dichotomy between "Sacraments" and "liturgy" in ecclesiastical discipline.

[F. R. MCMANUS]

SACRED COLLEGE

Recent papal documents have made two important changes in the governance of the College of Cardinals (12:817). The first deals with the selection of the dean and subdean of the College. According to Canon Law (CIC c. 237, n. 1) the cardinal who was first elevated to one of the seven suburbicarian dioceses (13:772) of Rome was to be dean of the College and was entrusted with the care of the Diocese of Ostia in addition to his own diocese. The dean takes precedence over all other cardinals and presides at their meetings. He is assisted by a subdean who is next in seniority as a cardinal bishop. Upon the death or resignation of the dean, the subdean immediately became dean (canon 237:2); and the next most senior cardinal bishop became subdean, and so on. The motu proprio of Paul VI, *Sacro cardinalium consilio* Feb. 22, 1965 (ActApS 57 [1965] 296–297) made the positions of dean and subdean elective by the cardinal bishops. The subdean or, in his absence, the senior cardinal bishop, presides over the election of the dean; the dean or, in his absence, the senior cardinal bishop, presides over the election of the subdean. The presiding officer informs the pope of the results of the election. The cardinal subdean no longer enjoys the right of succession; he only replaces the dean if the latter is impeded from acting.

Paul VI's motu proprio *Ingravescentem aetatem* Nov. 21, 1970 (ActApS 62 [1970] 810–813) dealt with mandatory retirement for cardinals. All must submit to the pope their resignations from all dicastery offices and curial institutes upon completing their 75th year. The pope then has the option of accepting the resignations. After his 80th birthday a cardinal can no longer be a member of a Roman dicastery or curial institute, nor can he enter the conclave and participate in a papal election. If he becomes eighty years old during the conclave, however, he continues to enjoy his right until the conclave is over. He retains all other privileges of cardinals until his death. If the Cardinal Camerlengo or the Grand Penitentiary completes his 80th year between the death of the pope and the conclave, the college is to elect his successor. If he completes his 80th year during the conclave, he continues in his office until the new pope is elected. Should the dean of the College be unable to attend the conclave because of age, the subdean fulfills his office. If the subdean, too, cannot attend, one of the senior cardinals is to be elected in his stead.

[J. G. JOHNSON]

ST. JOAN'S INTERNATIONAL ALLIANCE

St. Joan's International Alliance was founded in 1911 in London by Gabrielle Jeffery, May Kendall, and Beatrice Gadsby to work for women's rights. It has expanded into an international organization with sections in eight countries and members in a number of others. The United States Section was formed in 1965. The Alliance is an autonomous and politically neutral organization for Catholics, both men and women, and non-Catholics are admitted as associate members. Its goal is to secure legal and de facto equality between women and men in state, society, and Church. The Alliance has consultative status with the United Nations Economic and Social Council and UNESCO. Throughout the years of its existence, it has worked on such problems, among others, as the right of married women to choose their nationality, abolition of child marriages, admission of women to professions, the consular and diplomatic service, equal pay, and elimination of white slave traffic.

Since 1959 the Alliance has stressed the eradication of inequalities within the Church. A resolution adopted in 1961 asked that, if a diaconate was established as an independent ministry, it be open to women as well as men (see DIACONATE FOR WOMEN). It also asked that the laity, both men and women, be invited as observers and experts to Vatican Council II; requested that in the revision of Canon Law special attention be given to those provisions that refer to women (see WOMEN, CANON LAW ON), and for changes in the marriage liturgy. In 1964, the Alliance adopted a resolution at its annual meeting that "St. Joan's International Alliance reaffirms its loyalty and filial devotion, and expresses its conviction that should the Church in her wisdom and in her good time decide to extend to women the dignity of the priesthood, women would be willing and eager to respond." In 1977, the council of the Alliance adopted a resolution that the Congregation for the Doctrine of the Faith reexamine its Declaration on the Admission of Women to the Ministerial Priesthood, Oct. 15, 1976, in the light of studies by theologians, exegetes, and by the Pontifical Biblical Commission which challenge the arguments used in the Declaration.

The official publication of St. Joan's International Alliance is *The Catholic Citizen*, published from Geneva since 1915. The U.S. Section publishes a quarterly, *Bulletin of the United States Section of St. Joan's International Alliance*.

Bibliography: M. DALY, *The Church and the Second Sex* (New York 1968) 85–86. P. and W. PROCTOR, *Women in the Pulpit: Is God an Equal Opportunity Employer?* (New York 1976) 157–158.

[D. A. HAALAND]

SAINTS, MEMORIALS OF

The 1969 *Calendarium Romanum* distinguishes four degrees of celebration: solemnities, feasts, memorials, obligatory and optional (CalendRom 8–15). Solemnities and feasts are considered exceptional days; memorials are more simple observances or evocations of the servants of God. The term "memorial," traditional in liturgical history, is found in Vatican Council II's Constitution on the Sacred Liturgy as designating the feast of a saint (*Sacrosanctum Concilium* 104).

Obligatory Memorials. There are 63 obligatory memorials of the saints in the present calendar. The

*Sacramentary provides each with a proper Opening Prayer, a Prayer over the Gifts, and a Prayer after Communion. To preserve the unique character of the weekdays during Lent and the Easter season, only five obligatory memorials occur during March, April, and May. Moreover, whenever an obligatory memorial occupies a Lenten weekday, it may be celebrated as an optional memorial.

Optional Memorials. The calendar lists 95 optional memorials, i.e. those which, at the discretion of the celebrant, may be observed. At least one such Mass, however, should be celebrated when the saint is especially venerated in popular piety. A proper Opening Prayer is given in the Sacramentary, and the remaining texts are taken from the Common. At certain seasons (e.g., Advent weekdays after Dec. 17th), only the Opening Prayer may be used, the other texts being taken from the Proper of the Seasons. On Saturdays having no obligatory memorial, an optional memorial of the Blessed Virgin may be celebrated.

Bibliography: *Calendarium Romanum ex decreto Sacrosancti Oecumenici Concilii Vaticani II instauratum* (Typis Polyglottis Vaticanis 1969). GenInstrRomMissal 314–316.

[L. JOHNSON]

SECOND-CAREER VOCATIONS

In the severe and prolonged crisis of youth vocations which began in the U.S. in the early 1960s and has not yet worked itself out in the late 1970s attention is more and more being called to the fact that exclusive reliance on youth vocations is a very recent development.

Historical Background. The discipline of the Western Church requiring a life-commitment as a condition for public service in the Church developed from Christ's "conditions for discipleship" (cf. Lk 14.25–35). These conditions are obviously addressed to adults and all who respond in NT times were adults. Only in the Carolingian and medieval period with the foundation of monastery and cathedral schools was entrance into the dedicated life made possible for children and adolescents. The medieval universities, then the seminary legislation of Trent increased the flow of youth into the clerical and religious life. But it was not until the foundation of the teaching orders of the 18th and 19th centuries that exclusively or predominantly youth vocations became the objective and only in the 20th century with the universalization of compulsory schooling was the objective fully achievable.

A check on the age of entrance into the dedicated life in Butler's *Lives of the Saints* offers a useful point for evaluating the exclusive reliance on youth vocations. From the 5th through the 9th centuries about 19 percent of entrants into the priesthood or religious life were in their youth; 53 percent in the prime of life; about 28 percent in old age. In the four centuries preceding the above period practically all the saints had entered as adults; in the 20th century practically all entered as youths. On the single point of entrance age, the case with saints would seem to be as random as any others for purposes of a statistical sampling. The radical change in recent times, although initially remarkably successful in supplying dedicated personnel, now needs to be judged against the background of history.

Crisis in Vocations. In the U.S. in 1973 novices for religious life as sisters or brothers were down in numbers by 90 percent from 1962, then levelled off through

1977 to about 10 percent of the 1962 figure. Candidates for the diocesan priesthood fell by 60 percent from 1962 through 1977, in which year the number was still decreasing. Candidates for the priesthood in religious institutes dropped by some 70 percent between 1964 and 1977, in which year the number was falling even more sharply. The causes of so catastrophic a change will certainly prove to be complex. A great many indicators, however, point to a fear of life-commitment in the modern youth culture as the overwhelming cause. Another cause may be sought in the reliance on youth vocations. One response to Vatican Council II's call for renewal in the priestly and religious life has been a massive drive toward secular forms of life style and work; but there has also been a massive exodus from the dedicated to the secular life. There were 50,000 fewer religious women in the U.S. in 1977 than in 1966 (see RELIGIOUS INSTITUTES, DEPARTURES FROM). In the face of this remarkable phenomenon an obvious question arises: whether the renewal effort has been a conscious updating of the transcendent nature of the dedicated life or a subconscious striving by the first religious establishment in history lacking mature secular experience to explore and appropriate secular values. The question becomes particularly relevant when it is remembered that throughout history about 80 percent of priests and religious seem to have had mature secular experience before embracing the dedicated life.

The Second-Career Vocation Project. A de facto return to adult-entrance into the dedicated life is occurring as almost all novitiates and seminaries in the U.S. manifest a rapidly rising average entrance-age and a constantly increasing proportion of older men and women among their candidates. This spontaneous movement, however, is too slow to meet the worsening vocation crisis. The youthful fear of long-term commitment and the "change of consciousness" seem to be long-term phenomena. Thus a conscious and energetic return to the cultivation and acceptance of vocations at any age seems to be the right strategic response to the present crisis.

Origins. The Second-Career Vocation Project was begun at the University of Dayton in 1972 by the provincial of the Cincinnati Province of the Society of Mary as an attempt to bring these developments to the attention of the American Church and to begin research and experimentation for their solution. A comprehensive statistical study was inaugurated for every religious jurisdiction in the country for every year of the crisis, so as to establish conclusively the true dimensions of the phenomenon. All these jurisdictions were canvassed several times for reports on the research as it progressed and to try to arouse interest in exploiting the new "time of decision"—the after-forty period of life being created in post-industrial societies by an ever-lengthening life span and an ever-lowering age of retirement.

It was recognized that with all these efforts there would have to be a particular effort to encourage the continuation and even the intensification of youth recruitment, which had become, in recent generations, the exclusive object of effort. The new goal of youth recruitment, however, would be to keep options open into the college and adult years when fear of commitment would lessen with growing maturity. It developed that recruitment and formation personnel were so "locked in" on

youth recruitment, that the idea of centering expressly on older age groups made its way very slowly. What did make progress however, was a willingness to listen to older men and women who presented themselves on their own initiative to ask for admission into the religious life and the priesthood.

Objective. The specific objective of the Second-Career Vocation Project is to formalize the trend towards older candidates as much as possible by promoting the appointment of a special Second-Career Vocation Director in any diocese or religious institute sufficiently aware of the problem and opportunity. The work itself must be seen in two phases. First of all there is the attempt, simply by advertising, to "cream off" the vocations which have perdured among older people despite the universal insistence in recent times that after twenty-five years or so it was too late to apply. The second phase consists of reintroducing into the Christian consciousness the fact that one can follow the invitation of Christ at any age and that it should always be on the agenda in any career change. This was a normal part of Christian consciousness all through history, but has been very effectively removed since the 19th century. Such a broader effort on Christian reeducation will evidently take some time, but it is likely to be a very much easier task than trying to restore the pre-crisis, flourishing state of youth vocations. For this reason alone it is likely that the second-career effort will succeed.

Strategy. The indicated strategy is to accept readily any late vocations into the youth period before twenty-five and into the second-career period after forty. As a matter of fact, the fairly numerous late-vocation projects which have been set up, especially for admission to the priesthood, are gradually approaching the time when most of their candidates will be forty and over in age. The moderate number of prime-of-life vocations will increasingly find their place in the normal programs of recruitment and formation, since these latter will be handling a considerably older clientele than they had been used to before the crisis.

An awareness of these issues is important to the institutional life of the Church, since a collapse of recruitment of the magnitude indicated is a veritable time bomb whose effects will not be felt until it is too late to react. Existing personnel will be able to carry on, but their average age will increase with every passing year. About three decades (the time to pass from an average age of thirty-eight to an average age of sixty-eight) suffice to reach the point of no return; half of that time has already disappeared since the onset of the crisis.

Bibliography: The following are publications of the Second-Career Vocation Project. *Extent and Depth of the Present Crisis of Vocations in the Church.* (1976); *The Second-Career Vocation Project: Purposes, Constraints, Practical Exigencies.* (1977); *National Organization for Second-Career Vocations* (1977).

[W. J. FERREE]

SECONDARY EDUCATION, CATHOLIC

In October 1974 the Secondary School Department of the *National Catholic Educational Association published the following statement regarding Catholic secondary education:

Catholic high schools which achieve their specific purposes as religious and social educational institutions will survive the crisis of these days. We are firm in the belief that Catholic secondary education will endure today's discrimination and rejection in order to preserve and strengthen the intellectual and moral well being of tomorrow's world.

Lest anyone misunderstand our position, Catholic high school administrators are not absorbed with concerns of survival. We are concerned about our increased effectiveness in bringing about a world blessed by peace and justice because that is the mission of the Catholic Church and thus ours as well.

This statement came at a time of growing anxiety about the future of Catholic secondary schools. In a six-year period beginning 1965–66 and ending in 1971–72, there had been dramatic declines in the number of secondary schools. In 1971–72, 121 schools were closed. In the following five years, however, the number of high schools closed or consolidated has stabilized. In the year 1977–78, for instance, there were 24 schools closed, representing 1.5 percent of the total number of Catholic secondary schools. Several new schools were opened during this year. Likewise, during this period service at the secondary level of various ethnic groups increased sharply. For instance, enrollment of Black Americans increased from 3.7 percent in 1970–71 to 5.8 percent in 1976–77, and of Hispanic-surname students an increase of from 3.8 percent to 6.1 percent in the same period. Consideration of the context in which this progress and stabilization has occurred will resolve around heritage, purpose, curriculum, personnel, and finance. Finally, some projections for the future will be made.

The Heritage. The first schools to be structured apart from the home environment were the private academies. Prior to the Third Plenary Council of Baltimore held in 1884, support for Catholic elementary education was fostered by the first bishop in America, John Carroll. It was his hope that continued use would be made of the academies by Catholic high-school age youngsters. This hope gradually dimmed, however, as discrimination increased against Catholic immigrants and in 1799 the first Catholic secondary school was built. These early schools were built on sacrifice but expanded in number and enrollment rapidly, paralleling the pioneering spirit and westward movement of these early settlers. Catholic families found the public school environment generally to be Protestant and alien to their hopes and dreams.

Vocations to teaching congregations of men and women increased and the high schools, as well as the elementary parish schools, were generally staffed almost totally by members of these congregations. Gradually, as diocesan school offices and educational structures became more defined, fund-raising and building programs on a diocesan level came into being, with the result that the number of Catholic secondary schools expanded dramatically throughout the first half of the 20th century. In 1903 Bishop Conaty established the Catholic Education Association, later the National Catholic Educational Association, which was designed to provide professional leadership and service to Catholic schools, seminaries and colleges.

In 1925 the Supreme Court heard the case of *Pierce v. the Society of Sisters*, the Oregon School Case (10:738), and confirmed the right of parental choice in the selection of the type of schools for their youngsters. It also confirmed the right of the Church and of the various religious congregations to staff these schools. There was a general commitment to academic excellence and the promotion of Christian principles for family living in American society. As procedures for

accreditation of high schools were established by regional associations, the NCEA took the lead in promoting accreditation of Catholic high schools. The Commission on American Citizenship established at The Catholic University of America during this period developed curriculum materials in which the ideals and freedoms of the Bill of Rights and the Constitution were presented for Catholic schools and loyalty to America was stressed. Obedience to authority and to the teachings of the hierarchy were values highly esteemed in the secondary schools, and discipline was a hallmark. It would seem that this period was one of growth and expansion, although seeded from a base of minimal financial resources. A fledgling Catholic educational system was realizing maximum output. A frequently held goal by the schools was to develop Catholic leaders who would take their rightful place in American society.

By the middle of the 1960s the number of diocesan, private, and parish Catholic secondary schools was in excess of 2,000 and still expanding. At this point Vatican Council II was called, and the Church entered a period of questioning, declining financial support, and a sharp drop in the number of religious teachers and religious vocations for the staffing of the Catholic schools. Unions also in the large urban areas were becoming more powerful and militant. This period extended through the early 1970s, when solutions to the very pressing problems of financial support and personnel began to emerge.

Purpose. The 1972 pastoral letter of the American bishops entitled *To Teach As Jesus Did* focused the attention of Catholic secondary educators on the threefold purpose of Catholic education—communication of the authentic message of the Gospel and of the Church, establishment of a community of faith atmosphere, the rendering of service within the school community and to the large community in which it is located. This purpose fulfilled the first recommendation of the final report of the President's Panel on Nonpublic Education, chaired by Dr. Clarence C. Walton, which asked each nonpublic school to "clarify its unique identity as a voluntary enterprise...." The structure in which this purpose is identified and fostered will vary in its emphasis. The Catholic secondary schools today reflect the pluralism in the Roman Catholic Church itself. Some are more traditional; others are more humanistic; others, communitarian; and others, more service-oriented. These types do not exist in isolation, and indeed most schools demonstrate some of all four of these types with an accent on one.

Curriculum. As pointed out by Otto Kraushaar in his analysis of his study of nonpublic-school parents, there is a sense that nonpublic schools treat the student more as an individual than might be possible in the public school. This has been reflected over the last decade in a general focus on the needs of individual students as preeminent over prestige and achievement of the total student body. There has been, therefore, an accent on individualized instruction in Catholic secondary schools as evidenced in the continued and successful participation of Catholic secondary schools in the Model Schools Project sponsored by the Danforth Foundation and directed by the National Association of Secondary School Principals. This individualization, however, while utilizing team approaches, group presentation, and independent study, in addition to the more traditional lecture approach to teaching, has tended to reinforce the basis skills needed to live responsibly in American society. There also has been room for the experiential in the nine basic areas of the Catholic secondary school curriculum: (1) Religious Education; (2) Mathematics; (3) Science; (4) Fine Arts; (5) Language Arts; (6) Social Studies; (7) Vocational Education; (8) Physical Education; and (9) Foreign Language. The experiential element is also included in service programs involving the students immediately in such social issues as caring for the elderly, the sick, the hungry, the poor.

Measures of evaluation of these skills and experiences are undergoing change. There is a concerted effort to insure that students exhibit the required competencies before they graduate from the school. Movement toward competency-based graduation requirements on a state level has generally been perceived favorably by superintendents, boards, and administrators of Catholic secondary schools. Some schools have added their own measures of competency which go beyond those required by the state and may include religious education.

Catholic secondary schools have also been concerned that there be continuing self-evaluation of the school program. Such self-evaluation instruments as those developed by the Jesuits, by the Sisters of St. Joseph of Carondolet, the Sacred Heart Brothers, and other religious congregations are in use in the high schools of the religious orders, and sometimes in other Catholic secondary schools, as is the publication for Catholic secondary schools of the National Catholic Educational Association called *Giving Form to the Vision*. In some cases, evaluation teams have been developed to aid the schools in the evaluative process. Likewise, the motivation to achieve and to maintain regional accreditation continues to be quite strong.

Personnel. Two-thirds of the current Catholic secondary schools staff are lay teachers, the other third, clergy or religious. Ten percent of the administrators are lay persons; ninety percent are religious or clerics. A growing concern for salary scales and working conditions in the schools for and by lay faculty has led to a growth of Catholic *teachers unions, particularly in large dioceses and at the secondary school level. Some have affiliation, with American Federation of Teachers (AFT) and a few with the National Education Association (NEA); others are independent. Most allow membership only of lay faculty, but a few independent teacher organizations include religious faculty as well.

In this connection there is an important difference among schools. In diocesan secondary schools sponsorship and at least some financial support come from a central school office and such organizations may include all the teachers of the diocese. In private or interparochial secondary schools an individual faculty may have its own organization and funding may be the responsibility of a religious community, an individual parish or group of parishes, or more recently, a board of trustees.

The concern for articulating and demonstrating a uniqueness of purpose has led to an assessment of the philosophical, theological and spiritual formation of faculty members, as well as of their professional competency. Programs of spiritual formation for faculty are developing throughout the country in individual dioceses and schools. This need was expressed in the 1977 Statement of the Congregation for Catholic Education entitled, *The Catholic School*: "The school must be a community whose values are communicated through the interpersonal and sincere relationships of its members and through both individual and corporate adherence to the outlook on life that permeates the school."

Finance. The major concern for the survival of Catholic secondary schools over the past decade and a half has been that of financial support. Repeated efforts at obtaining increased levels of support from federal and state sources have been thwarted by the decisions of the U.S. Supreme Court. Legislation for programs at the national and state level of tax credits and vouchers continue to be proposed and voted on (*see* CHURCH AND STATE [U.S.]).

In general, the accounting procedures and financial management in individual schools are improving dramatically and more accurate data is being provided to diocesan-school planners and development personnel. In some areas, endowment funds are being established in an effort to hold tuition at a realistic level. Otherwise, there is a fear that Catholic secondary schools will become elitist, enrolling only youngsters of the upper classes.

In a special report on tuition for the NCEA, Rev. Frank Bredeweg set forth data illustrating the current disparity between operating revenue and operating cost. For instance, in the case of private secondary schools, (enrollment, 750–1,000) there is a difference between tuition and cost of $250.00 per pupil. For diocesan secondary schools a difference of $307.00 per pupil and for parish secondary schools a difference of $334.00 per pupil. Such deficits have to be made up through fund raising and subsidies. A study conducted in 1973 by Andrew Greeley and his colleagues at the National Opinion Research Center indicated a continuing willingness on the part of Catholic parents to support their Catholic schools. It would seem, however, that without planning for the future and good stewardship on the part of administrators and policy-making groups that a tipping point would be reached beyond which current sources of support and funding would not be adequate to maintain the schools.

Future. Catholic secondary schools continue to be a significant educational force in American society and are increasingly selected by non-Catholic as well as Catholic parents, in the tradition of parental choice in American education. Certain trends seem clear: (1) continuing increase in the number of lay teachers and lay administrators in Catholic secondary schools; (2) continued involvement of these schools in political and social issues; (3) growing concern for good financial management and a search for new sources of funding for the schools; (4) focus on human interdependence: experiential learning through service to the poor and the needy; (5) development of a sense of contemplation in students and the ability to reflect on the issues of the day; (6) increase of religious vocations to teaching apostolate; (7) pluralism in ecclesiologies, values and moral issues; (8) new understandings and relationships between educators and the hierarchy; (9) constructive self-criticism; broad use of research; and (10) realization of a new humanism in education through: increasing priority of learning skills over specific content; a learning environment supportive of affective and cognitive growth; greater opportunity for intensive human interaction; personalized education stressing variations in human motivation and learning style; and the preparation of students for life in a rapidly changing world.

This future is summed up in a forecast statement issued by the Secondary School Department, NCEA, in the Fall of 1977 which anticipated the following: "The Catholic high school will be a community of believers in Jesus Christ and of learners seeking to build a better world—a new earth of truth and justice—committed to enhancing the oneness of humankind in a plurality of life styles, religious customs, laws and patrimony."

See also PAROCHIAL SCHOOLS, CATHOLIC ELEMENTARY.

Bibliography: F. BREDEWEG, ed., *Catholic High Schools and Their Finances.* NCEA Special Report (Washington, D.C. 1978). Congregation for Catholic Education, "The Catholic School," Origins 7 (1977) 113–123 (also USCC Publ. Office, Washington D.C. 1977). G. ELFORD, *The Catholic School in Theory and Practice* (Washington D.C. 1973). W. GANLEY, ed., *Catholic Schools in the United States* (Denver 1978). A. GREELEY, W. C. MCCREADY and K. MCCOURT, *Catholic Schools in a Declining Church* (Kansas City, Mo. 1976). Jesuit Secondary Education Association, *Self-Evaluation Instrument for Jesuit Schools* (Washington D.C. 1975). O. F. KRAUSHAAR, *American Nonpublic Schools—Patterns of Diversity* (Baltimore 1972). E. J. MCDERMOTT, "Social Action Programs in Jesuit High Schools," *The Jesuit* (1977). National Catholic Educational Association Publications: *Giving Form to the Vision* (1974); *Secondary School Department Statement* (1974); *Heritage—Horizons: Secondary School Department Statement* (1977); *NCEA Notes: Convention Reporter* (1978). NCCB, *To Teach as Jesus Did* (USCC Publ. Office, Washington D.C. 1972). President's Committee on School Finance, *Nonpublic Education and the Public Good* (Washington D.C. 1972).

[J. D. OLSEN]

SECRETARIAT FOR PROMOTING CHRISTIAN UNITY

Founded in 1960 as a preparatory committee for Vatican Council II, the Secretariat became a conciliar commission in 1962 and was actively engaged in developing the ecumenical aspects of the Council's work.

Permanent organ of the Roman Curia since 1966, the Secretariat has as one important function service to the ecumenical movement within the Catholic Church. It sees to the proper interpretation and carrying out of principles of ecumenism, executes the decisions of the Council concerning ecumenism, establishes or fosters and coordinates the work of Catholic groups for promoting Christian unity. The Secretariat keeps the worldwide field in view. It works with the other organs of the Roman Curia to ensure that the ecumenical concern is given proper weight in the decisions and activities of these bodies. It fosters regional and international meetings which promote ecumenism.

However, work for Christian unity must essentially involve also the local Churches. Therefore the Secretariat has prepared documents to guide and develop this work. Its *Ecumenical Directory*, Part I (1967) and Part II (1970) consider organization for ecumenical work, validity of Baptism, sharing spiritual activity and resources with other Christians, prayer and worship in common, principles for ecumenical education, and especially theological education, cooperation between institutions of higher education. A number of documents on *Eucharistic sharing were published, particularly the *Instruction* of 1972. In 1970 appeared a fundamental document on *Reflections and Suggestions concerning Ecumenical Dialogue.* In 1975 *Ecumenical Collaboration at the Regional, National and Local Levels* was published to give information and orientations to help the local Catholic Churches in determining the form to be given to local ecumenical cooperation with other Christians and their Churches. The Secretariat is also open for consultation by episcopal conferences, ecumenical commissions, bishops, and individual Catholics.

The other principal function of the Secretariat is to be a "top-level" point of contact between the Catholic Church and other Christian Churches and organizations. With the Orthodox Churches this takes place through reciprocal visits, common declarations with heads of Churches, and theological conversations, where the emphasis is on deepening the already profound communion in faith and sacramental life existing with them. With the world Confessional Families there have been joint commissions touching upon doctrinal and pastoral questions whose published results are being evaluated by the Churches at large. There are frequent exchanges of observers and consultants even for business once considered strictly "denominational," e.g. church congresses.

A Joint Working Group with the World Council of Churches helps coordinate work of prayer for unity, joint Christian witness and practical collaboration in fields of common pastoral concern. The Secretariat is also involved in the expanding work of cooperation with Bible Societies in translating and affording easy access to the Scriptures.

This work is carried on by a small permanent staff with an assembly of thirty episcopal members meeting annually to determine general policy and a group of consultors, all under the direction of a Cardinal President.

No studies on the Secretariat exist. It publishes an *Information Service* three or four times a year which contains a chronicle of its activities and its various documents. Similar materials are found regularly in such publications as *Irénikon* (Belgium) and *One-in-Christ* (England).

[J. F. LONG]

SECULAR INSTITUTES

The past ten years have seen a tremendous development in the concept of the place in the life of the Church held by secular institutes (13:34), as they become increasingly aware of their essential nature. Earlier comparisons with religious institutes concluded that secular institutes constitute a third form of religious perfection, and therefore pertain to the religious life. Today it is recognized that secular institutes offer a new way to become totally consecrated to God.

There are secular institutes composed of diocesan priests, who seek the total gift of self through the evangelical counsels, and give support and spiritual assistance to their brother diocesan priests who are not members of the institute. But the great majority of institutes are composed of consecrated lay men and women, living ordinary lives and engaged in all those activities that are directed toward the human growth of the world according to God's plan.

Definition. Through the documents of Vatican Council II, the function and mission of the ordinary layman became clear, especially in the Constitution on the Church (*Lumen gentium* 31). Pope Paul VI, in his address to the directors general of secular institutes in Feb. 1972 (ActApS 64 [1972] 615–620), stressed the fact that they are indeed consecrated lay people whose way of being Church is to be engaged in secular values, "an advanced wing of the Church in the world, . . . a manifestation of what the Church wishes to do to construct the world described and desired by *Gaudium et spes*" (618).

Pius XII's apostolic constitution, *Provida mater ecclesia* (1947), emphasized three characteristics of secular institutes: consecration, apostolate, secularity. These three are interrelated and essential to the vocation. Through their consecration, expressed in profession of the evangelical counsels of chastity, obedience, and poverty, the members commit themselves totally to Christ and to the Church. Their entire lives are directed toward the apostolate of full responsibility for a transforming presence and action within the world in order to mould, perfect, penetrate, and sanctify it. Through their secularity, they take the natural order seriously and are committed to "illumine and organize temporal affairs in such a way that they may always start out, develop and persist according to Christ's mind" (*Lumen gentium* 31). They reflect a specific way in which the mystery of Christ can be lived in the world and the mystery of the Church manifested. Thus they are specialized, exemplary witnesses of the attitude and mission of the Church in the world today.

History. These institutes first came into existence in Europe, in answer to the needs and problems which developed from the French Revolution, from the changing times and conditions caused by the 19th-century industrialization and mechanization of the workaday world, and, more recently, from the suppression of religion by modern dictators. It was in this fertile ground that lay men and women of this century recognized the call to dedicate their lives according to the evangelical counsels while remaining lay persons among other lay persons, working and sharing with them the insecurities, joys, and sorrows of everyday secular life, in order to bring Christ to the world and the world to Christ.

By 1977 there were no less than 119 approved secular institutes of diocesan or pontifical right. Membership stands (1978) at approximately 54,000 throughout the world. Because of the hidden nature of the vocation, growth is not dramatic. In 1967 there were 16 secular institutes in the U.S.; ten years later there are 20, all but two of which have their roots in other lands, mainly in Europe.

World Conference of Secular Institutes. In 1970 higher officials of approved secular institutes were invited to participate in the first World Congress of Secular Institutes in Rome; there were more than 400 delegates. At this Congress delegates voted endorsement of the existing pluralism observed in organization, apostolate, way of life, and discretion of various institutes, and of the great latitude allowed, so long as the three essentials are maintained.

From this Congress in 1970 came the World Conference of Secular Institutes (*Conférence Mondiale des Instituts Séculiers*—CMIS) in 1972, with headquarters in Rome. It is designed to make this way of life better known and understood, to study the problems and implications of this new vocation, and to provide sharing of experiences. Individual institutes remain completely free and autonomous. The CMIS proposes study questions for national and regional Conferences. In 1976 the CMIS held its second international meeting, electing representative officers from member groups.

Since 1973 it has published a bimonthly, *Dialogue*, currently appearing in six languages.

Way of Life. There is a great variety in organization and customs among secular institutes, including all modes of living—from groups living together, although without common life, to such strict discreetness that members may be unaware of the identity of other members. The great majority of institutes are not involved in apostolates within the Church, since their call is precisely to influence the secular world. Individual members, however, may elect to serve the Church in some capacity, either professionally or in their spare time.

Members are indistinguishable from other lay persons, mainly living alone or with their families, working at all sorts of professions or occupations, personally called by God to live an ordinary life in an extraordinary way. Their lives are hidden and prayerful yet intensely active, and their intimate union with the Lord makes it possible for them to live a life of professional and social involvement in the world without following its spirit. Emphasis is on personal responsibility, service to fellow men, and the total gift of self to God.

Bibliography: J. BEYER, *Religious Life or Secular Institute* (Rome 1970). CMIS, *Dialogue* (Rome 1973–); *Secular Institutes in the Magisterium of the Church* (Rome 1974). International Congress of Secular Institutes, *Acta* (Rome 1970). F. MORLOT, *Bibliographie sur Instituts Séculiers* (années 1891–1972) (Rome 1974). National Center for Church Vocations, *Directory of Secular Institutes with Foundations in the U.S.A.* (Washington D.C. 1975). A. OBERTI et al., The Secular Institute," WaySuppl 12 (1971). PAUL VI, Address to Clerical and Lay Secular Institutes Feb. 2, 1972, Eng. tr. *Pope Speaks* 17 (1972) 26–32.

[M. P. IRWIN]

SECULARISM

Secularism has appeared with nuanced meanings in three distinctive, recent settings: Vatican Council II documents; the secular city process; the evangelical and the charismatic movements.

(1) The Dogmatic Constitution on the Church placed a positive emphasis on the vocation of the laity to work within secular affairs to which they bring a Christian dimension; nonetheless, "that ominous doctrine must rightly be rejected which attempts to build a society with no regard whatever for religion . . ." (*Lumen gentium* 36). The text did not contain the term "secularism" so as to avoid confusion with "laicism" (sometimes called "laicization"), which suggests either a positive role in the Church for the laity or the negative meaning (found in English and German) of freeing the laity from ecclesiastical control.

(2) Not to be confused with secularism is notion of the Secular City (H. Cox), a process of desacralization through emancipation: aware of his potentialities and responsibilities, man must make life possible in the world, which becomes his city under the care of his providence. Within this framework, the social sciences, especially sociology, become a principal source for the development of theology (*see* THEOLOGY AND SOCIOLOGY). Reaction has included accusations of: establishing a Christian elite without concern for the typical lay person; ignoring further developments in which Christians are not supposed to despise the world but rather lift it up, consecrate it and fulfill it. Less apparent but more critical in this process is the parallel growth of rationalism (in the strict sense) wherein internal consistency, rather than authority and faith, increasingly becomes

the principal criterion for personal and social values and thus eliminates any religious dimension in the evaluating procedure.

(3) Supplanting institutional values (both ecclesiastical and nonreligious) with personal values based on an identification with diverse public and private interest groups, causes, communities, and movements has frequently occasioned the juxtaposition (if not interpenetration) of secular and religious values within the same social setting. In addition, the lack of adequate criteria for evaluating seems to have contributed to two subsequent changes: the "reappropriation" of distinctive Catholic values among certain theologians (*e.g.*, Rahner); and a turning towards a fundamentalist view of Scripture in some Christian assemblies and in charismatic groups within the more structured Churches. The fundamentalists or evangelicals and the charismatics pursue the distinction between "the world" (as evil) and "the born again" through the Spirit (as saved). The secular, whether personal, institutional, or social, thus becomes synonymous with secularism (irreligious) and is therefore rejected as a value for the "born again" Christian, who has Christ as his personal Savior and sole criterion of value.

Bibliography: D. CALLAHAN, ed., *The Secular City Debate* (New York 1966). Y. CONGAR, *Christians Active in the World* (New York 1968); "The Role of The Church in the Modern World," in Vorgrimler 5:202–223. H. COX, *The Secular City* (New York 1965). C. GEFFRÉ, ed., *Humanism and Christianity. Concilium* 86 (New York 1973). K. HECKER, "Humanism," SacrMundi 3:74–78. F. KLOSTERMANN, "The Laity," Vorgrimler 1:231–259. E. NIERMANN, "Laity," SacrMundi 3:259–263.

[T. MCMAHON]

SEQUENCE

In liturgical usage, the Sequence is a musical setting of a text that in Latin is rhymed poetry. In origins, it was a trope, a musical extension of the Alleluia (13:100).

The revision of the Lectionary which was promulgated by Paul VI in 1969, has brought about some changes in the use of the Sequence. Prior to the revision, the following Sequences were used: Easter, *Victimae paschali laudes* (obligatory for the feast and its octave); Pentecost, *Veni, Sancte Spiritus* (obligatory for the feast and its octave); Corpus Christi, *Lauda Sion* (obligatory on the feast, optional during the octave, suppressed since 1960); Requiem Masses, *Dies irae*; Friday after Passion Sunday and Sept. 15, Feast of Our Lady of Sorrows, *Stabat Mater* (obligatory on both days).

The General Instruction of the Roman Missal says quite simply: "Except on Easter Sunday and Pentecost the sequences are optional" (GenInstrRomMissal 40). This means, in practice, that the Easter Sequence is optional during its octave; the calendar has eliminated the Pentecost octave, leaving the Sequence for the feast alone; the *Lauda Sion* is optional for the feast of Corpus Christi; the calendar revision has eliminated duplicate feasts, leaving the feast of Our Lady of Sorrows to be celebrated only on September 15, with its Sequence also optional; the *Dies irae* has been dropped completely from *Masses for the Dead (see OFFICE OF THE DEAD).

Three further points are to be noted in the revision: the Sequence is now placed *before* the Alleluia and the Verse before the Gospel, since this acclamation properly belongs to the Gospel proclamation. No official

musical settings are now available in English, but work is being done in this area by the International Commission on English in the Liturgy (ICEL). Finally, to aid choral recitation without singing, provision is made in the Lectionaries of the United States for prose translations of the four remaining Sequences.

[L. DURST]

SEX EDUCATION

The methods whereby young people have learned about sex have changed drastically in recent years (13:151; 16:413). In an urban society, fewer children can learn about reproduction through farm life; with smaller families, fewer children have young brothers and sisters. On the other hand, sexual appeals flood the mass media. The *Planned Parenthood Federation of America has begun "A Five-Year Plan: 1976–1980," aimed at bringing total sex freedom to teenagers. The Congregation for the Doctrine of the Faith in 1975 noted "the growing difficulties experienced by the faithful in obtaining knowledge of wholesome moral teaching, especially in sexual matters..." (*Declaration on Certain Questions concerning Sexual Ethics* 2). The same document stressed the need for sex education within Church teaching (ibid. 13).

Just as the family first teaches about basic human relationships, the family should first teach about a child's sexuality. At a time, however, when sex stimuli bombard the child from many directions, most parents recognize that no single source can balance the effect, and they welcome appropriate assistance.

In many cases, public school parents oppose school sex-education programs because the schools must use an amoral approach and sometimes present Planned Parenthood materials. When provided with opportunities for advanced information and involvement, Catholic school parents generally accept and appreciate programs which support the information, values, and behavior accepted in their homes. Not merely a study unit on reproduction, a sex education program should help young people view themselves in a positive way as total persons and respect others in all relationships.

The Sacred Congregation's *Declaration* supports a total approach: "Parents, in the first place, and also teachers of the young must endeavor to lead their children and their pupils, by way of a complete education, to the psychological, emotional, and moral maturity befitting their age. They will therefore prudently give them information suited to their age; and they will assiduously form their wills in accordance with Christian morals, not only by advice but above all by the example of their own lives..." (ibid. 13).

As the U.S. bishops affirmed in *Teach Them*, this integrated approach is more easily achieved in a fulltime Catholic education which can facilitate "the integration of religious truth and values with the result of life." Ideally, sex education is integrated with religion, health, biology, physical education, family life, home economics, sociology, psychology, and counseling. A total program of sex education should provide knowledge, help to develop values, and assist with moral decision-making. Topics like sterilization, birth control, abortion, and homosexuality should be included.

The 1977 Synod of Bishops, in a document prepared for Pope Paul VI, recommended a "more positive" presentation of sexual and social moral norms. Reflecting on the bishops' experience that youths accept strict moral codes regarding social justice, but often reject Catholic views on sexuality, the Synod asked that moral teachings be presented "in an especially positive way and with convincing arguments." Sexual morality, they said, should be seen as "evolving from the dignity of the human person and leading to true Christian freedom" (NC News Service, 10/31/77).

Bibliography: Congregation for the Doctrine of the Faith, *Declaration on Sexual Ethics*, Eng. tr. (USCC Publ. Office, Washington, D.C. 1977). USCC, *Teach Them*, Statement on Catholic Education (USCC Publ. Office, Washington, D.C. 1975).

[C. J. RECK]

SEXISM

Sexism refers primarily to the belief that persons are superior or inferior to one another on the basis of their sex. It includes, however, attitudes, value systems, and social patterns which express or support this belief. It is a contemporarily coined term, rising out of the women's movement, and not ordinarily used neutrally in its application to men or women. Rather, it indicates almost always the belief that it is men who are superior and women who are inferior because of their sex. As an evaluative term it includes the judgment that this belief is false and that formal and informal social patterns which support it are unjust.

There is dispute regarding the labelling of certain social patterns as sexist. Some argue that what is called sexist is merely the differentiation of social roles for men and women. Others argue that what makes all social, sexual role-differentiation sexist is the inevitable inequity entailed in the assignment of roles to persons on the basis of sex. Whatever the articulated beliefs regarding "different but equal" roles for women and men, women's gender-assigned roles have invariably been subordinate, passive, and/or restricted to the private sphere.

Christian Theology. Christian theology has played an important part in both establishing and challenging sexist beliefs and structures. Centuries of Christian theology continued to justify cultural patterns of hierarchy and subordination in relationships between men and women. Though early Christian experience had offered a glimpse of equality between the sexes, the order of inequality was too entrenched to be changed. Primitive Christian insights that "in Christ there is neither Jew nor Greek, slave nor free, neither male for female" (Gal 3.28) were soon obscured by their transposition into the dominant patterns of the time and into theologies of an eschatological future.

Two strains of thought within Christian theology have served to undergird sexism in particularly enduring ways. On the one hand, women have been associated with symbols of evil; on the other hand, the innate inferiority of women has been affirmed, even to the point of denying to them full identity as human images of God. Ancient myths associating woman with chaos, darkness, mystery, matter, and sin echoed in Christian interpretations of concupiscence, of sexuality as a dangerous source for evil, and thence of woman as temptress, as a symbol of sin. The texts of Justin Martyr, Irenaeus, Tertullian, of Origen, Augustine, Jerome, of Thomas Aquinas and Bonaventure, of Luther, John Knox, and the Puritans, all bear witness to the fact that woman appears throughout the centuries as

a special agent of evil. Instead of losing an identification with pollution and evil through the development of Christian thought, the notion of woman became theoretically intertwined with theologies of original sin and anthropological dualisms of higher and lower nature, mind and body, rationality and desire. Even when women were extolled, paradoxically, as paragons of virtue, their inferiority was reinforced. Placed on a pedestal, given ideals impossible of attainment, women experienced failure and a sense of guilt and evil.

The identification of woman with evil has perhaps been overshadowed as a cause of the practical inequality between the sexes by the refusal of Christian theology to attribute the fullness of the *imago Dei* to women. It is not only in the order of sin but in the order of nature and the order of grace that women have been declared lesser humans. Though all persons were considered to have been created in the image and likeness of God, men partook of that image primarily and fully, while women shared in it only derivatively and partially. Thus, men could fill roles as representatives of God, but women only as lovers of God and followers of men.

Contemporary Theological Evaluation. In the 20th century theology has generally ceased to affirm explicitly the inferiority of women. No longer is it argued that women are intellectually inferior to men or that wholly passive roles should be assigned to women either biologically or theologically. Doctrines of creation which place persons in graded hierarchies according to sex have been challenged and generally revised. The dignity of the human person which Christian theology has always affirmed has been shown to ground the principle of equality as a fundamental principle of justice. Nonetheless, at least one theory remains which continues to support gender-role differentiation in a way that limits women's roles to the private sphere and makes them subordinate to roles open to men. This is the theory that women and men are essentially complementary in a way that justifies distinction of social roles without violating the principle of equality. This argument is used in the Roman Catholic tradition to maintain a "proper sphere" for women which essentially excludes them from leadership roles in the legislative, judicial, and sacramental life of the Church, It is challenged by those who argue that though there are important differences between women and men, these are not morally relevant to the circumscription of social roles. Traditional efforts to delineate distinctive characteristics have proved distortive to the understanding of persons and injurious to human relations. Efforts to apply certain traits exclusively to one sex result in vague listings which are importantly culture-conditioned and subject to serious exceptions. Hence, exclusion of persons from major roles in the Church or society on the basis of sex constitutes unjust discrimination, the perpetuation of sexism in thought and social structure.

Bibliography: S. BUTLER, ed., Catholic Theological Society of America, *Research Report: Women in Church and Society, 1978* (Bronx, N.Y. 1978). J. CORIDEN, ed., *Sexism and Church Law* (New York 1977). J. ENGLISH, ed., *Sex Equality* (Englewood Cliffs, N.J. 1977). M. FARLEY, "Sources of Sexual Inequality in the History of Christian Thought," JRel 56 (1976) 162–176. A. L. HAGEMAN, ed., *Sexist Religion and Women in the Church* (New York 1974). R. RUETHER, ed., *Religion and Sexism* (New York 1974). L. and A. SWIDLER, eds., *Women Priests: A Catholic Commentary on the Vatican Declaration* (New York 1977).

[M. A. FARLEY]

SEXUAL MORALITY (IN THE BIBLE)

It is still widely assumed that the Bible is a final court of appeal in judgements concerning the morality of human acts. However, neither OT nor NT can be used in a simplistic way as a sourcebook for the Christian ethic.

Appeals to Texts on Morality. Critical exegesis has shown up the fragility of many proof-texts in Christian moral catechesis—e.g., the prohibition of coveting the neighbor's wife (Ex 20.17: Dt 5.21) as bearing on the morality of sexual fantasies; the fate of Onan son of Judah as a warning against the evil of masturbation (Gn 38.8–10); the death penalty for homosexual practice (Lv 18.22; 20.13) which passed into European civil codes from that of Justinian. As in this last case, the meaning and intent of ancient legal stipulations may not be immediately apparent, while the fact that certain laws happen to occur in the OT does not necessarily make them relevant to or incumbent on the Christian today (most obviously, but not exclusively, ritual and cultic regulations, e.g., those governing menstruation and other bodily discharges—Lv 12; 15; 18.19; 20.18; Dt 23.10–11). It would also be imprudent to accept as universally valid a perception recorded in the Bible as to what is or is not according to nature. Paul, e.g., excludes homosexuality as against nature (Rom 1.24–27) but also forbids men to wear their hair long on the same grounds (1 Cor 11.14). Hence natural law, a theory borrowed by Paul from Stoicism, and one which has been particularly influential in Catholic moral teaching, must on any showing leave room for such empirical data as: the cultural molding of sex roles; profound changes that have occurred in the structuring and understanding of the family and the institution of marriage; and a great deal of clinical, psychological, and sociological data bearing on the way moral issues are perceived and formulated. Thus certain recommendations directed at women in the NT—that they keep silent in church (1 Cor 14.34–36), wear a veil (11.5–16) or refrain from wearing pearls (1 Tim 2.9)—are rightly seen as perhaps relevant for the first but not necessarily for subsequent centuries; and similar discernment is called for in cases which are not so obvious.

Evaluation of Biblical Texts. These examples of appeal to the Bible illustrate the fact that Christian, and especially Catholic, ethical teaching has taken as its primary task to specify the moral status of individual acts and in doing so has generally assumed that OT laws continue to law claim on the Christian life (ritual laws have not always been excluded; e.g. the requirement of sexual abstention prior to the Eucharist based on Ex 19.15 and of "churching" for women based on Lv 12).

NT Prescriptions. Few would doubt the legitimacy of defining in some detail what kind of conduct is or is not consistent with the Christian vocation. In the apostolic and subapostolic periods Christian communities did not hesitate to specify certain acts or types of conduct as inconsistent with the Christian life—e.g., homosexual practice (Rom 1.24–27; 1 Cor 6.9; 1 Tim 1.10), frequenting of prostitutes (1 Cor 6.12–20); divorce, with one possible exception (Rom 7.2–3; 1 Cor 7.10–16); incest (1 Cor 5.1–5). Sometimes the specifying prescinded explicitly from the situation of non-Christians (1 Cor 5.12–13); sometimes it took the form of a universally binding obligation or prohibition (Rom 1.24–27).

Early Christian tradition, however, assumes that such specific judgments have meaning only in the context of the Christian calling, which takes its meaning from the covenant. Since this covenant presages the formation of a new community in a world alienated from God's purposes, it would seem to follow that Christian ethics is basically relational and communitarian (e.g. the metaphor of temple is used of the local Church, 1 Cor 3.16–17, and also of the individual member in his bodily existence, 1 Cor 6.19). It bears on the individual Christian primarily as a call to a new life lived, in Paul's terms, according to the Spirit not the flesh (Rom 8.1–17; 1 Cor 2.14–16; Gal 5.16–26). An important implication is the imperative of an ongoing transformation (Rom 12.2), already strongly suggested in the biblical life-stories familiar to Christians from their liturgy (e.g. Jacob, Gn 25–35, esp. 32.22–32).

Context. It is important to emphasize this context of moral decisions in view of an act-centered and objectivistic approach to sexuality which has been passed on through the penitentials, conciliar decrees, and the work of the canonists, reaching the individual Catholic Christian by way of the seminary manuals and catechisms.

Early Christian teaching brought to bear on the exercise of the sexual function, as on other matters, a high moral seriousness. The need for discipline and vigilance is stressed by the use of military and athletic metaphors (Rom 13.11–14; 1 Cor 9.24–27; 2 Tim 4.7–8) that are reminiscent of Stoic moral teaching, which also featured lists of virtues and vices (cf. Gal 5.19; 1 Cor 6.9–10; 1 Tim 1.9–10). The reality of moral culpability, and therefore of freedom, is affirmed. One can deviate from the goal—the etymological sense of sin (*hatta, avon*) in Hebrew—by the abuse of sexuality as in other ways, necessitating a return (*teshuvah,* repentance) to the point where the way was lost. Here as elsewhere early Christianity betrays its Jewish roots, the differentiating factor being the belief that the last age marked by the presence of the Spirit had been inaugurated by the death and resurrection of Jesus. It should be added that insistence on the reality of authentic guilt allows for the reality of inauthentic or premoral guilt, the admission, that is, that our moral perceptions also contain archaic elements which must be overcome if we are to attain maturity as persons.

In view of the atmosphere of eschatological crisis reflected in much of the NT there should be no expectation of a sustained treatment of the expansive and unitive potential of sexuality. It is this atmosphere, one suspects, that has led to unfounded allegations of misogyny directed at Paul, whose teaching is in fact, given the situation and the propensities of many Christians he is addressing, remarkably realistic and open-minded. The note of healthy realism is heard more frequently in the subapostolic period with respect to the decision to marry or remarry (e.g. 1 Tim 5.14) and in response to an exaggerated asceticism often based on suspect philosophical ideas (e.g. Col 2.20–23; 1 Tim 4.3–5). Yet it is difficult to avoid the conclusion that this sense of crisis, together with the polemical nature of much early Christian literature, has created some serious problems for Christian ethics. Nowhere is this more in evidence than in the central tenet of official Catholic teaching which restricts the exercise of the sexual function to marriage and, within marriage, to acts capable of procreation (a view, incidentally, shared by

Stoicism). While Catholic teaching has generally recognized both procreation and the mutual love and support between man and wife as the legitimate finality of sex relations together with procreation, the need to come out strongly against sexual permissiveness has tended to put the weight on the first rather than on the second purpose.

Current Church Teaching. In the modern period traditional positions about sexual morality have been challenged by a new sexual freedom created by the possibility of overcoming the age-old dangers of infection, conception, and detection. Faced with this situation, papal pronouncements in recent decades have reaffirmed traditional Christian values with great vigor. Pius XI's *Casti connubii* (1930) condemned the use of artificial means of contraception as unnatural and intrinsically immoral, a position reiterated in an address of Pius XII to a group of midwives (1951) and in the encyclical *Humanae vitae* of Paul VI (1968). This last signified a rejection of the majority report of a commission set up by John XXIII to study population, the family and birth, which suggested that the moral character of a marriage should not be determined by the potential or actual fecundity of each individual marital act. Since the findings of this commission were not ready when Vatican Council II's Constitution on the Church in the Modern World was promulgated, this text took up a tone of studied ambiguity on the matter (cf. *Gaudium et spes* 49–51).

In the tradition of these official directives the *Declaration on Certain Questions concerning Sexual Ethics* issued in 1975 by the Congregation for the Doctrine of the Faith stressed the dignity and vocation of the human subject, the abiding value of the institution of marriage faced with a variety of alternative life-styles, and the permanent validity of moral criteria independent of cultural and sociological data. While the value of these observations must be clearly acknowledged, it is equally clear that the last word has not been spoken on these matters. That so many practising Catholics do not follow the official teaching on birth control raises in an acute form the question of the place of empirical data in moral decision-making, while the need for effective population control on a global scale raises in an agonizing way the issue of conflicting responsibilities. Only a more profound grasp of the Christian Gospel combined with a greater sensitivity to the problems of the Christian living in today's world will allow for a satisfactory solution.

Bibliography: Congregation for the Doctrine of the Faith, *Declaration on Sexual Ethics*, Eng. tr. (USCC Publ. Office, Washington, D.C. 1977). C. E. CURRAN, ed., *Contraception, Authority and Dissent* (New York 1969); *Contemporary Problems in Moral Theology* (Notre Dame, Ind. 1970). G. F. GILDER, *Sexual Suicide* (New York 1973). R. HOYT, ed., *The Birth Control Debate* (Kansas City, Mo. 1968). J. NOONAN, *Contraception* (Cambridge, Mass. 1965). G. OUTKA and P. RAMSEY, *Norm and Content in Christian Ethics* (London 1963).

[J. BLENKINSOPP]

SEXUAL MORALITY
(MORAL THEOLOGY)

Sexual morality cannot be separated from a total view of Christian morality. The Christian is called to follow Christ, to love others as he loved them. So morality contains a call for that personal integration of vital drives that allows sexuality to participate in and mediate the love that is self-donating. Sexual teaching can be synthesized in the central paradox of Christian personal-ism: the deepest self is found in self-transcending love of the other. "For anyone who wants to save his life will lose it; but anyone who loses his life for my sake, that man will save it" (Lk 9.24).

Away from Dualisms. Contemporary Catholic reflection on sexual morality must come to grips with past influences that have been less than healthy. While Augustine's sexual pessimism may often be exaggerated, it is safe to say that a distrust of pleasure did dominate much of Western thought. Stoic as well as Alexandrian strains within Christian ascetical teaching were strong enough to nurture at times a repression of bodily instincts. In America the sociocultural impact of a Puritan dominant-class weighed heavily on the immigrant Catholic and provided at least a fertile soil for Jansenist tendencies to grow.

The sexual itself is a bodily expression by which one person communicates a special human outreach to another. The act of intercourse is a unique bodily symbol of loving self-donation. This symbolization is not that of Cartesian dualism. The body is not a neutral instrument; it contains meaning in itself (McCabe). Even psychologically the bodily act has an intentionality all its own (Rollo May). The meaning contained in bodily acts of sexuality is no more arbitrarily changeable than is the meaning of human facial expressions, laughter, or tears. There is clear teaching in the Church proclaiming that the bodily symbol of intercourse contains the meanings of unitive and procreative love.

The relationship between these two meanings has not always been clearly balanced. For so long a time the procreative meaning unduly dominated the understanding of marriage. Moral theologians spoke almost exclusively in terms of "rights and debts" without emphasizing the moral necessity of tenderness and respect required by the unitive meaning. The imbalance shows how extraordinary is the contribution of the more comprehensive theology of Vatican Council II: "This love is uniquely expressed and perfected through the marital act. The actions within marriage by which the couple are united intimately and chastely are noble and worthy ones. Expressed in a manner which is truly human, these actions signify and promote that mutual self-giving by which spouses enrich each other with a joyful and thankful will" (*Gaudium et spes* 49).

Marriage as the Normative Context. Sexual morality in Catholic thinking gives a basic norm, namely, that all genital sexual expression take place only within marriage. The reason for such an ethic is not legalistic, rather the norm is intrinsic to the unitive meaning of intercourse itself. In other words the characteristics of married love are clearly implied in the very meaning of intercourse itself. By its very bodily intimacy sexual love has its way of crying out for exclusivity. Since the human partners are historical, their bodily being-together implies a waking up in responsibility for one another tomorrow and tomorrow (fidelity). The bodily-expressed love is rendered more assuredly truthful to the degree that it risks embracing the beloved in the beloved's fragile becoming. Moreover, the human person is social, public, and ritual; vowed love in public ritual brings a privately expressed love and fidelity into external proclamation. The love is as it were "named" into deepest reality. Finally this lasting, exclusive public love shadows forth God's perduring love of his people "consummated" in the incarnation, death, and resurrection of his Only Son (*Gaudium et spes* 48). Requiring the marriage bond, then, is not only a law but rather a congruous honoring of what the bodily action of intercourse actually is—in itself matrimonial.

The Procreative Meaning Personalistically Related. Intercourse should take place in a procreative context not merely because seed can fertilize ovum; something deeper is at issue. The concern is rather that the human quality of openness to life be seen as integral to true love. Von Hildebrand articulates this by seeing life as a "superabundant finality" of intercourse. This openness to an overflow into life is seen phenomenologically as part and parcel of the very union of love. Such teaching is not easily heard today, but it is a wise intuition that avoids the tendency of erotic love to settle into a false utopia of egoistic privacy. It is in a love that opens its circle to a new creation that a couple is pulled into history (Jeannière). Such open love avoids the pitfalls of narcissism and becomes ever more assuredly self-transcending.

The procreative meaning of intercourse is not then *merely* biologistic or stoic, but personalistic, that is, intrinsically related to the quality of the interpersonal union of love. (Whether or not such life-orientedness must be present in full actuality in every act of intercourse constitutes some of the controversy surrounding Paul VI's *Humanae vitae*. Many who dissent from *Humanae vitae* would still wish to keep the sexual love ethic organically tied to a general structure of love-life.) But seeing a life structure as inherent to love itself has a deep and often-overlooked theological point. It is this: the human is made in the image of God. Sexual love's bond with procreativity is not an evolutionary accident (W. May). Human love is creative precisely because it is in the image of God's love.

Developmental Dimension. Of the many advances in recent Catholic moral reflection one of the most significant is the recognition of the developmental aspects of sexual morality. Catholic personalist thought recognizes that achievement of personhood is a task to be carried out; so also then is the personalization of the erotic. Moral teaching today discerns better than yesterday that sexual behavior cannot be evaluated statically; that similar behavior at different periods of life will be measured differently according to the significance of the behavior on the psycho-sexual growth process.

This reflects the idea that there can be no dichotomy between Christian spiritual-moral growth and the psychological growth of sexual integration. Irenaeus's oft-cited phrase *Gloria Dei vivens homo* gives voice to a Catholic tradition that recognizes human growth not as identical with but at least as integral to the life of grace. Thus the moralist's dialogue with the behavioral sciences can be genuine; the moralist can listen to psychology's insights into elements of the personal-growth process. The listening is one of critical discernment. A particular behavior may be judged as "wrong," i.e., not manifesting the full outwardness of integrated personal self-donation. Yet the same behavior may also embrace a certain "on-the-way" characteristic that has to qualify moral evaluation. If the behavioral sciences see certain behaviors as peculiar to growth phases (e.g., masturbation, adolescent petting), moral reflection need not surrender its core insight into the basic outward and other-centered norm for all sexual behavior. A knowing, statistical expectation can allow for a more understanding pastoral judgment. Statistics do not make morality, but critical reflection on the cultural, and anthropological meaning of certain behaviors can ground moral qualifications. Seeing someone in incipient stages of growth processes, for example, can lead to balanced conjecture that even though behavior may be essentially disordered, there still may be very minimal personal or existential engagement in that disorder.

Decision-Making in the Church. To find if a tradition is really a *Tradition*, to find if a teaching is normative for now and future, inquiry into an abstract meaning is not enough. The primary test is the experience of Christian living. Faith is not philosophy nor ideology, even if always joined inevitably with both. A sexual ethic in the Church must spring from a faith-reflection on the individual's and the community's life and experience of the Spirit. This requires a communal and individual discernment of spirits according to the ecclesiological norms of decision-making in systematic theology and spirituality.

Whatever the difficulties of this process of discernment, it is clear that the contemporary pastoral magisterium has maintained marriage to be the normative human setting of genital sexual expression. It is clear that premarital and homosexual as well as autosexual activity continues to be judged as a violation of the human and divine meanings of sexual love.

Moreover, despite significant controversy on many issues, a careful analysis would indicate that there is in the Church wide theological support for the broad lines of sexual teaching. There is frequently divergence and discussion in language, rationale, measuring of the degrees of seriousness, disagreements on borderline and conflict-of-value situations, controversies over theories of growth and compromise, discussion on the meaning of the single *human act. Yet in all this disagreement Catholic theology still manifests a remarkable convergence in the basic heterosexual, matrimonial, life-and-love moorings of human sexual expression. There are exceptions but the convergence is enough to be a theological source that gives support to teachings of the pastoral magisterium. Through all of this teaching, there is one other Gospel word, which the Church brings to the human struggle to live this morality. It is the single yet all important word, "compassion."

Bibliography: Documentation: Congregation for the Doctrine of the Faith, *Persona humana*, ActApS 68 (1976) 77–96; tr. *Declaration on Certain Questions Concerning Sexual Ethics* (USCC Publ. Office Washington, D.C. 1977) with commentary BP. FRANCIS MUGAVERO, Diocese of Brooklyn, Pastoral Letter of Feb. 11, 1976, "Sexuality: God's Gift," Origins 5 (1976) 485–494. NCCB, *To Live in Christ Jesus* (USCC Publ. Office, 1976); "Statement of the Committee on Doctrine concerning Human Sexuality," Origins 7 (1977) 376–378. Paul VI HumVitae.
Studies: J. FUCHS, *De castitate et ordine sexuali* (Rome 1963). J. GRÜNDEL, "SacrMundi 6:73–86. A. GUINDON, *The Sexual Language* (Ottawa 1976). R. HAUGHTON, *The Mystery of Sexuality* (Paramus, N.J. 1972). A. JEANNIÈRE, *Anthropology of Sex* (New York 1967). P. KEANE, *Sexual Morality* (Paramus, N.J. 1978). A. KOSNICK et al. *Human Sexuality* (New York 1977). R. MAY, *Love and Will* (New York 1969). W. MAY, *The Nature and Meaning of Chastity* (Chicago 1976). H. MCCABE, *What is Ethics All About* (Washington, D.C. 1969). R. MCCORMICK. "Notes on Moral Theology," ThSt 30 (1969) 635–692; 32 (1971) 66–122; 38 (1977) 57–114. J. NOONAN, *Contraception* (Cambridge, Mass. 1965). A. PLÉ, *Chastity and the Affective Life* tr. M. C. THOMPSON (New York 1966). D. VON HILDEBRAND, *In Defense of Purity* (New York 1935).   [F. X. MEEHAN]

SEXUALITY, HUMAN (IN THE BIBLE)

One of the most difficult problems for Christian theology has been the interpretation of sexual experience and the integration of the erotic into a total vision of human life. Much has been made of the fact that the NT uses ἀγάπη, a word rarely attested elsewhere, for the love which God shows mankind and which, consequently, should be characteristic of the Christian, but never uses ἔρως, attested often in classical antiquity (the discourse on *eros* of the priestess Diotima in Plato's *Symposium* being a specially significant case) and in Hellenistic romances. The consequent dichotomy between agapitic and erotic love (e.g. in Anders Nygren's *Agapē and Eros*), corresponding to Aquinas's distinction between *amor benevolentiae* and *amor concupiscentiae* (ST 1a2ae, 26.4), had the unfortunate tendency of blocking sexuality out of a total vision of the Christian life. Following on a standard interpretation of Gn 2–3 and some related biblical texts, the autonomous exercise of the sexual function was seen as characteristic of fallen man; it could find its place in the redeemed order only within the covenant of Christian Marriage; and it would be entirely absent from the final state destined for mankind in which "they neither marry nor are given in marriage" (Mt 22.30).

The Old Testament. A Christian evaluation of human sexuality would naturally begin with the doctrine of creation, especially since creation myths often had the function of validating and sacralizing sexuality (creation by means of procreation).

Creation Account. In Gn 1.1–2.4 (P) mankind is created in a state of sexual differentiation (1.27), which state participates in the goodness of the entire created order. There is no divine sexual couple—behind which it is often possible to detect a primordial androgynous being—but a deity who transcends sexual differentiation and refuses to be worshipped by sexual rites. By separating decisively the moment of creation from that of the emergence of evil (Gn 2.15–3.24) the tradition further emphasizes the primordial goodness of the first and prototypal sexual partnership and at the same time, by implication, demythologizes the sexual act. The narrative then goes on to relate how this first couple, referred to simply as the Man and the Woman, is seduced by the Snake into disobeying Yahweh's command not to eat the fruit of the wisdom tree and is consequently expelled from the Garden of Eden. While the ambient of this act is clearly sexual—eating as a common biblical euphemism for coition (the Snake punningly referred to as cunning and naked, the same word in Hebrew); the consequent shame at nakedness—the implications of the story carry beyond other "original sins," e.g., of Canaan in Gn 9.20–27 and Moab and Ammon in Gn 1930–38, which are frankly sexual in character. For the context of Gn 1–11 suggests that this mutual betrayal is the first step in a progressive deviation which renders impossible a genuine life-project and the formation of community. Emphasis on the paradigmatic and diagnostic character of the story provides a necessary counterbalance to the doctrine of original sin derived from it, especially in its Augustinian and Tridentine formulation.

The Life of Israel. The relation between religion and sex, familiar today from psychoanalytic theory and clinical practice, is evident in the OT mostly because of the struggle against Canaanite fertility rituals, which, however, were widely practised in Israel. This circumstance has helped create the impression of biblical religion as antisexual and anti-instinctual in general; the biblical attitude in its turn has contributed to a deterrent attitude towards sexuality throughout Christian history. In point of fact, however, sex is accorded no particular emphasis in the OT by being either hypostatized or down graded. Contrary to an often repeated Freudian critique, neither the legislation nor the prophetic accusations stress the suppression of the instinctual life; indeed, laws governing sexual mores are for the most part indistinguishable from stipulations in other and older law codes of the ancient Near East. Vocabulary covering sexual matters, some of it euphemistic, is not particularly revealing. The Hebrew word *ahavah*, love, is used of many different kinds of relationships; *hesed*, translated "steadfast love" in the Revised Standard Version, connotes not another kind of love, the agapitic kind, but a quality of relationship which allows love, wherever it emerges, to realize its full potential (hence its frequent use in covenant contexts). The transposition of this covenant love between Yahweh and his people into that between man and woman in Hos 1–3 opened up a new and powerful metaphorical field which was to exert an enduring influence on Jewish and Christian religious thinking. Without it the Song of Songs—fountainhead of a long mystical tradition in Judaism and Christianity—would not have found its place in the biblical canon, nor would it have been possible to speak of the sacramental nature of Christian marriage (Eph 5.32).

The high estimation in the OT of bodily existence and of the man-woman relationship had however to contend with certain cultural factors shared with the environment in which early Israel came into existence. These include a patriarchal marriage-institution according to which the husband in effect owned his wife as the result of a purchase (Hos 3.2, the *mohar*, marriage price), could divorce her at will (Dt 24.1–4), and annul vows made by her (Num 30). Moreover, the OT reflects, especially in the sapiential and gnomic literature, something of the widespread fear and distrust in which women were held by men almost everywhere in the literature of antiquity, e.g., warnings against the "foreign women" in Prov 1–9 not entirely offset by praise of the "valiant woman" in Prov 31.10–31. Whatever the reasons for this state of affairs (the widespread practice of cultic prostitution, taboos governing the woman's menses, even deeper psychological fears and anxieties), such factors have helped produce a deterrent attitude towards sexuality throughout Christian history, reinforced by dubious interpretations of Gn 2–3 as antifeminist (e.g. 1 Tim 2.14–15; cf. Sir 25.23) and the perseverance of ritual taboos governing menstruation and childbearing, e.g., the practice of "churching" after childbirth based on Lev 12.

The New Testament. Even less than the OT can the NT be expected to furnish a "theology of sexuality." The task of reaching back critically to the teaching of Jesus and his first disciples is beset with many difficulties. Critical study shows that on this as on other matters early Christian writings attest to more than one view and it remains to be determined to what extent and in what ways the practice of early Christian communities is mandatory for the Christian of today. The impression given by the teaching of Jesus recorded in the Gospels is that the demands of Torah, summated in the command to love God and the neighbor (Mt 22.34–40; cf. Dt 6.4–9, the *Shema*, and Lv 19.18), call for radical obedience both in deed (Mt 5.17–20; 19.16–19) and in the inner dispositions to which actions are traceable. Lust is therefore the moral equivalent of adultery (Mt 5.27–30; 15.19–20) and the primordial divine command binding man and woman in the covenant of marriage has priority over all later accommodations (Mt 5.31–32; 19.3–9; Mk 10.2–12). While the traditions recording Jesus' dealings with those who had sinned sexually emphasize his compassion and capacity for acceptance (Lk 7.36–50; Jn 7.53–8.11), nothing in early Christian tradition justifies the view that Jesus abrogated the Law in favor of love as an all-encompassing and all-sufficient principle of the moral life. It is therefore not surprising to find early Christian teachers condemning sexual sins, in some instances with clear reference to OT laws (e.g. 1 Cor 5.1–13; cf. Lv 18.7–8; Dt 17.2–7), insisting on marriage as a permanent bond (Rom 7.2–3; 1 Cor 7.10–16), and emphasizing the biblical association between fornication and idolatry (Rom 1.24–27; 1 Cor 10.6–22; 2 Pet 2.1–22).

A major problem in interpreting the teachings of Jesus, of Paul and of early Christianity in general is the atmosphere of eschatological crisis in which nascent Christianity developed. The celibacy practised by Jesus and some of his followers has to be understood as a response to this situation and not as the outcome of a negative attitude to sex relations. Moreover celibacy in several cases refers not to the total exclusion of marriage but to separation between spouses, which appears to have been practised in early Christian Churches and in other eschatological and prophetic conventicles (Mk 10.29; Lk 14.26; 18.29–30; 1 Cor 9.5; the Messianic Rule of the Qumran Community). However, a suspect ascetical extremism was already emerging in the subapostolic period (Col 2.20–23; 1 Tim 4.3–5) and continued to influence many sectors of Christianity, as with Encratism, Manicheism, Catharism. The flowering of monasticism also had the unfortunate side-effect of downgrading the marital state in the eyes of many. The resulting ambivalence towards sexuality remains a problem for the Christian Church and the task of reconciling its procreative finality with its broader potential for human fulfillment within the Christian vision of man's and woman's vocation is as urgent as ever.

Bibliography: D. S. BAILEY, *Homosexuality and the Western Christian Tradition* (New York 1955). J. BLENKINSOPP, *Celibacy, Ministry, Church* (New York 1968); *Sexuality and the Christian Tradition* (Dayton 1969). D. VON HILDEBRAND, *In Defense of Purity* (Baltimore 1962). A. KOSNIK et al., *Human Sexuality. New Directions in American Catholic Thought* (New York 1977). R. PATAI, *Sex and Family in the Bible and the Middle East* (New York 1959). C. R. TABOR, "Sex, Sexual Behavior," IntDictBiblSuppl (Nashville 1976) 817–820. M. TAYLOR, ed., *Sex: Thoughts for Contemporary Christians* (Garden City, N.Y. 1972).

[J. BLENKINSOPP]

SHERIDAN, TERENCE JAMES

Jesuit writer and editor, b. Dublin, Ireland, Sept. 16, 1908; d. Manila, Philippines, Dec. 11, 1970. Educated at Belvedere College, Dublin, he entered the Jesuit novitiate in 1927. During juniorate and philosophy studies, he began his lifetime career as a writer of plays and topical sketches. Assigned to Hong Kong in 1934, he studied Cantonese at Shiuhing, got his first taste for the Cantonese opera, and did a fair amount of writing for *The Rock*, a Hong Kong literary periodical. From 1935–37, he was on the teaching staff of Wah Yan College, Hong Kong. After theology in Dublin, he was ordained priest in 1940 and stayed to give missions and retreats in Ireland till he returned to Wah Yan in 1946.

Almost immediately he became involved in the cul-

tural life of post-war Hong Kong. He began his annual series of Cantonese operas in English, witty translation-adaptations of the well-known themes of Cantonese opera. His productions were always alive, exciting, very colorful. The most famous was *A Lizard Is No Dragon.* In 1951 he launched both a Chinese magazine for young people and *Outlook*, a literary and current affairs magazine. He was a leading member and producer for the Hong Kong Stage Club. He wrote a number of religious plays, film scripts and scenarios as well as pageants for the Marian Year and on the history of Hong Kong and Macao.

In the early 60s he was assigned to Singapore to edit the *Malaysian Catholic News* which became a lively paper in his hands, and he was quickly involved in radio, drama, and TV in the city. In 1966, after difficulties about his editorship of the newspaper, he resigned from the post and was sent to Manila to work towards an Overseas Program in Radio Veritas. After some months he left it and joined the staff of the East Asian Pastoral Institute. Here he taught communications and film and helped in editing *Teaching All Nations* and *Good Tidings*. He took part in the Fifth International Catechetical Study-Week in Manila (1967), in the Sixth at Medellín, Colombia (1968) and the subsequent meeting in San Antonio (1969) on the application of mass media to catechetics. Everywhere he was he brightened life by the exuberant cheerfulness of his presence. He lectured in the Philippines and in Chicago (Loyola Institute of Pastoral Studies) on the study, evaluation, and use of film, and spent time in Saigon in 1969 training the staff of a community development TV enterprise. He was working on the official film record of Pope Paul's visit to Manila when he died suddenly of cardiac failure.

Bibliography: T. J. SHERIDAN, *Letters to Bart* (London 1938); *Seven Chinese Stories* (London 1959); *Four Short Plays* (London 1960). J. HOFINGER and T. J. SHERIDAN, eds., *The Medellín Papers* (Manila 1969).

[T. O'NEILL]

SHUSTER, GEORGE N.

American journalist, author, and educator, b. Lancaster, Wis., 1894, d. South Bend, Ind., Jan. 25, 1977. Editor of *Commonweal* 1928–40, president of Hunter College, assistant to the president of the University of Notre Dame, and director of the Center for the Study of Man in Contemporary Society, Shuster was a towering Catholic figure of the 20th century. In World War I he served as a sergeant in Army intelligence. He was later educated at Notre Dame, the Universities of Poitiers and of Berlin, and at Columbia. He was head of the English department at Notre Dame (1920–24), then taught at Brooklyn Polytechnic Institute and St. Joseph's College for Women (1924–34). When he began his 20-year tenure at Hunter (1940), it was the largest public college for women in the world. He returned to Notre Dame as assistant to the president (1961–71), then as professor emeritus of English. In his early career he was interested in the Catholic influence in English literature, a concern reflected in *Catholic Spirit in Modern English Literature* (1922), *English Literature: a Textbook* (1926), *Catholic Church in America* (1927), and *Catholic Church in Current Literature* (1930). He edited *The World's Great Catholic Literature* (1942; rev. ed. 1964). In the 1930s he became alarmed at the rise of Hitler, as reflected in his *Germans: An Inquiry and an*

Estimate (1932), *Strong Man Rules* (1934), *Like a Mighty Army: Hitler versus Established Religion* (1935), and, with Arnold Bergstraesser, *Germany, a Short History* (1944). He was an American delegate to the United Nations Conference on International Education (1945) and thus helped create UNESCO. His book *Cultural Co-operation and the Peace* (1953) was a sympathetic account of UNESCO's failures and successes. Shuster's chagrin at aspects of the Communist regimes in Eastern Europe is reflected in his *Religion behind the Iron Curtain* (1954) and in his account of the ordeal of Cardinal Mindzenty, *In Silence I Speak* (1956, in collaboration with Tibor Horanyi). Shuster's reflections on a life-time career in education are found in *Education and Moral Wisdom* (1960) and *The Ground I Walked on; Reflections of a College President* (1961). He wrote numerous topical articles in the confusion following Vatican Council II. Special mention, however, should be made of two works he edited, containing the results of conferences held at Notre Dame: *Freedom and Authority in the West* (1967); and *Evolution in Perspective: Commentaries in Honor of Pierre Lecomte du Noüy* (1968). More controversial was his *Catholic Education in a Changing World* (1967), his reflections on the results of surveys conducted by Notre Dame and the National Opinion Research Center as part of a study of Catholic education. He recommended that elementary schools be abandoned in order to strengthen other parts of the system and that parochial schools be seen as a matter of lay rather than of clerical concern. At about the same time, he was chairman of a group of 37 scholars who conducted the first population-control research done under Catholic auspices. The group gave qualified endorsement to the use of contraceptives and suggested a change in the Church's traditional position on the subject.

Bibliography: G. N. SHUSTER, *On the Side of Truth: George N. Shuster, an Evaluation with Readings*, ed. W. P. LANNIE (Notre Dame, Ind. 1974).

[E. J. DILLON]

SILENCE IN WORSHIP

"In the liturgy God speaks to his people and we reply in song and prayer" (*Sacrosanctum Concilium* 33). Dialogue between God and his people is of the essence of worship. With the implementation of the Constitution on the Liturgy, a formerly silent people have found their voices and now respond to God at the liturgical assemblies (13:213). However, care must be taken that every moment of worship is not filled with words. There is need for times of silence: time to rest quietly and experience the mystery of God, time to listen to him, time to meditate on his Word. Accordingly, the Constitution states that "at the proper times a reverent silence should be observed" (ibid. 30).

This directive is explained in the General Instruction of the Roman Missal. Silence is to be observed at the designated times, and, furthermore, "the character of the silence will depend on the time when it occurs in the particular celebration" (GenInstrRomMissal 23). Not all silence is of the same kind. Liturgical silence is not merely a time when nothing is done; it is a time of interior process. Consequently it must be created; it does not just happen.

The beginning of the liturgy is a time to prepare, time to become aware of the need for God's salvation (ibid.

23). The invitation, "Let us pray," calls for reflection on needs and placing them before God. The one presiding can help focus the prayer; for example, "Let us pray for the grace to follow Christ more closely" (ibid. 23, 88).

Each member of the community is responsible for the attentive silence that must prevail during the proclamation of the Word. "When peaceful stillness compassed everything, your all-powerful word leapt down from heaven" (Wis 18.14–15). Children are often unable to help create this silence. The Directory for *Masses with Children suggests that infants be left in a separate room in the charge of parish helpers and that the older children have a special Liturgy of the Word and homily (Directory 17). A time of meditation is appropriate after the homily (GenInstrRomMissal 23). The quality of this period of silence is a good criterion for judging how well the Word was proclaimed and received.

Silence can be used as a response to the intentions proposed in the General Intercessions or Universal Prayer (ibid. 47). Silence during the Preparation of the Gifts can create an atmosphere of reflection and expectation. Noise, whether of collection baskets or missalette pages, should never disturb the Eucharistic Prayer. After Communion there is need for silence to praise God inwardly and to gather strength from the Eucharist to carry out God's Word (ibid 23, 56).

Bibliography: G. SMITH, "Liturgical Silence," *Carmelus* 23 (1976) 1–20.

[T. RICHSTATTER]

SIN (THEOLOGY)

Sin is both a reality and a mystery. It is one of the central themes of the Bible as well as one of the basic presuppositions which makes the whole drama of salvation both necessary and possible. Nevertheless, it remains an inscrutable mystery; it escapes every attempt to capture its full meaning in a theological formulation. There are many theologies of sin and yet none of them is able to articulate its nature in a manner which is perfect and complete (13:241).

The history of religions seems to indicate that any endeavor to investigate the nature of sin is rooted in one of three possible approaches: the dynamistic, the moralistic, or the personalistic. The dynamistic approach would see sin as the transgression of a taboo or an offense against mysterious supernatural beings and forces. The moralistic approach would see sin as the breaking of some external norm or law. The personalistic approach would see sin as the violation of an interpersonal relationship with the deity.

For a long period of time, it would seem that Roman Catholic efforts to set forth a basic theology of sin tended to focus in on the moralistic approach. Great emphasis was placed on sin as a "violation of the Law of God." In recent times, however, there has been an inclination on the part of the theologians to return to the personalistic approach. As a result, sin is often defined in contemporary theological writing as a "failure to respond to the initiatives of a loving God with whom one has entered into an interpersonal relationship." The moralistic approach tended to place emphasis on the deed that was done; the personalistic approach tends to place emphasis on the doer. Actually both emphases are needed: too much stress on the deed to the detriment of a consideration of the doer can be as misleading as too much stress on the doer to the detriment of the deed.

Fundamental Option Theory. Much of the contemporary theological writing on the nature of sin lays heavy stress on the so-called Fundamental Option Theory. This is an articulation of the personalistic approach and it attempts to envision sin as something located more in a process and in an orientation than in an individual action. The development of such a theory at this particular time in the history of theology seems to be rooted in a rediscovery of the biblical notion of sin, which, though often moralistic in tone, appears to favor a more personalistic orientation. Also to be acknowledged are the contributions of depth psychology to the contemporary theologizing about the nature of sin. Studies in this particular empirical discipline have emphasized the incompleteness with which the personal core of one's being is expressed in one's ordinary actions.

Basis and Nature of Sin. Development of the Fundamental Option Theory seems to be in direct proportion to the growing realization among moralists that personal conversion is the basic element in the Christian life. To become a Christian in the proper sense of the term is to adopt a new life style, to do an about-face from the self-centeredness dominant because of Adam's sin, to put off the "old man" and put on the "new man" (Eph 4.22–24; Col 3.9–10), to stop trying to "play God" as Adam did and become "the servant of all" in the manner indicated by Jesus in the act of his death. For the Christian, the act of conversion is constituted by an in-depth acceptance of a loving God realized through a loving acceptance of Jesus, who, in his paschal mystery, is the permanent incarnation and proof of God's abiding love for members of the human race.

Taking as its point of departure a more biblical and depth-psychology oriented view of conversion, the Fundamental Option Theory seeks to evaluate the Christian's particular actions within the context of his or her whole life stance. In this attempt to theologize about sin, the particular concrete action is no longer judged in isolation from the person acting; rather, it is evaluated in relation to the fundamental life-stance and basic attitude on the part of an individual subject. In this theory, all particular choices are to be referred to the primary criterion: they are to be judged in comparison with the fundamental option for God begun in the act of conversion and measured in regard to their degree of harmony or disharmony with it.

Kinds of Sin. A change in the basic theory of sin leads inevitably to a change in the understanding of the two traditional forms of sin. Accordingly, mortal sin is often described by proponents of this new approach as "not only a refusal to give something to God but a refusal to give him myself in an action in which I am fully engaged and really involved as a person"; venial sin is seen also as a refusal to give oneself but "a refusal which does not go to the heart of the person, a refusal which is not realized at the center of one's person."

Some proponents of the theory see the necessity of a threefold distinction of sins: "mortal," which is a forceful option for evil or the conclusion of a process that leads to a radical break with God; "serious," which betrays evil tendencies in a person's heart but does not necessarily bring about a radical reversal of the fundamental option; and "venial" which is a refusal to grow or a failure to attend to the implications of conversion as a life-long process.

Recently some imprecise reporting suggested that the *Declaration on Certain Questions Concerning Sexual Ethics* issued by the Sacred Congregation for the Doctrine of the Faith (December 29, 1975) voiced a condemnation of the Fundamental Option theory. It should be noted that what the Congregation did state was the following: ". . . it is wrong to say that particular acts are not enough to constitute mortal sin" (n. 10). It is obvious that no responsible Catholic theologian could hold such an opinion. It is quite possible in theory for a particular act to constitute a mortal sin; however, in actual practice, it can be extremely difficult.

It would be a mistake to see the Fundamental Option Theory as something entirely new and as a creation of contemporary theology. Rather, it is something which is being rediscovered from the "return to the sources" which marks the renewal in moral theology. In that connection, it is of interest to take note of an observation made over seven hundred years ago by St. Thomas Aquinas.

> Now the difference between venial and mortal sin is consequent upon the diversity of that lack of order which constitutes the nature of sin. For lack of order is twofold, one that destroys the principle of order, and another which, without destroying the principle of order, causes lack of order in the things which follow the principle . . . . When the soul is so disordered by sin as to turn away from its last end, viz., God, to Whom it is united by charity, there is mortal sin; but when it is disordered without turning away from God, then there is venial sin . . . . In practical matters, he who by sinning turns away from his last end, if we consider the nature of this sin, falls irreparably, and therefore is said to sin mortally and to deserve eternal punishment. But when a man sins without turning away from God, by the very nature of his sin his disorder can be repaired, because the principle of the order is not destroyed; and therefore he is said to sin venially, because, namely, he does not sin so as to deserve to be punished eternally (ST 1a1ae, 72.5).

Like every other theological attempt to articulate the meaning of that mysterious reality that sin is, the Fundamental Option Theory has advantages and disadvantages. It does help to overcome the excessive stress on the moralistic understanding of sin earlier so prevalent. However, it can be very seriously misunderstood by a generation which has been brought up on the "it's *only* a venial sin" syndrome. Nevertheless, the understanding of the root of moral activity which the Fundamental Option Theory rests on is of considerable help in the attempt to establish a proper understanding of the nature of mortal sin as well as the difference between mortal and venial sin.

Bibliography: E. BRUNO, "Contemporary Theological Understanding of Sin," *Living Word* 81 (1975) 207–222; 291–318; 406–449. E. COOPER, "A New Look at the Theology of Sin," LouvSt 3 (1971) 259–307; "The Fundamental Option," IrTheolQ 39 (1972) 383–392. S. FAGAN, *Has Sin Changed* (Wilmington, Del. 1977). J. FUCHS, "Sin and Conversion," TheolDig 14 (1966) 292–301. V. GENOVESI, "The Death of Love: A Radical Theology of Sin," AmEcclRev 169 (1975) 87–101. J. GLASER, "Transition between Grace and Sin: Fresh Perspectives," ThSt 29 (1968) 260–274. B. HÄRING, *Sin in the Secular Age* (New York 1974). T. HART, "Sin in the Context of the Fundamental Option," HomPastRev 71 (1970) 47–50. E. MALY, *Sin: Biblical Perspectives* (Dayton 1973). M. MCDONAGH, "The Moral Subject," IrTheolQ 39 (1972) 3–22. D. O'CALLAGHAN, "What is mortal Sin," *Furrow* 25 (1974) 71–87.   [J. A. O'DONOHOE]

SINGLE PEOPLE

The term "single people" as used in this article is a general heading, including the widowed and divorced as well as the never-married (13:250). Despite marked differences in the situations of each of these groups, they share common experiences and problems arising from living outside the institutional structures of married, priestly, and religious life, and thus should be considered together, at least initially.

The Fathers of Vatican Council II affirm the role of the single person in the life of the Church when they declare that witness to Christ is given not only by those in the clerical, religious, and married states, but also, "in a different way," by "widows and single people, who are able to make great contributions toward holiness and apostolic endeavor in the Church" (*Lumen gentium* 41).

The Pastoral Issues. Until recently, the Church has devoted little attention to single people, pastorally or theologically. Over the last twenty years, however, the number of single Catholics has risen sharply, because of changing social attitudes regarding the importance and stability of the institutions of marriage, priesthood, and religious life. Thus, the Council's statement takes on important new dimensions: (1) it enjoins the Church as a whole to incorporate single people fully into her life and mission; (2) it calls upon theologians to reflect on the religious and ecclesial significance of the single life; and (3) it actively enlists the participation of single people in the work of the Church.

People are single for various reasons, often including one or more of the following: (1) transition from the married or clerical states; (2) the responsibility of caring for aged or infirm parents or relatives; (3) circumstances that prevent them from marrying or from finding a suitable marriage partner; (4) the need for greater physical, social, and psychological freedom than marrieds, religious, or priests; (5) a fundamental orientation towards solitude; (6) in some cases, fear of lifelong commitments and responsibility toward others; (7) the relative importance in their lives of a career or a special cause.

Some of the issues confronting single Catholics today include: (1) defining and clarifying their role in a Church and a society primarily oriented toward the nuclear family; (2) the need to remedy the indifference and even suspicion that many churchmen and married people hold toward singles as a group; (3) urban alienation, loneliness, and the need for intimacy; (4) the need to reflect upon the nature of personal relationships and sexuality outside of marriage or a religious calling; (5) the social, economic, and political instability of many singles; (6) prejudice and exploitation in careers, housing, and financial matters; and (7) anxiety created by an open and uncertain future.

Ministry to Singles. Ministry to singles in the Church is still in its beginning stages. Most parishes are fundamentally family-oriented, even though there may be large numbers of single people living in their boundaries. Sermons and parish activities rarely seek to include singles, and many, justifiably dissatisfied, leave the institutional Church until they marry.

Especially in urban areas where most singles live, special ministries are now being established, some affiliated with parishes and others independent. Primarily, such ministries should provide a serious and spiritually-oriented environment with a strong communal dimension, to counteract the isolation and exploitation of urbanized, commercialized life, and to allow intimacy to grow. It should encourage development of the Christian single life through prayer and spiritual direction, and frank discussion of spiritual, social, and moral issues with an approach that is non-judgmental and theologically informed. It is important too that such a single ministry strive to integrate singles into the Christian community as a whole, bringing them into social contact with married people and families, and inviting them to assume positions of parish and diocesan leadership which are now almost exclusively filled by married people and religious.

Theological Issues. Theological reflection on the single life becomes increasingly necessary as the number of singles grows. Of special importance is the need to affirm single people in their present lives, emphasizing singleness in itself as a true vocation or calling from God, not as simply an interim state leading to marriage or a religious vocation, or as the unfortunate result of circumstance. This view of single life takes as its basis the Council's insistence that all Christians have in fact one and the same vocation, to holiness (*Lumen gentium* 5), and that the "states in life" are simply the means of living out the primary commitment to Christ made at Baptism. Regardless of whether or not they intend to remain single for life, this theology of the single vocation can be a great encouragement to singles to see their lives as meaningful and valuable apart from a decision to marry or enter the priesthood or religious life.

Other important matters deserving theological attention concern sexual relationships, intimacy, the nature of a commitment to Christ in a life without vows, the meaning of freedom in the single life, such alternative, Christian life styles as small communities of prayer and service, the use of time and money, solitude and ways of prayer as a single person, and the significance of the single person's open future in relation to the eschatological dimension of the Christian Church.

Bibliography: M. ADAMS, *Single Blessedness* (New York 1976). N. B. CHRISTOFF, *Saturday Night, Sunday Morning: Singles in the Church* (New York 1978). R. A. DOW, *Ministry with Single Adults* (Valley Forge, Pa. 1977). W. LYON, *A Pew for One, Please* (New York 1977). M. MCGINNIS, *Single* (New York 1976). N. PARENT, "Developing an Effective Adult Singles Program," LivLight, 12 (1975) 228–238. R. REPOHL, "The Spirituality of Singleness," *America* 135 (1976) 365–367. P. STEIN, *Single* (Englewood Cliffs, N.J. 1976). E. WAKIN, *Single Catholics and the Church* (Chicago 1978).

[R. REPOHL]

SOCIAL ACTION

Social action may be defined as any or all activities intended to promote the common good of society, understanding the latter term, with Vatican Council II, as "the sum total of those conditions of social life which enable human beings to achieve a fuller measure of perfection with greater ease" (*Dignitatis humanae* 6). Inasmuch as it is the right of all human beings to seek their perfection, justice requires that they be accorded the exercise of the right, or at least that impediments be removed from their path. Social action, then, is action for justice.

Basis for Church Social Action. This reasoning, admittedly a clarification that has emerged in our time, has progressed even further. The 1971 Synod of Bishops, gave social action a scriptural and theological base. The bishops pointed out that the God of the Old Testament "revealed himself to us as the liberator of the oppressed and the defender of the poor, the one who asked human beings to believe in themselves and to practice justice toward their neighbor," while Christ "lived his existence in the world as a total gift of himself to God for the salvation and liberation of men. In his preaching he proclaimed the fatherhood of God over all humanity and the intervention of God's justice for the poor and the oppressed" (Synod JustWorld p. 41). In impressive and (except in Vatican II's Constitution on the Church in the Modern World) rather unprecedented language, the bishops continue: "According to the Christian message, the attitude of human beings toward one another is at one with their attitude toward God; their response to the love of God which saves us through Christ becomes efficacious only in the love and service of humanity. So Christian love of neighbor and justice cannot be separated. In fact, love implies a radical demand for justice, and that involves a recognition of the dignity and rights of one's neighbor.... The actual situation of the world, in the light of faith, appears as a new event in the history of salvation. It calls us to return to the essential core of the Christian message.... The mission to preach the gospel requires that all of us dedicate ourselves today to the total liberation of humankind" (ibid. p. 42).

Clearly the Synod draws from rich sources in order to arrive at its oft quoted conclusion: "Action on behalf of justice and participation in the transformation of the world fully appear to us as a constitutive dimension of the preaching of the Gospel, or, in other words, of the Church's mission for the redemption of the human race and its liberation from every oppressive situation" (ibid. p. 34).

Clarifications. The term "a constitutive dimension" was novel in ecclesiastical documents and open to misinterpretation or exaggeration. Evidently Pope Paul thought so, for in both his opening and closing addresses to the *Synod of Bishops, 1974, he was at pains to establish proper priorities. Those engaged in social ministry, he said, are today often urged "to forget the priority that the message of salvation must have, and thus to reduce their own action to mere sociological activity." The Church today "believes firmly that the promotion of human rights is required by the gospel and is central to her ministry"; nonetheless, he continued, "the totality of salvation is not to be confused with one or another aspect of liberation, and the Good News must preserve all of its own originality: that of a God who saves us from sin and death and brings us to divine life. Hence, human advancement, social progress, etc., is not to be excessively emphasized on a temporal level to the detriment of the essential meaning which evangelization has for the Church of Christ: the announcement of the Good News."

Further refinement of the concept of Christian social action, or at least of social action sponsored officially by the Church, was provided by Avery Dulles, SJ, in "testimony" before the first bicentennial consultation on justice, conducted by NCCB in 1975 (see CALL TO ACTION). Fr. Dulles indicated two dilemmas confronting the Church's social ministry. The first—a tension between the abstract and the concrete—confronts the Church with two unacceptable alternatives. If it sticks to generalities, the Church is accused of timidity or ineffectiveness; yet when it espouses specific political, social, or economic causes, it is accused of wandering outside its sphere of competence. The second dilemma is a tension between the secular and the religious. If the Church becomes heavily involved in social and political issues, it does not satisfy those who turn to it for an experience of the transcendent. But if it withdraws from these issues it is "conniving with the oppressors." Fr. Dulles recommended that the Church pursue a middle road in both cases, and he included a list of "cautions"

Church leaders should consider in applying the Gospel to issues of justice.

Implementations. If the teaching Church must sometimes be tentative in its pronouncements on specific social issues, no such limitation is imposed on the active involvement by Christians high and low in efforts to rectify sinful social structures and to assist those suffering from them. The language employed by the Vatican Council II's Constitution on the Church in the Modern World in ch. 3, 4, and 5 makes it clear that Christians are not to be content only with "education for justice": "Christians *engaged actively* in modern economic and social progress and in the struggle for justice and charity must be convinced that they have much to contribute to the prosperity of mankind and to world peace" (*Gaudium et spes* 72). "Mindful of the words of the Lord: 'By this everyone will know that you are my disciples, if you have love for one another' (Jn 13.35), Christians can yearn for nothing more ardently than to *serve* the people of this age with an overgrowing generosity and success.... Not everyone who says 'Lord, Lord' will enter the kingdom of heaven, but those who do the will of the Father, and who manfully *put their hands to the work*. It is the Father's will that we should recognize Christ our brother in every person and *love them with an effective love*" (ibid. 93; emphases added).

One example of how literally these instructions are understood is the establishment by Pope Paul of the Pontifical Commission for Studies on *Justice and Peace, to coordinate international and national undertakings and to cooperate, through *SODEPAX with similar efforts by non-Catholics. Another example, on the American scene, is found in the six regional "justice hearings" conducted by the bishops of the United States, which climaxed in the Call to Action, national justice conference held in Detroit in 1976.

The forms of social action are as varied as the human needs they seek to satisfy. Sometimes the Church sets up its own organizations, sometimes it missions workers into existing structures, sometimes clerics or laypeople take on responsibilities over and above their primary occupations. The laity go into political life in order to promote justice, and the American bishops elected to go in 1975 into direct political action in order to secure, in opposition to legalized abortion, an amendment to the Constitution. Centers for research (the *Catholic Committee on Urban Ministry, at the University of Notre Dame and the Woodstock Theological Center in Washington, D.C.) were established. Professional surveys are commissioned: on women in positions of authority in the Church, on education for ministry, on alcoholism among the clergy. Journals and newspapers carry press releases, interviews, or articles on social issues; television and radio are utilized as means of "conscientization," i.e., of raising the awareness both of the oppressed and their oppressors. Community organizers, social workers, urban planners, counsellors in prisons and hospitals and old-age centers, the staff of agencies for youth, for unwed mothers, for nursing and health services, for refugees, for minorities, for the handicapped, for legal services to the poor, for children—all these (and many more categories could be listed) may be rightfully considered as working for justice.

Perhaps, however, the motivation could be more

conscious and explicit in many cases, and the words of Cardinal John Dearden, speaking to the American bishops at the end of his presidency of the NCCB in 1971 have their application here: "We need as a Conference to deepen and strengthen the theological dimension of much that we do. The motivation of our many activities is, after all, not pragmatism. We act instead out of deep religious conviction and an abiding love of the Church. We know this to be a fact. But at the same time we now lack the means by which it would be possible visibly and consistently to infuse with this understanding of its *raison d'être* all our Conference's manifold undertakings."

Laity in Ministry of Justice. Tangent to the question of motivation is the growing awareness of many laypeople that their apostolate is not just a participation in the mission of the hierarchy, as Pope Pius XI defined *Catholic Action. Nor, as Vatican Council II indicated (*Apostolicam actuositatem* 6), are they to confine their activities to the purely secular sphere, leaving "spiritual" or "churchly" tasks to the clergy. The laity are coming to see that there is only one apostolate, one ministry, that of the Church. "Lay people have an explicit vocation to Christianize the world, to nourish it, to promote justice and practice charity. They do not have lesser vocations than priests and religious. They have the same vocations, the same responsibilities. As full members of the Church, they are called to precisely the same apostolate.... All this is not to advocate the laity's simply taking over the functions of the clergy. Instead, we must bring to life a Church where ministry is nothing less and nothing more than the common coin of the community. We have to bring to life a Church in which all members are expected to be ministers as a price of their membership, where sharing is a lived experience, not just a sacramental one. We must form communities that constantly summon people to serve, identify areas of need, discern the talents of their members and put the explicit stamp of Christian ministry on people's attempts to help each other and their neighborhoods. In the long run we have to develop a spirituality that leads people to realize that all helping activity is ministerial and priestly" (Brophy 77).

Bibliography: D. BROPHY, "Lay Ministers for Tomorrow's Church," *America* 138, n. 4 (Feb. 4, 1978) 75–78. A. DULLES, "Dilemma Facing the Church in the World," *Origins* 4 (1975) 548–551. J. C. HAUGHEY, *The Faith That Does Justice* (New York 1977). R. LAURENTIN, *Liberation, Development, and Salvation* (Maryknoll, N.Y. 1972). V. P. MAINELLI, *Social Justice: The Catholic Position* (Gaithersburg, Md. 1975). B. L. MASSE, *The Church and Social Progress* (Milwaukee 1966). M. A. NEAL, *A Socio-theology of Letting Go* (New York 1977). J. NEWMAN, *The Christian in Society* (Baltimore 1962). PAUL VI, "Addresses to the Synod of Bishops," *Origins* 4 (1974) 241–245; 309–313. Third Synod of Bishops, *Origins* 4 (1974) 305–309. B. A. WREN, *Education for Justice* (Maryknoll, N.Y. 1977).

[W. J. LEONARD]

SOCIAL DEVELOPMENT AND WORLD PEACE, USCC COMMITTEE ON

The Social Development and World Peace Committee is one of three departmental committees of the United States Catholic Conference (USCC), the national-level executive agency of the American bishops. The twenty-one member Committee is responsible for reviewing and making recommendations to the USCC Administrative Board and Board of Trustees on objectives, programs, and policies of the USCC that relate to the social order. The Committee is chaired by a bishop elected by the general body of bishops to fill a three-year term. Committee membership is comprised of equal numbers of bishops and non-bishops. National Catholic organizations, including National Conference of Catholic Charities, National Catholic Rural Life Conference, National Office of Black Catholics, and the Catholic Committee on Appalachia, maintain observer status at the Committee meetings.

Origins and Programs. The Social Development and World Peace Committee was first established in 1972, the result of a merger of two episcopal advisory committees, the Committee on International Affairs and the Committee on Social Development. Prior to the establishment of the USCC in 1967 and the creation of these two Committees, matters pertaining to the social order were handled by the Social Action Department of the National Catholic Welfare Conference, the predecessor organization of the USCC. The Department was under the supervision of one episcopal chairman and it was responsible for American episcopal pronouncements on unemployment, labor, unionization, racial injustice, and other questions. Since the inception of the Committee on Social Development and World Peace a number of policies bearing on contemporary social issues have been developed and at the recommendation of the Committee, the United States Catholic Conference has adopted positions on a range of topics. These have included unemployment, human rights, world hunger, prison reform, capital punishment, disarmament, political responsibility, civil rights, the Panama Canal Treaty, Southern Africa and Eastern Europe (*see* PUBLIC POLICY ISSUES AND THE CHURCH). The positions developed by the Committee do not bind individual bishops to particular social or political stances but USCC policies usually inspire diocesan support of such positions in educational programs as well as pastoral and legislative activities.

Workings of the Committee. Policies adopted through the Committees' work govern the activities of the USCC itself. These activities may include the representation of the USCC before governmental bodies, educational or advocacy programs or other efforts. The Committee identifies an item of social concern through a variety of means. It may be that an individual bishop will encourage Committee attention to a particular social issue during one of two general meetings of the American episcopal conference held each year. Consultations involving groups of Catholics may also dictate some form of action by the Committee. The Call to Action assembly, a gathering of laity, priests and religious from 132 dioceses, in October of 1976 precipitated a range of initiatives by the Committee.

In the past, USCC department staff have been the primary source of Committee involvement. The Department is composed of two offices, one for domestic social policy and the other for questions dealing with international affairs. A 13-member staff serves the department with specialists in economics, political affairs, urban and rural issues, and health and welfare among other areas. Staff recommendations are periodically evaluated and acted upon by the Committee and from time to time the Committee serves in turn as a catalyst for staff action. Although credited with inviting Catholic involvement in efforts ranging from diocesan housing sponsorship to participation in international treaty ratifications, the Committee's work remains relatively unknown to most

Catholics, a fact documented during the American bishops' bicentennial observance, a consultation program devoted to the theme of justice (*see* CALL TO ACTION).

Although the Committee through the staff structure maintains regular communications with the diocesan social apostolate, USCC findings indicate that there has yet to be developed an effective method through which the social policies of the USCC can be communicated to the Catholic community. Significant improvements in developing mechanisms for greater participation in the affairs of the Committee and the USCC are expected in the near future with the promulgation of a five-year program drawn up by the bishops in response to the bicentennial Call to Action (*see* BISHOPS' JUSTICE PROGRAM).

Despite present developmental deficiencies, the Committee has involved many elements of the Catholic Church in a serious and sustained discussion and action on critically important social issues of the 1970s. With its wide range of participants and through its consultation efforts, it has provided a mechanism for Catholics and others who wish to engage or influence church leadership on matters pertaining to the social order.

[F. J. BUTLER]

SOCIAL HISTORY

Writing in 1964 Henry May noted that "for the study and understanding of American culture, the recovery of American religious history may well be the most important achievement of the last thirty years," (May 79). May went on to note that the two groups that had contributed least were atheists and Roman Catholics. Strange bedfellows indeed, but as far as Catholics were concerned, May's assessment was accurate. The same statement could not be made in 1978, however. The last 15-year period has witnessed a renewal in the historical study of American Catholicism and the principal reason for this is the emergence of social history as a major field of specialization.

Meaning. Social history is not easy to define. The name is used in reference to the history of the lower classes, to the study of human activities or the manners, customs, and everyday life of a particular community of people, and, finally, to the study of economics. Briefly put, it is the history of society—its people, culture and economy. It is a relatively new area of specialization that only began to develop seriously in the 1950s. Since its emergence in the 1950s the bulk of work in social history has centered on the following topics: the family, urban studies, classes and social groups, the culture of communities, and social movements. Methodologically social history has popularized the use of the computer because of its usefulness in quantitative research; conceptually it has adopted theories and ideas from the social sciences. In the process it has revolutionized the historical disciplines.

Study of Catholicism. The development of social history has also changed the historical study of Catholicism. Both in Europe and America there has emerged a new approach to the history of the Church which parallels the development of social history. Reinforcing this is the ecclesiology which emerged from Vatican Council II. Both these tendencies, one historical and the other theological, have led to a revitalization of the historical study of Catholicism.

Focus on the Parish. Social history with its emphasis on people and their culture and the new ecclesiology with its understanding of the Church as the People of God have refocused attention on the local parish community as the most appropriate setting to study the history of the Catholic community. Since the 1960s an increasing number of studies have emerged in the U.S. which bear the mark of this new approach to the history of Catholicism. Many of these studies have been done by a new breed of social historians trained in secular universities, while others have been written by historians educated in Catholic universities. In Europe the renaissance in the history of Catholicism has been even more significant.

The new angle of vision in church history has unveiled many aspects of the Catholic tradition which were hitherto unknown or at least not widely recognized. By focusing on the local parish community historians have begun to uncover the richness of popular piety and the role which religion exercised in the community. The religious behavior of ordinary Catholics is becoming better understood as historians explore the history of confraternities, shrines, pilgrimages, and religious festivals. Sermons, catechisms, and parish missions are other areas of study that also reveal the culture of Catholicism. The study of such topics not only answers the question of what it meant to be a Catholic in a given time and place, but it also assists in measuring the level of religious commitment prevalent in a particular community.

Focus on the Family. The history of the family is another area of study where the persistence or absence of religious values can be observed. The size of families, sexual mores, and patterns of marriage strikingly reflect the popular perception of Catholic morality. The parish also furnishes a basis for comparison between different ethnic communities. The ethnic or national parish was an important transitional institution in the lives of immigrants coming to the U.S.; studies of these communities are becoming more numerous and they reveal not only the continuities and changes which immigrants experienced in their adopted homeland, but also the differences and similarities between various immigrant communities. Differences in piety, class structure, institutional development, economic mobility, and family life can all be investigated through a study of the local parish. From such studies the plurality of the Catholic culture and the richness of this tradition are strikingly revealed.

Significance of Studies. The recovery of religious history among Catholics since the 1960s has been a significant development. Not only is it unveiling neglected areas of the Catholic tradition, but it also is increasing the understanding of this heritage. Most importantly the emphasis on social history or the history of society in its totality has forced historians of Catholicism to study the Church in relation to, not in isolation from the rest of society. A narrow denominational history has been supplanted by a more comprehensive approach which studies the People of God in the totality of their social environment.

A new history and a new ecclesiology have become two fundamental resources for a better appreciation of the Catholic heritage both past and present. Such topics as piety, the family, and the parish, together with the constellation of themes clustered around these topics are issues of enduring importance. Social history has underscored the importance of such themes in understanding the meaning of Catholicism both in the past and, of necessity, in the present.

See also CATHOLICISM, CULTURAL.

Bibliography: J. P. DOLAN, *The Immigrant Church: New York's Irish and German Catholics, 1815–1865* (Baltimore 1975); *Catholic Revivalism: The American Experience, 1830–1900* (Notre Dame, Ind. 1978). F. GILBERT and S. R. GRAUBARD, eds., *Historical Studies Today* (New York 1972). H. F. MAY, "The Recovery of American Religious History," AmHistRev 70 (1964) 79–92. *Ricerche di storia sociale e religiosa,* n.s. anno 5 n. 10 (July–December 1976) entire issue. S. TOMASI, *Piety and Power: The Role of Italian Parishes in the New York Metropolitan Area, 1880–1930* (Staten Island, N.Y. 1975).

[J. P. DOLAN]

SOCIAL WORK, CATHOLIC

Social work has been an expression of society's attempts to aid its members towards increased social functioning and to make experiences for greater dignity and well-being more available. Social work took shape as a profession in the 20th century. Within ever-broadening parameters of service, social workers have, over the decades, used a variety of means to offer their expanding knowledge and experience to people with problems and people in problem situations (13:361).

Development of Catholic Social Work in the U.S. In the practice of social work, the social functioning of persons is a primary concern; often, however, it is an impoverishment of resources which brings the action of social workers to bear on situations. Whether in activities to assist those in need directly, or in activities geared to change social institutions, the expected outcome of social-work activities is that the well-being of all people be enhanced. The organized expression of caring for people and helping them has many of its roots in groups formed to worship God and to serve him. For instance, by 1728 in the U.S. the Ursuline Sisters were offering organized social services to the children of New Orleans. The St. Vincent de Paul Society and Ladies of Charity, organizations of lay people, were early organized expressions of caring for others. Many who were committed to a religious communal life were also serving the poor, the ill, and children.

A national effort to come together and to learn from each other led to the convening of social service groups in the Catholic Church in 1910. The National Conference of Catholic Charities (NCCC), with a goal to keep a "theology of charity in touch with a profession of social work," gave direction to the continuing development of knowledgeable, skilled groups of social workers whose professional work was rooted in charity, i.e. in God's love. The NCCC was to coordinate and to perfect the activity of individual and institutional efforts in the apostolate of charity in the Church. So that its distinct identity would never be lost in the wider development of the social welfare field, the objective was that Catholic philosophy, doctrine and supernatural motivation and inspiration be maintained and supplemented by progress in method (Gavin 27–28).

In 1970, the NCCC initiated a study of its direction and renewal efforts were urged in the Report to the Conference in 1972, *Towards a Renewed Catholic Charities Movement.* Referred to as the Cadre Study, the report urged three major goals for the Conference and its member agencies: Continuing Commitment to Service, Humanizing and Transforming the Social Order, and Convening the Christian Community. The Cadre Study gave impetus and direction to the emerging need, once again, to speak of the "distinct identity" of social work in Catholic settings.

The Catholic Rationale. The essence of this distinct social work is its public acknowledgement of a transcendent God. This acknowledgement of God occurs through the presence of a Catholic agency in the social-welfare community and through the work of the staff of the agency—a work which seeks to bring forth the justice and liberation of the Kingdom of God. This social-work practice under Catholic auspices attests to man's origin in God his Creator and man's completion in Jesus Christ, the new creation (Rom 5.12–21). Through Jesus, God is in creative communion with his people and becomes Father to them. In Jesus, God has united himself with every person, sharing a love that transcends legal obligations. With Jesus, God values each person individually and acknowledges each person as a participant in the creative history of the world.

Social work in a Catholic setting is a ministry of the Church through which individuals carry forth the work of Jesus Christ under the guidance of the Holy Spirit. Catholic social workers find that their practice has guiding principles rooted in the love and mercy of Jesus; he is the ultimate model of humanity for them. Christian social work is informed by the theological tradition of the Church which has been interpreting salvation history for centuries. The tradition extends from St. Paul and his exposition of selfless love to Dorothy Day who has made a vocation of demonstrating the congruence of Catholic belief with service to the poor and oppressed.

A theological heritage helps Christian social work to understand the complexity of problems and to discover possible directions when it encounters resistance. In this dialogue, there is a dialectic in which questions and answers are mixed and reshaped by the interaction of heritage and contemporary problems. Without this interchange, heritage is discounted and social problems become one-dimensional. Archbishop Jean Jadot, Apostolic Delegate to the U.S., in speaking to the 63d Annual Meeting of the NCCC, stressed the need for increased theological study by the Christian social work agencies. A key to building a *community of service* is the exchange between theologians and social activists. This community, he said, "is a community built on the person and the example of Jesus, united in prayer and liturgical celebrations as it leads a life of action in the world, giving witness to its inner life of faith and distinctive moral values. Essential to this witness is the pursuit of justice, undertaking the works of charity, and leading a life of service to others" (Jadot 55).

Christian social work accepts that man, a creature and sacrament of God, is violated in all his humanity by poverty and oppression and recognizes the many times God has intervened with "social outcasts." Notably, in the Old Testament we see the concern of God for his people in the here and now situation when he acted through Moses. God's intention is clear, "I have seen the suffering of my people... and have come down to rescue them...." (Ex 3.7–8). Further, Moses joins his people in their struggle from suffering to liberation.

Christian social work also looks at the person of Jesus Christ. As Jesus entered into the lives of the disliked and downtrodden with love and solidarity (Lk 5.29–32), so Christian social work attempts to develop a humble tone that can carry a message to the seats of power. Instead of separating the social worker from the historical experience of the poor, this identification with the poor produces a spiritual bond of joy and hope. Further, there is the recognition that encountering the poor in solidarity and encountering Christ are inseparable elements of the faith of Christian social workers (Mt 25.34–40).

Christian social workers attempt to understand their own role in the oppression of others and examine their ability to change patterns of consumption and its absorption of wealth (Lk 14.28–33). Social work which is directed by a theology of charity cannot effectively agitate for the poor while maintaining an attitude of superiority to them. Identification with the poor allows workers and clients to come together as brothers and sisters. As an illustration of God's equal caring for all, the distinctions between professionals and consumers of service are minimized. Decision-making powers, participation in the planning process, and staff development are occasions for convening and out of this process grows a community of mutual love and support.

Pope Paul VI, quoting from *Lumen gentium*, stated that "without putting themselves in the place of the institutions of civil society, they (Christian organizations) have to express, in their own way and rising above their particular nature, the concrete demands of the Christian faith for a just, and consequently necessary, transformation of society." The Pope added, "today more than ever, the Word of God will be unable to be proclaimed and heard unless it is accompanied by the witness of the power of the Holy Spirit working within the action of Christians in the service of their brothers, at the points in which their existence and their future are at stake" (Paul VI OctogAdven 51).

Bibliography: R. A. ALVES, *A Theology of Human Hope* (Washington, D.C. 1969). *Encyclopedia of Social Work* v. 1–3 (Washington, D.C. 1977). J. H. GALPER, *The Politics of Social Services* (Englewood Cliffs, N.J. 1975). D. P. GAVIN, *The National Conference of Catholic Charities, 1910–1960* (Milwaukee 1962). G. GUTIERREZ, *A Theology of Liberation*, tr. C. INDA and J. EAGLESON (New York 1973). J. JADOT, "Building a Community through Faith and Service," *Social Thought* 3 n. 4 (1977) 51–58. NCCC, *Towards a Renewed Catholic Charities Movement* (Cadre Study) (Washington, D.C. 1972).

[P. DI LORENZO; M. GATZA]

SOCIALIZATION

Socialization, at times erroneously confused with socialism, was taken up in Vatican Council II following the initial and celebrated treatment of the concept by John XXIII (*Mater et magistra* 59–67). The Constitution on the Church in the Modern World first alludes to the multiplication of social relationships deriving from such modern forces as technology, *urbanization, and rapid communication (*Gaudium et spes* 6). With *Mater et magistra*, the conciliar statement recognizes that people create such association, not driven by blind forces but responding to natural inclinations.

Socialization does not always "promote personal development" nor freedom of the individual (ibid. 6); but "a wholesome socialization" will do so (ibid. 42). This is a socialization, including needed state intervention, which "does not hamper the development of family and social and cultural groups . . ." but promotes the common good, true autonomy, and community (ibid. 75).

With *Mater et magistra* (53), *Gaudium et spes* links socialization to subsidiarity. This requires that, where needed, state intervention not be at the expense of rightful autonomy of "intermediate bodies or organizations and their constructive activity . . ." or indeed of individuals (*Gaudium et spes* 75). Individuals and lesser bodies must be encouraged to do for themselves what they can.

The building of family associations, neighborhoods, and broader communities is widely recognized among Catholics today as an indispensable new ministry. Such ministry is consonant with current secular thinking of such authors as E. F. Schumacher in his *Small Is Beautiful* (1973).

[W. F. RYAN]

SOCIETAS LITURGICA

Societas Liturgica came into existence by the initiative of Wiebe Vos, a pastor of the Netherlands Reformed Church. In 1962 he had found *Studia liturgica*, "an international ecumenical quarterly for liturgical research and renewal." In 1965 he called a conference of twenty-five liturgists from Europe and North America at the Protestant community of Grandchamp, in Neuchâtel, Switzerland. With J. J. von Allmen in the chair, the conference discussed Christian initiation and resolved to found a Societas Liturgica, "an association for the promotion of ecumenical dialogue on worship, based on solid research, with the perspective of renewal and unity."

The foundation meeting of Societas Liturgica took place at Driebergen, Holland, in 1967. That meeting studied Vatican Council II's Constitution on the Liturgy and recent work on worship by the World Council of Churches' Faith and Order (5:807). Thereafter the Societas has held congresses at two-yearly intervals. The 1969 meeting at Glenstal Abbey, Ireland, took liturgical language as its theme. In 1971 the Strasbourg conference was devoted to contemporary worship, with an emphasis on new forms. The 1973 congress was housed by the Benedictines of Montserrat, Spain, and it studied contemporary forms of common prayer today. At Trier in 1975 attention was given to current work in the revision and composition of Eucharistic Prayers. The Canterbury congress of 1977 returned to the theme of Christian initiation; a new feature was the opportunity for short communications on work away from the main subject of the meeting. It is expected that the 1979 meeting will be held in the United States. Most of the papers delivered at meetings of the Societas have been published in English in *Studia liturgica* over the years; the following numbers are particularly noteworthy: 4, n. 1 (1965); 6, n. 1 (1969); 10, nn. 3–4 (1974); 11, nn. 3–4 (1976); 12, nn. 2–4 (1977).

Membership of Societas Liturgica is open to teachers of liturgy and to members of liturgical commissions. On the rolls there are now over 200 members. The international and ecumenical character of the society is illustrated by the list of its successive presidents, who hold office for two years: Placid Murray, OSB, Ireland (Roman Catholic); Dean R. C. D. Jasper, England (Anglican); P. M. Gy, OP, France (Roman Catholic); Professor J. J. von Allmen, Switzerland (Reformed); Professor B. Fischer, Germany (Roman Catholic); Professor T. J. Talley, U.S. (Episcopal). Since 1977 the secretary has been John E. Rotelle, OSA.

[G. WAINWRIGHT]

SOCIETIES, CONDEMNED (CANON LAW)

On July 18, 1974 a letter was sent from the Congregation for the Doctrine of the Faith to the president of the National Conference of Catholic Bishops in the U.S. concerning membership in Masonic societies and other societies of the same kind. Because many bishops had questioned the Congregation about the force and interpretation of CIC c. 2335, the Congregation responded that after extensive consultation and study of the diversity of such societies in the different nations it was agreed there would be no change in the general legislation until the revision of the Code of Canon Law is ready for publication. However, the Congregation noted that in particular cases, the penal law of the Church is subject to a strict interpretation. Consequently the opinion of those authors who hold that c. 2335 refers only to Catholics who enroll in associations that actually plot against the Church may be safely taught and applied. The prohibition, however, remains in force in every case against enrollment by clerics, religious, and members of secular institutes in any kind of masonic association.

Bibliography: O'Connor-Suppl c. 2335.

[R. J. MURPHY]

SOCIETY (THEOLOGY)

In the Constitution on the Church in the Modern World Vatican Council II outlined some general principles for a theology of society. They concerned the social nature of man, the interrelationship between individual and community and between the primacy of the person and a notion of the common good as "the sum total of social conditions which allow people, either as groups or as individuals, to reach their fulfilment more fully and more easily" (*Gaudium et spes* 25–26).

Resources: The Social Sciences. For these very general observations to become the subject of a systematic reflection on society, theologians must make use of the resources and conclusions of the social sciences. They will, first of all, have to take account of the almost bewildering variety which empirical research has discovered in social relationships and orders both across generations and across cultures. Secondly, they will have to reflect on what might be called "the dialectic of social existence," by which the very societies which men have produced themselves become the producers of men.

The latter interest will first see societies as human products, produced and constituted by shared meanings and values. Social relationships and orders are the effects of exercises of human intelligence and freedom, and not the inevitable products of a preconscious "human nature" nor of a cosmic or merely "natural" order.

Such social orders have their own "objectivity." They confront the individual born or reared within them with a massive inertial force. The "real world" into which he is introduced is the world as it has been shaped and interpreted by earlier generations and his own possibilities for self-realization are limited by the resources of his society and its communities. It is their language through which the world is mediated to him and which moulds and orients his own consciousness. It is their taken-for-granted stock of knowledge which constitutes the largest part of what he comes to "know." It is in

terms of their roles and institutions and in pursuit of the values they honor that he learns to orient his freedom. In all these ways, the individual is a social product; the self is socially mediated.

Society: Theological Object. So understood, the social order itself becomes an object of theological investigation and evaluation. The society, policy, economy are not premoral givens within which individuals privately live, and the Christian message does not concern only their privatized lives. The social order is another of the ambiguous works of man, and its moulding and orienting influence on those born and reared within it is no less ambiguous. The Gospel does not address individuals in the abstract, but only the persons who exist, all of whom are social products. Thus, for example, contemporary theologians speak of "sinful social structures" or of "social sin" to describe the larger context of evil to which the Gospel must be addressed, and seek to explain how the "reign of sin" shows itself there as well as in the minds and hearts of individuals.

Such reflections lead easily enough into a *political theology. This is not simply a "theology of politics," but an attempt to rethink the Christian message in terms of the fundamental and even constitutive role which societies play in the development of individuals. The search for meaning and value, which defines man, is seen to be a "political" enterprise, first in the sense that this search, like every other human endeavor, is inescapably marked by the social conditions under which it is undertaken, and, secondly, in the sense that the discovery of the revealed meanings and values of the Gospel has immediate political and social implications.

A critical theology of society, then, must: (1) start from the social matrix of individual existence; (2) critically explore the relationship between that essential freedom which the Church has always defended as "free will" and its effective realization in concrete individuals; (3) interpret the meaning of the Gospel and the role of the Church in the light of the social dialectic; (4) elaborate effective hermeneutical principles by which the Gospel may be made to evaluate social orders; and (5) learn how to collaborate with the social sciences in bringing the Gospel's redemptive truth and power to bear upon concrete social orders and situations.

Bibliography: P. BERGER and T. LUCKMANN, *The Social Construction of Reality* (Garden City, N.J. 1967). J. GREMILLION, *The Gospel of Peace and Justice: Catholic Social Teaching since Pope John* (Maryknoll, N.Y. 1976). G. GUTIERREZ, *A Theology of Liberation: History, Politics and Salvation,* tr. C. INDA and J. EAGLESON (Maryknoll, N.Y. 1973). B. LONERGAN, *Method in Theology* (New York 1972). J. B. METZ, tr., W. GLEN-DOEPEL, *A Theology of the World* (New York 1969).

[J. A. KOMONCHAK]

SOCIOLOGY

The importance of sociology to the Church was given emphasis in Vatican Council II's Pastoral Constitution on the Church in the Modern World, (*Gaudium et spes* 62). Sociologists have produced some important recent works clarifying the impact of modern society on the Church.

A foremost contribution is Robert Bellah's collection of essays, *Beyond Belief*. He argues that social change in every nation has produced a search for new modes of religious symbolization and hence new movements are emerging everywhere. The alleged decline of belief in modern society is largely a rejection of external authority and hierarchy in the name of personal autonomy.

The whole trend of today's culture is toward reducing external constraints and leaving more to the individual's discretion. A result is a crisis of institutional church authority, whereas religious commitment of the personal and individual sort is pervasive. To look exclusively at church dogma, or only at the realm of cognitive beliefs, is to miss many powerful dimensions of religious life.

A second important contribution is the work of Peter Berger and Thomas Luckmann. Their books include *The Social Construction of Reality* by Berger and Luckmann, *The Sacred Canopy* by Berger, and *The Invisible Religion* by Luckmann. In the last of these, Luckmann analyzes social changes which have altered the transcendent-meaning systems in industrial societies. Religion, functionally seen, provides the meaning-structures which give coherence to life and integrate the society. In a differentiated modern society the overall traditional meaning-structures cannot survive. In place of the single canopy there emerges an "assortment of ultimate meanings" grounded in different institutional sectors. The integration of these into a single meaningful whole is no longer provided by the society but becomes the burden of the individual, who tries to compose a coherent meaning–structure from available options. Luckmann contrasts the European and American Churches. Whereas in Europe the newly emerging sources of meaning are self-consciously separate from traditional Christian Churches, in America the Churches have included the new elements, with the result that the American Churches have achieved institutional strength at the cost of less distinct meaning–structures.

Several fruitful empirical studies have been done. *Catholic Schools in a Declining Church* by Andrew Greeley, William McCready, and Kathleen McCourt is important. It contains trend information on the upward social mobility of American Catholics, showing that the Irish Catholics have risen fastest and now exceed the average level of Protestants in socioeconomic status. It shows how American Catholics have welcomed the changes brought by Vatican II, but have been much troubled by birth control questions. It probes the strengths and weaknesses of Catholic schools, emerging with a strong argument for their ability to grow and their importance to Catholicism (*see* PAROCHIAL SCHOOLS, CATHOLIC ELEMENTARY). The book takes strong stands on some issues and goes beyond the empirical data on several, but even shorn of these advocacies it still is a major sociological contribution to understanding the situation of the Church in society today.

The past decade has seen many sociological studies of new religious movements. Two major works are edited by Glock and Bellah and by Zaretsky and Leone. Sociological analyses of the Catholic Pentecostal movement have been done by Harrison, McGuire, and Fichter.

See also THEOLOGY AND SOCIOLOGY.

Bibliography: R. BELLAH, *Beyond Belief* (New York 1970). P. BERGER and T. LUCKMANN, *The Social Construction of Reality* (Garden City, N.Y. 1966). P. BERGER, *The Sacred Canopy* (Garden City, N.Y. 1969). T. LUCKMANN, *The Invisible Religion* (New York 1967). A. GREELEY, W. MCCREADY, and K. MCCOURT, *Catholic Schools in a Declining Church* (Kansas City 1976). H. ABRAMSON, *Ethnic Diversity in Catholic America* (New York 1973). C. GLOCK and R. BELLAH, eds., *The New Religious Consciousness* (Berkeley 1976). I. ZARETSKY and M. LEONE, eds., *Religious Movements in Contemporary America* (Princeton 1974). M. HARRISON, "Sources of Recruitment to Catholic Pentecostalism," JScStRel 13 (1974) 49–64; "The Maintenance of Enthusiasm: Involvement in a New Religious Movement," *Sociological Analysis* 36 (1975) 150–160. M. MCGUIRE, "Toward a Sociological Interpretation of the Catholic Pentecostal Movement," RevRelRes 16 (1975) 94–104; "The Social Context of Prophecy: 'Word-Gifts' of the Spirit Among Catholic Pentecostals," RevRelRes 18 (1977) 134–147. J. FICHTER, *The Catholic Cult of the Paraclete* (New York 1975).

[D. R. HOGE]

SODEPAX

SODEPAX is the working name of the Committee on Society, Development and Peace of the Programme Unit *Justice and Service* of the World Council of Churches (WCC) and the Pontifical Commission *Justice and Peace* of the Holy See, which are its official parent bodies and contribute to its support. SODEPAX is a liaison body whose task is to promote development, justice, and peace by means of study and reflection programs. Based on the social thinking and teachings of the WCC, these programs are for ecumenical use in the Churches and are developed in close conjunction with the WCC and the Catholic Church. In this way, SODEPAX is intended to be a significant ecumenical instrument of the WCC's and the Catholic Church's common witness to Christian concern for development, justice, and peace in the world. In fact, it is the only joint endeavor undertaken by Rome and Geneva that operates on a continuous basis, and is thus an index of ecumenical collaboration, since the Roman Catholic Church is not a member of the World Council of Churches.

SODEPAX was established on an experimental basis in 1968, in the spirit of Vatican Council II and the WCC's Geneva Conference on Church and Society (1966). Its offices are in the Ecumenical Centre in Geneva and the General Secretary has customarily been a Catholic priest, the Associate General Secretary a Protestant. In its first phase, 1968–71, SODEPAX organized a number of large international conferences on development and peace, in addition to sponsoring many regional meetings and organizing national chapters in several countries. Its second mandate, 1972–75, was notable for activity in the Far East on development and an important conference which brought together Protestant and Catholic representatives from Northern Ireland to discuss avenues to peace. The third mandate of SODEPAX, 1976–78, saw the launching of an ecumenical program entitled *In Search of a New Society: Christian Participation in the Building of New Relations among Peoples.* Since 1973, SODEPAX has published a journal of documentation, news and articles, in French and English, called *Church Alert*.

In addition to its program function of reaching out to the Churches and the world, SODEPAX carries on a continuous liaison function between its parent bodies, seeking to draw them closer together in both reflection and action. It keeps in close touch with the Secretariat for the Promotion of Christian Unity and the *Joint Working Group of the World Council of Churches and the Roman Catholic Church, while acting as a kind of ecumenical and social conscience for the Churches, and especially its parent bodies. Perhaps most important of all, it attempts, despite its slim resources, to be the effective symbol of the Churches' commitment to unity and to the Christian service of mankind.

[J. LUCAL]

SOLEMN BLESSING AND PRAYER OVER THE PEOPLE

If the primitive Eucharist ended with the reception of Communion, it was not long before the rite included a period of prayer and meditation followed by a prayer by the one presiding. The congregation was then dismissed. The formula for this dismissal, *Ite missa est*, in the Roman rite gave rise to the name "Mass" in the West. (See: Jungmann 1:173. *Missa-missio-dimissio*-dismissal-Mass). However, this simple dismissal has undergone many variations in the history of the Roman rite.

One of the earliest embellishments was the "Prayer over the People." Often described as a prayer of inclination (from the invitation "Bow your heads for God's blessing"), the prayer is a parallel to the prayers that were said at the end of the Liturgy of the Word to bless the catechumens or penitents who were to leave at that point. The Prayer over the People was a prayer of blessing for those who are now leaving the assembly and returning to their work. The theme of the prayers was often temporal wants and material needs. In the Roman rite prior to the Missal of Paul VI, the Prayer survived only during Lent, introduced by *Humiliate capita vestra Deo* after the Postcommunion.

After the formal dismissal, as the papal or episcopal procession left the church, the bishop blessed the people as he passed by. In the 11th century priests, also, began to give this blessing; and the custom spread, apparently from France, but not very quickly, during the Middle Ages (see Dix 522). Other prayers were added to this blessing so that the Mass no longer ended with the dismissal.

Vatican Council II's Constitution on the Liturgy called for the rites to be restored so that the structure of the rite is evident (*Sacrosanctum Concilium* 21, 34, 50). Consequently the ending of the Mass was simplified and clarified. The Communion rite ends with the Prayer after Communion. There is a pause and a new movement is begun. If there are any announcements, they are made at this time. The one presiding then says: "The Lord be with you..." and gives the blessing. The deacon (or priest) then dismisses the assembly.

However, this simple blessing can be enriched and enlarged at the discretion of the one presiding by formulas which find their roots in the former Prayer over the People and the Solemn Blessings of the Gallican rite. The new Roman Missal offers 20 texts for the Solemn Blessings and 26 examples of the Prayer over the People. "They are printed together to allow complete freedom of choice. Either the solemn blessing or the prayer over the people may be chosen. During Lent the prayer over the people is principally used. Some of the texts of the blessings and prayers are very general; others are specified for particular seasons or occasions" (Sacramentary, "Foreword" 14*).

In addition to the texts given in the Latin edition, the English Language Sacramentary suggests formulas for the Solemn Blessing or the Prayer over the People for the Sundays in the principal seasons and for other special occasions. While the use of these prayers must not foster a new "clericalism" by emphasizing a priestly blessing immediately after the reception of Communion, the tasteful selection and use of these texts will give a joyful variety to the Dismissal Rite. Furthermore, they are to serve as the model for ending any liturgical celebration, as we see from the rubric which introduces the blessings: "These blessings and prayers may be used at the end of Mass, or after the Liturgy of the Word, after the Liturgy of the Hours, or the celebration of the Sacraments."

Bibliography: G. DIX, *The Shape of the Liturgy* (London 1945). J. JUNGMANN, *The Mass of the Roman Rite*, 2 v., tr. F. A. BRUNNER (New York 1951–55).   [T. RICHSTATTER]

SOLIDARITY, HUMAN

Solidarity, a cornerstone of Catholic social thought, was up to Vatican Council II based exclusively on the social nature of the human person (e.g. in Pius XI's *Quadragesimo anno* and John XXIII's *Mater et magistra, Pacem in terris*) as a reflection of human need for social life. With the Constitution on the Church in the Modern World there is a shift from the natural foundations to emphasize theological and scriptural foundations; also, solidarity becomes concretized as community.

As proof that "Christian revelation contributes to this community..." the Constitution argues that: (1) revelation helps understand the laws of social life; (2) God willed brotherhood and sisterhood, uniting love of God and neighbor in one commandment; (3) Jesus prayed that "all be one" and thereby—a striking comparison—"implied a certain likeness between the union of the divine persons and of God's children..." (*Gaudium et spes* 23 and 24). The document goes still further and insists on the communitarian character of salvation itself. God makes us a "single people... his people" (ibid. 32). Here the Sinai Covenant is cited. But Jesus, who develops and consummates this communitarian character in his life and work and preaching, "founded a new brotherly community... through His Body the Church... a family beloved of God and of Christ their Brother" (ibid. 32).

See also COMMUNITY OF MANKIND.

[W. F. RYAN]

SOUTHERN BAPTIST/ROMAN CATHOLIC CONSULTATIONS

Since 1971 there have been five regional Southern Baptist/Roman Catholic Conferences sponsored by the *Bishops' Committee for Ecumenical and Interreligious Affairs (BCEIA) and the Department of Interfaith Witness of the Home Mission Board of the Southern Baptist Convention.

The Regional Conferences. The first conference took place February 1–3, 1971 at Daytona Beach, Florida. Nearly 100 participants gathered from 10 Southeastern states to inaugurate the first in a series of regional contacts between the two groups. Among those attending were bishops, Baptist officials, pastors, ecumenical chairpersons, lay men and women. The theme chosen was "Issues and Answers." Major addresses on the topic, "Salvation: Its Meaning and Relation to Christian Social Responsibility," were given by Roman Catholic Bishop John May and Southern Baptist Dr. Cecil Sherman.

The jointly sponsored conference was widely hailed as an icebreaker in, at that time, relatively frozen Southern Baptist/Roman Catholic relationships. The two groups represent the two largest Christian Churches in the U.S. with Roman Catholics estimated to number 50 million and Southern Baptists, 13 million.

A second regional conference was held in Houston, Texas, Oct. 16–18, 1972, which had similar representation from the Southwestern part of the nation. "Living the Faith in Today's World" was chosen as the conference topic. After the conference ended a leading member of the Southern Baptist delegation, Dr. M. Thomas Starkes, wrote as follows: "Almost five centuries of ignorant fear, simplistic stereotyping and prejudicial aloofness are being shattered. In the last third of the 20th century Baptists and Catholics are actually meeting—in the open—with openness. ...Pioneers are often not recognized until they have gone, but they know the worth of what they chance. The risk at Houston was worth it, as Catholics and Baptists continued to marvel at the mercy of God working through each group urging His salvation through human vessels to human vessels. May there be more such risks" (Starkes, *Foreword*).

Marriottsville, Md. was the scene of the third regional conference, Feb. 4–6, 1974, which discussed the topic entitled "The Church Inside and Out." Representatives came from the Northeastern section of the U.S. for the three-day sharing at the Marriottsville Retreat Center near Baltimore.

Continuing the dialogical process between the formerly estranged Christian communities, a fourth regional conference met at the Vallombrosa Center, Menlo Park, Cal., Oct. 27–29, 1975. "Conversion to Christ and Life-Long Growth in the Spirit" was the theme. Once again, invited representatives came from Western and Northwestern states to exchange ideas and experiences, which served to dispel, to a large extent, misconceptions and caricatures frequently held by members of both groups toward each other.

The dialogical process, employed in these and similar conferences, is geared to erase such deterrents to understanding, appreciation, and acceptance. A guiding principle in dialogue is that those engaging in the process be firmly committed to the truth as they understand and accept it in their own tradition. With this anchor to a position, the participants in the dialogue express their convictions to each other. There is an honest search for truth and understanding with a willingness to recommend change in any church position found to be deficient or not in conformity with the Gospel, tradition, or right reason.

The last in the series of regional conferences took place at Kansas City, Mo., Nov. 28–30, 1977 when approximately 75 Southern Baptists and Roman Catholics from nine Midwestern states gathered for a three-day reflection on the "Theology and Experience of Worship." As in the other conferences, small groups were formed to discuss the theme in greater detail from various perspectives. In the course of the gathering a Roman Catholic Mass and a Southern Baptist worship service were conducted. For many of the participants this was the first time they had witnessed the other group at worship. Immense goodwill and sharing marked this assembly. Considerable expressions were made that smaller convocations of a similar type should be inaugurated in local areas in the midwest.

Future Plans. A long series of negotiations between the BCEIA and the Southern Baptist Convention Home Mission Board's Department of Interfaith Witness has resulted in the establishing of a Southern Baptist/ Roman Catholic Scholars' Dialogue commencing in April of 1978. First among the topics to be discussed by scholars from seminaries and institutions of learning from both traditions at the opening session is the theme of "The Church." Because of the independent character of each Southern Baptist congregation in Southern Baptist Convention policy no joint statements, or agreements, from the Scholars' Dialogue are to be forthcoming.

Bibliography: M. T. STARKES, *Living the Faith in Today's World* (Atlanta 1972).

[J. P. SHEEHAN]

SPIRITUALITY, CONTEMPORARY

The most striking and perhaps also the most significant effect of the renewal inaugurated by Vatican Council II has been an intensified interest and desire to share in the spiritual life.

Liturgy and Spirituality. The average practicing Catholic has been most affected by the reform of the liturgy. The Mass was always fairly central in Catholic spiritual practice, but its pervasive influence in the lives of the faithful has been greatly enhanced with the general introduction of the vernacular and other reform measures. Previous to Vatican II a relatively small number were directly nourished by the liturgical texts and action. When the priest came down from the high altar to a small table facing the people and invited them to sing popular hymns, do the readings, lead the congregation, bring the gifts, generally plan the liturgy, and sometimes even have the liturgy in their own living rooms, more and more of the faithful began effectively to hear the Word of God proclaimed and to interiorize the sentiments of the liturgical action. One result has been a renewed study and use of the Scriptures in the private devotional lives of Catholics. Concomitantly with the renewal of the Mass form came a more independent attitude on the part of the lay Catholic in moral judgment leading to an increased freedom in receiving the Eucharist. The emphasis on this as a shared meal rather than an awesome communion with the Transcendent has also greatly affected the role the Eucharist plays in Catholic spirituality today, reducing those practices which largely emphasized adoration: exposition, benediction, processions. In great measure what elements remained in the Western liturgy of mystery and awe before the Almighty have been eliminated and spirituality has been centered more on an incarnate God within community. The renewal of the Sacraments with their emphasis on communal participation and celebration has fostered the same attitude. The transformation of Extreme Unction into the Sacrament of the Sick has even brought the lonely act of dying more into the supportive presence of the Christian community and opened the way to communal healing services (*see* HEALING, CHRISTIAN). The most recent reform, the new rites of Penance, which has become the Sacrament of Reconciliation, has not yet had impact, but may, especially in its communal celebration, help the Catholic community to refind ways of expressing conversion and self-denial that have generally been lost with the end of most of the common obligations of fast and abstinence. More important perhaps is the opportunity this renewed rite offers to refind the value of the personal guidance and care of a spiritual father, the need for which many Christians have been discovering in the charismatic community with its emphasis on "headship," in Eastern religious traditions, or just in a sincere quest for a deeper prayer life. The American Jesuits especially have been trying to respond to the need through the establishment of several programs for the formation of competent spiritual guides.

The Charismatic Movement. Undoubtedly the liveliest spiritual movement in the American Catholic Church since Vatican II has been the charismatic movement. The ecumenical impetus which opened the Catholic community to a wide use of Protestant hymns in the renewed liturgy and a greater emphasis on scriptural reading, study and prayer, also opened a certain segment of people to a particular form of evangelical enthusiasm that broke in on American Protestantism early in this century—the willingness to receive and use certain of the gifts of the Spirit commonly seen among the faithful since the first days of the Church, praying and singing in tongues, prophecy, healing. The renewal for the most part has for Catholics blended well with the renewal of liturgical piety. The communal element has been greatly emphasized, the place of Scripture in spiritual formation and prayer is almost exaggerated, and Mass and the Sacraments are celebrated with an unparalleled fullness (*see* CHARISMATIC RENEWAL, CATHOLIC).

The Meditation Movement. Only a segment of the Catholic community has been attracted to the lively, extraverted form of piety that has characterized the charismatic movement in the Church. Unfortunately little was being offered to those who were attracted to a more quiet, interior experience of the Transcendent. Catholic retreat centers had suffered a period of decline and are only now beginning to experience new vitality as centers of prayer. Contemplative monasteries have been attracting large numbers but their teaching programs are virtually nonexistent. The result has been that large numbers of young Christians, and those not so young, have turned to Eastern religions and traditions to satisfy their desires in this direction. The movement is having one notable semantic effect. For the Catholic "meditation" has usually signified a discursive process of reflecting on a truth to evoke affective and volitional response, while "contemplation" meant a quiet, loving "presence to." In the Eastern traditions the words are used in the opposite sense, contemplation being a discursive process and meditation involving the silent presence, though not usually including love because of the absence of interpersonal relationship. So pervasive has been the influence of the Eastern meditation movements in the West that now even among Christians, the term "meditation" is coming to be the prevalent name used for inner prayer and presence and the term "contemplation" is falling somewhat by the wayside.

Only gradually is the Christian community beginning to recover its contemplative dimension, which was largely lost in the 16th century, and respond to this spiritual attraction. The Cistercians as the strongest contemplative group in the Church have been taking a lead. To foster the return to Christian sources they began publishing the great 12th-century spiritual and mystical texts that stand at the head of their tradition (*The Cistercian Fathers Series*) and the classic texts of monastic spirituality through the centuries (from Evagrius Ponticus and Dorotheos of Gaza to Jules Monchanin—*The Cistercian Studies Series*) to comple-

ment the *Fathers of the Church* series (The Catholic University of America) and the *Ancient Christian Writers* series (Newman-Paulist). The way has thus been prepared for the very significant series inaugurated by the Paulist Press in January 1978: *The Classics of Western Spirituality*. In 1973 in collaboration with Western Michigan University the Cistercians established the Institute for Cistercian Studies and three years later the Center for Contemplative Studies. In the following year the Paulists joining hands with the Jesuits opened in Boston the Isaac Hecker Institute of Applied Spirituality to come to grips with the notion and reality of a distinctive American spirituality and also to further the integration of the values and methods of Eastern traditions that have come to be very present in America.

The Cistercians, especially those of Saint Joseph's Abbey, Spencer, Massachusetts, had been pioneering in this area of integration of spiritualities, bringing to America the fruits of the study and experience of Jean-Marie Déchanet, OSB, (*Christian Yoga*), Francis Ancharya, Dom Bede Griffiths, OSB, Abhisktananda (Father Henri Le Saux), William Johnston, SJ (Christian Zen) and E. Lassalle, and working in collaboration with Swami Satchidananda (Integral Yoga Institute), Joshua Sasaki Roshi (Mount Baldy Zen Center), and the Transcendental Meditation movement of the Maharishi Mehesh Yogi. In June, 1977 at the request of the Secretariat for Non-Christian Religions the Spencer monks organized the Petersham Meeting, which led to the establishment of the North American Board for East-West Dialog. A symposium of spiritual masters West and East was held in June 1978 and an international seminar on the use of Eastern methods in Christian prayer is scheduled for August 1979. The aim of all these activities is not only to foster the evolution of a global spiritual culture to give a base to worldwide political, economic and ethical accord, but also to help the large number of Christians who have found values in Eastern spirituality to integrate these in a renewal of their Christian faith.

Perhaps the most significant contribution of the Spencer monks to the recent evolution of Catholic spirituality in America has been the promotion in collaboration with the *Conference of Major Superiors of Men USA and other similar Catholic organizations of a Christian meditation movement. A simple method for entering into nonconceptual prayer which belongs to Western Christian tradition is now being taught in centers across the country. This particular method arises from Saint John Cassian, finds its most popular expression in *The Cloud of Unknowing* and is commonly called Centering Prayer, a name drawn from the writings of Thomas Merton—undoubtedly the most popular and influential Catholic spiritual writer in English of the age. The English Benedictines have taken up this method and are teaching it in centers in England and Canada. It is gradually moving into other language areas within the Church and other similar methods are being developed (*see* PRAYER OF CENTERING).

Balancing Factors. Within the Christian meditation movement much of the emphasis in the quest for spiritual perfection has centered on the search for experience of the Transcendent, with the conviction that such experience will humble, enlighten, and lead to the growth of all the virtues. But side by side with this popular current there remains a faithful and strong advocacy of the ways of the Carmelite Doctors of the 16th century, of Saint Ignatius Loyola—whose more contemplative methods are being rediscovered and whose thirty-day program is quite popular at the moment, especially among religious—and some of the other particular schools of spirituality. Centers of Jesuit, Carmelite, and Franciscan studies have been established and programs for publishing the classics of these traditions and studies on them are actively being carried out.

George Maloney, SJ, of the John XXIII Center, Fordham University, has been a leader in promoting a balanced and fruitful use of Eastern Christian prayer within the American Catholic Community. The Jesus Prayer especially has become popular through the publication of *The Way of the Pilgrim*. Very valuable insights from the behavioral sciences, especially from the field of psychology have been effectively applied to the spiritual life in a popular way by such writers as John Powell, SJ, Henri Nouwen, a psychologist lecturing at Yale Divinity School, and Morton Kelsey, an Anglican priest and Jungian psychiatrist at the University of Notre Dame. At the same time there are those who look upon this emphasis on prayer and spiritual development as excessive and insist on the Christian way of fraternal love and service as having if not the primacy at least a predominent role in the quest for spiritual perfection. This is found especially among the active religious of the U.S. and has led recently to a fraternal warning from their brother and sister religious of Canada who have affirmed that "Religious life has a future among us if it is *the experience of God shining forth in all we do* . . ." (Third Interamerican Conference of Religious, Montreal, November 1977).

In theory there is no controversy as to what spiritual perfection ultimately means for the Christian, but there is relatively little theorizing today. The way to attaining it is centered in practice and experience. The social and political emphasis of the 1960s expressed itself in an emphasis on finding God in creation, in one's brethren who are to be loved and served. With the waning of the hopes of the 1960s there has been a turning to seeking the transcendent, immediate experience of God in himself. Meditation, prayer, is seen as the surer and more practical way to right action, universal brotherhood, peace on earth—whatever perfection man can hope to attain. As usual the large institutions—the hierarchy, the clerical ministry, the religious orders—are slow in moving with these popular shifts. In this they help the Christian community to preserve a more balanced outlook so that the pendulum does not swing to extremes and a truer picture of what integral Christian holiness is remains to guide the faithful and have its overflowing effect on all persons of good will.

See also CONTEMPLATION; PRAYER.

Bibliography: ABISHIKTANANDA (H. LE SAUX), *Prayer* (Philadelphia 1973); *Saccidananda* (Delhi 1974). R. BAILEY, *Thomas Merton on Mysticism* (New York 1975). W. CAPPS, *From Hope to Hope: From Moltmann to Merton in One Theological Decade* (Philadelphia 1976). J. M. DÉCHANET, *Christian Yoga*, tr. R. HINDMARSH (London 1960). J. GALLEN, ed., *Christians at Prayer* (Notre Dame, Ind. 1977). D. GOLEMAN, *The Varieties of the Meditative Experience* (New York 1977). B. GRIFFITHS, *Vedanta and Christian Faith* (Lower Lake, Cal. 1973); *Return to the Center* (Springfield, Ill. 1977). J. HIGGINS, *The Still Point* (New York 1970); ed., *The Cloud of Unknowing* (New York 1973); *Silent Music* (New York 1974); *The Mysticism of the Cloud of Unknowing* (Saint Meinrad, Ind. 1975). G. A. MALONEY, *The Breath of the Mystic* (Denville, N.J. 1974; *Inward Stillness* (Denville, N.J. 1976). H. NOUWEN, *Reaching Out* (New York 1975); *The Spirituality of Compassion* (New Haven, Conn. 1977). M. B. PENNINGTON, "Looking East-Seeing West," *America* 134 (1976) 180–182; "Spirituality for a World Culture," *America* 137 (1977) 100–103; *Daily We Touch Him* (New York 1977); ed., *Prayer and Liberation* (Canfield, Ohio 1977). J. POWELL, *Why I Am Afraid to Love* (Niles, Ill. 1972). L. J. SUENENS, *A New Pentecost?* (New York 1974).

[M. B. PENNINGTON]

SPONSORS

The revision of the Sacraments of Initiation following Vatican Council II has involved some significant shifts in the understanding of the role of the sponsor and in the expectations of those chosen to fill that role. Directives in the new rites supplant any previous canonical requirements (13:615).

Role of Sponsors. The General Introduction to Christian Initiation speaks of godparents as: assisting in the preparation for Baptism, testifying to the faith of the adult candidate or professing the Church's faith with the parents of a child to be baptized, and helping the new Christian persevere in faith after Baptism (ChrInitGenIntrod 8–9).

The Introduction to the Rite of Confirmation speaks in similar terms of the role of the sponsor before, during and after the celebration of the sacrament (ConfIntrod 5).

The Introduction to the Rite of Christian Initiation of Adults is more explicit in its explanation of the role of the sponsor. The sponsor accompanies the candidate when he asks to be admitted to the catechumenate. "This sponsor is to be a man or woman who knows the candidate, helps him, and witnesses to his morals, faith, and intention" (ChrInitAd 42). The rite notes that this sponsor may also fulfill the role of godparent or another may be chosen as godparent who takes on the responsibility for the candidate. In either case, the godparent "is close to the candidate because of his example, character and friendship" and is officially "delegated by the local Christian community and approved by the priest. He accompanies the candidate on the day of election, in the celebration of the sacraments, and during the period of postbaptismal catechesis. It is his responsibility to show the catechumen . . . the place of the gospel in his own life and in society, to help him on doubts and anxieties, to give public testimony for him, and to watch over the progress of his baptismal life" (ibid. 43).

Requirements. Such a view of the sponsor's role leads also to some shifts in the requirements for sponsors. For Baptism the godparent should: "(1) be mature enough to undertake this responsibility; (2) have received the three Sacraments of Initiation, Baptism, Confirmation and the Eucharist; (3) be a member of the Catholic Church canonically free to carry out this office. A baptized and believing Christian from a separated Church or Community may act as a godparent or Christian witness along with a Catholic godparent" (ChrInitGenIntrod 10).

For Confirmation, the same requirements are set forth (ConfIntrod 5). It is also recommended that the godparent at Baptism also be the sponsor at Confirmation, in order to stress the unity of the two Sacraments, though a special sponsor may be chosen and even parents may be sponsors for their children (ibid. 5).

Underlying these changes in requirements is a shift in the understanding of the sponsor's role. The sponsor is expected not only to answer for the candidate (see

13:615), but to share life and faith with the candidate before, during and after the ceremony. The sponsor takes on a responsibility not only for the sacramental rituals, but also for the whole process of growth and conversion involved in the extended period of initiation. The shift in the role of the sponsor corresponds to and is dependent on the shift in the understanding of the initiation process as exemplified in the new Rite of Christian Initiation of Adults. Further development in the role of the sponsor and in the way sponsors are chosen by the community may be expected as the contemporary Church gains experience with this renewed rite. The instructions concerning the new rites speak of one sponsor; the custom of having two godparents, however, continues and the directives apply to both.

See also CATECHUMENATE FOR ADULTS; CHRISTIAN INITIATION, SACRAMENTS OF.

[L. MICK]

STAFFA, DINO

Cardinal; b. Aug. 14, 1906, Santa Maria (Ravenna), Italy; d. Aug. 7, 1977, Rome. He was ordained for the diocese of Imola, May 25, 1929, and the same year received the doctorate of theology, at the Theological College of Bologna. On achieving the JUD (doctor of both laws) at the Pontifical Institute *Utriusque Juris*, in Rome, in 1932, he was assigned to the Sacred Congregation for Oriental Churches. In 1944, he was named an Auditor of the Roman Rota, two years later becoming Director of Rotal Studies. Pope John XXIII, in 1960 made him Secretary of the Congregation of Studies and Universities, and ordained him Archbishop of Palestrina. In 1967 Paul VI appointed Staffa Pro-Prefect of the Apostolic Signatura and created him a cardinal. In 1969, he was named Prefect of the Signatura and President of the Court of Cassation for the Vatican City State. These posts he held until his death.

During Vatican Council II, Staffa was Vice-President of the Commission for Seminaries and Catholic Schools. He is commonly labelled an "integralist" on the basis of his concern that the advance of a forward-looking present be integrated with the perceptions of the inspired past. In the first session of the Council he espoused a cause rapidly becoming unpopular, the maintenance of Latin in the liturgy. In the third session, he was more deeply involved in the issue of episcopal *collegiality, to the point of circulating among the Council Fathers mimeographed pamphlets. These papers reflected his concern lest the full power attributed to the pope, notably by Vatican Council I, be compromised by collegiality. He questioned that "college" could be used to describe the relationship between the pope and the other bishops, because of the inequalities between them defined by Vatican I. By his interventions he contributed largely to the eventual text of the Constitution on the Church. The concern which inspired his activity was met by the precise words that the discussion hammered out: "... together with their head and never apart from him the bishops have supreme and full authority over the universal Church" (*Lumen gentium* 22).

His attempts to influence the Decree on Priestly Formation, on the training of the clergy, were less successful. He sought to obtain for St. Thomas Aquinas a greater place than the one given him in the proposed text. His efforts, combined with those of Cardinal Rossi did not prevail against the eloquence of Cardinal Paul Léger, and this part of the decree was voted as it stood (cf. *Optatam totius* 16).

Staffa died in his Roman residence. Following Requiem Masses in St. Peter's, Aug. 9, and in the cathedral at Imola, Aug. 10, he was interred there. In addition to numerous articles (generally on Canon Law) in reviews and newspapers, his important published works include: *Commento al primo libro del Codice di Diritto*, with Cardinal Amleto Cicognani (2 v., Rome 1939–42); *Le Delegazioni apostoliche*, a history of papal representatives without diplomatic rank; *De conditione contra Matrimonii substantiam* (2d ed., Rome 1955).

Bibliography: OssRom Aug. 8–9, 1977. H. FESQUET, *The Drama of Vatican II*, tr. B. MURCHLAND (New York 1967).

[P. F. MULHERN]

STERILIZATION

During the period of widespread dissent subsequent to Vatican Council II's reconfirmation of Catholic teaching on contraception (*Gaudium et spes* 51) and the reiteration of the same teaching by Pope Paul VI's encyclical *Humanae vitae* (July 25, 1968), some Catholic hospitals in the U.S. began to admit the practice of surgical contraceptive sterilization (13:403). Defense of this practice was sought either in the fact of theological dissent itself, in an unsound extrapolation of the principle of totality (14:211), or under the rubric of legitimate material cooperation (13:245) in the admittedly wrong action of another.

Ultimately the National Conference of Catholic Bishops (NCCB) referred the matter to the Holy See for clarification and guidance and on March 13, 1975 the Vatican Congregation for the Doctrine of the Faith issued a statement addressed to the NCCB (ActApS 68 [1976] 738–740; Origins 6 [1976] 33–35). This statement reiterated the teaching of the Church on contraceptive sterilization and declared that "notwithstanding any subjectively right intention of those whose actions are prompted by the care or prevention of physical or mental illness which is foreseen or feared as a result of pregnancy, such sterilization remains absolutely forbidden according to the doctrine of the Church." The Congregation further rejected the extension of the principle of totality as a defense of contraceptive sterilization as unsound, and while making reference to "the dissent against this teaching from many theologians" denied that such dissent could constitute "a theological source which the faithful might invoke and thereby abandon the authentic teaching authority of the Church and follow the opinions of private theologians which dissent from it."

The Congregation added, with regard to the management of Catholic hospitals, that: "the official approbation of direct sterilization and, a fortiori, its management and execution in accord with hospital regulations is a matter which, in the objective order, is by its very nature (or intrinsically) evil. The Catholic hospital cannot cooperate with this for any reason." The document deals primarily with institutional policy of Catholic hospitals and points out: "Any cooperation so supplied is totally unbecoming the mission entrusted to this type of institution and would be contrary to the necessary proclamation and defense of the moral order." Finally the document makes reference to the principles of material cooperation, but only after ruling out "any cooperation which involves the approval or consent of the hospitals" and in such restrictive terms as to envision the possibility of such material cooperation only in rare and extreme circumstances and never as being in accord with hospital policy or regulations.

See also MEDICAL PERSONNEL, MORAL OBLIGATIONS OF.

[T. J. O'DONNELL]

STEWARDSHIP

Stewardship is not only a simple term, it is an uncomplicated solution to significant portions of major social problems. In practice, stewardship is an instrument of social justice. "The earth is the Lord's, and the fulness thereof" (Ps 24.1). All of material creation, as well as all wealth flowing from it, belongs to God. Wealth possessed or produced by human persons is owned by God. We own nothing absolutely; all we have we hold in trust. This is the faith foundation of the stewardship concept. All we have is held in trust for others—for those who inhabit this planet with us now, for those who will live here in the future. Stewardship has inescapable societal obligations.

The ownership of a particular share of material creation may be private but that private share cannot be used without regard for others. There are two considerations here: one of equity, the other of responsibility. Is my share a fair one relative to the needs and claims of others? Put another way, does my share represent an unfair gain at the expense of others? If the consideration of equity is broadened from the individual person to a larger group (as, for instance, one's race or nation) the equity issue is this: does one group's share represent an unfair gain taken at the expense of other groups?

The responsibility consideration looks to the future. Resources (wealth held in trust) and to be used now in a way that will provide for future generations a secure material basis for their existence. The depletion of oil, for example, will leave others with the problem of finding an alternative source of energy. To pollute lakes and streams now is to deprive others of water to drink. To fail to sustain the soil, is to deprive others of bread to sustain their lives. What we refer to as "our" resources are also theirs, for they, like us, are sons and daughters of the sole owner, the Lord, who has entrusted his material creation to our care and for our use. We are stewards.

Ultimately, stewardship is best explained in terms of love. Divine love created both the stewards and the resources over which stewardship is to be exercised. Similarly, love directs the responsible steward: "If a man that was rich enough in this world's goods saw that one of his brothers was in need, but closed his heart to him, how could the love of God be living in him? Dear children, our love is not to be just words or mere talk, but something real and active" (1 Jn 3.17–18).

The exercise of stewardship, if it were real and active in these times, could help to feed the hungry, assist the poor, and free the oppressed. Stewardship thus becomes an instrument of social justice. The concept of stewardship is pre-Christian. Stewards are guardians and managers who are held accountable to owners or masters. The steward exercises stewardship not dominion, which is proper only to the lord. There is a familial or family-service link between the steward and the one who holds true dominion over the property. The steward is in charge of a household which he does not own. The story of the "unjust steward" or "dishonest manager" (Lk 16.1–8) describes a social arrangement that was quite familiar to the disciples of Jesus. The arrangement was familiar in more ancient civilizations as well. Jesus used that familiar social context to teach a moral lesson, namely, that unjust stewardship is both a misuse of property and a violation of trust.

There is a clear social, as opposed to individualistic perspective associated with the contemporary revival of the notion of stewardship. It is, moreover, closely linked with the notion of economic justice and not unrelated to worldwide ecological and environmental concerns. If we waste or otherwise abuse resources, we are violating a trust. If we retain unfair portions of this world's wealth so that others are deprived of what is their due, our stewardship is characterized by the moral flaw of injustice. Hence, accompanying the revival of stewardship in the Christian community are signs of a return to a spare-and-share ethic.

In the recent past the concept of stewardship was commonly and almost exclusively applied, particularly in Protestant circles, to the management of parish property and income. This usage, while still common, is not at all opposed to the broader social application.

Bibliography: W. BYRON, *Toward Stewardship* (New York 1975); "The Ethics of Stewardship," *New Catholic World* 220 (1977) 230–237. D. HESSEL, ed., *Beyond Survival: Bread and Justice in Christian Perspective* (New York 1977). M. E. JEGEN and B. MANNO, eds., *The Earth is the Lord's: Essays on Stewardship* (New York 1977). W. KEECH, *The Life I Owe* (Valley Forge, Pa. 1963). National Catholic Stewardship Conference, *Stewardship of Money . . .*, Washington, D.C. (1975); *Stewardship of Time and Talent . . .* (1976); *Stewardship: Symbolic Presence of the Christ Event for the Church Today* (1976).

[W. BYRON]

STIPENDS

The postconciliar period has seen little change in the law on Mass stipends (CIC cc. 824–844; 13:175). However, several recent documents have considered the practical impossibility of adequately fulfilling Mass obligations; furthermore, Mass stipends were considered in a 1975 draft revising sacramental law provided by the Pontifical Commission for the Revision of the Code of Canon Law.

Firma in Traditione. On Nov. 29, 1971 the papal Secretariat of State issued a *Notificatio* that the pope was temporarily reserving to himself deliberation on the criteria for reducing, condoning, and commuting Mass stipends (ActApS 63 [1971] 841). All prior faculties were suspended except those granted bishops in the motu proprio *Pastorale munus* (ActApS 56 [1964] 5–12), 11–12. On June 13, 1974 Paul VI issued a motu proprio, *Firma in traditione* (ActApS 66 [1974] 308–311). It viewed stipends in relationship to the religious and ecclesial awareness of the faithful desiring to associate themselves more intimately with the Eucharistic Sacrifice. The preservation of this awareness and the precluding of abuses are key values underlying church law in this area.

Changing circumstances have brought it about that sometimes Mass obligations cannot be fully discharged. Accordingly they must be modified appropriately. Yet this must be done with scrupulous respect for the will of those offering the stipends. The motu proprio withdraws all prior faculties and determines that henceforth only the Congregations of the Roman Curia and the bishops may modify Mass obligations. Special faculties for the Roman Congregations were granted in a private communication dated June 13, 1974.

The faculties of bishops specified in *Pastorale munus*, 11–12, and in the *List of Faculties* customarily given to bishops and papal legates remain operative. *Firma in traditione* further empowers bishops to permit priests binating or trinating to take a stipend for each Mass to be applied to needs specified by the bishop or according to the intentions for which a condonation or reduction would otherwise have to be sought. The bishop may also reduce the conventual obligations of cathedral/ collegiate chapters proportionate to their diminished income. Finally he may transfer Mass obligations to days, churches, or altars different from those determined in foundations.

The Code Commission. The proposed Code Commission revision of Eucharistic discipline basically retains the CIC institute of stipends. Twenty-one norms (109–129) deal with the following issues: the legitimacy and purpose of stipends; the avoidance of abuses; the responsibilities of the individual celebrant in fulfilling Mass obligations; the amount of stipends; the supervision of the fulfillment of Mass obligations; the recording of the reception of stipends and the fulfillment of Mass obligations.

Various professional canonical societies have reacted differently to the proposed revision. Neither the British nor the Canadian Canon Law Societies question the relevance of stipends. However they favor a more limited treatment of stipends in universal law and greater particular-law discretion. On the contrary, the Canon Law Society of America critique raises basic questions about the viability of stipends. They seem based on a theology of merit and the fruits of the Mass unacceptable to contemporary sacramental theologians in light of conciliar Eucharistic theory and subsequent liturgical experience. The long history of the custom of stipends and their importance for clergy support should not preclude reflection on other ways of church support less open to clergy abuse and possible scandal on the part of the faithful. At present the draft *De sacramentis* is being reworked by the Commission in light of evaluations from around the world. There is no word on when or whether it will be promulgated.

Bibliography: *Communic* 4 (1972) 57–59, report on work of the Code Commission committee revising the law on stipends. T. BARBARENA, "El motu proprio 'Firma in traditione' de Misas," *Revista espanola de Derecho Canonico* 31 (1975) 83–102. T. GREEN, "Reflections on Other Parts of the Proposed Draft *De Sacramentis*," ProcCLSA 37 (1975) 194–205. PAUL VI, *Firma in traditione*, Eng. tr. Origins 4 (1974) 112; *Pastorale manus*, Eng. tr. Bousc-O'Connor 6:370–378. Pontificia Commissio Codici Iuris Canonici Recognoscendo, *Schema documenti pontificii quo disciplina canonica de sacramentis recognoscitur* (Typis Polyglottis Vaticanis, 1975). Secretaria Status, *Notificatio*, Eng. tr. O'Connor 7:644. P. TOCANEL, "Adnotations on the Motu Proprio Firma in Traditione 6/13/74 Dealing with the Faculty of Adjusting Mass Obligations," *Apollinaris* 47 (1974) 289–296.

[T. GREEN]

SUNDAY

Vatican Council II's Constitution on the Sacred Liturgy contains an expanded description of the significance of Sunday in the life of the faithful. The description focuses on the day itself and the action of the Church community. "By an apostolic tradition which took its origin from the very day of Christ's resurrection, the Church celebrates the paschal mystery every eighth day" (*Sacrosanctum Concilium* 106). Thus the Council Fathers articulated the memorial nature of the Sunday observance. The description continues: "For on this day Christ's faithful should come together into one place so that, by hearing the word of God and taking part in the Eucharist, they may call to mind the passion, the resurrection, and the glorification of the Lord Jesus" (ibid.). The document further notes that: "[the faithful] may thank God who 'has begotten us again, through the resurrection of Jesus Christ from the dead, unto a living hope'" (ibid.). The consequence of such a memorial day with its community action makes the Lord's day the original feast day. The Council urges that this observance should be part of the piety of the faithful in order that Sunday would become in fact a day of joy and freedom from work. Drawing these thoughts into a specific norm, the document continues: "Other celebrations, unless they be of overriding importance, must not have precedence over this day, which is the foundation and nucleus of the whole liturgical year" (ibid.).

The revised Roman Calendar (1969) translated these guiding thoughts of the Constitution on the Sacred Liturgy into practical norms. The calendar's table of liturgical days according to their order of precedence ranks the Sundays of the year sixth (CalendRom 4). The following specific norms are presented.

(1) "Because of its special importance, the celebration of Sunday is replaced only by solemnities or feasts of the Lord. The Sundays of Advent, Lent and the Easter season, however, take precedence over all solemnities and feasts of the Lord" (ibid. 5).

(2) "By its nature, Sunday excludes the permanent assignment of another celebration" (ibid. 6). Nevertheless, the document continues to note two categories of exceptions.

"Nevertheless (a) Sunday within the octave of Christmas is the feast of the Holy Family; (b) Sunday following January 6 is the feast of the Baptism of the Lord; (c) Sunday after Pentecost is the solemnity of the Holy Trinity; (d) the last Sunday of the liturgical year is the solemnity of Christ the King (ibid. 6). In those areas where the solemnities of Epiphany, Ascension and Corpus Christi are not observed as holydays of obligation, they are assigned to a Sunday" (ibid. 7).

(3) Sundays of the year do yield their place to feasts of the Lord which are found in the general calendar, proper solemnities, solemnities of the Lord, the Blessed Virgin Mary and saints listed in the general calendar (ibid. 59).

(4) "For the pastoral advantage of the people, it is permissible to observe on the Sundays of the year those celebrations which occur during the week and which are popular with the faithful, provided they take precedence over these Sundays in the table of liturgical days" (ibid. 58).

The revised calendar contains three directives for the development of particular (local) calendars. Among these there is an insistence that "the temporal cycle . . . in which the mystery of the redemption is unfolded during the liturgical year must be preserved intact and maintain proper preeminence over particular celebrations" (ibid. 50). The framers of the revised general calendar indicate strongly that the particular calendars are not to be enlarged disproportionally.

Hence saints are to have only one feast in the liturgical calendar (ibid.; *see* CALENDARS, PARTICULAR).

The expanded description of Sunday found in the Constitution on the Sacred Liturgy and the practical norms of the revised calendar move in the direction of recognizing Sunday as "the original feast day" (ibid. 4; *Sacrosanctum Concilium* 106). This is very consistent with current liturgical spirituality, which is centered on the person of Jesus in his passion, resurrection and glorification, i.e. on the paschal mystery.

[P. R. COONEY]

SYNOD OF BISHOPS
(THIRD GENERAL ASSEMBLY, 1974)

The fourth Synod of Bishops met in Rome from Sept. 27 through Oct. 26, 1974. The new structure, a gathering of bishops, is the realization of the idea for a regularly scheduled meeting of bishops to assist the pope by advice and counsel that was discussed in Vatican Council II (*Christus Dominus* 5). On Sept. 15, 1965, Pope Paul VI with the motu proprio, *Apostolica sollicitudo* (Act-ApS 57 [1965] 775–780), reestablished as an ecclesial institution the Synod of Bishops and gave it what was, in effect, its constitution. The document notes that the aims of the Synod are: (1) to encourage close union and valued assistance between the sovereign pontiff and the bishops of the entire world; (2) to insure that direct and real information is provided on the questions involving the internal action of the Church and its necessary action in the world today; (3) to facilitate agreement on essential points of doctrine and on methods of procedure in the life of the Church.

The first Synod met in 1967 and was followed by one in 1969 and 1971. All of these, except for the 1969 meeting, are called a "General Assembly of the Synod." The 1969 meeting was an extraordinary meeting and it is not numbered in the sequence of General Assemblies. Thus, the 1974 Synod, though the fourth in number, is designated the "Third General Assembly of the Synod of Bishops."

The Synod Body. The 1974 Synod meeting brought together 208 cardinals, bishops and heads of religious communities of men to discuss "Evangelization," the theme selected by Paul VI. Of the total number of members, 159 were bishops representing national episcopal conference around the world and from the Eastern Churches in communion with the Apostolic See. In addition, there were seventeen cardinals from the various departments of the Roman Curia, 10 delegates of the Unions of Superiors General, 21 members appointed by the Pope, and the Secretary General of the Permanent Secretariat of the Synod. Nine members were from the U.S.: four selected by the NCCB (Cardinals John J. Krol, John F. Dearden, and John J. Carberry and Archbishop Joseph L. Bernardin), two metropolitans of the Eastern rite (Archbishop Ambrose of the Ukrainian Rite, and Archbishop Stephen Kosicsko of the Byzantine Rite); one religious superior (Abbot Rembert Weakland, now abp. of Milwaukee), Archbishop John R. Quinn; appointed by the Holy Father, and the American-born prefect of the Vatican Congregation for the Clergy, Cardinal John J. Wright. The three Synodal presidents were Cardinals Juan Landazuri-Ricketts, archbishop of Lima, Franz Koenig, archbishop of Vienna, and Paul Zoungrana, archbishop

of Ouagadougou, Upper Volta. The 1974 Synod was the first to concentrate its entire activity on the Church's mission to the world. In this it differed from the first three assemblies, which had emphasized some aspect of church structure, discipline, or internal affairs. The 1974 Synod also modified the direction of the deliberations of earlier meetings. The thrust reflected a growing awareness that the Church must turn its attention to matters other than its internal operation, which had monopolized most of its energies since Vatican II.

Synod Concerns. There were many reasons that counseled this shift in emphasis and the Synod was faced with some of these as it began deliberating. Probably more sobering than any other single background awareness was the realization that there are whole sections of the earth where other faiths or ethical systems dominate. As the Synod met it became more aware that a large portion of the world has yet to receive the message of Christ as the source of man's happiness now and salvation in the life to come.

Other trends that surely preoccupied the Synodal Fathers were the resurgence of a new racism and a new nationalism. Across the earth, groups united by blood or culture are finding it more and more difficult to relate to other groups. This new racism is certainly appearing in Asia and Africa. The new nationalism perhaps is seen not only in the African nations but now in the whole subcontinent of India which, in its quest for national identity, has not only greatly restricted the evangelization efforts of "outside religions," but has not hesitated to use military force on numerous occasions to extend national frontiers and impose religious and ethical convictions. The Synod's *Declaratio* (see Caprile 1011–16) also notes as obstacles to the work of evangelization the present-day phenomena of secularization—which "completely excludes God from the horizon of human life and therefore from the profound meaning of existence"—and atheism "in its manifold forms which is widespread in many countries" (*Declaratio* 8). The Synod working paper (*Instrumentum laboris;* see Caprile 911–930) included sections on the situation of the particular local Churches and the special problems that confront each Church as it tried to spread the faith. It then presented some conclusions of the various episcopal conferences on how to approach the teaching of the faith in areas where it is hindered by some outside forces. Finally the draft touched on the difficult problem of the extent of the legitimate adaptation of the Gospel's message to meet present-day problems, thought patterns, conditions, and structures.

Special Problems. Problems of language and semantics became evident during the daily discussions. Many terms, such as "liberation," "indigenization," and "class alienation" were found to have several meanings. From the interventions of some of the Synodal Fathers, it became apparent that several words were used with one meaning, whereas they could be interpreted to mean something quite different than a speaker intended in the context of his intervention. Some words were ambiguous because they bore one interpretation in the light of the Christian faith and traditions and a very different one when viewed according to present political usage.

"Liberation." The ambiguity in the use of the word "liberation" was particularly striking. Certainly the Synod had to study the issue of liberation. For a considerable time a dispute over whether the Gospel is

to be preached in terms of political liberation, including as some writers propose, the Marxist dialectic and violent revolution, or exclusively in terms of man's liberation from sin and its consequences, has haunted missionary effort. However, in the bishops' speeches and discussions, the word "liberation" was used without an explicit and clear definition. The result was that when it came time to prepare a final document on evangelization the Synodal Fathers found that there was considerable negative reaction to this word.

The final *Declaratio* set "liberation" in the perspective of the Gospels and therefore gave it a Christian interpretation. The Synod's document explain in detail that every type of liberation must be rooted in Christian liberation from sin. It recognized the constant need to keep a proper balance between the spiritual orientation of the Gospels and the need to apply to today's problems the good news of Christ's redemptive love. The Gospel must be made concrete. Its preaching speaks of liberation of the evils of this world: for the Church is "at the service of all men but particularly the poor, the oppressed, the weak" (*Declaratio* 12). Her mission must include, then, liberation in the wider area of injustices found in social and political institutions. But this temporal liberation, the Synod continues, must be seen in the fuller and wider context of Christian liberation from sin, from egoism, and from alienation from God. Salvation of men includes their integral liberation, and Christian liberation-salvation is first rooted in the Church's essential and primary mission of bringing all men to the knowledge and love of God.

"*Indigenization.*" Another word that required definition by the Synodal Fathers was "indigenization." It was widely used in the halls of Synod '74, but, once again, the term was used ambiguously in the working paper and discussions. This lack of precision probably in great part accounts for the Synod's inability to reach early agreement on a final statement. The final document avoids the term altogether; rather it speaks of the conditions which "impel the particular Churches toward an appropriate 'translation' of the evangelical message. According to the principle of Incarnation [the local Churches] must devise new but faithful 'ways to take root'... in keeping with the way today's people think and act" (ibid. 9).

The essential problem of all indigenization is touched on in paragraph 8 where the problems of how to make the faith attractive while maintaining its purity are mentioned. Here the Synod comes to grip with the fundamental problem of diversity in unity. The faith is one; the doctrine of the Church is one. Human cultures and societies are many. The adaptation of the one faith to various cultures must be such that it at no time compromises the purity of the faith.

On Evangelization. The *Declaratio* sees evangelization in the context of the Church's mission to carry on Christ's work in the world. The Church herself is to be the witness to the truth that Jesus, the founder, revealed. The Church's function is to proclaim to all men that Jesus is the Lord, that his Father loves all men and would gather them into His Church and then into his final Kingdom. The document defines evangelization as the "announcement of the good news of Christ." This announcement is to result in the "foundation of the Church... in all peoples and places." The same text points out that this "mandate to evangelize all men

constitutes the essential mission of the Church" (*Declaratio* 4).

The Holy Father at the conclusion of the Synod spoke of the evangelization as "the teaching of the faith, a faith that is centered in the Blessed Trinity, our sharing in the Divine Nature, and the eternal Salvation of the world now and in the future" (Caprile 765).

Since the Church is by nature and intent missionary, all her members share the duty to spread the faith. The role of missionary falls to each believer "worthy of the name" (*Declaratio* 5). This witness, the document insists, must be carried out by example, not just by words. The lives of individual believers should compel others to want to examine the faith closely. Those outside the Church should see in it a true, living, fruitful teacher. Developing this point, the Synod noted that evangelization is centered in personal Christian witness, which requires a continued, internal conversion of individual Christians (ibid. 2). The Spirit must first be active in believers before he can reach out to others (ibid. 6).

The force of evangelization is the Holy Spirit. Without the Spirit the mission of Christ dies. For this reason, the *Declaratio* insists that at the root of every missionary effort and every individual witness there must be a personal union with God that comes only from prayer. The document notes that it is necessary that we be joined to God in assiduous prayer, meditation and contemplation of the Word of God (ibid. 7).

The Gospel must be translated by word and deed into the language of action which all men can see and hear. The difficult challenge of adapting the faith to a local environment must always be guided by the need to preserve its integrity. It is not evangelization merely to offer another form of secularized ethics or a watered down Gospel which leaves out much of Christ's message (ibid. 12).

Assessment. We can conclude from the 1974 Synod's *Declaratio*, which was not published as such by the Synod but given to the Holy Father for his use and study, and from his remarks at the Synod, that the Third General Assembly of Bishops made progress towards reaffirming the Church's ancient role of evangelizer and adapting it to today's needs. It affirmed that evangelization is still the essential mission of the Church. That mission must be carried out in vital and dynamic fashion, ready to adapt to meet new and local circumstances, quick to attack evils—social, political and personal—and aware that the first aim of all the Church's efforts is to bring men soon and safely to God.

On December 8, 1975, Pope Paul VI issued the apostolic exhortation *Evangelii nuntiandi* (On Evangelization in the Modern World). The document is obviously, in part, the fruit of the deliberations of the 1974 Synod and, in a sense, fills out the outline on missionary activity the Synod prepared. The document stresses the Christocentric nature of the Church's doctrine and mission, the need to bring the full message of Christ's redemptive love to all men, the place of method in teaching the faith, and the role that every believer has in the Church's work of evangelization.

See also EVANGELIZATION.

Bibliography: G. CAPRILE, *Il Sinodo dei Vescovi. Terza assemblea generale* (Rome n.d.).

[D. W. WUERL]

SYNOD OF BISHOPS
(FOURTH GENERAL ASSEMBLY, 1977)

The fifth Synod of Bishops met in Rome, Sept. 29–Oct. 28, 1977, the meeting occurring on the tenth anniversary of the first Synod, 1967. Since the second of these meetings, the 1969 Synod, was an extraordinary one, the 1977 gathering became the Fourth General Assembly of the Synod of Bishops. As in the case of all the Synods to date, the members were those cardinals and bishops selected by episcopal conferences throughout the world, representatives of the Eastern Churches, those appointed by the pope, the heads of the major offices of the Roman Curia, and representatives of various religious orders of men. The American members of this Synod included four elected by the National Conference of Catholic Bishops (Cardinal John J. Carberry, Archbishops Joseph L. Bernardin and John F. Whealon and Bishop Raymond A. Lucker), two Metropolitans of the Eastern Rites (Archbishop Stephen Kocisko and Bishop Joseph Schmondiuk), Cardinal Timothy Manning appointed by the pope, Abbot (now Archbishop) Rembert Weakland, Primate of the Benedictines, and Cardinal John J. Wright, Prefect of the Congregation for the Clergy, the Vatican office responsible, among other things, for worldwide catechetics. Cardinal Wright is the only American to have participated in all of the Synods since their establishment in 1967.

Theme: Catechesis. The 1977 Synod had as its theme Catechetics. Catechesis comes from the Greek word "to make resound" or "to echo." It is a precise word for what the Church has been doing since the days of the Apostles. It refers to the witnessing, proclaiming, preaching, or teaching of Christ's message, the "Good News," in such a way as to produce an "echo" of Christ in those who hear it. Catechetics is the art or discipline concerned with the what and the how of catechesis. Catechesis implies more than religious education, which has come to refer to the academic discipline of religion. In this sense religious education can mean the intellectual appreciation of a subject much like one would learn mathematics or biology. The Synod spoke of catechesis rather than religious education. As urged by the Synod, the term refers to every activity intended to help people grow and mature in the faith.

Another way of defining catechesis is to call it the active witnessing of Christ by word and deed. When catechesis is described as witness it is easy to see that it is not limited to bishops and priests. It is true, as the Synod documents point out, that all individual testimony to the truth revealed in Jesus Christ must find its touchstone of authenticity in terms of the teaching of the Church through her official witness. But it is also correct to say that the obligation to bear testimony concerning all that Jesus did and said falls to every believer. Hence all the faithful are called to be catechists (*Message to the People of God*, Synod 1977, 12; hereafter Message).

Deliberations. When the bishops faced the issue in the Synod aula, they seemed intent on moving beyond immediate controversies regarding methods of teaching the faith to confront underlying issues and point to the solutions. To some extent this tended to give the meeting in the eyes of the press a rather bland coloring. Yet the bishops, it must be remembered, were tackling church problems that are not always headline-catchers or the stuff of daily reporting. The Synod began its deliberations with a study of the working paper that grew out of earlier episcopal consultations. The Synod Office prepared a draft document and sent it to all the episcopal conferences. Reactions and suggestions to this paper were followed by the second paper that was sent to the synodal members in time for them to study it before they met in Rome to open the discussions.

Catechizing. In particular, the Bishops examined catechetics with a special reference to the teaching of the faith to children and young people. As the meeting's original Working Draft (*Instrumentum laboris*; hereafter Draft) pointed out "it is precisely children that can often be one of the most powerful reminders to the whole Christian community and individual members of the faithful to be attentive to their own vocation and their own educational responsibilities" (Draft 7). The Synod here spoke of the essential teaching mission which reaches out to all, young and old. In the words of the working paper, "in our time, even more than ever, there is needed a catechetics that accompanies Christians throughout their lives with due regard to their concrete situation of faith" (ibid. 6). In turn, catechetics is seen as one aspect of the great evangelical mission of the Church, the bringing of Christ to all men and women. For this reason there is a strong relationship between the work of the 1974 Synod on evangelization and the 1977 Synod on catechetics. The Synod's final public document, *Message to the People of God*, states that "it is the Church's task to proclaim and accomplish Christ's salvation in the whole world. This is the work of evangelization of which catechetics is an aspect. It is centered in the mystery of Christ. Christ, true God and true Man, and His saving work carried out in His Incarnation, Life and Death and Resurrection, is the center of the message" (Message 7).

Content or Method? By the time the 1977 Synod met, some of the polarization and polemics that had marked the field of catechetics since Vatican Council II had waned. The division in theory and approach that plagued much of the work in teaching the faith, particularly to the young in many of the European nations and North America, was not so much in evidence in the discussions in this Synod. The Synod had behind it the experience of many bishops who found themselves caught in the rather pronounced differences a few years earlier between those who were more inclined to concentrate on the method by which the faith was taught. Part also of this division was the school of thought that insisted that experience was the primary factor in reaching the child who was to be taught the faith. Thus the content element—the doctrine of the faith—was to receive less emphasis than the living out of an "experienced" Christianity.

Synod Message to the People of God. The general assumption that seemed to support nearly all of the speeches made from the floor and certainly reflected in the final public text was that catechetics as instruction of others in faith is essentially the handing on of a message. Thus, the document, issued in the name of the bishops of the Synod, tends to stress primarily the idea of content. But it must be remembered that content includes the understanding that living out the faith is a part also of the Church's teaching. Method, techniques, and pedagogical devices are only tools in the much more important task of telling others of the teaching of Christ (Message 7 and 8). The Synod insists that this teaching is to be in its fullness, for otherwise the learner, the instructed, would be left with an incomplete faith. "Fidelity in handing on the integral Gospel message and the authenticity of the catechetical mode of communication through which faith is transmitted are both to be discerned through the reverent attentiveness to the magisterial and pastoral ministry of the Church" (Message 8). The Synod's public document considers catechesis as the manifestation of the salvation of Christ. The center of catechetics is the mystery of Christ: "The Church insists that it is the bearer of the message of salvation destined for all mankind . . . [that] Jesus Christ is the focal point and foundation of our faith and source of our life" (Message 7). According to the Synod, catechetics has as its primary function the proclamation of the faith, the mystery of Christ. The communication of faith in and knowledge of Christ, the central reality of the Church's proclamation, can be seen, according to the Synod's text, under three headings; word, memory, and witness.

Catechesis as Word. As word, catechetics is concerned with the message received from Christ and taught in his Church. "The integral, vital substance handed down through the Creed provides the fundamental nucleus of the mystery of the one and triune God as it is revealed to us through the mystery of God's Son, the Incarnate Savior living always in His Church" (Message 8). The model for catechesis as word is found in the preparation for adult Baptism. The liturgical exemplar of this manner of teaching the faith is found in the special formation which prepares an adult convert for the profession of faith during the Paschal Vigil. During this preparation the catechumen receives the Word of God in the form of the Gospels and its ecclesial expression, the Creeds (*see* CATECHUMENATE FOR ADULTS).

Catechesis as Memory. As memory, catechetics is concerned with the action by which the Church recalls in each age the Good News about Christ. For this reason the Synod insists that certain elements of the Church's belief and heritage can be committed to memory and that religious education contain this element that has always formed a part of the way the Church passes on her message. The Synod notes that "normally, things should be memorized as part of the formation; such as biblical texts, especially from the New Testament, certain liturgical formulae which are the privileged expressions of these texts, and other prayers. Believers should also make their own expressions of faith, the living fruit of the reflections of Christians over the centuries, that have been gathered in the creeds and principal documents of the Church" (Message 9).

The aspect of catechesis shows its connection with the whole life of the believing community. For it is precisely as in living, effective memory of Christ that the Church celebrates the Eucharist. The value of words and actions today or at any time within the Christian family have effect and lasting meaning only inasmuch as they show forth the Lord Jesus and unite men and women with him. Thus, in doing so through the collective and individual memory of him, catechesis is connected with the entire sacramental and liturgical life of Christ's Church.

Catechesis as Witness. As witness, catechesis translates the word "which is rooted in living tradition" into the "living word for our times" (Message 10). At this point the Synod indicates that the faith cannot remain without fruit. By the believer—by the one who bears the Word of God—there must be not only a faith-acceptance of it but a translation of that faith into action. Thus, there is required a serious commitment. The believer must follow the law

of Christ in terms of moral action. Because this is so the Synod text continues: "We must affirm without ambiguity that there are laws and moral principles which catechesis must teach. In addition, we must affirm that the moral doctrine of the Gospel has a specific nature which goes far beyond the demands of mere natural ethics" (Message 10).

The three realities, faith, witness, and the Church are inseparable. None can function in a vacuum. Witness must be a constant declaration of the faith and this implies a communion with all those who hold the same faith. That community is the Church. Witness is always founded upon what it receives within the Church and falls back on that same Church for the authentication of the content of all to which it testifies. As the one principal witness, the Church has the obligation to testify to the faith and see that it is spread over the face of the earth. In the Church's unique witness as the extension of Christ, all believers are called to participate. Some share this ministry as official spokesmen for the Church, local or universal, others as believers whose personal witness is united to the Church. The communion and unity of their witness rests on the one Spirit who gives life and truth to his one Church (Message 10).

The Synod Propositions. In addition to its public document, *Message to the People of God*, the 1977 Synod offered to the Holy Father a series of 34 considerations or propositions (Prop.) related to catechetics. This material was forwarded to the Pope in the hope that he would use it in the preparation of his own public statement, an apostolic exhortation or encyclical (Prop. 1). The propositions were the principal points of reflection and concern that grew out of the discussions within the Synod. And although they are not presented as a complete text, they do offer a good summary of what had preoccupied the bishops during the month-long meeting. The 34 propositions were arrived at after several votations and consensus-gathering procedures. They form, together with the *Message to the People of God*, the fruit of the 1977 Synod.

In the propositions the bishops note the existence of new catechetical methods and the reasons for or scope of catechetics (Prop. 2–3). According to the propositions, the faith must be understood as living in Christ. For this reason, commitment to the faith is most important in those who are to teach others the way of the Lord. (Prop. 4–6). Authentic catechesis requires, however, more than just commitment. It must be founded on a clear and complete knowledge and presentation of the faith—which in turn is centered in the person of Christ (Prop. 7–8). Proper catechesis implies the presentation of the full and entire faith content and its implications for Christian living. It must also inspire one to want to live the Christian way of life in all its ramifications (Prop. 10–13). Teaching the faith takes into consideration the situation of the listener and attempts to use available methods that will help reach him or her (Prop. 14–20). Every believer is by nature a catechist—a teacher of the faith—but parents have a special role to play as they are the first teacher of the faith in the life of the child. Those who prepare the young in the grasp of the faith also have a special place in the mission of the Church (Prop. 21–25). The Christian community of believers is the home of the faith; it is, therefore, within the community that the believer learns the faith. The next section of propositions speaks of the role of the larger Christian community, the Church itself, in teaching the faith, and then of the place of smaller cells of community life. It notes that the family, the parish, the schools, and still other smaller communities are natural places for learning the faith (Prop. 26–29). There are various problems that arise in teaching within a given diocese and all should remember that the ultimate responsibility for the proper catechesis of the local Church rests with the bishop who is the principal teacher of the faith in that Church. Those who undertake this task do so in collaboration with him (Prop. 30–34).

Particular Issues. In the document made public for all the Church, *Message to the People of God*, the Synod stressed the need for catechesis to help families face the contemporary cultural breakdown. It speaks of the need to catechize couples before and after marriage concerning their responsibilities to each other and for special programs to assist parents in giving catechesis to their children.

Another major theme was the importance of small communities of faith as settings for catechesis. The hope expressed is to form small groups of Christians who support and encourage one another to live out more fully their faith (*see* BASIC CHRISTIAN COMMUNITIES).

In his final address Pope Paul emphasized that he looked to the Synodal Fathers to be a leaven inspiring their fellow bishops to action. He also referred to the General Catechetical Directory, issued in 1971 by the Congregation for the Clergy and sent to all episcopal conferences with the hope that it would be made the basis for catechetical texts and teaching. He also called upon the faithful to take up the task of catechetics—the mission of passing on the faith.

Assessment. Of particular value in this Synod was the frank appreciation of the problems that had divided catechists in the years following the Council. The Synod noted the two areas of emphasis, content and method, and opted for a statement that insisted on content-conscious catechetics while also urging the adoption of relevant techniques in teaching the faith. The Synod's balance is seen in its call for content—the knowledge of the faith—as well as an understanding of the need for methods of teaching that reach men and women, young and old, where they are today. The theme of catechetics as word, memory, and witness adopted by the Synod offers a brief summary of the way the Synod approached its subject and is a tool for understanding the nature of catechetics as it is lived within today's Church.

Bibliography: LivLight 15 (1978) 1–127, contains a summary of the working draft, as well as the text of "Message to the People of God" and the 34 Propositions of the Synod. USCC, "Message to the People of God, in *Synod of Bishops* 1977 (USCC Publ. Office, Washington D.C. 1978) 5–16.

[D. W. WUERL]

SYNODS, DIOCESAN

In the Decree on the Pastoral Office of Bishops in the Church Vatican Council II expressed the hope that the institutes of synods and councils would flourish with renewed vigor "so that the growth of religion and the maintenance of discipline in the various churches may increasingly be more effectively provided for in accordance with the needs of the times" (*Christus Dominus* 36). In response to this hope, the Sacred Congregation for Bishops, in its Directory for the Pastoral Ministry of Bishops (February 22, 1973), recommended the diocesan synod as a matter of extraordinary importance in the ministry of the bishops. In the Directory, the synod is no longer to be an assembly only of clerics; clergy, religious, and laity are to be invited. In the synod, the laws of the universal Church are to be adapted to local conditions; policies and programs are to be pointed out; problems resolved; and any errors in doctrine or morals corrected. The synod also offers an occasion for sacred celebrations which do much to renew faith, piety, and apostolic zeal in the diocese.

Bibliography: Congregation for Bishops, *Directory on the Pastoral Ministry of Bishops* (Ottawa 1974). J. A. CORIDEN, "The Diocesan Synod: An Instrument of Renewal for the Local Church," *Jurist* 34 (1974) 68–93 with selected bibliog.; F. B. DONNELLY, "The New Diocesan Synod," *Jurist* 34 (1974) 396–402.

[G. P. GRAHAM]

T

TABERNACLE

In 1966 Pope Paul VI publicly raised the question of an appropriate location of the tabernacle (13:908) for Eucharistic reservation. Since then there has been a gradual change in official documents on the subject; Roman misgivings about locating the tabernacle in a place distinct from the altar where Mass is celebrated have disappeared. The section of the revised Roman Ritual on Eucharistic cult (*De sacra communione extra Missam...*, June 21, 1973) returns to the exposition offered by the Congregation for the Sacraments in 1949: the primary purpose of Eucharistic reservation is to permit the giving of viaticum to the dying; the secondary purposes are to provide for Holy Communion outside Mass (i.e., when the Eucharist cannot be or is not celebrated) as well as Eucharistic adoration and devotion (HolyCommIntrod 5).

With this basic distinction of reservation and celebration, the ritual reasserts the close relationship (Eucharistic cult as the consequence of the Eucharistic celebration), but strongly urges that the tabernacle be located in a chapel separate and distinct from the body of the church. It leaves to the local bishop's judgment whether the tabernacle is to be on an altar or, according to older traditions, in some other position that is suitably adorned and prominent (ibid. 6; 9–10).

The rationale for the placement of the tabernacle, if possible, in an area distinct from the place of Eucharistic celebration had been developed officially in the May 25, 1967, instruction on Eucharistic worship (*Eucharisticum mysterium*) of the Congregation of Rites (ActApS 59 [1967] 539–573): "In the celebration of Mass the modes by which Christ is present in his Church become successively clearer: first he appears present in the very body of the faithful assembled in his name; then in his Word, when Scripture is read and explained; next, in the person of the minister; lastly, in a special manner under the eucharistic species [see *Sacrosanctum Concilium* 7]. From the viewpoint of sign, therefore, it is in better accord with the nature of liturgical celebration that the eucharistic presence of Christ not be at the altar where Mass is celebrated, since this presence is the result of the consecration and must appear to be such..." (55).

Thus new and renovated churches have located the tabernacle in separate chapels or distinct areas where it will not distract the attention of the liturgical assembly during the Eucharistic celebration; the place should be suited for private devotion and the tabernacle should be given every dignity, beauty, and prominence in that place.

As for the form and design of the tabernacle, this is left to local usage and the creativity of artists, provided it is a secure and becoming container for the reserved Sacrament (HolyCommIntrod 10). Experiments with designs similar to the lectern (and located for balance and symmetry within the sanctuary area) have not succeeded; the tabernacle has a function quite different from that of the lectern from which the Word of God is proclaimed and is not part of the Eucharistic celebration. Other designs that respect the function of the tabernacle as the house and container of the reserved Sacrament, whether located on a pedestal or table or recessed in a wall niche, have proved more fitting and beautiful.

[F. R. MCMANUS]

TAX EXEMPTION OF CHURCH PROPERTY

It is clear that the sovereign (state governments and to the extent delegated by the Constitution, the federal government) has the inherent right to impose taxes. The states may impose, or delegate to municipal governments the right to impose, direct taxes on property. The federal government may not impose direct taxes on property without apportioning the revenue derived from the taxes among the several states. But since the 16th Amendment to the Constitution (ratified in 1913) overturned the Supreme Court decision in *Pollock v. Farmers' Loan and Trust Company*, 157 U.S. 429, 15 S. Ct. 673, 39 L. Ed. 759 (1895), "The Congress shall have the power to lay and collect taxes on income, from whatever source derived, without apportionment among the several states, and without regard to any census or enumeration" (16th Amendment).

The Tradition of Exemption. The sovereign is not obliged to exercise its right to impose taxes. From time immemorial at the state level churches and church property (including rectories, parsonages, schools, cemeteries, etc.) have, by legislative grace, been exempt from property taxes. The reasons for such exemption are often vague but likely spring from the public policy that an organization that performs a function (relief of the poor, education of the ignorant, etc.) which in its absence might be required to be performed by the sovereign, should be exempt from taxes as to such functions. Moreover, a collection taken up by churches for such purposes can be construed to be a nontaxable event, i.e. merely a means whereby as a group, those contributing to the collection expend money in the way they would if they spent it individually. But the reasons for exemption for taxation at the state and federal levels are by no means clear.

There is in federal tax law and in the judicial decisions surrounding it no clear definition of "church." The First Amendment to the Constitution is an obvious reason why "church," among the myriad other organizations defined in federal and state codes, is left undefined. The First Amendment, among other provisions, says that "Congress shall make no law respecting an establishment of religion, or prohibiting the free exercise thereof....." Since the U.S. Constitution applies to the states, there is a reluctance at that level, as well, to define "church." The result has been that some organizations that are unworthy of the classification, "church," have nevertheless, seemingly for tax purposes alone, defined themselves to be churches and have, at least sporadically, driven the federal courts a step away from their "hands off" attitude (*U.S. v. Kuch*, 288 F. Supp. 439, 443–444 [D.D.C. 1968]; the Neo-American Church Case which held that psychedelic substances were the true "host" of the church and required "frequent communion"). The court has at times declared a "religion" not to be a religion.

Trend against Exemption. Such abuses apart, at the state and local levels the need for additional tax revenues has driven authorities to examine the level and extent of tax exemptions. Agencies of government are clearly exempt (parks, public buildings, elementary and secondary schools, etc.) since to tax them would, as Chief Justice Holmes put it, transfer funds from one pocket to the other in the same pair of pants. But other tax exempt properties (churches, private schools, cemeteries, private hospitals, etc.) become political "fair game" when the choice is either to "tax" them or to raise the citizen's (voter's) tax rates or assessments. California's Proposition 13 (1978) illustrates the political dynamics involved. But First Amendment prohibitions raise certain cloudy legal issues. Is it constitutionally permissible to tax a church (however defined) or its property? Is it possible to redefine a school as a "church auxiliary" and thereby subject it to local taxation while keeping from it federal or state support? Or, as some communities have done, should the existing definitional relationship be left intact but a fee imposed on church property "for services in lieu of taxation," for police and fire protection (including pension liabilities), street repairs, and lighting, garbage removal, etc. Attempts have been made to charge churches a "fee," sometimes amounting to 25 percent of full taxation for such services.

At the federal level, developments in the past several years could have impact upon the tax exemption of church property. One is the increasing scrutiny by the federal agencies of the activities of exempt organizations, together with administrative decisions purporting to implement the intent of Congress in passing laws of general applicability. An example of this is the administrative decision that churches must pay unemployment insurance on behalf of its employees, a tax from which churches were previously exempt. Another example is the restrictive and complex laws enacted in 1969 to govern private foundations and the subsequent regulations promulgated by the Internal Revenue Service. The laws and regulations are so complex that accountants and attorneys must be employed by even the smaller foundations to ensure compliance, thereby reducing the amount of foundation income available for distribution as grants.

Another development at the federal level that could have a long term impact on support of churches and their properties by charitable contributions is the concept of "tax expenditures" adopted by the Congressional Budget Act of 1974. Tax expenditures are defined there to be "revenue losses attributable to provisions of the Federal tax laws which allow a special exclusion, exemption, or deduction from gross income or which provide a special credit, a preferential rate of tax, or a deferral of tax liability." The *Special Analyses* of the budget of the U.S. Government (*Federal Yearbook*, 1979) states that tax expenditures are one means by which the Federal Government pursues public-policy objectives and, in most cases, can be viewed as alternatives to budget outlays, credit assistance, or other policy instruments. If "tax expenditures" should at some future date be considered as equivalent to budget outlay and as real expenditures of the Federal government, there could be a difficult First-Amendment issue regarding the more than five billion dollars annually listed as a tax expenditure because of the deductibility of charitable contributions made chiefly to churches.

The tax structure of the United States at all levels of government has become so sophisticated and pervasive, and the need for tax revenues so acute, that further attempts to erode statutory exemptions from taxation for churches and other charitable organizations are likely.

Bibliography: J. C. CHOMMIE, *The Law of Federal Income Taxation* (2d. ed., St. Paul, Minn. 1973). B. R. HOPKINS and J. H. MYERS, *The Law of Tax-Exempt Organizations* (Washington, D.C. 1975). *Special Analyses of the Budget of the Government of the United States of America, 1979* (Government Printing Office, Washington, D.C. 1978).

[J. P. WHALEN]

TEACHERS, LAY

The lay teacher has been a part of Catholic education from its beginnings in the United States. Catholic schools, organized by missionary priests and staffed primarily by lay teachers, were opened in Maryland and Pennsylvania throughout the 18th century. The bulk of the teaching in these parish schools was done by lay teachers well into the 19th century, until the teaching sisters and brothers gradually replaced them. Throughout the remainder of the 19th century and the first half of the 20th, lay teachers served in something of a substitute or back-up role, teaching only when sisters or brothers were not available (O'Donnell).

A Quiet Transition. Since 1950 a quiet transition from religious- to lay-staffing of Catholic schools has been underway. The transition has been quiet in that it has received comparatively little attention in the literature on Catholic education and virtually no public discussion within the Church. This transition has dealt mainly with the day-to-day operation of the schools. Despite a sharp increase in the number of lay principals and the appointment of lay administrators at the diocesan level, the control of Catholic education has remained in the hands of clergy and religious.

TABLE: Catholic School Religious and Lay Staffs, 1920–1980 (NCEA Data Bank)

Year	Elementary			Secondary		
	Religious	Lay	% Lay	Religious	Lay	% Lay
1920	38,592	2,989	7%	6,971	953	12%
1930	53,384	4,861	8	12,271	2,090	15
1940	56,438	3,643	8	17,522	3,454	16
1950	61,778	4,747	7	23,147	4,623	17
1960	79,119	29,050	27	32,910	10,823	25
1970	52,505	59,710	53	28,425	26,155	48
1975	35,434	63,885	64	19,684	30,273	61
1980	24,858*	71,033*	75*	15,286*	33,679*	70*

*Projections made in 1976.

From 1920 through 1950 the number of lay teachers as a percentage of the total Catholic school staff remained both constant and small, below 10 percent in the elementary schools and below 20 percent in the secondary schools (see Table). During this period, the religious teacher, "moulded in the spiritual life, with singleness of purpose and unselfish aims" was affirmed as the ideal teacher for the Catholic school (Larkin 235).

A Two-Staged Transition. Amid the post-war expansion of the Catholic schools from 1950 to 1960, the total staff increased from 94,235 to 151,902. The increased dependence on lay staff during this period resulted from the inability of religious communities, despite their own growth, to keep pace with the demand created by the expansion of Catholic schools. While the ideal of the Catholic school staffed by religious was not questioned, it became less and less attainable, even though the number of teaching religious increased from 84,925 to 113,795 between 1950 and 1965.

After 1965, the steadily increasing dependence on lay staff resulted not from growth but from a decline in the numbers of teaching religious, from 113,795 in 1965 to a projected 40,144 in 1980. During this period, changes in life styles of religious, increasing contact with and dependence on lay teachers and the Vatican Council II affirmation of the role of the laity led to the acceptance of lay teachers as full-fledged participants in Catholic education. In 1974, a National Catholic Educational Association (NCEA) study of 150 schools staffed entirely by lay personnel showed these schools to be faring as well as their Catholic school counterparts (Elford and Harrington). This study and a national survey of Catholics by the National Opinion Research Center (Greely, McCready, McCourt 37) both reported confidence in lay teachers' ability to carry on the work of Catholic schools.

During this same period, lay staff began to be appointed to diocesan-level administrative posts. By 1978 twenty laymen were serving as superintendents of schools or vicars of education and another twenty served in diocesan level administrative positions. In 1977 the NCEA chief-administrators division elected its first lay president.

Teacher Organizations. Increase in lay involvement took place during a period in American education marked by the increasing influence of teacher unions at all levels in education. In 1970, the National Labor Relations Board (NLRB) extended its jurisdiction to include the larger Catholic school systems. This decision came at a time when Catholic educational officials were emphasizing the secular services provided by Catholic schools in an effort to obtain state aid. Only after the U.S. Supreme Court in 1971 rejected the secular-services concept did Catholic officials begin to challenge the NLRB on the grounds of separation of Church and State. In 1972 the American Federation of Teachers established a Department of Nonpublic School Teachers with a full-time director. By 1976, 25 diocesan school systems were involved in formal negotiations over salary and working conditions with teacher organizations, either independent or affiliated with national organizations. During this period, the U.S. bishops publicly affirmed the right of teachers to organize (see TEACHERS' UNIONS, CATHOLIC), despite occasional conflicts between individual bishops and lay teachers over the issue of teacher unions. (NCEA 1976).

Preparation and Salaries. The increase in the number of lay teachers was accompanied by an increase in the level of academic preparation of both lay and religious teachers in Catholic elementary schools. In 1962 two-thirds of the lay staff and two-fifths of the sisters did not have college degrees (Neuwien 85–87). By 1970, 83 percent of the religious and 66 percent of the lay staff in elementary schools held at least a B.A. degree (NCEA 1971, 20). Catholic high schools have consistently employed credentialed personnel over the years. With the advent of better qualified staff and, in larger cities, Catholic-teacher unions, salaries for Catholic-school lay teachers increased steadily, though these salaries, as a rule, remained well below public school salaries. The costs of religious teachers rose even more sharply with fewer sisters in each convent and with the mounting cost of retirement funds for religious communities. A 1972 Los Angeles study showed the average cost per sister ($5,962) to be greater than the U.S. average salary for lay teachers. The 1974 NCEA study of all-lay schools showed a per pupil cost of $420, only $100 above the comparable figure for the typical Catholic school (Elford and Harrington).

Unfinished Work. In 1977, efforts were made to provide for representation within the Church of Catholic teachers, both lay and religious, under Catholic leadership. The NCEA leadership quietly explored several possibilities. Meetings were held among Catholic school union officials to form a national association of Catholic school teachers, prompted largely by the vigorous opposition of the American Federation of Teachers to a bill providing tax credit for parents of private school students. Throughout the 1970s, in articles and workshops, Catholic educators advanced the concept of the school as a "faith community." The 1972 NCCB message on education placed community "at the heart of Christian education not simply as a concept to be taught but as a reality to be lived" (To Teach 23). Thus, in place of religious communities, Catholic schools were now to be staffed by "faith communities" made up of a few religious and a majority of lay members. The implications of this change and other aspects of the quiet transition from religious to lay staffing have not received sufficient attention. As late as 1978, the establishment of national or diocesan scholarship funds for the professional development of lay staff members, who do not enjoy the benefits of a supporting community, the development of effective channels for the representation of lay-teacher needs within the Church, and a clear formulation and affirmation of the ministry of Catholic school lay teachers and administrators remained on the agenda of unfinished business in Catholic education (*see* TEACHERS, MINISTRY OF).

Catholic Higher Education. Throughout the history of Catholic higher education in the United States, lay staff have played a large role resembling that of their counterparts in other private and public institutions. In higher education, lay staff have also increased in number and influence with the decline in numerical strength of religious communities. The increasing lay image of Catholic college and universities has occasioned a productive examination of the mission of the Catholic college and university (*see* HIGHER EDUCATION, CATHOLIC; HIGHER EDUCATION, CHURCH AND).

Bibliography: G. ELFORD and E. HARRINGTON, "All-Lay Catholic Schools: A Promising Alternative," *Momentum* (NCEA) 5 (Feb. 1974) 27–38. A. M. GREELY, W. C. MCCREADY, and K. MCCOURT, *Catholic Schools in a Declining Church* (Kansas City, Mo. 1976). M. J. LARKIN, "The Place of the Lay Teacher in Parish Schools," *NCEA Proceedings* 19 (1922) 234–239. NCCB, *To Teach as Jesus Did: A Pastoral Message on Catholic Education* (USCC Publ. Office Washington, D.C. 1972). NCEA, *A Report on U.S. Catholic Schools, 1970–71* (Washington, D.C. 1971); *Unionism in Catholic Schools—A Symposium* (Washington, D.C. 1976). R. A. NEUWIEN, *Catholic Schools in Action* (Notre Dame, Ind. 1976). H. J. O'DONNELL, "The Lay Teacher in Catholic Education," *Notre Dame Journal of Education* 2 (1971–72) 84–96.

[G. ELFORD]

TEACHERS, MINISTRY OF

Teaching within the framework of the Church has for many centuries been termed an apostolate or a vocation. In recent years, however, and with increasing frequency teaching has been described as a ministry. This article will consider whether teaching is indeed a genuine ministry or whether the term has been misapplied in an attempt to add dignity and support to today's teachers. The term's meaning and implications will also be considered.

Basis in Scripture. The actions of Jesus Christ strongly support the concept of teaching as ministry, for Christ began his own ministry by teaching, trained his followers as they accompanied him on his trips of teaching and other service, then sent them out as ministers with the command to "teach" (Mt 28.20). Christ's major task, as that of most of the founders of the world's great religions, was teaching. This would seem to indicate that teaching is one of the most basic forms of religious ministry.

Bearing in mind that the root meaning of "minister" is "servant" or "one who serves or cares for another," the words of Jesus support the basic concept of ministry: "Anyone among you who aspires to greatness must serve the rest; whoever wants to rank first among you must serve the needs of all. The Son of Man has not come to be served but to serve . . ." (Mk 10.43–45).

St. Paul refers to teaching as a specific form of service or ministry within the Church: "It is he [Christ] who gave apostles, prophets, evangelists, pastors, and teachers in roles of service for the faithful to build up the body of Christ . . ." (Eph 4.11–12); ". . . God has set up in the Church first apostles, second prophets, third teachers . . ." (1 Cor 12.28). Although these passages basically confirm the concept of teaching as ministry, one other text should be noted. In his letter to the Romans, Paul seems to indicate some distinction between ministry and teaching: "One's gift may be prophecy; its use should be in proportion to his faith. It may be the gift of ministry; it should be used for service.

One who is a teacher should use his gift for teaching . . ." (Rom 12.6–7).

The Concept through Church History. Teaching in the early Church usually occurred during informal gatherings, especially at the breaking of the bread. The teaching function belonged originally to disciples, then passed to those taught by the disciples. The role of teacher was not a formal office, but rather emerged from the practical needs of the community—much as the role of elder. In his extensive work, *Ministry to Word and Sacrament*, Bernard Cooke traces the concept: "Early Christianity had possessed a somewhat distinct ministry of teaching, but this was very rapidly absorbed (along with prophecy) into the episcopal function. At the time of Nicaea there is certainly no explicit prohibition of teaching by others than the bishops. But it seems to be increasingly taken for granted that teaching of the faith should be done within episcopally directed circumstances, which practically means that it is to be done by clerics" (Cooke 260). Through the years, views differed about whether the ministry of teaching belonged only to the clergy (e.g., Origen wanted to be ordained a presbyter so that he could teach, yet Clement taught with no apparent role in the official ecclesiastical structure).

Nevertheless, by the Middle Ages, the clerical role in education was dominant and the teaching ministry was identified with the priestly ministry. Although the humanist influence around 1500 secularized education, the Reformers in the following century returned the trend to a religious one. The end of the 18th century witnessed another movement away from church control—followed again by a reversal, a demand for education under religious auspices. The number of students to be taught at that time necessitated increasing the number of nonclerical teachers, usually through the service of religious orders. This movement to religious, coupled with the gradual increase of lay teachers since the 1950s, has reestablished a distinct ministry of teaching.

One of the most positive assessments of the teaching ministry appears in Henri Nouwen's *Creative Ministry*: "The most universal and most appreciated role of the Christian ministry through the ages has been teaching. Wherever Christians went to be of service, they always considered teaching as one of the primary tasks because of their conviction that increasing insight in man and his world is the way to new freedom and new ways of life" (Nouwen 3).

Teaching in Recent Church Documents. Just as the emphasis on a distinct ministry of teaching appears and disappears during the history of the Church, so too the use of the term in Church documents is somewhat irregular.

Documents of Vatican Council II. These clearly identify the formal teaching service with the clergy alone: "As successors of the apostles, bishops receive from him the mission to teach all nations and to preach the gospel to every creature, so that all men may attain to salvation . . . . Now, that duty, which the Lord committed to the shepherds of his people, is a true service, and in sacred literature is significantly called *diakonia* or ministry" (*Lumen gentium* 24).

The tone becomes a bit more open in the Declaration on Christian Education. First the Council stresses that teaching is a vocation as well as an occupation: "Beautiful, therefore, and truly solemn is the vocation of all those who assist parents in fulfilling their task, and who represent human society as well, by undertaking the role of school teacher" (*Gravissimum educationis* 5). Nevertheless, the document is very sparing with the concept of teaching as ministry. Only once, in a section on the Catholic school, is the phrase clearly stated: "This holy Synod asserts that the ministry of such teachers is a true apostolate which our times make extremely serviceable and necessary, and which simultaneously renders an authentic service to society" (ibid. 8).

NCCB Statements. In 1972 the United States Bishops issued *To Teach as Jesus Did*, a pastoral replete with references to teaching as ministry. The preface alone refers to education as ministry four times, and the pastoral itself habitually makes such statements as: "... Catholic elementary and secondary schools are the best expression of the educational ministry to youth" (To Teach 84); and "... religious education programs for Catholic students who do not attend Catholic schools are an essential part of the Church's total educational ministry ..." (ibid. 93).

The succeeding statement of the U.S. Bishops in 1976, *Teach Them*, again freely uses the ministry concept: "... we affirm our debt to these dedicated ministers of education, sisters, brothers, priests and lay people, who teach by what they are" (Teach Them 3). Moreover, the bishops in *Teach Them* clarify and broaden the list of participants in the ministry: "There has been increased recognition that all share in the educational ministry, not just those specifically assigned to 'teach religion'" (ibid. 4). In fact, the document refers to other specific groups involved in the educational ministry: parents, teachers, administrators, pastors and the community. (ibid. 6–8).

With this increasing use of the term in church documents, one could look for frequent references to the educational ministry in the 1977 statement from the Congregation for Catholic Education, *The Catholic School*. On the contrary, the document consistently avoids the term.

Recent church documents do not show a simple chronological development. The only pattern that seems to emerge is that Vatican sources tend to avoid references to teaching as ministry while the United States bishops freely use the term ministry to describe teaching and education.

Meaning and Implications. In the Church there is common agreement that whatever form ministry takes, it exists for the sake of the community as a whole (*see* MINISTRY [ECCLESIOLOGY]). For the teacher, this requires that the ministry be focused on others—the students, the school, and the broader community. For the educational minister, there can be no consideration of teaching as "only a job." As Jean Vanier phrases it, the teaching minister finds that formal teaching is only the beginning, an entry point, "a commitment to people, whatever may happen" (Vanier 67).

Focus on the person is the reason that the ministry of teaching has never limited itself to the teaching of religion. Henri Nouwen explains: "Education is not primarily ministry because of what is taught but because of the nature of the educational process itself. Perhaps we have paid too much attention to the content of teaching without realizing that the teaching relationship is the most important factor in the ministry of teaching" (Nouwen 3–4).

All four of the recent documents point out the necessity of the teachers' witnessing to their own faith in Christ, not only in word, but by their lives. For the educational minister three elements are essential: message, fellowship, and service (see, To Teach 14–32). The message cannot remain only verbal, but must overflow to one of Christian living and liturgy (cf. *Gravissimum educationis* 2, 4). Community, which is central to Christian education, is not only a concept to be taught, but also a reality to be lived—among faculty as well as students (ibid 12). With so many unique resources, educational ministers in the Church must offer service to others and to each other by ways imitative of Jesus Christ: concern for the weak and poor; use of some time for reassuring and being available—rather than only for direct teaching; extended hours of service; ability to see talents and to build on them; respect for the right of others to make choices.

The distinct ministry of teaching—evident in the early Church and in recent documents of the U.S. bishops—does seem to be a genuine ministry with a scriptural basis. To emphasize this fact—for teachers themselves as well as for the broader community—a variety of commissioning ceremonies and recommitment services has been initiated on local as well as diocesan levels. In 1978 the National Catholic Educational Association made available a medal for distribution to educational ministers. Such recognition and support can strengthen a continuing ministry of teaching in the Church.

Bibliography: Congregation for Catholic Education, *The Catholic School* (USCC Publ. Office, Washington, D.C. 1977). B. COOKE, *Ministry to Word and Sacrament* (Philadelphia 1976). NCCB, *To Teach as Jesus Did* (USCC Publ. Office, Washington, D.C. 1972); *Teach Them* (USCC Publ. Office, Washington, D.C. 1976). H. J. M. NOUWEN, *Creative Ministry* (New York 1971). J. VANIER, *Be Not Afraid* (New York 1975).

[C. J. RECK]

TEACHERS' UNIONS, CATHOLIC

In the mid-1960s, a new phenomenon began to attract the attention of Catholic school administrators and the church hierarchy. With the increasing number of lay teachers entering Catholic-school classrooms, there was a growing awareness by these teachers of the need for status, security, improved benefits, and upgraded conditions of employment. Lay teachers began to group together and led to the formation of Teacher Organizations, whose goals included recognition and collective bargaining to achieve teacher needs. These organizations were, in reality, unions.

Origins and Litigation. The first such union was the Association of Catholic Teachers, begun in Philadelphia in 1966, and which, in April 1967, had staged the first system-wide strike by a group of Catholic lay teachers in the history of the United States. Since then, the number of Catholic teacher organizations has grown so that some form of collective bargaining can be found in over twenty dioceses. The union movement, although strongest in those dioceses with a well-established system of diocesan high schools, has moved into elementary schools and single schools in many locations throughout the country.

The movement of lay teachers toward organizations to represent them in dealings with their employers has not been without problems and as Monsignor George G. Higgins warned, it is approaching a public scandal in some diocesan sectors. Teachers accepting the Church's teachings on the right to organize, to select representatives of their own choosing, and to bargain collectively, were astounded to learn that these basic rights, long taught by the Church, did not apply to them when the Church was the employer. Teachers found diocesan officials thwarting and frustrating efforts to organize, even resorting to the firing of teachers for union activity. The National Labor Relations Board (NLRB) eventually found the Los Angeles and Gary, Ind. dioceses guilty of unfair labor practices in this area.

Since 1975, lay teachers in Chicago, Gary, Ft. Wayne, Los Angeles, and in the Philadelphia elementary schools have approached diocesan officials on the question of representation and have been denied this right. The Teachers Organizations then sought relief in the civil sector by petitioning NLRB. The findings of NLRB upheld the right of lay teachers to select representatives of their own choosing, by secret ballot election, for the purpose of engaging in collective bargaining. In the dioceses involved, the Church then instituted litigation in Federal court on the question of NLRB jurisdiction in Catholic schools. The Church views the intervention of the NLRB as entanglement of the State in the affairs of the Church, and a violation of the first Amendment to the U.S. Constitution. Teacher-union leaders, on the other hand, maintain that the issues are: the refusal of diocesan officials to recognize the rights of workers to organize and the necessity of protecting these rights under civil law, since diocesan officials refuse meaningful representation to their employees.

In all cases presently before the Courts on the question of NLRB jurisdiction in Catholic schools, it should be noted that teacher representatives first approached their diocesan officials and requested recognition. Only after they were refused did they seek assistance under civil statutes through the NLRB. The precedent for recourse to NLRB was established by lay teachers for Baltimore, who in 1975 successfully petitioned for and won a NLRB-run election. They were certified as the exclusive bargaining agent and negotiated a collective bargaining agreement without the diocese's raising any constitutional issues.

USCC Recognition. As teachers became more frustrated in their efforts to gain recognition, unrest grew and relations became more acrimonious. The question of Catholic Teacher Organizations was finally addressed by the American hierarchy in 1977. A Subcommittee of the United States Catholic Conference was created to explore the area of Teacher Organizations in Catholic schools. The Subcommittee met with groups and individuals involved in Catholic schools and lay-teacher organizations. They used as a guideline a Working Paper which concerned itself with the subject of collective bargaining and Teacher Organizations. On March 31, 1977 leaders of the lay teachers met with members of the Subcommittee in Chicago. For the first time, a representative national group of teacher leaders had the opportunity for an open and candid discussion with a Subcommittee representing the country's bishops.

On Sept. 15, 1977, the Subcommittee released its report. Among its findings:

The teacher-union question is a manageable one for the Catholic community.

Although experience to date has at times been characterized as acrimonious and contentious . . . the Subcommittee has noted on all sides reservoirs of good will and concern which, if tapped and given the benefit of good communication, will result in a meaningful realization or restoration of such a community.

The . . . question of the relationship of government to Catholic-school management is capable ultimately of a solution which will be satisfactory to all concerned parties (USCC Subcommittee 8).

In spite of the Subcommittee's report, which seems to offer at least the basis for dialogue, coupled with public statements by teacher leaders requesting good-will discussions based on the social-justice teachings of the Church, there has been little or no movement by church officials in many dioceses.

At the present time, the resolution of the NLRB issue lies in the hands of the United States Supreme Court which on October 30, 1978, heard oral arguments on an appeal of a Seventh Circuit Court decision concerning whether the NLRB has jurisdiction over lay teachers in Catholic schools of the Chicago and Fort Wayne-South Bend dioceses. The remarks made by the attorney representing the Catholic archbishop of Chicago once again point to the plight of lay teachers employed by Catholic schools. The attorney emphasized that the Minimum Wage Law should not apply to lay teachers in religious schools. He further stated that because lay teachers are subject to the Ordinary of the diocese, who has absolute and final say over them as employees, they should not be covered by the NLRB, even though the same NLRB has every right to organize the maintenance staff in the same schools.

The issue has become more exacerbated through statements during the November 1978 NCCB meeting in Washington on resistance by church officials against so-called government intrusion into Catholic schools in the areas of unemployment compensation and the right of teachers to organize because they work in Catholic schools. Bishop William McManus of Fort Wayne-South Bend, Ind., Chairman of the USCC Education Committee, defended some government intervention in church institutions by pointing out that as far as he knew, none of the Catholic school teachers were covered by unemployment compensation until the whole controversy arose. The bishop remarked that the situation seemed to amount to a claim of exemption from the Church's own social teaching. Bishop McManus also stated that when the USCC Subcommittee asked unions of teachers in Catholic schools why they became involved with the NLRB, the usual answer was that they could not bargain with their employers and so had to appeal to the NLRB.

The controversy continues on whether the Church's teaching on social justice applies to teachers in Catholic schools. The U.S. Supreme Court decision, however it is resolved, will not settle the problems in this complex area. The final resolution will come about only when both parties are willing to discuss the problems in an open and honest manner using the social teachings of the Church as a foundation.

Bibliography: G. C. HIGGINS, "Teacher Unions," *The Catholic Standard* (Washington, D.C. Oct. 21, 1976). USCC Subcommittee on Teacher Organizations, *Teacher Organizations in Catholic Schools* (Washington, D.C. 1977).

[J. J. REILLY]

TEACHING AUTHORITY OF THE CHURCH (MAGISTERIUM)

Vatican Council II briefly outlined the Catholic Church's position on the teaching authority of the

Church (*Lumen gentium* 25). That position, exposed and developed in the original article in the *New Catholic Encyclopedia* (13:959) remains substantially the same. Within the community of faith and witness, which lives by and is sent to proclaim the Gospel of salvation revealed and realized in Jesus Christ, God's definitive self-communication and gift, there exists a stable, authoritative, and, in specific circumstances, infallible ministry of the Word, first committed to the Apostles, and now possessed and exercised by their legitimate successors, the college of bishops in communion with the pope. As the official leaders of the Church, they have both the right and the obligation to speak with juridical authority in the name of the Church, proclaiming and teaching the Church's present understanding of the faith. Their pastoral oversight and authority in matters of doctrine extends to all the members of the Church, not excluding the professional theologian.

However, the concrete situation has changed considerably since Vatican II, and there has been a great deal of theological reflection and debate on questions that seriously concern and affect the understanding and exercise of the teaching authority of the Church. Much of this was put in motion or at least occasioned by Vatican II itself, though subsequent events, in particular the birth control debate subsequent upon Paul VI's encyclical *Humanae vitae* (1968), the continuing ecumenical dialogue with other Churches, and the general climate of the times have had their influence on the issues involved. The theological discussion regarding the meaning, nature, and scope of *infallibility is a central issue. In the context of the dialogue with other Churches, considerable research and theological reflection have been done concerning the origins and continuation of the apostolic ministry (*see* APOSTOLIC SUCCESSION; COLLEGIALITY). This issue is vital to the Catholic understanding of the teaching authority of the Church, but is not treated here *ex professo*. Attention will rather be focused primarily on the concrete situation and theological positions regarding the role and function of the magisterium within the community, its relationship to the other members of the Church, especially theologians, and the related issue of obedience to and dissent from official teaching.

Dissent since Vatican II. In the era preceding Vatican II, the Church in its theology, structures, and practice was almost exclusively hierarchically centered. The term "magisterium" bore reference exclusively to members of the hierarchy. Absolute and unquestioning obedience to their teaching, whether definitively and infallibly taught or not (few Catholics thought of making any distinction) was looked upon as the hallmark of the Catholic. The primary, if not exclusive, role of the professional theologian was seen as that of defending and explaining the teaching of the official magisterium; theological debate was confined to questions to which the magisterium had not yet addressed itself.

The current situation is in several respects quite different. No longer a serenely monolithic, hierarchically centered Church in self-assured possession of the truth, the present-day Church often appears to be uncertain of itself, torn by conflict and distrust, especially in the relationship between the hierarchy and theologians. Respectful dissent from official teaching is seen by many as a legitimate Catholic stance, at least when the teaching is not proposed as definitive. Some theologians feel free to question present official teaching in several areas and to present positions at variance with that teaching. It is also questioned whether the bishops are the only authentic teachers in the Church. Pluralism in theological thought makes it quite difficult to discern whether a particular theological position is at variance with Revelation and hence the hierarchy tends to exercise great caution in repudiating or condemning theological positions.

Towards an Ecclesiology of the Magisterium. Any evaluation of the present situation will necessarily depend upon the evaluator's theological position. There are several models of the Church that can serve as the focal point of a particular ecclesiology and the consequent understanding of the teaching authority. In a balanced approach, these models are seen to be mutually complementary rather than contradictory, yet in each the stress on specific issues is quite different (*see* CHURCH [THEOLOGY]). The theology of the magisterium that has held sway for the past 150 years is based on the model of the Church as a hierarchical society with a strong, almost exclusive, emphasis on juridical structures and authority. While acknowledging the central affirmations so strongly emphasized in this theology, many theologians, using other models, would maintain that other factors must be emphasized today in order to work toward a more balanced theology of the magisterium, and so to a more effective exercise of teaching authority in the Church. Some of these factors are briefly outlined here.

The Word of God and Its Formulations. The Church, and within the Church all teaching authority, is entirely relative to and in the service of the Revelation committed to the Church; the authority of the Word is absolute (cf. *Dei Verbum* 10). Emphasis on the *juridical* authority which proclaims the Word (a development that began only in the Middle Ages) can lead to an obscuring of this fact. One unfortunate result can be that greater emphasis is placed on the juridical aspect (e.g., whether a particular teaching has been solemnly defined) than on the value of the teaching itself (e.g. whether it is an adequate or balanced presentation of the truth; whether it can be understood today or needs reformulation).

All the Church's formulations of its faith (even its solemn definitions) are reformable in the sense that they are time-bound, human expressions of the faith, couched in the thought forms and theology of a particular culture or time, and hence always inadequate and subject to development. It is imperative that the Church constantly rethink its past teaching and address itself to present problems and challenges. While this is true even of definitive teaching, it is especially so of ordinary pastoral teaching that may be seriously defective. It is recognized that this task falls mainly upon theologians with scholarly competence.

Responsibility of the Theologian. To exercise this function adequately the theologian must have a deep awareness of his responsibility toward the official magisterium and the whole Church, and remember that he, too, is only a servant of the Word. He must also be assured of the confidence and cooperation of the bishops and be granted responsible freedom to pursue his research and propose his findings, even when they seem to conflict with official teaching. Though the bishops have the right and responsibility to oversee the teaching of the Church's scholars, this should be done with a clear awareness of the complexity and difficulty of the questions raised. A thesis that appears to be in contradiction to Revelation when judged from the viewpoint of one particular theology may in fact not be so. The complexity and difficulty is especially acute today when a pluralism in theological thought is becoming more of a reality (*see* PLURALISM, THEOLOGICAL) and the emerging Churches in non-Western cultural situations are seeking to express the Gospel in the thought forms of their own culture (*see* INCULTURATION, THEOLOGICAL). In this situation theologians must be aware of their special responsibility to challenge and question their peers, and not leave this to the bishops, who are often not competent to do so.

Teachers in the Church. Discussion of the role of theologians leads to the question: who are the teachers of the Church? Those who propose as basic model of the Church that of a hierarchical society would maintain that only those who have *juridical* authority are the teaching authority of the Church commissioned by Christ through the Apostles. Others may be associated with the bishops in carrying out their teaching office, but they participate in the magisterium only in a derivative way. This position is challenged today. Recent studies tend to show that it would be difficult to establish from Scripture and tradition that the bishops were always the only acknowledged teachers in the Church. The association of the magisterium with the bishops alone is of rather recent origin. In the early Councils theologians who were not bishops fully participated and would seem to have had a deliberative voice in the conciliar teachings.

Thus, it is proposed that there is no sharp distinction between the teaching and believing Church (*ecclesia docens et ecclesia discens*): all believers share in some way in proclaiming and teaching the faith; all are in some way both teachers and taught. Within the community, however, there are special gifts and ministries, each with its role. Of special importance is the stable pastoral ministry of the Word given to the bishops and the pope (with whom are associated the priests and deacons). As the commissioned leaders of the Church, a community of faith, they have the pastoral responsibility of guarding and teaching Revelation, and of officially expressing the Church's living faith in doctrinal statements. Theologians, however, are also teachers in the Church, not by virtue of a special commission, but because of their scholarly competence. Their role is also indispensable. Like any other member of the community, they receive from the bishops, and owe allegiance to, the Church's credal formulations and official teachings. Yet they also have a vital role to play in doctrinal formulations, as well as in the further understanding and development (including revision) of doctrinal formulas. Though conflict and tensions are apt to persist between bishops and theologians, the ideal to be worked toward is one of mutual respect and cooperation, each seeking to safeguard the other's responsibility and competence. This cooperation does not rule out responsible dissent by theologians from official teaching, in fact in specific circumstances it may be demanded, provided there is present throughout openness and readiness to understand and accept the teaching proposed by the bishops.

In carrying out its mission, the Church rests its confidence in the guidance and assistance of the Spirit promised by Christ. The guidance of the Spirit is promised in a special way to those who have a teaching function in the Church, first to the bishops and pope, but not excluding theologians and others. Yet all, bishops and theologians alike, need constantly to recall that the Spirit demands the docility and cooperation of those to whom he is sent. The efficacy, indeed the authority, of any teaching depends in great measure on the degree in which it is truly a teaching "in the Spirit." The teacher who in any way closes himself to the action of the Spirit, wherever that may be present, is failing in his responsibility as teacher in the service of the living Word.

Bibliography: R. BROWN, "Bishops and Theologians: 'Dispute' Surrounded by Fiction," Origins 7 (1978) 675–682. Y. CONGAR, "Pour une histoire sémantique du terme 'magisterium'"; "Bref historique des formes du 'magistère' et de ses relations avec les docteurs," RevScPhilTh 60 (1976) 85–112. A. L. DESCAMPS, "Théologie et magistère," EphemThLov 56 (1976) 82–133. A. DULLES, "What is Magisterium," Origins 6 (1976) 81–87. International Theological Commission, *Theses on the Relationship between the Ecclesiastical Magisterium and Theology* (USCC Publ. Office, Washington, D.C. 1977). R. MCCORMICK, "Notes on Moral Theology: 1976," ThSt 38 (1977) 84–100; "The Teaching of the Magisterium and Theologians," CathThSoc 24 (1969) 239–254.

[J. R. LERCH]

TEAM MINISTRY

Team ministry may be defined in various ways. From an organizational viewpoint, it describes a ministerial group who share equally pastoral responsibilities and authority. From a theological viewpoint, it refers to a core Gospel community who invite and foster renewed ecclesial commitment from the larger community they serve. In its make-up, team ministry can comprise priests alone or priests, religious, and laity; in either case the members are united by their shared work and, sometimes, by their communal life. Historically, pioneer team ministries, like that of St. Séverin in Paris, often adopted communal life styles based on models of religious life even though the members were diocesan priests. Many teams have evolved from being clerical to becoming a mixed group, some also sharing communal life.

Theological Import. To speak of team ministry only in organizational terms is to rob it of its theological meaning and pastoral symbolic value. The whole thrust of pastoral ministry is ecclesial and eschatological. The ecclesial concern of ministry is to build a credible church community that constantly renews itself by the way it evokes the charisms of all its members. This involves a growing eschatological responsibility for building the Kingdom. Such complementary concerns restore a scriptural sense of salvation, rooted in the shared redemptive needs of the world as well as those of the individual.

Given such a twofold task, team ministry must, first of all, be a model of what it proclaims: a core community shaped by Gospel values and concerns. Such a disciple community provides the necessary and challenging symbol of Gospel commitment constantly renewed. For it is not only sociologically but theologically true that the characteristic of a healthy religious community is renewed commitment. Team ministry must be tested by its ability to evoke such commitment from its own members and thus be a credible symbol to the larger Christian community. Otherwise, an organizational model may be substituting for the disciple-community model that is typical of the development of ministries in both the apostolic and subapostolic Church.

All of this suggests that a team ministry must share more than work-goals and problem-solving. Team ministry must include some type of shared life in which communal prayer and a dynamic for deepening commitment are priorities. If such values are respected, they provide a viable and flexible model for the larger church community, whether that be traditional, modular, or a variant of these.

Psychosocial Corollaries. There seems to be a correlation in the sparse testing done (e.g., the Hartford Study) between team effectiveness and ministerial effectiveness. Among the factors influencing team success are the self-image of its members, as affected by their work-role, and actively, communally-shared religious values. Although there is not enough hard data to permit categorical statements, experience suggests that satisfactory work-role achievement alone will not be sufficient for a more congruent self-image. Shared religious values do assure ongoing challenge to conversion and ecclesial responsibility for personal giftedness. Team success, then, would be best tested where satisfying ministerial work is constantly redefined by deepening religious and interpersonal values shared and challenged within a team. This would not only ensure renewable organizational structures of ministry but credible and communicable proclamation of Gospel conversion from the shared experience of the ministering team.

Bibliography: CARA Study, "Team Ministry/The Hartford Model," Origins 5 (1975) 193–202 with bibliography. D. DONNELLY, *Team: Theory and Practice of Team Ministry* (New York 1977). R. DUFFY, "A Test for Communitas: Team Ministry," *Worship* (1974) 566–579. B. THOMAS, "Corporate Ministry: A Reflection," ChSt 16 (1977) 213–217.

[R. A. DUFFY]

TECHNOLOGY, SOCIAL EFFECTS OF

A consistent, underlying theme of Vatican Council II is the importance of considering the specific qualities of culture and society shaping the contemporary world in its uniqueness. The Council directed its considerations to the concrete world of the 20th century, not to some abstract world without specific temporal definition. The concentration on this particular moment in space and time was to assure a proper understanding and embodiment of the reality of the Christian God who is appreciated as One who is immanent in transcendence, incarnate in divinity. The Lord is now present to and active in this world with all its uniqueness and particularities. The Constitution on the Church in the Modern World describes the present moment in human history as one profoundly unique in both social and cultural dimensions, so much so that one can speak of "a new age in human history" (*Gaudium et spes* 54). The range of change which brought about this new era is so pervasive that the Council admits that culture has taken a new form which in turn creates new ways of thinking and acting. To be a vital presence and force in this new context, the Church must understand this new situation and express its life in accordance with the dynamics of this new cultural setting.

Specific reference is made (ibid.) to the developments in modern technology because of its central influence on patterns of thought and action. Human thinking is more and more in the form of a "technological mentality," a way of thinking that emphasizes analysis, planning, the use of specific techniques and, above all, the control of all the components in the situation. Besides the mind-set which dominates a technological society, there are also the tangible results of that thinking in certain systems of operation and in the products created by research, planning, and production. From a religious point of view, the total range of technology deserves serious consideration and critical evaluation in terms of whether it enhances or detracts from the realization of the Kingdom of God on earth.

Impact of the Technological Mentality. This assessment takes on decided critical importance when the investigation concerns the effect of a particular aspect of technology on the human person. The technological mentality tends, for instance, to approach the human as object, number, an element of a process, a mere part of a material whole. If the human subject is reduced to the lesser proportions of object, if the sacred dignity of each person is judged worthwhile only to the extent that it contributes to some desired goal, then something God-given and essential is lost.

A further area of concern is the potential modification of the biological substratum of the human person through the rearrangement of the basic components of the living organism. Needed for this kind of assessment is an open and knowledgeable discussion between theologians, scientists, and informed citizens as to the ramifications of that kind of technological modification. In general, what is becoming clear with the profundity and rapidness of technological changes is that the possibilities for both good and evil are enhanced with the passage of time. Teilhard de Chardin pointed to this enhancement in his reflections on developments in science and technology. The harnessing of nuclear energy clearly gives evidence of the heightened ambivalence inherent in much of contemporary technology.

A more developed technology can be appreciated as incremental to the human ability to accomplish desires and plans effectively. The contemporary phenomenon of energy-consciousness brings to mind the dependence on energy sources outside ourselves that are needed in order to survive in the contemporary world. With more energy at their disposal, people can accomplish more, are more freed from a certain type of limitation. Their work can be done in more suitable surroundings. The products created can be mass-produced, thus making them potentially available to a greater number of users.

Perhaps in no other area has the impact of modern technology been more felt than in that of communication and travel. People have been brought closer together in a spatial sense which creates at least the possibility of a greater sense of community and an appreciation of the commonness of humanity throughout the earth. Of itself, technology does not create interpersonal closeness but it helps to create the conditions out of which real community can be established.

Yet the ambivalence of modern technology can be shown in referring to how technology makes people more self-sufficient, more able to accomplish their goals by themselves. They can travel alone in automobiles, be entertained in the privacy of their own dwellings by their own media center. Food can be prepared without outside assistance. It might be argued that modern technology has contributed to the ironic situation that people live in a time when community is facilitated by many inventions, yet persons feel quite alone and alienated from their sisters and brothers.

Impact of Technological Products. Much the same can be said about the products of technology. With a general expectation that all persons could benefit from possession of these products, many, in fact, do not. This raises questions of social justice, particularly with reference to the equitable distribution of goods and services. Part of the prophetic role of the Church is to alert its members and the world at large as to violations in the area of social justice. As life in the world becomes more dependent on the products of technology, sensitivity to availability and distributions becomes more a moral issue.

As humanity grows more dependent on and enamored of its technological might, it can tend to assume a practical autonomy from any other sources of energy outside itself and its tools. The need for God is eclipsed or considered meaningless because the areas of health, wealth, and happiness are now dominated by human creations. While this result is not at all mandated by an expanding technology, it must be admitted that many areas once of religious concern are now under the influence of a more effective technology.

Implied in the general cultural changes that accompany an ever-expansive technology is a requirement, therefore, that the proper range of religious interests be reexamined. Technological developments of the last century have given a new shape to the world, but it need not be said that the world is necessarily Godless. It can be argued that the extension of human ingenuity into ever-more effective technologies is part of the God-given human capacity to further bring the world into the dynamics of life in the Kingdom of God. This can be particularly so when the results of technology are a more successful feeding of the hungry, sheltering of the homeless, or implanting of knowledge where ignorance formerly held sway. The perception brought forward in *Gaudium et spes* was that a careful distinction should be made between human progress and the realization of the Kingdom of God (39). Nevertheless, where human progress serves "to a better ordering of human society," the concerns of the Kingdom are being realized. The world is given to humanity by God as a trust. Like good stewards humans must respect the wishes of the owner while at the same time using whatever resources there are to extend the love of God into the perfecting of the world for the enrichment of the human spirit and in the service of our common humanity.

Bibliography: I. G. BARBOUR, *Science and Secularity: The Ethics of Technology* (New York 1970). D. CALLAHAN, *The Tyranny of Survival* (New York 1973). L. GILKEY, *Religion and the Scientific Future* (New York 1970). B. MILLER, *Religion in a Technical Age* (Cambridge, Mass. 1978). G. VAHANIAN, *God and Utopia: The Church in a Technological Civilization* (New York 1977).

[D. M. THOMAS]

TECHNOLOGY, TRANSFER OF

Technology is practical knowledge systematically applied with a view to gaining control over nature and over human processes of every kind. It is, for the most part, derived from scientific knowledge and its usefulness in producing an object, facilitating a process, or organizing a task has been tested. Technology is, obviously, a precious resource with which to create new wealth. In 1970 U Thant, then Secretary-General of the United Nations, called technology the single most important resource for development. Many questions must be asked, however, before one assumes that technology can abolish human misery.

Can technology "deliver" on its implicit promise to bring development to Third World countries? Is modern technology truly the key to successful development, or must its basic assumptions about the advantages of large scale be challenged in the light of E. F. Schumacher's philosophy of "small is beautiful"? Can technologies, whether they are concretely embodied in products, processes, or the minds of expert consultants be "transferred" from one cultural setting to another in ways which are more beneficial than destructive? Finally, does not the very term "technology transfer" erroneously imply that technology, like science, is the common patrimony of humankind and can circulate internationally as a free good?

The Control of Technology. According to one UN estimate, 98 per cent of industrial technology produced outside the socialist countries is generated in Research and Development (R & D) laboratories controlled by the rich, developed countries and only 2 per cent in developing countries. Technology is an expensive commodity and it is not so much "transferred" internationally as sold at high prices in highly competitive markets. Lord Ritchie-Calder explains why the advantages supposedly accruing to latecomers in the arena of technology transfer may be illusory:

> It is true that one does not have to re-invent the wheel in order to ride a bicycle. It is true that each country that undertakes the modernization of its economy relies partly on the heritage of others. It is also true that there is a great deal of knowledge and know-how freely available for transmission from one country to another, but many of the less developed countries do not know how to go shopping in the supermarket of science (Nobel Laureate Patrick Blackett's phrase) nor how to get the free samples or generally available technology. The term "transfer" in this sense is a euphemism because technology and know-how is being bought and sold like a commodity, but there is no world market nor a world exchange nor world prices for technology. The "latecomers" in this case are like spectators arriving at the last moment at a cup final and having to buy tickets from speculators at excessive prices (Ritchie-Calder 11).

Some technologies are transferred across national boundaries thanks to a subsidy from a development agency like the International Bank for Reconstruction and Development (*World Bank) or the United Nations. Even in these cases, however, technology does not circulate free of charge; its cost is simply paid by some third party rather than by the purchaser.

Because it is a powerful weapon in marketing strategy, technology confers a strong competitive edge on those who own it. In general, those who supply technology (*multinational corporations, consultant firms, governmental agencies, international technical bodies, universities, research associations) to firms or governments in "less-developed" countries (LDCs) are reluctant to relinquish control over the source of technological creation, the R & D laboratory. The most profitable technology is the ability to generate new technology; indeed, a laboratory is a factory to produce new technology.

The Developing Nations. LDC leaders criticize prevailing modes of technology transfer on four grounds: their countries do not enjoy full access to the whole range of available technologies—pricing structures are unfair and discriminatory—technology is often sold as part of a "package deal" which obliges purchasers to acquire materials and services along with the technology, thereby impeding the optimum use of local resources, and—patterns of dependency are reinforced. The best way to devise an acceptable technology policy is to create a "vital nexus" which links preferred social values to specific development strategies, to criteria for adopting different scales and modes of technological application. When this nexus is absent, many technological decisions will prove incompatible with broader development objectives and impose undue value sacrifices on the societies making them. This is why Third World technology policies ought to include efforts to regulate the importation of technology, to encourage new local suppliers, to engage in concerted action among LDCs (the United Nations does this largely through its TCDC program—Technical Cooperation Among Developing Countries), and political pressure to change existing international patent and licensing agreements. Recent years have witnessed growing demands for the international acceptance of a Code of Conduct for Technology Transfers.

There is no simple way to reconcile the conflicting values and interests that are at play. Technology is not only a resource, but also a powerful instrument used by its creators to exercise social control. Even as it helps solve problems, it exacts high social and human costs. In an increasingly interdependent world, technology will continue to be "transferred" or to circulate across national borders. The basic issue is to conduct such "transfers" in ways that promote sound development and keep human costs down. Technology is a two-edged sword, simultaneously the creator and destroyer of values. Can its circulation help meet priority human needs, and enable non-expert communities to gain control over the social processes that affect their lives? These are key issues in the conflict-laden arena of technology transfers.

See also DEVELOPING NATIONS; NEW INTERNATIONAL ECONOMIC ORDER.

Bibliography: W. A. CHUDSON, *The International Transfer of Commercial Technology to Developing Countries* (New York, United Nations Institute for Training and Research, 1971). P. F. GONOD, *Clés pour le transfert technologique* (Washington, D.C., Economic Development Institute, International Bank for Reconstruction and Development, 1974). D. GOULET, "The Paradox of Technology Transfer," *Bulletin of the Atomic Scientists* 31 n. 6 (June 1975) 39–46; *The Uncertain Promise: Value Conflicts in Technology Transfer* (New York 1977). E. P. HAWTHORNE, *The Transfer of Technology* (Paris, Organization for Economic Co-operation and Development, 1971). LORD RITCHIE-CALDER, *Report on the Role of Modern Science and Technology in the Development of Nations* (New York, UN Document E/5238/Add 1 Jan. 23, 1973). E. F. SCHUMACHER, *Small is Beautiful: Economics as if People Mattered* (New York 1973).

[D. GOULET]

TEMPORAL VALUES

The Roman Catholic Church has a long tradition of natural law which recognizes both the inherent value of humanity and the concrete expression of this humanity in temporal forms. This tradition also provided a theoretical basis for Christian involvement in the world. There tended to be, however, a twofold division of reality which sharply disjoined the natural from the supernatural order. Because the natural realm was viewed as not in continuity with the supernatural, there arose an unfortunate dichotomy between the order of creation and the order of redemption. For instance, it was not sufficiently appreciated that people truly experience grace through natural human experience.

Vatican Council II's Constitution on the Church in the Modern World reflects a notable shift in the understanding of natural law. The Council Fathers state: "Nothing that is genuinely human fails to find an echo in the heart of the followers of Christ" (*Gaudium et spes* 1). Human experience, then, is not impervious to the reality of grace. Christian truth, saving truth, is not something opposed to, or even apart from, human truth and human values. There is only one order in which Christians can work out their salvation and, "the mission of the Church will show itself to be supremely human by the very fact of being religious" (ibid. 11). Since "the things of the world and the things of faith derive from the same God" (ibid. 36), the Christian life is open to all truly human values. So convinced were the Council Fathers of the interrelation between faith and the world, they claimed that to neglect temporal duties is to neglect God and to put salvation in jeopardy (ibid. 43). Christians, then, must integrate aesthetic, domestic, professional, scientific, and technical enterprises with religious values.

The Church recognizes a rightful autonomy to earthly affairs, as well as a reciprocity between the world and itself. On the one hand, the Church can contribute much to humanizing the world; on the other hand, the Church receives considerable and varied help from the world in preparing the ground for the Gospel (ibid. 40).

Contemporary theology overcomes the dichotomy between faith and daily life by insisting on the deeply human meaning of Christianity: the transcendent God is present in all areas of human value; God's grace pervades the entire fabric of human life; indeed, the Christian message provides incentive for building up the world. Contemporary movements in defense of the human person—for instance, to eliminate racial, sexual and economic oppression—can be firmly rooted in the Christian affirmation of the dignity of the human person. Such activity on behalf of the human family transforms society and fulfills those who develop and transcend themselves in the process (ibid. 35).

The acknowledgment of the deep significance of human activity on behalf of humankind need not entail a naive acceptance of everything about the world as salvific and good. The world has been redeemed, but it does and always will suffer from the limitations of its own finitude and sinfulness. For that reason, Christians and all persons of good will must strive to realize the Kingdom ever more perfectly, i.e., humanly (ibid. 37).

See also HOPE, THEOLOGY OF; PROGRESS.

[A. NEALE]

TERRORISM, POLITICAL

Terrorism is a systematic use of violence and coercive intimidation as an established policy intended to strike with fright, intense fear, or dread those against whom it is directed. In this sense, many forms of violence of group against group could be classified as terrorism, e.g., when during a labor dispute in a modern industrialized society, hoodlums succeed in dominating the scene by their intimidations and force. Acts of intimidation, or even murders, in such cases are violations of law and the perpetrators, if caught, are brought to court to be tried, since in the eyes of authorities and populace alike, they have committed crimes against society. Immediate economic gain is the motive for such crimes. Banditry in the countryside during earlier centuries and organized crime in modern cities are other examples of people practicing widespread coercion and intimidation to gain economic rewards.

Political terrorism, however, is perpetrated for an idea or a cause not for the financial gain of the individual revolutionary. Political terrorism becomes the ultimate and often desperate form of conflict between opposing *Weltanschauungs* or philosophies of life. In this kind of terrorism the individual person matters not as an individual, but only as one identified and affiliated with a group or social segment. Terrorism enters the political scene for the first time in the past century when revolutionary groups resorted to terror in their struggle against absolutist rule because of impatience with more reasonable but slower and sometimes corrupt democratic processes.

Regimes of Terrorism. Political terrorism can be exercised by the party or group in power as well as by the group attempting to acquire it. The first case is a "reign of terror," a government maintaining itself in power by intimidation and force. The Reign of Terror describes the period of the French Revolution from June 2, 1793, when the Jacobins came to power, to the execution of Maximilien Robespierre and his closest collaborators on July 23, 1794. At the instigation of the Jacobins, the National Convention decreed terror as the policy of government. The Red Terror was later followed by the White Terror, the period of royalist reprisals during the Second Restoration under Louis XVIII (1815–18). In 20th-century Russia, after the seizure of power by the Soviets, the Bolsheviks also established terror as the policy of government during the period of "War Communism," and the same happened under Stalin. In parts of the world dictatorial regimes continue to maintain power through terrorism.

Terrorism against Governments. If a regime of violence can be instituted by ruthless governments, so too a dedicated group of people can resort to terror in an attempt to challenge the established authority. The second half of the last century and the turn of this century offer many instances of this kind of political terrorism. In the Balkans, the *komitadji* were the most dreadful; in Italy the *carbonari*, the most active (and romanticized). In the rest of Western Europe terrorists were called "anarchists" and in Russia, "nihilists." Because of the antipathy of anarchists to organization and the discipline required for a systematic planning of prolonged terrorism, the anarchists practiced individual terrorism by sporadic acts of political assassination.

The two main intellectual pillars of anarchism, Pierre Proudhon (1809–65) and Prince Michael Bakunin (1814–76) were both staunch advocates of terror. Together with another Russian terrorist, Nechayev, Bakunin wrote a handbook on terrorism, "The Revolutionary Catechism," and organized a secret society of terrorists with the task of putting into practice his teachings. Whatever their name, such terrorists believed their way to be the only available option; their preferred method consisted of attempts on the lives of prominent governmental personages. Central Europe was the least affected by terrorism, Russia the most. First, there was *Zemlya i Volya* (Land and Will), a secret organization of the 1860s and 1870s, and later the *Narodnaya Volya* (Will of the People) that organized some of the most spectacular acts of terrorism, the greatest in 1881, the killing of Czar Alexander II. After that the *narodniki*, as they came to be known, increased their terrorist activities but were replaced by the Marxists with the coming of revolution.

In the U.S., anarchists committed various terrorist acts; among them the assassination of President William McKinley. Emma Goldman, Johan Most, and Herbert Marcuse (born in Germany) were the best known American advocates and theoreticians of anarchism. In the period between the two World Wars, political terrorism continued, but with less glamor, and was restricted to specific national areas, e.g., the Sinn Feiners (1919–21) in Ireland for the cause of unification and independence from the British, or the terrorism bordering on war in Armenia.

Current Transnational Terrorism. Following World War II, political terrorism renewed in intensity and during the 1960s drew world attention. In 1970 political terrorism became transnational in its dimension and perspective. Among its present day forms, one is a continuation of the terrorism familiar from the past. Terror tactics in Palestine and Northern Ireland have a clear objective: nationalism and independence. But a new kind of terrorist is emerging in some Latin American countries, like Argentina and Uruguay, and in the democracies of Western Europe, particularly in West Germany and Italy.

Here the terrorists seem to lack definite and coherent ideological or political purpose. For the new breed of terrorists, recruited from alienated youth who join radical underground groups of the left (and sometimes of the right), violence itself is the end, not the means. Terror is, as it were, deified and the terrorists become its worshipers. For the terrorists of the "Weatherman" organization in the U.S. or of the Baader-Meinhof type in Germany there is no political theory to guide them, no vision for a better future. Even when they talk vaguely of socialism, it is not known what they really mean since they themselves do no know or do not consider it important to have clear ideas. What matters is the terror. They are bent on destruction of the existing systems and not on the construction of a new one. The common bond is the "politics of hatred," hatred of Judaeo-Christian morality and tradition; hatred of middle-class aspirations and economic affluence; hatred of political stability and order. For the most part, the terrorists come from upper-middle and lower-upper class homes where successful parents provided them with comfort and security; yet they claim to speak for the working class. Needless to say, working-class people oppose terrorist tactics as much as anyone else.

In addition to such "traditional" tactics of terrorism as political assassinations and bombing, kidnapping and skyjacking are current weapons. These two, the most spectacular acts of terrorism, are designed mainly to fulfill one of the terrorists chief objectives: to gain public notoriety and the world's attention for their cause. In this they succeed because modern communications assure terrorists of a worldwide audience. With the ever-present television cameras, even a thwarted attempt becomes an instant success. It could easily be said that the degree of success of a terrorist operation depends almost entirely on the amount of publicity it receives. For this reason, the mass media are considered to be the reluctant partner of terrorism (a kind of public relations force) and television coverage to be the particularly necessary collaborator and helper.

Industrial democratic societies are becoming increasingly aware of their vulnerability to terrorist attacks. With the most modern weapons readily available—

stolen, bought, or supplied by governments sympathetic to the cause—terrorists can wreak havoc on any city they choose. Using heat-seeking rockets or delayed caps and fuses that fire photoelectrically, they can attack communication or transportation hubs, public utility installations, or any similar facility and so paralyze entire communities by their tactics.

Present-day political terrorism is also characterized by a much higher level of organization and financial support. Individual terrorist organizations in different countries are establishing contacts across national borders; they exchange information, cooperate, and coordinate their activities internationally. It is correct to speak of a "transnational terrorism," in which a kind of loose and shifting alliance does exist. As a consequence, various temporary coordinating committees function with such purposes as joint fund-raising, strategy, preparation of training manuals and subversive literature, forgery of passports and other identification papers.

Some of the terrorist organizations in Western Europe and Latin America oppose any kind of existing political systems, including the Soviet Union and the Peoples Republic of China, while the others are for the most part opposed to the Western capitalistic democracies only. But while the totalitarian states are for all practical purposes immune from any organized (counterrevolutionary) terrorism activity, the democracies find themselves at the terrorists' mercy.

Control of Terrorism. Being an open society, a democracy provides terrorists with everything they need: free and detailed information about buildings or persons selected to become the object of attack; constitutional guarantees of free speech and assembly; free movement and demonstration; bail; a permissive judicial system. Not a single terrorist was executed in Western democracies in the 1960s and 1970s. Democracies, in fact, are ill-prepared to defend themselves. To control terrorists harsher laws would be needed, due process set aside, and many constitutional guarantees suspended—in short democracies would have to renounce the very fundamentals on which they were established. They would become oppressive regimes and drive people into radical extremes of left and right and so provoke a violent polarization that would put an end to democracy and introduce some type of totalitarian state. The elimination of terrorism would thus result in the destruction of democracy, which is exactly what terrorists want.

To counter terrorism with success democracies will have to undertake more creative measures. In the first place, they will have to eliminate the grievances in which many terrorists find their justification. Most urgently needed is the creation of a more humane social order in which wealth will be more justly redistributed both within each country and between highly industrialized societies and developing countries. The scandalous gulf between the super-affluent and the destitute has to be abolished. Since all earthly goods are intended for the use of all human beings, the democracies must use their superior organizing skill to secure a system in which this universal purpose of goods and natural resources will be given paramount attention. Vatican Council II reaffirmed the traditional Christian teaching on private property, but at the same time made it clear that the rights of private property are not absolute, but relative and always subordinated to the common good (*Gaudium et spes* 69).

Another important measure to counter terrorism would be active and intensified participation of all citizens in public life. It is certainly not enough to have rights and not to use them. People must realize that they have not only the right of political participation, but also the duty of exercising this right and playing a far greater and decisive part in organizing the structures and life of the political community. There can be no place for political apathy within the framework of democracies. In an unusually long passage in dealing with the life of the political community, Vatican II considers citizens responsible for active participation in all spheres and levels as a requirement of modern politics and as a necessary corollary of human dignity (ibid. 73–75).

Enlightened political participation on a large scale by the citizenry will be of great help to government in creating a better social system with justice, bread, and freedom for all. This will reduce terrorist causes and activities substantially. Many terrorists even without cause will still agitate and they will have to be dealt with in the best manner possible. Clearly an unprecedented degree of international cooperation will be necessary, since the prospects of terrorist use of atomic weapons is a threat to the entire world community.

The 1971 Synod of Bishops, after analyzing different revolutionary ideologies, insisted once again on the need for freeing man and societies from every kind of oppression. But the Synod felt compelled unequivocally to state that the Church rejects any oppressive ideology and any violence as a means of achieving liberation. This decision rejects any liberation theology that endorses the possibility of revolution and violence in the fight for social liberation, as some regard the 1968 *Medellín Documents to have done. Also, the Synod corrects an erroneous interpretation by some Catholics of a passage of *Gaudium et spes* (74) as "a cautious nod in the direction of the right of Revolution" (D. Campion, in W. M. Abbott, *Documents of Vatican II*, p. 93). No such right is given or exists.

Bibliography: J. B. BELL, *Transnational Terror* (Washington 1975). W. Z. LAGEUR, *Terrorism* (Boston 1977). W. P. LINEBERRY, ed., *The Struggle against Terrorism* (New York 1977).

[T. MELADY and S. A. MIKOLIC]

THEISM AND PROCESS THOUGHT

During the last few years the principal challenge to traditional Christian theism has come from process philosophy and theology, one of the most lively and creative movements of contemporary philosophical and religious thought. A growing number of Catholic thinkers have also been drawing inspiration from the writings of this school. The *New Catholic Encyclopedia* contains an excellent account, by Lewis Ford, himself a leading process thinker, of contemporary process philosophy and process theology (16:363; 365). The purpose here is to reflect critically, from the point of view of Catholic thought, on the two main questions regarding process philosophy: What are the main contributions of process thought on the nature of God and his relations with the world which, without betraying their own traditions, Catholic philosophy and theology can fruitfully assimilate? What positions cannot be thus assimilated but remain incompatible with Catholic tradition, or at least are a source of serious difficulty until further clarification or adaptation is provided?

The responses to be given, summarily stated, are that a number of *basic insights* can and should be fruitfully assimilated by Catholic theism; process thought *as a system*, however—at least in the established systems of Alfred North Whitehead and Charles Hartshorne—is incompatible, or at least in serious tension, with traditional Catholic teaching on several key points. It would be unwise, however, to lay down any unbridgeable incompatibilities of principle with future possible developments of the process stream of thought, since it itself is now in full evolution—and must in principle continuously be open to such.

A very significant evolution has already taken place. The early Whiteheadian disciples tended to form a somewhat closed school, interested mainly in the internal working out and clarification of the system rather than in creative adaptations. When confronted with apparent oppositions between the system and traditional Christian teaching, they tended to bend their acceptance or interpretation of Revelation to fit their philosophy, rather than bend their philosophy to fit Revelation, as has always been the hallmark of the orthodox Christian theologian. Now this "scholastic period" of Whiteheadian thought, as some of the school have described it, is for the most part over or rapidly passing away. Neo-Whiteheadians are appearing, especially among Christian theologians and philosophers, who exhibit a new spirit of creative adaptation or even significant revision of the system where they feel it necessary to their Christian belief or human experience. Catholic thinkers can only welcome this trend, since it promises a much more open and creative context for dialogue enriching to both parties. Acceptance of the open-ended possibility of development among sincere Christians whose faith is seeking understanding is the context of what here follows.

Points of Apparent Incompatibility. What seems at present not to be compatible with the Catholic tradition of thought about God and His relations to the world? Three points are the denial of creation by God, of God's transcendence, and of personal immortality.

1. *God, the Cocreator Only.* In the original Whiteheadian system, God is not the creator of the universe out of nothing, i.e. out of no preexisting material or subject. The universe is an ongoing system that has always been and always will be. God does play an important and indeed, indispensable role in this ongoing system. God is source of the "eternal objects," i.e. possible intelligible forms or structures which he presents for integration by the momentary "actual occasions" or events, the sole realities outside of God himself. God provides the initial "subjective aim" or ideal goal of each newly arising actual occasion. God is providentially guiding the universe towards the greatest possible realizable good. God eternally preserves in his memory the values achieved by the perpetually-perishing, actual entities. But God is not the ultimate source of the very being (for Whitehead, becoming) of the universe, and for two reasons. First, his activity always presupposes the universe as somehow already present, at least in inchoate form, as subject of his action, somewhat like the Platonic demiurge injecting ideal forms into eternally preexisting matter. Secondly, each actual occasion (= actual entiry) *is* a self-creative act—not out of nothing but as a novel integration of the prior actual occasions in its environment that present themselves

passively to it for integration as they pass away. "Creativity," which really means self-creativity, is a universal attribute of all actual entities, of which God is the supreme but not the only instance. The concrete act of self-creative integration, which is the very being (becoming) of each actual occasion, must be, as existential act, its own act and not received from another. At best God might be called cocreator of each actual occasion in collaboration with the entity's own partially self-determining act. Thus there is really no answer in Whitehead as to why there is a universe in the first place or why the stream of internal self-creativity continues to bubble up endlessly in each new actual occasion. Creativity for Whitehead is a generalized description of a fact about the world, but not an explanation of the existence or source of this fact.

A simple example, drawn from a perceptive article by Ford, will help to show how it would be impossible for God to be a Creator (in the strict sense) of any actual entity in the Whiteheadian system. Take an act of freedom, for example. It would be intelligible to say that God can create a free *agent* or subject having a nature that has the God-given power to produce its own free act. But this would presuppose a distinction between the agent and its act. It would not make sense, however, to say that God created the very free *act* itself of another being, for then he, not the finite agent, would be responsible for it. Now process philosophy cannot admit any distinction between the agent and its act. There is no other being of the free agent save the momentary free act itself. The agent *is* the act. Hence the act must be its own, if it is free, and cannot be given by God, although God can cooperate with it and contribute to it. Furthermore, every actual occasion, as a novel, not entirely predetermined act of integration, has something analogous to freedom within it; hence none of them could possibly have been directly created by God. In a word, if all actual entities are nothing but their act, then even God cannot create the act, let alone the free act, of another being. He can create agents, not acts (Ford 1977).

Such a conception of God falls far short of the fullness of the traditional Judaeo-Christian belief in God as radical creator or ultimate source of the very being of the universe—a belief professed by all major Christian creeds: "I believe in one God, maker of all things...." From the early Church Fathers down to the present this has been traditionally interpreted as creation out of nothing (*ex nihilo*), so that all being is totally dependent on God for its very existence (a dependence mediated through other created agents after the initial radical beginning). Process theologians generally admit that the Whiteheadian conception of God as cocreator differs significantly from the traditional Christian interpretation. Some conclude that the latter, especially the notion of an absolute beginning, is a mythological image which should be dropped. Others, like John Cobb, wish to push the process conception closer to the tradition by drawing out the implications of the Whiteheadian doctrine that God alone gives the initial subjective aim to each new actual occasion; since this constitutes the initial phase of the latter's being-becoming, it might be likened to an initial gift of being, an overflow from the divine creativity. Others insist that any exercise of direct efficient causality by God would destroy one of the keystones of the system. Catholic thinkers can only welcome and encourage the creative adaptation of Whiteheadian thought along the lines of John Cobb. But they should be very slow to abandon the great philosophical and religious strength and richness of the traditional Christian conception of God as creator on whom the universe depends totally for its origin and being. The root of the difficulty lies in the fact that, as ordinarily understood in the Whiteheadian system, creativity *is not itself an actuality*. It is not an actually existing reservoir of power in the universe that can be drawn upon, since the only existent actualities are the individual actual occasions. Hence the individual bursts of self-creativity which characterize each newly arising actual entity, and which are the only ground for the generalized, abstracted description expressed by the term "creativity," seem literally to emerge out of nothing, with no prior ground for their *actuality* whatsoever (though there is ground for their form). The doctrine of creativity is admittedly obscure and undeveloped in Whitehead, but until this difficulty is cleared up the process theory of God remains philosophically and theologically inadequate to express the Christian conception of God as Creator, i.e. ultimate source of the very existence of the universe, as well as of its intelligible structures.

2. *A Dependent God.* The second point of incompatibility, or at least severe tension, with traditional Christian thought is that the process God seems to need the world for his own fulfillment, just as the world needs him. God's whole conscious life and satisfaction seem to come not from his own inner life but from leading the world to value and gathering it in his memory. God would be thoroughly incomplete and lacking full actuality without it. The meaning is a world-dependent God as well as a God-dependent world. Furthermore, the infinity of God, which some Whiteheadians like Lewis Ford are willing to concede to the primordial nature of God, seems finally to boil down to an infinity only of extrinsic attribution, in that the *object* of his thought—the total set of all possibilities which he eternally envisages—is infinite *in number*. The infinity does not seem to lie in the intrinsic inner fullness of God's own being in himself. But this falls far short of the traditional belief in the infinite perfection or fullness of God's own life within himself first, which out of love he then shares. This is where the Christian doctrine of the Trinity of Persons within God, with all its dynamism of internal processions and relations, takes on distinct philosophical relevance as a corrective to what appears as the onesidedly "extroverted" or world-absorbed consciousness of the Whiteheadian God. This point has been tellingly made by Ewert Cousins and other Catholic thinkers. Once God has expressed himself with infinite fullness in the gift of himself as Father to the Son and of both to the Holy Spirit, the divine self-expression has already been fulfilled and the finite world can be freely created as an overflow of divine altruistic love.

3. *Personal Immortality Denied.* The third point of incompatibility or tension is the apparent denial by Whitehead of any strictly individual, personal immortality. The reason is that all actual entities (=occasions), which are the only real things or subjects, endure only for a moment and then perish—all save God, the only exception to his metaphysical law. What ordinary language calls the enduring "I" is for Whitehead and Hartshorne only a "society" of successive "I"s, closely bound together in space, time, and the successive reincarnating of the same, defining, abstract, intelligible form. But this ongoing society, which some Christian process thinkers postulate as continuing into a future life with God, is not itself a new real subject or actual entity with personal moral acts proper to it *as a society*. The individual, responsible, moral "I"s of this life, who responded in personal faith and love to God's call, simply are not present in any subjective existential way in a future life with God; only the objective values they have achieved in their momentary flashes of existence are preserved forever in God's memory.

Yet a belief in a future life with God for the same individual subjective "I" that existed in this life and was redeemed by Christ and responded freely to his grace has always been an essential tenet of traditional Christian belief, presupposed throughout the whole of the New Testament in the doctrines of final judgment (with consequent reward and punishment), the resurrection of the redeemed, and life with God in the heavenly kingdom, and so understood by the Church Fathers and the ongoing tradition not only of the Catholic but of all the Christian Churches. Immortality is also one of the deepest and most universal natural desires of the human spirit. It seems, therefore, that here as elsewhere a Christian should adapt his philosophy to fit the richness of his faith and human intuition, not adapt his faith to fit his philosophy.

Christian process thinkers are well aware of this difficulty. Some have been willing to settle for objective immortality in the memory of God alone—which seems to be definitely less than a Christian position. Others have suggested that the system should be adapted to allow for an exception, in the case of the identity of human persons, to the law of momentary existence and perishing. This would indeed be a welcome move in itself, but it is quite a drastic revision of the Whiteheadian system: it leads right back to the notion of a subject distinct from its successive acts—a version of the classic substance doctrine which process philosophy began by rejecting. (In fact Whitehead gives no evidence of being familiar with the dynamic Aristotelian-Thomistic version of substance but only with the self-sufficient type of Descartes and the static type of Locke.) And once an exception is made for man, why not for the higher animals, and so on down the line? Thus the whole system would unravel.

Other Christian process thinkers have recently made quite a new and interesting creative adaptation of the system: they suggest that God preserves or recreates the last moment in the society of "I"s in its very subjective immediacy (not merely in objective memory) within his own life at the resurrection, now no longer limited to its own narrow personal environment of this life but sharing in the full vision and love of the divine life, thus participating in God's own victory over evil (see Suchocki). Such a move should be warmly welcomed by Catholic thinkers as a basis for further constructive dialogue, which would not compromise this nonnegotiable part of traditional Christian belief but show how process thought can be drawn into it in its own distinctive way.

Points for Assimilation. What now are the positive contributions of process thought that can be fruitfully assimilated by Catholic theism? The major contribution of process thought is the insistence that philosophical concepts do justice to the biblical revelation of God as involved in deeply personal, mutual relations of love and responsiveness with his creatures; this requires affirming that God is not only really related to the world but really affected by what happens in it in his own knowledge, love, compassion, joy. Process thinkers also claim that the traditional metaphysical concept of God put forward by Catholic thinkers like St. Thomas Aquinas cannot do justice to the "religiously available" God of Revelation because of its twin doctrines of the divine immutability and the absence of any real relations in God toward the world. What is needed is a new concept of the divine perfection that would include mutability and mutual real relations. Thus God's fullness of perfection is unsurpassed at any moment but constantly being surpassed by himself as his knowledge, love, joy in the value achieved by his creatures grow constantly, in tune with the world's changing history. God is in time as much as the world.

This challenge to traditional Catholic theism must be met. The following steps enter into such a response.

God Truly Related to Creatures. It must be candidly admitted that St. Thomas and other Catholic philosophers have left a gap between the metaphysical concept of God as infinite and immutable and the religious concept of God as involved in mutually responsive personal loving relations with his creatures; and they have not shown how to close this gap. The main contribution of process thought may turn out to be not the displacement of theistic metaphysics but the stimulation given towards creative adaptations of the theistic system from within its own latent resources.

It must be admitted that God is truly related to the world in personal relations of love and mutual responsiveness and that therefore he is positively affected by what happens in the world (i.e. different in his consciousness than he would have been had he not created or had acted otherwise). What happens in the world makes a significant, conscious difference to God. To make this intelligible to the contemporary world of thought and language, the Thomistic metaphysical doctrine that there are no "real relations" in God to the world should be dropped—not denied perhaps but quietly shelved as being no longer illuminating. The term "real relations" carries a very narrow technical meaning in St. Thomas, implying an intrinsic change in the real intrinsic (nonrelative) perfection of the subject of relation and the independent existence of the other term—neither of which requirement can be applied to God. What St. Thomas does allow—a point usually overlooked—is what might be called "intentionality relations" in the purely relational order of knowledge and love in God towards the world. His consciousness is determinately *different* both because of his decision to create this world and because of what happens in it, than it would have been otherwise. But St. Thomas refuses for technical reasons to call these "real relations." Such a position could perhaps be technically defended, but it is so narrow and imcomplete a perspective and so difficult to convey in modern thought forms that this major point of conflict with process thought should simply be dropped. Unambiguously it should be stated that God is *truly* ("really") *personally related* to the world by relations of knowledge and mutual love and *affected*–in his consciousness, not his

abiding intrinsic perfection of nature—by what happens in the world. A number of responsible Thomists have already been moving in that direction (see Clarke, Hill, Kelly, Wright).

Rethinking God's Immutability. Do the above affirmations require that the notion of *mutability* be introduced into the concept of divine perfection, as process thinkers insist? (One of their arguments is that no mind can know an as-yet-nonexistent, free future, hence God's knowledge must increase as the world goes on.) There seem to be two possible ways of responding. One is the simplest and most conciliatory; though not traditional, it could, if carefully qualified, be an orthodox Catholic position, remaining close to biblical language.

The approach would be to distinguish two kinds of immutability. One would be appropriate to God as the infinite perfection of personal being: i.e. immutability in his own intrinsic, absolute (nonrelative) perfection of nature, the eternally faithful God of Revelation, unchanging in his love and in the interior richness of his own Trinitarian life. Being already infinite, the divine perfection could never rise higher or fall lower. The second mode of immutability would imply total lack of alteration or difference of any kind even in the relative sphere of God's knowledge and love of others, as in the impassively self-contemplating Prime Mover of Aristotle or the Plotinian One. This would be inappropriate to the fulness of perfection proper to a truly personal, loving being, hence to the concept of the Christian God. Thus God could be said to be mutable in this relative dimension of knowledge, love, compassion, joy. He would be immutable in the absolute order, mutable in the relative order. The difference from the Whiteheadian notion of God as immutable in his "primordial nature" and mutable in his "consequent nature" (consequent to creation and the world's response) is that God would not need the world for his own completion and that, as properly the creator or ultimate source of all finite being, all the novelty of knowledge, love, joy he would receive from the world would still be only new finite participations and expressions of his already infinite fullness of being and thus not strictly increase this fullness by rising higher than their source. If a new, finite joy be added to an infinite, does the latter strictly increase or change? In one sense, yes; in another, no. The logic of the infinite transcends Aristotelian categories of change modeled on the physical and biological.

The second approach would be more traditional, and, if properly understood, can still be maintained, might even in the end be the better because more in accord with the transcendent mystery of God, though it would be far less palatable to process thinkers and the contemporary mind in general. This approach points out that the fact that God's consciousness is *different* for every response creatures make, *because* of this response—which must be held and St. Thomas himself holds (ST 1a, 14.5, 7, 9, 13, 15)—does not require that God *change* over time, first not responding, then *later* responding, as creatures do. All these differences could be present in God without temporal succession—which implies some real succession in the knower's own real internal being—in his eternal "Now," which includes and is correlated with all of successive and mutually exclusive "nows" but cannot be situated anywhere along the line among them. In this light, all questions of the type, "Does God know *now* (i.e. now, at 3 P.M. today, which excludes all future nows) a free act that will happen tomorrow?" the answer must be negative; no mind can know with certainty what does not yet exist and is not determined in its causes. What can be said is "God knows in *his* Now what is actually going on at time X, because he sees it as it is actually taking place, not in the future." But since his Now is incommensurable with any created nows and hence cannot be situated at *any* of them, the two "nows" are equivocal and their meanings cannot be interchanged. It would be more accurate to say simply that "God knows X," with no time specification at all. Most logical difficulties of process thinkers and others against this position collapse—cannot even be formulated correctly—in the light of this basic, but persistently ignored, rule of language about God in traditional theism. The traditional teaching leaves the *unimaginable* mystery of God's Now, but without contradiction in the thought or language which argue to and express it.

Which of the two paths of explanation outlined above should be preferred—that of limited *mutability* in God's knowledge and love relations or only inner *difference* without temporal succession—or whether both are alternate viable ways, can be a fruitful topic for further dialogue.

Bibliography: (1) Process Thought: D. BROWN, R. JAMES, G. REEVES, eds., *Process Philosophy and Christian Thought* (Indianapolis 1971). J. COBB, *A Christian Natural Theology* (Philadelphia 1965). E. COUSINS, ed., *Process Theology* (New York 1971). L. FORD and M. SUCHOCKI, "A Whiteheadian Reflection on Subjective Immortality," *Process Studies* 7 (1977) 1–13; (and the further development of M. SUCHOCKI, "The Question of Immortality: *Journal of Religion* 57 [1977] 288–306). L. FORD, "The Viability of Whitehead's God for Christian Theology," ProcAmerCathPhilAs 44 (1970) 130–140, with a negative rejoinder by R. NEVILLE, "The Impossibility of Whitehead's God for Christian Theology," *ibid.* 141–151; "Can Freedom Be Created?" Hor 4 (1977) 183–188. R. MELLERT, *What Is Process Theology?* (New York 1975) a sympathetic Catholic exposition.

(2) Catholic critical reflection: W. N. CLARKE, "A New Look at the Immutability of God," in R. ROTH, ed., *God Knowable and Unknowable* (New York 1973). M. D'ARCY, "The Immutability of God," ProcAmerCathPhilAs 41 (1967) 19–26. W. HILL, "Does the World Make a Difference to God?" Thomist 38 (1974) 148–164; "Does God Know the Future? Aquinas and Some Moderns," ThSt 36 (1975) 3–18. A. KELLY, "God: How Near a Relation?" Thomist 34 (1970) 191–229. W. STOKES, "Is God Really Related to the World?" Thomist 39 (1965) 145–150. J. WRIGHT, "Divine Knowledge and Human Freedom: The God Who dialogues," ThSt 38 (1977) 450–477.

See also the illuminating discussion, L. FORD and W. HILL, "In What Sense Is God Infinite? A Process and a Thomist View," Thomist 42 (1978) 1–27.

[W. N. CLARKE]

THEOLOGIAN

Although expressions of faith in Jesus of Nazareth are registered in the Scriptures and have been called "theologies," explicit interest in the theologian has emerged only with a recent philosophical "turn to the subject." It will be helpful therefore to discuss: (1) the role and notion of theologian at crucial moments in the Catholic tradition; (2) some problems which have recently appeared concerning the theologian's responsibilities; and (3) the major areas of discussion which require consideration in determining the qualifications of the theologian.

Notion and Role of the Theologian. It was only in the 4th century that Christians applied the noun "theologian" to Christian writers; before that in classical usage the term referred to poets and mythologizers, e.g. Hesiod. Most teachers of Christian religion during

the period either became or were bishops—although an important pre-Nicene exception is Origen of Alexandria (185–253). After the collapse of the classical educational system, Christian teachers primarily exercised their reflection in the context of missionary persuasion or of monastic piety.

Emergence of Academic Criteria. It is significant that the use of the world "theology" as a discipline distinct from meditation, preaching, or prayer (and thus the role of the theologian) coincides with the 12th-century rise of dialectics (notably in Peter Abelard [1079–1142]), the development of alternatives to monastic education, and the question of public authorization to teach theology (the *licentia docendi*). It was the master of the diocesan or cathedral school (the *scholasticus*) or eventually the chancellor of the university who granted the license to teach theology. The requirement to have a license was not to regulate the content of the candidate's teaching, but rather, owing to the increase in the number of students, to extend teaching in an orderly fashion beyond the one *magister* of a school. Regulation of teaching occurred on the local academic level until intervention by Pope Alexander III (1159–81). Although his interventions confirmed the chancellor or the *scholasticus* in the granting of licenses and their judging of a candidate's fitness, he maintained that the *scholasticus* could not demand a fee for the license nor could he refuse a license to those who were properly equipped by their learning. These decisions to prohibit academic simony were confirmed by the Lateran Council III (1179). Only in the 13th century did the licensed masters as a corporate body insist upon a consultative role in the examination of qualifications of applicants for the license.

In the medieval world, this external, institutional criterion paralleled the personal qualifications which were expected of the theologian. The theologian was not simply a thinker upon any body of knowledge, but rather one who was informed by faith and the intellectual gifts of the Holy Spirit. Since theology was the highest wisdom, it intimately involved the moral and religious status of the theologian.

Substitution of Juridic Criteria. Because the internal criteria specifying the theological *habitus* were somewhat difficult to ascertain, it is not surprising that public, institutional norms prevailed as the operative definition of the theologian. Thus, although the medieval license and the canonical mission to teach have different origins—the former in educational expansion; the latter in relation to jurisdiction for preaching and the need to control heterodox opinion (Conc. Trident., sess. V., *De ref.*, c. 1; CIC c. 398–400)—both have functioned as the public ecclesial identification of the theologian. Successive centuries have confirmed the proper ecclesiastical authority as the designator of the theologian within the Church.

Eventually, however, not only was authority viewed as the formal agency of legitimation for the theologian, but also authority became the material content of the theologian's teaching as well. Thus in the doctrine of Pope Pius XII, theologians appear as the mediators of the episcopal and papal magisterium to the faithful (see, for example, the encyclical *Humani generis* ActApS [1950] 565–9; *Si Diligis*, allocution at the canonization of St. Pius X ActApS 46 [1954] 314–317). Theologians have recently bridled under this definition.

Responsibilities of the Theologian: Recent Problems.
What has become clear in recent controversy is that the magisterium is not the only public to which the theologian is responsible. By outlining four of those responsibilities, one can ascertain certain of the elements which identify the theologian in the contemporary Church.

Magisterium. Probably because the theologian was defined in the dominant ecclesiological position by an adherence to magisterial pronouncements, recent difficulties of theologians with or dissent from ordinary, noninfallible papal teaching (*see* DISSENT, THEOLOGY OF 16:127) have proved to be the focus for redefinition of the theologian's task. The ensuing dialogue has made clear that although theologians have a responsibility to weigh authoritative pronouncements, assent to such teaching is nuanced according to the intent, contents, arguments, and promulgating authority of the position.

In 1976, The International Theological Commission (ITC) presented a number of theses concerning the relationship between theologians and the magisterium. (i) The role of the theologian is to study the Word of God and to teach it by virtue of a canonical mission. (ii) Both theologians and the magisterium have the common task of preserving the deposit of faith. (iii) Both must adhere to the Word of God, the *sensus fidei*, the documents of the tradition, and a pastoral and missionary concern. (iv) Both theologians and magisterium are actualized collegially; but they have (v) different functions, (vi) different authorities within the ecclesial body, (vii) differing ecclesiastical references; and (viii) different roles in the establishment and enactment of their freedom. The commission argued that although some tension between the scholarly community and the magisterium may be inevitable, it should appear as a sign of life, and should not prohibit a unified operation. Despite certain emphases in the document on the function of theologian as mediator of magisterial teaching to the faithful (v), the document marks a notable official shift from theology as an organ of the magisterium to a theology as an independent, responsible science whose authority rests upon its argumentation and the shared expertise of its clerical and nonclerical practitioners.

In keeping with this irenic tone, the response of the USCC's Committee on Doctrine to the Catholic Theological Society of America's report, *Human Sexuality* (A. Kosnik et al., eds., 1977) was measured in tone. It argued that the authors of the theological statement had not paid proper attention to the Scriptures as norm for theology and that the use of social scientific research in the report had disregarded an important dialogical distinction between the data of empirical research and the assertion of values. The statement of the Committee on Doctrine encouraged theologians to continue to work out positions on sexual ethics which would respect all the values the tradition has espoused. Theological faithfulness to the Tradition means attention to all the traditions.

Sciences. The ITC recognition of the scientific character of theological inquiry supports theologians who wish to find their place within the academic community at large. Classical culture knew an ascending series of scientific endeavors which culminated in theology; the contemporary notion of science emphasizes partial perspectives, particular, controlled, and repeatable experiments, probable results, and a continuing revision of method. As a member of an academic community, the theologian is required to speak to colleagues whose notion of honest intellectual inquiry does not seem to rest upon faith, history, and revealed, inspired texts. The dialogue concerning method in theology, the role of the observer in the "hard" sciences, the function of imagination in scientific experiment, the developing notion of tradition in the social sciences and the role of noninductive logics in scientific paradigm-shifts is proving to be a fruitful source of reexamination for classical formulations of both science and theology.

Politics and Practice. Criticism of speculative philosophies uninvolved in the ordinary affairs of the world has overflowed, a fortiori, into theology. Can a theology which does not have its roots in Christian practice and which does not return to enrich Christian living count as a study of the God of the Christian tradition? This argument has taken a characteristic form in Latin and South American *Liberation Theology, which has argued that theologians must involve themselves in the concrete emancipation of human beings. Theology which believes that its scientific status requires "objective" investigation without affective or moral contexts is mistaken. To argue for the disinterested character of speculative science is tacitly to affirm the cultural position of a theologian whose warrants may be unexamined. Some acculturated norms may be important to retain; others may need to be discarded as detrimental to human freedom. Critical responsibility for the social context defines one aspect of the theologian's operation.

Faith. Responsibility for the social context raises a question about a theologian's responsibility as a person. Need the theologian be a believer? This question has again been asked in the new pluralist context of apologetics. Apologetic theology places the theologian in dialogue with viewpoints that are frequently ignorant of the traditional formulae, occasionally hostile to apologetics' previous cultural usage, and/or more often simply apathetic toward its questions. The once-presumed cultural heritage in such discussions has shifted into an incommensurable pluralism in which participants cannot be assured a common understanding.

In this context, some theologians have maintained that honest intellectual inquiry requires the non-inclusion of the personal faith stance of the theologian. No explicitly Christian adherence need be the basis or warrant for the discussion. Opponents argue that this position has "rationalist" overtones and is not a recognizable reflection upon Christian faith. Though there seems to be some undifferentiated vocabulary in this debate (e.g. the meaning of faith), it is likely that the question will be resolved in terms of some of the wider categories now to be set out.

The Qualifications of the Theologian. From the above précis of recent problems it is clear that the qualifications of theologians are inextricably tied to the development of ecclesiology. The responsibilities of the individual theologian or of theologians as a body are multiple: to themselves as believers; to their immediate social group and its religious and social development; to scholars in non-Catholic, non-Christian, and non-religious disciplines; to the ecclesial tradition and its magisterium; to the relevant sociopolitical body; and to each of these as they mediate responsibility to God.

But the elaboration of this individual and social

position of the theologian, both within the local, national, and international Church and society asserts that the relationship is dialectical: the theologian is neither propagandist for, nor the dictator to, other elements of the polity, whether magisterial, academic, or parochial. Just as in the medieval Church, the status of theologian was only clarified in the course of socio-political and ecclesiastical developments, so too the contemporary position of the theologian will appear more clearly when the various social bodies to which the theologian belongs have begun to establish a new equilibrium. The theologian, however, has an active role to play in the establishment of that new secular and ecclesiastical polity.

Thus there are three major areas of consideration which will determine the future discussion of the role of the theologian: (1) the role of theory in experience; (2) the relation between traditional symbolic expressions and thought; and (3) the relationship between thought, preaching, and spirituality. All three are in some way reformulations of the first, but for the purposes of exposition will be treated separately.

Role of Theory in Experience. Science is a discipline which must ultimately return to the matrix of ordinary experience. The theologian at present is a target of much of the exasperation given in the stigmatizations of modern science. The more complicated and conceptually abstruse formulations of science seem alien to a society experiencing socio-economic problems of some magnitude. Thus, not only must the theologian be responsible for a socially-transforming theory, but that theory is expected to have its origins in a personally-transforming praxis. The debate concerning both politics and the faith of the theologian arises in this wider context. If the debate is fruitfully resolved, the theologian may have some critical insight to contribute to the discussion of the nature of the human sciences.

Symbolic Expressions and Thought. Systematic theology, whether about the good or about the true, clarifies itself by specification of concepts. Yet the earliest expressions of Christianity are in story, image, and symbol. An important issue, therefore, which specifies the theory/experience problem, concerns the ways in which concepts emerge from the ordinary forms of religious speech and how theology as reflective discourse emerges from theology as symbol and prayer. Questions which remain to be resolved in this context include: the relationship between the theologian and the particular confessional tradition with its credal and magisterial formulas; the "canonical mission" as legitimate recognition by the ecclesial body that an individual faithfully reflects a particular religious tradition; and the role of peers in the judgment of theological error.

Thought, Preaching, Spirituality. On the practical level of the individual ecclesial community, the conflict or ir-resolution in current society concerning behavior and thought becomes a division between the thinker, the preacher, and the saint. Where the classical theological world could find in Augustine or Aquinas an integration of all three and ideally demanded that integration of the theologian, the contemporary Christian community still struggles to discern their de facto relationship in society. The thinker's conceptual clarity, the preacher's missionary intent, and the saint's ascetical, even mystical desire for the Holy One all enter into discovering a definition of the theologian. The major contributions of

the last few years have recognized that no one structure of the ecclesial body has a monopoly in determining the theologian's emergent role.

Bibliography: "Bishops' Doctrinal Committee Responds to Book on Sexuality," Origins 7 (1977) 376–378. R. COFFY, "Magisterium and Theology," IrTheolQ 43 (1976) 247–259. Y. CONGAR, *A History of Theology,* tr. H. GUTHRIE (Garden City, N.Y. 1968) 260–275. J. CONNELLY, "The Task of Theology" (Paper and responses), CathThSoc 29 (1974) 1–75. P. DELHAYE, "L'organisation scolaire au xiie siècle," *Traditio* 5 (1947) 211–268. A. DULLES, "What is Magisterium," Origins 6 (1976) 81–88. International Theological Commission, *Theses on the Relationship between the Ecclesiastical Magisterium and Theology,* with commentary by O. Semmelroth and K. Lehmann (Washington, D.C. 1977). J.-P. JOSSUA, "From Theology to Theologian," *Catholic Mind* 68 (Dec. 1970) 5–10. J. KOMONCHAK, "*Humanae vitae* and Its Reception," ThSt 39 (1978) 221–257. G. PHILIP, "À propos du pluralisme en théologie" 46 (1970) 149–169. PIUS XII, *Si diligis, Pope Speaks* 1 (1954) 153–158. J. QUINN, "The Magisterium and the Field of Theology," Origins 7 (1978) 341–343 K. RAHNER, "Pluralism in Theology and the Unity of the Creed in the Church," *Theological Investigations* v. 11, tr. D. BOURKE (New York 1974) 3–23; "Possible Courses for the Theology of the Future," *Theological Investigations* v. 13, tr. D. BOURKE (New York 1975) 32–60; "The Congregation of the Faith and the Commission of Theologians," *Theological Investigations* v. 14, tr. D. BOURKE (New York 1976) 98–115. M. SECKLER, "Die Theologie als kirchliche Wissenschaft nach Pius XII und Paul VI," ThQschr 249 (1969) 209–234.

[S. HAPPEL]

THEOLOGICAL FIELD EDUCATION

Field Education is a relatively new component of seminary curricula. The name came into common usage in theological schools of the United States as a result of a study in 1966 by Charles F. Fielding sponsored by the American Association of Theological Schools in the United States and Canada. He was asked to make a study of practical training for the ministry with special attention to supervision. His work, *Education for Ministry,* gave a major impetus to this part of preparation for ministry in theological schools through the country. The program within the Catholic Church's seminaries was encouraged and supported by two documents. In 1970 the Sacred Congregation for Catholic Education issued its *Basic Plan for Priestly Formation (Ratio fundamentalis institutionis sacerdotalis),* which stressed the importance of special pastoral training for seminarians. Then in 1971 the National Conference of Catholic Bishops in *The Program of Priestly Formation* proposed that all Catholic seminaries have a program of field education which is to be integrated into the academic sphere. They describe the purpose of the program as follows:

> The custom of engaging in apostolic works is a common feature in seminaries today, but the essential role that this endeavor should play in the total educational and formative process has recently been recognized in a fuller way. This dimension of learning through active engagement in the ministry must be seen as an integral part of the total formation of the future priest, drawing from the academic and spiritual aspects and, in turn, feeding back into and enriching them. Active pastoral involvement, if carefully designed and properly supervised—an absolute necessity—is just as educational in nature as is classroom work. The latter provides the necessary theoretical background for the priest on mission; the former, a laboratory for learning through practice. Such a Field Education Program, therefore, is by no means an endorsement of a fallacious activism.

The 1976 edition of the NCCB *Program for Priestly Formation* repeats this paragraph (185).

While all field education programs involve pastoral education with learning sites outside the seminary, the goals and approaches differ widely. A recent survey of field education programs by Whitehead and Whitehead around the country found three different perspectives in the various programs: (1) field education as the application of academic theology in the practice of ministry; (2) field education as the acquisition and development of ministerial skills; (3) field education as a locus of learning theology. In the first of these approaches the theological tradition is taught in the academic classroom and applied to pastoral situations. In the second, field education is not directly theological; instead it consists of skill-development in such areas as counseling, evangelization, catechesis, and social services. In its third form field education is a source for learning theology inductively from the living experience of the Church, which interfaces with the Church's tradition taught in the classroom. One way of contrasting the first and third approaches is to see the theologian as the academic person in the first and the student as the one who applies theology to ministry; in the third both the academic person and the student are theologians but deriving theology from two different sources—both necessary for a full understanding of pastoral theology. Probably most seminaries include elements of all three approaches in their programs, but usually have a predominant emphasis on one direction.

The Association of Theological Field Educators is an interfaith national professional organization of program directors and others engaged in this part of seminary education.

Bibliography: Congregation for Catholic Education, *The Basic Plan for Priestly Formation*, Eng. tr. (USCC Publ. Office, Washington, D.C. 1971); C. R. FIELDING, *Education for Ministry* (Dayton, Ohio 1966). NCCB, *The Program of Priestly Formation* (Washington, D.C. 1971; 2d ed. 1976). J. and E. WHITEHEAD, eds., "Educational Models in Field Education," in *Theological Field Education—A Collection of Key Resources* (Kansas City, Mo. 1977).

[E. F. HARNETT]

THEOLOGY

Like faith, theology as a discipline has entered a period of crisis in which negatively its own identity is called into question and positively it faces the challenge of creative renewal (14:39). The history of its recent past gives evidence of a radical metamorphosis in which metaphysical thinking (Neoscholasticism; 10:337) has given way first to existential thinking (e.g. Bultmann and Rahner) and subsequently to historical thinking (e.g. Pannenberg and Metz). The approach to God has shifted from the objectivity of the cosmos, to an anthropocentric emphasis upon the immanence of thought and thence to radical historicality and *praxis*. The present altered status of the discipline can perhaps be schematically displayed in the following eleven considerations: (1) theology's scientific status; (2) theology and Revelation; (3) theology and the Bible; (4) foundational theology; (5) the crisis of language; (6) theology as transcendental anthropology; (7) theology as method; (8) theology as hermeneutics; (9) theology as eschatology; (10) theology as process thinking; (11) additional characteristics.

(1) **Scientific Status.** Neoscholasticism transformed Thomas Aquinas's notion of theology as a subalternated science (ST 1a, 1.3) into an exaggerated distinction between faith and reason, and extenuated the Aristotelian notion of science (*epistēmē*) employed by Aquinas, in terms of Cartesian rationalism. This introduced a ruinous separation between the *fact* of God's revealing (acknowledged by faith and on the authority of the Church) and its *content* and meaning (appropriated by way of logically deducing conclusions from

premises of faith). Theology became a science employing two distinct methodologies: the historical as "positive theology," and the rational as "speculative theology." In the first, it had two functions: to articulate the present teaching of the Church, and then to seek the foundations for such in Scripture and *tradition. In speculative theology the function was to attempt a reasoned elaboration of such doctrine. In the modern era, these two elements were so dissociated that their complementarity was lost, with a resulting collapse of theology as a viable scientific enterprise in this sense. Among the factors in that demise were, preeminently: (1) a growing awareness, since Kant, of the historicity of man and of all knowledge, which relativized the dogmatic and ecclesiastical character of the formulae of faith; (2) a shift in the understanding of the revelation-event, which altered the notion of religious truth; and (3) the transition from the intellectualism of classical culture to the empiricism of modern culture, in which rational certitude cedes to dialectical probability and priority is given to the experiential. In the face of this breakdown of an earlier structure, Rudolf Bultmann allowed a scientific function to exegesis alone and reduced theology to *kērygma*. More radically, Matthias Gatzenmeir (*Theologie als Wissenschaft*, 1974) has claimed recently that its reliance upon an esoteric source of information (revelation) which appeals to authority and defies all rational testing gives theology an exclusively confessional character and denies it the criteria and the name of science. Serious theologians have countered by insisting that theology retains its claim to science, not on analogy with the natural sciences (*Naturwissenschaften*) but with the humane sciences (*Geisteswissenschaften*, in the sense of the word since W. Dilthey). It is rational and public discourse on the symbols of Christianity and as such interprets a depth dimension to common human experience, with its own critically employed criteria for both meaning and truth. It readily acknowledges its confessional character but maintains—in light of the principle generally recognized today, in reaction to the ideal of the Enlightenment, that all thought involves some commitment by way of a preunderstanding on the part of the investigator—that this does not mean it is without empirically verifiable grounding. Obviously, such grounding cannot be absolutized so as to limit theology to only the empirically verifiable. The truth it seeks to articulate is that proper to the human person, whose being is rooted in freedom and so is indigenously historical and linguistic.

(2) **Theology and Revelation.** The religious crisis that developed between the two World Wars precipitated a radical revision in the understanding of the nature of Christian belief and especially of divine Revelation as its source. Revelation came to be looked upon not as God's imparting of truths about himself otherwise unattainable, but as the self-communication of a living God in present address to men. Faith response to this then appeared not as assent to propositions on the basis of authority (truth as *adaequatio*), but as existential encounter with the God who unveils himself to men (truth as *alētheia*). The locus of such encounter is human consciousness, which is indigenously historical; thus, it involves both the a priori conditions of consciousness and the a posteriori conditions of historical occurrence. The linguisticality of man means the spontaneous articulation of this religious experience into

language, of which the Bible is the privileged and normative instance. Originally, in the two thinkers most responsible for this revised understanding, the historical character of Revelation was compromised. Karl Barth's "Theology of the Word" hypostatized that Word into God in his primal history with mankind (*Ursgeschichte*); Rudolf Bultmann reduced it to a divine summons to the existential decision of faith within human subjectivity (*kērygma*). A succeeding generation led by Ernst Käsemann recovered the relevance of history for faith by viewing history not as chronology or literal biography but as a record of intentions and life-commitments of the participants underlying the events. Present meaning is thus safeguarded from subjectivity in that it arises only out of tradition. More recent theories of revelation, inaugurated by Wolfhart Pannenberg and others, tend to move a step further in rejecting outright the distinction between fact and meaning (that is between *Historie*, as what the historian establishes by historical, critical method as actually having happened, and *Geschichte*, as the impact of past events upon present consciousness) that underlies the earlier position. Meaning, while distinct from event, is ingredient in events themselves; Revelation is not the Word of God somehow above history but is itself universal history. While appropriating both developments, Catholic theology at the same time has resisted the collapse into existential subjectivity, on the one hand, and the absolutizing of universal history on the other; the former by an emphasis on the concrete historical character of God's acts, the latter by an insistence upon the normative interpretation of such history both in the apostolic and the postapostolic Church. There is growing agreement, at any rate, on setting aside a priori concepts of general revelation in favor of an approach that begins with the Christ-event itself as a bearer of meaning on the basis of its concrete origin. Revelation is thus the opening up of possibilities for human existence (P. Ricoeur); its credibility is not so much rational as integrally human in kind (P. A. Liégé). The literary documents in which such experience issues are depositivized and not so much read for any "objective" truth they contain as (in a move beyond the Protestant principle of *sola scriptura* and the Catholic reliance upon Church magisterium) they are interpreted in a search for the meaning they bear for man today. Out of this arise theories of continuing development whose common note is an ever new thematization into language of a primal understanding that either transcends language or (more likely) at least cannot be exhausted in former language expressions. K. Rahner, for example, distinguishes between a "transcendental revelation" that is preconceptual and preverbal, and a "categorical revelation" that is the concrete thematization of the former in event and word. It is the texts themselves that in an objective way *communicate* truth not explicitly *stated* in words.

(3) **Theology and the Bible.** The recovery of the hermeneutical role clearly signals the end to the divorce between exegesis and theology. Earlier, exegesis had tended to assume an overly positivistic character, resistant to the schemas of theology that were becoming more and more rationalistic and "speculative" in the pejorative sense. Sacred Scripture is now viewed not as a deposit of truths but as a culturally and historically determined witness to the revelatory event. Exegesis, then, is not a neutral and naively objective historical study, because it demands a faith commitment and a preunderstanding on the part of the investigator. Faith is thus understood as not mere assent but as already initial interpretative understanding (E. Schillebeeckx); a gradual awareness of its indispensible role in appropriating both the fact and the contents of Revelation has led to a recovery of the primacy of Scripture and its function in theology as a *norma non normata*. As signs of this: any serious contention of a second autonomous source of Revelation existing alongside Scripture has disappeared; later formulations of Christian truth appearing in postbiblical tradition are viewed as "the history of the effects of Scripture" (B. van Iersel). Noteworthy, too, is the emergence of biblical theology as a speculative act beyond, yet under the control of exegesis. None of this has meant the surrender by exegesis of its proper object and task—the recovery of the text in its original setting and the meaning it held for its author. But this function is put into the context of being a privileged moment in the larger hermeneutical task, which acknowledges that the text yields up its fullest meaning only in the perspective of an ongoing tradition.

(4) **Foundational Theology.** Theology is presently engaged in a critical reexamination of its own foundations in an attempt to provide itself with an epistemology, a method, and a set of categories for its interpretative work. This has meant the emergence of what is properly designated "foundational theology" to replace an earlier "fundamental theology," with a corresponding eschewing of prior procedures in the area of natural theology and apologetics, both concerned with seeking the rational grounds for, respectively, the existence of a Transcendent Cause and the credibility of Revelation. Both remain legitimate pursuits but as conducted within the ambiance of revealed theology, i.e. the *point de départ* is the properly theological one of Revelation understood as illumining the meaning of human existence. *Foundational theology, thus functioning analogously to philosophy in the latter's critical function, has thus become markedly anthropocentric and, in part, the believer's act of self-understanding. Foundational theology takes cognizance of the truth that knowledge of reality is available only on the basis of the structure of the particular being who questions it (Heidegger's *Dasein*) and takes historicity not as an accidental factor but as an essential constituent of human beingness. Further, all understanding is viewed as rooted in experience, the latter concept being broadened out to include "faith" as some sort of preunderstanding. Experience thus conditions both contact with the symbols of Revelation and their interpretation. Exploration focuses on the relationship between the formulas of Christian faith and common human experience, even secular experience in its very secularity. In this way, theology retreats from being a science of God and man in the divine self-communicative act. Interest thus centers on the sacred texts as the language event emerging from tradition and theology becomes hermeneutics. Contemporary theology is thereby rendered unavoidably pluralistic, resting on the two poles of religious pluralism and philosophical *pluralism. The first means a climate of ecumenism not only in the sense of an irenic spirit but in the sense of theologians crossing confessional lines in doctrinal matters. The second is most obvious in the wide spectrum of

epistemological options ranging from strict empiricism and linguistic analysis (Wittgenstein) to neoclassical metaphysics (Whitehead). The pluralism proper to theology is illustrated by David Tracy's discernment of five contemporary viable "models": orthodox, liberal, neo-orthodox, radical, and revisionist (Tracy 1975). There is clearly discernible a refusal of commitment to any one metaphysical system, a factor that gives rise to conceptual confusion, and not infrequently betrays an antimetaphysical bias, which undermines a traditional notion of theology as working under the sign of *logos*.

(5) **Crisis of Language.** At the bottom of theology's critical work lies the vexing problem of language. The "God is Dead" phenomenon of the 1960s graphically indicated that discussion had moved beyond the problem of believing in the reality of the Transcendent to the question as to whether it was possible to attach any meaning at all to speech that claimed to refer to what lay beyond the empirical order. The principle of empirical verification as employed in early Logical Positivism (8:964) came to be qualified in attending to the distinctive consciousness from which religious language arose. This led to an understanding of how meaning is determined by the way language is used and so allowed a genuine cognitive character to the speech of believers. Also, the principle of verifiability has given way to that of falsifiability, in which theoretical refutability is seen as strengthening the case for belief (K. Popper). Nevertheless, the question of truth tends still to be bracketed as something dependent entirely upon faith-commitment and not susceptible of critical mediation—though Catholic theology remains sanguine about finding rational support for credibility. The modes of linguistic expression are multiple and varied, though all God-talk is recognized to be indirect, oblique, and relational. Emphasis falls heavily today on nonliteral modes of speech, divided basically into the mythical and the symbolic, both understood as vehicles of truth, though often truth not translatable into literal terms. Resource to literal (as opposed to figurative) language, however, is still deemed necessary as long as the literal retains its indirect, nonunivocal character; without this the truth function of myth and symbol seemingly becomes arbitrary. Theology as narration, employing story, autobiography, and self-ascriptive language is now regarded as indispensable to the discipline, though by itself it can offer no criteria for truth or falsity and stands in need of conceptual language. The latter continues to be used primarily in the context of analogy, i.e. as concepts whose proper reference is to either realities of the cosmos (metaphysical analogy), or to subjective self-understanding (analogy in existential ontology), by means of which God is designated without being conceptually grasped. More frequently, concepts are used as hypothetical categories, as descriptive paradigms, and as disclosure models. Still, the necessity for an ontological undergirding of religious language continues to urge itself; metaphor and analogy are thus taken to be complementary in theological discourse. Much of the metaphysics deployed in theology is descriptive in kind, but of itself this raises the question of an interpretative metaphysics, of the move beyond language to being.

(6) **Theology as Transcendental Anthropology.** The dialectical theology of the Barth-Bultmannian axis sought to recoup the relevance of Christian faith by emphasizing respectively supernaturalism and existential decision, but in a way that radically reduced the significance of human nature on the one hand and history on the other. Attempts to surmount this, in a use of the transcendental philosophy of E. Husserl and M. Heidegger, led to a recasting of the discipline as theological anthropology, most notably in the work of Karl Rahner (*Theological Investigations*, 1961–). The a priori (structure of human existence) and a posteriori (events of history) elements in religious encounter were thereby seen as illuminating each other. Scripture and church doctrine are shown to be the thematizations, in culturally determined images and concepts, of a prior awareness of God that is nonobjective and preconceptual, while still forming part of conscious existence. This latter "prehension" is not indigenous to man's nature but is an existential structure thereof, due entirely to grace and constituting a supernatural existential in which man stands open to the God of a possible revelation (13:816). The vigor of this revised "theology of mediation" continues to assert itself, although reservations have been expressed on its anthropomorphism which runs the risk of measuring the mysteries of God by the meaning they bear for men. Hans Urs von Balthasar has strongly argued for the option of conceiving theology as aesthetics, in which God's concrete action in history, in its own splendor (*Herrlichkeit*), interprets itself to man in ways impossible to surmise from the latter's own existence.

(7) **Theology as Method.** Bernard Lonergan has employed the transcendental method differently, arguing that theology is less a discipline with its own nature than a method of thought. So transformed, it is isomorphic with the other humane sciences and rooted in the invariant structure of human consciousness as a dynamism of self-transcendence. Theology, on this view, comprises eight distinct but interrelated functional specialties: research, interpretation, history, dialectics, foundations, doctrines, systematics, and communications (Lonergan 1972). What has precipitated this alteration is the transition from the classical culture of antiquity to the empirical culture of modernity. Here genuine objectivity lies not in naive realism but in the subjectivity of the believer as he structures his own world of meaning. Theology attends not to truths but to the acts of theologians striving to understand and respond to truth.

(8) **Theology as Hermeneutics.** In abandoning its former procedures and becoming an interpretation of the encounter with God, mediated through Christian symbols of the past, theology has been enormously influenced by the seminal work of Hans-Georg Gadamer and his insisting that language is the basis of all understanding. Hermeneutics is nothing more than a theory of the very process of understanding itself, as the uncovering of the hiddenness of things through the tradition of language. Understanding is neither naive objectivity on one hand, nor subjective behavior on the other, but a coordination of subject and object in which understanding "belongs to the being of that which is understood" (Gadamer xix). Hermeneutics allows for the gradual emergence of meaning in the very process of reinterpretation that is tradition. The text possesses a life of its own wherein it meets the present interpreter and so "can assert its truth against one's own foremeanings" (ibid. 238). This dialogic "fusing of the

horizons" is the merging of past and present in language; it enables one to hear *in the text* what was previously unheard. The past comes alive as the life of a community giving meaning to the present; historical events are known in an authentic way that unleases their meaning for the present.

(9) **Theology as Eschatology.** As hermeneutics, theology has developed from a hermeneutic of existence (in Bultmann's separation of meaning from event), to a hermeneutic of language (in the merging of fact and meaning in language-event by Gadamer and E. Fuchs), and, finally, to a hermeneutic of history (in which revelation occurs not merely in history but precisely as history: Pannenberg and Moltmann). In this latter stage, meaning is ingredient in events themselves insofar as they anticipate the end of history and so its final meaning. Revelation is here history itself in its universality (*Universalsgeschichte*), whose end has already appeared proleptically in the Resurrection of Jesus of Nazareth. This awareness of the end of history remains provisional because it is only anticipated in the destiny of Jesus; thus, theology moves beyond Hegel's absolutizing of history. At work here is an ideosyncratic reversal of time, in which the present comes to us not from the past but out of the future. This ontological priority of the future means that God lies not "above", nor "within", but "ahead"; his actions in history have the character of promise, to which the preeminent Christian response is hope, not faith. Thus, one views "the world as history, history as the history of the end, faith as hope, and theology as eschatology" (J. B. Metz: "L'Église et le monde" in *Théologie d'aujourd'hui et de demain* [1967] 140). Of recent date, this use of universal history as hermeneutical key has tended to give way to a different emphasis on historical efficacy, in which *praxis* becomes at once a source and method for theology. Here the goal is not the interpretation of history from its end, but the transformation of a history still in the making, with concern centering upon the Church as mission (J. Moltmann, *The Church in the Power of the Spirit*, 1977). The underlying methodology owes much to the "critical theory of knowledge" of the *Frankfort School (J. Habermas and T. Adorno) which equates truth with intersubjective consensus achieved in unrestricted dialogue and societal action; recently it has received a Catholic adaptation (E. Schillebeeckx). Sometimes called "political theology," its offspring is *liberation theology, which advances Christianity as primarily committed to fostering liberation from political, racial, or sexual oppression.

(10) **Theology as Process Thinking.** The Anglo-Saxon, especially the American scene has witnessed the rise of a distinct theological style committed to the primacy of change and becoming over being. Taking its inspiration from A. Whitehead's philosophy of actualism, becoming is understood not as history but as the foundational category of a neoclassical metaphysics. It delivers to theology the focal concept of a dipolar God, at once infinite and finite, eternal and temporal, engaged with the world in an endless process of creative becoming. The ultimate category is not God (who is one actual entity among others) but creativity, to which God and world are subordinate but which is not itself actual (*see* THEISM AND PROCESS THOUGHT). Obviously, this necessitates a radical reinterpretation of all the Christian mysteries; a Catholic parallel to it, in a limited respect,

is to be found in Teilhard de Chardin's re-presentation of Christianity in terms of universal evolution.

(11) **Additional Characteristics.** Its new ambiance has enabled theology to begin developing a suggestion made at Vatican Council II into a theory of the hierarchy of truths of Christian doctrine (*Unitatis redintegratio* 2). This represents an alternative to former concern with "theological notes" (10:523) and both Y. Congar and C. Dumont urged it at the Council as able to claim the authority of Aquinas. Order among the revealed truths is determined on the basis of proximity to the foundational truth who is Jesus the Christ. Basically, this allows differentiating primary truths (Trinity, Incarnation, Redemption, etc.) from subordinate truths concerning the means of salvation (Church, Sacraments, Apostolic Succession, etc.). Another characteristic is the transfer of theology from the seminary to the university setting with the regaining of free inquiry. Also at work is an awareness of the need for dialogue with the nonbelieving world, in which theology attends to the genuine questions of contemporary mankind both within the believing community and outside it, including in the latter instance such questions as that of contemporary *atheism. Finally, mention should be made of attempts just getting under way to develop a genuine pastoral theology as a "moment" within theology proper, in which recourse would be had to the experience of Christians themselves and to the findings of the social sciences as rethought within a properly theological perspective (*see* THEOLOGICAL FIELD EDUCATION; THEOLOGY AND SOCIOLOGY).

Bibliography: H. U. VON BALTHASAR, *Love Alone* (New York 1969). I. BARBOUR, *Myths, Models and Paradigms* (New York 1974). D. BROWN, R. JAMES, and G. REEVES, *Process Philosophy and Christian Thought* (Indianapolis 1971). D. CARROLL, "Hierarchia Veritatum," IrTheolQ 44 (1977) 125–133. Y. CONGAR et al., *Pluralisme et Oecuménisme en Recherches Théologiques* (Paris 1976). H.-G. GADAMER, *Truth and Method*, tr. G. BARDEN and J. CUMMING (New York 1975). J. GILL, *I. Ramsey: To Speak Responsibility of God* (London 1976). C. GREFFRÉ, *A New Age in Theology* (New York 1974). W. KASPER, *The Methods of Dogmatic Theology* (New York 1969). B. LONERGAN, *Method in Theology* (New York 1972). A. NYGREN, *Meaning and Method* (Philadelphia 1972). W. PANNENBURG, "Hermeneutics and Universal History," *History and Hermeneutics* (New York 1967); *Theology and the Philosophy of Science* (Philadelphia 1976). K. RAHNER, *Grundkurs des Glaubens: Einführung in den Begriff des Christentums* (Freiburg–im–Breisgau 1976). E. SCHILLEBEECKX, *The Understanding of Faith* (New York 1974). T. TORRANCE, *Theological Science* (London 1969). D. TRACY, *Blessed Rage for Order* (New York 1974).

[W. J. HILL]

THEOLOGY AND HISTORY

Early Christianity was characterized by a strong sense of linear history in which God "economized" all that was to happen in light of his own intentions to bring history itself to its consummation in and as God's Kingdom.

Classical Theology. Augustine's *City of God*, however, transposed this lived grasp of divine providence to an ahistorical realm rooted in divine election of those who would participate in God's eternal glory. Augustine's view necessitated distinguishing between events in their dissolving temporality (in the city of man) and in their acquiring through grace a relationality to eternity (in the city of God). History as such was rendered neutral; nonetheless, salvation occurred only within time in which divine providence worked through, and not contrary to, man's free activity. This vision went unchallenged in the theologies of the later, medieval Church, where its meaning was deepened by articulation into the integral conceptual systems of the medievals. At the Reformation, John Calvin extenuated the Augustinian theory into a doctrine of predestinationism, but with the novel addition of calling for a transformation by the elect under God's rule of a history vitiated by sin.

The Enlightenment and its issue, liberal Protestantism, abandoned Calvin's view of history as sinful, and as such resistant to God's sovereignty, and reconceptualized it as progressive in a way that allowed for an eventual coincidence of God's aims and the direction given to history by men. Since God's acts in Christ established that coincidence, Schleiermacher and Ritschl were able to promote an understanding of theology as "thoroughly historicized eschatology" (L. Gilkey 153), in which the Kingdom, inaugurated and manifest in Christ, was a this-worldly one, lying in the temporal future. This contributed to the rise of modern historical consciousness in which the being of man is understood as essentially temporal and self-determinative, autonomous vis-à-vis the past and so oriented creatively towards the future. Within such thinking, any doctrine of providence is an embarrassment; paradoxically, such substitute forces of stabilization came to the fore as the law of Darwinian determinism.

Neo-Orthodoxy. In the period after World War I the relevancy of Christian faith began to erode under the impact of this new historical consciousness, precipitating the Neo-Orthodoxy movement in Protestantism (10:332), which capitulated to the modern notion of history as entirely secular and of itself devoid of any sacral dimension. God's act above time, however, intersects each moment and event, but in a time-transcending way hidden to the world and available only on the basis of faith in the Christ-event. This initial ahistorical cast, in which faith is rescued from historical criticism by being reduced to existential decision (Bultmann), was later compromised by allowing for a hidden sovereignty of God over the world (e.g. in Karl Barth's *Church Dogmatics*). But still history (and along with it, nature) was relativized to the point that it was no longer itself a bearer of divine purposes, but only an occasion in which God's Word confronts individuals. The inadequacies of this view appear in its ahistorical character, its fideism, and its individualism. Two major attempts to meet this objection have been: Oscar Cullmann's doctrine of *Heilsgeschichte*, a sacred history superimposed upon world history in which the purposes of God are unfolded; and the advocacy by the post-Bultmannians of a revised notion of New Testament history as the existential life-commitment of Jesus undergirding the events recounted.

The Eschatological View. Reaction began with an emphasis upon *eschatology, understood now not as the vertical dimension of eternity in every temporal moment (Neo-Orthodoxy), but as a thrust within history itself towards its own consummation and occurring within the present course of history rather than at the end of time. Divine revelation is universal history (Pannenberg), whose unity appears only from its end, anticipated in the destiny of Jesus. Reality is thus structured as time, in which the future is accorded ontological priority and impinges efficaciously upon the present. Thus, the transformation of history occurs not developmentally out of the past but in novel ways out of the future. This is not the *telos* of Aristotle and

Aquinas, in which the end preexists in divine intentionality, because the mode of God's being is also future. Nor is it Hegelianism, since the future lacks all logical determination and remains open, giving rise to the religious response of hope. For Jürgen Moltmann, God's action in history continually contradicts man's own achievements (*Theology of Hope*, 1967); thus the Church is summoned to the cause of liberation under the Holy Spirit as the divine power of futurity (*The Church in the Power of the Spirit*, 1977). This emphasis upon eschatology as the decisive element in Christianity is motivated in part by a desire to meet the charges of contemporary *atheism, especially in dialogue with Marxists (e.g. Ernst Bloch). Questionable in all this are the ontologizing of history, the conceiving of God in terms of futurity so that he ceases to be a God of the present, an arbitrary identifying of the future with freedom and the past with sin.

Process Thought. A radical alternative is operative in the theological use of Whitehead's ontology of process, represented by C. Hartshorne, S. Ogden, J. Cobb, L. Ford, D. D. Williams, N. Pittenger, and a host of younger American, mostly Protestant, theologians. Here, the basic category is becoming, applicable not just to history but to all reality, which ultimately consists of a plurality of "occasions" that are self-creative actualizations of eternal ideas. God himself is dipolar, at once temporal (necessarily interacting with the world in time) and eternal (in the sense that nothing of his being perishes in his becoming). History thus becomes God's supplying of subjective aims to actual occasions, by way of his envisioning of infinite possibilities, luring them to maximum actualization. A Catholic approximation to this, in some respects only, appears in Teilhard de Chardin's theology within an evolutionary worldview. Serious reservations towards this thought arise because of its dismissal of the events of history in their particularity, which, collapsing into pure becoming, possess no perduring significance. The centrality of Christ and his resurrection are necessarily relativized and lose all claim to uniqueness (*see* THEISM AND PROCESS THOUGHT).

Current Catholic Theology. Catholic theological views of history focus upon the Christ-event as neither exclusively incarnational nor exclusively eschatological. History is concerned with events of the past primarily in light of events in the making, involving man and God in dialogue. Karl Rahner sees the actions of God in history as supplying content to the transcendental, (objectless) capacities of man for knowledge and love; Hans Urs von Balthasar, by contrast, insists that God's Word in its very historicity interprets itself to men. Concern for the afterlife has given way to concern for the temporal future of mankind under God insofar as the *eschaton* is understood as taking shape only in the depths of earthly history (E. Schillebeeckx). Thus, the "promise–fulfillment" schema of futurist eschatology is qualified so as to give more weight to past tradition as ingredient in present self-understanding. The Church is the primal Sacrament of God's dealings with men in history; the primacy of the future is thereby not allowed to negate the actual relationship with God in the present. The vector of history runs from the present, by way of the past, into the future—not from the future into the present (K. Rahner). The appropriation of history by believers is less a private affair than something social that issues in public *praxis* (J. B. Metz), while the phenomenon of secularity has tended to put sacred history into richer perspective with world history.

Bibliography: R. ANDERSON, *Historical Transcendence and the Reality of God* (Grand Rapids, Mich. 1975). H. U. VON BALTHASAR, *A Theology of History* (New York 1963). L. GILKEY. *Reaping the Whirlwind* (New York 1976). J. B. METZ, *Theology of the World* (New York 1969). W. PANNENBERG, *Theology and the Kingdom of God* (Philadelphia 1969). K. RAHNER, "The Hermeneutics of Eschatological Assertions," *Theological Investigations* 6, tr. K. H. and B. KRUGER (Baltimore 1969). D. SOELLE, *Political Theology* (Philadelphia 1971). E. SCHILLEBEECKX, "The Interpretation of Eschatology," in L. COGNET, ed., *Post-Reformation Spirituality. Concilium* 41 (1969).

[W. J. HILL]

THEOLOGY AND LITURGY

A complex relationship exists between liturgy and theology, which it is the task of *liturgical theology to analyze and explore. One important focus on this relationship is the formative influence of the liturgy on theology implied in several documents of Vatican Council II. Aiming their remarks at students of theology, the Fathers urge an intimate link between the spiritual life and the intellectual, and suggest that the mystery of salvation revealed in Scripture guide the planning of the entire theological program: spiritual, intellectual, and pastoral. They further note: "This mystery of Christ and of man's salvation they should discover and live in the liturgy" (*Ad gentes* 16; cf. *Sacrosanctum Concilium* 17). The mystery of Christ with which theology grapples is actualized in the Church's liturgy. There the students are to discover experientially what reflectively they seek to understand.

The accent on *discovery* signals a radical shift in the relation of liturgy to theology. For centuries the liturgy has been viewed as an entity whose meaning was to be learned from dogmatic and scriptural sources. Now the implication is that liturgy speaks its own meaning to those who participate in it. The further implication is that theological truth cannot completely be grasped unless its meaning is discovered experientially in the liturgy itself.

The accent on *discovery* also signals a shift in the relation of people to the liturgy. Liturgy is a locus of experience where the saving action of God in Christ is both manifested and accomplished (*Sacrosanctum Concilium* 7). People have the right and duty to seek that experience within the liturgy itself. Awareness of God's saving action and consent to its claim are constitutive elements in a mature, explicit faith. To discover the mystery of Christ and salvation in the liturgy is to find the experience which theology names and amplifies.

Only in the light of Vatican II's radical shift can the formative influence of liturgy on theology be properly understood. Theology is reflection on faith and can only take shape as faith dictates. Theology, moreover, remains dependent on the input of faith, and can never achieve a life of its own. Experience of the mystery of Christ in the liturgy not only informs theological reflection, but imposes a limit upon it. Theology must recognize that the truth it examines and seeks to understand continues to unfold in the life of the Church: it happens *somewhere* and it looks like *something*. When theology forgets its dependence on liturgy, its very lifeblood is cut off. It loses an element crucial to its own integrity and incurs the mortal illness of imagining that it needs no human experience to animate its meaning and discourse. Theology and liturgy alike will be weakened.

By stressing the importance of discovery in the liturgy, Vatican II has restated a fundamental priority in the liturgy-theology relationship. Not only does liturgy speak its own meaning to experience, it speaks theology's meaning to experience as well. Liturgy, not theology, is the more primitive mode of communication by which God's saving action is spoken to us and accomplished for us. No one need be theologically acute to discover the mystery of Christ and salvation in the liturgy; no one, however, can be theologically acute without that discovery.

Bibliography: W. BURGHARDT, "A Theologian's Challenge to Liturgy," ThSt 35 (1974) 233–248. M. COLLINS, "Liturgical Methodology and the Cultural Evolution of Worship in the United States," *Worship* 49 (1975) 85–102; J. EMPEREUR, "The Theological Experience," ChSt 16 (1977) 45–62. P. FINK, "Towards a Liturgical Theology," *Worship* 47 (1973) 601–609. J. GALLEN, "American Liturgy: a Theological Locus," ThSt 35 (1974) 302–311; "Liturgical Reform: Product or Prayer," *Worship* 47 (1973) 580–591. L. GILKEY, "Symbols, Meaning, and the Divine Presence," ThSt 35 (1974) 249–267. R. KEIFER, "Liturgical Text as Primary Source for Eucharistic Theology," *Worship* 51 (1977) 186–196. P. REGAN, "Liturgy and the Experience of Celebration," *Worship* 47 (1973) 592–600. D. SALIERS, "Prayer and Emotion: Shaping and Expressing Christian Life," *Worship* 49 (1975) 461–475. A. SCHMEMANN, *Introduction to Liturgical Theology* (London 1966).

[P. FINK]

THEOLOGY AND PHILOSOPHY

In their attempt to articulate the changing theological scene signalled by Vatican Council II's call for renewal, contemporary Catholic theologians have found four quite different philosophical orientations appropriate and helpful. The four may be called transcendental, phenomenological, process, and linguistic. The first two, transcendental and phenomenological, refer more properly to methods or approaches to theology, which could as easily be applied to the study of literature. "Process" names a philosophy as well as a method. The last, linguistic, indicates more a theological style than either a method or a philosophy.

The Transcendental Direction. The transcendental orientation is evident in both of the major post-Vatican II Catholic theologians, Karl Rahner and Bernard Lonergan, despite deep differences in their approaches. The transcendental orientation, as manifest in both their writings, is marked by an interest in establishing the fundamental conditions necessary to make religious and theological claims. This approach is particularly helpful for appreciating the meanings of theological claims when the historical context within which they were first made may have passed away.

The Phenomenological Approach. The phenomenological orientation is to be found in one form or another in the writing of theologians who address a more popular audience. Gabriel Moran and Rosemary Haughton, despite great differences of style and focus, are alike in beginning as closely as possible to persons' experiences before relating those experiences to more traditional theological doctrines. The orientation is classified as phenomenological in order to underscore the relative significance given to the experiencing subject as distinct from the ontological object, the faithful seeker or converted Christian as distinct from the object of faith or divine Revelation.

The Process Approach. The process orientation in Catholic theology is more to be noted as an advocacy of followers of Teilhard de Chardin than of Whitehead, the process philosopher who has profoundly influenced Protestant theologians like John Cobb and Schubert Ogden. Above all, the hallmark of the process orientation is its optimism regarding the direction of a world that is ever coming to be, when the world is itself regarded as intimately related to the reality of God. The notion of a God in process of becoming who enters into the suffering and pain of life is one of the most attractive features of this orientation (*see* THEISM AND PROCESS THOUGHT).

The Linguistic Approach. The linguistic orientation can best be characterized by a quotation from D. Z. Phillips: "Philosophy is neither for nor against religious beliefs. After it has sought to clarify the grammar of such beliefs, its work is over." While individuals may disagree about the self-imposed limits expressed by Phillips, there is general agreement about philosophy's role in clarifying the grammar of religious belief as an integral part of the project of determining the truthfulness of religious claims. David Burrell remains the outstanding representative of this style of theology.

Clearly the list of prominent Catholic theologians includes many who have not been mentioned here, and assuredly not every theologian is to be as rigidly classified as is suggested here. The works of John Dunne and David Tracy, for example, represent two quite different blends of the transcendental and phenomenological methods. It might also be argued that each of the above orientations springs from the transcendental; notable in them all is a "shift to the subject." What cannot be denied, is that, as Catholic theology confronts modernity, the notion of conversion has become as important currently as the notion of Revelation was for theology in the Middle Ages.

See also PLURALISM, PHILOSOPHICAL. PLURALISM, THEOLOGICAL.

Bibliography: D. BURRELL, *Exercises in Religious Understanding* (Notre Dame 1974). J. DUNNE, *Reasons of the Heart* (New York 1978). R. HAUGHTON, *The Theology of Experience* (New York 1972). B. LONERGAN, *Method in Theology* (New York 1972). G. MORAN, *The Present Revelation* (New York 1975). K. RAHNER, *Theological Investigations*, v. 1–14 (Baltimore 1961–76). D. TRACY, *Blessed Rage for Order* (New York 1975).

[W. J. O'BRIEN]

THEOLOGY AND SOCIOLOGY

Concern for the connection between theology and sociology as methodologically distinct but related disciplines is relatively recent. It is rooted, however, in a much older question about the relation of religion and society. In that sense, the appropriate literature on theology and sociology would include such classic works, which predate the differentiation of academic disciplines, as Plato's *Republic*, Augustine's *City of God* and the writings of Montesquieu and de Tocqueville.

Historical Background. More precise methodological reflection on the relation between theology and sociology began in the Protestant theological world in 19th-century Germany as part of the discussion about the relation of faith and history, since sociology was primarily understood as a branch of history. Ernst Troeltsch (14:313) is the major figure in this discussion. Troeltsch transformed theology by his attention to the institutional prerequisites and correlates of Christianity and the way Christian ideas become world-historical, shaping forces only by their elective affinity with ascendant carrier groups and the transmutation and exfoliation of these ideas through their contact with pregiven societal structures, groups, and culture. Troeltsch scholars in the U.S., e.g., H. Richard Niebuhr (10:462) and James Luther Adams, continued his theoretical impulse. On a more practical level the disciplines were related by the use of sociology for pastoral planning in Protestant seminaries and church research agencies. On its part, the American Sociological Association, especially under the early leadership of Lester Ward and Albion Small, was much influenced by the social gospel movement (5:100).

Prior to 1960, Catholics did little methodological reflection on the relation between the two disciplines, although the American Catholic Sociological Association (*see* ASSOCIATION FOR THE SOCIOLOGY OF RELIGION) operated in its early years on the assumption that there was a specifically Catholic sociology. In Europe, church sociology, in the tradition of Gabriel Le Bras, was seen as a pretheoretical, ancillary, "fact-finding" discipline, useful for pastoral theology. In the aftermath of Vatican Council II, Catholic theologians began to dialogue with the proponents of sociology of knowledge and to inquire into new social action models to relate Church and society. Increasingly, dogma and theology are understood as strategic responses to pressing needs and claims of very particular times and places. Sociological analysis becomes an essential tool for hermeneutics in understanding the context and meaning of reactive dogmatic statements.

Evaluation of the Relationship. Many theologians now insist on social analysis as a necessary component in theological reflection. Sociology is essential for theology's task of ideology-critique and for delineating such key theological concepts as social sin, the Kingdom of God, liberation, and reading the signs of the times. Theologians turn to sociology to understand such processes as secularization and the privatization of religion. Sociology is no longer understood as a value-free purveyor of "facts," in accord with a naive realism or positivism, but is seen to include a worldview, a special imagination, and a model of human understanding. Theology has shifted from an older hierarchical understanding of the division between the sciences with its notion of "input" disciplines to a new framework of interdisciplinary creative collaboration.

Bases of Relationship. Neither theology nor sociology is, strictly speaking, a unified discipline. Both are conflictive fields of competing theoretical and methodological positions, some of them simply contradictory. Every theology contains, implicitly, a sociology and a theory of the self. Theology must raise questions about the societal implications of God's law and Kingdom and the personality implications of sanctification and love. Every theological performance claim about this-worldly transformations of self and society is subject to empirical test. Every *ecclesiology is also a theory about society. In the writings of some theologians, explicit theological motifs control the understanding of self and society. In others, secular theories of self and society determine theology. Thus, in choosing George Herbert Mead's understanding of self and society, H. Richard Niebuhr precludes certain theological options. Not every theology and sociology is compatible. It seems possible to draw up a taxonomy of the logical affinities between definite theological options and corresponding social theories.

On its part, sociology is not, in any simple sense, value-free. It includes hermeneutical presuppositions about the locus of the real, the flow of causality, and the power of value. Sociology sometimes slips from descriptive to prescriptive modes of analysis, since some vision of the future and the good society is operative in sociological and historical research.

Possible responses of Theology to Sociology in Dialogue. (1) The relevance of sociology to theology may be rejected. This response is possible only for those who rigidly separate nature and grace, e.g., Karl Barth, or who maintain idealistic epistemological positions about the unbridgeable gap between fact and value. If religion is a social fact and society has a religious dimension, theology and sociology must be correlated.

(2) Selective elements from sociology can be added as ancillary motifs for theology. Selective borrowing is usually eclectic and runs the risk that data of sociology may be either distorted in the translation process or irrelevant to the theologian's questions.

(3) A reductionist position may be taken that destroys the autonomy of sociology by subjecting it to theology. Creative collaboration between disciplines demands making distinctions between them as autonomous modes of knowing.

(4) A dialogue would mean corroboration of conclusions reached and grounded on theological premises. This is mere illuminative exemplification by means of sociological evidence rather than true interdisciplinary collaboration.

(5) Sociological language can be translated into theological discourse and vice versa. Care must be exercised to respect the varying language games of the different disciplines.

(6) A reciprocal transformation of disciplines is possible by a two-way dialogue and mutual interpenetration and critical correlation of both modes of knowing. The Catholic theological bias, drawing upon assumptions of the ultimate unity of truth in God and the analogical unity of knowledge, would seem to favor the sixth strategy for relating the disciplines. Perhaps, however, there are some contradictions among and between the disciplines of knowledge which cannot be removed because they reflect the brokenness of society. Only when the cleavages in social life resulting from sin are overcome will science be one. In the meantime, Christians strive for the goal of unifying sociology and theology.

Bibliography: J. L. ADAMS, *On Being Human Religiously* (Boston 1976). G. BAUM, *Religion and Alienation* (New York 1975). R. N. BELLAH, *Beyond Belief* (New York 1970). J. A. COLEMAN, "Theology and Sociology," CathThSoc 32 (1977) 55–71. H. R. NIEBUHR, *The Responsible Self* (New York 1963). E. TROELTSCH, *The Social Teaching of the Christian Churches,* tr. O. WYON (2 v., New York 1960). G. WINTER, *Elements for a Social Ethic* (New Work 1968). S. WOLIN, *Politics and Vision* (Boston 1960).

[J. A. COLEMAN]

THEOLOGY IN AMERICA

Theology in America has a complex and vital history. In fact the religious dimension is so intertwined with the secular in American history that Sidney E. Mead could with justice entitle his book, *Nation with the Soul of a Church* (1975). For a nation so overwhelmingly concerned with the divine and its own salvation it is little wonder that every public issue threatens to become embroiled in theological controversy—and that very many have. The history of American public life is thick with theologians and theology. Much of the theological literature is not of high quality, but then very little of any literature is. American theologians easily hold their own in the world of theological scholarship.

An American Theology? The issue of theology in America raises the questions of whether there is an American theology or, indeed, whether any national theology is possible, and what such a theology might be. There are American theologians and American Churches. There is clearly an "American experience" in the sense that the United States has a concrete and unique history, its own institutions and literature. Is there an American way of doing theology? The answer will depend in part on the way of conceiving the relation between theology and culture and the specific cultural conditions of theological reflection. In the classicist conception, reflection is acultural or supracultural; in a contemporary conception, reflection is transcultural, yet culturally founded and conditioned. Like physics, theology is transcultural in the sense that it aims at speaking truly, but such speaking invariably goes on within a cultural matrix and, unlike physics, is a mediation between a religion and a culture. The matrix provides the data and problems for reflection, the categories of expression, and ways of organizing the understanding achieved.

Cultural Influences. Some few characteristics of American culture have shaped that theological work. Space and movement, American social and political institutions, achievements in science and technology, industry and finance, religious and theological pluralism, and the peculiar events of American history contribute the range of data, set the problems, direct the attention, and limit the concerns of American theologians. From early Puritan attempts at identification of Church and town to more recent castigations of the nation in the name of a reforming Gospel in connection with the war in Vietnam, American theology has been riveted by the question of the relation of the divinity to national experience. The history of social and religious freedom and oppression, the issues of national grace and sin, the role of the Church in political and social reform etc. have engrossed theologians since the nation's inception.

Theological Language. It should be noted also that American theological solutions tend to be framed not in the language of an overarching technical philosophy but in a mode of speech close to the ordinary language of the American people. Although it is often said that American theology has been influenced by European philosophy and theology, it is also the case that an American theological language, wary of technical precision and nicety, fluid and expanding, fresh and direct, has evolved. This language may be dismissed as popular and nontechnical but it is effective and has appeal. The style of Jonathan Edwards' *Nature of True Virtue*, the controversial writings of the Boston Unitarians, or the work of such diverse figures as Horace Bushnell, Charles Finney, Walter Rauschenbusch, John Courtney Murray, or the Niebuhrs clearly show how close American theological prose is to ordinary American speech. American theological language is "arena" language precisely because historically theology in America has been done in the marketplace and town meeting rather than the academy. The language is vigorous, largely independent of European linguistic models and rhetoric, pragmatic, a language of commonsense, an organic part of the development of an American prose. The style is molded by concern for "experiential religion" dating from Jonathan Edwards and the First Awakening (1734) and for such vital social issues as religious liberty, slavery, national destiny, and, lately, sex and ecology. Finally, it is characterized by a constant and persistent revision of the traditional languages of religious and theological expression. The style shares the informality, urgency, and flexibility of American life at its best and most typical.

Issues in American Theology. Some of the issues of American theology have been mentioned. They have been characterized globally by one church historian as "public issues" addressed by and in turn shaping a "public theology" (Marty).

Protestant and Jewish Theologians. Among Protestant and Jewish authors of this century, for example, the reflection has centered on the relations between religion and culture. The question of liberal theology from Bushnell to Harvey Cox has been how inherited Christianity can contribute to and criticize American political and social experience. Protestant Neo-Orthodoxy, best represented by H. R. and Reinhold Niebuhr, brought Christian symbols to life in an effort to understand and interpret both the promise and the limits of American political and social experience. More recently, several authors, some not immediately identifiable as theologians, have continued this effort: Will Herberg, Sidney Mead, Robert Bellah. Those theologians who tend to philosophically technical reflection, such as Langdon Gilkey, John Cobb, Schubert Ogden, have engaged in a far-ranging critique of the Christian tradition in the light of American language and experience.

Catholic Theologians. On the Catholic side the issues and emphases are somewhat different but no less public. An overriding Catholic interest with the place of the Church and the Catholic in American political and social life has been both constructive and apologetic. The issues of religious liberty, of the relation between Church and State, of being Catholic and being American, have preoccupied Catholic thinkers since the colonization of Maryland. Politics has set the problem for Catholic theologians: for the Catholic colonists; for the great churchmen of the 19th century (Kenrick, Spalding, Keane, Ireland, England); and for the two outstanding Catholic apologists and publicists of that century, Orestes Brownson and Isaac Hecker. It remained true for 20th-century churchmen (Spellman) and theologians (Fenton, Murray, Weigel). The interest culminated in the Declaration of Religious Freedom of Vatican Council II (1965). Although American theology was much hampered by the post-Modernist doctrinal and organizational tightening, it has showed renewed vigor centering around broad cultural and ecclesial issues in the work of Avery Dulles, John Dunne, Andrew Greeley, Michael Novak, David Tracy, and others.

Common Contemporary Issues. The same public tendency of American theology surfaces in the culture criticism by both Catholics and Protestants in recent debates on civil religion, black religion, women's rights, and the more general movement in Christian thought called *liberation theology. It is not incorrect, in the light of the history and present state of American theology, to say that it has been dominated by issues

of practice. Its recognizable failure in systematic and speculative essays is balanced by its valuable interpretations of ordinary experience, if that experience is understood as political and social as well as individual.

Current Status. The present state of American theology can be gauged in several ways. From the point of view of method or the understanding of theology under which a theologian operates, American theology is as volatile as American life. In most theological traditions there are represented several basic methodological stances such as Orthodox, Liberal, Neo-Orthodox, Radical, and Revisionist (David Tracy, *Blessed Rage for Order*, 1975). The strains within and between denominations on this score are not inconsiderable. They were recently expressed in two cross-denominational documents issued by theologians, the "Harford Appeal for Theological Affirmation" (1975) and the "Boston Affirmations" (1976). The documents restate in a contemporary framework quite distinct, if conplementary, theological emphases on transcendence and immanence and represent the history of American theology over the past two hundred years and more in its fascination with the relationship between religious belief and social and political practice.

Other developments bear promise for the future of American theology. Since Vatican II, Catholic theologians have engaged in an ecumenical scholarly cooperation with Protestant and Jewish theologians and social scientists on interfaith committees, on faculties of theology and philosophy, in a series of distinguished publishing ventures of importance to theology and religious studies and, in general, in forming a national ecumenical community of theological scholarship. Catholic students of theology and ministry now form the largest single denominational group at several major Protestant divinity schools. The interchange between Catholic theologians and their bishops, while far from ideal, has increased, and there is hope for an expanding contribution of theological scholarship to the Church. There has grown up as well as expanding nonconfessional academic establishment devoted to the study of religion (American Academy of Religion, Council on the Study of Religion) which sometimes includes properly theological components and with which are affiliated professional theological organizations (Catholic Theological Society of America, Catholic Biblical Association). Through meetings and professional journals theologians and students of religion have considerable access to one another's work. The "nation with the soul of a Church" is spawning a large-scale, highly professional, and ecumenical body of scholars. Such developments as listed here and many others are bound to influence the future of American theology and, ultimately, of American religious bodies.

Bibliography: J. J. CAREY, "An Overview of Catholic Theology," *Theology Today* 30 (1973) 25–41. D. W. FERM, "American Protestant Theology," *Religious Life* 44 (1975) 59–72. J. J. HENNESSEY, "Roman Catholic Theology in the United States," LouvSt 6 (1976) 11–22. M. E. MARTY, "American Protestant Theology," LouvSt 6 (1976) 23–34. H. RICHARDSON, *Toward An American Theology* (New York 1967). J. J. WRIGHT, "Is there an American Theology," Communio 3 (1976) 136–150.

[W. M. SHEA]

THEOLOGY IN CATHOLIC COLLEGES

The teaching of theology in Catholic colleges has changed dramatically in the last two decades. If it was once possible to regard theology as a unitary science whose principles could be mastered and whose conclusions were secure, the current practice of theologians indicates general recognition of a deep-seated pluralism which can neither be ignored nor responsibly engaged in the manner that marked the theology of the 1940s and 1950s.

Contributing Factors. A number of factors have contributed to the present situation. Vatican Council II was not so much cause as symptom of fundamental changes in the spirit of Catholicism. For the first time the cultural forces which had rocked Protestantism to its foundations in the 19th century were absorbed and integrated into the life of Catholicism. Scholarly investigations into the composition of the Scriptures, once mistrusted, were affirmed and encouraged. The Vatican II documents also suggest that the generations of historical research encouraged by Leo XIII when he called for a return to Thomas Aquinas in the encyclical, *Aeterni Patris* (1879) have prepared the present generation for the intellectual challenges of "historical consciousness" that does not rest easy with absolute claims. Hence, the present theological context is one of dialogue with other Christians, with Judaism, with other religious traditions, and with atheism.

A second factor contributing to the present situation of theological *pluralism is the student. Catholic colleges have just begun to live with the situation produced by the decisions of many bishops in the late 1960s to close parochial schools in their dioceses. The change was gradual, since the factors, mainly economic, which led to a decline in support of parochial schools and eventually to their closing also moved more and more Catholic children into public schools at ever earlier ages. As a result, a different kind of student is present in the college classroom. In studies undertaken at the University of Notre Dame between 1975 and 1977, for example, it was discovered that less than half of the incoming students had four years of Catholic high school education and 20 per cent had had no religious instruction of any kind during those years. While most of those entering indicated strong interest in taking courses in theology at the college level, it appears that the number of students entering college largely ignorant of their religious traditions is growing.

The third factor contributing to theological pluralism is faculty. The ecumenical impulse of Vatican II encouraged colleges to insure dialogue with persons of other confessions and religions, and most faculties now reflect a diversity of religious convictions. Furthermore, as more and more Catholics, both lay and clerical, have been trained in Protestant divinity schools, diversification in approaches to theological education has deeply marked the teaching of theology in Catholic colleges.

Identity Crisis. Each of these factors has produced something like an identity crisis within departments of theology. In fact, in the majority of Catholic colleges, the department title "religious studies" has been adopted, indicating a differentiation within the discipline. In general, those departments which retain the name "theology" give more attention to investigating the particularities of the Catholic tradition and contemporary thought, simply assuming the faith commitment that is essential to the educational institution as a whole. Those departments which have adopted the title "religious studies," on the other hand, tend to be more attentive to religious differences among students and faculty and approach the study of religion more descrip-

tively than confessionally. However, since theology today is more often than not taught with an eye to the diversity of religious convictions present in any classroom, the ecumenical, comparative, and interdisciplinary elements are included in both situations and the lines of distinction between theology and religious studies are somewhat blurred (*see* RELIGIOUS EDUCATION).

Approaches to Theology. The factors influencing departments to change their names have also led to quite different approaches in the study of theology. Because the present theological context is one of ecumenical dialogue in the widest sense, the methods of theology have become interdisciplinary in an unprecedented way. The study of theology is carried out not only in dialogue with its age-old partner, philosophy, but courses relating theology to literature, psychology, sociology, anthropology, the natural sciences, and the *history of religions are to be found in virtually every college curriculum.

Because recent students have often not known the close parochial bonds of church, school, and neighborhood, they tend to be more critical and questioning of inherited forms of religion and regard Catholicism and Christianity as options. Therefore, their study of theology takes on a new form of personal quest as they explore the individual and social dimensions of religious experience. Teachers frequently accommodate students by designing courses that relate religious classics to the students' quite personal religious questions. In this way students are led to discover the personal meaning of the articles of faith that have been handed down to them by their parents or religious educators. In other instances, courses are designed to enlarge the vision of students so that they may recognize that religion is not simply a personal matter but one also deeply at issue in social problems—hunger, racism, war, poverty, injustice. The concern for both the personal and the social is to clarify the meaning of religious witness; the emphasis has shifted from questions about the object of faith to the meaning of religious witness. Because of the plurality of convictions present in the current classroom situation, the study of theology has relied more heavily on those disciplines which serve to clarify both the convictions of individual students and the fact of their diversity.

The Future. In the future, theology in Catholic colleges may take yet another turn as more and more students ask not so much about the meaning of their religious heritage as for information about it. If the number of students increase who have never read the Bible nor heard of Vatican II, theologians will need to rethink what is involved in insuring that students "come to vivid appreciation of their own heritage, not in an insular way, but as it lives in dialogue with the pluriform world culture in which they live" (A. Carr in Gaffney and O'Brien 34).

Bibliography: J. COULSON, ed., *Theology and the University* (Baltimore 1964). J. P. GAFFNEY and W. J. O'BRIEN, eds., *Occasional Papers on Catholic Higher Education* 1 (Washington, D.C. 1975). R. MASTERSON, ed., *Theology in the Catholic College* (Dubuque, Iowa 1961).

[W. J. O'BRIEN]

THEOLOGY IN SEMINARIES

Renewal in the Church, as envisioned at Vatican Council II, depends in great measure on the ministry of priests. The Council's Decree on Priestly Formation gives this truth emphatic expression in its opening and closing paragraphs. The quality of priestly ministry in the Church depends in great measure on the quality of programs of priestly formation. Renewal in the Church, therefore, is intimately linked with the renewal of seminaries, especially in view of the Council's teaching "that major seminaries are necessary for priestly formation" (*Optatam totius* 4).

A seminary is more than a school of theology. Professional formation for priestly ministry demands programs for the personal and spiritual development of seminarians and for their pastoral formation as well. However, a seminary cannot be anything less than a school of theology. A first-class theological education is an absolute necessity for those who aspire to serve in the ministerial priesthood in today's world. Seminaries enjoy no monopoly in the teaching of theology; many colleges and universities have excellent departments of theology. However, because of the critical role theology must play in the formation of future priests, there does exist a reality called "theology in seminaries." This expression might cause some misunderstanding, as though "theology in seminaries" were to suggest a theology of lessened academic rigor. On the contrary, this expression is intended to place theology in its properly pastoral context; it in no way connotes a theology diminished in intellectual seriousness.

This article has a twofold purpose. It seeks to present in summary form the implementation of *Optatam totius* in the seminaries of the United States, as this implementation is expressed in the documents that are presently normative for the work of priestly formation. It seeks also to provide a modest evaluation of the wider latitude given today to seminary programs of theology in the light of the complex issue of the legitimacy and limits of the theological *pluralism acceptable within the scope of Catholic theology.

Church Documents. Vatican Council II intended the Decree on Priestly Formation to function in the Church of today the way the seminary decree of the Council of Trent functioned in the Church of its day. The Decree's first article constitutes a historic breaking away from Tridentine seminary legislation and enunciates an operative principle of decentralization: "Since only general laws can be made where there exists a wide variety of nations and regions, a special program of priestly formation is to be undertaken by each country or rite. It must be set up by the episcopal conferences, revised from time to time and approved by the Apostolic See. In this way will the universal laws be adapted to the particular circumstances of times and localities so that the priestly training will always be in tune with the pastoral needs of those regions in which the ministry is to be exercised" (*Optatam totius* 1). In 1970 the Congregation for Catholic Education, in response to a request from the 1967 Synod of Bishops, made public *The Basic Plan for Priestly Formation* (*Ratio fundamentalis institutionis sacerdotalis* (ActApS 62 [1970] 321–384)). The aim of this document, in service to the episcopal conferences, was "to omit nothing that seemed useful; to add nothing superfluous; to lay down nothing that was not universally valid; always to pay attention to modern conditions" (7). In 1971 the *Bishops' Committee on Priestly Formation issued *The Program of Priestly Formation* as the official document for the renewal of seminaries implementing *Optatam totius*; in 1976 a second, revised edition became the normative guidelines presently in force. Also in 1976 the Sacred Congregation

for Catholic Education issued a valuable document on *The Theological Formation of Future Priests.*

Directions in Theological Education. First of all, theological education in seminaries of the United States is considered as graduate study. Graduate study is of two kinds, graduate academic study, primarily directed to preparing the student for teaching and research, and graduate professional study, directed to prepare a student to practice a profession. Even though the ministerial priesthood transcends the character of a profession, it demands graduate professional education for its exercise. The academic aspects of such professional education is the concern of this article. The Church also needs graduate academic programs to prepare scholars and teachers in theology; however, this is not the focus of a program of priestly formation. Secondly, theological education today, if it is to be in the spirit of Vatican II, must be ecumenical in dimension. This major emphasis concerns but transcends the academic aspect and touches all other areas of a seminary program. The pertinent documents treat this important matter at great length. Thirdly, a new and significant development in the Catholic seminaries of the United States now is *theological field education. This program is given powerful support in the Bishops' Committee document, which envisions field education as a stimulating and integrating force at work in the spiritual and academic maturation of the seminarians. Field education, while not concerned directly with the academic curriculum, is to be coordinated with and integrated into the academic sphere. The *Program* asserts that the active pastoral involvement provided by field education, if carefully designed and properly supervised, is just as educational as classroom work (185).

Foundational Principles. The renewal of seminary academic programs can profitably be examined in the light of principles that are foundational for the specific instructions on the distribution of theological courses.

Faith and Theology. The first principle concerns the relation between faith and theology, a relationship not of identity or of separation but of distinction (*Program* 97–100). Theology is described in the normative documents as faith seeking understanding. This first principle, then, insists on the necessary role and importance of faith for the work of theology. At the present time, however, there are some who do not support the notion that theology is *faith* seeking understanding. In the American theological community some intend to separate faith and theology, either in a laudable effort to defend theology's right to scientific existence, or because they reject the possibility of reconciling a commitment of faith and the freedom of intellectual inquiry. On the other hand, there are some who really do not support the notion that theology is faith seeking *understanding.* In the American Catholic community some give primacy not to understanding but to theology's role of justifying and defending official church teaching. *The Program of Priestly Formation* boldly champions the position on intelligence serving faith that was regained by Vatican Council I (Denz 3016); however, article 100 of the *Program* must be examined with care. The document rightly encourages the effort to discern the validity as well as the limitations of the human expression of God's truth in history. Article 100 states that "seminarians should be formed to distinguish the truths revealed by God from their theological mode of expression." This statement can be understood as describing the difference between the substance of a teaching and its formulation, as explicitly taught by John XXIII (cf. ActApS 54 [1962] 785–796), and by *Gaudium et spes* (62; cf. *Unitatis redintegratio* 6). However, if this statement is meant to suggest that revealed truths can be found somehow or somewhere untouched by theological modes of expression, this would change distinction into separation and undermine the very principle the document is defending.

Experience. A second basic principle of the *Program* concerns the fact that the priestly office "as essentially defined by the Church is today carried out in an entirely new situation and style, due to mankind's new needs and the nature of modern civilization" (101). This principle focuses on the necessary relation between the riches of the tradition and the experiences and insights of the believing community today. In other words, experience is an essential ingredient of theology. Theology is the correlation of the normative tradition and contemporary human experience. As a result, a theological curriculum must take into account "the needs of a multi-cultured society, be adapted to the needs of an ecumenical age, be geared to a global awareness of reality, a unified concept of humanity and a universal vision of faith" (102).

Historical Consciousness. A third basic principle is recognition that modern methods of historical study have profoundly changed the face of theology (Program 103–104). Pastoral in orientation, graduate professional study is not geared to the historical ideal of critically evaluating all the available evidence. However, it is imperative that seminarians come to appreciate the historical dimension as an essential moment in the theological study. A critical sense of history will protect the student from the excessive relativism that would destroy continuity with the past and from an ahistorical immutability that leaves no room for doctrinal development.

Adaptation. A fourth basic principle is the maxim, "whatever is received is received according to the manner of the recipient." The theological curriculum considers the experience, the interests, the needs of the student as a person (*Program* 109–111). In this way the academic program builds on what the student knows and leads him to inquire about the deeper truths of Revelation, especially seen in the social, political, moral, and ecclesial contexts of today. This principle calls for renewal in methods of theological instruction. Seminars, discussions, programs of independent study can supplement the lectures and thus help to bring experience and reflection into a working harmony.

Unity and Pluralism. The crucial issue of unity and pluralism in theology leads to a fifth basic principle (*Program* 107–108). That there are many theologies through which the one faith of the Catholic Church is expressed is evident both within the canon of the Scriptures and in the history of theology. These many theologies constitute a genuine wisdom "whose unity is established on the Word of God who is one, on the Gospel of Christ which is one, and on the Catholic Church which is one" (*Program* 107). Such a vision of unity demands a theological curriculum in which the different disciplines cooperate effectively so that the student comes to appreciate the inner unity, the coherence, and the harmony of the many theological tasks. This vision of unity is not shared in the global theological community. The pluralism that presently prevails is vastly different from the form of pluralism familiar to scholars of earlier ages. The development of the historical-critical method, the many turns of philosophy in the modern and contemporary periods, varying approaches to the question of interpretation have led today to bewildering diversification. Academic competence and Christian prudence are demanded of teachers so that teachers and students may appreciate both the legitimacy and the limits of pluralism within the context of theology's essential unity and the unity of faith.

These basic principles constitute the foundation for the new orientations that characterize the academic programs now in progress and still in development in the seminaries of the United States. The full implications of these principles, hidden from those who authored *The Program of Priestly Formation* and hidden still from those seminary authorities who are implementing it, should not be a cause of concern as long as the principles are set in their properly Catholic context. This context is well described in the *Program*: "In preparation for his ministry of service to the Word of God, the priestly candidate should understand and appreciate God's message as it is proclaimed in Sacred Scripture and reflected in the living tradition of the Church. He should appreciate the role of theology in advancing theological research and accept with wholehearted fidelity the college of bishops in union with the Roman Pontiff as the authentic magisterium in witnessing to the faith and giving pastoral guidance" (117).

The Curriculum. With regard to particular disciplines and their arrangement in the theological curriculum, pride of place goes to the study of Sacred Scripture which, as the inspired Word of God, ought to function as the soul of theology (*Dei Verbum* 24). There is more to theology than biblical theology but any theology not ultimately grounded in the Scriptures cannot claim the name of theology at all. It is essential that the professional character and the relative autonomy of Scripture study be recognized and that Scripture be taught by those qualified in the modern biblical approach. The tasks of the professor are to initiate the students in the method of exegesis, to familiarize the students with the problems of biblical criticism, and to help them understand and apply the rules for the proper interpretation of the Bible. As the *Program* exhorts: "Throughout his entire seminary training the candidate shall acquire a loving familiarity with the Word of God in the text of the Bible as fundamental to his Christian faith" (123).

The study of Sacred Scripture readies the student for the work of systematic theology. This demands thorough analysis and synthesis of the Christian faith in continuity with the heritage of the past and in the contemporary cultural context of the Church in the modern world. Divine Revelation does not come in ready-made theses but in a history of salvation. The rich theological tradition, in Scripture and in the development of dogma, must be studied in the context of the history of the Church. By means of this genetic-historical approach the student grasps his roots in history and develops a catholic view of doctrine by discerning the Gospel message in its many expressions in history. An integral experience in systematic reflection demands a measure of competency in many areas of traditional concern: fundamental theology, Christology, ecclesiology, sacramental theology, the Christian concept of God, and eschatology. The documents mention other areas in some detail. Moral theology, for example, with clear awareness of the Christian's sublime vocation and concerned about the Christian's responsibilities in and for the world, must be renewed on the basis of sound scriptural and doctrinal scholarship. Liturgy—its theology, its history, its juridical aspects—ought to be a major course in the curriculum and so taught that the student realizes how the mysteries of salvation are made present and operative in liturgical celebration (*see* LITURGICAL EDUCATION IN SEMINARIES; THEOLOGY AND LITURGY). Finally, insistence is placed on such pastoral studies as Canon Law, homiletics, catechetics, pastoral counseling, and the communication arts. To do systematic theology in today's world and thus in a contemporary manner, the student requires deeper understanding of contemporary philosophical movements. No serious work can be done in systematic theology and therefore no serious preparation for the preaching and teaching tasks of the priestly ministry can be had if the student is insufficiently aware of the new situations created in theology by contemporary philosophical concerns, anthropological, existential, personalist, sociopolitical, and hermeneutical. Theology today faces problems which touch the very foundations of theological knowledge, such as the very possibility of doctrinal definitions of permanent value. The student of systematic theology stands helpless in the face of contemporary challenges to his discipline if he remains without the philosophical skills that enable him to deal with the epistemological and ontological issues that are foundational for the theological task (*see* PHILOSOPHY IN SEMINARIES).

The renewal of the seminary academic program is vital to the task of priestly formation. The task of priestly formation is vital to the work of renewal in the Church. Whether this renewal is conceived in terms of the Church's inner life or in terms of the Church's outward vitality, so much depends on the ministry of priests. The quality of their ministry will reflect the quality of their seminary formation.

Bibliography: Bishops' Committee on Priestly Formation, *The Program of Priestly Formation* (2d ed., USCC Publ. Office, Washington, D.C. 1976). Congregation for Catholic Education, *Ratio fundamentalis . . .* tr., *The Basic Plan for Priestly Formation* (USCC Publ. Office, Washington, D.C. 1970); *The Theological Formation of Future Priests* (USCC Publ. Office, Washington, D.C. 1976).

[J. J. CONNELLY]

THIRD WORLD, CHURCH AND

The rapid emancipation of the colonial peoples of Asia and Africa from Western rule since 1945, followed by efforts on the part of both Western and Communist great powers to dominate them by neocolonialism, has led to the self-assertion of a group of nations collectively known as the "Third World." Though differing widely among themselves in culture, they, together with the economically dependent countries of Latin America, generally share the common denominator of being nations "still seeking the means to escape from the domination of the great powers and to develop freely." These efforts to achieve national independence, economic and cultural as well as political, have had repercussions in the life and theology of the Church since Vatican Council II. That about half of all baptized Catholics live today in the Third World is a fact that itself forces the Church, in accordance with the insistence of Vatican II on the need to discern the signs of the times as a source of theological reflection, to reflect on the relevance that the conditions and aspirations of the Third World have for understanding its own

nature and mission. It is no longer acceptable theologically to consider the Churches of "mission countries," as simply branches of the European and American Churches, destined to follow models and patterns operative there.

The Church's Active Ministry for Development. The nations of the Third World are characterized, first, by economic underdevelopment, which makes them dependent on the First and Second Worlds; and second, by a political, and especially cultural, dependence, largely the result of their economic dependence. This economic dependence in turn is seen to be ultimately due to a gross imbalance in the distribution of this world's wealth and the means to acquire it, both within the developing nations themselves and in relation to the economically developed countries (*see* WEALTH, DISTRIBUTION OF). In this unjust situation the Church, as witness to and servant of the Word of God, is called upon to denounce not only individual injustices, as she has so often done in the past, but likewise, and perhaps more especially, structural injustice, the national and international economic orders which perpetuate this situation and continue to accelerate this gap between the nations or classes who possess and those who do not and who cannot acquire the means of doing so within the present structures (*see* NEW INTERNATIONAL ECONOMIC ORDER).

In accordance with the teaching of Vatican II's *Gaudium et spes* and Paul VI's *Populorum progressio*, however, in this situation of massive injustice the task of the Church cannot be merely the prophetic one of denunciation. The Church must actively involve herself as well in the effort to change the conditions which cause so many to suffer injustice by actively promoting the economic development of the Third-World peoples and their liberation from the forces which oppress them. This work of development and liberation, however, must not be seen merely as a means to attract people to the Gospel, nor even as simply a kind of pre-evangelization in which the conditions necessary to preach the Gospel effectively may be established. Rather, as recognized by the 1971 Synod of Bishops (Synod of JustWorld p. 34) and stated more explicitly by Paul VI in *Evangelii nuntiandi* (Paul VI EvangNunt 31), the work of development and liberation is a necessary part of evangelization today and integral to the mission of the Church. Hence, even in situations in which there is no possibility of actually preaching the Word or administering the Sacraments, the Church must fulfill her mission of working for the coming of God's Kingdom by her contribution to human development, including that economic development necessary to make total human development possible.

The Church and the Local Churches. Such a concern for total human development, and even for the economic welfare of peoples, is not totally new in the Church. The evangelization of Latin America by the Iberian Churches in the 16th century and of the Asian and African peoples in the 19th century was accompanied by the introduction of European civilization, new methods of agriculture, and even technology. These benefits, however, came about as a result of conquest and colonization and were characterized by a cultural imperialism which had little respect for the indigenous cultures. Today the achievement of political independence has been followed by a desire to be free of other forms of imperialism as well, not only economic but also cultural. Just as the Church must assist the Third World peoples in achieving a just international economic structure in the world, and within these nations themselves must work that the wealth of the country be not concentrated in the hands of a small elite, so too she is obliged not to perpetuate herself in the carrying out of her mission by the imposition of Western cultural forms and values on non-Western peoples. This means not only the recognition of and respect for truly Christian values immanent in the cultures of Third World peoples, but also the right of these Churches to create their own modes of expression of God's Word (cf. *Ad gentes* 11–12; 19–22). The Church universal can no longer concern itself only with the theological problematics and pastoral formulations of the West, whether past or contemporary. Nor can it be assumed that the forms of church order and worship which have prevailed or are currently in use in the older Churches of the West are in any sense preferred modes of worshipping or ordering the universal Church. Though numerous measures have been taken toward the recognition of a legitimate pluralism in forms of worship and, more tentatively, toward accepting the principle of diverse theological expressions of the Gospel, it cannot be said that all the implications of Vatican II's recognition of cultural and theological pluralism have yet been recognized in practice. Not only in cultures with ancient and well developed philosophical and religious traditions of their own, like India and China, must such pluralism be acknowledged, but in other peoples too, even if possessing less developed systems of thought and values, an indigenous theology is demanded if the Gospel is truly to speak to all men (*see* INCULTURATION, THEOLOGICAL).

See also LITURGY AND LOCAL CHURCHES; MISSION (NEW TRENDS); MISSIONARY ADAPTATION.

Bibliography: G. H. ANDERSON, ed., *Asian Voices in Christian Theology* (Maryknoll, N.Y. 1976). G. H. ANDERSON and T. F. STRANSKY, eds., *Mission Trends No. 1: Crucial Issues in Mission Today* (New York 1974); *Mission Trends No. 2: Evangelization* (New York 1975); *Mission Trends No. 3: Third World Theologies* (New York 1976).

[J. N. SCHUMACHER]

THOMISM

The term Thomism is used to designate either the systematic teaching of St. Thomas Aquinas or what others have made of that teaching in their attempts to comprehend it and relate it to the problems and needs of later centuries (14:126). In both understandings there have been significant developments since Vatican Council II. This article sketches the major recent changes and trends.

Editions and Studies. The writings and thought of Aquinas himself (14:102) have received considerable attention because of the progress of editing and other research projects initiated in the pre-Vatican II era and because of the commemorative studies published on the occasion of the seventh centenary of Aquinas's death, March 7, 1974. The *Leonine Commission, charged with preparing critical editions of all the works of St. Thomas, had its period of greatest productivity since its foundation by Pope Leo XIII during the years 1965–77, publishing in that period 11 folio volumes of text and two smaller volumes listing codices containing manuscripts of Aquinas's writings. By 1976 Robert Busa, SJ, with the assistance of IBM computer technology, had produced his *Index Thomisticus*—8 massive volumes of indices together with a 23-volume "first concordance" of Latin terms occurring in all of Aquinas's vast literary output, with further concordances planned. At the time of his death in December

1975, Thomas Gilby, OP, its general editor, had sent to press the last of the 60-volume English-Latin edition of the *Summa theologiae* (1965–76). During 1974 the Pontifical Institute of Mediaeval Studies in Toronto published its two volumes of *Commemorative Studies* on Aquinas; the American Catholic Philosophical Association devoted its annual convention and its 48th *Proceedings* to studies on Aquinas and Bonaventure; and such scholarly quarterlies as *The Thomist, New Scholasticism, International Philosophical Quarterly, Review of Metaphysics,* and *Southwestern Journal of Philosophy* had special commemorative issues featuring studies on Thomism. Numerous conferences were also held, the most significant being the International Thomistic Congress in Rome and Naples, April 17–24, 1974, attended by Pope Paul VI and with 1674 subscribers from all over the world; by the end of 1977 six volumes of *Acts* from this congress had been published, with two more yet to come. Thus there has been no dearth of scholarly activity relating to Aquinas and his thought in the past decade.

Systematic Thomism. Systematic Thomism, in the sense of the use made by others of St. Thomas's thought, is more difficult to evaluate. Since it is historically conditioned there is some advantage in dividing this into three phases: First or Early Thomism, from the death of Aquinas to the beginning of the Protestant Reformation; Second or Middle Thomism, from the Reformation to the 19th-century revival; and Third Thomism, sometimes referred to as Neothomism (10:337), from the 1879 encyclical, *Aeterni Patris* (1:165), to the present. The first phase is of interest mainly to historians of philosophy and has not received significant scholarly attention in the past decade. The second phase, that of such classical commentators as Cajetan and John of St. Thomas and such recent thinkers as Jacques Maritain (14:135; 16:275), has suffered a decline of interest since Vatican II; generally the thought is too scholastic and too technical in formulation to be studied by other than experts, and not even Dominicans, who traditionally have cultivated this type of classical Thomism, have been promoting it. The third phase is perhaps more aptly characterized as developmental Thomism, and this has shown some growth. The movements that were flourishing in the mid-60s, mainly the existential Thomisms of Étienne Gilson (14:137, 5:726) and Cornelio Fabro (5:720), have continued to attract adherents; but the greatest development has come from confronting Thomas's thought with currents deriving from Kant, Hegel, and Heidegger, under the general rubric of transcendental Thomism (16:449). Where systematic theology is being done in the U.S., it is generally under the impetus provided by Joseph Maréchal, Karl Rahner, and Emerich Coreth, all European Jesuits who may be classified as transcendental Thomists. A related thinker is the Canadian Jesuit, Bernard Lonergan, whose Thomism has been influenced by a philosophy of science of the Kantian type. Americans who are identifiable as Thomists are publishing in the history and philosophy of science, the phenomenology of Husserl and Heidegger, those types of linguistic philosophy that permit an emphasis on analogy and hermeneutics, process thought of the Whiteheadian variety, and ethics and social studies that are rooted in man's nature. World-wide the writings of all Thomists in both theology and philosophy are listed in the *Rassegna di Letteratura Tomistica*, an annual publication of the University of St. Thomas Aquinas in Rome, the first volume of which appeared in 1966; this is a continuation (new series) of the *Bulletin Thomiste* (12 vols., 1924–65) previously published by the Dominicans of the Paris province.

Thomism in Catholic Education. In Catholic colleges and seminaries there has been a noticeable decline in Thomistic studies, mainly because of the abandonment of required courses in philosophy and theology at the college level, and because the training of future priests is now more oriented toward the ministerial, the liturgical, and the scriptural than toward the systematic and the metaphysical. Vatican Council II's Decree on Priestly Formation, however, stressed that seminarians be exercised in systematic theology "under the tutelage of St. Thomas," and otherwise made reference to the encyclical, *Humani generis* (7:215), as providing sure guidelines for seminary education (*Optatam totius* 16; cf. *Gravissimum educationis* 10). More recently, a document issued by the Sacred Congregation for Catholic Education in 1976 on *The Theological Formation of Future Priests* reaffirmed the singular value of Aquinas's philosophical synthesis for ongoing work in systematic theology. Also noteworthy is a study by J. R. Fenili in 1974, which showed that the philosophical preference of professors in Catholic theological seminaries in the U.S. still inclines heavily toward the Thomistic (*see* PLURALISM, PHILOSOPHICAL). Perhaps the most significant changes are that Thomism is no longer the monolithic system it was once believed to be in Catholic education and that studies in Thomism are now becoming the domain of the specialist working in the university or research center. The decline in Catholic institutions has been somewhat offset by a growth of interest in Aquinas and in medieval studies generally in non-Catholic academic circles.

Bibliography: Congregation for Catholic Education, *The Theological Formation of Future Priests*, (USCC Publ. Office, Washington 1976). J. R. FENILI, "The Role of Philosophy as a Preparation for Theological Studies for Catholic Seminarians" (Ph.D. dissertation, Marquette University 1974). W. A. WALLACE, "The Case for Developmental Thomism," ProcAmerCathPhilAs 44 (1970) 1–16. J. A. WEISHEIPL, *Friar Thomas d'Aquino: His Life, Thought, and Work* (Garden City, N.Y. 1974).

[W. A. WALLACE]

THORMAN, DONALD JOSEPH

American journalist, author, publisher of the *National Catholic Reporter*; b. Cicero, Ill., Dec. 23, 1924; married, Barbara Lisowski, 1952, seven children; d. Kansas City, Mo., Nov. 30, 1977. He was the third and last child of Harry and Adophine Leverman Thorman; his father died when Thorman was two. The young Thorman, growing up during the Depression, early worked to help support himself. He attended public elementary schools in Oak Park, Ill. and Oak Park High School. He spent his senior year at St. Philip's High School, Chicago, run by the Servite Fathers, and, upon graduation, entered the Servites' Mount St. Philip Monastery, Granville, Wisconsin for a year, then (1942) joined the U.S. Marine Corps. He left the Marines in 1946, joined the Viatorian Fathers for a year and then entered De Paul University. He next began teaching at Loyola University from which, in 1950 (during which year he spent a period at the University of Fribourg in Switzerland) he received an M.A. in sociol-

ogy. He enrolled in Fordham University to begin work on a doctorate, but returned to Chicago after one year to help his family when his brother-in-law was stricken with terminal cancer.

In 1952, he became managing editor of *The Voice of St. Jude* (now the *U.S. Catholic*). That same year, he married Barbara Lisowski. In 1956, Thorman became managing editor of *Ave Maria* magazine; in 1962, publisher and director of development for the Spiritual Life Institute of America; and in 1963, formed his own company, Catholic Communications Consultants. In December 1965, he became publisher of the *National Catholic Reporter*, which was then just over a year old.

Author of *The Emerging Layman* (Garden City, N.Y. 1962), Thorman was a major figure in the post-Vatican II U.S. Church, especially as publisher of the *Reporter*. (A group of lay people, with Robert G. Hoyt as editor, founded the newspaper in 1964 in the belief that an independent press is a vital and healthy asset to the Church.) Thorman and the newspaper's role were important also in ecumenical and interreligious affairs, and he was active in the National Conference of Christians and Jews. To a generation of Catholics, especially those familiar with the Chicago Catholic tradition arising from the social encyclicals, the Catholic labor movement, and the Christian Family Movement (whose journal he and his wife edited for 10 years), he epitomized that era and helped establish the positive, active role of the laity in the Church. His other books included *Christian Union* (Garden City, N.Y. 1967), *American Catholics Face the Future* (Wilkes Barre, Pa. 1968), and *Power to the People of God* (Paramus, N.J. 1970).

[A. JONES]

TOLERANCE

Vatican Council II gave the theory and practice of tolerance a meaning quite different from that of the formerly common Catholic position. The 19th-century "thesis-hypothesis" theory had in effect denied a positive right to religious freedom to any but Catholics (14:193). While liberal Catholics held the earlier view to be misguided, non-Catholics considered it arrogant and a threat. With Leo XIII the Church had started to take a new approach to Church-State relations, but it was only with Vatican II that the thesis-hypothesis position was officially laid aside. In its Declaration on Religious Freedom the Council explicitly acknowledged it to be a natural right that as rational and free agents all men should be able to respond, freely and responsibly, to the truth as each perceives it (*Dignitatis humanae* 2–4).

The implication is that tolerance is not the issue so much as fellowship: in fraternal dialogue, all should seek to understand and learn from each other. In a polarized society tolerance may be the minimal safeguard against injustice, but such is not the ideal or the norm. Instead of merely tolerating each other, religious groups should have remorse over their divisions and accept one another with respect and affection. The function of the State is not to *tolerate* any Church but to guarantee the full freedom of all within the requirements of the common good (cf. ibid. 6).

Bibliography: J. MARITAIN, *Truth and Human Fellowship* (Princeton, N.J. 1957).

[G. J. DALCOURT]

TOOLEN, THOMAS JOSEPH

Archbishop; b. Baltimore, Md., Feb. 28, 1886; d. Mobile, Ala., Dec. 4, 1976. Ordained to the priesthood by Cardinal James Gibbons in Baltimore, Sept. 27, 1910, after studies at St. Mary's Seminary there, he spent a year studying Canon Law at The Catholic University of America and then served St. Bernard's Parish, Baltimore, for fifteen years. Toolen was appointed archdiocesan director of the Society for the Propagation of the Faith in 1925, and on May 4, 1927 consecrated by Archbishop Michael Curley as the sixth bishop of Mobile.

The Diocese of Mobile in 1927 contained sixty-six counties in Alabama and ten in northwest Florida with a Catholic population of 48,000 served by 48 diocesan and 94 religious priests. Diocesan schools had a census of 7,800 and from eleven communities 339 sisters staffed schools, hospitals and orphanages. The forty-three years of Toolen's leadership saw the diocese grow threefold. When in 1968 the Florida counties were detached, Catholics numbered 134,600, and clergy, 200 diocesan, 210 religious. The bishop gave priority to Catholic education so that diocesan schools enrolled 23,000 and Confraternity of Christian Doctrine programs were organized for both children and adults. Religious communities of women active in the diocese grew to thirty-seven, and 885 sisters worked not only in traditional ministries but also in such new fields as centers for social service at Mobile, Birmingham, Pensacola, Montgomery, and Huntsville. As the South emerged from the Depression, Toolen set about a program of rebuilding and expansion. More than 700 units of new construction marked his administration including 189 churches, 112 elementary and high schools, and twenty-three health care facilities. Missions were opened and parishes established in rural areas to bring Catholic life for the first time to twenty-eight counties.

A strong spokesman for Catholics in the face of Ku Klux Klan attacks in the late 1920s, the bishop also championed racial justice in a segregated society. Parochial facilities and educational opportunities for Blacks were improved and pioneer efforts in social service and hospital care made racial history in Alabama. Both Pius XII and John XXIII cited Toolen for this work, the former pontiff conferring upon him the title of "Archbishop *ad personam*" in 1954. He took forceful action by ordering the integration of all Catholic schools in the diocese in 1964, stating in a pastoral letter, "I know this will not meet with the approval of many of our people, but in justice and charity, this must be done." The archbishop's refusal to endorse Black activism often connected with violence in the 1960s diminished his effectiveness in the eyes of many.

Upon Toolen's resignation in 1969 his see, designated in 1954 as "Mobile-Birmingham," was divided to form a new diocese for north Alabama. The archbishop remained active in religious, civic, and social affairs until his death. Flags flew at half-mast throughout the state to mark his funeral in Mobile.

[O. H. LIPSCOMB]

TOYNBEE, ARNOLD

English historian; b. London, April 14, 1889; d. York, Oct. 22, 1975. Toynbee's 12-volume *A Study of History* is perhaps the most widely read and certainly the most widely discussed historical work of the 20th century. Although other historians criticized the work on various scholarly grounds, its enormous detail and skillful prose make it an impressive literary accomplishment. Because it is so well known, Toynbee's work has provided the focus for many searching discussions of the philosophy of history. It is distinguished by its erudition, its universal scale, its modified cyclical view of history, and its emphasis on the role of religion in civilization.

Toynbee's erudition revealed his impressive academic background. After studies at Oxford and in Athens, he became a tutor of ancient history at Oxford. His post in the Foreign Office during World War I initiated his lifelong involvement in international affairs, which included thirty years as Director of Studies at the Royal Institute of International Affairs. This simultaneous study of the past and the present led to Toynbee's conviction that whole civilizations are the only intelligible unit of study and that a comparative examination of civilizations demonstrates general laws of human evolution.

This conviction pervaded *A Study of History*. It argues through an imposingly profuse narrative that civilizations arise and grow by making creative responses to a series of challenges, but the eventual failure of creativity leads to breakdown and a social schism culminating in disintegration. Toynbee modified this cyclical view of history, however, by asserting that higher religions emerge from the breakdown of civilizations. Instead of predicting the downfall of Western Civilization, he believed in the imminence of one world, in which "sectarianism is going to be subordinated to ecumenicalism; ... nationalism is going to be subordinated to world government; and ... specialization is going to be subordinated to a comprehensive view of human affairs." In this view, civilizations have merely provided the breeding ground for the higher religions, which "bring human beings into direct communion with absolute spiritual reality as individuals" rather than through the medium of a particular society. The coalescence of the four existing "Universal churches," Hinduism, Buddhism, Christianity, and Islam, seemed possible to Toynbee because of their great similarity. Although he found value in each of these faiths, he "couldn't swallow any one of them whole." He never repudiated his membership in the Church of England, but he admitted that "I should not pass the most elementary tests of Christian orthodoxy." Even so, his belief in an ultimate spiritual reality raised the comparative study of religion to a dominant place in his work.

Bibliography: E. T. GARGAN, ed., *The Intent of Toynbee's History* (Chicago 1961). M. F. A. MONTAGU, ed., *Toynbee and History* (Boston 1956). R. N. STROMBERG, *Arnold J. Toynbee* (Carbondale, Ill. 1972). A. J. TOYNBEE, *A Study of History* (New York 1934–61); *An Historian's Approach to Religion* (New York 1956); *Change and Habit* (New York 1966); *Surviving the Future* (New York 1971); A. J. TOYNBEE and G. R. URBAN, *Toynbee on Toynbee* (New York 1974). K. WINETROUT, *Arnold Toynbee* (Boston 1975).

[R. J. GIBBONS]

TRADITION (IN THEOLOGY)

Vatican Council II narrowed the gap between Protestant and Catholic thought over the nature of tradition and its relation to Scripture (14:225). The Dogmatic Constitution on Divine Revelation states that the two together flow from "the same divine wellspring" (Revelation) and form "one sacred deposit of the word of God, which is committed to the Church." Tradition itself "which comes from the apostles develops in the Church with the help of the Holy Spirit" (*Dei Verbum* 8, 9, 10).

Coincidentally with Vatican II a World Council of Churches Faith and Order Study Commission at its Montreal Conference in 1963 issued a special report stating, "Christians exist by the Tradition of the Gospel (the *paradōsis* of the *kērygma*) testified in Scripture, transmitted in and by the Church through the power of the Holy Spirit" (*Montreal Report* 45).

Recognition of Tradition. Catholics and Protestants agree that tradition as a process is an inevitable and necessary part of human life, a human phenomenon intimately connected with history. The Tradition (with a capital T) which Christians received and handed down in the course of centuries lent itself to the various traditions even as early as apostolic times (cf. 2 Thes 2.15; 1 Cor 11.2). Vatican II also declares, "It has had a varied development in various places, thanks to a similar variety of natural gifts and conditions of life" (*Unitatis redintegratio* 14; cf. 13, 17).

In addition to the ecumenical rapprochement Catholic theology has for the past century investigated the traditionary process itself, and not merely its noetic content, the deposit of faith. What is to explain the continuity and diversity within tradition, and how to deal with the *then* and *now*, the antithesis between tradition and progress? Somehow the *then* and *now* must be kept in paradoxical unity or else the traditionary process results in disintegration and falsification. The trend is to equate tradition with progress, to understand it not so much as a stable, unchanged and unchangeable heritage, but as a force eschatologically moving the Church into the future.

The revision of the liturgy ordered by Vatican II exemplifies how the Church coalesces with the traditionary process, how it operates "in the light of sound tradition" with an eye of adaptation to "the circumstances and needs of modern times." "For the liturgy is made up of unchangeable elements divinely instituted, and elements subject to change." The purpose of revision is "that sound tradition may be retained, and yet the way be open for legitimate progress" (*Sacrosanctum Concilium* 4, 21, 23). Thus the provenance of a liturgical tradition shapes its future at the same time as historical change belongs to and is the progressive factor in it.

Hermeneutics and Tradition. Literary tradition appears no longer as a mere theological problem but as a historical and cultural phenomenon. As biblical scholars have adopted form- and redaction-criticism for an understanding and interpretation of the Bible, so theologians have sought to formulate a hermeneutic of dogma. The philosophical-theological work of Hans-Georg Gadamer, Gerhard Ebeling, Ernst Fuchs, Edmund Schlink—key figures in the German hermeneutical discussion—and of theologians Piet Schoonenberg, Bernard Lonergan, Karl Rahner, Walter Kasper, has helped to clarify the basic structure of historical understanding, with its implications for the interpretation of dogma (*see* THEOLOGY; THEOLOGY AND HISTORY). The question they raise is that of the impact of the interpreter, given his subjective, historical situation and his faith standpoint, on a tradition handed down

from the past. There is no one moment in the historical movement of tradition but a variety of levels of tradition. To span the time difference between himself and a text, the interpreter must bring to bear on it a critico-historical method which differentiates the meaning of the text in its original historical setting, assesses its meaning in the full flow of tradition, and applies it to his own time horizon. A complete hermeneutic calls for a "mediation" or "fusion" of the past into a living tradition, not simply a recourse to the past of a text and its meaning.

The new hermeneutic is crucial for the interpretation of dogma. Such dogma as the *virgin birth, transubstantiation, justification, papal infallibility, for example, are not frozen in text and meaning but open to reformulation in the light of reinterpreting them within their own past and the present horizon of reality, faith, and understanding. The critico-historical study of a dogma, then, exposes its relativity—to what degree it reflects polemical, linguistic, cultural, and historical color, and where it stands in the hierarchy of Christian truths (16:208). Catholic tradition always recognized a differentiation of dogmas but, contrariwise, the notion of the infallibility of dogmas tends to reduce them to the same level of importance.

Authority and Tradition. With the introduction of the infallibility or truth of dogmas, a further element in tradition appears—authority. Without some kind of charismatic authority to support it, the *truth* of tradition cannot survive. It must have a guarantee or touchstone, whether that be, as in the case of apostolic tradition, a sense of unity in the faith and an acceptance of the apostolic deposit, or, when apostolic tradition passed into ecclesiastical tradition, the collection of Scriptures and the teaching authority, magisterium, endowed by the Holy Spirit with the charism of *infallibility.

Whether an infallible magisterium *alone* can be the test of an authentic tradition is a moot question. Though Vatican II reiterated the dogma of papal infallibility, it laid stress on the *sensus fidelium*, that "supernatural sense of the faith which characterizes the People as a whole," by which they "cannot err in matters of belief" (*Lumen gentium* 12). Thus Christian tradition upholds the value of the human capability to preserve and interpret the word of God.

Bibliography: P. BENOIT, R. E. MURPHY, and B. VAN IERSEL, eds., *The Dynamism of Biblical Tradition.* Concilium 20 (New York 1967). J. R. GEISELMANN, *The Meaning of Tradition* (New York 1966). T. B. OMMEN, "The Hermeneutic of Dogma," ThSt 35 (1974) 605–631. J. RATZINGER, "Tradition," LexThK[2] 10:293–299. J. WALGRAVE, *Unfolding Revelation: The Nature of Doctrinal Development* (Philadelphia 1972). K.-H. WEGER, "Tradition," SacrMundi 6:269–274.

[J. FICHTNER]

TRADITIONALIST MOVEMENT, CATHOLIC

Traditionalism may be defined as "the doctrines, principles, or practices, of those who follow or accept tradition or traditions; specifically: a. Acceptance of tradition or orally transmitted revelation. b. The beliefs of those opposed to modernism, liberalism, radicalism, etc., sometimes fundamentalism" (*Webster's International Dictionary*, 2d ed.). Of traditionalists in the Church St. Pius X wrote in the era of Modernism "The true friends of the people are not the revolutionaries or the innovators, but the traditionalists." Since few if any Catholics would deny they follow tradition, or that they part company in significant ways with the ideologies mentioned by Webster, it can safely be said that all Catholics are in some sense traditionalists, at least according to the root meaning of the word. This is not to beg the question of the Catholic traditionalist movement; it is simply to suggest that no onus need be attached to the word "traditionalism." In itself it is a good thing; like any good thing it is subject to abuse. If not everyone who rides under its banner enjoys full amity with church authority, this does not call into question the basic soundness of the instinct to conserve what is good.

The major changes in the Church's liturgy brought by Vatican Council II's historic Constitution on the Sacred Liturgy (*Sacrosanctum Concilium*, Dec. 4, 1963) seem in retrospect to have been too much for some people to accept. But in view of the fact that numerous studies have shown that an overwhelming majority of Catholics approve the changes, others would say the cause of the original friction was not the changes themselves but the callous and ill-prepared way in which they were sometimes implemented.

The Catholic Traditionalist Movement, Inc. Whatever the truth of the matter, as the changes began to be felt, most dramatically at first in the change of prayers and readings from Latin to the vernacular, the first signs of a Catholic traditionalist movement came to public attention in Spring 1965. Its chief proponent, and the man most closely associated with the phenomenon in the public mind, at least in the U.S., remains Rev. Gommar A. De Pauw, Founder-President of the Catholic Traditionalist Movement, Inc. (CTM). The Movement was founded, according to its official literature, after "a few concerned Roman Catholic men and women from various states" participated in a colloquium given by Fr. De Pauw, a Belgian-born priest who at that time was on the staff of Mt. St. Mary's Seminary, Emmitsburg, Md., on "present day conditions in the Church." Having examined the situation they "decided to do something to stop the forces of subversion which, under the pretext of *aggiornamento*, updating, were actually destroying our Catholic identity by undermining our traditional beliefs in the supremacy of the Roman Pontiff, the devotion to the Blessed Virgin Mary, the sacrificial nature of the Mass, and the Real Presence of Our Lord in the Holy Eucharist." The official literature states: "The primary goal of the CTM is educational: to acquaint the people with the true teachings of Vatican II, and the Roman Catholic bishops with the true sentiments of the people." On March 20, 1965 the organization made public a *Catholic Traditionalist Manifesto*, which placed major emphasis on the continued use of Latin in the liturgy. The document asked that "the centuries-sanctioned Latin form of the Mass not be banned, but, if not given full priority, at least be allowed to coexist with the new vernacular forms, so that priests and people be given full option and adequate opportunity to celebrate and assist at Mass in the traditional Latin form on Sundays as well as weekdays."

Indeed Latin was never banned (in 1978 it seems to be making a comeback and several dioceses have announced the regular scheduling of Masses in Latin)—but something far more "radical" occurred. When Pope Paul VI in 1969 replaced the Order of the Mass as decreed by Pope Pius V shortly after the Council of Trent, the so-called Tridentine Mass, with the new Order of the Mass, CTM had a new bone of contention and, in a sense, a more simplified cause: keeping alive the "true" Mass. "We of the CTM have been saying for the past twelve years," Father De Pauw wrote (CTM Newsletter Aug. 30, 1976)

that "No one on earth—not even a subsequent pope—has the right and authority to stop any priest from offering the traditional Latin Mass authorized 'in perpetuity' and 'for all times' by St. Pope Pius V, using the 'fullness of his supreme apostolic authority,' in his decree *Quo primum* of July 19, 1570." To this day Father De Pauw still celebrates the superseded Tridentine Mass at the organization's Ave Maria chapel in Westbury, N.Y. and the Mass is reportedly heard on some 17 radio stations each Sunday. He has vigorously disclaimed any connection with the Society of St. Pius X headed by Archbishop Marcel Lefebvre.

Other groups—concerned not only with celebrating the Tridentine Mass but with launching virulent attacks upon the new Order of Mass—also sprang up. The "true" Order of St. John, Knights of Malta (not to be confused with the Church-recognized Knights of Malta, a charitable group) tried to form traditionalist parishes free from the jurisdiction of local bishops. Tan Books and Publishers, founded in 1967 by a person associated with this group, publishes and promotes literature strongly attacking the new Order of the Mass. Typical of the 150 titles which Tan Books has available is *The Great Betrayal* in which the author states in regard to the new Mass that "in altering the words of Christ, it surely makes vernacular Mass invalid, beyond any possibility of argument."

The Society of St. Pius X. The man who has emerged within the past two years as the foremost proponent of the movement which began under the banner of traditionalism is Archbishop Marcel Lefebvre, former archbishop of Dakar, Senegal and of Tulle, France, founder of the Society of St. Pius X. The Archbishop was suspended from all priestly functions by Pope Paul VI in 1976. He has said publicly that the new Mass which he calls the "Catholic-Protestant Mass" and "a poisoned spring" is responsible for "defections from the Church, abandonment of the true faith, sacrilege, wounding of church unity and the spread of every type of unworthy cult." But no one, including Father Gommar de Pauw, believes that the Archbishop's concerns are limited to the survival of the Tridentine Mass. He has denounced virtually every development since Vatican Council II, including church efforts at dialogue with Communists and other nonbelievers. But while Archbishop Lefebvre, in defiance of the papal suspension, has collected funds, erected traditionalist seminaries, and ordained priests who work in several countries including the United States, he has thus far refused to ordain a bishop saying, "I do not want to do something which would appear as a rupture with the Catholic Church. I hope that continuity will be assured by other means, and I put my faith in providence."

Although few would deny that *The Wanderer* newspaper, published in St. Paul, Minn., is an extremely conservative organ, the fact remains that the newspaper, at some cost to itself, vigorously urged its readers to have nothing to do with the potential schism of Archbishop Lefebvre's group. A *Wanderer* editorial said that to reject "magisterial authority in the name of tradition is no less erroneous than to reject it in the name of theological modernism." Furthermore, "either the Council's teachings are erroneous or they are not," the editorial stated. "Once one examines the actual documents of the Council, rather than lazily accepting ... vague and secondhand ideas of what they contain, there is simply no way to get around the riches of dogmatic teaching for which Vatican Council II is responsible," *The Wanderer* said. The paper called on Catholic traditionalist parishes to try celebrating the Latin Mass in the new Order, rather than hardening their position. *The Wanderer* also refused to carry advertisements for Tan Publications and wrote to a number of other Catholic newspapers warning them against the Tan ads.

Loyal Traditionalists. *Catholics United for the Faith is an organization of Catholic lay people founded in 1968 and dedicated to defending the orthodoxy of Catholic doctrine. It has never been associated in any way with insisting on the Tridentine Mass or with defiance of ecclesiastical authority, although it is undeniable that a certain friction has sometimes existed between CUF and some church leaders. But in recent years the organization has become quite conciliatory concerning the efforts of the American bishops. In November 1977, following a meeting between the Bishops' Committee for Liaison with Priests, Religious and Laity, and CUF representatives, leaders of the organization issued a statement expressing "support and gratitude" to the bishops for the 1976 pastoral letter *To Live in Christ Jesus: A Pastoral Reflection on the Moral Life.* "Speaking as an association of Catholic lay people," the statement said, "Catholics United for the Faith would like to go on record as expressing to our bishops our appreciation for the firm, yet compassionate, moral guidance provided in this Pastoral to the faithful, and the example of what the Church stands for provided to the world at large."

The *Latin Liturgy Association, a non-Lefebvrist group, promotes the use of the approved Latin Mass but not the Tridentine Mass. "The position of the Latin Liturgy Association," according to its president, Dr. James Hitchcock, history professor at St. Louis University and editor of the quarterly *Communio*, "is simply that people who love the Latin liturgy should have an opportunity to hear it."

Many traditionalist groups which have surfaced over the years have withered away. Others, like Father De Pauw's movement, continue to thrive. Perhaps he could be allowed the last word on the subject. When asked by the *National Observer* in 1976 whether he was in touch with traditionalists in other countries, Father De Pauw replied: "Very much. Even with all the splinter groups. Even in this country. That, of course, is the weakness. There are so many splinter groups—that is the weakness of the traditionalist movement" (*National Observer*, Sept. 11, 1976).

Bibliography: R. DI VEROLI, "Archbishop Lefebvre Has Few Followers in U.S." *Clovis, New Mexico News-Journal* (Jan. 13, 1978). J. FILTEAU, "Liturgical Reform Created Church Dropouts," *National Catholic News Service*, (Washington, D.C., Dec. 5, 1973). T.C.FOX, "Lefebvre's Tridentine Pace in U.S. Quickens," *National Catholic Reporter*, (Kansas City, Mo., Dec. 10, 1976). M. HYER, "Battling Catholic Church Modernism," *Washington Post*, (Washington, D.C., July 30, 1977). Religious News Service, "Archbishop Lefebvre Issues New Blast Against Pope Paul, Vatican Council," (*RNS*, Paris, Dec. 29, 1977); "Archbishop Lefebvre Explains Why He Hasn't Ordained Bishops," (*RNS*, Paris, Feb. 6, 1978). H. R. WILLIAMSON, *The Great Betrayal* (Rockford, Ill., 1970).

[W. A. RYAN]

TURNER, THOMAS WYATT

Biologist, educator, pioneer leader of Black Catholics; b. March 16, 1877, Hughesville, Md.; d. April 21, 1978, Washington, D.C. In the preface to his unpublished autobiography, Thomas Wyatt Turner captured in simple language the meaning of a life which spanned more than a century: "For me, my color was my earliest handicap. Doors would be closed, opportunities lacking,

barriers erected because I was black. The American dream would be a dream only—to become a train engineer, a wealthy farmer, a storekeeper or whatever. But if I just had a chance, I would exert every effort to push open the door, tear down the barriers, seek every opportunity to become a man with dignity, respected for my personal worth." In May 1976 The Catholic University of America recognized that personal worth in bestowing an honorary doctor of science degree on this remarkable Catholic educator. The award came seventy-five years after Turner had left the University as a graduate student because of insufficient funds and more than forty years after he had received an ironic letter of refusal to his appeal for the admission of Black students to the institution.

Poverty and racism were battles which Turner waged most of his life. He was born in a sharecropper's cabin in Charles Co., Southern Maryland, the fifth of the nine children of Eli and Linnie (nee Gross) Turner. Baptized as an infant, he once remarked that he had "remained baptized ever since." The phrase was fitting, for Turner discovered early in life that the color barrier existed in church as elsewhere. While sitting in the old slave gallery for Sunday Mass as a child young Thomas vowed he would change such immoral practices. He received his early education in the county schools and in the fields as a sharecropper, completing his studies at an Episcopalian school in Charlotte Hall, Maryland. As graduation neared, this young student known as "Lawyer" was offered a college scholarship on condition that he became an Episcopalian. Accepting the advice of a friendly Quaker woman, Turner chose to "stick with" his Church instead. Shortly thereafter, he set out for Howard University in Washington, D.C., penniless but ambitious. Working his way through school, Turner obtained his BA degree in 1901. He accepted a scholarship for graduate study in science at Catholic University, but soon ran out of funds. About that time Turner received a request from Booker T. Washington to teach at Tuskegee Institute, which the young man eagerly accepted.

In 1902 Turner returned to Maryland to join the faculty of the Baltimore High and Training School, among the first Black teachers to staff Black schools in the state. He joined the fledgling NAACP as the first secretary of its Baltimore branch in 1910. Three years later he moved to Howard University as a biologist in the School of Education. Continuing his civil-rights activities, he organized the first city-wide membership drive for the Washington NAACP in 1915.

At the same time Turner directed his attention to the racist practices in his own Church. With fellow Black Catholics he organized the Committee against the Extension of Race Prejudice in the Church, which wrote to bishops letters of protest against discrimination in churches, schools, hospitals, orphanages, and seminaries. Racism in seminaries and convents was a primary concern to the committee. Finally, in 1924 the group adopted a constitution, established a permanent organization, Federated Colored Catholics (5:875) and elected Turner its first president.

Although Turner saw the organization as representative of the interests of Black Catholics in America, he welcomed the support of all groups, including white priests. One of the earliest such advocates was John LaFarge, SJ (8:314), editor of *America* magazine.

Another was William Markoe, SJ of St. Louis, who became editor of the Federation's official journal. For a time the three men worked harmoniously to keep the cause of racial justice before the American hierarchy through annual Federation conventions, letters to bishops, and local efforts at change. When William Markoe sought to transform the organization into a more "interracial" group, however, Turner balked. As an older Black Catholic who remembered stories of the earlier Afro-American Catholic Congress movement (1889–94) and its demise because of militancy, Turner feared a white domination which would reduce the Federation to mere discussion. The controversy between Turner and Markoe (with LaFarge largely silent) was waged, often bitterly, in private correspondence, meetings, and the press from 1931–32.

Finally, the organization split into two factions, with Turner as president of a small Eastern Group of Federation members. This organization functioned until 1952, with Turner often at the helm. Throughout this period the Federation president combined his church activities with a strenuous career as a professional educator. Receiving his master's degree from Howard in 1905 and his Ph.D. in botany from Cornell University in 1921, Turner served as acting dean of the School of Education at Howard (1914–20) and went to Hampton Institute in Virginia as first chairman of the biology department in 1924. He retired from that institution in 1945 after a distinguished career. The author of numerous published articles, he was the first Black man to present a paper before the Virginia Academy of Science and to serve as a research cytologist for the U.S. Department of Agriculture. He was honored by Hampton Institute in 1978 when its new natural sciences building was named Turner Hall. His pioneer work for equal rights in the Church is memorialized in the Dr. Thomas Wyatt Turner Award, given yearly to a deserving individual by the Secretariat of the National Office of Black Catholics in Washington, D.C. Beside his unpublished autobiography Turner also left in manuscript a history of Afro-American Catholicism.

Bibliography: M. W. NICKELS, "The Federated Colored Catholics: A Study in the Variant Perspectives on Racial Justice as Represented by John LaFarge, William Markoe, and Thomas Turner" (Ph.D. dissertation, Catholic University, 1975); "Journey of a Black Catholic," *America* 135 (July, 1976) 6–8. M. W. NICKELS et al., "NOBC Pioneer Dies in 102nd Year," *Impact!* 8 (April–May, 1978) 2–3.

[M. W. NICKELS]

TWOMEY, LOUIS J.

Pioneer in interracial and labor relations; b. Tampa, Fla., Oct. 5, 1905; d. New Orleans, La., Oct. 8, 1969. He graduated from Sacred Heart College (now known as Jesuit High School) in 1923, after which he attended Georgetown University, then entered the Society of Jesus at Grand Coteau, La. in 1926. His father's health led him to return home the following year, but he reentered the novitiate in 1929 and took vows there Feb. 2, 1931. The next two years he spent studying philosophy at St. Louis University; from 1933 to 1936 he taught at Spring Hill College (Mobile, Ala.), resuming his seminary studies in theology at St. Mary's College (St. Marys, Kan.), where he was ordained priest, June 21, 1939.

While at St. Mary's College, Twomey became vitally interested in social problems and published his first articles on the subject, drawing heavily from *Qua-*

dragesimo anno and *Rerum novarum*, the significant papal encyclicals. He served for a time as principal in his old Alma Mater, Jesuit High School in Tampa, returning to St. Louis University's Institute of Social Order in 1945, where he worked under the labor relations expert, Leo C. Brown, SJ; later, in 1962–63, he would serve as editor there of *Social Order* magazine.

He returned to the South in 1947 to set up the Institute of Industrial Relations (later called Institute of Human Relations) at Loyola University in New Orleans. He was named Regent of the Loyola Law School (a close associate of the dean) and lectured there on philosophy of law. He was instrumental at the time in integrating the Law School in 1952, one of the first black students being Norman Francis, later president of Xavier University (New Orleans). During the 1950s and 1960s, in fact, Twomey was in the vanguard of the movement toward interracial justice in the South. His Institute's direct focus was on social justice and much of its work dealt with trade unionism and management-labor relations. In the South, however, this meant the constant handling of racial issues. Closely associated with Twomey, though working in somewhat different ways, were two Jesuit colleagues, Joseph H. Fichter and Albert S. Foley, and Vincent O'Connell, SM. During the troubles marking integration in the New Orleans area, Archbishop Joseph F. Rummell leaned considerably on Louis Twomey.

While often attacked by Citizens' Councils and other extreme right-wing groups for being "soft" on Communism, Twomey was, in fact, constantly at pains to demonstrate that Christian social justice was the most effective answer to Communism. He lectured on the subject continually, not least during the Summer School for Catholic Action sessions all over the U.S. and Canada, starting in 1947 and ending two decades later. In 1964 he established at Loyola University an Inter-American Center "to train younger leadership groups in . . . building democratic, social institutions." Between 1964 and 1971, this Center trained an average of 250 Latin Americans per year.

Much of Twomey's most effective work, however, was done in the press, in *Social Order* and other such journals. Perhaps most important, however, was *Christ's Blueprint of the South* (later titled *Blueprint for the Christian Reshaping of Society*), which he started in 1948 and wrote singlehandedly almost until his death. (The *Blueprint* continues to be published at Loyola under the Institute's director, Rev. David A. Boileau.) It started as a mimeographed letter to Southern Jesuits, but quickly became national and international. By 1958 it went out to 2,000 Jesuits in 44 countries and elicited a strong letter of approval from the Jesuit superior général, John Baptist Janssens, SJ. In 1967, Janssens' successor, Pedro Arrupe, SJ. summoned Twomey to Rome to help prepare an official letter to all Jesuits "On the Interracial Apostolate." It is generally acknowledged that this letter, coupled with the monthly *Blueprint*, had most to do with shaping Jesuit social attitudes for a generation.

Bibliography: J. H. FICHTER, *One Man Research: Reminiscences of a Catholic Sociologist* (New York 1973). C. J. MCNASPY, *At Face Value: A Biography of Father Louis J. Twomey, SJ*, with a preface by W. Persy and afterword by D. A. Boileau (Institute of Human Relations, Loyola Univ. of New Orleans 1978). J. R. PAYNE, "A Jesuit Search for Social Justice: The Public Career of Louis J. Twomey, S.J." (Ph.D. dissertation, Univ. of Texas, 1976).

[C. J. MCNASPY]

U

UKRAINIAN RITE

The most pressing current issue for Ukrainian Rite Catholics (14:372) is their being granted the status of a patriarchate. The issue, which Cardinal Josef Slipyj, Primate of the Ukrainian Catholic Church, raised during the Second Session of Vatican II, on Oct. 11, 1963, has a long history.

Early History of the Issue. After the Ukraine embraced Christianity during the rule of Vladimir (Volodymyr) the Great in 988, the Ukrainian Church, although a part of the patriarchate of Constantinople, nevertheless had great autonomy. The Archbishop of Kiev and All of Rus, once appointed by the patriarch of Constantinople, had full jurisdiction over his metropoly. There were attempts to be independent of the patriarch of Constantinople even in the matter of the appointment of the metropolitan. As early as 1051 the bishops of the Kievan Metropoly appointed Hilarion as their metropolitan against the will of the patriarch of Constantinople. The same happened in 1147 when the bishops selected Klement Smolatych as metropolitan of Kiev without the consent of the patriarch of Constantinople. The metropolitan of Kiev had almost patriarchal rights in his metropoly. He had the right, with his synod of bishops, to appoint new bishops, to create new eparchies, to judge his bishops, and settle disputes between them. But still he lacked the title of patriarch and some privileges connected with it.

Before the Union of Brest (1596) the question of the creation of a patriarchate was raised in 1583 during the pontificate of Gregory XIII. His envoy to the court of the Polish King, Stephen Báthory and Tsar Ivan the Terrible, the Jesuit Antonio Possevino (11:627) discussed this problem with the princes of Sluck and Ostroh. The aim was to unite with Rome all the Orthodox subjects of the Polish Kingdom. The apostolic nuncio to Poland, Bp. Albert Bolognetti (1581–85), considered this problem to be of great importance, as did his superior, Papal Secretary of State Cardinal Ptolemy Galti. The Chancellor of Poland, Jan Zamoyski (1542–1605) wanted to transfer the Patriarchate of Constantinople to Kiev or some other Ukrainian city. Patriarch Jeremias II agreed to Zamoyski's project, but the Ukrainian magnate Prince Ostrogsky, who was the protector of Ukrainians in the Polish-Lithuanian Kingdom, hesitated to support it. The project was stimulated by political motives. The creation of a prestigious center for the Orthodox within the boundaries of the Polish-Lithuanian Kingdom would be of great importance. Moscow recognized the value of such an honor and, by bribery and coercion, forced Jeremiah II, who was visiting Moscow, to create a patriarchate in Moscow (1589).

By the terms of the Union of Brest, through which the Kievan Metropoly was united with Rome, the Apostolic See confirmed the broad, almost patriarchal rights of the Kievan Metropolitan, including the right to appoint bishops and create new eparchies. Because one group of the faithful, under the leadership of Prince Ostrogsky, refused to follow their bishops into the Union, the creation of the patriarchate in Kiev would promote unification of those separated from Rome. The Uniate Metropolitan Joseph Rutsky of Kiev (1613–37) and the Orthodox Metropolitan of Kiev, Peter Moghila (1596–1646) agreed on unification with Rome under the condition that Rome would create a patriarchate in Kiev. Pope Urban VIII received this proposal favorably. The Polish King Wladyslaw IV supported this idea for political reasons. However, because of the premature death of Metropolitan Rutsky (1637) and then of the Orthodox Metropolitan Moghila (1646), and the Cossack revolution against Poland under Bohdan Khmelnytsky (1648), the realization of this project had to be temporarily suspended. The problem of a Kievan patriarchate was raised again after the death of Khmelnytsky when Ivan Vyhowsky was elected Hetman of the Cossack State.

Because one of the provisions of the Treaty of Hadiach (1658) between the Cossacks and Poland was the liquidation of the Uniate Church, the papal nuncio Pietro Vidoni informed Pope Alexander VII about it, and the Pope reprimanded the Polish Primate V. Leschynsky for allowing the treaty to take place. Results were favorable for the Uniate Church. Hetman Ivan Vyhowsky, now decided to revive the question of the patriarchate. Pope Alexander VII declared through Vidoni that he was ready to create a patriarchate for the Ukrainian and Byelorussian Church. However, political conditions in the Ukraine resulted in Vyhowsky's resignation and again frustrated this plan, but it did not die entirely.

The question of a patriarchate was renewed under Pope Clement IX (1667–69). The Orthodox Metropolitans, Dionysius Balaban and Joseph Nelubowych-Tukalsky, were in favor and helped the Uniate Metropolitan Kolenda in this regard. And again, the partition of Ukraine between Moscow and Poland (1667) prevented the realization of their attempts. The Polish King Jan Sobieski proposed to the papal nuncio the creation of a patriarchate in place of the Kievan Metropoly (1673–74), but at the time the Apostolic See was totally occupied with the Turkish invasion of Europe.

The Ukrainian Church under Austria. The Uniate Church was liquidated by force in the Russian Empire in 1839, and its last segment was liquidated in 1875. But the Uniate dioceses which found themselves under the Austrian Empire of the Habsburgs after the partition of Poland received protection from the government and became treated as equal with the Latin Rite Church. Being part of the suppressed Church, the Ukrainian Catholic clergy realized that to raise the spirit of their own faithful and of those oppressed under Russian rule it would be necessary to crown this Church with the dignity of a cardinalate or to raise it to the rank of a patriarchate. This question was raised by the Prefect of Studies of the Halych Metropoly, Canon Mykhaylo Malynowsky, in 1842. Pope Gregory XVI carefully studied the project of Canon Malynowsky and at the April 27, 1843 session of the Congregation for Extraordinary Ecclesiastical Affairs himself proposed the creation of a Ukrainian patriarchate for Eastern Rite Catholics in the Austrian Empire. The Apostolic See informed the Austrian Government about it because the Emperor had the privilege of creating new ecclesiastical administrative units. Secretary of State Cardinal Luigi Lambruschini submitted the project to Chancellor Klemens Metternich. Papal Nuncio Altieri informed Cardinal Lambruschini (June 8, 1843) that Metternich was delighted with this project, although he saw very strong opposition from the Hungarian parliament to subordination of the Carpatho-Ruthenians to the Patriarch residing in the capital of Halychyana, Lviv. Opposition from the Hungarian chauvinists and the revolution of 1848 against Vienna, then the revolution against absolutism in Vienna in 1848, overturned the regime of Prince Metternich. With his fall the idea of the creation of a Ukrainian patriarchate collapsed, but it was again revived by Rev. Hipolit Terlecky, a descendant of a Polonized Ukrainian family. In early 1848, Fr. Terlecky sent a memo to Pope Pius IX, recommending the creation of a Ukrainian patriarchate. In order to promote the unification of the Orthodox of the East, Pius IX received the idea favorably, but again opposition of the Hungarian hierarchy and the Austrian government under the influence of the Polish nobility, which dominated political life in Galicia, changed his attitude towards this problem.

Another attempt to create a Ukrainian Catholic patriarchate was made by Pope Leo XIII in 1886. Again, strong protest by the Hungarian Primate Cardinal Janos Simor forced the Pope to abandon the plan. Pope Pius X took a practical step by giving the Metropolitan of Lviv powers equal to those of a patriarch, although without the title itself. During an audience with Pope Pius X, the Metropolitan of Lviv-Halych, the Servant of God Andriĭ Count Sheptytskyĭ (13:170) informed the Pope of the situation of his Church and his plan to organize the Catholic Church in the Russian Empire, stating that he was the rightful successor of the metropolitans of Kiev and Halych and had jurisdiction over the entire territory of the former Ruthenian Church, which includes Ukraine and Byelorussia. The answer of the Pope to the presentation of the Metropolitan was: "*Utere iure tuo*" ("Make use of your right"). By those words, Pius X confirmed all rights which were recognized in the Union of Brest by the papal bull *Decet Romanum Pontificem* (Feb. 23, 1596). Metropolitan Sheptytskyĭ exercised those rights by consecrating a bishop without consultation with Rome (Bishop Joseph Bocian), nominating a bishop (Rev. Dr. Demetrius Yaremko), and appointing an exarch for the Russian Catholics (Rev. Leonid Fiodorov).

The 20th-Century Controversy. All those rights of the Kievan metropolitan were, throughout history, curtailed by Polish kings, Austrian emperors, and the Roman See. But the idea of a patriarchate and some kind of autonomy was always alive. The question of jurisdiction became acute when Ukrainians emigrated from their homeland, and many settled in the U.S., Canada, Argentina, Brazil, and other countries. They needed spiritual care and the metropolitan of Lviv provided such care by sending priests, monks, and nuns to serve the people. Metropolitan Sheptytskyĭ as archbishop of Lviv twice visited the U.S., Canada, Argentina, and Brazil (in 1910 and in 1921–22). With establishment of the hierarchy for the Ukrainian Catholics in Exile, the Roman Curia claimed authority over them. Pope Pius XII promulgated, motu proprio, June 11, 1957 to be effective March 25, 1958, *Cleri sanctitati*, part of a code of Canon Law, which in 558 canons gives norms concerning the law on persons for the Eastern Catholic Churches (ActApS 49 [1957] 433–603). Canons 216–357 legislate on patriarchs, major archbishops, and their synods. *Cleri sanctitati* established the principle that Eastern patriarchs possess jurisdiction only within the territorial limits of their patriarchates and that, as a rule, they have no authority over the faithful of their rite outside these limits, except in expressly determined instances.

When the Ukrainian Primate Archbishop Metropolitan Josyf Slipyj was freed by the Soviet government from eighteen years of forced labor, he raised the issue of a Ukrainian patriarchate, as had been noted, at Vatican II. The Congregation for the Oriental Churches issued a declaration, Dec. 23, 1963, that "the Ukrainian Catholic Metropolitan of Lviv is to be regarded as major archbishop in accordance with cc. 324–339 . . . *Cleri sanctitati* . . ." (ActApS 56 [1964] 214). It was not an elevation of the Metropolitan of Lviv, but a recognition that the Metropolitan and his See already possessed this status.

Vatican II. In the Decree on the Eastern Churches Vatican II gave a great boost to the autonomous aspirations of the Ukrainian Catholic Church and the creation of a patriarchate:

The institution of the patriarchate has existed in the Church from the earliest times and was recognized by the first ecumenical Synods. By the name Eastern Patriarch is meant the bishop who has jurisdiction over all bishops (including metropolitans), clergy, and people of his own territory or rite, in accordance with the norms of the law and without prejudice to the primacy of the Roman Pontiff. Wherever an Ordinary of any rite is appointed outside the territorial bounds of its patriarchate, he remains attached to the hierarchy of the patriarchate of that rite, in accordance with the norm of law (*Orientalium Ecclesiarum* 7).

The Patriarchs with their synods constitute the superior authority for all affairs of the patriarchate, including the right to establish new eparchies and to nominate bishops of their rite within the territorial bounds of the patriarchate, without prejudice to the inalienable right of the Roman Pontiff to intervene in individual cases (ibid. 9).

What has been said of Patriarchs applies as well, under the norm of law, to major archbishops, who preside over the whole of some individual Church or rite (ibid. 10).

Yet the application of this principle to the only existing Catholic major archiepiscopate, the Ukrainian Church, appears to be suspended.

Of great importance in the question of creation of the Ukrainian patriarchate is the following:

Inasmuch as the patriarchal office is a traditional form of government in the Eastern Church, this Sacred and Ecumenical Council earnestly desires that where needed, new patriarchates should be erected. The establishment of such is reserved to an ecumenical Synod or to the Roman Pontiff (ibid. 11).

There is no question that the Ukrainian Catholic Church is in need of being united under a patriarch.

Arguments for a Patriarchate. The best leaders of the Ukrainian Church throughout the centuries strove to establish a patriarchate. Now in recent times, Cardinal Slipyj was supported in his attempts by the bishops, priests, and faithful.

In addition, the Ukrainian Catholic Church is numerically the largest of the Eastern Churches. Before the forceful liquidation of the Church by the Soviet regime in 1945–46 it counted over 4 million faithful and outside Ukraine there are now more than one million (see Tables 1 and 2 for statistics). Among the other Eastern Catholic Churches the largest numerically is the Malabarian in India with some 1.85 million; the largest patriarchate is that of the Maronites with 800,000; the Armenians have 100,000 faithful; the Syrian and the Coptic patriarchates, each has 80,000 faithful. With Ukrainian Catholics now dispersed around the globe, the unifying effect of a patriarchate is of vital importance, and it would be of great

TABLE 1: Status of the Ukrainian Church outside the Ukraine

	Parishes	Priests	Faithful
NORTH AMERICA:			
Chicago, St. Nicholas Eparchy	36	36	29,869
Edmonton Eparchy	47	62	52,560
New Westminister, B.C. Eparchy	10	9	25,000
Philadelphia Archeparchy	101	118	166,815
Saskatoon Eparchy	46	46	34,175
Stamford, Conn. Eparchy	57	53	87,250
Toronto Eparchy	71	94	83,200
Winnipeg Archeparchy	41	49	60,000
ELSEWHERE:			
Argentina	12	18	110,000
Australia	6	14	30,000
Austria	3	3	5,000
Brazil	15	46	99,000
France	13	13	17,200
Germany	20	25	32,000
Great Britain	15	16	25,000
Benelux	9	9	5,000
Krizevci Eparchy (Yugoslavia)	52	52	43,000
Total	554	663	905,069

[1]The 4,354,160 faithful (1943) in 6 eparchies of the Ukraine were forcefully incorporated into the Russian Orthodox Church by Stalin in 1945–46. The 1943 figures are from *AnnPont* (1978).

TABLE 2: Ruthenian Munhall—Pittsburgh Metropoly

	Parishes	Priests	Faithful
Parma, Ohio Eparchy	48	57	30,304
Passaic Eparchy	48	98	96,940
Pittsburgh Archeparchy	83	103	150,715
Total	215	258	277,959

[1]The Ukrainian and Ruthenian Catholics of the Eastern Rite number 1,183,028.

moral support for the Church in the catacombs in Ukraine. Regardless of severe persecutions the Ukrainian Catholic Church exists and is active. Cardinal Slipyj has made several requests for a patriarchate to the Holy Father and three times his requests have been denied. The denial has aroused bitterness among the Ukrainian faithful, expressed in publications and demonstrations.

The Ukrainian Catholic Church certainly deserves such a recognition as the creation of a patriarchate. No other Eastern Catholic Church suffered more in the last century for its Catholicism. With their steadfastness in suffering, Cardinal Slipyj and all the other martyred Ukrainian bishops, hundreds of priests and religious, and thousands of faithful have shown their allegiance to the Catholic Church headed by the Roman Pontiff. If they had joined the Russian Orthodox Church of Moscow, they would have avoided this suffering; Cardinal Slipyj was offered Moscow's Patriarchial See if he would renounce his allegiance to the pope.

The Holy See's Refusal. Pope Paul in a letter to Cardinal Slipyj, July 7, 1971 stated: "We have come reluctantly again to the conclusion that it is impossible, at least at this time, to establish a Ukrainian patriarchate." In response to this Cardinal Slipyj addressed the whole Ukrainian hierarchy and faithful: "Unfortunately, in the meantime new, unfavorable ecclesiastical and political circumstances have arisen, in consequence of which the Holy Father gave, for the time being, a negative reply."

The political circumstances are viewed as pressure from Moscow, with which the Vatican has entered into diplomatic dialogue (*see* DIPLOMACY, PAPAL). Regardless of those negative responses of the Holy See, Cardinal Slipyj assumed the title of patriarch (1974), without papal authorization. Cardinal Slipyj prepared the Constitution of the Patriarchal System and, with the signature of other bishops, submitted it for approval to the Holy Father. Cardinal Slipyj is of the opinion that he is the head of the Ukrainian Catholic Church and in his opinion such a right was granted by Vatican II in *Orientalium Ecclesiarum*. He convoked a synod of bishops, a title which the Congregation for the Eastern Churches denied, calling it simply a conference.

The controversy is continuing. Ukrainian Catholics make the accusation that the Vatican, under pressure of Moscow, is denying Ukrainians the right to govern their Church by themselves. They allege as the other reason for denial the desire of the Congregation for the Oriental Churches to keep the control of the Eastern Churches which it has had since 1917 (from 1622 the Ukrainian Church had been under Propaganda). As a rule (with the exception of Cardinal Coussa, nominated by Pope John XXIII) a Latin Rite Cardinal is head of the Congregation and other high officials are also of the Latin Rite. It remains to be seen whether the new Canon Law for the Oriental Churches, now in preparation, will solve this problem.

The Ukrainian Catholics accepted with regret the decision of Rome to separate the Ruthenians from the Major Archiepiscopate and to create for them the separate, Munhall-Pittsburgh Metropoly. Ruthenians are descendants of the immigrants from Carpatho-Rus (now Carpatho-Ukraine), are of the same ethnic extraction, and use the same liturgical rite and language as the Ukrainians.

Despite all those setbacks in the quest for Ukrainian autonomy in the form of a patriarchate, Ukrainian Catholics are loyal to the Holy See and this has many times been emphasized by Cardinal Slipyj. In his opinion, however, a patriarchate is the only security for the preservation of the Ukrainian Catholic Church.

Bibliography: A. M. AMMAN, *Abriss der Ostslavischen Kirchengeschichte* (Vienna 1950). M. ANDRUSIAK, *Sprawa Patriarchatu Kijowskiego za Wladyslawa IV* (Lwow 1934) (The Problem of the Kievan Patriarchate under Ladislaw IV). A. BARAN, *The Question of Ukrainian Patriarchate in the Times of M. Shashkewych* (Winnipeg 1974). W. LENCYK, "Actio pro unione Ecclesiarum in vita et operibus S.D. Metropolitae Andreae Szeptyckyj," *Bohoslovia* 35 (1971). H. LUZNYCKY, *The Quest for a Ukrainian Catholic Patriarchate,* (Philadelphia 1971). J. MADEY, *Le Patriarcat Ukrainien vers la perfection de l'état juridique actuel,* in Opera Theologicae Societatis Scientificae Ucrainorum v. 19 (Rome 1971). I. NAHAYEVSKY, *Patriarchates, Their Origin and Significance and the Ukrainian Patriarchate* (The Ukrainian Theological Society, New York, Munich, Toronto 1973). A. G. WELYKYJ, *Documenta Pontificum Romanorum historiam Ucrainae illustrantia,* 2v (Rome 1953).

[W. LENCYK]

UNDA

UNDA (Latin for "wave") is the international professional Catholic association for radio and television. It began as the International Catholic Committee for Radio, founded in 1928 in Cologne, Germany. It is recognized by the Holy See. UNDA's members internationally are not individuals but national and continental Catholic organizations (UNDA-USA and UNDA-ASIA, for example) which share UNDA's objectives, while retaining responsibility for their own activities. UNDA's headquarters are in Brussels.

UNDA's objectives are: to help coordinate professional and apostolic activities of Catholics in radio and television; to promote collaboration among members, through conferences, publications, information exchanges, research; to represent internationally the interests of members; to help meet communications needs of members; to help meet communications needs of the Third World; and to collaborate with non-Catholic organizations having similar objectives.

At the continental and national levels, UNDA conducts a variety of activities and programs suited to individual needs of each region. Development programs in broadcasting, planned, subsidized and executed under the auspices of UNDA, are primarily in the Third World countries of Africa, Asia, Latin America, and Oceania. Projects prepared at the local level are presented to the Congregation for the Evangelization of People in Rome and to other world funding agencies. In the past the Congregation has allotted through UNDA more than two million U.S. dollars. UNDA publishes a monthly newsletter, in English and in French, and a documentation quarterly.

UNDA-USA. UNDA-USA is a national professional Catholic Association for broadcasters and allied com-

municators. Organized in 1972, it succeeded the Catholic Broadcasters Association of America, which in 1948 had replaced the Catholic Forum of the Air, founded in 1939. UNDA-USA's Board of Directors includes representatives of the 12 USCC Regions, Catholic Television Network, Association of Catholic Radio and Television Syndicators, USCC Department of Communication, and media and government. Approximately 300 individuals and organizations are members.

UNDA-USA's objectives are: to encourage cooperation among diocesan communications directors, religious program syndicators, instructional television personnel and the USCC Department of Communications; to cooperate with all commercial and religious broadcasters whenever possible; to help develop a discerning audience for social communications; to assess the sources and influences of media; to be concerned with media government relations and the preservation of freedom of expression; to assess the impact of U.S. media upon other nations and peoples, and to help develop a sensitive awareness and mutual understanding among peoples of various cultures.

"Gabriel Awards" are made annually to national and local radio and TV programs in which commercial, educational, or religious broadcasters have best entertained, enriched, or informed with a vision of life reflecting basic religious principles. Awards are also given to a radio and TV station for consistently high quality programming, and to a person who has provided outstanding leadership in the field of national or local broadcasting.

UNDA-USA annually holds a General Assembly for all members. A newsletter for members is published six times a year. Headquarters in the United States are in Los Angeles.

[A. SCANNELL]

UNEMPLOYMENT

Unemployment continues to be a vexing problem (16:392). In the United States it has ranged from a low in full employment of under 4 percent of the labor force in the late 1960s to a high of 8.5 percent in 1975, declining to 6.4 percent at the close of 1977. Among the other industrial nations, only Canada has had a problem of comparable severity and persistence.

Paradoxically, although the unemployment rate has remained high, the level of employment has increased steadily over the past twenty years from 63 million in 1958 to 92 million in late 1977.

Part of the paradox is explained by the unbroken annual rise in the labor force (nearly 3 million in 1977 alone), new job seekers for whom jobs must be created in addition to those needed by the already unemployed. Especially significant in this respect is the spectacularly growing participation of women in the labor market; 49 percent of all adult women are currently employed or actively seeking work, representing 37 percent of the total work force. The impact of this growth in the number of women workers is evidenced by an unemployment of rate consistently higher than that of men, 8 percent in 1977, compared with 6 percent for males. Added to this is the somber employment status of youths, now 10 percent of the labor force, whose unemployment rate has varied from 12 percent to 19 percent in the past decade (over 30 percent for blacks).

Unemployment Theories. The search for greater understanding of these trends and of the contemporary nature of unemployment has generated new ideas and lively controversy among labor-market specialists. Among the more prominent of these are the following.

1. Efforts to Refine or Redefine the Meaning of Unemployment. For example, the Bureau of Labor Statistics now publishes five distinct measures of unemployment. These are in response to contentions that the unemployment rate, expressed as that percentage of the labor force actively but fruitlessly seeking work, either understates the problem by excluding both the "discouraged workers" (those who have dropped out of the labor force, convinced that no suitable jobs now exist), and part-time workers (those who work part-time because unable to find full-time employment); or that it overstates the problem by giving undue weight to "secondary workers" those who are not principal family breadwinners—frequently women and teenagers—but whose unemployment rates are higher than that of married men who constitute the core of the labor force.

2. Analyses Stressing Deficiencies in Segments of the Labor Supply rather than the Inadequacy of Demand for Labor. These concede that in recessions an inadequate demand for products, and hence for labor, is the salient problem, calling for the accepted remedies of credit ease, increased government spending, or tax reduction. However, noting the persistence of abnormal employment following economic recovery, several schools of thought have emerged which center their attention upon the need to improve the functioning of labor-market institutions so as to achieve a better balance between the supply of unemployed labor and job vacancies. These include the following.

a. Structuralists. Led by Professor Charles C. Killingsworth, this school contends that changing technology, shifting location of industry, and obsolescence of skills can cause an imbalance between supply and demand for labor. The imbalance necessitates steps to lessen geographic and occupational immobility of workers through retraining, vocational education and counselling, and relocation allowances, to reduce the unemployment rate;

b. Human Capital Theorists. Arguing that a workers' lack of "investment" in themselves has resulted in many of them having too little education or training to be readily employable, Professor Gary Becker and others also advocate expansion of special education and training programs to increase the employability of marginal workers.

3. A "Dual Labor-Market" Hypothesis. The hypothesis is that the labor market, like the economy, is stratified into a primary and a secondary sector. The former is characterized by high and stable employment under favorable conditions, the latter by irregular and unstable employment, which is ill-paid and generally unattractive. Legal restrictions such as licensing, union regulations, and sexual and racial discrimination raise almost insurmountable barriers to movement from the secondary into the primary sector, thus entrapping many women and minorities in a chronically-unstable employment situation. The remedy, according to such proponents as Professors Peter Doeringer and Michael Piore, is strict enforcement of existing antidiscrimination laws, coupled with additional legislation to compel employers to convert "secondary" type jobs into "primary" ones.

Fundamental to the success of these measures is a firmer long-run commitment by government to a policy of stable full employment.

Policies. In the aftermath of the Great Depression full employment became a primary objective of economic policy in the industrial nations. Substantial acceptance of this responsibility in the U.S. has occurred through the Employment Act of 1946. However, the goal of full employment envisioned by its sponsors has been elusive, particularly in much of the recent past. It has been made the more so by the emergence of severe and sustained inflation, which has blunted or made perilous the use of traditional, expansionary economic measures. The "Phillips-Curve" thesis which posits a necessary trade-off between increments of employment and inflation, although not universally accepted, highlights the policymakers' dilemma.

As a consequence, despite the misgivings of influential mainstream economists, the structuralists and their allies have won a hearing sufficient to see some of their prescriptions translated into public policy during the past fifteen years. The array of programs is extensive, including vocational education, on-the-job training, skill upgrading, expanded labor-market services, public-service employment, antidiscrimination laws, and area economic development. Most of these have now been subsumed under the Comprehensive Employment and Training Act (CETA) of 1973 ($9 billion expended in 1976).

More recently, a 3 percent rate of unemployment has been proposed as a target of public policy. Under the best known of these proposals, "The Full Employment and Balanced Growth Act of 1976" (known as the Humphrey-Hawkins bill), the Federal Government would become the employer of "last resort," for those whom private industry does not employ. Current debate centers on the philosophical propriety of government expansion of its role as employer, and on the inflationary potential of such a commitment.

Bibliography: G. S. BECKER, *Human Capital* (New York 1964). P. DOERINGER and M. PIORE, *Internal Labor Markets and Manpower Analysis* (Lexington, Mass. 1971). *Employment and Training Report of the President* (Washington 1978). R. E. HALL, "Why is the Unemployment Rate so High at Full Employment?" in *Brookings Papers on Economic Activity*, n. 3 (Washington 1970). J. KREPS and R. CLARK, *Sex, Age, and Work: The Changing Composition of the Labor Force* (Baltimore 1975). G. L. MANGUM, "Manpower Policies and Worker Status since the Thirties," in J. P. GOLDBERG et al., eds., *Federal Policies and Worker Status since the Thirties* (Madison, Wis. 1976). C. R. PERRY et al., *The Impact of Government Manpower Programs in General and on Minorities and Women* (Philadelphia 1975). J. SHISKIN, "Employment and Unemployment: the Doughnut or the Hole?" *Monthly Labor Review* 99 (Feb. 1976) 3–10. R. A. SOLOW, "What Happened to Full Employment?" *Quarterly Review of Economics and Business* 13 (1973), repr. in L. REYNOLDS et al., eds., *Readings in Labor Economics and Labor Relations* (2d ed. Englewood Cliffs, N.J. 1978) 95–103. S. P. ZELL, "Recent Developments in the Theory of Unemployment," *Monthly Review*, Federal Reserve Bank of Kansas City (1975), repr. in S. COHEN, ed., *Issues in Labor Policy* (Columbus, Ohio 1977) 227–235.

[L. F. CAIN]

UNICITY OF THE CHURCH

The unicity of the Church—that there is but one Church of Christ and that this unique Church is to be undivided in itself—is accepted by most Churches which consider themselves Christian (14:395). Historically widespread disagreement has existed, however, on the elements that constitute the one Church of Christ and on the fact and place of its continued existence. A growing consensus on these points is emerging as can be seen by an examination of two similar models for *organic union: that of a *conciliar fellowship*, gaining acceptance by members of the World Council of Churches and that of a *communion (communio) of Churches (typoi)*, gaining acceptance in Roman Catholic circles.

Both models assume that the unity of the Church has been *given* by God in Jesus Christ and has had continuous existence, but that it must be constantly rediscovered and expressed anew in history. This unity is in need of being made visible where it has been obscured, recovered to the extent that it has been lost, maintained where it is threatened, and brought to full conformity with the will of Christ. The one Church of Christ subsists in the historical Churches in varying degrees.

The proposed models presuppose that the organically united Church has as constitutive elements both the *invisible* gifts of faith, grace, virtues, and charisms, and their *visible* expression in the proclamation of the Word, celebration of the Sacraments, and in ministries for mission. Both the invisible gifts and their visible expression are to be *integrally united*. These two models accept the need for diversity-in-unity and unity-in-diversity as opposed to uniformity. Both models assume that there must be a visible unity of one faith expressed in a variety of forms, in worship and Eucharistic sharing, in common life in Christ, and in Christian witness and service to the world. Both models envision a universal communion (*communio*) or conciliar fellowship of local Churches united by a diversity of organizational patterns.

While the above comments stand in principle, the exact understanding of the elements varies from Church to Church. Such issues are debated as: the relationship between the local communities and the universal community; the meaning of "local Church" and "conciliar fellowship"; authority; legitimate diversity; the relationship between Church and Eucharist; the nature of the Church and its mission; the place of experience vis-à-vis the sources of Revelation; and the relationship of the unity of the Church to the unity of mankind. Developments at the grass-roots levels, the bilateral and multilateral consultations, in church union negotiations, and in the various councils of Churches offer the hope that these issues may be solved to the extent necessary for full union.

Bibliography: Committee on Purposes and Goals of Ecumenism, Massachusetts Council of Churches, *Odyssey Toward Unity: Foundations and Functions of Ecumenism and Conciliarism* (Newburyport, Mass. 1977). Faith and Order, *What Kind of Unity?*, paper n. 69 (Geneva 1974); *Uniting in Hope*, paper n. 72 (Geneva 1974). E. LANNE, "Pluralism and Unity: the Possibility of a Variety of 'Typologies' within the same Ecclesial Allegiance," *One-in-Christ* 6 (1970) 430–451; "The Unity of the Church in the Work of Faith and Order," *One-in-Christ* 12 (1976) 34–57. J. MACQUARRIE, *Christian Unity and Christian Diversity* (Philadelphia 1975). Roman Catholic/Presbyterian Reformed Consultation, U.S.A., Statement, *One-in-Christ* "The Unity We Seek," 13 (1977) 258–279. J. WILLEBRANDS, "Address in Cambridge, England," *Documents on Anglican/Roman Catholic Relations*, I (Washington, D.C. 1972) 32–41.

[A. LAUBENTHAL]

UNION OF SUPERIORS GENERAL (MEN)

The Union of Superiors General (USG) was established by the Sacred Congregation for Religious in 1955 to promote the life of religious institutes or societies of common life towards a more efficacious collaboration among themselves and in view of a more fruitful contact with the Holy See and the hierarchy. All superiors general of religious institutes or of societies of common life of pontifical right, as well as abbots primate and presidents of monastic congregations are members of the Union. Superiors of institutes of diocesan right may also belong to the Union as aggregated members. The Union functions through its various departments: the General Assembly, the Council of the Union, the Council for Liaison between the Sacred Congregation for Religious and Secular Institutes and the Union, Commissions, and the General Secretariat.

The usefulness of the USG has been manifested in numerous areas of concern. Prior to and during the several Synods of Bishops, superiors general have met to discuss synodal topics and to help the USG delegates to the Synods prepare their interventions. There has been collaboration, through one or more delegates, with the dicasteries and other institutions of the Holy See and the Vicariate of Rome. The latter has asked the collaboration of religious institutes to help to resolve the grave religious and social problems of the city of Rome. Several years ago, the USG Commission on Formation undertook a vast inquiry on religious formation. About 15,000 young religious and 1,900 religious engaged in formation the world over, provided the 550 replies to 800 copies of the questionnaire sent out.

There are contacts with the *International Union of Superiors General, and when feasible both unions work together. The USG, through its Secretariat, has relations with the Confederación Latino Americano de Religiosos (CLAR) and the national conferences of major superiors. It is presently in contact with 72 such conferences. There are also contacts with members of other Churches, especially with those committed to the religious life of their Churches. Besides the official organisms provided for in the Statutes, others have arisen spontaneously such as the biannual (three-day) and the monthly (one-afternoon) meetings, which are unofficial in character, but nevertheless provide a fraternal atmosphere for common reflection and prayer, the exchange of opinion, mutual acquaintance, and encouragement.

Bibliography: USG General Secretariat, Informational Notes (Rome, April 8, 1975).

[R. L. EVERY]

UNITED METHODIST/ROMAN CATHOLIC DIALOGUE

Contacts initiated at Vatican Council II promptly led to the inauguration of a Methodist-Roman Catholic dialogue in the United States. The first session was held in June 1966, under the cochairmanship of Bishop Joseph E. Brunini, representing the U.S. Bishops Committee for Ecumenical and Interreligious Affairs (BCEIA), and Bishop F. Gerald Ensley, representing the Commission on Ecumenical Relations of the Methodist Church.

By the time of the second session, held in December 1966, the positive character of the dialogue was well established. At the conclusion of that session the participants issued a Summary Memorandum recording their impressions. "The Catholic participants," they wrote, "were especially impressed by the role and influence of the early church tradition which is characteristic of early Methodism." For their part "the Methodists were edified and encouraged by the absence of both polemical and intellectualist emphases in the

Catholic presentations and discussions. They were pleasantly surprised, for example, to hear that the—to them—painful anathemas of Trent and Vatican I represent a judgment on doctrines held to be false and not the damnation of persons who may, on the grounds of conscience and convictions, hold those doctrines in one form or another whatever their historical circumstance. They were assured that this particular rhetoric of condemnation may now safely be regarded as 'historical'." Looking toward the future, the participants saw that "both Methodism and Catholicism are regularly involved in a constant dialectical tension between tradition and development, and never more than at the present time. They are bound to the assured truths of revelation as the foundation and warrant for their teaching and preaching in their churches. They are bound to the earnest effort to speak meaningfully to 'modern man,' and to correlate Christian truth and 'modern' knowledge in ways that are faithful to both. Their hope in this endeavor springs from their faith that God is the source and ground of all truth, that God's will for his children is that they shall come to the knowledge of the truth that shall make them free and blessed."

From its inception until 1970 the dialogue engaged participants from many levels of church life: bishops, pastors, women religious, professors, and lay people. The topics discussed ranged broadly, including "Salvation, Faith and Good Works," "The Spirit in the Church and Individuals," "Government Aid for Church Related Elementary and Secondary Schools," and "Shared Convictions on Education." The last subject resulted in a request that the bishops of the two Churches convene a national conference on religious concerns and the education crisis.

During this initial period, other events had an effect on the dialogue. In April 1968 The Methodist Church and the Evangelical United Brethren Church joined to form The United Methodist Church. This ecumenical event enlarged the number of Christians served by the dialogue.

In 1970 the General Conference of The United Methodist Church adopted "A Resolution of Intent" stating its present attitude toward the Roman Catholic Church and toward the seven anti-Roman Articles of Religion which John Wesley had retained from Anglicanism in the founding period of Methodism. The resolution read: "It is one of the virtues of historical insight that it enables men in a later age to recognize the circumstances of earlier events and documents without being slavishly bound to their historical evaluation, especially in a subsequent epoch when relationships have been radically altered. Such a transvaluation will enable us freely to relegate the polemics in these articles (and the anathemas of Trent as well) to our memories of *old, unhappy, far-off tales and battles long ago* and to rejoice in the newly positive relationships that are being developed between the United Methodist Church and the Roman Catholic Church, at levels both official and unofficial." The resolution concluded with the "heartiest offer of goodwill and Christian brotherhood to all our Roman Catholic brethren, in the avowed hope of the day when all bitter memories (ours and theirs) will have been redeemed by the gift of the fullness of Christian unity, from the God and Father of our common Lord, Jesus Christ."

Albert C. Outler, chairman of the Theological Study Commission on Doctrine and Doctrinal Standards wrote a letter conveying this resolution to Cardinal Jan Willebrands, President of the Secretariat for Promoting Christian Unity. Dr. Outler explained in his letter that "We will not deny or repudiate our past, nor expect this of anyone else. But we do reject for ourselves, as a church, any further continuance of those polemical attitudes that once characterized our past. The General conference adopted this Resolution of Intent unanimously—which makes of it a formal and official statement of the ecumenical position and policy of the United Methodist Church."

In 1971 the dialogue gained two new chairmen, Bishop James W. Malone of the BCEIA and Bishop Paul W. Washburn. Bishop Washburn served until 1972 when he was in turn succeeded by Bishop James K. Mathews, both representing the ecumenical office of the Board of Global Ministries of the United Methodist Church.

Beginning in 1971 the U.S. dialogue narrowed its field of discussion to focus on the ministry of the Church. Specifically it discussed the "Holiness and Spirituality of the Ordained Ministry." The subject held importance in the Methodist tradition of the itinerancy of its ministers in full connection as well as the various spiritual disciplines of the Catholic priest. A report of the dialogue's findings was published in 1976.

In 1977 the dialogue turned to a discussion of the Eucharist, giving attention to the contribution of other ecumenical consultations reporting agreements on this mystery, and also to the traditions of worship which express Methodist and Catholic faith concerning the Eucharist. The timeliness of the subject is underscored by the fact that in both Churches the traditions of worship are being renewed.

Bibliography: *Holiness and Spirituality of the Ordained Ministry* (USCC Publ. Office, Washington, D.C. 1976).

[J. F. HOTCHKIN]

UNITED NATIONS, HOLY SEE AND THE

The particular interest of the Holy See in the United Nations (UN) and the Specialized Agencies is based on a convergence of general aims: the maintenance of international peace and security; the development of friendly relations among nations; the promotion of international economic, social, and cultural cooperation; and the commitment to protect the basic rights of man.

In his encyclical *Pacem in terris* (1963) Pope John XXIII expressed the wish that the United Nations "become even more equal to the magnitude and nobility of its tasks, and that the day may come when every human being will find therein an effective safeguard for the rights which derive directly from his dignity as a person (John XXIII PacTerr 145)."

Although the Holy See has not become a member of the UN, it participates actively in the most important specialized agencies and bodies of the UN family. The Holy See is a member of the IAEA (International Atomic Energy Agency); it maintains permanent observers to the UN in New York and in Geneva, to UNESCO (United Nations Educational, Social, Cultural Organization) in Paris, to FAO (Food and Agriculture Organization) in Rome, to UNIDO (United Nations Industrial Development Organization) in Vienna and the Council of Europe in Strasbourg. Vatican representatives attend many international conferences initiated by the UN and its specialized agencies and has been participating in the elaboration of important multilateral conventions and treaties such as the Geneva Sea Conventions (1958); the Vienna Convention on the Law of Treaties (1969); the Vienna Conventions on Diplomatic and Consular Relations (1961, 1962); the International Convention on the Elimination of all Forms of Racial Discrimination (1966); and the Convention on Narcotics Drugs (1961).

The Holy See's participation, which was trebled during the pontificate of Pope Paul VI, in a wide range of international meetings, conventions and permanent organizations reflected Pope Paul's firm belief in diplomacy as a means of advancing Gospel ideals.

Bibliography: H. E. CARDINALE, *The Holy See and the International Order* (London 1976).

[R. A. O'NEILL]

UNITED NATIONS, PERMANENT VATICAN OBSERVER AT

The appointment of a permanent observer was the logical consequence of the favorable attitude towards the United Nations expressed by Pope John XXIII in his encyclical *Pacem in terris*, April 11, 1963. The encyclical received unprecedented quotation in various UN bodies and elicited a surge of hope among diplomats.

Although a member of UN entities, such as the High Commissioner for Refugees, the IAEA (International Atomic Energy Agency), and maintaining observers to the UNESCO (United Nations Educational, Social, Cultural Organization), FAO (Food and Agriculture Organization), and UNIDO (United Nations Industrial Development Organization), the Holy See has not established permanent membership in the UN. Full membership would involve it in matters of a political nature which would be in contrast with the Holy See's spirit and mission.

On March 21, 1964, a communication of the Cardinal Secretary of State informed U Thant, the Secretary-General of the United Nations, of the appointment of a Permanent Observer of the Holy See to the United Nations. Msgr. Alberto Giovannetti served as the first observer, beginning in 1964, until Msgr. Giovanni Cheli, the present Vatican diplomat, was appointed in 1973. The appointment of a Permanent Observer, who has limited voice but no vote in UN proceedings, provides the opportunity of following closely UN activities, especially in such fields of church concern as the pursuit of peace, disarmament, progress, the concerns of the developing countries, the protection of basic human rights, elimination of all forms of discrimination.

The Holy See Mission in New York has taken a more active role at the United Nations as evidenced by its statements during committee meetings of the Thirty-second General Assembly on the role of disarmament, on youth, on support for the idea of a UN university, on the aged. One of the Mission's activities is its annual celebration for World Peace Day for the UN community.

Bibliography: John XXIII PacTerr 142–145. R. KIRCHSCHLAGER, "The Presence of the Holy See as a Factor of Peace in the International Community," address delivered in Vienna at Headquarters of IAEA, Jan. 21, 1974.

[R. A. O'NEILL]

UNITED STATES CATHOLIC MISSION COUNCIL

The coordinating entity that in 1969 succeeded the Mission Secretariat (9:906).

Origin. The formation of three mission committees of the NCCB Conferences of Major Superiors of Men (CMSM) and of Women (now the Leadership Conference of Women Religious—LCWR) in 1967 was the first step in the establishment of a national Mission Council as recommended by the documents of Vatican Council II (*Ad gentes* 30; cf. Paul VI EcclSanct III). The three committees at their first meeting, on Jan. 31, 1968, moved to invite lay missionary organizations to form a fourth committee and to initiate a study of the functional relationship between the Mission Secretariat and the mission committees. On June 18, 1968, the committee chairpersons met in New York and after reviewing the self-study report of the Mission Secretariat, requested the participating mission committees to prepare proposals for structuring a new body more in keeping with Vatican II directives and able to provide better service to the mission efforts of the U.S. Church.

Proposals were drawn up in a full three-way meeting of these committees on June 28, 1968. The following Sept. 11, a resolution was passed to request the NCCB to dissolve the Mission Secretariat in favor of the new structure. In October 1968, delegates to the annual meeting of the Mission Secretariat supported the proposed changes and voted to phase out the Mission Secretariat in favor of a new Mission Council. The following Spring, at a meeting in Detroit, April 10, 1969, attended by Cardinal John Dearden, Bishop Joseph Bernardin, national director of the Pontifical Mission Aid Societies, members of the laity, and the three mission committees, the following resolution was formulated and adopted: "Be It Resolved That the National Council of Catholic Bishops Recommend the Establishment of a National Mission Council." This resolution was presented at the April meeting of the NCCB in Houston and approved. On August 20, 1969, at a meeting in New York, the Pontifical Mission Aid Societies organized themselves into still another committee. Thus the five member-committees of the U.S. Catholic Mission Council were established.

The first general assembly of the newly formed Mission Council took place in Washington, D.C., Nov. 7, 1969. The Bylaws were discussed and approved. During the second assembly of the Mission Council at Maryknoll, New York, June 1–3, 1970, the members chose Washington, D.C. as headquarters for the Council, elected the first executive secretary in the person of Rev. Joseph Connors, SVD, and established a budget for its operations. On Sept. 1, 1970, the Mission Council opened its National Office, located presently at 1302 Eighteenth Street, N.W., Washington, D.C.

Purpose. The purpose of the Mission Council is to serve as a forum and organ for the evaluation, coordination, and fostering of American Catholic participation in the worldwide missionary efforts of the Church. To carry out its purpose, the Council is designed to represent all Catholic groups and agencies throughout the country devoted to missionary activity. As a forum it assists intercommunication of these groups on individual efforts to further the common goal. As an organ, it enables them to take collective action on major common problems and projects.

Structure. The Council is composed of five constitutive committees, representing respectively the NCCB, CMSM, LCWR, the laity, and the mission agencies. The five seven-member committees make up the Council, which meets at least once a year to determine major policies and programs. The five chairpersons of the committees comprise the executive board. An Executive Secretary is responsible for the Council's day-to-day activities.

Activities. All that comes within the scope of evaluating, coordinating, and fostering the American Catholic missionary effort is a proper concern of the Mission Council. The Council participates in mission-oriented meetings and conventions, gathers and transmits useful information in this field, alerts constituents to national events and policies which affect their interests. It influences statements and policies of the NCCB; it keeps data on American missionaries overseas; it publishes *Intercom*, a newsletter with pertinent, up-to-date information; it offers seminars for furloughed missionaries, for teachers, and for mission coordinators; and in general, it assists in development of new policies which affect the preparation of missionaries, as it helps educate the American Church to become more open and universal.

Bibliography: Archives of the United States Catholic Mission Council, 1968–1977.
[A. BELLAGAMBA]

UNITED STATES CENTER FOR THE CATHOLIC BIBLICAL APOSTOLATE

An entity within the Department of Education of the United States Catholic Conference (USCC) to promote the pastoral biblical apostolate. Established by the USCC in 1971 in response to an invitation to membership from the World Catholic Federation for the Biblical Apostolate (WCFBA), it shares the Federation's purpose of implementing the Vatican Council II Constitution on Divine Revelation, requiring bishops to provide the Christian faithful with easy access to sacred Scripture (*Dei Verbum* 22); suitable instruction in the right use of the divine books, especially translations from the original languages with adequate explanations (ibid. 22, 25); a sharing of the wealth of the Scriptures through the ministers of the Word particularly in the liturgy (ibid.).

Activities. The Center serves the U.S. Bishops in biblical matters by working for the integration of the Bible into the daily life of the faithful. It provides the texts of Scripture for the documents issued by the NCCB/USCC. It promotes: wide use of the Bible among the faithful; authorship by scholars of popular biblical works, books, cassettes, and audio-visual materials; Bible study groups and programs for adult education; distribution of lower-than-cost copies of the NT in English and Spanish among people in poverty areas; close association with the WCFBA in an exchange of ideas, information, projects, and consultation on mutual problems; publication of bibliographies of popular biblical works; cooperation with the inter-confessional Laymen's Bible Committee in bringing the annual observance of National Bible Week to the diocesan and parish level, and with the American Bible Society.

The U.S. Center represents the USCC at Assemblies of the WCFBA and councils of the above-mentioned inter-confessional Bible organizations.   [S. J. HARTDEGEN]

UNITED STATES CONFERENCE OF SECULAR INSTITUTES

Forerunner of this organization was the Conference of the Life of Total Dedication in the World (CLTDW), originating in 1952 with members from various forms of consecrated life. In 1969 the Executive Board of the then inactive CLTDW resolved to participate in the 1970 World Congress of Secular Institutes in Rome as the U.S. Association of Secular Institutes (ASI). Following the establishment of the World Conference of Secular Institutes in 1972, the ASI revised its Statutes and adopted the name of United States Conference of Secular Institutes (CSI). In 1976 Rome approved the Statutes for six years.

Purposes of the CSI are: (1) to make better known and understood the call to consecrated secularity; (2) to make known the secular institutes existing in the U.S.; (3) to interchange ideas and experiences among U.S. secular institutes; (4) to represent the Conference officially in the World Conference of Secular Institutes and other national and international bodies; (5) to offer resources of the CSI to groups aspiring to become secular institutes; and (6) to do research to help the Church carry out her mission today. Annual meetings keep these purposes alive.

A quarterly, *Communications*, is published for member institutes, of which there are thirteen out of the twenty approved secular institutes in the United States.

See also SECULAR INSTITUTES.   [M. P. IRWIN]

UNITED STATES OF AMERICA

As preparation for the 1974 International Synod of Bishops, the National Conference of Catholic Bishops (NCCB) authorized a study, "A Review of the Principal Trends in the Life of the Catholic Church in the United States," which attempted to give an account of a post-Vatican II Church in a post-Vietnam and post-Watergate nation. The study reported "a disturbing degree of polarization, confusion, self-doubt and uncertainty about fundamental values and purposes" in both the religious and secular spheres of current U.S. society and noted that problems in one area tended to reinforce and aggravate those in the other. It emphasized, however, that simply cataloging problems, however real, did not exhaust the reality of current U.S. Catholicism, which also showed signs of underlying strength. Other observers of the American Catholic scene saw the conflict and confusion within the Church in the U.S. as offering a promise of vitality that could have a tremendous impact both on the Church and on American society, but offering as well the possibility of failure and the gradual erosion of institutional relevance and personal commitment. However unclear the future course of events for American Catholicism, it is safe to predict that a return to the monolithic unity of the past seems out of the question (14:425).

Inner Renewal. As the U.S. moved into its third century of nationhood, the emergence of significant new beginnings in the American Catholic community offered a basis for cautious optimism which, however, was still far from being shared by all the members of that community.

Liturgy, Ministry. By the mid '70s a majority of American Catholics had come to accept, and in many cases to prefer, the changes in liturgy which, when introduced after Vatican II, had caused widespread disorientation. The effort to promote fuller and more active participation of the people in the life of the Church brought additional changes in rites, practices, and pastoral ministries. Included in these was a revised liturgy for the private form of Penance or Reconciliation which emphasized Scripture and face-to-face prayerful dialogue between penitent and priest, but permitted the anonymity of the old form of confession for those preferring it. Communal celebrations of *Penance in various forms, with general absolution often followed by a Eucharistic Liturgy, were also employed more frequently and were viewed by some as a viable way to effect the reconciliation of alienated Catholics with the Church. A new optional practice of receiving *Communion in the hand was introduced in 1977 with a program of instruction on Eucharistic belief and practice. Perhaps the most significant postconciliar development in the area of pastoral ministry was the restoration of the permanent diaconate (16:123) and the use of *extraordinary ministers of the Eucharist, a practice that spread rapidly throughout dioceses in the United States. Formal Roman approval in 1977 of the ministries of catechist and minister of music (director) petitioned by the NCCB still left the need to further expand a wide range of officially commissioned ministries that would be diocesan, parochial, and familial in scope (see MINISTRY; MINISTRY, UNORDAINED). Among these, the need to identify and open up new ministerial and decision-making roles for women in the Church (see WOMEN IN MINISTRY) became more urgent following the 1977 declaration of the Vatican Congregation for the Doctrine of the Faith reaffirming its opposition to the ordination of *women as priests. Since the Vatican declaration omitted any discussion of the ordination of women to the diaconate, it left open the possibility of implementing a 1974 recommendation of the *Canon Law Society of America (CLSA) to develop a rationale to permit restoring the *diaconate for women. Within the general area of ministry, other tasks for the future include the study and reform of the life styles of ministers in the American Church to conform to Gospel values, and an even stronger commitment of the Church's resources for continued dialogue with other Christian groups in this country and abroad (see BILATERAL CONSULTATIONS).

In this continuing process of renewal, the revitalization and updating of liturgical forms and ministries became the concern of a variety of agencies. Headed by the NCCB, these included the various diocesan *liturgical committees, the *Bishops' Committee on the Liturgy, as well as the several institutes for pastoral liturgy such as those established at The Catholic University of America (Washington, D.C.), St. John's Abbey and University (Collegeville, Minn.) and the Notre Dame Center (Notre Dame University, Ind.). The new dialogue engaged in by the United States Lutheran/Roman Catholic dialogue group resulted in 1974 in a joint statement on papal primacy that reflected a growing Lutheran awareness of the need for a specific ministry serving the Church's unity and universal mission as well as a developing Catholic understanding of the need for a more nuanced understanding of the role of the papacy within the universal Church. The January 1975 "Appeal for Theological Affirmation," issued by an ecumenical group of theologians meeting in Hartford, Conn., was not an attempt to summarize basic dogmas held in common, but rather to identify certain current assumptions or "themes" present in both academic and popular culture. The unifying element in the thirteen Hartford themes was concern for the apparent loss of the sense of the transcendent and the consequent problems presented to all the Churches. In 1976, the jointly sponsored statement of the United Methodist/Roman Catholic dialogue group, "The Holiness and Spirituality of the Ordained Ministry," constituted the first major statement of the group since the two denominations began their ecumenical dialogue in 1966.

Opposition to church reform and other attempts at renewal has found its strongest expression in the Catholic *traditionalist movement. Its clerical and lay supporters in the U.S., in defiance of ecclesiastical authorities, have denounced Vatican-II reforms and continued to celebrate the old Latin Tridentine Mass (see LATIN MASS), and to use other religious customs declared obsolete by the Council. Among the traditionalist chapels established, one in Dickinson, Texas, was consecrated in July 1977 by Abp. Marcel Lefebvre, the French prelate and leader of the movement who became the object of widespread publicity in various parts ot Europe and the U.S. after his suspension by Pope Paul VI in 1976.

Church Governance. Efforts to renew church law and the administrative machinery of church governance have thus far not been notably successful in achieving Council goals. Since 1963, the Pontifical Commission for the Revision of the Code of Canon Law, established by John XXIII and continued by Paul VI, has been engaged in a revision of the 1917 Code of Canon Law. At the October 1977 meeting of the CLSA, the members adopted a statement critical of much that has been done by the Commission. The CLSA statement took issue with the confidential nature of the commission's overall procedures and the lack of sufficient consultation. Questioning whether codification itself should be retained as the most appropriate instrument for ordering the life and mission of the Church, the CLSA urged that further steps towards revision be worked out in consultation with the Synod of Bishops. Throughout the postconciliar years, the CLSA has exercised an effective influence on developments in the American Church, both in a research capacity for the NCCB and in an advocacy role for church renewal. The numerous studies of the CLSA have included several proposals developing norms, procedures and processes later adopted by the American hierarchy. In its 1974 report, "A Master Plan for the Next Decade," the CLSA pointed out that obsolete structures had impeded the implementation of the Council's ideal of authority as service exercised through subsidiarity and coresponsibility. It stressed the need to evaluate existing structures for effectiveness in exercising an authority understood as functional and diffused among the People of God. The report also suggested that bishops, clergy, and laity alike need to be educated in the science and art of government so as to acquire some understanding of the process involved in formulating policy, solving problems, making decisions, shaping organizations, maintaining community, resolving conflict, deploying personnel, and establishing laws.

Call to Action. Had the need identified by the CLSA for such education been effectively addressed, the problems inherent in the NCCB's *Call to Action conference held in Detroit, Oct. 21–23, 1976, as part of the American Church's observance of the nation's bicentennial, might not have been so formidable. However, despite its defects and problems, the justice conference, with its preparatory, two-year, nationwide consultation and its six regional justice-hearings, constituted one of the more diversified deliberative assemblies in the history of the American Church. In the words of Cardinal John Dearden, chairman of the Bishops Ad Hoc Committee for the Bicentennial which sponsored the conference, it was "a learning process which cannot fail to be helpful to ... the whole Church in the United States .... This process ... has been a marked success as a speaking and listening process .... We must struggle to continue this process of speaking and listening and find even more effective mechanisms for deliberation, decision, collaborative action." When, at its Spring 1977 meeting, the NCCB voted to repeal the penalty of excommunication that was imposed in the United States, but not elsewhere, on divorced Catholics who remarried, the action addressed one of the recommendations approved by the delegates to the Call to Action conference in their consideration of ways to improve family life. Whatever the immediate or future success associated with the Detroit conference, American Catholic experience with parish councils, priests' senates, and diocesan *pastoral councils has yet to demonstrate that they are the panacea many expected. It seems clear that the need remains for continued effort to improve all structures of shared responsibility in the American Church to the satisfaction of both pastors and people.

Catechetics. The Church's need to modernize its manner of understanding and presenting the faith, another task set by Vatican II, became more urgent with the dramatic increase within the last decade in the number of American Catholics who receive no formal education in the faith. At the 1977 *Synod of Bishops, a paper submitted by the NCCB stressed the need for catechists to give an accurate account of other religious beliefs, develop an appreciation for the contributions of other religions, promote joint social action projects, make known common values, and encourage dialogue and prayer in common. Work on a national catechetical directory to address these needs and supply norms and guidelines for Catholics in the United States in these times was begun in 1972, constituting the most significant undertaking in religious education in this century. Completed and approved by the NCCB in 1977, the *National Catechetical Directory, *Sharing the Light of Faith*, was sent to the Congregation for the Clergy for Vatican approval. The Directory emphasized the need for diverse approaches in catechizing people of differing ages and life experiences, underscoring the contribution the behavioral sciences can make to *catechetics. When this work becomes available it will serve a not inconsiderable need if, indeed, it provides adequately for the diversity in the present American Church. Concurrently, in response to Paul VI's *Evangelii nuntiandi* a program of *evangelization was inaugurated at the 1977 Fall meeting of NCCB and the *Bishops' Committee on Evangelization established (*see* MISSIONS, CATHOLIC).

Meanwhile the *charismatic renewal and *Marriage Encounter continue to grow and, although not attractive to all Catholics, manifest sources of vitality in the Church. The 41st International Eucharistic Congress held in Philadelphia, Aug. 1–8, 1976, brought bishops, priests, religious, and laity from many parts of the United States and the world for the celebration and discussion of "The Eucharist and the Hunger of the Human Family." World justice, contemporary spirituality, religious life, the role of women in the Church, and many other issues affecting Christian life were examined. Other occasions of celebration for the American Church during these years included one in 1975 when on September 14, Elizabeth Ann Bayley Seton, foundress of the first religious congregation of women in the U.S., was canonized by Paul VI, becoming the first American-born saint of the Roman Catholic Church. Another followed on June 19, 1977, when John Nepomucene Neumann, fourth bishop of Philadelphia, became the first American male to be named a saint.

Social Mission and Action. In contrast to its more timid stance of earlier years, the postconciliar Church in the United States increasingly concerned itself with a wide range of public policy issues in support of *human rights and social justice.

Church and Public Policy Issues. However, the complexity of applying the values of the Gospel in the social arena was reflected in the 1976 statement of the United States Catholic Conference (USCC), "Political Responsibility: Reflections on an Election Year," which emphasized that the mission of the Church must be seen as advocating the critical values of human rights and human justice and not as an effort to form a confessional or sectarian voting bloc intent on endorsing political parties or candidates, or on instructing people on how they should vote. During the ensuing presidential campaign, however, widespread controversy was aroused by the position of the Church on the abortion issue. In a letter to the episcopal chairman of Bishops' Ad Hoc Committee for Pro-Life Activities, the Executive Board of the National Federation of Priests' Councils expressed concern that the U.S. hierarchy had stressed abortion "to the neglect of other important social issues" creating the impression "that the one issue on which candidates are being judged is their legal approach to the issue of abortion." The controversy over the charges of "one-issue Church," prompted Cardinal John Dearden, former president of the NCCB, to restate the role of the Church in a pluralistic society and to remind Catholics that they "must accept the fact that public policy will not always reflect the Catholic position" ... that "in a pluralistic society public consensus cannot be determined by one religious group" ... nor should it be realized "in a vacuum of moral discourse." The shaping of public consensus, the Cardinal added, was a "delicate task" which necessitated drawing upon the resources of various religious traditions.

Advocacy of Human Rights. In this role as advocate of human rights and human justice, the Church gave strong expression to its concern over the moral aspects of public policy in such domestic issues as the right of life; *health care; full employment; income during *unemployment; collective bargaining; adequate housing; prison reform; justice for minority groups, particularly Blacks, Hispanic Americans, American Indians and women; amnesty for illegal aliens; welfare reform; rights for the aged; economic reform, including a challenge to growing consumerism, and many others.

Catholic involvement in the civil discourse for a consensus on international problems included statements on such issues as war, armaments, foreign aid, the Arab-Israeli conflict, the proposed Panama Canal Treaty, and a host of others. In 1977 a representative of the USCC testified before a House Subcommittee, urging a ban on Rhodesian chrome to "disassociate the United States from the Ian Smith regime and demonstrate to the African nations where the United States stands in the struggle for human rights."

By presidential appointment of Theodore Hesburgh, CSC, as ambassador to chair the U.S. delegation to the United Nations Conference on Science and Technology for Development scheduled for 1979, Fr. Hesburgh became the first U.S. priest to hold the rank of ambassador. Msgr. Geno Baroni's appointment as Assistant Secretary of the Department of Housing and Urban Development likewise marked the first appointment of a Catholic priest to a cabinet-level position in the United States. Such were some of the ways in which the public face of contemporary Catholicism became better known and appreciated in this country.

Conclusion. As the Church moves into the future, many problems remain to be dealt with, one of which was described in a resolution on sexuality passed at the Call to Action conference asking "That the Church in the United States acknowledge that it is living in a state of conflict and anguish arising from tension between the common understanding of the church teaching on contraception and the current practice of many Catholics, and that the . . . American bishops should . . . affirm more clearly the right and responsibility of married people to form their own consciences and to discern what is morally appropriate within the context of their marriage in view of historical church teaching . . . contemporary theological reflection, biologican and social scientific research, and those factors influencing the spiritual and emotional quality of the marital and family lives."

However, despite its present deep crisis over this and other issues, the contemporary Catholic Church is seen by some, such as Langdon Gilkey, as "presenting the possibility of immense new creativity and new relevance . . . that can redeem both herself and the Christian Church as a whole."

Bibliography: P. L. BERGER and R. J. NEUHAUS, eds., *Against the World* (New York 1976). R. E. BROWN, *Crises Facing the Church* (New York 1975). A. DULLES, *The Resilient Church* (New York 1977). A. GREELEY, *The Communal Catholic* (New York 1976); A. GREELEY, W. MCCREADY, K. MCCOURT, *Catholic Schools in a Declining Church* (New York 1976). A. KOSNIK et al., *Human Sexuality, New Directions in American Catholic Thought* (Ramsey, N.J. 1977). R. P. MCBRIEN, *Has the Church Surrendered* (Denville, N.J. 1974). M. MARTY, "E Pluribus Unum: The Religious Dimension Today," *Catholic Mind* 74 (Sept. 1975) 11–25. R. J. NEUHAUS, *Christian Faith and Public Policy* (Minneapolis, Minn. 1977). See also bibliog. for Canon Law Society of America; *Origins*, NC Documentary Series (Washington, D.C. 1974–).

[M. CARTHY]

UNITY OF THE CHURCH

The fragmentation of Christianity is so evident a hindrance to its propagation that the unity of the Church might be sought solely on pragmatic grounds. Church unity would no doubt increase the effectiveness of the Church's mission, but even if it did not, it would still be necessary to strive for it. The Church's central purpose is to witness to God's unifying and reconciling love in Christ. Therefore the unity of all human beings and their communion with

God is the goal towards which the Church is directed (Vatican II, *Lumen gentium* 1). The Church's own unity, consequently, is an intrinsic necessity and indeed a given object of faith. Like other gifts of grace, it is also a never-ending task to utilize and manifest the gift of unity in the Church's life.

Two problems have commanded the most attention in recent years. The first arises over the choice of a starting point. Given the centrality of the Eucharistic celebration to the meaning of the word, "Church," should the unity be conceived primarily in terms of the local Church rather than of the Church universal? Then, what kind of diversity can and should be welcomed, and what sort of unity must be envisaged to make room for all the legitimate diversities of a truly catholic Church? (*See* CATHOLICITY.) Cardinal Jan Willebrands, for example, noted that various existing "types" (traditions) of Church Bodies would not necessarily have to be abandoned in the event of union. The *Presbyterian-Reformed/Roman Catholic Consultation in the U.S. has described the ecumenical goal as a "communion of communions"; each Communion would preserve its own traditions intact, as long as the latter remain vital and are compatible with the broader unity of the whole Church.

The International Lutheran/Roman Catholic Working Group is considering various "models of unity," elaborated on the basis of interconfessional experiences to date and of extrapolations therefrom. "Organic unity," for example, is the express ultimate goal of the Anglican/Roman Catholic conversations, although the model of "sister Churches in communion" also finds application. The World Council of Churches has put forth the strategy of working toward a "genuinely ecumenical council" to crown the ecumenical movement of the 20th century; the term "conciliar fellowship" describes this model. "Reconciled diversity" and "concord" are two further models. The latter, exemplified in the Continental Lutheran and Reformed Churches' Leuenberg Concord (Sept. 30, 1974; named for the Swiss Reformed academy where it was drafted in March, 1973, it is an agreement to full pulpit and altar fellowship), finds Churches healing their rifts by formally recognizing that their mutual condemnations of each other's doctrine in the past no longer have any relevance.

Bibliography: T. BACHMANN et al., on the Leuenberg Agreement, *Lutheran World* 21 (1974) 328–348. Y. CONGAR, "Die Einekirche," in J. FEINER and M. LOHRER, eds., *Mysterium Salutis*, v. 4 pt. 1, (Einsiedeln 1972) 368–457. Consultation on Church Unity (COCU), "In Quest of a Church of Christ Uniting: A Statement of Emerging Theological Consensus," *Mid-Stream* 16 (1977) 49–92. N. EHRENSTROM, ed., *Confessions in Dialogue* (Geneva 1975) 196–211; What Unity Requires (Geneva 1976). E. LANNE, "The Unity of the Church in the Work of Faith and Order," *One-in-Christ* 12 (1976) 34–57. Secretariat for Promoting Christian Unity, *Information Service*, n. 31 (1976) (on Lutheran/Catholic Commission) 11–12. E. L. UNTERKOEFLER and A. HARSONYI, eds., *The Unity We Seek: A Statement by the Roman Catholic/Presbyterian-Reformed Consultation* (New York 1977). J. WILLEBRANDS, "Moving Toward a Typology of Churches," *Catholic Mind* 68 (1970) 35–42; "Models for Reunion," *One-in-Christ* 7 (1971) 115–123.

[P. MISNER]

URBANIZATION

Urbanization is a complex phenomenon including not only the physical growth of cities, but also that set of social structures, institutions, relationships, attitudes, ideas, and personalities involved in the kind of behavior that has come to be called urban. It refers to the process which world civilization is following regarding those issues usually associated with dense concentrations of populations. Paul VI's apostolic letter, a "Call to Action"

(*Octogesima adveniens*) devotes special attention to the topic.

Growth of Cities. Cities exert a greater influence upon world civilization than indicated by the number of urban inhabitants. The growth of cities, particularly within the last century, has led to the reorganization of civilization to the extent that rural life is now dependent on urban centers. The city is the initiating and controlling center of economic, political, cultural, and social life.

Urbanization appears inevitable because cities are the most efficient technique humans have developed for the control of the earth. The dominance of cities can be attributed to their concentration of industrial, commercial, financial, administrative, transportation, communication, social, cultural, and recreational facilities and activities. This sovereign status of cities has been abetted by the current energy crisis, for the cities, through their concentration of resources, are great conservers of energy.

Urban population statistics are indicative of the accelerating growth of urbanization. In 1900, 9.2 per cent of the world population lived in cities of 20,000 or more. By 1950, that figure had more than doubled and by 1970 increased to 27.8 per cent. Projections for the year 2000 put the world urban population at 48.3 per cent. In the U.S. 68 per cent of the population lived in cities in 1975.

The phenomenon of megalopolitization gives a more accurate picture of the urbanization process. The Boston-Washington megalopolis is six hundred miles long and thirty to one hundred miles wide, encompassing rural areas as well as urban centers. In 1960, it had a population of 37 million people dependent in livelihood and affected in life style and social behavior by the major urban centers, and a density of 53,000 people per square mile.

Marks and Problems of Urbanization. The characteristics of urbanization are numerous, not generally agreed upon, and of varying moral value. They include social, scientific, technological, cultural, economic, and political factors.

Many of the social characteristics result from density, the concentration of human and other resources in restricted geographical areas. They are: an increase in secondary rather than primary social contacts; greater dependence on more people for the satisfaction of life's needs; new forms of social integration based on segmented grouping around common interests; freedom from personal and emotional control of intimate groups; increased heterogeneity in life style; dissociation of work-place from place of residence; the growth of such formal social controls as law, police, courts, and traffic regulations.

Science, industry and technology, whose advances have been influenced by urbanization, have contributed the following characteristics: rapid tempo; complicated machinery; mass and instantaneous communication; multiple-dwelling units; improved sanitation and medical facilities; and computerization. Economic and financial factors that may be associated with urbanization are: a greater division of labor; the development of the human-services industries; bureaucratization; monopolistic capitalism; the corporation as a style of conducting business; and the rise of the middle class.

These factors and characteristics have generated a concatenation of social problems, the most critical of which have to do with the cities, the focal points of urbanization. Soaring crime rates, interracial tensions, loss of jobs, evanescing fiscal solvency, "redlining," panic peddling, inflation, inequitable tax burdens, housing-stock deterioration have made the cities huge reservations of the impoverished, disadvantaged, and involuntarily dependent.

The Church. Churches and synagogues, much more than government or big business, are the key to saving the cities and purging the process of urbanization of its malevolent side effects. The urban problem results from the fractured nature of community life and the disregard of the creative potential of human beings living in the city.

Historically, the Church has conceived its mission as community-building, though this has often meant building up the Christian community of faith through the dispension of spiritual services—the preaching of the Gospel and the dispensing of the Sacraments. Recently the Church, through the 1971 Synod of Bishops document, taking its lead from *Gaudium et spes*, has recognized that it is a community sent into the world to help create the conditions of true community that foreshadow the Kingdom of God (Synod JustWorld p. 52).

Community-building extends to the whole person, for the promised redemption includes freedom from all wants and oppression. Integral to the restoration of community is the revitalizing of the creative potential of the human person as the image of God the Creator, which is also a presupposition for community-building.

In the U.S., of prime importance to the upbuilding of the human community is the rediscovery of the human scale of the neighborhood, as the basic building block in the revival of the city. Neighborhoods are natural communities, networks of human relationships. They provide the appropriate geographical, political, social, and cultural settings for the maintenance of community life in a chaotic urban situation. Neighborhoods are of the scale whereby persons can take control of their lives and environment to produce conditions in which they can act decently, warmly and caringly to each other in the common pursuit of justice and love. Pope Paul VI, recognizing this, declared: "To build up the city, the place where men and their expanded communities exist, to create new modes of neighborliness and relationships ... is a task in which Christians must share" (Paul VI OctogAdven 12).

The function of the Church, as institution, is to use its institutional preponderance to inform the public moral sense of the necessity and importance of community. As local Church it can act as facilitator for neighborhood groups to obtain federal and business assistance to take the means to stop decline and deterioration in their neighborhoods, which are their basic communities and the basic building blocks of cities. The resources for this are the Catholic social ethic of personalism, pluralism, and subsidiarity. Personalism respects the dignity of the individual human person. Pluralism recognizes the importance of cultural diversity in the formation of community, and subsidiarity respects the creative potential of persons and social infra-groups.

See also COMMUNITY.

Bibliography: G. C. BARONI and G. GREEN, *Who's Left in the Neighborhood?* (Washington, D.C. 1976). A. M. GREELEY, *No Bigger Than Necessary* (New York 1977). P. K. HATT and A. J. REISS, JR., *Cities and Society* (Glencoe, Ill. 1957). U.S. Office of Federal Statistical Policy, *Social Indicators 1976* (Washington, D.C. 1977).

[R. D. PASQUARIELLO]

V

VAN DER VELDT, JAMES H.

Franciscan psychologist, scholar, b. Sloten, Holland March 15, 1893, d. Washington, D.C., Aug. 18, 1977. He was christened Herman, but during his adult life he was known nationally and internationally as James, the name given him at his reception into the Order of Friars Minors in 1912. He made his profession in 1918 and was ordained May 30, 1919. His early education was in Amsterdam, where also his ecclesiastical studies began at the seminary of the Franciscans. His university studies were carried on at Nijmegen in Holland and at Milan, where he studied with the renowned Agostino Gemelli (6:318); Fr. Van der Veldt received the Ph.D. at the University of Louvain in 1926. Two years later he became the *agrégé de philosophie* at the same university. His dissertation, written under the direction of the famed Professor Albert Michotte, was titled: "*L'Apprentissage du mouvement et l'automatisme, étude expérimentale,*" published in Paris, 1928.

Fr. Van der Veldt devoted his life to priestly and scholarly pursuits. The outstanding quality of his contributions is attested by the many honors awarded him. The Queen of the Netherlands knighted him in the Order of Orange, Nassau; pontifical decorations included Commander in Order of Merit in the Sovereign Military Order of Malta, of which he was chaplain of the Washington, D.C., Chapter, Lateran Cross of the Holy See First Degree, and Commander Imperial of the Order of St. George. Academic honors included on honorary doctorate of letters and membership in the Society of Sigma Xi.

Immediately upon completion of his studies at Louvain in 1928, Van der Veldt commenced his teaching career in Rome where, for twelve years, he taught at the Pontifical University of the Propagation of the Faith, where he was head of the psychological laboratory and at the Pontifical Athenaeum Sancti Antonii, where he was dean of philosophy. The remainder of his teaching career was in the United States. He came to St. Joseph's, Dunwoodie, the major seminary of the Archdiocese of New York in 1940. In 1945 he joined the faculty of The Catholic University of America as a member of the department of psychology and psychiatry, then under the chairmanship of Thomas Verner Moore (16:300). Fr. Van der Veldt became

Ordinary Professor in 1952 and after retirement was elected professor emeritus.

His great legacy to his students was the integration of new scientific findings with the basics of philosophy. He was able to do this with a wit and clarity which made him a teacher from whom both young and old could learn. In the classroom these interests are evidenced by a sample of his courses: Advanced General Psychology, Philosophical Concepts of Psychotherapy; History of Psychology, Development of Personality. He was an accomplished linguist. He traveled widely and was so proficient in languages that he was able to give scholarly lectures in the Netherlands, France, Spain, Italy, and the United States. At St. Matthew's Cathedral in Washington, D.C., his last assignment, he was very much in demand as a confessor because of his language skills.

In the style of the scholar of yesteryear, Fr. Van der Veldt combined interests in both the classics and science. He was an author of note; left close to 100 articles and several books, some of which are representive of his scientific studies, while others represent his classical interests and knowledge of history and of literature. His books include *The City Set on a Hill* (New York 1945); *Exploring the Vatican* (London 1947); *Psychiatry and Catholicism*; with Robert P. Odenwald (New York 1952), which was translated into several languages, and *Psychology for Counselors* (Chicago 1971). *The Ecclesiastical Orders of Knighthood* (Washington, D.C. 1956), is the definitive work in this field; requests for copies of this unique work were still being received·20 years after its publication. He also translated into English two books authored by Bishop Jan Olav Smit, Canon of St. Peter's, *The Angelic Shepherd, The Life of Pius XII* (New York 1950) and *St. Pius X, Pope* (Boston 1975).

This scholar in the true sense was a man of wit and humor, whose love for God, for people, and for life provided the will and zest to accomplish much and still maintain a vast coterie of friends and human relationships with the great and not so great.

[H. E. PEIXOTTO]

VATICAN COUNCIL II

Pope John XXIII's announcement, Jan. 25, 1959, less than three months after his election, that he intended to convoke an ecumenical council caught the world by surprise. There was no immediately obvious crisis requiring such an extraordinary measure and, except for those areas of the world where Christianity was suffering overt persecution, the Church gave considerable evidence of vigor and self-confidence in the decade and a half following World War II. The generic reasons John gave for convoking the Council—"affirming doctrine" and "ordering discipline"—cast little light on what he intended and on the course the Council might take. A generally pastoral purpose seemed to be what the Pope had principally in mind.

Development of the Spirit of Change. Once the Council was announced, however, certain problems and even grievances began to surface to which relatively little advertence had been given until the possibility of resolving them was offered by the Council. In Western Europe and North America, especially, there was a desire to end the religious and cultural isolation in which better-educated Catholics sometimes felt themselves confined. In Germany and Holland the experience of cooperation with Protestants during World II resulted in a desire for more active participation by the Church in the ecumenical movement. The American political experience seemed to tally ill with official Catholic teaching on the Church-State issue and some theologians hoped for a revision of that teaching. In missionary countries there was a developing sense of the inadequacy of methods of evangelization indissolubly conjoined to Westernization. The insistence upon Latin as the language of the liturgy was symptomatic of this problem. Even aside from the special problems in missionary lands, liturgists were frustrated that the general reform of the liturgy for which they had been preparing for several decades had not received a more favorable hearing in Rome. Some members of the episcopacy, moreover, had begun to express concern that over the course of the centuries their office had gradually been deprived of many of its rightful prerogatives and that the bishops had been reduced to simple executors of decisions of the Roman Curia.

Preparatory Stages. The vague purposes for an announced council thus evoked a wide range of expectations, hopes, and fears in the three and one-half years between the Pope's announcement of his decision and Vatican Council II's beginning. From the membership of the Preparatory Commissions and the work the Commissions accomplished a conservative bias became apparent. Though Pope John remained immensely popular during this period, he permitted certain occurrences interpreted by some as reactionary and even repressive. There was discouragement or alarm among those who hoped the Council would be innovative in resolving the problems emerging and already openly discussed. Among the causes of uneasiness were the conservative statutes enacted by the Roman Synod of 1960, the publication of the apostolic constitution *Veterum sapientia* in 1962 (promoting Latin), and the peremptory measure of the Holy Office in suspending from teaching two professors of the Pontificio Istituto Biblico—M. Zerwick, SJ and S. Lyonnet, SJ. These and similar actions began to create in some circles a decided animus against the Roman Curia, generally held to be directly or indirectly responsible for them. They also fostered the emergence of an ill-defined but well-publicized and very visible division among those who

were to participate in the Council between "progressives" and "conservatives."

Distinctive Features. When the Council finally opened, Oct. 11, 1962, there was no clear indication of what direction it would take and which of the two wings would dominate. However, the Council was already distinguished by a number of features unique, or at least extraordinary, in the history of such assemblies. These features would contribute to the eventual domination of the Council by the progressive wing and give the Council a character quite different from that of any which preceded it.

First of all, the 2,540 churchmen with right to vote who attended the opening session vastly exceeded the 700 or so who attended the opening session of Vatican I, and the number at Vatican I was more than triple the number present at the best attended sessions of Trent. Second, the missionary countries of Asia and Africa were considerably better represented by Western and native churchmen than was the case at Vatican I, whereas there had been none present at Trent and only three at Lateran V, 1512–17. Third, the vagueness of the purposes for which the Council was convoked encouraged an examination of all aspects of ecclesiastical life and thus gave the Council an open-ended agenda.

Fourth, the decision to admit non-Catholic "observers" to the sessions of the Council was unique, allowing the deliberations of the Council to be reviewed by scholars and churchmen who did not share basic assumptions upon which Catholic theology and discipline were based. As events would prove, this decision stimulated a more searching scrutiny of conciliar documents than would otherwise have been the case, and it was important for turning the attention of the Council to the large issue of the Church's general relationship to the contemporary world. Hans Küng's *The Council, Reform, and Reunion* (New York 1961), originally published in German (Vienna 1960), was the most influential among the many publications in the preparatory years that evoked a sense of the dramatic possibilities for change.

Fifth, the interest in the Council of the communications media was aggressive. Until the Council of Trent, the deliberations of councils were almost the private concern of those who participated in them. With the invention of printing, Trent and especially Vatican I had to contend with a more general and rapid dissemination of information and propaganda, but this dissemination was still confined to a very small percentage of the world's population. Radio and television, however, were now capable of thrusting news about the Council upon the world at large almost at the very moment any newsworthy event occurred. The actions of the Council would thus be discussed and debated in the public forum on a day-to-day basis and the members of the Council would be forced to explain and justify their actions to a public which did not always understand or have sympathy with the complex questions being raised. There is no doubt that the attempt to satisfy some of the objections and problems raised by the media affected the Council's direction and imparted confidence to those members of the Council who were more progressive in outlook.

Finally, the mentality with which many of the progressive theologians and other experts approached their task was more historical than in any previous council. This mentality was the result of the revival of historical studies in the 19th century and the consequent application of historical methods to sacred subjects, particularly to the history of doctrine, discipline, and liturgy. Theologians were thus much more aware of the profound changes that had taken place in the long history of the Church than were their counterparts in earlier councils. They were also aware that many of these changes could be adequately explained in merely human terms as expressions of a given culture and that they were therefore not necessarily irreversible. This keener sense of history thus permitted greater freedom in judgment that some practices or traditions might be simply anachronistic and should be modified or even eliminated. Moreover, it was now obvious from historical studies that many of the doctrines taught by the Church in the 20th century were unknown as such in the Church of the apostolic or patristic periods. The Immaculate Conception of Mary would be an example. Theologians could not escape facing issues like these, and John Courtney Murray, SJ, one of the *periti* at the Council, stated that "development of doctrine" was "*the* issue underlying all issues" at Vatican II. For the first time in an ecumenical council, therefore, doctrinal positions had to be formulated with as much concern for historical context and process as for their validity in terms of traditional metaphysics.

Spirit of the Documents. All these factors contributed to the most striking characteristic of the documents the Council produced: the great scope of their concerns. The Council wished to speak "to all men," as the Constitution on the Church in the Modern World succinctly stated (*Gaudium et spes* 2). In a word, Vatican II took greater note of the world around it than any previous council, and it assumed as one of its principal tasks colloquies or conversations with that world. The Council's pastoral concerns were thus broadened far beyond the confines of the Catholic Church to a universal horizon. The Council was fully aware, therefore, that the Church was in history and in the world, and it wanted the Church to act in accordance with that awareness.

From such an awareness of history and the world, it was an easy step to the decision to make some changes in the Church in order to put it into a more effective relationship with the contemporary situation. This awareness, indeed, was the psychological matrix capable of sustaining the idea of *aggiornamento*, which came to be the theme of the Council. The decrees of the Council by and large determined that religious practice and the expression of religious doctrine should be changed by the "new era" in order to meet the needs of the "new era," as the members of the Council perceived them. Previous councils had generally insisted on the stability of religious practice and doctrinal formulas and on the necessity of eradicating anything that would threaten that stability. *Aggiornamento* took the opposite position; in the breadth of its application and the depth of its implications, it was a revolution in the mentality with which previous councils had addressed their problems.

Vatican II Influences for Change in the Church. Even in the short time that has elapsed since the close of the Council in December 1965, it is clear that the Council had a dramatic impact on the life of the Church. This impact is principally due to three factors, already described. (1) The decisions of the Council were communicated to the Church and to society in general with an effectiveness inconceivable without modern developments in the media of communication. (2) The open-ended agenda resulted in a series of documents which touched every aspect of ecclesiastical life, including public and private expressions of piety. (3) The historical mentality which accepted change as a normal feature of religion reversed the common persuasion among Catholics that their cult and formulations of belief were immune to change.

Changes Legislated. The changes which resulted were in part legislated by the Council or by other authoritative documents which later implemented conciliar decrees. A series of documents emanating from the Holy See, for instance, greatly modified liturgical and sacramental practice, especially for the Eucharist and the Sacrament of Penance or Reconciliation (*see* LITURGICAL BOOKS OF THE ROMAN RITE). Religious orders revised, sometimes radically, their dress, their discipline, and even the apostolic scope of their activities (*see* RELIGIOUS LIFE, RENEWAL OF).

Changes Motivated by Vatican II. Other changes were due to the initiatives and experimentations which the Council encouraged without being overly specific as to what forms these initiatives and experiments might take. The Council's affirmation of the *ecumenical movement and its concern for justice and peace in the world resulted, for example, in more effective collaboration of Catholics and Catholic organizations with others. On a deeper level, Catholic religious instruction attempted to renew what was distinctive of Roman Catholicism by stressing, *inter alia*, those beliefs and values which Catholics shared with others. There was considerable effort in seminaries and elsewhere to base the teaching of theology more directly on the text of Scripture, and the Scholastic base on which Catholic theology had rested for centuries was decidedly challenged (*see* PLURALISM, PHILOSOPHICAL; THOMISM).

Turmoil in the Church. Despite the public debate on individual issues during the Council, the changes in practice and the change in mentality which the Council seemed to demand were thrust upon a Church not wholly prepared to understand or receive them. Although the progressive wing eventually came to dominate the Council and generally seemed to enjoy public approbation during the course of the Council, its viewpoints often could not be translated into action without offending the religious sensibilities even of many who felt sympathetic to the general direction the Council took. The faithful, as a body, remained conservative, and their expectations of the Church were sometimes far removed from what *aggiornamento* in its sweeping breadth seemed to require.

Thus, a period of considerable turmoil ensued in the years immediately following the Council. In some parts of the Church, there was a marked decrease in candidates for the priesthood and religious life, and, to a degree unprecedented since the Reformation, mature men and women left the priesthood and religious orders. Certain countries registered a decrease in attendance at the liturgy and a general decline in religious practice. The very viability of the so-called institutional Church was called into question by some scholars and responsible observers.

The disquiet in the Church was in part symptomatic of

a more widespread disquiet throughout the world which erupted unexpectedly towards the end of the 1960s and which sometimes resorted to violence in its protest against various institutions, programs, and ideologies. Nonetheless, the unrest in the Church testified to the perception many Catholics had that a very significant change had been effected in their religion as they had known it. From the viewpoint of church history, it can be asserted that never before in the history of Catholicism had so many and such sudden changes been legislated and implemented which immediately touched the lives of the faithful, and never before had such a radical adjustment of viewpoint been required of them.

Evaluation. If these changes are located in the broad course of Church history, they can be assessed as attempting the following reforms. (1) There was a reversal of the process of centralization of authority in the Holy See which originated with the Gregorian Reform of the 11th and 12th centuries (6:761) and which continued until the opening of Vatican II, with a moment of special strength achieved by the definition of papal infallibility at Vatican I. (2) There was a moderation of that influence of Greek metaphysics on the formulation of beliefs which had been operative since the patristic era and sanctioned by the Scholastic enterprise of the High Middle Ages. (3) There was a concomitant attempt to insert into doctrinal formulations some considerations of a more biblical and historical character. (4) A more appreciative attitude developed towards other religious communities, and especially towards the Christian Churches with origins in the crisis of the Protestant Reformation in the 16th century. (5) Catholics became more deeply engaged in problems of justice and peace in the world at large, thus complementing their engagement in more narrowly ecclesiastical enterprises. (6) A style of piety was fostered based more directly on biblical sources and on the public liturgy of the Church, to replace the so-called "devotionalism" and the paraliturgical practices that had characterized the late Middle Ages and had showed great vitality in the 19th and early 20th centuries. (7) There was a deemphasis of the distinction between clergy and laity, which had received particularly sharp formulation during the Gregorian Reform and its aftermath, and which tended in practice to reduce the role and dignity of the laity in the Church. (8) There emerged a greater sensitivity to local needs and customs, especially in missionary lands, and an effort to abandon the presupposition of European cultural superiority dominant in missionary efforts since the Chinese-Rites controversy of the 17th century (3:611).

With certain qualifications, therefore, it can be asserted that the Council dealt with a number of issues whose origins dated from the Middle Ages and the Counter Reformation and that it tried to reverse or to moderate considerably positions that crystallized at those crucial periods of Church history. No previous council had ever been so ambitious in its program.

See also CHANGE IN THE CHURCH.

Bibliography: W. J. BURGHARDT, "A Theologian's Challenge to Liturgy," ThSt 35 (1974) 233–248. C. DOLLEN, ed., *Vatican II: A Bibliography* (Metuchen, N.J. 1969). M. A. FAHEY, "Continuity in the Church amid Structural Changes," ThSt 35 (1974) 415–440. G. A. LINDBECK, *The Future of Roman Catholic Theology* (Philadelphia 1969). R. P. MCBRIEN, *The Remaking of the Church* (New York 1973). P. MISNER, "A Note on the Critique of Dogmas," ThSt 34 (1973) 690–700. J. W.

O'MALLEY, "Reform, Historical Consciousness, and Vatican II's Aggiornamento," ThSt 32 (1971) 573–601.

[J. W. O'MALLEY]

VERNACULAR IN LITURGY

There is ample evidence that the language of the people to whom Christianity was preached from the beginning was also the language used in their liturgy (cf. O. Korolevsky). However, only three languages were of importance in the development of the liturgy: Syro-Aramaic, Greek, and Latin. Syro-Aramaic was used in Jerusalem, in the Judaeo-Christian communities of Palestine, and in those territories to the north and east which had not come under hellenistic influence. Thus Edessa became the centre of a national Aramaic or Syrian Christianity. The Syriac liturgy has survived to the present day, though much of it is a translation from the Greek. Until the 4th century Greek was the *lingua franca* in the whole of the eastern half of the Roman Empire and was therefore the language of the liturgy in those areas. Even in Rome Greek was the common language. It was not until *c.* 250 A.D. that Latin predominated there and gradually became the official language of the Western Church.

In the East the principle of retaining the Byzantine liturgy in Greek as the official liturgical language was not maintained so rigidly as Latin in the West. When the Melkites around Antioch adopted Arabic as their vernacular, their liturgy was accordingly translated into Arabic. The Georgians in the Caucasus used Georgian. The Byzantine liturgy is also celebrated in Hungarian, Finnish, Chinese and Japanese. Other Oriental liturgies are celebrated in Syriac, Coptic, and Armenian.

In the West Latin was retained as the liturgical language of the Catholic Church in spite of strong protests at the time of the Reformation. The Council of Trent ruled that "it was not expedient" that Mass should be celebrated in the vernacular language (sess. 22, ch. 8; Denz 1749). The beginnings of a change are discernible in the Encyclical *Mediator Dei* (Nov. 20, 1947) which, while reiterating the statement that the use of Latin is a sign of the Church's unity, admitted that the use of the mother tongue was frequently of great advantage to the people. It did not specify what parts of the liturgy could be rendered in the mother tongue, and in fact hardly any permissions were given until after Vatican Council II, with the notable exception of the *Deutches Hochamt* (high Mass) in Germany.

Even the Council did not envisage an entire vernacular liturgy. It decreed that though existing special exemptions are to remain in force, the use of the Latin language is to be preserved in the Latin rites. However, in view of the advantage accruing to the people through the use of the mother tongue, in the first place the readings and directives and some of the prayers and chants could be translated at the discretion of the competent local authority (*Sacrosanctum Concilium* 36). This decree was later clarified by the Instruction of the Congregation of Rites *Inter oecumenici* (40; ActApS 56 [1964] 897–900). It was left to the episcopal conferences to decide which texts were to be translated. Permission was not given for the translation of the Roman Canon until June 29, 1967, with the Instruction *Tres abhinc annos* (ActApS 59 [1967] 442–448). Thus gradually in the whole of the liturgy the vernacular became permissible as pastoral needs became evident. At the same time the Sacred Congregation for Divine Worship continues to insist in the General Instruction on the Roman Missal that "since nowadays the faithful of different languages come together with ever increasing frequency, it is desirable that all should be able to sing together in Latin at least some parts of the Order of Mass, especially the Creed and the Lord's Prayer (GenInstrRomMissal 19).

All translations have to be authorized, i.e. confirmed, by the Congregation for Divine Worship before use in the liturgy and on June 25, 1969 the Consilium for the Implementation of the Constitution on the Sacred Liturgy published important guidelines for liturgical translators in an *Instruction on Translation of Liturgical Texts* (*see* LITURGICAL TEXTS, TRANSLATION OF). The Instruction furthermore recognises that texts translated from another language are not sufficient for the celebration of a fully renewed liturgy. New texts need to be created, though these new forms should "in some way grow organically from forms already in existence" (43). It is in accordance with this principle that the *International Commission for English in the Liturgy has composed alternative Opening Prayers and is in process of composing other alternative texts.

See also LATIN MASS.

Bibliography: D. ATTWATER, *Eastern Catholic Worship* (New York 1945). F. E. BRIGHTMAN, *Liturgies Western and Eastern* (Oxford 1896). J. A. JUNGMANN, *The Early Liturgies to the Time of Gregory the Great* (Notre Dame, Ind. 1959). A. A. KING, *Liturgies of the Primatial Sees* (Milwaukee 1957). C. KOROLEVSKY, *Living Languages in Catholic Worship* (Westminster 1957). A. RAES, *Introductio in Liturgiam Orientalem* (Rome 1947). H. SCHMIDT, *Liturgie et langue vulgaire* (Rome 1950).

[H. E. WINSTONE]

VIRGIN BIRTH

The perpetual virginity of Mary, the mother of Jesus, is a dogma of Catholic faith by the teaching of the Church's universal and ordinary magisterium (14:692). Nevertheless, certain aspects concerning the mystery have been the special subject of theological discussion during recent years. Difficulties have been raised by biblical scholars, Roman Catholic exegetes among them, regarding the historicity of the virginal conception of Christ as recorded in the infancy narratives of Matthew and Luke. New theories have been proposed about the interpretation of Mary's virginity in parturition, of her "vow" to remain a virgin throughout life, and also about the interpretation of the NT references to "*brothers* of the Lord," the ancient objection against her perpetual virginity. Some important developments have also taken place in the Christological symbolism and spiritual significance of Mary's virginity.

Historicity. The problems regarding the historicity of Mary's virginal conception center around three main issues: (1) the dubious historical meaning of the infancy narratives in general; (2) the fact that the rest of the NT is silent in the matter; and (3) the implication in virginal conception of a "high" Christology, since knowledge that he had no human father would have meant a premature realization of his divine origins, a diminution of his humanness according to modern Christological theories. Consequently it has been proposed that the virginal conception is a theologoumenon, i.e. a theological symbol, to support the later Christological belief that Jesus was God's Son from the moment of his conception.

Other Catholic exegetes and theologians have responded to such difficulties in accord with such lines of argumentation as the following. In principle historicity is compatible with any literary genre and the evangelists indeed record the virginal conception as a fact. If Joseph were the human father of Jesus, this certainly would have been made clear in a *Jewish* narrative which attaches great importance to paternity. Likewise, the silence in the rest of the NT is to be interpreted in favor of the virginal conception's being a fact because reference is never made to Joseph but only to Mary as the parent of Jesus. Further, to exegete the virginal conception as a Christological theologoumenon invented by the early Christians and evangelists is to create the even greater problems of determining whence they derived the notion and how they would reconcile it with their belief that Jesus as the Messiah must be "of the seed of David." They could have come to accept it only on faith in divine Revelation and so there is good reason to interpret Jesus' being conceived of the Holy Spirit and the Virgin as a historical fact with profound Christological symbolism.

Virgin In Partu. Concerning the virginity of Mary in giving birth to Christ, more recent theologizing avoids the concrete details of birthpangs, etc. as quite irrelevant to the religious meaning of the revealed mystery. Rather the emphasis is upon Mary as the subject of a unique act of childbearing. She bore her Son as the virginal Mother of God (*theotokos*) and the immaculate woman of faith filled with divine grace and free from the influence of any sin and concupiscence. Such an interpretation of the Fathers' sayings about the genetic details represents a development of the dogma. Similarly there is a growing tendency to interpret Lk 1.34, "And Mary said to the angel, 'How can this be, since I have no husband?'," as a Lucan literary device to give Gabriel an opening for the second part of his message, that Mary's conception will be virginal. Unlike these who hold the traditional theory that Mary had vowed to remain a virgin all her life prior to the Annunciation, an increasing number of exegetes are of the opinion that she realized only after it that God willed her perpetual virginity as a total consecration to the service of his Son. Thus Mary is the first person in salvation history, and her spouse Joseph is the second, to choose lifelong virginity out of love for Jesus.

"Brothers of the Lord." St. Jerome's theory that "brothers of the Lord" in the NT refers to the cousins of Jesus can no longer stand the test of textual criticism. In fact Jerome abandoned it himself later in life. Recently the hypothesis has been offered that the reference is to brothers but not to blood-brothers. They were the sons of Joseph's sister and were brought up with Jesus after their own father died. Thus, although they were in fact the first cousins of Jesus, the NT could readily refer to them as his brothers.

Symbolism of the Virgin Birth. The interpretation of Mary's virginity as a historical reality is in complete conformity with its rich symbolic value, especially in relation to Christ. The theological tradition from Augustine through Aquinas abounds with such reasons of fittingness for Mary's virginity as Christ's having but one Father in heaven and that his members are born of a virgin Church through the spiritual regeneration of Baptism. This Christocentric and ecclesio-typical emphasis is characteristic of contemporary Mariology. Concerning Mary's virginity it helps preclude any interpretation of it as a negative attitude toward sexual love in marriage. At the same time the religious significance of her virginal Motherhood of God is being developed to deepen the Christian doctrines of grace revealed in the complete gratuitousness of the Incarnation and of the eschatological value of consecrated virginity for the sake of God's reign.

Bibliography: R. E. BROWN, *The Virginal Conception and Bodily Resurrection of Jesus* (New York 1973). R. E. BROWN et al., *Mary in the New Testament* (New York, Philadelphia, Toronto 1978). J. F. CRAGHAN, "The Gospel Witness to Mary's 'Ante Partum' Virginity" *Marian Studies* 21 (1970) 28–68. J. A. FITZMYER, "The Virginal Conception of Jesus in the New Testament," ThSt 34 (1973) 541–575. F. M. JELLY, "Mary's Virginity in the Symbols and Councils," *Marian Studies* 21 (1970) 69–93. J. MCHUGH, *The Mother of Jesus in the New Testament* (New York 1975). M. MIGUENS, *The Virgin Birth: An Evaluation of Scriptural Evidence* (Westminister, Md. 1975). K. RAHNER, "*Virginitas in Partu*: A Contribution to the Problem of the Development of Dogma and of Tradition," *Theological Investigations* 4, tr. K. SMYTH (Baltimore 1966) 134–162.

[F. M. JELLY]

VIRGINITY, CONSECRATION TO (RITE)

The *Rite of Consecration to a Life of Virginity* was revised in accord with the directive of Vatican Council II (*Sacrosanctum Concilium* 80); the Latin text of the revision was promulgated on May 31, 1970 by the Congregation for Divine Worship and became effective Jan. 6, 1971. The approved English translation, together with the *Rite of Blessing of an Abbot or Abbess*, was published by the International Commision on English in the Liturgy (ICEL) in 1975. (For the 1970 Rite of Religious Profession [English version, 1974] see 16:385).

The Introduction to the Rite notes that the antiquity of the consecration is a sign of the Church's high esteem for the life of virginity as a sign of the Church's love of Christ and an eschatological witness (Introduction 1). The daily praying of the Liturgy of the Hours is urged for those who receive Consecration (ibid. 2). The most notable innovation regards those who may be consecrated. The earlier Rite in the Roman Pontifical was for nuns in the proper sense, cloistered religious women. In the new Rite provision is made not only for all women religious, active as well as contemplative, but also for women living in the world (ibid. 3).

The first form of the Rite is for women living in the world. The Ordinary of the diocese decides on conditions for admitting such women to consecration. They must have always been unmarried, of a character consonant with consecration, and dedicated to a life of prayer and service (ibid. 5). The consecrator is the bishop of the place. The rite itself consists of: the calling of the candidates; homily; examination of the candidates as to readiness and intent to persevere; litanies; renewal of the intention of perpetual chastity; solemn blessing or consecration; conferral of veil (optional), ring, and the book of the Liturgy of the Hours as signs of dedicated life. There is a Mass for Consecration to a Life of Virginity in the Sacramentary among the ritual Masses; the Mass of the day may also be used (ibid. 8); white vestments are worn (ibid. 10). The times recommended for the celebration are the Octave of Easter or other solemnities, Sundays, feasts of Mary or of holy virgins (Rite 1). It is recommended that the celebration take place in the cathedral and that the faithful be invited to be present (Rite 3, 4). The Rite itself takes place within the Liturgy of the Word after the Readings.

The renewal of intention, made in the hands of the bishop, is a resolution to follow Christ in perfect chastity.

The solemn consecratory prayer by the bishop refers to it as a vow (ibid. 24). The prayer of consecration as well as the prayers accompanying bestowal of the insignia reflect a rich theology of the meaning of virginity in the Church's life.

The form of consecration for religious women is combined with the making of final religious profession (see 16:385). Use of the Rite is for religious in communities where consecration has been customary or after permission has been obtained from competent authority (Introduction 5c). Those admitted must also have never been married and either be making or have made final profession (ibid. 5 a–b). When conjoined to the Rite of Religious Profession the consecration follows the candidate's pronouncement of profession (Rite 62–64), which of its nature is an intention of perpetual chastity. Certain other adaptations are made appropriate to the integration of profession and consecration.

To date (1978) the revised rite has not been widely known or used in the United States.

Bibliography: ICEL, *Rite of Blessing of an Abbot or Abbess, and Rite of Consecration to a Life of Virginity* (Washington, D.C. 1975).

[T. C. O'BRIEN]

VOCATION, CLERICAL

The word "vocation" means call. Every person is called by God by the fact that he has been created with unique possibilities and has undergone a unique history that has gifted him with unique modifications of the basic human openness to other creatures and to the infinite Creator. Each person has at each moment an inner dynamism to develop further the powers given him by God toward the condition of total acceptance in love of himself, his neighbor, and ultimately his maker. What has been freely given him in the past and what God freely gives him in the present and the future constitute his call and invites a free response. That free response is one of utilizing what has been given to him for his sake and for the sake of all others.

The Christian Vocation. Israel's vocation was constituted by its election as the people who were able to recognize that Yahweh was the one true God and that he was active in all of history, calling first Israel and then all men to himself. Israel was thus called to a mission of spreading the truth of the one God to all mankind. The fulfillment of the Israelite vocation, the Christian vocation, became possible with the Incarnation. That Christian vocation is achieved when one becomes aware that the intrinsic openness of all persons to the Creator now includes an openness to the risen humanity of Jesus through whom all nations have personal access to the Father (*see* HOLINESS, UNIVERSAL CALL TO).

The Clerical Vocation. Within the general Christian vocation there are many specialized vocations. Each one involves the reception of a gift from God, a special mode of realization of the general Christian vocation. To possess a priestly or clerical vocation means, first of all, to possess the basic qualities of the mature and healthy human and Christian vocation: bodily health adequate to render service, psychological maturity, a clear intellect, a free and generous will, and a profound faith orientation toward God in Christ. Secondly, it requires the achievement of the specific qualities that pertain to the priestly state. What these qualities are has not, unfortunately, been spelled out clearly in the

Church's tradition. In accord with the nature of the priesthood (*see* PRIEST AND PRIESTHOOD), it would seem that these qualities are the abilities: (1) to internalize the basic values of the Christian tradition and to grasp them in an articulate fashion; (2) to discern where the people to be served are in terms of these values; and (3) to lead in the process of building the Christian community in its inner life and in its mission to the world by facilitating the shared internalization of these values through such appropriate means as good example, teaching, individual spiritual direction, social leadership, presiding at the liturgy and the Sacraments. Thirdly, the priestly vocation demands, as does every specific vocation, the existence of free and adequate motivation. The candidate must freely will to accept the intrinsic orientation in his life that exists by reason of the possession, achieved historically by his responses to God's free gifts over time, of the human, Christian, and priestly qualities indicated above. He must will to accept this orientation for its own intrinsic goodness and not for such extrinsic reasons as the desire to please a parent or the belief that he is obliged to remain faithful to a rash promise made when he was immature. Finally, since a priestly vocation is essentially one that involves a relationship of service to the Christian community, it requires the acceptance by those who have charge of the community. The "marriage" or mutual commitment of priest and community takes place in ordination by a bishop.

Discernment of a Priestly Vocation. Such discernment is not a logical process but an awareness that one has achieved the qualities that constitute the priestly call. Such discernment demands, therefore, a knowledge both of the traditional values and of the candidate. It is best achieved by a frank exchange between the candidate and skilled persons who know the priestly values and who have had the opportunity of observing the candidate in individual relationships and in pastoral situations which have demanded of him the expression of those values.

Bibliography: C. A. BERNARD, "L'Idée de vocation," Greg 49 (1968) 479–509. J. C. HAUGHEY, *Should Anyone Say Forever?* (Garden City, N.Y. 1975). R. HOSTIE, *The Discernment of Vocations* (London 1963). H. H. ROWLEY, *The Biblical Doctrine of Election* (London 1950). D. S. SCHULLER et al., *Readiness for Ministry* v. 1, *Criteria* (Vandalia, Ohio 1975).

[P. CHIRICO]

VOCATION, PSYCHOLOGY OF

A priestly or religious vocation is an invitation by God that takes hold of the whole person, not as a profession or avocation, but as a penetration of the person's very essence and existence. The call is gratuitous and so must be the human response. Since supernatural grace builds on human nature, it follows that human nature, in order to manifest the reality of Christ, should be potentially healthy. The psychology of vocation to priesthood and religious life helps in the understanding that vocation involves the total person as spiritual, bodily, knowing, and affective being.

The present reflection centers on the psychology of vocation from the viewpoint of health rather than from that of the problematic. It is based on the teaching of Vatican Council II wherein the Fathers encourage "not only the use of theological principles but also of the findings of the secular sciences, especially of psychology and sociology" (*Gaudium et spes* 62).

Descriptive Definition. This attempt to define a psychology of vocation is guided by the works of Rulla and Van Kaam and by the clinical findings of the *House of Affirmation, International Therapeutic Center for Clergy and Religious (see bibliography). The psychology of vocation is the study of the human behavior, actions, traits, attitudes, and thoughts of persons and their familial/environmental influences in relationship to a call to the ordained ministry or religious life and to the continuing development under grace toward maturity in the chosen way of life. These aspects of the person, which constitute partial data for assessing suitability for commitment, can be revealed by tools developed from the science of psychology.

Principles of Psychological Evaluation of Candidates. Psychological evaluation of candidates for vocational commitment should include testing as well as personal, familial, and environmental investigations. Although psychological instruments employed in diagnostic testing are of proven clinical assistance, the role of the vocational director, the spiritual director, and other persons who have a relationship and/or knowledge of the candidate is of equal importance. The clinician who does the psychological testing should not be the one who decides the candidate's acceptability. The clinician's data is only one avenue of knowledge pertaining to the overall suitability of the candidate. The ultimate decision is that of the ecclesiastical authorities.

Diagnostic Psychological Testing. Several clinicians (Rulla, Coville, Kane) have pointed to the urgent need for ecclesiastical authorities to employ psychological testing. Many ethical testing instruments, objective and projective, can be employed as two-pronged tools to rule out psychologically unsuitable candidates and to provide information that helps seminary or formation directors in turn to help the candidates to mature in their overall development toward ordination and/or final commitment. A three-way conversation among the psychologist, the candidate, and the respective vocation or formation director is encouraged.

Since the values of the clinician do influence the results of the candidate-assessment report, the clinician should not only understand the client's right to self-determination but also have a thorough knowledge of the contemporary structures and responsibilities of the priesthood and religious life.

Psychological Interview. The psychological interview is essential to the assessment process. The House of Affirmation model employs not only a battery of tests, but also a psychological interview and, most importantly, a pastoral interview by a person experienced in the religious life or priesthood. There is referral to a psychiatrist when evidence from the psychological testing or the clinical or pastoral interview indicates the need for further professional, clinical investigation. In all instances, however, the psychological testing and interview reports are reviewed in conference with a psychiatrist sensitive to the candidate's religious values.

Candidate Qualities. It is important to secure a thorough history of a candidate's family background and to know what factors are presently influencing the candidate. Questionable data should not immediately disqualify a candidate, but careful observation should be made so as to judge what influences are motivating the candidate's decision. Full maturity should not be a prerequisite for entrance, but the potential for such maturity should be present. The candidate, of course, should be devoid of any evidence of psychosis, character disorders, and mental retardation.

The candidate should show signs of growing, or the capacity to grow, toward greater comfort with self, others, and God, and show reasonable security with vocational choice. The candidate's personality profile should reflect at least the beginning of an awareness of the need and personal desire for affectivity, of a capacity to profit from insight so as to grow in self-knowledge and self-acceptance, and of personal responsibility and assertiveness. The candidate should exhibit basic common sense; a willingness to live and cooperate with others; the beginnings of prayer, both personal and ecclesial; a capacity to cope with human emotions; and the desire to follow Jesus Christ in the Roman Catholic Church. This desire for the Roman Catholic priesthood/religious life should be reasonable, and the candidate should be comfortable with this vocational choice.

Negative Indicators. If a candidate who desires ministry nevertheless displays serious evidence of discomfort with self and/or of psychosexual confusion without the opportunity for psychosocial maturation, these findings should be reason enough for delay and perhaps disqualification. Excessively manipulative behavior (sometimes disguised as leadership ability) or excessive timidity (sometimes disguised as humility or prayerfulness) reflect the need for further maturation to take place prior to any permanent commitment or ordination.

The Interpersonal Network. A candidate's interpersonal-relationship network should be observed. The ability to maintain sustaining intimate relationships (Bush, Rulla, Agudo) without an obsessive need for numerous superficial friendships is important, as is an appreciation of marriage and other vocational choices. An inordinate fear of marriage or of the responsibilities of other life choices usually indicates a lack of the personality traits needed to live the celibate life style and to be involved in the accountability of ordained or professed discipleship. Excessive and consistent withdrawal from group behavior should be noted as a factor to be corrected prior to entering or during the formation period and to be resolved before permanent commitment or ordination is allowed. The candidate should be encouraged to see the necessity of spiritual direction and the importance of spiritual behavior, e.g., prayer, participation in liturgy, spiritual-growth programs. Should a candidate display absence of growth in the signs of the Spirit (Gal 5), then his or her suitability should be seriously questioned.

Obstacles to Psychological Growth in Vocation. Vocational obstacles are many, serious, and complex. Low (nonaffirmed) self-esteem is an obvious obstacle among persons whose behavior is often that of an alienated individual with neurotic characteristics of serious consequence—including excessive anxieties, exaggerated phobias, obsessive–compulsive behavior, and somatic complaints. Often professional psychiatric or psychological counseling is necessary to help alleviate the pain of these sufferers. All such persons need the consistent affirmation of other persons significant to them—family members, associates, and superiors.

Work Satisfaction. Low self-esteem can be related to low work satisfaction. Acute work frustration (Kinnane, Polcino, Bush) occurs when there is not adequate outlet for the priest or religious to express values, needs, and interests. Perpetuating the functionalistic model of society rather than exemplifying a countercultural position that would give priority to time and space for spiritual realities remains a problem. Diocesan and religious structures should integrate the life values and work values of ministerial personnel.

The Issue of Celibacy. Celibacy and its implications also point to a potential obstacle for perseverence. Candidates should clearly understand the official ecclesiastical position concerning celibacy so that they can freely choose celibacy and then ministry with a sense of adult responsibility and accountability (*see* CELIBACY, FORMATION IN).

Authority Conflicts. Lack of affirmation from authority figures can be a serious obstacle to vocational development. Priests and religious are often in conflict with and confused by the abrasive relationships that exist between subordinates and superiors, who generally represent church structures and administration. Vocational commitment constantly readjusts to emotional needs as well as to the influences and pressures of the environment. If persons feel that their vocational efforts are not appreciated, then the quality of their work, their capacity to cope with its pressure, and their interest in vocation diminish. However, priests and religious who feel that their superiors are understanding and supportive of their efforts enjoy a needed security. Their capacity for coping with pressure is strengthened and their vocational commitment becomes more meaningful, satisfying, and enduring. Only affirmed persons capable of affirming others should be chosen as bishops or major superiors.

Psychological Growth in Vocation. While good programs of candidate-assessment are needed to sustain the quality of persons who respond to a vocational call, a healthy environment of personal experiences and of quality leadership that will insure the candidate's personal and vocational maturation is equally essential. The structures of everyday living must allow for the exercise of individual accountability and responsibility. The psychodynamic processes, conscious and unconscious, present not only in the candidate but in those in leadership positions, should be conducive to healthy maturation. It is important therefore that persons in leadership positions have integrated personalities (for a better understanding of this concept, see Rulla and Newbold).

The first two or three years in ministerial life are extremely important, since this adult period of life is embraced with energy, enthusiasm, and dedication. These years are a time of life during which the minister (priest/religious) attempts to secure a satisfaction from work, an interesting development of leisure, a zeal for spiritual realities and productive relationships with peers, superiors, and laity. The experience of these pursuits and relationships will determine, in large part, the psychological nature of subsequent commitment to the priesthood or religious life.

Vocational commitment must be permanent from a theological viewpoint. Yet from a psychological viewpoint vocation is manifestly contingent upon many internal factors of personality as well as upon external environmental factors. Vocational commitment is a slow process whereby maturing persons continue to deepen their commitment at each life crisis in the development of their personal histories.

Bibliography: AQUINAS, ST. THOMAS, ST, 1a2ae, 50.3. B. J. BUSH, ed., *Coping: Issues of Emotional Living in an Age of Stress for Clergy and Religious* (Whitinsville, Mass. 1976). W. J. COVILLE, "The Psychological Development of Tentative Commitment to the Priesthood and the Religious Life," *Seminary Department Relevant Report*, National Catholic Educational Association (Washington, D.C. 1972). V. E. FRANKL, "Beyond Self-Actualization and Self-Expression," *Journal of Existential Psychology* Vol. 1, 1960. A. M. GREELEY, "Report of Subcommittee on Sociology," *Study on Priestly Life and Ministry* NCCB (Washington, D.C. 1971) 23–69. A. GREELEY and E. KENNEDY, *American Priests* (Chicago 1971). V. J. HECKLER and E. C. KENNEDY, *The Loyola Psychological Study of the Ministry and Life of the American Priest*, NCCB (Washington, D.C. 1971). T. A. KANE, *The Healing Touch of Affirmation* (Whitinsville, Mass. 1976); *Who Controls Me?* (Hicksville, N.Y. 1974). J. F. KINNANE, *Career Development for Priests and Religious* (Washington, D.C. 1970); *Vocational Motivation* (Washington, D.C. 1970). J. P. MADDEN, ed., *Loneliness: Issues of Emotional Living in an Age of Stress for Clergy and Religious* (Whitinsville, Mass. 1978). T. M. NEWBOLD, "Depth Psychology and Vocation," *Seminary Newsletter* Supplement, National Catholic Educational Association (Washington, D.C. Nov. 1973). J. PIEPER, *About Love*, tr. R. and C. WINSTON (Chicago 1972). A. POLCINO, ed., *Intimacy: Issues of Emotional Living in an Age of Stress for Clergy and Religious* (Whitinsville, Mass. 1978); "Mental Health and Religious Life," *Pakistan Sister's Bulletin* (Karachi, Pakistan 1963). K. RAHNER, *L'Évêque et le diocèse, Mystère de l'Église et action pastorale* (Paris 1969). L. M. RULLA, *Depth Psychology and Vocation: A Psychosocial Perspective* (Rome and Chicago 1971). L. M. RULLA, J. RIDICK, and F. IMODA, *Entering and Leaving Vocation: Intrapsychic Dynamics* (Rome and Chicago 1976). C. F. TAGESON, *The Relationship of Self Perceptions to Realism of Vocational Preference* (Washington, D.C. 1960). *The Program of Priestly Formation of the National Conference of Catholic Bishops* (2d ed. Washington, D.C. 1976). A. VANKAAM, *Personality Fulfillment in the Religious Life* (Denville, N.J. 1967). J. WRIGHT, "Priestly Maturity," *Seminarium* 22 (1970) 810–823. D. W. WUERL, *The Catholic Priesthood Today* (Chicago 1976).　　　　　　　　　　　　　　　　　[A. POLCINO]

VOCATION, RELIGIOUS

Vatican Council II provides one context through which we can come to an understanding of the nature and challenge of contemporary religious life. Consequently, it is within the major themes of conciliar and postconciliar documents that we look to discover an authoritative and compelling introduction to the call to religious life, religious vocation.

Universal Call to Holiness. Reminding the Church of the life of holiness to which all persons are summoned in Baptism, council documents situate both priestly and religious vocation within the mystery of Christ's redeeming love. "It is quite clear that all Christians in any state or walk of life are called to fulness of Christian life and to the perfection of love" (*Lumen gentium* 40). Religious life is a specification of the universal call to holiness; an expression of baptismal consecration (*Perfectae caritatis* 5) proper to those bound to the Church by profession and practice of the counsels. Proceeding from the initiative of the Holy Spirit, religious life provides evidence of the free and dynamic action whereby "some Christians, clerical and lay, are called by God" (*Lumen gentium* 43). Among both ordained and nonordained Christians, then, there are some who receive an invitation in faith to manifest the presence of God through their lives as religious, observing the evangelical counsels either by vows or by "other sacred ties of a similar nature" (ibid. 44).

The eloquence of the Council's documents commending the beauty and eminence of the universal call to holiness has occasionally prompted discussion of whether the traditional forms of religious life—the way of "perfect charity" or "perfection"—have not been displaced by more contemporary expressions of Christian vocation. Evidence, however, is to the contrary. Despite the evolution of new leadership and service roles for organizing, stimulating and sustaining the Christian community, there continue to be men and women distinguished by a life which has traditionally come to be called "religious." The Spirit continues to call each person as he wills; i.e., to that expression of the life of the Father that pleases him (Mk 9.33–35). The mystery of vocation, then, remains. The fidelity of the baptized person is—initially and throughout life—the fidelity of a careful listener: "My mother and my brother are those who hear the word of God, and do it" (Lk 8.21). The attitude of the faithful listener reflects that of Mary who is presented in the Gospel as prototype of all whose lives are spent in response to a call, pondering the implications (Lk 2.51).

Vocation: Call, Climate, Context. It is the role of the Christian community, called as it is to a holiness in keeping with baptismal grace, to provide an atmosphere of listening conducive to the growth in faith of each member. Husbands and wives are urged to be "cooperators of grace and witnesses of the faith" (*Apostolicam actuositatem* 11) offering understanding, support and wise counsel to their children. In matters of vocation, parents frequently play a uniquely significant role, enabling each child to make mature life-choices, decisions animated by a wholesome self-esteem and a growing awareness of the Lord laboring with many hands among his people. Church documents place particular emphasis on the role of the mother and father educating their children to understand and respect life-choices open to them and providing all due encouragement for any who seem destined for a religious vocation (ibid.).

But the family is not able to assume these responsibilities alone. The Church, therefore, calls its dioceses as well as its regional and national offices to "coordinate and systematize all pastoral work for vocations" (*Optatam totius* 2). Urging both "discretion" and "zeal" the Church challenges individuals within her organizations to develop a "generous" sense of vocation, a truly Catholic appreciation for God's call which crosses "the boundaries of individual dioceses, countries, religious congregations and rites [and] with the needs of the universal Church in view" (ibid.).

Call to Religious Life. Among Christian vocations, religious life has been acknowledged from early times as the life of a prophet-servant of the Church; a gift bestowed through the dynamic movement of the Spirit (*Perfectae caritatis* 1) to increase the Church's holiness of life and to ensure full pastoral care of the Church's members. The litany of greater founders and foundresses recalls to mind the Spirit who, over the centuries, animates the Church not only through the magisterium but also and perhaps most startlingly through many apparently very ordinary men and women intimately consecrated to God's service as religious:

> From the very beginning of the Church there were men and women who set out to follow Christ with greater liberty, and to imitate him more closely by practicing the evangelical counsels. They led lives dedicated to God, each in his own way. Many of them, under the inspiration of the Holy Spirit, became hermits or founded religious families. These the Church, by virtue of her authority, gladly accepted and approved. Thus, in keeping with the divine purposes, a wonderful variety of religious communities came into existence (ibid. 1).

Nor is the day of founding and refounding religious communities at an end. Recent times have given religious throughout the world a unique, if generally unanticipated, opportunity. By mandate of the Church all have been urged to undertake adaptations and expressions of renewal in keeping with the Gospel, the spirit of the founder, and a "new age of history" (*Gaudium et spes* 4).

Showing characteristic energy and zeal, men and women religious, priests, brothers, and sisters throughout the world, have responded to this mandate, examining practices, structures, life styles, prayer forms, and spirituality. The rewriting of constitutions, and establishment of new communities demonstrate a kind of fidelity congruent with the spirit of religious down through the centuries.

Response to the Call. Like other vocations to holiness, the religious vocation involves a process of recognition and response. Initially, an awareness or perception of the call to practice the counsels as a brother, priest, or sister prevails. Whether this first experience of a call involves a series of impressions, and a gradually maturing conviction, or a more focused and immediate realization, the consequences are similar. Sensing that a new life-direction may be required, the person may enter upon a time of weighing and assessing alternatives. If he or she arrives at a point of assent to what is perceived as the action of the Spirit, there is usually an effort to translate this spiritual assent into a practical plan of life. But the call of the Spirit, strong and compelling as this may be, is not to itself a vocation, but an invitation. Pondering what is being asked, the Christian is influenced by the gracious deference of a God who loves, engages, and urges, but never compels. It is evident that, although built upon human dispositions and natural gifts, a religious vocation is not the result of a simple career choice but is a personal response to the urgings of the Holy Spirit. Every person so called is witness to the gentle, deferential, and creative care of this Spirit, beckoning to a life marked by specific charisms. These are usually designated as chastity, poverty, and obedience, terms which attempt to describe not the gift itself but the consequences of the gift.

Just as the Church guides and supports religious communities as they strive to be faithful to their role in the life and mission of Jesus, so too the person discerning his or her vocation to religious life turns to the Church and to the religious community for assistance in ascertaining with some certainty what the call of the Lord might entail. The religious vocation involves a fourfold action: the call or subtle invitation; the inclination of the prospective candidate; the confirmation of a specific life-orientation by a religious "family" and by the Church; and a lifelong exchange of pledges with the God whose initiative has been instrumental in creating a bond and whose faithfulness sustains it.

> Besides giving legal sanction to the religious form of life and thus raising it to the dignity of a canonical state, the Church sets it forth liturgically also as a state of consecration to God. She herself, in virtue of her God-given authority, receives the vows of those who profess this form of life, asks aid and grace for them from God in her public prayer, commends them to God and bestows on them a spiritual blessing, associating their self-offering with the sacrifice of the Eucharist (*Lumen gentium* 45).

The call to religious life inevitably moves from the inclination of a man or woman to the solemn, public, and prayerful affirmation of the person as one called. Between these aspects of vocation there is a time of prayer, of reflection, and of testing and orientation, a kind of "internship" required by the Church and adapted by each religious community to allow the greatest possible latitude for individual and institute as partners in the discernment of vocation.

Call within a Specific Tradition. So concerned has the Church been about the quality and depth of this orientation to religious life that it has devoted a great deal of attention to the matter in documents organically linked with the conciliar process. The novitiate is established in an irreplaceable and privileged [position] as the first initiation into religious life (*Renovationis causam* 4). But the goals of the novitiate are unattainable unless the candidate brings to that experience "A minimum of human and spiritual preparation which must not only be verified but, very often, also completed" (ibid.).

To this end the Church has enlisted the help of major religious superiors of men and women, vocation and formation personnel, to take means to provide for a suitable time of prenovitiate probation ensuring a more mature and fully responsible choice on the part of the candidate and facilitating a more responsible and informed decision toward admission on the part of the religious community and the Church. "During this probationary period it is particularly necessary to secure assurance that the candidate for religious life be endowed with such elements of human and emotional maturity as will afford grounds for hope that he [she] will be able to progress towards fuller maturity" (ibid. 11.2). Those responsible for admission of candidates are cautioned to admit to novitiate only those evidencing "aptitudes and elements of maturity regarded as necessary for commitment to religious life as lived in the institute" (ibid. 14). Implicit in this directive is the Church's consciousness of the diversity of gifts demonstrated by religious communities, the differences of spirit, life and mission that distinguish one from another.

Also implicit in this as in other guidelines of the kind is a recognition of the religious vocation as a gift to be lived for the sake of others, rather than for one's own sake. The ministry dimension of the life is as explicit in the response of a contemplative as in the assent of one called to active apostolic life. ". . . the spiritual life of these followers should be devoted to the welfare of the whole Church. Thence arises their duty of working to implant and strengthen the kingdom of Christ in souls and to extend that kingdom to every land. This duty is to be discharged to the extent of their capacities and in keeping with the form of their proper vocation. The chosen means may be prayer or active undertakings. It is for this reason that the Church preserves and fosters the special character of her various religious communities" (*Lumen gentium* 44).

In Summary. Religious vocation evolves from the invitation of God, of the Church, and of the religious family or order. It is best understood in retrospect, *i.e.*, at the close of a life given over to the opportunity, the intensity, the asceticism, and the joy of response to God. One has only to page through the Old and New Testaments to perceive that prophet and apostle alike knew the meaning of vocation not through an initial "yes," but through lifetimes of questioning, considering, doubting, fearing, refusing, and assenting. Religious vocation is not a matter of desire or of worthiness, of right or of privilege, of intelligence or of competence. Its significance is of another order. Ultimately, its meaning is discovered only in the Christian's capacity to reckon with the meaning of grace, of gift, and of mystery.

Bibliography: Congregation for Religious and Secular Institutes, Instruction, *Renovationis causam*, Jan. 6, 1969, ActApS 61 (1969) 103–120; tr. *On Renewal of Religious Formation* (USCC Publ. Office, Washington, D.C. 1969); also Flannery 645–652.

[D. M. CARR]

VOW (PRACTICE AND THEOLOGY)

Few institutions in the Church have been as profoundly and pervasively affected by the spirit and content of Vatican Council II as religious life. The ground-work for the reform and renewal of religious life began decades before the Council, in the crisis of significance that followed World War II, but the Council gave impetus to and legitimized the renewal movement. So extensive, radical, and diverse has the renewal been that it is virtually impossible to speak of *the* theology and practice of the vows. Although most religious have responded eagerly to the Council's challenge to renew their life in response to the signs of the times and according to the norms of the Gospel and the particular charisms of the diverse institutes (*Perfectae caritatis* 2), there has been a marked difference in depth and extent of renewal between male and female religious, between clerical and lay religious, and among national groups. Furthermore, even within the group which, on the whole, has made the most notable progress in renewal, namely, American women religious, there is a relatively small but powerful and articulate traditionalist movement which has its counterparts in other countries. These diversities must be allowed to relativize the following paragraphs which will indicate the sources and the main directions of contemporary theology and practice of the vows as it is developing among the progressive majority.

Sources of Contemporary Theological Reflection. The contemporary theology of the vows is no longer synonymous with, nor generative of, the theology of religious life. Rather, the latter is context and matrix of the former. At least three major sources of contemporary theological reflection on religious life (and therefore on the vows) can be clearly discerned.

Primacy of Theology. First, there has been a reversal in the relationship between canonical legislation and the theology of religious life. Prior to Vatican II the theology of religious life in general, and of the vows in particular, was almost wholly derived from Canon Law. The Council's invitation to religious to renew their institutes led to wide experimentation, much of it contrary to common law and custom. This experimentation rapidly produced a vast body of experience which has become the subject matter of continuing, biblically guided, theological reflection on the meaning of religious life and how it should be lived today. The theory emerging from this reflection is now being critically brought to bear on existing and proposed legislation concerning religious life. Thus, theologically criticized praxis rather than canonical legislation is becoming the primary source of the evolving theology and practice of religious life, including the vows.

The Ecclesial Dimension. Secondly, following the inspired lead of the Council which placed the theological treatment of religious life within the Dogmatic Constitution on the Church (see *Lumen gentium* 39–47), religious are developing a deepened sense of the ecclesial character of their life. They have appropriated the implications of the Pastoral Constitution on the Church in the Modern World (*Gaudium et spes*), in which the Church renounced her centuries-old adversary stance toward the world and reaffirmed her solidarity with all humankind in the task of transforming this world into a just and peaceful context for human life and growth. Religious have, in many ways, outdistanced the hierarchical Church in their practical commitment to the mission of being in, with, and for the world, and in accepting the implications of this commitment for per-

sonal and corporate involvement in the cause of social justice. Thus, the emerging theology of religious life tends to speak less about the "works" of institutes (often in the past dichotomized from the "spiritual life") and to speak of the life of the institute as essentially missionary. Religious profession, as a particular actualization of Baptism, the true source of Christian ministry, is coming to be understood less as the assumption of personal obligations and more as consecration for ministry within, and as an expression of, the mission of the institute.

The Call to Holiness. Thirdly, the theology of religious life, and especially of profession, is being deeply affected by the revalidation of the universal Christian vocation to holiness (*Lumen gentium* 39–41). The realization of the incompatibility between recognizing that all Christians are called to the perfection of charity and claiming that religious are called to the "state of perfection" or to an intrinsically "higher life" has led to a progressive renunciation of elitist interpretations of profession and of the use of such status symbols as special dress and titles, special domiciles, and social privileges. This deliberate reintegration of religious into the People of God and thus into the world in which that People are pilgrims has created a challenge to reinterpret religious life as a way rather than as a caste, and to search for an understanding of the vows that does not imply a separation of religious from other Christians or exalt them above their sisters and brothers in the Christian community.

Directions in Contemporary Theological Reflection. The act of religious profession is currently the object of considerable theological reflection; many question whether religious profession is necessarily constituted by the three traditional vows of poverty, chastity, and obedience.

Religious Profession. There is a discernible tendency to regard profession, regardless of which vows are made, as the act of consecration by which one enters the religious state. Thus it is understood less as the assumption of a specific set of obligations and more as a personal commitment whose primary effect is to structure the life of the religious by a particular set of stable relations, namely, to Christ, to the Church, and to the institute whose life and mission the religious will share. This type of reflection has led to experimentation with a variety of forms for profession even within the same institute. There is widespread discussion of the desirability of replacing multiple vows with a single, all-inclusive vow that would emphasize the unity given to a person's life by religious commitment rather than the multiplicity of obligations assumed. Finally, without denying that the consecration constituted by religious profession is ideally life-long and that definitive commitment is possible and life-enhancing for those whose gift it is, there is increasing discussion of the possibility that not every religious profession need be perpetual. It is significant that contemporary reflection on profession is concerned with fundamental issues and not merely with legal or juridical problems.

Poverty. The theology of evangelical poverty, the object of the religious vow, is rooted in the Gospel values of joyous dependence on God and open-hearted sharing of God's gifts within the human community. In the course of history the understanding of this vow has varied widely. In modern times it has been understood as obliging the religious to renounce the independent use and/or ownership of all material goods. In practice, this renunciation was expressed by obtaining the permission of superiors for the use of whatever material goods were necessary for life or work.

Contemporary reflection on and practice of poverty is being deeply affected primarily by two factors. First, there is the psychological fact that total dependence upon superiors for one's material well-being is experienced by many religious as trivial in itself, unrelated to evangelical poverty, and conducive to immaturity and irresponsibility. The second factor is the increasing awareness on the part of many religious of the extent and severity of real destitution in the world and a consequent sense of inauthenticity in claiming to practice poverty while enjoying a disproportionate share of this world's goods and virtual freedom from material insecurity. These factors have led to considerable modification in the practice of poverty. Members are participating more directly and extensively in the handling of the finances of their local communities and institutes and assuming increasing responsibility for the ordinary economic affairs of their own lives.

These two factors have also had a profound influence on the theology of religious poverty. Many religious are coming to see the vow of poverty as a public commitment to responsible stewardship of the goods of the earth and to the struggle for a just economic order in which an equitable sharing of limited resources will hasten the end of the oppression of the poor by the rich. The implications of such an understanding of poverty reach from voluntary simplification of personal and communal lifestyles to individual and corporate participation in the politics of social justice.

Chastity. Chastity, or celibacy freely chosen for evangelical reasons, has been explained theologically in many ways in the course of history. Most of these explanations are considered unsatisfactory today because they involve, explicitly or implicitly, a negative attitude toward sexuality and a denigration of marriage as a Christian vocation. The practice flowing from such theologies though admirable in many respects, is often seen today as overly characterized by fear, guilt, and repression and as leading to serious affective underdevelopment in many religious.

The contemporary realization of the importance of sexuality in human life and of the irreplaceable role in affective growth of friendship with members of one's own and the other sex has led to a serious revision of both the theology and the practice of religious celibacy. This reflection has been influenced by the increasingly open discussion of sexuality in general, and particularly of homosexuality and of the relation of sexual expression to monogamous marriage. The focus of attention, both theologically and in practice, is still largely on personal development, the improvement of the affective quality of community life, and the consequent growth of religious in interpersonal effectiveness. Increasingly, however, religious are realizing the corporate significance of their chosen lifestyle as a witness complementary to that of Christian marriage. They are tending to see their celibacy less as a renunciation of marriage and more as a commitment to growth in love dedicated to the development of a world characterized by unselfish service and mutual care.

Obedience. In modern times obedience has been the vow whose theology and practice has had the greatest impact on the daily life of religious. Although it represented a sincere, and at times heroic, effort to discern and fulfill God's will in imitation of Christ who was obedient unto death, the traditional practice of obedience, which responded to the superior's will as the will of God, tended to diminish the responsibility of the "subject." The contemporary renewal of the theology and practice of religious obedience has been fostered by many factors, among the most important of which are the following: the realization of the psychological underdevelopment that often results from the life-long surrender of personal decision making and responsibility; the insight into the moral immaturity which often results from the possibility of regarding another as ultimately responsible for one's choices and actions; the sociological data on the superiority of shared leadership in voluntary societies; the positive political experience of many societies with democratic government; the relativizing in many institutes of an excessive task-orientation which led to an overdependence on the efficiency of command-obedience relations and the subservience of persons to work. Most important, perhaps, has been the theological realization that the Spirit speaks through all the members of the community and that to assign the role of "speaking for God" to a single member is to impoverish the community's efforts to discern the will of God. In the last analysis, the theological viability of the principle of hierarchy is being brought into question. This probably accounts for the extreme strain that developments in the area of obedience are causing.

In practice, and despite explicit official opposition, many institutes, especially of religious women, have moved steadily away from hierarchical organization. They have adopted participative procedures for the conduct of government; democratized elections; desacralized and in some cases abolished the role of local superior; instituted congregational policies which allow individuals in consultation with community leadership to choose their own ministerial commitments; and made leadership accountable to the membership as well as vice versa.

At the basis of these developments in practice are profound theological convictions about the dignity and equality of persons, the inalienability of personal freedom and responsibility, the right of every individual to justice, and the irreplaceable value for community life of full participation by the members. Many religious envision the building of communities in which authority is the function of truth and is neither confused with power nor buttressed by force, in which justice is the climate for mutual service, and in which all the members participate fully, freely, and equally as a prophetic participation in the Church's mission of liberation and reconciliation.

In summary, the theology and practice of the religious vows is in a state of rapid and profound transformation. This transformation is a function both of cultural evolution and of the theological awakening of the 20th century. The understanding and practice of the vows is moving away from an emphasis on the assumption of obligations and toward an emphasis on commitment to personal spiritual growth and to participation in the world-transforming mission of the Church.

Bibliography: E. CARROLL et al., *Journeying ... Resources* (LCWR,

Washington, D.C. 1977). Contains six position papers requested as resource material for the Leadership Conference of Women Religious (LCWR) Task Force for Contemporary Theology of Religious Life. *Documents on Renewal for Religious* (Boston: St. Paul Editions 1974). Contains English translations of all the official documents on the renewal of religious life issued since Vatican II. Leadership Conference of Women Religious, LCWR Recommendations: *Schema of Canons on Religious Life* (Washington, D.C. 1977). Contains the tabulated results of survey of US major superiors of women on the proposed schema and rationale for objections to 53 of the 242 articles of the draft. Pontifical Commission for the Revision of the CIC, *Schema of Canons on Institutes of Life Consecrated by Profession of the Evangelical Counsels* (Draft) tr. S. M. NOFFKE, J. I. O'CONNOR, and E. J. STOKES (USCC Publ. Office, Washington, D.C. 1977).   [S. SCHNEIDERS]

W

WAR, MORALITY OF

While there was almost universal condemnation of Christian participation in war by the early Fathers of the Church, this witness took a dramatic turn in the thought of St. Augustine of Hippo. One of the first major Christian thinkers to abandon any hope for Christian perfection in this life, St Augustine argued a position which would tolerate Christian participation in warfare while he denied Christians the possibility of personal self-defense. His thought was later developed by St. Thomas Aquinas, Fr. Vitoria, and Fr. Suárez and resulted in the following principles: (1) war must be declared by a legitimate authority; (2) it must be fought for a just cause; (3) it can be fought only after all peaceful means of settlement have been exhausted; (4) it must be fought with the intention of restoring peace—not to gain vengeance; (5) it must be fought in the proper manner—innocent civilians may not be attacked; (6) the principle of proportionality—that the good to be achieved must outweigh the evil inflicted—must be followed; and (7) only defensive wars, not wars of aggression may be waged (see 14:302).

Contemporary Teaching. These principles have been later commented on, or alluded to, by Popes Pius XII, John XXIII, Paul VI as well as by the Fathers of Vatican Council II, the 1971 Synod of Bishops, national episcopal conferences, the testimony of the Holy See on disarmament at the United Nations (1976), and also by individual theologians. The horrors of modern war, the ever-escalating arms race, the spread of nuclear weapons, and the prospects that even conventional wars could result in a major nuclear exchange have caused a dramatic reconsideration of the applicability of the just war principles in the latter half of the 20th century.

The nuclear "storm that threatens every moment" caused Pope John XXIII to speak vigorously against war and call for disarmament (John XXIII PacTerr 109–119). The Fathers of Vatican II urged "an evaluation of war with an entirely new attitude" and stated: "Any act of war aimed indiscriminately at the destruction of entire cities or of extensive areas along with their population is a crime against God and man himself. It merits unequivocal and unhesitating condemnation" (*Gaudium et spes* 80). This statement is particularly notable since it was the only explicit condemnation pronounced by Vatican II. The Council also called the

arms race "an utterly treacherous trap for humanity, and one which injures the poor to an intolerable degree" and urged us to "find means for resolving our disputes in a manner more worthy of man" (ibid. 81).

Pope Paul VI, in his address to the UN (Oct. 4, 1965), stated: "If you want to be brothers, let the weapons fall from your hands. You cannot love with weapons in your hands" (Paul VI 54). While Pope Paul tolerated the possession of "defensive" weapons, he also consistently called for an international public authority to regulate disputes between peoples in a nonviolent manner. The 1971 Synod of Bishops asserted that "it is absolutely necessary that international conflicts should not be settled by war" and urged that "a strategy of nonviolence" be fostered along with the right to conscientious objection (Synod JustWorld p. 49). Pope Paul called for an end to "the senseless cold war" which is a major cause of the arms race and the testimony of the Holy See to the UN (submitted in April–May 1976) condemned the arms race and called it "a danger," "an injustice," "a violation of law," "a form of theft," "a mistake," "a wrong," and a "folly" (Holy See).

Implications for a "Just-War" Theory. The following points are clear from recent papal, conciliar, and episcopal statements: (1) the use of nuclear weapons is clearly immoral; (2) the armaments race is in itself a danger to human survival; and (3) an international authority must be established to replace war as a normal means of settling disputes. It is quite clear that the just-war theory cannot apply to contemporary weapons of mass destruction and even conventional wars must be morally questioned since they can provoke the resort to nuclear weapons. While the moral issue involved in the possession of nuclear weapons for deterrence purposes is still unresolved, it is clear that contemporary church teaching does not regard deterrence as a steady or sure way to preserve peace. The reality of contemporary weapons is causing the Church to question the morality of war and violence in general and there is a greater tendency to endorse nonviolence as the Christian response to the immorality of contemporary war.

See also DISARMAMENT.

Bibliography: R. H. BAINTON, *Christian Attitudes toward War and Peace* (Nashville, Tenn. 1960). J. J. FAHEY, *Peace, War, and the Christian Conscience* (Christophers Publ., New York 1969). J. GREMILLION, *The Gospel of Peace and Justice* (Maryknoll, N.Y. 1976). HOLY SEE, "The Role of the United Nations and Disarmament" (1976 Testimony to the

UN) *Catholic Mind* 75 (April 1977) 46–55; also in *Pope Speaks* 22 (1977) 243–259. PAUL VI, "Address to the General Assembly of the United Nations," *Pope Speaks* 11 (1966) 47–57; World Day of Peace Messages, *Pope Speaks* 12 (1967) 329–330; 14 (1969) 311–315; 16 (1971) 349–352; 17 (1972–73) 11–15; 18 (1973) 352–356; 19 (1974–75) 341–346; 22 (1977) 38–45; 23 (1978) 35–41.

[J. J. FAHEY]

WARD, JUSTINE BAYARD CUTTING

Musician and educator; b. Aug. 7, 1879, Morristown, N.J. daughter of William Bayard and Olivia Murray Cutting; d. November 27, 1975, Washington, D.C. After her conversion to Roman Catholicism in 1904, she devoted herself to the cause of church music, inspired by the motu proprio, *Tra le sollecitudini*, on sacred music of Pius X (1903), which called for a revival of interest in Gregorian chant and classic polyphony.

Mrs. Ward was convinced that any reform in church music had to begin at the earliest stages of the child's education with proper training in music. In 1910 Dean Thomas E. Shields of Sisters' College, The Catholic University of America asked her to prepare a music curriculum for the parochial schools. With the collaboration of J. Young, SJ she published *Music First Year* of the Ward Method in 1916. That same year she introduced her Method in the Annunication School, in New York, assisted by Mother G. Stevens, a Religious of the Sacred Heart, and in 1917 she endowed a Pius X Chair of Liturgical Music at Manhattanville College. This later became known as the Pius X School of Liturgical Music. For many years, Mrs Ward taught at Sisters' College as well as at the Pius X School.

In 1920, Mrs. Ward, Secretary of the Auxiliary Committee for the Pontifical School of Sacred Music, Rome, joined forces with the St. Gregory Society of America to organize an International Congress of Gregorian Chant in New York. Dom André Mocquereau and Dom Augustin Gatard, Benedictine monks of the Solesmes Congregation, conducted the services at St. Patrick's Cathedral where hundreds of adults and children trained in the Ward Method sang the Gregorian chants. She was responsible, too, for the 1922 summer session at Manhattanville, where Dom Mocquereau taught the chant and Dom Hebert Desrocquettes, Gregorian accompaniment, both courses according to the principles of Solesmes.

The Ward Method spread quickly throughout the U.S. and Canada; teachers trained at Pius X introduced the Method in Europe, Australia, New Zealand, and in the mission lands of the Orient. Mrs. Ward reached a wide audience with her lectures on the chant illustrated with examples sung by the Pius X Choir, whose training she carefully supervised. In the early 1930s the partnership of Mother Stevens and Mrs. Ward was dissolved, but both continued to work zealously for the reform of church music. Mrs. Ward continued to write and/or revise her books: Mother Stevens continued as Director of the Pius X School until her death in 1948. The Pius X School was a center of liturgical music until 1969 when a unilateral administrative decision combined the function of the School with that of the music department of Manhattanville College, where a church music program is still offered.

In 1929 Mrs. Ward established the Dom Mocquereau *Schola Cantorum* Foundation for the teaching and the dissemination of Gregorian Chant and in 1930, she founded a *schola cantorum* at Catholic University. For her long service to church music Mrs. Ward received many honors: decorations from the Italian and Netherland governments: the *Croce di Benemerenza*, Order of Malta: the Cross, *Pro Ecclesia et pontifice* from Pius XII; honorary degrees from the Pontifical School of Sacred Music and Catholic University. The liturgical reforms of Vatican II with the emphasis on the vernacular deemphasized the Gregorian chant but Mrs. Ward, until her death, continued to support Solesmes in its research and study of Gregorian chant.

Bibliography: J. B. WARD, "The Reform in Church Music," *Atlantic Monthly* 97 (1906) 455–463; "Music in the Parochial Schools," *Catholic Choirmaster* 2 (Apr. 1916) 6–8; "School Music in Its Relation to Church Music," *Catholic Choirmaster* 4 (Jan. 1918) 2–9; *Hymnal* (Washington, D.C. 1918 rev. ed. 1930); *Gregorian Chant*, v. 1 and 2, Catholic Education Series (Washington, D.C. 1923 and 1949); "Ex ore infantium," *Commonweal* 2 (1925) 450–451; *That All May Sing* (Washington, D.C. 1956, rev. ed. New York 1976).

[C. A. CARROLL]

WARD, MAISIE

Author, publisher; b. Shanklin, Isle of Wight, England, Jan. 4, 1889; d. New York City, Jan. 28, 1975. Maisie Ward was the daughter of Wilfrid Ward (14:809), and granddaughter of William George ("Ideal") Ward. Her mother was Josephine Mary Ward, the novelist, daughter of James Robert Hope-Scott of Abbotsford. Maisie's education was entrusted to governesses and later to the Mary Ward nuns at Cambridge until 1907. She grew up in a family with many eminent friends and visitors, among them Chesterton, Belloc, George Windham, and the Baron von Hügel. During World War I Miss Ward served as a Red Cross nurse. After the war she became a charter member of the Catholic Evidence Guild; she and a scrubwoman were its first two women speakers. In 1926 she married Frank Sheed, a young Australian with whom she had worked at the Guild. Together they founded the publishing house, Sheed & Ward, and they were parents of two children, Wilfrid Sheed, the novelist and critic, and Rosemary Sheed Middleton, the columnist and translator.

Into Catholic publishing, a hitherto rather heavy and unimaginative business, Sheed & Ward brought a fresh and bracing spirit, considerable excitement, style, and wit. In the first number of their house organ, *The Trumpet*, was the notice: "In answer to many inquiries, we do not sell crucifixes, statues, rosary beads or medals; we sell books." Their goal was to lift the awareness of Catholic readers. They aimed, they said, "just above the middle of the brow," and introduced to readers not only new works in English, but such continental writers as Claudel, Karl Adam, Henri Ghéon, François Mauriac and others, up to and including Hans Küng. By 1933 the firm had opened a branch in New York City and Maisie Ward and her husband "commuted" from London. In 1939 the couple moved to the U.S. and Frank Sheed "commuted" the other way. The London office was completely destroyed in the World War II bombings; Sheed, in London at the time, rented a new office the following day. In 1960 Christopher Dawson remarked that the foundation of Sheed & Ward marked "an epoch in the history of English Catholicism," and "had changed the whole climate." The venture continued into the early 1970s and was then sold. It had belonged to an era, the era between the final conflicts and agonies of Modernism and Vatican Council II. During those years Sheed & Ward helped many Catholics keep their minds open and their hopes up.

Besides being a lecturer and publisher, Maisie Ward was the author of a number of books. Possibly the most important were *The Wilfrid Wards and the Transition* (1934) and *Insurrection and Resurrection* (1937). "Transition" in the first title refers to what her father, the eminent editor of the *Dublin Review*, saw as the shift of the Church from a 19th-century state of siege and its accompanying "siege mentality" to an opening to the world outside the Church. "Insurrection" in the second title was the Modernist revolt, and "Resurrection," the survival and renewed life of the Church after the crisis had passed. Both books are livened by the author's own recollections of many of the principals involved in that history. Other works of hers were a full biography, *Gilbert Keith Chesterton* (1943) and her own favorite, *Young Mr. Newman* (1948).

Besides lecturing, writing and publishing she was also actively interested in such humane projects as the Catholic Housing Aid Society, the Grail, and the Catholic Worker. She was a person of remarkable energy, intellectual vigor, wit, and humanity.

Bibliography: M. HOEHN, ed., *Catholic Authors: Contemporary Biographical Sketches: 1930–1947* (Newark, N.J. 1948). C. MORITZ, ed., *Current Biography Yearbook: 1966* (New York 1966). W. ROMIG, ed., *The Book of Catholic Authors* (4th Series) (Grosse Point, Mich. 1948). M. WARD, *Unfinished Business* (New York 1964); *To and Fro on the Earth* (New York 1974).

[E. D. CUFFE]

WEALTH, DISTRIBUTION OF

So long as mankind lived in primitive hunting and fishing societies, there were relatively small differences in the amounts of wealth held by individual households and other social groupings. But with the rise of the great agricultural civilizations of antiquity, the size of the economic surplus the social systems could produce grew substantially and with it disparities among various social units in the amount of that surplus to which they could lay claim. Territorial conquest and looting, the imposition of tribute obligations on subjugated peoples, and the institution of slavery exaggerated further the inequalities of income and wealth that typified societies of that era. Occasional concern over the extent of this inequality was expressed, as by Plato, and the virtues of charitable giving (i.e., some redistribution of income) were proclaimed in the Judaeo-Christian religious tradition. Yet, as a practical matter most social systems, both Western and non-Western, managed with little difficulty to tolerate quite considerable discrepancies in the distribution of wealth and income among their members. And since the class structure of society was taken as part of the natural order, wide variations in levels of income and holdings of wealth were accepted as a socially appropriate reflection of differences in status and worth.

During the Middle Ages doctrines of the just price and the just wage seemed somewhat to temper economic inequality by suggesting that distributive justice required that people be remunerated in a manner appropriate to their station in life. Reciprocal feudal obligations and almsgiving may also have blunted the harshness of interclass distinctions. Yet, here too the gap between rich and poor was as conspicious as ever, and, indeed, the economic growth that accompanied the Renaissance simply heightened the contrast between the privileged orders of society and those of lower social station. Down through the ages sporadic manifestations of social discontent—crime, violence, even uprisings—gave indication that not all the population found the prevailing distribution of riches agreeable. For the most part, though, the poor were powerless to effect any fundamental changes in the systems in which they lived.

Mercantilism and the Growth of Wealth. Over the past several centuries, commercial expansion, agricultural improvements, and technical progress in various industrial fields combined to increase steadily and considerably the economic surplus available to those who lived in Europe and, in due course, in North America. Under the system of capitalism, which displaced feudalism, those who owned the means of production benefitted especially. With the overseas extension of European rule—in Africa, Asia, and the New World—the favored areas (and classes) of the globe managed to boost their real incomes even higher by laying claim to resources located in other people's lands. Mercantilist policies were, in fact, designed to increase national economic strength at the expense of other countries and regions. The net effect of these developments was therefore to accentuate distributional disparities both within and among the various world regions. To some extent, the colonial insurrections that began in the Americas in 1776 were instigated by dissatisfaction with the international or interregional distribution of wealth.

What is important to realize, however, is that international inequalities in the distribution of wealth came about not merely through military conquest and political domination, nor even on account of the strategies of mercantilism. The rise of the market economy with its gradual spread throughout the world provided, once the Industrial Revolution was underway, an even more pervasive means for transferring resources out of territories inhabited by poor and technologically archaic peoples and placing them at the disposition of the wealthier and more technically advanced. Thanks to this massive transfer and to advances in productivity, it was eventually possible for even the working classes in the industrial economies to experience significant improvement in their material lot. An elaborate rationale or justification for this global process of wealth concentration was, in effect, provided by classical theories of international trade.

To be sure, from the 14th century onward occasional "Utopian" critics stressed the moral and social defects of what was to them an unacceptable distribution of income and wealth. John Wycliffe, Thomas More, Henri de Saint-Simon, Charles Fourier, and Robert Owen exemplify the range of this criticsm. Indeed, for some of these, inequality was more than inequity; it was seen as an iniquity. Here and there, peasant revolts revealed a less intellectual, more experimental form of social protest. But it is perhaps not an exaggeration to say that it was really not until the 18th and 19th centuries that the domestic distribution of wealth and income became a public–policy issue of some moment and continuing concern within various sovereign jurisdictions.

"The Social Question." By the 19th century, economic inequality became an issue for sustained and acrimonious argument, with outright revolt widespread in the Europe of 1848. Referred to most often as "the social question," it was the political, social, and equity aspects of the matter that received so much attention. Marx and his followers, the social democrats, and the British Fabians were particularly active in this great debate, joined, in time, by various social Christian reformers as well. Papal encyclicals, the solidarists, Social-Gospel proponents, Christian socialists, and Catholic activists all joined in decrying the lopsided distribution of riches. Thanks to growing interest in the subject, it became clear that the distribution of wealth and income was intimately tied in with other inequality systems (information and knowledge, political power, prestige, and status) that derive from the social structure in all its operations. A few economists—Marx, Hobson, and Veblen especially—laid stress on adverse economic consequences of the maldistribution of wealth, but it was in the 1930s that the economic dimension came most forcefully to the forefront of public policy discussion. J. M. Keynes provided the refined analysis which linked excessive economic inequality with recession and depression and this, together with social-welfare considerations, made the redistribution of wealth and income a preoccupation of governmental action through fiscal and monetary policy.

Current Protest. The focus of attention up to World War II was largely on the intranational distribution of wealth. Since then, it is gross international inequality that has attracted much analytical attention and policy concern. Yet various global economic assistance programs have made relatively little headway in reducing the enormous and possibly growing disparties in per-capita-income levels that separate the so-called Third World from the industrialized economies of both East and West. Moreover, inequality in the distribution of wealth within some developing countries has quite possibly become even more lopsided as a result of development schemes. While some have argued that economic development in these countries requires income inequality, recent critical thinking has called this strategy into question and it has become increasingly doubtful that the consumption standards of the affluent countries can ever be generalized to the world at large. As recent papal encyclicals have indicated, the structure of the world economic system must be significantly altered if real progress is to be achieved in reducing mass poverty.

See also LAND REFORM; NEW INTERNATIONAL ECONOMIC ORDER.

[W. GLADE]

WEEK OF PRAYER FOR CHRISTIAN UNITY

An annual eight-day period of prayer for Christian Unity is observed by all Christians, usually Jan. 18–25. Its origin is in the Chair of Unity Octave founded in 1908 by Fr. Paul Wattson of Graymoor, NY, and in the efforts of Abbé Paul Couturier of Lyons, France to modify the intentions of the Unity Octave so that all Christians could pray together for Christian Unity (3:422). The Chair of Unity Octave had a distinctly Roman Catholic orientation and development that paralleled Fr. Wattson's religious experience. For many other Christians it was too restrictive, and for some a conscience problem.

In 1935 Abbé Couturier renamed the Unity Octave "The Universal Week of Prayer for Christian Unity" and altered its prayers so that Christians interceded, not for the return of all to Rome, but for the unity Christ wills through the means he chooses. Many Roman Catholics were critical at the time of this approach, but no one argued with its aim, which was to stir up the spirit of prayer as a means for spiritual development. In 1939 Couturier wrote, "the whole fabric of Christendom must be shaken to its very depths by the universal prayer for Christians; it must experience a supernatural shock which will break down its prejudices, rectify its superficial and false ideas, cause hearts to grow into one another, and finally unite minds in the eternal light of the one Christ."

In the meantime some Anglicans developed various organizations whose aims were related to the Chair of Unity Octave. The Faith and Order Movement, an antecedent to the World Council of Churches, had, since 1920, promoted a "week of prayer" for church unity at Pentecost. Roman Catholics in England, acting on Pope Leo XIII's suggestion, developed a Pentecost novena for the reunion of Christians; in the U.S., Canada, other English-speaking countries, and in Latin nations the Unity Octave was promoted by the Atonement Friars. Orthodox Christians retained a cautious posture about all these happenings.

In 1941 the Faith and Order Movement changed the dates of its "week of prayer" to coincide with Couturier's, by then widespread in France, Germany, and the Netherlands. This brought about the first experience of Christians praying for unity together and at the same time. When the World Council of Churches was constituted in 1948 the Week of Prayer for Christian Unity was formally sponsored by its Faith and Order Commission. With the publication of Vatican Council II's Decree on Ecumenism the difficulties some Roman Catholics had with the Week of Prayer were resolved; with all Christians they could now participate in one observance. This possibility became a reality in 1966 when one prayer leaflet for all was prepared by an interdenominational committee and distributed universally. This committee became the permanent *Joint Working Group of the World Council of Churches and the Roman Catholic Church, which annually chooses the theme and prepares the basic materials for the annual Week of Prayer for Christian Unity. In the U.S. this basic material is adapted and distributed for American use by the Atonement Friars of the Graymoor Ecumenical Institute. This project is sponsored by the Faith and Order Department of the National Council of Churches of Christ and is endorsed by the Roman Catholic Bishops' Commission for Ecumenical and Interreligious Affairs.

Bibliography: C. ANGELL and C. LAFONTAINE, *Prophet of Reunion* (New York 1975). G. CURTIS, *Paul Couturier and Unity in Christ* (Westminster, Md. 1964). H. FEY, ed., *A History of the Ecumenical Movement*, v. 2 (Philadelphia 1970). R. MERCER, *What is this "Week of Prayer for Christian Unity"?* (London, SPCK and CTS, 1977).

[T. HORGAN]

WILLGING, EUGENE PAUL

Librarian; b. Dubuque, Iowa, Aug. 17, 1909; d. Washington, D.C., Sept. 20, 1965. Educated at Columbia College, he received his library degree from the University of Michigan. As cataloger at The Catholic University of America, he worked with the newly received Clementine Library collection. From 1933 to 1946 he was at the University of Scranton where he began the publication of the *Index to Catholic Pamphlets in the English Language* (1937–53), put out *A Handbook of American Catholic*

Societies with Dorothy Lynn (1940), and was the first editor of the reviewing journal *Best Sellers* (1940–). He was particularly interested in Catholic publishing as a vital factor in education and focused this interest in bibliographic control of popular publishing.

Moving to Catholic University in 1946 and becoming Director of Libraries in 1949, Willging was able to continue his editorial and bibliographic work, and to use these talents to enrich the library holdings. Card services for libraries and book dealers appeared, including the *Weekly List of Catholic Books.* As paperbacks grew in popularity, he published *Catalogue of Catholic Paperback Books* (1959–65). These attempts to control ephemera were significant, but his lasting work in the 16-part *Catholic Serials of the Nineteenth Century in the United States* (1959–68), coauthored with Herta Hatzfeld. As director of numerous theses in library science, Willging was preparing the groundwork for a complete bibliography of American Catholic publishing before 1900. Mullen Library now holds many of the volumes of this period in its Catholic Americana section. While involved in this research he was instrumental in procuring microfilms of many journals and newspapers for the library, as well as providing films for other institutions. Willging's interest in publishing as an educational medium and his interest in Catholic action brought a clearing-house activity to the University library under the auspices of the Mission Secretariat. Thousands of books were collected and sent to missions throughout the world during his directorship. Finally, his work in the evolution and realization of the *New Catholic Encyclopedia* should be noted, since he was instrumental in its founding and in making the editorial work easier by opening the resources of the library to the *Encyclopedia* staff.

A man of his time, Willging in his life epitomized the role of the layman working for Church-related activities. He was well known for these efforts, was made a Knight of the Holy Sepulcher, received citations acknowledging his contributions to the life of the Church, and, in 1957, was awarded an honorary degree from his alma mater, Loras College in Dubuque.

[C. LEE]

WITNESS, CHRISTIAN

Witness is personal testimony and involves the commitment of a person to a fact, or to a truth, or to another person. It may be made by words, by deeds, by dying. Christian witness, a term once generally confined to Protestant usage, has, especially since Vatican Council II, been adopted in Catholic circles, in the process achieving a newer meaning. In one important sense, witness expresses the whole of the Christian commitment in that to be a Christian is to give witness to Christ.

Jesus as Witness. Jesus is the prime, the sublime witness. The Father and the Holy Spirit give witness to Jesus (Jn 5.31; Lk 3.22) and he is a witness to them of what he has seen and heard in the presence of the Father (Jn 3.11–12); the promised Spirit will be the principal witness to him before the world (Acts 1.8).

To the witness that the Spirit will give of Jesus is closely joined the witness that will be given by those who were with him from "the beginning" (Jn 15.26). Thus, as Jesus is the witness par excellence to the Father and the Holy Spirit, so the Apostles will be the prime human witnesses to him. They are the eye- and ear-witnesses of the risen Lord (Acts 1.21); the facts to which they testify include everything in the life of Jesus, "all that he did" (Acts 10.39).

Early Christians. This witness of the Apostles was carried on by the early Christians. They, too, were called to give witness. Their witness does not rest on the same foundation as that of the Apostles, a direct acquaintance with Jesus and the events of His life, but their witness is concerned with the same person and, at times, must be exercised to the same heroic extent, the giving of their lives.

The basic Greek word for witness, μάρτυς occurs 34 times in the NT. In early persecution and martyrdom Christian witness shone out in its ultimate purity; the word "witness" thus came to take on a meaning from its extreme expression. Acts 22.20 speaks of the shedding of the blood of Stephen who was "a witness." He did not witness to the facts of the Lord's life as the Apostles had done but, by the shedding of his blood, he attested to his belief in that to which the Apostles had attested. With the arrival of persecution, the *martus* came to mean one who had witnessed by his dying. Until the Edict of Milan changed things, martyrdom was seen to be the highest achievement of the Christian life precisely because it was the strongest evidence the witness could give of accepting the Good News preached by its first human witnesses. When the age of the martyrs ended, the emphasis was transferred to the Christian witness of living for Christ rather than dying for him. This would remain the emphasis in the centuries ahead; it is the force of designating saints as "confessors."

Witness in the Church. Jesus, by his life and mainly by his death and resurrection, had testified to the Trinity's everlasting love for the human family. That witness of Jesus continues on, witnessed, in turn, by the Church. In its very *being* the Church is witness. In it, as Vatican II says, "The Spirit dwells...prays...and gives witness" (*Lumen gentium* 4). The Church "...is in the nature of sacrament" (ibid. 1); in all its life, then, the Church is witness. Each Sacrament administered or received, each word preached, each sick person tended, each poor person helped is a continuing witness to the first, the prime witness, Jesus. This witness is always, at least implicitly, a witness to the fatherhood of God; in the faithful, the Spirit bears witness "...to their adoptive sonship" (ibid. 4).

The first concrete witness the Church gives, therefore, must be holiness, and Vatican II, with insistent repetition, requires this witness of every member of the Church. Demanded of the chief pastors, even to the laying down of their lives, and of all the Church's ministers, this witness is not confined to them. Married couples and parents, for example, "...stand as witnesses and cooperators of the fruitfulness of Mother Church" (ibid. 41). After considering each class of Christian, the Council emphasizes that all are invited to a life of holiness and "...the perfection of their own state of life" (ibid. 43). All are called to Christian witness (*see* HOLINESS, UNIVERSAL CALL TO).

Liturgy. The chief means which the Council proposes for the realization of the witness of holiness is itself another witness, that is, the liturgy. To no other subject did Vatican II devote more time and space. Through the liturgy "...the faithful are enabled to express in their own lives and manifest to others [i.e. witness to] the mystery of Christ" (*Sacrosanctum Concilium* 1). This has particular application to the liturgy of the Sacraments, most especially to the Eucharist ".... through which," Pope Paul VI said, "we do not cease to proclaim [another equivalent of "witness"] the death and resurrection of the Lord" (Paul VI EvangTest 48).

Religious Life. Another strong witness is religious life, which traces "... its origins to the teaching and example of the divine Master" and so is "... a very clear symbol of the heavenly kingdom" (*Perfectae caritatis* 1). Throughout this decree on the up-to-date renewal of religious life Vatican II recommends the adaptation of the customs of the various religious institutes precisely so that they may be recognized by their contemporaries as witnesses to the principle that inspires them, the imitation of Christ. Particularly in the area of poverty, whose sign-value is powerful and yet can easily be obscured, the Council encourages a search for new forms, since "... voluntary poverty, in the footsteps of Christ, is a symbol much esteemed nowadays" (ibid. 13).

Cooperation among Christians. A new and forceful appeal to witness is found in the Decree on Ecumenism. It desires some common witness through action with other Christian, but non-Catholic, bodies. The readiness of the conciliar Fathers to admit a common guilt for the divisions of Christendom (a readiness which is also new) shows a consciousness of the need for such a confession, i.e. a witness, before the whole world (cf. *Unitatis redintegratio* 3, 7). "All Christians ... united in their efforts" should "... bear witness to our common hope" (ibid. 12). This has particular application to social matters. Cooperation among Christians in this area "expresses [i.e. witnesses to] "... the bond that already unites them" (ibid.). Thus the Council unites two basic NT ideas, viz., the Church as a community bearing witness to Christ and as a community of service in the imitation of Christ.

[P. F. MULHERN]

WOMEN, CANON LAW ON

Although in the Canon Law of the Church there is no specific canon, decree, or other legislation directly antifeminist, there is evidence that women's dignity is ignored and their opportunity for service in the Church severely limited.

Existing Legislation. The phrasing of canons in paternalistic or protective language suggests the subordination of women to men. Preferences are conceded to men but not to women. Thus legislation on the Privilege of the Faith, allows a man, after his Baptism, in specific circumstances to choose one of many wives he had, simultaneously or successively, before his Baptism; no corresponding option is given to women (CIC c. 1125). Norms for Christian burial give preference to a husband's choice (CIC c. 1229).

A similar attitude is present in canons based on past cultures and traditions. Thus women are separated from men in church buildings (CIC c. 1262). If religious women sing in their own church or public oratory, they are to do so from a place hidden from public view (CIC c. 1264n2). With regard to religious life, there is legislation on nuns' dowries (CIC c. 547), but no corresponding canon on religious men. Similarly one-sided is the regulation that a woman religious may not leave the convent without a companion (CIC c. 607). Two canons deal with confessors of men religious (CIC cc. 518–519); eight, minutely, with those of women

religious (CIC cc. 520–527). Regulations on the place where confessions may be heard (CIC cc. 909–910) apply only to women.

Both pre- and post-Vatican Council II legislation excludes women from administrative and juridical offices (CIC c. 1574; Paul VI, motu proprio *Causas matrimoniales*); from the Sacrament of Orders (CIC c. 968) and from institution into lay ministries (Paul VI MinQuaedam VII). A man has precedence over a woman as a minister of private Baptism in an emergency (CIC c. 747); and also as server at the Eucharistic Liturgy (CIC c. 813). Only men may receive the power of Order, ecclesiastical *jurisdiction, benefices, or pensions (CIC c. 108). In the composition of plenary, provincial, or diocesan synods major superiors only of male religious communities or other male groups are to be consulted or appointed to committees for preparation of the synods (CIC c. 282, 286, 358).

In principle everyone baptized enjoys fundamental rights in regard to juridical status as a person in the Church (CIC c. 87). But the factors conferring such status are described primarily in reference to men —legitimacy of birth, Baptism, age, place of origin, domicile, marital status, proper bishop, exercise of rights, consanguinity affinity, and rite (CIC cc. 87–98). The juridical status of a married woman is determined by reference to her husband; if she is an unmarried minor, by reference to her father. A single, adult woman has juridic status as a person, but loses it once she marries.

Current State of the Issue. Although some of the canons have been abrogated by postconciliar legislation, e.g., in the matter of confessors of religious, many have not, especially in the areas of administrative and juridical offices. The challenge from within the Catholic Church in this century calling for justice is expressed by Pope John XXIII (*Pacem in terris* 41), and again by the 1971 Synod of Bishops: "We also urge that women should have their own share of responsibility and participation in the community life of society and likewise of the Church" (Synod JustWorld p. 44). New, positive trends in the law are witnessed in the principles of Vatican Council II which emphasized the dignity of persons (*Gaudium et spes* 13–15); rejected discrimination among persons (*Lumen gentium* 32); and stressed the universality of the call to holiness (ibid. 39).

Inequities still exist in postconciliar legislation in regard to administrative and juridical offices. Also, as stated in the motu proprio, *Venite seorsum*, the requirement of papal cloister is maintained for contemplative orders of women, but is not for men (*see* CLOISTER).

The serious inadequacies regarding women in Canon Law, their being barred from ordination, some ministries, and administrative positions, require and are receiving theological as well as canonical study. Certain presuppositions especially regarding ministry and its relationship to the Church need to be and are being examined in their historical and theological settings, so as to evaluate the implications of the current practices of the Church.

Bibliography: Committee on the Status of Women in the Church Report, *Women, the Catholic Church and Canon Law*, ProcCLSA (1975) 185–192; Consensus Statement from the Symposium of Women and Church Law—*Report*, ProcCLSA (1976) 183–193. J. CORIDEN, ed., *Sexism and Church Law* (New York 1977), entire volume concentrates on special studies on women in the Church. A. M. GARDENER, ed., *Women and Catholic Priesthood: An Expanded Vision* (New York 1976).

J. RANGE, "Legal Exclusion of Women from Church Office," *Jurist* 33 (1974) 112–127. C. SAFILIOS-ROTHSCHILD et al., ThSt 36 n. 4 (1975) 577–765, entire volume concentrates on special studies on women in the Church. L. VASQUEZ, "The Position of Women according to the Code," *Jurist* 34 (1974) 128–142.

[J. A. BARNHISER]

WOMEN, ORDINATION OF

In the last decade, the ordination of women to the priesthood has surfaced as a major issue in many Christian Churches which traditionally have been opposed to the idea. After lengthy studies in recent years, several of these Churches have ruled in favor of admitting women to the priesthood. Examples include the United Methodist Church, the United Presbyterian Church, and some Lutheran Churches; several provinces of the Anglican Communion including the Episcopal Church of the United States of America have accepted women's ordination (the Lambeth Conference of 1978 voted to leave the issue up to the member Churches). The Roman Catholic Church, while it officially opposes the admission of women to Orders including the diaconate, has also been engaged internationally in theological reflection on the question.

Reasons for Interest in the Question. Several reasons emerge as causes of the interest in the question at this time. Some cluster around a new historical awareness in theology; others derive from anthropology.

Theological Reflections. Critical biblical and historical studies are revealing a much broader concept of ministry, leading to understanding ordained ministry itself as historically conditioned and not the exclusive form of ministry, as it had been considered during the last several centuries of the Church's history. This leads to critical reflection on the present form of the Sacrament of Order in such a way as to open up the question of some change in the current practice. Another consequence of critical-historical study is the rediscovery of the fact that women exercised a rather extensive public ministry in the early Church and received ordination to the diaconate. Even though the study of the tradition thus far does not show any instances of admitting women to priesthood, theological speculation on the question is encouraged by the new historical awareness. Some hold that as the Church's doctrine and discipline have evidenced development in other matters, so also it may show itself capable of change with regard to admitting women to Orders.

Cultural Antropology. Other reasons center around this century's keener awareness of cultural anthropology and its influence on theological understanding and formulation. Historical studies show conclusively that throughout the ages women have been excluded from many public roles, in both society and Church, because of the anthropological attitude that women are inferior by nature and thus must be subordinate to men—the accepted norm of societal and ecclesiastical functioning. Theological excesses of this cultural attitude have included the judgments that women are inferior at the very order of creation and thus have no status as individuals and also that they are saved only through grace mediated by men, who are more fitting subjects of divine action by reason of their superiority in nature.

These cultural and religious attitudes are changing, however, because of the widespread emphasis on human rights and equality for all as universally proclaimed today by both society and Church. Instead of hierarchical subordination and assigned cultural roles, both the social

sciences and contemporary theological reflection speak today of equality and of the complementarity of the sexes, with the aim of developing partnership as the model of relationship and mediation. The issue of women's roles in society and Church, in other words, cannot be isolated from the wider question of human liberation in its many facets, a concern that is one of the signs of the times. To the extent that women are judged unfit for ordained public ministry as based upon latent inferiority or subordinationist anthropology, to that extent this change in contemporary cultural awareness is significant for the question of the admission of women to Orders.

Pastoral Realities. Other reasons for attending to the question of women and priesthood group themselves around the present pastoral reality. In many parts of the world, women are in fact already exercising many forms of pastoral leadership, evidence that they are both called by the communities they serve and recognized as fit and competent for public ministry. This fact, coupled with the shortage of ordained ministers in several of these communities, leads to looking for new ways to serve the sacramental needs of these communities. While this pastoral situation does not constitute a positive reason for ordaining women, it does generate interest in a reexamination of the issue, with a view responding more creatively to urgent pastoral needs. This approach receives support from the renewed biblical understanding of ministry as service diversified to meet the needs of the believing community gathered in the Eucharist around the name of Jesus the Lord.

State of the Question in the Roman Catholic Church. The present official position of the Roman Catholic Church upholds the exclusion of women from ordination. The most recent official statement of this position is contained in the *Declaration on the Question of the Admission of Women to the Ministerial Priesthood (Inter insigniores)*, published Jan. 27, 1977 by the Congregation for the Doctrine of the Faith. While the Declaration intends to be authoritative in some sense and in fact argues positively in favor of maintaining the present position, theological discussion of the question continues within the Catholic Church.

Before the publication of the Declaration, in the U.S. the NCCB Committee on Pastoral Research and Practices published a short report (1972) calling for an "exhaustive study" of the question. Also before the Declaration came the study of the Pontifical Biblical Commission, informally published July 1, 1976. The Commission, having been asked for its opinion on Scripture and the ordination of women by the Congregation for the Doctrine of the Faith, concluded that the New Testament by itself alone cannot "settle in a clear way and once and for all the problem of the possible accession of women to the presbyterate."

Since the publication of the Declaration, international theological study and debate of the issue has increased significantly at both the formal and informal levels. Theologians, canonists, exegetes, and scholars of other disciplines working both individually and collaboratively have published numerous studies and critical reactions to the Declaration. Further, many study commissions and committees have been organized by such groups as the Canon Law Society of America, the Catholic Theological Society of America, and the NCCB. Some progress reports of these groups have already been published. Finally, the *Women's Ordination Conference, a grass-roots movement which organized and met for the first time in 1975, convened a second international assembly in November 1978 in order to continue to probe the issue.

The Arguments. The Declaration by the Congregation for the Doctrine of the Faith offers a succinct summary of the arguments used to oppose the admission of women to the priesthood. There is first the evidence of Scripture. The Declaration teaches that Jesus did not entrust the apostolic mission to women, even though in many other respects he acted against cultural prejudices in favor of women. Thus, it is argued, it is of the divine order that women are not to be ordained priests.

There is secondly the argument of tradition. The Declaration points out that it has been the unbroken tradition of the Church to ordain only men to the priesthood and this practice is normative, resting as it does on solid and indisputable apostolic tradition.

There are thirdly the arguments drawn from theological reasoning, especially the argument of fittingness regarding the nature of symbolism in Sacrament requiring natural resemblance (maleness) in the priest who acts *in persona Christi* when he pronounces the words of Eucharistic consecration.

The Declaration has performed a service in drawing together the traditional arguments against the ordination of women and in making clear the reasons for maintaining the present practice. But continuing studies show that scholars and teachers of the Church, with the benefits of the critical-historical method in Scripture and theological hermeneutics, are willing to carry the tradition further by performing the necessary work of critical judgment in the light of new data and methods as applied to the tradition. Such effort has always been sanctioned by the Church in its function of authentic development in fidelity to the Gospel and tradition. The ordination of women will continue to be an issue in the Roman Catholic Church, and perhaps in the even wider context of elaborating new forms of ordained ministry that are both faithful to the richness of the tradition and responsive to the needs of our new age.

Bibliography: Reports and the Declaration: NCCB Committee on Pastoral Research and Practices, *Theological Reflections on the Ordination of Women* (USCC Publ. Office, Washington, D.C. 1972); NCCB Ad Hoc Committee for Women in Society and the Church, *The Role of Women in Ecclesial Ministry: Biblical and Patristic Foundations*, A. CUNNINGHAM, ed. (Washington, D.C. 1976). Pontifical Biblical Commission, Unofficial Report, *Can Women be Priests?*, Origins 6 (1976–77) 92–96. Congregation for the Doctrine of the Faith, *Inter insigniores* ActApS 69 (1977) 98–116; tr. *Declaration on the Question of the Admission of Women to the Ministerial Priesthood and Commentary* (USCC Publ. Office, Washington, D.C. 1977).
Studies: R. T. BARNHOUSE, et al., "The Ordination of Women to the Priesthood: An Annotated Bibliography," *Anglican Theological Review*, Supplement Series, 6 (June 1976) 81–106. S. BUTLER, ed., *Research Report: Women in Church and Society 1978* (CTSA, Bronx, N.Y. 1978). J. A. CORIDEN, ed., *Sexism and Church Law: Equal Rights and Affirmative Action* (New York 1977). A. M. GARDINER, ed., *Women and Catholic Priesthood: An Expanded Vision* (New York 1976). R. GRYSON, *Le Ministère des femmes dans l'église ancienne* (Gembloux, Belgium 1972), tr., J. LAPORTE and M. L. HALL, *The Ministry of Women in the Early Church* (Collegeville, Minn. 1976). Jesuit School of Theology of Berkeley, California, *Women's Ordination: An Open Letter to the Apostolic Delegate*, Origins 6 (1976–1977) 661, 663–665. H. M. LEGRAND, "Views on the Ordination of Women," Origins 6 (1976–1977) 459–468. J. E. LYNCH, "The Ordination of Women: Protestant Experience in Ecumenical Perspective," JEcumSt 12 (1975) 173–197. K. RAHNER, "Priestertum der Frau?," StZeit 195 (1977) 291–301. J. RANGE, "Legal Exclusion of Women from Church Office," Jurist 34 (1974) 128–142. L. and A. SWIDLER, eds., *Women Priests: A Catholic Commentary on the Vatican Declaration* (New York 1977). G. TAVARD, *Women in Christian Tradition* (Notre Dame, Ind. 1973). H. VAN DER MEER, *Priestertum der Frau?* (Freiburg 1969), tr., A. and L. SWIDLER, *Women Priests in the Catholic Church?* (Philadelphia 1973).

[M. E. SHEEHAN]

WOMEN, RIGHTS OF

It is judicious to view the issue of women's rights under the general rubric of the Church's ministry of social justice. Christian justice, reflecting Jesus' ministry to the poor and lowly, the disenfranchised, and the outcasts, including women, is revolutionary in that it recognizes the inalienable rights of all. The history of Christianity is marked by the Church's continued struggle to realize the implications of this universal range of justice. The contemporary Church demonstrates an increasing interest in the rights of women at a time when the many changes in the ways women perceive themselves and are perceived demand responsible theological and pastoral reflection.

Theological Dimensions. The Vatican-Council II impetus towards justice for all has prompted various disciplines to contribute to a more mature ecclesial reflection on the rights and roles of women in the Church. Scripture scholars show that Christ affirmed women in a way that was remarkable for his own times and that still presents a lesson for ours. Historical studies indicate the Church's constancy in teaching that women no less than men are created in the image of God (e.g., Augustine, *De Trinitate* 12.7). Revisions of the theology of the Sacraments have provided broader opportunities for men and women alike to participate more fully in Church and ministry. Stressing a holistic approach to human sexuality, moral theology advances the Church's teaching on such matters as sexual ethics, reciprocity in marriage, the dignity of the individual, and the potential of women to define themselves as responsible Christians in a pluralistic world.

NCCB Declaration. Their proper rights, it must be stressed, are owed to women not because they are a special minority or category of persons, but because they are human beings and baptized Christians. The National Conference of Catholic Bishops (NCCB) affirmed that the following are among the rights of baptized Christians, according to Vatican Council II's documents, *Lumen gentium* and *Gaudium et spes*: to hear the Word of God and participate in the sacramental life of the Church; to exercise the apostolate and share in the mission of the Church; to speak and be heard ...regarding the pastoral needs and affairs of the Church; to enjoy education, freedom of inquiry, and freedom of expression in the sacred sciences; to be protected from arbitrary deprival of any right or office in the Church (see bibliog., NCCB).

The compelling feature of this remarkable enumeration of rights is its universality. The basic questions the Church must now address are whether these rights pertain only to some Christians but not to others, whether, in fact, they can actually be exercised by all, and whether any or all distinctions between men and women regarding these rights are in violation of more fundamental human and Christian rights. If some persons have been arbitrarily denied any or all of these rights, the right to an effective remedy must be added to the above enumeration. It is paradoxical that, although there has never been a serious question about the validity of baptizing females (cf. Gal 3.28), the implications of women's rights as baptized Christians is still in the process of being recognized even within the Church itself.

The Church's ministry of *justice must be universal if

it is to be credible. In this context the issues raised in the current debate about the ordination of women to the priesthood are particularly challenging. Anything less than a radical reexamination of the theology of Orders which currently excludes women by virtue of their sex, would be inconsistent with the Church's ministry of justice. The 1977 Declaration on the Question of the Admission of Women to the Ministerial Priesthood by the Congregation for the Doctrine of the Faith correctly identified priestly ordination as a "vocation" rather than any individual's "right." However, perhaps the real issue could be stated differently: the "right" involved is that of every Christian to respond to a divinely inspired vocation and to have this vocation tested in the Church. Otherwise, what the American bishops call the right to "exercise the apostolate and to share in the mission of the Church" does not apply to some Christians.

The Women's Rights Movement. The Church's concept of rights goes beyond any enumeration of human rights because the Church is called to empower, to recognize as right what human society might deem privilege. The Church can find encouragement in the advances being made in contemporary society regarding women's rights. These advances also bring a certain challenge to the Church to keep stride with social and political developments. Feminist organizations, for example, raise consciousness and sensitivity about the situation of women in a variety of sectors. In 1967 the UN agreed to amend its 22-year-old Human Rights Declaration with a resolution to eliminate discrimination against women, an action implying that some remedy is needed wherever women are not allowed the rights that can properly be called "human." The UN designation of 1975 as International Women's Year will have reverberations for decades as regional and national conferences show that "equal rights" is easier said than understood. Ecumenical discussions contribute their challenge to any Christian Church whose policies restrict, abridge, or circumvent the rights of women.

As Christians, women also have the right to education in justice, a right that could involve challenging the status quo. Currently the official policy-making and legislative positions in the Church are controlled by those with Orders. While this situation prevails, together with the exclusion of women from the priesthood, principles of equality and collegiality are compromised and the effectiveness of women's ministries is limited arbitrarily (i.e., because of sexual differences). Fidelity to Christ's ministry and to that tradition which preserves universal justice as the goal, compels the Church to continue striving to eliminate discrimination against women and to assure all baptized persons full Christian rights.

Bibliography: A. M. GARDINER, ed., *Women and the Catholic Priesthood: An Expanded Vision* (New York 1976). A. MAIDA, "Rights in the Church," ChSt 15 (1976) 255–267. NCCB, "Report of the Canon Law Society of America to the NCCB on the Subject of Due Process" in *A Summary of Actions Taken by the NCCB on the Subject of Due Process* II, A (Washington, D.C. 1969). PAUL VI, "Women/Disciples and Co-Workers," Origins 4 (1975) 718–719. R. R. RUETHER, ed., *Religion and Sexism: Images of Woman in the Jewish and Christian Traditions* (New York 1974). L. and A. SWIDLER, ed., *Women Priests. A Catholic Commentary on the Vatican Declaration* (New York 1978).

[M. A. GETTY]

WOMEN, THEOLOGICAL FORMATION OF

The traditional understanding of the role of women in the Church and in society probably accounts for the limited exposure women received in theological formation until the last quarter century. During their childhood and adolescence, women learned the rudiments of their faith through parochial schools or parish catechetical programs. Such learning was considered adequate to enable them to enter the marriage state and to be a good wife and mother. For the women who chose religious life, theological formation was somewhat more extensive. But the conviction, so well documented in the writings of the Fathers, that women lacked any capacity to engage in the speculative sciences, seriously limited their theological education.

Beginnings. However, events in the first decades of the twentieth century were to bring about the gradual disintegration of this myth. The impact of the Industrial Revolution and two World Wars on Western society forced women out of their homes and into the public forum of work. Soon they were entering professional fields hitherto reserved for men, such as law and medicine. Their entrance into professional roles in the Church was to come more slowly. It began primarily in the departments of theology in European universities, although St. Mary's College in Indiana pioneered a doctoral program for women in the first half of the century. Many degree and non-degree programs in formal theology flourished in the U.S. during the 1940s and 1950s. In 1948, the study department of the World Council of Churches completed a research project on the life and work of women in the Church. It showed that, in Germany alone, there were 400–500 women graduates of theology from distinguished universities.

It is difficult to discern how much this development in the Protestant tradition influenced the Roman Catholic tradition. The fact is, nevertheless, that in 1952, an International Pontifical Institute, Regina Mundi, was founded in Rome for the theological education of women. Pope Pius XII explained that the main purpose of such a school was the preparation of women to teach theology in women's Catholic colleges (Pius XII). In thus restricting women to teaching women, the separation of women from the male clerical world seemed to have been kept intact. However, such a restriction was shortlived.

The way was opened in 1965 for women to become theologians in their own right by the Pastoral Constitution on the Church in the Modern World. Vatican Council II called for many lay people to receive theological education and expressed the hope that "some would develop and deepen these studies by their own labors" (*Gaudium et spes* 62).

Current Status. In the decade following Vatican II, women have received advanced degrees in almost every branch of the sacred sciences from biblical studies to Canon Law, and they are beginning to produce creative, scholarly work in their respective fields. They are studying and teaching in pontifical institutions such as the Gregorian University and the Pontifical Biblical Institute as well as in the departments of theology and religious studies in major universities in Europe, Asia, and North America.

But the desire to teach or to do scholarly research has not been the only cause of women's seeking a theological formation. Statistics show that a decade after Vatican II, there were nearly one thousand women enrolled in Catholic seminary programs in the United States. Significantly, there are nearly equal numbers of religious (458) and lay women (477) in these programs (CARA). Although many of them are part-time students, some of these women are pursuing a program identical with that of the candidates for priestly ordination. Statistics issued by the Association of Theological Schools (ATS) show that, in 1976, in Canada and the U.S., there were 102 Catholic women enrolled in a master of divinity program (ATS). Many of them are hoping to work in a parish in a pastoral ministerial capacity, collaborating closely with the efforts of the ordained priests. Some are testifying to their sense of call to priesthood and are preparing to ask the Church to test their call. Some will probably move into developing countries. In Latin America and Africa as well as in parts of Asia, women are testifying to the need for women with theological and pastoral skills to assume responsibility in building up Christian communities in these areas of the world. Many women, out of the exigency of the times, are struggling to assume the role of pastor for the people.

Impact. The import of this extraordinary emergence of women into formal theological formation is hard to predict for a Church in transition. It is clear that, in the name of tradition, the movement is being strongly resisted by the official Church, especially when it aspires to Holy Orders. But the opening to the doors of the rich biblical and theological tradition of Christianity to women has already brought the Church to a new awareness in some ways. No longer can such an education be seen as the sole possession of the ordained minister; the Church is beginning to realize that it has a responsibility to enable every member of the Church to go as far as possible in plumbing the mystery of God. No longer can the Church honestly view women as inferior human beings. Evidence is growing that they can stand before God's Truth in faith and proclaim God's Word in love.

It is possible that the effect of women's long history of subordination in the Church on theological formation will produce new forms of discipleship, new forms of ministry with a special predilection for the poor and the oppressed. Hopefully, the Church's relinquishment of the gift of theological education as the special possession of the ordained minister, the Church's sharing of that gift with all God's people, will help to create a new Church, modeled on the first Christian communities who shared all things in trust and love.

Bibliography: ATS, *Fact Book of Theological Education, 1976–77* (Dayton, Ohio 1977). CARA, *Seminary Directory* (Washington, D.C. 1977). PIUS XII, motu proprio, *Nihil Ecclesiae antiquius*, ActApS 48 (1956) 189–192. World Council of Churches, "Report of Committee IV: 1. The Life and Work of Women in the Church," *Man's Disorder and God's Design*, v. 5., *The First Assembly of the World Council of Churches* (London 1949) 146–152 (summary of the Report).

[H. M. WRIGHT]

WOMEN AND PREACHING

Though women have moved into many new positions in the Church and are bringing their gifts to meet the needs of the Church in varied ministries today, they have not as yet official access to the pulpit.

History and Canon Law. All baptized Christians share in the priesthood of Christ; yet some of the faithful are called to be officially designated leaders in a ministerial priesthood. All baptized Christians are called to witness to the Good News, but some are mandated or commissioned to proclaim publicly and to interpret the Gospel of Jesus Christ, continuing his mission: "Let us go elsewhere, so that I can preach there too, because that is why I came" (Mk 1.38). This official preaching, at least after 100 A.D., was seen as the perogative of the bishop and those delegated by him. There is no evidence that women were ever so delegated, though there is little doubt that women prophets, at times, addressed the assembly.

Current Canon Law makes it clear that the ministerial office of preaching belongs to the Roman Pontiff and to the bishops for their diocese, though they may employ other qualified persons to assist them (CIC c. 1327). Even though c. 1342 bars all lay persons, men and women alike, from being among those to assist the bishop, cc. 1327 and 1328 indicate that is within the competency of the local Ordinary, for the spiritual good of his people, to commission individuals within his diocese to preach. In terms of the law barring women, Vatican Council II's Decree on the Pastoral Office of Bishops makes clear that the "individual diocesan bishops have the power to dispense from the general law of the Church in particular cases those faithful over whom they normally exercise authority. It must, however, be to their spiritual benefit and may not cover a matter which has been specifically reserved by the supreme authority of the Church" (*Christus Dominus* 8). This particular statement is implemented by the motu proprio *De Episcoporum muneribus* of June 15, 1966 (ActApS 58 [1966] 467–472), which lists twenty specific cases reserved to the Holy See, none of which is related to having women share in the official preaching of the Church (IX, 1–20).

Current Developments. Many women today are discerning a call to a ministry of the Word for the spiritual good of the faithful. Women are preaching retreats, preaching on college campuses, as hospital chaplains, on evangelical teams, and preaching to the "unchurched" and in priestless areas. Most of these women have degrees in theology; some, a master of divinity degree. In some seminaries today, homiletics classes are equally divided between women and men. In December 1977, a Catholic woman, for the first time in its thirteen-year history, became a member of the Academy of Homiletics, a professional organization for teachers of homiletics. Women, in other words, have the necessary theological background requisite for preaching.

Aware of what this gift could mean for the vitality of the Church, there have been several resolutions made in the past few years to legitimate the ministry of the Word for women. In January 1973, at the General Synod of the Bishops of West Germany, a request to introduce participation by the laity in preaching was sent to the prefect of the Congregation for the Clergy and permission for a three-year experimentation period was granted with certain conditions maintained (cf. *Unless They Be Sent: A Theological Report on Dominican Women Preaching* [November, 1977] 10). The term "lay persons" used throughout the document included men and women. The Dominican Leadership Conference in their report on Dominican women preaching saw this as an important precedent and petitioned the National Council of Catholic Bishops (NCCB) to recommend officially "that canon 1342 be rewritten to include priests, deacons, and qualified women and men" (ibid. 11). They also urged the

NCCB to encourage local Ordinaries in the meantime to dispense from the prescription of c. 1342 and to open preaching to qualified women and men. At the 1976 annual convention of the Canon Law Society of America, Recommendation 4 stated: "Qualified lay women and men should be commissioned to preach the Word of God" ("Women and Church Law," *Jurist*, 37 [1977] 321). Again, at the Detroit Call to Action in October 1976, Resolution 1, paragraph 4a states: "In order to move toward this goal [bringing women to greater participation in the life and ministry of the Church], the NCCB should initiate or open the office of preaching to women."

What seems evident, then, is a movement of the Spirit to free the gift that women can bring to the ministry of the Word. This is being called forth and affirmed with the realization that somehow the ecclesial community is impoverished when denied the added dimension that woman brings to her reflection on God's Word. Although few today would venture to label definitively the way in which woman's preaching is different from man's, there are few who would deny that there is a difference. Woman breaks open the Word and proclaims how its power touches the human experience as she knows it, and she knows it as woman.

The Vatican report "Women's Role and Evangelization" acknowledges that ". . . . much remains to be done before the immense resources of women are fully used for the Kingdom of God" (Origins, 5 [1976] 707). Since the ministry of preaching, however, is linked to jurisdiction and not Orders, since Vatican II's thrust was of pastoral concern for the People of God, and since there seems to be very little canonical difficulty, the legitimating and commissioning of women to preach could soon become a reality.

See also PREACHING; WOMEN IN MINISTRY.

Bibliography: E. CARROLL, "Women in Ministry," ThSt 36 (1975) 680–687. Congregation for the Doctrine of the Faith, Pastoral Commission, "Women's Role and Evangelization," Origins 5 (1976) 702–707. H. CROTWELL, ed., *Women and the Word: Sermons* (Philadelphia 1978). D. GRASSO, *Proclaiming God's Message* (Notre Dame, Ind. 1965). E. A. HAENSIL, "Preaching," SacrMundi 5:81–88. PAUL VI, *De Episcoporum muneribus*, tr. *On the Power to Grant Dispensations* (USCC Publ. Office, Washington, D.C. 1966). J. REESE, *Preaching God's Burning Word* (Collegeville, Minn. 1975).

[J. DELAPLANE]

WOMEN IN CAMPUS MINISTRY

Campus ministry has become the presence of the Church in higher education and women have made a significant contribution to that presence and ministry. In campus ministry women are actually involved in the Church's formal ministry.

History. The year 1959 witnessed the arrival of the first women on the campus scene. Two School Sisters of St. Francis from Milwaukee were hired for the Newman Center at the University of Colorado at Boulder and two Sisters of St. Joseph of New Orleans joined the staff of the Catholic Student Center at Louisiana State University at Baton Rouge. These Sisters immediately joined the Newman Chaplains' Association, but were greeted with less than enthusiasm by the majority of those in the previously all-clerical association. There was a gradual willingness to include them in all business and matters directed to those who were considered chaplains. Final integration came at the meeting at Rutgers in 1968 when the chaplains voted to include the Sisters in the traditional cocktail hour. A more rapid integration took place at the University of Colorado at

Boulder where, by 1961, the Sisters were referred to as Pastoral Associates and by 1963 as Associate Pastors. An important date to mention was April 1968, when Sister Sheila Doherty, SND de Namur was elected to the Executive Committee of the National Newman Chaplains' Association, the first woman to hold such a position.

From the very beginning of the *Catholic Campus Ministry Association (CCMA), an outgrowth of the National Newman Chaplains' Association, women have had a major role in its leadership and development. In fact, in 1977 the Catholic Campus Ministry Association elected as its first woman president, Ms. Jennifer Konecny, Associate Chaplain at the University of Santa Clara and hired as its first Executive Director, Sister Margaret M. Ivers, IBVM. Sister Anne Kelley, OP received a Danforth Grant for the study of women in campus ministry and in the Fall of 1972 regional meetings were held across the country for the purpose of this study. There was agreement with the general aims of the study, i.e. the coming together for support, sharing, and solidarity; the development of some guidelines for such matters as preparation, selection, and placement; and the exploration of job descriptions and new models for women in ministry. Presently, CCMA has a working task force on women with subcommittees for the East Coast and the Midwest. Hence, the discussion and study of women in ministry will probably be an evolutionary process for many future days.

Women are involved in campus ministry for all denominations and now have an organization for mutual support. Campus Ministry Women is a national organization of Catholic, Protestant, and Jewish women, working full and part time, paid and volunteer, as program staff, secretaries, directors, office managers, professors, clergy, spouses, students, and board members in ministry to higher education. Any women active in the work of campus ministry can belong to the organization. Men are welcomed as associate members.

Significance. Largely because of the presence of women, campus ministry is an area where collegial and nonhierarchical models of ministry have developed, have been successful, and can be applied to other areas of church ministries. Women as valued resources is evidenced by the fact of the increased numbers becoming active in campus ministry over the last several years. They have been "legitimized" in recent years by appointments as diocesan directors of campus ministry, as directors of campus ministry in Catholic universities and colleges, and in other roles traditionally retained for priests. Women in campus ministry have made significant contributions in the pastoral areas of spiritual direction and counseling, prayer groups, and paraliturgical celebrations; they have exerted leadership in both education and programming. Some of the religious and lay women who pioneered in this one area of a "clergy world" endured many hardships and scaled many barriers in the early days. The fruits of their labors can be seen across the country where team ministry is a reality. Sisters, priests, and laity are working together as coequal partners, serving the People of God in the arena of higher education.

Campus ministry is to the Church as higher education is to culture—a cutting edge. Those involved in campus ministry and higher education have the additional responsibilities that leadership implies. Women with their fine feminine gifts of warmth, caring, and gentleness have greatly enhanced this ministry the Church provides for the university community.

[M. M. IVERS]

WOMEN IN MINISTRY

The topic, women in ministry, is in one sense new for the Church, while in another it is a reality which has existed for centuries. It is new because ministry is a term undergoing an evolution in usage in the Roman Catholic Church (*see* MINISTRY [ECCLESIOLOGY]).

Vatican II on Ministry. The documents of Vatican Council II witness to a narrow definition of "ministry" and "minister." They occur almost exclusively in the Decree on the Ministry and Life of Priests and in the Decree on Priestly Formation. The first states that the office of sacred ministers "... should be understood as any function which has been permanently assigned and is to be exercised for a spiritual purpose" (*Presbyterorum ordinis* 20; cf. *Optatam totius* 4). Episcopal, priestly, and diaconal offices clearly fit this definition; it has also been extended to include those of reader and acolyte. Lay men may be installed in these two ministries officially. Episcopal petitions to the effect that ministers of music and catechists might be similarly installed in lay ministries have been granted in Rome. On the level of official teaching ministry is linked, either intrinsically or derivatively, to priesthood and episcopacy, or in other words to the Sacrament of Order (*Presbyterorum ordinis* 7). The extension of ministry in this context pertains primarily to services rendered within a liturgical setting or in the area of religious education.

The term customarily used in the documents of Vatican II for other kinds of Christian service performed by laity and religious is "apostolate." The laity "... exercise their apostolate both in the Church and in the world, in both the spiritual and the temporal orders" (*Apostolicam actuositatem* 5; *see* APOSTOLATE OF THE LAITY [DECREE]). There are also a great number of clerical and lay institutes "devoted to various aspects of the apostolate" (*Perfectae caritatis* 8).

Generally, though not entirely, in these documents the setting of ministry is sacramental functions in the building up of the Church; the apostolate encompasses those Christian services that are an extension of the Church into the social, economic, and political spheres of contemporary life. So long as the distinction is maintained there is difficulty even in speaking of women in ministry, since women are categorically excluded from the sacramental ministry. Nonetheless a glimmer of change is evident in a few places in the conciliar documents. The Decree on Ecumenism alludes to the variety of "spiritual gifts and ministries" with which God has endowed the Church "in order to perfect the saints for a work of ministry, for building up the Body of Christ" (*Unitatis redintegratio* 2).

Ministries of Women. In this more comprehensive understanding it is clear that women have been performing ministry within the Church since its beginning.

Church History. Current research points out the number of women mentioned by Paul as cooperators in his work. The fact that a female diaconate existed in the Eastern Church and to a lesser extent in the Western Church in the first six centuries has been clearly established. The later multiplication of religious con-

gregations of women devoted to apostolic work is further evidence of women carrying out services of education, health care, and social work in response to needs. These women particularly, along with lay women who have been associated with them or who have independently engaged in such work, attest to a continuing *diakonia* of women within the Church, even though that term is not customarily used to designate their apostolic endeavors. Whatever the terminology, however, women in ministry has been a consistent hallmark of the Church.

A Broadening Concept. Since Vatican Council II the wider and more inclusive understanding of ministry has gained currency. This development stems in part from the emphasis on ecclesiology which has dominated this period among theologians and church leaders. In part, too, it is explained by the remarkable expansion of ministries in local-Church situations, a movement to which women have contributed immeasurably. With the acknowledgment that the Church's mission is shared by all its members, that in fact Christians are baptized into mission, that mission is the responsibility of the whole Church to effect reconciliation in the world, that the Gospel imperative of working for human development and social justice engages all Christians—there has come a new ecclesial preoccupation with the nature of ministry. The meaning has widened so that many understand it as Bishop P. Francis Murphy of Baltimore defines it: "Ministry is what we do, in the name of Jesus, to accomplish our mission."

Religious Women. The point is illustrated by religious congregations of women who once narrowly defined their apostolates as education, health care, and social service. Today women religious present a varied profile of women in ministry. They continue their work of education, with its many specializations, in parochial, diocesan, and congregation-owned schools and colleges; but they are also found as ministers in other private and state-owned institutions. They are in many such institutions formally designated campus ministers. They teach, too, in seminaries and divinity schools. They are experts and consultants in the many forms of special education in the private and public spheres. Their work in the health-related fields and in social service extends beyond administration and other forms of service in institutions under Catholic sponsorship. They assume major roles in diocesan offices as supervisors of schools in various capacities, coordinators of religious education, directors of liturgy and music, pastoral-ministry planners, vicars of religious, directors of communications, organizers of programs for the permanent diaconate, specialists in youth ministry and ministry to the elderly, canon lawyers in marriage tribunals and other work. In Canada a sister has been named chancellor of the Diocese of Nelson, British Columbia.

At the parochial level women religious assume comparable responsibilities and are found in many forms of pastoral ministry—in parishes, hospitals, private and secular universities, high-rise housing developments, hospitals, nursing homes, prisons, juvenile homes, homes for unwed mothers, residences for the elderly, homes for the mentally retarded. They have pioneered in new ministries such as political action, legal aid to the poor, alcoholism rehabilitation, community organization and development, work for responsibility in corporate investment, and other forms of advocacy for issues of social justice in urban and rural areas.

Women religious are found on preaching teams and mission bands (*see* WOMEN AND PREACHING), in spiritual direction and retreat work. They conduct *houses of prayer and reflection and engage in creative ministries in art, music, and literature. In Third World countries they administer parishes, baptize, witness marriages, and preside at funerals.

Lay Women. The ministry of women religious, because of their organization and visibility within the Church, is easier to document than that of lay women. Yet lay women are found carrying out all of these developing forms of ministry in increasing numbers. They work through national, diocesan, and parish structures, in institutions sponsored by women and men religious, and in other volunteer agencies and organizations associated with the Church. The growing number of young lay women pursuing seminary education for ministry is an index of a trend which cannot be fully assessed at the present time. There is, however, a new awareness of the need to tailor educational programs in colleges and seminaries to accommodate women who are searching for ways in which to respond to their sense of vocation to Christian ministry.

Ecclesiological Issues. The many trends evident as women engage in ministry have given rise to some fundamental questions pertinent to ecclesiology. They arise from women's experience and address some of the ambiguities present in the current teaching about the nature of ministry.

Divorce of Ministry and Sacraments. Many women in their service to others find themselves at the "threshold of sacramental ministry." In caring for the sick and elderly, in counseling and spiritual direction, in pastoral ministry generally, women experience frustration in their inability to be bearers of the Sacraments of the Sick and of Reconciliation. In ministries such as work with the mentally retarded, which require special training and communications skills, they come to question the competence of the unskilled to be celebrators of Eucharist. These and other experiences illustrate the problem, namely, that their ministry which ought to culminate in a sacramental completion is truncated. It is this kind of *experience* of women in ministry, multiplied in many ways, that leads them to seek ordination in order to be complete ministers of the Gospel.

The problem, however, is not a "woman's issue," as it is frequently called. It is rather a question of the relation between what is sometimes called evangelization and the celebration of the Sacraments. It is the same problem to which the American bishops alluded in their document *The Ministerial Priesthood* (1972), which urged priests to maintain the mutual relationship between evangelization and celebration of the Sacraments. They stated, "A separation between the two would divide the heart of the Church to the point of imperilling the faith, and the priest, who is dedicated to the service of unity in the community, would be gravely distorting his ministry" (Part II, 1.b).

If ministry divorced from the celebration of Sacraments can "divide the heart of the Church," then the potential for such division in the growing diversification of ministries among women today is great. The division is not merely theoretical. Women know it deeply as they minister to others and their experience calls the whole Church to examine ministry as all the People of God are called upon to exercise it in the Church's mission of reconciliation within the world.

Mission and Ministry of the Laity. New movements in the ministry of women today give rise to questions about the involvement of the laity in ministry. The issue is complicated by the fact that women religious are not laity in the strict sense, nor are they clerics, a confusion present even in the documents of Vatican II. Women religious nonetheless have a readier entrée into ministry because of their unique status within the Church.

While official teaching suggests that the ministry of the Church is carried out under its mandate and through its recognized channels, women religious are developing work through avenues that have no clear affiliation with the Church in many of the instances cited above. Those whom they serve are people in need who may or may not be members of the Church. In all of these areas they speak of their work as ministry, especially out of a consciousness that the Church has a mission beyond itself, to the world. This growing consciousness is shared and acted upon also by many priests and lay people. As a result distinctions between ministry and apostolate are breaking down.

While women religious can extend their credibility as ministers into the secular sphere, this same possibility seems not so clear for lay women who may be performing the same service. While lay people are called to ". . . seek the kingdom of God by engaging in secular affairs and by ordering them according to the plan of God" (*Lumen gentium* 31), the degree to which their activities in this respect may be called ministry in any authorized sense is unclear. The remarkable work of such a woman as Dorothy Day is a case in point. Hers is an extraordinary witness of a woman serving the poor from a sense of Christian vocation and responsibility. The Gospel is its own authentication for such work. But to what extent it is not the "ministry of the Church" is a question for clarification in the Church's teaching.

Conclusion. History records the foundation of religious congregations by lay women, such as Angela Merici in Italy and Elizabeth Seton in the United States, who were inspired to organize groups of women for ministries of mercy in the face of human needs evident in their times. Though they may not have felt constrained, they still knew that to serve in the name of the Church required that they seek canonical approbation as an apostolic religious institute. Implicit in this longstanding requirement is the association of celibacy with ministry. Questioning the necessity of this association is one of the by-products of women's increased participation in ministry today. Lay women, as they experience the freedoms of contemporary life, aspire to recognition of their readiness and capacity for ministry in the Church. They view women religious as privileged in this respect. They appeal to them for the "bonding of women" to address the issues related to ministry that need reexamination for the sake of a more functional church discipline.

Women in ministry is therefore a long-standing reality of the Church which is taking on new dimensions. As it does it poses some questions for the continued renewal of the Church and exploration into the nature of ministry, which has been acknowledged by the American bishops as the gravest question confronting the Church today.

Bibliography: E. CARROLL, "Women and Ministry," ThSt 36 (1975) 660–687. N. FOLEY, "Women Religious, Diaconal Communities," Origins 5 (1975) 180–187. K. GILFEATHER, "Women and Ministry," *America* 135 (Oct. 2, 1976) 191–194. R. GRYSON, *The Ministry of Women in the Early Church*, tr. J. LAPORTE and M. L. HALL (Collegeville, Minn. 1976). H. LEGRAND, "Ministries: Main Lines of Research in Catholic Theology," Pro Mundi Vita *Bulletin* 50 (1974) 7. P. F. MURPHY, "Women in Ministry. The Future Based on the Present, New Experiences," Origins 7 (1977) 267–272. G. WOOD, "The Church as Ministering Community," Liturgy 22 (1977) 7–12.

[N. FOLEY]

WOMEN IN SOCIETY

Because the status of women is multidimensional and ongoing changes follow uneven and different paths, its assessment is necessarily complex. The complexity of the assessment of the status of women is further confounded by the nature of the American society, its heterogeneity, and its increasing tolerance of very different life styles, value sets, and options. The *women's liberation movement and ideology have considerably lessened the universality and validity of sex-role stereotypes so as to open up many new options for women and men. At the same time, however, many women and men feel less constrained and more comfortable to venture into previously "sex-inappropriate" options; others feel anxious and uncomfortable with the fact that their lives are not "set"; instead they can (and must) choose from among several alternatives. The malaise explains why well-educated women join groups that help them delimit their options such as the Krishna religious sect, which legitimizes the return to strict sex-role stereotypes.

The issues of equal educational and employment opportunities also create in women anticipation that, once such rights are granted, they must perform at levels comparable to those achieved by men. In fact lingering informal sex-discriminatory practices still require women to be many times more competent and high-achieving than men before they can enter prestige and well-paying "masculine" occupations or before they can occupy high-level, powerful positions (Safilios-Rothschild 1974; 1978). Such unequal requirements place a great burden on women. But even standing on their own feet is a new experience and carries considerable responsibility for many women and achievement within the present climate of harsh competition for a few positions is highly anxiety-provoking. Within this climate of anxiety and insecurity, partly created by continuing sex discrimination and partly by such social structural-factors as high unemployment rates, some women retreat and find "The Total Women" and "The Fascinating Womanhood" strategies quite attractive. For they still perceive less struggle and anxiety, and fewer pitfalls in investing their energies in a successful man than in their own status achievements.

Overall, it can be said that much of the overt, institutional sex discrimination has been eliminated. Very often, however, sex discrimination still persists but has gone "underground" and is manifested only in informal, more or less subtle strategies and techniques (Safilios-Rothschild, "Sex Discrimination").

Women's Marital and Familial Options. Over the last decade some important changes have taken place in women's range of marital and familial options. The single state for the first time is becoming socially acceptable for women. In 1976, 42.6 per cent of women 20–24 years of age were single, mainly because they postponed marriage (*1977 Statistical Abstract* and Stein). Furthermore, 45.3 per cent of all women below 35 were single in 1976, mainly because long or permanent singlehood is increasingly chosen after divorce, an option more often taken by divorced women with 5 or more years of education (Glick). While there are significant structural factors which limit the number of eligible men, these women seem to also prefer and opt for singlehood (Safilios-Rothschild, *Love*).

As the number of married working women who can support themselves grows, divorce initiated by women is an increasing option and leads to a significant increase of female-headed households, which now number one out of every eight families. Over the past 15 years, the number of divorced women heading families tripled, especially among white women, while the number of single (never married) women doubled, mainly among black women (McEaddy).

Married women increasingly come to view parenthood as well as the number of children to bear as options, although childlessness has not been an entirely acceptable choice for women who have completed the childbearing phase (*Current Population Reports*). Women do bear fewer children in the 70s than they did in the 60s, since the average number of children per couple is now two instead of the earlier three children (ibid.) and it has become somewhat more socially acceptable to have only one child (ibid.).

With regard to married woman's status in the family in terms of family power and division of labor, it is difficult to generalize, because there is a great variety by social class, working status of the woman, her level of income, the husband's sex-role attitudes and values, and the extent to which the woman negotiates for more equality. What is a definite change is the degree of legitimacy attached to such negotiations initiated by wives.

Women and Education. While it cannot be claimed that sex discrimination has been eliminated from the educational sector or that women have equal access, a number of significant gains have been made. At the elementary and high school level, Title IX in Education is a milestone; it prohibits schools from discriminating against students on the basis of sex in admissions, course entrance (including physical and vocational education), student rules and regulations, student services and benefits, financial aid, policies regarding marital and parental status, counseling and guidance, competitive sports, and employment (Sadner). To the extent that Title IX is widely implemented, the most important implications for women are: (1) preparation for trades now stereotyped as "masculine"; (2) increasing enrollment in math and science courses and, through special programs, assistance and encouragement to do well, so that the way will be opened for a variety of educational and occupational options now stereotyped as "masculine"; (3) increased awareness of available educational and occupational choices; and (4) the establishment of friendships between boys and girls through coeducational competitive athletics. The effects of many of these recent changes will not, however, become apparent until the early 1980s.

Some important changes have already taken place at the college level. In 1977, 49 per cent of all students enrolled in colleges were women, as compared to 40 per cent in 1967. Thus, women account for 93 per cent of the 1977 college-enrollment growth. This growth has taken place despite the fact that the earning potential of a woman's college education is still quite low, namely $980 extra yearly earnings for the college-educated woman as compared to $2,950 for the college-educated man (Magarell). Structural and informal sex discrimination still is operating so as to reduce the earning potential of even well-educated women.

With regard to fields of work choices have been broadened. In 1974–75, 54.4 per cent of the women graduating from college received their bachelor's degree in female-dominated fields, while the other nearly one half ranged from fields with an almost equal percentage of men and women to those dominated by males. The trends were particularly interesting in such fields as mathematics (in which 42 per cent of the graduates were women), biology (33 per cent), pharmacy (27 per cent women), chemistry (22 per cent), economics, geology, and business-management (16–17 per cent women in each) (HEW, *Earned Degrees*).

At the graduate-school level, the picture is less bright. Even in 1974, the attrition of women graduates beyond the first year was high. From 45.8 per cent of all graduate students, after the first year women dropped to 35 per cent (HEW, *Students*), most probably because a number of negative, discriminatory processes are in operation which "freeze women out" of graduate school. Available research studies list: lack of interest and sponsorship by a professor; less access to financial aid (particularly research assistantships); psychological harassment and intimidation (Solmon; Robin; Wiley and Sells). Some fields which are relatively open to women at the undergraduate level such as chemistry and business-management, do not seem to be open at the graduate level (HEW, *Earned Degrees*). Despite considerable sex discrimination at that level, the percentage of women receiving PhDs has increased from 14.3 in 1970–71 to 21.3 in 1974–75 (ibid.). With regard, finally, to the prestigious professional schools, some gains have been made in medicine, law, and veterinary medicine, while dentistry together with engineering remain the fields most inhospitable for women (HEW, *Students Enrolled*).

Women's Employment and Occupational Options. The option to work has definitely become socially acceptable for women and increasingly more married women not only can but are expected to work. In 1977, 48.5 per cent of all women 16 years old and over were in the labor force, while 37.7 per cent of all women 16 years old and over were in the labor force in 1960 (Labor Statistics). Beyond the considerable increase in the percentage of women working, what represents an even more important change is the normalization of working women with respect to age, marital and family status, race, and education. The working woman is no longer the atypical, nonaverage woman. She is married, has children, even young ones, and she has a husband who is not necessarily unemployed or at the lowest income bracket. In 1975, 58 per cent of the women in the labor force were married and living with their husbands (while only 31.5 per cent were in this category in December 1959) and in 1977, 37.4 per cent of married women with children under age six were in the labor force as compared to 18.6 per cent in 1960 (Blau). Despite, however, this normalization of work for American women, the earning gap between men and women has

not diminished; it has, on the contrary, widened, especially for some categories of workers (*Current Population Reports*; Labor, Women's Bureau). While the status of women has improved to some extent and in some areas more than others, women are still a long way from equality.

Bibliography: F. D. BLAU, "The Data on Women Workers, Past, Present, and Future," in A. H. STROMBERG and S. HARKESS, eds., *Women Working* (Palo Alto, Cal. 1978) 29–62. *Current Population Reports*, Series P-60, n. 90 (Washington, D.C. 1973). P. C. GLICK, "A Demographer Looks at American Families," *Journal of Marriage and the Family* 31 (1975) 15–26. B. J. MCEADDY, "Women Who Head Families: A Socioeconomic Analysis," *Monthly Labor Review* (June 1976) 3–9. J. MAGARRELL, "Women Account for 93 per cent of Enrollment Gain," *Chronicle of Higher Education* 15, n. 17 (Jan. 1978) 1. HEW (U.S. Dept. of Health, Education and Welfare, National Center for Education Statistics), *Earned Degrees Conferred: 1974–75*, Table 113; *Students Enrolled for Advanced Degrees* (1967–68 through 1974–75). Labor Statistics (U.S. Dept. of Labor Statistics), "Employment and Earnings, January, 1977," (Washington, D.C. 1977); Labor, Women's Bureau (U.S. Dept. of Labor, Women's Bureau: Employment and Standards Administration), *1975 Handbook on Women Workers* (Washington, D.C. 1975) 126–182. S. ROBIN, "The Female in Engineering," in R. PERRUCI and J. E. GERSTL, eds., *The Engineers and the Social System* (New York 1969) 203–218. M. SADNER, *A Student Guide to Title IX* (National Foundation for the Improvement of Education, Washington, D.C. 1977). C. SAFILIOS-ROTHSCHILD, *Women and Social Policy* (Englewood Cliffs, N.J. 1974); *Love, Sex, and Sex Roles* (Englewood Cliffs, N.J. 1977) 103–104; "Sex Discrimination: Theory and Research," in Foundation for the Study of Plural Societies, ed., *Gross-National Survey of Minority Problems* v. 5 (The Hague 1977); "Women and Work: Policy Implications and Prospects for the Future," in A. H. STROMBERG and S. HARKESS, eds., *Women Working* (Palo Alto, Cal. 1978) 419–432. L. W. SELLS, "Sex Differences in Graduate School Survival," paper, American Sociological Association meetings, New York, Aug. 28, 1973. L. SOLMON, "Do Women Graduate Students Get a Raw Deal?" paper, Public Choice Society, March 21, 1974. *1977 Statistical Abstract of the United States* (Washington, D.C. 1977). P. J. STEIN, "Singlehood: An Alternative to Marriage," *The Family Coordinator* 24, n. 4 (1975) 489–503.

[C. SAFILIOS-ROTHSCHILD]

WOMEN IN THE CHURCH

From a variety of viewpoints women in the Church today are asking questions about themselves which are opening up ecclesial issues related not only to women but to all persons in the Church. As women in the spirit of contemporary liberation movements seek a greater participation in social, economic, and political life, they are led to consider their estate within the Church, especially as they internalize the liberating message of the Gospel.

The Contemporary Church Experience of Women. The influence of the human-potential movement has awakened women, as well as men, to the values inherent in human personhood and in interpersonal relationships. As individuals come to appreciate themselves and their personal gifts more fully, they look for ways in which to utilize their gifts in service. Those who reflect upon the Gospel and the Christian imperative of discipleship in service to others, look to the Church as the channel for realizing their aspirations. Women who do often meet obstacles that surprise them; they encounter ideas and attitudes in conflict with their own developing self-concepts.

Liturgical Ministries. In local parishes with greater frequency than in the past young girls are asking to serve as acolytes. Parents, who are often not proponents of women's liberation, find themselves at a loss to explain to their young daughters why this role is not open to them. Parent groups who bring the question to public discussion meet with differing responses. In a number of situations girls are quietly admitted to the ranks of the parish acolytes; in other places the option remains closed on the grounds that service at the altar is the prerogative of males.

On the adult level the problem is compounded. In many parishes women are readily included as readers and extraordinary ministers of the Eucharist. In other places, usually because of the decree of the pastor or the regulation of the bishop, women are not permitted to serve in these capacities. The issue in this case received publicity in the public press when in 1972 the apostolic letter *Ministeria quaedam* restored the offices of acolyte and reader to the laity with the careful provision that formal commissioning of persons for these offices is reserved to men (Paul VI MinQuaedam VII). This stipulation is in evident conflict with the declared reason for the revision in church discipline. The document had cited as its purpose: to involve *all the faithful* in more active participation in the liturgy because *the Christian people* are a royal priesthood "*by reason of their baptism*" (ibid., quoting *Sacrosanctum Concilium* 14). Women found cause for wonder about the effects of Baptism in them.

The Diaconate. Similar questions arise in relation to the permanent diaconate. Diocesan programs for the preparation of permanent deacons have been developed since the 1967 motu proprio *Sacrum diaconatus ordinem* (ActApS 59 [1967] 697–704) following Vatican Council II. Women are directors of and teachers in permanent diaconate programs. In a number of dioceses women have applied for admission to these training programs but have been excluded. More recently some women have been admitted to the diocesan programs as candidates, although they have no assurance that they will be ordained as permanent deacons along with their male counterparts (*see* DIACONATE FOR WOMEN). One of the regulations governing permanent deacons raises another type of question about women. The current discipline dictates that should the wife of a permanent deacon die, he may not remarry. A prescription of this kind seems to disparage by implication both women and marriage in relation to ministry.

Issues of Morality. Questions of quite a different kind arise in the area of the Church's moral teaching. The official church position on birth control touches the lives of women uniquely. Studies, such as those summarized by Andrew Greeley in *The American Catholic*, show the gradual increase in women's departure from the position taken by *Humanae vitae* on artificial birth control. The evidence points to the fact that women are making their own judgments on the morality of using various means of artificial birth control. An unwillingness to accept moral direction from men in an area so intimate to the lives of women is advanced as the reason by some.

On the issue of abortion many women, along with numbers of men, have joined the Right-to-Life Movement across the U.S. and are active in pressuring the agencies of government to reverse the pro-abortion decision of the United States Supreme Court. Yet a significant number of other women who support the Church's teaching on abortion find themselves poorly served by the Church in instances of problem pregnancies. They find the Church's moral stance on the issue deficient in the practical circumstances of their lives.

Revisions of Law and Liturgy. Questions arise too about the Church's exclusion of women from deliberative processes whose outcomes affect them directly. A case in point is the current international project for the redrafting of Canon Law (*see* CODE OF CANON LAW, REVISION OF). Women religious, governed by Canon Law for religious institutes, and married women, subject to the canons regulating marriage, question the fact that exclusively male commissions are engaged in the process of preparing the schemata for the revision.

A particularly pervasive problem to which women are developing a growing sensitivity is that of sexist language in liturgical and doctrinal texts. In liturgical celebration the consistent use of allusions to "fathers," "sons," and "brothers" tends to attribute even to generic terms and pronouns a male connotation. On this account the Eucharistic Liturgy becomes for some women not a source of community-building but an exercise in alienation.

Sacramental Ministry. As women engage in ministry today they come to question their exclusion from sacramental ministry. Their work with people in pastoral settings often finds them receiving the anguished disclosures of people's pain and sin. Out of the desire to be the bearers of the Lord's reconciliation they ask themselves why it is that they are not acceptable candidates for ordination. This question came into the public forum in the national conference "Women in Future Priesthood Now: A *Call for Action" held in Detroit, Michigan in November 1975. Of the 837 women at that gathering who responded to a questionnaire, 289 expressed a desire for ordination to priesthood. In the face of the official Church's insistence that no one has a right to ordination, they and others ask rather for recognition that they have a right to have their sense of vocation to ordained ministry tested.

The importance of experience as a starting point for theological reflection is recognized today in the various forms of *liberation theology. Women theologians who engage in the theological enterprise from the base of their own experience find themselves in conflict with the prevailing doctrine on women.

Church Doctrine on Women. The earlier article of women in the *New Catholic Encyclopedia* (14:998) points out that church doctrine on women, long a disorganized mass of ideas, was synthesized in the writings and allocutions of Pope Pius XII. His teaching accentuates the equality of women with men on the one hand and the critical difference between them on the other. Women are viewed primarily as having a unique nature, dignity, and destiny, stemming from the essential vocation to motherhood. Because of it, the operative index in assessing the respective relations of men and women is *complementarity*.

Recognition of Women's Rights. The period from the time of Pius XII to the present, including the years of Vatican Council II, has been one of rapid development in the movement toward women's liberation. This movement is often addressed in terms of the evident change in the social, economic, and political roles of women as they take more prominent positions in secular affairs. In *Pacem in terris* Pope John XXIII cited women's growing participation in public life as one of the three significant characteristics of the times calling for a response from the Church. Pope John noted that the phenomenon of changing roles for women stemmed from their growing consciousness of human dignity (John XXIII PacTerr 41). He saw the ascendancy of the working classes, the emergence of new independent nations from situations of colonialism, and the change in the *socialization of women as evidence of the desire of many human beings to change the inferiority/superiority relations that have controlled their lives for centuries.

As church documents have continued to speak of women from the time of Pope John to the present certain themes are consistent: (1) the roles of women in society are changing; (2) the Church promotes the recognition of the civil rights of women as full equals of men; (3) new social roles for women must be consistent with the special prerogatives of women rooted in their childbearing function; (4) women should also play a more active part in the Church according to their proper nature and complementary relation to men.

In 1971 in his apostolic letter "A Call to Action" Paul VI addressed the injustice of discrimination against women and spoke approvingly of national charters for women to establish relationships of equality in rights and of respect for the dignity of women (Paul VI OctogAdven 13). In 1974 the Holy Father in an address to the Italian Catholic jurists, "Role of Women in Contemporary Society," listed the essentials which must be achieved for women in a renewed society: (1) the recognition of the civil rights of women as full equals of men; (2) laws that will enable women to fulfill the same professional, social, and political roles as men, according to their individual capacities; (3) acknowledgment, respect, and protection of the special prerogatives of women in marriage, family, education, and society; (4) the maintenance and defense of the dignity of unmarried women, wives, and widows, especially when, due to death or incapacity, they are deprived of the assistance of husbands (see Paul VI, 1974, 314).

Interpretation of Women's Role. These concerns for the social well-being of women are conditioned in church statements by expressions of care that the essential role of the woman as childbearer and mother be safeguarded. In "The Right to Be Born" Pope Paul wrote, "Women's authentic liberation does not consist in a formalistic or materialistic equality with the other sex, but in recognizing what the female personality has that is essentially specific to it: woman's vocation to be a mother" (see Paul VI, 1973, 335).

Reference to woman's proper role, her special nature, her complementary relation to man is a consistent thread running through church pronouncements on women with the assertion that the reality is rooted in the divine order of creation. The Congregation for the Evangelization of Peoples', "The Role of Women in Evangelization" (Oct. 19, 1975), states, "In noting that God created human beings male and female, Genesis, at the beginning of the sacred text, indicates briefly but clearly the complementary nature of the two sexes; that is to say, their likeness, difference and convergence in every human enterprise, including therefore evangelization" (see Congregation for the Evangelization of Peoples, 1976).

Complementarity of the sexes is seemingly carried to its ultimate in the *Declaration on the Question of the Admission of Women to the Ministerial Priesthood* (ActApS 69 [1972] 98–116). Referring to "symbols printed upon the human psychology," the Declaration affirms the inability of women to symbolize Christ in presiding at the Eucharist. "The same natural resemblance is required for persons as for things: when Christ's role in the Eucharist is to be expressed sacramentally, there would not be this 'natural resemblance' which must exist between Christ and the minister if the role of Christ were not taken by a man: in such a case it would be difficult to see in the minister the image of Christ. For Christ was and remains a man" (5).

Doctrinal Difficulties. The evident problems with this traditional approach to a doctrine of women are being raised in a growing body of literature.

Biblical Issues. First, the biblical interpretation based upon Genesis is simplistic in assuming that the creation accounts decree fixed roles for men and for women. The report of the Pontifical Biblical Commission on the ordination of women (see bibliog.) states that in Genesis 1 man and woman are called together to be the image of God on equal terms and in a community of life; and that in Genesis 2 they are placed on equal terms whereby in a community of love they become "the two of them one body." A number of biblical scholars today see the partnership or community aspect of the creation of humankind as the bearer of God's image rather than the human nature differentiated as male and female. Despite ecclesiastical insistence upon the complementarity of the female, the interpretation often suggests that the role of women is subordinate and auxiliary to man. It is only one step further to the implication that woman is an inferior or derivative person and that only in man is the image of God complete. The Declaration on women and ministerial priesthood seems to make such an interpretation explicit.

Philosophical Issues. The philosophical background of church teaching on women in the Scholastic treatment of natures as revealed and distinguished through specific or proper activities. Childbearing in this context, as it is apparently interpreted, becomes the specific function of woman and accordingly is revelatory of a proper nature. All other activities of women are interpreted as conditioned by this one biological function. The qualities of sensitivity, patience, endurance, devotion, fidelity, etc. attributed to woman are viewed as proceeding from the proper feminine nature and intrinsically connected to the role of motherhood. Individual women may in fact never have borne children but even when that capacity is dormant the nurturing qualities are regarded as uniquely theirs to be expressed maternally in whatever social, economic, or political roles they may fill.

Stress in this way upon the proper nature of woman suggests that there are two human natures rather than one. Yet classically in Scholastic thought there is one human nature shared by both men and women whose specific and identifying activities are those associated with rationality. Intelligence and will in humans distinguish them from other animals and allow them to bring under control the so-called lower appetites which they share with other animals. These would include sexuality both male and female. In the view of the Church, however, the function of woman in procreation seems to take precedence over rationality in identifying her. Whatever qualities of personhood woman may have are irreducibly linked to her role as mother. To the extent also that custom long associated woman with passivity in procreation, a less-active intellectual ability was attributed to her. By inference the presumed superior exercise of reason in man is associated with male sexuality.

The Sexism of Idealization. In addition to the scholastic approach to sexual differences the tradition of the Church inherits the ancient Semitic notions of the woman as evil, as temptress and seductress. Ideas about her contaminating influence stem from the blood tabus observed in the cultures of the ancient Near East. Because of the presumed natural propensities of women toward degradation the Church has honored the states of consecrated virginity and marriage as redemptive and protective of them. Mary, virgin and mother, epitomizes the ideal for women in these respects. In her all women are offered an example of the exaltation possible to them.

Pope Paul in "The Role of Women in Contemporary Society" spoke of this: "As We see her, Woman is a reflection of transcendent beauty, a symbol of limitless goodness, a mirror of the ideal human being as God conceived it in his own image and likeness. As We see her, Woman is a vision of virginal purity that revitalizes the highest affective and moral sentiments of the human heart. As We see her, she is, for man in his loneliness, the companion whose life is one of unreserved loving dedication, resourceful collaboration and help, courageous fidelity and toil, and habitual heroic sacrifice. As We see her, she is the Mother—let us bow in reverence before her—the mysterious wellspring of life, through whom nature still receives the breath of God, creator of the immortal soul.... As We see her, she symbolizes mankind itself" (see Paul VI, 1974, 316).

Women today reject this kind of laudatory description as in itself demeaning. They experience themselves as persons, neither evil nor divine, with very human capabilities and with ordinary inclinations to sin and virtue. They ask to be viewed as individuals with unique complements of gifts that are not to be stereotyped. Men are similarly not served by exalted descriptions of women. When all the finest qualities of human personhood are attributed to women the humanness of men becomes enigmatic. They become victims of a peculiar kind of oppression by implication and may readily ask about their own identity in the context of church teaching.

In all the authoritative allusions to women they are treated as a class without distinction. Such statements as "the Church owes women a debt of gratitude" and "the Church cannot thank women enough," which have appeared in official texts, reinforce the notion that women as an undifferentiated class of persons are perceived as marginal in a Church which is normatively male. The breach between the experience of women today and the prevailing church doctrine on women shows clearly the need for a new exploration into theological anthropology, utilizing the insights and conclusions from contemporary biblical scholarship and the human sciences. Incarnational theology requires it, as does a Church which preaches that Gospel wherein all are called to the freedom of the children of God.

Current Developments. While the importance of the theological project awaits recognition by those who are charged with the magisterium, a number of current developments show promise. In the face of growing agitation on the question of the ordination of women, Archbishop Joseph L. Bernardin, speaking as president of the National Conference of Catholic Bishops (Oct. 3, 1975), affirmed that women are called today to a greater leadership role in the Church. He stated that "their contributions are needed in the decision-making process at the parochial, diocesan, national, and universal levels."

In November 1977 Bishop Michael McAuliffe, chairman of the *Bishops' Committee on Women in Society and the Church, issued a summary of what his committee had gathered through a survey on the decision-making roles held by women in diocesan structures. Described as informal, the survey drew its conclusions from responses received from 100 dioceses. Though limited in scope, the study showed that both women religious and lay women are present in representative number in diocesan, educational, and social-services offices. Fewer women are involved in such areas as planning and finances, communications, marriage tribunals, liturgy and music, seminary training, and in such offices as vicars for religious (*see* NATIONAL CONFERENCE OF VICARS FOR RELIGIOUS). The report was tentative in tone and carried no recommendation for further action.

At the *Call for Action conference, sponsored by the NCCB in observance for the American bicentennial, Oct. 21–23, 1976 in Detroit, the delegates passed a series of recommendations on women in the Church. These are appropriately found within the section on Justice in the Church. They address a range of issues: promotion of the full participation of women in the life and mission of the Church; development of an informed position on the ordination of women; affirmative action by local Ordinaries to insure representation of women in diocesan and local decision-making bodies; equal access of women to professional and theological education and training; elimination of sexist language in liturgical and other church publications; full participation of women in roles of leadership, service, and authority in the Church; elimination of sexual discrimination in liturgical roles, including that of acolyte.

In October 1976, as well, the Canon Law Society of America sponsored a symposium on women. It adopted the consensus statement that resulted from that conference and committed itself to further studies of the *jus divinum*; of the relation between theory and practice as they pertain to law and ministries in the Church; of the juridical effects of charisms among the baptized; of new and contradictory developments in the Church on the relation between the power of Orders and of jurisdiction.

In January 1976 the *International Commission on English in the Liturgy passed a resolution to begin the project of reediting the official liturgical texts to eliminate discriminatory language. It set up a subcommittee to work in conjunction with its advisory committee to achieve this end.

A number of American Catholic bishops have issued pastoral letters on women. Among them are Bishop Charles A. Buswell of Pueblo, Col.; Bishop Carroll Dozier of Memphis, Tenn.; Bishop Leo Maher of San Diego, Cal.; Bishop Thomas McDonough of Louisville, Ky.; Archbishop William Borders and Auxiliary Bishop P. Francis Murphy of Baltimore, Maryland.

Women in the Church is a critical question of historical moment in the Church in 1979. It has demonstrated its potential for opening basic questions of ecclesiology and for bringing the Church to new self-awareness and relevance. Its central issue is Church, not women. It will be resolved when women are fully and completely members of the Church and when articles on women in the Church are archaisms.

See also WOMEN IN MINISTRY.

Bibliography: J. CHITTISTER, "'Brotherly Love' in Today's Church," *America* 136 (March 19, 1977) 233–236. Congregation for the Doctrine of the Faith, *Declaration on the Question of the Admission of Women to the Ministerial Priesthood*, Origins 6 (1977) 517–524. Congregation for the Evangelization of Peoples, Pastoral Commission, "The Role of Women in Evangelization," Origins 5 (1976) 702–707. N. FOLEY, "Woman in Vatican Documents, 1960 to the Present," *Sexism and Church Law* (New York 1977) 82–108. A. M. GARDINER, ed., *Women and Catholic Priesthood: An Expanded Vision* (New York 1976). A. GREELEY, *The American Catholic* (New York 1977). P. S. KEANE, *Sexual Morality* (New York 1977). E. J. KILMARTIN, "Full Participation of Women in the Life of the Church," *Sexism and Church Law* (New York 1977) 109–133. Leadership Conference of Women Religious, *New Visions, New Roles: Women in the Church* (Washington, D.C. 1975); *The Status and Roles of Women: Another Perspective* (Washington, D.C. 1976). M. MCAULIFFE, "The Positions Women Now Hold in the Church," Origins 7 (1977) 381–384. C. MILLER and K. SWIFT, *Words and Women* (Garden City, N.Y. 1976). M. A. O'NEILL, "Toward a Renewed Anthropology," ThSt 36 (1975) 725–736. PAUL VI, "The Right to Be Born," *The Pope Speaks* 17 (1973) 333–335; "The Role of Women in Contemporary Society," *The Pope Speaks* 19 (1974) 314–318; "The role of Women in Church and Society: Disciples and Co-Workers," Origins 4 (1975) 718–719. Pontifical Biblical Commission, "Can Women Be Priests?" Origins 6 (1976) 92–96. R. R. RUETHER, *New Woman New Earth* (New York 1975); ed., *Religion and Sexism* (New York 1974). L. M. RUSSELL, "Theological Aspects of Women and in Christian Communities," *Bulletin International: Femmes et hommes dans l'Église* 17 (April, 1976) 4–9. L. and A. SWIDLER, eds., *Women Priests. A Catholic Commentary on the Vatican Declaration* (New York 1977).

[N. FOLEY]

WOMEN IN THE MINISTRY OF JUSTICE

The ministry of justice springs from the Gospel record of Jesus' love command: "Love one another as I have loved you." It depends upon the realization that poverty and human misery are not merely an affliction of unfortunate individuals but frequently result from deep-rooted, unjust political and economic systems.

Through the centuries women have responded in personal and institutional ways to the immediate evidences of wretchedness. Catholic laywomen in the United States organized innumerable groups, such as the Ladies of Charity and the charitable outreach of the National Council of Catholic Women. Women religious staffed schools for the poor and provided for needy persons in hospitals and social services. In these ways the charitable undertakings of women proclaimed a Christlike concern to heal and enable, but did not actively question the established order of Church, economy, and state.

In the 1960s and 70s several factors served to broaden women's focus in living the love command—from almsgiving to justice. Through participation in the antiwar movement of the Viet Nam era and the Civil Rights Movement, women came to perceive the need for their own Women's Liberation Movement—thus becoming sensitized to the systemic nature of the ills being protested. Experience indicated that the gap between rich and poor both within and among countries was growing; that power inhered in structures rooted in the evils of racism, sexism, militarism; that the rights of profit and power ranked above each human being's right to have basic needs satisfied. Social teachings of recent popes, Vatican Council II, and the 1971 Synod of Bishops' *Justice in the World*, in analyzing such issues, aroused a strong, experientially-based response from women in the Church, especially women religious.

Vatican-II mandated renewal of religious life had involved women religious in a struggle for freedom to establish their own identity, define their mission, and impact the world. Their official national organization, the *Leadership Conference of Women Religious (LCWR), as well as groups like the *National Assembly of Women Religious (NAWR), *National Black Sisters Conference (NBSC), *National Coalition of American Nuns (NCAN), and *Las Hermanas, served as catalysts to involve and motivate congregations toward deeper involvement in justice issues. A conceptual framework for justice-related action, the *Quest for Justice* (1972) was published by the *Center of Concern of Washington. These initiatives, along with the further impetus given by Paul VI's apostolic letter "Call to Action" (1971), led a small group of sisters to establish *Network, a nationwide lobbying organization, based in Washington, D.C., to research and promote legislative issues affecting justice. Meanwhile a new spirituality fostered the integration of working for justice with a deep prayer life. Ministries—on parish, diocesan, neighborhood, or state levels—brought women into immediate contact with the problems of poor and marginated people and caused them to develop roles of advocacy, community organization, and enablement. For these women the *Catholic Committee on Urban Ministry, established primarily to facilitate the work of priests, offered a convenient forum for comparing experience and for bonding. Justice and Peace Centers, often on the initiative of women religious, but drawing together men and women, lay and religious, animated justice work in many cities and drew together in a loose national network called Convergence of Justice and Peace Centers.

Convictions about personal dignity, participation in decision making, and the theological imperatives of the Gospel served to draw women's attention to the injustice of their own position within the Church. A group of lay and religious women organized a national conference on Women in Future Priesthood Now, which proved so successful that it grew into the *Women's Ordination Conference, a national core group working for the promotion of women to priestly ordination within a renewed ministry.

When the bishops of the U.S. proposed to celebrate the country's bicentennial with parish, diocesan, and regional, processes and a national conference soliciting widespread witnessing to injustices, it was the women, especially the women religious, who most strongly supported it. As a consequence women participated as equals in the *Call to Action national conference (1976), and helped to recommend to the bishops a broad array of justice issues, including those of justice to women in society and Church. Women's commitment to the ministry of justice has effectively changed the women involved and has presented a serious challenge to the Church to be credible in its espousal of justice.

[E. CARROLL]

WOMEN'S LIBERATION MOVEMENT

Feminism and the struggle for full equality and participation of women in society and Church are not new to the late 20th century. Since the mid-1960s, however, the phenomenon labelled "women's liberation movement" appears to have acquired new momentum and a clear self-definition. The movement is not confined to any single part of the world; according to

Juliet Mitchell (*Woman's Estate*), there exists an identifiable women's movement in all but a handful of nations.

Aims and Themes. The aims of the women's movement are multiple. In poorer countries emphasis falls on such basic ends as eradicating female illiteracy, prolonging life expectancy, ameliorating work conditions for rural women, dealing with reproductive and child-care problems, widening access to primary education. In more affluent nations the women's movement seeks greater participation of women in policy-making positions at all levels of government, their entrance into graduate and professional fields—hitherto reserved almost exclusively for males—and parity in civil and social rights in such areas as marriage, citizenship, and business. In all countries efforts are made to increase employment opportunities for women and to eliminate discrimination in the terms and conditions of employment.

Underlying these reforms are fundamental themes: the central importance of person, the nature of social roles, the challenging of traditional assumptions about the "nature" of man and woman, the meaning of liberation, the evil of dominance/subservience patterns.

In 1975 the United Nations, recognizing the special urgency of the question, declared an International Year of Women, calling for widespread study of women's concerns and for commitment by government at all levels to improve the condition of women in every sphere. The World Conference for the International Women's Year in Mexico City that year resulted in a world plan of action outlining many of the problems that affect women.

Church Teachings and the Women's Movement. Paralleling these developments, the Church has recently directed its attention to the equality of women and their right to full participation in society and Church. In 1963 Pope John XXIII, commenting on the principal characteristics of the times, stated that women, increasingly conscious of their human dignity, "will not tolerate being treated as mere material instruments, but demand rights befitting a human person both in domestic and in public life" (John XXIII PacTerr 1). Three Vatican II documents comment briefly on the question. The Constitution on the Church insists that inequality arising from social condition, race, nationality, and sex should not exist (*Lumen gentium* 32). The Constitution on the Church Today states more strongly that "forms of social or cultural discrimination in basic personal rights on the grounds of sex, race, color, social conditions, language or religion, must be curbed and eradicated as incompatible with God's design" (*Gaudium et spes* 29). The document further states that women are to play their rightful part in society (ibid. 60). The Decree on the Laity adds that, since women are sharing more actively in the whole life of society, "their participation in the various sectors of the Church's apostolate should likewise develop" (*Apostolicam actuositatem* 9).

Other church documents since Vatican II reiterate this position. Paul VI's "Call to Action" urges recognition of the independence of woman "as a person with equal rights to participate in the political, social, economic and cultural life" (Paul VI OctogAdven 13). The 1971 Synod of Bishops' document, in a section declaring that the Church, if it ventures to speak to others of justice, must first be just in their eyes, urges that "women should have their own share of responsibility and participation in the community life of society

and likewise of the Church" (Synod JustWorld p. 44).

Because the Church has stated such principles and challenged itself to examine its own life and practice in light of principles of justice, there is growing action within the Church to sensitize members to the serious discrepancy between its teachings on the dignity and worth of every human person and its often misogynist traditions and practices. In a number of ways attention has been called to the almost total exclusion of women from preaching, liturgy, and government in the Church.

Although it cannot be said that the Church initiated or has been a strong force in the women's liberation movement, some of its teachings reinforce the aims of the movement and have provided the theoretical base for many who are active in the cause of women.

Bibliography: W. H. CHAFE, *The American Woman: Her Changing Social, Economic, and Political Roles, 1920–1970* (New York 1972). J. HOLE and E. LEVINE, *The Rebirth of Feminism* (New York 1971). E. JANEWAY, *Man's World, Woman's Place* (New York 1971). L. RUSSELL, *Human Liberation in a Feminist Perspective—a Theology* (Philadelphia 1974). G. TAVARD, *Woman in Christian Tradition* (Notre Dame, Ind. 1973).

[L. A. QUINONEZ]

WOMEN'S ORDINATION CONFERENCE

The Women's Ordination Conference (WOC) is a group whose main goal is the ordination of women from all states of life to a renewed priestly ministry in the Roman Catholic Church. WOC spearheads a movement which believes priestly ministry should have as its main function the calling forth of the gifts of all the People of God, thus fostering growth of adult Christian communities. The community and the individual person together with the hierarchy of the Church should test and ratify the call. WOC believes the ordination of women will bring about renewal in present priestly structures; it seeks to eliminate existing patriarchal structures, which by reinforcing sexism and promoting classism oppresses both women and men.

History. In 1975, called by Mary B. Lynch, a group of 33 persons met to plan the first conference on women's ordination. The time had come to analyze the question publicly, thus moving it to the level of an issue. The goal was accomplished before the Conference opened: envisioned originally for 700 participants, the event drew more than double that number. The conference concluded that present theological, scriptural, and traditional understandings of the priesthood in the Church are not sufficient grounds to exclude women from priestly ordination. The formation of an organization to move the issue was approved. In 1976 an Ad Hoc Committee, using a discernment process, after nationwide consultation selected 19 women to serve as Core Commissioners for two years. The Core Commission was defined as a policy-making/working body committed to a circular model of leadership. The organizational structure, considered to be secondary, was to be determined by the tasks envisioned as necessary to accomplish the goal. From 400 original members WOC's membership tripled in a year. Though individual membership is the main form of participation, several national organizations and religious congregations have joined WOC. Several bishops have contributed monetarily to the organization. Local satellite groups endorsing WOC's actions have become the key to the organization's vitality.

Tasks. WOC cosponsors sociological and psychological studies of different aspects of the issue initiated by the Quixote Center (Mt. Ranier, Md., a Catholic center devoted to spirituality and to justice and equality in the Church). WOC actively supports the ordination of women in the Episcopal Church. Represented at the *Call to Action Conference (1976) sponsored by the American bishops, WOC was instrumental in the passing of recommendations dealing with the ordination of women. In 1977 WOC's "Project Priesthood" identified over 350 women who believe themselves called to priestly ministry. Following the Congregation for the Doctrine of Faith's Declaration on the Question of Admitting Women to the Ministerial Priesthood (1977) WOC sponsored protest actions throughout the nation and welcomed the support of theologians and bishops who recognized the injustice of the Declaration's arguments that women cannot be ordained because they do not physically resemble Jesus. WOC joined that Women's Seminary Fund and the economic boycott of states which have not ratified the Equal Rights Amendment initiated by the National Organization of Women. At the NCCB Spring meeting of 1977, WOC organized a coalition to assure implementation of the Call to Action recommendations. WOC announced the Second Women's Ordination Conference to take place in November 1978. A preconference process sought to analyze priestly ministry as envisioned by the People of God upon reflection on its lived experience. WOC's Core Commission began a process to replace its members, while laying the groundword for a broadening of tasks according to the results of the Second Women's Ordination Conference.

This Conference, held in Baltimore, Md., Nov. 10–12, 1978, had some 2,000 participants, with a considerable international representation. Over 60% of those attending were women religious; also were present members of Priests for Equality and one bishop. A principal emphasis of the Conference was the Exercise of Ministries actually going on in the U.S. and accepted by ecclesial communities. Specific recommendations included: recognition of the call of women to permanent diaconate; greater implementation of team ministry; opening of preaching to women; support for women actually exercising priestly ministries; admission of male and female homosexuals to public ministry; access of women to seminaries that are financed by all the faithful.

Strategies were outlined for keeping the issue of women's ordination before the bishops and the public. A delegation to Pope John Paul II was recommended, as well as an International Women's Ordination Conference in Rome to coincide with the 1980 meeting of the Synod of Bishops. Other strategies included boycott days, both economic and of Eucharistic liturgies presided over by male priests, and a women's strike. There was also an ultimatum: "We recommend that unless the priestly ministries of women are officially recognized by the Institutional Church in the next five years that [sic] we ourselves will publicly celebrate the Church's affirmation of the call of women to priestly ministry." The Conference envisioned adopting a new name, "Women for a New Church."

[A. M. ISASI-DIAZ]

WORD OF GOD INSTITUTE

The Word of God Institute was founded as a result of the National Congress on the Word of God in 1972, the first congress in the history of the Church held specifically to celebrate the power of God's Word as revealed in the sacred Scriptures. The purpose of the Word of God Institute is to promote, support, conduct, and assist in any way educational, liturgical, and remedial programs and activities, public or private, through the use of any and all media, in order to further effective communication of the revealed Word of God as the primary pastoral work of the Church. The Institute is comprised of a Board of Directors, Episcopal Advisory Board, and Associates. Its center is at 487 Michigan Ave., Washington, D.C. 20017.

[J. BURKE]

WORLD BANK

The World Bank, formal title, the International Bank for Reconstruction and Development, an international institution whose objective is to assist the less developed countries raise the living standards of their people, is the largest single source of financial and technical assistance to the developing world.

Founded at a conference of 44 governments at Bretton Woods, N.H. toward the close of World War II, the Bank, by mid-1978, had a membership of 131 nations, was supervising some 1300 projects in 114 developing countries, and committing new funds at a level of about $8.5 billion a year. The Bank has its headquarters in Washington, D.C., but is owned and operated by its member countries, and is staffed by international civil servants comprising over a hundred nationalities. Its chief sources of funds are the paid-in capital subscriptions of its membership, the sale of World Bank bonds in the principal capital markets of the world, and the proceeds of past lending operations.

The Bank's Articles of Agreement provide that it lend only for high-priority productive purposes; that the loan's repayment must be guaranteed by the government concerned; that procurement must be open to international competitive bidding; and that the Bank's decision to lend must be based exclusively on economic rather than on political considerations. World Bank loans are repaid, on average, over a 20-year period. There has never been a default. The rate of interest is somewhat lower, but related to, market rates, and profits are turned back into lending operations.

A World Bank affiliate, the International Development Association (IDA), was established in 1960 for the purpose of assisting the very poorest developing countries, which need assistance on more liberal terms than the Bank itself is able to provide. IDA credits are extended for a period of 50 years, at no interest, and with only a small charge to cover administrative costs. Funding for IDA operations derive from three sources: transfers from World Bank earnings; capital subscribed by IDA member governments; and direct contributions from the Association's richer member countries.

Another World Bank affiliate, the International Finance Corporation (IFC), promotes the growth of productive private enterprise in developing countries both through its own investments, and the mobilization of local and foreign sources of private funds. Though IFC will invest in a project only when there is no objection on the part of the host government, it does not require a government guarantee of repayment.

Under Robert S. McNamara, President since 1968, the World Bank has very substantially expanded its overall development assistance and has evolved strategies specifically designed to help the absolute poor become more productive. In the three-year period

1975–1977 alone, it financed projects calculated to double the incomes of 40 million of the poorest people in the developing countries.

Bibliography: The World Bank, *World Development Report* (Washington, D.C. 1978).

[J. L. MADDUX]

WORLD HUNGER

The United Nations Food and Agricultural Organization (FAO) has estimated that approximately 460 million people in the world suffer severe malnutrition. Especially afflicted are small children, for whom protein deficiency is particularly harmful, since it hinders mental development. Such a high incidence of malnutrition, concentrated primarily in the developing countries of Asia, Africa, and Latin America but prevalent also among the poor in the industrialized world, is not only a physical scourge on the human family but is also a moral scourge.

Speaking at the UN World Food Conference in 1974, Pope Paul VI said that the present crisis of world hunger "appears in fact above all to be a crisis of civilization and of solidarity." According to the Pope, it is a crisis of civilization in that an overemphasis is placed on industrialization and purely technical solutions, while fundamental human values are neglected. The crisis also shows itself "when the accent is placed on the quest for mere economic success deriving from the large profits of industry." The crisis of solidarity appears in the unwillingness to share in a better distribution of resources, especially with the hungry, poor nations.

Causes. What are the causes of world hunger? One cause is the instability of a sufficient production of food. The world output of basic feed grains declined in the early 1970s, because of fluctuating weather patterns (e.g., droughts in the Soviet Union, India, and parts of Africa) and the shortage and rising price of fertilizers. Declining availability of low-cost arable lands and scarcity of fresh-water resources are additional production constraints. Moreover, the annual increase in the world's fish catch—an important source of high quality protein—peaked in 1970, impacted by the competitive over-fishing practices of several major nations.

Despite some minor improvement in food production in the past few years, it has still not been sufficient to meet the growing demand for more food—the second cause of world hunger. This growing demand is brought about both by rising population and by rising affluence. The world's population of four billion people is now growing at a rate of nearly two percent annually (which means a doubling every 37 years) and the bulk of this growth is concentrated in the developing countries. World production of food increases approximately 2.8 percent annually, but because of various physical and social constraints it is questionable whether food production can continue to keep up with the demand created by population growth. Moreover, rising affluence means even greater demand for available food and also a shift toward less efficient use of protein supplies, such as greater preference for grain-fed livestock.

A third cause of world hunger is inefficient and inequitable socio-economic patterns of production and distribution. Inefficient patterns are demonstrated, for example, in the commitment of many developing countries to a cash-crop agriculture (cotton, sugar, coffee, rubber, etc.). This commitment (a legacy of previous colonial dominance) means the developing nation imports rather than produces basic food stuffs. Inequitable patterns exist, for example, in the operation of a "free-market" principle which means scarce food stuffs go to those who can pay for them and not necessarily to those who have the greatest need for them.

Solutions Proposed. Approaches to meeting the challenge of the world hunger crisis were outlined at the World Food Conference: (1) in the short-term, increase and improve food aid, i.e., relief assistance from the rich countries to the poor countries; (2) in the middle-term, establish a global food reserve to meet severe emergencies whenever and wherever they arise; and (3) in the long-term, improve agricultural production, especially in the developing countries. If the international cooperation necessary for such approaches is undertaken, the global community will go a long way toward overcoming the crises of civilization and solidarity of which Pope Paul spoke.

Bibliography: L. R. BROWN with E. P. ECKHOLM, *By Bread Alone* (New York 1974). Food and Agricultural Organization, *Population, Food Supply and Agricultural Development* (Rome 1975). J. GREMILLION, ed., *Food/Energy and the Major Faiths* (Maryknoll, N.Y. 1978). F. M. LAPPE and J. COLLINS, *Food First* (Boston 1977). PAUL VI, "Address to the UN World Food Conference," *Pope Speaks* 19 (1974–75) 208–215. P. SIMON, *Bread for the World* (New York 1975).

[P. J. HENRIOT]

WORLDWIDE MARRIAGE ENCOUNTER

Worldwide Marriage Encounter emerged from the leadership group of *Marriage Encounter within the Diocese of Rockville Centre, New York. As Charles Gallagher, SJ and the team couples became sensitive to the capacity for the Marriage Encounter weekend to renew the Church, no longer could they confine themselves to the area of metropolitan New York. Within a seven-year period Worldwide Marriage Encounter has presented the weekend to more than seven-hundred thousand couples, spreading through North America as well as into more than thirty foreign countries. As affiliates of Worldwide Marriage Encounter ten different faith traditions offer the same weekend, with their own theology of marriage and Church adapted to their own purposes.

The leadership group of Worldwide Marriage Encounter is comprised of a National Board, with geographical representation, and an Executive Secretary Team, who are annually elected from among the Board membership.

See also NATIONAL MARRIAGE ENCOUNTER.

[F. L. GUTHRIE]

WORSHIP, COMMUNAL

Worship, the act of recognizing the worth of God (the Holy; the Absolute) and the ritual expression of this recognition, is traditionally deemed a part of religion. Religion, in general, is the perceived and accomplished relationship of man to God. Hence, both religion and worship depend upon the ontology (cosmology, anthropology, theology) of any given population: they are ultimately expressions of the understanding of what it means to be. For Christian worship the ontology of the Church as Communion is decisive (*see* CHURCH AND COMMUNIO). Thus, the worship of Christians is different from that of the Jains, for example, who venerate the Tirthankaras, so distant from the earthly that they can neither perceive nor reward the acts of worship given them.

Christian Worship. Since Christians do not worship a distant and alien god who is hostile, indifferent or even merely recalcitrant, Christian worship need not, indeed, cannot, try to "make contact" with a separated deity. Furthermore, the Christian priest is not properly a "mediator *between* God and man," no matter how often such an expression occurs in sermons. As is clear from the whole Letter to the Hebrews, this mediation has already, definitively, and unsurpassably taken place and in a precisely *human* mode (cf. 1 Tm 2.5). Through this mediation the world, although it still groans and awaits (Rom 8.18–25), has already been transfigured. Hence, Christian worship is both exultation and petition. This Christic status of the world's and humanity's relationship to God makes more than a metaphor Vatican Council II's statement that "the liturgy is . . . an exercise of the priest and of His Body the Church . . . In the earthly liturgy, by way of foretaste, we share in that heavenly liturgy . . ." (*Sacrosanctum Concilium* 7, 8).

For Christians, worship is the recognition and celebration that the entire world is "priestly"—already in creation (Gn 2.3; 8.20) and the "old" Covenant (Ex 19.5, 6) as well as the new (1 Pt 2.5, 9), whereby the particular chosen people acts as the Sacrament of salvation of and for the entire world (*Lumen gentium* 1, 48). All other Sacraments, sacramentals, rituals, and blessings are but the more definite and immediately tangible experiences of this consecrated cosmos. Already in Judaism it was clear that "Two that sit together occupied in the law have the presence among them" (*Pirique Aboth*, 3, 3). Hence, once more, Jesus' assertion in Mt 18.20, "Where two or three are gathered in my name I am there in the middle of them" is but the eschatological intensification of God's already abiding presence in the nongodly (for nature, see Wis 13. 1–9 and Rom 1–3).

Communal Worship. Such an insight, with its consequences for worship, is possible and necessary because of the Judaeo-Christian ontology. By its very nature Being is communion, both in God and in God's relationship with the creation. "All beings are by their nature symbolic, because they necessarily 'express' themselves in order to attain their own nature" (K. Rahner, 1966, 224). Likewise, and consequently, grace, a special mode of being, is by its very nature incarnational. This is crucial, for frequently public (communal) worship is justified solely on anthropological grounds, whether more psychological (man is soul and body; the interior expresses itself in the exterior) or sociological (man is a social or political animal). Although necessary, such a grounding is quite inadequate. Public, ritual worship is not an aid or help. It is, rather, in accord with the Judaeo-Christian ontology, the inevitable and necessary maturation of the religious act.

Thus, the Judaeo-Christian tradition is neither idolatrous nor iconoclastic. Image and sacrament neither compel nor encompass God. Rather, as in the creation itself, by the divine initiative they mediate the divine presence to the nondivine, but equally nondemonic world. Thus the Shekinah is able to be experienced by human beings, whether in the rainbow by Noah or at the Red Sea by all Israel—even the lowliest maidservants (cf. the midrash *Mekilta de-Rabbi Ishmael*, ed. J. Z. Lauterbach [Philadelphia 1933, 1949] II, 24 F.), or in the burning bush by Moses, or in the breaking of bread by the Emmaus disciples or the burning tongues by the apostolic Church. Such mediation is further participated in by human beings in life and liturgy, in service and symbol.

For Christians worship is the way the world in its condition of the Christly inaugurated "new creation" (2 Cor 5.17) behaves. This "new" Christian worship neither annuls nor denigrates natural and Jewish worship, for neither the Natural (Adam, Noah) nor the "Old" Covenants (Abraham, Moses, David) have been annulled, for God does not repent of his promises (Rom 9.6; 11.29). Practically, this is of great consequence as the grounds for the almost total adaptability and flexibility of Christian worship in common. The old Roman Ritual is to be reformed, not suppressed. In liturgical reform only that must be avoided which would lead the community to mirror itself rather than respond and reflect the glory-gift of God. The liturgy must always remain a signal of transcendence, a refusal to allow any particular historical state of affairs to be absolutized. Worship in common must always summon the believer, individual and community, to surpass (transcend) self. For this reason the Eucharist will always remain the acme of Christian worship, for it most memorably (1 Cor 11.25) illustrates the Christic transfiguration of the world. At the same time the admonition of K. Rahner must always be kept in mind: "The Church's union with Christ's sacrifice could and can be manifested and achieved in other ways as well as in the sign of the Eucharistic celebration. Indeed, in certain circumstances it can only be convincingly demonstrated in other signs—in acts of charity to relieve urgent need, in devout prayer, etc." (Rahner and Häussling 33). This clearly indicates that worship is not merely ritual.

Sacraments are not esoteric and spasmodic vertical intrusions of grace from above and beyond into this world. They are, rather, the intensified and here-and-now localized celebrations of "the fact that God wished to treat grace as the good of the (human) race as such." (Scheeben 564). Hence, all Sacraments presume that the same grace (of the Sacrament) is present and being lived by both Church and believers, both before and after the precisely sacramental action (Rahner 1963, 109–134). Neither superstition nor magic, the Sacraments (and all ritual) are the natural (logical) outcome of the symbol and incarnation ontology and salvation-history professed by the Judaeo-Christian tradition. Thus, Sacraments must always be understood as neither "instead of" nor "apart from" life and faith. The Scholastics were right when they invariably spoke of the "Sacraments of Faith" (*Sacramenta fidei*, e.g., cf. ST 3a, 48. 6 ad 2), for Sacraments are indeed the public, ritual celebrations of that faith which understands the relationship of God and world to be one of gift-ness. As the great mystic and theologian, Julian of Norwich so deftly said, "For he (Holy Spirit) regards us so tenderly that he sees all our life here to be penance; for the loving longing in us for him is a lasting penance in us, and he makes this penance in us, and mercifully he helps us to bear it" (Colledge and Walsh, ch. 81). This life-penance and sacrament-penance are not opposition, but supposition and manifestation, as Julian herself hints in chapters 57, 60. Likewise, St. Paul does not allow a dichotomy between Sacrament and life; nor can the one substitute for the other. The Lord's Supper is to be celebrated equally in both Sacrament and life (1 Cor 11.17–34). Indeed, Jesus himself, in the long tradition of both the law and the prophets, sanctions not separation, but circumincession of Sacrament, faith, and life (Mt 5.23; Lk 11.25).

In its greatest act of worship the Church assembles (*ekklēsia*), not like the Greek *polis* to deliberate its own self, but like the Jewish Qahal to hear the Word of God and to experience his presence. More intensely, though, for the Word of God has become flesh and the Bread of Life (Jn 1.14, 6.26–69) so that the world may have more abundant life, indeed, life that is everlasting (Jn 10.10; 6.27, 50, 54, 68).

"Worship in common" is, then, the way the Church as the Sacrament of God's salvation for the world celebrates its faith that God is not a destroyer, but a gift-giver. The gift is life and being. And so Christian worship is neither only ritual nor only life, but both. For Christian mysticism is neither denial of nor flight from the world. It is, rather, communion in creation's being and its transfiguration from natural creation to supernatural grace and glory wherein, as St. Augustine, in anticipation of Vatican II, asserted, the entire creation begins to become that "one man (theandric) who reaches to the ends of earth, to the end of time" (On Ps 142; Ps 85). Communal worship is the celebration, enjoying and effecting, of the congeniality of God and humanity.

Bibliography: E. COLLEDGE and J. WALSH, eds., *Showings* (New York 1978). J. JUNGMANN, *The Place of Christ in Liturgical Prayer*, tr. A. PEELER (London 1965). J. PIEPER, *Leisure the Basis of Culture*, tr. A. DRU (New York 1963); *In Tune with the World*, tr. R. and C. WINSTON (Chicago 1973). K. RAHNER, "Personal and Sacramental Piety," *Theological Investigations* 2, tr. K. H. KRUGER (Baltimore 1963) 109–134; "The Theology of the Symbol." *Theological Investigations* 4, tr. K. SMITH (Baltimore 1966) 221–250. K. RAHNER and A. HÄUSSLING, *The Celebration of the Eucharist* (New York 1968). A. M. ROGUET et al., *Études de pastorale liturgique* (Paris 1944). M. SCHEEBEN, *The Mysteries of Christianity*, tr. C. VOLLERT (St. Louis 1946). C. VAGAGGINI, *Theological Dimensions of the Liturgy*, tr. L. J. DOYLE and W. A. JURGENS (Collegeville, Minn. 1976).   [R. KRESS]

YOGA, CHRISTIAN

Yoga is based on the classical Indian philosophy, *Samkhya*, wherein the goal of the meditator is an isolation and disengagement of the self from earthly bondage. Freed from all entanglements, the initiate attains to an ultimate separation from all which is other than the self. This freedom demands rigorous bodily and mental discipline. First the disciple must put off external wickedness and such internal dispositions as anger, jealousy, cynicism, which lead to evil actions. Long years of practice in bodily movements and postures coordinated with proper breath-control enable the disciple to overcome physical and mental sluggishness and attain the appropriate psychosomatic freedom. The faculties of the mind are focused by hours of concentration on a single object. Certain lengthy exercises force the meditator to be rid of human vagaries and arrive at a "one-pointedness" or unity of consciousness. All of these preparatory efforts bring the disciple to the time of meditation.

The strict requirements of Yoga impress on the Christian meditator the years of discipline that go into the exercise and the fact that each person is a psychosomatic unity. To disregard this truth is to endanger a healthy spiritual life. Christians, however, cannot embrace the philosophical presuppositions of Yoga in their totality, since the Christian understanding of Revelation demands engagement, involvement, and relationship to God and humankind. Certain teachers of Yoga have attempted to adapt it to Christian audiences, suggesting that complete disengagement is only the other side of the coin of total engagement. It is this paradox that underlies the term "Christian Yoga."

See also PRAYER.

Bibliography: J. M. DÉCHANET, *Christian Yoga*, tr. R. HUNDMARCH (New York 1960). M. ELIADE, *Yoga; Immortality and Freedom*, tr. W. R. TRASK (Princeton 1969). J. PEREIRA, "Epiphanies of Revelation" *Thought* 51, n. 201 (1976) 185–204.

[B. DOHERTY]

YOUTH MINISTRY

As one among many ministries of the Church, youth ministry must be understood in terms of the mission and ministry of the whole Church, the community of persons who believe in Jesus Christ and continue his saving work through the action of the Holy Spirit. The Church's mission is threefold: to proclaim the Gospel of salvation; to offer itself as a group of people transformed by the Spirit into a community of faith, hope, and love; and to bring God's justice and love to others through service in its individual, social, and political dimensions.

As a manifestation of the Church's mission, youth ministry has many characteristics in common with other ministries of the Church, but also its own particular history and process, its own "story," which guides those who exercise this ministry. A Gospel account that especially captures the dynamics of youth ministry is the story of the disciples on the road to Emmaus (Lk 24.13–35).

To follow the Emmaus model, youth ministry is the Church's mission of reaching into the daily lives of modern young people and showing them the presence of God. It marks a return to the way Jesus taught, putting ministry before teaching and people over institutions. In this ministry, religious content is a way of life for the person ministering and the young person touched, through a sequential development of faith, dependent on the readiness and need of the adolescent.

To, with, by, and for Youth. Youth ministry is the response of the Christian community to the needs of young people, and the sharing of the unique gifts of youth with the larger community.

Youth ministry is *to* youth when the Christian community exercises its pastoral role in meeting young people's needs. Ministry to youth draws on the resources and gifts of the adult community to provide opportunities for growth that young people need but cannot always attain on their own. Ways in which the ministry to youth is currently being carried out include: guidance counseling; catechetical programs; organized sports activities; leadership training and job placement for disadvantaged youth; parish youth centers; family-life programs; camping opportunities; Catholic schools.

Youth ministry is *with* youth because young people share with adults a common responsibility to carry out the Church's mission. When youth have the opportunity to exercise this responsibility jointly with adults recognition is given to the particular gifts and insights which these young people bring to their family parish, or neighborhood. Ministry with youth occurs when they participate as members of parish councils, serve as catechists, readers, and extraordinary ministers of the Eucharist, and share with adults a responsibility for retreats, community service, or action for justice.

Youth ministry is *by* youth when young people exercise their own ministry to others, particularly to their peers. The operation of peer-counseling programs for drug abuse and other problems, tutoring, and many forms of community service are all parts of ministry by youth. Youth also minister to others when they serve as team members for youth retreats, teachers in catechetical programs, and leaders of youth activities.

Youth ministry is *for* youth in that adult youth-ministers attempt to interpret the needs of youth and act as advocates in articulating youth's legitimate concerns to the wider community. The adult involved in youth ministry has special access to the views of youth, and ordinarily has a degree of credibility, influence, and resources unavailable to young people. This places a responsibility on the adult to speak for youth and to sensitize and motivate other adults where youth needs are concerned. Ministers for youth might alert parish or diocesan councils to a desire for youth liturgies, work with community leaders to resolve gang problems, or help parents and children to work out misunderstandings and communication difficulties.

Diversity of Programs. The great diversity in youth ministry is reflected in the above examples, and owes its existence to the importance of each distinct dimension of the ministry to, with, by, and for youth.

Youth ministry is a multidimensional reality, but all of its varied facets are brought into focus by a common dedication to the following goals. (1) Youth ministry works to foster the total personal and spiritual growth of each young person. (2) Youth ministry seeks to draw young people to responsible participation in the life, mission, and work of the faith community.

In all places, youth ministry occurs within a given social, cultural, and religious context which shapes the specific form of the ministry. Youth culture, secular society, family, and the local church community are some of the institutions which form the context within which youth ministry must be carried out. Each of these environments exerts an important influence on young people, a consideration which should be reflected appropriately in balanced youth-ministry programs.

To examine the concrete dimensions of such programs, seven components of youth ministry can be identified which describe distinct aspects of youth ministry work: Word, Worship, Creating Community, Guidance and Healing, Justice and Service, Enablement, and Advocacy. Each of these is an expression of the ministry of the Christian community and acts to fulfill the Church's mission. The number and order of these components are not absolutes; however, they do represent a consensus on the part of persons involved with youth ministry and are useful as a working description of the most important elements of youth ministry.

Youth ministry today presents the challenge of helping to reveal the Christ of the Gospel and to exhibit faith in community and in personal relationships. This is a time of hope and building for the future. More than ever, it is evident today that youth genuinely hunger for the good news of Jesus Christ, and that faith communities are equipped to share it with them if their vision is broad and creative.   [P. O'NEILL]

CONTRIBUTORS

ADAMS, Donald E., J.C.D., Diocese of Harrisburg.
Article: Laity in Canon Law.

ADRIAZOLA, Maria, Assistant Professor of Theology, The Catholic University of America.
Article: Lay Spirituality.

AHERN, Barnabas, CP, Consultor, Congregation for the Doctrine of the Faith.
Articles: Doctrine of the Faith, Congregation for the; International Theological Commission.

ALLEN, Horace T., M.Div., M.Phil., Union Theological Seminary; Member ICET and Consultation on Common Texts.
Article: Consultation on Common Texts.

AMALORPAVADASS, D. S., Director, National Biblical Catechetical and Liturgical Centre, Bangalore, India.
Article: Missionary Adaptation.

ANTONSEN, Conrad, OP, Phoenix Blackfriars.
Article: Prayer.

ASHLEY, Benedict M., OP, Aquinas Institute of Theology, Dubuque, Iowa.
Articles: Euthanasia; Life, Prolongation of.

BACIGALUPO, Leonard F., OFM, St. Anthony Friary, Catskill, N.Y.
Article: Activism (Spiritual Life).

BALDWIN, Elizabeth, Coordinator for Health and Welfare, USCC.
Article: Health Care and the Church.

BARNHISER, Judith A., OSU, J.C.D.
Articles: Episcopal Vicar; Women, Canon Law on.

BARTELL, Ernest, CSC, Director, Fund for the Improvement of Post-Secondary Education, Department of Education, HEW, Washington, D.C.
Article: Higher Education and Government Funds.

BASSETT, William W., Professor of Law, School of Law, University of San Francisco.
Article: Code of Canon Law, Revision of.

BELLAGAMBA, Antonio, IMC, Executive Director, U.S. Catholic Mission Council, Washington, D.C.
Articles: Lay Missionaries; Missions, Catholic (U.S.); United States Catholic Mission Council.

BERNADICOU, Paul J., SJ, Associate Professor of Theology, University of San Francisco.
Article: Laity (Theology).

BEUSSE, Robert B., Secretary of Communication, Department of Communication, USCC, New York, N.Y.
Article: Communication, USCC Committee on.

BIECHLER, James E., Associate Professor of Religion, La Salle College, Philadelphia, Pa.
Article: Mysticism.

BILLINGS, Cora M., RSM, Coordinator, National Black Sisters Conference.
Article: National Black Sisters' Conference.

BILTON, William, CJM, Executive Secretary, National Assembly of Religious Brothers, Buffalo, N.Y.
Article: National Assembly of Religious Brothers.

BISSONNETTE, Tomás G., M.A., Cert., Instituto Pastoral Latinoamericano, Quito; Hispanic Ministry, Mundelein College; Teacher, Midwest Hispanic Center, Chicago, Ill.
Article: Basic Christian Communities.

BLENKINSOP, Joseph, Professor of Theology, University of Notre Dame.
Articles: Sexual Morality (In the Bible); Sexuality, Human (In the Bible).

BLUM, Virgil C., SJ, Jesuit Community, Marquette University; President, Catholic League for Religious and Civil Rights, Milwaukee, Wis.
Article: Catholic League for Religious and Civil Rights.

BOBERG, John T., SVD, Secretary-Treasurer, Association of Professors of Missions, Catholic Theological Union, Chicago, Ill.
Article: Association of Professors of Missions.

BOULTWOOD, Alban, OSB, Former Abbot, St. Anselm's Abbey, Washington, D.C.
Article: Hayden, Jerome.

BOWMAN, David J., SJ, Director, Ireland Program and Associate Director for Europe, National Council of the Churches of Christ in the U.S.A., New York, N.Y.
Articles: National Council of Churches of Christ in the U.S.A.; Northern Ireland.

BRAXTON, Edward K., Professor of Theology, University of Notre Dame.
Article: Black Theology.

BRENNAN, Margaret, IHM, Associate Professor of Pastoral Theology, Regis College, Toronto, Canada.
Articles: Nuns, Contemplative; Religious Life, Adaptation of.

BRODERICK, Most Rev. Edwin B., D.D., Executive Director, Catholic Relief Services, USCC, New York, N.Y.
Article: Catholic Relief Services.

BRODERICK, Joseph A., OP, Professor of Law, North Carolina Central University, Durham, N.C.
Articles: Civil Disobedience, Civil Law.

BROOKS, Robert McK. OPraem, St. Norbert Abbey Seminary, De Pere, Wis.
Article: Leakage in Church Membership.

BRUNEAU, Thomas, Ph.D., Associate Professor of

Political Science, McGill University, Montreal, Canada.
Article: Latin America, Church in.

BRYCE, Mary C., OSB, Associate Professor, Department of Religious Studies/Religious Education, Catholic University of America, Washington, D.C.
Articles: Catechesis; Catechesis, Adult; Catechetics; Catechisms.

BURGHARDT, Walter J., SJ, S.T.D., Theologian in Residence, Georgetown University, Washington, D.C.
Article: Historical Theology.

BURKE, Dennis M., OPraem, St. Norbert College, De Pere, Wis.
Article: Office, Ecclesiastical.

BURKE, John, OP, Executive Director, Word of God Institute, Washington, D.C.
Articles: Evangelization; Evangelization, Programs of; Word of God Institute.

BURKE, Mary, Staff Associate, Center of Concern, Washington, D.C.
Article: International Women's Year, World Conference for the.

BURKE, Redmond A. Ph.D., School of Library Science, University of Wisconsin-Oshkosh, Oshkosh, Wis.
Articles: Archives, Ecclesiastical; Catholic Press (U.S.).

BURNS, Hugh D., OP, Dominican House of Studies, Washington, D.C.
Article: Beatifications and Canonizations.

BURRELL, David B., CSC, Chairman, Department of Theology, University of Notre Dame.
Articles: Conservatism and Liberalism, Theological; Relativism.

BURROUGHS, Joseph A., CM, Ph.D., St. Mary Seminary, Perryville, Mo.
Article: Reason, Age of.

BUTLER, Francis J., Ph.D., Associate Secretary for Domestic Social Development, USCC.
Articles: Bishops' Justice Program; Call to Action Conference; Social Development and World Peace, USCC Committee on.

BUTLER, Richard J., Past-Director, Center for Pastoral Liturgy, Catholic University of America, Washington, D.C., Priest of the Archdiocese of Boston.
Article: Pastoral Liturgy, Institutes for.

BUTLER, Sara, MSBT.
Articles: Convert Apostolate; Ecumenical Marriages, Pastoral Care of.

BYRN, Robert, School of Law, Fordham University, New York, N.Y.
Article: Abortion (U.S. Law).

BYRON, William J., SJ, President, University of Scranton, Scranton, Pa.
Article: Stewardship.

CAIN, Leonard F., Ph.D., Executive Assistant to the

President, Catholic University of America, Washington, D.C.
Article: Unemployment.

CARLEN, Claudia, IHM, Head Librarian, St. John's Provincial Seminary, Plymouth, Mich.
Article: Appendix: Documents on Change in the Church.

CARR, Deanna M., BVM, National Director, National Sisters Vocation Conference, Chicago, Ill.
Articles: National Sisters Vocation Conference; Vocation, Religious.

CARROLL, Catherine A., RSC, Ph.D., A.A.G., Professor of Music, Manhattanville College, Purchase, N.Y.
Article: Ward, Justine.

CARROLL, Eamon R., OCarm, S.T.D., Whitefriars Hall, Washington, D.C.
Article: Mariology

CARROLL, Elizabeth, RSM, Staff Associate, Center of Concern, Washington, D.C.
Article: Women in the Ministry of Justice.

CARTER, Martin, SA, St. Francis Mission, Jamaica, West Indies.
Article: Religious Freedom.

CARTHY, Margaret, OSU, Ph.D., Dean, Graduate School, College of New Rochelle, New Rochelle, N.Y.
Article: United States of America.

CASTAÑEDA, Margarita, CND, Las Hermanas, New York, N.Y.
Article: Las Hermanas.

CAUWELAERT, Most Rev. Jan van, CICM, D.D., Former Bishop of Inongo (Zaire); Consultor, Congregation for the Evangelization of Peoples; Chairman, Commission for Catechesis and Catechetics, 1970–72; Pastoral Mission Animation; Congregation of the Immaculate Heart of Mary, Antwerp, Belgium.
Article: Catechists, Missionary.

CEROKE, Christian P., OCarm., S.T.D. Professor, Dept. of Religion and Religious Education, Catholic University of America, Washington, D.C.
Articles: Biblical Theology; Resurrection Narratives in the New Testament.

CHAMPLIN, Joseph M., Pastor, Holy Family Church, Fulton, N.Y.; Author; Columnist; Lecturer.
Articles: Benediction and Exposition of the Blessed Sacrament; Forty Hours Devotion; Holy Communion, Rites of.

CHESTER, Ann E., IHM, Contemplative Living in the Contemporary World Clearing Center, Detroit, Mich.
Articles: Community, Forms of; Houses of Prayer.

CHIRICO, Peter, SS, St. Thomas Seminary, Kenmore, Washington.
Articles: Infallibility; Priest and Priesthood, Christian; Priestly Formation; Vocation, Clerical.

"CHRISTOPHERS, The," New York, N.Y.
Article: Keller, James G.

CLARE, Mary, St. Benedict Center, Still River, Mass.
Article: Feeney, Leonard.

CLARK, Francis X., SJ, S.T.D., Professor of Missiology, East Asian Pastoral Institute of Ateneo de Manila University, Manila, Philippines.
Article: East Asian Pastoral Institute.

CLARKE, W. Norris, SJ, Department of Philosophy, Fordham University, Bronx, N.Y.
Article: Theism and Process Thought.

CLINE, William R., Senior Fellow, The Brookings Institution, Washington, D.C.
Article: Land Reform.

COLEMAN, John A., SJ, Jesuit School of Theology at Berkeley, Berkeley, Cal.
Article: Theology and Sociology.

COLESS, Gabriel M., OSB, St. Mary's Abbey, Norristown, N.J.
Article: Liturgical Reform.

COLLINS, Mary, OSB, Associate Professor of Religion, Department of Religious Studies, The University of Kansas, Lawrence, Kansas.
Article: Liturgy and Anthropology.

COLLINS, Patrick W., Director of Campus Ministry, Catholic University of America, Washington, D.C.
Article: Campus Ministry.

CONNELLY, John J., S.T.D., Professor of Theology, St. John's Seminary, School of Theology, Brighton, Mass.
Articles: Philosophy in Seminaries; Theology in Seminaries.

CONNERY, John J., SJ, Jesuit Community at Loyola, Chicago, Ill.
Article: Abortion (U.S. Law and Morality).

CONROY, Donald, S.T.L., Ph.D., Representative, Family Life, USCC, Washington, D.C.
Articles: Family; Family (Educational Role).

COONEY, Patrick R., Director, Department of Christian Worship, Archdiocese of Detroit, Detroit, Mich.
Article: Sunday.

CORCORAN, Rev. Msgr. Lawrence J., Executive Director, National Conference of Catholic Charities, Washington, D.C.
Article: Catholic Charities.

CORNELL, Thomas C., Executive Secretary, Catholic Peace Fellowship; Director, International Affairs, Fellowship of Reconciliation.
Article: Catholic Peace Fellowship; Fellowship of Reconciliation.

CORNIDES, Augustine W., OSB, Monasterio San Antonio Abad, Humacao, Puerto Rico.
Articles: All Souls' Day; Catafalque; Concelebration; Masses for the Dead.

CORRIGAN, John T., CFX, Catholic Library Association, Haverford, Pa.
Article: Catholic Library Association.

COSTA, Francis D., SSS, Associate Professor and Chairman, Department of Religious Studies, John Carroll University, Cleveland, Ohio.
Article: Eucharistic Devotions.

COSTELLO, Gerald, Managing Editor, *The Beacon,* Pequannock, N.J.
Article: Latin America, Evangelization in.

CROSBY, Michael H., OFMCap, Justice and Peace Center, Milwaukee, Wis.
Articles: Church Investments; Corporate Social Responsibility; National Catholic Coalition for Responsible Investment.

CROWE, Frederick E., SJ, Regis College, Toronto, Canada.
Article: Foundational Theology.

CROWLEY, Patty, Co-Foundress Christian Family Movement, Chicago, Ill.
Article: International Confederation of Christian Family Movements.

CUFFE, Edwin D., SJ, America House, New York, N.Y.
Article: Ward, Maisie.

CUNNINGHAM, Joseph L., Executive Secretary, Liturgy, Music, Art and Architecture, Diocese of Brooklyn, Brooklyn, N.Y.
Articles: Federation of Diocesan Liturgical Commissions (FDLC); Liturgical Committees, Parish; Liturgical Movement, Catholic; Parish (Community of Worship).

CUNNINGHAM, Madonna M., OSF, Ph.D., President and Associate Professor of Psychology, Our Lady of Angels College, Aston, Pa.
Article: Counseling, Pastoral.

DALCOURT, Gerard J., Ph.D., Professor of Philosophy, Seton Hall University, South Orange, N.J.
Articles: Conscience, Freedom of; Tolerance.

DALLEN, James, S.T.D., Professor of Theology, Rosemont College, Rosemont, Pa.
Articles: Altar Breads; Baptismal Water, Blessing of; Chrism Mass; Exorcism; Holy Oils and Chrism; Litany (Liturgical Use); Reconciliation with the Community.

DAVIS, Cyprian, OSB, St. Meinrad's Archabbey, St. Meinrad, Ind.
Article: Black Catholics (U.S.).

DAVIS, Joseph M., SM, Association for Education, The Marianists, Dayton, Ohio.
Articles: Bishops' Committee for Liaison with the National Office of Black Catholics; National Office for Black Catholics.

DECHERT, Charles R., Ordinary Professor of Politics, Catholic University of America, Washington, D.C.
Article: Political Communities; Politics, Church and.

DEDEK, John F., Associate Professor of Moral Theology, Department of Theology, Catholic University of America, Washington, D.C.
Articles: Circumstances, Moral; Consequences, Morality of.

DEHNE, Carl A., SJ, Instructor in Theology, Loyola University of Chicago, Chicago, Ill.
Articles: Devotions, Popular; Liturgical Catechesis.

DELAPLANE, Joan, OP, Aquinas Institute of Theology, Dubuque, Iowa.
Article: Women and Preaching.

DE PRIEST, Ellis L., SM, Rector, Professor of Liturgy, Notre Dame Seminary, New Orleans, La.
Article: Kingdom of God.

DILL, Edwin, ST, Mission Procurator, Missionary Servants of the Holy Trinity, Trinity Missions, Silver Spring, Md.
Article: National Catholic Development Conference.

DILLON, Edward J., Ph.D., Philadelphia, Pa.
Articles: Bibles, Common; Capital Punishment; "Cor Unum," Pontifical Council; Hildebrand, Dietrich von; Hutchins, Robert Maynard; Justice and Peace, Pontifical Commission for; Laity, Pontifical Council for the; Latin America, Pontifical Commission for; Lunn, Arnold; Medellín Documents; Missionaries of Charity; Pontifical Biblical Commission; Religious Relations with Judaism, Pontifical Commission for; Shuster, George N..

DI LORENZO, Paul, M.S.W., Catholic Social Services, Archdiocese of Philadelphia, Philadelphia, Pa.
Article: Social Work, Catholic.

DLOUHY, Maur, OSB, St. Procopius Abbey, Lisle, Ill.
Articles: Abbey *Nullius*; Abbot/Abbess, Blessing of.

DOHERTY, Barbara, SP, Ph.D., St. Joseph Provincial House, Park Ridge, Ill.
Articles: Contemplation; Yoga, Christian.

DOLAN, Jay P., Department of History, University of Notre Dame, Notre Dame, Ind.
Article: Social History.

DONAHUE, John A., Secretary-Treasurer, National Catholic Vocation Council, Chicago, Ill.
Article: National Catholic Vocation Council.

DOUGHERTY, James E., Ph.D., Professor of Political Science, St. Joseph's College, Philadelphia, Pa.
Article: Disarmament.

DOYLE, Joan P., BVM, President, Sisters of Charity of the Blessed Virgin Mary, Dubuque, Iowa; Former President, Leadership Conference of Women Religious.
Article: Religious (Women).

DRESSLER, Hermigild, OFM, Professor Emeritus, Classical Languages, Quincy College, Quincy, Ill.; Editorial Director, *Fathers of the Church*, CUA Press, Catholic University of America, Washington, D.C.
Article: Campbell, James Marshall.

DRISCOLL, Donald T., President, Association for Religious and Value Issues in Counseling, Iona College, New Rochelle, N.Y.
Article: Association for Religious and Value Issues in Counseling.

DUBAY, Thomas, SM, Marist Administration Center, Washington, D.C.
Articles: Holiness, Universal Call to: Holiness of the Church; Retreats.

DUFF, Edward, SJ, Professor Emeritus, Political Science, College of the Holy Cross, Worcester, Mass.
Article: Property, Private.

DUFFY, Regis A., OFM, S.T.D., Associate Professor, Washington Theological Union, Silver Spring Md.
Article: Team Ministry.

DULLES, Avery, SJ, Ph.L., S.T.D., Professor of Theology, Catholic University of America, Washington, D.C.
Article: Revelation, Fonts of.

DUMM, Demetrius R., OSB, Rector, St. Vincent Seminary, Latrobe, Pa.
Article: Monasticism, Contemporary.

DUNNING, James B., Ph.D., President, The National Organization for Continuing Education of Roman Catholic Clergy, Oakland, Cal.
Article: National Organization for Continuing Education of Roman Catholic Clergy.

DURBIN, Paul T., Ph.D., Professor, Department of Philosophy, University of Delaware, Newark, Del.
Article: Agnosticism.

DURST, Luanne, OSF, Administrative Assistant, Bishops' Committee on Liturgy, Washington, D.C.
Articles: Minister of Music; Profession of Faith (The Creed); Sequence.

DYER, George B., OP, Mexican American Cultural Center, San Antonio, Texas.
Articles: Migrant Farmworkers (U.S.); Migration, Right of.

EARLY, Tracy, Religious Journalist, New York, N.Y.
Article: Conway, William.

ECKSTEIN, Jean, President, National Council of Catholic Laity, Iowa City, Iowa.
Article: National Council of Catholic Laity.

EFROYMSON, David P., Ph.D., Professor, Department of Religion, La Salle College, Philadelphia, Pa.
Article: Patristics; Judaism and the Early Church.

EGAN, Keith J., Associate Professor, Department of Theology, Marquette University, Milwaukee, Wis.
Article: Knowles, David.

EGAN, Willis J., SJ, M.A., S.T.D., Professor of Theology, Loyola-Marymount University, Los Angeles, Cal.
Article: Laity, Theology of.

EHR, Donald J., SVD, Divine Word Seminary, Bordentown, N.J.
Articles: Creation; Monogenism and Polygenism.

ELFORD, George, Ph.D., Director, Educational Testing Service, Regional Office, Wellesley Hill, Mass.
Article: Teachers, Lay.

ELIZONDO, Virgil, Director, Mexican American Cultural Center, San Antonio, Texas.
Articles: Culture, Church and; Latin American Consultation for Theology in the Americas; Mexican-American Cultural Center.

ELLEBRACHT, Mary P., CPPS, St. Mary's Institute, Inc., O'Fallen, Mo.
Article: Liturgical Gestures.

EMPEREUR, James L., SJ, Assistant Professor of Systematic Theology, Jesuit School of Theology at Berkeley, Berkeley, Cal.
Articles: Celibacy, Formation in; Equality in the Church; Priesthood, Universal.

ENOCH, Elizabeth M., OSC, Association of Contem-

plative Sisters, Bronx, N.Y.
Article: Association of Contemplative Sisters.

ENZLER, Kathleen C., Director, Family Life Bureau, Archdiocese of Washington, Washington, D.C.
Articles: Clemens, Alphonse Henry; Family Services, Catholic.

EVANS, Bernard, Campaign for Human Development, Washington, D.C.
Article: Human Development.

EVERY, Louis, OP, Assistant to the Master General of the Order of Preachers, Convento S. Sabina, Rome.
Article: Union of Superiors General (Men).

FAHEY, Joseph A., Ph.D. Director, Peace Studies Institute, Manhattan College, Riverdale, N.Y.
Articles: Pacem in Terris Convocation; Pax Christi; Peace, International; War, Morality of.

FAHEY, Michael A., SJ, Concordia University, Montreal, P.Q., Canada.
Articles: Change in the Church; Eucharistic Sharing (Intercommunion).

FALARDEAU, Ernest R., SSS, Blessed Sacrament Fathers and Brothers, Cleveland, Ohio.
Article: Religion, Virtue of.

FARLEY, Margaret A., RSM, The Divinity School, Yale University, New Haven, Conn.
Article: Sexism.

FARRAHER, Joseph J., SJ, Jesuit Community, University of Santa Clara, Santa Clara, Cal.
Articles: Moral Theology (Contemporary Trends); Morality.

FAUCHER, Thomas, Pastor, Sacred Heart Church, Emmett, Idaho.
Articles: Children, Religion and; Liturgical Commissions, Diocesan and National.

FEIL, Carl M., OSM, M.A., S.T.L., Administrative Assistant, U.S. Catholic Mission Council, Washington, D.C.
Article: Mission (New Trends).

FERREE, William J., SM, Director, Second Career Vocation Project, University of Dayton, Dayton, Ohio.
Article: Second-Career Vocations.

FICHTNER, Joseph, OSC, S.T.D., Department of Theology, Mt. St. Mary's College, Emmitsburg, Md.
Articles: Faith, Act of; Tradition (In Theology).

FIEDLER, Rev. Msgr. Ernest J., Executive Director, Bishops' Committee on the Permanent Diaconate, Washington, D.C.
Article: Bishops' Committee on the Permanent Diaconate.

FINK, Peter E., SJ, Ph.D., Professor of Sacramental and Liturgical Theology, Weston School of Theology, Cambridge, Mass.
Articles: Liturgical Theology: Liturgiology; Theology and Liturgy.

FINN, James, Editor, *Worldview*, New York, N.Y.
Article: Middle East, Church and.

FIORENZA; Francis P. Schüssler, Ph.D., Department of Theology, Villanova University, Villanova, Pa.
Articles: Liberation Theology: Political Theology.

FISHER, Eugene J., Ph.D., Executive Secretary, Secretariat for Catholic-Jewish Relations, NCCB, Washington, D.C.
Articles: Catholic-Jewish Relations, NCCB Secretariat for; Jewish/Roman Catholic Relations.

FITZGERALD, Allan D., OSA, Department of Theology, Catholic University of America, Washington, D.C.
Articles: Chasuble; Chasuble-Alb; Furnishings, Sacred; Liturgical Vessels; Liturgical Vestments.

FITZPATRICK, Joseph P., SJ, Department of Sociology and Anthropology, Fordham University, Bronx, N.Y.
Articles: Pluralism, Social and Cultural; Prejudice.

FLEMING, David A., SM, Assistant to the Provincial, Society of Mary Provincialate, St. Louis, Mo.
Article: Religious Superiors.

FLYNN, Mary J., Ph.D., Assistant Professor, National Catholic School of Social Service; Director, Center for the Study of Pre-retirement and Aging, Catholic University of America, Washington, D.C.
Article: Aged, Care of.

FOLEY, Gertrude, SC, Sisters of Charity of Seton Hill, Greensburg, Pa.
Article: Charisms in Religious Life.

FOLEY, M. Nadine, OP, Ph.D., S.T.M., Vicaress, Adrian Dominican Sisters, Adrian, Mich.; Visiting Lecturer, Spring 1979, Ecumenical Affairs, Harvard Divinity School.
Articles: Diaconate for Women; Women in Ministry; Women in the Church.

FORD, John T., CSC, Chairman, Department of Theology, Catholic University of America, Washington, D.C.
Articles: Laity, Formation of; Ministry, Education for.

FREEDMAN, David N., Ph.D., Director, Program on Studies in Religion, University of Michigan, Ann Arbor, Mich.
Article: Ebla Tablets.

FUNK, Virgil, President, The National Association of Pastoral Musicians, Washington, D.C.
Articles: Mass, Music of; Music, Sacred (Legislation); National Association of Pastoral Musicians.

GAFFIGAN, Aloysius J., OSFS, A.B., J.C.D., Oblates of St. Francis De Sales, Hyattsville, Md.
Article: Common Life (Canon Law).

GALANTE, Joseph A., J.C.D., President, National Conference of Vicars for Religious, Philadelphia, Pa.
Article: National Conference of Vicars for Religious.

GALLAGHER, Eugene V., M.A., Lecturer, Religious Studies, Indiana University at Indianapolis, Indianapolis, Ind.
Articles: History of Religions; Religions, Comparative Study of.

GALLIN, Alice, OSU, Associate Executive Director, Association of Catholic Colleges and Universities, NCEA, Washington, D.C.
Article: Education, Human Right to.

GASTÓN, María Luisa, ACJ, Communications/Education Specialist, NCCB/USCC Secretariat for Hispanic Affairs, Washington, D.C.
Articles: Hispanic Affairs, NCCB/USCC Secretariat for; Hispanics in the U.S.

GEANEY, Dennis J., OSA, Director of Field Education, Catholic Theological Union, Chicago, Ill.
Articles: Apostolate of the Laity (Decree); Catholic Action; Ministry, Unordained.

GEORGE, A. Raymond, Tutor, Wesley College, Bristol, England.
Article: International Consultation on English Texts (ICET).

GERHARDT, Bernard C., S.T.L., J.C.D., Officialis, The Tribunal, Washington, D.C.
Articles: Monsignor; Prelates, Honorary.

GETTY, Mary A., RSM, S.T.D., Chairman, Theology Department, Carlow College, Pittsburgh, Pa.
Article: Women, Rights of.

GIBBONS, Robert J., Ph.D., Director, Administrative Research and Development, American Institute for Property and Liability Underwriters, Malvern, Pa.
Articles: Belgrade Conference; Developing Nations; Helsinki Agreement; La Pira, Giorgio: Mindszenty, József; Toynbee, Arnold.

GILBERT, Edward J., CSSR, Vice President and Academic Dean, Redemptorist Seminary, Esopus, N.Y.
Article: Marriage, Indissolubility of.

GLADE, William, Director, Institute of Latin American Studies, The University of Texas at Austin, Austin, Texas.
Article: Wealth, Distribution of.

GOULET, Dennis, Senior Fellow, Overseas Development Council, Washington, D.C.
Article: Technology, Transfer of

GRABNER, Donald, OSB, Conception Abbey, Conception, Mo.
Article: Preface.

GRAHAM, George P., J.C.D., Officialis of the Tribunal, Diocese of Rockville, Centre, N.Y.
Articles: Curia, Diocesan; Diocese (Eparchy); Dioceses, Revision of; Province and Region, Ecclesiastical; Synods, Diocesan.

GRAHAM, Robert A., SJ, La Civiltà cattolica, Rome.
Article: Diplomacy, Papal.

GREEN, Thomas J., J.C.D. Assistant Professor, Department of Canon Law, Catholic University of America, Washington, D.C.
Articles: Marriage Tribunals, Experimental Norms for; Penal Law, Draft of; Stipends.

GROVER, Veronica, SHCJ, Consultant, National Center for Justice and Peace Education, National Catholic Educational Association, Washington, D.C.
Article: Justice, Education for.

GRUENBERG, Gladys, Ph.D., Professor of Economics, St. Louis University, St. Louis, Mo.
Article: Brown, Leo Cyril.

GURRIERI, John A., Associate Director, NCCB Committee on the Liturgy, Washington, D.C.
Articles: Acolyte, Ministry of; Lay Ministers (Rite of Institution); Liturgy of the Hours (Pastoral Adaptation and Celebration); Reader, Ministry of.

GUTHRIE, Frederick L., M.Ed., Associate Director of Resource Community, Worldwide Marriage Encounter, Washington, D.C.
Article: Worldwide Marriage Encounter.

HAALAND, Dorothy A., President, U.S. Section, St. Joan's International Alliance, Anchorage, Alaska.
Article: Saint Joan's International Alliance.

HALLER, Robert B., OP, Providence College, Providence, R.I.
Articles: Congregational Singing; Hymnology; Liturgical Music; Musicology, Sacred.

HALLIGAN, Nicholas, OP, S.T.M., S.T.D., Archivist-Secretary, Apostolic Delegation, Washington, D.C.
Articles: Burial (Canon Law); Clerical Dress; Confession, Frequency of.

HALTON, Thomas, Chairman, Department of Greek and Latin, Catholic University of America, Washington, D.C.
Article: Deferrari, Roy J.

HAPPEL, Stephen, Professor of Theology, St. Meinrad's School of Theology, St. Meinrad, Ind.
Article: Theologian.

HARNETT, Edward F., Director, Theological Field Education, St. Mary of the Lake Seminary, Mundelein, Ill.
Article: Theological Field Education.

HARRINGTON, Jeremy, OFM, Editor-Publisher, *St. Anthony Messenger*, Cincinnatti, Ohio.
Article: Media of Social Communication and the Church.

HARTDEGEN, Stephen J., OFM, Director, U.S. Center for the Catholic Biblical Apostolate, Washington, D.C.
Article: United States Center for the Catholic Biblical Apostolate.

HARTIGAN, Patricia M., OP, National Coordinator, Movement for a Better World, Silver Spring, Md.
Article: Movement for a Better World.

HARVEY, John F., OSFS, De Sales Hall School of Theology, Hyattsville, Md.
Article: Homosexuality.

HASTINGS, Adrian C., Department of Religious Studies, University of Aberdeen, Aberdeen, Scotland.
Article: African Christianity.

HEADLEY, William R., CSSp, Coordinator of Social Science Research, Mission Research and Planning Department, Maryknoll, N.Y.
Article: Mission Planning.

HEARNE, Brian, CSSp, Lecturer in Pastoral Theology, Pastoral Institute, Gaba; Editor, *AFER*, Association of the Episcopal Conferences in Eastern Africa (Amecea), Eldoret, Kenya.
Article: Liturgy and Local Churches.

HEHIR, Brian, Associate Secretary for International Peace and Development, USCC, Washington, D.C.
Article: Justice and Peace, Ministry of.

HEINTSCHEL, Donald E., Executive Coordinator, Canon Law Society of America, Toledo, Ohio; Chairman, Joint Committee of Catholic Learned Societies, Toledo, Ohio.
Articles: Canon Law Society of America; Joint Committee of Catholic Learned Societies and Scholars.

HENLE, Robert J., SJ, St. Louis University, St. Louis, Mo.
Article: Planned Parenthood.

HENRIOT, Peter J., SJ, Director, Center of Concern, Washington, D.C.
Article: World Hunger.

HERR, Dan, President, The Thomas More Association, Chicago, Ill.
Article: Publishing, Catholic (U.S.).

HILL, Jeanne, OP, Retreat Director, Benedictine Abbey, Pecos, N.M.
Article: Healing, Christian.

HILL, Morton A., SJ, President, Morality in Media, Inc., New York, N.Y.
Article: Morality in Media, Inc.

HILL, Thomas, OFMCap, Executive Secretary Team, National Marriage Encounter, St. Paul, Minn.
Articles: Marriage Encounter; National Marriage Encounter.

HILL, William J., OP, Associate Professor of Systematic Theology, Catholic University of America. Washington, D.C.
Articles: Theology; Theology and History.

HINTON, Thomas D., Director, Finance and Administration, USCC, Washington, D.C.
Article: American Board of Catholic Missions.

HITCHCOCK, James, Ph.D., Professor of History, St. Louis University; Chairman, Latin Liturgy Association.
Articles: Higher Education, Catholic; Latin Liturgy Association.

HOFINGER, Johannes, SJ, Associate Director in Charge of Adult Education, Archdiocese of New Orleans, New Orleans, La.; Member, East Asian Pastoral Institute, Manila, Phillipines.
Articles: Jungmann, Josef Andreas; Religion, Teacher of.

HOFFMAN, Dennis, National Conference of Diocesan Vocation Directors, Duluth, Minn.
Article: National Conference of Diocesan Vocation Directors (NCDVD)

HOGAN, Most Rev. James J., D.D., Bishop of Altoona-Johnstown, Pa.
Article: Institute of Religious Life.

HOGE, Dean R., Ph.D., Associate Professor, Sociology, Catholic University of America, Washington, D.C.
Articles: Church Membership (U.S.); Sociology.

HOLLAND, Joseph, SJ, Center of Concern, Washington, D.C.
Article: Labor Movement.

HOLLENBACH, David, SJ, Assistant Professor of Theological Ethics, Weston School of Theology, Cambridge, Mass.
Article: Human Rights.

HOPKINS, Martin, K., OP, M.A., S.T.L., S.S.L., St Thomas Aquinas Priory, River Forest, Ill.
Articles: Eschatology; People of God.

HORGAN, Thaddeus, SA, Co-Director, Greymoor Ecumenical Institute, Greymoor/Garrison, N.Y.
Articles: Covenant Relationships; Ecumenical Institutes and Centers; Ecumenism, Regional and Local; Week of Prayer for Christian Unity.

HORVATH, Tibor, SJ, Professor of Systematic Theology, Regis College, Toronto, Canada.
Article: Preambles of Faith.

HOTCHKIN, John F., Ph.D., Executive Director, Committee on Ecumenical and Interreligious Affairs, NCCB, Washington, D.C.
Articles: Bilateral Consultations; Bishops' Committee for Ecumenical and Interreligious Affairs (BCEIA); United Methodist/Roman Catholic Dialogue.

HOVDA, Robert W., Editorial Director, The Liturgical Conference, Washington, D.C.
Article: Liturgical Conference.

HUBBARD, Anne M., MMM, Regional Superior, Medical Missionaries of Mary, Bronx, N.Y.
Article: Martin, Mary.

HUGHES, Gerald P., Executive Director, Cursillo Movement, National Center, Dallas, Texas.
Article: Cursillo Movement.

HUGHES, John C., MS, Chairman of Promotion and Membership, Catholic Preaching Ministry International, Cheshire, Conn.
Article: Catholic Preaching Ministry International.

HUNT, Joseph I., Professor, Old Testament, Nashotah House, Nashotah, Wis.
Articles: Bible Versions for Liturgy; Psalmody; Psalters, Vernacular (Liturgy).

HÜSSLER, Msgr. George, President, Caritas Internationalis, Freiburg/Br., Germany.
Article: Caritas Internationalis.

ILLIG, Alvin, Staff Director, Ad Hoc Committee on Evangelization, NCCB, Washington, D.C.
Article: Bishops' Committee on Evangelization.

IRWIN, Mary P., U.S. Assistant, Society of Our Lady of the Way, San Francisco, Cal.
Articles: Secular Institutes; United States Conference of Secular Institutes.

ISASI-DIAZ, Ada M., Women's Ordination Conference, Rochester, N.Y.
Article: Women's Ordination Conference.

IVERS, Margaret M., IBVM, M.A., Executive Director, Catholic Campus Ministry Association, Detroit, Mich.
Articles: Catholic Campus Ministry Association; Women in Campus Ministry.

JELLY, Frederick M., OP, Academic Dean, School of Theology, Pontifical College, Josephinum, Worthington, Ohio.
Articles: Mary and the Church; Virgin Birth.

JEWITT, Bernard C., St. Thomas More Rectory, Tulsa, Okla.
Article: Parish.

JOHNSON, John G., M.A., J.C.L., Diocese of Columbus, Columbus, Ohio.
Articles: Curia, Roman: Incardination and Excardination; Legates, Papal; Papal Secrecy; Sacred College.

JOHNSON, Lawrence, Executive Director, Office for Divine Worship, Diocese of Wilmington, Wilmingon, Del.
Articles: Blessings, Liturgical; Calendar, Liturgical (U.S.); Calendars, Particular; Churches, Dedication of; Saints, Memorials of.

JONES, Arthur, Editor and Publisher, *National Catholic Reporter*, Kansas City, Mo.
Article: Thorman, Donald.

KANE, Lawrence J., Executive Director, Human Life and Natural Family Planning Foundation, Washington, D.C.
Articles: Human Life and Natural Family Planning Foundation; Natural Family Planning.

KANE, Thomas A., Ph.D., D.P.S., International Executive Director and Psychotherapist, House of Affirmation, International Therapeutic Center for Clergy and Religious, Whitinsville, Mass.
Articles: House of Affirmation; Psychotheological Therapy.

KAY, Hugh, Jesuit Information Officer, London, England.
Articles: Corbishley, Thomas; D'Arcy, Martin.

KEATING, Kathleen SSJ, National Chairperson, National Association of Women Religious Chicago, Ill.
Article: National Assembly of Women Religious (NAWR).

KEEFE, Jeffry, OFMConv, Ph.D., Professor of Pastoral Psychology, St. Anthony-on-Hudson, Rensselaer, N.Y.; Training Staff, Onondaga Pastoral Counseling Center, Syracuse, N.Y.; Consultant, Tribunal, Diocese of Syracuse.
Article: Religion, Psychology of.

KEIFER, Ralph A., Ph.D., Catholic Theological Union, Chicago, Ill.; Associate Editor, *Worship.*
Articles: Eucharistic Prayers: Eucharistic Prayers for Special Occasions.

KELLEY, Joseph T., OSA, Professor in Religious Studies, Merrimack College, North Andover, Mass.
Articles: Latin Mass; Masses, Votive.

KELLY, Geffrey, B., S.T.D., La Salle College, Philadelphia, Pa.
Article: Communion of Saints.

KELLY, Patrick J., OP, St. Peter Martyr Priory, Los Angeles, Cal.
Article: Meagher, Paul Kevin.

KELLY, Most Reverend Thomas C., OP, General Secretary, NCCB/USCC, Washington, D.C.
Article: Episcopacy (Spiritual Theology).

KENNEDY, Diane, OP, Executive Director, PARABLE, Minneapolis, Minn.
Article: Apostolic Spirituality.

KENNEDY, Malcolm M., Opus Dei. New York, N.Y.
Article: Escrivá de Balaguer y Albás, José María.

KENNY, Michael, Ph.D., Professor, Anthropology, Catholic University of America, Washington, D.C.
Article: Culture, Development of.

KOMONCHAK, Joseph A., Assistant Professor, Department of Religion and Religious Education, Catholic University of America, Washington, D.C.
Articles: Authority, Ecclesiastical; Church and World; Community of Mankind; Society (Theology).

KONERMAN, Edward H., SJ, Secretary, Catholic Theological Society of America; Professor, St. Mary of the Lake Seminary, Mundelein, Ill.
Article: Catholic Theological Society of America.

KRAMER, Thomas E., Cathedral of the Holy Spirit, Bismarck, N. Dak.
Article: Collins, Joseph Burns.

KRESS, Robert, M.A., Ph.D., S.T.L., Professor, Department of Philosophy and Religion, University of Evansville, Evansville, Ind.
Articles: Catholicity; Church, Local (Theology); Church and Communio; Collegiality; Frankfurt School; Jaeger, Lorenz; Journet, Charles; Worship, Communal.

KREYCHE, Gerald F., Ph.D., Chairman, Department of Philosophy, De Paul University, Chicago, Ill.
Article: Metaphysics.

KRITZECK, James, Ph.D., University of Notre Dame, Notre Dame, Ind.
Article: Islamic/Roman Catholic Dialogue.

KROSNICKI, Thomas A., SVD, Associate Director, NCCB Committee on the Liturgy, Washington, D.C.
Article: Bishops' Committee on the Liturgy.

KROUSE, Dennis W., S.T.D., Director, Center for Liturgy and Prayer, Diocese of San Diego; Assistant Professor of Religious Studies, University of San Diego, San Diego, Cal.
Articles: Liturgical Education in Seminaries; Liturgy.

LA BARGE, Joseph A., Ph.D., Associate Professor of Religion, Bucknell University, Lewisburg, Pa.
Article: Death (Theology).

LA FONTAINE, Charles, V., SA, Co-Director, Graymoor Ecumenical Institute, Graymoor/Garrison, N.Y.: Editor, *Ecumenical Trends.*
Articles: Ecumenical Movement; Ecumenics.

LA GATZA, Marie, D.S.W., A.C.S.W., Catholic Social Services, Archdiocese of Philadelphia.
Article: Social Work, Catholic.

LAMBERT, Rollins E., Specialist for African Affairs, Office of International Peace and Justice, USCC, Washington, D.C.
Article: Africa, Southern.

LAND, Philip, SJ, Center of Concern, Washington, D.C.
Article: New International Economic Order.

LANE, Ralph, Jr., Ph.D., Professor of Sociology, University of San Francisco, San Francisco, Cal.
Article: Parish, Sociology of.

LARKIN, Ernest E., OCarm, President, Kino Institute, Phoenix, Ariz.
Article: Priestly Spirituality.

LAUBENTHAL, Allan, St. Mary Seminary, Cleveland, Ohio.
Articles; Organic Union; Reunion of Churches; Unicity of the Church.

LAVIN, Martin E., J.C.D., St. Mary Magdalen de Pazzi Church, Philadelphia, Pa.; Vice-Officialis, Archdiocese of Philadelphia.
Article: Rota, Roman.

LE BLANC, Paul J., St. Pius V Church, New York, N.Y.
Articles: Charisms in Ministry; Ministries, Lay; Ministries, Sacred.

LECKEY, Dolores R., Executive Director, NCCB Secretariat for the Laity, Washington, D.C.
Article: Bishops' Committee on the Laity.

LEE, Andrea, President, National Coalition of American Nuns, University Park, Pa.
Article: Prisons and Prisoners.

LEE, Carolyn T., Head, Theology, Philosophy, Canon Law Library, Catholic University of America, Washington, D.C.
Article: Willging, Eugene Paul.

LENCYK, Wasyl, Ph.D., St. Basil's Seminary, Stamford, Conn.
Article: Ukrainian Rite.

LENZ, Rev. Msgr. Paul A., Executive Director and Treasurer, Bureau of Catholic Indian Missions, Washington, D.C.
Articles: American Indian Catholic Missions; Bureau of Catholic Indian Missions.

LEONARD, William J., SJ, Professor Emeritus, Department of Social Sciences, Boston College; Superior, America House, New York, N.Y.
Article: Social Action.

LERCH, Joseph R., SJ, M.A., S.T.L., Professor of Systematic Theology, Jamshedpur, Bihar, India.
Article: Teaching Authority of the Church (Magisterium).

LINSCOTT, Mary, SNDdeN, President, International Union of Superiors General (UISG), Rome, Italy.
Articles: Council for Relations between the CRSI and IUSG; International Union of Superiors General (Women).

LIPSCOMB, Rev. Msgr. Oscar H., Chancellor, The Chancery, Diocese of Mobile.
Article: Toolen, Thomas.

LONG, John, SJ, M.A., S.T.L., Chief of Bureau, Secretariat for Promoting Christian Unity, Rome, Italy.
Article: Secretariat for Promoting Christian Unity.

LOWERY, Daniel L., CSSR, Mt. St. Alphonsus Seminary, Esopus, N.Y.
Articles: Advertising (Moral Aspect); Employees/Employers, Moral Obligations of.

LUCAL, John A., SJ, General Secretary, SODEPAX, Geneva, Switzerland.
Articles: SODEPAX; Joint Working Group of the World Council of Churches and the Roman Catholic Church.

LUNDY, George F., Editor, *Extension:* Director of Communications, Catholic Church Extension Society, Chicago, Ill.
Article: Catholic Church Extension Society.

LUZBETAK, Louis J., SVD, President, Divine Word College, Epworth, Iowa.
Articles: Missiology; Mission of the Church.

LYNCH, William A., M.D., President, National Federation of Catholic Physicians Guilds, Milton, Mass.
Article: National Federation of Catholic Physicians Guilds.

MacDONALD, Rev. Msgr. Colin A., Executive Director, Office of Priestly Life and Ministry, NCCB, Washington, D.C.
Article: Bishops' Committee on Priestly Life and Ministry.

McBRIEN, Richard, Institute for the Study of Religious Education and Service, Boston College, Chestnut Hill, Mass.
Articles: Apostolic Succession; Apostolicity.

McCARTHY, Donald G., Professor of Christian Ethics, Mt. St. Mary's Seminary, Norwood, Ohio; Member Presbyterian-Reformed/Roman Catholic Consultation.
Article: Presbyterian-Reformed/Roman Catholic Consultation.

McCARTHY, John D., Associate Professor, Department of Sociology, Catholic University of America, Washington, D.C.
Article: Public Opinion.

McCARTHY, John E., Director, Migration and Refugee Affairs, USCC, Washington, D.C.
Article: Migration and Refugee Services of the USCC.

McCASLIN, Patrick, President, National Association of Permanent Diaconate Directors; Director, Permanent Diaconate Program, Archdiocese of Omaha, Omaha, Neb.
Article: National Association of Permanent Diaconate Directors.

McDERMOTT, Brian O., SJ, Ph.D., Professor of Systematic Theology, Weston School of Theology, Cambridge, Mass.
Article: Original Sin.

McDONELL, Ruth, IHM, Specialist in Adolescent Catechesis, USCC Department of Education, Washington, D.C.
Articles: Catechesis, Adolescent; Media in Education.

McFADDEN, Thomas M., S.T.D., Department of Theology, St. Joseph's College, Philadelphia, Pa.
Articles: Christocentrism; Christology; College Theology Society.

McGOVERN, Arthur F., SJ, University of Detroit, Detroit, Mich.
Article: Marxism and Christianity.

McGRATH, Rev. Msgr. James, Officialis, The Tribunal, Archdiocese of Philadelphia.
Article: Good Conscience Procedures.

McHUGH, Rev. Msgr. James T., Director, Secretariat, NCCB ad hoc Committee for Pro-Life Activities, Washington, D.C.
Article: Bishops' Committee on Pro-Life Activities.

McKENNA, John C., CM, Department of Theology, St. John's University, Jamaica, N.Y.
Article: Communion in the Hand.

MACKEY, James, Ph.D., Department of Theology and Religious Studies, University of San Francisco, San Francisco, Cal.
Article: Religion, Philosophy of.

McMAHON, Thomas F., CSV, Professor, Socio-Legal Studies Department, Loyola University of Chicago, Chicago, Ill.
Articles: Indifferentism; Secularism.

McMANUS, Frederick R., J.C.D., LL.D., Vice Provost and Dean of Graduate Studies, Catholic University of America, Washington, D.C.
Articles: Altar; Sacraments and Divine Worship, Congregation for the; Tabernacle.

McNAMARA, Robert J., Ph.D., Executive Secretary, Association for the Sociology of Religion, Loyola University, Chicago, Ill.
Article: Association for the Sociology of Religion.

McNASPY, Clement J., SJ, University Professor, Loyola University, New Orleans, La.
Articles: Lavanoux, Maurice Émile; Twomey, Louis J.

MADDUX, John L., Office of the President, World Bank, Washington, D.C.
Article: World Bank.

MAGUIRE, Marjorie Reiley, Ph.D., Lecturer, Milwaukee, Wis.
Article: Dying, Care of.

MAHOWALD, Rev. Msgr. Richard J., Rome Office, Pontifical Mission for Palestine, Vatican City.
Articles: Continuing Education for Ministry; Institute for Continuing Theological Education.

MALDOON, Dorothy and Raymond, Executive Directing Couple, Christian Family Movement, Calumet College Center, Whiting, Ind.
Article: Christian Family Movement.

MARTHALER, Bernard L., OFMConv., Chairman, Department of Religious Studies/Religious Education, Catholic University of America, Washington, D.C.
Article: Religious Education.

MARTÍ, Thomas J., MM, Coordinator, Maryknoll Justice and Peace Office, Maryknoll, N.Y.
Article: Philippines, Church in.

MARTINEZ, Manuel, OFM, Executive Director, PADRES, San Antonio, Tx.
Article: PADRES.

MAY, William E., Department of Theology, Catholic University of America, Washington, D.C.
Articles: Law, Christian; Morality, Christian; Natural Law.

MEEHAN, Francis X., Associate Professor of Moral Theology, St. Charles Borromeo Seminary, Philadelphia, Pa.
Article: Sexual Morality (Moral Theology).

MEEHAN, John P., MM, President, Maryknoll Seminary, Maryknoll, N.Y.
Articles: Missionary; Missionary Formation.

MEINBERG, Cloud H., OSB, St. John's Abbey, Collegeville, Minn.
Articles: Baptismal Font; Baptistery; Chapel of Reconciliation; Communion Table.

MELADY, Thomas Patrick, Ph.D., Professor, Political Science and President, Sacred Heart University, Bridgeport, Conn.
Article: Terrorism, Political.

MENARD, Clarence, C., OMI, Eccl.Hist.D., Professor of Historical and Ascetical Theology, Notre Dame Seminary, New Orleans, La.; Member, Orthodox/Roman Catholic Consultation.
Article: Orthodox/Roman Catholic Consultation.

MEYER, Robert T., Ph.D., Professor Emeritus, Celtic Languages, Catholic University of America, Washington, D.C.
Article: Peebles, Bernard.

MEYERS, John F., President, National Catholic Educational Association, Washington, D.C.
Article: National Catholic Educational Association (NCEA).

MICK, Lawrence, Office for Worship, Dayton, Ohio.
Articles: Catechumenate for Adults; Catechumens (Juridic Status); Infant Baptism and Communion; Post-Baptismal Catechesis (Mystagogia); Sponsors.

MIKOLIC, Stephen, Professor of History, Sacred Heart University, Bridgeport, Conn.
Article: Terrorism, Political.

MILLER, Frances A., Foundress and International Director, Júdean Society, Inc., Mountain View, Cal.
Article: Júdean Society.

MISNER, Paul, Ph.D., Everett, Mass.
Articles: Church (Theology); Ecclesiology; Lutheran/Roman Catholic Dialogue; Lutheran-Reformed/Roman Catholic Study Commission; Primacy of the Pope; Unity of the Church.

MITCHELL, Leonel L., Professor of Liturgics, Seabury-Western Theological Seminary, Evanston, Ill.
Articles: Baptized Christians (Rite of Reception); Catechesis for Confirmation and Eucharist; Catechumenate (Rite of Admission); Christian Initiation, Sacraments of; Initiation of Children of Catechetical Age (Rite).

MITCHELL, Nathan, OSB, Assistant Professor of Liturgy, St. Meinrad Seminary, St. Meinrad, Ind.
Articles: Candidacy for Ordination (Rite of Admission); Celibacy (Rite of Commitment); Institution of Readers and Acolytes (Rite).

MODDE, Margaret Mary, OSF, J.C.D., Assisi Heights, Rochester, Minn.
Articles: Discipline, Ecclesiastical; Noncanonical Communities; Religious Institutes, Departures from.

MOELLER, William, FSC, Chairman, Department of Pastoral Education, Washington Theological Union, Silver Spring, Md.
Article: Brother, Religious.

MOLDAVER, Stephen M., A.P.R., Director of Public Relations, Catholic Hospital Association, St. Louis, Mo.
Article: Catholic Hospital Association.

MOLONEY, Joseph, OSF, Executive Director, National Apostolate for the Mentally Retarded, Brooklyn, N.Y.
Article: National Apostolate for the Mentally Retarded.

MONDIN, P. Gianbattista, SX, Dean of Philosophy, Pontificia Universitas Urbaniana, Rome; Director, Institute for the Study of Atheism.
Articles: Atheism; Institute for the Study of Atheism.

MONTAGUE, George P., SM, Marianist American Seminary, St. Basil's College, Toronto, Canada.
Articles: Charismatic Prayer; Holy Spirit.

MORACEZEWSKI, Albert S., OP, Ph.D., President, Pope John XXIII Medical-Moral Research and Education Center, St. Louis, Mo.
Articles: Experimentation, Medical; Fetal Research; Medical Ethics.

MORRISEY, Francis G., OMI, Dean, Faculty of Canon Law, Saint Paul University, Ottawa, Canada.
Article: Pope, Election of.

MULHERN, Philip F., OP, S.T.M., University of St. Thomas Aquinas, Rome.
Articles: Attwater, Donald; Baptismal Promises; Döpfner, Julius; Hollis, Christopher; Office of the Dead; Staffa, Dino; Witness, Christian.

MURNION, Philip J., Director, Pastoral Research Office, Archdiocese of New York, New York, N.Y.
Articles: Community; Parish (Community).

MURPHY, Francis X., CSSR, Rector, Holy Redeemer College, Washington, D.C.
Article: Paul VI, Pope.

MURPHY, Rev. Msgr. John F., Executive Director, Association of Catholic Colleges and Universities, NCEA, Washington, D.C.
Articles: Higher Education, Church and; Higher Education and Ecumenism.

MURPHY, John J., Ph.D., Department of Economics, Catholic University of America, Washington, D.C.
Article: Economic Aid, International.

MURPHY, Richard J., OMI, J.C.D., Oblate College, Washington, D.C.
Articles: Papal Household; Societies, Condemned (Canon Law).

NEAL, Marie Augusta, SNdeN., Professor of Sociology, Emmanuel College, Boston, Mass.
Article: Civil Religion.

NEALE, Ann, GNSH, Ph.D., Executive Director, Bishops' Committee for Human Values, Washington, D.C.
Articles: Bishops' Committee for Human Values; Temporal Values.

NEASON, Frances L., Executive Director, Secretariat, NCCB Committee for the Church in Latin America, Washington, D.C.
Article: Bishops' Committee for the Church in Latin America.

NELSEN, Hart M., Ph.D., Professor of Sociology, Catholic University of America, Washington, D.C.
Article: Religion, Sociology of.

NESSEL, William J., OSFS, M.A., J.C.D., Director of Pastoral Ministries, Allentown College of St. Francis de Sales; Director of Personnel, Oblates of St. Francis de Sales, Wilmington-Philadelphia Province, Wilmington, Del.
Article: Censorship of Books.

NICKELS, Marilyn W., Ph.D., Education Specialist, Bureau of the Census, Washington, D.C.
Article: Turner, Thomas Wyatt.

NOVAK, Francis A., CSSR, Executive Director, National Catholic Stewardship Council, Washington, D.C.
Articles: Fund Raising and Accountability; National Catholic Stewardship Council.

NOVAK, Michael, Ledden-Watson Chair of Religious Studies, Syracuse University, Syracuse, N.Y. (on leave); Resident Scholar, American Enterprise Institute for Public Policy Research, Washington, D.C.
Article: Catholicism (Cultural).

NOVAK, Vincent M., SJ, Jesuit Community, Fordham University, Bronx, N.Y.
Article: Catechetical Centers.

O'BRIEN, Thomas C., Executive Editor, *New Catholic Encyclopedia*, Vol. 17, Catholic University of America, Washington, D.C.
Articles: Conversion; Gilby, Thomas; John Paul I, Pope; John Paul II, Pope; Leonine Commission; Lercaro, Giacomo; Mass, Conventual/Community; Pontifical, Roman; Ritual, Roman; Virginity, Consecration to (Rite).

O'BRIEN, William James, Ph.D., Assistant Professor, Department of Theology, University of Notre Dame, Notre Dame, Ind.
Articles: Pluralism, Theological; Theology and Philosophy; Theology in Catholic Colleges.

O'BRIEN, William V., Ph.D., Professor of Government, Georgetown University, Washington, D.C.
Article: Genocide.

O'CONNELL, Timothy E., Ph.D., Associate Professor of Moral Theology, St. Mary of the Lake Seminary, Mundelein, Ill.
Articles: Personalism; Relativism, Moral.

O'CONNOR, Edward D., CSC, Department of Theology, University of Notre Dame, Notre Dame, Ind.
Articles: Charismatic Renewal, Catholic; Charismatic Renewal and Ecumenism.

O'CONNOR, James I., SJ, J.C.D., Professor Emeritus, Canon Law, Jesuit School of Theology in Chicago; Chaplain; Publisher, *Canon Law Digest*, St. Mary of the Lake Seminary, Mundelein, Ill.
Articles: Religious, Constitutions for; Religious, Exemption of.

O'CONNOR, John V., SJ, Executive Director, CARA, Washington, D.C.
Article: Center for Applied Research in the Apostolate (CARA).

O'CONNOR, Mary Alice, CSJ, Assistant Professor and Director, Liturgical Music Program, Catholic University of America, Washington, D.C.
Articles: Mass, Latin Chants for; Sacramentary, Music of.

O'DONNELL, Thomas, SJ, Pontificia Università Gregoriana, Rome.
Articles: Impotence; Sterilization.

O'DONOHOE, James A., J.C.D., Professor of Theological Ethics, St. John's Seminary, Brighton, Mass.
Articles: Human Act; Sin (Theology).

O'GARA, James, Editor, *Commonweal*, New York, N.Y.
Article: Cogley, John.

O'HANLON, Daniel J., SJ, Profesor of Fundamental and Systematic Theology, Jesuit School of Theology at Berkeley, Berkeley, Cal.
Article: Buddhism, Church and.

O'HARE, Joseph A., SJ, AMERICA, New York, N.Y.
Article: Roberts, Thomas D'Esterre.

OLSEN, John D., CFX, Ph.D., Executive Director, Secondary School Department, National Catholic Educational Association, Washington, D.C.
Article: Secondary Education, Catholic.

O'MALLEY, John W., SJ, Professor of History, University of Detroit, Detroit, Mich.
Articles: History, Philosophy and Theology of; Vatican Council II.

O'NEILL, James C., Catholic Relief Services, USCC, New York, N.Y.
Article: Norris, James Joseph.

O'NEILL, Mary Aquin, RSM, Department of Theology, Loyola College, Baltimore, Md.
Article: Feminism and Christian Theology.

O'NEILL, Patrick H., OSA, Representative for Campus and Young Adult Ministry, Washington, D.C.
Articles: Campus and Young Adult Ministry (USCC); Youth Ministry; Campus Ministry.

O'NEILL, Rae Ann, MM, Assistant Attaché, Office of the Permanent Observer of the Holy See to the United Nations, New York, N.Y.
Articles: United Nations, Holy See and; United Nations, Permanent Vatican Observer to.

O'NEILL, Thomas, SJ., East Asian Pastoral Institute, Manila, Phillipines.
Article: Sheridan, Terence.

O'ROURKE, Kevin D., OP, J.C.D., Vice-President,

Medical-Moral Affairs and Pastoral Care Services, Catholic Hospital Association, St. Louis, Mo.
Articles: Hospitals, Catholic; Medical Personnel, Moral Obligations of.

ÖRSY, Ladislas M., SJ, School of Religious Studies, Catholic University of America, Washington, D.C.
Articles: Canonical Studies; Jurisprudence, Canonical.

OSBORNE, Kenan B., OFM, President and Dean, Franciscan School of Theology, Berkeley, Cal.; Professor, Systematic Theology, Graduate Union, Berkeley, Cal.
Articles: Sacramental Theology, Sacraments (Theology).

OVERMAN, Conleth, CP, Holy Cross Center, Cincinnati, Ohio.
Article: Chapters, Religious; Prayer, Community.

PABLE, Martin, OFMCap, Master of Novices, St. Felix Friary, Huntington, Ind.
Article: Pastoral Psychology.

PAGE, John R., Associate Executive Secretary, International Commission on English in the Liturgy (ICEL), Washington, D.C.
Article: International Commission on English in the Liturgy (ICEL).

PAKENHAM, Daniel J., Executive Director, Bishops' Committee on Vocations, NCCB, Washington, D.C.
Articles: Bishops' Committee on Priestly Formation; Bishops' Committee on Vocations.

PANIKKAR, Raimondo, Ph.D., Professor, Department of Religious Studies, University of California, Santa Barbara, Cal.
Article: Hinduism, Church and.

PAREDES, Mario, Executive Director, Northeast Regional Pastoral Center for Hispanics, New York, N.Y.
Article: Ethnics, Rights of; Northeast Regional Pastoral Center for Hispanics.

PARADIS, Rev. Msgr. Wilfrid H., Project Director, National Catechetical Directory, NCCB, Washington, D.C.: Secretary for Education, USCC.
Article: National Catechetical Directory (U.S.).

PARATORE, Matthew R., Executive Secretary, International Liaison, U.S. Catholic Coordinating Center for Lay Volunteer Ministries, Washington, D.C.
Article: International Liaison.

PARSONAGE, Robert Rue, Membership Secretary, National Campus Ministry Association, New York. N.Y.
Article: National Campus Ministry Association.

PASQUARIELLO, Ronald D., National Center for Urban Ethnic Affairs, Washington, D.C.
Articles: Catholic Conference on Ethnic and Neighborhood Affairs; Ethnicity; National Center for Urban Ethnic Affairs (NCUEA); Urbanization.

PATER, Giles H., Ph.D., Professor of Liturgy, Mt. St. Mary's Seminary, Norwood, Ohio.
Article: Liturgy (Historical Development).

PATRICK, Ann E., SNJM, University of Chicago Divinity School, Chicago, Ill.
Article: Bishops' Committee on Women in Society and the Church.

PATRICK, James, Ph.D., Chairman, Department of Theology, University of Dallas, Irving Tex. Member, Disciples of Christ/Roman Catholic Consultation.
Articles: Christian; Disciples of Christ/Roman Catholic Consultation.

PEACHEY, Paul, Ph.D., Professor, Department of Sociology, Catholic University of America, Washington, D.C.
Article: Church in Communist Countries.

PEIFER, Claude, OSB, St. Bede Abbey, Peru, Ill.
Articles: Bible and Liturgy; Bible Services.

PEIXOTTO, Helen, Ph.D., Department of Psychology, Catholic University of America, Washington, D.C.
Article: Van der Veldt, James H.

PENNINGTON, M. Basil, OCSO, Monk of St. Joseph's Abbey, Spencer, Mass.
Articles: Concilium Monasticum Iuris Canonici; Perfection, Spiritual; Spirituality, Contemporary.

PERELLA, Frederick J., Director, Office of Urban Affairs of the Archdiocese of Hartford, New Haven, Conn.
Article: Poverty.

PHILIBERT, Paul J., OP, Boys Town Center for the Study of Youth Development, Department of Religious Studies/Religious Education, Catholic University of America, Washington, D.C.
Articles: Moral Development; Moral Education.

PIERRE, Kenneth J., Rector, St. John Vianney Seminary, St. Paul, Minn.
Article: Person, Dignity of.

PIGNONE, Mary Margaret, SND, Director, Office of Community Development, Diocese of Wheeling-Charleston, Williamston, W.Va.
Article: Core Appalachian Ministries (CAM).

POEL VAN DER, Cornelius, CSSp, St. John's Provincial Seminary, Plymouth, Mich.
Article: Juristiction (Canon Law).

POLCINO, Anna, SCMM, M.D., Psychiatrist, Lecturer, International Psychiatric Director, House of Affirmation, Whitinsville, Mass.
Article: Vocation, Psychology of.

POSEY, Teresa B., Secretary, U.S. Catholic Bishops' Advisory Council, Washington, D.C.
Article: Bishops' Advisory Council, U.S. Catholic.

POSPISHIL, Rev. Msgr. Victor J., J.C.D., Pastor, St. Mary's Ukrainian Catholic Church, Carteret, N.J.
Article: Eastern Catholic Churches.

POWER, David N., OMI, Associate Professor of Systematic Theology, Catholic University of America, Washington, D.C.
Articles: Hierarchy; Ministry (Ecclesiology).

PROVOST, James Harrison, S.T.D., M.A., J.C.D., Chancellor and Presiding Judge, Diocese of Helena, Helena, Montana.
Articles: Censures, Ecclesiastical; Penal Power of the Church.

PRUFER, Thomas, Ph.D., Associate Professor of Philosophy, Catholic University of America, Washington, D.C.
Article: Heidegger, Martin.

PRZYBILLA, Carla, OSF, Executive Director, Religious Formation Conference, Washington, D.C.
Articles: Religious Formation; Religious Formation Conference.

PURCELL, Theodore V., SJ, Department of Economics, Georgetown University, Washington, D.C.
Article: Business Ethics.

PURDY, Rev. Msgr. William F., Secretariat for Promoting Christian Unity, Vatican City, Italy.
Article: Joint Roman Catholic/World-Methodist Commission.

QUINN, A. James, J.D., J.C.D., Financial Secretary, Diocese of Cleveland, Financial and Legal Office, Cleveland, Ohio.
Article: Faculties, Bishops'.

QUINN, Frank C., OP, M.A., Ph.D., Assistant Professor, Aquinas Institute of Theology, Dubuque, Iowa.
Articles: Gregorian Chant; Liturgy of the Hours, Chants of.

QUINN, William, FSC, La Salle College, Philadelphia, Pa.
Articles: Community, Religious; Religious (Men).

QUIÑONEZ, Lora Ann, CPD, Ph.D., Generalate, Sisters of Divine Providence, Helotes, Texas.
Article: Women's Liberation Movement.

RECK, Carleen J., SSND, Executive Director, Department of Elementary Schools, NCEA, Washington, D.C.
Articles: Sex Education; Teachers, Ministry of.

REGAN, Patrick J., OSB, St. Joseph Abbey, St. Benedict, La.
Article: Celebration and Liturgy.

REGAN, Richard J., SJ, Associate Professor, Department of Political Science, Fordham University, Bronx, N.Y.
Article: Church and State (U.S.).

REID, Jay H., Director, Information Office, International Monetary Fund (IMF), Washington, D.C.
Article: International Monetary Fund.

REILLY, John, President, Association of Catholic Teachers, Philadelphia, Pa.
Articles: Association of Catholic Teachers; Teachers' Unions, Catholic.

REPOHL, Roger F., SJ, Department of Religious Studies, University of Santa Clara, Santa Clara, Cal.
Article: Single People.

RICHSTATTER, Thomas, OFM, Th.D., Liturgy Teacher, St. Leonard Franciscan Seminary, Dayton, Ohio.
Articles: Liturgical Experimentation; Liturgical Laws, Authority of; Liturgical Rites; Liturgy (Structural Elements); Rubrics; Silence in Worship; Solemn Blessing and Prayer over the People.

RIGALI, Norbert J., SJ, Associate Professor and Chairman, Department of Religious Studies, University of

San Diego, San Diego, Cal.
Article: Love (Theology).

RISK, James E., SJ, J.C.D., The Fairfield Jesuit Community, Fairfield, Conn.; Chancery, Diocese of Bridgeport.
Article: Commissions, Papal.

ROACH, Peggy, Member, Board of Directors, Catholic Committee on Urban Ministry, University of Notre Dame, Notre Dame, Ind.
Article: Catholic Committee on Urban Ministry (CCUM).

RONDEAU, Marie-J., Professor, University of Caen, France; Vice President, Amis du Cardinal Daniélou.
Article: Daniélou, Jean.

ROUTLEY, Erik, Skillman, N.J.
Article: Hymns and Hymnals.

ROVER, Thomas D., OP, Providence College, Providence, R.I.
Articles: Homily; Preaching.

RYAN, Herbert J., SJ, Ph.D., Jesuit Community, Loyola-Marymount University, Los Angeles, Cal.
Articles: Anglican Orders; Anglican/Roman Catholic Consultation (U.S.); Anglican/Roman Catholic International Commission (ARCIC).

RYAN, John Barry, Ph.D., former Director Notre Dame Center for Pastoral Liturgy, University of Notre Dame, Notre Dame, Ind.; Assistant Professor of Religious Studies, Manhattan College, Bronx, N.Y.
Articles: Extraordinary Ministers of the Eucharist; Extraordinary Ministers of the Eucharist (Rite of Institution); Masses With Children; North American Academy of Liturgy.

RYAN, Richard R., CM, J.C.D., Assistant Professor of Canon Law, St. Thomas Seminary, Denver, Colorado.
Article: Dispensations.

RYAN, Thomas J., Ph.D., Department of Theology, St. Joseph's College, Philadelphia, Pa.
Articles: Bultmann, Rudolf; Demythologizing; Dead Sea Scrolls; Revelation, Concept of (In the Bible).

RYAN, William A., Director, National Catholic Office for Information, NCCB/USCC, Washington, D.C.
Article: Traditionalist Movement, Catholic.

RYAN, William B., OP, S.T.M., J.C.D., Mt. St. Dominic, Caldwell, N.J.
Articles: Cloister; Confessors of Religious; Novitiate.

RYAN, William F., SJ, Former Director, Center of Concern, Washington, D.C.; Provincial, Jesuit Fathers of Upper Canada, Toronto, Canada.
Articles: Center of Concern; Multinational Corporations; Socialization; Solidarity, Human.

SAFILIOS-ROTHSCHILD, Constantine, Ph.D., Professor of Sociology, University of California at Santa Barbara, Santa Barbara, Cal.
Article: Women in Society.

ST. JAMES, Charles, FIC, Executive Director, National Conference of Religious Vocation Directors of Men, Chicago, Ill.
Article: National Conference of Religious Vocation Directors of Men.

SATTLER, Henry V., CSSR, Ph.D., Professor of Theology, University of Scranton, Scranton, Pa.
Article: Fellowship of Catholic Scholars.

SCANLAN, Margaret Shawn, SND, Director, Catholic Committee of Appalachia, Prestonburg, Ky.
Article: Catholic Committee of Appalachia.

SCANNELL, Anthony, OFMCap, President, UNDA-USA, Los Angeles, Cal.
Article: UNDA.

SCHAFTER, André, Les Publications de la vie Catholique, Paris, France.
Article: Conference of International Catholic Organizations.

SCHELLMAN, James M., Assistant to the Executive Secretary, International Commission on English in the Liturgy, Washington, D.C.
Article: Liturgical Books of the Roman Rite.

SCHEMELFENING, Marie A., Executive Director, National Federation of Christian Life Communities, St. Louis, Mo.
Article: Christian Life Communities.

SCHEPERS, Maurice, OP, Department of Religion, La Salle College, Philadelphia, Pa.
Article: Laity, Vocation of.

SCHNEIDERS, Sandra, IHM, Assistant Professor of New Testament Studies and Spirituality, The Jesuit School of Theology at Berkeley, Graduate Theological Union, Berkeley, Cal.
Article: Vow (Practice and Theology).

SCHUMACHER, John N., SJ, Professor of Church History, Ateneo de Manila University, Manila, Phillipine Islands.
Article: Third World, Church and.

SHAUGHNESSY, James D., Former Director, Notre Dame Center for Pastoral Liturgy, University of Notre Dame, Notre Dame, Ind.
Articles: Penance (Rite); Penance, Communal Celebration of.

SHAW, Russell, Secretary for Public Affairs, NCCB/USCC, Washington, D.C.
Articles: Media of Social Communication and Evangelization; Public Policy Issues and the Church.

SHEA, William M., Assistant Professor of Religion, Catholic University of America, Washington, D.C.
Articles: Pluralism, Theological; Theology in America.

SHEEHAN, J. Peter, Associate Director, Bishops' Committee on Ecumenical and Religious Affairs (BCEIA), Washington, D.C.
Article: Southern Baptist/Roman Catholic Consultations.

SHEEHAN, Mary Ellen, IHM, Assistant Professor of Theology, Toronto School of Theology, University of St. Michael, Toronto, Canada.
Article: Women, Ordination of.

SHEEHAN, Michael J., Holy Trinity Seminary, Irving, Texas.
Article: Pastoral Councils, Regional and National.

SHORTER, Aylward, WF, Kipalapala Seminary, Tabora, Tanzania.
Article: African Independent Church movement.

SHUDA, Rev. Msgr. Robert, Ph.D., Director of Education, Diocese of Greenburg, Greensburg, Pa.
Article: Parochial Schools, Catholic Elementary.

SIXEAS, Virginia, SNDdeN, Editor, NETWORK, Washington, D.C.
Articles: Activism, Political and Social; NETWORK.

SKEHAN, Joseph T., Ph.D., Associate Professor of Economics, Penn State University, Bloomsburg, Pa.
Article: National Association of Laity.

SKWOR, Donald P., Associate Secretary, Conference of Major Superiors of Men Religious, Washington, D.C.
Article: Conference of Major Superiors of Men (CMSM).

SMITH, Robert F., Ph.D., National Right To Work Committee, Fairfax, Va.
Article: Right to Work.

SPIERS, Rev. Msgr. Edward, Executive Director, Citizens for Educational Freedom, Washington, D.C.
Article: Citizens for Educational Freedom.

STAMSCHROR, Robert, Director, Religious Education/CCD, USCC, Washington, D.C.
Article: Religious Education/CCD.

STEEMAN, Theodore M., OFM, Department of Theology, Boston College, Chestnut Hill, Mass.
Article: Population Explosion.

STEICHEN, Alan J., OSB, Headmaster, St. John's Preparatory School, Collegeville, Minn.
Article: Homiletics.

STEINDL-RAST, David, OSB, Monastery of Mt. Saviour, Pine City, N.Y.
Article: Counsels, Evangelical.

STRANSKY, Thomas F., CSP, Former President Paulist Fathers, Paulist Generalate, Scarsdale, N.Y.
Article: Missions, Ecumenism and.

SULLIVAN, Edward M., Ph.D., Director of Research, CARA, Washington, D.C.
Articles: National Pastoral Planning Conference: Parish Councils; Pastoral Councils, Diocesan; Pastoral Ministries; Pastoral Planning.

SULLIVAN, John, OCD, Discalced Carmelite Fathers, Washington, D.C.
Articles: General Intercessions; Presidential Prayers; Sacramentary.

SULLIVAN, Thomas F., School of Religious Studies, Catholic University of America, Washington, D.C.
Article: First Confession.

SWEETSER, Thomas P., SJ, Parish Evaluation Project, Chicago, Ill.
Article: Parish Renewal.

TALLEY, Thomas J., Th.D., Professor of Liturgics,

The General Theological Seminary, New York, N.Y.
Articles: Calendar, Common Liturgical; Lectionaries; Liturgical Movement and Ecumensim.

TETLOW, Joseph A., SJ, Associate Editor, AMERICA, New York, N.Y.
Article: Inculturation, Theological.

TETREAU, Richard D., Ph.D., Director of Library, St. Peter's College, Jersey City, N.J.
Article: Focolare Movement.

THOMAN, Elizabeth, Executive Director, National Sisters Communication Service, Los Angeles, Cal.
Article: National Sisters Communication Service.

THOMAS, David M., Ph.D., Professor, School of Theology, St. Meinrad's Seminary, St. Meinrad, Ind.
Articles: Family Ministry; Parents and Children; Technology, Social Effects of.

THOMSON, Paul van K., Ph.D., Academic Vice-President and Professor of English, Providence College, Providence, R.I.
Article: Higher Education, Liberal Arts in.

TILLARD, Jean M. R., OP, Catholic Faculty of Theology and Philosophy, Dominican Priory, Ottawa, Canada.
Article: Incorporation into the Church (Membership).

TRAXLER, Margaret, SSND, president, National Coalition of American Nuns, Chicago, Ill.
Article: National Coalition of American Nuns (NCAN).

TRIPOLE, Martin R., SJ, Assistant Professor, Theology, St. Joseph's College, Philadelphia, Pa.
Articles: Hope, Theology of; Progress.

TROESTER, John W., President, National Federation of Spiritual Directors, Plymouth, Mich.
Article: National Federation of Spiritual Directors.

TURNER, Mary Daniel, SNDdeN, Superior General, Rome; former Executive Director, Leadership Conference of Women Religious.
Article: Leadership Conference of Women Religious (LCWR).

UNTENER, Kenneth E., S.T.D., Rector, St. John's Provincial Seminary, Plymouth, Mich.
Article: Reconciliation, Ministry of.

VILLOTTI (Biedrzycke), Joy, St. Paul, Minn.
Article: First Communion, Celebration of.

WAINWRIGHT, Geoffrey, M.A., B.D., Ph.D. in Theology; Methodist Minister; Professor of Systematic Theology, The Queen's College, Birmingham, England.
Article: Societas Liturgica.

WALL, A. E. P., Editor, *The Chicago Catholic,* Chicago, Ill.
Articles: International Union of the Catholic Press; Journalism, Catholic.

WALLACE, William A., OP, Ph.D., S.T.M., Professor of the Philosophy and History of Science, Catholic University of America, Washington, D.C.
Articles: Pluralism, Philosophical; Thomism.

742   CONTRIBUTORS

WASSMUTH, William, President, National Conference of Diocesan Directors of Religious Education/CCD, Boise, Idaho.
Article: National Conference of Diocesan Directors of Religious Education/CCD.

WEILAND, Duane J., S.T.D., Director, Permanent Diaconate Program, Diocese of Des Moines, Iowa.
Article: Permanent Diaconate, Formation for.

WELSH, Aloysius J., S.T.D., Executive Director, National Catholic Conference for Interracial Justice, Washington, D.C.
Articles: Interracial Justice; National Catholic Conference for Interracial Justice (NCCIJ).

WHALEN, John P., S.T.D., J.D., Consortium of Universities, Washington, D.C.
Article: Tax Exemption of Church Property.

WHALEN, Joseph M., S.T.L., Chancery Office, Allentown, Pa.
Article: Raimondi, Luigi.

WHITEHEAD, K. D., Executive Vice President, Catholics United for the Faith, Inc., New Rochelle, N.Y.
Article: Catholics United for the Faith.

WINKLER, Elizabeth, Ph.D., Secretary General, International Migration Commission, Geneva, Switzerland.
Articles: International Catholic Migration Commission; Migration, International.

WINSTONE, Harold, St. Thomas More Centre for Pastoral Theology, London, England.

Articles: Liturgical Texts, Translation of; Vernacular in Liturgy.

WOELFL, Paul A., SJ, Professor of Political Science, John Carroll University, Cleveland, Ohio.
Article: Equality.

WORLAND, Stephen T., Ph.D., Department of Economics, University of Notre Dame, Notre Dame, Ind.
Article: Association for Social Economics.

WREN, Carol, SSJ, M.A., College of Our Lady of the Elms, Chicopee, Mass.
Article: Commitment.

WRENN, Lawrence G., the Metropolitan Tribunal, Archdiocese of Hartford, Hartford, Conn.
Article: Marriage (Canon Law).

WRIGHT, Helen, SND, Assistant Professor, Sacramental/Ecclesial/Liturgical Theology, Washington Theological Union, Silver Spring, Md.
Article: Women, Theological Formation of.

WUERL, Rev. Donald, Sacred Congregation for the Clergy, Rome.
Articles: Synod of Bishops (Third General Assembly, 1974); Synod of Bishops (Fourth General Assembly, 1977).

YOUNG, James J., CSP, Rector and Director of Religious Formation, St. Paul's College, Washington, D.C.
Article: Divorced and Separated Catholics.

YUHAUS, Cassian, CP, Director of Religious Life, CARA, Washington, D.C.
Article: Religious Life, Renewal of.

BIBLICAL ABBREVIATIONS

The following abbreviations have been used throughout the Encyclopedia for biblical books and versions of the Bible.

BOOKS

Acts	Acts of the Apostles
Abd	Abdia
Ag	Aggai
Am	Amos
Ap	Apocalypse
Bar	Baruch
1–2 Chr	1 and 2 Chronicles (1 and 2 Paralipomenon in Septuagint and Vulgate)
Col	Colossians
1–2 Cor	1 and 2 Corinthians
Ct	Canticle of Canticles
Dn	Daniel
Dt	Deuteronomy
Eccl	Ecclesiastes
Eph	Ephesians
Est	Esther
Ex	Exodus
Ez	Ezechiel
Ezr	Ezra (Esdras B in Septuagint; 1 Esdras in Vulgate)
Gal	Galatians
Gn	Genesis
Hab	Habacuc
Heb	Hebrews
Is	Isaia
Jas	James
Jb	Job
Jdt	Judith
Jer	Jeremia
Jgs	Judges
Jl	Joel
Jn	John
1–3 Jn	1, 2, and 3 John
Jon	Jona
Jos	Josue
Jude	Jude
3–4 Kgs	3 and 4 Kings
Lam	Lamentations
Lk	Luke
Lv	Leviticus
Mal	Malachia
1–2 Mc	1 and 2 Machabees
Mi	Michea
Mk	Mark
Mt	Matthew

Na	Nahum
Neh	Nehemia (2 Esdras in Septuagint and Vulgate)
Nm	Numbers
Os	Osee
Phil	Phillippians
Phlm	Philemon
Prv	Proverbs
Ps	Psalms
1–2 Pt	1 and 2 Peter
Rom	Romans
Ru	Ruth
Sir	Sirach (Ecclesiasticus in Septuagint and Vulgate)
1–2 Sm	1 and 2 Samuel (1–2 Kings in Septuagint and Vulgate)
So	Sophonia
Tb	Tobia
1–2 Thes	1 and 2 Thessalonians
Ti	Titus
1–2 Tm	1 and 2 Timothy
Wis	Wisdom
Za	Zacharia

VERSIONS

Apoc	Apocrypha
ARV	American Standard Revised Version,
ARVm	American Standard Revised Version, margin
AT	American Translation
AV	Authorized Version (King James)
CCD	Confraternity of Christian Doctrine
DV	Douay-Challoner Version
ERV	English Revised Version
ERVm	English Revised Version, margin
EV	English Version(s) of the Bible
LXX	Septuagint
MT	Masoretic Text
NEB	New English Bible
NT	New Testament
OT	Old Testament
RSV	Revised Standard Version
RV	Revised Version
RVm	Revised Version, margin
Syr	Syriac
Vulg	Vulgate

BIBLIOGRAPHICAL ABBREVIATIONS

The following abbreviations (sigla) have been used for works frequently cited throughout Volume 17. The first list of standard reference works, periodical publications, and other sources combines selected abbreviations from Volume 15 for the reader's convenience and abbreviations from works that have appeared since publication of Volume 15. The other lists include documents of Paul VI, Vatican Council II, the Synod of Bishops, the American episcopal conference, and liturgical instructions; all the citations are to paragraph numbers whenever available in editions.

Reference Works, Periodicals, Other Sources:

Abbott	W. M. ABBOTT, ed., *The Documents of Vatican II*, translation ed., J. GALLAGHER (New York 1966).
ActApS	*Acta Apostolicae Sedis* (Rome 1909–).
AmBenRev	*American Benedictine Review* (Newark, N.J. 1950–).
AmEcclRev	*American Ecclesiastical Review* (Washington, D.C. 1889–1975).
AmHistRev	*American Historical Review* (New York 1896–).
AmSocRev	*American Sociological Review* (1936–).
AnalGreg	*Analecta Gregoriana* (Rome 1930–).
AnnPont	*Annuario Pontificio* (Rome 1912–).
BTB	*Biblical Theology Bulletin* (Rome 1971–).
Bousc-O'Connor	T. L. BOUSCAREN and J. I. O'CONNOR, comps., *Canon Law Digest* v. 1–6 (Milwaukee 1934–1960).
CathBiblQuart	*Catholic Biblical Quarterly* (Washington, D.C. 1939–).
CathHistRev	*American Catholic Historical Review* (Washington, D.C. 1916–).
CathTheolSoc	*Catholic Theological Society of America. Proceedings* (New York 1946–).
CE	*The Catholic Encyclopedia*, ed. C. G. HEBERMANN, et al., 16 v. (New York 1907–14; Suppl. 1922).
ChSt	*Chicago Studies: An Archdiocesan Review* (Mundelein, Ill. 1962–).
CIC	*Codex iuris canonici* (Rome 1918).
CivCatt	*La Civiltà cattolica* (Rome 1950–).
ClergyRev	*Clergy Review* (London 1931–).
ClerSanct	Pius XII, "Cleri sanctitati," *Acta Apostolicae Sedis* 49 (1957) 433–603, motu proprio.
ComRel	*Commentarium pro religiosis* (Rome 1920–).
CommunLiturg	*Communautés et liturgies* (Ottignies, Belgium 1975– ; formerly *Paroisses et liturgie*).
Communic	Commissio Codicis iuris canonici Recognoscendo. *Communicationes* (Vatican City 1969–).
Communio	*Communio; International Catholic Review.* American ed. (Spokane 1974–).
Concilium	*Concilium: Theology in an Age of Renewal*, v. 1–60 (New York 1965–60); *Religion in the Seventies*, v. 61– (New York 1971–).
Crux	*Crux of the News* (Albany 1967–).
Denz	H. DENZINGER, *Enchiridion symbolorum*; A. SCHÖNMETZER (32d ed. Freiburg-im-Br. 1963).
Diakonia	*Diakonia* (Bronx, N.Y. 1966–).
Dimension	*Dimension; Journal of Pastoral Concern* (Philadelphia 1969–).
DocCath	*La Documentation Catholique* (Paris 1919–).
DocLife Suppl	*Doctrine and Life. Supplement* (Dublin 1963–).
DTC	*Dictionnaire de théologie catholique*, ed. A. VACANT et al., 15 v. (Paris 1903–50; Tables générales 1951–).
Ecumenist	*Ecumenist* (New York 1962–).
EcumRev	*Ecumenical Review* (Geneva and New York, World Council of Churches 1948/49–).
EcumTr	*Ecumenical Trends* (Garrison, N.Y. 1972–).
EncCatt	*Enciclopedia cattolica*, ed. P. PASCHINI, et al. 12 v. (Rome 1949–54).
EnchCler²	Sacra Congregatio pro Institutione Catholica, *Enchiridion clericorum* (2d ed., Vatican City 1975).
EncTheol	*Encyclopedia of Theology: The Concise Sacramentum Mundi*, ed. K. RAHNER (New York 1975).
EnchLiturg	*Enchiridion documentorum instaurationis liturgicae* I (1963–1973), ed. R. KACZYNSKI (Rome 1976).
EphemLiturg	*Ephemerides liturgicae* (Rome 1887–).
EphemThLov	*Ephemerides Theologicae Lovanienses* (Bruges 1924–).
EsprVie	*Esprit et vie. l'ami du clergé* (Langres 1969–).
Flannery	A. FLANNERY, ed., *Vatican Council II: The Conciliar and Post Conciliar Documents* (New York 1975).

Greg	*Gregorianum* (Rome 1920–).
HarvThRev	*Harvard Theological Review* (Cambridge, Mass. 1908–).
HeythropJ	*Heythrop Journal* (Oxford 1960–).
HomPast Rev	*The Homiletic and Pastoral Review* (New York 1900–).
Hor	*Horizons: Journal of the College Theology Society* (Villanova, Pa. 1974–).
IDOC	*IDOC Bulletin* (Rome 1972–).
IDOC NA	*IDOC International Documentation. North American Edition* (New York 1970–).
Informationes SCRIS	*Informationes Sacrae Congregationis pro Religiosis et Institutionibus Saecularibus* (Vatican City, 1975–). English version *Consecrated Life* (Jamaica Plain, Mass. (1977–).
IntDictBibl	G. A. BUTTRICK, ed., *The Interpreter's Dictionary of the Bible*, 4v. (New York 1962).
IntDictBiblSuppl	K. CRIM et al., eds., *The Interpreter's Dictionary of the Bible*, Supplementary Volume (Nashville 1976).
IrEcclRec	*The Irish Ecclesiastical Record* (Dublin 1863–).
IrTheolQ	*The Irish Theological Quarterly* (Dublin 1906–22; 1951–).
JBiblLit	*Journal of Biblical Literature* (Philadelphia 1881–).
JEcumSt	*Journal of Ecumenical Studies* (Pittsburgh 1964–).
John XXIII MatMagis	JOHN XXIII, "Mater et Magistra," *Acta Apostolicae Sedis* 53 (1961) 401–464, encyclical.
JohnXXIII PacTerr	John XXIII, "Pacem in terris," *Acta Apostolicae Sedis* 55 (1963) 257–304, encyclical.
JRel	*Journal of Religion* (Chicago 1921–).
JScStRel	*Journal for the Scientific Study of Religion* (Wetteren, Holland 1961–).
JThSt	*Journal of Theological Studies* (London 1899–1949; new series 1950–).
Jurist	*The Jurist* (Washington, D.C. 1941–).
Kittel ThW (Eng)	G. KITTEL, ed., *Theological Dictionary of the New Testament*, tr. and ed. G. W. BROMILEY 10 v. (Grand Rapids, Mich. 1964–76).
LADOC	*LADOC: Bimonthly Publication of Latin American Documentation— USCC* (Washington, D.C. 1970–).
LexThK²	*Lexikon für Theologie und Kirche*, ed. J. HOFER and K. RAHNER, 10 v. (2d ed., Freiburg-im-Br. 1957–65).
LexThK²Suppl	*Lexikon für Theologie und Kirche. Das zweite vatikanische Konzil.* H. BRECHTER, et al., eds., pt. 1–3 (Freiburg-im-Br. 1966–68).
LiturgJB	*Liturgisches Jahrbuch* (Münster 1951–).
Liturgy	*Liturgy: Journal of the Liturgical Conference* (Washington, D.C. 1956–).
LivLight	*The Living Light: An Interdisciplinary Review of Christian Education* (Washington, D.C. 1964–).
LivWor	*Living Worship* (Washington, D.C. 1965–).
LouvSt	*Louvain Studies* (Louvain, American College, 1966–).
LumenEng	*Lumen Vitae*. English ed. (v. 5, Brussels 1950–).
LumEtVie	*Lumière et vie* (Bruges 1951–).
LumV	*Lumen Vitae* (Brussels 1946–).
Maison-Dieu	*La Maison-Dieu* (Paris 1945–).
Mansi	G. D. MANSI, *Sacrorum Conciliorum nova et amplissima collectio*, 31 v. (Florence-Venice 1757–98); reprinted and continued by L. PETIT and J. B. MARTIN, 53 v. in 60 (Paris 1889–1927; repr., 54 v. in 59, Graz (1960–61).
Month	The Month (London 1864–).
MusGG	*Die Musik in Geschichte und Gegenwart*, ed. F. BLUME (Kassel-Basel 1949–).
NCE	*New Catholic Encyclopedia*, 15 v. (Washington, D.C. 1967); Suppl. v. 16 (Washington, D.C. 1974).
Notitiae	*Notitiae. Commentarii ad nuntia et studia de re liturgica* v. 1–6, Consilium ad exsequendam Constitutionem de Sacra Liturgia (Vatican City 1965–69); v. 7–12, Sacra Congregatio pro Cultu Divino (1970–75); v. 13– cura Sectionis Cultu Divino, Sacrae Congregationis pro Sacramentis et Cultu Divino (1976–).
NouvRevTh	*Nouvelle revue théologique* (Tournai-Louvain-Paris 1869–).
NTSt	*New Testament Studies* (Cambridge-Washington, D.C. 1954–).
O'Connor 7	J. I. O'CONNOR, comp., *Canon Law Digest*, 1968–72, v. 7 (Chicago 1975).
O'Connor Suppl	J. I. O'CONNOR, comp., *Canon Law Digest, Supplements* through 1973, 1974, 1975, 1976 (Chicago 1975–77).
Origins	*Origins. National Catholic Documentary Service* (Washington, D.C. 1971–).
OssRom	*L'Osservatore Romano* (Rome 1849–).
OssRomEng	*L'Osservatore Romano*. Weekly English ed. (Rome 1968–).
Pauly-Wiss RE	*Paulys Realenzyklopädie der klassischen Altertumswissenschaft*, ed., G. WISSOWA et al. (Stuttgart 1893–).
PeriodicaMorCan-Liturg	*Periodica de re morali, canonica, liturgica* (Rome 1912–).

PG   *Patrologiae cursus completus ... Series graeca*, ed. J. P. MIGNE, 111 v. in 166 (Paris 1857–66).

PL   *Patrologiae cursus completus ... Series latina*, ed. J. P. MIGNE, 221 v. (Paris 1878–90).

ProcAmCathPhilAs   *American Catholic Philosophical Association. Proceedings of the Annual Meeting* (Baltimore 1926–).

ProcCLSA   *Canon Law Society of America. Proceedings of the Annual Convention* (1969–); from the 31st; prior Proceedings were published in the *Jurist*.

QuestLiturgParoiss   *Questions liturgiques et paroissiales* (Louvain 1921–).

RevRel   *Review for Religious* (Topeka, Kansas 1942–).

RevRelRes   *Review of Religious Research* (New York 1950–).

RevScPhilTh   *Revue des sciences philosophiques et théologiques* (Paris 1907–).

RevUnOttawa   *Revue de l'Université d'Ottawa* (Ottawa 1931–).

Righetti   M. RIGHETTI, *Manuale di storia liturgica*, 4 v. (Milan): v. 1 (2d ed. 1950), v. 2 (2d ed. 1955), v. 3 (1949), v. 4 (1953).

SacrMundi   *Sacramentum Mundi. An Encyclopedia of Theology*, ed. K. RAHNER, C. ERNST, et al., 6 v. (New York 1968–70).

ScriptBull *Scripture Bulletin* (London 1969–).

Sem   *Seminarium. Rivista per i seminari e per le vocazioni ecclesiastiche.* Congregation for Catholic Education (Vatican City 1950–).

Sisters   *Sisters Today*; formerly *Sponsa Regis* (Collegeville, Minn., v. 37, 1965–).

SourcesChr *Sources Chrétiennes*, ed. H. DE LUBAC, et al. (Paris 1941–).

StCan   *Studia Canonica* (Ottawa 1967–).

ST Lat-Eng *Saint Thomas Aquinas, Summa theologiae.* Latin text and English translation, Introductions, Notes, Appendices, and Glossaries. ed. T. GILBY (London and New York 1964–76).

StLiturg   *Studia Liturgica* (Nieuwendam, Holland 1962–).

StTest   *Studi e testi* (Rome 1900–).

StZeit   *Stimmen der Zeit* (Freiburg-im-Br. 1871–).

Supplément   *Le Supplément* (Paris, v. 23, 1970–) replaces *La Vie spirituelle. Supplément* (Paris v. 1–22, 1947–69).

TheolDig   *Theology Digest* (Kansas City, Mo. 1953–).

Thomist   *The Thomist* (Washington, D.C. 1939–).

ThPraktQ   *Theologisch-praktische Quartalschrift* (Linz 1848–).

ThQschr   *Theologische Quartalschrift* (Tübingen 1819– ; Stuttgart 1946–).

ThSt   *Theological Studies* (Woodstock, Md. 1940–).

ThZ   *Theologische Zeitschrift* (Basel 1945–).

UnaS   *Una sancta* (Meitingen-Augsburg 1962–).

VieSpirit   *La Vie spirituelle* (Paris 1919–).

VieSpiritSuppl   *La Vie spirituelle. Supplément* (Paris v. 1–22 1947–69) continued by *Le Supplément*.

Vorgrimler H. VORGRIMLER et al., eds., *Commentary on the Documents of Vatican II*, 5 v. (New York 1967–69).

Way   *The Way* (London 1961–).

WaySuppl   *The Way Supplement* (London 1966–).

Worship   *Worship* (Collegeville, Minn. 1951–); supersedes *Orate Fratres* (1926–51).

ZKathTh   *Zeitschrift für katholische Theologie* (Vienna 1877–).

ZTheolKirche   *Zeitschrift für Theologie und Kirche* (Tübingen 1891–).

Papal Documents, Paul VI:

Paul VI AdPasc   *Ad Pascendum* (1972), motu proprio on diaconate. ActApS 64 (1972) 534–540.

Paul VI ApSoll   *Apostolica sollicitudo* (1965), motu proprio, Synod of Bishops. ActApS 57 (1965) 775–780.

Paul VI DeEpMun   *De Episcoporum muneribus* (1966), motu proprio on bishops' faculties. ActApS 58 (1966) 467–472.

Paul VI EcclSanct   *Ecclesiae Sanctae* (1966), motu proprio implementing Vatican II decrees. ActApS 58 (1966) 757–787).

Paul VI EcclSuam   *Ecclesiam Suam* (1964), encyclical on the paths for the Church. ActApS 55 (1964) 609–659.

Paul VI EvangNunt   *Evangelium nuntiandi* (1976), apostolic exhortation on evangelization. ActApS 68 (1976) 5–76.

Paul VI EvangTest   *Evangelica testificatio* (1971), apostolic exhortation on religious life. ActApS 63 (1971) 497–526.

Paul VI HumVitae   *Humanae vitae* (1968), encyclical on the regulation of births. ActApS 60 (1968) 481–503.

Paul VI IndDoct   *Indulgentiarum doctrina* (1967), apostolic constitution on indulgences. ActApS 59 (1967) 5–24.

Paul VI LaudCant   *Laudis canticum* (1970), apostolic constitution on the Liturgy of the Hours. ActApS 63 (1971) 527–535.

Paul VI MatrMixta   *Matrimonia mixta* (1970), motu proprio on ecumenism and marriage. ActApS 62 (1970) 257–263.

Paul VI MinQuaedam	*Ministeria quaedam* (1972), motu proprio on Orders. ActApS 64 (1972) 529–534.
Paul VI MissRom	*Missale Romanum* (1969), apostolic constitution promulgating the revised Missal. ActApS 61 (1962) 217–222.
Paul VI MystFid	*Mysterium fidei* (1965), encyclical on the Eucharist. ActApS 57 (1965) 753–774.
Paul VI MystPasch	*Mysterii paschalis* (1969), motu proprio on the liturgical year. ActApS 61 (1969) 222–226.
Paul VI OctogAdven	*Octogesima adveniens* (1971), apostolic letter on the 80th anniversary of *Rerum novarum*, a "Call to Action." ActApS 63 (1971) 401–441.
Paul VI Paenitemini	*Paenitemini* (1966), apostolic constitution on penance, laws of fast and abstinence. ActApS 58 (1967) 177–198.
Paul VI PastMun	*Pastorale munus* (1964), motu proprio on bishops' faculties. ActApS 56 (1964) 5–12.
Paul VI PatBenev	*Paterna cum benevolentia* (1974), apostolic exhortation on reconciliation. ActApS 67 (1975) 5–23.
Paul VI PontDomus	*Pontificalis domus* (1968), motu proprio on changes in the papal household. ActApS 60 (1968) 305–315.
Paul VI PontRom	*Pontificalis Romani* (1968), apostolic constitution on new ordination rites. ActApS 60 (1968) 369–373.
Paul VI PopProgr	*Populorum progressio* (1967), encyclical on human development. ActApS 69 (1967) 257–299.
Paul VI RegEccl	*Regimini Ecclesiae universalis* (1967), apostolic constitution on reorganization of the Roman Curia. ActApS 59 (1967) 885–928.
Paul VI SacCael	*Sacerdotalis caelibatus* (1967), encyclical on priestly celibacy. ActApS 59 (1967) 657–697.
Paul VI SacrDiac	*Sacrum diaconatus ordinem* (1967), motu proprio on restoring permanent diaconate. ActApS 59 (1967) 697–704.

Documents of Vatican Council II (chronologically; translations, Abbott or Flannery at authors' discretion).

Sacrosanctum Concilium	(Constitution on the Sacred Liturgy) ActApS 56 (1964) 97–138.
Inter mirifica	(Decree on the Instruments of Social Communication) ActApS 56 (1964) 145–157.
Lumen gentium	(Dogmatic Constitution on the Church) ActApS 57 (1965) 5–71.
Orientalium Ecclesiarum	(Decree on Eastern Catholic Churches) ActApS 57 (1965) 76–89.
Unitatis redintegratio	(Decree on Ecumenism) ActApS 57 (1965) 90–112.
Christus Dominus	(Decree on the Bishops' Pastoral Office in the Church) ActApS 58 (1966) 673–701.
Perfectae caritatis	(Decree on the Appropriate Renewal of the Religious Life) ActApS 58 (1966) 702–712.
Optatam totius	(Decree on Priestly Formation) ActApS 58 (1966) 713–727.
Gravissimum educationis	(Declaration on Christian Education) ActApS 58 (1966) 728–739.
Nostra aetate	(Declaration on the Relationship of the Church to Non-Christian Religions) ActApS 58 (1966) 740–744.
Dei Verbum	(Dogmatic Constitution on Divine Revelation) ActApS 58 (1966) 817–835.
Apostolicam actuositatem	(Decree on the Apostolate of the Laity) ActApS 58 (1966) 837–864.
Dignitatis humanae	(Declaration on Religious Freedom) ActApS 58 (1966) 929–946.
Ad gentes	(Decree on the Church's Missionary Activity) ActApS 58 (1966) 947–990.
Presbyterorum ordinis	(Decree on the Ministry and Life of Priests) ActApS 58 (1966) 990–1024.
Gaudium et spes	(Pastoral Constitution on the Church in the Modern World) ActApS 58 (1966) 1025–1120.

Synod of Bishops, 1971:

Synod MinPr	Synod of Bishops, *The Ministerial Priesthood* (USCC publ. V, 375; references are to page).
Synod JustWorld	Synod of Bishops, *Justice in the World* (USCC publ. V, 375; references are to page).

NCCB Documents:

BCEIA Newsletter	National Conference of Catholic Bishops: Committee for Ecumenical and Interreligious Affairs, *Newsletter* (Washington, D.C. 1972–).
BCL Environment and Art	Bishops' Committee on the Liturgy, *Environment and Art in Catholic Worship* (Washington, D.C. 1978).
BCL Music	National Conference of Catholic Bishops' Committee on the Liturgy, *Music in Catholic Worship* (Washington, D.C. 1972).
BCL Newsletter	National Conference of Catholic Bishops' Committee on the Liturgy, *Newsletter* (Washington, D.C. 1965–).
CathHosp	National Conference of Catholic Bishops: Ad Hoc Committee Pro Life, *Pastoral Guidelines for Catholic Hospitals and Catholic Health Care Personnel* (Washington, D.C. 1975).
TeachThem	*Teach Them*, USCC Statement on Catholic Education (Washington, D.C. 1975).
ToLive	National Conference of Catholic Bishops, *To Live in Christ Jesus*, Pastoral Letter on Moral Values (Washington, D.C. 1976).
ToTeach	National Conference of Catholic Bishops, *To Teach as Jesus Did*, Pastoral Message on Catholic Education (Washington, D.C. 1973).

Liturgical Instructions:

With the exception of *Musicam sacram*, the following are part of the revised liturgical books of the Roman rite. Latin title and date of promulgation are followed by the title of the official English version, copyrighted and issued by The International Commission on English in the Liturgy (ICEL), Washington, D.C. There are various editions of the ICEL texts, e.g. in the U.S., *The Rites of the Catholic Church as Revised by the Second Vatican Ecumenical Council* (Pueblo Publishing Co., New York 1976); *The Sacramentary* (Liturgical Press, Collegeville, Minn. 1974); *Liturgy of the Hours* (Catholic Book Publishing Co., New York 1975–76). Bibliographical data include title and date of issue for the Latin *editio typica*, and of the ICEL version.

BaptCh	*Ordo baptismi parvulorum* (May 15, 1969; 2d ed. March 27, 1977). ICEL Rite of Baptism for Children (1969).
CalendRom	Sacred Congregation of Rites, "Normae generales de anno liturgico et de calendario," March 21, 1969, *Notitiae* 5 (1969) 163–176; also published as *Calendarium Romanum* (Vatican City 1969). ICEL, "General Norms for the Liturgical Year and the Calendar," Roman Missal (Sacramentary, 1973).
ChrInitAd	*Ordo initiationis christianae adultorum* (Jan. 6, 1972). ICEL, Rite of Christian Initiation of Adults, provisional text (1974).
ChrInitGenIntrod	"De institutione christiana. Praenotanda generalia, *Ordo baptismi parvulorum* ICEL, "Christian Initiation. General Introduction," Rite of Baptism for Children (1969).
ConfIntrod	*Ordo confirmationis* (Aug. 22, 1971). ICEL, Rite of Confirmation (1975).
FuneralIntrod	*Ordo exsequiarum* (April 15, 1969). ICEL, Rite of Funerals (1970).
GenInstrLitHor	"Institutio generalis de Liturgia Horarum," *Liturgia Horarum* (April 11, 1971). ICEL, "General Instruction on the Liturgy of the Hours," Liturgy of the Hours (1973).
GenInstrRomMissal	"Institutio generalis Missalis Romani," *Missale Romanum* (April 2, 1969; 2d ed. March 25, 1975). ICEL, "General Instruction on the Roman Missal," Roman Missal (Sacramentary, 1973).
HolyCommIntrod	*De sacra communione et cultu Mysterii Eucharistiae extra missam* (June 21, 1973). ICEL, Holy Communion and Worship of the Eucharist outside Mass (1974).
Institution	*De institutione lectorum et acolythorum de sacro caelibatu amplectendo, de admissione inter candidatos ad diaconatum et presbyteratum* (Dec. 3, 1972). ICEL, Institution of Readers and Acolytes, Admission to Candidacy for Ordination as Deacons and Priests, Commitment to Celibacy (1976).
LectIntrod	"Praenotanda," *Ordo lectionum missae* (May 25, 1969). ICEL, "Introduction," Lectionary for Mass (1969).
MarriageIntrod	*Ordo celebrandi matrimonium* (March 19, (1969). ICEL, Rite of Marriage (1969).
MusicamSacram	Sacred Congregation of Rites, *Musicam Sacram*, "Instructio de musica in sacra liturgia," March 5, 1967, ActApS 59 (1967) 300–320... *On Music in the Liturgy* (USCC Publ. Office, Washington, D.C. 1967).
Penance	*Ordo paenitentiae* (Dec. 2, 1973). ICEL, Rite of Penance (1974).

GENERAL ABBREVIATIONS/ACRONYMS

The few abbreviations used in Vol. 17 are in common use and are obvious. (There is a list of general abbreviations in NCE, v. 15.) The following acronyms, however, occur frequently:

BCEIA	Bishops' Committee for Ecumenical and Interreligious Affairs (National Conference of Catholic Bishops).
BCL	Bishops' Committee on the Liturgy (National Conference of Catholic Bishops).
CMSM	Conference of Major Superiors of Men.
FDLC	Federation of Diocesan Liturgical Commissions.
ICEL	International Commission on English in the Liturgy.
LCWR	Leadership Conference of Women Religious.
NCCB	National Conference of Catholic Bishops.
USCC	United States Catholic Conference.

Other acronyms are used only in the article on the corresponding organization.

APPENDIX

CATALOGUE AND INDEX OF DOCUMENTS ON CHANGE IN THE CHURCH

Documents of Pope Paul VI
1966–1978

Number	Year	Month	Day	Title and Subject
1.	1966	Jan.	3	*Finis Concilio* (apostolic letter motu proprio): postconciliar commissions to continue work of Vatican II. ActApS 58 (1966) 37–40
2.	1966	Jan.	25	*Verbi Dei* (apostolic letter motu proprio): yearly Lenten meetings at St. Mary Major to continue dialogue begun by Council with mankind. ActApS 58 (1966) 113–114
3.	1966	Feb.	17	*Paenitemini* (apostolic constitution): excellence of the virtue of penance; new laws of fast and abstinence. ActApS 58 (1966) 117–198 TPS 11(1966) 362–371
4.	1966	Mar.	24	*Hac in Urbe* (joint declaration) Paul VI and His Grace, Michael Ramsey, Abp. of Canterbury; inauguration of Anglican/Roman Catholic dialogue aimed at unity in Christ. ActApS 58 (1966) 286–288 (English and Latin) TPS 11 (1966) 166–167
5.	1966	May	3	*Summi Dei beneficio* (apostolic letter motu proprio): extending postconciliar jubilee until Dec. 8, 1966. ActApS 58 (1966) 337–341
6.	1966	June	10	*Munus apostolicum* (apostolic letter motu proprio): postponement of legislation promulgating final conciliar decrees and declarations ActApS 58 (1966) 465–466
7.	1966	June	15	*De Episcoporum muneribus* (apostolic letter motu proprio): enlarging bishops' power of dispensation. ActApS 58 (1966) 467–472 *Jurist* 26 (1966) 485–492
8.	1966	Aug.	6	*Ecclesiae Sanctae* (apostolic letter motu proprio): implementing *Christus Dominus*, *Presbyterorum ordinis*, *Perfectae caritatis*, and *Ad gentes*. ActApS 58 (1966) 757–787 TPS 11 (1966) 376–400
9.	1967	Jan.		*Praesentia vestra* (letters): asking Pres. Johnson, Gen. Nguyen Van Thieu, and Dr. Ho Chi Minh for armistice in Viet Nam. ActApS 59 (1967) 160–161 (English and French)
10.	1967	Jan.	1	*Indulgentiarum doctrina* (apostolic constitution): changes regarding indulgences. ActApS 59 (1967) 5–24 TPS 12 (1967) 124–135
11.	1967	Jan.	6	*Catholicam Christi Ecclesiam* (apostolic letter motu proprio): establishing Council on the Laity and Pontifical Commission for Justice and Peace. ActApS 59 (1967) 25–28 TPS 12 (1967) 103–106

Number	Year	Month	Day	Title and Subject
12.	1967	Mar.	26	*Populorum progressio* (encyclical): on the development of peoples.
				ActApS 59 (1967) 257–299 TPS 12 (1967) 144–172
13.	1967	May	2	*Episcopalis potestatis* (apostolic letter motu proprio): faculties of Eastern Rite bishops
				ActApS 59 (1967) 385–390 *Diakonia* 2 (1967) 293–296
14.	1967	May	13	*Signum magnum* (letter): to all bishops on Marian devotion.
				ActApS 59 (1967) 465–475 TPS 12 (1967) 278–286
15.	1967	June	8	*Moved by the duty* (telegram): asking Israeli and Arab heads of state for cessation of war. ActApS 59 (1967) 642 (English)
16.	1967	June	18	*Sacrum diaconatus ordinem* (apostolic letter motu proprio): restoring deacon's role.
				ActApS 59 (1967) 697–704 TPS 12 (1967) 237–243
17.	1967	June	24	*Sacerdotalis caelibatus* (encyclical letter): priestly celibacy.
				ActApS 59 (1967) 657–697 TPS 12 (1967) 291–319
18.	1967	Aug.	6	*Pro comperto sane* (apostolic letter motu proprio): Curia reforms.
				ActApS 59 (1967) 881–884
19.	1967	Aug.	15	*Regimini Ecclesiae universae* (apostolic constitution): reorganizing Roman Curia.
				ActApS 59 (1967) 885–928 TPS 12 (1967) 393–420
20.	1967	Oct.	28	*Le Pape Paul VI* (joint declaration): Paul VI and Patriarch Athenagoras I on Roman Catholic/Orthodox cooperation.
				ActApS 59 (1967) 1054–55
21.	1967	Dec.	8	*Ci rivolgiamo a tutti* (written message): plea for World Day of Peace Observance each New Year's Day.
				ActApS 59 (1967) 1097–1102 (Italian) *Catholic Mind* 66 (Feb. 1968) 55–58
22.	1968	Mar.	28	*Ponificalis domus* (apostolic letter motu proprio): restructuring papal household.
				ActApS 60 (1968) 305–315
23.	1968	June	18	*Pontificalis Romani* (apostolic constitution): on new rites approved for ordination of bishop, priest, deacon.
				ActApS 60 (1968) 369–373
24.	1968	June	21	*Pontificalia insignia* (apostolic letter motu proprio): use of pontifical insignia.
				ActApS 60 (1968) 374–377
25.	1968	June	30	*Sollemni hac Liturgia* (solemn profession of faith): Credo of the People of God, at end of the Year of Faith.
				ActApS 60 (1968) 433–435 TPS 13 (1968) 224–228
26.	1968	July	25	*Humanae vitae* (encyclical): the regulation of birth.
				ActApS 60 (1968) 481–503 *Catholic Mind* 66 (Sept. 1968) 35–48

Number	Year	Month	Day	Title and Subject
27.	1969	Feb.	14	*Mysterii paschalis* (apostolic letter motu proprio): the reordering of the liturgical year and the new Roman calendar. ActApS 61 (1969) 222–226 TPS 14 (1969) 181–184
28.	1969	Mar.	19	*Sanctitas clarior* (apostolic letter motu proprio): beatifications and canonizations. ActApS 61 (1969) 149–153
29.	1969	Apr.	3	*Missale Romanum* (apostolic constitution): promulgating the Roman Missal revised by Decree of Vatican II. ActApS 61 (1969) 217–222 TPS 14 (1969) 165–169
30.	1969	April	15	*Ad hoc usque tempus* (apostolic letter motu proprio): cardinals' titular churches. ActApS 61 (1969) 226–227
31.	1969	May	8	*Sacra Rituum Congregatio* (apostolic constitution): replacing Congregation of Rites with Congregations for Divine Worship and for Causes of Saints. ActApS 61 (1969) 297–305 TPS 14 (1969) 174–180
32.	1969	June	24	*Sollicitudo omnium Ecclesiarum* (apostolic letter motu proprio): papal representatives. ActApS 61 (1969) 473–484 TPS 14 (1969) 260–267
33.	1969	Aug.	15	*Pastoralis migratorum* (apostolic letter motu proprio): pastoral care of migrants. ActApS 61 (1969) 601–603 *Catholic Mind* 67 (Dec. 1969) 35–37
34.	1970	Mar.	19	*Apostolicae caritatis* (apostolic letter motu proprio): establishing Pontifical Commission for the Spiritual Care of Migratory and Itinerant People. ActApS 62 (1970) 193–197 OssRomEng 1970 n. 16 [107] 5
35.	1970	Mar.	31	*Matrimonia mixta* (apostolic letter motu proprio): norms for mixed marriages. ActApS 62 (1970) 257–263 TPS 15 (1970) 134–140.
36.	1970	May	12	*Paul VI, Evêque* (joint declaration): Paul VI and Vasken I, Patriarch of the Armenian Church, on Christian unity. ActApS 62 (1970) 416–417 (French)
37.	1970	Aug.	6	*Sancti Stephani ortum* (apostolic letter): to the Hungarian nation on the occasion of the 10th centenary of the Church in Hungary and in commemoration of the birth and Baptism of St. Stephen of Hungary. ActApS 62 (1970) 577–587 OssRomEng (1970) n.37 [128] 6
38.	1970	Sept.	27	*Multiformis Sapientia Dei* (apostolic letter): St. Teresa of Avila made a Doctor of the Church. ActApS 63 (1971) 185–192
39.	1970	Oct.	4	*Mirabilis in Ecclesia* (apostolic letter): St. Catherine of Siena made a Doctor of the Church. ActApS 63 (1971) 674–682
40.	1970	Nov.	1	*Laudis canticum* (apostolic constitution): the revised Liturgy of the Hours. ActApS 63 (1971) 527–535 TPS 16 (1971) 129–135

Number	Year	Month	Day	Title and Subject
41.	1970	Nov.	21	*Ingravescentem aetatem* (apostolic letter motu proprio): age limit for the exercise of major functions by cardinals.
				ActApS 62 (1970) 810–813 *Jurist* 31 (1971) 667–668
42.	1970	Dec.	8	*Quinque iam anni* (apostolic exhortation): to all bishops on the 5th anniversary of the closing of Vatican II.
				ActApS 63 (1971) 97–106 TPS 15 (1970) 324–332
43.	1971	Mar.	28	*Causas matrimoniales* (apostolic letter motu proprio): norms for expediting marriage cases.
				ActApS 63 (1971) 441–446 TPS 16 (1971) 233–237
44.	1971	May	14	*Octogesima adveniens* (apostolic letter): to Card. Maurice Roy, Pres. of the Council for the Laity and the Commission for Justice and Peace, on the occasion of the 80th anniversary of *Rerum novarum*.
				ActApS 63 (1971) 401–441 TPS 16 (1971) 137–164
45.	1971	June	27	*Sedula cura* (apostolic letter motu proprio): new laws for regulation of the Pontifical Biblical Commission.
				ActApS 63 (1971) 665–669 TPS 16 (1971) 96–99
46.	1971	June	29	*Evangelica testificatio* (apostolic exhortation): renewal of religious life according to the teachings of Vatican II.
				ActApS 63 (1971) 497–526 TPS 16 (1971) 108–128
47.	1971	July	15	*Amoris officio* (letter): to Card. Jean Villot, Secretary of State, establishing the Pontifical Council "Cor Unum."
				ActApS 63 (1971) 669–673 TPS 16 (1971) 284–287
48.	1971	Aug.	15	*Divinae consortium naturae* (apostolic constitution): the Sacrament of Confirmation.
				ActApS 63 (1971) 657–664 TPS 16 (1971) 223–228
49.	1971	Oct.	17	*Divinum illud* (apostolic letter): beatification of Fr. Maximilian Kolbe, OFM.
				ActApS 64 (1972) 401–407
50.	1971	Oct.	27	*Before this assembly* (address): to Mar Ignatius Jacob III, Syrian-Orthodox Patriarch of Antioch, and the Patriarch's reply.
				ActApS 63 (1971) 830–831 (English)
51.	1971	Oct.	27	*As they conclude* (joint declaration): of Paul VI and Mar Ignatius Jacob III at the conclusion of their visit.
				ActApS 63 (1971) 814–815 (English)
52.	1971	Dec.	8	*Noi riprendiamo* (written message): World Day of Peace, Jan. 1, 1972.
				ActApS 63 (1971) 865–868 *Tablet* (London) 225 (1971) 1231
53.	1972	June	4	*L'occasion* (address): on the publication of the exchange of letters between Paul VI and Athenagoras I, Patriarch of Constantinople.
				ActApS 64 (1972) 193–195 (French) OssRomEng (1972) n. 29 [225] 3–4

Number	Year	Month	Day	Title and Subject
54.	1972	Aug.	15	*Ad pascendum* (apostolic letter motu proprio): norms regarding the sacred Order of diaconate.
				ActApS 64 (1972) 534–540 TPS 17 (1972) 234–240
55.	1972	Aug.	15	*Ministeria quaedam* (apostolic letter motu proprio): reforming the discipline of first tonsure, minor orders, and subdiaconate.
				ActApS 64 (1972) 529–534 TPS 17 (1972) 257–261
56.	1972	Nov.	30	*Sacram unctionem* (apostolic constitution): the Sacrament of Anointing of the Sick.
				ActApS 65 (1973) 5–9 TPS 17 (1973) 578–581
57.	1973	Feb.	8	*Vivissima gioia* (address): to the Sacred Roman Rota; canonical equity.
				ActApS 65 (1973) 95–103 Origins 2 (1972–73) 567–568; 593–595
58.	1973	May	10	*Paul VI* (joint declaration): of Paul VI and Shenouda III, Pope of Alexandria and Patriarch of the See of St. Mark, affirms Chalcedon's Christology.
				ActApS 65 (1973) 299–301 (English)
59.	1973	Sept.	8	*Cum matrimonialium* (apostolic letter motu proprio): for marriage cases, norms established with the approval of the Eastern Catholic Churches.
				ActApS 65 (1973) 577–581
60.	1973	Dec.	10	*Poussé par la conscience* (written message): letter to the President of the 28th General Assembly of the UN, on the 25th anniversary of the UN Universal Declaration of Human Rights.
				ActApS 65 (1973) 673–677 TPS 18 (1974) 304–307
61.	1974	Feb.	2	*Marialis cultus* (apostolic exhortation): to all bishops, for the right ordering and development of devotion to Mary.
				ActApS 66 (1974) 113–168 TPS 19 (1974) 49–87
62.	1974	Feb.	4	*Secreta continere* (instruction): papal secrecy
				ActApS 66 (1974) 89–92
63.	1974	May	23	*Apostolorum limina* (bull of indiction): Holy Year, 1975.
				ActApS 66 (1974) 289–307 TPS 19 (1974) 5–11
64.	1974	June	13	*Firma in traditione* (apostolic letter motu proprio): norms on Mass stipends.
				ActApS 66 (1974) 308–311 RevRel 33 (1974) 1250–52
65.	1974	Dec.	8	*Paterna cum benevolentia* (apostolic exhortation): reconciliation within the Church.
				ActApS 67 (1975) 5–23 TPS 19 (1975) 319–332
66.	1975	May	9	*Gaudete in Domino* (apostolic exhortation): Christian joy.
				ActApS 67 (1975) 289–322 TPS 20 (1975) 4–28
67.	1975	July	11	*Constans Nobis* (apostolic constitution): formation of the Congregation for the Sacraments and Divine Worship, combining Congregations for the Discipline of the Sacraments and for Divine Worship.
				ActApS 67 (1975) 417–420 OssRomEng (1975) n. 31 [383] 8

Number	Year	Month	Day	Title and Subject
68.	1975	Sept.	14	*Omnes homines* (decretal letter): canonization of Bl. Elizabeth Ann Bayley Seton.
				ActApS 68 (1976) 689–693
69.	1975	Oct.	1	*Romano Pontifici eligendo* (apostolic constitution): vacancy of the Apostolic See and the election of the Roman Pontiff.
70.	1975	Oct.	12	*Christi splendor* (decretal letter): canonization of Bl. Oliver Plunket.
				ActApS 69 (1977) 65–74
71.	1975	Nov.	30	*We write* (letter): to His Grace Frederick Donald Coggan, Abp. of Canterbury on the ordination of women.
				ActApS 68 (1975) 599–600 (English)
72.	1975	Dec.	8	*Evangelii nuntiandi* (apostolic exhortation): to the episcopate, clergy, and faithful of all the world on evangelization in the modern world.
				ActApS 68 (1976) 5–76 TPS 21 (1976) 4–51
73.	1976	June	30	*Romani sermonis* (chirograph document): Foundation *Latinitas* established in order to preserve the excellence and extend the use of the Latin language.
74.	1976	Oct.	11	*To our esteemed* (private letter): to Marcel Lefebvre, former Archbishop-Bishop of Tulle.
				OssRomEng 1976 n.50 [454]6–8 TPS 22 (1977) 47–48
75.	1976	Oct.	17	*Omnis martyrii* (decretal letter): canonization of Bl. John Ogilvie.
				ActApS 69 (1977) 305–311
76.	1976	Oct.	23	*Catholica Ecclesia* (apostolic letter motu proprio): on abbeys *nullius* reorganized.
				ActApS 68 (1976) 694–696 TPS 22 (1977) 35–37
77.	1976	Dec.	10	*Apostolatus peragendi* (apostolic letter motu proprio): Council of the Laity restructured and named Pontifical Council for the Laity.
				ActApS 68 (1976) 696–700 TPS 22 (1977) 26–29
78.	1976	Dec.	10	*Iustitiam et pacem* (apostolic letter motu proprio): Pontifical Commission for Justice and Peace restructured.
				ActApS 68 (1976) 700–703 TPS 22 (1977) 30–33
79.	1977	Apr.	29	*This is* (joint declaration): Paul VI and His Grace, Frederick Donald Coggan, Abp. of Canterbury, on Anglican/Roman Catholic relations.
				ActApS 69 (1977) 286–289 (English) TPS 22 (1977) 269–272
80.	1977	June	19	*Regni Caelorum* (decretal letter): canonization of Bl. John Nepomucene Neumann.
				ActApS 70 (1978) 217–223
81.	1977	June	29	*C'est avec une joie* (letter): to the (Orthodox) Ecumenical Patriarch Demetrios I.
				ActApS 69 (1977) 449–450 (French) OssRomEng (1977) n. 28 [485] 10
82.	1977	Oct.	9	*Quamvis Libanus* (decretal letter): canonization of Sharbel Makhlouf.
				ActApS 70 (1978) 224–230
83.	1978	May	11	*Inter eximia* (apostolic letter motu proprio): on conferring the Sacred Pallium.
				ActApS 70 (1978) 441–442 OssRomEng (1978) n. 32 [541] 3

**Acts of the Sacred Congregations, Tribunals
and Secretariats (1966–1978)***

Number	Year	Month	Day	Title and Subject
84.	1966	Jan.	27	*Cum Nostra aetate* (SRC: decree): editions of liturgical books.
				ActApS 58 (1966) 169–171 *Jurist* 26 (1966) 366–368 (excerpt)
85.	1966	Feb.	14	*Cum hac nostra* (SRC: decree): administration of Holy Communion in hospitals.
				ActApS 58 (1966) 525–526 *Jurist* 26 (1966) 492 (summary)
86.	1966	Mar.	18	*Matrimonii sacramentum* (SCDF: instruction): mixed marriages.
				ActApS 58 (1966) 235–239 TPS 11 (1966) 114–118
87.	1966	May	31	*Religionum laicalium* (SCRel: decree): granting faculties to general superiors of religious congregations of pontifical rank.
				ActApS 59 (1967) 362–364
88.	1966	June	6	*Sanctissimus Dominus* (SCEO: declaration) suspension of the law in *Christus Dominus* 8b.
				ActApS 58 (1966) 523
89.	1966	June	14	*Post Litteras Apostolicas* (SCDF: notification): abrogation of ecclesiastical penalties attached to the Index.
				ActApS 58 (1966) 445 *Catholic Mind* 64 (Oct. 1966) 4
90.	1966	July	24	*Cum Oecumenicum* (SCDF: letter): to the presidents of episcopal conferences on the abuses in the interpretation of Vatican II
				ActApS 58 (1966) 659–661 Bousc-O'Connor 6:260–263

*Abbreviations:

CAP	Council for the Public Affairs of the Church
CL	Pontifical Council for the Laity
CNC	Commission of Cardinals on the "Dutch Catechism"
PBC	Pontifical Biblical Commission
PCCS	Pontifical Commission for Social Communication
PCSM	Pontifical Commission for Migration and Tourism
PCIV	Pontifical Commission for Interpretation of the Decrees of the Second Vatican Council
SC	Sacred Consistorial Congregation (since 1967 . . . for Bishops)
SCC	Sacred Congregation of the Council (since 1967 . . . for the Clergy)
SCC	Sacred Congregation for the Clergy (after 1967)
SCCD	Sacred Congregation for Divine Worship (since 1975 . . . for the Sacraments and Divine Worship)
SCCS	Sacred Congregation for the Causes of Saints
SCDF	Sacred Congregation for the Doctrine of the Faith
SCDS	Sacred Congregation for the Discipline of the Sacraments
SCE	Sacred Congregation for Bishops
SCEO	Sacred Congregation for the Oriental Churches
SCIC	Sacred Congregation for Catholic Education (before 1967 . . . of Seminaries and Universities)
SCRel	Sacred Congregation of Religious (after 1967 . . . of Religious and Secular Institutes)
SCRIS	Sacred Congregation for Religious and Secular Institutes
SCSCD	Sacred Congregation for the Sacraments and Divine Worship
SCSU	Sacred Congregation for Seminaries and Universities (after 1967 . . . for Catholic Education)
SNC	Secretariat for Nonbelievers
SPA	Sacred Apostolic Penitentiary
SRC	Sacred Congregation of Rites
SS	Secretariat of State
SSAT	Supreme Tribunal of the Apostolic Signatura
SUC	Secretariat for Christian Unity
SYB	Synod of Bishops

Number	Year	Month	Day	Title and Subject
91.	1966	Nov.	15	*Post editam* (SCDF: decree): explicitly revoking CIC cc. 1399 and 2318 (on the censure of books)
				ActApS 58 (1966) 1186 Bousc-O'Connor 6:817–818
92.	1966	Dec.	8	*Summi Pontificis* (SS: approval): regulations for conducting the Synod of Bishops.
				ActApS 59 (1967) 91–103 Bousc-O'Connor 6:400–412
93.	1967	n.d.		*Ego N. firma fide* (SCDF: formula): new formula for profession of faith and oath against Modernism.
				ActApS 59 (1967) 1058
94.	1967	Feb.	22	*Crescens matrimoniorum* (SCEO: decree): on marriage of Catholics with the baptized of non-Catholic Eastern Churches.
				ActApS 59 (1967) 165–166 TPS 12 (1967) 122–123
95.	1967	Feb.	24	*Tricenario Gregoriano* (SCC: declaration): Gregorian Masses: continuity of celebration.
				ActApS 59 (1967) 229–230 Bousc-O'Connor 6:559
96.	1967	Feb.	24	*Quaesitum est* (SCC: response): substantial observance of days of penance.
				ActApS 59 (1967) 229 Bousc-O'Connor 6:684–685
97.	1967	Mar.	5	*Musicam sacram* (SRC: instruction): music in the liturgy.
				ActApS 59 (1967) 300–320 TPS 12 (1967) 173–186
98.	1967	May	4	*Tres abhinc annos* (SRC: second instruction): implementation of the principles for liturgical renewal set forth in the Constitution on the Sacred Liturgy.
				ActApS 59 (1967) 442–448 TPS 12 (1967) 244–249
99.	1967	May	14	*Ad totam Ecclesiam* (SUC: directory): guidelines for implementing the decrees promulgated by Vatican II on ecumenism: Part I.
				ActApS 59 (1967) 574–592 TPS 12 (1967) 250–263
100.	1967	May	25	*Eucharisticum mysterium* (SRC: instruction): Eucharistic worship.
				ActApS 59 (1967) 539–573 TPS 12 (1967) 211–236
101.	1967	Dec.	30	*Cum notae causae* (SS: rescript): delay of date for the law in *Regimini Ecclesiae universae*, 12.
				ActApS 60 (1968) 50
102.	1968	Feb.	22	*La Curia Romana* (SS: regulation): on the Roman Curia.
				ActApS 60 (1968) 129–176 (Italian) O'Connor 7:147–176
103.	1968	June	6	*Domus Dei* (SRC: decree): the title of minor basilica.
				ActApS 60 (1968) 536–539 O'Connor 7:28–31
104.	1968	Jur		*Pontificales ritus* (SRC: instruction): simplification of pontifical rites and insignia.
				ActApS 60 (1968) 406–412 USCC, *On the Papal Household* (Washington, D.C. 1968) 23–30

Number	Year	Month	Day	Title and Subject
105.	1968	June	29	*In Constitutione Apostolica* (SPA: decree): new edition of *Enchiridion Indulgentiarum* (1967).
				ActApS 60 (1968) 413–414 O'Connor 7:675
106.	1968	Au		*Humanae personae* (SNC: norms): for dialogue with nonbelievers.
				ActApS 60 (1968) 692–704 Flannery 1002–14
107.	1968	Sept.	12	*Ad solemnia* (SRC: instruction); celebrations in honor of saints and beati newly elevated.
				ActApS 60 (1968) 602 O'Connor 7:32–33
108.	1968	Oct.	15	*Cum in Neerlandia* (CNC: declaration): the Dutch Catechism.
				ActApS 60 (1968) 685–691 *Catholic Mind* 67 (Jan. 1969) 1–3
109.	1969	Jan.	6	*Renovationis causam* (SCRel: instruction): the renewal of religious formation.
				ActApS 61 (1969) 103–120 TPS 14 (1969) 61–77
110.	1969	Mar.	31	*Ut sive sollicite* (SS: instruction): dress of cardinals, bishops, and other prelates.
				ActApS 61 (1969) 334–335 O'Connor 7:137–143
111.	1969	Apr.	4	*Patres Pontificiae* (PCIV response): the functions of a deacon (*Lumen gentium* 22).
				ActApS 61 (1969) 348 O'Connor 7:133
112.	1969	Apr.	30	*Peregrinans in terra* (SCC: directory): pastoral ministry to tourists.
				ActApS 61 (1969) 361–384 (Calendar in Index gives April 29) TPS 14 (1970) 380–397
113.	1969	May	15	*Ordinem Baptismi* (SCCD: decree): rite for Baptism of children.
				ActApS 61 (1969) 548 O'Connor 7:594–595
114.	1969	May	25	*Ordinem lectionum* (SCCD: decree): the order of Readings at Mass.
				ActApS 61 (1969) 548–549
115.	1969	May	29	*Memoriale Domini* (SCCD: instruction): the administration of Holy Communion. Communion in the hand may be petitioned by bishops.
				ActApS 61 (1969) 541–547 (with sample of letter to bishops petitioning) Flannery 148–153
116.	1969	June	24	*Summi Pontificis* (CAP: rescript): revised regulation for conducting the Synod of Bishops.
				ActApS 61 (1969) 525–539 O'Connor 7:322–341
117.	1969	July	3	*Patres Pontificiae* (PCIV: response): competent authority in *Ecclesiae Sanctae* I.21.
				ActApS 61 (1969) 551 O'Connor 7:133
118.	1969	July	10	*Petentibus nonnullis* (SCCD: decree): extension of period of suspension of time for revised baptismal rite.
				ActApS 61 (1969) 549–550 O'Connor 7:595–596

Number	Year	Month	Day	Title and Subject
119.	1969	July	12	*Commissio Theologica* (SCDF: statutes): International Theological Commission, experimental statutes.
				ActApS 61 (1969) 540–541
				O'Connor 7:180–181
120.	1969	Aug.	15	*Venite seorsum* (SCRIS: instruction): the contemplative life and the enclosure of nuns.
				ActApS 61 (1969) 674–690
				TPS 14 (1969) 268–282
121.	1969	Aug.	22	*Novo migrationum* (SCE: instruction): pastoral care of migrants.
				ActApS 61 (1969) 614–643
				O'Connor 7:190–220
122.	1969	Oct.	20	*Constitutione Apostolica* (SCCD: instruction): the gradual application of the new Missal; women liturgical readers permitted.
				ActApS 61 (1969) 749–753
				TPS 14 (1969) 375–379
123.	1969	Nov.	4	*Inter ea* (SCC: circular letter): to presidents of episcopal conferences on the permanent formation of the clergy.
				ActApS 62 (1970) 123–134
				TPS 15 (1970) 75–83
124.	1969	Nov.	27	*Clericalia Instituta* (SCRIS: decree): participation by lay religious in government of clerical institutions.
				ActApS 61 (1969) 739–740
				O'Connor 7:468–469
125.	1969	Nov.	27	*Cum Superiores* (SCRIS: decree); the delegated faculty of superiors general of lay religious institutes to grant secularization to members under temporary vows.
				ActApS 61 (1969) 788–739
				O'Connor 7:77
126.	1970	Jan.	6	*In Synodo Episcopali* (SCIC: program); outline of basic program for priestly formation.
				ActApS 62 (1970) 321–384
				TPS 15 (1970) 264–314
127.	1970	Jan.	7	*Dans ces derniers* (SUC: declaration): the position of the Catholic Church on the celebration of the Eucharist in common by Christians of different confessions.
				ActApS 62 (1970) 184–188 (French)
				TPS 15 (1970) 59–63
128.	1970	Feb.	2	*Professionis ritus* (SCCD: decree): new rite for religious profession.
				ActApS 62 (1970) 553
				O'Connor 7:515–516
				The norms were not published in the ActApS but are appended to the decree as it appears in *Notitiae* 6 (1970) 114–117. English in O'Connor 7:516–522.
129.	1970	Mar.	25	*Apostolica Sedes* (SCEO: declaration): hierarchs outside patriarchal territory.
				ActApS 62 (1970) 179
				O'Connor 7:9–10
130.	1970	Mar.	26	*Celebrationis eucharisticae* (SCCD: decree): the new Roman Missal.
				ActApS 62 (1970) 554
				O'Connor 7:632
131.	1970	Apr.	11	*Presbyteri sacra* (SCC: circular letter): to the presidents of episcopal conferences with guidelines for establishing priests' councils.
				ActApS 62 (1970) 459–465
				TPS 15 (1970) 157–162

Number	Year	Month	Day	Title and Subject
132.	1970	Apr.	16	*Spiritus Domini* (SUC: directory): guidelines for implementing the decrees promulgated by Vatican II on ecumenism: Part II. ActApS 62 (1970) 705–724 TPS 15 (1970) 171–185
133.	1970	May	31	*Consecrationis virginum* (SSCD: decree): new rite of consecration of virgins. ActApS 62 (1970) 650 *Jurist* 31 (1971) 686
134.	1970	June	4	*Clausuram papalem* (SCRIS: declaration): papal enclosure of religious orders of men. ActApS 62 (1970) 548–549 O'Connor 7:536
135.	1970	June	4	*Ad instituenda experimenta* (SCRIS: decree): according certain faculties to religious institutes. ActApS 62 (1970) 549–550 O'Connor 7:80–82
136.	1970	June	24	*Calendaria particularia* (SCCD: instruction): particular calendars and the selection of Mass and Office. ActApS 62 (1970) 651–653 USCC, *Instruction on Particular Calendars* (Washington, D.C. 1970)
137.	1970	June	29	*Sacramentali Communione* (SCCD: instruction): the extension of the faculty to distribute Holy Communion under both kinds. ActApS 62 (1970) 664–666 TPS 15 (1970) 245–248
138.	1970	July	19	*Patres Pontificiae* (PCIV: responses): general delegation for deacons assigned to a parish. ActApS 62 (1970) 571 O'Connor 7:752
139.	1970	July	25	*Litteris Apostolicis* (SCC: decree): the obligation of celebrating Mass for the people (*Missa pro populo*). ActApS 63 (1971) 943–944 Jurist 30 (1970) 500 (summary)
140.	1970	Sept.	5	*Liturgicae instaurationes* (SCCD: third instruction): correct implementation of the Constitution on the Sacred Liturgy. ActApS 62 (1970) 692–704 Flannery 209–221
141.	1970	Sept.	30	*Ordine lectionum* (SCCD: decree): the Latin edition of the Mass Lectionary. ActApS 63 (1971) 710
142.	1970	Nov.	9	*Abbatem et Abbatissam* (SCCD: decree): revised rite for blessing of abbot and abbess. ActApS 63 (1971) 710–711 O'Connor 7:554–555
143.	1970	Dec.	3	*Ritibus Hebdomadae* (SCCD: decree): the revised rite of blessing oils and consecrating chrism. ActApS 63 (1971) 711 O'Connor 7:590–591
144.	1970	Dec.	8	*Dum canonicarum* (SCBIS: decree): directions on the Sacrament of Penance, particularly for women religious. ActApS 63 (1971) 318–319 *Jurist* 31 (1971) 683–684

Number	Year	Month	Day	Title and Subject
145.	1970	Dec.	28	*Ut causarum* (SSAT: norms): interdiocesan or regional or interregional tribunals.
				ActApS 63 (1971) 486–492 O'Connor 7: 920–926
146.	1970	Dec.	28	*Inter cetera* (SSAT: circular letter): ecclesiastical tribunals: status and activity.
				ActApS 63 (1971) 480–486 O'Connor 7: 913–919
147.	1971	Jan.	13	*Antequam causam* (SCDF: norms): procedural norms on reduction to the lay state.
				ActApS 63 (1971) 303–308 *Jurist* 31 (1971) 672–680
148.	1971	Jan.	13	*Litteris Encyclicis* (SCDF: circular letter): to Ordinaries regarding laicization.
				ActApS 63 (1971) 309–312 O'Connor 7:110–117
149.	1971	Jan.	15	*Sacra Congregatio* (SCDF: regulation): new procedural norms for the examination of doctrine.
				ActApS 63 (1971) 234–236 *Jurist* 31 (1971) 680–681
150.	1971	Feb.	1	*Instructio a Sacra* (SCIC: declaration): co-education in secondary schools under religious auspices.
				ActApS 63 (1971) 250–251 Flannery 678–679
151.	1971	Feb.	14	*Patres Pontificiae* (PCIV: response): on the motu proprio *Causas Matrimoniales* (1971 Mar. 28)
				ActApS 66 (1974) 463
152.	1971	Apr.	11	*Ad normam* (SCC: directory): General Catechetical Directory.
				ActApS 64 (1972) 97–176 USCC, *General Catechetical Directory* (Washington, D.C. 1971)
153.	1971	Apr.	11	*Horarum Liturgia* (SCCD: decree): Latin edition of the Liturgy of the Hours according to the Roman Rite declared to be the *editio typica*.
				ActApS 63 (1971) 712
154.	1971	Apr.	11	*Opera artis* (SCC: circular letter): to the presidents of episcopal conferences on the historic-artistic heritage of the Church.
				ActApS 63 (1971) 315–317 O'Connor 7:821–824
155.	1971	May	23	*Communio et progressio* (PCCS: instruction): the proper application of the media of social communication, written at the order of Vatican Council II.
				ActApS 63 (1971) 593–656 TPS 16 (1971) 245–283
156.	1971	June	14	*Instructione* (SCCD: notification): the Roman Missal, Liturgy of the Hours, and Calendar.
				ActApS 63 (1971) 712–715 *Jurist* 31 (1971) 692–693 (summary)
157.	1971	July	1	*Patres Pontificiae* (PCIV: responses): founded Masses: reduction and extinction of obligation; recourse in case of a procedure to remove a pastor.
				ActApS 63 (1971) 860 O'Connor 7: 643; 1023
158.	1971	Aug.	20	*Conferentiae Episcopales* (CAP rescript): changes in the revised order of the celebration of the Synod of Bishops.
				ActApS 63 (1971) 702–704 O'Connor 7:338–341

Number	Year	Month	Day	Title and Subject
159.	1971	Aug.	22	*Peculiare Spiritus* (SCCD: decree): revised rite of Sacrament of Confirmation. ActApS 64 (1972) 77
160.	1971	Nov.	13	*Patres Pontificiae* (PCIV: response): faculties of deacons. ActApS 66 (1974) 667
161.	1971	Nov.	29	*Quo clarius* (SS: notification): the celebration and application of Masses. ActApS 63 (1971) 841 O'Connor 7:644
162.	1971	Nov.	30	*Beatissimus Pater* (SYB: rescript): introducing publication of the two documents of the 1971 Synod. ActApS 63 (197) 897 O'Connor 7:341–342
163.	1971	Nov.	30	*Ultimis temporibus* (SYB: document): *The Ministerial Priesthood.* ActApS 63 (1971) 898–922 TPS 16 (1971) 359–376
164.	1971	Nov.	30	*Convenientes* (SYB: document): *Justice in the World.* ActApS 63 (1971) 923–942 TPS 16 (1971) 377–389
165.	1971	Dec.	3	*Le Motu Proprio* (CL: directory): Catholic international organizations defined. ActApS 63 (1971) 948–956 (French) O'Connor 7:569–578
166.	1972	Jan.	6	*Ordinis Baptismi* (SCCD: decree): the rite of Christian initiation of adults. ActApS 64 (1972) 252 O'Connor 7:569
167.	1972	Feb.	2	*Experimenta circa* (SCRIS: decree): the form of government of secular institutes. ActApS 64 (1972) 393–394 RevRel 31 (1972) 593
168.	1972	Feb.	11	*Patres Pontificiae* (PCIV: response): dispensation from canonical form of celebrating mixed marriage. ActApS 64 (1972) 397 O'Connor 7:750
169.	1972	Feb.	11	*Patres Pontificiae* (PCIV: response): interpretation of competent authority for the erection of the national or regional seminary (*Optatam totius* 7). ActApS 64 (1972) 397 O'Connor 7:136–137
170.	1972	Feb.	21	*Mysterium Filii Dei* (SCCD: declaration): safe-guarding the belief in the mysteries of the Incarnation and the Holy Trinity against some recent errors. ActApS 64 (1972) 237–241 TPS 17 (1972) 64–69
171.	1972	Mar.	7	*Dispensationis matrimonii* (SCDS: instruction): procedure in cases of nonconsummation of marriage. ActApS 64 (1972) 244–252 O'Connor 7:988–997
172.	1972	Mar.	25	*Episcoporum delectum* (CAP: norms): selection of candidates for the episcopacy in the Latin Church. ActApS 64 (1972) 386–391 O'Connor 7:366–373 (Norms appended to document)
173	1972	June	1	*In quibus rerum* (SUC: instruction): admission of non-Catholic Christians to Holy Communion. ActApS 64 (1972) 518–525 O'Connor 7:583–590

Number	Year	Month	Day	Title and Subject
174.	1972	June	9	*Patres Pontificiae* (PCIV: response): the laying on of hands by minister of Confirmation.
				ActApS 64 (1972) 526 O'Connor 7:611
175.	1972	June	16	*Sacramentum Paenitentiae* (SCDF: pastoral norms): for the administration of general sacramental absolution.
				ActApS 64 (1972) 510–514 TPS 17 (1972) 280–284
176.	1972	June	24	*Thesaurum cantus* (SCCD: decree): the chants of the Roman Gradual.
				ActApS 65 (1973) 274 O'Connor 7:58
177.	1972	June	26	*Die XIII Ianuarii* (SCDF: declaration): laicization procedures.
				ActApS 64 (1972) 641–643 *National Catholic Reporter* 8 (Oct. 6, 1972) 18
178.	1972	June	27	*Orientalium Religiosorum* (SCEO: decree): faculties granted to Oriental-rite religious.
				ActApS 64 (1972) 738–743 O'Connor 7:19–24
179.	1972	Aug.	7	*In celebratione Missae* (SCCD: declaration): concelebration before or after Mass of ministry.
				ActApS 64 (1972) 561–563 ClergyRev 58 (1973) 222–223
180.	1972	Oct.	9	*Cum de nomine* (SCCD: decree): citing the name of the bishop in the Eucharistic Prayer.
				ActApS 64 (1972) 692–694 O'Connor 7:59–60
181.	1972	Dec.	3	*Ministeriorum disciplina* (SCCD: decree): institution as reader and acolyte; admission to candidacy for Orders; commitment to sacred celibacy.
				ActApS 65 (1973) 274–275 O'Connor 7:705
182.	1972	Dec.	7	*Infirmis cum* (SCCD: decree): publication of the rite of Anointing the Sick.
				ActApS 65 (1973) 275–276 O'Connor 7:686–687
183.	1973	Jan.	8	*Patres Pontificiae* (PCIV): response: the right of attacking the validity of a marriage.
				ActApS 65 (1973) 59
184.	1973	Jan.	29	*Immensae caritatis* (SCCD: instruction): facilitating sacramental Eucharistic Communion in particular circumstances; extraordinary ministers.
				ActApS 65 (1973) 264–271 TPS 18 (1973) 45–51
185.	1973	Mar.	19	*Patronus, liturgica* (SCCD: norms): establishing patron saints.
				ActApS 65 (1973) 276–279 DocCath 70 (1973) 1037–38 (French)
186.	1973	Mar.	23	*Sacra Congregatio* (SCDF: declaration): safeguarding the dignity of the Sacrament of Penance.
				ActApS 65 (1973) 678
187.	1973	Mar.	24	*Sanctus Pontifex* (SCDS/SCC: joint declaration): first reception of the Sacrament of Penance before first reception of the Eucharist.
				ActApS 65 (1973) 410 *Jurist* 33 (1973) 416–417 (summary)

Number	Year	Month	Day	Title and Subject
188.	1973	Apr.	18	*Patres Pontificiae* (PCIV: response): excommunication of religious; cessation of positions in the Roman Curia. ActApS 65 (1973) 220–221
189.	1973	Apr.	27	*Eucharisticae participationem* (SCCD: circular letters): to the presidents of episcopal conferences on Eucharistic Prayers. ActApS 65 (1973) 340–347 TPS 18 (1973) 132–129
190.	1973	May	24	*Sanctus Pontifex* (SCDS/SCC: joint declaration): children's reception of the Sacrament of Penance before First Communion. ActApS 65 (1973) 410 RevRel 33 (1974) 20–21
191.	1973	June	21	*Eucharistiae sacramentum* (SCCD: decree) rite for Holy Communion and worship of the Eucharist outside Mass recognized as the *editio typica*. ActApS 65 (1973) 610
192.	1973	June	24	*Mysterium Ecclesiae* (SCDF: declaration): in defense of the Catholic doctrine of the Church against certain errors of the present day. ActApS 65 (1973) 396–408 TPS 18 (1973) 145–147
193.	1973	July	15	*Exorta quaestione* (SCC: rescript): transfer of competence in marriage cases of nonconsummation to the one Congregation—that for the Discipline of the Sacraments. ActApS 65 (1973) 602
194.	1973	Sept.	20	*Patres Sacrae* (SCCD: decree): Christian burial; CIC C. 1241.1 abrogated. ActApS 65 (1973) 500 DocCath 70 (1973) 1006 (French)
195.	1973	Sept.	24	*E.mus Cardinalis* (SPA: decree):stipulation of the requirements for gaining the Holy Year indulgence in various local churches. ActApS 65 (1973) 615
196.	1973	Oct.	17	*Dopo la pubblicazione* (SUC: communication): interpreting the Instruction on admitting other Christians to Eucharistic Communion under certain circumstances. ActApS 65 (1973) 616–619 Flannery 560–563
197.	1973	Oct.	25	*Dum toto* (SCCD: circular letter): to the bishops and archbishops stating that the Holy Father reserves to himself the power to approve directly all vernacular translations of formulas for Sacraments. ActApS 66 (1974) 98–99 DocCath 71 (1974) 507–508 (French)
198.	1973	Nov.	1	*Pueros baptizatos* (SCCD: directory): Masses with Children. ActApS 66 (1974) 30–46 TPS 18 (1973) 317–331
199.	1973	Dec.	2	*Reconciliationem* (SCCD: decree): revising the liturgy of the Sacrament of Penance. ActApS 66 (1974) 172–173 *National Catholic Reporter* 10 (Feb. 15, 1974) 5 (excerpts)
200.	1974	Jan.	10	*Constitutio Apostolica* (SCCD: decree): postponing effective date of the apostolic constitution *Sacrum Unctionem Infirmorum*, because of translation technicalities. ActApS 66 (1974) 100 OssRomEng (1974) n. 5 305 12

Number	Year	Month	Day	Title and Subject
201.	1974	Jan.	25	*Instauratio liturgica* (SCCD: declaration): the approved versions of sacramental formulae. ActApS 66 (1964) 661 Flannery 271–272
202.	1974	Mar.	2	*Processus iudicialis* (SCRIS: decree): the release of religious priests who have taken perpetual vows. ActApS 66 (1974) 215–216 RevRel 33 (1974) 1249–50
203.	1974	Nov.	18	*Quaestio de abortu* (SCDF: declaration): abortion. ActApS 66 (1974) 730–747 TPS 19 (1975) 250–262
204.	1974	Dec.	1	*Datée du 28* (SUC: instruction): suggestions for the application of the conciliar declaration *Nostra Aetate* 4. ActApS (1975) 73–79
205.	1974	Dec.	7	*Ad baccalaureatum* (PBC: instruction): norm for degree examinations in biblical studies. ActApS 67 (1975) 153–158
206.	1975	Feb.	15	*Sacra Congregatio* (SCDF: declaration): two works of Hans Küng. ActApS 67 (1975) 203–204 OssRomEng n. 10 (March 6, 1975) 2
207.	1975	Mar.	19	*Ecclesiae pastorum* (SCDF: decree): censorship of books and pastoral vigilance. ActApS 67 (1975) 281–184 TPS 20 (1975) 78–81
208.	1975	Sept.	8	*Sacra Congregatio* (SCDF: monitum): regarding matrimony. ActApS 67 (1975) 559
209.	1975	Dec.	29	*Persona humana* (SCDF: declaration): On Certain Questions concerning Sexual Ethics. ActApS 68 (1976) 77–96 TPS 21 (1976) 60–73
210.	1976	June	11	*Accidit in diversia* (SCSCD: decree): the public celebration of Mass in the Catholic Church for other Christians who have died. ActApS 68 (1976) 621–622 TPS 21 (1976) 321–322
211.	1976	Sept.	17	*Exc. mus et Rev. mus* (SCDF: decree): certain unlawful priestly and episcopal ordinations. ActApS 68 (1976) 623 OssRomEng (1976) n. 40 [444]1
212.	1976	Oct.	15	*Inter insigniores* (SCDF: declaration): On the Question of the Admission of Women to the Ministerial Priesthood. ActApS 69 (1977) 98–116 TPS 22 (1977) 108–122
213.	1977	May	13	*Sacra Congregatio* (SCDF: decree): male impotence and sterility with regard to marriage ActApS 69 (1977) 426
214.	1977	May	20	*Utrum liceat* (SCC: response): on permitting First Communion before the reception of the Sacrament of Penance. ActApS 69 (1977) 427 TPS 22 (1977) 203

Number	Year	Month	Day	Title and Subject
215.	1977	Sept.	2	*Apostolatus Maris* (PCSM: decree): the pastoral care of migrant and itinerant people.
				ActApS 69 (1977) 737–738 Origins 8 (1978) 60–63 (excerpts) Norms ActApS 69 (1977) 738–746
216.	1977	Dec.	13	*Canon* 1569 (SSAT: circular letter): to diocesan archbishops and bishops on judicial recourse to the Supreme Pontiff.
				ActApS 70 (1978) 75
217.	1978	May	14	*Mutuae relationes* (SCRIS/SCE: directives) the relationship of bishops and religious orders.
				ActApS 70 (1978) 473–506 Origins 8 (1978) 161–175
218.	1978	May	26	*Conferenze Episcopali* (PCSM: circular letter): to the episcopal conferences on the pastoral aspects of human mobility in our day.
				ActApS 70 (1978) 357–378 TPS 23 (1978) 236–257
219.	1978	July	7	*Propositum dubium* (PCIV: response): procedures for the removal of pastors.
				ActApS 70 (1978) 534

[M. C. CARLEN]

GUIDE TO THE USE OF THE INDEX

The Index to Volume 17 of the *New Catholic Encyclopedia* is a guide to specific information contained in the more than 750 articles of the text. Each reference is followed by page number and quadrant letter showing location on the page (the letters a,b,c,d indicating respectively the upper and lower halves of the left and right columns of the page). The Index does not catalog every item of information, but does give access to the information most significant to the purposes of the Volume.

Scope. The scope of the Index corresponds to the purposes of the Volume: the intrinsic aim of developing the theme, Change in the Church; the further aim of supplementing those entries in the *New Catholic Encyclopedia* affected by Change in the Church. Consequently the Index includes, first, every article title in Volume 17 (indicated by capitals), most of which have a counterpart in an earlier volume; references to these same subjects occurring in other articles. The Index's other entries are on subjects or persons for which there is no separate article; such entries include: titles of articles in earlier volumes of the *New Catholic Encyclopedia;* significant subjects and personal names in Volume 17, as well as titles of Church documents—papal, conciliar, curial, episcopal; publications; religious and other relevant associations, learned societies, and organizations. Vatican II documents are indexed under their official, Latin title; their English designations are given as cross references to the Latin titles. For information on a particular topic the reader should first consult the general article and then pursue the additional references. Specific topics will be found as or under specific entries; e.g. the apostolic exhortation, *Evangelii nuntiandi,* is listed under title, but not under Paul VI.

Arrangement. The sequence in the Index, as in the *Encyclopedia* itself, is basically a dictionary arrangement. Entries are filed word by word; words are filed letter by letter according to the order of the English alphabet, without regard for any foreign-language diacritical marks. The order is familiar to most readers, since it is that generally used in telephone directories. Hyphenated words are treated as two separate terms unless the first part of the word is a prefix. Articles at the beginning of a title (a, an, the, and their foreign equivalents) are disregarded in order arrangement; in the case of papal documents, however, the article is retained for filing purposes, since it is an integral part of the *incipit* from which the title is derived.

Angola, People's Republic of 8b
Annales musicologiques (journal) 441d
Anniversary Masses
    Masses for the dead 397a
Annuarium statisticum Ecclesiae 92c
Annulment of marriages
    divorce mentality 388b
    improper convalidation 387d
    invalidating conditions 388a
    marriage tribunals, experimental norms
      390b
    psychological grounds 589a
    suspension of mandatory appeal 386a;
      390c
    tribunal practice 386a
    U.S. tribunals, statistics 385d; 387c
Annulments (series)
    Canon Law Society of America 70c
Anointing, baptismal
    omission 269c
Anointing and Pastoral Care of the Sick
    (BCL Study Text) 50a
Anointing and Pastoral Care of the Sick
    (Rite) 269b
Anointing of the Sick
    Christian healing 246d
    ministry of healing 247b
    parish celebration 595d
    theology of forgiveness 595d
Anonymous Christians
    missiology 418b
Anthropocentrism
    love (theology) 379c; 380b
Anthropology, cultural
    comparative study of religions 562d
    development of culture 169a
    history of religions 264c
    natural law 460c
Anthropology, theological
    feminist critique 230d
    transcendental 654c
Apartheid
    South Africa 6a
Apocrypha
    common Bibles 40b
    Dead Sea Scrolls 176b
Apologetics
    foundational theology 653d
    recent trends 235b
Apostles
    model for ministry 412d
    resurrection witnesses 577d
Apostles' Creed
    ecumenism 359d
    translation 153d; 296c
    use, optional 542d
Apostolate
    Vatican II terminology 711b

APOSTOLATE OF THE LAITY
  (DECREE) 22a
    Catholic Action 81b
    holiness, call to 265d
    implementation 327d
    laity (theology) 327a; 328d
    see also Apostolicam actuositatem

Apostolatus peragendi (motu proprio, 1976)
    Committee for the Family 226a
    Council for the Laity 327d
Apostolic Camera 171b
Apostolic Delegate 349a
Apostolic Signatura 171a
    marriage decisions 387b

APOSTOLIC SPIRITUALITY 22c
    activism 4a; 539c
    laity, vocation of 344d
    Optatam totius 539b

APOSTOLIC SUCCESSION 23c
    collegiality 139c
    Eucharistic sharing 216b
    ministry (ecclesiology) 414a
    Presbyterian-Reformed/Roman Catholic
      Consultation 534c

Apostolic Tradition (Hippolytus)
    ecumenical use 370d
    Eucharistic Prayers 214b; 370d
Apostolica sollicitudo (motu proprio, 1965)
  314c
    Synod of Bishops 627d
Apostolicae caritatis (motu proprio, 1970)
    migrants 409a
Apostolicae curae (papal bull, Leo XIII)
    Anglican Orders 20b
Apostolicam actuositatem (Decree on the
  Apostolate of the Laity)
    "domestic Church" 477a
    family 225d
    marriage bond 388c
    "ministry"/"apostolate" 712b
    parents as catechists 477a
    pastoral councils 486b
APOSTOLICITY 24b
    apostolic succession 24a
    charisms in ministry 107a
    martyria, diakonia, koinōnia 413a
    ministry (ecclesiology) 412d
Appalachia
    Core Appalachian Ministries 163c
    Glenmary Sisters 463c
    justice and peace ministry 85b
    This Land is Home for Me (pastoral,
      1975) 85b
Appalachian Regional Commission 85a
Appropriate Renewal of the Religious Life,
  Decree on the *see Perfectae caritatis*
Aristotle
    liberal arts 253c
Aristotelian-Thomistic philosophy
    Catholic philosophers 511a
ARCIC *see* Anglican/Roman Catholic
  International Commission (ARCIC)
Archiv für Musikwissenschaft 441d
ARCHIVES, ECCLESIASTICAL 25a
Armenian Apostolic Church
    Catholic dialogue 44c
Arms race
    immorality 188b
Ascension, Feast of 62d
Ascetical theology
    precepts and counsels 379a
Asceticism
    holiness, universal call to 266d
    Penance (Rite) 621d
Assistants at the Pontifical Throne 476c
Association for Clinical Pastoral Education
    Catholic seminaries 165b
ASSOCIATION FOR RELIGIOUS AND
  VALUE ISSUES IN COUNSELING 26c
ASSOCIATION FOR SOCIAL
  ECONOMICS 26d
ASSOCIATION FOR THE SOCIOLOGY
  OF RELIGION 27a
    theology and sociology 658c
Association of Catholic Colleges and
  Universities (NCEA) 452b
    ecumenism 255b
ASSOCIATION OF CATHOLIC
  TEACHERS 27b
    Catholic teachers' unions 637d
Association of Catholic Television and Radio
  Syndicators 402a
Association of Catholic Trade Unionists 325b
ASSOCIATION OF CONTEMPLATIVE
  SISTERS 27c
Association of Interchurch Families
  (England) 202d
Association of Ladies of Charity in the U.S.
  83c
Association of Major Religious Superiors of
  the Philippines
    human rights 506d
    rebuke by Rome 507b
Association of Professors and Researchers in
  Religious Education 77b
ASSOCIATION OF PROFESSORS OF
  MISSIONS 28a
    missiology 418a

Association of Theological Field Education
  652a
Association of Theological Schools
    women in theology programs 710a
Assumption of Mary
    ecclesiology 394a
Athanasian Creed 542d
ATHEISM 28b
    "absence of God" 328d
    agnosticism 17c
    conversion 159d
    faith, act of 224c
    Institute for the Study of Atheism 293a
    laity, vocation of 343d
    Marxism 391b; 392d
    philosophy of religion 557d
    postulatory/militant 290d
    practical/theoretical 293a
    symptoms 159d
    Synod of Bishops (1974) 627d
Atheists, dialogue with 29d; 421c; 656c
Athenagoras I
    ecumenism 101c; 472c
At-One-Ment (newsletter) 201c
Attività della Santa Sede (ann.) 92c
ATTWATER, DONALD 30d
Augustine, St.
    catechetics 76d
    Catholicity 96c
    "just war" theory 701a
    political theology 516c
    sexual morality 606c
    "two cities" 518b
AUTHORITY, ECCLESIASTICAL 31b
    apostolicity 24c
    ARCIC 21c
    charismatic renewal and ecumenism
      106d
    crisis 619a
    decentralization 690a
    ecclesiology 199b
    ecumenical dialogue 43a
    ecumenical movement 204b
    Joint Roman Catholic/World Methodist
      Commission 307c
    jurisdiction, power of 314a
    ministry (ecclesiology) 414a
    participative decision making 484d
    penal power 496d
    preaching 270c
    theological pluralism 513c; 514a
    tradition 343d; 688c
    Vatican II ecclesiology 209d
Authors, Catholic 550a

B

Bakunin, Michael 644b
Balthasar, Eulalio 54d
Balthasar, Hans Urs von
    atheism 30b
    historicity of God's Word 656d
    theology as aesthetics 654c
Baltic countries
    vacant sees 186d
Baltimore, Third Plenary Council
    parochial schools 483b; 599a
Baltimore Catechism 77d
Bangladesh
    genocide 242b
Baptism
    basis for ecclesiastical office 469a
    basis for Christian morality 437d
    basis for ministry 712c
    Christian Initiation 111b
    community bond 480c
    conditional 34c
    Easter 33d
    equality in the Church 708d; 716a
    incorporation into the Church 288c

C

CELAM see Consejo Episcopal Latino
Americano (CELAM)
Celebrant
chair of 240a
CELEBRATION AND LITURGY 97d
liturgical reform 363d
Celibacy
African Christianity 12b
deacons 412b
holiness of the Church 267d
ministry and 713a
Orthodox/Roman Catholic Consultation
474a
psychotheological therapy 546a; 547b
CELIBACY (RITE OF COMMITMENT)
98b
CELIBACY, FORMATION IN 98d
interpersonal relationships 694c
priestly formation 538c
vocation, psychology of 694c
CENSORSHIP OF BOOKS 99b
CENSURES, ECCLESIASTICAL 99c
Christian burial, denial of 60d
latae sententiae 497a, c
pastoral purpose 497b
pastoral revision 496c
CENTER FOR APPLIED RESEARCH IN
THE APOSTOLATE (CARA) 100a
liturgical education in seminaries,
survey 357b
mission planning 421b
pastoral-planning study 486a
religious life 573d
Center for Contemplative Studies
(Kalamazoo) 622c
Center for Pastoral Liturgy (Catholic
University) 487c
Center for Pastoral Liturgy (Univ. of Notre
Dame) 487c
CENTER OF CONCERN 100c
justice ministry of women 719c
Central African Empire 8b
Centre chrétien d'études Maghrebines
El-Biar, Algeria) 201a; 205a
Centre d'études oecuméniques (Strasbourg)
200d
Centre d'oecuménisme (Montreal) 201a
Centre national de pastorale liturgique
(Paris) 487a
liturgical music 284c
Centro de Pastoral Hispana para El
Nordeste see Northeast Regional Pastoral
Center for Hispanics
Chad, Republic of 8b
Chair, celebrant's 240a
Chair of Unity Octave see Week of Prayer
for Christian Unity
Chalcedon, Council of
contemporary Christology 113d; 116a
Chalice and paten
blessing 367a
material, design 367b
Chancery of Apostolic Letters 169c
CHANGE IN THE CHURCH 100d
Catholic behavioral attitudes 347d
charismatic renewal 105d
continuity and development 264b
post-Vatican II turmoil 689d
pre-Vatican II 688a
sociological analyses 560b
structural and institutional 24d
Vatican II view 264a; 689b
CHAPEL OF RECONCILIATION 103c
BCL directives 50a
Chaplains, prison 541d
Chaplains of His Holiness 476b
Chapter, cathedral 185d
CHAPTERS, RELIGIOUS 103d
Character, sacramental see Sacramental
character
CHARISMATIC PRAYER 104b
apostolicity 24d
charismatic renewal, Catholic 105c

prayer 528b
prayer, community 529d
CHARISMATIC RENEWAL, CATHOLIC
104d
apostolicity 24d
Christian healing 245d; 402d
Church, local 416b
community, forms of 147a
contemporary spirituality 622a
evangelization, programs of 219d
fundamentalism 603a
gift of tongues (glossalalia) 104b, c
Holy Spirit 269d
Mariology 383b
reaction to secularism 603a
sociological analysis 560a; 619b
CHARISMATIC RENEWAL AND
ECUMENISM 106b
ecumenical prayer 245d
Charismatic Renewal Services, Inc. 105c
Charismatic Retreats see Retreats
Charisms
charismatic renewal 105b
gifts of healing 246a
grace of words 531b
holiness of the Church 267c
Houses of Prayer 277a
institutional Church 106c
perfection, spiritual 501d
renewal in the Holy Spirit 269d
sanctifying grace and 269d
spirituality 341d
theology of 107d
CHARISMS IN MINISTRY 107a
ministry 412c
New Testament 536a
unordained ministry 415d
Word, sacrament, care 413b
CHARISMS IN RELIGIOUS LIFE 107c
charisms in ministry 107b
community, religious 147d
religious superiors 576a
Charities, U.S.A. (journal) 84d
Charities Congress (NCCC) 83d
Charity see Love (Theology)
Chastity
common life (Canon Law) 141d
homosexuality 272d
Chastity, Vow of
community life 547d; 698b
contemporary understanding 698b
witness value 698b
CHASUBLE 108b
CHASUBLE-ALB 108c
Chavez, Cesar
migrant farmworkers 407d
Chevetogne (Belgium)
Orthodox/Roman Catholic relations
200d
Child development see Moral Development
Child labor
migrant farmworkers (U.S.) 407b
Children, Masses with see Masses with
Children
CHILDREN, RELIGION AND 108d
adult catechesis 74d
age of reason 554a
catechesis 561d
children's liturgies 398a
First Communion celebrations 232b
first confession 234a
Masses with children 397b
moral education 433b
China, People's Republic of
genocide 242b
Chirau, Jeremiah
Rhodesia 8c
Chirico, P.
infallibility 291d
Chrism see Holy Oils and Chrism
CHRISM MASS 109d
renewal of priestly commitment 98c
Christ see Jesus Christ

Christ the King, Feast of
Calendar, Common Liturgical 65c
date 626c
CHRISTIAN 110a
Judaism and the early Church 310c
Christian Democracy 519b
Christian Education, Declaration on see
Gravissimum educationis
Christian Family Mission Vacation 111a
CHRISTIAN FAMILY MOVEMENT 110d
adult catechesis 75d
CHRISTIAN INITIATION, SACRAMENTS
OF 111b
baptismal promises 33b
baptismal water, blessing of 34a
basis for ministry 413a
charisms 269a
children of catechetical age 292c
Easter celebration 80a
exorcism 220b
infant Baptism and Communion 292b
integral view 370d
liturgical catechesis 354d
new models for catechesis 73c
pastoral and doctrinal implications 80b
postbaptismal catechesis 524d
sponsors 623c
Christian Life Communicator (period.) 113a
CHRISTIAN LIFE COMMUNITIES 112c
Christian morality see Morality, Christian
Christian Peace Conference
Church in Communist countries 127b
Christian Prayer
Liturgy of the Hours 376c
Christian Trade Unions
labor movement 325b
Christians for Socialism 333b; 391b
CHRISTOCENTRISM 113a
catechesis 630a, d
Evangelii nuntiandi 628d
Mariology 393c
salvation history 554c
theology of history 264a
CHRISTOLOGY 113c
catholicity 96c
Church and communio 122d
Dead Sea Scrolls 177d
demythologizing 211b
ecumenical aspect 205a
eschatology 210c
patristics 490d
resurrection narratives 576c; 580b
sacramental theology 591a
virgin birth 691b
Christophers, The 321d
Christus Dominus (Decree on Bishops)
abrogation of CIC c. 81 191b
bishops' powers 190d
catechetical renewal 73b
CHURCH (THEOLOGY) 116c
analogy of "Church" 119a
apostolic community 80b
authority, ecclesiastical 31c
bishops' authority 313d
Body of Christ 412d
called to conversion 156c
Canon Law 69c
Catholic and Protestant views 289b
Catholicity 96c
Christian Initiation 111d
Church and communio 121c
collegiality 138c; 540c
communitarian nature 415d
ecclesia docens/discens 640b
educational role 226d
Ekklēsia 118d
equality in the Church 209a
eschatological model 413a
eschatalogical process 102c
evangelization 218d
faith, act of 225b
family 225d
holiness, universal call to 267a
holiness of the Church 267b

Commission for Education in Ecumenism (BCEIA) 44a
Commission of Catholic Missions Among the Colored and Indian People 19b
Commission on Aging
  Catholic Charities 16c
Commission on American Citizenship 599c
Commission on Religion in Appalachia (CORA) 85a
Commission on the Year 2000 17b
COMMISSIONS, PAPAL 140a
COMMITMENT 141a
  infant Baptism and Communion 292b
  vocation, psychology of 694d
Committee against the Extension of Race Prejudice in the Church 670d
Committee on the Lay Apostolate (NCCB)
  see Bishops' Committee on the Laity
Common Catechism, The
  ecumenical cooperation 78a; 501b
Common Eucharistic Prayer
  ecumenical use 359d
Common good 319b; 515a; 612d
  advertising (moral aspect) 5d
  civil law 131b
  definition (Gaudium et spes) 131c
  international 181a; 522a
  personal rights 570b
  political communities 514d
  right to education 206c
  social justice 299c
  world community 515b
COMMON LIFE (CANON LAW) 141c
Common of saints
  Sacramentary 597c
"Communal Catholics" 481c
Communication
  homiletics 270d
COMMUNICATION, USCC COMMITTEE ON 142c
  Church and the media 401d
  media in evangelization 400d
  UNDA-USA 676c
Communicationes (period.) 93a; 681c
Comunidades de base see Basic Christian Communities
Communio et progressio (instr., 1971)
  advertising (moral aspect) 5b
  Catholic journalism 308c
  Church and the media 401a
  media in evangelization 400a; 401a
Communion bowl 367b
COMMUNION IN THE HAND 143b
  catechesis for 228d
  Immensae caritatis 222a
  symbolism 370d
  United States 682a
COMMUNION OF SAINTS 143d
  Church and communio 122c
  ecclesial communion 215d
  holiness, universal call to 266c
  holiness of the Church 267c
Communion of the Mass
  elements 593b
Communion for the sick see Holy Communion for the sick
COMMUNION TABLE 144d
Communion tube/spoon 367b
Communion under both kinds 144d; 372a
Communism
  atheism 28c
  papal repudiation 519c
Communist Countries see Church in Communist Countries
COMMUNITY 144d
  African Independent Church Movement 14a
  basic Christian communities 34d
  catechesis 561d; 630d
  Catholic education 599d
  Christian education 637b
  Christian Initiation 112a
  Church and urbanization 685c
  convening 83d

  development 454a
  human rights 319b
  love (theology) 380b
  ministerial and sacramental elements 478d
  neighborhood 685d
  parish 478c; 479c
  parish (community of worship) 480c
  political communities 514d
  psychotheological therapy 546c
  reconciliation 555b
  Sacraments and 591d
  team ministry 640d
COMMUNITY, FORMS OF 146a
  campus ministry 68b
  East Asian Pastoral Institute 195b
  houses of prayer 277a
  monasticism, contemporary 431a
  noncanonical communities 463b
  prayer groups 105c
COMMUNITY, RELIGIOUS 147b
  chapters, religious 104a
  common life (Canon Law) 142a
  community, forms of 146c
  formative communities 569a
  group dynamics 490a
  intercommunity living 564c
  new forms 573a; 574c
  participation and accountability 576a
  personal development 547a
  prayer, community 529d
  religious men 563c
  religious superiors 575d
Community Mass see Mass, Conventual/Community
COMMUNITY OF MANKIND 148a
  business ethics 62b
  Christian Initiation 112a
  Church and 117c
  education for justice 316a
  Gaudium et spes 22c; 146c
  interdependence 181a
  interracial justice 299c
  justice ministry 643d
  labor movement 326d
  Lumen gentium 22c
  technology 641d
  universal common good 181a; 515b
Community prayer see Prayer, Community
Community Response to Crime (USCC) 541c
Comparative Study of Religions see Religions, Comparative Study of
Compromise, theology of
  morality 434b
CONCELEBRATION 149c
  collegiality 371b
  community Mass 395a
  Sacramentary 593c
  vestments 108c
Concilium (Religion in the Seventies) (publ.) 93b
CONCILIUM MONASTICUM IURIS CANONICI 149d
Conclave
  cardinal electors 596d
  papal election 523c
Condemned societies see Societies, Condemned
Conditae a Christo (apostolic constitution, 1900) 571c
Cone, Cecil W. 54d
Cone, James H. 54d
Confederación Latino-Americana de Religiosos (CLAR) 573c
Conférence Mondiale des Instituts Séculiers 602b
CONFERENCE OF INTERNATIONAL CATHOLIC ORGANIZATIONS 150c
CONFERENCE OF MAJOR SUPERIORS OF MEN (CMSM) 150d
  Bishops' Committee on Priestly Life and Ministry 47a
  missiology 417c

  renewal 547a
  vocations 50d
Conference of Major Superiors of Women
  houses of prayer 276d
  see also LCWR
Conference on International Economic Cooperation (1975-77) 182a
Confession
  general absolution 498b
  necessity 499b
  Rite of Penance 497d; 499a
Confession, first see First Confession
CONFESSION, FREQUENCY OF 151b
  conversion process 499b
  theological problem 595b
Confession, general
  Rite of Penance 498b
Confessional
  Chapel of Reconciliation 103c
CONFESSORS OF RELIGIOUS 151c
  women in Canon Law 706b
Confirmation
  age for reception 111d; 595a
  catechesis 76a
  Christian Initiation 111c
  link with Baptism 595a; 623d
  sponsors 623d
  witness 531b
Confirmation, infant
  Christian Initiation 292b
  history 292b
Confiteor
  communal penitential rite 352c
Confraternity of Christian Doctrine see Religious Education/CCD
Confraternity Version
  Bible versions for liturgy 40a
Congar, Y.
  hierarchy of truths 655c
Congo, People's Republic of 8b
CONGREGATIONAL SINGING 151d
  BCL directives 361a
  chant books 395c
  hymnology 283c
  legislation on music 440b
  Sacramentary music 593d
Congregations of the Roman Curia see Curia, Roman
Congressional Comment (quarterly) 84d
Conscience, examination of
  Rite of Penance 498a
Conscience, formation of
  moral education 433b
  psychology of religion 559a
  role of the Church 243a
CONSCIENCE, FREEDOM OF 152c
  dialogue as mission 421b
  Dignitatis humanae 533d
  dignity of the person 504c
  evangelization 416d
  Helsinki Agreement 249c
  missiology 418b
  moral education 433b
  penal power of the Church 497c
Conscience clause
  Catholic Hospital Association 87a
  (Sen.) Church Amendment 404a
Conscientious objectors
  Church and State (U.S.) 124b
Consecrated life see Religious Life; Secular Institutes
Consecrated Life (period.) 93a; 293d
Consejo Episcopal Latino-Americano (CELAM)
  Bishops' Committee for the Church in Latin America 45c
  formation 332c; 336a
  Medellín Documents 399a
  missiology 417b
  mission planning 424c
  study on evangelization 336b
CONSEQUENCES, MORALITY OF 152d
  consequentialism 434b
CONSERVATISM AND LIBERALISM, THEOLOGICAL 153b

D

G

Hofinger, Johannes
  catechetics 76b
  East Asian Pastoral Institute 195a
HOLINESS, UNIVERSAL CALL TO 265b
  Baptism 342a
  charisms in ministry 107b
  Christian witness 705d
  commitment 141b
  communion of saints 144c
  contemplation 154d
  holiness of the Church 267a
  laity, vocation of 329a
  laity in Canon Law 329c
  lay spirituality 342d
  Methodist/Roman Catholic dialogue
    307d
  perfection, spiritual 501d
  single people 612c
  theology of religious life 697c
  unordained ministry 415d
  vocation, Christian 692d
  vocation, religious 659b
Holiness Movement 106b; 158c
HOLINESS OF THE CHURCH 267a
  communion of saints 144b
  Ecclesia reformata, semper reformanda
    123b
  episcopacy 208c
  holiness, universal call to 265d
  Pilgrim Church 123b, c
  religious life 564b
HOLLIS, (MAURICE) CHRISTOPHER
  268b
Holocaust Studies (Temple University) 303c
HOLY COMMUNION, RITES OF 268d
  Benediction and exposition of the Bl.
    Sacrament 37b
  Eucharist, worship and custody,
    instruction on 222b
  sign of unity 396c
Holy Communion and the Worship of the
  Eucharist Outside Mass (instr., 1973)
  212d
Holy Communion for the sick 222c; 269b
  acolyte 294a
  reservation of the Eucharist 633a
  viaticum 213a
Holy Communion outside Mass
  Holy Communion, Rites of 269a
  reservation of Eucharist 213a; 633a
Holy, Holy, Holy (*Sanctus*)
  music 360d
  translation 296c
Holy hour 213a
HOLY OILS AND CHRISM 269b
  blessing by priest 55d
  Chrism Mass 109d
Holy Orders *see* Orders, Sacrament of
Holy See, U.S. representative to 186b
HOLY SPIRIT 269d
  catholicity 96b
  charismatic prayer 104c, d
  charismatic renewal 105d
  charismatic renewal and ecumenism
    106d
  Christian Initiation 111c
  Church, local 423a
  communion of saints 144c
  ecclesiology 394b
  evangelization 416c
  faith, act of 585c
  force of evangelization 628c
  holiness of the Church 268a; 267b
  incorporation into the Church 288c
  indwelling 106a
  infallibility of the Church 31d
  inspiration of 106a
  life of the Church 105a
  ministry (ecclesiology) 413a
  preaching 531d
  presence in the Church 103b
  sanctification 344b
  Spirit Christology 114b
  spirituality 341c

  teaching authority of the Church 640b
  vocation, religious 696a
Holy Spirit, gifts of
  affective experience 158b
Holy Trinity, Solemnity of 626d
Holy water
  Masses for the dead 397b
Holy Week
  liturgical revision 370c
  music 593d
HOMILETICS 270b
HOMILY 271a
  homiletics 270d; 271a
  liturgical rites 530c
  Liturgy of the Word 363c
  Masses for the dead 397b
  preaching 530c
  silence following 610c
Homily Service (period.) 356a
HOMOSEXUALITY 271c
  ecumenical movement 204a
  homosexuals' rights 272c
  morality 607c
  NT proscription 605b
Honorary Palatine Guard 476b
Honorary Prelates of His Holiness 476b
HOPE (House of Prayer Experience) 276d
HOPE, THEOLOGY OF 273b
  Church and world 126b
  eschatology 211b
  Kingdom of God 322b
  progress 543b
  theology as eschatology 655b
Horizons (journal, College Theology Society)
  138a
Horkheimer, Max
  Frankfurt School 237d
Hospices
  care of the dying 194c; 247d
Hospital Progress (period.) 403a
HOSPITALS, CATHOLIC 274d
  Catholic identity 87d
  health care and the Church 247b
  shared services programs 87b
  sterilization 624c
Host *see* Altar Breads
HOUSE OF AFFIRMATION 276a
  psychotheological therapy 546a
  vocation, psychology of 693c
HOUSES OF PRAYER 276c
  community, religious 148a
  prayer community 530a
Housing
  interracial justice 300a
Hugh of St. Victor
  liberal arts 253d
HUMAN ACT 277b
  intrinsic value 557a
  love (theology) 379c
  morality 435c
  objective goodness/evil 435d
  sexual morality 607d
HUMAN DEVELOPMENT 278b
  Catholic Relief Services 93c
  Church and Third World 325d
  community of mankind 149a
  conversion and 159b
  "Cor Unum" 162c
  Core Appalachian Ministries 163c
  evangelization and 126a
  human rights 281c
  labor movement 326d
  missionary 426b
  Paul VI 494b
  political communities 515c
  Synod of Bishops (1971) 281c
HUMAN LIFE AND NATURAL FAMILY
  PLANNING FOUNDATION 278d
  research and education 459d
Human Life and states' rights amendments
  abortion (U.S. Law) 2b
Human Life Center 402d
Human Life Foundation
  origin 459d

HUMAN RIGHTS 280a
  Belgrade Conference 37a
  Bishops' Justice Program 52b
  Church and 521a
  Church in Latin America 332c
  corporate social responsibility 164b
  dignity of the person 504d
  ecumenical collaboration 430b
  education for justice 316a
  freedom of conscience 152c
  genocide 241d
  Helsinki Agreement 249b
  international migration 408b
  Latin America 334b
  medical ethics 402a
  migrant farmworkers 408a
  migration 409c
  military regimes 333c
  necessities of life 527c
  Philippines 506d
  political communities 516a
  Pontifical Commission for Justice and
    Peace 320a
  Presbyterian-Reformed/Roman Catholic
    Consultation 535a
  prolongation of life 351d
  right to education 206a
  right to work 207d
  social action 612d
  social ministry 319b
  technology and 402a
  women in the Church 708d
  world community 515c
Human Sexuality (publ.) 94b
  Bishops' Committee on Doctrine 650b
Human Solidarity *see* Solidarity, Human
Humanae salutis (apostolic constitution,
  1961)
  convocation of Vatican II 263c
Humanae vitae (encycl., Paul VI)
  authority crisis 31d
  Catholic women and 716b
  Cogley, John 137b
  intercourse as procreative 607a
  natural family planning 279d
  population explosion 524d
  sexual morality 606a
  theological dissent 433d; 639a
Humani generis (encycl., Pius XII)
  monogenism 431c
  theologians 649d
Humanism, secular
  agnosticism 17c
  atheism 28c
  Gospel and 29c
  medical ethics 402b
  moral theology (contemporary trends)
    433d
  repudiation 513a
  science and technology 17c
Humanist Manifestos I and II 17a
Humeral veil 367b
  Benediction and exposition of the Bl.
    Sacrament 37c
Humphrey-Hawkins Bill 677c
Hungarian Byzantine Rite 196d
Hungary
  Church in Communist countries 126c
Hunt v. McNair 125b
Husband
  rights regarding abortion 2d
Husserl, E. 654c
HUTCHINS, ROBERT MAYNARD 283a
Hymn
  definition 283c
Hymn, The (period.) 283d
Hymnal, national (U.S.) 285a
HYMNOLOGY 283c
HYMNS AND HYMNALS 284a
  congregational singing 152b
  Federation of Diocesan Liturgical
    Commissions 229a
  Liturgy of the Hours 375c

homiletics 270c
media in education 399c
Media of Social Communications, Pontifical
Commission for
advertising 5b
formation 140c
MEDIA OF SOCIAL COMMUNICATION
AND THE CHURCH 401a
American Indians 20a
Catholic journalism 308c
Catholic Press (U.S.) 90c
Communication, USCC Committee on
142c
media influence on Vatican II 688d
public opinion 548c
UNDA 676c
Mediator Dei (encycl., Pius XII)
liturgical laws 358b
liturgy (historical development) 370b
meaning of evangelization 218a
vernacular in liturgy 690d
Medical care
ordinary/extraordinary means 352a
MEDICAL ETHICS 402a
Catholic Hospital Association 86d
medical experimentation 220d
moral theology 434d
National Federation of Catholic
Physicians' Guilds 457a
ordinary/extraordinary means 352a
Medical Experimentation *see*
Experimentation, Medical
Medical-Moral Newsletter 403a
MEDICAL PERSONNEL, MORAL
OBLIGATIONS OF 403b
abortion (U.S. law and morality) 2d
medical vs. personal values 402c
prolongation of life 352a
sterilization 624d
uses of technology 402c
Meditation
contemplation 154b
contemporary methods 528d
Eastern influence 622a
prayer 528a
Meek v. Pittenger 125a; 485b
Melchisedek
Qumram Cave 11 177a
Melkite Rite 197a
Membership in the Church *see* Incorporation
into the Church (Membership)
Memorial Acclamation *see* Anamnesis
Memoriale Domini (instr., 1969)
Communion in the hand 143b
Memorials of the Saints *see* Saints,
Memorials of the
Mental retardation
National Apostolate for the Mentally
Retarded (NAMR) 445a
Menti nostrae (apostolic exhortation, Pius
XII)
activism 4a
Mercy killing *see* Euthanasia
Merton, Thomas
contemplative spirituality 444c; 622d
houses of prayer 276d
Message to the People of God (1977 Synod
of Bishops) 75b; 629d
Metanoia
conversion 156c
METAPHYSICS 404c
hostility to 508c
preambles of faith 532b
theological methodology 653d
Metz, Johannes
Kingdom of God 543a
political theology 517a; 657a
theology as eschatology 655a
theology of hope 273b
MEXICAN-AMERICAN CULTURAL
CENTER 405b
liturgical movement 359b
musicology, sacred 442d
PADRES 475c
pastoral liturgy 487c

Meyer, Albert (card.)
Unitatis redintegratio 43c
MIDDLE EAST, CHURCH AND 405d
Eastern Catholic Churches 195d
Islamic/Roman Catholic Dialogue 301c
Jewish/Roman Catholic relations 304b
papal diplomacy 186d
Paul VI 494c
MIGRANT FARMWORKERS (U.S.) 406d
Hispanic Affairs, Secretariat for 259b
Hispanics in the U.S. 260a
labor movement 326c
Las Hermanas 332a
right of migration 409c
undocumented aliens 326c
MIGRATION, INTERNATIONAL 408b
Catholic charities 82d
Third World peoples 462a
MIGRATION, RIGHT OF 409a
MIGRATION AND REFUGEE SERVICES
OF THE USCC 409d
Migration and Tourism, Pontifical
Commission for 408d
Military-Industrial Complex
economic inequality 326d
Mindanao-Sulu Pastoral Conference and
Secretariat (MSPCS)
justice ministry 506b
MINDZENTY, JÓSZEF 410b
papal diplomacy 186c
Paul VI 492c
MINISTER OF MUSIC 411a
lay ministries 412a
parish liturgical committees 355c
Minister of the Interior (Papal) 476a
Ministeria quaedam (motu proprio, 1972)
expansion of ministries 414b
lay ministries 293d; 411c
liturgical ministries 340a
minor orders 3c
reader 553a
subdiaconate, suppression 98c
women in ministry 716a
Ministerial Priesthood (Synod of Bishops,
1971) 539a
MINISTRIES, LAY 411c
acolyte 3c; 293d
activism, political and social 4b
basic Christian communities 336d
Bishops' Committee on the Laity 49b
Bishops' Committee on Vocations 51a
Catholic hospitals 274d
change in the Church 101c
charismatic renewal 106a
education for 414d
Eucharistic ministers 221d
evangelization 218a
expansion 414b
family ministry 227c
lay missionaries 341b
liturgy (historical development) 371b
missions (U.S.) 429b
new forms 340b
parish community 480a
parish worship 480d
preaching 531b
reader 293d; 553a
religious brothers 56d
religious education/CCD 568a
team ministry 488a
youth in ministry 725d
MINISTRIES, SACRED 412a
candidacy for ordination 69a
community and 416b
distinction 413d
evangelization 218a
ministry (ecclesiology) 412c
ordination of religious brothers 56c
threefold order 371b
universal priesthood 537d
MINISTRY (ECCLESIOLOGY) 412b
accountability 210b
ARCIC 20b; 21c
apostolicity 24d

charismatic/institutional 107c; 537d
charisms in ministry 107a
Decree on the Apostolate of the Laity 22b
early Church 536c
ecumenical understanding 43a; 203b
hierarchy and service 249d
liturgical reform 363b
Lutheran/Roman Catholic dialogue 381d
meaning of term 414c; 712c
missionary formation 428a
models 69c
Order, Sacrament of 595d, 707a
Order and jurisdiction 31c
ordination of women 707a
Orthodox/Roman Catholic agreement 473b
parish 478c, d
Penance (Rite) 371a
preaching 531d
Presbyterian-Reformed/Roman Catholic
Consultation 534c
priest and priesthood 536d
priesthood NT 535c
priestly ministry survey 487d
reconciliation 555b
religious brothers 56b
religious in the Church 574b
Sacraments and 713b
shared responsibility 487d
Unitatis redintegratio 712b
United Methodist/Roman Catholic
dialogue 679c
universal priesthood 537c
women in ministry 706d; 713b
Ministry, Continuing Education for *see*
Continuing Education for Ministry
MINISTRY, EDUCATION FOR 414c
permanent deacon formation 503c
MINISTRY, UNORDAINED 415c
Decree on the Apostolate of the Laity 22b
Ministry and Life of Priests, Decree on *see*
Presbyterorum ordinis
Ministry of charity
lay ministries 412a
Minor orders
suppression 293d; 340a
Minorities, Rights of
Black Theology 54c
capital punishment 71d
Church advocacy 300a
ethnics 212b
Minors
right to abortion 3b
Missale Romanum see Sacramentary
Missale Romanum (1570)
votive Masses 396c
Missale Romanum (1975)
editio typica 593c
Missale Romanum (apostolic constitution, 1969)
338b
MISSIOLOGY 416c
inculturation, theological 290b
intercultural experience 428a
Missiology (journal) 28b; 418b
MISSION (NEW TRENDS) 419b
African Christianity 11d
African Independent Churches 15b
inculturation 290b; 426d
lay missionaries 341b
local Churches 690b
missiological literature 417d
Pro Mundi Vita 542a
Third World 664b
Mission Churches
African Independent Church Movement
13d; 14d
MISSION OF THE CHURCH 422a
Ad gentes 419b
apostolicity 24c
Christian Initiation 111b
Church and culture 167c
commitment 141b
communion of giving and forgiving 123c
contemplative life 154c
evangelization 218a, b; 219a

N

Nag Hammadi
  patristics 490c
Nairobi Assembly (1975)
  human rights 282b
Namibia (South-West Africa) 6d
  church jurisdiction 9b
National Advisory Board of Diocesan
  Directors of Campus Ministry 68a
NATIONAL APOSTOLATE FOR THE
  MENTALLY RETARDED (NAMR) 445a
NATIONAL ASSEMBLY OF RELIGIOUS
  BROTHERS (NARB) 446a
NATIONAL ASSEMBLY OF WOMEN
  RELIGIOUS (NAWR) 446b
National Association of Diocesan
  Ecumenical Directors
  ecumenism, regional and local 205d
NATIONAL ASSOCIATION OF LAITY
  446c
NATIONAL ASSOCIATION OF
  PASTORAL MUSICIANS (NPM) 446d
  liturgical movement 359c
  renewal in liturgical music 361c
NATIONAL ASSOCIATION OF
  PERMANENT DIACONATE
  DIRECTORS 447b
National Biblical, Catechetical and
  Liturgical Centre (Bangalore) 487b
NATIONAL BLACK SISTERS'
  CONFERENCE 447b
  women in the ministry of justice 719c
NATIONAL CAMPUS MINISTRY
  ASSOCIATION 448a
NATIONAL CATECHETICAL
  DIRECTORY 448c
  catechesis defined 567d
  catechisms 78a
  family 227a
  family education 226d
NATIONAL CATHOLIC COALITION FOR
  RESPONSIBLE INVESTMENT 450c
  church investments 128c
  corporate social responsibility 164b
NATIONAL CATHOLIC CONFERENCE
  FOR INTERRACIAL JUSTICE (NCCIJ)
  451c
NATIONAL CATHOLIC DEVELOPMENT
  CONFERENCE 451c
NATIONAL CATHOLIC EDUCATIONAL
  ASSOCIATION (NCEA) 452a
  Catholic elementary schools 484d
  Catholic schools 485b
  Catholic Schools in a Declining Church,
    critique 484d
  church authority and higher education
    252b
  founding 599b
  Giving Form to the Vision (publ.) 600a
  lay teachers 635b
  lay teachers' salaries 635c
  school revenues/costs 600c
  secondary education 598d
  teaching ministry 637c
National Catholic News Service
  Communication, USCC Committee on
  142d
National Catholic Pharmacists Guild 402d
National Catholic Reporter (newspaper)
  551a
  editorial policy 308d
  Thorman, D. J. 666b
NATIONAL CATHOLIC STEWARDSHIP
  COUNCIL 452c
NATIONAL CATHOLIC VOCATION
  COUNCIL (NCVC) 453c
NATIONAL CENTER FOR
  URBAN ETHNIC AFFAIRS (NCUEA)
  453d
  community 145c

National Conference on Ethnic and
  Neighborhood Affairs 86a
National Center of the Confraternity of
  Christian Doctrine *see* Religious
  Education/CCD
National Christ Child Society 83c
NATIONAL COALITION OF AMERICAN
  NUNS (NCAN) 454b
  prisons and prisoners 541a
  justice ministry 719c
National Commission on Civil Disorders
  (Kerner Report) 300a
National Conference of Catholic Bishops
  (NCCB)
  aged, care of 16b
  altar girls 3d
  American Catholicism 681d
  arms control 189b
  Call to Action Conference 66d
  capital punishment 71c
  catechetics 683b
  Catholic hospitals and sterilization
    624c
  Church and the media 401d
  divorced Catholics 192a
  ecumenical marriages 202b
  excommunication of divorced Catholics
    683a
  first confession 233c
  marriage tribunals 386c
  media and evangelization 400b
  medical ethics, directives 403b
  mixed marriages, norms 385c
  National Catechetical Directory 449b
  origin and organization 544d
  *Pastoral Plan of Action for Family
    Ministry* 227b
  *Principles and Guidelines for Fund
    Raising* 238d
  public policy issues 549d
  public policy statements 683d
  secondary education 599d
  sex education 603d
  Statement on Catholic Jewish Relations
    (1965) 88b
  teachers' unions 635d; 638d
  teaching ministry 637d
  theological scholarship 660c
  U.S. Catholic Bishops' Advisory Council
    43b
  U.S. Catholic Mission Council 680c
  women in Church and society 718c
  women in the Church 708d
National Conference of Catholic Charities
  (NCCC)
  Cadre Study (1972) 82c; 616b
  foundation 616b
  history 82b
  programs 83a
National Conference of Catholic Guidance
  Councils *see* Association for Religious and
  Value Issues in Counseling
NATIONAL CONFERENCE OF
  DIOCESAN DIRECTORS OF
  RELIGIOUS EDUCATION/CCD 454d
NATIONAL CONFERENCE OF
  DIOCESAN VOCATION DIRECTORS
  (NCDVD) 455a
NATIONAL CONFERENCE OF
  RELIGIOUS VOCATION DIRECTORS
  OF MEN 455b
NATIONAL CONFERENCE OF VICARS
  FOR RELIGIOUS 455c; 573d
National Congress on Evangelization (1977)
  219b
NATIONAL COUNCIL OF CATHOLIC
  LAITY (NCCL) 456a
  Bishops' Committee on the Laity 48d
National Council of Catholic Men
  autonomy 48d
  National Council of Catholic Laity 456a
National Council of Catholic Women
  autonomy 48d
  evangelization, programs of 220a
  National Council of Catholic Laity 456a

National Council of Churches Center for the
  Study of Japanese Religions (Kyoto) 205a
NATIONAL COUNCIL OF CHURCHES
  OF CHRIST, U.S.A. (NCCC-USA) 456b
  BCEIA 43d
  Catholic participation 203c
  Week of Prayer for Christian Unity
    704d
National Council of Churches of Christ in
  the USA Ireland Program 465d
National Council on Aging 15d
National Council on the Study of Religion
  College Theology Society 138a
National Farm Worker Ministry 407d
NATIONAL FEDERATION OF
  CATHOLIC PHYSICIANS' GUILDS
  456d
  medico-moral problems 402d
NATIONAL FEDERATION OF
  SPIRITUAL DIRECTORS 457b
National Forum of Catholic Parent
  Organizations 452b
National Forum of Religious Educators
  76c; 452b
*National Guidelines for Diocesan Directors
  and Campus Ministers*
  Campus and Young Adult Ministry
    (USCC) 68a
National Institute of Child Health and
  Human Development 279b
National Labor Relations Board (NLRB)
  Catholic Teachers' Unions 638a
  lay teachers 635b
National Liturgical Office (Ottawa) 487b
NATIONAL MARRIAGE ENCOUNTER
  457b
National Neighborhood Commission 454b
National Neighborhood Training Institute
  454a
NATIONAL OFFICE FOR BLACK
  CATHOLICS 457c
  Dr. Thomas Wyatt Turner Award 671b
  liturgical music 442d
  origin 52d
NATIONAL ORGANIZATION FOR
  CONTINUING EDUCATION OF
  ROMAN CATHOLIC CLERGY
  (NOCERCC) 458a
NATIONAL PASTORAL PLANNING
  CONFERENCE 458b
National Plan for Church Vocations
  Bishops' Committee on Vocations 50d
National Race Crisis (NCCB Statement)
  300a
National Research Act
  medical experimentation 220d
National Secretariat for Social Action
  Church in the Philippines 506a
NATIONAL SISTERS COMMUNICA-
  TIONS SERVICE 458b
NATIONAL SISTERS VOCATION
  CONFERENCE (NSVC) 458d
National Women's Conference, Houston,
  1977
  abortion (U.S. law) 2b
Nationalism
  African Independent Church Movement
    15b
  Synod of Bishops (1974) 627c
Native American Catholic Congresses 19d
Native clergy
  evangelization 218b
NATURAL FAMILY PLANNING 459a
  family services 228c
  Human Life and Natural Family
    Planning Foundation 279b
Natural Family Planning Federation of
  America 279b
NATURAL LAW 460a
  Catholic social thought 282a
  Gaudium et spes 643c
  moral theology (contemporary trends)
    434b
  personalism 505b

right to work 587a
theology of marriage 596b
Nebreda, Alphonso
catechetics 76d
Neo-Chalcedonianism
Christology 114a
Neo-orthodoxy
ahistorical 656a
Neo-Pentecostalism *see* Charismatic
Renewal, Catholic
Neoscholasticism
concept of theology 652c
NETWORK 461a
Neuhaus, R.
community 145d
Native American Native Religious 19d
Neumann, John Nepomucene, Bp., St.
canonization 683c
proper Mass (U.S.) 66a
New American Bible
Bible versions for liturgy 38c; 39d
New Catholic Encyclopedia
Willging, E. P. 705a
New Covenant (period.) 105c
New English Bible
Bible versions for liturgy 39d
New Eve
NCCB pastoral on Mary 394b
typology 394b
New Family Movement 234d
New Humanity Movement 234d
NEW INTERNATIONAL ECONOMIC
ORDER 461b
Center of Concern 100d
international cooperation 181a
international economic aid 200b
International Monetary Fund 297b
labor movement 325c
Pontifical Commission for Justice and
Peace 320a
"New Left" Catholics 391b
New Oxford Annotated Bible
Bible versions for liturgy 39c
New Sower (period.) 77b
New Testament literature
Dead Sea Scrolls 177d
New Vulgate, Pontifical Commission for the
formation 141a
Newman Apostolate *see* Catholic Campus
Ministry Association
Newman, John H. (card.)
Development of Christian Doctrine
264b
Idea of a University 254b
Newspapers, Catholic 90d; 91a
table: circulation 90d
Nicene Creed
liturgical movement and ecumenism
359d
translation 153d; 296c
use 542c
see also Profession of Faith (The Creed)
Niebuhr, H. R.
theology and sociology 658c
Nigeria, Federal Republic of 9b
Church's growth 12a
genocide 242a
Nirvana
theology of negation 58c
Nisbet, Robert
community 145c
Noble Guard 476b
Nocturnal adoration 213a
Nonbelievers
atheism 29a
dialogue with 293b
Nonbelievers, Secretariat for *see* Secretariat
for Nonbelievers
NONCANONICAL COMMUNITIES 463b
development 574c
Non-Catholic observers
Vatican II 101c; 688d
Non-Christian Religions
Buddhism, Church and 57d

dialogue 423c
Hinduism 257d
sources of holiness 101d
Non-Christians, Secretariat for *see*
Secretariat for Non-Christians
NORRIS, JAMES JOSEPH 463d
NORTH AMERICAN ACADEMY OF
LITURGY 464b
liturgical movement 359b
music 361c
pastoral liturgy studies 487b
North American Area Council of the World
Alliance of Reformed Churches 534b
North American Conference of Separated
and Divorced Catholics (NACSDC) 191d
NORTHEAST REGIONAL PASTORAL
CENTER FOR HISPANICS 464d
NORTHERN IRELAND 465b
Conway, William (card.) 162b
terrorism 644c
Nostra aetate (Declaration on the Relation
of the Church to Non-Christian Religions)
discrimination 258b
Hinduism 258a
Islam 301a
Judaism 533b
prejudice 533c
Notes, theological
hierarchy of truths 655c
Notes de Pastorale Liturgique (period.)
487a
Notitiae (period.) 93b
NOVITIATE 466a
vocation, religious 696c
Nuclear deterrence
morality 187d
Nuclear weapons
morality 187a; 701d
Vatican II debate 186a
Nuncio, papal 349a
NUNS, CONTEMPLATIVE 466c
Association of Contemplative Sisters
27c
cloister 134b
Concilium Monasticum Iuris Canonici
150a
Nurses *see* Medical Personnel, Moral
Obligations of
Nyerere, Jules
community 145a
Ujamaa 13b
Nyquist decision 124d

O

Obedience, vow of
contemporary understanding 575c;
698b
women religious 565a
Oberburg, Bernard H. 77a
Octogesima adveniens (apostolic letter, 1971)
activism, political and social 4c
"Call to Action" 66c
community building 685d
discrimination against women 717a;
720b
economic injustices 440
human development 494b; 515d
Marxism 319a
new social issues 319a
political communities 148b
politics 519c
politics and common good 515a
urbanization 685d
Offertory
term changed 593a
OFFICE, ECCLESIASTICAL 469a
ecclesiology 123b
episcopal vicar 208d
unordained ministries 416b
women in Canon Law 706c

Office for Film and Broadcasting
Church and the media 401d
Communication, USCC Committee on
142d
OFFICE OF THE DEAD 469d
Official Catholic Directory 92d
Church statistics 128d; 347a
Official Development Assistance (ODA)
199d
Oficina Nacional de Información Social
(Peru) 333b
Oil of Catechumens
blessing 269b
Chrism Mass 109d
Oil of the Sick
blessing 269b
Chrism Mass 109d
permission to carry 269c
Oils *see* Holy Oils and Chrism
Old Testament Churches
African Independent Church Movement
13d
One in Christ (period.) 93a
ecumenism 601d
ministry to ecumenical marriages 202d
O'Neill, W. L.
community 145d
Oosthuizen, G. C.
African Independent Church Movement
15b
Opening Prayer
Mass music 395c
Opinion polls
church membership 347b
Optatam totius (Decree on Priestly
Formation)
biblical theology 40c
philosophy in seminaries 508a
priestly formation 537d
priestly spirituality 539b
seminaries 662a
"tutelage of St. Thomas Aquinas"
509a; 666a
vocations 50d
Opus Dei 211c
Oratio super populum see Solemn Blessing
and Prayers over the People
Order, Sacrament of
contemporary theology 595d
ecclesiastical office 469c
ecumenism 596a
episcopal ordination 138c
liturgy (historical development) 371b
ministry (ecclesiology) 413d
preaching office 531a
theology 414a; 415d
women in Canon Law 706a
Order of St. John, Knights of Malta
traditionalists 669b
Order of the faithful
parish (community of worship) 480d
Ordination
institution of readers and acolytes 293d
sacred ministries 412a
universal/special priesthood 537c
Ordination, episcopal
holiness of the Church 208c
Ordination, Rites of
revision 371b
Ordo cantus Missae (1972) 395b; 594a
Oregon School Case 599b
Organ
liturgical music 360c
location 360c
ORGANIC UNION 470b
conciliar fellowship 585a
ecumenical movement 203a
meanings 584d
models 678a
Oriental Churches, Congregation for the
169d
Ukrainian Rite 675d
ORIENTAL CODE OF CANON LAW,
REVISION OF 470d
Eastern Church criticism 196b

Schlette, R.
  missiology 418b
Schlink, Edmund 668b
Schmalzgrueber, Franz
  jurisprudence, canonical 387b
Scholastic theology
  natural-law theories 460b
  positive theology 652c
  Sacraments 556a
  speculative thought 652c
School District v. Schempp 125c
Schoonenberg, Piet 668b
  hermeneutics 668b
  Spirit Christology 114b
Schumacher, E. F. 617c; 642c
Science and technology
  agnosticism 17b
  Bishops' Committee for Human Values
    44c
Scripture
  criterion of theology 41a
  fonts of Revelation 586a
  integration of theology 41a
  primacy of 586b
  "theologies" in 41d
  tradition 586a
Scrutinies
  catechumenate for adults 80a
SECOND-CAREER VOCATIONS 597c
  Conference of Major Superiors of Men
    150d
Second-Career Vocation Project (Univ. of
  Dayton) 598b
Second Development Decade
  New International Economic Order
    461d
SECONDARY EDUCATION, CATHOLIC
  598d
  Association of Catholic Teachers 27c
  government aid 125b
  moral education 433a
Secrecy, papal *see* Papal Secrecy
Secretariat for Nonbelievers 140b; 171d
  study of atheism 293a
Secretariat for Non-Christians 170d
  formation 140b; 301b
SECRETARIAT FOR PROMOTING
  CHRISTIAN UNITY 601a
  ecumenism, regional and local 205b
  formation 140b
  Joint Roman Catholic/World Methodist
    Commission 307b
  Orthodox/Roman Catholic relations
    474c
  World Council of Churches 308b
Secretariat of State (Papal)
  organization and competence 169c
  papal legates 349b
  papal secrecy 476c
Secretariats of the Roman Curia *see* Curia,
  Roman
SECULAR INSTITUTES 601d
  common life (Canon Law) 142b
  U.S. Conference of Secular Institutes
    681c
SECULARISM 602c
  Catholic higher education 250b
  cultural Catholicism and 95d
  faith, act of 224d
  medical ethics 402b
  Synod of Bishops (1974) 627d
Secularity, theology of
  laity (theology) 327b
  laity, vocation of 328c; 345c
  sacred/world history 657a
  secular institutes 602a
Secularization
  Enlightenment, The 519a
Sedula cura (motu proprio, 1971)
  Pontifical Biblical Commission 523a
Segregation
  ethnics, rights of 212c
  interracial justice 300a
Self-defense
  abortion 3a

Seminaries
  evaluation 538c
  integrative program 538d
  liturgical education 356c
  need for 538b
  postconciliar education 414c
  priestly formation 538b
  theology courses 662a
Seminaries and Universities, Congregation
  of *see* Catholic Education, Congregation
  for
Seminary professors
  table: preferred philosophies 511c
Senegal, Republic of 10a
Sensitivity training
  pastoral psychology 490b
Sensus fidelium
  tradition 668d
Separated brethren
  catholicity 97b
  Christian Initiation 112a
  holiness of the Church 267c
  unity of the Church 97b
  Vatican II 106c
SEQUENCE 603b
Servizio di Documentazione e Studi
  (SEDOS) 421b
Seton, Elizabeth, St.
  canonization 683c
SEX EDUCATION 603c
  Planned Parenthood 509d
  parents and children 477b
Sex therapy
  marriage counseling 227d
SEXISM 604a
  Christian theology 230c
  cultural anthropology 707b
  idealization of women 718a
  institutional 714b
  language of liturgy and doctrine 716c
  occupational options 715a
  women in society 714b
  Women's Ordination Conference 720c
  women's rights 709b
SEXUAL MORALITY (IN THE BIBLE)
  605a
  homosexuality 272b
SEXUAL MORALITY (MORAL
  THEOLOGY) 606b
  contemporary trends 434d
  marriage and conjugal love 477b
  moral absolutes 436d
  sex therapy 227d
SEXUALITY, HUMAN (IN THE BIBLE)
  607d
  homosexuality 272b
  women in the Church 717c
Sharbel, Youssef Makhlouf, St.
  canonization 197a
Shared prayer
  prayer 528b
  prayer, community 529d
Shared responsibility for ministry
  pastoral councils 486c
  pastoral ministries 487d
  pastoral planning 489a
Sharing the Light of Faith see National
  Catechetical Directory (U.S.)
SHERIDAN, TERENCE JAMES 609b
SHUSTER, GEORGE N. 609d
Si diligis (allocution, Pius XII)
  theologians 649d
Sierra Leone, Republic of 10a
Sign of Peace *see* Kiss (Sign) of Peace
Sign of Peace (publ.) 50a
Signatura, Apostolic *see* Apostolic
  Signatura
Signs of the times
  theological source (*locus*) 586d
SILENCE IN WORSHIP 610b
  Liturgy of the Word 395d
SIN (THEOLOGY) 610d
  alienation 343b
  Christian morality 437c; 438a
  ecclesial dimension 556b

  NT meaning 605c
  objective morality 130c
  offense against community 500d
  original/personal 472a
  postbaptismal reconciliation 556b
  reconciliation 499b
  social dimension 149a
Sin, cooperation in
  medical personnel 624c
Sin, mortal
  fundamental option 611b
Sin, social
  equality 209b
  human development 149b
  Latin America 417b
  liberation theology 351b
  Sacrament of Reconciliation 595b
  society (theology) 618c
  theological critique 658d
Sin, venial
  confession, frequency of 151b
  meaning 611b
  Penance, Sacrament of 556b
Singing, congregational *see* Congregational
  Singing
SINGLE PEOPLE 611d
  women 714b
Sister Formation Conference *see* Religious
  Formation Conference
Sisters for Christian Community (SFCC)
  463c
Sisters Survey
  religious women 346b
Sisters Uniting
  Association of Contemplative Sisters
    27d
  Leadership Conference of Women
    Religious 346c
Sistersharing (newsletter) 458c
Sithole, Ndabaningi
  Rhodesia 8c
Situation Ethics
  moral theology 434a
Slater, Philip
  community 146a
Slavery
  interracial justice 299d
Slipyj, Joseph (card.)
  papal diplomacy 186c
  Oriental Code of Canon Law 196c
  Ukrainian patriarchate 674d; 675a
  Ukrainian Rite 492c
Slovak Catholic Church 197b
Smith, Ian
  Rhodesia 8a
SOCIAL ACTION 612d
  activism, political and social 4c
  Catholic charities 83d
  Catholic Conference on Ethnic and
    Neighborhood Affairs 86a
  Center of Concern 100d
  ecumenism, regional and local 205c
SOCIAL DEVELOPMENT AND WORLD
  PEACE, USCC COMMITTEE ON 614b
  sub-committee on health 403a
Social Gospel
  Protestant theology 658c
SOCIAL HISTORY 615a
  labor movement 325a
  sociology of the parish 481c
Social justice
  activism, political and social 4d
  basis 527d
  Bishops' Justice Program 52a
  business ethics 62a
  Call to Action 66d
  Catholic hospitals 275b
  Catholic social thought 315d
  Center of Concern 100d
  Christian Life Communities 112c
  civil disobedience 131a
  community of mankind 148c
  crime 541c
  dignity of the person 504d
  education for justice 316c

Suenens, Leo J. (card.)
  charismatic renewal 105c
Suicide
  burial (Canon Law) 60d
Summi Pontificis electio (motu proprio, 1962)
  papal elections 523c
SUNDAY 626b
  "little Eaaster" 34b
  liturgy (historical development) 371c
  General Norms of the Roman Calendar 65d
Sunday and Holy Day observance
  decline in Mass attendance 347c
Sundkler, Bengt (bp.)
  African Independent Church Movement 14b
Supernatural
  natural and 122c
Supernatural existential
  possibility of Revelation 654c
Supernatural order
  temporal values 643c
Supreme Court (U.S.)
  abortion (US law and morality) 2d
  abortion decisions 1c; 2c
  capital punishment 71b
  Doe v. Bolton 47c
  right to privacy 3a
  Roe v. Wade 47c
Surplice 367d
Suspension
  censures, ecclesiastical 99c
SWAPO (South West Africa Peoples' Organization)
  Namibia 7a
Swaziland
  Catholic Church 7c
Syllabus of Errors
  Church and State 519a
Symbolism, theological
  liturgical theology 366d
Symbols, liturgical
  authenticity 371d
  liturgical gestures 358a
  liturgy (structural elements) 372a
Syncretism, religious
  African Independent Church Movement 14c
  Santeria 261b
Synod, Roman (1960)
  conservatism 688b
Synod of Bishops
  constitution 627a
  ecclesiastical discipline 190a
  enumeration 627a; 629a
  papal elections 523d
  Paul VI 493c; 627a
Synod of Bishops (1967)
  International Theological Commission 297d
  Masses with children 397c
  revision of Canon Law 135b; 136a
Synod of Bishops (1971)
  conversion 156d
  education for justice 207a; 316a
  evangelization and development 419c; 612d
  International Theological Commission 318a
  justice and the Gospel 527d; 544c
  justice within the Church 164b
  morality of war 701c
  priests and politics 555c
  redemption and liberation 148d
  right to development 281c
  social ministry 317b
  women in ministry 719b
  women in the Church 706d
  women's rights 720b
SYNOD OF BISHOPS (THIRD GENERAL ASSEMBLY, 1974) 627a
  catechesis 73b
  debate on evangelization and development 317c

evangelization 24d
evangelization's link with development 159c
inculturation, theological 290b
John Paul II 305b; 306b
media in evangelization 400b
missiology, state of 416d, 418c
political terrorism 645c
revolution 645c
SYNOD OF BISHOPS (FOURTH GENERAL ASSEMBLY, 1977) 629a
  adult catechesis 75b
  catechetics and catechesis 76d
  sex education 603d
  U.S. Bishops on catechesis 76b; 226d
SYNODS, DIOCESAN 631c
  functions 185c
  women religious 706a
Synoptic Gospels
  resurrection narratives 579c, d
Systematic theology
  philosophical foundation 508c
  philosophical pluralism 510d
  theology in seminaries 663d
Szasz, Thomas
  medical ethics 402c

T

TABERNACLE 633a
  placement 18b
Table for gifts (liturgical)
  furnishings, sacred 240b
Tanzania, United Republic of 10b; 12a
  African Independent Church Movement 15b
  community 145a
TAX EXEMPTION OF CHURCH PROPERTY 633d
  Church and State 124c
  Citizens for Educational Freedom 130d
Taylor, E. B.
  cultural anthropology 168c
Te Deum
  Gregorian chant 243c
  translation 296c
Teach Them (NCCB)
  moral values 603d
  teaching ministry 637a
TEACHERS, LAY 634d
  Association of Catholic Teachers 27c
  Catholic secondary education 600b
  Catholic teachers' unions 637d
  formation 560d
  parochial schools 483c
  teachers of religion 560d
TEACHERS, MINISTRY OF 636a
  heralds and witnesses 561c
  lay teachers 635d
  ministry of the Word 561b
TEACHERS' UNIONS, CATHOLIC 637d
  Association of Catholic Teachers 27b
  Catholic secondary education 600b
  lay teachers 635c
  membership 600b
Teaching All Nations (period.) 77c; 93a; 195d
TEACHING AUTHORITY OF THE CHURCH (MAGISTERIUM) 638d
  authority, ecclesiastical 31b
  biblical theology 42b
  Congregation for the Doctrine of the Faith 192b
  discipline, ecclesiastical 190b
  "fallible magisterium" 32c
  formal/material components 32a
  formation of conscience 438a
  Humanae vitae 433d
  infallibility 291a
  jurisdiction (Canon Law) 313d
  measured by Word of God 31d

moral issues 437d
multiform 31d; 32d
ordinary magisterium 291c
pastoral decisions 607c
religion, teacher of 561d
theologian 650a
theological pluralism 513d
tradition (in theology) 668d
value of pronouncements 32b
TEAM MINISTRY 640c
  CARA study 488a
  religious brothers 56b
  women in campus ministry 711d
TECHNOLOGY, SOCIAL EFFECTS OF 641b
  agnosticism 17a
  eschatology 210d
  medical ethics 402d
Technology, medical 220c
TECHNOLOGY, TRANSFER OF 642b
  developing nations 544b
  economic aid, international 461c
  economic injustices 181c
  Third World poverty 526c
Teilhard de Chardin, Pierre
  atheism 29d
  influence on Vatican II 264b
  mysticism 443d
  process and morality 434a
  technology 641c
  universal evolution 655c; 656c
Tekakwitha Conference 19c
Television
  ally of terrorism 644d
  Church programs 401d
  decline in Catholic publishing 551b
  media in education 399d
  USCC criticisms 143a
TEMPORAL VALUES 643b
  Bishops' Committee for Human Values 44d
  Church and world 125d
  creation 166d
  eschatology 210d
  faith, act of 224d
  laity, vocation 327b; 328c; 614a
  monasticism, contemporary 431c
  progress 542d
Teresa of Calcutta, Mother
  Missionaries of Charity 425c
TERRORISM, POLITICAL 643d
  Middle East 406c
  Northern Ireland 465c
  Populorum progressio 399b
Tertullian
  political theology 516c
Testamentum Domini 370a
Testem benevolentiae (letter, Leo XIII)
  Americanism 4a
THEISM AND PROCESS THOUGHT 645d
  Christology 113d
  theology of hope 273d
THEOLOGIAN 649b
  competence 640b
  Congregation for the Doctrine of the Faith 193a
  dissent 32c
  distinct from religion teacher 560d
  fallible teaching 32c
  opinions not authoritative 624d
  responsibility 639d
  theological pluralism 514b
THEOLOGICAL FIELD EDUCATION 651c
  education for ministry 415b
  missionary formation 428c
  theology in seminaries 662c
Theological methodology
  liberation theology 350d
  praxis 351b
Theological Pluralism *see* Pluralism, Theological
THEOLOGY 652b
  authority, ecclesiastical 32a